Putting the Pieces Together:
An Integrated, Interactive Approach

Du605777

AN INTEGRATED APPROACH

T his book is designed so that the concepts build upon one another, with early chapters providing a strong foundation for understanding concepts in later chapters. The authors go beyond an uncritical presentation of text material to debate the strengths and weaknesses and advantages and disadvantages of various strategic management techniques, strategies, and structures. This approach demonstrates that in the real world, strategic issues are complex and involve a consideration of pros and cons and a willingness to accept tradeoffs. In addition, the authors draw not only on strategic management literature, but also on the literature of economics, marketing, organizational theory, operations management, finance, and international business to deliver a perspective that is truly strategic in that it integrates the contributions of these diverse disciplines into a comprehensive whole. Finally, a case selection *par excellence* (see the Table of Contents for a complete list) gives students the ultimate opportunity to explore the application of concepts.

An Interactive Approach

Extensive pedagogy including numerous examples and hands-on activities enhances learning and makes studying *Strategic Management* an interactive experience. Every chapter begins with an overview outline and ends with a **Chapter Summary** and **Discussion Questions.**

Other features in every chapter include:

OPENING CASES

Strategy at Yahoo! (Ch. 1)
Chainsaw Al Dunlap Gets the Ax (Ch. 2)
On-line Firms Revolutionize the Stockbrokerage Industry (Ch. 3)
Cisco Systems (Ch. 4)
Levi's Original Spin (Ch. 5)
How E*Trade Uses the Internet to Gain a Low-Cost Advantage (Ch. 6)
How eBay Revolutionized the Auction Business (Ch. 7)
Global Strategy at General Motors (Ch. 8)
Bombardier (Ch. 9)
Changing the Focus at Hewlett-Packard (Ch. 10)
Microsoft's New E-Structure (Ch. 11)
Oracle's New Approach to Control (Ch. 12)
Compaq's New Internet Strategy (Ch. 13)
From Reengineering to E-Engineering at Bank of America (Ch. 14)

STRATEGY IN ACTION FEATURES

1.1 Larry Bossidy, CEO
1.2 A Strategic Shift at Microsoft
1.3 Strategic Planning at Royal Dutch/Shell
1.4 Groupthink at Imperial Tobacco
2.1 Bill Agee at Morrison Knudsen
2.2 Engineering a Strategic Vision at AT&T
2.3 A Short-Term Emphasis Costs U.S. Companies the Lead in Flat Panel Displays
2.4 The Jack-in-the-Box Poisonings—Questionable Ethics?
3.1 Entry Barriers in the Japanese Brewing Industry
3.2 The Great European Soap War
3.3 The Failure of Digital's Alpha Chip
3.4 Finland's Nokia
4.1 Competitive Advantage in the U.S. Department Store Industry
4.2 Productivity in the Automobile Industry
4.3 Continental Airlines Goes from Worst to First
4.4 Value Creation at Pfizer
4.5 Microsoft's Luck
4.6 The Road to Ruin at DEC
5.1 Chemical and Chase Banks Merge to Realize Scale Economies
5.2 Too Much Experience at Texas Instruments
5.3 Toyota's Lean Production System
5.4 General Electric's Six Sigma Quality Improvement Process
5.5 Total Quality Management at Intermountain Health Care
5.6 Whatever Happened to the Digital Compact Cassette?
5.7 Slow Cycle Time at Apollo Computer
6.1 Who Wants an American Express Card?
6.2 Ford's Difficult Balancing Act
6.3 Finding a Niche in the Outsourcing Market

2002 Update

INTRODUCTION

One problem any management text faces is that events in the real world often move more rapidly than the typical three-year textbook revision cycle. Even annual update editions have difficulty keeping up with the pace of change in the real world. For example, since the last annual update edition of this text Kmart announced Chapter 11 bankruptcy, the closing of over 200 of its stores, and the replacement of three of its top executives including the CEO— all within a three-month cycle. The objective of this update is to bring selected cases up-to-date by relaying major changes in the circumstances and/or strategies of the companies profiled in these cases. In addition, we again provide the material related to new research streams that appeared in the first Annual Update.

The cases are arranged alphabetically followed by the case number from the text. The case material that appeared in the first Annual Update—Wizards of the Coast, America On-line, Amazon.com, Microsoft's Windows CE, The Home Video Game Industry, Monsanto, and Pharmacia & Upjohn—can now be found on the student textbook web site.

NEW RESEARCH STREAMS AND THEIR IMPLICATIONS FOR STRATEGY

In this section of the Annual Update, we review four streams of research in the strategy literature that have received increasing attention over the last two years and are having an important influence on management practice. The first stream of research, which we will consider under the heading "The Innovator's Dilemma," is based on the work of Clayton Christensen, among others. This work deals with the manner in which technological innovations can revolutionize industry structure and present incumbent enterprises with difficult strategic challenges while giving new ventures that pursue the correct strategy the opportunity to rise to market dominance. This is a relevant topic for review given the rapid rate of technological change that now confronts modern businesses. New technologies, including Internet-based commerce, optical communications equipment, hand-held computers, wireless technologies, biotechnology, and genomics, are upsetting the status quo in many industries. The work of Christensen and others can help us understand the implications of these events and hence make better strategic decisions.

The second stream of research we will review looks at how companies faced with uncertainty about the future can maintain their strategic flexibility by taking a real options approach to strategic decision making. It is linked to the first stream of research, for rapid technological change is a major producer of uncertainty in the real world. The exploration of real options is a topic that initially was confined to the academic literature. However, in recent years companies like Merck and Microsoft have embraced a real options methodology and are using it to evaluate their strategic decisions and maintain flexibility in the face of the uncertainty generated by technological change.

The third stream of research looks at the strategies that companies need to pursue to win a format war. A **format war** occurs when two competing and incompatible technologies vie for market acceptance and different companies are backing different technologies. A classic example was the format war between Sony and Matsushita to establish their rival formats for videocassette recorders as the dominant design in the marketplace. Sony championed the Betamax format and Matsushita the VHS format. In the end, Matsushita won this format war, and Sony was left with zero market share. Format wars are an increasingly important aspect of competition in many high-technology industries, including consumer electronics, computers, and telecommunications. In this Annual Update, we draw on recent research to discuss the strategies companies can adopt to win a format war.

Finally, we explore some specific ways in which new information technologies affect strategy formulation and implementation. We focus on how new computer software and hardware are changing the way organizations operate and the nature of the value chain they confront. Recent developments both inside and among organizations are reviewed.

These four streams of research cover material that assumes knowledge of many of the topics covered in the first half of the book. To get the most out of this new material, we suggest that you read this update after you have worked your way through at least the first six chapters of the text.

■ The Innovator's Dilemma

Clayton Christensen explores how new technologies cause great firms to fail.[1] Christensen's approach is historical; he has carefully documented the development of a number of industries over long periods of time. The patterns he has uncovered are quite alarming and have important implications for strategy.

Innovation as the Engine of Change   Christensen's starting point is the widely accepted observation that technological innovations can revolutionize industry structure and may lead to the decline of incumbent firms. A well-known example is the computer industry. The arrival of the personal computer in the late 1970s triggered a number of changes in the industry that ultimately led to the demise of incumbents such as IBM, Digital Equipment Corporation (DEC), and Wang Computers, and the rise of new entrants such as Microsoft, Intel, Seagate, Micron Technology, Apple, Dell, and Compaq. Prior to the arrival of the personal computer, the industry was dominated by vertically integrated enterprises such as IBM that sold mainframe or mid-range computers, to corporate or government buyers. These enterprises manufactured many of the hardware components that went into the computers, including central processing units, memory chips, and storage devices such as disk drives. They also developed proprietary operating systems and applications software to go with those computers, and sold the machines directly to customers using their own sales force.

The PC changed all of this. Because it was based on "open standards," the PC led to the fragmentation (de-integration) of the industry, with different companies focusing on different segments of the industry value chain. Thus, Microsoft produced the operating system and applications software, Seagate produced storage devices (disk drives), Intel manufactured microprocessors, Micron manufactured memory chips, and Dell and Compaq assembled the personal computers and also the servers that sat at the hubs of networks. The PC was initially sold through a new distribution channel (retail stores) to a new customer group (individuals or departments in businesses rather than centralized corporate buyers). The PC subsequently grew up to become an indispensable business tool and a mass market consumer appliance that was connected with other PCs and servers through networks based on Internet protocols. As this process unfolded, the incumbent firms of the pre-PC era went into decline, while new entrants rose to dominance with the growth of the new technology.

The Decline of Incumbents   One question Christensen focuses on is "Why do incumbent firms often decline following the introduction of radical new technology?" The answer uncovered through his research is that such incumbent firms listen closely to their customers, and their customers do not want the new technology, at least not initially. Thus, the incumbents decide not to invest in the new technology, or to make it a low priority. Subsequently, the new technology often increases rapidly in functionality so that ultimately the firms' customers change their minds and decide they do want it. By this point, however, it is not the incumbent firms that lead in the development and commercialization of the new technology, but the new entrants. At this juncture, the long-established customers of the incumbents turn to the new entrants, leaving the incumbents to play catch-up.

The mechanical excavator industry provides a good example of this process. Excavators are used to dig out foundations for large buildings, create trenches to lay large pipes for sewers and the like, and dig out foundations and trenches for residential construction and small trenches for farm work. Prior to the 1940s, the dominant technology used to manipulate the bucket on a mechanical excavator was based on a system of cables and pulleys. Although these mechanical systems could lift large buckets of earth, the excavators themselves were quite large, cumbersome, and expensive. Thus, they were rarely used to dig small trenches for house foundations, irrigation ditches for farmers, and the like. In most cases, these small trenches were dug by hand.

In the 1940s a new technology made its appearance—hydraulics. In theory, hydraulic systems had certain advantages over the established cable-and-pulley systems. Most important, their energy efficiency was higher. This meant that for a given bucket size, a smaller engine would be required using a hydraulic system. However, the initial hydraulic systems also had drawbacks. The seals on hydraulic cylinders were prone to leak under high pressure, effectively limiting the size of bucket that could be lifted using hydraulics. Notwithstanding this drawback, when hydraulics first appeared many incumbent firms in the mechanical excavation industry took the technology seriously enough to ask their primary customers whether they would be interested in products based on hydraulics. Since the primary customers of incumbents needed excavators with large buckets to dig out the foundations for buildings and large trenches, their reply was negative. For this customer set, the hydraulic systems of the 1940s were not reliable enough or powerful enough. Consequently, after consulting their customers, incumbent firms took the strategic decision not to invest in hydraulics. Instead, they continued to produce excavation equipment based on the dominant cable-and-pulley technology.

It was left to a number of new entrants to pioneer hydraulic excavation equipment. Because of the limits on bucket size imposed by the "seal problem," these companies initially focused on a poorly served niche in the market that could make use of small buckets—residential contractors and farmers. These new entrants included J. I. Case, John Deere, and Caterpillar. Over time, these new entrants were able to solve the engineering problems associated with weak hydraulic seals. As they did so, they manufactured excavators with larger buckets. Ultimately, these companies invaded the market niches served by the old-line incumbents—general contractors who dug the foundations for large buildings, sewers, and so on. At this point, Case, Deere, Caterpillar, and their kin rose to dominance in the industry, while the majority of incumbents from the prior era lost share. Most ultimately went out of business.

The message of this story is that the incumbent manufacturers of mechanical excavation equipment went out of business partly because they listened to their customers too closely! Neither they nor their customers appreciated the fact that like all new technologies, the efficacy of hydraulics would improve over time, allowing the technology to be used for applications that initially were out of reach. Thus, it was left to new entrants to commercialize the new technology. Over time, these new entrants moved into the market segments once dominated by incumbents.

Disruptive Technology   The story of the mechanical excavation industry is not unique. Christensen has documented similar developments in a number of other industries, including the computer and steel industries. Christensen uses the term **disruptive technology** to refer to a technology that gets its start outside the mainstream of a market and then, as its functionality improves over time, invades the main market. Such a technology is disruptive because it revolutionizes industry structure, reshaping the industry value chain and leading to the decline of incumbent firms.

Generalizing from industry studies, Christensen makes a number of points. First, he notes that initially, the functionality of new technologies is often very limited. Thus, the early hydraulic excavators could lift only small buckets. Similarly, the limited power of the early personal computers reduced their appeal to information system professionals in large corporations. However, as in the case of hydraulics and the personal computer, the performance of new technologies typically improves rapidly over time as basic engineering problems are solved.

Richard Foster has formalized the relationship between the performance of a technology and time in terms of what he calls the *technology S-curve* (see Figure 1).[2] This curve shows the relationship over time of *cumulative* investments in R&D and the performance (or functionality) of a given technology. Early in its evolution, R&D investments in the new technology tend to yield rapid improvements in performance as basic engineering problems are solved. After a time, however, diminishing returns to R&D begin to set in, the rate of performance improvement slows down, and the technology starts to approach its natural limit where further advances are not possible. For example, one can argue that there was more improvement in the first fifty years of the commercial aerospace business following the pio-

FIGURE 1:

The Technology S-Curve

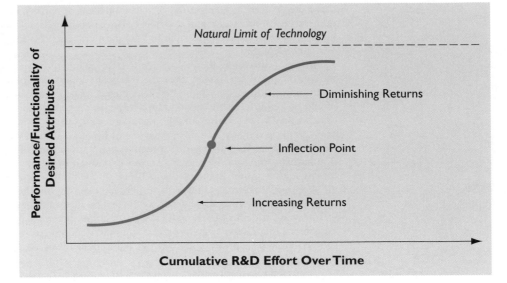

neering flight by the Wright Brothers than there was in the second fifty years. Indeed, the world's largest commercial jet aircraft, the Boeing 747, is based on a 1960s design, as is the world's fastest commercial jet aircraft, the Concorde.

Christensen argues that initially, many incumbents tend to ignore or underinvest in new technologies. One reason is negative feedback from established customers, who themselves cannot see a need for the new technology given its limited functionality. In terms of the technology S-curve, the new technology initially delivers fewer of the desired performance benefits than the established technology (see Figure 2) and thus is not favored by established customers. Because the new technology initially has limited appeal to established customers, the revenue stream from products incorporating that technology is projected to be very small and, consequently, not worth going after. The dominant attitude of incumbents seems to be: "It's a small market, it's not worth our bother."

As a consequence, it is often left to new entrants to commercialize new technologies. New entrants typically do so by focusing on small, out-of-the-way niches that are poorly served by incumbent enterprises and where customers are looking for different attributes. Thus, Caterpillar, now the dominant firm in the market for excavation equipment, got its start

FIGURE 2:

Technology S-Curves

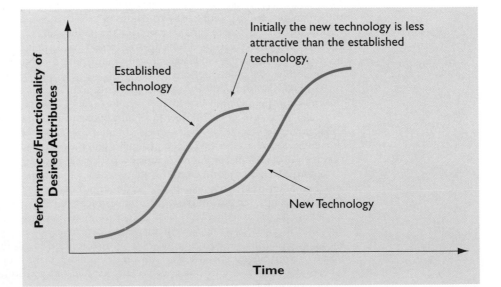

by focusing on the needs of farmers, a niche that the incumbent firms of the time generally ignored. Similarly, Microsoft got its start in 1975 by writing computer-programming software for hobbyists to run on the early personal computers, which again was a market of no interest to dominant enterprises of the mainframe era such as IBM. However, as the functionality of a technology improves over time, its performance attributes improve, its applications broaden, and it begins to attract the attention of the customer set that originally ignored it. Thus, by the 1960s general contractors were suddenly expressing interest in hydraulic excavators, and by the early 1990s chief information officers had as their major priority the establishment of companywide computer networks based on the personal computer and servers that used PC technology. At this point, it is the new entrants that are best positioned to serve the needs of this long-established customer set, not the old incumbents that failed to invest in the new technology.

Christensen takes this argument one step further, however. He notes that a new network of suppliers and distributors—a new value chain—typically grows up around the new entrants. Just as incumbent firms often initially ignore disruptive technology, so do their suppliers and distributors. This creates an opportunity for new suppliers and distributors to enter the market to serve the new entrants. As the new entrants grow, so does the associated network. Ultimately, Christensen suggests, the new entrants and their network may replace not only established enterprises, but also the entire value chain associated with incumbent enterprises. So, for example, as the PC grew in importance in the computer industry, not only did the primary PC manufacturers grow with the market; so did their network of component part suppliers, distributors, and providers of complementary products such as application software, printers, and modems. Taken to its logical extreme, this view suggests that disruptive technologies may result in the demise of the entire industry value chain associated with incumbent enterprises and the emergence of a new value chain associated with the new entrants.

Strategic Implications for Incumbents   What are the strategic implications of this story for incumbents? First, it is important to recognize that while Christensen has uncovered an important tendency, it is by no means written in stone that all incumbents are doomed to fail when faced with disruptive technologies. After all, although IBM was the dominant firm in the pre-PC era, it was also one of the early movers in the PC market. True, despite its entry into the PC marketplace, IBM remained focused on mainframes, and true, as Christensen's arguments would lead us to expect, the company went through several years of severe financial turmoil. However, IBM was able to cross the abyss created by the emergence of the PC and today has reinvented itself as a provider of e-business software, hardware, and consulting services.

If incumbents are not doomed to failure, what can they do to meet the challenges created by the emergence of disruptive technologies? First, knowledge about how disruptive technologies can revolutionize markets is itself a valuable strategic asset. Many of the incumbents Christensen examined failed because they took a myopic view of the new technology and because they asked their customers the wrong question. Instead of asking, "Are you interested in this new technology?" they should have recognized that the new technology was likely to improve rapidly over time and asked their customers, "Would you be interested in this new technology if it improves its functionality over time?" If they had done this, they might have made very different strategic decisions.

Second, following on from this, it is clearly important for incumbent enterprises to invest in newly emerging technologies that may ultimately become disruptive technologies. Companies have to hedge their bets about new technology. At any given point in time, there may be a swarm of emerging technologies, any one of which might ultimately become a disruptive technology (see Figure 3). Large incumbent companies that are generating significant cash flows can, and often should, establish and fund central R&D operations to invest in and develop such technologies. In addition, they may wish to acquire newly emerging companies that are pioneering potentially disruptive technologies. Cisco Systems, a dominant provider of Internet network equipment, is famous for pursuing this strategy. At the heart of this strategy must lie a recognition by the incumbent enterprise that it is better for the company to develop a disruptive technology, and then cannibalize its established sales base, than to have that sales base taken away by new entrants.

However, Christensen makes the very valid point that even when incumbents do undertake R&D investments in potentially disruptive technologies, they often fail to commercialize

FIGURE 3:

New Technology Swarms

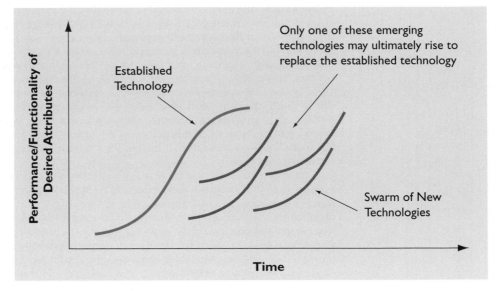

those technologies because of internal inertia forces. Christensen argues that in many cases, because the new technology initially promises only incremental revenues, when internal capital resources are constrained, R&D investments aimed at developing the new technology are limited by a lack of capital. While the company may intend to invest in the new technology, in practice those parts of the business that are currently generating the most cash may also claim that they need the greatest R&D investment to maintain their market position. Particularly early on in the development of a new technology, when it is very unclear what its long-term prospects may be, this can be a powerful argument. The consequence, however, may be that the incumbent fails to build a sufficient competence in the new technology and, if and when the technology emerges as a disruptive technology, the incumbent is successfully challenged by new entrants.

In addition, Christensen states that the commercialization of a new disruptive technology typically requires a radically different value chain with a completely different cost structure. In effect, he is saying that a new disruptive technology requires a new business model. It may require a different manufacturing system, and a different distribution system, a different price structure, and involve very different gross margins and operating margins. Christensen argues that it is almost impossible for two distinct business models to co-exist within the same organization. When companies try to do that, almost inevitably the established business model will suffocate the business model associated with the disruptive technology.

The solution to this problem: Separate out the disruptive technology and place it in its own autonomous operating division. For example, during the early 1980s, Hewlett-Packard (HP) built a very successful laser jet printer business. Then along came ink jet technology. Some in the company believed that ink jet printers would cannibalize sales of laser jets, and consequently argued that HP should not produce ink jets. Fortunately for HP, senior management at the time saw ink jet technology for what it was—a potentially disruptive technology. Far from not investing in this technology, they allocated significant R&D funds toward the commercialization of ink jets. Furthermore, when the technology was ready for market introduction, they established an autonomous ink jet division at a different geographical location with its own manufacturing, marketing, and distribution activities. They accepted that the ink jets division might take sales away from the laser jet division. They decided that it was better to have an HP division cannibalize the sales of another HP division than have those sales cannibalized by another company. Happily for HP, it turns out that ink jets cannibalize only sales of laser jets on the margin, and both have profitable market niches. This happy outcome, however, does not detract from the message of the story: If your company is developing a potentially disruptive technology, the chances of success will be enhanced if it is placed in a stand-alone product division and given its own mandate.

Strategic Implications for New Entrants   This stream of work also holds implications for new entrants. The new entrants, or attackers, have several advantages over incumbent enterprises. Internal inertia forces do not hamstring the new entrants. They do not have to worry about product cannibalization issues. They do not have to worry about their established customer base or existing value network. Instead, they can focus like a laser beam on the opportunities offered by the new disruptive technology, ride the S-curve of technology improvement, and grow rapidly with the market for that technology. But this does not mean the new entrants are without problems. They may be constrained by a lack of capital; they have to manage the organizational problems associated with rapid growth; and, perhaps most important, they need to find a way to take their technology from an out-of-the-way niche into the mass market.

Geoffrey Moore has referred to this problem as one of *crossing the chasm*.[3] Moore's point is that a chasm exists between the resources and capabilities required to succeed in a small, emerging market, where disruptive technologies typically take root, and the resources and capabilities required to succeed in the mass market that disruptive technologies invade once they start to mature. A major reason for this is that customers in the mass market are very different from the early adopters typically found in small, emerging markets. They have different needs, look for different things in the product, are often reached by different distribution channels, require different selling techniques and different marketing messages, and demand a different level of after-sales service and support. Again, a good example of this is the development of the market for personal computers. MITS, Southwest Technical Products, Digital Microsystems, and IMSAI dominated the early market for personal computers.[4] If you haven't heard of these companies, that is not surprising. All of them failed to cross the chasm to the mass market and instead went out of business. The reason is that they all produced personal computers that were designed to be used by individuals who could write programming languages. The mass market wanted personal computers that were easy to use, and the early personal computers were anything but that. It was left to Apple Computer to cross the chasm and market the first personal computer designed for the nontechnical user, the Apple II. Subsequently, Compaq, Dell Computer Corporation, and IBM, all of which focused on the mass business and consumer market, dominated the industry.

The message here is that if they are to succeed, new entrants need to focus not just on the niche where the disruptive technology first takes root, but also on the needs of the future mass market. Geoffrey Moore recommends that new entrants try to identify "beachheads" into the mass market. For example, Apple's beachhead into the mass market for personal computers was the educational market, where many of the first adopters of user-friendly personal computers were to be found. At the same time, new entrants need to be careful not to become locked into that beachhead. Again, Apple became so attuned to the needs of the educational market that it failed to build the resources and capabilities—such as a direct corporate sales force—required to succeed in the mass business market. New entrants, therefore, need to pay great attention to the resources and capabilities they are building, and must make sure they are able to serve the needs not only of small, out-of-the-way niches, but also of the emerging mass market. Paradoxically, just as incumbents may be hamstrung by internal inertia forces, so may new entrants be handicapped if they focus myopically on the very early adopters of their technology and fail to recognize the different needs of the mass market as it emerges.

■ Strategic Flexibility and Real Options

In Chapter 1 of this book, we note that one reason strategic planning often fails to deliver good results is that the real world is characterized by significant uncertainty and complexity. The future, by definition, cannot be known; it can only be guessed at; and even the best-laid strategic plans can run aground on the rocks of unforeseen changes in industry conditions. Uncertainty about the future is always there; it cannot be eradicated. One main source of uncertainty in the modern world, of course, is the rapid rate of technological progress. As should be clear from the last section, rapid technological change can give rise to disruptive technologies that revolutionize industry structure and threaten the very existence of incumbent enterprises. Other common sources of uncertainty are unanticipated moves by competitors, changing political conditions, changing regulatory regimes, or unanticipated macroeconomic shocks, such as the 1997–1998 Asian currency crises and the 2000 oil price shock. The question we will explore in this section is: What can companies do to manage uncertainty and improve their odds of pursuing viable strategies? As we will see, a technique called *real options* can be used to help manage uncertainty.[5]

Uncertainty, Commitments, and Opportunity Costs   Uncertainty significantly complicates the process of strategic decision making. The essence of the problem is that pursuing a course of action—a strategy—may require significant *irreversible* commitments, both financial and nonfinancial, before the uncertainty is resolved or reduced to acceptable levels. For example, Airbus is currently evaluating whether to build a super-jumbo jet, the A3XX.[6] If built, this aircraft, the largest commercial jet ever, will carry between 550 and 650 people and compete against Boeing's 747, which can carry a maximum of 520 people. The plane will cost $12 billion to develop. To generate a decent economic return, Airbus will have to sell some 600 A3XX planes by 2020. Airbus estimates worldwide demand for aircraft of more than 400 seats to be 1,200 between 2000 and 2020. On the basis of this estimate, it believes it can sell at least 600 A3XXs. Boeing estimates total worldwide demand for aircraft of more than 400 seats to be about 400 over the same period. Clearly there is a significant difference between the two estimates of market size. This difference is due to uncertainties about a number of variables, including future economic growth rates, fuel prices, and future travel patterns. Boeing assumes that in the future, more people will fly point to point, which reduces demand for very large aircraft; Airbus assumes that a significant number of flights will still be routed through hubs, which increases demand for very large aircraft.

It is also worth noting that Airbus is currently slated to receive $4 billion in European Union subsidies to help build the A3XX. Uncertainties exist here too. The legality of the subsidies may be challenged by the United States at the World Trade Organization. If the subsidies are reduced, Airbus will have to sell significantly more aircraft to make a profit, making the future of the subsidies another source of uncertainty.

At this point in time, these various uncertainties are irreducible. It will be several years before we know whether Boeing or Airbus is right. Thus, Airbus faces the prospect of making a major irreversible commitment now—one that totals $12 billion—long before it knows whether its assumptions are correct! If Airbus is right, the current managers will no doubt be lauded twenty years from now for betting the farm on the A3XX, just as Boeing management is now lauded for betting the company on the 747 in the 1960s. But if Airbus is wrong, the consequence could be financially disastrous. And sometimes companies are wrong.

In the early 1990s, Motorola made a similar bet in the face of uncertainty when it launched the Iridium project.[7] Billed as the world's first global wireless telephone service, Iridium was based on a network of seventy-seven satellites placed in low earth orbit. Motorola believed that the service could be sold to globetrotting business executives. Equipped with a suitable satellite telephone, they would be able to place and receive calls anywhere in the world, whether in the heart of New York City or deep in the Amazon jungle. In November 1998, Iridium switched on the service. By this time, the Iridium project had consumed $5.5 billion in investment and Iridium itself had been spun out of Motorola as an independent company in which Motorola held an 18 percent stake. Iridium's business plan called for 100,000 customers to be signed on by the end of 1998 and 500,000 by late 1999. However, customers were scarce from the outset. By the summer of 1999, Iridium had only 20,000 customers, well short of the half-million it needed to break even. On August 17 1999, Iridium filed for Chapter 11 bankruptcy protection after it defaulted on scheduled payments for $3 billion in bank loans and bonds.

Why did Iridium fail? One problem was that unlike wireless phones, Iridium phones did not work well among high buildings. Another problem was the design of the telephones themselves. The Iridium phones were cumbersome and difficult to use, and came with several attachments whose functions were not immediately obvious. The comparison with miniature wireless phones was not favorable. Then there was the cost of the service. The phones went for $3,000 apiece, and call time was billed at $4 to $9 per minute. Again, the comparison with wireless phones was unfavorable. Most important, in the decade since Iridium was originally conceived, wireless phones had become an attractive, inexpensive, and ubiquitous alternative technology. By 1999, wireless phone service was available in more than 60 countries and there were 300 million cell phone users worldwide. Why did anyone need a cumbersome, expensive, and inefficient Iridium phone when a wireless phone would suffice? As it turned out, nobody did.

As these two examples illustrate, future uncertainties about technology, demand conditions, and the like can scuttle expensive strategic initiatives. Worse still, one must consider the opportunities that a company must forgo once it makes an irreversible commitment to a course of action. Any strategy has associated opportunity costs. If Airbus does decide to invest $12 billion in the A3XX, the investment will obviously limit the firm's ability to pursue other projects. Similarly, Motorola's investment in Iridium limited its ability to invest in other technologies. In a world of limited resources, whenever a company pursues one course of action, it constrains or shuts off other possible courses of action; that is the opportunity cost. Yet, faced with uncertainty, it may be impossible to know which course of action will ultimately turn out to be the best.

Look again at Figure 3, and what do you see? A swarm of emerging technologies. It is quite possible that only one of these technologies will succeed and replace the dominant technology in the industry. This places a company deciding which technology to pursue in a difficult conundrum: In which of the four technologies shown in Figure 3 should it invest? There is no easy answer. At the time the decision must be made, the fog of uncertainty inevitably clouds the decision. So is there a way out of such a conundrum? Is there a way that Airbus can reduce the uncertainty associated with investing in the A3XX? Is there a way that Motorola might have reduced the uncertainty it confronted in 1991 when it initiated the Iridium project? Well, uncertainty cannot be eliminated, but it can be managed. Real options are a tool for managing uncertainty and reducing opportunity costs, thereby maintaining strategic flexibility.

Real Options   In financial terms, an **option** is simply the right to purchase an asset at some future date and at a predetermined price. The most familiar use of options is in stock options. For example, imagine the current price of Microsoft stock is $60 a share. Suppose I want to buy 1,000 shares of Microsoft, but I won't have the $60,000 in cash for three months until I receive my royalties from the sale of this book. Imagine also that I think the price of Microsoft stock will be a lot higher in three months; in fact, I think it might be trading at $100 a share in three months. Ideally, I'd like to lock in today's low price and then pay for the stock in three months when I get my next book royalty check. Can I do that? Yes! All I have to do is purchase an option to buy 1,000 shares of Microsoft at $60 a share in three months. Of course, I will have to pay for this option. Let's say it costs $6 a share for a total of $6,000. So it will cost me $66 a share to buy the 1,000 shares in three months, for a grand total of $66,000. If I'm correct about the stock going up to $100, this is a great deal. In effect, it will cost me $66,000 to purchase something worth $100,000.

Of course, the world is full of uncertainties, and I might be wrong. The stock might go a lot higher, in which case I will look really smart! But it could also go a lot lower. Let's say it goes to $30 a share. What then? Do I still have to buy the stock? No, I don't! And here is the important point: *The option gives me the right, but not the obligation, to buy the stock.* Obviously, if the stock falls, I will have lost the $6,000 I paid for the options, but I won't have to pay $60 for a $30 stock. In effect, the purchase of the option allows me to participate in the upside potential of the stock while limiting my downside risk to the cost of the option. The option buys me time—in this case, three months—before I have to make a purchase decision. With time comes flexibility, for if things don't turn out the way I planned due to some uncertain event that would have been hard to predict, I can put my $60,000 elsewhere. If Microsoft stock declines, I don't have to buy it. Or perhaps I can find a better use for my $60,000 in three months, in which case, even if Microsoft goes up somewhat, I may still not want to buy the stock, but instead invest the $60,000 in another company. The option allows me to wait for more information before making my investment decision. It gives me time during which some of the key uncertainties surrounding the future of the company may be resolved due to the unfolding of events. It puts off for three months the opportunity cost associated with sinking $60,000 into Microsoft, as opposed to some other, possibly better investment. The option allows me to keep my options open! It gives me flexibility. Of course, I have to pay for this luxury, but few things in life are free.

Real Options and Strategy   So what has all of this to do with strategy? As it turns out, quite a lot. The principal reason is that many strategic investment decisions have characteristics that are similar to an investment in a financial asset, such as a stock, and it might pay to take an options approach toward such a strategic investment.[8] To illustrate this issue, let's consider a pharmaceutical company such as Merck. Let's imagine that Merck has identified a small biotechnology company, BioHope, that is developing a promising drug that might eventually be used to cure Alzheimer's disease. The drug, which is given the name Recall, is just entering phase I clinical trials in human patients. (There are three phases in human clinical trials: phase I, II, and III. Each subsequent phase is bigger and more expensive to undertake. A drug must show beneficial effects in a phase III trial and a favorable safety profile for the Food and Drug Administration to approve its sale.)

Alzheimer's disease is a terrible affliction with no known cure. A treatment for Alzheimer's disease would probably generate sales of several billion dollars a year and profits approaching $1 billion. Merck knows it can purchase BioHope for $600 million. Sounds like a bargain, right? Well, hang on a minute. First, we need to ask: What are the unknowns here? It turns out there are several huge uncertainties. For one thing, history tells us that only one in ten drugs that enters human clinical trials actually makes it through the clinical process and is approved by the Food and Drug Administration (FDA) and marketed (this is the true figure). The hard fact is that when tested in humans, most promising drugs turn out to either not work very well or have nasty side effects. So there is a 90 percent chance that Recall may never see the light of day. Moreover, history also tells us that on average, taking a drug from early clinical trials to market approval can take ten years and cost $500 million in investment (these figures are true too).

Now let's rethink this decision. If Merck purchases BioHope for $600 million, it will then have to pay another $500 million to take the drug through clinical trials and the FDA approval process, and the probability that Recall will actually work is only about 10 percent! Suddenly this does not seem like such a great investment. Paying $1.1 billion and waiting ten years to get a 10 percent chance of something paying off doesn't look like very good odds. Of course, the $500 million will be spread out over ten years, but even so, the total investment is large. Also, we have to think about the opportunity cost here. What else might Merck have done with that $1.1 billion while waiting to see if Recall actually works? Ten years is a long time; all sorts of other opportunities might arise. Does Merck really want to sink $1.1 billion into Recall? That's one heck of an opportunity cost to bear! But wait a minute—let's not forget the upside here. Recall may not work—in fact, it probably won't if history is any guide—but if it does, this will be a huge financial boon to Merck worth billions of dollars. Can we afford to pass on this investment?

At this point, the smart people at Merck are probably asking themselves if there is a better way to deal with this problem. The answer is that there is: real options. In reality, under the leadership of its CFO, Judy Lewent, Merck was one of the very first companies to apply a real options perspective to evaluate decisions like this.[9] The people at Merck realized that investment decisions such as the one about BioHope have characteristics that are analogous to those of straight financial options, such as stock options. Specifically, the upside potential is large, the uncertainties are significant, and making an irreversible commitment to this venture today involves significant opportunity costs. In such cases, rather than making an irreversible commitment today, the company might try to structure a series of sequential investments over time that allow it to participate in the potential upside while minimizing short-term commitments. The idea is to gain more information, thereby reducing uncertainty, and make subsequent investment decisions on the basis of that information.

So here is what Merck could do with BioHope. Rather than purchase BioHope outright, Merck might go to the company and offer an options contract. This contract might be structured as follows. Merck commits to paying $10 million up front to BioHope and a further $290 million in milestone payments spread out over ten years. Then, Merck requests the exclusive right to manufacture, market, and sell Recall if the FDA approves the drug and commit to paying a 20 percent royalty on all sales of Recall to BioHope. The milestone payments might be associated with major events such as the successful completion of phase II clinical trials, the initiation of phase III trials, the successful completion of phase III trials, filing a new-drug application with the FDA, and marketing approval for Recall by the FDA. The milestone payments will get larger as Recall moves through this process and gets closer to the market—that is, as the uncertainty about the eventual outcome is reduced. Merck will reserve the right to terminate the contract if Recall does not successfully pass through any of these milestones (that is, if it fails to show efficacy in one of the trials).

This is an option contract because Merck has to invest only a relatively small amount (initially just $10 million) to get the right to participate in the upside for Recall while hedging against the uncertainty associated with the drug's development. The downside risk is limited to the size of the milestone (option) payments made at any one point in time. Because the contract is structured as an option contract, Merck is able to wait for more information before deciding whether to invest more, thereby maintaining Merck's strategic flexibility and allowing the company to pursue other ventures in the future if a more attractive opportunity comes along. In fact, because Merck does not have to invest too much initially in this venture, it can better leverage its available R&D resources, investing them in a number of different biotech companies that are pursuing different product opportunities.

Of course, just as with a financial option contract, there is a price to be paid here. In this example, Merck will ultimately bear three-fifths of all development costs for Recall, incur all manufacturing, sales, and marketing costs, and be required to pay a 20 percent royalty to BioHope on sales of Recall. Despite these costs, the deal still will bear major benefits for Merck if Recall ultimately makes it to market. The contract also represents a good deal for BioHope, since Merck picks up the majority of the development costs and all the manufacturing, sales, and marketing costs while still giving BioHope a substantial share in the potential upside from Recall.

Although beyond the scope of this book, it should be noted that in practice, sophisticated financial models can be and are used to work out a fair value for real options contracts such as our example.[10] What is important to note here is that a real options perspective can lead management to structure their strategic decisions and investments in a very different way. The perspective forces management to think about the uncertainties associated with a strategic investment (which is always a useful exercise), focuses attention on the opportunity costs of pursuing a strategy, places a premium on gathering more information to reduce uncertainty, and encourages managers to think of different ways to structure strategic investments so that additional commitments are made only after new information reduces uncertainty. Thus, a real options perspective encourages Merck to think about alternatives to purchasing BioHope outright. In fact, like Merck, many pharmaceutical companies now use a real options perspective to structure their investments in biotechnology firms, which helps explain why strategic alliances are so prevalent in this sector of the economy. Many of these "alliances" are based on option contracts that have as their central element a mix of upfront payments and successive milestone payments that are made only if additional information shows that further investment may bear fruit.

Nor is this approach confined to the pharmaceutical and biotechnology sectors of the industry. It is in fact being used by an increasing number of companies in a wide variety of sectors, from oil drilling to computer software. For example, Microsoft now trains all of its financial analysts in real options techniques. To return to the earlier examples of Airbus and Motorola, both of these companies have taken an options perspective. Airbus, for example, will not commit to building the A3XX until it has sixty firm orders for the aircraft. In other words, so far Airbus has only taken an option on producing the A3XX. The cost of that option is the price of all the development work done to date, which runs to about $1 billion. Airbus will commit to spending the other $11 billion only if it gets additional information—in the form of sixty orders—that reduces some of the uncertainties associated with the project. Similarly, Motorola reduced the costs associated with Iridium by spinning out the venture as an independent entity in which Motorola held an 18 percent stake and other investors held the rest. This strategy allowed Motorola to participate in the potential upside associated with Iridium while hedging against the downside risk, which turned out to be substantial.

One final point worth emphasizing here is that a real options perspective encourages companies to not shut down potential investment opportunities too early. It encourages companies to keep their options open until they can collect more information and resolve the uncertainty. Thus, if you look one more time at Figure 3, you will see that four alternative technologies are depicted as vying to replace the established technology. What if only one of these technologies ultimately wins out while the remainder fall by the wayside? A real options perspective would tell us that due to uncertainty, we cannot know early in the game which technology will win out. Therefore, we should try to buy an option on each technology, winnowing down the options only when more information becomes available. What we should not do, according to this perspective, is commit entirely to a single technology too early in the game. Doing so involves a double jeopardy, for not only might our choice be wrong, but by committing to one technology we risk failing to build a capability in the other emerging technologies that might ultimately win. We may be at a distinct disadvantage if our preferred choice fails to come through. Thus, at its core, a real options perspective is about how best to hedge bets among alternative courses of action when confronted with substantial uncertainty about the future. This makes it a very useful technique for evaluating real-world strategic decisions.

Competitive Strategy in Format Wars

As noted earlier, a *format war* occurs when two or more competing and incompatible technological formats vie for market acceptance and different companies back different technologies. Format wars are becoming increasingly common in technology-driven industries where technological standards (that is, formats) are required to ensure a product works seamlessly with its complements. This is the case in the personal computer industry, where it is important for a computer to work well with complements such as software, printers, and modems. In the PC industry, we currently have two formats: a dominant one based on an Intel microprocessor and a Windows operating system, which accounts for about 90 percent of the installed base (the so-called "Wintel" standard or format), and a niche format based on the Macintosh operating system, which accounts for much of the remainder. As most people realize, the two formats are incompatible: Software written for the Mac will not run on a Windows machine, and vice versa. We see the same phenomenon in the video game industry, where games for the Sony PlayStation will not run on a Nintendo game player (again, vice versa). Similarly, a wireless telephone that works in one region of the country may not work in another because of different technological standards.

In Chapter 3 of this book, we explored the topic of network economics. There we noted that in industries where standards are required to ensure that a product works well with its complements, positive feedback loops tend to operate. Specifically, the greater the installed base of a format (such as Wintel PCs), the greater the supply of complementary products, such as application software to run on that format, and the greater the value of that format to consumers, which tends to reinforce demand for the format. Thus, demand begets further demand (see Figure 3.7 in Chapter 3 and the related discussion for further details). Such positive feedback loops reinforce the dominance of the format with the greater installed base and can lead to concentrated market structures. Many argue that it is because of the positive feedback loop at work in the personal computer industry that Microsoft and Intel currently enjoy dominant positions in the markets for PC software and microprocessors, respectively.

More generally, in industries where standards are important and positive feedback loops operate, the market will often "lock in" to a single format or a limited number of formats. If a single company owns the technological format or key aspects of the format, as Microsoft does with the Windows operating system, that company alone can achieve market dominance. In other cases, several companies may jointly develop the format. This occurred with DVD players: Several companies collaborated in an industry association called the DVD Forum to establish a technological standard for DVD equipment.

Winning a Format War   From the perspective of a company pioneering a new technological format in a marketplace where positive feedback loops operate, the key question becomes "What strategy should we pursue to establish our format as the dominant one?" Potential competitors to the Wintel standard in computers, such as companies producing PCs and computer servers based on the Linux operating system, must grapple with this question. So must video game producers when they introduce a new format, such as Sony with the PlayStation II, Sega with the Dreamcast, and Microsoft with its X Box. Telecommunications equipment companies have to grapple with this issue when deciding to promote a certain format, such as Qualcomm, which is trying to get a technological format it developed, CDMA, adopted as a global standard for next-generation wireless telephones. Companies selling hand-held computers must grapple with this question; Palm, for example, is trying to establish its Palm operating system for hand-held computers, like the popular Palm series, as the dominant global format against stiff competition from Microsoft with its rival Windows CE format.

At the core, winning a format war requires a company to build the installed base for its format as rapidly as possible, thereby leveraging the positive feedback loop and locking customers into its design. Put differently, it requires the company to somehow jump-start and then accelerate demand for its format to establish it as the industry standard quickly as possible, thereby locking out competing formats. How can a company do this? A number of key strategies and tactics can be adopted to try to achieve this.[11]

Ensure a Supply of Complements   It is important for the company to make sure that in addition to the product itself, there is an adequate supply of complements. For example, no one will buy the Sony PlayStation II unless there is an adequate supply of games to run on that machine. Similarly, no one will purchase a Palm VII hand-held computer unless there are enough software applications to run on the Palm VII. Companies normally take two steps to ensure an adequate supply of complements.

First, they may diversify into the production of complements and seed the market with sufficient supply to help jump-start demand for their format. For example, before Sony produced the original PlayStation in the early 1990s, it established its own in-house unit to produce video games for the PlayStation. Then, when it launched the PlayStation, Sony also simultaneously issued sixteen games to run on the machine, giving consumers a reason to purchase the format.

Second, companies may create incentives or make it easy for independent companies to produce complements. Again, consider Sony's tactics with the original PlayStation. Sony licensed the right to produce games to a number of independent game developers, charged game developers a lower royalty than they had to pay to competitors such as Nintendo and Sega, and provided developers with software tools that made it easier for them to develop the games. Thus, the launch of the Sony PlayStation was accompanied by the simultaneous launch of thirty or so games, which quickly helped to stimulate demand for the machine.

Aggressive Pricing and Marketing   A common tactic is to adopt a razor-and-razor-blades pricing strategy. This involves pricing the product low to stimulate demand and grow installed base, and then trying to make large profits on the sale of complements, which are priced relatively high. For example, consider Hewlett-Packard's popular ink jet printers. To operate these printers, you must use Hewlett-Packard's ink jet cartridges. Hewlett-Packard typically sells its printers at cost, but it makes significant unit profits on the subsequent sale of replacement cartridges. In this case, the printer is the "razor," which is priced low to stimulate demand, while the cartridges are the "blades," which are priced high to make profits. It is important to realize that the ink jet printer represents a proprietary technological format because only Hewlett-Packard cartridges can be used with the printers and not cartridges designed for competing ink jet printers, such as those sold by Canon. A similar strategy is used in the video game industry, where manufacturers price video game consoles at cost, making profits on the royalties they receive from the sales of games that run on their systems.

With regard to marketing, again the trick is to try to jump-start demand to get an early lead in installed base. Substantial upfront marketing and point-of-sales promotion techniques are often used to try to get potential early adopters to buy a format and set the ball rolling with regard to a positive feedback loop. Again, the Sony PlayStation provides a good example, for Sony co-linked the introduction of the PlayStation with nationwide television advertising aimed at its primary demographic (eighteen- to thirty-four-year-olds) and in-store displays that allowed potential buyers to play games on the machine before making a purchase.

Cooperation with Competitors   In several cases, a number of companies have come close to simultaneously introducing competing and incompatible technological formats. A good example is the compact disk. Initially three companies—Sony, Philips, and Telefunken—were developing CD players using different variations of the underlying laser technology. If this situation had persisted, the three companies might have ultimately introduced incompatible technologies into the marketplace. In such a scenario, a CD made for a Philips CD player would not play on a Sony CD player. The near simultaneous introduction of such incompatible technologies can create significant confusion among consumers, and often leads them to delay their purchases. When this happens, the technologies may not take in the marketplace. Recognizing this problem, Sony and Philips decided to join forces and cooperate on development of the technology. Sony contributed its error correction technology, while Philips contributed its laser technology. The result of this cooperation was that momentum among other players in the industry value chain shifted toward the Sony/Philips alliances, and Telefunken was left with little support. Most important, record labels announced that they would support the Sony/Philips format but not the Telefunken format. Telefunken subsequently decided to abandon its efforts to develop CD technology. The cooperation was important because it reduced confusion in the industry and allowed a single format to rise to the fore, which in turn reduced confusion among consumers and speeded up adoption of the technology. The cooperation was a win-win for both Philips and Sony, which eliminated the third competitor (Telefunken) and were able to share in the success of the format.

Licensing of the Format   Another often-adopted strategy is to license the format to other enterprises so that they can produce products based on the format. The company that pioneered the format gains from the licensing fees that flow back to it and from the enlarged supply of the product, which in turn can stimulate demand and help accelerate market adoption. This was the strategy that Matsushita adopted with its VHS format for the videocassette recorder. In addition to producing VCRs at its own factory in Osaka, Matsushita let a number of other companies produce VHS format players under license. In direct contrast, Sony decided not to license its competing Betamax format, and produced all Betamax format players itself. One effect of this very different strategy was that VHS players became more widely available. This meant that more people purchased VHS players, which created an incentive for film companies to issue more films on VHS tapes (as opposed to Betamax tapes), which in turn further increased demand for VHS players and hence helped Matsushita to lock in VHS as the dominant format in the marketplace. Meanwhile, Sony, which ironically was first to market, saw its position marginalized by the reduced supply of the critical complement, prerecorded films, and ultimately withdrew Betamax players from the consumer marketplace.

Summary   In summary, the correct strategy to pursue in a particular scenario requires that the company consider all of these different strategies and tactics, and pursue those that seem most appropriate given the competitive circumstances prevailing in the industry. While there is no one best mix of strategies and tactics to pursue, it is critical for the company to keep the goal of rapidly growing installed base at the front of its mind. What matters is that the company pick strategies that help to jump-start demand for its format and leverage any positive feedback process that may exist. It is also important for the company not to pursue strategies that have the opposite effect. For example, pricing high to capture profits from early adopters, who tend to be less price sensitive than later adopters, can have the unfortunate effect of slowing down demand growth and letting a more aggressive competitor pick up share and establish its format as the dominant design.

■ Strategy and Information Technology (IT)

While we have discussed the effects of new information technology on organizations in many of our book's chapters, the rate at which changes in information systems and technologies are affecting organizational strategy and structure deserves more consideration. Total spending on computers and related services doubled from approximately $80 billion in 1984 to more than $160 billion in 1998, and continues to soar. Much of the increase in corporate profits and soaring stock prices in the 1990s has been attributed to its effects.[12] Information systems include many varieties of software platforms and databases. These encompass enterprisewide systems designed to manage all major functions of the organization, provided by companies such as SAP, PeopleSoft, JD Edwards, and so on, to more general-purpose database products targeted toward specific uses, such as the products offered by Oracle, Microsoft, and many others. Information technologies encompass a broad array of communication media and devices that link information systems and people, including voice mail, e-mail, voice conferencing, videoconferencing, the Internet, groupware and corporate intranets, car phones, fax machines, personal digital assistants, and so on. Information systems and information technologies are often inextricably linked and, since it has become conventional to do so, for the rest of this update we will refer to them jointly as information technology (IT).

Information technology affects all aspects of an organization's competitive strategy. First, IT is instrumental in both shaping core capabilities and integrating capabilities into the organization context, making them apparent at all organizational levels. Moreover, IT capabilities can be difficult to imitate since they are present not just in physical information systems but in the organization-specific information technologies developed inside the organization over time. Hence, Wal-Mart's ability to protect what it regards as a core competency in IT by legally blocking the movement of some of its key programmers to dot.coms like Amazon.com.

Second, competitive strategy and the ability to pursue a low-cost and/or differentiation strategy ultimately depends on a firm's ability to increase efficiency, quality, innovation, and customer responsiveness[13]—and IT has a major impact on these sources of competitive advantage. For example, one advantage of IT is knowledge leveraging, which involves sharing and integrating cross-functional expertise through appropriate forms of technology.[14] Benefits from knowledge leveraging include the development of synergies and delivery to customers of value-added services and products, which in turn may result in competitive advantage in the form of product or service differentiation. The way in which Citibank implemented an organizationwide IT to increase responsiveness to customers is instructive. In 2000, Citibank set its goal to be the premier global international financial company. Studying its business processes, it was clear that the main customer complaint was the amount of time customers had to wait for a response to their request, so Citibank set out to solve this problem. Teams of managers examined the way Citibank's current IT worked and then redesigned it to empower employees and reduce the "handoffs" between people and functions. Employees were then given extensive training in operating the new IT system. Citibank has been able to document significant time and cost savings as well as an increase in the level of personalized service it is able to offer its clients, which has led to a significant increase in the number of global customers.[15]

At the corporate level, IT, by reducing the bureaucratic costs associated with managing the relationships between corporate headquarters and divisions and among divisions, has allowed organizations to grow in the sense that the number of decision-making units has increased. IT also facilitates the sharing of knowledge and information not just inside divisions but also among divisions, which may lead to a broader product range for single-business firms and the ability to reap synergies or "product opportunities" for firms engaged in related diversification, such as AOL–Time Warner or Sony.

IT has very important effects on an organization's ability to innovate, an ability that is very important today, as discussed earlier. IT improves the base of knowledge that employees draw on when they engage in problem solving and decision making; it provides a mechanism to promote collaboration and information sharing both inside and across functions and divisions. However, knowledge or information availability alone will not lead to innovation; it is the ability to creatively use knowledge that is the key to promoting innovation and creating competitive advantage. Prahalad and Hamel, for example, suggest that it is not the absolute level of knowledge a firm possesses that leads to competitive advantage, but the speed with which it circulates in the firm.[16] IT produces information synergies and reallocates knowledge resources to the place where they can add the highest value to the organization.

Project-based work provides a vivid example of this process. As a project progresses, the need for particular team members waxes and wanes. Some employees will be part of a project from beginning to end, and others will be asked to participate only at key times when their expertise is required. IT provides management with the real-time capability to monitor project progress and needs and allocates knowledge resources accordingly in an effort to optimize the overall value added of each employee. Traditionally, product design has involved sequential processing across functions, with handoffs as each stage of the process is completed (see Chapter 4). This linear process is being replaced by parallel, concurrent engineering made possible through the application of IT, allowing employees to work simultaneously with continual interaction through electronic communication, which can promote innovation.

At the level of organizational structure, IT is changing organizational forms and promoting innovation inside virtual organizational forms. The real power of IT-enabled virtual organizations emerges when relationships among electronically connected people or firms produce new and/or qualitatively different communication that yields product or process innovation. For example, one type of IT-enabled interorganizational relationship noted by Venkatraman is knowledge leveraging, the sharing and integrating of expertise within a team or partnership through real-time, interconnected IT.[17] Some benefits from these arrangements include the development of cross-functional synergies that may result in competitive advantage in the form of product or service differentiation. Unlike more rigid bureaucratic organizational forms, new IT-enabled forms are viewed as more innovatively responsive to varied environmental pressures such as heightened market volatility or the globalization of business.

IT's effects on interorganizational relations such as joint ventures or strategic alliances is becoming an increasingly important topic given the promise that business-to-business networks hold for increasing organizational efficiency and innovation. For example, four categories of IT-enabled interorganizational relationships are transaction processing (such as EDI), inventory movement (use of IT to move materials or information about inventories across organizational boundaries), process links (connection of interdependent processes such as design and engineering across organizational boundaries), and knowledge leveraging (focuses on sharing and leveraging expertise within a partnership).[18] Similar to the situation inside an organization, one of the most obvious benefits from IT is the cost savings that stem from the ease with which information can be transmitted and utilized between organizations. Interorganizational electronic networks reduce the information costs associated with the search, evaluation, and monitoring of competing suppliers, often making strategic alliances more attractive than vertical integration. In addition, firms that use electronic networks not only reduce costs but, because they increase the pool of potential suppliers, reduce their exposure to opportunism.

It also affects strategic alliances in other ways. For instance, aside from electronically linking backward with suppliers, firms may use IT to link forward in the value chain to connect their operations with those of customers, which reduces their costs and creates a disincentive for customers to seek other suppliers. Increasingly, IT is being used in strategic alliances to break down barriers between industries and to link divergent value chains.[19] An additional perspective on how IT can enhance the effects of interorganizational relationships can be seen in how firms manage various structural parameters of partnerships. Also, specialization between organizations can be facilitated through IT that allows firms to transfer technical knowledge and other resource exchanges.[20]

A final important factor concerns the way IT is implemented in the strategy-making process. The appropriateness of the IT system chosen (and firms do make mistakes), the time needed to implement a technology, the supporting training and other learning processes that facilitate the technology, and so on affect IT's impact on efficiency and innovation. For example, an organization's ability to effectively train its work force to use a given IT will vary widely with its complexity, something many firms have failed to consider.

Thus, in conclusion, the implications of IT for strategy formulation and implementation are still evolving and will continue to do so as new software and hardware reshape competitive strategy. IT is changing the nature of value chain activities both inside and between organizations, affecting all four building blocks of competitive advantage—efficiency, quality, innovation, and responsiveness to customers.

CASE UPDATES

All of these case updates should be treated as an adjunct to the material contained in the original cases, not as stand-alone cases in their own right. They assume knowledge of the material discussed in the original cases.

■ Airborne Express (Case 20)

Founded in 1946, Airborne Express is currently the third largest air express delivery company in the U.S. As of March 2002, the company employs 22,527 people and delivers to almost any destination in the U.S. and more than 200 foreign countries.[1] Airborne Express has its own airport, located in Wilmington, Ohio, and a fleet of approximately 120 airplanes. In addition, about 60 airplanes are chartered for daily operations.[2] The company is known as the low-cost provider in the mail sector.[3]

During the last five years, the air cargo business has been subjected to several challenges and constraints. Nonetheless, 1997–1999 were excellent years for the industry. An overall growth of almost 12 percent in 1997 and about 9 percent in 1999 generated high earnings for air cargo carriers.[4] The year 1998 was Airborne Express's best ever. The company reported $137,285,000 in net earnings—the highest in the company's history. Airborne's success was reflected in a stock price high of about $40 at the beginning of 1999.[5]

1999   As mentioned previously, Airborne generated high revenues in 1999. However, due to a lack of domestic growth and rising fuel prices, the company was unable to achieve the

Airborne's Performance, 1997–2000[6]

	2000	1999	1998	1997
Operating results				
Revenues				
Domestic	$2,895,818	$2,772,782	$2,712,344	$2,514,737
International	380,132	366,342	361,440	397,672
Total	3,275,950	3,139,124	3,073,784	2,912,409
Net Earnings	28,492	91,201	137,285	120,072
Earnings per common share				
Basic	0.30	1.88	2.77	2.68
Diluted	0.30	1.85	2.72	2.44
Dividends per common share	0.16	0.16	0.16	0.15
Financial structure				
Property and equipment	$1,314,758	$1,115,712	$1,010,721	$ 901,303
Total assets	1,745,919	1,643,250	1,501,577	1,365,973
Long-term debt	322,230	314,707	249,149	250,559
Shareholder's equity	862,855	858,207	769,152	670,915
Number of shipments				
Domestic	322,493	316,391	316,590	297,032
International	6,558	7,038	6,451	5,699
Total	329,051	323,429	323,041	302,731

previous year's profitability.[7] With the growing acceptance of the Internet as a medium of communication, increasing numbers of people send documents by e-mail instead of express mail. This, among other factors, resulted in a stagnation of the domestic market.

At the same time, the rising number of households having Internet access had positive effects for Airborne and created new opportunities. The company entered the e-commerce world by creating airborne@home and forming an alliance with the U.S. Postal Service. This new service is especially designed for those firms that sell though catalogs. Packages are picked up by Airborne Express and transported to one of the approximately 22,000 delivery centers of the USPS. The Postal Service then delivers the packages to the customer. This new service is beneficial for both organizations. Airborne is able to take advantage of the established distribution network of the USPS, and the Postal Service gets additional business without investing in the development of new business segments.[8] The service was successfully tested during the second half of 1999 and established at the beginning of 2000.

The company's strategy of extension into new markets has likewise been successful. In cooperation with Airborne Logistics Services, a new center, Optical Village, was created near the company's airport in Wilmington. This center for optical devices allows eyeglass and contact lens manufacturers to reduce costs related to inventory and distribution. Companies all along the supply chain for eyeglass and contact lens production have established production facilities next to each other and are working closely together. Airborne Express serves as the primary shipper for Optical Village. Given that Airborne's airport is virtually "next door," companies are able to ship products faster, safer, and cheaper.[9]

During the last few years, Airborne Express was also successful in reducing its costs by improving the number of on-time arrivals of its airplanes. Compared to 1998, 5,000 more flights arrived on time in 1999.[10] The company continues its efforts to reduce delays as this is an efficient means of cost reduction. Additional improvements have been achieved in the mail sorting area, thus increasing the productivity of this process by 4 percent.[11] To increase overall operating efficiency, the company replaced several of its DC-8 planes with Boeing 767s acquired from Nippon Airlines. By buying passenger airplanes and converting them to cargo airplanes, the company is able to further reduce costs.[12]

2000   Overall, 2000 was a difficult year for the company. In order to stay competitive, Airborne Express had to add a fuel surcharge of 3 percent to its prices in April and an additional 1 percent in September. This was necessitated by significant increases in gasoline prices. Further stagnation in the company's core business, the domestic air cargo market, and a general economic recession negatively influenced the company's annual performance. Moreover, Airborne invested about $368 million to further increase and modernize its aircraft fleet and to acquire nine Boeing 767s.[13]

In order to attract additional business, Airborne began to concentrate more on small businesses and infrequent shippers. Traditionally, the company's focus had been primarily on large corporations. However, the Internet offers new possibilities to keep costs low in the small business and infrequent shipper sectors. The company also began plans to establish a small business center to better serve this market segment.[14]

The introduction of airborne@home at the beginning of the year was quite successful, and the company was able to gain additional market share in this sector. Furthermore, Airborne Express created a new product: Ground Delivery Service (GDS). This new door-to-door service was introduced primarily to extend and strengthen the company's ground shipping facilities and to further improve its services. In addition, the company put added emphasis on multi-service operations specifically designed for its customers. Due to strong long-term relationships with several large companies, Airborne is better able to custom-design its products. This was especially important for the development of new logistic solutions by Airborne Logistics. This division's service is designed to improve the performance of warehousing, inventory management, and distribution for its customers. It offers a complete menu of logistics and outsourcing options around the world.[15]

2001   The year 2001 was yet another difficult one for the industry. The overall economic situation was in a slump, and Airborne's business declined significantly. Although fuel prices had recovered, Airborne Express—along with other mail carriers—increased its shipping rates.[16] The attacks of September 11 caused an additional decline in the demand for air cargo services and an additional loss of business. The Federal Aviation Administration (FAA) grounded all commercial airplanes immediately after the attacks. Nonetheless, Airborne was able to keep most of its operations going by switching to ground transportation. Furthermore, the company, because it had its own airport, was able to resume its air transport business immediately after the FAA loosened restrictions.[17] Although the company was able to keep costs low, all these events resulted in severe losses. Accordingly, the company received compensation of $8.8 million from the U.S. government under the Air Transportation Safety and System Stabilization Act.[18]

Overall, the company's revenues dropped by 2 percent in 2001 after compensation for September 11 was included. Revenues from international operations declined by 5.2 percent. The domestic market's revenues fell by a comparatively small 1.6 percent.[19]

2002   The year 2002 will be another challenging one for Airborne Express, even though the economy is showing signs of improvement. The company's primary weakness is its ground distribution system, GDS. Airborne tried to improve its overall operations by the introduction of GDS. However, compared to its competitors, Airborne still delivers a high proportion of its mail by plane.[20] Another weakness is Airborne's international business. This declined significantly in 2001 in spite of investments the company made when it established new offices in Birmingham, England, and Amsterdam, Netherlands in 1999.[21] In addition, the company expects operational costs, especially insurance costs, to rise significantly.

According to AirCargo World Online, Airborne is currently negotiating with DHL Airways, the American division of DHL, about a possible purchase.[22] DHL's presence in the American market is rather weak, and the acquisition of a minority interest in Airborne Express could help the European-based company to gain further ground in the U.S. market.[23] Thus, it seems that the year 2002 will potentially be an important one for Airborne Express.

■ ATL Ultrasound, 2001 (Case 14)

ATL Ultrasound is one of the leading ultrasound equipment producers worldwide. The company was founded in 1969 and has its headquarters in Washington State. In 1998, ATL was the third largest company in the U.S. ultrasound market and number five worldwide.

Acquisition by Philips   In September 1998, Royal Philips Electrics, Netherlands, acquired ATL for $800 million.[24] This merger was seen as advantageous for both companies. By adding ATL's ultrasound equipment to its offerings, Philips Medical Systems, a division of Royal Philips Electronics, completed its medical imaging technique product line. The company is now able to offer high-quality products of all major four imaging techniques: x-ray diagnostics, magnet resonance, computed tomography, and ultrasound. If Philips was to become one of the global market leaders in diagnostic imaging systems, this acquisition was strategically important for the firm.

For ATL, the merger with Philips Medical Systems offered new possibilities in two areas: research and distribution. As one of the largest global electronic companies, Philips provided ATL with the necessary financial background and distribution network to serve a broader international market.

Although affiliated with Philips Medical Systems, ATL continues to operate under its own brand name. There are two major reasons for this. First, ATL has a reputation for high-quality products and innovative systems. Second, brand recognition and acceptance are especially important in the medical equipment market. ATL's major market remains the U.S. market. The company generates about 50 percent of its revenues in the U.S. The remaining 50 percent comes from sales to about 100 other countries.[25]

Because of the merger, the two companies have been able to achieve important synergistic effects in research and development. By combining experience and know-how, both firms have achieved significant product developments. For example, the launching of ATL's SonoCT in 2000 Real-time was a major step in the improvement of detection of fetal anomalies. Another breakthrough for the company occurred when the National Aeronautics and Space Administration (NASA) sent the company's HDI5000 ultrasound system to the International Space Station in March 2001. This equipment is helping NASA to gain important insight on how living without gravity affects organs and blood flow.

The collaborative efforts between Philips and ATL have brought about many innovations in the medical imaging market. And they have strengthened Philips Medical System's and ATL's positions in a highly competitive marketplace.

Royal Philips Electronics   Royal Philips Electronics is one of the world's largest electronics companies. It ranks ninth in the global electronics industry. Founded in 1891 by Gerard Philips, the company currently employs about 190,000 people worldwide. It has operating facilities in more than sixty countries and sells its products through an extensive net of worldwide distributors. Philips reported 32.1 billion Euro (about U.S.$30.2 billion) in sales for 2001.

The company's most important division is consumer electronics. Sales from this category accounted for 34 percent of the firm's revenues in 2001. Lighting is its second most important group. The medical systems division is Philips's third largest and generates 15 percent of the company's total sales.[26] The following table illustrates Philips's market position in its different business divisions.

Philips's Market Ranking, 2001[27]

	World	Europe
Lighting	1	1
Consumer electronics (audio/video)	3	2
Monitors (units)	3	2
Shavers	1	1
Steam irons	2	1
Semiconductors	11	4
Color picture tubes	2	1
Optical CD-R/RW drives and modules	1	1
Large LCD displays	1	1
Mobile LCD displays	1	1
Medical imaging equipment	3	2
Dental care (electric toothbrushes)	2	2

Philips Medical Systems is a division of Royal Philips Electronics and currently has about 19,000 employees (10 percent of the total number of employees of Royal Philips Electronics). Philips Medical Systems operates in over 100 countries. Through a large-scale acquisition strategy, Philips Medical Systems has been able to almost double its size over the past few years. Due to the acquisition of high-quality companies such as ATL in 1998 and Marconi Medical Systems in 2001, the medical division of Philips has become the market leader in many areas of medical imaging and patient monitoring systems.

■ Carnival Cruises, 2002 (Case 17)

In terms of passenger volume, Carnival Cruises is the largest cruising company worldwide. The company and its five subsidiaries currently operate forty-three ships, and an additional fourteen ships are under construction (see table). Three "fun ships" will begin operating in 2002 in America and Europe.[28]

Over the past few years, Carnival Cruises has continued its strategic expansion. In 1998, the company acquired 50 percent of Cunard Cruises, thus strengthening its market position in Europe.[29] With this acquisition, Carnival Cruises entertained more than 2 million passengers on its ships during 1998.[30] In addition, Carnival Cruises continued its innovative course and launched the MS *Paradise*, the world's first smoke-free cruising ship. On this vessel the company offers, among many other packages, cruises including seminars for people who would like to stop smoking.

The year 1998 was a successful one for Carnival Cruises. Its stock traded at more than $40 in July, and earnings per share rose from $1.12 in 1997 to $1.40.[31] However, the company faced several difficulties. Two powerful hurricanes hit the Caribbean, one of the com-

Ships Under Construction for Carnival and Subsidiaries[32]

Ship	Expected Service Date	Passenger Capacity	Estimated Total Cost (in millions)
Carnival			
Carnival *Legend*	8/02	2,124	$ 375
Carnival *Conquest*	12/02	2,974	500
Carnival *Glory*	8/03	2,974	500
Carnival *Miracle*	4/04	2,124	375
Carnival *Valor*	11/04	2,974	500
Total Carnival		15,294	2,625
Holland American			
Zuiderdam	12/02	1,848	$ 410
Oosterdam	7/03	1,848	410
Newbuild	5/04	1,848	410
Newbuild	11/05	1,848	410
Total Holland Amercia		7,392	1,640
Costa			
Costa *Mediterranea*	7/03	2,114	$ 335
Costa *Fortuna*	1/04	2,720	390
Costa *Magica*	12/04	2,720	390
Total Costa		7,554	1,115
Cunard			
Queen Mary 2	12/03	2,620	$ 780
Newbuild	2/05	1,968	410
Total Cunard		4,588	1,190
Total		34,828	$6,570

pany's main destinations. Hurricane George and Hurricane Mitch had a devastating impact on some of the Caribbean islands. As a result, the company was forced to quickly reschedule its travel itineraries.[33] In addition, the MS *Ecstasy* caught fire when it left the port of Miami in July. Although no one suffered severe injury, the company had to cope with negative publicity concerning its on-board safety.[34]

In 1999, Carnival Cruises acquired the remaining 50 percent of Cunard Cruise Lines. Carnival thus became the world's largest cruise line. With this acquisition, Carnival had secured its position in what it sees as *the* three segments of the cruise market: contemporary, premium, and luxury.[35] In 2000, the company continued its expansion in the European market: Carnival bought the remaining portion of Italy's Costa Cruise Line, the leading European cruise line. In the spring of 2001, Carnival Cruises repositioned several ships from America to Europe.[36] This move was the company's response to the growing European market.[37] Europeans typically take longer vacations than Americans, and cruises have become more popular among Europeans over the past few years. Costa and Cunard are well-established brands in many European countries and enjoy an excellent reputation. Combined with these actions, Carnival is attempting to further strengthen its brand names by increasing the number of ships in its fleets and by designing more attractive travel itineraries. Despite the European Union, which some refer to as the "United States of Europe," the European market remains very diverse. Carnival Cruises is attempting to meet the differing wants and needs of this market by offering special packages tailored to the preferences of the vacationers of the various countries.[38]

Contrary to Europeans, Americans typically prefer shorter vacations. And cruising is becoming increasingly popular among Americans. So for the U.S. market, Carnival Cruises redesigned the travel itineraries of several ships to meet the rising demand for short vacations. The company offered more three-, four-, and five-day cruises during 1999 and 2000. Furthermore, it decided to relocate some of its fleet and operate from additional U.S. ports in order to make access to its cruise ships more convenient to customers. In spite of a general decline of demand in the overall vacation industry, Carnival Cruises was able to generate respectable results for the years 1999 and 2000.

A Recessive Economy and the Terrorist Attacks of September 11   In general, 2001 was a hard year for the entire vacation industry. A recession decreased demand, and companies had to reduce prices in order to attract travelers. Cruise lines had to lower prices substantially to stimulate bookings.

To strengthen its financial position, Carnival Cruises sold its 25 percent of Airtours for $500 million and two smaller vessels of the luxury segment.[39] Due to the sale of the com-

Carnival Income Statement and Other Data (in thousands, except per-share data)[40]

	2001	2000	1999	1998
Revenues	$4,535,751	$3,778,542	$3,497,470	$3,009,306
Operating income before (loss) income from affiliated operations	935,755	945,130	943,941	819,792
Operating income	891,731	982,958	1,019,699	896,542
Net income	926,200	965,458	1,027,240	835,885
Earnings per share				
Basic	1.58	1.61	1.68	1.40
Diluted	1.58	1.60	1.66	1.40
Dividends per share	0.420	0.420	0.375	0.315
Cash from operations	1,238,936	1,279,535	1,329,724	1,091,840
Capital expenditures	826,568	1,003,348	872,984	1,150,413
Available lower berth days	20,685	15,888	14,336	12,237
Passengers carried	3,385	2,669	2,366	2,045
Occupancy percentage*	104.7%	105.4%	104.3%	106.3%

*Percentages in excess of 100 percent indicate that more than two passengers occupied some cabins.

pany's shares in Airtours and the reduction in the overall costs per available berth day, Carnival Cruises' third quarter results were favorable. With a net income of $495 million during the third quarter ($396.2 million in the same period a year before), the company was expecting a very positive annual result.[41]

However, the attacks of September 11 substantially altered expectations. The terrorist attacks were a major blow for the firm as well as the entire tourism industry. Many small companies in the industry, such as small travel agencies, had to go out of business.[42] During this period, the larger companies were forced to reduce their operations. Carnival Cruises attempted to face the blow by bringing ships closer to the domestic market and by instituting additional price reductions on cruise packages.[43] In addition, the company doubled the commission for travel agents.[44] This strategy was successful. In spite of the financial burden that September 11 represented to the industry, Carnival Cruises was able to close fiscal year 2001 with positive results (see table). Due to its expansion during the past few years and an aggressive pricing policy in the aftermath of September 11, Carnival entertained more than 3 million guests for this fiscal year (up from more than 2 million during 1998).[45]

The Possible Merger of P&O Princess and Royal Caribbean   In December 2001 Carnival Cruises publicly expressed its interest in the acquisition of P&O Princess Cruise Lines. Carnival's initial offer for P&O was £3.1 billion ($4.4 billion).[46] Prior to this offer, P&O and Royal Caribbean Cruise Line had announced a possible merger.[47] Either way, this merger would be one of the largest in the industry and would boost the resulting company to the top of the vacation industry.[48] However, despite recommendations by the P&O board of directors in favor of the merger with Royal Caribbean, the company's shareholders voted in February 2002 for a postponement of a decision.[49] As of the middle of March 2002, the outcome of this head-to-head race between the two competitors, Royal Caribbean and Carnival, was yet to be decided. It is, however, almost certain that the winner of this race will be the market leader of the future. This, of course, assumes that the relevant regulatory bodies permit either of the proposed mergers.

Expectations for 2002   All in all, Carnival Cruises has positive expectations for the year 2002. Customers are increasingly regaining confidence in traveling. The first quarter of 2002 brought a rise in prices compared to the drastically low prices of post–September 11. The higher prices are very much welcomed by the weakened vacation industry. Additionally, the number of cruise bookings substantially increased during the first quarter of the year.[50]

However, the cruise travel market is highly competitive as well as particularly vulnerable to economic and political changes. Furthermore, customers have learned to expect more convenience, luxury, and entertainment for less money. In order to stay competitive, cruise lines are forced to constantly refurbish ships and improve technical standards.

The recent past has shown that size is crucial in this industry. Only the larger companies are able to achieve cost reductions and to remain profitable while offering competitive prices. The lower prices have weakened smaller companies. Thus, further mergers and acquisitions may be expected.

■ Caterpillar (Case 23)

After the recession of the 1980s in the construction and mining industry, Caterpillar's recovery in the 1990s was quite spectacular. The *Fortune* 100 company had managed to become, in line with its strategic goals, the industry leader in most markets in which it operated.[51] While approaching the new millennium, Caterpillar continued its commitment to constantly improve, diversify its operations, and expand into foreign markets. Due to a restructuring of its manufacturing process, cost reductions, quality improvements, and the abovementioned diversification and expansion, the company managed to return to its former top position in the global market.

Due to the recession that began at the end of the 1990s, the years 2000 and 2001 were not good ones for the majority of investors. Most stocks experienced serious price decreases. After the attacks of September 11, the Dow Jones plummeted. Caterpillar, however, managed to improve its performance during these two years. The company was able to increase its sales revenues from $19,702 million in 1999 to $20,400 million in 2001 (see the following table for the company's performance).

Caterpillar's Financial Data, 1998–2001 (in millions, except per-share data)[52]

	Years Ended December 31			
	2001	*2000*	*1999*	*1998*
Sales and revenues	$ 20,450	$20,175	$19,702	$20,977
Sales	19,027	18,913	18,559	19,972
% inside USA	49%	50%	50%	51%
% outside USA	51%	50%	50%	49%
Revenues	1,423	1,262	1,143	1,005
Profit	805	1,053	946	1,513
As a % of sales and revenues	3.9%	5.2%	4.8%	7.2%
Profit per common share	2.35	3.04	2.66	4.17
Dividends per common share	1.390	1.345	1.275	1.150
Return on average common stock equity	14.4%	19.0%	17.9%	30.9%
Capital expenditures				
Property, plant, equipment	1,100	928	913	982
Equipment leased to others	868	665	490	344
Depreciation and amortization	1,169	1,063	814	893
Research and engineering expenses	898	854	490	838
As a % of sales and revenues	4.4%	4.2%	4.1%	4.0%
Average number of employees	70,678	67,200	66,225	64,441
Total assets	30,657	28,464	26,711	25,128
Long-term debts due after one year	11,291	11,334	9,928	9,404
Total debt	16,602	15,067	13,802	12,452
% of total debt to total debt and stockholder's equity (machinery and engines)	40%	38%	38%	38%

Diversification and Expansion: Keys to Success In Caterpillar's annual report for 2001, CEO and Chairman Glen Barton stated that one of the main reasons for the company's success in fiscal year 2001 was its diverse business structure.[53] Nevertheless, several of Caterpillar's core business segments performed rather poorly. Truck engine sales fell sharply, and construction operations decreased. The energy sector, however, experienced a boom. During the last few years, the coal mining, oil, gas, and other power sectors increased significantly. Sales of Caterpillar's Power Rent division increased by 24 percent during 2000.[54] The world's energy consumption is rapidly growing and thus creating a profitable business sector for Caterpillar.[55] Among others achievements, the company successfully helped to ease the California power shortage in 2000/2001 and expanded its energy business in Brazil.[56]

Equally successful during the past few years were subsidiaries Cat Financial and Cat Logistics. Cat Financial was formed in 1981 to offer financing alternatives for companies purchasing Caterpillar products. In 2001, Cat Financial helped finance 60 percent of all Caterpillar machinery purchased worldwide.[57] Cat Logistics is successfully offering solutions to logistical problems ranging from warehousing to operations management. This subsidiary has grown over the years to become one of the world's largest logistics organizations. It has thus become an important part of Caterpillar's product portfolio.[58]

Other important subdivisions and services are Cat Insurance, Cat Rent, Caterpillar Investment Management, and Cat Merchandise. Caterpillar has, for example, its own footwear collection produced by a shoe manufacturing company under a license agreement.

Caterpillar's expansion efforts, directed primarily at the Asian, Australian, and Latin American market, have proved successful. For instance, several joint venture manufacturing facilities established over the last few years have considerably strengthened Caterpillar's position in China. Sales in this market were almost $300 million in 2000, and the company is expecting future growth.[59] In Japan, Caterpillar further extended its joint venture with Mitsubishi. Shin Caterpillar Mitsubishi has successfully penetrated the Japanese market and is the second largest supplier of construction equipment in the country. In Australia, Caterpillar is expanding its mining equipment enterprise.[60] The company is the only heavy machinery seller operating a production facility in that country.[61]

Caterpillar also formed a number of strategically important alliances over the last few years. In December 2000, Caterpillar and DaimlerChrysler entered into agreements related to engine supply and technological cooperation. The two companies are cooperating in hopes of creating synergistic effects and lowering costs in the development of low-emission engines.[62] And in 2001, Caterpillar signed a software development agreement with Ford Motor Company to improve the car manufacturer's distribution network.[63]

Commitment to Improvement   Caterpillar's success during the last decade is based on the company's commitment to improvement in every business sector and to the future. The company is constantly looking for ways to improve its operations, cut costs, and outsource businesses that do not meet its strategic or profitability goals. For example, in 2001 the company sold its MT tractor line because it did not mesh well with the company's core businesses.[64]

E-business is another major focus of the company. Through the use of the Internet, customers now find it more convenient to access services, order parts, and get product information. The company is pushing e-business by establishing electronic stores. Currently, the company has 220 dealers worldwide and is selling its products in almost 200 countries. But the Internet allows the company to increase its geographic coverage area more easily and thus to extend its existing distribution network beyond what would otherwise be feasible.[65]

Another concern of Caterpillar is improving customer satisfaction. In 2001, the company started the Six Sigma program to significantly increase customer satisfaction and product quality.[66] Six Sigma is a business model requiring a company's commitment to zero defects.[67] Moreover, it is designed to leverage profitability by reducing costs and inefficiencies. According to the company's 2001 Annual Report, the first signs of success were noted shortly after Six Sigma's introduction. Both production defects and costs had been reduced even more than had been expected.[68]

Besides its concern for constant improvement within the company, Caterpillar has introduced several concepts to improve the environment. Over the last several years, the company has tried to continually decrease pollutant emissions from its engines and to meet the emission standards of the future. This is consistent with the company's commitment to the concept of sustainable development, which is the responsible use of resources in such a way that future generations will be able to enjoy life and still be able to meet their needs.[69]

Caterpillar's business environment is changing rapidly, and competition is high. As the recent recession has shown, the mining and construction business is very vulnerable to economic change. Also, the political environment heavily influences the company's performance. Recent steel tariffs will almost certainly affect the company because Caterpillar uses a great deal of steel in its products.[70] And since the company has most of its manufacturing facilities within the U.S., limits on steel imports and steel tariffs could hurt the company's competitiveness.

Given the current economic situation, the company's projections for fiscal year 2002 are modest.[71] However, Caterpillar is well prepared to remain an industry leader. The 2001 Annual Report clearly maps out the company's future path: Caterpillar will continue to follow its strategic course of improvement and expansion.

■ Enron International in India (Case 32)

Enron's bankruptcy   When Enron filed bankruptcy in the fall of 2001, America's economy stood still for a brief moment. The shocking collapse of Enron, a *Fortune* 500 company, was the largest bankruptcy ever filed in the nation's history.[72] It was obvious that this case would make history. In fact, many doubt if business will ever be as it was. Faith in U.S. capitalism has been thoroughly shaken in the eyes of some. Many people could not believe that a company like Enron, praised as outstanding only half a year before its fall, was no longer able to pay its creditors.[73] The weeks following the bankruptcy declaration quickly revealed the Enron business practices that were apparently the reason for the energy giant's collapse.

Enron was one of Wall Street's darlings.[74] In just fifteen years, the company grew from a regional energy provider to a large multinational trading company. By 2000, the company was ranked number seven in the U.S. and had 20,000 employees in thirty countries.[75] Its speed in creating new markets was amazing, and the firm's operations seemed very profitable.[76] In August 2000, Enron's stock was traded at more than $90, and by the end of the year shares were still traded at over $84.[77] The company's shares were part of almost every major portfolio. Revenues were outstanding, and nobody doubted the company's success story.[78] Enron was cited in many business publications as one of America's most successful companies. The following table shows Enron's success in numbers.

The corporation was very powerful. Many feel that this was in no small part due to its good political relationships. In fact, Enron's CEO, Kenneth Lay, supported President George W. Bush's election campaign substantially in 2000. In addition, he supported congressional members of both the Republican and the Democratic parties.[79] And it is alleged that Lay tried repeatedly to exert power over the political decision-making process.[80]

Enron's collapse took the business world by surprise. The company's bankruptcy was not only large but also very rapid.[81] When Enron reported its first quarterly loss in more than four years in mid-October 2001, the first doubts about the company's business practices appeared. By the end of October, following the revelation of some of Enron's previously unknown partnerships, investors' faith in Enron was severely damaged.[82] In November, Enron and Dynegy entered an agreement regarding Enron's acquisition by the rival.[83] However, by the end of November, Enron bonds were rated at "junk" status and the value of Enron shares had plunged to $9.[84]

Employees who had invested in their employer's stock were kept from selling their shares and lost millions. The company's contribution to the 401(k) retirement plan was made primarily in shares. In addition, most employees commonly invested their own contributions in company shares. Instead of warning employees about future losses, at the end of September Kenneth Lay encouraged employees to buy Enron's stock when he stated, "My personal belief is that Enron stock is an incredible bargain at current prices and we will look back in a couple of years from now and see the great opportunity that we currently have." At the time he made that statement, Lay had already sold about 600,000 of the shares he owned.[85]

At the beginning of December 2001, Enron filed for bankruptcy. A few days later, Congress began hearings on the Enron case. In January 2002, the Justice Department commenced a criminal investigation into Enron's business and accounting practices.[86]

The fall of the energy giant shed a pall over the business world. Some feel that off-balance-sheet financing methods and unconventional accounting practices are used by many companies to hide losses or decrease tax payments.[87] In Enron's case, the firm was able to avoid any government supervision in its derivative business.[88] By creating hundreds of partnerships, the company was able to keep many debts off its balance sheet and increase revenues for years. After the shock of the firm's collapse, it is understandable that certain institutions are asking for more governmental control of businesses.

At the beginning of 2002, it was alleged that Arthur Andersen (Enron's official auditor) employees had destroyed important documents to hide information. Andersen has suffered greatly from Enron's collapse. It is still not clear to what extent the auditors hid information from Enron's shareholders. Anderson's involvement in Enron's collapse will be the subject of a trial scheduled for May 2002. In the meantime, this "Big Five" auditing firm is trying to keep

Enron's Growth, 1985–2000[89]

	1985	*2000*
Employees	15,076	18,000 (worldwide)
Countries in which Enron operates	4	30+
Assets	$12.1 billion	$33 billion
Miles of pipeline owned	37,000	32,000
Power projects under construction	1	14 in 11 countries
Power projects in operation	1	51 in 15 countries
Fortune 500 ranking	Not ranked	18

its own business from falling apart. A growing number of important clients have dismissed the company.[90]

Enron's collapse will certainly continue to intrigue the business world and many in the general public. Almost every day new disclosures are made about how the company managed to fool investors. The company has substantially downsized its operations and its workforce. Regardless of the future of Enron, it is such an intriguing story that a number of film companies are expressing their interest in turning it into a movie.[91]

Enron International in India   Although Enron's project in India had a promising start, problems with Dabhol's only client, the Maharashtra State Electricity Board, MSEB, soon clouded the company's future in this country. In summer 2000, some individuals associated with the Maharashtra government started to question the project. Their concern was that the price of power from the plant was too high. This resulted in a cessation of payments by the MSEB to Enron for power supply for the months of November and December 2000. The government also officially announced a revision of tariffs. In May, the MSEB stopped buying power from the Dabhol plant and Enron issued a preliminary notice of the termination of the contract. At the time, Enron owned 65 percent of the $2 billion power plant. The MSEB, General Electric, and Bechtel owned the remaining 35 percent.[92] As is apparently the case with many Enron projects, the company's business practices were quite unconventional with this enterprise. In spite of Enron's promises, this project never generated any profit. Moreover, the company had to face several lawsuits for bribery. According to *Business Week International,* Enron did not hesitate to use its political connections to influence the Indian government.[93]

The Dabhol project has incited criticism of American business practices in Asia. Traditionally very different from the Western world, most Asian countries only recently opened their markets. Enron's project in India and the collapse of the company as a whole have certainly damaged the reputation of American companies in Asia.[94]

■ Kmart (Case 22)

Due to poor performance for a number of years, one of America's best-known retail companies was forced to file for Chapter 11 bankruptcy in January 2002.[95] When Kmart's most important food supplier, Fleming, stopped delivering in January due to Kmart's liquidity problems, filing for bankruptcy seemed to be an appropriate way out.[96] Although the bankruptcy court controls every step the company takes, Chapter 11 often makes it easier for companies to start anew.

Effects of Chapter 11 Bankruptcy   Kmart had 240,000 employees and operated 2,114 stores nationwide at the beginning of 2002.[97] However, in March 2002 the firm announced the closing of 284 stores in forty states and Puerto Rico, thus eliminating about 22,000 jobs as part of its Chapter 11 bankruptcy restructuring. [98] According to chief executive Chuck Conway, "The decision to close these underperforming stores, which do not meet our financial requirements going forward, is an integral part of the company's reorganization effort. While the business rationale supporting this action is compelling, we deeply regret the impact these store closings will have on our associates, our customers and the communities where these stores are located."[99]

Kmart expects that store closings and related cost savings will enhance its cash flow by about $550 million in 2002 and $45 million annually after that. The firm expects to record a charge in the range of $1.1–1.3 billion for the closings. But the closings are expected to improve its earnings before interest, taxes, and depreciation by about $31 million a year. The bankruptcy court approved $2 billion in fresh financing for Kmart and up to $150 million in bonuses for employees who help the company get back on track.[100]

Kmart's bankruptcy did not come out of the blue. The company had faced problems for a number of years. Due to the lack of an appropriate marketing strategy, Kmart failed to clearly position itself in the market.[101] While Wal-Mart, Kmart's primary competitor, was able to record constant increases in sales, Kmart's revenues decreased. Kmart earned around $3.8 billion in profits over fourteen years—a sum Wal-Mart earns in about six months.[102] Over the past few years, Kmart constantly lost ground to Wal-Mart and Target, a discounter selling upscale products.[103]

Strategy for 2000 and 2001 In 2000, Chuck Conaway joined Kmart as CEO. The former CVS Corporation restructurer immediately started his transformation program for Kmart. He reinstated the "BlueLight Special" and was able to extend the contract with celebrity Martha Stewart, Kmart's lifestyle consultant. Martha Stewart's product line is highly successful and contributes substantially to Kmart's revenues. The BlueLight Special is an old Kmart strategy, originally introduced in the 1960s. "BlueLight Always" signs point out products on sale throughout the store. With this strategy, Kmart hoped to capitalize on nostalgia and to emotionally address its shoppers. After the launching of the $25 million advertising campaign, Kmart's stock enjoyed a short rise in 2001. However, the campaign backfired. When Kmart reduced prices on about 38,000 items, Wal-Mart lowered prices even more and attracted additional sales. As a result, Kmart's Christmas sales declined while its rival reported significant sales increases.[104]

After the disappointing Christmas sales, Kmart's stock dropped drastically and the company was forced to increase its debt.[105] Although Kmart's managers are desperately working to get the company back on the road to success, the consumer's image of Kmart is not favorable. Badly maintained stores, items out of stock, and a consumer perception that Kmart is not up-to-date have increasingly kept consumers from returning to Kmart stores.[106] Further-

Kmart's Financial Performance, 1998–2000 (in thousands)[107]

	2000	1999	1998
Sales	$37,028	$35,925	$33,674
Assets	14,630	15,104	14,166
Net income	(244)	633	518

Kmart's Balance Sheet (in thousands)[108]

	January 31, 2000	January 26, 1999
Current Assets		
Cash and cash equivalents	$ 401	$ 344
Merchandise Inventory	6,412	7,101
Other current assets	811	715
Total current assets	7,624	8,160
Property and equipment, net	6,557	6,410
Other assets and deferred charges	449	534
Total assets	$14,630	$15,104
Current liabilities		
Long-term debt due within one year	$ 68	$ 66
Trade accounts payable	2,288	2,204
Accrued payroll and other liabilities	1,256	1,574
Taxes other than income taxes	187	232
Total current liabilities	3,799	4,076
Long-term debts and notes payable	2,084	1,759
Capital lease obligations	943	1,014
Other long-term liabilities	834	965
Company obligated mandatorily redeemable convertible preferred securities of a subsidiary trust holding	887	986
Common stock, $1 par value, 1,500,000,000 shares authorized	487	481
Capital in excess of par value	1,578	1,555
Retained earnings	4,018	4,268
Total liabilities and shareholders equity	$14,630	$15,104

more, the company has been unable to establish a clear image. According to a consumer survey conducted in 2001, Kmart has no real identity. Because of this discovery, Kmart hired Spike Lee, a well-known filmmaker, to brush up its image with a new series of TV advertisements. His "The Stuff of Life" campaign tries to reposition the company in the consumers' minds by moving away from a low-price strategy and establishing it as a company that has always been there for families. The TV spots regularly target African-American and Hispanic consumers, who make up a large proportion of Kmart customers. It is hoped that the $40 million campaign will create an emotional link to customers.[109]

Instead of focusing on attacking Wal-Mart's market share, this new campaign tries to create an even stronger bond with the 30 million weekly customers already shopping at Kmart.[110] However, creating an image that will be strong enough to get Kmart out of its troubles is a challenge. The company has set July 2003 as the date by which it will finish its restructuring process and emerge from bankruptcy. In the meanwhile, the company is planning to reduce costs by closing unprofitable stores. Furthermore, the company wants to improve the promotion of the Martha Stewart Everyday brand and other featured brands such as Route 66, Sesame Street, and Kathy Ireland.[111]

In addition, in February 2002 Kmart introduced a new fashion collection in cooperation with Disney. This colorful clothing collection for children is meant to attract more families.[112] The company has also started to put more effort into renewing the look of its stores and improving inventory control.[113] By introducing self-scanner checkouts in some stores in fall 2001, Kmart attempted to bring the latest technical standards to its stores and to attract customers who do not like to wait in line. However, due to a decreased marketing budget, the new self-scanner checkouts were insufficiently promoted and thus did not have the expected impact.[114]

Should Kmart eventually collapse, it would be among the biggest failures ever in the retail industry. Moreover, it would be a blow for the entire economy. Not only would more than 200,000 Kmart employees lose their jobs, but also many small and middle-sized companies working with Kmart could find themselves in trouble. Larger vendors would also be affected, as this would leave Wal-Mart as the only huge retailer of its type. Wal-Mart already exerts considerable pressure on suppliers to cut prices. Vendors are thus profiting from the competition between Wal-Mart and Kmart. This could help Kmart because vendors are interested in keeping the company alive.[115]

Although the company seems to have finally realized its underlying problems, Kmart's fate depends on several factors. Perhaps the most important factor is the consumer. Will the success of Kmart's new strategy be persuasive enough to rejuvenate within months the reputation the company has earned over years? Some analysts fear that this transformation process has come too late.[116] Others think that there is no place for another major discount retailer and that Kmart simply lost the battle with Wal-Mart.[117]

■ Eastman Kodak (Case 28)

Kodak, the American photo-imaging giant, was forced to face several problems during the last two decades. At the end of the 1980's, Kodak's executives realized that the company was on a dramatic downslide. New technology, globalization, and more aggressive competition found the seemingly invulnerable company unprepared.

Kodak's Struggle with New Market Conditions   Despite the restructuring process the company underwent at the end of the 1980s and beginning of the 1990s, Kodak's revenues continued to decline during the following years. Overall, sales dropped from 19.4 billion in 1991 to $13 billion in 2001. And Kodak dramatically reduced the number of its employees from 97,500 in 1997 to 78,400 in 2000 (see table for additional employee and financial information).[118]

To adapt to new market conditions, Kodak made several strategically important changes in the 1990s. The company reduced the number of plants, keeping only its largest facilities open. Moreover, it modernized and automated its production processes to cut manufacturing costs.[119]

Kodak also changed its reseller program. The new strategy was primarily sales oriented and incentive based. By setting sales goals and providing retailers with better customer training and marketing support, the company hoped that it would increase resellers' margins and thus enlarge its network of distributors. As a result of the more attractive reseller program, 120 additional companies became affiliated with Kodak from 1996 to 1998.[120] Kodak further improved its reseller program by offering additional support services such as business consulting and technical training.[121]

In 2001, Kodak introduced a different operating model. The new model was designed to reduce the company's operating complexity, thus making Kodak more flexible. In addition, product managers got more independence in decision-making, along with increased responsibility for product performance. By creating cross-functional work teams, the company hoped to better address customers' preferences and to enhance product innovation. Kodak expects the new operating model to reduce costs in the long run and to make the company adjust more easily to changing market conditions.[122]

To improve its performance, Kodak decided to increase investment in foreign markets, especially in China. During the late 1990s, the company pursued an aggressive marketing strategy in the Chinese market. By the end of the decade, Kodak had overtaken Fuji in terms of market share and had successfully established its brand in the Chinese market. To keep costs low, the company built film-manufacturing plants in China and was thus able to avoid high import tariffs. The strategy was successful. In July 2000, Kodak celebrated the opening of its 5000th Kodak retail store in China. This strong market position was, however, attainable only because Kodak had successfully lobbied the Chinese government for years.[123]

Developing markets like China is important for Kodak because the traditional photography business is still growing in such markets. According to estimates, only every sixth or seventh household in China has a camera.[124] China has become Kodak's second largest market, surpassed only by the U.S.[125] The company's expectations of future growth of the Chinese market are high.

Selected Kodak Financial Data (in millions, except per-share earnings) and Employee Data for Kodak[126]

	2000	1999	1998	1997	1996
Sales from continuing operations	$ 13,994	$ 14,089	$ 13,406	$ 14,538	$ 15,968
Earnings from operations	2,214	1,990	1,888	130	1,845
Basic earnings per share	4.62	4.38	4.30	.01	3.82
Diluted earnings per share	4.59	4.33	4.24	.01	3.76
on common shares	533	560	570	577	539
per common share	1.76	1.76	1.76	1.76	1.60
Common shares outstanding at year end	290.5	310.4	322.8	323.1	331.8
Shareholders at year end	113,308	131,709	129,495	135,132	137,092
Working capital	1,482	838	939	909	2,089
Total assets	14,212	14,370	14,733	13,145	14,438
Short-term borrowings	2,206	1,163	1,518	611	541
Long-term borrowings	1,166	936	504	585	559
Total shareholders' equity	3,428	3,912	3,988	3,161	4,734
Sales per business segment					
Consumer imaging	7,406	7,411	7,164	7,681	7,659
Kodak professional	1,706	1,910	1,840	2,272	2,367
Health imaging	2,185	2,120	1,526	1,532	1,627
Other imaging	2,697	2,648	2,876	3,053	4,315
Research & development costs	784	817	922	1,230	1,028
Employees					
in the U.S.	43,200	43,300	46,300	54,800	53,400
Worldwide	78,400	80,650	86,200	97,500	94,800

To better serve the domestic market and to increase its presence, Kodak entered into strategic alliances with several other firms. In 1998, the company introduced its "You've got pictures" and PhotoNet online Web sites in cooperation with AOL. Customers drop their films at a store and get their pictures online. They can then download or process them in other ways. Subsequently, additional important agreements to support the company's position in the digital imaging market were made with AT&T, Cisco Systems, and Hewlett Packard.[127]

Overall, the company has been able to keep its market position by increasing its portfolio and adding additional services. Furthermore, the company has expanded its retailer base and been able to gain market presence in Asia. The Asian market had been dominated primarily by Fuji, Kodak's strongest competitor. Thus, a strong position in China was strategically important for the company. According to Kodak, for years the Japanese company had tried to keep the American film manufacturer out of its domestic market by using its influence with the Japanese government. A lawsuit filed at the World Trade Organization by the U.S. government on behalf of Kodak, however, was decided in favor of Japan.[128]

The Digital Revolution and Kodak's EasyShare   The photography business was revolutionized in the 1990s by the introduction of digital cameras. While produced only for the professional market at the beginning, digital cameras soon conquered private households. When digital cameras became affordable in the mid-1990s, revenue from the traditional photography business started to decline.

Kodak rapidly became one of the main players in the digital imaging market. In 1990, the company introduced its first professional digital camera. In 1992, the company developed a new photo CD system. During the following years, Kodak installed printing kiosks in many retail stores. In 1995, the company sold its first digital camera for less than $1000. In spring 2001, the company successfully launched its EasyShare product line.[129]

Because of the constant decline of its traditional core business, Kodak increasingly invested in the development of consumer-friendly digital imaging products and services. Indeed, with EasyShare Kodak managed to solve a problem digital camera producers had faced—the very complex downloading process. With the EasyShare system, downloading and picture processing have become simpler than ever.[130] In addition, the company started a support Web site for EasyShare users that allows them to download and store pictures directly at the firm's company Web site. Consisting of six different camera models and a set of accessories, the EasyShare product line became an immediate success. Kodak digital cameras topped the bestselling lists for Christmas 2001 and made the company the market leader in this segment.[131]

Although the company's performance in the digital market is excellent, Kodak's main business remains traditional photography. The shift from traditional photography to digital photography was, overall, a financial blow for the company. In the long run, it is unlikely that digital imaging will provide the same high profit margins.[132] Consumers print only an estimated 15–20 percent of all pictures they take.[133] Thus, revenue generated from selling new film and from printing pictures is decreasing dramatically. Revenue in Kodak's traditional core business declined an estimated $2.1 billion in 2001, while revenue from digital imaging accounted for just $500 million.[134]

Furthermore, competition in the digital imaging sector is even tougher than in the traditional photography market. To remain the market leader, Kodak must stay ahead of innovative companies such as Sony, Canon, and Olympus.[135] Timing and innovation are crucial for the future success in this highly competitive and changing business.

Despite its strong position in digital imaging, Kodak's expectations for the year 2002 are, in the light of the current market situation, modest.[136] A recessive economy and the attacks of September 11 had a negative impact on the whole industry. Consumers cut back on traveling significantly and reduced their expenses for items like cameras. This, in turn, caused a decline in the purchase of film and printed pictures. In October 2001, Kodak announced the elimination of an additional 4,000 jobs. According to CEO David Carp, this was a move to strengthen the company's balance sheet for the coming years.[137]

Whether the company will be able to fully recover its old strength during the beginning of the new millennium will depend on several factors. These include economic conditions and the company's ability to sustain its current competitive advantage in digital imaging over the long run. However, new agreements such as a strategic partnership between Microsoft and Kodak's online photo printing service Ofoto.com seem to be a good start.[138]

■ Komatsu (Case 24)

Komatsu has pursued the strategic goals of expansion and cost reduction over the last decade. The company successfully acquired overseas companies and entered into several joint ventures and strategic alliances to further diversify its businesses.[139] As a result, the company was able to continually improve its fiscal results during the 1990s and became one of the major companies in the mining equipment and heavy machinery industry.

As of March 2001, the company employs more than 32,000 people and has operating facilities in twenty-seven countries around the globe. The company has 128 subsidiaries and owns an interest in more than 40 other companies. Operations range from the production of mining, construction equipment, and industrial machinery to electronics and integrative logistics systems.[140] Komatsu's diverse business holdings were one of the main reasons for its successful growth during the 1990s.

Over the past two years, however, the company's performance declined. The construction industry experienced a recession in most markets, and the electronics business produced disappointing results. The demand for semiconductors fell sharply, and sales were at a historic low. However, the mining sector improved slightly worldwide. And during this time the fastest growing geographic market continued to be China.[141]

The "G" to the 21st Mid-range Management Strategy   Despite Komatsu's emphasis on cost reduction and expansion throughout the last decade, management realized that additional improvements had to be made to remain profitable. Due to the worldwide economic recession, both sales and earnings declined. In 1999, the company reported a net loss of $104.9 million. However, the company recovered during the following years. Fiscal results for the years 2000 and 2001 were $130 million and $54.9 million, respectively (see table).[142]

The negative results for fiscal year 1999 were caused primarily by the worldwide decline in electronics sales and the continuing, long-term recession of the Japanese economy. To regain economic strength, the Japanese government began structural reforms in 1997 that, among other moves, included a sharp decrease in public spending.[143] This hit the construction business especially hard because governments traditionally are important customers of this industry.

Komatsu's Performance, 1994–2001 (in millions*)

	Year Ended March 31							
	2001	*2000*	*1999*	*1998*	*1997*	*1996*	*1995*	*1994*
Net sales	$8,701.3	10,249.1	8,996.6	8,301.3	8,862.2	9,339.5	10,562.2	8,292.7
Cost of sales	6,386.5	7,736.1	6,841.1	6,215.2	6,674.7	7,131.3	8,073.7	6,367.8
Net income (loss)	54.9	130.0	(104.9)	144.7	146.5	133.6	117.5	12.8
As percentage of sales	0.6%	1.3%	(1.2%)	1.7%	1.7%	1.4%	1.1%	0.2%
Capital expenditures	629.4	560.5	973.5	925.0	569.4	443.9	476.9	294.4
Total assets	11,136.5	13,352.2	12,920.3	11,741.8	12,199.4	14,887.9	17,723.8	13,489.9
Working capital	1,612.9	2,150.7	2,169.8	1,594.7	1,842.0	2,432.7	2,930.9	2,169.4
Property, plant, equipment	3,482.5	3,859.6	3,734.8	2,959.4	2,412.1	2,475.2	2,956.5	2,556.1
Long-term debt	1,891.7	238.1	2,476.7	1,480.4	1,319.3	1,310.4	1,615.5	1,397.8
Shareholders' equity	3,763.9	4,761.7	4,200.4	3,941.4	4,074.7	5,667.8	6,615.3	4,959.5
Net income (loss) per share								
Basic	0.057	0.134	(0.108)	0.147	0.137	0.133	0.117	0.013
Diluted	0.057	0.133	(0.108)	0.145	0.135	0.132	0.117	0.013
Cash dividends	0.048	0.058	0.059	0.060	0.065	0.075	0.092	0.078
Exchange rate* $1	¥126	103	118	133	124	107	87	102

* $ converted from ¥ at fiscal period end rate[144]

To bring the company back on track, in 2000 Komatsu embarked on a new strategy called the "G" to the 21st Mid-range Management Strategy.[145] Through this strategy the company plans to substantially increase return on equity and return on assets through March 2003. The strategy has four core elements:[146]

- A new growth strategy for the construction and mining equipment business

- A reduction of environmental stress, along with an expansion of the environmental business

- Attention focused on businesses in which Komatsu can maintain a technological edge on a global scale

- The attainment of a competitive advantage by deploying information technology (IT), or e-KOMATSU

Besides the decline noted in the construction industry in Japan, there has been a major decline in geographic regions outside of Japan during the past few years. Sales have dropped considerably in Komatsu's other two most important markets: North America and Europe.[147] To increase sales, the company plans to place more emphasis on the construction sector. And the company will focus its efforts on business sectors in which it already enjoys technological leadership. For example, Komatsu introduced its GALEO (Genuine Answers for Land and Environment Optimization) product line in May 2001. GALEO is a new brand of construction and mining equipment integrating the company's core concepts of environmental responsibility, safety, quality, reliability, and optimal use of information technology.[148]

IT is one of Komatsu's main areas of interest. The company sees the integration of IT into its products and daily business life as an opportunity to reinvent the way business is done. The company is focusing on the integration of e-KOMATSU into all its product lines and business segments. Moreover, e-KOMATSU has been designed to generate improved efficiencies and enhanced teamwork within and among the company's divisions and business units.[149]

The company is also committed to environmental protection. Recycling, the effective use of resources, energy conservation, and emissions reduction are key words at Komatsu. The firm is trying to restructure its operations so that costs are reduced to a minimum while resources are used optimally. The company's flagship operation regarding minimal environmental impact is the Oyama plant in Japan. This plant achieved Komatsu's zero emission goal (defined by the organization as "99% recycling of general and industrial waste") in 2000.[150] Along with environmental improvement programs for its own plants, the company will increasingly focus on the development of environmentally friendly products and environmental solutions for its customers—for example, recycling plants or construction equipment incorporating environmental conservation.[151]

Although the new "G" strategy has already brought a number of improvements, Komatsu's management wants to progress even further. The company continues to introduce additional cost-cutting measures to improve profits.

Changes in Management Structure and Further Cost Reductions
To further improve operations, Komatsu restructured its management in 1999, reducing the number of board members. Executive officers for the divisions in Japan and global officers for its overseas divisions and subsidiaries are now appointed directly by the upper management of the divisions and the subsidiaries, respectively. The new structure is intended to support a more flexible decision-making process and to allow more autonomy in the company's divisions and subsidiaries.[152]

According to the firm's semi-annual report for 2002, Komatsu's fixed costs are higher than those of its competitors. Further cost reductions are therefore essential if the firm is to stay competitive. Komatsu has calculated several ways to reduce both its fixed costs and its manufacturing costs. The company plans to reduce its overhead and to cut workforce costs by offering early retirement to selected employees. In addition, Komatsu expects to reduce its selling and administrative expenses through cost-related restructuring and other means.[153]

Regarding manufacturing costs, the company has developed successful, cost-efficient methods in its Japanese plants. Komatsu plans to introduce these to its overseas divisions. Moreover, Komatsu is planning to form additional strategic and other types of alliances to increase synergistic effects. For example, the company is exploring a possible strategic alliance with Volvo Construction Equipment.[154]

The future of the construction and mining industry is currently rather uncertain and will depend largely on the global economic situation. Komatsu's efforts to diversify its business have made the company less vulnerable to economic downturns in its core businesses. This will almost certainly be beneficial to the firm's future.

■ Nestlé (Case 33)

Nestlé S.A. is the largest food company in the world. The Swiss company employs more than 220,000 people in 479 factories all around the globe. Nestlé sells its products in almost every country in the world.[155]

During the last few years, Nestlé has grown considerably through strategic expansion and has diversified its businesses. The company, perhaps most famous for its chocolate and instant coffee, today produces more than just food. With its brand L'Oreal, Nestle also operates in the cosmetics market. And the company serves the pharmaceutical market.[156]

Strategic Expansion in Key Markets   Through strategic expansion the company significantly strengthened its market position and its presence in several business sectors. In 1997, the company bought the Perrier Vittel Group and thus became a major player in the mineral water market. In 2000, Nestlé bought Power Bar, an energy bar producer.[157]

In 2001, the company merged with Ralston Purina, an American pet food company. With this merger, Nestlé and Ralston Purina achieved a 39 percent market share of the American pet food market.[158] This created concern about antitrust violations, and federal approval took eleven months. It is said that Procter & Gamble, along with Mars, both major pet food producers, tried to turn the Federal Trade Commission against the merger.[159]

The combined Nestlé and Ralston Purina is now America's largest pet food producer. With a projected annual sales increase of 6.5 percent, twice that of human food, the pet food sector has become a key market for Nestlé.[160] Given the merger of the two similar companies, management is expecting synergistic effects will be forthcoming. Nestlé and Ralston Purina expect to reduce costs by at least $260 million in the near future. Consequently, the merged company will have to reorganize its business to create efficiencies. This reorganization process is projected to include a number of layoffs. In addition, Nestlé Purina anticipates making use of the food giant's international presence and the company's efficient distribution channels—of significance given that the international pet food market is estimated to be worth $25 billion.[161]

In addition to these acquisitions, in 2001 Nestlé obtained the exclusive rights to distribute Häagen-Dazs ice cream in the U.S. Under the agreement Nestlé has entered into with General Mills, the Swiss food company gained a 50 percent interest in the ice cream company. Moreover, it will be the sole distributor of Häagen-Dazs ice cream in North America for ninety-nine years.[162] In Europe, Nestlé bought the Schöller Holding from Germany's Südzucker. Both acquisitions further strengthen the company's position in the ice cream and frozen food market. The acquisition of Schöller was strategically important for the company because Schöller possesses a strong market position in such countries as Germany, France, and Spain. Furthermore, Schöller holds the exclusive rights for the distribution of the upscale Mövenpick ice cream.[163]

In Brazil, Nestlé further expanded its operations by acquiring the chocolate manufacturer Garoto. The Brazilian market is important for Nestlé, especially in the country's milk food business. Brazil's annual sales growth in this sector is 12.6 percent. The French food company Danone is competing with Nestlé to gain leadership in this market. The overall stronger presence of Nestlé in Brazil is thus important for the company.[164]

2001, an Excellent Year for Nestlé   The company's performance in the year 2001 surpassed even Nestlé's stated growth target. With an increase in net profits of 16 percent, the company seemed unaffected by the problems caused by the overall recession. Nestlé's efforts to strengthen its worldwide market position through strategic acquisitions and further cost reductions helped the company to perform well during a recessive economic period. The following table shows Nestlé's performance in 2001 compared to the previous year.

Nestlé's most important markets are Europe and America, with sales of $16,110 million and $16,023 million, respectively, in 2001. In Europe, the Eastern European market grew especially rapidly during the last few years. And the company was also able to report sales increases in strategically important Asian countries such as China and India.

Nestlé's Performance, 2000 and 2001
(in millions, except per-share data)[165]

	2001	*2000*
Sales	$51,022.9	$49,049.4
EBITA	5,851.2	5,783.1
Trading profit (EBIT)	5,553.0	5,533.7
Net profit	4,024.7	3,471.7
EPS	10.39	8.98
Dividend proposal	3.84	3.31
Real internal sales Growth	4.4%	4.4%

Considering its various businesses, the company generates most of its sales in the beverage market, with $14,472 million. Its second most important sector is its milk products (including ice cream) market, with $13,827 million. The prepared dishes, cooking aids, and pet care market follow this with $12,846 million.

Because of Nestlé's core principles of acquisitions and expansion in strategic markets, the company's future looks bright. Its sales increases are expected to continue. Another core principle is the company's focus on long-term profit and business development. Also, Nestlé is very successful in integrating new companies into its overall corporation. Nonetheless, most of its business divisions have a high degree of independence from the parent organization—thus helping to ensure flexibility and rapid decision-making. In addition, the company puts an emphasis on research and development.[166]

Nestlé is known for high-quality products and innovative ideas. This and the company's plans for cost reduction and reorganization to streamline its business operations and to increase efficiencies are likely to help the multinational food giant to continue its success. Nestlé is likely to maintain its market leadership in many business segments and to remain the world's largest food company.

■ Nucor (Case 27)

Nucor is America's second largest steel producer and largest steel recycling company. The North Carolina–based company has about 7,000 employees and operates facilities in nine U.S. states.[167] For a number of years, the company has focused strongly on expansion and on cost reduction through process improvement.[168]

Although the company has lately experienced a considerable decrease in earnings due to low steel prices, Nucor is still by far the most successful steel manufacturer of the entire U.S. steel industry. From 2000 to 2001, the company actually increased sales from 11,189,000 tons to 12,237,000 tons of steel. However, total revenues declined from $4,586,146,000 in 2000 to $4,139,249,000 in 2001, and earnings before taxes dropped from $478,308,000 in 2000 to $173,861,000 the same year (see table). This was reflected in lower earnings per share in 2001 of $1.45 compared to $3.80 per share in 2000.[169]

Accordingly, Nucor's share prices decreased during 2001 and fell to less than $35. However, Nucor's firm market position and the implementation of steel tariffs on foreign imports brought the company's stock back up to more than $60 in March 2002.[170]

Strategies at Nucor   Nucor's market position and increasing growth have attracted much attention in the business world. In fact, considering the overall industry performance during the last several years, the company's achievements stand out. The late 1990s were difficult for the U.S. steel industry. Prices fell by almost 50 percent over five years. More than thirty companies—half of the steel producers in the U.S.—have filed for bankruptcy under Chapter 11 since 1997.[171] Plunging revenues and rising energy costs at the beginning of the new millennium have changed the industry completely.[172] Many companies have been unable to compete with the less expensive steel imported from foreign countries. As a result, buyouts of struggling companies by bigger competitors have reduced the number of U.S. steel makers considerably.

Nucor, however, was able not only to survive these difficulties, but also to stay profitable. While other steel companies tumbled into bankruptcy, Nucor declared its 115th consecutive

Nucor's Steel Production, 1990–2001[173]

Year	Total Tons of Steel	Net Sales	Composite Sales Price/Ton	Earnings Before Income Taxes	Total per Ton
2001	12,237,000	4,139,249,000	338	173,861,000	16
2000	11,189,000	4,586,146,000	410	478,308,000	48
1999	10,176,000	4,009,346,000	394	379,189,000	42
1998	9,612,000	4,151,232,000	432	415,309,000	49
1997	9,786,000	4,184,498,000	428	460,182,000	53
1996	8,459,000	3,647,030,000	431	387,769,000	52
1995	7,943,000	3,462,046,000	436	432,335,000	62
1994	7,081,000	2,975,596,000	420	356,933,000	57
1993	5,891,000	2,253,738,000	383	187,110,000	35
1992	4,378,000	1,169,235,000	370	117,326,000	30
1991	3,905,000	1,465,457,000	375	95,816,000	28
1990	3,648,000	1,481,630,000	406	111,215,000	35

cash dividend in December 2001.[174] The firm's history of success has become a model over the years. Indeed, Nucor seems to have something that many other steel companies lack: a clearly defined business strategy.

Over the years, the company has continued its commitment to improvement, modernization, and expansion. Nucor's plants are well equipped, and the firm's production technology meets or exceeds modern standards.[175] With an emphasis on technological improvement, the steel manufacturer has managed to keep costs low while increasing efficiency. In addition, the company has continued its dedication to research and to the development of more efficient ways of production. In 2001, Nucor, BHP (an Australian mining company), and Japan's Ishikawa-Harima Heavy Industries started the construction of a steel sheet production plant in Indiana. This will be the first plant to use a promising new production process called strip casting. This new technology is intended to cut production costs. It is also designed to considerably shorten the traditionally long lead time, which in turn will decrease inventory costs.[176] Strip casting could revolutionize the steel industry and once again confirm Nucor's technical leadership.

Nucor's attitude toward its employees is another key factor in the company's success and one of the company's core principles. Based on performance, its compensation system helps to ensure a high work ethic and increased productivity throughout all operating facilities and organizational levels. Workers are assigned to teams, and efficiency is measured on a team basis. Besides relatively high wages due to incentives, the company provides a secure workplace by following a no-layoff policy. Over the past thirty-three years, Nucor has never laid off workers.[177] This is exceptional for an industry that traditionally is subject to cyclical depressions and thus has high layoff and turnover rates. Nucor's no-layoff policy is made possible by flexible working time. Overtime is accumulated during economic booms, and vacation time is taken during stagnating or recessive periods.[178] Furthermore, to keep workers on the payroll continually, repair work and other improvements are made during economic downturns.[179]

In spite of the company's growth, management has stayed lean and the overall company structure is decentralized. Thus, the different divisions are rather autonomous and flexible in decision-making.[180] The company's management has also maintained a close relationship with employees over the years. Nucor's employees are an integral part in the entire decision-making process. This emphasis on the integration and compensation of employees has worked well for the company. Nucor is known for its highly skilled and efficient workforce. Employee satisfaction is high, and turnover rates, as a result, are low.

An additional key to Nucor's success is its concentration on strategic expansion. In recent years, the company has been able to expand its operations by acquiring the assets of several struggling competitors. Among others, the company bought the assets of Auburn Steel in spring 2000 and of Trico Steel at the beginning of 2002[181]. Furthermore, Nucor has announced its intention to acquire Birmingham Steel for $500 million.[182]

Within the last few years, Nucor has managed to become one of the market leaders in steel production. Although the steel industry has experienced difficulties over the last five years, Nucor's market position is as strong as ever. The company's overall business strategy and somewhat unconventional approach toward its employees have proven successful. They have made the company into one of the top players in its field.

Import Tariffs and the Steel Industry   For several years, the U.S. steel industry lobbied heavily for tariffs, arguing that the absence of such tariffs in the U.S. was unfair trade because many foreign steel companies were heavily subsidized by their governments and were therefore able to keep prices artificially low.[183] Most steel producers were unable to lower their costs enough to stay competitive. Low prices and an economic recession brought many steel producers to the brink of bankruptcy. Financially strong companies such as Nucor took advantage of this situation and increased their holdings.

These lobbying efforts finally achieved success when on March 6, 2002, the Bush administration announced the implementation of steel tariffs.[184] The tariffs were meant to give the industry an opportunity to recover from past losses and to regain some strength.[185] The implementation of steel tariffs was very much welcomed by all American steel producers. Shortly after the announcement, most steel producers raised their prices significantly. Nucor, for example, announced a price increase of $20 per ton.[186] Also, investors reacted immediately, and the sector's stock prices improved considerably.

However, import tariffs are traditionally a very controversial political and economic issue. The recent implementation of steel tariffs has additionally fueled the debate about free trade and protectionism. Many experts feel that, overall, tariffs levied to protect domestic industries are counterproductive in the long run.

■ Outback Steakhouse (Case 26)

With about new 50 restaurants opened annually worldwide, Outback Steakhouse is among the fastest growing companies in the restaurant business.[187] As of December 2000, Outback operated more than 750 restaurants in over twenty nations worldwide (see first table on page 37) and was planning to open more during 2001 and 2002 (see second table on page 37).[188] The company had planned to open as many as 55 restaurants in 2001. But it was forced to cut back due to unfavorable market conditions.[189]

Net income increased during fiscal year 2000 by 13.5 percent compared to 1999, rising from $124,323,000 to $141,130,000.[190] In 2001, same-restaurant sales were down by 1.5 percent during the fall. But the company's operating results experienced overall growth for that year.[191] Despite the recession, the restaurant chain was able to increase sales and profits. This was reflected in the strong price per share at the end of 2001.[192]

Expansion and Diversification   Outback Steakhouse has successfully developed its operations through expansion of direct ownership, joint ventures with other restaurant chains, and franchise agreements. Currently, the restaurant chain offers eight different restaurant concepts, from steakhouses to seafood restaurants. The company operates about 600 original Outback Steakhouse restaurants worldwide.[193] The casual, relaxing atmosphere of its Australian-themed eateries has attracted a growing number of customers. Outback Steakhouses offer good-quality food at affordable prices. Although the restaurant is known for its big steaks and ribs, customers can also get pasta and salads.[194]

In 1999, Outback Steakhouse introduced its Curbside Take-Away service. According to studies, the take-away food sector is constantly growing due to the number of women who are working outside the home. Thus, the average family spends less time cooking and the demand for take-away food is experiencing constant growth. As a result, most restaurant chains have added a take-away service during the past several years to satisfy the growing demand in this area of the business.[195] Outback Steakhouse, however, went a step farther with Curbside Take-Away. Outback's version allows customers to remain seated in their car while picking up an order. This concept has been increasingly successful, growing from 4.7 percent of total sales in the first quarter of 2000 to 7 percent of total sales a year later.[196] To further expand its range of services, the company introduced a catering service providing food and beverages for any type of festivities and parties.[197]

Outback's fun concept is also successful internationally. Currently, the company operates restaurants in North America, Europe, Asia, and South America, with additional stores planned worldwide.[198] For example, Outback operates five restaurants in Mexico and plans a major

Outback Steakhouse and Subsidiary Restaurants[199]

	Year Ended December 31		
Restaurant	*2000*	*1999*	*1998*
Outback Steakhouse			
Company owned, domestic and international	521	478	436
Domestic franchised and joint venture	103	96	81
International franchised and joint venture	40	37	23
Total Outback Steakhouse	664	611	540
Carrabba's Italian Grill			
Company owned	60	56	52
Joint venture	21	16	12
Total Carrabba's Italian Grill	81	72	64
Fleming's Prime Steakhouse and Wine Bar			
Company owned	3	3	
Joint venture	2		
Total Fleming's Prime Steakhouse and Wine Bar	5	3	
Roy's Restaurants			
Company owned	1		
Joint venture	2		
Total Roy's Restaurants	3		
Zazarac			
Company owned	1		
Lee Roy Selmon's			
Company owned	1		
Total systemwide	755	686	604

Planned Outback Steakhouse and Related Restaurant Openings[200]

Restaurant	*2001*	*2002*
Outback Steakhouse, domestic		
Company owned	40–45	40–45
Franchised or joint venture	8–10	8–10
Outback Steakhouse, international		
Company owned	4–5	4–5
Franchised or joint venture	18–20	18–20
Carrabba's Italian Grill		
Company owned	6–8	6–8
Joint venture	10–12	10–12
Fleming's Prime Steakhouse and Wine Bar		
Joint venture	5–6	5–6
Roy's Restaurants		
Joint venture	5–6	5–6
Zazarac		
Company owned	1	1
Systemwide total	97–113	97–113

expansion in this country. In November 2001, the company announced its intentions to open twenty additional restaurants there. [201]

Outback Steakhouse's second largest restaurant chain is Carrabba's Italian Grill. Originally a joint venture agreement, more than half of the Carrabba's Italian Grills are now company owned. The Italian-style restaurants were particularly successful at the beginning of the millennium. For instance, Carrabba's increased same-store sales by 11.8 percent in 2000 compared to the same period a year earlier.[202]

In 2000, Outback Steakhouse, diversified further by entering into additional joint ventures.[203] The company added Fleming's Prime Steakhouse and Wine Bar and Roy's Restaurants. Fleming's Prime Steakhouse and Wine Bar, with restaurants mainly in California and Texas, offers upscale dining. The restaurant is particularly famous for its wine list, offering more than 100 domestic and international wines.[204] Roy's Restaurants is a chain operating primarily in Hawaii, mainland U.S., and Japan. It offers European-style food with an Asian-Pacific flavor in an upscale atmosphere.[205]

Outback Steakhouse has additional agreements with Zazarac, a Louisiana-style restaurant; Lee Roy Selmon's, famous for its southern-style barbecue dishes; Jimmy Buffet's Cheeseburger in Paradise; and Bonefish Grill.[206] Bonefish Grill is based in Florida and primarily offers high-quality seafood dishes. The agreement with Bonefish Grill adds seafood to Outback's existing concepts and is thus an important move toward increased diversification.[207]

Besides its unit expansion strategy, Outback Steakhouse is trying to increase same-store sales by offering additional services and improving customer satisfaction. This strategy allows Outback to increase sales without investing money in new restaurants.[208]

Customer and Employee Satisfaction   Constant improvement in customer service is another key to Outback's success. In addition to maintaining a well-trained and supervised staff, the company offers a number of consumer-oriented services, such as splitting meals without a surcharge. Furthermore, Outback Steakhouse is known for its employee-friendly environment. Obviously, the restaurant business is heavily service oriented. Thus, competent, motivated, and friendly staff members are part of any firm's success. By improving working conditions and changing hiring methods, the company reduced workforce turnover significantly. This, in turn, resulted in improved customer satisfaction.[209] In addition, Outback regularly conducts customer and employee surveys to be able to make further improvements as warranted.

The Future   Despite the slow emergence from the recent recession, experts expect growth for the casual restaurant business in the coming year. However, profit expectations are lower because operating costs are increasing.[210] Furthermore, the restaurant business is very much influenced by a range of unpredictable factors such as changes in input prices, in employee costs, and even in the political-legal environment. Outback Steakhouse, for example, experienced a rise in the price for baby back ribs in 2001. Due to the health risks associated with mad cow disease and the mouth-and-foot disease, the U.S. government had banned meat imports from Europe at the beginning of 2001. Outback had formerly been getting its baby pork ribs from Denmark. After the U.S. ban, it had to change suppliers and thus faced higher costs.[211] To add to the firm's problems, the chain's steakhouses in Europe experienced a significant decrease in demand due to these cattle diseases.[212]

Nevertheless, the company seems to be optimistic about its future. Through its diversification and expansion strategy, Outback Steakhouse has continually gained market share. Apparently, it almost certainly will continue to do so in the future.

■ RealNetworks, 2002 (Case 11)

Founded in 1994 under the name Progressive Networks, this firm was able to establish itself as a leader in the streaming media market within a very short time. RealNetworks' operations expanded quickly as the number of Internet users increased rapidly during the second half of the 1990s.

However, despite the company's swift growth during that period, the new millennium brought difficulties for the company. The Internet industry is rapidly changing, with many competitors penetrating the market. In addition, Microsoft and McIntosh, among other companies, launched their own versions of RealPlayer: Windows Media Player and Apple Quick Time, respectively. Although RealPlayer remained the most widely used streaming software,

Microsoft's Windows Media Player quickly gained market share. According to a report by Jupiter Media Metrix in November 2001, 28 percent of U.S. consumers using streaming software used RealPlayer, while 22 percent used Windows Media Player.[213] Within a short time, Microsoft was able to become number two in this market by bundling its Windows Media Player with Internet Explorer. As a result, the former partner had become RealNetworks' primary competitor in the streaming media market.[214]

Strategy of Expansion and Innovation   In order to strengthen market position and expand operations, RealNetworks pursued a strategy of expansion and acquired several business during the last few years. These included:

- Vivo Software in 1998 (streaming media)
- Xing Technology in 1998 (digital audio and video encoding and decoding technology, including MP3 software)
- NetZip in 2000 (Internet download management and utility software)
- Aegisoft in 2000 (secure digital media software)[215]

Furthermore, the company tried to develop new products and new markets. In March 2000, RealNetworks launched Real.com Games. Through several agreements with leading game producers, the company was able to offer a number of new games exclusively with Real.com Games.[216] In addition, the company constantly upgraded its existing products RealPlayer and RealJukebox and offered new services. In August 2000, the company introduced RealPlayer GoldPass, giving subscribers access to a combination of premium services, and RealOne, offering users premium news and entertainment.[217] Both services are available for monthly subscription fees and contribute considerably to the company's revenues. Furthermore, the company focused on forming strategic alliances with, among others, Sun Microsystems, Hewlett Packard, and Cisco Systems to distribute its products.[218] A promising invention is RealSystem iQ, launched in December 2000, a new delivery system primarily designed "to reduce network congestion by decentralizing the data stream."[219]

However, despite all efforts to stay competitive and innovative, RealNetworks had to reduce its workforce in July 2001 due to considerably reduced revenues. Hurt by the recession, many companies suspended possible deals. This had a negative effect on RealNetworks' financial performance.[220]

Restructuring Sources of Income   During the last three years, RealNetworks has substantially changed the sources of its income. Whereas previously the company had focused almost exclusively on the revenues of license agreements, advertising revenues and subscription fees are now a substantial part of its income.[221] Although the company still offers free downloading of the basic versions of most of its software, full or upscale versions have a monthly fee of about $10. RealPlayer GoldPass and RealOne allow subscribers to get news from CNN and ABC, sports from FoxSports, and entertainment from various other channels. As of December 2001, the two services had more than 500,000 subscribers and confirmed RealNetworks strong position in this niche market. In fact, experts judge the new RealOne service as the company's strongest advantage over competitors like Microsoft.[222]

Over a recent annual period, revenues from subscription fees rose by 24 percent and were at $18.3 million during fourth quarter 2001 compared with only $14.8 million during the same period a year earlier.[223]

RealNetworks' Revenue Sources, 1998–2000[224]

Net Revenues	Year Ended December 31		
	2000	1999	1998
Software license fee	61.3%	69.0%	73.0%
Service revenues (including subscription fees)	21.7	20.2	22.2
Advertising	17.0	10.8	4.8
Total	100.0	100.0	100.0

RealNetworks' Financial Performance, 1998–1999 (in thousands except per-share data)[225]

	Year Ended December 31		
	2000	*1999*	*1998*
Net revenues			
Software license fees	$148,091	$90,627	$48,487
Service revenues	52,505	26,446	14,742
Advertising	40,942	14,149	3,148
Total revenues	241,538	131,242	66,377
Cost of revenues	38,688	22,491	12,666
Operating expenses	328,876	111,791	77,700
Net income (loss)	(110,121)	6,926	(19,953)
Comprehensive income (loss)	(122,602)	6,149	(19,917)
Earnings (loss) per share			
Basic	(0.72)	0.05	(0.15)
Diluted	(0.72)	0.05	(0.15)
Total assets	578,408	411,124	n.a.
Shareholder's equity	480,812	330,559	n.a.

According to some analysts, streaming media is the technology of the future and likely to surpass television. Events such as the presidential election of 2000, the Superbowl, and the Olympics helped to increase the streaming video market substantially.[226] By supporting high-profile streaming events such as the Webcast of a Victoria's Secret fashion show in Paris, RealNetworks wants to help ensure that it will play a major role in this growing market.[227] Such events, including a U2 concert in October 2001 broadcast live over the Internet, tremendously increase users of streaming media. According to RealNetworks, 5 million people watched the pop concert.[228]

RealNetworks' future will depend on the company's ability to extend and maintain its advantage in the streaming media market. Thus, the company's products must gain an even broader market acceptance. In addition, RealNetworks has to continue its product development. With RealSystem iQ, the company wants to enter the mobile market by gaining the cooperation of worldwide mobile operators like AT&T. In addition, RealNetworks and Nokia announced an alliance in their efforts to make audio and video accessible for mobile users.

The Internet industry is extremely competitive, and timing is a very important factor. New competitors continually enter the market, and the number of companies mushrooms. Sustainable advantages are hard to create due to the constant imitation of products. In order to be successful in such a rapidly changing and competitive market, RealNetworks will have to continue to be more innovative than its competitors.

■ Sandvik (Case 39)

Sandvik is Sweden's largest exporter and one of the most successful steel companies worldwide. The firm has 35,000 employees and operates facilities in 130 countries. Sandvik is oriented toward the international market to a much larger extent than many multinational firms. In fact, the company generates 95 percent of its revenues outside of Sweden. The company's most important markets are Europe, North America, and Asia (see table).[229]

Sandvik's Split of Invoiced Sales by Market Region, 2001[230]

Europe	47%
NAFTA (the U.S., Canada, Mexico)	24
South America	4
Asia/Australia	20
Africa/Middle East	5

The company has successfully pursued a reorganization and development program over the past few years. In keeping with this program, the company has placed serious emphasis on furthering strategic expansion, continuing its efforts in research and development, creating synergetic effects, and improving its production efficiencies. In addition, Sandvik has increasingly tried to integrate information technology within its organization and products. Recognizing the importance of e-business as an opportunity to further increase market presence and to support relationships with customers, the company acquired one-fifth of Endorsia.com—a European-based e-business marketplace for industrial goods. Endorsia.com allows customers to quickly and easily obtain information on industrial goods products, prices, and innovations. The acquisition of an interest in Endorsia.com was a logical step in Sandvik's search for complementary products and services.[231]

As a whole, the company's performance remained strong in 2000 and 2001. While the recessive economy had little impact on the company's results for fiscal year 2000, Sandvik experienced a slowdown toward the end of 2001. However, the company's performance in 2001 taken as a whole was good. It reported a sales increase of 3 percent worldwide at fixed exchange rates. But as the table below reveals, while sales in Europe were up, the company recorded an 8 percent sales decline in North America and a 6 percent decline in South America.

Expansion   Growth and strategic expansion have been part of the firm's business strategy for a long time. As a result, Sandvik acquired over thirty companies during the last ten years.[232] These acquisitions not only increased the company's market share, but also diversified its product portfolio. Thus, over the years Sandvik has become an international high-tech engineering firm mainly producing high-quality steel products and machinery for mining and construction.

The South American market has become increasingly important over the past few years. Sandvik has increased its market share in South America by making several acquisitions, such as Hurth-Infer SA in 2001 and Bafco Mineria y Servidios S.A., the leading company in mining services in Chile in the same year.[233] In addition, at the beginning of 2002 the company invested over $18 million in its mining and construction machinery business in Brazil. This investment is part of Sandvik's strategy to specialize its operating facilities in order to increase economies of scale.

Despite the company's expressed strategy of expansion, during 2001 Sandvik also sold several subsidiaries, and minority interests in other companies and shut down selected production facilities as part of its restructuring process. Among the companies sold were Sterling Tubes in the UK and the dental-technology company Procera-Sandvik. As a result, Sandvik decreased its workforce by 800 employees at the end of the year.

Sandvik's Development by Market Area (invoiced sales in millions)[234]

Market Area	Fourth Quarter 2001*			Full-Year 2001*		
	Invoiced Sales	Share %	Change %	Invoiced Sales	Share %	Change %
EU	$ 507.63	41	−3	$1,927.40	40	+2
Rest of Europe	89.24	7	+19	348.92	7	+27
Europe total	596.87	48	−1	2,276.32	47	+4
NAFTA	269.96	22	−14	1,129.45	24	−8
South America	54.89	4	−3	196.97	4	−6
Africa/Middle East	66.63	5	+23	245.69	5	+28
Asia/Australia	262.13	21	+8	936.30	20	+10
Total	1,250.49	100	−3	4,784.73	100	+3

*Conversion rate as of March 25, 2002, SEK (Krona) 10.22 = $1.00[235]

Research and Development   Known for innovations, Sandvik invests about 4 percent of its annual sales in research and development. Around 1,400 people work in the company's R&D departments. At the beginning of 2002, Sandvik held 3,500 patents.[236] One of its core divisions, Sandvik Coromant, a tooling division, launches around 1,000 new products or product variations every year.[237] This emphasis on research and development has created a distinct competitive advantage for the company.

Through a close cooperation among the firm's various R&D departments, Sandvik has been able to achieve important synergetic effects that have helped to decrease costs. It has also been able to increase its output of innovations. For example, Sandvik Coromat and Sandvik Steel are extensively sharing knowledge and information. This has proven advantageous for both business divisions and has resulted in innovative products with improved quality.[238]

Flow groups   The company invested heavily in improving its production processes during the 1990s. By introducing more modern and innovative machinery, often developed by the company's own R&D departments, Sandvik achieved higher efficiency and productivity. However, the company also enhanced human resource systems and management. Since the creation at Sandvik Saws and Tools of "flow groups," they have contributed to the company's overall success. These groups are small teams of employees responsible for the production of a specific product. This responsibility includes planning, manufacturing, and quality control. As a result, the members of a specific flow group become experts in the production of their particular product. They are thus more likely to find ways to improve production. In addition, workers are more motivated since they are completely responsible for their product's production process. In other words, every flow group is responsible for the productivity and efficiency of its own production process.[239]

Since the introduction of flow groups, Sandvik's Saws and Tools division has been able to eliminate its planning and quality control departments. These activities are now part of each flow group's responsibility. The system worked so well that other Sandvik business units have adopted similar production groups.[240]

Sandvik's performance has been good in large part due to its commitment to organizational changes and innovation. However, for 2002 the company has projected a further slowdown in sales, a continuation of a trend begun in the fourth quarter of 2001.[241] As a result, the company will attempt to further increase productivity and efficiency by restructuring and expanding its organization.

■ Wal-Mart (Case 21)

The year 2001 was one of the most difficult years in recent history for America's retailers. A recession had already brought a considerable slowdown in sales when the terrorist attacks on September 11 occurred and took their toll on consumer confidence. A major decline in sales followed. Most retailers launched major advertising campaigns to bring consumers back to their stores, but the results were mixed. Although consumers eventually regained their confidence, most retail firms reported a decrease in revenues for fiscal year 2001. Even the holiday season, traditionally the most important period for retailers, was unable to make up what most companies had lost earlier in the year. In addition, the retail industry witnessed one of the biggest disappointments in retailing history: Kmart, Wal-Mart's primary competitor in the discount store sector, filed for bankruptcy in early 2002.

Wal-Mart, however, seemed to be quite resistant to the recession and the September events.[242] Indeed, 2001 was one of Wal-Mart's most successful years.[243] The company enjoyed double-digit sales increases and outperformed even the mammoth ExxonMobil in terms of revenues. While this enormous oil company reported sales of $213 billion, Wal-Mart's revenues were $217.8 billion—up by 13.8 percent.[244] Furthermore, the company's net income exceeded $6 billion for the first time.[245]

Part of Wal-Mart's success in 2001 was due to the company's strong market position. In addition, despite its size the company is able to quickly react to changing market conditions. For instance, in July 2001, because of declining sales, the company reduced its inventory and thus trimmed associated inventory costs by more than $1 billion.[246] Wal-Mart's size and market position as the world's biggest discounter also enabled the company to reduce prices substantially in order to attract customers. This proved particularly important during the 2001 Christmas selling season when Kmart, in an unsuccessful attempt to attract customers, lowered many of its prices. Wal-Mart reacted quickly by reducing many of its prices. The result: Kmart's sales continued to decline while Wal-Mart's increased.

The Wal-Mart retail division was not the only one that performed well in 2001. The company's wholesale division, Sam's Warehouse Club, was successful that year. The number of Sam's Club members was at a historic high, generating a significant growth in sales in this division. During the past few years, the company has added new services to Sam's offerings and thus upgraded the warehouse club's product line. For example, customers are now able to print their photos, buy gasoline, and have their prescriptions filled at Sam's.[247]

Wal-Mart's international stores performed equally well. The company currently operates more than 1,100 stores in Canada, Puerto Rico, Mexico, Argentina, Brazil, the United Kingdom, Germany, China, and Korea. The company's biggest international market presence is in Mexico, followed by the United Kingdom and Canada.[248]

Continuing Expansion and Diversification

For 2002, Wal-Mart plans to continue its expansion strategy. Domestically, the company will open 50 new discount stores, 180–185 Supercenters (including the expansion of some existing stores into Supercenters), and 50–55 new Sam's Clubs. As of March 2002, the company had already opened 37 of these planned stores.[249]

Wal-Mart also plans to open 120–130 additional stores internationally. All store openings will be in countries in which the company is already operating.[250] And the company announced plans to make its debut in the Japanese market through the acquisition of an interest in the Japanese Seiyu supermarket chain. Wal-Mart's long-term objective is to eventually gain control over Seiyu and thus create a solid market position in Japan. However, two major Japanese supermarket chains recently went bankrupt, thus raising doubts about the potential of the Japanese market.[251]

In terms of diversification, Wal-Mart finally managed, after some initial difficulties, to introduce its Web site www.walmart.com.[252] With this Web site, the company successfully entered the e-business market. In 2000, Wal-Mart's Web site was ranked number six in the list of the top "E-tailers" for the Christmas season, with 18,007,889 shopping visits.[253]

In addition, at the beginning of 2002 Walmart.com further expanded its services by offering cruises to Alaska and the Bahamas in cooperation with Carnival Cruises.[254] For these offerings, Wal-Mart is offering its "best-price" guarantee, for which the company is well known.

Wal-Mart: More Than Just Shopping

In 2001, Wal-Mart added a new concept that it calls the Store of the Community. Based on demographic data, evaluations about preferences, and sales data, Wal-Mart is able to draw conclusions about the buying behavior of a Wal-Mart store in a particular area. Accordingly, inventories for products that are in high demand in given stores will be increased in those stores. Also related to the new concept, store managers now submit an annual survey regarding their communities' year-round activities as well as geographic information. Thus, for example, the location of a nearby hospital, lake, or mountain influences the store's product portfolio. The Store of the Community concept is intended to help each Wal-Mart store fine-tune its inventory and provide more products that its customers really want, when they want it. Wal-Mart stores thus will reflect the communities' preferences and different lifestyles as well as seasonal events.[255]

Furthermore, during the coming year Wal-Mart will increasingly focus on its concept of "Retailtainment" to create a more enjoyable and a more relaxed shopping atmosphere. This concept includes anything that makes shopping at Wal-Mart more attractive, such as decorations, exhibits set up by community organizations, safety seminars put on by local police, or visits by area schools. In addition, the company is featuring events such as concerts and movie releases. In 2001, the company exclusively broadcast in its stores concerts by Ricky Martin, Garth Brooks, Faith Hill, and the Backstreet Boys.[256]

Another of Wal-Mart's major concerns is its link to local communities. By supporting local organizations, participating in fund-raising, and sponsoring local events, Wal-Mart tries to be more than just a store or employer for local communities. In 2001, the company raised more than $190 million through events and activities designed to create and support different projects; these included community matching grants for local organizations, the Children's Miracle Network, and support for children's hospitals or other local charity organizations. In addition, the company grants college scholarships for gifted students and created a teacher of the year award.[257]

The story of Wal-Mart is a success story in virtually every sense. The company has rewritten the history of the retailing industry. It is not only the world's largest discount chain, but also among the world's largest employers, with more than 1.3 million "associates."[258] In 2001, *Fortune* magazine ranked the company as the third most admired American company. In *Fortune* magazine's list of "100 Best to Work For," Wal-Mart was ranked number 94 at the beginning of 2002.[259]

However, the firm also has its detractors. Despite the admiration Wal-Mart receives from the business world, the company has faced criticism concerning its business practices in Third World countries. The company has been accused of paying less than minimum wage and of providing poor working conditions in such countries as Bangladesh and Honduras.[260]

However, despite the criticism of some, Wal-Mart has almost become a synonym for the American entrepreneurial spirit and for success. With its expansion plans and new concepts, the company appears to be well positioned for future success.

ENDNOTES: NEW RESEARCH STREAMS AND THEIR IMPLICATIONS FOR STRATEGY

1. See C. M. Christensen, *The Innovator's Dilemma* (Boston: Harvard Business School Press, 1997); C. M.Christensen and M. Overdorf,"Meeting the Challenge of Disruptive Change," *Harvard Business Review* (March–April 2000), 66–77.
2. R. N. Foster, *Innovation: The Attacker's Advantage* (New York: Summit Books, 1986).
3. G. A. Moore, *Crossing the Chasm* (New York: Harper-Collins, 1991); G. A. Moore, *Living on the Fault Line* (New York: HarperBusiness, 2000).
4. P. Freiberger and M. Swaine, *Fire in the Valley* (New York: McGraw-Hill, 2000).
5. See T. A. Luehrman,"Strategy as a Portfolio of Real Options," *Harvard Business Review* (September–October, 1998), 89–99; E. D. Beinhocker,"Robust Adaptive Strategies," *Sloan Management Review,* 40 (1999). R. G. McGrath and I. C. MacMillan."Assessing Technology Projects Using Real Options Reasoning," *Research Technology Management,* 43 (July–August 2000); F. P. Boer,"Valuation of Technology Using 'Real options,'" *Research Technology Management,* 43 (July–August 2000). T. Copland and V. Antikarov, *Real Options: A Practitioner's Guide* (Monitor Books, 2001).
6. "Super-Jumbo Trade War Ahead," *Economist,* May 6, 2000, pp. 63–64.
7. J. N. Sheth and R. Sisodia,"Why Cell Phones Succeeded Where Iridium Failed," *Wall Street Journal,* August 23, 1999, p. A14.
8. See Luehrman,"Strategy as a Portfolio"; Beinhocker."Robust Adaptive Strategies". McGrath and MacMillan, Assessing Technology Projects"; Boer,"Valuation of Technology"; Copland and Antikarov,"Real Options."
9. N. A. Nichols,"Scientific Management at Merck: An Interview with Judy Lewent," *Harvard Business Review* (January–February 1994) 89–95.
10. For details, see Copland and Antikarov,"Real Options"; Nichols,"Scientific Management at Merck."
11. See C. Shapiro and H. R.Varian, *Information Rules* (Boston: Harvard Business School Press, 1999); Charles W. L. Hill, Establishing a Standard: Competitive Strategy and Technological Standards in Winner Take All Industries," *Academy of Management Executive,* 11 (1997) 7–25, M. A. Shilling,"Technological Lockout: An Integrative Model of the Economic and Strategic Factors Driving Technology Success and Failure," *Academy of Management Review* 23 (1998), 267–285.
12. G. H. Taylor,"Knowledge Companies," In W. E. Halal, ed., *The Infinite Resource* 97–109.
13. M. E. Porter,"What Is Strategy?" *Harvard Business Review* 74 (November–December, 1996); 61–78. C. K. Prahalad, & G. Hamel,"The Core Competence of the Corporation," *Harvard Business Review,* 68 (May-June 1990) 43–59.
14. N. Venkatraman, N."IT-Enabled Business Transformation: From Automation to Business Scope Redefinition,"*Sloan Management Review,* 35 (Winter 1994), 73–87.
15. R. Rucker,"*Citibank Increases Customer Loyalty with Defect-Free Processes,"Journal for Quality and Participation* (Fall 2000), 32–36.
16. Prahalad and Hamel,"Core Competence."
17. Venkatraman,"IT-Enabled Business Transformation."
18. Ibid.
19. J. Fulk and G. DeSanctis,"Electronic Communication and Changing Organizational Forms," *Organization Science,* 6 (1996), 337–349.
20. N. Nohria and R. Eccles, Face-to-Face: Making Network Organizations Work," N. Nohria and R. G. Eccles, eds., *Networks and Organizations: Structure, Form, and Action* (Boston: Harvard Business School Press, 1992), 28–908.

ENDNOTES: CASE UPDATES

1. Airborne Express Company Web Site, <http://www.airborne.com>.
2. Ibid.
3. Beth M. Schwartz,"Air Cargo Make-Over," *Penton,* 40, February 1, 1999 (as from eLibrary.com).
4. AirCargo World Online, <http://www.aircargoworld.com>.
5. Airborne Express Company Web Site, Annual Report 1998, <http://www.airborne.com>.
6. Airborne Express Company Web Site, Annual Report 2000, <http://www.airborne.com>.
7. Airborne Express Company Web Site, Annual Report 1999, <http://www.airborne.com>.
8. Airborne Express Company Web Site.

9. Airborne Express Company, Annual Report 1999.
10. Ibid.
11. Ibid.
12. Schwartz, "Air Cargo Make-Over."
13. Airborne Express, Annual Report 2000.
14. Ibid.
15. Ibid.
16. Airborne Express Company Web Site, Press Release, "Airborne Express Announces New Rates with Expanded Service Portfolio; Airborne Remains Best Value in Industry," November 29, 2000, <http://www.airborne.com>.
17. Airborne Express Company Web Site, Press Release, "Airborne Express Reinstates Service Guarantee—"Business-as-Usual" for Global Carrier," September 17, 2001, <http://www.airborne.com>.
18. Airborne Express Company Web Site, Press Release, "Airborne Express Receives Compensation Under the U.S. Air Transportation Safety and System Stabilization Act," October 9, 2001, <http://www.airborne.com>.
19. Airborne Express Company Web Site, 2001 Statistical Report, <http://www.airborne.com>.
20. Paul Page, "The Economy Is Sliding and Traffic Is Falling, but Why Let a Little Recession Get in the Way of a Good Price Increase?" *AirCargo World Online,* 2001, <http://www.aircargoworld.com>.
21. Airborne Express, Annual Report 1999.
22. Page, "The Economy Is Sliding."
23. Gene G. Marcial, "BusinessWeek Investor: Inside Wall Street: DHL Could Help Airborne Take Off...," *Business Week,* July 9, 2001, p. 117.
24. Royal Philips Company Web Site, <http://www.philips.com>.
25. J. M. Barella, "ATL and Philips Medical Systems," *Medica Mundi,* 43, September 1999, p. 3.
26. Royal Philips Company Web Site.
27. Ibid.
28. Carnival Corporation Company Web Site, Annual Report 2001, <http://www.carnivalcorp.com>.
29. Carnival Corporation Company Web Site, Annual Report 1998, <http://www.carnivalcorp.com>.
30. Ibid.
31. Ibid.
32. Carnival Corporation Company Web Site, Annual Report, 2001, <http://www.carnivalcorp.com>.
33. Ibid.
34. Brendan Farrington, "Passengers Say They Reported Smoke Long Before Ship Announcement," *AP Online,* July 22, 1998 (as from eLibrary.com).
35. Business Search Engine, Carnival Corporation Information, <http://www.business.com>.
36. Carnival, Annual Report 2001.
37. Michael Connor, "Carnival Sees Expansion in European Cruise Market," *Reuters Business Report,* April 4, 2001 (as from eLibrary.com).
38. Ibid.
39. Ibid.
40. Carnival, Annual Report 2001.
41. Ibid.
42. Michael Connor, "Big Cruise Lines Hike Commissions for Travel Agents," *Reuters Business Report,* October 12, 2001 (as from eLibrary.com).
43. Ibid.
44. Connor, "Big Cruise Lines Hike Commissions."
45. Carnival, Annual Report 2001.
46. P&O Princess Cruises plc Company Web Site, Press Release, "P&O Princess Cruises plc ('P&O Princess') Rejection of Pre-conditional Proposal from Carnival Corporation ('Carnival')," December 16, 2001 <http://www.poprincesscruises.com>.
47. P&O Princess Cruises plc Company Web Site, <http://www.poprincesscruises.com>.
48. Scheherazade Danehkhu, "P&O Fights to Salvage Royal Merger—Leisure Postponement Vote Seen as Victory for Carnival," *Financial Times,* February 16, 2002, <http://www.ft.com>.
49. Ibid.
50. Carnival Corporation Company Web Site, Press Release, "Carnival Corporation Provides Updates on Wave Season Bookings," February 12, <http://www.carnivalcorp.com>.
51. Caterpillar Company Web Site, <http://www.cat.com>.
52. Caterpillar Company Web Site, Annual Report 2001, <http://www.cat.com>.
53. Ibid.
54. Caterpillar Company Web Site, Press Release, "Caterpillar's Engine Division Offers Solutions to Critical Energy Situation," February 2, 2001, <http://www.cat.com>.
55. Caterpillar Company Web Site.
56. Ibid.; Caterpillar Company Web Site, Press Release, "Caterpillar Inc. Expands Electric Power Product Offering in Latin America," July 6, 2002, <http://www.cat.com>.
57. Caterpillar, Annual Report 2001.
58. Caterpillar Company Web Site.
59. "Caterpillar: Business Might Be Hurt," *AP Online,* April 12, 2001 (as from e-Library.com).
60. "New Beginning," *Toronto Star,* July 4, 2000 (as from eLibrary.com).
61. Caterpillar Company Web Site.
62. Bob Edwards, "Analysis: Caterpillar and DaimlerChrysler Planning to Work Together to Build Large Engines," *Morning Edition* (NPR News), December 7, 2001 (as from eLibrary.com).
63. "Ford, Caterpillar Form Alliance," *AP Online,* November 31, 2001 (as from eLibrary.com).
64. "Update 1—Caterpillar to Sell MT Tractor Line to AGCO," *Reuters Business Report,* December 17, 2001 (as from eLibrary.com).
65. Caterpillar Company Web Site.
66. Ibid.
67. QPR, "What Is Six Sigma?" <http://www.qpronline.com>.
68. Caterpillar, Annual Report 2001.
69. "What Is Sustainable Development?" *IISDnet,* <http://iisd1.iisd.ca/sd/default.htm>.
70. "Trade Issues Limiting Steel Imports: J. B. (Jack) Porter," *Congressional Testimony,* March 23, 1999 (as from eLibrary.com).
71. Caterpillar Company Web Site, Annual Report 2002, <http://www.cat.com>.
72. Joe Stephens and Ellen Nakashima, "Senators Say White Broke Ethics Vow; Ex-Enron Official Hit on Stock Disclosure," *Washington Post,* March 7, 2002, p. A1.
73. "Answers About Enron," *Gannett News Service,* January 20, 2002 (as from eLibrary.com).

74. Robert Siegel and Jacki Lyden,"Analysis: How Enron Was Able to Keep the Analyst Community Bullish for So Long," *All Things Considered* (NPR), February 19, 2002 (as from eLibrary.com).

75. "Q&A: Facts Behind Collapse of the Company," *The Mirror*, January 30, 2002, p. 2.

76. Siegel and Lyden,"Analysis."

77. "Chronology—Rise and Fall of Energy Giant Enron," *Reuters,* January 20, 2002 (as from eLibrary.com).

78. Siegel and Lyden,"Analysis."

79. "Answers About Enron."

80. "Campaign Finance After Enron," *Washington Post*, January 23, 2002, p. A16.

81. Neal Conan,"Analysis: Rise and Fall of Enron," *Talk of the Nation* (NPR), January 3, 2002 (as from eLibrary.com).

82. "Chronology."

83. Kristen Hays,"Enron to Sell Off Money-Losing Assets," *AP Online,* November 14, 2001 (as from eLibrary.com).

84. Peter Behr, "Enron Raised Funds in Private Offering; Shareholders in Dark, Documents Show," *Washington Post*, January 22, p. A1.

85. Christine Dugas,"Employees' Faith in Enron Cost Them Dearly," *USA Today*, January 21, 2002, p. B1.

86. "Chronology."

87. Behr, "Enron Raised Funds."

88. "Campaign Finance After Enron."

89. Enron Company Web Site, <http://www.enron.com>.

90. "Enron Auditor Faces Criminal Charges," *BBC News*, March 15, 2002, <http://www.bbc.com>.

91. "Hollywood Battles for Enron Story," *BBC News*, March 14, 2002, <http://www.bbc.news>.

92. Ted C. Fishman,"Enron Past Returns to Burn Us All," *USA Today*, January 29, 2002, p. A1.

93. Mark L. Clifford and Pete Engardio,"The Corporation: Commentary: Enron Hasn't Made Many Friends in the Third World," *Business Week International,* February 12, 2002, p. 52.

94. Regan Morris,"Enron Collapse Casts Doubt on American Model for Deregulating Energy in Asia," *AP Worldstream*, January 24, 2002.

95. Kmart Company Web Site, Press Release,"Kmart Secures $2 Billion Financing Package and Files for Chapter 11 Reorganization to Aggressively Address Financial and Operational Challenges," January 22, 2002, <http://www.kmartcorp.com>.

96. David Koenig,"Fleming Cuts Shipments to Kmart," *AP Online*, January 21, 2001 (as from eLibrary.com.).

97. Bruce Horowitz,"Kmart Hopes Spike Lee Ads Do the Right Thing," *USA Today*, February 22, 2002, p. B3.

98. "Kmart to Cut 22,000 Jobs, Close 284 Stores," *USAToday.com,* March 8, 2002, <http://www.usatoday.com/money/retail/2002-03-08-kmart.htm>.

99. Ibid.

100. Ibid.

101. Horowitz,"Kmart Spike Lee Ads."

102. Patricia Sellers,"It's (Not) a Good Thing Kmart's Woes Threaten to Taint Martha Stewart's Image—and Business. Anyone Need a Potholder?" *Fortune*, February 4, 2002, p. 22.

103. Horowitz,"Kmart Spike Lee Ads."

104. Keith Naughton, Joan Raymond, and Franco Ordonez,"Crisis at Kmart: Not a Good Thing," *Newsweek,* January 28, 2002, p. 38.

105. Joann Muller,"The Corporation: Strategies: Kmart: The Flood Waters Are Rising," *Business Week*, January 28, 2002, p. 106.

106. Bruce Horowitz and Theresa Howard,"With Image Crumbling, Kmart Files Chapter 11," *USA Today,* January 23, 2001, p. B1.

107. Company Web Site, Annual Report 2000, <http:// www.kmartcorp.com>.

108. Ibid.

109. Horowitz,"Kmart Spike Lee Ads."

110. Ibid.

111. Muller,"The Corporation."

112. "Disney, Kmart Announce Direct-to-Retail Agreement for New Disney-Branded Clothing; Retailer to Develop, Sell Exclusive Line of Disney Apparel," *Business Wire*, February 6, 2001 (as from eLibrary.com).

113. Joann Muller and Ann Therese Palmer,"Marketing: Makeover: Kmart's Bright Idea," *Business Week*, April 9, 2001, p. 50.

114. Dina El-Boghadady,"Checking It Out at Kmart; Chain Uses Do-It-Yourself Scanners to Try to Gain Ground on Rivals," *Washington Post*, December 8, 2001, p. E1.

115. Angela Moore,"Feature—Kmart Tries Survival Path—but Which One?" *Reuters*, February 12, 2002 (as from eLibrary.com).

116. Horowitz,"Kmart Spike Lee Ads."

117. Horowitz and Howard,"With Image Crumbling."

118. Eastman Kodak Company Web Site, Annual Report 2001, <http://www. kodak.com>.

119. David Milstead,"Kodak Refocusing for the Future," *Denver Rocky Mountain News*, May 11, 2001, p. 7B.

120. "KODAK: Revamped Reseller Program Offers Higher Margins," *M2 PressWire*, May 12, 1998 (as from eLibrary.com).

121. "Eastman Kodak: Kodak Announces New, Modular Kodak Retail Solutions to Fulfill Specific Infrastructure Needs of Retailers and Grow Profit Potential; Retailers Can Leverage Kodak's Expertise through A. R.," *M2 PressWire*, February, 25, 2002 (as from eLibrary.com).

122. "Kodak Announces New Operating Model, Business Alignment to Build Profitable Growth," *Business Wire*, November 14, 2001 (as from eLibrary.com).

123. Clay Chandler,"China's Kodak Moment: Company's Focus Begins to Pay Off," *Washington Post*, June 7, 2000, p. E1.

124. Ibid.

125. "Kodak Looks to Digital Salvation," *BBC News*, June 21, 2000, <http://www.bbc.com>.

126. Eastman Kodak, Annual Report 2001.

127. Eastman Kodak Company Web Site, <http://www. kodak.com>.

128. "Kodak-Fuji Ruling," *BBC News*, April 1, 1998, <http://www.bbc.com>.

129. Eastman Kodak Company Web Site.

130. "Kodak Expands EasyShare System with New Family of Digital Cameras and Enhanced Picture Software for Better Home Printing," *Business Wire*, August 14, 2001 (as from eLibrary.com).

131. Ibid.

132. Andy Serwer,"Kodak in the Noose," *Fortune*, February 4, 2002, p. 147.

133. Geoffrey Smith and Faith Keenan,"News: Analysis & Commentary: Cameras: Kodak Is the Picture of Digital Success," *Business Week*, January 14, 2002, p. 39.

134. Ibid.
135. Serwer, "Kodak in the Noose."
136. "Kodak Earnings Slump," *BBC News,* <http://www.bbc>.
137. Ibid.
138. Smith and Keenan, "News."
139. Komatsu Company Web Site, <http://www.komatsu.com>.
140. Ibid.
141. Komatsu Company Web Site, Semi-Annual Report 2002, <http://www.komatsu.com>.
142. Komatsu Company Web Site, Annual Report 2001, <http://www.komatsu.com>.
143. Ibid.
144. Ibid.
145. Komatsu Company Web Site.
146. Komatsu Company Web Site, Annual Report 2000, <http://www.komatsu.com>.
147. Komatsu, Semi-Annual Report 2002.
148. Komatsu Company Web Site.
149. Komatsu, Annual Report 2001.
150. Ibid.
151. Ibid.
152. Komatsu Company Web Site.
153. Komatsu, Semi-Annual Report 2002.
154. Ibid.
155. Nestlé Company Web Site, <http://www.nestle.com>.
156. Ibid.
157. Ibid.
158. "Nestlé Buying Ralston Purina; Combined, the Two Companies Would Have 39% Market Share of the Pet Food Industry," *Atlanta Constitution*, January 16, 2001, p. E1.
159. Thomas Lee, "Nestlé-Purina Merger Will Make Mark in Pet-Food Industry Quickly; Company Will Exploit Vast Distribution System in Eastern Markets and Clout with Retailers to Gain Best Shelf Space," *St. Louis Post Dispatch*, December 16, 2001, p. G1.
160. "Nestlé in $10.3bn Pet Food Buy," *BBC News*, January 16, 2001, <http://www.bbc.ncws>.
161. Lee, "Nestlé-Purina Merger."
162. "Nestlé Pays $641M for Stake in Haagen-Dazs," *United Press International*, December 26, 2001 (as from eLibrary.com).
163. Nestlé Company Web Site, Press Release, "Nestlé and Südzucker in Negotiation About Schöller," June 29, 2001, <http://www.nestle.com>.
164. "Brazil: Danone and Nestlé Struggle for Leadership," *South American Business Information*, September 24, 2001 (as from eLibrary.com).
165. Nestlé Company Web Site, Annual Report 2001, <http://www.nestle.com>.
166. Nestlé Company Web Site.
167. Nucor Company Web Site, <http://www.nucor.com>.
168. Nucor Company Web Site, Annual Report 2000, <http://www.nucor.com>.
169. Nucor Company Web Site
170. Ibid.
171. Doug Palmer, "U.S. Steel Firms Plead for Import Relief," *Reuters*, February 13, 2002 (as from eLibrary.com); Jan Hopkins, "Nucor Corporation—Pres. & CEO, CNNfn," *Street Sweep (CNNfn)*, March 1, 2002 (as from eLibrary.com).
172. Brett Nelson, "An All-New Cast," *Forbes Magazine*, April 16, 2001, p. 318.
173. Nucor Company Web Site, News Release, "Nucor Announces One-Hundred Fifteenth (115th) Consecutive Cash Dividend," December 4, 2001, <http://www.nucor.com>.
174. Ibid.
175. Nucor, Annual Report 2000.
176. Nelson, "An All-New Cast."
177. Kim Clark, "No Pink Slips at This Plant," *U.S. News & World Report*, February 18, 2002, p. 40.
178. Ibid.
179. Ibid.
180. John H. Sheridan, "The Best vs. the Rest: A Glimpse at the Strategies, Strengths, and Management Styles Behind the Numbers," *Industry Week*, 246, August 18, 1997, pp. 70, 79.
181. Nucor Company Web Site, News Release, "Nucor Acquires Auburn Steel Assets," March 19, 2001, <http://www.nucor.com>; Nucor Company Web Site, News Release, "Nucor Obtains Approval to Purchase TRICO Steel Assets," January 25, 2002, <http://www.nucor.com>.
182. Nucor Company Web Site, News Release, "Nucor Offers to Purchase Substantially All Assets of Birmingham Steel for $500 Million in Cash," February 14, 2002, <http://www.nucor.com>.
183. Hopkins, "Nucor Corporation."
184. Palmer, "U.S. Steel Firms Plead."
185. Ibid.
186. Jamie LaReau, "Update 2—U.S. Steel, Nucor Raises Steel Prices," *Reuters Business Report*, February 26, 2001 (as from eLibrary.com).
187. Outback Steakhouse Company Web Site, Annual Reports, <http://www.outback.com>.
188. "Outback Steakhouse Says Earnings Expected Lower," *Reuters Business Report*, June 25, 2001 (as from eLibrary.com).
189. "Update 1—Outback Steakhouse Plans More Restaurants," *Reuters Business Report*, April 23, 2001 (as from eLibrary.com).
190. Outback Steakhouse Company Web Site, Annual Report 2000, <http://www.outback.com>.
191. "Outback Steakhouse Oct. Same-Store Sales Fall 1.5 pct.," *Reuters Business Report*, November 1, 2001 (as from eLibrary.com).
192. Outback Steakhouse Company Web Site, <http://www.outback.com>.
193. Ibid.
194. Ibid.
195. Rachel Brand, "Appetite for Takeout Grows; More Restaurants Offer to-Go Dinners to Meet the Consumer Demand," *Denver Rocky Mountain News*, December 12, 2000, p. B8.
196. "Update 1—Outback.
197. Outback Steakhouse Company Web Site.
198. Ibid.
199. Outback Steakhouse Company Web Site, Annual Report 2000, <http://www.outback.com>.
200. Ibid.
201. "Mexico: Outback Steakhouse Inc. Takes a Huge Bite," *South American Business Information*, November 26, 2001 (as from eLibrary.com).
202. Outback Steakhouse, Annual Report 2000.
203. Ibid.
204. Fleming's Prime Steakhouse and Wine Bar Company Web Site, <http://www.flemingssteakhouse.com>.

205. Roy's Restaurants Company Web Site, <http://www.roysrestaurant.com>.
206. Outback Steakhouse Company Web Site.
207. Andrea Meadows, "Outback Hooks Bonefish Grill," *Tampa Tribune*, August 28, 2001, p. 4.
208. "NPD Foodservice Information Group Reports 1999 Restaurant Sales Up, Unit Growth Flat," *Business Wire*, February 10, 2000 (as from eLibrary.com).
209. Vicky Uhland, "Cooking Up a Rare Approach, Springs Consultants Help Restaurant Hire, Keep Good Employees," *Denver Rocky Mountain News*, January 4, 2002, p. B8.
210. David Baily, "U.S. Casual Restaurants Seen Beating Rising Costs," *Reuters Business Report*, July 9, 2001 (as from eLibrary.com).
211. "Outback Steakhouse Says Earnings Expected Lower," *Reuters Business Report*, June 25, 2001 (as from eLibrary.com).
212. "Outback Steakhouse Immune to Europe Health Scares," *Reuters*, April 2, 2001 (as from eLibrary.com).
213. Shannon Dorey, "Streaming Media," *The-Surfs-Up*, 2001, <http://www.the-surfs-up.com>.
214. RealNetworks Company Web Site, Annual Report 2000, <http://www.realnetworks.com>.
215. Ibid.
216. RealNetworks Company Web Site, Press Release, "RealNetworks Launches Real.com Games," March 27, 2000, <http://www.realnetworks.com>.
217. RealNetworks Company Web Site <http://www.realnetworks.com>.
218. Ariana Eunjung Cha, "Microsoft's Problem Child; Former Ally RealNetworks Has Dominant Role in Internet Media," *Washington Post*, June 22, 2001, p. E1.
219. Dorey, "Streaming Media."
220. Franklin Paul, "Update 2—RealNetworks Profit Dips, 2001 View Trimmed," *Reuters Business Report*, January 30, 2001 (as from eLibrary.com).
221. Cha, "Microsoft's Problem Child."
222. Brent Schlender, "The Real Deal," *Fortune*, March 4, 2002, <http://www.fortune.com>.
223. Scott Hillis, "Update 2—RealNetworks Q4 Net Loss Falls, Sees Growth Ahead," *Reuters Business Report*, January 29, 2002 (as from eLibrary.com).
224. RealNetworks, Annual Report 2000.
225. RealNetworks, Annual Report 2000.
226. Dorey, "Streaming Media."
227. Ibid.
228. "Tiscali: Tiscali, U2.com and RealNetworks Today Announced That 5 Million Fans Watched the Live U2 Webcast from All Over the World," *M2 PressWire*, November 15, 2001 (as from eLibrary.com).
229. Sandvik Company Web Site, <http//www.sandvik.com>.
230. Ibid.
231. "Sandvik Becomes Part-Owner of Endorsia e-Business Marketplace," *Business Wire*, January 10, 2001 (as from eLibrary.com).
232. Sandvik Company Web Site.
233. "Sandvik Acquires Manufacturing of Cemented-Carbide Tools in Brazil," *Business Wire,* May 15, 2001 (as of elibrary.com); "Sandvik Expands in South America— Acquires Leading Service Company in the Mining Industry in Chile," *Business Wire*, June 5, 2001 (as from eLibrary.com).
234. Sandvik Company Web Site, Year End Report 2001, <http://www.sandvik.com>.
235. Foreign Exchange, *New York Times*, March 25, 2002, p. C10.
236. Sandvik Company Web Site.
237. Patricia L. Smith, "More Than Just the Sum of Its Parts," *American Machinist*, 142, July 1, 1998, pp. 50, 54.
238. Ibid.
239. Ibid.
240. Ibid.
241. Sandvik, Year End Report 2001.
242. "Wal-Mart Defies Recession," *BBC News*, February 19, 2002, <http://www.bbc.com>.
243. Wal-Mart Company Web Site, Annual Report 2001, <http://www.walmart.com>.
244. Linda Saigol, "Wal-Mart Sales Push It to World's Top," *Financial Times*, February 19, 2002, <http://www.ft.com>.
245. Wal-Mart, Annual Report 2001.
246. Ibid.
247. Ibid.
248. Ibid.
249. Wal-Mart Company Web Site, <http://www.walmart.com>.
250. Ibid.
251. "Wal-Mart Takes on Japan," *BBC News*, March 14, 2002, <http://www.ft.com>.
252. Wendy Zellner, "The Corporation: Strategies: Will Walmart.com Get It Right This Time?" *Business Week*, November 6, 2000, p. 104.
253. "Nielsen/NetRatings Announces Top E-Tailers of the 2000 Holiday Season," *Business Wire*, January 2, 2000 (as from eLibrary.com).
254. Dawn Gilbertson, "Walmart.com Goes Cruising," *Arizona Republic*, January 20, 2002, p. T1.
255. Wal-Mart, Annual Report 2001.
256. Ibid.
257. Ibid.
258. Wal-Mart Company Web Site.
259. Ibid.
260. Boycott International, <http://www.1worldcommunication.org/Walmart.htm>.

Strategic Management

AN INTEGRATED APPROACH

Fifth Edition

Charles W. L. Hill
University of Washington

Gareth R. Jones
Texas A&M University

HOUGHTON MIFFLIN COMPANY
Boston   New York

For Alexandra, Elizabeth, Charlotte, and Michelle

    C.W.L.H.

For Jennifer, Nicholas, and Julia

    G.R.J.

Sponsoring Editor: *George Hoffman*
Senior Associate Editor: *Susan M. Kahn*
Senior Project Editor: *Maria Morelli*
Editorial Assistants: *Cecilia Molinari, Tanius Stamper*
Production/Design Coordinator: *Jennifer Meyer Dare*
Manufacturing Coordinator: *Sally Culler*
Marketing Manager: *Melissa Russell*

Cover image and design: Harold Burch, Harold Burch Design, New York City

Netscape Communicator browser window copyright © 1999 Netscape Communication Corporation. Used with permission.

Printed in the U.S.A.

Library of Congress Catalog Card number: 00-133871

ISBN: 0-618-24126-4

123456789-QWV-03 02

Brief Contents

Contents

| Chapter 7 | Competitive Strategy and the Industrial Environment | 233 |

Chapter 8   Strategy in the Global Environment   265

Chapter 9   Corporate Strategy: Vertical Integration, Diversification, and Strategic Alliances   311

Chapter 10 Corporate Development: Building and Restructuring the Corporation

Chapter 13   Matching Structure and Control to Strategy   450

Preface

In its fourth edition, *Strategic Management: An Integrated Approach* became the most widely used strategic management textbook on the market. In every edition we have attracted new users who share with us the concern for currency in text and examples to ensure that cutting edge issues and theories in strategic management are addressed. The increased support for and acceptance of our integrated approach to strategic management has led us to revise the fifth edition of our book to explore the most important current new development affecting strategic management: the effects of the growing use of the Internet and new information technologies on all aspects of strategic management. In addition, the enthusiasm that greeted our interactive approach to involving students in strategic management has also led us to refine our hands-on approach in the section at the end of each chapter called Practicing Strategic Management.

We are grateful to the many instructors using our text, and we have continued to use feedback from them as well as from instructors not using our text to increase the value of *Strategic Management*. We have continued to update our coverage of all the flourishing strategic management literature while keeping the text readable. We have also written or collected a new set of strategic management cases that we believe are our best ever. Finally, we have broadened the offerings in our supplements package for both students and instructors. We believe that together, the text, cases, interactive teaching approach in our Practicing Strategic Management sections, and supplements package provide students and instructors with a learning and teaching experience that is second to none.

COMPREHENSIVE AND UP-TO-DATE COVERAGE

■ Significant Content Changes

The overall organization of this edition, as noted in Figure 1.1 on page 6, reflects that of previous editions and is designed so that the concepts build upon one another, with early chapters providing a strong foundation for later ones. Though the organization remains familiar, nearly every chapter in the fifth edition has been significantly revised to include coverage of issues related to the effects of new information technologies on company strategy and structure. This theme of the ***new economy***—the information technology complex in all of its facets, including computing, communications, and most obviously, the Internet—is emphasized throughout the text. The ongoing revolution in computing and communications technology, as embodied most vividly by the emergence of the Internet, has major strategic implications for the strategy of enterprises in a wide range of industries, from computers and communications, through financial services, to manufacturing and retailing. The Internet in particular represents a competitive paradigm shift of major proportions.

In this edition we draw on recent contributions to the academic literature to explain the implications of the new economy for competitive strategy. In addition, we have used numerous examples throughout the text to illustrate how the Internet affects businesses in a wide range of industries. Finally, a number of the cases in this edition focus explicitly on enterprises that compete in the new economy arena. For examples of the changes made in this edition to reflect the new economy theme, consider the following.

■ The chapter-opening cases and Strategy in Action features in many of the chapters look at enterprises competing in the Internet space and highlight the way new information technologies and the Internet are changing the way companies compete and do business today. For example, Chapter 1 opens with a review of the strategy pursued by Yahoo!; Chapter 3 opens with a discussion of how the Internet is revolutionizing the stockbrokerage industry; and Chapter 4 opens with a discussion of how Cisco Systems has used the Internet to automate much of its customer and service interface, in the process taking hundreds of millions of dollars annually out of its cost structure.

■ Within the text, we discuss the changes taking place in the information technology environment. For example, in Chapter 3, which deals with the environment, we now analyze the effects of market externalities on the competitive environment and how these externalities influence business- and corporate-level strategy. We also analyze how externalities affect the ***sources of competitive advantage***—efficiency, quality, innovation, and customer responsiveness—and have continued to revise our explanation of how organizations build strengths in these areas through functional-, business-, and corporate-level strategy. In this chapter, we have also added a section on ***network economics***. We explain how network effects, positive feedback loops, and switching costs can result in a market being dominated by a single enterprise. A good example is Microsoft's domination of the market for desktop computer operating systems.

■ In Chapter 5, which deals with operations, we look at how companies are using Internet-based information systems to dramatically increase their productivity and customer responsiveness.

■ In Chapter 7, we look at the strategies that firms can adopt to exploit network effects and establish themselves as market leaders.

■ Chapter 10, "Corporate Development," continues to provide students with a clear picture of the major changes that have been taking place in contemporary corporate strategy.

■ The chapters on strategy implementation now analyze how new information technologies influence organizational design and build competitive advantage.

■ In the case section of this edition, we have included new cases on America Online, Amazon.com, Real Networks, Microsoft, Sun Microsystems, and the Home Video Game Industry. All of these cases look at the strategy of enterprises competing in the "new economy" arena.

This new focus on the Internet and new information technologies brings our integrated picture of the strategic management process up to date.

Although we have included a large amount of theoretical and anecdotal material that relates to the new economy, it is also important to stress that we have continued to update other sections of the book to include recent advances in the literature and to use recent examples. For example:

- In Chapter 1 we have drawn on the work of Daniel Goldman in the new section on *emotional intelligence* and its relevance to strategic leadership.

- Also in Chapter 1, we have added a section on the role of *serendipity and strategy*. We explore the way serendipitous events can drive the strategy of an enterprise.

- In Chapter 3 we have expanded Porter's famous five-forces model to include a sixth force now recognized to be extremely important in many technology-driven industries: the power and vigor of enterprises that supply products that are *complements* to those produced by the industry. Porter focuses on substitutes, but ignores complements. See the section on **A Sixth Force: Complementors.**

- In Chapter 5 we have expanded the section on innovation in recognition of the important role that *continuous innovation* plays in sustaining a competitive advantage in the modern economy.

- Almost all of the opening cases for each chapter and many of the Strategy in Action features are either completely new or significantly revised.

Throughout the revision, we have been careful to preserve the *balanced and integrated* nature of our account of the strategic management process. Moreover, as we added new material, we deleted less current or less important concepts and information to ensure that students would concentrate on the core concepts and issues in the field. We have also paid close attention to retaining the book's readability.

Finally, it is important to emphasize that we have overhauled the case selection. Only seven of the forty-one cases in this edition have been retained from the prior edition, and most of these seven have been updated. As noted before, many of these cases emphasize new economy themes, but we continue to carry a good number of old economy cases. As always, we believe that the selection of cases we offer is the best on the market.

PRACTICING STRATEGIC MANAGEMENT: AN INTERACTIVE APPROACH

We hope you are excited by the hands-on learning possibilities provided by the exercises and assignments in the end-of-chapter *Practicing Strategic Management* sections. Following the Chapter Summary and Discussion Questions, each chapter contains the following assignments/exercises:

Small Group Exercise This short (20-minute) experiential exercise asks students to divide into groups and discuss a scenario concerning some aspect of strategic management. For example, the scenario in Chapter 11 asks students to discuss how they would reengineer the structure of a greeting cards company to increase the speed of product innovation.

Exploring the Web   The Internet exercise requires students to explore a particular web site and answer chapter-related questions. For example, the Chapter 8 assignment requires students to go to IBM's web site and analyze the company's strategy for competing in the global marketplace. This section also asks students to select a web site and answer questions relevant to the chapter.

Article File   As in the last edition, this exercise requires students to research business magazines to identify a company that is facing a particular strategic management problem. For instance, students are asked to locate and research a company pursuing a low-cost or a differentiation strategy, and to describe this company's strategy, its advantages and disadvantages, and the core competencies required to pursue it. Students' presentations of their findings lead to lively class discussions.

Strategic Management Project   Students in small groups choose a company to study for the whole semester and then analyze the company using the series of questions provided at the end of every chapter. For example, students might select Ford Motor Co. and, using the series of chapter questions, they will collect information on Ford's top managers, mission, ethical position, domestic and global strategy and structure, and so on. Eventually, students write a case study of their company and present it to the class at the end of the semester. We typically had students present one or more of the cases in the book early in the semester, but now in our classes we tend to treat the students' own projects as the major class assignment and their case presentations as the climax of the semester's learning experience.

Closing Case Study   A short closing case provides an opportunity for a short class discussion on a chapter-related theme.

In creating these exercises it is not our intention to suggest that they should *all* be used for *every* chapter. For example, over a semester an instructor might combine a group strategic management project with five to six article file assignments and five to six exploring the web exercises, while doing eight to ten small group experiential exercises in class.

We have found that our interactive approach to teaching strategic management appeals to students. It also greatly improves the quality of their learning experience. Our approach is more fully discussed in the *Instructor's Resource Manual*.

STRATEGIC
MANAGEMENT CASES

The 41 cases that we have selected for this edition will appeal, we are certain, to students and professors alike, both because these cases are intrinsically interesting and because of the number of strategic management issues they illuminate. The organizations discussed in the cases range from large, well-known ones, for which students can do research in order to update the information, to small, entrepreneurial businesses that illustrate the uncertainty and challenge of the strategic management process. In addition, the selections include many international cases, and most of the other cases contain some element of global strategy. Refer to the table of contents for a complete listing of the cases with brief descriptions.

We feel that our entire selection is unrivaled in breadth and depth, and we are grateful to the other case authors who have contributed to this edition.

Jacqueline M. Abbey
Georgetown University

Frank C. Barnes
University of North Carolina, Charlotte

M. Edgar Barrett
Thunderbird—The American Graduate School of International Management

Christopher A. Bartlett
Harvard Business School

Julian Birkinshaw
Richard Ivey School of Business, The University of Western Ontario (Canada)

Brad Brown
University of Virginia

Lew G. Brown
University of North Carolina at Greensboro

James W. Camerius
Northern Michigan University

Kristen M. Cashman
University of North Carolina at Greensboro

Lisa Chadderdon
Harvard Business School

James W. Clinton
University of Northern Colorado

Isaac Cohen
San Jose State University

Harold Dyck
California State University—San Bernardino

Michael I. Eizenberg
Bentley College

Vidya Gargeya
University of North Carolina at Greensboro

Madelyn Gengelbach
University of Missouri at Kansas City

Sue Greenfeld
California State University—San Bernardino

Irene Hagenbuch
Bentley College

Alan N. Hoffman
Bentley College

Harold F. Hogan, Jr.
Harvard Business School

Margaret Johnston
University of Washington

Javad Kargar
North Carolina Central University

Mike Keeffe
Southwest Texas State University

Robert Kennedy
Harvard Business School

Charles A. Kivett
University of North Carolina at Greensboro

Suresh Kotha
University of Washington

Jeffrey A. Krug
University of Illinois at Urbana-Champaign

Sharon Ungar Lane
Bentley College

Kevin B. Lowe
University of North Carolina at Greensboro

Michael Lubatkin
University of Connecticut

John H. Lundin
University of North Carolina at Greensboro

Stewart C. Malone
University of Virginia

Bill Middlebrook
Southwest Texas State University

Cynthia Montgomery
Harvard Business School

Richard Moxon
University of Washington

Karen L. Newman
Georgetown University

Stanley D. Nollen
Georgetown University

George M. Puia
Indiana State University

Krishnan Ramaya
University of Southern Indiana

John K. Ross III
Southwest Texas State University

Frank T. Rothaermel
Michigan State University

Don K. Sowers
University of North Carolina at Greensboro

Marilyn L. Taylor
University of Missouri at Kansas City

Robin Teigland
Richard Ivey School of Business, The University of Western Ontario (Canada)

Jorge Touché
Thunderbird—The American Graduate School of International Management

Suzanne Uhlen
Lund University (Sweden)

Roderick E. White
Richard Ivey School of Business, The University of Western Ontario (Canada)

Tony R. Wingler
University of North Carolina at Greensboro

To help students learn how to effectively analyze and write a case study, we continue to include a special section on this subject. This section includes a checklist and explanation of areas to consider, suggested research tools, tips on financial analysis, and guidelines for using the Strategic Management Project.

TEACHING AND LEARNING AIDS

Taken together, the teaching and learning features of *Strategic Management* provide a package that is unsurpassed in its coverage and that supports the integrated approach, which we have taken throughout the book.

■ For the Instructor

■ The **Instructor's Resource Manual**, which users liked so much in the first four editions of *Strategic Management*, has been completely revised. For each chapter we provide a *synopsis*, a list of *teaching objectives,* a *comprehensive lecture outline,* and *answers to discussion questions.* Each of the chapter opening cases also has a corresponding *teaching note* to help guide class discussion. Furthermore, the lecture outlines include summaries of the material in the *Strategy in Action* boxes. Finally, the manual includes comments on the Practicing Strategic Management sections and suggested answers to the Closing Case Discussion Questions.

■ **Instructor's Resource Manual: Cases** Because of the comprehensive nature of the Instructor's Resource Manual, the length of the manual has become a bit difficult to manage. To make the manual easier to handle, we have split it into two volumes with this edition. The cases volume includes a complete list of Case Discussion Questions as well as a *comprehensive teaching note* for each case, which gives a complete analysis of case issues.

■ The **Test Bank** (in the *Instructor's Resource Manual*) has been revised and offers a set of comprehensive true/false and multiple-choice questions, and the answers to them, for each chapter in the book. The **Computerized Test Bank** allows instructors to generate and change tests easily on the computer. Instructors can edit or add questions, select questions, or generate randomly selected tests. The program will print an answer key appropriate to each version created, and it lets instructors customize the printed appearance of the text. A call-in test service is also available through Faculty Services. The program also includes the Online Testing System and Gradebook. This feature allows instructors to administer tests via a network system, modem, or personal computer. It also includes a grading function that lets instructors set up a new class; record grades; analyze grades; and produce class and individual statistics.

■ A package of **color transparencies** accompanies the book. These include nearly all the figures found in the chapters.

■ Accompanying this edition is a set of **PowerPoint**® **slides**. This lecture tool combines clear, concise text and art to create a total presentation package that follows the concepts found in the text. Instructors with PowerPoint can edit slides and customize them to fit their own course needs; a viewer is included for those without. Slides can also be printed for lecture notes and class distribution.

■ **Videos** pertaining to several of the cases and concepts in the text are available to instructors. They help highlight many issues of interest and can be used to spark class discussion.

■ An extensive **Web site** contains many features to aid instructors including downloadable files for the text and case materials from the Instructor's Resource Manuals, the downloadable PowerPoint slides, the Video Guide, and sample syllabi. Additional materials on the student Web site may also be of use to instructors.

■ For the Student

■ A student **Web site** provides help for students as they make their way through the course. The Web site features links to the companies highlighted in each chapter's boxes and opening and closing cases as well as the full-length cases, links to other sites of general interest while studying strategic management, the Exploring the Web exercises with any updates as necessary to account for the inevitable changes that occur to the relevant sites, case discussion questions to guide students as they analyze the in-depth cases, and ACE self-tests related to each chapter.

■ The Real Deal UpGrade **CD-ROM** includes a glossary of key terms, chapter learning objectives to guide student study, and quizzes to test their understanding of the major concepts.

ACKNOWLEDGMENTS

This book is the product of far more than two authors. We are grateful to George Hoffman, our executive editor, and Melissa Russell, our marketing manager, for their help in promoting and developing the book and for providing us with timely feedback and information from professors and reviewers that have allowed us to shape the book to meet the needs of its intended market. We are also grateful to Susan Kahn, senior development editor, for ably coordinating the planning of our book and for managing the creation of the ancillary materials, and to Maria Morelli for her adept handling of production. We are also grateful to the case authors for allowing us to use their materials. We also want to thank the departments of management at the University of Washington and Texas A&M University for providing the setting and atmosphere in which the book could be written, and the students of these universities who reacted to and provided input for many of our ideas. In addition, the following reviewers of this and earlier editions gave us valuable suggestions for improving the manuscript from its original version to its current form:

Ken Armstrong
Anderson University

Kunal Banerji
West Virginia University

Glenn Bassett
University of Bridgeport

Thomas H. Berliner
The University of Texas at Dallas

Richard G. Brandenburg
University of Vermont

Steven Braund
University of Hull

Philip Bromiley
University of Minnesota

Geoffrey Brooks
Western Oregon State College

Lowell Busenitz
University of Houston

Gene R. Conaster
Golden State University

Steven W. Congden
University of Hartford

Catherine M. Daily
Ohio State University

Robert DeFillippi
Suffolk University Sawyer School of Management

Helen Deresky
SUNY—Plattsburgh

Gerald E. Evans
The University of Montana

John Fahy
Trinity College, Dublin

Patricia Feltes
Southwest Missouri State University

Mark Fiegener
Oregon State University

Isaac Fox
Washington State University

Craig Galbraith
University of North Carolina at Wilmington

Scott R. Gallagher
Rutgers University

Eliezer Geisler
Northeastern Illinois University

Gretchen Gemeinhardt
University of Houston

Lynn Godkin
Lamar University

Robert L. Goldberg
Northeastern University

Graham L. Hubbard
University of Minnesota

Tammy G. Hunt
University of North Carolina at Wilmington

James Gaius Ibe
Morris College

W. Grahm Irwin
Miami University

Jonathan L. Johnson
University of Arkansas Walton College of Business Administration

Marios Katsioloudes
University of South Carolina Coastal Carolina College

Robert Keating
University of North Carolina at Wilmington

Geoffrey King
California State University—Fullerton

Rico Lam
University of Oregon

Robert J. Litschert
Virginia Polytechnic Institute and State University

Franz T. Lohrke
Louisiana State University

Lance A. Masters
California State University—San Bernardino

Robert N. McGrath
Embry-Riddle Aeronautical University

Charles Mercer
Drury College

Van Miller
University of Dayton

Joanna Mulholland
West Chester University of Pennsylvania

Francine Newth
Providence College

Paul R. Reed
Sam Houston State University

Rhonda K. Reger
Arizona State University

Malika Richards
Indiana University

Ronald Sanchez
University of Illinois

Joseph A. Schenk
University of Dayton

Brian Shaffer
University of Kentucky

Pradip K. Shukla
Chapman University

Dennis L. Smart
University of Nebraska at Omaha

Barbara Spencer
Clemson University

Lawrence Steenberg
University of Evansville

Kim A. Stewart
University of Denver

Ted Takamura
Warner Pacific College

Bobby Vaught
Southwest Missouri State

Robert P. Vichas
Florida Atlantic University

Daniel L. White
Drexel University

Edgar L. Williams, Jr.
Norfolk State University

Finally, thanks are due to our families for their patience and support during the revision process. We especially thank our wives, Alexandra Hill and Jennifer George, for their ever increasing support and affection.

Charles W. L. Hill
Gareth R. Jones

The Strategic Management Process

OPENING CASE

Strategy at Yahoo!

BACK in 1993, Jerry Yang and David Filo were two graduate engineering students at Stanford University. Instead of writing their dissertations, which they probably should have been doing, the two were spending a lot of time surfing the World Wide Web and building lists of their favorite sites. On a whim, they decided to post their list on the Web. They dubbed the site "Jerry's Guide to the World Wide Web." Almost by accident, they had created one of the first Web directories. In doing so, they had solved a pressing need: how to find things on the Web. In 1994, they changed the name of the directory to Yahoo! (http://www.yahoo.com), which is supposed to stand for "Yet Another Hierarchical Officious Oracle," although Filo and Yang insist they selected the name because they considered themselves "yahoos."

By late 1994, Yahoo! was drawing more than 100,000 people a day. The directory had outgrown the limited ca-

pacity of the Stanford site, and Yahoo! was borrowing server space from nearby Netscape. Yang and Filo had decided to put their graduate studies on hold while they turned their attention to building Yahoo! into a business. One of their first hires, Srinija Srinivasan, or "ontological yahoo" as she is known within the company, refined and developed the classification scheme that has become the hallmark of Yahoo!'s Web directory. Yang and Filo's business model was to derive revenues from renting advertising space on the pages of the fast-growing directory.

To grow the business, however, they needed capital to fund investments in servers, software development, and classification personnel. A solution came in the form of an investment from Sequoia Capital, a Silicon Valley venture capital firm. As part of the investment package, Sequoia required Yang and Filo to hire an experienced chief executive officer (CEO). The man chosen for the job was Andrew

Koogle, a forty-five-year-old engineer with fifteen years experience in the management of high technology firms, including a stint as president of InterMec, a Seattle-based manufacturer of bar code scanning equipment.

By mid 1996, Koogle was heading a publicly traded company that listed 200,000 Web sites under 20,000 different categories and was being used by 800,000 people per day. This, however, was just the beginning. In conjunction with Yang, Filo, and another "gray-haired" hire—the chief operating officer, Jeffrel Mallett—Koogle crafted a vision of Yahoo! as a global media company whose principal asset would be a major Internet gateway, or portal, that would enable anyone to connect with anything or anybody. Koogle's ambition was to transform Yahoo!'s simple directory service into a conduit for bringing together buyers and sellers, thereby facilitating commercial transactions over the Web (e-commerce). In this vision, Yahoo! would continue to generate revenues from the sale of advertising space on its directory pages, but it would also garner significant revenues from e-commerce transactions by taking a small slice of each transaction executed over its service. The service, Yahoo! Store (http://store.yahoo.com), enables businesses to quickly create, publish and manage secure on-line stores to market and sell goods and services. After launching their store, merchants are included in searches on Yahoo! Shopping (http://shopping.yahoo.com), Yahoo!'s Internet shopping service.

To make this vision a reality, Yahoo! had to become one of the most useful and well-known locations on the Web—in short, it had to become a megabrand. A directory alone would not suffice, no matter how useful. So in order to increase traffic, Yahoo! began to add features that enhanced its appeal to Web users. One aspect of this was to supplement the directory with compelling content. Another was to allow registered users to customize Yahoo! pages to best match their needs. For example, registered Yahoo! users can customize a page in Yahoo!'s financial area so that they can track the value of their personal stock portfolio. The page provides links to message boards, where individual investors can discuss a company's prospects. Other links connect investors to valuable content pertaining to the companies in their stock portfolio, including news reports and commentary, research reports, detailed financial data and each company's Web site.

To build brand awareness, Yahoo! spent heavily on advertising, using radio and television ads targeted at mainstream America. To expand the reach of the service, Yahoo!

embarked on a strategy of opening up Yahoo! services around the world. Yahoo! also began to work with content providers and merchants to build their on-line presence, and by extension, to increase the value of Yahoo!'s site to users who could access the content and merchants through Yahoo! Moreover, Yahoo! increased its value to advertisers by enabling them to better target their advertising message to certain demographics. For example, the on-line broker E*Trade advertises heavily on Yahoo!'s financial pages. Such targeted advertising increases the conversion rate or yield associated with advertisements.

The results of this strategy have been quite spectacular. By 1998, the company had 50 million unique users, up from 26 million in the prior year. Some 35 million of these were registered with Yahoo! These users were accessing 167 million Yahoo! pages per day in December 1998. By the end of 1998, 3,800 companies were advertising on Yahoo!'s pages, up from 2,600 in 1997 and 700 in 1996. As of May 1999, some 5,000 merchants were selling products over Yahoo! Shopping, up from 3,500 in December 1998. At the same time, there were eighteen Yahoo!s outside the United States, and Yahoo! could be accessed in twelve languages. The company's revenues had grown from $21.5 million in 1996 to $203 million in 1998. Meanwhile, Yahoo!'s stock price soared from $5 a share in 1996 to a high of $244 a share in early 1999, effectively valuing Yahoo! at a staggering $45 billion and making Yang and Filo billionaires.

Going forward, Yahoo!'s strategy has been characterized by Koogle as "Yahoo! everywhere." To facilitate this, Yahoo! has been developing technology that will enable users to access Yahoo! over a wide range of digital devices, from conventional personal computers to hand-held personal assistants, smart cellular phones, television equipment with set top boxes, and hand-held Web tablets. Yahoo! has also continued to enhance the value of its service and brand by acquiring valuable Web properties. For example, in March 1999, Yahoo! acquired GeoCities, a popular Web service that allows individuals to publish their own home pages and related material on the Web. This was followed in April by the acquisition of Broadcast.com inc, the Web's leading aggregator and broadcaster of streaming audio and video programming. The Broadcast.com acquisition should allow Yahoo! to broadcast audio and video content over the Web, in addition to text, making Yahoo!'s network even more valuable to users.[1]

OVERVIEW

Why do some organizations succeed while others fail? In the fast-evolving world of the Internet, for example, how is it that companies like Yahoo! and AOL have managed to build a strong presence, whereas others, such as Prodigy, Excite, and Compuserve, have not had the same degree of success? In the retail industry, what distinguishes successes such as Wal-Mart from failures such as rival American discount retailer Kmart? Why has Wal-Mart consistently outperformed the industry, even in difficult years, whereas Kmart found itself facing the possibility of bankruptcy in the mid 1990s? In the personal computer industry, what are the factors that differentiate successful firms, such as Dell and Gateway 2000, from the failures, such as AST and Packard Bell, both of which saw their market share slump during the late 1990s? In the market for database software, why have Oracle and Microsoft managed to build strong market positions, whereas rivals such as Informix and Sybase have lost significant market share? In the airline industry, how is it that Southwest Airlines has managed to keep growing its revenues and profits through both good times and bad, whereas TWA has repeatedly flirted with bankruptcy? In the toy industry, what differentiates the successful firms such as Mattel and Hasbro from failures such as Coleco, which rode to fame with the Cabbage Patch Kids only to see sales slump as its brand lost appeal among America's young? How did Sony come to dominate the market for video games with its highly successful PlayStation, whereas former industry leader Sega saw its market share slump from 60 percent in the early 1990s to the low single digits by the end of the decade?

This book argues that the strategies an organization pursues have a major impact on its performance relative to its peers. A **strategy** is an action a company takes to attain one or more of its goals. For most if not all organizations, an overriding goal is to achieve superior performance. Thus, a strategy can often be defined more precisely as *an action a company takes to attain superior performance*. The overriding goal of Yahoo!, for example, is to achieve significant revenue and earnings growth. Yahoo!'s strategies for attaining this goal include maximizing the value of its service to individual Web users, thereby attracting a large volume of Web traffic, which in turn allows the company to garner significant revenues from renting advertising space to merchants and facilitating e-commerce transactions. The company has taken various actions that are consistent with maximizing the value of its service. These include building the best directory on the Web, enabling Yahoo! users to customize their Yahoo! service and post their own home page on the service (hence the acquisition of GeoCities) and providing valuable text, audio, and video content. Yahoo! has been more successful than its peers because it has a well-thought-out and well-executed strategy.

Much of this book is devoted to identifying and describing the pros and cons of the various strategies a company can pursue. Many of these strategies are generic— that is, they apply to all organizations, large or small, manufacturing or service, and profit-seeking or not-for-profit. The aim is to give you a thorough understanding of the analytical techniques and skills necessary to identify and exploit strategies successfully. The first step toward achieving this objective is to give you an overview of the **strategic management process,** that is, the process by which managers choose a set of strategies for the enterprise. By the end of this chapter, you will understand the processes managers use to select strategies for their company, and you will have an appreciation of these processes' strengths and weaknesses.

STRATEGIC PLANNING

Ask the average person in the street how an organization chooses its strategy, and the answer will probably be that the strategy is the result of a *rational planning* process orchestrated, if not dominated, by the *top management* of the organization. To a certain extent, this emphasis on a rational planning process dominated by top management reflects the military roots of strategy, with its imagery of generals clustered around a map table with their staff plotting out a strategy for defeating the enemy. This imagery has been propagated in the business literature by a number of writers, who have emphasized that strategy is the outcome of a formal planning process and that top management plays the most important role in this process.[2] The story of Yahoo!, discussed in the Opening Case, provides us with an example of the role of top management in strategy formulation. Koogle, Yahoo!'s CEO, seems to have been the principal strategic architect behind Yahoo!'s transformation from a Web directory into a compelling on-line destination that will connect anyone to anybody or anything.

Although the view of strategy as the product of a rational planning process driven by top management has some basis in reality, it is not the whole story. As we shall see later in the chapter, not all of an organization's strategies result from formal strategic planning exercises. Valuable strategies often emerge from deep within the organization without prior planning. Nevertheless, a consideration of planning is a useful starting point for our journey into the world of strategy. Accordingly, in this section we consider what might be described as a stereotypical strategic planning model.

■ A Basic Planning Model

The strategic planning process can be broken down into five main steps illustrated in Figure 1.1. You might want to think of Figure 1.1 as a plan of the book, for it also shows how the different chapters relate to the different steps of the strategic planning process. The five steps are (1) selection of the corporate mission and major corporate goals; (2) analysis of the organization's external competitive environment to identify **opportunities** and **threats**; (3) analysis of the organization's internal operating environment to identify the organization's **strengths** and **weaknesses**; (4) selection of strategies that build on the organization's strengths and correct its weaknesses in order to take advantage of external opportunities and counter external threats; and (5) strategy implementation. The task of analyzing the organization's external and internal environment and then selecting an appropriate strategy is normally referred to as **strategy formulation**. In contrast, **strategy implementation** typically involves designing appropriate organizational structures and control systems to put the organization's chosen strategy into action.

Each component illustrated in Figure 1.1 constitutes a *sequential* step in the strategic planning process. Each *cycle* of the planning process begins with a statement of the corporate mission and major corporate goals. The mission statement is followed by external analysis, internal analysis, and strategic choice. The process ends with the design of the organizational structure and control systems necessary to implement the organization's chosen strategy.

Some organizations go through this kind of process every year, although this should not be taken to imply that the organization chooses a new strategy each

FIGURE 1.1

The Main Components
of the Strategic
Planning Process

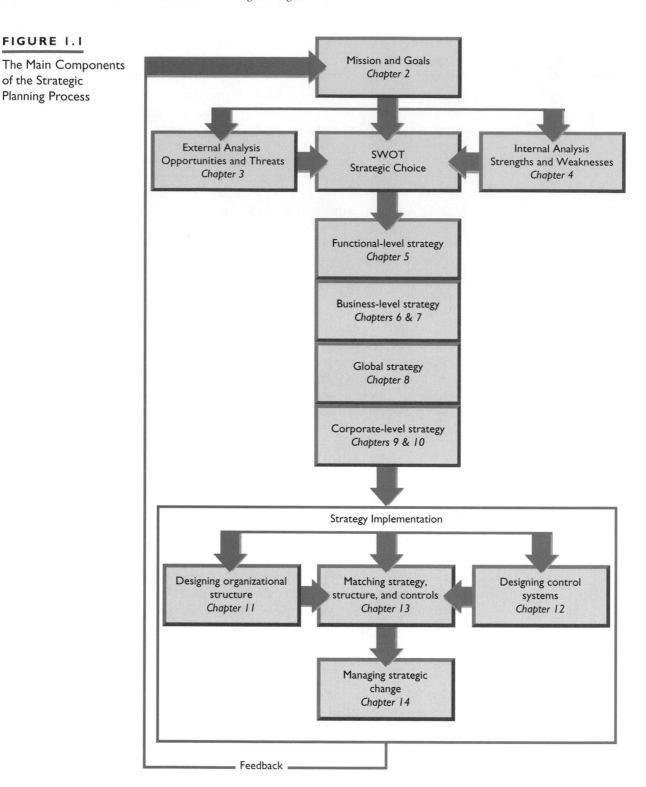

year. In many instances, the result is simply to reaffirm a strategy and structure that is already in place. The strategic plans generated by this kind of process generally cover a one-to-five-year period, with the plan being updated, or "rolled forward," every year. In many organizations, the results of the annual strategic planning process are used as input into the budget process for the coming year. Thus, strategic planning shapes resource allocation within the organization.

■ Mission and Major Goals

The first component of the strategic management process is defining the mission and major goals of the organization. This topic is covered in depth in Chapter 2. The mission and major goals of an organization provide the context within which strategies are formulated.

The **mission** sets out why the organization exists and what it should be doing. For example, the mission of a national airline might be defined as satisfying the needs of individual and business travelers for high-speed transportation at a reasonable price to all the major population centers of North America. Similarly, the mission of Yahoo! might be defined as "connecting anyone to anybody or anything."

Major goals specify what the organization hopes to fulfill in the medium to long term. Most profit-seeking organizations operate with a hierarchy of goals, in which attaining superior performance is placed at or near the top. Secondary goals are objectives judged necessary by the company if it is to attain superior performance. For example, under the leadership of Jack Welch, General Electric has operated with a secondary goal of being first or second in every major market in which it competes. This secondary goal reflects Welch's belief that building market share is the best way to achieve superior performance. Similarly, a major goal of Coca-Cola has been to put a Coke within an arm's reach of every consumer in the world. If Coca-Cola achieves this goal, superior performance is likely to follow. Not-for-profit organizations typically have a more diverse set of goals.

■ External Analysis

The second component of the strategic management process is the analysis of the organization's external operating environment. This topic is covered in detail in Chapter 3. The objective of external analysis is to identify strategic *opportunities* and *threats* in the organization's operating environment. Three interrelated environments should be examined at this stage: the immediate, or industry, environment in which the organization operates, the national environment, and the wider macroenvironment.

Analyzing the industry environment requires an assessment of the competitive structure of the organization's industry, including the competitive position of the focal organization and its major rivals, as well as the stage of industry development. Since many markets are now global markets, analyzing the industry environment also means assessing the impact of globalization on competition within an industry. Analyzing the national environment requires an assessment of whether the national context within which a company operates facilitates the attainment of a competitive advantage in the global marketplace. If it does not, then the company might have to consider shifting a significant part of its operations to countries where the national context does facilitate the attainment of a competitive advantage. Analyzing the macroenvironment consists of examining macroeconomic, social, government, legal, international, and technological factors that may affect the organization.

■ Internal Analysis

Internal analysis, the third component of the strategic management process, serves to pinpoint the *strengths* and *weaknesses* of the organization. Such issues as identifying the quantity and quality of resources available to the organization are considered in Chapter 4, where we probe the sources of competitive advantage. We look at how companies attain a competitive advantage, and we discuss the role of distinctive competencies (unique company strengths), resources, and capabilities in building and sustaining a company's competitive advantage. One conclusion that we reach in Chapter 4 is that building and maintaining a competitive advantage requires a company to achieve superior efficiency, quality, innovation, and customer responsiveness. Company strengths lead to superiority in these areas, whereas company weaknesses translate into inferior performance.

■ SWOT and Strategic Choice

The next component requires generating a series of strategic alternatives, given the company's internal strengths and weaknesses and its external opportunities and threats. The comparison of **s**trengths, **w**eaknesses, **o**pportunities, and **t**hreats is normally referred to as a **SWOT** analysis.[3] The central purpose of the SWOT analysis is to identify strategies that *align, fit,* or *match* a company's resources and capabilities to the demands of the environment in which the company operates. To put it another way, the purpose of the strategic alternatives generated by a SWOT analysis should be to build on company strengths in order to exploit opportunities and counter threats and to correct company weaknesses.

Strategic choice is the process of choosing among the alternatives generated by a SWOT analysis. The organization has to evaluate various alternatives against each other with respect to their ability to achieve major goals. The strategic alternatives generated can encompass business-level, functional-level, corporate-level, and global strategies. The process of strategic choice requires the organization to identify the set of business-level, functional-level, corporate-level, and global strategies that would best enable it to survive and prosper in the fast-changing and globally competitive environment that characterizes most modern industries.

Business-Level Strategy   The business-level strategy of a company encompasses the overall competitive theme that a company chooses to stress, the way it positions itself in the marketplace to gain a competitive advantage, and the different positioning strategies that can be used in different industry settings. The various strategic options available are first introduced in Chapter 4 and then discussed in more detail in Chapter 6. In Chapter 6, we review the pros and cons of three generic business-level strategies: a strategy of **cost leadership**, a strategy of **differentiation**, and a strategy of **focusing** on a particular market niche. Yahoo! pursues a differentiation strategy: the overall competitive theme the company has chosen is to stress differentiating its brand from those of competitors through a combination of marketing and product offering.

In Chapter 7, we build on Chapter 6 to consider the relationship between business-level strategy and industry structure. We concentrate on the different strategic options confronting companies in radically different industry settings, such as the benefits and drawbacks of establishing a first-mover advantage in a newly formed or embryonic industry. We also discuss the role of market signaling, price leadership, and product differentiation for sustaining a competitive advantage in mature industries, and we explore the different strategic options that a company can choose from in a declining industry.

Functional-Level Strategy   Competitive advantage stems from a company's ability to attain superior efficiency, quality, innovation, and customer responsiveness—a point made in Chapter 4. In Chapter 5, we examine the different functional-level (operations) strategies that can be employed to achieve these four crucial aims. By functional-level strategies, we mean strategies directed at improving the effectiveness of *operations* within a company, such as manufacturing, marketing, materials management, product development, and customer service.

Global Strategy   In today's world of global markets and global competition, achieving a competitive advantage and maximizing company performance increasingly require a company to expand its operations outside its home country. Accordingly, a company must consider the various global strategies it can pursue. In Chapter 8, we assess the benefits and costs of global expansion and examine four different strategies—multidomestic, international, global, and transnational—that a company can adopt to compete in the global marketplace. In addition, that chapter explores the benefits and costs of strategic alliances between global competitors, the different entry modes that can be used to penetrate a foreign market, and the role of host-government policies in influencing a company's choice of global strategy.

Corporate-Level Strategy   We deal with the issue of corporate-level strategy in Chapters 9 and 10. An organization's corporate-level strategy must answer this question: What businesses should we be in to maximize the long-run profitability of the organization? For many organizations, competing successfully often means **vertical integration**—integrating its operations either backward into the production of inputs for the company's main operation or forward into the disposal of outputs from the operation. Beyond this, companies that succeed in establishing a sustainable competitive advantage may find that they are generating resources *in excess* of their investment requirements within their primary industry. For such organizations, maximizing long-run profitability may entail **diversification** into new business areas. Accordingly, in Chapter 9, we look closely at the costs and benefits of different diversification strategies. In addition, we examine the role of **strategic alliances** as alternatives to diversification and vertical integration. In Chapter 10, we review the different vehicles that companies use to achieve vertical integration and diversification, including **acquisitions** and **new ventures**. We also consider how diversified companies can **restructure** their portfolio of businesses in order to improve company performance.

■ Strategy Implementation

Once a company has chosen a strategy to achieve its goals, that strategy then has to be put into action. In this book, we break down the topic of strategy implementation into four main components: (1) designing appropriate organizational structures; (2) designing control systems; (3) matching strategy, structure, and controls; and (4) managing conflict, politics, and change.

Designing Organizational Structure   Implementing a strategy requires the allocation of roles and responsibilities for different aspects of that strategy to different managers and subunits within the company. A company's organizational structure maps out roles and responsibilities, along with reporting relationships. In this sense, strategy is implemented through structure. At the toy company Mattel, for example, under CEO Jill Barad, there is a product group for each of Mattel's major brands: Barbie, Hot Wheels, Fisher Price, and Disney license products. Each of these subunits is headed by a vice president, who reports directly to Barad, and each vice president is responsible for ensuring that his or her product group successfully implements the company's brand extension strategy for that particular brand. If an organization's existing structure is not appropriate, given the company's strategy, a new structure may have to be designed. In Chapter 11, we discuss the different kinds of organizational structures that managers can use to implement strategy.

Designing Control Systems   Besides choosing a structure, an organization must also establish appropriate organizational control systems. It must decide how best to assess the performance and control the actions of subunits. The options range from market and output controls to bureaucratic controls and control through organizational culture, all of which we tackle in Chapter 12. An organization also needs to decide what kind of reward and incentive systems to set up for employees. Chapter 12 reviews those options as well.

Matching Strategy, Structure, and Controls   If it wants to succeed, a company must achieve a *fit*, or *congruence,* among its strategy, structure, and controls.[4] Chapter 13 focuses on the various means toward this end. Since different strategies and environments place different demands on an organization, they call for different structural responses and control systems. For example, a strategy of cost leadership demands that an organization be kept simple (so as to reduce costs) and that operations and controls stress productive efficiency. On the other hand, a strategy of differentiating a company's product by unique technological characteristics generates a need for integrating the company's activities around its technological core and establishing control systems that reward technical creativity.

Managing Strategic Change   We live in a world in which the only constant is change. Much of this change is the result of technological progress. In recent years, the way in which technological change can impact established markets has been vividly illustrated by the rise of the Internet and the associated World Wide Web. Web-based commerce is providing a host of new opportunities, while simultaneously threatening to make established business models obsolete. In the stockbrokerage industry, for example, the ability to use the Internet as a conduit for individuals to directly buy and sell stocks without the aid of a stockbroker has propelled the growth of companies such as E*Trade and Charles Schwab. Simultaneously, this change has threatened the established business model of "full-service" stockbrokerage companies such as Merrill Lynch, which have traditionally employed stockbrokers to buy and sell stocks for individuals. Because change is so pervasive, companies that succeed in the long run are those that are able to adapt their strategy and structure to a changing world. In 1999, for example, Merrill Lynch embraced an on-line strategy, even though this will effectively reduce the need for its vast network of stockbrokers. In Chapter 14, we take a close look at the process of managing strategic change and discuss the different tactics that managers can utilize to successfully implement such change.

■ The Feedback Loop

The feedback loop in Figure 1.1 indicates that strategic planning is an ongoing process. Once a strategy has been implemented, its execution must be monitored to determine the extent to which strategic objectives are actually being achieved. This information passes back to the corporate level through feedback loops. At the corporate level, it is fed into the next round of strategy formulation and implementation. It serves either to reaffirm existing corporate goals and strategies or to suggest changes. For example, when put into practice, a strategic objective may prove to be too optimistic, and so the next time more conservative objectives are set. Alternatively, feedback may reveal that strategic objectives were attainable but implementation was poor. In that case, the next round in strategic management may concentrate more on implementation. Because feedback is an aspect of organizational control, it is considered in detail in Chapter 12.

STRATEGIC MANAGERS

We have already alluded to the fact that, within the context of the traditional strategic planning model, the major responsibility for orchestrating the planning process rests on the shoulders of top managers. But who are these top managers, and what precisely is their strategic role? What about lower-level managers within the organization? What is their role in the strategic management process? In this section, we look at the strategic role of managers at different levels in the organization *through the lens of traditional strategic management theory*. Later in the chapter, we shall modify this view somewhat, but for now it constitutes a useful starting point.

In most modern organizations, there are two types of managers: **general managers** and **operations managers**. General managers are individuals who bear responsibility for the overall performance of the organization or of one of its major self-contained divisions. Their overriding concern is for the health of the *total* organization under their direction. This responsibility puts them in the unique position of directing the total organization in a strategic sense. Operations managers, on the other hand, bear responsibility for specific business functions or operations, such as human resources, purchasing, production, sales, marketing, product development, customer service, accounts, and so on. Their sphere of authority is normally confined to one organizational activity.

A typical multibusiness company has three main levels of management: the corporate level, the business level, and the operational level (see Figure 1.2). General managers are found at the first two of these levels, but their strategic roles differ depending on their sphere of responsibility. Operations managers, too, have a strategic role, though of a different kind. We now examine each of the three levels and the strategic roles assigned to managers within them.

■ Corporate-Level Managers

The corporate level of management consists of the chief executive officer (CEO), other senior executives, the board of directors, and corporate staff. These individuals occupy the apex of decision making within the organization. The CEO is the main general manager at this level. In consultation with other senior executives, he or she has the strategic role *to oversee* the development of strategies for the total organization. This role includes defining the mission and goals of the organization, determining what businesses it should be in, allocating resources among the different businesses, formulating and implementing strategies that span individual businesses, and providing leadership for the organization.

Consider General Electric. The company is active in a wide range of businesses, including lighting equipment, major appliances, motor and transportation equipment, turbine generators, construction and engineering services, industrial electronics, medical systems, aerospace, and aircraft engines. The main strategic responsibilities of its CEO, Jack Welch, include setting overall strategic objectives, allocating resources among the different business areas, deciding whether the firm should divest itself of any of its businesses, and determining whether it should

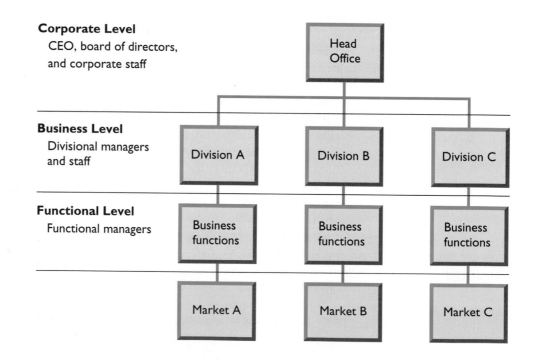

FIGURE 1.2

Levels of Strategic Management

Corporate Level
CEO, board of directors, and corporate staff

Head Office

Business Level
Divisional managers and staff

Division A   Division B   Division C

Functional Level
Functional managers

Business functions   Business functions   Business functions

Market A   Market B   Market C

acquire any new ones. In other words, it is up to Welch to develop strategies that span individual businesses. He is concerned with building and managing the corporate portfolio of businesses. It is not his specific responsibility, however, to develop strategies for competing in the individual business areas, such as aeroengines or financial services. The development of such strategies is the responsibility of business-level strategic managers.

Besides overseeing resource allocation and managing the divestment and acquisition processes, corporate-level general managers also provide a link between the people who oversee the strategic development of a firm and those who own it (stockholders). Corporate-level general managers, and particularly the CEO, can be viewed as the guardians of stockholder welfare. It is their responsibility to ensure that corporate strategies pursued by the company are consistent with maximizing stockholder wealth. If they are not, then the CEO is likely to be called to account by the stockholders.

For another look at the roles and responsibilities of a general manager, see Strategy in Action 1.1, which discusses Larry Bossidy, the hard-driving hard-nosed CEO of AlliedSignal. Bossidy sets the overall goals and strategic direction for AlliedSignal, but because the company is a diversified one, with more than twenty different business units, he leaves it up to individual business managers to decide the best strategy for their particular operation. Bossidy's involvement is limited to vigorously probing managers with questions to test the logic underlying their strategic decisions.

■ Business-Level Managers

In a multibusiness company, such as General Electric or AlliedSignal, the business level consists of the heads of individual business units within the organization and their support staff. In a single-industry company, the business and corporate levels are the same. A business unit is an organizational entity that operates in a distinct business area. Typically, it is self-contained and has its own functional departments (for example, its own finance, buying, production, and marketing departments). Within most companies, business units are referred to as **divisions**.

The main strategic managers at the business level are the heads of the divisions. Their strategic role is to translate general statements of direction and intent from the corporate level into concrete strategies for individual businesses. Thus, while corporate-level general managers are concerned with strategies that span individual businesses, business-level managers concentrate on strategies that are specific to a particular business. At General Electric, Jack Welch has committed the company to the objective of being first or second in every business in which the corporation competes. However, it is up to the general managers who head each division to work out for their business the details of a strategy that is consistent with this objective. Similarly, at AlliedSignal it is up to the heads of each division to work out how they are going to meet Bossidy's demanding goals of 15 percent earnings growth, 8 percent sales growth, and 6 percent productivity growth "forever" (see Strategy in Action 1.1).

■ Operations Managers

Operations managers bear responsibility for specific business functions or processes, such as human resources, manufacturing, materials management, marketing, research

1.1 STRATEGY *in* ACTION

Larry Bossidy, CEO

Larry Bossidy, the CEO of the diversified engineering company AlliedSignal, is reputed to be one of the most sought-after CEOs in corporate America. Since leaving the number two spot at General Electric in 1991 to join AlliedSignal, Bossidy has been approached by IBM, Merck, Kodak, and Westinghouse, all of which were looking for a new CEO. The reasons for so much attention are not hard to find. When Bossidy joined AlliedSignal, the company was widely perceived as a poorly performing enterprise based in a number of dull businesses in aerospace, auto parts, and engineered materials. At around $3.50 per share, the stock price was no higher than it had been in 1984, while the 1991 net profit of $342 million was well below the peak profit of $559 million earned in 1986. Under Bossidy's leadership, however, earnings surged to over $1.33 billion in 1998, while the stock price climbed to $60 per share by early 1999.

How has Bossidy done it? He has articulated a handful of challenging goals that he wants AlliedSignal to attain and then relentlessly pushed the managers of each of AlliedSignal's twenty-odd businesses, or divisions, to find ways of meeting those goals. The primary goal of AlliedSignal under Bossidy has been profitable growth. Bossidy wants to increase earnings per share by 15 percent annually. To achieve that, he reckons that AlliedSignal must grow sales of existing businesses by 8 percent per annum, increase productivity at an annual rate of 6 percent "forever," and achieve operating profit margins of at least 15 percent. These are challenging "stretch" goals for a company such as AlliedSignal, which is based in ma-

ture low-growth industries. To reach these goals, Bossidy has been pushing his managers to do four things: (1) enter foreign markets, particularly in Asia; (2) make selected niche acquisitions that can help to round out the product line of a business; (3) focus effort on improving efficiencies by driving waste and defects out of the manufacturing process; and (4) develop new products that can boost earnings growth, a particularly difficult challenge in a company that was once known for its aversion to new ideas.

Technically, Bossidy "negotiates" goals with the head of each of AlliedSignal's twenty businesses, but the reality is that he pushes them to accept goals that require a significant improvement in the performance of their businesses. He then tirelessly monitors his managers to make sure they follow through. Nearly every week, Bossidy visits at least one of AlliedSignal's businesses. He is known for vigorously probing managers in all-day meetings to find out what strategies they are adopting to meet the goals he has set for them. And if they fail? Well, they had better not. Bossidy bestows an award on business units that do not meet their cost of capital—it is called the "leaky bucket" award. More significantly, when people fail to meet his stretch targets, he fires them. In the automotive division, which makes brake parts and where profits are below par, Bossidy fired or transferred six of the top ten executives in the course of a year. Bossidy admits that he is demanding, relentless, and tough, but in his view this management style offers the only way forward for companies such as AlliedSignal that have to compete with aggressive low-cost foreign enterprises.[5]

and development (R&D), customer satisfaction, and product development. While they are not responsible for the overall performance of the organization, they do have a major strategic role. Their responsibility is to develop functional strategies in manufacturing, marketing, R&D, and so on, that help fulfill the strategic objectives set by business- and corporate-level general managers. In the case of General Electric's financial services business, for instance, manufacturing managers are responsible for developing manufacturing strategies consistent with the corporate objective of being first or second in that industry. Moreover, operations managers provide most of the information that makes it possible for business- and corporate-level general managers to formulate realistic and attainable strategies. Indeed, because they are closer to the customer than the typical general manager, operations managers may themselves generate important strategic ideas, which subsequently become major strategies for the company. Thus, it is important for general managers to listen closely to the ideas of their operations managers. An equally great responsibility for managers at the operational level is strategy implementation—the execution of corporate- and business-level decisions.

STRATEGIC LEADERSHIP

One of the key strategic roles of managers, whether they are general or operations managers, is to provide strategic leadership for their subordinates. **Strategic leadership** refers to the ability to articulate a strategic vision for the company, or a part of the company, and to motivate others to buy into that vision. An enormous amount has been written about leadership, and it is beyond the scope of this book to review this complex topic in detail. However, a few key characteristics of good leaders have been identified by several authors, and we discuss them here.[6] These characteristics are (1) vision, eloquence, and consistency; (2) commitment; (3) being well informed; (4) willingness to delegate and empower; (5) astute use of power; and (6) emotional intelligence.

■ Vision, Eloquence, and Consistency

One of the key tasks of leadership is to give the organization a sense of direction. Strong leaders seem to have a vision of where the organization should go. Moreover, they are eloquent enough to communicate this vision to others within the organization in terms that can energize people, and they consistently articulate their vision until it becomes part of the culture of the organization.[7] John F. Kennedy, Martin Luther King, Jr., and Margaret Thatcher have all been held up as examples of visionary leaders. All three had their own clear vision of the society they would like to see, and all were able to communicate it eloquently to people using evocative language that energized the audience. Think of the impact of Kennedy's challenge, "Ask not what your country can do for you; ask what you can do for your country" and of King's "I Have a Dream" speech. Kennedy and Thatcher were also able to use their political office to push for governmental actions that were consistent with their vision, whereas King was able to pressure the government from outside to make changes in society. In the world of business, examples of strong business leaders include Microsoft's Bill Gates, Jack Welch of General Electric, Herb Kelleher of Southwest Airlines, and Larry Bossidy of AlliedSignal, who is profiled in Strategy in Action 1.1.

■ Commitment

A strong leader is someone who demonstrates commitment to his or her particular vision, often leading by example. Consider the case of Nucor's recently retired CEO, Ken Iverson. Nucor is a very efficient steel maker, with perhaps the lowest cost structure in the steel industry. The company has turned in twenty-five years of profitable performance in an industry where most companies have lost money. It has done so by relentlessly focusing on cost minimization. In his tenure as CEO, it was

Iverson who set the example here. Iverson answered his own phone, employed only one secretary, drove an old car, flew coach class, and was proud of being one of the lowest-paid CEOs in the *Fortune* 500. This kind of commitment was a powerful signal to employees within Nucor that Iverson was serious about doing everything possible to minimize costs. It earned him the respect of Nucor employees, which in turn made them more willing to work hard. Although Iverson has retired, his legacy lives in the cost-conscious organizational culture that has been built at Nucor. Like all great leaders, Iverson has had an impact that goes beyond his tenure as a leader.

■ Being Well Informed

Good leaders do not operate in a vacuum. Rather, they develop a network of formal and informal sources that keep them well informed about what is going on within their company. They develop back-channel ways of finding out what is going on within the organization so that they do not have to rely on formal information channels. Herb Kelleher at Southwest Airlines, for example, was able to find out a lot about the health of his company by dropping in unannounced on aircraft maintenance facilities and helping workers there perform their tasks. Using informal and unconventional ways to gather information is wise, since formal channels can be captured by special interests within the organization or by gatekeepers, who may misrepresent the true state of affairs within the company to the leader. People like Kelleher, who are constantly interacting with their employees at all levels within the organization, are better able to build informal information networks than leaders who closet themselves in remote corporate headquarters and never interact with lower-level employees.

■ Willingness to Delegate and Empower

Good leaders are skilled delegators. They recognize that unless they do delegate they can quickly become overloaded with responsibilities. They also recognize that empowering subordinates to make decisions is a good motivational tool. Delegating also makes sense when it results in decisions being made by those who must implement them. At the same time, good leaders recognize that they need to maintain control over certain key decisions. Thus, although they will delegate many decisions to lower-level employees, they will not delegate those that they judge to be critical to the future success of the organization under their leadership.

■ Astute Use of Power

In a now classic article on leadership, Edward Wrapp notes that good leaders tend to be very astute in their use of power.[8] By this he means three things. First, good leaders play the power game with skill, preferring to build consensus for their ideas rather than use their authority to force ideas through. They act as members or democratic leaders of a coalition, rather than as dictators. Second, good leaders often hesitate to commit themselves publicly to detailed strategic plans or precise objectives, since in all probability the emergence of unexpected contingencies will require adaptation. Thus, a successful leader might commit the organization to a particular vision, such as minimizing costs or boosting product quality, without stating precisely how or when this will be achieved. It is important to note that good leaders often have precise private objectives and strategies that they would like to see the organization pursue. However, they recognize the futility of public commitment, given the likelihood of change and the difficulties of implementation. Third, Wrapp claims that good leaders possess the ability to push through programs in a piecemeal fashion. They recognize that, on occasion, it may be futile to try and push total packages or strategic programs through an organization, since significant objections to at least part of such programs are likely to arise. Instead, the successful leader may be willing to take less than total acceptance in order to achieve modest progress toward a goal. The successful leader tries to push through his or her ideas one piece at a time, so that they appear as incidental to other ideas, though in fact they are part of a larger program or hidden agenda that moves the organization in the direction of the manager's objectives.

Jeffery Pfeffer has articulated a similar vision of the politically astute manager who gets things done in organizations by intelligent use of power.[9] In Pfeffer's view, power comes from control over resources—including budgets, positions, information, and knowledge that is important to the organization. Politically astute managers use these resources to acquire another critical resource: allies. Allies can then help the managers attain their strategic objectives. Pfeffer stresses that one does not need to be a CEO to assemble power in an organization. Sometimes quite junior operations managers can build a surprisingly effective power base and use it to influence organizational outcomes.

■ Emotional Intelligence

Emotional intelligence is a term coined by Daniel Goleman to describe a bundle of psychological attributes that many strong leaders exhibit.[10] They include self-awareness, self-regulation, motivation, empathy, and social skills. Self-awareness refers to the ability to understand one's moods, emotions, and drives, as well as their effect on others. Self-regulation is the ability to control or redirect disruptive impulses or moods—to think before acting. Motivation refers to a passion for work that goes beyond money or status and a propensity to pursue goals with energy and persistence. Empathy means understanding the feelings and viewpoints of subordinates and taking those into account when making decisions. Goleman defines social skills as "friendliness with a purpose."

According to Goleman, leaders who possess these attributes—who exhibit a high degree of emotional intelligence—tend to be more effective than those who lack them. Their self-awareness and self-regulation help elicit the trust and confidence of subordinates. In Goleman's view, people respect leaders who, through self-awareness, recognize their own limitations and, because of self-regulation, don't shoot from the hip but consider decisions carefully. Goleman also argues that self-aware and self-regulating individuals tend to be more self-confident and therefore better able to cope with ambiguity and more open to change. A strong motivation exhibited in a passion for work can also be infectious, persuading others to join together in pursuit of a common goal or organizational mission. Finally, strong empathy and social skills can help leaders earn the loyalty of subordinates. Empathetic and socially adept individuals tend to be skilled at managing disputes between managers, better able to find common ground and purpose among diverse constituencies, and more likely to move people in a desired direction than leaders who lack these qualities. In short, Goleman argues that the psychological makeup of a leader matters.

STRATEGY AS AN EMERGENT PROCESS

The planning model we reviewed earlier in the chapter suggests that an organization's strategies are the result of a plan, that the strategic planning process itself is rational and highly structured, and that the process is orchestrated, and indeed dominated, by top management. In recent years, several scholars have advocated an alternative view of strategy making, which has called into question the traditional view centered on planning.[11] These scholars have three main criticisms of the planning model: one focuses on the unpredictability of the real world; the second emphasizes the role lower-level managers can play in the strategic management process; and the third points out that many successful strategies are often the result of serendipity, not rational strategizing.

■ Strategy Making in an Unpredictable World

Critics of formal planning systems argue that we live in a world in which uncertainty, complexity, and ambiguity dominate and in which small chance events can have a large and unpredictable impact on outcomes.[12] In such circumstances, they claim, even the most carefully thought-out strategic plans are prone to being rendered useless by rapid and unforeseen change in the environment. This is something that military historians and thinkers have long recognized. Carl von Clausewitz, the famous Prussian military strategist of the early 1800s, once noted that "the principles, rules, or even systems of strategy must always fall short, undermined by the world's endless complexities . . . in strategy most things are uncertain and variable."[13] Although von Clausewitz was talking about military strategy, his observations are just as relevant to business strategy. Witness, for example, how Microsoft was caught off guard by the rapid rise of the Internet and the sudden emergence of companies such as Netscape and Sun Microsystems as potential competitors (see Strategy in Action 1.2 for details).

In an unpredictable world, there is a premium on being able to respond quickly to changing circumstances, altering the strategies of the organization accordingly (as Microsoft did in response to the threat posed by Netscape—see Strategy in Action 1.2). According to critics, such a flexible approach to strategy making is not possible within the framework of the traditional strategic planning process, with its implicit assumption that an organization's strategies need to be reviewed only during the annual strategic planning exercise.

■ Strategy Making by Lower-Level Managers

Another criticism leveled at the rational planning model of strategy is that too much importance is attached to the role of top management.[15] An alternative view now gaining wide acceptance is that individual managers deep within an organization can and often do exert a profound influence on the evolution of strategy.[16] Writing with Robert Burgelman of Stanford University, Andy Grove, the CEO of Intel, has recently described how many important strategic decisions at Intel were initiated not by top managers, but by the autonomous action of mid-level managers deep within Intel.[17] These strategic decisions included the decision to exit an important market (the DRAM memory chip market) and the decision to develop a certain class of microprocessors (RISC-based microprocessors) in direct contrast to the stated strategy of Intel's top managers.

Another famous example of autonomous action occurred at 3M corporation back in the 1920s. At that time, 3M was primarily a manufacturer of sandpaper. Richard Drew, who was then a young laboratory assistant, came up with what he thought would be a great new product, a glue-covered paper. Drew saw applications for the product in the automobile industry, where it could be used to mask parts of a vehicle during painting. He presented the idea to the company's president, William McKnight. An unimpressed McKnight suggested that Drew drop the research. Drew didn't; instead, he developed the paper and then went out and got endorsements from potential customers in the auto industry. Armed with this information, he approached McKnight again. A chastened McKnight reversed his original position and gave Drew the go-ahead to start developing what was to become one of 3M's main product lines—sticky tape, a business it dominates to this day.[18] The point of this story, of course, is that it illustrates how autonomous action by a lower-level employee can shape the strategic destiny of a company.

■ Serendipity and Strategy

Business history is replete with examples of accidental events that helped push companies in new and profitable directions. What these examples suggest is that many successful strategies are not the result of well-thought-out plans, but of serendipity. One such example occurred at 3M during the 1960s. At that time, 3M was producing fluorocarbons for sale as coolant liquid in air conditioning equipment. One day, quite by accident, a researcher working with fluorocarbons in a 3M lab spilled some of the liquid on her shoes. Later that day, the same researcher spilled coffee over her shoes. She watched with interest as the coffee formed into little beads of liquid and then ran off her shoes without leaving a stain. Reflecting on this phenomenon, she realized that a fluorocarbon-based liquid might turn out to be useful for protecting fabrics from liquid stains—and so the idea for Scotch Guard was born. Subsequently, Scotch Guard became one of 3M's most profitable products and took the company into the fabric protection business, an area it had never planned to participate in.[19]

A similar example of serendipitous discovery occurred at the Seattle-based biotechnology company ICOS. During the mid 1990s, ICOS was testing a potential drug candidate for the treatment of hypertension on a sample of males in their fifties. The drug candidate, code-named IC351, was a small molecule product that could be taken orally. Early on, ICOS researchers noted an unusual aspect of the trial: there was a very high compliance rate among the patient sample. Patients were not dropping out of the trials, as often happens in these studies. After some months of testing, the company reviewed the clinical data and concluded that the drug had no effect on hypertension. They decided to halt the trials and asked the patients to return their unused pills. It was at this point that they encountered a highly unusual reaction: some of the patients protested at having to give the surplus pills back to ICOS. Curious to discover why, the ICOS researchers held a series of interviews with the patients. What soon became apparent was that several of the patients who had been taking IC351, as opposed to a placebo, were reporting a dramatic improvement in their sex life. It turned out that these patients has been suffering from male erectile dysfunction (MED), or impotence, as it is commonly called. By inhibiting the production of a selected enzyme, IC351 appeared to relax blood vessels, allowing increased blood flow to tissues and resulting in an improved sexual

STRATEGY in ACTION

A Strategic Shift at Microsoft

In the early 1990s, Microsoft emerged as the dominant software company in the desktop computing market. By 1995, Microsoft's Windows operating system was to be found on 90 percent of all personal computers, while the company enjoyed a market share in excess of 50 percent for a large number of popular desktop computing applications, including word processing, presentation software, and spreadsheets. So complete was Microsoft's dominance, that in 1993 several of its competitors filed complaints with the U. S. Department of Justice, alleging that Microsoft engaged in unfair trade practices—a charge that Microsoft vigorously denies. Meanwhile, the business press hailed the company's founder and CEO, Bill Gates, as one of the greatest strategic thinkers in the computer industry. The linchpin of Gates's strategy was to ensure the continued dominance of Microsoft's Windows operating system as the standard of choice in the personal computer environment.

In mid 1995, however, Microsoft suddenly began to look vulnerable when it was blind-sided by two related and unexpected developments. The first of these was the explosive growth of the global network of interlinked computers known as the Internet and the associated World Wide Web, or WWW, that sits on top of the Internet. In the late 1980s, Tim Bernes Lee, a physicist at the CERN research institute for particle physics in Switzerland, de-veloped a method for encoding, displaying, and transmitting text and graphics over the Internet using HTML (hypertext markup language). In effect, Bernes Lee had invented the World Wide Web. In 1993, a young computer programmer at the University of Illinois, Mark Andreessen, masterminded the development of a "browser" that could be used to travel the Internet, read HTML documents, and display them on a personal computer screen. In 1994, he left Illinois to help found Netscape, a software company that produced an improved version of the HTML browser, Netscape Navigator, along with "Web server software," which could be placed on the computer servers that were the nodes of the rapidly developing WWW to manage Web files and handle Web traffic. The growth of the WWW was nothing short of stunning. In 1990, fewer than 1 million users were connected to the Internet. By late 1995, largely as a result of the popularity of the WWW, the figure was approaching 80 million, and Netscape, not Microsoft, had supplied more than 70 percent of all Web browsers and Web server software.

The second development was the invention of the Java computer programming language at Sun Microsystems, one of the leading suppliers of computer workstations and servers. A program written in Java can be stored anywhere on the WWW and accessed by anyone with a Web browser that contains a Java interpreter—and by 1995, versions of Netscape Navigator did. Java is indifferent to

response. ICOS had stumbled on a powerful potential treatment for MED, a serious condition that affects approximately 20 million males in the United States alone. By 1999, ICOS had entered into a joint venture with Eli Lilly to develop the product and was close to initiating final clinical trials. In late 1998, Pfizer introduced a similar product, Viagra, and was experiencing rapid sales growth. Many analysts thought that the ICOS product was even more effective than Viagra and were predicting rapid market acceptance if it successfully cleared regulatory hurdles and made it to the market.[20]

As suggested by the 3M and ICOS examples, serendipitous discoveries are often the unintended consequence of scientific endeavor. This is not always the case, however. In the mid 1980s, for example, an employee at a small software company, WRQ, wanted to access the company's Hewlett-Packard computer from home by turning his personal computer into an HP terminal. Since no software existed to perform this task, he wrote a program for his personal use that enabled his personal computer to emulate a Hewlett-Packard terminal. Some of his colleagues thought that other companies might want to buy this software, so WRQ tried to sell it as a

the operating system of the personal computer on which a Web browser resides. So in theory, users of a current version of Netscape Navigator can access a word-processing program placed somewhere on the Web as and when they need it. Instead of purchasing the program outright for hundreds of dollars, all they need do is pay a few cents for the "run time" during which they use the program.

This development represented a potential body blow to Microsoft. It raised the possibility that people would no longer need to purchase expensive software applications from Microsoft and store them on their computers. Nor would they need a machine that utilized Microsoft's operating system. All they needed was a simple and inexpensive machine that was able to run a Netscape browser with a Java interpreter. They could then use this machine to access programs on the Web whenever they wanted, using the computing power of a remote server. As Scott McNealy, the CEO of Sun Microsystems, was fond of saying at the time, in this vision of the future "the network is the computer," while the standard is based not on Microsoft's Windows, but on Netscape and Java.

Microsoft's initial response to this unanticipated threat was to dismiss it. Bill Gates called Netscape's browser technology trivial. But by late 1995, it was clear that Microsoft had decided to respond to the unexpected threat posed by Netscape and Java by shifting its own strategic focus toward the WWW. Microsoft was to continue focusing on being the dominant software player in the desktop computing business, but its strategy for at-

taining this objective would start to change. In an all-day Internet conference, Microsoft stated that it would give away its own Web browser—Internet Explorer—and Web server software for free. Furthermore, the company promised that future software applications produced by Microsoft would contain "browser functions," which would enable users to roam the Web for information, and that new versions of its popular word-processing program would enable users to convert their documents into HTML format, which could be transmitted over the Web. Microsoft also declared that it would license Java from Sun and incorporate Java interpreters into some of its own products. In subsequent weeks, Microsoft announced an alliance with America Online (AOL), the world's largest on-line service, which would allow AOL's 5 million subscribers to use Microsoft's browser. This was followed by a deal with Intel to develop technology that would make video, voice, and data conferencing via the WWW as commonplace as placing a telephone call. By quickly abandoning its prior strategy and developing a new Internet strategy on the fly in response to an unanticipated threat, Microsoft suddenly positioned itself as a viable alternative to Netscape. The shift turned out to be remarkably successful. By late 1998, Microsoft's Internet Explorer was enjoying wide market acceptance while Netscape, facing shrinking demand for its products, agreed to be acquired by America Online.[14]

product. To its surprise, the company found that the demand was strong. Personal computers were starting to make their way onto the desks of many people in business, but these people still wanted to access data stored on mainframe computers, so they needed software that would transform their personal computers into mainframe terminals. For the next fifteen years, the company found it was generating sales of over $100 million from terminal emulation software.

The point is that serendipitous discoveries and events are commonplace and can open up all sorts of profitable avenues for a company. As a result, the strategy of many profitable firms is the product not of planning, but of the exploitation of serendipity. By the same token, some companies have missed out on profitable opportunities because serendipitous discoveries or events were inconsistent with their prior (planned) conception of what their strategy should be. In one of the classic examples of such myopia, a century ago the telegraph company Western Union turned down an opportunity to purchase the rights to an invention made by Alexander Graham Bell. The invention was the telephone, a technology that subsequently made the telegraph obsolete.

■ Intended and Emergent Strategies

Henry Mintzberg has incorporated the ideas discussed above into a model of strategy development that provides us with a more encompassing view of what strategy actually is. According to this model, which is illustrated in Figure 1.3, a company's **realized strategy** is the product of whatever planned, or **intended, strategies,** are actually put into action *and* of any unplanned, or **emergent, strategies.** In Mintzberg's view, emergent strategies are the unplanned responses to unforeseen circumstances. They often arise from autonomous action by individual managers deep within the organization (such as Richard Drew at 3M), or from serendipitous discoveries or events (such as those discussed at 3M, ICOS, and WRQ). They are *not* the product of formal top-down planning mechanisms.

Mintzberg maintains that emergent strategies are often successful and may be more appropriate than intended strategies. Richard Pascale has described how this was the case for the entry of Honda Motor into the U.S. motorcycle market.[21] When a number of Honda executives arrived in Los Angeles from Japan in 1959 to establish a U.S. subsidiary, their original aim (intended strategy) was to focus on selling 250-cc and 350-cc machines to confirmed motorcycle enthusiasts, rather than 50-cc Honda Cubs, which were a big hit in Japan. Their instinct told them that the Honda 50s were not suitable for the U.S. market, where everything was bigger and more luxurious than in Japan.

However, sales of the 250-cc and 350-cc bikes were sluggish, and the bikes themselves were plagued by mechanical failure. It looked as if Honda's strategy was going to fail. At the same time, the Japanese executives were using the Honda 50s to run errands around Los Angeles, attracting a lot of attention. One day they got a call from a Sears, Roebuck buyer who wanted to sell the 50-cc bikes to a broad market of Americans who were not necessarily already motorcycle enthusiasts. The Honda executives were hesitant to sell the small bikes for fear of alienating serious bikers, who might then associate Honda with "wimpy" machines. In the end, they were pushed into doing so by the failure of the 250-cc and 350-cc models. The rest is history. Honda had stumbled onto a previously untouched market segment that was to prove huge: the average American who had never owned a motorbike. Honda had also found an untried channel of distribution: general retailers rather than specialty motorbike stores. By 1964, nearly one out of every two motorcycles sold in the United States was a Honda.

The conventional explanation of Honda's success is that the company redefined the U.S. motorcycle industry with a brilliantly conceived *intended* strategy. The fact was that Honda's intended strategy was a near disaster. The strategy that *emerged* did so not through planning, but through unplanned action taken in response to unforeseen circumstances. Nevertheless, credit should be given to the Japanese management for recognizing the strength of the emergent strategy and for pursuing it with vigor.

The critical point demonstrated by the Honda example is that—in contrast to the view that all strategies are planned—successful strategies can emerge within an organization without prior planning, often in response to unforeseen circumstances. As Mintzberg has noted, strategies can take root in all kinds of strange places, virtually wherever people have the capacity to learn and the resources to support that capacity.

In practice, the strategies of most organizations are probably a combination of the intended (planned) and the emergent. The message for management is that it needs to recognize the process of emergence and to intervene when appropriate, killing off bad emergent strategies but nurturing potentially good ones.[22] To make

FIGURE 1.3

Emergent and
Deliberate Strategies

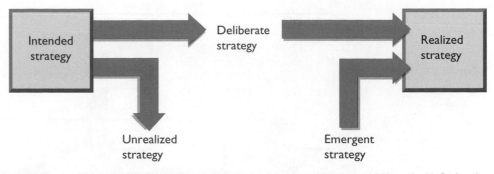

Source: Reprinted from "Strategy Formation in an Adhocracy," by Henry Mintzberg and Alexandra McGugh, published in *Administrative Science Quarterly,* Vol. 30, No. 2, June 1985, by permission of *Administrative Science Quarterly.*

such decisions, however, managers must be able to judge the worth of emergent strategies. They must be able to think strategically. Even though emergent strategies arise from within the organization without prior planning—that is, without going through the steps illustrated in Figure 1.1 in a *sequential* fashion—top management still has to evaluate emergent strategies. Such evaluation involves comparing each emergent strategy with the organization's goals, external environmental opportunities and threats, and the organization's internal strengths and weaknesses. The objective is to assess whether the emergent strategy fits the organization's needs and capabilities. In addition, Mintzberg stresses that an organization's capability to produce emergent strategies is a function of the kind of corporate culture fostered by the organization's structure and control systems.

In other words, the different components of the strategic management process are just as important from the perspective of emergent strategies as they are from the perspective of intended strategies. The essential differences between the strategic management process for intended and for emergent strategies are illustrated in Figure 1.4. The formulation of intended strategies is basically a top-down, planning-driven process, whereas the formulation of emergent strategies is a bottom-up process. In successful organizations, both processes are often at work.[23]

STRATEGIC PLANNING IN PRACTICE

Even the most vocal critics of formal strategic planning concede that it has a role. For example, Mintzberg's model of the strategy-making process, as illustrated in Figure 1.4, maintains a role for formal strategic planning, while simultaneously pointing to the importance of unplanned emergent strategies. Given that formal strategic planning is still widely practiced, and rightly so, it is pertinent to ask whether formal planning systems do actually help an organization attain superior performance.

On balance, the research evidence seems to indicate that formal planning systems do help companies make better strategic decisions. For example, a recent study analyzed in detail the results of twenty-six previously published studies of the relationship between strategic planning and company performance.[24] The study came to the conclusion that, on average, strategic planning does indeed have a positive impact on company performance, suggesting that strategic planning is a valuable activity.

Despite such results, many informed observers have increasingly questioned the use of formal planning systems as an aid to strategic decision making. Thomas J.

The Strategic Management Process for Intended and Emergent Strategies

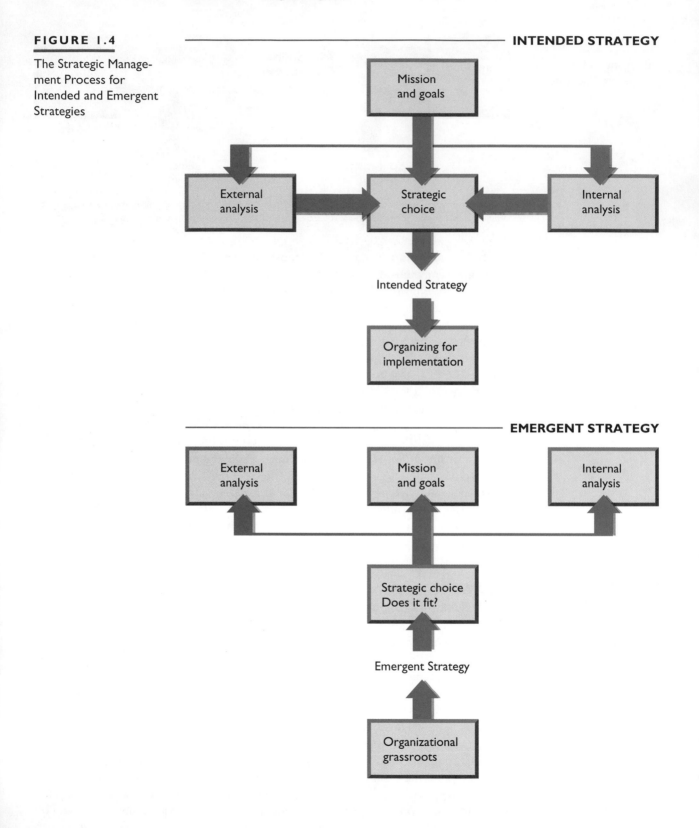

Peters and Robert H. Waterman, authors of the bestseller *In Search of Excellence*, were among the first to call into question the usefulness of formal planning systems, and the antiplanning rhetoric continues to be a theme in the more recent works of Peters.[25] Similarly, Mintzberg argues that business history is filled with examples of companies that have made poor decisions on the basis of supposedly comprehensive strategic planning.[26] For instance, Exxon's decisions to diversify into electrical equipment and office automation and to offset shrinking U.S. oil reserves by investing in shale oil and synthetic fuels resulted from a 1970s planning exercise that was overly pessimistic about the demand for oil-based products. Exxon foresaw ever higher prices for oil and predicted sharp falls in demand as a result. But oil prices actually tumbled during the 1980s, invalidating one of the basic assumptions of Exxon's plan. In addition, Exxon's diversification failed because of poor acquisitions and management problems in office automation.

Four explanations can be offered as to why formal strategic planning systems do not always produce the desired results. We consider three of them here and offer ways of dealing with them. We take up the fourth explanation, which focuses on decision-making biases among managers, in the next section. The three explanations are as follows: (1) planning under uncertainty; (2) top-down ivory tower planning; and (3) planning for the present, as opposed to the future.

■ Planning Under Uncertainty

One reason for the poor reputation of strategic planning is that many executives, in their initial enthusiasm for planning techniques, forgot that the future is inherently unpredictable. As at Exxon, a common problem was that executives often assumed it was possible to forecast the future accurately. But in the real world, the only constant is change. Even the best-laid plans can fall apart if unforeseen contingencies occur, and, as we noted earlier, in the real world unforeseen contingencies occur all the time.

Scenario Planning The recognition that in an uncertain world the future cannot be forecast with sufficient accuracy led Royal Dutch/Shell to pioneer the scenario approach to planning discussed in the Strategy in Action 1.3. Rather than try to forecast the future, Shell's planners attempt to model the company's environment and use that model to predict a range of possible scenarios. Executives are then asked to devise strategies to cope with the different scenarios. The objective is to get managers to understand the dynamic and complex nature of their environment, to think through problems in a strategic fashion, and to generate a range of strategic options that might be pursued under different circumstances.[27]

The scenario approach to planning seems to have spread quite rapidly among large companies. According to one survey, more than 50 percent of the *Fortune* 500 companies use some form of scenario-planning methods.[28] Although a detailed evaluation of the pros and cons of scenario planning has yet to appear, work by Paul Schoemaker of the University of Chicago seems to suggest that scenario planning does expand people's thinking, and as such it may lead to better plans, as seems to have occurred at Royal Dutch/Shell. However, Schoemaker cautions that forcing planners to consider extreme scenarios that are unbelievable can discredit the approach and cause resistance on the planners' part.

Strategic Planning at Royal Dutch/Shell

Royal Dutch/Shell, the world's largest oil company, is well known for its addiction to strategic planning. Despite the fact that many management gurus and CEOs now consider strategic planning an anachronism, Shell is convinced that long-term strategic planning has served the company well. Part of the reason for this success is that at Shell planning does not take the form of complex and inflexible ten-year plans generated by a team of corporate strategists far removed from operating realities. Rather, the planning process generates a series of "what if" scenarios, whose function is to try to get general managers at all levels of the corporation to think strategically about the environment in which they do business.

The strength of Shell's scenario-based planning system was perhaps most evident during the early 1980s. At that time, the price of a barrel of oil was hovering around $30. With exploration and development costs running at an industry average of around $11 per barrel, most oil companies were making record profits. Moreover, industry analysts were generally bullish; many were predicting that oil prices would increase to around $50 per barrel by 1990. Shell, however, was mulling over a handful of future scenarios, one of which included the possibility of a breakdown of the OPEC oil cartel's agreement to restrict supply, an oil glut, and a drop in oil prices to $15 per barrel. In 1984, Shell instructed the managers of its operating companies to indicate how they would respond to a $15-per-barrel world. This "game" set off some serious work at Shell to explore the question, "What will we do if it happens?"

By early 1986, the consequences of the "game" included efforts to cut exploration costs by pioneering advanced exploration technologies, massive investments in cost-efficient refining facilities, and a process of weeding out the least-profitable service stations. All this planning occurred at a time when most oil companies were busy diversifying outside the oil business rather than trying to improve the efficiency of their core operations. As it turned out, the price of oil was still $27 per barrel in early January 1986. But the failure of the OPEC cartel to set new production ceilings in 1985, new production from the North Sea and Alaska, and declining demand due to increased conservation efforts had created a growing oil glut. In late January, the dam burst. By February 1, oil was priced at $17 per barrel, and by April, the price was $10 per barrel.

Because Shell had already visited the $15 per barrel world, it had gained a head start over its rivals in its cost-cutting efforts. As a result, by 1989 the company's average oil and gas exploration costs were less than $2 per barrel, compared with an industry average of $4 per barrel. Moreover, in the crucial refining and marketing sector, Shell made a net return on assets of 8.4 percent in 1988, more than double the 3.8 percent average of the other oil majors: Exxon, BP, Chevron, Mobil, and Texaco.[29]

■ Ivory Tower Planning

A serious mistake made by many companies in their initial enthusiasm for planning has been to treat planning as an exclusively top-management function. This *ivory tower* approach can result in strategic plans formulated in a vacuum by planning executives who have little understanding or appreciation of operating realities. As a consequence, they formulate strategies that do more harm than good. For example, when demographic data indicated that houses and families were shrinking, planners at General Electric's appliance group concluded that smaller appliances were the wave of the future. Because the planners had little contact with home builders and retailers, they did not realize that kitchens and bathrooms were the two rooms that were not shrinking. Nor did they appreciate that working women wanted big refrigerators to cut down on trips to the supermarket. The result was that General Electric wasted a lot of time designing small appliances for which there was only limited demand.

The ivory tower concept of planning can also lead to tensions between planners and operating personnel. The experience of General Electric's appliance group is again illuminating. Many of the planners in this group were recruited from consulting firms or from topflight business schools. Many of the operating managers took this pattern of recruitment to mean that corporate executives did not deem them smart enough to think through strategic problems for themselves. They felt shut out from the decision-making process, which they believed to be unfairly constituted. Out of this perceived lack of procedural justice grew an us-versus-them state of mind, which quickly escalated into hostility. As a result, even when the planners were right, operating managers would not listen to them. In the early 1980s, the planners correctly recognized the importance of the globalization of the appliance market and the emerging Japanese threat. However, operating managers, who then saw Sears, Roebuck as the competition, paid them little heed.

Involving Operating Managers   Correcting the ivory tower approach to planning requires recognizing that, to succeed, strategic planning must encompass managers at *all* levels of the corporation. It is important to understand that much of the best planning can and should be done by operating managers. They are the ones closest to the facts. The role of corporate-level planners should be that of facilitators, who help operating managers do the planning both by setting the broad strategic goals of the organization and by providing operating managers with the resources required to identify the strategies that might be necessary to attain those goals.

Procedural Justice   It is not enough just to involve lower-level managers in the strategic planning process. They also need to perceive that the decision-making process is just. Chan Kim and Renee Mauborgne have written extensively about the importance of procedural justice in strategic decision making.[30] They define **procedural justice** as the extent to which the dynamics of a decision-making process are judged to be fair. If people perceive the decision-making process to be unjust, they are less likely to be committed to any resulting decisions and less likely to voluntarily cooperate in activities designed to implement those decisions. Consequently, their performance is likely to be below par. In short, a strategy chosen on the basis of a decision-making process that was perceived to be procedurally unjust might fail for lack of support among those who must implement it at the operating level.

Three criteria have been found to influence the extent to which strategic decisions are seen as just: engagement, explanation, and clarity of expectations.[31] *Engagement* means involving individuals in the decision-making process, both by asking them for their input and by allowing them to refute the merits of one another's ideas and assumptions. *Explanation* means that everyone involved and affected should be told the underlying rationale for strategic decisions, and explanations should be given as to why the ideas and inputs of individuals may have been overridden in reaching a decision. *Clarity of expectations* requires that before, during, and after strategic decisions are made managers have a solid understanding of what is expected of them and what the new "rules of the game" are. By paying close attention to engagement, explanation, and clarity of expectations, managers can greatly increase the likelihood that the strategic decision-making process is perceived as just, even when individuals have had their ideas and input overridden. In turn, this increases the probability that individuals will cooperate as fully as possible in the process of implementing those decisions. Consequently, company performance is likely to be higher than would have otherwise been the case.

■ Planning for the Present: Strategic Intent

The traditional strategic planning model we reviewed earlier has been characterized as the *fit model* of strategy making because it tries to achieve a fit between the internal resources and capabilities of an organization, and external environmental opportunities and threats. Gary Hamel and C. K. Prahalad have attacked the fit model as being too static and limiting.[32] They argue that adopting the fit model to strategy formulation leads to a mindset in which management focuses too much on the degree of fit between the *existing* resources of a company and *current* environmental opportunities, and not enough on building *new* resources and capabilities to create and exploit *future* opportunities. Strategies based on the fit model, say Hamel and Prahalad, tend to be more concerned with today's problems than with tomorrow's opportunities. As a result, companies that rely exclusively on the fit approach to strategy formulation are unlikely to be able to build and maintain a competitive advantage. This is particularly true in a dynamic competitive environment, where new competitors are continually arising and new ways of doing business are constantly being invented.

As Hamel and Prahalad note again and again, U.S. companies using the fit approach have been surprised by the ascent of foreign competitors that initially seemed to lack the resources and capabilities needed to make them a real threat. This happened to Xerox, which ignored the rise of Canon and Ricoh in the photocopier market until they had become serious global competitors; to General Motors, which initially overlooked the threat posed by Toyota and Honda in the 1970s; and to Caterpillar, which ignored the danger Komatsu posed to its heavy earthmoving business until it was almost too late to respond.

Strategic Intent   The secret of the success of companies such as Toyota, Canon, and Komatsu, according to Hamel and Prahalad, is that they all had bold ambitions that outstripped their existing resources and capabilities. All wanted to achieve global leadership, and they set out to build the resources and capabilities that would enable them to attain this goal. Consequently, the top management of these companies created an obsession with winning at all levels of the organization and then sustained that obsession over a ten- to twenty-year quest for global leadership. It is this obsession that Hamel and Prahalad refer to as **strategic intent**. At the same time, they stress that strategic intent is more than simply unfettered ambition. They argue that strategic intent also encompasses an active management process, which includes "focusing the organization's attention on the essence of winning; motivating people by communicating the value of the target; leaving room for individual and team contributions; sustaining enthusiasm by providing new operational definitions as circumstances change; and using intent consistently to guide resource allocations."[33] Thus, underlying the concept of strategic intent is the notion that strategy formulation should involve setting ambitious goals, which stretch a company, and then finding ways to build the resources and capabilities necessary to attain those goals.

Although Hamel and Prahalad aptly criticize the fit model, they note that in practice the two approaches to strategy formulation are not mutually exclusive. All the components of the strategic management process that we discussed earlier, and that are summarized in Figure 1.1, are important. Managers do have to analyze the external environment to identify opportunities and threats. They do have to analyze the company's resources and capabilities to identify strengths and weaknesses. They need to be familiar with the range of functional-level, business-level, corporate-level, and global strategies that are available to them. And they need to have an appreciation for the structures required to implement different strategies. What Hamel and Prahalad seem to be saying is that the strategic management process should begin with challenging goals—such as attaining global leadership—that stretch the organization. Then, throughout the process the emphasis should be on finding ways (strategies) to develop the resources and capabilities necessary to achieve these goals, rather than on exploiting *existing* strengths to take advantage of *existing* opportunities. The difference between strategic fit and strategic intent, therefore, may just be one of emphasis. Strategic intent is more internally focused and is concerned with building new resources and capabilities. Strategic fit focuses more on matching existing resources and capabilities to the external environment.

IMPROVING STRATEGIC DECISION MAKING

Even the best-designed strategic planning systems will fail to produce the desired results if strategic decision makers do not use the information at their disposal effectively. There is in fact a good deal of evidence that many managers are poor strategic decision makers.[34] The reasons have to do with two related psychological phenomena: cognitive biases and groupthink. We discuss each of them in turn and then consider techniques for improving decision making.

■ Cognitive Biases and Strategic Decisions

The rationality of human decision makers is bounded by our own cognitive capabilities.[35] We are not supercomputers, and it is difficult for us to absorb and process large amounts of information effectively. As a result, we tend to fall back on certain rules of thumb, or heuristics, when making decisions. Many of these rules of thumb are actually quite useful, since they help us to make sense of a complex and uncertain world. However, sometimes they also lead to severe and systematic errors in the decision-making process.[36] Systematic errors are errors that appear time and time again. These systematic errors seem to arise from a series of **cognitive biases** in the way that human decision makers process information and reach decisions. Because of cognitive biases, many managers end up making poor strategic decisions.

Figure 1.5 presents five well-known cognitive biases. These biases have been verified repeatedly in laboratory settings, so we can be reasonably sure that they exist and that we are all prone to them.[37] The **prior hypothesis bias** refers to the fact

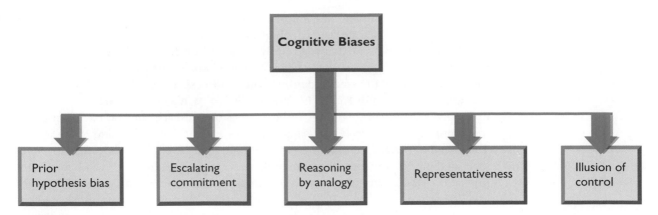

FIGURE 1.5

Five Well-Known
Cognitive Biases

that decision makers who have strong prior beliefs about the relationship between two variables tend to make decisions on the basis of these beliefs, even when presented with evidence that their beliefs are wrong. Moreover, they tend to seek and use information that is consistent with their prior beliefs, while ignoring information that contradicts these beliefs. To put this bias in a strategic context, it suggests that a CEO who has a strong prior belief that a certain strategy makes sense might continue to pursue that strategy, despite evidence that it is inappropriate or failing.

Another well-known cognitive bias is referred to as **escalating commitment**.[38] Escalating commitment occurs when decision makers, having already committed significant resources to a project, commit even more resources if they receive feedback that the project is failing. This may be an irrational response; a more logical response would be to abandon the project and move on (that is, to cut your losses and run), rather than escalate commitment. Feelings of personal responsibility for a project apparently induce decision makers to stick with a project, despite evidence that it is failing. One of the most famous examples of escalating commitment is U.S. policy during the Vietnam War. President Lyndon B. Johnson's reaction to information that U.S. policy in Vietnam was failing was to commit ever more resources to the war.[39] To draw on a business example, during the 1960s and 1970s the response of large U.S. steel makers to cost-efficient competition from minimills and foreign steel makers was to increase their investments in the technologically obsolete steel-making facilities they already possessed, rather than invest in new cutting-edge technology.[40] This was irrational; investments in such obsolete technology would never enable them to become cost efficient.

The bias of **reasoning by analogy** involves the use of simple analogies to make sense of complex problems. U.S. policy toward Vietnam in the 1960s, for example, was guided by the analogy of falling dominoes. U.S. policymakers believed that if Vietnam fell to the Communists the rest of Southeast Asia would also fall. The danger of using such analogies is that by oversimplifying a complex problem they can mislead. For example, several companies have relied on the analogy of a three-legged stool to justify diversifying into business areas of which they had little prior knowledge. The analogy suggests that a stool with fewer than three legs—and by extension, a company that is active in fewer than three different businesses—is unbalanced. Chrysler applied this analogy to justify its decision in the mid 1980s to diversify into the aerospace industry by acquiring Gulfstream, a manufacturer of executive jets. Five years later, Chrysler admitted that the diversification move had been a mistake and divested itself of this activity.

Representativeness is a bias rooted in the tendency to generalize from a small sample, or even a single vivid anecdote. This bias, however, violates the statistical law of large numbers, which says that it is inappropriate to generalize from a small sample, let alone from a single case. An interesting example of representativeness occurred after World War II, when Seawell Avery, the CEO of Montgomery Ward, shelved plans for national expansion to meet competition from Sears because he believed that a depression would follow the war. He based his belief on the fact that there had been a depression after World War I. As it turned out, there was no depression, and Sears went on to become a nationwide retailer, whereas Montgomery Ward did not. Avery's mistake was to generalize from one postwar experience and assume that depressions always follow wars.

The final cognitive bias is referred to as the **illusion of control**. It is the tendency to overestimate one's ability to control events. Top-level managers seem to be particularly prone to this bias. Having risen to the top of an organization, they tend to be overconfident about their ability to succeed. According to Richard Roll, such overconfidence leads to what he has termed the **hubris hypothesis** of takeovers.[41] Roll argues that senior managers are typically overconfident about their abilities to create value by acquiring another company. Hence, they end up making poor acquisition decisions, often paying far too much for the companies they acquire. Subsequently, servicing the debt taken on to finance such an acquisition makes it all but impossible to profit from the acquisition.

■ Groupthink and Strategic Decisions

The biases just discussed are individual biases. However, most strategic decisions are made by groups, not individuals. Thus, the group context within which decisions are made is clearly an important variable in determining whether cognitive biases will operate to adversely affect the strategic decision-making processes. The psychologist Irvin Janis has argued that many groups are characterized by a process known as groupthink and that as a result many groups do make poor strategic decisions.[42] **Groupthink** occurs when a group of decision makers embarks on a course of action without questioning underlying assumptions. Typically, a group coalesces around a person or policy. It ignores or filters out information that can be used to question the policy and develops after-the-fact rationalizations for its decision. Thus, commitment is based on an emotional, rather than an objective, assessment of the correct course of action. The consequences can be poor decisions.

This phenomenon may explain, at least in part, why companies often make poor strategic decisions in spite of sophisticated strategic management. Janis traced many historical fiascoes to defective policymaking by government leaders who received social support from their in-group of advisers. For example, he suggested that President John F. Kennedy's inner circle suffered from groupthink when the members of this group supported the decision to launch the Bay of Pigs invasion of Cuba, even though available information showed that it would be an unsuccessful venture and would damage U.S. relations with other countries.

Janis has observed that groupthink-dominated groups are characterized by strong pressures toward uniformity, which make their members avoid raising controversial

| 1.4 | STRATEGY *in* ACTION |

Groupthink at Imperial Tobacco

An example of groupthink concerns the 1979 acquisition of Howard Johnson by Britain's Imperial Group. In 1979, Imperial was the third largest tobacco company in the world, after British American Tobacco and Philip Morris. In the 1970s, Imperial began a diversification program designed to reduce its dependence on the declining tobacco market. Part of this program included a plan to acquire a major U.S. company. Imperial spent two years scanning the United States for a suitable acquisition opportunity. It was looking for an enterprise in a high-growth industry that had a high market share, a good track record, and good growth prospects and that could be acquired at a reasonable price. Imperial scanned more than 30 industries and 200 different companies before deciding on Howard Johnson.

When Imperial announced its plans to buy Howard Johnson for close to $500 million in 1979, the company's shareholders threatened rebellion. They were quick to point out that at $26 per share Imperial was paying double what Howard Johnson had been worth only six months previously, when share prices stood at $13. The acquisition hardly seemed to be at a reasonable price. Moreover, the motel industry was entering a low- rather

than a high-growth phase, and growth prospects were poor. Besides, Howard Johnson did not have a good track record. Imperial ignored shareholder protests and bought the lodging chain. Five years later, after persistent losses, Imperial was trying to divest itself of Howard Johnson. The acquisition had been a complete failure.

What went wrong? Why, after a two-year planning exercise, did Imperial buy a company that so patently did not fit its own criteria? The answer would seem to lie not in the planning, but in the quality of strategic decision making. Imperial bought Howard Johnson in spite of its planning, not because of it. The CEO decided independently that Howard Johnson was a good buy. A rather authoritarian figure who was overconfident of his ability (a case of hubris), the CEO surrounded himself with subordinates who agreed with him. In a clear sign that groupthink was at work, once he had made his choice his advisers concurred with his judgment and shared in developing rationalizations for it. No one questioned the decision itself, even though information was available to show that it was flawed. Instead, strategic planning was used to justify a decision that in practice did not conform with strategic objectives.[43]

issues, questioning weak arguments, or calling a halt to softheaded thinking. An interesting example of groupthink in a business context, the acquisition of Howard Johnson by the Imperial Group, is highlighted in Strategy in Action 1.4. Note that in this case groupthink seemed to exacerbate a number of other cognitive biases, including the illusion of control and prior hypothesis bias.

■ Techniques for Improving Decision Making

The existence of cognitive biases and groupthink raises the issue of how to bring critical information to bear on the decision mechanism so that strategic decisions made by the company are realistic and based on thorough evaluation. Two techniques known to counteract groupthink and cognitive biases are devil's advocacy and dialectic inquiry.

Devil's advocacy and dialectic inquiry have been proposed as two means of improving decision making.[44] **Devil's advocacy** requires the generation of both a plan and a critical analysis of the plan. One member of the decision-making group acts as the devil's advocate, bringing out all the reasons that might make the proposal unacceptable. In this way, decision makers can become aware of the possible

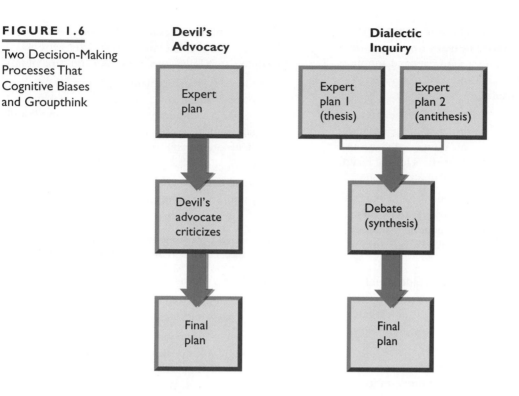

perils of recommended courses of action. **Dialectic inquiry** is more complex, for it requires the generation of a plan (a thesis) and a counterplan (an antithesis). According to R. O. Mason, one of the early proponents of this method in strategic management, the plan and the counterplan should reflect plausible but conflicting courses of action.[45] Corporate decision makers consider a debate between advocates of the plan and counterplan. The purpose of the debate is to reveal problems with definitions, recommended courses of action, and assumptions. As a result, corporate decision makers and planners are able to form a new and more encompassing conceptualization of the problem, which becomes the final plan (a synthesis).

Both of these decision-making processes are illustrated in Figure 1.6. If either of them had been used in the Imperial case, very likely a different (and probably a better) decision would have been made. However, there is considerable dispute over which of the two methods is better.[46] Researchers have reached conflicting conclusions, and the jury is still out on this issue. From a practical point of view, however, devil's advocacy is probably the easier method to implement because it involves less commitment in terms of time than dialectic inquiry.

SUMMARY OF CHAPTER

✔ A strategy is an action that a company takes to attain one or more of its goals.

✔ A central objective of strategic management is to identify why some organizations succeed while others fail.

✔ Traditional definitions of strategy stress that an organization's strategy is the outcome of a rational planning process.

✔ The major components of the strategic management process include defining the mission and major goals of the organization; analyzing the external and internal environments of the organization;

choosing strategies that align, or *fit,* the organization's strengths and weaknesses with external environmental opportunities and threats; and adopting organizational structures and control systems to implement the organization's chosen strategy.

✔ General managers are individuals who bear responsibility for the overall performance of the organization or of one of its major self-contained divisions. Their overriding strategic concern is for the health of the total organization under their direction.

✔ Operating managers are individuals who bear responsibility for a particular business function or operation. Although they lack general management responsibilities, they do play a very important strategic role.

✔ The key characteristics of good leaders include vision, eloquence, and consistency; commitment; being well informed; a willingness to delegate and empower; astute use of power; and emotional intelligence.

✔ A revision of the concept suggests that strategy can emerge from deep within an organization in the absence of formal plans as lower-level managers respond to unpredicted situations.

✔ Strategic planning often fails because executives do not plan for uncertainty and because ivory tower planners lose touch with operating realities.

✔ Hamel and Prahalad have criticized the fit approach to strategy making on the ground that it focuses too much on the degree of fit between existing resources and current opportunities and not enough on building new resources and capabilities to create and exploit future opportunities.

✔ Strategic intent refers to an obsession with achieving an objective that stretches the company and requires it to build new resources and capabilities.

✔ In spite of systematic planning, companies may adopt poor strategies if their decision-making processes are vulnerable to groupthink and if individual cognitive biases are allowed to intrude into the decision-making process.

✔ Techniques for enhancing the effectiveness of strategic decision making include devil's advocacy and dialectic inquiry.

DISCUSSION QUESTIONS

1. What do we mean by *strategy?*
2. What are the strengths of formal strategic planning? What are its weaknesses?
3. The book "Barbarians at the Gate" by Bryan Burroughs and John Helyar (Harper & Row, 1990) contains a detailed description of the acqusition of RJR Nabisco by KKR. Using the book as your source, evaluate KKR's decision to acquire RJR Nabisco. Do you think cognitive biases were at work here, and would managers at KKR have reached a different decision if they had employed devil's advocacy? Was the acquisition of RJR an intended or an emergent strategy? (Note: Answering this question requires a fair amount of reading.)
4. Evaluate President Bill Clinton against the leadership characteristics discussed in the text. On the basis of this comparison, do you think that President Clinton is a good strategic leader?

Practicing Strategic Management

SMALL-GROUP EXERCISE
Designing a Planning System

Break up into groups of three to five people, and discuss the following scenario:

You are a group of senior managers working for a fast-growing computer software company. Your product allows users to engage in interactive role-playing games over the Internet (World Wide Web). In the last three years, your company has gone from being a start-up enterprise with 10 employees and no revenues to a company with 250 employees and revenues of $60 million. The company has been growing so rapidly that you have not had time to create a strategic plan, but now your board of directors tells you that it wants to see a plan and that it wants the plan to drive decision making and resource allocation at the company. The board wants you to design a planning process that will have the following attributes:

1. It will be democratic, involving as many key employees as possible in the process.

2. It will help build a sense of shared vision within the company about how to continue to grow rapidly.

3. It will lead to the generation of three to five key strategies for the company.

4. It will drive the formulation of detailed action plans, and these plans will be subsequently linked to the company's annual operating budget.

Design a planning process for presentation to your board of directors. Think carefully about who should be included in this process. Be sure to outline the strengths and weaknesses of the approach you choose, and be prepared to justify why your approach might be superior to alternative approaches.

ARTICLE FILE 1

At the end of every chapter in this book, you will find an Article File task. The task requires you to search newspapers or magazines in the library for an example of a real company that satisfies the task question or issue. Your first article file task is to find an example of a company that has recently changed its strategy. Identify whether this change was the outcome of a formal planning process or an emergent response to unforeseen events occurring in the company's environment.

STRATEGIC MANAGEMENT PROJECT
Module 1

To give you a practical insight into the strategic management process, we provide a series of strategic modules—one at the end of every chapter in this book. Each module asks you to collect and analyze information relating to the material discussed in that chapter. By completing these strategic modules, you will gain a clearer idea of the overall strategic management process. The first step in this project is to pick a company to study. We recommend that you focus on the same company throughout the book. Remember also that we will be asking you for information about the corporate and international strategy of your company, as well as its structure. We strongly recommend that you pick a company for which such information is likely to be available.

There are two approaches that can be used to select a company to study, and your instructor will tell you which one to follow. The first approach is to pick a well-known company that has a lot of information written about it. For example, large publicly held companies such as IBM, Microsoft, and Southwest Airlines are routinely covered in the business and financial press. By going to the library at your university, you should be able to track down a great deal of information on such companies. Many libraries now have electronic data search facilities such as *ABI/Inform*, *Wall Street Journal Index*, *F&S Index*, and *Nexis*. These enable you to identify any article that has been written in the business press on the company of your choice within the last few years. If you do not have electronic data search facilities at your university, we suggest that you ask your librarian about data sources. A number of nonelectronic data sources are available. For example, *F&S Predicasts* publishes an annual list of articles relating to major companies that appeared in the national and international business press. You will also want to collect full financial information on the company that you pick. Again, this can be accessed from electronic databases such as *Compact Disclosure*. Alternatively, your library might have the annual financial reports, 10-K filings, or proxy statements pertaining to the company you pick. Again, ask your librarians; they are the best source of information.

A second approach is to pick a smaller company in your city or town to study. Although small companies are not routinely covered in the national business press, they may be covered in the local press. More importantly, this approach can work well if the management of the company will agree to talk to you *at length* about the strategy and structure of the company. If you happen to know somebody in such a company or if you yourself have worked there at some point, this approach can be very worthwhile. However, we *do not* recommend this approach unless you can get a *substantial* amount of guaranteed access to the company of your choice. If in doubt, ask your instructor before making a decision. The key issue is to make sure that you have access to enough interesting information to complete the strategic modules.

Your assignment for Strategic Management Project, Module 1, is to choose a company to study and to obtain enough information about that company to carry out the following instructions and answer the questions asked.

1. Give a short account of the history of the company, and trace the evolution of its strategy over time. Try to determine whether the strategic evolution of your company is the product of intended strategies, emergent strategies, or some combination of the two.

2. Identify the mission and major goals of the company.

3. Do a preliminary analysis of the internal strengths and weaknesses of the company and of the opportunities and threats that it faces in its environment. On the basis of this analysis, identify the strategies that you think the company should pursue. (Note: You will need to perform a much more detailed analysis later in the book.)

4. Who is the CEO of the company? Evaluate the CEO's leadership capabilities.

 EXPLORING THE WEB
Visiting Dell Computer

Go to the Web site of Dell Computer (http://www.dell.com) and find the section that describes Dell's history. Using the information contained there, map out the evolution of strategy at Dell from its establishment in the 1980s until the present day. To what degree do you think that the evolution of strategy at Dell was the result of detailed long-term strategic planning, and to what degree was it the result of unplanned actions taken in response to unpredictable circumstances?

Search the Web for a company site where there is sufficient information to map out the evolution of that company's strategy over a significant period of time. What drove the evolution of strategy at this company? To what degree was the evolution of strategy the result of detailed long-term strategic planning, and to what degree was it the result of unplanned actions taken in response to unpredictable circumstances?

CLOSING CASE

Jill Barad's Strategy for Mattel

On August 22, 1996, Jill Barad was named the next chief executive officer (CEO) of Mattel. At forty-five years of age, she had become one of the few women to head a major U.S. corporation. For Barad, the announcement was the fulfillment of a fifteen-year career at Mattel, during which she was best known for transforming Mattel's flagging line of Barbie dolls into the most profitable toy brand in the world. As product manager for Barbie, she had pioneered a brand extension strategy that had tripled Barbie sales to $1.4 billion between 1988 and 1995. In the process, she had gained a reputation for be-

ing a hard-driving manager and skilled marketing visionary. As CEO, one of Barad's first tasks was to decide on a strategy that would enable Mattel to grow earnings per share in line with the company's stated goal of 15 percent per annum compounded before the effects of any acquisitions.

Mattel is the world's largest toymaker, with 1995 revenues of $3.64 billion. Historically, the company's strengths have been in its Barbie brand, its Fisher-Price line of toys for young children (which generated 1995 revenues of more than $1 billion), the Hot Wheels brand, and its Disney licenses. Negotiated in 1988, the

Disney licenses give Mattel exclusive rights to make products based on Disney's movies for children. In 1995, Mattel earned revenues of $450 million from its Disney connection. Between 1988 and 1995 these four core product areas helped power Mattel to a compound annual growth rate of 20 percent for sales and 38 percent for operating income. By 1996, Mattel commanded about 16 percent of the market share for toys sold in the United States, although its share in Europe, the other great toy market, was less than 8 percent.

Despite Mattel's glittering past and Jill Barad's own starring role in it, many knowledgeable observers of the toy industry believed that the company's goal of 15 percent growth in earnings *before acquisitions* represented a difficult challenge for the new CEO. Barad took over the top spot at a time when Mattel's growth rate appeared to be slowing. In June 1996, Mattel reported that sales for its most recent quarter would be "approximately the same as last year," marking the first time quarterly results had been flat in eight years. To be sure, part of the slowdown was due to lackluster sales of its toys based on Disney's latest film, *The Hunchback of Notre Dame.* This shortfall could have easily been made up by a strong showing from toys linked to future Disney films. However, critics charged that the toy industry seemed to be suffering from a chronic lack of creativity. Of the fifteen top-selling toys in 1996, only three were toy company inventions that originated within the previous year. Mattel was very much a case in point. The Barbie brand had been around since 1959, Hot Wheels and Fisher-Price had been acquired rather than developed internally, and the creative impulse behind the Disney line of toys clearly came from that company, not Mattel.

Of course, it can be argued that given the fickle nature of the toy business, where last year's megahit can become this year's bust (remember Cabbage Patch Kids?), Mattel was right to focus on established and enduring brands. Nevertheless, by emphasizing established brands over innovations, Mattel ran the risk of missing successful new blockbusters. That is what happened with video games. Having given up after some early forays into video games, Mattel watched Japanese companies like Nintendo and Sega take that business from zero to $6 billion in sales.

As articulated in 1996, Barad's initial strategy for Mattel had four main elements. First, she made it clear that she would continue with the highly profitable practice of extending the company's existing brands. For example, she had plans to further develop a line of collectible Barbie dolls. Second, she would develop new product cate-

gories, particularly in boys' toys and board games, two areas where Mattel had traditionally been weak. That could be accomplished through internal product development or by acquiring an emerging company and then growing its business through further investments. Third, she would focus more effort on expanding overseas markets, where Mattel's presence was more limited than in the United States. Her stated goal was to increase overseas sales to more than 50 percent of Mattel's total—up from 40 percent in 1995. Finally, she would try to increase earnings by driving down costs. Cost reductions were to be achieved by outsourcing production to low-cost foreign factories in places such as China, a major shift for Mattel, which in 1995 manufactured two-thirds of its core product lines in its own plant.

Three years into her tenure, Barad's strategy for Mattel was increasingly being questioned by stockholders. After peaking at $44 a share in early 1998, the stock fell to $23 per share by June 1999 despite a record bull market in American stocks. The catalyst for the decline had been Barad's announcement that Mattel's profit growth would fall below the 15 percent goal during 1998 and 1999. The slowing growth was due to a number of problems that had stymied Barad's strategy. Parents were buying fewer toys and more computer software and video games for their children. Total U.S. toy sales were flat in 1998, while sales of video games increased by 20 percent and sales of software for children rose by 7 percent. Disney's most recent animated movies had been less successful than expected, and related toy sales had suffered accordingly. Moreover, most significantly, the popularity of the Barbie brand had declined, partly because of changing fashions. Parents were shifting their spending to computer software for girls and competing dolls, such as Pleasant Company's highly successful line of American Girl dolls. However, missteps by Mattel also contributed to the decline.

Throughout the 1990s, a big driver of Mattel's sales growth had been a line of Barbie collectibles known as Holiday Barbie—a line that Barad had introduced in 1988. Priced at $30 to $35 each, compared with less than $10 for a regular Barbie, by 1997 Holiday Barbie was generating $700 million of the total $1.7 billion in Barbie sales. In 1996, Barad had stated that she believed Holiday Barbie sales could exceed $1 billion. Accordingly, at Barad's insistence, in 1997 production of the Holiday Barbie line was set at 3 million dolls, a 1 million increase from 1996. However, much of the rise in demand during 1996 and 1997 stemmed from double ordering by retailers that had suffered from shortages in prior years. When the expected demand growth failed to materialize in 1998, retailers were left with excess stock of Holiday Barbie and started to discount, while putting new orders on hold. Consequently, after years of growth, Barbie sales fell by 15 percent in the first half of 1998. More significantly perhaps, overproduction had destroyed the collectible value of Holiday Barbie, and it was unclear whether Mattel could rebuild it.

To try to salvage her growth strategy, Barad took several actions in 1998 and 1999. In mid 1998, Mattel acquired the Pleasant Company for $700 million. By this point, the Pleasant Company was the number two doll maker in the United States. According to Barad, the Pleasant Company's highly successful American Girl brand was targeted at girls aged seven to twelve and was thus a perfect complement to Barbie, where the demographic was two- to seven-year-olds. This acquisition was followed in late 1998 by the acquisition of computer software maker The Learning Company for $3.5 billion. The Learning Company's software titles include the popular Reader Rabbit series, Carmen Sandiego, and Myst. In April 1999, after the announcement of a 2 percent decline in sales and a first-quarter loss of $18 million, Barad also laid out plans to cut 3,000 jobs in order to realize cost savings of $400 million over three years. Around the same time, she announced the formation of an on-line venture, www.mattel-store.com, to tap into the growing volume of on-line sales. Barad believed that this venture would generate revenues of $60 million in its first year alone. The company also stated that it had entered into an alliance with Intel to develop a generation of interactive toys.[47]

Case Discussion Questions

1. What was Jill Barad's primary goal for Mattel in 1996? What strategies did she choose in order to pursue these goals?

2. Why did Barad's strategies fail to generate the profit growth she had planned? Could better planning have helped Barad anticipate market trends?

3. Could better decision-making techniques have helped Barad avoid the decline in sales of Holiday Barbie?

4. How would you describe Mattel's strategy as of mid 1999? Does this strategy make sense, given changing conditions in the toy market? Would you describe this strategy as an emergent strategy or a planned strategy?

End Notes

1. S. G. Steinberg. "Seek and Ye Shall Find (Maybe)," *Wired*, release 4.05 (May 1996); L. Himelstein, H. Green, and R. Siklos, "Yahoo! The Company, The Strategy, The Stock," *Business Week*, September 7, 1998, p. 66; S. Moran, "For Yahoo, GeoCities May Only Be the Start," *Internet World*, March 15, 1999; Yahoo! 1998 Annual Report.

2. K. R. Andrews, *The Concept of Corporate Strategy* (Homewood, Ill.: Dow Jones Irwin, 1971); H. I. Ansoff, *Corporate Strategy* (New York: McGraw-Hill, 1965); C. W. Hofer and D. Schendel, *Strategy Formulation: Analytical Concepts* (St. Paul, Minn.: West, 1978).

3. Andrews, *The Concept of Corporate Strategy;* Ansoff, *Corporate Strategy;* Hofer and Schendel, *Strategy Formulation*.

4. M. E. Porter. "What Is Strategy?" *Harvard Business Review* (November–December 1996), 7, 61–90.

5. S. Tully, "So Mr. Bossidy, We Know You Can Cut. Now Show Us How to Grow," *Fortune*, August 21, 1995, pp. 70–80; E. G. Randall, "AlliedSignal," *Value Line*, February 9, 1999, p. 1353; "Chief Executive of the Year 1998: AlliedSignal's Larry Bossidy," *Chief Executive* (U.S.), November 1998, p. 32; J. P. Dolan, "The CEO's CEO," interview with Allied Signal CEO Larry Bossidy, *Chief Executive*, July 17, 1998, p. 28.

6. For a summary of research on strategic leadership, see D. C. Hambrick, "Putting Top Managers Back into the Picture," *Strategic Management Journal,* Special Issue, 10 (1989), 5–15. See also D. Goleman, "What Makes a Leader?" *Harvard Business Review* (November–December 1998), 92–105; and H. Mintzberg, "Covert Leadership," *Harvard Business Review* (November–December 1998), 140–148.

7. N. M. Tichy and D. O. Ulrich, "The Leadership Challenge: A Call for the Transformational Leader," *Sloan Management Review* (Fall 1984), 59–68; F. Westley and H. Mintzberg, "Visionary Leadership and Strategic Management," *Strategic Management Journal,* Special Issue, 10 (1989), 17–32.

8. E. Wrapp, "Good Managers Don't Make Policy Decisions," *Harvard Business Review* (September–October 1967), 91–99.

9. J. Pfeffer, *Managing with Power* (Boston: Harvard Business School Press, 1992).

10. Goleman. "What Makes a Leader?" pp. 92–105.

11. For details see R. A. Burgelman, "Intraorganizational Ecology of Strategy Making and Organizational Adaptation: Theory and Field Research," *Organization Science*, 2 (1991), 239–262; H. Mintzberg, "Patterns in Strategy Formulation," *Management Science*, 24 (1978), 934–948; S. L. Hart, "An Integrative Framework for Strategy Making Processes," *Academy of Management Review*, 17 (1992), 327–351; G. Hamel, "Strategy as Revolution," *Harvard Business Review* (July–August 1996), 74, 69–83.

12. This is the premise of those who advocate that chaos theory should be applied to strategic management. See R. Stacey and D. Parker, *Chaos, Management and Economics* (London: Institute for Economic Affairs, 1994); and H. Courtney, J. Kirkland, and P. Viguerie, "Strategy Under Uncertainty," *Harvard Business Review* (November–December 1997), 75, 66–79.

13. C. von Clausewitz, *On War*, translated and edited by M. Howard and P. Paret, (Princeton: 1976), pp. 134, 136.

14. "The Accidental Superhighway: A Survey of the Internet," *Economist*, July 1, 1995; G. Gilder, "The Coming Software Shift," *Forbes ASAP*, August 28, 1995, pp. 147–162; R. D. Hof, K. Rebello, and P. Burrows, "Scott McNealy's Rising Sun," *Business Week*, January 22, 1996, pp. 66–73. A. Cortese, J. Verity, K. Rebello, R. D. Hof, "The Software Revolution," *Business Week*, December 4, 1995, pp. 78–90; informal interviews by Charles Hill with key personnel at Microsoft.

15. Hart, "An Integrative Framework," pp. 327–351; Hamel, "Strategy as Revolution," pp. 74, 69–83.

16. See Burgelman, "Intraorganizational Ecology," pp. 239–262; Mintzberg, "Patterns in Strategy Formulation," pp. 934–948.

17. R. A. Burgelman and A. S. Grove, "Strategic Dissonance," *California Management Review* (Winter 1996), 8–28.

18. M. Dickson, "Back to the Future," *Financial Times*, May 30, 1994, p. 7.

19. Story was related to Charles Hill by George Rathmann, the head of 3M's research activities at the time.

20. Story related to the author by various employees of ICOS.

21. Richard T. Pascale, "Perspectives on Strategy: The Real Story Behind Honda's Success," *California Management Review*, 26 (1984), 47–72.

22. This viewpoint is strongly emphasized by Burgelman and Grove, "Strategic Dissonance," pp. 8–28.

23. Burgelman and Grove, "Strategic Dissonance," pp. 8–28.

24. C. C. Miller and L. B. Cardinal, "Strategic Planning and Firm Performance: A Synthesis of More than Two Decades of Research," *Academy of Management Journal*, 37, (1994), 1649–1665. See also see P. R. Rogers, A. Miller, and W. Q. Judge, "Using Information Processing Theory to Understand Planning/Performance Relationships in the Context of Strategy," *Strategic Management Journal*, 20 (1999), 567–577.

25. T. J. Peters and R. H. Waterman, *In Search of Excellence* (New York: Harper & Row, 1982); T. J. Peters, *Liberation Management: Necessary Disorganization for the Nanosecond Nineties* (New York: Knopf, 1992).

26. H. Mintzberg, "The Design School: Reconsidering the Basic Premises of Strategic Management," *Strategic Management Journal*, 11 (1990), 171–196; H. Mintzberg, *The Rise and Fall of Strategic Planning* (New York: Free Press, 1994).

27. Courtney, Kirkland, and Viguerie, "Strategy Under Uncertainty," pp. 66–79.

28. P. J. H. Schoemaker, "Multiple Scenario Development: Its Conceptual and Behavioral Foundation," *Strategic Management Journal*, 14 (1993), 193–213.

29. "According to Plan," *Economist,* July 22, 1989, pp. 60–63. A. P. de Geus, "Planning as Learning," *Harvard Business Review* (March–April 1988), 70–74; P. Wack, "Scenarios: Uncharted Waters Ahead," *Harvard Business Review* (September–October 1985), 73–89; T. Mack, "It's Time to Take Risks," *Forbes,* October 6, 1986, pp. 125–133.

30. W. C. Kim and R. Mauborgne, "Procedural Justice, Strategic Decision Making, and the Knowledge Economy," *Strategic Management Journal*, 19 (1998), 323–338; W. C. Kim and R. Mauborgne, "Fair Process: Managing in the Knowledge Economy," *Harvard Business Review*, July–August 1997), 75, 65–76.

31. Kim and Mauborgne, "Procedural Justice," pp. 323–338.

32. G. Hamel and C. K. Prahalad, *Competing for the Future* (New York: Free Press, 1994).

33. See G. Hamel and C. K. Prahalad, "Strategic Intent," *Harvard Business Review* (May–June 1989), p. 64.

34. For a review of the evidence, see C. R. Schwenk, "Cognitive Simplification Processes in Strategic Decision Making," *Strategic Management Journal*, 5 (1984), 111–128; and K. M. Eisenhardt and M. Zbaracki, "Strategic Decision Making," *Strategic Management Journal*, Special Issue, 13 (1992), 17–37.

35. H. Simon, *Administrative Behavior* (New York: McGraw Hill, 1957).

36. The original statement about this phenomenon was made by A. Tversky and D. Kahneman, "Judgment Under Uncertainty: Heuristics and Biases," *Science,* 185 (1974), 1124–1131.

37. Schwenk, "Cognitive Simplification Processes," pp. 111–128.

38. B. M. Staw, "The Escalation of Commitment to a Course of Action," *Academy of Management Review*, 6 (1981), 577–587.

39. Ibid.

40. M. J. Tang, "An Economic Perspective on Escalating Commitment," *Strategic Management Journal,* 9 (1988), 79–92.

41. R. Roll, "The Hubris Hypotheses of Corporate Takeovers," *Journal of Business,* 59 (1986), 197–216.

42. I. L. Janis, *Victims of Groupthink,* 2nd ed. (Boston: Houghton Mifflin, 1982). For an alternative view, see S. R. Fuller and R. J. Aldag, "Organizational Tonypandy: Lessons from a Quarter Century of the Groupthink Phenomenon," *Organizational Behavior and Human Decision Processes*, 73 (1998), 163–184.

43. The story ran on an almost daily basis in the *Financial Times* of London during the autumn of 1979.

44. See R. O. Mason, "A Dialectic Approach to Strategic Planning," *Management Science,* 13 (1969), 403–414; R. A. Cosier and J. C. Aplin, "A Critical View of Dialectic Inquiry in Strategic Planning," *Strategic Management Journal,* 1 (1980), 343–356; and I. I. Mintroff and R. O. Mason, "Structuring III—Structured Policy Issues: Further Explorations in a Methodology for Messy Problems," *Strategic Management Journal,* 1 (1980), 331–342.

45. Mason, "A Dialectic Approach," pp. 403–414.

46. D. M. Schweiger and P. A. Finger, "The Comparative Effectiveness of Dialectic Inquiry and Devil's Advocacy," *Strategic Management Journal* 5 (1984), 335–350.

47. Lisa Bannon, "Mattel Names Jill Barad Chief Executive," *Wall Street Journal*, August 23, 1996, p. B3; L. Sandler, "Mattel's Marriage to Disney Falters," *Wall Street Journal*, August 16, 1996, p. C2; "Mattel Growth Strategy to Pursue Acquisitions, Overseas Expansion," *Wall Street Journal*, June 15, 1996, p. B10; E. Schine, "Toys R Her,*" Business Week*, September 2, 1996, p. 47; L. Bannon. "Mattel Tries to Adjust as Holiday Barbie Leaves Under a Cloud," *Wall Street Journal,* June 7, 1999, p. A1, A10; "Toys Were Us," *Financial Times*, December 19, 1998, p. 9.

2 Stakeholders and the Corporate Mission

OPENING CASE

Chainsaw Al Dunlap Gets the Ax

IN JULY 1996, Sunbeam, a troubled maker of small appliances, announced that it had hired Al Dunlap as its chief executive officer. Sunbeam's stock jumped 50 percent at the news, to $18 5/8 as investors eagerly anticipated the gains that the legendary "Chainsaw Al" would bring to Sunbeam. Dunlap's reputation was built on a highly successful career as a turnaround specialist. Before joining Sunbeam, Dunlap had engineered a tough turnaround at Scott Paper. There he had laid off 31 percent of the work force, including 70 percent of all upper-level managers. The stock market valuation of Scott tripled during his tenure. After only eighteen months at Scott, Dunlap walked away with $100 million in salary, bonus, stock gains, and perks. Dunlap claimed that this reward was richly deserved, given the gains that he engineered in the stock of Scott Paper. Now investors hoped that he would work the same magic at Sunbeam.

Upon arrival at Sunbeam, Dunlap quickly fired seven of Sunbeam's top executives. Then he spent three months formulating his strategy, which he unveiled at an analyst meeting in November 1996. It was classic Dunlap. He stated that Sunbeam's work force would be cut in half, to just 6,000, and that eighteen of the company's twenty-six factories would be closed, four divisions disposed of, and the number of products offered by Sunbeam reduced by 81 percent to 1,500. Together, these measures were projected to produce annual savings of $225 million. Dunlap also laid out ambitious growth goals for Sunbeam: doubling revenues to $2 billion (after divestitures), raising operating profit margins to 20 percent from 2.5 percent, launching at least 30 new products a year, and increasing international sales to $600 million. "Our growth mission," he proclaimed, "is to become the dominant and most profitable small household appliance and outdoor cooking company in North America, with a leading share of Latin American and Asian Pacific markets."

Right from the start there were questions about the feasibility of this strategy. Several securities analysts who followed Sunbeam wondered how the company could possibly grow revenues, given the depth of the cuts in employment and products, particularly since the North American market for small appliances was experiencing no growth. Initially, however, Sunbeam's results seemed to suggest that Dunlap could indeed pull off this trick. Sunbeam's revenues grew by 18 percent in 1997, while operating margins income rose to $109.4 million and the stock price surged to around $50 a share. It looked like Dunlap was about to prove once again that tough guys finish first.

Under the surface, though, there were problems at Sunbeam. To grow revenues, Dunlap was urging Sunbeam's managers to engage in a "bill and hold" strategy with retailers. This arrangement allowed Sunbeam's products to be purchased at large discounts and then held at third-party warehouses for delivery later. In effect, Dunlap was shifting sales from future periods into the current period. Although the approach was not illegal, its ethics were questionable. Later, Dunlap defended the practice, claiming that it was an effort to extend the selling season and better meet surges in demand. Sunbeam's auditors, Arthur Anderson & Co., also insisted that the practice met accounting standards.

In early March 1998, Dunlap announced that Sunbeam would acquire three companies, including Coleman, the manufacturer of outdoor camping stoves. The market responded enthusiastically, and the stock hit an all-time high of $53. Some critics wondered, however, if this implied that Sunbeam could not reach its growth goals from internally generated sales. Shortly afterward, Dunlap announced that the company would book a first-quarter loss of $44.6 million. He blamed the loss on underlings who had offered "stupid, low-margin deals," and he insisted that it would "never happen again." To drive home his point, he fired a number of senior managers who, he claimed, were responsible for those deals. Among the dismissed was Donald Uzzi, Sunbeam's well-regarded executive vice president for worldwide consumer products. Around the same time, Dunlap announced that he would cut 5,100 more jobs at the acquired companies and at Sunbeam.

The layoff announcement did not stop the fall in Sunbeam's stock price, which had been declining ever since the announcement of a first-quarter loss and now stood under $20. The decline in the stock price accelerated in late May 1998, when the highly regarded financial newspaper *Barron's* published a scathing analysis of Sunbeam. In the article, *Barron's* alleged that Dunlap had employed $120 million of artificial profit boosters in 1997, without which Sunbeam would have recorded a loss.

Dunlap was so concerned about the *Barron's* article that he called a special meeting of the company's board of directors on June 9, 1998. The board had been supportive of Dunlap up to this point, and he could count several long-time friends among its members. What began as a straightforward meeting rebutting the *Barron's* article took a strange turn when one director asked Sunbeam's chief financial officer, Russ Kersh, if the company would make its next quarter's numbers. Kersh admitted that they were "challenging." At this point, Dunlap asked the outside advisers to step out and then told the board that he and the CFO would resign unless they got the right level of support from the board. "I have all of the necessary documents in my briefcase," Dunlap was reported to have said. Dunlap then stormed out of the room.

Over the next few days, the board members started to dig deeper into the Sunbeam situation. One director placed a call to several top executives. He quickly discovered that many of them had lost confidence in Dunlap, whom they characterized as abusive and unethical. He was also disturbed to hear that not only would Sunbeam miss its growth goals in the coming quarter, but that revenues would probably come in $60 million *below* the $290 million recorded in the same quarter a year earlier.

Armed with this information, the board convened a second meeting on June 13. At that meeting, the directors all agreed that Dunlap had to go. Most of the directors were Dunlap's friends, but they felt betrayed by him, misled about the company's financial condition, its second-quarter earnings, and its yearly numbers. That day they placed a call to Dunlap and told him that he had been dismissed. Three days later, the board also fired Russ Kersh, the CFO. Commenting on Dunlap's demise, the CEO of a Sunbeam competitor stated that Dunlap "is the logical extreme of an executive who has no values, no loyalty, no honor, no ethics. And yet he was held up as a corporate god in our culture. It greatly bothers me." A former plant manager fired by Dunlap remarked: "I guess the house of cards came tumbling down. When you reduce your work force by 50 percent, you lose your ability to manage. You can survive like that for months, not years." After the announcement that Dunlap had been fired, Sunbeam stock fell to under $8 a share, lower than it had been before Dunlap joined the company.[1]

OVERVIEW

The Opening Case tells the story of how Al Dunlap's career as a turnaround special-ist came to an abrupt end at Sunbeam. Dunlap failed for a number of reasons. He lacked a strategic vision that went beyond cutting costs. He did not know how to pursue a growth strategy, and to disguise this fact, he pursued ethically suspect ac-counting policies. He also misled investors and the board of directors about the true financial condition of the company. Consequently, he lost the support of important constituencies in the company, most notably other senior managers and the board of directors. Ultimately, the board could no longer tolerate him as CEO and fired both him and his CFO, Russ Kersh. It should also be noted that long before Dunlap lost the support of the board and other senior managers, he had already lost the support of numerous employees, many of whom had seen their colleagues fired and plants shut down.

This chapter is concerned with how companies can maintain the support of key constituencies—or stakeholders. A company's **stakeholders** are individuals or groups that have an interest, claim, or stake in the company, in what it does, and in how well it performs.[2] We begin by looking at the relationship between stakehold-ers and a company. Then we move on to consider the corporate mission statement, which is the first key indicator of how an organization views the claims of its stake-holders. The purpose of the mission statement is to establish the guiding principles for strategic decision making. We then explore the issue of corporate governance. By **corporate governance**, we mean the mechanisms that are used to "govern" managers and ensure that the actions they take are consistent with the interests of key stakeholder groups. The board of directors is a very important corporate gover-nance mechanism. As we saw in the Opening Case, the board has the power to re-move a CEO who is not satisfying the interests of key stakeholders.

The chapter closes with a look at the ethical dimension of strategic decisions and at the relationship between ethics and stakeholders' welfare. The Opening Case of-fers a good illustration of the importance of ethics. Dunlap's questionable ethics al-lowed him to mislead investors about the true financial state of the company, which helped bring about his removal. By the end of this chapter you will have a good grasp of how stakeholders, corporate governance mechanisms, and ethical considerations all influence the strategies that managers choose for their organizations.

STAKEHOLDERS

A company's stakeholders can be divided into internal stakeholders and external stakeholders (see Figure 2.1). **Internal stakeholders** are stockholders and em-ployees, including executive officers, other managers, and board members. **Exter-nal stakeholders** are all other individuals and groups that have some claim on the company. Typically, this group comprises customers, suppliers, governments, unions, local communities, and the general public.

All stakeholders are in an exchange relationship with the company. Each of the stakeholder groups listed in Figure 2.1 supplies the organization with important re-sources (or contributions), and in exchange each expects its interests to be satisfied

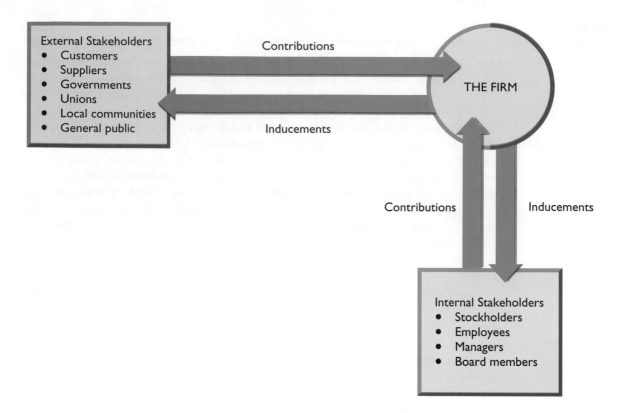

FIGURE 2.1

Stakeholders and the
Enterprise

(by inducements).[3] Stockholders provide the enterprise with capital and in exchange expect an appropriate return on their investment. Employees provide labor and skills and in exchange expect commensurate income, job satisfaction, job security, and good working conditions. Customers provide a company with its revenues and in exchange they want high-quality, reliable products that represent value for money. Suppliers provide a company with inputs and in exchange seek revenues and dependable buyers. Governments provide a company with rules and regulations that govern business practices and maintain fair competition and in exchange want companies that adhere to these rules. Unions help to provide a company with productive employees and in exchange want benefits for their members in proportion to their contributions to the company. Local communities provide companies with local infrastructure and in exchange want companies that are responsible citizens. The general public provides companies with national infrastructure and in exchange seeks some assurance that the quality of life will be improved as a result of the company's existence.

A company must take these claims into account when formulating its strategies, or stakeholders may withdraw their support. For example, stockholders may sell their shares, employees leave their jobs, and customers buy elsewhere. Suppliers may seek more dependable buyers. Unions may engage in disruptive labor disputes. Communities may oppose the company's attempts to locate its facilities in their area, and the general public may form pressure groups, demanding action against companies that impair the quality of life. Any of these reactions can have a disastrous effect on an enterprise, as Strategy in Action 2.1 illustrates. It shows how Bill Agee, the former CEO of Morrison Knudsen, lost his job because he failed to satisfy the interests of two important stakeholder groups: the company's employees and its stockholders.

A company cannot always satisfy the claims of all stakeholders. The goals of different groups may conflict, and in practice few organizations have the resources to manage all stakeholders.[5] For example, union claims for higher wages can conflict with consumer demands for reasonable prices and stockholder demands for acceptable returns. Often the company must make choices. To do so, it must identify the most important stakeholders and give highest priority to pursuing strategies that satisfy their needs. Stakeholder impact analysis can provide such identification. Typically, stakeholder impact analysis follows these steps:

1. Identifying stakeholders

2. Identifying stakeholders' interests and concerns

3. As a result, identifying what claims stakeholders are likely to make on the organization

4. Identifying the stakeholders who are most important from the organization's perspective

5. Identifying the resulting strategic challenges[6]

Such an analysis enables a company to identify the stakeholders most critical to its survival and to make sure that the satisfaction of their needs is paramount. Most companies that go through this process quickly reach the conclusion that there are three stakeholder groups the company must satisfy if it is to survive and prosper: customers, employees, and stakeholders. Both Al Dunlap and Bill Agee lost their CEO positions because they failed to satisfy the demands of stockholders for a good return on their investment. Agee also failed to satisfy the demands of employees for income, job satisfaction, job security, and good working conditions (and one could argue that the same was true of Dunlap). More generally, any company that fails to satisfy the needs of its customers will soon see its revenues fall and will ultimately go out of business.

THE MISSION STATEMENT

As noted earlier, the corporate mission statement is a key indicator of how an organization views the claims of its stakeholders. It describes how a company intends to incorporate stakeholder claims into its strategic decision making and thereby reduce the risk of losing stakeholder support. Thus, in its mission statement, a company makes a formal commitment to its stakeholders, sending out the message that its strategies will be formulated with the claims of those stakeholders in mind.

Most corporate mission statements are built around three main elements: (1) a declaration of the overall vision, or mission, of the company; (2) a summing-up of the key philosophical values that managers are committed to and that influence the

---

2.1   STRATEGY *in* ACTION

Bill Agee at Morrison Knudsen

Bill Agee made his name as a whiz kid who became the chief financial officer of paper-maker Boise Cascade during the 1970s while still in his early thirties. Agee left Boise Cascade after the company was forced to write down its profits by $250 million due to earlier overstatements of the value of timberland sales. At the time, the write-downs were the largest in corporate history, but this did not stop Agee from being appointed CEO of defense contractor Bendix in 1976, when he was only thirty-eight years old. At Bendix, Agee became involved in a famous corporate soap opera, which began when he promoted a young manager, Mary Cunningham, to a senior post, over the heads of other, more experienced, executives. At the time, many felt the promotion came about because the two were romantically involved. Both denied this, but in 1982 Agee divorced his wife and married Cunningham, who by this time had left Bendix.

In 1988, Agee became CEO of Idaho-based Morrison Knudsen (MK—a seventy-five-year-old construction company, which had made its name as the prime contractor on a number of large western construction projects, including the Hoover Dam and the trans-Alaska pipeline. By the time Agee joined MK, it was perceived as a venerable institution that wasn't quite living up to its performance potential. Agee's strategy for improving performance was to sell off some of MK's assets and invest the proceeds in the securities of other companies. He also pushed MK to aggressively pursue large construction projects and to grow its railcar manufacturing business. At one time, the railcar manufacturing business had been a major success at MK, but in recent years it had fallen on hard times, unable to hold its own against Japanese competition.

On the surface, MK appeared to be prospering under Agee's leadership. In 1993, the company earned $35.8 million, and Agee proclaimed it a "banner year" and a "watershed period" for MK's drive into railroad and mass-transit industries. Beneath the surface, however, things were unraveling for Agee. For one thing, 62 percent of MK's profits in 1993 came from Agee's financial plays in securities trading and capital gains on asset sales. Strip out these one-time gains, and it was clear that MK's operating performance was poor. The prime reason seems to have been Agee's insistence that in order to win new business MK should be the low bidder on large contracts. For instance, when MK bid on a contract to build eighty transit cars for the Bay Area Rapid Transit District (BART) in Oakland, California, Agee knocked down the bid to $142 million. According to one insider, the result was that "we were looking at a $14 million loss on the contract the day we won it." In the second quarter of 1994, MK announced a $40.5 million loss after taking a $59.4 million charge for underbidding various transit-car contracts. In the third quarter of 1994, MK took a $9.2 million charge against profits for underbidding on a $100 million contract to rebuild locomotives for Southern Pacific.

---

decisions they make; and (3) the articulation of key goals that management believes must be adhered to in order to attain the vision, or mission, and that are consistent with the values to which managers are committed.[7]

■ Vision, or Mission

The **vision,** or **mission,** of a company is what the company is trying to achieve over the medium to long term as formally declared in its mission statement. In practice, the terms *vision* and *mission* are often used interchangeably, and some companies use the term *purpose* instead. Boeing states that its mission is "to be the number one aerospace company in the world and among the premier industrial

To compound these problems, Agee's leadership had sparked significant employee opposition. In an anonymous letter sent to MK's board in November 1994, a group of MK executives calling themselves the MK Committee for Excellence leveled a slew of charges at Agee. Right off, they claimed, Agee had irked subordinates by removing the portrait of MK's founder from the headquarters and replacing it with a nearly life-sized portrait of himself and his wife, Mary Cunningham, paid for by the company. Agee further estranged insiders by quietly moving the CEO's office to his Pebble Beach estate in California and by scoffing at the company's engineering-oriented culture. Several old-hand MK engineering executives—people who had top reputations in their field—were fired, usually after crossing swords with Agee over his policies.

There was also the matter of Agee's pay and perks. At $2.4 million, Agee's 1993 compensation was equal to 6.8 percent of MK's net income, more than that of any other CEO of a company with earnings in the same range, according to a *Forbes* magazine list. According to insiders, MK paid $4 million a year for a corporate jet for Agee, equal to 13 percent of the company's general and administrative budget. The company also paid for landscaping services at Agee's Pebble Beach estate.

Things came to a head on February 1, 1995, when MK's board announced that the company would record a large loss for 1994. The board also announced that Agee would be stepping down as CEO, although initial indications were that he would stay on as chairman of the board. Preliminary figures suggested that MK would have to take a $179.6 million pretax charge in its 1994 fourth quarter, which would result in a net loss of $141 million for the quarter. At the same time, Standard & Poor's downgraded MK's long-term debt to junk bond rating, signaling that a significant risk of default existed.

The announcement gave rise to a blizzard of shareholder lawsuits and criticism, not only of Agee, but also of MK's board for acting so slowly. Many commentators wondered why it took a huge loss and an anonymous letter from MK executives to prod the board to action. Privately, several board members—most of whom were Agee's appointees and long-time friends—indicated that they were led astray by Agee, who repeatedly urged them not to worry about poor results. Still, many felt that the audit committee of the board of directors had not done a good job of vetting MK's financial accounts under Agee's leadership. Stung by this criticism, by the growing evidence of financial mismanagement under Agee's leadership, and by the Standard & Poor's downgrading of MK's debt, the board reversed its earlier position and decided to strip Agee of all posts at MK.

The shareholders' lawsuits were settled in September 1995. The settlement required MK to pay out $63 million in cash and stock to shareholders and to strengthen its board by adding seven new directors over the next two years. As part of the settlement, Agee agreed to relinquish rights to about $3 million in severance pay and to a cut in his MK pension from $303,000 a year for life to $99,750 a year for life.[4]

concerns in terms of quality, profitability, and growth."[8] The vision set forth by Weyerhaeuser, the world's largest forest products company, is to simply be "the best forest products company in the world."[9] Pfizer, one of the world's premier pharmaceutical companies, defines its mission as "helping humanity and delivering exceptional financial performance by discovering, developing and providing innovative health care products that lead to healthier and more productive lives."[10] The vision enunciated by Intel, the world's largest manufacturer of microprocessors, is "to get to a billion connected computers worldwide. . . .by providing the building blocks of the Internet.[11] Applied Materials, which manufactures the machines that make semiconductor chips, has as its mission to be "the leading supplier of semiconductor wafer processing systems and services worldwide through product innovation and enhancement of customer productivity."[12]

2.2   ° STRATEGY *in* ACTION

Engineering a Strategic Vision at AT&T

When Michael Armstrong was appointed CEO of AT&T in late 1997, he took over the reins of a company that seemed to be letting the rapid development of communications in the Internet age pass it by. The company still generated 90 percent of its revenues from its core long-distance phone business, but the growth in the communication market was in the wireless and Internet access arenas. Moreover, AT&T's core long-distance business was under threat. New entrants into this market, such as the Baby Bells, and aggressive newcomers, such as Qwest Communications, were driving down prices in an attempt to gain market share. Analysts predicted that prices for long-distance phone service could fall from an average of 15 cents per minute in 1998, to 5 cents per minute by 2002. As a result of new entry, some believed that AT&T's market share could decline from 50 percent to under 30 percent over the same period.

Surveying the competitive landscape, Armstrong was struck by the speed of the revolution sweeping the communications industry. He noted that it took radio thirty years to reach 50 million people. It took thirteen years for television to do the same. But the World Wide Web reached twice as many users in half the time. By 1998, more than 100 million people had logged on to the Internet. Projections suggested that there would be 250 million Internet users around the world by 2002. Commerce on the Internet, barely a blip a few years previously, was projected to surpass $300 billion by 2002. Wireless phones, once a novelty, were rapidly becoming a necessity, with 1 million Americans signing up for wireless service every month.

The conclusion that Armstrong drew from this analysis was that AT&T needed to shift rapidly from being a long-distance phone company to a company that could deliver high-speed and capacity (broadband) communications to business and residential consumers around the world, and do so profitably. Going forward, Armstrong stated, AT&T's strategic vision would be "to enrich our customers' personal lives and to make their businesses more successful by bringing to market exciting and useful communications services, building shareowner value in the process." By articulating this vision, Armstrong was signaling that AT&T intended to move aggressively into new communications markets. In January 1998, Armstrong announced that AT&T would move beyond the

---

What you may notice about these statements is that they all commit the corporation to an ambitious goal. To "be number one," "the best," to deliver "exceptional financial performance," "to get to a billion connected computers worldwide," and to be "the leading supplier." All these mission statements are examples of **strategic intent**.

Strategic Intent   We encountered the concept of strategic intent in Chapter 1. As you recall, underlying it is the notion that managers should set an overarching ambitious goal that stretches a company.[13] Often, the vision, or mission, statement articulates the company's strategic intent. Thus, Boeing's strategic intent is to remain the number one aerospace company in the world, while that of Applied Materials is to become the leading supplier of specific product and services. The argument for setting an overarching stretch goal is that (1) it gives a sense of direction and purpose to those within the company; (2) it helps drive strategic decision making and resource allocation; and (3) it forces managers within the company to look for significant improvements in the way they run the business, since that is the only way to attain stretch goals. Put differently, as Jack Welch, the CEO of General Electric, has observed:

> If you don't demand something out of the ordinary, you won't get anything but ordinary results. . . . We used to say nudge the peanut along, moving from, say, 4.73 inventory turns to 4.91. Now we want big stretch results like ten turns or fifteen turns.[14]

long-distance phone business and make major investments in local wireless and Internet-based phone services. He also stated that AT&T would take $1.6 billion out of its cost structure that year. Fine words indeed, but skeptical investors had heard this kind of rhetoric before and wanted to see action.

They didn't have to wait long. By the end of 1998, AT&T had reduced its work force by 18,000 and reached its cost-reduction goals. The employment cuts came from voluntary buyouts, a hiring freeze, and normal attrition. Soon after, AT&T announced its Digital One Rate for wireless customers. This rate carries no long-distance or roaming charge for cellular telephone customers. Although per minute charges have declined as a result, increased usage has more than made up for this. By early 1999, the average subscriber bill was up to $60 per month, an increase of $10 from six months earlier.

However, AT&T's biggest strategic moves under Armstrong have been aimed at acquiring cable television networks. In June 1988, Armstrong announced that AT&T would purchase TCI, America's largest cable television provider, in a $48 billion stock swap. The goal was to offer local phone service and high-speed Internet access over cable TV networks. With the TCI purchase came a recently acquired TCI subsidiary, @Home Corp, which specializes

in providing high-speed Internet access over cable TV networks. AT&T announced that it would use the cable network to begin delivering local phone service over the Internet by the end of 1999. To do this, AT&T stated that it would be using Internet Protocol switching, rather than the traditional circuit switch approach.

In May 1999, these developments were followed by the purchase for $58 billion of MediaOne Group, another large cable group. Simultaneously, AT&T announced that Microsoft would invest $5 billion in AT&T in return for a 3.9 percent ownership stake. For its part, AT&T agreed to use Microsoft's Windows CE as the operating system for set-top boxes.

From these deals it is now clear that AT&T's goal is to provide both local phone service and a broad array of Internet and multimedia services over its newly acquired cable network. Moreover, many of these services will be bundled together, with AT&T charging consumers a single rate for access to the entire range of services. The combination of TCI and MediaOne should enable AT&T to deliver these services to some 26 million homes in the United States. By acting on its vision, AT&T is in the process of evolving from a provider of long-distance phone service to a broad-based provider of communications services.[15]

However, managers must also make sure that the vision does not become so grandiose that it cannot be realized and thus loses credibility among employees. A stretch goal has to be attainable, even though it may require managers to strive for extraordinary performance improvements.

Strategy in Action 2.2 offers a detailed example of a vision that has driven the subsequent development of strategy. It examines CEO Michael Armstrong's process of selecting a strategic vision for AT&T, which is now guiding the repositioning of AT&T. The example illustrates how a new vision—a new articulation of strategic intent—can drive the strategic development of a company, even one as large as AT&T.

Customer Orientation and Business Definition   An important first step in the process of formulating a mission statement is to define the organization's business. Essentially, the definition should answer these questions: "What is our business? What will it be? What should it be?"[16] The responses guide the formulation of a mission statement.

To answer the first question—"What is our business?"—Derek F. Abell has suggested that a company should define its business in terms of three dimensions: who is being satisfied (what customer groups), what is being satisfied (what customer

FIGURE 2.2

Abell's Framework for
Defining the Business

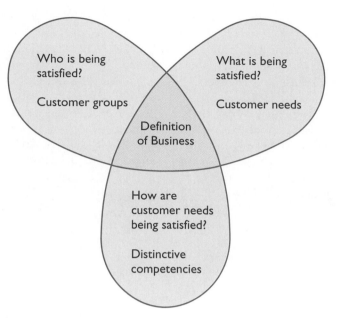

Source: Derek F. Abell, *Defining the Business: The Starting Point of Strategic Planning* (Englewood Cliffs, N.J.: Prentice-Hall, 1980), p. 17.

needs), and how are customer needs being satisfied (by what skills or distinctive competencies)?[17] Figure 2.2 illustrates these three dimensions.

Abell's approach stresses the need for a **consumer-oriented,** rather than a **product-oriented,** business definition. A product-oriented business definition focuses just on the products sold and the markets served. Abell maintains that such an approach obscures the company's function, which is to satisfy consumer needs. A product is only the physical manifestation of applying a particular skill to satisfy a particular need for a particular consumer group. In practice, that need can be served in different ways. A broad consumer-oriented business definition that identifies these ways can safeguard companies from being caught unaware by major shifts in demand. Indeed, by helping anticipate demand shifts, Abell's framework can assist companies in capitalizing on the changes in their environment. It can help answer the second question: "What will our business be?"

However, the need to take a customer-oriented view of a company's business has often been ignored. Consequently, history is littered with the wreckage of once great corporations that did not define their business or that defined it incorrectly. These firms failed to see what their business would become, and ultimately they declined. Theodore Levitt described the fall of the once mighty U.S. railroads in terms of their failure to define their business correctly:

> The railroads did not stop growing because the need for passenger and freight transportation declined. That grew. The railroads are in trouble today not because the need was filled by others (cars, trucks, airplanes, even telephones), but because it was not filled by the railroads themselves. They let others take customers away from them because they assumed themselves to be in the railroad business rather than in the transportation business. The reason they defined their industry wrong was because they were railroad oriented instead of transport oriented; they were product oriented instead of customer oriented.[18]

If the railroads had used Abell's framework, they might have anticipated the impact of technological change and decided that their business was transportation. In that case, they might have transferred their early strength in rail into dominance in today's diversified transport industry. But most railroads stuck to a product-oriented definition of their business and went bankrupt.

In contrast, for a long time IBM correctly foresaw what its business would be. Originally, IBM was a leader in the manufacture of typewriters and mechanical tabulating equipment using punch-card technology. However, IBM defined its business as providing a means for information processing and storage, rather than just supplying mechanical tabulating equipment and typewriters.[19] Given this definition, the company's subsequent moves into computers, software systems, office systems, and printers seem logical. It might also be argued that IBM's problems in the late 1980s and early 1990s arose because the company lost sight of the fact that increasingly consumer needs for information processing and storage were being satisfied by low-cost personal computers, and not by the mainframe computers produced by its core business.

The third question—"What should our business be?"—can also be answered using Abell's framework. Thus, IBM decided that its business should be information processing—that was its vision—and this vision drove its development of computers and office systems, all extensions of its original mechanical tabulating punch-card business. A similar kind of consumer-oriented thinking about "What our business should be" underlies AT&T's recent strategic moves (see Strategy in Action 2.2 for details). AT&T has clearly decided that it is in the communications services business, not the long-distance phone service business. Moreover, AT&T has recognized that changing technology—and particularly the rise of digital wireless networks and the Internet—is altering the way in which communications services will be delivered, including long-distance phone service. Hence AT&T's acquisition of cable TV networks and the introduction of its Digital One Rate for wireless customers.

Another company that has redefined its mission after taking a close look at the needs of its customers is Kodak, which used to see itself as a supplier of photographic equipment. More recently, Kodak has decided that it is in the "imaging business"—the business of providing any technology that allows customers to capture, process, manipulate, and display images. Thus the business includes not just photographic technology based on silver halide applications, which has been Kodak's mainstay, but also new digital imaging technology. Building on this new customer-oriented view of its business and having asked itself "What should our business be?" Kodak has articulated a new corporate vision, which is to be *the world leader in imaging*.[20]

■ Values

The values of a company state how managers intend to conduct themselves, how they intend to do business, and what kind of organization they want to build. Insofar as they direct behavior within a company, values are seen as the bedrock of a company's organizational culture and a driver of its competitive advantage.[21] Chapter 12 deals in depth with the issue of organizational culture.) For example, at General Electric, CEO Jack Welch has in recent years repeatedly articulated a set of values that includes "boundaryless behavior." He stressed its importance in a letter to shareholders:

Boundaryless behavior, an odd awkward phrase just a few years ago, is increasingly a way of life at GE. It has led to an obsession for finding a better way—a better idea—be its source a colleague, another GE business, or another company across the street or on the other side of the globe that will share its ideas and practices with us.[22]

Stated in this manner, boundaryless behavior is the antithesis of the "not invented here" syndrome, which causes managers to ignore ideas from outside the organization. It is a value that encourages managers to look outside their own particular function, business, or organization for ideas and solutions to problems. According to Welch, the institutionalization of boundaryless behavior within GE has shaped the culture of GE and helped improve the competitive position of the enterprise. He gives an example in his letter to shareholders:

Yokogawa, our partner in the Medical Systems business, has been using "Bullet Train Thinking" to take 30–50 percent out of product costs over a two-year period. This technique, which employs "out-of-the-box" thinking and cross-functional teams dedicated to removing obstacles to cost reduction, is now fully operational in our Aircraft Engines business. This effort should lead this business to double digit profitability growth in 1995, despite less than robust market conditions.[23]

Like GE, many companies articulate a set of values to emphasize their own distinctive outlook on business. The values of Lincoln Electric, for instance, emphasize that productivity increases should be shared with customers and employees through lower prices and higher wages. This belief distinguishes Lincoln Electric from many other enterprises and affects its goals and strategies.[24]

Another company whose values are famous is health care giant Johnson & Johnson. Its credo—a statement of its values—is reproduced in Figure 2.3. This credo expresses Johnson & Johnson's belief that the company's first responsibility is to the doctors, nurses, and patients who use J&J products. Next come its employees, the communities in which these employees live and work, and finally the stockholders. The credo is prominently displayed in every manager's office, and according to the Johnson & Johnson managers, it guides all important decisions. Strong evidence of the credo's influence was apparent in the company's response to the 1982 Tylenol crisis. Seven people in the Chicago area died after taking Tylenol capsules that had been laced with cyanide. Johnson & Johnson immediately withdrew all Tylenol capsules from the U.S. market, at an estimated cost to the company of $100 million. At the same time, the company embarked on a comprehensive communication effort targeted at the pharmaceutical and medical communities. By such means, Johnson & Johnson successfully presented itself to the public as a company that was willing to do what was right, regardless of the cost. Consequently, the Tylenol crisis enhanced rather than tarnished Johnson & Johnson's image. Indeed, because of its actions, the company was able to regain its status as a market leader in painkillers in a matter of months.[25]

In one study of organizational values, researchers identified a set of values associated with "high performing organizations" that, through their impact on employee behavior, help companies achieve superior financial performance.[26] Not surprisingly, these values include respect for the interest of key organizational stakeholders—particularly customers, employees, suppliers, and stockholders. They also include respect and encouragement of the assumption of leadership and entrepreneurial

FIGURE 2.3

Johnson & Johnson's
Credo

Our Credo

We believe our first responsibility is to the doctors, nurses and patients,
to mothers and fathers and all others who use our products and services.
In meeting their needs everything we do must be of high quality.
We must constantly strive to reduce our costs
in order to maintain reasonable prices.
Customers' orders must be serviced promptly and accurately.
Our suppliers and distributors must have an opportunity
to make a fair profit.

We are responsible to our employees,
the men and women who work with us throughout the world.
Everyone must be considered as an individual.
We must respect their dignity and recognize their merit.
They must have a sense of security in their jobs.
Compensation must be fair and adequate,
and working conditions clean, orderly and safe.
We must be mindful of ways to help our employees fulfill
their family responsibilities.
Employees must feel free to make suggestions and complaints.
There must be equal opportunity for employment, development
and advancement for those qualified.
We must provide competent management,
and their actions must be just and ethical.

We are responsible to the communities in which we live and work
and to the world community as well.
We must be good citizens — support good works and charities
and bear our fair share of taxes.
We must encourage civic improvements and better health and education.
We must maintain in good order
the property we are privileged to use,
protecting the environment and natural resources.

Our final responsibility is to our stockholders.
Business must make a sound profit.
We must experiment with new ideas.
Research must be carried on, innovative programs developed
and mistakes paid for.
New equipment must be purchased, new facilities provided
and new products launched.
Reserves must be created to provide for adverse times.
When we operate according to these principles,
the stockholders should realize a fair return.

Johnson & Johnson

Source: Courtesy of Johnson & Johnson.

behavior by mid- and lower-level managers, and respect for and a willingness to support efforts at change within the organization. According to the authors of such studies, Hewlett-Packard, Wal-Mart, and PepsiCo are among the companies that apparently emphasize such values consistently throughout their organization.

The study mentioned above also identified the values of poorly performing companies. These values, as might be expected, are *not* articulated in company mission statements. They include arrogance, particularly in regard to ideas from outside the company; a lack of respect for key stakeholders such as customers, employees, suppliers, and stockholders; and a history of resisting efforts at change and "punishing" mid- and lower-level managers who showed "too much leadership." The authors depict General Motors as one such organization, noting that mid- and lower-level managers there who showed too much leadership and initiative were not promoted.

■ Goals

Having stated a vision founded on a consumer-orientated definition of the company's business and having articulated some key values, the company can take the next step in the formulation of a mission statement: establishing major goals. A **goal** is a desired future state that a company attempts to realize. In this context, the purpose of setting goals is to specify with precision what must be done if the company is to attain its mission. For example, consistent with its mission of remaining the number one aerospace company in the world, the Commercial Aerospace Group of the Boeing Corporation set itself a number of goals in 1992. The first goal was to maintain a global market share of at least 60 percent in the large commercial jet aircraft business. The second was to cut in half by 1997 the time it took to build an aircraft, and the third was to bring down the cost of building an aircraft by 30 percent by the same year.

Goal Characteristics   To be meaningful, goals should have four main characteristics.[27] First, well-constructed goals are *precise and measurable*. If a goal cannot be stated precisely and measured, the company will be unable to assess its progress toward attaining that goal. Measurable goals give managers a yardstick for judging their performance.

Second, well-constructed goals *address important issues*. To maintain focus, an organization should operate with a limited number of major goals. Thus, the goals that are selected should all be important ones. In Boeing's case, the goals of reducing costs and "build time" focus managerial attention on two issues that are of critical significance if Boeing is to establish a competitive advantage in the commercial aircraft business: costs and customer responsiveness. The goal of attaining a minimum market share of 60 percent defines explicitly what it means to be an industry leader in commercial aircraft.

Third, well-constructed goals should be *challenging but realistic*. Challenging goals give managers an incentive to look for ways of improving the operations of an organization. However, if a goal is unrealistic in the challenges it poses, employees may give up, whereas a goal that is too easy may fail to motivate managers and other employees.[28] Again, Boeing can serve as an example. Reducing unit costs by 30 percent will require significant improvements in the efficiency of Boeing's operations, and this goal is challenging. Furthermore, experience at other companies has shown that it is possible to achieve 30 percent unit cost reductions over a six-year period; therefore, the goal is not unrealistic.[29]

Fourth, well-constructed goals should, when appropriate, *specify a time period* in which they ought to be achieved. Boeing committed itself to achieving its goals of cost and build-time reduction by 1997. Time constraints are important because they tell employees that success requires a goal to be attained by a given date, not after that date. Deadlines can inject a sense of urgency into the pursuit of a goal and act as a motivator. However, not all goals require time constraints. Boeing's goal of having a market share of at least 60 percent has no time period attached to it because Boeing already has around 60 percent of the market. By articulating this goal, management is saying that Boeing must not let its share slip below this critical level.

A final point worth emphasizing here is that well-constructed goals provide a means of evaluating the performance of managers. Again, the Boeing example is useful here, for the company *did not* attain its goals for build-time and cost reduction. Because of poor management of a production increase during 1997 and 1998, Boeing's unit costs *increased*, not decreased. This led to unanticipated financial losses and the removal of several key managers at Boeing's Commercial Airplane Group, including its head. These managers were dismissed because they failed to attain the goals that were set out in 1992. Goals, thus, are a very important element of a company's internal control systems. (This issue is condsidered further in Chapters 11 and 12.)

Maximizing Stockholder Returns   Although most profit-seeking organizations operate with a variety of corporate goals, within a *public* corporation—at least in theory—many of these goals are directed toward maximizing stockholder returns. A company's stockholders are its legal owners. Consequently, an overriding goal of most corporations is to maximize stockholder returns, which means increasing the long-run returns earned by stockholders from owning shares in the corporation.

Stockholders receive returns in two ways: from dividend payments and from capital appreciation in the market value of a share (that is, by increases in stock market prices). A company can best maximize stockholder returns by pursuing strategies that maximize its own profitability, as measured by the rate of return that the company achieves on its investments in plant, equipment, R&D, and the like—that is, its rate of return on investment (ROI). In general, the more efficient a company becomes, the higher will be its ROI; moreover, its future prospects will look better to stockholders, and it will have a greater ability to pay dividends. Furthermore, higher ROI leads to greater demand for a company's shares. Demand bids up the share price and leads to capital appreciation.

The Short-Term Problem   There is an important danger associated with overemphasizing a return on investment goal.[30] The overzealous pursuit of ROI can encourage managers to maximize short-run rather than long-run returns. A short-run orientation may encourage such misguided managerial action as cutting expenditures that are judged to be nonessential in the short run—for instance, expenditures for research and development, marketing, and new capital investments—but are vital in the long run. Although cutting current expenditures increases current ROI, the resulting underinvestment, lack of innovation, and poor market awareness jeopardize long-run ROI. Despite these negative consequences, managers may make such decisions because the adverse effects of a short-run orientation may not materialize and become apparent to stockholders for several years, or because they are under extreme pressure to achieve short-term ROI goals.

In a now famous *Harvard Business Review* article, Robert H. Hayes and William J. Abernathy argue that, historically, the widespread focus on short-run ROI was a major contributing factor in the loss of international competitiveness by U.S. companies.[31] Massachusetts Institute of Technology economist Lester Thurow likewise faulted the short-run orientation of many U.S. businesses for some of their problems. Thurow claims that many U.S. companies are unwilling to make long-run investments for fear of depressing their short-run ROI. He cites declining expenditures for research and development and reduced innovative activity within U.S. enterprises as evidence of this orientation.[32] Similarly, after a detailed study of productivity problems in U.S. industry, the MIT Commission on Industrial Productivity concluded that the short time horizons of many corporations placed them at a competitive disadvantage vis-à-vis their foreign rivals.[33] One of the consequences of short-term horizons, according to the MIT Commission, was the loss of U.S. leadership to Japanese companies in the videocassette recorder industry. The videocassette recorder was pioneered in the 1950s by the U.S.-based Ampex Corporation, primarily for use in the broadcasting industry. Ampex did try to produce a consumer variant of the product for a mass market but pulled out in 1970, when it decided it could not afford the R&D investment. Similarly, RCA, which also tried to develop a consumer videocassette recorder, pulled out in 1975 in the face of high development costs and manufacturing problems. This left the field open for Sony and Matsushita, both of which had been investing heavily during the 1970s to develop their own technology. Today the videocassette market is a multibillion-dollar market dominated by Matsushita. No U.S. company competes in this market.

As recounted in Strategy in Action 2.3, a similar story of short-term behavior seems to have hurt U.S. companies in the rapidly expanding market for active matrix liquid crystal displays (AM-LCDs). The AM-LCD technology, too, was originally developed in the United States, but the market is now dominated by Japanese companies.

Long-Term Goals   To guard against short-run behavior, managers need to ensure that they adopt goals whose attainment will increase the long-run performance and competitiveness of their enterprise. Long-term goals are related to such issues as customer satisfaction, employee productivity and efficiency, product quality, and innovation. The thinking here is that in order to attain such goals companies have to make long-term investments in plant, equipment, R&D, people, and processes. Only by doing so can a company improve its customer satisfaction, productivity, product quality, and innovation. Moreover, insofar as the attainment of such goals enhances a company's competitive position and boosts its *long-term* profitability, attaining such goals will help the company maximize the returns to be had from holding its stock.

CORPORATE GOVERNANCE AND STRATEGY

We noted that one of a company's major goals is to give its stockholders a good rate of return on their investment. In most publicly held corporations, however, stockholders delegate the job of controlling the company and selecting its strategies to corporate managers, who become the agents of the stockholders.[35] As the agents of stockholders, managers should pursue strategies that maximize *long-run* returns for stockholders. Although most managers are diligent about doing so, not all act in this fashion, and this failure gives rise to the corporate governance problem: managers pursuing strategies that are not in the interest of stockholders.

2.3 STRATEGY *in* ACTION

A Short-Term Emphasis Costs U.S. Companies the Lead in Flat Panel Displays

Active matrix liquid crystal displays (AM-LCDs) are the flat-top color displays used in laptop and notebook personal computers. In addition to computer displays, the screens are also critical components in camcorders, medical instruments, high-definition television, auto dashboards, aerospace instruments, factory control devices and instrumentation for the military. Global sales of AM-LCDs increased from $250 million in 1990 to around $8 billion in 1998, and projections suggest the market will grow by 20 percent per annum compounded for the foreseeable future.

The AM-LCD technology was pioneered during the 1960s at two U.S. companies, RCA and Westinghouse. However, neither company succeeded in commercializing the technology. One reason for this was that corporate management at both companies balked at the development costs and long pay-back periods and so they cut funding. The principal Westinghouse researcher, Jim Fergason, subsequently left the company and set up a venture to manufacture AM-LCDs. However, few U.S. companies were willing to utilize the technology, and Fergason found it difficult to raise sufficient capital. Ultimately, his venture failed.

With no large U.S. company undertaking primary AM-LCD research, it was left to the Japanese to emerge as the major producers. Sharp, NEC, and Toshiba now dominate the market; in 1998, they were responsible for 80 percent of worldwide production. Unlike their major U.S. competitors, these firms made massive investments in AM-LCD research and production facilities in that period. Sharp alone reportedly spent more than $1 billion on developing the technology during the 1980s. Although a number of small U.S. companies are in this business, they tend to focus on highly specialized niches (such as supplying the Defense Department) and have made investments to support only limited production. With the exception of IBM, which has a joint venture with Toshiba in Japan to manufacture AM-LCDs, no major U.S. company has a presence in this industry, and no U.S. company is capable of mass production.[34]

■ The Corporate Governance Problem

Why should managers want to pursue other strategies than those consistent with maximizing stockholder returns? Some writers have argued that, like many other people, managers are motivated by the desire for status, power, job security, and income.[36] By virtue of their position within the company, certain managers, such as the CEO, can use their authority and control over corporate funds to satisfy this desire. For example, CEOs might use their position to invest corporate funds in various perks that enhance their status—executive jets, lavish offices, and expense-paid trips to Hawaii—instead of investing those funds in ways that increase stockholder returns. Economists have termed such behavior **on-the-job consumption**.[37] Bill Agee is an example of a CEO who appeared to engage in excessive on-the-job consumption (see Strategy in Action 2.1).

Besides engaging in on-the-job-consumption, CEOs, along with other senior managers, might satisfy their desire for greater income by awarding themselves excessive pay increases. Critics of U.S. industry claim that extraordinary pay has now become an endemic problem. They point out that CEO pay has been increasing far more rapidly than the pay of average workers, primarily due to very liberal stock option grants, which enable a CEO to earn huge pay bonuses in a rising stock market, even if his company under-performs the market and competitors.[38] For example, in 1980 the average CEO earned 42 times what the average blue-collar worker earned. In 1990, this figure had increased to 85 times. By 1998, the average CEO earned 419 times the pay of the average blue-collar worker.[39] In 1987, the average compensation of the CEOs in the largest 200 companies on the list compiled by *Fortune* magazine increased to $8.7 million.[40] According to a study by the compensation consultants, Towers Perrin, in 1998 CEOs in the United States, as a group, earned 185 times the average pay of *all* employees in their enterprises, including managers.[41]

What rankles critics is the size of some CEO pay packages and their apparent lack of relationship to company performance.[42] In 1998, for example, Disney CEO Michael Eisner earned $575 million, mostly in the form of stock options, despite the fact that Disney did not do particularly well that year and the stock price fell 10 percent. Stanford Weill, CEO of Citigroup, earned $166 million. Jack Welch, CEO of General Electric, earned $83 million. The critics felt that the size of these pay awards was out of all proportion to the CEOs' achievement.[43]

A further concern is that in trying to satisfy the desire for status, security, power, and income, a CEO might engage in "empire building"—buying many new businesses in an attempt to increase the size of the company through diversification.[44] Although such growth may do little to enhance the company's profitability, and thus stockholder returns, it increases the size of the empire under the CEO's control, and by extension, the CEO's status, power, security, and income (there is a strong relationship between company size and CEO pay). To quote Carl Icahn, a famous corporate raider of the 1980s:

> Make no mistake, a strongly knit corporate aristocracy exists in America. The top man, what's more, usually finds expanding his power more important than rewarding owners (stockholders). When Mobil and USX had excess cash, did they enrich shareholders? Of course not. They bought Marcor and Marathon—disastrous investments, but major increases in the size of the manor.[45]

Thus, instead of maximizing stockholder returns, some senior managers may trade long-run profitability for greater company growth by buying new businesses. Figure 2.4 graphs profitability against a company's growth rate. A company that does not grow is probably missing out on some profitable opportunities.[46] A growth rate of G_0 in Figure 2.4 is not consistent with maximizing profitability ($P_1 < P_{max}$). A moderate growth rate of G_1, on the other hand, does allow a company to maximize profits, producing profits equal to P_{max}. Achieving a growth rate in excess of G_1, however, requires diversification into areas that the company knows little about. Consequently, it can be achieved only by sacrificing profitability (that is, past G_1, the investment required to finance further growth does not produce an adequate return, and the company's profitability declines). Yet G_2 may be the growth rate favored by an empire-building CEO, for it will increase his or her power, status, and income. At this growth rate, profits are equal only to P_2. Because $P_{max} > P_2$, a company growing at this rate is clearly not maximizing its profitability, nor the wealth of its stockholders. However, a growth rate of G_2 may be consistent with attaining managerial goals of power, status, and income.

FIGURE 2.4

The Tradeoff Between
Profitability and
Growth Rate

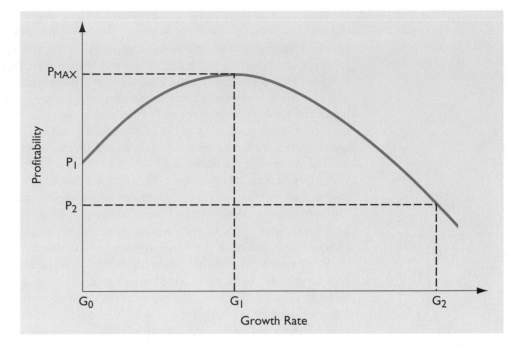

■ Corporate Governance Mechanisms

It must be stressed that by no means do all managers behave in the way just outlined. The vast majority are good stewards who consciously act to increase stockholder returns. Moreover, while some critics charge that CEOs are overpaid, one can
argue that many deserve their high pay and rich bonuses from stock options. At Disney, for example, Michael Eisner has been responsible for transforming that company
from an entertainment has-been into one of the most dynamic entertainment companies in the world. During his tenure, the stock price increased from $3 a share in
1985 to over $30 in 1998. Viewed this way, his 1998 earnings of $575 million, mostly
from the exercise of stock options, were his just reward for the creation of billions of
dollars in shareholder value. Similarly, the $83 million earned by Jack Welch in 1998
can be seen as the reward for the extraordinary increases in GE's share price over
Welch's tenure; the price rose from $1 in 1980 when Welch started to $100 by 1998.

Nevertheless, given that some managers put their own interests first, the problem facing stockholders is how to govern the corporation so that managerial desire
for on-the-job consumption, excessive salaries, or empire-building diversification is
held in check. There is also a need for mechanisms that let stockholders remove in-
competent or ineffective managers. A number of **governance mechanisms** allow
stockholders to exert some control over managers. They include the board of directors, stock-based compensation schemes, corporate takeovers, and the exchange of
equity for debt in leveraged buyouts.

Board of Directors Stockholders' interests are looked after within a company by
the board of directors. Board members are directly elected by stockholders, and, under corporate law, they represent the stockholders' interests in the company. Thus,

the board can be held legally accountable for the company's actions. Its position at the apex of decision making within the company allows the board to monitor corporate strategy decisions and ensure that they are consistent with stockholders' interests. If the board's sense is that corporate strategies are not in the best interest of stockholders, it can apply sanctions such as voting against management nominations to the board of directors or submitting its own nominees. In addition, the board has the legal authority to hire, fire, and compensate corporate employees, including, most importantly, the CEO.[47] One factor that led to the dismissal of Al Dunlap at Sunbeam and Morrison Knudsen's CEO, Bill Agee, was that their strategies had lost the support of the board.

The typical board of directors comprises a mix of inside and outside directors. Inside directors are senior employees of the company, such as the CEO. They are required on the board because they have valuable information about the company's activities. Without such information, the board cannot adequately perform its monitoring function. But since insiders are full-time employees of the company, their interests tend to be aligned with those of management. Hence, outside directors are needed to bring objectivity to the monitoring and evaluation processes. Outside directors are not full-time employees of the company. Many of them are full-time professional directors who hold positions on the boards of several companies. The need to maintain a reputation as competent outside directors gives them an incentive to perform their tasks as objectively and effectively as possible.[48]

Critics charge, however, that inside directors may be able to dominate the outsiders on the board. Insiders can use their position within the management hierarchy to exercise control over what kind of company-specific information the board receives. Consequently, insiders can present information in a way that puts them in a favorable light. In addition, insiders have the advantage of intimate knowledge of the company's operations. Because superior knowledge and control over information are sources of power (see Chapter 12), insiders may be better positioned to influence boardroom decision making than outsiders. The board may become the captive of insiders and merely rubber-stamp management decisions, instead of guarding stockholders' interests.

Some observers contend that many boards are dominated by the company CEO, particularly in those cases where the CEO is also the chairman of the board.[49] To support this view, they point out that both inside and outside directors are often the personal nominees of the CEO. The typical inside director is subordinate to the CEO in the company's hierarchy and therefore unlikely to criticize the boss. Since outside directors are frequently the CEO's nominees as well, they can hardly be expected to evaluate the CEO objectively. Thus, the loyalty of the board may be biased toward the CEO and not the stockholders. Moreover, when the CEO is also chairman of the board, he or she may be able to control the agenda of board discussions in such a manner as to deflect any criticisms of his or her leadership. That was a problem in the case of Bill Agee, who was both CEO and chairman of the board at Morrison Knudsen.

Today, there are clear signs that many corporate boards are moving away from merely rubber-stamping top-management decisions and are beginning to play a much more active role in corporate governance. One catalyst has been an increase in the number of lawsuits filed by stockholders against board members. The trend started in 1985, when a Delaware court ruled that the directors of Trans Union Corporation had been too quick to accept a takeover bid. The court held the directors personally liable for the difference between the offer they accepted and the price the company might have fetched in a sale. The directors then agreed to make up the $23.5 million difference. Since that ruling, a number of major lawsuits have been filed by stockholders against board members. These include suits directed against board members at Holly Farms, Northrup, Lincoln Savings & Loan, Lotus Development, and RJR Nabisco.[50]

Another catalyst has been the growing willingness of some institutional investors, such as the managers of large pension funds or index-linked mutual funds, to use their stockholding in a company, and the voting power it gives them, to gain seats on the board of directors, in order to pressure managers to adopt policies that improve the performance of the company's stock and to pressure the board to replace the CEOs of poorly performing companies. For example, in late 1995, officials of New York City's five major pension funds stated that they would nominate three candidates for seats on the board of Ethyl, a maker of petroleum additives that has performed poorly in recent years. Their objective was to use these board seats to push management harder to improve Ethyl's performance, and hence the value of their stock in Ethyl.[51]

Spurred on by the threat of legal action and pressures from powerful institutional shareholders, an increasing number of boards have started to assert their independence from company management in general and from corporate CEOs in particular. During the 1990s, boards of directors have engineered the removal or resignation of CEOs at a number of major companies, including American Express, Compaq Computer, Digital Equipment, General Motors, IBM, and Sunbeam. Another trend of some significance is the increasing tendency for an outside director to be made chairman of the board. In 1997, according to estimates from the National Association of Corporate Directors, 40 to 50 percent of big companies had an outside director as chairman, up from less than half that figure in 1990.[52] Such appointments limit the ability of corporate insiders, and particularly of the CEO, to exercise control over the board. It is notable that the removal of Robert Stempel as the CEO of General Motors followed the appointment of an outside director, John Smale, as chairman of the GM board.

Stock-Based Compensation   As another way to align the interests of managers with those of stockholders, and thus solve the corporate governance problem, stockholders have urged many companies to introduce stock-based compensation schemes for their managers. In addition to their regular salary, managers are given stock options in the company. Stock options give managers the right to buy the company's shares at a predetermined (strike) price, which may often turn out to be less than the market price of the stock. The idea behind stock options is to motivate managers to adopt strategies that increase the share price of the company, for in doing so they will also increase the value of their own stock options.

As noted earlier, many top managers often earn huge bonuses by exercising stock options that were granted several years before. While not denying that these options do motivate managers to improve company performance, critics claim that they are often too generous. A particular cause for concern is that stock options are often granted at such low strike prices that CEOs can hardly fail to make a significant amount of money by exercising them, even if the companies they run underperform the stock market by a significant margin. Other critics, including the famous investor Warren Buffet, complain that huge stock option grants, by increasing the outstanding number of shares in a company, unjustifiably dilute the equity of stockholders and accordingly should be shown in company accounts as a charge against profits. Buffet has noted that when his investment company, Berkshire Hathaway, "acquires an option issuing company, we promptly substitute a cash compensation plan having an economic value equivalent to that of the previous option plan. The acquiree's true compensation cost is therefore brought out of the closet and charged, as it should be, against earnings."[53] Buffet's point is that stock options are accounted for incorrectly in company financial statements. They are not listed as a cost, and therefore result in an understating of true employee costs and a corresponding overstatement of net profits.

On the other hand, several academic studies suggest that stock-based compensation schemes for executives—such as stock options—can align management and stockholder interests. For instance, one study found that managers were more likely to consider the effects of their acquisition decisions on stockholder returns if they themselves were significant shareholders.[54] According to another study, managers who were significant stockholders were less likely to pursue strategies that would maximize the size of the company rather than its profitability.[55] More generally, it is difficult to argue with the proposition that the chance to get rich from exercising stock options is the primary reason for the fourteen-hour days and six-day workweeks that many employees of fast-growing high technology firms put in.

Corporate Takeovers   If the board of directors is loyal to management rather than to stockholders, or if the company has not adopted stock-based compensation schemes, then a corporate governance problem may exist, and managers may pursue strategies that are inconsistent with maximizing stockholder wealth. However, stockholders still have some residual power, for they can always sell their shares. If they start doing so in large numbers, the price of the company's shares will decline. If the share price falls far enough, the company might be worth less on the stock market than the book value of its assets, at which point it may become an attractive acquisition target and runs the risk of being purchased by another enterprise, against the wishes of the target company's management.

The risk of being acquired by another company is known as the **takeover constraint**. The takeover constraint limits the extent to which managers can pursue strategies and take actions that put their own interests above those of stockholders. If they ignore stockholder interests and the company is acquired, senior managers typically lose their independence and probably their jobs as well. So the threat of takeover can constrain management action.

During the 1980s and early 1990s, the threat of takeover was often enforced by corporate raiders. **Corporate raiders** are individuals or corporations that buy up large blocks of shares in companies that they think are pursuing strategies inconsistent with maximizing stockholder wealth. Corporate raiders argue that if these underperforming companies pursued different strategies, they could create more wealth for stockholders. Raiders buy stock in a company either to take over the business and run it more efficiently, or to precipitate a change in the top management, replacing the existing team with one more likely to maximize stockholders' returns. Raiders, of course, are motivated not by altruism but by gain. If they succeed in their takeover bid, they can institute strategies that create value for stockholders—including themselves. Even if a takeover bid fails, raiders can still earn millions, for their stockholdings will typically be bought out by the defending company for a hefty premium. Called **greenmail**, this source of gain stirred much controversy and debate about its benefits. While some claim that the threat posed by raiders has had a salutary effect on enterprise performance by pushing corporate management to run their companies better, others claim there is little evidence of this.[56]

Leveraged Buyouts   Whereas in a typical takeover attempt a raider buys enough stock to gain control of a company, in a leveraged buyout (LBO) a company's own managers are often among the buyers. The management group undertaking an LBO raises cash by issuing bonds and then uses that cash to buy the company's stock. In effect, the company replaces its stockholders with creditors (bondholders), transforming the corporation from a public into a private entity. However, often the same institutions that were major stockholders before an LBO are major bondholders afterward. The difference is that as stockholders they were not guaranteed a regular dividend payment from the company; as bondholders they do have such a guarantee.

During the 1980s, the number and value of LBOs undertaken in the United States increased dramatically. The value of the 76 LBOs undertaken in 1979 totaled $1.4 billion (in 1988 dollars). In comparison, the value of the 214 LBOs undertaken in 1988 exceeded $77 billion. Since then, however, the LBO business in the United States has slowed considerably, with only a handful of transactions being executed each year. In 1997, for example, the total value of all leveraged buyouts was $29 billion. The LBO's demise, though, may be only temporary. Takeovers tend to go in cycles, and it is quite possible that leveraged buyouts will return in the United States in the near future. On the other hand, the popularity of LBOs is increasing in Europe. In 1998, for example, LBO transactions completed within the European Union hit a record $38 billion, and European LBO funds reportedly have access to $100 billion of capital.[57]

Supporters of the LBO technique, most notably Michael Jensen, claim that the LBO should be viewed as yet another governance mechanism that keeps management discretion in check.[58] Jensen believes that LBOs solve many of the problems created by imperfect corporate governance mechanisms. According to Jensen, a major weakness and source of waste in the public corporation is the conflict between stockholders and managers over the payout of free cash flow (**free cash flow** is cash flow in excess of that required to fund all investment projects with positive net present values when discounted at the relevant cost of capital). Since free cash flow is cash that cannot be profitably reinvested within the company, Jensen argues that it should be distributed to stockholders, but he notes that managers resist such distributions of surplus cash. Instead, for reasons discussed earlier, they tend to invest such cash in empire-building strategies.

Jensen sees LBOs as a solution to this problem. Although management does not have to pay out dividends to stockholders, it must make regular debt payments to bondholders or face bankruptcy. Thus, according to Jensen, the debt used to finance an LBO helps limit the waste of free cash flow by compelling managers to pay out excess cash to service debt rather than spending it on empire-building projects with low or negative returns, excessive staff and perquisites, and other organizational inefficiencies. Furthermore, Jensen sees debt as a way of motivating managers to seek greater efficiencies; high debt payments can force managers to slash unsound investment programs, reduce overhead, and dispose of assets that are more valuable outside the company. The proceeds generated by these restructurings can then be used to reduce debt to more sustainable levels, creating a more competitive organization.

Not all commentators are as enthusiastic about the potential of LBOs as Jensen. The former secretary of labor in the Clinton administration, Robert Reich, is one of the most vocal critics of LBOs.[59] Reich sees two main problems with LBOs. First, he argues that the necessity of paying back large loans forces management to focus on the short term and cut back on long-term investments, particularly in R&D and new capital spending. The net effect is likely to be a decline in the competitiveness of LBOs. Second, Reich believes that the debt taken on to finance an LBO significantly increases the risk of bankruptcy.

The studies that have been done on this issue, although they are limited in number, suggest that LBOs do have some beneficial effects.[60] Companies that undergo an LBO do seem to be more diversified than their peers, suggesting that they had at one time been run by empire-building CEOs. After the LBO, they tend to divest business units and narrow the scope of the company's activities, thereby undoing the excessive diversification of the past. Moreover, there is some evidence that after an LBO, the productivity of the company increases, primarily because it sells off poorly performing business units and simplifies its management structures to reduce bureaucracy.

STRATEGY AND ETHICS

Any strategic action taken by a company inevitably affects the welfare of its stakeholders: employees, suppliers, customers, stockholders, the local communities in which it does business, and the general public. While a strategy may enhance the welfare of some stakeholder groups, it may harm others. For example, faced with falling demand and excess capacity, a steel producer may decide to close down a steel-making facility that is the major source of employment in a small town. Although this action might be consistent with maximizing stockholders' returns, it could also result in thousands of people losing employment and the death of a small town. Is such a decision ethical? Is it the right thing to do, considering the likely impact on employees and the community in which they live? Managers must balance these competing benefits and costs. They must decide whether to proceed with the proposed strategy in the light of their assessment not only of its economic benefits, but also of its ethical implications, given the potentially adverse effect on some stakeholder groups.[61]

■ The Purpose of Business Ethics

The purpose of business ethics is not so much to teach the difference between right and wrong as to give people the tools for dealing with moral complexity, tools that they can use to identify and think through the moral implications of strategic decisions.[62] Most of us already have a good sense of what is right and wrong. We already know that it is wrong to lie, cheat, and steal. We know that it is wrong to take actions that put the lives of others at risk. Such moral values are instilled in us at an early age through formal and informal socialization. The problem, however, is that although most managers rigorously adhere to such moral principles in their private life, some fail to apply them in their professional life, occasionally with disastrous consequences.

The sorry history of Manville Corporation illustrates such failure. (Strategy in Action 2.4 offers another example, that of Jack-in-the-Box). Two decades ago, Manville (then Johns-Manville) was solid enough to be included among the giants of U.S. industry. By 1989, however, 80 percent of the equity of Manville was owned by a trust representing people who had sued the company for liability in connection with one of its principal former products, asbestos. More than forty years ago, information began to reach the medical department of Johns-Manville—and through it the company's managers—suggesting that inhalation of asbestos particles was a major cause of asbestosis, a fatal lung disease. Manville's managers suppressed the research. Moreover, as a matter of company policy, they apparently decided to conceal the information from affected employees. The company's medical staff collaborated in the cover-up. Somehow, managers at Manville persuaded themselves that it was more important to cover up the situation than to take steps to improve working conditions and find safer ways to handle asbestos. They calculated that the cost of improving working conditions was greater than the cost of health insurance to cover those who became ill, and so the best "economic" decision was to conceal the information from employees.[63]

The key to understanding the Manville story is the realization that the men and women at Manville who participated in the cover-up were not amoral monsters, but just ordinary people. Most of them would probably never dream of breaking the law or of physically harming anyone. And yet they consciously made a decision that led directly to great human suffering and death. How could this happen? What seemed to have occurred was that the decision to suppress information was considered on purely economic grounds. Its moral dimension was ignored. Somehow, the managers involved at Manville were able to convince themselves that they were engaged in making a rational business decision, which should be subjected to an economic cost-benefit analysis. Ethical considerations never entered into this calculation. Such behavior is possible only in an environment where business decisions are viewed as having no ethical component. But as the Manville example shows, business decisions *do* have an ethical component.

The task of business ethics, therefore, is to make two central points: (1) that business decisions do have an ethical component and (2) that managers must weigh the ethical implications of strategic decisions before choosing a course of action. Had managers at Manville been trained to think through the ethical implications of their decision, it is unlikely that they would have chosen the same course of action.

■ Shaping the Ethical Climate of an Organization

To foster awareness that strategic decisions have an ethical dimension, a company must establish an organizational climate that emphasizes the importance of ethics. This requires at least three steps. First, top managers have to use their leadership position to incorporate an ethical dimension into the values they stress. At Hewlett-Packard, for example, Bill Hewlett and David Packard, the company's founders,

The Jack-in-the-Box Poisonings—Questionable Ethics?

I n January 1993, several hospitals in Seattle started to notice a dramatic increase in the number of cases of E. coli bacterial infections. The E. coli bacteria are found in under-cooked meat. The symptoms of infection include severe fever, diarrhea, and vomiting. In the case of young people, the infection can be life threatening. Most of the victims of this outbreak were young, and many were in very serious condition. Epidemiologists quickly found a common element: almost all of the victims had eaten hamburgers at local Jack-in-the-Box restaurants shortly before falling ill.

Foodmaker, the parent company of Jack-in-the-Box, was quick to issue a statement denying that the meat served in its restaurants was undercooked. At the same time, it blamed the outbreak on a batch of bad meat that had been delivered from a supplier. The supplier responded by placing blame on Jack-in-the-Box. While Foodmaker and its supplier traded insults, the number of those infected rose to 200, and several children became seriously ill. Then Washington State health inspectors revealed that local Jack-in-the-Box restaurants were cooking meat at 140 degrees Fahrenheit, 15 degrees below the 155-degree state standard that had been in force since March 1992. Foodmaker responded by claiming that it had never received notification of the increase in standards. When Health Department officials came up with a copy of the notification that had been sent to local Jack-in-the-Box restaurants, Foodmaker changed its position. According to Robert Nugent, president of Jack-in-the-Box, the company had received the notification but the vice president whose responsibility it was to notify local area restaurants hadn't done so. Jack-in-the-Box indicated that it would take disciplinary action against the vice president, whom it refused to name.

Meanwhile the number of children infected had soared to 450, one had died, several were in a coma, and a number of others were listed as being in critical condition. At this stage Jack-in-the-Box offered to pay the hospital costs for those infected. But there was a catch; in return for paying medical costs, the company's lawyers asked the parents of the infected children to sign forms waiving their rights to subsequently file a lawsuit against Jack-in-the-Box. This request was greeted with outrage, and Jack-in-the-Box once more had to shift its position. This time the company agreed to pay the full hospital costs without requiring a waiver.

By February 1993, the worst of the outbreak was over. However, for Foodmaker the impact was only just becoming apparent. Nationwide sales at Jack-in-the-Box restaurants had plunged 35 percent in the first two weeks of February, the company's stock price had lost 30 percent of its value, and the company announced that it had put on hold plans to open eighty-five new Jack-in-the-Box stores in 1993. In the next two years, Foodmaker recorded nine consecutive quarters of losses, totaling $167 million, while revenues dropped 18 percent. It cost the company a reported $44 million to settle lawsuits from angry franchisees, who blamed their falling sales on Foodmaker, and $4 million to settle a stockholder lawsuit. The company also reportedly ended up paying $90 million in damages to victims and their families.

What seems to have hurt Jack-in-the-Box most was not the outbreak itself, but the company's repeated attempts to shift responsibility for the outbreak onto others, and its cynical attempt to link the offer of financial help to victims with lawsuit waivers. As a result, Jack-in-the-Box came out of the crisis with its reputation tarnished and its sales slumping. Compare this to Johnson & Johnson, which came out of the Tylenol crisis with its reputation for ethical behavior enhanced. It should be noted, though, that the lesson was not lost on Foodmaker. The company has completely overhauled its food distribution and preparation system to make sure this kind of thing does not happen again. Now Foodmaker's system is reportedly the best in the industry. Moreover, the company has explicitly recognized that it responded inappropriately to the crisis and has vowed never to make the same mistake again.[64]

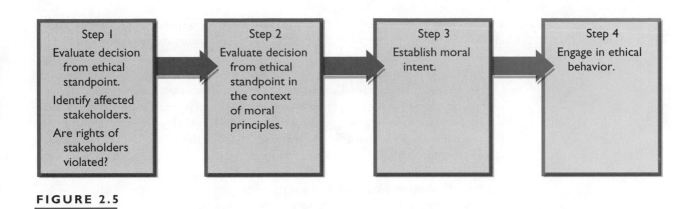

FIGURE 2.5

A Model of Ethical
Decision Making

propagated a set of values known as The HP Way. These values, which shape the
way business is conducted both within and by the corporation, have an important
ethical component. Among other things, they stress the need for confidence in and
respect for people, open communication, and concern for the individual employee.
Had these values been operational at Manville, they would have helped managers
there avoid their catastrophic mistake.

Second, ethical values must be incorporated into the company's mission statement. As noted earlier, Johnson & Johnson's credo helped the company respond to
the Tylenol crisis in an ethical manner. Third, ethical values must be acted on. Top
managers have to implement hiring, firing, and incentive systems that explicitly recognize the importance of adhering to ethical values in strategic decision making. At
Hewlett-Packard, for example, it has been said that although it is difficult to lose
your job (because of the concern for individual employees), nothing gets you fired
more quickly than violating the ethical norms of the company as articulated in The
HP Way.[65]

■ Thinking Through Ethical Problems

Besides establishing the right kind of ethical climate in an organization, managers
must be able to think through the ethical implications of strategic decisions in a systematic way. A number of different frameworks have been suggested as aids to the
decision-making process. The four-step model shown in Figure 2.5 is a compilation
of the various approaches recommended by several authorities on this subject.[66]

Step 1—evaluating a proposed strategic decision from an ethical standpoint—
requires managers to identify which stakeholders the decision would affect and in
what ways. Most importantly, managers need to determine whether the proposed
decision would violate the rights of any stakeholders. The term *rights* refers to the
fundamental entitlements of a stakeholder. For example, we might argue that the
right to information about health risks in the workplace is a fundamental entitlement of employees. It is also an entitlement that Manville ignored.

Step 2 involves judging the ethics of the proposed strategic decision, given the
information gained in step 1. This judgment should be guided by various moral principles that should not be violated. The principles might be those articulated in a
corporate mission statement or other company documents (such as Hewlett-
Packard's The HP Way). In addition, certain moral principles that we have adopted
as members of society—for instance, the prohibition on stealing—should not be

violated. The judgment at this stage will also be guided by the decision rule that is chosen to assess the proposed strategic decision. Although long-run profit maximization is rightly the decision rule that most companies stress, it should be applied subject to the constraint that no moral principles are violated.

Step 3, establishing moral intent, means that the company must resolve to place moral concerns ahead of other concerns in cases where either the rights of stakeholders or key moral principles have been violated. At this stage, input from top management might be particularly valuable. Without the proactive encouragement of top managers, middle-level managers might tend to place the narrow economic interests of the company before the interests of stakeholders. They might do so in the (usually erroneous) belief that top managers favor such an approach.

Step 4 requires the company to engage in ethical behavior. Clearly, Johnson & Johnson fulfilled this requirement during the Tylenol poisoning scare by pulling all its product off retail store shelves at great cost to the company.

■ Corporate Social Responsibility

Corporate social responsibility is the sense of obligation on the part of companies to build certain social criteria into their strategic decision making. The concept implies that when companies evaluate decisions from an ethical perspective, there should be a presumption in favor of adopting courses of action that enhance the welfare of society at large. The goals selected might be quite specific: to enhance the welfare of communities in which a company is based, improve the environment, or empower employees to give them a sense of self-worth.

In its purest form, social responsibility can be supported for its own sake simply because it is the right way for a company to behave. Less pure but perhaps more practical are the arguments that socially responsible behavior is in a company's self-interest and can lead to better financial performance.[67] Economic actions have social consequences affecting a company's outside stakeholders. Therefore, to retain the support of these stakeholders, the company must take those social consequences into account when formulating strategies. Otherwise, it may generate ill will and opposition. For example, if a community perceives a company as having an adverse impact on the local environment, it may block the company's attempts to build new facilities in the area.

Still, there are those who argue that a company has no business pursuing social goals. Nobel laureate Milton Friedman, for one, insists that social responsibility considerations should not enter into the decision process:

> What does it mean to say that the corporate executive has a social responsibility in his capacity as a businessman? If this statement is not pure rhetoric, it must mean that he is to act in some way that is not in the interests of his employers. For example . . . that he is to make expenditures on reducing pollution beyond the amount that is in the best interests of the corporation or that is required by law in order to contribute to the social objective of improving the environment. . . . Insofar as his actions in accord with his social responsibility reduce returns to stockholders, he is spending their money. Insofar as his actions raise the price to customers, he is spending the customers' money. Insofar as the actions lower the wages of some employees, he is spending their money.[68]

Friedman's position is that a business has only one kind of responsibility: to use its resources for activities that increase its profits, so long as it stays within the rules of the game, which is to say, so long as it engages in open and free competition without deception or fraud.

On the other hand, Edward H. Bowman of the University of Pennsylvania's Wharton School argues that social responsibility is actually a sound investment strategy.[69] He maintains that a company's social behavior affects the price of its stock; thus socially responsible policy can also benefit a company's important inside claimants, the stockholders. According to Bowman, many investors see companies that are not socially responsible as riskier investments. Moreover, many institutional investors, such as churches, universities, cities, states, and mutual funds, pay attention to corporate social behavior and thus influence the market for a company's stock.

Evidence can certainly be found in favor of Bowman's arguments. For example, the withdrawal of U.S. assets from South Africa by companies such as IBM and General Motors in 1986 can at least in part be attributed to a desire to create a favorable impression with investors. At that time, for social or political reasons, many investors were selling any stock they held in companies that maintained a substantial presence in South Africa. Similarly, Union Carbide saw its market value plunge more than 37 percent in 1984, in the aftermath of the gas leak at its Bhopal plant in India (which killed 2,000 people and left 150,000 seriously injured) and subsequent revelations concerning poor safety procedures at many Union Carbide plants. For Union Carbide, the consequence was a takeover bid from GAF (which ultimately failed), extended litigation, and a negative image problem.

SUMMARY OF CHAPTER

The primary purpose of this chapter has been to identify the various factors that influence and shape the organizational context within which strategies are formulated. Normally, these factors are explicitly recognized through the corporate mission statement. The mission statement thus sets the boundaries within which strategies must be contained. Specifically, this chapter makes the following points:

✔ Stakeholders are individuals or groups, either within or outside an organization, that have some claim on the organization. They include customers, suppliers, employees, and stockholders. If an organization is to survive and prosper, it must pay attention to the interests of these different stakeholder groups.

✔ The mission statement describes how a company intends to incorporate stakeholder claims into its strategic decision making and thereby reduce the risk of losing stakeholder support.

✔ The mission statement contains three broad elements: (a) a declaration of the overall vision of the company; (b) a summing-up of the key philosophical values that managers are committed to; and (c) the articulation of key goals that management believes must be adhered to.

✔ An important step in the process of formulating a mission statement is to come up with a definition of the organization's business. Defining the business involves focusing on consumer groups to be served, consumer needs to be satisfied, and the technologies by which those needs can be satisfied.

✔ The values of a company state how managers intend to conduct themselves, how they intend to do business, and what kind of organization they want to build. Values can become the bedrock of a company's organization culture and a driver of its competitive advantage.

✔ The goals of a company specify what must be done if the company is to attain its mission.

Well-constructed goals are precise and measurable, address important issues, are challenging but realistic, and specify a time period within which they should be achieved.

✔ Stockholders are among a company's most important stakeholders. Maximizing stockholder wealth is one of the most important goals of a company. A corporate governance problem arises when managers pursue strategies that are not consistent with this goal.

✔ A number of governance mechanisms serve to limit the ability of managers to pursue strategies that are at variance with maximizing stockholder wealth. These include stockholder meetings, the board of directors, stock-based compensation schemes, and the threat of a takeover.

✔ Many strategic decisions have an ethical dimension. Any action by a company inevitably has an impact on the welfare of its stakeholders.

✔ The purpose of business ethics is not so much to teach the difference between right and wrong, as to give people the tools for dealing with moral complexity—for identifying and thinking through the moral implications of strategic decisions.

DISCUSSION QUESTIONS

1. Why is it important for a company to take a consumer-oriented view of its businesses? What are the possible shortcomings of such a view?

2. What are the strategic implications of a focus on short-run returns? Discuss these implications in terms of the impact on product innovation, marketing expenditure, manufacturing, and purchasing decisions.

3. Are corporate raiders a positive or negative influence on the U.S. economy? How can companies reduce the risk of a takeover?

4. "Companies should always behave in an ethical manner, whatever the economic cost." Discuss this statement.

Practicing Strategic Management

SMALL-GROUP EXERCISE
Constructing a Mission Statement

Break up into groups of three to five people, and perform the tasks listed:

1. Define the business of your educational institution.

2. Use this business definition to guide the construction of a mission statement for your educational institution. Be sure that the mission statement contains a long-term vision, a set of values, and a number of important precise and measurable goals. Be prepared to articulate the logic behind your choice of vision, values, and goals.

3. Try to identify a number of key strategies that your educational institution needs to pursue in order to attain the vision and goals outlined in your mission statement. Be sure that these strategies are consistent with the values you set down in the mission statement.

STRATEGIC MANAGEMENT PROJECT
Module 2

This module deals with the relationships your company has with its major stakeholder groups. With the information you have at your disposal, perform the tasks and answer the questions listed.

1. Find out whether your company has a formal mission statement. Does this statement define the business, identify major goals, and articulate the corporate philosophy?

2. If your company lacks a mission statement, what do you think its mission statement should be like?

3. If your company has a mission statement, do you see it as appropriate, given the material discussed in this chapter?

4. Identify the main stakeholder groups in your company. What claims do they place on the company? How is the company trying to satisfy those claims?

5. Evaluate the performance of the CEO of your company from the perspective of (a) stockholders, (b) employees, (c) customers, and (d) suppliers. What does this evaluation tell you about the ability of the CEO and the priorities that he or she is committed to?

6. Try to establish whether the governance mechanisms that operate in your company do a good job of aligning the interests of top managers with those of stockholders.

7. Pick a major strategic decision made by your company in recent years and consider the ethical implications of that decision. In the light of your review, do you think that the company acted correctly?

ARTICLE FILE 2

Find an example of a company that ran into trouble because it failed to take into account the rights of one of its stakeholder groups when making an important strategic decision.

EXPLORING THE WEB
Visiting Merck

Go to the Web site of Merck, the world's largest pharmaceutical company (http://www.merck.com/), and find the mission statement posted there.

1. Evaluate this mission statement in light of the material contained in this chapter. Does the mission state clearly what Merck's basic strategic goal is? Do the values listed provide a good guideline for managerial action at Merck?

2. Follow the hypertext link "benefits humanity." Read the section on corporate responsibility, and then answer the following question: How does Merck try to balance the goals of providing stockholders with an adequate rate of return on their investment, and at the same time developing medicines that benefit humanity and that can be acquired by people in need at an affordable price? Do you think that Merck does a good job of balancing these goals?

General Task. Using the World Wide Web, find an example of a company mission statement that you think exemplifies many of the issues discussed in this chapter.

Body Shop International

THE BRITISH-BASED RETAILER, Body Shop International, is often viewed as a prime example of a company committed to being ethical and socially responsible in its business dealings. The company's founder and CEO, Anita Roddick, has become an energetic spokesperson for the importance of ethics and social responsibility. Body Shop competes in the international cosmetics and toiletries market but offers unique products derived from natural ingredients. The company has based its success on the claim that none of its products is tested on animals, contains artificial ingredients, or is elaborately packaged. The products appeal to consumers who are concerned about animal rights and the environment. Under a program called "Trade not Aid," Body Shop claims to purchase many of the ingredients for its products from Third World producers, and the company maintains that it pays its suppliers well. It also makes a point of plowing money back into the communities where its suppliers are based to support a variety of health and educational projects. This commitment to social responsibility helped propel Body Shop from a single store in 1976 to a global enterprise with 1,100 stores in forty-five countries and annual revenues of more than $700 million in 1995. According to Roddick,

> You can run a business differently from the way most businesses are run, you can share your prosperity with employees, and empower them without being in fear of them. You can rewrite the book in terms of how a company interacts with the community, on third world trade, global responsibility, and the role of educating customers and shareholders, and you can do all this and still play the game according to the City [the British version of Wall Street], still raise money, delight the Institutions and give shareholders a wondrous return on their investment.

Roddick's philosophy helped turn Body Shop into the darling of the business ethics community. However, the good feeling was rudely shattered in the fall of 1994 when a journalist, Jon Entine, published an article highly critical of Body Shop in the *Business Ethics* magazine. Among other things, Entine made the following claims:

- Body Shop uses many outdated, off-the-shelf product formulas filled with nonrenewable petrochemicals.

- Many of its products are contaminated and contain formaldehyde, an artificial ingredient.

- Body Shop has used ingredients in its products that have been tested on animals.

- Contrary to its claims, Body Shop sources only a tiny amount of ingredients through its Trade not Aid program. Moreover, Body Shop does not pay "first world wages for third world products," as it claims in its publicity.

- The company's charitable contributions and progressive environmental standards fall short of it's claims. Until 1994, the company never contributed more than 1.24 percent of its pretax profits to charitable organizations.

- The company invented stories about the exotic origins of some of its products.

Entine's article drew a vigorous response from Gordon Roddick, the chairman of Body Shop International. In a ten-page letter sent to all subscribers of *Business Ethics* magazine, Roddick claimed that Entine's article was filled with "many lies, distortions, and gross inaccuracies. . . . I am at a loss to find anything balanced or fair in this article." Roddick went on in the letter to give a detailed rebuttal of Entine's charges. For example, with regard to the Trade not Aid program, Roddick observed that Entine's article

> goes after our Trade not Aid program, building its attack around an utterly irrelevant statistic—the percentage of our ingredients that come from Trade not Aid projects. What is this number supposed to reveal? It certainly tells us nothing about the effectiveness of our efforts. Or the amount of time we have put into nurturing these projects. Or the obstacles we have had to overcome due to the lack of infrastructure in disenfranchised Third World communities. . . . One single ingredient, such as Brazil nut oil or cocoa butter, may take two years or more to source and develop. Believe me, there are much easier ways to do business than by taking on the problems of such projects. . . . We do it because we are asked to help by the disenfranchised communities themselves. The only significant measure of our success is the number of people who are directly beneficially affected by our activities. That is a number, I am proud to say, that runs into the thousands.

Body Shop followed up Entine's attack by commissioning an independent "ethics audit" by the New Economics Foundation, a London-based ethics business consultant. Issued in January 1996, the audit reported that

93 percent of Body Shop's employees feel the company lives up to its mission to be socially and environmentally responsible and that the purchases from suppliers in developing countries or poor communities increased by more than 30 percent during 1995. The audit also noted that less than 2 percent of the company's raw material inputs came from the Trade not Aid program in 1995, although about 17.8 percent of the accessories sold in Body Shop stores—such as brushes and sponges—came from the program. The company donated 2.3 percent of its pretax profits to charity in 1995.[70]

Case Discussion Questions

1. Is Anita Roddick correct when she claims that it is possible to run a business in a very ethical and socially responsible manner and still "give shareholders a wondrous return on their investment"?

2. Is the percentage of ingredients that come from Trade not Aid projects an irrelevant statistic, as Gordon Roddick claims?

3. In light of the ethics audit report, evaluate Body Shop's claims to be ethically responsible.

End Notes

1. J. Byrne, "How Al Dunlap Self-Destructed," *Business Week*, July 6, 1998, p. 58; G. DeGeorge, "Al Dunlap Revs Up His Chainsaw," *Business Week*, November 25, 1996, p. 37; "Exit Bad Guy," *Economist*, June 20, 1998, p. 70; E. Pollock and M. Brannigan, "Mixed Grill: The Sunbeam Shuffle," *Wall Street Journal*, August 19, 1998, p. A1.
2. E. Freeman, *Strategic Management: A Stakeholder Approach* (Boston: Pitman Press, 1984).
3. C. W. L. Hill and T. M. Jones, "Stakeholder-Agency Theory," *Journal of Management Studies*, 29 (1992) 131–154; J. G. March and H. A. Simon, *Organizations* (New York: Wiley, 1958).
4. J. E. Rigdon and J. S. Lubin, "Why Morrison Board Fired Agee," *Wall Street Journal*, February 13, 1995, p. B1; C. McCoy, "Worst 5 and 1 year Performer: Morrison Knudsen," *Wall Street Journal*, February 29, 1996, p. R2; "Morrison Knudsen Settles Most Shareholder Lawsuits," *Wall Street Journal*, September 21, 1995, p. B8; J. E. Rigdon, "William Agee to Leave Morrison Knudsen," *Wall Street Journal*, February 2, 1995, p. B1.
5. Hill and Jones, "Stakeholder-Agency Theory," pp. 131–154.
6. I. C. Macmillan and P. E. Jones, *Strategy Formulation: Power and Politics* (St. Paul, Minn.: West, 1986).
7. D. F. Abell, *Defining the Business: The Starting Point of Strategic Planning* (Englewood Cliffs, N.J.: Prentice-Hall, 1980); K. Andrews, *The Concept of Corporate Strategy* (Homewood, Ill.: Dow Jones Irwin, 1971); J. A. Pearce, "The Company Mission as a Strategic Tool," *Sloan Management Review* (Spring 1982), 15–24.
8. Boeing's World Wide Web home page (http://www.boeing.com).
9. Weyerhaeuser Annual Report, 1995.
10. Information from www.pfizer.com/pfizerinc/about/vision/visionfrm.html ( ).
11. Information from www.intel.com/intel/annual98/vision.html ( ).
12. Information from http://www.appliedmaterials.com/about/mission.html ( ).
13. G. Hamel and C. K. Prahalad, *Competing for the Future* (Boston: Harvard Business School Press, 1994). Also see J. C. Collins and J. I. Porras, "Building Your Company's Vision," *Harvard Business Review* (September–October, 1996), pp. 65–77.
14. Quoted in S. Tully, "Why Go for Stretch Targets," *Fortune*, November 14, 1995, pp. 145–158.
15. Speech given by Michael Armstrong to the Executives Club of Chicago, May 21, 1999, (archived at www.atl.com/speaches/99/990521_cma.html); P. Elstrom, "Mike Armstrong's Strong Showing," *Business Week*, January 25, 1999, p. 94; J. Rendleman, "The Morphing of a New AT&T," *PC Week*, May 10, 1999, p. 20; K. Kaplan, "AT&T Lays Out Bold Plan for Its Future," *Los Angeles Times*, January 27, 1998, p. D1.
16. These three questions were first proposed by P. F. Drucker. See P. F. Drucker, *Management—Tasks, Responsibilities, Practices* (New York: Harper & Row, 1974), pp. 74–94.
17. D. F. Abell, *Defining the Business.*
18. T. Levitt, "Marketing Myopia," *Harvard Business Review* (July–August 1960), 45–56.
19. P. A. Kidwell and P. E. Ceruzzi, *Landmarks in Digital Computing* (Washington D.C.: Smithsonian Institute, 1994).
20. Kodak's World Wide Web site (http://www.kodak.com) 1998.
21. Collins and Porras, "Building Your Company's Vision," pp. 65–77.
22. J. Welch, "To Our Share Owners." Letter in GE's 1994 Annual Report.
23. Ibid.
24. M. D. Richards, *Setting Strategic Goals and Objectives* (St. Paul, Minn.: West, 1986).
25. For details, see "Johnson & Johnson (A)," *Harvard Business School Case* No. 384-053, Harvard Business School.
26. See J. P. Kotter and J. L. Heskett, *Corporate Culture and Performance* (New York, Free Press, 1992). For similar work, see Collins and Porras, "Building your Company's Vision," pp. 65–77.
27. Richards, *Setting Strategic Goals.*
28. E. A. Locke, G. P. Latham, and M. Erez, "The Determinants of Goal Commitment," *Academy of Management Review*, 13 (1988), 23–39.
29. M. Hammer and J. Champy, *Reengineering the Corporation* (New York: Harper Business, 1993).
30. R. E. Hoskisson, M. A. Hitt, and C. W. L. Hill, "Managerial Incentives and Investment in R&D in Large Multiproduct Firms," *Organization Science*, 3 (1993), 325–341.
31. R. H. Hayes and W. J. Abernathy, "Managing Our Way to Economic Decline," *Harvard Business Review* (July–August 1980), 67–77.
32. L. C. Thurow, *The Zero Sum Solution* (New York: Simon & Schuster, 1985), 69–89.
33. M. L. Dertouzos, R. K. Lester, and R. M. Solow, *Made in America* (Cambridge, Mass.: MIT Press, 1989).
34. "Flat out in Japan," *Economist*, February 1, 1992, pp. 79–80; H. Nomura, "IBM, Apple Fight LCD Screen Tariffs: US Decision Forcing Assembly Offshore," *Nikkei Weekly*, October 26, 1992; A. Tanzer, "The New Improved Color Computer," *Forbes*, July 23, 1990, pp. 276–280; J. Ascierto, "A Death of a Dream?" *Electronic News*, April 5, 1999, p. 1.
35. M. C. Jensen and W. H. Meckling, "Theory of the Firm: Managerial Behavior, Agency Costs and Ownership Structure," *Journal of Financial Economics*, 3 (1976), 305–360.
36. For example, see R. Marris, *The Economic Theory of Managerial Capitalism* (London: Macmillan, 1964), and J. K. Galbraith, *The New Industrial State* (Boston: Houghton Mifflin, 1970).
37. E. F. Fama, "Agency Problems and the Theory of the Firm," *Journal of Political Economy*, 88 (1980), 375–390.
38. A. Rappaport, "New Thinking on How to Link Executive Pay with Performance," *Harvard Business Review* (March–April 1999) pp. 91–105.
39. E. Goodman, "CEO Pay Cap: Why Not Try It for Size?" *Houston Chronicle*, April 18, 1999, p. 6.

40. S. Tully, "Raising the Bar," *Fortune*, June 8, 1998, pp. 272–278.

41. A. Fisher, "CEO Pay," *Fortune*, June 8, 1998, p. 296.

42. For academic studies that look at the determinants of CEO pay, see M. C. Jensen and K. J. Murphy, "Performance Pay and Top Management Incentives," *Journal of Political Economy*, 98 (1990), 225–264; C. W. L. Hill and P. Phan, "CEO Tenure as a Determinant of CEO Pay," *Academy of Management Journal*, 34 (1991), 707–717; H. L. Tosi and L. R. Gomez-Mejia, "CEO Compensation Monitoring and Firm Performance," *Academy of Management Journal*, 37 (1994), 1002–1016; J. F. Porac, J. B. Wade, and T. G. Pollock, "Industry Categories and the Politics of the Comparable Firm in CEO Compensation," *Administrative Science Quarterly*, 44 (1999) 112–144.

43. Goodman, "CEO Pay Cap," p. 6.

44. For recent research on this issue, see P. J. Lane, A. A. Cannella, and M. H. Lubatkin, "Agency Problems as Antecedents to Unrelated Mergers and Diversification: Amihud and Lev Reconsidered," *Strategic Management Journal,* 19 (1998), 555–578.

45. C. Icahn, "What Ails Corporate America—and What Should Be Done?" *Business Week*, October 27, 1986, p. 101.

46. E. T. Penrose, *The Theory of the Growth of the Firm* (London: Macmillan, 1958).

47. O. E. Williamson, *The Economic Institutions of Capitalism* (New York: Free Press, 1985).

48. E. F. Fama, "Agency Problems and the Theory of the Firm," pp. 375–390.

49. S. Finkelstein and R. D'Aveni, "CEO Duality as a Double-Edged Sword," *Academy of Management Journal*, 37 (1994), 1079–1108; B. Ram Baliga and R. C. Moyer, "CEO Duality and Firm Performance," *Strategic Management Journal*, 17 (1996), 41–53; M. L. Mace, *Directors: Myth and Reality* (Cambridge, Mass.: Harvard University Press, 1971; S. C. Vance, *Corporate Leadership: Boards of Directors and Strategy* (New York: McGraw Hill, 1983).

50. M. Galen, "A Seat on the Board Is Getting Hotter," *Business Week*, July 3, 1989, pp. 72–73.

51. J. S. Lublin, "Irate Shareholders Target Ineffective Board Members," *Wall Street Journal*, November 6, 1995, p. B1.

52. G. Fuchsberg, "Chief Executives See Their Power Shrink," *Wall Street Journal*, March 15, 1993, pp. B1, B3.

53. Quoted in G. Morgenson, "Stock Options are Not a Free Lunch," *Forbes*, May 18, 1998, pp. 212–217.

54. W. G. Lewellen, C. Eoderer, and A. Rosenfeld, "Merger Decisions and Executive Stock Ownership in Acquiring Firms," *Journal of Accounting and Economics*, 7 (1985), 209–231.

55. C. W. L. Hill and S. A. Snell, "External Control, Corporate Strategy, and Firm Performance," *Strategic Management Journal*, 9 (1988), pp. 577–590.

56. J. P. Walsh and R. D. Kosnik, "Corporate Raiders and Their Disciplinary Role in the Market for Corporate Control," *Academy of Management Journal*, 36 (1993), 671–700.

57. S. Reed, "Buyout Fever," *Business Week*, June 14, 1999, p. 24.

58. See M. C. Jensen, "Agency Costs of Free Cash Flow, Corporate Finance, and Takeovers," *American Economic Review* (1986), 323–329; and M. C. Jensen, "The Eclipse of the Public Corporation," *Harvard Business Review* (September–October 1989), 61–74.

59. R. B. Reich, "Leveraged Buyouts: America Pays the Price," *New York Times Magazine*, January 29, 1989, pp. 32–40.

60. P. H. Pan and C. W. L. Hill, "Organizational Restructuring and Economic Performance in Leveraged Buyouts," *Academy of Management Journal*, 38 (1995), 704–739; M. F. Wiersema and J. P. Liebskind, "The Effects of Leveraged Buyouts on Corporate Growth and Diversification in Large Firms," *Strategic Management Journal*, 16 (1995), 447–460; J. P. Liebskind, M. F. Wiersema, and G. Hansen, "LBOs, Corporate Restructuring, and the Incentive Intensity Hypothesis," *Financial Management*, 21 (1992), 50–57.

61. R. E. Freeman and D. Gilbert, *Corporate Strategy and the Search for Ethics* (Englewood Cliffs, N.J.: Prentice-Hall, 1988).

62. R. C. Solomon, *Ethics and Excellence* (Oxford: Oxford University Press, 1992).

63. S. W. Gellerman, "Why Good Managers Make Bad Ethical Choices," *Ethics in Practice: Managing the Moral Corporation,* ed. Kenneth R. Andrews (Boston: Harvard Business School Press, 1989).

64. B. Holden, "Foodmaker Delays Expansion Plans in Wake of Food-Poisoning Outbreak," *Wall Street Journal*, February 16, 1993, p. B10; B. Holden, "Foodmaker, Struggling After Poisonings, Breaks with Its Public Relations Firm," *Wall Street Journal*, February 12, 1993, p. A4; R. Goff, "Coming Clean," *Forbes*, May 17, 1999, pp. 156–160.

65. K. O. Hanson and M. Velasquez, "Hewlett-Packard Company: Managing Ethics and Values," in *Corporate Ethics: A Prime Business Asset,* The Business Roundtable, February 1988.

66. For example, see Freeman and Gilbert, *Corporate Strategy and the Search for Ethics*; T. Jones, "Ethical Decision Making by Individuals in Organizations," *Academy of Management Review,* 16 (1991), 366–395; and J. R. Rest, *Moral Development: Advances in Research and Theory* (New York: Praeger, 1986).

67. S. A. Waddock and S. B. Graves, "The Corporate Social Performance–Financial Performance Link," *Strategic Management Journal*, 8 (1997), 303–319.

68. M. Friedman, "A Friedman Doctrine: The Social Responsibility of Business Is to Increase Its Profits," *New York Times Magazine,* September 13, 1970, p. 33.

69. E. D. Bowman, "Corporate Social Responsibility and the Investor," *Journal of Contemporary Business* (Winter 1973), 49–58.

70. T. P. Poe, "Body Shop Comes Clean About Audit of Its Operation," *Wall Street Journal*, January 26, 1996, p. B12; "Storm in a Bubble Bath," *Economist*, September 3, 1994, p. 56; J. Entine, "Shattered Image," *Business Ethics Magazine* (September–October 1994), 23–28; G. Roddick, letter to *Business Ethics* subscribers, September 22, 1994, Body Shop International.

PART TWO

The Nature of Competitive Advantage

3

External Analysis: The Identification of Industry Opportunities and Threats

OPENING CASE

On-line Firms Revolutionize the Stockbrokerage Industry

FOR YEARS, although trading on the stock market has been electronic, only professional stockbrokers with expensive computer hardware could trade on-line. If an individual investor wanted to buy or sell a stock, she had to call her stockbroker and place an order. The stockbroker would charge a commission for this service. At full-service stockbrokers such as Merrill Lynch—which offered their clients detailed research reports, stock recommendations, and financial planning services—these commissions could run to 2.5 percent of the value of the order. Thus, an order worth $10,000 could generate $250 in commissions.

The situation began to change in 1994 when a small discount broker, K. Aufhauser, took advantage of new technology to become the first to offer its clients the ability to trade on-line over the Internet, effectively bypassing stockbrokers. The offering allowed Aufhauser to operate with fewer personnel. The cost saving was passed on to consumers in the form of lower commissions. Initially, on-line trading was merely a curiosity, but several things changed this. First, the Internet started to make rapid inroads into the homes of individual Americans. Second, within a short space of time, a vast amount of investment information was being offered on the Internet. Individual investors soon found that they could go to sites such as the Motley Fool at America Online or Yahoo!'s finance site and get much of the information that they needed to make informed investment decisions. No longer did they have to call their stockbrokers to ask for information. Third, a number of small companies quickly followed Aufhauser's lead and took advantage of the Internet to offer their clients on-line trading for commissions that were significantly below those offered by full-service stockbrokers in the physical world. Finally, America's long bull market attracted ever more individuals to the stock market, particularly among America's large baby-boom generation, who were drawn to investing in order to build up funds for retirement. Increasingly, these newcomers set up on-line trading accounts.

The effects of these trends were dramatic. By 1999, there were 70 firms offering on-line trading via the Internet. Many of these companies did not even exist in 1994. The arrival of the Internet had lowered barriers to entry and allowed these companies to enter the stockbrokerage industry and compete against incumbents such as Merrill Lynch. As the competition for the business of on-line investors started to heat up, commissions started to fall. By early 1999, on-line brokerages such as E*Trade were charging deep discount fees of $14.95 per market order for trades of up to 5,000 shares. Thus, while an order for 1,000 shares of a stock trading at $20 a share could cost the client of a full-service broker as much as $500 in

commission, the same trade could be executed vie E*Trade for $14.95! Attracted by such low prices, from little more than a trickle in 1994, the volume of on-line trades grew to account for 30–35 percent of all stock trades by individuals as of mid 1999.

At first, full-service brokers derided on-line trading as dangerous and justified their high commissions by claiming that they offered their clients sound financial advice and proprietary research reports. However, with as many as 40 percent of all stockbrokers lacking much in the way of experience, and with the rapid increase in the amount of investment information that could be accessed on-line, such arguments sounded increasingly shrill and self-serving. By early 1999, it was becoming apparent that full-service brokers need to adapt to the new technology or risk seeing their client base evaporate. The landmark event occurred in June 1999, when Merrill Lynch, the world's largest full-service broker, bowed to the inevitable and announced that it, too, would soon offer its clients the ability to trade on-line for a fee of $29.95 for trades of up to 1,000 shares. An internal Merrill report estimated that as a result its army of 14,800 well-paid stockbrokers, who were paid chiefly in commissions, might initially see their incomes decline by 18 percent as a result of this move. Merrill knew that it faced a potential rebellion from its stockbrokers, but it also knew that it had no choice, given the forecasts suggesting that more than 50 percent of stock trades by individuals would be on-line by 2001.[1]

OVERVIEW

The Opening Case illustrates the impact that changing market conditions can have on prices and strategies in an industry. The rise of a new technology, the Internet, has lowered barriers to entry into the stockbrokerage industry, allowing upstarts like E*Trade and Ameritrade to compete head-to-head with incumbents such as Merrill Lynch for the business of individual investors. As hordes of these new enterprises entered the industry, prices (fees and commissions) plunged and demand shifted from high-priced full-service stockbrokers toward discount on-line brokers. The revolutionary nature of this process was illustrated by Merrill Lynch's decision in June 1999 to offer its clients on-line trading for a flat fee of $29.95 per trade of 1,000 shares or less. In effect, Merrill substantially reduced the price it charged individual investors and altered the way it delivered its service so that it might maintain its revenues and profits in the face of a fundamental change in the environment of the stockbrokerage industry.

Consistent with the theme introduced in the Opening Case, in this chapter we consider the influence of the industry environment in which a company competes on its performance. First, we discuss a number of models that can assist managers in analyzing the environment. The models provide a framework for identifying environmental opportunities and threats. **Opportunities** arise when a company can take advantage of conditions in its external environment to formulate and implement strategies that enable it to earn higher profits. Thus, the advent of the Internet provided an opportunity for discount stockbrokers to capture business from full-service brokers by offering services on-line. **Threats** arise when conditions in the external environmental endanger the integrity and profitability of the company's business. On-line stock trading threatened incumbent full-service stockbrokers such as Merrill Lynch. Second, we consider the competitive implications that arise when groups of companies within an industry pursue similar strategies. Third, we examine the nature of industry evolution and discuss in detail how the globalization of the world economy is affecting the competitive forces at work in an industry environment. Finally, we assess the impact of conditions within a nation on competitive advantage. By the end of the chapter, you will understand that to succeed a company must either fit its strategy to the industry environment in which it operates or be able to reshape the industry environment to its advantage through its chosen strategy.

ANALYZING INDUSTRY STRUCTURE

An **industry** can be defined as a group of companies offering products or services that are close substitutes for each other. Close substitutes are products or services that satisfy the same basic consumer needs. For example, the metal and plastic body panels used in automobile construction are close substitutes for each other. Despite different production technologies, auto supply companies manufacturing metal body panels are in the same basic industry as companies manufacturing plastic body panels. They are serving the same consumer need, the need of auto assembly companies for body panels.

The task facing managers is to analyze competitive forces in an industry environment in order to identify the opportunities and threats confronting a company. Michael E. Porter of the Harvard School of Business Administration has developed a framework that helps managers in this analysis.[2] Porter's framework, known as the **five forces model,** appears in Figure 3.1. This model focuses on five forces that shape competition within an industry: (1) the risk of new entry by potential competitors; (2) the degree of rivalry among established companies within an industry; (3) the bargaining power of buyers; (4) the bargaining power of suppliers; and (5) the threat of substitute products.

Porter argues that the stronger each of these forces, the more limited is the ability of established companies to raise prices and earn greater profits. Within Porter's framework, a strong competitive force can be regarded as a threat since it depresses profits. A weak competitive force can be viewed as an opportunity, for it allows a company to earn greater profits. The strength of the five forces may change through time as industry conditions change, as illustrated by the Opening Case. The task facing managers is to recognize how changes in the five forces give rise to new opportunities and threats, and to formulate appropriate strategic responses. In addition, it is possible for a company, *through its choice of strategy*, to alter the strength of one

FIGURE 3.1

The Five Forces Model

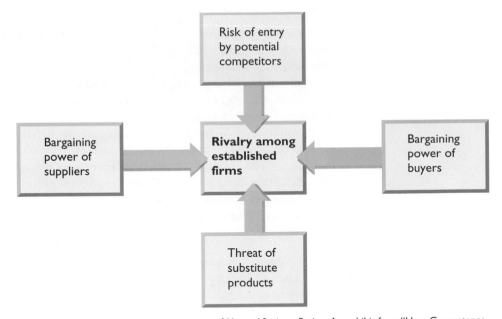

or more of the five forces to its advantage. This is discussed in the following chapters. In this section, we focus on understanding the impact that each of the five forces has on a company.

■ Potential Competitors

Companies that are not currently competing in an industry but have the capability to do so if they choose are **potential competitors**. For example, electric utilities are potential competitors to telecommunications companies in the markets for phone service and Internet access. In order to be able to deliver electricity to residential and commercial property, many electric utilities have been granted rights of way by state and local governments. They have laid electric cables down these rights of way, but there is nothing to stop them from putting in fiber-optic lines along these rights of way and offering high-bandwidth communication services to residential and commercial customers. In fact, a number of utilities have started to do this. For example, Tacoma City Light in Washington State has used its rights of way to run fiber-optic lines to several commercial buildings in the city of Tacoma and take away business from the dominant telecommunications service provider in the region, US West. Tacoma City Light is also laying coaxial cable to homes in its service region and offering a cable television service in direct competition with the local cable provider, TCI.[3]

   Incumbent companies (those already operating in an industry) try to discourage potential competitors from entering the industry, since the more companies enter, the more difficult it becomes for established companies to hold their share of the market and to generate profits. For example, TCI's response to the potential entry of Tacoma City Light into the cable TV business in Tacoma was to threaten intense competition on both price and service offerings. Thus, a high risk of entry by potential competitors represents a threat to the profitability of established companies. On the other hand, if the risk of new entry is low, incumbent companies can take advantage of this opportunity to raise prices and earn greater returns.

The strength of the competitive force of potential rivals is largely a function of the height of barriers to entry. **Barriers to entry** are factors that make it costly for companies to enter an industry. The greater the costs that potential competitors must bear to enter an industry, the greater are the barriers to entry. High entry barriers keep potential competitors out of an industry even when industry returns are high. The classic work on barriers to entry was done by economist Joe Bain. He identified three main sources of barriers to new entry: brand loyalty, absolute cost advantages, and economies of scale.[4] To Bain's list we can add two more entry barriers of considerable significance in many situations: switching costs and government regulation.

Brand Loyalty   Buyers' preference for the products of incumbent companies is termed **brand loyalty**. A company can create brand loyalty through continuous advertising of brand and company names, patent protection of products, product innovation achieved through company research and development programs, an emphasis on high product quality, and good after-sales service. Significant brand loyalty makes it difficult for new entrants to take market share away from established companies. Thus, it reduces the threat of entry by potential competitors since they may see the task of breaking down well-established consumer preferences as too costly.

Absolute Cost Advantages   Sometimes incumbent companies have an absolute cost advantage relative to potential entrants. **Absolute cost advantages** seem to derive from three main sources. These are (a) superior production operations, due to past experience, patents, or secret processes; (b) control of particular inputs required for production, such as labor, materials, equipment, or management skills; and (c) access to cheaper funds because existing companies represent lower risks than companies that are not yet established. If incumbent companies have an absolute cost advantage, then the threat of entry decreases.

Economies of Scale   The cost advantages associated with large company output are known as **economies of scale**. Sources of scale economies include cost reductions gained through mass-producing a standardized output, discounts on bulk purchases of raw-material inputs and component parts, the advantages gained by spreading of fixed costs over a large production volume, and economies of scale in advertising. If these cost advantages are significant, then a new entrant faces the dilemma of either entering on a small scale and suffering a significant cost disadvantage or taking a very large risk by entering on a large scale and bearing significant capital costs. A further risk of large-scale entry is that the increased supply of products will depress prices and result in vigorous retaliation by established companies. Thus, when established companies have economies of scale, the threat of entry is reduced.

Switching Costs   When it costs a consumer to switch from the product offering of an incumbent company to the product offering of a new entrant, **switching costs** arise . When these costs are high, consumers can be **locked in** to the product offerings of incumbents, even if new entrants offer better products.[5] A familiar example of switching costs concerns the costs associated with switching from one computer operating system to another. If an individual currently uses Microsoft's Windows operating system, and has a library of related software applications (such as word-processing software, spreadsheet, games) and document files, it is expensive for that individual to switch to another computer operating system, such as the Macintosh OS produced by Apple Computer. The reason is simple; to effect the change the individual will have to buy a new set of software applications because applications written for Windows will not run on the Macintosh OS. Moreover, the individual will have to devote considerable time and effort to convert her document files so that they can be used by applications written for the Macintosh OS. Faced with such an expense of money and time, most people are unwilling to make the switch *unless* the competing operating system offers a *substantial* leap forward in performance (and arguably, the Mac OS does not). Thus, at this point one might argue that high switching costs have created barriers to entry into the market for a personal computer operating system and that competing operating systems have been locked out of the market. At the same time, it is important to understand that if a competitor offers an operating system that represents a substantial improvement over Windows, then users will switch to that operating system. In this regard, the Linux operating system, which is being sold by Red Hat Software, is viewed by some as a potential threat to Microsoft's market dominance.

Government Regulation Historically, government regulation has constituted a major entry barrier in many industries. For example, until recently in the United States, government regulation prohibited providers of long-distance telephone service, such as AT&T, MCI, and Sprint, from competing for local telephone service with the Regional Bell Operating Companies (RBOCs) such as US West and Bell Atlantic. Moreover, the RBOCs were prohibited from entering the long-distance telephone market. Other potential providers of telephone service, including cable television service companies such as TCI Communications and Viacom (which could in theory use their cables to carry telephone traffic as well as TV signals), were prohibited from entering the market altogether. These regulatory barriers to entry significantly reduced the level of competition in both the local and long-distance telephone markets, enabling telephone companies to earn higher profits than might otherwise have been the case. All this changed in January 1996 when the U.S. government deregulated the industry, removing all barriers to entry. In the months that followed this announcement, the RBOCs, long-distance companies, and cable TV companies all announced their intention to enter each other's markets. A significant increase in competitive intensity is to be expected. A similar move toward deregulating telephone service can be seen in many other countries. The member states of the European Union, for example, deregulated their telephone markets on January 1, 1998.

Entry Barriers and Competition If established companies have built brand loyalty for their products, have an absolute cost advantage with respect to potential competitors, have significant scale economies, are the beneficiaries of high switching costs, or enjoy regulatory protection, the risk of entry by potential competitors is greatly diminished. When this risk is low, established companies can charge higher prices and earn greater profits than would have been possible otherwise. Clearly, it is in the interest of companies to pursue strategies consistent with raising entry barriers. Indeed, empirical evidence suggests that the height of barriers to entry is one of the most important determinants of profit rates in an industry.[6] Examples of industries where entry barriers are considerable include pharmaceuticals, household detergents, and commercial jet aircraft. In the first two cases, product differentiation achieved through substantial expenditures for research and development and for advertising has built brand loyalty, making it difficult for new companies to enter these industries on a significant scale. So successful have the differentiation strategies of Procter & Gamble and Unilever been in household detergents that these two companies dominate the global industry. In the case of the commercial jet aircraft industry, the barriers to entry are primarily due to the enormous fixed costs of product development (it cost Boeing $5 billion to develop its new wide-bodied jetliner, the 777) and the scale economies enjoyed by the incumbent companies, which enable them to price below a potential entrant's costs of production and still make a significant profit. A more detailed example of entry barriers appears in Strategy in Action 3.1, which discusses the barriers to entry in the Japanese brewing industry.

■ Rivalry Among Established Companies

The second of Porter's five competitive forces is the extent of rivalry among established companies within an industry. If this rivalry is weak, companies have an opportunity to raise prices and earn greater profits. But if rivalry is strong, significant price competition, including price wars, may result. Price competition limits profitability by reducing the margins that can be earned on sales. Thus, intense rivalry among established companies constitutes a strong threat to profitability. The extent of rivalry among established companies within an industry is largely a function of three factors: (1) industry competitive structure, (2) demand conditions, and (3) the height of exit barriers in the industry.

Competitive Structure   Competitive structure refers to the number and size distribution of companies in an industry. Structures vary from **fragmented** to **consolidated** and have different implications for rivalry. A fragmented industry contains a large number of small or medium-sized companies, none of which is in a position to dominate the industry. A consolidated industry may be dominated by a small number of large companies (in which case it is referred to as an oligopoly), or in extreme cases, by just one company (a monopoly). Fragmented industries range from agriculture, video rental, and health clubs to real estate brokerage and sun tanning parlors. Consolidated industries include aerospace, automobiles, and pharmaceuticals.

Many fragmented industries are characterized by low entry barriers and commodity-type products that are hard to differentiate. The combination of these traits tends to result in boom-and-bust cycles as industry profits rise and fall. Low entry barriers imply that whenever demand is strong and profits are high there will be a flood of new entrants hoping to cash in on the boom. The explosion in the number of video stores, health clubs, and sun tanning parlors during the 1980s exemplifies this situation.

Often the flood of new entrants into a booming fragmented industry creates excess capacity. Once excess capacity develops, companies start to cut prices in order to utilize their spare capacity. The difficulty companies face when trying to differentiate their products from those of competitors can worsen this tendency. The result is a price war, which depresses industry profits, forces some companies out of business, and deters potential new entrants. For example, after a decade of expansion and booming profits, many health clubs are now finding that they have to offer large discounts in order to hold on to their membership. In general, the more com-

3.1 STRATEGY *in* ACTION

Entry Barriers in the Japanese Brewing Industry

In 1565, an English visitor to Japan noted that the Japanese "feed moderately but they drink largely." This is still the case today; the Japanese have one of the highest levels of beer consumption per capita of any country in the world. In 1998, for example, fifty liters of beer were sold for every man, woman, and child in the country, making Japan's level of beer consumption per capita similar to that of big beer-drinking nations such as Australia, Britain, and Germany.

The Japanese market is dominated by four companies: Kirin, Asahi, Sapporo, and Suntory. In 1998, these four had a combined market share of around 97 percent. Collectively, these companies enjoy one of the highest profit rates of any industry in Japan. Despite this high level of profitability, however, there has been very little entry into this industry over the last three decades. Suntory has been the only successful new entrant in the last thirty years, and its market share stands at no more than 6 percent.

Normally, a lack of new entry into a profitable industry indicates the presence of high entry barriers, and that is certainly the case here. Like large brewers all over the world, Japan's big four spend heavily on advertising and promotions. Moreover, Japan's big brewers have been aggressive in the area of product development. During the 1990s, Asahi gained significant share from its competitors by pushing its "Super Dry" beer. The resulting product differentiation and brand identification have certainly helped to limit the potential for new entry. But some argue that there is more to it than this. Japan's big brewing companies have also benefited from significant regulatory barriers to entry. Brewers in Japan must have a license from the Ministry of Finance (MOF). Prior to 1994, the MOF would not issue a license to any brewer producing less than 2 million liters annually. This restriction represented an imposing hurdle to any potential new entrant. Interestingly enough, the reason for the licensing scheme was bureaucratic convenience rather than a desire to protect brewing companies from new entry; it is easier to collect tax from 4 companies than from 400.

Another significant barrier to entry has been Japan's distribution system. In Japan, there are often close ties between distributors and manufacturers, and this is the case in the brewing industry. Roughly half the beer consumed in Japan is sold in bars and restaurants. Their owners appear to be loyal to the big brewers and reluctant to take on competing brands that might alienate their main supplier. Small liquor stores are another main distribution outlet for beer, and they, too, have traditionally maintained close ties with the big brewers and are unwilling to sell the products of new entrants for fear that their main suppliers might "punish" them by denying them access to adequate supplies.

However, it now appears that some of the barriers to entering Japan's brewing industry are being lowered. As part of an economic liberalization plan, in 1994 the MOF reduced the production threshold required to gain a license from 2 million liters to 60,000 liters. This was low enough to allow the entry of microbreweries using the same technology that is now found in many brew pubs in the United States and Britain. Moreover, regulatory changes have also permitted the establishment of large new discount stores in Japan. (Until 1994, small retailers could effectively block the establishment of a large discount store in their region by appealing to the local authorities). Unlike traditional small retailers, large discount retailers are motivated more by price and profit than by loyalties to an established supplier and seem willing to sell the beer of foreign companies and microbreweries, in addition to that of Japan's big four.

Given the decline in barriers to entry associated with regulation and distribution channels, many observers thought that Japan's big four brewers would have to face new competitors in the years after 1994. So far, however, that has not happened. Instead, Japan's big four brewers continue to dominate the domestic market—a testament perhaps to the significance of advertising, promotions, and product differentiation as barriers to entry. On the other hand, Japan's brewers are facing indirect competition from an alternative alcoholic beverage, wine, which is starting to become fashionable among younger people.[7]

modity-like an industry's product, the more vicious will be the price war. This bust part of the cycle continues until overall industry capacity is brought into line with demand (through bankruptcies), at which point prices may stabilize again.

A fragmented industry structure, then, constitutes a threat rather than an opportunity. Most booms will be relatively short-lived because of the ease of new entry and will be followed by price wars and bankruptcies. Since it is often difficult to differentiate products in these industries, the best strategy for a company to pursue may be cost minimization. This strategy allows a company to rack up high returns in a boom and survive any subsequent bust.

The nature and intensity of rivalry in consolidated industries is much more difficult to predict. Because in consolidated industries companies are *interdependent,* the competitive actions of one company directly affect the profitability of others in the industry, and the impact on the market share of its rivals forces a response from them. The consequence of such competitive interdependence can be a dangerous competitive spiral, with rival companies trying to undercut each other's prices, pushing industry profits down in the process. The fare wars that have racked the airline industry in the early 1990s provide a good example. When demand for airline travel fell during 1990 as the U.S. economy slipped into a recession, airlines started cutting prices to try to maintain their passenger loads. When one airline serving a particular route cut its prices, its competitors would soon follow. The result was a particularly severe downward price spiral. So intense did price competition become that between 1990 and 1992 the industry lost a staggering $7.1 billion, more than had been made during its previous fifty years, and some long-established carriers, such as Pan American, disappeared into bankruptcy.

Clearly, high rivalry between companies in consolidated industries and the possibility of a price war constitute a major threat. Companies sometimes seek to reduce this threat by following the price lead set by a dominant company in the industry. However, they must be careful, for explicit price-fixing agreements are illegal, although tacit agreements are not. (A tacit agreement is one arrived at without direct communication). Instead, companies watch and interpret each other's behavior. Often tacit agreements involve following the price lead set by a dominant company.[8] However, tacit price-leadership agreements often break down under adverse economic conditions, as is beginning to occur in the beer industry. For most of the 1980s, Anheuser-Busch was the acknowledged price leader in this industry. The resulting absence of price competition helped keep industry profits high. However, slow growth in beer consumption during the late 1980s and early 1990s put pressure on the earnings of all beer majors and persuaded Miller Brewing—a division of Philip Morris—and Adolph Coors to break ranks and institute a policy of deep and continuous discounting for most of their beer brands. In 1990, market leader Anheuser-Busch announced that it would start offering similar discounts in order to protect its sales volume. Thus, after the breakdown of a tacit price-leadership agreement, the beer industry seemed to be sliding toward a price war.

More generally, when price wars are a threat, companies tend to compete on nonprice factors such as advertising and promotions, brand positioning, and product quality, functionality, and design. This type of competition constitutes an attempt to differentiate the company's product from those of competitors, thereby building brand loyalty and minimizing the likelihood of a price war. The effectiveness of this strategy, however, depends on how easy it is to differentiate the industry's product. Although some products (such as cars) are relatively easy to differentiate, others (such as airline travel) are difficult. Moreover, as Strategy in

Action 3.2 demonstrates, in practice nonprice competition in consolidated industries can often be as vigorous, expensive, and damaging as price competition.

Demand Conditions   An industry's demand conditions are another determinant of the intensity of rivalry among established companies. Growing demand stemming from new customers or from additional purchases by existing customers, tends to moderate competition by providing greater room for expansion. Growing demand tends to reduce rivalry because all companies can sell more without taking market share away from other companies, and high profits are often the result. Conversely, declining demand results in more rivalry as companies fight to maintain revenues and market share. Demand declines when consumers are leaving the marketplace or when each consumer is buying less. In that situation, a company can grow only by taking market share away from other companies. Thus, declining demand constitutes a major threat, for it increases the extent of rivalry between established companies. Moreover, as we saw in the Opening Case, a slowdown in the rate of growth of demand can also create problems.

Exit Barriers   Exit barriers are economic, strategic, and emotional factors that keep companies in an industry even when returns are low. If exit barriers are high, companies can become locked into an unprofitable industry where overall demand is static or declining. Excess productive capacity can result. In turn, excess capacity tends to lead to intensified price competition, with companies cutting prices in an attempt to obtain the orders needed to utilize their idle capacity.[10] Common exit barriers include the following:

1. Investments in plant and equipment that have no alternative uses and cannot be sold off. If the company wishes to leave the industry, it has to write off the book value of these assets.

2. High fixed costs of exit, such as severance pay to workers who are being made redundant.

3. Emotional attachments to an industry, as when a company is unwilling to exit from its original industry for sentimental reasons.

4. Economic dependence on the industry, as when a company is not diversified and so relies on the industry for its income.

The experience of the steel industry illustrates the adverse competitive effects of high exit barriers.[11] A combination of declining demand and new low-cost sources of supply created overcapacity in the global steel industry during the late 1980s. U.S. companies, with their high-cost structure, were on the sharp end of this decline. Demand for U.S. steel fell from a 1977 peak of 160 million tons to 70 million tons in 1986. The outcome was excess capacity amounting to an estimated 45 million tons in 1987, or 40 percent of total productive capacity. In order to try to utilize this capacity, many steel companies slashed their prices. As a consequence of the resulting price war, industry profits were low, and several of the majors, including LTV Steel and Bethlehem Steel, faced bankruptcy.

Since the steel industry was characterized by excess capacity for most of the 1980s, why did companies not reduce that capacity? The answer is that many tried to, but the costs of exit slowed this process and prolonged the associated price war. For example, in 1983 USX shut down 16 percent of its raw steel-making capacity at a cost of $1.2 billion. USX had to write off the book value of these assets; they could

The Great European Soap War

The European retail detergents market, like the global detergents market, is dominated by the products of just two companies, Unilever, the Anglo-Dutch concern, and the American consumer products giant, Procter & Gamble (P&G). Both companies sell a broad product line of detergents to consumers; both spend heavily on advertising, promotions, and brand positioning; and both de-emphasize price-based competition. The net result is that historically both companies have benefited from a relatively benign competitive environment, which has enabled them to earn higher profit margins than would be the case in a more price-competitive industry.

This cozy situation was rudely shattered in early 1994 after the Pan-European launch of a new detergent by Unilever. The product in question was Omo Power, which Unilever promoted as the biggest technical advance in fabric detergents in fifteen years. According to Unilever, Omo Power contained a powerful cleansing agent that washed clothes cleaner than any other product on the market. Consumers seemed to agree; sales of Omo Power surged in every country in which it was introduced during the first few months of 1994. P&G was alarmed by this development. The introduction of Omo Power seemed to violate a tacit understanding between the two companies that they would share technical information with each other. Moreover, Unilever was gaining market share at P&G's expense for the first time in two decades.

P&G's initial response was to try and discover what the secret ingredient in Omo Power might be. After extensive laboratory studies, P&G discovered that Unilever had used crystals of manganese. This surprised P&G, for although manganese could speed the bleaching process, P&G also knew from its own research that manganese attacked fabrics, which was why P&G had abandoned work on manganese ten years earlier. After submitting Omo Power to its own tests, P&G found that clothes washed repeatedly in the powder did indeed develop holes. Armed with this information, P&G decided to counterattack. Top executives from P&G visited top management at Unilever and stated bluntly that Omo Power was fundamentally flawed and should be pulled off the market. Unilever executives chose to discount this private warning. After two years of market testing with no complaints from consumers, Unilever saw no need to withdraw the product and believed P&G was overstating the problem because it was losing market share. It was at this point that P&G broke with the industry tradition of not criticizing the products of competitors and launched a ruthless public relations campaign pointing out the flaws of Omo Power. P&G gave the press a set of color pictures showing clothes purportedly suffering the ill effects of Omo Power—including shots of some tattered boxer shorts that were duly reproduced by the press all over Europe.

Unilever initially tried to dismiss P&G's claims, but a growing number of independent research institutes backed up P&G's findings. After several months of increasingly bitter public recriminations between the two companies, Unilever was eventually forced to concede that there was a problem. Unilever repositioned Omo Power in the market place from a product with broad applicability to a niche product for use with white fabrics and low water temperatures (conditions that minimized the damage problems).

In the end, Unilever was forced to admit that its $300 million investment in Omo had been a washout. By the end of 1994, Unilever's market share had fallen back to the level the company had attained prior to the launching of Omo Power. Moreover, executives from both companies admitted that the rules of the game in the industry had changed as a result of the dispute. Gone was the cozy agreement of sharing technical information and forbearing from directly attacking the products of a competitor. Nonprice competition in the industry would now be much more difficult than before. P&G fully expected Unilever to try and get its revenge by attacking any new product launch that it might try.[9]

not be sold. In addition, it had to cover pensions and insurance for 15,400 terminated workers. Given such high exit costs, companies such as USX have remained locked into this unprofitable industry. The effect of impeded exit has been more intense price competition than might otherwise have been the case. Thus, high exit barriers, by slowing the speed with which companies leave the industry, threaten the profitability of all companies within the steel industry.

■ The Bargaining Power of Buyers

The third of Porter's five competitive forces is the bargaining power of buyers. A company's buyers may be the customers who ultimately consume its products (its end users), but they may also be the companies that distribute its products to end users, such as retailers and wholesalers. For example, while Unilever sells its soap powder to end users, the major buyers of its products are supermarket chains, which then resell the product to the end users. Buyers can be viewed as a competitive threat when they are in a position to demand lower prices from the company, or when they demand better service (which can increase operating costs). On the other hand, when buyers are weak, a company can raise its prices and earn greater profits. Whether buyers are able to make demands on a company depends on their power relative to that of the company. According to Porter, buyers are most powerful in the following circumstances:

1. When the supply industry is composed of many small companies and the buyers are few in number and large. These circumstances allow the buyers to dominate supply companies.

2. When the buyers purchase in large quantities. In such circumstances, buyers can use their purchasing power as leverage to bargain for price reductions.

3. When the supply industry depends on the buyers for a large percentage of its total orders.

4. When the buyers can switch orders between supply companies at a low cost, thereby playing off companies against each other to force down prices.

5. When it is economically feasible for the buyers to purchase the input from several companies at once.

6. When the buyers can use the threat to supply their own needs through vertical integration as a device for forcing down prices.

An example of an industry whose buyers are powerful is the auto component supply industry. The buyers here are the large automobile companies, such as General Motors, Ford, and Chrysler. The suppliers of auto components are numerous and typically small in scale. Their buyers, the auto manufacturers, are large in size and few in number. Chrysler, for example, does business with nearly 2,000 different component suppliers and normally contracts with a number of different companies to supply the same part. The auto majors have used their powerful position to play off suppliers against each other, forcing down the price they have to pay for component parts and demanding better quality. If a component supplier objects, then the auto major uses the threat of switching to another supplier as a bargaining tool.

Additionally, to keep component prices down, both Ford and General Motors have used the threat of manufacturing a component themselves rather than buying it from auto component suppliers.

Another issue is that the relative power of buyers and suppliers tends to change over time in response to changing industry conditions. For example, because of changes now taking place in the pharmaceutical and health care industries, major buyers of pharmaceuticals (hospitals and health maintenance organizations) are gaining power over the suppliers of pharmaceuticals and have been able to demand lower prices.

■ The Bargaining Power of Suppliers

The fourth of Porter's competitive forces is the bargaining power of suppliers. Suppliers can be viewed as a threat when they are able to force up the price that a company must pay for its inputs or reduce the quality of the inputs they supply, thereby depressing the company's profitability. On the other hand, if suppliers are weak, this gives a company the opportunity to force down prices and demand higher input quality. As with buyers, the ability of suppliers to make demands on a company depends on their power relative to that of the company. According to Porter, suppliers are most powerful in these circumstances:

1. When the product that suppliers sell has few substitutes and is important to the company.

2. When the company's industry is not an important customer to the suppliers. In such instances, the suppliers' health does not depend on the company's industry, and suppliers have little incentive to reduce prices or improve quality.

3. When suppliers' respective products are differentiated to such an extent that it is costly for a company to switch from one supplier to another. In such cases, the company depends on its suppliers and cannot play them off against each other.

4. When, to raise prices, suppliers can use the threat of vertically integrating forward into the industry and competing directly with the company.

5. When buying companies cannot use the threat of vertically integrating backward and supplying their own needs as a means of reducing input prices.

Manufacturers of personal computers exemplify an industry that depends on a very powerful supplier. In this case, the supplier is Intel, the world's largest manufacturer of microprocessors for personal computers (PCs). The industry standard for personal computers runs on Intel's X86 microprocessor family, such as the Pentium series microprocessors currently sold in most PCs. So PC manufacturers have little choice but to use an Intel microprocessor as the brains for their machines. Although several companies have tried to produce clones of Intel's microprocessors, their success has been limited, leaving Intel with about 85 percent of the market. This puts Intel in a very powerful position with regard to the PC manufacturers. The product it supplies has few substitutes and switching costs facing the buyers are high, which enables Intel to raise prices above the level that would prevail in a more competitive supply market.[12]

■ Substitute Products

The final force in Porter's model is the threat of substitute products. Substitute products are the products of industries that serve similar consumer needs as the industry being analyzed. For example, companies in the coffee industry compete indirectly with those in the tea and soft-drink industries. All three industries serve consumer needs for drinks. The prices that companies in the coffee industry can charge are limited by the existence of substitutes such as tea and soft drinks. If the price of coffee rises too much relative to that of tea or soft drinks, then coffee drinkers will switch from coffee to those substitutes. This phenomenon occurred when unusually cold weather destroyed much of the Brazilian coffee crop in 1975–1976. The price of coffee rose to record highs, reflecting the shortage, and consumers began to switch to tea in large numbers.

The existence of close substitutes presents a strong competitive threat, limiting the price a company can charge and thus its profitability. However, if a company's products have few close substitutes (that is, if substitutes are a weak competitive force), then, other things being equal, the company has the opportunity to raise prices and earn additional profits. Consequently, its strategies should be designed to take advantage of this fact.

■ A Sixth Force: Complementors

Andrew Grove, the former CEO of Intel, and a part-time teacher at Stanford's Graduate School of Business, has argued that Porter's five forces model ignores a sixth force—the power, vigor, and competence of complementors.[13] **Complementors** are companies that sell complements to the enterprise's own product offerings. For example, the complementors to Sony's popular home video game system, the Play Station, are the companies that produce and sell games that run on the Play Station. Grove's point is that without an adequate supply of complementary products, demand in the industry will be weak, and revenues and profits will be low. No one would purchase the Play Station if there were not enough games to play on it. For another example, consider the early automobile industry. When the automobile was first introduced at the beginning of the twentieth century, demand for the product was very limited. One reason for this was the lack of important complementary products, such as a network of paved roads and gas stations. An automobile was of limited use when there were few paved roads to drive on, and when gas stations were few and far between. As the supply of complementary products increased—as roads and gas stations started to spring up—so did the attractiveness of owning a car. With roads to drive on and an adequate supply of gas stations, owning a car became more practical, and so demand started to pick up. In turn, this created a demand for more roads and gas stations, setting up a self-reinforcing positive feedback loop.

Grove's argument has a strong foundation in economic theory. Most economic textbooks have long argued that *both* substitutes and complements influenced demand in an industry.[14] Moreover, recent research has emphasized the importance of complementary products in determining demand and profitability in many high-technology industries, such as the computer industry, in which Grove made his mark.[15] The basic point, therefore, is that when complements are an important determinant of demand in an industry, the health of the industry depends critically on there being an adequate supply of complementary products produced by complementors. It follows that if complementors are weak and lack attractive product offerings, this can be a threat for the industry (the converse holds true as well).

■ The Role of the Macroenvironment

So far we have treated industries as self-contained entities. In practice, they are embedded in a wider **macroenvironment:** the broader economic, technological, social, demographic, and political and legal environment (see Figure 3.2). Changes in the macroenvironment can have a direct impact on any one of the forces in Porter's model, thereby altering the relative strength of these forces and with it, the attractiveness of an industry. We briefly consider how each aspect of these macroenvironmental forces can affect an industry's competitive structure.

The Macroeconomic Environment   The state of the macroeconomic environment determines the general health and well-being of the economy. This in turn affects a company's ability to earn an adequate rate of return. The four most important factors in the macroeconomy are the growth rate of the economy, interest rates, currency exchange rates, and inflation rates.

Because it leads to an expansion in consumer expenditures, economic growth tends to produce a general easing of competitive pressures within an industry. This gives companies the opportunity to expand their operations and earn higher profits. Because economic decline leads to a reduction in consumer expenditures, it increases competitive pressures. Economic decline frequently causes price wars in mature industries.

FIGURE 3.2

The Role of the
Macroenvironment

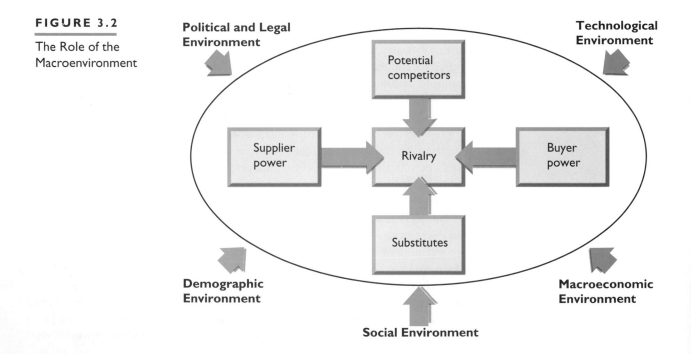

The level of interest rates can determine the level of demand for a company's products. Interest rates are important whenever consumers routinely borrow money to finance their purchase of these products. The most obvious example is the housing market, where the mortgage rate directly affects demand, but interest rates also have an impact on the sale of autos, appliances, and capital equipment, to give just a few examples. For companies in such industries, rising interest rates are a threat and falling rates an opportunity.

Currency exchange rates define the value of different national currencies against each other. Movement in currency exchange rates has a direct impact on the competitiveness of a company's products in the global marketplace. For example, when the value of the dollar is low compared with the value of other currencies, products made in the United States are relatively inexpensive and products made overseas are relatively expensive. A low or declining dollar reduces the threat from foreign competitors while creating opportunities for increased sales overseas. For example, the fall in the value of the dollar against the Japanese yen that occurred between 1985 and 1995, when the dollar/yen exchange rate declined from $1 = Y240 to $1 = Y85, sharply increased the price of imported Japanese cars, giving U.S. car manufacturers some degree of protection against the Japanese threat.

Inflation can destabilize the economy, producing slower economic growth, higher interest rates, and volatile currency movements. If inflation keeps increasing, investment planning becomes hazardous. The key characteristic of inflation is that it makes the future less predictable. In an inflationary environment, it may be impossible to predict with any accuracy the real value of returns that can be earned from a project five years hence. Such uncertainty makes companies less willing to invest. Their holding back in turn depresses economic activity and ultimately pushes the economy into a slump. Thus, high inflation is a threat to companies.

The Technological Environment Since World War II, the pace of technological change has accelerated,[16] unleashing a process that has been called a "perennial gale of creative destruction."[17] Technological change can make established products obsolete overnight, and at the same time it can create a host of new product possibilities. Thus, technological change is both creative and destructive—both an opportunity and a threat.

One of the most important impacts of technological change is that it can affect the height of barriers to entry and, as a result, radically reshape industry structure. This was clearly demonstrated in the Opening Case, when we saw how the spread of the Internet has lowered barriers to entry into the on-line stockbrokerage industry and produced a flood of new entrants and a more fragmented industry structure. In turn, these new entrants have driven down commission rates in the industry, just as theory would predict. In point of fact, the Internet represents a major technological change, and it appears to be in the process of unleashing a similar process of creative destruction across a wide range of industries. On-line retailers are springing up, selling everything from books and CDs to groceries and clothes, suggesting that the Internet has lowered entry barriers in the retail industry. The ability to buy airline tickets and book vacations on-line is a threat to established travel agents, while providing an opportunity for Internet-based start-ups that want to enter the travel industry. The rise of the Internet has also lowered barriers to entry into the news industry. For example, the providers of financial news now have to compete for advertising dollars and consumer attention with new Internet-based media organizations, which have sprung up in recent years, such as TheStreet.com, the Motley Fool, and Yahoo!'s financial section.

Another example of how technological change is reshaping an established industry can be found by considering the impact of biotechnology on the pharmaceutical industry. Although large companies such as Merck, Pfizer, and Eli Lilly have long dominated the pharmaceutical industry, a significant number of small biotechnology companies using recombinant DNA technology are threatening to change the competitive landscape. Between 1945 and 1990, only one new firm became a major player in the pharmaceutical industry, Syntex. Since 1990, a number of biotechnology companies have started to generate significant sales, including Amgen, Biogen, Genetech, Chiron, and Immunex. Moreover, there are now over 300 publicly traded companies in the United States developing novel medicines using biotechnology. The chance is that some of them will develop into significant companies in their own right, illustrating once again that technological change lowers entry barriers and allows new players to challenge the dominance of incumbents.

The Social Environment   Like technological change, social change creates opportunities and threats. One of the major social movements of the 1970s and 1980s was the trend toward greater health consciousness. Its impact has been immense, and companies that recognized the opportunities early have often reaped significant gains. Philip Morris, for example, capitalized on the growing health-consciousness trend when it acquired Miller Brewing and then redefined competition in the beer industry with its introduction of low-calorie beer (Miller Lite). Similarly, PepsiCo was able to gain market share from its rival, Coca-Cola, by introducing diet colas and fruit-based soft drinks first. At the same time the health trend has created a threat for many industries. The tobacco industry, for example, is now in decline as a direct result of greater consumer awareness of the health implications of smoking. Similarly, the sugar industry has seen sales decrease as consumers have decided to switch to artificial sweeteners.

The Demographic Environment   The changing composition of the population is another factor in the macroenvironment that can create both opportunities and threats. For example, as the baby-boom generation of the 1960s has aged, it has created a host of opportunities and threats. During the 1980s, many baby boomers were getting married and creating an upsurge in demand for the consumer appliances normally bought by couples marrying for the first time. Companies such as Whirlpool and General Electric capitalized on the resulting upsurge in demand for washing machines, dishwashers, spin dryers, and the like. The other side of the coin is that industries oriented toward the young, such as the toy industry, have seen their consumer base decline in recent years.

The Political and Legal Environment   Political and legal factors also have a major effect on the level of opportunities and threats in the environment. One of the most significant trends in recent years has been the move toward deregulation. By eliminating many legal restrictions, deregulation has lowered barriers to entry and led to intense competition in a number of industries. The deregulation of the airline industry in 1979 created the opportunity to establish low-fare carriers—an opportunity that Southwest Airlines, Value Jet, and others tried to capitalize on. At the same time, the increased intensity of competition created many threats, including, most notably, the threat of prolonged fare wars, which have thrown the airline industry into turmoil several times since 1979. The global telecommunications industry is now beginning to experience the same kind of turmoil following the deregulation of that industry in both the United States and the European Union.

STRATEGIC GROUPS WITHIN INDUSTRIES

■ The Concept of Strategic Groups

So far we have said little about how companies in an industry might differ from each other and what implications these differences might have for the opportunities and threats they face. In practice, companies in an industry often differ from each other with respect to factors such as the distribution channels they use, the market segments they serve, the quality of their products, technological leadership, customer service, pricing policy, advertising policy, and promotions. As a result of these differences, within most industries, it is possible to observe groups of companies in which each member follows the same basic strategy as other companies in the group, but a strategy that is *different* from that followed by companies in other groups. These groups of companies are known as **strategic groups**.[18]

Normally, a limited number of groups captures the essence of strategic differences between companies within an industry. For example, in the pharmaceutical industry, two main strategic groups stand out (see Figure 3.3).[19] One group, which includes such companies as Merck, Pfizer, and Eli Lilly, is characterized by heavy R&D spending and a focus on developing new proprietary blockbuster drugs. The companies in this *proprietary group* are pursuing a high-risk/high-return strategy. It is a high-risk strategy because basic drug research is difficult and expensive. Bringing a new drug to market can cost $100 million to $300 million in R&D money and a decade of research and clinical trials. The strategy is also a high-return one because a single successful drug can be patented, giving the innovator a seventeen-year monopoly on its production and sale. This lets the innovator charge a very high price for the patented drug, allowing the company to earn millions, if not billions, of dollars, over the lifetime of the patent.

The second strategic group might be characterized as the *generic drug* group. This group of companies, which includes Marion Labs, Carter Wallace, and ICN Pharmaceuticals, focuses on the manufacture of generic drugs—low-cost copies of drugs pioneered by companies in the proprietary group whose patents have now expired. The companies in this group are characterized by low R&D spending and an emphasis on price competition. They are pursuing a low-risk, low-return strategy. It is low risk because they are not investing millions of dollars in R&D. It is low return because they cannot charge high prices.

■ Implications of Strategic Groups

The concept of strategic groups has a number of implications for identifying threats and opportunities within an industry. First, a company's closest competitors are those in its strategic group—not those in other strategic groups. Since all the companies in a strategic group are pursuing similar strategies, consumers tend to view

FIGURE 3.3

Strategic Groups in
the Pharmaceutical
Industry

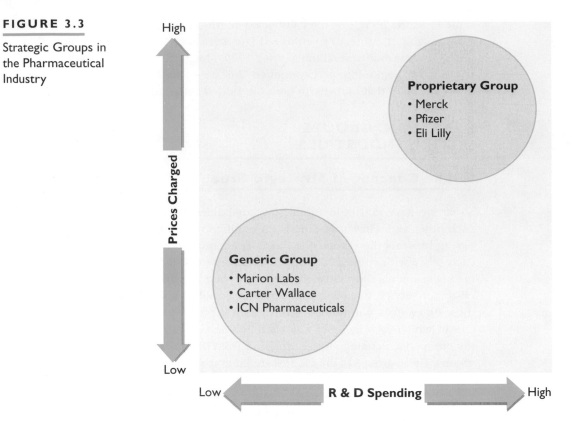

the products of such enterprises as direct substitutes for each other. Thus, a major threat to a company's profitability can come from within its own strategic group.

Second, different strategic groups can have a different standing with respect to each of the competitive forces. In other words, the risk of new entry by potential competitors, the degree of rivalry among companies within a group, the bargaining power of buyers, the bargaining power of suppliers, and the competitive force of substitute products can all vary in intensity among different strategic groups within the same industry.

For example, in the pharmaceutical industry, companies in the proprietary group have historically been in a very powerful position vis-à-vis buyers because their products are patented. Besides, rivalry within this group has been limited to competition to be the first to patent a new drug (so-called patent races). Price competition has been rare. Without price competition, companies in this group have been able to charge high prices and earn very high profits. In contrast, companies in the generic group have been in a much weaker position in regard to buyers since they lack patents for their products and since buyers can choose between very similar competing generic drugs. Moreover, price competition between the companies in this group has been quite intense, reflecting the lack of product differentiation. Thus, companies within this group have earned somewhat lower returns than companies in the proprietary group.

It follows that some strategic groups are more desirable than others, for they have a lower level of threats and greater opportunities. Managers must evaluate whether their company would be better off competing in a different strategic group. If the environment of another strategic group is more benign, then moving into that group can be regarded as an opportunity. Yet this opportunity is rarely without costs, mainly because of mobility barriers between groups. **Mobility barriers** are factors that inhibit the movement of companies between groups in an industry. They include both the barriers to entry into a group and the barriers to exit from a company's existing group. For example, Marion Labs would encounter mobility barriers if it attempted to enter the proprietary group in the pharmaceutical industry. These mobility barriers would arise from the fact that Marion lacks the R&D skills possessed by companies in the proprietary group, and building these skills would be an expensive proposition. Thus, a company contemplating entry into another strategic group must evaluate the height of mobility barriers before deciding whether the move is worthwhile.

Mobility barriers also imply that companies within a given group may be protected to a greater or lesser extent from the threat of entry by companies based in other strategic groups. If mobility barriers are low, the threat of entry from companies in other groups may be high, effectively limiting the prices companies can charge and the profits they can earn without attracting new competition. If mobility barriers are high, however, the threat of entry is low, and companies within the protected group have an opportunity to raise prices and earn higher returns without attracting entry.

LIMITATIONS OF THE FIVE FORCES AND STRATEGIC GROUP MODELS

The five forces and strategic group models provide useful ways of thinking about and analyzing the nature of competition within an industry to identify opportunities and threats. However, managers need to be aware of their shortcomings, for both models (1) present a static picture of competition that slights the role of innovation and (2) de-emphasize the significance of individual company differences while overemphasizing the importance of industry and strategic group structure as determinants of company profit rates.

■ Innovation and Industry Structure

Over any reasonable length of time, in many industries competition can be viewed as a process driven by innovation.[20] Companies that pioneer new products, processes, or strategies can often earn enormous profits. This prospect gives companies a strong incentive to seek innovative products, processes, and strategies. Consider, for example, the explosive growth of Apple Computer, Dell Computer, Toys 'R' Us, or Wal-Mart. In one way or another, all these companies were innovators. Apple pioneered the personal computer, Dell pioneered a whole new way of selling personal computers (by mail order), Toys 'R' Us pioneered a new way of selling toys (through large discount warehouse-type stores), and Wal-Mart pioneered the low-price discount superstore concept.

Successful innovation can revolutionize industry structure. In recent decades one of the most common consequences of innovation has been to lower the fixed costs of production, thereby reducing barriers to entry and allowing new, and smaller, enterprises to compete with large established organizations. Take the steel industry as an example. Two decades ago the industry was populated by large integrated steel companies such as U.S. Steel, LTV, and Bethlehem Steel. Dominated by a small number of large producers, the industry was a typical oligopoly, in which tacit price collusion was practiced. Then along came a series of efficient minimill producers such as Nucor and Chaparral Steel, which utilized a new technology—electric arc furnaces. Over the last twenty years, they have revolutionized the structure of the industry. What was once a consolidated industry is now much more fragmented and price competitive. The successor company to U.S. Steel, USX, now has only a 15 percent market share, down from 55 percent in the mid 1960s, and both Bethlehem and LTV have been through Chapter 11 bankruptcy proceedings. In contrast, as a group, the minimills now hold more than 30 percent of the market, up from 5 percent twenty years ago. Thus, the minimill innovation has reshaped the nature of competition in the steel industry.[21] A five forces model applied to the industry in 1970 would look very different from a five forces model applied in 1995.

In his more recent work, Michael Porter, the originator of the five forces and strategic group concepts, has explicitly recognized the role of innovation in revolutionizing industry structure. Porter now talks of innovations as "unfreezing" and "reshaping" industry structure. He argues that after a period of turbulence triggered by innovation the structure of an industry once more settles down into a fairly stable pattern. When the industry stabilizes in its new configuration, the five forces and strategic group concepts can once more be applied.[22] This view of the evolution of industry structure is often referred to as *punctuated equilibrium*.[23] The punctuated equilibrium view holds that long periods of equilibrium, when an industry's structure is stable, are punctuated by periods of rapid change when industry structure is revolutionized by innovation; there is an unfreezing and refreezing process

Figure 3.4 shows what punctuated equilibrium might look like for one key dimension of industry structure—competitive structure. From time t_0 to t_1 the competitive structure of the industry is a stable oligopoly, with a few companies sharing the market. At time t_1 a major new innovation is pioneered by either an existing company or a new entrant. The result is a period of turbulence between t_1 and t_2. After a while, however, the industry settles down into a new state of equilibrium, but now the competitive structure is far more fragmented. Note that the opposite could have happened: the industry could have become more consolidated, although this seems to be less common. In general, innovations seem to lower barriers to entry, allow more companies into the industry, and as a result lead to fragmentation rather than consolidation.

It is important to understand that during periods of rapid change, when industry structure is being revolutionized by innovation, value typically migrates to new business models.[24] In stockbrokerage, which we discussed in the Opening Case, value is currently migrating from the full-service broker model toward the on-line trading model. In the steel industry, the introduction of electric arc technology led to a migration of value from large integrated enterprises toward small minimills. In the book-selling industry, value may be beginning to migrate from "brick and mortar" booksellers toward on-line bookstores such as amazon.com (although it is still too early to state definitively how successful the on-line retail model will eventually be).

Because the five forces and strategic group models are static, they cannot adequately capture what occurs during periods of rapid change in the industry environment when value is migrating, but they are useful tools for analyzing industry

FIGURE 3.4

Punctuated Equilibrium
and Competitive
Structure

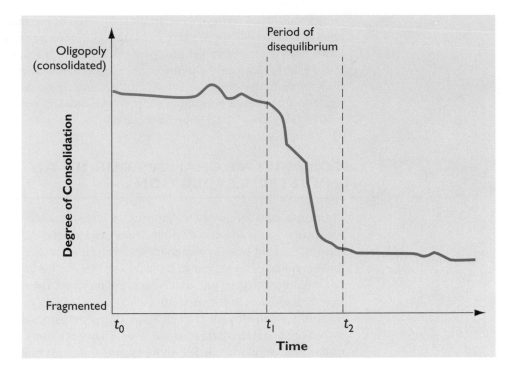

structure during periods of stability. Some scholars, though, question the validity of the punctuated equilibrium approach. Richard D'Avani has argued that many industries are **hypercompetitive**.[25] Hypercompetitive industries are characterized by permanent and ongoing innovation (the computer industry is often cited as an example of a hypercompetitive industry). The structure of such industries is constantly being revolutionized by innovation; there are no periods of equilibrium. When this is the case, some might argue that the five forces and strategic group models are of limited value since they represent no more than snapshots of a moving picture.

■ Industry Structure and Company Differences

The second criticism of the five forces and strategic group models is that they overemphasize the importance of industry structure as a determinant of company performance and underemphasize the importance of differences between companies within an industry or strategic group.[26] As we point out in the next chapter, there can be enormous variance in the profit rates of individual companies within an industry. Research by Richard Rumelt and others, for example, suggests that industry structure explains only about 10 percent of the variance in profit rates across companies.[27] The implication being that individual company differences explain much of the remainder. Other studies have put the explained variance closer to 20 percent, which is still not a large figure.[28] Similarly, a growing number of studies have found only very weak evidence of a link between strategic group membership and company profit rates, despite the fact that the strategic group model predicts a strong link.[29] Collectively, these studies suggest that the individual resources and capabilities of a company are far more important determinants of its profitability than is the industry or strategic group of which the company is a member. Although these findings do not make the five forces and strategic group models irrelevant, they do mean that the models have limited usefulness. A company will not be profitable just because it is based in an attractive industry or strategic group. As we discuss in Chapters 4 and 5, more is required.

COMPETITIVE CHANGES DURING AN INDUSTRY'S EVOLUTION

Over time, most industries pass through a series of stages, from growth through maturity and eventually into decline. These stages have different implications for the form of competition. The strength and nature of each of Porter's five competitive forces typically changes as an industry evolves.[30] This is particularly true regarding potential competitors and rivalry, and we focus on these two forces in our discussion. The changes in the strength and nature of these forces give rise to different opportunities and threats at each stage of an industry's evolution. The task facing managers is to *anticipate* how the strength of each force will change with the stage of industry development and to formulate strategies that take advantage of opportunities as they arise and that counter emerging threats.

The **industry life cycle model** is a useful tool for analyzing the effects of industry evolution on competitive forces. With it, we can identify five industry environments, each linked to a distinct stage of an industry's evolution: (1) an embryonic industry environment, (2) a growth industry environment, (3) a shakeout environment, (4) a mature industry environment, and (5) a declining industry environment (see Figure 3.5).

FIGURE 3.5

Stages of the Industry
Life Cycle

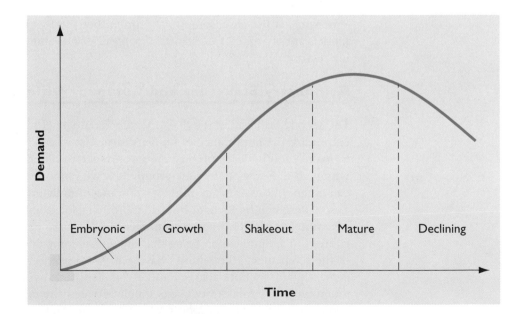

■ Embryonic Industries

An *embryonic* industry is one that is just beginning to develop (for example, personal computers in 1980). Growth at this stage is slow because of such factors as buyers' unfamiliarity with the industry's product, high prices due to the inability of companies to reap any significant scale economies, and poorly developed distribution channels. Barriers to entry at this stage in an industry's evolution tend to be based on access to key technological know-how rather than cost economies or brand loyalty. If the core know-how required to compete in the industry is complex and difficult to grasp, barriers to entry can be quite high and incumbent companies will be protected from potential competitors. Rivalry in embryonic industries is based not so much on price as on educating customers, opening up distribution channels, and perfecting the design of the product. Such rivalry can be intense, and the company that is the first to solve design problems often has the opportunity to develop a significant market position. An embryonic industry may also be the creation of one company's innovative efforts, as happened with personal computers (Apple), vacuum cleaners (Hoover), and photocopiers (Xerox). In such circumstances, the company has a major opportunity to capitalize on the lack of rivalry and build up a strong hold on the market.

■ Growth Industries

Once demand for the industry's product begins to take off, the industry develops the characteristics of a growth industry. In a *growth* industry, first-time demand is expanding rapidly as many new consumers enter the market. Typically, an industry grows when consumers become familiar with the product, when prices fall because experience and scale economies have been attained, and when distribution channels develop. The U.S. cellular telephone industry was in the growth stage for most of the 1990s. In 1990, there were only 5 million cellular subscribers in the nation. By 1998, however, this figure had increased to 70 million, and overall demand was still growing at a rate in excess of 25 percent per year. Similarly, in the United States the number of subscribers to on-line Internet services expanded from less than 1 million in 1990 to more than 60 million by the end of the decade.

Normally, the importance of control over technological knowledge as a barrier to entry has diminished by the time an industry enters its growth stage. Because few companies have yet achieved significant scale economics or differentiated their product sufficiently to guarantee brand loyalty, other entry barriers tend to be relatively low as well, particularly early in the growth stage. Thus, the threat from potential competitors is generally highest at this point. Paradoxically, however, high growth usually means that new entrants can be absorbed into an industry without a marked increase in competitive pressure.

During an industry's growth stage, rivalry tends to be relatively low. Rapid growth in demand enables companies to expand their revenues and profits without taking market share away from competitors. A company has the opportunity to expand its operations. In addition, a strategically aware company takes advantage of the relatively benign environment of the growth stage to prepare itself for the intense competition of the coming industry shakeout.

■ Industry Shakeout

Explosive growth of the type experienced by the cellular telephone or personal computer industries in the first half of the 1990s cannot be maintained indefinitely. Sooner or later the rate of growth slows, and the industry enters the shakeout stage. In the *shakeout* stage, demand approaches saturation levels. In a saturated market, there are few potential first-time buyers left. Most of the demand is limited to replacement demand.

As an industry enters the shakeout stage, rivalry between companies becomes intense. What typically happens is that companies that have become accustomed to rapid growth during an industry's growth phase continue to add capacity at rates consistent with past growth. Managers use historic growth rates to forecast future growth rates, and they plan expansions in productive capacity accordingly. As an industry approaches maturity, however, demand no longer grows at historic rates. The consequence is the emergence of excess productive capacity. This condition is illustrated in Figure 3.6, where the solid curve indicates the growth in demand over time and the broken curve indicates the growth in productive capacity over time. As you can see, past point t_1, demand growth becomes slower as the industry becomes mature. However, capacity continues to grow until time t_2. The gap between the solid and the broken lines signifies excess capacity. In an attempt to utilize this capacity, companies often cut prices. The result can be a price war, which drives many of the most inefficient companies into bankruptcy. This is itself enough to deter any new entry.

■ Mature Industries

The shakeout stage ends when the industry enters its *mature* stage. In a mature industry, the market is totally saturated and demand is limited to replacement de-

FIGURE 3.6

Growth in Demand and Capacity

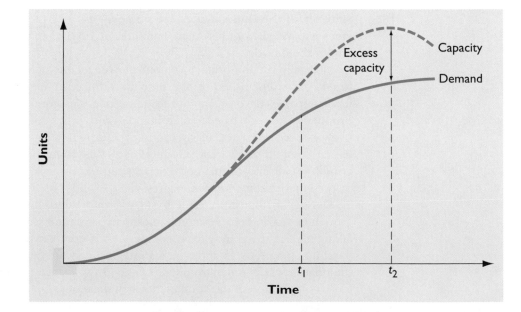

mand. During this stage, growth is low or zero. What little growth there is comes from population expansion bringing new consumers into the market.

As an industry enters maturity, barriers to entry increase and the threat of entry from potential competitors decreases. As growth slows during the shakeout, companies can no longer maintain historic growth rates merely by holding on to their market share. Competition for market share develops, driving down prices. Often the result is a price war, as happened in the airline industry during the 1988–1992 shakeout. To survive the shakeout, companies begin to focus both on cost minimization and on building brand loyalty. The airlines, for example, tried to cut operating costs by hiring nonunion labor and to build brand loyalty by introducing frequent-flyer programs. By the time an industry matures, the surviving companies are those that have brand loyalty and low-cost operations. Because both of these factors constitute a significant barrier to entry, the threat of entry by potential competitors is greatly diminished. High entry barriers in mature industries give companies the opportunity to increase prices and profits.

As a result of the shakeout, most industries in the maturity stage have consolidated and become oligopolies. In the airline industry, for example, because of the shakeout, the top five companies controlled 80 percent of the industry in 1995, up from only 50 percent in 1984. In mature industries, companies tend to recognize their interdependence and try to avoid price wars. Stable demand gives them the opportunity to enter into price-leadership agreements. The net effect is to reduce the threat of intense rivalry among established companies, thereby allowing greater profitability. However, as noted earlier, the stability of a mature industry is always threatened by further price wars. A general slump in economic activity can depress industry demand. As companies fight to maintain their revenues when demand flags, price-leadership agreements break down, rivalry increases, and prices and profits fall. The periodic price wars that occur in the airline industry seem to follow this pattern.

■ Declining Industries

Eventually, most industries enter a decline stage. In the *decline* stage, growth becomes negative for a variety of reasons, including technological substitution (for example, air travel for rail travel), social changes (greater health consciousness hitting tobacco sales), demographics (the declining birthrate hurting the market for baby and child products), and international competition (low-cost foreign competition pushing the U.S. steel industry into decline). Within a declining industry, the degree of rivalry among established companies usually increases. Depending on the speed of the decline and the height of exit barriers, competitive pressures can become as fierce as in the shakeout stage.[31] The main problem in a declining industry is that falling demand leads to the emergence of excess capacity. In trying to utilize this capacity, companies begin to cut prices, thus sparking a price war. As noted earlier, the U.S. steel industry experienced these problems because of the attempt of steel companies to utilize their excess capacity. The same problem occurred in the airline industry in the 1990–1992 period, as companies cut prices to ensure that they would not be flying with half-empty planes (that is, that they would not be operating with substantial excess capacity). Exit barriers play a part in adjusting excess capacity. The greater the exit barriers, the harder it is for companies to reduce capacity and the greater is the threat of severe price competition.

■ Variations on the Theme

It is important to remember that the industry life cycle model is a generalization. In practice, industry life cycles do not always follow the pattern illustrated in Figure 3.5. In some cases, growth is so rapid that the embryonic stage is skipped altogether. In other instances, industries fail to get past the embryonic stage. Industry growth can be revitalized after long periods of decline, either through innovations or through social changes. For example, the health boom brought the bicycle industry back to life after a long period of decline. The time span of the different stages can also vary significantly from industry to industry. Some industries can stay in maturity almost indefinitely if their products become basic necessities of life, as is the case for the automobile industry. Others skip the mature stage and go straight into decline. That is essentially what occurred in the vacuum tube industry. Vacuum tubes were replaced by transistors as a major component in electronic products while the industry was still in its growth stage. Still other industries may go through not one but several shakeouts before they enter full maturity.

NETWORK ECONOMICS AS A DETERMINANT OF INDUSTRY CONDITIONS

In recent years, there has been a growing realization that network economics are a primary determinant of competitive conditions in many high-technology industries, including computer hardware and software, consumer electronics, home video games, telecommunications, and Internet service providers.[32] **Network economics** arise in industries where the size of the "network" of *complementary* products is a primary determinant of demand for the industry's product. As argued earlier, the demand for automobiles early in the twentieth century was an increasing function of the *network* of paved roads and gas stations. Similarly, the demand for telephones is an increasing function of the number of other numbers that can be called with that phone; in other words, of the size of the telephone network (that is, the telephone network is the complementary product). When the first telephone service was introduced in New York City, only a hundred numbers could be called. The network was very small. There was only a limited number of wires and telephone switches. Consequently, the telephone was a relatively useless piece of equipment, nothing more than a technological curiosity. However, as more and more people got telephones and as the network of wires and switches expanded, the value of a telephone connection increased. This led to an increase in demand for telephone lines, which further increased the value of owning a telephone, setting up a positive feedback loop.

The same type of positive feedback loop is now at work in the Internet. The value of an Internet connection to individual users is an increasing function of the supply of useful information that they can access over the Internet and of the opportunity for engaging in commercial transactions through the medium of the Internet. The number of people with Internet connections drives forward the supply of such information and commercial services. The larger the number of people who are connected to the Internet, the greater is the opportunity for making money by supplying information and commercial services over the Internet. Thus, as more people connect to the Internet, this produces an increase in the supply of information and commercial services offered over the Internet. This increase, in turn, enhances the value of an Internet connection, which drives forward the demand for Internet connections, which leads to a further increase in the supply of information and services, and so on.

Why do network economics affect industry conditions? Well, for a start, once established, a positive feedback loop can help generate rapid demand growth, as we are now seeing in the Internet arena. The demand for Internet on-line services has been expanding at an exponential pace, primarily because a positive feedback loop is at work. Of course, such exponential surges in demand cannot go on forever, but while they are at work they make for very attractive industry conditions. Second, the operation of positive feedback loops can result in an industry becoming very concentrated and potential competitors being locked out by high switching costs. To understand this process, consider the history of the personal computer industry.

The value of a personal computer is an increasing function of the amount of software that is used on that computer and of the number of other complementary products that can be used with that computer, including printers, modems, and Internet connections. In other words, the value of a PC is an increasing function of the "network" of complementary products. In the late 1970s, a large number of different personal computers were on the market, and they used different operating systems and different microprocessors. Now the market is dominated by just one offering, the so-called Windows-Intel (or Wintel) standard. The only other viable product offering is that sold by Apple Computer, which has a small share of the market (in recent years, its share has never been more than 10 percent). The markets for personal computer operating systems and for microprocessors have become very concentrated, with Microsoft and Intel, respectively, dominating them. Moreover, high switching costs have raised entry barriers, making it extremely difficult for new enterprises to enter these markets.

This situation developed because IBM picked a Microsoft operating system (MS-DOS) and an Intel microprocessor to power its first personal computer, which was introduced in 1981. The IBM brand name had a lot of clout among businesses at the time, and demand for IBM PCs took off. As the *installed base* of IBM PCs grew, independent software developers faced a choice: whether to first write applications for the IBM PC or for competing products, such as that sold by Apple Computer. They were forced into making this choice because software written to run on one operating system and microprocessor will not run on another. As the sales of IBM PCs expanded, increasingly software developers wrote applications to run on an MS-DOS operating system powered by an Intel microprocessor, before turning their attention to applications for other computers, such as Apple's offering. Consequently, from early on, there was always more software available to run on the MS-DOS/Intel computers than on Apple computers. This increased the value of MS-DOS/Intel computers, relative to the alternatives, which led to a further increase in demand, and in turn, a more rapid increase in the supply of software to run on MS-DOS/Intel machines. In other words, the early lead gained by MS-DOS/Intel-based machines set up a positive feedback loop which resulted in the installed base of MS-DOS/Intel machines growing much faster than the installed base of alternative product offerings. This lead was sustained when Apple introduced its Macintosh operating system, which was arguably superior to Microsoft's MS-DOS offering, and continued when Microsoft replaced MS-DOS with Windows to create the Wintel standard (see Figure 3.7).

As a result of network economics, the markets for personal computer operating systems and microprocessors have become very concentrated. Microsoft and Intel

FIGURE 3.7

Positive Feedback in
the Computer Industry

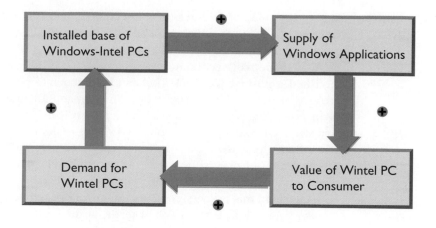

have tremendous bargaining power versus their suppliers and buyers, while switching costs have produced high barriers to entry. Because of these factors, as one might expect, Microsoft and Intel enjoy very high profit margins. Despite several attempts, new competitors have remained locked out of these profitable markets (see Strategy in Action 3.3 for an example). However, it would be wrong to assume that Microsoft and Intel are therefore immune to competition. If a new competitor should arise offering an operating system or microprocessor that is so superior that consumers are willing to bear switching costs, Microsoft and Intel could lose market share. The fact that this has not happened yet is partly a testament to the ability of Microsoft and Intel to improve continually the performance capabilities of the Windows operating systems and Intel's microprocessors.

In summary, a consideration of network economics leads to a number of important conclusions. First, in industries where network economics are important, positive feedback loops tend to operate. Once initiated, a positive feedback loop can lead to a rapid increase in demand. Second, markets where positive feedback loops operate tend to be winner-takes-all markets, with second- or third-string competitors being marginalized. This has occurred in the markets for computer operating systems and microprocessors. Third, enterprises that benefit from network economics tend to be in a powerful position relative to buyers and suppliers and tend to be protected from potential competitors by entry barriers arising from switching costs. From the perspective of an individual company, the trick is to find the right strategy that enables it to grow the installed base of its product rapidly in order to set up a positive feedback loop.

GLOBALIZATION AND INDUSTRY STRUCTURE

A fundamental change is occurring in the world economy.[34] We seem to be witnessing the globalization of production and of markets. With regard to the **globalization of production**, it has been observed that individual companies are increasingly dispersing parts of their production process to different locations around the globe to take advantage of national differences in the cost and quality of factors of production such as labor, energy, land, and capital. The objective is to lower costs and boost profits.

STRATEGY *in* ACTION

The Failure of Digital's Alpha Chip

In February 1992, Digital Equipment Corporation introduced the world's fastest microprocessor, the Alpha chip. Microprocessors are the brains of personal computers, workstations, and servers. The Alpha chip operated at more than twice the speed of Intel's best-selling microprocessors. Many at Digital had great hopes for the product, believing that it could ultimately grab a significant share of the booming market for microprocessors. By 1997, however, after Digital had spent $2.5 billion to develop the Alpha, the chip ranked dead last in market share, with an estimated 1 percent of the $18 billion microprocessor market. Intel's share stood at 92 percent.

The failure of the Alpha to gain market share despite its apparent performance advantage over existing microprocessors can be explained easily enough: there was never enough software to run on the Alpha. Hence, potential customers stayed away from investing in computers based on the Alpha chip. Digital was never able to get a positive feedback cycle going in which an increase in the supply of software configured to run on Alpha-based systems would have driven demand for Alpha-based computers, which would have meant that developers would have supplied more software for the Alpha, which would have further increased the demand for Alpha-based computers, and so on.

To be fair, Digital seemed to start off on the correct foot. In 1992, Microsoft agreed to adapt its next-generation operating system for corporate computers, Windows NT, so that it would run on the Alpha chip, in addition to Intel microprocessors. In return for this commitment from Microsoft, Digital agreed to make NT a central part of its own computer business. (Digital sold workstations, servers, and personal computers.) Following the agreement, Digital engineers devoted tremendous effort to fine-tuning the Alpha so that it would work with NT. However, when Digital engineers loaded tested versions of NT into

their computers, it became clear that NT needed far too much computer memory to run on a typical PC, putting Alpha beyond the reach of the mass market Digital had been hoping for.

In the spring of 1995, Digital tried again to kick start demand for the Alpha. Under the terms of a revised agreement with Microsoft, Digital agreed to provide network installation services for Microsoft. For its part, Microsoft agreed to continue to write a version of NT for the Alpha chip and to pay Digital up to $100 million to help train Digital NT technicians. Moreover, in October of that year, Microsoft stopped writing versions of NT for the IBM Power PC chip and Motorola's MIPS microprocessor, leaving the Alpha and Intel's Pentium series as the only chips that could run Windows NT.

Despite these developments, sales of the Alpha chip were still slow to take off. The Intel-based system now had such a huge lead in the Windows NT business that few developers were willing to take the risk and customize their software applications to run on the Alpha version of Windows NT, as opposed to Intel-based machines. To make matters worse, Digital hurt its own prospects by continuing to attach a premium price to Alpha machines, which slowed demand growth. By late 1994, Digital engineers had found a way to deliver Alpha workstations for $4,995. However, some of Digital's senior management vetoed the move because they feared that it would damage the 50 percent gross margins that Digital enjoyed in the high-end computer markets, which at the time was one of the few bright spots in Digital's business. In the end, when Digital did introduce its Alpha-based workstations for Windows NT, they were priced at $7,995, significantly above the price of high-end Intel-based machines. For corporate customers, this made the decision to go with Intel machines for Windows NT obvious—they were cheaper and more software applications were available for the Intel versions.[33]

For example, Boeing's new commercial jet aircraft, the 777, involves 132,500 engineered parts, which are produced around the world by 545 different suppliers. Eight Japanese suppliers make parts of the fuselage, doors, and wings; a supplier in Singapore makes the doors for the nose landing gear; three suppliers in Italy manufacture wing flaps; and so on. Part of Boeing's rationale for outsourcing so much production to foreign suppliers is that these various suppliers are the best in the world at performing their particular activity. Therefore, the result of having foreign suppliers build specific parts is a better final product.[35]

As for the **globalization of markets**, it has been argued that we are moving away from an economic system in which national markets are distinct entities, isolated from each other by trade barriers and barriers of distance, time, and culture, and toward a system in which national markets are merging into one huge global marketplace. Increasingly, consumers around the world demand and use the same basic product offerings. Consequently, in many industries it is no longer meaningful to talk about the German market, the U.S. market, or the Japanese market—there is only the global market. The global acceptance of Coca-Cola, Citigroup credit cards, Levi's blue jeans, the Sony PlayStation, McDonald's hamburgers, Nokia wireless phones, and Microsoft's Windows operating system exemplifies this trend.[36]

The trend toward the globalization of production and markets has several important implications for competition within an industry. First, it is crucial for companies to recognize that an industry's boundaries do not stop at national borders. Because many industries are becoming global in scope, actual and potential competitors exist not only in a company's home market, but also in other national markets. Companies that scan just their home market can be caught unprepared by the entry of efficient foreign competitors. The globalization of markets and production all imply that companies around the globe are finding their home markets under attack from foreign competitors. To illustrate, in Japan, Merrill Lynch and Citicorp are making inroads against Japanese financial service institutions. In the United States, Fuji has been taking market share from Kodak and Finland's Nokia has taken the lead from Motorola in the market for wireless phone handsets (see Strategy in Action 3.4). In the European Union, the once dominant Dutch company, Philips, has seen its market share in the consumer electronics industry taken by Japan's JVC, Matsushita, and Sony.

Second, the shift from national to global markets during the last twenty years has intensified competitive rivalry in industry after industry. National markets that were once consolidated oligopolies, dominated by three or four companies and subjected to relatively little foreign competition, have been transformed into segments of fragmented global industries, where a large number of companies battle each other for market share in country after country. This rivalry has driven down profit rates and made it all the more critical for companies to maximize their efficiency, quality, customer responsiveness, and innovative ability. The painful restructuring and downsizing that has been going on at companies such as Motorola and Kodak is as much a response to the increased intensity of global competition as it is to anything else. However, not all global industries are fragmented. Many remain consolidated oligopolies, except that now they are consolidated global, rather than national, oligopolies.

Third, as competitive intensity has increased, so has the rate of innovation. Companies strive to gain an advantage over their competitors by pioneering new products, processes, and ways of doing business. The result has been to compress product life cycles and make it vital for companies to stay on the leading edge of technology. In regard to highly competitive global industries, where the rate of innovation is accelerating, the criticism that Porter's five forces model is too static may be particularly relevant.

Finally, even though globalization has increased both the threat of entry and the intensity of rivalry within many formerly protected national markets, it has also created enormous opportunities for companies based in those markets. The steady decline in trade barriers has opened up many once protected markets to companies based outside them. Thus, for example, in recent years, western European, Japanese, and U.S. companies have accelerated their investments in the nations of eastern Europe, Latin America, and Southeast Asia as they try to take advantage of growth opportunities in those areas.

THE NATION-STATE AND COMPETITIVE ADVANTAGE

Despite the globalization of production and markets, many of the most successful companies in certain industries are still clustered in a small number of countries. For example, many of the world's most successful biotechnology and computer companies are based in the United States, many of the world's most successful consumer electronics companies are based in Japan, and many of the world's most successful chemical and engineering companies are based in Germany. This suggests that the nation-state within which a company is based may have an important bearing on the competitive position of that company in the global marketplace.

Companies need to understand how national factors can affect competitive advantage, for then they will be able to identify (1) where their most significant competitors are likely to come from and (2) where they might want to locate certain productive activities. Thus, seeking to take advantage of U.S. expertise in biotechnology, many foreign companies have set up research facilities in U.S. locations such as San Diego, Boston, and Seattle, where U.S. biotechnology companies tend to be clustered. Similarly, in an attempt to take advantage of Japanese success in consumer electronics, many U.S. electronics companies have set up research and production facilities in Japan, often in conjunction with Japanese partners.

In a study of national competitive advantage, Porter identified four attributes of a nation-state that have an important impact on the global competitiveness of companies located within that nation:

- *Factor endowments:* a nation's position in factors of production such as skilled labor or the infrastructure necessary to compete in a given industry

- *Local demand conditions:* the nature of home demand for the industry's product or service

- *Competitiveness of related and supporting industries:* the presence or absence in a nation of supplier industries and related industries that are internationally competitive

- *Strategy, structure, and rivalry:* the conditions in the nation governing how companies are created, organized, and managed and the nature of domestic rivalry[37]

Porter speaks of these four attributes as constituting *the diamond* (see Figure 3.8). He argues that firms are most likely to succeed in industries or industry segments

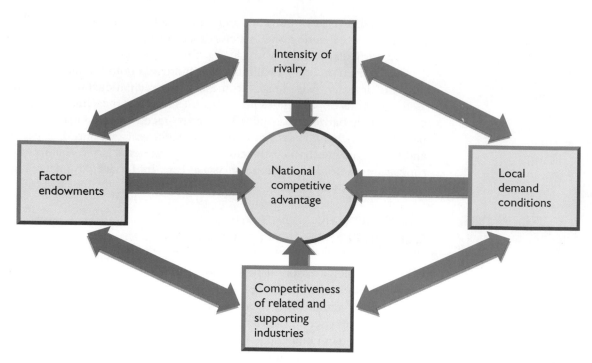

FIGURE 3.8

National Competitive
Advantage

where conditions with regard to the four attributes are favorable. He also argues
that the diamond's attributes form a mutually reinforcing system in which the effect
of one attribute is dependent on the state of others.

■ Factor Endowments

Porter follows basic economic theory in stressing that **factor conditions**—the
cost and quality of factors of production—are a prime determinant of the competitive advantage that certain countries might have in certain industries. Factors of
production include **basic factors,** such as land, labor, capital, and raw materials, and
advanced factors such as technological know-how, that is, managerial sophistication and physical infrastructure (such as, roads, railways, and ports). The competitive advantage that the United States enjoys in biotechnology might be explained by
the presence of certain advanced factors of production—technological know-how,
for instance—in combination with some basic factors, which might be a pool of relatively low-cost venture capital that can be used to fund risky start-ups in industries
such as biotechnology.

■ Local Demand Conditions

Porter emphasizes the role home demand plays in providing the impetus for "upgrading" competitive advantage. Companies are typically most sensitive to the needs
of their closest customers. Hence, the characteristics of home demand are particularly important in shaping the attributes of domestically made products and in creating pressures for innovation and quality. Porter argues that a nation's companies

gain competitive advantage if their domestic consumers are sophisticated and demanding. Sophisticated and demanding consumers pressure local companies to meet high standards of product quality and to produce innovative products. Porter notes that Japan's sophisticated and knowledgeable buyers of cameras helped stimulate the Japanese camera industry to improve product quality and to introduce innovative models. A similar example can be found in the cellular phone equipment industry, where sophisticated and demanding local customers in Scandinavia helped push Nokia of Finland and Ericsson of Sweden to invest in cellular phone technology long before demand for cellular phones took off in other developed nations. As a result, Nokia and Ericsson, together with Motorola, are today dominant players in the global cellular telephone equipment industry. The case of Nokia is reviewed in more depth in Strategy in Action 3.4.

■ Competitiveness of Related and Supporting Industries

The third broad attribute of national advantage in an industry is the presence in a country of suppliers or related industries that are internationally competitive. The benefits of investments in advanced factors of production by related and supporting industries can spill over into an industry, thereby helping it achieve a strong competitive position internationally. Swedish strength in fabricated steel products (for instance, ball bearings and cutting tools) has drawn on strengths in Sweden's specialty steel industry. Technological leadership in the U.S. semiconductor industry during the period up to the mid 1980s provided the basis for U.S. success in personal computers and several other technically advanced electronic products. Similarly, Switzerland's success in pharmaceuticals is closely linked to its previous international success in the technologically related dye industry. One consequence of this process is that successful industries within a country tend to be grouped into "clusters" of related industries. Indeed, this was one of the most pervasive findings of Porter's study. One such cluster is the German textile and apparel sector, which includes high-quality cotton, wool, synthetic fibers, sewing machine needles, and a wide range of textile machinery.

■ Strategy, Structure, and Rivalry

The fourth broad attribute of national competitive advantage in Porter's model is the strategy, structure, and rivalry of companies within a nation. Porter makes two important points here. His first is that different nations are characterized by different "management ideologies," which either help them or do not help them build national competitive advantage. For example, he notes the predominance of engineers on the top-management teams of German and Japanese companies. He attributes this to the companies' emphasis on improving manufacturing processes and product design. In contrast, Porter notes a predominance of people with finance backgrounds on the top-management teams of many U.S. companies. He links this to the lack of attention paid in many U.S. companies to improving manufacturing processes and product design, particularly during the 1970s and 80s. He also argues that the dominance of finance has led to a corresponding overemphasis on maximizing short-term financial returns. According to Porter, one consequence of these different management ideologies has been a relative loss of U.S. competitiveness in

3.4   STRATEGY *in* ACTION

Finland's Nokia

T he wireless phone market is one of the great growth stories of the 1990s. Starting from a very low base in 1990, annual global sales of wireless phones surged to 163 million units in 1998, representing an increase of 51 percent over the prior year. By 2000, some 300 million people worldwide will probably be using wireless phones. Four companies currently dominate the global market for wireless handsets: Motorola, Nokia, Ericsson, and Qualcomm. In 1998, the global market leader was Nokia, which had a 23 percent share, followed by Motorola with 20 percent and Ericsson with 15 percent. In the United States, the world's largest market, Nokia's dominance was even greater. The company had a 30 percent share of the U.S. market in 1998, compared with 23 percent for Motorola (which used to dominate the market), 11 percent for Ericsson, and 10 percent for Qualcomm.

Nokia's roots are in Finland, not normally a country that jumps to mind when we talk about leading-edge technology companies. Back in the 1980s, Nokia was a rambling Finnish conglomerate whose activities embraced tire manufacturing, paper production, consumer electronics and telecommunications equipment. How has this former conglomerate emerged to take a global leadership position in wireless handsets? Much of the answer lies in the history, geography, and political economy of Finland and its Nordic neighbors.

The story starts in 1981. It was then that the Nordic nations got together to create the world's first international wireless telephone network. Sparsely populated and inhospitably cold, they had good reason to become pioneers; it cost far too much to lay down a traditional wire line telephone service. Yet the very conditions causing the difficulty made telecommunications all the more valuable there; people driving through the Arctic winter and owners of remote northern houses needed a telephone to summon help if things went wrong. As a result, Sweden, Norway, and Finland became the first nations in the world to take wireless telecommunications seriously. They found, for example, that while it cost up to $800 per subscriber to bring a traditional wire line service to remote locations in the far north, the same locations could be linked by wireless cellular for only $500 per person.

Consequently, 12 percent of people in Scandinavia owned cellular phones by 1994, compared with less than 6 percent in the United States, the world's second most developed market. This lead continued during the decade. It is estimated that by 2000 more than 50 percent of Finland's phone users will have a wireless phone, compared with 25 percent in the United States, and the figure may reach 100 percent by 2010.

Nokia, a long-time telecommunications equipment supplier, was well positioned to take advantage of this development from the start, but there were also other forces at work in Finland that helped Nokia gain a competitive edge. Unlike virtually every other developed country, Finland has never had a national telephone monopoly. Instead, telephone service has long been provided by fifty or so autonomous local telephone companies, whose elected boards set prices by referendum (which, naturally, results in low prices). This army of independent and cost-conscious telephone service providers prevented Nokia from taking anything for granted in its home country. With typical Finnish pragmatism, its customers were willing to buy from the lowest-cost supplier, whether that was Nokia, Ericsson, Motorola, or someone else. This situation contrasted sharply with that prevailing in most developed nations up until the late 1980s and early 1990s, where domestic telephone monopolies typically purchased equipment from a dominant local supplier or made it themselves. Nokia responded to this competitive pressure by doing everything possible to drive down its manufacturing costs while staying at the leading edge of wireless technology.

The consequences of these forces are clear: the once obscure Finnish firm is now a global leader in the wireless market. Moreover, Nokia has emerged as the leader in digital wireless technology, which is the wave of the future. In no small part, Nokia has the lead because Scandinavia started switching over to digital technology five years before the rest of the world. In addition, spurred on by its cost-conscious customers, Nokia now has the lowest cost structure of any wireless handset equipment manufacturer in the world, and as a result, it is a more profitable enterprise than its global competitors.[39]

those engineering-based industries where manufacturing processes and product design issues are all-important (such as automobiles).

Porter's second point is that there is a strong association between vigorous domestic rivalry and the creation and persistence of competitive advantage in an industry. Vigorous domestic rivalry induces companies to look for ways to improve efficiency, which in turn makes them better international competitors. Domestic rivalry creates pressures to innovate, to improve quality, to reduce costs, and to invest in upgrading advanced factors. All this helps create world-class competitors. As an illustration, Porter cites the case of Japan:

> Nowhere is the role of domestic rivalry more evident than in Japan, where it is all-out warfare in which many companies fail to achieve profitability. With goals that stress market share, Japanese companies engage in a continuing struggle to outdo each other. Shares fluctuate markedly. The process is prominently covered in the business press. Elaborate rankings measure which companies are most popular with university graduates. The rate of new product and process development is breathtaking.[38]

A similar point about the stimulating effects of strong domestic competition can be made with regard to the rise of Nokia of Finland to global preeminence in the market for cellular telephone equipment (see Strategy in Action 3.4).

In sum, Porter's argument is that the degree to which a nation is likely to achieve international success in a certain industry is a function of the combined impact of factor endowments, domestic demand conditions, related and supporting industries, and domestic rivalry. He argues that for this "diamond" to have a positive impact on competitive performance usually requires the presence of all four components (although there are some exceptions). Porter also contends that government can influence each of the four components of the diamond either positively or negatively. It can affect factor endowments through subsidies, policies toward capital markets, policies toward education, and the like, and it can shape domestic demand through local product standards or with regulations that mandate or influence buyer needs. Government policy can also influence supporting and related industries through regulation, and influence rivalry through such devices as capital market regulation, tax policy, and antitrust laws.

As an example of Porter's theory, consider the U.S. computer hardware industry (personal computers, workstations, minicomputers, and mainframes). The existence of a world-class industry in the United States can be explained by the presence of advanced factors of production in the form of technological know-how; an intense rivalry among myriad competing computer companies; a strong local demand for computers (more personal computers have been sold in the United States than in the rest of the world combined); and internationally competitive supporting industries, such as the computer software and microprocessor industries.

Perhaps the most important implication of Porter's framework is its message about the attractiveness of certain locations for performing certain productive activities. For instance, many Japanese computer companies have moved much of their R&D activity to the United States so that they can benefit from the international competitiveness of the United States in this industry. Most U.S. financial service companies have substantial operations in London so that they can take advantage of London's central position in the world financial services industry. And many international textile companies have design operations in Italy so that they can take advantage of Italian style and design know-how. In all these cases, companies are trying to build a competitive advantage by establishing critical productive activities in the optimal location, as defined by the various elements highlighted in Porter's framework. This is an issue we discuss in depth in Chapter 8.

SUMMARY OF CHAPTER

This chapter details a framework that managers can use to analyze the external environment of their company, enabling them to identify opportunities and threats. The following major points are made in the chapter:

✔ For a company to succeed, either its strategy must fit the environment in which the company operates, or the company must be able to reshape this environment to its advantage through its choice of strategy. Companies typically fail when their strategy no longer fits the environment in which they operate.

✔ The main technique used to analyze competition in the industry environment is the five forces model. The five forces are (1) the risk of new entry by potential competitors, (2) the extent of rivalry among established firms, (3) the bargaining power of buyers, (4) the bargaining power of suppliers, and (5) the threat of substitute products. The stronger each force, the more competitive is the industry and the lower is the rate of return that can be earned.

✔ The risk of entry by potential competitors is a function of the height of barriers to entry. The higher the barriers to entry, the lower is the risk of entry and the greater are the profits that can be earned in the industry.

✔ The extent of rivalry among established companies is a function of an industry's competitive structure, demand conditions, and barriers to exit. Strong demand conditions moderate the competition among established companies and create opportunities for expansion. When demand is weak, intensive competition can develop, particularly in consolidated industries with high exit barriers.

✔ Buyers are most powerful when a company depends on them for business, but they themselves are not dependent on the company. In such circumstances, buyers are a threat.

✔ Suppliers are most powerful when a company depends on them for business but they themselves are not dependent on the company. In such circumstances, suppliers are a threat.

✔ Substitute products are the products of companies serving consumer needs that are similar to the needs served by the industry being analyzed. The greater the similarity of the substitute products, the lower is the price that companies can charge without losing customers to the substitutes.

✔ Some argue that there is a sixth competitive force of some significance—the power, vigor and competence of complementors. Powerful and vigorous complementors may have a strong positive impact on demand in an industry.

✔ Most industries are composed of strategic groups. Strategic groups are groups of companies pursuing the same or a similar strategy. Companies in different strategic groups pursue different strategies.

✔ The members of a company's strategic group constitute its immediate competitors. Since different strategic groups are characterized by different opportunities and threats, it may pay a company to switch strategic groups. The feasibility of doing so is a function of the height of mobility barriers.

✔ The five forces and strategic group models have been criticized for presenting a static picture of competition that de-emphasizes the role of innovation. Innovation can revolutionize industry structure and completely change the strength of different competitive forces.

✔ The five forces and strategic group models have been criticized for de-emphasizing the importance of individual company differences. A company will not be profitable just because it is based in an attractive industry or strategic group; much more is required.

✔ Industries go through a well-defined life cycle, from an embryonic stage, through growth, shake-out, and maturity, and eventually into decline. Each stage has different implications for the competitive structure of the industry, and each stage gives rise to its own set of opportunities and threats.

✔ In many high-technology industries, network economics are important and positive feedback loops tend to operate. Once initiated, a positive feedback loop can lead to a rapid increase in demand. Markets where positive feedback loops operate tend to be "winner takes all" markets. Enterprises that benefit from network economics tend to be in a powerful position relative to buyers and suppliers and tend to be protected from potential competitors by entry barriers arising from switching costs

✔ A fundamental change is occurring in the world economy: the globalization of production and of markets. The consequences of this change include more intense rivalry, more rapid innovation, and shorter product life cycles.

✔ There is a link between the national environment and the competitive advantage of a company in the global economy.

DISCUSSION QUESTIONS

1. Under what environmental conditions are price wars most likely to occur in an industry? What are the implications of price wars for a company? How should a company try to deal with the threat of a price war?

2. Discuss Porter's five forces model with reference to what you know about the U.S. airline industry. What does the model tell you about the level of competition in this industry?

3. Explain what impact network effects might have on demand and industry structure in the market for wireless handsets.

4. Identify a growth industry, a mature industry, and a declining industry. For each industry, identify the following: (a) the number and size distribution of companies; (b) the nature of barriers to entry; (c) the height of barriers to entry; and (d) the extent of product differentiation. What do these factors tell you about the nature of competition in each industry? What are the implications for the company in terms of opportunities and threats?

5. Assess the impact of macroenvironmental factors on the likely level of enrollment at your university over the next decade. What are the implications of these factors for the job security and salary level of your professors?

Practicing Strategic Management

SMALL-GROUP EXERCISE
Competing with Microsoft

Break up into groups of three to five people, and discuss the following scenario:

You are a group of managers and software engineers at a small start-up. You have developed a revolutionary new operating system for personal computers. This operating system offers distinct advantages over Microsoft's Windows operating system. It takes up less memory space on the hard drive of a personal computer. It takes full advantage of the power of the personal computer's microprocessor, and in theory can run software applications much faster than Windows. It is much easier to install and use than Windows. And it responds to voice instructions with an accuracy of 99.9 percent, in addition to input from a keyboard or mouse. The operating system is the only product offering that your company has produced.

1. Analyze the competitive structure of the market for personal computer operating systems. On the basis of this analysis, identify what factors might inhibit adoption of your operating system by consumers.

2. Can you think of a strategy that your company might pursue, either alone or in conjunction with other enterprises, in order to beat Microsoft? What will it take to successfully execute that strategy?

STRATEGIC MANAGEMENT PROJECT
Module 3

This module requires you to analyze the industry environment in which your company is based. Using the information you have at your disposal, perform the following tasks and answer the questions:

1. Apply the five forces model to the industry in which your company is based. What does this model tell you about the nature of competition in the industry?

2. Are there any changes taking place in the macroenvironment that might have an impact, either positive or negative, on the industry in which your company is based? If so, what are these changes and how will they affect the industry?

3. Identify any strategic groups that might exist in the industry. How does the intensity of competition differ across the strategic groups you have identified?

4. How dynamic is the industry in which your company is based? Is there any evidence that innovation is reshaping competition or has done so in the recent past?

5. In what stage of its life cycle is the industry in which your company is based? What are the implications of this for the intensity of competition, both now and in the future?

6. Is your company based in an industry that is becoming more global? If so, what are the implications of this change for competitive intensity?

7. Analyze the impact of national context as it pertains to the industry in which your company is based. Does national context help or hinder your company in achieving a competitive advantage in the global market place?

ARTICLE FILE 3

Find an example of an industry that has become more competitive in recent years. Identify the reasons for the increase in competitive pressure.

EXPLORING THE WEB
Visiting Boeing and Airbus

Visit the Web sites of Boeing (http://www.boeing.com) and of Airbus Industrie (http://www.airbus.com). Go to the news features of both sites and read through the press releases issued by both companies. Also look at the annual reports and company profile (or history features) contained on both sites. With this material as your guide, perform the following:

1. Use Porter's five forces model to analyze the nature of competition in the global commercial jet aircraft market.

2. Assess the likely outlook for competition during the next ten years in this market. Try to establish whether new entry into this industry is likely, whether demand will grow or shrink, how powerful buyers are likely to become, and what the impli-

cations of all this may be for the nature of competition ten years from now.

General Task Search the Web for information that allows you to assess the *current* state of competition

in the market for personal computers. Use that information to perform an analysis of the structure of the market in the United States. (Hint: Try visiting the Web sites of personal computer companies. Also visit Electronic Business Today at http://www.ebtmag.com).

CLOSING CASE

Boom and Bust in the Market for DRAMs

FOR MUCH OF THE FIRST HALF OF THE 1990s, the semiconductor industry seemed like one of the most extraordinary moneymaking machines ever invented. In no case has this been more true than in the market for dynamic random access memories (DRAMs), the memory devices used in personal computers (PCs), which account for about one-third of all semiconductor sales. In 1993, the global market for DRAMs was valued at $13.6 billion. In 1994, it increased to $23.1 billion, and in 1995 it surged to $55 billion. This rapid increase in demand for DRAMs was due to the confluence of a number of favorable factors.

First, stimulated by price cutting in the PC market, worldwide sales of personal computers grew at an annual average compound rate of 30 percent over the 1990–1995 period. Second, as more and more users of PCs switched to graphics-based software, such as Microsoft's Windows 95 operating system, the memory component of PCs increased. (Running graphics programs on a PC requires a large amount of memory.) Between 1991 and 1995, the average amount of DRAM contained in each PC sold increased from 2 megabytes to 12 megabytes. Third, other applications for DRAMs—particularly in telecommunications equipment and cellular phone handsets—also grew rapidly. For example, global shipments of cellular phones increased from 5 million to 50 million between 1991 and 1995.

As demand for DRAMs was surging during the 1990–1995 period, the supply was constrained. One reason for the shortage was the reluctance of many semiconductor companies to invest in new semiconductor fabricating plants. By 1995, a new fabrication facility could cost anywhere from $1 billion to $2.5 billion and take eighteen months to construct. Such enormous fixed costs made many companies wary of investing in the plants, particularly since demand conditions could change significantly in the eighteen months required to bring the new facility on line. Managers in this industry still remember the 1985–1987 period when a combination of slowing demand and massive capacity expansions by Japanese semiconductor companies led to an excess supply of DRAMs, plunging prices, and significant financial losses for most of the world's DRAM manufacturers. Indeed, it was during this period that a number of U.S. companies exited the DRAM market, including Intel, the company that invented the DRAM.

The combination of surging global demand for DRAMs and the constrained supply caused DRAM prices to rise dramatically between 1993 and 1995. In 1993, the average selling price for DRAM was $8.89 per megabyte, in 1994 it was $11.69, and by the middle of 1995 it was $14. This situation, however, benefited Micron Technology of Boise, Idaho—one of only two U.S. firms that remained in the DRAM market after the debacle of 1985–1987 (the other was Texas Instruments). In 1990, Micron had sales of under $300 million and was barely breaking even. Riding the industry wave, by 1994 the company had revenues of $1.63 billion and net income of $400 million. In 1995, its revenues rose to $2.95 billion and the net income to $844 million. Micron's gross profit margin for 1995 was 55 percent—an almost unheard of figure for a DRAM company—compared with 23 percent in 1990. Nor was Micron alone in achieving such impressive profit performance. By 1995, almost every DRAM company in the world was making record profits.

The huge profits became a signal for incumbent companies to expand their capacity and for new companies to enter the semiconductor industry. Starting in late 1994, more and more companies announced their intentions to invest in semiconductor fabrication plants. Micron Technology, too, jumped on the capacity expansion bandwagon; in June 1995, it unveiled plans to invest $2.5 billion in a new fabrication facility in Lehi, Utah, which was scheduled to begin production at the end of 1996. When Micron made its announcement, almost 100 new semiconductor fabrication facilities were being constructed around the world, many of them scheduled to come on stream in 1995 and 1996. Moreover, by the end of 1995, plans to build another 100 facilities had been announced.

In the fall of 1995, the other shoe dropped. After four years of rapid growth, there was a sudden slowdown in the growth rate of personal computer sales, particularly in the huge North American market. This slowdown occurred just as the new DRAM capacity was becoming operational. To make matters worse, throughout 1995 manufacturers of personal computers had been building up their inventories of DRAMs, both as a hedge against future price increases and to ensure an adequate supply of DRAMs for what they thought would be a very busy Christmas season. When the expected surge in Christmas sales of PCs failed to materialize, PC manufacturers found themselves holding too much inventory. They responded by drastically cutting back on their orders for DRAMs. The result: DRAM sales volume and prices slumped. Between late 1995 and March 1996, DRAM prices fell from $14 to $7 per megabyte. The consequences included falling profit margins for DRAM companies.

Reflecting the widespread perception that excess demand and rising prices had been replaced in short order by excess supply and plunging prices, the Philadelphia Semi-Conductor Index, a measure of the share price of American semiconductor companies, fell by 45 percent between September 1995 and March 1996. In February 1996, Micron Technology responded to this situation by dramatically slowing down the construction schedule for its Lehi facility, pushing out the start date for volume manufacturing another two to five years. Nor was Micron alone. By the spring of 1996, companies around the world were also announcing that they had put their capacity expansion plans on hold.[40]

Case Discussion Questions

1. Analyze the competitive structure of the DRAM market.

2. Using this analysis, explain why the industry has been characterized by boom and bust cycles.

3. If you were a company such as Micron Technology, what strategy might you adopt to deal more effectively with the boom-and-bust nature of the industry?

End Notes

1. C. Gasparino and R. Buckman, "Horning In: Facing Internet Threat, Merrill to Offer Trading Online for Low Fee," *Wall Street Journal*, June 1, 1999, p. A1; "Bears or Bulls, More and More People Are Trading Shares Online," *Economist*, October 17, 1998; L. N. Spiro and E. C. Baig, "Who Needs a Broker?" *Business Week*, February 22, 1999, p. 113.

2. M. E. Porter, *Competitive Strategy* (New York: Free Press, 1980).

3. Charles W. L. Hill has acted as an outside consultant to Tacoma City Light and evaluated the strategy on its behalf.

4. J. E. Bain, *Barriers to New Competition* (Cambridge, Mass: Harvard University Press, 1956). For a review of the modern literature on barriers to entry, see R. J. Gilbert, "Mobility Barriers and the Value of Incumbency," in R. Schmalensee and R. D. Willig, *Handbook of Industrial Organization*, (Amsterdam: North Holland, 1989), I.

5. A detailed discussion of switching costs and lock-in can be found in C. Shapiro and H. R. Varian, *Information Rules: A Strategic Guide to the Network Economy* (Boston, Mass: Harvard Business School Press, 1999).

6. Most of this information on barriers to entry can be found in the industrial organization economics literature. See especially Bain, *Barriers to New Competition;* M. Mann, "Seller Concentration, Barriers to Entry and Rates of Return in 30 Industries," *Review of Economics and Statistics,* 48 (1966), 296-307; W. S. Comanor and T. A. Wilson, "Advertising, Market Structure and Performance," *Review of Economics and Statistics,* 49 (1967), 423-440; and Gilbert, "Mobility Barriers and The Value of Incumbency"; K. Cool, L. H. Roller, and B. Leleux, "The Relative Impact of Actual and Potential Rivalry on Firm Profitability in the Pharmaceutical Industry," *Strategic Management Journal*, 20 (1999), 1-14.

7. "Only Here for the Biru," *Economist*, May 14, 1994, pp. 69-71; T. Craig, "The Japanese Beer Industry," in C. W. L. Hill and G. R. Jones, *Strategic Management: An Integrated Approach* (Boston: Houghton Mifflin, 1995); "Japan's Beer Wars," *Economist*, February 28, 1998, p. 68; A. Harney, "Japan's Favorite Beer Could Face Losing Its Sparkle," *Financial Times*, March 24, 1999, p. 27.

8. For a discussion of tacit agreements, see T. C. Schelling, *The Strategy of Conflict* (Cambridge, Mass.: Harvard University Press, 1960).

9. R. Oram, "Washing Whiter Proves a Murky Business," *Financial Times*, December 21, 1994, p. 6.

10. P. Ghemawat, *Commitment: The Dynamics of Strategy* (Boston, Harvard Business School Press, 1991).

11. For details, see D. F Barnett, and R. W. Crandall, 1986. "*Up from the Ashes*," (Washington D.C.: Brookings Institution, 1986); and F. Koelbel, "Strategies for Restructuring the Steel Industry," *Metal Producing, 33* (December 1986), pp. 28-33.

12. D. Kirkpatrick, "Why Compaq Is Mad at Intel," *Fortune*, October 31, 1994, pp. 171-178.

13. A.S.Grove, *Only the Paranoid Survive* (New York: Doubleday, 1996).

14. In standard microeconomic theory, the concept used for assessing the strength of substitutes and complements is the cross elasticity of demand.

15. For details and further references, see C. W. L. Hill, "Establishing a Standard: Competitive Strategy and Technology Standards in Winner Take All Industries," *Academy of Management Executive*, 11, (1997), 7-25; and C. Shapiro and H. R. Varian, *Information Rules: A Strategic Guide to the Network Economy* (Boston: Harvard Business School Press, 1999).

16. See M. Gort and J. Klepper, "Time Paths in the Diffusion of Product Innovations," *Economic Journal* (September 1982), 630-653. Looking at the history of forty-six different products, Gort and Klepper found that the length of time before other companies entered the markets created by a few inventive companies declined from an average of 14.4 years for products introduced before 1930 to 4.9 years for those introduced after 1949.

17. The phrase was originally coined by J. Schumpeter, *Capitalism, Socialism and Democracy* (London: Macmillan, 1950), p. 68.

18. The development of strategic-group theory has been a strong theme in the strategy literature. Important contributions include the following: R. E. Caves and M. E. Porter, "From Entry Barriers to Mobility Barriers," *Quarterly Journal of Economics* (May 1977), 241-262; K. R. Harrigan, "An Application of Clustering for Strategic Group Analysis," *Strategic Management Journal,* 6 (1985), 55-73; K. J. Hatten and D. E. Schendel, "Heterogeneity Within an Industry: Firm Conduct in the U.S. Brewing Industry, 1952-71," *Journal of Industrial Economics,* 26 (1977), 97-113; M. E. Porter, "The Structure Within Industries and Companies' Performance," *The Review of Economics and Statistics,* 61 (1979), 214-227. For an example of more recent work, see K. Cool and D. Schendel, "Performance Differences Among Strategic Group Members," *Strategic Management Journal*, 9 (1988), 207-233; and C. S. Galbraith, G. B. Merrill, and G. Morgan, "Bilateral Strategic Groups," *Strategic Management Journal*, 15 (1994), 613-626.

19. For details on the strategic group structure in the pharmaceutical industry, see K. Cool and I. Dierickx, "Rivalry, Strategic Groups, and Firm Profitability," *Strategic Management Journal*, 14 (1993), 47-59.

20. This perspective is associated with the Austrian school of economics. The perspective goes back to Schumpeter. For a recent summary of this school and its implications for strategy, see R. Jacobson, "The Austrian School of Strategy," *Academy of Management Review*, 17 (1992), 782-807; and C. W. L. Hill and D. Deeds, "The Importance of Industry Structure for the Determination of Industry Profitability, A Neo-Austrian Approach," *Journal of Management Studies*, 33 (1996), 429-451.

21. Barnett and Crandall, *Up from the Ashes*.

22. M. E. Porter, *The Competitive Advantage of Nations* (New York, Free Press, 1990).

23. The term *punctuated equilibrium* is borrowed from evolutionary biology. For a detailed explanation of the concept see M. L. Tushman, W. H. Newman, and E. Romanelli, "Convergence and Upheaval: Managing the Unsteady Pace of Organizational Evolution," *California Management Review*, 29 (1985), 29–44; and C. J. G. Gersick, "Revolutionary Change Theories: A Multilevel Exploration of the Punctuated Equilibrium Paradigm," *Academy of Management Review*, 16: (1991), 10–36.

24. A. J. Slywotzky, *Value Migration: How To Think Several Moves Ahead of the Competition* (Boston: Harvard Business School Press, 1996).

25. R. D'Avani, *Hypercompetition* (New York: Free Press, 1994).

26. Hill and Deeds, "The Importance of Industry Structure," 429–451.

27. R. P. Rumelt, "How Much Does Industry Matter?" *Strategic Management Journal*, 12 (1991), 167–185. See also A. J. Mauri and M. P. Michaels, "Firm and Industry Effects Within Strategic Management: An Empirical Examination," *Strategic Management Journal*, 19 (1998), 211–219.

28. See R. Schmalensee, "Inter-Industry Studies of Structure and Performance," in R. Schmalensee, and R. D. Willig, *Handbook of Industrial Organization*, Vol 1 (Amsterdam: North Holland, 1989). Similar results were found by A. N. McGahan and M. E. Porter, "How Much Does Industry Matter, Really?" *Strategic Management Journal*, 18 (1997), 15–30.

29. For example, see K. Cool and D. Schendel, "Strategic Group Formation and Performance: The Case of the U.S. Pharmaceutical Industry 1932–1992," *Management Science* (September 1987), 1102–1124.

30. C. W. Hofer has argued that life cycle considerations may be the most important contingency when formulating business strategy; see C. W. Hofer, "Toward a Contingency Theory of Business Strategy," *Academy of Management Journal*, 18 (1975), 784–810. There is also empirical evidence to support this view. See C. R. Anderson and C. P. Zeithaml, "Stages of the Product Life Cycle, Business Strategy, and Business Performance," *Academy of Management Journal*, 27 (1984), 5–24; and D. C. Hambrick and D. Lei, "Towards an Empirical Prioritization of Contingency Variables for Business Strategy," *Academy of Management Journal*, 28 (1985), 763–788. Also see G. Miles, C. C. Snow, and M. P. Sharfman, "Industry Variety and Performance," *Strategic Management Journal*, 14 (1993), 163–177.

31. The characteristics of declining industries have been summarized by K. R. Harrigan, "Strategy Formulation in Declining Industries," *Academy of Management Review*, 5 (1980), 599–604.

32. For details, see C. W. L. Hill, "Establishing a Standard," 7–25; Shapiro and Varian, *Information Rules*; B. Arthur, "Increasing Returns and the New World of Business," *Harvard Business Review* (July–August 1996), 100–109.

33. P. C. Judge and A. Reinhardt, "Why the Fastest Chip Didn't Win," *Business Week*, April 28, 1997, pp. 92–96.

34. P. Dicken, *Global Shift* (New York: Guilford Press, 1992).

35. I. Metthee, "Playing a Large Part," *Seattle-Post Intelligence*, April 9, 1994, p. 13.

36. T. Levitt, "The Globalization of Markets," *Harvard Business Review* (May–June 1983), 92–102.

37. M. E. Porter, *The Competitive Advantage of Nations* (New York: Free Press, 1990). See also R. Grant, "Porter's Competitive Advantage of Nations: An Assessment," *Strategic Management Journal*, 7 (1991), 535–548.

38. Porter, *The Competitive Advantage of Nations*, p. 121.

39. "Lessons from the Frozen North," *Economist*, October 8, 1994, pp. 76–77; G. Edmondson, "Grabbing Markets from the Giants," *Business Week*, Special Issue: 21st Century Capitalism, 1995, p. 156; Q. Hardy, "Bypassing the Bells—A Wireless World," *Wall Street Journal*, September 21, 1998, p. R16; Q. Hardy and G. Naik, "Nokia Takes the Lead as Wireless Makers Sell 162.9 Million Phones in 1998," *Wall Street Journal*, February 8, 1999, p. A1.

40. The World Wide Web page for Micron Technology (http://www.micron.com); "When the Chips Are Down," *Economist*, March 23, 1996, pp. 19–21; L. Kehoe, "U.S. Chip Makers Seek to Dispel the Gloom," *Financial Times*, April 20, 1996, p. 20; "Remind Me How to Make Money," *Economist*, August 26, 1995, pp. 55–56; Standard & Poor's Industry Surveys, *Electronics*, August 3, 1995.

4

Internal Analysis: Resources, Capabilities, Competencies, and Competitive Advantage

OPENING CASE STUDY

Cisco Systems

CISCO SYSTEMS is one of the great success stories of recent years. Two Stanford University computer scientists, Leonard Bosack and Sandra Lerner, founded the company in 1984. In the early 1980s, Stanford University had accumulated many separate computer networks—each using different machines and different electronic languages to communicate among themselves. The problem was that these networks could not talk to each other. Bosack and Lerner, who were married at the time, were the managers of separate networks. They worked on the problem of hooking these networks together, partly, so legend has it, in order to be able to send each other E-mail messages. Their solution was a specialized computer known as a router, which was able to connect different computer systems. Realizing that this device might have commercial value, they established Cisco and

shipped their first product in 1987. The company went public in 1990, with annual sales of around $70 million. Soon afterward, Cisco's sales started to increase exponentially as routers became a critical component of the rapidly expanding Internet. By 2000, Cisco had evolved into the dominant supplier of network equipment for the Internet—including routers, switches, and hubs—with annual sales in excess of $14 billion, no debt, a return on equity of around 24 percent and a return on assets of around 20 percent.

Cisco's rapid sales growth and high profitability owe much to its product innovation, which has continued at a fast pace since the company went public, but they are also due to the company's aggressive adoption of an e-business infrastructure. Here, too, Cisco has been an innovator. This infrastructure has enabled the company to reap major efficiency gains, while providing its customers with superior point-of-sales service and after-sales service and support. Cisco was one of the first companies to move much of its sales effort onto the Internet. The process began in 1996, when Cisco realized that its traditional sales infrastructure could not keep up with increasing demand. Rather than hire additional personnel to manage customer accounts, the company began to experiment with on-line sales. It developed a computer program to walk customers through the process of ordering equipment on-line. A critical feature of this program helps customers order exactly the right mix of equipment, thereby avoiding any ordering mistakes, such as the ordering of incompatible equipment. In 1997, the company sold $500 million worth of equipment on-line. By 1999, this figure had ballooned to $10 billion, or 80 percent of Cisco's total sales, making the company one of the most aggressive adopters of an on-line sales approach in the world.

Customers seem to love the automated order processing system, primarily because it minimizes ordering mistakes and allows quicker execution of orders. For example, at Sprint, which is a major customer, it used to take sixty days from the signing of a contract to complete a networking project. Now it takes thirty-five to forty-five

days, primarily because of the efficiency of Cisco's on-line ordering system. Moreover, Sprint has been able to cut its order-processing staff from 21 to 6, significantly saving costs. As for Cisco, the company has just 300 service agents handling all of its customer accounts, compared with the 900 it would need if sales were not handled on-line. The difference represents an annual saving of $20 million.

Cisco has also placed its customer support functions on-line. All routine customer service functions are now handled on-line by a computer program that can translate a customer's fuzzy inquiry into a standard description of a familiar problem; then it provides the four most likely explanations on screen, so that the customer might avoid blind alleys and not waste time. Since the company implemented the system in 1996, its sales have quadrupled, while its engineering support staff has merely doubled to 800. Without automated sales support, Cisco calculates that it would need at least 1,000 additional service engineers, which would cost around $75 million. Cisco has also moved to distributing all support software over the Internet, rather than transferring it to disks and mailing it to customers. This has saved Cisco another $250 million per year in annual operating costs.[1]

OVERVIEW

In Chapter 3, we discuss the elements of the external environment that determine an industry's attractiveness, and we examine how industry structure explains why some industries are more profitable than others. However, industry structure is not the only force that affects company profits. Within any given industry some companies are more profitable than others. For example, in the global auto industry, Toyota has consistently outperformed General Motors for most of the last twenty years. In the steel industry, Nucor has consistently outperformed U.S. Steel. In the U.S. retail clothing industry, The Gap has consistently outperformed JC Penney's, while in the Internet network equipment market, Cisco Systems has consistently outperformed competitors such as Bay Networks and 3Com. The question, therefore, is why within a particular industry do some companies outperform others? What is the basis of their competitive advantage?

Cisco provides some clues as to the sources of **competitive advantage**, that is, a company's ability to outperform its competitors. In the Opening Case, we saw how Cisco's competitive advantage stems partly from product innovation—after all, the company invented the router, one of the key pieces of equipment required to make the Internet work. Moreover, although the Opening Case does not dwell on this fact, Cisco has continued to remain at the leading edge of product innovation in the market for networking equipment. But there is more to Cisco's success than its excellent track record with regard to product innovation. As explained in the Opening Case, Cisco's aggressive approach to moving sales and customer service on-line has yielded huge dividends in terms of efficiency gains and customer satisfaction. Put differently, Cisco's process innovations in the area of on-line sales and customer service have also had a positive impact on its competitive advantage.

As you will see in this chapter, *innovation*, *efficiency*, and *customer responsiveness* can be regarded as three of the main building blocks of competitive advantage. *Quality* is a fourth building block. Cisco has a competitive advantage because it has skills in product and process innovation, because it is efficient, and because its on-line, or e-business, infrastructure has made it more responsive to customer needs. It would also not be surprising to find that Cisco's product quality is excellent. It is not surprising, then, that Cisco has become one of the great success stories of recent years.

In this chapter and the next, we look inside an organization at the strengths and weaknesses that determine its efficiency, innovative capability, product quality, and customer responsiveness. We explore how the strengths of an organization are grounded in its resources, capabilities, and competencies, and we discuss how these help a company attain a competitive advantage based on superior efficiency, innovation, quality, and customer responsiveness. We also discuss three critical questions. First, once it is obtained, what factors influence the durability of competitive advantage? Second, why do successful companies lose their competitive advantage? Third, how can companies avoid competitive failure and sustain their competitive advantage over time? When you have finished this chapter, you will have a good understanding of the nature of competitive advantage. This understanding will help you make better strategic decisions as a manager.

COMPETITIVE ADVANTAGE: VALUE CREATION, LOW COST, AND DIFFERENTIATION

We say that a company has a *competitive advantage* when its profit rate is higher than the average for its industry, and that it has a *sustained competitive advantage* when it is able to maintain this high profit rate over a number of years. In the U. S. department store industry, for example, Wal-Mart has had a sustained competitive advantage that has persisted for decades. This has been translated into a high profit rate (for details, see Strategy in Action 4.1). Two basic conditions determine a company's profit rate and hence whether it has a competitive advantage: the amount of value customers place on the company's goods or services, and the company's costs of production. In general, the more value customers place on a company's products, the higher the price the company can charge for those products. Note, however, that the price a company charges for a good or service is typically less than the value placed on that good or service by the customer because the customer captures some of that value in the form of what economists call a consumer surplus.[2] The customer gains this surplus because the company is competing with other companies for the customer's business, and so must charge a lower price than it

Competitive Advantage in the U.S. Department Store Industry

Figure 4.1 graphs the return on capital employed (ROK) earned by four companies active in the U.S. department stores industry between 1989 and 1998.[3] Their profitability is compared with the average profitability for the entire U.S. department store sector over the same time period. Figure 4.1 clearly illustrates that Wal-Mart and to a lesser degree, Nordstrom, had a sustained competitive advantage over the entire period. In contrast, the Hudson Bay company and Kmart were at a sustained competitive disadvantage most of the period. Among other things, the competitive advantage of Wal-Mart has been based on efficient logistics, high employee productivity, and excellent customer service. Moreover, Wal-Mart has led the industry in its *innovative* use of advanced information systems to manage everything, from its inventory and product mix to its pricing strategy. This process innovation has enabled Wal-Mart to reap substantial operating efficiencies while allowing the company to respond to differences in consumer demand across stores. Put differently, Wal-Mart excels on at least three of the building blocks of competitive advantage: innovation, efficiency, and customer responsiveness. Thus, it is not surprising that the company has consistently outperformed its peers.

Nordstrom too, has consistently outperformed its peers. This company's competitive advantage stems from the combination of a high-quality product offering linked with excellence in customer service, which has enabled the company to build a sustained competitive advantage on the basis of *quality* and *customer responsiveness*. In particular, Nordstrom is legendary for the attention that its salespeople devote to individual customers. For example, they will devote considerable time to assist "fashion-challenged" men to pick a stylish and matching combination of suit, shirts, shoes, and tie from the selection in a store. This differentiating factor has enabled Nordstrom to charge a high price for the products it sells.

In contrast, Kmart and Hudson Bay have been unable to build a strong competitive advantage, and both have underperformed the industry for years. Although Kmart has focused on the same discount niche that Wal-Mart has dominated, it lacks Wal-Mart's efficient operations and has a higher cost structure. Moreover, Kmart has generally followed Wal-Mart's lead in the adoption of information technology. Kmart has not been an innovator. As for Hudson Bay, this full-service department store chain has failed to build a significant differentiating feature that might enable it to mimic Nordstrom and charge a higher price for delivering excellent customer service. Indeed, both the product mix and customer service offered by Hudson Bay have left much to be desired, while operating margins have been further squeezed by operating inefficiencies and a high cost structure.

FIGURE 4.1

Return on Capital Employed for Selected U.S. Department Stores, 1989–1998

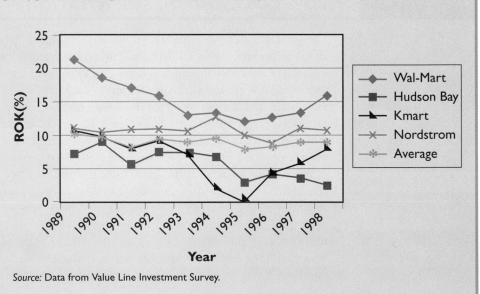

Source: Data from Value Line Investment Survey.

could as a monopoly supplier. Moreover, it is normally impossible to segment the market to such a degree that the company can charge each customer a price that reflects that individual's assessment of the value of a product—which economists refer to as a customer's reservation price. For these reasons, the price that gets charged tends to be less than the value placed on the product by many customers.

These concepts are illustrated in Figure 4.2. There you can see that the value of a product to a consumer may be V, the price that the company can charge for that product given competitive pressures may be P, and the costs of producing that product are C. The company's profit margin is equal to $P-C$, while the consumer surplus is equal to $V-P$. The company makes a profit so long as $P>C$, and its profit rate will be greater the lower C is *relative* to P. Bear in mind that the difference between V and P is in part determined by the intensity of competitive pressure in the marketplace. The lower the intensity of competitive pressure, the higher the price that can be charged relative to V.[4]

Note also that the value created by a company is measured by the difference between V and C ($V-C$). A company creates value by converting inputs that cost C into a product on which consumers place a value of V. A company can create more value for its customers either by lowering C, or by making the product more attractive through superior design, functionality, quality, and the like, so that consumers place a greater value on it (V increases) and, consequently, are willing to pay a high price (P increases). This discussion suggests that a company has high profits, and thus a competitive advantage, when it creates more value for its customers than do rivals. Put differently, *the concept of value creation lies at the heart of competitive advantage.*[5]

For a more concrete example, consider the case of the personal computer industry. In the mid 1990s, Compaq Computer was selling its top-of-the-line personal computers for about $2,600 each ($P$), while all of the costs associated with producing these computers (C)—including material costs, administrative costs, manufacturing costs, marketing costs, R&D costs, and capital costs—amounted to $2,300 per computer, giving Compaq a net profit margin (net of all costs) of $300 per computer. In contrast, one of its competitors, AST, was able to charge only $2,300 for its equivalent personal computer, while the cost of producing these machines was $2,400, giving AST a net loss of $100 per computer.

This comparison shows how a company's profit rate is jointly determined by the price it can charge for its products and by its cost structure. Compaq made

FIGURE 4.2

Value Creation

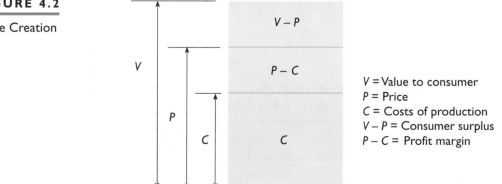

more profit per computer than AST in the mid 1990s because it could charge a higher price for its machines *and* because it had a lower cost structure. Compaq's lower cost structure came primarily from manufacturing efficiencies that AST lacked. As for its higher price, Compaq could command a higher price for its computers because consumers placed a higher value on a Compaq machine than on an AST machine, and therefore they were willing to pay more for a Compaq computer. Why did consumers place more value on Compaq machines? Primarily because they perceived Compaq products to be of a superior quality, functionality, and design relative to AST products. Put differently, Compaq had succeeded in differentiating its computers from those of AST (and various other producers) in the eyes of consumers. Thus, Compaq's competitive advantage in the mid 1990s came from a combination of low costs and differentiation. As a consequence of its superior cost and differentiation position, Compaq created more value for consumers than AST ($V - C$ was greater for Compaq than for AST). So one could say that Compaq's competitive advantage over AST was based on superior value creation.

We should note that superior value creation does not necessarily require a company to have the lowest cost structure in an industry or to create the most valuable product in the eyes of consumers, but it does require that the gap between perceived value (V) and costs of production (C) be greater than the gap attained by competitors. For example, as described in Strategy in Action 4.1, Nordstrom has had a sustained competitive advantage in the American department store industry. Although Nordstrom has a higher cost structure than many of its competitors, it was able to create more value because it successfully differentiated its service offering in the eyes of consumers so that consumers assigned a higher V to products purchased at Nordstrom. This perception of superior value was based on Nordstrom's obsession with customer service. It allowed Nordstrom to charge a higher price (P) for the products it sold than many competing full-service department stores. The higher price translated into a greater profit margin ($P - C$) for Nordstrom, as shown in Figure 4.1.

Michael Porter has argued that *low cost* and *differentiation* are two basic strategies for creating value and attaining a competitive advantage in an industry.[6] According to Porter, competitive advantage (along with higher profits) goes to those companies that can create superior value, and the way to create superior value is to drive down the cost structure of the business and/or differentiate the product in some way so that consumers value it more and are prepared to pay a premium price. But how can a company drive down its cost structure and differentiate its product offering from that of competitors so that it can create superior value? We tackle this question in both this chapter and the next one. In Chapter 6, we shall return to Porter's notions of low cost and differentiation strategies, when we examine his idea in more depth.

THE GENERIC BUILDING BLOCKS OF COMPETITIVE ADVANTAGE

As we have seen, four factors build competitive advantage: efficiency, quality, innovation, and customer responsiveness. They are the generic building blocks of competitive advantage that any company can adopt, regardless of its industry or the products

FIGURE 4.3

Generic Building Blocks
of Competitive
Advantage

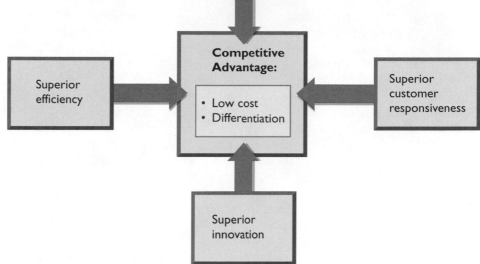

or services it produces (Figure 4.3). Although we discuss them separately below, they
are highly interrelated. For example, superior quality can lead to superior efficiency,
while innovation can enhance efficiency, quality, and customer responsiveness.

■ Efficiency

In one sense, a business is simply a device for transforming inputs into outputs. Inputs are basic factors of production such as labor, land, capital, management, and
technological know-how. Outputs are the goods and services that the business produces. The simplest measure of efficiency is the quantity of inputs that it takes to
produce a given output; that is, Efficiency = outputs/inputs. The more efficient a
company, the fewer the inputs required to produce a given output. For example, if it
takes General Motors thirty hours of employee time to assemble a car and it takes
Ford twenty-five hours, we can say that Ford is more efficient than GM. Moreover, so
long as other things are equal, such as wage rates, we can assume from these data
that Ford will have a lower cost structure than GM. Thus, efficiency helps a company attain a low-cost competitive advantage. In the Opening Case, you saw how
Cisco attained superior efficiency by pioneering the migration of sales and customer service functions to an on-line delivery model.

The most important component of efficiency for many companies is employee
productivity, which is usually measured by output per employee. Holding all else
constant, the company with the highest employee productivity in an industry will
typically have the lowest costs of production. In other words, that company will
have a cost-based competitive advantage. Strategy in Action 4.2 looks at the level of
employee productivity attained by volume manufacturers of automobiles based in

Productivity in the Automobile Industry

Every year since 1980, Harbor Associates, a consulting company founded by former Chrysler executive James Harbor, has issued a report on the level of productivity in assembly plants of U.S.-based volume manufacturers of automobiles. Until 1993, the report focused on just the big three U.S. companies, General Motors, Ford, and Chrysler (now DaimlerChrysler), but now it also includes data on the U.S.-based assembly operations of Nissan and Toyota, both of which have a significant manufacturing presence in this country. The following table shows the number of hours of labor it took to assemble a vehicle at each of these companies from 1988 to 1998. On this measure, Nissan and Toyota are the most efficient volume producers in the United States, whereas Ford is close behind, and General Motors is the least efficient.

The higher labor productivity of Nissan, Toyota, and Ford is attributed to their lean production systems, which are based on a large number of productivity-enhancing management techniques. For example, all three companies make extensive use of self-managing work teams. Each team is given the responsibility for performing a major assembly task, and the teams are also set challenging productivity and quality goals. At the same time, the teams are empowered to find ways to improve their productivity and quality control and are rewarded through the use of incentive pay if they exceed their productivity or quality goals. While GM and DaimlerChrysler have also tried to introduce self-managing teams into the workplace, diffusion of the technique has been held back by a long history of adversarial labor relations at these companies, which has made it difficult for management and labor to cooperate to introduce new concepts.

However, DaimlerChrysler in particular claims that the data given above present an incomplete picture of productivity, primarily because it ignores that company's low product-development costs. According to DaimlerChrysler, these are a source of superior productivity not recognized in the Harbor Report. Until the early 1990s, it took DaimlerChrysler at least four years and 1,400 design engineers to design a new car, or 5,600 engineer years. The Chrysler Neon, however, was designed in just thirty-three months and required only 740 design engineers, which translates into 2,035 engineer years, a more than 50 percent improvement in productivity and a saving in design costs of $45 million. DaimlerChrysler estimates

the United States. These data suggest that in their assembly operations Japanese manufactures still enjoy a productivity-based competitive advantage relative to their U.S. counterparts but that the gap has closed significantly since the late 1980s. Moreover, it would seem that DaimlerChrysler in particular has realized huge productivity gains in its product design process, which, when added to its assembly process, may make the company the most efficient volume manufacturer in the United States.

The interesting issue, of course, is how to achieve superior productivity. Later chapters examine in detail how a company can achieve high productivity (and quality, innovation, and customer responsiveness). For now, we just note that to achieve high productivity a company must adopt the appropriate strategy, structure, and control systems.

■ Quality

Quality products are goods and services that are reliable in the sense that they do the job they were designed for and do it well. This concept applies whether we are talking about a Toyota automobile, clothes designed and sold by The Gap, the cus-

that the design for its next major car project can be completed in two years by just 540 design engineers. James Harbor, the author of the Harbor Report, agrees that DaimlerChrysler's superior design capabilities are an important source of superior productivity. In his 1995 report, he concluded that when design costs are added to assembly costs, Chrysler emerged as the most productive automobile company in the United States.

How has DaimlerChrysler done this? Primarily by forming teams of design engineers, component suppliers, manufacturing personnel, and marketing staff to oversee the design process. These teams make sure that there is very tight integration in the design process among suppliers, engineering, manufacturing, and marketing. Cars are now designed for ease of manufacturing, and with input up front from marketing, while suppliers are brought into the process early on to ensure that their design for component parts interfaces well with Chrysler's design for the finished car. As a result, the amount of redesign work required has been dramatically reduced, and the design cycle time of four to six years has been decreased to under three years.[7]

Hours of labor required to assemble a vehicle

Company	1988	1994	1998
General Motors	39.02	30.26	30.32
DaimlerChrysler	36.64	27.8	32.15
Ford	26.0	25.0	22.85
Toyota	Not Available	19.30	21.20
Nissan	Not Available	18.3	17.07

tomer service department of Citibank, or the ability of an airline to have its planes arrive on time. The impact of high product quality on competitive advantage is twofold.[8] First, providing high-quality products increases the value of those products in the eyes of consumers. In turn, this enhanced perception of value allows the company to charge a higher price for its products. In the automobile industry, for example, companies such as Toyota not only have had a productivity-based cost advantage, but they have also been able to charge a higher price for their cars because of the higher quality of their products. Thus, compared with a company like General Motors, Toyota has had both lower costs and the ability to charge higher prices. As a result, historically Toyota has operated with a bigger profit margin than GM.

The second impact of high quality on competitive advantage comes from the greater efficiency and the lower unit costs it brings. Less employee time is wasted making defective products or providing substandard services and less time has to be spent fixing mistakes, which translates into higher employee productivity and lower unit costs. Thus, high product quality not only lets a company charge higher prices for its product, but also lowers costs (see Figure 4.4).

The importance of quality in building competitive advantage has increased dramatically during the last decade. Indeed, so crucial is the emphasis placed on quality

FIGURE 4.4

The Impact of Quality on Profits

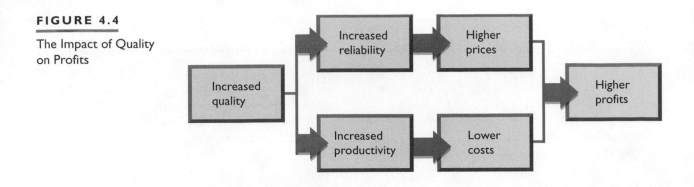

by many companies that achieving high product quality can no longer be viewed as just one way of gaining a competitive advantage. In many industries, it has become an absolute imperative for survival. Strategy in Action 4.3, which discusses the turnaround of Continental Airlines, illustrates the importance of quality in a service environment.

■ Innovation

Innovation can be defined as anything new or novel about the way a company operates or the products it produces. Innovation includes advances in the kinds of products, production processes, management systems, organizational structures, and strategies developed by a company. All of the following can be viewed as *innovations*: Intel's development of the microprocessor; the discounting strategy of Toys 'R' Us in the retail toy business; Toyota's lean production system for manufacturing automobiles; Cisco's development of the router and pioneering approach to on-line selling and customer service; and Wal-Mart's pioneering efforts to use information systems to manage its logistics, product mix, and product pricing. Successful innovation is about developing new products and/or managing the enterprise in a novel way that creates value for consumers.[10]

Innovation is perhaps the single most important building block of competitive advantage. In the long run, competition can be viewed as a process driven by innovation. Although not all innovations succeed, those that do can be a major source of competitive advantage because, by definition, they give a company something **unique**—something its competitors lack (until they imitate the innovation). Uniqueness lets a company differentiate itself from its rivals and charge a premium price for its product, or reduce its unit costs far below those of competitors.

As with efficiency and quality, we explore the issue of innovation more fully later in the book. A few examples can highlight the importance of innovation as the bedrock of competitive advantage. Consider Xerox's development of the photocopier, Cisco's development of the router, Intel's development of new microprocessors, Hewlett-Packard's development of the laser printer, Nike's development of high-tech athletic shoes, Bausch & Lomb's development of contact lenses, or Sony's development of the Walkman. All these product innovations helped build a competitive advantage for the pioneering companies. In each case, the company, by virtue of being the sole supplier of a new product, could charge a premium price. By the time competitors succeeded in imitating the innovator, the innovating com-

4.3 STRATEGY *in* ACTION

Continental Airlines Goes from Worst to First

When Gordon Bethune left Boeing to become the CEO of Continental Airlines in 1994, the company was the worst performing and least profitable of all major U.S. airlines. One of the main problems was the lack of reliability. In 1994, Continental planes arrived on time only 61 percent of the time, placing the company dead last in the influential Air Customer Satisfaction Study, produced by J.D. Power & Associates. To make matters worse, airline travelers ranked on-time performance as the most important factor when deciding which airline to fly on. Reliability was the primary metric passengers used to determine an airline's quality.

Bethune soon came to the conclusion that the prior management had cut costs so far that the service had suffered. In his words, "our service was lousy and nobody knew when a plane might land. We were unpredictable and unreliable, and when you are an airline, where does that leave you? It leaves you with a lot of empty planes. We had a lousy product, and nobody particularly wanted to buy it." Bethune's solution: he told Continental employees that if the airline's on-time performance improved, every employee would receive a $65 bonus. The total cost to the airline was $2.6 million. Bethune was proposing to improve performance by spending more money. It worked. When the program was launched in January 1995, 71 percent of the planes landed on time. By year-end, the figure was up to 80 percent, and Continental had risen to fifth in its on-time performance. For 1996, Bethune announced that the airline had to finish third or higher for employees to get the bonus, which he increased to $100. The airline finished second. It has not dropped out of the top three since then.

To support the drive toward greater reliability, Bethune also reorganized the way employees were managed. Out went the employee manual, to be replaced by a new set of guidelines, which gave front-line employees significant decision-making power to fix customer problems. For example, if a flight is canceled, a customer service agent might have to decide which passengers should receive priority to get on the next flight. Under the old system, the employee would have had to refer to the rule book, and if that did not provide an answer, ask a higher-level manager. This inflexible approach led to significant frustration among both passengers and employees. The new system allows customer service agents to fix problems as they see fit. According to Bethune, concentrating decision-making power in the hands of employees gave them the ability to solve customer problems in creative ways, which has had a dramatic impact on customers' perception of the quality of service they get at Continental.[9]

pany had built up such strong brand loyalty and supporting management processes that its position proved difficult for imitators to attack. Sony is still known for its Walkman, Hewlett-Packard for its laser printers, and Intel for its microprocessors.

■ Customer Responsiveness

To achieve superior customer responsiveness, a company must be able to do a better job than competitors of identifying and satisfying the needs of its customers. Consumers will then place more value on its products, creating a differentiation-based competitive advantage. Improving the quality of a company's product offering is consistent with achieving responsiveness, as is developing new products with features that existing products lack. In other words, achieving superior quality and innovation are an integral part of achieving superior customer responsiveness.

Another factor that stands out in any discussion of customer responsiveness is the need to customize goods and services to the unique demands of individual customers or customer groups. For example, the proliferation of different types of soft drinks and beers in recent years can be viewed partly as a response to this trend. Automobile companies, too, have become more adept at customizing cars to the demands of individual customers. For instance, following the lead of Toyota, the Saturn division of General Motors builds cars to order for individual customers, letting them choose from a wide range of colors and options.

An aspect of customer responsiveness that has drawn increasing attention is **customer response time,** which is the time that it takes for a good to be delivered or a service to be performed.[11] For a manufacturer of machinery, response time is the time it takes to fill customer orders. For a bank, it is the time it takes to process a loan or the time that a customer must stand in line to wait for a free teller. For a supermarket, it is the time that customers must stand in checkout lines. Customer survey after customer survey has shown slow response time to be a major source of customer dissatisfaction.[12]

Besides quality, customization, and response time, other sources of enhanced customer responsiveness are superior design, superior service, and superior after-sales service and support. All these factors enhance customer responsiveness and allow a company to differentiate itself from its less responsive competitors. In turn, differentiation enables a company to build brand loyalty and to charge a premium price for its products. For example, consider how much more people are prepared to pay for next-day delivery of Express Mail, as opposed to delivery in three to four days. In 1996, a two-page letter sent by overnight Express Mail within the United States cost about $10, compared with 32 cents for regular mail. Thus, the price premium for express delivery (reduced response time) was $9.68, or a premium of 3,025 percent over the regular price.

■ Summary

Efficiency, quality, customer responsiveness, and innovation are all important elements in obtaining a competitive advantage. Superior efficiency enables a company to lower its costs; superior quality lets it both charge a higher price and lower its costs; superior customer responsiveness allows it to charge a higher price; and superior innovation can lead to higher prices or lower unit costs (Figure 4.5). Together, these four factors help a company create more value by lowering costs or differentiating its products from those of competitors, which enables the company to outperform its competitors.

BUSINESS FUNCTIONS, THE VALUE CHAIN, AND VALUE CREATION

In this section, we consider the role played by the different functions of a company—such as production, marketing, R&D, service, information systems, materials management, and human resources—in the value creation process. Specifically, we briefly review how the different functions of a company can help in the process of driving down costs and increasing the perception of value through differentiation. As a first step, consider the concept of the value chain, which is illustrated in Figure

FIGURE 4.5

The Impact of Effi-
ciency, Quality, Cus-
tomer Responsiveness,
and Innovation on Unit
Costs and Prices

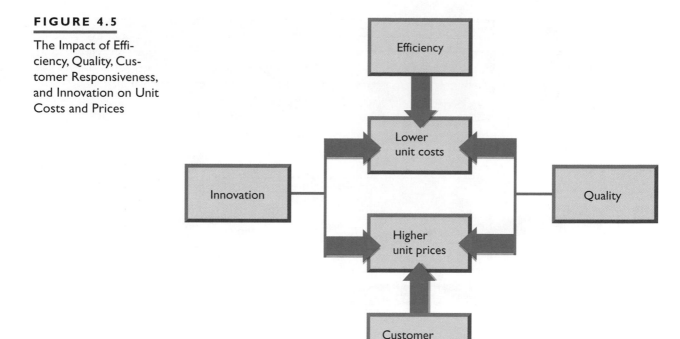

4.6. [13] The term ***value chain*** refers to the idea that a company is a chain of activities for transforming inputs into outputs that customers value. The process of transforming inputs into outputs comprises a number of primary and support activities.
Each activity adds value to the product.

■ Primary Activities

Primary activities have to do with the design, creation, and delivery of the product,
as well as its marketing and its support and after-sales service. In the value chain illustrated in Figure 4.6, the primary activities are broken down into four functions:
research and development, production, marketing and sales, and service.

   Research and development (R&D) is concerned with the design of products
and production processes. Although we think of R&D as being associated with the
design of physical products and production processes in manufacturing enterprises, many service companies also undertake R&D. For example, banks compete
with each other by developing new financial products and new ways of delivering
those products to customers. On-line banking and smart debit cards are two recent
examples of the fruits of new product development in the banking industry. Earlier
examples of innovation in the banking industry included ATM machines, credit
cards, and debit cards.

   By superior product design, R&D can increase the functionality of products,
which makes them more attractive to consumers. Alternatively, the work of R&D
may result in more efficient production processes, thereby lowering production

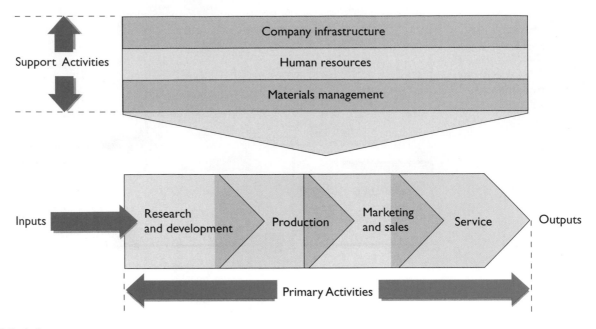

FIGURE 4.6

The Value Chain

costs. Either way, the R&D function of an enterprise can create value. At Intel, for example, R&D creates value both by developing ever more powerful microprocessors, and by helping to pioneer ever more efficient manufacturing processes (in conjunction with equipment suppliers).

Production is concerned with the creation of a good or service. For physical products, when we talk about production we generally mean manufacturing. For services such as banking or retail operations, production typically takes place when the service is actually delivered to the customer (for example, when a bank originates a loan for a customer, it is engaged in production of the loan). The production function of a company creates value by performing its activities efficiently so that lower costs result. Thus, as suggested by the data contained in Strategy in Action 4.2, the efficient production operations of Nissan, Ford, and Toyota are helping those automobile companies to create more value relative to competitors such as General Motors. Production can also create value by performing its activities in a way that is consistent with high product quality, which leads to differentiation and lower costs—both of which increase the value created by a company.

There are several ways in which the **marketing and sales** functions of a company can help create value. Through brand positioning and advertising, the marketing function can increase the value that consumers perceive to be contained in a company's product. Insofar as these activities help create a favorable impression of the company's product in the minds of consumers, they increase value. For example, in the 1980s the French company Perrier did a wonderful job of persuading U.S. consumers that slightly carbonated bottled water was worth $1.50 per bottle, rather than a price closer to the 50 cents that it cost to physically collect, bottle, and distribute the water. Perrier's marketing function increased the value that consumers ascribed to the product.

Marketing and sales can also create value by discovering consumer needs and communicating them back to the R&D function of the company, which can then design products that better match those needs. For another example of value creation by the marketing function of an enterprise, see Strategy in Action 4.4, which examines how the sales force of Pfizer increased the perception of the value associated with one of that company's main pharmaceuticals, Zoloft.

The role of the **service** function of an enterprise is to provide after-sales service and support. This function can create a perception of superior value in the minds of consumers by solving customer problems and supporting customers after they have purchased the product. For example, Caterpillar, the U.S.-based manufacturer

---

4.4   **STRATEGY** *in* **ACTION**

Value Creation at Pfizer

The antidepressant drug Prozac, introduced by Eli Lilly in 1988, has been one of the most lucrative mental health drugs in history. In 1995, U.S. consumers alone filled almost 19 million prescriptions for Prozac, hoping to mitigate the effects of a wide range of mental disorders including chronic depression, bulimia, and obsessive disorders. Worldwide sales of the drug topped $2 billion in 1995, making it a gold mine for Lilly.

But Prozac's market position is now under attack from an aggressive marketing and sales campaign by rival pharmaceutical company Pfizer. In 1992, Pfizer introduced its own antidepressant, Zoloft. According to medical experts, the differences between Prozac and Zoloft are slight at best. Both drugs function in the same basic manner, by boosting serotonin, a brain chemical believed to be in short supply in many depressed people. Both drugs also have a similar list of possible side effects: Prozac's label mentions nausea, nervousness, anxiety, insomnia, and drowsiness, and Zoloft's lists nausea and other stomach problems, diarrhea, sexual dysfunction, and sleepiness. As one expert noted, "these drugs are so similar that you have to be kidding yourself if you think one drug is going to be consistently superior to the other in treating patients."

Despite the similarity between the two products, however, Pfizer has been gaining share from Lilly in the antidepressant market. By 1998, Zoloft accounted for 40 percent of the market, up from little more than zero in 1992. The main reason for the success of Zoloft seems to be an aggressive marketing and sales campaign by Pfizer, which has given physicians the impression that Zoloft is a safer drug. Pfizer salespeople bill their product as a kind of Prozac Lite: just as effective but without Prozac's occasional downside, anxiety. The reference to anxiety seems carefully designed to remind doctors of a spate of failed lawsuits alleging that Prozac caused suicides and violent acts. Pfizer's sales force has also logged more "face time" with physicians than Lilly's. According to Scott-Levin and Associates, in 1995 Zoloft sales representatives made 660,000 sales visits to doctors—70,000 more than the Prozac sales force logged. About three-quarters of the visits by Zoloft representatives were not to psychiatrists but to primary care physicians, who increasingly prescribe antidepressants but presumably are less familiar with their more subtle properties. Doctors also claim that Pfizer salespeople play up Prozac's clinical reputation that it is more agitating than Zoloft. They also emphasize that unlike Zoloft, Prozac remains in the bloodstream for weeks after a patient stops taking it, raising the possibility of adverse drug interaction if a patient switches to other medications.

The important point here is that Pfizer's marketing and sales force is altering physicians' perceptions of the relative value of Prozac and Zoloft. For Pfizer, the payoff has come in terms of rapidly increasing revenues and market share and, of course, a greater return on the company's investment in developing Zoloft.[14]

of heavy earthmoving equipment, can get spare parts to any point in the world within twenty-four hours, thereby minimizing the amount of downtime its customers have to suffer if their Caterpillar equipment malfunctions. This is an extremely valuable support capability in an industry where downtime is very expensive. It has helped to increase the value that customers associate with Caterpillar products, and thus the price that Caterpillar can charge for them.

■ Support Activities

The **support activities** of the value chain provide inputs that allow the primary activities to take place (see Figure 4.6). The **materials management** (or logistics) function controls the transmission of physical materials through the value chain, from procurement through production and into distribution. The efficiency with which this is carried out can significantly lower costs, thereby creating more value. Wal-Mart, the U.S. retailing giant, reportedly has the most efficient materials management setup in the retail industry. By tightly controlling the flow of goods from its suppliers through its stores and into the hands of consumers, Wal-Mart has eliminated the need to hold large inventories of goods. Lower inventories mean lower costs, and hence greater value creation.

Similarly, there are a number of ways in which the **human resource** function can help an enterprise create more value. The human resource function ensures that the company has the right mix of skilled people to perform its value creation activities effectively. It is also the job of the human resource function to ensure that people are adequately trained, motivated, and compensated to perform their value creation tasks.

Information systems refer to the (largely) electronic systems for managing inventory, tracking sales, pricing products, selling products, dealing with customer service inquires, and so on. Information systems, when coupled with the communications features of the Internet, are holding out the promise of being able to alter the efficiency and effectiveness with which a company manages its other value creation activities. In the Opening Case, we saw how Cisco has used Internet-based information systems to profoundly alter the way its marketing, sales, and service functions are performed, realizing substantial efficiency gains in the process. Wal-Mart is another company that has used information systems to alter the way it does business. Wal-Mart's materials management function is able to track the sale of individual items very closely. This has enabled Wal-Mart to optimize its product mix and pricing strategy. Wal-Mart is rarely left with unwanted merchandise on its hands, which reduces costs, and the company is able to provide the right mix of goods to consumers, which increases the perception of value that consumers associate with Wal-Mart.

The final support activity is the **company infrastructure**. This has a somewhat different character from the other support activities. By infrastructure we mean the companywide context within which all the other value creation activities take place. The infrastructure includes the organizational structure, control systems, and culture of the company. Since top management can exert considerable influence on these aspects of a company, top management should also be viewed as part of a company's infrastructure. Indeed, through strong leadership, top management can consciously shape a company's infrastructure, and through it, the performance of all other value creation activities within the company.

■ Cross-Functional Goals

Achieving superior efficiency, quality, innovation, and customer responsiveness requires strategies that embrace several distinct value creation activities. Indeed, these goals can be regarded as *goals that cut across the different value creation functions of a company*; they are goals whose attainment requires substantial cross-functional integration. In Chapter 11, we consider in greater detail how to achieve cross-functional integration.

DISTINCTIVE COMPETENCIES, RESOURCES, AND CAPABILITIES

A **distinctive competency** is unique strength that allows a company to achieve superior efficiency, quality, innovation, or customer responsiveness and thereby to create superior value and attain a competitive advantage. A firm with a distinctive competency can differentiate its products or achieve substantially lower costs than its rivals. Consequently, it creates more value than its rivals and will earn a profit rate substantially above the industry average.

For example, it can be argued that Toyota has distinctive competencies in the development and operation of manufacturing processes. Toyota has pioneered a whole range of manufacturing techniques, such as just-in-time inventory systems, self-managing teams, and reduced setup times for complex equipment. These competencies have helped Toyota attain superior efficiency and product quality, which are the basis of its competitive advantage in the global automobile industry.[15]

■ Resources and Capabilities

The distinctive competencies of an organization arise from two complementary sources: its **resources** and **capabilities** (see Figure 4.7).[16] The financial, physical, human, technological, and organizational resources of the company can be divided into **tangible resources** (land, buildings, plant, and equipment) and **intangible resources** (brand names, reputation, patents, and technological or marketing know-how). To give rise to a distinctive competency, a company's resources must be both *unique* and *valuable*. A unique resource is one that no other company has. For example, Polaroid's distinctive competency in instant photography was based on a unique intangible resource: technological know-how in instant film processing protected from imitation by a thicket of patents. A resource is valuable if it in some way helps create strong demand for the company's products. Polaroid's technological know-how was valuable because it created strong demand for its photographic products.

Capabilities refer to a company's skills at coordinating its resources and putting them to productive use. These skills reside in an organization's routines; that is, in the way a company makes decisions and manages its internal processes in order to achieve organizational objectives. More generally, a company's capabilities are the product of its organizational structure and control systems. They specify how

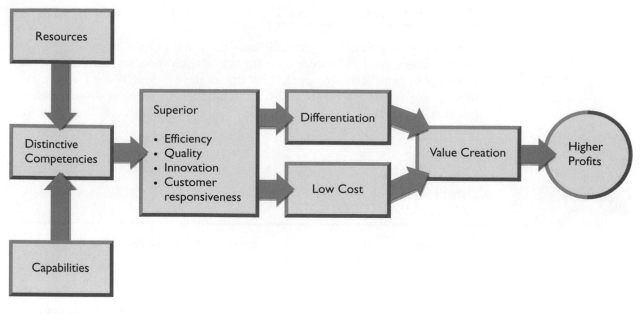

FIGURE 4.7

The Roots of
Competitive Advantage

and where decisions are made within a company, the kind of behaviors the company rewards, and the company's cultural norms and values. (We discuss in Chapters 11 and 12 how organizational structure and control systems help a company obtain capabilities.) It is important to keep in mind that capabilities are, by definition, intangible. They reside not so much in individuals as in the way individuals interact, cooperate, and make decisions within the context of an organization.[17]

The distinction between resources and capabilities is critical to understanding what generates a distinctive competency. A company may have unique and valuable resources, but unless it has the capability to use those resources effectively, it may not be able to create or sustain a distinctive competency. It is also important to recognize that a company may not need unique and valuable resources to establish a distinctive competency so long as it has capabilities that no competitor possesses. For example, the steel minimill operator Nucor is widely acknowledged to be the most cost-efficient steel maker in the United States. But Nucor's distinctive competency in low-cost steel making does not come from any unique and valuable resources. Nucor has the same resources (plant, equipment, skilled employees, and know-how) as many other minimill operators. What distinguishes Nucor is its unique capability to manage its resources in a highly productive way. Specifically, Nucor's structure, control systems, and culture promote efficiency at all levels of the company.

In sum, for a company to have a distinctive competency, it must at a minimum have either (1) a unique and valuable resource and the capabilities (skills) necessary to exploit that resource (as illustrated by Polaroid) or (2) a unique capability to manage common resources (as exemplified by Nucor). A company's distinctive competency is strongest when it possesses *both* unique and valuable resources and unique capabilities to manage those resources.

■ Strategy and Competitive Advantage

The primary objective of strategy is to achieve a competitive advantage. Attaining this goal demands a two-pronged effort. A company needs to pursue strategies that build on its existing resources and capabilities (its competencies), as well as strategies that build additional resources and capabilities (that is, develop new competencies) and thus enhance the company's long-run competitive position.[18] Figure 4.8 illustrates the relationship between a firm's strategies and its resources and capabilities. It is important to note that by *strategies* we mean *all* types of strategy—functional-level strategies, business-level strategies, corporate-level strategies, international strategies, or, more typically, some combination of them. We discuss the various strategies available to a company in detail throughout the next six chapters. What needs stressing here is that successful strategies often either build on a company's existing distinctive competencies or help a company develop new ones.

The history of The Walt Disney Company during the 1980s exemplifies the need to pursue strategies that build on a firm's resources and capabilities. In the early 1980s, Disney suffered a string of poor financial years. This culminated in a 1984 management shakeup, when Michael Eisner was appointed CEO. Four years later, Disney's sales had increased from $1.66 billion to $3.75 billion, its net profits from $98 million to $570 million, and its stock market valuation from $1.8 billion to $10.3 billion. What brought about this transformation was the company's deliberate attempt to exploit its existing resources and capabilities more aggressively. These resources and capabilities included Disney's enormous film library, its brand name, and its in-house filmmaking skills, particularly in animation. Under Eisner, many old Disney classics were rereleased, first in movie theaters, and then on video, earning the company millions in the process. Disney also started a cable television channel, the Disney Channel, to utilize this library and capitalize on the firm's brand name. In addition, under Eisner, the filmmaking arm of Disney flourished, first with a string of low-budget box-office hits under the Touchstone label and then with the reintroduction of the product that had originally made Disney famous, the full-length animated feature. Putting together its brand name and in-house animation capabilities, Disney produced three major box-office hits in four years: *The Little Mermaid, Beauty and the Beast,* and *Aladdin*.[19] In sum, Disney's transformation was based primarily on strategies that exploited the company's existing resource base.

FIGURE 4.8

The Relationship Between Strategies and Resources and Capabilities

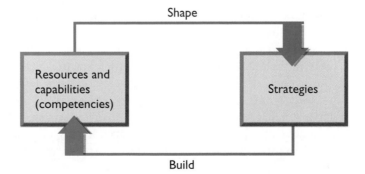

Other companies that have successfully exploited their resources and capabilities to create profitable opportunities include 3M and Honda. The former exploited its distinctive competency in sticky tape to create businesses as diverse as Post-it Notes, pressure-sensitive tapes, and coated abrasives. The latter exploited its distinctive competency in the design and manufacture of high-powered lightweight engines to move from motorcycles to cars, lawn mowers, and four-wheel off-road buggies. On the other hand, some of the most striking strategic failures have occurred at companies that have strayed too far from their distinctive competencies. For example, Exxon, which has distinctive competencies in oil exploration, extraction, and refining, spent much of the 1970s diversifying into areas such as office automation equipment, where it had no capabilities. The effort failed and Exxon sold off these diversified businesses during the 1980s.

As for the process of building resources and capabilities through strategies, consider Xerox. During the late 1970s, its market share in the photocopier business slumped by 50 percent because its main Japanese competitors, Canon and Ricoh, were paying close attention to their distinctive competencies, whereas Xerox was not. As a result, by the early 1980s, Canon and Ricoh were selling high-quality and technologically superior copiers at a price approximating that of Xerox. To recapture its lost market share, Xerox had to fundamentally rethink the way it did business. It launched a series of functional-level strategies designed to improve quality and product design, eliminate unnecessary inventory, and reduce new product development time (cycle time). The goal of these strategies was to develop the kind of resources and capabilities that had enabled Canon and Ricoh to take market share away from Xerox. Xerox was reasonably successful in this endeavor; its share of the U.S. copier market increased from a low of 10 percent in 1985 to 18 percent in 1991.[20] The company's renaissance stemmed from the successful implementation of functional-level strategies to build new distinctive competencies.

■ The Role of Luck

A number of scholars have argued that luck plays a critical role in determining competitive success and failure.[21] In its most extreme version, the luck argument devalues the importance of planned strategy. Instead, it states that in coping with uncertainty some companies just happened to stumble on the correct strategy. Put another way, they just happened to develop or possess the right kind of resources and capabilities by accident rather than by design.

Although luck may be the reason for a company's success in particular cases, it is an unconvincing explanation for the persistent success of a company. Recall our argument that the generic building blocks of competitive advantage are superior efficiency, quality, innovation, and customer responsiveness. Keep in mind also that competition is a process in which companies are continually trying to outdo each other in their ability to achieve high efficiency, quality, innovation, and customer responsiveness. It is possible to imagine a company getting lucky and coming into possession of resources that allow it to achieve excellence on one or more of these dimensions. However, it is difficult to imagine how *sustained* excellence on any of these four dimensions could be produced by anything other than conscious effort, that is, by strategy. Luck may indeed play a role in success, and Strategy in Action 4.5 discusses the role of luck in the early history of Microsoft. However, to argue that success is entirely a matter of luck is to strain credibility.

4.5 STRATEGY *in* ACTION

Microsoft's Luck

The product that launched Microsoft into its leadership position in the software industry was MS-DOS, the operating system for IBM and IBM-compatible PCs. The original DOS program, however, was not developed by Microsoft. Instead, it was developed by a company called Seattle Computer, where it was known as Q-DOS (which stood for "quick and dirty operating system"). When IBM was looking for an operating system to run its original PC, it made contact with a number of software companies, including Microsoft, asking them whether they could develop such a system. IBM did not, however, make contact with Seattle Computer. Bill Gates, a player in the emerging Seattle computer community, knew that Seattle Computer had already developed a disk operating system. Borrowing $50,000 from his father, a senior partner in a prominent Seattle law company, Gates went to see the CEO of Seattle Computer and offered to purchase the rights to the company's Q-DOS system. He did not, of course, reveal that

IBM was looking for a disk operating system. Since Seattle Computer was short of cash, the CEO quickly agreed. Gates then renamed the system MS-DOS, upgraded it somewhat, and licensed it to IBM. The rest, as they say, is history.

So was Microsoft lucky? Of course it was. It was lucky that Seattle Computer had not heard about IBM's request. It was lucky that IBM approached Microsoft. It was lucky that Gates knew about Seattle Computer's operating system. And it was lucky that Gates had a father wealthy enough to lend him $50,000 on short notice. On the other hand, to attribute all of Microsoft's subsequent success to luck would be wrong. While MS-DOS gave Microsoft a tremendous head start in the industry, it did not guarantee Microsoft continued worldwide success. To achieve that, Microsoft had to build the appropriate set of resources and capabilities required to produce a continual stream of innovative software, which is precisely what the company did with the cash generated from MS-DOS.[22]

THE DURABILITY OF COMPETITIVE ADVANTAGE

The question that we now need to address is, How long will a competitive advantage last once it has been created? What is the durability of competitive advantage given that other companies are also seeking to develop distinctive competencies that will give them a competitive advantage? The answer depends on three factors: barriers to imitation, the capability of competitors, and the general dynamism of the industry environment.

■ Barriers to Imitation

A company with a competitive advantage will earn higher than average profits. These profits send a signal to rivals that the company is in possession of some valuable distinctive competency that allows it to create superior value. Naturally, its competitors will try to identify and imitate that competency. Insofar as they are successful, they may ultimately surpass the company's superior profits.[23] How quickly will rivals imitate a company's distinctive competencies? This is an important question, because the speed of imitation has a bearing upon the durability of a company's competitive advantage. Other things being equal, the more rapidly competitors imitate a company's distinctive competencies, the less durable will be its competitive advantage and the more urgent the need to continually improve its competencies in order to stay one step ahead of the imitators. It is important to stress at the outset that ultimately almost any distinctive competency can be imitated by a competitor. The critical issue is *time*. The longer it takes competitors to imitate a distinctive competency, the greater the opportunity the company has to build a strong market position and reputation with consumers, which is then more difficult for competitors to attack. Moreover, the longer it takes to achieve an imitation, the greater is the opportunity for the imitated company to enhance its competency, or build other competencies, that will keep it ahead of the competition.

Barriers to imitation are a primary determinant of the speed of imitation. **Barriers to imitation** are factors that make it difficult for a competitor to copy a company's distinctive competencies. The greater the barriers to such imitation, the more sustainable is a company's competitive advantage.[24]

Imitating Resources   In general, the easiest distinctive competencies for prospective rivals to imitate tend to be those based on possession of unique and valuable tangible resources, such as buildings, plant, and equipment. Such resources are visible to competitors and can often be purchased on the open market. For example, if a company's competitive advantage is based on sole possession of efficient-scale manufacturing facilities, competitors may move fairly quickly to establish similar facilities. Although Ford gained a competitive advantage over General Motors in the 1920s by being the first to adopt an assembly line manufacturing technology to produce automobiles, General Motors quickly imitated that innovation. A similar process is occurring in the auto industry at present, as companies try to imitate Toyota's famous production system, which formed the basis for much of its competitive advantage during the 1970s and 1980s. GM's Saturn plant, for instance, is GM's attempt to replicate Toyota's production system.

Intangible resources can be more difficult to imitate. This is particularly true of brand names. Brand names are important because they symbolize a company's reputation. In the heavy earthmoving equipment industry, for example, the Caterpillar brand name is synonymous with high quality and superior after-sales service and support. Similarly, the St. Michael's brand name used by Marks & Spencer, Britain's largest retailer and one of the world's most profitable, symbolizes high-quality but reasonably priced clothing. Customers will often display a preference for the products of such companies because the brand name is an important guarantee of high quality. Although competitors might like to imitate well-established brand names, the law prohibits them from doing so.

Marketing and technological know-how are also important intangible resources. Unlike brand names, however, company-specific marketing and technological know-how can be relatively easy to imitate. In the case of marketing know-how, the movement of skilled marketing personnel between companies may facilitate the general dissemination of know-how. For example, in the 1970s, Ford was acknowledged as the best marketer among the big three U.S. auto companies. In 1979, it lost a lot of its marketing know-how to Chrysler when its most successful marketer, Lee Iacocca, joined Chrysler. Iacocca subsequently hired many of Ford's top marketing people to work with him at Chrysler. More generally, successful marketing strategies are relatively easy to imitate because they are so visible to competitors. Thus, Coca-Cola quickly imitated PepsiCo's Diet Pepsi brand with the introduction of its own brand, Diet Coke.

With regard to technological know-how, in theory the patent system should make technological know-how relatively immune to imitation. Patents give the inventor of a new product a twenty-year exclusive production agreement. Thus, for example, the biotechnology company Immunex discovered and patented a biological product that treats rheumatoid arthritis. Known as Enbrel, this product is capable of halting the disease-causing mechanism that leads to rheumatoid arthritis, whereas all prior treatments simply provided patients with some relief from the symptoms of the illness. Approved by the FDA in 1998, this product racked up sales of more than $400 million in its first year on the market and may ultimately generate revenues of $2 billion per year for Immunex. Despite the enormous market potential here, Immunex's patent stops potential competitors from introducing their own version of Enbrel. Many other inventions, however, are not as easily protected from imitation by the patent system as are biological products. In electrical and computer engineering, for instance, it is often possible to "invent around" patents. One study found that 60 percent of patented innovations were successfully invented around in four years.[26] This statistic suggests that, in general, distinctive competencies based on technological know-how can be relatively short-lived.

Imitating Capabilities   Imitating a company's capabilities tends to be more difficult than imitating its tangible and intangible resources, chiefly because a company's capabilities are often invisible to outsiders. Since capabilities are based on the way decisions are made and processes managed deep within a company, by definition it is hard for outsiders to discern them. Thus, for example, outsiders may have trouble identifying precisely why 3M is so successful at developing new products, why Nucor is such an efficient steel producer, or why Cisco is able to stay at the cutting edge of the market for network equipment.

On its own, the invisible nature of capabilities would not be enough to halt imitation. In theory, competitors could still gain insights into how a company operates by hiring people away from that company. However, a company's capabilities rarely reside in a single individual. Rather, they are the product of how numerous individuals interact within a unique organizational setting. It is possible that no one individual within a company may be familiar with the totality of a company's internal operating routines and procedures. In such cases, hiring people away from a successful company in order to imitate its key capabilities may not be helpful.

Consider a football team. Its success is the product not of any one individual but of the way individuals work together as a team and the unwritten or tacit understanding between them. Therefore, the transfer of a star player from a winning to a losing team may not be enough to improve the performance of the losing team. However, suppose you buy the whole team. This is what almost happened in 1993 to the German subsidiary of General Motors. It had to obtain an injunction from the German government to prevent Ignacio Lopez de Arriortua, the former GM vice president of operations and the new CEO of Volkswagen, from poaching forty of GM's managers by offering them very high salaries. His intent was to take all the managers who were expert in low-cost production to Volkswagen, which is desperately trying to reduce its costs to compete with the Japanese. Clearly, he was trying to imitate GM's new-found competency in efficiency by buying GM's capabilities through buying its managers.

To sum up, since resources are easier to imitate than capabilities, a distinctive competency based on a company's unique capabilities is probably more durable (less imitable) than one based on its resources. It is more likely to form the foundation for a long-run competitive advantage.

■ Capability of Competitors

According to work by Pankaj Ghemawat, a major determinant of the capability of competitors to rapidly imitate a company's competitive advantage is the nature of the competitors' prior strategic commitments.[26] By **strategic commitment**, Ghemawat means a company's commitment to a particular way of doing business—that is, to developing a particular set of resources and capabilities. Ghemawat's point is that once a company has made a strategic commitment it will find it difficult to respond to new competition if doing so requires a break with this commitment. Therefore, when competitors already have long-established commitments to a particular way of doing business, they may be slow to imitate an innovating company's competitive advantage. Its competitive advantage will thus be relatively durable.

The U.S. automobile industry offers an example. From 1945 to 1975, the industry was dominated by the stable oligopoly of General Motors, Ford, and Chrysler, all of whom geared their operations to the production of large cars—which was what American consumers demanded at the time. When the market shifted from large cars to small, fuel-efficient ones during the late 1970s, U.S. companies lacked the resources and capabilities required to produce these cars. Their prior commitments had built the wrong kind of skills for this new environment. As a result, foreign producers, and particularly the Japanese, stepped into the market breach by providing compact, fuel-efficient, high-quality, and low-cost cars. The failure of U.S. auto manufacturers to react quickly to the distinctive competency of Japanese auto companies gave the latter time to build a strong market position and brand loyalty, which subsequently proved difficult to attack.

Another determinant of the ability of competitors to respond to a company's competitive advantage is their **absorptive capacity**[27]—that is, the ability of an enterprise to identify, value, assimilate and utilize new knowledge. For example, in the 1960s and 1970s, Toyota developed a competitive advantage based on its innovation of lean production systems. Competitors such as General Motors were slow to imitate this innovation, primarily because they lacked the necessary absorptive capacity. General Motors was such a bureaucratic and inward-looking organization that it was very difficult for the company to identify, value, assimilate, and utilize the knowledge underlying lean production systems. Indeed, long after General Motors had identified and understood the importance of lean production systems, the company was still struggling to assimilate and utilize that new knowledge. Put differently, internal inertia can make it difficult for established competitors to respond to a rival whose competitive advantage is based on new products or internal processes—that is, on innovation.

Taken together, factors such as existing strategic commitments and low absorptive capacity limit the ability of established competitors to imitate the competitive advantage of a rival, particularly when that competitive advantage derives from innovative products or processes. This is why, when innovations reshape the rules of competition in an industry, value often migrates away from established competitors and toward new enterprises that are operating with new business models.

■ Industry Dynamism

A dynamic industry environment is one that is changing rapidly. We examined the factors that determine the dynamism and intensity of competition in an industry in Chapter 3 when we discussed the external environment. The most dynamic industries tend to be those with a very high rate of product innovation—for instance, the consumer electronics industry and the personal computer industry. In dynamic industries, the rapid rate of innovation means that product life cycles are shortening and that competitive advantage can be very transitory. A company that has a competitive advantage today may find its market position outflanked tomorrow by a rival's innovation.

In the personal computer industry, for example, the rapid increase in computing power during the last two decades has contributed to a high degree of innovation and a turbulent environment. Reflecting the persistence of innovation, in the late 1970s and early 1980s Apple Computer had an industrywide competitive advantage due to its innovation. In 1981, IBM seized the advantage with its introduction of its first personal computer. By the mid 1980s, however, IBM had lost its competitive advantage to high-power "clone" manufacturers such as Compaq, which had beaten IBM in the race to introduce a computer based on Intel's 386 chip. In turn, in the 1990s Compaq subsequently lost its competitive advantage to companies such as Dell and Gateway, which pioneered new low-cost ways of delivering computers to consumers utilizing the Internet as a direct selling device.

■ Summary

The durability of a company's competitive advantage depends on three factors: the height of barriers to imitation, the capability of competitors to imitate its innovation, and the general level of dynamism in the industry environment. When barriers to imitation are low, capable competitors abound, and the environment is very dynamic, with innovations being developed all the time, then competitive advantage is likely to be transitory. On the other hand, even within such industries, companies can achieve a more enduring competitive advantage if they are able to make investments that build barriers to imitation. During the 1980s, Apple Computer built a competitive advantage based on the combination of a proprietary disk operating system and an intangible product image (as noted earlier, intangible resources are difficult to imitate). The resulting brand loyalty enabled Apple to carve out a fairly secure niche in an industry where competitive advantage has otherwise proved to be very fleeting. However, by the mid 1990s, its strategy had been imitated, primarily due to the introduction of Microsoft's Windows operating system, which imitated most of the features that had enabled Apple to build brand loyalty. As a result, by 1996 Apple was in financial trouble, providing yet another example that no competitive advantage lasts forever. Ultimately, anything can be imitated. (Interestingly enough, though, Apple has shown remarkable resilience. In the late 1990s, it clawed its way back from the brink of bankruptcy to once again establish a viable position within its niche).

WHY DO COMPANIES FAIL?

In this section, we take the issue of why a company might lose its competitive advantage one step further and ask, Why do companies fail? We define a failing company as one whose profit rate is substantially lower than the average profit rate of its competitors. A company can lose its competitive advantage but still not fail. It may just earn average profits. Failure implies something more drastic. Failing companies typically earn low or negative profits; in other words, they are at a competitive disadvantage.

The question is particularly pertinent since some of the most successful companies of the twentieth century have at times seen their competitive position deteriorate. Companies such as IBM, General Motors, American Express, Digital Equipment, and Compaq Computer, all at one time held up as examples of managerial excellence, have gone through periods of poor financial performance, when they clearly lacked any competitive advantage. We explore three related reasons for failure: inertia, prior strategic commitments, and the Icarus paradox.

■ Inertia

The inertia argument says that companies find it difficult to change their strategies and structures in order to adapt to changing competitive conditions.[28] IBM is a classic example of this problem. For thirty years, it was viewed as the world's most successful computer company. Then, in the space of a few short years, its success turned into a disaster, with a loss of $5 billion in 1992 leading to layoffs of more than 100,000 employees. IBM's troubles were caused by a dramatic decline in the cost of computing power as a result of innovations in microprocessors. With the advent of powerful low-cost microprocessors, the locus of the computer market shifted from mainframes to small, low-priced personal computers. This left IBM's huge mainframe operations with a diminished market. Even though IBM had, and still has, a significant presence in the personal computer market, it had failed to shift the focus of its efforts away from mainframes and toward personal computers. This failure meant deep trouble for one of the most successful companies of the twentieth century (although IBM has now executed a successful turnaround, primarily by repositioning the company as a provider of e-commerce infrastructure and solutions).

Why do companies find it so difficult to adapt to new environmental conditions? One factor that seems to stand out is the role of an organization's capabilities in causing inertia. Earlier in the chapter, we argue that organizational capabilities can be a source of competitive advantage; their downside, however, is that they are difficult to change. Recall that capabilities are the way a company makes decisions and manages its processes. IBM always emphasized close coordination between different operating units and favored decision processes that stressed consensus among interdependent operating units as a prerequisite for a decision to go forward.[29] This capability was a source of advantage for IBM during the 1970s, when coordination among its worldwide operating units was necessary in order to develop, manufacture, and sell complex mainframes. But the slow-moving bureaucracy that it had spawned was a source of failure in the 1990s, when organizations had to adapt readily to rapid environmental change.

Capabilities are difficult to change because a certain distribution of power and influence is embedded within the established decision-making and management processes of an organization. Those who play key roles in a decision-making process clearly have more power. It follows that changing the established capabilities of an organization means changing its existing distribution of power and influence, and those whose power and influence would diminish resist such change. Proposals for change trigger turf battles. The power struggle and the political resistance associated with trying to alter the way in which an organization makes decisions and manages its process—that is, trying to change its capabilities—bring on inertia. This is not to say that companies cannot change. However, because change is so often resisted by those who feel threatened by it, in most cases change has to be induced by a crisis. By then the company may already be failing, as happened at IBM.

■ Prior Strategic Commitments

Ghemawat has argued that a company's prior strategic commitments not only limit its ability to imitate rivals, but may also cause competitive disadvantage.[30] IBM, for instance, had made major investments in the mainframe computer business. As a result, when the market shifted, it was stuck with significant resources that were specialized to that particular business. The company had manufacturing facilities geared to the production of mainframes, research organizations that were similarly specialized, and a mainframe sales force. Since these resources were not well suited to the newly emerging personal computer business, IBM's difficulties in the early 1990s were in a sense inevitable. Its prior strategic commitments locked IBM into a business that was shrinking. Shedding these resources was bound to cause hardship for all organization stakeholders.

■ The Icarus Paradox

In his book, Danny Miller has postulated that the roots of competitive failure can be found in what he termed the Icarus paradox.[31] Icarus is a figure in Greek mythology who used a pair of wings—made for him by his father—to escape from an island where he was being held prisoner. He flew so well that he went higher and higher, ever closer to the sun, until the heat of the sun melted the wax that held his wings together and he plunged to his death in the Aegean Sea. The paradox is that his greatest asset, his ability to fly, caused his demise. Miller argues that the same paradox applies to many once successful companies. According to Miller, many companies become so dazzled by their early success that they believe more of the same type of effort is the way to future success. As a result, however, a company can become so specialized and inner-directed that it loses sight of market realities and the fundamental requirements for achieving a competitive advantage. Sooner or later this leads to failure.

Miller identifies four major categories among the rising and falling companies. The "craftsmen," such as Texas Instruments and Digital Equipment Corporation

The Road to Ruin at DEC

DEC's original success was founded on the minicomputer, a cheaper more flexible version of its mainframe cousins that Ken Olson and his brilliant team of engineers invented in the 1960s. Olson and his staff improved their original minis until they could not be surpassed in quality and reliability. In the 1970s, their VAX series of minicomputers was widely regarded as the most reliable computers ever produced. DEC was rewarded by high profit rates and rapid growth. By 1990, DEC was number twenty-seven on the *Fortune 500* list of the largest corporations in America.

However, buoyed up by its own success, DEC turned into an engineering monoculture. Its engineers became idols; its marketing and accounting staff were barely tolerated. Component specifications and design standards were all that senior managers understood. Technological fine-tuning became such an obsession that the needs of customers for smaller, more economical, user-friendly

computers were ignored. For example, DEC's personal computers bombed because they were so out of touch with the needs of consumers. The company also failed to respond to the threat to its core market presented by the rise of computer workstations and client/server architecture. Indeed, Ken Olson was known for dismissing such new products. He once remarked, "We always say that customers are right, but they are not always right." That may be so, but DEC, blinded by its own early success, failed to remain responsive to its customers and to changing market conditions.

By the early 1990s, DEC was a company in deep trouble. Olson was forced out in July 1992, and the company lost billions of dollars between 1992 and 1995. It returned to profitability in 1996, primarily because of the success of a turnaround strategy aimed at re-orientating the company to serve precisely those areas that Olson had dismissed. In 1998, the company was acquired by Compaq Computer.[32]

(DEC) achieved early success through engineering excellence. But then the companies became so obsessed with engineering details that they lost sight of market realities. (The story of DEC's demise is summarized in Strategy in Action 4.6.) Then there are the "builders," for instance, Gulf & Western and ITT. Having built successful, moderately diversified companies, they then became so enchanted with diversification for its own sake that they continued to diversify far beyond the point at which it was profitable to do so. Miller's third group are the "pioneers," such as Wang Labs. Enamored of their own originally brilliant innovations they continued to search for additional brilliant innovations, but ended up producing novel but completely useless products. The final category comprises the "salesmen," exemplified by Procter & Gamble and Chrysler. They became so convinced of their ability to sell anything that they paid scant attention to product development and manufacturing excellence and as a result spawned a proliferation of bland, inferior products.

AVOIDING FAILURE AND SUSTAINING COMPETITIVE ADVANTAGE

How can a company avoid the traps that have snared so many once successful companies? How can it build a sustainable competitive advantage? We do not give a complete answer here as much of the remaining text deals with these issues. However, a number of key points can be made at this juncture.

■ Focus on the Building Blocks of Competitive Advantage

First, maintaining a competitive advantage requires a company to continue focusing on the four generic building blocks of competitive advantage—efficiency, quality, innovation, and customer responsiveness—and to develop distinctive competencies that contribute to superior performance in these areas. One of the messages of Miller's Icarus paradox is that many successful companies become unbalanced in their pursuit of distinctive competencies. DEC, for example, focused on engineering quality at the expense of almost everything else, including, most importantly, customer responsiveness. Other companies forget to focus on any distinctive competency. This was certainly the case at ITT, where an empire-building CEO, Harold Geneen, focused on diversification but lost sight of the need to focus on achieving excellence in efficiency, quality, innovation, and customer responsiveness at the level of business units within ITT.

■ Institute Continuous Improvement and Learning

The only constant in the world is change. Today's source of competitive advantage may soon be rapidly imitated by capable competitors, or it may be made obsolete by the innovations of a rival. In such a dynamic and fast-paced environment, the only way that a company can maintain a competitive advantage over time is to continually improve its efficiency, quality, innovation, and customer responsiveness. The way to do so is to recognize the importance of learning within the organization.[33] The most successful companies are not those that stand still, resting on their laurels. They are those that continually seek out ways of improving their operations and, in the process, are constantly upgrading the value of their distinctive competencies or creating new competencies. Companies such as General Electric and Toyota have a reputation for being learning organizations. What this means is that they are continually analyzing the processes that underlie their efficiency, quality, innovation, and customer responsiveness. Their objective is to learn from prior mistakes and to seek out ways to improve their processes over time. This has enabled Toyota, for example, to continually upgrade its employee productivity and product quality, allowing the company to stay one step ahead of imitators.

■ Track Best Industrial Practice and Use Benchmarking

One of the best ways to develop distinctive competencies that contribute to superior efficiency, quality, innovation, and customer responsiveness is to identify **best industrial practice** and to adopt it. Only by so doing will a company be able to build and maintain the resources and capabilities that underpin excellence in efficiency, quality, innovation, and customer responsiveness. What constitutes best industrial practice is an issue we discuss in some depth in Chapter 5. However, it requires tracking the practice of other companies, and perhaps the best way to do so is through **benchmarking**. This is the process of measuring the company against the products, practices, and services of some of its most efficient global competitors. For example, when Xerox was in trouble in the early 1980s, it decided to institute a policy of benchmarking as a means of identifying ways to improve the efficiency of its operations. Xerox benchmarked L.L. Bean for distribution procedures, Deere & Company for central computer operations, Procter & Gamble for marketing, and Florida Power & Light for total quality management processes. By the early 1990s, Xerox was benchmarking 240 functions against comparable areas in other companies. This process has been credited with helping Xerox dramatically improve the efficiency of its operations.[34]

■ Overcome Inertia

A further reason for failure is an inability to adapt to changing conditions because of organizational inertia. Overcoming the barriers to change within an organization is one of the key requirements for maintaining a competitive advantage, and we devote a whole chapter, Chapter 14, to this issue. Suffice it to say here that identifying barriers to change is an important first step. Once this step has been taken, implementing change requires good leadership, the judicious use of power, and appropriate changes in organizational structure and control systems. All these issues are discussed later in the book.

SUMMARY OF CHAPTER

The principal objective of this chapter is to identify the basis of competitive advantage by examining why, within a given industry, some companies outperform others. Competitive advantage is the product of at least one of the following: superior efficiency, superior quality, superior innovation, and superior customer responsiveness. Achieving superiority here requires that a company develop appropriate distinctive competencies, which in turn are a product of the kind of resources and capabilities that a company possesses. The chapter also examines issues related to the durability of competitive advantage. This durability is determined by the height of barriers to imitation, the capability of competitors to imitate a company's advantage, and the general level of environmental turbulence. Finally, the discussion of why companies fail and what they can do to avoid failure indicates that failure is due to factors such as organizational inertia, prior strategic commitments, and the Icarus paradox. Avoiding failure requires that a company constantly try to upgrade its distinctive competencies in accordance with best industrial practice and that it take steps to overcome organizational inertia. The main points made in this chapter can be summarized as follows:

✔ The source of a competitive advantage is superior value creation.

✔ To create superior value, a company must lower its costs, differentiate its product so that it can charge a higher price, or do both simultaneously.

✔ The four generic building blocks of competitive advantage are efficiency, quality, innovation, and customer responsiveness.

✔ Superior efficiency enables a company to lower its costs; superior quality allows it both to charge a higher price and to lower its costs; and superior customer service lets it charge a higher price. Superior innovation can lead to higher prices, particularly in the case of product innovations; or it can lead to lower unit costs, particularly in the case of process innovations.

✔ Distinctive competencies are the unique strengths of a company. Valuable distinctive competencies enable a company to earn a profit rate that is above the industry average.

✔ The distinctive competencies of an organization arise from its resources and capabilities.

✔ Resources refer to the financial, physical, human, technological, and organizational assets of a company.

✔ Capabilities refer to a company's skills at coordinating resources and putting them to productive use.

✔ In order to achieve a competitive advantage, companies need to pursue strategies that build on the existing resources and capabilities of an organization (its competencies), and they need to formulate strategies that build additional resources and capabilities (develop new competencies).

✔ The durability of a company's competitive advantage depends on the height of barriers to imitation, the capability of competitors, and environmental dynamism.

✔ Failing companies typically earn low or negative profits. Three factors seem to contribute to failure—organizational inertia in the face of environmental change, the nature of a company's prior strategic commitments, and the Icarus paradox.

✔ Avoiding failure requires a constant focus on the basic building blocks of competitive advantage, continuous improvement, identification and adoption of best industrial practice, and victory over inertia.

DISCUSSION QUESTIONS

1. What are the main implications of the material discussed in this chapter for strategy formulation?

2. When is a company's competitive advantage most likely to endure over time?

3. Which is more important in explaining the success and failure of companies, strategizing or luck?

Practicing Strategic Management

SMALL-GROUP EXERCISE
Analyzing Competitive Advantage

Break up into groups of three to five people. Drawing on the concepts introduced in this case, analyze the competitive position of your business school in the market for business education. Then answer the following questions:

1. Does your business school have a competitive advantage?

2. If so, on what is this advantage based and is this advantage sustainable?

3. If your school does not have a competitive advantage in the market for business education, identify the inhibiting factors that are holding it back.

4. How might the Internet change the way in which business education is delivered?

5. Does the Internet pose a threat to the competitive position of your school in the market for business education, or is it an opportunity for your school to enhance its competitive position? (Note: it can be both.)

ARTICLE FILE 4

Find an example of a company that has sustained its competitive advantage for more than ten years. Identify the source of the competitive advantage and describe why it has lasted so long.

STRATEGIC MANAGEMENT PROJECT
Module 4

This module deals with the competitive position of your company. With the information you have at your disposal, perform the tasks and answer the questions listed:

1. Identify whether your company has a competitive advantage or disadvantage in its primary industry. (Its primary industry is the one in which it has the most sales.)

2. Evaluate your company against the four generic building blocks of competitive advantage: efficiency, quality, innovation, and customer responsiveness. How does this exercise help you understand the performance of your company relative to its competitors?

3. What are the distinctive competencies of your company?

4. What role have prior strategies played in shaping the distinctive competencies of your company? What role has luck played?

5. Do the strategies currently pursued by your company build on its distinctive competencies? Are they an attempt to build new competencies?

6. What are the barriers to imitating the distinctive competencies of your company?

7. Is there any evidence that your company finds it difficult to adapt to changing industry conditions? If so, why do you think this is the case?

EXPLORING THE WEB
Visiting Johnson & Johnson

Visit the Web site of Johnson & Johnson (http://www.jnj.com). Read through the material contained on the site, paying particular attention to the features on the company's history, its credo, innovations, and company news. On the basis of this information, answer the following questions:

1. Do you think that Johnson & Johnson has a distinctive competency?

2. What is the nature of this competency? How does it help the company attain a competitive advantage?

3. What are the resources and capabilities that underlie this competency? Where do these resources and capabilities come from?

4. How imitable is Johnson & Johnson's distinctive competency?

Search the Web for a company site that goes into depth about the history, products, and competitive position of that company. On the basis of the information you collect, answer the following questions.

1. Does the company have a distinctive competency?

2. What is the nature of this competency? How does it help the company attain a competitive advantage?

3. What are the resources and capabilities that underlie this competency? Where do these resources and capabilities come from?

4. How imitable is the company's distinctive competency?

CLOSING CASE

Marks & Spencer

MARKS & SPENCER (M&S) is a British retailing institution. Founded in 1884 by Michael Marks, a Polish Jew who had emigrated to England, the company has been a national chain since the early 1900s. By 1926, the company had a branch in every major town in the country and had become Britain's largest retailer, a position it still holds in 2000. Primarily a supplier of clothing and foodstuffs, M&S is one of the world's most profitable retailers. In 1999, M&S's 300 United Kingdom stores had sales of over 7 billion pounds sterling, accounted for 15 percent of all retail clothing sales in the United Kingdom and 5 percent of all food sales. According to the *Guinness Book of Records,* in 1991 the company's flagship store at Marble Arch in London had a turnover of $3,700 per square foot—more than any other department store in the world.

M&S provides a selective range of clothing and food items aimed at rapid turnover. The firm sells all its products under its own St. Michael's label. M&S offers high-quality products at moderate rather than low prices. This combination of high quality and reasonable price encourages customers to associate M&S with value for money, and the firm's ability to deliver this combination consistently over the years has built up enormous customer goodwill in Britain. So strong is M&S's reputation among British consumers that the company does no advertising in that market.

To achieve the combination of moderate prices and high quality, M&S works very closely with its suppliers, many of whom have been selling a major portion of their output to M&S for generations. The focus on quality is reinforced by M&S's practice of having its technical people work closely with suppliers on product design. Suppliers are more than willing to respond to the firm's demands, for they know that M&S is loyal to its suppliers and as it grows so do they. The sales volume generated by M&S's strategy of providing only a selective range of clothing and food enables M&S's suppliers to realize substantial economies of scale from large production runs. These cost savings are then passed on to M&S in the form of lower prices. In turn, M&S passes on part of the savings to the consumer.

Crucial to M&S's effectiveness is a clear focus on the customer. The tone is set by top management. Each senior manager makes a habit of wearing M&S clothes and eating M&S food. Thus, managers develop an understanding of what it is that customers want and like about M&S products; by staying close to the customer, they can improve the quality and design of the products they offer. The customer focus is reinforced at the store level by store managers who monitor sales volume and quickly identify lines that are selling and those that are not. Then store managers can transmit this information to suppliers, which have the capacity to quickly modify their production, increasing the output of lines that are selling well and reducing the output of lines that are not moving.

Another central feature of M&S is its pioneering approach to human relations. Long before it became fashionable to do so, M&S had developed a commitment to the well-being of its employees. M&S has always viewed itself as a family business with a broad responsibility for the welfare of its employees. It offers employees medical and pension plans that provide benefits that are well above the industry average. The company pays its employees at a rate that is also well above the industry average, and it makes a practice of promoting employees from within, rather than hiring from outside. Furthermore, there are a series of in-store amenities for employees, including subsidized cafeterias, medical services, recreation rooms, and hairdressing salons. The reward for M&S is the trust and loyalty of its employees and, ultimately, high employee productivity.

Just as vital is the company's commitment to simplifying its operating structure and strategic control systems.

M&S has a very flat hierarchy; there is little in the way of intervening management layers between store managers and top management. The firm utilizes just two profit margins, one for foodstuff and one for clothing. This practice reduces bureaucracy and frees its store managers from worrying about pricing issues. Instead, they are encouraged to focus on maximizing sales volume. A store's performance is assessed by its sales volume. Control is achieved partly through formal budgetary procedures and partly through an informal probing process, in which top management drops in unannounced at stores and quizzes managers there about the store. In a typical year, just about every store in Britain will receive at least one unannounced visit from top management. This keeps store managers on their toes and constantly alert to the need to provide the kind of value-for-money products that customers have come to associate with M&S.[35]

Case Discussion Questions

1. What do you think is the source of Marks & Spencer's competitive advantage?

2. Marks & Spencer has managed to maintain its competitive advantage in British retailing for more than fifty years. Why, do you think, have rival firms found Marks & Spencer's competitive position so difficult to attack?

End Notes

1. "Cisco @ speed," *Economist*, June 26, 1999, Special report: Business and the Internet, p. 12; S. Tully, "How Cisco Mastered the Net," *Fortune*, August 17, 1997, p. 207–210; C. Kano, The Real King of the Internet, *Fortune*, September 7, 1998, 82–93.

2. The concept of consumer surplus is an important one in economics. For a more detailed exposition, see D. Besanko, D. Dranove, and M. Shanley. *Economics of Strategy* (New York: John Wiley, 1996).

3. The data is taken from the Value Line Investment Survey. The average ROK is the average of all 17 department stores followed continuously by Value Line over this time period.

4. However, *P = V* only in the special case where the company has a perfect monopoly and where it can charge each customer a unique price that reflects the value of the product to that customer (i.e., where perfect price discrimination is possible). More generally, except in the limiting case of perfect price discrimination, even a monopolist will see most consumers capture some of the value of a product in the form of a consumer surplus.

5. This point is central to the work of Michael Porter. See M. E. Porter, *Competitive Advantage* (New York: Free Press, 1985). See also Chapter 4 in P. Ghemawat, *Commitment: The Dynamic of Strategy* (New York: Free Press, 1991).

6. M. E. Porter, *Competitive Strategy* (New York: Free Press, 1980).

7. D. Lavin, "Chrysler Is Now Low-Cost Producer in the Automobile Industry," *Wall Street Journal*, June 23, 1994, p. B5; N. Templin, "The Auto Trade Fight," *Wall Street Journal*, May 18, 1995, p. A6; W. M. Bulkeley, "Pushing the Pace," *Wall Street Journal*, December 23, 1994, p. A1; D. Levin. "GM Would Have to Cut 20,000 Workers to Match Ford," *Wall Street Journal*, June 24, 1994, p. C22; The Harbor Report. Harbor & Associates, 1999.

8. See D. Garvin, "What Does Product Quality Really Mean," *Sloan Management Review*, 26 (Fall 1984), 25–44; P. B. Crosby, *Quality Is Free* (Mentor, 1980); and A. Gabor, *The Man Who Discovered Quality* (Times Books, 1990).

9. G. Bethune, "From Worst to First," *Fortune*, May 25, 1998, pp. 185–190.

10. W. Chan Kim and R. Mauborgne, "Value Innovation: The Strategic Logic of High Growth," *Harvard Business Review* (January–February 1997), 102–115.

11. G. Stalk and T. M. Hout, *Competing Against Time* (New York: Free Press, 1990).

12. Ibid

13. M. E. Porter, *Competitive Advantage*.

14. R. Langreth, "High Anxiety: Rivals Threaten Prozac's Reign," *Wall Street Journal*, May 9, 1996, pp. B1–B2.

15. M. Cusumano, *The Japanese Automobile Industry* (Cambridge, Mass.: Harvard University Press, 1989).

16. The material in this section relies on the so-called resource-based view of the firm. For summaries of this perspective, see J. B. Barney, "Firm Resources and Sustained Competitive Advantage," *Journal of Management*, 17 (1991), 99–120; J. T. Mahoney and J. R. Pandian, "The Resource-Based View Within the Conversation of Strategic Management," *Strategic Management Journal*, 13 (1992), 63–380; R. Amit and P. J. H. Schoemaker, "Strategic Assets and Organizational Rent," *Strategic Management Journal*, 14 (1993), 33–46; M. A. Peteraf, "The Cornerstones of Competitive Advantage: A Resource-Based View," *Strategic Management Journal*, 14 (1993), 179–191; and B. Wernerfelt, "A Resource Based View of the Firm," *Strategic Management Journal*, 5 (1994), 171–180.

17. For a discussion of organizational capabilities, see R. R. Nelson and S. Winter, *An Evolutionary Theory of Economic Change* (Cambridge, Mass.: Belknap Press, 1982).

18. R. M. Grant, *Contemporary Strategic Analysis* (Cambridge, Mass.: Blackwell, 1991). See also Chan Kim and Mauborgne, "Value Innovation," pp. 102–115.

19. "Disney's Magic," *Business Week*, March 9, 1987; "Michael Eisner's Hit Parade," *Business Week*, February 1, 1988.

20. D. Kearns, "Leadership Through Quality," *Academy of Management Executive*, 4 (1990), 86–89; J. Sheridan, "America's Best Plants," *Industry Week*, October 15, 1990, pp. 27–40.

21. The classic statement of this position was made by A. A. Alchain, "Uncertainty, Evolution, and Economic Theory," *Journal of Political Economy*, 84 (1950), 488–500

22. S. Manes and P. Andrews, *Gates* (New York: Simon & Schuster, 1993).

23. This is the nature of the competitive process. For more details see C. W. L. Hill and D. Deeds, "The Importance of Industry Structure for the Determination of Firm Profitability: A Neo-Austrian Perspective," *Journal of Management Studies*, 33, 1996, p. 429–452.

24. Like resources and capabilities, the concept of barriers to imitation is also grounded in the resource-based view of the firm. For details, see R. Reed and R. J. DeFillippi, "Causal Ambiguity, Barriers to Imitation, and Sustainable Competitive Advantage," *Academy of Management Review*, 15 (1990), 88–102.

25. E. Mansfield, "How Economists See R&D," *Harvard Business Review* (November–December 1981), 98–106.

26. P. Ghemawat, *Commitment: The Dynamic of Strategy* (New York: Free Press, 1991).

27. W. M. Cohen and D. A. Levinthal, "Absorptive Capacity: a New Perspective on Learning and Innovation," *Administrative Science Quarterly*, 35 (1990), 128–152.

28. M. T. Hannah and J. Freeman, "Structural Inertia and Organizational Change," *American Sociological Review*, 49 (1984), 149–164.

29. See "IBM Corporation," *Harvard Business School Case* No. 180-034, 1985.

30. Ghemawat, *Commitment*.

31. D. Miller, *The Icarus Paradox* (New York: HarperBusiness, 1990).

32. Ibid. Also P. D. Llosa, "We Must Know What We Are Doing," *Fortune*, November 14, 1994, p. 68.

33. P. M. Senge, *The Fifth Discipline: The Art and Practice of the Learning Organization* (New York: Doubleday, 1990).

34. D. Kearns, "Leadership Through Quality," pp. 86–89.

35. J. Thornhill, "A European Spark for Marks," *Financial Times*, July 13, 1992, p. 8; Marks & Spencer, Ltd. (A)," *Harvard Business School Case* No. 91-392-089, 1991; J, Marcom, "Blue Blazers and Guacamole," *Forbes*, November 25, 1991, pp. 64–68; M. Evans, "Marks & Spencer Battles On," *Financial Post*, December 11, 1989, p. 32.

PART THREE

Strategies

5 Building Competitive Advantage Through Functional-Level Strategy

OPENING CASE

LEVI STRAUSS is an American icon. For two generations, it has dressed the world in its fabled blue jeans. In recent years, however, Levi's luster has begun to fade even more rapidly than the blue dye on an old pair of 501s. The fast-moving fashion world seems to be leaving Levi's behind. In 1998, for example, Levi's sales declined by 13 percent, to $6 billion, while its share of the domestic blue jeans market fell from 16.3 percent in 1997 to 14.8 percent. Levi's problems have two sources. First, a combination of good design and savvy marketing has helped competitors such as The Gap take share from Levi's. Second, Levi's jeans are just too expensive. Unlike most of its competitors, which have moved the bulk of their manufacturing to Asia or central America, Levi continues to have a significant manufacturing presence in the United States. But the high cost of labor in the United States means that Levi has to charge higher prices to recoup its costs, and consumers just don't seem willing to pay a premium price for Levi's jeans anymore.

Levi's Original Spin

Levi's solution to this problems has been twofold. First, the company announced that it would close eleven of its twenty-two U.S. plants, laying off 5,900 domestic employees, and move manufacturing to low-cost locations. Second, in an attempt to keep its remaining eleven U.S. plants humming, the company announced that it would step up its Original Spin program to supply jeans that are custom-made for individual consumers. Levi's thinking is that if it can customize its jeans for each individual's body shape—and no two people are identical—it will be able to charge a premium price and therefore cover the costs of continuing to have a substantial manufacturing presence in the United States.

At the core of the Original Spin program is an attempt to use Web-based technology and computer-controlled production equipment to implement a strategy of mass customization that has as its goal a desire to give each customer a better-fitting pair of jeans in the customer's preferred style. The idea is that, with the help of a sales associate, customers will create the jeans they want by picking from six colors, three basic models, five different leg openings, and two types of fly. Their waist, rear, and inseam will be measured, and then they will try on a pair of plain "test-drive" jeans to make sure that they like the fit. If they do, the order will be punched into a Web-based computer terminal linked to the stitching machines in a Levi Strauss factory. Customers can even give the jeans a name—for example, "Rebel" for a pair of black jeans. At the factory, computer-controlled tools precision-cut the jeans and stitch an individual bar code inside. The jeans are then sewn and washed, identified by the code, and shipped to the customer's home. The whole process takes no more than two to three weeks. The bar code tag stores the measurements for simple reordering.

Today, a fully stocked Levi's store carries approximately 130 pairs of ready-to-wear jeans. With the Original Spin program, the number of choices available will leap to 750. Sanjay Choudhuri, Levi's director of mass customization, feels that 750 is about the right number of choices. Unlimited choice would create inefficiencies at the manufacturing plant. Levi's strategy is to offer enough choice to give the customer the illusion of infinite variety, yet make it feasible to produce the jeans with little or no additional cost penalty. Levi hopes to charge a premium price—about 20 percent higher—for this service. However, in the company's view, the real benefit of the program is that it changes the nature of the relationship between Levi Strauss and its customers from an anonymous relationship in which the customer walks out of the store with a pair of off-the-shelf jeans, to one in which Levi Strauss aims to become each customer's personal jeans adviser. If the program works, Levi might extend it to embrace several other apparel offerings, such as its Dockers line of pants for men. It may also roll out the program in international markets.

Further down the road, Levi might use a device that will scan the entire body. The machine, developed by an independent company, projects 300,000 pinpoints of light from head to toe and then photographs the body from six angles to produce a kind of three-dimensional portrait. These data result in a custom pattern that can be transmitted to a production plant to manufacture jeans, shirts, or any other item of clothing. Within five years, body-scanning equipment may be available in Levi stores.[1]

OVERVIEW

In Chapter 4, we discuss the central role played by efficiency, quality, innovation, and customer responsiveness in building and maintaining a competitive advantage. In this chapter, we consider what managers can do at the level of functions, or operations, within a company to attain superior efficiency, quality, innovation, and customer responsiveness. Functional-level strategies are strategies directed at improving the effectiveness of basic operations within a company, such as production, marketing, materials management, research and development, and human resources. Even though these strategies may be focused on a given function, as often as not they embrace two or more functions and require close cooperation among functions to attain companywide efficiency, quality, innovation, and customer responsiveness goals.

For example, the Opening Case describes how Levi Strauss is utilizing Web-based technology and computer-controlled equipment to pursue a strategy of mass customization. If successful, this innovative program will change the nature of Levi's relationship with its customers. By customizing its basic product offering to the idiosyncratic body shapes and tastes of individual customers, Levi aims to build a reputation for customer responsiveness, to gain share from its competitors, and to charge a premium price for its products.

To explore the issue of functional-level strategies further, in this chapter we look at how companies can increase their efficiency, quality, innovation, and customer responsiveness. Although in some cases we will focus on the contribution of a given function—such as production or marketing—toward attaining these goals, we will also emphasize the importance of strategies and policies that cut across functions. By the time you have finished this chapter, you should have a much clearer understanding of the actions that managers can take at the operating level to attain superior efficiency, quality, innovation, and customer responsiveness.

ACHIEVING SUPERIOR EFFICIENCY

A company is a device for transforming inputs into outputs. Inputs are basic factors of production such as labor, land, capital, management, technological know-how, and so on. Outputs are the goods and services that a company produces. The simplest measure of efficiency is the quantity of inputs that it takes to produce a given output; that is, Efficiency = outputs/inputs. The more efficient a company is, the fewer the inputs required to produce a given output and, therefore, the lower its cost structure. Put another way, an efficient company has higher productivity than its rivals and, therefore, lower costs.

We review here the various steps that companies can take at the functional level to boost their efficiency and thus lower their unit costs. After considering the primary functions of production and marketing, we move on to examine the various support functions of the enterprise. We must stress, however, that achieving superior quality plays a major role in achieving superior efficiency. We delay discussion of how to achieve superior quality until the next section.

■ Production and Efficiency: Economies of Scale

Economies of scale are unit-cost reductions associated with a large scale of output. One source of economies of scale is the ability to spread fixed costs over a large production volume. Fixed costs are costs that must be incurred to produce a product regardless of the level of output; they include the costs of purchasing machinery, the costs of setting up machinery for individual production runs, the costs of facilities, and the costs of advertising and R&D. For example, it is costing Microsoft approximately $1 billion to develop the next version of its Windows operating system, Windows 2000. Microsoft can realize substantial scale economies by spreading the fixed costs associated with developing a new operating system over the enormous unit-sales volume it expects for this operating system (90 percent of the world's personal computers use a Microsoft operating system). In Microsoft's case, these scale economies are even more significant due to the trivial incremental (or marginal) cost of producing additional copies of Windows 2000 (once the master copy has been produced, additional CDs containing the operating system can be produced for just a few cents).

Many high-technology companies face a similar cost structure: high fixed costs and trivial marginal costs. It costs telecommunications companies billions of dollars in infrastructure to build out their networks, but almost nothing to transmit additional signals down those networks. It costs Intel approximately $5 billion to build a new fabrication facility to produce microprocessors, but only a few cents to produce each chip. It can cost pharmaceutical companies as much as $500 million to develop a new drug, but only a few cents to produce additional units of that drug. For all of these companies, the key to their efficiency and profitability is to increase sales rapidly enough so that fixed costs can be spread out over a large unit volume, and substantial scale economies can be realized.

Another source of scale economies is the ability of companies producing in large volumes to achieve a greater division of labor and specialization. Specialization, in turn, is said to have a favorable impact on productivity, mainly because it enables employees to become very skilled at performing a particular task. The classic example of such economies is Ford's Model T automobile. The world's first mass-produced car, the Model T Ford was introduced in 1923. Until then, Ford had made cars using an expensive hand-built "craft production" method. By introducing mass-production techniques, the company achieved greater division of labor (that is, it split assembly into small, repeatable tasks) and specialization, which boosted employee productivity. Ford was also able to spread the fixed costs of developing an automobile and setting up production machinery over a large volume of output. As a result of these economies, the cost of manufacturing a car at Ford fell from $3,000 to less than $900 (in 1958 dollars).

Nor are scale economies relevant just to manufacturing enterprises such as Ford and Du Pont. Many service companies also benefit from realizing substantial scale economies. An example is given in Strategy in Action 5.1, which looks at the economies of scale realized from the merger between two large New York banks, Chemical Bank and Chase Manhattan Bank.

Some experts argue that after a certain minimum efficient scale (MES) of output is reached there are few, if any, additional scale economies to be had from expanding volume.[3] (**Minimum efficient scale** is the minimum plant size necessary to gain significant economies of scale.) In other words, as shown in Figure 5.1, the long-run unit-cost curve of a company is L-shaped. At outputs beyond MES in Figure 5.1, additional cost reductions are hard to come by. Another point worth bearing in mind is that diseconomies of scale can arise when large enterprises build up a substantial corporate bureaucracy, which increases corporate overhead without reducing unit costs.

■ Production and Efficiency: Learning Effects

Learning effects are cost savings that come from learning by doing. Labor, for example, learns by repetition how best to carry out a task. In other words, labor productivity increases over time, and unit costs fall as individuals learn the most efficient way to perform a particular task. Equally important, in new manufacturing facilities management typically learns over time how best to run the new operation. Hence, production costs decline because of increasing labor productivity and management efficiency.

Learning effects tend to be more significant when a technologically complex task is repeated, since there is more to learn. Thus, learning effects will be more significant in an assembly process involving 1,000 complex steps than in an assembly process involving 100 simple steps. Although learning effects are normally associated with the manufacturing process, as with economies of scale there are reasons for believing that they are just as important in many service industries. For example, one famous study of learning in the context of the health care industry found that

5.1   STRATEGY *in* ACTION

Chemical and Chase Banks Merge to Realize Scale Economies

In August 1995, two of the world's largest banks, Chemical Bank and Chase Manhattan Bank, both of New York, announced their intention to merge. The merger was officially completed on March 31, 1996. The combined bank, which goes under the Chase name, has more than $300 billion in assets, making it the largest bank in the United States and the fourth largest in the world. The new Chase is capitalized at $20 billion and is number one or two in the United States in numerous segments of the banking business, including loan syndication, trading of derivatives, currency and securities trading, global custody services, luxury auto financing, New York City retail banking, and mortgaging services.

The prime reason given for the merger was anticipated cost savings of more than $1.7 billion per year, primarily through the realization of economies of scale. The newly merged bank had good reason for thinking that these kinds of cost savings were possible. In a 1991 merger between Chemical and Manufacturers Hanover, another New York–based bank, cost savings of $750 million per year were realized by eliminating duplicated assets, such as physical facilities, information systems, and personnel.

The cost savings in the Chase-Chemical combination had several sources. First, significant economies of scale were possible by combining the 600 retail branches of the original banks. Closing excess branches and consolidating its retail business into a smaller number of branches allowed the new bank to significantly increase the capacity utilization of its retail banking network. The combined bank was able to generate the same volume of retail business from fewer branches. The fixed costs associated with retail branches—including rents, personnel, equipment, and utility costs—dropped, which translated into a substantial reduction in the unit cost required to serve the average customer.

Another source of scale-based cost savings arose from the combination of a whole array of back-office functions. For example, the combined bank now has to operate only one computer network instead of two. By getting greater utilization out of a fixed computer infrastructure—mainframe computers, servers, and the associated software—the combined bank was able to further drive down its fixed cost structure. Combining management functions also brought substantial savings. For example, the new Chase bank has doubled the number of auto loans and mortgage originations it issues, but because of office automation it can manage the increased volume with less than twice the management staff. This saving implies a big reduction in fixed costs and a corresponding fall in the unit costs of servicing the average auto loan or mortgage customer.[2]

more experienced medical providers posted significantly lower mortality rates for a number of common surgical procedures, suggesting that learning effects are at work in surgery.[4] The authors of this study used the evidence to argue for the establishment of regional referral centers for the provision of highly specialized medical care. These centers would perform many specific surgical procedures (for instance, heart surgery), replacing local facilities with lower volumes and presumably higher mortality rates.

In terms of the long-run average cost curve of a company, while economies of scale imply a movement along the curve (say from A to B in Figure 5.2), the realization of learning effects implies a downward shift of the entire curve (B to C in Figure 5.2) as both labor and management become more efficient over time at performing their tasks at each and every level of output. No matter how complex the task, however, learning effects typically die out after a limited period of time. Indeed, it has been suggested that they are really important only during the start-up period of a new process and cease after two or three years.[5]

FIGURE 5.1

FIGURE 5.1

A Typical Long-Run
Unit-Cost Curve

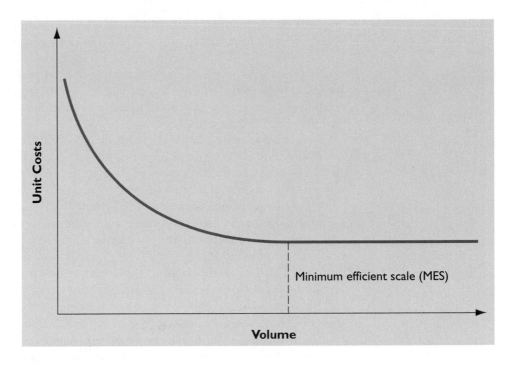

FIGURE 5.2

Economies of Scale and
Learning Effects

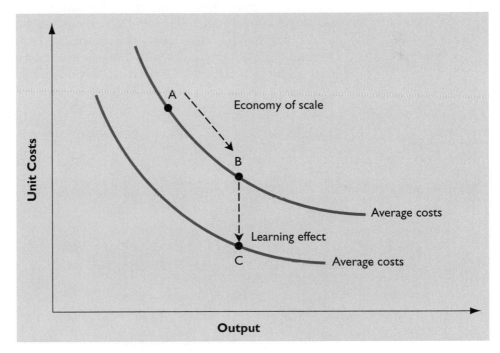

■ Production and Efficiency: The Experience Curve

The experience curve refers to the systematic unit-cost reductions that have been observed to occur over the life of a product.[6] According to the experience curve concept, unit manufacturing costs for a product typically decline by some characteristic amount each time accumulated output of the product is doubled (accumulated output is the total output of a product since its introduction). The relationship was first observed in the aircraft industry, where it was found that each time accumulated output of airframes was doubled, unit costs declined to 80 percent of their previous level.[7] Thus, the fourth airframe typically cost only 80 percent of the second airframe to produce, the eighth airframe only 80 percent of the fourth, the sixteenth only 80 percent of the eighth, and so on. The outcome of this process is a relationship between unit manufacturing costs and accumulated output similar to that illustrated in Figure 5.3.

Economies of scale and learning effects underlie the experience curve phenomenon. Put simply, as a company increases the accumulated volume of its output over time, it is able to realize both economies of scale (as volume increases) and learning effects. Consequently, unit costs fall with increases in accumulated output.

The strategic significance of the experience curve is clear. It suggests that increasing a company's product volume and market share will also bring cost advantages over the competition. Thus, company A in Figure 5.3, because it is further down the experience curve, has a clear cost advantage over company B. The concept is perhaps most important in those industries where the production process involves the mass production of a standardized output (for example, the manufacture of semiconductor chips). If a company wishes to become more efficient, and thereby attain a low-cost position, it must try to ride down the experience curve as quickly as possible. This means constructing efficient scale manufacturing facilities even before the company has the demand and aggressively pursuing cost reductions from learning effects. The company might also need to adopt an aggressive marketing strategy, cutting prices to the bone and stressing heavy sales promotions in order to build up demand, and hence accumulated volume, as quickly as possible. Once down the experience curve, because of its superior efficiency, the company is likely to have a significant cost advantage over its competitors. For example, it has

FIGURE 5.3

A Typical Experience Curve

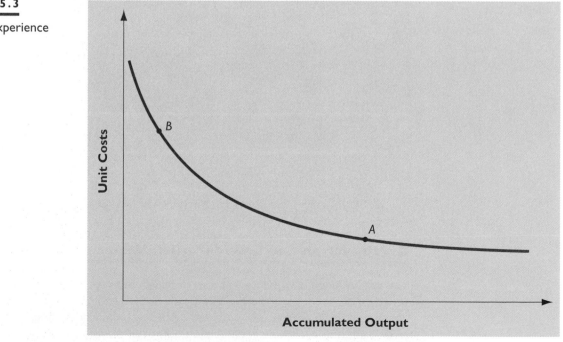

5.2

STRATEGY in ACTION

Too Much Experience at Texas Instruments

Texas Instruments (TI) was an early user of the experience curve concept. TI was a technological innovator, first in silicon transistors and then in semiconductors. The company discovered that with every doubling of accumulated production volume of a transistor or semiconductor, unit costs declined to 73 percent of their previous level. Building on this insight, whenever TI first produced a new transistor or semiconductor it would slash the price of the product to stimulate demand. The goal was to drive up the accumulated volume of production and so drive down costs through the realization of experience curve economies. As a result, during the 1960s and 1970s, TI hammered its competitors in transistors; then it moved on to prevail in semiconductors, and ultimately in hand-held calculators and digital watches. Indeed, for the twenty years up until 1982, TI enjoyed rapid growth, with sales quadrupling between 1977 and 1981 alone.

However, after 1982 things began to go wrong for TI. The company's single-minded focus on cost reductions, an outgrowth of its strategic reliance on the experience curve, left it with a poor understanding of consumer needs and market trends. Competitors such as Casio and Hewlett-Packard began to make major inroads into TI's hand-held calculator business by focusing on additional features that consumers demanded rather than on cost and price. TI was slow to react to this trend and lost substantial market share as a result. In the late 1970s, TI also decided to focus on semiconductors for watches and calculators, where it had gained substantial cost economies based on the experience curve, rather than develop metal-oxide semiconductors for computer memories and advanced semiconductors. As it turned out, however, with the growth in minicomputers and personal computers in the early 1980s, the market shifted toward high-power metal-oxide semiconductors. Consequently, TI soon found itself outflanked by Intel and Motorola. In sum, TI's focus on realizing experience curve economies initially benefited the company, but then it seems to have contributed toward a myopia that was to cost the company dearly.[9]

been argued that the early success of Texas Instruments was based on exploiting the experience curve (see Strategy in Action 5.2 for details); that Intel uses such tactics to ride down the experience curve and gain a competitive advantage over its rivals in the market for microprocessors; and that one reason Matsushita came to dominate the global market for VHS videotape recorders is that it based its strategy on the experience curve.[8]

However, the company farthest down the experience curve must not become complacent about its cost advantage. As Strategy in Action 5.2 points out, an obsession with the experience curve at Texas Instruments may have harmed the company. More generally, there are three reasons why companies should not become complacent about their efficiency-based cost advantages derived from experience effects. First, since neither learning effects nor economies of scale go on forever, the experience curve is likely to bottom out at some point; indeed, it must do so by definition. When this occurs, further unit-cost reductions from learning effects and economies of scale will be hard to come by. Thus, in time, other companies can catch up with the cost leader. Once this happens, a number of low-cost companies can have cost parity with each other. In such circumstances, a sustainable competitive advantage must rely on other strategic factors besides the minimization of production costs by utilizing existing technologies—factors such as better customer responsiveness, product quality, or innovation.

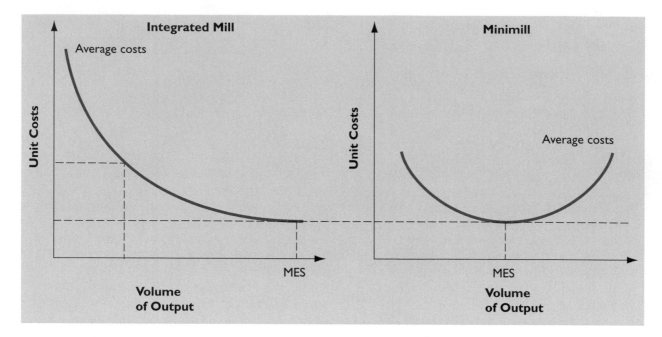

FIGURE 5.4

Unit Production Costs in an Integrated Steel Mill and a Minimill

Second, cost advantages gained from experience effects can be made obsolete by the development of new technologies. For example, the price of television picture tubes followed the experience curve pattern from the introduction of television in the late 1940s until 1963. The average unit price dropped from $34 to $8 (in 1958 dollars) in that time. The advent of color television interrupted the experience curve. Manufacturing picture tubes for color televisions required a new manufacturing technology, and the price for color TV tubes shot up to $51 by 1966. Then the experience curve reasserted itself. The price dropped to $48 in 1968, $37 in 1970, and $36 in 1972.[10] In short, technological change can alter the rules of the game, requiring that former low-cost companies take steps to reestablish their competitive edge.

A further reason for avoiding complacency is that high volume does not necessarily give a company a cost advantage. Some technologies have different cost functions. For example, the steel industry has two alternative manufacturing technologies: an integrated technology, which relies on the basic oxygen furnace, and a minimill technology, which depends on the electric arc furnace. As illustrated in Figure 5.4, the minimum efficient scale (MES) of the electric arc furnace is located at relatively low volumes, whereas the MES of the basic oxygen furnace is located at relatively high volumes. Even when both operations are producing at their most efficient output levels, steel companies with basic oxygen furnaces do not have a cost advantage over minimills.

Consequently, the pursuit of experience economies by an integrated company using basic oxygen technology may not bring the kind of cost advantages that a naive reading of the experience curve phenomenon would lead the company to expect. Indeed, there have been significant periods of time during which integrated companies have not been able to get enough orders to run at optimum capacity. Hence their production costs have been considerably higher than those of minimills.[11] More generally, as we discuss next, in many industries new flexible manufacturing technologies hold out the promise of allowing small manufacturers to produce at unit costs comparable to those of large assembly line operations.

■ Production and Efficiency: Flexible Manufacturing and Mass Customization

Central to the concept of economies of scale is the idea that the best way to achieve high efficiency, and hence low unit costs, is through the mass production of a standardized output. The tradeoff implicit in this idea is between unit costs and product variety. Producing greater product variety from a factory implies shorter production runs, which in turn imply an inability to realize economies of scale. That is, wide product variety makes it difficult for a company to increase its production efficiency and thus reduce its unit costs. According to this logic, the way to increase efficiency and drive down unit costs is to limit product variety and produce a standardized product in large volumes (see Figure 5.5a).

This view of production efficiency has been challenged by the rise of flexible manufacturing technologies. The term *flexible manufacturing technology*—or *lean production*, as it is often called—covers a range of manufacturing technologies designed to (1) reduce setup times for complex equipment, (2) increase the utilization of individual machines through better scheduling, and (3) improve quality control at all stages of the manufacturing process.[12] Flexible manufacturing technologies allow the company to produce a wider variety of end products at a unit cost that at one time could be achieved only through the mass production of a standardized output (see Figure 5.5b). Indeed, recent research suggests that the adoption of flexible manufacturing technologies may actually increase efficiency and lower unit costs relative to what can be achieved by the mass production of a standardized output, while at the same time enabling the company to customize its product offering to a much greater extent than was once thought possible. The term *mass customization* has been coined to describe the ability of companies to use flexible manufacturing technology to reconcile two goals that were once thought to be incompatible: low cost and product customization.[13]

Flexible manufacturing technologies vary in their sophistication and complexity. One of the most famous examples of a flexible manufacturing technology, Toyota's production system, is relatively unsophisticated, but it has been credited with making Toyota the most efficient auto company in the global industry. Toyota's flexible manufacturing system is profiled in Strategy in Action 5.3. **Flexible machine cells** are another common flexible manufacturing technology. A flexible machine cell is a grouping of various types of machinery, a common materials handler, and a centralized cell controller (computer). Each cell normally contains four to six machines capable of performing a variety of operations. The typical cell is dedicated to the production of a family of parts or products. The settings on machines are computer controlled, which allows each cell to switch quickly between the production of different parts or products.

Improved capacity utilization and reductions in work-in-progress (that is, stockpiles of partly finished products) and in waste are major efficiency benefits of flexible machine cells. Improved capacity utilization arises from the reduction in setup times and from the computer-controlled coordination of production flow between

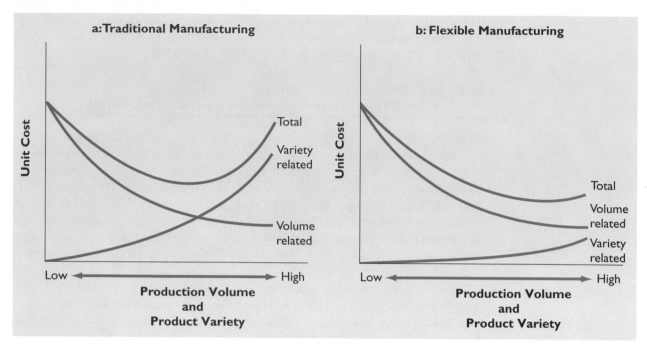

FIGURE 5.5

The Tradeoff Between
Costs and Product
Variety

machines, which eliminates bottlenecks. The tight coordination between machines also reduces work-in-progress. Reductions in waste are due to the ability of computer-controlled machinery to identify ways to transform inputs into outputs while producing a minimum of unusable waste material. Given all these factors, whereas free standing machines might be in use 50 percent of the time, the same machines when grouped into a cell can be used more than 80 percent of the time and produce the same end product with half the waste. This increases efficiency and results in lower costs.

The efficiency benefits of installing flexible manufacturing technology can be dramatic. W.L. Gore, a privately owned company that manufactures a wide range of products from high-tech computer cables to its famous Gore-Tex fabric, has adopted flexible cells in several of its forty-six factories. In its cable-making facilities, the effect has been to cut the time taken to make computer cables by 50 percent, to reduce stock by 33 percent, and to shrink the space taken up by the plant by 25 percent. Similarly, Compaq Computer, the manufacturer of personal computers, replaced three of the sixteen assembly lines in its Houston factory with twenty-one cells. As a result, employee productivity rose by 25 percent, and the cost of converting the three assembly lines to cells was recouped in six months. Lexmark, a producer of computer printers, has also converted 80 percent of its 2,700-employee factory in Lexington, Kentucky, to flexible manufacturing cells, and it too has seen productivity increase by around 25 percent.[14]

Besides improving efficiency and lowering costs, flexible manufacturing technologies also enable companies to customize products to the unique demands of small consumer groups—at a cost that at one time could be achieved only by mass-producing a standardized output. Thus, they help a company achieve mass cus-

STRATEGY *in* ACTION

Toyota's Lean Production System

Toyota's flexible manufacturing system was developed by one of the company's engineers, Ohno Taiichi. After working at Toyota for five years and visiting Ford's U.S. plants, Ohno became convinced that the mass-production philosophy for making cars was flawed. He saw numerous problems, including three major drawbacks. First, long production runs created massive inventories, which had to be stored in large warehouses. This was expensive, both because of the cost of warehousing, and because inventories tied up capital in unproductive uses. Second, if the initial machine settings were wrong, long production runs resulted in the production of a large number of defects (that is, waste). Third, the mass production system was unable to accommodate consumer preferences for product diversity.

Ohno looked for ways to make shorter production runs economical. He developed a number of techniques designed to reduce setup times for production equipment (a major source of fixed costs). By using a system of levers and pulleys, he was able to reduce the time required to change dies on stamping equipment from a full day in 1950 to three minutes by 1971. This made small production runs economical, which in turn allowed Toyota to respond better to consumer demands for product diversity. Small production runs also eliminated the need to hold large inventories, thereby reducing warehousing costs. Furthermore, small product runs and the lack of inventory meant that defective parts were produced only in small numbers and entered the assembly process immediately. This reduced waste and made it easier to trace defects to their source and fix the problem. In sum, Ohno's innovations enabled Toyota to produce a more diverse product range at a lower unit cost than was possible with conventional mass production.[15]

---

tomization, which increases its customer responsiveness. The Opening Case on Levi Strauss provides a good example of this. By linking flexible manufacturing technology with the power of the Web, Levi has been able to customize jeans to an individual's measurements and tastes.

■ Marketing and Efficiency

The marketing strategy that a company adopts can have a major impact upon the efficiency and cost structure of an enterprise. **Marketing strategy** refers to the position that a company takes with regard to pricing, promotion, advertising, product design, and distribution. It can play a major role in boosting a company's efficiency. Some of the steps leading to greater efficiency are fairly obvious. For example, we have already discussed how riding down the experience curve to gain a low-cost position can be facilitated by aggressive pricing, promotions, and advertising—all of which are the task of the marketing function. However, there are other aspects of marketing strategy that have a less obvious, though not less significant, impact on efficiency. One important aspect is the relationship between customer defection rates and unit costs.[16]

Customer defection rates are the percentage of a company's customers that defect every year to competitors. Defection rates are determined by customer loyalty, which in turn is a function of the ability of a company to satisfy its customers. Because acquiring a new customer entails certain one-time fixed costs for advertising, promotions, and the like, there is a direct relationship between defection rates and costs. The longer a company holds on to a customer, the greater is the volume of customer-generated unit sales that can be set against these fixed costs, and the lower the average unit cost of each sale. Thus, lowering customer defection rates allows a company to achieve substantial cost economies. This is illustrated in Figure 5.6, which shows that high defection rates imply high average unit costs (and vice versa).

One consequence of the relationship summarized in Figure 5.6 is a relationship, illustrated in Figure 5.7, between the length of time that a customer stays with the company and profit per customer. Because of the fixed costs of acquiring new customers, serving customers who stay with the company only for a short time before switching to competitors can often yield a negative profit. However, the longer a customer stays with the company, the more the fixed costs of acquiring that customer can be spread out over repeat purchases, which boosts the profit per customer. Thus, as shown in Figure 5.7, there is a positive relationship between the length of time that a customer stays with a company and profit per customer.

For an example of this phenomenon, consider the credit card business.[17] In 1990, most credit card companies spent an average of $51 to recruit a customer and set up a new account. These costs came from the advertising required to attract new customers, from credit checks required for each customer, and from the mechanics of setting up an account and issuing a card. These one-time fixed costs can be recouped only if a customer stays with the company for at least two years. Moreover, when customers stay a second year, they tend to increase their use of the credit card, which raises the volume of revenues generated by each customer over time. As a result, the average profit per customer in the credit card business increases from minus $51 in year 1 (that is, a loss of $51) to $44 in year 3 and $55 in year 6.

Another economic benefit of long-time customer loyalty is the free advertising that customers provide for a company. Loyal customers do a lot of talking, and they

FIGURE 5.6

The Relationship Between Average Unit Costs and Customer Defection Rates

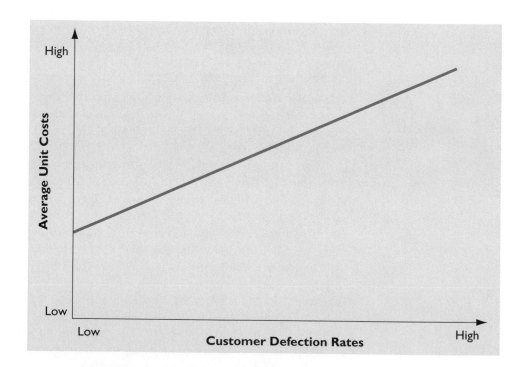

FIGURE 5.7

The Relationship
Between Customer
Loyalty and Profit per
Customer

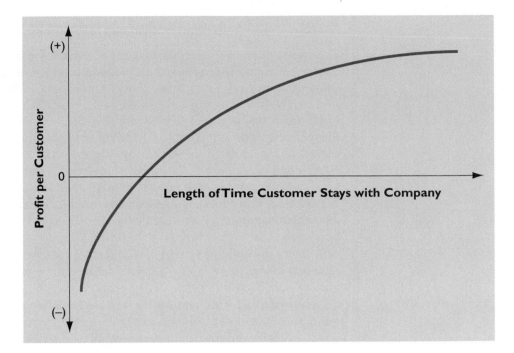

can dramatically increase the volume of business through referrals. A striking example of this is the clothing and food retailer Marks & Spencer, which is Britain's largest and most profitable retailer. Its success is built on a well-earned reputation for providing its customers with high-quality goods at a reasonable price. The company has generated such customer loyalty that it does not need to do much advertising in Britain—a major source of cost saving.

The key message, then, is that reducing customer defection rates and building customer loyalty can be a major source of cost saving. Because it leads to lower unit costs, reducing customer defection rates by just 5 percent can increase profits per customer anywhere from 25 percent to 85 percent, depending on the industry. For example, a 5 percent reduction in customer defection rates leads to the following increases in profits per customer over the average customer life: a 75 percent increase in profit per customer in the credit card business; a 50 percent increase in profit per customer in the insurance brokerage industry; a 45 percent increase in profit per customer in the industrial laundry business; and a 35 percent increase in profit per customer in the computer software industry.[18]

How can a company reduce customer defection rates? It can do so by building brand loyalty, which in turn requires that the company be responsive to the needs of its customers. We consider the issue of customer responsiveness later in the chapter. For now, note that a central component of developing a strategy to reduce defection rates is to spot customers who do defect, find out why they defected, and act on that information so that other customers do not defect for similar reasons in the future. To take these measures, the marketing function must have information systems capable of tracking customer defections.

Materials Management, JIT, and Efficiency

The contribution of materials management to boosting the efficiency of a company can be just as dramatic as the contribution of production and marketing. **Materials management** encompasses the activities necessary to get materials to a production facility (including the costs if purchasing material inputs), through the production process, and out through a distribution system to the end user.[19] The potential for reducing costs through more efficient materials management is enormous. In the average manufacturing enterprise, the materials and transportation costs account for 50 percent to 70 percent of revenues. Even a small reduction in these costs can have a substantial impact on profitability. According to one estimate, for a company with revenues of $1 million, a return on investment rate of 5 percent, and materials management costs that amount to 50 percent of sales revenues (including purchasing costs), increasing total profits by $15,000 would require either a 30 percent increase in sales revenues or a 3 percent reduction in materials costs.[20] In a saturated market, it would be much easier to reduce materials costs by 3 percent than to increase sales revenues by 30 percent.

Improving the efficiency of the materials management function typically requires the adoption of just-in-time (JIT) inventory systems. The basic philosophy behind JIT is to economize on inventory holding costs by having materials arrive at a manufacturing plant just in time to enter the production process, and not before. The major cost saving comes from increasing inventory turnover, which reduces inventory holding costs, such as warehousing and storage costs. For example, Wal-Mart uses JIT systems to replenish the stock in its stores at least twice a week. Many stores receive daily deliveries. The typical competitor—Kmart or Sears—replenishes its stock every two weeks. Compared with these competitors, Wal-Mart can maintain the same service levels with one-fourth the inventory investment, which is a major source of cost saving. Thus, faster inventory turnover has helped Wal-Mart achieve an efficiency-based competitive advantage in the retailing industry.[21]

The drawback of JIT systems is that they leave a firm without a buffer stock of inventory. Although buffer stocks of inventory are expensive to store, they can help tide a firm over shortages on inputs brought about by disruption among suppliers (for instance, a labor dispute at a key supplier). Buffer stocks can also help a firm respond quickly to increases in demand. However, there are ways around these limitations. For example, to reduce the risks linked to dependence on just one supplier for an important input, it might pay the firm to source inputs from multiple suppliers.

R&D Strategy and Efficiency

The role of superior research and development in helping a company achieve greater efficiency is twofold. First, the R&D function can boost efficiency by designing products that are easy to manufacture. By cutting down on the number of parts that make up a product, R&D can dramatically decrease the required assembly time, which translates into higher employee productivity and lower unit costs. For example, after Texas Instruments redesigned an infrared sighting mechanism that it supplies to the Pentagon, the company found that it had reduced the number of parts from 47 to 12, the number of assembly steps from 56 to 13, the time spent fabricating metal from 757 minutes per unit to 219 minutes per unit, and unit assembly time from 129 minutes to 20 minutes. The result was a substantial decline in production costs. Design for manufacturing requires close coordination between the production and R&D functions of the company, of course. Cross-functional teams that contain production and R&D personnel, so that they can work on the problem jointly, best achieve such coordination.

The second way in which the R&D function can help a company achieve greater efficiency is by pioneering process innovations. A process innovation is an innovation in the way production processes operate that improves their efficiency. Process innovations have often been a major source of competitive advantage. In the automobile industry, Toyota's competitive advantage is based partly on the company's invention of new flexible manufacturing processes, which dramatically reduced setup times. This process innovation enabled Toyota to obtain efficiency gains associated with flexible manufacturing systems years ahead of its competitors.

■ Human Resource Strategy and Efficiency

Employee productivity is one of the key determinants of an enterprise's efficiency and cost structure. The more productive the employees, the lower will be the unit costs. The challenge for a company's human resource function is to devise ways to increase employee productivity. It has three main choices: training employees, organizing the work force into self-managing teams, and linking pay to performance.

Employee Training   Individuals are a major input into the production process. A company that employs individuals with higher skills is likely to be more efficient than one employing less skilled personnel. Individuals who are more skilled can perform tasks faster and more accurately and are more likely to learn the complex tasks associated with many modern production methods than individuals with lesser skills. Training can upgrade employee skill levels, bringing the firm productivity-related efficiency gains.[22]

Self-Managing Teams   Self-managing teams are a relatively recent phenomenon. Few companies used them until the mid 1980s, but since then they have spread rapidly. The growth of flexible manufacturing cells, which group workers into teams, has undoubtedly facilitated the spread of self-managing teams among manufacturing enterprises. The typical team comprises five to fifteen employees who produce an entire product or undertake an entire task. Team members learn all team tasks and rotate from job to job. A more flexible work force is one result. Team members can fill in for absent coworkers. Teams also take over managerial duties such as work and vacation scheduling, ordering materials, and hiring new members. The greater responsibility thrust on team members and the empowerment it implies are seen as motivators. (Empowerment is the process of giving lower-level employees decision-making power.) People often respond well to being given greater autonomy and responsibility. Performance bonuses linked to team production and quality targets work as an additional motivator.

The net effect of introducing self-managing teams is reportedly an increase in productivity of 30 percent or more and a substantial increase in product quality. Further cost savings arise from eliminating supervisors and creating a flatter organizational hierarchy. In manufacturing enterprises, perhaps the most potent combination is that of self-managing teams and flexible manufacturing cells. The two seem designed for each other. For example, after the introduction of flexible manufacturing technology and work practices based on self-managing teams in 1988, a General

Electric plant in Salisbury, North Carolina, increased productivity by 250 percent compared with GE plants that produced the same products in 1984.[23] Still, teams are no panacea; in manufacturing enterprises, self-managing teams may fail to live up to their potential unless they are integrated with flexible manufacturing technology. More generally, teams thrust a lot of management responsibilities on team members, and helping the members to cope with these responsibilities often requires substantial training—a fact that many companies often forget in their rush to drive down costs, with the result that the teams don't work out as well as planned.[24]

Pay for Performance   People work for money, so it is hardly surprising that linking pay to performance can help increase employee productivity. However, the issue is not quite so simple as just introducing incentive pay systems; it is also important to define what kind of performance is to be rewarded and how. Some of the most efficient companies in the world, mindful that cooperation among employees is necessary to realize productivity gains, do not link pay to individual performance. Instead they link pay to group or team performance. For example, at Nucor, which is widely viewed as one of the most efficient steel makers in the world, the work force is divided into teams of thirty or so. Bonus pay, which can amount to 30 percent of base pay, is linked to the ability of the team to meet productivity and quality goals. This link creates a strong incentive for individuals to cooperate with each other in pursuit of team goals; that is, it facilitates teamwork.

■ Information Systems, the Internet, and Efficiency

With the rapid spread of computers, the explosive growth of the Internet and corporate Intranets (internal corporate computer networks based on Internet standards), and the spread of high-bandwidth communication conduits from fiber optics to digital wireless technology, the information system functions of enterprises are moving to center stage in the quest for operating efficiencies.[25] The impact of information systems on productivity is wide ranging and potentially affects all other activities of an enterprise. For example, in the Opening Case of Chapter 4, we saw how Cisco Systems has been able to realize significant cost savings by moving its ordering and customer service functions on-line. The company has just 300 service agents handling all its customer accounts, compared with the 900 it would need if sales were not handled on-line. The difference represents an annual saving of $20 million. Moreover, without automated customer service functions, Cisco calculates that it would need at least 1,000 additional service engineers, which would cost around $75 million.[26]

Dell Computer is famous for having been the first to implement on-line selling in the personal computer industry and now sells some 40 percent of its computers on-line. Dell has also put much of its customer service functions on-line, replacing telephone calls to customer service representatives. Each week some 200,000 people access Dell's troubleshooting tips on-line. Each of these hits at Dell's Web site saves the company a potential $15, which is the average cost of a technical support call. If just 10 percent of these people were to call Dell using a telephone, it would cost the company $15.6 million per year.[27]

More generally, what companies like Cisco and Dell are doing is using Web-based information systems to reduce the costs of coordination between the company and its customers, and the company and its suppliers. By using Web-based programs to automate customer and supplier interactions, a company can substantially reduce the number of people required to manage these interfaces, thereby decreasing costs and increasing productivity. Nor is this trend limited to high-technology companies such as Cisco or Dell Computer. Banks and financial service companies are finding that they can substantially reduce costs by moving customer accounts and support functions on-line. Such a move reduces the need for customer service representatives, bank tellers, stockbrokers, insurance agents, and so on. For example, while the average cost of executing a transaction at a bank, such as shifting money from one account to another, is about $1.07, executing the same transaction over the Internet costs $0.01.[28] Similarly, the whole theory behind Internet-based retailers such as Amazon.com is that significant costs can be taken out of the retailing system by replacing physical stores and their supporting personnel with an on-line virtual store and automated ordering and checkout processes. Cost savings can also be realized by using Web-based information systems to automate many internal company activities, from managing expense reimbursements to benefits planning and hiring processes, thereby reducing the need for internal support personnel.

For many years, skeptics questioned the impact that computer-based information systems were having on productivity, but recent productivity data from America suggest that the productivity gains are starting to appear. For the 1996–1998 period, U.S. nonfarm productivity growth accelerated from a historic average of 1 percent per year to 2.2 percent a year. In late 1998 and early 1999, it accelerated again to over 3 percent per annum. The productivity growth was greatest in the computer industry itself, which is not surprising, given the efforts by companies like Cisco and Dell to implement Web-based sales and service functions.[29]

■ Infrastructure and Efficiency

The infrastructure sets the context within which all other value creation activities take place. It follows that the infrastructure can help in achieving efficiency goals. Above all, the infrastructure can foster a companywide commitment to efficiency and promote cooperation among different functions in pursuit of efficiency goals.

A companywide commitment to efficiency can be built through the leadership of top management. The leadership task is to articulate a vision that recognizes the need for all functions of the company to focus on improving their efficiency. It is not enough just to improve the efficiency of production, or marketing, or R&D. Achieving superior efficiency requires a companywide commitment to this goal, and this commitment can be articulated only by top management.

A further leadership task is to facilitate cross-functional cooperation needed to achieve superior efficiency. For example, designing products that are easy to manufacture requires that production and R&D personnel communicate; integrating JIT systems with production scheduling requires close communication between material management and production; designing self-managing teams to perform production tasks requires close cooperation between human resources and production; and so on.

TABLE 5.1

The Primary Roles of Different Value Creation Functions in Achieving Superior Efficiency

Value Creation Function	Primary Roles
Infrastructure (Leadership)	1. Provide companywide commitment to efficiency. 2. Facilitate cooperation among functions.
Production	1. Where appropriate, pursue economies of scale and learning economics. 2. Implement flexible manufacturing systems.
Marketing	1. Where appropriate, adopt aggressive marketing to ride down the experience curve. 2. Limit customer defection rates by building brand loyalty.
Materials Management	1. Implement JIT systems.
R&D	1. Design products for ease of manufacture. 2. Seek process innovations.
Information Systems	1. Use information systems to automate processes. 2. Use information systems to reduce costs of coordination.
Human Resources	1. Institute training programs to build skills. 2. Implement self-managing teams. 3. Implement pay for performance.

■ Summary: Achieving Superior Efficiency

Table 5.1 summarizes the primary roles that various functions must take in order to achieve superior efficiency. Bear in mind that achieving superior efficiency is not something that can be tackled on a function by function basis. It requires an organizationwide commitment and an ability to ensure close cooperation among functions. Top management, by exercising leadership and influencing the infrastructure, plays a major role in this process.

ACHIEVING SUPERIOR QUALITY

We note in Chapter 4 that superior quality gives a company two advantages. The enhanced reputation for quality lets the company charge a premium price for its product, and the elimination of defects from the production process increases efficiency and hence lowers costs. In this section, we examine the means a company can use to achieve superior quality. The main one is **total quality management** (TQM), a management philosophy that focuses on improving the quality of a company's products and services and stresses that all company operations should be oriented toward this goal.[30] A companywide philosophy, it requires the cooperation of all the different functions if it is to be successfully implemented. We first consider the total quality management concept and then discuss the various steps needed to implement TQM programs. Throughout, we highlight the roles that different functions must play in this process.

■ The TQM Concept

The total quality management concept was first developed by a number of U.S. consultants, including H. W. Edwards Deming, Joseph Juran, and A. V. Feigenbaum.[31] Originally, these consultants won few converts in the United States. In contrast, the Japanese embraced them enthusiastically and even named their premier annual prize for manufacturing excellence after Deming. The philosophy underlying TQM, as articulated by Deming, is based on the following five-step chain reaction:

1. Improved quality means that costs decrease because of less rework, fewer mistakes, fewer delays, and better use of time and materials.

2. As a result, productivity improves.

3. Better quality leads to higher market share and allows the company to raise prices.

4. This increases the company's profitability and allows it to stay in business.

5. Thus, the company creates more jobs.[32]

Deming identified fourteen steps that should be part of any TQM program; they are summarized in Table 5.2. (Deming continually changed these points in line with his belief in the importance of continuous quality improvement; those given here are the latest—1990—version.) In essence, Deming urged a company to have a definite strategic plan for where it is going and how it is going to get there. He argued that management should embrace the philosophy that mistakes, defects, and poor-quality materials are not acceptable and should be eliminated. Quality of supervision should be improved by allowing more time for supervisors to work with employees and giving them appropriate skills for the job. Furthermore, management should create an environment in which employees will not fear reporting problems or recommending improvements. Deming also believed that work standards should not only be defined as numbers or quotas, but should also include some notion of quality to promote the production of defect-free output. He argued that management has the responsibility to train employees in new skills to keep pace with changes in the workplace and that achieving better quality requires the commitment of everyone in the company.

It took the rise of Japan to the top rank of economic powers to alert western business to the importance of the TQM concept. Since the early 1980s, TQM practices have spread rapidly throughout western industry. Strategy in Action 5.4 describes one of the most successful implementations of a quality improvement process, General Electric's six sigma program. Despite such instances of spectacular success, TQM practices are still not universally accepted. A study by the American Quality Foundation found that only 20 percent of U.S. companies regularly review the consequences of quality performance, compared with 70 percent of Japanese companies.[33] Another study by Arthur D. Little of 500 American companies using TQM found that only 36 percent believed that TQM was increasing their competitiveness.[34] A prime reason for this, according to the study, was that many companies had not fully understood or embraced the TQM concept.

TABLE 5.2

Deming's Fourteen Points to Quality

1. Create constancy of purpose toward improvement of product and service, with the aim to become competitive and to stay in business, and to provide jobs.

2. Adopt the new philosophy. We are in a new economic age. Western management must awaken to the challenge, must learn their responsibilities, and take on leadership for change.

3. Cease dependence on inspection to achieve quality. Eliminate the need for inspection on a mass basis by building quality into the product in the first place.

4. End the practice of awarding business on the basis of price tag. Instead, minimize total cost.

5. Improve constantly and forever the system of production and service, to improve quality and productivity, and thus constantly decrease costs.

6. Institute training on the job.

7. Institute leadership. The aim of leadership should be to help people and machines and gadgets do a better job. Leadership of management is in need of an overhaul, as well as leadership of production workers.

8. Drive out fear, so that everyone may work effectively for the company.

9. Break down barriers between departments. People in research, design, sales, and production must work as a team, to foresee problems of production and in use that may be encountered with the product or service.

10. Eliminate slogans, exhortations, and targets for the work force asking for zero defects and new levels of productivity. Such exhortations only create adversarial relationships. The bulk of the causes of low quality and low productivity belong to the system and thus lie beyond the power of the work force.

11. (a) Eliminate work standards on the factory floor. Substitute leadership. (b) Eliminate management by objective. Eliminate management by numbers, numerical goals. Substitute leadership.

12. (a) Remove barriers that rob hourly workers of their right to pride of workmanship. The responsibility of supervisors must be changed from sheer numbers to quality. (b) Remove barriers that rob people in management and in engineering of their right to pride of workmanship.

13. Institute a vigorous program of education and self-improvement.

14. Put everybody in the company to work to accomplish the transformation. The transformation is everybody's job.

"Deming's 14 Points to Quality," from Gabor, Andrea, *The Man Who Discovered Quality: Howard W. Edwards Deming Brought the Quality Revolution to America—The Stories of Ford, Xerox, & GM* (New York: Random House, 1990).

■ Implementing TQM

Among companies that have successfully adopted TQM, certain imperatives stand out. We discuss them in the order in which they are usually tackled in companies implementing TQM programs, and we highlight the role that the various functions play in regard to each precept. What cannot be stressed enough, however, is that implementing TQM requires close cooperation among all functions in the pursuit of

5.4 STRATEGY *in* ACTION

General Electric's Six Sigma Quality Improvement Process

Six sigma is a quality and efficiency program that has been adopted by several major corporations, such as Motorola, General Electric, and Allied Signal. It is a philosophy that aims to reduce defects, boost productivity, eliminate waste and cut costs throughout a company. The term *sigma* comes from the Greek letter that statisticians use to represent a standard deviation from a mean. The higher the number of sigmas, the smaller the number of errors. At sigma, a production process would be 99.99966 percent accurate, creating just 3.4 defects per million units. While it is almost impossible for a company to achieve such perfection, six sigma quality is a goal that several strive toward.

General Electric is perhaps the most fervent adopter of six sigma programs. Under the direction of long-serving CEO, Jack Welch, GE spent nearly $1 billion between 1995 and 1998 to convert all its divisions to the six sigma faith. Welch credits the six sigma program with raising GE's operating profit margins to 16.6 percent in 1998, up from 14.4 percent three years earlier.

One of the first products designed from start to finish using six sigma processes was a $1.25 million diagnostic computer tomography, or CT, scanner called the Lightspeed, which produces three-dimensional images of the human body. Introducing it in 1998, GE spent $50 million to run 250 separate six sigma analyses designed to improve the reliability and lower the manufacturing cost of the Lightspeed scanner. The new scanner captures multiple images simultaneously, requiring only twenty seconds to do full body scans that once took three minutes—important because patients must remain perfectly still during the scan. Not only is the Lightspeed fast, but the first customers also noticed that it ran without downtime from the start, a testament to the reliability of the product.

Achieving that reliability took a lot of work. GE's engineers deconstructed the scanner into its basic components and tried to improve the reliability of each through a detailed step-by-step analysis. For example, the most important part of CT scanners is the vacuum tubes, which focus x-ray waves. The tubes that GE used in previous scanners, which cost $60,000 each, had low reliability. Hospitals and clinics wanted the tubes to operate twelve hours a day for at least six months, but typically they lasted only half that long. Moreover, GE was scrapping some $20 million in tubes each year because they failed preshipping performance tests, while a disturbing number of faulty tubes were slipping past inspection only to be pronounced dead on arrival.

To try and solve the reliability problem, the six sigma team took the tubes apart. They knew that one problem involves a petroleum-based oil used in the tube to prevent short circuits by isolating the anode, which has a positive charge, from the negatively charged cathode. The oil often deteriorated after a few months, leading to short circuits, but the team did not know why. By using statistical "what if" scenarios on all parts of the tube, however, the researchers learned that the lead-based paint on the inside of the tube was adulterating the oil. Acting on this information, the team developed a paint that would preserve the tube and protect the oil.

By pursuing this and other improvements, the six sigma team was able to extend the average life of a vacuum tube in the CT scanner from three months to over a year. Although the improvements increased the cost of the tube from $60,000 to $85,000, the increased cost was outweighed by the reduction in replacement costs, making it an attractive proposition for customers.[35]

the common goal of improving quality; it is a process that cuts across functions. The role played by the different functions in implementing TQM is summarized in Table 5.3. Strategy in Action 5.5 at the end of this section describes the efforts of a service company to put TQM into practice and the benefits it has gained.

Build Organizational Commitment to Quality There is evidence that TQM will do little to improve the performance of a company unless it is embraced by

TABLE 5.3

The Role Played by Different Functions in Implementing TQM

Value Creation Function	Primary Roles
Infrastructure (Leadership)	1. Provide leadership and commitment to quality. 2. Find ways to measure quality. 3. Set goals and create incentives. 4. Solicit input from employees. 5. Encourage cooperation among functions.
Production	1. Shorten production runs. 2. Trace defects back to source.
Marketing	1. Focus on the customer. 2. Provide customer feedback on quality.
Materials Management	1. Rationalize suppliers. 2. Help suppliers implement TQM. 3. Trace defects back to suppliers.
R&D	1. Design products that are easy to manufacture.
Information Systems	1. Use information systems to monitor defect rates.
Human Resources	1. Institute TQM training programs. 2. Organize employees into quality teams.

everyone in the organization.[36] For example, when Xerox launched its quality program in 1983, its first step was to educate its entire work force, from top management down, in the importance and operation of the TQM concept. It did so by forming groups, beginning with a group at the top of the organization that included the CEO. The top group was the first to receive basic TQM training. Each member of this group was then given the task of training a group at the next level in the hierarchy, and so on down throughout the organization until all 100,000 employees had received basic TQM training. Both top management and the human resource function of the company can play a major role in this process. Top management has the responsibility of exercising the leadership required to make a commitment to quality an organizationwide goal. The human resource function must take on responsibility for companywide training in TQM techniques.

Focus on the Customer   TQM practitioners see a focus on the customer as the starting point, and indeed, the raison d'être, of the whole quality philosophy.[37] The marketing function, because it provides the primary point of contact with the customer, should play a major role here. It needs to identify what the customers want from the good or service that the company provides; what the company actually provides to customers; and the gap between what customers want and what they actually get, which could be called the quality gap. Then, together with the other functions of the company, it needs to formulate a plan for closing the quality gap.

5.5 STRATEGY *in* ACTION

Total Quality Management at Intermountain Health Care

Intermountain Health Care is a nonprofit chain of twenty-four hospitals operating in Idaho, Utah, and Wyoming. Intermountain first adopted TQM for certain sections of its system in the mid 1980s, and in 1990 it adopted TQM systemwide. The goal of TQM was to find and eliminate inappropriate variations in medical care—to provide the patient with better health care and, in the process, to reduce costs. The starting point was to identify variations in practice across physicians, particularly with regard to the cost and success rate of treatments. These data were then shared among physicians within the Intermountain system. The next step was for the physicians to take the data and use them to eliminate poor practices and to generally upgrade the quality of medical care.

The results have been quite striking. One early improvement was an attempt by Intermountain's hospital in Salt Lake City to lower the rate of postoperative wound infections. Before the effort began in 1985, the hospital's postoperative infection rate was 1.8 percent; this was 0.2 points below the national average, but still unacceptably high from a TQM perspective. By using a bedside computer system to make sure that antibiotics were given to patients two hours before surgery, the hospital dropped the infection rate in half, to 0.9 percent, within a year. Since then, the postoperative infection rate has dropped further still, to 0.4 percent compared with the national average of 2 percent. Given that the average postoperative infection adds $14,000 to a hospital bill, this constitutes a big cost saving.

Intermountain is now focusing on dozens of problems, including situations in which the wrong type or dose of medication is given, the top cause of poor medical care. Intermountain expects its efforts in this area to quickly eliminate at least 60 percent of such mistakes and to reduce medical related costs by up to $2 million a year per hospital.[40]

Find Ways to Measure Quality   Another imperative of any TQM program is to create some metric that can be used to measure quality. This is relatively easy in manufacturing companies, where quality can be measured by criteria such as defects per million parts. It tends to be more difficult in service companies, but with a little creativity suitable metrics can be devised. For example, one of the metrics Florida Power & Light uses to measure quality is meter reading errors per month. Another is the frequency and duration of power outages. L.L. Bean, the Freeport, Maine, mail-order retailer of outdoor gear, uses the percentage of orders that are correctly filled as one of its quality measures. For some banks, the key measures are the number of customer defections per year and the number of statement errors per thousand customers. The common theme that runs through all these examples is identifying what quality means from a customer's perspective and devising a method to gauge this. Top management should take primary responsibility for formulating different metrics to measure quality, but to succeed in this effort, it must receive input from the various functions of the company.

Set Goals and Create Incentives   Once a metric has been devised, the next step is to set a challenging quality goal and to create incentives for reaching that goal. Xerox again provides us with an example. When it introduced its TQM program, Xerox's initial goal was to reduce defective parts from 25,000 per million to 1,000 per million. One way of creating incentives to attain such a goal is to link rewards, such as bonus pay and opportunities for promotion, to the goal. Thus, within many companies that have adopted self-managing teams, the bonus pay of team members is determined in part by their ability to attain quality goals. The task of setting goals and creating incentives is one of the key tasks of top management.

Solicit Input from Employees   Employees can be a vital source of information regarding the sources of poor quality. Therefore, some framework must be established for soliciting employee suggestions as to the improvements that can be made. Quality circles—which are meetings of groups of employees—have often been used to achieve this goal. Other companies have utilized self-managing teams as forums for discussing quality improvement ideas. Whatever the forum, soliciting input from lower-level employees requires that management be open to receiving, and acting on, bad news and criticism from employees. According to Deming, one problem with U.S. management is that it has grown used to "killing the bearer of bad tidings." But, he argues, managers who are committed to the quality concept must recognize that bad news is a gold mine of information.[38]

Identify Defects and Trace Them to the Source   Product defects most often occur in the production process. TQM preaches the need to identify defects during the work process, trace them to their source, find out what caused them, and make corrections so that they do not recur. Production and materials management typically has primary responsibility for this task.

To uncover defects, Deming advocates the use of statistical procedures to pinpoint variations in the quality of goods or services. Deming views variation as the enemy of quality.[39] Once variations have been identified, they must be traced to their source and eliminated. One technique that helps greatly in tracing defects to their source is reducing lot sizes for manufactured products. With short production runs, defects show up immediately. Consequently, they can be quickly traced to the source and the problem can be fixed. Reducing lot sizes also means that when defective products are produced, their number will not be large, thus decreasing waste. Flexible manufacturing techniques, discussed earlier, can be used to reduce lot sizes without raising costs. Consequently, adopting flexible manufacturing techniques is an important aspect of a TQM program.

Just-in-time (JIT) inventory systems also play a part. Under a JIT system, defective parts enter the manufacturing process immediately; they are not warehoused for several months before use. Hence defective inputs can be quickly spotted. The problem can then be traced to the supply source and corrected before more defective parts are produced. Under a more traditional system, the practice of warehousing parts for months before they are used may mean that large numbers of defects are produced by a supplier before they enter the production process.

Build Relationship with Suppliers   A major source of poor-quality finished goods is poor-quality component parts. To decrease product defects, a company has to work with its suppliers to improve the quality of the parts they supply. The primary responsibility in this area falls on the materials management function, since it is the function that interacts with suppliers.

To implement JIT systems with suppliers and to get suppliers to adopt their own TQM programs, two steps are necessary. First, the number of suppliers has to be reduced to manageable proportions. Second, the company must commit to building a cooperative long-term relationship with the suppliers that remain. Asking suppliers to invest in JIT and TQM systems is asking them to make major investments that tie them to the company. For example, in order to fully implement a JIT system, the company may ask a supplier to relocate its manufacturing plant so that it is next door to the company's assembly plant. Suppliers are likely to be hesitant about making such investments unless they feel that the company is committed to an enduring, long-term relationship with them.

Design for Ease of Manufacture   The more assembly steps a product requires, the more opportunities there are for making mistakes. Designing products with fewer parts should make assembly easier and result in fewer defects. Both R&D and manufacturing need to be involved in designing products that are easy to manufacture.

Break Down Barriers Between Functions   Implementing TQM requires organizationwide commitment and substantial cooperation among functions. R&D has to cooperate with production to design products that are easy to manufacture, marketing has to cooperate with production and R&D so that customer problems identified by marketing can be acted on, human resource management has to cooperate with all the other functions of the company in order to devise suitable quality-training programs, and so on. The issue of achieving cooperation among subunits within a company is explored in Chapter 11. What needs stressing at this point is that ultimately it is the responsibility of top management to ensure that such cooperation occurs.

ACHIEVING SUPERIOR INNOVATION

In many ways innovation is the single most important building block of competitive advantage. Successful innovation of products or processes gives a company something unique that its competitors lack. This uniqueness may allow a company to charge a premium price or lower its cost structure below that of its rivals. Competitors, however, will try to imitate successful innovations. Often they will succeed, although high barriers to imitation can slow down the speed of imitation. Therefore, maintaining a competitive advantage requires a continuing commitment to innovation.

Many companies have established a track record for successful innovation. Among them are Du Pont, which has produced a steady stream of successful innovations such as cellophane, nylon, Freon (used in all air conditioners), and Teflon (nonstick pans); Sony, whose successes include the Walkman and the compact disk; Merck, the drug company that during the 1980s produced seven major new drugs; 3M, which has applied its core competency in tapes and adhesives to developing a wide range of new products; and Intel, which has consistently managed to lead in the development of innovative new microprocessors to run personal computers.

■ The High Failure Rate of Innovation

Although innovation can be a source of competitive advantage, the failure rate of innovative new products is high. One study of product development in sixteen companies in the chemical, drug, petroleum, and electronics industries suggested that only about twenty percent of R&D projects ultimately result in a commercially successful product or process.[41] Another in-depth case study of product development in three companies (one in chemicals and two in drugs) reported that about 60 percent of R&D projects reached technical completion, 30 percent were commercialized, and only 12 percent earned an economic profit that exceeded the company's cost of capital.[42] Similarly, a famous study by the consulting division of Booz, Allen, & Hamilton found that over one-third of 13,000 new consumer and industrial products failed to meet company-specific financial and strategic performance criteria.[43] Another study found that 45 percent of new products introduced into the marketplace did not meet their profitability goals.[44] In sum, this evidence suggests that many R&D projects do not result in a commercial product and that between 33 percent and 60 percent of all new products that do reach the marketplace fail to generate an adequate economic return. Two well-publicized product failures have been Apple Computer's Newton, a personal digital assistant, and Sony's Betamax format in the video player and recorder market. Although many reasons have been advanced to explain why so many new products fail to generate an economic return, five explanations for failure appear on most lists: uncertainty, poor commercialization, poor positioning strategy, technological myopia, and a lack of speed in the development process.[45]

Uncertainty   New product development is an inherently risky process. It requires testing a hypothesis whose answer is impossible to know prior to market introduction: namely, is there sufficient market demand for this new technology? Although good market research can minimize the uncertainty about likely future demand for a new technology, the uncertainty cannot be eradicated altogether. Therefore, a certain failure rate is to be expected.

We would expect that failure rate to be higher for quantum product innovations than for incremental innovations. A **quantum innovation** represents a radical departure from existing technology—the introduction of something that is new to the world. The development of the World Wide Web can be considered a quantum innovation in communications technology. Other quantum innovations include the development of the first photocopier by Xerox, the first videocassette recorder by AMPEX, and the first contact lenses by Bausch & Lomb. **Incremental innovation** refers to an extension of existing technology. For example, Intel's Pentium Pro microprocessor is an incremental product innovation because it builds on the existing microprocessor architecture of Intel's X86 series.

The uncertainty of future demand for a new product is much greater if that product represents a quantum innovation that is new to the world than if it is an incremental innovation designed to replace an established product whose demand profile is already well known. Consequently, the failure rate tends to be higher for quantum innovations.

Poor Commercialization   A second reason frequently cited to explain the high failure rate of new product introductions is **poor commercialization**—a condition that occurs when there is an intrinsic demand for a new technology, but the technology is not well adapted to consumer needs because of factors such as poor design and poor quality. For instance, many of the early personal computers failed to sell because one needed to be a computer programmer to use them. It took Steve Jobs at Apple Computer to understand that if the technology could be made user-friendly (if it could be commercialized), there would be an enormous market for it.

Hence the original personal computers marketed by Apple incorporated little in the way of radically new technology, but they made existing technology accessible to the average person. The failure of Apple Computer to establish a market for the Newton—the personal digital assistant or hand-held computer that Apple introduced in the summer of 1993—can be traced to poor commercialization of a potentially attractive technology. Apple predicted a $1 billion market for the Newton, but sales failed to materialize when it became clear that the Newton's software could not adequately recognize messages written on the Newton's message pad. Despite this failure, many companies believe that there is an intrinsic demand for this kind of technology, but only if the product can be better commercialized.

Poor Positioning Strategy   Poor positioning strategy arises when a company introduces an intrinsically attractive new product, but sales fail to materialize because it is poorly positioned in the market place. **Positioning strategy** is the position a company adopts for a product on four main dimensions of marketing: price, distribution, promotion and advertising, and product features. Apart from poor product quality, another reason for the failure of the Apple Newton was poor positioning strategy. The Newton was introduced at such a high initial price (close to $1,000) that probably there would have been few takers even if the technology had been adequately commercialized. Poor positioning strategy may have also affected the recent introduction of the digital compact cassette (DCC), discussed in Strategy in Action 5.6. The DCC suffered from high prices, poor promotion, and a failure by the innovating companies to produce products for the portable and car market.

Technological Myopia   Another reason why many new product introductions fail is that companies often make the mistake of marketing a technology for which there is not enough consumer demand. **Technological myopia** occurs when a company gets blinded by the wizardry of a new technology and fails to consider whether there is consumer demand for the product. This problem may have been a factor in the failure of the desktop computer introduced by NeXT in the late 1980s. (NeXT was founded by Steve Jobs, the founder of Apple Computer.) Technologically, the NeXT machines were clearly ahead of their time, with advanced software and hardware features that would not be incorporated into most personal computers for another decade. However, consumer acceptance was very slow, primarily because of the complete lack of applications software such as spreadsheet and word-processing programs to run on the machines. Management at NeXT was so enthusiastic about the technology of their new computer that they ignored this basic market reality. After several years of slow sales, NeXT eventually withdrew the machines from the marketplace.

Slowness in Marketing   Finally, companies fail when they are slow to get their products to market. The longer the time between initial development and final marketing—that is, the slower the "cycle time"—the more likely it is that someone else will beat the firm to market and gain a first-mover advantage.[47] By and large, slow innovators update their products less frequently than fast innovators. Consequently, they can be perceived as technical laggards relative to the fast innovators. In the automobile industry, General Motors has suffered from being a slow innovator. Its product development cycle has been about five years, compared with two to three years at Honda, Toyota, and Mazda, and three to four years at Ford. Because they are

Whatever Happened to the Digital Compact Cassette?

The Digital Compact Cassette (DCC) was developed by Philips, the Dutch consumer electronics company. The DCC is a recordable audio digital technology that offers sound qualities superior to those of analog cassette technology. The DCC was designed to replace analog cassette tapes in much the same way that digital compact disks have replaced analog long-playing records. An attractive feature of the technology was a design that allowed users to play their analog cassette tapes on the DCC, in addition to DCC digital tapes. The thinking at Philips was that this feature would make the product very attractive to users, who would not have to replace their existing collection of analog cassette tapes when they purchased a DCC player. To try and ensure initial acceptance of the technology, Philips lined up a number of recording companies—including MCA, Polygram, EMI, and Warner—all of whom agreed to issue prerecorded DCC tapes in conjunction with the launch by Philips of the tapes players.

Brought out in 1993, the DCC was hailed in the press as the biggest new product introduction in the consumer electronics industry since the introduction of the compact disk a decade earlier. However, as initial demand failed to materialize, retailers with unsold DCC tapes and decks on their hands refused to keep devoting valuable shelf space to DCC products, and recording companies soon stopped issuing prerecorded DCC tapes. It was obvious within a year that the product was stillborn in the marketplace.

Why did the DCC fail to gain market acceptance despite its apparently attractive features? Poor positioning strategy is probably part of the explanation. Philips introduced the technology at a very high price—around $1,000 for a basic home deck—out of the reach of most consumers. Moreover, Philips failed to introduce a portable model (to compete with Sony's Walkman) or a model for cars (most consumers still have analog tape players in their cars). To make matters worse, the original promotional advertising failed to mention one of the most attractive features of the technology—that DCC tape drives could play existing analog tapes. Finally, Philips implemented a very abstract advertising campaign, which left most consumers confused about the nature of the new technology.

Another reason for the poor market acceptance was the limited value placed on the technology by many consumers. Most consumers did not see the DCC as a big advance over CD players. True, CD technology did not have recording capability, but CD players were increasingly turning up in cars and Sony had marketed a very successful portable version of the CD (the Discman)—both market niches that were natural targets for the DCC. Consequently, few consumers valued the technology enough to pay $1,000 or so for a player. Whether Philips would have been able to build sales for the DCC had it entered the market at a lower price point, with better advertising and a broader range of models, remains an open question, but success would probably have been more likely.[46]

based on five-year-old technology and design concepts, GM cars are already out-of-date when they reach the market. Another example of the consequences of slow innovation, the demise of Apollo Computer at the hands of Sun Microsystems, is presented in Strategy in Action 5.7.

■ Building Competencies in Innovation

Companies can take a number of steps in order to build a competency in innovation and avoid failure. Three of the most important seem to be (1) building skills in basic and applied scientific research; (2) developing a good process for project selection and project management, and (3) integrating the different functions of the

Slow Cycle Time at Apollo Computer

In 1980, Apollo Computer created the market for engineering computer workstations. (Workstations are high-powered freestanding minicomputers.) Apollo was rewarded with rapid growth and a virtual monopoly position. Its first real competitor, Sun Microsystems, did not introduce a competing product until 1982. However, by 1988 Apollo had lost its lead in the workstation market to Sun. While Apollo was generating revenues of $600 million in 1988, Sun's revenues were more than $1 billion. Between 1984 and 1988, Sun's revenues from workstations grew at an annual rate of 100 percent, compared with Apollo's annual growth rate of 35 percent.

The cause of Apollo's slower growth was a slow cycle time. In the computer industry, innovations in microprocessor technology are proceeding at a furious pace. In order to stay abreast of new microprocessor technology, any manufacturer of computers must be continually updating their product. However, while Sun had succeeded in introducing a new product every twelve months and in doubling the power of its workstations every eighteen months on the average, Apollo's product development cycle had stretched out to more than two years. As a result, Apollo's products were regularly superseded by the more technologically advanced products introduced by Sun, and Apollo was falling further and further behind. Consequently, while Sun had increased its market share from 21 percent to 33 percent between 1985 and 1988, Apollo's fell from 41 percent to under 20 percent. In 1989, facing mounting problems, Apollo was acquired by Hewlett-Packard.[48]

company through cross-functional product development teams and partly parallel development processes.[49]

Building Skills in Basic and Applied Research   Building skills in basic and applied research requires the employment of research scientists and engineers and the establishment of a work environment that fosters creativity. A number of top companies try to achieve this by setting up university-style research facilities, where scientists and engineers are given time to work on their own research projects, in addition to projects that are linked directly to ongoing company research. At Hewlett-Packard, for example, the company labs are open to engineers around the clock. Hewlett-Packard even encourages its corporate researchers to devote 10 percent of company time to exploring their own ideas—and does not penalize them if they fail. Similarly, at 3M there is a "15 percent rule," which allows researchers to spend 15 percent of the workweek researching any topic they want to investigate, as long as there is the potential of a payoff for the company. The most famous outcome of this policy is the ubiquitous yellow Post-it Notes. The idea for them evolved from a researcher's desire to find a way to keep the bookmark from falling out of his hymn book. Post-it Notes are now a major 3M consumer business, with revenues of around $300 million.

Project Selection and Management   Project management is the overall management of the innovation process, from generation of the original concept, through development, and into final production and shipping. Project management requires three important skills: the ability to encourage as much generation of ideas as possible; the ability to select among competing projects at an early stage of development

FIGURE 5.8

The Development
Funnel

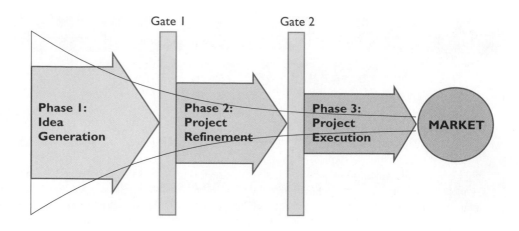

so that the most promising receive funding and potential costly failures are killed off; and the ability to minimize time to market. The concept of the development funnel, illustrated in Figure 5.8, summarizes what is required to build these skills.[50]

As Figure 5.8 shows, the development funnel is divided into three phases. The objective in phase 1 is to widen the mouth of the tunnel to encourage as much idea generation as possible. To this end, a company should solicit input from all its functions, as well as from customers, competitors, and suppliers.

At gate 1 the funnel narrows. Here ideas are reviewed by a cross-functional team of managers who were not involved in the original concept development. Those concepts that are ready to proceed then move on to phase 2 of the funnel, which is where the details of the project proposal are worked out. Note that gate 1 is not a go/no-go evaluation point. At this screen, ideas may be sent back for further concept development to be resubmitted for evaluation.

During phase 2, which typically lasts only one or two months, the data and information developed during phase 1 are put into a form that will enable senior management to evaluate proposed projects against competing projects. Normally, this requires the development of a careful project plan, complete with details of the proposed target market, attainable market share, likely revenues, development costs, production costs, key milestones, and the like. The next big selection point, gate 2, is a go/no-go evaluation point. Senior managers are brought in to review the various projects under consideration. Their task is to select those projects that seem likely winners and that make most sense from a strategic perspective, given the long-term goals of the enterprise. The overriding objective at this gate is to select projects whose successful completion will help maintain or build a competitive advantage for the company. A related objective is to ensure that the company does not spread its scarce capital and human resources too thinly over too many projects and that instead it concentrates resources on those projects where the probability of success and potential returns are most attractive. Any project selected to go forward at this stage will be funded and staffed, the expectation being that it will be carried through to market introduction. In phase 3, the project development proposal is executed by a cross-functional product development team.

Cross-Functional Integration   Tight cross-functional integration between R&D, production, and marketing can help a company to ensure that

1. product development projects are driven by customer needs.

2. new products are designed for ease of manufacture.

3. development costs are kept in check.

4. time to market is minimized.

Close integration between R&D and marketing is required to ensure that product development projects are driven by the needs of customers. A company's customers can be one of its primary sources of new product ideas. Identification of customer needs, and particularly unmet needs, can set the context within which successful product innovation takes place. As the point of contact with customers, the marketing function of a company can provide valuable information in this regard. Moreover, integration of R&D and marketing is crucial if a new product is to be properly commercialized. Without integration of R&D and marketing, a company runs the risk of developing products for which there is little or no demand.

The case of Techsonic Industries illustrates the benefits of integrating R&D and marketing. This Alabama company manufactures depth finders—electronic devices used in fishing to measure the depth of water beneath a boat and to track the prey. Techsonic had weathered nine new-product failures in a row when the company decided to conduct interviews across the country with those engaged in the sport of fishing to identify what they needed. It discovered an unmet need for a depth finder with a gauge that could be read in bright sunlight, so that is what Techsonic developed. In the year after the $250 depth finder hit the market, Techsonic's sales tripled to $80 million and its market share surged to 40 percent.[51]

Integrating of R&D and production can help a company ensure that products are designed with manufacturing requirements in mind, which lowers manufacturing costs and leaves less room for mistakes, thus increasing product quality. Such integration can also reduce development costs and speed products to market. If a new product is not designed with manufacturing capabilities in mind, it may prove too difficult to build, given existing manufacturing technology. In that case, it will have to be redesigned, and both overall development costs and the time it takes to bring the product to market may increase significantly. For example, making design changes during product planning could raise overall development costs by 50 percent and add 25 percent to the time it takes to bring the product to market.[52] Moreover, many quantum product innovations require new processes to manufacture them. That makes it all the more important to integrate R&D and production, since minimizing time to market and development costs may require the simultaneous development of new products and new processes.[53]

Product Development Teams One of the best way to achieve cross-functional integration is to establish cross-functional product development teams. These are teams composed of representatives from R&D, marketing, and production. The objective of a team should be to take a product development project through from the initial concept development to market introduction. Certain attributes seem particularly important for a product development team to have if it is to function effectively and meet all its development milestones.[54]

First, the team should be led by a "heavyweight" project manager, who has both high status within the organization and the power and authority to obtain the financial and human resources that the team needs to succeed. This "heavyweight" leader should be dedicated primarily, if not entirely, to the project. The leader should be someone who believes in the project—that is, a champion of the project—and should also be skilled at integrating the perspectives of different functions and at helping personnel from different functions work together for a common goal. Moreover, the leader must also be able to act as the team's advocate to senior management.

Second, the team should include at least one member from each key function. The team members should have an ability to contribute functional expertise, high standing within their function, a willingness to share responsibility for team results, and an ability to put functional advocacy aside. Generally, it is preferable for core team members to be 100 percent dedicated to the project for its duration so that their focus is on the project, not on the ongoing work of their function.

Third, the team members should be physically colocated to create a sense of camaraderie and to facilitate communication.

Fourth, the team should have a clear plan and clear goals, particularly with regard to critical development milestones and development budgets. The team should have incentives to attain those goals—such as pay bonuses when major development milestones are hit.

Fifth, each team needs to develop its own processes for communication and conflict resolution. For example, one product development team at Quantum Corporation, a California-based manufacturer of disk drives for personal computers, instituted a rule that all major decisions would be made and conflicts resolved at meetings that were held every Monday afternoon. This simple rule helped the team to meet its development goals.[55]

Partly Parallel Development Processes   One way in which a product development team can compress the time it takes to develop a product and bring it to market is to utilize a partly parallel development process. Traditionally, product development processes have been organized on a sequential basis, as illustrated in Figure 5.9a. A problem with this kind of process is that product development proceeds without consideration of manufacturing issues. Most significantly, since the basic design of a product is completed before the design of a manufacturing process and full-scale commercial production, there is no early warning system to indicate manufacturability. Consequently, the company may find that it cannot manufacture the product in a cost-efficient way and must send it back to the design stage for redesign. The result is that cycle time lengthens as the product iterates back and forth between stages.

To solve this problem, companies typically use a process similar to that illustrated in Figure 5.9b. In the partly parallel development process, development stages overlap so that, for example, work starts on the development of the production process before the product design is finalized. By reducing the need for expensive and time-consuming product redesigns, such a process can significantly reduce the time it takes to develop a new product and bring it to market.

What occurred after Intel introduced its 386 microprocessor in 1986 illustrates this point. A number of companies, including IBM and Compaq, were racing to be the first to introduce a 386-based personal computer. Compaq beat IBM by six months and gained a major share of the high-powered market, mainly because it used a cross-functional team and a partly parallel process to develop the product. The team included engineers (R&D) and marketing, production, and finance peo-

FIGURE 5.9

Sequential and Partly
Parallel Development
Processes

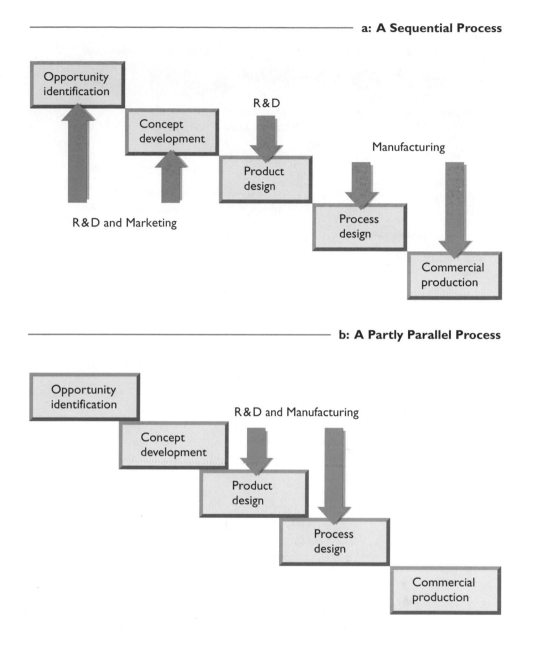

ple. Each function worked in parallel rather than sequentially. While the engineers
were designing the product, the production people were setting up the manufacturing facilities, the marketing people were working on distribution and planning
marketing campaigns, and the finance people were working on project funding.

■ Summary: Achieving Superior Innovation

The primary role that the various functions play in achieving superior innovation is
summarized in Table 5.4. Two matters, especially, need noting. First, top management must bear primary responsibility for overseeing the whole development

TABLE 5.4

The Role Played by Various Functions in Achieving Superior Innovation

Value Creation Function	Primary Roles
Infrastructure (Leadership)	1. Manage overall project (i.e., manage the development function). 2. Facilitate cross-functional cooperation.
Production	1. Cooperate with R&D on designing products that are easy to manufacture. 2. Work with R&D to develop process innovations.
Marketing	1. Provide market information to R&D. 2. Work with R&D to develop new products.
Materials Management	No primary responsibility.
R&D	1. Develop new products and processes. 2. Cooperate with other functions, particularly marketing and manufacturing, in the development process.
Information Systems	1. Use information systems to coordinate cross-functional and cross-company product development work.
Human Resources	1. Hire talented scientists and engineers.

process. This entails both managing the development funnel and facilitating cooperation between functions. Second, while R&D plays a central role in the innovation process, the effectiveness of R&D in developing new products and processes depends on its ability to cooperate with marketing and production.

ACHIEVING SUPERIOR CUSTOMER RESPONSIVENESS

To achieve superior customer responsiveness, a company must give customers what they want when they want it—so long as the company's long-term profitability is not compromised in the process. The more responsive a company is to the needs of its customers, the greater the brand loyalty it can command. In turn, strong brand loyalty may allow a company to charge a premium price for its products or to sell more goods and services to customers. Either way, the company that is responsive to its customers' needs will have a competitive advantage.

Achieving superior customer responsiveness means giving customers value for money, and steps taken to improve the efficiency of a company's production process and the quality of its output should be consistent with this aim. In addition, giving customers what they want may require the development of new products with new features. In other words, achieving superior efficiency, quality, and innovation are all part of achieving superior customer responsiveness. There are two other prerequisites for attaining this goal. The first is to focus on the company's customers and their needs, and the second, to find ways to better satisfy those needs.

■ Customer Focus

A company cannot be responsive to its customers' needs unless it knows what those needs are. Thus, the first step in building superior customer responsiveness is to motivate the whole company to focus on the customer. The means to this end are demonstrating leadership, shaping employee attitudes, and using mechanisms for bringing customers into the company.

Leadership   Customer focus must start at the top of the organization. A commitment to superior customer responsiveness brings attitudinal changes throughout a company that can ultimately be built only through strong leadership. A mission statement (see Chapter 2) that puts customers first is one way to send a clear message to employees about the desired focus. Another avenue is top management's own actions. For example, Tom Monaghan, the founder of Domino's Pizza, stays close to the customer by visiting as many stores as possible every week, running some deliveries himself, insisting that other top managers do the same, and eating Domino's pizza regularly.

Employee Attitudes   Achieving a superior customer focus requires that all employees see the customer as the focus of their activity. Leadership alone is not enough to attain this goal. All employees must be trained to focus on the customer, whether their function is marketing, manufacturing, R&D, or accounting. The objective should be to make employees think of themselves as customers—to put themselves in the customers' shoes. At that point, employees will be better able to identify ways to improve the quality of a customer's experience with the company.

To reinforce this mindset, incentive systems within the company should reward employees for satisfying customers. For example, senior managers at the Four Seasons hotel chain, who pride themselves on their customer focus, like to tell the story of Roy Dyment, a doorman in Toronto who neglected to load a departing guest's briefcase into his taxi. The doorman called the guest, a lawyer, in Washington D.C., and found that he desperately needed the briefcase for a morning meeting. Dyment hopped on a plane to Washington and returned it—without first securing approval from his boss. Far from punishing Dyment for making a mistake and for not checking with management before going to Washington, the Four Seasons responded by naming him Employee of the Year.[57] This action sent a powerful message to Four Seasons employees about the importance of satisfying customer needs.

Bringing Customers into the Company   "Know thy customer" is one of the keys to achieving superior customer responsiveness. Knowing the customer not only requires that employees think like customers themselves; it also demands that they listen to what their customers have to say, and, as much as possible, bring them into the company. While this may not involve physically bringing customers into the company, it does mean bringing in customers' opinions by soliciting feedback from customers on the company's goods and services and by building information systems that communicate the feedback to the relevant people.

For an example, consider mail-order clothing retailer Lands' End. Through its catalog and customer service telephone operators, Lands' End actively solicits comments from its customers about the quality of its clothing and the kind of merchandise they want Lands' End to supply. Indeed, it was customers' insistence that prompted the company to move into the clothing segment. Lands' End used to supply equipment for sailboats through mail-order catalogs. However, it received so many requests from customers to include outdoor clothing in its offering that it responded by expanding the catalog to fill this need. Soon clothing became the main business and Lands' End dropped the sailboat equipment. Today, the company still pays close attention to customer requests. Every month a computer printout of customer requests and comments is given to managers. This feedback helps the company to fine-tune the merchandise it sells. Indeed, frequently new lines of merchandise are introduced in response to customer requests.[58]

■ Satisfying Customer Needs

Once a focus on the customer has been achieved, the next task is to satisfy the customer needs that have been identified. As already noted, efficiency, quality, and innovation are all crucial to satisfying those needs. Beyond that, companies can provide a higher level of satisfaction if they customize the product, as much as possible, to the requirements of individual customers and if they minimize the time it takes to respond to customer demands.

Customization   Varying the features of a good or service to tailor it to the unique needs of groups of customers or, in the extreme case, individual customers is known as **customization**. It used to be thought that customization raised costs. However, as noted earlier in this chapter, the development of flexible manufacturing technologies has made it feasible to produce a far greater variety of products than could previously be done without suffering a substantial cost penalty. Companies can now customize their products to a much greater extent than they could ten to fifteen years ago, particularly when flexible manufacturing technologies are linked with Web-based information systems. The Opening Case illustrates how Levi Strauss is using Web-based systems in conjunction with flexible manufacturing technology to customize its blue jeans for individual consumers. The same is true of service companies. For example, on-line retailers such as Amazon.com have used Web-based technologies to develop a home page for their stores that is customized for each individual user. When customers access Amazon.com, they are confronted with a list of recommendations for books or music to purchase that is based on an analysis of their prior buying history.

The trend toward customization has fragmented many markets, particularly consumer markets, into ever smaller niches. An example of this fragmentation occurred in Japan in the early 1980s, when Honda dominated the motorcycle market there. Second-place Yamaha decided to go after Honda's lead. In 1981, it announced the opening of a new factory, which, when operating at full capacity, would make Yamaha the world's largest manufacturer of motorcycles. Honda responded by proliferating its product line and stepping up its rate of new-product introduction. At the start of what became known as the "motorcycle wars," Honda had 60 motorcycles in its product line. Over the next eighteen months, Honda rapidly increased its range to 113 models, customizing them to ever smaller niches. Honda was able to accomplish this without bearing a significant cost penalty because it was a flexible manufacturer. The flood of Honda's customized models pushed Yamaha out of much of the market, effectively stalling its bid to overtake Honda.[59]

Response Time   Giving customers what they want when they want it requires speed of response to customer demands. To gain a competitive advantage, a company must often respond to consumer demands very quickly, whether the transaction is a furniture manufacturer's delivery of a product once it has been ordered, a bank's processing of a loan application, an automobile manufacturer's delivery of a spare part for a car that broke down, or the wait in a supermarket checkout line. We live in a fast-paced society, where time is a valuable commodity. Companies that can satisfy customer demands for rapid response can build brand loyalty and set a higher price for the product or service.

Increased speed lets a company charge a significant premium, as the mail delivery industry illustrates. The air express niche of the mail delivery industry is based on the notion that customers are often willing to pay considerably more for overnight Express Mail, as opposed to regular mail. Another example of the value of rapid response is Caterpillar, the manufacturer of heavy earthmoving equipment, which can get a spare part to any point in the world within twenty-four hours. Since downtime for heavy construction equipment is very costly, Caterpillar's ability to respond quickly in the event of equipment malfunction is of prime importance to its customers. As a result, many of them have remained loyal to Caterpillar despite the aggressive low-price competition from Komatsu of Japan.

In general, reducing response time requires (1) a marketing function that can quickly communicate customer requests to production, (2) production and materials management functions that can quickly adjust production schedules in response to unanticipated customer demands, and (3) information systems that can help production and marketing in this process.

■ Summary: Achieving Superior Customer Responsiveness

Table 5.5 summarizes the steps different functions must take if a company is to achieve superior customer responsiveness. Although marketing plays the critical role in helping a company attain this goal, primarily because it represents the point

TABLE 5.5

The Primary Role of Different Functions in Achieving Superior Customer Responsiveness

Value Creation Function	Primary Roles
Infrastructure (Leadership)	1. Through leadership by example, build a companywide commitment to customer responsiveness.
Production	1. Achieve customization by implementing flexible manufacturing. 2. Achieve rapid response through flexible manufacturing.
Marketing	1. Know the customer. 2. Communicate customer feedback to appropriate functions.
Materials Management	1. Develop logistics systems capable of responding quickly to unanticipated customer demands (JIT).
R&D	1. Bring customers into the product development process.
Information Systems	1. Use Web-based information systems to increase customer responsiveness.
Human Resources	1. Develop training programs that get employees to think like customers.

of contact with the customer, Table 5.5 shows that the other functions also have major roles to perform. Moreover, like achieving superior efficiency, quality, and innovation, achieving superior customer responsiveness requires top management to lead in building a customer orientation within the company.

SUMMARY OF CHAPTER

This chapter discusses the role that functional-level strategies play in achieving efficiency, quality, innovation, and customer responsiveness. It examines in detail the different steps that lead to this end and makes the following main points:

✔ A company can increase efficiency through a number of steps. These include exploiting economies of scale and learning effects, adopting flexible manufacturing technologies, reducing customer defection rates, implementing just-in-time systems, getting the R&D function to design products that are easy to manufacture, upgrading the skills of employees through training, introducing self-managing teams, linking pay to performance, building a companywide commitment to efficiency through strong leadership, and designing structures that facilitate cooperation among different functions in pursuit of efficiency goals.

✔ Superior quality can help a company both to lower its costs and to differentiate its product and charge a premium price.

✔ Achieving superior quality demands an organizationwide commitment to quality and a clear focus on the customer. It also requires metrics to measure quality goals and incentives that emphasize quality; input from employees regarding ways in which quality can be improved; a methodology for tracing defects to their source and correcting the problems that produce them; rationalization of the company's supply base; cooperation with the suppliers that remain to implement TQM programs; products that are designed for ease of manufacturing; and substantial cooperation among functions.

✔ The failure rate of new-product introductions is high due to factors such as uncertainty, poor commercialization, poor positioning strategy, technological myopia, and slow cycle time.

✔ To achieve superior innovation, a company must build skills in basic and applied research; design good processes for managing development projects; and achieve close integration between the different functions of the enterprise, primarily through the adoption of cross-functional product development teams and partly parallel development processes.

✔ Achieving superior customer responsiveness often requires that the company achieve superior efficiency, quality, and innovation.

✔ To achieve superior customer responsiveness, a company needs to give customers what they want when they want it. It must ensure a strong customer focus, which can be attained through leadership; training employees to think like customers; bring customers into the company by means of superior market research; customizing the product to the unique needs of individual customers or customer groups; and responding quickly to customer demands.

DISCUSSION QUESTIONS

1. How are the four generic building blocks of competitive advantage related to each other?

2. What role can top management play in helping a company achieve superior efficiency, quality, innovation, and customer responsiveness?

3. In the long run, will adoption of TQM practices give a company a competitive advantage, or will it be required just to achieve parity with competitors?

4. In what sense might innovation be called the single most important building block of competitive advantage?

Practicing Strategic Management

 SMALL-GROUP EXERCISE
Identifying Excellence

Break up into groups of three to five people, and discuss the following scenario:

You are the management team of a start-up company, which will produce disk drives for the personal computer industry. You will sell your product to manufacturers of personal computers (original equipment manufacturers). The disk drive market is characterized by rapid technological change, product life cycles of only six to nine months, intense price competition, high fixed costs for manufacturing equipment, and substantial manufacturing economies of scale. Your customers—the original equipment manufacturers—issue very demanding technological specifications that your product has to comply with. The original equipment manufacturers also pressure you to deliver your product on time so that it fits in with their own product introduction schedule. In this industry, what functional competencies are the most important for you to build? How will you design your internal processes to ensure that those competencies are built within the company?

 STRATEGIC MANAGEMENT
PROJECT
Module 5

This module deals with the ability of your company to achieve superior efficiency, quality, innovation, and customer responsiveness. With the information you have at your disposal, answer the questions and perform the tasks listed:

1. Is your company pursuing any of the efficiency-enhancing practices discussed in this chapter?

2. Is your company pursuing any of the quality-enhancing practices discussed in this chapter?

3. Is your company pursuing any of the practices designed to enhance innovation discussed in this chapter?

4. Is your company pursuing any of the practices designed to increase customer responsiveness discussed in this chapter?

5. Evaluate the competitive position of your company in the light of your answers to questions 1–4. Explain what, if anything, the company needs to do to improve its competitive position.

 ARTICLE FILE 5

Find an example of a company that is widely regarded as excellent. Identify the source of its excellence and relate it to the material discussed in this chapter. Pay particular attention to the role played by the various functions in building excellence.

 EXPLORING THE WEB
Visiting Applied Materials

Visit the Web site of Applied Materials, the world's largest manufacturer of semiconductor fabrication equipment at (http://www.appliedmaterials.com). Find and read the company's mission statement. What does this mission statement tell you about the kind of competitive advantage that Applied Materials is trying to build? How important are efficiency, quality, innovation, and customer responsiveness to this company?

Now go to the sections of Applied's Web site that detail the company's financial results, products, and press releases. Read through these sections and try to establish how successful Applied has been at meeting the objectives set down in its mission statement. What do you think the company has done at the functional level to increase its efficiency, customer responsiveness, innovative ability, and product quality?

Search the Web for a company whose home page describes in some detail its approach to achieving one of the following: superior productivity, product quality, customer service, or innovation. Using this information, document the company's functional-level strategy and assess whether the strategy makes sense, given what you have learned so far in this book.

CLOSING CASE

Reengineering Lloyds Bank

LLOYDS BANK is one of the largest banks in Britain, with 29,000 employees and 1,800 branches nationwide. It is also one of Britain's most profitable banks, with one of the lowest ratios of operating costs to income in the British banking industry. Lloyds' senior management gives much of the credit for the bank's recent performance to its Service Quality Improvement Program (SQIP), an exercise in business process reengineering. Business process reengineering is an attempt to reorganize companies around their core processes as opposed to their traditional functions, such as the production department, marketing department, or human resource department. The term *core processes* has been defined as "a collection of activities that takes one or more kinds of input and creates an output that is of value to the customer." Processes often include activities such as customer service, order fulfillment, and product development.

Lloyds Bank turned to process reengineering in September 1992 in an attempt to increase the quality of its service and drive down the cost structure of its retail branch banking network. The catalyst was the growing competition from Britain's building societies (which are similar to U.S. savings and loans). The building societies had aggressively pursued Lloyds' retail customers following the deregulation of the British financial services industry, which had allowed banks and building societies to enter each other's markets for the first time. The bank was also worried about the impact of service expansion on its cost structure. During the 1980s, each time the bank entered a new service market (for example, home mortgage financing), it simply added more staff to a retail branch. As a result, by the early 1990s, branch costs were beginning to spiral out of control.

Under the traditional system at Lloyds, staff were given narrowly defined functional responsibilities within the context of a rigid hierarchical structure. One set of people would be responsible for managing checking accounts, another for reviewing a customer's credit, and still another for issuing credit cards, and so on. One consequence was that countless people and bits of paper were involved in what, from the customers' point of view, was a single process. For example, under the old system for opening an account at a Lloyds branch, an application form could spend a month wandering from desk to desk as different staff ordered bank cards, reviewed credit details, ordered checkbooks, opened savings accounts, and so on. Under Lloyds' new system, a single person is now responsible for a largely paperless "quality welcome" process, which entails reviewing the customer's credit history, setting up an account, and issuing credit cards, ATM cards, and checkbooks. With this new process, it usually takes less than a week for a new account to be fully functional.

Besides the "quality welcome" process, Lloyds identified five other core processes within its branches, including "lending control," "periodic payments," and "customer retention."

Each process was assigned a process owner, whose job it was to make sure that the process was reengineered to achieve Lloyds' goals of driving down costs and increasing the quality of customer service. The processes were tested in a make-believe branch before being introduced across the bank's network of retail branches in a series of waves starting in July 1993. The indications are that SQIP is having the desired effect. Lloyds' managers claim that the reengineering project has comfortably cleared the 12 percent return on capital hurdle required of business ideas. For example, the number of faulty checkbook orders fell by 30 percent in the first two months of the program—producing savings large enough to pay for the computers that monitor this activity under the new process. There is also evidence that the bank is meeting its central aim of improving customer service. Lloyds' own measure of customer satisfaction rose from 73 percent in mid 1993, when the project began, to 80 percent by mid 1995, putting the bank comfortably ahead of its two largest British rivals. Having said that, however, a 7 percent improvement in customer satisfaction is less than stunning.

Also on the down side, Lloyds has had to deal with morale problems in many of its branches, where the reengineering process is often perceived to be a subtle way of cutting jobs and, in some cases, closing down branches altogether. The bank closed 300 branches between 1990 and 1995, although management claims that this effort was independent of the reengineering process, which focuses on what is happening within branches.

Management does not question the fact that 200 jobs have been lost as a result of the reengineering process but points out that all these losses were voluntary. Those hit hardest by the reengineering effort seem to be middle-level managers, as opposed to branch employees. Between mid 1993 and mid 1995, the bank reduced the number of area directors from 80 to 41, largely because the reengineering effort enabled the bank to do more with less. Whatever the true cause of the job losses, there are concerns that employee morale problems are inhibiting Lloyd's ability to realize the full benefits of its reengineering efforts.[60]

Case Discussion Questions

1. What are the goals of the reengineering project at Lloyds Bank? If successful, how will this project affect the efficiency, quality, and customer responsiveness of Lloyds Bank?

2. Is the kind of process reengineering described here consistent with Deming's approach to total quality management, as described in this chapter?

3. Can you see a down side to Lloyds' reengineering effort? What is it? How might the impact of this down side be limited?

End Notes

1. E. Schonfeld, "The Customized, Digitized, Have It Your Way Economy," *Fortune*, September 28, 1998, p. 117; M. Knight, "Levi's to Close 11 Plants in Shift to Offshore Manufacturing," *Business and Industry*, February 24, 1999, p. 6; "The View from the Outside, Levi's Needs More Than a Patch," *New York Times*, February 28, 1999, p. 4.

2. *Chase press release*, "Chase and Chemical Merger Creating Largest Banking Company in the United States," March 21, 1996, (http://www.chase.com); S. Lipin, "Joining Fortunes," *Wall Street Journal*, August 28, 1995, p. 1; G. B. Knecht, "Chemical Merger with Chase Echoes Earlier Alliance," *Wall Street Journal*, September 1, 1995, p. 4.

3. For example, see F. M. Scherer, A. Beckenstein, E. Kaufer, and R. D. Murphy, *The Economies of Multiplant Operations* (Cambridge, Mass.: Harvard University Press, 1975).

4. H. Luft, J. Bunker, and A. Enthoven, "Should Operations Be Regionalized?" *New England Journal of Medicine*, 301 (1979) 1364–1369.

5. G. Hall and S. Howell, "The Experience Curve from an Economist's Perspective," *Strategic Management Journal*, 6 (1985), 197–212; M. Lieberman, "The Learning Curve and Pricing in the Chemical Processing Industries," *RAND Journal of Economics*, 15 (1984), 213–228.

6. Boston Consulting Group, *Perspectives on Experience* (Boston: Boston Consulting Group, 1972); Hall and Howell, "The Experience Curve,"; W. B. Hirschmann, "Profit from the Learning Curve," *Harvard Business Review* (January–February 1964), 125–139.

7. A. A. Alchian, "Reliability of Progress Curves in Airframe Production," *Econometrica*, 31 (1963), 679–693.

8. M. Borrus, L. A. Tyson, and J. Zysman, "Creating Advantage: How Government Policies Create Trade in the Semi-Conductor Industry," *Strategic Trade Policy and the New International Economics*, ed. P. R. Krugman (Cambridge, Mass.: MIT Press, 1986); S. Ghoshal and C. A. Bartlett, "Matsushita Electrical Industrial (MEI) in 1987," *Harvard Business School Case* No. 388-144, 1988.

9. G. Stalk and T. M. Hout, *Competing Against Time* (New York: Free Press, 1990); D. Miller, *The Icarus Paradox* (New York: Harper Business, 1990).

10. Abernathy and Wayne, "Limits of the Learning Curve," *Harvard Business Review*, pp. 109–119, 1980.

11. D. F. Barnett and R. W. Crandall, *Up from the Ashes: The Rise of the Steel Minimill in the United States* (Washington, D.C.: Brookings Institution, 1986).

12. See P. Nemetz and L. Fry, "Flexible Manufacturing Organizations: Implications for Strategy Formulation," *Academy of Management Review*, 13 (1988), 627–638; N. Greenwood, *Implementing Flexible Manufacturing Systems* (New York: Halstead Press, 1986); J. P. Womack, D. T. Jones, and D. Roos, *The Machine That Changed the World* (New York: Rawson Associates, 1990); and R. Parthasarthy and S. P. Seith, "The Impact of Flexible Automation on Business Strategy and Organizational Structure," *Academy of Management Review*, 17 (1992), 86–111.

13. B. J. Pine, *Mass Customization: The New Frontier in Business Competition* (Boston: Harvard Business School Press, 1993); S. Kotha, "Mass Customization: Implementing the Emerging Paradigm for Competitive Advantage," *Strategic Management Journal*, 16 (1995), 21–42; J. H. Gilmore and B. J. Pine II, "The Four Faces of Mass Customization," *Harvard Business Review* (January–February, 1997), 91–101.

14. "The Celling Out of America," *Economist*, December 17, 1994, pp. 63–64.

15. M. A. Cusumano, *The Japanese Automobile Industry* (Cambridge, Mass.: Harvard University Press, 1989); Ohno Taiichi, *Toyota Production System* (Cambridge, Mass.: Productivity Press, 1990); Womack, Jones, and Roos, *The Machine That Changed the World*.

16. F. F. Reichheld and W. E. Sasser, "Zero Defections: Quality Comes to Service," *Harvard Business Review* (September–October 1990), 105–111.

17. The example comes from Reichheld and Sasser, "Zero Defections," 105–111.

18. Ibid.

19. R. Narasimhan and J. R. Carter, "Organization, Communication and Coordination of International Sourcing," *International Marketing Review*, 7 (1990) 6–20.

20. H. F. Busch, "Integrated Materials Management," *IJDP & MM*, 18 (1990) 28–39.

21. Stalk and Hout, *Competing Against Time*.

22. A. Sorge and M. Warner, "Manpower Training, Manufacturing Organization, and Work Place Relations in Great Britain and West Germany," *British Journal of Industrial Relations*, 18 (1980), 318–333; R. Jaikumar, "Postindustrial Manufacturing," *Harvard Business Review* (November-December 1986), 72–83.

23. J. Hoerr, "The Payoff from Teamwork," *Business Week*, July 10, 1989, pp. 56–62.

24. "The Trouble with Teams," *Economist*, January 14, 1995, p. 61.

25. T. C. Powell and A. Dent-Micallef, "Information Technology as Competitive Advantage: The Role of Human, Business, and Technology Resource," *Strategic Management Journal*, 18 (1997), 375–405; B. Gates, *Business @ the Speed of Thought* (New York: Warner Books, 1999).

26. "Cisco@Speed," *Economist*, Special Report: Business and the Internet, June 26, 1999, p. 12; S. Tully, "How Cisco Mastered the Net," *Fortune*, August 17, 1997, p. 207–210; C. Kano. "The Real King of the Internet," *Fortune*, September 7, 1998, pp. 82–93.

27. Gates, *Business@the Speed of Thought*.

28. Ibid.

29. "Work in Progress," *Economist*, July 24, 1999.

30. See the articles published in the special issue on total quality management, *Academy of Management Review*, 19 (1994). The following paper provides a good overview of many of the issues involved from an academic perspective: J. W. Dean and D. E. Bowen, "Management Theory and Total Quality," *Academy of Management Review*, 19 (1994),

392–418. Also see T.C.Powell,"Total Quality Management as Competitive Advantage," *Strategic Management Journal*, 16 (1995), 15–37.

31. For general background information, see "How to Build Quality," *Economist*, September 23, 1989, pp. 91–92; A. Gabor, *The Man Who Discovered Quality* (New York: Penguin, 1990); and P. B. Crosby, *Quality Is Free* (New York: Mentor, 1980).

32. W. E. Deming,"Improvement of Quality and Productivity Through Action by Management," *National Productivity Review*, 1 (Winter 1981–1982), 12–22.

33. J. Bowles,"Is American Management Really Committed to Quality?" *Management Review* (April 1992), 42–46.

34. O. Port and G. Smith,"Quality," *Business Week*, November 30, 1992, pp. 66–75. See also "The Straining of Quality," *Economist*, January 14, 1995, pp. 55–56.

35. C. H. Deutsch,"Six Sigma Enlightenment," *New York Times*, December 7, 1998, p. 1; J. J. Barshay,"The Six Sigma Story," *Star Tribune*, June 14, 1999, p. 1; D. D. Bak,"Rethinking Industrial Drives," *Electrical/Electronics Technology*, November 30, 1998, p. 58.

36. Bowles,"Is American Management Really Committed to Quality?"; "The Straining of Quality."

37. Gabor, *The Man Who Discovered Quality*.

38. Deming,"Improvement of Quality and Productivity."

39. W. E. Deming, *Out of the Crisis* (Cambridge, Mass.: MIT Center for Advanced Engineering Study, 1986).

40. J. F. Siler and S. Atchison,"The Rx at Work in Utah," *Business Week*, October 25, 1991, p. 113.

41. E. Mansfield."How Economists See R&D," *Harvard Business Review* (November–December, 1981), 98–106.

42. Ibid.

43. Booz, Allen, & Hamilton,"New Products Management for the 1980's," privately published research report, 1982.

44. A. L. Page,"PDMA's New Product Development Practices Survey: Performance and Best Practices." PDMA 15th Annual International Conference, Boston, October 16, 1991.

45. See S. L. Brown and K. M. Eisenhardt,"Product Development: Past Research, Present Findings, and Future Directions," *Academy of Management Review*, 20 (1995), 343–378; M. B. Lieberman and D. B. Montgomery,"First Mover Advantages," *Strategic Management Journal* (Special Issue 9, Summer 1988), 41–58; D. J. Teece,"Profiting from Technological Innovation: Implications for Integration, Collaboration, Licensing and Public Policy," *Research Policy*, 15 (1987), 285–305; G. J. Tellis and P. N. Golder,"First to Market,

First to Fail?" *Sloan Management Review* (Winter 1996), 65–75.

46. R. L. Hudson,"Philips Official Calls DCC Launch Flawed, Vows Division Comeback," *Wall Street Journal*, August 19, 1993, p. A7; (2) A. Kupfer,"The Next Wave in Cassette Tapes," *Fortune*, June 3, 1991, pp. 153–158; P. M. Reilly, "Sony's Digital Audio Format Pulls Ahead of Philips's, But Both Still Have Far to Go," *Wall Street Journal*, August 6, 1993, p. B1.

47. Stalk and Hout, *Competing Against Time*.

48. Ibid.; B. Buell and R.D. Hof,"Hewlett-Packard Rethinks Itself," *Business Week*, April 1, 1991, pp. 76–79.

49. Clark and Wheelwright, *Managing New Product and Process Development*.; M. A. Schilling and C. W. L. Hill."Managing the New Product Development Process," *Academy of Management Executive*, 12, (August 1998), 67–81.

50. Clark and Wheelwright, *Managing New Product and Process Development*.

51. P. Sellers,"Getting Customers to Love You," *Fortune*, March 13, 1989, pp. 38–42.

52. O. Port,"Moving Past the Assembly Line," *Business Week*, Special Issue: Reinventing America, 1992, pp. 177–180.

53. G. P. Pisano and S. C. Wheelwright,"The New Logic of High Tech R&D," *Harvard Business Review*, September–October 1995, 93–105.

54. K. B. Clark and T. Fujimoto,"The Power of Product Integrity," *Harvard Business Review* (November–December 1990), 107–118; Clark and Wheelwright, *Managing New Product and Process;* Brown and Eisenhardt,"Product Development: Past Research, Present Findings, and Future Directions"; Stalk and Hout, *Competing Against Time*.

55. C. Christensen,"Quantum Corporation—Business and Product Teams," *Harvard Business School Case* No. 9 692-023.

56. S. Caminiti,"A Mail Order Romance: Lands' End Courts Unseen Customers," *Fortune*, March 13, 1989, pp. 43–44.

57. Sellers,"Getting Customers to Love You."

58. Caminiti,"A Mail Order Romance."

59. Stalk and Hout, *Competing Against Time*.

60. "The Black Horse Goes to the Vet," *Economist*, July 22, 1995, pp. 71–72; J. Kelley,"London Calling," *Journal of Business Strategy*, (March–April 1995), 22–26; K. Waterhouse and A. Morgan,"Using Research to Help Keep Good Customers," *Marketing and Research Today* (August 1994), 181–194; M. Hammer and J. Champy, *Reengineering the Corporation* (New York: Harper Business, 1993).

6

Business-Level Strategy

How E*Trade Uses the Internet to Gain a Low-Cost Advantage

AS WE SAW IN CHAPTER 3, in many industries new entrants have taken advantage of the opportunities opened up by the Internet to overcome barriers to entry and compete successfully against market leaders. Consider the situation of E*Trade, the on-line brokerage firm. As we discussed, for many years large established brokerages like Merrill Lynch had dominated the industry and used their protected positions to charge exorbitant brokerage fees. E*Trade's managers bought and developed software and hardware that allowed its customers to make their own trades, and to do so at a price as low as $19.95.[1]

However, the low-cost competition story in the brokerage industry did not end there. By 1999, E*Trade itself came under pressure from a new generation of on-line brokerage houses, such as Suretrade, Ameritrade and DLJ, which began offering customers trades for only $9.95 and even $7.95, undercutting E*Trade's prices by 100 percent. How could a company like E*Trade, which had made its reputation by being the low-cost leader in the industry, compete against companies that saw themselves as the new cost leaders?

The answer for E*Trade was to enhance its differentiated appeal to its customers by offering them a higher quality of service and a broader product line. E*Trade introduced a brand-new software package that made it even easier for customers to use the Internet to trade shares. What was very important, the new software was more reliable in that customers could make their trades when they wanted. Previously, E*Trade, like other brokerage firms, had experienced many problems when too many customers made trades at once; often the overloaded system simply crashed and customers were unable to buy or sell shares. E*Trade's new package also offered customers more financial research tools and gave them access to more information about specific companies to aid them in their investment decisions. In addition, E*Trade offered customers increased access to real-time stock quotes so that they could take advantage of second-to-second changes in stock prices to make money. Finally, it gave customers the opportunity to invest in Initial Public Offerings (IPOs) of shares from new companies where both potential risks and returns are high.

Furthermore, in 1999 E*Trade decided to merge with an on-line bank, Telebank, to provide its customers with a broad range of on-line banking services, such as paying bills on-line, and thus to become a one-stop on-line shopping site for all of a customer's financial needs.[2] It also took over a variety of other insurance and financial service companies to offer its customers a broad financial service product line.

The realization that it could not just be a low-cost company but also had to create a differentiation advantage in the quickly evolving on-line financial services industry has paid off for E*Trade. Its customers did not switch to the new low-cost leaders because customers perceived that for the $19.95 price they were receiving extra value for money in terms of service and reliability. E*Trade's customer accounts have increased steadily, and its stock price has soared as investors see that the company's competitive advantage is sustainable and that the company is likely to remain a dominant player in the changed industry environment. Indeed, E*Trade has shown the other firms in the industry that to remain viable they must all pursue a simultaneous low-cost and differentiation strategy—something that has become possible only because of the emergence of the Internet, which has created external economies that firms can exploit to increase their performance and competitive advantage.

OVERVIEW

As the E*Trade case suggests, this chapter examines how a company can compete effectively in a business or industry and scrutinizes the various strategies that it can adopt to maximize competitive advantage and profitability. Chapter 3, on the external industry environment, provides concepts for analyzing industry opportunities and threats. Chapters 4 and 5 discuss how a company develops functional-level strategies to build internal strengths and distinctive competencies to achieve a competitive advantage. The purpose of this chapter is to consider the business-level strategies that a company can use to exploit its competitive advantage and compete effectively in an industry. By the end of this chapter, you will be able to identify and distinguish between the principal kinds of business-level strategies that strategic managers can develop to give their companies a competitive advantage over their rivals.

WHAT IS BUSINESS-LEVEL STRATEGY?

Business-level strategy refers to the plan of action that strategic managers adopt for using a company's resources and distinctive competencies to gain a competitive advantage over its rivals in a market or industry. In Chapter 2, we discuss Derek F. Abell's view that the process of business definition entails decisions about (1) customers' needs, or *what* is to be satisfied; (2) customer groups, or *who* is to be satisfied; and (3) distinctive competencies, or *how* customer needs are to be satisfied.[3] These three decisions are the basis for choosing a business-level strategy because they determine how a company will compete in a business or industry. Consequently, we need to look at the ways in which a company makes these three decisions to gain a competitive advantage over its rivals.

■ Customers' Needs and Product Differentiation

Customers' needs are desires, wants, or cravings that can be satisfied by means of the characteristics of a product or service. For example, a person's craving for something sweet can be satisfied by a carton of Ben & Jerry's ice cream, a Snickers bar, or a spoonful of sugar. **Product differentiation** is the process of creating a competitive advantage by designing products—goods or services—to satisfy customers' needs. All companies must differentiate their products to a certain degree in order to attract customers and satisfy some minimal level of need. However, some companies differentiate their products to a much greater degree than others, and this difference can give them a competitive edge.

Some companies offer the customer a low-priced product without engaging in much product differentiation. Others seek to create something unique about their product so that they satisfy customers' needs in ways that other products cannot. The uniqueness may relate to the physical characteristics of the product, such as quality or reliability, or it may lie in the product's appeal to customers' psychological needs, such as the need for prestige or status.[4] Thus, a Japanese car may be differentiated by its reputation for reliability, and a Corvette or a Porsche may be differentiated by its ability to satisfy customers' needs for status.

■ Customer Groups and Market Segmentation

Market segmentation is the way a company decides to group customers, based on important differences in their needs or preferences, in order to gain a competitive advantage.[5] For example, General Motors groups its customers according to the amount of money they want and can afford to spend to buy a car, and for each group it builds different cars, which range from the low-priced GEO Metro to the high-priced Cadillac Seville.

In general, a company can adopt three alternative strategies toward market segmentation.[6] First, it can choose not to recognize that different groups of customers have different needs and instead adopt the approach of serving the average customer. Second, a company can choose to segment its market into different constituencies and develop a product to suit the needs of each. For example, in a recent catalog, Sony offered twenty-four different 19-inch color television sets, each targeted at a different market segment. Third, a company can choose to recognize that the market is segmented but concentrate on servicing only one market segment, or niche, such as the luxury-car niche pursued by Mercedes-Benz.

Why would a company want to make complex product/market choices and create a different product tailored to each market segment rather than create a single product for the whole market? The answer is that the decision to provide many products for many market niches allows a company to satisfy customers' needs better. As a result, customers' demand for the company's products rises and generates more revenue than would be the case if the company offered just one product for the whole market.[7] Sometimes, however, the nature of the product or the nature of the industry does not allow much differentiation, as is true, for instance, of bulk chemicals or cement.[8] These industries afford little opportunity for obtaining a competitive advantage through product differentiation and market segmentation because there is little opportunity for serving customers' needs and customer groups in different ways. Instead, price is the main criterion by which customers evaluate the product, and the competitive advantage lies with the company that has superior efficiency and can provide the lowest-priced product.

■ Distinctive Competencies

The third issue in business-level strategy is deciding which distinctive competencies to pursue to satisfy customers' needs and customer groups.[9] As we discuss in Chapter 4, there are four ways companies can obtain a competitive advantage: superior efficiency, quality, innovation, and responsiveness to customers. The Four Seasons hotel chain, for example, attempts to do all it can to provide its customers with the highest-quality accommodations and the best customer service possible. In making business strategy choices, a company must decide how to organize and combine its distinctive competencies to gain a competitive advantage. The source of these distinctive competencies is examined at length in Chapter 5.

CHOOSING A GENERIC BUSINESS-LEVEL STRATEGY

Companies pursue a business-level strategy to gain a competitive advantage that allows them to outperform rivals and achieve above-average returns. They can choose from three basic generic competitive approaches: cost leadership, differentiation, and focus, although, as we will see, these can be combined in different ways.[10] These strategies are called *generic* because all businesses or industries can pursue them regardless of whether they are manufacturing, service, or not-for-profit enterprises. Each of the generic strategies results from a company's making consistent choices on product, market, and distinctive competencies—choices that reinforce each other. Table 6.1 summarizes the choices appropriate for each of the three generic strategies.

■ Cost-Leadership Strategy

A company's goal in pursuing a **cost-leadership strategy** is to outperform competitors by doing everything it can to produce goods or services at a cost lower than theirs. Two advantages accrue from a cost-leadership strategy. First, because of its lower costs, the cost leader is able to charge a lower price than its competitors yet make the same level of profit. If companies in the industry charge similar prices for their products, the cost leader still makes a higher profit than its competitors because of its lower costs. Second, if rivalry within the industry increases and companies start to compete on price, the cost leader will be able to withstand competition

TABLE 6.1

Product/Market/Distinctive-Competency Choices and Generic Competitive Strategies

	Cost Leadership	Differentiation	Focus
Product Differentiation	Low (principally by price)	High (principally by uniqueness)	Low to high (price or uniqueness)
Market Segmentation	Low (mass market)	High (many market segments)	Low (one or a few segments)
Distinctive Competency	Manufacturing and materials management	Research and development, sales and marketing	Any kind of distinctive competency

better than the other companies because of its lower costs. For both these reasons, cost leaders are likely to earn above-average profits. How does a company become the cost leader? It achieves this position by means of the product/market/distinctive-competency choices that it makes to gain a low-cost competitive advantage (see Table 6.1).

Strategic Choices The cost leader chooses a low level of product differentiation. Differentiation is expensive; if the company expends resources to make its products unique, then its costs rise.[11] The cost leader aims for a level of differentiation not markedly inferior to that of the differentiator (a company that competes by spending resources on product development), but a level obtainable at low cost.[12] The cost leader does not try to be the industry leader in differentiation; it waits until customers want a feature or service before providing it. For example, a cost leader does not introduce stereo sound in television sets. It adds stereo sound only when it is obvious that consumers want it.

The cost leader also normally ignores the different market segments and positions its product to appeal to the average customer. The reason the cost leader makes this choice is, again, that developing a line of products tailored to the needs of different market segments is an expensive proposition. A cost leader normally engages in only a limited amount of market segmentation. Even though no customer may be totally happy with the product, the fact that the company normally charges a lower price than its competitors attracts customers to its products.

In developing distinctive competencies, the overriding goal of the cost leader must be to increase its efficiency and lower its costs compared with its rivals. The development of distinctive competencies in manufacturing and materials management is central to achieving this goal. Companies pursuing a low-cost strategy may attempt to ride down the experience curve so that they can lower their manufacturing costs.

Achieving a low-cost position may also require that the company develop skills in flexible manufacturing and adopt efficient materials-management techniques. (As you may recall, Table 5.1 outlines the ways in which a company's functions can be used to increase efficiency.) Consequently, the manufacturing and materials-management functions are the center of attention for a company pursuing a cost-leadership strategy; the other functions shape their distinctive competencies to meet the needs of manufacturing and materials management.[13] For example, the sales function may develop the competency of capturing large, stable sets of customers' orders. In turn, this allows manufacturing to make longer production runs and so achieve economies of scale and reduce costs. The human resource function may focus on instituting training programs and compensation systems that lower costs by enhancing employees' productivity, and the research and development function may specialize in process improvements to lower the manufacturing costs. We saw in the Opening Case, for example, how E*Trade took advantage of advances in information technology to lower the costs associated with exchanging goods between buyers and sellers. Similarly, Dell Computer uses the Internet to lower the cost of selling its computers—Internet sales now account for more than 30 percent of its sales.

Many cost leaders gear all their strategic product/market/distinctive-competency choices to the single goal of squeezing out every cent of costs to sustain their competitive advantage. A company such as H. J. Heinz is another excellent example of a cost leader. Because beans and canned vegetables do not permit much of a markup, the profit comes from the large volume of cans sold. Therefore, Heinz goes to extraordinary lengths to try to reduce costs—by even one-twentieth of a cent per can—because this will lead to large cost savings and thus bigger profits over the long run. As you will see in the chapters in Part Four on strategy implementation, another source of cost savings in pursuing cost leadership is the design of the organizational structure to match this strategy, since structure is a major source of a company's costs. As we discuss in Chapter 12, a low-cost strategy usually implies tight production controls and rigorous use of budgets to control the production process.

Advantages and Disadvantages   The advantages of each generic strategy are best discussed in terms of Porter's five forces model, which is introduced in Chapter 3.[14] The five forces are threats from competitors, powerful suppliers, powerful buyers, substitute products, and new entrants. The cost leader is protected from *industry competitors* by its cost advantage. Its lower costs also mean that it will be less affected than its competitors by increases in the price of inputs if there are *powerful suppliers* and less affected by a fall in the price it can charge for its products if there are *powerful buyers*. Moreover, since cost leadership usually requires a big market share, the cost leader purchases in relatively large quantities, increasing its bargaining power over suppliers. If *substitute products* start to come into the market, the cost leader can reduce its price to compete with them and retain its market share. Finally, the leader's cost advantage constitutes a *barrier to entry*, since other companies are unable to enter the industry and match the leader's costs or prices. The cost leader is, therefore, relatively safe as long as it can maintain its cost advantage and price is the key for a significant number of buyers.

The principal dangers of the cost-leadership approach lurk in competitors' ability to find ways to produce at lower cost and beat the cost leader at its own game. For instance, if technological change makes experience-curve economies obsolete, new companies may apply lower-cost technologies that give them a cost advantage over the cost leader. The steel minimills discussed in Chapter 5 gained this advantage. Competitors may also draw a cost advantage from labor-cost savings. Foreign competitors in the Third World have very low labor costs; for example, wage costs in the United States are roughly 600 percent more than they are in Malaysia, China, or Mexico. Many U.S. companies now assemble their products abroad as part of their low-cost strategy; many are forced to do so simply to compete.

Competitors' ability to imitate easily the cost leader's methods is another threat to the cost-leadership strategy. For example, the ability of IBM-clone manufacturers to produce IBM-compatible products at costs similar to IBM's (but, of course, to sell them at a much lower price) was a major factor contributing to IBM's troubles.

Finally, the cost-leadership strategy carries a risk that the cost leader, in its single-minded desire to reduce costs, may lose sight of changes in customers' tastes. Thus, a company might make decisions that decrease costs but drastically affect demand for the product. For example, Joseph Schlitz Brewing lowered the quality of its beer's ingredients, substituting inferior grains to reduce costs. Consumers immediately caught on, with the result that demand for the product dropped dramatically. As mentioned earlier, the cost leader cannot abandon product differentiation, and even low-priced products, such as Timex watches, cannot be too inferior to the more expensive watches made by Seiko if the low-cost, low-price policy is to succeed.

■ Differentiation Strategy

The objective of the generic **differentiation strategy** is to achieve a competitive advantage by creating a product (good or service) that is perceived by customers to be *unique* in some important way. The differentiated company's ability to satisfy a customer's need in a way that its competitors cannot means that it can charge a *premium price* (a price considerably above the industry's average). The ability to increase revenues by charging premium prices (rather than by reducing costs as the cost leader does) allows the differentiator to outperform its competitors and gain above-average profits. The premium price is usually substantially above the price charged by the cost leader, and customers pay it because they believe the product's differentiated qualities are worth the difference. Consequently, the product is priced on the basis of what the market will bear.[15]

Thus, Mercedes-Benz cars are much more expensive in the United States than in Europe because they confer more status here. Similarly, a BMW is not a lot more expensive to produce than a Honda, but its price is determined by customers who perceive that the prestige of owning a BMW is something worth paying for. Similarly, Rolex watches do not cost much to produce; their design has not changed very much for years, and their gold content represents only a fraction of the price. Customers, however, buy a Rolex because of the unique quality they perceive in it: its ability to confer status on its wearer. In stereos, the name Bang & Olufsen of Denmark stands out; in jewelry, Tiffany; in airplanes, Learjets. All these products command premium prices because of their differentiated qualities.

Strategic Choices   As Table 6.1 shows, a differentiator chooses a high level of product differentiation to gain a competitive advantage. Product differentiation can be achieved in three principal ways, which are discussed in detail in Chapter 4: quality, innovation, and responsiveness to customers. For example, Procter & Gamble claims that its product quality is high and that Ivory soap is 99.44 percent pure. Maytag stresses reliability and the best repair record of any washer on the market. IBM promotes the quality service provided by its well-trained sales force.

Innovation is very important for technologically complex products, for which new features are the source of differentiation, and many people pay a premium price for new and innovative products, such as a state-of-the-art computer, stereo, or car.

When differentiation is based on responsiveness to customers, a company offers comprehensive after-sales service and product repair. This is an especially important consideration for complex products such as cars and domestic appliances, which are likely to break down periodically. Companies such as Maytag, Dell Computer, and BMW all excel in responsiveness to customers. In service organizations, quality-of-service attributes are also very important. Why can Neiman Marcus, Nordstrom, and Federal Express charge premium prices? They offer an exceptionally high level of service. Similarly, firms of lawyers or accountants stress the service aspects of their operations to clients: their knowledge, professionalism, and reputation.

Finally, a product's appeal to customers' psychological desires can become a source of differentiation. The appeal can be to prestige or status, as it is with BMWs and Rolex watches; to patriotism, as with Chevrolet; to safety of home and family, as with Prudential Insurance; or to value for money, as with Sears and JC Penney. Differentiation can also be tailored to age groups and to socioeconomic groups. Indeed, the bases of differentiation are endless.

A company that pursues a differentiation strategy strives to differentiate itself along as many dimensions as possible. The less it resembles its rivals, the more it is protected from competition and the wider is its market appeal. Thus, BMWs do not offer only prestige. They also offer technological sophistication, luxury, and reliability, as well as good, although very expensive, repair service. All these bases of differentiation help increase sales.

Generally, a differentiator chooses to segment its market into many niches. Now and then a company offers a product designed for each market niche and decides to be a **broad differentiator**, but a company might choose to serve just those niches in which it has a specific differentiation advantage. For example, Sony produces twenty-four models of television, filling all the niches from mid-priced to high-priced sets. However, its lowest-priced model is always priced about $100 above that of its competitors, bringing into play the premium-price factor. You have to pay extra for a Sony. Similarly, although Mercedes-Benz has filled niches below its old high-priced models with its S and C series, until recently it made no attempt to produce a car for every market segment. In 1996, however, it announced that it was planning to introduce a new line of less expensive cars to appeal to a wider market, and analysts were at once concerned that this would affect its differentiated appeal.

Finally, in choosing which distinctive competency to pursue, a differentiated company concentrates on the organizational function that provides the sources of its differentiation advantage. Differentiation on the basis of innovation and technological competency depends on the R&D function, as discussed in Chapter 5. Efforts to improve service to customers depend on the quality of the sales function. A focus on a specific function does not mean, however, that the control of costs is not important for a differentiator. A differentiator does not want to increase costs unnecessarily and tries to keep them somewhere near those of the cost leader. However, since developing the distinctive competency needed to provide a differentiation advantage is often expensive, a differentiator usually has higher costs than the cost leader.

Still, it must control all costs that do not contribute to its differentiation advantage so that the price of the product does not exceed what customers are willing to pay. Since bigger profits are earned by controlling costs and by maximizing revenues, it pays to control costs, though not to minimize them to the point of losing the source of differentiation.[16] The owners of the famous Savoy Hotel in London faced just this problem in the 1990s. The Savoy's reputation has always been based on the incredibly high level of service it offers its customers. Three hotel employees attend to the needs of each guest, and in every room a guest can summon a waiter, maid, or valet by pressing a button at the bedside. The cost of offering this level of service has been so high that the hotel makes less than 1 percent net profit every year.[17] Its owners are trying to find ways to reduce costs to increase profits. However, their problem is that if they reduce the number of hotel staff (the main source of the Savoy's high costs), they may destroy the main source of its differentiated appeal.

Advantages and Disadvantages   The advantages of the differentiation strategy can now be discussed in the context of the five forces model. Differentiation safeguards a company against competitors to the degree that customers develop *brand loyalty* for its products. Brand loyalty is a very valuable asset because it protects the company on all fronts. For example, powerful suppliers are rarely a problem because the differentiated company's strategy is geared more toward the price it can charge than toward the costs of production. Thus, a differentiator can tolerate moderate increases in the prices of its inputs better than the cost leader can. Differentiators are unlikely to experience problems with powerful buyers because the differentiator offers the buyer a unique product. Only it can supply the product, and it commands brand loyalty. Differentiators can pass on price increases to customers because customers are willing to pay the premium price. Differentiation and brand loyalty also create a barrier to entry for other companies seeking to enter the industry. New companies are forced to develop their own distinctive competency to be able to compete, and doing so is very expensive.

Finally, the threat of substitute products depends on the ability of competitors' products to meet the same customers' needs as the differentiator's products and to break customers' brand loyalty. This can happen, as when IBM-clone manufacturers captured a large share of the home computer market, but many people still want an IBM, even though there are many IBM clones available. The issue is, how much of a premium price a company can charge for uniqueness before customers switch products?

The main problems with a differentiation strategy center on the company's long-term ability to maintain its perceived uniqueness in customers' eyes. We have seen in the last ten years how quickly competitors move to imitate and copy successful differentiators. This has happened in many industries, such as computers, autos, and home electronics. Patents and first-mover advantages (the advantages of being the first to market a product or service) last only so long, and as the overall quality of products produced by all companies goes up, brand loyalty declines. The story of the way American Express lost its competitive advantage, told in Strategy in Action 6.1, highlights many of the threats that face a differentiator.

A strategy of differentiation, then, requires the firm to develop a competitive advantage by making choices about its product, market, and distinctive competency that reinforce each other and together increase the value of a good or service in the eyes of consumers. When a product has uniqueness in customers' eyes, differentiators can charge a premium price. However, the disadvantages of a differentiation strategy are the ease with which competitors can imitate a differentiator's product and the difficulty of maintaining a premium price. When differentiation stems from the design or physical features of the product, differentiators are at great risk because imitation is easy. The risk is that over time products such as VCRs or stereos become *commoditylike* products, for which the importance of differentiation diminishes as customers become more price sensitive. When differentiation stems from quality of service or reliability or from any *intangible source*, such as Federal Express's guarantee of fast delivery or the prestige of a Rolex, a company is much more secure. It is difficult to imitate intangibles, and the differentiator can reap the benefits of this strategy for a long time. Nevertheless, all differentiators must watch out for imitators and be careful that they do not charge a price higher than the market will bear.

■ Cost Leadership *and* Differentiation

Recently, changes in production techniques—in particular, the development of flexible manufacturing technologies (discussed in Chapter 5)—have made the choice between cost-leadership and differentiation strategies less clear-cut. With techno-

Who Wants an American Express Card?

American Express Company's green, gold, and platinum credit cards used to be closely linked with high status and prestige. Obtaining an American Express (AmEx) card required a high income, and obtaining a gold or platinum card required an even higher one. AmEx carefully differentiated its product by using famous people to advertise the virtues—exclusivity and uniqueness—of possessing its card. Consumers were willing to pay the high yearly fee to possess the card, even though every month they were required to pay off the debit balance they had accumulated. AmEx's cards were a premium product that allowed the company to charge both customers and merchants more because it offered quality service and conferred status on the user. For many years, its credit card operation was the money spinner of AmEx's Travel Related Services (TRS) Division, and the company's stock price soared as its profits surpassed $200 million by 1990.[18]

AmEx's differentiated strategy began to suffer in the 1990s, however. Rival companies such as MasterCard and Visa advertised that their cards can be used at locations where AmEx's are not accepted. Moreover, as these companies make clear, anybody can own a MasterCard or a Visa gold card; it is not just for the fortunate elite. In addition, various companies and banks have banded together to offer the consumer many other benefits of using their particular credit cards. For example, banks and airlines formed alliances that allow consumers to use a bank's credit card to accumulate miles toward the purchase of an airline's tickets. By 1995, thousands of other companies—among them, AT&T, General Motors, Yahoo!, Kroger's, and Dell—began issuing their own credit cards, which offer customers savings on their products, often without a yearly fee. The emergence of all these new credit cards broke the loyalty of AmEx customers and shattered the card's unique image. It lost its differentiated appeal and become one more credit card in an overcrowded market. More than 2 million of its users deserted Amex, and the firm lost hundreds of millions of dollars in the early 1990s.

However, Amex strove to fight back and restore profitability to its division. To reduce costs, it laid off more than 5,000 employees in the TRS division, started its own airline mileage program to entice its previous cardholders back, and made its card more available to potential users, such as college students. By lowering the fees it charges merchants, it also increased the number of outlets that accept the card. For example, the card can now be used at Kmart. Furthermore, in 1998, it spent $1.13 billion on marketing and promotion to rebuild its brand name.[19] Finally, in 1999, it announced that it was developing the "ultimate travel card," a new electronic smart card that it intended to make the global standard for travel and entertainment transactions. Among other things, this card permits electronic ticketing and boarding passes, automated car rental check-in, Internet identification and access, and payment functions, which include an electronic purse.[20] In this way, AMEX hopes to promote its differentiated image and once again become the credit card that everyone wants to use.

logical developments, companies have found it easier to obtain the benefits of both strategies. The reason is that the new flexible technologies allow firms to pursue a differentiation strategy at a low cost: that is, companies can combine these two generic strategies.

Traditionally, differentiation was obtainable only at high cost because the necessity of producing different models for different market segments meant that firms had to have short production runs, which raised manufacturing costs. In addition, the differentiated firm had to bear higher marketing costs than the cost leader because it was serving many market segments. As a result, differentiators had higher costs than cost leaders, which produced large batches of standardized products. However, flexible manufacturing may enable a firm pursuing differentiation to manufacture a range of products at a cost comparable to that of the cost leader. The use of robots and flexible manufacturing cells reduces the costs of retooling the production line and the costs associated with small production runs. Indeed, a factor promoting the current trend toward market fragmentation and niche marketing in many consumer goods industries, such as mobile phones, computers, and appliances, is the substantial reduction of the costs of differentiation by flexible manufacturing.

Another way that a differentiated producer may be able to realize significant economies of scale is by standardizing many of the component parts used in its end products. For example, in the 1990s Chrysler began to offer more than twenty different models of cars and minivans to different segments of the auto market. However, despite their different appearances, all twenty models were based on only three different platforms. Moreover, most of the cars used many of the same components, including axles, drive units, suspensions, and gear boxes. As a result, Chrysler was able to realize significant economies of scale in the manufacture and bulk purchase of standardized component parts.

A company can also reduce both production and marketing costs if it limits the number of models in the product line by offering packages of options rather than letting consumers decide exactly what options they require. It is increasingly common for auto manufacturers, for example, to offer an economy auto package, a luxury package, and a sports package to appeal to the principal market segments. Package offerings substantially lower manufacturing costs because long production runs of the various packages are possible. At the same time, the firm is able to focus its advertising and marketing efforts on particular market segments so that these costs are also decreased. Once again, the firm is getting gains from differentiation and from low cost at the same time.

Just-in-time inventory systems, too, can help reduce costs, as well as improve the quality and reliability of a company's products. This benefit is important to differentiated firms, for whom quality and reliability are essential ingredients of the product's appeal. Rolls-Royces, for instance, are never supposed to break down. Improved quality control enhances a company's reputation and thus allows it to charge a premium price, which is one object of TQM programs.

Taking advantage of the new production and marketing developments, some firms are managing to reap the gains from cost-leadership and differentiation strategies simultaneously. Since they can charge a premium price for their products compared with the price charged by the pure cost leader and since they have lower costs than the pure differentiator, they are obtaining at least an equal, and probably a higher, level of profit than firms pursuing only one of the generic strategies. Hence the combined strategy is the most profitable to pursue, and companies are quickly moving to take advantage of the new production, materials-management, and marketing techniques. Indeed, U.S. companies must take advantage of them if they are to regain a competitive advantage, for the Japanese pioneered many of these new developments. This explains why firms such as Toyota and Sony are currently much more profitable than their U.S. counterparts, General Motors and Zenith, respectively. However, American firms such as McDonald's, Motorola, and Ford, which is profiled in Strategy in Action 6.2, are pursuing both strategies simultaneously with great success.

Ford's Difficult Balancing Act

In the 1990s, Alex Trotman, Ford Motor's CEO at the time, faced the problem of how best to compete in an increasingly competitive car industry. On the one hand, Ford, like other large U.S. carmakers, had been forced to find ways to reduce costs to compete effectively against low-priced competitors from Japan and Europe. On the other, Ford had to differentiate its cars and make them stand out so that customers would be attracted to them and would buy them rather than the cars of its rivals.

To reduce costs, Ford forged ahead with a global cost-cutting plan called Ford 2000. The plan included producing very similar models of cars and trucks that could be sold globally to customers in all the countries of the world in which Ford does business. It also meant centralizing all car design activities at five global design centers to reduce costs. Finally, the plan reduced the number of different car platforms (the frames on which the car models are based) and the number of component parts, again to decrease costs. For example, instead of the more than thirty different kinds of car horns, Ford decided to use only three, which it bought in bigger volume from a few manufacturers. Ford projected a $1 billion saving in engineering costs and $11 billion in reduced plant investment costs from this plan.[21]

To make Ford's products unique, Trotman also authorized a radically new program of car styling. Throughout the 1970s and 1980s, Ford had been known for the big, boxy, plain look of its cars, a look that had changed little in decades. From the mid 1980s on, Ford began to restyle all its cars. Trotman's multibillion-dollar program culminated in the radical redesign of the best-selling car in the United States, the Ford Taurus, which Ford launched in the fall of 1995. The accentuated curves and oval shape of the Taurus reflected the redesign of Ford's other cars, such as the Lincoln Continental, the Mustang, and the Mondeo, Ford's first world car.

By 1996, however, it became clear to Trotman and other top Ford executives that the dual push to reduce costs on a global level while launching a whole new series of redesigned global cars was not working. The enormous development costs of the new cars had raised costs dramatically and forced up car prices. The typical well-equipped Taurus, for example, was retailing for more than $20,000, more than $3,000 above the old model, and customers were experiencing sticker shock. In essence, all the cost savings brought about by the Ford 2000 plan were being eaten up by the high costs associated with its push to produce a radically new, differentiated line of cars. By mid 1996 the Honda Accord had once again become the best-selling car in the United States, Ford's profits had plunged 58 percent, its stock price was flat, and many analysts were worried that Ford's new strategy was not working.[22]

In May 1996, Trotman announced a new plan to bring together the cost and differentiation sides of Ford's business-level strategy. He argued that Ford's basic strategy was correct and that all the benefits of the launch of new cars and the saving in costs would be reaped well into the next century. In the short term, however, to boost sales, Ford announced that it would bring out stripped-down models of the Taurus and other cars to reduce the price and attract more customers. In addition, recognizing that its new cars were costing too much to develop, Ford announced that it would close two of its global design centers and further consolidate its design program to reduce development costs. Trotman and his top management team continued to search for ways to align both the cost and differentiation sides of the business-strategy equation to provide Ford's customers with a well-designed car at a price they are willing to pay.

In 1999, a new CEO, Jacques Nasser, took control of the company and announced new moves to further the company's competitive advantage. First, he orchestrated Ford's purchase of Volvo to increase its product range. He also announced a new global push to reduce costs, including a new move to decentralize control to each of Ford's business units so that they might search out innovative ways to streamline their operations and increase efficiency.[23] By the end of the 1990s, Ford's strategy paid off as its sales and profits rose to record levels.

■ Focus Strategy

The third generic competitive strategy, the **focus strategy**, differs from the other two chiefly because it is directed toward serving the needs of a *limited customer group* or *segment*. A focus strategy concentrates on serving a particular market niche, which can be defined geographically, by type of customer, or by segment of the product line.[24] For example, a geographic niche can be defined by region or even by locality. Selecting a niche by type of customer might mean serving only the very rich, the very young, or the very adventurous. Concentrating only on a segment of the product line means focusing only on vegetarian foods, on very fast automobiles, on designer clothes, or on sunglasses. In following a focus strategy, a company is *specializing* in some way.

Once it has chosen its market segment, a company pursues a focus strategy through either a differentiation or a low-cost approach. Figure 6.1 shows these two different kinds of focused strategies and compares them with a pure cost-leadership or differentiation strategy.

In essence, a focused company is a specialized differentiator *or* a cost leader. If a company uses a focused low-cost approach, it competes against the cost leader in the market segments in which it has no cost disadvantage. For example, in local lumber or cement markets, the focuser has lower transportation costs than the low-cost national company. The focuser may also have a cost advantage because it is producing complex or custom-built products that do not lend themselves easily to economies of scale in production and, therefore, offer few experience-curve advantages. With a focus strategy, a company concentrates on small-volume custom products, for which it has a cost advantage, and leaves the large-volume standardized market to the cost leader.

If a company uses a focused differentiation approach, then all the means of differentiation that are open to the differentiator are available to the focused company. The point is that the focused company competes with the differentiator in only one or in just a few segments. For example, Porsche, a focused company, competes against General Motors in the sports car segment of the car market, not in other market segments. Focused companies are likely to develop differentiated product qualities successfully because of their knowledge of a small customer set (such as sports car buyers) or knowledge of a region.

FIGURE 6.1

Types of Business-Level Strategies

	Offers products to only one group of customers	Offers products to many kinds of customers
Offers low-priced products to customers	Focused Cost-Leadership Strategy	Cost-Leadership Strategy
Offers unique or distinctive products to customers	Focused Differentiation Strategy	Differentiation Strategy

STRATEGY *in* ACTION

Finding a Niche in the Outsourcing Market

Outsourcing occurs when one company contracts with another to have it perform one of the value creation functions for it. Increasingly, many companies are finding it very difficult to keep up with the pace of technological change in the computer software industry and are outsourcing their data-processing needs to specialized software companies. For example, Electronic Data Systems (EDS), founded by Ross Perot, has grown into a $15 billion computer services giant that manages other companies' data-processing operations using its own proprietary software. IBM is another large company that has moved to exploit this developing market; in 1999, it signed many billion-dollar contracts with large computer makers such as Dell and Motorola to be their primary computer parts supplier.

As you can imagine, however, different kinds of organizations, such as universities, banks, insurance agencies, local governments, and utilities, have different kinds of data-processing needs and problems. Consequently, each kind of company requires a specialized kind of software system that can be customized to its specific needs. As a result, it is difficult for any one software company to serve the needs of a wide range of different companies, and the outsourcing market in data processing is very fragmented. Large companies such as EDS have only a small market share; for example, EDS had just 18 percent market share in 1996. Consequently, opportunities abound.

Increasingly, small, specialized software companies

have been springing up to manage the needs of particular kinds of clients. An example is Systems & Computer Technology, based in Malvern, Pennsylvania, which went head-to-head with EDS to secure a seven-year $35 million outsourcing contract to serve the data-processing needs of Dallas County. The company has yearly revenues of only $200 million, compared with EDS's $15 billion, but it won the contract because it specializes in servicing the needs of local government and institutions of higher education.[25] It could show Dallas County its twelve ongoing contracts with municipal clients, whereas EDS could offer its experience with only one, a hospital. The focused company won out over the differentiator.

Other focused companies are also springing up—for instance, the Bisys Group and Systematics Company, which serves the needs of banks and universities. It appears that in the data-processing industry, small, focused companies are strong competitors because of their ability to provide specialized, personal service to specific clients in a way that large differentiators cannot.[26] Indeed, EDS has run into problems in the late 1990s because of the emergence of agile, Internet-based competitors that can provide e-commerce solutions at a price much lower than EDS's.[27] In 1999, EDS replaced its CEO and announced the appointment of a new e-business chief to catch up and get back in the game.[28] Only time will tell if it can regain its dominant position in the fast-changing Internet services industry environment.

Furthermore, concentration on a small range of products sometimes allows a focuser to develop innovations faster than a large differentiator can. However, the focuser does not attempt to serve all market segments, for doing so would bring it into direct competition with the differentiator. Instead, a focused company concentrates on building market share in one market segment and, if successful, may begin to serve more and more market segments, chipping away the differentiator's competitive advantage. The emergence of small software companies to take advantage of specialized niches in the outsourcing market, discussed in Strategy in Action 6.3, illustrates how focused companies can obtain a competitive advantage.

Strategic Choices Table 6.1 illustrates the specific product/market/distinctive-competency choices made by a focused company. Differentiation can be high or low because the company can pursue a low-cost or a differentiation approach. As for customer groups, a focused company chooses specific niches in which to compete rather than going for a whole market, as a cost leader does, or filling a large number of niches, as a broad differentiator does. The focused firm can pursue any distinctive competency because it can seek any kind of differentiation or low-cost advantage. Thus, it might find a cost advantage and develop a superior efficiency in low-cost manufacturing within a region. Alternatively, it might develop superior skills in responsiveness to customers, based on its ability to serve the needs of regional customers in ways that a national differentiator would find very expensive.

The many avenues a focused company can take to develop a competitive advantage explain why there are so many small companies in relation to large ones. A focused company has enormous opportunity to develop its own niche and compete against low-cost and differentiated enterprises, which tend to be larger. A focus strategy provides an opportunity for an entrepreneur to find and then exploit a gap in the market by developing an innovative product that customers cannot do without.[29] The steel minimills discussed in Chapter 5 are a good example of how focused companies specializing in one market can grow so efficient that they become the cost leaders. Many large companies started with a focus strategy, and, of course, one means by which companies can expand is to take over other focused companies. For example, Saatchi & Saatchi DFS Compton, a specialist marketing company, grew by taking over several companies that were also specialists in their own markets, such as Hay Associates, the management consultants.

Advantages and Disadvantages   A focused company's competitive advantages stem from the source of its distinctive competency—efficiency, quality, innovation, or responsiveness to customers. The firm is protected from *rivals* to the extent that it can provide a product or service they cannot. This ability also gives the focuser power over its *buyers* because they cannot get the same thing from anyone else. With regard to *powerful suppliers*, however, a focused company is at a disadvantage, because it buys in small volume and thus is in the suppliers' power. However, as long as it can pass on price increases to loyal customers, this disadvantage may not be a significant problem. *Potential entrants* have to overcome the loyalty from customers the focuser has generated, and the development of customers' loyalty also lessens the threat from *substitute products.* This protection from the five forces allows the focuser to earn above-average returns on its investment. Another advantage of the focus strategy is that it permits a company to stay close to its customers and to respond to their changing needs. The difficulty a large differentiator sometimes experiences in managing a large number of market segments is not an issue for a focuser.

Since a focuser produces a small volume, its production costs often exceed those of a low-cost company. Higher costs can also reduce profitability if a focuser is forced to invest heavily in developing a distinctive competency—such as expensive product innovation—in order to compete with a differentiated firm. However, once again, flexible manufacturing systems are opening up new opportunities for focused firms because small production runs become possible at a lower cost. Increasingly, small specialized firms are competing with large companies in specific market segments in which their cost disadvantage is much reduced.

A second problem is that the focuser's niche can suddenly disappear because of technological change or changes in consumers' tastes. Unlike the more generalist differentiator, a focuser cannot move easily to new niches, given its concentration of resources and competency in one or a few niches. For example, a clothing manufacturer that focuses on heavy metal enthusiasts would find it difficult to shift to other segments if heavy metal loses its appeal, and a Mexican restaurant would find it difficult to move to Chinese food if customers' tastes change. The disappearance of niches is one reason that so many small companies fail.

Finally, there is the prospect that differentiators will compete for a focuser's niche by offering a product that can satisfy the demands of the focuser's customers; for example, GM's and Ford's new luxury cars are aimed at Lexus, BMW, and Mercedes-Benz buyers. A focuser is vulnerable to attack and, therefore, has to defend its niche constantly.

■ Stuck in the Middle

Each generic strategy requires a company to make consistent product/market/distinctive-competency choices to establish a competitive advantage. In other words, a company must achieve a fit among the three components of business-level strategy. Thus, for example, a low-cost company cannot strive for a high level of market segmentation, as a differentiator does, and provide a wide range of products because doing so would raise production costs too much and the company would lose its low-cost advantage. Similarly, a differentiator with a competency in innovation that tries to reduce its expenditures on research and development or one with a competency in responsiveness to customers through after-sales service that seeks to economize on its sales force to decrease costs is asking for trouble because it will lose its competitive advantage as its distinctive competency disappears.

Choosing a business-level strategy successfully means giving serious attention to all elements of the competitive plan. Many companies, through ignorance or through mistakes, do not do the planning necessary for success in their chosen strategy. Such companies are said to be **stuck in the middle** because they have made product/market choices in such a way that they have been unable to obtain or sustain a competitive advantage.[30] As a result, they have no consistent business-level strategy, experience below-average performance, and suffer when industry competition intensifies.

Some stuck-in-the-middle companies may have started out by pursuing one of the three generic strategies but then made wrong resource allocation decisions or experienced a hostile, changing environment. It is very easy to lose control of a generic strategy unless strategic managers keep close track of the business and its environment, constantly adjusting product/market choices to suit changing conditions within the industry. The experience of Holiday Inns in the 1980s, described in Strategy in Action 6.4, shows how a company can become stuck in the middle because of environmental changes.

As the experience of Holiday Inns suggests, there are many paths to being stuck in the middle. Quite commonly, a focuser can get stuck in the middle when it becomes overconfident and starts to act like a broad differentiator. People Express, the defunct airline, exemplified a company in this situation. It started out as a specialized air carrier serving a narrow market niche: low-priced travel on the eastern seaboard. In pursuing this focus strategy based on cost leadership, it was very successful, but when it tried to expand to other geographic regions and began taking over other airlines to gain a larger number of planes, it lost its niche. People Express became one more carrier in an increasingly competitive market, in which it had no special competitive advantage against the other national carriers. The result was financial troubles. People Express was swallowed up by Texas Air and incorporated into Continental Airlines. By contrast, Southwest Airlines, the focused low-cost company, has continued to focus on this strategy and has grown successfully.

Holiday Inns' Rough Ride

The history of the Holiday Inns motel chain is one of the great success stories in U.S. business. Its founder, Kemmons Wilson, vacationing in the early 1950s, found existing motels to be small, expensive, and of unpredictable quality. This discovery, along with the prospect of unprecedented highway travel that would come with the new interstate highway program, triggered a realization: There was an unmet customer need, a gap in the market for quality accommodations. Holiday Inns was founded to meet that need.

From the beginning, Holiday Inns set the standard for offering motel features such as air conditioning and icemakers while keeping room rates reasonable. These amenities enhanced the motels' popularity, and motel franchising, Wilson's invention, made rapid expansion possible. By 1960, Holiday Inns' motels dotted the U.S. landscape; they could be found in virtually every city and on every major highway. Before the 1960s ended, more than 1,000 of them were in full operation, and occupancy rates averaged 80 percent. The concept of mass accommodation had arrived.[31]

By the 1970s, however, the motel chain was in trouble. The service offered by Holiday Inns appealed to the average traveler, who wanted a standardized product (a room) at an average price. In essence, Holiday Inns had been targeting the middle of the hotel-room market. The problem was that travelers were beginning to make different demands on hotels and motels. Some wanted luxury and were willing to pay higher prices for better accommodations and service. Others sought low prices and accepted rock-bottom quality and service in exchange. Although the market had fragmented into different groups of customers with different needs, Holiday Inns was still offering an undifferentiated, average-cost, average-quality product.[32]

Holiday Inns missed the change in the market and thus failed to respond appropriately to it, but the competition did not. Companies such as Hyatt siphoned off the top end of the market, where quality and service sold rooms.

Chains such as Motel 6 and Days Inns captured the basic-quality, low-price end of the market. In between were many specialty chains that appealed to business travelers, families, or self-caterers (people who want to be able to cook in their hotel rooms). Holiday Inns' position was attacked from all sides. The company's earnings declined as occupancy rates dropped drastically, and marginal Holiday Inns motels began to close as competition increased.

Wounded but not dead, Holiday Inns began a counterattack. The original chain was upgraded to suit quality-oriented travelers. At the same time, to meet the needs of different kinds of travelers, Holiday Inns created new hotel and motel chains, including the luxury Crowne Plazas; the Hampton Inns, which serve the low-priced end of the market; and the all-suite Embassy Suites. Holiday Inns tried to meet the demands of the many niches, or segments, of the hotel market that have emerged as customers' needs have changed over time.[33]

These moves were successful in the early 1990s, and Holiday Inns grew to become one of the largest suppliers of hotel rooms in the industry. However, by 1996, it became clear that Holiday Inns was once again losing its differentiated appeal as its revenues and profits fell. A new CEO, Thomas R. Oliver, was brought in to remake Holiday Inns. His solution? To upgrade the Holiday Inns flagship chain with new furniture, food, and a large new advertising budget.

While this worked, other moves to restore profitability created new problems. Oliver also wanted to open other budget chains aimed at the business traveler. However, he wanted to use the Holiday Inns name on them to give them instant name recognition. Many of the regular Holiday Inns franchisees objected, since this would reduce the differentiated appeal of their chain. For example, Oliver plans to open a chain called the Staybridge Suites by Holiday Inns which are tailored to long-term business customers. Whatever the outcome of these efforts, one thing is clear: Holiday Inns needs to remake its image in the highly competitive hotel room industry.

Differentiators, too, can fail in the market and end up stuck in the middle if competitors attack their markets with more specialized or low-cost products that blunt their competitive edge. This happened to IBM in the large-frame computer market as personal computers became more powerful and able to do the job of the much more expensive mainframes. The increasing movement toward flexible manufacturing systems aggravates the problems faced by cost leaders and differentiators. Many large firms will become stuck in the middle unless they make the investment needed to pursue both strategies simultaneously. No company is safe in the jungle of competition, and each must be constantly on the lookout to exploit competitive advantages as they arise and to defend the advantages it already has.

To sum up, successful management of a generic competitive strategy requires strategic managers to attend to two main matters. First, they need to ensure that the product/market/distinctive-competency decisions they make are oriented toward one specific competitive strategy. Second, they need to monitor the environment so that they can keep the firm's sources of competitive advantage in tune with changing opportunities and threats.

STRATEGIC GROUPS AND BUSINESS-LEVEL STRATEGY

As implied by the preceding discussion, companies in an industry can pursue many different kinds of business-level strategies that differ from each other with respect to factors such as the choice of market segments to serve, product quality, technological leadership, customer service, pricing policy, and advertising policy. As a result, within most industries, strategic groups emerge, each of which is composed of companies pursuing the same generic strategy.[34] Thus, for example, all the companies inside an industry pursuing a low-cost strategy form one strategic group; all those seeking to pursue a broad differentiation strategy constitute another strategic group; and all those pursing a focus-differentiation strategy or a focused low-cost strategy form yet other strategic groups.

For instance, in the pharmaceutical industry, which we discuss in Chapter 3, there are two main strategic groups.[35] One group includes such companies as Merck, Eli Lilly, and Pfizer (see Figure 3.5), which pursue a differentiation strategy characterized by heavy R&D spending and a focus on developing new proprietary blockbuster drugs. The other strategic group might be characterized as the *low-cost strategic group* because it focuses on the manufacture of low-priced generic drugs. Companies in this group are pursuing a low-cost strategy because they are not investing millions of dollars in R&D, and, as a result, they cannot expect to charge a premium price.

The concept of strategic groups has a number of implications for business-level strategy. First, a company's immediate competitors are those companies pursuing the same strategy in its strategic group. Consumers tend to view the products of such enterprises as being direct substitutes for each other. Thus, a major threat to a company's profitability may arise primarily from within its own strategic group, not necessarily from the other companies in the industry pursuing different generic business-level strategies. For example, the main competition for Toyota comes from Honda, Ford, and GM, not from Rolls-Royce.

Second, different strategic groups can have a different standing with respect to each of Porter's five competitive forces because, as already discussed, the five forces affect companies in different ways. In other words, the risk of new entry by potential competitors, the degree of rivalry among companies within a group, the bargaining power of buyers, the bargaining power of suppliers, and the competitive force of substitute products can all vary in intensity among different strategic groups within the same industry.

In the pharmaceutical industry, for example, companies in the differentiation strategic group have historically been in a very powerful position vis-à-vis buyers because their products are patented. Besides, rivalry within this group has been limited to competition to be the first to patent a new drug and achieve a **first-mover advantage**, the advantage that a company that is first to market a new product is said to possess. In contrast, companies in the low-cost group have been in a much weaker position, since they lack patents for their products and buyers can choose among very similar competing generic drugs. Moreover, price competition among the companies in this group has been quite intense, reflecting the lack of product differentiation. Thus, companies within this group have earned somewhat lower returns than companies in the proprietary group.

As discussed in Chapter 3, mobility barriers are factors that inhibit the movement of companies between groups in an industry. The relative height of mobility barriers determines how successfully companies in one group can compete with companies in another. For example, can a differentiation strategic group also pursue a low-cost strategy and thus achieve the low-cost/differentiation strategy previously discussed? To the degree that companies in one group can develop or obtain the functional and financial resources they need to either lower their costs or embark on a major R&D expansion, they may be able to compete successfully with companies in another strategic group. In effect, they have created yet another strategic group—a combined low-cost and differentiation strategic group, which, as we have seen, has the strongest competitive advantage and the greatest ability to earn above-average profits. In fact, the need to pursue a simultaneous global low-cost/differentiation strategy has been the major driving force behind the wave of merger activities that swept through the large drug companies in the 1990s. For example, the U.S. company Upjohn merged with the Swedish company Pharmacia to pursue a global low-cost/differentiation strategy. Thus, the strategic group map in the pharmaceutical industry is changing dramatically as firms fight to survive in the rapidly consolidating global pharmaceutical industry. So far, Pfizer, Merck, and Eli Lilly are still pursuing a pure differentiated strategy, but the other merged companies are moving quickly to reposition themselves as low-cost differentiators.

CHOOSING AN INVESTMENT STRATEGY AT THE BUSINESS LEVEL

We have been discussing business-level strategy in terms of making product/market/distinctive-competency choices to gain a competitive advantage. There is a second major choice to be made at the business level, however—the choice of which type of investment strategy to pursue in support of the competitive strategy.[36]

An **investment strategy** sets the amount and type of resources—human, functional, and financial—that must be invested to gain a competitive advantage.

Generic competitive strategies provide competitive advantages, but they are expensive to develop and maintain. A simultaneous differentiation/cost-leadership strategy is the most expensive, because it requires that a company invest resources not only in functions such as R&D, sales, and marketing to develop distinctive competencies, but also in functions such as manufacturing and materials management to find ways to reduce costs. Differentiation is the next most expensive generic strategy and then cost leadership, which is less expensive to maintain once the initial investment in a manufacturing plant and equipment has been made. Cost leadership does not require such sophisticated research and development or marketing efforts as a differentiation strategy. The focus strategy is cheapest because fewer resources are needed to serve one market segment than to serve the whole market.

In deciding on an investment strategy, a company must evaluate the potential returns from investing in a generic competitive strategy against the cost. In this way, it can determine whether it is likely to be profitable to pursue a certain strategy and how profitability will change as competition within the industry changes. Two factors are crucial in choosing an investment strategy: the strength of a company's position in an industry relative to its competitors and the stage of the industry's life cycle in which the company is competing.[37]

■ Competitive Position

Two attributes can be used to determine the strength of a company's relative competitive position. First, the larger a company's *market share*, the stronger is its competitive position and the greater are the potential returns from future investment. A large market share provides experience-curve economies and suggests that the company has earned brand loyalty. One of the main reasons a wave of mergers has taken place in the pharmaceutical industry, for example, is that the merging of two or more different companies creates a much larger customer base that can be more efficiently served by one global sales force rather than the two global sales forces that previously existed. Thus, large market share may help an organization to lower its costs on a global, as well as a national, basis.

The uniqueness, strength, and number of a company's *distinctive competencies* are the second measure of competitive position. If it is difficult to imitate a company's research and development expertise, its manufacturing and marketing skills, its knowledge of particular customer segments, and its unique reputation or brand name capital, the company's relative competitive position is strong and its returns from the generic strategy increase. Once again, an attempt to build new and improved distinctive competencies has been a principal reason for the merger of pharmaceutical companies. For example, Ciba-Geigy and Sandoz, two giant Swiss pharmaceutical companies, recently merged because they were developing complementary kinds of drugs for treating the same broad range of diseases. By pooling their skills and abilities, they have created the second largest pharmaceutical company in the world, and they hope to use their combined distinctive competencies to compete head-to-head with U.S. companies such as Pfizer and Merck.

In general, companies with the largest market share and the strongest distinctive competencies are in the best position to build and sustain their competitive advantage. A unique distinctive competency leads to increased demand for the company's products, and, as a result of the revenues obtained from larger market share, the company has more resources to invest in developing its distinctive competency.

These two attributes reinforce one another and explain why some companies get stronger and stronger over time. Companies with a smaller market share and little potential for developing a distinctive competency are in a much weaker competitive position.[38]

■ Life Cycle Effects

The second main factor influencing the investment attractiveness of a generic strategy is the *stage of the industry life cycle.* Each life cycle stage is accompanied by a particular industry environment, presenting different opportunities and threats. Each stage, therefore, has different implications for the investment of resources needed to obtain a competitive advantage. Competition is strongest in the shakeout stage of the life cycle and least important in the embryonic stage, for example. The risks of pursuing a strategy change over time. The difference in risk explains why the potential returns from investing in a competitive strategy depend on the life cycle stage.

■ Choosing an Investment Strategy

Table 6.2 summarizes the relationship among the stage of the life cycle, the competitive position, and the investment strategy at the business level.

Embryonic Strategy   In the embryonic stage, all companies, weak and strong, emphasize the development of a distinctive competency and a product/market policy. During this stage, investment needs are great because a company has to establish a competitive advantage. Many fledgling companies in the industry are seeking resources to develop a distinctive competency. Thus, the appropriate business-level investment strategy is a **share-building strategy**. The aim is to build market share

TABLE 6.2

Choosing an Investment Strategy at the Business Level

	Strong Competitive Position	*Weak Competitive Position*
Stage of Industry Life Cycle		
Embryonic	Share building	Share building
Growth	Growth	Market concentration
Shakeout	Share increasing	Market concentration or harvest/liquidation
Maturity	Hold-and-maintain or profit	Harvest or liquidation/ divestiture
Decline	Market concentration or harvest (asset reduction)	Turnaround, liquidation, or divestiture

by developing a stable and unique competitive advantage to attract customers who have no knowledge of the company's products.

Companies require large amounts of capital to build research and development competencies or sales and service competencies. They cannot generate much of this capital internally. Thus, a company's success depends on its ability to demonstrate a unique competency to attract outside investors, or venture capitalists. If a company gains the resources to develop a distinctive competency, it will be in a relatively stronger competitive position. If it fails, its only option may be to exit the industry. In fact, companies in weak competitive positions at all stages in the life cycle may choose to exit the industry to cut their losses.

Growth Strategies At the growth stage, the task facing a company is to consolidate its position and provide the base it needs to survive the coming shakeout. Thus, the appropriate investment strategy is the **growth strategy**. The goal is to maintain a company's relative competitive position in a rapidly expanding market and, if possible, to increase it—in other words, to grow with the expanding market. However, other companies are entering the market and catching up with the industry's innovators. As a result, first movers require successive waves of capital infusion to sustain the momentum generated by their success in the embryonic stage. For example, differentiators need to engage in massive research and development to preserve their technological lead, and cost leaders need to invest in state-of-the-art machinery and computers to obtain new experience-curve economies. All this investment is very expensive.

The growth stage is also the time when companies try to consolidate existing market niches and enter new ones so that they can increase their market share. Increasing the level of market segmentation to become a broad differentiator is expensive as well. A company has to invest resources to develop a new sales and marketing competency. Consequently, at the growth stage, companies fine-tune their competitive strategy (which we discuss at length in the next chapter) and make business-level investment decisions about the relative advantages of a differentiation, low-cost, or focus strategy, given financial needs and relative competitive position. For instance, if one company has emerged as the cost leader, some companies may decide to compete head-to-head with it and enter this strategic group, whereas others will not. Instead, they will pursue a growth strategy using a differentiation or focus approach and invest resources in developing unique competencies. As a result, strategic groups start to develop in an industry as each company seeks the best way to invest its scarce resources to maximize its competitive advantage.

Companies must spend a lot of money just to keep up with growth in the market, and finding additional resources to develop new skills and competencies is a difficult task for strategic managers. Consequently, companies in a weak competitive position at this stage engage in a **market concentration strategy** to consolidate their position. They seek to specialize in some way and may adopt a focus strategy and move to a focused strategic group to reduce their investment needs. If very weak, they may choose to exit the industry and sell out to a stronger competitor.

Shakeout Strategies By the shakeout stage, demand increases slowly, and competition by price or product characteristics becomes intense. Companies in strong competitive positions need resources to invest in a **share-increasing strategy** to attract customers from weak companies that are exiting the market. In other words, companies attempt to maintain and increase market share despite fierce competition. The way companies invest their resources depends on their generic strategy.

For cost leaders, because of the price wars that can occur, investment in cost control is crucial if they are to survive the shakeout stage, and they must do all they can to reduce costs. Differentiators in a strong competitive position choose to forge ahead and become broad differentiators. Their investment is likely to be oriented toward marketing, and they are likely to develop a sophisticated after-sales service network. They also widen the product range to match the range of customers' needs. Differentiators in a weak position reduce their investment burden by withdrawing to a focused strategy—the **market concentration strategy**—to specialize in a particular niche or product. Weak companies exiting the industry engage in a **harvest** or **liquidation strategy**, both of which are discussed later in this chapter.

Maturity Strategies By the maturity stage, a relatively stable strategic group structure has emerged in the industry, and companies have learned how their competitors will react to their competitive moves. At this point, companies want to reap the rewards of their previous investments in developing a generic strategy. Until now, profits have been reinvested in the business, and dividends have been small. Investors in strong companies have obtained their rewards through the appreciation of the value of their stock, because the company has reinvested most of its capital to maintain and increase market share. As market growth slows in the maturity stage, a company's investment strategy depends on the level of competition in the industry and the source of the company's competitive advantage.

In environments where competition is high because technological change is occurring or where barriers to entry are low, companies need to defend their competitive position. Strategic managers need to continue to invest heavily in maintaining the company's competitive advantage. Both low-cost companies and differentiators adopt a **hold-and-maintain strategy** to support their generic strategies. They expend resources to develop their distinctive competency so as to remain the market leaders. For example, differentiated companies may invest in improved after-sales service, and low-cost companies may invest in the latest production technologies, such as robotics.

It is at this point, however, that companies realize they must begin to pursue both a low-cost and a differentiation strategy if they are to protect themselves from aggressive competitors (both at home and abroad) that are watching for any opportunity or perceived weakness to take the lead in the industry. Differentiators take advantage of their strong position to develop flexible manufacturing systems to reduce their production costs. Cost leaders move to start differentiating their products to expand their market share by serving more market segments. For example, Gallo moved from the bulk-wine segment and began marketing premium wines and wine coolers to take advantage of its low production costs. In 1996, Gallo's new premium brand, Falling Leaf, became the best-selling chardonnay in the United States. Similarly, in the fast-food industry in the 1990s, McDonald's experienced intense pressure to lower its costs after Taco Bell began to offer its $.99 tacos. To counter this competitive attack, McDonald's sought new ways to lower its costs and widen its menu.

Historically, however, many companies have felt protected from competition within the industry in the maturity stage. Consequently, they decide to exploit their competitive advantage to the fullest by engaging in a **profit strategy**. A company pursuing this strategy attempts to maximize the present returns from its previous investments. Typically, it reinvests proportionally less in improvement of its functional resources and increases returns to shareholders. The profit strategy works well only as long as competitive forces remain relatively constant, so that the company can maintain the profit margins developed by its competitive strategy. However, it must be alert to threats from the environment and must take care not to become complacent and unresponsive to environmental changes.

All too often market leaders fail to exercise vigilance in managing the environment, imagining that they are impervious to competition. Thus, General Motors felt secure against foreign-car manufacturers until changes in oil prices precipitated a crisis. Kodak, which had profited for so long from its strengths in film processing, was slow to respond to the threat of electronic imaging techniques. Paradoxically, the most successful companies often fail to sense changes in the market. As Strategy in Action 6.5 shows, Gucci is another example of a company that over time failed to pursue a hold-and-maintain strategy to manage the competitive environment.

6.5   STRATEGY *in* ACTION

Gucci Loses Its Grip

Gucci has one of the most readily recognized brand name of all luxury goods companies. Its leather products, such as shoes and handbags, and its clothes are global status symbols worn by the world's wealthiest people. However, the power of its brand name was put at great risk in the middle 1990s because its CEO, Maurizio Gucci, and its designers had lost track of its customers' desires and its industry environment. Unlike competitors such as Versace, Ferragamo, and Giorgio Armani, the company failed to innovate and offer styles that appealed to a new, more casual global audience. To save money as its losses mounted, Gucci reduced its advertising budget. This was a disastrous move, for it sharpened the perception that Gucci was outmoded and out of touch with the luxury market. The company became caught in a vicious cycle downward.

It was saved by a tragedy. Maurizio Gucci's wife arranged to have him gunned down in a Milan doorway in 1995; as a result Domenico De Sole became CEO, and he had a clear vision of what to do. Lacking money because of mounting losses, De Sole named a Texan, Thomas Ford, as Gucci's chief designer and invested all the company's resources in producing a revolutionary, new, Ford-designed line of clothes for both men and women to attract back Gucci's customers. An instant success, the clothes generated much attention and free advertising for Gucci. All of a sudden, customers flocked back to Gucci stores, and, as they bought clothes, they also bought Gucci's signature leather products, such as $500 shoes and handbags. The company's sales and profits increased, and De Sole invested the proceeds in advertising, tripling the advertising budget. He thus changed the vicious cycle downward into a virtuous cycle upward.

Gucci has gone from strength to strength under De Sole and Ford; it regained its status as one of the foremost brand names in the world. In fact, it became so successful that it attracted the attention of LVMH, the French luxury goods company that owns such brand names as Moet et Chandon, and Louis Vuitton. LVMH first bought a significant number of Gucci shares, and it looked like it might try to take over the company; however, De Sole fought back. In October 1999, it appeared that Gucci might take over Fendi, another Italian fashion house, as De Sole strove to keep Gucci under his control. No matter what happens, Gucci's global future looks bright indeed.

Decline Strategies   The decline stage of an industry's life cycle begins when demand for the industry's product starts to fall. There are many possible reasons for decline, including foreign competition and the loss of a company's distinctive competency as its rivals enter with new or more efficient technologies. Thus, a company must decide what investment strategy to adopt in order to deal with new circumstances within its industry. Table 6.2 lists the strategies that companies can resort to when their competitive position is declining.[39]

The initial strategies that companies can adopt are market concentration and asset reduction.[40] With a **market concentration strategy**, a company attempts to consolidate its product and market choices. It narrows its product range and exits marginal niches in an attempt to redeploy its resources more effectively and improve its competitive position. Reducing customer groups served may also allow a company to pursue a focus strategy in order to survive the decline stage. (As noted earlier, weak companies in the growth stage tend to adopt this strategy.) That is what International Harvester did as the demand for farm machinery fell. It now produces only medium-sized trucks under the Navistar name.

An **asset reduction strategy** requires a company to limit or decrease its investment in a business and to extract, or milk, the investment as much as it can. This approach is sometimes called a **harvest strategy** because a company will exit the industry once it has harvested all the returns it can. It reduces to a minimum the assets it employs in the business and forgoes investment for the sake of immediate profits.[41] A market concentration strategy, on the other hand, generally indicates that a company is trying to turn around its business so that it can survive in the long run.

Low-cost companies are more likely to pursue a harvest strategy simply because a smaller market share means higher costs, and they are unable to move to a focus strategy. Differentiators, in contrast, have a competitive advantage in this stage if they can move to a focus strategy.

At any stage of the life cycle, companies that are in weak competitive positions may apply **turnaround strategies**.[42] The questions that a company has to answer are whether it has the resources available to develop a viable business-level strategy to compete in the industry and how much that will cost. If a company is stuck in the middle, for example, it must assess the investment costs of developing a low-cost or differentiation strategy. Perhaps a company pursuing a low-cost strategy has not made the right product or market choices, or perhaps a differentiator has been missing niche opportunities. In such cases, the company can redeploy resources and change its strategy.

Sometimes a company's loss of competitiveness may be due to poor strategy implementation. If so, the company must move to change its structure and control systems rather than its strategy. For example, Dan Schendel, a prominent management researcher, found that 74 percent of the turnaround situations he and his colleagues studied were due to inefficient strategy implementation. The strategy-structure fit at the business level is thus very important in determining competitive strength.[43] We discuss it in detail in Chapter 13.

If a company decides that turnaround is not possible, either for competitive or for life cycle reasons, then the two remaining investment alternatives are **liquidation** and **divestiture**. As the terms imply, the company moves to exit the industry either by liquidating its assets or by selling the whole business. Both can be regarded as radical forms of harvesting strategy, because the company is seeking to get back as much as it can from its investment in the business. Often, however, it can only exit at a loss and take a tax write-off. Timing is important, because the earlier a company senses that divestiture is necessary, the more it can get for its assets. There are many stories about companies that buy weak or declining companies, thinking they can turn them around, and then realize their mistake as the new acquisitions become a drain on their resources. Often the acquired companies have lost their competitive advantage, and the cost of regaining it is too great. However, there have also been spectacular successes, such as that achieved by Lee Iacocca, who engaged in a low-cost strategy at Chrysler that set the scene for its success in the 1990s.

SUMMARY OF CHAPTER

The purpose of this chapter is to discuss the factors that must be considered if a company is to develop a business-level strategy that allows it to compete effectively in the marketplace. The formulation of business-level strategy means matching the opportunities and threats in the environment to the company's strengths and weaknesses by making choices about products, markets, and distinctive competencies, as well as the investments necessary to pursue the choices. All companies, from one-person operations to the strategic business units of large corporations, must develop a business strategy if they are to compete effectively and maximize their long-term profitability. The chapter makes the following main points:

- Business-level strategy refers to the way strategic managers devise a plan of action for using a company's resources and distinctive competencies to gain a competitive advantage over rivals in a market or industry.

- At the heart of developing a generic business-level strategy are choices concerning product differentiation, market segmentation, and distinctive competency.

- The combination of those three choices results in the specific form of generic business-level strategy employed by a company.

- The three pure generic competitive strategies are cost leadership, differentiation, and focus. Each has advantages and disadvantages. A company must constantly manage its strategy; otherwise, it risks being stuck in the middle.

- Increasingly, developments in manufacturing technology are allowing firms to pursue both a cost-leadership and a differentiation strategy and thus obtain the economic benefits of both strategies simultaneously. Technical developments also allow

small firms to compete with large firms on an equal footing in particular market segments and hence increase the number of firms pursuing a focus strategy.

- Companies can also adopt two forms of focus strategy: a focused low-cost strategy and a focused differentiation strategy.

- Most industries are composed of strategic groups. Strategic groups are groups of companies pursuing the same or a similar business-level strategy. The members of a strategic group constitute a company's immediate competitors.

- Since different strategic groups are characterized by different opportunities and threats, it may pay a company to switch strategic groups. The feasibility of doing so is a function of the height of mobility barriers.

- The second choice facing a company is an investment strategy for supporting the competitive strategy. The choice of investment strategy depends on two main factors: (1) the strength of a company's competitive position in the industry and (2) the stage of the industry's life cycle.

- The main types of investment strategy are share building, growth, share increasing, hold-and-maintain, profit, market concentration, asset reduction, harvest, turnaround, liquidation, and divestiture.

DISCUSSION QUESTIONS

1. Why does each generic competitive strategy require a different set of product/market/distinctive-competency choices? Give examples of pairs of companies in (a) the computer industry and (b) the auto industry that pursue different competitive strategies.

2. How can companies pursuing a cost-leadership, differentiation, or focus strategy become stuck in the

middle? In what ways can they regain their competitive advantage?

3. Over an industry's life cycle, what investment strategy choices should be made by (a) differentiators in a strong competitive position and (b) differentiators in a weak competitive position?

4. How do technical developments affect the generic strategies pursued by firms in an industry? How might they do so in the future?

5. Why is it difficult for a company in one strategic group to change to a different strategic group?

Practicing Strategic Management

SMALL-GROUP EXERCISE
Finding a Strategy for a Restaurant

Break up into groups of three to five people, and discuss the following scenario:

You are a group of partners contemplating opening a new restaurant in your city. You are trying to decide what business-level strategy would provide your restaurant with the best competitive advantage to make it as profitable as possible.

1. Create a strategic group of the restaurants in your city and define their generic strategies.

2. Identify which restaurants you think are the most profitable and why.

3. On the basis of this analysis, decide what kind of restaurant you want to open and why.

STRATEGIC MANAGEMENT PROJECT
Module 6

This part of the project focuses on the nature of your company's business-level strategy. If your company operates in more than one business, concentrate either on its core, or most central, business, or on its most important businesses. Using all the information you have collected on your company, answer the following questions:

1. How differentiated are the products/services of your company? What is the basis of their differentiated appeal?

2. What is your company's strategy toward market segmentation? If it segments its market, on what basis does it do so?

3. What distinctive competencies does your company have? (To answer this question, use the information from the module on functional-level strategy in the last chapter.) Is efficiency, quality, innovation, responsiveness to customers, or a combination of these factors the main driving force in your company?

4. Based on these product/market/distinctive-competency choices, what generic business-level strategy is your company pursuing?

5. What are the advantages and disadvantages associated with your company's choice of business-level strategy?

6. How could you improve its business-level strategy to strengthen its competitive advantage?

7. Is your company a member of a strategic group in an industry? If so, which group?

8. What investment strategy is your company pursuing to support its generic strategy? How does this match the strength of its competitive position and the stage of its industry's life cycle?

ARTICLE FILE 6

Find an example (or several examples) of a company pursuing one or more of the three generic business-level strategies. Which strategy is it? What product/market/distinctive-competency choices is it based on? What are its advantages and disadvantages?

EXPLORING THE WEB
Visiting the Luxury-Car Market

Enter the Web sites of three luxury-car makers such as Lexus (www.lexususa.com), BMW (www.bmwusa.com), or Cadillac (www.cadillac.com), all of which compete in the same strategic group. Scan the sites to determine the key features of each company's business-level strategy. In what ways are their strategies similar and different? Which of these companies do you think has a competitive advantage over the others? Why?

Search the Web for a company pursuing a low-cost strategy, a differentiation strategy, or both. What product/market/distinctive-competency choices has the company made to pursue this strategy? How successful has the company been in its industry using this strategy?

Liz Claiborne, Inc.

DESIGNER LIZ CLAIBORNE founded her company in 1976 with the help of three partners. By 1990, the company had more than $2 billion in annual sales, and its stock had become a Wall Street favorite. The secret of the company's success was Liz Claiborne's decision to focus on the rapidly growing professional women's segment of the clothing market. By 1976, women were entering the work force in rapidly increasing numbers, but relatively few companies were producing clothes for this segment. Those that did cater to it were very high-priced firms such as Ellen Tracy, Donna Karan, and Anne Klein. Liz Claiborne decided to find out what kinds of clothing professional women wanted. Then she used her considerable talents to create a design team to focus on providing attractively designed clothing for professional women at reasonable prices. In doing so, she tapped an unmet customer need, and the result was dramatic as sales boomed.

To protect her firm's image, Liz Claiborne sold her clothing through established retailers, such as Macy's, Bloomingdale's, and Dillard's. Retailers were required to buy at least $50,000 worth of her collection, and the company controlled the way its suits and dresses were sold in each store—for example, the way clothes were hung and displayed. This attention to detail was part of her strategy of focusing on the upscale professional clothing niche. To promote its growth, the company then started to find new outlets for its clothes and opened a chain of Liz Claiborne boutiques and factory outlets. The Liz Claiborne team also used its design skills to produce a line of men's sportswear and to develop new products such as perfume, shoes, and accessories. By 1988, the Liz Claiborne name had become famous.

However, by 1990 the company's growth had slowed, and the company was in trouble. Competitors, recognizing the niche pioneered by Liz Claiborne, had begun to offer their own lines of professional women's clothing. Expensive designers such as Anne Klein and Donna Karan had new lines of cheaper clothing, priced to compete directly with Liz Claiborne. In addition, low-cost manufacturers had begun to produce clothing lines that undercut Liz Claiborne's prices, often using look-alike designs. This competition from both the top and the bottom end of the market took sales away from the company.

Another problem for Liz Claiborne came from the retail end. Many of the company's best customers, retailers such as Macy's, were in deep financial difficulty and were cutting back on purchases to reduce their debt. At the same time, cost-conscious consumers were buying more and more clothing from stores such as Casual Corner and JC Penney and even from discount stores such as Kmart and Wal-Mart, which do not sell the Liz Claiborne line but carry the low-priced lines of competitors. As customers switched to both cheaper stores and cheaper lines, Liz Claiborne's sales suffered.

Given this deteriorating situation, the company moved quickly to change its strategy. Jerry Chazen, who replaced Liz Claiborne as CEO of the company on her retirement, decided to broaden the company's product line and produce low-cost lines of clothing. To do so and at the same time protect the Liz Claiborne brand name, he bought Russ Togs, a clothing maker that produces three brands of women's clothing: Crazy Horse, The Villager, and Red Horse. As part of the company's new strategy, each of these clothing makers' lines was redesigned and targeted at a different price range in the women's clothing market. For example, Russ Togs, a sportswear line, was upgraded to sell a new line of clothing for 20 to 30 percent less than the Liz Claiborne line. Moreover, this clothing is sold through discount merchandisers such as Wal-Mart and in low-priced department stores such as Sears and JC Penney. In this way, the Liz Claiborne company began to serve the general women's clothing market, not just the professional women's clothing niche.[44]

Top management found that this new strategy bolstered the company's sagging sales and it led to a new period of growth and expansion in the late 1990s. In addition, they have taken the company's existing design skills and capabilities and applied them in other new market segments. Now, however, the company is going head-to-head with low-cost producers and has had to find new ways to reduce costs in order to compete. In 1999, the company reported record operating profits due to a growth in sales in its main product lines. Liz Claiborne has turned the corner and is once again a major player in the volatile women's clothing industry.[45]

Case Discussion Questions

1. What factors led to the success of Liz Claiborne, Inc.?
2. What changes has the company recently made in its strategy? Why?

End Notes

1. www.E*trade.com (1999).
2. Press releases, www.E*trade.com (1999).
3. D. F. Abell, *Defining the Business: The Starting Point of Strategic Planning* (Englewood Cliffs, N.J.: Prentice-Hall, 1980), p. 169.
4. R. Kotler, *Marketing Management*, 5th ed. (Englewood Cliffs, N.J.: Prentice-Hall, 1984); M. R. Darby and E. Karni, "Free Competition and the Optimal Amount of Fraud," *Journal of Law and Economics*, 16 (1973), 67-86.
5. Abell, *Defining the Business*, p. 8.
6. M. E. Porter, *Competitive Advantage: Creating and Sustaining Superior Performance* (New York: Free Press, 1985).
7. R. D. Buzzell and F. D. Wiersema, "Successful Share Building Strategies," *Harvard Business Review* (January–February 1981), 135-144; L. W. Phillips, D. R. Chang, and R. D. Buzzell, "Product Quality, Cost Position, and Business Performance: A Test of Some Key Hypotheses," *Journal of Marketing*, 47 (1983), 26-43.
8. M. E. Porter, *Competitive Strategy: Techniques for Analyzing Industries and Competitors* (New York: Free Press, 1980), p. 45.
9. Abell, *Defining the Business*, p. 15.
10. Although many other authors have discussed cost leadership and differentiation as basic competitive approaches—e.g., F. Scherer, *Industrial Market Structure and Economic Performance*, 2nd. ed. (Boston: Houghton Mifflin, 1980)—Porter's model (Porter, *Competitive Strategy*) has become the dominant approach. Consequently, this model is the one developed here and the discussion draws heavily on his definitions. The basic cost-leadership/differentiation dimension has received substantial empirical support; see, for instance, D. C. Hambrick, "High Profit Strategies in Mature Capital Goods Industries: A Contingency Approach," *Academy of Management Journal*, 26 (1983), 687-707.
11. Porter, *Competitive Advantage*, p. 37.
12. Ibid., pp. 13-14.
13. D. Miller, "Configurations of Strategy and Structure: Towards a Synthesis," *Strategic Management Journal*, 7 (1986), 217-231.
14. Porter, *Competitive Advantage*, pp. 44-46.
15. C. W. Hofer and D. Schendel, *Strategy Formulation: Analytical Concepts* (St. Paul, Minn.: West, 1978).
16. W. K. Hall, "Survival Strategies in a Hostile Environment," *Harvard Business Review*, 58 (1980), 75-85; Hambrick, "High Profit Strategies," pp. 687-707.
17. J. Guyon, "Can the Savoy Cut Costs and Be the Savoy?" *Wall Street Journal*, October 25, 1994, p. B1.
18. L. Nathans Spiro and M. Landler, "Less-Than-Fantastic Plastic," *Business Week*, November 9, 1992, pp. 100-101; Edward Baig, "Platinum Cards: Move over, Amex," *Business-Week*, August 19, 1996, p. 84; John N. Frank, "American Express's Attention Getter," *Credit Card Management* (August 1996), 36-37.
19. L. Beyer, "Breaking Tradition," *Credit Card Management*, 12, (1999) pp. 57-60.
20. R. Rolfe, "The Smart Centurion," *Credit Card Management*, 12 (1999), pp. 132-136.
21. D. McGinn, "For Ford, Making Wall Street Happy Is Job One," *Newsweek*, April 8, 1996, p. 48.
22. O. Suris, "Ford's Earnings Plunged 58% in 1st Quarter," *Wall Street Journal*, April 18, 1996, p. 7.
23. K. Kerwin and K. Naughton, "Remaking Ford," *Business Week*, 1999, October 11, pp. 68-75.
24. Porter, *Competitive Strategy*, p. 46.
25. J. W. Verity, "They Make a Killing Minding Other People's Business," *Business Week*, November 30, 1992, p. 96.
26. M. Willis, "Outsourcing Benefits Administration: A Disciplined Process for Conducting a Thorough Cost-Benefit Analysis," *Compensation & Benefits Management* (Winter 1996), 45-53; J. Gebhart, "Beyond the Information Systems Outsourcing Bandwagon: The Insourcing Response," *Sloan Business Review* (Winter 1996), 177.
27. B. Caldwell and J. Mateyaschuk, "Reviving EDS," *Informationweek*, 742 (1999), 18-19.
28. W. Zellner, "Can EDS Catch Up With the Net," *Business Week*, May 17, 1999, p.112.
29. P. F. Drucker, *The Practice of Management* (New York: Harper, 1954).
30. Porter, *Competitive Advantage*, pp. 44-46.
31. "The Holiday Inns Trip; A Breeze for Decades, Bumpy Ride in the 1980s," *Wall Street Journal*, February 11, 1987, p.1.
32. Holiday Inns, Annual Report, 1985.
33. Bureau of Labor Statistics, *U.S. Industrial Output* (Washington, D.C., 1986); M. Gleason and A. Salomon, "Fallon's Challenge: Make Holiday Inn More 'In'," *Advertising Age*, September 2, 1996, p. 14; J. Miller, "Amenities Range from Snacks to Technology," *Hotel and Motel Management*, July 3, 1996, pp. 38-40.
34. The development of strategic group theory has been a strong theme in the strategy literature. Important contributions include R. E. Caves and M. Porter, "From Entry Barriers to Mobility Barriers," *Quarterly Journal of Economics* (May 1977), 241-262; K. R. Harrigan, "An Application of Clustering for Strategic Group Analysis," *Strategic Management Journal*, 6 (1985), 55-73; K. J. Hatten and D. E. Schendel, "Heterogeneity Within an Industry: Firm Conduct in the U.S. Brewing Industry, 1952-1971," *Journal of Industrial Economics*, 26 (1976), 97-113; M. E. Porter, "The Structure Within Industries and Companies' Performance," *Review of Economics and Statistics*, 61 (1979), 214-227.
35. For details on strategic group structure in the pharmaceutical industry, see K. Cool and I. Dierickx, "Rivalry, Strategic Groups, and Firm Profitability," *Strategic Management Journal*, 14 (1993), 47-59.
36. Hofer and Schendel, *Strategy Formulation*, pp. 102-104.
37. Our discussion of the investment, or posturing, component of business-level strategy draws heavily on Hofer and Schendel's discussion in *Strategy Formulation*, especially Chapter 6.

38. Hofer and Schendel, *Strategy Formulation*, pp. 75–77.

39. K. R. Harrigan, "Strategy Formulation in Declining Industries," *Academy of Management Review*, 5 (1980), 599–604.

40. Hofer and Schendel, *Strategy Formulation*, pp. 169–172.

41. L. R. Feldman and A. L. Page, "Harvesting: The Misunderstood Market Exit Strategy," *Journal of Business Strategy*, 4 (1985), 79–85.

42. C. W. Hofer, "Turnaround Strategies," *Journal of Business Strategy*, 1 (1980), 19–31.

43. Hofer and Schendel, *Strategy Formulation*, p. 172.

44. N. Darnton, "The Joy of Polyester," *Newsweek*, August 3, 1992, p. 61.

45. C. Miller, "Liz Claiborne Throws a Curve with New Brand for Gen Xers," *Marketing News*, July 1, 1996, pp. 1, 10; E. Underwood, "Claiborne Back in Media," *Brandweek*, January 15, 1996, p. 2.

7 Competitive Strategy and the Industry Environment

OPENING CASE

How eBay Revolutionized the Auction Business

IN THE 1990S, many entrepreneurs have tried to use new information technologies, and particularly the Internet, to provide new or improved services to customers. Their goal in exploring the potential of the new technology was to find ways of gaining a competitive advantage over existing firms in a particular industry environment. Nowhere has this been more evident than in the auction industry.

Traditionally, auctions have been events bringing buyers and sellers face to face to determine the fair market value of a product. Auction houses range from the most prestigious ones, such as Sotheby's and Christie's, which sell fine art and antiques, to small local auction companies that sell the contents of someone's house.

In the early 1990s, Pierre Omidyar had an idea for a new kind of auction company, an on-line one, which he believed would revolutionize the selling of all kinds of products—not just fine arts and antiques; but any kind of collectible, from cars to Beanie Babies—by bringing buyers and sellers together through the Internet. He left his job at Microsoft and began to write the software that would provide the platform for an on-line auction service. The result was eBay, launched on Labor Day 1995.[1]

On the eBay Web site, sellers are able to electronically describe their product, post a photograph, and set an initial price, which buyers can then bid up. The highest bidder wins. The company charges a modest fee to list the product plus a low percentage of the final sales price. Sellers have the advantage that their product appears before buyers in every part of the United States, as well as abroad—wherever someone has a computer and can log on to eBay's on-line auction site. Buyers enjoy access to a huge array of merchandise, which can be quickly scanned by using the appropriate keywords on eBay's search engine.

Thus, eBay provides a low-cost forum where buyers and sellers can meet to buy and sell products. The company makes its money from the sheer volume of products that it sells. Every day, millions are listed, so that even with low fees eBay is able to generate high profits.

As you can imagine, eBay's low-cost approach has generated many imitators; after all, it is relatively easy to write a software program and develop an on-line auction site. However, eBay's early start has also given it another major competitive advantage. As the first in the on-line auction business, it has developed a loyal following of both buyers and sellers, who will not switch to other on-line auction companies even when they provide the service for free. By 1999, for instance, Yahoo! and MSN, and hundreds of small specialized companies, had developed their own on-line auction businesses and decided to charge users nothing for their services. Most of them, however, including Yahoo!'s auction site, have not attracted many buyers and sellers. The reason is simple. Sellers know that eBay's site attracts many more buyers than does Yahoo!'s and consequently that they are likely to obtain the highest price there; and eBay buyers know that they will find the greatest selection at that site and so focus their search

there. Thus, besides achieving a low-cost competency, eBay has developed a substantial reputation, which has given it a differentiation advantage as well.

Other on-line companies, however, are not willing to give away the lucrative on-line auction market to eBay; they are searching for new ways to fight back. In June 1999, for example, bookseller Amazon.com announced that it was forming an alliance with Sotheby's to create an upmarket on-line auction service. Other companies have also been seeking partners. In October 1999, Yahoo!, Amazon.com, and others announced that they were banding together to combine their auction businesses and offer a credible alternative to eBay.[2]

After this announcement, eBay's price on the stock market fell. It had soared several thousand percent because investors thought that eBay's strategy had given it a sustainable competitive advantage over its rivals. Through his innovative use of new information technology, Omidyar had brought increased value for millions of buyers and sellers and in the meantime had created more than $1 billion of value for himself in his eBay stock. Now the question arises whether eBay can maintain this value.

OVERVIEW

Chapter 6 examines the different kinds of generic business-level strategies that companies can adopt to obtain a competitive advantage and outperform their rivals. If strategic managers do succeed in developing a successful generic business-level strategy, they face still another crucial task: choosing an appropriate competitive strategy to position their company so that it can sustain its competitive advantage over time in different kinds of industry environments. That is the issue we explore in this chapter.

First, we focus on how companies in *fragmented industries* try to develop competitive strategies that support their generic strategies. Second, we consider the challenges of developing a competitive advantage in *embryonic* and *growth industries.* Third, we probe the nature of competitive relations in *mature industries.* We concentrate here on how a set of companies that have been pursuing successful generic competitive strategies (such as the major burger chains) can use a variety of competitive tactics and gambits to manage the high level of competitive interdependence found in such industries. Finally, we assess the problems of managing a company's generic competitive strategy in *declining industries,* in which rivalry between competitors is high because market demand is slowing or falling. By the end of this chapter, you will understand how the successful pursuit of a generic strategy depends on the selection of the right competitive strategy to manage the industry environment.

STRATEGIES IN FRAGMENTED INDUSTRIES

A **fragmented industry** is one consisting of a large number of small and medium-sized companies. The video-rental industry, for example, is still very fragmented, as is the restaurant industry, the health-club industry, and the legal-services industry. There are several reasons why an industry may consist of many small companies rather than a few large ones.[3] Some industries offer few economies of scale, and so large companies do not have an advantage over smaller enterprises. Indeed, in some industries there are diseconomies of scale. For instance, many home buyers prefer to deal with local real estate agencies, which they perceive as having better local knowledge than national chains. Similarly, in the restaurant business, many customers prefer the unique style of a local restaurant. Because they lack economies of scale, fragmented industries are often characterized by low barriers to entry (and new entries keep the industry fragmented). That is the situation in the restaurant industry, since the costs of opening a restaurant are very moderate and can be borne by a single entrepreneur. High transportation costs, too, can keep an industry fragmented, for regional production may be the only efficient way to satisfy customers' needs, as in the cement business. Finally, an industry may be fragmented because customers' needs are so specialized that only small job lots of products are required, and thus there is no room for a large mass-production operation to satisfy the market.

For some fragmented industries, these factors dictate the competitive strategy to pursue, and the *focus strategy* stands out as the principal choice. Companies may specialize by customer group, customer need, or geographic region; consequently, many small specialty companies operate in local or regional market segments. All kinds of custom-made products—furniture, clothing, hats, boots, and so on—fall into this category, as do all small service operations that cater to particular customers' needs, such as laundries, restaurants, health clubs, and furniture-rental stores. Indeed, service companies make up a large proportion of the enterprises in fragmented industries because they provide personalized service to clients and, therefore, need to be responsive to their needs.

Strategic managers, however, are eager to gain the cost advantages of pursuing a low-cost strategy or the sales/revenue-enhancing advantages of differentiation by circumventing the problems of a fragmented industry. Because returns from consolidating a fragmented industry are often huge, during the last thirty years many companies have developed competitive strategies to achieve such consolidation. Among these companies are the large retailers Wal-Mart, Sears, and JC Penney; fast-food chains such as McDonald's and Burger King; video-rental chains such as Blockbuster Entertainment with its Blockbuster Video stores; and chains of health clubs, repair shops, and even lawyers and consultants. To grow, consolidate their industries, and become the industry leaders, these companies utilize three main competitive strategies: (1) chaining, (2) franchising, (3) horizontal merger and (4) using the Internet.

■ Chaining

Companies such as Wal-Mart and Midas International pursue a **chaining** strategy to obtain the advantages of cost leadership. They establish networks of linked merchandising outlets so interconnected that they function as one large business entity. The amazing buying power that these companies possess through their nationwide store chains allows them to negotiate large price reductions with their suppliers, which in turn promotes their competitive advantage. They overcome the barrier of high transportation costs by establishing sophisticated regional distribution centers, which can economize on inventory costs and maximize responsiveness to the needs of stores and customers. (This is Wal-Mart's specialty.) Last but not least, they realize economies of scale from sharing managerial skills across the chain and from advertising nationally rather than locally.

■ Franchising

For differentiated companies in fragmented industries, such as McDonald's or Century 21 Real Estate, the competitive advantage comes from a business strategy that employs franchise agreements. In **franchising** the franchisor (parent) grants the franchisee the right to use the parent's name, reputation, and business skills at a particular location or area. If the franchisee also acts as the manager, he or she is strongly motivated to control the business closely and make sure that quality and standards are consistently high so that customers' needs are always satisfied. Such motivation is particularly critical in a strategy of differentiation, for which a company's ability to maintain its uniqueness is very important. Indeed, one reason industries fragment is the difficulty of controlling the many small outlets that must be operated while at the same time retaining their uniqueness. Franchising solves this problem.[4] In addition, franchising lessens the financial burden of swift expansion and so permits rapid growth of the company. Finally, a differentiated large company can reap the advantages of large-scale advertising, as well as economies in purchasing, management, and distribution, as McDonald's does very efficiently. Indeed, McDonald's is able to pursue cost leadership and differentiation simultaneously only because franchising allows costs to be controlled locally and differentiation to be achieved by marketing on a national level.

■ Horizontal Merger

Companies such as Anheuser-Busch, Dillard Department Stores, and Blockbuster Entertainment have been choosing a business-level strategy of **horizontal merger** to consolidate their respective industries. For example, Dillard arranged the merger of regional store chains in order to form a national company. By pursuing horizontal merger, companies are able to obtain economies of scale or secure a national market for their product. As a result, they are able to pursue a cost-leadership or a differentiation strategy, or both.

■ Using the Internet

The latest means by which companies have been able to consolidate a fragmented industry is the Internet, and eBay, profiled in the Opening Case, is a good example of this approach. Before eBay, the auction business was extremely fragmented, and local auctions in cities were the usual way in which people could dispose of their antiques and collectibles. With the advent of eBay, sellers using it know that they are getting wide visibility for their collectibles, and therefore are likely to receive a higher price for their product. Amazon.com's success in the book market has led to the closing of many small bookstores, which simply cannot compete either by price or selection. The trend toward using the Internet seems likely to further consolidate even relatively oligopolistic industries.

The challenge in a fragmented industry is to choose the most appropriate means—franchising, chaining, horizontal merger, or Internet—of overcoming a fragmented market so that the competitive advantages associated with the different business-level strategies can be realized. It is difficult to think of any major service activities—from consulting and accounting firms to businesses satisfying the smallest consumer need, such as beauty parlors and car-repair shops—that have not been merged or consolidated by chaining, franchising, and now by the Internet.

STRATEGIES IN EMBRYONIC AND GROWTH INDUSTRIES

Embryonic industries are typically created by the innovations of pioneering companies that become the first movers in a new market. For example, Apple singlehandedly created the market for personal computers, Xerox created the market for photocopiers, and McDonald's created the market for fast food. In most cases, the pioneering company can initially earn enormous profits from its innovation because it is the only company in the industry for a time. For example, before the entry of IBM into the personal computer market in 1981, Apple enjoyed a virtual monopoly. Similarly, during the seventeen years before its patents expired, Xerox enjoyed a monopoly in the market for photocopiers, earning enormous profits as a result.[5]

However, innovators' high profits also attract potential imitators and second movers, as the companies that enter the market later are known. Typically, second movers enter during the growth stage of an industry and may cause the pioneering, first-mover company to lose its commanding competitive position. Figure 7.1 shows how the profit rate enjoyed by the innovator in an embryonic industry can decline as imitators crowd into the market during its growth stage. Thus, Apple's onetime monopoly position was competed away as hordes of other personal computer makers entered the market in the early and mid 1980s, trying to share in Apple's success. Once its patents expired, Xerox, too, faced many imitators, and some of them, such as Canon and Ricoh, were ultimately very successful in the photocopier market. In the fast-food market, the early success of McDonald's drew imitators, including Burger King, Wendy's, and Foodmaker, with its Jack-in-the-Box restaurants.

Although their market share has declined since their early days, companies such as Apple, Xerox, and McDonald's are still major competitors. Other early innovators were not so lucky. For example, in the mid 1970s, EMI pioneered the development of the CAT scanner. Widely regarded as the most important advance in radiology since the x-ray, the CAT scanner takes three-dimensional x-ray pictures of the body. Despite being the pioneer, however, EMI soon saw imitators such as General Electric capture the market. EMI itself withdrew from the CAT market in the early 1980s. Similarly, Bowman invented the pocket calculator, only to see Texas Instruments reap the long-run rewards of the innovation, and Royal Crown Cola pioneered the introduction of diet colas, but it was Coca-Cola and PepsiCo that made

FIGURE 7.1

How an Innovator's
Profits Can Be
Competed Away

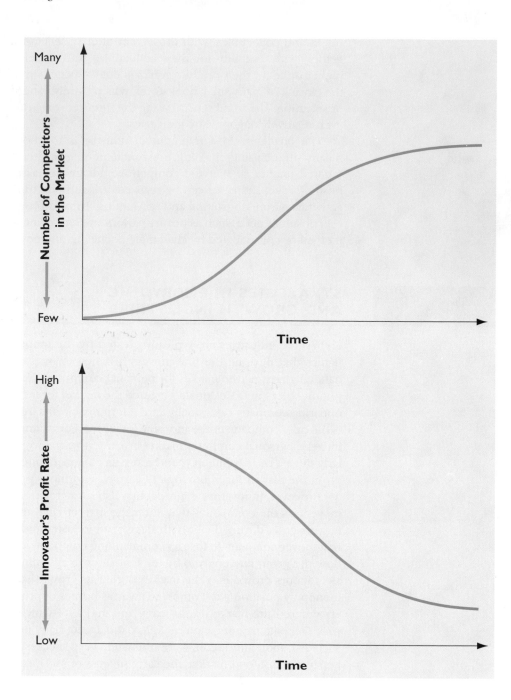

enormous profits from the concept. Thus, first movers often lose out to second movers as competition in an industry becomes intense.

Given the inevitability of imitation, the key issue for an innovating company in an embryonic industry is how to exploit its innovation and build an enduring long-run competitive advantage based on low cost or differentiation. Three strategies are available to the company: (1) to develop and market the innovation itself; (2) to develop and market the innovation jointly with other companies through a strategic alliance or joint venture; and (3) to license the innovation to others and let them develop the market.

The optimal choice of strategy depends on the answers to three questions. First, does the innovating company have the *complementary assets* to exploit its innovation and obtain a competitive advantage? Second, how difficult is it for imitators to copy the company's innovation—in other words, what is the *height of barriers to imitation?* And third, are there *capable competitors* that could rapidly imitate the innovation? Before we discuss the optimal choice of innovation strategy, we need to examine the answers to these three questions.

■ Complementary Assets

Complementary assets are those required to exploit a new innovation and gain a competitive advantage successfully.[6] Among the most important complementary assets are competitive manufacturing facilities capable of handling rapid growth in customers' demand while maintaining high product quality. State-of-the-art manufacturing facilities enable the innovator to move quickly down the experience curve without encountering production bottlenecks and/or problems with the quality of the product. The inability to satisfy demand because of these problems, however, creates the opportunity for imitators to enter the marketplace. For example, Compaq Computer was able to grow rapidly in the market for MS-DOS personal computers during the 1990s at the expense of the product's pioneer, IBM, largely because IBM lacked what Compaq possessed: the state-of-the-art manufacturing facilities to build low-cost computers.

Complementary assets also include marketing know-how, an adequate sales force, access to distribution systems, and an after-sales service and support network. Furthermore, the Internet is making it easier for small companies to develop a nationwide presence since it offers a low-cost way to advertise and sell products to customers. All these assets can help an innovator build brand loyalty. They also help the innovator achieve market penetration more rapidly.[7] In turn, the resulting increases in volume facilitate more rapid movement down the experience curve.

Developing such complementary assets can be very expensive, and embryonic companies often need large infusions of capital for this purpose. That is the reason first movers often lose out to late movers that are large, successful companies, often established in other industries, with the resources to develop a presence in the new industry quickly. Hewlett-Packard and 3M exemplify companies that can move quickly to capitalize on the opportunities arising when other companies open up new product markets, such as compact disks or floppy disks. For instance, Hewlett-Packard began producing personal computers that competed directly with those of Compaq, IBM, and Apple, the early movers.

■ Height of Barriers to Imitation

Barriers to imitation are introduced in Chapter 4, in the discussion of the durability of competitive advantage. As you may recall, **barriers to imitation** are factors that prevent rivals from imitating a company's distinctive competencies. Barriers to imitation also prevent rivals, particularly second or late movers, from imitating a company's innovation. Although ultimately any innovation can be copied, the higher the barriers, the longer it takes for rivals to imitate.

Barriers to imitation give an innovator time to establish a competitive advantage and build more enduring barriers to entry in the newly created market. Patents, for example, are among the most widely used barriers to imitation. By protecting its photocopier technology with a thicket of patents, Xerox was able to delay any significant imitation of its product for seventeen years. However, patents are often easy to "invent around." For example, one study found that this happened to 60 percent of patented innovations within four years.[8] If patent protection is weak, a company might try to slow imitation by developing new products and processes in secret. The most famous example of this approach is Coca-Cola, which has kept the formula for Coke a secret for generations. But Coca-Cola's success in this regard is an exception. A study of 100 companies has estimated that proprietary information about a company's decision to develop a major new product or process is known to its rivals within about twelve to eighteen months of the original development decision.[9]

■ Capable Competitors

Capable competitors are companies that can move quickly to imitate the pioneering company. Competitors' capability to imitate a pioneer's innovation depends primarily on two factors: (1) R&D skills and (2) access to complementary assets. In general, the greater the number of capable competitors with access to the R&D skills and complementary assets needed to imitate an innovation, the more rapid is imitation likely to be.

In this context, R&D skills refer to the ability of rivals to reverse-engineer an innovation in order to find out how it works and quickly develop a comparable product. As an example, consider the CAT scanner. GE bought one of the first CAT scanners produced by EMI, and its technical experts reverse-engineered it. Despite the product's technological complexity, GE developed its own version of it, which allowed GE to imitate EMI quickly and ultimately to replace EMI as the major supplier of CAT scanners.

With regard to complementary assets, the access that rivals have to marketing, sales know-how, or manufacturing capabilities is one of the key determinants of the rate of imitation. If would-be imitators lack critical complementary assets, not only do they have to imitate the innovation, but they may also have to imitate the innovator's complementary assets. This is expensive, as AT&T discovered when it tried to enter the personal computer business in 1984. AT&T lacked the marketing assets (sales force and distribution systems) necessary to support personal computer products. The lack of these assets and the time it takes to build them partly explain why four years after it originally entered the market AT&T had lost $2.5 billion and still had not emerged as a viable contender.

■ Three Innovation Strategies

The way in which these three factors—complementary assets, height of barriers to imitation, and the capability of competitors—influence the choice of innovation strategy is summarized in Table 7.1. The competitive strategy of *developing and marketing the innovation alone* makes most sense when (1) the innovator has the complementary assets necessary to develop the innovation, (2) the barriers to imitating a new innovation are high, and (3) the number of capable competitors is limited. Complementary assets allow rapid development and promotion of the

TABLE 7.1

Strategies for Profiting from Innovation

Strategy	Does Innovator Have All Required Complementary Assets?	Likely Height of Barriers to Imitation	Number of Capable Competitors
Going it alone	Yes	High	Few
Entering into alliance	No	High	Limited
License innovation	No	Low	Many

innovation. High barriers to imitation buy the innovator time to establish a competitive advantage and build enduring barriers to entry through brand loyalty and/or experience-based cost advantages. The fewer the capable competitors, the less likely it is that any one of them will succeed in circumventing barriers to imitation and quickly imitating the innovation. The availability of the Internet makes this strategy more viable since a company can promote an innovation much more easily and inexpensively.

The competitive strategy of *developing and marketing the innovation jointly with other companies through a strategic alliance or joint venture* makes most sense when (1) the innovator lacks complementary assets, (2) barriers to imitation are high, and (3) there are several capable competitors. In such circumstances, it makes sense to enter into an alliance with a company that already has the complementary assets, in other words, with a capable competitor. Theoretically, such an alliance should prove to be mutually beneficial, and each partner can share in high profits that neither could earn on its own. The attempt by Body Shop International, described in Strategy in Action 7.1, to go it alone in the effort to enter the U.S. market rather than to form an alliance with U.S. partners illustrates the benefit of alliances in quickly exploiting an innovation.

The third strategy, *licensing*, makes most sense when (1) the innovating company lacks the complementary assets, (2) barriers to imitation are low, and (3) there are many capable competitors. The combination of low barriers to imitation and many capable competitors makes rapid imitation almost certain. The innovator's lack of complementary assets further suggests that an imitator will soon capture the innovator's competitive advantage. Given these factors, since rapid diffusion of the innovator's technology through imitation is inevitable, by licensing out its technology the innovator can at least share in some of the benefits of this diffusion.[11]

STRATEGY IN MATURE INDUSTRIES

As a result of fierce competition in the shakeout stage, an industry becomes consolidated, and so a mature industry is often dominated by a small number of large companies. Although a mature industry may also contain many medium-sized

The Body Shop Opens Too Late

In 1976, Anita Roddick, a former flower child and the owner of a small hotel in southern England, had an idea. Rising sentiment against the use of animals in testing cosmetics and a wave of environmentalism that focused on "natural" products gave her the idea for a range of skin creams, shampoos, and lotions made from fruit and vegetable oils rather than animal products. Her products, moreover, would not be tested on animals. Roddick began to sell her line of new products from a small shop in Brighton, a seaside town, and the results surpassed her wildest expectations. Her line of cosmetics was an instant success, and to capitalize on it, she began to franchise the right to open stores called The Body Shop to sell her products. By 1993, there were more than 700 of these stores around the world, with combined sales of more than $250 million.

In Britain and Europe, to speed the growth of the company, Roddick mainly franchised her stores through alliances with other individuals and companies. In her push to enter the U.S. market in 1988, however, she decided to own her stores and forgo the rapid expansion that franchising would have made possible. This was a costly mistake. Large U.S. cosmetic companies such as Estée Lauder and entrepreneurs such as Leslie Wexner of The Limited were quick to see the opportunities that Roddick had opened up in this rapidly growing market segment. They moved fast to imitate her product lines, which was not technically difficult to do, and began to market their own natural cosmetics. For example, Estée Lauder

brought out its Origins line of cosmetics, and Wexner opened the Bath and Body Works to sell his own line of natural cosmetics. Both these ventures have been very successful and have gained a large share of the market.

Realizing the competitive threat from imitators, in 1990 Roddick began to move quickly to franchise The Body Shop in the United States, and by 1993 more than 150 stores had opened. Although the stores have been successful, the delay in opening them gave Roddick's competitors the opportunity to establish their own brand names and robbed her enterprise of the uniqueness that its products enjoy throughout Europe. Given that the United States is by far the world's biggest cosmetics market and natural cosmetics are its fastest-growing segment, this mistake cost Body Shop billions of dollars in lost revenues.

Roddick acknowledged that her strategy was a mistake; however, during the 1990s, she failed to energize her company, and in 1998 a new CEO, Patrick Gournay, took over. He moved quickly to revive flagging sales by opening new stores at a very fast rate, by increasing the level of product innovation, and by using the Internet to raise sales. In 1999, for example, he was aiming for product innovation growth of 60 percent as opposed to the 25 percent that the company had managed earlier.[10] Gournay has obviously learnt the lesson well: when an innovation is easy to imitate and there are many capable competitors, a company must do all it can to speed the development and sale of a new product.

companies and a host of small specialized ones, the large companies determine the nature of the industry's competition because they can influence the five competitive forces. Indeed, these are the companies that developed the most successful generic business-level strategies in the industry.

By the end of the shakeout stage, strategic groups of companies pursuing similar generic competitive strategies have emerged in the industry. As we discuss in Chapter 6, all the companies pursuing a low-cost strategy can be viewed as composing one strategic group; all those pursuing differentiation constitute another; and the focusers form a third. Companies in an industry constantly analyze each other's business-level strategies, and they know that if they move to change their strategies, their actions are likely to stimulate a competitive response from rivals in their strategic group and from companies in other groups that may be threatened by the change in strategy.

For example, a differentiator that starts to lower its prices because it has adopted a more cost-efficient technology not only threatens other differentiators in its group, but also threatens low-cost companies, which see their competitive edge being eroded. These other companies may now change their strategies in response—most likely by reducing their prices, too, as is currently happening in the personal computer industry. Thus, the way one company changes or fine-tunes its business-level strategy over time affects the way the other companies in the industry pursue theirs. Hence, by the mature stage of the industry life cycle, companies have learned just how *interdependent* their strategies are.

In fact, the main challenge facing companies in a mature industry is to adopt a competitive strategy that *simultaneously* allows each individual company to protect its competitive advantage and preserves industry profitability. No generic strategy will generate above-average profits if competitive forces in an industry are so strong that companies are at the mercy of each other, potential entrants, powerful suppliers, powerful customers, and so on. As a result, in mature industries, competitive strategy revolves around understanding how large companies try *collectively* to reduce the strength of the five forces of industry competition to preserve both company and industry profitability.

Interdependent companies can help protect their competitive advantage and profitability by adopting competitive moves and tactics to reduce the threat of each competitive force. In the next sections, we examine the various price and nonprice competitive moves and tactics that companies use—first, to deter entry into an industry, and second, to reduce the level of rivalry within an industry. We then discuss methods that companies can employ to gain more control over suppliers and buyers.

STRATEGIES TO DETER ENTRY IN MATURE INDUSTRIES

Companies can utilize three main methods to deter entry by potential rivals and hence maintain and increase industry profitability. As Figure 7.2 shows, these methods are product proliferation, price cutting, and excess capacity.

FIGURE 7.2

Strategies for Deterring Entry of Rivals

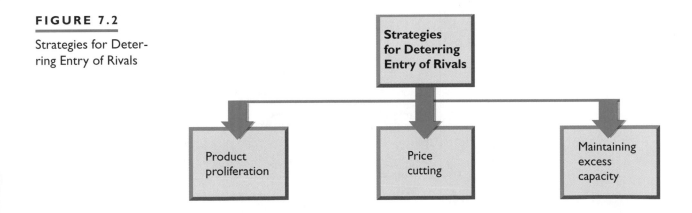

■ Product Proliferation

Companies seldom produce just one product. Most commonly, they produce a range of products aimed at different market segments so that they have broad product lines. Sometimes, to diminish the threat of entry, companies expand the range of products they make to fill a wide variety of niches. Such expansion creates a barrier to entry because potential competitors now find it harder to break into an industry in which all the niches are filled.[12] This strategy of pursuing a broad product line to deter entry is known as **product proliferation.**

Because the large U.S. carmakers were so slow to fill the small-car niches (they did *not* pursue a product proliferation strategy), they were vulnerable to the entry of the Japanese into these market segments in the United States. American carmakers had no excuse for this situation, for in their European operations they had a long history of small-car manufacturing. They should have seen the opening and filled it ten years earlier, but their view was that small cars meant small profits. In the breakfast-cereal industry, on the other hand, competition is based on the production of new kinds of cereal to satisfy or create new desires by consumers. Thus, the number of breakfast cereals proliferates, making it very difficult for prospective entrants to attack a new market segment.

Figure 7.3 indicates how product proliferation can deter entry. It depicts product space in the restaurant industry along two dimensions: (1) atmosphere, which ranges from fast food to candlelight dining; and (2) quality of food, which ranges from average to gourmet. The circles represent product spaces filled by restaurants located along the two dimensions. Thus, McDonald's is situated in the average quality/fast-food area. A gap in the product space gives a potential entrant or an existing

FIGURE 7.3

Product Proliferation in the Restaurant Industry

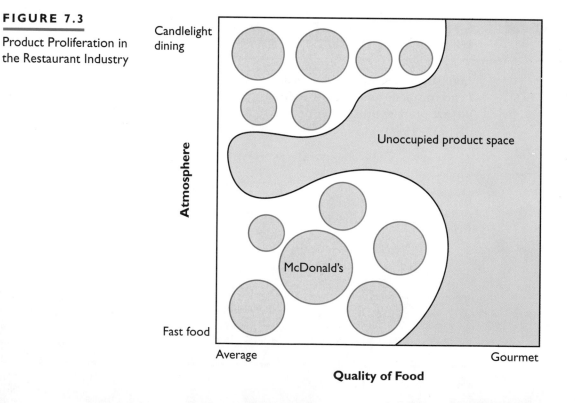

rival an opportunity to enter the market and make inroads. The shaded unoccupied product space represents areas where new restaurants can enter the market. Filling all the product spaces, however, creates a barrier to entry and makes it much more difficult for a new company to gain a foothold in the market and differentiate itself.

■ Price Cutting

In some situations, pricing strategies involving **price cutting** can be used to deter entry by other companies, thus protecting the profit margins of companies already in an industry. One price-cutting strategy, for example, is to charge a high price initially for a product and seize short-term profits but then to cut prices aggressively in order to build market share *and* deter potential entrants simultaneously.[13] The incumbent companies thus signal to potential entrants that if they enter the industry, the incumbents will use their competitive advantage to drive down prices to a level at which new companies will be unable to cover their costs.[14] This pricing strategy also allows a company to ride down the experience curve and obtain substantial economies of scale. Since costs fall with prices, profit margins could still be maintained.

This strategy, though, is unlikely to deter a strong potential competitor—an established company that is trying to find profitable investment opportunities in other industries. It is difficult, for example, to imagine that 3M would be afraid to enter an industry because companies there threaten to drive down prices. A company such as 3M has the resources to withstand any short-term losses. Hewlett-Packard also had few worries about entering the highly competitive personal computer industry because of its powerful set of distinctive competencies. Hence, it may be in the interest of incumbent companies to accept new entry gracefully, giving up market share gradually to the new entrants to prevent price wars from developing, and thus save their profits, if this is feasible.

Most evidence suggests that companies first skim the market and charge high prices during the growth stage, maximizing short-run profits.[15] Then they move to increase their market share and charge a lower price to expand the market rapidly; develop a reputation; and obtain economies of scale, driving down costs and barring entry. As competitors do enter, the incumbent companies reduce prices to retard entry and give up market share to create a stable industry context—one in which they can use nonprice competitive tactics, such as product differentiation, to maximize long-run profits. At that point, nonprice competition becomes the main basis of industry competition, and prices are quite likely to rise as competition stabilizes. Thus, competitive tactics such as pricing and product differentiation are linked in mature industries; competitive decisions are taken to maximize the returns from a company's generic strategy. The airline industry, discussed in Strategy in Action 7.2, offers an illustration of how and when companies use both price and nonprice competitive tactics to build barriers to entry that deter new entrants and reduce rivalry.

■ Maintaining Excess Capacity

The third competitive technique that allows companies to deter entry involves maintaining excess capacity, that is, producing more of a product than customers currently demand. Existing industry companies may deliberately develop some limited amount of excess capacity because it serves to warn potential entrants that if they enter the industry, existing firms can retaliate by increasing output and forcing

STRATEGY *in* ACTION

Ups and Downs in the Airline Industry

Before deregulation in 1978, competition over fares and ticket prices was not permitted in the airline industry, and the airlines had to find other ways to compete. Their response was to attract customers by offering more frequent flights and better service—a form of product differentiation. Since all airlines imitated one another, however, no airline was able to get a competitive advantage over its rivals, and each airline's costs rose dramatically because of the expense of extra flights, improved meals, and so on. To cover the higher costs, the airlines constantly applied for fare increases. As a result, customers paid higher and higher fares to compensate for the airlines' inefficiency. In an attempt to cure this problem, the U.S. Congress decided to deregulate the industry, permitting competition in ticket prices and allowing free entry into the industry. The airlines did not want deregulation. (Why should they? They were receiving a nice profit as a protected industry.) However, deregulation did take place in 1979, and the result was chaos.

Deregulation destroyed the old competitive tactics and maneuvers the airlines had long adopted. Before deregulation, the major airlines knew each other's competitive moves by heart. In the new world of price competition, entry into the industry was easy, and a host of small airlines entered to compete with the major companies. During regulation, no airline had had to develop a generic strategy. There had been no incentive to keep costs low because cost increases could be passed on to consumers. In addition, all firms had used the same means to differentiate themselves, so that no airline had a competitive advantage in being unique. With no rules to

tell them how to compete and no experience of free competition, the airlines waged a price war as new, low-cost entrants such as People Express and Southwest Airlines sought to gain market share from the major players.

To survive in this environment, the major airlines have adopted new competitive tactics to protect their business-level strategies. One of these tactics is the development of hub-and-spoke networks, which have allowed them to build national route structures at low cost. These networks also make it difficult for new firms to enter the industry, because the major airlines hold most of the available gates at large airports. Through nonprice means, the major companies have tried to create new barriers to entry, thereby reducing the threat of new entrants. They have tried to develop new competitive rules of the game to stabilize competition within the industry and prevent price competition.

The use of all these price and nonprice techniques did reduce the number of new entrants, and by 1995 the industry had become profitable, after losing billions of dollars in the early 1990s. However, since 1995, there have been increasing customer complaints about lost bags, poor quality or nonexistent food, cramped seats, and higher fares as the major airlines have sought to reduce their costs and increase their profits. In addition, the wave of strategic alliances in the industry, for example, between American Airlines and British Airlines and between Continental Airlines and Northwest Airlines have led many analysts to conclude that customers may see even more price hikes and cuts in quality as the airlines enjoy their strong bargaining position.

down prices until entry would become unprofitable. However, the threat to increase output has to be *credible,* that is, companies in an industry must collectively be able to raise the level of production quickly if entry appears likely.

STRATEGIES TO MANAGE RIVALRY IN MATURE INDUSTRIES

Beyond seeking to deter entry, companies also wish to develop a competitive strategy to manage their competitive interdependence and decrease rivalry. As we noted earlier, unrestricted competition over prices or output reduces the level of company and industry profitability. Several competitive tactics and gambits are available to companies to manage industry relations. The most important are price signaling, price leadership, nonprice competition, and capacity control.

■ Price Signaling

Most industries start out fragmented, with small companies battling for market share. Then, over time, the leading players emerge, and companies start to interpret each other's competitive moves. Price signaling is the first means by which companies attempt to structure competition within an industry in order to control rivalry among competitors.[16] **Price signaling** is the process by which companies increase or decrease product prices to convey their intentions to other companies and so influence the way they price their products.[17] There are two ways in which companies use price signaling to help defend their generic competitive strategies.

First, companies may use price signaling to announce that they will respond vigorously to hostile competitive moves that threaten them. For example, companies may signal that if one company starts to cut prices aggressively, they will respond in kind—hence the term **tit-for-tat strategy** is often used to describe this kind of market signaling. The outcome of a tit-for-tat strategy is that nobody gains. Similarly, as we note in the last section, companies may signal to potential entrants that if the latter do enter the market, they will fight back by reducing prices and the new entrants may incur significant losses.

A second, and very important, use of price signaling is to allow companies indirectly to coordinate their actions and avoid costly competitive moves that lead to a breakdown in the pricing policy within an industry. One company may signal that it intends to lower prices because it wishes to attract customers who are switching to the products of another industry, not because it wishes to stimulate a price war. On the other hand, signaling can be used to improve profitability within an industry. The airline industry is a good example of the power of price signaling. In the 1980s, signals of lower prices set off price wars, but in the 1990s, the airlines have used price signaling to obtain uniform price increases. Nonrefundable tickets, too, originated as a market signal by one company that was quickly copied by all other companies in the industry. In sum, price signaling allows companies to give one another information that enables them to understand each other's competitive product/market strategy and make coordinated competitive moves.

■ Price Leadership

Price leadership—the taking on by one company of the responsibility for setting industry prices—is a second tactic used to enhance the profitability of companies in a mature industry.[18] Formal price leadership, or price setting by companies jointly, is illegal under antitrust laws, so the process of price leadership is often very subtle. In the auto industry, for example, auto prices are set by imitation. The price set by the weakest company—that is, the one with the highest costs—is often used as the basis for competitors' pricing. Thus, U.S. carmakers set their prices, and Japanese carmakers then set theirs with reference to the U.S. prices. The Japanese are happy to do this because they have lower costs than U.S. companies and are making higher profits than U.S. carmakers without competing with them by price. Pricing is done by market segment. The prices of different auto models in the model range indicate the customer segments that the companies are aiming for and the price range they believe the market segment can tolerate. Each manufacturer prices a model in the segment with reference to the *prices* charged by its competitors, not by reference to competitors' costs. Price leadership allows differentiators to charge a premium price and also helps low-cost companies by increasing their margins.

Although price leadership can stabilize industry relationships by preventing head-to-head competition and thus raise the level of profitability within an industry, it has its dangers. Price leadership helps companies with high costs, allowing them to survive without becoming more productive or more efficient. Thus, it may foster complacency; companies may keep extracting profits without reinvesting any to improve their productivity. In the long term, such behavior will make them vulnerable to new entrants that have lower costs because they have developed new productive techniques. That is what happened in the U.S. auto industry after the Japanese entered the market. Following years of tacit price fixing, with General Motors as the leader, the carmakers were subjected to growing low-cost Japanese competition, to which they were unable to respond. Indeed, many U.S. auto companies have survived into the 1990s only because the Japanese carmakers were foreign firms. Had the foreign firms been new U.S. entrants, the government would probably not have taken steps to protect Chrysler, Ford, or General Motors, and they would be much smaller companies today.

■ Nonprice Competition

A third very important aspect of product/market strategy in mature industries is the use of **nonprice competition** to manage rivalry within an industry. Using various tactics and maneuvers to try to prevent costly price cutting and price wars does not preclude competition by product differentiation. Indeed, in many industries, product differentiation is the principal competitive tactic used to prevent competitors from obtaining access to a company's customers and attacking its market share. In other words, companies rely on product differentiation to deter potential entrants and manage rivalry within their industry. Product differentiation allows industry rivals to compete for market share by offering products with different or superior features or by applying different marketing techniques. In Figure 7.4, product and market segment dimensions are used to identify four nonprice competitive strategies based on product differentiation. (Notice that this model applies to new market segments, not new markets.)[19]

FIGURE 7.4

Four Nonprice
Competitive Strategies

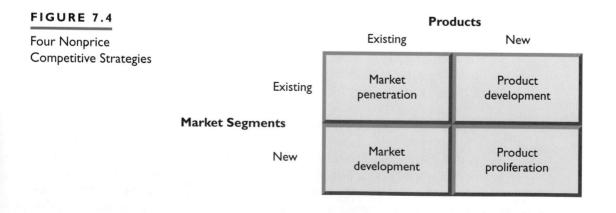

STRATEGY *in* **ACTION**

Warfare in Toyland

Toys 'R' Us, based in Paramus, New Jersey, grew at an astonishing 25 percent annual rate throughout the 1980s and today holds a 20 percent share of the $15 billion retail toy market, which makes it the industry leader. To reach its commanding position, the company used a strategy of market penetration based on developing a nationwide chain of retail outlets and a cost-leadership strategy. To lower costs, Toys 'R' Us developed efficient materials-management techniques for ordering and distributing toys to its stores. It also provided only a low level of customer service. Together, these moves allowed it to obtain a very low expense-to-sales ratio of 17 percent. Toys 'R' Us then used its low costs to promote a philosophy of everyday low pricing. The company deliberately set out to undercut the prices of its rivals, and it succeeded. In fact, its two largest competitors in the 1980s, Child World and Lionel, went bankrupt.[22] Pursuing a market-penetration strategy based on low cost thus brought spectacular results for Toys 'R' Us.

In the 1990s, however, the company's commanding position was threatened by a new set of rivals, which were also pursuing market-penetration strategies. Companies such as Wal-Mart, Kmart, and Target Stores rapidly expanded the number of their stores and beat Toys 'R' Us at its own game by selling toys at prices that were often below those of Toys 'R' Us. Indeed, Toys 'R' Us saw its sales fall from 25 percent in 1990 to 17 percent by 1999, and Wal-Mart is now the market leader with 18 percent.

The new competition squeezed profits for Toys 'R' Us and forced the company to turn to nonprice competition to attract customers. For example, Toys 'R' Us promoted its wide range of products as a competitive advantage; it made its stores more attractive; and it also increased the level of customer service by offering customers more personalized attention. In addition, it also went on-line and is in the process of developing a major Web presence. However, it was slow to do so and eToys, an Internet start-up, is the current leader in this market segment.[23] However, analysts feel that Toys 'R' Us, under newly appointed CEO Bob Moog, is rebuilding its brand name and that the company is poised to regain its leading position in the industry.

Market Penetration When a company concentrates on expanding market share in its existing product markets, it is engaging in a strategy of **market penetration.**[20] Market penetration involves heavy advertising to promote and build product differentiation. In a mature industry, the thrust of advertising is to influence consumers' brand choice and create a brand-name reputation for the company and its products. In this way, a company can increase its market share by attracting the customers of its rivals. Because brand-name products often command premium prices, building market share in this situation is very profitable.

In some mature industries—for example, soap and detergent, disposable diapers, and brewing—a market-penetration strategy becomes a way of life.[21] In these industries, all companies engage in intensive advertising and battle for market share. Each company fears that by not advertising it will lose market share to rivals. Consequently, in the soap and detergent industry, for instance, Procter & Gamble spends more than 20 percent of sales revenues on advertising, with the aim of maintaining and perhaps building market share. These huge advertising outlays constitute a barrier to entry for prospective entrants. As Strategy in Action 7.3 details, Toys 'R' Us rose to prominence in the retail toy market by pursuing a market-penetration strategy.

Product Development   **Product development** is the creation of new or improved products to replace existing ones.[24] The wet-shaving industry is another industry that depends on product replacement to create successive waves of consumer demand, which then create new sources of revenue for companies in the industry. Gillette, for example, periodically comes out with a new and improved razor—such as the Sensor shaving system—which often gives a massive boost to its market share. Similarly, in the car industry, each major car company replaces its models every three to five years to encourage customers to trade in their old models and buy the new one.

Product development is important for maintaining product differentiation and building market share.[25] For instance, the laundry detergent Tide has gone through more than fifty different changes in formulation during the past forty years to improve its performance. The product is always advertised as Tide, but it is a different product each year. The battle over diet colas is another interesting example of competitive product differentiation by product development. Royal Crown Cola developed Diet Rite, the first diet cola. However, Coca-Cola and PepsiCo responded quickly with their versions of the diet drink, and by massive advertising, they soon took over the market. Refining and improving products is an important competitive tactic in defending a company's generic competitive strategy in a mature industry, but this kind of competition can be as vicious as a price war because it is very expensive and raises costs dramatically.

Market signaling to competitors can also be an important part of a product development strategy. One company may let the others know that it is proceeding with product innovations that will provide a competitive advantage the others will be unable to imitate effectively because their entry into the market will be too late. For example, software companies such as Microsoft often announce new operating systems years in advance. The purpose of such an announcement is to deter prospective competitors from making the huge investments needed to compete with the industry leaders and to let its customers know that the company still has the competitive edge so important to retaining customers' loyalty. However, preemptive signaling can backfire, as IBM found out when it announced that its PS/2 operating system would not be compatible with the operating systems presently standard in the industry. Other companies in the industry collectively signaled to IBM and IBM's customers that they would band together to protect the existing operation systems, thus preserving industry standards and preventing IBM from obtaining a competitive advantage from its new technology. IBM subsequently backed down. If a preemptive move is to succeed, competitors must believe that a company will act according to its signals and stick to its position. If the threat is not credible, the signaling company weakens its position.

Market Development   **Market development** finds new market segments for a company's products. A company pursuing this strategy wants to capitalize on the brand name it has developed in one market segment by locating new market segments in which to compete. In this way, it can exploit the product differentiation advantages of its brand name. The Japanese auto manufacturers provide an interesting example of the use of market development. When they first entered the market, each Japanese manufacturer offered a car, such as the Toyota Corolla and the Honda Accord, aimed at the economy segment of the auto market. However, the Japanese upgraded each car over time, and now each is directed at a more expensive market segment. The Accord is a leading contender in the mid-size-car segment, while the Corolla fills the small-car segment that used to be occupied by the Celica, which is now aimed at a sportier market segment. By redefining their product offerings, Japanese manufacturers have profitably developed their market segments and successfully attacked their industry rivals, wresting market share from these companies. Although the Japanese used to compete primarily as low-cost producers, market development has allowed them to become differentiators as well. Toyota is an example of a company that has used market development to pursue simultaneously a low-cost and a differentiation strategy.

Product Proliferation **Product proliferation** can be used to manage rivalry within an industry and to deter entry. The strategy of product proliferation generally means that large companies in an industry all have a product in each market segment or niche and compete head-to-head for customers. If a new niche develops, such as sports utility vehicles, designer sunglasses, or Internet Web sites, then the leader gets a first-mover advantage, but soon all the other companies catch up, and once again competition is stabilized and rivalry within the industry is reduced. Product proliferation thus allows the development of stable industry competition based on product differentiation, not price—that is, nonprice competition based on the development of new products. The battle is over a product's perceived quality and uniqueness, *not* over its price.

■ Capacity Control

Although nonprice competition helps mature industries avoid the cutthroat price reductions that shrink both company and industry levels of profitability, in some industries price competition does periodically break out. This occurs most commonly when there is industry overcapacity—that is, when companies collectively produce too much output so that lowering the price is the only way to dispose of it. If one company starts to cut prices, the others quickly follow because they fear that the price cutter will be able to sell all its inventory and they will be left holding unwanted goods. **Capacity control** strategies are the last set of competitive tactics and maneuvers for managing rivalry within an industry that we discuss in this chapter.

Excess capacity may be caused by a shortfall in demand, as when a recession lowers the demand for cars and causes car companies to give customers price incentives to purchase a new car. In this situation, companies can do nothing except wait for better times. By and large, however, excess capacity results from companies within an industry simultaneously responding to favorable conditions: they all invest in new plants to be able to take advantage of the predicted upsurge in demand. Paradoxically, each individual company's effort to outperform the others means that collectively the companies create industry overcapacity, which hurts them all. Figure 7.5 illustrates this situation. Although demand is rising, the consequence of each company's decision to increase capacity is a surge in industry capacity, which drives down prices.

To prevent the accumulation of costly excess capacity, companies must devise strategies that let them control—or at least benefit from—capacity expansion programs. Before we examine these strategies, however, we need to consider in greater detail the factors that cause excess capacity.[26]

FIGURE 7.5

Changes in Industry
Capacity and Demand

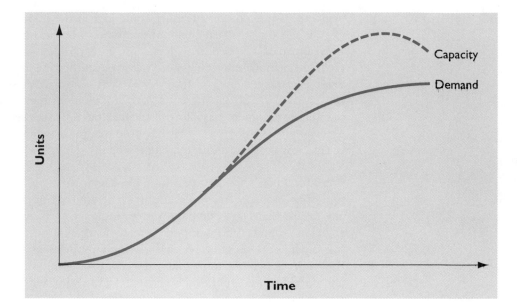

Factors Causing Excess Capacity   The problem of excess capacity often derives from technological factors. Sometimes new, low-cost technology is the culprit because, to prevent being left behind, all companies introduce it simultaneously. Excess capacity occurs because the new technology can produce more than the old. In addition, new technology is often introduced in large increments, which generate overcapacity. For instance, an airline that needs more seats on a route must add another plane, thereby adding hundreds of seats even though only fifty are needed. To take another example, a new chemical process may operate efficiently only at the rate of 1,000 gallons a day, whereas the previous process was efficient at 500 gallons a day. If all companies within an industry change technologies, industry capacity may double and enormous problems can result.

Overcapacity may also be caused by competitive factors within an industry. Entry into an industry is one such factor. Japan's entry into the semiconductor industry caused massive overcapacity and price declines for microchips. Similarly, the collapse of OPEC was due to the entry of new countries able to produce oil at competitive prices. Sometimes the age of a company's plant is the source of the problem. For example, in the hotel industry, given the rapidity with which the quality of hotel furnishings declines, customers are attracted to new hotels. The building of new hotel chains alongside the old chains, however, can cause excess capacity. Often companies are making simultaneous competitive moves based on industry trends, but those moves eventually lead to head-to-head competition. Most fast-food chains, for instance, establish new outlets whenever demographic data show population increases. However, the companies seem to forget that all chains use the same data. Thus, a locality that has no fast-food outlets may suddenly see several being built at the same time. Whether they can all survive depends on the growth rate of demand relative to the growth rate of the fast-food chains.

Choosing a Capacity-Control Strategy   Given the various ways in which capacity can expand, companies clearly need to find some means of controlling it. If they are always plagued by price cutting and price wars, companies will be unable to recoup the investments in their generic strategies. Low profitability within an industry caused by overcapacity forces not just the weakest companies but sometimes the major players as well to exit the industry. In general, companies have two strategic choices. Either (1) each company individually must try to preempt its rivals and seize the initiative, or (2) the companies collectively must find indirect means of coordinating with each other so that they are all aware of the mutual effects of their actions.

To *preempt* rivals, a company must foresee a large increase in demand in the product market and then move rapidly to establish large-scale operations that will be able to satisfy the predicted demand. By achieving a first-mover advantage, the company may deter other firms from entering the market since the preemptor will usually be able to move down the experience curve, reduce its costs, and therefore its prices as well, and threaten a price war if necessary.

This strategy, however, is extremely risky, for it involves investing resources in a generic strategy before the extent and profitability of the future market are clear. Wal-Mart, with its strategy of locating in small rural towns to tap an underexploited market for discount goods, preempted Sears and Kmart. Wal-Mart has been able to engage in market penetration and market expansion because of the secure base it established in its rural strongholds.

A preemptive strategy is also risky if it does not deter competitors and they decide to enter the market. If the competitors have a stronger generic strategy or more resources, such as AT&T or IBM, they can make the preemptor suffer. Thus, for the strategy to succeed, the preemptor must generally be a credible company with enough resources to withstand a possible price war.

To *coordinate* with rivals as a capacity-control strategy, caution must be exercised since collusion on the timing of new investments is illegal under antitrust law. However, tacit coordination is practiced in many industries as companies attempt to understand and forecast the competitive moves of each other. Generally, companies use market signaling and engage in a kind of tit-for-tat strategy to secure coordination. They make announcements about their future investment decisions in trade journals and newspapers. In addition, they share information about their production levels and their forecasts of demand within an industry to bring supply and demand into equilibrium. Thus, a coordination strategy reduces the risks associated with investment in the industry.

SUPPLY AND DISTRIBUTION STRATEGY IN MATURE INDUSTRIES

As you saw in Chapter 3, when an industry becomes consolidated and comprises a few large companies, it gains strength over its suppliers and customers. Suppliers become dependent on the industry for buying their inputs and on customers for obtaining the industry's outputs. By the mature stage, to protect their market share and improve product quality, many companies want to take over more of the distribution of their products and control the source of inputs crucial to the production process. When they seek ownership of supply or distribution operations, they are pursuing a strategy of *vertical integration,* which is considered in detail in Chapter 9. In this chapter, we discuss how the way a company controls its supplier and distributor relationships protects its generic strategy and helps it develop a competitive advantage.

By controlling supplier and distributor relationships, a company can safeguard its ability to dispose of its outputs or to acquire inputs in a timely, reliable manner. This in turn, can reduce costs and improve product quality. One way to analyze the issues involved in choosing a distribution/supplier strategy is to contrast the situation that exists between a company and its suppliers and distributors in Japan with the situation that exists in the United States.

In the United States, it is common for a company and its suppliers and distributors to have an anonymous relationship in which each party tries to strike the best bargain to make the most profit. Often purchasing and distribution personnel are routinely rotated to prevent kickbacks. In contrast, the relationship between a company and its suppliers and distributors in Japan is based on long-term personal relationships and trust. Suppliers in Japan are sensitive to the needs of the company, respond quickly to changes in the specification of inputs, and adjust supply to meet the requirements of a company's just-in-time inventory system. The results of this close relationship are lower costs and the ability to respond to unexpected changes in customers' demand. Developing close supplier/distributor relationships is a tactic that supports Japanese companies' generic strategies. Clearly, it pays a company to develop a long-term relationship with its suppliers and distributors, and more and more U.S. companies such as Xerox, Motorola, Kodak, McDonald's, and Wal-Mart have formed close linkages with their suppliers.

A company has many options to choose from in deciding on the appropriate way to distribute its products to gain a competitive advantage. It may distribute its products to an independent distributor, which in turn distributes them to retailers. Alternatively, a company might distribute directly to retailers or even to the final customer. More and more companies are using this option as they turn to the Internet to market and sell their products. Strategy in Action 7.4 illustrates this shift.

In general, the *complexity of a product* and the *amount of information* needed about its operation and maintenance determine the distribution strategy chosen. Car companies, for example, use franchisees rather than "car supermarkets" to control the distribution of their autos. The reason is the high level of after-sales service and support needed to satisfy customers. Carmakers are able to penalize franchisees by withholding cars from a dealership if customers' complaints rise, giving them effective control over franchisees' behavior.

On the other hand, large electronics manufacturers and producers of consumer durables such as appliances generally prefer to use a network of distributors to control distribution. To enhance market share and control the way products are sold and serviced, manufacturers choose five or six large distributors per state to control distribution. The distributors are required to carry the full line of a company's products and invest in after-sales service facilities. The result is that the manufacturer receives good feedback on how its products are selling, and the distributor becomes knowledgeable about a company's products and thus helps the company maintain and increase its control over the market. The company is able to discipline its distributors if they start to discount prices or otherwise threaten the company's reputation or generic strategy.

Large manufacturers such as Johnson & Johnson, Procter & Gamble, and General Foods typically sell directly to a retailer and avoid giving profits to a distributor or wholesaler. They do so in part because they have lower profit margins than the

---

7.4 STRATEGY *in* ACTION

Compaq and Dell Go Head-to-Head in Distribution

As new developments in technology alter the nature of competition in the personal computer industry, the distribution strategies of its major players are also changing. These changes are evident in the struggle between Dell Computer and Compaq Computer for domination of the personal computer market. Founded by a team of engineers, Compaq has from the start emphasized the engineering and research side of the PC business. For example, it was the first company to bring out a computer using Intel's new 486 chip. Its differentiation strategy was to produce high-end PCs based on the newest technology, which would command a premium price. Compaq specialized in the business market, and it developed a sophisticated, 2,000-strong dealer network to distribute, sell, and service its expensive PCs.[27]

Dell, on the other hand, focused from the beginning on the marketing and distribution end of the PC business. Its low-cost strategy was to assemble a PC and then sell it directly to consumers through mail-order outlets, cutting out the dealer in order to offer a rock-bottom price. The company was viewed by its managers primarily as a distribution or mail-order company, not as an engineering one.

As computers increasingly became commodity products and prices fell drastically, Compaq realized that its strategy of selling only through high-priced dealers would mean disaster. It changed its strategy to produce a low-cost computer, and in the 1990s began its own mail-order distribution, offering its machines directly to consumers, and more recently to businesses.

However, Compaq has not been as successful as Dell in its on-line distribution strategy, both because Dell was first to engage in such distribution and established a first-mover advantage, and because Dell has established a more customer-friendly Web site and enjoys the record for fewest customer complaints. Moreover, while each company offers next-day delivery and installation of computers, as well as extended warranties, Dell has reached ahead in providing the best on-line customer service, and indeed is making quality customer service, as well as price, a main focus of its competitive advantage.[28]

In 1999, Compaq's new CEO, Michael Capellas, announced a bold new Internet distribution and sales strategy to make Compaq the leader in on-line selling to businesses and consumers.[29] Clearly, the battle between these companies is not over.

---

makers of electronic equipment and consumer durables. However, this strategy also allows them to influence a retailer's behavior directly. For example, they can refuse to supply a particular product that a retailer wants unless the retailer stocks the entire range of the company's products. In addition, the companies are assured of shelf space for new products. Coca-Cola and PepsiCo are two companies that are able to influence retailers to reduce the shelf space given to competing products or even to exclude them. They can do so because soft drinks have the highest profit margins of any product sold in supermarkets. Gallo is one of the few winemakers that control the distribution and retailing of their products. This is one reason that Gallo is so consistently profitable.

In sum, devising the appropriate strategy for acquiring inputs and disposing of outputs is a crucial part of competitive strategy in mature industry environments. Companies can gain a competitive advantage through the means they choose to control their relationships with distributors and suppliers. By selecting the right strategy, they are able to control their costs, their price and nonprice strategies, their reputation, and the quality of their products. These are crucial issues in mature industries.

STRATEGIES IN DECLINING INDUSTRIES

Sooner or later many industries enter into a decline stage, in which the size of the total market starts to shrink. The railroad, tobacco, and steel industries are at this stage. Industries start declining for a number of reasons, including technological change, social trends, and demographic shifts. The railroad and steel industries began to decline when technological changes brought viable substitutes for the products these industries manufactured. The advent of the internal combustion engine drove the railroad industry into decline, and the steel industry fell into decline with the rise of plastics and composite materials. As for the tobacco industry, changing social attitudes toward smoking, which are themselves a product of growing concerns about the health effects of smoking, have caused decline.

There are four main strategies that companies can adopt to deal with decline: (1) a **leadership strategy,** by which a company seeks to become the dominant player in a declining industry; (2) a **niche strategy,** which focuses on pockets of demand that are declining more slowly than the industry as a whole; (3) a **harvest strategy,** which optimizes cash flow; and (4) a **divestment strategy,** by which a company sells off the business to others. Before examining each of these strategies in detail, it is important to note that the choice of strategy depends in part on the *intensity* of the competition.

■ The Severity of Decline

When the size of the total market is shrinking, competition tends to intensify in a declining industry and profit rates tend to fall. The intensity of competition in a declining industry depends on four critical factors, which are indicated in Figure 7.6. First, the intensity of competition is greater in industries in which decline is rapid as opposed to industries, such as tobacco, in which decline is slow and gradual.

Second, the intensity of competition is greater in declining industries in which exit barriers are high. As you recall from Chapter 3, high exit barriers keep compa-

FIGURE 7.6

Factors That Determine the Intensity of Competition in Declining Industries

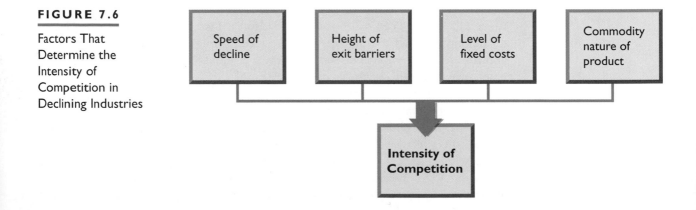

nies locked into an industry even when demand is falling. The result is the emergence of excess productive capacity, and hence an increased probability of fierce price competition.

Third, and related to the previous point, the intensity of competition is greater in declining industries in which fixed costs are high (as in the steel industry). The reason is that the need to cover fixed costs, such as the costs of maintaining productive capacity, can make companies try to utilize any excess capacity they have by slashing prices—an action that can trigger a price war.

Finally, the intensity of competition is greater in declining industries in which the product is perceived as a commodity (as it is in the steel industry) in contrast to industries in which differentiation gives rise to significant brand loyalty, as was true until very recently of the declining tobacco industry.

Not all segments of an industry typically decline at the same rate. In some segments, demand may remain reasonably strong, despite decline elsewhere. The steel industry illustrates this situation. Although bulk steel products, such as sheet steel, have suffered a general decline, demand has actually risen for specialty steels, such as those used in high-speed machine tools. Vacuum tubes provide another example. Although demand for them collapsed when transistors replaced them as a key component in many electronics products, for years afterward vacuum tubes still had some limited applications in radar equipment. Consequently, demand in this vacuum tube segment remained strong despite the general decline in the demand for vacuum tubes. The point, then, is that there may be *pockets of demand* in an industry in which demand is declining more slowly than in the industry as a whole or not declining at all. Price competition thus may be far less intense among the companies serving such pockets of demand than within the industry as a whole.

■ Choosing a Strategy

As already noted, four main strategies are available to companies in a declining industry: a leadership strategy, a niche strategy, a harvest strategy, and a divestment strategy. Figure 7.7 provides a simple framework for guiding strategic choice. Note that intensity of competition in the declining industry is measured on the vertical axis and that a company's strengths *relative* to remaining pockets of demand are measured on the horizontal axis.

Leadership Strategy   A leadership strategy aims at growing in a declining industry by picking up the market share of companies that are leaving the industry. A leadership strategy makes most sense (1) when the company has distinctive strengths that allow it to capture market share in a declining industry and (2) when the speed of decline and the intensity of competition in the declining industry are moderate. Philip Morris has pursued such a strategy in the tobacco industry. By aggressive marketing, Philip Morris has increased its market share in a declining industry and earned enormous profits in the process.

The tactical steps companies might use to achieve a leadership position include aggressive pricing and marketing to build market share; acquiring established competitors to consolidate the industry; and raising the stakes for other competitors, for

FIGURE 7.7

Strategy Selection in a
Declining Industry

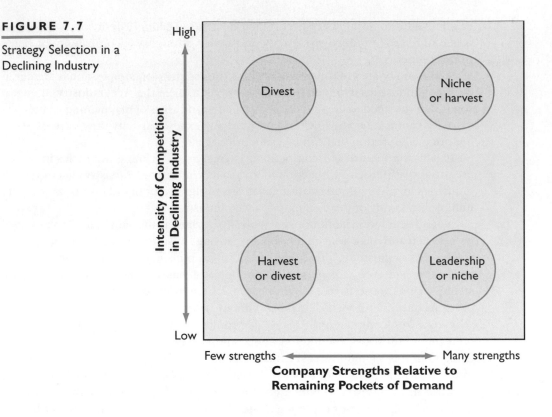

**Company Strengths Relative to
Remaining Pockets of Demand**

instance, by making new investments in productive capacity. Such competitive tactics signal to other competitors that the company is willing and able to stay and compete in the declining industry. These signals may persuade other companies to exit the industry, which would further enhance the competitive position of the industry leader. Strategy in Action 7.5 offers an example of a company, Richardson Electronics, that has prospered by taking a leadership position in a declining industry. It is one of the last companies in the vacuum tube business.

Niche Strategy   A niche strategy focuses on those pockets of demand in the industry in which demand is stable or declining less rapidly than the industry as a whole. The strategy makes sense when the company has some unique strengths related to those niches where demand remains relatively strong. As an example, consider Naval, a company that manufactures whaling harpoons, as well as small guns to fire them, and makes money doing so. This might be considered rather odd, since whaling has been outlawed by the world community. However, Naval survived the terminal decline of the harpoon industry by focusing on the one group of people who are still allowed to hunt whales, although only in very limited numbers—North American Eskimos. Eskimos are permitted to hunt bowhead whales, provided that they do so only for food and not for commercial purposes. Naval is the sole supplier of small harpoon whaling guns to Eskimo communities, and its monopoly position allows it to earn a healthy return in this small market.[31]

7.5

STRATEGY *in* ACTION

How to Make Money in the Vacuum Tube Business

At its peak in the early 1950s, the vacuum tube business was a major industry in which companies such as Westinghouse, General Electric, RCA, and Western Electric had a large stake. Then along came the transistor, making most vacuum tubes obsolete, and one by one all the big companies exited the industry. Richardson Electronics, however, not only stayed in the business but also demonstrated that high returns are possible in a declining industry. Primarily a distributor (although it does have some manufacturing capabilities), Richardson bought the remains of a dozen companies in the United States and Europe as they exited the vacuum tube industry. Richardson now has a warehouse that stocks more than 10,000 different types of vacuum tubes. The company is the world's only supplier of many of them, which helps explain why its gross margin is in the 35 percent to 40 percent range.

Richardson survives and prospers because vacuum tubes are vital parts of some older electronic equipment that would be costly to replace with solid-state equipment. In addition, vacuum tubes still outperform semiconductors in some limited applications, including radar and welding machines. The U.S. government and General Motors are big Richardson customers.

Speed is the essence of Richardson's business. The company's Illinois warehouse offers overnight delivery to some 40,000 customers, processing 650 orders a day, whose average price is $550. Customers such as GM don't really care whether a vacuum tube costs $250 or $350; what they care about is the $40,000 to $50,000 downtime loss that they face when a key piece of welding equipment isn't working. By responding quickly to the demands of such customers and by being the only major supplier of many types of vacuum tubes, Richardson has placed itself in a position that many companies in growing industries would envy—a monopoly position. In 1997, however, a new company, Westrex, was formed to take advantage of the growing popularity of vacuum tubes in high-end stereo systems, and by 1999 it was competing head-to-head with Richardson in some market segments.[30] Clearly, competition can be found even in a declining industry.

Harvest Strategy As we note in Chapter 6, a harvest strategy is the best choice when a company wishes to get out of a declining industry and perhaps optimize cash flow in the process. This strategy makes the most sense when the company foresees a steep decline and intense future competition or when it lacks strengths relative to remaining pockets of demand in the industry. A harvest strategy requires the company to cut all new investments in capital equipment, advertising, R&D, and the like. As illustrated in Figure 7.8, the inevitable result is that the company will lose market share, but because it is no longer investing in this business, initially its positive cash flow will increase. Essentially, the company is taking cash flow in exchange for market share. Ultimately, however, cash flows will start to decline, and at this stage it makes sense for the company to liquidate the business. Although this strategy is very appealing in theory, it can be somewhat difficult to put into practice. Employee morale in a business that is being run down may suffer. Furthermore, if customers catch on to what the company is doing, they may defect rapidly. Then market share may decline much faster than the company expected.

Divestment Strategy A divestment strategy rests on the idea that a company can maximize its net investment recovery from a business by selling it early, before the industry has entered into a steep decline. This strategy is appropriate when the

FIGURE 7.8

A Harvest Strategy

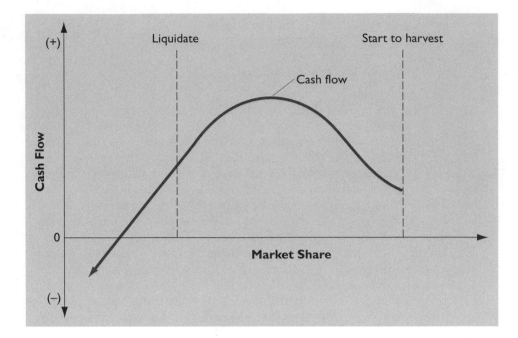

company has few strengths relative to whatever pockets of demand are likely to remain in the industry and when the competition in the declining industry is likely to be intense. The best option may be to sell out to a company that is pursuing a leadership strategy in the industry. The drawback of the divestment strategy is that it depends for its success on the ability of the company to spot accurately its industry's decline before it becomes serious and to sell out while the company's assets are still valued by others.

SUMMARY OF CHAPTER

The purpose of this chapter is to discuss the competitive strategies that companies can use in different industry environments to protect and enhance their generic business-level strategies. Developing a generic competitive strategy and an investment strategy is only the first part, albeit a crucial one, of business-level strategy. Choosing industry-appropriate competitive tactics, gambits, and maneuvers is the second part of successful strategy formulation at the business level. Companies must always be on the alert for changes in conditions within their industry and in the competitive behavior of their rivals if they are to respond to these changes in a timely manner. The chapter makes the following main points:

✔ In fragmented industries composed of a large number of small and medium-sized companies,

the principal forms of competitive strategy are chaining, franchising, horizontal merger, and using the Internet.

✔ In embryonic and growth industries, developing a strategy to profit from technical innovations is a crucial aspect of competitive strategy. The three strategies a company can choose from are (1) to develop and market the technology itself, (2) to do so jointly with another company, or (3) to license the technology to existing companies.

✔ Mature industries are composed of a few large companies whose actions are so highly interdependent that the success of one company's strategy depends on the responses of its rivals.

✔ The principal competitive tactics and moves used by companies in mature industries to deter entry are product proliferation, price cutting, and maintaining excess capacity.

✔ The principal competitive tactics and maneuvers used by companies in mature industries to manage rivalry are price signaling, price leadership, nonprice competition, and capacity control.

✔ Companies in mature industries also need to develop a supply-and-distribution strategy to protect the source of their competitive advantage.

✔ In declining industries, in which market demand has leveled off or is falling, companies must tailor their price and nonprice strategies to the new competitive environment. They also need to manage industry capacity to prevent the emergence of capacity expansion problems.

✔ There are four main strategies a company can pursue when demand is falling: leadership, niche, harvest, and divestment strategies. The choice of strategy is determined by the severity of industry decline and the company's strengths relative to the remaining pockets of demand.

DISCUSSION QUESTIONS

1. Why are industries fragmented? What are the main ways in which companies can turn a fragmented industry into a consolidated one?

2. What are the key problems involved in maintaining a competitive advantage in a growth industry environment? What are the dangers associated with being the leader?

3. Discuss how companies can use (a) product differentiation and (b) capacity control to manage rivalry and increase an industry's profitability.

Practicing Strategic Management

 SMALL-GROUP EXERCISE
How to Keep the Hot Sauce Hot

Break up into groups of three to five people, and discuss the following scenario:

You are the managers of a company that has pioneered a new kind of hot sauce for chicken that has taken the market by storm. The hot sauce's differentiated appeal is based on a unique combination of spices and packaging that allows you to charge a premium price. Within the last three years, your hot sauce has achieved a national reputation, and now major food companies such as Kraft and Nabisco, seeing the potential of this market segment, are beginning to introduce hot sauces of their own, imitating your product.

1. Describe the generic business-level strategy you are pursuing.

2. Describe the industry's environment in which you are competing.

3. What kinds of competitive tactics and maneuvers could you adopt to protect your generic strategy in this kind of environment?

4. What do you think is the best strategy for you to pursue in this situation?

 STRATEGIC MANAGEMENT PROJECT
Module 7

This part of the project continues the analysis of your company's business-level strategy and considers how conditions in the industry's environment affect the company's competitive strategy.

1. In what kind of industry environment (for example, embryonic, mature) does your company operate? (Use the information from Strategic Management Project: Module 3 to answer this question.)

2. Discuss how your company has attempted to develop a competitive strategy to protect its business-level strategy. For example, if your company is operating in an embryonic industry, discuss the ways it has attempted to increase its competitive advantage over time. If it is operating in a mature industry, discuss how it has tried to manage the five forces of industry competition.

3. What new strategies would you advise your company to pursue to increase its competitive advantage? For example, what kinds of strategy toward buyers or suppliers should it adopt? How should it attempt to differentiate its products in the future?

4. Based on this analysis, do you think your company will be able to maintain its competitive advantage in the future? Why or why not?

 ARTICLE FILE 7

Find examples of the ways in which a company or group of companies has adopted a competitive strategy to protect or enhance its business-level strategy.

 EXPLORING THE WEB
Visiting Wal-Mart

Enter the Web site of retailer Wal-Mart (www.wal.mart.com/). Click on "Corporate Information," and then click on "Corporate Timeline." Study the events in Wal-Mart's timeline, and from them outline the way Wal-Mart's competitive strategy in the retailing industry has developed over time.

Search the Web for a company that has recently changed its competitive strategy in some way. What precipitated the shift in its strategy? What strategy changes did the company make?

The
Burger Wars

DURING THE 1990S, in the mature and saturated fast-food industry, competition for customers between the different hamburger chains has been intense. McDonald's, the industry leader, has been under pressure to maintain its profit margins, because, as the price of fast food has fallen, price wars have periodically broken out. Taco Bell started a major price war when it introduced its $.99 taco, for instance, which pushed McDonald's and other burger chains such as Burger King and Wendy's to find ways to lower their costs and prices. As a result of price competition, all the burger chains were forced to learn how to make a cheaper hamburger, and they have been able to lower their prices.

With most fast-food restaurants now offering comparable prices, the focus of competition between the burger chains has shifted to other aspects of their products. First, the major chains are all introducing bigger burger patties. The battle was started by Burger King, which is still waging an aggressive campaign to increase its market share at the expense of McDonald's. In 1994, Burger King added a full ounce of beef to its 1.8 ounce regular patty and followed this with an intense advertising campaign based on the slogan, "Get Your Burger's Worth," directed at McDonald's burger, which was more than 40 percent lighter. The campaign worked for Burger King, and the chain's market share rose by 18 percent in 1995. As a result, in May 1996, McDonald's announced that it would enlarge its regular patty by 25 percent to beat back the challenge from Burger King and from Wendy's, which has always offered a larger burger (and whose "Where's the Beef?" slogan helped it gain market share in the 1980s).[32]

Developing bigger burgers is only one part of competitive strategy in the fast-food industry, however. The main burger chains are constantly experimenting with new and improved kinds of burgers to appeal to customers—burgers that add cheese, bacon, different kinds of vegetables, and exotic sauces. They are also trying whole-meal offerings, such as McDonald's "value meals," to provide a competitive package to attract customers.[33]

Furthermore, recognizing the competition from other kinds of fast-food chains, such as those specializing in chicken or Mexican food, the burger chains have moved to broaden their menus. McDonald's, for example, offers chicken dishes, pizza, and salads; it also allows restaurants to customize their menus to suit the tastes of customers in the region in which they are located. Thus, McDonald's restaurants in New England have lobster on the menu, and those in Japan serve sushi. Product development is a major part of competitive strategy in the industry.

Another major competitive strategy that Burger King and McDonald's have adopted is market penetration: opening up new restaurants to attract customers. Because all the big chains have thousands of restaurants each, many analysts thought that the market was saturated, meaning that it would not be profitable to open more restaurants. However, McDonald's in particular has opened hundreds of restaurants in new locations such as gas stations and large retail stores (for example, Wal-Mart), all of which are profitable and have helped it protect its market share and maintain its margins.

Finally, a major aspect of the burger chains' competitive strategy has been to take their core competencies and apply them on an international level by building global restaurant empires. Indeed, so important have global operations become that both McDonald's and Burger King earn a significant part of their profits from their foreign operations. In the mature fast-food industry, developing new competitive strategies to fend off attacks by other companies within the industry and to protect and enhance competitive advantage is a never-ending task for strategic managers. Even McDonald's is currently experiencing many problems because of the intense competition in the industry.[34]

Case Discussion Questions

1. Describe the nature of competition and the industry environment of the fast-food industry.

2. What strategies are fast-food restaurants pursuing today to protect their competitive position?

End Notes

1. *www.ebay.com* (1999).
2. Press releases, *www.amazon.com* (1999).
3. M. Porter, *Competitive Strategy: Techniques for Analyzing Industries and Competitors* (New York: Free Press, 1980), pp. 191–200.
4. S. A. Shane, "Hybrid Organizational Arrangements and Their Implications for Firm Growth and Survival: A Study of New Franchisors," *Academy of Management Journal,* 1 (1996), 216–234.
5. Much of this section is based on C. W. L. Hill, M. Heeley, and J. Sakson, "Strategies for Profiting from Innovation," *Advances in Global High Technology Management* (Greenwich, Conn.: JAI Press, 1993), III, 79–95.
6. The importance of complementary assets was first noted by D. J. Teece. See D. J. Teece, "Profiting from Technological Innovation," in *The Competitive Challenge,* ed. D. J. Teece (New York: Harper & Row, 1986), pp. 26–54.
7. M. J. Chen and D. C. Hambrick, "Speed, Stealth, and Selective Attack: How Small Firms Differ from Large Firms in Competitive Behavior," *Academy of Management Journal,* 38 (1995), 453–482.
8. E. Mansfield, M. Schwartz, and S. Wagner, "Imitation Costs and Patents: An Empirical Study," *Economic Journal,* 91 (1981), 907–918.
9. E. Mansfield, "How Rapidly Does New Industrial Technology Leak Out?" *Journal of Industrial Economics,* 34 (1985), 217–223.
10. "Reshaping the Body Shop," *Global Cosmetic Industry,* (July 1999), 10.
11. This argument has been made in the game theory literature. See R. Caves, H. Cookell, and P. J. Killing, "The Imperfect Market for Technology Licenses," *Oxford Bulletin of Economics and Statistics,* 45 (1983), 249–267; N. T. Gallini, "Deterrence by Market Sharing: A Strategic Incentive for Licensing," *American Economic Review,* 74 (1984), 931–941; and C. Shapiro, "Patent Licensing and R&D Rivalry," *American Economic Review,* 75 (1985), 25–30.
12. J. Brander and J. Eaton, "Product Line Rivalry," *American Economic Review,* 74 (1985), 323–334.
13. P. Milgrom and J. Roberts, "Predation, Reputation, and Entry Deterrence," *Journal of Economic Theory,* 27 (1982), 280–312.
14. S. M. Oster, *Modern Competitive Analysis* (New York: Oxford University Press, 1990), pp. 262–264.
15. D. A. Hay and D. J. Morris, *Industrial Economics: Theory and Evidence* (New York: Oxford University Press, 1979), pp. 192–193.
16. Porter, *Competitive Strategy,* pp. 76–86.
17. O. Heil, and T. S. Robertson, "Towards a Theory of Competitive Market Signaling: A Research Agenda," *Strategic Management Journal,* 12 (1991), 403–418.
18. Scherer, *Industrial Market Structure and Economic Performance,* Chapter 8.
19. The model differs from Ansoff's model for this reason. See H. I. Ansoff, *Corporate Strategy* (London: Penguin Books, 1984).
20. Ibid, pp. 97–100.
21. R. D. Buzzell, B. T. Gale, and R. G. M. Sultan, "Market Share—A Key to Profitability," *Harvard Business Review* (January–February 1975), 97–103; R. Jacobson and D. A. Aaker, "Is Market Share All That It's Cracked Up to Be?" *Journal of Marketing,* 49 (1985), 11–22.
22. M. Maremont and G. Bowens, "Brawls in Toyland," *Business Week,* December 21, 1992, pp. 36–37.
23. S. Eads, "The Toys 'R' Us Empire Strikes Back, *Business Week,* June 7, 1999, pp. 55–59.
24. Ansoff, *Corporate Strategy,* pp. 98–99.
25. S.L. Brown and K. M. Eisenhardt, "Product Development: Past Research, Present Findings, and Future Directions," *Academy of Management Review,* 20 (1995), 343–378.
26. The next section draws heavily on M. B. Lieberman, "Strategies for Capacity Expansion," *Sloan Management Review,* 8 (1987), 19–27; and Porter, *Competitive Strategy,* pp. 324–338.
27. K. Pope, "Out for Blood, For Compaq and Dell Accent Is on Personal in the Computer Wars," *Wall Street Journal,* February 13, 1993, pp. A1, A6.
28. M. Stepanek, "What Does No.1 Do for an Encore," *Business Week,* November 2, 1998, pp. 44–47.
29. A. Taylor III, "Compaq Looks Inside for Salvation," *Fortune,* August 16, 1999, pp. 124–129.
30. P. Haynes, "Western Electric Redux," *Forbes,* January 26, 1998, pp. 46–47.
31. J. Willoughby, "The Last Iceman," *Forbes,* July 13, 1987, pp. 183–202.
32. R. Gibson, "Bigger Burger By McDonald's: A Two-Ouncer," *Wall Street Journal,* April 18, 1996, p. B1.
33. D. Leonhardt, "McDonald's: Can It Regain Its Golden Touch?" *Business Week,* February 28, 1998, pp. 22–27.
34. D. Leonhardt and A. T. Palmer, "Getting Off Their McButts," *Business Week,* February 22, 1999, pp. 65–66.

8 Strategy in the Global Environment

OPENING CASE

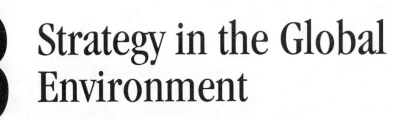

Global Strategy at General Motors

IN MANY RESPECTS, General Motors is one of the oldest multinational corporations in the world. Founded in 1908, GM established its first international operations in the 1920s. General Motors is now the world's largest industrial corporation and full-line automobile manufacturer, with annual revenues of more than $100 billion. The company sells 8 million vehicles per year, 3.2 million of which are produced and marketed outside of its North American base. In 1997, GM had a 31 percent share of the North American market and an 8.9 percent share of the market in the rest of the world.

Historically, the bulk of GM's foreign operations have been concentrated in Western Europe. Local brand names such as Opel, Vauxhall, Saab, and Holden, helped the company sell 1.7 million vehicles in 1997 and gain an 11.3 percent market share, second only to that of Ford. Although GM has long had a presence in Latin America and Asia, until recently sales there accounted for only a relatively small fraction of the company's total international business. However, GM's plans call for this to change rapidly over the next few years. Sensing that Asia, Latin America, and eastern Europe may be the automobile industry's growth markets early in the next century, GM has embarked on ambitious plans to invest $2.2 billion in four new manufacturing facilities in Argentina, Poland, China, and Thailand. One of the most significant things about this expansion is that it is going hand in hand with a sea change in GM's philosophy toward the management of its international operations.

Traditionally, GM saw the developing world as a dumping ground for obsolete technology and outdated models. Just a few years ago, for example, GM's Brazilian factories were churning out U.S.-designed Chevy Chevettes that hadn't been produced in North America for years. GM's Detroit-based executives saw this as a way of squeezing the maximum cash flow from the company's investments in aging technology. GM managers in the developing world, however, took it as an indication that the center did not view developing world operations as being of great significance. This feeling was exacerbated by the fact that most operations in the developing world were instructed to carry out manufacturing and marketing plans formulated in the company's Detroit headquarters, rather than being trusted to develop their own.

In contrast, GM's European operations were traditionally managed on an arm's length basis. The company's national operations were often being allowed both to design their own cars and manufacturing facilities and to formulate their own marketing strategies. This regional and national autonomy made it possible for GM's European operations to produce vehicles that were closely tailored to the needs of local customers. However, it also meant costly duplication of effort in design and manufacturing operations, as well as a failure to share valuable technology, skills, and practices across different national subsidiaries. Thus, while General Motors exerted tight control over its operations in the developing world, its control over operations in Europe was perhaps too lax. Clearly, the company's international operations lacked overall strategic coherence.

Now, in an effort to change this state of affairs, GM is switching from its Detroit-centric view of the world to a philosophy that centers of excellence may be found anywhere in the company's global operations. The company is consciously trying to tap these centers of excellence to provide its global operations with the very latest technology. The four new manufacturing plants being constructed in the developing world are an embodiment of this new approach. All four will be identical, incorporating state-of-the-art technology, and all have been designed not by Americans, but by a team of Brazilian and German engineers. By building identical plants, GM should be able to mimic Toyota, whose plants are so much alike that a change in a car in Japan can be quickly replicated around the world. The GM plants are modeled after GM's Eisenach facility in Germany, which is managed by the company's Opel subsidiary. It was at the Eisenach plant that GM figured out how to implement the lean production system pioneered by Toyota. The plant is now the most efficient auto-manufacturing operation in Europe and the best within GM, with a productivity rate at least twice that of most North American assembly operations. When com-

pleted, each of these new plants will produce state-of-the-art vehicles for local consumption.

In order to realize scale economies, GM is also trying to design and build vehicles that share a common global platform. Engineering teams located in Germany, Detroit, South America, and Australia are designing these common vehicle platforms. The idea is that local plants will be allowed to customize certain features of the vehicles to match the tastes and preferences of local customers. At the same time, adhering to a common global platform will enable the company to spread its costs of designing a car over greater volume and to realize scale economies in the manufacture of shared components—both of which should help GM lower its overall cost structure. The first fruits of this effort include the 1998 Cadillac Seville, which was designed to be sold in more than forty countries. GM's family of front-wheel-drive minivans was also designed around a common platform, which will allow the vehicles to be produced in multiple locations around the globe, as was the 1998 Opel Astra, GM's best-selling car in Europe.

Despite GM's bold moves toward greater global integration, numerous problems still loom on its horizon. Compared with Ford, Toyota, or the new Daimler/Chrysler combination, GM still suffers from high costs, low perceived quality, and a profusion of brands. Moreover, while its aggressive move into emerging markets may be based on the reasonable assumption that demand will grow strong in these areas, other automobile companies are also expanding their production facilities in the same markets, raising the specter of global excess capacity and price wars. Finally, and perhaps most significantly, there are those within GM who argue that the push toward "global cars" is misconceived. In particular, the engineering staff at Opel's Russelsheim design facility, which takes the lead on design of many key global models, has voiced concern that the distinctively European engineering features they deem essential to a car's local success may be dropped in the drive to devise what they see as blander "global" cars.[1]

OVERVIEW

This chapter examines the strategies companies adopt when they expand outside their domestic marketplace and start to compete globally. One option companies have is to sell the same basic product worldwide, that is, use a global strategy. For example, Intel sells the same basic microprocessors worldwide; it does not customize the product to take into account the tastes and preferences of consumers in different nations. By offering a standardized product worldwide, Intel can realize substantial scale economies and build a competitive advantage based on low cost. However, such a strategy often conflicts with the need to customize products to the tastes and preference of consumers in different marketplaces, primarily because customization tends to raise costs. The tension between how much to standardize and how much to customize is one of the fundamental conflicts that global companies have to resolve.

In this chapter, we explore the nature of this conflict and suggest some guidelines that companies can use to identify the best strategy, given their resources, capabilities, and the nature of the markets in which they compete. Toward this end, we consider the different strategies that companies use to compete in the global marketplace and discuss the advantages and disadvantages of each. We also scrutinize two closely related issues: (1) the decision as to which foreign markets to enter, when to enter them, and on what scale; and (2) the choice of entry mode, as well as the different means by which companies enter foreign markets, including exporting, licensing, setting up a joint venture, and setting up a wholly owned subsidiary. The chapter closes with a discussion of the benefits and costs of entering into strategic alliances with global competitors. By the time you have completed this chapter you will have a good understanding of the various strategic issues that companies face when they decide to expand their operations outside of their home country.

General Motors, which is profiled in the opening case, gives us a preview of some of the issues that we shall be dealing with in the current chapter. As described in the case, General Motor's international expansion is being driven by a belief that emerging markets offer the greatest potential for future demand growth. GM is not alone in this belief. Not only are many other automobile firms pursuing a similar expansion strategy, but so are firms from a wide range of industries. Although GM has long had operations overseas, until recently these took second place in the company's Detroit-centric view of the world. Now GM is recognizing that to compete successfully in emerging markets, it is no longer enough to transfer outdated technology and designs from Detroit. It must build a globally integrated corporation that draws on centers of excellence wherever they may be in the world to engineer global cars and state-of-the-art production systems. For all of its economic benefits, though, the trend toward greater integration of its global operations is clearly causing worry within GM's European units. They fear that an ability to respond to local market needs may be lost in the process. As we shall see in this chapter, GM's struggle with this issue is not unique. Many multinational enterprises are striving to find the right balance between global integration and local responsiveness.

PROFITING FROM GLOBAL EXPANSION

Expanding globally allows companies, large or small, to increase their profitability in ways not available to purely domestic enterprises. Companies that operate internationally can (1) earn a greater return from their distinctive competencies; (2) realize what we refer to as location economies by dispersing individual value creation activities to those locations where they can be performed most efficiently; and (3) ride down the experience curve ahead of competitors, thereby lowering the costs of value creation.

■ Transferring Distinctive Competencies

In Chapter 4, where the concept is first considered, **distinctive competencies** are defined as *unique strengths that allow a company to achieve superior efficiency, quality, innovation, or customer responsiveness*. Such strengths typically find their expression in product offerings that other companies find difficult to match or imitate. Thus, distinctive competencies form the bedrock of a company's competitive advantage. They enable a company to lower the costs of value creation and/or to perform value creation activities in ways that lead to differentiation and premium pricing.

Companies with valuable distinctive competencies can often realize enormous returns by applying those competencies, and the products they produce, to foreign markets where indigenous competitors lack similar competencies and products. For example, as described in Strategy in Action 8.1, McDonald's has expanded rapidly overseas in recent years to exploit its distinctive competencies in managing fast-food operations. These competencies have proved to be just as valuable in countries as diverse as France, Russia, China, Germany, and Brazil as they have been in the United States. Before McDonald's entry, none of these countries had U.S.-style fast-food chains, so McDonald's was bringing in unique skills and a unique product. The lack of indigenous competitors with similar competencies and products has greatly enhanced the profitability of this strategy for McDonald's.

In an earlier era, U.S. firms such as Kellogg, Coca-Cola, H. J. Heinz, and Procter & Gamble expanded overseas to exploit their competencies in developing and marketing branded consumer products. These competencies and the resulting products—which were developed in the U.S. market during the 1950s and 1960s—yielded enormous returns when applied to European markets, where most indigenous competitors lacked similar marketing skills and products. Their near-monopoly on consumer marketing skills allowed these U.S. firms to dominate many European consumer product markets during the 1960s and 1970s. Similarly, in the 1970s and 1980s, many Japanese firms expanded globally to exploit their skills in production, materials management, and new product development—competencies that many of their indigenous North American and European competitors seemed to lack at the time. Today, retail companies such as Wal-Mart and financial companies such as Citigroup, Merrill Lynch, and American Express are transferring the valuable competencies they developed in their core home market to other developed and emerging markets where indigenous competitors lack those competencies.

■ Realizing Location Economies

Location economies are the economies that arise from performing a value creation activity in the optimal location for that activity, wherever in the world that might be (transportation costs and trade barriers permitting). Locating a value creation activity in the optimal location for that activity can have one of two effects: (1) *lower the costs of value creation, helping the company achieve a low-cost position,* or (2) *enable a company to differentiate its product offering and charge a premium price.* Thus, efforts to realize location economies are consistent with the generic business-level strategies of low cost and differentiation. In theory, a company that realizes location economies by dispersing each of its value creation activities to its optimal location should have a competitive advantage over a company that bases all its value creation activities at a single location. It should be better able to differentiate its product offering and lower its cost structure than its single-location competitor. In a world where competitive pressures are increasing, such a strategy may well become an imperative for survival.

For an example of location economies, consider Swan Optical, a U.S.-based manufacturer and distributor of eyewear. With sales revenues only in the $20 million to $30 million range, Swan is hardly a giant, yet it manufacturers its eyewear in low-cost factories in Hong Kong and China that it jointly owns with a Hong Kong–based partner. Swan also has a minority stake in eyewear design houses in Japan, France, and Italy. Swan Optical, thus, is a company that has dispersed its manufacturing and design processes to different locations around the world in order to take advantage of the favorable skill base and cost structure found in other countries. Investments in Hong Kong and then China have helped Swan lower its cost structure, whereas investments in Japan, France, and Italy have helped it produce differentiated designer eyewear for which it can charge a premium price. The critical point is that by dispersing its manufacturing and design activities in this way, Swan has been able to establish a competitive advantage for itself in the global marketplace for eyewear.[3]

Boeing's strategy for manufacturing its new commercial jet aircraft, the 777, also illustrates location economies. The 777 uses 132,500 engineered parts produced around the world by 545 different suppliers. For example, eight Japanese suppliers make parts of the fuselage, doors, and wings; a supplier in Singapore makes the doors for the nose landing gear; and three suppliers in Italy manufacture wing flaps. Part of Boeing's rationale for outsourcing so much production to foreign suppliers is that these various suppliers are the best in the world at performing their particular activity when measured on the basis of cost and quality. Therefore, the result of having foreign suppliers build specific parts is a better final product and a competitive advantage for Boeing in the global marketplace.[4]

Generalizing from the Swan and Boeing examples, we can say that one result of this kind of thinking is the creation of a **global web** of value creation activities, with different stages of the value chain being dispersed to those locations around the globe where value added is maximized, or where the costs of value creation are minimized. To bring in still another example, consider the case of GM's Pontiac Le Mans cited in Robert Reich's *The Work of Nations*.[5] Marketed primarily in the United States, the car was designed in Germany; key components were manufactured in Japan, Taiwan, and Singapore; the assembly operation was performed in South Korea; and the advertising strategy was formulated in Great Britain. The car was designed in Germany because GM believed the designers in its German subsidiary had the skills most suited to the job at hand. (They were the most capable of producing a design that added value.) Components were manufactured in Japan, Taiwan, and Singapore because favorable factor conditions there—relatively low cost, skilled labor—suggested that those locations had a comparative advantage in the production of components (which helped reduce the costs of value creation). The car was assembled in South Korea because GM believed that the low labor costs there would minimize the costs of assembly (also helping to minimize the costs of value creation). Finally, the advertising strategy was formulated in Great

8.1 STRATEGY *in* ACTION

McDonald's Everywhere

Established in 1955, McDonald's faced a problem by the early 1980s. After three decades of rapid growth, the U.S. fast-food market was beginning to show signs of market saturation. McDonald's response to the slowdown was to expand abroad rapidly. In 1980, the chain opened 28 percent of its new restaurants abroad; in 1986, the figure reached 40 percent, in 1990 it was close to 60 percent, and in 1997 it surpassed 70 percent. Since the early 1980s, the firm's foreign revenues and profits have grown at the rate of 22 percent per year. By 1997, McDonald's had 10,752 restaurants in 108 countries, aside from the United States. Together, these restaurants generated $16.5 billion (53 percent) of the company's $31 billion in revenues. Moreover, McDonald's shows no signs of slowing down. Management notes that there is still only one McDonald's restaurant for every 500,000 people in the foreign countries where it currently does business. This compares with one McDonald's restaurant for every 25,000 people in the United States. The company's plans call for its foreign expansion to continue at a rapid rate. In England, France, and Germany combined, the chain opened 500 more restaurants between 1995 and 1997, for a total gain of 37 percent. In 1997, McDonald's announced that it would open 2,000 restaurants per year for the foreseeable future, the majority of them outside the United States. The plan includes major expansion in Latin America, where the company expects to invest $2 billion

over the next few years.

One of the keys to McDonald's successful foreign expansion is detailed planning. When the company enters a foreign country, it does so only after some very careful preparation. In what is a fairly typical pattern, before McDonald's opened its first Polish restaurant in 1992, the company spent eighteen months establishing essential contacts and getting to know the local culture. Locations, real estate, construction, supply, personnel, legal, and government relations were all worked out in advance. In June 1992, a team of fifty employees from the United States, Russia, Germany, and Britain went to Poland to help with the opening of the first four restaurants. One of their primary objectives was to hire and train local personnel. By mid 1994, all of these employees except one had returned to their home countries. They were replaced by Polish nationals, who had been trained up to the skill level required for running a McDonald's operation.

Another key to the firm's international strategy is the export not only of its fast-food products, but also of the management skills that spurred its growth in the United States. McDonald's U.S. success was built on a formula of close relations with suppliers, nationwide marketing might, tight control over store-level operating procedures, and a franchising system that encourages entrepreneurial individual franchisees. Although this system has worked flawlessly in the United States, some modifications must be made in other countries. One of the firm's biggest chal-

Britain, because GM believed a particular advertising agency there was the most able to produce an advertising campaign that would help sell the car. (This decision was consistent with GM's desire to maximize the value added.)

◼ Moving Down the Experience Curve

As you recall from Chapter 5, the experience curve refers to the systematic decrease in production costs that has been observed to occur over the life of a product. In Chapter 5, we point out that learning effects and economies of scale underlie the experience curve and that moving down the experience curve allows a company to lower the costs of value creation. The company that moves down the experience curve most rapidly will have a cost advantage over its competitors. Moving down the experience curve is therefore consistent with the business-level strategy of cost leadership.

lenges had been to infuse each store with the same culture and standardized operating procedures that have been the hallmark of its success in the United States. To aid in this task, in many countries McDonald's has enlisted the help of large partners through joint venture arrangements. The partners play a key role in learning and transplanting the organization's values to local employees.

Foreign partners have also played a key role in helping McDonald's adapt its marketing methods and menu to local conditions. Although U.S.-style fast food remains the staple fare on the menu, local products have been added. In Brazil, for instance, McDonald's sells a soft drink made from the guarana, an Amazonian berry. Patrons of McDonald's in Malaysia, Singapore, and Thailand savor milk shakes flavored with durian, a foul-smelling (to U.S. tastes, at least) fruit considered an aphrodisiac by the locals. In Arab countries, McDonald's restaurants maintain "Halal" menus, which signify compliance with Islamic laws on food preparation, especially beef. In 1995, McDonald's opened the first kosher restaurant in suburban Jerusalem. The restaurant does not serve dairy products. And in India, the Big Mac is made with lamb and called the "Maharaja Mac."

McDonald's greatest problem, however, has been to replicate its U.S. supply chain in other countries. U.S. suppliers are fiercely loyal to McDonald's; they must be, because their fortunes are closely linked to those of McDonald's. McDonald's maintains very rigorous specifications for all the raw ingredients it uses—the key to its consistency and quality control. Outside the United States, however, McDonald's has found suppliers far less willing to make the investments required to meet its specifications. In Great Britain, for example, McDonald's had problems getting local bakeries to produce the hamburger bun. After experiencing quality problems with two local bakeries, McDonald's built its own bakery to supply its stores there. In a more extreme case, when McDonald's decided to open a restaurant in Russia, it found that local suppliers lacked the capability to produce goods of the quality it demanded. The firm was forced to vertically integrate through the local food industry on a heroic scale, importing potato seeds and bull semen and indirectly managing dairy farms, cattle ranches, and vegetable plots. It also had to construct the world's largest food-processing plant, at a cost of $40 million. The restaurant itself cost only $4.5 million.

Now that it has a successful foreign operation, McDonald's is experiencing benefits that go beyond the immediate financial ones. Increasingly the firm is finding that its foreign franchisees are a source of valuable new ideas. The Dutch operation created a prefabricated modular store, which can be moved over a weekend and is now widely used to set up temporary restaurants at big outdoor events. The Swedes came up with an enhanced meat freezer, which is now used companywide. And satellite stores, or low-overhead mini McDonald's, which are now appearing in hospitals and sports arenas in the United States, were invented in Singapore.[2]

Many of the underlying sources of experience-based cost economies are to be found in the plant. This is true of most learning effects and of the economics of scale derived from spreading the fixed costs of building productive capacity over a large output. It follows that the key to riding down the experience curve as rapidly as possible is to increase the accumulated volume *produced by a plant* as quickly as possible. Since global markets are larger than domestic markets, companies that serve a global market *from a single location* are likely to build up accumulated volume faster than companies that focus primarily on serving their home market or on serving multiple markets from multiple production locations. Thus, serving a global market from a single location is consistent with moving down the experience curve and establishing a low-cost position.

In addition, to get down the experience curve quickly, companies need to price and market very aggressively so that demand expands rapidly. They also need to build production capacity capable of serving a global market. Another point to bear in mind is that the cost advantages of serving the world market from a single location will be all the more significant if that location is also the optimal one for performing that value creation activity—that is, if the company is *simultaneously* realizing cost economies from experience-curve effects *and* from location economies.

One company that has excelled in the pursuit of such a strategy is Matsushita. Along with Sony and Philips NV, in the 1970s Matsushita was in the race to develop a commercially viable VCR. Although Matsushita initially lagged behind both Philips and Sony, it was ultimately able to get its VHS format accepted as the world standard and to reap enormous experience-curve cost economies in the process. This cost advantage subsequently constituted a formidable barrier to new competition. Matsushita's strategy was to build global volume as rapidly as possible. To ensure that it could accommodate worldwide demand, it increased production capacity thirty-threefold, from 205,000 units in 1977 to 6.8 million units by 1984. By serving the world market from a single location in Japan, Matsushita was able to realize significant learning effects and economies of scale. These allowed it to drop its prices by 50 percent within five years of selling its first VHS-formatted VCR. As a result, by 1983 Matsushita was the world's major VCR producer, accounting for approximately 45 percent of world production and enjoying a significant cost advantage over its main competitors. The next largest company, Hitachi, accounted for only 11.1 percent of world production in 1983.[6]

■ Global Expansion and Business-Level Strategy

It is important to recognize that the different ways of profiting from global expansion are all linked to the generic *business-level strategies* of cost leadership and differentiation. Companies that transfer distinctive competencies to other countries are trying to realize greater gains from their low-cost or differentiation-based competitive advantage. Companies such as Swan Optical that attempt to realize location economies are trying to lower their costs and/or increase value added so that they can better differentiate themselves from their competitors. And companies that serve a global market in order to ride more quickly down the experience curve are trying to build a competitive advantage based on low cost, as Matsushita did with its VHS-formatted VCRs.

PRESSURES FOR COST REDUCTIONS AND LOCAL RESPONSIVENESS

Companies that compete in the global marketplace typically face two types of competitive pressures: *pressures for cost reductions* and *pressures to be locally responsive* (see Figure 8.1).[7] These competitive pressures place conflicting demands on a company. Responding to pressures for cost reductions requires that a company try to minimize its unit costs. To attain this goal, a company may have to base its productive activities at the most favorable low-cost location, wherever in the world that might be. It may also have to offer a standardized product to the global marketplace in order to ride down the experience curve as quickly as possible. On the other hand, responding to pressures to be locally responsive requires that a company differentiate its product offering and marketing strategy from country to country in an effort to accommodate the diverse demands arising from national differences in

FIGURE 8.1

Pressures for Cost Reduction and Local Responsiveness

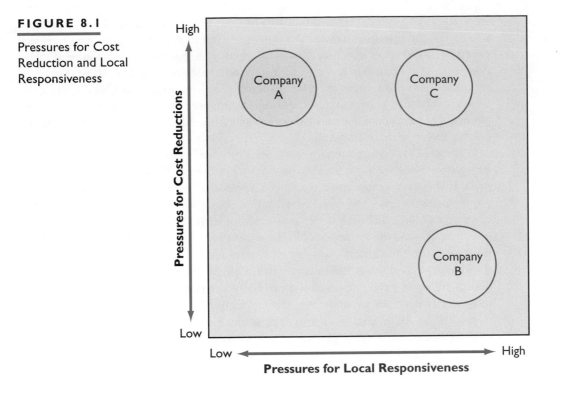

consumer tastes and preferences, business practices, distribution channels, competitive conditions, and government policies. Because differentiation across countries can involve significant duplication and a lack of product standardization, it may raise costs.

Whereas some companies, such as company A in Figure 8.1, face high pressures for cost reductions and low pressures for local responsiveness, and others, such as company B, face low pressures for cost reductions and high pressures for local responsiveness, many companies are in the position of company C. They face high pressures for *both* cost reductions and local responsiveness. Dealing with these conflicting and contradictory pressures is a difficult strategic challenge for a company, primarily because being locally responsive tends to raise costs. In the remainder of this section, we consider the sources of pressures for cost reductions and local responsiveness, and in the next section we examine the strategies that companies adopt in order to deal with these pressures.

■ Pressures for Cost Reductions

Increasingly, international companies must cope with pressures for cost reductions. Pressures for cost reductions can be particularly intense in industries producing commodity-type products, where meaningful differentiation on nonprice factors is difficult and price is the main competitive weapon. Products that serve universal needs tend to fall into this category. Universal needs exist when the tastes and preferences of consumers in different nations are similar, if not identical. This obviously applies to conventional commodity products such as bulk chemicals, petroleum, steel, sugar, and the like. It also tends to be true for many industrial and consumer products—for instance, hand-held calculators, semiconductor chips, and personal computers. Pressures for cost reductions are also intense in industries where major competitors are based in low-cost locations, where there is persistent excess capacity, and where consumers are powerful and face low switching costs. Many commentators have also argued that the liberalization of the world trade and investment environment in recent decades has generally increased cost pressures by facilitating greater international competition.[8]

Pressures for cost reductions have been intense in the global tire industry in recent years. Tires are a commodity product for which differentiation is difficult and price is the main competitive weapon. The major buyers of tires, automobile companies, are powerful and face low switching costs, so they have been playing tire companies off against each other in an attempt to get lower prices. And the decline in global demand for automobiles in the early 1990s has created a serious excess capacity situation in the tire industry, with as much as 25 percent of world capacity standing idle. The result has been a worldwide price war, with almost all tire companies suffering heavy losses in the early 1990s. In response to the cost pressures, most tire companies are now trying to rationalize their operations in a way consistent with the attainment of a low-cost position. They are moving production to low-cost facilities and offering globally standardized products in an attempt to realize experience-curve economies.[9]

■ Pressures for Local Responsiveness

Pressures for local responsiveness arise from differences in consumer tastes and preferences, differences in infrastructure and traditional practices, differences in distribution channels, and host government demands.

Differences in Consumer Tastes and Preferences   Strong pressures for local responsiveness emerge when consumer tastes and preferences differ significantly between countries, as they may for historical or cultural reasons. In such cases, the product and marketing messages have to be customized to appeal to the tastes and preferences of local consumers. This typically creates pressures for the delegation of production and marketing functions to national subsidiaries.

In the automobile industry, for example, there is a strong demand among North American consumers for pickup trucks. This is particularly true in the South and West, where many families have a pickup truck as a second or third car. In contrast, in European countries pickup trucks are seen purely as utility vehicles and are purchased primarily by companies rather than individuals. Consequently, the marketing message needs to be tailored to the different nature of demand in North America and Europe.

As a counterpoint, in a now famous article Professor Theodore Levitt of the Harvard Business School argued that consumer demands for local customization are on the decline worldwide.[10] According to Levitt, modern communications and transport technologies have created the conditions for a convergence of the tastes and preferences of consumers from different nations. The result is the emergence of enormous global markets for standardized consumer products. As evidence of the increasing homogeneity of the global marketplace, Levitt cites worldwide acceptance of McDonald's hamburgers, Coca-Cola, Levi Strauss blue jeans, and Sony television sets, all of which are sold as standardized products.

Levitt's argument, however, has been characterized as extreme by many commentators. For example, Christopher Bartlett and Sumantra Ghoshal have observed that in the consumer electronics industry buyers reacted to an overdose of standardized global products by showing a renewed preference for products that are differentiated to local conditions.[11] They note that Amstrad, the fast-growing British computer and electronics company, got its start by recognizing and responding to local consumer needs. Amstrad captured a major share of the British audio player market by moving away from the standardized inexpensive music centers marketed by global companies such as Sony and Matsushita. Amstrad's product was encased in teak rather than metal cabinets, with a control panel tailor-made to appeal to British consumers' preferences. In response, Matsushita had to reverse its earlier bias toward standardized global design and place more emphasis on local customization.

Differences in Infrastructure and Traditional Practices Pressures for local responsiveness arise from differences in infrastructure and/or traditional practices among countries, creating a need to customize products accordingly. Fulfilling this need may require the delegation of manufacturing and production functions to foreign subsidiaries. For example, in North America consumer electrical systems are based on 110 volts, whereas in some European countries 240-volt systems are standard. Thus, domestic electrical appliances have to be customized to take this difference in infrastructure into account. Traditional practices also often vary across nations. For example, in Britain people drive on the left-hand side of the road, creating a demand for right-hand drive cars, whereas in France people drive on the right-hand side of the road and therefore want left-hand drive cars. Obviously, automobiles have to be customized to take this difference in traditional practices into account.

Differences in Distribution Channels A company's marketing strategies may have to be responsive to differences in distribution channels among countries. This may necessitate the delegation of marketing functions to national subsidiaries. In the pharmaceutical industry, for instance, the British and Japanese distribution system is radically different from the U.S. system. British and Japanese doctors will not accept or respond favorably to a U.S.-style high-pressure sales force. Thus, pharmaceutical companies have to adopt different marketing practices in Britain and Japan compared with the United States, switching from hard sell to soft sell.

Host Government Demands Economic and political demands imposed by host country governments may necessitate a degree of local responsiveness. For example, the politics of health care around the world requires that pharmaceutical companies manufacture in multiple locations. Pharmaceutical companies are subject to local clinical testing, registration procedures, and pricing restrictions, all of which make it necessary that the manufacturing and marketing of a drug should meet local requirements. Moreover, since governments and government agencies control a significant proportion of the health care budget in most countries, they are in a powerful position to demand a high level of local responsiveness.

More generally, threats of protectionism, economic nationalism, and local content rules (which require that a certain percentage of a product should be manufactured locally) all dictate that international businesses manufacture locally. As an example, consider Bombardier, the Canadian-based manufacturer of railcars, aircraft, jet boats, and snowmobiles. Bombardier has twelve railcar factories across Europe. Critics of the firm argue that the resulting duplication of manufacturing facilities leads to high costs and helps explain why Bombardier makes lower profit margins on its railcar operations than on its other business lines. In reply, managers at Bombardier argue that in Europe informal rules with regard to local content favor people who use local workers. To sell railcars in Germany, they claim, you must manufacture in Germany. The same goes for Belgium, Austria, and France. To try and address its cost structure in Europe, Bombardier has centralized its engineering and purchasing functions, but it has no plans to centralize manufacturing.[12]

Implications   Pressures for local responsiveness imply that it may not be possible for a company to realize the full benefits from experience-curve effects and location economies. It may not be possible, for instance, to serve the global marketplace from a single low-cost location, producing a globally standardized product and marketing it worldwide to achieve experience-curve cost economies. In practice, the need to customize the product offering to local conditions may work against the implementation of such a strategy. As noted earlier, automobile companies have found that Japanese, U.S., and European consumers demand different kinds of cars, which means customizing products for local markets. In response, companies such as Honda, Ford, and Toyota are pursuing a strategy of establishing top-to-bottom design and production facilities in each of these regions so that they can better serve local demands. Although such customization brings benefits, it also limits the ability of a company to realize significant experience-curve cost economies and location economies. In addition, pressures for local responsiveness imply that it may not be possible to transfer wholesale from one nation to another the skills and products associated with a company's distinctive competencies. Concessions often have to be made to local conditions. For an example, take another look at Strategy in Action 8.1 and its description of the concessions to local conditions that McDonald's has had to make in different national markets.

STRATEGIC CHOICE

Companies use four basic strategies to enter and compete in the international environment: an international strategy, a multidomestic strategy, a global strategy, and a transnational strategy.[13] Each of these strategies has its advantages and disadvantages. The appropriateness of each varies with the extent of pressures for cost reductions and local responsiveness. Figure 8.2 illustrates when each of these strategies is most appropriate. In this section, we describe each strategy, identify when it is appropriate, and discuss its pros and cons.

FIGURE 8.2

Four Basic Strategies

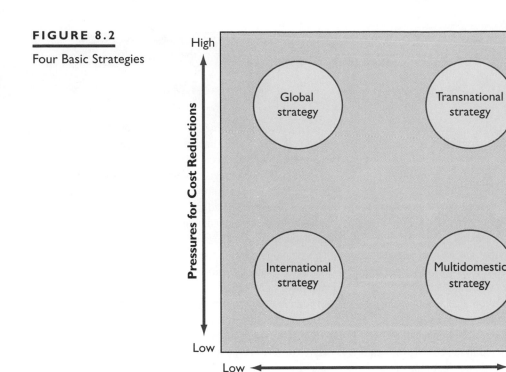

■ International Strategy

Companies that pursue an international strategy try to create value by transferring valuable skills and products to foreign markets where indigenous competitors lack those skills and products. Most international companies have created value by transferring differentiated product offerings developed at home to new markets overseas. Accordingly, they tend to centralize product development functions (for instance, R&D) at home. However, they also tend to establish manufacturing and marketing functions in each major country in which they do business. But although they may undertake some local customization of product offering and marketing strategy, this tends to be rather limited in scope. Ultimately, in most international companies the head office retains tight control over marketing and product strategy.

International companies include such enterprises as Toys 'R' Us, McDonald's, IBM, Kellogg, and Procter & Gamble. Indeed, the majority of U.S. companies that expanded abroad in the 1950s and 1960s fall into this category. Procter & Gamble, which is profiled in Strategy in Action 8.2, can serve as an example. Traditionally, the company has had production facilities in all its major markets outside the United States, including Britain, Germany, and Japan. These facilities, however, manufactured differentiated products that had been developed by the U.S. parent company and that were often marketed using the marketing message developed in the United States. Historically at least, while there has been some local responsiveness at P&G, it has been rather limited.

Procter & Gamble's International Strategy

Procter & Gamble (P&G), the large U.S. consumer products company, has a well-earned reputation as one of the world's best marketers. With more than eighty major brands, P&G generates more than $20 billion in revenues worldwide. Together with Unilever, P&G is a dominant global force in laundry detergents, cleaning products, and personal-care products. P&G expanded abroad in the post–World War II years by pursuing an international strategy: transferring brands and marketing policies developed in the United States to Western Europe, initially with considerable success. Over the next thirty years, this policy resulted in the development of a classic international firm in which new product development and marketing strategies were pioneered in the United States and only then transferred to other countries. Although some adaptation of marketing policies to accommodate country differences was pursued, by and large the adaptation was fairly minimal.

The first signs that this strategy was flawed began to emerge in the 1970s when P&G suffered a number of major setbacks in Japan. By 1985, after thirteen years in Japan, P&G was still losing $40 million a year there. After introducing disposable diapers in Japan and at one time commanding an 80 percent share of the market, by the early 1980s P&G had seen its share slip to a miserable 8 percent. In P&G's place, three major Japanese consumer products firms dominated the market. P&G's problem was that its diapers, developed in the United States, were deemed too bulky by Japanese consumers. Consequently, the Japanese consumer products firm Kao developed a line of trim-fit diapers more suited to the preferences of Japanese consumers. Kao supported the introduction of its product with a marketing blitz and was quickly rewarded with a 30 percent share of the market. As for P&G, only belatedly did it realize that it had to modify its diapers to accommodate the preferences of Japanese consumers. Once it did so, it managed to increase its share of the Japanese market to 30 percent. Moreover, in an example of global learning, P&G's trim-fit diapers, originally developed for the Japanese market, became a bestseller in the United States.

P&G's experience with disposable diapers in Japan prompted the company to rethink its new-product devel-

An international strategy makes sense if a company has a valuable distinctive competency that indigenous competitors in foreign markets lack and if the company faces relatively weak pressures for local responsiveness and cost reductions. In such circumstances, an international strategy can be very profitable. However, when pressures for local responsiveness are high, companies pursuing this strategy lose out to companies that place a greater emphasis on customizing the product offering and market strategy to local conditions. Moreover, because of the duplication of manufacturing facilities, companies that pursue an international strategy tend to incur high operating costs. Hence this strategy is often inappropriate in industries where cost pressures are high.

■ Multidomestic Strategy

Companies pursuing a multidomestic strategy orient themselves toward achieving maximum local responsiveness. The key distinguishing feature of multidomestic firms is that they extensively customize both their product offering and their marketing strategy to match different national conditions. Consistent with this approach, they tend to establish a complete set of value creation activities—including production, marketing, and R&D—in each major national market in which they do

opment and marketing philosophy. It had to admit that its U.S.-centered way of doing business would no longer work. Since the late 1980s, P&G has been attempting to delegate far more responsibility for new-product development and marketing strategy to its major subsidiary firms in Japan and Europe. The result has been the creation of a company that is more responsive to local differences in consumer tastes and preferences and more willing to admit that good new products can be developed outside the United States.

Despite the apparent changes at P&G, it is still not clear that it has achieved the revolution in thinking needed to alter its long-established practices. P&G's recent venture into the Polish shampoo market perhaps illustrates that the company still has some way to go. In the summer of 1991 P&G entered the Polish market with its Vidal Sasson Wash & Go, an all-in-one shampoo and conditioner that is a bestseller in the United States and Europe. The product launch was supported by a U.S.-style marketing blitz on a scale never before seen in Poland. At first, the campaign seemed to be working as P&G captured more than 30 percent of the market for shampoos in Poland, but in early 1992 sales suddenly plummeted. Then came the rumors that Wash & Go caused dandruff

and hair loss—allegations P&G strenuously denied. Next came the jokes. One doing the rounds in Poland ran as follows: "I washed my car with Wash & Go and the tires went bald." And when the then President Lech Walesa proposed that he also become prime minister, critics derided the idea as a "two-in-one solution, just like Wash & Go."

Where did P&G go wrong? The most common theory is that it promoted Wash & Go too hard in a country that has little enthusiasm for brash, American-style advertising. A poll by Pentor, a private market research company in Warsaw, found that almost three times as many Poles disliked P&G's commercials as liked them. Pentor also argues that the high-profile marketing campaign backfired because years of Communist Party propaganda led Polish consumers to suspect that advertising is simply a way to shift goods that nobody wants. Some also believe that Wash & Go, which was developed for U.S. consumers who shampoo daily, was far too sophisticated for Polish consumers who are less obsessed with personal hygiene. Underlying all these criticisms seems to be the idea that P&G was once again stumbling because it had transferred a product and marketing strategy wholesale from the United States to another country without modification to accommodate the tastes and preferences of local consumers.[14]

business. As a result, they generally cannot realize value from experience-curve effects and location economies. Accordingly, many multidomestic firms have a high-cost structure. They also tend to do a poor job of leveraging core competencies within the firm. General Motors, profiled in the Opening Case, is a good example of a company that has historically functioned as a multidomestic corporation, particularly with regard to its extensive European operations, which are largely self-contained entities.

A multidomestic strategy makes most sense when there are high pressures for local responsiveness and low pressures for cost reductions. The high-cost structure associated with the duplication of production facilities makes this strategy inappropriate in industries where cost pressures are intense (which is the case in the automobile industry, a fact that explains GM's current attempts to change its strategic orientation). Another weakness of this strategy is that many multidomestic companies have developed into decentralized federations, in which each national subsidiary functions in a largely autonomous manner. Consequently, after a time they begin to lose the ability to transfer the skills and products derived from distinctive competencies to their various national subsidiaries around the world. In a famous case that illustrates the problems this can cause, the failure of Philips NV to establish its V2000 VCR format as the dominant design in the VCR industry during the late 1970s, as opposed to Matsushita's VHS format, was due to the refusal of its U.S. subsidiary company to adopt the V2000 format. Instead, the subsidiary bought VCRs produced by Matsushita and put its own label on them.

■ Global Strategy

Companies that pursue a global strategy focus on increasing profitability by reaping the cost reductions that come from experience-curve effects and location economies. That is, they are pursuing a low-cost strategy. The production, marketing, and R&D activities of companies pursuing a global strategy are concentrated in a few favorable locations. Global companies tend not to customize their product offering and marketing strategy to local conditions. The reason is that customization raises costs, for it involves shorter production runs and the duplication of functions. Instead, global companies prefer to market a standardized product worldwide so that they can reap the maximum benefits from the economies of scale that underlie the experience curve. They also tend to use their cost advantage to support aggressive pricing in world markets.

This strategy makes most sense in those cases where there are strong pressures for cost reductions and where demands for local responsiveness are minimal. Increasingly, these conditions prevail in many industrial goods industries. In the semiconductor industry, for example, global standards have emerged, creating enormous demands for standardized global products. Accordingly, companies such as Intel, Texas Instruments, and Motorola all pursue a global strategy. However, as noted earlier, these conditions are not found in many consumer goods markets, where demands for local responsiveness remain high (as in the markets for audio players, automobiles, and processed food products). The strategy is inappropriate when demands for local responsiveness are high.

■ Transnational Strategy

Christopher Bartlett and Sumantra Ghoshal argue that in today's environment, competitive conditions are so intense that in order to survive in the global marketplace companies *must exploit experience-based cost economies and location economies, transfer distinctive competencies within the company, and at the same time pay attention to pressures for local responsiveness.*[15] Moreover, they note that in the modern multinational enterprise, distinctive competencies do not reside just in the home country but can develop in any of the company's worldwide operations. Thus, they maintain that the flow of skills and product offerings should not be all one way, from home company to foreign subsidiary, as in the case of companies pursuing an international strategy. Rather, the flow should also be from foreign subsidiary to home country, and from foreign subsidiary to foreign subsidiary—a process Bartlett and Ghoshal refer to as **global learning**. They term the strategy pursued by companies that are trying to achieve all of these objectives simultaneously a **transnational strategy**.

A transnational strategy makes sense when a company faces high pressures for cost reductions and high pressures for local responsiveness. In essence, *companies that pursue a transnational strategy are trying to simultaneously achieve low-cost and differentiation advantages.* As attractive as this sounds, in practice the strategy is not an easy one to pursue. As mentioned earlier, pressures for local responsiveness and cost reductions place conflicting demands on a company. Being locally responsive raises costs, which obviously makes cost reductions difficult to achieve. How then can a company effectively pursue a transnational strategy?

Some clues can be derived from the case of Caterpillar. The need to compete with low-cost rivals such as Komatsu of Japan has forced Caterpillar to look for greater cost economies. However, variations in construction practices and government regulations across countries mean that Caterpillar also has to be responsive to local demands. Therefore, as illustrated in Figure 8.3, Caterpillar confronts significant pressures for cost reductions and for local responsiveness.

To deal with cost pressures, Caterpillar redesigned its products to use many identical components and invested in a few large-scale component manufacturing facilities, sited at favorable locations, to fill global demand and realize scale economies. At the same time, the company augments the centralized manufacturing of components with assembly plants in each of its major global markets. At these plants, Caterpillar adds local product features, tailoring the finished product to local needs. Thus, Caterpillar is able to realize many of the benefits of global manufacturing while reacting to pressures for local responsiveness by differentiating its product among national markets.[16] Caterpillar started to pursue this strategy in 1979, and by 1997 had succeeded in doubling output per employee, significantly reducing its overall cost structure in the process. Meanwhile, Komatsu and Hitachi, which are still wedded to a Japan-centric global strategy, have seen their cost advantages evaporate and have been steadily losing market share to Caterpillar. (It should be noted that General Motors is trying to pursue a similar strategy with its development of common global platforms for some of its vehicles, as detailed in the Opening Case.)

FIGURE 8.3

Cost Pressures and Pressures for Local Responsiveness Facing Caterpillar

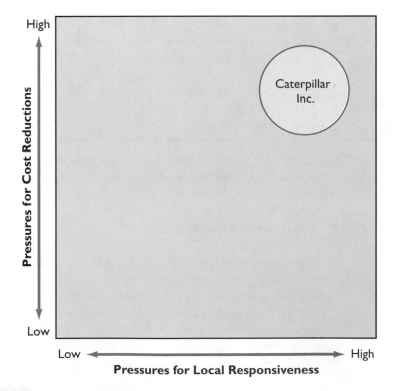

Examples such as Caterpillar and General Motors notwithstanding, Bartlett and Ghoshal admit that building an organization capable of supporting a transnational strategic posture is a complex and difficult task. The core of the problem is that simultaneously trying to achieve cost efficiencies, global learning, and local responsiveness places contradictory demands on an organization. Exactly how a company can deal with the dilemmas posed by such difficult organizational issues is a topic that we return to and discuss in more detail in Chapter 13, when we examine the structure of international business. For now, it is important to note that the organizational problems associated with pursuing what are essentially conflicting objectives constitute a major impediment to implementing a transnational strategy. Companies that attempt to pursue a transnational strategy can become bogged down in an organizational morass that only leads to inefficiencies.

It might also be noted that, by presenting it as the only viable strategy, Bartlett and Ghoshal may be overstating the case for the transnational. Although doubtless in some industries the company that can adopt a transnational strategy will have a competitive advantage, in other industries global, multidomestic, and international strategies remain viable. In the global semiconductor industry, for example, pressures for local customization are minimal and competition is purely a cost game, making a global strategy optimal. Indeed, this is the case in many industrial goods markets, where the product serves universal needs. On the other hand, the argument can be made that to compete in certain consumer goods markets, such as the consumer electronics industry, a company has to try and adopt a transnational strategy.

■ Summary

The advantages and disadvantages of each of the four strategies discussed above are summarized in Table 8.1. Although a transnational strategy appears to offer the most advantages, it should not be forgotten that implementing it raises difficult organizational issues. More generally, as already shown in Figure 8.2, the appropriateness of each strategy depends on the relative strength of pressures for cost reductions and for local responsiveness.

BASIC ENTRY DECISIONS

In this section, we look at three basic decisions that a firm contemplating foreign expansion must make: which markets to enter, when to enter those markets, and on what scale?

■ Which Foreign Markets?

There are more than 160 different nation-states in the world. They do not all hold out the same profit potential for a company contemplating foreign expansion. The choice among different foreign markets must be made on the basis of an assessment of their long-run profit potential. The attractiveness of a country as a potential market for an international business depends on balancing the benefits, costs, and risks associated with doing business in that country. The long-run economic benefits of doing business in a country are a function of factors such as the size of a market (in

TABLE 8.1

The Advantages and Disadvantages of Different Strategies for Competing Globally

Strategy	Advantages	Disadvantages
International	• Transfer of distinctive competencies to foreign markets	• Lack of local responsiveness • Inability to realize location economies • Failure to exploit experience-curve effects
Multidomestic	• Ability to customize product offerings and marketing in accordance with local responsiveness	• Inability to realize location economies • Failure to exploit experience-curve effects • Failure to transfer distinctive competencies to foreign markets
Global	• Ability to exploit experience-curve effects • Ability to exploit location economies	• Lack of local responsiveness
Transnational	• Ability to exploit experience-curve effects • Ability to exploit location economies • Ability to customize product offerings and marketing in accordance with local responsiveness • Reaping benefits of global learning	• Difficulties in implementation because of organizational problems

terms of demographics), the present wealth (purchasing power) of consumers in that market, and the likely future wealth of consumers. While some markets are very large when measured by numbers of consumers (for instance, China and India), low living standards may imply limited purchasing power and, therefore, a relatively small market when measured in economic terms. The costs and risks associated with doing business in a foreign country are typically lower in economically advanced and politically stable democratic nations, and greater in less developed and politically unstable nations.

The benefit-cost-risk calculator is complicated by the fact that the potential long-run benefits bear little relationship to a nation's current stage of economic development or political stability. Rather, they depend on likely future economic growth rates, and economic growth appears to be a function of a free market system and a country's capacity for growth (which may be greater in less developed nations). Thus, other things being equal, the benefit/cost/risk tradeoff is likely to be most favorable in politically stable developed and developing nations that have free market systems and do not have a dramatic upsurge in either inflation rates or private sector debt. It is likely to be least favorable in politically unstable developing nations that operate with a mixed or command economy, or in developing nations where speculative financial bubbles have led to excess borrowing.

By applying the type of reasoning processes indicated above, a company can come up with a ranking of countries in terms of their attractiveness and long-run profit potential.[17] Obviously, preference is then given to entering markets that rank high. The entry into foreign markets of the American financial services company

Merrill Lynch, whose situation is profiled in more detail in Strategy in Action 8.3, illustrates this approach. Merrill Lynch has recently expanded into the United Kingdom, Canada, and Japan. All three of these countries have a large pool of private savings and exhibit relatively low political and economic risks—so it makes sense that they would be attractive to Merrill Lynch. By offering its financial service products, such as mutual funds and investment advice, Merrill Lynch should be able to capture a large enough proportion of the private savings pool in each country to justify its investment in setting up business there. Of the three countries, Japan is probably the most risky given the fragile state of its financial system, which is still suffering from a serious bad debt problem. However, the large size of the Japanese market, and the fact that its government seems to be embarking on significant reform, explains why Merrill has been attracted to this nation.

One other factor of importance is the value that an international business can create in a foreign market. This depends on the suitability of its product offering to that market, and the nature of indigenous competition.[18] If the international business can offer a product that has not been widely available in that market and that satisfies an unmet need, the value of that product to consumers is likely to be much greater than if the international business simply offers the same type of product that indigenous competitors and other foreign entrants are already offering. In turn, greater value translates into an ability to charge higher prices and/or build up unit sales volume more rapidly. Again, on this count Japan is clearly very attractive to Merrill Lynch. Japanese households invest only 3 percent of their savings in individual stocks and mutual funds (much of the balance being in low-yielding bank accounts or government bonds). In comparison, over 40 percent of U.S. households invest in individual stocks and mutual funds. Moreover, Japan's own indigenous financial institutions have been very slow to offer stock-based mutual funds to retail investors, and other foreign firms have yet to establish a significant presence in the market. It follows that Merrill Lynch can create potentially enormous value by bringing Japanese consumers a range of products that they have not been offered previously, and that satisfy unmet needs for greater returns from their savings.

■ Timing of Entry

Once a set of attractive markets has been identified, it is important to consider the timing of entry. With regard to the **timing of entry**, we say that entry is early when an international business enters a foreign market before other foreign firms, and late when it enters after other international businesses have already established themselves in the market. Several first-mover advantages are frequently associated with entering a market early.[20] One is the ability to preempt rivals and capture demand by establishing a strong brand name. A second advantage is the ability to build up sales volume in that country and ride down the experience curve ahead of rivals. To the extent that this is possible, it gives the early entrant a cost advantage over later entrants. This cost advantage may enable the early entrant to respond to later entry by cutting prices below the (higher) cost structure of later entrants, thereby driving them out of the market. A third advantage is the ability of early entrants to create switching costs that tie customers into their products or services. Such switching costs make it difficult for later entrants to win business.

The case of Merrill Lynch in Japan, described in Strategy in Action 8.3, can be used to illustrate these concepts. By entering the private client market in Japan early, Merrill hoped to establish a brand name that later entrants would find difficult to match. Moreover, by entering early with a valuable product offering, Merrill hoped to build up its sales volume rapidly. That would enable the company to spread the fixed costs associated with setting up operations in Japan over a large volume, thereby realizing scale economies. These fixed costs include the costs of establishing a network of appropriately equipped branches in Japan. In addition, as Merrill trains its Japanese staff, their productivity should rise due to learning economies, which again translates into lower costs. Thus, Merrill should be able to ride down the experience curve, and this would give it a lower-cost structure than later entrants could have. Finally, Merrill's business philosophy is to establish close relationships between its financial advisers (that is, its stockbrokers) and private clients. These advisers are taught to find out what their clients need and so help manage their finances more effectively. People rarely change these relationships once they are established; in other words, because of switching costs, they are unlikely to shift their business to later entrants. This effect is likely to be particularly strong in a country such as Japan, where long-term relationships have traditionally been very important in business and social settings. For all of these reasons, Merrill Lynch may be able to capture first-mover advantages that will enable it to enjoy a strong competitive position in Japan for years to come.

It is important to realize that there can also be disadvantages associated with entering a foreign market before other international businesses—often referred to as **first-mover disadvantages**.[21] These disadvantages may give rise to **pioneering costs,** or costs that an early entrant has to bear but a later entrant can avoid. Pioneering costs arise when the business system in a foreign country is so different from that in a firm's home market that the enterprise has to devote considerable effort, time, and expense to learning the rules of the game. Pioneering costs include the costs of business failure if the firm, because of its ignorance of the foreign environment, makes some major mistakes. Put differently, there is a certain liability associated with being a foreigner, and this liability is greater for foreign firms that enter a national market early.[22] Recent research evidence seems to confirm that the probability of survival increases if an international business enters a national market *after* several other foreign firms have already done so.[23] The late entrant, it would appear, benefits by observing and learning from the mistakes made by early entrants.

Pioneering costs also include the costs of promoting and establishing a product offering, including the costs of educating customers. These costs can be particularly significant when the product being promoted is one that local consumers are not familiar with. In many ways, Merrill Lynch will have to bear such pioneering costs in Japan. Most Japanese are not familiar with the type of investment products and services that Merrill intends to sell, so Merrill will have to invest significant resources in customer education. In contrast, later entrants may be able to get a free ride on an early entrant's investments in learning and customer education by noting how the early entrant proceeded in the market, by avoiding costly mistakes made by the early entrant, and by exploiting the market potential created by the early entrant's investments in customer education.

■ Scale of Entry and Strategic Commitments

The final issue that an international business needs to consider when contemplating market entry is the scale of entry. Entering a market on a large scale involves the commitment of significant resources to that venture. While not all companies have

Merrill Lynch in Japan

Merrill Lynch, the U.S.-based financial services institution, is an investment banking titan. It is the world's largest underwriter of debt and equity and the third largest mergers and acquisitions adviser behind Morgan Stanley and Goldman Sachs. As one might expect, Merrill Lynch's investment banking operations have long had a global reach. The company has a dominant presence not only in New York, but also in London and Tokyo. However, until recently Merrill's international presence was limited to the investment banking side of its business. In contrast, its private client business—which offers banking, financial advice, and stockbrokerage services to individuals—has historically been concentrated in the United States. This is now changing rapidly. In 1995, Merrill purchased Smith New Court, the largest stockbrokerage firm in Britain. This was followed in 1997 by the acquisition of Mercury Asset Management, the United Kingdom's leading manager of mutual funds. Then, in 1998, Merrill acquired Midland Walwyn, Canada's last major independent stockbrokerage firm. The company's boldest moves, however, have probably been in Japan.

Merrill first started to establish a private client business in Japan in the 1980s but met with very limited success. At the time, it was the first foreign firm to enter Japan's private client investment market. The company found it extremely difficult to attract employee talent and customers away from Japan's big four stockbrokerage firms, which traditionally had monopolized the Japanese market. Moreover, restrictive regulations made it almost impossible for Merrill to offer its Japanese private clients the range of services it was offering clients in the United States. For example, foreign exchange regulations meant that it was very difficult for Merrill to sell non-Japanese stocks, bonds, and mutual funds to Japanese investors. In 1993, the company admitted defeat, closed its six retail branches in Kobe and Kyoto, and withdrew from the private client market in Japan.

Over the next few years, however, things started to change. In the mid 1990s, Japan embarked on a wide-ranging deregulation of its financial services industry. Among other things, this led to the removal of many of the restrictions that had made it so difficult for Merrill to do business in Japan. For example, the relaxation of foreign exchange controls meant that by 1998 it was possible for Japanese citizens to purchase foreign stocks, bonds, and mutual funds. Meanwhile, Japan's big four stockbrokerage firms continued to struggle with serious financial problems. These problems were the result of the 1991 crash of that country's stock market. Indeed, in November 1997, in what was a dramatic shock to many Japanese, one of these firms, Yamaichi Securities, declared that it was bankrupt due to $2.2 billion in accumulated "hidden losses" and would shut its doors. Recognizing that the country's financial system was strained and in need of fresh capital, know-how, and the stimulus of greater com-

the resources necessary to enter on a large scale, even some large enterprises prefer to enter foreign markets on a small scale and then build their presence slowly over time as they become more familiar with the foreign market. The original entry by Merrill Lynch into the private client market in Japan was on a small scale, involving as it did only a handful of branches. In contrast, Merrill's reentry into the Japanese market in 1997 was on a significant scale.

The consequences of entering on a significant scale are associated with the value of the resulting strategic commitments. [24] A **strategic commitment** is a decision that has a long-term impact and is difficult to reverse. Deciding to enter a foreign market on a significant scale is a major strategic commitment. Strategic commitments, such as large-scale market entry, can have an important influence on the nature of competition in a market. For example, by entering Japan's private client business on a significant scale, Merrill has signaled its commitment to the

petition, the Japanese government signaled that it would adopt a much more relaxed attitude toward foreign entry into its financial services industry. This attitude underlay Japan's wholehearted endorsement of a 1997 deal brokered by the World Trade Organization to liberalize global financial services. Among other things, the WTO deal made it much easier for foreign firms to sell financial service products to Japanese investors.

By 1997, it had become clear to Merrill Lynch that the climate in Japan had changed significantly. The big attraction of the market was still the same—the financial assets owned by Japanese households are huge, amounting to a staggering Y1,220 trillion in late 1997, only 3 percent of which were then invested in mutual funds (most are invested in low-yielding bank accounts and government bonds). However, attitudes were changing and it looked as if it would be much easier to do business in Japan. Accordingly, in mid 1997, Merrill started to consider re-entering the Japanese private client market. Initially, the company considered a joint venture with Sanwa Bank to sell Merrill's mutual fund products to Japanese consumers through Sanwa's 400 retail branches. The proposed alliance had the advantage of allowing Merrill to leverage Sanwa's existing distribution system, rather than having to build a distribution system of its own from scratch. However, in the long run, such a strategy would not have given Merrill the presence on the ground that it felt it needed to build a solid financial services business in Japan. Merrill's executives reasoned that it was important for them to make a major commitment to the Japanese market in order to establish its brand name as a premier provider of investment products and financial advice to individuals. This would enable the company to entrench itself as a major player before other foreign institutions entered the market—and before Japan's own stockbrokerages rose to the challenge. At the same time, given their prior experience in Japan, Merrill's executives were hesitant to go down this road because of the huge costs and risks involved.

The problem of how best to enter the Japanese market was solved by the bankruptcy of Yamaichi Securities. Suddenly Yamaichi's nationwide network of offices and 7,000 employees were up for grabs. In late December 1997, Merrill announced that it would hire some 2,000 of Yamaichi's employees, and acquire up to fifty of Yamaichi's branch offices. The deal, which was enthusiastically endorsed by the Japanese government, significantly lowered Merrill's costs of establishing a retail network in Japan. Merrill's goal for the new subsidiary was to have $20 billion under management by 2000. The company was off to a quick start. In February 1998, Merrill launched its first mutual fund in Japan and saw the value of its assets swell to $1 billion by April. The company now has a significant head start over other foreign financial service institutions that may be contemplating building a private client network in Japan. Indeed, Merrill's hope is that by the time other foreign institutions enter it will already have a commanding presence in Japan, which will be difficult to challenge.[19]

market. This will have several effects. On the positive side, it will make it easier for Merrill to attract clients. The scale of entry gives potential clients reason to believe that Merrill will remain in the market for the long run. The scale of entry may also give other foreign institutions considering entry into Japan's market pause for thought, since now they will have to compete not only against Japan's indigenous institutions, but also against an aggressive and successful U.S. institution. On the negative side, the move may wake up Japan's financial institutions and elicit a vigorous competitive response from them. Moreover, by committing itself heavily to Japan, Merrill may have fewer resources available to support expansion in other desirable markets. In other words, Merrill's commitment to Japan limits its strategic flexibility.

As suggested by this example, significant strategic commitments are neither unambiguously good nor bad. Rather, they tend to change the competitive playing field and unleash a number of changes, some of which may be desirable and some of which will not be. It is therefore important for a firm to think through the implications of large-scale entry into a market and act accordingly. Of particular relevance is trying to identify how actual and potential competitors might react to large-scale entry into a market. It is also important to bear in mind that there is a connection between large-scale entry and first-mover advantages. Specifically, the large-scale entrant is more likely than the small-scale entrant to capture the first-mover advantages associated with demand preemption, scale economies, and switching costs.

Although it is difficult to generalize, what seems clear is that the value of the commitments flowing from large-scale entry into a foreign market must be balanced against the resulting risks and lack of flexibility associated with significant commitments. At the same time, it is worth stressing that strategic inflexibility can also have value. A famous example from military history that illustrates the value of inflexibility concerns Hernando Cortés's conquest of the Aztec Empire in Mexico. When he landed in Mexico, Cortés ordered his men to burn all but one of his ships. Cortés reasoned that by eliminating their only method of retreat, his men had no choice but to fight hard to win—and ultimately they did fight hard and win.[25]

Balanced against the value and risks of the commitments associated with large-scale entry are the benefits of small-scale entry. Small-scale entry has the advantage of allowing a firm to learn about a foreign market while simultaneously limiting the firm's exposure to that market. In this sense, small-scale entry can be seen as a way of gathering more information about a foreign market before deciding whether or not to enter on a significant scale and how best to enter that market. Thus, by giving the firm time to collect information, small-scale entry reduces the risks associated with a subsequent large-scale entry. On the other hand, the lack of commitment associated with small-scale entry may make it more difficult for the small-scale entrant to build market share and to capture first-mover or early-mover advantages. The risk-averse firm that enters a foreign market on a small scale may limit its potential losses, but it may also miss the chance to capture first-mover advantages to another international business.

■ Summary

It is important to realize that there are no "right" decisions, here, but just decisions that are associated with different levels of risk and reward. Entering a large developing nation such as China or India before most other international businesses in the company's industry, and entering on a large scale, will be associated with high levels of risk. In such cases, the liability of being foreign is increased by the absence of prior foreign entrants, whose experience can be a useful guide. At the same time, the potential long-term rewards associated with such a strategy are great. The early large-scale entrant into a major developing nation may be able to capture significant first-mover advantages, which will bolster its long-run position in that market. In contrast, entering developed nations such as Australia or Canada after other international businesses in the company's industry, and entering initially on a small scale in order to first learn more about those markets, will be associated with much lower levels of risk. However, the potential long-term rewards are also likely to be lower since the company is forgoing the opportunity to capture first-mover advantages and since the lack of commitment to the market signaled by small-scale entry may limit its future growth potential.

THE CHOICE OF
ENTRY MODE

Considering entry into a foreign market raises the question of the best mode of such entry. There are five main choices: exporting, licensing, franchising, entering into a joint venture with a host country company, and setting up a wholly owned subsidiary in the host country. Each entry mode has its advantages and disadvantages, and managers must weigh these carefully when deciding which mode to use.[26]

■ Exporting

Most manufacturing companies begin their global expansion as exporters and only later switch to one of the other modes for serving a foreign market. Exporting has two distinct advantages: it avoids the costs of establishing manufacturing operations in the host country, which are often substantial, and it may be consistent with realizing experience-curve cost economies and location economies. By manufacturing the product in a centralized location and then exporting it to other national markets, the company may be able to realize substantial scale economies from its global sales volume. That is how Sony came to dominate the global television market, how Matsushita came to dominate the VCR market, and how many Japanese auto companies originally made inroads into the U.S. auto market.

On the other hand, there are a number of drawbacks to exporting. First, exporting from the company's *home* base may not be appropriate if there are lower-cost locations for manufacturing the product abroad (that is, if the company can realize location economies by moving production elsewhere). Thus, particularly in the case of a company pursuing a global or transnational strategy, it may pay to manufacture in a location where conditions are most favorable from a value creation perspective and then export from that location to the rest of the globe. This, of course, is not so much an argument against exporting as an argument against exporting from the company's *home* country. For example, many U.S. electronics companies have moved some of their manufacturing to Asia because low-cost but highly skilled labor is available there. They export from that location to the rest of the globe, including the United States.

Another drawback is that high transport costs can make exporting uneconomical, particularly in the case of bulk products. One way of getting around this problem is to manufacture bulk products on a regional basis. Such a strategy enables the company to realize some economies from large-scale production while limiting transport costs. Thus, many multinational chemical companies manufacture their products on a regional basis, serving several countries in a region from one facility.

Tariff barriers, too, can make exporting uneconomical, and the threat to impose tariff barriers by the government of a country the company is exporting to can make the strategy very risky. Indeed, the implicit threat from Congress to impose tariffs on Japanese cars imported into the United States led directly to the decision by many Japanese auto companies to set up manufacturing plants in the United States.

Finally, a common practice among companies that are just beginning to export also poses risks. A company may delegate marketing activities in each country in which it does business to a local agent, but there is no guarantee that the agent will act in the company's best interest. Often foreign agents also carry the products of competing companies and thus have divided loyalties. Consequently, they may not do as good a job as the company would do if it managed marketing itself. One way to solve this problem is to set up a wholly owned subsidiary in the host country to handle local marketing. By so doing, the company can both reap the cost advantages that arise from manufacturing the product in a single location and exercise tight control over marketing strategy in the host country.

■ Licensing

International licensing is an arrangement whereby a foreign licensee buys the rights to produce a company's product in the licensee's country for a negotiated fee (normally, royalty payments on the number of units sold). The licensee then puts up most of the capital necessary to get the overseas operation going.[27]

The advantage of licensing is that the company does not have to bear the development costs and risks associated with opening up a foreign market. Licensing, therefore, can be a very attractive option for companies that lack the capital to develop operations overseas. It can also be an attractive option for companies that are unwilling to commit substantial financial resources to an unfamiliar or politically volatile foreign market, where political risks are particularly high.

Licensing has three serious drawbacks, however. First, it does not give a company the tight control over manufacturing, marketing, and strategic functions in foreign countries that it needs to have in order to realize experience-curve cost economies and location economies—as companies pursuing both global and transnational strategies try to do. Typically, each licensee sets up its own manufacturing operations. Hence, the company stands little chance of realizing experience-curve cost economies and location economies by manufacturing its product in a centralized location. When these economies are likely to be important, licensing may not be the best way of expanding overseas.

Second, competing in a global marketplace may make it necessary for a company to coordinate strategic moves across countries so that the profits earned in one country can be used to support competitive attacks in another. Licensing, by its very nature, severely limits a company's ability to coordinate strategy in this way. A licensee is unlikely to let a multinational company take its profits (beyond those due in the form of royalty payments) and use them to support an entirely different licensee operating in another country.

A third problem with licensing is the risk associated with licensing technological know-how to foreign companies. For many multinational companies, technological know-how forms the basis of their competitive advantage, and they would want to maintain control over the use to which it is put. By licensing its technology, a company can quickly lose control over it. RCA, for instance, once licensed its color television technology to a number of Japanese companies. The Japanese companies quickly assimilated RCA's technology and then used it to enter the U.S. market. Now the Japanese have a bigger share of the U.S. market than the RCA brand.

There are ways of reducing this risk, however, and one of them is to enter into a cross-licensing agreement with a foreign firm. Under a **cross-licensing agreement**, a firm might license some valuable intangible property to a foreign partner, but in addition to a royalty payment, the firm might also request that the foreign partner license some of its valuable know-how to the firm. Such agreements are reckoned to reduce the risks associated with licensing technological know-how, since the licensee realizes that if it violates the spirit of a licensing contract (by using the knowledge obtained to compete directly with the licensor), the licensor can do the same to it. Put differently, cross-licensing agreements enable firms to hold each other hostage, which reduces the probability that they will behave opportunistically toward each other.[28] Such cross-licensing agreements are increasingly common in high-technology industries. For example, the U.S. biotechnology firm Amgen has licensed one of its key drugs, Nuprogene, to Kirin, the Japanese pharmaceutical company. The license gives Kirin the right to sell Nuprogene in Japan. In return, Amgen receives a royalty payment, but it also gained the right, through a licensing agreement, to sell certain of Kirin's products in the United States.

■ Franchising

In many respects, franchising is similar to licensing, although franchising tends to involve longer-term commitments than licensing. **Franchising** is basically a specialized form of licensing in which the franchiser not only sells intangible property (normally a trademark) to the franchisee, but also insists that the franchisee agree to abide by strict rules as to how it does business. Often, the franchiser will also assist the franchisee on an ongoing basis in running the business. As with licensing, the franchiser typically receives a royalty payment, which amounts to some percentage of the franchisee's revenues.

Whereas licensing is a strategy pursued primarily by manufacturing companies, franchising is a strategy employed chiefly by service companies. McDonald's is a good example of a firm that has grown by using a franchising strategy. McDonald's has set down strict rules as to how franchisees should operate a restaurant. These rules extend to control over the menu, cooking methods, staffing policies, and the design and location of a restaurant. McDonald's also organizes the supply chain for its franchisees and provides management training and financial assistance for them.[29]

The advantages of franchising are similar to those of licensing. Specifically, the franchiser does not have to bear the development costs and risks of opening up a foreign market on its own, for the franchisee typically assumes those costs and risks. Thus, using a franchising strategy, a service company can build up a global presence quickly and at a low cost.

The disadvantages, however, are less pronounced than in the case of licensing. Since franchising is a strategy used by service companies, a franchiser does not have to consider the need to coordinate manufacturing in order to achieve experience-curve effects and location economies. Nevertheless, franchising may inhibit a company's ability to achieve global strategic coordination.

A more significant disadvantage of franchising is the lack of quality control. The foundation of franchising arrangements is the notion that the company's brand name conveys a message to consumers about the quality of the company's product. Thus, business travelers booking into a Hilton International hotel in Hong Kong can reasonably expect the same quality of room, food, and service as they would receive in New York. The Hilton brand name is a guarantee of the consistency of product quality. However, foreign franchisees may not be as concerned about quality as they should be, and poor quality may mean not only lost sales in the foreign market, but also a decline in the company's worldwide reputation. For example, a bad experience at the Hilton in one location may cause the business traveler never go to another Hilton hotel anywhere and steer colleagues away as well. The geographic distance separating the franchiser from its foreign franchisees and the sheer number of individual franchisees—tens of thousands in the case of McDonald's—can make it difficult for the franchiser to detect poor quality. Consequently, quality problems may persist.

To obviate this drawback, a company can set up a subsidiary in each country or region in which it is expanding. The subsidiary might be wholly owned by the company or a joint venture with a foreign company. The subsidiary then assumes the rights and obligations to establish franchisees throughout that particular country or region. The combination of proximity and the limited number of independent franchisees that have to be monitored reduces the quality control problem. Besides, since the subsidiary is at least partly owned by the company, the company can place its own managers in the subsidiary to ensure the kind of quality monitoring it wants. This organizational arrangement has proved very popular in practice. It has been used by McDonald's, KFC, and Hilton Hotels to expand their international operations, to name just three examples.

■ Joint Ventures

Establishing a joint venture with a foreign company has long been a favored mode for entering a new market. One of the most famous long-term joint ventures, the Fuji-Xerox joint venture to produce photocopiers for the Japanese market, is discussed in Strategy in Action 8.4. The most typical form of joint venture is a 50/50 venture, in which each party takes a 50 percent ownership stake and operating control is shared by a team of managers from both parent companies (as is in the Fuji-Xerox joint venture). Some companies, however, have sought joint ventures in which they have a majority shareholding (for example, a 51/49 ownership split). This permits tighter control by the dominant partner.[30]

Joint ventures have a number of advantages. First, a company may feel that it can benefit from a local partner's knowledge of a host country's competitive conditions, culture, language, political systems, and business systems. Second, when the development costs and risks of opening up a foreign market are high, a company might gain by sharing these costs and risks with a local partner. Third, in some countries political considerations make joint ventures the only feasible entry mode.[31] For instance, historically, many U.S. companies found it much easier to get permission to set up operations in Japan if they went in with a Japanese partner than if they tried to enter on their own. Indeed, this was a prime motivation behind the establishment of the Fuji-Xerox joint venture.

Despite these advantages, joint ventures can be difficult to establish and run because of two main drawbacks. First, as in the case of licensing, a company that enters into a joint venture risks losing control over its technology to its venture partner. To minimize this risk, a company can seek a majority ownership stake in the joint venture, for as the dominant partner it would be able to exercise greater control over its technology. The trouble with this strategy is that it may be difficult to find a foreign partner willing to accept a minority ownership position.

The second disadvantage is that a joint venture does not give a company the tight control over its subsidiaries that it might need in order to realize experience-curve effects or location economies—as both global and transnational companies try to do—or to engage in coordinated global attacks against its global rivals. Consider the entry of Texas Instruments (TI) into the Japanese semiconductor market. When TI established semiconductor facilities in Japan, its sole purpose was to limit Japanese manufacturers' market share and the amount of cash available to them to invade TI's global market. In other words, TI was engaging in global strategic coordination. To implement this strategy, TI's Japanese subsidiary had to be prepared to take instructions from the TI corporate headquarters regarding competitive strategy. The strategy also required that the Japanese subsidiary be run at a loss if necessary. Clearly, a Japanese joint venture partner would have been unlikely to accept such conditions since they would have meant a negative return on investment. Thus, in order to implement this strategy, TI set up a wholly owned subsidiary in Japan instead of entering this market through a joint venture.

■ Wholly Owned Subsidiaries

A **wholly owned subsidiary** is one in which the parent company owns 100 percent of the subsidiary's stock. To establish a wholly owned subsidiary in a foreign market, a company can either set up a completely new operation in that country or acquire an established host country company and use it to promote its products in the host market (as Merrill Lynch did when it acquired various assets of Yamaichi Securities—see Strategy in Action 8.3).

Setting up a wholly owned subsidiary offers three advantages. First, when a company's competitive advantage is based on its control of a technological competency, a wholly owned subsidiary will normally be the preferred entry mode, since it reduces the company's risk of losing this control. Consequently, many high-tech companies prefer wholly owned subsidiaries to joint ventures or licensing arrangements. Wholly owned subsidiaries tend to be the favored entry mode in the semiconductor, electronics, and pharmaceutical industries. Second, a wholly owned subsidiary gives a company the kind of tight control over operations in different countries that it needs if it is going to engage in global strategic coordination—taking profits from one country to support competitive attacks in another. Third, a wholly owned subsidiary may be the best choice if a company wants to realize location economies and experience-curve effects. As you saw earlier, when cost pressures are intense, it may pay a company to configure its value chain in such a way that value added at each stage is maximized. Thus, a national subsidiary may specialize in manufacturing only part of the product line or certain components of the end product, exchanging parts and products with other subsidiaries in the company's

8.4   STRATEGY *in* ACTION

Fuji-Xerox

Originally established in 1962, Fuji-Xerox is structured as a 50/50 joint venture between the Xerox Group, the U.S. maker of photocopiers, and Fuji Photo Film, Japan's largest manufacturer of film products. With 1995 sales of more than $8 billion, Fuji-Xerox provides Xerox with more than 20 percent of its worldwide revenues. A prime motivation for the initial establishment of the joint venture was the fact that in the early 1960s the Japanese government did not allow foreign companies to set up wholly owned subsidiaries in Japan. The joint venture was originally conceived as a marketing organization to sell xerographic products that would be manufactured by Fuji Photo under license from Xerox. However, when the Japanese government refused to approve the establishment of a joint venture intended solely as a sales company, the joint venture agreement was revised to give Fuji-Xerox manufacturing rights. Day-to-day management of the venture was placed in the hand of a Japanese management team, which was given autonomy to develop its own operations and strategy, subject to oversight by a board of directors that contained representatives from both Xerox and Fuji Photo.

Initially, Fuji-Xerox followed the lead of Xerox in manufacturing and selling the large high-volume copiers developed by Xerox in the United States. These machines were sold at a premium price to the high end of the market. However, Fuji-Xerox noticed that in the Japanese market new competitors, such as Canon and Ricoh, were making significant inroads by building small low-volume copiers and focusing on the mid- and low-priced segments of the market. This led to Fuji-Xerox's development of its first "homegrown" copier, the FX2200, which at the time was billed as the world's smallest copier. Introduced in 1973, the FX200 hit the market just in time to allow Fuji-Xerox to hold its own against a blizzard of new competition in Japan, which followed the expiration of many of Xerox's key patents.

Around the same time, Fuji-Xerox also embarked on a total quality control (TQC) program. The aims of the program were to speed up the development of new products, reduce waste, improve quality, and lower manufacturing costs. Its first fruit was the FX3500. Introduced in 1977, by 1979 the FX3500 had broken the Japanese record for the number of copiers sold in one year. Partly because of the FX3500's success, in 1980 the company won Japan's prestigious Deming Prize. The success of this copier was all the more notable because at the same time Xerox was canceling a series of programs to develop low- to mid-level copiers and reaffirming instead its commitment to serving the high end of the market.

By the early 1980s, Fuji-Xerox was number two in the Japanese copier market, with a share in the 20 percent to

global system. Establishing such a global production system requires a high degree of control over the operations of national affiliates. Different national operations have to be prepared to accept centrally determined decisions as to how they should produce, how much they should produce, and how their output should be priced for transfer between operations. A wholly owned subsidiary would, of course, have to comply with these mandates, whereas licensees or joint venture partners would most likely shun such a subservient role.

On the other hand, establishing a wholly owned subsidiary is generally the most costly method of serving a foreign market. The parent company must bear all the costs and risks of setting up overseas operations—in contrast to joint ventures, where the costs and risks are shared, or licensing, where the licensee bears most of the costs and risks. But the risks of learning to do business in a new culture dimin-

22 percent range, just behind that of market leader Canon. In contrast, Xerox was running into all sorts of problems in the U.S. market. As its patents had expired, a number of companies, including Canon, Ricoh, Kodak, and IBM, had begun to take market share from Xerox. Canon and Ricoh were particularly successful by focusing on that segment of the market that Xerox had ignored— the low end. As a result, Xerox's market share in the Americas fell from 35 percent in 1975 to 25 percent in 1980, while its profitability slumped.

Seeking to recapture share, Xerox began to sell Fuji-Xerox's FX3500 copier in the United States. Not only did the FX3500 help Xerox halt the rapid decline in its share of the U.S. market, but it also opened Xerox's eyes to the benefits of Fuji-Xerox's TQC program. Xerox found that the reject rate for Fuji-Xerox parts was only a fraction of that for U.S. parts. Visits to Fuji-Xerox revealed another important truth: quality in manufacturing does not increase real costs; it lowers them by decreasing the number of defective products and reducing service costs. These developments forced Xerox to rethink the way it did business.

From being the main provider of products, technology, and management know-how to Fuji-Xerox, Xerox became in the 1980s the willing pupil of Fuji-Xerox. In 1983, Xerox introduced its Leadership Through Quality program, which was based on Fuji-Xerox's TQC program. As part of this effort, Xerox launched quality training for its suppliers and was rewarded when the number of defective parts from suppliers fell from 25,000 per million in 1983 to 300 per million by 1992.

In 1985 and 1986, Xerox began focusing on its new-product development process. One goal was to design products that, while customized to market conditions in different countries, also contained a large number of globally standardized parts. Another goal was to reduce the time it took to design new products and bring them to market. To achieve these goals, Xerox set up joint product development teams with Fuji-Xerox. Each team managed the design, component sources, manufacturing, distribution, and follow-up customer service on a worldwide basis. The use of design teams cut as much as one year from the overall product development cycle and saved millions of dollars.

The new approach to product development led to the creation of the 5100 copier—the first product designed jointly by Xerox and Fuji-Xerox for the worldwide market. Manufactured in U.S. plants, it was launched in Japan in November 1990 and in the United States the following February. The global design of the 5100 reportedly reduced overall time to market and saved the company more than $10 million in development costs.

Thanks to the skills and products acquired from Fuji-Xerox, Xerox's position improved markedly during the 1980s. The company was able to regain market share from its competitors and to boost its profits and revenues. Xerox's share of the U.S. copier market increased from a low of 10 percent in 1985 to 18 percent in 1991.[52]

ish if the company acquires an established host country enterprise. Acquisitions, though, raise a whole set of additional problems, such as trying to marry divergent corporate cultures, and these problems may more than offset the benefits. (The problems associated with acquisitions are discussed in Chapter 10).

■ Choosing Among Entry Modes

The advantages and disadvantages of the various entry modes are summarized in Table 8.2. Inevitably, there are tradeoffs in choosing one entry mode over another. For example, when considering entry into an unfamiliar country with a track record of nationalizing foreign-owned enterprises, a company might favor a joint venture

TABLE 8.2

The Advantages and Disadvantages of Different Entry Modes

Entry Mode	Advantages	Disadvantages
Exporting	• Ability to realize location and experience-curve economies	• High transport costs • Trade barriers • Problems with local marketing agents
Licensing	• Low development costs and risks	• Inability to realize location and experience-curve economies • Inability to engage in global strategic coordination • Lack of control over technology
Franchising	• Low development cost and risks	• Inability to engage in global strategic coordination • Lack of control over quality
Joint ventures	• Access to local partner's knowledge • Shared development costs and risks • Political dependency	• Inability to engage in global strategic coordination • Inability to realize location and experience-curve economies • Lack of control over technology
Wholly owned subsidiaries	• Protection of technology • Ability to engage in global strategic coordination • Ability to realize location and experience-curve economies	• High costs and risks

with a local enterprise. Its rationale might be that the local partner will help it establish operations in an unfamiliar environment and will speak out against nationalization should the possibility arise. But if the company's distinctive competency is based on proprietary technology, entering into a joint venture might mean risking loss of control over that technology to the joint venture partner, which would make this strategy unattractive. Despite such hazards, some generalizations can be offered about the optimal choice of entry mode.

Distinctive Competencies and Entry Mode   When companies expand internationally to earn greater returns from their distinctive competencies, transferring the skills and products derived from their competencies to foreign markets where indigenous competitors lack those skills, the companies are pursuing an international strategy. The optimal entry mode for such companies depends to some degree on the nature of their distinctive competency. In particular, we need to distinguish between companies with a distinctive competency in technological know-how and those with a distinctive competency in management know-how.

If a company's competitive advantage—its distinctive competency—derives from its control of proprietary *technological know-how*, licensing and joint venture arrangements should be avoided, if possible, in order to minimize the risk of losing control of that technology. Thus, if a high-tech company is considering setting up operations in a foreign country in order to profit from a distinctive competency in technological know-how, it should probably do so through a wholly owned subsidiary.

This rule, however, should not be viewed as a hard and fast one. For instance, a licensing or joint venture arrangement might be structured in such a way as to reduce the risks of a company's technological know-how being expropriated by licensees or joint venture partners (as was the case with the Fuji-Xerox venture). We consider this kind of arrangement in more detail later in the chapter when we discuss the issue of structuring strategic alliances. To take another exception to the rule, a company may perceive its technological advantage as being only transitory and expect rapid imitation of its core technology by competitors. In such a case, the company might want to license its technology as quickly as possible to foreign companies in order to gain global acceptance of its technology before imitation occurs.[33] Such a strategy has some advantages. By licensing its technology to competitors, the company may deter them from developing their own, possibly superior, technology. It also may be able to establish its technology as the dominant design in the industry (as Matsushita did with its VHS format for VCRs), ensuring a steady stream of royalty payments. Such situations apart, however, the attractions of licensing are probably outweighed by the risks of losing control of technology, and therefore licensing should be avoided.

The competitive advantage of many service companies, such as McDonald's or Hilton Hotels, is based on *management know-how*. For such companies, the risk of losing control of their management skills to franchisees or joint venture partners is not that great. The reason is that the valuable asset of such companies is their brand name, and brand names are generally well protected by international laws pertaining to trademarks. Given this fact, many of the issues that arise in the case of technological know-how do not arise in the case of management know-how. As a result, many service companies favor a combination of franchising and subsidiaries to control franchisees within a particular country or region. The subsidiary may be wholly owned or a joint venture. In most cases, however, service companies have found that entering into a joint venture with a local partner in order to set up a controlling subsidiary in a country or region works best because a joint venture is often politically more acceptable and brings a degree of local knowledge to the subsidiary.

Pressures for Cost Reduction and Entry Mode   The greater the pressures for cost reductions, the more likely it is that a company will want to pursue some combination of exporting and wholly owned subsidiaries. By manufacturing in the locations where factor conditions are optimal and then exporting to the rest of the world, a company may be able to realize substantial location economies and experience-curve effects. The company might then want to export the finished product to marketing subsidiaries based in various countries. Typically, these subsidiaries would be wholly owned and have the responsibility for overseeing distribution in a particular country. Setting up wholly owned marketing subsidiaries is preferable to a joint ventures arrangement or to using a foreign marketing agent because it gives the company the tight control over marketing that might be required to coordinate a globally dispersed value chain. In addition, tight control over a local operation enables the company to use the profits generated in one market to improve its competitive position in another market. Hence, companies pursuing global or transnational strategies prefer to establish wholly owned subsidiaries.

GLOBAL STRATEGIC ALLIANCES

Strategic alliances are cooperative agreements between companies that may also be competitors. In this section, we deal specifically with strategic alliances between companies from different countries. Strategic alliances run the range from formal joint ventures, in which two or more companies have an equity stake, to short-term contractual agreements in which two companies may agree to cooperate on a particular problem (such as developing a new product).

■ Advantages of Strategic Alliances

Companies enter into strategic alliances with actual or potential competitors in order to achieve a number of strategic objectives.[34] First, as noted earlier in this chapter, strategic alliances may be a way of facilitating entry into a foreign market. For example, Motorola initially found it very difficult to gain access to the Japanese cellular telephone market. In the mid 1980s, the company complained loudly about formal and informal Japanese trade barriers. The turning point for Motorola came in 1987, when it formed its alliance with Toshiba to build microprocessors. As part of the deal, Toshiba provided Motorola with marketing help—including some of its best managers. This aided Motorola in the political game of winning government approval to enter the Japanese market and obtaining allocations of radio frequencies for its mobile communications systems. Since then, Motorola has played down the importance of Japan's informal trade barriers. Although privately the company still admits they exist, with Toshiba's help Motorola has become skilled at getting around them.[35]

Second, many companies have entered into strategic alliances in order to share the fixed costs (and associated risks) that arise from the development of new products or processes. Motorola's alliance with Toshiba was partly motivated by a desire to share the high fixed costs associated with setting up an operation to manufacture microprocessors. The microprocessor business is so capital intensive—it cost Motorola and Toshiba close to $1 billion to set up their facility—that few companies can afford the costs and risks of going it alone.

Third, many alliances can be seen as a way of bringing together complementary skills and assets that neither company could easily develop on its own. For example, in 1990 AT&T struck a deal with NEC of Japan to trade technological skills. Under the agreement, AT&T transferred some of its computer-aided design technology to NEC. In return, NEC gave AT&T access to the technology underlying NEC advanced-logic computer chips. Such equitable trading of distinctive competencies seems to underlie many of the most successful strategic alliances.

Finally, it may make sense to enter into an alliance if it helps the company set technological standards for its industry and if those standards benefit the company. For example, in 1992 the Dutch electronics company Philips entered into an alliance with its global competitor, Matsushita, to manufacture and market the digital compact cassette (DDC) system pioneered by Philips. The motive for this action was that linking up with Matsushita would help Philips establish the DCC system as a new technological standard in the recording and consumer electronics industries. The issue is an important one because Sony has developed a competing minicompact disk technology, which Sony hopes to establish as a new technical standard. Since the two technologies do very similar things, there is probably room for only one new standard. The technology that becomes the new standard will be the one to succeed. The loser in this race will probably have to write off an investment worth billions of dollars. Philips sees the alliance with Matsushita as a tactic for winning the race, for it ties a potential major competitor into its standard.

■ Disadvantages of Strategic Alliances

The various advantages discussed above can be very significant. Nevertheless, some commentators have criticized strategic alliances on the grounds that they give competitors a low-cost route to gain new technology and market access. For example, Robert Reich and Eric Mankin have argued that strategic alliances between U.S. and Japanese companies are part of an implicit Japanese strategy to keep higher-paying, higher-value-added jobs in Japan while gaining the project-engineering and production-process skills that underlie the competitive success of many U.S. companies.[36] They have viewed Japanese success in the machine tool and semiconductor industries as largely built on U.S. technology acquired through various strategic alliances. They have also asserted that increasingly U.S. managers are aiding the Japanese in achieving their goals by entering into alliances that channel new inventions to Japan and provide a U.S. sales and distribution network for the resulting products. Although such deals may generate short-term profits, in the long run, according to Reich and Mankin, the result is to "hollow out" U.S. companies, leaving them with no competitive advantage in the global marketplace.

Reich and Mankin have a point; alliances do have risks. Unless it is careful, a company can give away more than it gets in return. On the other hand, there are so many examples of apparently successful alliances between companies, including alliances between U.S. and Japanese companies, that Reich and Mankin's position seems more than a little extreme. It is difficult to see how the Motorola-Toshiba alliance or Fuji-Xerox fits their thesis. In these cases, both partners seemed to have gained from the alliance. Since Reich and Mankin undoubtedly do have a point, the question becomes, *why do some alliances benefit the company, whereas in others it can end up giving away technology and market access and get very little in return?* The next section provides an answer to this question.

MAKING STRATEGIC ALLIANCES WORK

The failure rate for international strategic alliances seems to be quite high. For example, one study of forty-nine international strategic alliances found that two-thirds run into serious managerial and financial troubles within two years of their formation, and that although eventually many of these problems are solved, 33 percent are ultimately rated as failures by the parties involved.[37] Below we argue that the success of an alliance seems to be a function of three main factors: partner selection, alliance structure, and the manner in which the alliance is managed.

■ Partner Selection

One of the keys to making a strategic alliance work is to select the right kind of partner. A good partner has three principal characteristics. First, a good partner helps the firm achieve its strategic goals—whether they be achieving market access, sharing the costs and risks of new-product development, or gaining access to critical core competencies. In other words, the partner must have capabilities that the company lacks and that it values.

Second, a good partner shares the firm's vision for the purpose of the alliance. If two companies approach an alliance with radically different agendas, the chances are great that the relationship will not be harmonious and will end in divorce. This seems to have been the case with the alliance between GM and Daewoo, discussed in Strategy in Action 8.5. GM's agenda was to use Daewoo as a source of cheap labor to produce cars for the Korean and U.S. markets, whereas Daewoo wanted to use GM's know-how and distribution systems to grow its own business not just in Korea and the United States, but also in Europe. Different perceptions of the strategic role of the venture contributed to the dissolution of the alliance.

Third, a good partner is unlikely to try to opportunistically exploit the alliance for its own ends; that is, to expropriate the company's technological know-how while giving little in return. In this respect, firms that have a reputation for fair play and want to maintain it probably make the best partners. For example, IBM is involved in so many strategic alliances that it would not pay the company to trample roughshod over individual alliance partners. Such actions would tarnish IBM's hard-won reputation of being a good partner and would make it more difficult for IBM to attract alliance partners in the future. Similarly, their reputations lessen the likelihood that such Japanese companies as Sony, Toshiba, and Fuji, which have a history of alliances with non-Japanese firms, would opportunistically exploit an alliance partner.

To select a partner with these three characteristics, a company needs to conduct comprehensive research on potential alliance candidates. To increase the probability of selecting a good partner, the firm should collect as much pertinent, publicly available information about potential allies as possible; collect data from informed third parties, including companies that have had alliances with the potential partners, investment bankers who have had dealings with them, and some of their former employees; and get to know potential partners as well as possible before committing to an alliance. This last step should include face-to-face meetings between senior managers (and perhaps middle-level managers) to ensure that the chemistry is right.

■ Alliance Structure

Having selected a partner, the alliance should be structured so that the company's risk of giving too much away to the partner is reduced to an acceptable level. Figure 8.4 depicts the four safeguards against opportunism by alliance partners that we discuss here. (**Opportunism** includes the "theft" of technology and/or markets that Reich and Mankin describe.) First, alliances can be designed to make it difficult (if not impossible) to transfer technology not meant to be transferred. Specifically, the design, development, manufacture, and service of a product manufactured by an alliance can be structured so as to "wall off" sensitive technologies and thus prevent

8.5   ## STRATEGY *in* ACTION

General Motors and Daewoo

In June 1984, General Motors and Daewoo of Korea signed an agreement that called for each to invest $100 million in a Korean-based 50/50 joint venture, Daewoo Motor Company, which would manufacture a subcompact car, the Pontiac LeMans, based on GM's popular German-designed Opel Kadett. (Opel is GM's German subsidiary.) Daewoo executives would be in charge of the day-to-day management of the alliance, and a few GM executives would provide managerial and technical advice. Initially, the alliance was seen as a smart move for both companies. GM doubted that a small car could be built profitably in the United States because of high labor costs, and it saw enormous advantages in this marriage of German technology and Korean cheap labor. Roger Smith, then GM's chairman, told Korean reporters that GM's North American operation would probably end up importing 80,000 to 100,000 cars a year from Daewoo Motors. As for Daewoo, it saw itself getting access to the superior engineering skills of GM and an entrée into the world's largest car market—the United States.

Eight years of financial losses later, the joint venture collapsed in a blizzard of mutual recriminations between Daewoo and General Motors. From GM's perspective, things started to go seriously wrong in 1987, just as the first LeMans was rolling off Daewoo's production line. Korea had lurched toward democracy, and workers throughout the country demanded better wages. Daewoo was hit by a series of bitter strikes, which repeatedly halted LeMans production. To calm the labor troubles, Daewoo Motor more than doubled workers' wages, and suddenly it was cheaper to build Opels in Germany. (German wages were still higher, but German productivity was also much higher, which translated into lower labor costs.)

Equally problematic was the poor quality of the cars rolling off the Daewoo production line. Electrical systems often crashed on the LeMans, and the braking system had a tendency to fail after just a few thousand miles. The LeMans soon gained a reputation for poor quality, and U.S. sales plummeted to 37,000 vehicles in 1991, down 86 percent from their 1988 high point. Hurt by the reputation of LeMans as a lemon, Daewoo's share of the rapidly growing Korean car market also slumped from a high of 21.4 percent in 1987 to 12.3 percent in 1991.

If GM was disappointed in Daewoo, that was nothing compared with Daewoo's frustration with GM. Daewoo's chairman, Kim WooChoong, complained that GM executives were arrogant and treated him shabbily. He was angry that GM tried to prohibit him from expanding the market for Daewoo's cars. In late 1988, he negotiated a deal to sell 7,000 Daewoo Motor's cars in eastern Europe. GM executives immediately tried to kill the deal, telling Kim that Europe was the territory of GM's German subsidiary, Opel. To make matters worse, when Daewoo developed a new sedan and asked GM to sell it in the United States, GM refused. By this point, Kim's frustration at having his expansion plans for eastern Europe and the United States held back by GM was clear to all. Daewoo management also believed that poor sales of the LeMans in the United States were not due to quality problems, but to GM's poor marketing efforts.

Events came to a head in 1991 when Daewoo asked GM to agree to expand the manufacturing facilities of the joint venture. The plan called for each partner to put in another $100 million and for Daewoo to double its output. GM refused on the grounds that increasing output would not help Daewoo Motor unless the venture could first improve its product quality. The matter festered until late 1991, when GM delivered a blunt proposal to Daewoo: either GM would buy out Daewoo's stake, or Daewoo would buy out GM's stake in the joint venture. Much to GM's surprise, Daewoo agreed to buy out GM's stake. The divorce was completed in November 1992 with an agreement by Daewoo to pay GM $170 million over three years for its 50 percent stake in Daewoo Motor Company.[38]

FIGURE 8.4

Structuring Alliances to
Reduce Opportunism

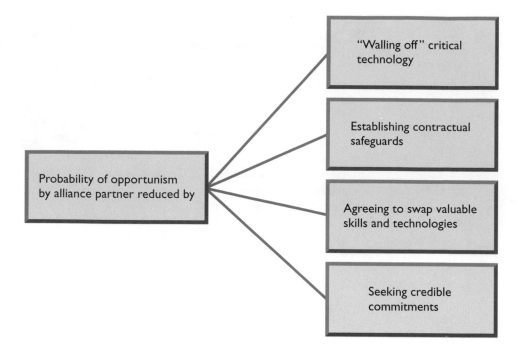

their leakage to the other participant. In the alliance between General Electric and Snecma to build commercial aircraft engines, for example, GE reduced the risk of "excess transfer" by walling off certain sections of the production process. The modularization effectively cut off the transfer of what GE regarded as key competitive technology, while permitting Snecma access to final assembly. Similarly, in the alliance between Boeing and the Japanese to build the 767, Boeing walled off research, design, and marketing functions considered central to its competitive position, while allowing the Japanese to share in production technology. Boeing also walled off new technologies not required for 767 production.[39]

Second, contractual safeguards can be written into an alliance agreement to guard against the risk of opportunism by a partner. For example, TRW has three strategic alliances with large Japanese auto component suppliers to produce seat belts, engine valves, and steering gears for sale to Japanese-owned auto assembly plants in the United States. TRW has clauses in each of its alliance contracts that bar the Japanese firms from competing with TRW to supply U.S.-owned auto companies with component parts. By means of these clauses, TRW is protecting itself against the possibility that the Japanese companies are entering into the alliances merely as a means of gaining access to the North American market to compete with TRW in its home market.

Third, both parties to an alliance can agree in advance to swap skills and technologies, thereby ensuring a chance for equitable gain. Cross-licensing agreements are one way to achieve this goal. For example, in the alliance between Motorola and Toshiba, Motorola has licensed some of its microprocessor technology to Toshiba, and in return Toshiba has licensed some of its memory chip technology to Motorola.

Fourth, the risk of opportunism by an alliance partner can be reduced if the firm extracts a significant credible commitment from its partner in advance. The long-term alliance between Xerox and Fuji to build photocopiers for the Asian market, discussed in Strategy in Action 8.4, perhaps best illustrates this approach. Rather than enter into an informal agreement or some kind of licensing arrangement (which Fuji Photo initially wanted), Xerox insisted that Fuji invest in a 50/50 joint venture to serve Japan and East Asia. This venture constituted such a significant investment in people, equipment, and facilities that Fuji Photo was committed from the outset to making the alliance work in order to earn a return on its investment. By agreeing to the joint venture, Fuji made a credible commitment to the alliance, and Xerox felt secure in transferring its photocopier technology to Fuji.[40]

■ Managing the Alliance

Once a partner has been selected and an appropriate alliance structure agreed on, the task facing the company is to maximize the benefits from the alliance. One important ingredient of success appears to be a sensitivity to cultural differences. Differences in management style can often be attributed to cultural differences. Managers need to make allowances for such differences when dealing with their partner. In addition, managing an alliance successfully means building interpersonal relationships among managers from the different companies—a lesson that can be drawn from the successful strategic alliance between Ford and Mazda to jointly develop cars for the global auto industry. This partnership has resulted in the development of such best-selling cars as the Ford Explorer and the Mazda Navajo. Ford and Mazda have set up a framework of meetings within which managers from Ford and Mazda not only discuss matters pertaining to the alliance but also have sufficient nonwork time to allow them to get to know each other better. The resulting personal friendships can help build trust and facilitate harmonious relations between the two companies. Moreover, personal relationships can create an informal management network between the companies, and this network can then be used to help solve problems that arise in more formal contexts, such as joint committee meetings between personnel from both firms.

A major factor determining how much a company gains from an alliance is its ability to learn from alliance partners. Gary Hamel, Yves Doz, and C. K. Prahalad reached this conclusion after a five-year study of fifteen strategic alliances between major multinationals. They focused on a number of alliances between Japanese companies and western (European or American) partners. In every case in which a Japanese company emerged from an alliance stronger than its western partner, the Japanese company had made a greater effort to learn. Indeed, few western companies seemed to want to learn from their Japanese partners. They tended to regard the alliance purely as a cost-sharing or risk-sharing device, rather than as an opportunity to learn how a potential competitor does business.[41] As a counterpoint, however, it is worth noting that Xerox clearly used the Fuji-Xerox joint venture to learn about "Japanese" manufacturing practices, such as total quality control and design for manufacturing (see Strategy in Action 8.4).

On the other hand, the joint effort of General Motors and Toyota to build the Chevrolet Nova exemplifies an alliance that reveals a clear learning asymmetry. Structured as a formal joint venture, called New United Motor Manufacturing, this alliance gives both parties a 50 percent equity stake. The venture owns an auto plant in Fremont, California. According to one of the Japanese managers, Toyota achieved most of its objectives from the alliance: "We learned about U.S. supply and transportation. And we got the confidence to manage U.S. workers." All that knowledge was then quickly transferred to Georgetown, Kentucky, where Toyota opened a plant of its own in 1988. By contrast, although General Motors got a new product, the Chevrolet Nova, some GM managers complained that their new knowledge was never put to good use inside GM. They say that they should have been kept together as a team to educate GM's engineers and workers about the Japanese system. Instead they were dispersed to different GM subsidiaries.[42]

When entering an alliance, a company must take some measures to ensure that it learns from its alliance partner and then puts that knowledge to good use within its own organization. One suggested approach is to educate all operating employees about the partner's strengths and weaknesses and make clear to them how acquiring particular skills will bolster their company's competitive position. For such learning to be of value, the knowledge acquired from an alliance has to be diffused throughout the organization—as did not happen at GM. To spread this knowledge, the managers involved in an alliance should be used as a resource in familiarizing others within the company about the skills of an alliance partner.

SUMMARY OF CHAPTER

This chapter examines the various ways in which companies can profit from global expansion and reviews the strategies that companies engaged in global competition can adopt. It also discusses the optimal choice of entry mode to serve a foreign market and explores the issue of strategic alliances. The chapter makes the following main points:

- ✔ For some companies, international expansion represents a way of earning greater returns by transferring the skills and product offerings derived from their distinctive competencies to markets where indigenous competitors lack those skills.

- ✔ Because of national differences, it pays a company to base each value creation activity it performs at the location where factor conditions are most conducive to the performance of that activity. We refer to this strategy as focusing on the attainment of location economies.

- ✔ By building sales volume more rapidly, international expansion can assist a company in the process of moving down the experience curve.

- ✔ The best strategy for a company to pursue may depend on the kind of pressures it must cope with: pressures for cost reductions or for local responsiveness. Pressures for cost reductions are greatest in industries producing commodity-type products, where price is the main competitive weapon. Pressures for local responsiveness arise

from differences in consumer tastes and preferences, as well as from national infrastructure and traditional practices, distribution channels, and host government demands.

- ✔ Companies pursuing an international strategy transfer the skills and products derived from distinctive competencies to foreign markets, while undertaking some limited local customization.

- ✔ Companies pursuing a multidomestic strategy customize their product offering, marketing strategy, and business strategy to national conditions.

- ✔ Companies pursuing a global strategy focus on reaping the cost reductions that come from experience-curve effects and location economies.

- ✔ Many industries are now so competitive that companies must adopt a transnational strategy. This involves a simultaneous focus on reducing costs, transferring skills and products, and local responsiveness. Implementing such a strategy, however, may not be easy.

- ✔ The most attractive foreign markets tend to be found in politically stable developed and developing nations with free market systems, but without a dramatic upsurge in either inflation rates or private sector debt.

- ✔ Entering a national market early, before other international businesses have established themselves, brings several advantages, but these advantages must be balanced against the pioneering costs that early entrants often have to bear, including the greater risk of business failure.

✔ Large-scale entry into a national market constitutes a major strategic commitment, which is likely to change the nature of competition in that market and limit the entrant's future strategic flexibility. The firm needs to think through the implications of such commitments before embarking on a large-scale entry. Although making major strategic commitments can yield many benefits, there are also risks associated with such a strategy.

✔ The five different ways of entering a foreign market are exporting, licensing, franchising, entering into a joint venture, and setting up a wholly owned subsidiary. The optimal choice of entry mode depends on the company's strategy.

✔ Strategic alliances are cooperative agreements between actual or potential competitors. The advantages of alliances are that they facilitate entry into foreign markets, enable partners to share the fixed costs and risks associated with new products and processes, facilitate the transfer of complementary skills between companies, and help companies establish technical standards.

✔ The drawbacks of a strategic alliance are that the company risks giving away technological know-how and market access to its alliance partner while getting very little in return.

✔ The disadvantages associated with alliances can be reduced if the company selects partners carefully, paying close attention to reputation, and if it structures the alliance so as to avoid unintended transfers of know-how.

DISCUSSION QUESTIONS

1. Plot the position of the following companies on Figure 8.1: Procter & Gamble, IBM, Coca-Cola, Dow Chemical, AOL, and McDonald's. In each case, justify your answer.

2. Are the following global industries or multidomestic industries: bulk chemicals, pharmaceuticals, branded food products, moviemaking, television manufacture, personal computers, airline travel, and Internet on-line services such as AOL and MSN?

3. Discuss how the need for control over foreign operations varies with the strategy and distinctive competencies of a company. What are the implications of this relationship for the choice of entry mode?

4. Licensing proprietary technology to foreign competitors is the best way to give up a company's competitive advantage. Discuss.

5. What kind of companies stand to gain the most from entering into strategic alliances with potential competitors? Why?

Practicing Strategic Management

SMALL-GROUP EXERCISE
Developing a Global Strategy

Break up into a group of three to five people and discuss the following scenario:

You work for a company in the soft-drink industry that has developed a line of carbonated fruit-based drinks. You have already establishing a significant presence in your home market, and now you are planning the global strategy development of the company in the soft-drink industry. You need to decide the following:

1. What overall strategy to pursue—a global strategy, multidomestic strategy, international strategy, or transnational strategy?

2. Which markets to enter first?

3. What entry strategy to pursue (for instance, franchising, joint venture, wholly owned subsidiary)?

What information do you need in order to make these kinds of decision? Based on what you do know, what strategies would you recommend?

STRATEGIC MANAGEMENT PROJECT
Module 8

This module requires you to identify how your company might profit from global expansion, the strategy that your company should pursue globally, and the entry mode that it might favor. With the information you have at your disposal, answer the questions regarding the following two situations:

ARTICLE FILE 8

Find an example of a multinational company that has switched its strategy in recent years from a multidomestic, international, or global strategy to a transnational strategy. Identify why the company made the switch and any problems that the company may be encountering while it tries to change its strategic orientation.

Your Company Is Already Doing Business in Other Countries

1. Is your company creating value or lowering the costs of value creation by realizing location economies, transferring distinctive competencies abroad, or realizing cost economies from the experience curve? If not, does it have the potential to do so?

2. How responsive is your company to differences between nations? Does it vary its product and marketing message from country to country? Should it?

3. What are the cost pressures and pressures for local responsiveness in the industry in which your company is based?

4. What strategy is your company pursuing to compete globally? In your opinion, is this the correct strategy, given cost pressures and pressures for local responsiveness?

5. What major foreign market does your company serve and what mode has it used to enter this market? Why is your company active in these markets, and not others? What are the advantages and disadvantages of using this mode? Might another mode be preferable?

Your Company Is Not Yet Doing Business in Other Countries

1. What potential does your company have to add value to its products or lower the costs of value creation by expanding internationally?

2. On the international level, what are the cost pressures and pressures for local responsiveness in the industry in which your company is based? What implications do these pressures have for the strategy that your company might pursue if it chose to expand globally?

3. What foreign market might your company enter and what entry mode should it use to enter this market? Justify your answer.

EXPLORING THE WEB
Visting IBM

IBM is the acronym of International Business Machines. Using the significant resources located at IBM's corporate Web site, including annual reports and company history, explain what "International" means in IBM. Specifically, how many countries is IBM active in? How does it create value by expanding into foreign markets? What entry mode does it adopt in most markets? Can you find any exceptions to this? How would you characterize IBM's strategy for competing in the global marketplace? Is the company pursuing a transnational, global, international, or multidomestic strategy?

General Task   Search the Web for a company site where there is a good description of that company's international operations. On the basis of this information, try to establish how the company enters foreign markets and what overall strategy it is pursuing (global, international, multidomestic, transnational).

CLOSING CASE

ESTABLISHED IN THE 1940S IN SWEDEN by Ingvar Kamprad, IKEA has grown rapidly in recent years to become one of the world's largest retailers of home furnishings. In its initial push to expand globally, IKEA largely ignored the retailing rule that international success requires tailoring product lines closely to national tastes and preferences. Instead, IKEA stuck with the vision, articulated by Kamprad, that wherever it ventures in the world the company should sell a basic product range that is "typically Swedish." The company also remained primarily production oriented; that is, the Swedish management and design group decided what it was going to sell and then presented it to the worldwide public, often with very little research as to what the public actually wanted. Moreover, the company emphasized its Swedish roots in its international advertising, even going as far as to insist on a "Swedish" blue and yellow color scheme for its stores.

Despite breaking some key rules of international retailing, the formula of selling Swedish-designed products in the same way everywhere seemed to work. Between 1974 and 1994, IKEA expanded from a company with 10 stores, only one of which was outside Scandinavia, and annual revenues of $210 million, to a group with 125 stores in twenty-six countries and sales of nearly $5 billion. In 1994, only 11 percent of its sales were generated in Sweden. Of the balance, 29.6 percent came from Germany, 42.5 percent from the rest of western Europe, and 14.2 percent from North America. IKEA's expansion in North America has been its most recent international venture.

The source of IKEA's success has been its ability to offer consumers good value for money. IKEA's approach

IKEA

starts with a global network of suppliers, which comprises 2,700 firms in sixty-seven countries. An IKEA supplier gains long-term contracts, technical advice, and leased equipment from the company. In return, IKEA demands an exclusive contract and low prices. IKEA's designers work closely with suppliers to build savings into the products from the outset by designing products that can be produced at a low cost. IKEA displays its enormous range of more than 10,000 products in cheap out-of-town stores. It sells most of its furniture as knocked-down kits for customers to take home and assemble themselves. The firm reaps huge economies of scale from the size of each store and the big production runs made possible by selling the same products all over the world. This strategy allows IKEA to match its rivals on quality, while undercutting them by up to 30 percent on price and still maintaining a healthy after-tax return on sales of around 7 percent.

This strategy has consistently worked well for IKEA until 1985, when the company decided to enter the North American market. Between 1985 and 1990 IKEA opened six stores in North America—but unlike the company's stores across Europe, the new stores did not quickly become profitable. Instead, by 1990 it was clear that IKEA's North American operations were in trouble. IKEA's unapologetically Swedish products, which had sold so well across Europe, jarred with U.S. tastes and sometimes with physiques as well. Swedish beds were narrow and measured in centimeters. IKEA did not sell the matching bedroom suites that U.S. consumers liked. Its kitchen cupboards were too narrow for the large dinner plates needed for pizza. Its glasses were too small for a nation that adds ice to everything. And the drawers in IKEA's bedroom chests were too shallow for American consumers, who tend to store sweaters in them.

In 1990, the company's top management came to the realization that if IKEA was to succeed in North America, it would have to customize its product offerings to North American tastes. The company set about redesigning its product range. The drawers on bedroom chests were made two inches deeper—and sales immediately increased by 30 to 40 percent. IKEA now sells U.S.-style king- and queen-size beds, measured in inches, and it sells them as part of complete bedroom suites. Currently, it is redesigning its entire range of kitchen furniture and kitchenware to better appeal to U.S. tastes. The company had also boosted the amount of products being sourced locally from 15 percent in 1990 to 45 percent in 1994, a move that has made it far less vulnerable to adverse movements in exchange rates.

This break with its traditional strategy has paid off for IKEA. Between 1990 and 1994, its North American sales tripled to $480 million, and the company claims that it has been making a profit in North America since early 1993, although it admits that profit margins are still lower in North America than in Europe. By 1995, the company had also expanded the number of North American stores to fifteen.[43]

Case Discussion Questions

1. How would you characterize IKEA's original strategy for profiting from foreign markets?

2. Why did the strategy work so well in Europe but break down in the United States?

3. How would you chacterize IKEA's post-1990 strategy? How successful has this strategy been? (Hint: Use the Web to collect details about IKEA's recent financial results. www.ikea.com)

End Notes

1. R. Blumenstein,"GM Is Building Plants in Developing Nations to Woo New Markets," *Wall Street Journal*, August 4, 1997, p. A1; H. Simonian,"GM Hopes to Turn Corner with New Astra," *Financial Times*, November 29, 1997, p. 15; D. Howes,"GM, Ford Play for Keeps Abroad," *The Detroit News*, March 8, 1998, p. D1.
2. K. Deveny et al.,"McWorld?" *Business Week*, October 13, 1986, pp. 78-86;"Slow Food," *Economist*, February 3, 1990, p. 64; H. S. Byrne,"Welcome to McWorld," *Barron's*, August 29, 1994, pp. 25-28; A. E. Serwer,"McDonald's Conquers the World," *Fortune*, October 17, 1994, pp. 103-116.
3. C. S. Tranger,"Enter the Mini-Multinational," *Northeast International Business* (March 1989),13-14.
4. I. Metthee,"Playing a Large Part," *Seattle-Post Intelligence*, April 9, 1994, p. 13.
5. R. B. Reich, *The Work of Nations* (New York: Knopf, 1991).
6. "Matsushita Electrical Industrial in 1987," in *Transnational Management*, ed. C. A. Bartlett and S. Ghoshal (Homewood, Ill.: Irwin, 1992).
7. C. K. Prahalad and Y. L. Doz, *The Multinational Mission: Balancing Local Demands and Global Vision* (New York: Free Press, 1987); also see J. Birkinshaw, A. Morrison, and J. Hulland,"Structural and Competitive Determinants of a Global Integration Strategy," *Strategic Management Journal*, 16 (1995), 637-655.
8. Prahalad and Doz, *The Multinational Mission*.
9. "The Tire Industry's Costly Obsession with Size," *Economist*, June 8, 1993, p. 65-66.
10. T. Levitt,"The Globalization of Markets," *Harvard Business Review*, (May-June 1983), 92-102.
11. C. A. Bartlett and S. Ghoshal, *The Transnational Solution: Managing Across Borders*, (Boston: Harvard Business School Press, 1989).
12. C. J. Chipello,"Local Presence Is Key to European Deals," *Wall Street Journal*, June 30, 1998, p. A15.
13. Bartlett and Ghoshal, *Managing Across Borders*.
14. G. de Jonquieres and C. Bobinski,"Wash and Get into a Lather in Poland," *Financial Times*, May 28, 1989, p. 2;"Perestroika in Soapland," *Economist*, June 10, 1989, pp. 69-71; "After Early Stumbles P&G Is Making Inroads Overseas," *Wall Street Journal*, February 6, 1989, p. B1; Bartlett and Ghoshal, *Managing Across Borders*; G. Das,"Local Memoirs of a Global Business Manager," *Harvard Business Review* (March 1993), 38-48.
15. Bartlett and Ghoshal, *Managing Across Borders*.
16. T. Hout, M. E. Porter, and E. Rudden,"How Global Companies Win Out," *Harvard Business Review*, (September-October, 1982), 98-108.
17. See C. W. L. Hill, *International Business: Competing in the Global Marketplace* (Burr Ridge, Ill.: 2000).
18. This can be reconceptualized as the resource base of the entrant, relative to indigenous competitors. For work that focuses on this issue, see W. C. Bogenr, H. Thomas, and J. McGee,"A Longitudinal Study of the Competitive Positions and Entry Paths of European Firms in the U.S. Pharmaceutical Market," *Strategic Management Journal*, 17 (1996), 85-107; D. Collis,"A Resource-Based Analysis of Global Competition," *Strategic Management Journal*, 12 (1991) 49-68; and S. Tallman,"Strategic Management Models and Resource-Based Strategies Among MNE's in a Host Market," *Strategic Management Journal*, 12 (1991), 69-82.
19. "Japan's Big Bang. Enter Merrill," *Economist*, January 3, 1998, p. 72; J. P. Donlon,"Merrill Cinch," *Chief Executive* (March 1998), p. 28-32; D. Holley,"Merrill Lynch to Open 31 Offices Throughout Japan," *Los Angeles Times*, February 13, 1998, p. D1; A. Rowley,"Merrill Thunders into Japan," *Banker* (March 1998), 6.
20. For a discussion of first-mover advantages, see M. Liberman and D. Montgomery,"First Mover Advantages," *Strategic Management Journal*, 9 (Special Issue on Strategy Content, Summer 1988), 41-58.
21. J. M. Shaver, W. Mitchell, and B. Yeung,"The Effect of Own Firm and Other Firm Experience on Foreign Direct Investment Survival in the United States 1987-92," *Strategic Management Journal*, 18 (1997), 811-824.
22. S. Zaheer and E. Mosakowski,"The Dynamics of the Liability of Foreignness: a Global Study of Survival in the Financial Services Industry," *Strategic Management Journal*, 18 (1997), 439-464.
23. Shaver, Mitchell, and Yeung,"The Effect of Own Firm and Other Firm Experience."
24. P. Ghemawat, *Commitment: The Dynamics of Strategy* (New York: Free Press, 1991).
25. R. Luecke, *Scuttle Your Ships Before Advancing* (Oxford: Oxford University Press, 1994).
26. This section draws on several studies including C. W. L. Hill, P. Hwang, and W. C. Kim,"An Eclectic Theory of the Choice of International Entry Mode," *Strategic Management Journal*, 11 (1990), 117-28; C. W. L. Hill and W. C. Kim,"Searching for a Dynamic Theory of the Multinational Enterprise: A Transaction Cost Model," *Strategic Management Journal*, 9 (Special Issue on Strategy Content, 1988), 93-104; E. Anderson and H. Gatignon,"Modes of Foreign Entry: A Transaction Cost Analysis and Propositions," *Journal of International Business Studies* 17 (1986), 1-26; F. R. Root, *Entry Strategies for International Markets* (Lexington, Mass.: D. C. Heath, 1980); A. Madhok,"Cost, Value and Foreign Market Entry: The Transaction and the Firm," *Strategic Management Journal*, 18 (1997), 39-61.
27. F. J. Contractor,"The Role of Licensing in International Strategy," *Columbia Journal of World Business* (Winter 1982), 73-83.
28. O. E. Williamson, *The Economic Institutions of Capitalism* (New York: Free Press, 1985).
29. A. E. Serwer,"McDonald's Conquers the World."
30. B. Kogut,"Joint Ventures: Theoretical and Empirical Perspectives," *Strategic Management Journal*, 9 (1988), 319-332.
31. D. G. Bradley,"Managing Against Expropriation," *Harvard Business Review* (July-August 1977), 78-90.

32. R. Howard, "The CEO as Organizational Architect," *Harvard Business Review* (September–October 1992), 106–123; D. Kearns, "Leadership Through Quality," *Academy of Management Executive*, 4 (1990), 86–89; K. McQuade and B. Gomes-Casseres, "Xerox and Fuji-Xerox," *Harvard Business School* Case No. 9-391-156; E. Terazono and C. Lorenz, "An Angry Young Warrior," *Financial Times*, September 19, 1994, p. 11.

33. C. W. L. Hill, "Strategies for Exploiting Technological Innovations," *Organization Science*, 3 (1992), 428–441.

34. See K. Ohmae, "The Global Logic of Strategic Alliances," *Harvard Business Review* (March–April 1989), 143–154; G. Hamel, Y. L. Doz, and C. K. Prahalad, "Collaborate with Your Competitors and Win!" *Harvard Business Review* (January–February 1988), 133–139; W. Burgers, C. W. L. Hill, and W. C. Kim, "Alliances in the Global Auto Industry," *Strategic Management Journal*, 14 (1993), 419–432.

35. "Asia Beckons," *Economist*, May 30, 1992, pp. 63–64.

36. R. B. Reich and E. D. Mankin, "Joint Ventures with Japan Give Away Our Future," *Harvard Business Review*, (March–April 1986), 78–90.

37. J. Bleeke and D. Ernst, "The Way to Win in Cross-Border Alliances," *Harvard Business Review* (November–December 1991), 127–135.

38. D. Darlin, "Daewoo Will Pay GM $170 Million for Venture Stake," *Wall Street Journal*, November 11, 1992, p. A6; D. Darlin and J. B. White, "Failed Marriage," *Wall Street Journal*, January 16, 1992, p. A1.

39. W. Roehl and J. F. Truitt, "Stormy Open Marriages Are Better," *Columbia Journal of World Business* (Summer 1987), 87–95.

40. K. McQuade and B. Gomes-Casseres, "Xerox and Fuji-Xerox."

41. Hamel, Doz, and Prahalad, "Collaborate with Your Competitors and Win!"

42. B. Wysocki, "Cross Border Alliances Become Favorite Way to Crack New Markets," *Wall Street Journal*, March 4, 1990, p. A1.

43. "Furnishing the World," *Economist*, November 19, 1994, pp. 79–80; H. Carnegy, "Struggle to Save the Soul of IKEA," *Financial Times*, March 27, 1995, p. 12.

9

Corporate Strategy: Vertical Integration, Diversification, and Strategic Alliances

OPENING CASE

Bombardier

BOMBARDIER is one of the great business success stories to come out of Canada in the second half of the twentieth century. A manufacturer of transportation equipment, including snowmobiles, railcars, and jet aircraft of seventy seats or less, the company has grown from sales of $10 million in the mid 1960s to around $7 billion in 1999, and it has posted consistent year-on-year growth in revenues and earnings. The key to this growth has been successful diversification.

Established in 1942 as a manufacturer of snowgoing equipment (tracked vehicles for crossing snow, such as snow cats), Bombardier expanded into the closely related market of snowmobiles in the 1960s. As oil prices surged in the early 1970s because of action by the Organization of Petroleum Exporting Countries (OPEC), demand for snowmobiles plummeted. Bombardier's response was to diversify into the manufacture of railcars. Laurent Beaudoin, the company's CEO for a thirty-three-year period that ended in 1999, reasoned that Bombardier's engineering skills and manufacturing capacity could be quickly converted from the manufacture of snowmobiles to the manufacture of railcars. In a make-or-break gamble, he purchased a French license for a subway car design and boldly bid on, and won, a huge contract to build cars for the Montreal subway system. This contract was followed by a 1982 deal to build 825 cars for the New York subway system. Today, Bombardier builds cars for mass-transit systems on four continents, ranking number two in the world railcar market. It also produces freight cars and locomotives. The railcar and locomotive business now accounts for around one-quarter of the company's business.

The next diversification move came in 1986, when Bombardier purchased Canadair from the Canadian government for what many viewed as a bargain basement price. A struggling manufacturer of small regional aircraft, Canadair had been saved from total collapse when it was bought by the Canadian government. The key asset that interested Bombardier was the design and manufacturing technology behind Canadair's small corporate jet, the Challenger. Shortly after the acquisition, Bombardier invested an amount equivalent to half the market capitalization of the company to develop a fifty-seat regional jet that just about everyone else thought the industry did not need. At the time, propeller-driven aircraft dominated the regional aircraft market. Just about everybody was wrong. The jet, and it successor aircraft, including a seventy-seat plane, have sold well. The Canadair acquisition was followed by several other purchases of troubled manufacturers of small aircraft, including Short Brother in Northern Ireland, de Havilland in Canada, and Learjet in the United States. In each case, Bombardier was able to purchase these companies for a relatively low price because of their financial troubles.

By imposing good management and tight financial discipline, and by developing a well-thought-out range of smaller jet aircraft in the twenty- to ninety-seat range, Bombardier has managed to weld this grab bag of companies into a coherent and significant force in the global aerospace market. Now the third largest civilian aerospace company in the world, behind Boeing and Airbus, Bom-

bardier has thrived by focusing on a niche where Boeing and Airbus do not compete. In 1998, it received a record 200 orders for its small regional jet aircraft. In total, the units now account for more than half of Bombardier's revenues and profits.

Bombardier's management attributes much of the company's success with diversification to a number of factors. It has entered only those niches where it thought it had a good chance of being the number one or two player in the world, and it has acquired valuable technology at a relatively low cost. Furthermore, it has managed its different businesses within a decentralized organizational structure, which gives the managers of business units the freedom to pursue what they think are the appropriate competitive and operations strategies, subject of course to a detailed review from the top. The company has deliberately taken big risks in its diversification moves. According to the current CEO, Bob Brown, Bombardier's key values are boldness and energy. "When you take action," he says, "take bold action. And when you decide to do something, do it 150 percent."[1]

OVERVIEW

The principal concern of corporate strategy is identifying the business areas in which a company should participate in order to maximize its long-run profitability. When choosing business areas to compete in, a company has several options. It can focus on just one business; it can diversify into a number of different business areas as Bombardier, discussed in the Opening Case, has done; or it can vertically integrate, either upstream to produce its own inputs or downstream to dispose of its own outputs. This chapter explores the various options in depth and examines their pros and cons. It also considers strategic alliances as alternatives to vertical integration and diversification.

As described in the Opening Case, Bombardier made diversification its corporate strategy. From the manufacture of snowgoing equipment such as snow cats, it diversified first into that of snowmobiles (and later skidoos, or water scooters), then into railcar and locomotive manufacture, and finally into the manufacture of small (less than 100-seat) commercial aircraft. The diversification into making snowmobiles was a successful attempt to apply the company's engineering skills in developing and producing snowgoing equipment for the recreational market. By diversifying into railcar manufacture, the company strove to reduce its dependence on the volatile snowmobile business, as well as utilize its excess capacity in manufacturing and engineering talent. The move into aerospace was a bold effort to take advantage of an unexploited opportunity in the market for small jet aircraft. In each case, Bombardier was able to create value. In snowmobiles, it created value by using its existing skill base to manufacture a revolutionary new recreational product. In railcars and locomotives, it initially created value by using diversification to profitably exploit its excess capacity in engineering talent and manufacturing capacity. In aerospace, it created value by consolidating a fragmented market and developing a successful family of innovative small jet aircraft aimed at the regional commuter market.

In this chapter, we repeatedly stress that to succeed, corporate-level strategies should *create value*. To understand what this means, we have to go back to the concept of value creation and the value chain, introduced in Chapter 4: *To create value, a corporate strategy should enable a company, or one or more of its business units, to perform one or more of the value creation functions at a lower cost, or perform one or more of the value creation functions in a way that allows for differentiation and a premium price.* Thus, a company's *corporate* strategy should help in the process of establishing a distinctive competency and competitive advantage *at the business level*. There is, therefore, a very important link between corporate-level strategy and competitive advantage at the business level.

CONCENTRATION ON A SINGLE BUSINESS

For many companies, the appropriate corporate-level strategy does not involve vertical integration or diversification. Instead, corporate strategy entails concentrating on competing successfully within the confines of a single business (that is, focusing on a single industry or market). Examples of companies that currently pursue such a strategy include McDonald's with its focus on the fast-food restaurant business; Coca-Cola, with its focus on the soft drink business; and Sears with its focus on department store retailing. Interestingly enough, both Coca-Cola and Sears at one time pursued diversification strategies. Coca-Cola once owned Columbia Pictures and a wine-producing business; Sears owned Allstate Insurance, Caldwell Banker (a real estate operation), and Dean Witter (a financial services enterprise). However, both companies found that diversification dissipated rather than created value and so they divested their businesses, refocusing on a single operation. They made the change because there are clear advantages to concentrating on just one business area.

One advantage is that the company can focus its total managerial, financial, technological, and physical resources and capabilities on competing successfully in a single area. This strategy can be important in fast-growing industries, where demands on the company's resources and capabilities are likely to be substantial, but where the long-term profits that flow from establishing a competitive advantage are also likely to be very significant. For example, it would make little sense for a company such as America Online to pursue a diversification strategy while the on-line industry still has many years of rapid growth ahead of it and while competing successfully in that marketplace is placing significant demands on the managerial, financial, and technological resources and capabilities of America Online. If it did diversify, America Online would probably run the risk of starving its fast-growing core business of necessary resources, which could quickly result in the decline of that operation.

Nor do just fast-growing companies benefit from focusing an organization's resources and capabilities on one business activity. Some diversified companies active in more mature businesses have also stretched scarce resources too thinly over too many activities, and their performance has declined as a consequence. Sears, for example, found that its diversification into financial services and real estate diverted top management's attention away from its core retailing business, which contributed to a decline in the profitability of that activity. Similarly, Coca-Cola's decision to divest Columbia Pictures was in part driven by a realization that running an entertainment business was diverting valuable top management attention from its core soft drink operation.

Another advantage of concentrating on a single businesses is that the company thereby "sticks to its knitting."[2] What this means is that the company sticks to doing what it knows best, and does not make the mistake of diversifying into areas that it knows little about and where its existing resources and capabilities add little value. Companies undertaking such diversification are likely to discover after the event that they are involved in a business they do not understand and that their uninformed decision making may have a serious and perhaps detrimental effect. For example, in 1991 the Japanese consumer electronics concern Matsushita acquired the U.S. movie and music group MCA. The senior executives at Matsushita, however, soon realized that they knew very little about either the music or the movie businesses. Matsushita's hamfisted attempts to give strategic guidance to top managers at MCA alienated those managers, several of whom left the organization; others engaged in what amounted to an open rebellion, ignoring attempts by Japanese executives to intervene in the running of MCA. At one time it was rumored in the financial press that as many as 100 top MCA managers were considering defecting from the organization. This proved to be very damaging in a business where one of the prime assets is people. Matsushita soon found itself trying to fix managerial problems in a business it did not understand. In 1995, it divested MCA, admitting at the time that it had made an expensive mistake. (Matsushita reportedly lost $2 billion on the deal.)[3]

Concentrating on just one business area, however, also has disadvantages. As the next section shows, a certain amount of vertical integration may be necessary to create value and establish a competitive advantage within a company's core business. Moreover, companies that concentrate on just one business may be missing out on opportunities to create value and make greater profits by leveraging their resources and capabilities to other activities. As Bombadier's success, described in the Opening Case indicates, diversification can help create value by allowing a company to leverage valuable resources and capabilities across businesses.

VERTICAL INTEGRATION

A strategy of **vertical integration** means that a company is producing its own inputs (backward, or upstream, integration) or is disposing of its own outputs (forward, or downstream, integration). A steel company that supplies its iron ore needs from company-owned iron ore mines exemplifies backward (upstream) integration. An automaker that sells its cars through company-owned distribution outlets illustrates forward (downstream) integration. Figure 9.1 shows the four *main* stages in a typical raw-material-to-consumer production chain. For a company based in the assembly stage, backward integration means moving into intermediate manufacturing

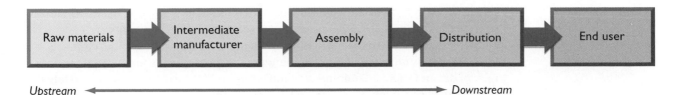

Upstream ←————————————————————————————→ Downstream

FIGURE 9.1

Stages in the Raw-
Material-to-Consumer
Value Chain

and raw-material production. Forward integration means moves into distribution. At each stage in the chain, *value is added* to the product. What this means is that a company at that stage takes the product produced in the previous stage and transforms it in some way so that it is worth more to a company at the next stage in the chain and, ultimately, to the end user.

As an example of the value-added concept, consider the production chain in the personal computer industry, illustrated in Figure 9.2. In this industry, the raw materials companies include the manufacturers of specialty ceramics, chemicals, and metals such as Kyocera of Japan, which makes the ceramic substrate for semiconductors. These companies sell their output to the manufacturers of intermediate products. The intermediate manufacturers, which include Intel, Seagate, and Micron Technology, transform the ceramics, chemicals, and metals they purchase into computer components such as microprocessors, memory chips, and disk drives. In doing so they *add value* to the raw materials they purchase. These components are then sold to assembly companies such as Apple, Dell, and Compaq, which take these components and transform them into personal computers—that is, *add value* to the components they purchase. Many of the completed personal computers are then sold to distributors such as Office Max and Computer World, or value-added resellers, which in turn sell them to final customers. The distributors also *add value* to the product by making it accessible to customers and by providing service and support. Thus, value is added by companies at each stage in the raw-materials-to-consumer chain.

Viewed this way, vertical integration presents companies with a choice about which value-added stages of the raw-material-to-consumer chain to compete in. In the personal computer industry, most companies have not integrated into adjacent

FIGURE 9.2

The Raw-Material-to-
Consumer Value Chain
in the Personal
Computer Industry

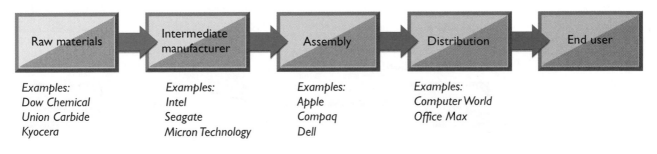

Examples:
Dow Chemical
Union Carbide
Kyocera

Examples:
Intel
Seagate
Micron Technology

Examples:
Apple
Compaq
Dell

Examples:
Computer World
Office Max

stages. However, there are some major exceptions. Intel, for one, has operated in both the intermediate manufacturer and assembly stage of the industry. It is a vertically integrated enterprise, not only producing microprocessors and chip sets for personal computers, but also assembling personal computers for computer companies under an Original Equipment Manufacturer (OEM) arrangement, which lets the downstream company put its brand label on an Intel PC.

Besides forward and backward integration, it is also possible to distinguish between **full integration** and **taper integration** (see Figure 9.3).[4] A company achieves full integration when it produces all of a particular input needed for its processes or when it disposes of all its output through its own operations. Taper integration occurs when a company buys from independent suppliers in addition to company-owned suppliers, or when it disposes of its output through independent outlets in addition to company-owned outlets. The advantages of taper integration over full integration are discussed later in the chapter.

■ Creating Value Through Vertical Integration

A company pursuing vertical integration is normally motivated by a desire to strengthen the competitive position of its original, or core, business.[5] There are four main arguments for pursuing a vertical integration strategy. Vertical integration (1) enables the company to build barriers to new competition, (2) facilitates investments in efficiency-enhancing specialized assets, (3) protects product quality, and (4) results in improved scheduling.

Building Barriers to Entry   By vertically integrating backward to gain control over the source of critical inputs or vertically integrating forward to gain control over distribution channels, a company can build barriers to new entry into its industry. To the extent that this strategy is effective, it limits competition in the company's industry, thereby enabling the company to charge a higher price and make greater profits than it could otherwise.[6] To grasp this argument, consider a famous example of this strategy from the 1930s.

At that time, commercial smelting of aluminum was pioneered by companies such as Alcoa and Alcan. Aluminum is derived from smelting bauxite. Although bauxite is a common mineral, the percentage of aluminum in bauxite is usually so low that it is not economical to mine and smelt. During the 1930s, only one large-

FIGURE 9.3

Full and Taper
Integration

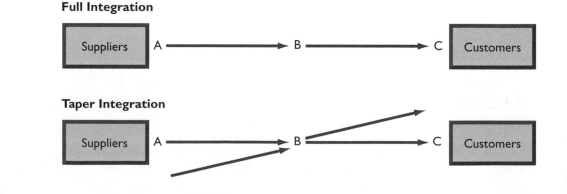

scale deposit of bauxite had been discovered where the percentage of aluminum in the mineral made smelting economical. This deposit was on the Caribbean island of Jamaica. Alcoa and Alcan vertically integrated backward and acquired ownership over this deposit. This action created a barrier to entry into the aluminum industry. Potential competitors were deterred from entry because they could not get access to high-grade bauxite; it was all owned by Alcoa and Alcan. Because they had to use lower-grade bauxite, those that did enter the industry found themselves at a cost disadvantage. This situation persisted until the 1950s, when new high-grade deposits were discovered in Australia and Indonesia.

During the 1970s and 1980s, a similar strategy was pursued by vertically integrated companies in the computer industry such as IBM and Digital Equipment. These companies manufactured the main components of computers such as microprocessors and memory chips, designed and assembled the computers, produced the software that ran the computers, and sold the final product directly to end users. The original rationale behind this strategy was that many of the key components and software used in computers contained proprietary elements. These companies reasoned that by producing the proprietary technology in-house they could limit rivals' access to it, thereby building barriers to entry. Thus, when IBM introduced its PS/2 personal computer system in the mid 1980s, it announced that certain component parts incorporating proprietary technology would be manufactured in-house by IBM.

While this strategy worked well from the 1960s until the early 1980s, it has been failing since then, particularly in the personal computer and server segments of the industry. In the early 1990s, the worst performers in the computer industry were precisely the companies that pursued the vertical integration strategy: IBM and Digital Equipment. What seems to have happened is that the shift to open standards in computer hardware and software has nullified the advantages for computer companies of being extensively vertically integrated. In addition, new personal computer companies such as Dell and Compaq found that they could quickly reverse-engineer and duplicate the proprietary components that companies such as IBM placed in their personal computers, effectively circumventing this barrier to entry.

Facilitating Investments in Specialized Assets A specialized asset is an asset that is designed to perform a specific task and whose value is significantly reduced in its next best use.[7] A specialized asset may be a piece of equipment that has very specialized uses, or it may be the know-how or skills that an individual or company has acquired through training and experience. Companies (and individuals) invest in specialized assets because these assets allow them to lower the costs of value creation and/or to better differentiate their product offering from that of competitors, thereby facilitating premium pricing. A company might invest in specialized equipment because that enables it to lower its manufacturing costs and increase its quality, or it might invest in developing highly specialized technological knowledge because doing so lets it develop better products than its rivals. Thus, specialization can be the basis for achieving a competitive advantage at the business level.

A company, however, may find it very difficult to persuade other companies in *adjacent* stages in the raw-material-to-consumer production chain to undertake investments in specialized assets. To realize the economic gains associated with such investments, the company may have to integrate vertically into the adjacent stages and make the investments itself. Imagine, for instance, that Ford has developed a new, high-performance, high-quality, and uniquely designed carburetor. The carburetor will increase fuel efficiency, which in turn will help differentiate Ford's cars from those of its rivals—that is, it will give Ford a competitive advantage. Ford has to decide whether to make the carburetor in-house (vertical integration) or contract out manufacturing to an independent supplier (outsourcing). Manufacturing these carburetors requires substantial investments in equipment that can be used only for this purpose. Because of its unique design, the equipment cannot be used to manufacture any other type of carburetor for Ford or any other auto firm. Thus, the investment in this equipment constitutes an investment in specialized assets.

An independent supplier that has been asked by Ford to make this investment might reason that once it has done so it will become dependent on Ford for business *since Ford is the only possible customer for the output of this equipment*. The supplier perceives the situation as putting Ford in a strong bargaining position and worries that Ford might use the position to squeeze down prices for the carburetors. Given this risk, the supplier declines to make the investment in specialized equipment.

Ford, too, might fear excessive dependence. It might reason that by contracting out production of these carburetors to an independent supplier it might have to rely on that supplier for a vital input. Because of the specialized equipment needed to produce the carburetors, Ford would not be able to switch its orders easily to other suppliers, since they would lack that equipment. Ford perceives the situation as increasing the bargaining power of the supplier and worries that the supplier might use its bargaining strength to demand higher prices.

The condition of ***mutual dependence*** that would be created by the investment in specialized assets makes Ford hesitant to contract out and makes any potential suppliers hesitant to undertake such investments. The real problem here is a lack of trust. Neither Ford nor the supplier completely trusts the other to play fair in this situation. The lack of trust arises from the **risk of holdup**, that is, of being taken advantage of by a trading partner after the investment in specialized assets has been made.[8] Because of this risk, Ford might reason that the only safe way to get the new carburetors is to manufacture them itself.

To generalize from this example, when achieving a competitive advantage requires one company to make investments in specialized assets in order to trade with another, the risk of holdup may serve as a deterrent, and the investment may not take place. In those circumstances, the potential for competitive gains from specialization would be lost. To prevent such loss, companies vertically integrate into adjacent stages in the value chain. This consideration has driven automobile companies to vertically integrate backward into the production of component parts, steel companies to vertically integrate backward into the production of iron, computer companies to vertically integrate backward into chip production, and aluminum companies to vertically integrate backward into bauxite mining. The rationale underlying vertical integration in the aluminum industry is explored in greater detail in Strategy in Action 9.1.

Protecting Product Quality   By protecting product quality, vertical integration enables a company to become a differentiated player in its core business. The banana industry illustrates this situation. Historically, a problem facing food companies that import bananas was the variable quality of delivered bananas, which often arrived on the shelves of American stores either too ripe or not ripe enough. To correct this problem, major U.S. food companies such as General Foods have integrated

9.1 **STRATEGY in ACTION**

Specialized Assets and Vertical Integration in the Aluminum Industry

Aluminum refineries are designed to refine bauxite ore and produce aluminum. The metal content and chemical composition of bauxite ore vary from deposit to deposit. Each type of ore requires a specialized refinery—that is, the refinery must be designed for a particular type of ore. Running one type of bauxite through a refinery designed for another type reportedly increases production costs by 20 percent to 100 percent.[9] Thus, the value of an investment in a specialized aluminum refinery and the cost of the output produced by that refinery depend on its receiving the right kind of bauxite ore.

Let us assume that an aluminum company has to decide whether to invest in an aluminum refinery designed to refine a certain type of ore and that this ore is produced only by a bauxite company at a single bauxite mine. Using a different type of ore would raise production costs by 50 percent. The value of the aluminum company's investment depends on the price it must pay the bauxite company for this bauxite. But once the aluminum company has made the investment in a new refinery, what is to stop the bauxite company from raising bauxite prices? The answer is nothing; once it has made the investment

the aluminum company is locked into its relationship with its bauxite supplier. The bauxite company can increase bauxite prices secure in the knowledge that as long as the resulting increase in the total production costs of the aluminum company is less than 50 percent, the aluminum company will continue to buy from it. Consequently, once the aluminum company has made the investment, the bauxite company can hold up the aluminum company.

How can the aluminum company reduce the risk of hold up? The answer is by purchasing the bauxite company. If the aluminum company can purchase the bauxite company, or that company's bauxite mine, it need no longer fear that bauxite prices will be increased after the investment in an aluminum refinery has been made. In other words, it makes economic sense for the aluminum company contemplating the investment to engage in vertical integration. By eliminating the risk of holdup, vertical integration makes the specialized investment worthwhile. In practice, it has been argued, these kinds of considerations have driven aluminum companies to pursue vertical integration to such an extent that, according to one study, 91 percent of the total volume of bauxite is transferred within vertically integrated aluminum companies.[10]

backward to gain control over supply sources. Consequently, they have been able to distribute bananas of a standard quality at the optimal time for consumption. Knowing they can rely on the quality of these brands, consumers are willing to pay more for them. Thus, by vertically integrating backward into plantation ownership, the banana companies have built consumer confidence, which enables them to charge a premium price for their product. Similarly, when McDonald's decided to open its first restaurant in Moscow, it found, much to its initial dismay, that in order to serve food and drink indistinguishable from that served in McDonald's restaurants elsewhere, it had to vertically integrate backward and supply its own needs. The quality of Russian-grown potatoes and meat was simply too poor. Thus, to protect the quality of its product, McDonald's set up its own dairy farms, cattle ranches, vegetable plots, and food-processing plant within Russia.

The same kind of considerations can result in forward integration. Ownership of distribution outlets may be necessary if the required standards of after-sales service for complex products are to be maintained. For example, in the 1920s Kodak owned retail outlets for distributing photographic equipment. The company felt that few established retail outlets had the skills necessary to sell and service its photographic equipment. By the 1930s, however, Kodak decided that it no longer needed to own its retail outlets because other retailers had begun to provide satisfactory distribution and service for Kodak products. The company then withdrew from retailing.

Improved Scheduling   It is sometimes argued that strategic advantages arise from the easier planning, coordination, and scheduling of adjacent processes made possible in vertically integrated organizations.[11] Such advantages can be particularly important to companies trying to realize the benefits of just-in-time inventory systems, discussed in detail in Chapter 5. For example, in the 1920s Ford profited from the tight coordination and scheduling that is possible with backward vertical integration. Ford integrated backward into steel foundries, iron ore shipping, and iron ore mining. Deliveries at Ford were coordinated to such an extent that iron ore unloaded at Ford's steel foundries on the Great Lakes was turned into engine blocks within twenty-four hours. Thus, Ford substantially lowered its cost structure by eliminating the need to hold excessive inventories.

The enhanced scheduling that vertical integration makes feasible may also enable a company to respond better to sudden changes in demand, or to get its product into the marketplace faster. A situation in the microprocessor industry of the early 1990s illustrates this point. Demand for microprocessors was running at an all-time high, and most microprocessor manufacturing plants were operating at full capacity. At that time, several microprocessor companies that specialized in chip design but contracted out manufacturing found themselves at a strategic disadvantage. For example, in 1991 Chips & Technologies succeeded in designing a clone of Intel's 386 microprocessor. Chips & Technologies sent its clone design to Texas Instruments (TI) to be manufactured, only to find that it had to wait fourteen weeks until TI could schedule time to manufacture that item. In that short span of time, the price for a 386 microprocessor fell from $112 to $50. By the time TI produced the 386 clone for Chips & Technologies, the company had missed the best part of the market. Had Chips & Technologies been vertically integrated into manufacturing, this loss would not have occurred.[12]

■ Arguments Against Vertical Integration

Vertical integration has its disadvantages. Most important among them are (1) cost disadvantages, (2) disadvantages that arise when technology is changing fast, and (3) disadvantages that arise when demand is unpredictable. These disadvantages imply that the benefits of vertical integration are not always as substantial as they might seem initially.

Cost Disadvantages   Although often undertaken to gain a production cost advantage, vertical integration can raise costs if a company becomes committed to purchasing inputs from company-owned suppliers when low-cost external sources of supply exist. For example, during the early 1990s General Motors made 68 percent of the component parts for its vehicles in-house, more than any other major automaker (at Chrysler the figure was 30 percent, and at Toyota 28 percent). That vertical integration caused GM to be the highest-cost producer among the world's major car companies. In 1992, GM was paying $34.60 an hour in United Auto Workers wages and benefits to its employees at company-owned suppliers for work that rivals could get done by independent nonunionized suppliers at half these rates.[13] Thus, vertical integration can be a disadvantage when a company's own sources of supply have higher operating costs than those of independent suppliers.

Company-owned suppliers might have high operating costs compared with independent suppliers because company-owned suppliers know that they can always sell their output to other parts of the company. Not having to compete for orders lessens the incentive to minimize operating costs. Indeed, the managers of the supply operation may be tempted to pass on any cost increases to other parts of the company in the form of higher transfer prices, rather than looking for ways to lower those costs. Thus, the lack of incentive to reduce costs can raise operating costs. The problem may be less serious, however, when the company pursues taper, rather than full, integration, since the need to compete with independent suppliers can produce a downward pressure on the cost structure of company-owned suppliers.

Technological Change When technology is changing fast, vertical integration poses the hazard of tying a company to an obsolescent technology.[14] Consider a radio manufacturer that in the 1950s integrated backward and acquired a manufacturer of vacuum tubes. When in the 1960s transistors replaced vacuum tubes as a major component in radios, this company found itself tied to a technologically obsolescent business. Switching to transistors would have meant writing off its investment in vacuum tubes. Therefore, the company was reluctant to change and instead continued to use vacuum tubes in its radios while its nonintegrated competitors were rapidly switching to the new technology. Since it kept making an outdated product, the company rapidly lost market share. Thus, vertical integration can inhibit a company's ability to change its suppliers or its distribution systems to match the requirements of changing technology.

Demand Uncertainty Vertical integration can also be risky in unstable or unpredictable demand conditions. When demand is stable, higher degrees of vertical integration might be managed with relative ease. Stable demand allows better scheduling and coordination of production flows among different activities. When demand conditions are unstable or unpredictable, achieving close coordination among vertically integrated activities may be difficult.

The problem is to balance capacity among different stages of a process. For example, an auto manufacturer might vertically integrate backward to acquire a supplier of carburetors that has a capacity exactly matching the auto manufacturer's needs. However, if demand for autos subsequently falls, the automaker will find itself locked into a business that is running below capacity. Clearly, this would be uneconomical. The auto manufacturer could avoid this situation by continuing to buy carburetors on the open market rather than making them itself. If demand conditions are unpredictable, taper integration might be somewhat less risky than full integration. When a company obtains only part of its total input requirements from company-owned suppliers, in times of low demand it can keep its in-house suppliers running at full capacity by ordering exclusively from them.

■ Bureaucratic Costs and the Limits of Vertical Integration

As already noted, although vertical integration can create value, it may also result in substantial costs caused by a lack of incentive on the part of company-owned suppliers to reduce their operating costs, by a possible lack of strategic flexibility in times of changing technology, or by uncertain demand. Together, these costs form a major component of what we refer to as the **bureaucratic costs** of vertical integration. Bureaucratic costs are simply the costs of running an organization. They include the costs that stem from bureaucratic inefficiencies, such as those we have just discussed. Bureaucratic costs place a limit on the amount of vertical integration that can be profitably pursued; it makes sense for a company to vertically integrate only if the value created by such a strategy exceeds the bureaucratic costs associated with expanding the boundaries of the organization to incorporate additional upstream or downstream activities.

Commonsense reasoning suggests that not all vertical integration opportunities have the same potential for value creation. Although vertical integration may initially have a favorable impact, the value created by additional integration into areas more distant from a company's core business is likely to become increasingly marginal. The more marginal the value created by a vertical integration move, the more likely it is that the bureaucratic costs associated with expanding the boundaries of the organization into new activities will outweigh the value created. Once this occurs, a limit to profitable vertical integration has been reached.[15]

It is worth bearing in mind, however, that the pursuit of taper rather than full integration may decrease the bureaucratic costs of vertical integration. The reason is that taper integration creates an incentive for in-house suppliers to reduce their operating costs and increases the company's ability to respond to changing demand conditions. Hence it reduces some of the organizational inefficiencies that raise bureaucratic costs.

ALTERNATIVES TO VERTICAL INTEGRATION: COOPERATIVE RELATIONSHIPS AND STRATEGIC OUTSOURCING

The disadvantages associated with vertical integration raise the question whether it is possible to reap the benefits of vertical integration without having to bear the associated bureaucratic costs. Can the benefits associated with vertical integration be captured through outsourcing activities to other companies? The answer seems to be a qualified yes. Under certain circumstances, companies can realize the gains linked with vertical integration, without having to bear the bureaucratic costs, if they enter into long-term cooperative relationships with their trading partners. Such long-term relationships are typically referred to as strategic alliances. However, companies will generally be unable to realize the gains associated with vertical integration if they enter into short-term contracts with their trading partners. To see why this is so, we first discuss the problems associated with short-term contracts. Then we look at strategic alliances and long-term contracts as an alternative to vertical integration and discuss how companies can build enduring, long-term relationships with their trading partners.

■ Short-Term Contracts and Competitive Bidding

A short-term contract is one that lasts for a year or less. Many companies use short-term contracts to structure the purchasing of their inputs or the sale of their outputs. A classic example is the automobile company that uses a **competitive bidding strategy** to negotiate the price for a particular part produced by component suppliers. General Motors for example, often solicits bids from a number of different suppliers for producing a component part and awards a one-year contract to the supplier submitting the lowest bid. At the end of the year, the contract is put out for competitive bid again. Thus, there is no guarantee that the company that won the contract one year will hold on to it the following year.

The benefit of this strategy is that it forces suppliers to keep down their prices. But GM's lack of long-term commitment to individual suppliers may make them very hesitant to undertake the type of investments in specialized assets that may be needed to improve the design or quality of component parts or to improve scheduling between GM and its suppliers. Indeed, with no guarantee that it would remain a GM supplier the following year, the supplier may refuse to undertake investments in specialized assets. GM then may have to vertically integrate backward in order to realize the gains associated with specialization.

In other words, the strategy of short-term contracting and competitive bidding, *because it signals a lack of long-term commitment to its suppliers on the part of a company*, will make it very difficult for that company to realize the gains associated with vertical integration. This is not a problem when there is minimal need for close cooperation between the company and its suppliers to facilitate investments in specialized assets, improve scheduling, or improve product quality. In such cases competitive bidding may be optimal. However, when this need is significant, a competitive bidding strategy can be a serious drawback.

Interestingly enough, there are indications that in the past GM, by adopting a competitive bidding stance with regard to its suppliers, placed itself at a competitive disadvantage. In 1992, the company instructed its part suppliers to cut their prices by 10 percent, regardless of prior pricing agreements. In effect, GM tore up existing contracts and tried to force through its policy by threatening to weed out suppliers that did not agree to the price reduction. Although such action may yield short-term benefits for companies, there is a long-term cost to be borne: the loss of trust and the hostility created between the company and its suppliers. According to press reports, several suppliers claimed that they cut back on research for future GM parts. They also indicated that they would first impart new ideas to Chrysler (now DaimlerChrysler) or Ford, both of which took a more cooperative approach to forging long-term relationships with suppliers.[16]

■ Strategic Alliances and Long-Term Contracting

Long-term contracts are long-term cooperative relationships between two companies. Such agreements are often referred to in the popular press as **strategic alliances**. Typically in these arrangements, one company agrees to supply the other, and the other company agrees to continue purchasing from that supplier; both make a commitment to jointly seek ways of lowering the costs or raising the quality of inputs into the downstream company's value creation process. If it is achieved, such a stable long-term relationship lets the participating companies share the value that might be created by vertical integration while avoiding many of the bureaucratic costs linked to ownership of an adjacent stage in the raw-material-to-consumer production chain. Thus, long-term contracts can substitute for vertical integration.

The cooperative relationships that many Japanese auto companies have with their component-parts suppliers (the *keiretsu* system) exemplify successful long-term contracting. These relationships often go back decades. Together, the auto companies and their suppliers work out ways to increase value added—for instance, by implementing just-in-time inventory systems or by cooperating on component-part designs to improve quality and lower assembly costs. As part of this process, the suppliers make substantial investments in specialized assets in order to better serve the needs of the auto companies. Thus, the Japanese automakers have been able to capture many of the benefits of vertical integration without having to bear the associated bureaucratic costs. The component-parts suppliers also benefit from these relationships, for they grow with the company they supply and share in its success.[17]

In contrast to their Japanese counterparts, U.S. auto companies historically tended to pursue formal vertical integration.[18] According to several studies, the increased bureaucratic costs of managing extensive vertical integration helped place GM and Ford at a disadvantage relative to their Japanese competition.[19] Moreover, when U.S. auto companies decided not to integrate vertically, they did not necessarily enter into cooperative long-term relationships with independent component suppliers. Instead, they tended to use their powerful position to pursue an aggressive competitive bidding strategy, playing off component suppliers against each other.[20] This mindset seems to be changing. Strategy in Action 9.2 details how DaimlerChrysler has tried to build long-term cooperative relationships with suppliers.

■ Building Long-Term Cooperative Relationships

Given the lack of trust and the fear of holdup that arises when one company has to invest in specialized asset in order to trade with another, how can companies achieve stable long-term strategic alliances with each other? How have companies such as Toyota managed to develop enduring relationships with their suppliers?

Companies can take some specific steps to ensure that a long-term cooperative relationship will work and to lessen the chances of a partner reneging on an agreement. One of those steps is for the company making investments in specialized assets to demand a hostage from its partner. Another is to establish a credible commitment on both sides to build a trusting long-term relationship.[22]

Hostage Taking   Hostage taking is a means of guaranteeing that a partner will keep its side of the bargain. The cooperative relationship between Boeing and Northrop illustrates this type of situation. Northrop is a major subcontractor for Boeing's commercial airline division, providing many component parts for the 747 and 767 aircraft. To serve Boeing's special needs, Northrop has had to make substantial investments in specialized assets. In theory, because of the sunk costs associated with such investments, Northrop is dependent on Boeing, and Boeing is in a position to renege on previous agreements and use the threat to switch orders to other suppliers as a way of driving down prices. However, in practice Boeing is unlikely to do so since the company is also a major supplier to Northrop's defense division, providing many parts for the Stealth bomber. Boeing has had to make substantial investments in specialized assets in order to serve Northrop's needs. Thus, the companies are *mutually dependent*. Boeing, therefore, is unlikely to renege on any pricing agreements with Northrop, since it knows that Northrop could respond in kind. Each company holds a hostage that can be used as insurance against the other company's unilateral reneging on prior pricing agreements.

Credible Commitments   A credible commitment is a believable commitment to support the development of a long-term relationship between companies. To understand the concept of credibility in this context, consider the following relation-

DaimlerChrysler's U.S. Keiretsu

Like many long established companies, Chrysler (now DaimlerChrysler) for most of its history managed suppliers through a competitive bidding process, in which suppliers were selected on the basis of their ability to supply components at the lowest possible cost to Chrysler. A supplier's track record on performance and quality was relatively unimportant in this process. Contracts were renegotiated every two years with little or no commitment from Chrysler to continue to do business with a particular supplier. As a result, the typical relationship between Chrysler and its suppliers was characterized by mutual distrust, suspicion, and the suppliers' reluctance to invest too much in that relationship.

Since the early 1990s, however, Chrysler has systematically reorganized its dealings with suppliers in an attempt to build stable long-term relationships. The aim of this new approach has been to try and get suppliers to help Chrysler develop new products and improve its production processes. To encourage suppliers to cooperate and make investments that are specific to Chrysler's needs, the company has moved sharply away from its old adversarial approach. The average contract with suppliers has been lengthened from two years to over four and a half years. Furthermore, Chrysler has given 90 percent of its suppliers oral commitments that business will be extended for at least the life of a model, if not beyond that. The company has also committed itself to share with suppliers the benefits of any process improvements they might suggest. The basic thinking behind offering suppliers such credible commitments is to align incentives between Chrysler and its suppliers—to create a sense of shared destiny, which would encourage mutual cooperation to increase the size of the financial pie available to both.

The fruits of this new approach are beginning to appear. By involving suppliers early on in product development and giving them greater responsibility for design

and manufacturing, DaimlerChrysler has substantially compressed its product development cycle and also taken a lot of cost out of the product development effort. DaimlerChrysler's U.S. operation has reduced the time it takes to develop a new vehicle from 234 weeks during the mid 1980s to about 160 weeks today. The total cost of developing a new vehicle has also fallen by 20 percent to 40 percent, depending on the model. With development costs in the automobile industry running between $1 and $2 billion, that translates into huge financial savings—often the direct result of engineering improvements suggested by suppliers, or of improved coordination between the company and suppliers in the design process. To facilitate this process, the number of resident engineers from suppliers who work side by side with DaimlerChrysler engineers in cross-company design teams increased from 30 in 1989 to more than 300 by 1996.

Beginning in 1990, Chrysler also implemented a program known internally as the Supplier Cost Reduction Effort (or SCORE). SCORE focuses on cooperation between DaimlerChrysler and suppliers to identify opportunities for process improvements. In its first two years of operation, SCORE generated 875 ideas from suppliers, which were worth $170.8 million in annual savings to suppliers. In 1994, suppliers submitted 3,786 ideas, which produced $504 million in annual savings. By December 1995, Chrysler had implemented a total of 5,300 ideas that have generated more than $1.7 billion in annual savings. One supplier alone, Magna International, had submitted 214 proposals by December 1995; Chrysler adopted 129 of them, for a total cost saving of $75.5 million. Many of the ideas have a relatively small financial impact in themselves—for example, a Magna suggestion to change the type of decorative wood grain used on minivans saved $0.5 million per year. But the cumulative impact of thousands of such ideas has been very significant on DaimlerChrysler's bottom line.[21]

ship between General Electric and IBM. GE is one of the major suppliers of advanced semiconductor chips to IBM, and many of the chips are customized to IBM's own requirements. To meet IBM's specific needs, GE has had to make substantial investments in specialized assets that have little other value. As a consequence, GE is dependent on IBM and faces the risk that IBM will take advantage of this dependence to demand lower prices. Theoretically, IBM could back up its demand with the threat to switch to another supplier. However, GE reduced this risk by having IBM enter into a contractual agreement that committed IBM to purchase chips from GE for a ten-year period. In addition, IBM agreed to share in the costs of developing the customized chips, thereby reducing GE's investments in specialized assets. Thus, by publicly committing itself to a long-term contract and by putting some money into the development of the customized chips, IBM has essentially made a *credible commitment* to continue purchasing those chips from GE.

Maintaining Market Discipline   A company that has entered into a long-term relationship can become too dependent on an inefficient partner. Since it does not have to compete with other organizations in the marketplace for the company's business, the partner may lack the incentive to be cost efficient. Consequently, a company entering into a cooperative long-term relationship must be able to apply some kind of market discipline to its partner.

The company holds two strong cards. First, even long-term contracts are periodically renegotiated, generally every four to five years. Thus, a partner knows that if it fails to live up to its commitments, the company may refuse to renew the contract. Second, some companies engaged in long-term relationships with suppliers use a **parallel sourcing policy**—that is, they enter into a long-term contract with two suppliers for the same part (as is the practice at Toyota, for example).[23] This arrangement gives the company a hedge against a defiant partner, for each supplier knows that if it fails to comply with the agreement, the company can switch all its business to the other. This threat is rarely made explicit, since that would be against the spirit of building a cooperative long-term relationship. But the mere awareness of parallel sourcing serves to inject an element of market discipline into the relationship, signaling to suppliers that if the need arises, they can be replaced at short notice.

Summary   By establishing credible commitments or by taking hostages, companies may be able to use long-term contracts to realize much of the value associated with vertical integration, yet not have to bear the bureaucratic costs of formal vertical integration. As a general point, note that the growing importance of just-in-time inventory systems as a way of reducing costs and enhancing quality is increasing the pressure on companies to enter into long-term agreements in a wide range of industries. These agreements thus might become much more popular in the future. However, when such agreements cannot be reached, formal vertical integration may be called for.

■ Strategic Outsourcing and the Virtual Corporation

The opposite of vertical integration is **outsourcing** value creation activities to subcontractors. In recent years, there has been a clear move among many enterprises to outsource noncore activities.[24] This process typically begins with a company identifying those value creation activities that form the basis of its competitive advantage (its distinctive or core competencies). The idea is to keep performing these core value creation activities within the company. The remaining activities are then reviewed to see whether they can be performed more effectively and efficiently by independent suppliers. If they can, these activities are outsourced to those suppliers. The relationships between the company and the suppliers are then often structured as long-term contractual relationships, although in some instances it may make sense to manage relationships on the basis of competitive bidding. The term **virtual corporation** has been coined to describe companies that have pursued extensive strategic outsourcing.[25]

In recent years, Xerox has been relying heavily on strategic outsourcing. The company has determined that its distinctive competencies lie in the design and manufacture of photocopying systems. To reduce the cost of performing noncore value creation activities, Xerox has outsourced the responsibility for performing many of them to other companies. For example, Xerox has a $3.2 billion contract with Electronic Data Systems (EDS) under which EDS runs all Xerox's internal computer and telecommunications networks. As part of this relationship, 1,700 Xerox employees have been transferred to EDS. Since the relationship involves substantial investments in specialized assets on the part of EDS, Xerox has structured it as a long-term cooperative alliance.[26]

To use another example, NIKE, the world's largest manufacturer of athletic shoes, has outsourced all its manufacturing operations to Asian partners, while keeping its core product design and marketing capabilities in-house.

Strategic outsourcing offers several advantages.[27] First, by outsourcing a noncore activity to a supplier that is more efficient at performing that particular activity, the company may be able to reduce its own cost structure. Second, by outsourcing a noncore value creation activity to a supplier that has a distinctive competency in that particular activity, the company may also be able to better differentiate its final product. For example, Cincinnati Bell has developed a distinctive competency in the customer care function (customer care includes activating accounts, billing customers, and dealing with customer inquiries). Accordingly, several other telephone companies, including AT&T Wireless and MCI Long Distance, outsource their customer care function to Cincinnati Bell. Both companies believe that Cincinnati Bell can provide a better customer care service than they can. Thus, outsourcing helps AT&T Wireless and MCI Long Distance to better differentiate their service offering. A third advantage of strategic outsourcing is that it enables the company to concentrate scarce human, financial, and physical resources on further strengthening its core or distinctive competencies. Thus, AT&T Wireless can devote all its energies to building wireless networks, secure in the knowledge that Cincinnati Bell can look after the customer care functions. Finally, it has been argued that strategic outsourcing enables a company to be more flexible and responsive to changing market conditions. The belief is that, unencumbered by commitments to internal suppliers, a company can switch more easily between providers of noncore value creation activities in response to changing market conditions than can a comparable company that undertakes those activities itself.

The disadvantages of strategic outsourcing need to be recognized as well. By outsourcing an activity, a company loses both the ability to learn from that activity and the opportunity to transform it into a distinctive competency. Thus, although outsourcing customer care activities to Cincinnati Bell may make sense right now for AT&T Wireless, one potential problem with this strategy is that AT&T Wireless will fail to build a valuable internal competency in customer care. Ultimately, there is a risk that this lack may place AT&T Wireless at a competitive disadvantage, in regard to wireless providers that have such a competency, particularly if customer care becomes an important feature of competition in the marketplace. A further drawback of outsourcing is that the company may become too dependent on a particular supplier. In the long run, this may hurt the company if the performance of that supplier starts to deteriorate, or if the supplier starts to use its power to demand higher prices from the company. Another concern is that in its enthusiasm for strategic outsourcing, a company might go too far and outsource value creation activities that are central to the maintenance of its competitive advantage. By doing so, the company might well lose control over the future development of a competency, and as a result its performance might ultimately decline. None of this is meant to imply that strategic outsourcing should not be pursued, but it does indicate that managers should carefully weigh the pros and cons of the strategy before pursuing it.

DIVERSIFICATION

The third major option for a company when it is choosing business areas to compete in is diversification. There are two main types of diversification: related diversification and unrelated diversification. **Related diversification** is diversification into a new business activity that is linked to a company's existing business activity, or activities, by commonality between one or more components of each activity's value chain. Normally, these linkages are based on manufacturing, marketing, or technological commonalities. The diversification of Philip Morris into the brewing industry with the acquisition of Miller Brewing is an example of related diversification because there are marketing commonalities between the brewing and tobacco business (both are consumer product businesses in which competitive success depends on brand-positioning skills). **Unrelated diversification** is diversification into a new business area, which has no obvious connection with any of the company's existing areas.

In this section, we first consider how diversification can create value for a company, and then we examine some reasons why so much diversification apparently dissipates rather than creates value. We also take into account the bureaucratic costs of diversification. Finally, we discuss some of the factors that determine the choice between the strategies of related and unrelated diversification.

■ Creating Value Through Diversification

Most companies first consider diversification when they are generating financial resources *in excess* of those necessary to maintain a competitive advantage in their original, or core, business.[28] The question they must tackle is how to invest the excess resources in order to create value. The diversified company can create value in three main ways: (1) through superior internal governance, (2) by transferring competencies among businesses, and (3) by realizing economies of scope.

Superior Internal Governance   The term *internal governance* refers to the manner in which the top executives of a company manage (or "govern") subunits and individuals within the organization. In the context of a diversified company, governance has to do with the effectiveness of senior managers in managing businesses. Diversification can create value when the senior executives of a company manage the different business units within the organization so well that they perform better than they would if they were independent companies.[29] That is not easy to accomplish. However, certain senior executives seem to have developed a skill for managing businesses and pushing the heads of those business units to achieve superior performance. Jack Welch at General Electric, Bill Gates and Steve Balmer at Microsoft, and Dennis Kozlowski at Tyco International stand out as examples. (See Strategy in Action 9.3 for details of Kozlowski at Tyco.)

An examination of companies that succeed at creating value through superior internal governance reveals a number of shared features. First, the company's different business units tend to be placed into self-contained divisions. For example, Tyco has different divisions for its disposable medical products, security systems, and electronic components businesses. Second, these divisions tend to be managed by senior executives in a very decentralized fashion. The executives do not get involved in the day-to-day operations of such divisions; instead, they set challenging financial goals for each division, probe the general managers of each division about their strategy for attaining these goals, monitor divisional performance, and hold the general managers accountable for that performance. Third, these internal monitoring and control mechanisms are linked with progressive incentive pay systems, which reward divisional personnel for attaining or surpassing performance goals. Although this strategy sounds like a relatively easy one to pursue, in practice it seems to require very good senior executives to carry it through.

A variant of this approach might be characterized as an **acquisition and restructuring** strategy, which is based on the presumption that a company with superior internal governance systems can create value by acquiring inefficient and poorly managed enterprises and improving their efficiency. This strategy can be considered diversification because the acquired company does not have to be in the same industry as the acquiring company.

The efficiency of the acquired company can be improved by various means. First of all, the acquiring company usually replaces the top management team of the acquired company with a more aggressive top management team. Then, the new top management team is prompted to sell off any unproductive assets, such as executive jets and elaborate corporate headquarters, and to reduce staffing levels. It is also encouraged to intervene in the running of the acquired businesses to seek out ways of improving their efficiency, quality, innovativeness, and customer responsiveness. Furthermore, to motivate the new top management team and other employees of the acquired unit to undertake such actions, increases in their pay may be linked to improvement in the unit's performance. In addition, the acquiring company often establishes performance goals for the acquired company that cannot be met without significant improvements in operating efficiency. It also makes the new top management aware that failure to achieve performance improvements consistent with these goals within a given amount of time will probably result in their losing their jobs. This system of rewards and punishments established by the acquiring company gives the new managers of the acquired enterprise every incentive to look for ways of improving the efficiency of the unit under their charge. Tyco International, discussed in Strategy in Action 9.3, exemplifies this approach.

Transferring Competencies Companies that base their diversification strategy on transferring competencies seek out new businesses related to their existing

STRATEGY in ACTION

Tyco International

Tyco International is a diversified U.S. conglomerate with operations in a broad range of industries, including medical supplies, electronic security and electrical components, flow control products, fire suppression and detection equipment, and environmental services. Between 1992 and 1998, Tyco's revenues grew at an annual rate of 26 percent, increasing from $3.6 billion to $12.3 billion. During that period, the company's profits grew even faster, expanding by an average of 52 percent every year—from $95.3 million to $1.2 billion. The key to Tyco's revenue growth has been a series of major acquisitions, including those of U.S. Surgical, a medical supplies company, and AMP, the global leader in electronic connectors. The key to the company's profit growth has been the management of the existing and acquired businesses in a way that improves their profitability beyond what they would generate as independent companies. The man who deserves most of the credit for this performance is Dennis Kozlowski, the company's CEO, whom many supporters compare with General Electric's legendary CEO, Jack Welch.

Kozlowski has a very clear methodology for managing existing and acquired businesses. He keeps Tyco very decentralized. Headquarters consists of fewer than seventy employees, most of whom are engaged in companywide functions such as taxation, legal services and investor relations. Each operating division is a self-contained and operationally autonomous entity. The heads of Tyco's divisions are to be found where the operations are located. Perks for senior managers, such as first-class air travel, country club memberships, extensive severance packages, and the like, are an anathema. Reporting requirements are minimal and limited to regular reporting of key financial and strategic indicators. Most of the conversations between Kozlowski and the general managers of operating divisions are unstructured one-on-one debates about the strategy that the division is pursuing. Kozlowski's goal in these debates is to test the thinking of the managers—and to push them to think through strategic decisions in a thorough manner.

Kozlowski has married this decentralized structure with a very performance-oriented set of incentive systems. No bonuses are paid out to anyone at Tyco unless annual net income growth exceeds 15 percent. However, bonus payouts ramp up quickly for each increment above that minimum and are unlimited for general managers. Other managers can also receive bonuses that are multiples of their salary. Supervisors down at the plant level get cash or stock option grants that can be worth as much as 40 percent of their salary. Even hourly factory workers share in the bonus system, receiving two to three weeks of extra pay a year in bonuses if their unit exceeds performance targets. To make sure that people don't engage in game playing to hit or exceed their performance targets, Kozlowski does check profit contribution against cash flow to ascertain that managers are not fiddling with accounting concepts such as asset write-downs, inventories, or receivables to make their numbers look better.

In Kozlowski's view, combining decentralization with progressive incentives and strategic probing on the part of top management makes for a very liberating and transforming system which has enabled Tyco to unlock much of the value in its acquisitions. The system encourages employees to control costs and look for ways to grow revenues. As a result, operating margins have soared at many newly acquired enterprises. At the security company ADT, for example, which Tyco acquired in 1996, operating margins increased from 12 percent to 22 percent in just two years under the Tyco banner. At AMP, acquired in 1998, the goal is to increase operating margins from 9 percent to 18 percent in just two years.[30]

business by one or more value creation functions—for example, manufacturing, marketing, materials management, and research and development. They may want to create value by drawing on distinctive skills in one or more of their existing value creation functions in order to improve the competitive position of the new business. Alternatively, they may acquire a company in a different business area in the belief that some of the skills of the acquired company can improve the efficiency of their existing value creation activities. If successful, such competency transfers can lower the costs of value creation in one or more of a company's diversified businesses or enable one or more of these businesses to perform their value creation functions in a way that leads to differentiation and a premium price. The transfer of marketing skills by Philip Morris to Miller Brewing, discussed earlier, is perhaps one of the classic examples of how value *can* be created by competency transfers. Drawing on its marketing and brand-positioning skills, Philip Morris pioneered the introduction of Miller Lite, the product that redefined the brewing industry and moved Miller from number six to number two in the market.

For such a strategy to work, the competencies being transferred must involve activities that are important for establishing a competitive advantage. All too often companies assume that any commonality is sufficient for creating value. The acquisition of Hughes Aircraft by General Motors, made simply because autos and auto manufacturing were going electronic and Hughes was an electronics concern, demonstrates the folly of overestimating the commonalities among businesses. To date, the acquisition has failed to realize any of the anticipated gains for GM, whose competitive position has not improved.

In the technology arena, there is a group of companies that have made leveraging competencies a way of life. They include 3M, Hewlett-Packard, Canon, and Thermo Electron (which is profiled in the Closing Case). Each of these companies has developed certain skill sets (competencies), which they then have leveraged to produce new products in diversified areas. For example, Canon began as a manufacturer of cameras. To succeed in this market, Canon had to develop skills in precision mechanics, optics, and microelectronics. Subsequently, Canon has drawn on these skill sets to produce a wide range of products that address diverse markets, including fax machines, laser jet printers, scanners, and copiers. The value here arises from applying skills developed to support one business opportunity and applying them to another opportunity.[31]

Economies of Scope   The sharing of resources such as manufacturing facilities, distribution channels, advertising campaigns, and R&D costs by two or more business units gives rise to **economies of scope**. Each business unit that shares resources has to invest less in the shared functions.[32] For example, the costs of General Electric's advertising, sales, and service activities in major appliances are low because they are spread over a wide range of products. Similarly, one of the motives behind the 1998 merger of Citicorp and Travelers to form Citigroup was that the merger would let Travelers sell its insurance products and financial services through Citicorp's retail banking network. Put differently, the merger allows the expanded group to better utilize an existing asset—its retail banking network.

It is important to understand that economies of scope are related to economies of scale. For example, by producing the components for the assembly operations of two distinct businesses, a component-manufacturing plant may be able to operate at greater capacity, thereby realizing *economies of scale* in addition to economies of scope. Thus, a diversification strategy based on economies of scope can help a company attain a low-cost position in each of the businesses in which it operates. Diversification to realize economies of scope can therefore be a valid way of supporting the generic business-level strategy of cost leadership.

However, like competency transfers, diversification to realize economies of scope is possible only when there are significant commonalities between one or more of the value creation functions of a company's existing and new activities.

Moreover, managers need to be aware that the bureaucratic costs of coordination necessary to achieve economies of scope within a company often outweigh the value that can be created by such a strategy.[33] Consequently, the strategy should be pursued only when sharing is likely to generate a *significant* competitive advantage in one or more of a company's business units.

Procter & Gamble's disposable diaper and paper towel businesses offer one of the best examples of the successful realization of economies of scope. These businesses share the costs of procuring certain raw materials (such as paper) and developing the technology for new products and processes. In addition, a joint sales force sells both products to supermarket buyers, and both products are shipped by means of the same distribution system. This resource sharing has given both business units a cost advantage that has enabled them to undercut their less diversified competitors.[34]

■ Bureaucratic Costs and the Limits of Diversification

While diversification can create value for a company, it often ends up doing just the opposite. For example, in a study that looked at the diversification of thirty-three major U.S. corporations over a thirty-five-year time period, Michael Porter observed that the track record of corporate diversification has been dismal.[35] Porter found that most of the companies had divested many more diversified acquisitions than they had kept. He concluded that the corporate diversification strategies of most companies have dissipated value instead of creating it. More generally, a large number of academic studies support the conclusion that *extensive* diversification tends to depress rather than improve company profitability.[36]

One reason for the failure of diversification to achieve its aims is that all too often the *bureaucratic costs* of diversification exceed the value created by the strategy. The level of bureaucratic costs in a diversified organization is a function of two factors: (1) the number of businesses in a company's portfolio and (2) the extent of coordination required between the different businesses of the company in order to realize value from a diversification strategy.

Number of Businesses   The greater the number of businesses in a company's portfolio, the more difficult it is for corporate management to remain informed about the complexities of each business. Management simply does not have the time to process all the information needed to assess the strategic plan of each business unit objectively. This problem began to occur at General Electric in the 1970s. As the then CEO Reg Jones commented,

> I tried to review each plan in great detail. This effort took untold hours and placed a tremendous burden on the corporate executive office. After a while I began to realize that no matter how hard we would work, we could not achieve the necessary in-depth understanding of the 40-odd business unit plans.[37]

The information overload in extensively diversified companies may lead corporate-level management to base important resource allocation decisions on only the most superficial analysis of each business unit's competitive position. Thus, for example, a promising business unit may be starved of investment funds, while other business units receive far more cash than they can profitably reinvest in their operations. Furthermore, the lack of familiarity with operating affairs on the part of corporate-level management increases the chances that business-level managers might deceive corporate-level managers. For instance, business-unit managers might blame poor performance on difficult competitive conditions, even when it is the consequence of poor management. Thus, information overload can result in substantial inefficiencies within extensively diversified companies that cancel out the value created by diversification. These inefficiencies include the suboptimal allocation of cash resources within the company and a failure by corporate management to successfully encourage and reward aggressive profit-seeking behavior by business-unit managers.

The inefficiencies arising from information overload can be viewed as one component of the bureaucratic costs of extensive diversification. Of course, these costs can be reduced to manageable proportions if a company limits the scope of its diversification. Indeed, a desire to decrease these costs lay behind the 1990s and 1980s divestments and strategic concentration strategies of highly diversified conglomerates created in the 1960s and 1970s, such as Esmark, General Electric, ITT, Textron, Tenneco, and United Technologies. For example, under the leadership of Jack Welch, GE switched its emphasis from forty main business units to sixteen contained within three clearly defined sectors.

Coordination Among Businesses The coordination required to realize value from a diversification strategy based on competency transfers or economies of scope can also be a source of bureaucratic costs. Both the transfer of distinctive competencies and the achievement of economies of scope demand close coordination among business units. The bureaucratic mechanisms needed for this coordination give rise to bureaucratic costs.

A more serious matter, however, is that substantial bureaucratic costs can result from a firm's inability to identify the unique profit contribution of a business unit that is sharing resources with another unit in an attempt to realize economies of scope. Consider a company that has two business units—one producing household products (such as liquid soap and laundry detergent) and another producing packaged food products. The products of both units are sold through supermarkets. In order to lower the costs of value creation, the parent company decides to pool the marketing and sales functions of each business unit. Pooling allows the business units to share the costs of a sales force (one sales force can sell the products of both divisions) and gain cost economies from using the same physical distribution system. The organizational structure required to achieve this might be similar to that illustrated in Figure 9.4. The company is organized into three divisions: a household products division, a food products division, and a marketing division.

Although such an arrangement may create value, it can also give rise to substantial control problems and hence bureaucratic costs. For example, if the performance of the household products business begins to slip, identifying who is to be held accountable—the management of the household products division or the management of the marketing division—may prove difficult. Indeed, each may blame the other for poor performance: The management of the household products division might blame the marketing policies of the marketing division, and the management of the marketing division might blame the poor quality and high costs of products produced by the household products division. Although this kind of problem can be resolved if corporate management directly audits the affairs of both divisions, doing so is costly in terms of both the time and the effort that corporate management must expend.

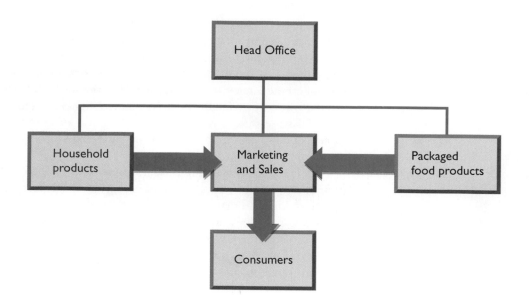

Now imagine the situation within a company that is trying to create value by sharing marketing, manufacturing, and R&D resources across ten businesses rather than just two. Clearly, the accountability problem could become far more severe in such a company. Indeed, the problem might become so acute that the effort involved in trying to tie down accountability might create a serious information overload for corporate management. When this occurs, corporate management effectively loses control of the company. If accountability cannot be sorted out, the consequences may include poor resource allocation decisions, a generally high level of organizational slack, and an inability by corporate management to encourage and reward aggressive profit-seeking behavior by business-unit managers. All these inefficiencies can be considered part of the bureaucratic costs of diversification to realize economies of scope.

Limits of Diversification   Thus, although diversification can create value for a company, it inevitably involves bureaucratic costs. As in the case of vertical integration, the existence of bureaucratic costs places a limit on the amount of diversification that can be profitably pursued. It makes sense for a company to diversify only as long as the value created by such a strategy exceeds the bureaucratic costs associated with expanding the boundaries of the organization to incorporate additional business activities.

It bears repeating that the greater the number of business units within a company and the greater the need for coordination among those business units, the larger the bureaucratic costs are likely to be. Hence a company that has twenty businesses, all of which are trying to share resources, incurs much larger bureaucratic costs than a company that has ten businesses, none of which is trying to share resources. The implications of this relationship are quite straightforward. Specifically, the greater the number of businesses already in a company's portfolio and the greater the need for coordination among those businesses, the more probable it is that the value created by a diversification move will be outweighed by the resulting increase in bureaucratic costs. Once this occurs, a profitable limit to the diversified scope of the enterprise will be reached. However, many companies continue to diversify past this limit, and their performance declines. To solve this problem, a company must reduce the scope of the enterprise through divestments. Strategy in Action 9.4 discusses a company—ICI—that overdiversified and subsequently had to divest itself of previously acquired businesses. In Chapter 10, we look at a number of other companies that have made the same mistake.

9.4 STRATEGY in ACTION

Diversification and Divestments at ICI

Formed in 1926 by the merger of a number of chemical concerns, Britain's Imperial Chemical Industries (ICI) has always been a diverse company, but in the 1980s ICI embarked on a new wave of diversified acquisitions aimed at expanding its presence in a broad range of high-value-added specialty chemicals operations. By the early 1980s, ICI was already involved in such markets as bulk chemicals, explosives, fertilizers, paints, commodity plastics, and pharmaceuticals. In 1985, it added to this portfolio the advanced plastics materials operations of the U.S. firm Beatrice Company, purchased for $750 million. In 1986, it bought Glidden, another American company, for $580 million. This acquisition made ICI the world's biggest paint manufacturer, and it was followed in 1987 by the acquisition of American Stauffer Chemical for $1.7 billion. ICI retained American Stauffer's specialty agrochemical business but sold off the rest. By the end of the 1980s, ICI was Britain's largest manufacturing enterprise and the world's fourth largest chemical company.

However, expanding the scope of ICI's business activities did little for the company's bottom line. In 1990, ICI saw its pretax profits drop by 36 percent to $1.7 billion on sales of $23 billion. Meanwhile, ICI's specialty chemicals operations did not do as well as the company had hoped. Paints and other specialty products had a profit margin of only 2.8 percent that year, compared with a margin of 5.7 percent in the company's more traditional bulk chemical operations.

In May 1991, these financial problems attracted the attention of Hanson PLC, one of Britain's best known corporate raiders. Hanson has thrived by purchasing conglomerates such as ICI and then breaking them up and selling the parts off to other companies, typically for a substantial profit. Hanson purchased a 4.1 percent stake

in ICI and threatened to make a full takeover bid. Although the full bid never materialized, and Hanson subsequently sold off its stake for a handsome profit, the threatened takeover started a debate in ICI as to the rationale behind its diversification strategy.

After much consideration, ICI's top management came to two main conclusions. First, although many of ICI's businesses were linked in some way to the chemical industry, there were far fewer synergies between its operations than management had initially thought. In the final analysis, ICI's top management concluded that there was little commonality between bulk chemicals and pharmaceuticals, between plastics and paint, and between explosives and advanced materials. Second, the company had become so diverse that top management found itself spread too thinly over too many different businesses. The company was simply unable to give the kind of top management attention and financial resources that many of its businesses required. In other words, the value created by the strategy of diversification was questionable, while the bureaucratic costs of managing a large and complex diversified entity were substantial. Thus, diversification at ICI dissipated rather than created value.

In 1992, ICI's top management decided to break the company into its constituent parts. The first stage in this process was completed in March 1993, when ICI was split into two parts. One part, which kept the name ICI, consists of industrial chemicals, paints, and explosives. According to the company, bits of this operation will probably be sold off in the future. The other part, which is now called Zeneca, has taken ICI's drugs, pesticides, seeds, and specialty chemicals businesses. ICI believes that the two companies will do better on their own than they did as part of a larger enterprise.[38]

■ Diversification That Dissipates Value

The failue of so much diversification to create value is also due to the fact that many companies diversify for the wrong reasons. This is particularly true of diversification to pool risks or to achieve greater growth, both of which are often given by company managers as reasons for diversification.

In the case of risk pooling, the benefits are said to come from merging imperfectly correlated income streams to create a more stable income stream. An example of risk pooling might be USX's diversification into the oil and gas industry in an effort to offset the adverse effects of cyclical downturns in the steel industry. According to advocates of risk pooling, the more stable income stream reduces the risk of bankruptcy and is in the best interests of the company's stockholders.

However, this simple argument ignores two facts. First, stockholders can easily eliminate the risks inherent in holding an individual stock by diversifying their own portfolios, and they can do so at a much lower cost than the company can. Thus, far from being in the best interests of stockholders, attempts to pool risks through diversification represent an unproductive use of resources. Second, research on this topic suggests that corporate diversification is not a very effective way to pool risks.[39] The business cycles of different industries are not easy to predict and in any case tend to be less important in terms of their impact on profits than a general economic downturn, which hits all industries simultaneously.

As for diversification to achieve greater growth, it is not a coherent strategy because growth on its own does not create value. Growth should be the *by-product*, not the objective, of a diversification strategy. However, companies sometimes diversify for reasons of growth alone, rather than to gain any well-thought-out strategic advantage. ITT under the leadership of Harold Geneen took this path. Geneen turned ITT from an international telecommunications company into a broadly based conglomerate comprising more than 100 separate businesses, with interests in such diverse areas as baking, car rental, defense electronics, fire hydrants, insurance, hotels, paper products, and telecommunications. The strategy had more to do with Geneen's desire to build an empire than with maximizing the company's value. After Geneen's departure in 1979, ITT's management divested many of the businesses acquired under his leadership in order to concentrate on insurance and financial services. This process reached its logical conclusion in 1996, when the remaining three businesses of ITT were spun off as independent entities.

■ Related Versus Unrelated Diversification

One issue a company must resolve is whether to diversify into totally new businesses or businesses related to its existing business by value-chain commonalities. The distinction is between related diversification and unrelated diversification. By definition, a related company can create value by resource sharing and by transferring competencies between businesses. It can also carry out some restructuring. In contrast, since there are no commonalities between the value chains of unrelated businesses, an unrelated company cannot create value by sharing resources or transferring competencies. Unrelated diversifiers can create value only by pursuing an acquisition and restructuring strategy.

Since related diversification can create value in more ways than unrelated diversification, one might think that related diversification should be the preferred strategy. In addition, related diversification is normally perceived as involving fewer risks because the company is moving into business areas about which top management has some knowledge. Probably because of those considerations, most diversified companies display a preference for related diversification.[40] However, research suggests that the average related company is, at best, only marginally more profitable than the average unrelated company.[41] How can this be, if related diversification is associated with more benefits than unrelated diversification?

The answer is quite simple. Bureaucratic costs arise from (1) the number of businesses in a company's portfolio and (2) the extent of coordination required among the different businesses in order to realize value from a diversification strategy. An unrelated company does not have to achieve coordination between business units and so it has to cope only with the bureaucratic costs that arise from the number of businesses in its portfolio. In contrast, a related diversified company has to achieve coordination between business units if it is to realize the value that comes from skill transfers and resource sharing. Consequently, it has to cope with the bureaucratic costs that arise *both* from the number of business units in its portfolio *and* from coordination among business units. Thus, although it is true that related diversified companies can create value in more ways than unrelated companies, they have to bear higher bureaucratic costs in order to do so. These higher costs may cancel out the higher benefits, making the strategy no more profitable than one of unrelated diversification. Table 9.1 lists the sources of value and costs for each strategy.

How then is a company to choose between these strategies? The choice depends on a comparison of the relative value added and the bureaucratic costs associated with each strategy. In making this comparison, it should be noted that the opportunities for creating value from related diversification are a function of the extent of commonalities between the skills required to compete in the company's core business and the skills required to compete in other industrial and commercial areas. Some companies' skills are so specialized that they have few applications outside the core businesses. For example, since the commonalities between steel making and other industrial or commercial operations are few, most steel companies have diversified into unrelated industries (LTV into defense contracting, USX into oil and gas). When companies have less specialized skills, they can find many more related diversification opportunities outside the core business. Examples include chemical companies (such as Dow Chemical and Du Pont) and electrical engineering companies (such as General Electric). Consequently, the opportunities available to them to create value from related diversification are much greater.

TABLE 9.1

Comparing Related and Unrelated Diversification

Strategy	*Ways of Creating Value*	*Source of Bureaucratic Costs*
Related diversification	• Restructuring • Transferring skills	• Number of businesses • Coordination among businesses • Economies of scope
Unrelated diversification	• Restructuring	• Number of businesses

Thus, it pays a firm to concentrate on related diversification when (1) the company's core skills are applicable to a wide variety of industrial and commercial situations and (2) the bureaucratic costs of implementation do not exceed the value that can be created through resource sharing or skill transfers. The second condition is likely to hold only for companies that are moderately diversified. At high levels of related diversification, the bureaucratic costs of additional diversification are likely to outweigh the value created by that diversification, and the strategy may become unprofitable.

By the same logic, it may pay a company to concentrate on unrelated diversification when (1) the company's core functional skills are highly specialized and have few applications outside the company's core business; (2) the company's top management is skilled at acquiring and turning around poorly run businesses (and many are not); and (3) the bureaucratic costs of implementation do not exceed the value that can be created by pursuing a restructuring strategy. However, the third condition is *unlikely* to hold for companies that are highly diversified. Thus, no matter whether a company pursues a related or an unrelated diversification strategy, the existence of bureaucratic costs suggests that there are very real limits to the profitable diversification of the company.

STRATEGIC ALLIANCES AS AN ALTERNATIVE TO DIVERSIFICATION

Diversification can be unprofitable because of the bureaucratic costs associated with implementing the strategy. One way of trying to realize the value associated with diversification, without having to bear the same level of bureaucratic costs is to enter into a strategic alliance with another company to start a new business venture.

In this context, strategic alliances are essentially agreements between two or more companies to share the costs, risks, and benefits associated with developing new business opportunities. Many strategic alliances are constituted as formal joint ventures, in which each party has an equity stake. Other alliances take the form of a long-term contract between companies in which they agree to undertake some joint activity that benefits both. Agreements to work together on joint R&D projects often take this form.

Strategic alliances seem to be a particularly viable option when a company wishes to create value from transferring competencies or sharing resources between diversified businesses in order to realize economies of scope. Alliances offer companies a framework within which to share the resources required to establish a new business. Alternatively, alliances enable companies to swap complementary skills to produce a new range of products. For example, consider the alliance between United Technologies and Dow Chemical to build plastic-based composite parts for the aerospace industry. United Technologies was already involved in the aerospace industry (it built Sikorsky helicopters), and Dow Chemical had skills in the development and manufacture of plastic-based composites. The alliance called for United Technologies to contribute its advanced aerospace skills and for Dow to contribute its skills in developing and manufacturing plastic-based composites to a joint venture in which each company would have a 50 percent equity stake. The joint venture was to undertake the task of developing, manufacturing, and marketing a new line of plastic-based composite parts for the aerospace industry. Through the alliance, both companies would become involved in new activities. They would, in short, be able to realize some of the benefits associated with related diversification without having to merge activities formally or bear the costs and risks of developing the new products on their own.

Bureaucratic costs have been reduced because neither Dow nor United Technologies actually expanded its own organization, nor did either company have to coordinate internal skill transfers. Rather, since incorporation, the joint venture has been operating as an independent company, and both Dow and United Technologies receive payment in the form of dividends.

Of course, there is a downside to such alliances. For one thing, profits must be split with an alliance partner, whereas with full diversification a company gets to keep all the profits. Another problem is that when a company enters into an alliance, it always runs the risk that it might give away critical know-how to its alliance partner, which might then use that know-how to compete directly with the company in the future. For example, having gained access to Dow's expertise in plastic-based composites, United Technologies might dissolve the alliance and produce these materials on its own. However, such risk can be minimized if Dow gets a *credible commitment* from United Technologies. By entering into a formal joint venture, rather than a more loosely structured alliance, United Technologies has given such a commitment because it has had to invest substantial amounts of capital. Thus, if United Technologies tried to produce plastic-based composites on its own, it would essentially be competing against itself.

SUMMARY OF CHAPTER

The purpose of this chapter is to examine the different corporate-level strategies that companies pursue in order to maximize their value. The chapter makes the following main points:

- Corporate strategies should *add value* to a corporation, enabling it, or one or more of its business units, to perform one or more of the value creation functions at a lower cost or in a way that allows differentiation and brings a premium price.

- Concentrating on a single business lets a company focus its total managerial, financial, technological, and physical resources and capabilities on competing successfully in just one area. It also ensures that the company sticks to doing what it knows best.

- The company that concentrates on a single business may be missing out on the opportunity to create value through vertical integration and/or diversification.

- Vertical integration can enable a company to achieve a competitive advantage by helping build

barriers to entry, facilitating investments in specialized assets, protecting product quality, and helping improve scheduling between adjacent stages in the value chain.

- The disadvantages of vertical integration include cost disadvantages if a company's internal source of supply is a high-cost one, and lack of flexibility when technology is changing fast or when demand is uncertain.

- Entering into a long-term contract can enable a company to realize many of the benefits associated with vertical integration without having to bear the same level of bureaucratic costs. However, to avoid the risks associated with becoming too dependent on its partner, a company entering into a long-term contract needs to seek a credible commitment from its partner or establish a mutual hostage-taking situation.

- The strategic outsourcing of noncore value creation activities may allow a company to lower its costs, better differentiate its product offering, and make better use of scarce resources, while also enabling it to respond rapidly to changing market conditions. However, strategic outsourcing may have a detrimental effect if the company outsources important value creation activities, or if it becomes too dependent on key suppliers of those activities.

✔ Diversification can create value through the pursuit of a restructuring strategy, competency transfers, and the realization of economies of scope.

✔ The bureaucratic costs of diversification are a function of the number of independent business units within the company and the extent of coordination between those business units.

✔ Diversification motivated by a desire to pool risks or achieve greater growth is often associated with the dissipation of value.

✔ Related diversification is preferred to unrelated diversification because it enables a company to engage in more value creation activities and is less risky. If a company's skills are not transferable, the company may have no choice but to pursue unrelated diversification.

✔ Strategic alliances can enable companies to realize many of the benefits of related diversification without having to bear the same level of bureaucratic costs. However, when entering into an alliance, a company does run the risk of giving away key technology to its partner. This risk can be minimized if a company gets a credible commitment from its partner.

DISCUSSION QUESTIONS

1. Why was it profitable for General Motors and Ford to integrate backward into component-parts manufacturing in the past, and why are both companies now trying to buy more of their parts from outside?

2. Under what conditions might concentration on a single business be inconsistent with the goal of maximizing stockholder wealth? Why?

3. General Motors integrated vertically in the 1920s, diversified in the 1930s, and expanded overseas in the 1950s. Explain these developments with reference to the profitability of pursuing each strategy. Why, do you think, vertical integration is normally the first strategy to be pursued after concentration on a single business?

4. What value creation activities should a company outsource to independent suppliers? What are the risks involved in outsourcing these activities?

5. When is a company likely to choose related diversification and when is it likely to choose unrelated diversification? Discuss with reference to an electronics manufacturer and an ocean shipping company.

Practicing Strategic Management

 SMALL-GROUP EXERCISE
Comparing Vertical Integration Strategies

Break up into a group of three to five people. Then read the following description of the activities of Quantum Corporation and Seagate Technologies, both of which manufacture computer disk drives. On the basis of this description, outline the pros and cons of a vertical integration strategy. Which strategy do you think makes most sense in the context of the computer disk drive industry?

Quantum Corporation and Seagate Technologies are both major producers of disk drives for personal computers and workstations. The disk drive industry is characterized by sharp fluctuations in the level of demand, intense price competition, rapid technological change, and product life cycles of no more than twelve to eighteen months. In recent years, Quantum and Seagate have pursued very different vertical integration strategies. Seagate is a vertically integrated manufacturer of disk drives, both designing and manufacturing the bulk of its own disk drives. Quantum specializes in design, while outsourcing most of its manufacturing to a number of independent suppliers, including, most importantly, Matsushita Kotobuki Electronics (MKE) of Japan. Quantum makes only its newest and most expensive products in-house. Once a new drive is perfected and ready for large-scale manufacturing, Quantum turns over manufacturing to MKE. MKE and Quantum have cemented their partnership over eight years. At each stage in designing a new product, Quantum's engineers send the newest drawings to a production team at MKE. MKE examines the drawings and is constantly proposing changes that make new disk drives easier to manufacture. When the product is ready for manufacture, eight to ten Quantum engineers travel to MKE's plant in Japan for at least a month to work on production ramp-up.

 STRATEGIC MANAGEMENT
Project Module 9

This module requires you to assess the vertical integration and diversification strategy being pursued by your company. With the information you have at your disposal, answer the questions:

1. How vertically integrated is your company? If your company does have vertically integrated operations, is it pursuing a strategy of taper or full integration?

2. How diversified is your company? If your company is already diversified, is it pursuing a related diversification strategy, an unrelated diversification strategy, or some mix of the two?

3. Assess the potential for your company to create value through vertical integration. In reaching your assessment, also consider the bureaucratic costs of managing vertical integration.

4. On the basis of your assessment in question 3, do you think your company should (a) outsource some operations that are currently performed in-house or (b) bring some operations in-house that are currently outsourced? Justify your recommendations.

5. Is your company currently involved in any long-term cooperative relationships with suppliers or buyers? If so, how are these relationships structured? Do you think that these relationships add value to the company? Why?

6. Is there any potential for your company to enter into (additional) long-term cooperative relationships with suppliers or buyers? If so, how might these relationships be structured?

7. Assess the potential for your company to create value through diversification. In reaching your assessment, also consider the bureaucratic costs of managing diversification.

8. On the basis of your assessment in question 7, do you think your company should (a) sell off some diversified operations or (b) pursue additional diversification? Justify your recommendations.

9. Is your company currently trying to transfer skills or realize economies of scope by entering into strategic alliances with other companies? If so, how are these relationships structured? Do you think that these relationships add value to the company? Why?

10. Is there any potential for your company to transfer skills or realize economies of scope by entering into (additional) strategic alliances with other companies? If so, how might these relationships be structured?

 ## ARTICLE FILE 9

Find an example of a company whose vertical integration or diversification strategy appears to have dissipated rather than created value. Identify why this has happened and what the company should do to rectify the situation.

EXPLORING THE WEB
Visiting Motorola

Visit the Web site of Motorola (http://www.motorola.com) and review the various business activities of the company. Using this information, answer the following questions:

1. To what extent is Motorola vertically integrated?

2. Does vertical integration help Motorola establish a competitive advantage, or does it put the company at a competitive disadvantage?

3. How diversified is Motorola? What diversification strategy is Motorola pursuing—related or unrelated diversification?

4. How, if at all, does Motorola's diversification strategy create value for the company's stockholders?

General Task   Search the Web for an example of a company that has pursued a diversification strategy. Describe that strategy and assess whether the strategy creates or dissipates value for the company.

CLOSING CASE

Thermo Electron

IN 1983, George Hatsopoulos, the founder and CEO of Thermo Electron, was puzzling over the future of the company. At the time, Thermo Electron was a $200-million-a-year manufacturer of energy and environmental equipment. Hatsopoulos noted that most new technology enterprises were not started by big companies. Rather, they were started by independent entrepreneurs working on their own. Yet most of these start-ups failed, crippled either by an inability to raise capital or by the high cost of capital they did raise. Hatsopoulos wondered whether there might be a way to combine the best of big and small companies.

The solution he came up with has been the diversification engine of Thermo Electron ever since. Thermo's strategy has been to draw on its R&D know-how to develop radically new products for discrete market niches not already addressed by the company or its subsidiaries. These products are then spun off as the core of stand-alone companies, in which Thermo holds a majority equity stake. Between 1983 and 1998, Thermo Electron produced twenty-three such spinoffs, all but three of which were publicly traded. In the process, Thermo diversified into a wide range of businesses, including power plants, artificial hearts, and laser hair removers, and grew its sales to more than $3.6 billion.

Although Thermo kept a majority stake in each spinoff, it would give the new companies far more freedom than a conventional subsidiary might have done. Day-to-day control of operations, along with aggressive stock option contracts, were typically handed over to each subsidiary. Each subsidiary also kept the capital that it raised through an initial public offering, using it in the way that made most sense for that particular business. To encourage the senior executives of spinoffs to couple their strategy with that of the entire family of companies, the stock options were split so that 40 percent were linked to the performance of the particular spinoff, 40 percent of them to that of the parent company, Thermo Electron, and 20 percent to that of its sibling.

Validating the strategy, the company's financial record of accomplishment during the 1983–1997 period was very strong, with the compound return to shareholders averaging 28 percent annually. However, the company has had its critics. Its multiplication of subsidiaries has given rise to a corporate structure that looks more like an intertwined strand of DNA than a typical chain of command. Such complexity can have a damping effect on share price. Some investors have complained that the corporate structure is to complicated. Having twenty-three public subsidiaries means producing twenty-three annual reports, and filing ninety-two quarterly earnings statements a year, a not inexpensive endeavor. The ongoing process of spinning off companies can spread scarce management and engineering talent too thinly over too many disparate businesses. In addition, bad performance by one subsidiary can cast a shadow over the whole company and adversely affect both revenues and share price. In July 1998, a Thermo subsidiary warned of lower-than-expected revenues, which would make just a small dent in the parent company's third-quarter profits—but Thermo's share price fell 17 percent. In addition, control by the parent can complicate any business that the spinoff may try to do with competitors of the parent or other subsidiaries.

In 1998 and 1999, the company's critics had a field day as Thermo Electron's performance began to slump. In the wake of a series of disappointed financial results, George Hatsopoulos admitted that the spinoff strategy may have been pushed too far and that the company had spun off business that did not meet its own criteria for growth and management depth. He also acknowledged that in

striving to boost their stock prices and realize stock option gains, some subsidiaries may have rushed to market products that were not adequately engineered or tested. The results have included slow sales and product recalls, which have reflected poorly on the entire corporation. In June 1999, Hatsopoulos stepped down as CEO. His replacement announced that the company would refocus its effort on a smaller number of subsidiaries—eleven—with the remainder being closed, sold, or consolidated into the larger entity. [42]

Case Discussion Questions

1. Historically, how has Thermo Electron's unusual diversification strategy created value for the company and its shareholders?

2. What are the significant drawbacks of this strategy?

3. Do the problems Thermo Electron experienced in 1998 and 1999 invalidate the strategy?

End Notes

1. W. H. Miller, "After 33 Years, New Leader," *Industry Week*, July 5, 1999, p. 41; "Subway to the Sky," *Economist*, August 23, 1997, p. 52; A. dePalma, "The Transportation Giant Up North," *New York Times*, December 25, 1988, p. 1.

2. T. J. Peters and R. H. Waterman, *In Search of Excellence* (New York: Harper & Row, 1982).

3. D. P. Hamilton, "Red-Faced Matsushita Gets Back to Basics," *Wall Street Journal*, April 10, 1995, p. A14.

4. K. R. Harrian, "Formulating Vertical Integration Strategies," *Academy of Management Review*, 9 (1984), 638–652.

5. This is the essence of the argument made by A. D. Chandler, *Strategy and Structure* (Cambridge, Mass.: MIT Press, 1962); the same argument is also made by Jeffrey Pfeffer and Gerald R. Salancik, *The External Control of Organizations*, (New York: Harper & Row, 1978). See also K. R. Harrigan, *Strategic Flexibility* (Lexington, Mass.: Lexington Books, 1985); K. R. Harrigan, "Vertical Integration and Corporate Strategy," *Academy of Management Journal*, 28 (1985), 397–425; and F. M. Scherer, *Industrial Market Structure and Economic Performance* (Chicago: Rand McNally, 1981).

6. This section is based on the transaction cost approach popularized by O. E. Williamson, *The Economic Institutions of Capitalism* (New York: Free Press, 1985).

7. Williamson, *Economic Institutions*. For recent empirical work that uses this framework, see L. Poppo and T. Zenger, "Testing Alternative Theories of the Firm: Transaction Cost, Knowledge-Based, and Measurement Explanations for Make or Buy Decisions in Information Services," *Strategic Management Journal*, 19 (1998), 853–878.

8. Williamson, *Economic Institutions*.

9. J. F. Hennart, "Upstream Vertical Integration in the Aluminum and Tin Industries," *Journal of Economic Behavior and Organization*, 9 (1988), 281–299.

10. Ibid.

11. A. D. Chandler, *The Visible Hand* (Cambridge, Mass.: Harvard University Press, 1977).

12. Julia Pitta, "Score One for Vertical Integration," *Forbes*, January 18, 1993, pp. 88–89.

13. J. White and N. Templin, "Harsh Regimen: A Swollen GM Finds It Hard to Stick with Its Crash Diet," *Wall Street Journal*, September 9, 1992, p. A1.

14. Harrigan, *Strategic Flexibility*, pp. 67–87.

15. For a detailed theoretical rationale for this argument see G. R. Jones and C. W. L. Hill, "A Transaction Cost Analysis of Strategy-Structure Choice," *Strategic Management Journal*, 9 (1988), 159–172.

16. K. Kelly, Z. Schiller, and J. Treece, "Cut Costs or Else," *Business Week*, March 22, 1993, pp. 28–29.

17. X. Martin, W. Mitchell, and A. Swaminathan, "Recreating and Extending Japanese Automobile Buyer-Supplier Links in North America," *Strategic Management Journal*, 16 (1995), 589–619; C. W. L. Hill, "National Institutional Structures, Transaction Cost Economizing, and Competitive Advantage," *Organization Science*, 6 (1995), 119–131.

18. Standard & Poor's "Autos—Auto Parts," *Industry Surveys*, June 24, 1993.

19. See J. Womack, D. Jones, and D. Roos, *The Machine That Changed the World* (New York: Rawson Associates, 1990); and J. Richardson, "Parallel Sourcing and Supplier Performance in the Japanese Automobile Industry," *Strategic Management Journal*, 14 (1993), 339–350.

20. R. Mudambi and S. Helper, "The Close but Adversarial Model of Supplier Relations in the U.S. Auto Industry," *Strategic Management Journal*, 19 (1998), 775–792.

21. J. H. Dyer, "How Chrysler Created an American Keiretsu," *Harvard Business Review* (July–August 1996), 42–56.

22. Williamson, *Economic Institutions*; see also J. H. Dyer, "Effective Inter-Firm Collaboration: How Firms Minimize Transaction Costs and Maximize Transaction Value," *Strategic Management Journal*, 18 (1997), 535–556.

23. Richardson, "Parallel Sourcing."

24. W. H. Davidow and M. S. Malone, *The Virtual Corporation* (New York: Harper & Row, 1992).

25. Ibid.

26. "The Outing of Outsourcing," November 25, 1995, pp. 57–58.

27. Davidow and Malone, *Virtual Corporation*; H. W. Chesbrough and D. J. Teece, "When is Virtual Virtuous? Organizing for Innovation," *Harvard Business Review* (January–February, 1996), 65–74.

28. This resource-based view of diversification can be traced to E. Penrose's seminal book, *The Theory of the Growth of the Firm* (Oxford: Oxford University Press, 1959).

29. See, for example, Jones and Hill, "A Transaction Cost Analysis"; and O. E. Williamson, *Markets and Hierarchies*, (New York: Free Press, 19), pp. 132–175.

30. J. R. Lang, "Tyco's Titan," *Barron's*, April 12, 1999, 27–32; M. Quan, "Connector Maker Eyes Expansion Under New Owner Tyco," *Electronic Engineering Times*, July 26, 1999; Web site (www.tycoint.com).

31. G. Hamel and C. K. Prahalad, *Competing for the Future* (Boston: Harvard Business School Press, 1994).

32. D. J. Teece, "Economies of Scope and the Scope of the Enterprise," *Journal of Economic Behavior and Organization*, 3 (1980), 223–247. For recent empirical work on this topic, see C. H. St. John and J. S. Harrison, "Manufacturing Based Relatedness, Synergy and Coordination," *Strategic Management Journal*, 20 (1999), 129–145.

33. For a detailed discussion, see C. W. L. Hill and R. E. Hoskisson, "Strategy and Structure in the Multiproduct Firm," *Academy of Management Review*, 12 (1987), pp. 331–341.

34. M. E. Porter, *Competitive Advantage: Creating and Sustaining Superior Performance* (New York: Free Press, 1985), p. 326.

35. M. E. Porter, "From Competitive Advantage to Corporate Strategy," *Harvard Business Review* (May–June 1987), 43–59.

36. For reviews of the evidence, see V. Ramanujam and P. Varadarajan, "Research on Corporate Diversification: A Synthesis," *Strategic Management Journal*, 10 (1989), 523–551; and G. Dess, J. F. Hennart, C. W. L. Hill, and A. Gupta, "Research Issues in Strategic Management," *Journal of Management*, 21 (1995), 357–392.

37. C. R. Christensen et al., *Business Policy Text and Cases* (Homewood, Ill.: Irwin, 1987), p. 778.

38. S. McMurray, "ICI Changes Tack and Splits Itself into Two Businesses," *Wall Street Journal*, March 5, sec. B, p. 3; "Hanson Likes the Look of ICI," *Economist*, May 18, 1991, pp. 69–70.

39. For evidence, see C. W. L. Hill, "Conglomerate Performance over the Economic Cycle," *Journal of Industrial Economics*, 32 (1983), 197–212; and D. T. C. Mueller, "The Effects of Conglomerate Mergers," *Journal of Banking and Finance*, 1 (1977), 315–347.

40. For example, see C. W. L. Hill, "Diversified Growth and Competition," *Applied Economics*, 17 (1985), 827–847; and R. P. Rumelt, *Strategy, Structure and Economic Performance* (Boston: Harvard Business School Press, 1974). See also Jones and Hill, "A Transaction Cost Analysis."

41. See H. K. Christensen and C. A. Montgomery, "Corporate Economic Performance: Diversification Strategy Versus Market Structure," *Strategic Management Journal*, 2 (1981), 327–343; and Jones and Hill, "A Transaction Cost Analysis"; G. Dess et al. "Research Issues"; C. W. L. Hill, "The Role of Headquarters in the Multidivisional Firm," in ed. R. Rumelt, D. J. Teece, and D. Schendel, *Fundamental Issues in Strategy Research* (Cambridge, Mass: Harvard Business School Press, 1994), pp. 297–321.

42. "Spinning It Out at Thermo Electron," *Economist*, April 12, 1997, pp. 57–58; B. Knestout, "Thermo Electron and All Its Children," *Kiplinger's Personal Finance Magazine,* 52 (October 1998), 36; R. Kerber, "Thermo Electron Announces Further Restructuring Moves; Will Take $450M Pretax Charge, Sell Units, Cut Jobs," *The Boston Globe*, May 25, 1999, p. D1.

10 Corporate Development: Building and Restructuring the Corporation

OPENING CASE

Changing the Focus at Hewlett-Packard

HEWLETT-PACKARD (HP) is a corporate legend. The company was established in 1938 by two Stanford University professors, William Hewlett and David Packard, who built their first product, an audio oscillator used to test sound, in a Palo Alto garage. Subsequently, the company grew to become the world's largest manufacturer of test and measurement equipment before diversifying into medical equipment in the early 1960s, and computers and peripherals in the mid 1960s. Along the way, former HP employees "seeded" numerous small start-ups, helping to create Silicon Valley.

By 1998, the company was generating revenues of $47 billion in a wide range of related businesses that spanned the test and measurement, medical equipment, and computer industries. However, the company had a problem: its growth rate had fallen below that of more focused computer industry rivals, such as Sun Microsystems and IBM. The perception in the industry was that HP was letting an opportunity pass it by to seize a leadership position in the fast-growing Internet arena. An internal business review undertaken by CEO Lewis Platt and his senior colleagues in late 1998 and early 1999 came to a similar conclusion. Over the previous two years, HP had tried to boost its profitability by a combination of job cuts and new-product introductions, such as a printer-copier hybrid, but to no avail. Platt and his colleagues decided that the key problem lay in a lack of corporate focus. The company had become too big and too diversified to respond effectively to new challenges, such as the challenge presented by the rapid emergence of the Internet. Moreover, because of problems in Asia and cutbacks in medical spending, the test and measurement and medical equipment businesses had performed quite poorly in recent years. Declining sales in these areas had dragged down the performance of the entire company and masked the respectable (although less than excellent) performance of the computer-related businesses. Moreover, senior managers found that they had to devote much of their time and energy to fixing problems in the non-computer businesses, to the detriment of the computer operation.

Platt decided that the time had come for bold action and a reconfiguration of the corporate portfolio. On March 3, 1999, the company announced that it would spin off its test and measurement and medical equipment businesses into an as yet unnamed independent company with revenues of around $7.6 billion. Once the spinoff is completed, HP will become a more focused manufacturer of printers, personal computers, and servers, a set of operations that have far more in common with each other than with those the company decided to spin off. The company reportedly also considered spinning off its printer business but decided against doing so because of the complex technology licensing arrangements that would be required between the computer and printer operations. At the same time, Platt announced that he would be stepping down as CEO and initiated a search for his successor.

This announcement was followed by another, in May 1999, that the core computer business would henceforth pursue a broad-based Internet-centric strategy, dubbed E-services. This strategy has two components. First, HP is developing software that will let companies search the Web for almost any service—for example, a database that will provide the best price on a microprocessor or the cheapest place to rent computing power to support a big on-line promotion. To gain the technology required for this strategy, HP has acquired a number of small Internet-based companies and invested more than $100 million in a dozen other Internet-related companies. Second, HP will move aggressively into the computer outsourcing market, renting out space and software on HP servers located at huge server farms, and providing technical support and consulting services. HP has calculated that many companies will prefer this approach, rather than invest millions of dollars to buy dedicated hardware and hire technical support staff. HP also plans to works closely with major software vendors, such as SAP and Oracle, and communications companies such as Qwest. For example, a partnership between HP, Qwest Communications, and SAP will charge mid-sized companies a few hundred dollars a month so that they can run SAP software on HP machines over Qwest's high-speed fiber optic communications network.

The final piece in the restructuring puzzle fell into place in July 1999, when HP announced that Carly Fiorina would become HPs new CEO. Prior to her appointment, Fiorina ran the global services division of Lucent. At forty-four, she is not only one of the youngest people to head one of the twenty largest public corporations in America, she is also the first woman to do so and the first outsider to head HP. Many viewed Fiorina's appointment as a clear indication that HP intended to break with its past and go full bore after opportunities in the Internet arena.[1]

OVERVIEW

Chapter 9 discusses the corporate-level strategies that companies pursue in order to become multibusiness enterprises. This chapter builds on Chapter 9 by addressing central issues of corporate development. **Corporate development** is concerned with identifying *which* business opportunities a company should pursue, *how* it should pursue those opportunities, and *how* it should exit from businesses that do not fit the company's strategic vision. The Opening Case touched on some of these issues. Historically, Hewlett-Packard's strategy has been to diversify into related areas through internal new ventures. This strategy took HP from test and measurement into medical equipment, then into computers, and finally into computer peripherals. More recently, senior executives at HP decided that they should pursue opportunities in the fast-developing Internet arena. They decided to pursue these opportunities through a combination of vehicles, including new-product offerings, acquisitions, and alliances, such as the alliance between HP, SAP, and Qwest Communications, described in the Opening Case. At the same time, they decided to restructure to company and spin off any business that could not be tied into the core computer and Internet operations and did not fit the new vision. The result was the spinoff of HP's test and measurement and medical equipment businesses.

In this chapter, we start by looking at approaches that companies can take to reviewing their portfolio of businesses. The objectives of such a review are to help determine which of its existing businesses a company should continue to participate in, which it should exit from, and whether the company should consider entering any new business areas. Then, we turn our attention to the different *vehicles*, or means, that companies use to enter and develop new business areas. The choice here is among acquisitions, internal new ventures, and joint ventures. **Acquisitions** involve buying an existing business; **internal new ventures** start a new business from scratch; and **joint ventures** typically establish a new business with the assistance of a partner.

The chapter closes with a look at restructuring and exit strategy. For reasons that we first touched on in Chapter 9 and discuss further in this chapter, during the 1970s and 1980s many companies became too diversified or too vertically integrated. In recent years, there has been a notable shift away from these strategies, with companies selling off many of their diversified activities and refocusing on their core businesses.

REVIEWING THE CORPORATE PORTFOLIO

A central concern of corporate development is identifying which business opportunities a company should pursue. A common starting point is to review a company's existing portfolio of businesses activities. As stated earlier, the purpose of such a review is to help determine which of its existing businesses a company should continue to participate in, which it should exit from, and whether the company should consider entering any new business areas. In this section, we discuss two different approaches to undertaking such a review.

The first approach utilizes a set of techniques known as "portfolio planning matrices."[2] Developed primarily by management consultants, these techniques are meant to compare the competitive position of the different businesses in a company's portfolio against each other on the basis of common criteria. Below, we argue that these techniques contain some flaws and that their application has produced some bad decisions.

The second approach we consider has been championed by Gary Hamel and C.K. Prahalad. This approach reconceptualizes a company as a portfolio of core competencies, as opposed to a portfolio of businesses.[3] Corporate development is oriented toward maintaining existing competencies, building new competencies, and leveraging competencies by applying them to new business opportunities. For example, according to Hamel and Prahalad, the success of a company such as 3M in creating new business has come from its ability to apply its core competency in adhesives to a wide range of businesses opportunities, from Scotch Tape to Post-it Notes.

■ Portfolio Planning

One of the most famous portfolio planning matrices is referred to as the growth-share matrix. This was developed by the Boston Consulting Group (BCG), principally to help senior managers identify the cash flow requirements of different businesses in their portfolio and to help determine whether they need to change the mix of businesses in the portfolio. We review the growth-share matrix in order to illustrate both the value and the limitations of portfolio planning tools. The growth-share matrix has three main steps: (1) dividing a company into strategic business units (SBUs); (2) assessing the prospects of each SBU and comparing them against each other by means of a matrix; and (3) developing strategic objectives for each SBU.

Identifying SBUs   According to the BCG, a company must create an SBU for each economically distinct business area that it competes in. Normally, a company defines its SBUs in terms of the product markets they are competing in. For example, Ciba Geigy, Switzerland's largest chemical and pharmaceutical company and an active user of portfolio planning techniques, has identified thirty-three strategic business units in areas such as proprietary pharmaceuticals, generic pharmaceuticals, seed treatments, reactive dyes, detergents, resins, paper chemicals, diagnostics, and composite materials (see Strategy in Action 10.1).

Assessing and Comparing SBUs   Having defined SBUs, top managers then assess each according to two criteria: (1) the SBU's relative market share and (2) the growth rate of the SBU's industry. **Relative market share** is the ratio of an SBU's market share to the market share held by the largest rival company in its industry. If SBU X has a market share of 10 percent and its largest rival has a market share of 30 percent, SBU X's relative market share is 10/30, or 0.3. Only if an SBU is a market leader in its industry will it have a relative market share greater than 1.0. For example, if SBU Y has a market share of 40 percent and its largest rival has a market share of 10 percent, then SBU Y's relative market share is 40/10, or 4.0. According to the BCG, market share gives a company cost advantages from economies of scale and learning effects. An SBU with a relative market share greater than 1.0 is assumed to be farther down the experience curve and therefore to have a significant cost advantage over its rivals. By similar logic, an SBU with a relative market share smaller than 1.0 is assumed to lack the scale economies and low-cost position of the market leader.

The growth rate of an SBU's industry is assessed according to whether it is faster or slower than the growth rate of the economy as a whole. BCG's position is that high-growth industries offer a more favorable competitive environment and better long-term prospects than slow-growth industries.

Given the relative market share and industry growth rate for each SBU, management compares SBUs against each other by way of a matrix similar to that illustrated in Figure 10.1. The horizontal dimension of this matrix measures relative market share; the vertical dimension measures industry growth rate. The center of each circle corresponds to the position of an SBU on the two dimensions of the matrix. The size of each circle is proportional to the sales revenue generated by each business in the company's portfolio. The bigger the circle, the larger is the SBU's revenue relative to total corporate revenues.

Portfolio Planning at Ciba-Geigy

Ciba-Geigy is a large Swiss-based company with interests in chemicals and pharmaceuticals and annual revenues in excess of $25 billion. Since 1984, the company has been using portfolio planning techniques as a tool to assist corporate management in the process of strategic planning, resource allocation, and performance assessment. Although the company looked closely at the growth-share matrix devised by the Boston Consulting Group, it decided to develop a customized portfolio planning tool that would better suit its needs.

Ciba had divided the company into thirty-three separate strategic business units, such as proprietary pharmaceuticals, generic pharmaceuticals, seed treatments, reactive dyes, detergents, resins, paper chemicals, diagnostics, and composite materials. At Ciba, each SBU is assessed according to two main criteria: the likely future growth rate of its industry, and the competitive position of the SBU relative to its rivals. In deriving a measure of competitive position, Ciba looks at relative market share, but unlike the original BCG growth-share matrix, the company also considers a range of other competitive factors, such as cost structure, product quality, core competencies, and relative profitability.

Using these data, Ciba classifies its SBUs into one of five categories: development, growth, pillar, niche, and core. Development businesses are in the early stage of their life cycle and usually require substantial R&D investments. Growth businesses are competitive SBUs based in large and/or growing markets. Ciba will commit substantial funds in order to build the competitive position of such a business. Pillar businesses are market leaders that are based in attractive industries, such as Ciba's pharmaceutical businesses. They typically receive a high priority in R&D funding and resource allocation in order to maintain their pillar status. Niche businesses are market leaders that are constrained because they serve a relatively small market (Ciba's animal health business, for example, was defined as a niche business). Core businesses are large SBUs that compete in mature industries (Ciba's dyes, polymers, and pigments SBUs are all classified as core). Core businesses are seen as generating excess cash that can be used to fund investments elsewhere within the company.

What is interesting about Ciba's approach is that these classifications are not taken as gospel. The company is quite willing to violate the investment rules associated with the different categories if that seems appropriate. For example, in 1994 Ciba committed itself to major new investments in its pigments SBU to upgrade its U.S. production facilities, even though its portfolio planning categories suggest that this was a mature low-growth core business that should be used to generate funds for investment elsewhere within the company. Ciba's view appears to be that the utility of portfolio planning lies not so much in its role as a guide to resource allocation, as it does in helping top managers set reasonable strategic expectations and objectives for the different SBUs within the company. Thus, Ciba's corporate managers will assign very different strategic and financial objectives to SBUs classified as growth businesses compared with those classified as pillars. Pillars would be expected to earn a higher return on assets, generate greater cash flow, and contribute more of their earnings to the corporate bottom line than a growth business. By the same token, however, growth businesses would be expected to grow their revenues and earnings at a faster rate than pillars. The performance of managers running these SBUs is then compared against these different expectations.[4]

The matrix is divided into four cells. SBUs in cell 1 are defined as **stars**, in cell 2 as **question marks**, in cell 3 as **cash cows**, and in cell 4 as **dogs**. BCG argues that these different types of SBUs have different long-term prospects and different implications for cash flows.

■ *Stars*. The leading SBUs in a company's portfolio are the stars. Stars have a high relative market share and are based in high-growth industries. Accordingly, they offer attractive long-term profit and growth opportunities.

FIGURE 10.1

The BCG Matrix

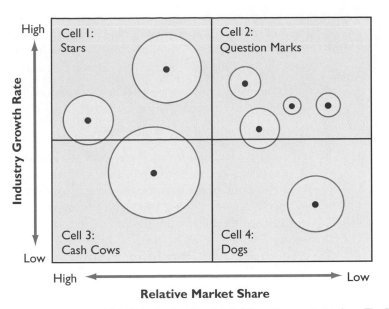

Source: Perspectives, No. 66, "The Product Portfolio." Adapted by permission from The Boston Consulting Group, Inc., 1970.

■ *Question marks.* Question marks are SBUs that are relatively weak in competitive terms (they have low relative market shares) but are based in high-growth industries and thus may offer opportunities for long-term profit and growth. A question mark can become a star if nurtured properly. To become a market leader, a question mark requires substantial net injections of cash; it is cash hungry. The corporate head office has to decide whether a particular question mark has the potential to become a star and is therefore worth the capital investment necessary to achieve stardom.

■ *Cash cows.* SBUs that have a high market share in low-growth industries and a strong competitive position in mature industries are cash cows. Their competitive strength comes from being farthest down the experience curve. They are the cost leaders in their industries. BCG argues that this position enables such SBUs to remain very profitable. However, low growth implies a lack of opportunities for future expansion. As a consequence, BCG argues that the capital investment requirements of cash cows are not substantial, and thus they are depicted as generating a strong positive cash flow.

■ *Dogs.* SBUs that are in low-growth industries but have a low market share are dogs. They have a weak competitive position in unattractive industries and thus are viewed as offering few benefits to a company. BCG suggests that such SBUs are unlikely to generate much in the way of a positive cash flow and indeed may become cash hogs. Though offering few prospects for future growth in returns, dogs may require substantial capital investments just to maintain their low market share.

Strategic Implications The objective of the BCG portfolio matrix is to identify how corporate cash resources can best be used to maximize a company's future growth and profitability. BCG recommendations include the following:

■ The cash surplus from any cash cows should be used to support the development of selected question marks and to nurture stars. The long-term objective is to consolidate the position of stars and to turn favored question marks into stars, thus making the company's portfolio more attractive.

■ Question marks with the weakest or most uncertain long-term prospects should be divested to reduce demands on a company's cash resources.

■ The company should exit from any industry where the SBU is a dog.

■ If a company lacks sufficient cash cows, stars, or question marks, it should consider acquisitions and divestments to build a more balanced portfolio. A portfolio should contain enough stars and question marks to ensure a healthy growth and profit outlook for the company and enough cash cows to support the investment requirements of the stars and question marks.

■ Limitations of Portfolio Planning

Though portfolio planning techniques may sound reasonable, if we take the BCG matrix as an example, there at least four main flaws. First, the model is simplistic. An assessment of an SBU in terms of just two dimensions, market share and industry growth, is bound to be misleading, for a host of other relevant factors should be taken into account. Although market share is undoubtedly an important determinant of an SBU's competitive position, companies can also establish a strong competitive position by differentiating their product to serve the needs of a particular segment of the market. A business having a low market share can be very profitable and have a strong competitive position in certain segments of a market. The auto manufacturer BMW is in this position, yet the BCG matrix would classify BMW as a dog because it is a low-market-share business in a low-growth industry. Similarly, industry growth is not the only factor determining industry attractiveness. Many factors besides growth determine competitive intensity in an industry and thus its attractiveness.

Second, the connection between relative market share and cost savings is not as straightforward as BCG suggests. High market share does not always give a company a cost advantage. In some industries—for example, the U.S. steel industry—low-market-share companies using a low-share technology (minimills) can have lower production costs than high-market-share companies using high-share technologies (integrated mills). The BCG matrix would classify minimill operations as the dogs of the U.S. steel industry, whereas in fact their performance over the last decade has characterized them as star businesses.

Third, a high market share in a low-growth industry does not necessarily result in the large positive cash flow characteristic of cash cow businesses. The BCG matrix would classify General Motors' auto operations as a cash cow. However, the capital investments needed to remain competitive are so substantial in the auto industry that the reverse is more likely to be true. Low-growth industries can be very competitive, and staying ahead in such an environment can require substantial cash investments.

To be fair, several companies and management consulting enterprises have recognized the limitations of the BCG approach and developed alternative approaches that address the weaknesses noted above. For example, Ciba-Geigy, whose use of portfolio planning techniques is reviewed in Strategy in Action 10.1, has devised a planning approach that recognizes a wider range of competitive factors needed to be taken into consideration when assessing an SBU's position. Similarly, the management consultants McKinsey and Company developed a portfolio matrix that uses a much wider range of factors to assess the attractiveness of an industry in which an SBU competes, as well as the competitive position of an SBU (see Figure 10.2). Included in the assessment of industry attractiveness are factors such as industry size, growth, cyclicality, competitive intensity, and technological dynamism. The assessment of competitive position relies on factors such as market share and an SBU's relative position with regard to production costs, product quality, price competitiveness, distribution, and innovation.

Although there is no doubt that the approaches adopted by Ciba and McKinsey represent a distinct improvement over the original BCG model, in general all portfolio planning techniques suffer from significant flaws. Most important, they fail to pay attention to the source of value creation from diversification. They treat business units as independent, whereas in fact they may be linked by the need to transfer skills and competencies or to realize economies of scope. Moreover, portfolio planning approaches tend to trivialize the process of managing a large diversified company. They suggest that success is simply a matter of putting together the right portfolio of businesses, whereas in reality it comes from managing a diversified portfolio to *create value*, whether by leveraging distinctive competencies across business units, by sharing resources to realize economies of scope, or by achieving

FIGURE 10.2

The McKinsey Matrix

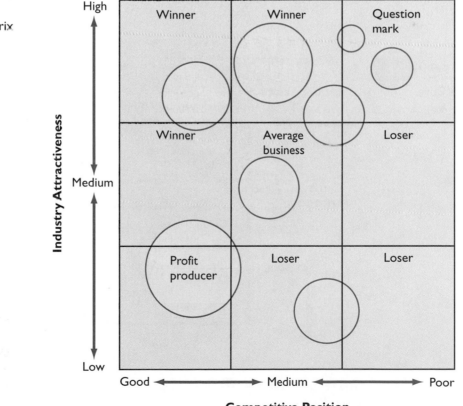

superior governance. In diverting top management's attention away from these vital tasks and legitimizing underinvestment in core business areas designated as cash cows, portfolio management techniques may have done a great disservice to the corporations that adopted them.

■ The Corporation as a Portfolio of Core Competencies

According to Gary Hamel and C.K. Prahalad, a more fruitful approach toward identifying the different business opportunities open to a company is to reconceptualize the company as a portfolio of core competencies—as opposed to a portfolio of businesses—and then consider how those competencies might be developed to sustain existing businesses and leveraged to create new business opportunities.[5] As you may recall, we introduce the concept of a *competency* in Chapter 4, when we discuss how distinctive competencies can form the bedrock of a company's competitive advantage. According to Hamel and Prahalad, **a core competency** is a central *value-creating* capability of an organization—a core skill. They argue, for example, that Canon, the Japanese concern best known for its cameras and photocopiers, has core competencies in precision mechanics, fine optics, microelectronics, and electronic imaging.

Hamel and Prahalad maintain that identifying *current* core competencies is the first step to take for a company engaged in the process of deciding which business opportunities to pursue. Once a company has identified its core competencies, Hamel and Prahalad advocate using a matrix similar to that shown in Figure 10.3 to establish an agenda for building and leveraging core competencies to create new business opportunities. This matrix distinguishes between existing and new compe-

FIGURE 10.3

Establishing a Core Competency Agenda

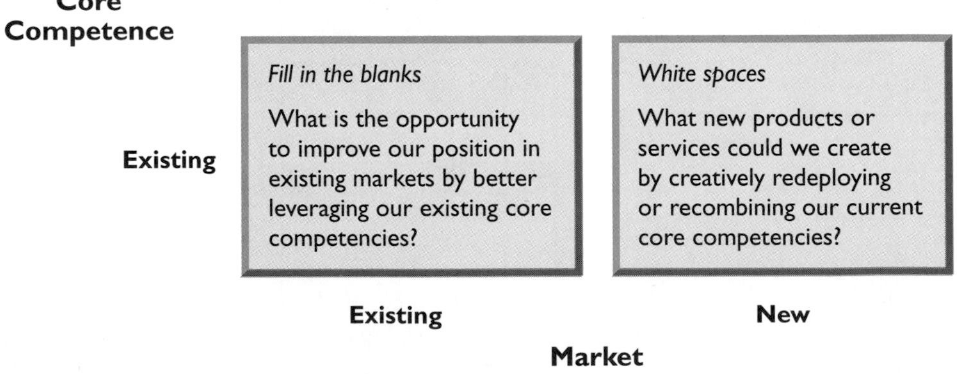

Core Competence

New

Premier plus 10

What new core competencies will we need to build to protect and extend our franchise in current markets?

Mega-opportunities

What new core competencies would we need to build to participate in the most exciting markets of the future?

Existing

Fill in the blanks

What is the opportunity to improve our position in existing markets by better leveraging our existing core competencies?

White spaces

What new products or services could we create by creatively redeploying or recombining our current core competencies?

Existing   **New**

Market

Source: G. Hamel and C. K. Prahalad, *Competing for the Future* (Cambridge, Mass.: Harvard Business School Press, 1994), p. 227.

tencies, and between existing and new-product markets. Each quadrant in the matrix has a title, the strategic implications of which are discussed in the following paragraphs.

Fill in the Blanks The lower left quadrant represents the company's existing portfolio of competencies and products. Ten years ago, for example, Canon had competencies in precision mechanics, fine optics, and microelectronics and was active in two basic businesses—producing cameras and photocopiers. The competencies in precision mechanics and fine optics were used in the production of basic mechanical cameras. These two competencies plus an additional competence in microelectronics were required to produce plain-paper copiers. The phrase *fill in the blanks* refers to the opportunity to improve the company's competitive position in existing markets by leveraging existing core competencies. So, for example, Canon was able to improve the position of its camera business by leveraging microelectronics skills from its copier business to support the development of cameras with electronic features, such as autofocus capabilities.

Premier Plus 10 The upper left quadrant is referred to as premier plus 10. The term is meant to suggest another important question: What new core competencies must be built today to ensure that the company remains a *premier* provider of its existing products in *ten* years' time? Canon, for example, decided that in order to maintain a competitive edge in its copier business, it was going to have to build a new competency in electronic imaging (which refers to the ability to capture and store images in a digital format, as opposed to using more traditional, chemical-based photographic processes). In turn, this new competency has subsequently helped Canon to extend its product range to include laser copiers, color copiers, and digital cameras.

White Spaces The lower right quadrant is referred to as white spaces. The question to be addressed here is how best to fill the white space by creatively redeploying or recombining current core competencies. In Canon's case, the company has been able to recombine its established core competencies in precision mechanics and fine optics and its recently acquired competency in electronic imaging to enter the market for fax machines and bubble jet printers.

Mega-Opportunities Opportunities represented by the upper right quadrant of Figure 10.3 do not overlap with the company's current market position, or its current competency endowment. Nevertheless, a company may choose to pursue such opportunities if they are seen to be particularly attractive, significant, or relevant to the company's existing business opportunities. For example, back in 1979 Monsanto was primarily a manufacturer of chemicals, including fertilizers. However, the company saw that there were enormous opportunities in the emerging field of biotechnology. Specifically, senior research scientists at Monsanto felt that it might be possible to produce genetically engineered crop seeds that would produce their own "organic" pesticides. That year, the company began a massive investment, which ultimately amounted to several hundred of millions of dollars, to build a world-class competency in biotechnology. This investment was funded by cash flows generated by Monsanto's core chemical operations. The investment started to bear fruit in the mid 1990s, when Monsanto introduced a series of genetically engineered crop seeds, including Bollgard, a cotton seed that is resistant to many common pests, including the bollworm, and Roundup resistant soybean seeds (Round up is a herbicide produced by Monsanto).[6]

Like more traditional tools for reviewing the corporate portfolio, such as the portfolio planning matrices discussed earlier, the framework advocated by Hamel and Prahalad helps to identify business opportunities and has clear implications for allocating resources (as exemplified by the Monsanto case just discussed). However, the great advantage of Hamel and Prahalad's framework is that it focuses explicitly on how a company can *create value* by building new competencies or by recombining existing competencies to enter new business areas (as Canon did with fax machines and bubble jet printers). Whereas traditional portfolio tools treat businesses as independent, Hamel and Prahald's framework recognizes the interdependencies between businesses and focuses on the opportunities for creating value by building and leveraging competencies. In this sense, their framework is far more "strategic" than the frameworks once advocated by the Boston Consulting Group and others like them.

■ Entry Strategy

Having reviewed the different businesses in the company's portfolio, corporate management might decide to enter a new business area, as Monsanto did when it decided in 1979 to enter the biotechnology field. There are three vehicles that companies use to enter new business areas: internal ventures, acquisition, and joint ventures. In the next three sections, we review the benefits and risks associated with each entry mode and consider how those risks can be minimized. Then we discuss the factors that influence the choice among these three modes in a given situation.

INTERNAL NEW VENTURING

■ Attractions of Internal New Venturing

Internal new venturing is typically employed as an entry strategy when a company possesses a set of valuable competencies (resources and capabilities) in its existing businesses that can be leveraged or recombined to enter the new business area. As a rule, science-based companies that use their technology to create market opportunities in related areas tend to favor internal new venturing as an entry strategy. Du Pont, for example, has created whole new markets with products such as cellophane, nylon, Freon, and Teflon—all internally generated innovations. Another company, 3M, has a near-legendary knack for shaping new markets from internally generated ideas. Hewlett-Packard moved into computers and peripherals by creating internal new ventures. Intel offers yet another example of a company that has leveraged its core competencies to enter new markets. Intel started off as a manufacturer of memory devices (DRAMs), but it subsequently built on its core competencies in semiconductor design and fabrication to enter the microprocessor business, and then the flash memory business. Interestingly enough, Intel exited the DRAM business in the late 1980s, but it remains the world's largest producer of microprocessors and flash memories.

Even if it lacks the competencies required to compete in a new business area, a company may pursue an internal venturing strategy when it is entering a newly emerging or embryonic industry in which there are no established players that possess the competencies required to compete in that industry. In such a case, the option of acquiring an established enterprise possessing those competencies is ruled out and the company may have no choice but to enter through an internal new venture. That was the position Monsanto found itself in when, in 1979, it contemplated entering the biotechnology field to produce herbicides and pest-resistant crop seeds. The biotechnology field was young at that time, and there were no incumbent companies focused on applying biotechnology to agricultural products. Accordingly, Monsanto established an internal new venture to enter the field, even though at the time it lacked the required competencies. Indeed, Monsanto's whole venturing strategy was developed around the notion that it needed to build competencies ahead of other potential competitors, thereby gaining a strong competitive lead in this newly emerging field.

■ Pitfalls of Internal New Venturing

Despite the popularity of the internal new venture strategy, its failure is reportedly very high. The evidence on the failure rate of new products indicates the scope of the problem, since most internal new ventures are associated with new product offerings. According to the evidence, somewhere between 33 and 60 percent of all new products that reach the marketplace fail to generate an adequate economic return.[7] Three reasons are often given to explain the relatively high failure rate of internal new ventures: (1) market entry on too small a scale, (2) poor commercialization of the new venture product, and (3) poor corporate management of the venture process.[8]

Scale of Entry   Research suggests that *on average* large-scale entry into a new business is often a critical precondition of new-venture success. Although in the short run, large-scale entry means significant development costs and substantial losses, in the long run (which can be as long as five to twelve years, depending on the industry) it brings greater returns than small-scale entry.[9] The reasons for this include the ability of large-scale entrants to more rapidly realize scale economies, build brand loyalty, and gain access to distribution channels, all of which increase the probability that a new venture will succeed. In contrast, small-scale entrants may find themselves handicapped both by high costs, due to a lack of scale economies, and by a lack of market presence, which limits their ability to build brand loyalties and gain access to distribution channels. These scale effects are probably particularly significant when a company is entering an established industry, where incumbent companies have scale economies, brand loyalties, and access to distribution channels, and the new entrant often has to match these in order to succeed.

Figure 10.4 plots the relationships among scale of entry, profitability, and cash flow over time for successful small-scale and large-scale ventures. The figure shows that successful small-scale entry incurs lower initial losses, but in the long run large-scale entry generates greater returns. However, perhaps because of the costs of large-scale entry and the potential losses if the venture fails, many companies prefer a small-scale entry strategy. Acting on this preference can be a mistake, for the company fails to build up the market share necessary for long-term success.

FIGURE 10.4

Scale of Entry, Profitability, and Cash Flow

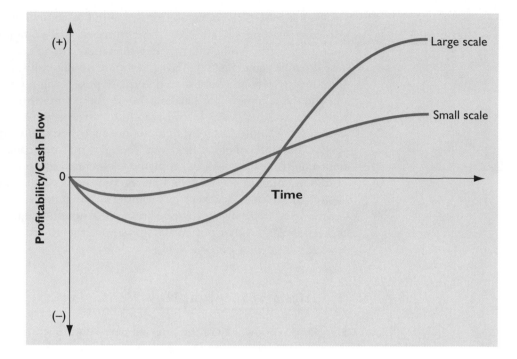

Commercialization   Many internal new ventures are high-technology operations. To be commercially successful, science-based innovations must be developed with market requirements in mind. Many internal new ventures fail when a company ignores the basic needs of the market. A company can become blinded by the technological possibilities of a new product and fail to analyze market opportunities properly. Thus, a new venture may fail because of a lack of commercialization or because it is marketing a technology for which there is no demand. One of the most dramatic new venture failures in recent years, that of the Iridium satellite communications system developed by Motorola, is discussed in Strategy in Action 10.2. As you will see, Iridium failed because, even though the technology was impressive, the market demand did not materialize and may never have been there in the first place.

The desktop computer marketed by NeXT, the company started by the founder of Apple, Steven Jobs, is another example of a new venture that miscarried. The NeXT system failed to gain market share because the computer incorporated an array of expensive technologies that consumers simply did not want—such as optical disk drives and hi-fi sound. The optical disk drives, in particular, turned customers off because they made it difficult to switch work from a PC with a floppy drive to a NeXT machine with an optical drive. In other words, NeXT failed because its founder was so dazzled by leading-edge technology that he ignored customer needs.

Poor Implementation   Managing the new-venture process raises difficult organizational issues.[11] Although we deal with the specifics of implementation in later chapters, we must note some of the most common mistakes here.[12] The shotgun approach of supporting many different internal new-venture projects can be a major error, for it places great demands on a company's cash flow and can result in the best ventures being starved of the cash they need for success.

STRATEGY in ACTION

10.2

Iridium Falls to Earth

The Iridium project was dreamed up by Motorola engineers back in the 1980s. The project was breathtaking in its scope. It called for sixty-six communications satellites to be placed in an orbital network. In theory, this network of flying telecommunications switches would enable anyone with an Iridium satellite phone to place and receive calls, no matter where the individual was on the planet—deep in the urban canyons of New York, at the bottom of the Grand Canyon, or in the most remote parts of the Amazon jungle. Motorola's CEO, Christopher Galvin, called the project the eighth wonder of the world. Five billion dollars later, Iridium went live on November 1, 1998. Motorola had spun the company off a few years earlier but still held 18 percent of the equity and several lucrative supply contracts with Iridium. Nine months later, Iridium declared bankruptcy after defaulting on scheduled debt service payments. Although Iridium had received 1.5 million inquiries from people interested in the service, only 20,000 subscribers had signed on, compared with a first-year target of 500,000. With so few customers, Iridium could not generate the income required to service its debt payments.

To its critics, the Iridium project was a classic case of a company being so blinded by the promise of a technology that it ignored market realities. The project had several serious shortcomings that limited its market acceptance. First, the phones themselves were large and heavy by current cell phone standards, weighing more than a pound. They were difficult to use and came with all sorts of attachments that perplexed many customers. Call clarity was poor and despite the "can be used anywhere" marketing theme, the phones could not be used inside cars or buildings—the favorite hangouts of the busy globetrotting executives at whom the service was aimed. Second, the service was expensive. The phones themselves cost $3,000 each, and airtime ranged from $4 to $9 per minute—placing the service way out of the reach of a mass market. Third, Iridium had a very poor sales and distribution system. Someone wishing to purchase a phone and sign up for the service would have had a hard time finding a distributor. And finally, the wide acceptance of a much cheaper and more convenient substitute, the conventional cell phone, limited the need for the Iridium Satellite phone. True, because of incompatible standards and limited coverage, cell phones cannot be used everywhere but nowadays an executive visiting a foreign country can easily rent a cell phone at the airport, and it will suffice for most, if not all, of his or her needs. Given this, who would pay $3,000 for the privilege of owning a phone the size and weight of a brick that would not work in places where cell phones do work—such as buildings and cars?[10]

Another common mistake is failure by corporate management to set the strategic context within which new-venture projects should be developed. Simply allowing a team of research scientists to do research in their favorite field may produce novel results, but these results may have little strategic or commercial value. It is necessary to be very clear about the strategic objectives of the venture and to understand how the venture will seek to establish a competitive advantage.

Failure to anticipate the time and costs involved in the venture process constitutes a further mistake. Many companies have unrealistic expectations regarding the time frame required. Reportedly, some companies operate with a philosophy of killing new businesses if they do not turn a profit by the end of the third year—clearly an unrealistic view, given the evidence that it can take five to twelve years before a venture generates substantial profits.

■ Guidelines for Successful Internal New Venturing

To avoid the pitfalls just discussed, a company should adopt a structured approach to managing internal new venturing. New venturing typically begins with R&D. To make effective use of its R&D capacity, a company must first spell out its strategic objectives and then communicate them to its scientists and engineers. Research, after all, makes sense only when it is undertaken in areas relevant to strategic goals.[13]

To increase the probability of commercial success, a company should foster close links between R&D and marketing personnel, for this is the best way to ensure that research projects address the needs of the market. The company should also foster close links between R&D and manufacturing personnel, to ensure that the company has the capability to manufacture any proposed new products.

Many companies successfully integrate different functions by setting up project teams. Such teams comprise representatives of the various functional areas; their task is to oversee the development of new products. For example, Compaq's success in introducing new products in the personal computer industry has been linked to its use of project teams, which oversee the development of a new product from its inception to its market introduction.

Another advantage of such teams is that they can significantly reduce the time it takes to develop a new product. Thus, while R&D personnel are working on the design, manufacturing personnel can be setting up facilities, and marketing personnel can be developing its plans. Because of such integration, Compaq needed only six months to take the first portable personal computer from an idea on the drawing board to a marketable product.

To use resources most effectively, a company must also devise a selection process for choosing only the ventures that demonstrate the greatest probability of commercial success. Picking future winners is a tricky business, since by definition new ventures have an uncertain future. One study found the uncertainty surrounding new ventures to be so great that it usually took a company four to five years after launching the venture to reasonably estimate the venture's future profitability.[14] Nevertheless, a selection process is necessary if a company is to avoid spreading its resources too thinly over too many projects.

Once a project has been selected, management needs to monitor the progress of the venture closely. Evidence suggests that the most important criterion for evaluating a venture during its first four to five years is market share growth rather than cash flow or profitability. In the long run, the most successful ventures are those that increase their market share. A company should have clearly defined market share objectives for an internal new venture and decide to retain or kill it in its early years on the basis of its ability to achieve market share goals. Only in the medium term should profitability and cash flow begin to take on greater importance.

Finally, the association of large-scale entry with greater long-term profitability suggests that a company can increase the probability of success for an internal new venture by thinking big. Thinking big means the construction of efficient-scale manufacturing facilities ahead of demand, large marketing expenditures to build a market presence and brand loyalty, and a commitment by corporate management to accept initial losses as long as market share is expanding.

ACQUISITIONS AS AN ENTRY STRATEGY

■ Attractions of Acquisitions

Companies often use acquisition to enter a business area that is new to them when they lack important competencies (resources and capabilities) required to compete in that area, but when they can purchase an incumbent company that has those competencies and do so at a reasonable price. Companies also have a preference for acquisitions as an entry mode when they feel the need to move fast. As discussed earlier, building a new business through internal venturing can be a relatively slow process. In contrast, acquisition is a much quicker way to establish a significant market presence and generate profitability. A company can purchase a market leader in a strong cash position overnight, rather than spend years building up a market-leadership position through internal development. Thus, when speed is important, acquisition is the favored entry mode.

Acquisitions are also often perceived to be somewhat less risky that internal new ventures, primarily because they involve less uncertainty. Because of the nature of internal new ventures, large uncertainties are associated with projecting future profitability, revenues, and cash flows. In contrast, when a company makes an acquisition, it is acquiring known profitability, known revenues, and known market share; thus it reduces uncertainty. An acquisition allows a company to buy an established business with a track record, and for this reason many companies favor acquisitions.

Finally, acquisitions may be the preferred entry mode when the industry to be entered is well established and incumbent enterprises enjoy significant protection from barriers to entry. As you may recall from Chapter 3, barriers to entry arise from factors associated with product differentiation (brand loyalty), absolute cost advantages, and economies of scale. When such barriers are substantial, a company finds entering an industry through internal new venturing difficult. To enter, a company may have to construct an efficient-scale manufacturing plant, undertake massive advertising to break down established brand loyalties, and quickly build up distribution outlets—all goals that are hard to achieve and likely to involve substantial expenditures. In contrast, by acquiring an established enterprise, a company can circumvent most entry barriers. It can purchase a market leader, which already benefits from substantial scale economies and brand loyalty. Thus, the greater the barriers to entry, the more likely it is that acquisitions will be the favored entry mode. (We should note, however, that the attractiveness of an acquisition is predicated on the assumption that an incumbent company can be acquired for less than it would cost to enter the same industry by way of an internal new venture. As we shall see in the next section, the validity of this assumption is often questionable.)

■ Pitfalls of Acquisitions

For the reasons just noted, acquisitions have long been a popular vehicle for expanding the scope of an organization into new business areas. Despite their popularity, however, there is ample evidence that many acquisitions fail to add value for the acquiring company and, indeed, often end up dissipating value. For example, a study by Mercer Management Consulting looked at 150 acquisitions, worth more than $500 million each, that were undertaken between January 1990 and July 1995.[15] The Mercer study concluded that 50 percent of these acquisitions ended up eroding, or substantially eroding, shareholder value, while another 33 percent created only marginal returns. Just 17 percent of the acquisitions were judged to be successful.

More generally, there is a wealth of evidence from academic research suggesting that many acquisitions fail to realize their anticipated benefits.[16] In a major study of the postacquisition performance of acquired companies, David Ravenscraft and Mike Scherer concluded that many good companies were acquired and, on average, their profits and market shares declined following acquisition.[17] They also noted that a smaller but substantial subset of those good companies experienced traumatic difficulties, which ultimately led to their being sold off by the acquiring company. In other words, Ravenscraft and Scherer's evidence, like that presented by McKinsey and Company, suggests that many acquisitions destroy rather than create value.

Why do so many acquisitions apparently fail to create value? There appear to be four major reasons: (1) companies often experience difficulties when trying to integrate divergent corporate cultures; (2) companies overestimate the potential economic benefits from an acquisition; (3) acquisitions tend to be very expensive; and (4) companies often do not adequately screen their acquisition targets.

Postacquisition Integration Having made an acquisition, the acquiring company has to integrate the acquired business into its own organizational structure. Integration can entail the adoption of common management and financial control systems, the joining together of operations from the acquired and the acquiring company, or the establishment of linkages to share information and personnel. When integration is attempted, many unexpected problems can occur. Often they stem from differences in corporate cultures. After an acquisition, many acquired companies experience high management turnover, possibly because their employees do not like the acquiring company's way of doing things.[18] Research evidence suggests that the loss of management talent and expertise, to say nothing of the damage from constant tension between the businesses, can materially harm the performance of the acquired unit.[19] For an example of what can occur, see Strategy in Action 10.3, which examines the high management turnover at The Boston Company, after it was acquired by Mellon Bank in 1993.

Overestimating Economic Benefits Even when companies achieve integration, they often overestimate the potential for creating value by joining together different businesses. They overestimate the strategic advantages that can be derived from the acquisition and thus pay more for the target company than it is probably worth. Richard Roll has attributed this tendency to hubris on the part of top management. According to Roll, top managers typically overestimate their ability to create value from an acquisition, primarily because rising to the top of a corporation has given them an exaggerated sense of their own capabilities.[21]

Coca-Cola's 1975 acquisition of a number of medium-sized winemaking companies illustrates the situation in which a company overestimates the economic benefits from an acquisition. Reasoning that a beverage is a beverage, Coca-Cola wanted to use its distinctive competency in marketing to dominate the U.S. wine industry. But after buying three wine companies and enduring seven years of marginal prof-

10.3   STRATEGY *in* ACTION

Postacquisition Problems at Mellon Bank

In the early 1990s, Frank Cahouet, the CEO of Philadelphia-based Mellon Bank, conceived of a corporate strategy that would reduce the vulnerability of Mellon's earnings to changes in interest rates. Cahouet's solution was to diversify into financial services in order to gain access to a steady flow of fee-based income from money management operations. As part of this strategy, in 1993 Mellon acquired The Boston Company for $1.45 billion. Boston is a high-profile money management company that manages investments for major institutional clients, such as state and corporate pension funds. In 1994, Mellon followed up its Boston acquisition with the acquisition of Dreyfus, a mutual fund provider, for $1.7 billion. As a result, by 1995 almost half of Mellon's income was generated from fee-based financial services.

However, in 1995 Mellon hit some serious bumps on the road in its attempt to become a money market powerhouse. Problems at Boston began to surface soon after the Mellon acquisition. From the start, there was a clear clash of cultures. At Mellon, many managers arrive at their mundane offices by 7 A.M. and put in twelve-hour days for pay that is modest by banking industry standards. They are also accustomed to a firm management hierarchy, carefully controlled by Frank Cahouet, whose management style emphasizes cost containment and frugality. Boston managers also put in twelve-hour days, but they expect considerable autonomy, flexible work schedules, high pay, ample perks, and large performance bonuses. In most years, the top twenty executives at Boston earn between $750,000 and $1 million each. Mellon executives who visited the Boston unit were dumbstruck by the country club atmosphere and opulence they saw. In its move to streamline Boston, Mellon insisted that Boston cut expenses and introduced new regulations for restricting travel, entertainment, and perks.

Things started to go wrong in October 1993, when the Wisconsin state pension fund complained to Mellon of lower returns on a portfolio run by Boston. In November, Mellon liquidated the portfolio, taking a $130 million charge against earnings. Mellon also fired the responsible portfolio manager, who, it claimed, was making "unathorized trades." At Boston, however, many managers saw Mellon's action as violating guarantees of operating autonomy that Mellon had given Boston at the time of the acquisition. They blamed Mellon for prematurely liquidating a portfolio whose strategy, they claimed, Mellon executives had approved—a portfolio, moreover, that could still prove a winner if interest rates fell (which they subsequently did).

Infuriated by Mellon's interference in the running of Boston, in March seven managers at Boston's asset management unit, including the unit's CEO, Desmond Heathwood, proposed a management buyout to Mellon. This unit was one of the gems in Boston's crown, with over $26 billion in assets under management. Heathwood had been openly disdainful of Mellon's bankers, believing that they were out of their league in the investment business. In April, Mellon rejected the buyout proposal, and Heathwood promptly left to start his own investment management company. A few days later Mellon asked employees at Boston to sign employment contracts that limited their ability to leave and work for Heathwood's competing business. Another thirteen senior employees refused to sign and quit to join Heathwood's new money management operation.

The defection of Heathwood and his colleges was followed by a series of high-profile client defections. The Arizona state retirement system, for example, pulled $1 billion out of Mellon and transferred it to Heathwood's firm, and the Fresno Country retirement system transferred $400 million in assets over to Heathwood. As one client stated, "We have a relationship with The Boston Co. that goes back over 30 years, and the people who worked on the account are the people who left—so we left too."

Reflecting on the episode, Frank Cahouet noted that "we've clearly been hurt. . . . But this episode is very manageable. We are not going to lose our momentum." Others weren't so sure. In this incident, they saw yet another example of how difficult it can be to merge two divergent corporate cultures, and how the management turnover that results from such attempts can deal a serious blow to any attempt to create value out of an acquisition.[20]

its, Coca-Cola finally conceded that wine and soft drinks are very different products, with different kinds of appeal, pricing systems, and distribution networks. In 1983, it sold the wine operations to Joseph E. Seagram & Sons for $210 million—the price Coca-Cola had paid and a substantial loss when adjusted for inflation.[22]

The Expense of Acquisitions Acquisitions of companies whose stock is publicly traded tend to be very expensive. When a company bids to acquire the stock of another enterprise, the stock price frequently gets bid up in the acquisition process. This is particularly likely to occur in the case of contested bids, where two or more companies simultaneously bid for control of a single target company. Thus, the acquiring company must often pay a premium over the current market value of the target. In the early 1980s, acquiring companies paid an average premium of 40 to 50 percent over current stock prices for an acquisition. Between 1985 and 1988, when takeover activity was at its peak, premiums of 80 percent were not uncommon. Indeed, in the giant contested takeover bid for RJR Nabisco during late 1988, the stock price of RJR was bid up from $45 per share prior to the takeover attempt to $110 per share by the time RJR was sold—a premium of over 200 percent! By the first half of the 1990s, the takeover premium was once more in the 40 to 50 percent range.

The debt taken on to finance such expensive acquisitions can later become a noose around the acquiring company's neck, particularly if interest rates rise. Moreover, if the market value of the target company prior to an acquisition was a true reflection of that company's worth under its management at that time, a premium of 50 over this value means that the acquiring company has to improve the performance of the acquired unit by just as much if it is to reap a positive return on its investment. Such performance gains, however, can be very difficult to achieve.

Inadequate Preacquisition Screening After researching acquisitions made by twenty different companies, a study by Philippe Haspeslagh and David Jemison concluded that one reason for the failure of acquisitions is management's inadequate attention to preacquisition screening.[23] It found that many companies decide to acquire other firms without thoroughly analyzing the potential benefits and costs. Then, after the acquisition has been completed, the companies discover that instead of a well-run business, they have bought a troubled organization. That was Xerox's experience when it purchased the Crum and Forster insurance business in the early 1980s. Only after completing the acquisition did Xerox learn that Crum and Forster was a high-cost and inefficient provider of insurance. Xerox subsequently divested the business at a significant financial loss.

■ Guidelines for Successful Acquisition

To avoid pitfalls and make successful acquisitions, companies need to take a structured approach with three main components: (1) target identification and preacquisition screening, (2) bidding strategy, and (3) integration.[24]

Screening Thorough preacquisition screening increases a company's knowledge about potential takeover targets, leads to a more realistic assessment of the problems involved in executing an acquisition and integrating the new business into the company's organizational structure, and lessens the risk of purchasing a potential problem business. The screening should begin with a detailed assessment of the strategic rationale for making the acquisition and identification of the kind of enterprise that would make an ideal acquisition candidate.

Next, the company should scan a target population of potential acquisition candidates, and evaluate each according to a detailed set of criteria, focusing on (1) financial position, (2) product market position, (3) competitive environment, (4) management capabilities, and (5) corporate culture. Such an evaluation should enable the company to identify the strengths and weaknesses of each candidate, the extent of potential economies of scope between the acquiring and the acquired companies, the compatibility of the two corporate cultures, and potential integration problems.

The company should then reduce the list of candidates to the most favored ones and evaluate them further. At this stage, it should sound out third parties, such as investment bankers, whose opinions may be important and who may be able to give valuable insights about the efficiency of target companies. The company that leads the list after this process should be the acquisition target.

Bidding Strategy   The objective of bidding strategy is to reduce the price that a company must pay for an acquisition candidate. The essential element of a good bidding strategy is timing. For example, Hanson PLC, one of the most successful takeover machines of the 1980s, always looked for essentially sound businesses that were suffering from short-term problems due to cyclical industry factors or from problems localized in one division. Such companies are typically undervalued by the stock market and thus can be picked up without payment of the standard 40 or 50 percent premium over current stock prices. With good timing, a company can make a bargain purchase.

Integration   Despite good screening and bidding, an acquisition will fail unless positive steps are taken to integrate the acquired company into the organizational structure of the acquiring one. Integration should center on the source of the potential strategic advantages of the acquisition—for instance, opportunities to share marketing, manufacturing, procurement, R&D, financial, or management resources. Integration should also be accompanied by steps to eliminate any duplication of facilities or functions. In addition, any unwanted activities of the acquired company should be sold. Finally, if the different business activities are closely related, they will require a high degree of integration. In the case of a company like Hanson PLC, the level of integration can be minimal, for the company's strategy is one of unrelated diversification. But a company such as Philip Morris requires greater integration because its strategy is one of related diversification.

JOINT VENTURES AS AN ENTRY STRATEGY

■ Attractions of Joint Ventures

A company may prefer internal new venturing to acquisition as an entry strategy into new business areas, yet hesitate to commit itself to an internal new venture because of the risks and costs of building a new operation from the ground up. Such a situation is most likely to occur when a company sees the possibility of establishing a new business in an embryonic or growth industry but the risks and costs associated with the project are more than it is willing to assume on its own. In these circumstances, the company may decide to enter into a joint venture with another company and use the joint venture as a vehicle for entering the new business area. Such an arrangement enables the company to share the substantial risks and costs involved in a new project.

To illustrate, in 1990 IBM and Motorola set up a joint venture with the aim of providing a service that allowed computer users to communicate over radio waves. Customers buying the service can use hand-held computers, made by Motorola, to communicate by means of a private network of radio towers that IBM has built across the United States. The venture targets the potentially enormous market of people who could benefit from using computers in the field—for instance, people who repair equipment in offices and insurance claims adjusters. Analysts estimate that the market for such a service is currently in the tens of millions of dollars but could reach billions over the next decade.[25]

Because of the embryonic nature of the industry, the venture faces substantial risks. A number of competing technologies are on the horizon. For example, laptop computers are being fitted with modems that can communicate with host computers through cellular telephone networks. Although cellular networks are more crowded and less reliable than radio networks, that state of affairs could change. Given this uncertainty, it makes sense for IBM and Motorola to combine in a joint venture and share the risks associated with building up this business.

In addition, a joint venture makes sense when a company can increase the probability of successfully establishing a new business by joining forces with another company. For a company that has some of the skills and assets necessary to establish a successful new venture, teaming up with another company that has complementary skills and assets may increase the probability of success.

Again, the venture between IBM and Motorola provides an example. Motorola dominates the market for mobile radios and already manufactures hand-held computers, but it lacks a nationwide radio network through which users of hand-held computers might communicate with each other. IBM lacks radio technology, but it does have a private network of radio towers (originally built for communicating with 20,000-plus IBM service people in the field), which covers more than 90 percent of the country. Combining Motorola's skills in radio technology with IBM's radio network in a single joint venture increases significantly the probability of establishing a successful new business.

■ Drawbacks of Joint Ventures

There are three main drawbacks to joint venture arrangements. First, a joint venture allows a company to share the risks and costs of developing a new business, but it also requires the sharing of profits if the new business succeeds. Second, a company that enters into a joint venture always runs the risk of giving critical know-how away to its joint venture partner, which might use that know-how to compete directly with the company in the future. As we point out in discussing global strategic alliances in Chapter 8, however, joint ventures can be structured to minimize this risk. Third, the venture partners must share control. If the partners have different business philosophies, time horizons, or investment preferences, substantial problems can arise. Conflicts over how to run the joint venture can tear it apart and result in business failure.

In sum, although joint ventures often have a distinct advantage over internal new venturing as a means of establishing a new business operation, they also have certain drawbacks. When deciding whether to go it alone or cooperate with another company in a joint venture, strategic managers need to assess carefully the pros and cons of the alternatives.

RESTRUCTURING

So far we have focused on strategies for expanding the scope of a company into new business areas. We turn now to their opposite: strategies for reducing the scope of the company by *exiting* business areas. In recent years, reducing the scope of a company through restructuring has become an increasingly popular strategy, particularly among the companies that diversified their activities during the 1960s, 1970s, and 1980s. In most cases, companies that are engaged in restructuring are divesting themselves of diversified activities in order to concentrate on their core businesses.[26] They include General Electric, which began restructuring when Jack Welch became its CEO, and Sears, which sold off Allstate Insurance, Coldwell Banker Real Estate, and the brokerage Dean Witter Reynolds, in order to focus more on its core retailing operations. (For details of restructuring at Sears, see Strategy in Action 10.4.)

The first question that must be asked is, why are so many companies restructuring at this particular time? After answering it, we examine the different strategies that companies adopt for exiting from business areas. Then we discuss the various turnaround strategies that companies employ to revitalize their core business area.

■ Why Restructure?

One reason for so much restructuring in recent years is overdiversification. There is plenty of evidence that in the heyday of the corporate diversification movement, which began in the 1960s and lasted until the early 1980s, many companies overdiversified.[27] More precisely, the bureaucratic inefficiencies created by expanding the scope of the organization outweighed the additional value that could be created, and company performance declined. As performance declined, the stock price of many of these diversified companies fell, and they found themselves vulnerable to hostile takeover bids. Indeed, a number of diversified companies were acquired in the 1980s and subsequently broken up. This is what happened to U.S. Industries and SCM, two diversified conglomerates that were acquired and then broken up by Hanson PLC. Similarly, after the diversified consumer products business RJR Nabisco was acquired by Kohlberg, Kravis & Roberts in a 1988 leveraged buyout, RJR sold off many of its diversified businesses to independent investors or to other companies.

A second factor driving the current restructuring trend is that in the 1980s and 1990s many diversified companies found their core business areas under attack from new competition. For example, due to deregulation AT&T now faces a much

The Restructuring of Sears

In 1981, Sears, which was then the largest retailer in the United States, announced in a single week that it would acquire Dean Witter Reynolds, the country's fifth largest stockbrokerage, and Coldwell Banker, the nation's biggest real estate broker, for a total of $800 million. The idea was to team those two financial service operations with Allstate Insurance, which Sears had acquired in 1934 and which was then the world's second largest personal property and casualty insurer. At the heart of this strategy was the desire on the part of Sears to leverage its fabled "bond of trust" with the consumer into the fast-growing financial services industry—a strategy its CEO, Edward Brennan, often referred to as "socks to stocks." Sears felt that its retail customers would be strongly attracted to financial services providers that were owned by Sears. Indeed, the company planned to locate offices for its financial services operations in Sears department stores, and to use its catalog mailing list as a channel for selling financial services.

However, the 1980s and early 1990s were not kind to Sears. While the financial services operations of the company did well, its core retailing operation ran into serious problems. During most of the 1980s, the earnings of the Sears retail group fell at an annual rate of 7 to 8 percent and its market share slumped. The share of department store merchandise accounted for by Sears fell from 9 percent in 1982 to 6 percent in 1992. More significantly, Sears did little to keep up with the growth of discount and niche retailers such as Wal-Mart, Costco, Home Depot, and Toys 'R' Us, all of which ate into Sears's blue-collar clientele. Critics charged that senior executives at Sears seemed more interested in new ventures and the potential for synergy than in the basic business of running the Sears stores. As a result, Sears was slow to respond to new competition and its sales stagnated.

The problems in the retail operations at Sears attracted the scorn of Wall Street and at least one abortive takeover attempt in early 1988, when rumors of a $50.2 billion takeover bid by Revlon's Chairman Ronald O. Perelman were making the rounds on Wall Street. Sears responded by announcing a decision to sell off its Chicago headquarters and introducing an "everyday low pricing" strategy at its stores. Both moves failed. After a year, Sears abandoned attempts to sell the Sears Tower. Furthermore, it never could convince consumers that it had the lowest prices in town—probably because it didn't.

Meanwhile, the stock continued to slump. To make matters worse, in 1992 Sears's fabled "bond of trust" with consumers was blown apart when it was revealed that its automobile services operation had been systematically overcharging consumers for repair services. At the same time, Moody's Investors Service, noting Sears's growing burden of debt, lowered the company's bond rating. The stock slumped further, and investors pushed the company to take drastic action. In September 1992, Sears announced plans to sell Dean Witter Reynolds and Coldwell Banker and to spin off 20 percent of Allstate to independent investors. In effect, Sears was turning its back on thirteen years of diversification and an investment of billions of dollars so that top management could devote more time to revitalizing its troubled retailing arm. This shift was a humiliating admission by top management, and particularly CEO Brennan, that they had mishandled the company's strategy.[28]

more competitive environment in its core long-distance business, which helped to drive its decision to exit from noncore activities. Similarly, Sears still faces profound competitive challenges in the retailing industry, where demand is shifting from department stores such as Sears to low-cost discounters such as Costco, or niche stores like The Gap (see Strategy in Action 10.4). The top management of these companies found that in order to devote the necessary attention to their troubled core business it had to shed its diversified activities, which had become an unwelcome distraction.

A final factor of some importance is that innovations in management processes and strategy have diminished the advantages of vertical integration or diversification. In response, companies have reduced the scope of their activities through restructuring and divestments. For example, ten years ago there was little understanding of how long-term cooperative relationships between a company and its suppliers could be a viable alternative to vertical integration. Most companies considered only two alternatives for managing the supply chain: vertical integration or competitive bidding. As we note in Chapter 9, however, if the conditions are right, a third alternative for managing the supply chain, *long-term contracting*, can be a strategy that is superior to both vertical integration and competitive bidding. Like vertical integration, long-term contracting facilitates investments in specialization. But unlike vertical integration, it does not involve high bureaucratic costs, nor does it dispense with market discipline. As this strategic innovation has spread throughout the business world, the relative advantages of vertical integration have declined.

■ Exit Strategies

Companies can choose from three main strategies for exiting business areas: divestment, harvest, and liquidation. You have already encountered all three in Chapter 7, where we discuss strategies for competing in declining industries. We review them briefly here.

Divestment   Of the three main strategies, divestment is usually favored. It represents the best way for a company to recoup as much of its initial investment in a business unit as possible. The idea is to sell the business unit to the highest bidder. Three types of buyers are independent investors, other companies, and the management of the unit to be divested. Selling off a business unit to independent investors is normally referred to as a **spinoff**. A spinoff makes good sense when the unit to be sold is profitable and when the stock market has an appetite for new stock issues (which is normal during market upswings, but *not* during market downswings). Thus, for example, in 1992 the timber products company Weyerhaeuser successfully spun off its Paragon Trade Brands to independent investors. Investors snapped up the stock of the new issue, which makes "own label" disposable diapers for supermarket chains and is highly profitable. However, spinoffs do not work if the unit to be spun off is unprofitable and unattractive to independent investors or if the stock market is slumping and unresponsive to new issues.

Selling off a unit to another company is a strategy frequently pursued when a unit can be sold to a company in the same line of business as the unit. In such cases, the purchaser is often prepared to pay a considerable amount of money for the opportunity to substantially increase the size of its business virtually overnight. For example, in 1987 Hanson PLC sold off its Glidden paint subsidiary, which it acquired six months earlier in the takeover of SCM, to Imperial Chemicals Industry (ICI). Glidden was the largest paint company in the United States, and ICI was the largest manufacturer of paint outside the United States, so the match made a good deal of sense from ICI's perspective, while Hanson was able to get a substantial price for the sale.

Selling off a unit to its management is normally referred to as a **management buyout (MBO)**. MBOs are very similar to leveraged buyouts (LBOs), discussed in

Chapter 2. In an MBO, the unit is sold to its management, which often finances the purchase through the sale of high-yield bonds to investors. The bond issue is normally arranged by a buyout specialist, such as Kohlberg, Kravis & Roberts, which, along with management, will typically hold a sizable proportion of the shares in the MBO. MBOs often take place when financially troubled units have only two other options: a harvest strategy or liquidation.

An MBO can be very risky for the management team involved, since its members may have to sign personal guarantees to back up the bond issue and may lose everything if the MBO ultimately fails. On the other hand, if the management team succeeds in turning around the troubled unit, its reward can be a significant increase in personal wealth. Thus, an MBO strategy can be characterized as a *high risk–high return* strategy for the management team involved. Faced with the possible liquidation of their business unit, many management teams are willing to take the risk. However, the viability of this option depends not only on a willing management team, but also on there being enough buyers of high yield–high risk bonds—so-called junk bonds—to be able to finance the MBO. In recent years, the general slump in the junk bond market has made the MBO strategy a more difficult one for companies to follow.

Harvest and Liquidation   Since the pros and cons of harvest and liquidation strategies are discussed in detail in Chapter 6, we note just a few points here. First, a harvest or liquidation strategy is generally considered inferior to a divestment strategy since the company can probably best recoup its investment in a business unit by divestment. Second, a harvest strategy means halting investment in a unit in order to maximize short- to medium-term cash flow from that unit before liquidating it. Although this strategy seems fine in theory, it is often a poor one to apply in practice. Once it becomes apparent that the unit is pursuing a harvest strategy, the morale of the unit's employees, as well as the confidence of the unit's customers and suppliers in its continuing operation, can sink very quickly. If this occurs, as it often does, then the rapid decline in the unit's revenues can make the strategy untenable. Finally, a liquidation strategy is the least attractive of all to pursue since it requires the company to write off its investment in a business unit, often at a considerable cost. However, in the case of a poorly performing business unit for which a selloff or spinoff is unlikely and an MBO cannot be arranged, liquidation may be the only viable alternative.

TURNAROUND STRATEGY

Many companies restructure their operations, divesting themselves of their diversified activities, because they wish to focus more on their core business area. As in the case of Sears, this often occurs because the core business area is itself in trouble and needs top management attention. An integral part of restructuring, therefore, is the development of a strategy for turning around the company's core or remaining business areas. In this section, we review in some detail the various steps that companies take to turn around troubled business areas. We first look at the causes of corporate decline and then discuss the main elements of successful turnaround strategies.

■ The Causes of Corporate Decline

Seven main causes stand out in most cases of corporate decline: poor management, overexpansion, inadequate financial controls, high costs, the emergence of powerful new competition, unforeseen shifts in demand, and organizational inertia.[29] Normally, several, if not all, of these factors are present in a decline. For example, IBM's decline in the early 1990s was brought on by a high-cost structure, powerful new low-cost competition from personal computer makers, a shift in demand away from mainframe computers (IBM's main business), and IBM's slow response to these factors due to organizational inertia.

Poor Management   Poor management covers a multitude of sins, ranging from sheer incompetence to neglect of core businesses and an insufficient number of good managers. Although not necessarily a bad thing, one-person rule often seems to be at the root of poor management. One study found that the presence of a dominant and autocratic chief executive with a passion for empire-building strategies often characterizes failing companies.[30] Another study of eighty-one turnaround situations found that in thirty-six cases troubled companies suffered from an autocratic manager who tried to do it all, but, in the face of complexity and change, could not.[31] In a review of the empirical studies of turnaround situations, Richard Hoffman identified a number of other management defects commonly found in declining companies.[32] These included a lack of balanced expertise at the top (for example, too many engineers), a lack of strong middle management, a failure to provide for orderly management succession by a departing CEO (which may result in an internal succession battle), and a failure by the board of directors to monitor adequately management's strategic decisions.

Overexpansion   The empire-building strategies of autocratic CEOs often involve rapid expansion and extensive diversification. Much of this diversification tends to be poorly conceived and adds little value to the company. As already noted in this chapter and Chapter 9, the consequences of too much diversification include loss of control and an inability to cope with recessionary conditions. Moreover, companies that expand rapidly tend to do so by taking on large amounts of debt financing. Adverse economic conditions can limit a company's ability to meet its debt requirements and thus precipitate a financial crisis.

Inadequate Financial Controls   The most common aspect of inadequate financial controls is the failure to assign profit responsibility to key decision makers within the organization. The lack of accountability for the financial consequences of their actions can encourage middle-level managers to employ excess staff and spend resources beyond what is necessary for maximum efficiency. In such cases, bureaucracy may balloon and costs spiral out of control. This is precisely what happened at Chrysler during the 1970s. As Lee Iacocca later noted, Jerry Greenwald, whom Iacocca brought in to head the finance function in 1980, "had a hell of a time finding anybody who could be identified as having specific responsibility for anything. They would tell him, 'Well, everyone is responsible for controlling costs.' Jerry knew very well what that meant—in the final analysis nobody was."[33]

High Costs   Inadequate financial controls can lead to high costs. Beyond this, the most common cause of a high-cost structure is low labor productivity. It may stem from union-imposed restrictive working practices (as in the case of the auto and steel industries), management's failure to invest in new labor-saving technologies, or, more often, a combination of both. Other common causes include high wage rates (a particularly important factor for companies competing on costs in the global marketplace) and a failure to realize economies of scale because of low market share.

New Competition   Competition in capitalist economies is a process characterized by the continual emergence of new companies championing new ways of doing business. In recent years few industries and few established companies have been spared the competitive challenge of powerful new competition. Indeed, many established businesses have failed or run into serious trouble because they did not respond quickly enough to such threats. Powerful new competition is a central cause of corporate decline. IBM has been hammered by powerful new competition from personal computer makers and Sears has been hard hit by powerful new competition from discount and niche stores (see Strategy in Action 10.4). In both these cases, the established company failed to appreciate the strength of new competitors until it was in serious trouble.

Unforeseen Demand Shifts   Unforeseen, and often unforeseeable, shifts in demand can be brought about by major changes in technology, economic or political conditions, and social and cultural norms. Although such changes can open up market opportunities for new products, they also threaten the existence of many established enterprises, necessitating restructuring. A recent example is the rapid rise of the Internet and the World Wide Web, which, among other things, blind-sided Microsoft, the dominant software company in the personal computer market. Although Microsoft has since responded to the rise of the Internet, doing so required the company to remake its strategy.

Organizational Inertia   On their own, the emergence of powerful new competition and unforeseen shifts in demand might not be enough to cause corporate decline. What is also required is an organization that is slow to respond to such environmental changes. As you saw in Chapter 4, where we first touched on the issue of corporate decline, organizational inertia stands out as a major reason why companies are often so slow to respond to new competitive conditions.

■ The Main Steps of Turnaround

There is no standard model of how a company should respond to a decline. Indeed, there can be no such model because every situation is unique. However, in most successful turnaround situations, a number of common features are present. They include changing the leadership, redefining the company's strategic focus, divesting or closing unwanted assets, taking steps to improve the profitability of remaining operations, and, occasionally, making acquisitions to rebuild core operations.

Changing the Leadership   Since the old leadership bears the stigma of failure, new leadership is an essential element of most retrenchment and turnaround situations. For example, as the first step in implementing a turnaround, IBM replaced CEO John Akers with an outsider, Lou Gerstner. To resolve a crisis, the new leader should be someone who is able to make difficult decisions, motivate lower-level managers, listen to the views of others, and delegate power when appropriate.

Redefining Strategic Focus   For a single-business enterprise, redefining strategic focus involves a reevaluation of the company's business-level strategy. A failed cost leader, for example, may reorient toward a more focused or differentiated strategy. For a diversified company, redefining strategic focus means identifying the businesses in the portfolio that have the best long-term profit and growth prospects and concentrating investment there.

Asset Sales and Closures   Having redefined its strategic focus, a company should divest as many unwanted assets as it can find buyers for and liquidate whatever remains. It is important not to confuse unwanted assets with unprofitable assets. Assets that no longer fit in with the redefined strategic focus of the company may be very profitable. Their sale can bring the company much-needed cash, which it can invest in improving the operations that remain.

Improving Profitability   Improving the profitability of the operations that remain after asset sales and closures requires a number of steps to improve efficiency, quality, innovation, and customer responsiveness. We discuss in Chapter 5 many of the functional-level strategies that companies can pursue to achieve these ends, so you may want to review that chapter for details. Note, though, that improving profitability typically involves one or more of the following: (1) laying off white- and blue-collar employees; (2) investing in labor-saving equipment; (3) assigning profit responsibility to individuals and subunits within the company, by a change of organizational structure if necessary; (4) tightening financial controls; (5) cutting back on marginal products; (6) reengineering business processes to cut costs and boost productivity; and (7) introducing total quality management processes.

Acquisitions   A somewhat surprising but quite common turnaround strategy is to make acquisitions, primarily to strengthen the competitive position of a company's remaining core operations. For example, Champion International used to be a very diversified company, manufacturing a wide range of paper and wood products. After years of declining performance, in the mid 1980s Champion decided to focus on its profitable newsprint and magazine paper business. The company divested many of its other paper and wood products businesses, but at the same time it paid $1.8 billion for St. Regis, one of the country's largest manufacturers of newsprint and magazine paper.

SUMMARY OF CHAPTER

This chapter builds on the material in Chapter 9 by addressing central issues of corporate development. **Corporate development** is concerned with identifying *which* business opportunities a company should pursue, *how* it should pursue those opportunities, and

how it should exit from businesses that do not fit the company's strategic vision. The chapter makes the following points:

✔ A common way for starting to identify which business opportunities to pursue is to review a company's existing portfolio of business activities. One approach to undertaking such a review utilizes a set of techniques known as portfolio planning matrices. The purpose of these techniques is to compare the competitive position of the different businesses in a company's portfolio on the basis of common criteria.

✔ A second approach to the corporate development process, championed by Gary Hamel and C.K. Prahalad, reconceptualizes a company as a portfolio of core competencies—as opposed to a portfolio of businesses. In this approach, corporate development is oriented toward maintaining existing competencies, building new competencies, and leveraging competencies by applying them to new business opportunities.

✔ The advantage of Hamel and Prahalad's framework is that it focuses explicitly on how a company can *create value* by building new competencies, or by recombining existing competencies to enter new business areas. While traditional portfolio planning matrices treat businesses as independent, Hamel and Prahald's framework recognizes the interdependencies between businesses and focuses on the opportunities for creating value by building and leveraging competencies.

✔ There are three vehicles that companies use to enter new business areas: internal ventures, acquisitions, and joint ventures.

✔ Internal new venturing is typically employed as an entry strategy when a company possesses a set of valuable competencies in its existing businesses that can be leveraged or recombined to enter the new business area.

✔ Many internal ventures fail because of entry on too small a scale, poor commercialization, and poor corporate management of the internal venture process. Guarding against failure involves a structured approach toward project selection and management, integration of R&D and marketing to improve commercialization of a venture idea, and entry on a significant scale.

✔ Acquisitions are often favored as an entry strategy when the company lacks important competencies (resources and capabilities) required to compete in an area, but when it can purchase an incumbent company that has those competencies and do so at a reasonable price. Acquisitions also tend to be favored when the barriers to entry into the target industry are high, and when the company is

unwilling to accept the time frame, development costs, and risks of internal new venturing.

✔ Many acquisitions fail because of poor postacquisition integration, overestimation of the value that can be created from an acquisition, the high cost of acquisition, and poor preacquisition screening. Guarding against acquisition failure requires structured screening, good bidding strategies, and positive attempts to integrate the acquired company into the organization of the acquiring one.

✔ Joint ventures may be the preferred entry strategy when (1) the risks and costs associated with setting up a new business unit are more than the company is willing to assume on its own and (2) the company can increase the probability of successfully establishing a new business by teaming up with another company that has skills and assets complementing its own.

✔ The current popularity of restructuring is due to (1) overdiversification by many companies in the 1970s and 1980s, (2) the rise of competitive challenges to the core business units of many diversified enterprises, and (3) innovations in the management process that have reduced the advantages of vertical integration and diversification.

✔ Exit strategies include divestment, harvest, and liquidation. The choice of exit strategy is governed by the characteristics of the relevant business unit.

✔ The causes of corporate decline include poor management, overexpansion, inadequate financial controls, high costs, the emergence of powerful new competition, unforeseen shifts in demand, and organizational inertia.

✔ Responses to corporate decline include changing the leadership, redefining the company's strategic focus, divestment or closure of unwanted assets, taking steps to improve the profitability of the operations that remain, and occasionally, acquisitions to rebuild core operations.

DISCUSSION QUESTIONS

1. Under what circumstances might it be best to enter a new business area by acquisition, and under what

circumstances might internal new venturing be the preferred entry mode?

2. IBM has decided to diversify into the cellular telecommunication business. What entry strategy would you recommend that the company pursue? Why?

3. Review the change in the composition of GE's portfolio of businesses under the leadership of Jack Welch (1981 to the present). How has GE's portfolio been reorganized? From a value creation perspective, what is the logic underlying this reorganization?

Practicing Strategic Management

SMALL-GROUP EXERCISE
Dun & Bradstreet

Break up into groups of three to five people. Then read the following news release from Dun & Bradstreet. On the basis of this information, identify the strategic rationale for the split and evaluate how the split might affect the performance of three successor companies. If you were a stockholder in the old Dun & Bradstreet, would you approve of this split? Why?

D&B TRANSFORMED INTO THREE INDEPENDENT PUBLIC COMPANIES

WILTON, CONN., Jan. 9, 1996—Dun & Bradstreet CEO Robert E. Weissman today announced a sweeping strategy that will transform the 155-year-old business information giant into three publicly traded, global corporations.

"This important action is designed to increase shareholder value by unlocking D&B's substantial underlying franchise strengths," said Weissman.

Building on preeminent Dun & Bradstreet businesses, the reorganization establishes three independent companies focused on high-growth information markets; financial information services; and consumer-product market research.

"Since the 1800s, D&B has grown by effectively managing a portfolio of businesses and gaining economies of scale," stated Weissman. "But the velocity of change in information markets has dramatically altered the rules of business survival. Today, market focus and speed are the primary drivers of competitive advantage. This plan is our blueprint for success in the 21st century," said Weissman.

The plan, approved today at a special meeting of D&B's board of directors, calls for D&B to create three separate companies by spinning off two of its businesses to shareholders. "D&B is the leader in business information," said Weissman. "By freeing our companies to tightly focus on our core vertical markets, we can more rapidly leverage this leadership position into emerging growth areas."

The three new companies are:

*   Cognizant Corporation, a new high-growth company, which includes IMS International, the leading global supplier of marketing information to the pharmaceutical and health care industries;

Nielsen Media Research, the leader in audience measurement for electronic media; and Gartner Group, the premier provider of advisory services to high-tech users, vendors and suppliers, in which Cognizant will hold a majority interest.

*   The Dun & Bradstreet Corporation, consisting of Dun & Bradstreet Information Services, the world's largest source of business-to-business marketing and commercial-credit information; Moody's Investors Service, a global leader in rating debt; and Reuben H. Donnelley, a premier provider of Yellow Pages marketing and publishing.

*   A. C. Nielsen, the global leader in marketing information for the fast-moving consumer packaged goods industry.

"These three separate companies will tailor their strategies to the unique demands of their markets, determining investments, capital structures and policies that will strengthen their respective global capabilities. This plan also clarifies D&B from an investor's perspective by grouping the businesses into three logical investment categories, each with distinct risk/reward profiles," said Weissman.

The Dun & Bradstreet Corporation is the world's largest marketer of information, software and services for business decision making, with worldwide revenue of $4.9 billion in 1994.

STRATEGIC MANAGEMENT PROJECT
Module 10

This module requires you to assess your company's use of acquisitions, internal new ventures, and joint ventures as strategies for entering a new business area and/or as attempts to restructure its portfolio of businesses.

ARTICLE FILE 10

Find an example of a company that has made an acquisition that apparently failed to create any value. Identify and critically evaluate the rationale used by top management to justify the acquisition at the time it was made. Explain why the acquisition subsequently failed.

A. If Your Company Has Entered a New Business Area During the Last Decade

1. Pick one new business area that your company has entered during the last ten years.
2. Identify the rationale for entering this business area.
3. Identify the strategy used to enter this business area.
4. Evaluate the rationale for using this particular entry strategy. Do you think that this was the best entry strategy to use? Justify your answer.
5. Do you think that the addition of this business area to the company has added or dissipated value? Again, justify your answer.

B. If Your Company Has Restructured Its Business During the Last Decade

1. Identify the rationale for pursuing a restructuring strategy.
2. Pick one business area that your company has exited from during the last ten years.
3. Identify the strategy used to exit from this particular business area. Do you think that this was the best exit strategy to use? Justify your answer.

4. In general, do you think that exiting from this business area has been in the company's best interest?

EXPLORING THE WEB
Visiting General Electric

Visit the Web site of General Electric (http://www.gc .com). Using the information contained within that Web site, answer the following questions:

1. Review GE's portfolio of major businesses. Does this portfolio make sense from a value creation perspective? Why?
2. What (if any) changes would you make to GE's portfolio of businesses? Why would you make these changes?
3. What (if any) core competencies do you think are held in common by one or more of GE's major business units? Is there any evidence that GE creates new businesses by leveraging its core competencies?

General Task   By searching through information sources on the Web, find an example of a company that has recently restructured its portfolio of businesses. Identify and evaluate the strategic rationale behind this restructuring. Does it make sense?

CLOSING CASE

Breaking Up AT&T

ON SEPTEMBER 20, 1995, AT&T, the world's largest telecommunications company, with annual revenues of $75 billion, announced that it would split itself into three independent companies. The largest of these, which was to retain the AT&T name, would manage the company's long-distance, international, and wireless telecommunications businesses. The new AT&T would retain its position as the largest provider of telecommunications service in the world, with 1995 revenues in excess of $50 billion. Second in size of the new companies was to be the network equipment business. Renamed Lucent Technologies, this business generated 1995 revenues of $21 billion and ranked as the third largest provider of telecommunication network equipment in the world after Germany's Alcatel and Motorola of the United

States. The smallest of the new companies was AT&T's Global Information Solutions business, a manufacturer of computer systems, with annual revenues of $9 billion. Global Information Solutions was built around NCR, a computer company that AT&T acquired in 1991 for $7.5 billion.

The decision to break up AT&T into three parts was the result of a number of factors that came to a head in the mid 1990s. First was the impending deregulation of the U.S. telecommunications industry. After deregulation, local and long-distance telephone companies would be free to enter each other's markets. AT&T would face more competition in its core long-distance business as the Regional Bell Operating Companies (RBOCs) tried to enter this market. At the same time, AT&T would be able to enter the local phone businesses and compete directly against the RBOCs. The second factor was the privatization of state-owned telephone companies around the world and the deregulation of many foreign telephone markets. These developments created enormous opportunities for AT&T, which for the first time saw the possibility of building a truly global telephone network by forming alliances with newly privatized telephone companies and by entering foreign markets. The third factor was rapid change in the telecommunications business as new technologies, such as wireless communications and the Internet, created significant opportunities and threats for AT&T. Faced with such changes in its operating environment, AT&T's management realized that it needed to focus all its energies and resources on the company's core telecommunications business, unencumbered by the distractions presented by the network equipment and computer businesses.

AT&T's management was also aware that the performance of the computer and network equipment businesses had suffered as a result of their association with AT&T. The equipment business was trying to sell products to companies that competed directly against AT&T, such as MCI and Sprint, or would compete against AT&T after deregulation, such as the RBOCs. These potential customers were increasingly reluctant to purchase equipment from a supplier that was also a competitor. For example, just before the breakup was announced, Motorola beat AT&T to a $800 million order for wireless telecommunications equipment from GTE. GTE had long been one of AT&Ts largest equipment customers, but now it faced the threat of competing against AT&T in the local phone business. Freed from its association with AT&T, the network equip-

ment business would have a greater chance of capturing business from other telephone service providers.

As for the computer business, this was forecast to lose around $1 billion in 1995. Although AT&T had always had some significant computer skills—after all, many network equipment products, such as digital switches, are essentially specialized computers—it had never been able to establish a profitable computer operation. During the 1980s, AT&T lost billions of dollars trying to establish a presence in the personal computer market through an internal new venture. Moreover, its 1991 acquisition of NCR—which was an attempt to strengthen this venture—turned out to be a disaster, partly because the computer market shifted away from the kind of customized equipment provided by NCR, and partly because there was a clash between the management cultures of the two companies, which led to high management turnover in the acquired unit. Many now felt that AT&T's deep pockets had kept the computer operation in markets that it should have exited years ago—such as the personal computer market. They believed that an independent computer operation might be more responsive to market demands and would not be burdened by the clashing cultural heritage of AT&T and NCR.[34]

Case Discussion Questions

1. What changes in AT&T's operating environment triggered its 1995 decision to break up the company into three entities?

2. How has the breakup created value for shareholders?

3. Does the 1995 breakup imply that AT&T's pre-1995 strategic vision was seriously flawed?

End Notes

1. "HP: No Longer Lost in Cyberspace?" *Business Week*, May 31, 1999, p. 124; I. J. Dugan, "Hewlett to Become 2 Companies," *Washington Post*, March 3, 1999, p. E1; D. P. Hamilton and S. Thurm, "HP to Spin Off Its Measurement Operations," *Wall Street Journal,* March 3, 1999, p. A3; D. P. Hamilton and R. Blumenstein, "HP Names Carly Fiorina, a Lucent Star, to Be CEO," *Wall Street Journal,* July 20, 1999, p. B1.

2. C. W. Hofer and D. Schendel, *Strategy Formulation: Analytical Concepts* (St. Paul, Minn.: West, 1979); R. A. Bettis and W. K. Hall, "Strategic Portfolio Management in the Multibusiness Firm," *California Management Review*, 24 (1981), 23–28.

3. G. Hamel and C. K. Prahalad, *Competing for the Future* (Cambridge, Mass: Harvard Business School Press, 1994).

4. D. J. Collis, "Portfolio Planning at Ciba Geigy and the Newport Investment Proposal," *Harvard Business School Case* No. 795-040, 1995; Ciba-Geigy's World Wide Web page (http://www.cina.com).

5. G. Hamel and C. K. Prahalad, *Competing for the Future.*

6. D. L. Barton and G. Pisano, "Monsanto's March into Biotechnology," *Harvard Business School Case* No. 690-009 (1990). See Monsanto's home page for details of its genetically engineered seed products (http://www.monsanto.com).

7. See Booz, Allen, & Hamilton, *New Products Management for the 1980's,* privately published research report, 1982; A. L. Page, *PDMA's New Product Development Practices Survey: Performance and Best Practices,* PDMA 15th Annual International Conference, Boston, October 16, 1991; and E. Mansfield, "How Economists See R&D," *Harvard Business Review* (November–December 1981), 98–106.

8. See R. Biggadike, "The Risky Business of Diversification," *Harvard Business Review* (May–June 1979), 103–111; R. A. Burgelman, "A Process Model of Internal Corporate Venturing in the Diversified Major Firm," *Administrative Science Quarterly,* 28 (1983), 223–244; and Z. Block and I. C. Macmillan, *Corporate Venturing* (Cambridge, Mass: Harvard Business School Press, 1993).

9. R. Biggadike, "The Risky Business of Diversification"; Block and Macmillan, *Corporate Venturing.*

10. R. O. Crockett and C. Yang, "Why Motorola Should Hang Up on Iridium," *Business Week*, August 30, 1999, p. 46; L. Cauley, "Iridium's Downfall: The Marketing Took a Back Seat to the Science," *Wall Street Journal,* August 18, 1999, p. A1; J. N. Seth and R. Sisodia, "Why Cell Phones Succeeded Where Iridium Failed," *Wall Street Journal*, August 23, 1999, p. A14.

11. I. C. MacMillan and R. George, "Corporate Venturing: Challenges for Senior Managers," *Journal of Business Strategy*, 5 (1985), 34–43.

12. See R. A. Burgelman, M. M. Maidique, and S. C. Wheelwright, *Strategic Management of Technology and Innovation* (Chicago: Irwin, 1996), pp. 493–507.

13. See Z. Block and I. C. Macmillan, *Corporate Venturing,* (Cambridge, Mass.: Harvard Business School Press, 1993); Burgelman, Maidique, and Wheelwright, *Strategic Management of Technology and Innovation.*

14. G. Beardsley and E. Mansfield, "A Note on the Accuracy of Industrial Forecasts of the Profitability of New Products and Processes," *Journal of Business,* 23 (1978), 127–130.

15. J. Warner, J. Templeman, and R. Horn, "The Case Against Mergers," *Business Week*, October 30, 1995, 122–134.

16. For evidence on acquisitions and performance, see R. E. Caves, "Mergers, Takeovers, and Economic Efficiency," *International Journal of Industrial Organization*, 7 (1989), 151–174; M. C. Jensen and R. S. Ruback, "The Market for Corporate Control: The Scientific Evidence," *Journal of Financial Economics*, 11 (1983), 5–50; R. Roll, "Empirical Evidence on Takeover Activity and Shareholder Wealth," in *Knights, Raiders and Targets,* ed. J. C. Coffee, L. Lowenstein, and S. Rose (Oxford: Oxford University Press, 1989); Schleifer and Vishny, "Takeovers in the 60s and 80s" and T. H. Brush, "Predicted Changes in Operational Synergy and Post Acquisition Performance of Acquired Businesses," *Strategic Management Journal,* 17 (1996), 1–24.

17. D. J. Ravenscraft and F. M. Scherer, *Mergers, Selloffs, and Economic Efficiency* (Washington, D.C.: Brookings Institution, 1987).

18. See J. P. Walsh, "Top Management Turnover Following Mergers and Acquisitions," *Strategic Management Journal*, 9 (1988), 173–183.

19. See A. A. Cannella and D. C. Hambrick, "Executive Departure and Acquisition Performance," *Strategic Management Journal*, 14 (1993), 137–152.

20. M. Murray and J. Rebello, "Mellon Bank Corp: One Big Unhappy Family," *Wall Street Journal*, April 28, 1995, pp. B1, B4; K. Holland, "A Bank Eat Bank World—With Indigeston," *Business Week*, October 30, 1995, p. 130.

21. R. Roll, "The Hubris Hypothesis of Corporate Takeovers," *Journal of Business,* 59 (1986), 197–216.

22. "Coca-Cola: A Sobering Lesson from Its Journey into Wine," *Business Week,* June 3, 1985, pp. 96–98.

23. P. Haspeslagh and D. Jemison, *Managing Acquisitions.* (New York: Free Press, 1991).

24. For views on this issue, see L. L Fray, D. H. Gaylin, and J. W. Down, "Successful Acquisition Planning," *Journal of Business Strategy*, 5 (1984), 46–55; C. W. L. Hill, "Profile of a Conglomerate Takeover: BTR and Thomas Tilling," *Journal of General Management,* 10 (1984), 34–50; D. R. Willensky, "Making It Happen: How to Execute an Acquisition," *Business Horizons* (March–April 1985), 38–45; Haspeslagh and Jemison, *Managing Acquisitions;* P. L. Anslinger and T. E. Copeland, "Growth Through Acquisition: A Fresh Look," *Harvard Business Review* (January–February 1996), 126–135.

25. P. B. Carroll, "IBM, Motorola Plan Radio Link for Computers," *Wall Street Journal*, January 29, 1990, pp. B1, B5.

26. For a recent review of the evidence, and some contrary empirical evidence, see D. E. Hatfield, J. P. Liebskind, and T. C.

Opler, "The Effects of Corporate Restructuring on Aggregate Industry Specialization," *Strategic Management Journal*, 17 (1996), 55–72.

27. For example, see A. Schleifer and R. W. Vishny, "Takeovers in the 60s and 80s: Evidence and Implications," *Strategic Management Journal*, 12 (Special Issue, Winter 1991), 51–60.

28. See G. A. Patterson, and F. Schwadel, "Back in Time," *Wall Street Journal*, September 30, 1992, p. 1; J. Flynn, "Smaller but Wiser," *Business Week*, October 12, 1992, pp. 28–29; B. Bremner, "The Big Store's Trauma," *Business Week,* July 10, 1989, pp. 50–55.

29. See J. Argenti, *Corporate Collapse: Causes and Symptoms* (New York: McGraw-Hill, 1976); R. C. Hoffman, "Strategies for Corporate Turnarounds: What Do We Know About Them?" *Journal of General Management*, 14 (1984), 46–66; D. Schendel, G. R. Patton, and J. Riggs, "Corporate Turnaround Strategies: A Study of Profit Decline and Recov-

ery," *Journal of General Management,* 2 (1976), 1–22; and S. Siafter, *Corporate Recovery: Successful Turnaround Strategies and Their Implementation* (Hammondsworth, England: Penguin Books, 1984), pp. 25–60.

30. D. B. Bibeault, *Corporate Turnaround* (New York: McGraw-Hill, 1982).

31. Hoffman, "Strategies for Corporate Turnarounds."

32. Ibid.

33. Lee Iacocca, *Iacocca: An Autobiography* (New York: Bantam Books, 1984), p. 254.

34. T. Jackson, "Giant Bows to Colossal Pressure," *Financial Times,* September 22, 1995, p. 13; "AT&T's Three Way Split," *The Economist,* September 23, 1995, pp. 51–52; "Fatal Attraction," *Economist,* March 23, 1996, pp. 73–74; A. Ramirez, "Opportunity and New Risk for a Spinoff," *New York Times*, September 22, 1995, pp. C1, C4.

Implementing Strategy

Designing Organizational Structure

II

OPENING CASE

Microsoft's New E-Structure

IN THE 1990s, Microsoft emerged as the dominant global company in the computer software industry. However, as it has grown it has run into management problems, many of them stemming from the growth of the Internet and e-commerce and their effect on Microsoft's main business, desktop computer software. So serious are these problems that in 1999 Microsoft moved to radically change its organizational structure.

Over time, Microsoft had developed a structure with five levels in the hierarchy. Given that it had only 30,000 employees, its structure was quite flat, and flat structures help speed decision making. However, the problem at Microsoft was that Bill Gates, Microsoft's CEO, and Steve Ballmer, its president had, over time, begun to increasingly involve themselves in all important organizational decision making and had developed a very centralized approach to management. As the challenges of keeping up with the Internet increased, managers lower down the hierarchy felt themselves under increasing scrutiny and complained that Microsoft was becoming excessively bureaucratic. What is

more, Gates and Ballmer's close involvement in decision making had seriously slowed down the decision-making process, and since the Internet business changes frequently and in unpredictable ways. The slow response to these changes threatened Microsoft's future.

To increase Microsoft's ability to respond to these changes Ballmer and Gates knew they had to alter its structure. Previously, the company had two main product divisions: the operating systems division responsible for developing Windows, and a product development division responsible for developing applied uses as varied as Microsoft Word and Internet Explorer. Within each division, employees were organized into product teams, in which they worked together on specific projects. In the new structure, the product development division is divided up into six different groups based on the needs of different kinds of customers. The six groups target corporate customers, knowledge workers, home PC users, computer game buyers, Web surfers, and cyber shoppers. In this new market structure, each group is responsible for interfacing with its customer group, researching customers' needs, and then developing state-of-the-art software applications to meet those needs.[1]

Recognizing that this change in structure would pay off only if they changed their management style, Gates and Ballmer also resolved to change their management style. Henceforth, they decided, they would not intervene in each division's strategy; they would decentralize control to the heads of the six market divisions and to the team leaders in each division.[2] In this way, they hoped to transfer authority down the line, and speed the decision-making process, something vital in a fast-changing environment.

So far, the effect of these changes is unknown. Some analysts think that Gates and Ballmer will have a difficult time stepping back from decision making and that at the first sign of danger they will rush in to take up the reins. However, analysts also agree that Microsoft had to take some action if it did not want to experience the same problems of inertia and bureaucracy that plagued other giants, such as IBM and GM.

OVERVIEW

As the Opening Case suggests, in this chapter we consider how a company should organize its activities to create the most value. In Chapter 1, we define *strategy implementation* as the way in which a company creates the organizational arrangements that allow it to pursue its strategy most effectively. Strategy is implemented through organizational design. **Organizational design** means selecting the combination of organizational structure and control systems that lets a company pursue its strategy most effectively—that lets it *create and sustain a competitive advantage.*

The primary role of organizational structure and control is twofold: (1) to *coordinate* the activities of employees so that they work together most effectively to implement a strategy that increases competitive advantage and (2) to *motivate* employees and provide them with the incentives to achieve superior efficiency, quality, innovation, or customer responsiveness. Microsoft's strategy, for example, was to speed decision making and new-product development by moving to a new decentralized organizational structure. This structure allowed lower-level managers and teams to make decisions and respond quickly to the ever changing nature of competition in the Internet industry.

Organizational structure and control shape the way people behave and determine how they will act in the organizational setting. If a new CEO wants to know why it takes a long time for people to make decisions in a company, why there is a lack of cooperation between sales and manufacturing, or why product innovations are few and far between, he or she needs to look at the design of the organizational structure and control system and analyze how it coordinates and motivates employees' behavior. An analysis of how structure and control work makes it possible to change them to improve both coordination and motivation. Good organizational design allows an organization to improve its ability to create value and obtain a competitive advantage.

In this chapter, we examine the organizational structures available to strategic managers to coordinate and motivate employees. In Chapter 12, we consider the strategic control systems that managers use in conjunction with their organizational structures to monitor, motivate, and reward corporate, divisional, and functional performance. In Chapter 13, we trace the ways in which different strategy choices lead to the use of different kinds of structure and control systems. After reading these three chapters, you will be able to understand the principles behind Microsoft's redesign of its organizational structure and control system and you will be able to choose the right organizational design for implementing a company's strategy.

THE ROLE OF ORGANIZATIONAL STRUCTURE

After formulating a company's strategy, management must make designing organizational structure its next priority, for strategy is implemented through organizational structure. The value creation activities of organizational members are meaningless unless some type of structure is used to assign people to tasks and connect the activities of different people and functions.[3] As we discuss in Chapter 4, each organizational function needs to develop a distinctive competency in a value creation activity in order to increase efficiency, quality, innovation, or customer responsiveness. Thus, each function needs a structure designed to allow it to develop its skills and become more specialized and productive. As functions become increasingly specialized, however, they often begin to pursue their own goals exclusively and lose sight of the need to communicate and coordinate with other functions. The goals of R&D, for example, center on innovation and product design, whereas the goals of manufacturing often revolve around increasing efficiency. Left to themselves, the functions may have little to say to one another, and value creation opportunities will be lost.

The role of organizational structure is to provide the vehicle through which managers can coordinate the activities of the various functions or divisions to exploit fully their skills and capabilities. To pursue a cost-leadership strategy, for example, a company must design a structure that facilitates close coordination between the activities of manufacturing and R&D to ensure that innovative products can be produced both reliably and cost effectively. To achieve gains from synergy between divisions, managers must design mechanisms that allow divisions to communicate and share their skills and knowledge. In pursuing a global or multidomestic strategy, managers must create the right kind of organizational structure for managing the flow of resources and capabilities between domestic and foreign divisions. In Chapter 13, we examine in detail how managers match their strategies to different kinds of structure and control systems. Our goal now is to examine the basic building blocks of organizational structure to understand how it shapes the behavior of people, functions, and divisions.

■ Building Blocks of Organizational Structure

The basic building blocks of organizational structure are differentiation and integration. **Differentiation** is the way in which a company allocates people and resources to organizational tasks in order to create value.[4] Generally, the greater the number of different functions or divisions in an organization and the more skilled and specialized they are, the higher is the level of differentiation. For example, a company such as General Motors, with more than 300 different divisions and a multitude of different sales, research and development, and design departments, has a much greater level of differentiation than a local manufacturing company or restaurant. In deciding how to differentiate the organization to create value, strategic managers face two choices.

First, strategic managers must choose how to distribute *decision-making authority* in the organization to control value creation activities best; these are **vertical differentiation** choices.[5] For example, corporate managers must decide how much authority to delegate to managers at the divisional or functional level. Second, corporate managers must choose how to divide people and tasks into functions and divisions to increase their ability to create value; these are **horizontal differentiation** choices. Should there be separate sales and marketing departments, for example, or should the two be combined? What is the best way to divide the sales force to maximize its ability to serve customers' needs—by type of customer or by region in which customers are located?

Integration is the means by which a company seeks to coordinate people and functions to accomplish organizational tasks.[6] As just noted, when separate and distinct value creation functions exist, they tend to pursue their own goals and objectives. An organization has to create an organizational structure that lets the different functions and divisions coordinate their activities to pursue a strategy effectively. An organization uses integrating mechanisms, as well as the various types of control systems discussed in the next chapter, to promote coordination and cooperation between functions and divisions. In the case of Microsoft, for instance, to speed innovation and product development, the company established teams so that employees could work together to effectively exchange information and ideas. Similarly, establishing organizational norms, values, and a common culture that supports innovation promotes integration.

In short, differentiation refers to the way in which a company divides itself into parts (functions and divisions), and integration refers to the way in which the parts are then combined. Together, the two processes determine how an organizational structure will operate and how successfully strategic managers will be able to create value through their chosen strategies.

■ Differentiation, Integration, and Bureaucratic Costs

Implementing a structure to coordinate and motivate task activities is very expensive. The costs of operating an organizational structure and control system are called **bureaucratic costs**. The more complex the structure—that is, the higher the level of differentiation and integration—the higher are the bureaucratic costs of managing it. The more differentiated the company, for example, the more managers there are in specialized roles and the more resources each manager requires to perform that role effectively. Managers are expensive, and the more managers a company employs, the higher are its bureaucratic costs.

Similarly, the more integrated the company, the more managerial time is spent in face-to-face meetings to coordinate task activities. Managerial time also costs money, and thus the higher the level of integration, the more costly it is to operate the structure. A large company such as IBM or GM spends billions of dollars a year to operate its structures: that is, to pay its managers and employees and to provide them with the resources—offices, computers, equipment, laboratories, and so forth—they need to create value.

The high bureaucratic costs associated with strategy implementation can reduce a company's profits as fast or faster than poor strategy formulation, and thus they directly affect bottom-line organizational performance. This is why good organizational design is so important. You will recall from Chapter 4 that profit is the difference between revenues and costs. Bureaucratic costs are a large component of the cost side of the equation. Thus, a poor organizational design (for instance, one that has too many levels in the hierarchy or a badly thought-out pattern of work relationships) results in high costs, which reduce profits. By contrast, good organizational design, which economizes on bureaucratic costs, can give a company a low-cost advantage, which raises profits.

Organizational design also affects the revenue side of the equation. If strategic managers choose the right structure to coordinate value creation activities, they enhance the company's ability to create value, charge a premium price, and thus increase revenues. Bill Gates hopes that Microsoft's new structure will increase its ability to create value and a stream of new Internet software products for the different customer groups. Thus, good design affects both the revenue and the cost side of the profit equation, as Figure 11.1 illustrates. This is why strategy implementation is such a vital issue. In today's competitive environment, more and more companies are restructuring or reengineering their organizations to improve bottom-line performance through good organizational design. Consequently, it is necessary to understand the principles behind organizational design. We start by looking at differentiation.

FIGURE 11.1

How Organizational
Design Increases
Profitability

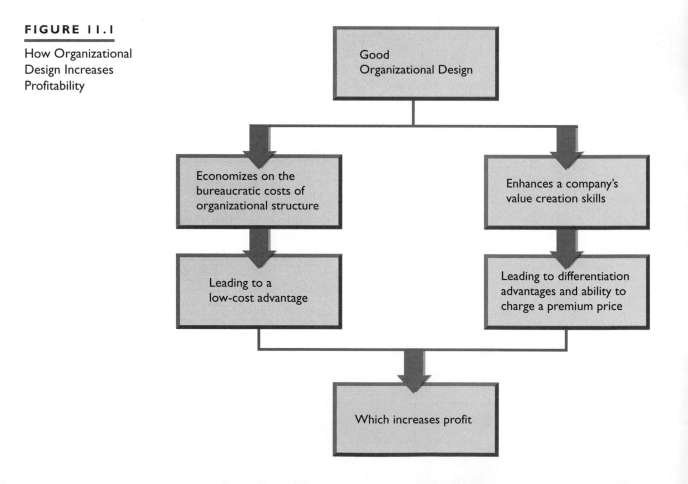

VERTICAL DIFFERENTIATION

The aim of vertical differentiation is to specify the reporting relationships that link people, tasks, and functions at all levels of a company. Fundamentally, this means that management chooses the appropriate number of hierarchical levels and the correct span of control for implementing a company's strategy most effectively.

The organizational hierarchy establishes the authority structure from the top to the bottom of the organization. The **span of control** is defined as the number of subordinates a manager directly manages.[7] The basic choice is whether to aim for a **flat structure**, with few hierarchical levels and thus a relatively wide span of control, or a **tall structure**, with many levels and thus a relatively narrow span of control (see Figure 11.2). Tall structures have many hierarchical levels relative to size; flat structures have few levels relative to size.[8] For example, research suggests that the average number of hierarchical levels for a company employing 3,000 persons is seven. Thus, an organization having nine levels would be called tall, and one having four would be called flat. With its 30,000 employees and five hierarchical levels, Microsoft, for instance, had a relatively flat structure.

Companies choose the number of levels they need on the basis of their strategy and the functional tasks necessary to achieve this strategy.[9] High-tech companies, for example, often pursue a strategy of differentiation based on service and quality. Consequently, these companies usually have flat structures, giving employees wide discretion to meet customers' demands without having to refer constantly to supervisors.[10] (We discuss this subject further in Chapter 12.) The crux of the matter is that the allocation of authority and responsibility in the organization must match the needs of corporate-, business-, and functional-level strategies.[11]

FIGURE 11.2

Tall and Flat Structures

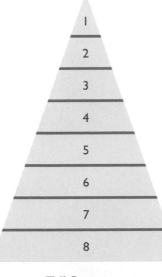

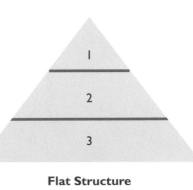

Tall Structure
(8 levels)

Flat Structure
(3 levels)

■ Problems with Tall Structures

As a company grows and diversifies, the number of levels in its hierarchy of authority increases to allow it to efficiently monitor and coordinate employee activities. Research shows that the number of hierarchical levels relative to company size is predictable as the size increases (see Figure 11.3).[12]

Companies with approximately 1,000 employees usually have four levels in the hierarchy: chief executive officer, departmental vice presidents, first-line supervisors, and shop-floor employees. Those with 3,000 employees have increased their level of vertical differentiation by raising the number of levels to eight. Something interesting happens to those with more than 3,000 employees, however. Even when companies grow to 10,000 employees or more, the number of hierarchical levels rarely increases beyond nine or ten. As organizations grow, managers apparently try to limit the number of hierarchical levels.

Managers try to keep the organization as flat as possible and follow what is known as the **principle of the minimum chain of command,** which states that an organization should choose a hierarchy with the minimum number of levels of authority necessary to achieve its strategy. Managers try to keep the hierarchy as flat as possible because when companies become too tall, problems occur, making strategy more difficult to implement and raising the level of bureaucratic costs.[13] Several factors that raise bureaucratic costs are illustrated in Figure 11.4 and discussed in the following paragraphs.

Coordination Problems Too many hierarchical levels impede communication and coordination between employees and functions and raise bureaucratic costs. Communication between the top and the bottom of the hierarchy takes much longer as the chain of command lengthens. This leads to inflexibility, and valuable

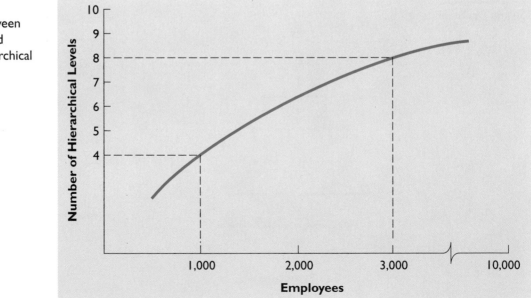

FIGURE 11.3

Relationship Between Company Size and Number of Hierarchical Levels

FIGURE 11.4

Sources of
Bureaucratic Costs

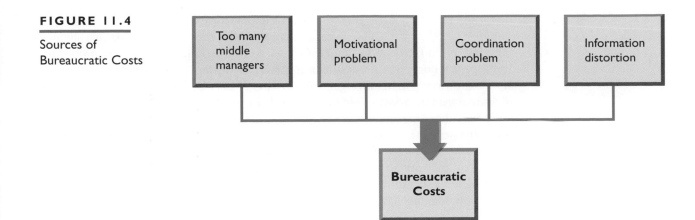

time is lost in bringing a new product to market or in keeping up with technological developments.[14] For Federal Express, communication and coordination are vital. Therefore, to avoid problems with them, the company allows a maximum of only five layers of management between the employee and the CEO.[15] In contrast, Procter & Gamble had a tall hierarchy, with the result that the company needed twice as much time as its competitors to introduce new products. To improve coordination and reduce costs, the company moved to streamline its structure and reduce its number of hierarchical levels.[16] Other companies have also taken measures to flatten their structures in order to speed communication and decision making. Strategy in Action 11.1 describes the changes made at General Electric and Alcoa.

Information Distortion   More subtle, but just as important, are the problems of information distortion that occur as the hierarchy of authority lengthens. Going

---

11.1   **STRATEGY *in* ACTION**

How to Flatten Structure

T all hierarchies cause such severe coordination and communications problems that many companies have been striving to shrink their hierarchies. For example, General Electric CEO Jack Welch has flattened the hierarchy from nine levels to four to bring him closer to his divisional managers and shorten the time it takes them to make decisions. At Alcoa, planning and decision making at the divisional level once were scrutinized by five levels of corporate management before divisional managers were allowed to proceed with their plans. Chairman Paul O'Neill wiped out these layers so that divisional managers would report directly to him. At both companies, these changes have brought top management closer to customers and provided divisional managers with the autonomy to be innovative and responsive to customers' needs. Moreover, flattening the hierarchy has saved these companies billions of dollars in managerial salaries and significantly reduced bureaucratic costs. Flattening their structures has clearly paid off for them.

down the hierarchy, managers at different levels (for example, divisional or corporate managers) may misinterpret information, either through accidental garbling of messages or on purpose, to suit their own interests. In either case, information from the top may not reach its destination intact. For instance, a request to share divisional knowledge to achieve gains from synergy may be overlooked or ignored by divisional managers who perceive it as a threat to their autonomy and power. This attitude among managers was one of the problems that led Lee Iacocca to reorganize Chrysler so that cost-cutting measures could be coordinated across divisions.

Information transmitted upward in the hierarchy may also be distorted. Subordinates may transmit to their superiors only information that improves their own standing in the organization. The greater the number of hierarchical levels, the more scope subordinates have to distort facts, so that the bureaucratic costs of managing the hierarchy increase. Similarly, bureaucratic costs increase if managers start to compete with each other. When they are free of close corporate supervision, they may hoard information to promote their own interests at the expense of the organization's. This also reduces coordination.

Motivational Problems   As the number of levels in the hierarchy increases, the amount of authority possessed by managers at each hierarchical level falls. For example, consider the situation of two identically sized organizations, one of which has three levels in its hierarchy and the other seven. Managers in the flat structure have much more authority, and greater authority increases their motivation to perform effectively and take responsibility for the organization's performance. Besides, when there are fewer managers, their performance is more visible and they can expect greater rewards when the business does well.

By contrast, the ability of managers in a tall structure to exercise authority is limited, and their decisions are constantly scrutinized by their superiors. As a result, managers tend to pass the buck and refuse to take the risks that are often necessary when new strategies are pursued. This increases the bureaucratic costs of managing the organization because more managerial time is spent coordinating task activities. Thus, the shape of the organization's structure strongly affects the motivation of people within it and the way in which strategy is implemented.[17]

Too Many Middle Managers   Another drawback of tall structures is that having many hierarchical levels implies having many middle managers, and employing managers is expensive. As noted earlier, managerial salaries, benefits, offices, and secretaries are a huge expense for an organization. If the average middle manager costs a company a total of $200,000 a year, then employing 100 surplus managers costs $20 million a year. Most large U.S. companies have recognized this fact, and in the 1990s companies such as IBM, GM, Compaq, and Procter & Gamble have moved to downsize their hierarchies, terminating thousands of managers. When these companies made billions of dollars in profits, they had little incentive to control the number of levels in the hierarchy and the number of managers. Once they grew aware of the cost of these managers, however, the companies ruthlessly purged the hierarchy, reducing the number of levels and thus the number of managers in order to lower bureaucratic costs and restore profitability.

To offer another example, when companies grow and are successful, they often hire personnel and create new positions without much regard for the effect of these actions on the organizational hierarchy. Later, when managers review that structure, it is quite common to see the number of levels reduced because of the disadvantages just discussed. Deregulation, too, prompts a reduction in levels and personnel. In a deregulated environment, companies must respond to increased competition. Since deregulation of the banking industry and the development of nationwide banks, banks like Bank of America and Chase Manhattan have reduced costs and streamlined their structures so that they could respond more rapidly to opportunities and threats brought about by increased competition. For example, Bank of America has laid off 20 percent of its work force.[18]

In sum, many problems arise when companies become too tall and the chain of command becomes too long. Strategic managers tend to lose control over the hierarchy, which means that they lose control over their strategies. Disaster often follows because a tall organizational structure decreases, rather than promotes, motivation and coordination between employees and functions and, as a result, bureaucratic costs escalate. One way to overcome such problems, at least partially, and to lessen bureaucratic costs is to decentralize authority—that is, vest authority in the hierarchy's lower levels as well as at the top. Because this is one of the most important implementation decisions a company can make, we discuss it next in more detail.

■ Centralization or Decentralization?

Authority is centralized when managers at the upper levels of the organizational hierarchy retain the authority to make the most important decisions. When authority is decentralized, it is delegated to divisions, functions, and managers and workers at lower levels in the organization. By delegating authority in this fashion, managers can economize on bureaucratic costs and avoid communication and coordination problems because information does not have to be constantly sent to the top of the organization for decisions to be made. There are three advantages to decentralization.

First, when strategic managers delegate operational decision-making responsibility to middle and first-level managers, they reduce information overload, enabling strategic managers to spend more time on strategic decision making. Consequently, they can make more effective decisions.

Second, when managers in the bottom layers of the organization become responsible for adapting the organization to suit local conditions, their motivation and accountability increase. The result is that decentralization promotes organizational flexibility and reduces bureaucratic costs because lower-level managers are authorized to make on-the-spot decisions. As AT&T has demonstrated, this can be an enormous advantage for business strategy. AT&T has a tall structure, but it is well known for the amount of authority it delegates to lower-level employees. Operational personnel can respond quickly to customers' needs and so ensure superior service, which is a major source of AT&T's competitive advantage. Similarly, to revitalize its product strategy, Westinghouse has massively decentralized its operations to give divisions more autonomy and encourage risk taking and a quick response to customers' needs.[19] Union Pacific also took that route, as detailed in Strategy in Action 11.2.

The third advantage of decentralization is that when lower-level employees are given the right to make important decisions, fewer managers are needed to oversee their activities and tell them what to do. Fewer managers mean lower bureaucratic costs.

If decentralization is so effective, why do not all companies decentralize decision making and avoid the problems of tall hierarchies? The answer is that centralization also has advantages. Centralized decision making allows easier coordination

Union Pacific Decentralizes to Increase Customer Responsiveness

In 1998, Union Pacific, one of the biggest rail freight carriers in the United States, was experiencing a crisis. The U.S. economic boom was causing a record increase in the amount of freight that the railroad had to transport, but the railroad was experiencing record delays in moving the freight. Union Pacific's customers were irate, complaining bitterly about the problem. Besides, the delays were costing the company a tremendous amount in penalty payments—$150 million.[20]

Why was there a problem? In its effort to cut costs, Union Pacific had developed a very centralized management approach. All the scheduling and route planning were handled centrally at its headquarters in the attempt to promote operating efficiency. The job of regional managers was largely to ensure the smooth flow of freight

through their regions. Recognizing that efficiency had to be balanced by responsiveness to customers, Union Pacific's CEO, Dick Davidson, announced a sweeping reorganization to the company's customers. Henceforth, regional managers were to have the authority to make operational decisions at the level at which it was most important—field operations. Regional managers would be able to alter scheduling and routing to accommodate customers' requests even if this raised costs, for the goal of the organization now was to "return to excellent performance by simplifying our processes and becoming easier to deal with."[21] In making this decision, the company was following the lead of its competitors, most of which had already moved to decentralize their operations, recognizing the many advantages of doing so.

of the organizational activities needed to pursue a company's strategy. If managers at all levels can make their own decisions, overall planning becomes extremely difficult, and the company may lose control of its decision making.

Centralization also means that decisions fit broad organization objectives. When its branch operations were getting out of hand, for example, Merrill Lynch increased centralization by installing more information systems to give corporate managers greater control over branch activities. Similarly, Hewlett-Packard centralized research and development responsibility at the corporate level to provide a more directed corporate strategy. Furthermore, in times of crisis, centralization of authority permits strong leadership because authority is focused on one person or group. This focus allows for speedy decision making and a concerted response by the whole organization.

Perhaps Lee Iacocca personifies the meaning of centralization in times of crisis. Iacocca provided the centralized control and vision needed for Chrysler's managers to respond creatively to the company's problems and move to the product-team structure, which has helped restore the company's profitability. On the other hand, Honda's experience with recentralizing authority, described in Strategy in Action 11.3, warns against going too far.

■ Summary

Managing the strategy-structure relationship when the number of hierarchical levels becomes too great is difficult and expensive. Depending on a company's situation, the bureaucratic costs of tall hierarchies can be reduced by decentralization. As company size increases, however, decentralization may become less effective. How then, as firms grow and diversify, can they economize on bureaucratic costs without

11.3 STRATEGY in ACTION

Honda's Change of Heart

In the early 1990s, Honda, like many other Japanese firms, found itself facing increased competition in a depressed global marketplace. It realized that its strategy of relying on product innovation to increase its sales growth had caused it to neglect the cost and efficiency side of the equation. As a result, its profit margins were eroding. Under its founder, Shoichiro Honda, the company had pioneered the concept of the Honda Way, based on a decentralized, participative, consensus approach to management. Teams led the decision-making process, and authority was decentralized throughout the company.

However, Honda's new president, Nobuhiko Kawamoto, concluded that this process had gone too far. He decided to recentralize authority in order to provide the control and direction needed to slash costs and increase efficiency. He began to give Honda's top managers more and more authority for corporatewide strategy and made them responsible for overseeing both the company's domestic and global strategy. The effect of this move was unexpected: Many of his top executives found it physically impossible to assume the extra responsibility that this new policy of centralization required. One key executive, Shoichiro Irimajiri, who was assigned responsibility for overseeing both Honda's global R&D *and* manufacturing operations, was forced to resign abruptly after his doctors told him that his extra workload had pushed him to the brink of a heart attack. As Kawamoto commented, maybe he had given Irimajiri too much responsibility.[22]

Since the new policy of centralization was not working, Kawamoto had to find another solution to the centralization-decentralization dilemma. He decided to delegate more authority down the hierarchy on a global basis. Managers in Honda's North American, European, and Japanese divisions would take over responsibility for managing strategy for their divisions. The role of Honda's corporate executives in Japan would be to provide coordination among divisions and facilitate the sharing of skills and resources to reduce costs. In this way, Honda hoped to strike a new balance between centralization and decentralization, so that the company could remain innovative and responsive to customers' needs in order to encourage sales growth but, at the same time, become more efficient in order to reduce costs.

Kawamoto's idea for a new structure for Honda has proved very successful. The new policy of decentralization has allowed divisional managers to form closer ties with Honda's suppliers and with its dealers, as well as make decisions faster. Suppliers are providing Honda with significantly lower cost inputs, and its close ties with dealers have allowed it to tailor its product line to better match customer needs.[23] The result has been that Honda's costs have fallen and its sales have risen dramatically, and by 1998 Honda was making record profits.[24] The company has returned to the Honda Way it pioneered.

becoming too tall or too decentralized? How can a firm such as Exxon control 300,000 employees without becoming too bureaucratic and inflexible? There must be alternative ways of creating organizational arrangements to achieve corporate objectives. The first of these ways is to choose the appropriate form of horizontal differentiation, that is, to decide how best to group organizational activities and tasks in order to create value.

HORIZONTAL DIFFERENTIATION

Whereas vertical differentiation concerns the division of authority, horizontal differentiation focuses on the division and grouping of tasks to meet the objectives of the business.[25] Because, to a large degree, an organization's tasks are a function of its strategy, the dominant view is that companies choose a form of horizontal differentiation or structure to match their organizational strategy. Perhaps the first person to address this issue formally was the Harvard business historian Alfred D. Chandler.[26] After studying the organizational problems experienced in large U.S. corporations such as Du Pont and General Motors as they grew and diversified in the early decades of this century, Chandler reached two conclusions: (1) that in principle organizational structure follows the growth strategy of a company, or, in other words, the range and variety of tasks it chooses to pursue and (2) that U.S. companies' structures change as their strategy changes in a predictable way over time.[27] The kinds of structure that companies adopt are discussed in this section.

■ Simple Structure

The simple structure is normally used by the small, entrepreneurial company producing a single product or a few related ones for a specific market segment. Often in this situation, one person, the entrepreneur, takes on most of the managerial tasks. No formal arrangements regarding organization exist, and horizontal differentiation is low because employees perform multiple duties.

A classic example of this structure is Apple Computer in its earliest stage, as a venture between two persons. Steven Jobs and Steven Wozniak worked together in a garage to perform all the necessary tasks to market their personal computer. They bought the component parts, assembled the first machines, and shipped them to customers. The success of their product, however, made this simple structure outdated almost as soon as it was adopted. To grow and perform all the tasks required by a rapidly expanding company, Apple needed a more complex form of horizontal differentiation. It needed to invest resources in creating an infrastructure to develop and enhance its distinctive competencies. Although developing a more complex structure raises bureaucratic costs, this is acceptable as long as the structure increases the amount of value a company can create.

■ Functional Structure

As companies grow, two things happen. First, the range of tasks that must be performed expands. For example, it suddenly becomes apparent that the services of a professional accountant or a production manager or a marketing expert are needed to take control of specialized tasks. Second, no one person can successfully perform more than one organizational task without becoming overloaded. The founder, for instance, can no longer simultaneously make and sell the product. The question that arises is what grouping of activities, or what form of horizontal differentiation, can most efficiently handle the needs of the growing company at least cost? The answer for most companies is a functional structure.

Functional structures group people on the basis of their common expertise and experience or because they use the same resources.[28] For example, engineers are grouped in a function because they perform the same tasks and use the same skills or equipment. Figure 11.5 shows a typical functional structure. Each of the rectangles represents a different functional specialization—research and development, sales and marketing, manufacturing, and so on—and each function concentrates on its own specialized task.

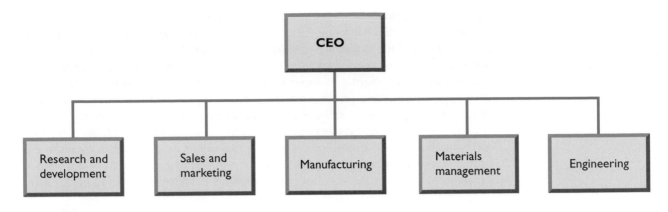

FIGURE 11.5

Functional Structure

■ Advantages of a Functional Structure

Functional structures have several advantages. First, if people who perform similar tasks are grouped together, they can learn from one another and become better—more specialized and productive—at what they do.

Second, they can monitor each other to make sure that all are performing their tasks effectively and not shirking their responsibilities. As a result, the work process becomes more efficient, reducing manufacturing costs and increasing operational flexibility.

A third important advantage of functional structures is that they give managers greater control of organizational activities. As already noted, many difficulties arise when the number of levels in the hierarchy increases. If people are grouped into different functions, however, each with their own managers, then *several different hierarchies are created*, and the company can avoid becoming too tall. There will be one hierarchy in manufacturing, for example, and another in accounting and finance. Managing the business is much easier when different groups specialize in different organizational tasks and are managed separately.

■ Disadvantages of a Functional Structure

In adopting a functional structure, a company increases its level of horizontal differentiation to handle more complex tasks. The structure allows it to keep control of its activities as it grows. This structure serves the company well until it starts to grow and diversify. If the company becomes geographically diverse and begins operating in many locations or if it starts producing a wide range of products, control and coordination problems arise that lower a company's ability to coordinate its activities and increase bureaucratic costs.[29]

Communications Problems   As separate functional hierarchies evolve, functions grow more remote from one another. As a result, it becomes increasingly difficult to communicate across functions and to coordinate their activities. This communication problem stems from **functional orientations**.[30] With greater differentiation, the various functions develop different orientations to the problems and issues facing the organization. Different functions have different time or goal orientations. Some, such as manufacturing, see things in a short time frame and concentrate on achieving short-run goals, such as reducing manufacturing costs. Others, such as research and development, see things from a long-term point of view, and their goals (that is, innovation and product development) may have a time horizon of several years. These factors may cause each function to develop a different view of the strategic issues facing the company. Manufacturing, for example, may see the strategic issue as the need to reduce costs, sales may see it as the need to increase customer responsiveness, and research and development may see it as the need to create new products. In such cases, the functions have trouble communicating and coordinating with one another, and bureaucratic costs increase.

Measurement Problems   As the number of its products proliferates, a company may find it difficult to gauge the contribution of a product or a group of products to its overall profitability. Consequently, the company may turn out some unprofitable products without realizing it and may also make poor decisions about resource allocation. This means that the company's measurement systems are not complex enough to serve its needs. Dell Computer's explosive growth in the early 1990s, for example, caused it to lose control of its inventory management systems; hence, it could not accurately project supply and demand for the components that go into its personal computers. Problems with its organizational structure plagued Dell, reducing efficiency and quality. As one manager commented, designing its structure to keep pace with its growth was like "building a high performance car while going around the race track."[31] However, Dell succeeded and today enjoys a 10 percent cost advantage over competitors such as Compaq in part because of its innovative organizational design.

Location Problems   Location factors may also hamper coordination and control. If a company is producing or selling in many different regional areas, then the centralized system of control provided by the functional structure no longer suits it because managers in the various regions must be flexible enough to respond to the needs of these regions. Thus, the functional structure is not complex enough to handle regional diversity.

Strategic Problems   Sometimes the combined effect of all these factors is that long-term strategic considerations are ignored because management is preoccupied with solving communication and coordination problems. As a result, a company may lose direction and fail to take advantage of new opportunities while bureaucratic costs escalate.

   Experiencing these problems is a sign that the company does not have an appropriate level of differentiation to achieve its objectives. A company must change its mix of vertical and horizontal differentiation if it is to perform effectively the organizational tasks that will enhance its competitive advantage. Essentially, these problems indicate that the company has outgrown its structure. It needs to invest more resources in developing a more complex structure, one that can meet the needs of its competitive strategy. Once again, this is expensive, but as long as the value a company can create is greater than the bureaucratic costs of operating the structure, it makes sense to adopt a more complex structure. Many companies choose a multidivisional structure.

■ Multidivisional Structure

The multidivisional structure possesses two main innovations over a functional structure, innovations that let a company grow and diversify yet overcome problems that stem from loss of control. First, each distinct product line or business unit is placed in its own *self-contained unit or division*, with all support functions. For example, PepsiCo has two major divisions—soft drinks and snack foods—and each has its own functions, such as marketing and research and development. The result is a higher level of horizontal differentiation.

Second, the office of *corporate headquarters staff* is created to monitor divisional activities and to exercise financial control over each of the divisions.[32] This staff contains corporate managers who oversee the activities of divisional and functional managers, and it constitutes an additional level in the organizational hierarchy. Hence, there is a higher level of vertical differentiation in a multidivisional structure than in a functional structure.

Figure 11.6 presents a typical multidivisional structure found in a large chemical company such as Du Pont. Although this company might easily have seventy operating divisions, only three—the oil, pharmaceuticals, and plastics divisions—are represented here. As a self-contained business unit, each division possesses a full array of

FIGURE 11.6

Multidivisional Structure

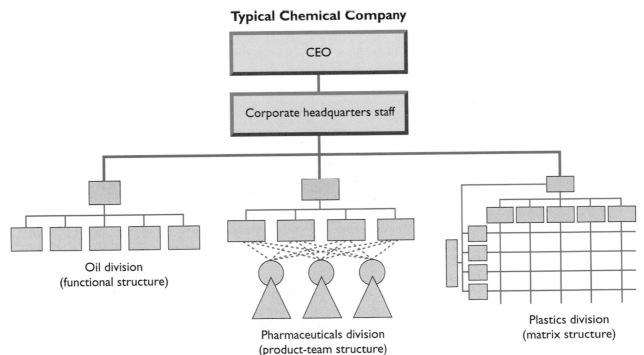

Typical Chemical Company

Oil division
(functional structure)

Pharmaceuticals division
(product-team structure)

Plastics division
(matrix structure)

support services. For example, each has self-contained accounting, sales, and personnel departments. Each division functions as a profit center, making it much easier for corporate headquarters staff to monitor and evaluate each division's activities.[33]

The bureaucratic costs of operating a multidivisional structure are very high compared with those at a functional structure. The size of the corporate staff is a major expense, and companies such as GM and IBM have thousands of managers on their corporate staffs even after their massive downsizing. Similarly, the use of product divisions, each with its own specialist support functions such as research and development and marketing, is a major expense. However, once again, if higher bureaucratic costs are offset by a higher level of value creation, it makes sense to move to a more complex structure.

Each division is also able to adopt the structure that best suits its needs. Figure 11.6 shows that the oil division has a functional structure because its activities are standardized; the pharmaceuticals division has a product-team structure; and the plastics division has a matrix structure. (The latter two structures are discussed in detail later in this chapter.) Similarly, General Motors operates the whole corporation through a multidivisional structure, but each auto division organizes itself into different product groups, based on the type of auto made.

In the multidivisional structure, day-to-day operations of a division are the responsibility of divisional management; that is, divisional management has **operating responsibility**. Corporate headquarters staff, however, which includes members of the board of directors as well as top executives, is responsible for overseeing long-term plans and providing the guidance for interdivisional projects. This staff has **strategic responsibility**. Such a combination of self-contained divisions with a centralized corporate management represents a higher level of both vertical and horizontal differentiation, as noted earlier. These two innovations provide the extra control necessary to coordinate growth and diversification. Because this structure, despite its high bureaucratic costs, has now been adopted by more than 90 percent of all large U.S. corporations, we need to consider its advantages and disadvantages in more detail.

■ Advantages of a Multidivisional Structure

When managed effectively at both the corporate and the divisional levels, a multidivisional structure offers several advantages. Together, they can raise corporate profitability to a new peak because they allow the organization to operate more complex kinds of corporate-level strategy.

Enhanced Corporate Financial Control   The profitability of different business divisions is clearly visible in the multidivisional structure.[34] Because each division is its own profit center, financial controls can be applied to each business on the basis of profit criteria. Typically, these controls cover establishing targets, monitoring performance on a regular basis, and selectively intervening when problems arise. Corporate headquarters is also in a better position to allocate corporate financial resources among competing divisions. The visibility of divisional performance means that corporate headquarters can identify the divisions in which investment of funds will yield the greatest long-term returns. In a sense, the corporate office is in a position to act as the investor or banker in an internal capital market, channeling funds to high-yield uses.

Enhanced Strategic Control   The multidivisional structure frees corporate staff from operating responsibilities. The staff thus gains time for contemplating wider strategic issues and for developing responses to environmental changes. The multidivisional structure also enables corporate headquarters to obtain the proper information to perform strategic planning functions. For example, separating individual businesses is a necessary prerequisite for portfolio planning.

Growth   The multidivisional structure lets the company overcome an organizational limit to its growth. By reducing information overload at the center, corporate managers can handle a greater number of businesses. They can consider opportunities for further growth and diversification. Communication problems are reduced because the same set of standardized accounting and financial control techniques can be used for all divisions. Also, corporate managers are able to implement a policy of management by exception, which means that they intervene only when problems arise.

Stronger Pursuit of Internal Efficiency   Within a functional structure, the interdependence of functional departments means that the *individual* performance of each function inside a company cannot be measured by objective criteria. For example, the profitability of the finance function, marketing function, or manufacturing function cannot be assessed in isolation because they are only part of the whole. This often means that within the functional structure considerable degrees of organizational slack—that is, functional resources that are used unproductively—can go undetected. For example, the head of the finance function might employ a larger staff than required for efficiency to reduce work pressures inside the department and to bring the manager higher status.

In a multidivisional structure, however, the individual efficiency of each autonomous division can be directly observed and measured in terms of the profit it generates. Thus, autonomy makes divisional managers accountable for their own performance; they can have no alibis for poor performance. The corporate office is thus in a better position to identify inefficiencies.

■ Disadvantages of a Multidivisional Structure

Probably because a multidivisional structure has a number of powerful advantages, it seems to be the preferred choice of most large diversified enterprises today. Indeed, research suggests that large companies that adopt this structure outperform those that retain the functional structure.[35] A multidivisional structure has its disadvantages as well, however. Good management can eliminate some of them, but others are inherent in the way the structure operates and require constant managerial attention. These disadvantages are discussed next.

Establishing the Divisional-Corporate Authority Relationship   The authority relationship between corporate headquarters and the divisions must be correctly established. The multidivisional structure introduces a new level in the hierarchy—the corporate level. The problem lies in deciding how much authority and control to assign to the operating divisions and how much authority to retain at corporate headquarters.

This problem was first noted by Alfred Sloan, the founder of General Motors. He introduced the multidivisional structure at General Motors, which became the first company to adopt it, and created General Motors' familiar five-automobile divisions: Chevrolet, Pontiac, Oldsmobile, Buick, and Cadillac.[36] What Sloan found, however, was that when headquarters retained too much power and authority, the operating divisions lacked sufficient autonomy to develop the business strategy that might best meet the needs of the division. On the other hand, when too much power was delegated to the divisions, they pursued divisional objectives, with little heed to the needs of the whole corporation. As a result, for example, not all of the potential gains from synergy discussed earlier could be achieved.

Thus, the central issue in managing the multidivisional structure is how much authority should be *centralized* at corporate headquarters and how much should be *decentralized* to the divisions. This issue must be decided by each company in reference to the nature of its business- and corporate-level strategies. There are no easy answers, and over time, as the environment changes or the company alters its strategies, the balance between corporate and divisional control will also change. Strategy in Action 11.4 illustrates this problem. It highlights the changes that Amoco, one of the largest U.S. oil companies, has made in its divisional structure.

Distortion of Information   If corporate headquarters puts too much emphasis on divisional return on investment—for instance, by setting very high and stringent return-on-investment targets—divisional managers may choose to distort the information they supply top management and paint a rosy picture of the present situation at the expense of future profits. That is, divisions may maximize short-run profits, perhaps by cutting product development or new investments or marketing expenditures. This may cost the company dearly in the future. The problem stems from too tight financial control. General Motors has suffered from this problem in recent years, as declining performance has prompted divisional managers to try to make their divisions look good to corporate headquarters. Managing the corporate-divisional interface requires coping with subtle power issues.

Competition for Resources   The third problem of managing a multidivisional structure is that the divisions themselves may compete for resources, and this rivalry prevents synergy gains or economies of scope from emerging. For example, the amount of money that corporate personnel has to distribute to the divisions is fixed. Generally, the divisions that can demonstrate the highest return on investment will get the lion's share of the money. Because that large share strengthens them in the next time period, the strong divisions grow stronger. Consequently, divisions may actively compete for resources and, by doing so, reduce interdivisional coordination.

Transfer Pricing   Divisional competition may also lead to battles over **transfer pricing**. As we discuss in Chapter 9, one of the problems with vertical integration or related diversification is setting transfer prices between divisions. Rivalry among divisions increases the problem of setting fair prices. Each supplying division tries to set the highest price for its outputs to maximize its own return on investment. Such competition can completely undermine the corporate culture and make a

11.4 STRATEGY *in* ACTION

Amoco's New Approach

As with most other global oil companies, Amoco is engaged in three major activities: oil exploration, refining, and chemicals manufacturing. To manage these activities, Amoco used a three-legged structure and created three independent operating subsidiaries to manage each of its three main activities. Each subsidiary had its own set of managers, who were responsible for overseeing all the many different business divisions inside each subsidiary. The managers of all three subsidiaries then reported to Amoco's corporate-level managers, who oversaw their activities and made the final decision on what each subsidiary should be doing. Thus, all important decision making at Amoco took place at the top of the organization. As a result, it often took a long time to make decisions because of the many managerial layers between Amoco's corporate managers and its divisional managers. Since divisional managers were responsible for developing an effective business-level strategy, the slow decision-making process hampered their attempts to build a competitive advantage.[37]

In the 1990s, however, Amoco, like other global oil companies such as Exxon, British Petroleum, and Mobil, experienced intense pressure to reduce costs because of flat gas prices. To try to boost profits, Amoco laid off more than one-quarter of its work force, but this did not have the desired effect. Therefore, Amoco's managers took a close look at the company's structure to see whether there was a way to increase its performance.

Amoco's chairman and CEO, H. Laurance Fuller, concluded that a massive reorganization of Amoco's structure was necessary. Fuller decided to eliminate Amoco's three-legged structure completely and to remove all the managers at the subsidiary level. The three subsidiaries were divided into seventeen independent business divisions, and Amoco changed to a multidivisional structure. Henceforth, decision-making authority was decentralized to the managers of each division, who could choose their own strategy for the division. Each division was to be evaluated on the basis of its ability to reach certain growth targets set by corporate managers, but the way the divisions achieved those targets would be determined by their own managers.

By 1996, it was clear that Fuller's idea for a new, flatter, decentralized product-division structure had worked. Managers were acting more entrepreneurially and the company was operating more efficiently. In 1998, in another attempt to increase efficiency, Fuller agreed to merge Amoco with British Petroleum (BP). The companies are still in the process of deciding how to combine the activities of their various divisions, many of whose activities overlap and duplicate one another, so that the company can compete effectively in the new century.[38]

company a battleground. Many companies have a history of competition among divisions. Some, of course, may encourage competition, if managers believe that it leads to maximum performance.

Short-Term Research and Development Focus If extremely high ROI targets are set by corporate headquarters, there is a danger that the divisions will cut back on research and development expenditures to improve the financial performance of the division. Although this inflates divisional performance in the short term, it reduces a division's ability to develop new products and leads to a fall in the stream of long-term profits. Hence, corporate headquarters personnel must carefully control their interactions with the divisions to ensure that both the short- and long-term goals of the business are being achieved.

Bureaucratic Costs   As noted earlier, because each division possesses its own specialized functions, such as finance or research and development, multidivisional structures are expensive to run and manage. Research and development is especially costly, and so some companies centralize such functions at the corporate level to serve all divisions. The duplication of specialist services is not a problem if the gains from having separate specialist functions outweigh the costs. Again, strategic managers must decide whether duplication is financially justified. Activities are often centralized in times of downturn or recession, particularly advisory services and planning functions; divisions, however, are retained as profit centers.

The advantages of divisional structures must be balanced against their disadvantages, but, as we already noted, the disadvantages can be managed by an observant, professional management team that is aware of the issues involved. The multidivisional structure is the dominant one today, which clearly suggests its usefulness as the means of managing the multibusiness corporation.

■ Matrix Structure

A matrix structure differs from the structures discussed so far in that it is based on two forms of horizontal differentiation rather than on one, as in the functional structure.[39] In the matrix design, activities on the vertical axis are grouped by *function,* so that there is a familiar differentiation of tasks into functions such as engineering, sales and marketing, and research and development. In addition, superimposed on this vertical pattern is a horizontal pattern based on differentiation by *product or project.* The result is a complex network of reporting relationships among projects and functions, as depicted in Figure 11.7.

This structure also employs an unusual kind of vertical differentiation. Although matrix structures are flat, with few hierarchical levels, employees inside the matrix have two bosses: a **functional boss**, who is the head of a function, and a **project boss**, who is responsible for managing the individual projects. Employees work on a project team with specialists from other functions and report to the project boss on project matters and the functional boss on matters relating to functional issues. All employees who work in a project team are called **two-boss employees** and are responsible for managing coordination and communication among the functions and projects.

Matrix structures were first developed by companies that are in high-technology industries such as aerospace and electronics—for example, TRW and Hughes Aircraft. These companies were developing radically new products in uncertain, competitive environments, and speed of product development was the crucial consideration. They needed a structure that could respond to this need, but the functional structure was too inflexible to allow the complex role and task interactions necessary to meet new-product development requirements. Moreover, employees in these companies tend to be highly qualified and professional and perform best in autonomous, flexible working conditions. The matrix structure provides such conditions.

For example, this structure requires a minimum of direct hierarchical control by supervisors. Team members control their own behavior, and participation in project teams allows them to monitor other team members and learn from each other. Furthermore, as the project goes through its different phases, different specialists from various functions are required. Thus, for example, at the first stage, the services of research and development specialists may be called for; then at the next stage, engi-

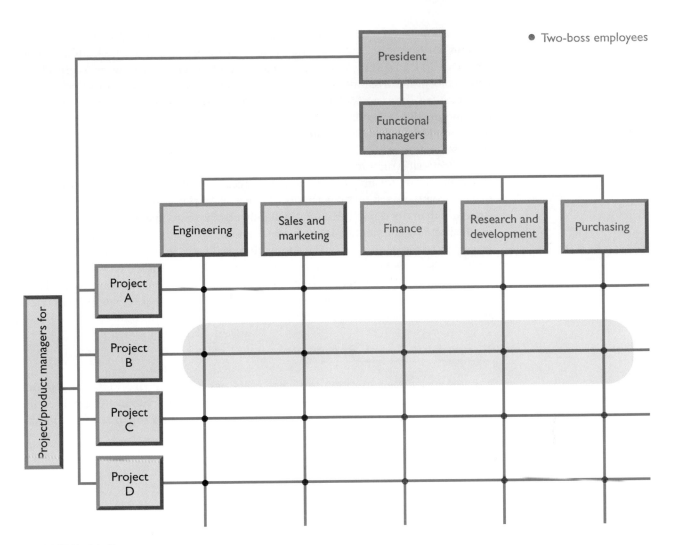

FIGURE 11.7

Matrix Structure

neers and marketing specialists may be needed to make cost and marketing projections. As the demand for the type of specialist changes, team members can be moved to other projects that require their services. The matrix structure, therefore, can make maximum use of employees' skills as existing projects are completed and new ones come into existence.

Finally, the freedom given by the matrix not only provides the autonomy to motivate employees, but also leaves top management free to concentrate on strategic issues, since they do not have to become involved in operating matters. On all these counts, the matrix is an excellent tool for creating the flexibility necessary for quick reactions to competitive conditions.

The matrix structure does have disadvantages, however.[40] First, the bureaucratic costs of operating this structure are very high compared with those of operating a functional structure. Because employees tend to be highly skilled, both salaries and overhead are high. Second, the constant movement of employees around the matrix means that time and money are spent establishing new team relationships and getting the project off the ground. Third, the two-boss employee's role, balancing as it does the interests of the project with those of the function, is difficult to manage, and care must be taken to avoid conflict between functions and projects over resources. Over time, it is possible that project managers will take the leading role in planning and goal setting, in which case the structure would work more like a product or multidivisional structure. If function and project relationships are left uncontrolled, they can lead to power struggles among managers, resulting in stagnation and decline rather than increased flexibility. Finally, the larger the organization, the more difficult it is to operate a matrix structure, because task and role relationships become complex. In such situations, the only option may be to change to a multidivisional structure.

Given these advantages and disadvantages, the matrix is generally used only when a company's strategy warrants it. There is no point in using a more complex structure than necessary because it will only cost more to manage. In dynamic product/market environments, such as biotechnology and computers, the benefits of the matrix in terms of flexibility and innovation are likely to exceed the high bureaucratic costs of using it, and so it becomes an appropriate choice of structure. However, companies in the mature stage of an industry's life cycle or those pursuing a low-cost strategy would rarely choose this structure because it is expensive to operate. We discuss matrix structure further in Chapter 13.

■ Product-Team Structure

A major structural innovation in recent years has been the **product-team structure**. Its advantages are similar to those of a matrix structure, but it is much easier and far less costly to operate because of the way people are organized into permanent cross-functional teams, as Figure 11.8 illustrates.

FIGURE 11.8

Product-Team Structure

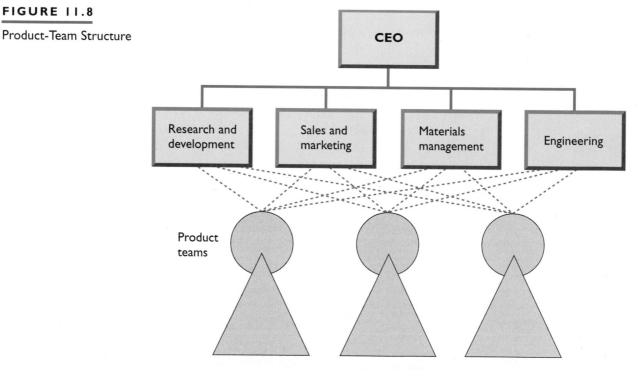

In the product-team structure, as in the matrix structure, tasks are divided along product or project lines to reduce bureaucratic costs and to increase management's ability to monitor and control the manufacturing process. However, instead of being assigned only *temporarily* to different projects, as in the matrix structure, functional specialists are placed in *permanent* cross-functional teams. As a result, the costs associated with coordinating their activities are much lower than in a matrix structure, in which tasks and reporting relationships change rapidly.

Cross-functional teams are formed right at the beginning of the product-development process so that any difficulties that arise can be ironed out early, before they lead to major redesign problems. When all functions have direct input from the beginning, design costs and subsequent manufacturing costs can be kept low. Moreover, the use of cross-functional teams speeds innovation and customer responsiveness because when authority is decentralized to the team, decisions can be made more quickly. Strategy in Action 11.5 profiles Lexmark, which shifted to a product-team structure to reduce costs and speed product development.

11.5 STRATEGY in ACTION

Restructuring at Lexmark

Lexmark, a printer and typewriter manufacturer, was a division of IBM until it was sold to a New York investment firm in 1992. As an IBM division, it had performed badly, and IBM sold it after years of losses brought on by high operating costs and an inability to produce new products that could compete with Hewlett-Packard and Japanese printer makers such as Epson. Its new top-management team, led by Marvin Mann, an ex-IBM executive, had the task of reengineering its structure to turn the company around.

Mann first destroyed the organizational structure that the company had developed under its former IBM management. Like the rest of IBM, the division had a tall, centralized structure, where all important decisions were made high in the organization by top managers. This slowed decision making and made it very difficult to communicate across functions because so many managers at different levels and in different functions had to approve new plans.

Moving quickly to change this system, Mann streamlined the company's hierarchy, which meant terminating 50 percent of its managers and eliminating all staff managers—that is, those with no direct-line responsibility.

This action cut out three levels in the hierarchy. He then decentralized authority to the product managers of the company's four product groups and told them to develop their own plans and goals. In addition, to continue the process of decentralization, product managers were instructed to develop cross-functional teams comprising employees from all functions, with the goal of finding new and improved ways of organizing task activities to reduce costs. The teams were to use competitive benchmarking and evaluate their competitors' products in order to establish new performance standards to guide their activities. Finally, as an incentive for employees to work hard at increasing efficiency, innovation, and quality, Mann established a company stock ownership scheme to reward employees for their efforts.

The reengineering of the organizational structure to a product-team structure has been very successful for Lexmark. The cost of launching new products has gone down by 50 percent and it has speeded up its new-product development cycle by 30 percent. The company's net income was $149 million in 1997 and increased to $243 million in 1998.[41] Since its share price has jumped from $20 a share in 1993 to more than $100 in 1999, its employees have shared in its success too.

■ Geographic Structure

When a company operates as a geographic structure, geographic regions become the basis for the grouping of organizational activities. For example, a company may divide its manufacturing operations and establish manufacturing plants in different regions of the country. This allows it to be responsive to the needs of regional customers and reduces transportation costs. Similarly, service organizations such as store chains or banks may organize their sales and marketing activities on a regional, rather than on a national, level to get closer to their customers.

A geographic structure provides more control than a functional structure because there are several regional hierarchies carrying out the work previously performed by a single centralized hierarchy. A company such as Federal Express clearly needs to operate a geographic structure to fulfill its corporate goal: next-day delivery. Large merchandising organizations, such as Neiman Marcus, Dillard Department Stores, and Wal-Mart, also moved to a geographic structure soon after they started building stores across the country. With this type of structure, different regional clothing needs (for example, sun wear in the Southwest, down coats in the East) can be handled as required. At the same time, because the purchasing function remains centralized, one central organization can buy for all regions. Thus, in using a geographic structure a company can both achieve economies of scale in buying and distribution and reduce coordination and communication problems.

Neiman Marcus developed a geographic structure similar to the one shown in Figure 11.9 to manage its nationwide chain of stores. In each region, it established a team of regional buyers to respond to the needs of customers in each geographic area—for example, the western, central, eastern, and southern regions. The regional

FIGURE 11.9

Geographic Structure

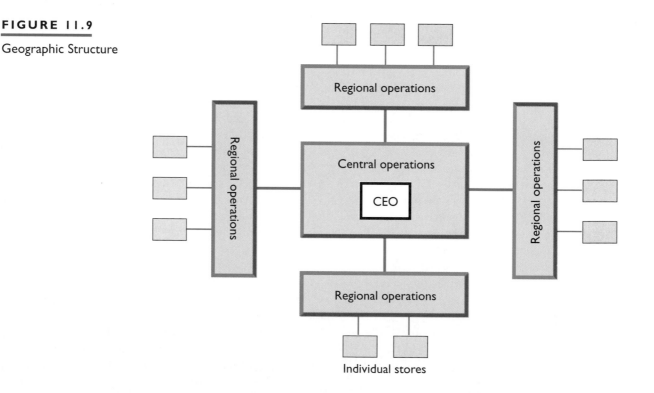

buyers then fed their information to the central buyers at corporate headquarters, who coordinated their demands to obtain purchasing economies and to ensure that Neiman Marcus's high-quality standards, on which its differentiation advantage depends, were maintained nationally.

The usefulness of the matrix, product-team, or geographic structure depends, however, on the size of the company and its range of products and regions. If a company starts to diversify into unrelated products or to integrate vertically into new industries, these structures cannot handle the increased diversity, and a company must move to a multidivisional structure. Only the multidivisional structure is complex enough to deal with the needs of the large, multibusiness company.

INTEGRATION AND INTEGRATING MECHANISMS

As just discussed, an organization must choose the appropriate form of differentiation to match its strategy. Greater diversification, for example, requires that a company move from a functional structure to a multidivisional structure. Differentiation, however, is only the first organizational design decision to be made. The second decision concerns the level of integration necessary to make an organizational structure work effectively. As noted earlier, *integration* refers to the extent to which an organization seeks to coordinate its value creation activities and make them interdependent. The design issue can be summed up simply: the higher a company's level of differentiation, the higher is the level of integration needed to make organizational structure work effectively.[42] Thus, if a company adopts a more complex form of differentiation, it requires a more complex form of integration to accomplish its goals. Federal Express, for example, needs an enormous amount of integration and coordination to allow it to fulfill its promise of next-day package delivery. It is renowned for its innovative use of integrating mechanisms, such as customer-liaison personnel, to manage its transactions quickly and efficiently.

■ Forms of Integrating Mechanisms

There is a series of integrating mechanisms a company can use to increase its level of integration as its level of differentiation increases.[43] These mechanisms—on a continuum from simple to complex—are listed in Table 11.1, together with examples of the individuals or groups that might perform these integrating roles. As is the case when increasing the level of differentiation, however, increasing the level of integration is expensive. There are high bureaucratic costs associated with using managers to coordinate value creation activities. Hence, a company only uses more complex integrating mechanisms to coordinate its activities to the extent necessary to implement its strategy effectively.

Direct Contact   The aim behind establishing direct contact among managers is to set up a context within which managers from different divisions or functions can work together to solve mutual problems. Managers from different functions have different goals and interests but equal authority, and so they may tend to compete rather than cooperate when conflicts arise. In a typical functional structure, for example, the heads of each of the functions have equal authority; the nearest common

TABLE 11.1

Types and Examples of Integrating Mechanisms

Direct contact	Sales and production managers
Liason roles	Assistant sales and plant managers
Task forces	Representatives from sales, production, and research and development
Teams	Organizational executive committee
Integrating roles	Assistant vice president for strategic planning or vice president without portfolio
Matrix	All roles are integrating roles

point of authority is the CEO. Consequently, if disputes arise, no mechanism exists to resolve the conflicts apart from the authority of the boss.

In fact, one sign of conflict in organizations is the number of problems sent up the hierarchy for upper-level managers to solve. This wastes management time and effort, slows down strategic decision making, and makes it difficult to create a cooperative culture in the company. For this reason, companies generally choose more complex integrating mechanisms to coordinate interfunctional and divisional activities.

Interdepartmental Liaison Roles   A company can improve its interfunctional coordination through the interdepartmental liaison role. When the volume of contacts between two departments or functions increases, one of the ways of improving coordination is to give one manager in *each* division or function the responsibility for coordinating with the other. These managers may meet daily, weekly, monthly, or as needed. Figure 11.10a depicts the nature of the liaison role, the small dot representing the manager inside the functional department who has responsibility for coordinating with the other function. The responsibility for coordination is part of a manager's full-time job, but through these roles a permanent relationship forms between the managers involved, greatly easing strains between departments. Furthermore, liaison roles offer a way of transferring information across the organization, which is important in large, anonymous organizations, whose employees may know no one outside their immediate department.

Temporary Task Forces   When more than two functions or divisions share common problems, direct contact and liaison roles are of limited value because they do not provide enough coordination. The solution is to adopt a more complex form of integrating mechanism called a task force. The nature of the task force is represented diagrammatically in Figure 11.10b. One member of each function or division is assigned to a task force created to solve a specific problem. Essentially, task forces are *ad hoc committees,* and members are responsible for reporting back to their departments on the issues addressed and solutions recommended. Task forces are temporary because, once the problem has been solved, members return to their normal roles in their own departments or are assigned to other task forces. Task force members also perform many of their normal duties while serving on the task force.

FIGURE 11.10

Forms of Integrating
Mechanisms

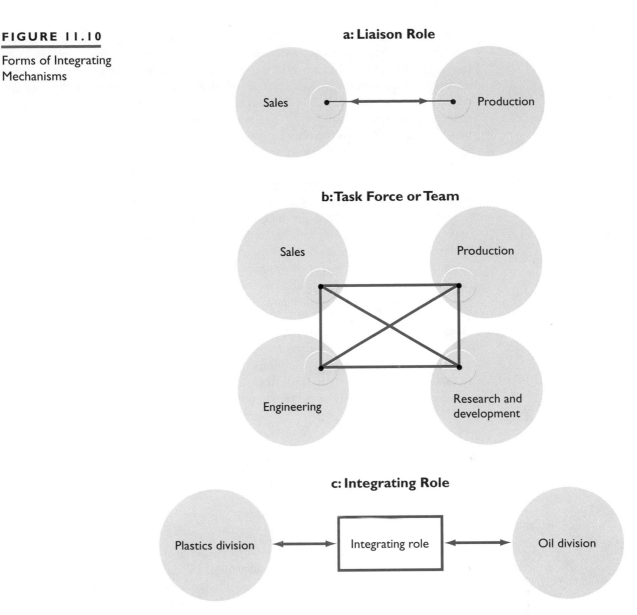

• Indicates manager with responsibility for integration

Permanent Teams In many cases, the issues addressed by a task force recur. To deal with these issues effectively, an organization must establish a permanent integrating mechanism, such as a permanent team. An example of a permanent team is a new-product development committee, which is responsible for the choice, design, and marketing of new products. Such an activity obviously requires a great deal of integration among functions if new products are to be successfully introduced, and establishing a permanent integrating mechanism accomplishes this. Intel, for instance, emphasizes teamwork. It formed a council system based on approximately ninety cross-functional groups, which meet regularly to set functional strategy in areas such as engineering and marketing and to develop business-level strategy.

The importance of teams in the management of the organizational structure cannot be overemphasized. Essentially, permanent teams are the organization's *standing committees,* and much of the strategic direction of the organization is formulated in their meetings. Henry Mintzberg, in a study of how the managers of corporations spend their time, discovered that they spend more than 60 percent of their time in these committees.[44] The reason is not bureaucracy but rather the fact that integration is possible only in intensive, face-to-face sessions, in which managers can understand others' viewpoints and develop a cohesive organizational strategy. The more complex the company, the more important these teams become. Westinghouse, for example, has established a whole new task force and team system to promote integration among divisions and improve corporate performance.

As discussed earlier, the product-team structure is based on the use of cross-functional teams to speed products to market. These teams assume the responsibility for all aspects of product development. The way in which AT&T made use of cross-functional teams to speed product development in its race to compete with Japanese manufacturers (described in Strategy in Action 11.6) illustrates how these teams can increase coordination and integration among functions.

Integrating Roles   The only function of the integrating role is to prompt integration among divisions or departments; it is a full-time job. As Figure 11.10c indicates, the role is independent of the subunits or divisions being integrated. It is staffed by an independent expert, who is normally a senior manager with a great deal of experience in the joint needs of the two departments. The job is to coordinate the deci-

---

11.6   STRATEGY *in* ACTION

Teamwork at AT&T

Like other large companies, AT&T had developed a very tall, centralized structure to manage its activities. While the telephone industry was regulated, AT&T cared little about the way its massive bureaucracy slowed down decision making. However, after deregulation a major problem facing the company was how to speed the development of new telephones and answering machines that could compete with those of Japanese companies such as Panasonic and Sony. These companies led the market in terms of both the features and the low price of telephone products, and AT&T was a poor third in the competitive marketplace.

AT&T's answer was to bypass the bureaucracy by creating cross-functional teams. Previously, AT&T had employed the usual functional approach to managing product development. The product started in engineering and then went to manufacturing, which in turn handed the product over to marketing. This was a slow and time-consuming process. In the new approach, John Hanley, the AT&T vice president of product development, decided to form teams of six to twelve people from all these functions to handle all aspects of the development process. Each team was given a deadline for the various project phases and then left to get on with the job. The results were astonishing. Product development time was reduced by 50 percent (for example, AT&T's new 4200 phone was produced in one year, not the usual two), costs went down, and quality went up. Today, AT&T's answering machines and cordless phones are the market leaders, and AT&T has extended the use of cross-functional teams throughout its business.

sion process among departments or divisions so that synergetic gains from cooperation can be obtained. One study found that Du Pont had created 160 integrating roles to provide coordination among the different divisions of the company and improve corporate performance.[45] Once again, the more differentiated the company, the more common are these roles. Often people in these roles take the responsibility for chairing task forces and teams, and this provides additional integration.

Integrating Departments   Sometimes the number of integrating roles becomes so high that a permanent integrating department is established at corporate headquarters. Normally, this occurs only in large, diversified corporations that see the need for integration among divisions. This department consists mainly of strategic planners and may indeed be called the strategic planning department. Corporate headquarters staff in a divisional structure can also be viewed as an integrating department from the divisional perspective.

Matrix Structure   Finally, when differentiation is very high and the company must be able to respond quickly to the environment, a matrix structure becomes the appropriate integrating device. The matrix contains many of the integrating mechanisms already discussed. The subproject managers integrate among functions and projects, and the matrix is built on the basis of temporary task forces.

■ Integration and Control

Clearly, firms have a large number of options open to them when they increase their level of differentiation as a result of increased growth or diversification. The implementation issue is for managers to match differentiation with the level of integration to meet organizational objectives. Note that while too much differentiation and not enough integration leads to a failure of implementation, the converse is also true. That is, the combination of low differentiation and high integration leads to an overcontrolled, bureaucratized organization, in which flexibility and speed of response are reduced rather than enhanced by the level of integration. Besides, too much integration is expensive for the company because it raises bureaucratic costs. For these reasons, the goal is to decide on the optimum amount of integration necessary for meeting organizational goals and objectives. A company needs to operate the simplest structure consistent with implementing its strategy effectively. In practice, integrating mechanisms are only the first means through which a company seeks to increase its ability to control and coordinate its activities; modern information systems are a second.

■ Information Systems and Organizational Structure

As we discuss throughout this book, advances in software information systems and Internet technology are having important effects on managers and organizations. By improving the ability of managers to coordinate and control the activities of the organization, and by helping managers make more effective decisions, modern computer-based information systems have become a central component of any organization's structure. Evidence is growing, too, that information systems can be a source of competitive advantage; organizations that do not adopt leading-edge information systems are likely to be at a competitive disadvantage. In this section, we examine how the rapid growth of computerized information systems is affecting organizational structure and competitive advantage.

Until the development of modern computer-based information systems, there was no viable alternative to the organizational hierarchy, despite the information problems associated with it discussed earlier. The rapid rise of computer-based information systems has been associated with a "delayering" (flattening) of the organizational hierarchy and a move toward greater decentralization and horizontal information flows within organizations.[46] By electronically providing managers with high-quality, timely, and relatively complete information, modern information systems have reduced the need for tall management hierarchies. Modern information systems have reduced the need for a hierarchy to function as a means of controlling the activities of the organization. In addition, they have reduced the need for a management hierarchy to coordinate organizational activities.

E-mail systems, the development of software programs for sharing documents electronically, and the development of the Internet has all increased horizontal information flows within organizations. The development of organizationwide computer networks is breaking down the barriers that have traditionally separated departments, and the result has been improved performance and superior efficiency, quality, innovation, and customer responsiveness.[47] One reason for an increase in efficiency is that the use of advanced information systems can reduce the number of employees required to perform organizational activities. At one time, for example, thirteen layers of management separated Eastman Kodak's general manager of manufacturing and factory workers. Now, with the help of information systems, the number of layers has been reduced to four. Similarly, Intel has found that by increasing the sophistication of its information systems it has been able to cut the number of hierarchical layers in the organization from ten to five.[48]

Moreover, by increasing horizontal information flows and helping to break down the barriers that separate departments, computer networks are allowing managers to boost quality, innovation, and responsiveness to customers. The experience of Lotus Development, the company that developed Lotus Notes, illustrates how information systems can speed product development. Using their own Notes technology, Lotus managers found that software writers in Asia and Europe can work almost in parallel with their U.S. counterparts, sharing documentation and messages among themselves on a real-time basis. As a result, a Japanese version of a new product can be introduced within three or four weeks of its English-language release, instead of the three or four months that were necessary before the adoption of Notes.[49]

Thus, state-of-the-art information technology can improve the competitiveness of an organization. Indeed, the search for competitive advantage is driving much of the rapid development and adoption of such systems. By improving the decision-making capability of managers, modern information systems help an organization enhance its competitive position. To facilitate the use of information software systems and to make organizational structure work, however, a company must create a control and incentive structure to motivate people and subunits to raise organizational performance. In the next chapter, we discuss the various kinds of strategic control systems that organizations can use to make their organizational structures work effectively.

SUMMARY OF CHAPTER

This chapter discusses the issues involved in designing a structure to meet the needs of a company's strategy. Companies can adopt a large number of structures to match changes in their size and strategy over time. The structure a company selects is the one whose logic of grouping activities (that is, whose form of horizontal differentiation) best meets the needs of its business or businesses. The company must match its form of horizontal differentiation to vertical differentiation. That is, it must choose a structure and then make choices about levels in the hierarchy and the degree of centralization or decentralization. It is the combination of both kinds of differentiation that produces internal organizational arrangements.

Once a company has divided itself into parts, however, it then must integrate itself. A company must choose the appropriate level of integration to match its level of differentiation if it is to coordinate its value creation activities successfully. Since differentiation and integration are expensive, a company's goal is to economize on bureaucratic costs by adopting the simplest structure consistent with achieving its strategy. We stress the following points:

✔ Implementing a strategy successfully depends on selecting the right organizational structure and control system to match a company's strategy.

✔ The basic tool of strategy implementation is organizational design. Good organizational design increases profits in two ways. First, it economizes on bureaucratic costs and lowers the costs of value creation activities. Second, it enhances the ability of a company's value creation functions to achieve superior efficiency, quality, innovation, and customer responsiveness and to obtain a differentiation advantage.

✔ Differentiation and integration are the two design concepts that govern how a structure will work. The higher the level of differentiation and integration, the higher are bureaucratic costs.

✔ Differentiation has two aspects: (1) vertical differentiation, which refers to how a company chooses to allocate its decision-making authority, and (2) horizontal differentiation, which refers to the way a company groups organizational activities into functions, departments, or divisions.

✔ The basic choice in vertical differentiation is whether to have a flat or a tall structure. Tall hierarchies have a number of disadvantages, such as problems with communication and information transfer, motivation, and cost. Decentralization, or delegation of authority, however, can solve some of these problems.

✔ As a company grows and diversifies, it adopts a multidivisional structure. Although a multidivisional structure has higher bureaucratic costs than a functional structure, it overcomes the control problems associated with a functional structure and gives a company the capability to handle its value creation activities effectively.

✔ Other specialized kinds of structures include the matrix, product-team, and geographic structures. Each has a specialized use and, to be chosen, must match the needs of the organization.

✔ The more complex the company and the higher its level of differentiation, the higher is the level of integration needed to manage its structure.

✔ The kinds of integrating mechanisms available to a company range from direct contact to matrix structure. The more complex the mechanism, the greater are the costs of using it. A company should take care to match these mechanisms to its strategic needs.

DISCUSSION QUESTIONS

1. What is the difference between vertical and horizontal differentiation? Rank the various structures discussed in this chapter along these two dimensions.

2. What kind of structure best describes the way your (a) business school and (b) university operate? Why is the structure appropriate? Would another structure fit better?

3. When would a company decide to change from a functional to a multidivisional structure?

4. When would a company choose a matrix structure? What are the problems associated with managing this structure, and why might a product-team structure be preferable?

Practicing Strategic Management

SMALL-GROUP EXERCISE
Speeding Up Product Development

Break up into groups of three to five people, and discuss the following scenario:

You are the top functional managers of a small greeting card company whose new lines of humorous cards for every occasion are selling out as fast as they are reaching the stores. Currently, your employees are organized into different functions such as card designers, artists, and joke writers, as well as functions such as marketing and manufacturing. Each function works on a wide range of different kinds of cards—birthday, Christmas, Hanukkah, Thanksgiving, and so on. Sometimes the design department comes up with the initial idea for a new card and sends the idea to the artists, who draw and color the picture. Then the card is sent to the joke writers who write the joke to suit the card. At other times, the process starts with writing the joke, which is sent to the design department to find the best use for the idea.

The problem you are experiencing is that your current functional structure does not allowing you to produce new cards fast enough to satisfy customers' demands. It typically takes a new card one year to reach the market, and you want to shorten this time by half to protect and expand your market niche.

1. Discuss ways in which you can improve the operation of your current functional structure to speed the product-development process.

2. Discuss the pros and cons of moving to a (a) multidivisional, (b) matrix, and (c) product-team structure to reduce card development time.

3. Which of these structures, do you think, is most appropriate and why?

STRATEGIC MANAGEMENT PROJECT
Module 11

This module asks you to identify the type of organizational structure used by your organization and to explain why your company has selected this form of differentiation and integration. If you are studying a company in your area, you will probably have more information about the company's structure than if you are studying a company using published sources. However, you can make many inferences about the company's structure from the nature of its activities, and if you write to the company, it may provide you with an organizational chart and other information.

1. How large is the company as measured by the number of its employees? How many levels in the hierarchy does it have from the top to the bottom?

2. Based on these two measures and any other information you may have, would you say your company operates with a relatively tall or flat structure? What effect does this have on people's behavior?

3. Does your company have a centralized or a decentralized approach to decision making? How do you know?

4. In what ways do the company's vertical differentiation choices affect the behavior of people and subunits? Do you think the company's choice of vertical differentiation is appropriate for its activities? Why or why not?

5. What changes (if any) would you make in the way the company operates in a vertical direction?

6. Draw an organizational chart showing the main way in which your company groups its activities. Based on this chart, what kind of structure (functional or divisional) does your company operate with?

7. Why did your company choose this structure? In what ways is it appropriate for its business? In what ways is it not?

8. What changes (if any) would you make in the way your company operates in a horizontal direction?

9. Given this analysis, does your company have a low or a high level of differentiation?

10. What kind of integration or integration mechanisms does your company use? Why? Does its level of integration match its level of differentiation?

11. Based on the analysis of your company's level of differentiation and integration, would you say your company is coordinating and motivating its people and subunits effectively? Why or why not?

12. What changes would you make in the company's structure to increase the firm's effectiveness? What changes has the company itself made to improve effectiveness? Why?

 ARTICLE FILE 11

Find an example (or examples) of a company that has recently changed its organizational structure. What changes did it make? Why did it make these changes? What effect did these changes have on the behavior of people and subunits?

**EXPLORING THE WEB
What Kind of Organizational Structure?**

Explore the Web to find a Web site that displays a company's organizational chart or that talks about a company's method of managing its structure. (For example, does it use a centralized or decentralized approach?) What kind of structure does the company use to manage its activities?

CLOSING CASE

Chrysler's Cross-Functional Product Teams

AFTER MANY YEARS of poor performance and mounting losses, Chrysler, the number three U.S. carmaker, has been experiencing a turnaround in the 1990s. Its new car models such as the Dodge Viper, the Stratus, and the cab-forward LH cars have been attracting many customers back to the company and away from Japanese imports. The company's profits and stock price have surged upward as a result. How has Chrysler achieved this turnaround? Chrysler's top management attributes its success to its new product-team structure, which uses cross-functional teams.

Like other U.S. car companies, Chrysler used to have a functional approach to designing and producing its cars. In the functional approach, the responsibility for the design of a new car was allocated to many different design departments, each of which was responsible for the design of one component, such as the engine or the body. Managers further up the hierarchy were responsible for coordinating the activities of the different design departments in order to ensure that the components were compatible with one another. Top managers were also responsible for coordinating the activities of support functions, such as purchasing, marketing, and accounting, with the design process as their contributions were needed. When the design process was finished, the new car was then turned over to the manufacturing department, which decided how best to produce it.

Chrysler's functional approach slowed down the product-development process and made cross-functional communication difficult and slow. Each function pursued its activities in isolation from other functions, and it was left to top management to provide the integration necessary to coordinate functional activities. As a result, it took Chrysler an average of five years to bring a new car to market, a figure that was well behind the record of the Japanese, who took two to three years. Chrysler's structure was raising its costs, slowing innovation, and making the company less responsive to the needs of its customers. The company's top managers began to search for a new way of organizing its value creation activities to turn the company around. To begin this process, top management looked at the way Japanese companies were organized, particularly at the way Honda structured its value creation activities. Chrysler sent fourteen of its managers to study Honda's system and report back on its operation.[50]

Honda had pioneered the Honda Way concept of organizing its activities. It created small teams, comprising members from various functions, and gave them the responsibility and authority to manage a project from its conception through all design activities to final manufacture and sale. Honda had found that when it used these cross-functional teams, product development time dropped dramatically because functional communication and coordination were much easier in teams. Moreover, design costs were much lower when different functions worked together to solve problems as they emerged, because to change a design later (for example, to add a second air bag) could cost millions of dollars. Honda had also found that its policy of decentralizing authority to the team kept the organization flexible, innovative, and able to take advantage of emerging technical opportunities.

CLOSING CASE *(continued)*

Chrysler decided to imitate Honda's structure and took the opportunity to do so when it chose to build an expensive luxury car called the Viper. To manage the development of this new car, Chrysler created a cross-functional product team consisting of eighty-five people.[51] It established the team in a huge new research and development center it had built in Auburn Hills, Michigan, and gave it the authority and responsibility to bring the car to market. The outcome was dramatic. Within one year, top management could see that the team had achieved what would have taken three years under Chrysler's old system. In fact, the team brought the car to market in just thirty-six months at a development cost of $75 million, results that compared favorably with those obtained by Japanese companies.

With this success in hand, Chrysler's top management moved to restructure the whole company according to the product-team concept. Top management divided up functional personnel and assigned them to work in product teams charged with developing new cars, such as those

with the cab-forward design. The number of levels in Chrysler's hierarchy decreased since authority was decentralized to managers in the product teams, who were responsible for all aspects of new-car development. Instead of having to integrate the activities of different functions, top managers could concentrate on allocating resources among projects, deciding future product developments, and continually challenging the teams to improve their efforts. Chrysler's efforts brought the reward of a dramatic drop in costs and an increase in quality and customer responsiveness. The price of the firm's shares soared during the 1990s as customers rushed to buy its cars.

Case Discussion Questions

1. What are the main differences between a functional and a product-team structure?

2. What are the advantages of Chrysler's new team structure, and what are some potential problems associated with it?

End Notes

1. Press release, www.microsoft.com (1999).
2. M. Moeller, S. Hamm, and T. J. Mullaney, "Remaking Microsoft: Why America's Most Successful Company Needed an Overhaul," *Business Week*, May 17, 1999, pp. 52–56.
3. J. R. Galbraith, *Designing Complex Organizations* (Reading, Mass.: Addison-Wesley, 1973).
4. J. Child, *Organization: A Guide for Managers and Administrators* (New York: Harper & Row, 1977), pp. 50–72.
5. R. H. Miles, *Macro Organizational Behavior* (Santa Monica, Calif.: Goodyear, 1980), pp. 19–20.
6. Galbraith, *Designing Complex Organizations*.
7. V. A. Graicunas, "Relationship in Organization," in *Papers on the Science of Administration,* eds. L. Gulick and L. Urwick (New York: Institute of Public Administration, 1937), pp. 181–185; J. C. Worthy, "Organizational Structure and Company Morale," *American Sociological Review*, 15 (1950), 169–179.
8. Child, *Organization*, pp. 50–52.
9. G. R. Jones, "Organization-Client Transactions and Organizational Governance Structures," *Academy of Management Journal*, 30 (1987), 197–218.
10. H. Mintzberg, *The Structuring of Organizations* (Englewood Cliffs, N.J.: Prentice-Hall, 1979), p. 435.
11. B. Woolridge and S. W. Floyd, "The Strategy Process, Middle Management Involvement, and Organizational Performance," *Strategic Management Journal*, 11 (1990), 231–241.
12. Child, *Organization*, p. 51.
13. R. Carzo Jr. and J. N. Yanousas, "Effects of Flat and Tall Organization Structure," *Administrative Science Quarterly*, 14 (1969), 178–191.
14. A. Gupta and V. Govindardan, "Business Unit Strategy, Managerial Characteristics, and Business Unit Effectiveness at Stratcgy Implementation," *Academy of Management Journal*, 27 (1984), 25–41; R. T. Lenz, "Determinants of Organizational Performance: An Interdisciplinary Review," *Strategic Management Journal*, 2 (1981), 131–154.
15. W. H. Wagel, "Keeping the Organization Lean at Federal Express," *Personnel* (March 1984), 4.
16. J. Koter, "For P&G Rivals, the New Game Is to Beat the Leader, Not Copy It," *Wall Street Journal*, May 6, 1985, p. 35.
17. G. R. Jones, "Task Visibility, Free Riding and Shirking: Explaining the Effect of Organization Structure on Employee Behavior," *Academy of Management Review*, 4 (1984), 684–695.
18. Press release, www.BankofAmerica.com (September, 1999).
19. "Operation Turnaround—How Westinghouse's New Chairman Plans to Fire Up an Old Line Company," *Business Week*, December 14, 1983, pp. 124–133.
20. "Union Pacific to Reorganize," cnnfn.com (August 20, 1998), p.20.
21. Press release, www.unionpacific.com (1998).

22. C. Chandler and J. B. White, "Honda's Middle Managers Will Regain Authority in New Overhaul of Company," *Wall Street Journal*, May 16, 1992, p. A2.
23. J. H. Sheridan, "Best of Everything," *Industry Week*, January 19, 1998, pp. 13–14.
24. T. Clark, "How Honda Thrives," *Industry Week*, October 5, 1998, pp. 50–54.
25. R. L. Daft, *Organizational Theory and Design*, 3rd ed. (St. Paul, Minn.: West, 1986), p. 215.
26. Alfred D. Chandler, *Strategy and Structure* (Cambridge, Mass.: MIT Press, 1962).
27. This discussion draws heavily on Chandler, *Strategy and Structure*; and B. R. Scott, *Stages of Corporate Development* (Cambridge, Mass.: Intercollegiate Clearing House, Harvard Business School, 1971).
28. J. R. Galbraith and R. K. Kazanjian, *Strategy Implementation: Structure System and Process*, 2nd ed. (St. Paul, Minn.: West, 1986); Child, *Organization;* R. Duncan, "What Is the Right Organizational Structure?" *Organizational Dynamics* (Winter 1979), 59–80.
29. O. E. Williamson, *Markets and Hierarchies: Analysis and Antitrust Implications* (New York: Free Press, 1975).
30. P. R. Lawrence and J. Lorsch, *Organization and Environment* (Boston: Division of Research, Harvard Business School, 1967).
31. K. Pope, "Dell Refocuses on Groundwork to Cope with Rocketing Sales," *Wall Street Journal*, June 18, 1993, p. B5.
32. Chandler, *Strategy and Structure*; Williamson, *Markets and Hierarchies*; L. Wrigley, "Divisional Autonomy and Diversification" (Ph.D. diss., Harvard Business School, 1970).
33. R. P. Rumelt, *Strategy, Structure, and Economic Performance* (Boston: Division of Research, Harvard Business School, 1974); Scott, *Stages of Corporate Development*; Williamson, *Markets and Hierarchies*.
34. The discussion draws on each of the sources cited in endnotes 20–27 and on G. R. Jones and C. W. L. Hill, "Transaction Cost Analysis of Strategy-Structure Choice," *Strategic Management Journal*, 9 (1988), 159–172.
35. H. O. Armour and D. J. Teece, "Organizational Structure and Economic Performance: A Test of the Multidivisional Hypothesis," *Bell Journal of Economics*, 9 (1978), 106–122.
36. Alfred Sloan, *My Years at General Motors* (New York: Doubleday, 1983), Chapter 3.
37. C. Soloman, "Amoco to Cut More Jobs and Radically Alter Its Structure" *Wall Street Journal*, July 22, 1995, p. B4.
38. "Shell Reorganizes for Speed and Profit," *Oil & Gas Journal*, December 21, 1998, p.31.
39. S. M. Davis and R. R. Lawrence, *Matrix* (Reading, Mass.: Addison-Wesley, 1977); J. R. Galbraith, "Matrix Organization Designs: How to Combine Functional and Project Forms," *Business Horizons*, 14 (1971), 29–40.
40. Duncan, "What Is the Right Organizational Structure?"; Davis and Lawrence, *Matrix*.

41. K. M. Kroll, "Making 4 Minus 3 Equal 2," *Industry Week*, March 1, 1999, pp. 46–51.

42. P. R. Lawrence and J. Lorsch, *Organization and Environment*, pp. 50–55.

43. Galbraith, *Designing Complex Organizations*, Chapter 1; Galbraith and Kazanjian, *Strategy Implementation*, Chapter 7.

44. H. Mintzberg, *The Nature of Managerial Work* (Englewood Cliffs, N.J.: Prentice-Hall, 1973), Chapter 10.

45. Lawrence and Lorsch, *Organization and Environment*, p. 55.

46. Davidow and Malone, *The Virtual Corporation* (Homewood, Ill: Irwin, 1996).

47. Ibid.

48. Ibid., p. 168.

49. Stewart, "Managing in a Wired Company," *Business Week*, September 16, 1998, pp. 40–44.

50. D. Woodruff and E. Lesly, "Surge at Chrysler," *Fortune*, November 9, 1992, pp. 88–96.

51. "Chrysler Reengineers Product Development Process," *Information Week*, September 7, 1992, p. 20.

12 Designing Strategic Control Systems

OPENING CASE

Oracle's New Approach to Control

ORACLE is the second largest independent software company after Microsoft. Like Bill Gates, Microsoft's chairman, Oracle's founder and chairman, Larry Ellison, recognized that his company had a major problem in 1999. Ellison woke up to the fact that his own company was not using the latest Internet software—software it had developed itself—to control its activities even though its customers were using it. As a result, Oracle was having a difficult time understanding its customers' needs; and, internally Oracle was not experiencing the cost savings that result from implementing its own database and financial control software. Ellison moved quickly to change Oracle's control systems so that they were Internet based.

One of the main advantages of Internet-based control software is that it permits the centralized management of a company's widespread operations. A company's corporate managers can easily compare and contrast in real time the performance of different divisions spread throughout the globe; as a result, they can quickly identify problems and take corrective action. However, to his embarrassment, Ellison discovered that Oracle's financial and human resource information was located on more than seventy different computing systems across the world. Tracking such basics as the size of the company's work force and the sales of its leading products required a lot of time and effort. Consequently, corrective action was unduly delayed, and many opportunities were being missed.

Recognizing the absurdity of the situation, Ellison ordered his managers to totally change the way the company controlled—that is, monitored and evaluated—its activities and to implement its new Internet-based control systems as quickly as possible. His goal was to have all of the company's sales, cost, profit, and human resource information systems consolidated in two, rather than forty locations, and to make this information available to managers throughout the company instantaneously with one click of a mouse. In addition, he instructed managers to investigate which kinds of activities were being monitored and controlled by people, and wherever possible to substitute Internet-based control. For example, previously Oracle had more than 300 people responsible for monitoring and managing such tasks as paper-based travel-planning and expense report systems. These tasks were automated into software systems and put on-line; and employees were then made responsible for filing their own. The 300 people displaced by this new approach were transferred into sales and consulting positions.[1] The savings for the company totaled more than $1 billion a year.

By using control systems based on Internet software, Oracle's managers are also able to get closer to their customers. In 1999, Oracle gave all its salespeople new customer-relationship management software and in-

OPENING CASE *(continued)*

structed them to enter into the system detailed information about the customers' purchases, future plans, web orders, and service requests. As a result, headquarters managers can track sales orders easily. If they see problems such as lost sales or multiple service requests, they can quickly contact customers to solve these difficulties and thus build better customer relations.

So amazed has Ellison been at the result of implementing Internet software systems that he has radically

rethought Oracle's management control systems. He now believes that, because of the advances of modern computer information systems, Oracle's employees should be doing only one of three things: building its products, servicing its products, or selling its products. All other activities should be automated by developing new information control systems, and it should be the job of the managers to use control only to facilitate one of these three frontline activities.

OVERVIEW

As we note in Chapter 11, strategy implementation requires selecting the right combination of structure and control for achieving a company's strategy. An organizational structure assigns people to tasks and roles (differentiation) and specifies how these are to be coordinated (integration). Nevertheless, organizational structure does not of itself provide or contain the mechanism through which people can be *motivated* to make it work. Hence the need for control. The purpose of strategic control is to provide managers with (1) a means of motivating employees to work toward organizational goals and (2) specific feedback on how well an organization and its members are performing. Structure provides an organization with a skeleton, but control gives it the muscles, sinews, nerves, and sensations that allow managers to regulate and govern its activities.

In this chapter, we first look in detail at the nature of strategic control and describe the main steps in the control process. We then discuss the main types of strategic control systems available to managers to shape and influence employees—financial controls, output controls, behavior controls, and control through the values and norms of an organization's culture. Finally, we discuss how the design of reward systems becomes an important part of the strategic control process. By the end of this chapter, you will appreciate the rich variety of different control systems available to managers and understand why developing an appropriate control system is vital to maximizing the performance of an organization and its members.

WHAT IS STRATEGIC CONTROL?

Strategic control is the process by which managers monitor the ongoing activities of an organization and its members to evaluate whether activities are being performed efficiently and effectively and to take corrective action to improve performance if they are not. First, strategic managers choose the organizational strategy and structure they hope will allow the organization to use its resources most effectively to create value for its customers. Second, strategic managers create control systems to monitor and evaluate whether, in fact, their organization's strategy and structure are working as the managers intended, how they could be improved, and how they should be changed if they are not working.

Strategic control does not just mean reacting to events *after* they have occurred; it also means keeping an organization on track, anticipating events that might occur, and responding swiftly to new opportunities that present themselves. As you will recall from Chapter 1, *strategic intent* refers to the obsession strategic managers have for building organizational resources and capabilities in order to dominate their environments, but it also involves "focusing the organization's attention on the essence of winning; motivating people by communicating the value of the target; leaving room for individual and team contributions; sustaining enthusiasm ... and using intent consistently to guide resource allocation."[2] Behind the concept of strategic intent is a vision of strategic control as a system that sets ambitious goals and targets for all managers and employees and then develops performance measures that stretch and encourage the mangers and employees to excel in their quest to raise performance.

Thus, strategic control is not just about monitoring how well an organization and its members are achieving current goals or about how well the firm is utilizing its existing resources. It is also about keeping employees motivated, focused on the important problems confronting an organization now and in the future, and working together to find solutions that can help an organization perform better over time.[3]

■ The Importance of Strategic Control

To understand the vital importance of strategic control, consider how it helps managers to obtain superior efficiency, quality, innovation, and responsiveness to customers, the four basic building blocks of competitive advantage.

Control and Efficiency To determine how *efficiently* they are using organizational resources, managers must be able to measure accurately how many units of inputs (raw materials, human resources, and so on) are being used to produce a unit of output. They must also be able to measure the number of units of outputs (goods and services) they produce. A control system contains the measures or yardsticks that allow managers to assess how efficiently they are producing goods and services. Moreover, if managers experiment with changing the way they produce goods and services to find a more efficient way of producing them, these measures tell managers how successful they have been.

Thus, for example, when managers at Chrysler decided to change to a product-team structure to design, engineer, and manufacture their new cars (See Closing Case, Chapter 11), they used such measures as time taken to design a new car and cost savings per car produced to evaluate how well this new structure worked. When they used these measures to compare the performance of the new structure with that of the old structure, they found that the new structure performed better. Without a control system in place, managers have no idea how well their organization is performing and how they can make it perform better, and such knowledge is becoming increasingly important in today's highly competitive environment.[4]

Control and Quality Today, much of the competition between organizations revolves around increasing the *quality* of goods and services. In the car industry, for example, within each price range, cars compete against one another in terms of their features, design, and reliability over time. So whether a customer buys a Ford Taurus, a GM Cavalier, a Chrysler Intrepid, a Toyota Camry, or a Honda Accord depends significantly on the quality of each company's product. Organizational control is important in determining the quality of goods and services because it gives managers feedback on product quality. If managers of an organization such as Chrysler consistently measure the number of customers' complaints and the number of new cars returned for repairs, they have a good indication of how much quality they have built into their product. That is, do they have a car that does not break down?

Strategic managers create a control system that consistently monitors the quality of goods and services so that they can make continuous improvements to quality over time—which gives them a competitive advantage. Total quality management, an organizationwide control system that focuses on improving quality and reducing costs, is discussed at length in Chapter 5.

Control and Innovation   Strategic control can also help to raise the level of *innovation* in an organization. Successful innovation takes place when managers create an organizational setting in which employees feel empowered to be creative and in which authority is decentralized to employees so that they feel free to experiment and take risks. Deciding on the appropriate control systems to encourage risk taking is a major management challenge, and, as discussed later in the chapter, an organization's culture becomes important in this regard. At Chrysler, for example, to encourage each product team to perform, top managers monitor the performance of each team separately (for instance, by examining how each team reduced costs or increased quality) and then pay each team on a bonus system related to its performance. The product team manager then evaluates each team member's individual performance, and the most innovative employees receive promotions and rewards based on their performance level.

Control and Responsiveness to Customers   Finally, strategic managers can help make their organizations more *responsive to customers* if they develop a control system that allows them to evaluate how well employees with customer contact are performing their jobs. Monitoring employees' behavior can help managers find ways to help increase employees' performance level, perhaps by revealing areas in which skill training can help employees or by finding new procedures that allow employees to perform their jobs better. When employees know their behaviors are being monitored, they may have more incentive to be helpful and consistent in the way they act toward customers. To help improve customer service, for example, Chrysler regularly surveys customers about their experiences with particular Chrysler dealers. If a dealership receives too many complaints from customers, Chrysler's managers investigate the dealership to uncover the sources of the problems and suggest solutions. If necessary, they can threaten to reduce the number of cars a dealership receives to force it to improve the quality of customer service.

■ A Balanced Scorecard Approach to Strategic Control

As just discussed, strategic control entails developing performance measures that allow managers both to evaluate how well they have utilized organizational resources to create value *and* to sense new opportunities for creating value in the future. One increasingly influential model that guides managers through the process of creating the right kind of strategic control systems to enhance organizational performance is the balanced scorecard model.[5]

According to the **balanced scorecard model**, strategic managers have traditionally relied on financial measures of performance such as profit and return on investment to evaluate organizational performance. But financial information, though important, is not enough by itself. If strategic managers are to obtain a true picture of organizational performance, financial information must be supplemented with performance measures that indicate how well an organization has been achieving the four building blocks of competitive advantage—efficiency, quality, innovation, and responsiveness to customers. This is so because financial results simply inform strategic managers about the results of decisions they have *already taken*; the other measures balance this picture of performance by informing managers about how accurately the organization has in place the building blocks that drive *future performance*.[6]

One version of the way the balanced scorecard operates is presented in Figure 12.1. Based on an organization's mission and goals, strategic managers develop a set of strategies to build competitive advantage to achieve these goals. They then establish an organizational structure to use resources to obtain a competitive advantage.[7] To evaluate how well the strategy and structure are working, managers develop specific performance measures that assess how well the four building blocks of competitive advantage are being achieved.

■ *Efficiency* can be measured by the level of production costs, the number of hours needed to produce a product, and the cost of raw materials.

■ *Quality* can be measured by the number of rejects, the number of defective products returned from customers, and the level of product reliability over time.

FIGURE 12.1

A Balance Scorecard Approach

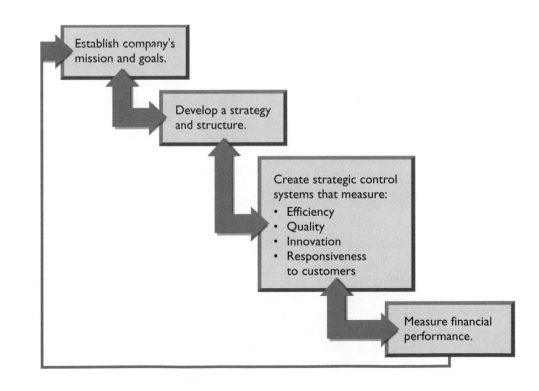

■ *Innovation* can be measured by the number of new products introduced, the time taken to develop the next generation of new products in comparison with the competition, and the expense or cost of product development.

■ *Responsiveness to customers* can be measured by the number of repeat customers, the level of on-time delivery to customers, and the level of customer service.

As R. S. Kaplan and D. P. Norton, the developers of this approach suggest,

> Think of the balanced scorecard as the dials and indicators in an airplane cockpit. For the complex task of navigating and flying an airplane, pilots need detailed information about many aspects of the flight. They need information on fuel, air speed, altitude, learning, destination, and other indicators that summarize the current and predicted environment. Reliance on one instrument can be fatal. Similarly, the complexity of managing an organization today requires that managers be able to view performance in several areas simultaneously.[8]

The way in which strategic managers' ability to build a competitive advantage translates into organizational performance is then measured using financial measures such as cash flow, quarterly sales growth, increase in market share, and return on investment or equity. Based on an evaluation of the complete set of measures in the balanced scorecard, strategic managers are in a good position to reevaluate the company's mission and goals. They can also take action to rectify problems or to exploit new opportunities by changing the organization's strategy and structure—which is the purpose of strategic control.

STRATEGIC CONTROL SYSTEMS

Strategic control systems are the formal target-setting, measurement, and feedback systems that allow strategic managers to evaluate whether a company is achieving superior efficiency, quality, innovation, and customer responsiveness and implementing its strategy successfully. An effective control system should have three characteristics. It should be *flexible* enough to allow managers to respond as necessary to unexpected events; it should provide *accurate information,* giving a true picture of organizational performance; and it should supply managers with the information in a *timely manner* because making decisions on the basis of outdated information is a recipe for failure.[9] As Figure 12.2 shows, designing an effective strategic control system requires four steps.

1. *Establish the standards and targets against which performance is to be evaluated.* The standards and targets managers select are the ways in which a company chooses to evaluate its performance. General performance standards often derive from the goal of achieving superior efficiency, quality, innovation, or customer responsiveness. Specific performance targets are derived from the strategy pursued by the company. For example, if a company is pursuing a low-cost strategy, then reducing costs by 7 percent a year might be a target. If the company is a service organization such as Wal-Mart or McDonald's, its standards might include time targets for serving customers or guidelines for food quality.

FIGURE 12.2

Steps in Designing an
Effective Control System

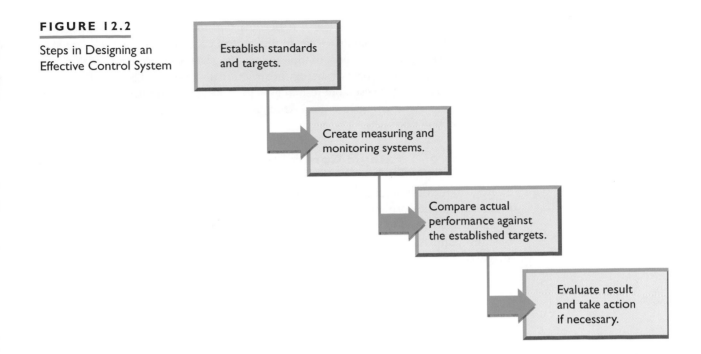

2. *Create the measuring and monitoring systems that indicate whether the standards and targets are being reached.* The company establishes procedures for assessing whether work goals at all levels in the organization are being achieved. In some cases, measuring performance is fairly straightforward. For example, managers can measure quite easily how many customers their employees serve by counting the number of receipts from the cash register. In many cases, however, measuring performance is a difficult task because the organization is engaged in many complex activities. How can managers judge how well their research and development department is doing when it may take five years for products to be developed? How can they measure the company's performance when the company is entering new markets and serving new customers? How can they evaluate how well divisions are integrating? The answer is that managers need to use various types of control systems, which we discuss later in this chapter.

3. *Compare actual performance against the established targets.* Managers evaluate whether and to what extent performance deviates from the standards and targets developed in step 1. If performance is higher, management may decide that it has set the standards too low and may raise them for the next time period. The Japanese are renowned for the way they use targets on the production line to control costs. They are constantly trying to raise performance, and they raise the standards to provide a goal for managers to work toward. On the other hand, if performance is too low, managers must decide whether to take remedial action. This decision is easy when the reasons for poor performance can be identified—for instance, high labor costs. More often, however, the reasons for poor performance are hard to uncover. They may stem from involved external factors, such as a recession, or from internal ones. For instance, the research and development laboratory may have underestimated the problems it would encounter or the extra costs of doing unforeseen research. For any form of action, however, step 4 is necessary.

4. *Initiate corrective action when it is decided that the standards and targets are not being achieved.* The final stage in the control process is to take the corrective action that will allow the organization to meet its goals. Such corrective action may mean changing any aspect of strategy or structure discussed in this book. For example, managers may invest more resources in improving R&D, or diversify, or even decide to change their organizational structure. The goal is to enhance continually an organization's competitive advantage.

■ Levels of Strategic Control

Strategic control systems are developed to measure performance at four levels in an organization: the corporate, divisional, functional, and individual levels. Managers at all levels must develop the most appropriate set of measures to evaluate corporate-, business-, and functional-level performance. As the balanced scorecard approach suggests, these measures should be tied as closely as possibly to the goals of achieving superior efficiency, quality, innovativeness, and responsiveness to customers. Care must be taken, however, to ensure that the standards used at each level do not cause problems at the other levels—for example, that the attempts of divisions to improve their performance do not conflict with corporate performance. Furthermore, controls at each level should provide the basis on which managers at the levels below can select their control systems. Figure 12.3 illustrates these links.

FIGURE 12.3

Levels of Organizational Control

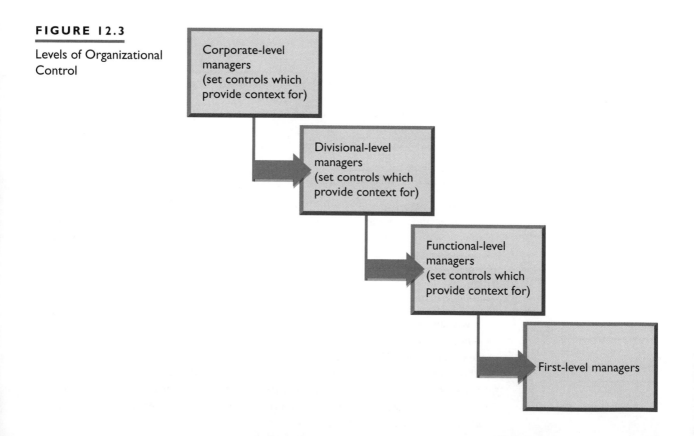

TABLE 12.1

Types of Control Systems

Financial Controls	Output Controls	Behavior Controls	Organizational Culture
Stock price	Divisional goals	Budgets	Values
ROI	Functional goals	Standardization	Norms
	Individual goals	Rules and procedures	Socialization

Table 12.1 shows the various types of strategic control systems managers can use to monitor and coordinate organizational activities. Each of these types of control and its use at various organizational levels—corporate, divisional, functional, and individual—is discussed in the next sections.

■ Financial Controls

As noted earlier, the most common measures managers and other stakeholders use to monitor and evaluate a company's performance are financial controls. Typically, strategic managers select financial goals they wish their company to achieve, such as growth, profitability, and return to shareholders, and then they measure whether or not these goals have been achieved. One reason for the popularity of financial performance measures is that they are objective. The performance of one company can be compared with that of another in terms of its stock market price, return on investment, market share, or even cash flow so that strategic managers and other stakeholders, particularly shareholders, have some way of judging their company's performance relative to that of other companies.

Stock price, for example, is a useful measure of a company's performance primarily because the price of the stock is determined competitively by the number of buyers and sellers in the market. The stock's value is an indication of the market's *expectations* for the firm's future performance. Thus, movements in the price of a stock provide shareholders with feedback on a company's and its managers' performance. Stock market price acts as an important measure of performance because top managers watch it closely and are sensitive to its rise and fall, particularly its fall. When, Ford Motor's stock price failed to increase in 1996, for example, CEO Alex Trotman took heed of the shareholders' complaint that Ford's product development costs and car prices were too high. In response, he took steps to reduce costs and boost the company's ROI and stock price. Finally, because stock price reflects the long-term future return from the stock, it can be regarded as an indicator of the company's long-run potential.

Return on investment (ROI), determined by dividing net income by invested capital, is another popular kind of financial control. At the corporate level, the performance of the whole company can be evaluated *against* that of other companies to gauge its relative performance. Top managers, for example, can assess how well their strategies have worked by comparing their company's performance with that of similar companies. In the personal computer industry, companies such as Dell, Compaq, and Apple use ROI to gauge their performance relative to that of their competitors. A declining ROI signals a potential problem with a company's strategy or structure. Apple's ROI, for example, has been falling in relation to Dell's and Compaq's. The reason, according to analysts, is that Apple has been rather slow both in product innovation and in reacting to the price-cutting moves of its rivals.

ROI can also be used inside the company at the divisional level to judge the performance of an operating division by comparing it with that of a similar freestanding business or other internal division. Indeed, one reason for selecting a multidivisional structure is that each division can be evaluated as a self-contained profit center. Consequently, management can directly measure the performance of one division against another. General Motors moved to a divisional structure partly because it could use this standard. It gave GM's corporate managers information about the relative costs of the various divisions, allowing them to base capital allocations on relative performance.

Similarly, manufacturing companies often establish production facilities at different locations, domestically and globally, so that they can measure the relative performance of one against the other. For example, Xerox was able to identify the relative inefficiency of its U.S. division by comparing its profitability with that of its Japanese counterpart. ROI is a powerful form of control at the divisional level, especially if divisional managers are rewarded on the basis of their performance vis-à-vis other divisions. The most successful divisional managers are promoted to become the next generation of corporate executives.

Failure to meet stock price or ROI targets also indicates that corrective action is necessary. It signals the need for corporate reorganization in order to meet corporate objectives, and such reorganization can involve a change in structure or liquidation and divestiture of businesses. It can also indicate the need for new strategic leadership. In recent years, the CEOs of American Express, Digital Equipment, Westinghouse, and GM have all been ousted by disgruntled boards of directors, dismayed at the declining performance of their companies relative to that of the competition.

■ Output Controls

While financial goals and controls are an important part of the balanced scorecard approach, it is also necessary to develop goals and controls that tell managers how well their strategies are creating a competitive advantage and building distinctive competencies and capabilities that will lead to future success. When strategic managers implement the balanced scorecard approach and establish goals and measures to evaluate efficiency, quality, innovation, and responsiveness to customers, they are using output control. **Output control** is a system of control in which strategic managers estimate or forecast appropriate performance goals for each division, department, and employee and then measure actual performance relative to these goals. Often a company's reward system is linked to performance on these goals, so that output control also provides an incentive structure for motivating employees at all levels in the organization.

Divisional Goals   Divisional goals state corporate managers' expectations for each division concerning performance on such dimensions as efficiency, quality, innovation, and responsiveness to customers. Generally, corporate managers set challenging divisional goals to encourage divisional managers to create more effective strategies and structures in the future. At General Electric, for example, CEO Jack Welch has set clear performance goals for GE's more than 150 divisions. He expects each division to be number one or two in its industry in terms of market share. Divisional managers are given considerable autonomy to formulate a strategy to meet this goal (to find ways to increase efficiency, innovation, and so on), and the divisions that fail are divested.

Functional and Individual Goals   Output control at the functional and individual levels is a continuation of control at the divisional level. Divisional managers set goals for functional managers that will allow the division to achieve its goals. As at the divisional level, functional goals are established to encourage development of competencies that provide the company with a competitive advantage. The same four building blocks of competitive advantage (efficiency, quality, innovation, and customer responsiveness) act as the goals against which functional performance is evaluated. In the sales function, for example, goals related to efficiency (such as cost of sales), quality (such as number of returns), and customer responsiveness (such as the time needed to respond to customer needs) can be established for the whole function.

Finally, functional managers establish goals that individual employees are expected to achieve to allow the function to achieve its goals. Sales personnel, for example, can be given specific goals (related to functional goals), which they in turn are required to achieve. Functions and individuals are then evaluated on the basis of achieving or not achieving their goals, and in sales compensation is commonly pegged to achievement. The achievement of these goals is a sign that the company's strategy is working and meeting organizational objectives. Strategy in Action 12.1 describes how Cypress Semiconductor's CEO, T. J. Rodgers, uses his company's information systems and intranet as a form of output control.

■ Management by Objectives

To use output control most effectively, many organizations implement management by objectives. **Management by objectives (MBO)** is a system of evaluating managers by their ability to achieve specific organizational goals or performance standards and to meet their operating budgets.[12] A management by objectives system requires these steps:

1. *Establishing specific goals and objectives at each level of the organization.* Management by objectives starts when corporate managers establish overall organizational objectives, such as specific financial performance goals already discussed. Then the objective setting cascades down the organization as managers at the divisional and functional levels set their objectives so as to achieve corporate objectives.[13]

2. *Making goal setting a participatory process.* An important part of a management by objectives system is that, at every level, managers sit down with their subordinate managers to determine jointly appropriate and feasible objectives and to decide on the budget that will be needed to achieve them. Thus, subordinates participate in the objective-setting process, which is a way of getting their commitment to achieve those goals and meet their budgets.[14]

12.1 **STRATEGY *in* ACTION**

Control at Cypress Semiconductor

I n the fast-moving semiconductor business, a premium is placed on organizational adaptability. At Cypress Semiconductor, CEO T. J. Rodgers was facing a problem. How could he control his growing, 1,500-employee organization without developing a bureaucratic management hierarchy? Rodgers believed that a tall hierarchy hinders the ability of an organization to adapt to changing conditions. He was committed to maintaining a flat and decentralized organizational structure with a minimum of management layers. At the same time, he needed to control his employees to ensure that they perform in a manner that is consistent with the goals of the company. How could he achieve this without resorting to direct supervision and the management hierarchy that it implies?

The solution that Rodgers adopted was to implement a computer-based information system through which he can manage what every employee and team is doing in his fast-moving and decentralized organization.[10] Each employee maintains a list of ten to fifteen goals, such as "Meet with marketing for new product launch" or "Make sure to check with customer X." Noted next to each goal is when it was agreed upon, when it is due to be finished, and whether it has been finished. All of this information is stored on a central computer. Rodgers claims that he can review the goals of all 1,500 employees in about four hours, and he does so each week.[11] How is this possible? He manages by exception and looks only for employees who are falling behind. He then calls them, not to scold but to ask whether there is anything he can do to help them get the job done. It takes only about half an hour each week for employees to review and update their lists. This system allows Rodgers to exercise control over his organization without resorting to the expensive layers of a management hierarchy.

---

3. *Periodic review of progress toward meeting goals.* Once specific objectives have been agreed upon for managers at each level, managers become accountable for meeting them. Periodically, they sit down with their subordinates and evaluate their progress. Normally, salary raises and promotions are linked to the goal-setting process, and managers who have achieved their goals receive the most rewards. The issue of how to design reward systems to motivate managers and other organizational employees is detailed later in the chapter.

One company that has spent considerable time developing an effective MBO system is Zytec, a leading manufacturer of power supplies for computers and other electronic equipment. All Zytec's managers and workers are involved in its goal-setting process. Top managers first set up six cross-functional teams to create a five-year plan for the company and to set broad goals for each function.[15] This plan is then reviewed by employees from all areas of the company, who evaluate its feasibility and make suggestions as to how it could be modified or improved. Each function then uses the broad goals in the plan to set more specific goals for each manager within each function, which are reviewed with top managers. At Zytec, the MBO system is organizationwide and fully participatory; performance is reviewed both from an annual and a five-year perspective in keeping with the company's five-year plan. So successful has Zytec's MBO system been that not only have its costs dropped dramatically but it also won the Baldrige Award for quality.

STRATEGY *in* ACTION

12.2

How Not to Use Output Control to Get Ahead

William J. Fife masterminded the turnaround of Giddings and Lewis, a manufacturer of automated factory equipment for companies such as GM, Boeing, AMR, and Ford. In 1988, the company was losing money and had a declining customer base. By 1993, Fife had made it the largest company in the industry, with sales that for every quarter exceeded year-earlier results and a stock price that had quadrupled since Fife sold its stock on the open market in 1989. Nevertheless, in April 1993, the board of directors decided that Fife was no longer a suitable leader and asked him to resign because, as the board saw it, his use of output controls was damaging the future of the company.

Fife's turnaround strategy relied on broadening the company's product base by innovating products to suit new kinds of customers, for example, airlines and consumer manufacturing companies. Then his goal was to increase sales by promoting customer responsiveness. As an example to his managers and employees, Fife would fly anywhere in the United States to solve customer problems personally. To promote his strategy of increasing sales through innovation and customer responsiveness, Fife made extensive use of output controls as the main way of evaluating the performance of his product and financial managers. Periodically, he would sit down with his executives to review the financial, sales, and cost figures for a product or product range.

However, when the figures failed to please him, he would verbally attack and abuse the executive concerned in front of his or her peers, who sat through the assault in embarrassed silence. Any attempts to fight back would merely prolong the attack, and top managers began to complain to board members that Fife was destroying working relationships. Moreover, top mangers claimed that Fife's preoccupation with the short-term bottom line was causing problems for the organization because his focus on sales and cost targets was forcing them to cut back on research and development or customer service to meet the stringent targets that he set. Eventually, they pointed out, this practice would hurt customer relations. Thus, Fife's managers claimed that his exclusive focus on output control goal setting was reducing flexibility and integration and threatening the company's future performance.

Whatever the truth in these claims, the board of directors (which Fife had appointed) listened to the disgruntled managers and decided that for the good of the organization they should ask Fife to resign. As Clyde Folley, the acting chairman put it, the board wanted, "nice, quiet, level leadership" and the reestablishment of good working relationships between managers at all levels. However, the stock market reacted differently to the news of Fife's departure, and the company's stock price plunged by more than 20 percent on the announcement. Clearly, shareholders liked the effect of Fife's output controls on the company's performance, even if his mangers did not.

While Zytec illustrates the advantages of MBO, the story of Giddings and Lewis, highlighted in Strategy in Action 12.2, illustrates some of the problems that can arise if it is used inappropriately.

The inappropriate use of output control can also promote conflict among divisions. In general, setting across-the-board output targets, such as ROI targets, for divisions can lead to destructive results if divisions single-mindedly try to maximize divisional profits at the expense of corporate objectives. Moreover, to reach output targets, divisions may start to distort the numbers and engage in strategic manipulation of the figures to make their divisions look good.[16]

In sum, strategic managers need to use the balanced scorecard approach to design the set of output controls that will best promote long-run profitability. In practice, output controls must be used in conjunction with behavior controls and organizational culture if the right strategic behaviors are to be encouraged.

■ Behavior Controls

The first step in strategy implementation is for managers to design the right kind of organizational structure. To make the structure work, however, employees must learn the kinds of behaviors they are expected to perform. Using managers to tell employees what to do lengthens the organizational hierarchy, is expensive, and raises bureaucratic costs; consequently, strategic managers rely on behavior controls. **Behavior control** is control through the establishment of a comprehensive system of rules and procedures to direct the actions or behavior of divisions, functions, and individuals.[17]

In using behavior controls, the intention is not to specify the goals, but to standardize the way of reaching them. Rules standardize behavior and make outcomes predictable. If employees follow the rules, then actions are performed and decisions handled the same way time and time again. The result is predictability and accuracy, the aim of all control systems. The main types of behavior controls are operating budgets and standardization.

Operating Budgets   Once managers at each level have been given a goal to achieve, operating budgets that regulate how managers and workers are to attain those goals are established. An **operating budget** is a blueprint that states how managers intend to use organizational resources to achieve organizational goals most efficiently. Most commonly, managers at one level allocate to managers at a lower level a specific amount of resources to use to produce goods and services.

Once they have been given a budget, managers must decide how they will allocate certain amounts of money for different organizational activities. These lower-level managers are then evaluated on the basis of their ability to stay within the budget and make the best use of it. Thus, for example, managers at GE's washing machine division might have a budget of $50 million to develop and sell a new line of washing machines, and they have to decide how much money to allocate to R&D, engineering, sales, and other areas so that the division generates the most revenue and hence makes the biggest profit.

Most commonly, large organizations treat each division as a stand-alone profit center, and corporate managers evaluate each division's performance by its relative contribution to corporate profitability. Strategy in Action 12.3 describes how Japanese companies have been using operating budgets and setting challenging goals to increase efficiency.

Standardization   **Standardization** refers to the degree to which a company specifies how decisions are to be made so that employees' behavior becomes predictable.[19] In practice, there are three things an organization can standardize: *inputs, conversion activities,* and *outputs.*

12.3 STRATEGY *in* ACTION

Japan Focuses on Budgets

In the 1990s, Japanese companies have been facing increasing problems in competing in the global marketplace because the rising value of the yen has made their products so expensive abroad. In addition, the Japanese have experienced difficulties because their global competitors have lowered their costs by imitating many of the cost-saving innovations in manufacturing that Japanese companies pioneered, such as total quality management. With their competitive advantage eroding because their foreign competitors' costs are as low or lower than theirs, Japanese companies have been seeking new ways to cut costs to increase their efficiency.

At the top of their list of ways to reduce costs is making ingenious use of budgets to increase efficiency, but to do so in a way that does not destroy innovation. One of the techniques is to decentralize the responsibility for meeting budgets targets right down to the level of the first-line supervisor and worker. At Kirin's brewery in Kyoto, for example, managers at all levels compete against one another to report the biggest profits, and information about costs is posted on the wall for all employees to see how their day-to-day performance affects progress toward meeting goals and budget targets.[18] Some companies have divided up their work force into small teams and even split into many divisions so that employees are more aware of how the level of their performance affects costs and profits. The high-tech Kyocera company, for example, divided itself up into more than 800 small units (nicknamed amoebas) that trade with each other and try to get the most value for what they do.

Furthermore, recognizing that a large proportion of their costs are payments for inputs such as components parts, Japanese companies work with their suppliers to help them reduce costs and raise product quality. Members of their research and development, engineering, and manufacturing functions become part of cross-company teams established to find new ways to reduce costs, not the least of which is to teach their suppliers how to use budgets and goals to lower their costs. This new focus on budgets as a control system has paid off, and companies such as Toyota and Honda have enjoyed enormous cost savings by developing in-depth relationships with non-Japanese suppliers that have led to record profits despite the high value of the yen.

1. *Standardization of inputs.* One way in which an organization can control the behavior of both people and resources is to standardize the inputs into the organization. This means that managers screen inputs according to preestablished criteria or standards and then decide which inputs to allow into the organization. If employees are the input in question, for example, then one way of standardizing them is to specify which qualities and skills they must possess and then to select only those applicants who possess them. Arthur Andersen, the accounting firm, is a very selective recruiter, as are most prestigious organizations.

   If the inputs in question are raw materials or component parts, then the same considerations apply. The Japanese are renowned for the high quality and precise tolerances they demand from component parts to minimize problems with the product at the manufacturing stage. Just-in-time inventory systems also help standardize the flow of inputs.

2. *Standardization of conversion activities.* The aim of standardizing conversion activities is to program work activities so that they are done the same way time and time again. The goal is predictability. Behavior controls, such as rules and procedures, are

among the chief means by which companies can standardize throughputs. Fast-food restaurants such as McDonald's and Burger King, for example, standardize all aspects of their restaurant operations; the result is standardized fast food.

3. *Standardization of outputs.* The goal of standardizing outputs is to specify what the performance characteristics of the final product or service should be—what dimensions or tolerances the product should conform to, for example. To ensure that their products are standardized, companies apply quality control and use various criteria to measure this standardization. One criterion might be the number of goods returned from customers or the number of customers' complaints. On production lines, periodic sampling of products can indicate whether they are meeting performance characteristics.

   Given the intensity of foreign competition, companies are devoting extra resources to standardizing outputs, not just to reduce costs but to retain customers. If the product's performance satisfies customers, they will continue buying from that company. For example, if a consumer purchases a Japanese car and has no problems with its performance, which car is he or she most likely to buy next time? That is why companies such as U.S. carmakers have been emphasizing the quality dimension of their products. They know how important standardizing outputs is in a competitive market.

Rules and Procedures   As with other kinds of controls, the use of behavior control is accompanied by potential pitfalls that must be managed if the organization is to avoid strategic problems. Top management must be careful to monitor and evaluate the usefulness of behavior controls over time. Rules constrain people and lead to standardized, predictable behavior. However, rules are always easier to establish than to get rid of, and over time the number of rules an organization uses tends to increase. As new developments lead to additional rules, often the old rules are not discarded, and the company becomes overly bureaucratized. Consequently, the organization and the people in it become inflexible and are slow to react to changing or unusual circumstances. Such inflexibility can reduce a company's competitive advantage by lowering the pace of innovation and by reducing customer responsiveness.

Inside the organization, too, integration and coordination may fall apart as rules impede communication between functions. Managers must therefore be continually on the alert for opportunities to reduce the number of rules and procedures necessary to manage the business and should always prefer to discard a rule rather than add a new one. Hence, reducing the number of rules and procedures to the essential minimum is important. Strategic managers frequently neglect this task, however, and often only a change in strategic leadership brings the company back on course.

ORGANIZATIONAL CULTURE

The first function of strategic control is to shape the behavior of organizational members to ensure they are working toward organizational goals and to take corrective action if those goals are not being met. The second function, however, is to keep organizational members focused on thinking about what is best for their organization in the future and to keep them looking for new opportunities to use organizational resources and competencies to create value. One important kind of strategic control system that serves this dual function is organizational culture.

■ What Is Organizational Culture?

Organizational culture is the specific collection of values and norms that are shared by people and groups in an organization and that control the way they interact with each other and with stakeholders outside the organization.[20] **Organizational values** are beliefs and ideas about what kinds of goals members of an organization should pursue and about the appropriate kinds or standards of behavior organizational members should use to achieve these goals. Jack Welch of General Electric is a CEO who is famous for the set of organizational values that he emphasizes, which include entrepreneurship, ownership, honesty, frankness, and open communication. By stressing entrepreneurship and ownership, Welch has been trying to get GE to behave less like a big bureaucracy and more like a collection of smaller and very adaptive companies. He has emphasized giving lower-level managers considerable decision-making autonomy and encouraged them to take risks—that is, to be more like entrepreneurs and less like corporate bureaucrats. The stress Welch places on values such as honesty, frankness, and open communication is a reflection of his belief that an open internal dialogue is necessary for successful operations at General Electric.[21]

From organizational values develop **organizational norms**, guidelines or expectations that *prescribe* appropriate kinds of behavior by employees in particular situations and control the behavior of organizational members toward one another. The norms of behavior for software programmers at Microsoft, the world's largest manufacturer of computer software, include working long hours and weekends, wearing whatever clothing is comfortable (but never a suit and tie), consuming junk food, and communicating with other employees via electronic mail and the company's state-of-the-art intranet.

Organizational culture functions as a type of control in that strategic managers can influence the kind of values and norms that develop in an organization—values and norms that specify appropriate and inappropriate behaviors and that shape and influence the way its members behave.[22] Strategic managers such as Jack Welch, for example, deliberately cultivate values that tell their subordinates they should perform their roles in innovative, creative ways. They establish and support norms dictating that, to be innovative and entrepreneurial, employees should feel free to experiment and go out on a limb even if there is a significant chance of failure. Top managers at organizations such as Intel, Microsoft, and Sun Microsystems also encourage their employees to adopt such values to support their commitment to innovation as a source of their competitive advantage.

Other managers, however, might cultivate values that say employees should always be conservative and cautious in their dealings with others, consult with their superiors before they make important decisions, and record their actions in writing so they can be held accountable for what happens. Managers of organizations such as chemical and oil companies, financial institutions, and insurance companies—any organization in which caution is needed—may encourage a conservative, wary approach to making decisions.[23] In a bank or mutual fund, for example, the risk of losing all of the investors' money makes a cautious approach to investing highly appropriate. Thus, we might expect that managers of different kinds of organizations will deliberately try to cultivate and develop the organizational values and norms best suited to their strategy and structure.

Organizational socialization is the term used to describe how people learn organizational culture. Through socialization, people internalize and learn the norms and values of the culture so that they *become* organizational members.[24] Control through culture is so powerful because, once these values have been internalized, they become a part of the individual's values, and the individual follows organizational values without thinking about them.[25] Very often the values and norms of an organization's culture are transmitted to its members through the stories, myths, and language that people in the organization use, as well as by other means (see Figure 12.4). This chapter's Closing Case, for example, mentions some of the stories that Wal-Mart's associates use to remind themselves about the values of the company. In addition, there are many stories about Sam Walton and about how frugal he was (for example, that he used to drive a thirty-year-old pickup truck and lived in a very modest home) to reinforce Wal-Mart's low-cost strategy and frugal approach. Some of the rites and ceremonies that Wal-Mart uses are the Wal-Mart cheer that happens every morning at the store and a huge extravaganza every year at the company's headquarters to which all high-performing associates are invited.

■ Culture and Strategic Leadership

Since both an organization's structure (the design of its task and reporting relationships) and its culture shape employees' behavior, it is crucial to match organizational structure and culture to implement strategy successfully. The ways that organizations design and create their structures are discussed in Chapter 11. The question that remains is, how do they design and create their cultures? In general, organizational culture is the product of strategic leadership.

The Influence of the Founder   First, organizational culture is created by the strategic leadership provided by an organization's founder and top managers. The organization's founder is particularly important in determining culture because the

FIGURE 12.4

Ways of Transmitting
Organizational Culture

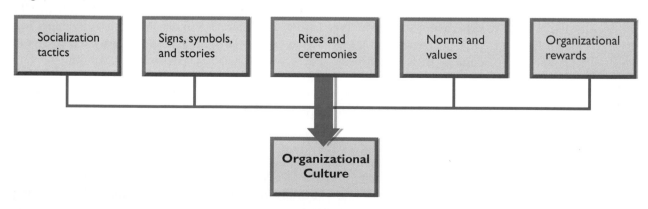

founder imprints his or her values and management style on the organization. For instance, Walt Disney's conservative influence on the company he established continued until well after his death. Managers were afraid to experiment with new forms of entertainment because they were afraid Walt Disney wouldn't like it. It took the installation of a new management team under Michael Eisner to turn around the company's fortunes and allow it to deal with the realities of the new entertainment industry.

As another example, consider Hewlett-Packard (HP), a recognized leader in the electronic instrumentation industry. The company was established in the 1940s, and its culture is an outgrowth of the strong personal beliefs of its founders, Bill Hewlett and Dave Packard. Bill and Dave, as they were known within the company, created HP's culture in a formal statement of HP's basic values: to serve everyone who had a stake in the company with integrity and fairness, including customers, suppliers, employees, stockholders, and society in general. Bill and Dave helped establish these values and build HP's culture by hiring like-minded people and by letting these values guide their own actions as managers. One outgrowth of their commitment to employees was a policy that HP would not be a "hire and fire company." This principle was severely tested on a couple of occasions in the 1970s, when declines in business forced the company to adopt the policy of a nine-day fortnight, under which all staff took a 10 percent pay cut and worked 10 percent fewer hours. While other companies laid off workers, HP kept its full complement of staff, thereby emphasizing the company's commitment to its employees.[26]

Thus, the values developed by HP's founders helped guide managerial action at HP and led directly to the policy of no layoffs. In turn, the commitment to employees that this action signaled has helped foster a productive work force at HP that is willing to go to great lengths to help the company succeed. The result has been superior company performance over time.

The leadership style established by the founder is transmitted to the company's managers, and as the company grows, it typically attracts new managers and employees who share the same values. Moreover, members of the organization typically recruit and select only those who do share their values. Thus, a company's culture becomes more and more distinct as its members become more similar. The virtue of these shared values and common culture is that it *increases integration and improves coordination among organizational members.* For example, the common language that typically emerges in an organization because people share the same beliefs and values facilitates cooperation among managers. Similarly, rules and procedures and direct supervision are less important when shared norms and values control behavior and motivate employees. When organizational members buy into cultural norms and values, this bonds them to the organization and increases their commitment to find new ways to help it succeed. That is, employees are more likely to commit themselves to organizational goals and work actively to develop new skills and competencies to help achieve those goals. Strategy in Action 12.4 details how Ray Kroc built a strong culture at McDonald's.

Organizational Structure   Strategic leadership also affects organizational culture through the way managers design organizational structure—that is, the way managers delegate authority and divide up task relationships. Michael Dell, chairman of Dell Computer, for example, has always tried to keep his company as flat as possible

12.4   STRATEGY *in* ACTION

How Ray Kroc Established McDonald's Culture

In the restaurant business, maintaining product quality is a major problem because the quality of the food, the service, and the restaurant premises varies with the chefs and waiters. If a customer gets a bad meal, poor service, or dirty silverware, the restaurant may lose not only that customer, but other potential customers, too, as negative comments travel by word of mouth. In this context, consider the problem Ray Kroc, the man who pioneered McDonald's growth, faced when McDonald's franchises began to open by the thousands throughout the United States. How could he maintain product quality to protect the company's reputation as it grew? Moreover, how could he try to build a corporate culture that made the organization responsive to the needs of customers to promote its competitive advantage? Kroc's answer was to develop a sophisticated control system, which specified every detail of how each McDonald's restaurant was to be operated and managed, in order to create an organizational culture.

First, Kroc developed a comprehensive system of rules and procedures for both franchise owners and employees to follow in running each restaurant. The most effective way to perform such tasks as cooking burgers, making fries, greeting customers, and cleaning tables was worked out in advance, written down in rule books, and then taught to each McDonald's manager and employee through a formal training process. Prospective franchise owners had to attend "Hamburger University," the company's training center in Chicago, where in an intensive, month-long program they learned all aspects of a McDonald's operation. In turn, they were expected to train their work force and make sure that employees understood operating procedures thoroughly. Kroc's goal in establishing this system of rules and procedures was to build a common culture so that whatever franchise customers walked into, they would always find the same level of quality in food and service. If customers always get what they expect from a restaurant, the restaurant has developed superior customer responsiveness.

However, Kroc's attempt to build culture went well beyond written rules and procedures specifying the performance of various tasks. He also developed McDonald's franchise system to help the company control its structure as it grew. Kroc believed that a manager who is also a franchise owner (and who receives a large share of the profits) is more motivated to buy into a company's culture than a manager paid a straight salary. Thus, McDonald's reward and incentive system allowed it to keep control over its operating structure as it expanded. Moreover, McDonald's was very selective in selling its franchises; the franchisees had to be people with the skills and capabilities that Kroc believed McDonald's managers should have.

Within each restaurant, franchise owners were also instructed that they should pay particular attention to training their employees and instilling in them the norms and values of quality service. Having learned about McDonald's core cultural values at their training sessions, franchise owners were expected to transmit McDonald's concepts of efficiency, quality, and customer service to their employees. The development of shared norms, values, and an organizational culture also helped McDonald's standardize employees' behavior so that customers would know how they would be treated in a McDonald's restaurant. Moreover, McDonald's tried to include customers in its culture. It had customers bus their own tables, but it also showed concern for customers' needs by building playgrounds, offering Happy Meals, and organizing birthday parties for customers' children. In creating its family-oriented culture, McDonald's was ensuring future customer loyalty because satisfied children are likely to remain loyal customers as adults.

and has decentralized authority to lower-level managers and employees, who are charged with striving to get "as close to the customer" as they can. As a result, he has created a customer-service culture at Dell in which employees go out of their way to provide high-quality customer service. By contrast, Henry Ford I designed his company to give him absolute control over decision making. He even scrutinized the actions of his top-management team, and his successor, Henry Ford II, continued to manage the company in a highly centralized way. The result for Ford Motor Car Company was an organizational culture in which managers became conservative and afraid to take risks, and the company was known for its slow pace of change and innovation. Thus, the way an organization designs its structure affects the cultural norms and values that develop within the organization. Managers need to be aware of this fact when implementing their strategies.

■ Adaptive and Inert Cultures

Few environments are stable for a prolonged period of time. Thus, if an organization is to survive, managers must take actions that enable an organization to adapt to environmental changes. If they do not take such action, they may find themselves faced with declining demand for their products. In the last section, we suggest that strategic managers can build an organizational culture that encourages employees to find new ways of developing organizational competencies to exploit new opportunities in the environment. Research evidence has largely confirmed this. In a study of 207 companies, John Kotter and James Heskett distinguished between adaptive cultures and inert cultures.[27] **Adaptive cultures** are those that are innovative and encourage and reward initiative by middle and lower-level managers. **Inert cultures** are those that are cautious and conservative, do not value initiative on the part of middle and lower-level managers, and may even actively discourage such behavior.

According to Kotter and Heskett, managers in organizations with adaptive cultures are able to introduce changes in the way the organization operates, including changes in its strategy and structure, that allow the organization to adapt to changes occurring in the external environment. This does not occur at organizations with inert cultures. As a result, organizations with adaptive cultures are more likely to survive in a changing environment and indeed should have higher performance than organizations with inert cultures. This, in fact, is exactly what Kotter and Heskett found among the 207 companies they examined.

When an organization has an inert culture, strategic problems can result. If, for example, top managers all accept the same set of norms and values, the danger arises that they will be unable to steer the organization in a new strategic direction should the environment change and new competitors or technology demand that the company change. Furthermore, having designed their structures, managers become used to the way they operate, and they rarely recognize the important effect structure has on cultural norms and values. Thus, organizational culture can promote inertia. At IBM, for instance, managers were unable to see, until it was too late, that the development of powerful personal computers and interactive, networking software would have long-term implications for IBM's cash cow, mainframe computers. Their blindness resulted from the tenets of IBM's culture that mainframes would always be the dominant product design and personal computers would only be appendages to mainframes. Moreover, IBM's tall, centralized structure slowed decision making and encouraged the development of conservative norms and values, making managers averse to risk and reluctant to challenge the status quo.

As Chapter 1 points out, cognitive biases can distort the decision-making process. Over time, the norms and values of an organization's culture can bias decision making and cause managers to misperceive the reality of the situation facing their company. To prevent these strategic leadership problems from arising, great care needs to be taken in composing the top-management team.

■ The Composition of the Top-Management Team

The composition of the top-management team helps determine the company's strategic direction, and the personalities and vision of the team's members establish the values and norms that lower-level managers will follow. Researchers have found that when a company has a diverse top-management team, with managers drawn from different functional backgrounds or from different organizations or national cultures, the threat of inertia and of faulty decision making is reduced and the culture becomes adaptive. One of the reasons for IBM's failure to change was that almost all its top managers came from inside IBM and from the mainframe computer division. They had all been exposed to the same set of learning experiences and had developed similar norms and values. When Coca-Cola concluded that its top-management team was becoming too inbred and homogeneous, it deliberately recruited a new top-management team, including the CEO, composed of several foreign nationals, to manage its global strategy. Like Coca-Cola, many organizations are paying increasing attention to planning for executive succession in the top-management team so that they can manage their cultures over time.

■ Traits of Strong and Adaptive Corporate Cultures

Several scholars in the field have tried to uncover the common traits that strong and adaptive corporate cultures share and to find out whether there is a particular set of values that dominates adaptive cultures but is missing from weak or inert ones. An early but still influential attempt is T. J. Peters and R. H. Waterman's account of the values and norms characterizing successful organizations and their cultures.[28] They argue that adaptive organizations show three common value sets.

First, successful companies have values promoting a *bias for action*. The emphasis is on autonomy and entrepreneurship, and employees are encouraged to take risks—for example, to create new products, even though there is no assurance that these products will be winners. Managers are closely involved in the day-to-day operations of the company and do not simply make strategic decisions while isolated in some ivory tower, and employees have a "hands-on, value-driven approach."

The second set of values stems from the *nature of the organization's mission*. The company must stick with what it does best and maintain control over its core activities. A company can easily get sidetracked into pursuing activities outside its area of expertise just because they seem to promise a quick return. Management should cultivate values so that a company sticks to its knitting, which means staying with the businesses it knows best. A company must also establish close relationships with customers as a way of improving its competitive position. After all, who knows more about a company's performance than those who use its products or services? By emphasizing customer-oriented values, organizations are able to learn customers' needs and improve their ability to develop the products and services that customers desire. All these management values are strongly represented in companies such as Microsoft, Hewlett-Packard, and Toyota, which are sure of their mission and take constant steps to maintain it.

The third set of values bears on *how to operate the organization*. A company should try to establish an organizational design that will motivate employees to do their best. Inherent in this set of values is the belief that productivity is obtained through people and that respect for the individual is the primary means by which a company can create the right atmosphere for productive behavior. As William Ouchi has noted, a similar philosophy pervades the culture of Japanese companies.[29] Many U.S. companies—for instance, Eastman Kodak, Procter & Gamble, and Levi Strauss—pay this kind of attention to their employees. An emphasis on entrepreneurship and respect for the employee leads to the establishment of a structure that gives employees the latitude to make decisions and motivates them to succeed. Because a simple structure and a lean staff best fit this situation, the organization should be designed with only the number of managers and hierarchical levels that are necessary to get the job done. The organization should also be sufficiently decentralized to permit employees' participation, but centralized enough for management to make sure that the company pursues its strategic mission and that cultural values are followed.

These three main sets of values are at the heart of an organization's culture, and management transmits and maintains them through strategic leadership. Strategic managers need to establish the values and norms that will help them bring their organizations into the future. When this is accomplished, only those people who fit the values are recruited into the organization, and, through training, they become a part of the organization's culture. Thus, the types of control systems chosen should reinforce and build on one another in a cohesive way. However, organizational culture cannot by itself make structure work. It must be backed by output and behavior controls and matched to a reward system so that employees will in fact cultivate organizational norms and values and pursue organizational goals.

STRATEGIC REWARD SYSTEMS

Organizations also strive to control employees' behavior by linking reward systems to their control systems.[30] Based on a company's strategy (low cost or differentiation, for example), strategic managers must decide which behaviors to reward. They then create a control system to measure these behaviors and link the reward structure to them. Determining how to relate rewards to performance is a crucial strategic decision because it determines the incentive structure that affects the way managers and employees at all levels in the organization behave. You learned earlier how structure and control shape employees' behavior. The design of the organization's incentive system is a vital element in the control process because it motivates and reinforces desired behaviors.

As Chapter 2 points out, top managers can be encouraged to work in the shareholders' interests by being rewarded with stock options linked to the company's long-term performance. Furthermore, companies such as Kodak and GM require managers to buy company stock. When managers are made shareholders, they are more motivated to pursue long-term rather than short-term goals. Similarly, in designing a pay system for salespeople, the choice is whether to motivate salespeople through straight salary or salary plus a bonus based on how much is sold. Neiman Marcus, the luxury retailer, pays employees a straight salary because it wants to encourage high-quality service but to discourage a hard-sell approach. Thus, there are no incentives based on quantity sold. On the other hand, the pay system for rewarding car salespeople encourages high-pressure selling; it typically contains a large bonus for the number and price of cars sold.

Since the design of a company's reward system affects the way managers and employees behave, the reward system also affects the *kinds of norms, values, and culture that develop in an organization.* Thus, top-management teams rewarded solely by salary and those rewarded by stock options linked to performance are likely to have different norms and values. Specifically, top-management teams rewarded with stock options may be more entrepreneurial and more concerned with increasing quality and innovation than those that lack this reward. Companies such as Sears, GM, Kodak, and Westinghouse, which previously made little attempt to link performance to rewards, had slow-moving, bureaucratic cultures. All these companies now require managers to own company stock.

We now take a closer look at the types of reward systems available to strategic managers.[31] Generally, reward systems are found at the individual and group or total organizational levels. Often these systems are used in combination; for example, merit raises at the individual level may be accompanied by a bonus based on divisional or corporate performance. Within each type, several forms of reward systems are available.

■ Individual Reward Systems

Piecework Plans   Piecework plans are used when outputs can be objectively measured. Essentially, employees are paid on the basis of some set amount for each unit of output produced. Piecework plans are most commonly used for employees on production lines, where individuals work alone and their performance can be directly measured. Because this system encourages quantity rather than quality, the company normally applies stringent quality controls to ensure that the quality is acceptable.

Commission Systems   Commission systems resemble piecework systems, except that they are normally tied not to what is produced, but to how much is sold. Thus, they are most commonly found in sales situations. Often the salaries of salespeople are based principally on commission to encourage superior performance. First-rate salespeople can earn more than $1 million per year in many industries.

Bonus Plans   Bonus plans at the individual level generally reward the performance of a company's key individuals, such as the CEO and senior vice presidents.[32] The performance of these people is visible to the organization as a whole and to stakeholders such as shareholders. Consequently, there is a strong rationale for paying these individuals according to some measure of functional or divisional performance. A company must proceed carefully, however, if it is to avoid problems such as emphasis on short-run rather than long-term objectives. For example, paying bonuses based on quarterly or yearly ROI rather than on five-year growth can have a markedly different effect on the way strategic managers behave. Insisting that members of a top-management team own stock in the company motivates managers and ties their interests to those of the shareholders.

Promotion   Last, but not least, promotion is an important source of reward for individuals at all organizational levels. Managers compete for promotion to the next level in the hierarchy; the highest-performing functional managers become the next generation of divisional managers, and the highest-performing divisional managers become the next generation of corporate managers. Promotion is so important because salary and bonuses rise sharply as managers ascend the hierarchy. The CEO often earns in salary alone 50 percent more than the person next in the chain of command. In 1996, for example, the average CEO in the top *Fortune* 200 companies earned nearly $4.7 million dollars, almost double the $2.4 million earned by the next highest-ranking executive.[33] The rewards from promotion are enormous, and this is why organizational career ladders are closely watched by aspiring managers. Some organizations deliberately encourage promotion tournaments, contests between managers for promotion, to motivate high performance.

■ Group and Organizational Reward Systems

Group and organizational reward systems provide additional ways in which companies can relate pay to performance. The increasing use of product-team structures and cross-functional teams has led many organizations to develop some form of group-based rewards system to encourage high team performance. The most common reward systems at these levels are group bonuses, profit sharing, employee stock options, and organization bonuses.

Group-Based Bonus Systems   Sometimes a company can establish project teams, or work groups, that perform all the operations needed to turn out a product or provide a service. This arrangement makes it possible to measure group performance and offer rewards on the basis of group productivity. The system can be highly motivating because employees are allowed to develop the best work procedures for doing the job and are responsible for improving their own productivity. For example, Wal-Mart supports a group bonus plan based on controlling shrinkage (that is, employee theft).

Profit Sharing Systems   Profit sharing plans are designed to reward employees on the basis of the profit a company earns in any one time period. Such plans encourage employees to take a broad view of their activities and feel connected to the company as a whole. Wal-Mart uses this method as well to develop its organizational culture.

Employee Stock Option Plans   Rather than reward employees on the basis of short-term profits, a company sometimes establishes an employee stock ownership plan (ESOP) and allows employees to buy its shares at below-market prices, heightening employees' motivation. As shareholders, the employees focus not only on short-term profits but also on long-term capital appreciation, for they are now the company's owners. Over time, if enough employees participate, they can control a substantial stock holding, as do the employees of United Airlines, and thus become vitally interested in the company's performance. ESOPs can be very important in developing an adaptive corporate culture because employees share in the profits that result.

Organization Bonus Systems   Profit is not the only basis on which a company can reward organizationwide performance. Rewards are also commonly based on cost savings, quality increases, and production increases obtained in the most recent time period. Because these systems usually require that outputs be measured accurately, they are most common in assembly-line organizations or in service companies, where it is possible to cost out the price of the services of personnel. The systems are mainly a backup to other forms of pay systems. In rare situations, however, they become the principal means of control. That is the case at Lincoln Electric, a company renowned for the success of its cost-savings group plan.

Control through organizational reward systems complements all the other forms of control we discuss in this chapter. Rewards act as the oil that makes a control system function effectively. To ensure that the right strategic behaviors are being rewarded, rewards should be closely linked to an organization's strategy. Moreover, they should be so designed that they do not lead to conflicts among divisions, functions, or individuals. Since organizational structure and organizational control and reward systems are not independent dimensions of organizational design but are highly interrelated, they must be compatible if an organization is to implement its strategy successfully. Matching structure and control to strategy is the issue we focus on in Chapter 13.

SUMMARY OF CHAPTER

Choosing a control system to match the firm's strategy and structure offers management a number of important challenges. Management must select controls that provide a framework to monitor, measure, and evaluate accurately whether or not it has achieved its goals and strategic objectives. Financial and output controls must be backed up with behavior controls and organizational culture to ensure that the firm is achieving its goals in the most efficient way possible. In general, these controls should reinforce one another, and care must be taken to ensure that they do not result in unforeseen consequences, such as competition among functions, divisions, and individuals. Many top managers point to the difficulty of changing organizational culture when they talk about reengineering their organization so that it can pursue new strategic goals. This difficulty arises because culture is the product of the complex interaction of many factors, such as top management, organizational structure, and the organization's reward and incentive systems. The chapter makes the following main points:

✔ Organizational structure does not operate effectively unless the appropriate control and incentive systems are in place to shape and motivate employees' behavior.

✔ Strategic control is the process of setting targets and monitoring, evaluating, and rewarding organizational performance. The balanced scorecard approach to strategic control suggests that managers should develop strategic control systems that measure all important aspects of their organization's performance.

✔ Control takes place at all levels in the organization—corporate, divisional, functional, and individual.

✔ Effective control systems are flexible, accurate, and able to provide quick feedback to strategic planners.

✔ Many kinds of performance standards are available to implement a company's strategy. The kinds of measures managers choose affect the way a company operates.

✔ Control systems range from those directed at measuring outputs to those measuring behaviors or actions.

✔ The two main forms of financial control are stock market price and return on investment (ROI).

✔ Output controls establish goals for divisions, functions, and individuals. They can be used only when outputs can be objectively measured and are often linked to a management by objectives system.

✔ Behavior controls are achieved through budgets, standardization, and rules and procedures.

✔ Organizational culture is the collection of norms and values that govern the way in which people act and behave inside the organization.

✔ An organization's culture is the product of a founder's or top-management team's values and attitudes, of the way managers choose to design the organization's structure, and of the strategic reward systems managers use to shape and motivate employees' behavior.

✔ An organization's reward systems constitute the final form of control. A company designs its reward systems to provide employees with the incentives to make its structure work effectively and to align their interests with organizational goals and objectives.

✔ Organizations use all these forms of control simultaneously. Management must select and combine those that are consistent with each other and with the strategy and structure of the organization.

DISCUSSION QUESTIONS

1. What are the relationships among differentiation, integration, and strategic control systems? Why are these relationships important?

2. For each of the structures we discuss in Chapter 11, outline the most suitable control systems.

3. What kind of control and reward systems would you be likely to find in (a) a small manufacturing company, (b) a chain store, (c) a high-tech company, and (d) a Big Five accounting firm?

Practicing Strategic Management

SMALL-GROUP EXERCISE
Creating a Strategic Control System

Break up into groups of three to five people, and discuss the following scenario:

You are managers in charge of project teams of design engineers, each of which is working on a different aspect of the design for a new generation of luxury sports sedans. You are meeting to design a control system that will be used to motivate and reward all the teams. Your objective is to create a control system that will help to increase the performance of each team separately and facilitate cooperation between the teams, something that is necessary since the various projects are interlinked and affect one another (the different parts of the car must fit together). Since competition in the luxury-car market is intense, it is imperative that the car be of the highest quality possible and incorporate all state-of-the-art technology.

1. Using the balanced scorecard approach, discuss what kind of output controls are most important for measuring the teams' performance.

2. Discuss what kinds of behavior controls you should establish to facilitate interactions both within the teams and between the teams.

3. Discuss how you might go about developing a culture to help promote high team performance.

STRATEGIC MANAGEMENT PROJECT
Module 12

For this part of your project, you need to obtain information about your company's control and incentive systems, which may be difficult to do unless your project pertains to a real company and you can interview managers directly. Some forms of information, such as compensation for top management, are available in the company's annual reports or 10-K. If your company is well known, magazines such as *Fortune* or *Business Week* frequently report on corporate culture or control issues. Nevertheless, you may be forced to make some bold assumptions to complete this part of the project.

1. What are the major kinds of control problems facing your company? How do these control problems relate to your organization's structure, which you identified in the last chapter?

2. With the information at your disposal, list the main kinds of control systems used by your organization to solve these problems. Specifically, what use does your company make of (a) financial controls, (b) output controls, (c) behavior controls, and (d) organizational culture?

3. What kinds of behaviors is the organization trying to (a) shape and (b) motivate through the use of these control systems?

4. What role does the top-management team play in creating the culture of your organization? Can you identify the characteristic norms and values that describe the way people behave in your organization? How does the design of the organization's structure affect its culture?

5. Collect the salary and compensation data for your company's top management from its annual reports. How does the organization use rewards to shape and motivate its managers? For example, how much of top managers' total compensation is based on bonuses and stock options, and how much is based on straight salary?

6. Does the organization offer other kinds of employees any incentives based on performance? What kinds of incentives? For example, is there an employee stock ownership plan in operation?

7. Based on this analysis, do you think that your organization's control system is functioning effectively? For example, is your organization collecting the right kinds of information? Is it measuring the right kinds of behavior? How could the control system be improved?

8. To what degree is there a match between your company's structure and its control and incentive systems? That is, are its control systems allowing it to operate its structure effectively? How could they be improved?

ARTICLE FILE 12

Find an example of a company that has recently changed one or more of its control and incentive systems. Which of its control systems did it change (for instance, output control or culture)? Why did it make the change? What does it hope to achieve by the change? How will changing the control system affect the way its structure operates?

EXPLORING THE WEB
What Kind of Control?

Search the Web for an example of a company that uses one or more of the types of control systems discussed in the chapter. What control system is it? Why does the company use it?

CLOSING CASE

Sam Walton's Approach to Control

WAL-MART, HEADQUARTERED IN BENTONVILLE, Arkansas, is the largest retailer in the world, with sales of almost $100 billion in 1996. Its success rests on the nature of the strategic control systems that its founder, the late Sam Walton, established for the company. Walton wanted all his managers and workers to have a hands-on approach to their jobs and to be fully committed to Wal-Mart's main goal, which he defined as total customer satisfaction. To motivate his employees, Walton created a strategic control system that gave employees at all levels continuous feedback about their and the company's performance.

First, Walton developed a financial control system that provided managers with day-to-day feedback about the performance of all aspects of the business. Through a sophisticated companywide satellite system, corporate managers at the Bentonville headquarters can evaluate the performance of each store, and even of each department in each store. Information about store profits and the rate of turnover of goods is provided to store managers on a daily basis, and store managers in turn communicate this information to Wal-Mart's 625,000 employees (who are called associates). By sharing such information, Walton's method encourages all associates to learn the fundamentals of the retailing business so they can work to improve it.[34]

If any store seems to be underperforming, managers and associates meet to probe the reasons and to find solutions to help raise performance. Wal-Mart's top managers routinely visit stores having problems to lend their expertise, and each month top managers use the company's aircraft to fly to various Wal-Mart's stores so they can keep their fingers on the pulse of the business. In addition, it is customary for Wal-Mart's top managers to spend their Saturdays meeting together to discuss the week's financial results and their implications for the future.[35]

Walton also insisted on linking performance to rewards. Each manager's individual performance, measured by his or her ability to meet specific goals or output targets, is reflected in pay raises and chances for promotion (promotion both to bigger stores in the company's 2,000-store empire and even to corporate headquarters, since Wal-Mart routinely promotes from within the company rather than hiring managers from other companies). While top managers receive large stock options linked to the company's performance targets and stock price, even ordinary associates receive stock in the company. An associate who started with Walton in the 1970s would by now have accumulated more than $250,000 in stock because of the appreciation of Wal-Mart's stock over time.

Walton also instituted an elaborate system of controls, such as rules and budgets, to shape employees' behavior. Each store performs the same activities in the same way, and all employees receive the same kind of training so they know how to behave toward customers. In this way, Wal-Mart is able to standardize its operations, which leads to major cost savings and allows managers to make storewide changes easily when they need to.

Finally, Walton was not content just to use output and behavior controls and monetary rewards to motivate his associates. To involve his associates in the business and encourage them to develop work behaviors focused on providing quality customer service, he established strong cultural values and norms for his company. Some norms that associates are expected to follow include the *ten-foot attitude*, which developed when Walton, during his visits to the stores, encouraged associates to "promise that whenever you come within 10 feet of a customer you will look him in the eye, greet him, and ask him if you can help him"; the *sundown rule,* which states that employees should strive to answer customers' requests by sundown on the day they receive them; and the *Wal-Mart cheer* ("Give me a *W*, give me an *A*," and so on), which is used in all its stores.

The strong customer-oriented values that Walton created are exemplified in the stories its members tell one another about the company's concern for its customers. They include stories such as the one about Sheila, who risked her own safety when she jumped in front of a car to prevent a little boy from being struck; about Phyllis, who

administered CPR to a customer who had suffered a heart attack in her store; and about Annette, who gave up the Power Ranger she had on layaway for her own son so a customer's son could have his birthday wish.[36] The strong Wal-Mart culture helps control and motivate its employees, spurring the associates to achieve the stringent output and financial targets the company has set for itself.[37]

Case Discussion Questions

1. What were the main elements of the control system created by Sam Walton?

2. In what ways will this control system facilitate Wal-Mart's present strategy of global expansion?

End Notes

1. M. Moeller, "Oracle: Practising What it Preaches," *Business Week*, August 16, 1999, pp. 1–5.

2. G. Hamel and C. K. Prahalad, "Strategic Intent," *Harvard Business Review* (May–June 1989), 64.

3. R. Simmons, "Strategic Orientation and Top Management Attention to Control Systems," *Strategic Management Journal*, 12 (1991), 49–62.

4. R. Simmons, "How New Top Managers Use Control Systems as Levers of Strategic Renewal," *Strategic Management Journal*, 15 (1994), 169–189.

5. R. S. Kaplan and D. P. Norton, "The Balanced Scorecard—Measures That Drive Performance," *Harvard Business Review* (January–February 1992), 71–79.

6. R. S. Kaplan and D. P. Norton, "Using the Balanced Scorecard as a Strategic Management System," *Harvard Business Review* (January–February 1996), 75–85.

7. R. S. Kaplan and D. P. Norton, "Putting the Balanced Scorecard to Work," *Harvard Business Review* (September–October 1993), 134–147.

8. Kaplan and Norton, "The Balanced Scorecard," p. 72.

9. W. G. Ouchi, "The Transmission of Control Through Organizational Hierarchy," *Academy of Management Journal,* 21 (1978), 173–192; W. H. Newman, *Constructive Control* (Englewood Cliffs, N. J.: Prentice-Hall, 1975).

10. Press release, www.cypress.com (1998).

11. B. Dumaine, "The Bureaucracy Busters," *Fortune*, June 17, 1991, 46.

12. P. F. Drucker, *The Practise of Management* (New York: Harper & Row, 1954).

13. S. J. Carroll and H. L. Tosi, *Management by Objectives: Applications and Research* (New York: Macmillan, 1973).

14. R. Rodgers and J. E. Hunter, "Impact of Management by Objectives on Organizational Productivity," *Journal of Applied Psychology*, 76 (1991), 322–326.

15. Bureau of Business Practice, *Profiles of Malcolm Baldrige Award Winners* (Boston: Allyn & Bacon, 1992).

16. E. Flamholtz, "Organizational Control Systems as a Managerial Tool," *California Management Review* (Winter 1979), 50–58.

17. O. E. Williamson, *Markets and Hierarchies* (New York: Free Press, 1975); W. G. Ouchi, "Markets, Bureaucracies, and Clans," *Administrative Science Quarterly,* 25 (1980), 129–141.

18. "In Praise of the Blue Suit," *Economist*, January 13, 1996, p. 59.

19. H. Mintzberg, *The Structuring of Organizations* (Englewood Cliffs, N.J.: Prentice-Hall, 1979), pp. 5–9.

20. L. Smircich, "Concepts of Culture and Organizational Analysis," *Administrative Science Quarterly,* 28 (1983), 339–358.

21. "General Electric," *Harvard Business School Case* No. 9-385-315, 1984.

22. Ouchi, "Markets, Bureaucracies, and Clans," p. 130.

23. G. R. Jones, *Organizational Theory* (Reading, Mass.: Addison-Wesley, 1997).

24. J. Van Maanen and E. H. Schein, "Towards a Theory of Organizational Socialization," in *Research in Organizational Behavior,* ed. B. M. Staw (Greenwich, Conn.: JAI Press, 1979), pp. 1, 209–264.

25. G. R. Jones, "Socialization Tactics, Self-Efficacy, and Newcomers' Adjustments to Organizations," *Academy of Management Journal,* 29 (1986), 262–279.

26. For details of The HP Way, see J. P. Kotter and J. L. Heskett, *Corporate Culture and Performance* (New York: Free Press, 1992), Chapter 5.

27. Kotter and Heskett, *Corporate Culture*.

28. T. J. Peters and R. H. Waterman, *In Search of Excellence: Lessons from America's Best-Run Companies* (New York: Harper & Row, 1982).

29. W. G. Ouchi, *Theory Z: How American Business Can Meet the Japanese Challenge* (Reading, Mass.: Addison-Wesley, 1981).

30. E. E. Lawler III, *Motivation in Work Organizations* (Monterey, Calif.: Brooks/Cole, 1973); J. Galbraith and R. Kazanjian, *Strategy Implementation* (St. Paul, Minn.: West, 1992), Chapter 6.

31. E. E. Lawler III, "The Design of Effective Reward Systems," in *Handbook of Organizational Behavior,* ed. J. W. Lorsch (Englewood Cliffs, N.J.: Prentice-Hall, 1987), 386–422; R. Mathis and J. Jackson, *Personnel,* 2nd ed. (St. Paul, Minn.: West, 1979), p. 456.

32. H. L. Tosi Jr. and L. R. Gomez-Mejia, "CEO Compensation and Firm Performance," *Academy of Management Journal*, 37 (1994), 1002–1016.

33. T. Y. Hausman, "Second Behind," *Wall Street Journal*, April 11, 1996, p. A4.

34. J. Pettet, "Wal-Mart Yesterday and Today," *Discount Merchandiser* (December 1995), 66–67.

35. M. Reid, "Stores of Value," *Economist*, March 4, 1995 pp. ss5–ss7.

36. www.walmart.com, 1999.

37. M. Troy, "The Culture Remains the Constant," *Discount Store News*, June 8, 1998, pp. 95–98.

13 Matching Structure and Control to Strategy

OPENING CASE

Compaq's New Internet Strategy

IN A BOOMING ENVIRONMENT, where computer firms such as Dell and IBM are reporting record profits, Compaq reported losses in 1999.[1] Why? Its new CEO, Michael Capellas, attributes its problems to three factors: (1) the difficulties associated with integrating Digital Equipment's operations into Compaq's after the takeover of Digital Equipment in 1998; (2) Compaq's slowness in developing an Internet strategy and reaching out to customers, both corporate and individual, on-line; and (3) its failure to control inventory costs at a time when rivals such as Dell and Gateway are perfecting ways to streamline their operations and gain a low-cost advantage. To solve these problems, Capellas and his top-management team implemented a new strategy and structure for Compaq in 1999.

As it had grown through the 1990s, Compaq had implemented a matrix structure to control its diverse businesses. Over time, however, the matrix structure resulted in increasingly slow decision making because geography—especially after the Digital acquisition—rather than product considerations drove strategy making.[2] The needs of the whole corporation were being ignored as the needs of each geographic business or division took precedence.

Consequently, Capellas decided to scrap the decentralized matrix structure. He replaced it with a multidivisional one, based on product line—for example, personal computers or high-end corporate workstations. At the same time, he made each business a profit center and gave each division's managers clear sales and profit objectives and the responsibility to achieve those objectives.[3]

Capellas then announced a new strategy for the company: henceforth, Compaq would pursue an Internet strategy, both to increase its direct sales to customers and to streamline and integrate its own operations in order to reduce costs and speed decision making. Capellas charged a team of corporate managers with establishing a series of Internet teams to speed the development of Internet-based software systems to facilitate direct sales to all types of customers—for example, commercial, individual, and education. Moreover, he demanded that these systems be standardized across business divisions. His aim was both to integrate the divisions' activities and to allow them to work together to provide large customers with a complete computer package consisting of mainframes and servers, as well as desktop and portable computers.

Recognizing that Compaq had been slow to use the Internet to facilitate the management of its value chain, Capellas also instructed managers to take Compaq's functional operations on-line. For example, Compaq was not closely connected to its suppliers on-line whereas Dell, its major competitor, was. Dell had achieved a 10 percent cost advantage over Compaq as a result of its ability to reduce inventory and warehousing costs by using a state-of-the-art Internet information system. Furthermore, Dell has also been leading the way in direct selling to customers over the Internet. Capellas recognized that Compaq must match Dell in this regard if it is to regain its competitive position. His goal is to raise direct sales from 15 percent of total sales to 25 percent by the end of 1999, and to increase this figure in the years ahead.

Although the effects of Compaq's new strategy and structure on its bottom-line performance are still unknown, analysts feel that Capellas has made many of the right moves. They worry, however, that Compaq waited too long to reinvent itself. With such strong and agile competitors in the market as Dell, IBM, and Sun Microsystems, it is not clear that Compaq will be able to recover its preeminent position in the marketplace.

OVERVIEW

At Compaq, Michael Capellas and his top-management team moved to implement the right mix of structure and control systems so that the company could pursue a new strategy to manage the competitive environment. In this chapter, we discuss how the nature of a company's corporate-, business-, and functional-level strategy affects the choice of structure and control systems—in other words, how strategic managers should match different forms of structure and control to strategy. As we emphasized in Chapter 1, the issue facing strategic managers is to match strategy formulation with strategy implementation. All the tools of strategy formulation and implementation are discussed in previous chapters. In this chapter, we put the two sides of the equation together and examine how strategic managers match strategy and structure to build competitive advantage.

First, we consider how functional-level strategy and the attempt to achieve superior efficiency, quality, innovation, and customer responsiveness affect structure and control. Second, we examine how a company's choice of generic business-level strategy influences the choice of structure and control for implementing the strategy. Third, we focus on the implementation of a global strategy and discuss how to match different global strategies with different global structures. Finally, we take up the special problems that different kinds of corporate-level strategy pose for strategic managers in designing a structure and note how changes in corporate-level strategy over time affect the form of structure and control systems adopted by a company. By the end of this chapter, you will understand how to match strategy to structure to create a high-performing organization.

STRUCTURE AND CONTROL AT THE FUNCTIONAL LEVEL

Chapter 5, on functional-level strategy, discusses how a company's functions can help it achieve superior efficiency, quality, innovation, and customer responsiveness—the four building blocks of competitive advantage. It also discusses how strategic managers can help each function to develop a distinctive competency. We now examine the way in which strategic managers can create a structure and control system to encourage the development of various distinctive functional competencies, or skills.

Decisions at the functional level fall into two categories: choices about the level of vertical differentiation and choices about monitoring and evaluation systems. (Choices about horizontal differentiation are *not* relevant here because we are considering each function individually.) The choices depend on the distinctive competency a company is pursuing.

■ Manufacturing

In manufacturing, functional strategy usually centers on improving efficiency, quality, and responsiveness to customers. A company must create an organizational setting in which managers can learn from experience-curve effects how to economize on costs. Traditionally, to move down the experience curve quickly, companies have exercised tight control over work activities and employees and developed tall, centralized hierarchies to squeeze out costs wherever possible. As part of their attempt to increase efficiency, companies have also made great use of behavior and output controls to reduce costs. Activities are standardized. For example, human inputs are standardized through the recruitment and training of skilled personnel, the work process is standardized or programmed to reduce costs, and quality control is used to make sure that outputs are being produced correctly. In addition, managers use output controls such as operating budgets to monitor and contain costs continuously.

Following the lead of Japanese companies such as Toyota and Sony, which operate total quality management (TQM) and flexible manufacturing systems, many U.S. companies have moved to change the way they design the manufacturing setting. As detailed in Chapter 5, successful TQM requires a different approach to organizational design. With TQM, the inputs and involvement of all employees in the decision-making process are necessary to improve production efficiency and quality. Thus, authority has to be decentralized in order to motivate employees to improve the production process. In TQM, work teams are created and workers are given the responsibility and authority to discover and implement improved work procedures. Quality control circles are formed to exchange information and suggestions about problems and work procedures. Frequently, a bonus system or employee stock ownership plan (ESOP) is established to motivate workers and allow them to share in the increased value that TQM often produces.

No longer are managers employed purely to supervise workers and make sure they are doing the job. Managers assume the role of coach and facilitator, and team members jointly take on the supervisory burden, reducing bureaucratic costs. Work teams are often given the responsibility of controlling and disciplining their members; they may even have to decide who should work in their team. Frequently, work teams develop strong norms and values, and work-group culture becomes an important means of control. This type of control matches the new decentralized team approach.

Although workers are given more freedom to control their activities, the extensive use of output controls and the continuous measurement of efficiency and quality ensure that the work team's activities meet the goals set for the function by management. Efficiency and quality increase as new and improved work rules and procedures are developed to raise the level of standardization. The aim is to find the right match between structure and control and a TQM approach, so that manufacturing develops the distinctive competency leading to superior efficiency and quality.

■ Research and Development

The functional strategy for a research and development department is to develop a distinctive competency in innovation and to develop technology that results in products that fit customers' needs. Consequently, the R&D department's structure and control systems should be designed to provide the coordination necessary for scientists and engineers to bring products quickly to market. Moreover, these systems should motivate R&D scientists to develop innovative products or processes.

In practice, R&D departments typically have flat, decentralized structures that group scientists into teams. Flat structures give research and development personnel the freedom and autonomy to be innovative. Furthermore, because the performance of scientists and engineers can typically be judged only over the long term (because it may take several years for a project to be completed), adding layers of hierarchy would simply raise bureaucratic costs and waste resources.[4]

By using teams, strategic managers can take advantage of scientists' ability to work jointly in solving problems and to enhance each other's performance. In small teams, too, the professional values and norms that highly trained employees bring to the situation promote coordination. A culture for innovation frequently emerges to control employees' behavior, as has occurred at Motorola and Intel, where the race to be first energizes the R&D teams. Strategy in Action 13.1 describes Intel's use of R&D teams to innovate and improve computer chips.

To spur teams to work effectively, the reward system should be linked to the performance of the team. If scientists, individually or in a team, do not share in the profits a company obtains from its new products or processes, they may have little motivation to contribute wholeheartedly to the team. To prevent the departure of their key employees and to encourage high motivation, companies such as Merck, Intel, and Microsoft give their researchers stock options and rewards tied to their individual performance, their team performance, and the company's performance. As a result, many of these scientists and engineers have become multimillionaires.

■ Sales

Like research and development, the sales function usually has a flat structure. Most commonly, three hierarchical levels—sales director, regional or product sales managers, and individual salespeople—can accommodate even large sales forces. Flat structures are possible because the organization does not depend on direct supervision for control. Salespeople's activities are often complex; moreover, because they are dispersed in the field, these employees are difficult to monitor. Rather than depend on the hierarchy, the sales function usually employs output and behavior controls.

Output controls, such as specific sales goals or goals for increasing responsiveness to customers, can be easily established and monitored by supervisors. Then output controls can be linked to a bonus reward system to motivate salespeople. Behavior controls—for instance, detailed reports that salespeople file describing their

Intel's R&D Department

I ntel is the world leader in the development of chips, the microprocessors that are the heart of all computers. Intel is very profitable, and throughout the 1990s it earned record profits because it had a monopoly on the production of the Pentium chip, which is still the industry standard. In the race to produce new and improved chips, Intel is constantly under attack from companies such as Motorola, IBM, and Japan's NEC and has to protect its competitive advantage. Consequently, the need to develop new chips or improved versions of existing ones (such as the Pentium Pro) forms the basis of Intel's differentiation strategy.

To speed product development, Intel has implemented a team structure in its R&D department. To try to ensure that it will always have the leading-edge technology, the company has six different teams working on the next generation of chips; each team's innovations can then be put together to create the final state-of-the-art product. However, it also has six teams working simultaneously on the subsequent generation of chips, and six teams working on the generation of chips to follow that one. In other words, to sustain its leading-edge technology and maintain its monopoly, the company has created a team structure in which its scientists and engineers work on the frontiers of chip research so that they can control the technology of tomorrow.[5] This approach has certainly paid off for Intel. The company's stock price has increased more than 600 percent in the 1990s. Indeed, Intel is expected to outperform the market for as long as its teams succeed in making the company the innovation leader in the chip industry.

interactions with customers—can also be used to standardize salespeople's behavior and make it easier for supervisors to review their performance.[6]

Similar design considerations apply to the other functions, such as accounting, finance, engineering, and human resource management. Managers must select the right combination of structure and control mechanisms to allow each function to contribute to achieving superior efficiency, quality, innovation, and responsiveness to customers. When, as now, reducing costs is often required for survival, more and more companies are flattening their functional hierarchies and decentralizing control to reduce bureaucratic costs. Strategic managers must develop control and incentive systems that align employees' interests with those of the organization and that motivate employees.

STRUCTURE AND CONTROL AT THE BUSINESS LEVEL

Building competitive advantage through organizational design starts at the functional level. However, the key to successful strategy implementation is a structure that *links and combines* the skills and competencies of a company's value creation functions, allowing it to pursue a business-level strategy successfully. In this section, we consider the organizational design issues for a company seeking to implement one of the generic competitive business-level strategies to build and sustain its competitive advantage.

Generic Business-Level Strategies

Designing the right mix of structure and control at the business level is a continuation of designing a company's functions. Having implemented the right structure and control system for each individual function, the company must then implement the organizational arrangements so that all the functions can be managed together to achieve business-level strategy objectives. Because the focus is on managing *cross-functional relationships*, the choice of horizontal differentiation (the grouping of organizational activities) and integration for achieving business-level strategies becomes very important.[7] Control systems must also be selected with the monitoring and evaluating of cross-functional activities in mind. Table 13.1 summarizes the appropriate organizational structure and control systems that companies can use when following a low-cost, differentiation, or focus strategy.

Cost-Leadership Strategy and Structure

The aim of the cost-leadership strategy is to make the company pursuing it the lowest-cost producer in the market.[8] At the business level, this means reducing costs not just in production, but across *all* functions in the organization, including research and development and sales and marketing.

If a company is pursuing a cost-leadership strategy, its research and development efforts probably focus on product and process development rather than on the more expensive product innovation, which carries no guarantee of success. In other words, the company stresses research that improves product characteristics

TABLE 13.1

Generic Strategy, Structure, and Control

	Strategy		
	Cost Leadership	**Differentiation**	**Focus**
Appropriate Structure	Functional	Product team or matrix	Functional
Integrating Mechanisms	Center on manufacturing	Center on R&D or marketing	Center on product or customer
Output Controls	Great use (e.g., cost control)	Some use (e.g., quality goals)	Some use (e.g., cost and quality)
Behavior Controls	Some use (e.g., budgets, standardization)	Great use (e.g., rules, budgets)	Some use (e.g., budgets)
Organizational Culture	Little use (e.g., quality control circles)	Great use (e.g., norms and values)	Great use (e.g., norms and values)

or lowers the cost of making existing products. Similarly, the company tries to decrease the cost of sales and marketing by offering a standard product to a mass market rather than by offering different products aimed at different market segments, which is also more expensive.[9]

To implement a cost-leadership strategy, the company chooses a structure and control system that has a low level of bureaucratic costs. As we discuss in earlier chapters, bureaucratic costs are those of managing a company's strategy through structure and control. Structure and control are expensive, and the more complex the structure—that is, the higher its level of differentiation and integration—the higher are bureaucratic costs. To economize on bureaucratic costs, a cost leader will, therefore, choose the simplest or least expensive structure compatible with the needs of the low-cost strategy.

In practice, the structure chosen is normally a functional structure. This structure is relatively inexpensive to operate because it is based on a low level of differentiation and integration. Even in a functional structure, cross-functional teams can be organized around the manufacturing function. For example, a TQM program implemented through task forces and teams can be developed to integrate the activities of manufacturing and the other functions. This allows for continuous improvements in the rules and procedures for standardizing task activities, which is a major source of cost saving.[10]

A cost-leadership company also tries to keep its structure as flat as possible to reduce bureaucratic costs, and functional structures are relatively flat. The cost leader constantly evaluates whether it needs that extra level in the hierarchy and whether it can decentralize authority (perhaps to the work group) to keep costs low. Seagate Technology, a producer of hard disks, exemplifies a cost leader that continually streamlines its structure to maintain a competitive advantage. It periodically reduces levels in the hierarchy and institutes strict production controls to minimize costs. This process has kept it ahead of its Japanese competitors. Similarly, John Reed, the chairman of Citicorp, flattened his organization's structure, wiping out two levels of management and terminating dozens of executives to reduce costs. His cost-cutting efforts helped turn a loss of $457 million in 1991 into record profits throughout the 1990s, and Citicorp's share price has soared as a result.[11]

To further reduce costs, cost-leadership companies try to use the cheapest and easiest forms of control available—output controls. For each function, a company adopts output controls that allow it to monitor and evaluate functional performance closely. In the manufacturing function, for instance, the company imposes tight controls and stresses meeting budgets based on production, cost, or quality targets.[12] In research and development, too, the emphasis falls on the bottom line. R&D personnel, eager to demonstrate their contribution to cost savings, may focus their efforts on improving process technology, where actual savings are calculable.

H. J. Heinz clearly illustrates such efforts. In following a cost-leadership strategy, it places enormous emphasis on production improvements that can reduce the cost of a can of beans. Like manufacturing and research and development, the sales function is closely monitored, and sales targets are usually challenging. Cost-leadership companies, however, are likely to reward employees through generous incentive and bonus plans to encourage high performance. Often their culture is based on values that emphasize the bottom line. Lincoln Electric and PepsiCo are other examples of such companies.

In short, pursuing a successful cost-leadership strategy requires close attention to the design of structure and control to limit bureaucratic costs. Managers, rules, and organizational control mechanisms cost money, and low-cost companies must try to economize when implementing their structures. When a company's competitive advantage depends on building and sustaining a low-cost advantage, adopting the right organizational arrangements is vital.

■ Differentiation Strategy and Structure

To pursue a differentiation strategy, a company must develop a distinctive competency in a function such as research and development or marketing and sales. As we have already discussed, doing so usually means that a company produces a wider range of products, serves more market niches, and generally has to customize its products to the needs of different customers. These factors make it difficult to standardize activities; they also increase the demands made on functional managers. Hence, the differentiated company usually employs a more complex structure—that is, a structure with a higher level of differentiation and integration—than the cost leader. The bureaucratic costs of a differentiator are higher than those of a cost leader, but these costs are recouped through the higher value it adds to its differentiated products.

To make its product unique in the eyes of the customer, for example, a differentiated company must design its structure and control system around the *particular source* of its competitive advantage.[13] Suppose that the differentiator's strength lies in technological competency; the company has the cutting-edge technology. In this case, the company's structure and control systems should be designed around the research and development function. Implementing a *matrix structure*, as Texas Instruments and TRW Systems have done, promotes innovation and speeds product development, for this type of structure permits intensive cross-functional integration. Integrating mechanisms, such as task forces and teams, help transfer knowledge among functions and are designed around the research and development function. Sales, marketing, and production targets are geared to research and development goals; marketing devises advertising programs that focus on technological possibilities, and salespeople are evaluated on their understanding of new-product characteristics and their ability to inform potential customers about them. Stringent sales targets are unlikely to be set in this situation because the goal is quality of service.

As detailed in Chapter 11, however, there are many problems associated with a matrix structure. The changing composition of product teams, the ambiguity arising from having two bosses, the use of more complex integration mechanisms, and the greater difficulty of monitoring and evaluating the work of teams greatly increase the bureaucratic costs necessary to coordinate and control task activities. Nevertheless, companies are willing to incur the higher bureaucratic costs of a matrix structure when it allows them to create more value from their differentiation strategy.

Sometimes the advantages of a differentiation strategy can be obtained from a less expensive structure. For example, when the source of the differentiator's competitive advantage is superior quality or responsiveness to customers, companies design a structure around their products, and a *product-team* or *geographic* structure may fit best. In a product-team structure, each product group can focus on the needs of a particular product market. Support functions such as research and development or sales are organized by product, and task forces and teams have a product, not a research, orientation.

If a company's differentiation strategy is based on serving the needs of a number of different market segments, a geographic structure becomes appropriate. Thus, if it focuses on types of customers, a differentiated company may use a geographic structure designed according to a regional logic or even according to different types of customers, such as businesses, individual consumers, or the government. Both Compaq and Rockwell International have reorganized their structures to concentrate on the needs of specific customers or regions. The new geographic structure allows them to become more responsive to the needs of specific groups of customers and to serve those needs better. For example, information about changes in customers' preferences can be quickly fed back to R&D and product design so that a company can protect its competitive advantage.

The control systems used to match the structure can also be geared to the company's distinctive competency. For the differentiator, it is important that the various functions do not pull in different directions; indeed, cooperation among the functions is vital for cross-functional integration. However, when functions work together, output controls become much harder to use. In general, it is much more difficult to measure the performance of people in different functions when they are engaged in cooperative efforts. Consequently, a company must rely more on behavior controls and shared norms and values when pursuing a strategy of differentiation.

That is why companies pursuing a differentiation strategy often have a markedly different kind of culture from those pursuing a low-cost strategy. Because human resources—good scientists, designers, or marketing people—are often the source of differentiation, these organizations have a culture based on professionalism or collegiality, a culture that emphasizes the distinctiveness of the human resource rather than the high pressure of the bottom line.[14] Hewlett-Packard, Motorola, and Coca-Cola, all of which emphasize some kind of distinctive competency, exemplify companies with professional cultures.

The bureaucratic costs of operating the structure and control system of the differentiator are higher than the cost leader's, but the benefits are also greater if companies can reap the rewards of a premium price. Companies are willing to accept a higher level of bureaucratic costs provided their structure and control systems lead to superior efficiency, quality, innovation, or responsiveness to customers.

■ Implementing a Combined Differentiation and Cost-Leadership Strategy

As we point out in Chapter 6, pursuing a combined differentiation and low-cost strategy is the most difficult challenge facing a company at the business level. On the one hand, the company has to coordinate its activities around manufacturing and materials management to implement a cost-reduction strategy. On the other, it must also coordinate its activities around the source of its differentiation advantage, such as R&D or marketing, to protect its competency in innovation or responsiveness to customers. For many companies in this situation, the answer has been the product-team structure, discussed in Chapter 11. It is far less costly to operate than a matrix structure but provides a much higher level of cross-functional integration than the functional structure.

As you recall from Chapter 11, a product-team structure groups tasks by product, and each product line is managed by a cross-functional team, which provides all the support services necessary to bring the product to market. The role of the product team is to protect and enhance a company's differentiation advantage and at the same time coordinate with manufacturing to lower costs. DaimlerChrysler, Hallmark

Cards, and Xerox are among the companies that have reorganized from a functional to a product-team structure so that they can simultaneously speed product development and control their operating costs.

John Fluke Manufacturing, a leader in electronic testing tools, is a good example of a company that has made use of product teams to speed product development. The company assembles "Phoenix teams," which are cross-functional groups that are given 100 days and $100,000 to identify a market need and a new product to fill it.[15] So far, these teams have led to the development of two successful new products. As Strategy in Action 13.2 shows, 3M also uses cross-functional teams to promote a culture of innovation.

13.2 STRATEGY *in* ACTION

How 3M Uses Teams to Build Culture

A company well known for product innovation, 3M aims to achieve at least 25 percent of its growth each year through new products developed within the last five years. To promote product development, 3M has always taken care to design its structure and culture so that employees are provided with the freedom and motivation to experiment and take risks. For example, 3M has an informal norm that researchers should use 15 percent of their time to develop projects of their own choosing. It was this norm that brought about the development of new products such as Post-it Notes. In addition, 3M has been careful to establish career ladders for its scientists in order to gain their long-term commitment, and it rewards successful product innovators with substantial bonuses. All these practices have gained the loyalty and support of its scientists and helped create a culture of innovation.

The company has also recognized the increasing importance of linking and coordinating the efforts of people in different functions to speed product development. As noted earlier, people in different functions tend to develop different subunit orientations and to focus their efforts on their own tasks to the exclusion of the needs of other functions. The danger of such tendencies is that each function will develop norms and values that suit its own needs but do little to promote organizational coordination and integration.

To avoid this problem, 3M has established a system of cross-functional teams composed of members of product development, process development, marketing, manufacturing, packaging, and other functions to create organizationwide norms and values of innovation. So that all groups have a common focus, the teams work closely with customers; customers' needs become the platform on which the different functions can then apply their skills and capabilities.[16] For example, one of 3M's cross-functional teams worked closely with disposable diaper manufacturers to develop the right kind of sticky tape for their needs.

To promote integration in the team and foster cooperative norms and values, each team is headed by a "product champion," who takes the responsibility for building cohesive team relationships and developing a team culture. In addition, one of 3M's top managers becomes a "management sponsor," whose job is to help the team get resources and to provide support when the going gets tough. After all, product development is a very risky process, and many projects do not succeed. Finally, 3M established the Golden Step Program, which gives employees substantial monetary bonuses to honor and reward cross-functional teams, to create a culture in which innovation is a valued activity, and to develop norms and values that support and reward the sharing of information among scientists and among people in different functions. Clearly, all this attention to creating a culture of innovation has paid off for 3M.

■ Focus Strategy and Structure

In Chapter 6, we define *focus strategy* as a strategy directed at a particular market or customer segment. A company focuses on a product or range of products aimed at one sort of customer or region. This strategy tends to have higher production costs than the other two strategies because output levels are lower, making it harder to obtain substantial economies of scale. As a result, a company using a focus strategy must exercise cost control. On the other hand, because some attribute of its product—possibly its ability to provide customers with high-quality, personalized service—usually gives such a company its unique advantage, a company using a focus strategy has to develop a unique competency. For both these reasons, the structure and control system adopted by a company following a focus strategy has to be inexpensive to operate but flexible enough to allow a distinctive competency to emerge.

A company using a focus strategy normally adopts a functional structure to meet these needs. This structure is appropriate because it is complex enough to manage the activities necessary to serve the needs of the market segment or produce a narrow range of products. At the same time, the bureaucratic costs of operating a functional structure are relatively low, and there is less need for complex, expensive integrating mechanisms. This structure permits more personal control and flexibility than the other two, and so it reduces bureaucratic costs while fostering the development of a distinctive competency.[17] Given its small size, a company using a focus strategy can rely less on output and behavior controls and more on culture, which is vital to the development of a service competency. Although output controls need to be used in production and sales, this form of control is inexpensive in a small organization.

The combination of functional structure and low cost of control helps offset the higher costs of production and at the same time allows the firm to develop unique strengths. It is little wonder, therefore, that there are so many companies using a focus strategy. Additionally, because such a company's competitive advantage is often based on personalized service, the flexibility of this kind of structure lets the company respond quickly to customers' needs and change its products in response to customers' requests. The structure then backs up the strategy and helps the firm develop and maintain its distinctive competency. The way in which Wang Laboratories reorganized itself, highlighted in Strategy in Action 13.3, shows how a company pursuing a focus strategy can achieve a strategy-structure fit.

■ Summary

Companies pursuing a generic business-level strategy must adopt the appropriate form of structure and control if they are to use their resources effectively to develop superior efficiency, quality, innovation, and responsiveness to customers. Companies are willing to bear the bureaucratic costs of operating organizational structure and control systems if these systems increase their ability to create value from lowering their costs or charging a premium price for their products. Hence, over time, companies must manage and change their structures to allow them to create value. However, many companies do *not* use the right forms of structure over time and fail to manage their strategies. These companies are not as successful and do not survive as long as those that do match their strategy, structure, and control systems.[20]

STRATEGY in ACTION

Wang's New Focused Strategy

In the 1980s, Wang Laboratories was one of the biggest and most successful computer companies in the world. But in the early 1990s, it almost went bankrupt because it could not compete against giants such as IBM and EDS. The company exists today only because a new CEO, Joseph Tucci, reorganized it, switched to a focus strategy, and radically altered Wang's structure so that the strategy could be pursued cost effectively.

Rather than compete head-to-head with IBM and EDS in providing software consulting services, Wang specializes in installing easy to use software systems based on Microsoft's Windows NT system. It has built up many contracts with small and large businesses to provide them

with the support they need when they install new or improved computer systems. To operate this new focus strategy Tucci was forced to wield the knife. He slashed Wang's work force from 20,000 to 5,300 and cut out four levels of management, reducing the number of hierarchical levels from seven to three.[18] He also decentralized authority to lower-level managers so that they could handle customer requests responsively and held them accountable and rewarded them based on quarterly reviews.

This combination of a focused software services strategy and a new streamlined structure has worked well. Wang is now the fourth largest services company in the United States, and by 1998, it once again employed more than 20,000 people.[19]

DESIGNING A GLOBAL STRUCTURE

In Chapter 8, we note that the strategies of most large companies have a global dimension if the firms produce and sell their products in international markets. Procter & Gamble and food companies such as H. J. Heinz, Kellogg, and Nestlé Enterprises, for example, have production operations throughout the world, as do the large automakers and computer makers. In this section, we examine how each of the four principal global strategies affects a company's choice of structure and control.

As you'll recall from Chapter 8, (1) a *multidomestic strategy* is oriented toward local responsiveness, and a company establishes semiautonomous national units in each country in which it operates to produce and customize products to local markets; (2) an *international strategy* is based on R&D and marketing being centralized at home and all the other value creation functions being decentralized to national units; (3) a *global strategy* is oriented toward cost reduction, with all the principal value creation functions centralized at the optimal global location; and (4) a *transnational strategy* is focused so that it can achieve local responsiveness as well as global integration, and therefore some functions are centralized at the optimal global location while others are decentralized, both to achieve local responsiveness and to facilitate global learning.

If a company is to operate each strategy successfully, the need to coordinate and integrate global tasks increases as the company moves from a multidomestic to an international to a global and then to a transnational strategy. The bureaucratic costs of managing a transnational strategy are much higher than those of managing a multidomestic strategy. To implement a transnational strategy, a company transfers its distinctive competencies to the global location where they can create the most value, and then it establishes a global network to coordinate its foreign and domestic divisions. This coordination involves managing global resource transfers to facilitate global learning. Compared with the other strategies, more managerial time has to be spent coordinating organizational resources and capabilities to achieve the global synergies that justify pursuing a transnational strategy.

By contrast, pursuing a multidomestic strategy does not require coordination of activities on a global level because value creation activities are handled locally, by country or world region. The international and global strategies fit between the other two strategies. Although products have to be sold and marketed globally, and hence global product transfers must be managed, there is less need to coordinate resource transfers than in the case of a transnational strategy.

The implication is that as companies change from a multidomestic to an international, global, or transnational strategy, they require a more complex structure and control system to coordinate the value creation activities associated with that strategy. Therefore, the bureaucratic costs increase at each stage. For a multidomestic strategy, they are low; for an international strategy, medium; for a global strategy, high; and for a transnational strategy, very high (see Table 13.2). In general, the choice of structure and control systems for managing a global business is a function of three factors:

1. The decision how to distribute and allocate responsibility and authority between domestic and foreign managers so that effective control over a company's foreign operations is maintained

2. The selection of a level of horizontal differentiation that groups foreign operations with domestic operations in a way that allows the best use of resources and serves the needs of foreign customers most effectively

TABLE 13.2

Global Strategy/Structure Relationships

	Multidomestic Strategy	International Strategy	Global Strategy	Transnational Strategy
	Low ←——————— Need for Coordination ————————→ High			
	Low ←——————— Bureaucratic Costs ————————→ High			
Centralization of Authority	Decentralized to national unit	Core competencies centralized, others decentralized to national units	Centralized at optimal global location	Simultaneously centralized and decentralized
Horizontal Differentiation	Global-area structure	International-division structure	Global product-group structure	Global-matrix structure, matrix in the mind
Need for Complex Integrating Mechanisms	Low	Medium	High	Very High
Organizational Culture	Not important	Quite important	Important	Very important

FIGURE 13.1

Global-Area Structure

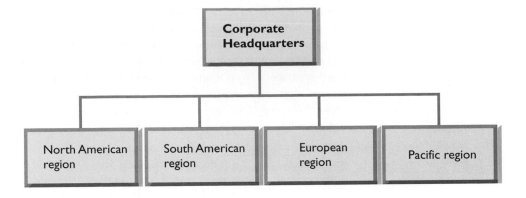

3. The selection of the right kinds of integration mechanism and organizational culture to make the structure function effectively

Table 13.2 summarizes the appropriate design choices for companies pursuing each of these strategies.

■ Multidomestic Strategy and Structure

When a company pursues a multidomestic strategy, it generally operates with a global-area structure (see Figure 13.1). When using this structure, a company duplicates all value creation activities and establishes a foreign division in every country or world area in which it operates. Authority is then decentralized to managers in each foreign division, and they devise the appropriate strategy for responding to the needs of the local environment. Because corporate headquarters managers are so far away from the scene of operations, it makes sense to decentralize control and grant decision-making authority to managers in the foreign operations. Managers at global headquarters use market and output controls, such as rate of return, growth in market share, and operation costs, to evaluate the performance of foreign divisions. On the basis of such global comparisons, they can make decisions about capital allocation and orchestrate the transfer of new knowledge among divisions.

A company that makes and sells the same products in many different markets often groups its foreign subsidiaries into world regions to simplify the coordination of products across countries. Europe might be one region, the Pacific Rim another, and the Middle East a third. Such grouping allows the same set of market and behavior controls to be applied across all divisions inside a region. Thus, companies can obtain synergies from dealing with broadly similar cultures because information can be transmitted more easily. For example, consumers' preferences regarding product design and marketing are likely to be more similar among countries in one world region than among countries in different world regions.

Because the foreign divisions themselves have little or no contact with each other, no integrating mechanisms are needed. Nor does a global organizational culture develop, since there are no transfers of personnel or informal contacts among managers from the various world regions. Car companies such as Chrysler, General Motors, and Ford all used to employ global-area structures to manage their foreign operations. Ford of Europe, for example, had little or no contact with its U.S. parent, and capital was the principal resource exchanged.

One problem with a global-area structure and a multidomestic strategy is that the duplication of specialist activities raises costs. Moreover, the company is not taking advantage of opportunities to trade information and knowledge on a global basis or of low-cost manufacturing opportunities. Multidomestic companies have chosen to keep behavior costs low; however, they lose the many benefits of operating globally.

■ International Strategy and Structure

A company pursuing an international strategy adopts a different route to global expansion. Normally, the company shifts to this strategy when it begins selling its domestically made products in foreign markets. Until recently, companies such as Mercedes-Benz and Jaguar made no attempt to produce in a foreign market; instead, they distributed and sold their domestically produced cars internationally. Such companies usually just add a **foreign operations department** to their existing structure and continue to use the same control system. If a company is using a functional structure, this department has to coordinate manufacturing, sales, and research and development activities with the needs of the foreign market. Efforts at customization are minimal, however.

In the foreign country, the company usually establishes a subsidiary to handle sales and distribution. For example, the Mercedes-Benz foreign subsidiaries allocate dealerships, organize supplies of spare parts, and, of course, sell cars. A system of behavior controls is then established to keep the home office informed of changes in sales, spare parts requirements, and so on.

A company with many different products or businesses operating from a multidivisional structure has the challenging problem of coordinating the flow of different products across different countries. To manage these transfers, many companies create an international division, which they add to their existing divisional structure[21] (see Figure 13.2).

International operations are managed as a separate divisional business, whose managers are given the authority and responsibility for coordinating domestic product divisions and foreign markets. The international division also controls the foreign subsidiaries that market the products and decides how much authority to delegate to foreign management. This arrangement permits the company to engage in more complex foreign operations at relatively low bureaucratic cost. However, managers in the foreign countries are essentially under the control of managers in the international division, and if the domestic and foreign managers compete for control of operations in the foreign country, conflict and lack of cooperation can result.

■ Global Strategy and Structure

A company embarks on a global strategy when it starts to locate manufacturing and all the other value creation activities in the lowest-cost global location to increase efficiency, quality, and innovation. In seeking to obtain the gains from global learning, a company must cope with greater coordination and integration problems. It has to find a structure that can coordinate resource transfers between corporate

FIGURE 13.2

International-Division
Structure

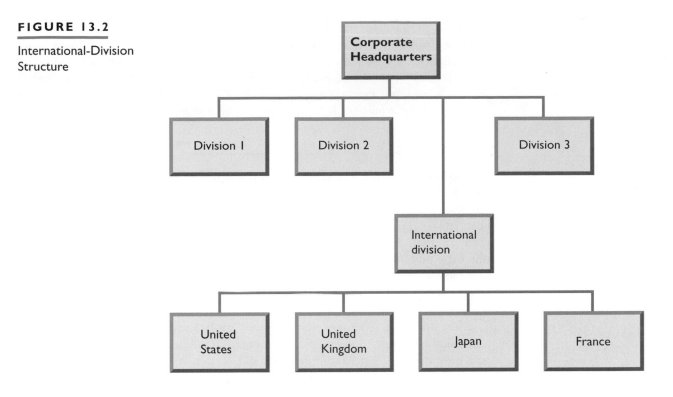

headquarters and foreign divisions and at the same time provide the centralized control that a global strategy requires. The answer for many companies is a **global product group structure** (see Figure 13.3).

In this structure, a product-group headquarters (similar to an SBU headquarters) is created to coordinate the activities of the domestic and foreign divisions within the product group. Product-group managers in the home country are responsible for organizing all aspects of value creation on a global basis. The product-group

FIGURE 13.3

Global Product-
Group Structure

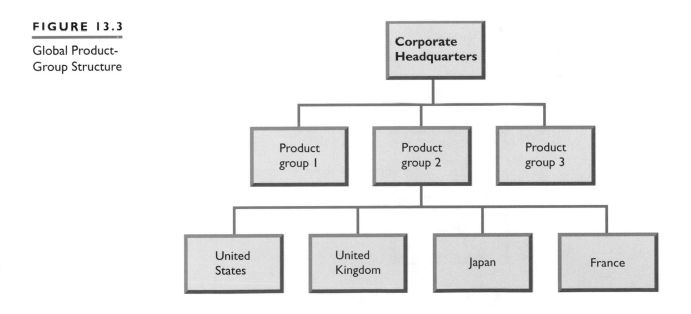

structure allows managers to decide how best to pursue a global strategy—for example, to decide which value creation activities, such as manufacturing or product design, should be performed in which country to increase efficiency. Increasingly, U.S. and Japanese companies are moving manufacturing to low-cost countries such as China but establishing product-design centers in Europe or the United States to take advantage of foreign skills and capabilities.

■ Transnational Strategy and Structure

The main failing of the global product-group structure is that while it allows a company to achieve superior efficiency and quality, it is weak when it comes to responsiveness to customers because the focus is still on centralized control to reduce costs. Moreover, this structure makes it difficult for the different product groups to trade information and knowledge and to obtain the benefits of cooperation. Sometimes the potential gains from sharing product, marketing, or research and development knowledge between product groups are very high, but because a company lacks a structure that can coordinate the groups' activities, these gains cannot be achieved.

More and more, companies are adopting **global matrix structures**, which let them simultaneously reduce costs by increasing efficiency *and* differentiate their activities through superior innovation and responsiveness to customers. Figure 13.4 shows such a structure, adopted by a large chemical company such as Du Pont or Amoco.

On the vertical axis, instead of functions, there are the company's *product groups,* which provide specialist services such as R&D, product design, and marketing information to the foreign divisions, or SBUs. For example, these might be the petroleum, plastics, pharmaceuticals, or fertilizer product groups. On the horizontal axis are the company's *foreign divisions, or SBUs,* in the various countries or world

FIGURE 13.4

Global-Matrix Structure

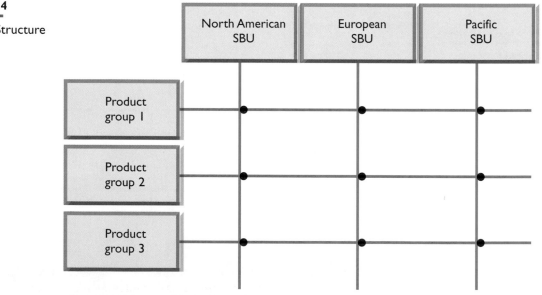

● Individual operating companies

regions in which it operates. Managers in the foreign subsidiary control foreign operations and through a system of behavior controls report to divisional personnel back in the United States. They are also responsible, together with U.S. divisional personnel, for developing control and reward systems that promote the sharing of marketing or research and development information to achieve gains from synergies.

This structure both provides a great deal of local flexibility and gives divisional personnel in the United States considerable access to information about local affairs. The matrix structure also allows knowledge and experience to be transferred among geographic regions and among divisions and regions. Since it offers many opportunities for face-to-face contact between domestic and foreign managers, the matrix facilitates the transmission of a company's norms and values and, hence, the development of a global corporate culture. This is especially important for an international company, for which lines of communication are longer and information is subject to distortion. Club Med, for instance, fully exploits these synergies in the way it manages its holiday resorts.

The matrix also lets each home division balance production so that, for example, a lack of demand in one region of the world can be compensated by increased demand in another. For example, Philip Morris balances cigarette production so that slumping demand in the United States is countered by expanding demand in other regions of the world. Similarly, Japanese car manufacturers plan their international strategy to compensate for import restrictions or currency changes in the world market.

To make these matrix structures work, many companies strive to develop a strong international organizational culture to facilitate communication and coordination among managers. For example, companies are increasingly transferring managers between foreign and domestic operations so that they can develop a global view. Furthermore, to improve integration, companies are trying to form global networks of managers so that they can turn to each other for help. The idea is to create a **matrix in the mind**—an information network that lets a company capitalize globally on the skills and capabilities of its personnel.[22]

To foster the development of the matrix-in-the-mind concept and promote co-operation, companies are also using electronic integrating devices such as on-line teleconferencing, E-mail, and global intranets between different parts of their operations, both globally and domestically. For example, Hitachi coordinates its nineteen Japanese laboratories by means of an on-line teleconferencing system, and both Microsoft and Hewlett-Packard make extensive use of electronic computer systems to integrate their activities.

These integration mechanisms provide the extra coordination that helps the global-matrix structure work effectively. It is a very complex structure to operate and carries a high level of bureaucratic costs. However, the potential gains for a company in terms of superior efficiency, quality, innovation, and responsiveness to customers make these costs worthwhile. In the complicated game of international competition, companies must increasingly adopt many of these elements of a global matrix to survive. Nestlé found itself in this situation, as Strategy in Action 13.4 details.

■ Summary

Most large companies have an international component in their organizational structures. The issue for international companies, as for all others, is to adopt the structure and control system that best fits their strategy. The need to implement

Reengineering Nestlé's Global Structure

Nestlé, based in Vevey, Switzerland, is the world's biggest food company. In 1996, its global sales passed $50 billion a year, a figure it wants to double by the year 2001. To achieve this goal, the company has been pursuing an ambitious program of global expansion by acquiring many famous companies—for instance, Perrier, the French mineral water producer, and Rowntree Mackintosh, the British candy maker. In the United States, Nestlé bought the giant Carnation Company in 1985, and it also purchased Stouffer Foods and Contadina, among other large food companies.

Traditionally, Nestlé pursued a multidomestic strategy and managed its operating companies through a global area structure. In each country, each individual company (such as Carnation) was responsible for managing all aspects of its business-level strategy: in other words, companies were free to control their own product development and marketing and to manage all local operations. Acquisitions, expansions, and corporate resource decisions, such as capital investment, were made at the Vevey headquarters by Nestlé's corporate executives. Because all important decisions were made centrally, the size of the corporate staff increased dramatically. In the early 1990s, Nestlé's chairman, Helmut Maucher, realized that the company had major problems.

Corporate managers had become very remote from the difficulties experienced by the operating companies, and the centralized operating structure slowed down decision making. Nestlé had trouble responding quickly to the changing environment. Moreover, the company was forfeiting all the gains from global learning and possible synergies from resource sharing between operating companies and world regions because each company was operated separately and corporate executives made no attempt to integrate across companies around the world. Maucher realized that the company could not increase its sales and profits through its existing operating structure. To create more value, it had to find a new way of organizing its activities.

Maucher started the reengineering of Nestlé's structure from the top down. He massively reduced the power of corporate management by decentralizing authority to the managers of seven product groups, which he created to oversee the company's major product lines (for example, coffee, milk, and candy) on a global level. The role of each product group was to integrate the activities of operating companies in its area in order to obtain synergies and the gains from global learning. After the change, managers in the candy product group, for instance, began orchestrating the marketing and sale of Rowntree candy products, such as After Eight Mints and Smarties, throughout Europe, and sales climbed by 60 percent.

Maucher then turned his attention to the way the operating companies worked in each country or world region. He grouped all the operating companies within a country or region into one SBU and then created a team of SBU managers to link and coordinate the activities of the various companies in that country. When the different companies or divisions started to share joint purchasing, marketing, and sales activities, major cost savings resulted. In the United States, the SBU management team, headed by Timm Krull, reduced the number of sales officers nationwide from 115 to 22 and decreased the number of suppliers of packaging from 43 to 3.

Finally, Maucher decided to use a matrix structure to integrate the activities of the seven global product groups with the operations of Nestlé's country- or region-based SBUs. The goal of this matrix structure is to have the company pursue a transnational strategy, allowing it to obtain the gains from global learning and cost reduction. For example, Timm Krull now spends one week every month in Vevey with product-group executives, discussing ways of exploiting and sharing the resources of the company on a global basis. Moreover, managers are also looking to strategic alliances as a way of obtaining cost savings from shared distribution networks.[23]

So far, this new decentralized matrix structure has speeded decision making and product development and has enabled the company to integrate the activities of its many new acquisitions. Maucher hopes that it will help Nestlé reach its ambitious sales goal by the year 2001.

international strategy successfully has put increasing pressures on corporate managers to design the company's structure and controls so that the firm can respond to the challenges of the world market.

STRUCTURE AND CONTROL AT THE CORPORATE LEVEL

At the corporate level, strategic managers need to choose the organizational structure that will allow them to operate a number of different businesses efficiently. The structure normally chosen at the corporate level is the multidivisional structure. The larger and more diverse the businesses in the corporate portfolio, the more likely the company is to have a multidivisional structure. The reason is that each division requires its own set of specialist support functions to operate efficiently, and a headquarters corporate staff is needed to oversee and evaluate divisional operations to ensure that corporate goals are being achieved. Once strategic managers select a multidivisional structure, they must then make choices about what kind of integrating mechanisms and control systems to use to make the structure work efficiently. Later in this chapter, we discuss how the corporate-level strategies of unrelated diversification, vertical integration, and related diversification affect the choice of structure and control systems.

As discussed in Chapter 9, the main reason a company pursues vertical integration is to achieve *economies of integration* among divisions.[24] For example, a company can coordinate resource-scheduling decisions among divisions to reduce costs and improve quality. This might mean locating a rolling mill next to a steel furnace to save the costs of reheating steel ingots and make it easier to control the quality of the final product. Similarly, the chief gains from related diversification come from obtaining synergies or *economies of scope* among divisions. Divisions benefit by transferring of core competencies such as R&D or by sharing distribution and sales networks. With both these strategies, the benefits to the company come from some *transfer of resources* among divisions, and so the company must coordinate activities among divisions to secure these benefits. Consequently, structure and control must be designed to handle the transfer of resources among divisions.

In the case of unrelated diversification, however, the benefits to the company come from restructuring and establishing of an *internal capital market,* which allows corporate personnel to make better allocations of capital than would be possible in an external capital market. With this strategy, there are no transactions or exchanges among divisions, each operates separately. Structure and control must therefore be designed to allow each division to operate independently.

A company's choice of structure and control mechanisms depends on the degree to which a company must control the interactions among divisions. The more interdependent the divisions—that is, the more they depend on each other for resources—the more complex are the control and integration mechanisms required to integrate their activities and make the strategy work.[25] Consequently, as the need for integration increases, so, too, does the level of bureaucratic costs, but a company is willing to bear the increased bureaucratic costs stemming from a more complex strategy if the strategy creates more value.[26] This is illustrated in Table 13.3, which also indicates what forms of structure and control companies should adopt to manage the three corporate strategies. We examine them in detail in the next sections.

TABLE 13.3

Corporate Strategy and Structure and Control

Corporate Strategy	Appropriate Structure	Need for Integration	Type of Control		
			Financial Control	*Behavior Control*	*Organizational Culture*
Unrelated diversification	Multidivisional	Low (no exchanges between divisions)	Great use (e.g., ROI)	Some use (e.g., budgets)	Little use
Vertical integration	Multidivisional	Medium (scheduling resource transfers)	Great use (e.g., ROI, transfer pricing)	Great use (e.g., standardization, budgets)	Some use (e.g., shared norms and values)
Related diversification	Multidivisional	High (acheiving synergies between divisions by integrating roles)	Little use	Great use (e.g., rules, budgets)	Great use (e.g., norms, values, common language)

■ Unrelated Diversification

Because there are *no linkages* among divisions, unrelated diversification is the easiest and cheapest strategy to manage; it is associated with the lowest level of bureaucratic costs. The main requirement of the structure and control system is that it allow corporate managers to evaluate divisional performance easily and accurately. Thus, companies use a multidivisional structure, and each division is evaluated by financial controls such as return on investment. A company also applies sophisticated accounting controls to obtain information quickly from the divisions so that corporate managers can readily compare divisions on several dimensions. Textron and Dover are good examples of companies that manage their structures by using sophisticated computer networks and accounting controls, which allow them almost daily access to divisional performance.

Divisions normally have considerable autonomy, unless they fail to reach their ROI objectives. Generally, corporate headquarters is not interested in the types of business-level strategy pursued by each division unless there are problems. If problems arise, corporate headquarters may step in to take corrective action, perhaps replacing managers or providing additional financial resources, depending on the reason for the problem. If corporate personnel see no possibility of a turnaround, however, they may just as easily decide to divest the division. The multidivisional structure allows the unrelated company to operate its businesses as a portfolio of investments, which can be bought and sold as business conditions change. Usually, managers in the various divisions do not know one another, and they may not know what companies are in the corporate portfolio.

The use of financial controls to manage a company means that no integration among divisions is necessary. This is why the bureaucratic costs of managing an unrelated company are low. The biggest problem facing corporate personnel is determining capital allocations to the various divisions so that the overall profitability of the portfolio is maximized. They also have to oversee divisional managers and make sure that divisions are achieving ROI targets. Alco Standard's way of managing its businesses, described in Strategy in Action 13.5, demonstrates how to operate a strategy of unrelated diversification.

■ Vertical Integration

Vertical integration is a more expensive strategy to manage than unrelated diversification because *sequential resource flows* from one division to the next must be coordinated. The multidivisional structure effects such coordination. This structure provides the centralized control necessary for the vertically integrated company to achieve benefits from the control of resource transfers. Corporate personnel assume the responsibility for devising financial and behavior controls to promote the efficient transfer of resources among divisions. Complex rules and procedures are

---

13.5   STRATEGY in ACTION

Alco Standard Gets It Right

Alco Standard, based in Valley Forge, Pennsylvania, is one of the largest office supply companies in the United States, distributing office and paper supplies and materials through a nationwide network of wholly owned distribution companies. It pursues a highly successful strategy of unrelated diversification. Since 1965, the company has bought and sold more than 300 different companies. It used to be involved in more than 50 different industries, but now it operates 50 businesses in only two main areas: office products and paper distribution. However, the corporate office makes no attempt to intervene in the activities of the different divisions.

The policy of Alco's top management is that authority and control should be completely decentralized to the managers in each of the company's businesses. Each business is left alone to make its own manufacturing or purchasing decisions even though some potential synergies, in the form of corporationwide purchasing or marketing, are being lost. Top management pursues this nonintervention policy because it believes that the gains from allowing its managers to act as independent entrepreneurs exceed any potential economies of scope that might result from coordinating interdivisional activities. It believes that a decentralized operating system allows a big company to act in a way that is similar to a small company, avoiding the problem of growing bureaucracy and organizational inertia.

At Alco, top management interprets its role as relieving the divisions of administrative chores, such as bookkeeping and accounting, and collecting market information on competitive pricing and products, which allows divisional managers to improve their business-level strategy. Centralizing these information activities reduces each division's bureaucratic costs and provides the standardization that lets top management make better decisions about resource allocation. Alco's division heads are regarded as partners in the corporate enterprise and are rewarded through stock options linked to the performance of their divisions. So far, Alco has been very successful with its decentralized operating structure and has achieved a compound growth rate of 19 percent a year.

instituted to manage interdivisional relationships and specify how exchanges are to be made; consequently, bureaucratic costs rise. As previously noted, complex resource exchanges can lead to conflict among divisions, and corporate managers must try to minimize divisional conflicts.

Centralizing authority at corporate headquarters must be done with care in vertically related companies. It carries the risk of involving corporate managers in operating issues at the business level to the point at which the divisions lose their autonomy and motivation. As we point out in Chapter 11, the company must strike the right balance of centralized control at corporate headquarters and decentralized control at the divisional level if it is to implement this strategy successfully.

Because their interests are at stake, divisions need to have input into scheduling and decisions regarding resource transfer. For example, the plastics division in a chemical company has a vital interest in the activities of the oil division, for the quality of the products it gets from the oil division determines the quality of its own products. Divisional integrating mechanisms can bring about direct coordination and information transfers among divisions.[27] To handle communication among divisions, a company sets up task forces or teams for the purpose; it can also establish liaison roles. In high-tech and chemical companies, for example, integrating roles among divisions is common. These integrating mechanisms also increase bureaucratic costs.

Thus, a strategy of vertical integration is managed through a combination of corporate and divisional controls. Although the organizational structure and control systems used for managing this strategy have higher bureaucratic costs than those used for unrelated diversification, the benefits derived from vertical integration often outweigh its extra costs.

■ Related Diversification

In the case of related diversification, divisions share research and development knowledge, information, customer bases, and goodwill to obtain gains from synergies. The process is difficult to manage, and so a multidivisional structure is used to facilitate the transfer of resources to obtain synergies. Even with this structure, however, high levels of resource sharing and joint production by divisions make it hard for corporate managers to measure the performance of each individual division.[28] If a related company is to obtain gains from synergy, it has to adopt more complicated forms of integration and control at the divisional level to make the structure work efficiently.

First, financial control is difficult to use because divisions share resources, so it is not easy to measure the performance of an individual division. Therefore, a company needs to develop a corporate culture that stresses cooperation among divisions and corporate, rather than purely divisional, goals. Second, corporate managers must establish sophisticated integrating devices to ensure coordination among divisions. Integrating roles and teams are crucial because they provide the context in which managers from different divisions can meet and develop a common vision of corporate goals. Hewlett-Packard, for instance, created three new high-level integrating teams to ensure that the new products developed by its technology group made their way quickly to its product divisions. All this extra integration is very expensive, however, and must be carefully managed.

An organization with a multidivisional structure must have the right mix of incentives and rewards for cooperation if it is to achieve gains from sharing skills and resources among divisions.[29] With unrelated diversification, divisions operate autonomously, and the company can quite easily reward managers on their division's individual performance. With related diversification, however, rewarding divisions is more difficult because they are engaged in joint production, and strategic managers must be sensitive and alert to achieving equity in rewards among divisions. The aim always is to design the structure so that it can maximize the benefits from the strategy at the lowest bureaucratic cost.

Managing a strategy of related diversification also raises the issue of how much authority to centralize and how much to decentralize. Corporate managers need to take a close look at how their controls affect divisional performance and autonomy. If corporate managers get too involved in the day-to-day operations of the divisions, they can endanger divisional autonomy and undercut divisional managers' decision making.[30] Corporate managers, after all, see everything from a corporate, rather than a divisional, perspective. For instance, in the Heinz example mentioned earlier, management tried to develop one form of competitive advantage, a low-cost advantage, in every division.[31] Although this approach may work well for Heinz, it may be markedly inappropriate for a company that is operating a totally diverse set of businesses, each of which needs to develop its own unique competency. Too much corporate control can put divisional managers in a straitjacket. When too many managers become involved in managing the business, performance suffers and bureaucratic costs escalate. Companies such as IBM and General Motors experienced this problem; their corporate staffs became top-heavy, slowing decision making and draining the company's profits.

SPECIAL ISSUES IN STRATEGY-STRUCTURE CHOICE

As noted in Chapter 10, today many organizations are changing their corporate-level strategies and restructuring their organizations to find new ways to use their resources and capabilities to create value. In this section we focus on three strategy structure issues that arise during the rebuilding or restructuring process: the management of mergers and acquisitions, the management of new ventures, and the management of outsourcing through the development of a network structure.

■ Mergers, Acquisitions, and Structure

In Chapter 10, we point out that mergers and acquisitions are the principal vehicles by which companies enter new product markets and expand the size of their operations.[32] Earlier we discuss the strategic advantages and disadvantages of mergers. We now consider how to design structure and control systems to manage new acquisitions. This issue is important because many acquisitions are unsuccessful, and one of the main reasons is that many companies do a very poor job of integrating the new divisions into their corporate structure, as happened at Compaq, profiled in the Opening Case.[33]

The first factor that makes managing new acquisitions difficult is the nature of the businesses a company acquires. If a company acquires businesses related to its existing businesses, it should find it fairly easy to integrate them into its corporate structure. The controls already being used in the related company can be adapted to the new divisions. To achieve gains from synergies, the company can expand its task forces or increase the number of integrating roles, so that the new divisions are drawn into the existing divisional structure.

If managers do not understand how to develop connections among divisions to permit gains from economies of scope, the new businesses will perform poorly.[34] Some authors have argued that this is why the quality of management is so important. A company must employ managers who have the ability to recognize synergies among apparently different businesses and so derive benefits from acquisitions and mergers.[35] For instance, Porter cites the example of Philip Morris, the cigarette producer, which took over Miller Brewing.[36] On the surface, these seem to be very different businesses. However, when their products are viewed as consumer products that are often bought and consumed together, the possibility of sales, distribution, and marketing synergies becomes clearer, and this merger was a great success. On the other hand, if companies acquire unrelated businesses only to operate them as a portfolio of investments, they should have no trouble managing the acquisitions.

Implementation problems are likely to arise only when corporate managers try to interfere in businesses they know little about or when they use inappropriate structure and controls to manage the new business and attempt to achieve the wrong kind of benefits from the acquisition. For example, if managers try to integrate unrelated companies with related ones, apply the wrong kinds of controls at the divisional level, or interfere in business-level strategy, corporate performance suffers as bureaucratic costs skyrocket. These mistakes explain why related acquisitions are sometimes more successful than unrelated ones.[37]

Therefore, strategic managers need to be very sensitive to the problems involved in taking over new businesses through mergers and acquisitions. Like other managers, they rarely appreciate the real issues inherent in managing the new business and the level of bureaucratic costs involved in managing a strategy until they have to deal with these issues personally. Even when acquiring closely related businesses, new managers must realize that each business has a unique culture, or way of doing things. Such idiosyncrasies must be understood in order to manage the new organization properly. Over time new management can change the culture and alter the internal workings of the company, but this is a difficult implementation task. Besides, the bureaucratic costs of changing a culture are often enormous because the top-management team and the organizational structure have to be changed in order to change the way people behave. We discuss this in detail in Chapter 14, which considers organizational politics and strategic change.

■ Internal New Ventures and Structure

The main alternative to growth through acquisition and merger is for a company to develop new businesses internally. In Chapter 10, we call this strategy internal *new venturing* and discuss its advantages for growth and diversification. Now we consider the design of the appropriate internal arrangements for encouraging the development of new ventures.

At the heart of new-venture design must be the realization by corporate managers that internal new venturing is a form of entrepreneurship. The design should encourage creativity and give new-venture managers the opportunity and resources to develop new products or markets. Hewlett-Packard, for example, gives managers a great deal of latitude in this respect. To encourage innovation, it allows them to work on informal projects while they carry out their assigned tasks.[38] More generally, management must choose the appropriate structure and controls for operating new ventures.[39]

One of the main design choices is the creation of **new-venture divisions**. To provide new-venture managers with the autonomy to experiment and take risks, the company sets up a new-venture division separate from other divisions and makes it a center for new product or project development. Away from the day-to-day scrutiny of top management, divisional personnel pursue the creation of new business as though they were external entrepreneurs. The division is operated by controls that reinforce the entrepreneurial spirit. Thus, market and output controls are inappropriate because they can inhibit risk taking. Instead, the company develops a culture for entrepreneurship in this division to provide a climate for innovation. Care must be taken, however, to institute bureaucratic controls that put some limits on freedom of action. Otherwise, costly mistakes may be made, and resources wasted on frivolous ideas.

In managing the new-venture division, it is important to use integrating mechanisms such as task forces and teams to screen new ideas. Managers from research and development, sales and marketing, and product development are heavily involved in this screening process. Generally, the champions of new products must defend their projects before a formal evaluation committee, consisting of proven entrepreneurs and experienced managers from the other divisions, to secure the resources for developing them. Companies such as 3M, IBM, and Texas Instruments are examples of successful companies that use this method for creating opportunities internally.

Care must be taken to preserve the autonomy of the new-venture division. As mentioned earlier, the costs of research and development are high, and the rewards uncertain. After spending millions of dollars, corporate managers often become concerned about the division's performance and introduce tight output controls or strong budgets to increase accountability. These measures hurt the entrepreneurial culture.

Sometimes, however, after creating a new invention, the new venture division wants to reap the benefits by producing and marketing it. If this happens, the division becomes an ordinary operating division and entrepreneurship declines.[40] Strategic managers must take steps to provide a structure that can sustain the entrepreneurial spirit.[41]

Hewlett-Packard has a novel way of dealing with new venturing. In the operating divisions, as soon as a new, self-supporting product is developed, a new division is formed to produce and market the product. By spinning off the product in this fashion, the company keeps all its divisions small and entrepreneurial. The arrangement also provides a good climate for innovation. However, Hewlett-Packard also found that having many new venture divisions was too expensive and so has merged some of them.

Internal new venturing is an important means by which large, established companies can maintain their momentum and grow from within.[42] The alternative is to acquire small businesses that have already developed some technological competency and to pump resources into them, which has been Microsoft's favored strategy in recent years as it enters the many different niches of the Internet software market. This approach can also succeed, and it obviously lessens management's burden if the company operates the new business as an independent entity.

By and large, companies are likely to operate in both ways, acquiring some new businesses and developing others internally. As increasing competition from abroad has threatened their dominance in existing businesses, companies have been forced to evaluate opportunities for maximizing long-term growth in new businesses, and many of them have made acquisitions.

■ Network Structure and the Virtual Organization

You will recall from Chapters 9 and 10 that the use of outsourcing is increasing rapidly as organizations recognize the many opportunities it offers to reduce costs and increase their flexibility. U.S. companies spent $100 billion on outsourcing in 1996, and this outlay reached $500 billion by 2000. Companies such as EDS, which manages the information systems of large organizations such as Xerox and Kodak, are major beneficiaries of this new organizing approach. On a global level, the development of a global network of strategic alliances between companies is an alternative to the use of the complex global-matrix structure.[43]

In order to implement outsourcing effectively, strategic managers must decide what organizational arrangements to adopt. Increasingly, a **network structure**— the set of strategic alliances that an organization creates with suppliers, manufacturers, and distributors to produce and market a product—is becoming the structure of choice to implement outsourcing. An example of a network structure is the series of strategic alliances that Japanese car companies—for instance, Toyota and Honda—formed with their suppliers of inputs such as car axles, gearboxes, and air conditioning systems. Members of the network work together on a long-term basis to find new ways to reduce costs and increase the quality of their products. Moreover, developing a network structure allows an organization to avoid the high costs of operating a complex organizational structure (the costs of employing many managers, for example).

Finally, a network structure allows a company to form strategic alliances with foreign suppliers, which gives managers access to low-cost foreign sources of inputs, keeping costs low. Strategy in Action 13.6 describes the network structure that NIKE uses to produce and market its sports shoes.

Some small companies that use a focus strategy go even further than NIKE and create a network structure to perform almost all their functional activities. Topsy Tail, a small Texas company that sells hair-styling gadgets such as false ponytails, has created strategic alliances with other companies that not only manufacture and distribute its products but also design, market, and package them. Apart from its CEO, Tomima Edmark, who orchestrates these alliances and is at the hub of the network, the company has almost no permanent employees—only outside companies and people who contract with Edmark to perform certain services, in return for which they receive a set fee.[46]

The ability of managers to develop a network structure to produce or provide the goods and services their customers want, rather than create a complex organizational structure to do so, has led many researchers and consultants to popularize the idea of the "virtual organization." The virtual organization is composed of people

13.6 STRATEGY *in* ACTION

NIKE's Network Structure

N IKE, located in Beaverton, Oregon, is the largest and most profitable sports shoe manufacturer in the world. The key to NIKE's success is the network structure that Philip Knight, NIKE's founder and CEO, created to allow his company to produce and market shoes. As discussed earlier, the most successful companies today simultaneously pursue a low-cost and a differentiation strategy. Knight realized this early on, and he created an organizational structure to allow his company to achieve this goal.

By far the largest function at NIKE's headquarters in Beaverton is the design function, staffed by talented designers who pioneer innovations in sports shoe design such as the air pump and Air Jordans that NIKE introduced so successfully. Designers use computer-aided design (CAD) to design their shoes, and all new-product information, including manufacturing instructions, is stored electronically. When the designers have done their work, they relay all the blueprints for the new products electronically to a network of suppliers and manufacturers throughout Southeast Asia with whom NIKE has formed strategic alliances.[44] Instructions for the design of a new sole, for example, may be sent to a supplier in Taiwan, and instructions for the leather uppers to a supplier in Malaysia. These suppliers produce the shoe parts, which are then sent for final assembly to a manufacturer in China with whom NIKE has established an alliance.

From China these shoes are shipped to distributors throughout the world. Of the 99 million pairs of shoes NIKE makes each year, 99 percent are made in Southeast Asia.

There are two main advantages to this network structure for NIKE. First, NIKE's costs are very low because wages in Southeast Asia are a fraction of what they are in the United States and this gives NIKE a low-cost advantage. Second, NIKE is able to respond to changes in sports shoe fashion very quickly. Using its global computer system, NIKE can, literally overnight, change the instructions it gives to each of its suppliers so that within a few weeks new kinds of shoes are being produced by its foreign manufacturers.[45] If any of its alliance partners fail to perform up to NIKE's standards, they are simply replaced with new partners, so NIKE has great control over its network structure. In fact, the company works closely with its suppliers to take advantage of any new developments in technology that can help it reduce costs and increase quality.

The ability of NIKE to outsource all its manufacturing abroad allows Knight to keep NIKE's U.S. structure small and flexible. NIKE is able to use a functional structure to organize its activities, and Knight decentralizes control of the design process to teams that are assigned to develop each of the new kinds of sports shoes for which NIKE is known.

who are linked by computers, faxes, computer-aided design systems, and video teleconferencing and who may rarely if ever see one another face to face. People come and go as and when their services are needed, much as in a matrix structure, but they are not formal members of an organization, just functional experts who form an alliance with an organization, fulfill their contractual obligations, and then move on to the next project.

Andersen Consulting, the global management consulting company, is becoming just such a virtual organization. CEO George Shaheen says the company's headquarters are wherever he happens to be at the time. (He spends 80 percent of his time traveling.)[47] The company's 40,000 consultants often work from their homes, traveling to meet the company's clients throughout the world and only rarely stopping in at one of Andersen's branch offices to meet their superiors and colleagues. The consultants all pool their knowledge in a massive internal database they can easily access through computer and the company's intranet.

SUMMARY OF CHAPTER

This chapter brings together strategy formulation and strategy implementation and examines how a company's choice of strategy affects the form of its structure and control systems. The reason that many companies such as IBM and General Motors experience problems with their structure should now be clear: they have lost control over their structure, and their bureaucratic costs are escalating. The challenge for a company is to manage its structure and control systems so that it can economize on bureaucratic costs and ensure that they match the potential gains from its strategy. The following are the main points of the chapter:

✔ Implementing strategy through organizational structure and control is expensive, and companies need to constantly monitor and oversee their structures in order to economize on bureaucratic costs.

✔ At the functional level, each function requires a different kind of structure and control system to achieve its functional objectives.

✔ At the business level, the structure and control system must be designed to achieve business-level objectives, which means managing the relationships among all the functions to permit the company to develop a distinctive competency.

✔ Cost-leadership and differentiation strategies each require a structure and control system that matches the source of the company's competitive advantage. Implementing a simultaneous cost-leadership and differentiation strategy is the problem facing many companies today.

✔ As a company moves from a multidomestic to an international, global, and transnational strategy, it needs to switch to a more complex structure that allows it to coordinate increasingly complex resource transfers. Similarly, it needs to adopt a more complex integration and control system that facilitates global learning. When there are gains to be derived from synergy, companies frequently adopt a global-matrix structure to share knowledge and expertise.

✔ At the corporate level, a company must choose the structure and control system that will allow it to operate a collection of businesses efficiently.

✔ Unrelated diversification, vertical integration, and related diversification require different forms of structure and control if the benefits of pursuing the strategy are to be realized.

✔ As companies change their corporate strategies over time, they must change their structure because different strategies are managed in different ways.

✔ The profitability of mergers and acquisitions depends on the structure and control systems that companies adopt to manage them and the way a company integrates them into its existing businesses.

✔ To encourage internal new venturing, companies must design a structure that gives the new-venture division the autonomy it needs in order to develop new products and protect it from excessive interference by corporate managers.

✔ Increasingly, the growth of outsourcing has led companies to develop network structures. The virtual corporation is becoming a reality as computer information systems become more sophisticated.

DISCUSSION QUESTIONS

1. How should (a) a high-tech company, (b) a fast-food franchise, and (c) a small manufacturing company design their functional structures and control systems to implement a generic strategy?

2. If a related company begins to buy unrelated businesses, in what ways should it change its structure or control mechanisms to manage the acquisitions?

3. How would you design a structure and control system to encourage entrepreneurship in a large, established corporation?

Practicing Strategic Management

SMALL-GROUP EXERCISE
Deciding on an Organizational Structure

Break up into groups of three to five people, and discuss the following scenario:

You are a group of managers of a major soft drinks company that is going head-to-head with Coca-Cola to increase market share. Your strategy is to increase your product range and offer a soft drink in every segment of the market to attract customers. Currently, you have a functional structure. What you are trying to work out now is how best to implement your strategy in order to launch your new products. Should you move to a more complex kind of product structure, and, if so, which one? Alternatively, should you establish new-venture divisions and spin off each kind of new soft drink into its own company so that each company can focus its resources on its market niche? There is also a global dimension to your strategy, because it is your intention to compete with Coca-Cola for market share worldwide, and you must consider what is the best structure globally as well as domestically.

1. Debate the pros and cons of the different possible organizational structures, and decide which structure you are going to implement.

2. Debate the pros and cons of the different types of global structures, and decide which is most appropriate and which will best fit in with your domestic structure.

STRATEGIC MANAGEMENT PROJECT
Module 13

This part of the Strategic Management Project requires you to take the information you have collected in the last two chapters on organizational structure and controls and link it to the strategy pursued by your company, which you identified in earlier chapters.

1. What are the sources of your company's distinctive competencies? Which functions are most important to it? How does your company design its structure at the *functional level* to enhance its (a) efficiency, (b) quality, (c) innovation, (d) and responsiveness to customers?

2. What is your company's business-level strategy? How does it design its structure and control systems to enhance and support its business-level strategy? For example, what steps does it take to further cross-functional integration? Does it have a functional, product, or matrix structure?

3. How does your company's culture support its strategy? Can you determine any ways in which its top-management team influences its culture?

4. What kind of international strategy does your company pursue? How does it control its global activities? What kind of structure does it use? Why?

5. At the corporate level, does your company use a multidivisional structure? Why or why not? What crucial implementation problems must your company manage in order to implement its strategy effectively? For example, what kind of integration mechanisms does it employ?

6. Based on this analysis, does your company have high or low bureaucratic costs? Is this level of bureaucratic costs justified by the value it can create through its strategy?

7. Can you suggest ways of altering the company's structure to reduce the level of bureaucratic costs?

8. Can you suggest ways of altering the company's structure or control systems to allow it to create more value? Would this change increase or decrease bureaucratic costs?

9. In sum, do you think your company has achieved a good fit between its strategy and structure?

ARTICLE FILE 13

Find an example(s) of a company that has changed its structure and control systems to manage its strategy better. What were the problems with its old structure? What changes did it make to its structure and control systems? What effects does it expect these changes to have on performance?

🧩 **EXPLORING THE WEB**
Matching Strategy and Structure

Search the Web for a company that is in the process of modifying or changing its organizational structure (do-

mestic or global) to manage its new strategy. What structure is it moving toward? Why is this structure more appropriate than the old one?

CLOSING CASE

Hughes Aircraft Reengineers Its Structure

HUGHES AIRCRAFT is one of the large U.S. defense companies that has been battered by the end of the cold war and the decline in the defense budget. Hughes had been accustomed to a protected environment in which lavish government revenues allowed it to develop advanced technology for military uses, such as missiles, satellites, and radar systems. However, by 1990 Hughes was confronted with a major strategic problem. How could it compete in the new environment in which government revenues were scarce? To survive, Hughes had to find a new strategy based on the development of new technology for nonmilitary uses—and find it fast.

As a first step in changing the company's direction, C. Michael Armstrong, an ex-IBM top manager, was appointed CEO of Hughes in 1991. In IBM's European division, Armstrong had developed a reputation as someone who could turn around a company and redeploy its resources quickly and effectively; investors hoped he could do so at Hughes.

Armstrong began his task by analyzing the company's strategy and structure. What he found was a firm pursuing a differentiated strategy based on developing advanced technological products. To pursue its differentiated strategy, Hughes had developed a divisional structure to lead its development efforts. It had created seven separate technology divisions, each responsible for a different kind of product—missiles, radar, and so forth. Over time, the organization had become very tall and centralized, as each technology division developed its own empire to support its efforts. The primary coordination between divisions took place at the top of the organization, where top divisional managers met regularly with corporate managers to report on and plan future product developments.

Armstrong recognized that this fit between strategy and structure might be appropriate for a company operating in a protected environment, in which money was not a problem. However, it was not appropriate for a company facing intense pressure to lower costs and develop prod-

ucts for nonmilitary applications, such as consumer electronics and home satellites. The divisional structure duplicated expensive R&D activities, and no mechanism was in place to promote the sharing of knowledge and expertise among the different divisions. Moreover, there were few incentives for managers to cut costs because scarce resources had not been a problem, and managers had been rewarded mainly for the success of their product development efforts. Armstrong realized that to make the company more competitive and improve the way it utilized its skills and resources, he had to find a new operating strategy and structure.

Armstrong began the process of change by focusing the company's strategy on customers and markets, not on technology and products. Henceforth, the needs of customers, not the needs of technology, would be the logic behind the organization of the company's activities. He changed the structure from a divisional one based on technology to one based on the needs of customers. The seven technology divisions were reengineered into five market groups according to the kinds of customers' needs they satisfied. Thus, consumer electronics became one market group, and industrial and commercial applications became another. Then technological expertise was reorganized to serve the needs of each kind of customer.

Continuing his reengineering program, Armstrong slashed the number of levels in the managerial hierarchy, eliminating two levels in order to bring managers closer to the customer. He continued this reengineering effort by decentralizing authority and pushing decision making down into the divisions, so that lower-level managers could better respond to customers' needs. In addition, he reorganized the company's international operations by transferring managers from the United States to foreign countries so that they would be closer to their customers.

To make this new customer-oriented structure work effectively, Armstrong also changed the organization's control systems. He created a system of output controls based on benchmarking competitors' costs to provide managers with standards against which to evaluate their performance and to force them to pay attention to costs and quality. He then set up new incentive programs for managers and workers at all levels, linking the programs to achievement of the new targets for efficiency, quality, and responsiveness to customers. Finally, he worked hard with his top management team to establish and promote the norms and values of a customer-oriented organizational culture across the new market divisions. Henceforth, at Hughes technology would be made to fit the customer, not vice versa.

Armstrong's efforts to engineer a new fit between strategy and structure at Hughes have been spectacularly successful. His top management team has fully bought into the new corporate culture, and divisional managers are adopting new entrepreneurial values based on meeting customers' needs. Some of the company's early successes include the launch of its RCA minidish satellite television system and the development of one of the largest private space-based satellite systems in the world.[48] Its stock price has soared as Hughes has used its leading-edge technology to provide customers with quality products at competitive prices. With its new simultaneous differentiation/low-cost strategy, Hughes is performing well in the new competitive environment.

Case Discussion Questions

1. What problems did Armstrong discover regarding strategy and structure with Hughes?

2. What steps did he take to reengineer the company?

End Notes

1. Press release, www.compaq.com, (September 1999).
2. M. Hays, "Compaq Maps Future," *Informationweek*, June 17, 1998, p.14.
3. A. Taylor III, "Compaq Looks Inside for Salvation," *Fortune*, August 16, 1999, pp. 124–128.
4. W. G. Ouchi, "The Relationship Between Organizational Structure and Organizational Control," *Administrative Science Quarterly,* 22 (1977), 95–113.
5. R. Bunderi, "Intel Researchers Aim to Think Big While Staying Close to Development," *Research-Technology Management* (March/April 1998), 3–4.
6. K. M. Eisenhardt, "Control: Organizational and Economic Approaches," *Management Science,* 16 (1985), 134–148.
7. J. R. Galbraith, *Designing Complex Organizations* (Reading, Mass.: Addison-Wesley, 1973); P. R. Lawrence and J. W. Lorsch, *Organization and Environment* (Cambridge, Mass.: Harvard University Press, 1967); D. Miller, "Strategy Making and Structure: Analysis and Implications for Performance," *Academy of Management Journal,* 30 (1987), 7–32.
8. M. E. Porter, *Competitive Strategy: Techniques for Analyzing Industries and Competitors* (New York: Free Press, 1980); D. Miller, "Configurations of Strategy and Structure," *Strategic Management Journal,* 7 (1986), 233–249.
9. D. Miller and P. H. Freisen, *Organizations: A Quantum View* (Englewood Cliffs, N.J.: Prentice-Hall, 1984).
10. J. Woodward, *Industrial Organization: Theory and Practice* (London: Oxford University Press, 1965); Lawrence and Lorsch, *Organization and Environment.*
11. C. J. Loomis, "The Reed That Citicorp Leans On," *Fortune,* July 12, 1993, pp. 90–93.
12. R. E. White, "Generic Business Strategies, Organizational Context and Performance: An Empirical Investigation," *Strategic Management Journal,* 7 (1986), 217–231.
13. Porter, *Competitive Strategy;* Miller, "Configurations of Strategy and Structure."
14. E. Deal and A. A. Kennedy, *Corporate Cultures* (Reading, Mass.: Addison-Wesley, 1985); "Corporate Culture," *Business Week,* October 27, 1980, pp. 148–160.
15. B. Saporito, "How to Revive a Fading Firm," *Fortune,* March 22, 1993, p. 80.
16. G. Imperato, "3M Expert Tells How to Run Meetings that Really Work," *Fast Company*, May 23, 1999, p. 18.
17. D. Miller, "Configurations of Strategy and Structure," in R. E. Miles and C. C. Snow, *Organizational Strategy, Structure, and Process* (New York: McGraw-Hill, 1978).
18. E. Nee, "Reboot," *Forbes*, May 4, 1998, pp. 23–25.
19. Annual Report, www.wang.com, (1999).
20. Lawrence and Lorsch, *Organization and Environment.*
21. J. Stopford and L. Wells, *Managing the Multinational Enterprise* (London: Longman, 1972).

22. C. A. Bartlett and S. Ghoshal, *Managing Across Borders: The Transnational Solution* (Cambridge, Mass.: Harvard Business School, 1991).
23. A. Edgecliffe-Johnson, "Nestle and Pillsbury Forge Ice Cream Alliance in U.S.," *Financial Times*, August 20, 1999, p. 15.
24. G. R. Jones and C. W. L. Hill, "Transaction Cost Analysis of Strategy-Structure Choice," *Strategic Management Journal,* 9 (1988), 159–172.
25. Ibid.
26. R. A. D'Aveni and D. J. Ravenscraft, "Economies of Integration Versus Bureaucracy Costs: Does Vertical Integration Improve Performance?" *Academy of Management Journal,* 5 (1994), 1167–1206.
27. Lawrence and Lorsch, *Organization and Environment;* Galbraith, *Designing Complex Organizations;* M. E. Porter, *Competitive Advantage: Creating and Sustaining Superior Performance* (New York: Free Press, 1985).
28. P. R. Nayyar, "Performance Effects of Information Asymmetry and Economies of Scope in Diversified Service Firm," *Academy of Management Journal*, 36 (1993), 28–57.
29. L. R. Gomez-Mejia, "Structure and Process of Diversification, Compensation Strategy, and Performance," *Strategic Management Journal*, 13 (1992), 381–397.
30. C. C. Markides, and P. J. Williamson, "Related Diversification, Core Competencies, and Corporate Performance," *Strategic Management Journal*, 15 (Special Issue, 1994), 149–165.
31. Porter, *Competitive Strategy.*
32. M. S. Salter and W. A. Weinhold, *Diversification Through Acquisition* (New York: Free Press, 1979).
33. F. T. Paine and D. J. Power, "Merger Strategy: An Examination of Drucker's Five Rules for Successful Acquisitions," *Strategic Management Journal,* 5 (1984), 99–110.
34. G. D. Bruton, B. M. Oviatt, and M. A. White, "Performance of Acquisitions of Distressed Firms," *Academy of Management Journal,* 4 (1994), 972–989.
35. C. K. Prahalad and R. A. Bettis, "The Dominant Logic: A New Linkage Between Diversity and Performance," *Strategic Management Journal,* 7 (1986), 485–501; Porter, *Competitive Strategy.*
36. Porter, *Competitive Strategy.*
37. H. Singh and C. A. Montgomery, "Corporate Acquisitions and Economic Performance," unpublished manuscript, 1984.
38. N. D. Fast, "The Future of Industrial New Venture Departments," *Industrial Marketing Management,* 8 (1979), 264–279.
39. R. A. Burgelman, "Managing the New Venture Division: Research Findings and the Implications for Strategic Management," *Strategic Management Journal,* 6 (1985), 39–54.
40. Fast, "The Future of Industrial New Venture Departments."
41. Burgelman, "Managing the New Venture Division."

42. R. A. Burgelman, "Corporate Entrepreneurship and Strategic Management: Insights from a Process Study," *Management Science,* 29 (1983), 1349–1364.

43. B. Kogut, "Joint Ventures: Theoretical and Empirical Perspectives," *Strategic Management Journal*, 9 (1988), 319–332.

44. G. S. Capowski, "Designing a Corporate Identity," *Management Review* (June 1993), 37–38.

45. J. Marcia, "Just Doing It," *Distribution* (January 1995), 36–40.

46. "The Outing of Outsourcing," *Economist*, November 25, 1995, p. 36.

47. "Andersen's Androids," *Economist*, May 4, 1996, p. 72.

48. J. Cole, "New CEO at Hughes Studied Its Managers, Got Them on His Side," *Wall Street Journal,* March 30, 1993, pp. A1, A8.

14 Implementing Strategic Change

OPENING CASE

From Reengineering to E-Engineering at Bank of America

BY 1999, Bank of America had grown to become the largest financial institution in the United States as a result of a series of mergers, most noticeably the merger with NationsBank in 1998.[1] As it has grown, Bank of America has been constantly changing its structure and control systems to help it operate more effectively. In the process it has made particular use of two change techniques: reengineering and E-engineering.

Reengineering is a change technique that helps an organization make better use of its resources; it involves changing task relationships and organizational structure. At Bank of America, for example, before the use of reengineering, it was quite common for customers to get passed around among four or five different bank employees for even routine banking matters. This was time consuming and tedious and often left customers feeling frustrated. Bank of America used reengineering to change and improve the customer-employee relationship.

Rather than having different employees be responsible for different aspects of the customer service encounter, it trained each customer service employee in all the multiple jobs needed to satisfy a customer's needs. In the process

of doing so, it pushed down responsibility to each employee, which flattened the hierarchy of authority. Bank of America also created teams of specialized customer service employees to handle the needs of specific groups of customers, such as commercial customers, so that employees could learn from one another and work together. As a result of this process, fewer employees were needed to serve customers and customer and employee satisfaction increased.

Since then, Bank of America has utilized another technique to improve its customer service operations: E-engineering. Change in E-engineering is brought about through the use of new information technologies to smooth and enhance customer service. As we have seen in previous chapters, it often involves the use of the Internet. Bank of America has taken advantage of the Internet to start on-line banking. Customers are able to access their accounts and analyze their transactions; when problems arise, they can communicate with customer service employees through E-mail and soon will also be able to use instant messaging. In addition, Bank of America is establishing systems that allow customers to pay their bills on-line and make deposits on-line so that in the future there are likely to be far fewer customer visits to banks. This frees up employees' time to pamper current customers and pursue new ones, such as college students entering the work force and people who have recently relocated to a new city. In a banking environment that is becoming dominated by a few large banks, finding new customers is very important.

Moreover, Bank of America is using E-engineering to streamline its internal operations. All employees now record the details and results of customer service operations on-line so that managers have instant access to daily operations. Managers also have access to immediate information from branches around the United States. In an en-vironment where banks can now provide other financial services—for instance, stockbroking, investment banking, and insurance—such information systems make it easier to tailor the bank's services to the needs of individual customers.[2] Finally, Bank of America is expanding globally because many of its large corporate clients, such as Alamo Rent-A-Car and Delta, have global operations, and a global Internet-based information system makes it easy to handle financial services on a worldwide scale.

In all these ways, E-engineering is allowing Bank of America to change its structure so that it can better pursue its strategy of differentiation in today's competitive banking environment.

OVERVIEW

In today's global environment, change rather than stability is the order of the day. Rapid changes in technology, competition, and customers' demands have increased the rate at which companies need to alter their strategies and structures to survive in the marketplace. As we discuss in Chapter 4, however, one of the principal reasons companies fail is their inability to change themselves and adapt to a new competitive environment because of *organizational inertia*.[3] Once an organization has been created and task and role relationships are defined, a set of forces is put into operation that makes an organization resistant to change. In considering *The Icarus Paradox* in Chapter 4, for example, we note the tendency of organizations to continue to rely on the skills and capabilities that made them successful even when those capabilities do not match the new competitive environment.[4] We also point out that there is another cause of organizational inertia: the conflict and power struggles that occur at the top of an organization as managers strive to influence decision making to protect and enhance their own positions.

In this chapter, we look at the issue strategic managers must deal with as they seek to overcome organizational inertia and change an organization's strategy and structure—the issue of how to implement strategic change. Until now in our study of strategic management, we have treated strategy formulation and implementation from an impersonal, rational perspective, one from which decisions are made coldly and logically. In reality, this picture of how strategic managers decide on and change strategy and structure is incomplete; it ignores the way power and political processes influence the decision-making process and the selection of organizational objectives.

This chapter discusses why it is difficult to change organizations and outlines the issues and problems that managers must address and solve if they are to succeed in changing a company's strategy and structure so that it matches new competitive environments. By the end of this chapter, you will understand the forces at play when strategic managers try to change their organizations and the role of power and politics in helping to implement change successfully.

STRATEGIC CHANGE

Strategic change is the movement of a company away from its present state toward some desired future state to increase its competitive advantage. In the last decade, most large *Fortune* 500 companies have gone through some kind of strategic change as their managers have tried to strengthen their existing core competencies and build new ones to compete more effectively.[5] Most of these companies have been pursuing one of three major kinds of strategic change: reengineering and E-engineering; restructuring; and innovation (see Figure 14.1).

■ Reengineering and E-Engineering

Often, because of drastic unexpected changes in the environment, such as the emergence of aggressive new competitors or technological breakthroughs, strategic managers need to develop a new strategy and structure to raise the level of their business's performance. One way of changing a company to allow it to operate more effectively is by reengineering. **Reengineering** is the "fundamental rethinking and radical redesign of business processes to achieve dramatic improvements in critical, contemporary measures of performance such as cost, quality, service, and speed."[6] As this definition suggests, strategic managers who use reengineering must completely rethink how their organization goes about its business. Instead of concentrating on a company's *functions*, strategic managers make *business processes* the focus of attention.

A **business process** is any activity (such as order processing, inventory control, or product design) that is vital to delivering goods and services to customers quickly or that promotes high quality or low costs. Business processes are not the

FIGURE 14.1

Three Major Types of
Strategic Change

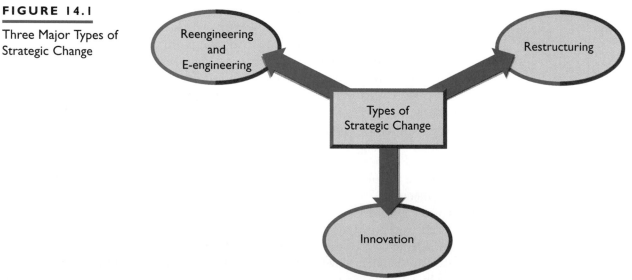

responsibility of any one function but *cut across functions*. Hallmark Cards, for example, reengineered its card-design process with great success. Before the reengineering effort, artists, writers, and editors worked in different functions to produce all kinds of cards. After reengineering, these same artists, writers, and editors were put in cross-functional teams, each of which now works on a specific type of card, such as birthday, Christmas, or Mother's Day. As a result, the time it took to bring a new card to market dropped from years to months, and Hallmark's performance increased dramatically.

Because reengineering focuses on business processes and not on functions, an organization that reengineers always has to adopt a different approach to organizing its activities. Organizations that take up reengineering ignore deliberately the existing arrangement of tasks, roles, and work activities. They start the reengineering process with the customer (not the product or service) and ask, How can we reorganize the way we do our work, our business processes, to provide the best quality and the lowest-cost goods and services to the customer?

Frequently, when companies ask this question, they realize that there are more effective ways to organize their activities. For example, a business process that currently involves members of ten different functions working sequentially to provide goods and services might be performed by one person or a few people at a fraction of the cost after reengineering. Often, individual jobs become increasingly complex, and people are grouped into cross-functional teams as business processes are reengineered to reduce costs and increase quality. This occurred at Eastman Chemicals as it reengineered itself to raise quality and responsiveness to customers.

Reengineering and total quality management (TQM), discussed in Chapter 5, are highly interrelated and complementary. After reengineering has taken place and the question, What is the best way to provide customers with the goods or service they require? has been answered, TQM takes over, focusing on the next question: How can we now continue to improve and refine the new process and find better ways of managing task and role relationships? Successful organizations examine both questions simultaneously and continuously attempt to identify new and better processes for meeting the goals of increased efficiency, quality, and customer responsiveness. Thus, they are always seeking to improve their visions of their desired future state. Another example of reengineering is the change program that took place at IBM Credit which is described in Strategy in Action 14.1.

As this example shows, the introduction of a new computer-based information system was an important aspect of change at IBM. So important has the development of new information systems been for a company's internal operations and for the way that it manages the external environment that the term E-engineering been coined to refer to change efforts centered on the introduction of new software systems. We have seen in previous chapters how the use of Internet-based systems can change the way a company's structure and control systems operate. For example, we saw how at Cypress Semiconductor the CEO uses the company's on-line management information system to monitor his managers' activities and help him keep the organizational hierarchy flat. We saw, too, how Oracle and Compaq are using Internet-based systems to streamline their operations and forge better links with their customers. E-engineering is likely to keep gaining in importance as it alters the way a company organizes its value creation functions and links them together to improve its performance.

14.1 STRATEGY *in* ACTION

A New Approach at IBM Credit

IBM Credit, a wholly owned division of IBM, manages the financing and leasing of IBM computers, particularly mainframes, to IBM's customers. Before the company's reengineering, when a financing request arrived at the division's headquarters in Old Greenwich, Connecticut, it went through a five-step approval process, involving the activities of five different functions. First, the IBM salesperson called up the credit department, which logged the request and recorded details about the potential customer. Second, this information was brought to the credit-checking department, where a credit check on the potential customer was made. Third, when the credit check was complete, the request was taken to the contracts department, which wrote the contract. Fourth, from there the request went to the pricing department, which determined the actual financial details of the loan, such as the interest rate and the term of the loan. Finally, the whole package of information was assembled by the dispatching department and was delivered to the sales representative, who gave it to the customer.

This series of cross-functional activities took an average of seven days to complete, and sales representatives constantly complained that this delay resulted in a low level of customer responsiveness, which reduced customer satisfaction. Also, potential customers were tempted to shop around for financing and even to look at competitors' machines. The delay in closing the deal caused uncertainty for all concerned.

The change process began when two senior IBM credit managers reviewed the whole finance-approval process. They found that the time spent by different specialists in the different functions actually processing a loan application was only ninety minutes. The approval process took seven days because of the delay in transmitting information and requests between departments. The managers also came to realize that the activities taking place in each department were not complex; each department had its own computer system containing its own work procedures, but the work done in each department was pretty routine.

Armed with this information, IBM managers concluded that the approval process could, in fact, be reengineered into one overarching process handled by one person with a computer system containing all the necessary information and work procedures to perform the five loan-processing activities. If the application proved to be very complex, a team of experts stood ready to help process it, but IBM found that after the reengineering a typical application could be finished in four hours rather than the previous seven days. A sales representative could go back to the customer the same day to close the deal, and all the uncertainty surrounding the transaction was removed. As reengineering consultants M. Hammer and J. Champy note, this *dramatic* performance increase was brought about by a *radical* change to the *process* as a whole.[7] Change through reengineering requires managers to go back to the basics and analyze each step in the work process to identify a better way of coordinating and integrating the activities necessary to provide customers with goods and services.

■ Restructuring

Strategic managers also turn to restructuring as a means of implementing strategic change aimed at improving performance. **Restructuring** has two basic steps. First, an organization reduces its level of differentiation and integration by eliminating divisions, departments, or levels in the hierarchy. Second, an organization *downsizes* by reducing the number of its employees to decrease operating costs. When Jack Smith took over as the head of General Motors, for example, GM had more than twenty-two levels in the hierarchy and more than 20,000 corporate managers. Describing his organization as a top-heavy bureaucracy, Smith quickly moved to slash costs and restructure the company. Today, while still tall, GM has only twelve levels in the hierarchy and half as many corporate managers.

Changes in the relationships between divisions or functions are common in restructuring programs. IBM, in an effort to cut development costs and speed cooperation among engineers, created a new division to take control of the production of microprocessors and memory systems. This restructuring move took engineers from IBM's thirteen divisions and grouped them in a brand-new headquarters in Austin, Texas, to increase their effectiveness.

There are many reasons why restructuring becomes necessary and why an organization may need to downsize its operations.[8] Sometimes an unforeseen change occurs in the business environment: perhaps a shift in technology makes a company's products obsolete, or a worldwide recession reduces the demand for its products. An organization may also find itself with excess capacity because customers no longer want the goods and services it provides, viewing them as outdated or of poor value for the money. Sometimes, too, organizations downsize because they have grown excessively tall and bureaucratic, and operating costs have skyrocketed. Even companies that hold a strong position may choose to restructure, simply to build and improve their competitive advantage and stay on top. Strategy in Action 14.2 illustrates the effort of a strong company, Quaker Oats, to improve its performance through restructuring.

All too often, however, companies must downsize and lay off employees because they have failed to continually monitor the operation of their basic business processes and have not made the incremental changes in strategies and structures that would help them contain costs and adjust to changing conditions. Paradoxically, because they have not paid attention to the need to reengineer themselves, they are forced into a position in which restructuring becomes the only way they can survive in an increasingly competitive environment.

14.2   **STRATEGY *in* ACTION**

Quaker Oats Wields the Ax

In six years, James F. Doyle, the head of the Gatorade division at Quaker Oats, had made the division the most profitable in the company. Each year sales and profits had increased despite the fact that the company as a whole was having a rough time because of its disastrous acquisition of the Snapple company, which it sold off in 1997 at a $1.4 billion loss. It was this fiasco that had led to the appointment of a new CEO, Robert S. Morrison, in 1998.

Imagine Doyle's surprise when, with no warning at all, Morrison told Doyle that he believed Quaker Oats had an unnecessarily complex structure and that he was eliminating the entire level of top management at Quaker Oats—the level that included Doyle. Morrison then promoted ten lower-level executives to head each of the company's food lines, such as Rice-a-Roni, Life Cereal, and Gatorade, and indicated that in the future they would report directly to him.[9] Morrison believes this move will allow him to better monitor and manage the performance of each business line and save Quaker Oats millions of dollars a year.

■ Innovation

As already noted, restructuring often may be necessary because changes in technology make an organization's technology, or the goods and services it produces, obsolete. For example, changes in technology have made computers both much cheaper to manufacture and more powerful and have affected what customers want. If organizations are to avoid being left behind in the competitive race to produce new goods and services, they must take steps to introduce new products or develop new technologies to produce those products reliably and at low cost.

You will recall from earlier discussions that **innovation** is the process by which organizations use their skills and resources to create new technologies or goods and services in order to change and respond better to the needs of their customers.[10] Innovation can bring a company spectacular success. Apple Computer, for instance, changed the face of the computer industry when it introduced its personal computer. Honda changed the face of the small motorbike market when it introduced 50-cc motorcycles, and Mary Kay cosmetics changed the way cosmetics were sold to customers when it introduced its at-home cosmetics parties and its personalized style of selling.

Along with change generated by innovation, however, comes a high level of risk because the outcomes of research and development activities are often uncertain.[11] Thus, while innovation can lead to the kind of change organizations want—the introduction of profitable new technologies and products—it can also usher in undesirable change—technologies that are inefficient and products customers don't want. In 1998, Informix, a software maker, almost went bankrupt when demand for its main database software plummeted because of competition from Oracle. It survived by developing Internet software for niche markets and by 1999 was profitable again.[12]

Innovation is one of the most difficult change processes to manage. As we discuss in previous chapters, when organizations rely on innovation as the source of their competitive advantage, they need to adopt flexible structures such as matrix or cross-functional team structures, which give people the freedom to experiment and be creative.[13] Functions need to coordinate their activities and work together if innovation is to be successful, and companies that rely on innovation have to facilitate the change effort and support the efforts of their members to be creative. For example, the term *skunkworks* was coined at Lockheed when that company set up a specialized unit, separate from its regular functional organization, to pioneer the development of a new spy plane, the U2. Creating a separate unit allowed managers to act more flexibly and autonomously. To try to increase the success rate of innovation and new-product development, many high-tech organizations have developed the role of "product champion" and appointed an expert manager to head a new team and lead a new project from its beginning to commercialization.[14] Of all the kinds of change programs that strategic managers can implement, innovation has the prospects for the greatest long-term success but also the greatest risks.

In order to understand the issues involved in implementing these kinds of strategic change, it is useful to focus on the series of distinct steps that strategic managers must follow if the change process is to succeed.[15] These steps are listed in Figure 14.2 and discussed in the rest of this chapter.

FIGURE 14.2

Stages in the
Change Process

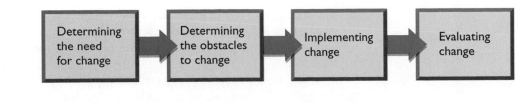

| Determining the need for change | → | Determining the obstacles to change | → | Implementing change | → | Evaluating change |

DETERMINING THE NEED FOR CHANGE

The first step in the change process is for strategic managers to recognize the need for change. Sometimes this need is obvious, as when divisions are fighting or when competitors introduce a product that is clearly superior to anything that the company has in production. More often, however, managers have trouble determining that something is going wrong in the organization. Problems may develop gradually, and organizational performance may slip for a number of years before it becomes obvious. At GM and IBM for example, profitability fell, but because these were reputable companies, the fall caused little stir. After a lapse of time, however, investors realized that these companies' stock was overvalued, and its price plunged when investors saw that managers were not taking the steps necessary to restructure the companies and turn around their performance quickly.

Thus, the first step in the change process occurs when a company's strategic managers or others in a position to take action recognize that there is a *gap between desired company performance and actual performance*.[16] Using measures such as a decline in profitability, ROI, stock price, or market share as indicators that change is needed, managers can start looking for the source of the problem. To discover it, they conduct a SWOT analysis.

Strategic managers examine the company's *strengths* and *weaknesses*. For example, management conducts a strategic audit of all functions and divisions and looks at their contribution to profitability over time. Perhaps some divisions have become relatively unprofitable as innovation has slowed without management's realizing it. Perhaps sales and marketing have failed to keep pace with changes occurring in the competitive environment. Perhaps the company's product is simply outdated. Strategic managers also analyze the company's level of differentiation and integration to make sure that it is appropriate for its strategy. Perhaps a company does not have the integrating mechanisms in place to achieve gains from synergy, or perhaps the structure has become tall and inflexible so that bureaucratic costs have escalated. Perhaps it is necessary to quickly implement a product-team structure to speed the process of product development.

Strategic managers then examine environmental *opportunities* and *threats* that might explain the problem, using all the concepts developed in Chapter 3 of this book. For instance, intense competition may have arisen unexpectedly from substitute products, or a shift in consumers' tastes or technology may have caught the company unawares. Perhaps the strategic group structure in the industry has changed and new kinds of competitors have emerged, such as one or more companies pursuing a simultaneous low-cost/differentiation strategy.

Once the source of the problem has been identified using SWOT analysis, strategic managers must determine the desired future state of the company—that is, how it should change its strategy and structure to achieve the new goals they have set for it. As occurred at IBM and Westinghouse, managers may decide to lower costs by restructuring operations. Alternatively, as happened at Merck and General Motors, the company may increase its research and development budget or diversify into new products to increase the rate of product innovation. Essentially, strategic managers apply the conceptual tools this book has described to work out the best strategy and structure for maximizing profitability. The choices they make are specific to each individual company, and, as noted earlier, there is no way that managers can determine their correctness in advance.

In sum, the first step in the change process involves determining the need for change, analyzing the organization's current position, and determining how to achieve the desired future state that strategic managers would like it to attain—by implementing a reengineering, restructuring, or innovation program, for example.

DETERMINING THE OBSTACLES TO CHANGE

Restructuring, reengineering, innovation, and other forms of strategic change are often resisted by people and groups inside an organization. Often, for example, the decision to restructure and downsize an organization requires the establishment of a new set of task and role relationships among organizational employees. Because this change may threaten the jobs of some employees, they resist the changes taking place, as happened at Eastman Chemicals profiled in the Closing Case. Many efforts at change, restructuring included, take a long time and often fail because of the strong resistance to change at all levels in the organization. Thus, the second step in implementing strategic change is to determine the obstacles or resistance to change that exists in a company.[17]

■ Types of Obstacles to Change

Strategic managers must analyze the factors that are causing organizational inertia and preventing the company from reaching its ideal future state. Obstacles to change can be found at four levels in the organization: corporate, divisional, functional, and individual.

Corporate Obstacles   At the corporate level, several potential obstacles must be considered. Changing strategy or structure, even in seemingly trivial ways, may significantly affect a company's behavior. For example, suppose that to reduce costs a company decides to centralize all divisional purchasing and sales activities at the corporate level. Such consolidation could severely damage each division's ability to develop a unique strategy for its own individual markets. Alternatively, suppose that, in response to low-cost foreign competition, a company decides to pursue a policy of differentiation. This action would change the balance of power among functions and lead to problems as functions start fighting to retain their status in the organization. A *company's present structure and strategy* may constitute powerful obstacles to change. They produce a massive amount of inertia, which has to be overcome before change can take place. This is why strategic change is usually a slow process.[18]

The *type of structure* a company uses can be another impediment to change. For example, it is much easier to change strategy if a company is using a matrix rather than a functional structure, or if it is decentralized rather than centralized, or if it has a high rather than a low level of integration. Decentralized, matrix structures are more flexible than highly controlled functional structures, and thus there is less potential for conflict between functions or divisions because people are used to co-operative cross-functional relationships.

Although some are easier to change than others, *corporate cultures* can present still another obstacle to change. For example, change is notoriously difficult in the military because obedience and the following of orders are deemed sacred. Some cultures, however, such as Hewlett-Packard's, thrive on flexibility or even change itself; they adapt much more easily when change becomes necessary.

Divisional Obstacles   Similar factors operate at the divisional level. Change at that level is difficult if divisions are *highly interrelated and trade resources,* because a shift in one division's operations affects other divisions. Consequently, it is harder to manage change if a company is pursuing a strategy of related, rather than unrelated, diversification. Furthermore, changes in strategy affect different divisions in different ways, because change generally favors the interests of some divisions over those of others. Managers in the different divisions may thus have *different attitudes to change*, and some will be less supportive than others. For example, existing divisions may resist the establishing of new product divisions because they will lose resources, and their status in the organization will diminish.

Functional Obstacles   The same obstacles to change exist at the functional level Like divisions, different functions have *different strategic orientations and goals* and react differently to the changes management proposes. For example, manufacturing generally has a short-term, cost-directed efficiency orientation; research and development is oriented toward long-term, technical goals; and sales is oriented toward satisfying customers' needs. Thus, production may see the solution to a problem as one of reducing costs, sales as one of increasing demand, and research and development as product innovation. Differences in functional orientation make it hard to formulate and implement a new strategy; they slow a company's response to changes in the competitive environment.

Individual Obstacles   At the individual level, too, people are notoriously *resistant to change* because change implies uncertainty, which breeds insecurity and fear of the unknown.[19] Because managers are people, this individual resistance reinforces the tendency of each function and division to oppose changes that may have uncertain effects on them. Restructuring and reengineering efforts can be particularly stressful for managers at all levels of the organization. During the 1990s, for example, AT&T announced the layoff of thousands of its managers every few years. Successive waves of layoffs spawn fear and anxiety about the future among the remaining employees, lessening their commitment to the organization and lowering their morale.

All these obstacles make it difficult to change organizational strategy or structure quickly. That is why U.S. car manufacturers took so long to respond to the Japanese challenge and why companies such as IBM and Digital Equipment were so slow to respond to the threat of powerful workstations and personal computers from companies such as Sun Microsystems and Dell Computer. These companies were accustomed to a situation of complete dominance in their industries and had developed inflexible, centralized structures, which inhibited risk taking and quick reaction.

Paradoxically, companies that experience the greatest uncertainty may become best able to respond to it. When companies have been forced to change frequently, strategic managers often develop the ability to handle change easily.[20] Strategic managers must understand potential obstacles to change as they design a new strategy and structure. Obstacles must be recognized, and the strategic plan must take them into account. The larger and more complex the organization, the harder it is to implement change because inertia is likely to be more pervasive. Strategy in Action 14.3, which tells how Michael Walsh overcame inertia at Tenneco, illustrates a way of overcoming obstacles to change in a large, complex organization.

■ Organizational Conflict: An Important Obstacle to Change

The obstacles to change just discussed can also dramatically reduce a company's ability to change when they spawn organizational conflict between functions and between divisions. **Organizational conflict** is the struggle that arises when the goal-directed behavior of one organizational group blocks the goal-directed behavior of another.[21] Different functions and divisions have different orientations, so if organizational change favors one division over another, organizational conflict can erupt, resulting in a failure to move quickly to exploit new strategic opportunities. A model developed by Lou R. Pondy helps show how conflict emerges in organizations and how it can become a powerful obstacle to change in its own right.[22]

The five stages in Pondy's model of the conflict process are summarized in Figure 14.3. The first stage in the conflict process is *latent conflict,* potential conflict that can flare up when the right conditions arise. All the obstacles to change just discussed are potential sources of conflict. For example, latent conflicts are frequently activated by changes in an organization's strategy or structure that affect the relationship among functions or divisions. Suppose a company has been producing one major product type but then decides to diversify and produce different kinds of products. To overcome problems of coordinating a range of specialist services over many products, the company moves from a functional to a divisional structure. The new structure changes task relationships among divisional managers, and this in turn changes the relative status and areas of authority of the different functional and product managers. Conflict between functional and product managers or among product managers is likely to ensue.

Because every change in a company's strategy and structure alters the organizational context, conflict can easily arise unless the situation is carefully managed to avoid it. Good strategic planning allows managers to anticipate problems that may emerge later so that they can move early to prevent them.[23] For example, when managers change a company's strategy, they should also consider the effect of these changes on future group relationships. Similarly, when changing organizational

The Shakeout at Tenneco

A sprawling conglomerate, Tenneco operates in such businesses as natural gas, shipbuilding, auto parts, chemicals, and farm equipment. In 1991, the company, which is based in Houston, Texas, was ranked twenty-seventh in the *Fortune* 500, with sales at more than $14 billion. Nevertheless, when Michael H. Walsh became president of Tenneco in 1991, he entered a company that had experienced falling earnings for years and was expected to post a net loss of $732 million in 1991. His mission was to turn Tenneco around and restructure its assets.

Walsh was used to the challenge of changing a large company. He had successfully turned around Union Pacific, a large railroad company, and it was on the basis of his reputation as a change agent that Tenneco's board of directors had hired him. When Walsh took over the restructuring effort, his first step was to analyze Tenneco's problems in order to find their causes. He uncovered serious flaws in the company's structure and culture, which had led to poor performance in the various operating divisions. For example, Case, the company's agricultural equipment maker, was in very poor financial shape and was a major contributor to poor corporate performance. To keep Case afloat, top management had continually siphoned off the profits of the chemicals and auto parts divisions, which were doing well. As a result, managers in these divisions had little incentive to improve divisional performance or to cooperate with one another and share resources or capabilities.

Over the years, top management had failed to institute a rigorous system of financial and output controls to monitor and control divisional performance. Divisional managers had been allowed to run their operations with little corporate oversight. Consequently, they had made investments that supported their own interests, not those of the corporation. With few checks on their activities, the divisions had become top-heavy and noncompetitive. Furthermore, as already mentioned, they lacked any incentive to cooperate and improve corporate performance together.

Walsh recognized that the way Tenneco's structure and culture were working had become a powerful obstacle to change. He realized that to change divisional managers' behavior and overcome the inertia, which had

brought the company continual losses, he would have to restructure the corporate-divisional relationship. He started from the top by changing managers' attitudes and behavior. First, he instituted a set of output controls and made it clear that these goals would be monitored and enforced. Second, he created a system of teams in which the managers from the different divisions met together to critique each other's performance. Third, he flattened the corporate hierarchy, wiping out three layers of corporate managers to bring him closer to the divisions and to let the heads of the divisions function as the company's top-management team. (Previously, divisional managers had met one-on-one with the CEO; now they operated as a corporate team.)

After this restructuring, Walsh decentralized more control to divisional managers. At the same time, he made them more accountable for their actions, since each manager's performance was now more visible to the CEO and to other top managers. As a result, top managers had more incentive to improve corporate performance. These changes effectively destroyed the inertia permeating Tenneco's old organizational structure and led to the evolution of a new culture, in which corporate, not divisional, goals and values guided divisional behavior.

Walsh continued these change efforts at all levels of the company. To change attitudes and behavior at the functional level, he instituted a system of quality teams in every division of the company. In these cross-functional teams, employees are expected to search for solutions to improve quality and reduce costs, and Walsh regularly videotapes messages to Tenneco's employees to exhort them to find new ways of improving performance. He also set an example by wiping out top management's perks such as private dining rooms, luxury yachts, jets, and cars.

Throughout the company, Walsh destroyed the old culture of apathy, which had made managers and other employees content to maintain the status quo and avoid confronting the company's problems. Walsh's efforts to change the company were spectacularly successful. Tenneco made record profits in the 1990s because of Walsh's restructuring efforts. Overcoming obstacles to change in a company may be a very difficult process, but as Tenneco's experience suggests, managers, employees, and shareholders can reap big dividends from it.

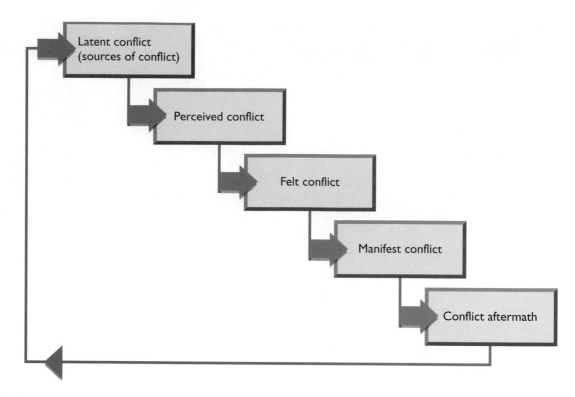

FIGURE 14.3

Stages in the
Conflict Process

structure, strategic managers should anticipate the effects of the changes on functional and divisional relationships. However, because avoidance is not always possible, latent conflict may quickly lead to *perceived conflict,* the second stage.

Perceived conflict occurs when managers become aware of the clashes. After a change in strategy and structure, managers discover that the actions of another function or group obstruct the operations of their group. Managers start to react to the situation, and from the perceived stage they go quickly to the third stage, *felt conflict.* It is at this point that managers start to personalize the conflict. Opinions polarize as one function or division starts to blame the others for causing the conflict. Production might blame the inefficiency of sales for a fall in orders, while sales might blame production for a fall in product quality. Typically, there is a marked lack of cooperation at this stage, and integration among functions or divisions breaks down as the groups start to develop an us-versus-them mentality. If not managed, this stage in the conflict process leads quickly to the fourth stage, *manifest conflict.*

At this point, the conflict among functions or divisions comes into the open, and each group strives to thwart the goals of the other. Groups compete to protect their own interests and block the interests of other groups. Naturally, this blocks change and prevents an organization from adapting to its environment. Manifest conflict can take many forms. The most obvious is fighting or a lack of cooperation among top managers as they start to blame the managers of other functions or divisions for causing the problem. Other forms of manifest conflict are transfer pricing battles between divisions and knowledge hoarding. If divisional managers refuse to share resources or information, a company cannot develop synergy between divisions, and all the benefits of changing to a strategy of related diversification will be lost.

At the functional level, the effects of conflict can be equally devastating. A company in trouble cannot change and pursue a low-cost strategy if its functions are competing. For example, if sales makes no attempt to keep manufacturing informed about customers' demands, manufacturing cannot maximize the length of production runs. Similarly, a struggling company trying to change and regain its differentiated appeal cannot do so if marketing does not inform research and development about changes in consumers' preferences or if product engineering and research and development are competing over product specifications. Most companies have experienced each of these conflicts at one time or another and suffered a loss in performance and competitive advantage when conflict has blocked their ability to change and adapt quickly to a changing environment.

Manifest conflict is also common in top-management circles. There managers fight for promotion to high office or for resources to enhance their status and prestige in the organization. But if top managers are all fighting, how can a company reengineer or restructure itself successfully?

The long-term effects of manifest conflict emerge in the last stage of the conflict process, the *conflict aftermath.* Suppose that in one company a change in strategy led to conflict among division managers over transfer prices. Then divisional managers, with the help of corporate personnel, resolved the problem to everyone's satisfaction and reestablished good working relationships. In another company, however, the conflict between divisions over transfer prices was settled only by the intervention of corporate managers, who *imposed* a solution on divisional managers. A year later, a change in the environment occurred that made the transfer pricing system in both companies inequitable, and prices had to be renegotiated. How would the two companies react to the need to change again? The managers in the company in which the conflict was settled amicably would likely approach this new round of negotiations with a cooperative, not an adversarial, attitude, and necessary changes could be achieved rapidly. However, in the company in which divisions never really established an agreement, a new round of intense clashes would be likely and change would be difficult to achieve.

Conflict aftermath sets the scene for the next round of conflict, which will certainly occur because the environment is constantly changing and so must companies. The reason some companies have a long history of bad relationships among functions or divisions is that their conflict has never been managed successfully. In companies in which strategic managers have resolved the conflict, a cohesive organizational culture develops. In these companies, managers adopt a cooperative, not a competitive, attitude when conflict occurs because of change. The question that needs to be tackled, then, is how best to manage conflict strategically to avoid its bad effects and to make changes in strategy and structure as smooth as possible. There are several tactics and techniques that strategic managers can use to overcome conflict and implement strategic change effectively. Perhaps the most important of these is the way they use power and political tactics to manage strategic change.

IMPLEMENTING STRATEGIC CHANGE AND THE ROLE OF ORGANIZATIONAL POLITICS

Decisions about strategy and structure and how to change strategy and structure are not made just by following a calculated, rational plan in which only shareholders' interests are considered. In reality, strategic decision making is quite different.

When evaluating alternative courses of action and choosing a new strategic direction, managers often make decisions that will further their personal, functional, or divisional interests. **Organizational politics** are tactics that strategic managers engage in to obtain and use power to influence organizational goals and change strategy and structure to further their own interests.[24] Top-level managers constantly come into conflict over what the correct policy decisions should be, and power struggles and coalition building are a major part of strategic decision making. In this political view of decision making, obstacles to change are overcome and conflicts over goals are settled by compromise, bargaining, and negotiation between managers and coalitions of managers and by the outright use of power.[25]

In this section, we examine the relationship between strategic change and organizational politics and the process of political decision making. First, we consider the sources of politics and why politics is a necessary part of managing the strategic change process. Second, we look at how managers or divisions can increase their power so that they can influence the company's strategic direction. Third, we explore the ways in which a company can manage politics to overcome inertia and implement strategic change.

■ Sources of Organizational Politics

To understand why politics is an integral part of strategic change, it is useful to contrast the rational view of organizational decision making with the political view of how strategic decisions get made (see Figure 14.4). The rational view assumes that

FIGURE 14.4

Rational and Political Views of Decision Making

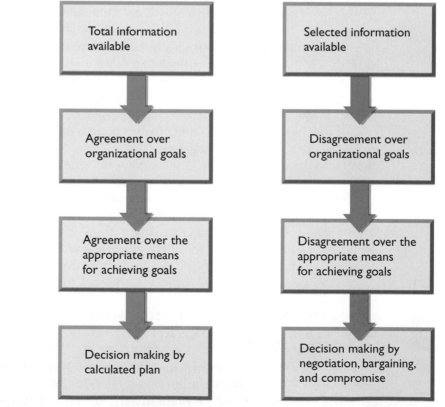

CHAPTER 14 *Implementing Strategic Change*

complete *information* is available and no uncertainty exists about outcomes, but the political view suggests that strategic managers can never be sure that they are making the best decisions. From a political perspective, decision making always takes place in uncertainty, in which the outcomes of strategic change are difficult to predict. According to the rational view, moreover, managers always agree about appropriate organizational *goals* and the appropriate *means*, or strategies, for achieving these goals. According to the political view, on the other hand, the choice of goals and means is linked to each individual's, function's, or division's pursuit of self-interest. Disagreement over the best course of action is inevitable in the political view because strategic change necessarily favors some individuals or divisions over others. For example, if managers decide to invest in resources to promote and develop one product, other products will not be created. Some managers win; others lose.

Given the political point of view, strategy choices are never right or wrong; they are simply better or worse. As a result, managers have to promote their ideas and lobby for support from other managers so that they can build up backing for a course of future action. Thus, coalition building is a vital part of managing strategic change.[26] Managers join coalitions to lobby for their interests because in doing so they increase their political muscle in relation to their organizational opponents.

Managers also engage in politics for personal reasons. Because organizations are shaped like pyramids, individual managers realize that the higher they rise, the more difficult it is to climb to the next position.[27] If their views prevail and the organization follows their lead, however, *and* if their decisions bear results, they reap rewards and promotions. Thus, by being successful at politics and claiming responsibility for successful change, they increase their visibility in the organization and make themselves contenders for higher organizational office.

The assumption that personal, rather than shareholder or organizational, interest governs strategic choice is what gives the word *politics* bad connotations in many people's minds. However, because no one knows for certain what will happen as a result of strategic change, letting people pursue their own interest may in the long run mean that the organization's interests are being followed. This is because competition among managers stemming from self-interest may lead to better strategic decision making and lead to an improved change plan, with successful managers moving to the top of the organization over time. If a company can maintain checks and balances in its top-management circles (by preventing any particular manager or coalition from becoming too powerful), politics can be a healthy influence, for it can prevent managers from becoming complacent about the status quo, promote strategic change, and thus avert organizational decline.

If politics grows rampant, however, and if powerful managers gain such dominance that they can suppress the views of managers who oppose their interests, major problems may arise. Checks and balances fade, organizational inertia increases, and performance suffers. For example, at Gulf & Western, as soon as its founder died, the company sold off fifty businesses that the new top management considered his pet projects and not suited to the company's portfolio. Ultimately, companies that let politics get so out of hand that shareholders' interests suffer are taken over by aggressive new management teams, which engage in major restructuring activities—often involving the layoff of thousands of employees—to turn around a company.

Figure 14.5 illustrates the effect of organizational politics on performance. The figure shows that up to point A, politics can increase organizational performance because it can *overcome inertia and induce needed organizational change*. After

FIGURE 14.5

Effect of Organizational
Politics on Performance

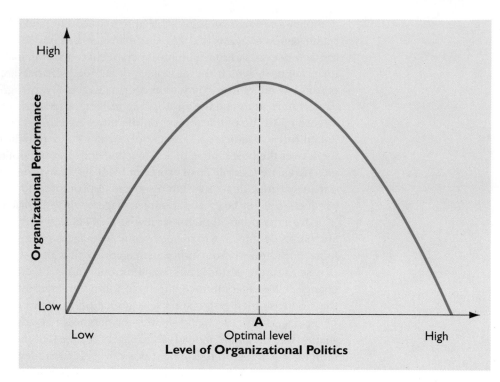

point A, however, an increase in the level of organizational politics can lead to a decline in performance, for politics gets out of control and the organization fragments into competing interest groups. Therefore, astute managers seek to keep the level of political behavior from passing the optimum point. If kept in check, politics can be a useful management tool for overcoming inertia and bringing about strategic change. The best CEOs recognize this fact and create a strategic context in which managers can fight for their ideas and reap the rewards from successfully promoting change in organizational strategy and structure. For example, 3M is well known for its top-management committee structure, in which divisional managers who request new funds and new-venture managers who champion new products must present their projects to the entire top-management team and lobby for support for their ideas. All top managers in 3M experienced this learning process, and presumably the ones in the top-management team are those who succeeded best at mobilizing support and commitment for their concepts.

■ Legitimate Power and Politics

To play politics and bring about the strategic change that they support, managers must have power. **Power** can be defined as the ability of one individual, function, or division to cause another individual, function, or division to do something that it would not otherwise have done.[28] Perhaps the simplest way to understand power is to look at its sources: legitimate power and informal power.

Legitimate power is the authority a manager possesses by virtue of holding a formal position in the hierarchy. This is why the CEO is so powerful. As the top manager of a company, he or she decides whom to delegate power to and how much to give. Authority also gives a manager the power to resolve conflicts and decide what needs to be done. This is the power that *gives a manager the ability to overcome obstacles to change.* For example, as discussed earlier, conflict often occurs between functions and divisions because they have different goals and interests. Because functional managers have equal authority, they cannot control each other, so when functional managers cannot solve their problems, these problems are often passed on to corporate managers or the CEO, who has the authority to impose a solution on the parties. The story of the way managers at BankAmerica took full control over another bank after a merger demonstrates the potency of legitimate power in bringing about strategic change, it helps reveal the steps that it took to become the biggest bank in the U.S. (See Opening Case.) Details are given in Strategy in Action 14.4.

■ Informal Sources of Power and Politics

While a considerable amount of a strategic manager's power derives from his or her level in the hierarchy, many other informal sources of power are crucial in determining what kinds of changes will be made in strategy and structure and thus in a company's future direction. To a large degree, how much informal power the managers of the different functions and divisions possess derives from a company's corporate- and business-level strategies. Different strategies make some functions or divisions, *and thus their managers*, more important than others in achieving the corporate mission and consequently confer a greater ability to implement strategic change. Figure 14.6 lists the informal sources of power that we discuss next.

Ability to Cope with Uncertainty   A function or division gains power if it can reduce uncertainty for another function or division.[29] Suppose that a company is pursuing a strategy of vertical integration. A division that controls the supply and quality of inputs to another division has power over it because it controls the uncertainty facing the second division. At the business level, in a company pursuing a low-cost strategy, sales has power over production because sales provides information about customers' needs that is necessary to minimize production costs. In a company pursuing a differentiation strategy, research and development has power over marketing at the early stages in a product's life cycle because it controls product innovations. However, once innovation problems have been solved, marketing is likely to be the most powerful function because it supplies research and development with information on customers' needs. Thus, a function's power depends on the degree to which other functions rely on it.

Centrality   Power also derives from the centrality of a division or function.[30] **Centrality** refers to the extent to which a division or function is at the center of resource transfers among divisions. For example, in a chemical company, the division supplying specialized chemicals is likely to be central because its activities are critical to both the petroleum division, which supplies its inputs, and the end-using divisions such as plastics or pharmaceuticals, which depend on its outputs. Its activities are central to the production process of all the company's businesses. Therefore, it can exert pressure on corporate headquarters to pursue policies in its own interest.

STRATEGY in ACTION

Who Has Power in a Merger?

When BankAmerica merged with Security Pacific in 1991, the merger was supposed to be a merger of equals, with the top management of both banks jointly running the new company. Richard Rosenberg, the chairman of BankAmerica, agreed to form an office of the chairman with Security Pacific's chairman, Robert Smith; it was also agreed that Smith would succeed Rosenberg as the chairman of the new bank when Rosenberg retired. Similarly, there was supposed to be a 50/50 board split between the directors of both companies, and BankAmerica agreed to name four of Security Pacific's top managers to the new top-management team.

After the merger, however, things did not work out as had been expected. BankAmerica had planned the merger hurriedly, without investigating the details of Security Pacific's financial condition thoroughly. After the merger, BankAmerica's managers began to find major flaws in the way Security Pacific's managers made loans, which had resulted in more than $300 million of write-offs for the company, with equally large sums to follow. BankAmerica's top-management team came to despise and ridicule the way Security Pacific's managers did business. They blamed a large part of the problem on Security Pacific's culture, which was decentralized and freewheeling and allowed top managers to loan large sums of money to clients on the basis of personal ties. By contrast, BankAmerica had developed a conservative, centralized decision-making style and curbed the autonomy of lower-level managers; loans were made according to company-wide criteria scrutinized by top management.

Believing that their culture was the one that had to be developed in the new organization, BankAmerica's managers began to use their legitimate power as the dominant party in the merger (Rosenberg as chairman of the bigger company had more legitimate power than Smith) to strip authority from Security Pacific's managers and to take control of the reins of the new organization. Less than two weeks after the merger, Smith found himself relieved of all important decision-making authority, which was transferred to Rosenberg and his top-management team. Similarly, whenever BankAmerica's top managers were negotiating with Security Pacific's managers over future task and authority relationships, they used their power to cut the authority of Security Pacific's managers and to drive them from the organization. After a few months, almost all of Security Pacific's top managers had left the new organization, followed by thousands of middle-level managers, who, BankAmerica managers felt, could not be trusted to maintain the company's new cultural standards and way of doing business.

At the functional level, the function that has the most centrality, and therefore power, is the one that provides the distinctive competency on which a company's business-level strategy is based.[31] Thus, at Apple Computer, the function with the greatest centrality is research and development because the company's competitive advantage rests on a technical competency. On the other hand, at Wal-Mart the purchasing and distribution function is the most central because Wal-Mart's competitive advantage depends on its ability to provide a low-cost product.

Control over Information Functions and divisions are also central if they are at the heart of the information flow—that is, if they can control the flow of information to other functions or divisions (or both).[32] Information is a power resource because, by giving or withholding information, one function or division can cause others to behave in certain ways. Sales, for instance, can control the way production operates. If sales manipulates information to satisfy its own goals—for example, responsiveness to customers—production costs will rise, but production may be un-

FIGURE 14.6

Informal Sources
of Power

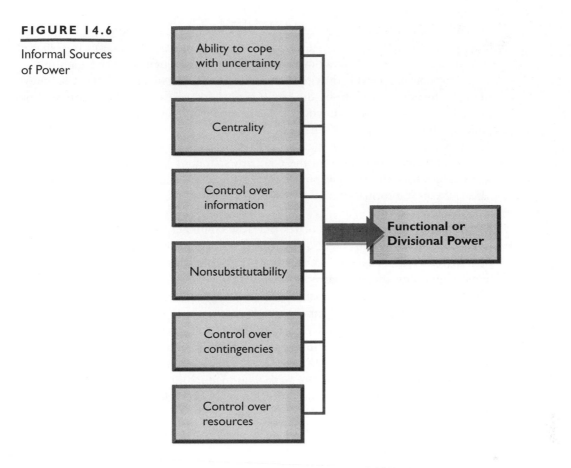

aware that costs could be lowered with a different sales strategy. Similarly, research
and development can shape managers' attitudes to the competitive prospects of different kinds of products by supplying favorable information about the products it
prefers and downplaying others.

In a very real sense, managers in organizations are engaging in a subtle information game when they form policies, set objectives, and influence the change
process. We discuss in Chapter 11 how divisions can disguise their performance by
providing only positive information to corporate managers. The more powerful a division, the more easily it can do this. In both strategy formulation and implementation, by using information to develop a power base, divisions and functions can
strongly influence policy changes that favor their own interests.

Nonsubstitutability   A function or division can accrue power proportionately to
the degree to which its activities are **nonsubstitutable**—that is, cannot be duplicated. For example, if a company is vertically integrated, supplying divisions are nonsubstitutable to the extent that the company cannot buy in the marketplace what
they produce. Thus, the petroleum products division is not very powerful if large
quantities of oil are available from other suppliers. In an oil crisis, the opposite is
true. On the other hand, the activities of a new-venture division—a division in
which new products are developed—are nonsubstitutable to the extent that a company cannot buy another company that possesses similar knowledge or expertise. If
knowledge or information can be bought, the division is substitutable.

The same holds true at the functional level. A function and the managers within it are powerful to the extent that no other function can perform their task. As in the case of centrality, which function is nonsubstitutable depends on the nature of a company's business-level strategy. If the company is pursuing a low-cost strategy, then production is likely to be the key function, and research and development or marketing has less power. However, if the company is pursuing a strategy of differentiation, then the opposite is likely to be the case.

Thus, the power that a function or division gains by virtue of its centrality or nonsubstitutability derives from the company's strategy. Eventually, as a company's strategy changes, the relative power of the functions and divisions also changes. This is the next informal source of power that we discuss.

Control over Contingencies   Over time, the contingencies—that is, the opportunities and threats—facing a company from the competitive environment change as the environment changes.[33] The functions or divisions that can deal with the problems confronting the company and allow it to achieve its objectives gain power. Conversely, the functions that can no longer manage the contingency lose power. For example, consider which functional executives rose to top management positions during the last fifty years. Generally, the executives who reached the highest posts did so from functions or divisions that were able to deal with the opportunities and threats facing the company.[34]

In the 1950s, for instance, the main contingency problem a company had to cope with was to produce goods and services. Pent-up demand from the years of World War II led to a huge increase in consumer spending for automobiles, homes, and durable goods. Goods needed to be produced quickly and cheaply to meet demand, and during this period the managers who rose to the top were from the *manufacturing* function or *consumer products* divisions.

In the 1960s, the problem changed. Most companies had increased their productive capacity, and the market was saturated. Producing goods was not as difficult as selling them. Hence, *marketing and sales* functions rose to prominence. The rise of executives in companies reflected this critical contingency, for greater numbers of them emerged from the sales function and from *marketing-oriented* divisions than from any other groups.

In the 1970s, companies began to realize that competitive conditions were permanent. They had to streamline their strategies and structures to survive in an increasingly hostile environment. As a result, *accounting and finance* became the function that supplied most of the additions to the top-management team. Today, a company's business- and corporate-level strategy determines which group gains preeminence.

Control over Resources   The final informal source of power examined here is the ability to control and allocate scarce resources.[35] This source gives corporate-level managers their clout. Obviously, the power of corporate managers depends to a large extent on their ability to allocate capital to the operating divisions and to allot cash to or take it from a division on the basis of their expectations of its future success.

However, the power of resources is not a function merely of the ability to allocate resources immediately; it also comes from the ability to *generate resources in the future.* Thus, individual divisions that can generate resources will have power in the corporation. For example, divisions that can generate high revenues from sales to consumers have great power. At the functional level, the same kinds of considerations apply. The ability of sales and marketing to increase customers' demand and generate revenues explains their power in the organization. In general, the function that can generate the most resources has the most power.

■ Summary

The most powerful division or function in a company, then, is the one that can reduce uncertainty for others, is most central and nonsubstitutable, has control over resources and can generate them, and is able to deal with the critical external strategic contingency facing the company. In practice, each function or division in a company has power from one or more of these sources, and so there is a distribution of power among functions and divisions.

At the level of individual managers, too, there are various informal ways to increase personal power. First, managers can try to make themselves *irreplaceable*.[36] For example, they may develop specialized skills—such as a knowledge of computers or special relationships with key customers—that allow them to solve problems or limit uncertainty for other managers in the organization. Second, they may specialize in an area of increasing concern to the organization so that they eventually control a crucial *contingency* facing the organization. Third, managers can also try to make themselves more *central* in an organization by deliberately accepting responsibilities that bring them into contact with many functions or managers. Finally, another tactic to obtain power is to be associated with powerful managers who are clearly on their way to the top. By supporting a powerful manager and being indispensable to him or her, it is possible to rise up the organizational ladder with that manager. Political managers cultivate both people and information, and they are able to build up a personal network of contacts in the organization that they can then use to pursue personal goals such as promotion.

■ Effects of Power and Politics on Strategic Change

Power and politics strongly influence a company's choice of strategy and structure, for a company has to maintain an organizational context that is responsive both to the aspirations of the various divisions, functions, and managers and to changes in the external environment.[37] The problem companies face is that the internal structure of power always lags behind changes in the environment because, in general, the environment changes faster than companies can respond. Those in power never voluntarily give up engaging in politics, but excessive politicking and power struggles reduce a company's flexibility, cause inertia, and erode competitive advantage.

To use politics to promote effective change, a company must devise organizational arrangements that create a **power balance** among the various divisions or functions so that no single one dominates the whole enterprise. If no power balance exists, power struggles proceed unchecked and change becomes impossible as divisions start to compete and to hoard information or knowledge to maximize their own returns. In such situations, exchanging resources among divisions becomes expensive, and gains from synergy are difficult to obtain. These factors in turn lower a company's profitability and reduce organizational growth.

In the divisional structure, the corporate headquarters staff plays the balancing role because they can exert power even over strong divisions and force them to share resources for the good of the whole corporation. In a single-business company, a strong chief executive officer is important because he or she must replace the corporate center and balance the power of the strong functions against the weak. The forceful CEO takes the responsibility for giving weak functions an opportunity to air their concerns and interests and tries to avoid being railroaded into decisions by the strong function pursuing its own interests. Thus, the CEO of a large corporation has great potential for exercising power to bring about change. The CEO also plays another important role, however: that of arbiter of acceptable political decision making.

Politics pervades all companies, but the CEO and top-level managers can shape its character. In some organizations, power plays are the norm because the CEOs themselves garnered power in that way. However, other companies—especially those founded by entrepreneurs who believed in democracy or in decentralized decision making—may not tolerate power struggles, and a different kind of political behavior becomes acceptable. It is based on a function or division manager's competency or expertise rather than on her or his ability to form powerful coalitions.

At PepsiCo, politics is of the cutthroat power play variety, and there is a rapid turnover of managers who fail to meet organizational aspirations. At Coca-Cola, however, ideas and expertise are much more important in politics than power plays directed at maximizing functional or divisional self-interest. Similarly, Intel does not tolerate politicking or lobbying for personal gain; instead, it rewards risk taking and makes promotion contingent on performance, not seniority.

To design an organizational structure that creates a power balance facilitating change, strategic managers can use the tools of implementation discussed in Chapters 11 and 12. First, they must create the right mix of integrating mechanisms so that functions or divisions can share information and ideas. A multidivisional structure offers one means of balancing power among divisions, and the matrix or product-team structure offers another among functions. A company can then develop norms, values, and a common culture that emphasize corporate, rather than divisional, interests and that stress the company's mission. In companies such as Microsoft or 3M, for instance, culture serves to harmonize divisional interests with the achievement of corporate goals.

Finally, as we note earlier, strong hierarchical control by a gifted chief executive officer can also create the organizational context in which politics can facilitate the change process. When CEOs use their expert knowledge as their power, they provide the strategic leadership that allows a company to overcome inertia and change its strategy and structure. Indeed, it should be part of the strategic manager's job to learn how to manage politics and power to further corporate interests, because politics is an essential part of the process of strategic change.

MANAGING AND EVALUATING CHANGE

Even with the political situation under control, implementing change—that is, managing and evaluating change—raises several questions. For instance, who should actually carry out the change: internal managers or external consultants?

Although internal managers may have the most experience or knowledge about a company's operations, they may lack perspective because they are too much a part of the organization's culture. They also run the risk of appearing to be politically motivated and of having a personal stake in the changes they recommend. Companies, therefore, often turn to external consultants, who can view a situation more objectively. Outside consultants, however, must spend a lot of time learning about the company and its problems before they can propose a plan of action. It is for both these reasons that many companies such as Quaker Oats, Tenneco, and IBM have brought in new CEOs from outside the company to spearhead their change efforts. In this way, companies can get the benefits of both inside information and external perspective.

Generally, a company can take two main approaches to managing change: top-down change or bottom-up change. With **top-down change**, a strong CEO such as a Morrison or Walsh or a top-management team analyzes how to alter strategy and structure, recommends a course of action, and then moves quickly to restructure and implement change in the organization. The emphasis is on speed of response and management of problems as they occur. **Bottom-up change** is much more gradual. Top management consults with managers at all levels in the organization. Then, over time, it develops a detailed plan for change, with a timetable of events and stages that the company will go through. The emphasis in bottom-up change is on participation and on keeping people informed about the situation, so that uncertainty is minimized.

The advantage of bottom-up change is that it removes some of the obstacles to change by including them in the strategic plan. Furthermore, the purpose of consulting with managers at all levels is to reveal potential problems. The disadvantage of bottom-up change is its slowness.

On the other hand, in the case of the much speedier top-down change, the problems may emerge later and may be difficult to resolve. Lumbering giants such as Tenneco and IBM often need top-down change because managers are so unaccustomed to and threatened by change that only a radical restructuring effort provides the momentum to overcome organizational inertia.

Managers at McDonnell Douglas learned this lesson when they sought ways to turn around their company's performance in the 1990s, after the huge cutbacks in defense spending brought about by the end of the cold war. To improve performance, managers started a program of bottom-up change and tried to involve employees in finding ways to cut costs and raise the level of innovation. After several months, they realized that nothing was changing, and so on a day that has gone down in McDonnell Douglas history as "The Monday Massacre" top managers instituted a radical program of top-down change.

They eliminated the positions of all 5,000 of McDonnell Douglas's managers and supervisors and restructured the company from seven layers in the hierarchy to five, so that in the future only 2,800 managers would be required. They then let the 5,000 managers and supervisors compete for the 2,800 new positions.[38] The placing of new managers in all-new positions totally destroyed the company's old culture and ways of operating and allowed top management to bring about needed changes in the organization quickly. The result for McDonnell Douglas was a complete turnaround of its business and, eventually, a higher rate of new-product innovation. However, for about a year after the change, the company was in upheaval as managers essentially had to create a new organizational structure to operate their business. The moral of the story is that organizations that change the most find change easiest because inertia has not yet built up and those such as McDonnell Douglas that do not change find change the most difficult.

The last step in the change process is to evaluate the effects of the changes in strategy and structure on organizational performance. A company must compare the way it operates after implementing change with the way it operated before. Managers use indexes such as changes in stock market price or market share to assess the effects of change in strategy. It is much more difficult, however, to assess the effects of changes in structure on a company's performance because they are so much harder to measure. Whereas companies can easily measure the increased revenue from increased product differentiation, they do not have any sure means of evaluating how a shift from a product to a divisional structure has affected performance. Managers can be surveyed, however, and over time it may become obvious that organizational flexibility and the company's ability to manage its strategy have increased. Managers can also assess whether the change has decreased the level of politicking and conflict and strengthened cooperation among the divisions and functions.

SUMMARY OF CHAPTER

Organizational change is a complex and difficult process for companies to manage successfully. The first hurdle is getting managers to realize that change is necessary and to admit that there is a problem. Once the need for change has been recognized, managers can go about the process of recommending a course of action and analyze potential obstacles to change. Strategic managers need to appreciate, however, that companies are not just rational decision-making systems in which managers coldly calculate the potential returns from their investments. Organizations are arenas of power, in which individuals and groups fight for prestige and possession of scarce resources. In the pursuit of their interests, managers compete and come into conflict. The very nature of the organization makes this inevitable. Managers have to deal with politics and conflict creatively to implement strategic change successfully and enhance or restore a company's competitive advantage. The most successful companies are those in which change is regarded as the norm and managers are constantly seeking to improve organizational strengths and eliminate weaknesses so that they can maximize future profitability. This chapter makes the following main points:

- ✔ Strategic change is the movement of a company away from its present state to some desired future state to increase its competitive advantage. Three main types of strategic change are reengineering and E-engineering; restructuring; and innovation.
- ✔ Strategic change is implemented through a series of steps that strategic managers must follow if the change process is to succeed.
- ✔ The first step in the change process is determining the need for change. Strategic managers must recognize a gap between actual performance and desired performance, use a SWOT analysis to define the company's present state, and then determine its desired future state.
- ✔ The second step in the change process is identifying the obstacles to change that may prevent a company from reaching its desired future state. Obstacles to change are found at the corporate, divisional, functional, and individual levels. Important obstacles include the inertia produced by an organization's present strategy, structure, culture and differences in divisional and functional goals and interests.
- ✔ Organizational conflict results from fights between divisions, functions, and individual managers pursuing different goals and interests. Conflict is also a major obstacle to change, and managers must seek ways to resolve conflict to implement strategic change successfully.
- ✔ Strategic managers play organizational politics to overcome obstacles to change, resolve conflicts,

and bring about strategic change. Organizational politics are the tactics that strategic managers engage in to use power and to influence goals and change strategy and structure to further their own interests.

✔ To play politics, managers must have power. Power is the ability of one party to cause another party to act in a way that it would not otherwise have done.

✔ Power available to strategic managers includes legitimate power and power from informal sources, such as coping with uncertainty, centrality, control over information, nonsubstitutability, and control over contingencies and resources.

✔ Power and politics influence a company's choice of strategy and structure and the nature of the strategic changes that are implemented.

✔ Strategic managers need to evaluate the results of each change process and use this analysis to define the organization's present condition so that they can start the next change process. Well-run

companies are constantly aware of the need to monitor their performance, and strategic managers institutionalize change so that they can continually realign their strategy and structure to suit the competitive environment.

DISCUSSION QUESTIONS

1. What is the difference between reengineering, E-engineering, and restructuring?

2. What are the main obstacles to change that a company pursuing a differentiation strategy would face if it should be forced to pursue a cost-leadership strategy?

3. Discuss how you would set up a plan for change for an unrelated company that is starting to pursue a strategy of related diversification. What problems will the company encounter? How should it deal with them?

4. How can using politics to overcome obstacles to change and to resolve conflict help to implement strategic change?

Practicing Strategic Management

SMALL-GROUP EXERCISE
Handling Change

Break up into groups of three to five people, and discuss the following scenario:

You are a group of top-level strategic managers of a large, well-established computer company that has traditionally pursued a strategy of differentiation based on research and development. Now, because of intense competition, your company is being forced to pursue a combined low-cost/differentiation strategy. You have been charged with preparing a plan to change the company's structure and strategy, and you have decided on two main changes. First, you plan to reengineer the company and move from a multidivisional structure to one in which cross-functional product teams become responsible for developing each new computer model. Second, to decentralize decision making and reduce costs, you propose to restructure the company and severely cut the number of corporate and top divisional managers.

1. Discuss the nature of the obstacles to change at the organizational, functional, and individual level that you, as internal change agents, will encounter in implementing this new strategy and structure. Which do you think will be the most important obstacles to change?

2. Discuss some ways by which you can overcome obstacles to change to help your organization move to its desired future state.

STRATEGIC MANAGEMENT PROJECT
Module 14

For the final part of the Strategic Management Project, your task is to examine how your organization has managed the process of strategic change.

1. Find some examples of recent changes in your company's strategy or structure. What kinds of change did your company implement? Why did your company make these changes?

2. What, do you think, are the major obstacles to change in your organization?

3. Given the nature of your organization's strategy and structure, is conflict a likely obstacle to change in your organization? Can you find any examples of conflicts that have occurred in your organization?

4. Is there any evidence of political contests or struggles between top managers or between divisions or functions in your organization? What can you find out about the power of the CEO and the top-management team?

5. Using the informal sources of power discussed in the chapter (for example, centrality, control over resources), draw a map of the power relationships between the various managers, divisions, or functions inside your organization. On the basis of this analysis, which are the most powerful managers or subunits? Why? How do managers in the powerful subunits use power to influence decision making?

6. How well do you think strategic managers have managed the change process? What other changes do you think your company should make in its strategy or structure?

ARTICLE FILE 14

Find an example of a company that has been implementing a major change in its strategy and/or structure. Why did managers think that change was necessary? What kind of change was implemented, and what were its effects?

EXPLORING THE WEB
Managing Change

Search the Web to find a company that has recently been involved in some major kind of change process. What was the nature of the change? Why did the change take place? What problems did the company experience during the change process?

EASTMAN CHEMICALS, a former division of Eastman Kodak, is one of the success stories of the 1990s. It has totally restructured and reengineered its operations to make product quality and responsiveness to customers its major goals. So successful has it been in its quest to increase quality that it won the prestigious Malcolm Baldrige National Quality Award.[39] How did Eastman's managers bring about this change?

First, top management decided to change from its old, centralized, product-oriented divisional structure to one that was based more on the needs of its customers. Prior to the restructuring, the managers at Eastman Chemicals viewed their job as creating new kinds of chemicals and worrying about who to sell them to later. After the change, the needs of customers became their paramount concern, and they saw their business as discovering what customers wanted and then marshaling organizational resources to create new products that satisfied those wants.

Second, with their new customer-oriented structure in place, top management sat down to reengineer the product-innovation process. Under Eastman's old product-oriented division structure, all divisions operated separately and there was little communication between them. Moreover, each division was organized on functional lines and made a separate and distinct contribution to product development. The result was that product development typically took a long time, and, as mentioned earlier, the product, not the customer, was the focus. Top managers decided to change totally the way their organization worked. Cooperation between divisions and functions to speed product development and to raise product quality and customer responsiveness became the goal. Therefore, management reengineered the organization on horizontal, not vertical, lines.

Third, inside each division the old functional structure was scrapped and new cross-functional product teams, composed of people from all relevant functions, were charged with the responsibility for bringing a new product to market. To understand customers' needs better, Eastman Chemicals contacted its major customers and asked them to appoint one of their managers to work with each team. Essentially, each team was empowered to take re-

Raising Quality at Eastman Chemicals

sponsibility for all aspects of the management of the project, and decision-making responsibility in the company was forced down to the team level. Fourth, top managers decided to change the reward system and introduce an employee stock ownership plan. The result of these changes, Eastman Chemicals top managers found, was an increase in motivation, faster communication and coordination, and, what they wanted most, an increase in quality and the rate of new-product innovation.

Fifth, top managers also reengineered the relationships between divisions to promote innovation, and new interdivisional teams composed of managers from each division were created. The level of cooperation and the number of new interdivisional projects started between divisions are now monitored closely by top managers, who measure performance on both a divisional and an interdivisional level. Indeed, with the new decentralized approach to decision making, corporate managers see one of their major roles as fostering integration between divisions, just as divisional managers see one of their major roles as acting as facilitators between the cross-functional teams in their respective divisions.

This dramatic change in strategy and structure at Eastman Chemicals has not been easily achieved. Many divisional managers were very skeptical of top management's efforts at change, as were managers inside each division. There was considerable resistance at all levels; managers who saw their jobs and their responsibilities shifting were afraid of the effects the changes might have on them. Nevertheless, top managers forced through the changes, and over time, as the positive effects were seen—in an increase in the number of satisfied customers, in higher profits, and in higher salaries and stock appreciation—the whole organization bought into the new philosophy. The performance of Eastman Chemicals has soared throughout the 1990s.

Questions for Discussion

1. What were the main steps in the change process?
2. What lessons can be learned by other companies from Eastman Chemicals' experiences?

End Notes

1. www.BankAmerica.com (1999).
2. B. Garrity, "BankAmerica Syndication Group's Biggest Challenge Comes from Within: How Do You Meld Philosophies of Five Different Locations?" *Investment Dealers Digest*, November 2, 1998, pp.5–6.
3. M. T. Hannan and J. Freeman, "Structural Inertia and Organizational Change," *American Sociological Review*, 49 (1984), 149–164.
4. D. Miller, *The Icarus Paradox* (New York: Harper Business, 1990).
5. J. Thackray, "Restructuring in the Name of the Hurricane," *Euromoney* (February 1987), 106–108.
6. M. Hammer and J. Champy, *Reengineering the Corporation* (New York: HarperCollins, 1993).
7. Ibid., p.39.
8. G. D. Bruton, J. K. Keels, and C. L. Shook, "Downsizing the Firm: Answering the Strategic Questions," *Academy of Management Executive* (May 1996), 38–45.
9. D. Leonhardt, "Stirring Things Up at Quaker Oats," *Business Week*, March 30, 1998, p.42.
10. G. R. Jones, *Organizational Theory;* R. A. Burgelman and M. A. Maidique, *Strategic Management of Technology and Innovation* (Homewood, Ill.: Irwin, 1988).
11. G. R. Jones and J. E. Butler, "Managing Internal Corporate Entrepreneurship: An Agency Theory Perspective," *Journal of Management*, 18 (1992), 733–749.
12. D. Callaghan, "Aint No Mountain High Enough," *Marketing Intelligence*, June 1999, pp.72–78.
13. R. A. Burgelman, "Designs for Corporate Entrepreneurship in Established Firms," *California Management Review*, 26 (1984), 154–166.
14. D. Frey, "Learning the Ropes: My Life as a Product Champion," *Harvard Business Review* (September–October 1991), 46–56.
15. R. Beckhard, *Organizational Development* (Reading, Mass.: Addison-Wesley, 1969); W. L. French and C. H. Bell Jr., *Organizational Development*, 2nd ed. (Englewood Cliffs, NJ.: Prentice-Hall, 1978).
16. Beckhard, *Organizational Development.*
17. L. C. Coch and R. P. French Jr., "Overcoming Resistance to Change," *Human Relations* (August 1948), 512–532; P. R. Lawrence, "How to Deal with Resistance to Change," *Harvard Business Review* (January–February 1969), 4–12.
18. J. O. Huff, A. S. Huff, and H. Thomas, "Strategic Renewal and the Interaction of Cumulative Stress and Inertia," *Strategic Management Journal*, 13 (Special Issue, 1992), 55–75.
19. P. Kotter and L. A. Schlesinger, "Choosing Strategies for Change," *Harvard Business Review* (March–April 1979), 106–114.
20. J. R. Galbraith, "Designing the Innovative Organization," *Organizational Dynamics* (Winter 1982), 5–25.
21. J. A. Litterer, "Conflict in Organizations: A Reexamination," *Academy of Management Journal*, 9 (1966), 178–186; S. M. Schmidt and T. A. Kochan, "Conflict: Towards Conceptual Clarity," *Administrative Science Quarterly*, 13 (1972), 359–370.
22. L. R. Pondy, "Organizational Conflict: Concepts and Models," *Administrative Science Quarterly*, 2 (1967), 296–320.
23. A. C. Amason, "Distinguishing the Effects of Functional and Dysfunctional Conflict on Strategic Decision Making: Resolving a Paradox for Top Management Teams," *Academy of Management Journal*, 1 (1996), 123–148.
24. R. H. Miles, *Macro Organizational Behavior* (Santa Monica, Calif.: Goodyear, 1980).
25. A. M. Pettigrew, *The Politics of Organizational Decision Making* (London: Tavistock, 1973).
26. J. G. March, "The Business Firm as a Coalition," *Journal of Politics*, 24 (1962), 662–678; D. J. Vredenburgh and J. G. Maurer, "A Process Framework of Organizational Politics," *Human Relations*, 37 (1984), 47–66.
27. T. Burns, "Micropolitics: Mechanisms of Institutional Change," *Administrative Science Quarterly*, 6 (1961), 257–281.
28. R. A. Dahl, "The Concept of Power," *Behavioral Science*, 2 (1957), 201–215; G. A. Astley and P. S. Sachdeva, "Structural Sources of Intraorganizational Power," *Academy of Management Review*, 9 (1984), 104–113.
29. This section draws heavily on D. J. Hickson, C. R. Hinings, C. A. Lee, R. E. Schneck, and D. J. Pennings, "A Strategic Contingencies Theory of Intraorganizational Power," *Administrative Science Quarterly* 16, (1971), 216–227; and C. R. Hinings, D. J. Hickson, J. M. Pennings, and R. E. Schneck, "Structural Conditions of Intraorganizational Power," *Administrative Science Quarterly*, 19 (1974), 22–44.
30. Hickson et al., "A Strategic Contingencies Theory."
31. H. Ibarra, "Network Centrality, Power, and Innovation Involvement: Determinants of Technical and Administrative Roles," *Academy of Management Journal*, 36 (1993), 471–501.
32. Pettigrew, *The Politics of Organizational Decision Making.*
33. Hickson et al., "A Strategic Contingencies Theory."
34. H. A. Landsberger, "The Horizontal Dimension in Bureaucracy," *Administrative Science Quarterly*, 6 (1961), 299–322.
35. G. R. Salancik and J. Pfeffer, "The Bases and Use of Power in Organizational Decision Making: The Case of a University," *Administrative Science Quarterly*, 19 (1974), 453–473.
36. Hickson et al., "A Strategic Contingencies Theory."
37. J. Pfeffer, *Managing with Power* (Boston: Harvard Business School Press, 1992).
38. J. F. McDonnell, "Learning to Think in Different Terms: TQM & Restructuring at McDonnell Douglas," *Executive Speeches* (June–July 1994), 25–28.
39. E. A. Deavenport Jr., "Winning the Balridge Award," *Management* (June 1994), 36–38.

PART FIVE

Cases in Strategic Management

INTRODUCTION

Analyzing a Case Study and Writing a Case Study Analysis

WHAT IS CASE STUDY ANALYSIS?

Case study analysis is an integral part of a course in strategic management. The purpose of a case study is to provide students with experience of the strategic management problems faced by actual organizations. A case study presents an account of what happened to a business or industry over a number of years. It chronicles the events that managers had to deal with, such as changes in the competitive environment, and charts the managers' response, which usually involved changing the business- or corporate-level strategy. The cases in Part V of this book cover a wide range of issues and problems that managers have had to confront. Some cases are about finding the right business-level strategy to compete in changing conditions. Some are about companies that grew by acquisition, with little concern for the rationale behind their growth, and how growth by acquisition affected their future profitability. Each case is different because each organization is different. The underlying thread in all the cases, however, is the use of strategic management techniques to solve business problems.

Cases prove valuable in a strategic management course for several reasons. First, cases provide you, the student, with experience of organizational problems that you probably have not had the opportunity to experience firsthand. In a relatively short period of time, you will have the chance to appreciate and analyze the problems faced by many different companies and to understand how managers tried to deal with them.

Second, cases illustrate the theory and content of strategic management—that is, all the information presented to you in the previous chapters of this book. This information has been collected, discovered, and distilled from the observations, research, and experience of managers and academicians. The meaning and implications of this information are made clearer when they are applied to case studies. The theory and concepts help reveal what is going on in the companies studied and allow you to evaluate the solutions that specific companies adopted to deal with their problems. Consequently, when you analyze cases, you will be like a detective who, with a set of conceptual tools, probes what happened and what or who was responsible and then marshals the evidence that provides the solution. Top managers enjoy the thrill of testing their problem-solving abilities in the real world. It is important to remember, after all, that no one knows what the right answer is. All that managers can do is to make the best guess. In fact, managers say repeatedly that they are happy if they are right only half the time in solving strategic problems. Strategic management is an uncertain game, and using cases to see how theory can be put into practice is one way of improving your skills of diagnostic investigation.

Third, case studies provide you with the opportunity to participate in class and to gain experience in presenting your ideas to others. Instructors may sometimes call on students as a group to identify what is going on in a case, and through classroom discussion the issues in and solutions to the case problem will reveal themselves. In such a situation, you will have to organize your views and conclusions so that you can present them to the class. Your classmates may have analyzed the issues differently from you, and they will want you to argue your points before they will accept your conclusions; so be prepared for debate. This mode of discussion is an example of the dialectical approach to decision making that you may recall from Chapter 1. This is how decisions are made in the actual business world.

Instructors also may assign an individual, but more commonly a group, to analyze the case before the whole class. The individual or group probably will be responsible for a thirty- to forty-minute presentation of the case to the class. That presentation must cover the issues involved, the problems facing the company, and a series of recommendations for resolving the problems. The discussion then will be thrown open to the class, and you will have to defend your ideas. Through such discussions and presentations, you will experience how to convey your ideas effectively to others. Remember that a great deal of managers' time is spent in these kinds of situations, presenting their ideas and engaging in discussion with other managers, who have their own views about what is going on. Thus, you will experience in the classroom the actual process of strategic management, and this will serve you well in your future career.

If you work in groups to analyze case studies, you also will learn about the group process involved in working as a team. When people work in groups, it is often difficult to schedule time and allocate responsibility for the case analysis. There are always group members who shirk their responsibilities and group members who are so sure of their own ideas that they try to dominate the group's analysis. Most of the strategic management takes place in groups, however, and it is best if you learn about these problems now.

ANALYZING A CASE STUDY

As just mentioned, the purpose of the case study is to let you apply the concepts of strategic management when you analyze the issues facing a specific company. To analyze a case study, therefore, you must examine closely the issues with which the company is confronted. Most often you will need to read the case several times— once to grasp the overall picture of what is happening to the company and then several times more to discover and grasp the specific problems.

Generally, detailed analysis of a case study should include eight areas:

1. The history, development, and growth of the company over time

2. The identification of the company's internal strengths and weaknesses

3. The nature of the external environment surrounding the company

4. A SWOT analysis

5. The kind of corporate-level strategy pursued by the company

6. The nature of the company's business-level strategy

7. The company's structure and control systems and how they match its strategy

8. Recommendations

To analyze a case, you need to apply the concepts taught in this course to each of these areas. Where to look for a review of the concepts you need to use is obvious from the chapter titles. For example, to analyze the company's environment, you would use Chapter 3, on environmental analysis.

To help you further, we next offer a summary of some of the steps you can take to analyze the case material for each of the eight points we have just noted.

1. *Analyze the company's history, development, and growth.* A convenient way to investigate how a company's past strategy and structure affect it in the present is to chart the critical incidents in its history—that is, the events that were the most unusual or the most essential for its development into the company it is today. Some of the events have to do with its founding, its initial products, how it made new-product market decisions, and how it developed and chose functional competencies to pursue. Its entry into new businesses and shifts in its main lines of business are also important milestones to consider.

2. *Identify the company's internal strengths and weaknesses.* Once the historical profile is completed, you can begin the SWOT analysis. Use all the incidents you have charted to develop an account of the company's strengths and weaknesses as they have emerged historically. Examine each of the value creation functions of the company, and identify the functions in which the company is currently strong and currently weak. Some companies might be weak in marketing; some might be strong in research and development. Make lists of these strengths and weaknesses. The table on page C14 gives examples of what might go in these lists.

3. *Analyze the external environment.* The next step is to identify environmental opportunities and threats. Here you should apply all the concepts from Chapter 3, on industry and macroenvironments, to analyze the environment the company is confronting. Of particular importance at the industry level is Porter's five forces model and the stage of the life cycle model. Which factors in the macroenvironment will appear salient depends on the specific company being analyzed. However, use each concept in turn (for instance, demographic factors) to see whether it is relevant for the company in question.

Having done this analysis, you will have generated both an analysis of the company's environment and a list of opportunities and threats. The table on page C14 also lists some common environmental opportunities and threats that you might look for, but the list you generate will be specific to your company.

4. *Evaluate the SWOT analysis.* Having identified the company's external opportunities and threats as well as its internal strengths and weaknesses, you need to consider what your findings mean. That is, you need to balance strengths and weaknesses against opportunities and threats. Is the company in an overall strong competitive position? Can it continue to pursue its current business- or corporate-level strategy profitably? What can the company do to turn weaknesses into strengths and threats into opportunities? Can it develop new functional, business, or corporate strategies to accomplish this change? *Never merely generate the SWOT*

analysis and then put it aside. Because it provides a succinct summary of the company's condition, a good SWOT analysis is the key to all the analyses that follow.

5. *Analyze corporate-level strategy.* To analyze a company's corporate-level strategy, you first need to define the company's mission and goals. Sometimes the mission and goals are stated explicitly in the case; at other times you will have to infer them from available information. The information you need to collect to find out the company's corporate strategy includes such factors as its line(s) of business and the nature of its subsidiaries and acquisitions. It is important to analyze the relationship among the company's businesses. Do they trade or exchange resources? Are there gains to be achieved from synergy? Alternatively, is the company just running a portfolio of investments? This analysis should enable you to define the corporate strategy that the company is pursuing (for example, related or unrelated diversification, or a combination of both) and to conclude whether the company operates in just one core business. Then, using your SWOT analysis, debate the merits of this strategy. Is it appropriate, given the environment the company is in? Could a change in corporate strategy provide the company with new opportunities or transform a weakness into a strength? For example, should the company diversify from its core business into new businesses?

Other issues should be considered as well. How and why has the company's strategy changed over time? What is the claimed rationale for any changes? Often it is a good idea to analyze the company's businesses or products to assess its situation and identify which divisions contribute the most to or detract from its competitive advantage. It is also useful to explore how the company has built its portfolio over time. Did it acquire new businesses, or did it internally venture its own? All these factors provide clues about the company and indicate ways of improving its future performance.

6. *Analyze business-level strategy.* Once you know the company's corporate-level strategy and have done the SWOT analysis, the next step is to identify the company's business-level strategy. If the company is a single-business company, its business-level strategy is identical to its corporate-level strategy. If the company is in many businesses, each business will have its own business-level strategy. You will need to identify the company's generic competitive strategy—differentiation, low cost, or focus—and its investment strategy, given the company's relative competitive position and the stage of the life cycle. The company also may market different products using different business-level strategies. For example, it may offer a low-cost product range and a line of differentiated products. Be sure to give a full account of a company's business-level strategy to show how it competes.

Identifying the functional strategies that a company pursues to build competitive advantage through superior efficiency, quality, innovation, and customer responsiveness and to achieve its business-level strategy is very important. The SWOT analysis will have provided you with information on the company's functional competencies. You should further investigate its production, marketing, or research and development strategy to gain a picture of where the company is going. For example, pursuing a low-cost or a differentiation strategy successfully requires a very different set of competencies. Has the company developed the right ones? If it has, how can it exploit them further? Can it pursue both a low-cost and a differentiation strategy simultaneously?

The SWOT analysis is especially important at this point if the industry analysis, particularly Porter's model, has revealed the threats to the company from the environment. Can the company deal with these threats? How should it change its business-level strategy to counter them? To evaluate the potential of a company's business-level strategy, you must first perform a thorough SWOT analysis that captures the essence of its problems.

Once you complete this analysis, you will have a full picture of the way the company is operating and be in a position to evaluate the potential of its strategy. Thus, you will be able to make recommendations concerning the pattern of its future actions. However, first you need to consider strategy implementation, or the way the company tries to achieve its strategy.

7. *Analyze structure and control systems.* The aim of this analysis is to identify what structure and control systems the company is using to implement its strategy and to evaluate whether that structure is the appropriate one for the company. As we discuss in Chapter 13, different corporate and business strategies require different structures. Chapter 13 provides you with the conceptual tools to determine *the degree of fit between the company's strategy and structure.* For example, does the company have the right level of vertical differentiation (for instance, does it have the appropriate number of levels in the hierarchy or decentralized control?) or horizontal differentiation (does it use a functional structure when it should be using a product structure?)? Similarly, is the company using the right integration or control systems to manage its operations? Are managers being appropriately rewarded? Are the right rewards in place for encouraging cooperation among divisions? These are all issues that should be considered.

In some cases there will be little information on these issues, whereas in others there will be a lot. Obviously, in writing each case you should gear the analysis toward its most salient issues. For example, organizational conflict, power, and politics will be important issues for some companies. Try to analyze why problems in these areas are occurring. Do they occur because of bad strategy formulation or because of bad strategy implementation?

Organizational change is an issue in most of the cases because the companies are attempting to alter their strategies or structures to solve strategic problems. Thus, as a part of the analysis, you might suggest an action plan that the company in question could use to achieve its goals. For example, you might list in a logical sequence the steps the company would need to follow to alter its business-level strategy from differentiation to focus.

8. *Make recommendations.* The last part of the case analysis process involves making recommendations based on your analysis. Obviously, the quality of your recommendations is a direct result of the thoroughness with which you prepared the case analysis. The work you put into the case analysis will be obvious to the professor from the nature of your recommendations. Recommendations are directed at solving whatever strategic problem the company is facing and at increasing its future profitability. Your recommendations should be in line with your analysis; that is, they should follow logically from the previous discussion. For example, your recommendations generally will center on the specific ways of changing functional, business, and corporate strategy and organizational structure and control to improve business performance. The set of recommendations will be specific to each case, and so it is difficult to discuss these recommendations here. Such recommendations

might include an increase in spending on specific research and development projects, the divesting of certain businesses, a change from a strategy of unrelated to related diversification, an increase in the level of integration among divisions by using task forces and teams, or a move to a different kind of structure to implement a new business-level strategy. Again, make sure your recommendations are mutually consistent and are written in the form of an action plan. The plan might contain a timetable that sequences the actions for changing the company's strategy and a description of how changes at the corporate level will necessitate changes at the business level and subsequently at the functional level.

After following all these stages, you will have performed a thorough analysis of the case and will be in a position to join in class discussion or present your ideas to the class, depending on the format used by your professor. Remember that you must tailor your analysis to suit the specific issue discussed in your case. In some cases, you might completely omit one of the steps in the analysis because it is not relevant to the situation you are considering. You must be sensitive to the needs of the case and not apply the framework we have discussed in this section blindly. The framework is meant only as a guide and not as an outline that you must use to do a successful analysis.

WRITING A CASE STUDY ANALYSIS

Often, as part of your course requirements, you will need to present your instructor with a written case analysis. This may be an individual or a group report. Whatever the situation, there are certain guidelines to follow in writing a case analysis that will improve the evaluation your work will receive from your instructor. Before we discuss these guidelines and before you use them, make sure that they do not conflict with any directions your instructor has given you.

The structure of your written report is critical. Generally, if you follow the steps for analysis discussed in the previous section, *you already will have a good structure for your written discussion.* all reports begin with an *introduction* to the case. In it you outline briefly what the company does, how it developed historically, what problems it is experiencing, and how you are going to approach the issues in the case write-up. Do this sequentially by writing, for example, "First, we discuss the environment of Company X. . . . Third, we discuss Company X's business-level strategy. . . . Last, we provide recommendations for turning around Company X's business."

In the second part of the case write-up, the strategic-analysis section, do the SWOT analysis, analyze and discuss the nature and problems of the company's business-level and corporate strategy, and then analyze its structure and control systems. Make sure you use plenty of headings and subheadings to structure your analysis. For example, have separate sections on any important conceptual tool you use. Thus, you might have a section on Porter's five forces model as part of your analysis of the environment. You might offer a separate section on portfolio techniques when analyzing a company's corporate strategy. Tailor the sections and subsections to the specific issues of importance in the case.

In the third part of the case write-up, present your solutions and recommendations. Be comprehensive, and make sure they are in line with the previous analysis so that the recommendations fit together and move logically from one to the next.

The recommendations section is very revealing because, as mentioned earlier, your instructor will have a good idea of how much work you put into the case from the quality of your recommendations.

Following this framework will provide a good structure for most written reports, though obviously it must be shaped to fit the individual case being considered. Some cases are about excellent companies experiencing no problems. In such instances, it is hard to write recommendations. Instead, you can focus on analyzing why the company is doing so well, using that analysis to structure the discussion. Following are some minor suggestions that can help make a good analysis even better.

1. Do not repeat in summary form large pieces of factual information from the case. The instructor has read the case and knows what is going on. Rather, use the information in the case to illustrate your statements, to defend your arguments, or to make salient points. Beyond the brief introduction to the company, you must avoid being *descriptive;* instead, you must be *analytical.*

2. Make sure the sections and subsections of your discussion flow logically and smoothly from one to the next. That is, try to build on what has gone before so that the analysis of the case study moves toward a climax. This is particularly important for group analysis, because there is a tendency for people in a group to split up the work and say, "I'll do the beginning, you take the middle, and I'll do the end." The result is a choppy, stilted analysis because the parts do not flow from one to the next, and it is obvious to the instructor that no real group work has been done.

3. Avoid grammatical and spelling errors. They make the paper sloppy.

4. Some cases dealing with well-known companies end in 1993 or 1994 because no later information was available when the case was written. If possible, do a library search for more information on what has happened to the company in subsequent years. Following are sources of information for performing this search:

   The Internet with its World Wide Web is the place to start your research. Very often you can download copies of a company's annual report from its Web site, and many companies also keep lists of press releases and articles that have been written about them. Thoroughly search the company's Web site for information such as the company's history and performance, and download all relevant information at the beginning of your project. Yahoo is a particularly good search engine to use to discover the address of your company's Web site, although others work as well.

   Compact disk sources such as Lotus One Source and InfoTrac provide an amazing amount of good information, including summaries of recent articles written on specific companies that you can then access in the library.

   F&S Predicasts provide a listing on a yearly basis of all the articles written about a particular company. Simply reading the titles gives an indication of what has been happening in the company.

   Annual reports on a Form 10-K often provide an organization chart.

   Companies themselves provide information if you write and ask for it.

   Fortune, BusinessWeek, and *Forbes* have many articles on companies featured in the cases in this book.

Standard & Poor's industry reports provide detailed information about the competitive conditions facing the company's industry. Be sure to look at this journal.

5. Sometimes instructors hand out questions for each case to help you in your analysis. Use these as a guide for writing the case analysis. They often illuminate the important issues that have to be covered in the discussion.

If you follow the guidelines in this section, you should be able to write a thorough and effective evaluation.

GUIDELINES FOR THE STRATEGIC MANAGEMENT PROJECT

The case study guidelines just discussed also can be followed to help you conduct research for the Strategic Management Project Modules that are at the end of every chapter in this book. In order to answer the questions contained in each module, for example, it is necessary to locate and access articles on your chosen company in the same way that you will update the information on companies highlighted in the case studies. Obviously, however, you need to collect more information on your chosen company because it is *your case.*

The guidelines also can be used to help you to write your Strategic Management Project. The experience you develop from analyzing one or more of the companies in the case studies and writing the resulting report should help you improve the analytical skills needed for the Strategic Management Project. Essentially, in your Strategic Management Project, you are writing about and analyzing a company at the same time to show how that company creates value through its strategy and structure.

THE ROLE OF FINANCIAL ANALYSIS IN CASE STUDY ANALYSIS

Another important aspect of analyzing a case study and writing a case study analysis is the role and use of financial information. A careful analysis of the company's financial condition immensely improves a case write-up. After all, financial data represent the concrete results of the company's strategy and structure. Although analyzing financial statements can be quite complex, a general idea of a company's financial position can be determined through the use of ratio analysis. Financial performance ratios can be calculated from the balance sheet and income statement. These ratios can be classified into five different subgroups: profit ratios, liquidity ratios, activity ratios, leverage ratios, and shareholder-return ratios. These ratios should be compared with the industry average or the company's prior years of performance. It should be noted, however, that deviation from the average is not necessarily bad; it simply warrants further investigation. For example, young companies will have purchased assets at a different price and will likely have a different capital structure than older companies. In addition to ratio analysis, a company's cash flow position is of critical importance and should be assessed. Cash flow shows how much actual cash a company possesses.

■ Profit Ratios

Profit ratios measure the efficiency with which the company uses its resources. The more efficient the company, the greater is its profitability. It is useful to compare a company's profitability against that of its major competitors in its industry. Such a comparison tells whether the company is operating more or less efficiently than its rivals. In addition, the change in a company's profit ratios over time tells whether its performance is improving or declining.

A number of different profit ratios can be used, and each of them measures a different aspect of a company's performance. The most commonly used profit ratios are as follows:

1. *Gross profit margin.* The gross profit margin simply gives the percentage of sales available to cover general and administrative expenses and other operating costs. It is defined as follows:

$$\text{Gross Profit Margin} = \frac{\text{Sales Revenue} - \text{Cost of Goods Sold}}{\text{Sales Revenue}}$$

2. *Net profit margin.* Net profit margin is the percentage of profit earned on sales. This ratio is important because businesses need to make a profit to survive in the long run. It is defined as follows:

$$\text{Net Profit Margin} = \frac{\text{Net Income}}{\text{Sales Revenue}}$$

3. *Return on total assets.* This ratio measures the profit earned on the employment of assets. It is defined as follows:

$$\text{Return on Total Assets} = \frac{\text{Net Income Available to Common Stockholders}}{\text{Total Assets}}$$

Net income is the profit after preferred dividends (those set by contract) have been paid. Total assets include both current and noncurrent assets.

4. *Return on stockholders' equity.* This ratio measures the percentage of profit earned on common stockholders' investment in the company. In theory, a company attempting to maximize the wealth of its stockholders should be trying to maximize this ratio. It is defined as follows:

$$\text{Return on Stockholders' Equity} = \frac{\text{Net Income Available to Common Stockholders}}{\text{Stockholders' Equity}}$$

■ Liquidity Ratios

A company's liquidity is a measure of its ability to meet short-term obligations. An asset is deemed liquid if it can be readily converted into cash. Liquid assets are current assets such as cash, marketable securities, accounts receivable, and so on. Two commonly used liquidity ratios are as follows:

1. *Current ratio.* The current ratio measures the extent to which the claims of short-term creditors are covered by assets that can be quickly converted into cash. Most companies should have a ratio of at least 1, because failure to meet these commitments can lead to bankruptcy. The ratio is defined as follows:

$$\text{Current Ratio} = \frac{\text{Current Assets}}{\text{Current Liabilities}}$$

2. *Quick ratio.* The quick ratio measures a company's ability to pay off the claims of short-term creditors without relying on the sale of its inventories. This is a valuable measure since in practice the sale of inventories is often difficult. It is defined as follows:

$$\text{Quick Ratio} = \frac{\text{Current Assets} - \text{Inventory}}{\text{Current Liabilities}}$$

■ Activity Ratios

Activity ratios indicate how effectively a company is managing its assets. The following two ratios are particularly useful.

1. *Inventory turnover.* This measures the number of times inventory is turned over. It is useful in determining whether a firm is carrying excess stock in inventory. It is defined as follows:

$$\text{Inventory Turnover} = \frac{\text{Cost of Goods Sold}}{\text{Inventory}}$$

Cost of goods sold is a better measure of turnover than sales, since it is the cost of the inventory items. Inventory is taken at the balance sheet date. Some companies choose to compute an average inventory, beginning inventory, plus ending inventory, but for simplicity use the inventory at the balance sheet date.

2. *Days sales outstanding (DSO), or average collection period.* This ratio is the average time a company has to wait to receive its cash after making a sale. It measures how effective the company's credit, billing, and collection procedures are. It is defined as follows:

$$\text{DSO} = \frac{\text{Accounts Receivable}}{\text{Total Sales}/360}$$

Accounts receivable is divided by average daily sales. The use of 360 is the standard number of days for most financial analysis.

■ Leverage Ratios

A company is said to be highly leveraged if it uses more debt than equity, including stock and retained earnings. The balance between debt and equity is called the *capital structure.* The optimal capital structure is determined by the individual company. Debt has a lower cost because creditors take less risk; they know they will get their interest and principal. However, debt can be risky to the firm because if enough profit is not made to cover the interest and principal payments, bankruptcy can occur.

Three commonly used leverage ratios are as follows:

1. *Debt-to-assets ratio.* The debt-to-asset ratio is the most direct measure of the extent to which borrowed funds have been used to finance a company's investments. It is defined as follows:

$$\text{Debt-to-Assets Ratio} = \frac{\text{Total Debt}}{\text{Total Assets}}$$

Total debt is the sum of a company's current liabilities and its long-term debt, and total assets are the sum of fixed assets and current assets.

2. *Debt-to-equity ratio.* The debt-to-equity ratio indicates the balance between debt and equity in a company's capital structure. This is perhaps the most widely used measure of a company's leverage. It is defined as follows:

$$\text{Debt-to-Equity Ratio} = \frac{\text{Total Debt}}{\text{Total Equity}}$$

3. *Times-covered ratio.* The times-covered ratio measures the extent to which a company's gross profit covers its annual interest payments. If the times-covered ratio declines to less than 1, then the company is unable to meet its interest costs and is technically insolvent. The ratio is defined as follows:

$$\text{Times-Covered Ratio} = \frac{\text{Profit Before Interest and Tax}}{\text{Total Interest Charges}}$$

■ Shareholder-Return Ratios

Shareholder-return ratios measure the return earned by shareholders from holding stock in the company. Given the goal of maximizing stockholders' wealth, providing shareholders with an adequate rate of return is a primary objective of most companies. As with profit ratios, it can be helpful to compare a company's shareholders returns against those of similar companies. This provides a yardstick for determining how well the company is satisfying the demands of this particularly important group of organizational constituents. Four commonly used ratios are as follows:

1. *Total shareholder returns.* Total shareholder returns measure the returns earned by time $t + 1$ on an investment in a company's stock made at time t. (Time t is the time at which the initial investment is made.) Total shareholder returns include both dividend payments and appreciation in the value of the stock (adjusted for stock splits) and are defined as follows:

$$\text{Total Shareholder Returns} = \frac{\text{Stock Price } (t + 1)\text{-Stock Price } (t) + \text{Sum of Annual Dividends per Share}}{\text{Stock Price } (t)}$$

Thus, if a shareholder invests $2 at time t, and at time $t +1$ the share is worth $3, while the sum of annual dividends for the period t to $t + 1$ has amounted to $0.2, total shareholder returns are equal to $(3 - 2 + 0.2)/2 = 0.6$, which is a 60 percent return on an initial investment of $2 made at time t.

2. *Price-earnings ratio.* The price-earnings ratio measures the amount investors are willing to pay per dollar of profit. It is defined as follows:

$$\text{Price-Earnings Ratio} = \frac{\text{Market Price per Share}}{\text{Earnings per Share}}$$

3. *Market to book value.* Another useful ratio is market to book value. This measures a company's expected future growth prospects. It is defined as follows:

$$\text{Market to Book Value} = \frac{\text{Market Price per Share}}{\text{Earnings per Share}}$$

4. *Dividend yield.* The dividend yield measures the return to shareholders received in the form of dividends. It is defined as follows:

$$\text{Dividend Yield} = \frac{\text{Dividend per Share}}{\text{Market Price per Share}}$$

Market price per share can be calculated for the first of the year, in which case the dividend yield refers to the return on an investment made at the beginning of the year. Alternatively, the average share price over the year may be used. A company must decide how much of its profits to pay to stockholders and how much to reinvest in the company. Companies with strong growth prospects should have a lower dividend payout ratio than mature companies. The rationale is that shareholders can invest the money elsewhere if the company is not growing. The optimal ratio depends on the individual firm, but the key decider is whether the company can produce better returns than the investor can earn elsewhere.

■ Cash Flow

Cash flow position is simply cash received minus cash distributed. The net cash flow can be taken from a company's statement of cash flows. Cash flow is important for what it tells us about a company's financing needs. A strong positive cash flow enables a company to fund future investments without having to borrow money from bankers or investors. This is desirable because the company avoids the need to pay out interest or dividends. A weak or negative cash flow means that a company has to turn to external sources to fund future investments. Generally, companies in strong-growth industries often find themselves in a poor cash flow position (because their investment needs are substantial), whereas successful companies based in mature industries generally find themselves in a strong cash flow position.

A company's internally generated cash flow is calculated by adding back its depreciation provision to profits after interest, taxes, and dividend payments. If this figure is insufficient to cover proposed new-investment expenditures, the company has little choice but to borrow funds to make up the shortfall or to curtail investments. If this figure exceeds proposed new investments, the company can use the excess to build up its liquidity (that is, through investments in financial assets) or to repay existing loans ahead of schedule.

CONCLUSION

When evaluating a case, it is important to be *systematic*. Analyze the case in a logical fashion, beginning with the identification of operating and financial strengths and weaknesses and environmental opportunities and threats. Move on to assess the value of a company's current strategies only when you are fully conversant with the SWOT analysis of the company. Ask yourself whether the company's current strategies make sense, given its SWOT analysis. If they do not, what changes need to be made? What are your recommendations? Above all, link any strategic recommendations you may make to the SWOT analysis. State explicitly how the strategies you identify take advantage of the company's strengths to exploit environmental opportunities, how they rectify the company's weaknesses, and how they counter environmental threats. Also, do not forget to outline what needs to be done to implement your recommendations.

TABLE 1

A SWOT Checklist

Potential internal strengths	Potential internal weaknesses
Many product lines?	Obsolete, narrow product lines?
Broad market coverage?	Rising manufacturing costs?
Manufacturing competence?	Decline in R&D innovations?
Good marketing skills?	Poor marketing plan?
Good materials management systems?	Poor material management systems?
R&D skills and leadership?	Loss of customer good will?
Information system competencies?	Inadequate human resources?
Human resource competencies?	Inadequate information systems?
Brand name reputation?	Loss of brand name capital?
Portfolio management skills?	Growth without direction?
Cost of differentiation advantage?	Bad portfolio management?
New-venture management expertise?	Loss of corporate direction?
Appropriate management style?	Infighting among divisions?
Appropriate organizational structure?	Loss of corporate control?
Appropriate control systems?	Inappropriate organizational structure and control systems?
Ability to manage strategic change?	High conflict and politics?
Well-developed corporate strategy?	Poor financial management?
Good financial management?	Others?
Others?	
Potential environmental opportunities	Potential environmental threats
Expand core business(es)?	Attacks on core business(es)?
Exploit new market segments?	Increases in domestic competition?
Widen product range?	Increase in foreign competition?
Extend cost or differentiation advantage?	Change in consumer tastes?
Diversify into new growth businesses?	Fall in barriers to entry?
Expand into foreign markets?	Rise in new or substitute products?
Apply R&D skills in new areas?	Increase in industry rivalry?
Enter new related businesses?	New forms of industry competition?
Vertically integrate forward?	Potential for takeover?
Vertically integrate backward?	Existence of corporate raiders?
Enlarge corporate portfolio?	Increase in regional competition?
Overcome barriers to entry?	Changes in demographic factors?
Reduce rivalry among competitors?	Changes in economic factors?
Make profitable new acquisitions?	Downturn in economy?
Apply brand name capital in new areas?	Rising labor costs?
Seek fast market growth?	Slower market growth?
Others?	Others?

A

Small Business, Entrepreneurship, and Ethics Cases

Artistic Impressions, Inc.: Developing An Entrepreneurial Growth Strategy

This case was prepared by James W. Camerius of Northern Michigan University and James W. Clinton of the University of Northern Colorado.

INTRODUCTION

"I think that there's plenty of opportunity out there and I don't think that we're scratching the surface in the African-American market," suggested Bart Breighner, president and chief executive officer of Artistic Impressions, Inc. "But the reality is that African-Americans make up only 10 percent of this country's population of close to 300 million. I want the whole shot, so we're going to do things to grow the Caucasian market."

Bart Breighner was excited and optimistic about the future of the company he had created. Artistic Impressions was a rapidly growing direct seller of affordable art works for the home and office. The firm had a plan to achieve sales of $25 million in 1998. Twice ranked in the top 500 fastest-growing private companies in the United States, according to *INC.* magazine, the company had its sales increase more than 962 percent in the past five years.

Artistic Impressions, with corporate offices and distribution center in Lombard, Illinois, a western suburb of Chicago, sold paintings and other art works through more than 2,700 salespeople in over forty states, primarily to African-Americans.

The selling was done by means of home art shows—a form of the direct marketing party plan. The corporate strategy was based on a perceived market need and a compensation system designed to reward salespeople with substantial commissions. Breighner was certain he had positioned the firm for future growth. Breighner called a meeting of his staff to discuss repositioning the firm for the future. He asked the staff to respond to the following issues: "What do we need to do to get us where we want to go, to reach the kind of customer we want to reach, and to recruit and maintain the kind of sales force that will grow the business?"

BART BREIGHNER

Bart Breighner had graduated from the University of Maryland. In 1962, he was making $4,500 a year as a teacher of high school math. Six years later, he earned $100,000 a year as a manager for World Book Encyclopedia. He had a thirty-year track record in the direct selling field, primarily with World Book Encyclopedia. In his twenty-one years with World Book, he had built field sales organizations. For the last seven of those years, he held the position of executive vice president and director of North American sales. Reflecting on that period, he said:

> They sent me through the Harvard University Advanced Management Program. As part of my job responsibility, I traveled around the world.... that was an exciting career. But the company

This case is intended to be used as a basis for class discussion rather than as an illustration of either effective or ineffective handling of the situation. This case was prepared by James W. Camerius, Northern Michigan University, and James W. Clinton, University of Northern Colorado. Used by permission.

was sold twice, and I wasn't politically adept at dealing with the paternalistic environment. I wasn't comfortable and I did move on. I decided to become an entrepreneur."

Breighner next entered the loan consulting business on a freelance basis, by starting a small but profitable financial planning company. He left after a short period of time to become a consultant to Bee Line Fashions, an $80 million company experiencing financial difficulties. Tiring again of the corporate environment, he left after six months because "We could not agree on how we were going to salvage [the company].... it was going way down. At that point, I said, Hey, who was I kidding? I'm too rambunctious to report to someone else."

After additional experience in training and recruiting programs, Breighner decided to return to direct selling. "I missed direct sales and the psychic rewards the business offers," he recalled. "I looked into possibilities and capital requirements." He surveyed the field to identify an unsatisfied market need. He felt that he wanted to "control his own destiny" at that midcareer point in his life. A number of fields in direct sales are relatively crowded—such as nutrition and cosmetic and facial products—but there are very few successful home enhancement companies. Consequently, he founded Artistic Impressions, Inc., in 1985.

In 1995, in his book, *Face to Face Selling*, Breighner detailed the steps individuals needed to take in order to get started and succeed in sales—steps such as setting goals, preparing mentally, and developing a sales presentation. The book also explored what Breighner called "the art of creative confrontation" to effectively deal with others. He used many of his own experiences throughout the book, citing creative sales techniques for new and experienced salespeople.

Breighner believed that his initial motivation to enter direct selling came from a popular platform speaker whom he had met early in his career. When asked why he was still working in the field at the age of seventy, the speaker said, "I need the money."

When Breighner started Artistic Impressions, he intended it to become the dominant company in the industry. "Success is intentional," he said. Breighner was a finalist several times for the Entrepreneur of the Year award sponsored by Ernst & Young, an accounting and consulting firm. He also created a comprehensive videotape series for training his sales force, with an emphasis on building confidence in even the most inexperienced new consultant. He also served on the board of directors of the Direct Selling Association, an industry organization located in Washington, D.C.

THE DIRECT SALES ENVIRONMENT

The direct selling industry consisted of a few well-established companies and many smaller firms that sold a broad range of products, such as toys, animal food, plant-care products, clothing, computer software, and financial services. Avon (cosmetics), Amway Corporation (home cleaning products), Shaklee Corporation (vitamins and health foods), World Book, Encyclopaedia Britannica, Tupperware (plastic dishes and food containers), Kirby (vacuum cleaners), and Mary Kay (cosmetics) dominated this market. By the 1980s, analysts believed that the industry was in a mature stage of development, including a high concentration of firms selling nutritional products (vitamins) and facial products (cosmetics).

Spectacular sales growth, characteristic of the 1960s and 1970s, had given way in most firms to a pattern of stagnant revenues and profits. The industry found it difficult to attract new salespeople, who were typically responsible for generating much of a company's sales growth. Industry problems were blamed on the increasing number of men and women who worked full time, which made it difficult to find enough recruits for part-time sales and to reach sales targets. An improved economy, too, was faulted, for it encouraged some potential customers to avoid purchasing items from part-time salespeople and shop instead at established retail stores for more expensive products. In addition, the marketplace had become more sophisticated, forcing manufacturers to develop new, more upscale, products and modify existing ones, which were outdated.

As Breighner saw it, Artistic Impressions offered a career in direct sales that would appeal to individuals who wanted to be independent, successful businesspeople,—and particularly to those in other careers who feared being displaced through corporate downsizing. Breighner also believed that successful professionals who were frustrated in their present positions and wanted a midcareer change would find satisfaction in selling his company's products. "Our people, who are independent contractors, see our company as a vehicle for obtaining financial independence," he suggested.

On reviewing the direct selling field in 1984, Breighner concluded that there were very few successful "home enhancement companies." A major competitor in the field was a firm called Home Interiors, with annual sales of about $500 million. Several smaller companies were less of a threat. Breighner indicated that while he respected their product lines and their business methods, he felt that the market would support and probably needed an art product for the home that was more upscale than what was available. He perceived an opening for a different kind of company.

THE ORGANIZATION

Artistic Impressions was a privately held, multilevel direct sales organization. A multilevel organization is one in which a hierarchical network of distributors is created to sell and distribute a product line. What distinguishes this approach is the fact that each distributor in the network is not only seeking to make retail sales of goods and services to the final consumer, but is also looking for distributors to join his or her distribution network. By recruiting and training new distributors, the recruiter becomes a master distributor who earns sales commissions and bonuses on the retail sales of all distributors within the network. Artistic Impressions' primary business was selling framed art by means of the party plan. The party plan method of at-home retailing requires a salesperson to make sales presentations in the home of a host or hostess who has invited potential customers to a "party." Usually, the party plan includes various games and other entertainment activities, in which participants receive small inexpensive gifts. Closing the sale occurs when the salesperson takes orders from the people attending the party.

According to the company's mission statement, "Artistic Impressions exists to provide quality art at affordable prices to enhance the American home." But, Breighner noted, the primary goal of the firm, or any company, was to survive, and the second goal was to be consistently profitable—"profit is not something that is left over."

Although Breighner was Caucasian, African-Americans made up 90 percent of his company's sales force, as well as 90 percent of its customers. As Breighner explained,

It wasn't intentional. It just went that way, because of the direction of the organization. We got some powerful management and sales people with exceptional educational and professional backgrounds who just happened to be African-American. I would like to have a blended company, that is, a company that reflects the population as a whole. Some people call this diversity.

Given the customer base, the primary focus of the company's product line was art that would appeal to African-Americans. "We have a very large African-American community," Deborah Thompson-Widmer, the company's director of promotions and communications, who is Caucasian, pointed out, adding that "It's very hard to find African-American art out there. We hit a gold mine . . . [in this area], and [our products] really met a need."

A former associate dean of admissions at Ripon College in Wisconsin, Thompson-Widmer oversaw three departments at Artistic Impressions. Field service processed new applications for sales representatives, monitored the productivity of sales representatives, and generated reports for team managers. Promotions sought to motivate the sales force by developing incentives such as contests, customer specials, and hostess specials. The third department, marketing, developed promotional materials and videos. Thompson-Widmer stressed the importance for the company of

a whole trend in the economy where people are staying home more, they're doing more things at home, they're entertaining in the home, and they want to decorate the home. That has helped us. So many people don't go to galleries because they don't think they can afford gallery art. So many people want to decorate but they don't get to the store, they don't know what to get.

Artistic Impressions discovered that religious art appealed greatly to the African-American community. In two paintings, *The Last Supper*, by the artist R. Williams, and *Praying Hands*, the flesh tones were darker than in other portrayals. The company's version appeared as a replica of an original painting, but done in darker flesh tones. The design was also available as a figurine. Other art works depicted African-Americans in various true-to-life situations. The product line also included landscapes, florals, still lifes, and abstracts that had a broader appeal and did not emphasize ethnic background as strongly.

Another emerging market niche that the company was just beginning to explore was Hispanic art. Thompson-Widmer noted that

> We have a very strong group of sellers in Puerto Rico. They're asking for more and more Hispanic art. We've started to branch into that because the marketplace is telling us that we have a segment of people saying this is what we need, and that's where we are going. We're in a really big growth spurt now. Sales for the year are up 30 percent. We're booming in the number of recruits coming in and the number of states we're in. It's a very exciting process. We really want to stay in the United States. We did Puerto Rico because it's easy to ship. If there was a direction we would go first, it probably would be Canada.

THE PROCESS

Identifying a Market Need

In the 1980s, marketing studies conducted by World Book Encyclopedia revealed that the field of home beautification was going to grow in the future. "I made a mental note at that time that the field was hot and was going to continue to be hot," Bart Breighner recalled. "I made lists of what business I could be in. Later that factor plus my more than twenty years of experience of recruiting, training, and developing direct sales people combined to show me a way to capitalize on my assets."

During his trips to Europe, Breighner came to enjoy art in general and accumulated a collection of moderately priced art works. While searching for a new residence in the western suburbs of Chicago, he observed that the art decorating people's homes was not very attractive. Often, ordinary posters served as the centerpiece of home decoration. He felt that he could provide products to the American public that would enhance their quality of life. Hence, he defined the nature of the business as "home enhancement." The core of his strategy was to (1) find a need, (2) develop a product to fill it, and (3) develop a compensation system that would allow the firm to fulfill its objectives and at the same time provide above average income for its sales force. Entry-level participants were to be known as consultants. The marketing program at Artistic Impressions was based on "consultants who take pride in making homes and offices more attractive by offering beautiful, affordable pieces of artwork in the comfort of a home or office."

Although first-year sales reached $500,000, the company lost $120,000. The following year's sales tripled to $1.5 million, doubled the next year to $3 million, were $5 million in the fourth year, and $6.5 million the fifth. The company currently recorded ninety-one months of consecutive increases over the previous month. Breighner anticipated doubling sales over the next three years.

THE PRODUCT LINE

The product line featured more than 375 hand-painted originals, serigraphs, lithographs and prints, with over 150 specialized framing options. The company also sold limited edition figurines and collector plates. These items were illustrated in a 100-page company catalog. The art came from thousands of artists from around the world. In addition, the company also sold a broad spectrum of art created by artists with whom it had contracted on an independent basis—for instance, H. Hargrove, a popular creator of Americana. As mentioned earlier, it also sold ethnic and religious art, which it felt could interest a diverse audience but appealed primarily to African-Americans and other ethnic groups.

Renee DeRosa was in charge of product development. She attended art shows around the country, and artists contacted her about their work. A product committee reviewed the art to evaluate its market potential. The committee also worked with regional managers to identify regional tastes. Customer tastes and preferences filtered up from the field to the product committee, which made the marketing decision. Committee members followed trends in decorating, color schemes, and styles, knowing that what was popular in California might not be in New York.

To introduce new products, Artistic Impressions' management periodically published new catalog supplements. The 1998 supplement showed several examples of a new process, developed by the company, called stochastic reproduction. It is a technique for producing tones and colors with sharper and clearer imaging. It allowed colors and images to "jump off the canvas" and provide a "life-like appearance."

As Breighner recalls:

We were in business only two years when a Korean-American, who was in the forefront of replicating painting on canvas from original oil paintings, came to work for Artistic. We started producing paintings on canvas, what we call lithographic canvas. That was the key. It revolutionized our business. Some people call them prints on canvas, because they're reproductions from an original oil painting. We also developed a studio and hired some foreign artists—Koreans, Chinese, and Russian. We have the technology to reproduce the same abstract painting over and over.

PROMOTION

As stated earlier, the marketing system of Artistic Impressions comprised approximately 2,700 salespeople, who operated in more than forty states. In 1997, representatives of the company conducted more than 40,000 art shows. They arranged with hosts to invite friends, relatives, and acquaintances into living rooms to view sixty or more paintings, many of which were originals. Guests were pre-screened before each home so that the show could be customized for them. Consultants could request any type of artwork. If the person hosting the show wanted contemporary works in burgundies and greens, he or she would be sent twenty to thirty paintings with these color schemes.

When a show was scheduled, the consultant arrived at the host's home and displayed the artwork on an easel with up to forty framed samples. After the show, the guests, often including both husbands and wives, had an opportunity to buy the paintings. Typically, five to ten people attended a show and the presentation lasted about an hour. Future hosts were often selected from guests at the show. Hosts were eligible to purchase paintings from the company's product line at substantial discounts.

A consultant could earn up to $50 an hour for a show. The person hosting it would get 10 percent of the show's sales, which averaged $1,000—or $100 off a piece of artwork. If two of his or her guests ask to do a show in the future, he or she would get another $100 off another piece of artwork for each hostess. The typical art consultant who worked one night a week earned more than $10,000 a year. Special incentives to motivate associates included discounts on art, prizes, and trips to London, Switzerland, Hawaii, and Acapulco, Mexico. Commissions for consultants started at 22 percent and increased, depending on sales volume. "The consultants get about $8,000 in inventory they can use and trade every week through resupply to get new paintings for the shows," Thompson-Widmer said. "Our consultants do nothing more than set up shows, sell, get the commission, recruit more people, and we take care of the other aspects of the business."

The corporate sales training program, called "The System Works," was provided free to consultants by corporate management. Sales consultants were encouraged to qualify for management opportunities by recruiting others to become consultants. In this multilevel organization, consultants were eligible to initially become sales directors after recruiting three people as consultants. As sales directors, they earned commissions and bonuses on sales made by their new recruits. "The sales director gets an override, a percentage payback for training the consultants under them. The override increases with each level. We always pay four levels down," Thompson-Widmer explained. "Everything is based on current production, team building and team sales volume."

The first level of management was the sales director, and the next level, the regional manager. The regional manager supervised two sales directors. A regional manager with a team of two sales directors and twenty-four consultants scheduling, on average, two weekly shows each, could earn more than $50,000 annually. Some of the senior managers supervised several hundred independent contractors. The next level, zone manager, included two regions with twelve people each plus six people under them plus the individual. The top level was the executive manager, who supervised four zones in the hierarchy: consultants, sales directors, regional managers, and zone managers. Commission and bonuses increased as one moved up the hierarchy. In 1998, the sales force was primarily African-American. It was headed by Cedric Hill, also an African-American, who was president of the sales division. Before joining the Artistic Impressions management team, Hill was an aerospace engineer working at NASA. Hill and his team generated $8 million worth of sales within five years of joining the company.

To motivate sales associates, the company held an annual convention at a hotel in the Chicago area. The three-day event was designed as a business and networking environment. It featured a series of meetings of active consultants, team competition, new product introduction, entertainment, motivational sessions, and sales performance recognition. The artists who created the artwork sold by the company attended the convention, displaying their latest work and meeting with the company's representatives. Each year, Artistic Impressions recognized top achievers at all levels in personal sales, number of shows given, recruiting of new consultants, and so forth. Those attending the convention paid their own expenses. "We hold two regional meetings every year for our managers and keep training them," said Thompson-Widmer. "We also send our trainers from our corporate office to help train in the field as well. We pretty much run our business interacting with about seventy to seventy-five regional and zone managers. Although we send out mailings to all our representatives, our focus is to hit the regional managers."

The company did no national or regional advertising. Publicity was limited to feature stories on the company and its activities in magazines such as *Black Enterprise.*

DISTRIBUTION

Sales associates were not required to purchase inventory or deliver merchandise. The company shipped all products by United Parcel Service (UPS) from a distribution center adjacent to corporate headquarters in Lombard, Illinois, to the show host, who delivered them to customers. Approximately 7,000 framed paintings per week were shipped to show hosts.

PRICE

Listed prices of art works included the choice of frame from a basic line of thirty frames. The price range for the majority of artwork sold was $69 to $149. The company was concerned that the price of its product be kept within an affordable range for its customers. If customers chose the artwork of an upscale designer or a specialized, higher-quality, museum frame, they paid additional charges. Designer frames ranged in price from $10 to $30 more, depending on the size of the frame. The museum line of frames was available in only two sizes and sold for either $60 or $80. Frame liners were also available and cost from $10 to $30, depending on the size of artwork selected. Limited editions of figurines and plates sold exclusively by Artistic Impressions started at $29.95. Some special figurines emulated original paintings also sold by the company. R. Williams's *The Last Supper* was one such work, priced at $159.

CORPORATE RESPONSIBILITY

Artistic Impressions created a partnership with the National Foundation for Teaching Entrepreneurship (NFTE). Breighner served as its chairman, maintaining that it was important to "donate your talents as well as money to organizations of this type." He had raised more than $500,000 in the last five years for NFTE. NFTE provided entrepreneurial and motivational training for inner city youth, along with a practical plan for exiting poverty. Breighner intended to sponsor about twelve summer camps, to be offered free to inner city youth from up to a dozen U.S. cities. The Direct Selling Association honored Artistic Impressions with the "Vision for Tomorrow" award in recognition of its "contribution to support and launch the careers of disadvantaged youth."

THE CHALLENGE

Breighner was certain that he had positioned Artistic Impressions for continued success by appealing to a wider market. Others on his executive team were not so sure. They felt that the company was already struggling in 1998 just to get 7,000 mostly African-American paintings out to current customers. Some thought that any attempt to enter new markets would distract from the highly successful niche strategy that the company had developed since its inception. But Breighner held his ground:

The business we're in is selling art, framed art, and we do it primarily with a party plan, the home show method. But we're going to redo the mission because frankly, we're an opportunity-driven company.

References

Artistic Impressions, Inc. "Share the Exciting World of Art." Company sales brochure, 1998.

Artistic Impressions, Inc. Catalog Supplement, 1998.

Breighner, Bart. *Face to Face Selling*. Indianapolis: Park Avenue Publications, 1995.

Camerius, J. W., and J. W. Clinton. Interview with Bart Breighner, founder and president of Artistic Impressions, Inc. Lombard, Ill., May 12, 1998.

———. Interview with Deborah Thompson-Widmer, director of promotions and communications, Artistic Impressions, Inc. Lombard, Illinois, May 12, 1998.

Kuratko, D. F., and R. M. Hodgetts, *Entrepreneurship: A Contemporary Approach*. Fort Worth: Dryden Press, 1998.

Pride, W. M., and O. C. Ferrell. *Marketing: Concepts and Strategies*. Boston: Houghton Mifflin Company, 1993.

CASE 2

Brithinee Electric Revisited: *"... Raising the Standards"*

This case was prepared by Harold Dyck and Sue Greenfeld of California State University, San Bernadino.

INTRODUCTION

As teenagers, identical twins Wallace Jr. and Don Brithinee helped when their father, Wallace Sr., started Brithinee Electric in 1963. Back then, the entire business consisted of repairing electric motors. Providing service to customers with critical motor repair needs became an enduring philosophy of Brithinee Electric. On occasion, this meant "working around the clock." Hard work eventually earned the twin brothers Ph.D.'s in mathematics from the University of California, Riverside, by the time they were twenty-three years old, and led to the success of the firm in the succeeding decades. This success is demonstrated by various industry and manufacturers' awards presented to Brithinee Electric, proudly displayed in the lobby. Upstairs in the entrance to the conference room are pictures of Wally and Don Brithinee with distinguished political figures, including former head of the Joint Chiefs of Staff, General Colin Powell, and former British Prime Minister Margaret Thatcher.

Brithinee Electric repairs industrial motors, distributes motor-control devices, and designs and builds control panels, primarily for municipalities

This case is intended to be used as the basis for class discussion rather than as an illustration of either effective or ineffective handling of the situation. This case was prepared by Harold Dyck, Ph.D., and Susan Greenfeld, D.B.A., California State University, San Bernardino. It was presented at North Armerican Case Research Association meeting, Sonoma, California, October 1999. Used by permission.

and other businesses. In 1988, when this Colton, California, firm marked its twenty-five years in business, it had twenty-three employees, and $4.6 million in revenue. In subsequent years, a case study about it appeared in three strategic management textbooks.[1] The most pressing issues facing the company then included employee development, job rotation, overdependence on the "Brithinee boys," and a possible expansion. As the company was located in the Inland Empire (about 50 miles directly east of Los Angeles), an expansion would have meant serving the San Diego area with a new facility there. At that time, the company had an implied mission based on quality and service but no formal mission statement.

By 1999, Brithinee Electric had made many improvements and experienced a number of market developments. The company had witnessed a recession, lost a $1 million per year customer, observed dramatic changes in its industry, and improved employee training. It was less concerned about job rotation, had solved most of the overdependence issues, and had decided not to expand to San Diego. The firm also formalized a mission statement that included "enabling the customer" as an aim. The Brithinee philosophy means empowering their multiethnic employees to "provide literature, materials, specifications, and some learning opportunities for our customers." In addition, the company recently added the words "Brithinee Electric ...Raising the Standards" to its "Customer Bill of Rights" (see Figures 1 and 2).

FIGURE I

Brithinee's Mission Statement

> **Brithinee Electric**
>
> **Our mission**
>
> *to delight our customers by delivering
> products and services of superior quality,
> thereby raising their expectations.*

Having grown their company to fifty employees and $6.7 million in revenues, Wally and Don Brithinee, sole owners of Brithinee Electric, now face different issues, many not foreseen in 1988. For example, the competition for selling electric motors is far more serious today than eleven years ago, and the market has changed toward more sophisticated control devices. Brithinee Electric faces these questions: How does an independent motor rewinding shop position itself for the twenty-first century? How can it distinguish itself from the competition? Can it position itself as a high-quality service provider when the customers don't understand the need for the standards? Figure 3 presents

FIGURE 2

Brithinee's Customer
Bill of Rights

CUSTOMER BILL OF RIGHTS

At Brithinee Electric, we believe both the customer and the supplier of electrical hardware and service will benefit if the purchase decision is an informed one. Assert your rights as customer by getting to know your vendor's business practices. Get maximum value by comparing the vendor's commitment as well as the price.

As a customer of Brithinee Electric, you have the right to expect:

RELIABILITY
* Stable workforce
* Work references
* Sound financial condition
* Environmental responsibility

QUALITY
* Qualified personnel
* Documentation
* Pride in workmanship
* Best available technology

COMMUNICATION
* Before and after tests reports
* Prompt and accurate quotations
* Product and service alternatives
* Accurate itemized invoices

COMMITMENT
* Service
* Investment in technology and our facility
* Investment in inventory
* Problem solving

*BRITHINEE
ELECTRIC
... Raising the Standards*

FIGURE 3

Brithinee Electric's Organization Chart

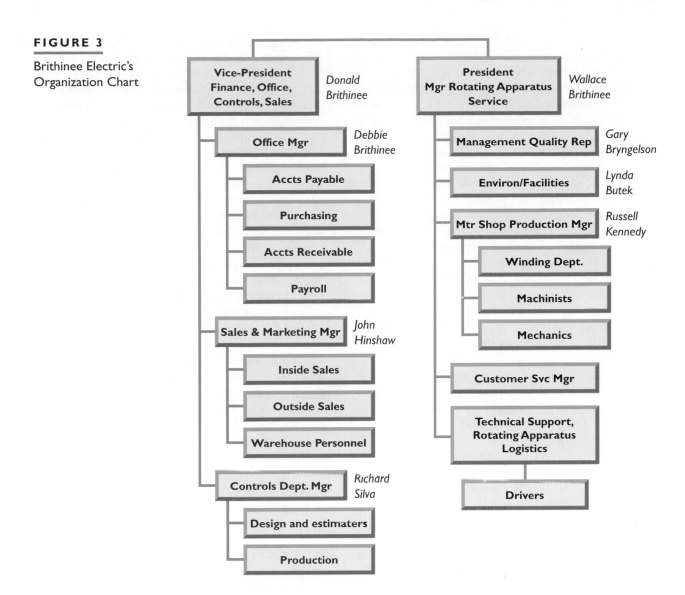

the current organizational chart, showing Wally and Don Brithinee and key Brithinee personnel.

COMPANY HISTORY

Wallace Brithinee Sr. started Brithinee Electric in 1963 after two previous ventures did not work out. However, these earlier ventures were the springboard for the formation of this third endeavor in repairing industrial motors. Even as young boys, Wally and Don Brithinee were learning the rewinding business and worked alongside their father in starting and developing the fledgling company.

In 1970, when Lincoln Electric, a large manufacturer of electric motors, came out with an appealing low-price motor, the Brithinees made a strategic decision to become distributors in addition to repairing motors. This allowed the company to offer a choice to the customer: replace or repair. By 1972, Brithinee Electric had seven employees and enough business to feel optimistic about the future—so it built a 10,000 square-foot facility, which was expanded to 16,750 square feet seven years later. By 1980, the company had twenty-three employees, and in 1982, Wallace Sr. stepped down, with Wally and Don Brithinee taking over the business.

In 1987, Brithinee had about $4.5 million in revenue, 75 percent of it from sales distribution (primarily for Toshiba and Baldor) and 25 percent from repair of motors. Building customized control panels, a new venture with one full-time employee, was not material enough to be listed as a separate category in the company's financial statements.

Various governmental agencies and utilities in the United States and Canada place the energy use of electric motors in industry at about 70 percent of total electrical energy consumption—roughly equivalent to the energy consumption of all passenger automobiles. Just as poor repair practices can increase gasoline consumption in an automobile, poor repair practices performed in the repair of an electric motor can decrease its energy efficiency. Thus, when Iraq invaded Kuwait in August 1990, threatening Western oil supplies, legislators in the United States and Canada revised energy legislation from the 1970s. Regulators, noting that the motor horsepower repaired far exceeds the horsepower sold new, studied the repair process for electric motors, as well as the purchasing practices of industrial firms. Although draconian measures such as licensing schemes or even the banning of motor repair in favor of replacement with new, energy-efficient models were being considered, the sentiment for less government intervention led to voluntary-compliance programs that seek to transform the market.

Besides trying to reduce U.S. dependence on foreign oil, the U.S. government signed several climate-change treaties (for instance, Rio de Janeiro and Kyoto) and agreed to reduce greenhouse gas emissions. Since fossil-fuel power plants are large contributors to such emissions, it will be necessary to decrease their loads to reach the targeted reductions, and electric motor-driven systems are a large component of the load. Hence, heightened environmental concerns can be seen as a further contributor to the pressure to improve electric motor repair practices.

While the industrial user of an electric motor–driven system may not be greatly motivated by the distant feel of U.S. treaties or global warming, such a user is highly motivated by both the potential for greater reliability of the machinery stemming from improved repair practices and by the prospect of lower power bills. Consequently, Wally Brithinee, as the chairman of the Engineering Committee of the Electrical Apparatus Service Association (EASA), took the lead in developing a set of standards and guidelines for repair of electric motors that met most of the regulators' objections. These became the "building blocks" for the motor repair industry, ushering in a "market transformation." These standards also became a marketing tool for Brithinee Electric.

In 1991, the company experienced its first significant decline in revenues. It "hit a brick wall," says Don Brithinee. The United States suffered a recession, which Brithinee weathered with some pain. The company also lost its $1 million per year customer, "through no fault of their own." This customer was lost because it could not accommodate the change in the size of the variable frequency drive that Brithinee was supplying. The total revenue declined further in 1992 before turning upward and resuming a growth mode. In 1996, revenue finally exceeded that of 1990. Brithinee takes pride in the fact that no one was laid off during the downturn, though some employees were asked to use their accumulated vacation time.

In 1992, Brithinee made three changes to accommodate the rebuilding of large quantities of locomotive motors from the Electro-Motive Division (EMD) of General Motors and to expand inventory space. First, it acquired a second 13,000 square-foot building (called the "680 Building" because of its address) about 100 yards south of the old site. This building cost $495,000, for which the company spent $141,000 for remodeling. Second, it moved $500,000 of inventory out of the main building into the new building, enlarged the winding machine shop areas, and dedicated special floor space to EMD. Third, it established more stringent quality procedures than had previously existed.

Acquiring the new building pushed Brithinee Electric in a new strategic direction: designing and building control panels. Previously, Brithinee "dabbled" in making control panels, but now that became a significant part of the business. The company prefers not to be dependent on one industry. Its main work is in water pumping and treatment, rock crushing, cement facilities, and the food industry, including wineries and breweries. The decline in aerospace and defense orders in the early 1990s taught many southern California businesses not to have all their eggs in one basket.

The expansion of control panels was a "Y in the road," says Don. "It is a different beast . . . it's a cleaner operation . . . it's not a repair operation at all. It is an assembly of new electronic components." As part of this new focus, in 1992, Brithinee hired Richard Silva, who was instrumental in attaining Underwriter Laboratories (UL) certification for the company. Consequently, Square D and Telemecanique, both subsidiaries of Groupe Schneider, a French multinational corporation, became major new customers.

In addition, Lynda Butek, the environmental/ facilities coordinator, who works directly for Wally Brithinee, was responsible for the 1992 installation of a closed-loop aqueous parts washer for loads weighing up to 20,000 pounds. Previously, the company had to dispose of large quantities of water from a washdown area. Figures 4 and 5 show the current facilities.

In 1997, the original "620 building" underwent a major renovation, costing $315,000. As he describes the changes Wally states the reasons for the remodeling:

> . . . to control the environment in the manufacturing area, and to make it reflect the quality of the products produced there. In that regard, we had specific goals and tasks. One was to reduce noise and increase the desirability of the eastern one-third of the building as a work area. That area has certain processes with air handlers and pumps that generate audible noise. These include

the paint booth exhaust; the sand-blast cabinet and dust collector; and the parts washer, with its array of pumps. We evaluated all the lighting in the building and greatly increased it. . . .

> At the same time, controls were centralized so that it would be easy to reduce lighting and electrical consumption when personnel were not in the work area. During the remodel, we added insulation with value of R–30 and covered the ceiling with a white plastic sheath. That moderated temperatures, further reduced noise, and increased the effectiveness of the light. The effects were dramatic.

> Shop offices were enlarged, allowing better supervisory control at the plant floor. A laser printer was added, with fax-modem, and the shop offices became much more efficient. There was far less cause for drivers, delivery persons, and shop personnel to come into the business office. The offices of this building were redone to eliminate the large, open office area. As we had grown, the open area seemed to create many

FIGURE 4

Layout of the 620 Building

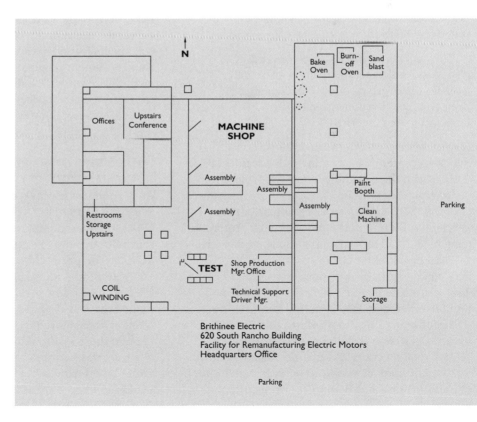

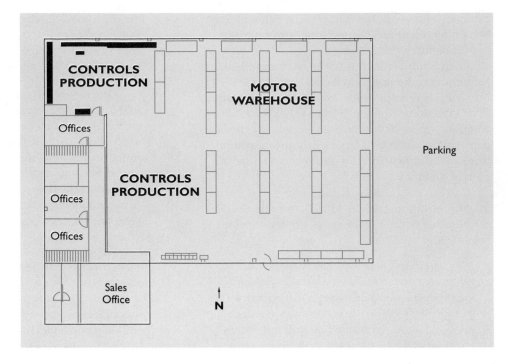

FIGURE 5

Layout of the
680 Building

distractions to the tasks at hand and to offer sound interference for telephone conversations.

The conference room that existed was re-shaped and enlarged, and today is fitted with a table for executive meetings. The decor has been completely redone from its early 1970s look, to a more modern look.

As other shops in Southern California have closed, larger motors are coming in for repairs at Brithinee. Wanting to handle larger stators and rotors, the company is adding a vacuum pressure impregnation (VPI) tank as an integral part of their repair facility. Putting in the new VPI tank required digging a 10- to 12-foot pit and getting various environmental protection permits.

Brithinee primarily uses personal selling to establish relationships, and it benefits from word-of-mouth advertising. In late 1997, the company hired Cyd Sandefur as an assistant to Don Brithinee to work on advertising and other special projects.

Today, total revenues are at $6.99 million, with 43 percent from repair work, 26 percent from motor sales, and the remaining 31 percent from custom-made control panel sales. Whereas eleven years earlier the accounting records were separated into statements for repairs and statements for sales, today there is a single consolidated statement. This system gives the company the flexibility to move people from one area to another but loses the detailed information concerning specific labor charges.

INDUSTRY DYNAMICS

At the end of the 1980s, sales of new motors grew at a 20 percent rate. As the industry edged into the 1990s, the market matured, prices came down and reliability went up. Features became more user-friendly. The product became more standardized, and was more widely sold in consumer markets. By the late 1990s, competition heated up to the point that twelve out of thirteen of Toshiba's top distributors in variable-frequency drives (inverters) decreased their year-to-year purchases. "What changed was better competition from some premium brand names," states Don. Brithinee Electric could not keep pace as a straight-forward distributor, and its market share of new motor sales dropped, contrary to its expectations.

The variable-frequency drives greatly changed the industry by increasing motor system efficiency, reducing energy consumption, and shifting market demand. These drives introduce high-voltage pulses, thousands each second, into the motor windings, resulting in "partial discharge" and corona. This produces highly corrosive ozone and charged particles that erode the organic insulation from the windings. These problems could cost customer goodwill while increasing costs to rework a motor. When a motor winding fails, the entire job must be redone. Previously, insulation life could be ten to twelve years without a failure, but with the new electronic frequency drives, wire failures could occur within a few hundred hours of operation.

Before the failure mechanism was known (and it is still under investigation), the Engineering Committee of the EASA met with researchers from various laboratories and from manufacturers of the basic building-block materials within a motor winding. The purpose was to make sure that the needs of the repair industry were known and to inform that there was an increase in winding failures not easily explained by inspection and analysis used in the past. If and when more resistant materials became available, the motor repair industry should not be the last to find out.

The development of the microprocessor-controlled variable-frequency drive paralleled that of the computer during the 1990s. This created opportunities for improved process control as well as energy efficiency of the driven system. Roughly during the same time, the Energy Policy Act of 1992 (EPACT) caused motor manufacturers to redesign industrial electric motors to be more energy-efficient. The design changes generally included increasing the active materials in the stator and rotor. In the stator (the part that is usually rewound), those active materials are the laminated steel sheets ("core iron") and the copper wire. In the case of the wire, the designer increases the cross-section of the conductor, while the length of the wire is reduced, thus reducing winding resistance. But these design changes usually result in increased difficulty for coil insertion (trying to stuff more copper into a very crowded frame and core). Thus, the repair industry needed thinner, tougher, slicker insulation in order to maintain the energy

efficiency of the motor, yet have resistance to the harsh electrical environment from the variable-frequency drive that may be applied.

Meetings with Du Pont's Nomex and Kevlar researchers and marketers in Richmond, Virginia, as well as with key industry suppliers of wire (Essex Group, Phelps Dodge) and resins (P. D. George Company), reiterated all these issues. Additionally, EASA's Engineering Committee met several times with the technical subsection of the NEMA Motors and Generators Committee, so that every effort was made to strengthen the information ties between manufacturers and the repair industry. The result was guidelines for motor rewinding that provide both an energy-efficient rewind and a winding that can give long life in the variable-frequency applications, using materials that are readily available.

While chairing the EASA committee, Wally Brithinee recognized that there were marketing issues for Brithinee Electric in winding an "inverter-duty" motor. It enhanced the relationship with several motor manufacturers, and helped to distinguish the windings coming out of his company's facility as perhaps superior to the new motors' windings.

In 1999, Brithinee Electric had less repair competition than it did in the eleven previous years. The large manufacturers with repair shops had withdrawn from Southern California. Don says, "The playing field is a lot more level when we are competing with another independent company than with the captive business of a major manufacturer. That has brought some positive changes for us because we don't have the pressure of competing with some of the majors."

The closings included ASEA Brown Boveri, a Swiss company, which was a 30,000 square foot shop, 30 miles to the west of Brithinee Electric. Electro-Motive Division of General Motors folded its motor repair facility in Los Angeles, while Reliance Electric shut its shop in Anaheim. Westinghouse had been gone for a number of years, and General Electric did little repair of high-voltage motors and no longer did rewind. The last big captive shop was owned by McGraw-Edison, which was sold to MagneTek. This company in turn sold the operation to Eastern Electric, which uses a much smaller staff. Since the majors have vanished, opportunities for independents in the industry have improved. Don wonders: Why did the "big boys" leave the market? Do they know something we don't know? How can Brithinee capitalize on these industry changes?

EXTERNAL AND GOVERNMENTAL INTERFACES

As part of their commitment to educating and raising the expectations of their customers, Wally Brithinee and Lynda Butek have taken on leadership roles within EASA. Wally, we saw earlier, became chair of the Engineering Committee. Lynda became chair of the Environmental Affairs Committee, renamed the Governmental Affairs Committee, and also serves on the Insurance and Safety Committee. She says that involvement in the EASA "really helped the business from a technical standpoint." This committee work has kept Brithinee abreast of the newest materials and technology and given it the opportunity to initiate and maintain contacts with wire, insulation materials, and equipment manufacturers.

In addition, the company works closely with several regulatory agencies, including the South Coast Air Quality Management District (SCAQMD) and the Air Resources Board (ARB) of California, to help streamline regulations. There are several agencies in California with overlapping jurisdictions, but they do not appear to communicate with each other. Every year, Lynda fills out three sets of forms with basically the same information for three different state agencies. For example, she recalls a report which took her half a day to prepare. Brithinee owed $6.95 for particulate matter emissions (for example, sulfur oxide, methane, hydrogen oxide, 1.1.1 trichloroethane and carbon monoxide). Lynda questions the reasonableness of all these agencies and considers how to best streamline the processes to minimize repetition and how to gather the information with the least disruptions of work. She believes, "that California is still the toughest state to get permits in." Wally adds that whatever happens in California is closely watched by the industry in other states. As Wally reflects on his involvement with EASA and various agencies, he ponders how to best influence government regulatory policies. Is there anything he can do to minimize agency overlap and duplication of effort for

the industry? How can EASA lobby state and federal agencies to become more business-friendly while also protecting society?

OPERATIONS

Motor Repair—"Your Emergencies Are Our Concern"

Brithinee repairs motors up to 1000 HP, 4000 volts, and currently up to 5 tons. According to Wally Brithinee, "95 percent of all motors 200 horsepower and above can be expected to be repaired once in their lifetime." Motor repair begins with the receiving of incoming electrical motors. Using contract drivers and its own fleet of trucks, Brithinee picks up and delivers customers' motors, or customers will bring the motors to the shop. The motors then undergo initial inspection and testing before being dismantled. The core is tested and the old windings are burned off in a temperature-controlled oven. Then a second core test is performed. The motors are rewound with new quadruple-build or inverter-duty magnet wire. Connections are made and an inspection performed before additional assembly and final testing. Approximately 70 percent of the motor is used in the remanufacture; most of the rest is recycled. The finished motor repair can maintain energy efficiency within ½ percent of what the motor was designed for. Finally the motor is prepared for shipping and delivery to the customer. Brithinee does not repair motors on site due to liability, the difficulty associated with burning off the old windings, the use of chemicals, rewinding, assembly, and bonding of the new wire inside the industrial motor (see Figure 6).

The Motor Repair Workflow

Russ Kennedy, production manager since 1988, oversees the workflow from start to finish. He makes the work assignments and ensures that finished goods are delivered in a timely fashion. He documents the initial conditions of incoming motors using one of three digital cameras, and the images are stored electronically on a Macintosh. This has improved the process "tremendously" over the previously used Polaroids. Benefits include lower

FIGURE 6

Flow Chart for
Motor Repair

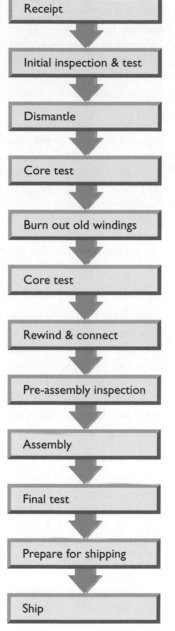

Receipt

Initial inspection & test

Dismantle

Core test

Burn out old windings

Core test

Rewind & connect

Pre-assembly inspection

Assembly

Final test

Prepare for shipping

Ship

Workers walk into Russ's office and pick up their assignments—with the photos on them. The motors are placed in bins both alphabetically and numerically. Supposedly, every job has a home, but with three shifts and uneven pallet sizes, workers on limited occasions will put a motor "wherever," and finding that motor "can become an Easter egg hunt," says Russ. Brithinee still has jobs in the shop from 1995. For example, a company that owns a $30,000 motor may not have sufficient funds in its budget to get it repaired immediately, so it just leaves the motor with Brithinee. Although Brithinee has cleared out a significant number of these older jobs, its management still wonders, "at what point do you provide service to your customers by storing the motors *gratis* vs. charging for that storage?"

A typical repair can range from $600 to $7,000. The job comes in, an estimate is made by fax or phone, and the customer is allowed to respond to the quote before the repair proceeds. Motors are scheduled for repair based on customer need as determined at a daily production meeting, at which the day and night shift production and customer service team discusses work-in-progress. At that time, the team determines the priority for open jobs and discusses what work will be performed during the night shifts. In the early 1990s, EASA created laminated charts with acceptable tolerance values to allow the workers to compare the fit of each part. These charts are placed at each workstation. Various agencies now recommend that customers patronize repair facilities using the guidelines developed by EASA.

Russ color codes the work orders: green for go, red for stop, and orange for a "hot" rush job. Orange jobs go to the head of the queue. Russ cites the case where the City of Riverside didn't have water for ten city blocks, and Brithinee Electric worked through the night to complete the rush job. The customer pays a premium for the overtime when that happens. Jobs may be assigned by worker's ability. A priority job can preempt another job, "by the minute," says Russ. The repair of a "hot" rush job from a very big customer may begin before a quote has been accepted, causing consternation in the accounts receivable department. This department has the responsibility to satisfy the customer's purchasing and accounting needs. Brithinee wonders: how to provide a procedure that meets the needs of the accounting department without holding up

costs, more flexibility, more views of each motor, and file-handling capability. Having a picture associated electronically with the work order has decreased the number of misunderstandings with workers and customers. For example, one customer, after delivery of the repaired motor, inquired about a missing part. A picture cleared up the problem.

emergency work? Besides, one of Wally's goals is to reduce Brithinee's overtime costs. Three-fourths of the costs of repair is labor while one-fourth goes for parts and material.

Layout and Work Stoppages

With from 75 to 110 work orders open at any one time and eighteen workers on the day shift, five on the swing shift, and three on graveyard shift, there is never any time a worker is idle. Occasionally, a machine may be idle when workers are pulled off a machine to work on a rush job. There used to be bottlenecks in the shop floor area and it was thought that more space would remedy the problem. A consultant hired to redesign the plant layout interviewed everyone and made suggestions about restructuring the work area to get a better workflow. She told them, Russ recalls, that "you don't need more room, you just need to change the way you do things." Previously, process work crossed paths too frequently from department to department. The company corrected the problem by relocating aisles and increasing their size, adding electrical outlets and lighting, and improving each workstation. The more hazardous repair operations were separated out to a specific area.

Other problems included work stoppages, which would occur when work crews ran out of propane gas. No one was monitoring the gas level. Regular deliveries by a propane gas vendor freed workers to concentrate on the task at hand. Russ wonders: what is the appropriate level of outsourcing? Besides the delivery of gas propane, are there any other areas which Brithinee should consider?

Customer Reports

Beginning in 1993, Brithinee Electric began providing to the customer a previously internal computer report on why a motor fails. Brithinee decided to share this information with its customers to add value to the service it provides, and to raise the level of their expectations.

This report explains what was found, how the motor tested when it came in, and how it tests when it goes out. Included are specifics about vibration, resistance of the winding, and types of bearings installed, which provide a baseline for the motor's performance. Wally says, "We don't expect [the customer] to even ask for what they really

need. . . . With our training and outreach programs through the Department of Energy, [we ask ourselves] 'how do you get the user of electrical motor systems to develop or purchase a good system—for both efficiency and reliability?' "

Lynda Butek says, "Brithinee Electric has always had a reputation for quality . . . and that reputation has tripled in the last nine to ten years. Wally has instituted a very rigorous testing and reporting system for our customers that they didn't even know they wanted." She indicates that at first customers appeared to ignore the report, but "now you try not to send it and you get a phone call. 'Where is my report? I need my report!' " Not only do customers expect to receive the report from Brithinee; now they also expect to obtain such a report from Brithinee's competitors.

Customized Control Panels

Customized control panels involve building industrial integrated systems, dealing with programmable logic controllers, motor controls, and variable frequency drives. Brithinee sees itself as neither a mass producer nor a low-price leader. From one employee in 1987, this department now has grown to eight employees. Sometimes the workload for control panels expands, and up to nine people are "borrowed" from the repair side to complete a project. Brithinee is a niche player, specializing in drives and soft-start applications, which reduce stresses associated with each motor start and increase the longevity of the motor. A control panel can cost $1,000 to $10,000 in labor time to design. Brithinee sometimes charges separately for designing the control panel and related software, and for manufacture.

When Brithinee hired Richard Silva, the controls department manager, in 1992, one of his first assignments was to establish the necessary procedures in order to manufacture control panels listed with Underwriters Laboratories, under UL Standard 508 and, later, UL845. While Underwriters Laboratories does not share liability, the UL label does convey that the listed product meets accepted safety standards in its construction, thereby reducing the risk of liability. "It legitimizes you. . . . It has been real good for our business. It has opened doors, and been a plus for us," says Richard Silva.

Richard indicates that Brithinee will "overdesign" a product, meaning that it builds to guarantee product performance. If the panel fails, it hurts the company in two ways: (1) the costs to send someone to fix the problem and (2) the company's reputation is damaged. "First time, every time we want it to work," says Richard. For example, Brithinee uses a larger-size wire and will dip it in tin to lessen problems associated with heat. Brithinee also investigates where the panel will be installed and serviced and it takes into account environmental conditions, such as heat, moisture, and wind. One panel shipped to the United Arab Emirates was designed with parts that would be available locally if the need should arise.

For the UL845, Richard works with several large companies, including Square D. Square D finds Brithinee's control panel operations very flexible. Brithinee can build control panels in a hurry, faster than Square D's own plant can do. As Richard describes the sales sequence, "Brithinee is a subcontractor to Square D who sells the product to a distributor who sells it to an electrical contractor who will sell it to the general contractor who actually sells to the municipality or utility company." Square D also supplies Brithinee with some control panel parts. Thus, Square D is both a supplier and a customer and represents major dollars with few billings.

Candace Winn, manager of Square D's Oceanside, California plant, describes her company's relationship with Brithinee as "unique." She says, "We talk to them all the time on the phone three to six times a day. . . . They have a real knack for educating the customer." She feels confident that when she gets a job from Brithinee it is done correctly, and she almost considers the firm to be a sister company. David Whitney, senior sales engineer at Square D, who calls on industrial-type end-users in Orange County and part of Los Angeles County, characterizes the Square D–Brithinee relationship as more like a partnership than as a customer-supplier one. He remarks, "There is a lot of trust and shared information. . . . Brithinee has a lot of product expertise. They will see what our customers want and design it for them."

AutoCAD drawing adds to Brithinee's flexibility and allows the company to get its product to the market faster by compressing the design phase. For a job with design specifications, the length of the project could be years, and they might not even win the bid. Once a project is approved, it typically takes four to six weeks to build a control panel. The longest lead time is acquiring the metal structure that houses the electrical components. Building the control panel might take only a week or two.

In scheduling a control panel job, Richard plans for unexpected delays, but the control panel department takes special pride in having so far met all the deadlines for shipping their products. Richard affirms that "we have never, ever, ever missed a ship date. Never. We will never miss a ship date. . . . I have been here Saturday and Sunday to make a ship date. . . . It is important to us. You are only as good as your reputation."

Richard explains that the UL508 directory looks "like a telephone directory," but there are only twenty companies in the United States with the UL845 certification. Other companies with the UL845 are very large corporations, such as Siemens, Allen-Bradley, and Square D. More than the UL508 certification, the UL845 has elevated the visibility of Brithinee Electric and helped it obtain more business.

Several Brithinee individuals mention that repair costs are well known and manageable, but a good system for determining the labor costs and profit on control panels has eluded them. Richard explains that "labor has been a real problem. Until recently, we did not have a good way to keep track of accounting hours." Sometimes Brithinee would not know for six months whether it made money on a job. For bidding on a job, Brithinee bases its estimates on historical data, but each job can be unique and variable. Richard ponders what it would take to get the feedback he needs to make better bids, win more contracts, and increase the profitability of the firm.

ISO AND EASA Q CERTIFICATIONS

The International Organization for Standardization (ISO) created worldwide guidelines to promote operational efficiency, improve productivity, and reduce costs. The ISO 9000 concept took off in the early 1990s and has helped to define world-class quality systems. Most large manufacturers (for instance, Toshiba, General Motors, and Square D) are ISO 9000.

There are three models of ISO 9000: 9001, 9002, and 9003. (However, a new revision is expected to have only one model.) The most rigorous of the ISO standards is the ISO 9001, which means that the company has certification in design, engineering, and manufacturing, whereas ISO 9002 means qualification in just manufacturing. The ISO standards guarantee a formalized system to create a product in a consistent manner. They do not guarantee quality in terms of customer satisfaction as measured against expectations.

The Electrical Apparatus Service Association (EASA) has initiated a related standard, the EASA Q. Lynda Butek asserts that this standard " is *more* than the ISO 9002 … [it is 9002] plus specific procedures only having to do with motor rewind. It also includes a customer satisfaction audit of certain selected customers, which the ISO 9002 does not have." The EASA Q was put together by the Technical Services Committee of EASA, chaired by Wally Brithinee.

Russ Kennedy says that movement toward EASA Q and ISO 9002 "makes my job easier with the documentation. Procedures are being implemented that everyone's following. It helps change the mindset of a 20-year mechanic to conform to today's standards and regulations.… It's a great adventure we're in right now. It makes work very interesting, and these guys [the Brithinee brothers] are behind it."

On the other hand, is ISO really necessary given the company's UL certification? Candace Winn, at Square D, says that it is the *UL* certifications that distinguish Brithinee from other control panel makers. Of the three certifications (that is, UL845, ISO 9002, and EASA Q), the UL845 is "drastically important," she says.

The pressure for achieving ISO 9002 is internally driven. "It is not a big market issue here in Southern California," says Wally. Other industries (i.e., paper and petroleum) are moving toward ISO 9000 certification, but there is no market pressure for Brithinee. "Most of our customers are not terribly concerned about [our being ISO 9002 certified]," says Don. "For our size business, it doesn't seem to be an expectation."

In some industries, ISO helps a company compete on the global scene, but none of Brithinee's repair work is international due to the high cost of transporting heavy industrial motors. A few international sales of control panels systems occur, though, since the value per pound is significantly higher.

Brithinee designed process flow charts for its jobs with GM's Electro-Motive Division, where procedures were more standardized than in their other rewinding business. These procedures include calibration of all measuring instruments. A byproduct of the GM work has been the addition of similar systems for Brithinee's other motor repair work.

While ISO 9000 certification is not a major issue for Brithinee (which already has a relationship with GM), GM uses it as a screen to prequalify when selecting new vendors.

According to Don, Brithinee Electric would like to avoid errors in office and administration (such as invoicing), in the repair shop, and in the control systems areas. It would like to develop systems in how to provide feedback, detection and prevention of errors. "Every point seems to be a spot in which we can make savings." For example, Brithinee sold a vehicle and verbally canceled the cellular telephone service associated with that vehicle. The provider stated it did not need anything in writing to cancel the telephone number. Debbie Brithinee, the firm's office manager and Don's wife, wrote a memo to staff members to watch out that no further charges came through on that telephone number. Something got lost in the procedure, and sixteen months later they realized that they had been charged $70 a month for a telephone number that had zero calls on it. The telephone company refused to refund the money. Don wonders whether it is worth the time and energy to change cellular telephone vendors, or could better procedures have prevented this error from occurring in the first place?

Another costly error occurred with a large customized control panel order when the individual quoting the price made a mistake in handling the spreadsheet. Accidentally, 18 percent of the materials were not added into the cost, virtually wiping out any profit—all because the line was not included in a summation. This was the largest job Brithinee has ever had. If a company has significant customized business, how does it create standardized systems and procedures? Can standardized procedures catch mistakes in Brithinee's processes? ISO certification of procedures may be one way to prevent procedural errors.

ISO 9000 certification is a popular movement in other industries, and Don and Wally Brithinee wonder if ISO certification could make their company more competitive in the electrical apparatus industry. Could it add value? David Whitney at Square D remarks that Brithinee would be smart to attain ISO 9000 as many big customers, such as Boeing, sometimes ask about quality programs, and "it certainly helps to be able to say 'we are working with customers with ISO.'"

Don wonders if achieving ISO 9002 would "awaken that interest" in the firm's customers?

Brithinee is getting virtually no external pressure from its customers to become ISO certified. The principal benefit would be the internal side—the savings associated with going through the process of developing these systems. "Our goal will eventually be to achieve ISO 9002, but we are still a ways off.... We are working on a number of fronts towards that end," says Wally. He also ponders the question: Is the year 2000 a realistic goal for achieving this certification?

THE VALUE CHAIN, RELATIONSHIP MARKETING, AND ADVERTISING

The value chain is defined as the sum of activities from start to finish that add value. These activities include procurement, design, assembly, remanufacture, distribution, marketing, and service. Relationship marketing involves creating and maintaining long-term relationships with external and internal customers. These concepts are part of Brithinee's long-term strategy.

Brithinee Electric is more engaged in value-added activities and in creating longer-term relationships with both suppliers and customers than it had been in 1987. Ten years ago, Brithinee did not have much value-added assembly. The contract with EMD Locomotive provided one value-added dimension in the repair shop. Most sales in 1987 were off-the-shelf packages for Toshiba and Baldor. Brithinee Electric was not good at retaining that type of sales. It lacked retail outlets and could not compete with aggressive discount houses entering this market in the early 1990s. However, control panels added new opportunities for its business, capitalizing on its interest in customized high-tech products and services in the electrical apparatus industry.

Relationship marketing is also evident with Square D, where Brithinee actually helps David Whitney (at Square D) sell to his customers. Brithinee becomes an extension of Square D's value-added chain, and vice versa. "My customer may be a water district and I may ask where do they get their motors repaired and suggest to the customer that they contact Brithinee," comments Dave.

Two outside salespeople generate business by calling on customers and identifying new prospects, whether in the repair area, sales, or control panels. Its competitors sometimes refer a customer to Brithinee, and it reciprocates on occasion when it cannot fulfill a customer's request. Bill Gaborko at C&M Electric, a small local competitor, receives telephone referrals from Brithinee to handle single-phase motors. C&M does not do large motors, and it refers those customers to Brithinee.

The Brithinee philosophy is to grow and maintain the business primarily with existing customers, but also go after new customers. "Getting a new customer is the most expensive part of a business," says John Hinshaw, the sales and marketing manager. The company looks for new "business starts" in the Inland Empire.

John confirms that the computer-generated repair reports given to customers on the problems found and the job done has helped raise customers' expectations and that those customers now require the same information from Brithinee's competitors. He also stresses, like Richard Silva, the value of the UL label and sees it as the most important certification in generating sales locally, especially for the control panel side of the business. For example, the city of Los Angeles does not care about ISO 9000. "For electrical safety, UL is it," John comments.

Brithinee is exploring new ways to generate sales because it would like to run its three shifts at full strength and to increase revenues and profit margins. Using a Dun & Bradstreet "Marketplace" CD-ROM set, it has identified hundreds of prospects that are like its client base. The company has also discovered that sometimes its repair customers don't know about the control side of the business, and vice versa.

In order to reach out to a new customer base, Don Brithinee and Cyd Sandefur have been attending a marketing class at a local community college. She helps Don create presentation material for seminars and find other ways as well to familiarize the public with the company and its work. The presentations have been given to groups of customers or through the EASA trade organization, both on-site and out in the field. These seminars cover such topics as how to hook up and safely use industrial motors, how to make the equipment run better, and how to do maintenance planning. Wally believes that, "customers are better customers when they know what we do."

Don and Cyd have also toyed with the idea of creating a supply chain to Arizona and northern California because there are carrier services that guarantee overnight delivery. Cyd says that they are still in the infancy stage of their marketing efforts and are considering what further steps Brithinee could take to market itself.

ACCOUNTING AND INFORMATION TECHNOLOGY

Before she was hired by Brithinee Electric, Debbie Brithinee, Don's wife, had worked for seventeen years in accounting, purchasing, and trust operations in a county government, overseeing a $70 million budget. Periodically, she helped on special projects for the Brithinee firm before becoming Brithinee's office manager in 1990. She is now responsible for Brithinee's general ledger and other types of accounting. Table 1 presents an eleven-year overview of Brithinee's financial status, including its balance sheet and income statement.

In 1998, at the request of employees, Brithinee introduced a 401(k) profit-sharing plan. It was implemented after companywide meetings and a vote. Until then, the company had placed annual bonuses into a guaranteed fund that could not be tapped by the employees. With the 401(k) plan, Brithinee is committing funds monthly, which is difficult since the company does not know how profitable it will be at year's end. Debbie says that

"our financial statements look very different month-to-month than they did in prior years. . . . it was a big step for us to go into the 401(k)." Employees are fully vested in the 401(k) the first day they begin work. The two advantages of the 401(k), as Wally sees it are that the employees are both aware of the plan throughout the year and control the funds. The question he wrestles with, however, is how to ensure that employees "understand a tie-in between . . . [their] performance and the company's performance," for if the employees "are to succeed, the company needs to succeed."

Another accounting issue is the difficulty of measuring labor associated with control panel projects. "We don't do cost accounting," Debbie says. "In the repair shop, we have done considerable analysis on what goes into a repair. . . . But in the control panel area, it's very, very difficult to get a handle on that. That's what we're working on now." She would like to know what systems would capture information to solve this problem. Could the company develop better methods to account for the dramatic differences that occur between initial estimates and the actual building of the control panel? These differences include labor uncertainty and changes in the prices of parts. Customer design changes can also complicate the process. Debbie wonders whether the firm can overcome its

TABLE 1

Brithinee Electric's Financial Statements, 1988–1998

	Balance Sheet			
	1988	1989	1990	1991
Assets				
Current assets	1,278,365	1,644,500	1,551,245	1,229,799
Fixed assets less accumulated depreciation	121,739	82,625	139,922	193,562
Other assets	14,716	14,716	14,716	7,876
Total	1,414,820	1,741,841	1,705,884	1,431,238
Liabilities and Shareholders' Equity				
Current liabilities	356,096	563,656	332,276	328,377
Longterm liabilities				
Shareholders' equity	1,058,724	1,178,184	1,373,607	1,102,860
Total	1,414,820	1,741,841	1,705,884	1,431,238
Income Statement				
Gross income	4,836,401	5,372,555	5,643,979	4,530,838
Cost of goods sold	3,349,853	3,766,378	3,751,243	3,013,072

reluctance to adjust the original estimate once changes occur. Tracking purchase orders is problematic, according to Cyd Sandefur, who is doing the tracking manually. She says that "things change in the middle of the project. Something will be quoted that doesn't work." This means renegotiation for parts and prices.

In terms of information technology, Don states, "We enjoy our computers . . . we probably have thirty computers scattered around . . . versus only one or two ten years ago. . . . This is a big plus." These computers include both Macintosh and Windows NT-based machines operating on the same network. The software they use allows both types of machines to work side by side entering orders, sending mail, accessing data files and exchanging data across the network. The company has created its local area network (LAN) and is on the Internet but does not have its own Web site. Don reflects, "I don't find that most of the customers we deal with would find their way to us through [a Web site] . . . not yet." The company is seeking lower-cost ways of reaching its customers.

Regarding the company's use of computers, Wally calls them "a shop tool." He created the spreadsheets that track progress of motors through the repair processes. "It is not universally acknowledged that you would put computers in the shop

area," he says. Don further elaborates that "we don't have an integrated system for our order entry and accounting." Brithinee has purchased some custom software to reduce paperwork and streamline processes, but it has yet to be implemented. The goal is to reduce the amount of hours devoted to accounting, and Don wonders how best to achieve it.

PERSONNEL ISSUES

Brithinee Electric's reputation for dealing with emergencies tends to attract more emergencies. "Always being in a panic mode" was wearing its personnel down. To respond to this problem and to create a less stressful organizational climate, Brithinee undertook two actions: it contracted with a psychological consultant who could assist the company in its hiring practices, and it added a second and third shift.

In 1996, the industrial psychologist began pretesting applicants, a process intended to comply with employment discrimination laws. "We have been trying to put together a company of more like-minded people," states Don. "We have managed to remove some personnel who were a problem for us. . . . This has made the organizational environment more pleasant and conveyed a better image

Balance Sheet						
1992	*1993*	*1994*	*1995*	*1996*	*1997*	*1998 (Proj)*
1,105,523	1,997,596	1,125,322	1,195,479	1,269,494	1,501,129	1,446,709
271,273	223,745	293,329	240,558	363,180	406,165	441,091
2,087	6,896	6,896	6,896	1,093	2,004	1,951
1,378,883	1,228,238	1,425,546	1,442,933	1,633,767	1,909,299	1,889,752
540,978	376,593	3,787,799	292,863	305,465	550,758	351,239
		28,079	19,036	26,708	36,106	27,662
837,905	851,644	1,018,668	1,131,034	1,301,593	1,322,434	1,510,850
1,378,883	1,228,237	1,425,546	1,442,933	1,633,767	1,909,299	1,889,752
4,405,211	4,968,783	5,127,066	5,995,404	5,696,261	6,490,431	7,027,731
3,045,850	3,260,598	3,344,487	2,854,561	3,525,998	4,370,105	4,483,012

to our customers and even our vendors." Brithinee profiled both potential employees and, with their permission, the existing employees. This has given the company insights as to why certain personalities work well together and others do not. As Russ Kennedy explains, "We want people to fit . . . the Brithinee profile."

Another aspect of the current employee tests resulted in people being moved around. "This seems to be working out a lot better," comments Lynda Butek. In addition, Brithinee has instituted drug testing for preemployment screening and created a "no-tolerance drug usage policy." Employees using illegal drugs were removed. Among them was an individual who had crashed a truck, and was creating morale problems. His dismissal boosted morale in the shop. While some may view such firings as harsh, one employee describes the management style at Brithinee as "very forgiving." For example, the company allows people the flexibility to make mistakes, and most employees seem to appreciate this.

In hiring additional personnel for a second and third shift, it was important to choose those with the "right characteristics." Brithinee used to have attrition due to employee burnout. Now, the work is shared by a broader group of workers with similar goals. In addition, the company has three or four "all purpose, no purpose" utility people at the entry level. "We have grown on all fronts . . . [and now] we take emergencies more in stride," says Russ.

Brithinee Electric suffers from some growth-related problems common to small, family-owned businesses. Long-time employees remember working side by side with Don and Wally and have difficulty following the chain of command. The psychologist has aided the company by redefining job descriptions and creating more fully and carefully documented employee manuals. He has also helped Wally and Don communicate better with each other. Wally mentions that he is sold on the value of using a psychologist to help managers better understand their staff and adopt a team approach.

As for pay increases—always a significant personnel issue—they are determined by Don and Wally, who factor in profitability, labor market conditions, and the value of the individual to the company. Employees cannot expect to get a yearly pay raise.

GROWTH AND THE FUTURE

As Brithinee looks into the future, Don and Wally consider how best to grow revenues by 10 to 15 percent in an industry predicted to shrink by 2 percent per year. Should they remain focused and expand their existing electrical motors, sales, and control panels departments, or should they diversify into other areas? The questioning involves not just growth, but also what areas the company should grow in. Predictions as to where the business will grow are hard to make. For example, since 1988 the rewinding portion of the business grew by 180 percent. Wally comments, "I would have never expected that. . . . We've never been good at predictions here." Brithinee Electric forecasts its earnings only one year at a time, but its consultant suggests that it set longer-term goals.

In reflecting on future business opportunities, Wally notes that the water industry nationwide is expected to spend $40 billion in upgrades of water and wastewater treatment facilities in the near future, a significant part of which will finance conversion to variable-frequency drives. "Upgrading fits our controls arena," he says. "This is our greatest potential area for growth." Brithinee already runs three shifts, but the second and third shift are skeleton crews. Should the firm expand to fully staffed crews, and if so, how soon? Expanding the repair side for handling larger-size motors, however, would require extensive capital investment. As Wally puts it, "everything would have to be upsized to another level greater than what we have." He sees the intensive struggle for capital and wonders where the capital might come from.

Another possibility for growth is to expand the facility by acquiring more land. The company has already acquired the vacant lot of about 5 acres between its two current buildings. According to Lynda Butek, it is a "strange piece of property" because it also wraps around the back of both buildings, a cul-de-sac, and extends to the next street. What would be the best use for it: expanding the warehouse, making it into a parking lot or a control panel area, or erecting another building in order to handle more repair work?

As the Brithinee brothers contemplate what will best prepare them for the twenty-first century, they ask whether quality is enough to ensure expansion for the company? Will attaining ISO 9000 and EASA Q enhance the business as much as they hope it will? Will educating its customers continue to create a niche for Brithinee? What other activities can Brithinee implement to "raise the standards" and "define the level of expectations" of its customers? Finally, as the brothers celebrate their fiftieth birthday, the issues of retirement and succession loom in the future.

If and when Don and Wally Brithinee should decide to limit their involvement in the business or leave it altogether, the typical exit strategies would include (1) closing the business; (2) being bought out by partners or employees; (3) selling to outsiders and relinquishing all ties to the business; (4) positioning the firm for a merger or acquisition but remaining as active board members and/or as employees; (5) passing the business to the next generation; (6) hiring a CEO/president to run the firm; (7) leasing the facilities and equipment; or (8) going public. A merger or acquisition by a large U.S. corporation would seem unlikely given that major U.S. players have essentially left the industry. However, there are some lesser known American, as

well as British, firms that might be interested in this company. As for the next generation, Don and Deborah Brithinee have one child, Nicole, aged ten, while Wally remains single. The brothers carry substantial life and disability insurance policies on each other.

References

Electrical Apparatus Service Association, Inc. (EASA), "Understanding A-C Motor Efficiency," pamphlet, 1994.
———, "How to Get the Most from Your Electric Motors," pamphlet, 1997.
———, "EASA AR 100 1998 Recommended Practice," pamphlet, 1998.
Greenfeld, S. "Brithinee Electric." Case study in Smith, Arnold and Bizzell, *Business Strategy and Policy.* Boston: Houghton-Mifflin, 1991, pp. 180–200. Also in Stahl and Grisby, *Strategic Management for Decision Making,* Boston: PWS-Kent Publishing Co., 1992, pp. 368–387; and in Dess & Miller, *Strategic Management.* New York: McGraw-Hill, 1993), pp. 393–410.
Nailen, Richard L. "Building A Service Company's Numbers with Higher Mathematics." *Electrical Apparatus,* December 1997.
"You Got It Off the Ground and Flying, Now How Do You Safely Land It?" *Los Angeles Times,* December 16, 1998, p. C8.

Wizards of the Coast

This case was prepared by Frank T. Rothaermel of Michigan State University and Suresh Kotha and Richard Moxon of the University of Washington.

The excitement was high among the top managers of Wizards of the Coast, the world's leading adventure gaming company, as they sat down to review progress over the first half of 1997. The company had just completed the acquisition of a major competitor, and with the opening of its first gaming entertainment center, it was pioneering a whole new retail concept. After three years of tremendous growth fueled by one hit product, followed by an unexpected downturn in revenues in 1996, Wizards looked to be on the rebound. But everyone knew that the company still had to prove that it had a sustainable growth strategy for the future.

CREATING THE MAGIC

In 1997, Wizards of the Coast was a privately held company best known for the world's leading adventure trading-card game, *Magic: The Gathering*®. Since its release in 1993, more than 5 million consumers worldwide had embraced the game, which was available in nine languages and played in over fifty-two countries. (See Appendix A for a description of *Magic*®.)

The Genesis

Wizards of the Coast was founded by Peter Adkison and a group of other young professionals in 1990

to develop role-playing games. Adkison had been intrigued by strategy and role-playing games ever since early childhood. He recalls playing games as a youngster all night long under the comforters of his bed using a flashlight, so that his mother would think he was asleep when she took a peek into the room during the early night hours. In high school, he developed a passion for the *Dungeons & Dragons*® *(D&D)* adventure role-playing game. (See Appendix B for a description of *D&D*.) It seemed natural to him to turn this hobby into a business. After graduating from college, Adkison worked for Boeing as a computer systems analyst but was eager to start his own venture. He recalls, "I was a small cog in a huge machine that itself was a small cog in a huge machine." Adkison and six of his friends kept their jobs but began developing role-playing games in their spare time.

In 1991, Adkison met Richard Garfield in a chat room on the Internet. At the time, Garfield was a doctoral student in combinational mathematics at the University of Pennsylvania and was known as an avid game player who had been designing his own games since he was a teenager. When the two got together at a game convention, the concept for *Magic*® was born. Adkison had the idea that there was a need for a fantasy role-playing game that was portable and could be played anywhere in no more than an hour. He thought that maybe it should be a card game. Garfield had also been interested in fantasy games since playing a game called *Cosmic Encounter* in the 1980s. One of the pieces in *Cosmic Encounter* had special powers. By invoking these powers, a player could change the rules of the game. This intrigued Garfield, and he wondered what would happen if all the pieces were magic, each one altering the game in some unique way. He believed that this idea could lead to a fantasy board game, but Adkison persuaded him to focus on cards instead and to think about a format in which players could trade cards.

Garfield came back a few weeks later with a prototype of *Magic: The Gathering®*. The idea was to combine a fantasy game concept, where players controlled the acts of mystical characters, with a trading-card format, where players could buy and sell collectible cards similar to those of their sports heroes. As Garfield remembers, "The concept of a trading-card game was one of the only 'Eureka!' experiences I've had." Adkison emphasizes the point that the first prototype of *Magic®* resembled very closely the later commercialized version of *Magic®*: "We still have the original, hand-drawn cards, and gosh, if you know how to play *Magic®*, you can play just fine with that very first game."

Operating out of the basement of Adkison's home as an eight-person company, Wizards of the Coast released *Magic: The Gathering®* in August 1993. The game became an overnight success. The first printing of 10 million cards, which was expected to last a year, sold out in just six weeks. According to one owner of a game store, "My initial order was for 24 units, my second order was for 572, and my third was to send everything you've got in the warehouse." With its sales success also came critical acclaim and the winning of several game and toy industry awards.

After *Magic's* instant splash, Garfield quit his new teaching position at Whitman College and began to pursue his true passion as a game inventor with Wizards of the Coast. Adkison made Garfield an equity partner in Wizards of the Coast and fully dedicated his then fledgling firm to creating fantasy card games. Adkison too quit his job at Boeing to become the president and CEO of Wizards of the Coast. (See Figure 1 for a timeline of Wizards of the Coast.)

Products and Customers

Magic® cards were sold in starter decks of sixty randomly selected cards for about $8.95, and booster packs of eight or fifteen cards for about $2.95 retail price. Even though these were the recommended retail prices, it was not uncommon for retailers to unbundle decks and to mark up the prices of highly demanded cards. The cards featured original artwork that appealed to fantasy-

game players and collectors. As a consequence, *Magic®* cards were both collected and traded, with a card's price determined by its strategic role and its collector value. Each deck was unique, so no two players had identical sets of cards. Players traded cards in order to create a deck with desired characteristics.

According to the chief game developer for Wizards of the Coast, twenty-seven-year old George Skaff Elias, the typical *Magic®* player is a person with a good education, disposable income, and an affinity for computers. While the game is most popular with males in their teens or twenties, the game also caught on with younger teens and with older men and women as well. College dormitories are a particular breeding ground for new "gamers." Compared with the typical player of a board game such as Monopoly, the player of *Magic®* sees the game more like a hobby, something on which to spend a significant amount of time and money.

Manufacturing and Distribution

Wizards contracted out the design, manufacturing, and packaging of its cards and other products. Most of its *Magic®* cards were designed by independent artists, who earned royalties from their sales by Wizards. The tremendous royalty payments due to the unexpected success of *Magic®* were initially a problem for Wizards, but it was solved in a friendly round of renegotiations with the artists. In the beginning, the company relied only on one supplier, Carta Mundi in Belgium, since no other firm could deliver the quality needed along with the ability to do the sophisticated card sorting that was required. During the first two years of booming popularity, manufacturing capacity was the single biggest constraint on the growth of Wizards. Carta Mundi was in 1997 still the largest supplier, but other suppliers were contracted as the game grew and as they were able to meet Wizards' standards.

Wizards built a widespread network to market its cards. Most adventure games were sold through small game, comic, or hobby shops, which were often mom-and-pop stores, supplied through relatively small distributors. These shops were critical for reaching the serious gamers and accounted for about 75 percent of the company's sales. Wizards allocated new card series to these stores, and there was often a feeding frenzy as consumers rushed to get an edge with new cards. As the popularity of *Magic®* rose, Wizards was able to enter national

FIGURE 3.1

Timeline of Wizards of the Coast

1990   Wizards of the Coast is formed as a sole proprietorship by Peter Adkison (May).

Wizards of the Coast is incorporated (December).

1991   Adkison meets Richard Garfield on the Internet.

First play-test version of *Magic: The Gathering®* is distributed.

Wizards acquires the Talislanta role-playing game line from Bard Games.

1992   Wizards releases its first new product, *The Primal Order®*.

Six other role-playing products are released.

Palladium sues Wizards for trademark infringement in its product *The Primal Order®*.

Garfield Games is formed to launch *Magic: The Gathering®*.

1993   Wizards lays off all its employees.

Everyone stays on to launch *Magic,* being paid in stock.

The Palladium lawsuit is settled.

Magic: The Gathering® is launched to record sales.

The *Duelist Convocation (DCI)* is started to provide tournament play for *Magic®*.

All employees are hired back.

The company moves from "the basement" to real offices.

The *Duelist* magazine is launched.

Garfield Games and Wizards of the Coast merge.

1994   Five expansions for *Magic* are released.

Jyhad®, the second trading-card game, based on the Vampire RPG, is released.

First world championships for *Magic* are held in Seattle.

First European office is opened in Glasgow.

1995   *Netrunner®*, WotC's third trading-card game, is released.

The Everyway® role-playing game is released.

Wizards buys Andon, a convention management company.

The *Magic: The Gathering®* computer game is released by Microprose.

More than thirty employees are laid off in company's largest downsizing.

All game divisions are divested except for trading-card games.

1996   The *Magic: The Gathering®* $1,000,000 Pro Tour is launched in New York.

The Wizards of the Coast tournament center opens at corporate headquarters.

The BattleTech trading-card game is released.

Wizards gains the contract to run Origins, the second largest game convention in the United States.

1997   The Wizards of the Coast Game Center opens in Seattle.

Wizards acquires TSR Inc.

Wizards acquires Five Rings Publishing Group.

First Wizards retail store opens in Seattle.

toy chains such as Toys 'R' Us, bookstores such as Barnes & Noble, and discounters such as Target. These stores did not have the same atmosphere and appeal as the small retailers but were more effective for reaching the mass market.

The Wizards Culture

While developing the systems needed to manage a much larger enterprise, Adkison was trying to preserve the creative culture that was present when the company was formed. Leading by example, for many years he refused to have his own office or even a cubicle. On his business cards and memos, his position and title was stated as "CEO and janitor." He saw the company as similar to a small software firm, with a casual, creative atmosphere that tolerated individualism and creativity, expressed, for example, in eccentric clothing, body piercing, and frequent nerf wars among employees. But over the years, the atmosphere had become more reserved, and Adkinson now even has a corner office.

Wizards' executives and employees tended to be very committed to the gaming concept. Garfield, the inventor of *Magic®*, sees adventure games as the "intellectual counterpart of sports—they keep you mentally fit." He believes that with playing *Magic®* comes "a lot of stealth education," whether it is art appreciation because of the beautiful cards or enhanced literacy because of the occasional quote from Shakespeare. Garfield also believes that *Magic®* is a strategic game that could be played successfully only when the player has a good understanding of strategy, probability, and chance.

Adkison, however, recognized that devoted gamers did not always make successful executives.

There's nobody in the company who's ever managed a company this size, including me. We're trying to balance the desire for top-notch people to take us to the next level with the desire to stay true to people who founded the company. And that is very, very tough. We faced a lot of organizational problems when hiring people on top of an existing layer. None of the people who reported to me in 1993 report to me now. Many of them are still here, but experienced managers have come into the organization between them and myself. Our board of directors has evolved also, going from a board

composed mainly of founders and management to a board with several outside directors, who have a lot of gray hair.

As Adkison pointed out, the firm hired experienced managers from established toy companies, used consultants on strategy and operational issues, and brought outsiders into its board of directors. In the meantime, Adkison himself completed an MBA degree in 1997 at the University of Washington Business School. He knew that he would need to continue strengthening the organization if it was to create a sustainable strategy for growth. Some of the newly hired professionals, who came with strong credentials, did not fit in well at Wizards and were asked to leave after a short time. Adkison made the transition from an entrepreneur to a traditional CEO as he deepened his theoretical understanding of business as well as his management skills and combined both with his intuitive feel for the gaming business.

THE ADVENTURE GAMING INDUSTRY

Wizards' executives defined the company as part of the adventure gaming industry, which is itself part of the much larger toy industry. They followed publications of the *Toy Manufacturers of America*, as well as the more specialized *Comics Retailer*, a monthly publication that had in-depth reports on gaming developments. Total U.S. toy industry sales in 1996 were estimated at more than $17 billion, of which the biggest single category was video games. Outside of video games, the games/puzzles category accounted for approximately $1.4 billion of sales. Role-playing, trading-card and war games, the segments in which Wizards competed most directly, accounted for about $350 million to $500 million in 1996 according to *Comics Retailer*, while the Game Manufacturers Association estimated gaming sales at $750 million.

The adventure gaming industry began in the 1960s with the development of a number of war games. The industry was revolutionized and began rapid growth in the early 1970s with the introduction of *Dungeons & Dragons®*, the first popular role-playing game. The game attracted players with its complexity and with the opportunity for players to exercise their creativity. The industry was revolutionized once again in the early 1990s with the introduction of *Magic*®. By 1997, *Dungeons & Dragons*® and *Magic*® were still the top-selling role-playing and trading-card games. The rest of the industry consisted of another major competitor, Games Workshop, a UK-based company with revenues of more than $100 million, and many smaller competitors. Industry observers estimated that the most serious potential future competition would come from companies invading adventure games from other industries.

Although there was no clear distinction between adventure and family games, what made adventure games unique was the fact that people pursued these games as a serious hobby, sometimes dedicating many hours a week to playing a certain game. In Adkison's words, "The Magic player is a hobby gamer, meaning it is a person that would rather game than do anything else. If this person could, he or she would play all the time. The constraint people are facing is the time they have to play." This commitment of hobby players led some critics to characterize players of *Dungeons & Dragons*® and *Magic*® as members of a cult.

Industry executives, however, feel that this is an unfair image and see most gamers as devoted to the intellectual and creative challenges offered by the games. According to a survey conducted by the *Game Manufacturers Association,* adventure game enthusiasts are young, literate and are doing well in scholastic endeavors. The survey results indicate that a majority of them are indeed very young—about 31 percent are between ten and fourteen years of age, about 37 percent are between fifteen and eighteen years old, and 32 percent are nineteen years or older. The survey also revealed that about 82 percent of the respondents indicated that they maintain a grade-point average of 3.0 or better in high school or college, and about 65 percent said that they read thirty-six or more books a year. About 80 percent described themselves as book readers.

Another issue facing the gaming industry is the rise of the Internet and of computer-based games. Most people in the industry regarded typical video games as representing completely different customer experiences: either lonely quests through fantasy worlds or "shoot-em-up" arcade-like games. But the Internet offered the possibility of role-playing and trading-cards in a virtual world.

GROWING THE MAGIC

The success of *Magic*® put Wizards on an explosive growth trajectory. Sales of about $200,000 in 1993 rocketed to $57 million in 1994 and $127 million in 1995. Adkison muses: "Our margins are fantastic, just like Microsoft's on software, because we basically sell intellectual property. We have basically zero marginal cost." Wizards and Adkison had become instant entrepreneurial superstars. The company grew to about 500 employees and in 1996 moved to a brand-new, 178,000-square-foot office complex down the street from Boeing's job center in Renton, Washington. It had also opened several international sales offices.

Growth, however, brought problems. Staffing became close to chaotic. For instance, Adkison found that someone who had been on the payroll for several months had never really been hired by anybody. According to Adkison, "I've made so many mistakes, it's not even funny, and that is not counting the mistakes I made last week." Many of the gamers who started with the company were not ready to move into managerial roles. On the other hand, some managers who were brought in from outside could not work well with the gamers.

As it was already the dominant adventure trading-card game, there was not much growth potential for *Magic*® in taking an increasing share of this market. Wizards focused instead on extending the *Magic*® brand name into other products and in reaching the mass market to increase the overall size of the adventure trading-card industry. At the same time, Wizards had begun promoting *Magic*® tournaments in an effort to give the game added legitimacy and defend it from competing games.

Extending the Brand

Adkison was now attempting to leverage the *Magic*® brand name through licensing into books, computer games, and other products. With the popularity of *Magic*®, Wizards was able to pick and choose its opportunities. For example, *Magic*® appeared as a book series, published by HarperCollins, with more than half a million copies sold. It was also out in two CD-ROM computer games. Wizards' executives felt that bookstores were a logical market for Wizards' products, since *Magic*® players tended to be heavy readers, and *Magic*® itself was often played in bookstores.

Magic® merchandise had been extended through licensing into prepaid phone cards, clothing, card albums and protectors, a *Magic*® strategy guide and encyclopedia, and calendars. Wizards had also reached an agreement with an Internet development and design company to develop interactive CD-ROM products to serve as guides to the fantasy worlds created by Wizards. Wizards had also received movie and television offers, but no agreements had been reached so far. Licensing revenues were estimated to be about $1 million annually.

Going for the Mass Market

The dream of Wizards and other adventure game developers was the mass-market role-playing game. Selling a normal board game was a one-shot revenue of less than $10 to a game company, but customers could spend up to $500 per year on a role-playing game. A mass-market hit could easily create a billion-dollar company.

In the summer of 1997, Wizards introduced a more mainstream version of *Magic*® named *Portal*®. The game was targeted at a broader audience, such as younger teens and families, and was launched with a media campaign of close to $5 million. The aim was to move toward a consumer other than the core gamer, who had made *Magic*® a magical success. *Portal*® would be distributed through mass-market retailers such as Toys 'R' Us and Target. Wizards also introduced the so-called Arc System games. The Arc System game is a generic trading-card game system, which allows the development of card decks based on a variety of popular characters from television, such as Xena, the Warrior Princess. Those decks can also be intermingled.

But Wizards saw risks in the mass market as well. *Magic*® gamers were attracted to the atmosphere of game stores and to the experience of the game, not just the game itself. Mass-market retailers, on the other hand, saw games as "boxes." And given their tremendous buying power, Wizards would not enjoy the same margins that it did on its *Magic*® sales.

Developing Tournaments

To sustain and increase *Magic*® sales, Wizards was attempting to professionalize the activity of playing *Magic*®, transforming it into a legitimate sport. Noted Adkison, "It's been proven that sports are very sustainable. They hold people's attention for a long time." One part of the strategy was to create players with celebrity standing who could then push the game's popularity in the mass market.

Tournaments had been organized informally in the first years of *Magic*®, many of them held in and sponsored by the game stores selling *Magic*®. And hundreds of tournaments were held each year. In 1996, the company organized a six-city professional tournament series that offered $1 million in prizes and scholarships. Wizards also created a computer-based global ranking for all professional players, accessible at the Wizards home page (www.wizards.com). In the United States, more than 50,000 tournament players competed in thirty leagues.

The *Magic*® World Championships generated such interest that they were carried on television by ESPN for the first time in 1997. Players from more than forty countries competed for individual and team titles and for $250,000 in prize money. Wizards was able to attract a corporate partner, MCI Telecommunications, to sponsor the world championships. According to one news analysis, the partnership gave legitimacy to Wizards and provided a mass audience, while MCI was able to tap an attractive audience by being associated with a "cool" event. According to the company that brokered the deal, *Magic*® players were especially attractive because of their passion for the game and their desire to collect everything associated with it. "You've never seen loyalty like this. It's unrivaled across any other product or service category," one analyst stated. MCI agreed to sponsor Wizard's *Magic*® tournaments in exchange for exclusive worldwide rights to produce and distribute *Magic*® prepaid telephone cards featuring the artwork of *Magic*® cards.

Wizards also published a variety of magazines connected with its games. *The Duelist* featured information on upcoming *Magic*® tournaments and articles and tips from celebrity players. The *Dragon* magazine, which came to Wizards with the acquisition of the *Dungeons & Dragons*® game, had been published since the 1970s.

Opening Game Centers

In May 1997, Wizards of the Coast opened its first retail and gaming store, a 34,000-square-foot Wizards of the Coast Game Center located in Seattle, close to the campus of the University of Washington. Figure 2 shows pictures of the game center. Designed as the first entertainment center solely aimed at adventure gamers, it offered an extensive array of arcade video games, sold games and associated merchandise, offered food and beverages, and provided a place to meet and compete with other trading-card gamers. It was also intended to be a site for tournaments. According to Adkison,

> The game center is sort of like Nike Town or Planet Hollywood. Playing is a serious hobby for the Magic player. Therefore, we decided to create the ultimate gaming and retail environment. This is a club, a hangout, a place for the devoted game players to go and know they can play any time. I was inspired by Starbucks' concept of the 'third place.' I wanted to create a third place for the gamer, a place between home and school or work. Starbucks inspired us but we want to make it even better.

Wizards hoped that game centers would create an even stronger game playing community. The company also hoped that game centers could expand the interest in games and encourage people to consider games as an entertainment choice, like going to the movies or out to dinner. Just as the Cineplex concept broadened to the moviegoing public, Wizards hoped that "gameplexes" could do the same thing for games. The first Wizards of the Coast Game Center carried many competitive games, but Wizards games were featured prominently.

Lisa Stevens, one of the original founders and vice president of Location-Based Entertainment, comments: "Our strategic intent was driven by the quest 'to make games as big as movies.' We were all inspired by that quest. And then we ask ourselves, what made the movies big? Basically, the invention of the Cineplex, where you could go as a group and see different movies. That is why we offer different games in our retail stores, even games from some of our competitors." Another objective behind game centers was to improve the retail distribution of the Wizards product line. The company was disappointed with the support given by traditional retail-

FIGURE 2

Wizards of the Coast Game Center in Seattle's University District

ers to the games and felt that it knew better than retailers how to retail and support its games.

Wizards knew that the success of game centers was not a sure thing. Other companies, such as Gameworks, had introduced family entertainment centers with very limited success. Wizards was encouraged, however, by the success of the U.K.-based Games Workshop, with its gaming centers featuring the popular game *Warhammer®*. Adkison pointed out: "We have the brand but we need to improve distribution. Target and other stores help sustain the sales but those stores don't create new players, that's what we do in our retail stores."

Product Development

Wizards had developed and marketed what was viewed as many great games, but none was able to replicate *Magic's®* success. Although Adkison remained optimistic, he realized that repeating that tremendous success would be difficult. "We have several things we're working on in R&D that could turn out to be like *Magic®*. But in the gaming business, you can't bank on that success. We have to learn to make money with smaller releases."

The adventure game industry had developed largely as a result of two runaway hits, first *Dungeons & Dragons®*, and then *Magic®*. Adkison expected that another hit would one day revolutionize the industry once again. But it seemed unlikely that the same company would be responsible for the next revolution. Wizards needed to position itself to succeed even if it was not the one to develop this next hit.

Besides aggressively promoting *Magic®*, Wizards of the Coast had applied for a patent on *Magic®*, covering not the design of the cards but the method of play. It was set on collecting royalty payments from imitators, which had blossomed in recent years. Entry barriers to the game industry were relatively low, and Wizards estimated that there were more than 100 games trying to compete with *Magic®*.

Adkison recognized that Wizards of the Coast was still a one-product company, whose future was tightly linked to the success of *Magic®*: "*Magic®* provides over 90 percent of our cash flow. It is obviously our primary focus. The big strategic issue with *Magic®* is to develop its potential to become a 'classic game' that yields steady profits year after year. I wouldn't mind being a $500 million to $1 billion company. We want to make games as big as the movies."

Acquisitions

Wizards had recently completed two major acquisitions: Five Rings Publishing, the developer of the *Legends of the Five Rings®* trading-card game; and TSR, the creator of the pioneering *Dungeons & Dragons®* adventure game. The latter acquisition brought the number one (Wizards) and number three (TSR) of the adventure gaming industry under one roof in 1997. The number two of the industry is the publicly traded company Games Workshop from the United Kingdom. Adkison comments on Wizards' acquisition strategy:

> Looking at hobby gaming industry means that you need to look at a horizontally narrowed focused segment. And there are only three games in the hobby category out there: 1) *Magic®*, 2) *Dungeons & Dragons®*, and 3) *Warhammer®* [owned by Games Workshop]. And the sweet thing is that we own two of those three. One thing I have learned in my competitive analysis course in MBA-school is that it may be better to be a big player in a small market than to be a small player in a big market. And we want to be a big player.

However, integrating these acquisitions had been a major challenge for Wizards. It had to sort out TSR's very serious financial difficulties, and it moved the TSR operations and many of its staff from Wisconsin to its Seattle area headquarters.

Wizards had also confirmed reports that it had held discussions with Westend Games, which had the license for a Star Wars role-playing game, and another for a DC Comics role-playing game. There were other small game companies that might also make attractive acquisition candidates.

Global Expansion

Wizards estimated that *Magic®* was played in more than fifty countries by more than 5 million players. The company now had international offices in Antwerp, London, and Paris, and it planned to open other offices in Europe and Asia soon. Adkison noted that international sales had been very important in sustaining the company during the downturn in U.S. sales in 1996. The international market still had a lot of expansion potential.

BEYOND *MAGIC*®: CHALLENGES FACING PETER ADKISON

In December 1995, Wizards had a round of downsizing as Adkison was attempting to focus the company on *Magic*®. Wizards divested itself of the product lines that were not primarily trading-card games. The company's growth came to a sudden halt in 1996, when sales fell off to $117 million. According to Adkison, while the cause was partly the inevitable leveling-off in the growth of *Magic's*® customer base, the downturn was also due to the fragmentation of the retail game stores. The success of *Magic*® had drawn many entrepreneurs into the game store business, but there was not enough room for all of them. The resulting shakeout caused some distributors to go under, and this hit Wizards too.

In addition, many imitators offered role-playing adventure games on-line, and Wizards' executives worried that such games might replace the face-to-face experience of Wizards' *Magic*® and *Dungeons & Dragons*®. Adkison recognized that the company would have to respond to the Internet challenge: "Currently, we are looking at e-commerce, and how to sell on-line. Should we ignore it or crush it?"

While sales in 1997 were expected to be close to the same level as in 1996, Adkison was aiming at future growth. "We certainly can operate at a slow growth mode and make nice profits," he said. "But we are focused on growing the company more rapidly in the future." Part of the pressure for growth was coming from its original investors. Many of them were friends of the original entrepreneurs, came from modest backgrounds, and had become rich from their investment in Wizards. But this wealth was all on paper, and many wanted to cash out some of their investments. But to take the company public at an attractive price, Wizards would need to have a good growth story for new investors. Hence it was critical to develop a sustainable growth strategy. This was the central issue facing Wizards' executives as they sat down in mid 1997 to discuss Wizards' future.

APPENDIX A: MAGIC: THE GATHERING®

The game *Magic: The Gathering*® combines elements of chess, bridge, and the 1970s role-playing game *Dungeons & Dragons.*® *Magic*® is a trading-card game in which the two players are rival wizards dueling for control of a magical "universe" called *Dominia.* Each player starts out with twenty life points, or lives. The goal is to reduce the opponent's life points from twenty to zero before the opponent has reduced your life points to zero.

Before starting the game, each player builds a deck of at least forty cards from his or her collection of cards and then plays that deck against the opponent's deck. Each player begins by shuffling his or her deck and drawing seven cards. The players take turns; each player's turn is made up of a series of actions, such as playing cards and attacking the opponent. There are several types of elaborately illustrated cards a player can chose from. For example, lands are the most basic, providing the magical energy a player needs to play all other cards. Creatures can fight for the player either by attacking the opponent or by fighting off the opponent's creatures. Other cards represent spells that a player can cast to hurt the opponent or help his or her creatures. The basic strategy of *Magic* lies in choosing when to play what card and when to use what creatures to attack the opponent or protect yourself. More complex strategies involve combining cards to make them more powerful and choosing which cards to use in the player's deck to make it most effective. Games usually last between fifteen minutes and half an hour; however, some games can last up to several hours.

One of the key features of *Magic*® is that each game played is unique since each player starts out with a deck of 40 cards individually selected from among the more than 4,000 different cards sold. It is not uncommon for a player to own several hundred or even thousands of cards. Each player tries to assemble his or her favorite 40 cards out of the pool he or she owns according to the player's intended strategy. This ingenious twist encourages players to buy or trade for new cards to enhance their powers and strategic game options.

In addition, the game is in permanent evolution since new cards are constantly released and older cards are retired by Wizards of the Coast. These retired cards gain instant status as collectibles to be bought, sold, and traded in hobby stores, on college campuses, and on the Internet. New cards are issued in different sets and limited editions; many cards are even printed in limited numbers. These perpetual expansions have kept the game novel and contributed to its phenomenal growth as players engage in frantic buying and trading of cards in a fantasy arms race to create a competitive advantage in their individualist starter deck. Since most of the strategy in *Magic*® is assembling the unassailable deck, serious players have spent hundreds, if not thousands, of dollars to create their dream deck. This has led to the criticism that affluent players are more likely to win than their poorer counterparts.

With each expansion, *Dominia,* the fantasy multiverse where the wizards battle, also expands. "Think of *Dominia* as a beach," says Wizards spokeswoman Sue-Lane Wood. "Each expansion is a grain of sand on that beach, each its own universe." Currently, *Magic*® has undergone just a dozen or so extensions. However, the possible number of expansions is limited only by the imagination and the players' willingness to remain bewitched. Here are samples of *Magic*® cards.

Samples of
Magic® Cards

APPENDIX B: DUNGEONS & DRAGONS®

The *Dungeons & Dragons*® role-playing game, commonly known as *D&D,* evolved from historical war gaming, in which armchair generals lined up armies of painted miniature figurines on tabletops, decorated to look like battlefields, and staged skirmishes that were either historical or theoretical. Troop movements were negotiated with the help of rulers, and combat was resolved through the roll of dice and consultation of tables. Role-playing began with an idea to put aside the role of an entire army and take up the role of an individual character, who would infiltrate a castle through the sewers below to open the drawbridge and let in the invading army. This scenario proved so popular that the designer ran it repeatedly, for numerous friends and fellow wargamers, eventually substituting fantasy monsters for castle guards as obstacles to be overcome. Eventually, one of the players, Gary Gygax, volunteered to create standard rules for the new game, and he added rules for playing spell-casting wizards to offer an alternative to role-playing a warrior. These new rules were first published in Gygax's wargaming periodical *Chainmail,* but in 1974 he developed a full set of rules and called them *Dungeons & Dragons*®.

Over the next twenty-five years, *D&D* would be distributed in twenty-two countries and translated into more than a dozen languages. The *Advanced Dungeons & Dragons*® game expanded on the original in 1978, and the second-edition *AD&D*® game hit the market in 1989. Over a dozen *campaign settings*—distinct worlds in which to play *D&D*—were published over the years, and novels, computer games, board games, cartoons, comic books, and other media built upon the brand. Throughout its life, the *D&D* game frequently has been misunderstood, condemned, associated with nerds, and given up for dead, yet it retains near-universal brand recognition even among people who have never played it, and sales of the game are rising.

How D&D Is Played

Although computer games are simulating the traditional game with increasing efficiency, *D&D* is played with paper, pencil, dice, and rulebooks. A character is created by rolling dice to determine his or her basic physical and mental attributes, then the player chooses the character's profession (for example, fighter or wizard), equips the character for the road, joins with a group of friends who also have created characters, and goes on an adventure. One of the players takes on the special role of *Dungeon Master.* This person presents the situation at hand to the rest of the players, who react in character to cooperatively tell a story and enjoy the adventure together. For example, the Dungeon Master may say something like this, "You cross the drawbridge and enter the Castle of Nightmares, ready to seek and recover the famed *Staff of the Magi,* but a group of creatures steps from the shadows within to block your way. What will you do?" Each of the players in turn declares what his or her character intends to do—call out a greeting or threat, draw a weapon and prepare for battle, cast a spell, or anything else the player imagines the char-

acter might do under the circumstances—and then dice are rolled to determine the order in which actions take place and whether or not they are successful. (The Dungeon Master plays the role of every person and creature met by the adventuring party). Rounds of action continue until the encounter is resolved. The player-characters then move on and continue to explore the castle until they achieve their goal (in this case, finding the Staff) or until their characters are either captured or killed by the inhabitants of the castle. Collectively, they tell the story of the adventure, and collectively they work to succeed (or fail). Assuming the party is successful, they gain *experience points,* grow more powerful, and move on to even more challenging scenarios. Ongoing campaigns may last for years, with groups playing every week for hours at a time.

CASE 4

American Council for International Studies (ACIS): Striving to Stay Small

This case was prepared by Michael I. Eizenberg, Sharon Ungar Lane, and Alan N. Hoffman of Bentley College.

In the spring of 1977 four young middle-level managers at American Leadership Study Groups (ALSG) concluded that they were unhappy with the way their company was being run. As they saw it, senior management was out of touch with the day-to-day activities of the company and with long-range planning. After thoroughly discussing their concerns, Michael Eizenberg, aged twenty-nine, John Hannyngton, aged twenty-five, Peter Jones, aged twenty-seven, and David Stitt, aged twenty-six, decided that they would leave ALSG and go out on their own. They were convinced that they had the right combination of skills, experience, expertise, and commitment to build their own organization.

They soon enlisted the support of Linda Van Huss, ALSG's leading field sales person. Clandestinely, they created a business plan, sought legal advice, and among them invested $100,000 in cash. In addition, their close working relationships with Djohn Andersen and Miriam Zumpolle secured them $200,000 in backing from the Scandinavian Student Travel Service.

This case is intended to be used as the basis for class discussion rather than as an illustration of either effective or ineffective handling of the situation. This case was prepared by Michael I. Eizenberg, Sharon Unger Lane, and Alan N. Hoffman, Bentley College. Used by permission.

ACIS: THE EARLY YEARS

The American Council for International Studies, or ACIS, was conceived as an educational travel organization that enabled teachers to lead their students on educational trips abroad. Its goal was to create a highly efficient hands-on infrastructure, which would foster close partnerships with teachers so that they would return each year with a new group of student travelers. Senior managers' involvement in the day-to-day running of the organization to forge these partnerships was crucial and differentiated ACIS from its competitors.

In August 1978, ACIS was launched with a mailing to high schools throughout the United States. Its first brochure was a simple 32-page black-and-white catalog, whose prices were only a few percentage points lower than those in the glossy 100-page brochures of their much more established competition. The founders were counting on their personal relations with teachers, as well as their expertise, to bring in an initial base of customers. Sales during the first few months were much lower than they expected. Clients felt some personal loyalty, but were finally influenced by a sense of stability they had in working with a well-established organization.

"We didn't really understand the risk we were taking until we were actually out on our own,"

TABLE I

Overview of Educational Travel Organizations in 1979

Name	Year Founded	Estimated Number of Clients	Estimated Revenue	Location
American Institute for Foreign Study (AIFS)	1965	15,000	$25 million	Greenwich, Conn.
CHA	1966	17,000	$27 million	Philadelphia, Pa.
American Leadership Study Group (ALSG)	1966	12,000	$20 million	Worcester, Mass.
American Council for International Studies (ACIS)	1978	2,300	$3 million	Boston, Mass.

Eizenberg, the ACIS president, recalls. "Within the organization we were extremely confident of ourselves and our abilities. It wasn't until we were actually in our own sparsely furnished offices that we understood how much we had depended on the infrastructure we had previously worked within. All of a sudden, we understood the risk we were taking. There was a moment of pause, but we became stronger and more focused. We pulled harder together, and there was added intensity and purpose to our work. We realized that if we were going to make it, it would be because we had the strength and determination to make it happen."

Business did not pour into ACIS. Van Huss drove to high schools all over the South, virtually collaring the teachers who, she knew, led groups. New leads were followed up immediately with unprecedented levels of personal service. Despite its best efforts, when the sales season ended in January, ACIS had signed up only 2,300 participants—roughly 16 percent of what the established organizations were carrying, and about 30 percent below their own worst-case projections.

AIRLINE DEREGULATION

Throughout the 1960s and 1970s, all tour operators, including organizations offering educational trips, relied upon the inexpensive flights to Europe offered by charter companies. Only when charter flights were full did organizations turn to the

scheduled airlines for a few seats at significantly higher rates. The managers at ACIS were stunned to discover that they did not have enough passengers to make even the smallest charter flight operation possible. They had never considered having to rely totally on the scheduled carriers. Now they assumed they were going to have to grab a few seats here and there from a variety of carriers, at rates well above their budgets.

However, by the end of the 1970s, travelers' disenchantment with charter flights and the Airline Deregulation Act of 1978 began to have an impact. The skies were opening up to new competition on routes between the United States and the United Kingdom. Laker Airways was already beginning to provide scheduled service between New York and London; and British Airways and the U.S. flag carriers were faced with significant low-priced competition in their most lucrative transatlantic market.

The ACIS managers had nurtured contacts at British Airways, but British Airways had in the past been reluctant to seek the lower-priced traffic of customers such as ACIS. In early December, a call came from British Airways indicating its willingness to reconsider its position. An exploratory breakfast the next day with district manager Jim Kivlehan turned into an all-day session. By lunchtime, they had established that ACIS passengers could fly from all thirteen British Airways gateways in the United States so that it would not be necessary for passengers to fly to New York to board a charter flight. By late afternoon, British Airways had decided it would be willing to provide service to points beyond London with convenient connections on British European Airways. By the end of the day, the majority of ACIS passengers were placed at rates below original budgets on British Airways' scheduled 747s. The remaining passengers were placed on other foreign flag carriers in groups of forty or fifty at higher rates. The end result was much better than originally anticipated.

Its early foothold in selling scheduled service at new competitive rates from gateways throughout the United States suddenly gave ACIS a significant competitive advantage. Its small size in 1979 allowed the company to shift its passengers easily from charters to scheduled flights, and direct scheduled airline service from multiple U.S. gateways quickly became a defining characteristic of ACIS. Larger, more established companies lacked the impetus to change, and their existing infrastructures made such a major change difficult to implement. They had thrived with charters and controlled significant market share; they would only gradually make the shift that ACIS had made in one morning.

IT'S GREAT TO BE SMALL

ACIS's organizational structure was simple. Eizenberg was president. He handled flights, general management, and corporate functions. Stitt and Jones were responsible for telephone sales in Boston, Van Huss was in charge of field sales throughout the Southeast, and Hannyngton directed overseas operations. All four were Vice Presidents. There were three other full-time employees.

When prospective trip leaders spoke to Jones, Stitt, or Van Huss, they had direct access to Hannyngton's strong organizational abilities overseas and Eizenberg's grasp of the emerging opportunities in the deregulated airline industry. All decisions were made within the small management group. When they disagreed, they considered various solutions until they found one that worked from all points of view. Everyone was on hand, accessible, and deeply committed to the common goal of doing their best for each customer.

The integration of sales, flight, and overseas arrangements was spontaneous. The whole organization, its customers, and suppliers benefited greatly from the fact that commitments were made

quickly and decisively. Active communication led to constant and thorough review.

Close partnerships were forged with teachers who led groups. Especially careful attention was paid to selecting staff in Europe, who would be ACIS's frontline representatives overseas and in day-to-day charge of all educational and operational components. ACIS executives were also always highly visible abroad, pitching in to ensure high levels of customer satisfaction. As the dollar strengthened during the early and mid 1980s, ACIS significantly improved hotel quality without passing on major price increases, adding substantially to its own bottom line. Teachers frequently commented that ACIS's programs kept improving every year.

The years from 1980 to 1985 were outstanding for ACIS. Enrollments grew 25 to 30 percent each year. Tangible excitement pulsed through the organization. Everything kept getting better. Airline seats were plentiful and the dollar had more and more purchasing power abroad. When Eurodollar interest rates soared to 20 percent, ACIS's bottom line rose substantially as well. Profitability was high enough each year to support building a larger organization with higher ongoing and infrastructure expenses. Most importantly, the word was spreading to high school teachers everywhere that ACIS offered a genuinely interesting educational experience, great quality, and exceptional personal service.

In 1981, ACIS began investing in a Data General computer system, and Mike Tenney was hired as system architect. He created an integrated database for sales, marketing, operations, and administration. Embedded "notepads" allowed sales and operations staff to make modifications to ACIS's expanding range of preplanned itineraries and keep track of special customer requests and sales commitments, permitting the selling process to remain responsive to special customers and changing market conditions. By 1983, there was E-mail throughout the Boston office and a modem link with Atlanta. By 1984, many ACIS managers had Macintoshes on their desks and used emulation software to access travel information in the Data General computer system.

1985: GROWTH AND PROSPERITY

In 1985, ACIS had acquired a historic brownstone building for its headquarters in Boston and opened sales offices in Atlanta, Chicago, and Los Angeles. In addition, it had acquired a small office building for its European headquarters in London, opened an operations office in Paris, and invested in start-up companies to handle arrangements in Madrid and Rome. Its customer base was loyal and solid and enthusiastically referred new customers to ACIS. The organization had excellent working relationships with all major airlines. The overseas network provided high-quality services, and the educational experience was beneficial to all involved. However, ACIS's core infrastructure in 1985 remained surprisingly small. Seventeen people worked in Boston, four in Atlanta, one in Chicago and Los Angeles, and two in London and Paris. Revenues were now in the same range as those of its largest competitors, and it provided superior service with many fewer staff members.

"Both 1984 and 1985 were incredible years," Eizenberg recalls. "The marketplace had a definite rhythm. The dollar was stronger than it had ever been. Suddenly it was 10 francs to the dollar, not 5. Everyone wanted to go to Europe, the airlines had plenty of seats to sell, and we had great trips to offer at very good prices. It was as if we were dancing to the beat of our customers and our suppliers. Each of us at ACIS had developed a lot of our own patterns, but we danced together. It felt like we all had parts in an amazing piece of choreography." ACIS's sales season for spring and summer 1986 ended just before the Christmas holidays of 1985 and had set another record. Everyone in the organization felt great heading home for the holiday break.

TERRORISM STRIKES THE ROME AIRPORT

On December 27, 1985, as terminals were jammed with hundreds of holiday travelers waiting at the check-in counters, Leonardo da Vinci Airport in Rome was attacked by terrorists. At 9:03 A.M. a man threw a grenade toward an espresso bar. Other terrorists showered the 820-foot-long terminal with bullets. Within five minutes the attack was over, leaving fifteen people dead and seventy-four wounded. Minutes later, the terror was repeated at Schwechat Airport in Vienna as terrorists opened fire with AK-47 automatic rifles and rolled three hand grenades across the floor like bowling balls toward their victims. The result: thirty-seven dead and forty-seven wounded. The entire civilized world was outraged and feared what terrorists might do next.

Airport authorities had been on guard because of a November 26, 1985, U.S. Federal Aviation Administration (FAA) alert for terrorist threats. Interpol, the international Paris-based anticrime organization, had issued a similar warning. But heightened security at the airports in both Rome and Vienna had not prevented the attacks because precautions had been taken mainly in the boarding areas and around the planes themselves, whereas the terrorists attacked places away from the boarding gates, where people were allowed to move freely. The aim clearly was to massacre innocent, defenseless civilians.

The impact on international travel was immediate. No one wanted to go to Europe. It seemed as though everyone who had signed up for an ACIS trip no longer had any intention of going. The switchboard was overwhelmed with phone calls insisting that trips be canceled and all monies refunded. ACIS received 7,000 cancellations and demands for refunds in just two days. Its remaining 8,000 passengers were likely to cancel as well.

For the first few days, everyone at ACIS was stunned trying to deal with the panic. "At first, we simply did our best to buy time and try to calm everybody down. We assured them that we were a responsible organization, and could be counted on in this difficult situation," Eizenberg explains. "No matter what we said, it was clear that the situation was far beyond anything we could control. A sense of panic prevailed that we increasingly felt helpless to do anything about. Cancellations kept streaming in, along with demands for full refunds."

Perhaps 30 percent of prospective participants were willing to take a wait-and-see attitude. The predominant view from the marketplace called for ACIS to cancel all trips and make full refunds. However, doing so would have had severe financial consequences. After all the work and money already expended, the whole of 1986 stood to be a total loss.

The ACIS participant contract contained clear language about cancellation penalties, entitling ACIS to keep $250 from the deposit of anyone who canceled. Enforcing these penalties would give ACIS the same level of income from those who chose to cancel as it would earn from those who chose to participate.

Although the U.S. State Department informed ACIS that there were no travel advisories indicating that travel to Europe was unsafe or that there was a significant threat of future terrorist attacks, ACIS

TABLE 2

Overview of Educational Travel Organizations in 1985

Name	Year Founded	Estimated Number of Clients	Estimated Revenue	Location
American Institute for Foreign Study (AIFS)	1965	14,000	$25 million	Greenwich, Conn.
CHA	1966	16,000	$27 million	Philadelphia, Pa.
American Leadership Study Group (ALSG)	1966	13,000	$21 million	Worcester, Mass.
American Council for International Studies (ACIS)	1978	15,300	$24 million	Boston, Mass.

could not sell this view in the marketplace. However, enforcing cancellation penalties would have alienated the goodwill ACIS had worked so hard to build up. After all its success and good luck, ACIS faced a no-win situation: either risk losing the market or face losing a significant percentage of its capital.

"After a week, even the most loyal ACIS teachers were growing impatient for answers. They needed an immediate solution that would work with students, parents, and school administrators," Eizenberg recalls. "On January 7, we announced we were amending the cancellation policies stated in our catalogue and were offering full refunds of all monies except for a $35 registration/processing fee and a $150 credit which could be used on a future trip abroad with ACIS."

Everyone at ACIS felt that the offer was an extremely fair and generous solution under the circumstances. Most parents, teachers, and school administrators also acknowledged the good faith the offer represented. Still, processing the 8,000 cancellations was discouraging to everyone at ACIS. ACIS's fine reputation had been thoroughly tested, but not tarnished.

ACIS had built up financial reserves during its good years, and they would have been dangerously drained had 1986 been a total loss. But the year turned out quite well. Retaining the $35 registration/processing fee guaranteed the organization $500,000 in 1986 income. Interest income on deposits and future credits contributed another $350,000. Six thousand passengers ended up travel-

ing, yielding $250,000 in operating income. Airlines eager to generate sales came through with $250,000 in promotional support. By the spring the dollar had dropped 12 percent in value, and the organization sold off $3 million in excess foreign exchange contracts. This brought in an additional $350,000. By year's end, ACIS both showed a respectable profit while preserving its greatest asset, the goodwill of its customers.

While ACIS withstood the unprecedented events of 1986 quite well, the feeling that it could not withstand two or three similar years in rapid succession persisted. When the sales season for 1987 began in September 1986, the market had not gotten over the shock either. The substantially weaker U.S. dollar and lower U.S. interest rates were not helping. By October, it was clear that the market would recover only to about 75 percent of its previous level and that profitability would be reduced to about half of what it was in 1985.

THE ACQUISITION OF ACIS

In late October of 1986, Eizenberg spoke with Bertil Hult, owner of EF, the world's largest educational travel organization. EF had begun as a small language school for Swedish students who wanted to study English in the United Kingdom. By 1986, EF was operating various language and exchange programs for more than 50,000 participants worldwide. Hult wanted to expand his position in the U.S. market and asked if ACIS would be interested in becoming part of his large and diversified organization. He suggested that they meet at his offices in Santa Barbara.

"I really didn't expect much when I flew out. There were four of us with significant ownership positions in ACIS, and I knew that it would take $5,000,000 for a deal to be worthwhile for all of us. I couldn't imagine anyone paying that much for ACIS in the current market environment. At the meetings, I was extremely impressed with Bertil and the other EF senior managers I met," Eizenberg recalls. "Late the following afternoon we got around to discussing the number. Bertil's jaw dropped when I mentioned the $5 million figure. He'd thought we were in bad financial shape after 1986, but we weren't. I remember his saying that with EF's management, worldwide resources, and marketing expertise, he could quickly build a company much larger and more competitive than ACIS for a lot less than $5 million. The meeting ended cordially, but I realized that EF was never going to pay the money it would take to make us all happy, and there was no way we were going to sell for less."

A week later, at the annual meeting of the Council for Standards in International Education (CSIET) in Washington, D.C., Eizenberg sat with one of the EF executives he had met in Santa Barbara. Hank Kahn, a divisional president of American Institute for Foreign Study (AIFS), observed Eizenberg's rapport with his EF colleagues and asked what was going on between him and EF. Eizenberg told Kahn that EF was interested in acquiring ACIS and added that the number being discussed was $5 million.

AIFS, Inc. had become a publicly traded company (NASDAQ) in February 1986. At that time, it was the parent company of the American Institute for Foreign Study, Inc. The institute operated a diversified group of programs all in the field of international education. These included College Semester Summer Study Abroad, High School Academic and Travel programs, and several inbound programs (including Camp America, Homestay in America, Academic Year in America, and Au Pair in America). It also owned Richmond College, a fully accredited American university in London. In November 1986, AIFS; Inc. acquired ELS English Language Schools as its second subsidiary. In the spring of 1987, Roger Walther, president and co-founder of AIFS; Inc., announced his intention to acquire ACIS, one of his largest competitors in the outbound high school market, in order to propel

the firm to dominance in the international student travel industry.

In June 1987, AIFS, Inc. acquired ACIS for $4.75 million combined cash and stock, plus earn-out incentives worth an additional $1.5 million over five years. ACIS thus became AIFS, Inc.'s third subsidiary. The management for all AIFS, outbound high school programs became the responsibility of the ACIS management team, and ACIS became the single brand name for all ACIS and AIFS outbound high school programs (see Figure 1).

Eizenberg remained as president and CEO of ACIS and also joined the board of AIFS, Inc., and the board of trustees of Richmond College. Jones, Hannyngton, and Van Huss retained their positions as senior managers at ACIS, keeping intact the entrepreneurial team that had created the company.

The late 1980s were a time of expansive growth for AIFS, Inc. With the acquisition of the two new subsidiaries sales volume grew from $33,049,000 in 1986 to $95,604,000 in 1988. The high school subsidiary accounted for approximately 40 percent of gross sales in 1988, and AIFS, Inc. returned to a leadership position in this important market area.

The original owners of ACIS stayed on as the management team of the organization. The ACIS subsidiary underwent regular review by the AIFS, Inc. board, but it continued to function with a great deal of autonomy. ACIS achieved all of the performance goals established in the original acquisition agreement and received the maximum amount payable under the terms of the earn-out. The 1990s brought new challenges and new opportunities for AIFS, Inc. and for the management team of the ACIS subsidiary.

1990: WAR IN IRAQ/KUWAIT

In August, 1990, Iraqi military forces invaded and occupied the small neighboring Kuwait, and in January 1991 Desert Storm was launched against Iraq. Iraq capitulated on February 28. ACIS enrollments in 1991 suffered much as they had in 1986. Enrollments had been low during the fall. When the war erupted in January, ACIS experienced a 50 percent cancellation rate. By the time the war ended, it was too late to renew interest in ACIS's 1991 programs. As in 1986, ACIS kept a small processing fee and refunded the balance of all monies paid except for

FIGURE I

Organizational Chart of AIFS, Inc. and Subsidiaries, 1997

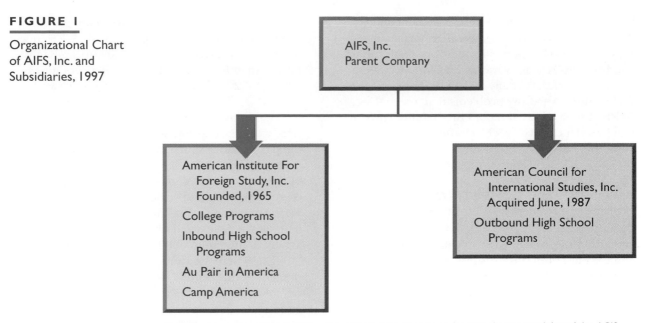

Note: the management for all AIFS outbound high school programs became the responsibility of the ACIS management team in 1988. ACIS became the single brand name for all ACIS and AIFS outbound high school programs in 1989.

$150, which could be used as a credit on a future trip with ACIS. However, ACIS recognized that the low participant numbers offered a chance to regroup and began looking at its 1992 planning with a new sense of urgency.

NEW LOOK, NEW IDEAS, NEW BUSINESS

In January 1992, Charlotte Dietz, the vice president of marketing, initiated a series of focus group meetings and several marketing initiatives that were destined to change the face of ACIS entirely. A "partnership committee" of twenty-five teachers came to Boston to discuss their views of international travel in general and ACIS in particular. The loyalty the teachers felt to ACIS was stronger than anyone within the organization had imagined. They reinforced the view that the quality of ACIS programs abroad and its level of personal service prior to departure was markedly superior to that of its competitors. The teachers genuinely wanted to help spread the word about the superiority of ACIS programs. The problem was that CHA, EF, ACIS and ALSG all had beautiful four-color brochures emphasizing the high quality each organization offered.

All that differentiated them was price; and in this regard, ACIS was at a disadvantage.

ACIS's marketing plan for 1992 was a strategic breakthrough. It focused on three key areas: (1) mobilizing ACIS's loyal customer base, (2) enhancing and differentiating ACIS's written materials, and (3) making ACIS's commitment to quality tangible and accessible to new teachers.

In early July, a personal letter of thanks was sent to the entire ACIS mailing list. The letter also solicited referrals, offering a $100 stipend per new teacher enrolled. The mailing yielded new leads, which in turn yielded a lot of new business.

The 1992 ACIS catalog was published in late August 1991. Its look was revolutionary. The presentation was of the highest quality; it looked more like a coffee-table book than a travel brochure. On the cover was a reproduction of Maximilien Luce's impressionist masterpiece "Le Quai St-Michel et Notre Dame." Beautiful four-color photographs adorned the inside pages. Interesting vignettes created exciting itineraries. Teacher testimonials expressed satisfaction and loyalty. ACIS's brochure finally conveyed its unique vision of educational travel.

Participant numbers skyrocketed in 1992. Flight costs were kept substantially below budget. More than 100 new couriers were selected and trained. All departments and overseas offices maintained very high levels of performance. Continuing airline and hotel overcapacity meant that suppliers were genuinely grateful for any and all business and willingly helped solve any problems that arose. ACIS finished the year with record profitability. The original founders of ACIS received the balance of their earn-out.

A LONG-TIME COMPETITOR EXITS

In September 1991, Milestone Educational Institute acquired the assets of ALSG. In June, 1993, Milestone went out of business leaving more than 5,000 students and teachers without trips at the last minute. The ACIS management team immediately set about helping the stranded travelers, supported by $100,000 of corporate funds for the cause to provide free or substantially reduced rates to the stranded groups. Continental Airlines provided free tickets for all passengers ALSG had booked with Continental. Several communities held local fund-raising events. EF also offered a reduced rate plan. Passports, a new entrant started by Gil Markle, the original founder of ALSG, provided support as well. Within ten days, the majority of stranded travelers were setting off on trips. ACIS benefited tremendously from the goodwill its actions created during the crisis, adding substantially to its bottom line for many years to come.

A GOOD IDEA

In 1993, ACIS managers read *Service Breakthroughs,* a book by James Heskett, Earl Sasser, and Christopher Hart, all Harvard Business School professors. ACIS was already committed to providing high quality. *Service Breakthroughs* made high quality crucial and insisted that a key step to achieving it was establishing parameters so that quality could be objectively measured. Questionnaires were individually prepared for each teacher to evaluate every service, measure overall satisfaction, and compare ACIS to other travel organizations.

The overall level of teacher satisfaction was exceptionally high: 96.5 percent indicated that they planned to travel with ACIS again, and 98 percent indicated they would recommend ACIS to a colleague. More than 75 percent of experienced teachers indicated that ACIS was "outstandingly better" than its lower-priced competitors, and an additional 20 percent indicated that ACIS was "better."

The reports also collated statistical data about satisfaction ratings for each hotel and every meal, the performance of the courier, and overall predeparture service, as well as the educational content of the trip. Overall ratings were high, although there were some disparities. Statistical standards were established according to type of service. To be retained, hotels and restaurants were required to achieve a minimum of 80 percent good/excellent ratings, 15 percent average, and not more than 5 percent poor. Couriers were required to achieve ratings of at least 80 percent excellent, 15 percent good, and 5 percent average. Educational content required an overall 95 percent rating of excellent.

The "Teacher Evaluation Report" was distributed to all ACIS staff and immediately became the standard by which the organization measured itself. Key numbers from this report were published in ACIS's 1994 teacher brochure to emphasize teacher satisfaction.

EVERYTHING IS GREAT, BUT . . .

ACIS's 1994 results were outstanding. It gained a significant portion of the market share that ALSG had previously controlled, and the dollar increased in value. Altogether, it made for an extremely impressive bottom line.

Each of the functional departments maintained high levels of performance even with all the growth. However, the significant increase in volume began to strain internal systems. In its 1994 brochure, ACIS offered ninety-two different programs, many of which could be modified with extra days or additional features. Sales staff also regularly made minor adjustments at the request of teachers. The notepad feature of the now ten-year-old database allowed the noting of these modifications and adjustments but did not integrate them into the actual database structure. At lower volume levels, it was feasible for all the departments to work with the notepads, but not as volume increased.

TABLE 3

Overview of Educational Travel Organizations in 1994

Name	Year Founded	Estimated Number of Participants	Estimated Revenue	Location
EF	1986	70,000	$120 million	Cambridge, Mass.
CHA	1966	35,000	$ 70 million	Philadelphia, Pa.
ACIS	1978	35,000	$ 80 million	Boston, Mass.
Passports	1993	2,300	$ 3 million	Spencer, Mass.

Until seventy-five days prior to departure, ACIS "free sold" from a wide-open inventory of more than ninety itineraries. Some teachers had groups as small as five or six participants; others as large as forty or fifty. For efficient operation in Europe, they all had to be divided into bus groups of thirty-five to forty-five. Eighty percent of the time this happened as part of the natural flow of demand. However, significant numbers of teachers were asked to switch dates or change their programs to fit a coherent operational structure. The large variety of programs offered by ACIS meant that this consolidation process became more complex as the number of participants and the number of itineraries offered grew.

Airline and hotel capacity was beginning to show signs of tightening, and it was extremely challenging to find the space needed during the peak demand periods. The premise of unlimited capacity was questioned.

Twice in 1994 the organization ground to a virtual halt while the issues surrounding consolidating groups and finding the required air and hotel capacity were resolved. ACIS was uncharacteristically performing like a large, unwieldy company. Often ACIS senior managers had to step in to solve problems that went beyond what staff members could address.

The hands-on work of ACIS senior staff during these periods helped maintain overall morale within the organization and a high satisfaction level among teachers. Teachers were frequently given extra benefits when their trip plans needed to be changed. Customer satisfaction results were extremely high in 1994, with nearly 99 percent of teachers saying that they would recommend ACIS to a colleague. Enrollment figures and profitability came in at record levels. By the time of the 1995 sales meeting in August 1994, the intense months of the previous year were a distant memory.

YIELD MANAGEMENT AND GLOBAL ALLIANCES

Before the Airline Deregulation Act of 1978, the U.S. government carefully regulated the number of scheduled flights allowed on all international and domestic routes, and all airlines were required to charge the same governmentally regulated rates. As soon as the Deregulation Act took effect, upstarts such as People's Express, Laker, New York Air, Southwest, and Midway moved into previously protected routes, and airline capacity more than doubled. The established carriers also scrambled to expand route systems. The extra capacity created a bonanza for travel industry wholesalers such as ACIS. Airlines needed help filling all the seats that were coming into the market. High-volume wholesalers were able to leverage huge discounts from carriers desperate for business. Wholesalers in every market segment prospered while the airlines themselves lost billions year after year.

In response, the established carriers began to develop yield management systems. The early systems lacked the sophistication and the computer capability to manage seat inventory for maximum yield. Carriers either sold too many cheap seats and didn't hold back sufficient seat inventory for higher-paying customers, or they held back too many high-priced seats and flew empty airplanes.

In 1988, Bell Laboratories patented a mathematical formula that could perform rapid calculations on fare problems with literally thousands of variables. During the next five years further advances in software enabled the yield and inventory control departments at major airlines to perform complicated passenger demand and rate-per-seat calculations on a flight by flight basis. Computer-driven yield-control calculations decided the number of cheap seats available on every flight.

In 1991, the U.S. government granted antitrust immunity to a global alliance between Northwest Airlines and KLM Royal Dutch Airlines. This global alliance permitted Northwest and KLM to code-share using the same aircraft on previously competitive routes, and to enter into joint marketing agreements that covered their entire route systems. Delta Airlines entered into a similar global alliance with Swiss Air and Sabena, and United Airlines entered an alliance with Lufthansa and SAS. An alliance between British Airways and American Airlines is awaiting government approval. These alliances reduced the amount of capacity partners made available on competitive routes to passenger demand.

By 1994, the unprecedented airline losses, which occurred in the first fourteen years after deregulation, had turned into record profits.

1995: UPGRADING ACIS INFORMATION SYSTEMS

In 1995, senior management recognized that the problem of communication between the strong functional departments needed to be addressed. A core inventory of trips was established, and the group reservations department was put in charge of overall coordination of the sales, flights, and overseas departments. But the two initiatives yielded only small improvements in overall coordination. The large variety of trips that ACIS offered made selling into the core inventory extremely difficult, especially in the competitive market in which ACIS was operating. Airlines were releasing less of their flight inventory to wholesale group sales. By the time the

ACIS group reservations department had the opportunity to provide overall coordination, a lot of the least expensive airline space was already gone.

Mike Tenney, a senior vice president at the company, was at work on writing the code for a new Oracle database system. In the meantime, each department was forced to find complex, inefficient, and undocumented "work-arounds" to cope with the limitations of the now twelve-year-old computer system. Annually, ACIS experienced two extremely difficult and stressful time periods, when the overall organizational flow stopped while the expectations and demands of groups were made to fit within available airline and hotel space. In 1995, the two periods lasted six weeks instead of four. For the first time, significant airlines cost overruns were incurred for about 3 percent of ACIS passengers. The dollar also weakened at a time when ACIS was "long" dollars. These two factors reduced ACIS profitability by about 20 percent from the record levels achieved the year before. Although 1995 was a good year, management was concerned that it would no longer always be easy to find the cheap airline seats that ACIS's budgeting depended on.

Stephen Cummings, also a senior vice president, installed a wide area network using frame relay technology. This gave all 100 ACIS employees in the United States and Europe instant access to the Business Basic database, as well as several secondary databases developed in Lotus Notes. The Microsoft Office Suite was installed on all ACIS servers worldwide. Lotus Notes Mail was used companywide and ACIS began gathering teacher E-mail addresses to facilitate electronic communication with teachers. A Web site was established with basic information about ACIS and its most popular programs.

But it was increasingly clear that the overall organizational design of the company did not work effectively within the constraints of limited airline and hotel capacity, and there was as much of a battle for cheap seats as there was for passengers. The organization was being stretched to its limits for longer periods of time than ever before.

NEW CHALLENGES FOR 1996

ACIS faced new challenges at every turn. EF already had a mailing out that guaranteed extremely low prices for 1996. In addition, experienced employees from Milestone created a new competitor, National Educational Travel Council (NETC), which had secured substantial backing from a group of U.K. investors and offered high-quality, small-company service at low prices.

ACIS senior managers also realized that the overall dynamics of the business were changing because cheap seats were becoming a scarce commodity and were often sold out, especially during busy periods. And it had become increasingly difficult to find well-located high-quality hotels within ACIS's budgets. ACIS's commitment to maintaining consistently high quality also drove trip fees up, because services receiving lower customer satisfaction had to be replaced with more expensive ones, increasing the price differential between ACIS and its lower-priced competitors. Customers willing to pay the larger price differential were harder to find. At the same time, the dollar was dropping in value in Europe, and ACIS was long dollars for the entire 1996 season.

Senior management was very concerned about losing market share, especially to NETC. Something had to be done to keep prices down. The best way to hold the line was to get more business in sooner to increase efficiency and ensure the best access to the maximum number of cheap seats and lowest-priced good-quality land arrangements.

ACIS: BEGINNING TO LOSE THAT "SMALL FEELING"

ACIS announced its most aggressive pricing strategy ever, contingent on participants meeting early enrollment deadlines. They did, and by October 15 enrollments were at record levels. The deluge of registrations stretched ACIS processing capabilities to their limits. The new enrollment deadlines added another degree of complexity to the already strained computer system. In processing early registration, there was definite advantage when the group reservations department could position groups so that they meshed well with the expectations of teachers and the availability of flights and overseas arrangements. Frequently, however, there was no readily apparent solution, and it became extremely complex to negotiate an outcome that was acceptable to the different functional departments, because each had limitations and requirements that it felt compelled to meet. In effect, this meant that 25 percent of all groups booked could not readily

flow through the system. This was further complicated by the notepad structure of the old database system, which dealt with minor modifications to itineraries by noting them as text in an "exceptions" field, and did not integrate them into the overall database structure.

The 1996 strategy worked only insofar as it preserved and expanded ACIS's market share. It kept NETC from gaining market share solely at the expense of ACIS. However, ACIS began to feel like a big company. The organization ground to a halt for extended periods to resolve discrepancies between teacher expectation and operational requirements. But as high quality remained a driving concern, ACIS again received extremely high teacher satisfaction ratings.

Despite the surge in enrollment numbers, profitability for 1996 dropped to its lowest level in several years: lower prices yielded decreased margins and high enrollment led to long dollars while the value of the dollar plummeted. In addition, the strategy of having participants book early so that ACIS would have better access to lower-priced airline seats was only partly successful. The cost savings were more than offset by cost overages on the last 5 percent of passengers booked, reducing profitability.

THE NEED TO GET SMALL AGAIN

January 1996 was a crucial month at ACIS. Eizenberg had returned after spending three months in the Advanced Management Program at Harvard Business School. Passenger numbers were at a record high, but airlines were increasingly imposing capacity limitations. Hotel space was tight. The twelve-year-old reservation and group management system was being stretched to its limits. Consolidating groups into a workable structure was more complex than ever before. Everyone in the organization displayed incredible dedication, but there was also more than enough stress and frustration.

ACIS had five major functional departments: administration, flights, group reservations, overseas, and sales. Meetings were held to consider the challenges the organization faced. They began with a strategic overview of the growth and development of ACIS, and proceeded to a discussion of how a combination of once extremely favorable external conditions had become much more challenging. Six common themes emerged:

■ Profitability needed to improve.

■ The database system caused a lot of problems.

■ There were difficulties in communicating between departments and offices.

■ The staff in one department did not know what the staff in another department did.

■ Competition made it hard to find new clients and low-cost airline seats.

■ Sometimes ACIS felt like a big, clumsy company.

"The problems we faced would have been unthinkable in the early days of ACIS," Eizenberg recalls. "Then profitability had increased year after year. In those days it was great when the computer had worked right, but we were close enough to what we were doing that it didn't matter as much when it didn't. Sure, we had written memos to document what we were doing, but the most important communication happened spontaneously when we simply spoke to each other every day. When there were seven, eight, nine, ten of us, we worked so closely together that we always knew what the other was doing. Selling was much easier when we had a smaller number of programs. We knew the exact details of each program so well that it was simple to convince potential clients about our superior product. Years before, we could move the whole organization in an instant to take advantage of inexpensive airline seats when they became available. Back then we proved that a highly motivated team working together with the right combination of capabilities and experience could accomplish just about anything. Peter Jones, my partner from the earliest days of the organization, was skeptical at first but he climbed on board when I told him it was time to reinvent the old ACIS. The only difference was this time we'd be coaches."

1997: ANOTHER DIFFICULT YEAR FOR EDUCATIONAL TRAVEL

Sales started slowly for 1997. The crash of TWA Flight 800 in July 1996 had cast a shadow over educational travel. In addition, the dollar was weak when ACIS entered into foreign exchange contracts to establish pricing rates for its 1997 programs. This forced the company to significantly increase prices to bring its margins back to workable levels. There were also difficulties in implementing the new Oracle database system. Together, all these factors contributed to a significant decline in 1997 sales compared with sales in the previous two years.

APPENDIX: AIFS, INC., 1997

Board of Directors
Cyril J.H. Taylor
Chairman of the Board

Robert N. Brennan
Vice Chairman
President and COO, American Institute for Foreign Study, Inc.

Michael I. Eizenberg
President and CEO, American Council for International Studies, Inc.

Walter McCann
President, Richmond College

Peter Tcherepnine
Executive Vice President
Loeb Partners Corporation

Headquarters
AIFS, Inc.
102 Greenwich Avenue
Greenwich, Connecticut 06830

Subsidiaries
American Institute for Foreign Study
102 Greenwich Avenue
Greenwich, Connecticut 06820

37 Queens Gate
London, SW7 5HR

American Council for International Studies
19 Bay State Road
Boston, Massachusetts 02181

Subsidiary Officers

American Institute for Foreign Study

Cyril J.H. Taylor
Chairman and CEO

Robert N. Brennan
President and COO

Peter Lasalandra
Senior Vice President

William Gertz
Senior Vice President

John Linakis
Senior Vice President

Robert Cristadoro
Vice President

Barbara Cartledge
Vice President

Dennis Regan
Vice President

Paul Moonves
Senior Vice President and Treasurer

American Council for International Studies

Michael I. Eizenberg
President and CEO

Peter Jones
Managing Director

Tom Jones
Executive Vice President

Rebecca Tabaczynski
Executive Vice President

Linda Van Huss
Executive Vice President

Charlotte Dietz
Senior Vice President

Stephen Cummings
Senior Vice President

Michael Tenney
Senior Vice President

CASE 5

Replacements, LTD.

This case was prepared by Lew G. Brown, Tony R. Wingler, Vidya Gargeya, John H. Lundin, Kevin B. Lowe, Don K. Sowers, Kristen M. Cashman, and Charles A. Kivett, of the Joseph M. Bryan School of Business and Economics, University of North Carolina at Greensboro.

A HOBBY BECOMES A BUSINESS

On September 5, 1997, just a little before 1:30 P.M., a group of faculty members and an undergraduate research fellow from the University of North Carolina at Greensboro assembled outside the front entrance to Replacements, Ltd. The company's headquarters was located just off Interstate highways 85 and 40 on Greensboro's eastern edge. As the group waited for everyone to arrive, a steady stream of customers entered and left the company's large, first-floor showroom.

Once everyone was present, the group entered the building, and Doug Anderson, the company's executive vice president, escorted the visitors to the second-floor conference room. Waiting there were Ron Swanson, the chief information officer; Scott Fleming, the vice president of operations; and Kelly Smith, the chief financial officer. (See Figure 1 for the company's organization chart.)

A few minutes later, Bob Page, the company's president, entered the conference room. Like all the officers, he was casually dressed, wearing a dark blue knit shirt that bore the Replacements, Ltd.,

This case is intended to be used as the basis for class discussion rather than as an illustration of either effective or ineffective handling of the situation. This case was prepared by Lew G. Brown, Tony R. Wingler, Vidya Gargeya, John H. Lundin, Kevin B. Lowe, Don K. Sowers, Kristen M. Cashman, and Charles A. Kivett, University of North Carolina at Greensboro. Used by permission.

logo. Following closely behind Page were his two miniature black and tan dachshunds, Trudy and Toby. Page always had the two dogs with him at work, and they had free run of the executive office area. It was not unusual for them to enter and leave meetings, perhaps carrying chew-toys with them.

After the introductions, Page began:

I'm not comfortable making speeches, but I do like to talk about the company's history. So I thought I would just do that as a way of helping you begin gathering information for your case.

I was born on a small tobacco farm in Rockingham County, near the city of Reidsville. I have two brothers and a sister. We grew up working on the farm. When the time came, I went to North Carolina State University. After two years, I decided to transfer to UNC Chapel Hill, where I majored in accounting. After graduation, the Army drafted me. I got out in 1970, went to work for an accounting firm, and later earned my CPA.

After about four years, for some reason, I took a job as an auditor with the State of North Carolina. From the first day, I hated the job. I just didn't like politics and all the rules and regulations. I was very unhappy.

About this time, I guess to get away from my unhappiness at work, I started going to flea markets, buying and selling things on consignment. It was not unusual for me to leave work on a

FIGURE I

Replacements, Ltd., Organizational Chart

Source: Replacements, Ltd.

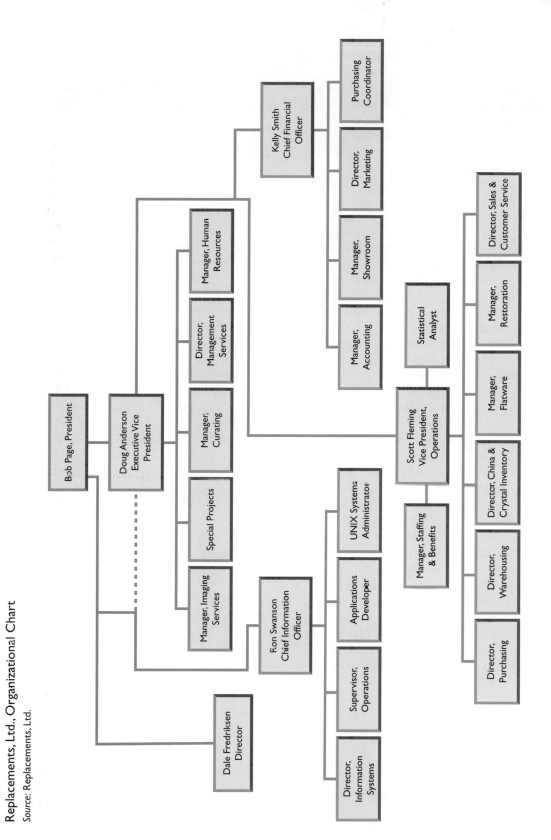

Friday afternoon and drive all night in order to be at a flea market, say, in Nashville, Tennessee, the next morning.

People learned about my hobby and began to ask me to keep an eye out for various things, especially china patterns. Perhaps they had broken a piece of their china and found that the manufacturer no longer made that pattern. Or, perhaps they had never had a full set and now wanted to complete it. When I got a request, I'd make a note on a 3-by-5 index card and put it in an old recipe box. When I was at a flea market and found a china pattern that someone needed, I'd buy it. When I got home, I'd drop them a line or give them a call.

I was still working for the state at this time. Word of my hobby spread, and I found myself getting more and more requests. I'd come home at night and find lots of mail and phone messages. I set up a card table in my bedroom to keep up with the paperwork. I packed orders for mailing on my kitchen floor.

By 1981, I was working late almost every night. I'd sold about $53,000 worth of china, etc., the previous year. I finally got up the nerve to quit my job with the state in March and to try to make a go of my hobby. My friends thought I was crazy to leave a good job with the state in order to sell used "dishes." But I wanted to do something enjoyable and fun. I thought I'd be better off in the long run.

The first thing I needed was more space, because I'd filled up my apartment. I rented about 500–600 square feet in a building in Greensboro. I needed some way to haul all the stuff I bought around, so I bought a used van for $3,000. Funny. I had to put up my old Toyota as collateral to buy the van. I hired a part-time college student to pack orders for me, and I did the rest. I still went on buying trips every weekend.

By September that year, 1981, I had incorporated the business as Replacements and bought a 2,000-square-foot building that the owner financed for me. I had several part-time employees by then, and it didn't take long to run out of space. So I started looking for another location. Zoning regulations were a real problem.

I found a place with 4,000 square feet. We filled it up in a year. This was sometime in 1982.

I got two more adjoining lots, and we built a 15,000-square-foot building.

Sometime around 1986, we moved again. This time to a place with 40,000 square feet, and the company was up to fifty employees. That same year, I was nearly killed in a car wreck while on one of my trips and had to spend nearly five months in a wheelchair.

By 1989, I realized we needed more space. This time I was going to look around to find a piece of land that was big enough so that we wouldn't have to move again. Moving is such a nightmare. A friend happened to see this 87-acre parcel where we are now. I bought it, and we built 105,000 square feet. It took two teams four months to move the inventory. It was 20 miles one way from the old place. Operating during that period was also a nightmare, because you were never sure where anything was. Often a piece you needed was still at the old place, and we'd have to make a special trip just to get it.

In 1994, we expanded, adding 120,000 square feet this time. As you'll see when you tour the building, we're about full again.

Today, we have about 500 employees here and about 1,500 dealers out scouring flea markets, auctions, etc., looking for stuff they can buy and then sell to Replacements so we can then sell it to our customers. We publish a quarterly index that lists 95,000 patterns and what we will pay a dealer, or an individual, for any of the pieces in those patterns. We have 4 million pieces in our inventory. We also buy from manufacturers when they discontinue a pattern, and we handle current lines. We also buy silverware and flatware, collectibles, and crystal. We now get about 26,000 calls in an average week. Our sales this year will be about $60 million. [See Figure 2] Not bad for selling used "dishes." And we're the largest company like this in the world. Our nearest competitor has less than $3 million in sales and ten employees. We really don't have any competition.

And, I'm happy. I'm the sole owner of this business, yet I still live in the same 1,300-square-foot house I have lived in since I bought it for $55,000 fourteen years ago. I drive a seven-year-old Ford Explorer. I really enjoy helping folks find and replace that piece that broke. China,

FIGURE 2

Replacements, Ltd.:
Total Sales
vs. Employees

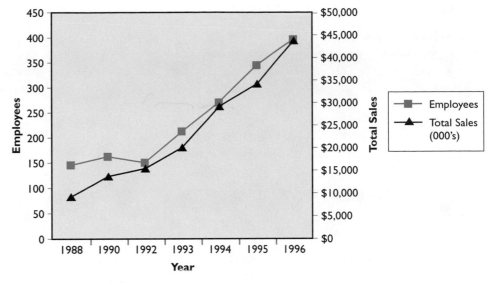

Source: Replacements, Ltd.

crystal, and all that is so personal. We have people come in here and bring their entire set of china and crystal. They may be going into a retirement home and don't have room for it and don't have family to give it to. They ask us to find one buyer so the set won't be broken up. And we do. I take customer calls every day. This business is all about helping people out and making them happy.

I know you folks are from the business school. We're glad you're here. We're always looking for new ideas. But, you need to understand, we don't have a business plan. We don't have a strategy. We don't have a marketing plan. We don't have budgets. We don't have much of that stuff you teach, but we've been pretty successful.

THE TABLETOP MARKET

Page had obviously identified a large, untapped market, but no one knew just how large the market for used china, crystal, and flatware was. There were no market studies or market research reports on it.

However, information was available on the retail "tabletop" market. *HFN* magazine presented an analysis of the industry in its September 1997 issue. Tables 1 and 2 give summary statistics from that report and information on the major manufacturers in the tabletop market. The tabletop market included dinnerware, glassware and crystal, and flatware. The dinnerware market included *housewares* (so-called "everyday" or casual dinnerware), sold by mass merchandisers, *upstairs casual* (casual or everyday dinnerware with somewhat higher prices than mass-market prices), and *upstairs formal* (including formal china). The term *upstairs* implies a higher-priced, more formal item. Crystal included stemware—crystal pieces with a base and a stem supporting the portion that would hold the beverage, such as a wine glass. Flatware included sterling silver, silverplate (utensils that were plated with silver), and stainless steel pieces.

The *HFN* article noted several industry trends:

- Lifestyle stores and home superstores such as Linens and Things and Bed, Bath, and Beyond were responsible for much of the industry's growth.

- There was a move to open-stock selling, that is, allowing customers to buy individual items rather than requiring that they buy full place settings or

TABLE 1

The Tabletop Industry, 1996

A. Total Market:		
Category	Retail Dollar Volume	Percent of Total
Dinnerware	$1.659 billion	40.3%
Glassware and crystal	$1.706 billion	41.4%
Flatware	$ .753 billion	18.3%
Total market	$4.117 billion	100% +3.3% from 1995

B. Dinnerware Analysis:		
Category	Retail Dollar Volume	Percent of Total
Housewares, mass market	$934.2 million	56.3%
Upstairs formal	$431.2 million	26% −2% from 1995
Upstairs casual	$293.6 million	17.7%
Total dinnerware	$1.659 billion	100% +2% from 1995

C. Crystal Analysis:		
Category	Retail Dollar Volume	Percent of Total
Crystal giftware	$455.7 million	68.1%
Crystal stemware	$175.3 million	26.2% +1.92% from 1995
Crystal barware	$ 38.1 million	5.7%
Total crystal	$669.2 million	100% +5% from 1995

D. Flatware Analysis:		
Category	Retail Dollar Volume	Percent of Total
Stainless steel	$535.9 million	72%
Sterling silver	$152.0 million	20% No Change from 1995
Silverplate	$ 65.0 million	8%
Total flatware	$752.9 million	100% +5% from 1995

sets of items. Some brides, for example, were requesting just dinner plates. Some consumers were mixing formal and casual tableware.

■ A shift from formal to casual was taking place, as evidenced by the switch to more casual dress in business settings. Color had become more important in casual china.

■ Baby boomers were saving for retirement and, at the same time, to deal with stressful lifestyles, were eating out more often and spending more on leisure.

■ In upstairs tabletop, upstairs casual dinnerware and crystal stemware were doing well, but analysts did not regard formal china as a growth

TABLE 2

Major Manufacturers of Upstairs Tableware

- ***Lenox, Inc.***   Estimated 1996 sales: $370 million.   Parent: Brown-Forman, Corp.   Subsidiaries: Dansk International Designs, Ltd.; Gorham, Inc.; Kirk Stieff Company.

- ***Mikasa, Inc.***   Estimated 1996 sales: $372.3 million.   Public company with headquarters in London.

- ***Noritake Company, Inc.***   Estimated 1996 sales: $51 million.   Parent: Noritake Company, Ltd.   Headquarters in London.

- ***Royal China and Porcelain Companies, Inc.***   Estimated 1993 sales: $30 million.   Parent: Royal Worcester Spode, Ltd.   Headquarters in London.

- ***Royal Doulton USA, Inc.***   Estimated 1992 sales: $8.4 million.   Parent Pearson, Inc.   Headquarters in London.

- ***Waterford Wedgwood PLC., Inc.***   Estimated 1996 sales: $636.7 million. (Wedgwood Group (china) = $378 million, Waterford Crystal = $259 million).

- ***Oneida Silversmiths Division.***   Estimated 1996 sales: $270 million.   Parent: Oneida, Ltd. (Oneida Ltd. 1997 sales = $376.9 million;   54% of sales from consumer tableware).

- ***Reed and Barton Corporation.***   Estimated 1995 sales: $43 million.   Private company with headquarters in London.

- ***Syratech Corporation.***   Estimated 1996 sales: $270.9 million.   Silver, silverplated, and sterling brands marketed under Wallace, International Silver, and Westmoreland brand names. Wallace Silversmiths, Inc., 1996 sales estimated at $75 million.   Corporate revenues include sale of casual furniture.

- ***Durand International.***   Estimated 1994 sales: $24 million.   Manufactures lead crystal.   Private subsidiary with headquarters in London.

Source: HFN Magazine, September 1997, pp. 5-29

opportunity. Noritake, the second largest formal china manufacturer, had targeted the self-purchase customer and the "encore" bride. Although manufacturers of formal tableware were responding to the casual trend, they were not neglecting the formal.

MARKETING AT REPLACEMENTS

"As Bob Page often says, 'We'll try anything—once,'" Kelly Smith observed as he discussed Replacements' marketing strategy. The company's chief financial officer, Smith also headed its marketing efforts. He had joined Replacements in 1995, af-

ter graduating from Wake Forest University with a degree in accounting, getting his CPA, and working for Arthur Anderson, Kayser Roth (a textile firm), and NationsBank.

For example, in June 1994, the company decided to try advertising in *Parade* magazine, the magazine that's inserted in Sunday newspapers all across the country. The people at *Parade* had been trying to get us to advertise. So we advertised only in the West Coast edition, thinking there'd be consumers, especially in California, who'd be interested in our service; and advertising in one region would give us a chance to see how *Parade* worked. It so happened that the first ad followed a major California earthquake by only a couple of months. Apparently there were a lot of people who'd lost some or all of their china and crystal in the quake. The Monday morning following the Sunday ad, our telephones rang off the hook. We had over 3,000 phone calls that day, which at that time was really a huge volume of calls for one day. It was by far our record day. And for a long time that record stood.

Just to give you an idea of how we have grown, yesterday we had—let me look at my daily call record a second—yes, we had 4,800 calls yesterday. That's a pretty normal day now.

I know you're interested in what I think the big issues are from a marketing perspective. Well, the first issue is how we can continue to find the right media to generate new leads, new customers. Historically, we've been space-ad driven. We've not done a lot of prospecting, direct mailing, buying lists, like a lot of direct marketing companies do. What little we've done, we've found to be unsuccessful if we didn't have the names of patterns associated with customer names; that is, we know what particular patterns each customer on the list owns. We've talked to bridal stores to try to get the list of clients who bought a certain pattern when we learn that a manufacturer has discontinued that particular pattern, but we really haven't had much luck with that. The big challenge is finding the right media to help us sustain our growth rate. We know it's out there; it's just a question of finding it.

A second problem we face is having a more defined customer contact strategy. Once we get a name on file, we tend to send them quotes several times a year. We have seasonal sales and sales on select patterns. We've some general controls on this; but in theory, we could send out lots of quotes for just a little bit of inventory. We don't do any analysis of our customers' buying histories, and we rarely purge our database. We need to come up with a strategy to generate sales without spewing quotes out of our building. But, we know how important quoting is. In July 1995, we stopped quoting for a month while we converted to a new computer system; and sales plummeted. We all became sensitized to how important the quoting process is to maintaining sales growth. But I

was doing some estimating just last week. If you're on file with one pattern, you'll probably get four to six mailings a year from us. If you, however, had eight patterns, you might get forty-eight mailings a year—and they'd all come in the same old, nice-looking envelope. So we've got to figure out what we call "smart quoting."

TARGET MARKET

Smith then described the market that Replacements goes after.

> Our target market is anyone who has china, crystal, sterling, or flatware patterns where they need to replace a broken or missing piece or just want to complete their set but the pattern is no longer produced. We also offer collectible items, like Hummel figurines, for people who like to collect those kinds of things.
>
> We had a study several years ago. We determined that our typical customer was between 45 and 75 years old and was generally an affluent female. I wish I could find that study, but I can't seem to put my hands on it.

FINDING THE PRODUCT

Obtaining the product requires intermediaries, Smith explained.

> I guess the first question a lot of people have is how do we get all the things we have to sell. Well, I said this is an unusual business. Unlike other retailers, we can't call up the manufacturer and say, send us 100 suits in assorted sizes.
>
> The primary source of our product is the 1,500 or so active independent, individual suppliers who buy china, etc., anywhere they can find it. It might be at a flea market, an estate auction, or an antique store. The supplier can look up a particular pattern and piece in that pattern in our index to see what we'll pay for it. [See Figure 3.] Then the supplier can buy the piece for something less than what we will pay. The supplier makes money on the spread, just as we do when we sell the piece for more than we paid the supplier.
>
> That supplier then boxes up any pieces he/she may have and sends them to us. Each morning we'll get from 300 to 500 boxes deliv-

FIGURE 3

Sample Line from a Page in Replacements' Supplier Index[1]

China

Pattern: Noritake	N	**Pla**	**CS**	**DP**	**LP**	**SP**	**BB**	**CR**	**SU**
Lilac Time	2483	13.5	1	11	9	1	.50	3	4
Lilac Time (con)		**OV**	**RV**	**PLI**	**PL2**	**PL3**	**FR**	**CER**	**SO**
		2	21	24	1	41	6	7	10
Lilac Time (con)		**CSS**	**GR**	**BD**	**S/P**	**TP**	**CP**	**CV**	**DE**
		17	27	23	15	45	45	49	9
Lilac Time (con)		**CH**	**REL**	**MUG**	**BOU**				
		33	10	10	12				

Code Key

Code	Description	Code	Description
PLA	Place setting, consisting of:	**CER**	Cereal bowl (rim or coupe)
CS	Cup and saucer	**SO**	Soup bowl (rim or coupe, 7"-9")
DP	Dinner plate (10" to 10-3/4")	**CSS**	Cream soup and saucer
SP	Salad plate (round, 8" to 8-3/4")	**GR**	Gravy boat with stand (1 or 2 pieces)
BB	Bread and butter (6" to 7-3/4")	**BD**	Butter dish with lid
LP	Luncheon plate (round, 9" to 9-1/2")	**S/P**	Salt and pepper set
CR	Creamer	**TP**	Tea pot with lid (short and stout)
SU	Sugar bowl with lid	**CP**	Coffee pot with lid (tall and thin)
OV	Oval vegetable bowl (9"-11")	**CV**	Covered vegetable (oval or round)
RV	Round vegetable bowl (8"-11")	**DE**	DemiTasse cup and saucer
PLI	Platter One (10" to 13-7/8")	**CH**	Chop plate (round platter, 12"-14")
PL2	Platter Two (14" to 15-7/8")	**REL**	Relish (7"-10")
PL3	Platter Three (16"-18")	**MUG**	Mug
FR	Fruit/Dessert bowl (4" to 5'3/4")	**BOU**	Bouillon soup & saucer

[1]Figures listed under the codes for type of piece are in dollars. For example, 13.5 listed for a place setting of Noritake Lilac Time means that Replacements will pay $13.50 for a four-piece place setting consisting of a cup and saucer, dinner plate, salad plate, and bread and butter plate.

ered to us in Greensboro—about 250,000 pieces a month. It's like Christmas every day. We never know what's coming until we open the boxes.

Once we open the box, we inspect the contents and compare them to the paperwork the supplier has completed and included with the shipment. That paperwork includes the supplier's statement as to what he/she expects us to pay. We grade the merchandise, enter it in the computer, and send it to inventory. The paperwork then goes to accounting so that we can pay the supplier. We pay the suppliers within fourteen days, and sometimes sooner. Some of the suppli-

ers just do this as a hobby. For others, it's their job. Last year we paid sixty-one different suppliers more than $20,000 each, with a few earning in the six-figure range. We want being a supplier to be a reliable and stable source of income.

One problem is that, as in any business, about 20 percent of the suppliers produce about 80 percent of the product. We have a lot of inactive suppliers. We had about 3,000 suppliers two years ago. All it cost was $15 a year to be a supplier and get our index, which we publish four times a year. But it cost us $25 a year just to publish the indexes for that supplier. The index contains general information for our suppliers and lists what we will pay for every piece of every china, crystal and glassware, flatware, and collectible item. The index is about two inches thick.

So in January 1996, we started the STAR supplier program. We raised the annual membership fee to $100. For this, the member got the indexes free, access to a special 800 number, twenty-four-hour turnaround on quotes, electronic payment to the supplier's bank account, and a 1 percent rebate on all sales to us once the supplier passed $5,000 in a year. The 1 percent rebate applied to all $5,000 plus the amount above that level. That program helped a little, but we still had too many people who didn't sell anything to us.

So we've just revised the program again. Now, you have to sell us at least $2,000 in the prior year in order to be a STAR supplier. If you sold less than $500, it will cost you $400 to be a member. We're probably down to about 1,500 suppliers now. They account for about 85 percent of our supply.

About 8 to 10 percent of our supply comes from manufacturers. When a manufacturer decides to discontinue a pattern, we will buy its inventory of that pattern. The manufacturers decided about five years ago that it was cheaper to let us handle the small orders for remnants. They'll also often sell active patterns to us as they would to any other dealer, with us getting a standard discount from their recommended retail price. We have active accounts with most manufacturers now. In fact, we are Noritake's biggest customer.

The final 5 to 7 percent of our supply comes from individuals. [Table 3 summarizes sales by product type.] People may just walk into our showroom and sell to us. Sometimes they have inherited the items and don't want them or would rather have the money. Other times, the person is going through a divorce and wants to sell the items.

We estimate that we have about 95,000 patterns and over 4 million pieces in inventory. We also offer collectibles like rare figurines, collectible plates, past Christmas ornaments, etc. For all our products, we offer a thirty-day, money-back, satisfaction guarantee.

We also have a couple of other 'products.' We offer a free pattern-identification service. We have several curators who work with customers to identify patterns. Often a person doesn't know the manufacturer's or the pattern's name. They can send us a picture, tracing, or an actual piece; and our staff will conduct the research to identify the pattern and manufacturer. We also offer a flatware restoration and cleaning service and have considered offering a china repair service. We repair china now for resale, but we have never offered that service to our customers.

PRICE

Smith next described the company's approach to pricing.

Bob understands supply and demand so well. From the very beginning he was developing his buying-pricing model so we can buy the inventory we need, not buy the inventory we don't need, and move the inventory that we have.

Bob uses a pricing matrix that has customer groups down one axis, that is, the number of customers we have for a pattern. For example, do we have one to ten customers or eleven to twenty, and so forth. The other axis is the number of pieces we have in stock. At the intersection of each row and column is the percentage of the retail price that we're willing to pay for an item. So if we have a lot of customers for a pattern and not much inventory, we'll pay 50 percent of retail, which is the most we'll pay for anything. At the other end of the scale, if we have lots of inventory and not many customers, we'll only pay 5 percent of retail. Bob set up these parameters years ago. We continue to find ways to add layers of screening to make pricing more advantageous for us. We have minimum/maximum/absolute pricing we set for particular patterns that can override the matrix based on all sorts of factors. There may be a particular pattern that we really want, and we'll pay a certain price for items in that pattern regardless of what the matrix might say.

Pricing is a continuous process. Literally every day, Bob's setting up special pricing scales for certain patterns or groups of patterns. By changing the retail prices, we automatically change the buying prices by action of the matrix. So, if we need more dinner plates in a pattern, we can raise the retail price to reflect

TABLE 3

Replacements, Ltd.: Sales by Product Type

Product Type	1995	1996	1997
China	$23,280,361	$29,180,113	$34,107,173
Crystal	2,911,824	3,594,419	4,134,168
Flatware	4,986,811	6,778,454	9,097,704
Collectibles	365,474	676,207	884,495
Showroom	1,128,235	1,665,924	1,573,174
Totals	$32,672,705	$41,895,117	$49,796,714

Source: Replacements, Ltd.

demand. This increases the buying price. At some price point, our buyers will seek out that pattern; or if they or others are holding that pattern, at some price they'll be willing to sell. We started getting away from the standardized pricing scales to more customized pricing about one and a half to two years ago. This is Bob's biggest time consumer and his most important job. Although there'll always need to be judgment in this, we need to systematize our pricing in order to reduce the amount of fine tuning or tweaking we do now.

THE SHOWROOM

The Replacements showroom, Smith noted, is more than a place for selling.

In addition to selling directly to our customers by mail, we also operate a showroom here so customers can stop by and make purchases. Bob started a showroom several years ago. It was probably only about 200 square feet—pretty much of an afterthought. But more and more people kept stopping by, so the showroom had to grow. Now it takes 12,000 square feet, and we have about 100,000 people per month visiting it. We also offer guided tours every half-hour from 8:30 A.M. to 8:00 P.M., seven days a week, year-round. Part of our showroom is our museum, which has over 2,000 unique pieces of china, crystal, and silver on display.

PROMOTION

Smith introduced Mark Klein and described his background and his duties as the company's director of marketing.

He's responsible for all our communications work. He directs a graphic artist, a media placement coordinator, a manufacturer's liaison, and a senior merchandising analyst who takes care of developing and placing all our ads. He also supervises our mailing operation, which involves a manager and seven employees. Before joining us last September, Mark worked ten years with Hecht's Department Stores as a buyer of housewares, china, and furniture, and then served as a field sales representative for a furniture company for six years. He has a degree in marketing and management from Virginia Tech.

Smith then asked Klein to discuss Replacements' advertising program. Klein responded:

Okay, Kelly. Our advertising's obviously very important in generating leads. We track our advertising very carefully so we can determine which are the best magazines to use for advertising.

I guess it'd be good to start by summarizing our print advertising program. I've prepared for you this table, which summarizes our print advertising program for September 1996 through August 1997. [See Figure 4.] During this period, we advertised in eighty-four magazines.

FIGURE 4

Advertising Analysis For Publications Advertised in 9/96–8/97

Publication*	Code	ROI	Ad Cost	Total Sales	New Clients
Better Homes & Gardens Ad-Monthly Pub-Monthly 1½" Listing 1/3 pg in 3/96	GB	$7.76	$62,295	$966,862	8,801
Colonial Homes Ad-Bimonthly Pub-Monthly 1/12 Pg BW	CH	$13.75	$8,444	$232,280	1,942
Country Living Ad-Monthly Pub-Bimonthly 1/3 Pg Masthead out May 96, 16M Classified Word Ad	CL	$35.40	$7,166	$507,273	4,208
Good Housekeeping Ad-Monthly Pub-Monthly 1" Listing remnant 7/96, 25M	GH	$7.91	$27,437	$433,917	3,735
Gourmet Ad-Monthly Pub-Monthly STF Calico blue starting in Dec 96 1/12 Page, BW	GT	$6.60	$23,099	$305,065	2,002
House Beautiful Ad-Monthly Pub-Monthly 1/12 Page 4-C	HB	$8.18	$41,889	$685,364	4,526
Martha Stewart Living Ad-Monthly Pub-Monthly Vil Holly in Dec 96 issue 1/12 Page 4/C, 10x/yr.	MS	$6.27	$30,490	$382,570	5,403
New Yorker Ad-Weekly Pub-Weekly 1½" weekly 1/6 thru 7/7/97	YO	$3.30	$54,137	$357,708	1,857
Smithsonian Ad-Monthly Pub-Monthly 2" Listing/makegood 3/97	SM	$5.71	$23,709	$270,819	1,605
Southern Living Ad-Monthly Pub-Monthly 39 words, Prepaid Oct-Dec 97 Prepay 3 mos. 10% discount	SL	$106.87	$9,567	$2,044.962	12,122
Sunset Ad-Monthly Pub-Monthly 4-C Test ad Oct, Nov, Dec 96, JB BW 1/12 pg 1/12 Page, 2/97 Coach Scenes	TU	$10.77	$18,117	$390,238	2,668
Victoria Ad-Monthly Pub-Monthly 1/3 4C in 3/96, 12M	VI	$6.94	$24,345	$337,898	5,286
Yankee Ad-Monthly Pub-Monthly	YA	$5.27	$27,417	$289,030	2,320
Subtotal—All but Parade		$8.39	$552,346	$9,265,633	75,286
Parade Ad-Monthly Pub-Monthly	—	$2.58	$1,049,263	$6,246,195	89,572
TOTAL—All publications		$4.84	$1,601,609	$15,511,828	164,858

*Specific publications listed are the top fourteen in terms of total sales. Subtotal and total figures include *all* publications.
Source: Replacements, Ltd.

This table summarizes the top fourteen magazines in terms of the sales dollars the advertising generated. It shows basic information on the magazine and our ad, the code our telemarketers use when they record that magazine as the source of a new customer, the return on investment from the ad, the cost of the ad, and the number of new sales and clients it generated in the period. We calculate the ROI measure by taking 50 percent of the total sales amount (which assumes an average 50 percent gross margin on sales) and dividing that by the cost of the ad. This figure then gives us the gross margin dollars generated for each dollar of ad cost. If this number drops below 1.0, then we drop that magazine unless there's some other factor working.

We also track sales for magazines in which we didn't advertise during the past twelve months. You see, once a person becomes a client and we include the client in our database, we designate the source of that client. Our operators ask the clients on their first call how they heard about Replacements. If a client says he/she saw our ad in the *New York Times Magazine*, then we put that code in the client's file. From then on, we credit all purchases that client may make to that magazine. Sometimes we may have discontinued our ads in that magazine, but we still track our sales for those customers by that magazine.

Many of these magazines also have sections where they list the advertisers in that edition and allow readers to circle a number on a card to request information from that advertiser. This information comes to us from the magazines, and we have to enter the information manually and then mail the person a Replacements' brochure. We track these inquiries and sales from the inquiries also.

At this juncture, Smith suggested that Klein also tell how the company keeps track of its other client sources. Klein agreed:

Good point. I also prepared a list of our top 16 client sources from other than publications. I took these from an overall list of about 150 such sources. For example, if a customer calls in and says he/she was referred to us by an antique store, we would code that customer as "AS." The exhibit shows that in the past twelve months we had over $462,000 in sales to such customers. This table also shows the sales we credit to our lists, that is, lists of customers we've purchased over the years. You'll see on the exhibit a listing for the "C.C.M. List" or the "W. D. C. List." You'll notice also the listing for "Department Store Referral." Many people will go to a department store if they break a piece of china or need additional pieces. If the store doesn't carry that pattern or if it's discontinued, often the store personnel will refer the customer to us. The Discovery Channel has a show called "Start to Finish" that runs about a five-minute segment on Replacements. It's run the segment about twelve to fifteen times over the past two years. Every time it runs, we get a burst of telephone calls. In fact, you can "see" the calls move across the country as the show airs in different time zones.

The largest total sales dollar item is the "friend or relative" entry. You can see the importance of word of mouth; but, frankly, we wonder if this entry isn't just a catch-all when our operators are busy. For example, when someone calls and indicates that she saw our ad in *American Country Collectibles* magazine, the operator may not know the code for that magazine. If not, he/she must go to another screen and scroll through a list to find the code. This takes time, and our operators are very busy. We think that in such a case it is easy just to enter the code for friend or relative (FR) and save the time and trouble of looking.

Smith confirmed that "having our operators get accurate information is one of our biggest concerns," as this information is crucial for tracking. Klein continued, focusing again on advertising.

I think Kelly mentioned earlier that we are space-ad driven. We've tried a little television and radio advertising, but they just don't seem to work very well for us. We've too much information we need to communicate, and we can't seem to do it effectively in thirty seconds or a minute. Plus, we find that people need to see sample items in the ad.

For example, here's a sample ad from *Parade*. [See Figure 5.] You'll notice the line of plates across the bottom. One might assume that we just pick some sample plates for the ad, but we select each individual plate/pattern very

FIGURE 5

Sample *Parade* Ad

Source: Replacements, Ltd.

carefully based on our inventory and the number of customers who might want that pattern. We'll have people call in who'll say that they recognize their pattern as being the fifth plate from the left in the ad. So our operators must have copies of the ads with pattern names noted so they can help the customers.

Our staff does all of the creative work in developing our ads. Until 1995, we used outside companies to do this. We think we can do it just as well; and by placing the ads ourselves, we save the 15 percent fee we'd have paid an advertising agency to do that.

Despite our focus on print ads, we're trying to get a TV ad with Visa, the credit card folks. You may remember that Visa has these ads in which it features unique or unusual businesses and notes that the establishments don't take American Express. We think we fit Visa's criteria, and Bob has a personal goal of getting Replacements in one of those ads. We even filmed a sample ad to show Visa. We haven't had any luck yet. Visa is also developing some radio ads with the same theme, but we're not sure Replacements will work as well on radio.

We're always looking for new home-and-shelter-type publications in which to advertise. Bob encourages us to try anything. One of the greatest things about working here is that we don't have an ad budget—so if we come up with an idea we like, we just try it. Although we don't have a budget, we spend about 3 to 4 percent of revenue on advertising. We just seem to hit that range. We could certainly spend more, but we find there is a "wear-out" factor with our advertising. For example, we only advertise once a month in *Parade*. Our ad is on the page with the 'Intelligence Report' feature, the second most-read page in the magazine. But our space is always the same size and our ads look alike even though we change them. If we advertised every week, we'd just speed up the wear-out factor.

Personal Selling

As telemarketing is very important to Replacements, Klein offered some specifics about the process, also describing how calls are followed up.

I've mentioned our telemarketing staff several times, so perhaps I should discuss this process in more detail. We've about seventy full-time staff in this area who operate from 8 A.M. to 10 P.M. daily, year-round. When we're not open, we record messages by voice mail and return the calls the next day. About 90 percent of our sales are by telephone, with the remaining 10 percent occurring in our showroom. Our operators will handle about 26,000 calls a week. We have five T-1 lines into the building, each T-1 being twenty-four lines. Even though you have to add twenty-four lines at a time, we'll add a T-1 before we really need it because we want customers to be able to get in. It is rare that all of our lines are busy, but it has happened. People can also E-mail us at ReplaceLtd@aol.com.

The first time a customer calls our 1–800-Replace number, he/she's typically seen one of our ads and is interested in getting a free list of patterns we carry and other basic information. Our operators try to establish rapport. Our goal in that first call is to get the customer's name and address and the names of any patterns he/she owns and a particular piece request. This is critical to us knowing how to price and how to adjust our pricing matrix. As I've noted, we also record how the customer came to call us, through an ad, a referral, or however. So our goal is to get that customer on file with as much specific information as possible. Finally, our operators are supposed to conclude the call by asking if the customer has any other china, crystal, silver, flatware, glassware, everyday stoneware, etc., needs that we can help them with. This is a way to educate the customer about our other offerings. So many customers think we only carry china.

We have over 2.5 million customers on file. However, one problem is that many records are so old that we are not sure if the information, such as which pieces they want, is still valid. If a customer calls in who is already on our system, the operator just punches in the customer's phone number to call up his/her information.

So we have a standard format that our operators follow. The typical operator will take 70 to 110 calls per day. We try to hire people with telephone experience. They need the ability to sit at a desk all day and take calls. We put them through a month's training. New employees can take monitored calls in about two weeks. They have to learn the computer screens and how to work them. They'll sit and listen as an experienced person takes calls.

Because we can get bursts of calls from time to time, we've developed a system so that other staff members working in other functional areas are trained to handle phone calls and take orders. Even our managers, including Bob, do this. When someone calls, our automatic system answers before the first ring and delivers a prerecorded message. At the end of the message, the call goes to an operator, depending on which number the customer selects from the menu. The computer monitors incoming traffic, and

whenever there are more than two calls in the queue, the queue beginning whenever the system answers a call, we have bells that ring in certain offices. For example, bells will ring in the accounting office, the mailroom, and other support departments. The bells also ring in several of the managers' offices like Kelly's and Bob's. A light in the telephone operators' room goes on so that an operator who's getting ready to go on a break, for example, knows to wait.

That's our standard system. We also have what we call a "Code 2." Anyone who is involved in the system can call a Code 2. They do this by announcing over the intercom that we have a Code 2. We don't have any specific rules about when to do this. For example, we've a display on our phones that tells us how many calls are in queue and what the maximum wait time is. If I notice that there are more than three calls in the queue and wait time is twenty seconds, I'll call a Code 2. We do this over the intercom rather than with bells so that backup staff will hear it even if they aren't at their desks.

As a result of this system, we can handle the peak-call periods. Our average wait time is *eight seconds*. If we do have calls that are blocked due to our lines being busy or customers abandon a call, we have a system that captures their phone numbers; and we'll call them the next day to see if we can help them.

We've five supervisors who monitor calls for quality-control purposes, and we produce daily reports that keep up with every detail. We know how many calls each person takes, the average talk time, and lots of other information. I noted that managers serve as Code 2 backups. Bob Page, for example, took sixty-nine calls yesterday. That's high, but he enjoys taking the calls. It allows him, and all of us, to keep in touch with customers.

We also have a similar phone system with twenty operators in our purchasing department. These folks deal with our suppliers. We have twelve people in our customer service area, handling questions, returns, or problem orders. We're considering consolidating all three groups and using the phone system to route calls to each operator based on that operator's skills and responsibilities.

Now once a person has called, talked to an operator, and been added to the system as a new client, we'll have their patterns on file. The next day, we send that person a quote that lists his/her patterns and the prices for the pieces that we have in stock. We send these letters first class because we found that bulk mail was too slow. We also can send just a brochure.

If the person calling wants a dinner plate in a certain pattern and we don't have that pattern in stock, we ask the customer if he/she would like to be in our "call collect first" program. This means the customer says he/she'll accept a collect call if the piece he/she is looking for comes in. We'll call them before we send out letters to other customers who're looking for that same pattern or piece. This used to be an actual collect call; but we found we were spending so much time trying to complete the collect call, so we just started paying for it ourselves. But by the customer saying he/she'll accept a collect call, we know we have a more serious customer.

When we get more pieces in on a pattern than we need to satisfy our "call collect" customers, we send out a mailing to others in the database who are looking for that pattern. These and all the other quotes we mail, with the exception of that first quote, go third class bulk, with about a ten-day delivery time. We have some decision rules that determine when and if we do a wider mailing.

Independent of these mailings are our sales runs. These account for the bulk of our mailings. We group patterns into various groups to balance the size of our mailings. Based on our sales history and inventory, the computer will calculate a discount and generate sales quotes. We go through that sales cycle about five times a year with each cycle being about three weeks and each mailing ranging from 240,000 to 375,000 letters. If we still have inventory after a sales run, we may discount the item even more the next time. One to two times a year, we go through the process of quoting everybody at full price. [See Figure 6.]

So you can see how, as I mentioned earlier, someone could get lots of mailings from us over the period of a year. This can get expensive, and we don't want to overwhelm people with quotes. So we have to work constantly on and think about our customer-contact strategy. Are there more efficient and effective ways to contact customers once we find them and get them on our system?

OPERATIONS MANAGEMENT AND INFORMATION SYSTEMS

Taking Inventory

Scott Fleming, Replacements' vice president for operations, had just left the inventory area and entered the company's first-floor showroom on his way back to his second-floor office. He noticed Ron Swanson, chief information officer, who had just finished talking to one of the sales associates who helped showroom customers. In the background, another group of visitors was departing on a Replacements' tour—as groups did every thirty minutes.

Fleming had worked for Replacements for seven years during the 1980s. He left the company for four years before returning in 1994. Swanson had joined Replacements in early 1996 as chief information officer. He brought twenty-seven years of experience, including twenty years with county government in Iowa; five years with Sara Lee; and two years with CMI, a textile manufacturer.

Fleming called out to Swanson:

I was just on the way up to see if I could catch you. I've just been back in the inventory area. As you know, we had a tremendous number of shipments come in yesterday, and the pieces are beginning to work their way back to inventory. The staff is really pushed. Bob has always believed that the more inventory we have, the more we can sell. But no matter how fast we grow, it seems that the inventory grows faster. I'm concerned that we need to tackle this problem strategically. I think keeping track of inventory is taxing our information system.

On an average day, Replacements' supplier network shipped 300 to 500 boxes via surface carriers (such as UPS), resulting in the company receiving more than 50,000 pieces in an average week. In turn, the company shipped about 35,000 pieces a week to meet customer orders. (See Figure 7.)

At the beginning of any given day, the company had no listing of the items that would be delivered

FIGURE 6

1997 Sales Cycle 4—Sales Run
Work Process Schedule

Group	Group's Previous Sale Ends	Sale Dates	Begin Process	Greenbar to Bob	Greenbar from Bob	Start Printing	Finish Printing	Finish Mailing	Number of Customers
11&13	6/18/97	7/16-8/7	6/24	6/25	6/27	6/30	7/6	7/7	271,568
15&2	6/25/97	7/23-8/14	6/26	6/27	6/30	7/7	7/12	7/13	239,821
1&3	7/2/97	7/30-8/20	6/27	6/30	7/1	7/13	7/19	7/21	261,169
4&5	7/9/97	8/6-8/27	7/1	7/2	7/3	7/20	7/26	7/28	313,466
6&7	7/16/97	8/13-9/3	7/21	7/22	7/24	7/27	8/2	8/4	314,709
8&9	7/23/97	8/20-9/10	7/28	7/29	8/1	8/3	8/9	8/11	317,805
10&11	7/30/97	8/27-9/17	8/4	8/5	8/7	8/10	8/16	8/18	360,137
16	8/6/97	9/3-9/24	8/11	8/12	8/14	8/17	8/23	8/25	371,760
17&14	8/13/97	9/10-10-1	8/18	8/19	8/21	8/24	8/31	9/1	375,468

Group 11 Hutchenreuter Crustal—Kaysons
          Lenox Crystal
Group 13 Ken Kraft China—Mauser Mfg. Co. Silver (omit Mikasa
          & Metlox China)
          International Silver (Lufberry—Zephyr)
Group 15 Moncrief—Oscar de la Renta Silver
Group 2   Royal Dalton
          Red Wing China—Royal Saxony
          Gorham Silver (252H—Imperial Chrysanthemum)
Group 1   Old Abbey—Rewcrest (omit Royal Doulton)
          Oneida (Modjeska)—Oneida (Young Love)
          Rosenthal
Group 3   Royal Sealy—Sheffield (omit RW)
Group 4   Shafford—Warwick China (omit Syracuse) (omit
          Towle)
Group 5   Gorham Silver (Imperial—Zodiac)
          Waterford—Zylstra (omit Wedgwood China)
          Allan Adler Silver—Booths

Group 6   Wedgwood
          Borsumy Fine Chila—Crown Empire (omit Castleton)
Group 7   Castleton
          Towle
          Ceralene Raynaud—Englishtown Crafts
Group 8   Enesco China—Freeman (omit Fostoria)
Group 9   Fostoria
          Frigast Silver—Hibbard, Spencer, Bart (omit Haviland)
Group 10 International Silver (1810—Lovelace)
          Haviland
          Johnson Brothers
Group 12 Lenox China
Group 16 Noritake, Wallace Silver
Group 17 Metlox, Royal Worcester, Syracuse
          Oneida/Heirloom Silver (Abington)—Oneida/
          Heirloom Monte Carlo
Group 14 Mikasa
          Spode China

Source: Replacements, Ltd.

to its docks that day. A shipment's contents were known only after warehouse employees opened the box. Once employees opened the boxes, they used computer terminals to enter data on the pieces received. They then sent the pieces to the appropriate area (china, crystal, or flatware), where other employees carefully inspected each piece and determined the amount that Replacements would pay to the supplier for each one. The employees then issued payment orders and sent them to the accounting department. They also assigned each piece to a specific location in one of more than 59,000 bins arranged in 16-feet-high shelves and then transferred the piece to inventory. Defective items were sent to appropriate areas for restoration and then placed in inventory.

The company stocked about 73,000 china patterns from 1,300 manufacturers; 12,500 crystal patterns from 265 manufacturers; and 9,600 flatware patterns from 439 manufacturers. The total

FIGURE 7

Layout of
Replacements, Ltd.

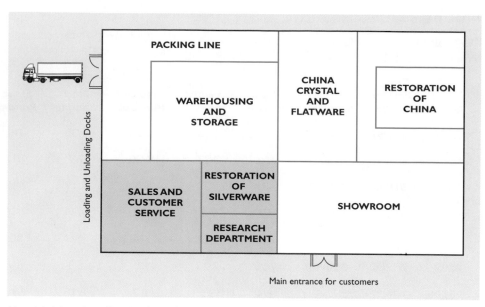

Note: Administration offices are located on the second and third floor above sales and customer service, restoration of silverware, and research department section of the building (as shown by the shaded area).

inventory amounted to more than 4 million individual pieces.

Fleming spoke about some of the problems:

> One of my concerns is that we have so many new people. They're good employees, but they don't yet know the patterns. Although they can quickly learn to find the more commonly ordered patterns, it's hard for them to find the rarer, less frequently ordered patterns. Further, I'm concerned that it is easy for a new employee who is working hard to put a piece in the wrong place. As a result, it could be lost forever! There's no telling how much lost inventory we have floating around on those shelves.
>
> And on top of that, we estimate that about 7 percent of the items we receive are broken in shipment; and we break another 2 percent while we are handling them. So we've got a quality problem on top of an information problem.

Swanson asked how his department could help. Fleming responded:

> I wish I had some new ideas, Ron. Frankly, I am at my wit's end trying to solve this inventory/ quality management problem without an accurate information system. And, to add to the

> confusion, we're unable to handle all the calls we receive from both our suppliers and customers.

Replacements received about 5,000 calls from customers and suppliers in a typical fourteen-hour day. About fifty-six salespeople and sixty-one purchasing employees handled most of the calls. In addition, there were more than eighty others who helped handle telephone calls when needed— including Page, as mentioned earlier. Jack Whitley Jr., the director of sales and customer service, felt that the company needed to add from four to fourteen full-time employees to handle the telephone calls. Fleming explained:

> Our phone records tell us that customers abandon about 1 percent of all calls. I wish we could do something about that. That translates to more than a half million dollars in revenue! Also, many times we find that a particular item sought by a customer is not available in our inventory. However, in all likelihood a supplier could find that item within a few months. But we have no system in place by which we can correlate the receipt of that item to the earlier customer request. I really have no idea how much money we may be losing on that account.

History of Replacements' Information Systems

The earliest system used to remember customers' names and patterns was simply Page's handwritten 3-by-5 file cards. After about three years, the manual system was unable to keep up with the growth in customers and inventory.

In 1985, Replacements purchased a Data General (DG) minicomputer. The installation automated both the china and flatware inventory and the customer list.

Two years later, the company hired an internal programming staff to develop both batch and data-entry functions to support the company's operations. This group subsequently developed the first on-line systems, which were referred to as "green screen-COBOL-interactive" systems.

In 1993, the company installed the first local area networks (LANs), and PCs began to replace the terminals. Even though the PCs possessed computing capability, they employed a "terminal emulation" interface, which used only a small portion of their total capability. Eventually, the DG system grew to 300 terminals, with 220 of them being PCs.

Later in 1993, the DG system's scalability (the ability to increase the system to meet demand) became an issue. Replacements' management decided to look into two alternative solutions:

1. Expanding the existing, proprietary DG platform by changing to the UNIX operating system using Oracle database software
2. Moving to a more "open" system of Hewlett-Packard hardware with the UNIX operating system and Sybase database software

Both options required a database conversion from the old INFOS database management system. Replacements hired an independent consulting firm to supply the project manager for the projected conversion. The task of translating the database structures from the hierarchical INFOS database to the relational Oracle database proved more difficult than the consulting firm had projected. The initial implementation date was delayed over nine months. During this period, many of the development staff left Replacements. After eighteen months of working to convert the database, the management team decided to implement the new system immediately. Managers had considered different cut-over approaches; but the main problem

was that only one computer was available, and it could only run one operating system and database at a time. The team decided that an immediate cut-over from the old to the new system would happen over a long holiday weekend: "Tomorrow we go live!" That holiday weekend was the July 4 weekend, 1995.

Problems riddled the changeover from the start. The new system lost recently entered orders. Critical inventory updates failed. Important data was lost somewhere in the system. The new system came apart, and system users rapidly lost confidence in its precision and reliability. In some instances, when a customer called to place an order, the order taker would run back into the warehouse to verify the existence of the inventory before confirming the order. Because of the problems with lost orders, some orders were handwritten and hand-filled to ensure inventory availability and delivery. One executive remarked, "This came as close as anything to completely destroying the business."

Eventually, the new system became more reliable, and the employees became more confident in its ability to reflect inventory and to execute necessary transactions accurately. During this period, Replacements' programmers found lots of errors in the programming modules. This revelation made the managers realize that they needed to be more proactive in their system's design and development.

It took the internal programmers almost a year to repair the system installed on July 4, 1995. By then, they had also implemented a limited fail-safe system that provided redundancy by making possible the operation of major functions if the primary system failed. The backup system did not have the capability to run the entire operation, but it would prevent a total shutdown. In order to keep the vital operations functioning, the group decided that the system would suspend noncritical operations in the event of a primary computer failure.

Toward the end of 1995, managers decided that they needed to take a more strategic view in the information systems area. A six-month search ensued to select a chief information officer (CIO), and Swanson was hired as Replacements' first CIO in May 1996. At this time, most of the information system's staff was also new on the job. The information services provided consisted of basic maintenance only—that is, keeping what was running operational.

After five months on the job, Swanson submitted his initial vision of what was needed. The report, entitled "A Proposal for Strategic Direction," recommended a change in hardware platform, a change to a new financial system, a change to database servers, and a change in application development tools. As a result, Replacements developed a new financial system on the IBM AS400, moved to a Microsoft NT Server on a 10/100 megabit local area network to provide access to data and images pertaining to china and flatware, and implemented Powerbuilder, a comprehensive application development tool. A new call center was implemented to enhance the capacity for handling incoming calls. Replacements also began leasing rather than purchasing hardware.

Information Systems Challenges

Replacements faced many questions and challenges in the information systems area. How could the functional areas integrate their operations, and how could the systems ensure that the data collected were current and accurate? What upgrade path should the company take to enhance the performance of the major processors (DGs and IBM)? Could operations and marketing help to design a more effective system to support their needs? Did Replacements have the information architecture to guide its processing and application decisions into the twenty-first century? In which IS competencies should Replacements invest? Should IS merely support the other functional areas at Replacements, or were there some areas where IS should take the lead?

CORPORATE STRATEGY

Finding Respect

Bob Page looked out his window toward Interstates 85/40. It was snowing heavily—very unusual for the first week of December in North Carolina. It was Friday, and everyone was exhausted but energized by the last two weeks' hectic activities. Sales on Monday had reached a record high of $417,000, smashing the previous one-day record of $286,000 set just a year ago, on December 5, 1996. Tuesday's sales had topped $375,000.

A reporter from the *Wall Street Journal* had visited Replacements earlier in the week and made several follow-up telephone calls about an article that the paper would publish in late December. An issue of *Southern Living* that included an article on Replacements had just hit the newsstands. The president of Wedgwood USA and a representative from the office in England had come to see Page. Five years ago, Page had gone to England to see someone at Wedgwood only to be stood up. Now, it was Wedgwood that approached Replacements.

Trudy, one of his two dachshunds, interrupted his thoughts, begging for a dog treat. Her puppies would arrive in three weeks. Several employees had already adopted them and, like their parents, the puppies would come to work every day.

Page had never envisioned it being like this. He had thought that he would be lucky to have six employees. Now there were 500 people in the Replacements family, 50 hired in the last two months. He had known there was demand, but he had never dreamed how much of a demand there was. He shared his view of the company and its strengths.

It's not something that business school professors would want to hear, but we really don't talk about the bottom line. That would almost never come up in a conversation here. Our philosophy is that we do the things that we believe in and the bottom line will take care of itself. We take care of our customers.

I think that just by doing the things that we're doing today, sales are going to continue to grow. The articles in *Southern Living* and in the *Wall Street Journal*—that's exposure. More and more people find out about us, yet half of our business still comes from word of mouth.

There are dozens and dozens of companies that've started up since I started Replacements, but they're still on a level like when I operated out of my attic. We recently bought out a competitor in Washington State, and its entire inventory and office furniture fit in two tractor-trailers. We ship out two tractor-trailer loads of merchandise daily.

We've established an impeccable reputation with our suppliers. They know that they can trust us to send them their money. I've heard some horror stories that when they've sent someone else something it would take them six months to get their money. In other cases, I've heard that the company said that it was going to pay one price and after they have shipped it the company said, "Well we're not going to pay that." I think that our real focus on computers and our index have made us different. We have one competitor who was sending out letters to our suppliers asking them to get our index but not let us know what they were doing. On certain items they would pay $2.00 or $5.00 per piece more—but then told the suppliers not to ship anything without telling them.

We recently purchased the mailing list of one of our former competitors. It also wanted to sell its inventory, but it had such depth in the pieces that it had. It had a fifty-year supply of cups and saucers in one pattern! What we look at is buying a lot of different pieces, but not in huge amounts. They just kept accumulating pieces, but it was their buying system that didn't work for them. They might pay $15 for a cup and saucer and then they would automatically pay $15 for the dinner plate because the system was so rigid. We may be paying $1 for the cup and saucer and $25 for the dinner plate based on demand or how much inventory we already have.

Our customers can't find the product anywhere else. Some of our patterns are more than 100 years old. We couple that with the level of customer service that we provide. What would it take for a substantial competitor to emerge? Money, experience, a customer list, inventory, and a period of time. At this time, I'm not really concerned about competitors, because if someone had all the money in the world, they wouldn't have the inventory. We have the largest stockpile in the world of discontinued products. It would take a competitor a period of time to accumulate the inventory.

When we put out our indexes, the first ones to buy them are our competitors. Of course, a lot of our competitors sell a good portion of their inventory to us. They don't have the client base that we do. It has taken us all these years to accumulate 2½ million customers. You couldn't do that overnight. If you had all the customers, what would you sell them? Now we have made lots of mistakes over the years. For example, we were buying a pattern called Sylvia from a German manufacturer. It turned out that Sylvia was a shape, not a pattern, and now we have 25 patterns with a Sylvia shape. This is something that was listed in our book, and if someone brought

a piece in we would buy it—but it wasn't what we thought we were buying. These are the kinds of things that other people are going to have to learn, too. We have knowledge here that nobody else would have. And we keep documenting things. We have over 2,200 old Noritake patterns, forty years old or older. When we publish our book, it's just going to be a killer book. This is doing a service to the world.

We are constantly adding patterns. We computer-image hundreds of patterns a week. We'd love for our customers and suppliers to have access to this knowledge. We have suppliers who fax things in here or bring a piece in or try to describe it over the phone. If they had access to some of this knowledge, it would make it easier. Here is an example of a pattern to which we have assigned a number. For our purposes, it is an identifiable pattern. This would save on our own research time. We may also want to have customers place their own orders.

We entered the silver business because we kept getting more and more requests from people asking why we didn't handle silver, too. And, of course, we already had our mailing list. It's fairly cost effective to add silver. With our supplier base, we just had to let them know we were in the silver business. It was a natural expansion of our business . . . all tableware.

Refurbishment is a business that we want to do at some point when we get caught up ourselves. We have a large new kiln that we're operating; and in the last couple of weeks, we have gotten fire polishing for beveling stemware. We lost some pieces before we perfected that. There's a lot of experimentation involved. With the china patterns, we keep records of the temperature to fire various patterns, which patterns we can fire, and which we can't. We get better at what we do as time goes on. We have the ability to launch the business now, but we are processing so many things that we already bought but can't sell until we refurbish. If someone came in right now, we could do it—but we don't have the manpower. It's very time consuming, and it's a real art.

I went to England four or five years ago to meet with people from Wedgwood, and the man who I had an appointment with was out of town. Now, they want us to be their worldwide distributor for closeouts. The president of Wedg-wood USA and another man from England were here. They approached us about this arrangement—we did not approach them. They have their own matching center for recently discontinued patterns (patterns discontinued within the last five years). They shared information with us on the total sales of various patterns in all markets. They gave us a breakdown of sales by those patterns in the United States, the United Kingdom, Japan, and Australia. They want to sell us all the company's discontinued inventory, and they would refer to us all the customers who are looking for discontinued merchandise. We would supply that from the United States.

Over the years, we've bought thousands of pieces of stemware from Lenox crystal in recent patterns that have been out of production for three or four years. We had such demand that they'd produce those just for us. They also would have produced some of their china patterns for us if they still had some of the decals to decorate the pieces. Once they've discontinued patterns, they'll sell them out to us because they want to dispose of them. They also have outlet stores, but we sell more Lenox pieces than all their outlet stores combined.

Back four or five years ago, we had a dip in employee morale. I'd say that now our employee morale is way up there. Everyone's working really hard. And we have people who're really thrilled to be here. It's really great. It's demanding, very demanding; but it's positive adrenaline for the most part. I really enjoy it.

I still try very hard to know everyone by name. I'd know 95 percent of them. We've got so many new ones. I get a picture of everybody, and they fill out a questionnaire giving a little bit of information about themselves, what attracted them to Replacements, and what's the most interesting thing about them. I took these home last night. In my spare time, I look at their pictures and read their comments. When we had twenty-five employees, I knew everybody and their brothers and sisters. I miss some of that, but I am still very close to a lot of people here. I like to think that this is my extended family.

It's our real intent to take care of our people. We've higher expectations of our employees than most places. Right now, they're over-worked because it's our busy season. I think that people either love it here, or they hate it. Typically, people who just want a job won't be here long. We have others who just couldn't think of working anywhere else. They just love being here. And it's a very diverse group. For example, there's a guy who we hired down in imaging who's a vegetarian and is really new-wave looking. But he wrote the nicest little thing. He started working here through a temporary agency. And he wrote that this is the neatest job that he'd ever worked at or heard about, and he had been looking for over a year. He's very enthusiastic about being here. We want people who are really glad to be here. We feel like attitude is the most important thing.

There's a learning curve. The new employees train for two or three weeks out in the warehouse before they ever have anyone on the phone, and then they are not proficient at what they do. It takes six months to a year to really get familiar with the products, and still they wouldn't have the depth of knowledge needed to put that customer on file and send them a list. There are so many times that I get a customer on the phone and think that if somebody else in phone sales had gotten that customer that they'd not be able to talk them through and get the information to put that customer on file and send them a list. I'm able to talk them through because of my product knowledge. Right now our employee is just looking at a computer screen; it will be very educational when we get pictures on the screen and he or she can see what the product looks like.

The thing I love to do is to go to flea markets and antique shops and buy things. What would I do if I didn't own Replacements? I love what I do. I really enjoy it. I'm overworked right now. I enjoy going out in the warehouse and working. I go out there every day. And, of course, I do a lot of the identification. There were 750 pieces of mail today. Some days there are 1,100 or 1,200, so it was fairly light today. I go through and I can identify up to $\frac{1}{2}$ of the pieces that come in. I love to take sales calls. I get ideas from everything I do, whether it's the mail or sales calls. If I'm out of town for a few days, I can hardly wait to get back. I'm always ready to get back."

CASE 6

The Scaffold Plank Incident

This case was prepared by Stewart C. Malone and Brad Brown of the University of Virginia.

What had started as a typically slow February day in the lumber business had turned into a moral dilemma. With 12 inches of snow covering the ground, construction (and lumber shipments) had ground to a halt and on the 26th of the month, the company was still $5,000 below break-even point. In the three years since he had been in the business, Bob Hopkins knew that a losing February was nothing unusual, but the country seemed to be headed for a recession, and as usual, housing starts were leading the way into the abyss.

Bob had gone to work for a commercial bank immediately after college but soon found the bureaucracy to be overwhelming and his career progress appeared to be written in stone. At the same time he was considering changing jobs, one of his customers, John White, offered him a job at White Lumber Company. The job was as a "trader," a position that involved both buying and selling lumber. The compensation was incentive-based and there was no cap on how much a trader could earn. White Lumber, although small in size, was one of the bank's best accounts. John White was not only a director of the bank but one of the community's leading citizens.

It was a little after 8:00 A.M. when Bob received a call from Stan Parrish, the lumber buyer at Quality Lumber. Quality was one of White Lumber's best retail dealer accounts, and Bob and Stan had established a good relationship.

"Bob, I need a price and availability on 600 pieces of 3 × 12 Doug fir-rough-sawn—2 & better

grade—16-feet long," said Stan, after exchanging the usual pleasantries.

"No problem, Stan. We could have those ready for pickup tomorrow and the price would be $470 per thousand board feet."

"The price sounds good, Bob. I'll probably be getting back to you this afternoon with a firm order," Stan replied.

Bob poured a third cup of coffee and mentally congratulated himself. Not bad, he thought—a two-truck order and a price that guaranteed full margin. It was only a half-hour later that Mike Fayerweather, his partner, asked Bob if he had gotten any inquiries on a truck of 16-foot scaffold plank. As Bob said he hadn't, alarm bells began to go off in his brain. While Stan had not said anything about scaffold plank, the similarities between the inquiries seemed to be more than coincidence.

While almost all lumber undergoes some sort of grading, the grading rules on scaffold plank were unusually restrictive. Scaffold planks are the wooden planks that are suspended between metal supports, often many stories above the ground. When you see painters and window-washers six stories in the air, they generally are standing on scaffold plank. The lumber had to be free of most of the natural defects found in ordinary construction lumber and had to have unusually high strength in flexing. Most people would not be able to tell certified scaffold plank from ordinary lumber, but it was covered by its own rules in the grading book, and if you were working ten stories above the ground, you definitely wanted to have certified scaffold plank underneath you. White Lumber did not carry scaffold plank, but its rough 3 × 12s certainly would fool all but the expertly trained eye.

This case is intended to be used as a basis for class discussion rather than as an illustration of either effective or ineffective handling of the situation. This case was prepared by Stewart C. Malone and Brad Brown, University of Virginia. Used by permission.

At lunch, Bob discussed his concerns about the inquiry with Mike.

"Look, Bob, I just don't see where we have a problem. Stank didn't specify scaffold plank, and you didn't quote him on scaffold plank," observed Mike. "We aren't even certain that the order is for the same material."

"I know all that, Mike," said Bob, "but we both know that four inquiries with the same tally is just too big a coincidence, and three of those inquiries were for Paragraph 171 scaffold plank. It seems reasonable to assume that Stan's quotation is for the same stuff."

"Well, it's obvious that our construction lumber is a good deal cheaper than the certified plank. If Stan is quoting based on our 2 & better grade and the rest of his competition is quoting on scaffold plank, then he will certainly win the job," Mike said.

"Maybe I should call Stan back and get more information on the specifications of the job. It may turn out that this isn't a scaffold plank job, and all of these problems will just disappear."

The waitress slipped the check between the two lumbermen. "Well, that might not be such a great idea, Bob. First, Stan may be a little ticked off if you were suggesting he might be doing something unethical. It could blow the relations between our companies. Second, suppose he does say that the material is going to be used for scaffolding. We would no longer be able to say we didn't know what it was going to be used for, and our best legal defense is out the window. I'd advise against calling him."

Bob thought about discussing the situation with John White, but White was out of town. Also, White prided himself on giving his traders a great deal of autonomy. Going to White too often for answers to questions was perceived as showing a lack of initiative and responsibility.

Against Mike's earlier warnings, Bob called Stan after lunch and discovered to his dismay that the material was going to be used as scaffold plank.

"Listen, Bob, I've been trying to sell this account for three months and this is the first inquiry that I've had a chance on. This is really important to me personally and to my superiors here at Quality. With this sale, we could land this account."

"But, Stan, we both know that our material doesn't meet the specs for scaffold plank."

"I know, I know," said Stan, "but I'm not selling it to the customer as scaffold plank. It's just regular construction lumber as far as we are both con-

cerned. That's how I've sold it, and that's what will show on the invoices. We're completely protected. Now just between you and me, the foreman on the job kinda winked at me and told me it was going to be scaffolding, but they're interested in keeping their costs down too. Also, they need this lumber by Friday, and there just isn't any scaffold plank in the local market."

"It just doesn't seem right to me," replied Bob.

"Look, I don't particularly like it, either. The actual specifications call for 2-inch thick material, but since it isn't actually scaffold plank, I'm going to order 3-inch planks. That is an extra inch of strength, and we both know that the load factors given in the engineering tables are too conservative to begin with. There's no chance that the material could fail in use. I happen to know that Haney Lumber is quoting a non-scaffold grade in a 2-inch material. If we don't grab this, someone else will and the material will be a lot worse than what we are going to supply."

When Bob continued to express hesitation, Stan said, "I won't hear about the status of the order until tomorrow, but we both know that your material will do this job OK—scaffold plank or not. The next year or two in this business are going to be lean for everyone, and our job—yours and mine—is putting lumber on job sites, not debating how many angels can dance on the head of a pin. Now if Quality can't count on you doing your job as a supplier, there are plenty of other wholesalers calling here every day who want our business. You better decide if you are going to be one of the survivors or not! I'll talk to you in the morning, Bob."

The next morning, Bob found a note on his desk telling him to see John White ASAP. Bob entered John's oak-paneled office and described the conversation with Stan yesterday. John slid a company sales order across the desk, and Bob saw it was a sales order for the 3 × 12s to Quality Lumber. In the space for the salesman's name, Bob saw that John had filled in "Bob Hopkins." Barely able to control his anger, Bob said, "I don't want anything to do with this order. I thought White Lumber was an ethical company, and here we are doing the same thing that all the fly-by-nighters do," sputtered Bob in concluding his argument.

John White looked at Bob and calmly puffed on his pipe. "The first thing you better do, Bob, is to calm down and put away your righteous superiority for a moment. You can't make or understand a good decision when you are as lathered up as you are. You are beginning to sound like a religious nut. What makes you think that you have the monopoly on ethical behavior? You've been out of college for four or five years, while I've been making these decisions for forty years. If you go into the industry or the community and compare your reputation with mine, you'll find out that you aren't even in the same league."

Bob knew John White was right. He had, perhaps, overstated his case, and in doing so, sounded like a zealot. When he relaxed and felt as though he was once again capable of rational thought, he said, "We both know that this lumber is going to be used for a purpose for which it is probably not suitable. Granted, there is only a very small chance that it will fail, but I don't see how we can take that chance."

"Look, Bob, I've been in this business for a long time, and I've seen practices that would curl your hair. Undershipping (shipping 290 pieces when the order calls for 300), shipping material a grade below what was ordered, bribing building inspectors and receiving clerks, and so on. We don't do those things at my company."

"Don't we have a responsibility to our customers, though?" asked Bob.

"Of course we do, Bob, but we aren't policemen, either. Our job is to sell lumber that is up to specification. I can't and won't be responsible for how the lumber is used after it leaves our yard. Between the forest and the final user, lumber may pass through a dozen transactions before it reaches the ultimate user. If we are to assume responsibility for every one of those transactions, we would probably have time to sell about four boards a year. We have to assume, just like every other business, that our suppliers and our customers are knowledgeable and will also act ethically. But whether they do or don't, it is not possible for us to be their keepers."

Bob interjected, "But we have reason to believe that this material will be used as scaffolding. I think we have an obligation to follow up on that information.

"Hold on, just a second, Bob. I told you once we are not the police. We don't even know who the final user is, so how are we going to follow up on this? If Stan is jerking us around, he certainly won't tell us. And even if we did know, what would we do? If we are going to do this consistently, that means we would have to ask every customer who the final end user is. Most of our customers would

interpret that as us trying to bypass them in the distribution channel. They won't tell us, and I can't blame them. If we carry your argument to its final conclusion, we'll have to start taking depositions on every invoice we sell.

"In the Quality Lumber instance, we are selling material to the customer as specified by the customer, Stan at Quality Lumber. The invoice will be marked, 'This material is not suitable for use as scaffold plank.' Although I'm not a lawyer, I believe that we have fulfilled our legal obligation. We have a signed purchase order and are supplying lumber that meets the specifications. I know we have followed the practices that are customary in the industry. Finally, I believe that our material will be better than anything else that could conceivably go on the job. Right now, there is no 2-inch dense 171 scaffold plank in this market, so it is not as though a better grade could be supplied in the time allotted. I would argue that we are ethically obligated to supply this lumber. If anyone is ethically at fault, it is probably the purchasing agent who specified a material that is not available."

When Bob still appeared to be unconvinced, John White asked him, "What about the other people here at the company? You're acting as though you are the only person who has a stake in this. It may be easy for you to turn this order down—you've got a college degree and a lot of career options. But I have to worry about all of the people at this company. Steve out there on the forklift never finished high school. He's worked here thirty years and if he loses this job, he'll probably never find another one. Janet over in bookkeeping has a disabled husband. While I can't afford to pay her very much, our health insurance plan keeps their family together. With the bills her husband accumulates in a year, she could never get him on another group insurance plan if she lost this job.

"Bob, I'm not saying that we should do anything and then try to justify it, but business ethics in the real world is not the same thing you studied in the classroom. There it is easy to say, 'Oh, there is an ethical problem here. We better not do that.' In the classroom, you have nothing to lose by taking the morally superior ground. Out here, companies close, people lose their jobs, lives can be destroyed. To always say, 'No, we won't do that' is no better than having no ethics at all. Ethics involves making tough choices, weighing costs and benefits. There are no hard-and-fast answers in these cases. We just have to approach each situation individually."

As Bob left John's office, he was more confused than ever. When he first entered his office, he had every intention of quitting in moral indignation, but John's argument had made a lot of sense to him, and he both trusted and respected John. After all, John White had a great deal more experience than he did and was highly respected in both the community and the lumber industry. Yet he was still uncomfortable with the decision. Was selling lumber to Quality merely a necessary adjustment of his ivory tower ethics to the real world of business? Or was it the first fork in the road to a destination he did not want to reach?

CASE 7

Royal Dutch Shell and the Execution of Ken Saro-Wiwa

This case was prepared by Charles W. L. Hill of the University of Washington.

INTRODUCTION

In 1995, a Nigerian military tribunal, in what most observers decried as a "sham trial," ordered the execution of noted author and playwright Ken Saro-Wiwa and eight other members of the Movement for the Survival of the Ogoni People. The Ogoni are a 500,000-member ethnic group of farmers and fishermen who live in an area of Nigeria's coastal plain. For several years, the Ogoni had been waging a vigorous political campaign against Nigeria's military rulers and the giant oil company, Royal Dutch Shell. They had been seeking greater self-determination, rights to the revenue stemming from oil exploration on traditional Ogoni lands, and compensation for the environmental degradation to their land caused by frequent oil spills from fractured pipelines. Shell had been pumping oil from Ogoni lands since the late 1950s. In 1994, four Ogoni chiefs who advocated cooperation rather than confrontation with Nigeria's military government were lynched by a mob of Ogoni youth. Though he was not present, Saro-Wiwa, a leader of the protest movement, was arrested and subsequently sentenced to death along with eight other Ogoni activists.

Despite intensive international pressure that included appeals to Shell to use its influence in the country to gain clemency for the convicted, the executions went ahead as scheduled on November

10, 1995. In the aftermath of the executions, Shell was roundly criticized in the Western media for its apparent unwillingness to bring pressure to bear on Nigeria's totalitarian regime. The incident started some soul-searching at Shell about the social and environmental responsibility of a multinational corporation in societies such as Nigeria that fall short of Western standards for the protection of human rights and the environment.

BACKGROUND

In 1961, the African nation of Nigeria won independence from Britain. At that time, many believed that Nigeria had the potential to become one of the engines of economic growth in Africa. The country was blessed with abundant natural resources, particularly oil and gas, was a net exporter of food stuffs, and had a large population that, by African standards, was well educated. (Today, Nigeria has the largest population in Africa—more than 110 million people.) By the mid 1990s, it was clear that much of that potential was still to be realized. Thirty-five years after winning independence, Nigeria still depended heavily on the oil sector. Oil production accounted for 30 percent of GDP, 95 percent of foreign exchange earnings, and about 80 percent of the government's budget revenues. The largely subsistence agricultural sector had failed to keep up with rapid population growth, and Nigeria, once a large net exporter of food, now had to import food. GDP per capita was a paltry $230, one quarter of what it had been in 1981, and the country was creaking under $40 billion of external debt. Nigeria had been unable to garner financial

This case is intended to be used as the basis for class discussion rather than as an illustration of effective or ineffective handling of the situation. This case was prepared by Charles W. L. Hill, University of Washington. Used by permission.

assistance from institutions such as the International Monetary Fund because of an unwillingness on the part of the government to account for how it used the revenues from oil taxes.

Political problems partly explained Nigeria's economic malaise. The country has suffered from internal strife between some of the more than 250 ethnic groups that constitute the nation. In the 1960s, the country was racked by a particularly nasty civil war. In December 1983, the civilian government of the country was replaced in a coup by a military regime, which proceeded to rule by decree. In 1993, democratic elections were held, but the military government nullified the results, declaring that there had been widespread ballot fraud.

Royal Dutch Shell is the main foreign oil producer operating in Nigeria. The company was formed at the turn of the century when Holland's Royal Dutch Company, which had substantial oil operations in Indonesia, merged with Britain's Shell Transport and Trading to create one of the world's first multinational oil companies. Shell is now the world's largest oil company, with annual revenues exceeding $130 billion. The company has been operating in Nigeria since 1937 and by the mid 1990s was pumping about half of Nigeria's oil. Nigerian oil accounts for about 11 to 12 percent of the company's global output and generates net income for Shell of around $200 million per annum.

PROBLEMS IN THE OGONI REGION

In 1958, Royal Dutch Shell struck oil on Ogoni lands. By some estimates, the company has extracted some $30 billion worth of oil from the region since then. Despite this, the Ogoni remain desperately poor. Most live in palm-roofed mud huts and practice subsistence agriculture. Of Shell's 5,000 employees in Nigeria, in 1995 only 85 were Ogoni. Because they are a powerless minority among Nigeria's 110 million people, the Ogoni are often overlooked when it comes to the allocation of jobs either in government or in the private sector.

Starting in 1982, the Nigerian government supposedly directed 1.5 percent of the oil revenue it received back to the communities where the oil was produced. In 1992, that percentage was increased to 3 percent. The Ogoni, however, claim that they have seen virtually none of this money. Most appears to

have been spent in the tribal lands of the ruling majority or has vanished in corrupt deals. Although there were ninety-six oil wells, two refineries, a petrochemical complex and a fertilizer plant in the Ogoni region in 1994, the lone hospital was an unfinished concrete husk, and the government schools, unable to pay teachers, were rarely open.

In addition to the lack of returns from oil production in their region, the Ogoni claim that their lands have suffered from environmental degradation, much of which could be laid at the feet of Shell. Ogoni activists claim that Shell's poor environmental safeguards have resulted in numerous oil spills and widespread contamination of the soil and ground water. A Shell spokesman, interviewed in 1994, seemed to acknowledge that there might be some basis to these complaints. He stated that "Some of the facilities installed during the last 30 years, while acceptable at the time, aren't as we would build them today. Given the age of some of these lines [oil pipelines], regrettably oil spills have occurred from time to time."[1] However, the same spokesman also blamed many of the more recent leaks in the Ogoni region on deliberate sabotage. The sabotage, he stated, had one of two motives— to back up claims for compensation or to support claims of environmental degradation.

On hearing of these claims, Ken Saro-Wiwa called them "preposterous." Saro-Wiwa argued that although uneducated youths, frustrated and angry, may have damaged some Shell installations in one or two incidents, "the people would never deliberately spill oil on their land because they know the so-called compensation is paltry and the land is never restored."[2] To support his position, Saro-Wiwa pointed to a spill from the 1960s near a settlement called Ebubu that still had not been cleaned up. In response, Shell stated that the spill occurred during the civil war in the 1960s, and cleanup work was completed in 1990. Subsequently, sunken oil reappeared at the surface, but Shell claims that it was unable to do anything about this because of threats made against its employees in the region. Indeed, in January 1993, out of concern for their safety, Shell barred its employees from entering the region.

In April 1993, the Ogoni organized their first protests against Shell and the government. Ogoni farmers stood in front of earthmoving equipment that was laying a pipeline for Shell through croplands. Although Shell stated that the land had been acquired by legal means and that full compensation had been paid to the farmers and local community, some of the locals remained unhappy about what they viewed as continuing exploitation of their land. Seeing a threat to the continuity of its oil operations, Shell informed the Nigerian government about the protest. Units from the Nigerian military soon arrived, and shots were fired into the crowd of protesters, killing one Ogoni man and wounding several others.

Subsequently, in a series of murky incidents, Nigerian soldiers stormed Ogoni villages, saying that they were quelling unrest between neighboring Ogoni tribes. For their part, the Ogoni claimed that the raids were punishment for obstructing Shell. They stated that the military had orders to use minor land disputes, which had long been settled with little violence, as an excuse to lay waste entire villages. A feared unit of the Mobile Police with the nickname "Kill and Go" conducted some of the raids. Although details are sketchy, it has been reported that hundreds of people lost their lives in the violence. In any event, the cycle of violence ultimately culminated in the killing of the Ogoni chiefs who argued for compromise with the Nigerian government. In turn, this provided the government with the justification it needed to arrest Ken Saro Wiwa and eight associates in the Movement for the Survival of the Ogoni People.

NIGERIA AND SHELL UNDER PRESSURE

Saro-Wiwa's arrest achieved the goal that the protests and bloodshed had not; it focused international attention on the plight of the Ogoni, the heavy-handed policies of the Nigerian government, and Shell's activities in Nigeria. Several human rights organizations immediately pressured Shell to use its influence to gain the release of Saro-Wiwa. They also urged Shell to put on hold plans to start work on a $3.5 billion liquefied natural gas project in Nigeria. The project was structured as a joint venture with the Nigerian government. Shell's central role in the project gave it considerable influence over the government, or so human rights activists believed.

For its part, Shell stated that it deplored the heavy-handed approach taken by the Nigerian government toward the Ogoni, and regretted pain and loss suffered by Ogoni communities. The company

also indicated that it was using "discreet diplomacy" to try and bring influence to bear on the Nigerian government. Nigeria's military leadership, however, was in no mood to listen to discreet diplomacy from Shell or anyone else. After a trial by a military tribunal that was derided as nothing more than a "kangaroo court," Saro-Wiwa and his associates were sentenced to death by hanging. The sentence was carried out shortly after sunrise on November 10, 1995.

AFTERMATH

In the wake of Saro-Wiwa's hanging, a storm of protest erupted around the world. The heads of state of the fifty-two nation British Commonwealth, meeting in New Zealand at the time of Saro-Wiwa's execution, suspended Nigeria and stated that they would expel the country if it did not return to democratic rule within two years. U.S. President Bill Clinton recalled the U.S. ambassador to Nigeria and banned the sale of military equipment, on top of aid cuts made in protest at Saro-Wiwa's arrest. British Prime Minister John Major banned arms sales to Nigeria and called for the widest possible embargo. Ambassadors from the fifteen nation European Union were recalled, and the EU suspended all aid to Nigeria.

On the other hand, no country halted purchases of Nigerian oil or sales of oil service equipment to Nigeria. The United States, which imports 40 percent of Nigeria's daily output of 2 million barrels, was silent on the question of an oil embargo. Similarly, no Western country—many of which had national companies working in the Nigerian oil industry—indicated that it would impose an embargo on sales to, or purchase from, the Nigerian oil industry. Alone among major public figures, South African President Nelson Mandela called for a ban on Shell. The call was echoed by several environment groups, including Greenpeace and Friends of the Earth, both of which urged their supporters to boycott Shell products. However, South Africa never did enact a formal ban, and the boycott calls met with only limited success.

For its part, Shell indicated that it would go ahead with its plans for a liquefied natural gas operation in Nigeria in partnership with the Nigerian government. In a public notice published in British newspapers, Shell stated that "it has been suggested that Shell should pull out of Nigeria's liquefied natural gas project. But if we do so now, the project will collapse. Maybe forever. So let's be clear who gets hurt if the project gets cancelled. A cancellation would certainly hurt the thousands of Nigerians who will be working on the project, and the tens of thousand benefiting in the local economy."[3]

In November 1996, the Center for Constitutional Rights filed a federal lawsuit in the U.S. District Court in Manhattan on behalf of relatives of Saro-Wiwa who now resided in the United States. The lawsuit accused Royal Dutch Shell of being part of a conspiracy that led to Saro-Wiwa's hanging. Shell denied the allegations and stated that they would be refuted in court.

In May 1997, at the annual general meeting of Shell Transport and Trading in London, a group of eighteen institutional investors tabled a resolution that would have required Shell to establish an independent external body to monitor its environmental and human rights policies. John Jennings, the outgoing chairman of the company, told reporters after the meeting that proxy votes from shareholders were running 10 to 1 against the resolution.

One reason for the defeat of the shareholder resolution was that the company had already indicated that it was taking steps to reform its culture and improve its own monitoring of environmental and human rights policies. Indeed, prior to the shareholder meeting, the company issued its own report on its policies in Nigeria, in which the company did admit that it needed to improve its monitoring of environmental and human rights policies. Under the leadership of its new head, Mark Moody-Stuart, Shell subsequently stated that it expected its companies to express support for fundamental human rights, in line with the legitimate role of business, and to give proper regard to health, safety, and the environment consistent with its commitment to sustainable development. The company also embraced the U.N. Universal Declaration of Human Rights, and pledged to set up socially responsible management systems and to develop training procedures to help management deal with human rights dilemmas.

Commenting on these steps, a spokesman for Human Rights Watch stated: "I'm prepared to give them some credit that they realized they had to look at what their own operations were and how to respond. They acknowledged that big companies have social responsibility, and that's a pretty big step for the multinational corporations."[4]

Endnotes

1. G. Brooks, "Slick Alliance," *Wall Street Journal*, May 6, 1994, p. A1.
2. G. Brooks, "Slick Alliance," *Wall Street Journal*, May 6, 1994, p. A1.
3. P. Beckett, "Shell Boldly Defends Its Role in Nigeria," *Wall Street Journal*, November 27, 1995, p. A9.
4. M. Hamilton, "Shell's New Worldview," *The Washington Post*, August 2, 1998, p. H1. Additional sources used in the preparation of this case are "Multinationals and Their Morals," *Economist,* December 2, 1995; R. Corzine, "Shell Discovers Time and Tide Wait for No Man," *Financial Times*, March 10, 1998, p. 17; R. Corzine, and Boulton, "Shell Defends Its Ethics on Eve of General Meeting," *Financial Times*, May 14, 1997, p. 29; J. Hoagland, "Shell's Game in Nigeria," *Washington Post*, November 5, 1995, p. C7; R. Hudson and M. Rose, "Shell Is Pressured to Scrap Its Plans for a New Plant in Nigeria Amid Protests," *Wall Street Journal*, November 14, 1995, p. A11; T. Kamm, "Executions Raise Sanction Threat," *Wall Street Journal*, November 13, 1995, p. A10.

Business Level: Domestic and Global Cases

America Online and the Internet (A)

This case was prepared by Charles W. L. Hill of the University of Washington.

Content, context, community, commerce and connectivity at a low cost.

—*Steve Case, CEO of America Online*

INTRODUCTION

As of June 1996, America Online (AOL) was the world's leading provider of commercial on-line services. Since its initial public offering in 1992, AOL had grown from an obscure on-line service with fewer than 200,000 subscribers and revenues of just $27 million into a titan in the fast-evolving world of cyberspace, with 6.2 million subscribers, revenues in excess of $1 billion, and strategic alliances with a slew of Internet software and service providers, including AT&T, Microsoft, and Netscape. Once seen as a distant third to its well-funded rivals, Prodigy and CompuServe, AOL was now clearly *the* major force in the commercial on-line market. Reflecting this, the stock had soared more than 100-fold since its initial public offering, hitting a peak of $71 per share in May 1996. At that price, AOL had a market capitalization of more than $6.4 billion! (See the financial data shown in Table 1.)

However, in the rapidly changing world of high technology, competitive advantage is often a fleeting thing. By the fall of 1996 there were wolves baying at AOL's door. One perennial problem cited by skeptics was AOL's high churn rate. (Churn rate refers to the number of subscribers who leave the service within a defined period of time, normally one year.) Estimates suggested that 30 to 40 per-

This case is intended to be used as a basis for class discussion rather than as an illustration of either effective or ineffective handling of the situation. This case was prepared by Charles W. L. Hill, University of Washington. Used by permission.

cent of subscribers quit the service within one, year of signing on. The reasons given to explain this high churn rate typically included uninspiring content and connection problems that frustrated subscribers. Another problem concerned a slow-down in the rate of subscriber growth, which became evident during the summer of 1996. AOL claimed that this slowdown reflected "normal" seasonal trends, but critical observers weren't so sure. There were also repeated allegations that AOL used questionable accounting practices, which understated the cost of acquiring new subscribers and overstated its operating profit. AOL was also facing increased price competition from Internet access providers and other on-line commercial services. To cap it all, many technophiles saw AOL's real competition as the World Wide Web, which they characterized as an ocean of content and information in comparison to AOL, which they dismissed as nothing more than a pond. Why on earth, they wondered, would consumers want to sign on with AOL, when for a flat fee of less than $20 per month they can sign on with any one of a growing number of Internet access providers and surf the Web at will using a Web browser downloaded for free from Netscape or Microsoft? Reflecting these concerns, AOL's stock price fell sharply from its May 1996 highs, hitting $24 per share by early October, a loss of more than 60 percent in less than four months. The investment community clearly had doubts about the ability of AOL to establish itself as a viable enterprise. How would AOL respond?

TABLE I

America Online Financial Data: 1991–1995

Per Share Data ($) (Year ended June 30)	1995	1994	1993	1992	1991
Tangible book value	$ 1.08	$ 1.70	0.51	0.43	–0.65
Cash flow	$ 0.57	$ 0.11	0.07	0.06	0.03
Earnings	$–0.50	$ 0.10	0.06	0.05	0.00
Dividends	Nil	Nil	Nil	Nil	Nil
Payout ratio	Nil	Nil	Nil	Nil	Nil
Prices—high	$ 44¼	$ 14⅝	$ 8¾	$ 3⅝	NA
—low	$ 12⅜	$ 6	$ 2¼	$ 1⅜	NA
P/E Ratio—high	NM	NM	NM	73	NA
—low	NM	NM	NM	27	NA
Income Statement Analysis (million $)					
Revenues	$ 394	$ 104	$40.0	$27.0	$21.0
Operating income	$ 103	$ 9.3	$ 5.1	$ 3.8	$ 2.0
Depreciation	$ 72.1	$ 1.3	$ 0.6	$ 0.5	$ 0.5
Interest expense	$ 1.0	NA	NA	NA	NA
Pretax income	$–18.5	$ 10.0	$ 5.0	$ 3.6	$ 1.5
Effective tax rate	NM	38%	38%	38%	38%
Net income	$–33.6	$ 6.2	$ 3.1	$ 2.2	$ 0.9
Balance Sheet & Other Financial Data (million $)					
Cash	$ 64.1	$ 67.7	$14.3	$14.0	$ 1.0
Current assets	$ 133	$ 105	$25.0	$19.0	$ 4.0
Total assets	$ 406	$ 148	$32.0	$24.0	$ 8.0
Current liability	$ 133	$ 40.4	$ 8.6	$ 4.4	$ 3.8
Long-term debt	$ 19.5	$ 5.8	Nil	Nil	$ 0.2
Common equity	$ 218	$ 99	$23.8	$18.9	$–6.0
Total capital	$ 273	$ 108	$24.0	$19.0	$ 4.0
Capital expense	$ 57.8	$ 17.5	$ 1.8	$ 0.7	$ 0.1
Cash flow	$ 38.4	$ 7.5	$ 3.7	$ 2.7	$ 0.5
Current ratio	1.0	2.6	3.0	4.4	1.0
% Long-term of capitalization	7.1%	5.4%	Nil	Nil	4.8%
% Net income of revenues	NM	5.9%	7.7%	8.3%	4.4%
% Return on assets	NM	6.6%	10.7%	7.4%	NA
% Return on equity	NM	9.7%	13.9%	NM	NA

Source: Company accounts.

CYBERSPACE

Cyberspace—that vast, hip, cool, creative, anarchic, digitally constructed visual and audio reality that is diffused throughout and embedded within the growing World Wide Web of interconnected computers—owes its origins to, of all things, cold war paranoia. The Internet, or the skeleton on which the flesh of cyberspace hangs, started its life in 1969 in a military laboratory under the sponsorship of the Pentagon's Advanced Research Projects Agency. The Internet was conceived as a means of allowing scientists working on military contracts all over America to share expensive computers and other resources. As an afterthought, a few of the original designers also came up with a way of sending messages between computers, and E-mail was born.

The design of the Internet displays its military origins.[1] At its most basic, the Internet is nothing more than a collection of computers linked to a network of high-speed telephone lines and switches (see Figure 1). To ensure easy connectivity, the Internet is based on a communications protocol known as TCP/IP, which is in the public domain (it is an open standard). Data traveling along the Internet are split into tiny packets of information; an Internet address is assigned to each packet; and, given their common addresses, the packets can take different routes to their destination. This makes it hard for anyone to eavesdrop on messages—an important source of comfort to the paranoid warriors of the cold war. Moreover, a "packet-switched" network can resist large-scale destruction. If one route is knocked out for some reason (for example, by a nuclear bomb), packets will simply travel along a route that remains intact.

Until the early 1980s, the Internet was tiny and very obscure, consisting of fewer than 500 "host" computers. However, academics were starting to take notice. They found the Internet to be a useful conduit for sharing information with their colleagues. Because the Internet utilized open standards, it was easy to hook into, and because the U.S. government had subsidized the building of much of the early infrastructure, it was inexpensive to use. Soon universities and research laboratories around the world were connecting their own internal networks of computers to the Internet, transforming it into a globally dispersed "network of networks," and by 1987 approximately 28,000 host computers were attached. The Internet, however, was still a very dry place, lacking in color, sound, and images. To become of interest to a wider audience, it needed to change.

The World Wide Web

The change, when it came, was accidental and explosive. In the late 1980s, Tim Bernes Lee, a physicist at the CERN research institute for particle physics in Switzerland, developed a method of organizing on-line scientific information. His insight was that documents stored in digital form could be cross-referenced, or linked, by using "hypertext." Associated with the hypertext would be an Internet

address. Users could select a hypertext term in a document they were reading on-line, and they would be linked electronically to a document associated with that term. For example, a physicist at CERN who was using her computer to read a research paper that cited a study undertaken by scientists in Los Alamos would simply have to click on the cite with her computer's mouse—assuming that it was formatted in hypertext—and she would be linked with the source document, which might be stored on a computer at Los Alamos, or for that matter, on any other computer linked to the Internet. Bernes Lee developed a simple computer code, known as hypertext markup language, or HTML, for formatting documents containing hypertext. Within HTML he also embedded instructions that could be used to display graphics files connected with a document on a computer screen. Without really knowing it, Bernes Lee had invented the World Wide Web (WWW).

In 1993, a young computer programmer at the University of Illinois, Mark Andreessen, masterminded the development of a browser that could be used to surf the Internet, read documents that had been formatted with HTML, and display the associated text and graphics on a personal computer screen. In 1994, he left Illinois to help establish Netscape, a software company that produced an improved version of the HTML browser he had developed at Illinois, Netscape Navigator. Netscape also produced Web server software that could be placed on the computer servers, which were the nodes of the rapidly developing WWW, to manage Web files and handle traffic.

Facilitated by the wide availability of browsers and Web server software and powered by the sudden rush of nontechnical users to get on-line, the growth of the WWW was nothing short of stunning. In 1990, less than 1 million users were connected to the Internet. By late 1995, largely as a result of the popularity of the WWW, the figure was approaching 80 million. Projections suggest there will be 160 million users by 1998, and perhaps as many as 500 million by early in the next century.[2]

A related development was the invention of the Java computer programming language at Sun Microsystems, one of the leading suppliers of computer workstations and servers. A program written in Java can be stored anywhere on the WWW and accessed by anyone with a Web browser on his or her personal computer that contains a Java interpreter. (The new versions of most Web browsers such as Netscape's Navigator and Microsoft's Internet Explorer include a Java interpreter.) Java is indifferent to the operating system of the personal computer on which a Web browser resides. Therefore, in theory, someone using a current version of Netscape Navigator can access a word processing program placed somewhere on the Web as and when it is needed. Instead of purchasing the program outright for hundreds of dollars, all the user needs to do is pay a few cents for the run time during which the program is used. To date, the main use of Java has been to run simple visual applications on downloaded Web pages.[3]

The Infrastructure of the Internet

The infrastructure of the Internet is composed of five key elements: a backbone, digital switches, dedicated computers known as servers, Points of Presence (POPs), and the computers of connected users (see Figure 2).[4] The backbone of the net is a system of fiber-optic telecommunications lines that can transfer 40 million bits of data per second between two nodes in the system at the speed of light. (In comparison, using "slow" telephone lines, the average modem transfers data at 28,800 bits per second.) Most backbone lines are owned by the telephone companies (AT&T, MCI, Sprint), which lease capacity wholesale to Internet users. Digital ATM switches are found at the nodes of the system, of which there are tens of thousands. These ATM switches, which are nothing more than specialized computers, direct the packets of data that flow along the Internet.

From the ATM switches, fiber-optic lines branch off to connect large users, such as universities and corporations. These larger users have their own internal networks (local area networks known as LANs), complete with local switches. Users within the organization can connect to the Internet from their personal computers by utilizing networking software such as Windows NT or Novell Netware. Most larger users also maintain servers where they store data that can be accessed by anyone connected to the Internet (for example, HTML documents such as WWW home pages).

Other lines branch off from ATM switches to connect smaller organizations and individuals to the Internet. These users must first dial a telephone number to connect to a POP, which is simply another switch connected to the ATM switch. (Anyone who uses AOL's service first has to dial a telephone number to connect to a POP before accessing the service.) From the POP, lines branch off to home users who connect through analog modems and ISDN lines. (An ISDN telephone line uses digital rather than analog signals to transmit data, which significantly increases transmission speed.) The local area networks of smaller organizations may also be connected to the Internet through a POP. Many of these smaller organizations also maintain their own Web servers.

Internet Service Providers

During the early 1990s, personal computers penetrated small businesses and the home market in record numbers. (By 1995, an estimated 30 percent of U.S. households owned a personal computer.) The rapid diffusion of PCs among the households and small businesses, when coupled with the development of HTML and Web browsers, created consumer demand for access to the World Wide Web. The initial demand was largely from academicians and students, who were using it to access the Web through various university networks and wanted similar access at home. Soon, however, demand mushroomed to include small businesses, many of which wanted to experiment with selling goods and services via the WWW, and individuals from a wide range of backgrounds.

Internet service providers (ISPs) emerged to serve this demand. There are literally hundreds of ISPs operating today in the United States, but they are increasingly dominated by a handful of big names, including all three major long-distance carriers (AT&T, MCI, and Sprint), along with some less familiar names (UUNet, Netcom Online, PSI Net, AGIS-Net99, BBN, and GNN—an ISP owned by AOL). Some of the Internet service providers have invested heavily in building the infrastructure of the Internet (UUNet and Sprint, for example), installing fiber-optic backbone lines, ATM switches, servers, and POPs. These ISPs often lease their surplus capacity to other ISPs. Most ISPs license Web browsers from Microsoft and/or Netscape, providing these for free to their customers.

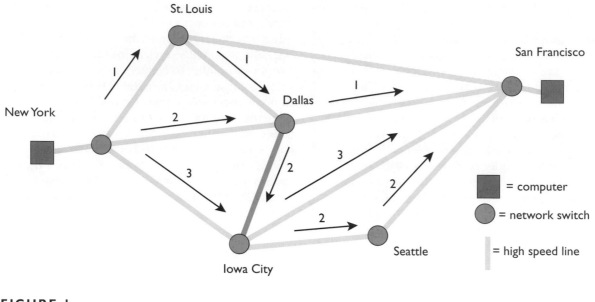

FIGURE I

How the
Internet Works

The emergence of ISPs is a relatively recent phenomenon. By early 1996, there were about 600,000 direct ISP subscribers in the United States, compared with 10.5 million subscribers for various proprietary on-line services such as AOL, Prodigy, MSN, and CompuServe.[5] However, the entry of companies such as AT&T into this business and the growing familiarity of users with the Web point toward a potentially dramatic increase in the number of ISPs over the next few years. Some observers speculate that over the next few years subscriber growth will be increasingly oriented toward ISPs, as opposed to the established on-line service.

By 1996, two trends were evident among ISPs—consolidation and intensifying price competition. The most dramatic example of consolidation was the acquisition for $2 billion of UUNet by MSF Communications, a competitive-access telephone service company with operations in the United States and Europe. According to the CEO of MSF Communications, "The combination of our fiber-optic network and UUNet's Internet services are a match made in heaven."[6] For UUNet, the great advantage of the acquisition was that it would reduce

UUNet's costs. ISPs normally have to pay substantial fees to local and long-distance telephone companies in order to access their networks. In 1995, more than 40 percent of UUNet's network expenses were for local communications service.[7] The acquisition would reduce these, putting UUNet on a level footing with the likes of AT&T and MCI.

By 1995, most ISPs were charging a basic monthly fee for access (usually in the $10-per-month range) plus an hourly rate that would kick in after the first five to ten hours of usage in a month (for example, $2.95 after the first five hours of access time). Under this pricing structure, it was not uncommon for active subscribers to run up bills in excess of $50 per month. By 1996, however, the pricing trend among ISPs seemed to be headed toward a flat rate monthly fee for a basic service. This development was driven by the entry of large telephone companies into the ISP business. In early 1996, AT&T entered the ISP business with the introduction of its WorldNet service. AT&T announced that it would provide its long-distance customers with five free hours of Internet access a month and charge $2.50 per hour for additional ac-

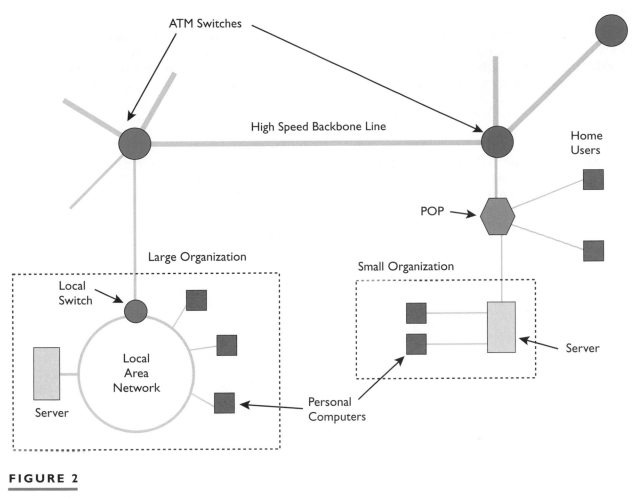

FIGURE 2

Internet Infrastructure

cess. It also offered unlimited Internet access for $19.95 per month. AT&T's announcement resulted in 212,000 customers signing up for the service by the time it went live on March 14, 1996. So strong was the demand that AT&T found itself without the network capacity (POPs and switches) and software to service the demand, and by mid-1996 there was a two-month waiting list before customers could connect to the service.[8]

MCI responded to AT&T's entry with a similar pricing structure, including the flat rate charge of $19.95 per month for unlimited access. MCI also announced that it would triple the capacity of its Internet access network and offer its customers high-speed ISDN Internet access. In announcing this move, a senior vice president at MCI noted that "MCI's pioneering efforts in the Internet market have resulted in a $100 million business that we expect to grow to $2 billion by 2000."[9]

Proprietary On-Line Services

Long before the ISPs had a notable presence, there were the proprietary on-line service providers (OSPs). The OSPs differ from the ISPs in that an OSP allows a fee-paying subscriber access to a private, closed network that contains exclusive content. ISPs simply grant access to the World Wide Web, but OSPs bundle exclusive content for their subscribers. Currently, subscribers have to use a proprietary interface to access these on-line services. In addition, OSP subscribers can use the service as a gateway to the WWW. An AOL subscriber, for example, can browse the Web using AOL's Web browser, Netscape Navigator, or Microsoft's Internet Explorer.

As of mid 1996, there were four major OSPs in the United States: America Online, CompuServe, Prodigy, and the Microsoft Network (MSN). AOL is discussed in detail later in this case. Prodigy is the oldest and smallest of these services, with around 1 million subscribers. Prodigy was established in 1984 as a joint venture between Sears, IBM, and CBS. IBM was to provide the technology, Sears wanted to experiment with on-line commerce, and CBS was to provide news and advertising. CBS pulled out after a short time, but IBM and Sears stuck with it until May 1996, pouring $1.2 billion into Prodigy. By that point it was clear that Prodigy was losing out to other OSPs, so IBM and Sears sold the service for $250 million to International Wireless, a Boston-based investment group. When discussing Prodigy's failure to grow, analysts often cited its clunky interface, poorly organized and uninspiring content, failure to embrace chat rooms and E-mail, and unimaginative distribution strategy.[10]

With 4.7 million subscribers, CompuServe is second only to AOL in the OSP market, although until two years ago it was substantially larger than AOL. CompuServe was established by H&R Block in an effort to diversify H&R Block's core tax return business (which has a pronounced seasonal fluctuation in revenues) and to provide an on-line conduit for Block's financial services business. In April 1996, H&R Block took the first step in the process of spinning off CompuServe to independent investors, selling 16 million shares, or a 17.7 percent stake in the service, for an average price of $30 per share, raising $454 million in the process.[11]

During 1995, CompuServe added new subscribers at the rate of about 100,000 per month, substantially less than AOL's subscriber acquisition rate of 400,000 per month.[12] CompuServe's inability to match AOL has been variously attributed to a confusing pricing scheme, poor marketing, and an interface that was less intuitive and appealing than that employed by AOL.

In August 1995, CompuServe took a number of steps that were designed to correct these problems. The pricing structure, which charged subscribers a different price for different aspects of the service, was revamped and replaced with a flat monthly fee of $9.95 for the first five hours and $2.95 for each subsequent hour. CompuServe also announced plans to introduce a new low-cost service aimed at Internet novices and children in an attempt to strengthen its network infrastructure by increasing the number of access points from 50,000 to 105,000 and to triple its spending on marketing to $115 million.[13]

CompuServe's new service, WOW, was introduced in the spring of 1996.[14] WOW was designed to challenge AOL on both price and child safety. Although WOW is produced by CompuServe, it is a completely different service. For a flat fee of $18 per month, WOW offers unlimited access to a mix of proprietary content and features, as well as to the Internet's World Wide Web and E-mail. WOW utilizes Microsoft's Internet Explorer as its Web browser. WOW was explicitly designed with features to protect children from accessing undesirable content on the Web (that is, pornography), and to give children a gateway to the on-line world. When a subscriber first signs onto WOW, a master account is set up for a parent and up to five subaccounts for other family members. If any of these accounts is designated as a children's account, it will see only a special kid's version of WOW, with child-oriented designs and features. It remains to be seen whether this new service can help break the lock that AOL apparently has on new-subscriber growth.

In August 1995, Microsoft launched its own proprietary on-line service, the Microsoft Network, or MSN. At the time, many thought that MSN would rapidly capture market share from the three established OSPs, partly because an icon that enabled PC users to connect with MSN was one of the first things people saw when they booted up Windows 95, Microsoft's new operating system. However, things turned out rather differently.

Although MSN did build up its subscriber base at a rapid rate (more than 1.6 million subscribers had signed up by October 1996, making MSN the world's largest on-line service), Microsoft abruptly changed its strategy in December 1995. The catalyst for the change in strategy was the growing popularity of Netscape and Java. The shift from desktop-centered to Web-centered computing promised by the fusion of Netscape and Java was perceived by many as a threat to Microsoft's core operating system and applications business.[15] In response, Microsoft changed its Internet strategy to embrace the Web and set itself up as a direct competitor to Netscape.

As one element of this strategy, MSN was to be recast as a Web site that would be built according to the Internet's software standards (including HTML and Java) as opposed to a proprietary software standard developed by Microsoft. Parts of the Web site were to be accessible for free by anyone with a Web browser. The free part of the site was to include MSNBC, a joint venture with NBC that offered a twenty-four-hour cable TV news service to compete with CNN and a regularly updated text-based news content on the MSN Web site. By October 1996, MSNBC could be accessed by 17 million cable TV viewers and anyone with a browser and access to the Web. Fee-paying MSN subscribers could also gain access to additional service offerings that would be closed to nonsubscribers.[16]

On October 10, 1996, Microsoft formally unveiled the new Web-based MSN. In addition to providing access to the Web like any ISP, MSN provided subscribers with a number of proprietary services, including a news and entertainment area; E-mail; chat rooms; bulletin boards; an Internet navigator to help MSN subscribers find useful content on the Web; and various other reference materials, such as an on-line version of Encarta, Microsoft's best-selling multimedia encyclopedia. MSN offered subscribers a choice of pricing structure. One scheme was based on $6.95 per month for five hours, with additional hours being priced at $2.50. The other scheme, aimed at heavy users, offered unlimited access for $19.95 per month.[17]

A final proprietary on-line service of some note was e*World, the on-line service offered by Apple to users of its computers. It turned out to be one of Apple Computer's spectacular failures, just like its personal digital assistant, the Newton. Apple pinned its hopes for e*World on interactive games. This strategy did little to whet the appetite of the world's 15 million or so Macintosh users, and subscriptions topped out at 100,000 in 1995 before heading downhill. In 1996, Apple announced that it would close down e*World. Why did e*World fail to garner more support? Reasons given for the failure of the service include poor marketing, high prices, the lack of a free trial period (most on-line services offer new subscribers one month of free access), narrow content, and a failure to open up e*World to the non-Macintosh computer owner.[18]

The Commercialization of Cyberspace

Many believe that the Internet will soon become a huge conduit for electronic commerce. The Web is a place where buyers and sellers can find each other and trade at a much lower cost than in the material world. For example, consider Lands' End, which sells casual clothing through mail-order catalogs. Two of the largest items in the cost structure of Lands' End are the cost of catalogs and postage. The extent to which the customers of Lands' End can be encouraged to browse for clothes at Lands' End's own Internet store (www.landsend.com) may ultimately limit the need for Lands' End to send out catalogs, significantly reducing the company's cost structure.

Another example is Amazon.com, which promotes itself as the world's largest bookstore. Established in the summer of 1995, Amazon.com sells more than 1.1 million titles (five times the inventory of the largest book superstore), yet it does not have a material retail presence. All of its business is conducted through the Web. This means that Amazon.com has a substantially lower cost structure than book retailers that operate physical stores, which in turn supports discounts of 10 to 30 percent on a wide range of books. Amazon.com will deliver popular books in two to three days, although more obscure titles can take three weeks.[19]

The software industry is perhaps the industry in which the migration to the Web is most natural. After all, software is nothing more than bits of information, and software programs can be easily downloaded over the Web. Among other things, this new channel of distribution might ultimately put traditional software retailers, such as Egghead Software, out of business.

According to International Data Corporation, as of early 1996 there were more than 100,000 retailers on the Web, although total revenues in 1995 amounted to just $324 million.[20] However, the volume of business is expected to grow exponentially. AT&T, for example, estimated that merchants would sell some $518 million worth of goods over the Internet in 1996 and that this figure would rise to $6.6 billion by the year 2000.[21] Other forecasts see slower growth. Price Waterhouse, for example, sees Internet sales of $1.4 billion by 1998.[22] By comparison, according to Forrester Research Inc., the mail catalog industry generated $53 billion in sales in 1995.[23]

On-line financial services, including on-line banking and on-line stock trading, are emerging as another potentially large segment of on-line commerce. A growing number of banks—among them giants such as Wells Fargo, Citicorp, and Chase—are embracing the concept of on-line banking, and many are working with software companies such as Microsoft and Intuit to develop an on-line presence. Stockbrokerage firms are also moving onto the Web. As of mid 1996, around 800,000 individual investors were trading stocks electronically, although many were still using proprietary software offered by institutions with a material retail presence such as Charles Schwab and Fidelity. However, a number of electronic brokerage firms, such as E*Trade, have recently set up operations on the Web, and the possibility exists that these firms might experience substantial growth in the future. The great attraction of on-line banking and stock brokering is that it reduces the need for maintaining a costly physical presence in the marketplace, including physical facilities and employees (such as bank tellers and stockbrokers).[24]

One of the great impediments to the growth of Internet commerce is doubt among consumers about the security of transactions executed over the Internet. There is a fear that computer hackers might be able to access credit card numbers transmitted over the Internet and use those numbers to run up large debts. To combat this problem, a number of software companies, such as CyberCash and VeriFone, have developed encryption technology that provides for more secure electronic transactions executed via the Web. Growing confidence in the security offered by encryption technology could significantly help to boost Internet commerce.[25]

Electronic Bottlenecks

Issues of security aside, a number of other factors are currently holding back the development of the Internet. An August 1996 survey of Internet users by *BusinessWeek* and Louis Harris & Associates reported that 73 percent found slow access to be a minor or major problem, 56 percent said that the high cost of access was a problem, 66 percent said

that the difficulty of locating useful information was a problem, 61 percent cited difficult connections as a problem, and 36 percent cited uninteresting content as a problem.[26]

Concerns about slow access point toward a major problem with the Internet—a lack of bandwidth. Bandwidth is related to the speed of data transmission. Many users have only low bandwidth and hence low speed links to the Internet (for instance, modems that transfer data at 14,400 bps or 28,800 bps). With these slow links, it can take a long time to download graphic-intensive Web pages. However, much faster modems are being developed. ISDN modems are already available that allow access to the Web at speeds of 128 bps. Cable modems that offer access speeds 1,000 times faster than conventional modems are currently being tested in the market and should be widely available by the year 2000. (Cable modems utilize the coaxial cable feeds that are currently used for cable TV.)

However, even with significantly faster modems, bandwidth problems will still persist on the Internet because of the vast volume of traffic now flowing through the infrastructure. Ultimately, large investments in infrastructure, including backbone fiber-optic links and ATM switches, as well as the development of data compression techniques, will be required to overcome the Internet's bandwidth problems. If the Internet develops into an economic force, however, these investments should be forthcoming.

AOL

The history of AOL is interwoven with that of the company's thirty-eight-year-old CEO, Steve Case. After a brief spell in marketing at Procter & Gamble and Pizza Hut, Case joined Control Video, the forerunner of AOL, in 1983 as a marketing assistant. At the time, Control Video was a gaming service for Atari computer owners. Case was introduced to the founders of Control Video by his older brother, Dan, who was then an associate with the San Francisco investment bank Hambrecht & Quist and represented the bank on the company's board. (Dan Case is now CEO of Hambrecht & Quist.)

Soon after Steve Case was hired, Control Video ran out of money. The board promptly fired the existing management team and brought in as CEO Jim Kimsey, an entrepreneur who had been working part-time at Control Video. Under Kimsey's direction Control Video was reborn in 1985 as Quantum Computer Services, an on-line service for owners of Commodore computers.

Right from the beginning, Kimsey groomed Case to succeed him. Case played a role in raising $5 million in venture capital for Quantum, and he was the prime mover in expanding Quantum's business. By the early 1990s, Quantum, which changed its name to America Online in 1991, was gunning for a share of the still small, but rapidly growing commercial on-line service business. The two market leaders at the time were Prodigy and CompuServe. In need of capital to expand its service, in 1992 AOL undertook an initial public offering, which raised $66 million. At the time, AOL had $27 million in annual revenues, 200,000 subscribers, and 250 employees.

Case's strategy for AOL has had three main elements: extensive marketing to generate rapid subscriber growth, the acquisition of desirable content to keep those subscribers interested in the service, and investment in a high-speed network infrastructure that will guarantee subscribers rapid access to AOL. Judged by subscriber and revenue growth, the strategy seems to have worked. Between 1994 and late 1996, AOL added 5 million customers, propelling AOL past Prodigy and CompuServe into the number one spot in the on-line industry. As of June 1996, AOL had more than 6.2 million customers (up from only 3 million a year earlier), annualized revenues in excess of $1.1 billion, and more than 4,500 employees. Moreover, with only 11 percent of households in the United States subscribing to on-line services as of 1996, the potential for further growth looked bright.[27]

The Service

When they sign on to AOL, subscribers are greeted with an attractively designed interface that allows them to access a wide range of services through twenty "channels." For example, someone interested in investing in stocks can click on the "personal finance" channel. Within this channel they can access a vast amount of useful investment information, including company stock reports, analysts' estimates of future corporate earnings, stock market quotes that are updated every fifteen minutes, industry and company news, investment advice from proprietary content providers such as the Motley Fool, stock bulletin boards where sub-

scribers post their thoughts on the prospects for individual companies, investment chat rooms, and much more.

Other channels allow subscribers to read on-line versions of many popular newspapers (for example, the *New York Times, Investors Business Daily*) and magazines (for example, *Business-Week, Scientific American, PC World, Time*); to access and download a vast library of computer software; to play interactive games on-line with other subscribers; to get regularly updated local, national, and international news and to discuss that news with other interested subscribers in dedicated chat rooms; to keep up with developments in their favorite sport; to browse through a wide array of entertainment offerings including on-line versions of Viacom's cable TV channels, MTV, Nickelodeon, and VH1; and to plan vacations and purchase airline tickets. AOL also has a "person to person" feature that contains a large number of chat rooms, each of which can accommodate more than thirty-nine users at any one time and which are devoted to topics that range from the general and mundane to the bizarre and strange (one popular chat room with the title "raiding the fridge" seems devoted to discussing the merits—culinary and otherwise—of SPAM). It is also possible for subscribers to create their own "private" chat room to converse with friends or family. Subscribers can send E-mail over the Internet, and they can use AOL's Web browser to access and surf the World Wide Web. (They can also use Microsoft's Internet Explorer and Netscape's Navigator if they so wish.)

According to AOL data, as of early 1996 the breakdown of an average subscriber's use of on-line time was as follows: 15 percent spent surfing the World Wide Web; 25 percent spent in chat rooms; 20 percent spent writing or reading E-mail; 30 percent spent viewing content on AOL; and 10 percent spent on other activities, such as interactive games.[28]

Content Providers

AOL has contracts with more than 1,000 content providers, including some of the biggest names in the media business (for example, Viacom, Time Warner, Capital Cities/ABC). AOL tracks the amount of time that individual subscribers spend visiting different content areas, assigns a dollar amount to that time, and offers content providers a percentage share of revenues generated during a subscriber's visit. So, for example, if a subscriber spends an hour in Viacom's MTV area at a rate of $2.95 per hour, AOL might keep 50 percent of that revenue and pass the remaining percent on to Viacom. The actual percentage revenue split varies significantly from provider to provider.

Initially, AOL adopted something of a laissez-faire attitude toward the presentation of content, letting providers make content and presentation decisions. More recently, the company has come to the realization that this approach often resulted in dull and uninspiring content. For example, having *Time* magazine repackage its print product for on-line consumers was not creating the desired excitement among subscribers. To try to improve the quality of content on AOL, the company developed two different models for working with content providers—cooperative joint ventures and the Greenhouse.[29]

The joint venture model explicitly recognizes that AOL will work cooperatively with well-established content providers to develop on-line content. Underlying this approach is a presumption that AOL can increase the value of a content offering by bringing its own experience to bear on the development of that offering. Some examples of the results of such partnerings include an expanded health channel jointly developed with Time Warner; fashion and lifestyles sites developed in collaboration with Capital Cities/ABC; and the MTV and Nickelodeon sites developed in cooperation with Viacom.

The Greenhouse takes entrepreneurial companies that would otherwise not have the capital, marketing, or distribution to function on their own and gives them a low-cost loan to start their business, a place on the AOL network, and the benefit of AOL's experience. The idea is to help create new content providers that are specifically geared to take advantage of the unique features and power of the on-line medium. In return for this backing, AOL reserves the right to purchase a portion of the equity of a Greenhouse partner if it so desires. One of the most successful products of the Greenhouse system has been the Motley Fool, an on-line investment forum run by two brothers, Tom and David Gardner. Located in AOL's personal finance channel, the Fool has expanded to become one of AOL's top ten content providers, and one of the most renowned of the new media companies to be found in cyberspace.

Infrastructure

Difficulty connecting to the service, the slow speed of data transmission, and frequent service breakdowns were among the biggest sources of dissatisfaction voiced by AOL subscribers during the 1993–1995 period. To a large degree, these problems were a result of AOL's subscriber growth outstripping the growth in its network capacity. In response, AOL has been investing heavily in network infrastructure.

In February 1995, AOL acquired Advanced Network Services (ANS) for $35 million. ANS has years of experience in building high-speed infrastructure for the Internet. With the help of ANS, in mid 1995 AOL launched AOLnet, a high-speed network that adheres to the Internet's TCP/IP communications standard and is wholly owned and operated by AOL. With the establishment of AOLnet, AOL now has access to one of the fastest TCP/IP backbones in the world, along with 500 Points of Presence (POPs). By owning many of its own POPs rather than leasing them from the likes of Sprint or MCI, AOL can guarantee access to subscribers and avoid the variable costs associated with leasing POPs.

By March 1996, around 50 percent of AOL's network traffic was funneled through AOLnet, and by mid 1997 the figure should be around 85 percent.[30] Apart from improving access, one of the advantages of a proprietary network is that over time it should allow AOL to shift from a variable-cost to a fixed-cost model for data communications, while the overall per-hour cost of providing data communications should decrease. The impact of AOLnet was evident in the last quarter of fiscal 1996 (ended June 30), when AOL's gross margin rose to 46.6 percent from 42.2 percent in the prior year. According to AOL, the improvement in gross margin was a direct result of more traffic being handled by AOLnet.[31] The buildup of AOLnet continues to require a substantial investment in telecommunications equipment, much of which AOL is financing through leasing.[32]

Despite its investments in infrastructure, AOL still does experience some connection problems. In August 1996, AOL's entire network was shut down for seventeen hours due to what the company called a "coincidental series of events that are unlikely to occur again." Whatever the cause, the shutdown was a major inconvenience, particularly for those business users who relied on AOL for E-mail and other data transmission services.[33]

In addition to network infrastructure, AOL has invested in data compression software in an attempt to push back some of the constraints on access speed in a world where most subscribers connect with modems that operate at the "slow" speed of 28,800 bps or less. In February 1996, AOL acquired Johnson-Grace, a software company known for its data-compression technology. Using high-speed data-compression technology, AOL has been able to reduce significantly the time it takes to download graphics onto a personal computer. As a result, according to Steve Case,

> We can provide a virtual broadband service to people with slow modems. . . . This displaces the need for high bandwidth connectivity. The bandwidth gap—the bandwidth haves and the bandwidth havenots—plays right into the hands of AOL. We're optimizing the service in recognition of the fact that consumers have slow modems and that the Internet was designed for people with high speed connectivity.[34]

Pricing, Marketing, and Churn

Through December 31, 1994, the standard monthly membership fee for AOL was $9.95 for five hours of access and $3.50 per hour thereafter. In January 1995, AOL reduced the per hour fee to $2.95, although it left the base fee unchanged. In May 1996, AOL announced an additional pricing plan for heavy users of the service. This included twenty hours of service for $19.95 per month and an hourly fee of $2.95 for use in excess of that. As of November 1996, the company was said to be considering a move toward a flat-rate fee for unlimited use of the service.

To get people to try out its service, AOL spends heavily on marketing. The company gives away the interface and connection software for free and frequently runs mass-mail promotions, sending out tens of thousands of AOL software disks at a time to potential subscribers in an attempt to lure them onto the service. All new subscribers get a one-month free trial period. In September 1996, Case announced

that AOL would spend $100 million on a fall quarter print-and-television-media campaign aimed at attracting new users. The company's goal called for 10.5 million AOL subscribers by June 1997.

Aggressive marketing does not come cheaply. For the nine months ending in March 31, 1996, AOL's marketing expenses were $145.9 million, an increase of 205 percent compared with the nine-month period ending March 31, 1995. Moreover, AOL's subscriber acquisition costs have been on an even steeper incline. Subscriber acquisition costs add other costs, such as the costs of software disks and postage for direct-mail campaigns, to marketing costs. For the nine months ending March 31, 1996, AOL's subscriber acquisition costs were $306.7 million, an increase of 368 percent over the $65.5 million spent in the nine-month period ending March 31, 1995. Estimates of AOL's cost of acquiring customers in the financial year ending June 1996 ranged from $40 to $110 per customer. Steve Case claims that the true cost is toward the low end of this range. In an interview given in September 1996, he noted that "right now we are spending $45 to get someone new on the system."[35] There is, however, some confusion as to exactly how the company calculates these figures, since there is a difference between getting people onto the system for a one-month free trial period and getting them to stay on the system as fee-paying subscribers. Some analysts claim that AOL's estimates of subscriber acquisition costs are calculated on the basis of those who try out the system and include those who don't stay after the first month. This approach understates the true cost of acquiring fee-paying subscribers. In any event, AOL does admit that the cost of acquiring new subscribers will increase to $50 to $60 per subscriber in fiscal 1997 as a result of an intensive marketing campaign to attract new subscribers.[36]

Whatever the true cost of acquiring customers, there is certainly controversy over how AOL has chosen to account for these costs. For accounting purposes, AOL has treated many of the costs of acquiring new subscribers as capital investment rather than as a current expense. These costs have then been amortized against earnings over twenty-four months. The effect has been to increase AOL's current earnings, but at the price of an increase in the level of deferred subscriber acquisition costs on AOL's balance sheet. (For the year ending June

TABLE 2

AOL's Income Under Different Accounting Assumptions ($millions)[37]

	1993	1994	1995
Total revenues	$52.4	$117.5	$397.3
Deferred subscriber acquisition expenses	$ 3.6	$ 19.5	$ 50.8
Total expenses reported	$52	$114.9	$431
Total income reported	$ 0.4	$ 2.6	–$ 33.6
Total expenses revised	$55.6	$134.4	$481.8
Net income revised	–$ 3.2	–$ 7.0	–$ 84.5

1996, deferred subscriber acquisition costs rose to $314 million, up from $50.8 million in the year ending June 1995.) Table 2 summarizes the results of a study, commissioned by *BusinessWeek,* which restated AOL's earnings using more conventional accounting practices. The table suggests that in 1995 AOL's loss would have more than doubled had it used more conventional accounting practices. (AOL's financial statements are given in Table 1.)

Part of the reason for AOL's high subscriber acquisition costs is the high churn rate associated with its service. It is difficult to pin down AOL's churn rate, and the company is less than forthcoming with estimates. However, most analyst estimates suggest that somewhere between 30 and 40 percent of AOL's fee-paying customers leave the service within the first year of signing on, a figure that Case does not dispute. (These figures exclude those who try the service for a free one-month trial period and drop off before receiving their first bill.)[38] In the quarter that ended June 1996 *BusinessWeek* reported that while AOL signed up about 1.8 million new members, 1.5 million dropped the service (many before receiving their first bill) for a net gain of 300,000.[39] A more detailed analysis of AOL's churn rate in the quarter that ended March 31, 1996, suggests that of the 1.1 million subscribers that dropped the service, 450,000 left before their first bill (they were never really subscribers), 300,000 left during the next three months, and 100,000 old subscribers departed.[40] Tom Gardner, cofounder of AOL's successful Motley Fool investment service, has speculated that the reasons for the high churn rate, in order of importance, are connection problems, uninspiring content, price, and customer service.[41]

Revenue Sources

For the year ending June 30, 1996, AOL earned revenues of $1,093 million compared with $394 million in the year ending June 30, 1995. Most of these revenues (around 91 percent) are generated from subscriber fees. Over the years, there has been a steady increase in the average monthly fee per subscriber, from about $15 per month in 1994, to $17 per month in 1995, and $19 per month by June 1996.[42] This average figure, however, hides wide variation. Some analysts believe that the top 15 percent of AOL's subscribers generate around 50 percent of the subscription revenue. In mid 1996, these on-line addicts had an average monthly bill of $63.[43]

AOL's other revenues are generated from the sale of merchandise, data network services (primarily to businesses), on-line transactions, and advertising. For the nine months ending March 31, 1996, these revenues totaled $70.9 million, an increase of 126 percent from the same period a year earlier.

Diversifying Revenue Sources

Although AOL aimed to have 10.5 million subscribers by June 1997, it also wanted to reduce its dependence on fees from subscribers by diversifying its revenue sources. Initiatives currently under way to attain this objective include attempts to increase advertising revenues, establish Enterprise AOL as a valuable service for large organizations, expand internationally, and enter the fast-growing ISP market.

Advertising   In 1996, Steve Case announced plans aimed at dramatically increasing the revenues generated from advertising and on-line merchandise sales. In early 1996, AOL hired an ex-advertising agency executive and gave him a staff of thirty-five dedicated people to sell ad space on AOL. AOL has 102 "screens" on which it is selling ad space. A screen lists a set of choices within a channel. For example, within AOL's personal finance channel, there is a screen that allows users to pull up stock quotes, check the current value of their portfolio, check market news, or utilize various company and market research options. Advertisements typically appear as banners on a screen. AOL is pricing the ad space on its screens on the basis of the number of impressions, or hits, a screen gets. The pricing is generally within the range of $30 to $60 per 1,000 impressions, although some deals are apparently being done above that price point. AOL anticipates generating annual advertising revenues of $500,000 to $3 million per screen.[44]

AOL envisions the on-line advertising market growing to about $1.5 billion to $2.0 billion by the year 2000. The company is aiming to get a 20 percent share of this market. AOL claims that advertisements on AOL have a conversion rate of 12.5 percent, compared with a normal direct mail conversion rate of 3 percent, meaning that AOL is better at targeting potential purchasers of an advertiser's goods or services. In mid 1996, AOL's 6.2 million subscribers had an average income of $68,000, making them a highly desirable audience for many advertisers.[45]

Enterprise AOL   Enterprise AOL, a division of AOL, focuses on selling private on-line services, known as PAOLs, to large users. Early clients of this service include Century 21 (the nationwide real estate company), Harvard Business School, and PIP Printing. PAOLs are best suited to large organizations that lack dedicated networks and franchise organizations that need to get a lot of information out to their franchisees. As of mid 1996, AOL had contracts to establish ten PAOLs.

International Services   In November 1995, AOL announced a joint venture with Bertelsmann, the large German publishing and media company, to establish on-line services in Europe, starting with Germany, France, and Britain. These services were to be localized and written in the dominant local tongue. AOL is something of a late entrant into this market. CompuServe, for example, has been running an on-line service in Germany for seven years and has 250,000 German subscribers. In addition,

there are a number of other local on-line services in Europe. By June 1996, AOL had 100,000 European customers, the majority in Germany.[46]

ISP Market   GNN, or Global Network Navigator, is an Internet service provider that AOL acquired in June 1995 for $11 million. AOL relaunched GNN as an ISP in October 1995, and by June 1996 the service had around 300,000 subscribers. GNN subscribers cannot access AOL's proprietary service, but for a flat fee they can use a standard browser (Microsoft's Explorer or Netscape's Navigator) to surf the Web. Unlike many other ISPs, GNN will have the advantage of a dedicated network infrastructure in AOLnet.

AOL's decision to establish GNN seems to indicate that the company might be hedging its bets with regard to the rapid rise of the World Wide Web as a potential alternative to AOL. Some of the thinking behind this move was contained in a confidential internal AOL memo that found its way into the hands of the press. According to the memo, AOL conducted a market trial of 260 people who accessed AOL and the Internet using high-speed cable modems. Of the 260, 170 elected to keep some form of on-line access and pay for it. Of the 170, about 11 percent chose to utilize just AOL's service, 29 percent chose to access both the Internet and AOL, and 60 percent chose the Internet without AOL.[47]

CONCLUSION

Much of 1996 was full of contradictions for AOL. On the one hand, AOL emerged as the dominant on-line service in the world, with 6.2 million subscribers and annual revenues in excess of $1 billion. On the other, critics of the company charged that the combination of high churn rate, questionable accounting practices, market saturation, and a real threat from low-priced Internet service providers left AOL increasingly vulnerable. Reflecting growing uncertainty about AOL's viability, the stock price had fallen from more than $71 per share in May 1996 to $24 in October of the same year.

In contrast, in an interview given in late 1996, Steve Case claimed that AOL's churn rate (with somewhere less than 40 percent of subscribers leaving before the end of their first year of paid-up subscription) was comparable with magazine publishing norms and nothing to be too concerned about. He also pointed out that with only 11 percent of U.S. homes hooked into an on-line service, there was still enormous room for growth at AOL. As for the Internet and World Wide Web, Case sees this not as a threat, but as an opportunity.

> The threat [of the Web] is more perception than reality. Certainly we run scared. If it weren't for that threat, we'd be pretty cocky and arrogant right now. We're responding to them [ISPs], but the vision for the company hasn't changed that much. . . . We haven't buried our heads in the sand and said the Web is irrelevant. We started providing Internet access a few years ago. . . . Let's imagine that AOL didn't exist, and the Net did. The Internet basically is this broken up world. Consumers would hook up with service providers and subscribe to services they want on an à la carte basis. Which is probably fine for a technologically astute early adopter but seems awfully complicated for the consumer market. If you want to reach a mainstream audience, you have to make it more plug and play. One stop shopping. One disk to install. One price to pay. One customer service number to call. Building web sites and hoping people will find them is a significant leap of faith.[48]

Endnotes

1. "The Accidental Superhighway: A Survey of the Internet," *Economist,* July 1, 1995, p. 7.
2. Raul Taylor, "Internet Users Likely to Reach 500 Million by 2000," *Financial Times,* May 13, 1996, p. 4.
3. George Gilder, "Telecoms: The Coming Software Shift," *Forbes ASAP,* August 1995, pp. 146-162.
4. Randy Befumo, "The Digital World," A Motley Fool Investment Report, March 1996.
5. Ibid.
6. Louise Kehoe, "Group Pays $2 Billion for Internet Service Provider," *Financial Times,* May 1, 1996, p. 1.
7. Ibid.
8. Alan Cane, "MCI Price Move Intensifies Internet Wars," *Financial Times,* March 19, 1996, p. 17.
9. Ibid.
10. Roger Lowenstein, "Being There First Isn't Good Enough," *Wall Street Journal,* May 16, 1996, p. C1.
11. Thomas Weber, "CompuServe Corp. Offering Is Priced at $30 a Share," *Wall Street Journal,* April 19, 1996, p. B6.
12. Befumo, "Digital World."
13. Jared Sandberg, "CompuServe to Revamp Service, Change Prices, Before Rival Microsoft Launch," *Wall Street Journal,* August 2, 1996, p. B3.
14. Walter Mossberg, "Cheaper, Kid Friendly On Line Service Will WOW PC Users," *Wall Street Journal,* March 21, 1996, p. B1.
15. George Gilder, "Telecoms: The Coming Software Shift."
16. Don Clark, "New Internet Model Leaves Some Content Providers Without Much of a Home," *Wall Street Journal,* April 12, 1996, p. A3.
17. Microsoft press release, "New Web Based Version of the Microsoft Network Debuts," October 10, 1996.
18. Befumo, "Digital World."
19. G. Bruce Knecht, "How a Wall Street Whiz Found a Niche Selling Books on the Internet," *Wall Street Journal,* May 16, 1996, p. A1.
20. Ibid.
21. AT&T home page, "Commerce on the Web" (http://www.att.com).
22. Alan Cane, "Net's Rivals Feel the Squeeze," *Financial Times,* February 26, 1996, p. 13.
23. Joan Rigdon, "Netscape and GE Join to Develop Internet Business Software for Internet Use," *Wall Street Journal,* April 10, 1996, p. B6.
24. Vanessa O'Connell, "Let the Buying Begin," *Wall Street Journal,* June 17, 1996, p. A8.
25. Don Clark, "Verifone Sets Internet Payment System for Banks to Sell, Lowering Web Barriers," *Wall Street Journal,* June 18, 1996, p. B4.
26. *BusinessWeek*/Harris Poll, "Internet Travelers Aren't Fed Up—Yet," *BusinessWeek,* August 26, 1996, p. 66.
27. Amy Cortese et al. "The Online World of Steve Case," *BusinessWeek,* April 15, 1996, pp. 78-87; Gene Koprowski, "AOL CEO Steve Case," *Forbes ASAP,* October 7, 1996, pp. 94-95.
28. Befumo, "Digital World."
29. Ibid.
30. Randy Befumo, "The Lunchtime News," Motley Fool, August 9, 1996.
31. America Online press release, August 8, 1996.
32. America Online 10K report, June 1996.
33. Thomas Weber, "AOL's Blackout and Loss of Subscribers Eclipse Jump in Fourth Quarter Profits," *Wall Street Journal,* August 9, 1996, p. B3.
34. Koprowski, "AOL CEO Steve Case," p. 96.
35. Ibid.
36. Befumo, "The Lunchtime News."
37. Koprowski, "AOL CEO Steve Case."
38. Amy Cortese et al., "The Online World of Steve Case."
39. Amy Barrett and Paul Eng, "AOL Downloads a New Growth Plan," *BusinessWeek,* October 14, 1996, pp. 85-86.
40. Tom Gardner, "How Do We Value America Online?" Motley Fool Online Forum, June 8, 1996.
41. Ibid.
42. America Online 10-K reports for 1996 and 1995.
43. Thomas Weber, "America Online May Face Long Hot Summer as Stock Wilts 10% on Some Bearish Reports," *Wall Street Journal,* June 6, 1996, p. C2.
44. Randy Befumo, "America Online Blitzed Analysts," The Evening News: Motley Fool Online Forum, June 14, 1996.
45. Ibid.
46. Douglas Lavin, "America Online Enters a Crowded Europe," *Wall Street Journal,* November 28, 1995, p. B6; Befumo, "America Online Blitzed Analysts."
47. Jared Sandberg, "America Online Agrees to Licensing Pact with AOL," *Wall Street Journal,* March 12, 1996, p. B5.
48. Koprowski, "AOL CEO Steve Case," pp. 94-96.

CASE 9

America Online (B)

This case was prepared by Charles W. L. Hill of the University of Washington.

INTRODUCTION

Nineteen hundred and ninety-six was a pivotal year for America Online (AOL). After four years of break-neck growth, AOL was now a major player in cyberspace. Subscribers had increased from 200,000 to more than 6 million. In June 1996, annual revenues passed the $1 billion mark. AOL was handling more than 11 million E-mail messages a day. It hosted 7,000 chat rooms nightly and featured more than 1,100 proprietary content sites on 21 "channels." An astounding one out of every three users on the Internet used AOL.[1] But for all its success, the on-line service provider was suddenly beset by problems from all sides.

The Internet was becoming increasingly well organized, leading some critics to question the need for a proprietary on-line service like AOL. Internet service providers (ISPs) from small mom-and-pop operations to telecommunications giants like AT&T and MCI had started offering unlimited access to the Internet for $19.95 a month. AOL's pricing plan charged users a fee of $9.95 per month plus $2.95 per hour, which meant that heaviest users could run up bills anywhere from $50 to $300 per month. Partly as a result, AOL's subscriber churn rate was unacceptably high. Estimates that by mid 1996 the monthly churn rate would be around 6 percent, implied that more than 70 percent of AOL's customers would leave the service within one year of joining![2] Increasingly, the customers who were leaving were long-time heavy users who were AOL's biggest spenders. Although

This case is intended to be used as the basis for class discussion rather than as an illustration of either effective or ineffective handling of the situation. This case was prepared by Charles W. L. Hill, University of Washington. Used by permission.

representing only one-third of the subscriber base, these heavy users were accounting for two-thirds of AOL's revenues.

To complicate matters, marketing costs associated with acquiring new customers were spiraling out of control, with many households receiving multiple packages of promotional material containing AOL software disks. Moreover, critics on Wall Street were blasting the company for its practice of amortizing the costs of acquiring new customers against earnings over twenty-four months, rather than treating them as a current expense—a practice that inflated AOL's current earnings. By June 1996, AOL had some $314 million in deferred costs on its balance sheet—enough to bury the $30 million pretax profit for fiscal 1996 under a sea of red ink. Shortly after the fiscal 1996 figures were released in June 1996, Bill Razzouck, AOL's president, resigned. Only four months previously, Razzouck had joined the company from Federal Express. His brief had been to bring order to AOL's operations. Wall Street interpreted his sudden departure as a sign that things at AOL were out of control. Reflecting these problems, AOL's stock price had tumbled from the $70 range to the $20 range by June 1996. Many now wondered if the service could survive.

SUMMER 1996

Throughout the summer of 1996, AOL's management team tried to grapple with these seemingly intractable problems. Solving the pricing and churn problems was at the top of their agenda. The big concern was that if the company adopted a flat-rate pricing scheme similar to that used by ISPs, the loss of revenue would be devastating (at the time, AOL was garnering 85 percent of its revenues from user fees). ISPs offered no more than access and a browser, which enabled them to operate with a low-cost structure. In comparison, as a proprietary service, AOL had to cover its overhead costs related to content, marketing, and personnel. Could AOL with its high-cost structure afford to move to a flat-rate pricing scheme?

In May 1996, AOL had announced its first response to the ISP threat, a new "20/20" pricing plan, which charged users a flat fee of $19.95 for the first twenty hours of use and $2.95 per hour thereafter. The plan did little to slow down customer defection rates. Moreover, the plan upset many of AOL's content providers, who depended on the $2.95 hourly fee for their income. (Most content providers received a cut of the dollar value of the time a user spent at their site on AOL.)

Throughout the summer, the internal debate within AOL continued. The primary issue was how to protect revenues if the switch to flat-rate pricing was adopted. The company was already pursuing a host of options, including increasing revenues from selling advertising space on the service, selling AOL merchandise, and taking a cut of on-line transactions executed over AOL. Among the other options considered was offering an "adult only" channel that would carry a surcharge.[3] The idea was to connect AOL users to an aggregation of adult content culled from the World Wide Web, restrict access to those over twenty-one, and charge a premium price for this option. The option was pulled after focus groups suggested that the inclusion of such a channel would outrage some users and might damage AOL's brand image.

One thing was clear—under any scenario AOL had to continue to grow, and it had to make its brand more compelling. If it did not, there was no way that the company would be able to command a high price for advertising space or offer businesses the opportunity to sell directly to AOL users through its service. For CEO Steve Case, a critical issue was identifying the right person to help build AOL's brand. By late summer, he seemed to have found a solution in the person of Bob Pittman.

Then forty-two years old, Pittman had already left his mark on global pop culture. A one-time radio disk jockey, in 1981, together with John Lack, Pittman started an all-music cable television channel called Music Television, or MTV. Charismatic,

photogenic and charming, Pittman was in many ways the ultimate marketing wunderkind. In addition to MTV, Pittman also had a hand in the creation of VH1 and the Nick at Nite cable TV channels.[4] Pittman had left MTV in 1985 and spent several years running Time Warner Enterprises, the business development unit of Time Warner. While there, he oversaw the purchase of the struggling Six Flags theme park chain. Pittman became CEO of Six Flags, masterminded its turnaround, and then sold 51 percent of the division to Boston Venture Partners for $1 billion (Pittman reportedly made $40 million on the deal).[5] In 1995, Pittman left Time Warner to run Century 21, a nationwide residential real estate chain. It was at this point that Steve Case began to court Pittman, sensing that he was the right person to build AOL's brand. Pittman joined AOL's board in October 1995, but Case was looking for closer involvement.

After Razzouck's departure in June 1996, Case stepped up his courting of Pittman. In early August, Pittman took a vacation to think things over. Then disaster hit AOL. On August 7, during a routine overhaul of some equipment at AOL's data center, the system inexplicably shut down. It took nineteen hours to get AOL back on line. The media was all over the story. The AOL blackout was the lead on CNN's *Headline News* that evening, ahead of a segment that signs of life had been detected in rocks from Mars. The next morning, the AOL blackout garnered front-page headlines in most newspapers. The media detailed stories of the inconvenience suffered by those who could not access their E-mail or surf the Internet, and noted the thousands of dollars in revenues lost by businesses that depended on AOL traffic. One story relayed the woes of the flower delivery service, 1–800-FLOWERS, which received a significant share of its orders over the Internet and which estimated that it lost $40,000 to $50,000 as a result of the blackout. Critics claimed that AOL's blackout was due to a failure to upgrade its infrastructure to keep pace with subscriber growth.[6] AOL claimed that the blackout occurred due to a highly unlikely series of event that were unlikely to ever occur again. Following the blackout, many investors turned sour on the already struggling company, and AOL's stock sunk further. Bob Pittman drew a different conclusion from these events. To Pittman, the media frenzy proved that AOL had become a mainstream company providing a valuable service. He formally joined AOL's management team in late October 1996.

FALL 1996

In September 1996, AOL held a pep rally for its 1,500 northern Virginia employees at a local convention center. The occasion was a $300 million marketing blitz intended to "relaunch" AOL. There were roller dancers and satellite hookups, theme songs, and a cheering crowd. Case, wearing jeans, sunglasses, and a leather jacket, addressed the crowd. Ted Leonsis, head of AOL's studio system, came out and shouted, "We can be like Coca-Cola! We can become like Disney, like Nike, like MTV!"[7]

On October 10, 1996, Microsoft's MSN announced that it would henceforth base its site on HTML—hypertext markup language—open up part of its site to anyone browsing the Web, and adopt a flat-rate pricing scheme of $19.95 per month for unlimited access to MSN's "proprietary content" and the Web. The move forced AOL's hand. On October 29, AOL responded with a number of announcements.[8]

First, Pittman was formally introduced as a member of AOL's management team. To better focus the enterprise and accommodate Pittman, Case split AOL into three operating divisions. These were ANS Communications, which would handle the access infrastructure under the leadership of Bruce Bind; AOL Studios, which would develop content under the leadership of Ted Leonsis; and AOL Networks, the flagship on-line service, which Pittman would run. In his remarks to the press, Pittman compared the on-line business with the cable TV industry he helped to create. Like the cable TV business in the 1980s, Pittman stated, "you have to convince people it's a real business. . . . but it's destined to be part of the American landscape. . . . I've seen this movie before, I've been here."[9]

Second, AOL announced that starting December 1, it too would offer unlimited access for $19.95 per month. Many of AOL's content providers greeted this announcement with trepidation. They were upset that AOL had not given them any warning that this was coming and were concerned about the implications of the move for their revenue stream. Until now, many content providers

had earned money from their share of AOL's hourly fees. (Content providers would typically receive a share of the hourly revenue generated while users were at their AOL site.) Now the hourly fees were going away, which indicated that revenues would have to come from advertising and transactions. The shift to flat-rate pricing also meant that controlling costs became an immediate issue. AOL announced that it would lay off 300 employees—the first layoffs in its history—and shut down its GNN Internet access division. The value of GNN, which was AOL's own Internet service provider, had been effectively obviated by the move to flat-rate pricing.

Third, AOL bit another bullet when Case announced that AOL would take a charge of $353.7 million against earnings to write off deferred subscriber acquisition costs. Henceforth, subscriber acquisition costs would be treated as an expense and accounted for when they were incurred, rather than amortized against earnings over twenty-four months. The write-off wiped out all of the profit that AOL had made up to this point and resulted in a loss of $3.80 per share in the first quarter of fiscal 1997. To the critics, this provided more proof that AOL was nothing more than a game of smoke and mirrors. To the company's supporters, it showed a new atmosphere of realism at the company.

TOO MUCH OF A GOOD THING

Anticipating increased usage after the December 1 introduction of unlimited access, AOL entered into an agreement with BBN Corporation under which BBN was to build out AOL's TCP/IP dial-up network, AOLNet, to ensure that AOL could handle the expected increase in demand for its service. Under the four-year, $340 million contract, AOL would add 70,000 modems per year to AOLNet. At the time, AOLNet had 170,000 modems, so the increase in capacity amounted to 40 percent per year. It wasn't enough. On December 1, usage surged to 2.5 million hours—up from an average of 1.6 million hours per day in October. Members trying to log on were frequently greeted with busy signals. On December 2, AOL responded by announcing that it would accelerate the buildout of its dial-up network, spending an additional $250 million by mid 1997.

After the announcement of the move to flat-rate pricing and unlimited access, AOL's membership surged. The service added more than half a million new members in December alone. By early January, close to 8 million people were using the service, exceeding both the company's expectations and the capacity of its network. By mid January, mail had doubled in three months to 24 million pieces a day and usage had increased to 4.5 million hours per day. Hundreds of thousands of new members were joining the service. The busy signals continued. Complaints from irritated members were overwhelming the capacity of AOL's customer service operation. On January 16, Case responded by announcing that AOL would invest an additional $100 million in its dial-up network over the next few months. The company also pledged to reduce its marketing expenditures and pull its TV ad campaign until the capacity of its network had been upgraded. The busy signals continued. A number of state attorneys general banded together and announced that they would sue AOL for deceptive selling practices, false advertising, and even fraud. By the end of January, Case agreed to give a refund to any member who requested it as compensation for the inability to access the network. In return, the states agreed to drop their lawsuit.[10]

RETHINKING AOL

While Case was busy trying to cope with the consequences of the unexpected surge in demand for AOL's service, Pittman was rethinking AOL's business model. It was clear to Pittman that AOL was a terrific brand. Despite all the gaffes over the last year, the service continued to grow at breakneck speed. With revenue growth from subscribers now constrained by flat-rate pricing, Pittman knew that it was time to leverage the brand in order to maximize revenues from advertising and e-commerce—and that AOL had to move quickly. Although AOL had already embarked on this road a year ago, Pittman gave the strategy a new impetus. Moreover, he sharpened the focus of the strategy. Prior to his arrival, AOL had been considering entering all sorts of businesses itself, from selling books to long-distance telephone service. Under Pittman's leadership, the emphasis changed to helping other organizations sell their goods and services to AOL members.

On February 25, 1997, Pittman announced the first of what was to become a steady stream of deals. Under this deal, Tel-Save Holdings, a long-

distance telephone service reseller, paid AOL $100 million for the privilege of being able to sell long-distance services to AOL's members. Prior to the deal, Tel-Save had 500,000 customers. The $100 million was an advance on future commission payments that would be due to AOL for members Tel-Save signed up. For Tel-Save, the deal had two big attractions. It was a cost effective way of reaching 8 million potential customers, and AOL would bill Tel-Save customers electronically and charge their credit cards for calls made using Tel-Save. Tel-Save estimated that electronic billing and credit card payments would reduce its unit costs by 30 percent, enabling it to offer customers long-distance rates 20 percent below those offered by rivals.[11] By March 1998, AOL and Tel-Save announced that the long-distance reseller had added 500,000 customers from AOL.[12]

On March 4, 1997, AOL opened to advertisers its 14,000 chat rooms, which logged 1 million hours daily. On June 10, CUC International agreed to pay AOL an advance of $50 million against future commissions in order to market its range of discount services directly to AOL subscribers. CUC expected to generate more than 1 million new interactive memberships per year from its AOL connection.[13] On July 7, Amazon.com, the Internet bookseller, agreed to pay AOL at least $19 million over three years in advances on commissions to be the featured bookseller on AOL's Web site, aol.com. If Amazon.com sales through AOL exceeded targets, this figure would be increased. Barnes & Noble paid a similar amount (later increased to $40 million) to be the bookseller on AOL's proprietary service. Also in July 1997, 1–800-FLOWERS agreed to pay AOL at least $25 million in advances on commissions over four years to sell on the service. The flower company expected the deal to produce $250 million in sales over four years.[14]

Around the same time, AOL began to charge retailers "rents" of at least $250,000 per year for their spots on AOL, in addition to commissions. This represented a shift from AOL's old practice of simply taking a cut of the revenues generated from sales over AOL. Revenues from this source had been disappointing, but Pittman felt that the change in incentive structure implied by the imposition of rents would yield significant dividends down the road.

In addition to taking a cut out of e-commerce transactions, during this period, AOL also began to change its relationship with content providers. Under the old pricing scheme, AOL *paid* content providers a fee based on the time members spent at their sites. With the hourly fee now gone, AOL had no incentive to pay content providers. Instead, the company started requiring content providers to pay it a fee in exchange for the privilege of being able to offer content through AOL. In one of the first deals, announced in July 1997, AOL stated that it had signed CBS Sportsline to serve as an "anchor tenant" for the service's sports channel.[15]

In addition to demanding fees, AOL started to weed out weak content providers, refusing to renew their contracts when they came due. For example, in August 1997, AOL refused to renew the contract for MetaCreations Inc., an on-line game company that created MetaSquares, a checkerslike game that could be played on-line at AOL. Prior to the new pricing regime, MetaCreations received 20 percent of the hourly fees generated for AOL while members were playing MetaSquares. When the contract came up for renewal, AOL sought to do away with the royalty arrangement, although the company did offer to buy the game outright. MetaCreations claimed the offer was too low and refused to sell. Aside from the game, MetaCreations had other content on AOL, including technical support sessions for people who used its software. That content was also removed, because MetaCreations refused to pay the $50,000 annual fee demand by AOL.[16]

The fruits of this change in strategy started to become apparent by 1998. In fiscal 1995, AOL generated some $6 million in revenues from advertising and commercial fees. This increased to $100.2 million in 1996, $180 million in 1997, and $511 million in 1998. The figure for 1999 seemed likely to exceed $1 billion out of total AOL revenues of more than $4 billion. Moreover, there was no sign of a slowdown in the flow of deals bringing cash into AOL's coffers. In early 1999, AOL entered into a five-year agreement valued at $500 million with First USA under which First USA became the exclusive marketer of credit card products and service on AOL. Similarly, in July 1999 drkoop.com, an Internet-based health care site established by Dr. Everett Koop, the former surgeon general of the United States, agreed to pay AOL $89 million over four years. This was an advance on commissions for the chance to sell to AOL's members, which by then exceeded 19 million.[17] As of March 31, 1999, AOL's *backlog* of advertising and commerce rev-

enues exceeded $1.3 billion (the *backlog* refers to future revenues guaranteed to AOL under the terms of agreements with content providers and on-line retailers).[18]

THE STUDIO SYSTEM

In October 1996, AOL established AOL Studios under the leadership of Ted Leonsis. The goal of AOL Studios was to turn AOL into a major producer of original on-line content that would generate direct revenues of $50 million to $100 million by 2000, and significantly more in indirect revenues from advertising on sites created by AOL Studios. Prior to AOL Studios, AOL attempted to develop compelling on-line content through the medium of its Greenhouse unit, which invested $50 million between 1994 and 1996 in start-up providers on on-line content. Other than that effort, however, AOL was primarily a distributor of other people's content.

With the establishment of AOL Studios, AOL seemed to be signaling that it wanted to get more involved in the creation of proprietary content. To Leonsis, the initiative made sense given that by 1997, on any night, as many people logged on to AOL as were watching MTV or CNN. At the same time, Leonsis had no illusions that AOL Studios would be able to do it all on its own, and he actively solicited proposals in search of ventures to seed, license, or buy outright. AOL Studios also posted its content on the Web, in addition to AOL's proprietary network.

In its first full year, AOL Studios invested in or created about fifty on-line properties, some of which were proprietary to AOL and some of which were Web based.[19] They included Digital Cities (a Web-based local content service, which can be accessed at http://home.digitalcity.com), Electra (an arena aimed at women's issues), Entertainment Asylum (a site for film, TV, and music fans), Real Fans Sports Network (a site for sports fans), and Xtream Games (an AOL channel for on-line gaming that charges a premium price of $1.99 per hour).

Critics charged that AOL Studios would have a tough time competing against established content providers in the areas it had targeted—entertainment, women, sports, and games. In the sports area for example, Disney's ESPN Sports-Zone and CBS's SportsLine both had a strong Web presence.[20] Moreover, other on-line providers were also moving into the same space, most notably Microsoft, whose MSN Network offers a similar range of content.

In practice, like any other content creator, AOL Studios seems likely to have its share of successes and failures. Real Fans Sports, for example, was pulled in favor of CBS's SportsLine. On the other hand, a Studios creation, Love@AOL, quickly evolved into one of the most popular destinations on the network, with 50 million or more hits (page views) per month. The area includes 50,000 personal ads, often accompanied by photographs, places to chat with guest star sex symbols and "Party Games." The area needs only about twelve AOL employees to keep it running, costs $2 million per year, but generates significantly more than that in advertising revenues from brand sponsors.[21] Digital Cities, Electra, and Entertainment Asylum have also turned out to be hits.

COMPUSERVE GOES AOL

While AOL continued to grow its member base, even through the troubled summer of 1996, its rivals continued to lag far behind. By 1997, Prodigy was almost extinct, CompuServe seemed stuck at 2.6 million customers and was losing money, and MSN was still far behind AOL with 2.3 million members. In September 1997, AOL took another big step toward establishing a sustainable position in cyberspace when in a three-way transaction with telecommunications provider WorldCom and CompuServe's parent, H&R Block, AOL acquired CompuServe's on-line network.[22]

Under the deal, WorldCom announced that it would buy CompuServe from H&R Block in a $1.3 billion stock swap. The deal, however, was engineered by AOL, which had been eyeing CompuServe's subscriber base for some time. WorldCom transferred CompuServe's 2.6 million subscribers, software, data centers, and content to AOL, while holding on to CompuServe's Internet infrastructure. In return for this and $175 million, AOL transferred its network infrastructure unit, ANS, to WorldCom. AOL also agreed to purchase its network services from WorldCom for at least five years. The price, agreed to in advance, was reported to be little more than what AOL was paying ANS in-house. As a result of the deal, AOL effectively exited the network services business, while increasing its membership roll to 11.6 million. After the deal, AOL commanded a 54 percent share of the U.S. on-line service market. [23]

After completing this acquisition, on February 8, 1998, AOL announced another reorganization of the company. In the new structure, Pittman was appointed president and chief operating officer of AOL, solidifying his position as number two at the company. Three divisions were put under Pittman—AOL Networks, CompuServe, and AOL Studios (implying that Leonsis, AOL's long-time number two, would now report to Pittman). AOL elected to continue running CompuServe as a separate service. The three divisions would share the same sales and marketing, customer service, and backroom functions.

On the same date, AOL also announced that it would be increasing its monthly fee for unlimited access by $2, to $21.95. The company's stock surged to an all-time high of $115 7/16 on February 11, 1998, whereas it had been in the $20 range during the summer of 1996. On February 12, AOL reported its earnings for the three months ending December 31, 1997: $20.8 million on record revenues of $592 million. AOL's balance sheet was also much improved. As a result of various deals, the company now had $750 million in cash. After having been written off by many commentators during 1996, AOL was rapidly evolving into the first blue chip Internet company.

ICQ

Although AOL remains primarily a proprietary on-line service, the company has been steadily moving offerings onto the Web. AOL has had a Web presence for several years at http//www.aol.com, its Internet gateway, or portal, that can be accessed either from the proprietary service or from the Web by anyone with a browser and Internet access, AOL member or not. Some of the offerings of AOL Studios, such as Digital Cities, are also Web based. In June 1998, AOL took another step in this direction when it acquired Mirabilis, an Israeli software company, for $287 million. The primary asset of Mirabilis was a little-known software package called ICQ (http://www.icq.com).

ICQ (which stands for "I seek you") is a sophisticated instant message system that can link individual users in real-time dialogue via the Internet. Anyone can subscribe to ICQ and download the software for free. ICQ can alert a subscriber when designated friends are on-line and let a user chat, transfer files, or play games, all while other applications are running on the user's computer. ICQ is a persistent program—it becomes active as soon as a subscriber turns on the computer and is the first thing to appear on a subscriber's screen, even before the user reaches an Internet portal site or activates a browser. The small rectangular ICQ screen stays on a user's monitor until the computer is turned off, running in the background whenever a user is on-line. Pop-up messages alert an ICQ subscriber to an incoming message or chat request.

Despite its low profile, at the time of the Mirabilis acquisition, 13 million people subscribed to ICQ—as many as subscribed to AOL's proprietary service.[24] The big difference between the two is that while most of AOL's members are located in North America, ICQ subscribers are scattered around the world. After the acquisition, AOL announced that it would continue to offer ICQ for free, and would let ICQ operate as a separate entity within AOL. By March 31, 1999, ICQ subscribers had grown to more than 32 million, 13 million of whom had used the service within the last thirty days. More than 7 million people used ICQ every day.[25] While AOL did not at this time rent out advertising space on ICQ's screen, the company was reportedly considering the option.[26] With the acquisition of ICQ, Bob Pittman began referring to AOL as a company with four brands—AOL, CompuServe, Digital Cities, and ICQ.[27]

AOL, NETSCAPE, AND SUN

AOL's acquisition spree continued in November of 1998 when the company announced that it had agreed to acquire Netscape in a stock swap valued at $4.3 billion. Netscape was one of the first Internet companies, and despite inroads from Microsoft's Internet Explorer, its browser, Netscape Navigator, was still the most widely used. Netscape also had a popular Web portal, Netscape Netcenter, but its most valuable asset was its e-commerce software, which was sold to businesses to help them manage on-line transactions and accounted for 70 percent of Netscape's revenues at the time of the purchase.[28]

Simultaneously, AOL reached a three-year agreement with Sun Microsystems, which manufactures computer workstations and servers, and has developed a popular version of the UNIX operating sys-

tem and two software languages geared toward the Web, Java and Jini. Under the agreement, Sun will market Netscape's business software and help develop versions of AOL for digital devices. In addition, AOL and Sun will jointly sell electronic commerce packages to businesses that want to market their wares on-line. AOL also committed to buying Sun computers and services valued at $500 million. For its part, Sun will pay AOL more than $350 million in licensing, marketing, and advertising fees.

According to a statement by Steve Case, the AOL-Netscape-Sun combination will facilitate the growth of electronic commerce by offering "end-to-end" solutions for those businesses that want to get into e-commerce, a market that Forester Research estimates will be worth $35 billion by 2002.[29] Companies that want to build stores in cyberspace could start with Sun's servers and operating system. Then they would add Netscape's software programs for building a virtual store and handling transaction processing. Finally, they could turn to AOL to market the stores to millions of consumers through AOL's service, Digital Cities, Netscape's Netcenter portal, and perhaps ICQ. Sun also brings its 7,000-person sales force to the table, and it can be used to sell Netscape's software and AOL's storefront locations in cyberspace.

As critics have been quick to point out, however, this deal takes AOL into new territory. Up to this point, AOL has been a consumer mass-market company, but the deal adds businesses to the mix. Moreover, the deal brings the AOL-Netscape-Sun troika into direct competition with a couple of very powerful companies that have already a strong hold on selling e-commerce solutions to businesses—Microsoft and IBM. Microsoft in particular, offers a compelling alternative, given the rapid market acceptance of its Windows NT operating system, transaction processing and back-office software. Moreover, despite AOL's success, there are plenty of other outlets for businesses in cyberspace, including Microsoft's MSN Network, and popular portals such as Yahoo! and Lycos.[30]

The Netscape acquisition closed in mid March 1999. Shortly afterward, AOL announced that it would be laying off 350 to 500 employees at Netscape and as many as 500 at AOL. The layoffs were presented as the consequence of greater efficiencies achieved by combining the two organizations. Simultaneously, AOL stated that it would split the company into four product groups: The Interactive Services Group, which includes the flagship AOL service, along with Netscape's Netcenter portal; the Netscape Enterprise Group, which will handle Netscape's corporate software offering; AOL Studios, which now includes ICQ; and AOL International.[31]

THE QUEST FOR BANDWIDTH

Pittman has frequently stated that in cyberspace "location, location, location" is the key. So far, he has been proved correct, but as 1999 progressed, it became increasingly clear that besides location AOL needed to be able to offer its members greater bandwidth. Bandwidth refers to the rate at which digital data can be transferred between two points. Currently, most consumers have only relatively low bandwidth connections to the Internet over standard telephone lines (a typical computer modem can transmit and receive data at 56 kilobits per second). Case has long argued that greater bandwidth connections would allow high-resolution video and audio data to be transmitted effectively to consumers over the Internet. In turn, this would dramatically expand the range of interactive service that consumers could access over the Internet, which could drive forward the growth in demand for AOL's various offerings.

There are various ways of delivering high bandwidth connections to the home, all of which are in the early stages of being rolled out.[32] One way utilizes DSL (digital subscriber line) technology to increase the bandwidth of standard copper telephone lines. DSL technology typically moves data at between 128K and 1.5 megabits per second, with 640K being the norm. This is the solution favored by telephone companies. By mid 1999, there were about 180,000 DSL subscribers in the United States. But DSL signals degrade with distance and typically will not work more than 3 miles from a phone switch.

Another solution involves adapting the coaxial cable used to transmit cable TV signals to carry two-way Internet traffic. Consumers with cable modems attached to their PCs would then be able to access the Internet at speeds up to 500 times faster than with a standard 56K telephone modem. TV cables run past 95 percent of homes in the United States. By mid 1999, 750,000 people in the United States were using services based on cable modems.

A third solution is to use digital satellite technology to beam down data at very high bandwidth rates. The problem with this solution right now is that the consumers can not beam data back at similar rates. Rather, they have to communicate requests for data through conventional telephone lines operating at 56K. This might change in a few years when new satellite systems, such as Teledesic, go into operation. Microsoft's Bill Gates and his Seattle neighbor, Craig McCaw, who owns Nextel, a large wireless company, are funding Teledesic. The service aims to put about 300 satellites in low earth orbit that can handle high bandwidth two-way communication. Consumers will not need a cable link or telephone line to communicate with a Teledesic satellite, just an antenna on their roof. By mid 1999, some 25,000 consumers were using satellite services to connect to the Internet.

Case is not the only one who believes that high bandwidth connectivity is the key to expanding demand for interactive services over the Internet. Gates also believes that high bandwidth connectivity is crucial, and sees high bandwidth driving forward demand for Microsoft software and services, including AOL rival, MSN.[33] In 1998, Microsoft began to invest in cable TV companies as part of a strategy to create incentives for the cable companies to speed up their moves to upgrade their coaxial cable networks so that they could carry Internet traffic.

Microsoft started the ball rolling with a $5 billion investment in Comcast, a nationwide cable operator. Soon afterward, AT&T jumped into the fray when it acquired the number one cable operator in the United States, TCI, for $75 billion. AT&T announced that it intended to provide phone service and Internet access over cable. Along with TCI came @Home, in which TCI had a controlling ownership stake and which was a leader in offering access to the Internet over coaxial cable. Then on May 10, 1999, AT&T acquired another major cable company, MediaOne, for $60 billion. MediaOne happened to be part-owner of Roadrunner, which was a major competitor to @Home. As part of the AT&T–MediaOne deal, Microsoft agreed to invest $5 billion in AT&T and to purchase a 30 percent stake in MediaOne's European cable TV operating subsidiary, TeleWest (at one point, Microsoft was rumored to be preparing a rival bid for MediaOne). In return for Microsoft's investment, AT&T agreed to put Microsoft's Windows CE operating system into the set-top boxes that will be used to pipe the Internet into existing TV sets. Some observers also wondered whether this meant that Microsoft's MSN portal would be the first thing to pop up on an Internet-enabled TV set.[34]

This flurry of deals led to speculation that AOL might be shut out of high bandwidth access to the Internet via cable. So far cable networks have been closed to AOL because federal regulators have ruled that cable operators have the exclusive right to market data services to their own subscribers. AOL has challenged this ruling but initially met with little success. As an alternative, in early 1999 AOL entered into strategic alliances with two of America's telephone giants, Bell Atlantic and SBC Communications, to use DSL technology to make available a high-speed upgrade connection to AOL subscribers starting in the summer of 1999. By the end of 1999, AOL planned to offer a high-speed broadband upgrade in areas covering nearly 16 million homes in 21 states. The company was rumored to be contemplating charging consumers a higher fee for broadband services.

The deals with the telephone companies were followed by a May 12 announcement that AOL would make a record $1.5-billion investment in Hughes Electronics and jointly introduce new consumer offerings with the Hughes DirecTV satellite service.[35] The proposed offerings include AOL-Plus, which will provide high-speed Internet connection over satellite, and AOL TV for such television-based functions as interactive shopping, Web surfing, E-mail and electronic chat, more commonly performed over the Internet. A set-top box, which the partners are developing jointly, will allow TV viewers to chat with friends, check their E-mail and engage in e-commerce. While this deal put AOL back in the broadband race, and positioned the company to enter the interactive TV market, the shortcomings of current satellite systems still leave AOL at a potential disadvantage.

NEXT MOVES?

For the three months ending March 31, 1999, AOL announced strong financial results. Revenues increased 66 percent over the same period a year earlier, to a record $1.3 billion. These results suggested that the company was likely to record revenues in excess of $4.5 billion in fiscal year 1999, which ended in June. After-tax profits increased to

$117 million for the quarter, up from $39 million for the same period a year earlier (these results exclude any contribution from the Netscape acquisition, which closed on March 17, 1999). Advertising and commerce revenues were $275 million, up 94 percent from a year earlier. Some 16.9 million people now subscribed to AOL's flagship service, and another 2 million to CompuServe. Some 3 million of these subscribers were outside North America—mostly in Europe, where AOL had a successful joint venture with the large German publishing company, Bertelsmann. ICQ had 32 million registered users, and Netscape's Netcenter portal, 15 million registered users. By early July, AOL's stock had surged to $130 a share, up from $17 a share in October 1998. At this price, AOL had a market value of $140 billion, making the company the twentieth most valuable enterprise on the planet. By comparison, General Motors had a market value of around $44 billion.

In many ways, AOL had never been stronger, and yet uncertainties still swirled around the company and its market space. The Internet continued to get more organized. Portals such as Yahoo!, Lycos, and MSN were increasingly becoming gateways of choice for consumers accessing the Web. AOL's proprietary service was also a gateway, but questions remained as to how valuable a portal it would be as Web users became increasingly sophisticated, particularly since some of AOL's strongest features, such as E-mail and chat, could now be found on the Web. Of course, AOL was also participating in this space with its ICQ chat and messaging service and its own Web-based portals, aol.com and Netcenter. Still, some questioned the long-term growth prospects of the proprietary service, particularly in view if the $140 billion valuation that investors had assigned to AOL.

This concern was heightened by signs that, after their initial enthusiasm, at least some advertisers had become disenchanted with the Web, casting doubt on the ability of AOL and others to grow revenues from Web advertising at the anticipated rates. For example, Levi Strauss pulled its Web advertising in 1999 after an internal analysis showed that it did not generate the traffic required to cover costs. According to a company spokesman, Levi Strauss was spending anywhere from $56 to $120 per paying customer in Web-based advertising fees to get customers to visit its Web site, but once they were there, spending did not even come close to covering the costs.[36] Part of the problem seems to

FIGURE I

AOL's Financial Data

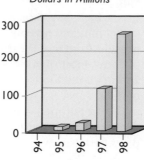

**Advertising and
Commerce Revenues**
Dollars in Millions

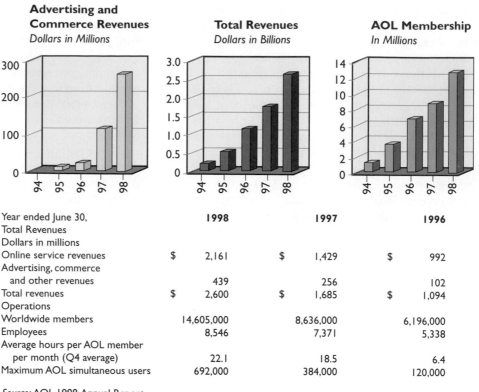

Total Revenues
Dollars in Billions

AOL Membership
In Millions

Year ended June 30, Total Revenues Dollars in millions		1998		1997		1996
Online service revenues	$	2,161	$	1,429	$	992
Advertising, commerce and other revenues		439		256		102
Total revenues	$	2,600	$	1,685	$	1,094
Operations						
Worldwide members		14,605,000		8,636,000		6,196,000
Employees		8,546		7,371		5,338
Average hours per AOL member per month (Q4 average)		22.1		18.5		6.4
Maximum AOL simultaneous users		692,000		384,000		120,000

Source: AOL 1998 Annual Report.

be that while television viewers are used to passively watching ads, Web surfers consider ads a distraction and tend to ignore them.

AOL's defenders point out that the elegant and intuitive design of the proprietary service's interface and the well-thought-out programming continued to give the service a big advantage over competing portals such as MSN and Yahoo!, which were far more intimidating to the on-line neophyte. Moreover, AOL still had huge growth prospects, both in its core North American market, where some 60 percent of homes were still not connected to the Internet, and internationally, where on-line usage lagged that in North America by several years. As for the sustainability of growth rates in on-line advertising revenue, it should be noted that while advertising spending on the Internet reached a record $1.9 billion in 1998, that was still only 5 percent of the figure spent on television advertising. Surely, there was room for growth here, many argued, particularly when high bandwidth connections make streaming audio and video more viable, which could change the form of much Web-based advertising.

Going forward, part of AOL's game plan is to offer AOL on a wide range of digital devices that can access the Internet, including hand-held devices, smart phones, and television sets equipped with set-top boxes. AOL hopes that this "AOL Anywhere" strategy will dramatically expand the company's role as a premier information mediator. Another AOL strategy is to turn tasks traditionally performed by personal computer software into services delivered on-line. Early efforts have focused on delivering E-mail without the need for E-mail software to reside on a personal computer. AOL members can now read and send E-mail from any Web browser. The next wave will focus on personal information applications, such as address books and calendars. In support of this strategy, in April 1999 AOL spent $150 million to acquire a small company, When.com, which provides calendar services over the Internet. The system operates much like the appointment book built into Microsoft's Outlook personal information manager, but with a twist—each time a user enters an appointment, the information travels across the Internet and gets stored on a server computer. This means that users can check and update their calendars from any Web-connected digital device, anywhere, anytime.[37]

Endnotes

1. F. Rose, "Keyword: Context," *Wired*, Release 4.12, December 1996.
2. K. Swisher, *AOL.COM: How Steve Case Beat Bill Gates, Nailed the Netheads, and Made Millions in the War for the Web* (New York: Random House, 1998).
3. Ibid.
4. D. Hilzenrath, "Turnaround Task at AOL," *Washington Post*, October 31, 1996, p. E1.
5. F. Rose, "Keyword."
6. R. Chandrasekaran and D. Hilzenrath, "Routine Maintenance Turned AOL Off," *Washington Post*, August 9, 1996, p. F1.
7. F. Rose, "Keyword."
8. D. Hilzenrath, "Emergency Overhaul for AOL," *Washington Post*, October 30, 1996, p. A1.
9. D. Hilzenrath, "Turnaround Task."
10. K. Swisher, *AOL.COM: How Steve Case Beat Bill Gates.*
11. J. Sandberg, "Firm Pays AOL $100 Million in Phone Pact," *Wall Street Journal*, February 26, 1997, pp. B4, B6.
12. "AOL and Tel-Save Approach Half a Million Long Distance Lines," AOL press release, March 25, 1998.
13. "AOL and CUC Announce Online Partnership," AOL press release, June 10, 1997.
14. J. Sandberg, "Retailers Pay Big for Internet Space," *Houston Chronicle*, July 13, 1997, 2 STAR Edition, p. 8.
15. "AOL/SportsLine Deal," *New Media Age*, July 10, 1997, p. 6.
16. G. Miller, "Heard on the Beat," *Los Angeles Times*, August 18, 1997, p. 3.
17. P. Tolme, "AOL, Koop in $89 Million Alliance," *Associated Press*, July 8, 1999.
18. "America Online Reports FY99 Third Quarter Income," AOL press release, April 27, 1999.
19. J. Sandberg, "Inside AOL's Bid to Develop Its Own Hot Sites," *Wall Street Journal*, November 21, 1997, p. B1.
20. C. Yang, "A Major Studio Named AOL?" *Business Week*, December 1, 1997, p. 173.
21. J. Sandberg, "Inside AOL's Bid."
22. "Opportunity Knocks," *Economist*, September 13, 1997, p. 63.
23. C. Yang, "Answered Prayers at America Online," *Business Week*, September 22, 1997, p. 30.
24. V. Baldwin Hick, "Passionate Members of ICQ Fear a Link with America Online," *St. Louis Post Dispatch*, June 15, 1998, p. 1.
25. "America Online Reports FY99 Third Quarter Income."
26. T. E. Weber, "America Online's Next Frontier: All AOL, All the Time," *Wall Street Journal*, March 19, 1999, p. B1.
27. C. Dubow, "AOL Beats Estimates, Adds 1.8 Million Subscribers," *Forbes Digital Tool*, www.forbes.com, (April 28, 1999).
28. T. E. Weber, "AOL Sets Accord to Purchase Netscape in a Stock Transaction for $4.3 Billion," *Wall Street Journal*, November 25, 1998, p. A3.
29. "Internet Riders," *Economist*, November 28, 1998, p. 63.
30. H. Green, "Not So Odd a Couple After All," *Business Week*, December 21, 1998, p. 77.
31. T. E. Weber, "AOL Unveils Job Cuts, Reorganization," *Wall Street Journal*, March 25, 1999, p. B4.
32. A. Reinhardt, "As the Web Spins," *Business Week*, May 24, 1999, p. 30.
33. Bill Gates interview with Charles W. L. Hill, June 1998.
34. A. Sloan, "AT&T-MediaOne Soap Opera Has Just About Everything," *Business Week*, May 11, 1999, p. 3.
35. S. Hofmeister, "AOL, Hughes Link Up to Challenge Cable," *Los Angeles Times*, June 22, 1999, p. 1.
36. J. Gaw, "Some Log Off the Web," *Seattle Times*, July 11, 1999, p. F1.
37. T. E. Weber, "Power Tools," *Wall Street Journal*, June 21, 1999, p. R23.

CASE 10

Amazon.com: Expanding Beyond Books

This case was prepared by Suresh Kotha of the University of Washington.

Jeff Bezos, the CEO of Amazon.com, was pleased that his three year-old on-line start-up, www. amazon.com, had gone from being an underground sensation for book lovers on the World Wide Web (WWW) to one of the most admired Internet retailers on Wall Street. To date, his attempts to transform the traditional book-retailing format through technology that taps the interactive nature of the Internet has been very successful. Although his company garnered rave reviews from respected Wall Street analysts, Bezos clearly understood that this was not the moment to dwell on the past. In the fast-moving world of the Internet, he and his firm continued to face many formidable challenges.

This case describes how Bezos has managed to build a rapidly growing retail business on the Internet and the challenges he and his top management face as other industry giants such as Barnes & Noble, and Bertelsmann, the German publishing conglomerate, attempt to imitate his model of competition.

COMPANY BACKGROUND

In 1994, Jeffrey Bezos, a computer science and electrical-engineering graduate from Princeton University, was the youngest senior vice president in the history of D. E. Shaw, a Wall Street–based investment bank. During the summer of 1994, one important statistic about the Internet caught his attention, and imagination—Internet usage was

growing at 2,300 percent a year. His reaction: "Anything that's growing that fast is going to be ubiquitous very quickly. It was my wake-up call."

He left his job at D. E. Shaw and drew up a list of twenty possible products that could be sold on the Internet. He quickly narrowed his prospects to music and books. Both shared a potential advantage for on-line sale: far too many titles for a single store to stock. He chose books.

> There are so many of them! There are 1.5 million English-language books in print, 3 million books in all languages worldwide. This volume defined the opportunity. Consumers keep demonstrating that they value authoritative selection. The biggest phenomenon in retailing is the big-format store—the "category killer"— whether it's selling books, toys, or music. But the largest physical bookstore in the world has only 175,000 titles.... With some 4,200 US publishers and the two biggest booksellers, Barnes & Noble and Borders Group Inc., accounting for less than 12% of total sales, there aren't any 800-pound gorillas in book selling.[1]

In contrast, the music industry had only six major record companies, which controlled the distribution of records and CDs sold in the United States. With such control, these firms had the potential to lock out a new business threatening the traditional record store format.

To start his new venture, Bezos left New York City to move west—to Boulder, Seattle, or Portland. As he drove west, he refined and fine-tuned his thoughts as well as his business plan. In doing so, he concluded that Seattle was his final destination. He recalls:

It sounds counterintuitive, but physical location is very important for the success of a virtual business. We could have started Amazon.com anywhere. We chose Seattle because it met a rigorous set of criteria. It had to be a place with lots of technical talent. It had to be near a place with large numbers of books. It had to be a nice place to live—great people won't work in places they don't want to live. Finally, it had to be in a small state. In the mail-order business, you have to charge sales tax to customers who live in any state where you have a business presence. It made no sense for us to be in California or New York.... Obviously Seattle has a great programming culture. And it's close to Roseburg, Oregon, which has one of the biggest book warehouses in the world.[2]

Renting a house in Bellevue, a Seattle suburb, Bezos started working out of his garage. Ironically, he held meetings with prospective employees and suppliers at a nearby Barnes & Noble superstore. Bezos also raised several million dollars from private investors. Operating from a 400-square-foot office in Bellevue, he launched his venture, Amazon.com, on the Internet in July 1995.

As word about his new venture spread quickly across the Internet, sales picked up rapidly. Six weeks after opening, Bezos moved his new firm to a 2,000-square-foot warehouse. Six months later, he moved once again, this time to a 17,000-square-foot building in an industrial neighborhood in Seattle. To fund further expansion, Bezos attracted $8 million from Kleiner, Perkins, Caufield & Byers, a venture-capital firm based in the Silicon Valley that has funded firms such as Sun Microsystems and Netscape.

By the end of 1996, his firm was one of the most successful Web retailers, with revenues reaching $15.6 million. (Revenues for a large Barnes & Noble superstore amount to about $5 million on average per year.) With revenues surging quarter after quarter, Bezos decided to take his company public. However, just days before the firm's initial public offering (IPO) of 3 million shares, Barnes & Noble—the nation's largest book retailer—launched its on-line store and sued Amazon.com for claiming to be the world's largest bookstore. To entice customers to visit its Web store, Barnes & Noble offered deeper discounts. Bezos retaliated with a counter lawsuit.[3]

On May 14, 1997, Bezos took Amazon.com public. The *Wall Street Journal* noted that "Amazon's May 1997 debut on the Nasdaq Stock Market came with no small amount of hype. On the first day of trading, investors bid the price of shares up to $23.50 from their offering price of $18. But the shares then fell, and within three weeks of the IPO they were below their offering price." Despite this, customers have continued to flock to Amazon.com's Web site. By October 1997, Amazon.com served its millionth "unique" customer. To keep pace with such growth, the firm expanded its Seattle warehouse and built a second 200,000-square-foot state-of-the-art distribution center in New Castle, Delaware. With these additions Amazon.com successfully increased its stocking and shipping capabilities to nearly six times its 1996 levels.

As the firm continued to expand its customer base, sales revenues have surged. The firm's revenues increased from $15.7 million in 1996 to $147 million in 1997 (see Tables 1 and 2 for the firm's balance sheet and income statements). They were expected to top $550 million for fiscal 1998. In response to this revenue growth, the company's stock and market capitalization have risen as well. As of July 1998, the capitalization was around $6.4 billion, a number that represents the combined value of the nation's two largest retailers, Barnes & Noble and Borders Books & Music, whose combined sales are about ten times those of Amazon.com.

THE BOOK PUBLISHING INDUSTRY

The United States is the world's largest market for books, with retail book sales accounting for $20.76 billion in 1997. Comprising more than 2,500 publishers, the U.S. book publishing industry is one of the oldest and most fragmented industries.[4] Figure 1 shows its structure.

The Sellers and the Buyers

The industry sells a variety of books, including trade, professional, mass-market, El-hi (elementary-high school) and college textbooks, and others, and each of these categories varies in terms of sales, competition, profitability, and volatility (see Tables 3 and 4).

Publishers Publishers sell books on a consignment basis and assume all the risk in this industry. They also accept returns on unsold books, guaranteeing their distributors a 100 percent refund on

TABLE 1

Amazon.com—Consolidated Balance Sheets, Unaudited
(in thousands, except share and per share data)

	June 30, 1998	December 31, 1997
Assets		
Current assets:		
Cash	$ 2,523	$ 1,567
Marketable securities	337,396	123,499
Inventories	17,035	8,971
Prepaid expenses and other	12,487	3,298
Total current assets	369,441	137,335
Fixed assets, net	14,014	9,265
Deposits and other	284	166
Goodwill and other purchased intangibles, net	52,398	—
Deferred charges	7,622	2,240
Total assets	$ 443,759	$ 149,006
Liabilities and Stockholders' Equity		
Current liabilities:		
Accounts payable	$ 47,556	$ 32,697
Accrued advertising	9,971	3,454
Other liabilities and accrued expenses	13,713	6,167
Current portion of long-term debt	684	1,500
Total current liabilities	71,924	43,818
Long-term portion of debt	332,225	76,521
Long-term portion of capital lease obligation	181	181
Stockholders' equity:		
Preferred stock, $0.01 par value:		
Authorized shares—10,000,000; issued and outstanding shares—none		
Common stock, $0.01 par value:		
Authorized shares—300,000,000 issued and outstanding		
shares—49,669,601 and 47,874,338 shares, resp	497	479
Additional paid-in capital	104,368	63,552
Deferred compensation	(1,301)	(1,930)
Other gains (losses)	(35)	—
Accumulated deficit	(64,100)	(33,615)
Total stockholders' equity	39,429	28,486
Total liabilities and stockholders' equity	$ 443,759	$ 149,006

TABLE 2

Amazon.com— Consolidated Statements of Operations, Unaudited

(in thousands, except per share data)

	Quarter Ended June 30		Six Months Ended June 30	
	1998	1997	1998	1997
Net sales	$ 115,977	$ 27,855	$ 203,352	$ 3,860
Cost of sales	89,786	22,633	157,840	35,117
Gross profit	26,191	5,222	45,512	8,743
Operating expenses:				
Marketing and sales	26,452	7,773	45,955	11,679
Product development	8,060	2,808	14,789	4,383
General and administrative	3,262	1,708	5,225	2,850
Amortization of goodwill and other purchased intangibles	5,413	—	5,413	—
Total operating expenses	43,187	12,289	71,382	18,912
Loss from operations	(16,996)	(7,067)	(25,870)	(10,169)
Interest income	3,334	366	4,974	430
Interest expense	(7,564)	(4)	(9,589)	(4)
Net interest income (expense)	(4,230)	362	(4,615)	426
Net loss	$ (21,226)	$ (6,705)	$ (30,485)	$ (9,743)
Basic and diluted loss per share	$ (0.44)	$ (0.16)	$ (0.64)	$ (0.24)
Shares used in computation of basic and diluted loss per share	47,977	42,634	47,299	40,719

them. They provide money and contracts to prospective authors and decide how many copies of a book to print. Typically, a first-run printing for a book varies from 5,000 to 50,000 copies. However, best-selling authors' first-run printings are generally set at around 300,000 copies.

In practice, however, trade (adult and juvenile books) and paperback publishers print far more copies than will be sold. About 25 percent of all books distributed to wholesalers are returned, and at times these percentages run as high as 40 percent for mass-market paperbacks. According to industry experts, 20 to 30 percent for hardcover book returns is judged acceptable and 30 to 50 percent is generally considered high. Anything above

50 percent is viewed as disastrous. In a process known as remaindering (offering books to discount stores, jobbers, and other vendors), publishers drastically reduce the price after a certain period. Apart from the material cost of returns and the lost revenue they represent, publishers spend millions of dollars each year transporting books back and forth. In this industry, profit margins are driven by book volume, which in turn hinges on the size of each print run. Generally about 10 percent of titles make a profit, with 90 percent barely breaking even. Table 5 indicates the margins on a typical hardcover book.

The "big three"—publishers Warner Books, Simon & Schuster, and Pearson—accounted for 21

FIGURE I

Book Publishing Market
Structure

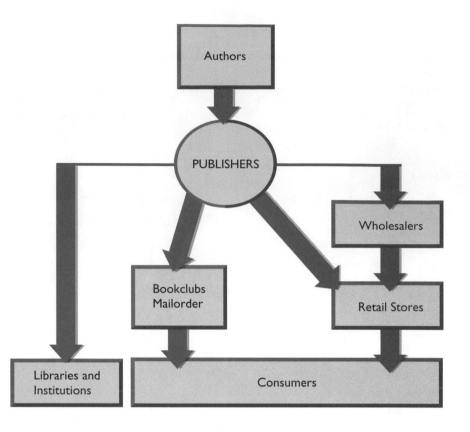

percent of sales in 1995. The twenty largest book-publishing companies in the United States command more than 60 percent of all retail sales. Warner Books, a subsidiary of Time Warner, the U. S. entertainment giant, was the largest publisher in 1995, with sales of $3.7 billion. Simon & Schuster, a division of Viacom Corporation, ranked second, with sales reaching $2.17 billion, and Pearson, a group that owns the *Financial Times*, ranked third, with revenues of $1.75 billion.

Wholesalers.   Wholesalers distribute books. They take orders from independent booksellers and chains, and consolidate them into lot-orders for publishers. Publishers supply wholesalers, who in turn supply the thousands of retail bookstores located throughout the country. Wholesalers accounted for almost 30 percent of publishers' sales in 1996. Unlike publishing and retailing, wholesaling is highly concentrated, with firms like Ingram Book Co. and Baker and Taylor commanding more than 80 percent of the market.

Competition in wholesaling revolves around the speed of delivery and the number of titles

stocked. Ingram, for instance, receives more than 70 percent of its orders electronically and offers one-day delivery to about 82 percent of its U.S. customers. In 1994, the average net profit per book for wholesalers was less than 1.5 percent. This figure was down from the traditional margins of about 2 percent a few years earlier.[5]

Technological advances have made warehouse operations more efficient, which in turn has made it possible for wholesalers to provide attractive discounts to retailers. Also, the types of books wholesalers are supplying to retailers are changing. Bookstores are increasingly relying on wholesalers for fast-selling titles and less-popular backlist books.[6] However, with the emergence of superstores, such large retailers as Barnes & Noble and Borders Books & Music are no longer using wholesalers for initial orders of major titles. For example, Borders Books & Music buys more than 90 percent of its titles directly from publishers.

Retail Bookstores   Bookstore chains and independent and general retailers accounted for between 35 and 40 percent of industry revenues in 1994

TABLE 3

The Various Product Categories

Trade Books.

This segment includes general interest hardcover and paperback books sold to adults and juveniles. Trade books accounted for almost 25 percent of book revenues in 1997. According to industry reports, books sold to adults increased by more than 30 percent between 1991 and 1995. Juvenile book sales, showed a double-digit growth rate in the late 1980s and early 1990s. However, juvenile hardcover book sales represented a 2.3 percent increase in 1997 over the previous year, and juvenile paperback book sales fell by as much as 18.6 percent during the same period. This slow growth was attributed to a decline in the number of popular titles and increased spending by children on toys and games.

Random House, Bantam Doubleday Dell, Simon & Schuster, HarperCollins, and Penguin are some of the leading firms that competed in this product category.

Professional Books.

More than 165 million profession books were sold in 1997, accounting for $4.15 billion, Since 1991, professional book sales have grown at a compound annual rate of 3.0 percent (in units). Legal publishing was the largest segment of the professional-books category, with the scientific and technical category coming in second place. The long-term outlook for this category was good because employment in the medical, legal, scientific, and business profession was expected to grow strongly.

Thomson Crops was the largest professional-books publisher, with sales of $1.99 billion. Professional book revenues made up 31 percent of Thomson's total revenues. Reed Elsevier ranked second with 1994 sales of $1.63 billion, and was followed by Wolters Kluwer and Times Mirror with $1.07 billion and $775 million in sales, respectively.

Mass-Market Books.

A large proportion of these books are sold through magazine wholesalers and outlets such as newsstands and drugstores. This category includes bestsellers that have shelf lives of about three to six weeks, and in 1997 they accounted for about 7 percent of all books sold. Although the cost of acquiring the paperback rights to a best-selling hardcover title can cost millions of dollars, the per-unit fixed costs for printing are small because print runs were as large as 500,000. However, when return rates, which typically exceed 40 percent, are factored in, profit margins tend to be less than 12 percent.

The largest publishers are Random House, Bantam Doubleday Dell, Simon & Schuster, and HarperCollins.

El-Hi Textbooks.

El-hi, or elementary–high school, books accounted for 14 percent of all books sold in 1997, (they used to represent 30 percent of all books sold in 1994). Sales in this segment rose nearly 14 percent in 1997, and forecasts suggest that are likely to increase by 4.8 percent in 1998. El-hi is driven by state adoption and enrollment levels, and the books are sold to school systems on a contract basis. The development of materials for schools is a capital-intensive process that typically takes up to five years for most new programs. Per pupil expenditures, as well as the number of students, are expected to grow through the year 2000, implying moderate growth (3 to 4 percent) for this segment.

The big publishers are owned by media conglomerates such as News Corp., Times Mirror, and Paramount. The largest el-hi publisher is McGraw-Hill, followed by Paramount (the parent company of Prentice-Hall and Silver Burdett), Harcourt Brace, and Houghton Mifflin.

College Textbooks.

College publishing is the most profitable category. The cost of producing a college text is lower than in the el-hi market, because the texts are typically prepared by university faculty members and used individually. However, the unit sales tend to be small and used textbook sales generally accounted for 20 to 40 percent of total sales. College textbook sales represented 12.8 percent of all book sales in 1997. Sales are estimated to increase 6.9 percent, to $2.85 billion, in 1998.

Prentice-Hall (owned by Paramount) is the largest college publisher, followed by HB College (owned by Harcourt General), International Thomson, McGraw-Hill, and Irwin (a division of Times Mirror).

TABLE 4

Unit Sales (in millions) and Dollar Sales (in millions) by Product Category

Product Category	1997 Units	1997 ($mill)	1998* Units	1998* ($mill)	Profit Margins in 1993
Trade books					
Adults (hardcover and paperbacks)	441.8	$4095.2	438.9	$4160.0	13.7%**
Juvenile (hardcover and paperbacks)	343.8	1358.0	355.9	1437.6	7.7%
Mass market	473.2	1433.8	472.3	1480.3	3.1%
Book clubs	137.7	1145.3	141.3	1207.2	
Mail order	85.7	521.0	81.8	504.7	
Religious	166.6	1132.7	170.3	1178.0	12.4%
Professional (business, medical, scientific, and technical)	165.2	4156.4	169.6	4404.6	8.0%
University press	17.8	367.8	18.0	382.1	
El-hi (elementary–high school)	286.5	2959.6	282.8	3102.4	14.9%
College (textbook and materials)	168.2	2669.7	173.7	2852.8	15.8%
Standard tests	—	191.4	—	204.3	
Subject reference	1.2	736.5	1.2	766.9	
Total	**2287.7**	**$20,767.4**	**2305.8**	**$21,680.9**	

*Projected sales.
**For hardcover books.
Source: Book Industry Study Group Trends, 1998.

TABLE 5

Profit Margins for a "Typical" Book

Book List Price	$19.95	
Revenue to publisher (i.e., price paid by wholesaler or bookstore)	$10.37	48% discount off suggested retail price
Manufacturing cost	$ 2.00	Printing, binding, jacket design, composition, typesetting, paper, ink
Publisher overhead	$ 3.00	Marketing, fulfillment
Returns and allowances	$ 3.00	
Author's royalties	$ 2.00	
Total publishing costs	$10.00	
Publisher's operating profit	$ 0.37	Returns amount for 3.7%

TABLE 6

Book Sales in 1994 by Various Distribution Channels

Channel	% of Total sales
Bookstore chains, independents and general retailers	35%–40%
Mail order and book clubs	21%
Sales to college book stores	17%
Schools	15%
Libraries and other institutions	10%

(see Table 6). From 1975 to 1995, the number of bookstores in the United States increased from 11,990 to 17,340. According to industry sources, the total sales for the nation's four largest bookstore chains—Barnes & Noble, Borders Books & Music, Books-A-Million, and Crown Books—rose 14.3 percent, to $5.68 billion, for the fiscal year ending in January 1998 (see Table 7). This figure represented about 24 percent of all book sales. Industry analysts point out that from 1992 through 1995, superstore bookstore sales grew at a com-

TABLE 7

Bookstore Chain Sales ($millions)

Chain	1998*	1997	% Change
Barnes & Noble	$2,797.0	$2448.0	14.2%
Borders Group	2,266.0	1,958.8	15.7
Books-A-Million	324.8	278.6	16.5
Crown Books	297.5	287.7	3.4
Total	$5685.3	$4,973.1	14.3%

*Estimates
Source: Publishers Weekly, March 23, 1998, p.17.

pounded rate of 71 percent while non-superstore sales grew at a rate of 4 percent.

With the increasing growth of these superstores, experts cautioned that in smaller markets a shakeout was inevitable.[7] Also, 1995 marked the first year in which bookstore chains sold more books than independents.[8] A spokesperson for the American Booksellers Association, noted that "In the three years from 1993 to 1995, 150 to 200 independent-owned bookstores went out of business—50 to 60 in 1996 alone.... By contrast in the same period, approximately 450 retail superstore outlets opened, led by Barnes & Noble and the Borders Group, with 348 openings."[9]

Independent booksellers believed, however, that the growth of superstores might be reaching a saturation point. Still, even as Barnes & Noble and Borders entered city after city, as many as 142 U.S. metropolitan markets did not have a book superstore. According to Amy Ryan, a Prudential Securities analyst, the current rate of expansion could continue at least through the year 2000, for the country could support about 1,500 such stores.

Institutions and Libraries There are more than 29,000 private, public, and academic libraries in the United States.[10] This market is crucial to publishers because of its stability and size. Since libraries order only what they want, this lowers the overhead costs associated with inventory and return processing, making this segment a relatively profitable one for publishers. Moreover, as hardcover trade books have become relatively expensive, many readers now borrow them from libraries instead of buying them. Industry experts observed that about 95 percent of general titles published in any year sold less than 20,000 copies; of that number, about 55 percent were purchased by libraries. Libraries also frequently repurchase titles to replace worn-out and stolen books. By doing so, they keep the backlist sales healthy.

Mail Order and Book Clubs The industry has witnessed a significant drop in the mail-order book business. This drop in sales was attributed to the growth of large discount-sale retailers. Publishers' book club sales on the other hand have risen steadily, gaining 9 percent in 1994 and in early 1995. This growth was attributed to the increasing popularity of specialized book clubs, which focus on favorite baby-boomer interests such as gardening and computers.

The Buying Public   A survey commissioned by American Booksellers Association found that some 106 million adults purchased about 456.9 million books in any given quarter. The survey, which looked at book-buying habits of consumers during the calendar year 1994, revealed that six in ten American adults say they purchased at least one book in the last three months. Annually, that corresponds to 1.8 billion books sold, an average of seventeen books per book-buying consumer a year. The average amount paid for the three most recent books purchased by consumers in the last thirty days was about $15. According to another report, by the Book Industry Study Group, "1996 was a year of major transition and flux in the publishing industry with buyer and seller alike reexamining standard operating procedures to work together in order to adapt to recent changes including growth of retail space and the impact of the Internet."

The Growing Presence of Virtual Bookstores

In its two hardest challenges—physically distributing the right number of books to bookstores and getting the word about serious books out to potential readers—bookselling is getting a more than trivial assist from the new on-line technologies. The rapid growth of the on-line businesses is spreading to book publishing and retailing. According to Larry Daniels, director of information technologies for the National Association of College Stores, "Booksellers' concern revolves around the potential for publishers to deal directly with consumers and the media on the Internet. . . . The phenomenon could mean the elimination of middlemen such as bookstores."[11] Daniels also notes the potential for publishers to be "disintermediated," because computer-literate writers can now publish and distribute their own works on-line. However, the leading publishing houses are skeptical of electronic book-publishing capabilities and remain uncertain about the Internet's future with regard to physical books.

Despite industry skepticism and concern, the Internet has a plethora of virtual bookstores selling books. A cursory search on an Internet search-engine such as Yahoo! produced a listing of 475 on-line bookstores operating on the World Wide Web as of August 1998. A search on Buyers Index (www.buyersindex.com), a mail-order buyers' search engine, yielded more than 234 on-line bookstores. Many of these firms are relatively unknown compared with such on-line retailers as Amazon.com and Barnes & Noble. These two firms in particular have been growing at the self-reported double-digit rates and are fast becoming a formidable presence on the Web. Book and music sales on-line accounted for $156 million in 1997. Although this amount represented a small percentage of the overall retail book sales in 1997, it is projected to reach about $1.1 billion in 2001.

COMPETING ON THE WORLD WIDE WEB

Operating a Virtual Bookstore

Unlike traditional bookstores, Amazon.com has no bookshelves for browsing. All contact with the company is either through its Web site [www.amazon.com] or by E-mail. At the firm's Web site, customers can search for a specific book, topic, or author, or they can browse their way through a book catalog featuring numerous subjects. Visitors can also read book reviews from other customers, the *New York Times,* the *Atlantic Monthly,* and Amazon.com's staff. Customers can browse, fill up a virtual shopping basket, and then complete the sale by entering their credit card information or by placing their order on-line and then phoning in their credit card information. Customer orders are processed immediately. Books in stock (mostly bestsellers) are packaged and mailed the same day. When their order has been shipped, customers are notified by E-mail. Amazon.com places orders for non-bestsellers with the appropriate book publisher immediately.

Shunning the elaborate graphics that clutter many Web sites on the Internet, the firm instead loads up its customers with information. For many featured books, it offers capsule descriptions, snippets of reviews and "self-administered" interviews posted by authors. The firm has found a way to use the technology to offer services that a traditional store or catalog can't match. As Bezos notes,

An Amazon customer can romp through a database of 1.1 million titles (five times the largest superstore's inventory), searching by subject or name. When you select a book, Amazon is programmed to flash other related titles you may also want to buy. If you tell Amazon about favorite authors and topics, it will send you by electronic mail a constant stream of recommendations. You want to know when a book comes out in paperback? Amazon will E-mail that too.[12]

Additionally, the firm offers space for readers to post their own reviews and then steps out of the way and lets its customers sell to each other. Bezos points out the advantages of cyberspace for book customers:

> There are so many things we can do on-line that can't be done in the real world. We want customers who enter Amazon.com to indicate whether they want to be "visible" or "invisible." If they choose "visible," then when they're in the science fiction section, other people will know they're there. People can ask for recommendations— 'read any good books lately?'—or recommend books to others. I'm an outgoing person, but I'd never go into a bookstore and ask a complete stranger to recommend a book. The semi-anonymity of the on-line environment makes people less inhibited.[13]

Value Propositions and Customer Service

When asked why people come to his site, Bezos responds:

> Bill Gates laid it out in a magazine interview. He said, "I buy all my books at Amazon.com because I'm busy and it's convenient. They have a big selection, and they've been reliable." Those are three of our four core value propositions: convenience, selection, service. The only one he left out is price: we are the broadest discounters in the world in any product category. . . . These value propositions are interrelated, and they all relate to the Web.[14]

At Amazon.com, almost all books are discounted. Bestsellers are sold at a 30 to 40 percent discount and the other books at a 10 percent discount. Bezos explains that "We discount because we have a lower cost structure than physical stores do and we turn our inventory 150 times a year. That's like selling bread in a supermarket. Physical bookstores turn their inventory only 3 or 4 times a year."

The firm's Seattle and Delaware warehouses are used to stock popular books items, and to consolidate and repack customer orders. Moreover, only after the firm receives a paid customer order does it

TABLE 8

Amazon.com's Customer Bill of Rights

Amazon.com specifies these rights for its customers:

1. No obligation.
Eyes & Editors Personal Notification Services are provided free of charge, and you are under no obligation to buy anything.

2. Unsubscribing.
You can unsubscribe or change your subscriptions at any time.

3. Privacy.
We do not sell or rent information about our customers. If you would like to make sure we never sell or rent information about you to third parties, just send a blank E-mail message to never@amazon.com.

request the appropriate publisher to ship the book to Amazon.com. The firm then ships the book to the customer.[15] It owns little expensive retail real estate and its operations are largely automated. Its distribution center in Delaware, for example, uses state-of-the-art technology to consolidate and package books for shipment.

To keep customers interested in Amazon.com, the firm offers two forms of E-mail-based service to its registered customers. "Eyes" is a personal notification service, in which customers can register their interests in a particular author or topic. Once customers register with Amazon.com, they receive information about new books published by their favorite author. "Editor's service" provides editorial comments about featured books via E-mail. Three full-time editors read book reviews, pore over customer orders, and survey current events to select the featured books. These, and other freelance editors employed by the firm, provide registered users with E-mail updates on the latest and greatest books they've been reading. These services are automated and are available free of charge, and customers subscribing to these services have certain guaranteed rights (see Table 8 for "Customer Bill of Rights"). According to Bezos, such services are vital for success on the Internet:

Customer service is a critical success factor for on-line merchants. If you make customers unhappy in the physical world, they might each tell a few friends. If you make customers unhappy on the Internet, they can each tell thousands of friends with one message to a newsgroup. If you make them really happy, they can tell thousands of people about that. I want every customer to become an evangelist for us. About 63 percent of the book orders come from repeat customers.

The firm's employees also compile a weekly list of the twenty most obscure titles on order, and Bezos awards a prize for the most amusing. Amazon.com drums up all these orders through a mix of state-of-the-art software and old-fashioned salesmanship. When asked to differentiate his firm from potential rivals, Bezos stresses the challenges of electronic marketing:

People who just scratch the surface of Amazon.com say—"oh, you sell books on the Web"—don't understand how hard it is to actually be an electronic merchant. We're not just putting up a Web site. We do 90 percent of our customer service by E-mail rather than by telephone. . . . There are very few off-the-shelf tools that help do what we're doing. We've had to develop lots of our own technologies. There are no companies selling software to manage email centers. So we had to develop our own tools. In a way this is good news. There are lots of barriers to entry.[16]

Culture and Philosophy

Amazon.com had 800 employees in August 1998. A significant portion of the firm's employees manage "content" on the firm's Web site, including such tasks as Web page updating and formatting book reviews for display. The firm also employs a large number of people to develop software tools for operating on the Internet, and a large group of employees do nothing but answer E-mails from customers. At Amazon.com, "ingenuity and problem-solving" are key, says Bezos

Almost nothing is off-the-shelf at Amazon.com: Our software engineers are developing programs that are the first of their kind; our editors create original content; our site team designs features that can't be found anywhere else. . . .

Also, we have some of the best programmers, and the best servers in the world.

According to Amazon.com insiders, "This is a very driven place. Hours are typically 8 to 8 and many people work weekends. Jeff spends every waking hour on this business." Bezos confirms that

Everyone at Amazon.com works hard, long, and smart. We act like owners because we are owners—stock options give each of us an equity stake in the company. We are passionate about what we're doing. Because of that, we have fun at work, and it makes it easy for us to work hard. What we're building is unprecedented. We're not aspiring to a corporate model—we are creating the model. This to me is the most compelling reason for people to come to work here.

As for his workers, Bezos points out that "There is no Amazon.com 'type.'"

There are Amazon.com employees who have three master's degrees and some who speak five languages. We have people who worked at Procter & Gamble and Microsoft, and people who worked at *Rolling Stone* and the *Village Voice*. We have a professional figure skater, two racecar drivers, a Rhodes scholar, a set of twins, a husband and wife, and their dog. We wear jeans to work, have meetings in the hallway, and we get excited about HTML-enabled E-mail.

He describes his firm's corporate philosophy as follows:

The Amazon.com corporate philosophy is simple: If it's good for our customers, it's worth doing. Our company mission is to leverage technology and expertise to provide the best buying experience on the Internet. Put another way, we want people to come to Amazon.com, find whatever they want, discover things they didn't know they wanted, and leave feeling they have a new favorite place to shop.

Operating Philosophy

The firm's operating philosophy is unlike that of traditional bookstores. At Amazon.com there are no salespeople. The firm is open for business twenty-four hours a day and has a global presence. More than 3 million customers from 160 countries have purchased books from the firm. The firm is devoid of expensive furnishings, and money is spent sparingly. "We made the first four desks we have here ourselves," Bezos recalls, adding that "all our desks are made out of doors and four-by-fours.... My monitor stand is a bunch of old phone books. We spend money on the things that matter to our customers and we don't spend money on anything else."[17]

Amazon.com spends a substantial amount on Web advertising and marketing. According to Jupiter Communications, the firm spent more than $340,000 in the first half of the 1996 and ranked thirty-fourth in Web ad spending. Since then, however, these expenses have gone up significantly. This is partly because Amazon.com has entered into multiyear advertising agreements with Internet aggregators, such as Yahoo!, Excite, and AOL. For the quarter ending June 1998, the firm spent $26.5 million on marketing, equivalent to 23 percent of sales.

Since Amazon.com is an Internet-only retailer, Web advertising gives it a unique opportunity to track the success of an ad by the number of click-throughs to the store's Web site and the number of Internet surfers who actually purchase something. Industry analysts estimate that between 2 and 3 percent of people who see an ad on the Web will actually click-through to see more.

The firm advertises mainly in such large-circulation newspapers as the *Wall Street Journal*, *New York Times*, and *San Jose Mercury News*, and on Internet search-engine sites such as Yahoo!, Lycos, the Microsoft Network (MSN), and Microsoft's *Slate* magazine. Amazon.com keeps its banner ads simple, with just a few words and a Web address. Recently, the firm has started advertising on radio and television (for example, CNN). It also hands out discount coupons in several cities to entice customers to use its services.

The decision to locate Amazon.com in Seattle appears to be paying off. The firm has been able to attract some Microsoft veterans and many highly qualified executives. Figure 2 illustrates how the firm is organized and the Appendix provides a brief description of the firm's top management.

Growth Through Micro-Franchising

Amazon.com has been growing at a rapid pace each quarter. Part of the reason for this fast growth is the firm's Associates Program. The program was designed to increase traffic to Amazon.com by creating a referral service from other Web sites to Amazon.com's 2.5-million book catalog. An associates Web site, such as Starchefs—which features cookbook authors— recommends books and makes a link from its Web page to Amazon.com's catalog page for the books. The associated Web site then earns referral fees for sales generated by these links. Partners receive weekly referral fee statements and a check for the referral fees earned in that quarter. More than 90,000 sites have already signed up for this program and earn a commission sometimes up to 15 percent of the value of books bought by the referred customer. The "Web technology," says Bezos, "has made it possible to set up micro-franchises, and with zero overhead."[18]

Since July 1995, Amazon.com has doubled in size every 2.4 months.[19] By August 1996, sales were growing at 34 percent a month. The firm posted revenues of $147.8 million for 1997, an 838 percent increase over the previous year. However,

FIGURE 2

Amazon.com's Organizational Structure

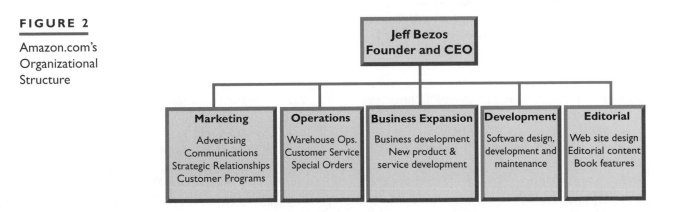

Jeff Bezos Founder and CEO				
Marketing	**Operations**	**Business Expansion**	**Development**	**Editorial**
Advertising Communications Strategic Relationships Customer Programs	Warehouse Ops. Customer Service Special Orders	Business development New product & service development	Software design, development and maintenance	Web site design Editorial content Book features

the net loss for fiscal 1997 was 27.6 million, compared with a net loss in fiscal 1996 of $5.8 million. When the company was founded in 1995, the plan was to be profitable in five years. The firm claims to have exceeded expectations and has made its business plan more aggressive. Despite continuing losses, Wall Street's interest in the new venture has remained strong. Furthermore, based on cybershare (and revenues), the firm is acknowledged to be the largest on-line bookstore on the Web.

Bezos is focused on expanding Amazon.com. "In the year 2000, our goal is to be one of the world's leading bookstores," he says. "We believe we're expanding the market for books. With this new way of selling books on the Web we can expose people to far more books than before. People buy books from us that they won't find in bookstores. And we're growing rapidly in this stagnant market."

CHALLENGES FACING AMAZON.COM

Although Bezos is pleased that Amazon.com is well regarded by analysts on Wall Street, he acknowledges that many strategic challenges remain. Three in particular demand his immediate attention: finding creative ways to fend off formidable new competitors; leveraging the firm's brand name to expand beyond just books; and integrating the new acquisitions made by the firm.

Fending Off Formidable Competitors

Competition between on-line book merchants is likely to become even more intense, with a growing number of publishers and retailers going online. For example, Ingram and other large publishers have begun experimenting with the World Wide Web. As the *Wall Street Journal* has reported, "In addition to Amazon and Barnes & Noble, publisher Random House Inc. sells books on-line and Viacom Inc.'s Simon & Schuster unit launched an Internet book-selling site grandly called 'The SuperStore.'"[20]

Barnes & Noble, the largest U.S. book retailer, launched its on-line store in May 1997, a little less than two years after Amazon.com opened for business. Although Barnes & Noble finds itself in the unusual position of trailing a competitor, it claims that it holds the unique distinction of operating in four different channels—retail stores, the Internet, 1-800-THE-BOOK, and mail order. Stephen Riggio,

vice chairman of Barnes & Noble, who is presiding over the new on-line venture, sees a rosy future: "How big is it [on-line sales] going to get? We're looking at $100 million in sales this year [1998]. We're not being speculative about that range. We're going to be there. It's going to be bigger than a billion dollar business." Barnes & Noble on-line sales for the year ending in 1997 amounted to $14 million, a small fraction of the firm's overall retail book sales. However, according to a report in *Business Week*, Leonard Riggio, CEO of Barnes & Noble, is dead serious about the on-line segment:

> Riggio plans to spend $40 million to ballyhoo the service in 1998. . . . Riggio is already thinking ahead of how to integrate this technology into the shelves of Barnes & Noble. In the bookstore of the future, he says, customers could tap into millions of titles and print any part from these works on the spot. He talks about software programs that could point customers to specific lines in various books, threaded by a single topic, or ones that could ferret out and print obscure texts that never made it into book form. In short, Riggio envisions modifying what constitutes a published work.[21]

In July 1998, Borders Group Inc. (the parent corporation of Borders Books & Music) entered the fray with Borders.com, a newly formed subsidiary. At the Borders Web site, customers can purchase books, music CDs, and videos. The firm's Web site described Borders' late entry as follows:

> We're not content with being just another on-line bookseller. We want to do it right. Anyone who's been to a Borders store knows that selling books, music, and videos isn't just a business, it's a passion. . . . At Borders.com, we aim to provide the same high level of expertise and vast selection customers have come to associate with the Borders name. No other on-line bookseller can offer 10 million books, CDs, and videos—in stock and available now.

In late 1997, Ingram, the largest U.S. distributor of books, started experimenting with on-line retailing. It began testing an experimental service to create new on-line retailers. According to a report in *Business Week*, "All the would-be retailers had to do was lure the shoppers. Ingram handled everything else, from maintaining the Web site to taking orders, processing credit-card billings, and shipping the books. In effect the virtual bookshops became little more than a retail façade of Ingram. However, after six months of test-marketing, Ingram quietly pulled the plug in early October."[22]

Undaunted by Ingram's failure, Bertelsmann, the German media conglomerate, announced in February 1998 that it planned to open an on-line store (tentatively called BooksOn-line) that will sell books in English, French, Spanish, German, and Dutch.[23] Bertelsmann hoped to ship books to customers in Europe and the United States through its extensive distribution in both countries. In October 1998, however, the firm announced it was buying a 50 percent share in Barnesandnoble.com for $200 million, and both Bertelsmann and Barnes & Noble are expected to spend another $100 million each to strengthen their joint operation. Furthermore, Bertelsmann will abandon the U.S. rollout of its BooksOn-line service. Maria Latour-Kadison, an on-line retail analyst at *Forrester Research*, calls the linking-up of the two firms a "real powerhouse combination: the retail power of Barnes & Noble and the fulfillment power of Bertelsmann. . . . They already have what Amazon is spending millions to acquire [a brand name and infrastructure]. There's a very steep learning curve associated with doing on-line retailing well, and Bertelsmann will be able to leapfrog some of it because of Barnesandnoble.com's experience.[24]

Bezos acknowledges that "Bertelsmann can be a formidable competitor. They have 50 percent stake in AOL's German operations, over 35 million active book and music club members and significant warehousing and book distribution assets spread out internationally." He points out, however, that Amazon.com is

. . . not competitor focused but customer focused. Figuring out what the customer wants is a never ending process. We differentiate along the following dimensions: selection (we are still the largest); ease of use; price; and discovery. Scale is important in e-commerce and so is 'ease of use.' Our innovations like '1-Click shopping' continue to make our Web site far more attractive than competitors. We are working with interesting features such as "book matcher," using the latest collaborative filtering technology that we acquired from Net Perceptions. We believe such things greatly enhance the customer experience at our store. Discovery means under-

standing customers as individuals and finding ways to accelerate their discovery process while they are at the store. We are working on software that increases the odds that customers will find the right book that they are looking for when searching in our store. Discovery is powerful for customers.

Consequently, Bezos's immediate concern centers on finding innovative ways to stay ahead of his competitors, and he acknowledges that this will remain a continuing challenge.

Leveraging the Amazon.com Brand Name

In June 1998, Amazon.com expanded its product line to include music. The music store offers more than 125,000 titles—ten times the CD selection of the typical music store—and everyday savings of up to 40 percent. The new music store features expert and customer reviews, interviews, an essentials lists, a list of the hottest CDs from around the country and the world, music news, and recommendations. Music fans can search for their favorite music by CD title, artist, song title, or label. Bezos describes the new venture as follows:

You can browse through nearly 300 styles ranging from Alternative to Zydeco (everything but Classical, which is on the way) or use "Essentials" (my favorite feature) to learn about the best CDs to help you start or build a collection in a particular style. And you can reduce guesswork by listening to some of our 225,000 song clips. . . . It's a music discovery machine. Using the power of technology and the Internet, we're enriching the music experience for everyone, from casual to devoted listeners alike.

Customers, he adds, had a large part in the store's creation:

The music store was designed with the help of more than 20,000 customers who responded to our invitation to "build the music store of your dreams." Many of the features in our new music store are the direct result of these suggestions. Our customers told us they wanted a site that is as rich in musical selection and content as the Amazon.com bookstore—with the same great prices, features, and customer service.

The launch of Amazon.com's music store was accompanied by a major update of the firm's Web site, and Bezos sums up the changes:

> We didn't focus only on music. We've also redesigned our store to make it even easier to find the books you want.... The new store design permits customers to move easily between the book and music areas, making it fast and simple to find what they are looking for and to discover new titles. We now provide an integrated shopping cart, 1-Click ordering, and consolidated shipping across both books and music.

Unlike book retailers, many on-line music stores such as cdnow.com (www.cdnow.com) and n2k.com (www.n2k.com) have been in operations for more than a few years. For example, cdnow.com claims that it is the world's leading on-line music store by offering more than 250,000 music related items, and n2k.com operates many music sites (called channels), including Music Boulevard on the World Wide Web (see Table 9 for a partial listing of on-line music stores). In response to Amazon.com's entry into the music business, Cdnow and N2K signed an agreement in October to merge their two companies. Bezos, however, says that "We don't really view existing on-line music stores as our direct competitors. We are more focused on parties that already have a large portion of music sales." Some analysts, though, take a skeptical view of Amazon.com's efforts to compete in music business, as a report in the *Wall Street Journal* illustrates:

> But the move [to offer music CDs] is risky too; Cyberspace is increasingly crowded with on-line superstores set up by Amazon's physical-world counterparts, companies with more marketing clout and track records of profitability. And Amazon could lose cachet with bibliophiles if its forays into other media dilute its reputation as a destination for booklovers.... [M]ail-order giants Columbia House, a joint venture of Time Warner Inc. and Sony Corp., and Bertelsmann AG's BMG Entertainment have made Internet selling a top priority. Columbia House is taking orders from music-club members on one site; on a separate super-store site, Total E, it's moving straight into Amazon territory with plans to add books and CD-ROMs to its existing catalogue of videos and CDs.[25]

Analysts have also pointed out that the music business is "somewhere between a no-margin and a low-margin business" and hence have questioned the firm's move into the music field. Bezos sees the situation differently:

> Amazon.com brand has to stand for something. For us the brand name means price, convenience, customer service, and a great selection. There is a huge advantage in expanding to other product categories. The customer acquisition costs are significantly lower and so are the costs related to the life time value of that customer. If we can successfully expand the brand, as we think we can, then there are significant economic benefits to expansion.... We recognize that the music business is a different environment than books. About half-a-dozen players control the entire distribution of music in this country and the likely implication of such control is lower margins. However, we like to emphasize the incremental dollar value of music sales to our existing customers.

Integrating New Acquisitions

Capitalizing on increased market value, Amazon.com acquired three companies, Bookpages, Telebook, and Internet Movie Database in April 1998. Bezos assesses the value of these additions as follows:

> With these we have accelerated our expansion into European e-commerce and acquired a foundation for a best-of-breed video store. These acquisitions will enable Amazon.com to offer a new set of consumers the same combination of selection, service and value that we now provide our U.S. book customers. Fortunately, we were able to build an international brand name as a by product of operating on the Internet. People in Japan, Germany, and UK are very familiar with the Amazon.com name (about 22 percent of the firm's sales come from outside the United States currently).

Although Bezos remains quiet about his intentions regarding Internet Movie Database, analysts speculate that *The Internet Movie Database* is likely to form the key underpinning for Amazon.com's eventual entry into on-line video sales.

TABLE 9

A Partial Listing of On-line Music Stores

Cdnow*

The idea for this store was conceived in the summer of 1994, and it was started by twin brothers Jason and Matt Olim in their parents' basement in 1994. In 1997, the firm posted sales of $15 million. It reported averages of about 18 percent in operating margins.

Music Boulevard (www.musicboulevard.com).

Owned by n2k, Music Boulevard operates transaction sites in English, French, German, Japanese, and Spanish. Started in September 1996, n2k.com bills itself as "the premier on-line music entertainment company and the Internet's only complete source for music content, community and comment." In 1997 it reported revenues of $11.7 million.

Musicspot (www.musicspot.com).

According to a recent 10,000-household PC-Meter survey, CUC's musicspot ranked top among the top "Hot Storefronts."

Tunes.com (www.tunes.com).

Tunes.com, based in Berkeley, California, was launched in November 1996. It features 200,000 thirty-second music clips backed by collaborative filter, which matches visitors' music interests to profiles created by people with similar tastes. The company plans to have 1 million samples on-line by mid 1998, which will make it the largest music sampling source on-line.

Records Clubs.

Record clubs are shaping up to be the Web's most powerful retailers. An estimated 16.5 million customers belong to record clubs in the United States. Columbia House and BMG both debuted Web sites in 1995. Their sites now handle all club chores, including administration, buying, status checking, and the commendable job of cyber-retailing.

*Cdnow and Music Boulevard signed an agreement on October 8, 1998, to merge their two companies.

In July 1998, Amazon.com signed agreements to acquire two additional firms. They include Junglee Corp and PlanetAll. PlanetAll, is a Cambridge, Massachusetts, firm that provides a unique Web-based address book, calendar, and reminder service. Junglee Corp., based in Sunnyvale, California, is a leading provider of advanced Web-based virtual database (VDB) technology that can help shoppers find millions of products on the Internet (see Table 10). Discussing his firm's intention to acquire these two firms, Bezos stressed their importance:

PlanetAll is the most innovative use of the Internet I've seen. It's simply a breakthrough in doing something as fundamental and important as staying in touch. The reason PlanetAll has over 1.5 million members—and is growing even faster than the Internet—is simple: it creates extraordinary value for its users. I believe PlanetAll

will prove to be one of the most important online applications.... Junglee has assembled an extraordinary team of people. Together we'll empower customers to find and discover the products they want to buy.

Commenting on the recent expansion and acquisitions, Bezos described his company's way of proceeding and the criteria it uses:

Our product extension and geographic expansion is better late than early. Why better late than early? We had to first focus on the book business and grow that until we were comfortable with it. There are always numerous opportunities to expand. We try to err on the side of being slow. Fortunately, we are not capital constrained, but we are definitely people constrained. We only pursue opportunities when

TABLE 10

Recent Acquisitions by Amazon.com

Bookpages (www.bookpages.co.uk).
As one of the largest on-line bookstores in the United Kingdom, the firm provides access to all 1.2 million UK books in print.*

Telebook (www.telebuch.de).
This firm, operating through its ABC Bücherdienst subsidiary, is Germany's number one on-line bookstore, with a catalog of nearly 400,000 German-language titles.

Internet Movie Database (www.imdb.com).
Originally launched in 1990, Internet Movie Database is a comprehensive repository for movie and television information on the Internet and is an excellent example of genuine community on the Internet.

PlanetAll.com (www.PlanetAll.com).
The firm launched in November 1996 reportedly has 1.5 million members and reports that thousands of new members are joining each day to use the secure, free service to organize and automatically update information about friends, business associates, relatives, and alumni. Users accessing PlanetAll service have complete control over their own contact information and decide what information they want to share with others on a person-by-person basis. Moreover, PlanetAll's service is compatible with personal information managers (PIMs) and personal digital assistants (PDAs), such as Microsoft Outlook and 3Com PalmPilot. Also, it has integrated its service within the sites of a number of Internet leaders, including Lycos and GeoCities, as well as numerous universities and professional associations. Amazon.com intends to operate PlanetAll as a wholly owned subsidiary located in Cambridge. Savage and the two cofounders will remain with the company.**

Junglee Corp (www.junglee.com).
The firm was founded in June 1996. The firm's breakthrough virtual database (VDB) technology derives from the founders' doctoral research carried out at Stanford University. Junglee's first deployment was CareerPost.com, the Washington Post Company's on-line recruitment site, in January 1997. Junglee carries more than 15 million items in the Junglee Shopping Guide and over 90,000 job listings in its Job Canopy. Junglee has developed breakthrough database technology that can dramatically enhance customers' ability to discover and choose from among millions of products on-line. To date, two of the markets it has targeted have been on-line retailing and on-line recruitment. Junglee's customers and partners in these markets include Yahoo!, Compaq, Snap!, six of the top seven newspaper companies, and many other new-media companies. All founders of Junglee are expected to remain with the company.

*Each of these three acquisitions, Bookpages, Telebook, and Internet Movie Database, will be accounted for under the purchase method of accounting. The company will incur total charges of approximately $55 million in connection with all three transactions. Consideration comprised of cash and common stock, and the company anticipates issuing an aggregate of approximately 540,000 shares of common stock as a result of these transactions.
**Amazon.com will acquire 100 percent of the outstanding shares and assume all outstanding options of Junglee and PlanetAll in exchange for equity having an aggregate value of approximately $280 million. Amazon.com will issue approximately 800,000 shares and assume all outstanding options in connection with the acquisition of PlanetAll; it anticipates accounting for this transaction as a pooling of interests. Amazon.com will issue approximately 1.6 million shares and assume all outstanding options in connection with the acquisition of Junglee and anticipates accounting for this transaction under the purchase method of accounting.

the people bandwidth is not constrained.... The single most important criterion that we use to acquire a new company is this: Who are the people behind this venture, and what is the people bandwidth of the acquired company going to be? We are looking for business athletes indoctrinated in this space and companies that have a culture that is common with ours.

The *Wall Street Journal*, however, casts some doubt on the company's prospects for success:

In the end, though, neither specialization nor branding may determine who succeeds in the on-line sales game. In the physical world, hard-core-comparison shopping has been left to a highly motivated faction of consumers willing to trudge between stores. But on the Web, it's become almost effortless. Today, a user can enter a title of a book on Yahoo! Inc.'s Visa Shopping Guide site which then queries multiple booksellers for prices and displays the result in a table. Hyperlink next to book prices lets users order the cheapest one at the click of a mouse. With comparison services proliferating elsewhere on the Web—and for dozens of other products—it's unclear whether a sterling brand like Amazon's will ultimately sway consumers when rock-bottom prices are so easy to spot.[26]

Bezos concedes that many challenges still confront him and his top-management team as they ponder the future moves by his firm:

It is hard to provide great customer service and experience for the customer. It is hard to grow the business. But when you combine these two, the complexity of operating increases exponentially. We are expanding our product line and broadening our geographic reach simultaneously, and there is a lot of execution risk when you try to do this. Moreover, many of our new initiatives will continue to require aggressive investment and entail significant execution challenges. However, that is the nature of this business.

APPENDIX: AMAZON.COM'S TOP-MANAGEMENT TEAM

Jeffrey P. Bezos, *Founder and Chief Executive Officer,* Jeff Bezos has always been interested in anything that can be revolutionized by computers. Intrigued by the amazing growth in the use of the Internet, Jeff created a business model that leveraged the Internet's unique ability to deliver huge amounts of information rapidly and efficiently. In 1994, he founded Amazon.com, Inc., an Internet retailer of books and other information-based products that offers what traditional retailers cannot: lower prices, authoritative selection, and a wealth of product information. Before heading west to start Amazon.com, Jeff worked at the intersection of computer science and finance, leading the development of computer systems that helped manage more than $250 billion in assets for Bankers Trust Company. He also helped build one of the most technically sophisticated quantitative hedge funds

on Wall Street for D. E. Shaw & Co. Jeff received a degree in electrical engineering and computer science, summa cum laude, from Princeton University in 1986. He is a member of Phi Beta Kappa.

George T. Aposporos, *Vice President, Business Development* George Aposporos joined Amazon.com in May 1997 as vice president of business development and is responsible for identifying and negotiating key strategic relationships for the company. Prior to joining Amazon.com, George was founder and president of Digital Brands, a strategic consulting and interactive marketing firm that has served clients such as Starbucks Coffee, Sybase, American Express, and BMG Entertainment. While at Digital Brands, he placed Starbucks in the first campaign to use animated advertising on America On-line. From March 1994 to August 1995, George was vice president of I.C.E., a Toronto-based multimedia developer and corporate communications firm, where he spearheaded involvement in interactive media, including development of the company's interactive television and Internet capabilities. From 1989 to 1994, he was an independent producer in a variety of media, including television, video, and CD-ROMs. George was an Olin Scholar at Wesleyan University.

Rick Ayre, *Vice President and Executive Editor* Rick Ayre joined Amazon.com in September 1996 as vice president and executive editor and is responsible for the editorial content and design of the Amazon.com Web site. Rick comes to Amazon.com from *PC Magazine*, the popular Ziff-Davis publication, where he served as executive editor for technology. Rick launched *PC Magazine* on the World Wide Web in March 1995. He was responsible for the print coverage of on-line technology, and he ran *PC Magazine*'s on-line services, including the *PC Magazine* on-line Web site and PC MagNet, part of ZD Net on Compuserve. During his five years at *PC Magazine*, Rick also held positions as the magazine's executive editor for software and as technical director for software in its labs, where he supervised all software product testing. Before joining the magazine, Rick served as chief of information resources management at the Highland Drive VAMC, a 750-bed hospital in Pittsburgh. He began his technology career while a Ph.D. candidate in psychiatric epidemiology at the University of Pittsburgh in the early 1980s. There he learned to program in Fortran to manipulate large data sets on an early DEC time-sharing system.

When the IBM PC was born, he quickly adopted one and taught himself to program in Pascal and to use dBASE. He was soon logging on to local BBS systems, and he's been working on-line ever since.

Joy D. Covey, *Chief Financial Officer* Joy Covey joined Amazon.com in December 1996 as chief financial officer and vice president of finance and administration. She is responsible for financial and management systems and reporting, and she also manages planning and analysis, legal, administrative, and investor relations, and human relations activities. Before joining Amazon.com, Joy was vice president of business development and vice president of operations, broadcast division, of Avid Technology, a leader in the digital media industry. From 1991 to 1995, she was the CFO of Digidesign, where she managed a successful IPO and eventual merger with Avid Technology. During her tenure, Digidesign achieved an annual growth of more than 50 percent and strong and consistent profitability and cash flow, and it strengthened its dominant position in the digital audio production systems market. Before she worked at Digidesign, Joy was a mergers and acquisitions associate at the investment bank of Wasserstein Perella & Co. and a certified public accountant with Arthur Young & Co. (currently Ernst & Young). She holds both a J.D. and an M.B.A. from Harvard, where she was a Baker Scholar, and a B.S. in business administration, summa cum laude, from California State University, Fresno.

Richard L. Dalzell, *Chief Information Officer* Richard Dalzell joined Amazon.com in August 1997 as chief information officer and is responsible for all Amazon.com information systems, including corporate networks, logistics, electronic buying, accounting, and data warehousing. Before joining Amazon.com, Rick was vice president of information systems for Wal-Mart Stores. He managed all merchandising and logistics systems, led the development of world-class supply chain systems, set the standard for international retailing and merchandising systems, and was instrumental in establishing the world's largest commercial decision-support and data-mining systems. From 1990 to 1994, Rick held several management positions within the information systems division at Wal-Mart. Prior to that, he spent three years as the business development manager for E-Systems and seven years as a teleprocessing officer in the U.S. Army. Rick re-

ceived a B.S. in engineering from the U.S. Military Academy, West Point, in 1979.

Mary Engstrom Morouse, *Vice President, Merchandising* Mary Engstrom Morouse joined Amazon.com in February 1997 as vice president of publisher affairs and became vice president of merchandising in April 1998. She is responsible for managing supplier relationships and direct purchasing. Before joining Amazon.com, Mary served as general manager of the security business unit and vice president of product marketing at Symantec Corporation, a developer of information management and productivity enhancement software. In these roles, she managed the development, production, testing, manufacturing, distribution, and marketing of Symantec's line of antivirus and security products, including the Norton AntiVirus line. From July 1989 to September 1994, she held several management positions at Microsoft Corporation, including group product manager for Microsoft Access, group product manager for Microsoft Project, and director of marketing in strategic relations. She received her B.A. in economics from the University of California, Berkeley, in 1984 and her M.B.A. from the Anderson Graduate School of Management at the University of California, Los Angeles, in 1989.

Sheldon J. Kaphan, *Chief Technology Officer* Shel Kaphan has served as Amazon.com's vice president and chief technology officer since March 1997. In this role, Shel is responsible for technical architecture and directing technical efforts. From October 1994 to March 1997, he was vice president of research and development for the company and was responsible for developing Amazon.com's core software and maintaining the company's Web site. Shel brings more than twenty years of experience in designing hardware and software systems and services to Amazon.com. Before joining the company, he held senior engineering positions at Kaleida Labs, Frox, and Lucid. He received a B.A. in mathematics, cum laude, from the University of California, Santa Cruz, in 1980.

John David Risher, *Senior Vice President, Product Development* David Risher joined Amazon.com in February 1997 as vice president of product development, responsible for developing new products and services. He was promoted to senior vice president of product development in December 1997 and now has overall responsibility for product development, marketing, editorial, and content licensing. Before joining Amazon.com, David was founder of and product unit manager for Microsoft Investor, Microsoft Corporation's Web site for personal investment. From 1991 to 1995, he held a variety of marketing and project management positions within the Microsoft Access product team, including Microsoft Access team manager. In this role, he managed all aspects of the product development team, including design, development, branding, advertising, and customer research, to produce Microsoft Access 95. From 1987 to 1989, David was an associate at the LEK Partnership, a corporate management consulting firm. He holds a B.A. in comparative literature, magna cum laude, from Princeton University and an M.B.A. from Harvard Business School.

Joel R. Spiegel, *Vice President, Engineering* Joel Spiegel joined Amazon.com in March 1997 as vice president of engineering and is responsible for all Web site software. From March 1995 to March 1997, Joel held several positions with Microsoft Corporation, including Windows 95 Multimedia development manager, Windows Multimedia group manager, and product unit manager for information retrieval. From June 1986 to March 1995, he held a variety of positions at Apple Computer, most recently as senior manager, and was responsible for new product development in the Apple Business Systems Division. Prior to that, he held software product development positions at a number of companies, including Hewlett-Packard and VisiCorp. During his career, Joel has had a hand in the development and delivery of a wide range of software products, including Windows 95 Multimedia, DirectX, Macintosh System 7 File Sharing, several versions of MacDraw, AppleSearch, Smalltalk–80 for the Macintosh, and VisiON. Joel holds a B.A. in biology, with honors, from Grinnell College.

Jimmy Wright, *Chief Logistics Officer* Jimmy Wright joined Amazon.com in July 1998 as vice president and chief logistics officer. He is responsible for all global supply chain activities, including managing the company's distribution centers, product purchasing, distribution, and shipping. Jimmy comes to Amazon.com with more than twenty-six years of experience in logistics management. He was recognized as one of the key logistics leaders within Wal-Mart Stores, the world's largest retailer

and a company globally known for its logistics excellence. He joined Wal-Mart in 1985 and served as vice president of distribution from 1990 until his retirement in 1998. During that time he was responsible for more than thirty regional and specialty distribution centers, which accounted for 38 million square feet of retail distribution space, staffed by more than 32,000 employees. Jimmy's career in logistics management began at the Fina Oil and Chemical Company, a branch of Petrofina S.A., based in Brussels. From 1972 to 1985, he held a variety of positions, including general manager of distribution. He received a B.B.A. in personnel management from the University of Texas in 1976.

Endnotes

1. "Who's Writing the Book on Web Business?" *Fast Company* (October–November 1996), 132–133.
2. Ibid.
3. In October 1997, Barnes & Noble and Amazon.com settled their respective lawsuits by saying that they would prefer to get back to business and compete in the marketplace rather than in the courtroom.
4. Much of the information discussed in this section, and the section that follows, is drawn from "Amazon.com," a Washington University Business School case, by Suresh Kotha and Emer Dooley, 1997.
5. *Publishers Weekly*, January 1, 1996.
6. Although the bestselling books get the bulk of the attention and marketing dollars, backlist books are considered the bread and butter of the industry. A backlist is the publishing company's catalog of books that have already appeared in print. Estimates indicated that as much as 25 to 30 percent of a publisher's revenues come from this source. Backlisted books have predictable sales, with occasional bumps, such as when a subject matter loses favor with consumers or when an author dies. Since these books require no editing and little promotion, they are generally profitable. Moreover, print runs are easier to predict, resulting in fewer returns to publishers.
7. *Publishers Weekly*, March 11, 1996. Superstores, originally confined to big metropolitan areas, were increasingly entering markets with populations of 150,000 or less. Industry estimates indicated that superstores had to make around $200 a square foot to turn a profit. For example, a typical Barnes & Noble superstore needed $3 million to $4 million in sales revenues to break even. Some industry observers questioned whether such cities can support these mammoth stores and whether superstores in these locations could sell enough books to turn a profit.
8. *Philadelphia Business Journal*, September 27, 1996.
9. "A Nonchain Bookstore Bucks the Tide," *New York Times*, September 8, 1996.
10. *Standard and Poor's Industry Surveys*, July 20, 1995.
11. *Christian Science Monitor*, September 18, 1996.

12. *Wall Street Journal,* May 16, 1996.
13. *Fast Company* (October–November 1996).
14. Ibid.
15. Industry observers note that although Amazon discounts most books, it levies a $3 service charge per order, plus 95 cents per book. Furthermore, it can take Amazon a week to deliver a book that isn't a bestseller, and even longer for the most esoteric titles. Also, some people don't like providing their credit card number over the Internet.
16. *Fast Company* (October–November 1996).
17. *Upside* (October 1996).
18. "Amazon.com forges new sales channel," *Web Week*, August 19, 1996.
19. *Financial Times*, October 7, 1996.
20. *Wall Street Journal*, October 21, 1997.
21. "The Baron of Books," *Business Week*, June 29, 1998.
22. Ingram's experimental foray into on-line retailing floundered because many of the new on-line entrants were unable to attract enough customers. Notes *Business Week*, "Ingram stirred a backlash among its existing clientele, who were clearly not happy with the prospect of having to compete with other low-cost clones."
23. Bertelsmann AG is the world's third largest media conglomerate, with $14 billion in sales in 1997. In July 1998, Bertelsmann acquired U.S.-based Random House Publishing. This single largest publisher of English-language books owns Doubleday, Bantam Books, Dell Publishing, and several other publishing companies.
24. *Internet World*, October 12, 1998.
25. "In Looking to Branch Out, Amazon Goes Out on a Limb," *Wall Street Journal*, May 12, 1998.
26. *Wall Street Journal*, May 12, 1998.

RealNetworks

This case was prepared by Margaret Johnston and Suresh Kotha of the University of Washington.

RealNetworks is a streaming-media software firm located in Seattle, Washington. The firm's streaming software products enable multimedia content developers and others to stream both audio and video content over the Internet and intranets to end-users.[1] End users, in turn, can view this content with the firm's "player" software, know as RealPlayer. Within three years of its founding, the firm has managed to create a strong demand for its streaming server software products and become a leader in this important segment. Many aspects of its business model are being imitated by competitors.

The firm permits users to download its Real-Player software for free at its Web site (http://www.real.com). With more than 40,000 downloads a day, the firm claims that more than 18 million RealPlayers have been distributed globally. Recently, the firm signed an exclusive licensing agreement with Microsoft, the world's dominant PC software firm, to bundle RealPlayer with every copy of the Internet Explorer that Microsoft distributes. Microsoft's Internet Explorer is the world's second most popular Internet browser software, after Netscape's Navigator. However, despite the rapid growth and well-entrenched position of RealNetworks, its top management faces a host of challenges.

This case discusses the genesis of RealNetworks, its rapid growth, and its approach to competition in audio and video streaming in the Internet and intranet markets. It highlights the issues that confront the firm as its top management formulates a strategy for continued rapid growth despite various uncertainties and challenges.

COMPANY BACKGROUND

Founded in April 1994 as Progressive Networks, the firm quickly established itself as a pioneer and industry leader in the delivery of real-time audio and video content over the Internet. The firm was the brainchild of Rob Glaser, a former Microsoft executive. Early in 1994, Glaser was toying with the idea of using interactive multimedia technology to create a "cable channel focused on politics and culture." Robert Reid, who has chronicled the early growth of the Web and Glaser's contributing role in its evolution, points out that

> The notion of interactive television (ITV) was by then [early 1994] all the rage. Many smug pundits were even viewing the PC as downright dowdy. For his part, Rob was at first agnostic about whether to use ITV or the PC as the medium for his half-formed vision. Then he encountered Mosaic—a 'total epiphany,' he remembers. He almost immediately concluded that 'interactive TV was going to be stillborn,' and that 'the whole mechanism that Mosaic had used to bootstrap itself, A, was a big deal in its own right, and B, once established, itself could be used as a bootstrapping mechanism for other stuff.' That *other stuff,* or rather some of it, turned out to be RealAudio.[2]

According to a report in the *Wall Street Journal,* "Mr. Glaser sank about $1 million of his own money into a start-up that would first produce software for compressing and transmitting sound. With additional funding from friends such as Lotus founder Mitch Kapor, RealAudio 1.0 quickly made its debut in April 1995."[3] That was exactly one year since Glaser founded the firm.

Despite some disdain from the Internet elite because of the tinny sound, which created an unsatisfying experience, RealAudio 1.0 broke the Web's sound barrier. Soon the product began to win industry favor. Notes Reid:

> RealAudio debuted on the Web on April 10, 1995, along with content from ABC News, National Public Radio (NPR), and others. Tiny Progressive was soon covered by such publications as the *New York Times*, the *Wall Street Journal*, and the *Economist*. *USA Today* characterized RealAudio as 'The technology of the '20s meeting the technology of the '90s,' while *Time* [magazine] meanwhile assured the image-conscious that 'Glaser's system is not just for geeks.'[4]

Within a month, Netscape, the world's largest browser software firm, began shipping RealAudio as part of its Navigator browser software. By August of that year, Progressive Networks had sold its server products to several large Internet media companies, including Starwave, Ziff-Davis, and ABC News.

Just a couple of months later, in October 1995, the firm released a newer and more advanced version of its server and player (RealAudio 2.0) products. Its player software won the *Internet World* magazine's "Outstanding Software Product of the Year" award in April 1996. By September 1996, Progressive Networks released yet another version, RealAudio 3.0. Shortly thereafter Prodigy, a leading on-line service provider, began bundling the firm's player software with its custom browser. Although a handful of other firms provided audio-streaming solutions, none matched the rapid growth of RealNetworks.

Having established itself as a leading provider of audio-streaming software, Progressive Networks turned its attention to video streaming. According to a report in *Wired*,

> In December 1995, while attempting to vacation in Hawaii, Glaser got some email from a two-person San Francisco company, FreeVu, which had an Internet videoconferencing tool under development. Glaser took a look, was impressed, and persuaded FreeVu's principals to sign on as Progressive employees. RealVideo's development effort had begun.[5]

In February 1997, the firm released a product that combined video and audio streaming, Real-Player 4.0. By then, however, several video-streaming providers—for instance, Xing Technologies, VDOnet, Vosaic, and VXtreme—were already marketing products on the World Wide Web. Recognizing this, Glaser signed an exclusive licensing agreement with Microsoft to bundle RealPlayer with Internet Explorer. With such an agreement, the firm has had little difficulty in achieving a dominant position in video streaming on the Internet.

In September 1997, the firm changed its name from Progressive Networks to RealNetworks and filed for an initial public offering (IPO). The IPO was undertaken to raise capital to continue funding product development. During this period, the firm also introduced the fifth major upgrade of its server (RealSystem) and player (RealPlayer) software.[6] On October 3, 1997, RealNetworks went public on the NASDAQ Stock Exchange with a 3.5 million share offering. The stock opened at $12.50 per share and then moved to $19 per share before settling around $16. Net proceeds for the offering were approximately $38.5 million. The stock has remained healthy throughout the fall of 1997, despite the slump in over-the-counter stocks of other Internet companies. Within a three-month time period, Glaser had successfully partnered with Microsoft, launched a major upgrade of the product system, and had taken RealNetworks public.

With frequent product upgrades, RealNetworks has garnered widespread support and won many industry awards. For example, writing about its latest product upgrade, Allen Weiner, an analyst with Dataquest, notes that the firm has demonstrated superiority in all areas of streaming:

> With the release of RealSystem 5.0, RealNetworks is taking the streaming media market by storm. . . . RealNetworks' emphasis on innovation, coupled with its cross-platform architecture, incredible brand recognition and majority market share, continues to place it at the forefront of the streaming media market."[7]

Most importantly, RealNetworks has managed to compile an impressive list of companies that use its server software to transmit multimedia content over the Internet. This list includes all three major U.S. television networks (NBC, ABC, and CBS), two major long-distance telephone carriers, the U.S. Senate, and many of the biggest companies in the music industry, including Sony. In just four years since its founding, RealNetworks had produced more than eight product varieties and grown to more than 350 employees. For 1997, the firm as a whole reported total revenue of $32.7 million, an increase of 134 percent from $14.0 million in 1996. However, the net loss was $11.2 million for 1997, compared with $3.8 million for the previous year (see Table 1).

PRODUCTS, MARKETS, AND COMPETITION

RealNetworks competes in two different markets—the Internet and the intranet markets. The potential Internet customers include the Web site creators and the end users that access those Web sites. The potential intranet customers include all businesses with internal networks that connect employees.

TABLE 1

Summary Consolidated Financial Data

	Period from February 9, 1994 (inception) to December 31, 1994	Year Ended December 31,		Nine Months Ended September 30,	
		1995	1996	1996	1997
	(in thousands, except per share data)				
Statement of Operations Data:					
Total net revenues	$ —	$ 1,812	$14,012	$ 8,274	$22,417
Total cost of revenues	—	62	2,185	969	4,609
Gross profit	—	1,750	11,827	7,305	17,808
Operating loss	(545)	(1,595)	(4,016)	(2,475)	(9,759)
Net loss	(545)	(1,501)	(3,789)	(2,315)	(8,575)
Pro forma net loss per share[1]			$ (0.14)		$ (0.32)
Shares used to compute pro forma net loss per share(1)			27,779		28,315

	December 31, 1996	September 30, 1997	
		Actual	As Adjusted[2]
		(in thousands)	
Balance Sheet Data:			
Cash, cash equivalents and short-term investments	$ 19,595	$ 67,648	$108,529
Working capital	16,893	50,762	91,643
Total assets	26,468	84,372	125,253
Redeemable, convertible preferred stock	23,153	49,278	—
Shareholders' equity (deficit)	(3,320)	(8,089)	82,070

1. For an explanation of pro forma net loss per share and the number of shares used to compute pro forma net loss per share, see Note 1 of Notes to Consolidated Financial Statements.

2. As adjusted to give effect to the (i) conversion of all outstanding shares of Series A Common Stock, Series B Common Stock, Series C Common Stock, Series A Preferred Stock, Series B Preferred Stock, Series C Preferred Stock and Series D Preferred Stock into Common Stock and Series E Preferred Stock into Special Common Stock, in each case on closing of the offering; (ii) sale by the Company of the 3,000,000 shares of Common Stock offered hereby at the initial public offering price of $12.50 per share; (iii) application of the estimated net proceeds of the offering; and (iv) issuance of 998,058 shares of Common Stock upon exercise of outstanding warrants at an average exercise price of $6.97 per share (for an aggregate of $6,956,000). Excludes up to 3,709,305 shares of Special Common Stock (representing additional cash and shareholders' equity of up to $50,001,431) issuable on exercise of the Series E Warrant.

Source: RealNetworks Prospectus, November 21, 1997.

TABLE 2

Major Features of RealSystem 5.0.

The RealSystem 5.0 software includes these major features:

- *Animation.* In addition to streaming videos and audio messages, customers could stream animation clips, such as cartoons and computer aided drawing (CAD) sequences. Animation sequences can be synchronized with RealAudio.

- *Ad Insertion and Rotation.* Moving advertisements can appear along with any video or animation sequence. If viewers use their mouse to click on the advertisement, they could be sent to the advertiser's Web site.

- *User Registration and Tracking.* For Web site creators who wish to offer video and audio streams to select viewers only, the server software can detect who is making the request and track usage. This is particularly useful to Web site developers who wish to charge a fee for viewing content.

- *Fast-Modem Optimization.* The 5.0 RealVideo system is designed for optimal use with the fast 56.6 Kbps modems that have appeared on the market.

The RealSystem 5.0-server software is priced from $700 to $21,000 depending on how many streams can be sent at one time. The lower-priced products target customers who want to make audio and video available on their Web site. The more expensive line of professional server products targets ISPs, commercial Web developers and content providers. The firm also offers a free trial version of the server software that streams to sixty viewers at one time. This free software can be downloaded directly from the firm's Web site.

The Internet Market

Core Products   The firm's core products include the RealPlayer and RealSystem server software. The RealSystem server software allows developers to display, or "stream," video content to viewers via the Internet. The RealPlayer software enables individuals to view a video clip being "streamed" from a server. The player software can be downloaded for free directly from the firm's Web site. The firm also offers RealPlayer Plus, an enhanced version, for $29. This version offers several easy to use features including memory buttons that are not included in the free version. It can be purchased separately in a retail software store or purchased bundled with products such as modems. It can also be downloaded and paid for directly from RealNetworks.

When using the RealSystem product, customers have the choice of either streaming video "live" or "on-demand." In order to stream video on-demand to Internet end users (viewers), customers or developers must take three steps. First, using the RealPublisher tool that is included with the RealSystem software they convert the video content into a digital-video file. Special video-editing equipment, not included with the RealSystem software, is needed for this process. Second, this file must be uploaded onto a server computer that end users can reach. When end users link to the server by means of a browser with RealPlayer software (a plug-in) properly installed, the player software will automatically begin streaming the video from the server onto the viewer's computer.[8]

As noted earlier, the most recent product release from RealNetworks is RealSystem 5.0. This version includes capabilities that were not part of earlier products (see Table 2). Since its release in the fourth quarter of 1997, the number of Web pages using streaming media has grown by 50 percent. According to industry experts, about 80 percent of those Web pages now use RealAudio, RealVideo, or RealFlash content.

Despite the growing popularity of video streaming, however, the quality of the video streamed over the Internet does not compare with that of broadcast TV.[9] Although the quality of the streaming video has improved with each new product release, the video images still look jerky when customers use a 28.8 Kbps modem to access such content. But for customers who use higher-bandwidth access lines such as an ISDN connection, the video quality is markedly better.

Other Products and Services   In addition to selling software products, RealNetworks offers a range of consulting services, which include training sessions on setting up and administering the firm's server software and on creating RealAudio and RealVideo content. For large customer installations, the RealNetworks consulting staff often assist in redesigning the customer's information systems to best adapt and incorporate its streaming technology. Although some of the consulting services offered by the firm are free, many are fee based, and charges for such services vary with individual client requirements.

An additional source of revenue for the firm is its content aggregation and hosting business on the Internet. On the firm's Web site, customers can view different types of content (audio or video) assembled on many different Web properties. Although many are managed by RealNetworks, some of them are owned and maintained by others. But all of these sites are hosted by RealNetworks (see Table 3 for a detailed list). By combining different sites, the firm hopes to demonstrate the capability and superior quality of its streaming technology solutions (relative to its competitors), provide exclusive access to interesting multimedia content to Web surfers, and generate revenues from advertisement sales based on the site's ability to attract traffic. Finally, the firm operates a virtual store called RealStore, where customers can purchase products such as content-creation utilities, training videos, modems, and other software products.

Competitive factors in this market include the quality and reliability of software; features provided for creating, editing and adapting multimedia content; the ease of use and interactive user features provided as part of the system; issues pertaining to scalability and cost per user; and compatibility with the user's existing network components and software systems.

Customers   The firm's Internet customers can be broadly segmented into two groups: server and player customers. These two segments can be further divided by customer requirements. For the player segment, there are three basic types of customers: beginner/light users, experienced/light

users, and advanced users. Beginner/light users are interested in a viewing solution that is easy to install and use. These customers are likely to choose the $29 RealPlayer Plus product over the free version distributed by the firm. This is because this Plus version includes a manual that provides installation and setup instructions. The more experienced/light users are likely to choose the free version of the RealPlayer product. Finally, the advanced users may or may not choose the Plus product depending on how much they value the extra features offered by that version relative to competitor products.

The Internet server customers can be divided into five specific segments:

- *Media companies* such as the *Wall Street Journal*, CBS, Fox News, and Warner Brothers, which create content and fund parts of the infrastructure for delivering that content.

- *Commercial Web site developers*, or businesses with Web sites used for revenue generation, such as Yahoo!, Lands' End, and numerous others. Some of these sites generate revenue through transactions, whereas others focus on generating advertising revenues based on the traffic attracted to the sites.

- *Noncommercial Web site developers*, or firms that operate Web sites to distribute information. Examples include government agencies, schools, and private clubs that could potentially include streaming content on their sites.

- *Internet service providers (ISPs)*, or businesses that sell access to the Internet and also frequently offer Web site development and management services to their customers. These types of businesses may wish to offer their customers streaming capabilities and thus purchase streaming server products directly from RealNetworks.

- *Streaming service providers*, or businesses that exist solely to develop and manage sites with streaming content. US-West Enterprise Networking and Digital Nation are examples of "hosting" service businesses.

As of December 1997, the estimated number of Internet users in the world was 40 million. According to NetRatings, a market research firm, by the year

TABLE 3

Content Offerings at RealNetworks

RealNetwork's offerings include the following:

- **Timecast,** a guide to RealAudio and RealVideo content and programming information. The site provides links to more than 2,500 Web sites, including more than 500 radio and television stations where customers can view multimedia content created using RealNetworks' software products.

- **MusicNet,** a preview site featuring more than 1,000 songs from nearly 400 artists. The site is organized in ten categories.

- **Daily Briefing,** the Internet's first personalized, on-demand audio and video newscast. It allows customers to design their own custom streaming media newscasts from more than thirty-five short programs in the areas of news, sports, entertainment, weather, and business/technology, and to receive custom newscasts daily. Daily Briefing providers include NBC News, The Weather Channel, CBS/SportsLine, and Warner Bros.

- **Film.com,** the leading source of professional movie reviews on the Internet, with more than sixty critics. The site provides in-depth information about, and streaming media clips of, movies, including reviews and previews.

- **LiveConcerts.com,** a Web site operated in cooperation with House of Blues. It offers live streamed music concerts, album previews, and archives containing streaming music. It also provides up-to-date concert schedules.

- **Web Active,** a Web site that focuses on giving a voice to progressive political and social opinion, news, and activism on the Internet.

- **Real Planet,** an international guide to RealAudio and RealVideo content. It has ongoing features of events from around the globe.

2000 this number should grow to 200 million. In January 1998, a little more than 21 percent of all U.S. households had access to the Internet. Of these, about a quarter had signed up only in the preceding six months. Hence, the size of the potential consumer market for the firm's products is growing rapidly, but so is the competition.

Competition   The market for software and services for the Internet (and intranet) is relatively new, constantly evolving, and becoming intensely competitive. In a broad sense, audio and video streaming technology faces competition from traditional media such as TV and radio broadcasting, and storage devices such as VCRs and CD-ROMs. A major limitation of current streaming technology is its inability to deliver the video quality similar to that of broadcast TV. Consequently, these existing alternatives limit the immediate market potential for streaming products. However, the appeal of

streaming media is its potential to deliver multimedia content directly to users *on demand*.

RealNetworks' direct competitors include companies such as Microsoft, VDOnet, Xing Technology, VivoActive Software, and Vosaic. All these companies offer products and services similar to those of RealNetworks (see Table 4 for third-party reviews of the products). Additionally, a large number of potential competitors such as media companies and browser developers may aggressively pursue this market.

A competitive threat to RealNetworks is the likely integration of streaming software with other widely used applications. Although Microsoft currently ships its Internet Explorer browser software with a RealNetworks' media player, it has announced that future versions of its operating systems will include a built-in streaming-viewer product. For example, a product labeled "Windows Media Player" is expected to be included in the

TABLE 4

Streaming Software Competitors

Company	Streaming Video Product	Server Price	Excerpts from Product Reviews
RealNetworks	RealVideo 5.0	$650 and up	"With RealSystem 5.0, RealNetworks continues the pattern of innovation started in 1994 when the company introduced multimedia to the Internet with RealAudio. RealSystem 5.0 features creative advanced functionality that will soon prove invaluable to high-volume video producers. At the same time, Real, facing competitive pressure from Microsoft's free product, NetShow, is offering free streaming audio and video to lower-volume producers who don't need the special features offered by RealSystem 5.0." (*PC Magazine,* October 10, 1997)
Microsoft	NetShow 2.0	Free	"It's very much a work in progress, offering average-quality video, a server with network-utilization safeguards, and a well-featured but slightly irritating player. It's all free, too." (*PC Magazine,* October 7, 1997)
VDOnet	VDOLive 2.1	$299 and up	"If you're looking for a stable, server-based technology for your intranet, consider VDOnet's VDOLive 2.1. This veteran of the nascent streaming-video market offers high-quality video and a wide array of configuration options, including the ability to limit network use by user number or stream count. Only the higher quality of RealVideo's and VivoActive's video and the better functionality of RealVideo make those products stand out above VDOLive. And if you're on a budget, you'll be pleased with VDOLive's price." (*PC Magazine,* October 7, 1997)
VivoActive Software	VivoActive 2.0	$695	"For users who don't want to worry about server maintenance, VivoActive Software's VivoActive 2.0 is an inexpensive, high-quality, serverless technology that emphasizes ease of use and simplicity over a mass of features. VivoActive 2.0 has no server component, so VivoActive can't protect network utilization by limiting users or video-transfer bandwidth. With a total implementation cost of $695 for an unlimited number of streams, VivoActive is an ideal, inexpensive choice for smaller companies." (*PC Magazine,* October 7, 1997)
Vosaic	MediaSuite 1.04	$150 and up	"Although a promising entry in the streaming-video market and particularly adept at high-motion video, Vosaic MediaSuite 1.04 ultimately can't compete with such products as RealVideo or VDOLive on most intranet applications. Vosaic ranked near the bottom on our talking-head tests, and though the server, player, and encoder are functional, they're not as polished or feature-rich as those of other systems. You don't have to pay for the server, but at $150 per stream, Vosaic's technology is still relatively expensive." (*PC Magazine,* October 7, 1997)
Xing Technology	StreamWorks 3.0	$3000 and up	"StreamWorks 3.0.252 produces high-quality video at high bandwidths but doesn't scale down well, resulting in last-place finishes on our jury tests. The $3,000 price for 50 seats is reasonable, but you probably shouldn't consider StreamWorks unless you transmit the bulk of your videos at bandwidths of 256 Kbps or higher." (*PC Magazine,* October 7, 1997)

forthcoming Windows '98. Furthermore, Microsoft has also announced plans to release a server product for video and audio streaming, known as Site-Server. It intends to provide its player and server products for free. Although some Web browsers already include a "media player" component, industry observers predict that all Web browsers will include a streaming-media viewer in the near future.

RealNetworks' products also compete, to a lesser degree, with nonstreaming audio- and video-delivery technologies such as AVI and QuickTime, and indirectly with delivery systems such as Flash, marketed by Macromedia, a leading producer of animation and multimedia authoring software. Flash is a product used for delivering text-based training content on the Internet.

The Intranet Market

Products   There are two basic products targeted at intranet customers: the server, and player products. Businesses interested in streaming video and audio content can purchase both the server and player as a bundle. Such bundles are available in five configurations. The low-end solution bundle is free, offering the ability to stream 10 video clips at one time. This product is called the Intranet Solution RealServer 5.0. The second bundle, the RealSystem Intranet Solution IS100, allows 100 simultaneous streams and is priced around $5,000. It offers features not available in the free version. The third bundle, the IS600, is priced at $25,000 and supports 600 streams. The two largest bundles, the IS2500 and the IS7500, support 2,500 and 7,500 streams and cost $50,000 and $100,000, respectively. These prices are for annual licensing fees. In addition to the licensing fees, customers have the option to purchase support and upgrade contracts ranging from $2,000 to $40,000, depending on the bundle purchased initially.

Customers   Although there are many types of businesses buying solutions from RealNetworks, the firm targets companies with an intranet. Intranets are private computer networks that use Internet technology to connect employees within the firm. Specifically, RealNetworks focuses on businesses that can afford a $50,000 solution and frequently create multimedia content for company-wide dissemination. Many businesses recognize the benefits of streaming multimedia content to em-

ployees in many different locations nationally and globally. RealNetworks promotes two streaming video applications for such firms:

- *Corporate Communications.* Businesses can use RealVideo and RealAudio to distribute companywide information. For example, Boeing uses RealVideo to provide employees with the latest information on their company, products, and industry. Boeing estimates that it saved nearly $1 million in 1997 on replication and distribution costs of multimedia content alone.

- *Training.* Businesses can use RealVideo to stream training material to employees. Such video training modules can be viewed on demand by employees in different locations. For example, General Electric uses RealVideo to create video-based interactive product training programs for new employees. Such programs are distributed over the firm's intranets.

RealNetworks sells RealSystem Intranet Solution products directly to customers. For large customers, RealNetworks has outside account executives and consultants available to visit the customers on site. These account executives and consultants study the customers' requirements before making a recommendation.

Competition   VDOnet, Xing Technologies, and Microsoft compete with RealNetworks in the intranet market. All three competitors have streaming-video products targeted at businesses with corporate networks. The technologies offered by VDOnet and Xing Technologies are designed specifically for higher-speed networks and thus are more of a threat to RealNetworks in the intranet market than in the Internet market.[10]

APPROACH TO COMPETITION

Glaser's objective is to build RealNetworks into a "leading media streaming company, providing software and services that enable the delivery of a broad range of multimedia content over the Internet and Intranet, thereby facilitating the evolution of the Internet into a mass communications and commerce medium." He and his top-management team plan to achieve this objective by (1) making the "Real" brand name ubiquitous on the Internet and corporate intranets; (2) developing and fostering alliances and partnerships to promote multimedia streaming; (3) shaping industry standards for streaming; and (4) funding innovation in streaming technology to stay ahead of the competition.

Brand Ubiquity

From its inception, RealNetworks has chosen to offer its RealPlayer software to individuals free of charge. RealNetworks has done so to promote the widespread adoption of its client (player) software and to speed up the acceptance of the Internet as a mass-communications medium for streaming multimedia content. Any person with a PC and an Internet connection could download a free copy of the firm's player software to view and listen to video and audio clips. "Our belief has always been that we benefit tremendously by pursuing the most rapid and broadest paths to growing the streaming-media market," Glaser says. "You can expect us to continue to be oriented towards ubiquity."[11] Glaser adds that he "was really struck by the fact that if you look at the long-term survivors against Microsoft—Novell, Oracle, even Intuit . . . they didn't try to make all their money on initial-use client software. They made their money on a mix of things."[12]

Reid offers an additional insight regarding the giveaways:

> The genesis of Rob's decision to give away his client software lay in his decade . . . [of experience at] Microsoft. There he learned that if you make your business beholden to making money from the initial-use client software, the result could be easily that Microsoft would just sort of suck away your core business, either by putting a feature in Windows, or by aggregating a set of things like with Office.[13]

According to Reid, although Glaser's business model appears similar to that pioneered by Netscape, it was in no way inspired by it. Indeed, Glaser settled on this model months before Netscape shipped the Navigator.[14]

To encourage free RealPlayer downloads and RealPlayer Plus sales, RealNetworks advertises heavily on the Internet and also promotes its brand name with many public relations activities. As mentioned earlier, it has managed to attract the attention of many mainstream journalists from newspapers and magazines including the *New York Times*, the *Wall Street Journal*, *USA Today*, *Time*, and *Wired*. Also, the firm's products have garnered many awards at industry trade shows, thus increasing its visibility. It is not surprising, therefore, that Glaser confidently calls the "Real" brand "one of the most widely recognized brands on the Internet."

Alliances and Partnerships

Under Glaser's leadership, RealNetworks has formed numerous partnerships and alliances. It has signed development partnerships with others to ensure that its products work well when integrated with their technologies. When using a streaming media solution, server customers in particular are mixing this technology with hardware and software products bought from others. For example, the firm partnered with Microsoft to ensure that the RealPlayer and RealSystem products work in Windows 95 and Windows NT environments. RealNetworks has also partnered with Sun Microsystems, the makers of the Solaris operating systems to ensure that its products would operate smoothly in a Unix environment. The firm also makes its products compatible with machines that use the Macintosh operating system. Additionally, the firm has agreements with Macromedia, the largest provider of animation-editing software, to transmit animated material over the Internet.

RealNetworks also partners with technology companies to create combined services. In August of 1997, for example, it signed a joint-venture agreement with MCI and launched the *Real Broadcast Network*. This pilot service, created by combining the RealSystem technology with MCI's worldwide Internet network infrastructure, offers broadcasting services for content developers to deliver tens of thousands of video streams simultaneously on the Internet. MCI, which owns a significant portion of the Internet infrastructure (or backbone), has upgraded its infrastructure to facilitate rapid streaming. This was done by strategically placing RealNetworks splitter and multicast technology throughout its network. Such devices eliminate bottlenecks by allowing computer users to access a video/audio feed from the closest of MCI's nine U.S. locations. RealNetworks and MCI are targeting media companies and *Fortune* 1000 companies that might use this service for internal employee training or to post new product announcements on the Web. ABC News' on-line service, for example, used the service to broadcast audio and video clips accompanying a text story of the 1997 UPS strike. Other customers include Atlantic Records, ESPN, and Home & Garden Television.[15] The service costs up to $8,500 a month. The cost is much higher for continuous broadcasting.

Shaping Evolving Industry Standards

The firm's efforts have also focused on shaping industry standards regarding streaming technology and protocols. An aspect of the firm's rapidly evolving marketplace is the trend toward open standards and protocols for streaming software. Until recently, only users with a RealNetworks viewer could watch video and audio clips streamed from the firm's server products. RealNetworks has also joined other important industry players (for example, Microsoft and Sun Microsystems) in their efforts to set protocol, transmission, and compression standards. RealNetworks and Microsoft, for instance, have taken special pains to define the industry standards for streaming products. Their goal is to ensure that any server software can send streams (audio and video) to any player. Emphasizing the need for common standards, Microsoft's soon-to-be-released Windows Media Player will be able to play streams from RealNetworks' server software. At that time, the NetShow, a Microsoft server product, will play video streaming from RealNetworks' server products. Similarly, RealPlayers could play video streaming from Microsoft's NetShow server.

On July 21, 1997, Microsoft acquired a 10 percent nonvoting minority stake in RealNetworks for $30 million. However, Microsoft's new NetShow product is a direct competitor to RealVideo, RealNetworks' video-streaming software. The two companies declared that the partnership was necessary if an industry standard was going to be formed. According to Glaser,

> We see a real pathway forward to turn the Internet into a mass medium. We have worked successfully with Microsoft in the past, and this agreement brings our relationship to a new level. The ultimate goal is for Microsoft's and Progressive's streaming formats to become fully compatible, allowing all on-line audio and video

broadcasts to be interpreted by both companies' players.

As Rich Tong, a Microsoft vice president points out: "The user only wants it to work.... So it is good business to work with RealNetworks to set standards for compatibility and expand the market for all of us."[16]

Several of the streaming technologies that RealNetworks has developed have been submitted to Internet standards committees for review. Although none of these standards have been fully accepted by the players in the industry so far, many are highly favored.[17] The firm aggressively pursues the acceptance of these standards in order to gain more industry recognition as well as more market share. However, because of RealNetworks' 80 percent market share, its approach to streaming has become the de facto industry standard.

Technological Innovation

Whenever a competitor releases a new product, the industry observers quickly rush to compare it with those of RealNetworks. Therefore, to stay ahead of competition, the firm must make frequent product upgrades and improvements. It devotes a substantial portion of its resources to developing new products and product features, expanding and improving its fundamental streaming technology, and strengthening its technological expertise. For example, during the fiscal year that ended December 31, 1996, and the six months that ended June 30, 1997, RealNetworks spent 34 percent and 41 percent of its total net revenues on research and development activities. As of August 1997, it had 90 employees, or 32 percent of its work force, engaged in research and development activities. RealNetworks' executives say that the firm must hire additional skilled software engineers to further its research and development efforts. Given its small size, such efforts are increasingly straining the firm's resources and capabilities.

Part of RealNetworks' R&D strategy is to hire the brightest, most experienced developers and executives in the world (see Appendix A for list of executives hired to assist Glaser in managing RealNetworks). Glaser sees this strategy as essential, for, he says, "In an industry where intellectual capital is the primary asset of the firm, the people you hire can make or break the firm. Developers must be constantly nurtured and trained in order to turn out new technology at the speed of light."

CHALLENGES IN GOING FORWARD

As the top management of RealNetworks looks to the future, it confronts several new challenges.

Bandwidth Constraints

The growth of the streaming-video market is hampered by bandwidth constraints of the Internet and World Wide Web. Most home users access the WWW with 28.8 kbps or slower modems. At these low-transmission speeds, users cannot play video without distortion. However, industry experts predict that this situation is likely to change as Internet service providers and telecommunications firms such as MCI and AT&T upgrade their infrastructure to provide customers with technologies that provide greater bandwidth to WWW surfers. Also, the increasing use of technologies such as ISDN telephone lines, cable modems, and direct-broadcast satellite services may help alleviate the current bandwidth constraints.

More troubling, however, is the fact that a majority of Web surfers are unwilling to pay for content (print, video or audio) offered on the Internet. Although a few exceptions such as the *Wall Street Journal Interactive* exist, most of the content providers have been unable to convert traffic on their Web sites into paying members.

Balancing Competition and Cooperation

Despite its large market share, RealNetworks still faces significant threats from Microsoft and others. When Microsoft acquired a minority stake in RealNetworks, a surprising aspect of this agreement was that Microsoft also licensed the RealAudio and RealVideo 4.0 programming code for an additional $30 million (see Appendix B for details of this agreement). Such a close relationship between RealNetworks and Microsoft has left many industry analysts wondering whether the firm might end up in the situation of trying to make money on technology that Microsoft gives away for free. Glaser offered this view of the situation:

If we don't execute well, it could turn out to be a bad deal. . . . But face it—if we don't execute well, we would have been in just as much trouble without the deal. And if we do execute— if we keep driving our standards forward independently and remain at the forefront of the market and the technology—it'll turn out to be an amazing deal. There are pitfalls. But if you want a sure thing, you should take a job at the post office, right?[18]

On August 5, 1997, just fifteen days after the Microsoft-RealNetworks partnership announcement, Microsoft purchased VXtreme, one of RealNetworks' biggest competitors on the Internet. Microsoft plans to use the acquired technology to further develop its products in this segment. For example, Microsoft is expected to release NetShow, its streaming server product later this year. Earlier in November of 1997, Microsoft had announced that it would include its streaming server software for free with all Microsoft NT server product.

The Department of Justice, along with several industry analysts, has expressed concerns about such tactics. It has been suggested that Microsoft is effectively trying to drive its streaming competitors out of the server business. Alan Weiner, an analyst with Dataquest, states that "Microsoft is taking dead aim at RealNetworks in terms of the dominance of the streaming video market. As the pipes get fatter, streaming media servers will be the backbone to serve all kinds of content in the future. It's important to establish dominance now."[19] To many analysts it is unclear whether RealNetworks can compete successfully with Microsoft's free and heavily marketed NetShow product. However, according to a *Wall Street Journal* report in early 1998, Microsoft "may decide to charge for the latest version of NetShow coming out this year, which would be good for RealNetworks. Microsoft will also continue to bundle RealNetworks' player software with Microsoft browser, which is good for RealNetworks. And the day after RealNetworks' Sun deal, Microsoft announced an agreement with RealNetworks' server software, also good for RealNetworks."[20]

Continuing to Innovate

It is in this uncertain environment that RealNetworks has begun planning yet another upgrade of its player and server software. The firm hopes that by incorporating new capabilities, such as animation, ad insertion, and pay-per-view features, it can maintain its dominant position for streaming software. However, such product enhancements cost money, which leads to the firm's most important challenge: improving its profitability to ensure acceptable financial returns for its new stockholders.

Despite rapid growth, RealNetworks remains unprofitable. The firm posted a $12 million deficit for 1997 and is unlikely to show a profit until the end of 1999."[21] With continuous losses, it is unclear whether the firm can continue to fund the future product developments. Compounding this issue is the ever-increasing cost of developing new upgrades to its existing software. Furthermore, finding sophisticated talent in an increasingly tight labor market is expensive.

As the novelty of the Internet wears off, customers may start demanding better-quality video streaming. The cost of funding new product developments to further advance streaming technology and add features is becoming expensive. In such an environment, management must decide whether a focus on winning market share can continue to be a viable strategy. Some at RealNetworks concede that the firm may have to look for partners to undertake joint-product development efforts in the future.

In light of these uncertainties facing the firm, Rob Glaser and his top-management team have to decide whether a shift in strategy is necessary.

APPENDIX A: REALNETWORKS' TOP-MANAGEMENT TEAM

Rob Glaser, chairman and CEO, is the founder of RealNetworks (Nasdaq: RNWK), the leader in streaming media products and services for the Internet. Since 1995, RealNetworks has played a pioneering and leadership role in media delivery over the Internet through its RealAudio, RealVideo, RealPlayer, and RealSystem products. Glaser is a member of several nonprofit boards and committees, including, most recently, his appointment by President Clinton to the Advisory Committee on Public Interest Obligations of Digital Television Broadcasters. Before founding RealNetworks, Glaser spent ten years at Microsoft, most recently attaining the position of vice president of multimedia and consumer systems and bringing to market successful pioneering products in the areas of multimedia, computer networking, and desktop applications.

Bruce Jacobsen has served as president and chief operating officer since February 1996 and as a director since August 1997. From April 1995 to February 1996, he was chief operating officer of Dreamworks Interactive, a joint venture between Microsoft and Dreamworks SKG, a partnership among Steven Spielberg, Jeffery Katzenberg and David Geffen. From August 1986 to April 1995, Jacobsen was employed at Microsoft in a number of capacities, including general manager of the Kids/Games business unit. He graduated summa cum laude with honors from Yale University and holds an M.B.A. from Stanford University.

Mark Klebanoff has served as chief financial officer since June 1996. From May 1992 to June 1996, he was vice president of finance and operations of Industrial Systems, a client/server process information management software vendor, which merged with Aspen Technology in 1995. From 1989 to 1992, Klebanoff worked in a number of general management capacities for the Japanese trading company Itochu. He has a B.A. from Yale University and a master's degree from the Yale School of Management.

Len Jordan has served as senior vice president, media systems since January 1997. From November 1993 to November 1996, he worked in a number of capacities at Creative Multimedia, a developer and publisher of CD-ROM/Internet products, and became its president. From September 1989 to November 1993, Jordan was employed at Central Point Software, a utility software publisher. Jordan graduated magna cum laude from Eccles School of Business at the University of Utah with B.S. degrees in finance and economics.

Phillip Barrett has served as senior vice president, media systems, since January 1997, and from November 1994 to January 1997, had been vice president, software development. From March 1986 to October 1994, Barrett was a development group manager at Microsoft, where he led development efforts for Windows 386, Windows 3.0, and Windows 3.1. He has an A.B. in mathematics from Rutgers University and an M.S. in computer sciences from the University of Wisconsin, Madison.

Maria Cantwell has served as senior vice president, consumer and e-commerce, since July 1997. From April 1995 to July 1997, she served as vice president, marketing of the company. From February 1995 to April 1995, Cantwell was a consultant to the company. Before that, she was a member of the 103rd Congress. She has a B.A. in public administration from Miami University.

James Higa has served as vice president, Asia/ROW, since September 1996. From January

1989 to August 1996, he was the director for Asia/Pacific for NeXT Software. From 1986 to 1989, Higa served as director of product marketing at Apple Japan. He has a B.A. in political science from Stanford University.

John Atcheson has served as vice president, media publishing, since January 1997. From March 1990 to May 1996, he was president and chief executive officer of MNI Interactive, a developer and distributor of consumer interactive services. Atcheson has a B.A. from Brown University and an M.B.A. from the Stanford Graduate School of Business.

Kelly Jo MacArthur has served as vice president and general counsel since October 1996. From January 1995 to March 1996, she was general counsel and director of business affairs for Compton's NewMedia, which was acquired by Learning Co. in 1996. From July 1989 to December 1994, MacArthur was an attorney at Sidley & Austin. She graduated summa cum laude from the University of Illinois at Champaign-Urbana and has a J.D. from Harvard Law School.

Erik Moris has served as vice president, marketing, since August 1997 and from April 1997 until then had been product manager. From September 1996 to April 1997, Moris was a consultant to the company. From May 1995 to August 1996, he was employed at Microsoft, where he managed advertising for the Windows 95 launch and was group manager for the Internet Platform and Tools Division. From 1985 to 1994, Moris was a senior vice president at McCann-Erickson Advertising. He has a B.A. in communications and business from Western Washington University.

Jeff Lehman has served as vice president, advertising sales, since October 1997. From September 1985 to September 1997, he was employed by Ziff-Davis/Softbank in a number of publishing positions, including those of vice president and director. He graduated cum laude from the University of Central Florida with a B.S.B.A. and an M.B.A. with honors.

Philip Rosedale has served as vice president, media systems, since October 1997. From February 1996 to October 1997, he had been the firm's general manager, software development. From June 1986 to February 1996, Rosedale was chief executive officer of Automated Management Systems, a developer and marketer of software applications, which he had founded. Rosedale graduated cum laude from the University of California, San Diego, with a B.S. in physics.

APPENDIX B: DETAILS OF REALNETWORKS' RELATIONSHIP AGREEMENT WITH MICROSOFT

In June 1997, RealNetworks entered into a strategic agreement with Microsoft, according to which RealNetworks granted Microsoft a nonexclusive license to substantial elements of the source code of the firm's RealAudio/RealVideo Version 4.0 technology, including its basic RealPlayer and elements of its EasyStart Server products, and related trademarks.

Under the agreement, Microsoft may sublicense its rights to the RealAudio and RealVideo Version 4.0 technology to third parties under certain circumstances. The agreement also provides for substantial refunds to Microsoft under prescribed circumstances that are solely within the firm's control. The amount of these refunds diminishes over time. The firm may not assign its obligations under the agreement without Microsoft's consent. Microsoft is obligated to distribute the firm's RealPlayer Version 4.0 for a defined term as long as the firm's player supports certain Microsoft architectures.

RealNetworks also agreed to work with Microsoft and several other companies to author and promote ASF as a standard file format for streaming media. The agreement also requires the firm to provide Microsoft with engineering consultation services, certain error corrections, and certain technical support over a defined term.

In connection with the agreement, Microsoft also purchased a minority interest in the firm. Microsoft currently offers its own streaming media product, NetShow. Additionally, Microsoft recently acquired VXtreme, a direct competitor of the firm in the market for streaming media software. Microsoft also owns a minority interest in VDOnet, a direct competitor of the firm in the market for streaming video software.

Endnotes

1. Streaming technology enables the transmission and playback of continuous "streams" of multimedia content, such as audio and video, over the Internet and intranets and represents a significant advancement over earlier technologies.
2. R. Reid, *Architects of the Web* (New York: Wiley, 19), p. 77.
3. "A Web Pioneer Does a Delicate Dance with Microsoft," *Wall Street Journal*, February 12, 1998.
4. Reid, *Architects*, p. 79.

5. R. Reid, "Real Revolution," *Wired* (October 1997).

6. When the firm releases a new product, it releases both the server and player versions simultaneously. For example, the most recent product released by the firm is the RealSystem 5.0. Customers can acquire either the server or the player version of the new software. The new RealVideo servers are always backward compatible with older server products and can stream audio only, or video *and* audio content.

7. "RealSystem 5.0 Experiences Rapid Market Adaptation," RealNetworks press release, December 1997.

8. The approach used for streaming media live is similar. The difference between live streaming and on-demand streaming is that the content is converted to streaming format as it is being created. For example, a customer could stream a live video of a conference speaker. To view the speech, a person would have to be at his or her computer at the time of the actual presentation. Live streaming media content can be recorded for on-demand viewing at a later time.

9. Television video (using NTSC standards) has a basic rate of roughly 100 megabits per second. Encoding this signal at 100 Kbs implies a compression ratio of 1000:1. By comparison, audio is typically compressed at a rate of roughly 15:1. Clearly, the process of video compression is challenging. Solutions typically involve dramatically reducing (subsampling) the size and frame rate of the images. However, such tactics induce visual artifacts in the reconstructed images. Artifacts are noticeable differences between the original images and the encoded images that can be identified and characterized.

10. One major difference between intranet and Internet customers is the speed of transmission. The transmission between an intranet server and a player is usually much faster. This is because businesses have network connections for their employees' computers that are faster than the modems typically used by home computer users. Faster transmission of data means that video clips are less distorted.

11. G. Welz and J. Carl, "Progressive Networks' CEO Talks About RealVideo," *Web Week*, March 17, 1997.

12. Reid, *Architects,* p. 80.

13. R. Reid, *Architects*, p. 79.

14. R. Reid, "Real Revolution."

15. "MCI and Progressive Team Up; Microsoft to Acquire VXtreme," *Wall Street Journal Interactive Edition*, August 10, 1997.

16. *Wall Street Journal*, February 12, 1998.

17. The firm has adopted RTSP (Real Transport streaming protocol), a proposed protocol for standardizing the control and delivery of streaming media over the Internet. The firm claims that RTSP is a unified standard for a broad range of media data types and is intended to promote a greater level of interoperability among various streaming media solutions. RTSP is built on top of a number of other Internet standard protocols such as HTTP, TCP/IP, and Real Transport protocol, and is complementary with ASF, a file format for streaming media that does not specify a method of client-server interaction. RTSP provides the client-server specification necessary to stream ASF and other file types. According to RealNetworks, its proposed RTSP was submitted to the IETF in October 1996 and this protocol was supported by more than forty companies.

18. R. Reid, "Real Revolution," *Wired* (October 1997), on-line version.

19. A. Orr, "Microsoft, Sun ride down stream," *ZDNet News Channel On-line*, January 26, 1998.

20. *Wall Street Journal*, February 12, 1998.

21. "RealNetworks Beats Estimates, but Investors Send Stock Lower," *Wall Street Journal*, January 30, 1998.

CASE 12

Microsoft's Windows CE: Digital Devices and the Next Computing Paradigm

This case was prepared by Charles W. L. Hill of the University of Washington.

INTRODUCTION

"Whisper it quietly, the personal computer—the machine of the 1990s—will be entering its twilight years by the beginning of the new millennium."[1] So claimed the influential newsmagazine, the *Economist*, in a recent article. Nor is the *Economist* alone in making this prediction. IDC, a forecaster of computing trends, recently issued a report entitled "The end of the PC-centric era." Similarly, Forrester Research, a consulting firm that focuses on high-technology businesses, has argued that the PC era may be "winding down." What these various visions of the future are depicting is a paradigm shift of potentially enormous dimensions. Ground zero of this shift is a concept known as ubiquitous computing.

Credit to coining the concept of ubiquitous computing is normally given to Mark Weiser, chief technologist at Xerox's Palo Alto research center.[2] Weiser argues that we are about to enter the third era in the evolution of computing.[3] The first era was the mainframe era. In this era, computers were rare and expensive, and we serviced them. The second era, in which we are still deeply immersed, is the personal computing era. The PC is a relatively inexpensive and commonplace general-purpose appliance. Our relationship to the personal computer is, well, personal. PCs are increasingly indispensable in our lives. They are also, according to Weiser (and a host of other critics) unwieldy, noisy, unreliable, and unfriendly machines that lack the elegance, simplicity, and performance of specialized appli-

ances. Some go as far as to argue that we are psychologically addicted to our PCs, and because of this, we put up with inefficiencies and inelegance that would not be tolerated in any other product.[4] Despite the limitations of the PC, Weiser argues that this second wave of computing will grow larger still, before it has its energy sapped on the shores of the third era of computing.

The third era, according to Weiser, will be the era of ubiquitous computing. This era will be characterized by a profusion of inexpensive computers that we will interact with on an almost constant basis. Computers, in the form of special-purpose embedded processors, can already be found in watches, ovens, cars, wallets, and cell phones. Inevitably, these computers will become more pervasive, will talk to one another, and will form the invisible computational infrastructure of our lives. So ultimately, says Weiser, "If your refrigerator watches you take the milk carton in and out every day, and if your refrigerator could talk to your wallet, then when you went to the store the wallet could tell the milk cartons that you need milk. And the milk cartons could then say to you, 'Hey buy me, you're out of milk.'"[5]

Although Weiser believes that his vision is still six to ten years off, the harbingers of the third era of computing are already with us. Small digital devices are proliferating, from palm devices and PC companions to smart phones, set-top boxes, digital cameras, and auto PCs. By using the communications protocols of the World Wide Web, these intelligent devices are being empowered with the ability to talk to each other across high-speed wireline and wireless networks.[6] In 1997, 96 percent of the devices hooked into the Internet were PCs, but according to recent predications by IDC, within four years close

This case is intended to be used as the basis for class discussion rather than as an illustration of either effective or ineffective handling of the situation. This case was prepared by Charles W. L. Hill, University of Washington. Used by permission.

to half of the total will be non-PC devices, including palm tops, set-top boxes, cell phones, and video game terminals. By 2002, IDC estimates that non-PC devices with Web capability will total 41 million units, up from 3.6 million in 1998.[7]

Where will Microsoft be in the era of ubiquitous computing? If some of the company's competitors have their way, nowhere to be seen. One vision of the future of computing depicts a world in which digital devices based on non-Microsoft operating systems "grow up" to replace the PC. These devices will run Java applications, be interconnected using Jini-networks built around Sun servers, access data from Oracle databases, and receive their service from AOL.

Leading Microsoft's charge against this potential reality is the latest component of the company's embrace-and-extend strategy, Windows CE. CE is Microsoft's operating system for digital devices. However, in attempting to get Windows CE established as the de facto standard for digital devices, Microsoft faces significant challenges. To drive forward adoptions, it must get the product attributes and the strategy right. It must out-maneuver competitors who are themselves becoming increasingly sophisticated with regard to standard building strategies. And it must validate the implicit assumption that the same basic business model that worked so spectacularly for PCs, also applies to the more fragmented world of digital devices.

DIGITAL DEVICES

The term *digital devices* refers to a bewildering array of products that perform a wide variety of applications. For purposes of taxonomy, they can be segmented into four main groups: hand-held de-

vices, smart phones, vertical application devices, and other devices (see Table 1). This segmentation is very rough since there is a significant degree of blurring across boundaries.

Hand-held Devices

Hand-held devices are normally defined to include palm-sized devices—for example, 3Com's popular PalmPilot and Palm III personal information organizers; "Clamshell" PC companions such as Hewlett-Packard's 660LX; and larger "Mondo" PC companions that use Microsoft's "Jupiter" Windows CE 2.11 operating system such as HP's Jornada 820. These devices range in price from $300 to $1,000. The initial growth in demand for such devices was driven by the spectacular success of the PalmPilot. Within eighteen months of its launch in April 1996, more than 1 million PalmPilots were shipped, making for a faster product ramp-up than occurred with the first cell phones and pagers. By late 1998, more than 2 million units had been sold.

Hand-helds are used for personal information management (scheduling, address books, and so forth), note taking, E-mail, word processing, and expense tracking. According to Sherwood Research, the five most popular hand-held applications of "mobile professionals" who used both a hand-held and a notebook PC are personal information management (87 percent), note taking (42 percent), E-mail (31 percent), word processing (28 percent), and expense tracking (23 percent).[8]

Estimates from Sherwood Research of the market segmentation and near term growth prospects in the *United States* for certain hand-held devices are given in Table 2.[9]

Another market research group, IDC, expects the total *worldwide* hand-held companion market

---

TABLE 1

A Simple Taxonomy of Digital Devices

Hand-helds	Smart Phones	Vertical Application Devices	Other Devices
Palm devices		Pen tablet	Set-top Boxes
PC companions		Pen notepad	Auto PCs
PDAs		Keypad hand-held	Game terminal
			Digital cameras
			Digital books
			Point of sale terminals

TABLE 2

Growth Forecasts for Hand-held Devices

	1998	1999	2000
Palm	1,433,000	2,054,000	2,724,000
Clamshell	523,000	628,000	756,000
Mondo (Jupiter)	54,000	295,000	869,000
Total	2,010,000	2,977,000	4,349,000

to grow from 3.1 million units in 1997, to 13.1 million units in 2001, a compound annual growth rate of around 44 percent.[10] IDC notes, however, that customer confusion over the price and benefits of hand-held devices may inhibit adoption of the technology. Moreover, the multiplicity of choices with regard to form factors and operating systems may further confuse consumers and slow down adoption rates. Competition from low-priced/low-weight notebooks may also cut into growth in the hand-held device market.

Smart Phones

Smart phones represent a fusion of the attributes of digital cell phones and hand-held devices. Smart phones can handle data as well as voice traffic. They function both as a cell phone and as a personal digital assistant, thereby limiting the number of devices that people have to carry. The Nokia 9110 Communicator—which has a flip-up screen and is capable of composing and sending faxes, E-mail and Web browsing—is at the leading edge of smart phone technology.

According to Dataquest, global sales of mobile phones will rise from 100 million in 1997 to around 360 million in 2002. Of these, Dataquest estimates that 15 to 20 percent will be smart phones. A more conservative view of likely diffusion of smart phone technology comes from IDC. IDC believes that adoption of smart phone technology will take off first in the European and Japanese markets, primarily because they have a critical complement in place: a universal wireless communications infrastructure (for example, GSM in Europe).[11] Alternatively, the lack of a universal

wireless standard in the United States will slow down adoption rates.

IDC believes that smart phone technology is still in the early adopter growth phase. Growth is being held back by high price and lack of customer education. Consumers are confused as to the difference between smart phones and advanced digital cell phones. IDC estimates that 0.437 million smart phones were shipped worldwide in 1997. The research group forecasts that the market will expand to 5.898 million units by 2001 as demand for the device begins to take off. The European Union and Japan are forecasted to account for 1.65 million units and 1.32 million units, respectively, while the United States will account for 0.899 million units.[12]

Vertical Application Devices

Vertical application devices (VADs) are hand-held pen- or keypad-based devices used to gather data from the field or in other mobile situations and transmit it to a central point. Familiar examples include the keypad-based handsets used by FedEx delivery and pickup drivers to collect tracking data for packages. Other uses of VADs include collecting inventory information from a warehouse, and bedside accessing of a patient's records in a hospital setting.

IDC estimates that the VAD market amounted to 2 million units in 1998 and forecasts that it will grow to 3.5 million by 2001.[13] IDC believes that small pen-based notepads using a Windows CE operating system will present themselves as inexpensive alternatives to traditional devices and start to gain share. Connectivity with corporate data systems that run on Windows NT servers may facilitate this trend.

Other Devices

The "other device" category represents a diverse grab bag of digital devices including set-top boxes, auto PCs, and game terminals.

Set-Top Boxes Set-top boxes add functionality to cable service (for instance, movies on demand or additional information linked to programming). They also bring Web browsing capabilities to the TV, and promise to transform TVs into interactive communication devices (for example, E-mail, home shopping). The potential market for set-top boxes is huge. There are 250 million TV sets in the United States alone ready for upgrade. Then again, sales of *WebTV* have been slow, and it is unclear at this point how interested consumers are in using the TV to access the Web.

In the United States, the Telecom Act of 1996 mandated that by July 1, 2000, consumer premise equipment (such as set-top boxes) must be available to consumers from sources other than their cable operator or the vendor from whom the service is obtained. In other words, the FCC has ruled that all set-top boxes must be made available for retail sale. The ruling requires manufacturers to build set-top boxes based on standards that allow the devices to connect with any number of headends (servers) and be compatible with any cable system. This implies that all new set-top boxes must be interoperable. Device manufacturers and cable operators alike are moving aggressively in order to deliver affordable devices that act like a cable converter box, cable modem, and network computer all rolled into one.

A number of companies are developing or already marketing set-top box operating systems. Microsoft is in the market with its Windows CE product. Others include Sun (Java), Apple, Oracle, Sony, and Psion, which is preparing to license its EPOC operating system to set-top box device manufacturers and cable operators.[14]

AutoPCs   In December 1998, Clarion started to sell its AutoPC, an in-dashboard personal computer and audio system with voice control.[15] The AutoPC utilizes a Windows CE operating system. It follows voice commands and has the capability to talk back, reading E-mail that can be received via a special radio broadcast. It can also use its address book to dial an in-car cell phone. The basic system retails for about $1,300 and fits into the space of a traditional car radio. The voice recognition software homes in on syllables rather than complete words and responds only to a limited range of commands, which improves accuracy.

For consumers, the promised benefits of a voice-controlled auto PC are convenience and safety. Instead of having to fumble to dial an in-car cell phone, figure out how to turn down the air conditioner, or change the track on a CD, the words "phone dial 555–1212," "temperature 70 degrees," or "play disk two, track three" should suffice.

Ford will begin to incorporate the AutoPC in its top of the line Jaguar car range in Spring 1999. Although it will probably be several years before the technology penetrates the mass market, the poten-

tial market is clearly immense. There are 15 million automobiles sold each year in the United States alone, and 50 million worldwide.

Game Terminals   As of late 1998, the video game terminal market was dominated by hardware from Sony and Nintendo. There are now more than 20 million Sony PlayStations and Nintendo 64 consoles in U.S. homes and more than 50 million worldwide.[16] Sony reportedly has 70 percent of the market and Nintendo 30 percent.[17] If the history of the industry is any guide, however, there could be a sea change in market share when the next generation of more powerful game machines debuts.

The first of the next generation machines, Sega's Dreamcast, was introduced in Japan in November 1998 and was scheduled for U.S. introduction in late 1999. This was to be followed by a new Sony machine in 2000, and the next generation Nintendo machine in 2001. All three of these machines are expected to come with Internet capability, allowing for multiplayer games over the Web.

Sega led the video game industry with its 16-bit system Sega Genesis in the early 1990s. However, Sega disappeared almost completely from the market when the 32-bit Sega Saturn failed to gain consumer acceptance in the face of strong competition from Sony. Sega hopes that the Dreamcast will reverse its humiliation. The new machine is based on a 128-bit processor, boasts leading-edge 3D graphics capabilities, comes equipped with Internet capability, and utilizes a version of Microsoft's Windows CE operating system.

Sega's decision to go with CE was based on a calculation that the choice will make it easier for Sega to win back game developers, who now focus on developing games for the Sony and Nintendo systems or for the PC game market. Because of the commonalities between Windows and Windows CE, developers who write games for the PC based on Windows operating system protocols will have an easier time adapting their games to Sega's Windows CE system than to a proprietary operating system.

Additional Products   Set-top boxes, auto PCs, and game terminals represent just three examples of the wide range of intelligent devices that will increasingly populate our world. Other examples include digital cameras, Web phones, digital books, car navigation systems, DVD players, digital wallets, home thermostats that can be monitored and adjusted from remote locations, and perhaps one day, even Weiser's intelligent refrigerator. Indeed, it is in the nature of technological progress that many of the future applications of embedded microprocessors cannot yet be foreseen. When these unforeseen applications do emerge, however, the question remains, "What operating system will they use?"

MICROSOFT'S STRATEGY: WINDOWS CE

At the forefront of Microsoft's strategy for ubiquitous computing is an attempt to extend its Windows franchise into the world of digital devices. Leading the charge is the Windows CE 2.0 operating system, which the company is trying to license to as many device manufacturers as possible. The goal is to get CE established as the de facto standard for digital devices. In theory, standardization on a single operating system, by expanding the market for applications written to that operating system, lowers the risk and increases the potential payoff associated with developing applications, thereby increasing the supply of applications. Standardization, in other word, sets up a self-reinforcing virtuous cycle, in which lower development risk leads to increased supply of applications, which increases the demand for digital devices and drives further expansions of supply and demand. By such a process, standardization can help to create the market.

So far, Microsoft has registered some significant wins for CE. Versions of Windows CE 2.0 have been licensed to manufacturers of hand-held PCs and palm PCs such as Hewlett-Packard, Sharp, NEC, Casio, and Philips. CE has been licensed to TCI for use in its set-top boxes, to Samsung for use in smart phones, to Clarion as the OS for its AutoPC, and to Sega for its Dreamcast video game player. Moreover, Windows CE seems likely to move into new devices. Hewlett-Packard is studying CE to see if it can be used in HP printers. Atlanta based Radiant Systems plans to sell Windows CE point-of-sale devices to fast-food restaurants (customers press buttons on a screen to select the food and drinks they want). Intermec, a leader in bar code technology, is developing a Windows CE vertical application device for data collection that is designed for use in inventory-tracking applications.[18] Microsoft has also entered into a joint venture with Qualcomm to develop wireless devices and services based on CE

and Qualcomm's CDMA digital cellular technology.[19]

Windows CE 2.0 runs on a number of central processing units, including the MIPS R3000 and R4000, Motorola PowerPC, Hitachi SH3, Intel X86, and ARM chips. CE resides in read-only memory chips, not random access memory, which reduces the likelihood of a crash. As would be expected for a digital device operating system, CE requires relatively little memory and can be stored in 4.0 megabytes of ROM.

Windows CE is modular and can be customized to suit needs of customers, thereby enabling CE to function as the operating system on a wide variety of divergent devices. Modularity means that device manufacturers can pick the elements of CE that they need to use. A manufacturer can choose among 120 options, mixing and matching features as needed. For example, if the device has no display, there is no need for the display code. Thus, for embedded-type applications without a display, a customer might choose to use just the kernel, which takes up less space than the complete operating system. Or a manufacturer could use the kernel and one or more Windows CE components for applications such as set-top boxes. The next version of CE, code-named Cedar, will include modular components that will enable OEMs to create a true Windows CE–based cellular phone OS.[20]

Windows CE communicates effortlessly with standard Microsoft applications, making data sharing and synchronization with desktop PCs easy. Hand-held PCs have pocket versions of Microsoft's Office suite programs, which can be quickly swapped with a PC, as well as a pocket version of Internet Explorer and a pocket Outlook. Synchronization with a desktop computer or server is accomplished using Windows CE Services 2.1, which is included with each Windows CE handheld product and runs only on Windows 95/98 or NT systems.

An attraction of CE is that developers can use Microsoft Windows development tools and Win 32 APIs to write applications. This leverages the skill base of the large Windows development community. It is estimated that some 5 million developers around the world are currently writing software for Windows 95 and NT, so in theory there is a huge reservoir of talent out there ready to write software for Windows CE, and programs for other systems can be quickly modified for CE.[21]

On October 8, 1998, Microsoft introduced Windows CE 2.11 Hand-held PC Professional Edition. This version of CE is aimed at larger-form-factor PC companion hardware, known as the H/PC Pro platform (formally known as Jupiter). The format has a larger keyboard and LCD screen than other hand-held PCs. These devices are targeted at corporate users who are mobile and need "Windows lite" functionality. The device is a PC companion, however, and not a PC, in that it lacks the functionality of desktops, such as support for off-the-shelf Windows applications, CD-ROM drives, and so forth. Twelve vendors have announced that they are supporting the H/PC Pro platform. IDC believes that the product suffers from poor market positioning.[22] There is some concern that ultimately this platform will cannibalize low-end notebook sales.[23]

A clear advantage of Windows CE is that it leverages Microsoft's existing brand recognition amongst end users. Adopters of hand-held devices, such as PC companions and palm PCs, find it intuitively appealing to use an interface that has so many commonalities with the familiar desktop environment. This preference for the familiar, and for a device that is easy to synchronize with desktop PCs, might be expected to produce a presumption in favor of Windows CE. This presumption seemed to be confirmed in a recent IDC market survey, which asked potential and actual corporate adopters what operating system should run on a hand-held device they selected. The results, which are given in Table 3, suggest that Windows CE has significant appeal.

While the worldwide market for digital devices running Windows CE could clearly be immense—within a few years outnumbering by a factor of five to ten the number of PCs sold per year—the licensing revenue per unit will probably be significantly less than that derived from a PC.[25] Still, it is important to understand that the diffusion of Windows CE could drive demand for Windows NT data bases, electronic commerce, and transaction servers, thereby enabling Microsoft to gain substantial indirect revenue contributions from CE.

To this end, Microsoft is positioning Windows CE as part of a total solution strategy. The company is creating bundles that allow service providers to easily link Windows CE devices with NT-based services. As an example, Microsoft is reportedly working with CableData to sell NT-based billing and customer service products that let cable customers with Windows CE set-top boxes order movies or check account balances via their remote control units.[26] Thus, the diffusion of CE will help Microsoft sell complementary products such as NT, on which it earns larger margins.

DOUBTS ABOUT CE

Despite Microsoft's dominance in the desktop world, and its deep pockets, many industry participants and observers are skeptical about the company's ability to dominate the digital device arena in the same way that it has dominated the PC arena.

A frequently heard argument is that the digital device arena lacks the same compelling need for standardization that Microsoft exploited in the PC arena.[27] The world of digital devices is far more fragmented than that of PCs, so the argument goes, hence standards are naturally less important. This

---

TABLE 3

Operating System Preferences for Hand-held Devices[24]

Operating System	Super PC Companion (H/PC Pro)	PC Companion	Personal Companion
Windows CE	71.9%	64.8%	38.7%
Palm OS	4.3%	6.8%	33.8%
Java	12%	19.3%	16.7%

view is reflected in the following quote from Jerry Fidler, CEO of Wind River Systems, whose VxWorks operating system kernel for embedded processors competes in some of the same space as Windows CE. Fidler has suggested that "It's going to be tough for Microsoft. This isn't a one size fits all market. Applications are specific, not standard like they are in the PC world. This world is chaos."[28] Similarly, Forrester Research has argued that operating system conformity isn't as important in the digital device arena because, unlike PCs, most devices do not have to run thousands of applications. More than 90 percent of 3Com's PalmPilot users, for example, rely entirely on a handful of embedded applications such as the contact list and calendar.[29]

A big driver for standardization in the PC world is the need to ensure that data flows easily between software applications, and between the PC and a wide range of peripherals. In the digital device arena, however, it has been argued that Internet connectivity and standard data formats such as HTML and the emerging Web access protocol will provide the lingua franca for devices. Moreover, synchronization tools from companies such as Puma Technologies and Starfish software will tap into PCs and Internet resident databases to ensure that phone lists and preferences on smart appliances are kept in sync, regardless of the underlying operating system.

Other critics have focused more on the shortcomings of Windows CE than on any actual or perceived flaws in Microsoft's strategy. A big issue with Windows CE is that it currently does not offer strong real time operating system (RTOS) capabilities. With its response time of 250 microseconds, CE is just too slow to be used for applications that must be choreographed to the microsecond, such as the motion of a print head on an ink-jet printer, factory floor automation systems, or precision robotics, all of which require thread latencies of below 50 microseconds.[30] RTOS capabilities are also required for many wireless applications. However, Windows CE should have RTOS capabilities by the fall of 1999. This should help Windows CE to penetrate the embedded systems market.

Another issue is related to the reported size of the RTOS for Windows CE. Major RTOS vendors, such as Wind River Systems and Integrated Systems, offer scalable systems that start with kernels of around 1 kilobyte. Frugal use of memory is a key requirement for many embedded system designs.

However, current reports suggest that Windows CE RTOS will need at least 2 megabytes of ROM to hold the CE operating system. This is far more memory allocation than developers for embedded systems normally have to account for. If true, many potential users will be repelled by the need to squander so much memory.[31]

COMPETITORS

As might be expected, competitors offer a significant threat to market acceptance of Windows CE. This threat is enhanced by the fact that many important suppliers of complements, such as TCI in the set-top box arena, have a vested interest in ensuring that the market for digital device operating systems remains fragmented. (TCI licensed Windows CE for 5 million of the 12 million set-top boxes it is planning to build. At the same time, TCI has licensed Personal-Java from Sun for all its boxes). One of the biggest fears of device manufacturers and suppliers of complement services, such as cable, is that Microsoft will dominate the digital device world in much the same way as it has dominated the PC world. If this were to occur, Microsoft could conceivably capture much of the economic value in the marketplace, leaving device manufacturers and service providers to compete with each other in a commodity world. In the words of TCI president, Leo Hinderly, many device manufacturers and complement suppliers "don't want to be a Bill Gates download."[32] This fear adds momentum to any offering that helps to keep Microsoft's ambitions in check. In other words, there is something of a presumption in favor of non-Microsoft solutions on the part of many other participants in the digital device value chain.

There is certainly an abundance of non-Microsoft solutions, including 3Com's Palm OS, Psion's EPOC, Sun Microsystems' Java OS, and Wind River System's VxWorks (see Table 4). Several of these alternatives are discussed in detail below.

3Com's PalmPilot and Palm OS

The PalmPilot was the brain child of Jeff Hawkins and Donna Dubinsky. Their vision was to produce a simple electronic device that would have four basic functions: a calendar, an address book, a to-do list, and memo writing function. They believed that

TABLE 4

OS Competitors for Digital Devices[33]

Vendor	OS	Comments
3Com	Palm OS	Used in Palm Computing devices sold by 3Com and its licensees; also targeting smart phones
Integrated Systems	PSOS	Ships in car navigation systems, digital cameras, phones, and Sony's satellite set-top box
Lucent	Inferno	Focuses on phones and network devices like firewalls and routers.
Microsoft	Windows CE	Currently targeting set-top boxes, DVD players, game consoles, phones, and hand-held devices
Power TV	Power TV OS	Aimed at set-top boxes, TVs, network computers, and DVD players; used in Scientific Atlanta's digital set top
Psion	EPOC	Targeting hand-held devices, smart phones, and set-top boxes
QNX	QNX Software	Targeting set-top boxes, DVD players, VCRs and phones.
Sun Micro	Java OS	Built by coupling real time OS and Java virtual machine; dependent on new Java applications; licensed for use in TCI set-top boxes
Wind River Systems	VxWorks	Ships in satellite set tops and digital cameras; targeting DVD and wireless phones

the main competitor for the Pilot would not be computers, but paper. Accordingly, they tried hard to make the Pilot a model of simplicity. For example, looking up the day schedule is no more difficult than opening a date book: one push of a button and there it is.

This was not a vision that sold easily in Silicon Valley. Dubinsky and Hawkins repeatedly tried to raise venture capital money but kept running up against objections that the device was too simple and lacked important attributes, such as a PC card, or functions, such as a spreadsheet. After eighteen months of their effort, U.S. Robotics, a Midwest company, emerged as the "angel" backer (U.S. Robotics later merged with 3Com).[34]

The PalmPilot was launched in April 1996. An electronic address book and calendar/date book that recognizes handwriting and communicates with any PC, it retailed for $200–$400. For the first four months sales were painfully slow; then demand started to increase exponentially as the Pilot suddenly became a "hip" device for busy execu-

tives. Within eighteen months of the initial launch, more than 1 million PalmPilots were shipped, making for a faster demand ramp-up than the first cell phones and pagers. By the end of 1998, more than 2 million units had been sold.

Benefiting from early mover advantages, 3Com built a large community of developers that now offer applications for the PalmPilot and its successor, the Palm III (the Palm III incorporates a larger screen and built-in infrared beam to share data—such as electronic business cards—with other users). There are now more than 5,000 developers making add-on products for the Palm devices, such as PilotMail and PilotClock. By late 1998, there were some 1,600 applications for the PalmPilot and Palm III, versus 300 for Windows CE hand-held devices. An abundance of shareware and freeware is helping to drive market acceptance of the PalmPilot. Sales for applications are also being driven by alternative distribution channels, such as the Web.

As with any successful new product, competitors soon imitated the Pilot's form and functions.

The most notable imitator was Microsoft's "Palm PC," with its Windows CE operating system. Several other companies have licensed Windows CE to produce Palm PC devices, including Casio and Philips. Windows CE Palm PC devices have more built-in features than 3Com's PalmPilot and Palm III, but they take longer to load data and consume battery power more rapidly.

In 1998, IDC calculated that the PalmPilot accounted for 78 percent of the $980 million a year hand-held market. Trying to build installed base, 3Com is licensing the Palm OS as fast as it can to companies such as IBM and Qualcomm. Qualcomm is adapting the Palm OS for use in a smart phone, the pdQ, which is scheduled to ship in 1999.

IDC expects that the global market for palm devices will grow from 1.2 million units in 1997 to 8.2 million units in 2001.[35] Sherwood Research estimates that U.S. sales of palm computing devices utilizing 3Com's Palm OS will hit 1.433 million in 1998, and grow to 2.724 million by 2000. Sherwood's sales forecasts appear in Table 5.

Some observers doubt that the Palm OS can survive over the long term in the corporate area, primarily because the keyboards on hand-held PCs are better input devices for most corporate users. Moreover, some argue that the PalmPilot, which uses an aging 16-bit processor, suffers from a lack of standardized programming tools. They predict that the major portion of the back-end enterprise market will eventually connect to CE devices because they run the most commonly used 32-bit code.[37]

Sherwood Research believes that "3Com will continue to dominate the palm-sized market, and by default the entire handheld PC market. The form

factor and functionality, combined with a powerful set of developer applications, means that 3Com really only faces competition from itself as it cannibalizes its own product line with the introduction of new products that incorporate enhanced or new features."[38]

Support for this position can be found in the fact that major corporate applications providers, such as SAP, Oracle, Sybase, and Computer Associates, are all working on ways to deliver their enterprise resource planning, database, and management software to Palm OS platforms. For example, SAP's mobile R/3, introduced in mid 1998, runs on a version of the 3Com PalmPilot sold by Symbol, as well as on 3Com's PalmPilot and IBM's WorkPad version of the PalmPilot.[39] Similarly, Oracle is planning to enter the mobile database market. In mid 1998, Oracle announced a partnership with 3Com to integrate a 150-kilobyte version of the Oracle Lite client database into Palm OS units. Oracle states that this integration will let Palm OS applications and data be replicated, synchronized, and shared with Oracle8 databases. However, the company also plans to run Oracle Lite betas on Windows CE. Indeed, most applications companies are hedging their bets by developing applications for *both* the Palm OS and Windows CE platforms.

Psion and EPOC

Psion is a British company that was an early leader in the market for hand-held computers. Its Series 5 machine was introduced in mid 1997, a full six months before similar devices utilizing Windows CE. The Series 5 was greeted with critical and popular acclaim, especially in Europe. The Series 5, which is a derivative of Psion's popular Series 3 machine, uses Psion's EPOC operating system, and a novel and highly usable keyboard, which offers far more than the tiny-buttoned keyboards usually associated with hand-held computers. The Psion Series 5 comes with a set of built-in applications, which share data formats with popular Microsoft desktop applications. These include a Word-compatible word processor. Psion provides excellent desktop connectivity with Windows through its PsiWin product.[40]

Despite beating Windows CE hand-held devices to the market by some time, Psion had been facing an uphill struggle as CE gained momentum. Indeed,

TABLE 5

Sales Forecasts for Palm Devices[36]

Type	1998	1999	2000
Palm OS	995,000	1,435,000	1,780,000
Palm size PCs/CE	344,000	547,000	654,000
Other	94,000	72,000	290,000
Total	1,433,000	2,054,000	2,724,000

many were ready to write the company off—that is until Psion pulled an ace out of the hole in the form of Symbia. Symbia is a joint venture with cellular telephone giants Ericsson, Nokia, and Motorola. The objective of the venture is to adopt Psion's EPOC operating system as the OS for the next generation of "smart cellular phones." According to Dataquest, by 2002 roughly 50 million smart phones will be sold every year—equivalent to the number of PCs sold today. Psion's partners in Symbia account for more than 70 percent of the sales of mobile phones. If their share holds and smart phone sales grow as predicted, Psion's EPOC could still emerge as a significant competitor to Windows CE.[41]

Symbia will license EPOC to all comers for a fee of around $5 to $10 per phone, which compares favorably with the $25 per unit that Microsoft reportedly charges to license CE.[42] Psion claims that EPOC is better suited than CE to cell phones, where long battery life and efficient use of memory are more important than links to a PC desktop. Be that as it may, EPOC has another attribute that attracts Psion's partners and any potential licensees—it is not a Microsoft product. Psion's founder, David Potter, underscored this point as he outlined the thinking behind Symbia: "We looked at the cellular industry, an industry selling 100 million units a year, and asked: 'Are these guys really going to allow the mighty Bill to come in and take their businesses?' It's absolutely obvious that there is no way they are going to do that. We looked at their needs and said, let's make these guys secure."[43] Building on this success, Potter has announced his intentions to license EPOC to other electronic hardware manufacturers, such as set-top box manufacturers.

Wind River Systems

Wind River Systems is a long-time participant in the market for embedded system operating systems with its VxWorks real-time operating system and its set of Tornado development tools for embedded system applications. As of 1998, Wind River controls about 33 percent of the market for third-party RTOS for embedded processors. Wind River has been involved in more than 10,000 customer products and projects, from Cisco routers to Kodak digital cameras. VxWorks is considered so reliable that NASA used it on the Mars Pathfinder.[44]

Wind River does not intend to go head-to-head with Microsoft. Indeed, the company seems to be de-emphasizing embedded markets, such as hand-held

PCs, where Microsoft has already established a strong position. Rather, Wind River intends to compete by finding new uses for its technology, such as GUIs and Internet connections on a wide range of products, including camcorders, copiers, printers and retail kiosks. Toward that end, the company has made a number of acquisitions designed to boost its graphic interface and Internet capabilities.[45] Despite Wind River's attempts to avoid head-to-head competition with Microsoft, adding GUI and Internet functionality to VxWork seems likely to bring the company into conflict with Microsoft at some point.

Sun Micro: Dreams of Java and Jini

Sun Microsystems is trying to position Java as a threat to Windows CE in all of its markets. The great strength claimed for Java is its platform independence—the same compiled Java code will run on any processor or operating system with a compatible Java Virtual Machine (JVM). The Java concept of "write once run anywhere" is obviously very attractive to developers—and if it works it will reduce the imperative for standardizing on a single operating system. Sun is also pushing its own Java operating system for embedded applications, JavaOS.

Java has certainly made some inroads into the digital device world. For example, Hitachi and TCI have both licensed Java for use in their respective set-top boxes. A wide range of other companies are offering Java support for embedded system applications. Wind River Systems offers a version of its own operating systems for embedded processors, VxWorks, that runs Java. Other competitors in the embedded system space, including Integrated Systems, Mentor Graphics, and Cygnus Solutions, also offer embedded system tools for Java.[46]

Jini is the latest addition to Sun's Java vision. What Java aims to do for software, Jini hopes to do for the machines that run it: provide an overarching universal platform—a distributed operating system, in effect, in which devices of every description can meet. Jini is about trying to create an architecture, a universal language, a set of super protocols—to knit together the emerging global computer and communications network, and make everything work with and make it accessible by everything else.[47]

The basic point of Jini is to simplify user interaction with the network. The key to Jini is Java's platform independence and its own innate ability to work over existing network software and protocols. As an extension of Java code, along with the federation of Java Virtual Machines (JVMs), Jini becomes the universal language for disparate devices. The core of Jini's architecture lies in a "lookup service," known as JavaSpace. The lookup service acts as an electronic bulletin board that monitors the devices attached to a network. So the combination of Java's ability to run on different computers and the ability of Jini-enabled devices to send their own software code to the lookup service and receive instructions from other devices is what gives a Jini network its potential magic.[48]

To consumers this means the ability to connect, power, and control through the network any appliance with an embedded processor, including handheld devices, smart phones, set-top boxes, and home thermostats. Once connected, the device announces itself to the network, indicates what it is there to do, and then carries out its task.

On a corporate scale, Jini has potential for altering the way networks operate, without changing the underlying structure. Computing power would be distributed among devices connected to the computer, letting them share each other's resources. If Jini works, you will be able to sit with your laptop, it will be able to reach out across the network, and for the moments that you need the power, it will become the largest supercomputer in the world.[49] Instead of a platform designed to provide all capabilities in all cases, Jini provides only what is needed. And by using Java as the standard platform, interoperability is achieved. Basically, any device with a link to the network and a programmable ROM can be a network device with Jini.[50]

Sun is trying to position the Java/Jini combination as the offering that will make Weiser's vision of ubiquitous computing a reality. To this end, Sun is reportedly going to license Jini for free to diffuse the technology as rapidly as possible. If successful, Sun's vision will lead to a world in which a myriad of digital devices running Java connect and communicate with each other via Jini networks. In this vision of the future of computing, there is no imperative for standardization on a particular operating system, and the dominance of Microsoft will evaporate.

The problem with this vision is that so far it has promised far more than has been delivered. The Java/Jini combination may make for great press, but while it is widely supported, there is little evidence of overwhelming momentum in favor of Java in the digital device arena. Meanwhile, Jini remains a re-

search project. One Microsoft spokesman claimed that Jini does little more than reinvent the kinds of network services—such as file and print—that are already in widespread use in non-Java environments. Sun needs Jini, so the argument goes, because Java does not provide any services of this kind, and Java-only devices, therefore, have no way of connecting to network services.[51]

Even Windows CE skeptics, such as Forrester Research, believe that a dearth of Java applications and Microsoft's existing tools and developer community will make CE rather than Java the leader in the high-end "net visible" space, which includes set-top boxes and hand-held PC companions. Like CE, Java is also too slow for many embedded system applications that require real time capabilities.[52]

Perhaps more troubling for Sun, there are signs that the Java community is beginning to fragment, raising the specter that Java may go the way of UNIX, which fragmented into a set of partly incompatible versions. Hewlett-Packard has developed its own clone of Java, Chai, that HP claims is a better alternative to "real" Java in many embedded system applications. Elsewhere, much to Sun's chagrin, a breakaway group of companies has banded together to form a version of Java that is suitable for real time applications.[53]

KEY STRATEGIC ISSUES

The competitive situation in the digital device arena is still unfolding daily. Huge uncertainties abound as to the future direction of the market. How will the technology evolve? Will Weiser's vision of ubiquitous computing come to pass? What are the attributes of the technology required to facilitate this development? Will standards be important in the digital device arena, or in segments of that arena? What kind of products will be demanded by mass-market consumers, as opposed to technophiles? Where will the growth be? What product attributes in terms of form factors and functions will be required to drive forward expansions of demand? What is the correct technological, product development and competitive strategy for Microsoft to pursue in order for the company to help grow the market and to position itself to profit from that growth, irrespective of how critical uncertainties resolve themselves? How can Microsoft gain a major share in a market where not only competitors, but also suppliers of important complements, have a vested interest in seeing the company's market share bounded?

Endnotes

1. "After the PC," *Economist,* September 12, 1998, p. 79.
2. E. Wasserman, "Electronics Guru Predicts Ubiquitous Computing," *Arizona Republic*, January 19, 1998, p. E1.
3. M. Weiser, "The Future of Ubiquitous Computing on Campus," *Communications of the ACM*, 4 (January 1998), 41.
4. T. K. Landauer, *The Trouble with Computers* (MIT Press, 1995).
5. Wasserman, "Electronics Guru," p. E1.
6. J. Markoff, "Taking a Step Towards Converting the Home into a Supercomputer," *New York Times*, July 15, 1998, p. 1.
7. E. W. Desmond and J. Hodges, "Microsoft's Big Bet on Small Machines," *Fortune*, July 20, 1998, p. 86.
8. Sherwood Research, "Effects Handhelds Will Have on Notebook PCs," February 16, 1998.
9. Sherwood Research, "Handheld Forecast Update: Breakout of the Palm Sized Market," September 14, 1998.
10. IDC, "Boom or Bust? Worldwide Smart Handheld Devices Market Review and Forecast Update," 1997–2001, 1998.
11. Ibid.
12. Ibid.
13. Ibid.
14. Sherwood Research, "Consumer CE-Based Appliances, Set Top Boxes," August 31, 1998.
15. G. L. White, "Cars That Listen Promise a New Direction in Driving," *Wall Street Journal*, December 28, 1998, p. B1; S. Manes, "Compute While You Are Driving," *Forbes*, January 11, 1999, p. 112-114.
16. N. Weinberg, "Sega's New Dimension," *Forbes*, September 7, 1998, p. 206-208.
17. D. Takahashi, "Video Game Makers See Soaring Sales Now—and Lots of Trouble Ahead," *Wall Street Journal*, June 15, 1998, p. A10.
18. J. G. Spooner, "Windows CE Goes Vertical," *PC Week*, November 9, 1998, p. 39.
19. J. G. Spooner, "Alliance to Bolster CE," *PC Week*, November 9, 1998, p. 16.
20. A. Fiebus, "WinCE: Your Next OS?" *Information Week*, November 16, 1998, p. 127.
21. J. Jurvis, "Business Support Grows for Windows CE," *Information Week*, March 2, 1998.
22. IDC, "Smart Hand-held Devices: Jupiter—Not for Many Moons," October 1998.
23. Sherwood Research, "Effects Handhelds Will Have on Notebook PCs," February 16, 1998.
24. IDC, "U.S. Customer Directions and Buying Behavior: The 1998 Smart Handheld Devices Survey," 1998, Table 14.
25. The estimate of five to ten times as many CE digital devices and Windows PCs was given by Craig Mundie in a recent *Fortune* article, E.W. Desmond and J. Hodges, "Microsoft's Big Bet on Small Machines," *Fortune*, July 20, 1998, p. 86.
26. "Windows CE Falls Short."
27. Ibid.
28. Desmond and Hodges, "Microsoft's Big Bet."
29. "Windows CE Falls Short."
30. T. Foremski, "Microsoft Gets Real," *Electronics Weekly*, May 6, 1998, p. 34.
31. Ibid.
32. S. Hamm, "Microsoft's Future: A Band of Powerful Foes Is Determined to Slow the Gates Juggernaut," *Business Week,* January 19, 1998, p. 58.
33. Compiled from various sources, including "Windows CE Falls Short," *Forrester Report*, 5 (May 1998).
34. D. S. Jackson, "Palm-to-Palm Combat," *Time Magazine*, March 16, 1998, p. 42.
35. IDC, "Boom or Bust?"
36. Sherwood Research, "Handheld Forecast Update."
37. R. Levin and T. Davey, "Handhelds—Mobile Evolution," *Information Week*, June 15, 1998, p. 20.
38. Sherwood Research, "Handheld Forecast Update."
39. Levin and Davey, "Handhelds."
40. N. Clayton and S. Vogel, "Palmistry," *Scotsman*, September 9, 1998, p. 8.
41. Wallace, "The Man Bill Gates Fears Most," *Fortune*, November 23, 1998, p. 257.
42. D. Gillmor, "Formidable Force Aims at Microsoft," *San Jose Mercury News*, July 7, 1998, p. E1.
43. Wallace, "The Man Bill Gates Fears Most."
44. D. Diamond, "Lord of the Toasters," *Wired* (September 1998).
45. P. Coffee, "Wind River, Zinc to Duel Win CE," *PC Week*, July 6, 1998, p. 16.
46. "Major Embedded Tool Companies Turn Towards Java," *Java World* (January 1998).
47. K. Kelly and S. Reiss, "One Huge Computer," *Wired* (August 1998).
48. "Net Watch: Sun Microsystems and Jini Architecture," *Izarek Shopper* (October 1998).
49. Ibid.
50. A. Goldberg, "I Dream of Jini, and So Should You," *PC Week*, August 3, 1998.
51. "Microsoft Says Jini Is Old Hat," *Computergram International*, July 17, 1998.
52. "Windows CE Falls Short."
53. D. Lyons, "Java in Jeopardy," *Forbes*, January 11, 1999, p. 110-111.

Sun Microsystems, Inc.

This case was prepared by Irene Hagenbuch and Alan N. Hoffman of Bentley College.

The Network is the computer's means to make all the systems work together like one big resource. Sun has always seen our customers' computing needs answered by a variety of computing resources in a heterogeneous network.

—*Scott G. McNealy, CEO, April 1987*

COMPANY BACKGROUND

John Doerr, of Klein Perkins, has described Sun Microsystems with world headquarters in Palo Alto, California, as "the last standing, fully integrated computing company adding its own value at the chip, OS and systems level."

The company's history started in 1982, when Andreas Bechtolsheim, Bill Joy, Vinod Khosla, and Scott McNealy founded Sun Microsystems for Stanford University Network. Within a month after the introduction of the business plan, which Bechtolsheim, an electrical engineering whiz, had built it for Stanford's computer network. The same year, the first Sun system, the Sun-1, a high-performance computer based on readily available, inexpensive components and UNIX, was produced. After a rocky two-year start, McNealy, who started out as vice president for manufacturing and operations, was appointed president in 1984 when Khosla left the company. Today, Sun has emerged as a global *Fortune* 500 leader in enterprise network computing, with operations in 150 countries and more than $8 billion in revenues.

The company's philosophy is to enable customers to create breakaway business strategies by using their network computing products, solutions, and services. Sun further states that in an age

This case is intended to be used as the basis for class discussion rather than as an illustration of either effective or ineffective handling of the situation. This case was prepared by Irene Hagenbuch and Alan N. Hoffman, Bentley College. Used by permission.

where information is power it provides the technology, innovation, and partnerships that enable individuals or entire organizations to access information from anywhere to anything on any device allowing users to better differentiate and more effectively create breakaway business products and services.

Supporting and enforcing their philosophy where everything they bring to the market is predicated upon the existence of the network, where Java is on every client and every server, Sun has a vision statement. It says that its "vision is for a networked computing future driven by the needs and choices of the customer. It is a vision in which every man, woman and child has access to the collective planetary wisdom that resides on the network." Sun further explains that the Internet represents the first environment through which the company's vision can actually start to be achieved. They see their role as one of making the most of the opportunity, by delivering open, affordable and useful products to help as many people as possible share in the power of the network around the world.

COMPETITION

Sun's competitors in the technical and scientific markets are primarily Hewlett-Packard (HP), International Business Machines Corporation (IBM), Compaq Computer (CPQ) and Silicon Graphics, Inc. (SGI).

The information technology industry, the market for Sun's services and products, is extremely competitive. The industry is characterized by rapid, continuous change, frequent product performance improvements, short product life cycles and price reductions. This environment forces Sun to rapidly and continuously develop, introduce, and deliver in quantity new systems, software, and service products, in addition to new microprocessor technologies, to offer its customers improved performance at competitive prices. The company has begun to improve, change, and implement a number of new business practices, processes, and a series of related information systems. Jim Moore from GeoPartners Research in Cambridge, Massachusetts, compares Sun with IBM in its glorious days, when customers viewed it as the repository of wisdom and competence: "Sun has suddenly become a thought leader for the whole industry."

Compared with previous years, Sun has become increasingly dependent on the ability of its suppliers. Their competence in designing, manufacturing, and delivering advanced components required for the timely introduction of new products is crucial to Sun's future competitiveness. The failure of any of these suppliers to deliver components on time or in sufficient quantities or the failure of any of Sun's own designers to develop innovative products on a timely basis could also have a serious impact on the company's operating results. To prevent any adverse effect on its net revenues and operating results, Sun frequently makes advanced payments to specific suppliers and often enters into non-cancelable purchase contracts with vendors early in the design process. The commitments help secure components for the development, production, and introduction of new products. The distribution of the computer systems sold by Sun is accomplished through the company's own systems. No customer accounted for more than 10 percent of Sun's revenues in fiscal 1997, 1996, or 1995. Sun's vision and strategy have stayed constant. With more market opportunities, an increasing number of companies are realizing the benefits of open network computing.

After Sun observed that sharing data between computers was crucial to key business tasks, McNealy worked extensively to transform Sun's product line in order to capitalize on networking. Today, its main products can be divided into six categories: servers and workstations, Solaris and Solstice, SunSpectrum, WorkShop and NEO, UltraSparc and Java processors, and Java software (see Table 1). This wide variety of products is used to implement the McNealy philosophy: "The network is the computer." Sun was refiguring its UNIX operating system for workstations, called Solaris, to run servers that coordinate work and store data on networks.

The year 1994 was marked as a big year in the computer industry. Sun faced the dramatic expansion of the Internet's World Wide Web. Millions of users came to believe that the network was indeed the computer. Since this statement has been accepted by Sun for a long time, the company had been faster in making the transition compared with its UNIX rivals IBM and Hewlett-Packard. This led to many customers turning to Sun for their workstations. According to Computer Intelligence, a research firm located in La Jolla, California, 26 percent of all Web servers in use in the United States were made by Sun—that is more than by any other company.

By 1998, Sun was the leading provider of UNIX-based servers. Java has helped increase sales, even though the language does nothing yet to make Sun's servers better than any of its competitors. Using Java to sell servers is a necessity, since the workstation, the computer Sun was built on, is going the way of the minicomputer. The more expensive machines made by Sun and others are being replaced by PCs incorporating cheaper Intel microprocessors. While companies are having inexpensive Windows NT servers handle their simpler networking tasks, they still rely on UNIX for their most critical applications since Solaris servers crash a lot less than NT servers. Nonetheless, the PCs that run Microsoft's Windows NT operating system, Compaq, Dell and others will soon take over the market for workstations priced under $10,000.

In January 1998, however, Sun announced sweeping innovations made to its award-winning power desktop line. This move, designed to capture new growth within the $19 billion market for high-end personal computers and powerful workstations, allows the company to grow market share at both the low end (less than $5,000) and high end (more than $15,000) of the workstation market. Putting its expertise in high-performance system design has enabled the company to bring down the price of advanced workstations and graphics technologies. Sun's announcement of new graphics capabilities, as well as of the fastest workstation, the

TABLE 1

Sun Microsystems Products

- ***Servers and Workstations.*** The company offers a full line of Ultra Enterprise servers to support an immense database and mission-critical business applications. With its Netra server family, Sun delivers preconfigured solutions for intranet and Internet publishing. Its Ultra workstation series combines accelerated graphics, high-bandwidth networking, and fast processing to provide outstanding performance for technical applications.

- ***Solaris and Solstice.*** With Sun's installed base of more than 2 million systems, Solaris software is the leading operating environment for open client-server networks. The Solstice products consist of a highly scalable and comprehensive suite of Intranet management software, helping organizations securely access, administer, and manage rapidly changing Intranet computing environments.

- ***SunSpectrum.*** This newly developed portfolio of enterprisewide support services connects Sun's customers to a highly responsive organization that supports more than half a million systems worldwide. That combination of hardware, system software, and application support with premium account-level services maximizes both system availability and customer satisfaction.

- ***Workshop and NEO.*** The Workshop family, which includes the new Java WorkShop solution, delivers visual development tools that quickly and easily create multiplatform applications for the Internet, intranets, and enterprise networks. NEO delivers system administration tools, object-oriented development tools, and transparent networking in order to reduce the cost of creating, customizing, and maintaining applications.

- ***UltraSPARC and Java Processors.*** Well-developed UltraSPARC microprocessors accelerate multimedia and networking applications with their innovative architecture and VIS media instruction set through powering networked systems from routers to supercomputers. The planned JavaChip microprocessor family will be optimized for Java-powered applications.

- ***Java Software.*** It is the first software platform planned from the start for the Internet and corporate intranets that will run on any computer.

Source: (Form-10k)

Ultra 60 multiprocessing system, ideally positioned the company to take market share from competitors such as Hewlett-Packard, IBM, DEC, and Silicon Graphics at the high end of the market. Sun is pushing Silicon Graphics' technology to the limits with its new price/performance levels and intends to overtake SGI's market share in the $25,000+ workstation market, which was approximately $3 billion in 1996. These new workstations allowed the users to run the most popular Microsoft Windows 95 applications alongside the Solaris applications. This meant that users could run the more than 12,000 Solaris applications, which offered proven UNIX reliability/uptime, handled larger data sets and delivered faster real-world modeling capabilities than the NT environment, in addition to the PC applications like Microsoft office.

The new Darwin line was designed to appeal to the growing base of desktop users who were demanding more reliability and power. When the Darwin systems are coupled with new accelerated graphics, it allows Sun to focus more on the needs of the rapidly growing base of digital contents creators. This desktop line sets a new low-price point for workstation functionality, enabling Sun to grasp market share from Compaq and other PC vendors at the lower end of the market. Part of this move into the desktop markets was the announcement of a worldwide trade-in program designed to ensure investment protection for existing Sun customers and to attract new customers currently using other PCs and workstations that compete with the Sun platform. To specifically draw the attention of Silicon Graphics, Apple Computer, and

Compaq customers, as well as those of other PC vendors, toward the performance and speedy graphics advantages of Sun systems, Sun designed its "Jurassic-Back," "Mac-Back," and "Paq-Back" trade-in promotions.

FINANCIAL PERFORMANCE

Even though Sun's industry is fast changing and highly competitive, the company has managed to

have at least 10 percent sales growth over the last several years across its product line. Its net revenue in fiscal 1998 increased to $9.7 billion, or 13 percent compared with $8.6 billion in fiscal 1997 (see Table 2). Net income was flat for 1998—at $762 million for fiscal 1998, the same as for fiscal 1997. However, the product's gross margin was 53.8 percent for fiscal 1998, compared with 51.1 percent for fiscal 1997. Research and development expenses increased by $188 million, or 22.7 percent,

TABLE 2

Sun Microsystems' Consolidated Statements of Income
(In thousands, except per share amounts)

	Years ended June 30		
	1998	1997	1996
Net avenues:			
Products	$8,603,259	$7,747,115	$6,392,358
Services	1,187,581	851,231	702,393
Total net revenues	9,790,840	8,598,346	7,094,751
Costs and expenses:			
Cost of sales—products	3,972,283	3,790,284	3,468,416
Cost of sales—services	721,053	530,176	452,812
Research and development	1,013,782	825,968	653,044
Selling, general and administrative	2,777,264	2,402,442	1,787,567
Purchased in-process research and development	176,384	22,958	57,900
Total costs and expenses	8,660,766	7,571,828	6,419,739
Operating income	1,130,074	1,026,518	675,012
Gain on sale of equity investment	—	62,245	—
Interest income	47,663	39,899	42,976
Interest expense	(1,571)	(7,455)	(9,114)
Income before income taxes	1,176,166	1,121,207	708,874
Provision for income taxes	413,304	358,787	232,486
Net income	$ 762,862	$ 762,420	$ 476,388
Net income per common share—basic	$ 2.04	$ 2.07	$ 1.28
Net income per common share—diluted	$ 1.93	$ 1.96	$ 1.21
Shares used in the calculation of net income per common share—basic	373,728	368,426	371,134
Shares used in the calculation of net income per common share—diluted	394,274	388,967	393,380

in fiscal 1998. Sun has one of the strongest balance sheets in the industry, with $822 million in cash in the bank (see Table 3.) Having been the world leader in workstation sales (with 39 percent in unit sales and 35 percent in revenues, per Dataquest), the company is successfully transforming itself into an enterprise-computing firm with a focus on global network computing. This was a necessary move as Sun's workstation sales started to slip and its server sales to gain.

Over the last ten years, the company's revenues have grown an average of 34.1 percent annually as the demand for its open network computing products and services has risen. The revenues by geography are well balanced. Approximately 49 percent of the total revenue is generated from outside the United States. The company's net income has grown 41 percent annually on average over the same time period.

CORPORATE GOVERNANCE

Scott G. McNealy

The life story of Sun's current chairman of the board, president, and chief executive officer, Scott G. McNealy, is not very typical for a Silicon Valley entrepreneur. He didn't drop out of college to realize his idea for the PC business, nor did he work his way up through engineering. His background in manufacturing makes McNealy a fierce competitor who knows his business fundamentals, always keeps score, and has good moves. He is smart, complex, and fiercely ambitious. Over the many years at Sun, McNealy has become one of the industry's most respected managers. Lawrence J. Ellison, CEO of Oracle says, "There are two things I think about Scott. One is passionate leadership, and the other is his rigorous financial management. And that's uncommon to find in one person" (*Fortune,* October 13, 1997). Those talents, along with his competitive instinct and nonstop drive, have kept Sun rolling through a decade of tremendous change in the computer industry.

McNealy grew up in a house where hard work and a fast-paced environment were part of everyday life. As a child, McNealy learned a great deal about manufacturing. His curiosity about his father's work (his father was vice chairman of American Motors) led the gradeschooler to look into his dad's briefcase at night to inspect its contents.

Many Saturdays, he went along to the plant and snooped around while his father caught up on paperwork. By the time he reached his teenage years, McNealy was spending evenings with his father reading over memos and playing golf with industry leaders such as Lee A. Iacocca.

Graduating from Harvard University in economics, McNealy took a job for two years as a foreman at a Rockwell International Corp. plant in Ashtabula, Ohio, which made body panels for semi tractors. In 1978, he enrolled in Stanford University's business school, where he focused on manufacturing at a time when finance and information technologies were the ways to the top. While many of his classmates wanted to launch a Digital Age business, McNealy signed on as a manufacturing trainee for FMC Corp. The company assigned him to a factory in Silicon Valley where it was building Bradley fighting vehicles for the U.S. Army.

McNealy's career in the computer world started in 1981, when his mentor from Harvard asked him for help in the troubled production department of a workstation company called Onyx Systems. After only ten months at Onyx, he was contacted by a former Stanford classmate, Vinod Khosla, and asked to join him and Bechtolsheim in starting Sun. In 1982, he joined Sun to head its manufacturing and operations. His manufacturing skills enabled the new company to keep up with the high demand as sales went from $9 million in 1983 to $39 million in 1984. Nonetheless, the high amount of new orders surpassed the cash available for expansion. McNealy then asked their customer Eastman Kodak to invest $20 million. As a condition of the investment, Kodak insisted that McNealy take over as president. In 1984, he was officially named CEO of the company.

McNealy showed his ability as a CEO over the coming years. After the company went public in 1986, it took two years for Sun to outgrow its production capacities, which led to the company's first quarterly loss. Its troubled production facilities were reason enough for McNealy to move from Sun's executive suite to the floor of Sun's biggest factory and revamp the company's manufacturing. In the months after production was rolling again, he showed skills nobody expected. He deliberately pruned the product line, sharpening Sun's focus to workstations built around a high-powered processor of its own design. The realization that fixing problems on the factory floor was no job for the

TABLE 3

Sun Microsystems' Consolidated Balance Sheets

(In thousands, except share and per share amounts)

	At June 30	
	1998	1997
Assets		
Current assets:		
Cash and cash equivalents	$ 822,267	$ 660,170
Short-term investments	476,185	452,590
Accounts receivable, net of allowances of $235,563		
in 1998 and $196,091 in 1997	1,845,765	1,666,523
Inventories	346,446	437,978
Deferred tax assets	371,841	286,720
Other current assets	285,021	224,469
Total current assets	4,147,525	3,728,450
Property, plant and equipment:		
Machinery and equipment	1,251,660	1,057,239
Furniture and fixtures	113,636	93,078
Leasehold improvements	256,233	166,745
Land and buildings	635,699	341,279
	2,257,228	1,658,341
Accumulated depreciation and amortization	(956,616)	(858,448)
	1,300,612	799,893
Other assets, net	262,925	168,931
	$5,711,062	$4,697,274
Liabilities and Stockholders' Equity		
Current liabilities:		
Short-term borrowings	$ 7,169	$ 100,930
Accounts payable	495,603	468,912
Accrued payroll-related liabilities	315,929	337,412
Accrued liabilities and other	810,562	625,600
Deferred service revenues	264,967	197,616
Income taxes payable	188,641	118,568
Note payable	40,000	——
Total current liabilities	2,122,871	1,849,038
Deferred income taxes and other obligations	74,563	106,299
Commitments and contingencies		
Stockholders' equity:		
Preferred stock, $0.001 par value, 10,000,000 shares		
authorized; no shares issued and outstanding	—	—
Common stock, $0.00067 par value, 950,000,000 shares authorized;		
issued: 430,311,441 shares in 1998 and 430,535,886 shares in 1997	288	288
Additional paid-in capital	1,345,508	1,229,797
Retained earnings	3,150,935	2,409,850
Treasury stock, at cost: 54,007,866 shares in 1998 and		
60,050,380 shares in 1997	(1,003,191)	(915,426)
Currency translation adjustment and other	20,088	17,428
Total stockholders' equity	3,513,628	2,741,937
	$5,711,062	$4,697,274

CEO of a company of Sun's size led McNealy to reorganize the company's structure. He pushed profit-and-loss responsibility down to individual product organizations, called planets, which let them feel the troubles if things went wrong.

At Sun's headquarters, McNealy, having an image in the industry of being brash, was building a corporate culture based on his own motto: "Kick butt and have fun." Soon after that, the company became known for its aggressive marketing, featuring Network, McNealy's Greater Swiss Mountain dog, and various juvenile behavior taking place within Sun's headquarters.

This humor had an important effect on the culture. During these competitive times in the computer industry when good positions and good workers were hard to find, it helped employees live with their demanding jobs and bound the company. Both Carol A. Bartz, former sales vice president of Sun, and Thomas J. Meredith, former Sun treasurer, agree that McNealy has a special gift. Using humor and a tremendous amount of energy, McNealy has the ability to raise employees enthusiastically to their feet.

Sun does not consist of McNealy alone, however. According to Ellison, McNealy has complemented his leadership with very capable people. "You don't find Scott surrounded by dummies. You find Scott surrounded by real smart people, like Bill Joy and Eric Schmidt [chief technology officer] and others who do wonderful work."

JAVA—THE PROGRAMMING LANGUAGE

Java originated in a 1990 programming language, code-named Oak, that would enable all computerized devices to run simple programs distributed to them over a network. At one point, Oak was part of the effort to develop a two-way interactive cable TV system (which Sun lost out to Silicon Graphics). By the end of 1994, Oak seemed to be going nowhere. During one last presentation of Oak, McNealy recognized the potential of the programming language—how to reach his ultimate goal of harnessing the Internet to stop Microsoft from swallowing all of them—and became its biggest supporter. Soon after that, the language was renamed Java, a colloquial word for "coffee." The fact that the name was informal and generic compared with previous programming language names which were obscure and somewhat daunting, implied that normal people should also care about Java, whether they knew what it did or not. By May 1995, McNealy informed the public about the new concept, but at that point the public did not know what to make of it. On January 12, 1996, Sun officially released Java, its new network software, and Sun entered a new era with a tremendous amount of public exposure and a heightened interest in the company.

The brand name Java refers both to a programming language and to a set of components and tools. It was originally viewed as a language that would jazz up Web pages with graphic animations—dancing icons, for example. To Microsoft's dismay, Java has evolved to trick people into thinking it is a computing platform. What makes Java a self-sufficient computing system is the Java Virtual Machine, or JVM—a piece of software that imitates all the functions of the computing device. This gives Java the possibility to run on any machine with a JVM, insensitive to the underlying operating system (Windows, Macintosh, UNIX, and so forth), and allows applications written in Java to run on all machines without being changed. The Java digital language is the first universal software that would allow all computerized devices to share programs and communicate over a network. It makes possible the rapid development of versatile programs for communicating and collaborating on the Internet.

Compared with ordinary software applications, Java applications, or "applets," are little programs that reside on the network in centralized servers. The network delivers the programs to the user's machine when needed. Because the applets are so much smaller, they require comparably less time to download. In other words, Java lets programmers write small applications that can zip across the World Wide Web. Without leaving the browser, the user will then be able to print out attractive text and charts. The user always gets the latest version of the applets. As the software is stored in only one place, corporations can keep it updated more easily. Java's designers believed that in this new environment, the program's speed would be measured by how fast a program ran on a network and not by how fast a program ran on an individual computer. In this sense, being object oriented versus speed oriented makes programs run faster, or at least appear to. Java was developed to have its objects move quickly into and out of different machines and merge with other Java objects on the network, even when these objects appeared unexpectedly.

With the immense growth of the World Wide Web, Java's introduction was one of those magic moments where place and time seemed perfect. It appeared to be the language best suited for Internet computing. Besides applying to all PCs, Java is inherently virus-proof, because the language was designed so that applets cannot alter data in the user's computer's files or on its hard disk. Silicon Graphics and Macromedia partnered with Sun to jointly define a new set of open multimedia formats and application programming interfaces (APIs) to extend Sun's Java. The companies believe that these new API formats will enhance Java's capabilities for providing animation and interactivity, especially in the area of 3D rendering and multimedia over the Internet or corporate networks.

With the increasing importance of the Internet, McNealy once more is convinced that Java will alter the dynamics of the business. "Java opens up a whole new world for Sun," he says. It can be said that a part of the new world has already come into view. Java is well on its way to becoming the Internet software standard, which would put Sun as the leader in Internet computing. Millions of personal computer owners already have access to Java because the software was built into the 1996 release of Netscape's Web browser. As the "intelligent network" starts to include mobile phones, smart pagers, and hand-held electronic assistants, along with the traditional computers, Java is set to become a standard language for these far-flung devices.

Although Sun is planning eventually to donate the software language to the computer world through publicizing all the specifications and letting anybody use them, Java should continue to spur profitable growth for the company. According to management, Java will increase Sun's sale of Internet servers, priced at $25,000, and starts its new line of JavaStation network computers. Java will also raise the demand for Sun's software development tools and for special Sun chips, which other computer makers can incorporate into their machines to run Java faster.

McNealy's view of the future is not shared universally, however. It is very unlikely that Java will change computing so soon. The programming language is still at a fairly immature stage and its programs run considerably more slowly than programs written specifically for a particular computer oper-

ating system. Furthermore, there have been security issues raised by a system of distributing software on the Net.

The Java Controversy

By the first week of December 1995, many of the top names in computing—from Netscape, Oracle, and Apple to BulletProof, Wind River Systems, Toshiba, and IBM—had endorsed Java. IBM had 2,500 programmers working to improve Java because it saw Java as the glue that can finally link its many lines of computers seamlessly. Because Java programs run on any hardware or operating system, Java could bypass, and therefore break, Microsoft's cash cow, Microsoft Office. So that Java might be on further PCs, Sun tried to persuade Microsoft to incorporate a Java interpreter right into the Windows operating systems. After four months of negotiations, Sun received a fax from Microsoft in March 1996 agreeing to license Java on Sun's terms. Microsoft had changed its strategy of writing its own software for any interface or function (unless customers demanded that Microsoft adopt another) because of a software language. In its many years of business, Microsoft had rarely adopted anyone else's software or hardware standards. The company had agreed to license a product from Sun because it did not have a lot of choices.

On October 7, 1997, however, Sun Microsystems announced that the company had filed a lawsuit in U.S. District Court, Northern District of California, San Jose Division, against Microsoft Corporation for breaching its contractual obligation to deliver a compatible implementation of Java technology on its products. The complaint also charged Microsoft with trademark infringement, false advertising, unfair competition, interference with prospective economic advantage, and inducing breach of contract. Sun claimed that Microsoft has deliberately violated its licensing agreement in an attempt to reduce the cross-platform compatibility made possible by the Java technology and deliver a version of the technology that worked only with Microsoft's products. Additionally, Sun charged that Microsoft illegally placed Sun's software code on its World Wide Web site. Sun asked for $35 million in damages over that one issue.

Even though there have been threats about revoking Microsoft's Java licensing agreement, Sun did not plan to cancel Microsoft's license. The company's goal was to pressure Microsoft to fulfill the obligations created in that license. Sun was seeking a court order to prevent Microsoft from improperly using the Java Compatible logo and deceiving the marketplace. The logo appeared in different locations in and on Microsoft's consumer packaging and promotional materials. Sun was further seeking to prevent Microsoft from misleading Java developers and from delivering anything but fully compatible Java technology implementations. Sun felt it had the responsibility to defend the integrity of Java. Michael Morris, Sun's vice president and general counsel, stated that "nowhere is the sanctity of a trademark more important than in the field of computer software. Our customers rely on the reputation and the goodwill of the trademark to make informed, efficient decisions about the technology they are using."

One of any of Java licensee's most significant contractual obligations is to pass the Java compatibility tests. These tests determine if a licensee's technology conforms to the Java specifications and APIs. In Microsoft's case, the products that failed were the new Internet Explorer 4.0 browser and the Software Development Kit for Java (SDKJ). The new technology did not pass Sun's compatibility tests because of an improper modification of the products by Microsoft. Hence, applications written using Microsoft's development tools do not run on all machines without some necessary adjustments.

For the two companies the stakes are high. McNealy is convinced that Sun can win a lawsuit against Microsoft, the most powerful software company in the world, by having a court that looks at the case, and not at the companies involved. Winning the suit would enable Sun to live up to the CEO's idea behind his drive to develop Java: to free the world of the duopolistic grip of Microsoft and Intel, or so-called Wintel. It would open the market for Sun and other computer companies. As Microsoft is fully aware of McNealy's concept, its strategy is to encourage developers to write Java programs that are tied to Windows. This would block Sun's efforts to expand the language into a possibly full-blown operating system.

Sun and its CEO are very confident that the court will see the merits of the complaint and move to a speedy resolution. Sun seems to ignore, however, that Microsoft, Intel, Digital Equipment, and Compaq Computer have all signed an open letter on September 11, 1997, urging Sun to turn con-

trol of Java over to the International Standards Organization (ISO). This demand would put the Java logo in the public domain. Sun seems to have missed the point that this suit is not solely about Microsoft. It is about whether Sun can respond to the standards body. If Sun loses, its previously forwarded plan where the ISO would have some oversight over Java might not get accepted and Sun would have to give up control of the key components of Java and the Java brand. This, in turn, would lead to a huge future loss in revenue and a decline in investments by many trustworthy companies such as IBM, which have partnered with Sun in the development of Java. Furthermore, it would enable Microsoft to establish a Windows-only variant of Java—one that would benefit just Wintel (PCs based on Intel's microprocessor using the Windows operating system) machine users—as a competing standard that would block Sun from creating a uniform Java that can run equally well on any type of computer.

The Feud with Microsoft

The suit had developed into a public fight between Sun Microsystems and Microsoft, two extremely successful companies. This sniping between Sun and Microsoft is more about who controls the future of computing than the surface spat over the Java Internet programming language. Microsoft has brought its weight into play to slow Sun down further. Microsoft is using its power, market visibility and market presence to try to reposition Java as "just another programming language."

The rivalry between the two companies has become so shrill that Aaron Goldberg, of Computer Intelligence in La Jolla, California, calls it a "urinary Olympics." After winning out over Apple, Lotus, and WordPerfect, Microsoft is convinced that it is on its way to win the browser war as well. Although Netscape is still growing and finding new customers, it may lose out to Microsoft as well. Thinking that Sun will succeed where others have failed is probably irrational.

At the same time, it has to be said that it may be smart to be perceived as the one company that is attacking Microsoft. Many CIOs have started to worry about the increasing costs of information technology systems and software and their dependence on Microsoft and Intel. The incredibly high sums spent on equipment and maintenance increased the CIOs' willingness to support new alternatives. In addition to the CIOs, customers have always liked to apply pressure to the market leaders in the hope of driving down prices. Consumers like the concept that no user of Java needs to buy the software in a retail store or from an electronic catalogue; it is part of the economic transaction. There is also a willingness and availability of money in the industry to help anyone who might loosen Microsoft's control over the way things will be in the future. This is why there has been so much support for Java, even more than McNealy originally expected.

McNealy soon will have to decide if this almost personal vendetta against Microsoft to break its power in the computer industry is in the best interest of Sun's shareholders and if it is a healthy path for Sun in the future. He could have considered cooperating with Microsoft. This would have opened up Java to the masses and could have helped Sun sell even more highly profitable servers and workstations. Stating Sun's point of view that Java does not have to make money for the company as long as it helps the company break Microsoft's business model shows McNealy's intent. Sadly enough, this might really not be in the public's best interest. McNealy is convinced that "if Java catches on big, the software lock-in of the Microsoft Windows/Intel design will end. Then, computer and software companies will once again be able to differentiate their products. Indeed, they will have to." If Java does not catch on or especially, if Sun loses the suit, no one, including McNealy, will know what Sun's future will look like in the computer technology industry—especially if one considers that the lawsuit, as well as Java itself, does not affect Microsoft as much as originally thought. The fact that many people like Java does not change how customers want to use those computers on their desks. They still want to calculate spreadsheets, process words, hold presentations, and manage personal information by using software that allows them to do all of it as conveniently as possible. It does not seem to make a difference that the new programmers will use Java to create new software. Many of the present programmers will continue using conventional languages to develop commercial software as all the new languages will end up running on Windows machines anyway, because these are the machines the majority of the users already have.

Sun Microsystems Faces Revolt over Java Control

On November 3, 1998, the *Financial Times* proclaimed in a front-page article:

> Sun Microsystems is facing an industry revolt against its control of Java, the computer language which allows programs to run on any system. On November 2, 1998, 14 companies, including Hewlett-Packard, Microsoft, Siemens and Rockwell, announced they would start setting their own standards for creating Java programs which control devices such as cellphones and printers. The move follows several months of negotiations with Sun over industry complaints that it was being too slow at developing new software standards and was charging too much in licensing fees.
>
> Joe Beyers, general manager of Internet Software at Hewlett-Packard, said, "We are trying to respond to customer needs but Sun has been unwilling to relinquish control of Java. If they want to go in a different direction they can, but I hope they can join us."
>
> Sun has focused on developing Java for mainstream computer programming to the frustration of companies wishing to develop other uses. Sun has yet to start selling its own system for running Java programs on embedded processors.
>
> Hewlett-Packard this year broke Sun's grip on Java by developing its own system for operating Java programs called Chai, which does not require a license from Sun.
>
> Mr. Beyers says several other companies are developing similar systems.

On November 24, 1998, America Online announced that it was purchasing Netscape Communications for $4.2 billion and entering into a multi-layered strategic partnership with Sun Microsystems to develop new Internet access devices.

References

Alsop, S. "Warning to Scott McNealy: Don't Moon the Ogre." *Fortune.* October 13, 1997.

——. "Sun's Java: What's Hype, What's Real." *Fortune.* July 7, 1997.

Bank, D. "Sun Lawsuit Is Latest Shot at Microsoft." *Wall Street Journal.* October 9, 1997.

——. "Sun Suit Says Microsoft Disrupts Java." *Wall Street Journal.* October 10, 1997.

Fitzgerald, Michael. "Sun's Threat: Microsoft Could Lose Java License." *ZDNet.* September 23, 1997.

Gomes, L. "Sun Microsystems 1st-Period Net, Sales Miss Expectations Due to Currency Rates." *Wall Street Journal.* October 17, 1997.

———. "Profits at Sun Microsystems Increases 56%." *Wall Street Journal.* April 16, 1997.

Gomes, L., and D. Clark. "Java Is Finding Niches But Isn't Yet Living Up to Its Early Promises." *Wall Street Journal,* August 27, 1997.

Hamm, S., with R. Hof. "Operation Sunblock: Microsoft Goes to War." *Business Week,* October 27, 1997.

Hof, R. D., with P. Burrows and K. Rebello. "Scott McNealy's Rising Sun." *BusinessWeek,* January 22, 1996.

Hof, Robert D., with J. Verity. "Now, Sun Has to Keep Java Perking." *BusinessWeek,* January 22, 1996.

Indiana Rigdon, J. "Sun Microsystems' Earnings Soar 41% Due to Strength at Top of Product Line." *Wall Street Journal,* January 16, 1997.

Kirkpatrick, D. "Meanwhile, Back At Headquarters. . . ." *Fortune,* October 13, 1997.

Mitchell, R. "Extreme Fighting, Silicon Valley Style." *U.S. News & World Report,* October 20, 1997.

Schlender, B. "The Adventures of Scott McNealy." *Fortune,* October 13, 1997.

———. "Sun's Java: The Threat to Microsoft Is Real." *Fortune,* November 11, 1996.

Seminerio, M. "Java Jive: Microsoft vs. Sun Draws No Blood—Yet." *ZDNet,* September 23, 1997.

Sun Microsystems, Inc., home page (www.sun.com).

"Sun Microsystems, Silicon Graphics and Macomecia Intend to Define a New Set of Open 3D and Multimedia Interfaces for Java and the Web," from Sun Microsystems, Inc., home page (www.sun.com).

Sun Microsystems, Inc., Annual Report 1996.

Sun Microsystems, Inc., Annual Report 1997.

"Wind River System's Tornado for Java Passes Sun Microsystems' Java Compatibility Tests," biz.yahoo.com/prnews/980121/ca_wind_ri_1.html. (January 21, 1998)

"BulletProof Releases JdesignerPro 2.32—Advanced RAD Application Development System for Java," biz.yahoo.com/prnews/980120/ca_bulletp_1 html. (January 20, 1998).

"Sun Unveils Plans to Grow Desktop Market at Expense of Compaq, H-P and SGI," www.sun.dom/smi/Press/ sunflash/9801/sunflash.980113.3.html. (January 13, 1998).

"Sun Sues Microsoft for Breach of Java Contract": www.sun.com/smi/Press.sunflash/9710/sunflash/. 971007.10.html (October 7, 1997).

"Sun Microsystems Seeks to Bar Microsoft from Unauthorized Use of 'Java Compatible' Logo," www.java.sun.com/pr/1997/nov/sun.pr97118.html. (November 18, 1997).

CASE 14

ATL: Strategic Positioning

This case was prepared by Charles W. L. Hill of the University of Washington.

INTRODUCTION

In early July 1998, the top-management team of ATL Ultrasound, a leader in the medical ultrasound business, gathered in the bucolic surroundings of the Columbia Winery in Washington State for its annual two-day strategic planning retreat. Its task was to discuss several key strategic issues that had been confronting the company for some time and had yet to be resolved to anyone's satisfaction.

ATL was established in 1969 in order to commercialize technology developed at the University of Washington's health sciences complex. The company was one of the early pioneers in the market for medical ultrasound equipment. Over the next quarter of a century, it established a reputation for technological leadership. This reputation was solidified in 1988, when ATL introduced the world's first digital ultrasound equipment. By 1997, ATL had established itself as one of the top four ultrasound manufacturers in the world, along with Acuson, Hewlett-Packard, and Toshiba. Each of these companies had about 15 percent to 17 percent of the global market. In 1997, ATL generated record revenues of $431 million and near record net profits of $21.2 million. Almost half of its revenues were booked outside the United States.

In November 1997, the company had launched its latest product, the HDI 5000, a high-end digital ultrasound unit priced around $250,000. The HDI 5000 represented ATL's fifth generation of all-digital

technology and, in something of a public relations coup, was selected by NASA for use by astronauts to perform sophisticated medical diagnostics aboard the international space station when it is launched in 2001. Essentially a specialized computer, the HDI 5000 can perform more than 14 billion operations per second. It incorporates a range of advanced diagnostic features, including a patented new Doppler blood flow imaging technology and adaptive system intelligence. The product garnered strong reviews from radiologists and gained rapid market acceptance. By July 1998, it was apparent that the HDI 5000 would sell more than 1,000 units in its first year alone, exceeding the company's prelaunch goal.

Despite the success of the HDI 5000, as ATL's top managers gathered at the Columbia Winery, they knew they faced some major challenges. There was significant disagreement within the company about the appropriate strategic focus. ATL offered a broad product line, spanning all major clinical applications of ultrasound technology, from the premium- to mid-price range. Some questioned the wisdom of such a broad market strategy; they believed that ATL lacked the technical and financial resources to pursue it successfully. In their view, the company would be better served by focusing its development efforts on premium machines targeted at the radiology or general imaging market. Others embraced the goal of offering a broad product line aimed at the premium and mid-range price segments, but believed that ATL had yet to identify and clearly articulate the appropriate strategy for attaining this goal.

To complicate matters, in recent years General Electric and Siemens had moved aggressively into the medical ultrasound market. These companies

This case is intended to be used as the basis for class discussion rather than as an illustration of either effective or ineffective handling of the situation. This case was prepared by Charles W. L. Hill, University of Washington. Used by permission.

C178

already had a strong position in medical diagnostic imaging equipment, selling everything from x-ray machines and computed tomography (CT) scanners to magnetic resonance imaging (MRI) machines. Both GE and Siemens seemed intent on adding ultrasound equipment to their product portfolio. To this end, in early 1988 General Electric Medical Systems (GEMS) purchased a second-tier ultrasound company, Diasonics. This purchase, when combined with GE's existing ultrasound sales, gave GE potential 1998 revenues in the $460 million range. In 1997, Siemens had worldwide ultrasound revenues of $267 million, and it, too, was reportedly on the lookout for acquisition candidates. ATL's managers had to decide how best to respond to this new competitive threat. A particular cause for concern was that by bundling together a diverse range of imaging products and offering deep price discounts to hospitals and multihospital systems that purchase the entire bundle, multimodality firms such as GE and Siemens might be able to capture share from dedicated ultrasound companies such as ATL.

Although the worldwide market for medical ultrasound equipment was projected to grow, some worried that these new competitors might accelerate the erosion in average selling price that ATL and its competitors had experienced. During the first half of the 1990s, average retail prices for ultrasound equipment had fallen by around 10 percent to 15 percent per annum. Since 1997, the decline had been reversed by the introduction of new "super-premium" machines such as ATL's HDI 5000 and Acuson's Sequoia. However, ATL was forecasting some weakening of average retail prices after 2000 as these products aged. To maintain gross margins against the background of falling prices, ATL would have to find ways to drive down its cost structure.

MEDICAL IMAGING

Medical imaging is a critical step in the diagnosis of many ailments. For eighty years, the business of taking pictures of the inside of the body was routine: send x-rays through the body and record an image on film. Over the last quarter of a century, however, a number of different imaging technologies have made their way into the medical mainstream. Where once there were only x-rays, now there are CT scanners, MRI machines, and ultrasound. Each

of these techniques is transforming diagnosis of disease, and each has its strengths and weaknesses. Competition among these different imaging techniques is growing.

Computed tomography is closest to x-rays. It uses a series of x-ray pictures taken by a camera orbiting the body. A computer combines these to form a detailed cross-sectional image. A problem with x-rays is that they distinguish between body areas of different density—though that makes them useful for studying the skeleton, for example. A problem with the CT scan is that it produces much more radiation than an x-ray. That is not considered dangerous, but receiving hundreds of CT scans may be inadvisable. Both these problems are dealt with by magnetic resonance imaging, which takes a picture of where water is in the body without using x-rays. It distinguishes clearly between skin, fat, and muscle. The technology is based on the fact that water molecules can behave like tiny magnets. An MRI scanner bathes the body in a powerful magnetic field and the water molecules in the body line up. The molecules are jarred by a radio wave pulse, and as they realign with the magnetic field, they emit their own radio pulse. The pattern of that return pulse is turned into a cross section of the body by a computer. But MRI has three drawbacks: the machinery required costs about $2 million and fills a room (a CT scanner costs about $1 million); the powerful magnets wipe magnetic storage media such as credit cards and floppy disks and may harm patients with heart pacemakers; and, like CT, all it provides are snapshots.

This is where ultrasound imaging comes in. A noninvasive procedure, ultrasound uses the reflection of high frequency sound waves to create images of the body's soft tissue, organs, and blood flow in real time on a television monitor. The principle is very similar to the echo sonar by which dolphins, bats, and submarines navigate. Ultrasound systems include three major components: a scanhead, which transmits sound waves into the body of a patient, receives returning echoes from the patient, and converts the echoes into electrical signals; a computer processing unit, which processes the electrical echo signals into images or measurements of physiological conditions within the patient's body; and a monitor, which displays the resulting images or measurement information. The scanhead is held by the ultrasound operator and passed over the area being imaged. Because of the real-time capability of ultrasound, one can, for example, watch a heart beat or a fetus move in a woman's womb.

In the hands of a skilled operator, an ultrasound image may be as clear as a CT scan or an x-ray, but in general, the image quality is inferior. The best images are of structures near the surface of the body, up to a depth of about 10 centimeters. The images show a smaller area than MRI or CT scans. However, increases in the clarity and power of ultrasound equipment is enabling ultrasound operators to distinguish between different types of tissue and, therefore, do some of the work previously allocated to CT and MRI specialists. Radiologists are also increasingly making use of contrast agents in ultrasound to increase image precision and show various structures within the body more clearly.

A cost-effective procedure, ultrasound can eliminate the need for more invasive and expensive procedures. Ultrasound machinery is small enough to be wheeled about on a trolley and costs between $250,000 and $30,000, depending on the sophistication of the machine. Although the image quality is lesser than that produced by CT or MRI, the lower cost of ultrasound equipment is facilitating market adoption, particularly in countries where MRI and CT machines are viewed as prohibitively expensive.

Recent advances in ultrasound have emphasized enhancing the diagnostic properties of the technology. Among the areas of intense research are tissue harmonic imaging, contrast imaging, and three-dimensional imaging. Tissue harmonic imaging involves using broadbeam scanheads to detect and image echoes that are reflected off tissue at a higher frequency than those originally transmitted. The shifting from one frequency to another is called harmonics. Tissue harmonic imaging enables a dramatic reduction in image artifacts, reduces haze and clutter, and significantly increases contrast resolution. Contrast imaging involves using contrast agents, microbubbles of which reflect ultrasound waves at a different frequency than the surrounding tissue. When used in conjunction with harmonic imaging, contrast agents enable the physician to gain a clearer image of specific soft tissue. Three-dimensional imaging—such as a 3D view of a beating heart—can provide more information for a diagnostic decision.

Scanhead technology represents another area of research in ultrasound. As mentioned earlier, scanheads are held by the ultrasound operator over the area to be imaged, and they transmit and receive sound waves. In addition to having broadbeam capability, so that they can transmit and receive signals of a different frequency (necessary for harmonic imaging), modern scanheads come in a wide range of specialized design for different diagnostic tasks.

THE MEDICAL ULTRASOUND MARKET

In 1997, more than $8 billion was spent on medical imaging equipment worldwide. Diagnostic ultrasound products, upgrades, and accessories sold for use in hospitals, clinics, and physicians' offices accounted for an estimated $2.8 billion of this total, a 5.5 percent increase over the prior year. Ultrasound sales booked in the United States totaled around $853 million. Western Europe accounted for another $765 million, Japan for $400 million, the rest of Asia for $330 million, and Latin America for $225 million. After several slow years, the ultrasound market was predicted to grow steadily over the next few years, particularly in the United States, where new product introductions were projected to drive growth. Most industry sources forecast growth of 6 to 8 percent between 1997 and 2002; they see the global market for ultrasound closing in on around $3.5 billion by 2002, and expect the U.S. market to exceed $1.2 billion.

The medical ultrasound business is divided into different market segments based on medical specialty and price. The main medical segments, in order of importance, are radiology, cardiology, obstetrics-gynecology, and vascular surgery. Figure 1 summarizes the 1997 market segment data in the United States and Figure 2 summarizes the 1997 international data. The definitions of market segments differ slightly since in the international market, general imaging is taken to include both radiology *and* internal medicine. In radiology, ultrasound is used to obtain diagnostic information on organs and soft tissue, particularly in the abdominal area. It is also used to ascertain fetal development, guide tissue biopsies, and visualize blood flow. In cardiology, ultrasound is used to capture real-time images of the heart and its valves. Referred to as echocardiography, these images help the physician assess heart function, as well as congenital and valvular disease. Echocardiography is a useful tool for the detection and assessment of coronary

FIGURE I

1997 U.S. Sales by
Market Segment
(in $ millions)

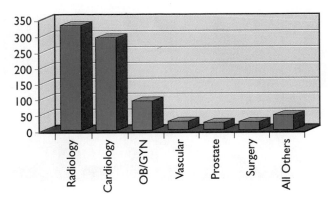

artery disease. In ob-gyn, ultrasound is the preferred imaging technique for the assessment of fetal development, because it is noninvasive and involves no ionizing radiation. Ultrasound is also used for general gynecological and infertility examinations. In vascular surgery, ultrasound is used to identify plaque deposits and their characteristics, clots, and valve competence in blood vessels. In the United States, the number of radiology exams using ultrasound grew from 25.8 million in 1996 to 27.5 million in 1997. The ultrasound exam figures for cardiology were 13.4 million in 1996 and 14.8 million in 1997. For ob-gyn, they increased from 10.8 million exams to 11.4 million.

Customers in each segment demand machines that have diagnostic features appropriate for their specialty. Cardiologists, for example, are more interested in 3D imaging capabilities and advanced quantitative data output than radiologists. It should be noted, however, that a substantial proportion of the radiology market also requires machines that have cardiac imaging capabilities. Often referred to

as the shared service market, many community or smaller hospitals in the United States fall into this category.

The ultrasound market can be segmented not only according to medical specialty, but also on the basis of price (see Figure 3). Its four main price segments are premium-performance, high-performance, mid-range, and low-end machines. Premium-performance machines make up about 18 percent of the world market and cost more than $160,000, with the super-premium machines fetching as much as $250,000. These powerful systems provide the physician with superior color definition of subtle tissue characteristics and incorporate an array of advanced features, such as tissue harmonic imaging and 3D imaging capability. They also come equipped with a wide variety of specialized scanheads for specific imaging tasks. High-performance machines, which are priced between $100,000 and $160,000 and constitute about 30 percent of the world market, also include many advanced color-imaging capabilities and a variety of scanheads.

FIGURE 2

1997 International
Sales by Market
Segment (in $ millions)

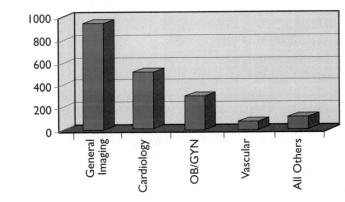

FIGURE 3

Ultrasound Price
Segments in 1997

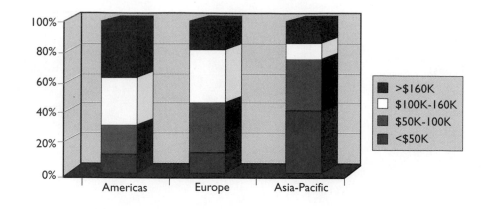

Generally, however, they lack cutting-edge diagnostic technology, such as tissue harmonic imaging. Mid-range ultrasound systems sell for between $50,000 and $100,000 and make up about 28 percent of the world ultrasound market. These systems produce a basic low-resolution color image and utilize a limited number of scanheads. Low-end machines sell for under $50,000 and constitute 24 percent of the world market. This market segment is characterized by basic black-and-white imaging systems, and a limited selection of scanheads. These machines provide limited diagnostic information.

What is clear from Figure 3 is that the international markets are far more price sensitive than the U.S. market. Some 62 percent of all units sold in 1997 in the Americas—the bulk of them in the United States—were priced at more than $100,000, whereas 77 percent of all units sold in the Asian Pacific region were priced at under $100,000. These differences reflect not only differences in the wealth of a region, but also societal differences in the proportion of resources devoted to health care. The international market is primarily a mid-range and low-end market.

Toshiba is the largest manufacturer of ultrasound equipment in the world, with 14.7 percent of the global market as measured by combined product and service revenues in 1997 (see Figure 4). However, Toshiba's position reflects its dominance in Japan and parts of Asia. Elsewhere, it is a relatively weak player. GE, after its early 1988 acquisition of Diasonics, has catapulted into second place, followed closely by HP, Acuson, and ATL. In the important U.S. market, which is the lead market for new generation ultrasound products, Acuson, HP, ATL, and GE/Diasonics dominate. (See Figure 5,

which shows market share data based on revenues from equipment sales and upgrades; service revenues are excluded.) The relative ranking of the three companies has historically been driven by the age of their product offerings. In 1996, HP led the market, but Acuson captured the lead in 1997 due to strong sales of its new generation premium product, the Sequoia. ATL had a relatively weak year in 1997 because its lead product, the HDI 3000, had been introduced in October 1994 and was now aging. ATL was expected to come on strong in 1998 following the successful launch of its latest product, the HDI 5000.

Although HP is number two in the U.S. market, its strong showing is primarily due to a dominant position in the cardiology market—a market HP pioneered—where it held a 55 percent share of equipment sales and upgrades in 1997. Acuson was second with a 22 percent share, and ATL third with 12 percent. In the U.S. radiology market, Acuson led the way with a 41.5 percent share of equipment sales and upgrades, followed by ATL (20.2 percent), and GE (14.3 percent). HP had only a 3.2 percent share of this market.

The ultrasound market is a high-technology business with relatively short product life cycles and continuing pressures to develop new products that incorporate new or improved diagnostic features. Competition between the major players is intense and based on technological features, price, and service support. Hospitals are the major customers, accounting for 71 percent of unit shipments by value in the United States in 1997. Demand for equipment in the private sector (clinics and doctors' offices) is, however, growing somewhat faster than demand from hospitals.

FIGURE 4

1997 Worldwide
Market Share (%) of
Ultrasound Companies

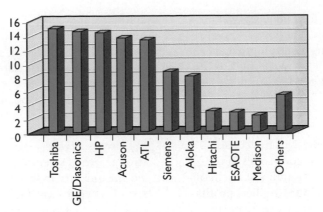

Within the United States, most large companies sell directly, while smaller companies typically turn over distribution to multiproduct distributors. According to industry data, Acuson had a seventy-person sales force in 1997, of which twenty-eight were dedicated to the cardiology market. ATL had a seventy-seven person sales force, with twenty-three dedicated to cardiology and fourteen to women's health. HP had a fifty-eight person sales force, fifty of whom were dedicated to cardiology. Internationally a mix of direct sales and distributors is used. ATL, for example, uses direct sales in fifteen major foreign markets but utilizes distributors elsewhere. The large companies also maintain their own customer support and service operations in those countries where they have a direct-sales presence. Dealers provide service and support in other markets.

The whole industry was characterized by low profitability in the mid 1990s as companies struggled with a combination of aging products, slowing demand growth, falling prices, and intense competition. An emphasis on health care cost containment in the United States also had a negative impact on market demand and prices for ultrasound equipment during the mid 1990s. Acuson lost $10.6 million in 1997, but made $22.4 million in 1997 as sales for its new Sequoia and Aspen products began to take off. ATL reported record net income of $21.2 million in 1997, but its profit margin was only 5 percent. HP's ultrasound business was estimated to be profitable but suffering from margin pressure. Both GE and Diasonics probably did no better than break even in 1997. Toshiba's ultrasound business was reportedly

FIGURE 5

1997 U.S. Market
Share (%)

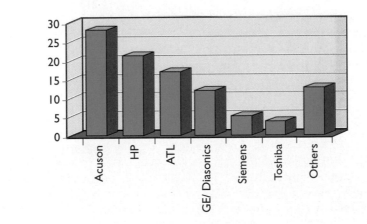

barely profitable, while the ultrasound operations of Siemens were unprofitable. There was some hope that prices and margins might improve in 1998–2000 as additional new products such as ATL's HDI 5000 gained market acceptance.

ATL

Since its establishment in 1969, ATL has consistently been among the leading companies in the medical ultrasound business. Located just north of Seattle, ATL had 1997 sales of $431 million, profits of $21.2 million, and 2,700 employees. Some 49 percent of its revenues were generated outside of the United States. (See Table 1 for financial statements.) The company has direct sales and service subsidiaries in fourteen nations, including Australia, Canada, China, France, Germany, India, Italy, Sweden, the United Kingdom, and Singapore. The Chinese subsidiary, the most recent, was established in May 1997. In other parts of the world, ATL has a presence through an extensive network of independent distributors.

In 1980, ATL was acquired by Squibb, a large pharmaceutical and medical equipment enterprise. In 1986, Squibb spun off its medical equipment operations under a separate company, Westmark Holdings. Denis Fell moved from Squibb to head Westmark. In 1992, Westmark split itself into two entities, ATL and Spacelabs, a manufacturer of patient-monitoring systems. Fell became ATL's CEO. Throughout this period, ATL retained its own separate identity, first within Squibb and then within Westmark.

Always a technology-driven company with a strong core of scientific talent, back in 1988 ATL led the industry in the development of digital ultrasound when it introduced the first digital ultrasound product. Similarly, in the 1990s ATL pioneered harmonic imaging technology, introducing, in 1996, the first machine with harmonic imaging capability, a version of the HDI 3000. Reflecting its focus on technological leadership, traditionally ATL's strongest position has been in the premium and high-end segments of the market. Nevertheless, given that half of the world market is for units priced under $100,000, ATL has long looked for a way to compete effectively in the mid-range. To this end, in May 1994 ATL acquired Interspec, a smaller Pennsylvania-based ultrasound company that had a presence in the mid range and cardiology market segments.

TABLE I

ATL's Financial Data
(in thousands, except per share data)

	1997	1996	1995
Results of Operations			
Revenues	$431,244	$419,157	$399,446
Gross profit	213,819	204,982	184,525
Selling, general and administrative expenses	128,739	122,990	119,955
Research and development expenses	59,710	53,969	50,255
Net income (loss)	$ 21,171	$ (828)	$ 12,002
Net income, excluding nonrecurring items	$ 21,171	$ 21,829	$ 10,617
Net income (loss) per share—diluted	$ 1.41	$ (0.06)	$ 0.88
Net income per share, excluding nonrecurring items—diluted	$ 1.41	$ 1.47	$ 0.78
Balance Sheet			
Cash and short-term investments	$ 30,821	$ 63,262	$ 35,654
Total assets	361,810	380,201	353,448
Long-term debt	12,307	12,936	14,837
Shareholders' equity	229,721	211,250	210,923
Common Shares Outstanding	14,413	14,023	13,610

Current Product Offerings

In mid 1998, ATL offered four main products: the HDI 5000, targeted at the premium price segment of the market; the older HDI 3000, targeted at the high-performance price segment; the HDI 1000, targeted at the mid-range price segment; and the Ultramark 400, targeted at the mid- to low-end price segment.

HDI 5000   The HDI 5000 was ATL's fifth generation digital ultrasound machine. First sold in November 1997, the HDI 5000 is a state-of-the-art system that incorporates a wide range of advanced diagnostic features and can be equipped with a wide range of high-performance ATL broadband scanheads, three of which are new to this model. In addition, the HDI 5000 comes with networking capability, which will allow physicians to share ultrasound images with each other via the Web. A variant of the HDI 5000, the HDI 5000cv, is targeted at the cardiology marketplace and comes equipped with the diagnostic features and scanheads demanded by cardiologists. Priced as high as $250,000 depending on features, the HDI 5000 seemed to be garnering significant market acceptance and was on track to sell more than 1,000 units in under twelve months. With the sales boost provided by the HDI 5000, in May 1998 ATL announced that it had shipped more than 10,000 all-digital HDI ultrasound systems since the product family was first introduced in 1988. ATL estimated that the worldwide installed base of all-digital systems numbered 14,000 by mid 1998, giving ATL a market share of more than 70 percent. To improve market acceptance of the HDI 5000, ATL offered the product both as a new system, and as an on-site upgrade to the older HDI 3000 system. This was made possible by the fact that the two products shared the same basic platform. The HDI 5000 could also make use of scanheads designed for the HDI 3000.

Despite the success of the HDI 5000, some within the company noted that the HDI 5000cv lacked the detailed quantification data capabilities that came with Hewlett-Packard's SONOS 5500 and SONOS 2500 dedicated cardiology ultrasound products. Quantification data were viewed by cardiologists as an important diagnostic tool. According to one manager, HP was about a year ahead of ATL with regard to quantification features. On the other hand, the harmonic imaging and contrast agent features of the HDI 5000 were at the forefront of ultrasound technology. Still, others noted that while ATL remains a leader in digital ultrasound technology and the beam-forming required for harmonic imaging, the company's principal competitors had narrowed the performance gap and were fast catching up. Yet another view was offered by one executive, who feared that the current push to add additional cardiology features to the HDI 5000cv might divert scarce scientific talent away from radiology and general imaging. This executive noted that "around 80 percent of the new features planned for the HDI 5000 and 3000 focus on cardiology applications such as quantification and 3D imaging—we are not paying sufficient attention to our core general imaging market. We lack the depth of scientific talent to focus on all of these market opportunities. We need to prioritize better."

HDI 3000   The HDI 3000 was ATL's fourth generation digital machine, and had been sold since October 1994. Originally sold as a premium machine, the product had been repositioned toward the high-performance price segment. Although this machine lacked the raw processing power of the HDI 5000, ATL had continued adding advanced features to it—such as tissue harmonic imaging, which was added in March 1997. A variant of the HDI 3000, the HDI 3000cv, was targeted at the cardiology marketplace.

HDI 1000   In early 1997, ATL introduced the HDI 1000, a product that was conceived as ATL's internally developed and produced digital offering for the mid-range marketplace. This was a market segment in which ATL had long struggled to develop a strong product offering. Although the mid-range market accounted for 28 percent of global ultrasound sales by value, ATL accounted for less than 10 percent of all sales to this segment. Some felt that if ATL was to meet Wall Street's growth expectations, the company needed to develop a viable mid-range offering. ATL's previous offering, the Apogee 800, which was introduced in October 1994, was acquired as part of the 1994 Interspec acquisition. The Apogee system had not lived up to expectations.

The HDI 1000 began as a controversial development project within ATL. Some internal critics believed that the HDI 1000 demonstrated all too well the long standing problem that the company was having not only in developing a viable mid-range offering, but also in making the difficult choice about what to focus on. A key problem ATL faced was how to design and produce an ultrasound system that built on ATL's strengths in digital ultrasound technology, but could be produced at a cost that would make it a profitable product offering in the mid range. The HDI 1000 was based on a revolutionary design philosophy. The design concept, as first articulated in the early 1990s, was to take advantage of the increasing power and falling cost of computer processing in order to replace many hardware components within ultrasound machines with software. The thinking was that by replacing specialized hardware with software, the unit cost of manufacturing the HDI 1000 could be driven down, enabling ATL to cost-effectively produce a powerful all-digital mid-range unit. Fell, the company's CEO, referred to the HDI 1000 design concept as a second inflection point in the ultrasound market, comparable in importance to the introduction of the first digital system back in 1988 (the first inflection point).

At the time the HDI 1000 project was launched, some voiced concern that the project would divert scarce engineering resources from ATL's core product offerings, and dedicate them to a complex project with a low probability of success. Moreover, they argued that the project was driven by a technological vision, as opposed to market needs. Despite such reservations, the promoters of the project had some important allies on the board, including the founder of the company and the current CEO, so the project was given the go-ahead.

Developing the HDI 1000 turned out to be a daunting task. The engineering problems inherent in replacing custom hardware with software had been underestimated, and ATL lacked the engineers required to work out the problems in an expeditious manner. Despite these constraints, ATL did manage to replace more than fifty percent of the hardware components in a conventional ultrasound machine with software, which in the HDI 1000 performs more than 70 percent of the functions of the ultrasound system. At the heart of this software-intensive system is a proprietary multitasking software management technology, developed by the HDI 1000 team, which utilizes object-oriented software architecture to perform self-contained software tasks that replace conventional hardware.

When the HDI 1000 was eventually introduced in 1997, the project was already two years over

schedule, it cost more to manufacture than initially planned, and it suffered from some software reliability problems. Moreover, the product lacked several critical shared-service features, particularly those required by cardiologists. Although development continued and a new version of the HDI 1000 scheduled for release in January 1999 included an expanded feature set, initial sales were below expectations. The product did find a niche, but it was as an ob-gyn machine in the United States market. As of June 1998, the HDI 1000 had not given ATL the presence in the global mid-range market that the company had been looking for.

Ultramark 400   The failure of the HDI 1000 to match ATL's expectations in the global mid-range market was the catalyst behind a strategic partnership, announced in May 1998, between ATL and Medison, a South Korean ultrasound company. Medison had been building a reputation as a highly competitive manufacturer of basic ultrasound products in the $30,000 to $50,000 price range. Under the deal announced, ATL agreed to start marketing Medison's basic black-and-white digital ultrasound system throughout its global direct sales and distribution network. The product, referred to as the Ultramark 400, is to be manufactured for ATL by Medison in South Korea. In the U.S. market, ATL indicated that it would target the Ultramark 400 system at the office-based ob-gyn market, while continuing to sell the more sophisticated HDI 1000 color imaging system to the ob-gyn departments in hospitals and larger clinics.

The announcement of the Medison deal caught many of ATL's own managers by surprise. They wondered whether the deal signaled a shift in the strategic thinking of top management at ATL away from the philosophy of developing mid-range offerings in house, or whether the deal was nothing more than a temporary solution to a problem caused by the failure of the HDI 1000 to live up to its initial promise.

HDI 1500   The Ultramark 400 marketing deal was conceived as the first step in a deeper collaboration between ATL and Medison. The next step involves codevelopment of a new product, based on ATL technology, that will be aimed at the mid-range market, manufactured by Medison in South Korea, and sold through ATL's global network. Referred to as the HDI 1500, this all-digital color system is scheduled for introduction in late 1998 and seems likely to replace the HDI 1000 and Ultramark 400 as ATL's primary mid-range offering. The HDI 1500 will have the advantage of sharing common platform features with the HDI 5000 and HDI 3000 and of being able to utilize most HDI broadband scanheads.

The Product Development Process

At ATL, product development is the responsibility of the product generation function (engineering). The product generation function is organized as a conventional matrix, with basic engineering functions on one side and projects on the other (see Figure 6). Two committees play an important role in driving the activities of the product generation organization: the senior technology staff and the product generation council.

The senior technology staff is a committee of fifteen engineers, selected by their peers, who are responsible for developing the technology strategy of ATL. The fifteen engineers elect a chief, and for two years this individual is accorded VP status and serves on both the product generation council and the executive management committee of ATL. The product generation council is responsible for product strategy. Its members include the heads of the various engineering functions and projects, along with key marketing and manufacturing personnel. The council is responsible for the new product generation strategy at ATL and for the integration of cross-functional requirements within the product generation organization.

Technology Strategy   At ATL, technology strategy is concerned with identifying, understanding, and developing technologies that are essential to the development of diagnostic ultrasound. ATL divides technology into two broad categories: (1) ultrasound-specific technologies, including the physics and engineering knowledge used in ultrasound and a basic understanding of its clinical application, and (2) supporting technologies, which are not necessarily specific to diagnostic ultrasound. Examples of the former technologies include the physics of harmonic imaging and the use of contrast agents and 3D imaging in diagnostic ultrasound. Examples of the latter include software and hardware architectural issues, communications technologies, and issues related to manufacturing.

ATL's goals in developing its technology strategy are to differentiate its products on the basis of superior proprietary diagnostic ultrasound technology, to bring reliable products to market in a reasonable time span, and to do so in a manner that does not increase manufacturing costs. An ideal goal is to bring product to market two to three years ahead of competitors, or when there is a competitive release, to be able to respond within a year. Five guiding principles govern all areas of technical strategy: (1) leveraging commonality across products so as to reduce time to market and system costs (the HDI 5000 and 3000 machines, for example, share the same basic hardware platform and many software features); (2) influencing and embracing broad industry standards; (3) using commercially available technology wherever appropriate; (4) developing and maintaining key ultrasound tools where commercial tools are not available; and (5) maintaining awareness of progress in key technological areas through contacts with academic institutions, research publications, academic conferences, and the like.

An example of technology strategy at work at ATL is the company's evolving competence in harmonic contrast imaging. Contrast agents are used to highlight certain tissue structures. ATL was the first to demonstrate that the microbubbles in different contrast agents reflect sound waves at different frequencies, and that in conjunction with broadband scanners this feature could be used to enhance image quality and diagnostic value. ATL is continuing to pursue microbubble physics research and is working closely with the manufacturers of contrast agents. The knowledge gained should enable ATL to optimize ultrasound images for specific contrast agents. ATL is also devoting considerable effort to developing a good quantification package for echocardiogram applications.

New Product Strategy   New product generation strategy is developed by the product generation council and implemented through the product generation organization. ATL's top executives had committed the company to the goal of becoming the global market share leader in the ultrasound business, with products that served all major price segments. The product development strategy of the company called for the development of a family of digital ultrasound products aimed at the premium

FIGURE 6

ATL's Product
Generation Organization

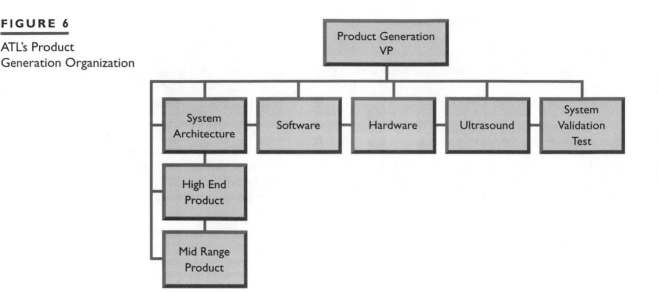

to mid-range price segments of the market and containing the feature sets appropriate for radiology, cardiology, ob-gyn, and vascular surgery. The family of products, which would be based on a common platform to reduce manufacturing costs, was scheduled for market introduction between late 2000 and early 2001. It was not clear whether the mid-range offerings in this family would be manufactured by ATL, or by a partner such as Medison.

Commenting on this strategy, one insider noted that "It's typical ATL. Once again we are trying to be all things to all people. We need to prioritize better. We do not have the resource to simultaneously pursue all of these product opportunities." Fell disagreed. "I know people say these things," he commented, "but we really have no choice. We cannot achieve our growth objective and boost our stock price unless we participate in the major segments of the market, and that includes the mid range. Anyway, part of my job is to push people to achieve goals that they do not think are possible."

The product generation council uses a number of mechanisms to control and drive the product development process. To begin with, the council has developed an aggregate product plan, which describes all development activities, including the resources needed, estimated development costs, and time lines. This plan is reviewed by the council on a quarterly basis. The council is responsible for prioritizing the development activities listed in the plan. To become part of the aggregate plan, a proj-

ect charter and contract must be reviewed and approved by the council. The project charter contains a brief description of the project and identifies the core team members and the project sponsor. The project contract—which is a contract between the council, core team members, and the project sponsor—contains detailed goals and objectives, and estimates development costs and the development schedule, including important calendar milestones. Once the contract is agreed on, any change must be reviewed and approved by the council. Once allocated to a development team, core team members are 100 percent accountable to the project, not to their function. There is also an incentive program, which links the bonus pay of core team members to development team results.

After the project is initiated, ATL utilizes a phase gate process to review and control its development (see Figure 7). This process contains a limited number of gates, which are either decision points or review points; some of them are optional, depending on the nature of the product being developed. For example, new platform projects have to go through a more rigorous process than simple derivative projects. The criteria for moving on to the next stage of development also vary, depending on the nature of the project.

FDA Regulations   Because ATL produces medical equipment, its product development processes are closely monitored and regulated by the Federal

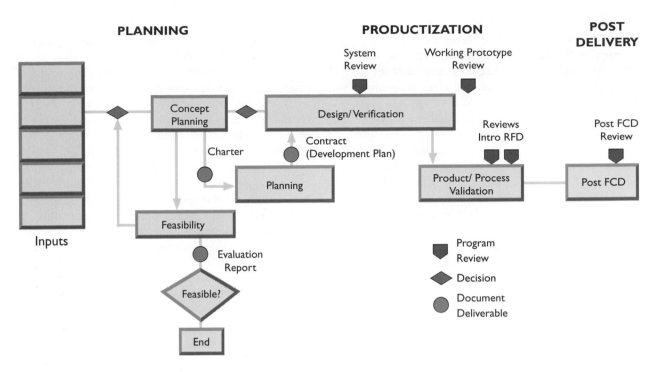

FIGURE 7

ATL's Stage Gate
Process

Drug Administration. The FDA must approve all new products and major modifications before marketing can begin. FDA regulations now also embrace monitoring and approval of manufacturing and service activities. Product design processes, too, are open to rigorous FDA inspection and critique. The FDA requires that all medical devices introduced into the market be preceded either by a premarket notification clearance order (referred to as a 510k), or an approved premarket application (PMA). An approved PMA application indicates that the FDA has determined that the device has been proven, through the submission of clinical trial data and manufacturing quality assurance information, to be safe and effective for its labeled indications. The process of obtaining a 510k typically takes six to nine months, whereas a PMA approval typically takes more than one year.

Manufacturing

ATL manufactures both ultrasound systems and scanheads. The exceptions are the Ultramark 400

and upcoming HDI 1500, which are manufactured by Medison. Since the early 1990s, ATL has aggressively implemented a number of improvements in its internal manufacturing processes in order to drive down system costs, increase quality, and reduce build time. For example, build time for ultrasound systems has been reduced from 140 days in 1988 to just 15 days in 1997, enabling ATL to implement a "build to order" strategy, which minimizes inventory. Build time for scanheads has been reduced from 25 days in 1988 to 16 days in 1997. ATL builds scanheads utilizing a "make to stock" strategy, putting items into finished goods inventory.

Materials account for the largest portion of system and scanhead costs (about 70 percent and 50 percent, respectively), followed by labor (5 percent and 12 percent, respectively), and overhead (20 percent and 38 percent, respectively). Materials costs are driven down each year by focusing on design cost reductions (design for manufacturing) and by negotiating aggressively with suppliers for volume discounts. Until 1990, ATL purchased finished circuit boards for its systems from external vendors. Dissatisfied with the costs it had to pay, in the early 1990s ATL began to move surface mount technology in-house (surface mount technology refers to the process of mounting electronic components onto circuit boards). At the time, ATL was paying as much as 21.5 cents per placement to purchase circuit boards from external manufacturers. By optimizing capacity utilization through better production scheduling, ATL has driven per placement costs from 17.5 cents in 1990, when it first started to finish circuit boards in-house, to just more than 5 cents per placement in 1997. As a result of moving production in-house, ATL now builds and assembles as much as 90 percent of the major modules within its ultrasound systems and scanheads. This level of in-house production is unusual among high-technology companies.

Organization and Management

The bulk of ATL employees are to be found in one of three main functions: product generation (engineering), worldwide sales and marketing, and operations. Three smaller functions—finance, human resources, and legal affairs—perform important support roles. Overall management of ATL is provided by an executive committee composed of the vice presidents of these functions, along with Fell, the CEO. The worldwide marketing and sales organization is divided into three main geographical regions—the Americas, Asia/Pacific, and Europe. Sales and marketing also has a unit dedicated to the U.S. cardiology business. There is no formal cross-functional matrix structure, although as discussed earlier, product generation is organized as a matrix.

In interviews with this case writer, several managers within ATL voiced concerns about the general organization and management of the company. Internal critics believed that ATL has been too technology driven. The failure of the HDI 1000 was repeatedly mentioned as an example of this phenomenon. The critics believed that ATL's three core functions—product generation, operations, and sales and marketing—were silos that did not communicate sufficiently with each other. They expressed concern that the personalities of some of the key players in the company made matters worse. Fell was nearing seventy, and although he was unquestionably a strong advocate for the company on Wall Street and had led ATL well, some felt that it was time for him to step down and pass on the reins of leadership. They noted that Fell delegated significant decision-making authority to the executive committee, but the executive committee itself seemed reluctant to make difficult choices, to set overall strategic direction, or to effectively prioritize between competing claims on resources. In the words of one manager, "Failure to focus and prioritize is a real problem within the company. We do not ask whether a dollar spent here yields a greater return than a dollar spent elsewhere. Top management needs to do a better job of communicating priorities." Moreover, the vice president for worldwide sales and marketing was viewed by some of his colleagues on the executive committee as being overly protective of his turf and not enough of a team player. This helped to stymie any attempts by the executive committee to make difficult choices. As a result, according to one internal critic, "This is a company run by the middle management. The executive committee doesn't drive the workings of the company."

At the same time, most managers interviewed acknowledged that the company did have strong technical skills, perhaps stronger than most of its competitors, and that its employees were both excellent and loyal. To quote one, "This is a company with a strong employee base. There is a lot of intellectual horsepower at ATL. People stay here. The employee turnover is low." Another notable feature of the company was the cosmopolitan nature of its management. For example, Fell was English, as was the head of the technology staff, and the executive team included a Frenchman and a Spaniard.

Key Strategic Issues Going Forward

As senior managers met for the 1998 strategic planning review, a number of issues had made their way to the top of the agenda. A key issue was the appropriate strategic focus for ATL. Specifically, should the company continue to participate in the cardiology and mid-range market segments, particularly given its limited resources, and if so, what should the appropriate strategy be? There were some within the company who felt that focusing on the cardiology and mid-range segments pulled scarce resources away from the company's core premium and high-end radiology franchise. Others believed that if the company was to grow, it needed to find some way to participate successfully in these important segments.

The question surrounding the mid-range strategy had been thrown into sharp relief by the failure if the HDI 1000 system to meet its original expectations and by the recent, and to many surprising, deal with Medison. Several managers wondered whether the Medison deal marked a new strategic departure for ATL, or whether it was simply an opportunistic way of maintaining a position in the mid-range market while ATL again tried to develop its own product offering for this segment.

Also high in people's minds was the question of how to respond to the emergence of multi-modality competitors in the medical imaging space, such as GE and Siemens, both of which could bundle ultrasound products with other imaging and medical products in their efforts to make purchases more attractive to hospitals. How big a threat would GE prove to be, and how should ATL respond to this threat?

CASE 15

Cooper Tire & Rubber Company, 1998

This case was prepared by Javad Kargar of North Carolina Central University.

INTRODUCTION

Cooper Tire & Rubber Company is one of only a few companies to achieve both consistent and high growth and strong returns for more than a decade. It's future looks bright as well, although top managers must confront threats from the increased competition in the replacement tire market and the recent major changes in the new products, such as run-flats, and production systems announced by the big three tire companies. In addition, foreign low-cost production and sales opportunities have been created with the passage of the North American Free Trade Agreement (NAFTA) and the conclusion of the General Agreement on Tariffs and Trade (GATT).

The Early Years: Rubber Meets Road

Cooper was founded in 1914 as a manufacturer of patches, cement, and repair kits for tires. By 1920, Ira J. Cooper had broadened the scope of the firm, repositioning it as a tire manufacturer. At that time, Cooper had more than 130 domestic competitors, 40 in Ohio alone. The corporation's founder emphasized three principles: good merchandise, fair play, and a square deal. This so-called "Cooper Creed" remains a well-known corporate doctrine.[1]

In 1930, the Cooper Corporation and Giant Tire & Rubber merged with the Falls Rubber Company to form the Master Tire & Rubber Company. Within

a year, the combined production of the three plants totaled 2,850 tires per day. In 1946, the firm's name was changed to Cooper Tire & Rubber Company, in recognition of Ira J. Cooper's contribution.[2]

The Middle Years: Pumping Up Production

Several converging growth factors made the postwar era one of expansion for the tire industry. More disposable income enabled more Americans to own cars. The expansion of the interstate highway system and the trend toward suburbanization meant more wear and tear on tires and an increasing demand for replacement tires. Furthermore, buses, taxis, and trucks were rapidly supplanting the rail system for local and long-distance transportation. Cooper's expansion included the 1956 acquisition and refurbishment of a plant from the Dismuke Tire and Rubber Company in Clarksdale, Mississippi, which enabled Cooper to meet the growing demand for inner tubes and tread rubber. In addition, between 1947 and 1964, Cooper Tire developed its own national wholesaling system. The company attracted private-label customers and earned retailer loyalty by pledging not to open its own sales outlets—a strategy that also allowed it to avoid the headaches of the retail market.[3]

In 1960, the company went public with a listing on the New York Stock Exchange, and its distribution of shares facilitated another decade of growth. That year Cooper also acquired a plant in Auburn, Indiana, where all its automotive and custom-engineered rubber parts were produced. In 1964, an industrial rubber products division was established, and production was expanded with the acquisition of a second industrial product plant near

El Dorado, Arkansas. Other capital improvements at Cooper's corporate headquarters during the 1960s included a new warehouse at the Findlay, Ohio, plant and a research and engineering building to accommodate testing, laboratory, tire design, engineering, and sales training operations. Before the decade had ended, Cooper had completed a new tire plant in Texarkana, Arkansas.

By 1973, Cooper had completed research and development of its own radial tire building equipment and in-house product testing. Full-scale production of steel-belted radial passenger tires at the Findlay and Texarkana plants began the following year. A plant in Bowling Green, Ohio, was purchased in 1977 to manufacture reinforced hose and extruded rubber products.

The 1980s and 1990s: Wheeling and Dealing

The 1980s were years of significant change for Cooper. The company's strong financial condition has enabled it to expand tire production capacity while most of the industry has been contracting. Research and development at Cooper were enhanced by several capital investments during the 1980s. By mid decade, its warehousing capacity had increased to accommodate 3.2 million units of tires. In 1983, Cooper made the *Fortune* 500 list of America's largest industrial companies. In the following year, its net sales exceeded $500 million, and its net income was more than $24 million. In 1985, Cooper made its first foreign acquisition—a manufacturer of inner tubes in Mexico. That same year, Cooper was named one of the *101 Best Performing Companies in America*. In 1988, the Findlay plant and the Moraine distribution center were granted foreign trade subzone status by the U.S. Department of Commerce, which reduced and deferred the company's duty payments on imported raw materials.

As Cooper celebrated its seventy-fifty anniversary in 1989, the company's emphasis on the replacement tire market was rewarded. In the same year, the Tupelo, Mississippi, plant's tire-finishing operations were automated, reducing production costs, and a new building was added to the Bowling Green plant for warehousing. Warranty coverage on Cooper's premium radial was also expanded that year to include treadwear protection. In 1990, Cooper purchased its fourth tire-manufacturing facility, a 1.8-million-square-foot plant in Albany, Geor-

gia. Other expansions of existing plants were made in 1991 and 1992. Cooper acquired British-based Avon Tyres in early 1997. Cooper's capital investment has continued to grow during the 1990s, reaching $194.89 million in 1995, $193.69 million in 1996, and $107.52 million in 1997.

OVERVIEW OF THE TIRE INDUSTRY

Tire manufacturing became an important industry in the first half of the twentieth century as motor vehicles became the dominant mode of transportation. Tire industry comprises two major market segments: (1) the original equipment (OE) market, and (2) the replacement market. Both markets include passenger car tires; light, medium, and heavy truck tires; and farm vehicle tires.

The demand for OE tires is directly related to the number of new vehicles produced. However, demand for replacement tires depends on such factors as the average age of a car, the durability of tire tread, the number of cars in circulation, the average number of miles driven, and gasoline prices. Any reduction in new car sales is considered good news in the replacement market because it means that drivers are hanging on to their cars longer. Even in a strong economy, used car sales rise along with those of new cars, and motorists also spend more time on the road, further increasing the demand for replacement tires. Over the past four years, worldwide production of motor vehicles has remained steady at around 48 million units per year. However, the demand for OE passenger-car tires rose about 10 percent in 1996, to about 57.1 million units, and this demand is expected to continue to rise, reaching 58.1 million in 1998.[4]

The Original Equipment Market Segment

Auto manufacturers buy all of their tires directly from tire manufacturers. No auto producers have integrated backward into tire manufacturing as they have into other component vehicle parts.[5] Competition among the tire manufacturers to supply tires to the auto manufacturers has been fierce. Since tires are such a small cost item in the overall price of new vehicles, changes in OE tire prices have virtually zero effect on total OE tire demand.[6] However, the demand for OE tires, is highly elastic to the ease with which motor vehicle manufacturers could switch to other tire manufacturers' brands. All the major tire manufacturers were eager to have new vehicles equipped with their own brands in order to enhance replacement tire sales. The sale of OE tires was thus seen as strategically important, not only as a way to strengthen sales in the more profitable replacement segment but also to achieve economies of scale in manufacturing.

Vehicle manufacturers set detailed tire specifications for each of their vehicle models, and tire producers must meet those specifications if their tires are to be considered original equipment. It was typical for auto/truck manufacturers to establish higher quality standards for the OE tires they purchased than was the case for replacement tires. The automobile companies buy tires in large quantities and, since the number of buyers is low, they can usually negotiate low prices. Using this leverage over the years, the automakers have managed to negotiate an average price for an OE tire that was several dollars below what wholesale distributors paid tire manufacturers for a replacement tire of somewhat lower quality. In effect, the auto companies bought OE tires for roughly half the retail price commanded by replacement tires. As a result, the original equipment market has become a low-margin one relative to the replacement tire market.

According to the latest forecast by the Tire Market Analysis Committee (TMAC) of the Rubber Manufacturers Association, demand for OE passenger tires is expected to increase a modest 1.2 percent in 1998, rising to 58.1 million units, compared with 57.4 million units predicted in 1997. But OE shipments of light truck tires will remain relatively flat—at or below the 1997 shipment level of 6 million tires, the TMAC predicted.[7]

The Replacement Tire Market Segment

Demand for replacement tires during the 1970s and early 1980s was weak, partly because of the higher gasoline prices, which reduced the average number of miles driven annually per vehicles. In the United States, the average number of miles driven annually per vehicle dropped from 10,800 before the gasoline shortage era to 9,500 miles in 1993.[8] Recently, stable gasoline prices had contributed to a rise in the annual mileage rate per vehicle. Every 100-mile change in the average number of miles traveled per vehicle produced a 1-million unit change in replacement tire production.[9] Since 1991, unit shipments of replacement tires have increased every year (see Table 1 for volume trends in the United States by segment). In 1996, the replacement tire market in the passenger car and light truck in the United States was three times larger than the original equipment market, with a projected 2 percent annual growth rate.[10] During its useful life, a vehicle may require between two and six sets of replacement tires.

Tire manufacturers produce a large variety of grades and lines of tires for distribution under both

TABLE I

Trends in U.S. Tire Shipments, 1993–1998 (in millions of units)

Type of Tire	1993	1994	1995	1996	1997	1998
Passenger car:						
Replacement	165.2	170.0	171.0	175.3	178.5	180.0
OE	52.2	58.5	55.0	57.1	57.4	58.1
Retread	6.6	5.9	5.0	4.2	3.5	3.1
Light truck, truck, bus:						
Replacement	34.4	37.8	36.6	39.2	41.5	42.8
OE	8.5	10.8	11.6	10.2	10.9	10.9
Retread	22.8	23.3	23.0	23.5	24.2	24.8

Source: Tire Business, December 8, 1997, p. 14.

manufacturers' brand names and private labels. Branded replacement tires are manufactured to the tire producer's own specifications, which are usually below those required by auto manufacturers for OE tires. Some private-label tires supplied to wholesale distributors and large chain retailers are manufactured to the buyer's specifications rather than to the manufacturer's standards. There are often subtle differences in trade depth, grades of rubber, and component construction such that many replacement tires on the market are not equal to the quality and durability of OE tires.[11] As a consequence, replacement tires have a somewhat shorter life span than OE tires. By 1992, most tire manufacturers provided a guaranteed mileage warranty to the buyers of replacement tires. Moreover, nearly all branded replacement tires now carry lifetime warranties against manufacturing defects.

The major tire producers often use network TV campaigns to promote their brands, introduce new types of tires, and pull customers to their retail dealer outlets. Their network TV ad budgets commonly run from $10 million to $30 million a year, and their budgets for cooperative ads with dealers run from $20 million to $100 million a year. Several tire companies also sponsor auto racing events to promote the performance capabilities of their tires.

Replacement tires are marketed to vehicle owners through a variety of retail channels, including independent tire dealers, service stations, manufacturer-owned retail stores, major department stores with auto centers, retail chains, automobile dealerships, and warehouse clubs. Independent tire dealers usually carry the brands of several different major manufacturers as well as a discount-priced private-label brand, providing replacement buyers with a full assortment of brands with varying tread design, widths, durability, quality, and price attributes. Over the years, independent tire dealers handled about 66 percent of replacement tire segments. Surveys have shown that dealers were able to influence a car owner's choice of replacement tires, both as to brand and as to type of tire. Studies have also shown that most replacement tire buyers do not have strong tire brand preferences, making it easy for tire salespeople to switch customers to tire brands and grades with the highest dealer margins.[12] Dealers normally push their private-label tires because their profit margins on them are higher than they are on the name-brand tires of major manufacturers. Dealer margins on re-

placement tires are typically in the 35 to 40 percent range. Independent tire dealers frequently run price promotion ads in the local newspapers, making it easy for price-sensitive buyers to watch for sales and buy at off-list prices.

Service stations stock one or two manufacturers' brand tires and maybe a private-label brand. Retail tire outlets owned and franchised by the tire manufacturers carry only the manufacturer's name brands and perhaps a private-label made by the manufacturer. Department stores and the major retail chains usually market their own private-label brands, but occasionally carry also manufacturers' label tires.

In the past, retread tires have been widely used, and retreaded tire buyers were very price conscious. Retreaded tires were made from tires with worn treads. In 1996, the retreaded tire segment was very small and declining partly because buyers could purchase a new, more reliable set of tires for about $100 more than the cost of retreads. The size of the U.S. passenger car retread market dropped from 6.6 million units in 1993 to about 3.1 million units in 1996 (see also Table 1).

According to TMAC, dealers can look forward during 1998 to continued market growth in the wake of the previous year's expected record of 178.5 million passenger tires and 29 million light truck units. It is forecasting replacement shipments of 12.6 million tires in 1998, up less than 1 percent from 1997's anticipated 12.5 million units.[13]

Securities analyst Harry Millis of Fundamental Research in Willoughby, Ohio, also is upbeat about the industry's prospects in 1998. His forecast calls for slightly higher shipments to the replacement market—182.2 million units of passenger tires and 30.4 million light truck tires. He expects replacement shipments of medium truck tires to reach 13.4 million units during 1998, up 6.3 percent from his last year's estimate. Overall, Millis looks for OE and replacement shipments of all tires to rise about 1.9 percent in 1998 to 293.8 million units.[14]

Raw Material Supplies

More than 200 raw materials are used in manufacturing tires. The most important are natural rubber, synthetic rubber, fabric and fabric cord, polyvinyl alcohol, sulfur, crude oil, carbon black, and high-carbon steel bead wire. Crude oil is the largest raw

TABLE 2

North American Market Leaders 1996

Company/Plant Location	Year Opened	Unionized	Employees	Estimated Capacity
Goodyear				
Medicine Hat, Alberta	1960	Yes	230	8,200 units/day
Napanee, Ontario	1990	No	550	17,000 units/day
Valleyfield, Quebec	1964	Yes	1,300	26,000 units/day
Akron, Ohio	1983	Yes	600	2,000 units/day
Danville, VA	1966	Yes	2,300	13,000 units/day
Gadsden, AL	1929	Yes	2,300	33,000 units/day
Lawton, OK	1978	No	2,300	59,000 units/day
Topeka, KA	1944	Yes	2,000	8,100 units/day
Union City, TN	1968	Yes	3,000	53,100 units/day
Kelly-Springfield Tire, Fayetteville, NC	1969	Yes	2,900	62,000 units/day
Kelly-Springfield Tire, Freeport, III, IL	1964	Yes	1,700	30,000 units/day
Tyler, TX	1962	Yes	1,500	37,500 units/day
Compania Hulera Goodyear	1941	Yes	2,150	18,000 units/day
			22,830	366,900 units/day
Michelin				
Granton, Nova Scotia	1971	No	1,300	9,000 units/day
Waterville, Nova Scotia	1982	No	900	2,000 units/day
Bridgewater, Nova Scotia	1973	No	1,200	11,000 units/day
Uniroyal Goodrich, Kitchene, Ontario	1962	Yes	1,050	17,000 units/day
Michelin Aircraft Tire, Norwood, NC	1989	No	455	12,500 units/day
Dothan, AL	1979	No	700	4,500 units/day
Greenville, SC	1975	No	2,000	23,000 units/day
Lexington, SC	1981	No	1,300	15,000 units/day
Spartanburg, SC	1978	No	1,500	5,000 units/day
Uniroyal Goodrich, Opelika, AL	1963	Yes	1,625	26,000 units/day
Uniroyal Goodrich, Ardmore, OK	1969	No	1,975	32,000 units/day

material cost; the manufacture of an average-size passenger car radial tire consumes about 10 gallons of crude oil. Raw material costs for a typical passenger car radial were about $16, about half of a tire manufacturing cost in 1993.[15]

All of the raw materials are commodities, available in bulk from a variety of sources on world markets.[16] Several manufacturers had integrated backward into rubber manufacturing and tire fabrics, and supply all or part of their production needs for these materials. However, there is no evidence that these manufacturers have gained a meaningful cost advantage or have better ability to differentiate their products on the basis of quality.[17]

The overall price of tire materials has climbed about 8 percent in 1993.[18] Most notable is the rise in the cost of natural rubber, resulting from supply shortages at Asian producers. Those shortages caused an increase in the use of other materials, but that situation has subsequently worsened because of production snags and some facilities going off-line temporarily. Natural rubber will likely remain in short supply for some time, since increasing production is a relatively slow process. Synthetic material prices, however, may decline because the shortage is more a function of production capacity than material availability.[19]

Labor Costs

Although tire manufacturing is relatively capital intensive, there is significant labor content. Labor

TABLE 2 *(continued)*

Company/Plant Location	Year Opened	Unionized	Employees	Estimated Capacity
Uniroyal Goodrich, Fort Wayne, IN	1961	Yes	1,500	29,000 units/day
Uniroyal Goodrich, Tuscaloosa, AL	1945	Yes	2,000	30,000 units/day
			17,505	216,000 units/day
Bridgestone				
Bridgestone/Firestone, Joliette, Quebec	1965	Yes	880	12,500 units/day
Bridgestone/Firestone, Bloomington, Ill	1965	Yes	515	300 units/day
Bridgestone/Firestone, Decature, Ill, IL	1963	Yes	1,945	24,000 units/day
Bridgestone/Firestone, Des Moines, IOWA	1945	Yes	1,741	12,100 units/day
Bridgestone/Firestone, Oklahoma City	1969	Yes	1,032	34,500 units/day
Bridgestone/Firestone, Warren County, TN	1990	Yes	851	5,500 units/day
Bridgestone/Firestone, Wilson, NC	1973	No	2,181	41,000 units/day
			9,145	129,900 units/day
Cooper Tire & Rubber				
Albany, GA	1991	No	900	22,000 units/day
Findlay, Ohio	1919	Yes	1,000	26,000 units/day
Texarkana, Ark	1964	Yes	1,300	39,000 units/day
Tupelo, Miss.	No	No	1,100	39,000 units/day
			4,300	126,000 units/day
Continental/General Tire				
Bryan, Ohio	1967	Yes	350	300 units/day
Charlotte, NC	1967	Yes	1,848	29,000 units/day
Mayfield, KY	1960	Yes	350	5,000 units/day
Mount Vernon, Ill	1974	No	1,961	27,000 units/day
			4,509	87,600 units/day

Source: *Tire Business*, December 8, 1997, p.15

costs run from about 15 to 40 percent of total costs, depending on wage rates and labor productivity.[20] Industry observers are predicting greater worldwide sourcing of tires from countries having the lowest labor costs, with Korea, Mexico, and Brazil becoming increasingly attractive production locations.[21] Several major tire manufacturers were said to be considering plant locations in low-wage countries. Shipping costs for tires made in foreign countries and then marketed in the United States were approximately $1 per tire in 1992.[22]

Efforts to reduce labor costs at U.S. plants focused mainly on unionized plants and generally took the form of boosting worker productivity through both automation and the elimination of costly work rules.[23] Tire producers' relations with the United Rubber Workers Union (URW) had historically been stormy. URW over the years had won, sometimes after long strikes, an excellent wage and fringe benefit package.[24] Each local union had also negotiated plant work rules that in many cases held down labor productivity. The URW in the past has struck several foreign-owned facilities located in the United States, and the negotiation process appears to be increasingly acrimonious. Herein lies an opportunity for the other tire manufacturers, since demand for OE and replacement tires is already strong.[25] Table 2 shows the North American plants of the various tire producers, their unionized status, and their production capacities.

COMPETITION IN THE REPLACEMENT TIRE MARKET

In recent years, competition in the replacement tire market has centered mainly on price and tire performance. The recession and the uncertainty about job security had forced many consumers to become more price conscious and less brand loyal. Furthermore, since the demand for cars declined between 1988 and 1995, the market for OE tires has shrunk, making competition fiercer in the replacement market. Thus, many tire producers have dumped entire inventories into the replacement market, lowering prices and making profit margins even leaner. Many of the vehicles on the road are old—the average age of the U.S. vehicle fleet is now more than eight years. While these cars and trucks are maintained, the owners often do not want to spend a lot of money on them because there is a new car in the future. This mentality, fostered by the prevailing economical climate, plays right into the hands of the low-cost tire producers.

Tire producers had long emphasized performance characteristics such as traction, handling, and braking. Overall, tire quality and performance were on the upswing. The longer tread life of OE and replacement tires threatened to radically reduce the number of sets of replacement tires needed per vehicle in service.

Cooper's Competitors

Even with sales more than $1.8 billion, Cooper is still relatively small in an industry dominated by a few giant firms. Over the last few years, Cooper's major competitors in the replacement tire market have been Goodyear, Michelin, Bridgestone, and Continental/General Tire. As can be seen in Table 3, the five largest tire manufacturers collectively accounted for approximately 83 percent of the North American's $19.9 billion tire sales in 1996.

Goodyear   Goodyear Tire Company, headquartered in Akron, is the largest rubber producer in the world, with about 91,750 employees. Together with its subsidiary, Kelly-Springfield Tire Company, Goodyear can produce in its North American plants approximately 489,300 units of tires a day, which represents more than 35 percent of the North American tire production capacity (see

TABLE 3

Tire Market Leaders, 1996 *(in thousands)*

Company	Sales	Market Share (%)
Goodyear	$5,815	29.2%
Michelin	4,200	21.1%
Bridgestone	3,900	19.6%
Cooper	1,300	6.3%
Continental	1,250	6.5%
Others	3,435	17.3%
	$19,900	100%

Source: Tire Business, December 8, 1997, p. 14.

Table 4). It leads both the North American tire market and Latin American, but ranks second in the world tire market (see Table 5). Its market share accounted for 29.2 percent of North American's $19.9 billion tire sales in 1996.

Goodyear's reputation for tire quality has been considered strong, generally on a par with Michelin and slightly ahead of Bridgestone. Goodyear has had the broadest line of tire products of any manufacturer. Over the years, Goodyear has been among the top fifty national advertisers, promoting its tires. Its distinctive blimps are among the best-known advertising symbols in the United States. Goodyear's R&D expenditures for 1996 were about

TABLE 4

World Top Tire Producers

Company	Units (millions)	Average Price/Unit
Goodyear	178.6	$66
Michelin	171.3	76
Bridgestone	169.0	73
Continental	76.1	61
Sumitomo	61.5	65
Pirelli	48.0	65
Yokohama	21.0	n.a.
Cooper	37.0	43

Source: National Tire Dealers Retreaders Association.

TABLE 5

Tire Market Profitability, 1996 *(in millions)*

Company	Sales	Net Earnings	% of Sales
Bridgestone	$17,993	$646.3	3.6
Goodyear	13,110	101.7	0.78
Michelin	13,943	609.0	4.4
Continental	6,952	128.3	1.8
Sumitomo	5,353	43.0	0.8
Yokohama	3,700	34.5	0.93
Pirelli	6,636	300.0	4.5
Toyo	2,417	9.8	0.41
Cooper	1,615	107.9	6.7
Kumho	1,517	7.7	0.51
Hankook	1,267	12.6	1.0
Ohtsu	944	2.8	0.3

Source: Tire Business, December 8, 1997, p. 14.

$375 million, with a capital investment of more than $618 million (see Table 6).

The company's problems have been aggravated by heavy interest payments (more than $1 million per year) on debts incurred for fending off a hostile takeover in 1986 and by continuing losses on its "All American" oil transport unit. In early 1991, Goodyear reported a $38 million loss on its 1990 operations, the company's first money-losing year since the De-

pression. In June 1991, Goodyear's board of directors hired S.G. Gault as the company's new CEO. Gault immediately made Goodyear's program to become a low-cost producer a high priority, with the goal of reducing costs by $350 million within three years. In addition, Gault set up programs to boost sales by introducing new types of tires. Goodyear became very active in purchasing multi-outlet retailers, while its sales force attempted to convert independent tire dealers to Goodyear brands and to win new accounts for Kelly-Springfield and Lee Tires.

Goodyear's strategy in acquiring large-volume independent dealerships that carried three or four brands was to increase the share of Goodyear tires being sold in these outlets. Later in 1991, Wal-Mart agreed to market Douglas brand radial car and light-truck tires made by Goodyear's Kelly-Springfield subsidiary. Goodyear also recruited Sears to sell seven lines of its tires at Sears's 850 auto centers after research showed that some 2 million Goodyear tires a year were being replaced by tires bought at Sears. In early 1992, Goodyear introduced its Aqua-tred line, with a tread design that prevented hydroplaning, and a new Invicta tire designed to produce less friction and to boost fuel economy by 4 percent. Goodyear made an impressive turnaround, with earnings of $97 million in 1991.

In 1993, tires and tubes represented about 83 percent of Goodyear's 11.60 billion in sales. The company's total profitability that year was $1.16

TABLE 6

R&D and Capital Expenditures in 1996 (in millions)

Company	R & D Expenditures	% of Sales	Capital Investment	% of Sales
Michelin	$697	5.0	$802	5.8
Goodyear	375	2.9	618	4.7
Bridgestone	336	1.9	1,169	6.5
Continental	278	4.0	368	5.3
Pirelli	204	3.1	351	5.3
Sumitomo	161	3.0	423	7.9
Yokohama	123	3.3	na	na
Toyo	76	3.1	163	6.7
Hankook	55	4.3	55	8.3
Cooper	20	1.2	194	12

Source: Tire Business, December 8, 1997, p. 17.

billion. Foreign sales accounted for about 42 percent of its revenues. The OE tire market accounted for approximately 40 percent of Goodyear's tire sales, with the remaining 60 percent made in the replacement market.

In the last decade, Goodyear and its subsidiaries have increased their share of the U.S. replacement tire market from about 15.5 percent to about 29 percent. Goodyear's North American market share in the passenger car replacement market was 17 percent in 1996. In the original equipment tire market, where Goodyear is a major supplier to auto manufacturers, its share has grown from about 27 percent to 36 percent.[26]

Goodyear will likely suffer less of the impact of the supply shortages than other companies because it grows most of its own natural rubber. In 1994, Goodyear led the year's second round of price hikes with 2 to 4 percent increases in October. Other companies followed the higher rates.[27] The company's strategy was to position its more expensive product at a better relative value to attract more interest in the replacement market.[28]

There is no question as to who's in charge at Goodyear in 1998. Sam Gibara continues to hold all three of the company's top jobs—chairman, CEO, and president. He says that's not because he wants to be all-powerful, but because he feels obligated to directly oversee implementation of Goodyear's strategic plan. Gibara was assigned the key role in mapping Goodyear's strategy by Stan Gault, his predecessor, while Gault helped Goodyear survive the financial devastation caused by raider James Goldsmith's hostile attempt to take over the company. Calling on his experience with Goodyear in many parts of the world, Gibara has truly globalized the company and emphasized growth overseas. He has placed heavy emphasis on technology. This is evidenced by the hiring of some 200 scientists and technicians and by the company's development of all-steel ultra-tensile steel (UTS) tire construction and run-flat extended mobility tire (EMT) and by the introduction of its automated IMPACT tire-building system.

The introduction of EMT in July 1997 and UTS technology for tire construction and automated IMPACT tire-production system in February 1998 certainly indicate the company's commitment to providing its dealers and their customers with the very best products available. According to Gibara,

EMT and run-flat tires are top of the line tires that are relatively expensive. He expects that by the end of 1999 about 15 percent of total Goodyear tire production will be run-flat tires and that by the year 2003 it will be 70 percent. Meanwhile, a significant portion of the company's capital budget for 1999 will be devoted to expansion and implementation of the IMPACT system. It takes up to twenty-four months to install the system and to train people to operate it, but the company expects that by 2003, about 15 percent of its tires will be produced by IMPACT.

Goodyear plans to reduce the number of tires it produces, reversing a trend among tire makers of expanding the lines and sizes offered. Over the next three years, Goodyear will introduce at least twenty-one new tires, Marco Molinnari, vice president of sales and marketing, told dealers attending the company's national dealer conference in Nashville, on February 9–12, 1998. But, during that same period, Goodyear will cut the number of lines it offers by 38 percent. Reducing the number of lines will simplify the selling proposition. Fewer lines will also improve the inventory mix and cash flow.

Celebrating its 100th year in business, Goodyear told dealers about two technological innovations that will lead the company into its second century of business: a new low-cost, highly efficient manufacturing process; and a new steel wire cord that is 40 percent stronger than conventional tire reinforcement.

Management at Goodyear also believes in product differentiation. In its centennial year, the Akron-based tire maker has introduced four innovative tires designed to keep it and its dealers ahead of the pack in the competitive North American tire marketplace: (1) Wrangler RF-A (rotation-free aqua-tred), a 60,000-mile light truck tire package that eliminates the need for tire rotation; (2) Eagle F1 Steel ultra light performance tire; (3) Eagle Aquasteel EMT run-flat performance tire; and (4) Integrity, an OE tire now being offered to the replacement market.[29]

Groupe Michelin   Groupe Michelin, a French tire producer, is the acknowledged leader in radial tire technology. The company has about 120,000 employees, and its plants are reputed to be among the most highly automated in the industry. Michelin operates seventy tire plants in fifteen countries in Europe, the U.S., Africa, and Asia. In North America,

Michelin has thirteen tire plants with a total production capacity of 216,000 units per day; eight plants (all nonunion) make Michelin brand tires, while five plants (one nonunion) produce Uniroyal and Goodrich brand tires (see Table 2).

With its 1989 acquisition of Uniroyal-Goodrich, Groupe Michelin became the global market share leader. The company ranked second, behind Goodyear, in market share throughout the North American market. In 1993, its total market share accounted for over 21 percent of North America's tire sales. However, its North American market share in the passenger replacement tire market was 15 percent in the same year. The B.F. Goodrich brand is being positioned to focus on performance and targets the light-truck sector of the U.S. replacement tire market. But the Uniroyal brand is being aimed at the OE sector and at the middle of the replacement tire sector, targeting vehicle owners seeking a medium-grade tire at a medium or average price.

Michelin is represented by nearly 8,000 dealers operating in most cities and many towns. Its Michelin brand tires appeal mainly to quality-sensitive buyers who drive relatively expensive cars. The tire's high performance has permitted the company to claim that children are safer riding on Michelins and, because of this reputation, it can charge top dollar. In 1992, Michelin introduced its XH4 line of tires, guaranteed to deliver 80,000 miles of treadwear. According to one company official, "if new vehicles come equipped with 80,000-mile tires, by the time the owner replaces the OE tires, he won't be planning to keep the car much longer, and he won't be looking at first-line replacement tires."

It has always been Michelin's mission to be a leader in finding new solutions with new tire products. For example, Michelin recently developed a new concept and PAX technology. It is a major step in tire technology because the PAX provides outstanding zero-pressure (run-flat) performance without sacrificing anything in its operation while fully inflated. Present run-flat tires are heavier than standard tires. With heavier side walls capable of supporting the weight of the vehicle, you have a higher rolling resistance that reduces fuel economy. Even with a hole in it with the size of a golf ball, the Michelin Zero Pressure tire will take you up to 50 miles at 55 mph. Recently, Michelin said it would introduce its MXV4 ZP—a broad-market, run-flat passenger tire—to the aftermarket.

Like any totally new concept, the PAX will require changes not only in technology, but also in thinking. Vehicles have carried a spare tire for 100 years and the present tire and rim design has not changed in 40 years. According to Edouard Michelin, there has been tremendous interest in PAX technology from new-vehicle manufacturers. At present the company has about fifty projects worldwide in which it is working with OE automakers on possible PAX applications. Michelin is open to the idea of licensing PAX technology for use by others. The PAX clearly sets a whole new performance standard, which can not be duplicated with the present tire/wheel system and, therefore, will not face the same marketing problem. Over time and with mass production, it is believed that the PAX system will not add cost to the vehicle, specifically since it will require only four tires instead of five by eliminating the spare. It is also believed that this system will be fully successful. However, there is always a risk with any new concept.

Michelin plans to increase its supply of tires for North America by 10 million units per year over the next eighteen months, by increasing both production in North American plants and exports. Overall, its plan is to increase sales by 3 to 5 percent in the next three to five years.

Michelin has always maintained a great deal of secrecy about the C3M automated tire-making facilities. The C3M process results in excellent products with a great degree of uniformity. In addition, the flexibility of this process is outstanding. The C3M can be set up in two or three days. A single machine replaces twenty to thirty machines required in a normal tire-making process, and tire lines can be switched quickly to meet the company's needs. Michelin has eight C3M facilities—one in Sweden, two in the United States, four in France, and one in Brazil. Recently, Michelin announced that it had begun producing tires at a plant in Greenville, S.C., using its new C3M advanced manufacturing process. The highly flexible manufacturing process uses one-third the energy and needs much less factory space than traditional tire plants.

Michelin's Reno plant in the United States is right next to its tire distribution center. The company can switch tire lines being produced to quickly replace tires shipped from inventory, as needed to efficiently maintain its supplies on hand.

For the first half of 1998, Michelin's net earnings fell 11.8 percent, to $290.4 million, while operating profits went down 8.5 percent, to $453.2 million. The company expects the numbers to rebound in the second half of 1998 because of several factors, including recent price increases in North America and Europe, greater truck tire manufacturing capacity across Europe, and productivity gains.

The company's capital spending in the first half of 1998 rose 16 percent, to $526 million, putting it on a pace to exceed the full year expenditures record set last year at $1.05 billion. Among new projects is a medium truck tire plant in China, built adjacent to the existing Michelin Shen Yang Tire Co. Ltd. car and light truck tire plant.

Bridgestone   Bridgestone was the first Japanese tire company to produce tires in the United States. It began manufacturing truck tires in the United States in 1984, when it acquired a truck tire plant from Firestone. Between 1984 and 1988, Bridgestone worked hard to expand its network of retail dealers in order to enhance its U.S. replacement tire market share. In 1988, Bridgestone bought what remained of Firestone for $2.6 billion. The Bridgestone/Firestone subsidiary gave the Japanese tire manufacturer a seven-plant production base and a network of more than 4,000 retail tire outlets and MasterCare auto service centers in North America.

Nevertheless, its acquisition of Firestone has been costly for Bridgestone. Having failed to survey Firestone's plants prior to the purchase, Bridgestone has spent more than anticipated on upgrading its tire plants. The company's president, Akira Yeiri, has installed a new management at the money-losing Bridgestone/Firestone subsidiary, and the new team seems to have made a lot of changes. Bridgestone dominated the Japanese tire market, ranked third in the U.S. market, and was the second top tire producer worldwide in 1993, with sales of $14.4 billion. The company's total profitability in that year was $1.15 billion.[30] Of the 20.5 percent of its North American market share in 1993, about 12 percent was in the replacement tire market. The company's R&D budget for 1996 was $336 million, with a capital investment of more than $1.1 billion. Bridgestone employed more than 9,000 people in its seven North American plants in 1996.[31]

Continental AG   Continental is Germany's largest tire producer and the second largest company in Europe (behind Michelin). Its acquisition of Gen-

eral Tire in 1987 made it the world's fourth largest producer. Immediately after the acquisition of General Tire, Continental launched a five-year, $670 million program to modernize General's U.S. and Canadian plants. Continental supplies OE tires to Mercedes-Benz, BMW, Audi, Volkswagen, Porsche, and Volvo.[32] In 1996, Continental had twenty-four tire plants in sixteen countries. Continental is committed to product development and research. In 1996, Continental spent $278 million in R&D, which represents about 4 percent of its total sales. Its tires are viewed as premium quality and offer independent tire dealers attractive profit margins.

In 1991, Continental merged its sales force for the Continental and General brands under General Tire management at the subsidiary's Akron headquarters.[33] The plan was to position General tires in the mainstream portion of the market, target Continental brands for the upscale segments, and offer dealers more models to better cover the price-quality spectrum. This program also offered dealers the advantages of combined delivery, common purchase terms, and more economical cooperative advertising packages.

The management at Continental believes that the best way to gain market share is by acquiring more dealers rather than through a merger of producers. For this reason, in recent years, Continental had strengthened its access to the replacement tire market by buying a 400-unit retail chain in Great Britain and buying a minority interest in 400 additional retail outlets in Germany, Scotland, Canada, and the United States.[34]

According to Frangengerg, the company's CEO, cost reduction and dealer development have been two of the four pillars of the company's strategy. The others are advancement of innovation and technology and improving the motivation of employees.[35]

COOPER OPERATIONS

Corporate Structure and Top Management

The early 1970s were very troubled times at Cooper; its very survival was in question.[36] In 1972, certified public account Ivan W. Gorr was an employee of Arthur Young & Co. assigned to the Cooper account, and Cooper was looking for a corporate controller. Gorr was offered the job. For Gorr, the decision to join Cooper in the face of adversity was a challenge. He became president and chief operating officer of the company in 1982 and chairman and chief executive officer in 1989.[37]

According to Gorr, "The company turned itself around by embracing one of the fundamental tenets of modern quality management: Listen to your employees. The company had a lot of highly capable people at that time, and top management gave them a chance to stand up and say what the company should be doing and what they could do to help it get there."[38] Moreover, Gorr says: "The cornerstone of Cooper's *customer need* orientation and the driving force behind its goals and objectives is the company's corporate philosophy: to produce value and quality, as defined by the customer. To leverage its core competencies in product quality, efficient production methods, and outstanding service to the distribution channel, Cooper has charted a more aggressive strategic plan, entitled "Cooper 21,"[39] with these key elements:

1. Commitment to rapid global expansion
2. Increased awareness of the Cooper brand
3. Acceleration of already successful cost reduction efforts
4. Greater emphasis on product innovation

A high level of free-flowing communication has been developed among all employees concerning company strategies and objectives. Top management deeply believes that the success of the organization is based on the success of its individual members, and vice versa. Cooper emphasizes a strong commitment to customer service and to quality, both of which demand a high degree of loyalty and an integrated effort among all employees.[40] To foster this integration, Cooper maintains very short lines in the organization of its staffing. Information needed for decision making is accessed quickly, without unnecessary bureaucratic protocols, and communications are direct. The company's stated goals and objectives are well communicated all the way down the line. The bureaucratic layering is said to be so thin that it is difficult to find anyone who bears the title of *assistant*.

Production

Cooper specializes in the manufacturing and marketing of rubber products for consumers and for industrial uses. These products include automobile and truck tires, inner tubes, vibration control prod-ucts, hose and tubing, and automotive body sealing products. Production takes place in two divisions: the tire division and the engineered rubber products division.[41] Tire products represent about 85 percent of the company's production and sales. Cooper runs its tire plants at 100 percent capacity, while others operate at around 80 percent capacity.[42] In a capital-intensive industry, that creates a lot of leverage.

Cooper's engineered products division (which accounted for about 16 percent of revenues) manufactures a variety of products primarily for the original equipment automotive market. Engineered products division is a relatively fractured area, with competition spread widely among both rubber and plastics companies. Since improving profitability in the tire industry is becoming increasingly difficult, many companies are turning to engineered products.[43] Automakers, in their own efforts to reduce costs, have been pushing suppliers to lower prices. This is creating opportunities for those companies that have the economies of scale needed to manufacture products cheaply and still remain profitable. Cooper, with its low-cost production know-how, will be in a good position to grab a lot of new contracts. According to Cooper's management, the company has received high service ratings from customers for its engineered products and is planning to take full advantage of these opportunities. Cooper is constantly introducing several new tire product lines each year.

In July 1993, Cooper opened a purchasing office in Singapore for raw materials, such as crude rubber. According to management, this move put Cooper closer to the suppliers for better control of the quality and consistency of materials. Cooper's inventory-control policies and procedures are believed to be very efficient—buying ahead on occasion to get the best deals, but no hedging on raw materials.

Cooper's tire operations position it as North America's fourth largest replacement tire maker, and ninth worldwide. With a mix equally divided between proprietary house brand and private customers, Cooper markets its tires in more than 100 countries around the globe.

Cooper's engineered products operations serve virtually every North American light vehicle manufacturer, as well as an expanding number of European-based original equipment manufacturers. With more than 1,800 specific parts, primary product categories for the engineered products operation include vibration control systems to help minimize vehicle vibrations; automotive sealing products to help seal the vehicle from outside elements; and hoses and assemblies to transport fluids, fuels, and gases.

Spurred by trends such as outsourcing and source consolidation, Cooper has steadily strengthened its position as a partner with major OEMs in vehicle design and system problem solving. All six engineered products manufacturing facilities have earned the QS–9000 certification as required by the Big Three automakers. Reflecting the commitment to world-class manufacturing, Cooper's plants have received numerous quality awards, including the Gold Pentastar from Chrysler, the Certified Supplier Award from Eaton Yale Suspension Division, and the Q1 award from Ford Motor. Cooper also received the Source Award as the top supplier in the automotive division.[44]

Historically, Cooper has generated the highest operating margins in the U.S. industry. A key element of the "Cooper 21" plan is to achieve efficiencies across all operating areas. Based on results today, management expects to exceed its 1998 cost savings target of $30 million, and has set a goal of $40 million in cost savings for 1999.[45]

Market Positioning

One factor in Cooper's success is its confining itself to the replacement tire market. Although Cooper is a midget among the world's tire makers, it is the only major U.S. producer that steers clear of the low-margin business of making OE tires for new cars. Instead, it concentrates on the replacement tire market, which is about four times larger than the OE market, and growing faster because the owners of today's highly durable cars are keeping them longer.[46] Although the major competitors control 57 percent of the replacement market, Cooper doubled its share of the balance between 1986 and 1993 to 23 percent. In fact, Cooper made about 8 percent of the 230 million replacement tires sold in North America in 1996.

Research and Development

The second resoundingly correct decision involves R&D. While other tire makers incur high R&D expenses to capture a share of the OE tire market segment, Cooper has been able to produce tires with a proven track record and sell them to value-oriented customers. Instead of pioneering its own designs, the company often waits to see what sells well as original equipment. Gorr says, "All we have to do is produce the winners."[47] Original tires on new cars normally last up to four years. Therefore, the company has been able to reduce speculative research and development expenditures and has had ample time to produce its own versions. It does not just copy others' designs, however; it has very active R&D departments in both its tire and its engineered rubber products divisions. There is very good communication between the R&D departments and other organizational units. Engineers in R&D are crossed-trained in manufacturing procedures and spend a lot of time on the floor so that they will not be working in isolation. In 1996, Cooper spent $20 million on R&D, more than the $15.1 million spent in 1993. This represents about 1.2 percent of 1996 sales, compared with about 2.9 percent for Goodyear, 1.9 percent for Bridgestone, 4 percent for Continental, and 5 percent for Michelin.

Cooper continues to make progress in the efficiency and productivity of its manufacturing process. According to the management, the major thrust in Cooper has been to reduce the time it takes to develop and produce tires. Speed to market is, and will continue to be, very important to the customers. In early 1998, Cooper expanded its research and engineering capabilities, including a 73,500-square-feet addition to its facility in Findlay, Ohio, and a 900-acre test site near San Antonio.

Computer technology is used in product design and development, machine design, and mold design. Cooper's innovative application of advanced computer technology provides the company with a competitive advantage in bringing new, high-quality products to market quickly. Data collection devices on a wide range of equipment throughout the production process provide accurate information on the components being made. Comparing the component data with product orders from customers ensures that the proper tires are scheduled for production.[48]

A state-of-the-art material handling system to transport materials between the component production and tire assembly areas was introduced at the Tupelo plant in 1992. Automating "high handling" functions has improved efficiency and safety.

Cooper's equipment design engineers continually work to improve existing production equipment or to design custom machines when commercial models are unavailable or are inadequate for the company's requirements. Current projects include developing total systems for tire assembly and component production, as well as collateral equipment and machine modifications to increase efficiency and productivity.[49] Employee teams, comprising production, technical, and marketing employees, are often involved in machine design and process improvements.

In 1995, Cooper entered into an agreement with the ContiTech group of Hanover, Germany, to share technologies in the design and development of original equipment products for the world car market.

Pampering Employees

Much of the credit for Cooper Tire's success, says Alec Reinhardt, the company's chief financial officer, should go to a work force motivated in a way that fits nicely with management's unending search for new ways to hold down costs.[50] Under the direction of Gorr, the company has made great strides in developing a participative, cooperative, and less hierarchical work climate. Cooper's management has long recognized that the performance of dedicated employees can make a difference in a market where one or more competitors sell products with very little difference among them. Therefore, Cooper is always seeking motivated employees who are team players and good communicators and who have the right attitude toward their jobs. Employees become involved at all levels of the organization, especially in the areas of productivity, quality assurance, and customer service. Monthly meetings are held in each department to update workers on new developments and to solicit their suggestions and information about problems. Gorr has recently cited employee recommendations in the key areas of business positioning, product distribution, dealer relations, and quality assurance as the cornerstones on which Cooper's current success rest.[51]

Cooper's employee recruiting process operates by examining applicants through a series of screening procedures. Those applicants who pass the initial screening are motivated people—team players and good communicators—with the right attitude and personality to fit the job for which they have applied. Then they take two pencil-and-paper tests, one of which is keyed to a video tape, followed by a one-on-one behavioral-type interview with a supervisor. Those who make it through the preliminary screening are placed in groups, where *teams* work on problem solving in situations involving some stress.

All new Cooper employees undergo a basic, two-week training and orientation course. Each new employee's spouse is also asked to come in to learn what it means to work for Cooper and why the company considers an employee's spouse to be part of the team. Training courses are designed to meet the specific needs of each employee. After the two weeks' basic course, an employee's training can continue for anywhere from three days to over a year. Cooper's management schedules working hours and shifts so as to allow employees ample days off for participating in community activities and to develop a family atmosphere at the plants.

Incentive is a driving force for Cooper's employees. Cooper's innovative compensation system, in which the earnings of everyone from the CEO to line workers rise and fall with the individual performance and contribution to productivity, instills loyalty. In fact, although incentive programs are offered to every Cooper employee, none of them is based on market share. According to Reinhardt, "Market share is not something that drives our company at all. We are very oriented to return on assets."[52] Executives' compensation provides for cuts as well as raises of up to 30 percent. Profit sharing opportunities and paid incentives also augment paychecks of Cooper's blue-collar and clerical workers. Hourly workers get paid extra for producing more, and salaried employees can earn bonuses of up to 7.5 percent on the return on assets they handle.

Employee turnover is discouraged by Cooper's stock option plan. Cooper has a very low (3.1 percent) turnover rate, and absenteeism is at one-tenth of 1 percent.[53] For staff and management alike, a long tenure with the company is the norm. At the age of sixty-three, Gorr himself ranked as a newcomer because of having put in only twenty-one years with the company. President Patrick W. Rooney has been with Cooper for forty-one years, and even Reinhardt—the most junior member of the top-management team—joined the company almost twenty-two years ago. The company feels that all jobs are important, and its management has good relations with the workers. According to Gorr, "Dedicated workers help. We grow our talent and we motivate them with ownership, identity, and pride. The non-performed leaves us very quick."[54] All of Cooper's managers are substantial stockholders, as are many workers. Reinhardt estimates that employees hold 20 percent of Cooper's stock. Cooper's stock purchase program has been very rewarding for many employees. If the company's matching contributions are included, those workers who began faithfully investing 6 percent of their salary in Cooper stock when Gorr joined Cooper would have an equity share of well over $1 million.[55]

About 15 percent of Cooper's employees are unionized, a figure considerably lower than that of its rivals. The company had a new contract at one of its two unionized plants in 1994, and the other plant's contracts were reviewed in 1995. According to management, this facility has not posed a serious threat to output. Also, union health care issues were resolved in 1990. Furthermore, a strike probably would not materially affect Cooper's earnings since the company can shift production to nonunionized facilities.

Choosing a Location

Another possible factor in Cooper's superior performance lies in its small-town locations. Cooper wastes no money on frills, not even on utilization of its headquarters in the small town of Findlay, Ohio. When Cooper wants to expand its capacity, it does so cheaply by buying old plants and refurbishing them. This has been made possible by the fact that more than thirty-five tire plants have been shut down since the 1970s.[56] Cooper has a good engineering department, which designs and builds the company's own production equipment, as well as adapts and modifies other equipment to meet its own needs and specifications. This engineering team also continually monitors advances in new technology for possible incorporation in Cooper's manufacturing processes.[57]

Cooper's tire plants are in places such as Tupelo, Mississippi, and Texarkana, Arkansas, where the company is a master employee and where people have a strong work ethic. In these small towns, Cooper employees at all levels and their families constantly interact in community churches and organizations. A feeling seems to develop that everyone has a stake in the future of the company. Analysts say that Cooper's small-town locations permit it to pay lower salaries and to reap other savings over companies in urban sites. Most Cooper

employees grew up in and around the rural areas where the company's four tire plants are located. Employees drawn from these smaller communities tend to make a more long-term commitment to the firm and to exhibit a stronger work ethic than employees from larger and more mobile communities. According to Reinhardt, "There's a different work ethic in smaller communities."[58]

Quality Control

Cooper's quality control policies and procedures are managed by specific staff, but a great deal of the responsibility for quality rests with the individual worker, who is trained to do his own quality-assurance checks. Cooper's employee-centered organization results in high product quality. Employees receive as many as 900 hours of training, and signs bearing such slogans as "Quantity is Important, but Quality is MORE Important" hang from factory walls. To symbolize a personal commitment to quality, each tire carries not only a brand name, but also a sticker identifying the worker who built it. This helps foster pride in workmanship among Cooper's employees and the company hopes, creates a bond with the consumers buying the tires.[59]

According to an industry analyst, Cooper is far ahead of the curve in emphasizing quality products and services. Quality has become such a big part of Cooper's culture that it is not talked about anymore.[60] As a leader of the 215,000-member U.S. Chamber of Commerce, Gorr plans to travel frequently, carrying the message that there is no substitute for producing quality products and being sensitive to customer needs in today's competitive global marketplace. He will be able to point to the difference in performance that adopting this culture has made in his own company.[61]

Distribution and Marketing

Cooper markets its products nationally and internationally through well-established channels of distribution. Among its customers are automotive manufacturing companies, independent tire dealers and wholesale distributors, and large retail chains. Independent dealers and distributors remain crucial to the company's success. Rather than selling through its own retail chains as Goodyear and Bridgestone/Firestone do, Cooper continues to sell about half of its production as private labels to the store chains, mass merchants, and discounters. Private-label customers include Sears, TBC, Hercules, Pep Boys, Del-Nat, Parrish, and Nokian. The other half of the production is primarily sold under the company's Cooper, Mastercraft, Starfire, and Roadmaster house brand through independent tire dealers, which, according to *Modern Tire Dealer*, as a distribution channel represented 71 percent of all passenger tires sold in 1997.[62] According to industry research, customers buy the tires recommended by the dealer more than 50 percent of the time.[63] And according to the tire trade press, dealers love Cooper because it provides them with the highest gross margins in the industry and does not have company retail stores that compete against them. Says Gorr, "Our aim is to assist our dealers, who are our valued customers, not compete against them."[64] Cooper's ten largest customers accounted for approximately 90 percent of its total 1996 sales. Net sales in 1996 reached more than $1.6 billion, increasing 8.4 percent over the prior year's sales.

Product shipments to customers are directed through a strategic, nationwide network of distribution centers, which ensures timely deliveries to customers. A new management information system was introduced to further streamline inventory and order-processing operations and to provide even better service to customers.

Cooper focuses its relatively modest marketing budget on supporting its independent dealers, mainly by providing superior service and delivery and by offering a value-priced product on which the dealers generally make larger profits. Cooper advertising programs assist dealers and distributors with promotional materials in their local markets. Cooperative advertising allowances are based on annual dealer purchases and are applicable to all types of media.[65] Cooper's 1993 marketing and general administrative expenses were about 5 percent of sales, compared with Goodyear's 17 percent. The "American-Owned, American-Made" theme, introduced during 1992, gained much publicity for the company. A variation of this theme was used in 1993: "Put your trust in American hands." Cooper has no active advertising or promotion for its engineered products because these are targeted to industrial users (auto manufacturers), who comprise a small market.

Cooper's house brands are growing a little faster than its private-label business. To broaden brand awareness among customers, at the beginning of 1997 Cooper signed Arnold Palmer as company spokesman and stepped up its media advertising expenditures. It is believed that these moves are beginning to pay off, with all four house brands showing healthy sales increases and the Cooper brand making the strongest showing.

Over the past few years, price pressure on private-label tires has increased, squeezing the price differential between major brands and private-labels. But Cooper management believes that private-label tires still play a very important role in the replacement tire market. Private-label tires are an excellent value and provide independent tire dealers with the ability to call their marketing shots and maintain product control in their local markets. The strong private brands with distributors and dealers who provide good service will continue to prosper.[66]

Cooper has expanded exports for its products over the past several years. Its new acquisition of British-based Avon Tyres has added $169 million to annual sales, increasing Cooper's international sales exposure from its 8 percent preacquisition level and providing a strong base for future global expansion. Management has set a goal of achieving 25 to 30 percent of total sales from international operations within five years, with the growth planned to come from tires and engineered products.[67]

In 1997 and 1998, Cooper was honored by private brand customer Sears and also received high marks from independent dealers. The Company received the Sears Partners in Progress Award out of more than 10,000 vendors vying for this recognition. Additionally, Cooper and Mastercraft house brands were ranked at the top of a national survey of tire dealers conducted by *Tire Review*, with dealers ranking Mastercraft first and Cooper second.[68]

Financial Performance

Over the past decade, Cooper has demonstrated that a company does not have to lead its industry to generate enormous wealth for its owners. The company has posted impressive profits over the years as other tire makers have struggled to regain profitability. Its average return on equity between 1988 and 1994 was more than 22 percent. In 1997, the company's net income reached $122.4 million, up 13.5 percent from net income in 1996 of $107.9 million. Net income for 1995 reached 112.8 million, down about 14 percent from 1994. Return on stockholders' equity was about 14.7 percent in

1997 and averaged 19.5 percent over the past five years. Cooper's stock price increased dramatically in the last decade, rising by 3,800 percent. Stock reached a high of $28.44 versus a low of $15.75 during 1997. Cooper's financial statements are shown in Tables 7 and 8.

Cooper's strong operating cash flows provided funds for investment in capacity expansion and technological advances and contributed to growing financial strength. The company's capital expenditures during 1997 amounted to $107.5 million, compared with $193.7 million in 1996, and $194.9 million in 1995. The cash flow from operations after capital spending has been very good, and Cooper has been able to reduce its debt over several years. Its long-term debt-to-equity ratio was about 1 to 4 in 1997, up from 1 to 20 in 1994.

Toward the Future

There are a number of issues to be considered. Cooper has always operated under a *price umbrella* created by the OE tire manufacturers; therefore, as that umbrella rises, so does Cooper's profitability. However, the industry is becoming extremely competitive as major tire makers recognize the attractiveness of the replacement tire market. Cooper will not have the luxury of watching how a tire performs for two or three years before deciding whether to copy it. Furthermore, Cooper's competitors have recently narrowed the gap on this low-cost producer, and the closer rivalry is likely to cause the company's margins to rise more slowly than in the past years. This may signal the beginning of heightened price competition. More tire manufacturers have started providing guaranteed longer mileage warranties to the buyers of replacement tires, and the longer warranties of 60,000 to 80,000 miles are likely to create an intermediate-term demand problem. Therefore, Cooper may find it difficult to maintain its growth rate. Finally, with the passage of NAFTA and the conclusion of GATT, foreign sales opportunities appear to be increasingly meaningful.

What should Cooper do to ensure its continued growth? Some managers suggest that Cooper should develop new-model tires and aggressively expand capacity in its OE manufacturing business in the United States and Mexico. Few managers believe that Cooper's performance could be made stronger by increased output. They argue that the expansion recently completed should enable the

TABLE 7

Consolidated Statements of Income (dollars in thousands, except per share)

| | Year Ended December 31 | | | |
	1997	1996	1995	1994
Net sales	$ 1,813,005	$ 1,619,345	$ 1,493,622	$ 1,403,243
Cost of goods sold	1,403,968	1,289,729	1,179,582	1,070,375
Gross income	314,573	252,796	250,727	277,265
Selling, Admin. and GE	105,532	79,874	73,796	68,748
Depreciation and amort.	94,464	76,820	63,313	55,603
Operating income	209,041	172,922	176,931	208,517
Other income (expenses)	1,406	824	3,836	2,282
Interest expenses	17,283	5,969	4,212	3,850
Pretax income	194,792	172,092	180,070	208,119
Income taxes	72,381	64,208	67,250	79,600
Net income	122,411	107,884	112,820	128,519
Net income per share	1.55	1.30	1.35	1.54
Average shares outstanding	77,442,158	81,581,768	83,510,732	83,623,000

Source: Cooper Tire & Rubber Company, 1997, Annual Report.

33333333333333333333333333333333333333333333333333333333 Help

TABLE 8

Consolidated Balance Sheet (in thousands)

	1997	1996	1995	1994
Assets				
Current assets:				
Cash and cash equivalents	$ 52,910	$ 19,459	$ 23,187	$ 103,285
Accounts receivable	292,416	267,149	257,049	221,237
Inventories	191,684	141,618	137,964	116,523
Prepaid expenses	17,602	15,399	12,384	13,666
Total current assets	$ 554,612	$ 443,625	$ 430,584	$ 454,711
Properties and plants, net	860,448	792,419	678,876	549,601
Other assets	80,896	36,965	34,241	35,419
Total assets	$1,495,959	$1,273,009	$1,143,701	$1,039,731
Liabilities and Shareholders' Equity				
Current liabilities				
Accounts payable—trade	$ 100,135	$81,571	$ 78,823	$83,864
Notes payable and current long-term debt	11,273	37,081	5,035	5,112
Accrued payables	40,311	32,299	29,422	58,324
Income taxes payable	6,477	3,116	10,834	6,049
Total current liabilities	$ 200,331	$ 187,495	$ 158,368	$ 151,608
Long-term debt	205,525	69,489	28,574	33,614
Provision risks/charges	144,566	139,070	132,963	127,347
Deferred taxes	73,608	52,768	36,656	29,737
Other long-term liabilities	38,351	37,575	38,341	35,348
Shareholders' equity	833,575	786,612	748,799	662,077
Total liabilities and equity	$1,495,956	$1,273,009	$1,143,701	$1,039,731

Source: Cooper Tire & Rubber Company, 1997 Annual Report.

company to boost annual sales of $2.5 billion, while more than doubling profits within five years. However, some other managers want to challenge such projections. They argue that the company could not handle such rapid expansion and strongly believe that the key success factor for Cooper is to achieve more efficiencies across all the existing operations. Some even suggest that the company stop growing. They argue that the tire industry is mature and that currently North America has 16 percent more capacity for making car tires. Some managers also argue that the company's product identifiability should be aggressively im-

proved. In light of these arguments, it is left to management to find concrete answers to these and other strategic question.

Endnotes

1. Cooper Tire & Rubber Company, "Our History," 1997.
2. Ibid.
3. Ibid.
4. *Tire Business*, December 8, 1997. A Crain publication.
5. A. A. Thompson, Jr., "Competition in the World Tire Industry, 1993," *Strategic Management*, 7th ed., (Irwin, 1993), pp. 581–614
6. Ibid.

7. *Tire Business,* December 8, 1997
8. Thompson, "Competition in the World Tire Industry."
9. Ibid.
10. *Tire Business,* December 8, 1997.
11. Thompson, "Competition in the World Tire Industry."
12. Ibid.
13. *Tire Business,* January 5, 1998. A Crain publication.
14. Ibid.
15. Thompson, "Competition in the World Tire Industry."
16. Ibid.
17. Ibid.
18. E. B. Lusk, "Tire & Rubber Industry," *Value Line,* September 16, 1994.
19. Ibid.
20. Thompson, "Competition in the World Tire Industry."
21. Ibid.
22. Ibid.
23. Ibid.
24. Ibid.
25. Lusk, "Tire & Rubber Industry."
26. *Tire Business,* December 8, 1997.
27. Lusk, "Tire & Rubber Industry."
28. Ibid.
29. *Tire Business,* December 8, 1997.
30. Ibid.
31. Ibid.
32. Thompson, "Competition in the World Tire Industry."
33. *Tire Business,* November 4, 1991, p. 12. A Crain publication.
34. Thompson, "Competition in the World Tire Industry."
35. *Modern Tire Dealer* (August 1998), 79, A Bill publication.
36. A. G. Holzinger, "A Successful Competition," *Nation's Business* (April 1993).
37. Ibid.
38. Ibid.
39. Cooper's home page (http://www.coopertire.com/profilepage2.htm).
40. Holzinger, "A Successful Competition."
41. Cooper Tire & Rubber Company, 1993 Annual Report, February 1993.
42. A. Taylor, "Cooper Tire & Rubber: Now Hear This Jack Welch!" *Fortune,* April 6, 1992.
43. Lusk, "Tire & Rubber Industry."
44. Cooper's home page.
45. Ibid.
46. Holzinger, "A Successful Competition."
47. Taylor, "Cooper Tire & Rubber."
48. Holzinger, "A Successful Competition."
49. Cooper Tire & Rubber Company, 1993 Annual Report, February 1993.
50. *Tire Business,* December 8, 1997.
51. Holzinger, "A Successful Competition."
52. Taylor, "Cooper Tire & Rubber."
53. Holzinger, "A Successful Competition."
54. Ibid.
55. H. Byrne, "Cooper Tire and Rubber: Ready to Accelerate," *Barron's,* March 21, 1994.
56. Ibid.
57. Holzinger, "A Successful Competition."
58. Ibid.
59. Byrne, "Cooper Tire and Rubber."
60. Ibid.
61. Holzinger, "A Successful Competition."
62. *Modern Tire Dealer.*
63. Holzinger, "A Successful Competition."
64. Thompson, "Competition in the World Tire Industry."
65. Holzinger, "A Successful Competition."
66. Cooper's home page.
67. Ibid.
68. Ibid.

CASE 16

The Home Video Game Industry: From *Pong* to Dreamcast

This case was prepared by Charles W. L. Hill of the University of Washington.

AN INDUSTRY IS BORN

In 1968, Nolan Bushnell, the twenty-four-year-old son of a Utah cement contractor, graduated from the University of Utah with a degree in engineering.[1] After graduation, he moved to California, where he briefly worked in the computer graphics division of Ampex. At home, Bushnell turned his daughter's bedroom into a laboratory (the little girl was expelled to the living room couch). There he created a simpler version of *Space War*, a computer game that had been invented in 1962 by an MIT graduate student, Steve Russell. Bushnell's version of Russell's game, which he called *Computer Space*, was made of integrated circuits connected to a 19-inch black-and-white television screen. Unlike a computer, Bushnell's invention could do nothing but play the game, but that also meant that unlike a computer, it could be produced cheaply.

Bushnell envisioned video games like his standing next to pinball machines in arcades. With hopes of having his invention put into production, Bushnell left Ampex for a small pinball company that manufactured 1,500 copies of his video game. The game never sold, primarily because players had to read a full page of directions before they could play the game—far too complex for an arcade game. Bushnell left the pinball company and, together with a friend, Ted Dabney, put in $500 to start a company that would develop a simpler video game. They wanted to call the company Syzygy, but the name was already taken, so they set-

This case is intended to be used as the basis for class discussion rather than as an illustration of either effective or ineffective handling of the situation. This case was prepared by Charles W. L. Hill, University of Washington. Used by permission.

tled on Atari, a Japanese word that was the equivalent of *check* in the *go*.

In his home laboratory, Bushnell built the simplest game he could think of. People knew the rules immediately, and it could be played with one hand, which, according to Bushnell, had the virtue of enabling a player to hold a beer in the other. In the game, which was modeled on table tennis, a ball was batted back and forth by paddles that could be moved up and down sides of a court by twisting knobs. He named the game *Pong* after the sonarlike sound that was emitted every time the ball connected with a paddle.

In the fall of 1972, Bushnell installed his prototype for *Pong* in Andy Capp's tavern in Sunnyvale, California. The only instructions were "avoid missing the ball for a high score." In its first week, 1,200 quarters were deposited in the casserole dish that served for a coin box in Bushnell's prototype. Bushnell was ecstatic; his simple game had brought in $300 in a week. The pinball machine that stood next to it averaged $35 a week.

Lacking the capital to mass-produce the game himself, Bushnell approached established amusement game companies, only to be repeatedly shown the door. Down but hardly out, Bushnell cut his hair, put on a suit, and talked his way into a $50,000 line of credit from a local bank. With this, he set up a production line in an abandoned roller skating rink. He hired a motley collection of long-haired geeks and put them to work assembling machines while Led Zeppelin and the Rolling Stones were played at full volume over the speaker system of the rink. Among his first batch of employees was a skinny seventeen-year-old named Steve Jobs, who would later found a few companies of his own, including Apple Computer, NeXT, and Pixar. Like others, Jobs had been attracted by a help wanted ad that read: "Have Fun and Make Money."

In no time at all, Bushnell was selling all of the machines that his small staff could make—about ten per day—but to really grow, he needed additional capital. While the ambiance at the rink, with its mix of freaks, rock music, and marijuana fumes, put off most potential investors, Don Valentine, one of the country's most astute and credible venture capitalists, was impressed with the growth story. Armed with Valentine's money, Atari began to ramp up production and expand its range of games. New games included *Tank* and *Breakout*—the latter designed by Jobs and a friend of his, Steve Wozniak, who had left Hewlett-Packard to work at Atari.

By 1974, 100,000 *Pong*-like games were sold worldwide. Although only 10 percent of those were manufactured by Atari, the company still made $3.2 million that year. With the *Pong* clones coming on strong, Bushnell decided to make a *Pong* system for the home. In fact, Magnavox had been marketing a *Pong*-type game for the home since 1972, although sales had been modest.[2] Bushnell's team managed to compress Atari's coin-operated *Pong* game down to a few inexpensive circuits, which were contained in the game console. Atari's *Pong* had a sharper picture and more sensitive controllers than the Magnavox machine; it also cost less. Bushnell then went on a road show, demonstrating *Pong* to toy store buyers, but met with an indifferent response and no sales. Dejected, he returned to Atari with no idea of what to do next. Then the buyer for the sports goods department at Sears came to see Bushnell, reviewed the machine, and offered to buy every home *Pong* game Atari could make. With the backing of Sears, Bushnell boosted production. Sears ran a major television ad campaign to sell home *Pong*, and Atari's sales soared, hitting $450 million in 1975. The home video game had arrived.

BOOM AND BUST

Nothing attracts competitors like success, and by 1976 some twenty different companies were crowding into the home video game market, including National Semiconductor, RCA, Coleco, and Fairchild. It was the last of these companies that was to revolutionize the industry. Recognizing the limitations of existing home video game designs, in 1976 Fairchild came out with a home video game system capable of playing multiple games. The Fairchild system consisted of three components—a console, controllers, and cartridges. The console was a small computer optimized for graphics processing capabilities. It was designed to receive information from the controllers, process it, and send signals to a TV monitor. The controllers were hand-held devices used to direct on-screen action. The cartridges contained chips encoding the instructions for a game. They were designed to be inserted into the console.

In 1976, Bushnell sold Atari to Warner Communications for $28 million. Bushnell stayed on to run Atari. Backed by Warner's capital, in 1977 Atari developed and bought out its own cartridge-based system, the Atari 2600. The 2600 system was sold for $200, and associated cartridges retailed for $25 to $30. Sales surged during the 1977 Christmas season. However, a lack of manufacturing capacity on the part of market leader Atari and a very cautious approach to inventory by Fairchild led to shortages and kept sales significantly below what they could have been. Fairchild's cautious approach was the result of prior experience in consumer electronics. A year earlier, it had ramped up demand for its digital watches, only to get severely burnt by a buildup of excess inventory that had caused the company to take a $24.5 million write-off.[3]

Coming out of the 1977 Christmas season, Atari claimed to have sold around 400,000 units of the 2600 VCA, about 50 percent of all cartridge-based systems in American homes. Atari had also racked up more than $100 million in sales of game cartridges. By this point, second-place Fairchild sold around 250,000 units of its system. Cartridge sales for the year totaled about 1.2 million units, with an average selling price of around $20. Fresh from this success, and fortified by market forecasts predicting sales of 33 million cartridges and an installed base of 16 million machines by 1980, Bushnell committed Atari to manufacturing 1 million units of the 2600 for the 1978 Christmas season. Atari estimated that total demand would reach 2 million units. Bushnell was also encouraged by signals from Fairchild that it would again be limiting production to around 200,000 units. At this point, Atari had a library of around nine games. Fairchild had seventeen.[4]

Atari was not the only company to get excited by the growth forecasts. In 1978, a host of other companies entered the market with incompatible cartridge-based home systems. They included Coleco, National Semiconductor, Magnavox, General Instrument, and around a dozen others. However, the multitude of choices did not seem to entice consumers, and the 1978 Christmas season brought unexpectedly low sales. An industry shakeout followed in which only Atari and Coleco survived. Atari lost Bushnell, who was ousted by Warner executives (Bushnell went on to start Chuck E. Cheese Pizza Time Theater, a restaurant chain that had 278 outlets by 1981). Bushnell later stated that part of the problem was a disagreement over strategy. Bushnell wanted Atari to price the 2600 at cost and make money on sales of software; Warner wanted to continue making profits on hardware sales.[5]

Several important developments occurred in 1979. Several game producers and programmers defected from Atari to set up their own firm, Activision, to make games compatible with the Atari 2600. Their success encouraged others to follow suit. Second, Coleco developed an expansion module that allowed its machine to play Atari games. Atari and Mattel (which entered in 1979) did likewise. Third, 1979 saw the introduction of three new games into the home market—*Space Invaders*, *Asteroids*, and *Pac-Man*. All three were adapted from popular arcade games and all three helped drive demand for players.

Demand recovered strongly in late 1979 and kept growing for the next three years. In 1981, U.S. sales of home video games and cartridges hit $1 billion. In 1982, they surged to $3 billion, with Atari accounting for half of this amount. It seemed as if Atari could do no wrong. The 2600 was everywhere. Some 20 million units were sold, and by late 1982, there were now hundreds of games available for it. A large number of independent companies were now producing games for the 2600, including Activision, Imagic, and Epyx. Second-place Coleco was also doing well, partly based on a highly popular arcade game, *Donkey Kong*, that it had licensed from a Japanese company called Nintendo.

Atari was also in contact with Nintendo. In 1982, the company very nearly licensed the rights to Nintendo's Famicom, a cartridge-based video game system machine that was a big hit in Japan. Atari's successor to the 2600, the 5200, was not

selling well and the Famicom seemed like a good substitute. However, the negotiations broke down when Atari discovered that Nintendo had extended its *Donkey Kong* license to Coleco. This allowed Coleco to port a version of the game to its home computer, which was a direct competitor to Atari's 800 home computer.[6]

Coming off a strong 1982, the industry hoped for continued growth in 1983. Then the bottom dropped out of the market. Sales of home video games plunged to $100 million. Atari lost $500 million in the first nine months of the year, causing the stock of the parent company, Warner Communications, to drop in half. Part of the blame for the collapse was laid at the feet of an enormous inventory overhang of unsold games. Some 15 to 20 million surplus game cartridges were left over from the 1982 Christmas season (in 1981 there were none). On top of this, around 500 new games hit the market in 1993. The average price of a cartridge plunged from $30 in 1979 to $16 in 1982, and then $4 in 1983. As sales slowed, retailers cut back on the shelf space allocated to video games. It proved difficult for new games to make a splash in a crowded market. Atari had to bulldoze 6 million *ET: The Extraterrestrial* games. Meanwhile, big hits from previous years, such as *Pac-Man*, were bundled with game players and given away free to try to encourage system sales.[7]

Surveying the rubble, commentators claimed that the video game industry was dead. The era of dedicated game machines was over, they said. Personal computers were taking their place.[8] It seemed to be true. Mattel sold off its game business, Fairchild moved on to other things, Coleco folded, and Warner decided to break up Atari and sell its constituent pieces—at least those for which it could find a buyer. No one in America seemed to want to have anything to do with the home video game business—no one except Minoru Arakawa, the head of Nintendo's U.S. subsidiary, Nintendo of America (NOA). Picking through the rubble of the industry, Arakawa noticed that there was one group of people who seemed to be oblivious to the obituaries. Video arcades were still packed, bringing in $7 billion a year—more money than the entire movie industry. Perhaps it was not a lack of interest in home video games that had killed off the industry. Perhaps it was bad business practice.

THE NINTENDO MONOPOLY

Nintendo was a century-old Japanese company that had built up a profitable business making playing cards before diversifying into the video game business. Based in Kyoto and still run by the founding Yamauchi family, in the late 1970s the company started to diversify into the video game business. The first step was to license video game technology from Magnavox. In 1977, Nintendo introduced a home video game system in Japan based on this technology that played a variation of *Pong*. In 1978, the company began to sell coin-operated video games. It had its first hit with *Donkey Kong*, designed by Sigeru Miyamoto.

The Famicom

In the early 1980s, the company's boss, Hiroshi Yamauchi, decided that Nintendo had to develop its own video game machine. He pushed the company's engineers to develop a machine that combined superior graphics-processing capabilities with a low price. Yamauchi wanted a machine that could sell for $75, less than half the price of competing machines at the time. He dubbed the machine the "Family Computer," or Famicom. The machine his engineers designed was based on the controller, console, and plug-in cartridge format pioneered by Fairchild. It contained two custom chips: an 8-bit central processing unit and a graphics-processing unit. Both chips had been scaled down to perform only essential functions. A 16-bit processor was available at the time, but to keep costs down, Yamauchi refused to use it.

Nintendo approached Ricoh, the electronics giant, which had spare semiconductor capacity. The chips, they said, had to cost no more that 2,000 yen. Ricoh thought that the 2,000 yen price point was absurd. Yamauchi's response was to guarantee Ricoh a 3-million-chip order within two years. Since the leading companies in Japan were selling at most 30,000 video games per year at the time, many within the company viewed this as an outrageous commitment, but Ricoh went for it.[9]

Another feature of the machine was its memory; 2,000 bytes of RAM (random access memory) as opposed to the 256 bytes of RAM in the Atari machine. The result was a machine with superior graphics-processing capabilities and faster action that could handle far more complex games than Atari games. Nintendo's engineers also built a new set of chips into the game cartridges. In addition to chips that held the game program, Nintendo developed memory map controller (MMC) chips, which took over some of the graphics-processing work from the chips in the console and enabled the system to handle more complex games. With the addition of the MMC chips, the potential for more sophisticated and complex games had arrived. Over time, Nintendo's engineers developed more powerful MMC chips, enabling the basic 8-bit system to do things that originally seemed out of reach. The engineers also figured out a way to include a battery backup system in cartridges, which allowed some games to store information independently—to keep track of where a player had left off or to track high scores.

The Games

Yamauchi recognized that great hardware would not sell itself. The key to the market, he reasoned, was great games. When developing the hardware, Yamauchi had instructed the engineers to make sure that "it was appreciated by software engineers." Moreover, Nintendo decided that Nintendo would become a haven for game designers. "An ordinary man," he said, "cannot develop good games no matter how hard he tries. A handful of people in this world can develop games that everyone wants. Those are the people we want at Nintendo."[10]

Here Yamauchi had an ace in the hole in the person of Sigeru Miyamoto. Miyamoto, a graduate of Kanazawa Munici College of Industrial Arts, had joined Nintendo at the age of twenty-four. Yamauchi had hired Miyamoto as a favor to his father, an old friend, although he had little idea what he would do with an artist. For three years, Miyamoto worked as Nintendo's staff artist. Then in 1980, Yamauchi called Miyamoto into his office. Nintendo had started selling coin-operated video games, but one of the new games, *Radarscope*, was a disaster. Could Miyamoto come up with a new game? Miyamoto was delighted. He had always spent a lot of time drawing cartoons, and as a student, he had played video games constantly. Miyamoto believed that video games could be used to bring cartoons to life.[11]

The game Miyamoto developed was nothing short of a revelation. At a time when most coin-operated video games lacked characters or depth,

Miyamoto created a game around a story that had both. At a time when most games involved battles with space invaders or heroes shooting lasers at aliens, Miyamoto's game did neither. Based loosely on *Beauty and the Beast* and *King Kong*, Miyamoto's game has a pet ape run off with his master's beautiful girlfriend. His master is an ordinary carpenter, called Mario. Neither handsome nor heroic, Mario has a bulbous nose, a bushy mustache, a pair of large, pathetic eyes, and a red cap (which Miyamoto added because he was not good at hairstyles). He does not carry a laser gun. The ape runs off with the girl to get back at his master, who was not especially nice to the beast. The man, of course, has to get the girl back. To do that, the little man has to run up ramps, climb ladders, jump off elevators, and the like, while the ape throws objects at the hapless carpenter. Since the main character is an ape, Miyamoto called him *Kong*, and because he was as stubborn as a donkey, he called the game *Donkey Kong*.

Released in 1981, *Donkey Kong* was a sensation in the world of coin-operated video arcades and a smash hit for Nintendo. In 1984, Yamauchi again summoned Miyamoto to his office. He needed more games, this time for the Famicom. Miyamoto was made the head of a new R&D group. He was told to come up with the most imaginative video games ever.

Miyamoto began with Mario from *Donkey Kong*. A colleague had told him that Mario looked more like a plumber than a carpenter, so a plumber he became. Miyamoto gave Mario a brother, Luigi, who was as tall and thin as Mario was short and fat. They became the *Super Mario Brothers*. Since plumbers spend their time working on pipes, large green sewer pipes became obstacles and doorways into secret worlds. Mario and Luigi's task was to search for the captive Princess Toadstool. Mario and Luigi are endearing bumblers, unequal to their task yet surviving. They shoot, squash, or evade their enemies—a potpourri of Dr. Seuss–like inventions that include flying turtles and stinging fish, man-eating flowers and fire-breathing dragons— while they collect gold coins, blow air bubbles, and climb vines into smiling clouds.[12]

Super Mario Brothers was introduced in 1985. For Miyamoto, this was just the beginning. Between 1985 and 1991, he produced eight *Mario* games. Some 60 to 70 million were sold worldwide, making Miyamoto the most successful game designer in

the world. After adapting *Donkey Kong* for the Famicom, he went on to create other top-selling games, including another classic, *The Legend of Zelda*. While Miyamoto drew freely on folklore, literature, and pop culture, the main source for his ideas was his own experience. The memory of being lost among a maze of sliding doors in his family's home was recreated in the labyrinths of the *Zelda* games. The dog that attacked him when he was a child attacks Mario in *Super Mario*. As a child, Miyamoto had once climbed a tree to catch a view of far-off mountains and got stuck. Mario gets himself into a similar fix. Once Miyamoto went hiking without a map and was surprised to stumble across a lake. In the *Legend of Zelda*, part of the adventure is to walk into new places without a map and be confronted by surprises.

Nintendo in Japan

Nintendo introduced the Famicom into the Japanese market in May 1983. The Famicom was priced at $100, more than Yamauchi wanted, but significantly less than the products of competitors. When he introduced the machine, Yamauchi urged retailers to forgo profits on the hardware because it was just a tool to sell software, and that is where they would make their money. Backed by an extensive advertising campaign, 500,000 units of the Famicom were sold in the first two months. Within a year, the figure stood at a million, and sales were still expanding at a rapid clip. With the hardware rapidly finding its way into Japanese homes, Nintendo was besieged by calls from desperate retailers frantically demanding more games.

It was at this point that Yamauchi told Miyamoto to come up with the most imaginative games ever. However, Yamauchi also realized that Nintendo alone could not satisfy the growing thirst for new games, and so he initiated a licensing program. To become a Nintendo licensee, companies had to agree to an unprecedented series of restrictions. Licensees could issue only five Nintendo games per year, and they could not write those titles for other platforms. The licensing fee was set at 20 percent of the wholesale price of each cartridge sold (game cartridges wholesaled for around $30). It typically cost $500,000 to develop a game and took around six months. Nintendo insisted that games did not contain any excessively violent or sexually suggestive material and reviewed every game before allowing it to be produced.[13]

Despite these restrictions, six companies agreed to become Nintendo licensees, not least because millions of customers were now clamoring for games. They were Bandai, Capcom, Konami, Namco, Taito, and Hudson. Bandai was Japan's largest toy company. The others already made either coin-operated video games or computer software games. Because of these licensing agreements, they saw their sales and earnings surge. For example, Konami's earnings went from $10 million in 1987 to $300 million in 1991.

After the six licensees began selling games, reports of defective games began to reach Yamauchi. The original six licensees were allowed to manufacture their own game cartridges. Realizing that he had given away the ability to control the quality of the cartridges, Yamauchi decided to change the contract for future licensees. Future licensees were required to submit all manufacturing orders for cartridges to Nintendo. Nintendo charged licensees $14 per cartridge, required that they place a minimum order for 10,000 units, and insisted on cash payment in full when the order was placed (later the minimum order was raised to 30,000). Nintendo outsourced all manufacturing to other companies, using the volume of its orders to get rock-bottom prices. The cartridges were estimated to cost Nintendo between $6 and $8 each. The licensees then picked up the cartridges from Nintendo's loading dock and were responsible for distribution. In 1985, there were seventeen licensees; by 1987, there were fifty. At this point, 90 percent of the home video game systems sold in Japan were Nintendo systems.

Nintendo in America

In 1980, Nintendo established a subsidiary in America to sell its coin-operated video games. The subsidiary was headed by Yamauchi's American-educated son-in-law, Minoru Arakawa. All of the other essential employees were Americans, including Ron Judy and Al Stone. Based originally in Seattle, for its first two years Nintendo of America (NOA) struggled to sell second-rate games such as *Radarscope*. The subsidiary seemed on the brink of closing. NOA could not even make the rent payment on the warehouse. Then they received a large shipment from Japan: 2,000 units of a new coin-operated video game. Opening the box, they discovered *Donkey Kong.* After briefly playing the game, Judy exclaimed that is was a disaster. Stone walked out of the building, declaring that "its over."[14] The managers were appalled. They could not imagine a game less likely to sell in video arcades. The only promising sign was that a twenty-year employee, Howard Philips, rapidly became glued to the machine. They had to pry him off.

Arakawa, however, knew he had little choice but to try to sell the game. Judy persuaded the owner of the Spot Tavern near Nintendo's office to take one of the game on a trial basis. After one night, Judy discovered there was $30 in the coin box, a phenomenal amount. The next night there was $35, and $36 the night after that. NOA had a hit on its hands.

By the end of 1982, NOA had sold more than 60,000 copies of *Donkey Kong* and booked sales in excess of $100 million. Having outgrown its Seattle location, the subsidiary moved to a new site in Redmond, a Seattle suburb, where it located next to a small but fast-growing software company run by an old school acquaintance of Howard Philips, one Bill Gates.

By 1984, NOA was riding a wave of success in the coin-operated video-game market. Arakawa, however, was interested in the possibilities of selling Nintendo's new Famicom system in the United States. Throughout 1984, Arakawa, Judy, and Stone met with numerous toy and department store representatives to discuss the possibilities, only to be repeatedly rebuffed. Still smarting from the 1983 debacle, they wanted nothing to do with the home video-game business. They also met with former managers from Atari and Coleco to gain their insights. The most common responses they received was that the market collapsed because the last generation of games "sucked."

Arakawa and his team decided that if they were going to sell the Famicom in the United States, they would have to find a new distribution channel. The obvious choice was consumer electronics stores. Thus, Arakawa asked the R&D team back in Kyoto to redesign the Famicom for the U.S. market so that it looked less like a toy (the Famicom was encased in red and white plastic), and more like a consumer electronics device. The redesigned machine was renamed the Nintendo Entertainment System (NES).

Another major issue was how to avoid the "suck factor" with games. Arakawa's big fear was that illegal, low-quality, Taiwanese games would flood the U.S. market if the NES was successful. To stop counterfeit games being played on the NES, Arakawa asked Nintendo's Japanese engineers to design some kind of security system into the U.S. version of the Famicom, so that only Nintendo-approved games could be played on the NES. The Japanese engineers responded by designing a security chip that was to be embedded in the game cartridges. The NES would not work unless the security chips in the cartridges connected with a chip in the NES. Since the code embedded in the security chip was proprietary, the implication of this system was that no one could manufacture games for the NES without Nintendo's specific approval.

To overcome the skepticism and reluctance of retailers to stock a home video-game system, in late 1985 Arakawa decided to make an extraordinary commitment. Nintendo would stock stores and set up displays and windows. Retailers would not have to pay for anything they stocked for ninety days. After that, retailers could pay Nintendo for what they sold and return the rest. The NES was bundled with Nintendo's best-selling game in Japan, *Super Mario Brothers*. It was essentially a risk free proposition for retailers, but even with this, most were skeptical. Ultimately, thirty Nintendo personnel descended on the New York area. Referred to as the Nintendo SWAT team, after an extraordinary blitz that involved eighteen-hour days, they persuaded some stores to stock the NES. To support the New York product launch, Nintendo also committed itself to a $5 million advertising campaign, heavily concentrated at the seven- to fourteen-year-old boys, who seemed to be Nintendo's likely core audience.

By December 1985, between 500 and 600 stores in the New York area were stocking Nintendo systems. Sales were moderate—about half of the 100,000 NES machines shipped from Japan were sold—but it was enough to justify going forward. The SWAT team then moved on—first Los Angeles, then Chicago, and then Dallas. As in New York, sales started at a moderate pace, but by late 1986 they were starting to accelerate rapidly, and Nintendo went national with the NES.

In 1986, around 1 million NES units sold in the United States. In 1987, the figure increased to 3 million. In 1988, it jumped to more than 7 million. In the same year, 33 million game cartridges were sold. Nintendo mania had arrived in the United States. To expand the supply of games, Nintendo licensed the rights to produce up to five games per year to thirty-one American software companies. Nintendo continued to use a restrictive licensing agreement that gave it exclusive rights to any games, required licensees to place their orders through Nintendo, and insisted on a 30,000-unit minimum order.[15]

By 1990, the home video-game market was worth $5 billion worldwide. Nintendo dominated the industry with a 90 percent share of the market for game equipment. The parent company was now deemed by some to be the most profitable company in Japan. By 1992, it was netting more than $1 billion in gross profit annually, or more than $1.5 million for each employee in Japan. The company's stock market value exceeded that of Sony, Japan's premier consumer electronics firm. Indeed, the company's net profit exceeded that of all the American movie studios combined. Nintendo games, it seemed, were bigger than the movies.

As of 1991, there were more than 100 licensees for Nintendo, and more than 450 titles were available for the NES. In the United States, Nintendo products were distributed through toy stores (30 percent of volume), mass merchandisers (40 percent of volume), and department stores (10 percent). Nintendo tightly controlled the number of game titles and games that could be sold, quickly withdrawing titles as soon as interest appeared to be declining. In 1988, retailers requested 110 million cartridges from Nintendo. Market surveys suggested that perhaps 45 million could have been sold, but Nintendo only allowed 33 million to be shipped.[16] Nintendo claimed that the shortage of games was in part due to a worldwide shortage of semiconductor chips.

A number of companies had tried to reverse-engineer the code embedded in Nintendo's security chip, which competitors characterized as a "lock-out" chip. Nintendo successfully sued them. The most notable was Atari Games, one of the successors of the original Atari, which in 1987 sued Nintendo of America for anticompetitive behavior. Atari claimed that the purpose of the security chip was to monopolize the market. At the same time, Atari announced that it had found a way around Nintendo's security chip and would begin to sell unlicensed games.[17] NOA responded with a countersuit. In a March 1991 ruling, Atari was found to have obtained Nintendo's security code illegally and ordered to stop selling NES-compatible games. However, Nintendo did not always have it all its own way. In 1990, under pressure from Congress, the Department of Justice, and a number of other lawsuits, Nintendo rescinded its exclusivity requirements, freeing up developers to write games for other platforms. However, developers faced a problem: what platform could they write for?

SEGA'S SONIC BOOM

Back in 1954, David Rosen, a twenty-year-old American, left the U.S. Air Force after a tour of duty in Tokyo.[18] Rosen had noticed that Japanese people needed lots of photographs for ID cards, but that local photo studios were slow and expensive. He formed a company, Rosen Enterprises, and went into the photo-booth business. The booths were a big success, and by 1957 Rosen had established a successful nationwide chain. At this point, the Japanese economy was booming so Rosen decided it was time to get into another business—entertainment. As his vehicle, he chose arcade games, which were unknown in Japan at the time. He picked up used games on the cheap from America and set up arcades in the same Japanese department stores and theaters that typically housed his photo booths. Within a few years, Rosen had 200 arcades nationwide. His only competition came from another American-owned firm, Service Games (or SeGa), whose original business was jukeboxes and fruit machines.

By the early 1960s, the Japanese arcade market had caught up with the U.S. market. The problem was that game makers had run out of exciting new games to offer. Rosen decided that he would have to get into the business of designing and manufacturing games, but to do that he needed manufacturing facilities. SeGa manufactured its own games, so in 1965 Rosen approached the company and suggested a merger. The result was Sega Enterprise, a Japanese company that had Rosen as the CEO.

Rosen himself designed Sega's first game, *Periscope*, in which the objective was to sink chain-mounted cardboard ships by firing torpedoes, represented by lines of colored lights. *Periscope* was a big success not only in Japan, but also in the United States and Europe, and allowed Sega to build up a respectable export business. Over the years, the company continued to invest heavily in game development, always using the latest electronic technology.

Gulf and Western, a U.S. conglomerate, acquired Sega in 1969, with Rosen running the subsidiary. In 1975, Gulf & Western took Sega public in the United States, but left Sega Japan as a G&W subsidiary. Hayao Nakayama, a former Sega distributor, was drafted as president. In the early 1980s, Nakayama pushed G&W to invest more in Sega Japan, so that the company could enter the then booming home video-game market. When G&W refused, Nakayama suggested a management buyout. G&W agreed, and in 1984, for the price of just $38 million, Sega became a Japanese company once more (Sega's Japanese revenues were around $700 million, but by now the company was barely profitable).

Sega was caught off guard by the huge success of Nintendo's Famicom. Although it released its own 8-bit system in 1986, the machine never commanded more than 5 percent of the Japanese market. Nakayama, however, was not about to give up. From years in the arcade business, he understood that great games drove sales. Nevertheless, he also understood that more powerful technology gave game developers the tools to design games that are more appealing. This philosophy underlay Nakayama's decision to develop a 16-bit game system, the Genesis.

To do this, Sega took the design of its 16-bit arcade machine and adapted it for the Genesis. Compared with Nintendo's 8-bit machine, the 16-bit machine was able to boast an array of superior technological features. These included high-definition graphics and animation, a full spectrum of colors, two independent scrolling backgrounds that created an impressive depth of field, and near CD-quality sound. The design strategy also made it easy to port Sega's catalog of arcade hits over to the Genesis.

The Genesis was launched in Japan in 1989, and in the United States in 1990. In the United States, the machine was priced at $199. The company hoped that sales would be increased by the popularity of its arcade games, such as the graphically violent *Altered Beast*. Sega also licensed other companies to develop games for the Genesis platform. In an effort to recruit licensees, Sega asked for lower royalty rates than Nintendo, and it gave licensees the right to manufacture their own cartridges. However, independent game developers were slow to climb on board, while the $200 price tag for the player held back sales.

One of the first independent game developers to sign up with Sega was Electronic Arts. Established by Trip Hawkins, Electronic Arts had focused on designing games for personal computers, and consequently, had missed the Nintendo 8-bit era.

Now Hawkins was determined to get a presence in the home video-game market, and hitching his company's wagon to Sega seemed to be the best option. The Nintendo playing field was already excessively crowded, and besides, Sega was offering a far less restrictive licensing deal than Nintendo. Electronic Arts subsequently wrote a number of big-selling games for the Genesis, including *John Madden Football*, and several gory combat-type games.[19]

Nintendo had not been ignoring the potential of the 16-bit system. Nintendo's own 16-bit system, the Super NES, was ready for market introduction in 1989—at the same time as Sega's Genesis. Nintendo did introduce the Super NES in Japan in 1990, where it quickly established a strong market presence and beat out Sega's Genesis. However, in the United States the company decided to hold back longer in order to reap the full benefits of the dominance it enjoyed with the 8-bit NES system. Yamauchi was also worried about the lack of backward compatibility between Nintendo's 8-bit and 16-bit systems. (The company had tried to make the 16-bit system able to play 8-bit games but concluded that the cost of doing so was prohibitive.) These concerns may have led the company to delay market introduction until the 8-bit market was saturated.

Meanwhile, in the United States, the Sega bandwagon was beginning to gain momentum. One development that gave the Genesis a push was the introduction of a new Sega game, *Sonic the Hedgehog*. Developed by an independent team contracted to Sega, the game featured a cute hedgehog that impatiently tapped his paw when the player took too long to act. Impatience was Sonic's central feature—he had places to go, and quickly. He zipped along, collecting brass rings when he could find them, before rolling into a ball and flying down slides with loops and through underground tunnels. Sonic was Sega's Mario.

In mid 1991, in an attempt to jump-start slow sales, Tom Kalinske, head of Sega's American subsidiary, decided to bundle *Sonic the Hedgehog* with the game player. He also reduced the price for the bundled unit to $150, and relaunched the system with an aggressive advertising campaign aimed at teenagers. The campaign was built around the slogan "Genesis does what Nintendon't." The shift in strategy worked, and sales accelerated sharply.

Sega's success prompted Nintendo to launch its own 16-bit system. Nintendo's Super NES was intro-

duced at a $200 price point. However, Sega now had a two-year head start in games. By the end of 1991, about 125 game titles were available for the Genesis, compared with 25 for the Super NES. In May 1992, Nintendo reduced the price of the Super NES to $150. At this time, Sega was claiming a 63 percent share of the 16-bit market in the United States, and Nintendo a 60 percent share. By now, Sega was cool. As it became cool, Sega took more chances with mass media–defined morality. When Acclaim Entertainment released its bloody *Mortal Kombat* game in September 1992, the Sega version let players rip off heads and tear out hearts. Reflecting Nintendo's image of its core market, the Nintendo version was sanitized. Sega version outsold Nintendo's two to one.[20] Therefore, the momentum continued to run in Sega's favor. By January 1993, there were 320 titles available for the Sega Genesis, and 130 for the Super NES. In early 1994, independent estimates suggested that Sega had 60 percent of the U.S. market and Nintendo 40 percent. Nintendo disputed this.

3DO TRIES TO DO IT

Trip Hawkins, whose first big success was Electronic Arts, founded 3DO in 1991.[21] His vision for 3DO was to shift the home video-game business from the existing cartridge-based format toward a CD-ROM-based platform. The original partners in 3DO were Electronic Arts, Matsushita, Time Warner, AT&T, and the venture capital firm Kleiner Perkins. Collectively, they invested more than $17 million in 3DO, making it the best-capitalized start-up in the history of the home video-game industry. In May 1993, 3DO went public at $15 per share. By October of that year, the stock had risen to $48 per share, valuing 3DO at $1 billion—not bad for a company that had yet to generate a single dollar in revenues.

The basis for 3DO's $1 billion market cap was patented computer system architecture and copyrighted operating system that allowed for much richer graphics and audio capabilities. The system was built around a 32-bit RISC microprocessor and proprietary graphics processor chips. The 3DO system stored games on a CD-ROM instead of a cartridge. It could hold up to 600 megabytes of content, sharply up from the 10 megabytes of content found in the typical game cartridge of the time. The slower access time of a CD-ROM compared with that of a cartridge was finessed somewhat by using a double-speed CD-ROM drive.[22]

The belief at 3DO—a belief apparently shared by many investors—was that the superior storage and graphics-processing capabilities of the 3DO system would prove very attractive to game developers, allowing them to be far more creative. In turn, better games would rapidly attract customers away from Nintendo and Sega. Developing games to take advantage of the capabilities of a CD-ROM system altered the economics of game development. Estimates suggested that it would cost approximately $2 million to produce a game for the 3DO system and could take as long as twenty-four months to develop the game. However, at $2 per disk, a CD-ROM cost substantially less to produce than a cartridge.

The centerpiece of 3DO's strategy was to license its hardware technology for free. Game developers paid a royalty of $3 per disk for access to the 3DO operating code. Disks typically retailed for $40 each.

Matsushita introduced the first 3DO machine into the U.S. market in October 1993. Priced at $700, the machine was sold through electronic retailers that carried Panasonic high-end electronics products. Commenting on the machine, Sega's Kalinske noted that "It's a noble effort. Some people will buy 3DO, and they'll have a wonderful experience. It's impressive, but it's a niche. We've done the research. It does not become a large market until you go below $500. At $300, it starts to get interesting. We make no money on hardware. It's a cutthroat business. I hope Matsushita understands that."[23] CD-ROM disks for the 3DO machine retailed for around $75. The machine came bundled with *Crash n Burn*, a high-speed combat racing game. However, only 18 titles for the 3DO were available by the crucial Christmas period, although reports suggested that 150 titles were being developed.[24]

Sales of the hardware were slow, reaching only 30,000 by January 1994.[25] In the same month, AT&T and Sanyo both announced that they would begin to manufacture the 3DO machine. In March, faced with continuing sluggish sales, 3DO announced that it would give hardware manufacturers two shares of 3DO stock for every unit sold at or below a certain retail price. Matsushita dropped the price of its machine to $500. About the same time, Toshiba, LG, and Samsung all announced that they would start to produce 3DO machines.

By June 1994, cumulative sales of 3DO machines in the United States stood at 40,000 units. Matsushita announced plans to expand distribution beyond its 3,500 outlets to include the toy and mass merchandise channels. Hawkins and his partners announced that they would invest another $37 million in 3DO. By July, there were 750 licensees of 3DO software, but only forty titles were available for the format. Sales continued at a very sluggish pace and the supply of new software titles started to dry up.[26]

In September 1996, 3DO announced that it would either sell its hardware system business or move it into a joint venture.[27] It also announced that about 150 people, or one-third of the work force, would probably lose their jobs in the restructuring. According to Hawkins, 3DO would now focus on developing software for on-line gaming. Hawkins stated that the Internet, and Internet entertainment, constituted a huge opportunity for 3DO. The stock dropped $1.375, to $6.75, on the news.

SEGA'S SATURN

Both Sega and Sony also introduced CD-ROM–based systems in the mid 1990s. Sega had in fact beaten 3DO to the market with its November 1992 introduction of the Sega CD, a $300 CD-ROM add-on to the 16-bit Genesis. Sega sold 100,000 units in its first month alone. However, sales then slowed down, and by December 1993 were standing at just 250,000 units. One reason for the slowdown, according to critics, was a lack of strong games. Sega was also working on a 32-bit CD-ROM system, the Saturn, which was targeted for a mid 1995 introduction in the United States. In January 1994, Sega announced that Microsoft would supply the operating system for the Saturn.[28]

In March 1994, Sega announced the Genesis Super 32X, a $150 add-on cartridge, designed to increase the performance of Genesis cartridge and CD-ROM games. The 32X contained the 32-bit Hitachi microprocessor that was to be used in the Saturn. Sega called the 32X "the poor man's 32-bit machine" because it sold for a mere $149. Introduced in the fall of 1994, the 32X never lived up to its expectations. Most users appeared willing to wait for the real thing, the Sega Saturn, promised for release the following year.

In early 1995, Sega informed the press and retailers that it would release the Saturn on "Sega

Saturn Saturday, Sept 2nd." Actually, Sega released the 32-bit Saturn in May 1995. It was priced at $400 per unit and accompanied by the introduction of just ten games. Sega apparently believed that the world would be delighted by the May release of the Saturn. However, the Saturn was released without the industry fanfare that normally greets a new game machine. Moreover, only four retail chains received the Saturn in May, while the rest were told they would have to wait until September. This move alienated retailers, who responded by dropping Sega products from their stores.[29] Sega, it appeared, had made a marketing blunder.[30]

SONY'S PLAYSTATION

In the fall of 1995, Sony entered the fray with the introduction of the Sony PlayStation.[31] The PlayStation used a 32-bit RISC microprocessor running at 33 MHz and a double-speed CD-ROM drive. The PlayStation cost an estimated $500 million to develop. The machine had actually been in development since 1991, when Sony decided that the home video-game industry was getting too big to ignore. Initially, Sony was in an alliance with Nintendo to develop the machine, but when Nintendo walked away from the alliance in 1992 after a disagreement over who owned the rights to any future CD-ROM games, Sony went it alone.[32]

Right from the start, Sony felt that it would be able to leverage its presence in the film and music business to build a strong position in the home video-game industry. A consumer electronics giant with a position in the Hollywood movie business and the music industry (Sony owned Columbia Pictures and the Columbia record label), Sony believed that it had access to significant intellectual property that could form the basis of many popular games.

In 1991, Sony established a division in New York, Sony Electronic Publishing, that was to serve as an umbrella organization for Sony's multimedia offerings. Headed by Iceland native Olaf Olafsson, then just twenty-eight years old, this organization ultimately took the lead role in both the market launch of the PlayStation, and in developing game titles.[33] In 1993, as part of this effort, Sony purchased a well-respected British game developer, Psygnosis. By fall 1995 launch, this unit had twenty games ready to complement the PlayStation. These included *The Haldeman Diaries*, *Mickey Mania* (developed in collaboration with Disney), and

Johnny Mnemonic, based on William Gibson's short story. To entice independent game developers such as Electronic Arts, Namco, and Acclaim Entertainment, Olafsson used the promise of low royalty rates. The standard royalty rate was set at $9 per disk, although those that signed on early enough were given a lower royalty rate. Sony also provided some 4,000 game development tools to licensees in an effort to help them speed games to market.[34]

To distribute the PlayStation, Sony set up a retail channel separate from Sony's consumer electronics sales force and marketed the PlayStation as a hip and powerful alternative to the outdated Nintendo and Sega cartridge-based systems. Sony worked closely with retailers before the launch to find out how it could help them sell the PlayStation. To jump start demand, Sony set up in-store displays to allow potential consumers to try the equipment. Just before the launch, Sony had lined up an impressive 12,000 retail outlets in the United States.[35]

Sony targeted its advertising for the PlayStation at males in the eighteen to thirty-five age range. The targeting was evident in the content of many of the games. One of the big hits for the PlayStation was *Tomb Raider*, whose central character, Lara Croft, combined sex appeal with savviness and helped to recruit an older generation to the PlayStation.[36] The PlayStation was initially priced at $299, and games retailed for as much as $60. Sony's Tokyo-based executives had reportedly been insisting on a $350-$400 price for the PlayStation, but Olafsson pushed hard for the lower price. Because of the fallout from this internal battle, in January 1996 Olafsson resigned from Sony. By then, however, Sony was following his script.[37]

Sony's prelaunch work was rewarded with strong early sales. By January 1996, more than 800,000 PlayStations, as well as 4 million games, had been sold in the United States. In May 1996, with 1.2 million PlayStations shipped, Sony reduced the price of the PlayStation to $199. Sega responded with a similar price cut for its Saturn. The prices on some of Sony's initial games were also reduced to $29.99. The weekend after the price cuts, retailers reported that PlayStation sales were up by between 350 and 1,000 percent over the prior week.[38] The sales surge continued through 1996. By the end of the year, sales of the PlayStation and associated software amounted to $1.3 billion, out of total U.S. sales of $2.2 billion for all video-game hardware and software. In March 1997, Sony cut the price of the PlayStation again, this time to $149. It also reduced its suggested retail price for games by $10, to $49.99. By this point, Sony had sold 3.4 million units of the PlayStation in the United States, compared with Saturn's 1.6 million units.[39] Worldwide, the PlayStation had outsold the Saturn 13 million to 7.8 million units, and Saturn sales were slowing.[40] The momentum was clearly running in Sony's favor, but the company now had a new challenge to deal with: Nintendo's latest generation game machine, the N64.

NINTENDO STRIKES BACK

In July 1996, Nintendo launched the Nintendo 64 (N64) in the Japanese market. This was followed by a late fall introduction in the United States. The N64 is a 64-bit machine developed in conjunction with Silicon Graphics. Originally targeted for introduction a year earlier, the N64 had been in development since 1993. The machine used a plug-in cartridge format rather than a CD-ROM drive. According to Nintendo, cartridges allow for faster access time and are far sturdier than CD-ROMs (an important consideration with children).[41]

The most striking feature of the N64 machine, however, was its 3D graphics capability. The N64 provides fully rounded figures that can turn on their heels, rotating through 180 degrees. Advanced ray tracing techniques borrowed from military simulators and engineering workstations added to the sense of realism by providing proper highlighting, reflections, and shadows.

The N64 was targeted at children and young teenagers, priced at $200, and launched with just four games. Despite the lack of games, initial sales were very robust. Indeed, 1997 turned out to be a strong year for both Sony and Nintendo. The overall U.S. market was robust, with sales of hardware and software combined reaching a record $5.5 billion. According to estimates, the PlayStation accounted for 49 percent of machines and games by value. The N64 captured a 41 percent share, leaving Sega trailing badly with less than 10 percent of the market. During the year, the average price for game machines had fallen to $150. By year-end, there were 300 titles available for the PlayStation compared with 40 for the N64. Games for the PlayStation retailed for $40, on average, compared with more than $60 for the N64.[42]

By late 1998, there were signs that the PlayStation was widening its lead over the N64. In the crucial North American market, the PlayStation was reported to be outselling the N64 by a 2 to 1 margin, although Nintendo retained a lead in the under-twelve age category. At this point, there were 115 games available for the N64, against 431 for the PlayStation.[43] Worldwide, Sony had now sold close to 55 million PlayStations. The success of the PlayStation had a major impact on Sony's bottom line. In fiscal 1998, the PlayStation business generated revenues of $5.5 billion for Sony, 10 percent of its worldwide revenues, but accounted for $886 million, or 22.5 percent, of the company's operating income.[44]

THE NEXT GENERATION

After almost vanishing from the marketplace in 1998, Sega made a bold attempt to retake a leadership position with the late 1998 Japanese introduction of its Dreamcast home video game machine. The Dreamcast is the most powerful home video-game machine yet with the capability to display advanced 3D graphics. The Dreamcast runs on a 128-bit microprocessor that runs at 200 MHz and uses a Microsoft Windows CE operating system. The games are stored on a CD-ROM, and the machine comes equipped with a 56K modem to facilitate multiplayer on-line game playing. Priced at $240, and launched with only a handful of games, the Dreamcast still sold more than 1 million units in its first few months on the Japanese market.

Sega has scheduled a September 1999 date for the U.S. launch of the Dreamcast. The machine will be priced at $199. Up to 12 games will be available at launch, including a new version of *Sonic the Hedgehog,* which cost an estimated $30 million to produce. By Christmas 1999, there should be 30 games, and 100 by mid 2000. Sega has licensed some 100 independent developers to work on Dreamcast games. The company has plans to spend some $100 million on advertising to launch the system in the United States. Sega has already struck distribution agreements with some of the largest chains in the United States, including Toys "R" Us, Wal-Mart, and Sears. Some 20,000 stores should be carrying the Dreamcast. As of the spring of 1999, advanced orders for the Dreamcast stood at 300,000.[45]

Sony also has plans to launch a 128-bit machine, dubbed the PlayStation II, in 2000. Reportedly, the company is investing $1 billion in the development of the PlayStation II. The machine is expected to have graphics capabilities 200 times faster than the original PlayStation and will utilize a DVD disk for storage. In an attempt to leverage its huge global installed base, Sony plans to make its new machine backward compatible with the original PlayStation.[46] Nintendo is also reportedly working on a 128-bit machine, although details are sketchy.

Going forward, the great unknown is the threat that the personal computer poses to the video-game industry. The threat has been discussed for years, but until recently general purpose PCs have lacked the capabilities of specialized game machines. This may now be changing. Microsoft has provided a direct interface between Windows applications and three-dimensional graphics technology with a variation on its Active X technology, Direct X. According to game developers, the combination of Direct X, fast Pentium microprocessors, faster CD-ROM drives, and graphics accelerator chips has made the PC a much more appealing platform for which to write games. Another attraction of writing for the PC is that game developers do not have to pay royalties to PC manufacturers for the privilege of supplying compatible games.

Since early 1997, most new PCs have been sold with 3D graphics capability. Moreover, with prices dropping to under $1,000 for high powered entry-level PCs, industry estimates suggest that more than 100 million PCs may be sold in 1998, all of them with a high enough specification to run advanced games. Indeed, game software may be the only application that really stretches the modern PC.[47]

Endnotes

1. A good account of early history of Bushnell and Atari can be found in S. Cohen, *Zap! The Rise and Fall of Atari* (New York: McGraw-Hill, 1984).

2. R. Isaacs, "Video Games Race to Catch a Changing Market," *Business Week*, December 26, 1977, p. 44B.

3. P. Pagnano, "Atari's Game Plan to Overwhelm Its Competitors," *Business Week*, May 8, 1978, p. 50F.

4. Isaacs, "Video Games."

5. P. Pagnano, "Atari's Game Plan"; D. Sheff, *Game Over* (New York: Random House, 1993).

6. Cohen, *Zap!*

7. L. Kehoe, "Atari Seeks Way Out of Video Game Woes," *Financial Times*, December 14, 1983, p. 23.

8. M. Schrage, "The High-Tech Dinosaurs: Video Games, Once Ascendant, Are Making Way," *Washington Post*, July 31, 1983, p. F1.

9. Sheff, *Game Over.*

10. Quoted in Sheff, *Game Over.*

11. Sheff, *Game Over.*

12. D. Golden, "In Search of Princess Toadstool," *Boston Globe*, November 20, 1988, p. 18.

13. N. Gross, and G. Lewis, "Here Comes the *Super Mario Bros,*" *Business Week*, November 9, 1987, p. 138.

14. Sheff, *Game Over.*

15. Golden, "In Search of Princess Toadstool."

16. "Marketer of the Year," *Adweek*, November 27, 1989, p. 15.

17. C. Lazzareschi, "No Mere Child's Play," *Los Angeles Times*, December 16, 1988, p. 1.

18. For a good summary of the early history of Sega, see J. Battle and B. Johnstone, "The Next Level: Sega's Plans for World Domination," *Wired*, release 1.06, December 1993.

19. Sheff, *Game Over.*

20. Battle and Johnstone, "The Next Level."

21. For background details, see J. Flower, "3DO: Hip or Hype?" *Wired,* release 1.02, May/June 1993.

22. R. Brandt, "3DO's New Game Player: Awesome or Another Betamax?" *Business Week*, January 11, 1993, p. 38.

23. Flower, "3DO: Hip or Hype?"

24. S. Jacobs, "Third Time's a Charm (They Hope)," *Wired*, release 2.01, January 1994.

25. A. Dunkin, "Video Games: The Next Generation," *Business Week,* January 31, 1994, p. 80.

26. J. Greenstein, "No Clear Winners, Though Some Losers: The Video Game Industry in 1995," *Business Week*, December 22, 1995, p. 42.

27. "3DO Says 'I Do' on Major Shift of its Game Strategy," *Los Angeles Times*, September 17, 1996, p. 2.

28. Battle and Johnstone, "The Next Level."

29. Greenstein, "No Clear Winners."

30. D. P. Hamilton, "Sega Suddenly Finds Itself Embattled," *Wall Street Journal*, March 31, 1997, p. A10.

31. S. Taves, "Meet Your New Playmate," *Wired*, release 3.09, September 1995.

32. I. Kunni, "The Games Sony Plays," *Business Week*, June 15, 1998, p. 128.

33. C. Platt, "WordNerd," *Wired*, release 3.10, October 1995.

34. Kunni, "The Games Sony Plays."

35. J. A. Trachtenberg, "Race Quits Sony Just Before U.S. Rollout of Its PlayStation Video-Game System," *Wall Street Journal*, August 8, 1995, p. B3.

36. S. Beenstock, "Market Raider: How Sony Won the Console Game," *Marketing*, September 10, 1998, p. 26.

37. J. A. Trachtenberg, "Olafsson Calls It Quits as Chairman of Sony's Technology Strategy Group," *Wall Street Journal*, January 23, 1996, p. B6.

38. J. Greenstein, "Price Cuts Boost Saturn, PlayStation Hardware Sales," *Video Business*, May 31, 1996, p. 1.

39. J. Greenstein, "Sony Cuts Prices of PlayStation Hardware," *Video Business*, March 10, 1997, p. 1.

40. Hamilton, "Sega Suddenly Finds Itself Embattled."

41. "Nintendo Wakes Up," *Economist*, August 3, 1996, p. 55–56.

42. D. Takahashi, "Game Plan: Video Game Makers See Soaring Sales Now—and Lots of Trouble Ahead," *Wall Street Journal*, June 15, 1998, p. R10.

43. D. Takahashi, "Sony and Nintendo Battle for Kids Under 13," *Wall Street Journal*, September 24, 1998, p. B4.

44. Kunni, "The Games Sony Plays."

45. D. Takahashi, "Sega Is Pricing Game Machine on the Low Side," *Wall Street Journal*, April 16, 1999, p. B6.

46. J. Paradise, "Sony to Launch New PlayStation in Coming Year," *Wall Street Journal*, March 3, 1999, p. B1.

47. B. Fitzgerald, "Pieces of the Puzzle—Closer to Reality," *Wall Street Journal*, November 16, 1998, p. R33.

Carnival Corporation, 1998

This case was prepared by Mike Keeffe, John K. Ross III, and Bill Middlebrook of the Southwest Texas State University.

In terms of passengers carried, revenues generated, and available capacity, Carnival Corporation is the largest cruise line in the world and considered the leader and innovator in the cruise travel industry. Though its beginnings were inauspicious, Carnival has grown from two converted ocean liners to an organization with two cruise divisions (and a joint venture to operate a third cruise line), as well as a chain of Alaskan hotels and tour coaches. Corporate revenues for fiscal 1997 reached $2.4 billion, with net income of $666 million from operations. The growth continues, with May 1998 revenues up $100 million over the same quarter in 1997—to $1.219 billion. Carnival has several firsts in the cruise industry including these two: more than 1 million passengers carried in a single year, and being the first cruise line to carry 5 million total passengers by fiscal 1994. Currently, their market share of the cruise travel industry stands at approximately 26 percent overall.

Carnival Corporation's CEO and Chairman, Micky Arison, and Carnival Cruise Lines' President, Bob Dickinson, are prepared to maintain their reputation as the leader and innovator in the industry. They have assembled one of the newest fleets catering to cruisers and introduced several superliners built specifically for the Caribbean and Alaskan cruise markets. By the year 2002, the company expects to invest more than $3 billion in new ships. The company has also expanded its Holland America Lines fleet to cater to more established cruisers

This case is intended to be used as the basis for class discussion rather than as an illustration of either effective or ineffective handling of the situation. This case was prepared by Dr. Mike Keeffe, Dr. John K. Ross III, and Dr. Bill Middlebrook, Southwest Texas State University. Used by permission.

and plans to add three of the new ships to its fleet in the premium cruise segment. Strategically, Carnival Corporation seems to have made the right moves at the right time, sometimes in direct contradiction to industry analysts and cruise trends.

Cruise Lines International Association (CLIA), an industry trade group, has tracked the growth of the cruise industry for more than twenty-five years. In 1970, approximately 500,000 passengers took cruises for three consecutive nights or more, reaching a peak of 5 million passengers in 1997—an average annual compound growth rate of approximately 8.9 percent. (This growth rate has declined to approximately 2 percent per year over the period from 1991 to 1995.) At the end of 1997, the industry had 136 ships in service, with an aggregate berth capacity of 119,000. CLIA estimates that the number of passengers carried in North America increased from 4.6 million in 1996 to 5 million in 1997, or approximately 8.7 percent. CLIA expects the number of cruise passengers to increase to 5.3 million in 1998; and with new ships to be delivered, the North American market will have roughly 144 vessels, with an aggregate capacity of 132,000 berths.

Carnival has exceeded the recent industry trends, and its growth rate in the number of passengers carried was 11.2 percent per year over the 1992–1996 period. The company's passenger capacity in 1991 was 17,973 berths and had increased to 31,078 at the end of fiscal 1997. More capacity will be added with the delivery of several new cruise ships already on order, such as the *Elation,* which went into service in early 1998, adding 2,040 to the passenger capacity.

Even with the growth in the cruise industry, the company believes that cruises represent only 2 percent of the applicable North American vacation market, defined as persons who travel for leisure purposes on trips of three nights or longer, involving at least one night's stay in a hotel. The Boston Consulting group, in a 1989 study, estimated that only 5 percent of the people in the North American target market have taken a cruise for leisure purposes and that the market potential was in excess of $50 billion. Carnival Corporation (1996) believes that only 7 percent of the North American population has ever cruised. Various cruise operators, including Carnival Corporation, have based their expansion and capital spending programs on the possibility of capturing part of the 93 to 95 percent of the North American population who have yet to take a cruise vacation.

THE EVOLUTION OF CRUISING

The replacement of ocean liners by aircraft in the 1960s as the primary means of transoceanic travel created the opportunity for developing the modern cruise industry. No longer needed to ferry passengers from destination to destination, ships became available to investors with visions of a new vacation alternative to complement the increasing affluence of Americans. Cruising, once available mainly to the rich and the leisure class, was targeted to the middle class, with service and amenities similar to the grand days of first-class ocean travel.

According to Robert Meyers, editor and publisher of *Cruise Travel* magazine, the increasing popularity of taking a cruise as a vacation can be traced to two serendipitously timed events. First, television's *Love Boat* series dispelled many myths associated with cruising and depicted people of all ages and backgrounds enjoying the cruise experience. This show was among the top ten shows on television for many years, according to Nielsen ratings, and provided extensive publicity for cruise operators. Second, the increasing affluence of Americans and the increased participation of women in the work force gave couples and families more disposable income for discretionary purposes, especially vacations. As the myths were dispelled and disposable income grew, cruising attracted younger couples and families as a vacation alternative, creating a large new target market for the cruise product which accelerated the growth in the number of Americans taking cruises as a vacation.

CARNIVAL HISTORY

In 1972, Ted Arison, backed by American Travel Services, Inc. (AITS), purchased an aging ocean liner from Canadian Pacific Empress Lines for $6.5 million. The new AITS subsidiary, Carnival Cruise Line, refurbished the vessel from bow to stern and renamed it the *Mardi Gras* to capture the party spirit. (Also included in the deal was another ship later renamed the *Carnivale*.) The company's start was not promising, however, as on the first voyage the *Mardi Gras*, with more than 300 invited travel agents aboard, ran aground in Miami Harbor. The ship was slow and guzzled expensive fuel, limiting the number of ports of call and lengthening the minimum stay of passengers on the ship to break even. Arison then bought another old ocean vessel from Union Castle Lines to complement the *Mardi Gras* and the *Carnivale* and named it the *Festivale*. To attract customers, he began adding diversions on board such as planned activities, a casino, nightclubs, discos, and other forms of entertainment designed to enhance the shipboard experience.

Carnival lost money for the next three years, and in late 1974 Arison bought out the Carnival Cruise subsidiary of AITS, Inc., for $1 cash and the assumption of $5 million in debt. One month later, the *Mardi Gras* began showing a profit and through the remainder of 1975 operated at more than 100 percent capacity. (Normal ship capacity is determined by the number of fixed berths available. Ships, like hotels, can operate beyond this fixed capacity by using rollaway beds, pullmans, and upper bunks.) Arison (then chairman), along with Bob Dickinson (who was then vice president of sales and marketing) and his son Micky Arison (then president of Carnival), began to alter the approach to cruise vacations. Carnival went after first-time and younger cruisers with a moderately priced vacation package that included airfare to the port of embarkation and home after the cruise. Per diem rates were very competitive with other vacation packages and Carnival offered passage to multiple exotic Caribbean ports, several meals provided daily with premier restaurant service, and all forms of entertainment and activities included in the base fare. The only things not included in the fare were items of a personal nature, liquor purchases, gambling, and tips for the cabin steward, table waiter, and busboy. Carnival continued to enhance the shipboard experience with a greater variety of activities, nightclubs, and other forms of entertainment, and varied ports of call to increase its attractiveness to potential customers. It was the first modern cruise operator to use multimedia advertising promotions, and it established the theme of "fun ship" cruises, primarily promoting the ship as the destination and ports of call as secondary. Carnival told the public that it was throwing a shipboard party and everyone was invited. The "fun ship" theme still permeates all Carnival Cruise ships.

Throughout the 1980s, Carnival was able to maintain a growth rate of approximately 30 percent, about three times that of the industry as a whole, and between 1982 and 1988 its ships sailed with an average of 104 percent capacity (currently, they operate at 104 to 105 percent capacity, depending on the season). Targeting younger, first-time passengers by promoting the ship as a destination proved to be extremely successful. Carnival's 1987 customer profile showed that 30 percent of the passengers were between the ages of twenty-five and thirty-nine, with household incomes of $25,000 to $50,000.

In 1987, Ted Arison sold 20 percent of his shares in Carnival Cruise Lines and immediately generated more than $400 million for further expansion. In 1988, Carnival acquired the Holland America Lines, which had four cruise ships with 4,500 berths. Holland America was positioned to the higher-income travelers, with cruise prices averaging 25 to 35 percent more than similar Carnival cruises. The deal also included two Holland America subsidiaries, Windstar Sail Cruises and Holland America Westours. This success, and the foresight of management, allowed Carnival to begin an aggressive "superliner" building campaign for their core subsidiary. By 1989, the cruise segments of Carnival Corporation carried more than 750,000 passengers in one year, a first in the cruise industry.

Arison relinquished the role of chairman to his son Micky in 1990, a time when the explosive growth of the 1980s began to subside. Higher fuel prices and increased airline costs began to affect the industry as a whole, and the Persian Gulf War caused many cruise operators to divert ships from European and Indian ports to the Caribbean area of operations, increasing the number of ships competing directly with Carnival. Carnival's stock price fell from $25 in June 1990 to $13 late in the year. The company also incurred a $25.5 million loss during fiscal 1990 for the operation of the Crystal Palace Resort and Casino. In 1991, Carnival reached a settlement with the Bahamian government (effective March 1, 1992) to surrender the 672-room Riveria Towers to the Hotel Corporation of the Bahamas in exchange for the cancellation of some debt incurred in constructing and developing the resort. The corporation took a $135 million write-down on the Crystal Palace for that year.

The early 1990s, even with industrywide demand slowing, were still a very exciting time. Carnival took delivery of its first two superliners: the *Fantasy* (1990) and the *Ecstasy* (1991), which were to further penetrate the three- and four-day cruise market and supplement the seven-day market. In early 1991, Carnival took delivery of the third superliner, the *Sensation* (inaugural sailing November 1, 1993) and later in the year contracted for the fourth one, to be named the *Fascination* (inaugural sailing 1994).

In 1991, Carnival attempted to acquire Premier Cruise Lines, which was then the official cruise line for Disney World in Orlando, Florida, for approximately $372 million. The deal was never consummated since the parties involved could not agree on price. In 1992, Carnival acquired 50 percent of Seabourn, gaining the cruise operations of K/S Seabourn Cruise Lines, and formed a partnership with Atle Byrnestad. Seabourn serves the ultraluxury market with destinations in South America, the Mediterranean, Southeast Asia, and the Baltic area.

The 1993–1995 period saw the addition of the superliner *Imagination* for Carnival Cruise Lines and the *Ryndam* for Holland America Lines. In 1994, the company discontinued operations of Fiestamarina Lines, which had attempted to serve a Spanish-speaking clientele. Fiestamarina was beset with marketing and operational problems and never achieved continuous operations. Many industry analysts and observers were surprised at the failure of Carnival to successfully develop this market. In 1995, Carnival sold a 49 percent interest in the Epirotiki Line, a Greek cruise operation, for $25 million and purchased $101 million (face amount) of senior secured notes of Kloster Cruise Limited, the parent of competitor Norwegian Cruise Lines, for $81 million. Kloster was having financial difficulties and Carnival could not obtain common stock of the company in a negotiated agreement. If Kloster were to fail, Carnival Corporation would be in a good position to acquire some of the assets of Kloster.

Carnival Corporation is expanding through internally generated growth as evidenced by the

TABLE 1

Carnival and Holland America Ships Under Construction

Vessel	Expected Delivery	Shipyard	Passenger Capacity*	Cost (millions)
Carnival Cruise Lines				
Elation	03/98	Masa-Yards	2,040	$300
Paradise	12/98	Masa-Yards	2,040	300
Carnival Triumph	07/99	Fincantieri	2,640	400
Carnival Victory	08/00	Fincantieri	2,640	430
CCL newbuild	12/00	Masa-Yards	2,100	375
CCL newbuild	2001	Masa-Yards	2,100	375
CCL newbuild	2002	Masa-Yards	2,100	375
Total Carnival Cruise Lines			15,912	$2,437
Holland America Lines				
Volendam	6/99	Fincantieri	1,440	274
Zaandam	12/99	Fincantieri	1,440	286
HAL newbuild	9/00	Fincantieri	1,440	300
Total Holland America Lines			4,260	$860
Windstar Cruises				
Wind Surf	5/98	Purchase	312	40
Total for all Vessel's			20,484	$3,337

*In accordance with industry practice, all capacities indicated here are calculated based on two passengers per cabin, even though some cabins can accommodate three or four passengers. 10Q–5/31/98.

number of new ships on order (see Table 1). Additionally, Carnival seems to be willing to continue with its external expansion through acquisitions if the right opportunity arises.

In June 1997, Royal Caribbean made a bid to buy Celebrity Cruise Lines for $500 million and assumption of $800 million in debt. Within a week, Carnival had responded by submitting a counter offer to Celebrity for $510 million and the assumption of debt, then two days later raising the bid to $525 million. However, Royal Caribbean seems to have had the inside track and announced on June 30, 1997, the final merger arrangements with Celebrity. The resulting company would have seventeen ships with approximately 30,000 berths.

However, not to be thwarted in its attempts at continued expansion, Carnival announced in June 1997 the purchase of Costa, an Italian cruise company and the largest European cruise line, for $141 million. External expansion continued when on May 28, 1998, Carnival announced the acquisition of Cunard Line for $500 million from Kvaerner ASA. Cunard was then merged with Seabourn Cruise Line (50 percent owned by Carnival), with Carnival owning 68 percent of the resulting Cunard Line Limited.

THE CRUISE PRODUCT

Ted and Mickey Arison envisioned a product where the classical cruise elegance along with modern convenience could be had at a price comparable to land-based vacation packages sold by travel agents. Carnival's all-inclusive package, when compared with resorts or a theme park such as Disney World, often is priced below these destinations—especially when the array of activities, entertainment, and meals is considered.

A typical vacation on a Carnival cruise ship starts when the bags are tagged for the ship at the airport. Upon arriving at the port of embarkation, passengers are ferried by air-conditioned buses to the ship for boarding, and luggage is delivered by the cruise ship staff to the passenger's cabin. Waiters dot the ship offering tropical drinks to the backdrop of a Caribbean rhythm, while the cruise staff orients passengers to the various decks, cabins, and public rooms. In a few hours (most ships sail in the early evening), dinner is served in the main dining rooms, where wine selection rivals the finest restaurants and the variety of main dishes is designed to suit every palate. Diners can always order double portions if they decide not to save room for desserts and after-dinner treats.

After dinner, cruisers can choose between many forms of entertainment, including live music, dancing, nightclubs (most ships have five or more distinct nightclubs), and a selection of movies; or they can sleep through the midnight buffet until breakfast. During the night, a daily program of activities arrives at the passengers' cabins. The biggest decisions to be made for the rest of the vacation will be what to do (or not to do), what to eat and when (usually eight separate serving times, not including the twenty-four-hour room service), and when to sleep. Service in all areas, from dining to housekeeping, is upscale and immediate. The service is so good that a common shipboard joke says that if you leave your bed during the night to visit the head (sea talk for bathroom), your cabin steward will have made the bed and placed chocolates on the pillow by the time you return.

After the cruise, passengers are transported back to the airport in air-conditioned buses for the flight home. Representatives of the cruise line are on hand at the airport to help cruisers in meeting their scheduled flights. When all amenities are considered, most vacation packages would be hard-pressed to match Carnival's per diem prices, which range from $125 to $250 per person, depending on accommodations. (Holland America and Seabourn are higher, averaging $300 per person/per day.) Occasional specials offer even lower prices, and special suite accommodations can be had for an additional payment.

CARNIVAL OPERATIONS

Carnival Corporation, headquartered in Miami, is composed of Carnival Cruise Lines, Holland America Lines which includes Windstar Sail Cruises as a subsidiary, Holland America Westours, Westmark Hotels, Airtours, and the newly created Cunard Line Limited. Carnival Cruise Lines, Inc., is a Panamanian corporation, and its subsidiaries are incorporated in Panama, the Netherlands Antilles, the British Virgin Islands, Liberia, and the Bahamas. The ships are subject to inspection by the U.S. Coast Guard for compliance with the Convention for the Safety of Life at Sea (SOLAS), which mandates specific structural requirements for safety of passengers at sea, and by the U.S. Public Health Service for sanitary standards. The company is also regulated in some aspects by the Federal Maritime Commission.

At its helm, Carnival Corporation has Micky Arison, the CEO and chairman of the board and Bob Dickinson, the president and COO of Carnival Cruise Lines. A. Kirk Lanterman is the president and CEO of the Holland America cruise division, which includes Holland America Westours and Windstar Sail Cruises. (A list of the corporate officers appears in Figure 1.)

The company's product positioning stems from its belief that the cruise market actually comprises three primary segments with different passenger demographics, passenger characteristics, and growth requirements: the contemporary, premium, and luxury segments. The contemporary segment is served by Carnival ships for cruises that last seven days or less and feature a casual ambiance. The premium segment, served by Holland America, offers seven-day and longer cruises and appeals to the more affluent consumers. The luxury segment, while considerably smaller than the others, caters to experienced cruisers for seven-day and longer sailings and is served by Seabourn. Specialty sailing cruises are provided by Windstar Sail Cruises, a subsidiary of Holland America.

The corporate structure is built around the "profit center" concept and is updated periodically, as needed for control and coordination. Carnival's cruise subsidiaries give it a presence in most of the major cruise segments and make possible worldwide operations.

Carnival has always placed a high priority on marketing in an attempt to promote cruises as an alternative to land-based vacations. It wants customers to know that the ship in itself is the destination and the ports of call are important, but secondary, to the cruise experience. Education and the creation of awareness are critical to corporate marketing efforts. Carnival was the first cruise line

FIGURE I

Corporate Officers of Carnival Corporation

Micky Arison, chairman of the board and CEO, Carnival Corporation

Howard S. Frank, vice chairman and COO, Carnival Corporation

Gerald R. Cahill, senior vice president, finance, and CFO, Carnival Corporation

Roderick K. McLeod, senior vice president, marketing, Carnival Corporation

Lowell Zemnick, vice president and treasurer, Carnival Corporation

Robert H. Dickinson, president and COO, Carnival Cruise Lines

Meshulam Zonis, senior vice president, operations, Carnival Cruise Lines

A. Kirk Lanterman, chairman of the board and CEO, Holland America Lines

Peter T. McHugh, president and COO, Holland America Lines

Source: Carnival Corporation, 1998

to successfully break away from traditional print media and use television to reach a broader market. Even though other lines have followed Carnival's lead in selecting promotional media and are near in total advertising expenditures, the organization still leads all cruise competitors in advertising and marketing expenditures.

Carnival wants to remain the leader and innovator in the cruise industry and intends to do this through sophisticated promotional efforts and by gaining the loyalty of former cruisers, refurbishing ships, varying activities and ports of call, and being innovative in all aspects of ship operations. Given the company's historical success with this promotional effort, management intends to build on the theme of the ship as a destination. The company capitalizes and amortizes direct-response advertising and expenses other advertising costs as incurred. Advertising expenses totaled $112 million in 1997; $109 million in 1996; $98 million in 1995; and $85 million in 1994.

FINANCIAL PERFORMANCE

Carnival retains Price Waterhouse as independent accountants, the Barnett Bank Trust Company–North America as the registrar and stock transfer agent, and its Class A common stock trades on the New York Stock Exchange under the symbol CCL. In December 1996, Carnival amended the terms of its revolving credit facility primarily to combine two facilities into a single $1 billion unsecured revolving credit facility due 2001. The borrowing rate on the One Billion Dollar Revolver is a maximum of LIBOR* plus fourteen basis points and the facility fee is six basis points.

In October 1996, Carnival initiated a commercial paper program which is supported by the One Billion Dollar Revolver. As of November 30, 1996, the Company had $307 million outstanding under its commercial paper program and $693 million

*"LIBOR Rate" means, for an Interest Period for each LIBOR (London Interbank Offer Rate) Rate Advance comprising part of the same Borrowing, the rate determined by the Agent to be the rate of interest per annum (i) rounded upward to the nearest whole multiple of 1/100 of 1% per annum, appearing on Telerate screen 3750 at 11:00 A.M. (London time) two Business Days before the first day of such Interest Period for such Interest Period and in an amount substantially equal to such portion of the Loan, or if the Agent cannot so determine the LIBOR Rate by reference to Telerate screen 3750, then (ii) equal to the average (rounded upward to the nearest whole multiple of 1/100 of 1% per annum, if such average is not such a multiple) of the rate per annum at which deposits in United States Dollars are offered by the principal office of each of the Reference Lenders in London, England, to prime banks in the London interbank market at 11:00 A.M. (London time) two Business Days before the first day of such Interest Period for a term equal to such Interest Period and in an amount substantially equal to such portion of the Loan. In the latter case, the LIBOR Rate for an Interest Period shall be determined by the Agent on the basis of applicable rates furnished to and received by the Agent from the Reference Lenders two Business Days before the first day of such Interest Period, subject, however, to the provisions of Section 2.05. If at any time the Agent shall determine that by reason of circumstances affecting the London interbank market (i) adequate and reasonable means do not exist for ascertaining the LIBOR Rate for the succeeding Interest Period or (ii) the making or continuance of any Loan at the LIBOR Rate has become impracticable as a result of a contingency occurring after the date of this Agreement which materially and adversely affects the London interbank market, the Agent shall so notify the Lenders and the Borrower. Failing the availability of the LIBOR Rate, the LIBOR Rate shall mean the Base Rate thereafter in effect from time to time until such time as a LIBOR Rate may be determined by reference to the London interbank market.

TABLE 2

Carnival Corporation, Consolidated Statements of Operations (in thousands)

	Six-Month Comparison	
	May 31, 1998	*May 31, 1997*
Revenues	$1,219,196	$1,117,696
Costs and expenses:		
Operating expense	669,951	634,622
Selling and administrative	163,784	156,219
Depreciation and amortization	89,266	82,658
	923,000	493,564
Operating income before affiliated	296,195	244,197
Income from affiliated	(13,034)	11,694
Operating income	283,161	232,503
Other income (expense):		
Interest income	5,885	3,382
Interest expense, net of capitalized interest	(24,735)	(31,536)
Other income (expense)	(662)	2,105
Income tax expense	6,861	6,353
	(12,651)	(19,696)
Income before extraordinary item	270,510	212,807
Extraordinary item		
Loss on early extinguishment of debt		
Discontinued operations		
Hotel casino operating loss		
Loss on disposal of hotel casino		
Net income	$270,510	$212,807

available for borrowing under the One Billion Dollar Revolver.

The consolidated financial statements for Carnival Cruise Lines, Inc., are shown in Tables 2 and 3, and selected financial data are presented in Table 4.

Customer cruise deposits, which represent unearned revenue, are included in the balance sheet when received and recognized as cruise revenues on completion of the voyage. Customers are required to pay the full cruise fare (minus deposit) sixty days in advance, with the fares being recognized as cruise revenue on completion of the voyage.

Property and equipment on the financial statements are listed at cost. Depreciation and amortiza-

tion are calculated using the straight-line method over the following estimated useful lives: vessels twenty-five to thirty years, buildings twenty to forty years, equipment two to twenty years, and leasehold improvements at the "term of lease" or "related asset life," whichever is shorter. Goodwill of $275 million resulting from the acquisition of HAL Antillen, N.V. (Holland America Lines) is being amortized using the straight line-method over forty years.

During 1995, Carnival received $40 million from the settlement of litigation with Metra Oy, the former parent company of Wartsila Marine Industries, related to losses suffered in connection with

1997	1996	1995	1994	1993	1992	1991
$2,447,468	$2,212,572	$1,998,150	$1,806,016	$1,556,919	$1,473,614	$1,404,704
1,322,669	1,241,269	1,131,113	1,028,475	907,925	865,587	810,317
296,533	274,855	248,566	223,272	207,995	194,298	193,316
167,287	144,987	128,433	110,595	93,333	88,833	85,166
1,786,489	1,661,111	1,508,112	1,362,342	1,209,253	1,148,718	1,088,799
660,979	551,461					
53,091	45,967					
714,070	597,428	490,038	443,674	347,666	324,896	315,905
8,675	18,597	14,403	8,668	11,527	16,946	10,596
(55,898)	(64,092)	(63,080)	(51,378)	(34,325)	(53,325)	(65,428)
5,436	23,414	19,104	(9,146)	(1,201)	2,731	1,746
(6,233)	(9,045)	(9,374)	(10,053)	(5,497)	(9,008)	(8,995)
(48,020)	(31,126)	(38,947)	(61,909)	(29,496)	(43,123)	(62,081)
666,050	566,302	451,091	381,765	318,170	281,773	253,824
					(5,189)	
						(33,173)
						(135,463)
$666,050	$566,302	$451,091	$381,765	$318,170	$276,584	$84,998

Years Ended November 30

the construction of three cruise ships. (Wartsila had declared bankruptcy in late 1994.) Of this amount, $14.4 million was recorded as "other income," with the remainder used to pay legal fees and reduce the cost basis of the three ships.

On June 25, 1996, Carnival reached an agreement with the trustees of Wartsila and creditors for the bankruptcy; it resulted in a cash payment of approximately $80 million. Of the $80 million received, $5 million was used to pay certain costs, $32 million was recorded as other income and $43 million was used to reduce the cost basis of certain ships that had been affected by the bankruptcy.

By May 31, 1998, Carnival had outstanding long-term debt of $1.55 billion, with the current portion being $58.45 million. This debt consists primarily of $306.8 million in commercial paper and a number of unsecured debentures and notes of less than $200 million, each at rates ranging from 5.65 to 7.7 percent.

According to the Internal Revenue Code of 1986, Carnival is considered a "controlled foreign corporation (CFC)" since 50 percent of its stock is held by individuals who are residents of foreign countries and its countries of incorporation exempt shipping operations of U.S. persons from income tax. Because of CFC status, Carnival expects

TABLE 3

**Carnival Corporation, Consolidated Balance Sheets
(in thousands)**

		Years Ended November 30		
	May 31, 1998	1997	1996	1995
Assets				
Current assets:				
Cash and cash equivalents	$120,600	$139,989	$111,629	$53,365
Short-term investments	9,414	9,738	12,486	50,395
Accounts receivable	66,503	57,090	38,109	33,080
Consumable inventories (average cost)	76,226	54,970	53,281	48,820
Prepaid expenses and other	102,754	74,238	75,428	70,718
Total current assets	375,497	336,025	290,933	256,378
Property and equipment (at cost)				
Less accumulated depreciation and amortization	5,469,814	4,327,413	4,099,038	3,414,823
Other assets				
Goodwill (less accumulated amortization)	403,077	212,607	219,589	226,571
Long-term notes receivable				78,907
Investment in affiliates and other assets	425,715	479,329	430,330	128,808
Net assets of discontinued operations	37,733	71,40|	61,998	
	6,711,836		5,101,888	$4,105,487
Liabilities and shareholders' equity:				
Current liabilities:				
Current portion of long-term debt	58,457	59,620	66,369	$72,752
Accounts payable	187,897	106,783	84,748	90,237
Accrued liabilities	169,048	154,253	126,511	113,483
Customer deposits	755,890	420,908	352,698	292,606
Dividends payable	44,619	44,578	32,416	25,632
Reserve for discontinued operations				
Total current liabilities	121,911	786,142	662,742	594,710
Long-term debt	1,557,016	1,015,294	1,277,529	1,035,031
Convertible notes			39,103	115,000
Other long-term liabilities	23,907	20,241	91,630	15,873
Shareholders' equity:				
Class A common stock (1 vote share)	5,949	2,972	2,397	2,298
Class B common stock (5 votes share)			550	550
Paid in capital	871,676	866,097	819,610	594,811
Retained earnings	2,912,499	2,731,213	2,207,781	1,752,140
Other	1,799	4,816	546	(4,926
Total shareholders' equity	3,791,923	3,605,098	3,030,884	2,344,873
	$6,711,836	$5,426,775	$5,101,888	$4,105,487

Source: 1997 and 1998 10k and 10Qs.

	Years Ended November 30		
	1994	*1993*	*1992*
Assets			
Current assets:			
Cash and cash equivalents	$54,105	$60,243	$115,014
Short-term investments	70,115	88,677	111,048
Accounts receivable	20,789	19,310	21,624
Consumable inventories (average cost)	45,122	37,245	31,618
Prepaid expenses and other	50,318	48,323	32,120
Total current assets	240,449	253,798	311,424
Property and equipment (at cost)			
Less accumulated depreciation and amortization	3,071,431	2,588,009	1,961,402
Other assets			
Goodwill (less accumulated amortization)	233,553	237,327	244,789
Long-term notes receivable	76,876	29,136	
Investment in affiliates and other assets	47,514	21,097	38,439
Net assets of discontinued operations		89,553	89,553
	$3,669,823	$3,218,920	$2,645,607
Liabilities and shareholders' equity:			
Current liabilities:			
Current portion of long-term debt	$84,644	$91,621	$97,931
Accounts payable	86,750	81,374	71,473
Accrued liabilities	114,868	94,830	69,919
Customer deposits	257,505	228,153	178,945
Dividends payable	21,190	19,763	19,750
Reserve for discontinued operations		34,253	36,763
Total current liabilities	564,957	549,994	474,781
Long-term debt	1,046,904	916,221	776,600
Convertible notes	115,000	115,000	
Other long-term liabilities	14,028	10,499	9,381
Shareholders' equity:			
Class A common stock (1 vote share)	2,276	2,274	1,136
Class B common stock (5 votes share)	550	550	275
Paid in capital	544,947	541,194	539,622
Retained earnings	1,390,589	1,089,323	850,193
Other	(9,428)	(6,135)	(6,381)
Total shareholders' equity	1,928,934	1,627,206	1,384,845
	$3,669,823	$3,218,920	$2,645,607

TABLE 4

**Carnival Corporation, Selected Financial Data by Segment
(in thousands)**

	Years Ended November 30					
	1997	*1996*	*1995*	*1994*	*1993*	*1992*
Revenues						
Cruise	$2,257,567	$2,003,458	$1,800,775	$1,623,069	$1,381,473	$1,292,587
Tour	242,646	263,356	241,909	227,613	214,382	215,194
Intersegment revenues	(52,745)	(54,242)	(44,534)	(44,666)	(38,936)	(34,167)
	2,447,468	2,212,572	1,998,150	1,806,016	1,556,919	1,473,614
Gross Operating Profit						
Cruise	1,072,758	913,880	810,736	726,808	598,642	552,669
Tour	52,041	57,423	56,301	50,733	50,352	55,358
	1,124,799	971,303	867,037	777,541	648,994	608,027
Depreciation and Amortization						
Cruise	157,454	135,694	120,304	101,146	84,228	79,743
Tour	8,862	8,317	8,129	9,449	9,105	9,090
Corporate	971	976				
	167,287	144,987	128,433	110,595	93,333	88,833
Operating Income						
Cruise	656,009	535,814	465,870	425,590	333,392	310,845
Tour	13,262	21,252	24,168	18,084	14,274	23,051
Corporate	44,799	40,362				
	714,070	597,428	490,038	443,674	347,666	333,896
Identifiable Assets						
Cruise	4,744,140	4,514,675	3,967,174	3,531,727	2,995,221	2,415,547
Tour	163,941	150,851	138,313	138,096	134,146	140,507
Discontinued resort and casino	518,694				89,553	89,553
Corporate	5,426,775	436,362				
		5,101,888	4,105,487	3,669,823	3,218,920	2,645,607
Capital Expenditures						
Cruise	414,963	841,871	456,920	587,249	705,196	111,766
Tour	42,507	14,964	8,747	9,963	10,281	11,400
Corporate	40,187	1,810				
	$497,657	$858,645	$465,667	$597,212	$715,477	$123,166

Source: 1997 and 1998 10k and 10Qs.

that all of its income (with the exception of U.S. source income from the transportation, hotel, and tour businesses of Holland America) will be exempt from U.S. federal income taxes at the corporate level.

The primary financial consideration of importance to Carnival management involves the control of costs, both fixed and variable, for the maintenance of a healthy profit margin. Carnival has the lowest break-even point of any organization in the cruise industry (ships break even at approximately 60 percent of capacity) due to operational experience and economies of scale. However, fixed costs, including depreciation, fuel, insurance, port charges, and crew costs, which represent more than 33 percent of the company's operating expenses, cannot be significantly reduced in relation to decreases in passenger loads and aggregate passenger ticket revenue. (Major expense items are airfares (25–30 percent), travel agent fees (10 percent), and labor (13–15 percent) Increases in these costs could negatively affect the profitability of the organization.

PRINCIPAL SUBSIDIARIES

Carnival Cruise Line

At the end of fiscal 1996, Carnival operated eleven ships with a total berth capacity of 20,332. Carnival operates principally in the Caribbean and has an assortment of ships and ports of call serving the three-, four-, and seven-day cruise markets (see Table 5).

Each ship is a floating resort, including a full maritime staff, shopkeepers and casino operators, entertainers, and complete hotel staff. Approximately 14 percent of corporate revenue is generated from shipboard activities such as casino operations, liquor sales, and gift shop items. At various ports of call, passengers can also take advantage of tours, shore excursions, and duty-free shopping at their own expense.

Shipboard operations are designed to provide maximum entertainment, activities, and service. The size of the company and the similarity in design of the new cruise ships have allowed Carnival to achieve various economies of scale, and management is very cost-conscious.

Although the Carnival Cruise Lines division is increasing its presence in the shorter cruise markets, its general marketing strategy is to use three-,

four-, or seven-day moderately priced cruises to fit the time and budget constraints of the middle class. Shorter cruises can cost less than $500 per person (depending on accommodations), up to roughly $3,000 per person in a luxury suite on a seven-day cruise, including port charges. (Per diem rates for shorter cruises are slightly higher, on average, than per diem rates for seven-day cruises.) Average rates per day are approximately $180, excluding gambling, liquor and soft drinks, and items of a personal nature. Guests are expected to tip their cabin steward and waiter at a suggested rate of $3 per person/per day, and the bus boy at $1.50 per person/per day.

Around 99 percent of all Carnival cruises are sold through travel agents, who receive a standard commission of 10 percent (15 percent in Florida). Carnival works extensively with travel agents to help promote cruises as an alternative to a Disney or European vacation. In addition to training travel agents from nonaffiliated travel and vacation firms to sell cruises, a special group of employees regularly visit travel agents posing as prospective clients. If the agent recommends a cruise before another vacation option, he or she receives $100. If the travel agent specifies a Carnival cruise before other options, the reward is $1,000 on the spot. During fiscal 1995, Carnival took reservations from about 29,000 of the approximately 45,000 travel agencies in the U.S. and Canada, and no one travel agency accounted for more than two percent of Carnival revenues.

On-board service is labor intensive. Carnival employs help from some fifty-one nations—mostly Third World countries—with reasonable returns to employees. For example, waiters on the *Jubilee* can earn approximately $18,000 to $27,000 per year (base salary and tips)—significantly more than could be earned in their home country for similar employment. Waiters typically work ten hours per day, with approximately one day off per week for a specified contract period (usually three to nine months). Carnival records show that employees remain with the company for approximately eight years and that applicants exceed the demand for all cruise positions. Nonetheless, the American Maritime Union has cited Carnival (and other cruise operators) several times for exploitation of its crew.

Holland America Lines

On January 17, 1989, Carnival acquired all the outstanding stock of HAL Antillen N.V. from Holland

TABLE 5

The Ships of Carnival Corporation

	Registry	Built	First in company	Service cap*	Gross tons	Length/ Width	Areas of operation
Carnival Cruise Lines							
Carnival Destiny	Panama	1996	1997	2,642	101,000	893/116	Caribbean
Inspiration	Panama	1996	1996	2,040	70,367	855/104	Caribbean
Imagination	Panama	1995	1995	2,040	70,367	855/104	Caribbean
Fascination	Panama	1994	1994	2,040	70,367	855/104	Caribbean
Sensation	Panama	1993	1993	2,040	70,367	855/104	Caribbean
Ecstasy	Liberia	1991	1991	2,040	70,367	855/104	Caribbean
Fantasy	Liberia	1990	1990	2,044	70,367	855/104	Bahamas
Celebration	Liberia	1987	1987	1,486	47,262	738/92	Caribbean
Jubilee	Panama	1986	1986	1,486	47,262	738/92	Mexican Riviera
Holiday	Panama	1985	1985	1,452	46,052	727/92	Mexican Riviera
Tropicale	Liberia	1982	1982	1,022	36,674	660/85	Alaska, Caribbean
Total Carnival ships' capacity: 20,332							
Holland America Line							
Veendam	Bahamas	1996	1996	1,266	55,451	720/101	Alaska, Caribbean
Ryndam	Netherlands	1994	1994	1,266	55,451	720/101	Alaska, Caribbean
Maasdam	Netherlands	1993	1993	1,266	55,451	720/101	Europe, Caribbean
Statendam	Netherlands	1993	1993	1,266	55,451	720/101	Alaska, Caribbean
Westerdam	Netherlands	1986	1988	1,494	53,872	798/95	Canada, Caribbean
Noordam	Netherlands	1984	1984	1,214	33,930	704/89	Alaska, Caribbean
Nieuw Amsterdam	Netherlands	1983	1983	1,214	33,930	704/89	Alaska, Caribbean
Rotterdam IV	Netherlands	1997	1997	1,316	62,000	780/106	Alaska, Worldwide
Total HAL ships' capacity: 10,302							
Windstar Cruises							
Wind Spirit	Bahamas	1988	1988	148	5,736	440/52	Caribbean, Mediterranean
Wind Song	Bahamas	1987	1987	148	5,703	440/52	Costa Rica, Tahita
Wind Star	Bahamas	1986	1986	148	5,703	440/52	Caribbean, Mediterranean
Total Windstar ships' capacity: 444							
Total capacity: 31,078							

*In accordance with industry practice, passenger capacity is calculated based on two passengers per cabin even though some cabins can accommodate three or four passengers.

America Lines N.V. for $625 million in cash. Carnival financed the purchase through $250 million in retained earnings (cash account) and borrowed the other $375 million from banks at 0.25 percent over the prime rate. Carnival received the assets and operations of the Holland America Lines, Westours, Westmark Hotels, and Windstar Sail Cruises. Holland America has seven cruise ships, with a capacity of 8,795 berths, and new ships are to be delivered in the future.

Founded in 1873, Holland America Lines is an upscale line (it charges an average of 25 percent more than similar Carnival cruises), with principal destinations in Alaska during the summer months and the Caribbean during the fall and winter. It also offers some worldwide cruises of up to ninety-eight days. Holland America targets an older, more sophisticated cruiser and has fewer youth-oriented activities. On its ships, passengers can dance to the sounds of the Big Band era and avoid the discos of Carnival ships. Passengers on Holland America ships enjoy more service (a higher staff-to-passenger ratio than Carnival offers) and have more cabin and public space per person; in addition, there is a "no tipping" shipboard policy. Although Holland America has not experienced the spectacular growth of Carnival cruise ships, it has had constant growth over the decade of the 1980s and early 1990s, with high occupancy. The operation of these ships and the structure of the crew resemble the Carnival cruise ship model, and the acquisition of the line gave the Carnival Corporation a presence in the Alaskan market, where it had none before.

Holland America Westours is the largest tour operator in Alaska and the Canadian Rockies and provides vacation synergy with Holland America cruises. The transportation division of Westours includes more than 290 motor coaches, consisting of the Gray Line of Alaska, the Gray Line of Seattle, Westours motorcoaches, the McKinley Explorer railroad coaches, and three day boats for tours to glaciers and other points of interest. Carnival management believes that Alaskan cruises and tours should increase in the future due to a number of factors, such as the aging population wanting relaxing vacations with scenic beauty and Alaska being a U.S. destination.

Westmark Hotels comprises sixteen hotels in Alaska and the Yukon Territory, and also provide synergy with cruise operations and Westours. Westmark is the largest group of hotels in the region, offering moderately priced rooms for the vacationer.

Windstar Sail Cruises was acquired by Holland America Lines in 1988 and consists of three computer-controlled sailing vessels, with a berth capacity of 444. Windstar is very upscale and offers an alternative to traditional cruise liners with a more intimate, activity-oriented cruise. The ships operate primarily in the Mediterranean and the South Pacific, visiting ports not accessible to large cruise ships. Although catering to a small segment of the cruise vacation industry, Windstar helps fulfill Carnival's commitment to participate in all segments of the cruise industry.

Seaborn Cruise Lines

In April 1992, the company acquired 25 percent of the capital stock of Seabourn. As part of the trans-

action, the company also made a subordinated secured ten-year loan of $15 million and a $10 million convertible loan to Seabourn. In December 1995, the $10 million convertible loan was converted by the company into an additional 25 percent equity interest in Seabourn.

Seabourn targets the luxury market with three vessels, providing 200 passengers per ship with all-suite accommodations. Seabourn is considered the "Rolls-Royce" of the cruise industry and in 1992 was named the "World's Best Cruise Line" by the prestigious Condé Nast Traveler's Fifth Annual Readers Choice poll. Seabourn cruises the Americas, Europe and the Mediterranean, and the Far East.

Airtours

In April 1996, the company acquired a 29.5 percent interest in Airtours for approximately $307 million. Airtours, along with its subsidiaries, is the largest air-inclusive tour operator in the world and is publicly traded on the London Stock Exchange. Airtours provides air-inclusive packaged holidays to the British, Scandinavian, and North American markets. It serves approximately 5 million people per year and owns or operates thirty-two hotels, two cruise ships, and thirty-one aircraft.

Airtours operates eighteen aircraft (one additional aircraft is scheduled to enter service in the spring of 1997) exclusively for its U.K. tour operators, meeting a large proportion of their flying requirements. In addition, Airtours' subsidiary Premiair operates a fleet of thirteen aircraft (one additional aircraft is also scheduled to enter service with Premier in the spring of 1997), which meets most of the flying requirements for Airtours' Scandinavian tour operators.

Airtours owns or operates thirty-two hotels (6,500 rooms), which provide rooms to Airtours' tour operators principally in the Mediterranean and the Canary Islands. In addition, Airtours has a 50 percent interest in Tenerife Sol, a joint venture with Sol Hotels Group of Spain, which owns and operates three additional hotels in the Canary Islands, providing 1,300 rooms.

Through its subsidiary Sun Cruises, Airtours owns and operates two cruise ships. Both the 800-berth MS *Seawing* and the 1,062-berth MS *Carousel* commenced operations in 1995. Recently, Airtours acquired a third ship, the MS *Sundream*, which is the sister ship of the MS *Carousel*. The MS *Sundream* is expected to commence operations in

May 1997. The ships operate in the Mediterranean, the Caribbean, and around the Canary Islands and are booked exclusively by Airtours' tour operators.

Costa Crociere S.p.A.

In June 1997, Carnival and Airtours purchased the equity securities of Costa from the Costa family at a cost of approximately $141 million. Costa is headquartered in Italy and is considered Europe's largest cruise line, with seven ships and 7,710 passenger capacity. Costa operates primarily in the Mediterranean, Northern Europe, the Caribbean, and South America. The major market for Costa is southern Europe, mainly Italy, Spain, and France. In January 1998, Costa signed an agreement to construct an eighth ship, with a capacity of approximately 2,100 passengers.

Cunard Line

Carnival's most recent acquisition has been the Cunard Line, announced on May 28, 1998. Comprising five ships, the Cunard Line is considered a luxury line with strong brand name recognition. Carnival purchased 50 percent of Cunard for an estimated $255 million, with the other 50 percent being owned by Atle Brynestad. Cunard was immediately merged with Seabourn, and the resulting Cunard Cruise Line Limited (68 percent owned by Carnival), with its now eight ships, will be headed by the former president of Seabourn, Larry Pimentel.

Joint Venture with Hyundai Merchant Marine Co. Ltd.

In September 1996, Carnival and Hyundai Merchant Marine Co. Ltd. (HMM) signed an agreement to form a 50/50 joint venture to develop the Asian cruise vacation market. Each has contributed $4.8 million as the initial capital of the joint venture. In addition, in November 1996, Carnival sold the cruise ship *Tropicale* to the joint venture for approximately $95.5 million cash. Carnival then chartered the vessel from the joint venture until the joint venture is ready to begin cruise operations in the Asian market, targeting a start date in or around the spring of 1998. The joint venture borrowed the $95.5 million purchase price from a financial institution and Carnival and HMM each guaranteed 50 percent of the borrowed funds.

This arrangement was, however, short-lived as in September 1997 the joint venture was dissolved and Carnival repurchased the *Tropicale* for $93 million.

FUTURE CONSIDERATIONS

Carnival's management will have to continue monitoring several strategic factors and issues for the next few years. The industry itself should see further consolidation through mergers and buyouts, and the expansion of the industry could negatively affect the profitability of various cruise operators. Another factor of concern to management is how to reach the large North American market, of which only 5 to 7 percent have ever taken a cruise.

With the industry maturing, cruise competitors have become more sophisticated in their marketing efforts, and price competition is the norm in most cruise segments. (For a partial listing of major industry competitors, see Appendix A.) Royal Caribbean Cruise Lines has also instituted a major shipbuilding program and is successfully challenging Carnival Cruise Lines in the contemporary segment. The announcement of the Walt Disney Company that it would enter the cruise market with two 80,000-ton cruise liners by 1998 should significantly affect the family cruise vacation segment.

With competition intensifying, industry observers believe the wave of failures, mergers, buyouts and strategic alliances will swell. Regency Cruises ceased operations on October 29, 1995, and has filed for Chapter 11 bankruptcy. American Family Cruises, a spinoff from Costa Cruise Lines, failed to reach the family market, and Carnival's Fiestamarina failed to reach the Spanish-speaking market. EffJohn International sold its Commodore Cruise subsidiary to a group of Miami-based investors, which then chartered one of its two ships to World Explorer Cruises/Semester at Sea. Sun Cruise Lines merged with Epirotiki Cruise Line under the name of Royal Olympic Cruises, and Cunard bought the Royal Viking Line and its name from Kloster Cruise Ltd., with one ship of its fleet being transferred to Kloster's Royal Cruise Line. All of these failures, mergers, and buyouts occurred in 1995, which was not an unusual year for changes in the cruise line industry.

The increasing industry capacity is also a source of concern to cruise operators. The slow growth in industry demand is occurring during a period when industry berth capacity continues to grow. The entry of Disney and the ships already on order by current operators will increase industry berth capacity by more than 10,000 per year for the next three years—a significant increase. (See Appendix B for new ships under construction.) The danger lies in cruise operators using the price weapon in their marketing campaigns to fill cabins. If cruise operators cannot make a reasonable return on investment, they will have to reduce operating costs to remain profitable, and that will affect the quality of service. In these circumstances, further industry acquisitions, mergers, and consolidations would become more likely. The worst-case scenario would be the financial failure of weaker lines.

Still, Carnival's management believes that demand should increase during the remainder of the 1990s. Considering that only 5 to 7 percent of the North American market has taken a cruise vacation, reaching more of the North American target market would improve industry profitability. Industry analysts point out, however, that an assessment of market potential is only an educated guess. What will happen if the current demand figures foreshadow the future?

APPENDIX A:
MAJOR INDUSTRY COMPETITORS

Celebrity Cruises, 5200 Blue Lagoon Drive, Miami, FL 33126
Celebrity Cruises operates four modern cruise ships on four-, seven-, and ten-day cruises to Bermuda, the Caribbean, the Panama Canal, and Alaska. Celebrity attracts first-time as well as seasoned cruisers. Purchased by Royal Caribbean on July 30, 1997.

Norwegian Cruise Lines, 95 Merrick Way., Coral Gables, FL 33134
Norwegian Cruise Lines (NCL), formerly Norwegian Caribbean Lines, was the first to base a modern fleet of cruise ships in the Port of Miami. It operates ten modern cruise liners on three-, four-, and seven-day eastern and western Caribbean cruises and cruises to Bermuda. A wide variety of activities and entertainment attracts a diverse array of customers. NCL has just completed reconstruction of two ships and is building the *Norwegian Sky*, a 2,000-passenger ship to be delivered in the summer of 1999.

Disney Cruise Line, 500 South Buena Vista Street, Burbank, CA 91521

Disney has just recently entered the cruise market with the introduction of the *Disney Magic* and *Disney Wonder*. Both ships will cater to both children and adults and will feature 875 staterooms each. Each cruise will include a visit to Disney's private island, Castaway Cay. Although Disney currently has only two ships and the cruise portion of Disney is small, the company's potential for future growth is substantial. It had more than more than $22 billion in revenues and $1.9 billion net profits in 1997.

Princess Cruises, 10100 Santa Monica Boulevard, Los Angeles, CA 90067
Princess Cruises, with its fleet of nine "Love Boats," offers seven-day and extended cruises to the Caribbean, Alaska, Canada, Africa, the Far East, South America, and Europe. Its primary market is the upscale fifty-plus experienced traveler, according to Mike Hannan, senior vice president for marketing services. Princess ships have an ambiance best described as casual elegance and are famous for their Italian-style dining rooms and onboard entertainment.

Royal Caribbean Cruise Lines, 1050 Caribbean Way, Miami, FL 33132
The nine ships have consistently been given high marks by passengers and travel agents over the past twenty-one years. The ships are built for the contemporary market, are large and modern, and offer three-, four-, and seven-day, as well as extended, cruises. The company prides itself on service and exceptional cuisine. With the purchase of Celebrity, RCCL becomes the largest cruise line in the world, with seventeen ships and a passenger capacity of more than 31,100. Plans include the introduction of six additional ships by 2002. In 1997, RCCL had a net income of $175 million on revenues of $1.93 billion.

Other Industry Competitors (Partial List)

American Hawaii Cruises, two ships—Hawaiian Islands
Club Med, two ships—Europe, Caribbean
Commodore Cruise Line, one ship—Caribbean
Cunard Line, eight ships—Caribbean, worldwide
Dolphin Cruise Line, three ships—Caribbean, Bermuda
Radisson Seven Seas Cruises, three ships—worldwide
Royal Olympic Cruises, six ships—Caribbean, worldwide

Royal Cruise Line, four ships—Caribbean, Alaska, worldwide

Source: Cruise Line International Association, 1996, and company 10k's and annual reports.

APPENDIX B:
CURRENT AND FUTURE LINERS

Liners Completed and Placed in Service During the Past Three Years

Carrier and Vessel (Year), Number of Passengers
Carnival Cruise Lines, *Elation* (1998), 2040
Carnival Cruise Lines, *Destiny* (1997), 2642
Carnival Cruise Lines, *Inspiration* (1996), 2040
Celebrity Cruises, *Mercury* (1997), 1870
Celebrity Cruises, *Galaxy* (1996), 1870
Costa Cruises, *Costa Victoria* (1996), 1950
Holland America Line, *Veendam* (1996), 1266
Holland America Line, *Rotterdam VI* (1997), 1316
Princess Cruises, *Dawn Princess* (1997), 1950
Princess Cruises, *Grand Princess* (1998), 2600
Radisson Seven Seas Cruises, *Paul Gaugin* (1997), 320
Royal Caribbean Cruises, *Rhapsody of the Seas* (1997), 2000
Royal Caribbean Cruises, *Enchantment of the Seas* (1997), 1950
Royal Caribbean Cruises, *Splendour of the Seas* (1996), 1800
Royal Caribbean Cruises, *Grandeur of the Seas* (1996), 1850
Royal Caribbean Cruises, *Vision of the Seas* (1998), 2000

Future Liners Now Under Construction

Carrier and Vessel (Expected Launch), Number of Passengers
Disney Cruise Line, *Disney Magic* (1998), 1740
Carnival Cruise Lines, *Paradise* (1998-99), 2040
Disney Cruise Line, *Disney Wonder* (1998-99), 1740
Carnival Cruises Lines, *Triumph* (1999), 2758
Holland America Line, *Volendam* (1999), 1440

Holland America Line, *Zaandam* (1999), 1440
Norwegian Cruise Line, *Norwegian Sky* (1999), 2000
Princess Cruises, *Sea Princess* (1999), 1950
Princess Cruises, *Ocean Princess* (1999), 2022
Radisson Seven Seas, unnamed (1999), 490
Renaissance Cruises, *R3* (1999), 684
Renaissance Cruises, *R4* (1999), 684
Royal Caribbean Cruises, *Voyager of the Seas* (1999), 3114
Carnival Cruise Lines, *Victory* (2000), 2642
Carnival Cruise Lines, unnamed (2000), 2100
Costa Cruises, unnamed (2000), 1950
Celebrity Cruises, unnamed (2000), 1950
Delta Queen Steamboat Co., unnamed (2000), 225
Holland America Line, unnamed (2000), 1380
P & O Cruises, unnamed (2000), 1840
Royal Caribbean Cruises, *Project Eagle* (2000), 3114
Silversea Cruises, unnamed (2000), 396
Celebrity Cruises, unnamed (2001), 1950
Princess Cruises, unnamed (2001), 2600
Princess Cruises, unnamed (2001), 2600
Royal Caribbean Cruises, unnamed (2001), 2000
Silversea Cruises, unnamed (2000), 396
Royal Caribbean Cruises, unnamed (2002), 3114
American Hawaii Cruises, 2 unnamed, undetermined
Source: Cruise News @http://www.cruise-news.com/.

References

Cruise Lines International Association (CLIA) 1996–1998 (www.cruising.com).
Carnival Corporation (www.carnival.com).
Carnival Corporation Annual Reports, 1996–1998.
Carnival Corporation 1997 and 1998 10k, retrieved from EDGAR database (http://www.sec.gov/edaux/formlynx.htm).
Carnival Corporation 1997 and 1998 10Qs, retrieved from EDGAR database (http://www.sec.gov/edaux/formlynx.htm).
Celebrity Cruises (www.celebrit-cruises.com).
Celebrity Cruises 1997 and 1998 10k, retrieved from EDGAR database (http://www.sec.gov/edaux/formlynx.htm).
Celebrity Cruises 1997 and 1998 10Qs, retrieved from EDGAR database (http://www.sec.gov/edaux/formlynx.htm).
Disney Cruise Line (www.disney.go.com/DisneyCruise).
Norwegian Cruise Lines (www.ncl.com).
Princess Cruises (www.princess.com).
Royal Caribbean Cruise Lines (www.rccl.com).

CASE 18

Circus Circus Enterprises, Inc., 1998

This case was prepared by John K. Ross III, Mike Keeffe, and Bill Middlebrook of the Southwest Texas State University.

We possess the resources to accomplish the big projects: the know-how, the financial power and the places to invest. The renovation of our existing projects will soon be behind us, which last year represented the broadest scope of construction ever taken on by a gaming company. Now we are well-positioned to originate new projects. Getting big projects right is the route to future wealth in gaming; big successful projects tend to prove long staying power in our business. When the counting is over, we think our customers and investors will hold the winning hand.

Circus Circus Annual Report, 1997

INTRODUCTION[1]

Big projects and a winning hand—Circus Circus does seem to have both. And big projects they are, with huge pink-and white-striped concrete circus tents, a 600-foot-long riverboat replica, a giant castle, and a great pyramid. Its latest project, Mandalay Bay, will include a 3,700-room hotel/casino, an 11-acre aquatic environment with beaches, a snorkeling reef, and a swim-up shark exhibit.

Circus Circus Enterprises, Inc.—hereafter Circus—describes itself as in the business of entertainment and has been one of the innovators in the theme resort concept popular in casino gaming. Its areas of operation are the glitzy vacation and convention meccas of Las Vegas, Reno, and Laughlin, Nevada, as well as other locations in the United States and abroad. Historically, Circus's marketing of its products has been called "right out of the bargain basement," and has catered to low rollers. Circus has continued to broaden its market and now aims more at the middle-income gambler and family-oriented vacationers, as well as the more up-scale traveler and player.

Circus was purchased in 1974 for $50,000 as a small and unprofitable casino operation by partners William G. Bennett, an aggressive cost-cutter who ran furniture stores before entering the gaming industry in 1965, and William N. Pennington. The partners were able to rejuvenate Circus with fresh marketing, went public with a stock offering in October 1983, and experienced rapid growth and high profitability over time. Within the period 1993–1997, the average return on invested capital was 16.5 percent and Circus had generated more than $1 billion in free cash flow. Circus has become one of the major players in the Las Vegas, Laughlin, and Reno markets in terms of square footage of casino space and number of hotel rooms—despite the incredible growth in both markets. In 1997, for

This case is intended to be used as the basis for class discussion rather than as an illustration of either effective or ineffective handling of the situation. This case was prepared by Dr. John K. Ross III, Dr. Mike Keeffe, and Dr. Bill Middlebrook of the Southwest Texas State University. Used by permission.

the first time in the company's history, casino gaming operations provided slightly less than one half of total revenues, and that trend continued into 1998 (see Table 1). On January 31, 1998, Circus reported a net income of approximately $89.9 million on revenues of $1.35 billion. This was down slightly from the 1997 net income of more than $100 million on revenues of $1.3 billion. During that same year Circus invested more than $585.8 million in capital expenditures and another $663.3 million was invested in fiscal year 1998.

CIRCUS CIRCUS OPERATIONS

Circus defines entertainment as pure play and fun, and it goes out of the way to see that customers have plenty of opportunities for both. Each Circus location has a distinctive ambiance. Circus Circus–Las Vegas is the world of the big top, where live circus acts are performed free every thirty minutes. Kids may cluster around video games while the adults migrate to nickel slot machines and dollar game tables. Located at the north end of the Vegas strip, Circus Circus–Las Vegas sits on 69 acres of land with 3,744 hotel rooms, shopping areas, two specialty restaurants, a buffet with seating for 1,200, fast-food shops, cocktail lounges, video arcades, and 109,000 square feet of casino space. It also includes the Grand Slam Canyon, a 5-acre glass-enclosed theme park with a four-loop roller coaster. Approximately 384 guests may also stay at nearby Circusland RV Park. The company had invested $126.7 million in this property for new rooms and remodeling in the year ending January 31, 1997, and another $35.2 million in fiscal year 1998.

The Luxor, hotel and casino complex with an Egyptian theme, opened on October 15, 1993, when 10,000 people entered to play the 2,245 slot and video poker games and 110 table games in the 120,000-square-foot casino in the hotel atrium (reported to be the world's largest). By the end of the opening weekend, 40,000 people per day were visiting the thirty-story bronze pyramid that encases the hotel and entertainment facilities.

Besides the pyramid, the Luxor features two new twenty-two-story hotel towers containing 492 suites and is connected to Excalibur—a giant, colorful medieval castle—by a climate-controlled skyway with moving walkways. Situated at the south end of the Las Vegas strip on a 64-acre site adjacent to the Excalibur, the Luxor features a food and entertainment area on three different levels beneath the hotel atrium. The pyramid's hotel rooms can be reached from the four corners of the building by state-of-the-art "inclinators" which travel at a 39-degree angle. Parking is available for nearly 3,200 vehicles; approximately 1,800 of those spaces are in a covered garage.

Luxor underwent major renovations, costing $323.3 million during fiscal 1997 and another $116.5 million in fiscal 1998. The resulting complex contains 4,425 hotel rooms, extensively renovated casino space, an additional 20,000 square feet of convention area, an 800-seat buffet, a series of IMAX attractions, five theme restaurants, seven cocktail lounges, and a variety of specialty shops. Circus expects to draw significant walk-in traffic to the newly refurbished Luxor and is one of the principal components of the Masterplan Mile.

Located next to Luxor, Excalibur is one of the first sights travelers see as they exit Interstate 15 (management was confident that the castle would make a lasting impression on mainstream tourists and vacationing families arriving in Las Vegas). Guests cross a drawbridge over a moat, onto a cobblestone walkway where multicolored spires, turrets, and battlements rise above them. The castle walls are four twenty-eight story hotel towers containing a total of 4,008 rooms. Inside is a medieval world containing a Fantasy Faire filled with strolling jugglers, fire eaters, and acrobats, as well as a Royal Village complete with peasants, serfs, and ladies-in-waiting around medieval theme shops. The 110,000-square-foot casino encompasses 2,442 slot machines, more than 89 game tables, a sports book, and a poker and keno area. There are twelve restaurants, capable of feeding more than 20,000 people daily, and a 1,000-seat amphitheater. Excalibur, which opened in June 1990, was built for $294 million and primarily financed with internally generated funds. In the year ending January 31, 1997, it contributed 23 percent of the organization's revenues, down from 33 percent in 1993. Yet 1997 was a record year, generating the company's highest margins and more than $100 million in operating cash flow. In fiscal 1998, Excalibur underwent $25.1 million in renovations and was connected to the Luxor by enclosed, moving walkways.

Situated between the two anchors on the Las Vegas strip are two smaller casinos owned and operated by Circus. The Silver City Casino and Slots-A-Fun primarily depend on the foot traffic along the strip for their gambling patrons. Combined, they offer more than 1,202 slot machines and 46 gaming tables on 34,900 square feet of casino floor.

Circus owns and operates ten properties in Nevada and one in Mississippi. It also has a 50 percent ownership in three others (see Table 2).

All of the Circus operations do well in the city of Las Vegas. However, Circus Circus 1997 operational earnings for the Luxor and Circus Circus–Las Vegas were off 38 percent from the previous year. Management blames the disruption in services due to renovations for this decline. However, Circus's combined hotel-room occupancy rates had remained above 90 percent, partly because of low room rates ($45 to $69 at Circus Circus–Las Vegas) and popular buffets. Each of the major properties contains large, inexpensive buffets that management believe make staying with Circus more attractive. Recently results, though, show a room occupancy rate of 87.5 percent, partly because of the building boom in Las Vegas.

The company's other big-top facility is Circus Circus–Reno. With the addition of Skyway Tower in 1985, this big top now offers a total of 1,605 hotel rooms, 60,600 square feet of casino, a buffet which can seat 700 people, shops, video arcades, cocktail lounges, midway games, and circus acts. Circus Circus–Reno had several marginal years, but has become one of the leaders in the Reno market. Circus anticipates that recent remodeling, at a cost of $25.6 million, will increase this property's revenue-generating potential.

The Colorado Belle and The Edgewater Hotel are located on the banks of the Colorado River, in Laughlin, Nevada, a city 90 miles south of Las Vegas. The Colorado Belle, opened in 1987, features a huge paddle-wheel riverboat replica, buffet, cocktail lounges, and shops. The Edgewater, acquired in 1983, has a southwestern motif, a 57,000-square-foot casino, a bowling center, buffet, and cocktail lounges. Combined, these two properties contain 2,700 rooms and more than 120,000 square feet of casino. The two operations contributed 12 percent of the company's revenues in the year ended January 31, 1997, and again in 1998—down from 21 percent in 1994. The extensive proliferation of casinos throughout the region, primarily on Indian land, and the development of mega-resorts in Las Vegas have seriously eroded outlying markets such as Laughlin.

Three properties purchased in 1995 and located in Jean and Henderson, Nevada, represent continuing investments by Circus in outlying markets. The Gold Strike and Nevada Landing service

the I-15 market between Las Vegas and southern California. These properties have more than 73,000 square feet of casino space, 2,140 slot machines and 42 gaming tables combined. Each has limited hotel space (1,116 rooms total) and depends heavily on I-15 traffic. The Railroad Pass is considered a local casino and is dependent on Henderson residents as its market. This smaller casino contains only 395 slot machines and 11 gaming tables.

Gold Strike–Tunica (formerly Circus Circus–Tunica) is a dockside casino in Tunica, Mississippi, opened in 1994 on 24 acres of land along the Mississippi River, approximately 20 miles south of Memphis. In 1997, its operating income declined by more than 50 percent due to the increase in competition and lack of hotel rooms. Circus decided to renovate this property and add a 1,200 room tower hotel. Total cost for all the remodeling was $119.8 million.

Joint Ventures

Circus is engaged in three joint ventures through the wholly owned subsidiary Circus Participant. In Las Vegas, Circus joined with Mirage Resorts to build and operate the Monte Carlo, a hotel-casino with 3,002 rooms designed along the lines of the grand casinos of the Mediterranean. It is located on 46 acres (with 600 feet on the Las Vegas strip) between the New York–New York casino and the soon to be completed Bellagio, with all three casinos to be connected by monorail. The Monte Carlo features a 90,000-square-foot casino containing 2,221 slot machines and 95 gaming tables, along with a 550-seat bingo parlor, high-tech arcade rides, restaurants and buffets, a microbrewery, approximately 15,000 square feet of meeting and convention space, and a 1,200-seat theater. Opened on June 21, 1996, the Monte Carlo generated $14.6 million as Circus's share in operating income for the first seven months of operation.

In Elgin, Illinois, Circus is in a 50 percent partnership with Hyatt Development Corporation in The Grand Victoria. Styled to resemble a Victorian riverboat, this floating casino and land-based entertainment complex includes some 36,000 square feet of casino space, containing 977 slot machines and 56 gaming tables. The adjacent land-based complex contains two movie theaters, a 240-seat buffet, restaurants and parking for approximately 2,000 vehicles. Built for a total of $112 million, The Grand Victoria returned to Circus $44 million in operating income in 1996.

TABLE 1

Circus Circus Enterprises, Inc.
Sources of Revenues as a Percentage of Net Revenues

	1998	1997	1996	1995
Casinos	46.7%	49.2%	51.2%	52.3%
Food and beverage	15.9	15.8	15.5	16.2
Hotel	24.4	22.0	21.4	19.9
Other	10.5	11.0	12.2	14.2
Unconsolidated	7.3	6.5	3.5	.5
Less: complimentary allowances	4.8	4.5	3.8	3.1

Source: Circus Circus 10-K, January 31, 1995–1998

The third joint venture is a 50 percent partnership with Eldorado Limited in the Silver Legacy. Opened in 1995, this casino is located between Circus Circus–Reno and the Eldorado Hotel and Casino on two city blocks in downtown Reno, Nevada. The Silver Legacy has 1,711 hotel rooms, 85,000 square feet of casino, 2,275 slot machines and 89 gaming tables. Management seems to believe that the Silver Legacy holds promise; however, the Reno market is suffering, and the opening of the Silver Legacy has cannibalized the Circus Circus–Reno market.

Circus was engaged in a fourth joint venture to penetrate the Canadian market, but on January 23, 1997, announced it had been bought out by Hilton Hotels Corporation, one of three partners in the venture.

Circus has achieved success through an aggressive growth strategy and a corporate structure designed to enhance that growth. A strong cash position, innovative ideas, and attention to cost control have allowed Circus to satisfy the bottom line during a period when competitors were typically taking on large debt obligations to finance new projects (see Tables 3 through 6). Yet the market is changing. Gambling of all kinds has spread across the country. No longer does the average individual need to go to Las Vegas or New Jersey; instead, gambling can be found as close as the local quick market (lottery), bingo hall, many Indian reservations, the Mississippi River, and other places. There are now almost 300 casinos in Las Vegas alone, 60 in Colorado, and 160 in California. In order to maintain a competitive edge, Circus has con-

tinued to invest heavily in renovation of existing properties (a strategy common to the entertainment/amusement industry) and continues to develop new projects.

New Ventures

Circus has three new projects planned for opening in the near future. The largest project, Mandalay Bay, is scheduled for completion in the first quarter of 1999, and its cost is estimated at $950 million (excluding land). Circus owns a contiguous mile of the southern end of the Las Vegas strip, which it calls its Masterplan Mile and which currently contains the Excalibur and Luxor resorts. Located next to the Luxor, Mandalay Bay will aim for the upscale traveler and player and will be styled as a South Seas adventure. The resort will contain a forty-three story hotel-casino with more than 3,700 rooms and an 11-acre aquatic environment. The aquatic environment will have a surfing beach, swim-up shark tank, and snorkeling reef. A Four Seasons Hotel with some 400 rooms will complement the remainder of Mandalay Bay. Circus anticipates that the rest of the Masterplan Mile will eventually comprise at least one additional casino resort and a number of stand-alone hotels and amusement centers.

Circus also plans three other casino projects, provided all the necessary licenses and agreements can be obtained. In Detroit, Michigan, Circus has combined with the Atwater Casino Group in a joint venture to build a $600 million project. Negotiations with the city to develop the project have been completed; however, the rest of the appropri-

TABLE 2

Circus Circus Enterprises, Inc.
Properties and Percent of Total Revenues

Properties	Percent of Revenues			
	1998	*1997*	*1996*	*1995*
Las Vegas, Nevada				
Circus Circus–Las Vegas	25[1]	24[1]	27[1]	29[1]
Excalibur	21	23	23	25
Luxor	23	17	20	24
Slots-A-Fun and Silver City				
Reno, Nevada				
Circus Circus–Reno				
Laughlin, Nevada				
Colorado Belle	12[2]	12[2]	13[2]	16[2]
Edgewater				
Jean, Nevada				
Gold Strike	6[3]	6[3]	4[3]	NA
Nevada Landing				
Henderson, Nevada				
Railroad Pass				
Tunica, Mississippi				
Gold Strike	4	4	5	3
50% ownership:				
Silver Legacy, Reno, Nevada	7.3	6.5[4]	3.5[4]	.5[4]
Monte Carlo, Las Vegas, Nevada				
Grand Victoria Riverboat Casino, Elgin, Illinois				

[1] Combined with revenues from Circus Circus-Reno.
[2] Colorado Belle and Edgewater have been combined.
[3] Gold Strike and Nevada Landing have been combined.
[4] Revenues of unconsolidated affiliates have been combined.
Revenues from Slots-A-Fun and Silver City, management fees, and other income were not separately reported.

ate licenses will need to be obtained before construction begins.

Along the Mississippi Gulf, at the north end of the Bay of St. Louis, Circus plans to construct a casino resort containing 1,500 rooms at an estimated cost of $225 million. Circus has received all necessary permits to begin construction, but these approvals have been challenged in court, delaying the project.

In Atlantic City, Circus has entered into an agreement with Mirage Resorts to develop a 181-acre site in the Marina District. Land title has been transferred to Mirage, but Mirage has purported to cancel its agreement with Circus. Circus has filed suit against Mirage seeking to enforce the contract, while others have filed suit to stop all development in the area.

Most of Circus's projects are being tailored to attract mainstream tourists and family vacationers. However the addition of several joint ventures and the completion of the Masterplan Mile will also attract the more upscale customer.

TABLE 3

Circus Circus Selected Financial Information

	FY98	*FY97*	*FY96*	*FY95*	*FY94*	*FY93*	*FY92*	*FY91*
Earnings Per Share	0.40	0.99	1.33	1.59	1.34	2.05	1.84	1.39
Current Ratio	.85	1.17	1.30	1.35	.95	.90	1.14	.88
Total Liabilities/								
Total Assets	.65	.62	.44	.54	.57	.48	.58	.77
Operating Profit Margin	17.4%	17%	19%	22%	21%	24.4%	24.9%	22.9%

Sources: Circus Circus Annual Reports and 10-Ks, 1991–1998.

THE GAMING INDUSTRY

By 1997 the gaming industry had captured a large amount of the vacation and leisure-time dollars spent in the United States. Gamblers lost more than $44.3 billion on legal wagering in 1995 (up from $29.9 billion in 1992), including wagers at race-tracks, bingo parlors, lotteries, and casinos. This figure does not include dollars spent on lodging, food, transportation, and other expenditures associated with visits to gaming facilities. Casino gambling accounts for 76 percent of all legal gambling expenditures, far ahead of second-place Indian reservation gambling at 8.9 percent, and lotteries at 7.1 percent. The popularity of casino gambling may be credited to a more frequent and somewhat higher payout as compared with lotteries and racetracks; however, as winnings are recycled, the multiplier effect restores a high return to casino operators.

Geographic expansion has slowed considerably as no additional states have approved casino-type gambling since 1993. Growth has occurred in developed locations, with Las Vegas, Nevada, and Atlantic City, New Jersey, leading the way.

Las Vegas remains the largest U.S. gaming market and one of the largest convention markets, with more than 100,000 hotel rooms hosting more than 29.6 million visitors in 1996, up 2.2 percent over 1995. Casino operators are building to take advantage of this continued growth. Recent projects include the Monte Carlo ($350 million), New York–New York ($350 million), Bellagio ($1.4 billion), Hilton Hotels ($750 million), and Project Paradise ($800 million). Additionally, Harrah's is adding a 989-room tower and remodeling 500 current rooms, and Caesar's Palace has expansion plans to add 2,000 rooms. Las Vegas hotel and casino capacity is expected to continue to expand, with some 12,500 rooms opening within a year, beginning in the fall of 1998. According to the Las Vegas Convention and Visitor Authority, Las Vegas is a destination market, with most visitors planning their trip more than a week in advance (81 percent), arriving by car (47 percent) or airplane (42 percent), and stay-

TABLE 4

Circus Circus Twelve-Year Summary of Revenues and Net Income

FY	Revenues (in thousands)	Net Income (in thousands)
98	$1,354,487	$89,908
97	1,334,250	100,733
96	1,299,596	128,898
95	1,170,182	136,286
94	954,923	116,189
93	843,025	117,322
92	806,023	103,348
91	692,052	76,292
90	522,376	76,064
89	511,960	81,714
88	458,856	55,900
87	373,967	28,198
86	306,993	37,375

Sources: Circus Circus Annual Reports and 10-Ks, 1986–1998.

TABLE 5

Circus Circus Enterprises Inc., Annual Income (in thousands)

	Year Ended January 31				
	1998	1997	1996	1995	1994
Revenues					
Casino	$ 632,122	$ 655,902	$ 664,772	$ 612,115	$538,813
Rooms	330,644	294,241	278,807	232,346	176,001
Food and beverage	215,584	210,384	201,385	189,664	152,469
Other	142,407	146,554	158,534	166,295	117,501
Earnings of unconsolidated affiliates	98,977	86,646	45,485	5,459	—
	1,419,734	1,393,727	1,348,983	1,205,879	984,784
Less complimentary allowances	(65,247)	(59,477)	(49,387)	(35,697)	(29,861)
Net revenue	1,354,487	1,334,250	1,299,596	1,170,182	954,923
Costs and expenses					
Casino	316,902	302,096	275,680	246,416	209,402
Rooms	122,934	116,508	110,362	94,257	78,932
Food and beverage	199,955	200,722	188,712	177,136	149,267
Other operating expenses	90,187	90,601	92,631	107,297	72,802
General and administrative	232,536	227,348	215,083	183,175	152,104
Depreciation and amortization	117,474	95,414	93,938	81,109	58,105
Preopening expense	3,447	—	—	3,012	16,506
Abandonment loss		48,309	45,148	—	—
	1,083,435	1,080,998	1,021,554	892,402	737,118
Operating profit before corporate expense	271,052	223,252	278,042	277,780	217,805
Corporate expense	34,552	31,083	26,669	21,773	16,744
Income from operations	236,500	222,169	251,373	256,007	201,061
Other income (expense)					
Interest, dividends and other income (loss)	9,779	5,077	4,022	225	(683)
Interest income and guarantee fees from unconsolidated affiliate	6,041	6,865	7,517	992	—
Interest expense	(88,847)	(54,681)	(51,537)	(42,734)	(17,770)
Interest expense from unconsolidated affiliate	(15,551)	(15,567)	(5,616)	—	—
	(88,578)	(58,306)	(45,614)	(41,517)	(18,453)
Income before provision for income tax	147,922	163,863	205,759	214,490	182,608
Provision for income tax	58,014	63,130	76,861	78,204	66,419
Income before extraordinary loss		—	—	—	116,189
Extraordinary loss		—	—	—	—
Net income	$ 89,908	$ 100,733	$ 128,898	$ 136,286	$116,189
Earnings per share					
Income before extraordinary loss	.95	.99	1.33	1.59	1.34
Extraordinary loss	—	—	—	—	—
Net income per share	$ .94	$ .99	$ 1.33	$ 1.59	$ 1.34

Sources: Circus Circus Annual Reports and 10-Ks, 1994–1998.

TABLE 6

Circus Circus Enterprises, Inc., Consolidated Balance Sheets (in thousands)

	Year Ended January 31				
	1998	*1997*	*1996*	*1995*	*1994*
Assets					
Current assets:					
Cash and cash equivalents	$ 58,631	$ 69,516	$ 62,704	$ 53,764	$ 39,110
Receivables	33,640	34,434	16,527	8,931	8,673
Inventories	22,440	19,371	20,459	22,660	20,057
Prepaid expenses	20,281	19,951	19,418	20,103	20,062
Deferred income tax	7,871	8,577	7,272	5,463	
Total current	142,863	151,849	124,380	110,921	87,902
Property, equipment	2,466,848	1,920,032	1,474,684	1,239,062	1,183,164
Other assets					
Excess of purchase price over fair market value	375,375	385,583	394,518	9,836	10,200
Notes receivable	1,075	36,443	27,508	68,083	
Investments in unconsolidated affiliates	255,392	214,123	173,270	74,840	
Deferred charges and other assets	21,995	21,081	17,533	9,806	16,658
Total other	653,837	657,230	612,829	162,565	26,858
Total assets	$3,263,548	$2,729,111	$2,213,503	$1,512,548	$1,297,924
Liabilities and Stockholders' Equity					
Current liabilities:					
Current portion of long-term debt	3,071	379	863	106	169
Accounts and contracts payable					
Trade	22,103	22,658	16,824	12,102	14,804
Construction	40,670	21,144	—	1,101	13,844
Accrued liabilities					
Salaries, wages and vacations	36,107	31,847	30,866	24,946	19,650
Progressive Jackpots	7,511	6,799	8,151	7,447	4,881
Advance room deposits	6,217	7,383	7,517	8,701	6,981
Interest payable	17,828	9,004	3,169	2,331	2,278
Other	33,451	30,554	28,142	25,274	25,648
Income tax payable					3,806
Total current liabilities	166,958	129,768	95,532	82,008	92,061
Long-term debt	1,788,818	1,405,897	715,214	632,652	567,345
Other liabilities					
Deferred income tax	175,934	152,635	148,096	110,776	77,153
Other long-term liabilities	8,089	6,439	9,319	988	1,415
Total other liabilities	184,023	159,074	157,415	111,764	78,568
Total liabilities	2,139,799	1,694,739	968,161	826,424	737,974
Redeemable preferred stock		17,631	18,530		
Temporary equity		44,950			
Commitments and contingent liabilities					
Stockholders' equity					
Common stock	1,893	1,880	1,880	1,607	1,603
Preferred stock					
Additional paid-in capital	558,658	498,893	527,205	124,960	120,135
Retained earnings	1,074,271	984,363	883,630	754,732	618,446
Treasury stock	(511,073)	(513,345)	(185,903)	(195,175)	(180,234)
Total stockholders' equity	1,123,749	971,791	1,226,812	686,124	559,950
Total liabilities and stockholders' equity	$3,263,548	$2,729,111	$2,213,503	$1,512,548	$1,297,924

Sources: Circus Circus Annual Reports and 10-Ks, 1994–1998.

ing in a hotel (72 percent). Gamblers are typically return visitors (77 percent), who like playing the slots (65 percent) and average 2.2 trips per year.

The primary difference between the Las Vegas market and that of Atlantic City is the type of consumer frequenting these markets. While Las Vegas attracts overnight resort-seeking vacationers, Atlantic City's clientele comprises predominantly day-trippers traveling by automobile or bus. Gaming revenues are expected to continue to grow, perhaps to $4 billion in 1997 split between ten casino/hotels currently operating. Growth in the Atlantic City area will be concentrated in the Marina section of town, where Mirage Resorts has entered into an agreement with the city to develop 150 acres of the Marina as a destination resort. This development will include a resort wholly owned by Mirage, a casino/hotel developed by Circus, and a complex developed by a joint venture with Mirage and Boyd Corp. Currently in Atlantic City, Donald Trump's gaming empire holds the largest market share—30 percent—with Trump's Castle, Trump Plaza, and the Taj Mahal. The next closest in market share is Caesar's (10.3 percent), Tropicana and Bally's (9.2 percent each), and Showboat (9 percent).

A number of smaller markets exist around the United States, primarily in Mississippi, Louisiana, Illinois, Missouri, and Indiana. Each state has imposed various restrictions on the development of casino operations within it. In some cases—for example, in Illinois, where there are only ten gaming licenses available—the restrictions have limited the growth opportunities and hurt revenues. But in Mississippi and Louisiana, revenues are up 8 percent and 15 percent, respectively, in riverboat operations. Native American casinos continue to be developed on federally controlled Indian land. These casinos are not publicly held but do tend to be managed by publicly held corporations. Overall, these other locations present a mix of opportunities and generally constitute only a small portion of total gaming revenues.

MAJOR INDUSTRY PLAYERS

Over the past several years, mergers and acquisitions have reshaped the gaming industry. As of the end of 1996, the industry was a combination of corporations ranging from those engaged solely in

gaming to multinational conglomerates. The largest competitors, in terms of revenues, combined multiple industries to generate both large revenues and substantial profits (see Table 7). However, those engaged primarily in gaming could also be extremely profitable.

In 1996, Hilton began a hostile acquisition attempt of ITT Corporation. As a result of this attempt, ITT has merged with Starwood Lodging Corporation and Starwood Lodging Trust. The resulting corporation is one of the world's largest hotel and gaming companies, owning the Sheraton, The Luxury Collection, the Four Points Hotels, and Caesar's, as well as communications and educational services. In 1996, ITT hosted approximately 50 million customer nights in locations worldwide. Gaming operations are located in Las Vegas, Atlantic City, Halifax and Sydney (Nova Scotia), as well as elsewhere in Canada, Lake Tahoe, Tunica (Mississippi), Lima (Peru), Cairo (Egypt), and Australia. In 1996, ITT's net income was $249 million on revenues of $6.579 billion. In June 1996, the company had announced plans to join with Planet Hollywood to develop casino/hotels with the Planet Hollywood theme in both Las Vegas and Atlantic City. However, these plans may be deferred as ITT becomes fully integrated into Starwood and management has the opportunity to refocus on the operations of the company.

Hilton Hotels owned (as of February 1, 1998) or leased and operated 25 hotels and managed 34 hotels partially or wholly owned by others, along with 180 franchised hotels. Eleven of the hotels are also casinos, 6 of which are located in Nevada, 2 in Atlantic City, and the other 3 in Australia, and Uruguay. In 1997, Hilton had net income of $250 million on $5.31 billion in revenues. Hilton received some 38 percent of total operating revenues from gaming operations and continued to expand in the market. Recent expansions included the Wild Wild West theme hotel casino in Atlantic City, the completed acquisition of all the assets of Bally's, and construction of a 2,900-room Paris Casino resort located next to Bally's in Las Vegas.

Harrah's Entertainment, Inc., is primarily engaged in the gaming industry with casino/hotels in Reno, Lake Tahoe, Las Vegas, and Laughlin, Nevada, as well as Atlantic City, New Jersey; riverboats in Joliet, Illinois, and Vicksburg and Tunica, Mississippi, Shreveport, Louisiana, and Kansas City,

TABLE 7

**Major U.S. Gaming, Lottery and Pari-mutuel Companies
1996 Revenues and Net Income (in millions)**

	1997 Revenues	*1997 Income*	*1996 Revenues*	*1996 Net Income*
Starwood/ITT			$6597.0	$249.0
Hilton Hotels	$5316.0	$250.0	3940.0	82.0
Harrah's Entertainment	1619.0	99.3	1586.0	98.9
Mirage Resorts	1546.0	207	1358.3	206.0
Circus Circus	1354.4	89.9	1247.0	100.7
Trump Hotel and Casino, Inc.	1399.3	−42.1	976.3	−4.9
MGM Grand	827.5	111.0	804.8	74.5
Aztar	782.3	4.4	777.5	20.6
Int. Game Technology	743.9	137.2	733.5	118.0

Sources: Individual companies' annual reports and 10-Ks, 1996.

Kansas; two Indian casinos; and a casino in Auckland, New Zealand. In 1997, it operated a total of approximately 774,500 square feet of casino space, with 19,835 slot machines and 934 table games. From this and some 8,197 hotel rooms, the company had a net income of $99.3 million on $1.619 billion in revenues.

All of the Mirage Resorts gaming operations are currently located in Nevada. The company owns and operates the Golden Nugget–Downtown, Las Vegas, the Mirage on the strip in Las Vegas, Treasure Island, and the Golden Nugget–Laughlin. Additionally, it is a 50 percent owner of the Monte Carlo with Circus Circus. Net income for Mirage Resorts in 1997 was $207 million on revenues of $1.546 billion. Current expansion plans include the development of the Bellagio in Las Vegas ($1.6 billion estimated cost) and the Beau Rivage in Biloxi, Mississippi ($600 million estimated cost). These two properties would add a total of 265,900 square feet of casino space to the current Mirage inventory and an additional 252 gaming tables and 4,746 slot machines. Still another project is the development of the Marina area in Atlantic City, New Jersey, in partnership with Boyd Gaming.

MGM Grand Hotel and Casino is located on approximately 114 acres at the northeast corner of Las Vegas Boulevard, across the street from the New York–New York Hotel and Casino. The casino covers approximately 171,500 square feet, and is one of the largest casinos in the world. It has 3,669 slot machines and 157 table games. Current plans call for extensive renovation, costing $700 million. Through a wholly owned subsidiary, MGM owns and operates the MGM Grand Diamond Beach Hotel and a hotel/casino resort in Darwin, Australia. Additionally, MGM and Primadonna Resorts, Inc., each own 50 percent of the New York–New York Hotel and Casino, a $460 million architecturally distinctive themed destination resort, which opened on January 3, 1997. MGM also intends to construct and operate a destination resort hotel/casino—an entertainment and retail facility in Atlantic City on approximately 35 acres of land on the Atlantic City Boardwalk.

THE LEGAL ENVIRONMENT

Within the gaming industry, all current operators must consider compliance with extensive gaming regulations as a primary concern. Each state or country has its own specific regulations and regulatory boards and extensive reporting and licensing requirements. For example, in Las Vegas, Nevada, gambling operations are subject to regulatory control by the Nevada State Gaming Control Board, by the Clark County Nevada Gaming and Liquor Licensing Board, and by city government regulations. The laws, regulations and supervisory procedures of virtually all gaming authorities are based on public policy primarily concerned with preventing unsavory or unsuitable persons from having a direct or indirect involvement with gaming at any time or in any capacity and the establishment and maintenance of responsible accounting practices. Additional regulations typically cover the following: maintenance of effective controls over the financial practices of licensees, including the establishment of minimum procedures for internal fiscal affairs and the safeguarding of assets and revenues; providing reliable record keeping and requiring the filing of periodic reports; prevention of cheating and fraudulent practices; and providing a source of state and local revenues through taxation and licensing fees. Changes in such laws, regulations, and procedures could have an adverse effect on any gaming operation. All gaming companies must submit detailed operating and financial reports to authorities. Nearly all financial transactions, including loans, leases, and the sale of securities must be reported. Some financial activities are subject to approval by regulatory agencies. As Circus moves into other locations outside of Nevada, it will need to adhere to local regulations.

FUTURE CONSIDERATION

According to Circus Circus, it is "in the business of entertainment, with . . . core strength in casino gaming," and it intends to focus its efforts in Las Vegas, Atlantic City, and Mississippi. The company also believes that the "future product in gaming . . . is the entertainment resort" (Circus Circus 1997 Annual Report).

Circus was one of the innovators of the gaming resort concept and has continued to be a leader in that field. However, the mega-entertainment resort industry operates differently than the traditional casino gaming industry. In the past consumers would visit a casino to experience the thrill of gambling. Now they not only gamble, but expect to be dazzled by enormous entertainment complexes that are costing billions of dollars to build. The competition has continued to increase at the same time that growth rates have been slowing.

For years, analysts have questioned the ability of the gaming industry to continue high growth in established markets as the industry matures. Through the 1970s and 1980s the gaming industry experienced rapid growth. Through the 1990s, the industry began to experience a shakeout of marginal competitors and consolidation phase. Circus Circus

has been successful through this turmoil but now faces the task of maintaining high growth in a more mature industry.

APPENDIX A: CIRCUS CIRCUS ENTERPRISES, INC., TOP MANAGEMENT

Board of Directors

Clyde T. Turner, 59, chairman of the board and CEO
Michael S. Ensign, 59, vice chairman of the board and COO
Glenn Schaeffer, 43, president and CFO
William A. Richardson, 50, vice chairman of the board and executive vice president
Richard P. Banis, 52, former president and COO
Arthur II. Bilger, 44, former president and COO of New World Communications Group International
Richard A. Etter, 58, former chairman and CEO of Bank of America–Nevada
William E. Bannen, M.D., 48, vice president/chief medical officer of Blue Cross Blue Shield of Nevada
Donna B. More, 40, partner in the law firm of Freeborn & Peters
Michael D. McKee, 51, executive vice president of The Irving Company

Officers

Clyde T. Turner, chairman of the board and CEO
Michael S. Ensign, vice chairman of the board and COO
Glenn Schaeffer, president, CFO, and treasurer
William A. Richardson, vice chairman of the board and executive vice president
Tony Alamo, senior vice president, operations
Gregg Solomon, senior vice president, operations
Kurt D. Sullivan, senior vice president, operations
Steve Greathouse, senior vice president, operations
Yvett Landau, vice president, general counsel, and secretary
Les Martin, vice president and chief accounting officer
Sources: Annual Report 1998; Proxy Statement May 1, 1998.

References

Anderson, "Economic Impacts of Casino Gaming in the United States." American Gaming Association, May 1997.
Aztar Corp., 1997 and 1998 10-K. Retrieved from EDGAR database (http://www.sec.gov/Archives/edgar/data/).

"Circus Circus Announces Promotion." *PR Newswire*, June 10, 1997.

Circus Circus Enterprises, Inc. Annual Report to Shareholders, January 31, 1989, January 31, 1990, January 31, 1993, January 31, 1994, January 31, 1995, January 31, 1996, January 31, 1997, and January 31, 1998.

Corning, Blair. "Luxor: Egypt Opens in Vegas." *San Antonio Express News*, October 24, 1993.

Harrah's Entertainment, Inc., 1997 and 1998 10-K. Retrieved from EDGAR database (http://www.sec.gov/Archives/edgar/data/).

"Harrah's Survey of Casino Entertainment." Harrah's Entertainment, Inc., 1996.

Hilton Hotels Corp., 1997 and 1998 10-K. Retrieved from EDGAR database (http://www.sec.gov/Archives/edgar/data/).

"ITT Board Rejects Hilton's Offer as Inadequate, Reaffirms Belief That ITT's Comprehensive Plan Is in the Best Interest of ITT Shareholders." Press release, August 14, 1997.

ITT Corp., 1997 10-K. Retrieved from EDGAR database (http://www.sec.gov/Archives/edgar/data/).

Lalli, Sergio. "Excalibur Awaiteth." *Hotel and Motel Management*, June 11, 1990.

Mirage Resorts, Inc., 1997 and 1998 10-K. Retrieved from EDGAR database (http://www.sec.gov/Archives/edgar/data/).

MGM Grand, Inc., 1997 and 1998 10-K. Retrieved from EDGAR database (http://www.sec.gov/Archives/edgar/data/).

Standard & Poor's. "Casinos Move into New Areas." *Industry Surveys*, March 11, 1993, pp. L35–L41.

———— "Industry Surveys—Lodging and Gaming," *Industry Surveys*, June 19, 1997.

CASE 19

The Evolution of the Air Express Industry

The case was prepared by Charles W.L. Hill of the University of Washington.

INTRODUCTION

The air express industry is that segment of the broader air cargo industry that specializes in rapid (normally overnight) delivery of small packages. It is generally agreed that the air express industry in the United States began with Fred Smith's vision for Federal Express Company, which started operations in 1973. Federal Express transformed the structure of the existing air cargo industry and paved the way for rapid growth in the overnight package segment of that industry. A further impetus to the industry's development was the 1977 deregulation of the U.S. air cargo industry. For the first time this allowed Federal Express (and its emerging competitors) to buy large jets. The story of the industry during the 1980s was one of rapid growth and new entry. Between 1982 and 1989, air express cargo shipments in the United States grew at an annual average rate of 31 percent. In contrast, shipments of air freight and air mail grew at an annual rate of only 2.7 percent.[1] This rapid growth attracted new entrants such as United Parcel Service (UPS) and Airborne Freight (which operates under the name Airborne Express). The entry of UPS triggered severe price cutting, which ultimately drove some of the weaker competitors out of the market and touched off a wave of consolidation in the industry.

By the mid 1990s, the industry structure had stabilized, with three firms—Federal Express, UPS, and Airborne Express—accounting for around 70 percent of U.S. air express shipments. (See Table 1 for a comparison of the three companies.)[2] During

This case is intended to be used as a basis for class discussion rather than as an illustration of either effective or ineffective handling of the situation. This case was prepared by Charles W. L. Hill, University of Washington. Used by permission.

the first half of the 1990s, the air express industry continued to grow at a healthy rate, with express shipments expanding from 4,404 million ton miles in 1990 to 7,042 million ton miles in 1994, an annual growth rate of slightly more than 16 percent (see Figure 1).[3] Despite this growth, the industry was hit by repeated rounds of price cutting as the three biggest firms battled to capture major accounts. In addition to price cutting, the big three also competed vigorously on the basis of technology, service offerings, and the global reach of their operations.

THE INDUSTRY IN 1973

In 1973, roughly 1.5 billion tons of freight were shipped annually in the United States. Most of this was carried by surface transport, with airfreight accounting for less than 2 percent of the total.[4] While shipment by airfreight was often quicker than shipment by surface freight, the high cost of airfreight had kept down demand. The typical users of airfreight at this time were suppliers of time-sensitive, high-priced goods, such as computer parts and medical instruments, which were needed at dispersed locations but which were too expensive for their customers to hold as inventory.

The main cargo carriers in 1973 were major passenger airlines, which operated a number of all-cargo planes and carried additional cargo in the bellies of their passenger planes. There was also a handful of all-cargo airlines, such as Flying Tiger. From 1973 onward, the passenger airlines moved steadily away from all-cargo planes and began to concentrate cargo freight in the bellies of passenger planes. This was a response to increases in fuel

TABLE 1

Main U.S. Air Express Operators, 1995

	Federal Express	*UPS*	*Airborne Express*
U.S. Market Share*	35%	26%	9%
Revenues	$10.3 billion	$21 billion	$2.2 billion
Aircraft fleet	559	184	109
Employees	122,000	335,000	19,000
Delivery vehicles	36,000	65,000	12,800

*Market share figures refer to share of U.S. domestic airfreight and express mail delivery. Figures for just express mail delivery are higher.
Source: All of the data come from the company Web sites with the exception of market share data, which are from Standard & Poor's, "Aerospace and Air Transport," *Industry Surveys* (February 1996).

costs, which made the operation of many older cargo jets uneconomical.

With regard to distribution of cargo to and from airports, in 1973 about 20 percent of all airfreight was delivered to airports by the shipper and/or picked up by the consignee. The bulk of the remaining 80 percent was accounted for by three major intermediaries: (1) Air Cargo Incorporated, (2) freight forwarders, and (3) the U.S. Postal Service. Air Cargo Incorporated was a trucking service, wholly owned by twenty-six airlines, which performed pickup and delivery service for the airlines' direct customers. Freight forwarders were trucking carriers that consolidated cargo going to the airlines. They purchased cargo space from the airlines and retailed this in small amounts. They dealt primarily with small customers, providing pickup and delivery services in most cities, either in their own trucks or through contract agents. The U.S. Postal Service used air service for transportation of long-distance letter mail and air parcel post.[5]

FIGURE 1

Volume Growth of the U.S. Air Express Market, 1985–1994 (millions of air cargo ton miles)

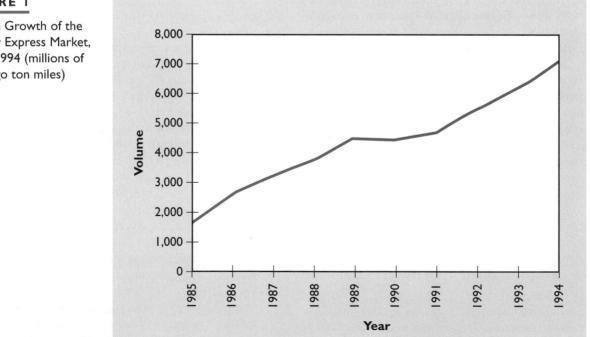

THE FEDERAL EXPRESS CONCEPT

Federal Express, founded by Fred Smith, Jr., was incorporated in 1971 and began operations in 1973. At that time, a significant proportion of small package airfreight flew on commercial passenger flights. Smith believed that there were major differences between packages and passengers, and he was convinced that the two had to be treated differently. Most passengers moved between major cities and wanted the convenience of daytime flights. Cargo shippers preferred nighttime service to coincide with late-afternoon pickups and next-day delivery. Because small package airfreight was subservient to the requirements of passengers' flight schedules, it was often difficult for the major airlines to achieve next-day delivery of airfreight.

Smith's aim was to build a system that could achieve next-day delivery of small package airfreight (less than 70 pounds). He set up Federal Express with his $8 million family inheritance and $90 million in venture capital. Federal Express established what was at that time a unique hub-and-spoke route system. The hub of the system was Memphis, chosen for its good weather conditions, central location, and the fact that it was Smith's hometown. The spokes were regular routes between Memphis and shipping facilities at public airports in the cities serviced by Federal Express. Every weeknight, aircraft would leave their home cities with a load of packages and fly down the "spokes" to Memphis (often with one or two stops on the way). At Memphis, all packages were unloaded, sorted by destination, and reloaded. The aircraft then returned to their home cities in the early hours of the morning. Packages were ferried to and from airports by Federal Express couriers driving the company's vans and working to a tight schedule. Thus, from door to door the package was in Federal Express's hands. This system guaranteed that a package picked up from a customer in New York at 5 P.M. would reach its final destination in Los Angeles (or any major city) by noon the following day. It enabled Federal Express to realize economies in sorting and to utilize its air cargo capacity efficiently. Federal Express also pioneered the use of standard packaging, with an upper weight limit of 70 pounds and a maximum length plus girth of 108 inches. This helped Federal Express to gain further efficiencies from mechanized sorting at its Memphis hub. Later entrants into the industry copied Federal Express's package standards and hub-and-spoke operating system.

To accomplish overnight delivery, Federal Express had to operate its own planes. However, restrictive regulations enforced by the Civil Aeronautics Board (CAB) prohibited the company from buying large jet aircraft. To get around this restriction, Federal Express bought a fleet of twin-engine executive jets, which it converted to mini-freighters. These planes had a cargo capacity of 6,200 pounds, which enabled Federal Express to get a license as an air taxi operator.

After 1973, Federal Express quickly built up volume. By 1976, it had an average daily volume of 19,000 packages, a fleet of 32 aircraft, 500 delivery vans, and 2,000 employees, and it had initiated service in seventy-five cities. Moreover, after three loss-making years, the company turned in a profit of $3.7 million on revenues of $75 million.[6] However, volume had grown to the point at which Federal Express desperately needed to use larger planes to maintain operating efficiencies. As a result, Smith's voice was added to those calling for Congress to deregulate the airline industry and allow greater competition.

DEREGULATION AND ITS AFTERMATH

In November 1977, Congress relaxed regulations controlling competition in the air cargo industry, one year before passenger services were deregulated. This involved a drastic loosening of standards for entry into the industry. The old CAB authority to name the carriers that could operate on the various routes was changed to the relatively simple authority to decide which among candidate carriers was fit, willing, and able to operate an all-cargo route. In addition, CAB controls over pricing were significantly reduced. The immediate effect was an increase in rates for certain types of shipments, particularly minimum- and high-weight categories, suggesting that prices had been held artificially low by regulation. As a result, the average yield (revenue per ton mile) on domestic airfreight increased 10.6 percent in 1978 and 11.3 percent in 1979.[7]

Freed from the constraints of regulation, Federal Express immediately began to purchase larger jets and quickly established itself as a major carrier of small-package airfreight. However, despite the increase in yields, new entry into the air cargo industry was limited, at least initially. This was mainly due to the high capital requirements involved in establishing an all-cargo carrier. Indeed, by the end of 1978, there were only four major all-cargo carriers serving the domestic market: Airlift International, Federal Express, Flying Tiger, and Seaboard World Airlines. While all of these had increased their route structure following deregulation, only Federal Express specialized in next-day delivery for small packages. Demand for a next-day delivery service continued to boom. Industry estimates suggest that the small-package priority market had grown to about 82 million pieces in 1979, up from 43 million in 1974.[8]

At the same time, in response to increasing competition from the all-cargo carriers, the passenger airlines continued their retreat from the all-cargo business (originally begun in 1973 as a response to high fuel prices). Between 1973 and 1978, there was a 45 percent decline in the mileage of all-cargo flights by the airlines. This was followed by a 14 percent decline between 1978 and 1979. Instead of all-cargo flights, the airlines concentrated their attentions on carrying cargo in the bellies of passenger flights. This practice hurt the freight forwarders badly. The freight forwarders had long relied on the all-cargo flights of major airlines to achieve next-day delivery. Now the freight forwarders were being squeezed out of this segment by a lack of available lift at the time needed to ensure next-day delivery.

It was this problem that led to one of the major postderegulation developments in the industry: the acquisition and operation by freight forwarders of their own fleets of aircraft. Between 1979 and 1981, five of the six largest freight forwarders became involved in this activity. The two largest of these were Emery Air Freight and Airborne Express. Emery operated a fleet of sixty-six aircraft at the end of 1979, the majority of which were leased from other carriers. In mid 1980 this fleet was providing service to approximately 129 cities, carrying both large-volume shipments and small-package express.

Airborne Express acquired its own fleet of aircraft in April 1980 with the purchase of Midwest Charter Express, an Ohio-based all-cargo airline. Then, in 1981, Airborne opened a new hub in Ohio, which became the center of its small-package express operation. This enabled Airborne to provide next-day delivery for small packages to 125 cities in the United States.[9] Other freight forwarders that moved into the overnight mail market

included Purolator Courier and Gelco, both of which offered overnight delivery by air on a limited geographic scale.

INDUSTRY EVOLUTION, 1980–1986

New Products and Industry Growth

In 1981, Federal Express expanded its role in the overnight market with the introduction of an overnight letter service, with a limit of 2 ounces. This guaranteed overnight delivery service was set up in direct competition with the U.S. Postal Service's Priority Mail. The demand for such a service was illustrated by its expansion to about 17,000 letters per day within its first three months of operation.

More generally, the focus of the air express industry was changing from being predominantly a conduit for goods to being a distributor of information—particularly company documents, letters, contracts, drawings, and the like. As a result of the growth in demand for information distribution, new product offerings such as the overnight letter, and Federal Express's own marketing efforts, the air express industry enjoyed high growth during the early 1980s, averaging more than 20 percent per annum.[10] Indeed, many observers attribute most of the growth in the overnight delivery business at this time to Federal Express's marketing efforts. According to one industry participant, "Federal Express pulled off one of the greatest marketing scams in the industry by making people believe they absolutely, positively, had to have something right away."[11]

Increasing Price Competition

Despite rapid growth in demand, competitive intensity in the industry increased sharply in 1982 following the entry of UPS into the overnight-delivery market. UPS was already by far the largest private package transporter in the United States, with an enormous ground-oriented distribution network and revenues in excess of $4 billion per annum. In addition, UPS had for a long time offered a second-day air service for priority packages, primarily by using the planes of all-cargo and passenger airlines. In 1982, UPS acquired a fleet of twenty-four used Boeing 727-100s and added four DC-8 freighters from Flying Tiger, enabling it to introduce next-day air service in September of that year—at roughly half the price Federal Express was charging at the time.[12]

Federal Express countered almost immediately by announcing that it would institute 10:30 A.M. priority overnight delivery (at a cost to the company of $18 million). However, none of the other carriers followed suit, reasoning that most of their customers are usually busy or in meetings in the morning hours, so delivery before noon was not really that important. Instead, by March of 1983 most of the major carriers in the market were offering their high-volume customers contract rates that matched the UPS price structure (including Federal Express). Then three new services introduced by Purolator, Emery, and Gelco Courier pushed prices even lower.

What followed was something of a competitive free-for-all, with constant price changes and volume discounts being offered by all industry participants. Not surprisingly, these developments began to hit the profit margins of the express carriers. Between 1983 and 1984, Federal Express saw its average revenue per pack fall nearly 14 percent, while Emery saw a 15 percent decline in its yield on small shipments.[13]

A further factor driving price down at this time was the growing tendency of customers to group together and negotiate for lower prices. For example, Xerox set up accounts with Purolator and Emery that covered not only Xerox's express packages but also those of fifty other companies, including Mayflower Corp., the moving company, and the Chicago Board of Trade. By negotiating as a group, these companies were able to achieve prices as much as 60 percent lower than those they could get on their own.[14]

The main beneficiary of the price war was UPS, which by 1985 had gained the number two spot in the industry, with 15 percent of the market. Federal Express, meanwhile, had seen its market share slip back to 37 percent from around 45 percent two years earlier. The other four major players in the industry at this time were Emery Air Freight (with 14 percent of market share), Purolator (with 10 percent of market share), Airborne Express (with 8 percent of market share), and the U.S. Postal Service (with 8 percent of market share).[15] The survival of all four of these carriers in the air express business was in question by 1986. Emery, Purolator, and the U.S. Postal Service were all reporting losses on their air express business, while Airborne had seen its profits slump 66 percent in the first quarter of 1986 and now had razor-thin margins.

The Specter of Fax

To make matters worse, by the mid 1980s there were increasing concerns that electronic mail would take much of the information distribution business away from the air express operators. In particular, as the speed and quality of facsimile machines improved and the price of the equipment fell, fax emerged as a very real threat to the volume of document traffic handled by the air express carriers.

Federal Express responded to this perceived threat by its 1984 entry into the electronic mail business with its ZAPMAIL product. The company established fax equipment in its retail outlets, as well as in some of its trucks. Federal's existing courier service would pick up documents and then transmit them by fax to a Federal Express receiver. The document would then be delivered to its destination by the courier service. The aim was to provide door-to-door service within two hours. Unfortunately for Federal Express, fax technology developed rapidly, making it cost effective for corporate clients to buy their own equipment, rather than use Federal's. In 1986, after two years of large losses, Federal Express admitted its mistake and abandoned ZAPMAIL.

The growth of facsimile continued to be a threat, however, and undoubtedly squeezed the growth rate in the document traffic. Federal Express's experience in this category is illuminating. During 1986, its year-to-year gains in monthly overnight document traffic were in the 50 to 60 percent range. By late 1988, the gains were down in the 9 to 10 percent range.[16] However, a 1988 study by Airborne Express of the impact of fax machines puts this threat in some perspective. Eighty-one percent of executives contacted for a study by Airborne said that their use of fax had increased over the past year. However, those same executives said that fax is having a limited impact on air express; approximately 77 percent said that their use of air express had either remained constant or increased during the same period.[17]

INDUSTRY EVOLUTION, 1987–1996

Industry Consolidation

A slowdown in the growth rate of the air express business due to increasing geographic saturation and inroads made by electronic transmission stimulated further price discounting in 1987 and early

1988. Predictably, this created problems for the weakest companies in the industry. The first to go was Purolator Courier, which had lost $65 million during 1985 and 1986. Purolator's problems stemmed from a failure to install an adequate computer system. The company was unable to track shipments, a crucial asset in this industry, and its best corporate customers were billed 120 days late.[18] In 1987 Purolator agreed to be acquired by Emery. The latter was unable to effect a satisfactory integration of Purolator and itself sustained large losses in 1988 and early 1989.

In April 1989, Consolidated Freightways, a major trucking company and parent of CF Air Freight, the third largest heavy shipment specialist in the United States, acquired Emery for $478 million. However, CF Air Freight soon found itself struggling to cope with Emery's problems. In its first eleven months with CF, Emery lost $100 million. One of the main problems was Emery's billing and tracking system, described as a "rat's nest" of conflicting tariff schedules, which caused overbillings of customers and made tracking packages en route a major chore. In addition, CF enraged corporate customers by trying to add a "fuel surcharge" of 4 to 7 percent to prices in early 1989. Competitors held the line on prices and picked up business from CF/Emery.[19]

As a result of the decline of the CF/Emery/Purolator combination, the other firms in the industry were able to pick up market share. By 1994, the industry's estimates suggested that Federal Express accounted for 35 percent of domestic airfreight and air express industry revenues; UPS had 26 percent, Airborne Express was third with 9 percent; and Emery, DHL (a large Brussels-based international air express carrier), and the U.S. Postal Service each held on to 4 percent of the market. The remainder of the market was split between numerous small cargo carriers and several combination carriers, such as Evergreen International and Atlas Air. (Combination carriers specialize mostly in heavy freight but do carry some express mail.)[20]

The other major acquisition in the industry during this time was the purchase of Flying Tiger by Federal Express for $880 million in December 1988. Although Flying Tiger had some air express operations in the United States, its primary strength was as a heavy cargo carrier with a global route structure. The acquisition was part of Federal Express's goal of becoming a major player in the in-ternational air express market (more of this later). However, the acquisition was not without its problems. For one thing, many of Flying Tiger's biggest customers, including UPS and Airborne Express, are Federal's competitors in the domestic market. These companies have long paid Tiger to carry packages to those countries where they have no landing rights. It seemed unlikely that these companies would continue to push international business to their biggest domestic competitor. Further problems arose in the process of trying to integrate the two operations. These included the scheduling of aircraft and pilots, the servicing of Tiger's fleet, and the merging of Federal's nonunionized pilots with Tiger's unionized pilots.[21]

During the late 1980s and early 1990s, there were also hints of further consolidations. TNT Ltd., a large Australian-based air cargo operation with a global network, made an unsuccessful attempt to acquire Airborne Express in 1986. TNT's bid was frustrated by opposition from Airborne and by the difficulties inherent in getting around U.S. law, which currently limits foreign firms from having more than a 25 percent stake in U.S. airlines. In addition, DHL Airways, the U.S. subsidiary of DHL International, was reportedly attempting to enlarge its presence in the United States and was on the lookout for an acquisition.[22]

Pricing Trends

In October 1988, UPS offered new discounts to high-volume customers in domestic markets. For the first time since 1983, competitors declined to match the cuts. Then in January 1989, UPS announced a price increase of 5 percent for next-day air service, its first price increase in nearly six years. Federal Express, Airborne, and Consolidated Freightways all followed suit with moderate increases. Further rate increases of 5.9 percent on next-day air letters were announced by UPS in February 1990. Federal Express followed suit in April, and Airborne also implemented selective price hikes on noncontract business of 5 percent or 50 cents a package on packages up to 20 pounds.[23]

However, just as prices were beginning to stabilize, along came the 1990–1991 recession. For the first time in the history of the U.S. air express industry, there was a decline in year-on-year shipments, with express freight falling from 4,455 million ton miles in 1989 to 4,403 million ton miles in 1990. This decline triggered another round of competitive price cuts, and yields plummeted. Although demand rebounded strongly, repeated attempts to raise prices in 1992, 1993, and 1994 simply did not stick.[24] Much of the price cutting was focused on large corporate accounts, which by this time were generating 75 percent by volume of express mail shipments. For example, as a result of deep price discounting in 1994, UPS was able to lure home shopping programmer QVC and computer mail-order company Gateway 2000 away from Federal Express. However, at about the same time, Federal Express used discounting to capture retailer Williams-Sonoma away from UPS.[25] This prolonged period of price discounting depressed profit margins and contributed to losses at all three major carriers during the early 1990s. Bolstered by a strong economy, prices finally began to stabilize during late 1995, when price increases announced by UPS were followed by those at Federal Express and Airborne.[26]

Product Trends

Second-Day Delivery   Having seen a slowdown in the growth rate of the next day document delivery business during the early 1990s, the major operators in the air express business began to look for new product opportunities to sustain their growth and margins. One trend has been to move into the second-day delivery market, or deferred services as it is called in the industry.[27] The move toward second-day delivery was started by Airborne Express in 1991, and it was soon imitated by its major competitors. Second-day delivery commands a substantially lower price point than first-day delivery. In 1994, for example, Federal Express made an average of $9.23 on second-day deliveries, compared with $16.37 on priority overnight service.

The express mail operators see deferred services as a way to utilize excess capacity at the margin, thereby boosting revenues and profits. Since many second-day packages can be shipped on the ground, the cost of second-day delivery can more than compensate for the lower price. Still, in some ways the service has been almost too successful. During the mid 1990s the growth rate for deferred services was significantly higher than for priority overnight mail, as many corporations came to the realization that they could live with a second-day service. At Airborne Express, for example, second-

day delivery accounted for 42 percent of total volume in 1996, up from 37 percent in 1995.[28]

Premium Services   Another development has been a move toward a premium service. In 1994, UPS introduced its Early AM service, which guaranteed delivery of packages and letters by 8:30 A.M. in select cities. UPS aimed Early AM at a range of businesses that need documents or materials before the start of the business day. These include hospitals, which are expected to use the service to ship critical drugs and medical devices; architects who need to have their blueprints sent to a construction site; and salespeople. Although demand for the service is predicted to be light, the premium price makes for high profit margins. In 1994, UPS's price for a letter delivered at 10:30 A.M. was $10.75, while it charge $40 for an equivalent Early AM delivery. UPS believes that it can provide the service at little extra cost because most of its planes arrive in their destination cities by 7:30 A.M. Federal Express and Airborne initially declined to follow UPS's lead.[29]

Logistics Services   A further development of some note has been the move by all major operators into third-party logistics services. Since the later half of the 1980s, more and more companies have been relying on air express operations as part of their just-in-time inventory control systems. As a result, the content of packages carried by air express operators has been moving away from letters and documents and toward high-value, low-weight products. By 1994, less than 20 percent of Federal Express's revenues came from documents.[30] To take advantage of this trend, all of the major operators have been moving into logistics services that are designed to assist business customers in their warehousing, distribution, and assembly operations. The emphasis of this business is on helping customers reduce the time involved in their production cycles and gain distribution efficiencies.

In the late 1980s, Federal Express set up a business logistics services (BLS) division. The new division evolved from Federal Express's Parts Bank. The Parts Bank stores critical inventory for clients, most of whom are based in the high-tech electronics and medical industries. On request, Federal Express will ship this inventory to its client's customers. The service saves clients from having to invest in their own distribution systems; it also allows them to achieve economies of scale by making large production runs and then storing the inventory at the Parts Bank.

The BLS division has expanded this service to include some assembly operations and customs brokerage and to assist in achieving just-in-time manufacturing. Thus, for example, one U.S. computer company relies on BLS to deliver electronic subassemblies from the Far East as a key part of its just-in-time system. Federal Express brings the products in on its aircraft, clears them through customs with the help of a broker, and manages truck transportation to the customer's dock.[31]

UPS moved into the logistics business in 1993 when it established UPS Worldwide Logistics, which it positioned as a third-party provider of global supply chain management solutions, including transportation management, warehouse operations, inventory management, documentation for import and export, network optimization, and reverse logistics. UPS's logistics business is based at its Louisville, Kentucky, hub. In 1995 the company announced that it would invest $75 million to expand the scope of this facility, bringing total employment in the facility to 2,200 by the end of 1988.[32]

Airborne Express has also made a significant push into this end of the business. A number of Airborne's corporate accounts utilize a warehousing service called Stock Exchange. As with Federal Express's Parts Bank, clients warehouse critical inventory at Airborne's hub in Wilmington, Ohio, and then ship those items on request to their customers. In addition, Airborne has set up a commerce park on 1,000 acres around its Wilmington hub. The park is aimed at companies that want to outsource logistics to Airborne and can gain special advantages by locating at the company's hub. Not the least of these is the ability to make shipping decisions as late as 2 A.M. Eastern time.

Information Systems

Since the late 1980s, the three major U.S. air express carriers have devoted ever more attention to competing on the basis of information technology. The ability to track a package as it moves through an operator's delivery network has always been an important aspect of competition in an industry where reliability is so highly valued. Given this, all of the major players in the industry have invested heavily in bar code technology, scanners, and computerized tracking systems. More recently, UPS, Federal Express, and Airborne have all invested in Internet-based technology that allows customers to order pickups, print shipping labels, and track deliveries on-line.

Globalization

Perhaps the most important development for the long-run future of the industry has been the increasing globalization of the airfreight industry. The combination of a healthy U.S. economy, strong and expanding East Asian economies, and the move toward ever closer economic integration in Western Europe all offer opportunities for growth in the international air cargo business. Moreover, the increasing globalization of companies in a whole range of industries, from electronics to autos and from fast food to clothing, is beginning to dictate that the air express operators follow suit.

Global manufacturers want to keep inventories at a minimum and deliver just-in-time as a way of keeping down costs and fine-tuning production, which requires speedy supply routes. Thus, some electronics companies will manufacture key components in one location, ship them by air to another for final assembly, and then deliver them by air to a third location for sale. This is particularly true among industries producing small high-value items (for example, electronics, medical equipment, and computer software) that can be economically transported by air—industries for which just-in-time inventory systems are crucial for keeping down costs. It is also true in the fashion industry, where timing is all important. For example, the clothing chain The Limited manufactures clothes in Hong Kong and then ships them by air to the United States to keep from missing out on fashion trends.[33] In addition, an increasing number of wholesalers are beginning to turn to international air express as a way of meeting delivery deadlines.

The emergence of integrated global corporations is also increasing the demand for the global shipment of contracts, confidential papers, computer printouts, and other documents that are far too bulky for fax machines to handle. Major U.S. corporations are increasingly demanding the same kind of service that they receive from air express operators within the United States for their far-flung global operations.

As a consequence of these trends, rapid growth is predicted in the global arena. According to recent forecasts, the market for international air express is expected to grow at around 18 percent annually from 1996 through to 2016.[34] Faced with an increasingly mature market at home, the race is on among the major air cargo operators to build global air and ground transportation networks that will enable them to deliver goods and documents between any two points on the globe within forty-eight hours.

Currently, the company with the most extensive international operations is DHL. As of 1995 DHL enjoyed a 44 percent share of the worldwide market for international air express services (see Table 2).[35] Started in California in 1969 and now based in Brussels, DHL is smaller than many of its rivals, but it has managed to capture as much as an 80 percent share in some markets, such as documents leaving Japan, by concentrating solely on international air express. The strength of DHL was enhanced in mid 1992 when Lufthansa, Japan Airlines, and the Japanese trading company, Nisho Iwai, announced that they intended to invest as much as $500 million for a 57.5 percent stake in DHL. Although Lufthansa and Japan Airlines are primarily known for their passenger flights, they also are among the top five airfreight haulers in the world, both because they carry cargo in the holds of their passenger flights and because they each have a fleet of all-cargo aircraft.[36]

TNT Ltd., a $6 billion Australian conglomerate, is another big player in the international air express market, with courier services from 184 countries as well as package express and mail services. In 1995, its share of the international air express market was 12 percent, down from 18 percent in 1990.[37]

TABLE 2

International Air Express Market, Market Share—1995

Company	Market Share
DHL International	44%
Federal Express	21%
UPS	12%
TNT	12%
Others	11%

Source: Standard & Poor's, "Aerospace and Air Transport," *Industry Surveys*, February 1996.

Among U.S. carriers, Federal Express was first off the blocks in the race to build up a global air express network. Between 1984 and 1989, Federal Express purchased seventeen other companies worldwide in an attempt to build up its global distribution capabilities, culminating in the $880 million purchase of Flying Tiger. The main asset of Flying Tiger was not so much its aircraft, as its landing rights overseas. The Flying Tiger acquisition gave Federal Express service to 103 countries, a combined fleet of 328 aircraft, and revenues of $5.2 billion in fiscal 1989.[38]

However, Federal Express has had to suffer through years of losses in its international operations. Start-up costs were heavy, due in part to the enormous capital investments required to build an integrated air and ground network worldwide. Between 1985 and 1992, Federal Express spent $2.5 billion to build an international presence. In addition, faced with heavy competition, Federal Express found it difficult to generate the international volume required to fly its planes at above break-even capacity on many international routes. Since the demand for outbound service from the United States is greater than the demand for inbound service, planes that would leave New York full often returned half-empty.

Moreover, trade barriers have also proved very damaging to the bottom line. Customs regulations require a great deal of expensive and time-consuming labor, such as checking paperwork and rating package contents for duties. This obviously inhibits the ability of international air cargo carriers to effect express delivery. Federal Express has been particularly irritated by Japanese requirements that each inbound envelope be opened and searched for pornography, a practice that seems to be designed to slow down the company's growth rate in the Japanese market.

Federal Express has also found it extremely difficult to get landing rights in many markets. For example, it took three years to get permission from Japan to make four flights per week from Memphis to Tokyo, a key link in the overseas system. Then in 1988, just three days before the service was due to begin, the Japanese notified Federal that no packages weighing more than 70 pounds could pass through Tokyo. To make matters worse, until 1995 Japan limited Federal's ability to fly on from Tokyo and Osaka to other locations in Asia. The Japanese claimed, with some justification, that due to government regulations, the U.S. air traffic market is difficult for foreign carriers to enter, so they see no urgency to help Federal build a market presence in Japan and elsewhere in Asia.[39]

After heavy financial losses, in 1992 Federal abruptly shifted its international strategy, selling off its expensive European ground network to local carriers in order to concentrate on intercontinental deliveries. Under the new strategy, Federal will rely on a network of local partners to deliver its packages. Also, Federal entered into an alliance with TNT to share space on Federal's daily transatlantic flights. Under the agreement, TNT will fly packages from its hub in Cologne Germany, to Britain, where they will be loaded onto Federal's daily New York flight.[40]

UPS has also moved to build up an international presence. In 1988, UPS bought eight smaller European airfreight companies and Hong Kong's Asian Courier Service, and it announced air service and ground delivery in 175 countries and territories. However, it has not been all smooth sailing for UPS either. UPS had been using Flying Tiger for its Pacific shipments. The acquisition of Flying Tiger by Federal Express left UPS in the difficult situation of shipping its parcels on a competitor's plane. UPS was concerned that it could get its shipments pushed to the back of the aircraft. Since there were few alternative carriers, UPS pushed for authority to run an all-cargo route to Tokyo, but approval was slow in coming. Moreover, "beyond rights" to carry cargo from Tokyo to further destinations (such as Singapore and Hong Kong) were also difficult to gain.

In March 1996, UPS sidestepped years of frustrations associated with building an Asian hub in Tokyo by announcing that it would invest $400 million in a Taiwan hub, which would henceforth be the central node in its Asian network. The decision to invest in an Asian hub followed close on the heels of a 1995 decision by UPS to invest $1.1 billion to build a ground network in Europe. In September 1996, UPS went one step further toward building an international air express service when it announced that it would start a Pan-European next-day delivery service for small packages. UPS hopes that its recent moves will finally push its international operations into the black after eight years of losses.[41]

The other U.S. carrier that is making a determined push overseas is Airborne Express. However, right from the start Airborne's strategy differs from that of Federal Express and UPS insofar as it decided not to invest in its own international air-

fleet and ground operations. Airborne's strategy has two aspects. First, it will continue to fly its own planes in the United States but book space on other air carriers for shipments going overseas. Second, it has been looking for strategic alliances with foreign companies that would give it market access and ground operations overseas. In 1989, the company announced an alliance with Mitsui & Co., a $125 billion-a-year Japanese trading and finance firm, and Tonami Transportation Co., operators of a ground-based express delivery service in Japan called Panther Express. The deal calls for Mitsui to purchase $40 million worth of Airborne's stock and to provide $100 million in aircraft financing over the next five years and for the partners to collaborate in building volume in the lucrative Japan-U.S. air express market. Non-Japanese firms currently only handle 15 percent of the air shipments going in and out of Japan, but now that Mitsui owns part of Airborne, the Seattle-based company is counting on getting the inside track on the other 85 percent of the market.[42]

Endnotes

1. Standard & Poor's, "Aerospace and Air Transport," *Industry Surveys* (February 1996).
2. Ibid.
3. Ibid.
4. C. H. Lovelock, "Federal Express (B)," *Harvard Business School Case* No. 579-040, 1978.
5. Standard & Poor's, "Aerospace and Air Transport," *Industry Surveys* (January 1981).
6. Lovelock, "Federal Express (B)."
7. Standard & Poor's, "Aerospace and Air Transport," *Industry Surveys* (January 1981).
8. Ibid.
9. Ibid.
10. Standard & Poor's, "Aerospace and Air Transport," *Industry Surveys* (January 1984).
11. C. Hall, "High Fliers," *Marketing and Media Decisions,* August 1986, p. 138.
12. Standard & Poor's, "Aerospace and Air Transport," *Industry Surveys* (January 1984).
13. Standard & Poor's, "Aerospace and Air Transport," *Industry Surveys* (December 1984).
14. B. Dumaine, "Turbulence Hits the Air Couriers," *Fortune,* July 21, 1986, pp. 101–106.
15. Ibid.
16. Standard & Poor's, "Aerospace and Air Transport," *Industry Surveys* (May 1989).
17. "Are Faxes Putting the Whammy on Air Express? This Study Says No," *Distribution* (January 1989), 22.
18. C. Hawkins, "Purolator: Still No Overnight Success," *Business Week,* June 16, 1986, pp. 76–78.
19. J. O'C. Hamilton, "Emery Is One Heavy Load for Consolidated Freightways," *Business Week,* March 26, 1990, pp. 62–64.

20. Standard & Poor's "Aerospace and Air Transport," *Industry Surveys* (February 1996).

21. "Hold That Tiger: FedEx Is Now World Heavyweight," *Purchasing,* September 14, 1989, pp. 41–42.

22. Standard & Poor's, "Aerospace and Air Transport," *Industry Surveys* (April 1988).

23. R. G. Blumenthal, "UPS Move to Lift Rates Could Spur Increases by Rivals," *Wall Street Journal,* February 13, 1990, pp. B1, B4.

24. Standard & Poor's, "Aerospace and Air Transport," *Industry Surveys* (February 1996).

25. David Greising, "Watch Out for Flying Packages," *Business Week,* November 1994, p. 40.

26. "UPS to Raise Its Rates for Packages," *Wall Street Journal,* January 9, 1995, p. C22.

27. R. Frank, "Federal Express Grapples with Changes in U.S. Market," *Wall Street Journal,* July 5, 1994, p. B6.

28. M. Royce, "Airborne Freight," *Value Line Investment Survey,* September 20, 1996.

29. R. Frank, "UPS Planning Earlier Delivery," *Wall Street Journal,* September 29, 1994, p. A4.

30. Frank, "Federal Express Grapples with Changes in U.S. Market."

31. P. Bradley, "Good Things Come in Small Packages," *Purchasing,* November 9, 1989, pp. 58–64.

32. Company press releases (http://www.ups.com/news/).

33. J. M. Feldman, "The Coming of Age of International Air Freight," *Air Transport World,* June 1989, pp. 31–33.

34. Standard & Poor's, "Aerospace and Air Transport," *Industry Surveys* (February 1996).

35. Ibid.

36. P. Greiff, "Lufthansa, JAL, and a Trading Firm Acquire a Majority Stake in DHL," *Wall Street Journal,* August 24, 1992, p. A5.

37. Standard & Poor's, "Aerospace and Air Transport," *Industry Surveys* (February 1996).

38. "Hold That Tiger."

39. D. Blackmon, "FedEx Swings from Confidence Abroad to a Tightrope," *Wall Street Journal,* March 15, 1996, p. B4.

40. D. Pearl, "Federal Express Plans to Trim Assets in Europe," *Wall Street Journal,* March 17, 1992, p. A3.

41. Company press releases (http://www.ups.com/news/).

42. Byron Acohido, "Expansion Express," *Seattle Times,* June 30, 1990, pp. E1, E6.

CASE 20

Airborne Express

This case was prepared by Charles W. L. Hill of the University of Washington.

INTRODUCTION

Airborne Freight, which operates under the name Airborne Express, is an integrated air express transportation company, providing next-morning delivery of small packages (less than 70 pounds) and documents throughout the United States. The company owns and operates an airline and a fleet of ground-transportation vehicles to provide complete door-to-door service. It is also an airfreight forwarder, moving shipments of any size on a worldwide basis. As of 1996 Airborne Express held third place in the U.S. air express industry, with 9 percent of the market. Its main domestic competitors are Federal Express, which has 35 percent of the market; United Parcel Service (UPS), which has 24 percent of the market; and Consolidated Freightways (CF) and the U.S. Postal Service, each of which holds a 4 percent market share.[1]

The evolution of the air express industry and the state of competition in the industry are discussed in the preceding case, "The Evolution of the Air Express Industry." This case focuses on the operating structure, competitive strategy, organizational structure, and cultures of Airborne Express.

HISTORY OF AIRBORNE EXPRESS

Airborne Express was originally known as Pacific Air Freight when it was founded in Seattle at the close of World War II by Holt W. Webster, a former

Army Air Corps officer. (See Table 1 for a listing of major milestones in the history of Airborne Express.) The company was merged with Airborne Freight Corporation of California in 1968, taking the name of the California company but retaining management direction by the former officers of Pacific Air Freight. Airborne was initially an exclusive airfreight forwarder. Freight forwarders such as Airborne arrange for the transportation of air cargo between any two destinations. They purchase cargo space from the airlines and retail this in small amounts. They deal primarily with small customers, providing pickup and delivery services in most cities, either in their own trucks or through contract agents.

Following the 1977 deregulation of the airline industry, Airborne entered the air express industry by leasing the airplanes and pilots of Midwest Charter, a small airline operating out of its own airport in Wilmington, Ohio. However, Airborne quickly became dissatisfied with the limited amount of control it was able to exercise over Midwest, which made it very difficult to achieve the kind of tight coordination and control of logistics that was necessary to become a successful air express operator. Instead of continuing to lease Midwest's planes and facility, in 1980 Airborne decided to buy "the entire bucket of slop; company, planes, pilots, airport and all."

Among other things, the Midwest acquisition put Airborne in the position of being the only industry participant to own an airport. Airborne immediately began the job of developing a hub-and-spoke system capable of supporting a nationwide distribution system. An efficient sorting facility was established at the Wilmington hub. Airborne upgraded Midwest's fleet of prop and propjet aircraft, building a modern fleet of DC-8s, DC-9s, and YS-11

The case is intended as a basis for classroom discussion rather than as an illustration of either effective or ineffective handling of the situation. This case was prepared by Charles W. L. Hill, University of Washington. Used by permission.

TABLE I

Fifty Years of Airborne Express

1946	Airborne Flower Traffic Association of California founded to fly fresh flowers from Hawaii to the mainland.
1968	Airborne of California and Pacific Air Freight of Seattle merge to form Airborne Freight Corporation, with headquarters in Seattle, Washington.
1979–1981	Airborne Express is born. Airborne purchases Midwest Air Charter and then purchases Clinton County Air Force Base in Wilmington, Ohio, becoming the only carrier to own and operate an airport. The package sort center opens, creating the hub for the hub-and-spoke system.
1984–1986	Airborne is first carrier to establish a privately operated Foreign Trade Zone in an air industrial park.
1987	Airborne opens the Airborne Stock Exchange, a third-party inventory management and distribution service. New service provided to and from more than 8,000 Canadian locations.
1988	Airborne is first air express carrier to provide same-day delivery through the purchase of Sky Courier.
1990	Airborne named at the International Cargo Forum and Exposition as the carrier with the most outstanding integrated cargo system over the previous two years.
1991	Airborne is first transportation company to receive Volvo-Flying Motors' Excellent Performance Award. Ranked "most effective user of information systems in the U.S. transportation industry" by Computerworld. Receives "Spread the Word!" electronic data interchange (EDI) award for the largest number of EDI users worldwide in the air express and freight-forwarding industry.
1992	Airborne introduces the first prepurchased Express Letters and Packs with Flight-Ready SM.
1993	Airborne introduces Advanced Logistics Services (ALS), a new subsidiary providing outsourced warehousing and distribution services. IBM consolidates its international shipping operation with Airborne.
1994	Airborne is first express carrier to introduce ocean-shipping services with opening of Ocean Service Division. Advanced Logistics services (ALS) establishes the first new film distribution program for the movie industry in fifty years. Airborne is the first to provide on-line communication to Vietnam.
1995	Airborne Alliance Group, a consortium of transportation, logistics, third-party customer service operations, and high-tech companies providing value-added services, is formed. Airborne opens a second runway at its hub, the largest privately owned airport in the United States. Expanded fleet with acquisition of Boeing 767-200 aircraft.
1996	Airborne Express celebrates fifty years of providing distribution solutions to businesses.

aircraft. These planes left major cities every evening, flying down the spokes carrying letters and packages to the central sort facility in Wilmington, Ohio. There the letters and packages were unloaded, sorted according to their final destination, and then reloaded and flown to their final destination for delivery before noon the next day.

During the late 1970s and early 1980s, dramatic growth in the industry attracted many competitors. (See Figure 1 for data on Airborne's domestic shipment growth.) As a consequence, despite a high-growth rate, price competition became intense, forcing a number of companies to the sidelines by the late 1980s. (See Figure 2 for data on revenues per shipment.) Airborne was able to survive this period by pursuing a number of strategies that increased productivity and drove costs down to the

lowest levels in the industry. (See Figure 3 data on operating costs per shipment.) As a consequence, by the late 1980s Airborne had pulled away from a pack of struggling competitors to become one of the top three companies in the industry, a position it still held in the mid 1990s.

AIR EXPRESS OPERATIONS

The Domestic Delivery Network

As of 1996, Airborne Express had 265 ground stations within the United States. The stations are essentially the ends of the spokes in Airborne's hub-and-spoke system (the hub being Wilmington, Ohio—see Figure 4). In each station there are about 50 to 55 or so drivers plus staff. About 80

FIGURE 1

Shipment Growth,
1984–1995

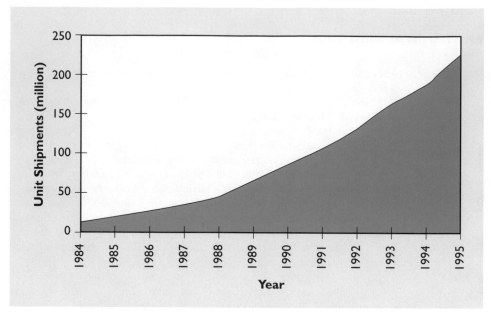

Source: Airborne Express

FIGURE 2

Unit Revenues per
Domestic Shipment,
1984–1995

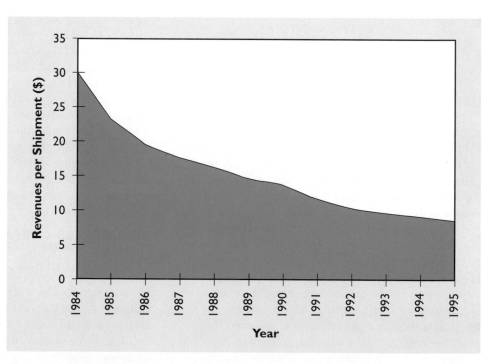

Source: Airborne Express

FIGURE 3

Operating Costs per
Shipment

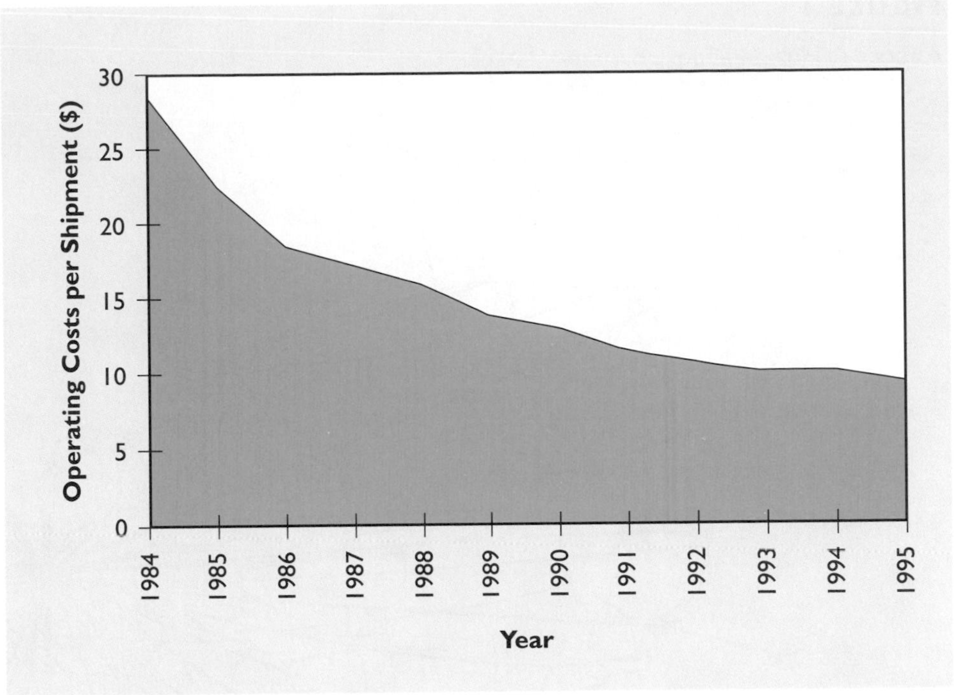

Source: Airborne Express

percent of Airborne's 19,500 full-time and part-time employees are found at this level. The stations are the basic units in Airborne's delivery organization. Their primary task is to ferry packages between clients and the local air terminal. Airborne utilizes approximately 12,800 radio-dispatch delivery vans and trucks to transport packages, of which 4,500 are owned by the company. Independent contractors under contract with the company provide the balance of the company's pickup and delivery services.

Airborne's drivers make their last round of major clients at 5 P.M. The drivers either collect packages directly from clients or from one of the company's 9,800 plus drop boxes. The drop boxes are placed at strategic locations, such as in the lobbies of major commercial buildings. To give clients a little more time, in most major cities there are also a few central drop boxes that are not emptied until 6 P.M. If a client needs still more time, so long as the package can be delivered to the airport by 7 P.M., it will make the evening flight.

When a driver picks up a package, he or she will read a bar code that is attached to the package with a hand-held scanner. This information is then fed directly into Airborne's proprietary FOCUS (Freight, On-Line Control and Update System) computer system. The FOCUS system, which has global coverage, records shipment status at key points in the life cycle of a shipment. Thus, a customer can call Airborne on a twenty-four-hour basis to find out where in Airborne's system a package is. FOCUS also allows a customer direct access to shipment information through the Internet. All a customer needs to do is access Airborne's Web site and key the code number assigned to a package, and the FOCUS system will tell the customer where in Airborne's system the package is currently.

When the driver has completed the pickup route, she or he takes the load to Airborne's loading docks at the local airport. (Airborne serves all ninety-nine major metropolitan airports in the United States.) There the packages are loaded into C-containers (discussed later in this case study). Several C-containers are then towed by hand or by tractor to a waiting aircraft, where they are loaded onto a conveyer belt and in turn pass through the passenger door of the aircraft. Before long, the aircraft is loaded and takes off. It will either fly directly to the company's hub at Wilmington, or it

FIGURE 4

Airborne's Hub-and-Spoke System

may make one or two stops along the way to pick up more packages.

Sometime between midnight and 2 A.M., most of the aircraft will have landed at Wilmington. An old strategic air command base, Wilmington lies within a 600-mile radius (an overnight drive or one-hour flying time) of 60 percent of the U.S. population. Wilmington has the advantage of a good-weather record. In all the years that Airborne has operated at Wilmington, air operations have been "fogged out" on only a handful of days. In 1995, Airborne opened a second runway at Wilmington. Developed at a cost of $60 million, the second runway makes Wilmington the largest privately owned airport in the country. The runway expansion was part of a $120 million upgrade of the Wilmington sorting facility.

After arrival at Wilmington, the plane taxis down the runway and parks alongside a group of aircraft that are already disgorging their load of C-containers. Within minutes the C-containers are unloaded from the plane down a conveyer belt and towed to the sort facility by a tractor. The sort facility has the capacity to handle 980,000 packages per night. During 1995, the facility handled an average of 835,000 packages a night. The bar codes on the packages are read, and then the packages are directed through a labyrinth of conveyer belts and sorted according to final destination. The sorting is partly done by hand and partly automated. At the end of this process, packages are grouped together by final destination and loaded into a C-container. An aircraft bound for the final destination is then loaded with C-containers, and by 5 A.M. most aircraft have taken off.

Upon arrival at the final destination, the plane is unloaded and the packages sorted according to their delivery points within the surrounding area.

Airborne couriers then take the packages on the final leg of their journey. Packages have a 75 percent probability of being delivered to clients by 10:30 A.M., and a 98 percent probability of being delivered by noon.

Regional Trucking Hubs

Although about 75 percent of packages are transported by air and pass through Wilmington, Airborne has also established ten regional trucking hubs that deal with the remaining 25 percent of the company's domestic volume. These hubs sort shipments that originate and have a destination within approximately a 300-mile radius. The first one opened was in Allentown, Pennsylvania, which is centrally located on the East Coast. This hub handles packages that are being transported between points within the Washington, D.C., to Boston area. Instead of transporting packages by air, packages to be transported within this area are sorted by the drivers at pickup and delivered from the driver's home station by scheduled truck runs to the Allentown hub. There they are sorted according to destination and taken to the appropriate station on another scheduled truck run for final delivery.

One advantage of ground-based transportation through trucking hubs is that operating costs are much lower than for air transportation. The average cost of a package transported by air is more than five times greater than the cost of a package transported on the ground. However, this cost differential is transparent to the customer, who assumes that all packages are flown. Thus, Airborne can charge the same price for ground-transported packages as for air-transported packages, but the former yields a much higher return. The trucking hubs also have the advantage of taking some of the load off the Wilmington sorting facility, which is currently operating at about 90 percent capacity.

International Operations

In addition to its domestic express operations, Airborne is also an international company, providing service to more than 200 companies worldwide. International operations currently account for about 16 percent of total revenues, although this share is expected to increase with the forecasted growth in the international air express industry. (See "The Evolution of the Air Express Industry, 1973–1996," Case 19.)

Airborne offers two international products: freight products and express products. Freight products are commercial-sized, larger-unit shipments. This service provides door-to-airport service. Goods are picked up domestically from the customer and then shipped to the destination airport. A consignee or an agent of the consignee gets the paperwork and must clear the shipment through customs. Express packages are small packages, documents, and letters. This is a door-to-door service, and all shipments are cleared through customs by Airborne.

Airborne does not fly any of its own aircraft overseas. Rather, it contracts for space on all-cargo airlines or in the cargo holds of passenger airlines. Airborne owns facilities overseas in Japan, Taiwan, Hong Kong, Singapore, Australia, New Zealand, and London. These function in a manner similar to Airborne's domestic stations. (That is, they have their own trucks and drivers and are hooked into the FOCUS tracking system.) The majority of foreign distribution, however, is carried out by foreign agents. Foreign agents are large, local, well-established surface delivery companies. Airborne has entered into a number of exclusive strategic alliances with large foreign agents. These include alliances with Purolator (Canada) and Mitsui (Japan). The rationale for entering strategic alliances, along with Airborne's approach to global expansion, is discussed in greater detail later in this case.

Another aspect of Airborne's international operations has been the creation at its Wilmington hub of the only privately certified Foreign Trade Zone (FTZ) in the United States. While in an FTZ, merchandise is tax free and no customs duty is paid on it until it leaves. Thus, a foreign-based company may store critical inventory in the FTZ and have Airborne deliver it just-in-time to U.S. customers. This allows the foreign company to hold inventory in the United States without having to pay customs duty on it until the need arises.

Aircraft Purchase and Maintenance

As of 1996, Airborne Express owned a fleet of 105 aircraft, including 33 DC-8s, 61 DC-9s, and 11 YS-11 turboprop aircraft. In addition, approximately 70 smaller aircraft are chartered nightly to connect smaller cities with company aircraft that then operate to and from the Wilmington hub. To keep down capital expenditures, Airborne has traditionally purchased only used planes. Airborne converts the planes to suit its specifications at a maintenance facility based at its Wilmington hub. Once it gets a plane, Airborne typically guts the interior and installs state-of-the-art electronics and avionics equipment. The company's philosophy is to get all of the upgrades that it can into an aircraft. Although this can cost a lot up front, there is a payback in terms of increased aircraft reliability and a reduction in service downtime. Airborne also standardizes cockpits as much as possible. This makes it easier for crews to switch from one aircraft to another if the need arises. According to the company, the total purchase and modification of a secondhand DC-9 costs about $10 million, compared with an equivalent new plane cost of $40 million. An additional factor reducing operating costs is that Airborne's DC-9 and YS-11 aircraft require only a two-person cockpit crew, as opposed to the three-person crews required in most Federal Express and UPS aircraft.

After conversion, Airborne strives to keep aircraft maintenance costs down by carrying out virtually all of its own fleet repairs. (It is the only all-cargo carrier to do so.) The Wilmington maintenance facility can handle everything except major engine repairs and has the capability to machine critical aircraft parts if needed. The company sees this in-house facility as a major source of cost savings. It estimates that maintenance labor costs run $16 per hour versus an industry standard of $65 per hour for subcontracted labor.

In December 1995, Airborne announced a deal to purchase twelve used Boeing 767-200 aircraft between the years 1997 and 2000, and it announced plans to purchase a further ten to fifteen used 767-200s between the years 2000 and 2004. These will be the first wide-bodied aircraft in Airborne's fleet. The cost of introducing the first twelve aircraft will be about $290 million, and the additional aircraft will cost a further $360 million. The shift to wide-bodied aircraft was prompted by an internal study, which concluded that with growing volume, wide-bodied aircraft would lead to greater operating efficiencies.

C-Containers

C-containers are uniquely shaped 60-cubic-foot containers, developed by Airborne Express in 1985 at a cost of $3.5 million. They are designed to fit through the passenger doors of DC-8 and DC-9 aircraft. They replaced the much larger A-containers,

widely used in the air cargo business. At six times the size of a C-container, A-containers can be loaded only through specially built cargo doors and require specialized loading equipment. The loading equipment required for C-containers is a modified belt loader, similar to that used for loading baggage onto a plane, and about 80 percent less expensive than the equipment needed to load A-containers. The use of C-containers also means that Airborne does not have to bear the $1 million per plane cost required to install cargo doors that will take A-containers. The C-containers are shaped to allow maximum utilization of the planes' interior loading space. Fifty of the containers fit into a converted DC-9, and about 83 fit into a DC-8-62. Moreover, a C-container filled with packages can be moved by a single person, making them easy to load and unload. Airborne Express has taken out a patent on the design of the C-containers.

Information Systems

Airborne utilizes three information systems to help it boost productivity and improve customer service. The first of these systems is referred to as the LIBRA II system. LIBRA II equipment, which includes a metering device and PC computer software, is installed in the mailroom of clients. With minimum data entry, the metering device weighs the package, calculates the shipping charges, generates the shipping labels, and provides a daily shipping report. As of early 1996, the system was in use at approximately 8,200 domestic customer locations. Its use not only benefits the customers but also lowers Airborne's operating costs since LIBRA II shipment data are transferred into Airborne's FOCUS shipment tracking system automatically, thereby avoiding duplicate data entry.

FOCUS is the second of Airborne's three main information systems. As discussed earlier, the FOCUS system is essentially a worldwide tracking system. The bar codes on each package are read at various points (for example, at pickup, at sorting in Wilmington, at arrival, and so forth) using handheld scanners, and this information is fed into Airborne's computer system. Using FOCUS, Airborne can track the progress of a shipment through its national and international logistics system. The major benefit is in terms of customer service. Through an Internet link, Airborne's customers can track their own shipment through Airborne's system on a twenty-four-hour basis.

For its highest-volume corporate customers, Airborne has developed Customer Linkage, an electronic data interchange (EDI) program and the third information system. The EDI system is designed to eliminate the flow of paperwork between Airborne and its major clients. The EDI system allows customers to create shipping documentation at the same time they are entering orders for their goods. At the end of each day, shipping activities are transmitted electronically to Airborne's FOCUS system, where they are captured for shipment tracking and billing. Customer Linkage benefits the customer by eliminating repetitive data entry and paperwork. It also lowers the company's operating costs by eliminating manual data entry. (In essence, both LIBRA II and Customer Linkage push off a lot of the data-entry work into the hands of customers.) The EDI system includes electronic invoicing and payment remittance processing. Airborne also offers its customers a program known as Quicklink, which significantly reduces the programming time required by customers to take advantage of linkage benefits.

Logistics Services

Although small-package express mail remains Airborne's main business, through its Advanced Logistics Services Corp. (ALS) subsidiary the company is increasingly promoting a range of third-party logistics services. These services provide customers with the ability to maintain inventories in a 1-million-square-foot "stock exchange" facility located at Airborne's Wilmington hub or at sixty smaller "stock exchange" facilities around the country. The inventory can be managed either by the company or by the customer's personnel. Inventory stored at Wilmington can be delivered utilizing either Airborne's airline system or, if required, commercial airlines on a next-flight-out basis. ALS's central print computer program allows information on inventories to be sent electronically to customers' computers located at Wilmington, where Airborne's personnel monitor printed output and ship inventories according to customers' instructions.

For example, consider the case of Data Products Corp., a producer of computer printers. Data Products takes advantage of low labor costs to carry out significant assembly operations in Hong Kong. Many of the primary component parts for its printers, however, such as microprocessors, are manufactured in the United States and have to be shipped to Hong Kong. The finished product is then shipped back to the United States for sale. In setting up a global manufacturing system, Data Products had a decision to make: either consolidate the parts from its hundreds of suppliers in-house and then arrange for shipment to Hong Kong, or contract out to someone who could handle the whole logistics process. Data Products decided to contract out, and they picked Airborne Express to consolidate the component parts and arrange for shipments.

Airborne controls the consolidation and movement of component parts from the component part suppliers through to the Hong Kong assembly operation in such a way as to minimize inventory-holding costs. The key feature of Airborne's service is that all of Data Products' materials are collected at Airborne's facility at Los Angeles International Airport. Data Products' Hong Kong assembly plants can then tell Airborne what parts to ship by air as and when they are needed. Airborne is thus able to provide inventory control for Data Products. In addition, by scheduling deliveries so that year-round traffic between Los Angeles and Hong Kong can be guaranteed, Airborne is able to negotiate a better air rate from Japan Air Lines (JAL) for the transportation of component parts.

STRATEGY

Positioning Strategy

In the early 1980s Airborne Express tried hard to compete head-to-head with Federal Express. This included an attempt to establish broad market coverage, including both frequent and infrequent users. Frequent users are those that generate more than $20,000 of business per month, or more than 1,000 shipments per month. Infrequent users generate less than $20,000 per month, or less than 1,000 shipments per month.

To build broad market coverage, Airborne followed Federal Express's lead of funding a television advertising campaign designed to build consumer awareness. However, by the mid 1980s Airborne decided that this was an expensive way of building market share. The advertising campaign bought recognition but little penetration. One of the principal problems was that it was expensive to serve infrequent users. Infrequent users demanded the same level of service as frequent users, but Airborne would typically only get one shipment per pickup with an infrequent user, compared with ten or more shipments per pickup with a frequent user, so far more pickups were required to generate the same volume of business. Given the extremely competitive nature of the industry at this time, such an inefficient utilization of capacity was of great concern to Airborne.

Consequently, in the mid 1980s Airborne decided to become a niche player in the industry and focused on serving the needs of high-volume corporate accounts. The company slashed its advertising expenditure, pulling the plug on its TV ad campaign, and invested more resources in building a direct sales force, which is now 300 strong. By focusing upon high-volume corporate accounts, Airborne was able to establish scheduled pickup routes and use its ground capacity more efficiently. This enabled the company to achieve significant reductions in its unit cost structure. Partly due to this factor, Airborne executives reckon that their cost structure is as much as $3 per shipment less than that of their primary competitor, Federal Express.

Of course, there is a downside to this strategy. High-volume corporate customers have a great deal more bargaining power than infrequent users, so they can and do demand substantial discounts. For example, in March 1987 Airborne achieved a major coup when it won an exclusive three-year contract to handle all of IBM's express packages weighing less than 150 pounds. However, to win the IBM account, Airborne had to offer rates up to 84 percent below Federal Express's list prices. Nevertheless, so far the strategy seems to have worked for Airborne. As of 1995, approximately 80 percent of Airborne's revenues have come from corporate accounts, most of them secured through competitive bidding. The concentrated volume that this business represents has helped Airborne to drive down costs.

Delivery Time, Reliability, and Flexibility

A further feature of Airborne's strategy was the decision not to try to compete with Federal Express on delivery time. Federal Express and UPS currently guarantee delivery by 10:30 A.M. Airborne guarantees delivery by midday, although it offers a 10:30 guarantee to some very large corporate customers. Guaranteeing delivery by 10:30 A.M. would mean stretching Airborne's already tight scheduling system to the limit. To meet its 10:30 A.M. deadline, Federal Express has to operate with a deadline for the previous day's pickups of 6:30 P.M. Airborne can

afford to be a little more flexible and can arrange pickups at 6:00 P.M. if that suits a corporate client's particular needs. Later pickups clearly benefit the shipper, who is, after all, the paying party.

In addition, Airborne executives feel that a guaranteed 10:30 A.M. delivery is unnecessary. The extra hour and a half does not make a great deal of difference to most clients, and they are willing to accept the extra time in exchange for lower prices. In addition, Airborne stresses the reliability of its delivery schedules. As one executive put it, "a package delivered consistently at 11:15 A.M. is as good as delivery at 10:30 A.M." This reliability is enhanced by Airborne's ability to provide shipment tracking through its FOCUS system.

Deferred Services

With a slowdown in the growth rate of the express mail market toward the end of the 1980s, in 1990 Airborne decided to enter the deferred-delivery business with its Select Delivery Service (SDS) product. The SDS service provides for next-afternoon or second-day delivery. Packages weighing 5 pounds or less are generally delivered on a next-afternoon basis, with packages of more than 5 pounds being delivered on a second-day basis. SDS shipment comprised approximately 42 percent of total domestic shipments in 1995. They are priced lower than overnight express products, reflecting the less time-sensitive nature of these deliveries. The company utilizes any spare capacity on its express flights to carry SDS shipments. In addition, Airborne uses other carriers, such as passenger carriers with spare cargo capacity in the bellies of their planes, to carry less urgent SDS shipments.

Early in 1996, Airborne began to phase in two new services to replace its SDS service. Next Afternoon Service is available for shipments weighing 5 pounds or less, and Second Day Service is offered for shipments of all weights.

International Strategy

One of the major strategic challenges currently facing Airborne (along with the other express mail carriers) is how best to establish an international service that is comparable to its domestic service. Many of Airborne's major corporate clients are becoming ever more global in their own strategic orientation. As this occurs, they are increasingly demanding a compatible express mail service. In addition, the rise of companies with globally dispersed manufacturing operations that rely on just-in-time delivery systems to keep their inventory holding costs down has created a demand for a global air express service that can transport critical inventory between operations located in different parts of the world. (Consider the example of Data Products discussed earlier in this case study.)

The initial response of Federal Express and UPS to this challenge was to undertake massive capital investment to establish international airlift capability and international ground operations based on the U.S. model. (For details, see "The Evolution of the Air Express Industry," Case 19). Their rationale was that a wholly owned global delivery network was necessary to establish the tight control, coordination, and scheduling required for a successful air express operation. More recently, however, Federal Express pulled out of its European ground operations, while continuing to fly its own aircraft overseas.

Airborne has decided on a quite different strategy. In part born of financial necessity (Airborne lacks the capital necessary to imitate Federal Express and UPS), Airborne has decided to pursue what it refers to as a *variable cost strategy.* This involves two main elements: (1) the utilization of international airlift on existing air cargo operators and passenger aircraft to get its packages overseas, and (2) entry into strategic alliances with foreign companies that already have established ground delivery networks. In these two ways, Airborne hopes to be able to establish global coverage without having to undertake the kind of capital investments that Federal Express and UPS have made.

Airborne executives defend their decision to continue to purchase space on international flights rather than fly their own aircraft overseas by making a number of points. First, they point out that Airborne's international business is currently 70 percent outbound and 30 percent inbound. If Airborne were to fly its own aircraft overseas, this would mean flying them back half-empty. Second, on many routes Airborne simply doesn't yet have the volume necessary to justify flying its own planes. Third, currently national air carriers are giving Airborne good prices. If Airborne began to fly directly overseas, the company would be seen as a competitor and might no longer be given price breaks. Fourth, getting international airlift space is currently not a problem. While space can be limited in the third and fourth quarters of the year, Airborne is such a big customer that it usually has few problems getting lift.

On the other hand, the long-term viability of this strategy is questionable, given the rapid evolution in the international air express business. Flying Tiger was once one of Airborne's major providers of international lift. However, following the purchase of Flying Tiger by Federal Express, Airborne has reduced its business with Flying Tiger. (The business Airborne gave to Flying Tiger dropped from $27 million in 1988 to $14 million in 1989.) Apart from concerns about giving business to a competitor, Airborne fears that its packages will be "pushed to the back of the plane" whenever Flying Tiger has problems of capacity overload.

A further, potentially adverse, development occurred in June 1990, when the trio of JAL, Lufthansa, and the Japanese trading company Nisho Iwai purchased a 57.5 percent stake in DHL, a major international delivery operator with an extensive ground network in many industrialized nations, and announced intentions to invest $500 million in DHL. Since JAL has been a major carrier of Airborne's packages around the Pacific Rim, this could have negative implications for the company.

With regard to strategic alliances, Airborne currently has major alliances with Purolator (Canada) and Mitsui (Japan). The Purolator alliance dates back to October 1987. Purolator is primarily a ground service with 2,200 delivery vehicles, 5,600 employees, and delivery to 8,000 points within Canada. Airborne flies directly to a number of Canadian destinations, while Purolator handles the ground deliveries.

The alliance with Mitsui was announced in December 1989. Mitsui is one of the world's leading trading companies. Together with Tonami Transportation Co., Mitsui owns Panther Express, one of the top five express carriers in Japan and a company with a substantial ground network. The deal calls for the establishment of a joint venture between Airborne, Mitsui, and Tonami. To be known as Airborne Express Japan, the joint venture will combine Airborne's existing Japanese operations with Panther Express. Airborne will handle all of the shipments to and from Japan. The joint venture will be owned 40 percent by Airborne, 40 percent by Mitsui, and 20 percent by Tonami. The agreement specifies that board decisions must be made by consensus between the three partners. A majority of two cannot outvote the third. In addition, the deal calls for Mitsui to invest $40 million in Airborne Express through the purchase of a new issue of nonvoting 6.9 percent cumulative convertible preferred stock and a commitment to Airborne from Mitsui of up to $100 million for aircraft financing. There is no doubt that Airborne executives see the Mitsui deal as a major coup, both financially and in terms of market penetration into the huge Japanese market. The primary advantage claimed by Airborne executives for expanding via strategic alliances is that the company gets an established ground-based delivery network overseas without having to make capital investments.

ORGANIZATION

The Top-Management Team

The organizational structure of Airborne Express is flat (to keep lines of communication short) and is arranged on a functional basis. The top level is shown in Figure 5. Robert Cline, the CEO, and

Robert Brazier, the president and COO, have been with the company since the early 1960s. Carl Donaway bears primary responsibility for the ABX Air, Inc., subsidiary. He specializes in airline operations, which includes managing the Wilmington hub, the package sorting facility, and all aircraft and flight maintenance operations. Working under him are 2,800 employees—300 pilots, and 2,500 airport, aircraft maintenance, and sorting workers.

Roy Liljebeck's responsibilities center on the finance and administrative functions. His departments include treasurer, controller, accounting, purchasing, information systems, data processing, and archiving. Of the approximately 1,100 people working at headquarters, 700 to 800 fall within these areas.

Richard Goodwin handles all human resource functions. Since there are no field personnel officers (except at Wilmington), everything related to employment is handled through the Seattle head office.

FIGURE 5

Airborne's Organizational Structure

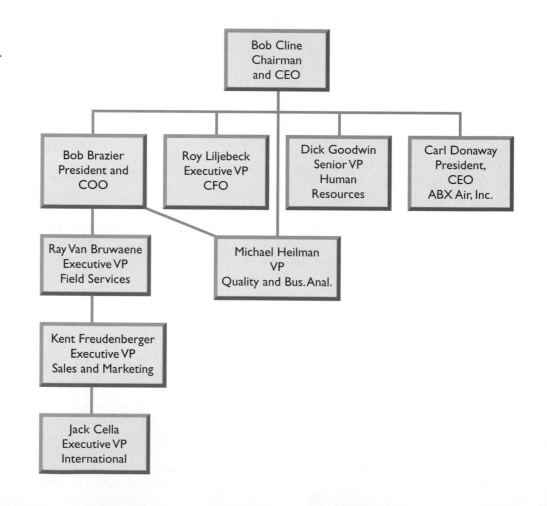

This includes recruiting, hiring, compensation and benefits, training, and employee communications.

The following three senior managers report directly to Brazier: Kent Freudenberger, executive vice president for marketing and sales; Ray van Bruwaene, executive vice president for field services; and Jack Cella, executive vice president for international.

Freudenberg's concern is marketing the express product (not freight), both nationally and internationally, and making direct pricing decisions. The 300-person direct sales force is responsible to Freudenberger.

Van Bruwaene deals with operations, that is, the service that Airborne sells. This includes picking up the package, getting it to Wilmington, and delivery to the final destination. He is responsible for managing the delivery network and for the associated functions such as customer service and data entry in the field. The stations, along with the drivers and station staff, are under Van Bruwaene's control.

Cella deals with international issues such as joint venture agreements, marketing agreements, agent and broker relations, pricing decisions, and so forth.

A striking feature of this top-management team is its longevity of service. The most recent arrival has been with Airborne for twenty-one years, while many of the top officers have spent their entire careers with the company. Despite their long service, several of the senior managers still have five to ten years to go before retirement. The advantage of a long-serving top-management team is that the members know each other well, having established a solid working relationship over a long number of years. Among other things, this consistency means that many of the interpersonal and communications difficulties that can plague top-management teams have been worked out long ago. One potential disadvantage is that the top-management team could become somewhat inbred and myopic. Another is that several promising younger managers have been frustrated by the lack of promotion opportunities at Airborne and have moved on to other organizations.

Decision Making, Control, and Culture

The philosophy at Airborne is to keep the organizational structure as flat as possible, to shorten lines of communication and allow for a free flow of ideas within the managerial hierarchy. The top managers generally feel that they are open to ideas suggested by lower-level managers. At the same time, the decision-making process is fairly centralized. The view is that interdependence between functions makes centralized decision making necessary. To quote one executive, "Coordination is the essence of this business. We need centralized decision making in order to achieve this."

Control at Airborne Express is geared toward boosting productivity, lowering costs, and maintaining a reliable high-quality service. This is achieved through a combination of budgetary controls, pay-for-performance incentive systems, and a corporate culture that continually stresses key values.

For example, consider the procedure used to control stations (which contain about 80 percent of all employees). Station operations are reviewed on a quarterly basis using a budgetary process. Control and evaluation of station effectiveness stress four categories. The first is service, measured by the time between pickup and delivery. The goal is to achieve 95 to 97 percent of all deliveries before noon. The second category is productivity, measured by total shipments per employee hour. The third category is controllable cost, and the fourth is station profitability. Goals for each of these categories are determined each quarter in a bottom-up procedure that involves station managers in the goal-setting process. These goals are then linked to an incentive pay system whereby station managers can earn up to 10 percent of their quarterly salary just by meeting their goals, with no maximum on the upside if they go over the goals.

The direct-sales force also has an incentive pay system. The target pay structure for the sales organization is 70 percent base pay and a 30 percent commission. There is, however, no cap on the commissions for salespeople. So in theory, there is no limit to what a salesperson can earn. There are also contests that are designed to boost performance. For example, there is a so-called Top Gun competition for the sales force, in which the top salesperson for each quarter wins a $20,000 prize.

Incentive pay systems apart, however, Airborne is not known as a high payer. The company's approach is not to be the compensation leader. Rather, the company tries to set its salary structure to position it in the middle of the labor market. Thus, according to Dick Goodwin, "We target our pay philosophy (total package—compensation plus benefits) to be right at the 50th percentile plus or minus 5 percent."

A degree of self-control is also achieved by trying to establish a corporate culture that focuses employees' attention on the key values required to maintain a competitive edge in the air express industry. The values continually stressed by top managers at Airborne, and communicated throughout the organization by the company's newspaper and a quarterly video, emphasize serving customers' needs, maintaining quality, doing it right the first time around, and excellent service. There is also a companywide emphasis on productivity and cost control. One executive, when describing the company's attitude to expenditures, said, "We challenge everything.... We're the toughest sons of bitches

on the block." Another noted that "among managers I feel that there is a universal agreement on the need to control costs. This is a very tough business, and our people are aware of that. Airborne has an underdog mentality—a desire to be a survivor."

FINANCIAL STRATEGY

A summary of Airborne's financial situation is given in Table 2. Airborne's principal source of liquidity for capital expenditures has been through internally generated cash flows. Management has set a self-imposed limit of senior debt to total capital of 40 percent and total long-term debt to capital of 50 percent. Airborne issues new equity shares as debt

TABLE 2

Selected Financial Data
(in thousands)

	1995	1994	1993	1992
Operating Results				
Revenues				
Domestic	$1,871,163	$1,660,003	$1,484,787	$1,259,792
International	368,188	310,756	235,194	224,524
Total	2,239,351	1,970,759	1,719,981	1,484,316
Operating Expenses	2,170,370	1,881,821	1,636,861	1,456,450
Earnings from Operations	68,981	88,938	83,120	27,866
Interest, Net	29,347	24,663	24,093	18,779
Earnings Before Taxes	39,634	64,275	59,027	9,087
Income Taxes	15,814	25,440	23,738	3,930
Net Earnings Before Changes in Accounting	23,820	38,835	35,289	5,157
Cumulative Effect of Changes in Accounting	——	——	3,828	——
Net Earnings	23,820	38,835	39,117	5,157
Preferred Stock Dividends	276	894	2,760	2,760
Net Earnings Available to Common Shareholders	$ 23,544	$ 37,941	$ 36,357	$ 2,397
Financial Structure				
Working Capital	$ 91,599	$ 66,871	$ 56,521	$ 50,276
Property and Equipment	842,703	766,346	733,963	730,937
Total Assets	1,217,384	1,078,506	1,002,866	964,739
Long-Term Debt	364,621	279,422	269,250	303,335
Subordinated Debt	115,000	118,580	122,150	125,720
Redeemable Preferred Stock	3,948	5,000	40,000	40,000
Shareholders' Equity	406,315	387,398	318,824	285,639

levels reach these limits. Its last equity issue was in July 1990. Other sources of financing for Airborne are sales and leasebacks of aircraft and the joint venture with Mitsui (which provided $40 million and a commitment of $100 million in aircraft financing). During 1989 Airborne sold and leased back nine planes. This reduced the company's debt and generated $83 million in cash. Airborne wants to continue to lease back 20 to 30 percent of their aircraft.

AN INTERVIEW WITH ROBERT CLINE

Robert Cline is the CEO of Airborne Freight, the parent company of Airborne Express. Below are selections from an interview with Cline conducted by Charles Hill in 1990.

Hill: The margins in this business are often described as razor thin. Airborne is already an efficient operation. Do you see any hope of margins widening in the future?

Cline: I do see hope. The industry is consolidating, which is resulting in much greater price stability. Instead of ten viable players, in our portion of the industry there are now really just three. Last year we saw the most stable pricing environment in a decade, and I think it's going to continue. The reason I say this is that we are seeing UPS raise rates, and there is a very good chance from all we hear that Federal Express will follow. So that with price stability and our continued ability to bring down costs, it should lead to continued margin improvement.

Hill: Do you ever fear being squeezed out in a price war between Federal Express and UPS? While Airborne has the lowest cost structure, does the company still lack the financial resources to compete head-to-head with Federal Express and UPS in a price war?

Cline: That's always been a concern that we have had . . . that the two elephants will wrestle around in the grass and accidentally roll over us. Our best guess is that won't happen. One, because at this point in time UPS has not decided to discount. They are not really bidding for corporate accounts. Now, will they eventually get into it? It's a difficult one to say. We take the position that we don't think they will, but we'd better be prepared for it. But you know, if UPS does get into discounting in the air, they'd better be prepared to do it on the ground as well.

As for FedEx, you never now; they might. I would feel more comfortable against FedEx, quite honestly, than I would against UPS because of their size, and they have this surface element to subsidize air. Our costs are definitely lower than FedEx's. Sure, if they went to an all-out price war, it would be difficult to match them, but their balance sheet is not that strong.

Hill: Why do you think FedEx is losing money internationally?

Cline: I think it's a tough nut to crack. They are flying their planes over there, and they don't have enough volume to justify it. The volume just isn't there, especially the backhaul. I'm sure it's killing them. They have built this enormous overhead, and now the volume has to catch up with it. Because of their international problems, it wouldn't make much sense for them to get into a domestic price war and erode the only good margins they have.

Hill: How do you see the global market for express mail developing over the next decade?

Cline: It's in its infancy. It's where the U.S. market was eight to ten years ago. There will be very rapid growth, I think, especially in the smaller package business. Who the players will be has yet to be decided. UPS and Federal have got the resources and have leapt in with direct service, flying their aircraft and operating stations. Then you have the guys who aren't flying planes: ourselves; DHL, who probably has the biggest franchise going right now; and TNT, the Australian firm that owns 15 percent of us is also a very big player, especially in Europe.

We will remain an indirect carrier. We are not flying. We don't intend to fly—we don't really need to fly—there are all kinds of capacity available. Take Europe. UPS goes into Cologne and Federal goes into Brussels. We use scheduled airlines, so we have a choice. If it's to Paris, we go direct. If it's to London, we go direct. Whereas they have to go into a hub and redistribute. So actually, in many cases we have a service advantage over them. The only advantage they are going to have over us is if they can fill their aircraft with high-yielding freight—then their cost structure will be lower.

Hill: Fred Smith [CEO of Federal Express] says that to succeed internationally you have to fly your own planes and build your own ground network to get tight control over distribution.

Cline: That was his whole theory in the U.S., and he was right because we didn't have the service. But I don't know if that's necessary internationally. I mean, there are so many flights, a lot of capacity. Now once we develop enough volume both ways on a consistent basis we might fly. The only problem with flying the scheduled airlines is that you are subject to their pricing schedules, and their prices do go up and down.

Hill: Where would you like Airborne to be in the global market by the year 2000?

Cline: Our global program is to develop strategic alliances. Our deal with Mitsui is a major step in that direction. The advantage is what they can bring to the table in the way of business, their knowledge of the area [Japan], their ability to get into markets that we as an American company cannot. Federal Express is kidding themselves if they think they are ever really going to make a dent in the Japanese market.

Hill: It's often said that the prime motive that Japanese companies have for entering into joint ventures is that they want to learn from their U.S. partners, and once they have learned what they want to learn they often quit. Do you think there is any danger of this occurring?

Cline: I doubt it. I don't think Mitsui could ever develop its own U.S. airline system due to the foreign ownership problem [foreign ownership of U.S. airlines is limited to 25 percent]. We have a unique franchise, and there is really nobody else they can go to. So I don't worry about that too much. Besides, we did get a commitment from them for $140 million. If they walk away from this thing, they also walk away from a pretty big investment.

Hill: What is the current state of your relationship with TNT? Are they likely to try another takeover bid?

Cline: It's an uneasy relationship. We actually do work together in certain areas of the world . . . but those are arm's-length transactions. I know that TNT would like a stronger relationship with Airborne, but we do not see any economic advantage in a closer relationship. I think that TNT has backed away from any future takeover bid, primarily due to the foreign ownership rule.

Hill: What is the impact on your margins of rising fuel costs?

Cline: Fuel costs amount to 4 percent of our total costs, so it's not a major impact. On the other hand, if fuel costs go up by 50 percent, it will knock down our margins by 2.5 percent. And since our margins are only 5 percent, it does have an effect.

CONCLUSION

As Airborne Express approaches the year 2000, a number of key strategic opportunities and emerging threats confront the company. These include (1) the rapid globalization of the air express industry; (2) the development of logistics services based on rapid air transportation; (3) the growth potential for a second-day air service; (4) capacity constraints (Airborne is currently utilizing 90 percent of its airlift capacity, which leaves little margin for error should aircraft need repairs); (5) an economic recession in the United States; and (6) the increase in fuel costs that seems sure to follow a worldwide surge in oil prices during 1996 (oil prices rose from $18 a barrel in mid 1995 to $25 a barrel in late 1996). The company must decide how to position itself with regard to each of these opportunities and threats.

Endnote

1. Standard & Poor's "Aerospace and Air Transport," *Industry Surveys* (February 1996).

CASE 21

Wal-Mart Stores: Strategies for Continued Market Dominance

This case was prepared by James W. Camerius of Northern Michigan University.

David Glass assumed the role of president and chief executive officer at Wal-Mart, the position previously held by Sam Walton. Known for his hard-driving managerial style, Glass gained his experience in retailing at a small supermarket chain in Springfield, Missouri. He joined Wal-Mart as executive vice president for finance in 1976 and was named president and chief operating officer in 1984. In 1998, as he reflected on growth strategies of the firm, he offered this comment: "Seldom can you count on everything coming together as well as it did this year. We believe we could always do better, but we improved more this year than I can ever remember in the past. If Wal-Mart had been content to be just an Arkansas retailer in the early days, we probably would not be where we are today."

A MATURING ORGANIZATION

In 1998, Wal-Mart Stores, Inc., Bentonville, Arkansas, operated mass-merchandising retail stores under a variety of names and retail formats, including the following: Wal-Mart discount department stores; Sam's Wholesale Clubs, wholesale/retail membership warehouses; and Wal-Mart Supercenters, large combination grocery and general merchandise stores in all fifty states. Its international division operated in Canada, Mexico, Ar-

This case is intended to be used as a basis for class discussion rather than to illustrate either effective or ineffective handling of the situation. This case was prepared by James W. Camerius of Northern Michigan University. Used by permission.

gentina, Brazil, Germany, and Puerto Rico, and through joint ventures in China. It was not only the nation's largest discount department store chain, but had surpassed the retail division of Sears, Roebuck, and Co. in sales volume as the largest retail firm in the United States. The McLane Company, a support division with over 36,000 customers, was the nation's largest distributor of food and merchandise to convenience stores and served selected Wal-Marts, Sam's Clubs, and Supercenters. Wal-Mart also continued to operate a small number of discount department stores called Bud's Discount City. A financial summary of Wal-Mart Stores, Inc., for the fiscal years ended January 31, 1997 and 1998 appears in Table 1.

THE SAM WALTON SPIRIT

Much of the success of Wal-Mart was attributed to the entrepreneurial spirit of its founder and chairman of the board, Samuel Moore Walton (1918–1992). Many considered him one of the most influential retailers of the century.

Sam Walton, or "Mr. Sam" as some referred to him, traced his down-to-earth, old-fashioned, home-spun, evangelical ways to growing up in rural Oklahoma, Missouri, and Arkansas. Although he was remarkably blasé about his roots, some suggested that it was the simple belief in hard work and ambition that had "unlocked countless doors and showered upon him, his customers, and his employees ... the fruits of ... years of labor in building [this] highly successful company."

TABLE I

Wal-Mart Stores, Inc., Financial Summary

Consolidated Statements of Income (in millions except per share data)			
	Fiscal Years Ended January 31		
	1998	1997	1996
Revenues:			
Net sales	$117,958	$104,859	$93,627
Other income—net	1,341	1,319	1,146
	119,299	106,178	94,773
Costs and expenses:			
Cost of sales	93,438	83,510	74,505
Operating, selling and general and administrative expenses	19,358	16,946	15,021
Interest costs:			
Debt	555	629	692
Capital leases	229	216	196
	113,580	101,301	90,414
Income before income taxes, minority interest and equity in unconsolidated subsidiaries	5,719	4,877	4,359
Provision for income taxes			
Current	2,095	1,974	1,530
Deferred	20	(180)	76
	2,115	1,794	1,606
Income before minority interest and equity in unconsolidated subsidiaries	3,604	3,083	2,753
Minority interest and equity in unconsolidated subsidiaries	(78)	(27)	(13)
Net income	$3,526	$3,056	$2,740
Net income per share—basic and dilutive	$1.56	$1.33	$1.19

Consolidated Balance Sheets (in millions)		
	January 31, 1998	January 31, 1997
Assets		
Current assets:		
Cash and cash equivalents	$1,447	$883
Receivables	976	845
Inventories		
At replacement cost	16,845	16,193
Less LIFO reserve	348	296
Inventories at LIFO cost	16,497	15,897
Prepaid expenses and other	432	368
Total current assets	19,352	17,993
Property, plant and equipment, at cost:		
Land	4,691	3,689
Building and improvements	14,646	12,724
Fixtures and equipment	7,636	6,390
Transportation equipment	403	379
	27,376	23,182
Less accumulated depreciation	5,907	4,849
Net property, plant and equipment	21,469	18,333

Consolidated Balance Sheets (in millions)	January 31, 1998	January 31, 1997
Property under capital lease:		
Property under capital lease	3,040	2,782
Less accumulated amortization	903	791
Net property under capital leases	2,137	1,991
Other assets and deferred charges	2,426	1,287
Total assets	$45,384	$39,604
Liabilities and Shareholders' Equity		
Current liabilities:		
Accounts payable	$9,126	$7,628
Accrued liabilities	3,628	2,413
Accrued income taxes	565	298
Long-term debt due within one year	1,039	523
Obligations under capital leases due within one year	102	95
Total current liabilities	14,460	10,957
Long-term debt	7,191	7,709
Long-term obligations under capital leases	2,483	2,307
Deferred income taxes and other	809	463
Minority interest	1,938	1,025
Shareholders' equity		
Preferred stock ($.10 par value; 100 shares authorized, none issued)		
Common stock ($.10 par value; 5,500 shares authorized, 2,241 and 2,285 issued and outstanding in 1998 and 1997, respectively)	224	228
Capital in excess of par value	585	547
Retained earnings	18,167	16,768
Foreign currency translation adjustment	(473)	(400)
Total shareholders' equity	18,503	17,143
Total liabilities and shareholders' equity	$45,384	$39,604

Source: Company Annual Reports.

"Our goal has always been in our business to be the very best," Sam Walton said in an interview, "and ... we believe that in order to do that, you've got to make a good situation and put the interests of your associates first. If we really do that consistently, they in turn will cause ... our business to be successful, which is what we've talked about and espoused and practiced." "The reason for our success," he said, "is our people and the way that they're treated and the way they feel about their company." Many have suggested that this "people first" philosophy, which guided the company through the challenges and setbacks of its early years, has allowed it to maintain its consistent record of growth and expansion in later years.

There was little about Sam Walton's background that foretokened his amazing success. He was born in Kingfisher, Oklahoma, on March 29, 1918, to Thomas and Nancy Walton. Thomas Wal-

ton was a banker at the time and later entered the farm mortgage business and moved to Missouri. Growing up in rural Missouri in the depths of the Great Depression, Sam Walton discovered early on that he "had a fair amount of ambition and enjoyed working," he once noted. He completed high school at Columbia, Missouri, and received a bachelor of arts degree in economics from the University of Missouri in 1940. "I really had no idea what I would be," he said, adding as an afterthought, "at one point in time, I thought I wanted to become president of the United States."

An enthusiastic and positive individual, Sam Walton was "just your basic home-spun billionaire," a columnist once suggested, noting that "Mr. Sam is a life-long small-town resident who didn't change much as he got richer than his neighbors." Walton had tremendous energy, enjoyed bird hunting with his dogs, and flew a corporate plane. When the company was much smaller, he could boast that he personally visited every Wal-Mart store at least once a year. A store visit usually included Walton leading Wal-Mart cheers that began, "Give me a W, give me an A. . . ." To many employees he had the air of a fiery Baptist preacher. Paul R. Carter, a Wal-Mart executive vice president, was quoted as saying, "Mr. Walton has a calling." He became the richest man in America, and by 1991 had created a personal fortune for his family in excess of $21 billion.

Sam Walton's success was widely chronicled. He was selected by the investment publication *Financial World* in 1989 as the CEO of the Decade. He had honorary degrees from the University of the Ozarks, the University of Arkansas, and the University of Missouri. He also received many of the most distinguished professional awards of the industry such as Man of the Year, Discounter of the Year, and Chief Executive Officer of the Year, and was the second retailer to be inducted into the Discounting Hall of Fame. In 1984, he received the Horatio Alger Award and in December 1989 was acknowledged by *Discount Stores News* as Retailer of the Decade. "Walton does a remarkable job of instilling near-religious fervor in his people," said analyst Robert Buchanan of A. G. Edwards. "I think that speaks to the heart of his success." In late 1989, Sam Walton was diagnosed as having multiple myeloma, or cancer of the bone marrow. He planned to remain active in the company as chairman of the board of directors.

THE MARKETING CONCEPT

Genesis of an Idea

Sam Walton started his retail career in 1940 as a management trainee with the J. C. Penney Company in Des Moines, Iowa. He was impressed with the Penney method of doing business and later modeled the Wal-Mart chain on "The Penney Idea" (see Table 2). The Penney Company found strength in calling employees "associates" rather than clerks. Penney's, founded in Kemerer, Wyoming, in 1902, located stores on the main streets of small towns and cities throughout the United States.

Following service in the U.S. Army during World War II, Sam Walton acquired a Ben Franklin variety store franchise in Newport, Arkansas. He operated this store successfully with his brother, James L. "Bud" Walton (1921–1995), until losing the

TABLE 2

The Penney Idea, 1913

1. To serve the public, as nearly as we can, to its complete satisfaction.

2. To expect for the service we render a fair remuneration and not all the profit the traffic will bear.

3. To do all in our power to pack the customer's dollar full of value, quality, and satisfaction.

4. To continue to train ourselves and our associates so that the service we give will be more and more intelligently performed.

5. To improve constantly the human factor in our business.

6. To reward men and women in our organization through participation in what the business produces.

7. To test our every policy, method, and act in this wise: "Does it square with what is right and just?"

Source: Vance H. Trimble, *Sam Walton: The Inside Story of America's Richest Man* (New York: Dutton, 1990).

lease in 1950. When Wal-Mart was incorporated in 1962, the firm was operating a chain of fifteen stores. Bud Walton became a senior vice president of the firm and concentrated on finding suitable store locations, acquiring real estate, and directing store construction.

The early retail stores owned by Sam Walton in Newport and Bentonville, Arkansas, and later in other small towns in adjoining southern states, were variety store operations. Relatively small (6,000 square feet), they were located on the main street and displayed merchandise on plain wooden tables and counters. Bearing the Ben Franklin name and supplied by Butler Brothers of Chicago and Saint Louis, they were characterized by a limited price line, low gross margins, high merchandise turnover, and concentration on return on investment. The firm, operating under the Walton 5 & 10 name, was the largest Ben Franklin franchisee in the country in 1962. The variety stores were phased out by 1976 to allow the company to concentrate on the growth of Wal-Mart discount department stores.

Foundations of Growth

The original Wal-Mart discount concept was not a unique idea. Sam Walton became convinced in the late 1950s that discounting would transform retailing. He traveled extensively in New England, the cradle of off-pricing. After he had visited just about every discounter in the United States, he tried to interest Butler Brothers executives in Chicago in the discount store concept. The first Kmart—described as a "conveniently located one-stop shopping unit where customers could buy a wide variety of quality merchandise at discount prices"—had just opened in Garden City, Michigan. Walton's theory was to operate a similar discount store in a small community, and in that setting he would offer name brand merchandise at low prices and would add friendly service. Butler Brothers executives rejected the idea. The first Wal-Mart Discount City opened in late 1962 in Rogers, Arkansas.

Wal-Mart stores would sell nationally advertised, well-known brand merchandise at low prices in austere surroundings. As corporate policy, they would cheerfully give refunds, credits, and rain checks. Management conceived the firm as a "discount department store chain offering a wide variety of general merchandise to the customer." It sought opportunistic purchases of merchandise from whatever sources were available, and strongly emphasized health and beauty aids in the product line, as well as the "stacking it high" way of presenting merchandise. By the end of 1979, there were 276 Wal-Mart stores located in eleven states.

The firm developed an aggressive expansion strategy. New stores were located primarily in towns with a population of 5,000 to 25,000. The stores ranged in size from 30,000 to 60,000 square feet, with 45,000 as the average. The firm also expanded by locating stores in contiguous areas, town by town, state by state. When its discount operations came to dominate a market area, it moved to an adjoining area. While other retailers built warehouses to serve existing outlets, Wal-Mart built the distribution center first and then spotted stores all around it, pooling advertising and distribution overhead. Most stores were less than a six-hour drive from one of the company's warehouses. The first major distribution center, a 390,000 square-foot facility, opened in Searcy, Arkansas, outside Bentonville, in 1978.

National Perspectives

At the beginning of 1991, the firm had 1,573 Wal-Mart stores in thirty-five states, with expansion planned for adjacent states. Wal-Mart became the largest retailer and the largest discount department store in the United States.

As a national discount department store chain, Wal-Mart Stores, Inc., offered a wide variety of general merchandise to the customer. The stores were designed to offer one-stop shopping in thirty-six departments, which included family apparel, health and beauty aids, household needs, electronics, toys, fabric and crafts, automotive supplies, lawn and patio supplies and furnishings, jewelry, and shoes. In addition, at certain store locations, the company also operated a pharmacy, an automotive supply and service center, a garden center, or a snack bar. Instead of stressing special promotions, which called for multiple newspaper advertising circulars, Wal-Mart prided itself on its "everyday low price." It also expected its stores to "provide the customer with a clean, pleasant, and friendly shopping experience."

Although Wal-Mart carried much the same merchandise as the competition, offered similar prices, and operated stores that resembled those of its rivals, there were many differences. In the typical Wal-Mart store, employees wore blue vests to identify themselves, aisles were wide, apparel departments were carpeted in warm colors, a store employee followed customers to their cars to pick up their shopping carts, and the customer was welcomed at the door by a "people greeter," who gave directions and struck up conversations. In some cases, merchandise was bagged in brown paper sacks rather than plastic bags because customers seemed to prefer them. A simple Wal-Mart logo in white letters on a brown background on the front of the store served to identify the firm. In consumer studies, it was determined that the chain was particularly adept at striking the delicate balance needed to convince customers that its prices were low without making people feel that its stores were too cheap. In many ways, competitors such as Kmart sought to emulate Wal-Mart by introducing people greeters, upgrading interiors, developing new logos and signage, and introducing new inventory response systems.

A "satisfaction guaranteed" refund and exchange policy was introduced to make customers trust Wal-Mart's merchandise and quality. Technological advancements such as scanner cash registers, hand-held computers for ordering of merchandise, and computer linkages of stores with the general office and distribution centers improved communications and merchandise replenishment. Each store was encouraged to initiate programs that would make it an integral part of the community in which it operated. Associates were encouraged to "maintain the highest standards of honesty, morality, and business ethics in dealing with the public."

THE EXTERNAL ENVIRONMENT

Industry analysts labeled the 1980s and early 1990s as eras of economic uncertainty for retailers. Many retailers were negatively affected by increased competitive pressures, sluggish consumer spending, slower-than-anticipated economic growth in North America, and recessions abroad. In 1995, Wal-Mart management felt that the high consumer debt level caused many shoppers to reduce or defer spending on anything other than essentials and that the lack of exciting new products or apparel trends reduced discretionary spending. Fierce competition resulted in lower margins, and the lack of inflation stalled productivity increases. By 1998, the country had returned to prosperity. Unemployment was low, total income was relatively high, and interest rates were stable. Combined with a low inflation rate, buying power was perceived to be high and consumers were generally willing to buy.

Many retail enterprises confronted heavy competitive pressure by restructuring. Sears, Roebuck and Co., based in Chicago, became a more focused retailer by divesting itself of Allstate Insurance Company and its real estate subsidiaries. In 1993, the company announced it would close 118 unprofitable stores and discontinue the unprofitable Sears general merchandise catalog. It eliminated 50,000 jobs and began a $4 billion, five-year remodeling plan for its remaining multiline department stores. After unsuccessfully experimenting with an "everyday low price" strategy, management chose

to realign its merchandise strategy to meet the needs of middle-market customers, who were primarily women, by focusing on product lines in apparel, home, and automotive. The new focus on apparel was supported with the advertising campaign "The Softer Side of Sears." A later company-wide campaign broadened the appeal: "The many sides of Sears fit the many sides of your life." Sears completed its return to its retailing roots by selling off its ownership in Dean Witter Financial Services, Discovery Card, Coldwell Banker Real Estate, and Sears mortgage banking operations.

By the early 1990s, the discount department store industry had changed in a number of ways and many analysts thought it had reached maturity. Several formerly successful firms, such as E. J. Korvette, W. T. Grant, Atlantic Mills, Arlans, Federals, Zayre, Heck's, and Ames, had declared bankruptcy and as a result either liquidated or reorganized. Venture announced liquidation in early 1998. Regional firms such as Target Stores and Shopko Stores began carrying more fashionable merchandise in more attractive facilities and shifted their emphasis to national markets. Specialty retailers such as Toys 'R' Us, Pier 1 Imports and Oshmans were making big inroads in toys, home furnishing, and sporting goods. The "superstores" of drug and food chains were rapidly discounting increasing amounts of general merchandise. Some firms, such as May Department Stores Company, with Caldor and Venture, and Woolworth Corporation, with Woolco, had withdrawn from the field by either selling their discount divisions or closing them down entirely. The firm's remaining 122 Woolco stores in Canada were sold to Wal-Mart in 1994. All remaining Woolworth variety stores in the United States were closed in 1997.

Several new retail formats had emerged in the marketplace to challenge the traditional discount department store format. The superstore, a 100,000–300,000-square-foot operation, combined a large supermarket with a discount general-merchandise store. Originally a European retailing concept, these outlets were known as "malls without walls." Kmart's Super Kmart Centers, American Fare, and Wal-Mart's Supercenter Store were examples of this trend toward large operations. Warehouse retailing, which involved some combination of warehouse and showroom facilities, used warehouse principles to reduce operating expenses and thereby offer discount prices as a primary customer appeal. Home Depot combined the traditional hardware store and lumber yard with a self-service home improvement center to become the largest home center operator in the nation.

Some retailers responded to changes in the marketplace by selling goods at price levels (20 to 60 percent) below regular retail prices. These off-price operations appeared as two general types: (1) factory outlet stores such as Burlington Coat Factory Warehouse, Bass Shoes, and Manhattan's Brand Name Fashion Outlet, and (2) independents such as Loehmann's, T. J. Maxx, Marshall's, and Clothestime which bought seconds, overages, closeouts or leftover goods. Other retailers chose to dominate a product classification. Some super specialists, such as Sock Appeal, Little Piggie, and Sock Market, offered a single narrowly defined classification of merchandise with an extensive assortment of brands, colors, and sizes. Others, as niche specialists, such as Kids Mart, a division of Woolworth Corporation, and McKids, a division of Sears, targeted an identified market with carefully selected merchandise and appropriately designed stores. Certain retailers, such as Silk Greenhouse (silk plants and flowers), Office Club (office supplies and equipment), and Toys 'R' Us (toys) were called "category killers" because they had achieved merchandise dominance in their respective product categories. Stores such as The Limited, Limited Express, Victoria's Secret, and The Banana Republic became minidepartment specialists by showcasing new lines and accessories alongside traditional merchandise lines.

Kmart Corporation, headquartered in Troy, Michigan, became the industry's third largest retailer after Sears, Roebuck and second largest discount department store chain in the United States in the 1990s. It had 2,136 stores and $32,183 million in sales at the beginning of 1998. The firm was perceived by many industry analysts and consumers in several independent studies as a laggard. It had been the industry sales leader for a number of years and had recently announced a turnaround in profitability. In the same studies, Wal-Mart was perceived as the industry leader even though, according to the *Wall Street Journal*, "they carry much the same merchandise, offer prices that are pennies apart and operate stores that look almost exactly alike." "Even their names are similar," the newspaper pointed out. The original Kmart concept of a "conveniently located, one-stop shopping unit where customers could buy a wide variety of quality merchandise at discount prices" had lost its competitive edge in a changing market. As one analyst noted in an industry newsletter, "They had done so well for the past 20 years without paying attention to market changes, now they have to." Kmart acquired a new chairman, president and chief executive officer in 1995. Wal-Mart and Kmart sales growth over the period 1987–1997 is summarized in Table 3, and a competitive analysis of four major retail firms is presented in Table 4.

Some retailers, such as Kmart, had initially focused on appealing to professional, middle-class consumers who lived in suburban areas and who were likely to be price sensitive. Other firms, such as Target (Dayton Hudson), which had adopted the discount concept early, generally attempted to go after an upscale consumer who had an annual household income of $25,000 to $44,000. Still other firms, such as Fleet Farm and Menard's, served the rural consumer, while those like Chicago's Goldblatt's Department Stores and Ames Discount Department Stores chose to serve blacks and Hispanics in the inner city.

In rural communities, Wal-Mart's success often came at the expense of established local merchants and units of regional discount store chains. Hardware stores, family department stores, building supply outlets, and stores featuring fabrics, sporting goods and shoes were among the first either to close or to relocate elsewhere. Regional discount retailers in the Sunbelt states—for instance, Roses, Howard's, T.G.&Y., and Duckwall-ALCO, which once enjoyed solid sales and earnings—were forced to reposition themselves by renovating stores, opening bigger and more modern units, re-merchandising assortments, and offering lower prices. In many cases, stores such as Coast-to-Coast, Pamida, and Ben Franklin closed upon a Wal-Mart announcement that it was planning to build in a specific community. As a local newspaper editor put it, "Just the word that Wal-Mart was coming made some stores close up."

CORPORATE STRATEGIES

The corporate and marketing strategies that emerged at Wal-Mart were based on a set of two main objectives that had guided the firm through its growth years. The first objective featured the

TABLE 3

Competitive Sales and Store Comparison, 1987–1997 (in $ millions)

	Kmart			Wal-Mart	
Year	Sales	Stores[1]		Sales	Stores[1]
1997	$32,183,000	2,136		117,958,000	3,406
1996	31,437,000	2,261		104,859,000	3,054
1995	34,389,000	2,161		93,627,000	2,943
1994	34,025,000	2,481		82,494,000	2,684
1993	34,156,000	2,486		67,344,000	2,400
1992	37,724,000	2,435		55,484,000	2,136
1991	34,580,000	2,391		43,886,900	1,928
1990	32,070,000	2,350		32,601,594	1,721
1989	29,533,000	2,361		25,810,656	1,525
1988	27,301,000	2,307		20,649,001	1,364
1987	25,627,000	2,273		15,959,255	1,198

[1]Number of general merchandise stores.

customer: "customers would be provided what they want, when they want it, all at a value." The second objective emphasized team spirit: "treating each other as we would hope to be treated, acknowledging our total dependency on our Associate-partners to sustain our success." The strategies included aggressive plans for new store openings; expansion to additional states; upgrading, relocation, refurbishing and remodeling of existing stores; and opening new distribution centers. The plan was to not have a single operating unit that had not been updated in the past seven years. For Wal-Mart management, the 1990s became "A new era for Wal-Mart; an era in which we plan to grow into a truly nationwide retailer, and should we continue to perform, our sales and earnings will also grow beyond where most could have envisioned at the dawn of the 80s."

In the decade of the 1980s, Wal-Mart had developed a number of new retail formats. The first SAM's Club opened in Oklahoma City, Oklahoma, in 1983. The wholesale club was an idea which had been developed by other firms earlier but which found its greatest success and growth in acceptability at Wal-Mart. SAM's Clubs featured a vast array of product categories with limited selection of brand and model, cash-and-carry business with limited hours,

large (100,000-square-foot), bare-bones facilities, rock-bottom wholesale prices, and minimal promotion. The limited-membership plan permitted not only wholesale members who bought membership to shop there, but also nonmembers, who usually paid a percentage above the ticket price of the merchandise. At the beginning of 1998, there were 483 SAM's Clubs in operation. A revision in merchandising strategy resulted in fewer items in the inventory mix, with more emphasis on lower prices.

Wal-Mart supercenters were large combination stores. They were first opened in 1988 as Hypermarket*USA, a 222,000-square-foot superstore that combined a discount store with a large grocery store, a food court of restaurants, and other service businesses such as banks or video tape rental stores. A scaled-down version of Hypermarket*USA was called the Wal-Mart SuperCenter—similar in merchandise offerings, but with about half the square footage of hypermarts. These expanded-store concepts also included convenience stores and gasoline distribution outlets to "enhance shopping convenience." The company proceeded slowly with these plans and later suspended its plans for building any more hypermarkets in favor of the smaller supercenter. In 1998, Wal-Mart operated 502 supercenters. It also announced plans to build

TABLE 4

An Industry Comparative Analysis, 1997

	Wal-Mart	Sears[1]	Kmart	Target
Sales (in millions)	$117,958	$36,371	$32,183	$20,368
Net income (in thousands)	$ 3,526	$ 1,188	$ 249	$ 1,287
Net income per share	$ 1.56	$ 3.03	$ .51	$ n/a
Dividends per share	$ .27	$ n/a	$ n/a	$ n/a
Percent of sales change	12.0 percent	8.0 percent	2.4 percent	14 percent

Number of stores

Wal-Mart and subsidiaries
  Wal-Mart stores: 2,421
  SAM's Clubs: 483
  Supercenters: 502

Kmart Corporation
  General merchandise: 2,136

Dayton Hudson Corporation
  Target: 796
  Mervyn's: 269
  Department stores: 65

Sears, Roebuck (all divisions)[1]
Sears Merchandise Group
  Department stores: 833
  Hardware stores: 255
  Furniture stores: 129
  Sears dealer stores: 576
  Auto/tire stores: 780
  Auto parts stores
    Western Auto: 39
    Parts America: 576
  Western Auto dealer stores: 800

Source: Corporate Annual Reports.

several full-fledged supermarkets called Wal-Mart Food and Drug Express, with a drive-through option, as "laboratories" to test how the concept would work and what changes would be required before making a decision to proceed with additional units.

In 1991, Wal-Mart acquired The McLane Company, a provider of retail and grocery distribution services for retail stores. It was not considered a major segment of the total Wal-Mart operation.

On the international level, Wal-Mart management had a goal to be the dominant retailer in each country it entered. With the acquisition of 122 former Woolco stores in Canada, the company exceeded expectations in sales growth, market share, and profitability. With a tender offer for shares and mergers of joint ventures in Mexico, the company had a controlling interest in Cifra, Mexico's largest retailer. Cifra operated stores with a variety of con-cepts in every region of Mexico, ranging from the nation's largest chain of sit-down restaurants to a softline department store. Plans were also proceeding with start-up operations in Argentina and Brazil as well as China. The acquisition of 21 hypermarkets in Germany at the end of 1997 marked the company's first entry into Europe, which management considered "one of the best consumer markets in the world." These large stores offered one-stop shopping facilities similar to Wal-Mart Supercenters. The international expansion accelerated management's plans for the development of Wal-Mart as a global brand along the lines of Coca-Cola, Disney, and McDonald's. "We are a global brand name," said Bobby Martin, president of the international division of Wal-Mart. "To customers everywhere it means low cost, best value, greatest selection of quality merchandise and highest standards of customer service." Some changes were mandated in Wal-Mart's international operations to meet local tastes and intense competitive conditions. "We're building companies out there," said Martin. "That's like starting Wal-Mart all over again in South America or Indonesia or China." Although stores in different international markets would coordinate purchasing to gain leverage with suppliers, developing new technology and planning overall strategy would be done from Wal-Mart headquarters in Bentonville, Arkansas. At the beginning of 1998, Wal-Mart's international division operated 500 discount stores, 61 supercenters, and 40 SAM'S Clubs.

The company launched several programs to "highlight" popular social causes. The "Buy American" program was a Wal-Mart retail program initiated in 1985. The theme was "Bring It Home To The USA" and its purpose was to communicate Wal-Mart's support for American manufacturing. The company exerted substantial influence to encourage manufacturers to produce goods in the United States rather than import them. Vendors were attracted into the program by encouraging manufacturers to initiate the process by contacting the company directly with proposals to sell goods that were made in the United States. Buyers also targeted specific import items in their assortments on a state-by-state basis to encourage domestic manufacturing. According to Haim Dabah, president of Gitano Group, Inc., a maker of fashion discount clothing, which imported 95 percent of its clothing and now makes about 20 percent of its products here, "Wal-Mart let it be known loud and clear that if you're going to grow with them, you sure better have some products made in the U.S.A." Farris Fashion, Inc. (flannel shirts), Roadmaster Corporation (exercise bicycles), Flanders Industries, Inc. (lawn chairs), and Magic Chef (microwave ovens) were among the vendors that chose to participate in the program.

From the Wal-Mart standpoint, the "Buy American" program centered on value—producing and selling quality merchandise at a competitive price. The promotion included television advertisements featuring factory workers, a soaring American eagle, and the slogan: "We buy American whenever we can, so you can too." Prominent in-store signage and store circulars were also included. One store poster read: "Success Stories—These items formerly imported, are now being purchased by Wal-Mart in the U.S.A."

Wal-Mart was one of the first retailers to embrace the concept of "green" marketing. The program offered shoppers the option of purchasing products that were better for the environment in three respects: manufacturing, use, and disposal. It was introduced through full-page advertisements in the *Wall Street Journal* and *USA Today*. In-store signage identified those products that were environmentally safe. As Wal-Mart executives saw it, "customers are concerned about the quality of land, air, and water, and would like the opportunity to do something positive." To initiate the program, Wal-Mart notified 7,000 vendors that it had a corporate concern for the environment and was seeking their support. Wal-Mart television advertising showed children on swings, fields of grain blowing in the wind, and roses. Green-and-white store signs, printed on recycled paper, marked products or packaging that had been developed or redesigned to be more environmentally sound.

Wal-Mart had become the channel commander in the distribution of many brand name items. As the nation's largest retailer and, in many geographic areas, the dominant distributor, it exerted considerable influence in negotiation for the best price, delivery terms, promotion allowances, and continuity of supply. Many of these benefits could be passed on to consumers in the form of quality name brand items available at lower than competitive prices. As a matter of corporate policy, management often insisted on doing business only with a producer's top sales executives rather than going through a manufacturer's representative. Wal-Mart had been accused of threatening to buy from other producers if firms refused to sell to it directly. In the ensuing power struggle, Wal-Mart executives refused to talk about the controversial policy or admit that it existed. As a member of an industry association representing a group of sales agencies suggested, "In the Southwest, Wal-Mart's the only show in town." An industry analyst added, "They're extremely aggressive. Their approach has always been to give the customer the benefit of a corporate saving. That builds up customer loyalty and market share."

Another key factor in the mix was an inventory-control system that was recognized as the most sophisticated in retailing. A high-speed computer system linked virtually all the stores to headquarters and the company's distribution centers. It electronically logged every item sold at the checkout counter, automatically kept the warehouses informed of merchandise to be ordered, and directed the flow of goods to the stores and even to the proper shelves. Most important for management, it helped detect sales trends quickly and speeded up market reaction time substantially. According to Bob Connolly, executive vice president of merchandising, "Wal-Mart has used the data gathered by technology to make more inventory available in the key items that customers want most, while reducing inventories overall."

DECISION MAKING IN A MARKET-ORIENTED FIRM

One principle that distinguished Wal-Mart was the unusual depth of employee involvement in company affairs. Corporate strategies emphasized human resource management. Wal-Mart employees became associates, a term borrowed from Sam Walton's early association with J.C. Penney. Input was encouraged at meetings at the store and corporate level. The firm hired employees locally and provided training programs. In addition, through a "Letter to the President" program, management encouraged employees to ask questions and made words such as "we," "us," and "our" part of the corporate language. A number of special award programs recognized individual, department, and division achievement. Stock-ownership and profit-sharing programs were introduced as part of a "partnership" concept.

The corporate culture was acknowledged by the editors of the trade publication *Mass Market Retailers* when it recognized all 275,000 associates collectively as the Mass Market Retailers of the Year. "The Wal-Mart associate," the editors noted, "in this decade that term has come to symbolize all that is right with the American worker, particularly in the retailing environment and most particularly at Wal-Mart." The "store within a store" concept, as a Wal-Mart corporate policy, trained individuals to be merchants by being responsible for the performance of their own departments as if they were running their own businesses. Seminars and training programs afforded them opportunities to grow within the company. "People development, not just a good 'program' for any growing company but a must to secure our future," is how Suzanne Allford, vice president of the Wal-Mart people division explained the firm's decentralized approach to retail management development.

"The Wal-Mart Way," was a phase that was used by management to summarize the firm's unconventional approach to business and the development of the corporate culture. As noted in a report referring to a recent development program, "We stepped outside our retailing world to examine the best managed companies in the United States in an effort to determine the fundamentals of their success and to 'benchmark' our own performances. The name Total Quality Management (TQM) was used to identify this vehicle for proliferating the very best things we do while incorporating the new ideas our people have that will assure our future."

THE GROWTH CHALLENGE

And what of Wal-Mart without Mr. Sam? "There's no transition to make," said Glass, "because the principles and the basic values he used in founding this company were so sound and so universally accepted." "As for the future," he suggested,

There's more opportunity ahead of us than behind us. We're good students of retailing and we've studied the mistakes that others have made. We'll make our own mistakes, but we won't repeat theirs. The only thing constant at Wal-Mart is change. We'll be fine as long as we never lose our responsiveness to the customer.

Management identified four key legacies of Sam Walton to guide the company's "quest for value" in the future: (1) everyday low prices, (2) customer service, (3) leadership, and (4) change.

For more than twenty-five years, the company experienced tremendous growth and, as one analyst put it, "has been consistently on the cutting edge of low-markup mass merchandising." Much of the forward momentum had come from the entrepreneurial spirit of Samuel Moore Walton. The company announced on Monday, April 6, 1992, following Walton's death, that his son, S. Robson Walton, vice chairman of Wal-Mart, would succeed his father as chairman of the board. Glass would remain president and CEO. The Wal-Mart board of directors and executive officers in 1998 are listed in the appendix.

A new management team was in place. Management felt that it had positioned the firm as an industry leader. However, a number of new challenges had to be met. It had been predicted as early as 1993 that Wal-Mart's same-store growth would likely slip into the 7 to 8 percent range in the near future. Analysts were also concerned about the increased competition in the warehouse club business and the company's move from its roots in southern and midwestern small towns to the more competitive and costly markets of the Northeast. Wal-Mart supercenters faced more re-silient rivals in the grocery field. Unions represent-ing supermarket workers delayed and in some cases killed expansion opportunities. Some analysts said:"the company is simply suffering from the high expectations its stellar performance over the years has created." In early 1996, management ac-knowledged that 1995 had not been a "Wal-Mart year." After ninety-nine consecutive quarters of earnings growth, Wal-Mart management said profit for the fiscal fourth quarter, ending January 31, would decline as much as 11 percent from the year before. Much of the company's sales growth in 1996 and 1997 was attributed to the opening of new stores in an expansion program. Same-store sales growth in 1996 and 1997 was 5 percent and 6 percent, respectively, when compared with the pre-vious year's sales performance.

APPENDIX: WAL-MART STORES, INC., BOARD OF DIRECTORS AND CORPORATE OFFICERS, 1998

Directors: Jeronimo Arango, Paul R. Carter, John A. Cooper, Jr., Stephen Friedman, Stanley C. Gault, David D. Glass, Frederick S. Humphries, E. Stanley Kroenke, Elizabeth A. Sanders, Jack C. Shewmaker, Donald G. Soderquist, Dr. Paula Stern, John T. Walton, S. Robson Walton; *Chairman of the Board:* S. Robson Walton; *CEO, President:* David D. Glass; *Vice Chairman, COO:* Donald G. Soderquist; *Executive VP, President-Wal-Mart Realty:* Paul R. Carter; *Executive VP Merchandising:* Bob Con-nolly; *Executive VP, COO-Operations, Wal-Mart Stores Division:* Thomas M. Coughlin; *Executive VP-Specialty Division:* David Dible; *Executive VP, President-Sam's Club Division:* Mark Hansen; *Executive VP, President-International Division:* Bob L. Martin; *Executive VP, CFO:* John B. Menzer; *Executive VP, President-Wal-Mart Stores Division:* H. Lee Scott; *Executive VP-Supercenter:* Nick White; *Senior VP, Secretary-General Counsel:* Robert K. Rhoads; *Senior VP, Finance-Treasurer:* J. J. Fitzsimmons

References

"A Supercenter Comes to Town." *Chain Store Age Executive*, De-cember 1989, 23–30.

Barrier, Michael. "Walton's Mountain." *Nation's Business*, April 1988, 18–20.

Bergman, Joan. "Saga of Sam Walton." *Stores,* January 1988, 129–130.

Blumenthal, Karen. "Marketing with Emotion: Wal-Mart Shows the Way." *Wall Street Journal*, November 20, 1989, B3.

Bragg, Arthur. "Wal-Mart's War on Reps." *Sales & Marketing Man-agement*, March 1987, 41–43.

Brauer, Molly. "Sam's: Setting a Fast Pace." *Chain Store Age Execu-tive*, August 1983, 20–21.

Corwin, Pat, Jay L. Johnson, and Renee M. Rouland. "Made in U.S.A." *Discount Merchandiser*, November 1989, 48–52.

"David Glass's Biggest Job Is Filling Sam's Shoes." *Business Month*, December 1988, 42.

Fisher, Christy, and Patricia Sternad. "Wal-Mart Pulls Back on Hy-permart Plans." *Advertising Age*, February 19, 1990, 49.

Fisher, Christy, and Judith Graham. "Wal-Mart Throws 'Green' Gauntlet." *Advertising Age*, August 21, 1989, 1.

Friedland, Johnathan, and Louise Lee. "The Wal-Mart Way Some-times Gets Lost in Translation Overseas." *Wall Street Journal*, October 8, 1997, A1, A12.

"Glass Is CEO at Wal-Mart." *Discount Merchandiser*, March 1988, 6.

Helliker, Kevin. "Wal-Mart's Store of the Future Blends Discount Prices, Department-Store Feel." *Wall Street Journal*, May 17, 1991, B1, B8.

Helliker, Kevin, and Bob Ortega. "Falling Profit Marks End of Era at Wal-Mart." *Wall Street Journal*, January 18, 1996, B1.

Huey, John. "America's Most Successful Merchant." *Fortune*, Sep-tember 23, 1991, 46–48.

Johnson, Jay L. "Are We Ready for Big Changes?" *Discount Mer-chandiser*, August 1989, 48, 53–54.

——— "Hypermarts and Supercenters—Where Are They Head-ing?" *Discount Merchandiser*, November 1989, 60.

——— "Internal Communication: A Key To Wal-Mart's Success." *Discount Merchandiser*, November 1989, 68.

——— "The Supercenter Challenge." *Discount Merchandiser*, August 1989, 70.

Kelly, Kevin. "Sam Walton Chooses a Chip Off the Old CEO." *Business Week*, February 15, 1988, 29.

Kerr, Dick. "Wal-Mart Steps Up 'Buy American.'" *Housewares*, March 7–13, 1986, 1.

Lee, Louise. "Discounter Wal-Mart Is Catering to Affluent to Maintain Growth." *Wall Street Journal*, February 7, 1996, A1.

Lee, Louise, and Joel Millman. "Wal-Mart to Buy Majority Stake in Cifra." *Wall Street Journal*, June 4, 1997, A3.

"Management Style: Sam Moore Walton." *Business Month*, May 1989, 38.

Marsch, Barbara. "The Challenge: Merchants Mobilize to Battle Wal-Mart in a Small Community." *Wall Street Journal*, June 5, 1991, A1, A4.

Mason, Todd. "Sam Walton of Wal-Mart: Just Your Basic Home-spun Billionaire." *Business Week*, October 14, 1985, 142–143.

Nelson, Emily. "Wal-Mart to Build a Test Supermarket in Bid to Boost Grocery-Industry Share." *Wall Street Journal*, June 19, 1998, A4.

"Our People Make the Difference: The History of Wal-Mart." Bentonville, Ark.: Wal-Mart Video Productions, 1991. Video cassette.

Peters, Tom J., and Nancy Austin, *A Passion for Excellence*. New York: Random House, 266–267.

Rawn, Cynthia Dunn. "Wal-Mart vs. Main Street." *American Demographics*, June 1990, 58–59.

Reier, Sharon. "CEO of the Decade: Sam M. Walton." *Financial World*, April 4, 1989, 56–57.

"Retailer Completes Purchase of Wertkauf of Germany." *Wall Street Journal*, December 31, 1997, B3.

Rudnitsky, Howard. "How Sam Walton Does It." *Forbes*, August 16, 1982, 42–44.

——— "Play It Again, Sam." *Forbes*, August 10, 1987, 48.

"Sam Moore Walton." *Business Month*, May 1989, 38.

Schwadel, Francine. "Little Touches Spur Wal-Mart's Rise." *Wall Street Journal*, September 22, 1989, B1.

Sheets, Kenneth R. "How Wal-Mart Hits Main St." *U.S. News & World Report*, March 13, 1989, 53–55.

Smith, Sarah. "America's Most Admired Corporations." *Fortune*, January 29, 1990, 56.

Sprout, Alison L. "America's Most Admired Corporations." *Fortune*, February 11, 1991, 52.

"The Early Days: Walton Kept Adding 'a Few More' Stores." *Discount Store News*, December 9, 1985, 61.

Thurmond, Shannon. "Sam Speaks Volumes About New Formats." *Advertising Age*, May 9, 1988, S26.

Trimble, Vance H. *Sam Walton: The Inside Story of America's Richest Man*. New York: Dutton, 1990.

"Wal-Mart Spoken Here." *Business Week*, June 23, 1997, 138.

Wal-Mart Stores, Inc. Annual Reports, 1996, 1997, and 1998.

"Wal-Mart's 'Green' Campaign to Emphasize Recycling Next." *Adweek's Marketing Week*, February 12, 1990, 60–61.

"Wal-Mart Rolls Out Its Supercenters." *Chain Store Age Executive*, December 1988, 18–19.

"Wal-Mart: The Model Discounter." *Dun's Business Month*, December 1982, 60–61.

"Wal-Mart to Acquire McLane, Distributor to Retail Industry." *Wall Street Journal*, October 2, 1990, A8.

"Wholesale Clubs." *Discount Merchandiser*, November 1987, 26.

"Work, Ambition—Sam Walton." press release, Wal-Mart Stores, Inc.

Zweig, Jason. "Expand It Again, Sam." *Forbes*, July 9, 1990, 106.

Kmart: A Corporate Strategy Dilemma

This case was prepared by James W. Camerius of Northern Michigan University.

Floyd Hall, chairman, president, and chief executive officer of Kmart Corporation since June 1995, was pleased with Kmart's financial results reported in the first quarter of fiscal 1998. Earnings had more than tripled from the previous year's levels. Net income for the quarter ended April 29 rose to $47 million from $14 million a year earlier. Hall was very optimistic about the company's future. The financial information convinced him that a new corporate strategy that he had introduced recently would revitalize Kmart's core business, its 2,136 discount stores, and put the company on the road to recovery. Industry analysts had noted that Kmart, once an industry leader, had posted eleven straight quarters of disappointing earnings and had been dogged by persistent bankruptcy rumors. Analysts cautioned that much of Kmart's growth reflected the strength of the consumer economy and that the company's future in a period of slower economic growth still looked uncertain.

Kmart was one of the world's largest mass-merchandise retailers. After several years of restructuring, it comprised mainly general merchandise businesses in the form of traditional Kmart discount department stores and Big Kmart (consumables and convenience) stores, as well as Super Kmart Centers (food and general merchandise). It operated in all fifty states and in Puerto Rico, Guam, and the U.S. Virgin Islands. It also had equity

interests in Meldisco subsidiaries of Melville Corporation, which operated Kmart footwear departments. Measured in sales volume, Kmart was the third largest retailer and the second largest discount department store chain in the United States.

The discount department store industry was perceived to have reached maturity. Kmart, as part of that industry, had a retail management strategy that was developed in the late 1950s and revised in the early 1990s. The company was in a dilemma regarding its corporate strategy. The problem was how to stop Kmart's financial decline and provide a new direction that would reposition the company in a fiercely competitive environment.

THE EARLY YEARS

Kmart grew out of an organization founded in 1899 in Detroit by Sebastian S. Kresge. The first S. S. Kresge store represented a new type of retailing: it featured low-priced merchandise for cash in low-budget, relatively small buildings (4,000 to 6,000 square feet) with sparse furnishings. The adoption of the "5¢ and 10¢" or "variety store" concept, pioneered by F. W. Woolworth Company in 1879, led to rapid and profitable development of what was then the S. S. Kresge Company.

Kresge believed it could substantially increase its retail business through centralized buying and control, the development of standardized store operating procedures, and expansion in heavy traffic areas by opening new stores there. When the firm was incorporated in 1912, in Delaware, it had eighty-five stores, with sales of $10,325,000, and, next to Woolworth's, was the largest variety chain in the world. In 1916, it was reincorporated in Michigan. Over the next forty years, it experimented with mail-order catalogues, full-line department stores, self-service, a number of price lines, and the opening of stores in planned shopping centers. However, it continued to emphasize variety stores.

By 1957, corporate management became aware that the development of supermarkets and the expansion of drugstore chains into general merchandise lines had made inroads into market categories previously dominated by variety stores. It also became clear that a new form of store with a discount merchandising strategy was emerging.

THE CUNNINGHAM CONNECTION

In 1957, in an effort to save the company and make it competitive again, Frank Williams, the then president of Kresge, nominated Harry B. Cunningham as general vice president. He did so to free Cunningham, who had worked his way up the ranks in the organization, from operating responsibility. Cunningham was being groomed for the presidency and was given the assignment to study existing retailing businesses and recommend marketing changes.

In his visits to Kresge stores, and those of the competition, Cunningham became interested in discounting—particularly in a new operation in Garden City, Long Island. Eugene Ferkauf had recently opened large discount department stores called E. J. Korvette. The stores emphasized discount mass merchandising and featured low prices and margins, high turnover, large free-standing departmentalized units, and ample parking space. Typically, they were located in the suburbs.

Cunningham was impressed with the discount concept, but he knew he had first to convince the Kresge board of directors, whose support would be necessary for any new strategy to succeed. He studied the company for two years and presented it with the following recommendation:

We can't beat the discounters operating under the physical constraints and the self-imposed merchandise limitations of variety stores. We can join them—and not only join them, but with our people, procedures, and organization, we can become a leader in the discount industry.

In a speech delivered at the University of Michigan, Cunningham made his management approach clear by concluding with an admonition from the British author, Sir Hugh Walpole: "Don't play for safety, it's the most dangerous game in the world."

The board of directors had a difficult job. Change is never easy, especially when the company has established procedures in place and a proud heritage. Before the first presentation to the board could be made, rumors were circulating that one shocked senior executive had said:

We have been in the variety business for 60 years—we know everything there is to know about it, and we're not doing very well in that, and you want to get us into a business we don't know anything about.

Nevertheless, the board accepted Cunningham's recommendations. When Williams retired, Cunningham became the new president and chief executive officer and was directed to proceed with his recommendations.

THE BIRTH OF KMART

Management conceived the original Kmart as a conveniently located one-stop shopping unit where customers could buy a wide variety of quality merchandise at discount prices. The typical Kmart had 75,000 square feet, all on one floor. It generally stood by itself in a high-traffic, suburban area, with plenty of parking space. All stores had a similar floor plan.

The company made an $80 million commitment in leases and merchandise for thirty-three stores before the first Kmart opened in 1962 in Garden City, Michigan. As part of this strategy, management decided to rely on the strengths and abilities of its own people to make decisions rather than employing outside experts for advice.

The original Kresge 5 & 10 variety store operation was characterized by low gross margins, high turnover, and concentration on return on investment. The main difference in the Kmart strategy would be the offering of a much wider merchandise mix.

The company had the knowledge and ability to merchandise 50 percent of the departments in the planned Kmart merchandise mix and contracted for operation of the remaining departments. In the following years, Kmart took over most of those departments originally contracted to licensees. Eventually, all departments, except shoes, were operated by Kmart.

By 1987, the twenty-fifth anniversary of the opening of the first Kmart store in America, sales and earnings of Kmart Corporation were at an all-time high. The company was the world's largest discount retailer, with sales of $25,627 million, and operated 3,934 general merchandise and specialty stores.

On April 6, 1987, Kmart Corporation announced that it agreed to sell most of its remaining Kresge variety stores in the United States to Mc-Crory Corporation, a unit of the closely held Rapid American Corporation of New York.

THE NATURE OF THE COMPETITIVE ENVIRONMENT

A Changing Marketplace

The retail sector of the United States economy went through a number of dramatic and turbulent changes during the 1980s and early 1990s. Retail analysts concluded that many retail firms were negatively affected by increased competitive pressures, sluggish consumer spending, slower-than-anticipated economic growth in North America, and recessions abroad. As one retail consultant noted,

> The structure of distribution in advanced economies is currently undergoing a series of changes that are as profound in their impact and as pervasive in their influence as those that occurred in manufacturing during the 19th century.

This changing environment affected the discount department store industry. Nearly a dozen firms, including E. J. Korvette, W. T. Grant, Arlans, Atlantic Mills, and Ames, passed into bankruptcy or reorganization. Some firms, such as Woolworth (Woolco Division), withdrew from the field entirely after years of disappointment. Saint Louis–based May Department Stores sold its Caldor and Venture discount divisions, each with annual sales of more than $1 billion. Venture announced liquidation in early 1998.

As senior management at Kmart saw it, most of the firms facing difficulties in the industry had this situation in common: they had been very successful five or ten years ago but had not changed and, therefore, had become somewhat dated. Manage-

ments that had a historically successful formula, particularly in retailing, found it hard to adapt to change, especially at the peak of success, and would wait too long when faced with threats in the environment. Then they were forced to scramble to regain competitiveness.

Wal-Mart Stores, Inc., based in Bentonville, Arkansas, was an exception. Growth-oriented, it had emerged in 1991 as the nation's largest retailer and retained that position through 1997. It was also the largest discount department store chain in sales volume. Operating under a variety of names and formats, nationally and internationally, the company included Wal-Mart stores, Wal-Mart Supercenters, and SAM's Warehouse Clubs. The firm found early strength in cultivating rural markets, merchandise restocking programs, "everyday low pricing," and the control of operations through companywide computer programs that linked cash registers to corporate headquarters.

Among other companies, Sears, Roebuck, and Co., in a state of stagnated growth for several years, completed a return to its retailing roots by spinning off to shareholders its $9 billion controlling stake in its Allstate Corporation insurance unit and by the divestment of financial services. After unsuccessfully experimenting with an "everyday low-price" strategy, management chose to refine its merchandising program to meet the needs of middle-market customers, who were primarily women, by focusing on apparel, home, and automotive product lines.

Many retailers such, as Target (Dayton Hudson), which adopted the discount concept, attempted to go after the upscale customer—that is, someone with an annual household income of $25,000 to $44,000. Other pockets of population were served by firms such as Zayre, which had focused on consumers in the inner city before being acquired by Ames Department Stores, and Wal-Mart, which initially served the needs of the more rural consumer in secondary markets.

Kmart executives found that discount department stores were being challenged by several retail formats. Some retailers were assortment oriented, offering a much greater depth of assortment within a given product category. For example, Toys 'R' Us operated 20,000-square-foot toy supermarkets. Its prices were very competitive within an industry that was very competitive. When consumers entered a Toys 'R' Us facility, they usually had no doubt that if the product wasn't there, no one else had it. In 1997, however, Toys 'R' Us was challenged by industry leader Wal-Mart and other firms that offered a higher level of service and had more aggressive pricing practices.

Some retailers were experimenting with the "off price" apparel concept—that is, selling name brands and designer goods at 20 to 70 percent discounts. Others, such as Home Depot and Menard's, operated home improvement centers that were warehouse-style stores with a wide range of hard-line merchandise for both do-it-yourselfers and professionals. Still others opened drug supermarkets that offered a wide variety of high-turnover merchandise in a convenient location. In these cases, competition was becoming more risk oriented by putting $3 million or $4 million in merchandise at retail value in an 80,000-square-foot facility and of-

fering genuinely low prices. Jewel-Osco stores in the Midwest, Rite Aid, and a series of independents exemplified the organizations that employed an entirely new concept of the drug supermarket.

Thus, competition was offering something that was new and different in terms of depth of assortment, competitive price image, and format. Kmart management perceived the changes as a threat because these were viable businesses and they were hindering it in its ability to improve and maintain market share in specific merchandise categories. An industry competitive analysis is shown in Table 1.

EXPANSION AND CONTRACTION

When Joseph E. Antonini was appointed chairman of Kmart Corporation in October, 1987, he was charged with the responsibility of maintaining and eventually

TABLE 1

An Industry Competitive Analysis, 1997

	Kmart	Wal-Mart	Sears	Dayton Hudson
Sales (in millions)	$32,183	$117,958	$41,296	$27,757
Net income (in millions)	$249	$3,526	$1,188	$751
Sales growth	2.4%	12%	8%	9%
Profit margin	.8%	2.9%	2.9%	2.7%
Sales/sq.ft	211	N/A	318	226
Return/equity	5%	19.8%	20%	16.8%

Number of Stores
Kmart Corporation
    Kmart traditional discount stores: 2,037
    Super Kmart centers: 99

Wal-Mart Stores, Inc. (includes international)
    Wal-Mart discount stores: 2,421
    Supercenters: 502
    SAM'S Clubs: 483

Sears, Roebuck and Company
    Full-line stores: 833
    Hardware stores: 255
    Homelife furniture stores: 129

    Sears dealer stores: 576
Sears tire group
    Sears Auto Centers: 780
    National Tire & Battery stores: 326
Sears Parts Group
    Parts America stores: 576
    Western Auto stores: 39
    Western Auto (locally owned): 800

Dayton Hudson Corporation
    Target: 796
    Mervyn's: 269
    Department store division: 65

Source: Company Annual Reports.

accelerating the chain's record of growth, despite a mature retail marketplace. He moved to link experimental formats into profitable chains. As he noted, it was essential to embrace change:

> Our vision calls for the constant and never-ceasing exploration of new modes of retailing, so that our core business of U.S. Kmart stores can be constantly renewed and reinvigorated by what we learn from our other businesses.

In the mid 1970s and throughout the 1980s, Kmart became involved in the acquisition or development of several smaller new operations. For instance, Kmart Insurance Services, Inc., acquired as Planned Marketing Associates in 1974, offered a full line of life, health, and accident insurance at centers located in twenty-seven Kmart stores, primarily in the South and Southwest.

In 1982, Kmart initiated its own off-price specialty apparel concept, called Designer Depot. That year it opened twenty-eight Designer Depot stores to appeal to customers who wanted quality upscale clothing at a budget price. A variation of this concept, called Garment Rack, was opened to sell apparel that normally would not be sold in Designer Depot. A distribution center was added in 1983, to supplement them. Neither venture proved successful.

Kmart also attempted a joint venture with the Hechinger Company of Washington, D.C., a warehouse home center retailer. However, after much deliberation, Kmart chose instead to acquire, in 1984, Home Centers of America of San Antonio, Texas, which operated 80,000-square-foot warehouse home centers. The new division, renamed Builders Square, had grown to 167 units by 1996. It capitalized on Kmart's real estate, construction, and management expertise and Home Centers of America's merchandising expertise. Builders Square was sold in 1997.

Waldenbooks, a chain of 877 bookstores, was acquired from Carter, Hawley Hale, Inc., in 1984. Part of Kmart's strategy was to capture a greater share of the market with a product category that it already had in its stores. Kmart had been interested in the book business for some time and took advantage of an opportunity in the marketplace to build on its common knowledge base. Borders Books and Music, an operator of 50 large-format superstores,

became part of Kmart in 1992 to form the Borders Group, a division that would include Waldenbooks. The Borders Group, Inc., was sold in 1995.

The Bruno's, Inc., joint venture in 1987 formed a partnership to develop large combination grocery and general merchandise stores, or "hypermarkets," called American Fare. The giant one-stop-shopping facilities of 225,000 square feet traded on the grocery expertise of Bruno's and the general merchandise of Kmart to offer a wide selection of products and services at discount prices. A similar venture, called Super Kmart Center, represented later thinking on combination stores with a smaller size and format. In 1998, Kmart operated ninety-nine Super Kmart Centers, all in the United States.

In 1988, the company acquired a controlling interest in Makro, Inc., a Cincinnati-based operator of warehouse club stores. Makro, with annual sales of about $300 million, operated member-only stores, which were stocked with low-priced fresh and frozen groceries, apparel, and durable goods in suburbs of Atlanta, Cincinnati, Washington, and Philadelphia. PACE Membership Warehouse, Inc., a similar operation, was acquired in 1989. The "club" stores were sold in 1994.

PayLess Drug Stores, which operated superdrugstores in a number of western states, was sold in 1994 to Thrifty PayLess Holdings, Inc., an entity in which Kmart maintained a significant investment. Interests in The Sport Authority, an operator of large-format sporting goods stores, which Kmart acquired in 1990, were disposed of during 1995.

On the international level, an interest in Coles Myer, Ltd, Australia's largest retailer, was sold in November 1994. At the beginning of 1996, interests in thirteen Kmart general merchandise stores in the Czech and Slovak Republics were sold to Tesco PLC, one of the United Kingdom's largest retailers. In February 1998, Kmart stores in Canada were sold to Hudson's Bay Co., a Canadian chain of historic full-service department stores. The interest in Kmart Mexico, S.A. de C.V., was disposed of in fiscal year 1997.

Founded in 1988, OfficeMax, with 328 stores, was one of the largest operators of high-volume, deep discount office products superstores in the United States. In 1991, it became a Kmart unit in which Kmart had ownership of more than 90 percent. Kmart sold its interest in OfficeMax in 1995.

In 1998, Kmart maintained an equity interest in Meldisco subsidiaries of Melville Corporation, operators of Kmart footwear departments.

THE MATURATION OF KMART

Early corporate research revealed that 80 percent of the population found it convenient to shop at Kmart. One study concluded that one out of every two adults in the United States shopped at a Kmart at least once a month. Despite this popular appeal, strategies that had allowed the firm to have something for everybody were no longer felt to be appropriate for the 1990s. Kmart found that it had a broad customer base because it operated on a national basis. Its strategies had assumed that the company was serving everyone in the markets where it was established.

Kmart was often perceived as aiming at the low-income consumer. The financial community believed that Kmart catered to the blue-collar, low-income and upper-lower-class customers. Actually, though, Kmart was serving the professional and middle-class market because its stores were initially in suburban communities, where that population lived.

In more recent years, Kmart has made a major commitment to secondary or rural markets, but these were areas it had not previously cultivated. When developing its initial strategies, the firm perceived the rural consumer as different from the urban or suburban customer. In re-addressing the situation, it discovered that its assortments in rural areas were too limited and that there were too many preconceived notions regarding what the Nebraska farmer really wanted. Kmart discovered that the rural consumer didn't always shop for bib overalls and shovels but was looking for microwave ovens and the same things everyone else shopped for.

Kmart's goal was not to attract more customers but to get customers to spend more. Customers were thought of as categories demonstrating divergent tastes and needs. The upper-income consumer would buy more health and beauty aids, cameras, and sporting goods, whereas the lower-income consumer would buy toys and clothing.

As it sought to capture a larger share of the market and get people to spend more, Kmart began to recognize a market that was more upscale. When consumer research was conducted and management examined the profile of the trade area and

the profile of the person who shopped at Kmart in the previous month, they were found to be identical. Kmart was predominately serving the suburban consumer in suburban locations. In 1997, Kmart's primary target customers were women between the ages of twenty-five and forty-five, with children at home and with annual household incomes of $20,000 to $50,000. The core Kmart shopper averaged 4.3 visits to a Kmart store per month. The purchase amount per visit was $40, and the purchase rate during a store visit was 95 percent. The firm estimated that 180 million people shopped at Kmart in an average year.

Through research on lifestyle in the markets it served, Kmart determined that there were more two-income families, that families were having fewer children, that there were more working wives, and that customers tended to be homeowners. Customers were very careful how they spent their money and were perceived as seeking quality. This was a distinct contrast to the 1960s and early 1970s, which tended to have the orientation of a throw-away society. Now the customer said, "What we want is products that will last longer. We'll have to pay more for them but we'll still want them and at the lowest price possible." Thus, prices had to be competitive, but the insistence on better quality was the new element. According to a Kmart Annual Report, "Consumers today are well educated and informed. They want good value and they know it when they see it. Price remains a key consideration, but the consumers' new definition of value includes quality as well as price."

Corporate management at Kmart considered the discount department store to be a mature idea. Although maturity was sometimes looked on with disfavor, Kmart executives did not think that maturity had to mean a lack of profitability or a lack of opportunity to increase sales. The industry was perceived as being "reborn." It was in this context, in 1990, that a series of new retailing strategies were developed with the aim of upgrading the Kmart image.

THE RENEWAL PROGRAM

The strategies that emerged to confront a changing environment resulted from an overall reexamination of existing corporate strategies. The new program included the following: accelerated store expansion and refurbishing; capitalizing on dominant lifestyle departments; centralized merchandising; more capital investment in retail automation; aggressive and focused advertising; and continued growth through new specialty retail formats.

This five-year, $2.3 billion program involved virtually all Kmart discount stores. There would be approximately 250 new full-size Kmart stores, 620 enlargements, 280 relocations and 30 closings. In addition 1,260 stores would be refurbished to bring their layout and fixtures up to new store standards.

Product displays received a good deal of attention early on, for they needed improvement. The traditional Kmart layout was by product category, and the locations for specific departments were often holdovers from the variety store. Many departments would not give up prime locations. As part of its new marketing strategy, the company introduced the shop concept. The concept resulted in a variety of new departments such as Soft Goods for the Home, Kitchen Korners, and Home Electronic Centers. They carried goods that were complementary—to entice shoppers to buy several interrelated products rather than just one item. The goal of each of these "do-it-yourself" departments, as management called them, was to sell a lifestyle-oriented approach to consumers.

Kmart's five-year program also focused on utilizing and revitalizing the space that the company already had under its control. The remodeling and updating of existing properties gave virtually all U.S. Kmart discount stores a new look: a broad poppy-red-and-gold band around interior walls as a "horizon," and new round, square, and honeycomb racks that displayed the full garment. Other changes included the relocation of jewelry and women's apparel to areas closer to the entrance, and the redesigning of counters to make them look more upscale and hold more merchandise.

Name brands were added in soft and hard goods as management recognized that the customer transferred the product quality of branded goods to perceptions of private-label merchandise. "If you sell Wrangler, there is good quality. Then the private label must be good quality"—that, in the view of Kmart management, would be the customer's way of thinking. Consequently, the company increased its emphasis on trusted national brands such as Rubbermaid, Procter & Gamble, and Kodak and stressed major strategic vendor relationships. In addition, it began to enhance its private-

label brands such as Kathy Ireland, Jaclyn Smith, Route 66, and Sesame Street in apparel. Additional private-label merchandise included K Gro in home gardening, American Fare in grocery and consumables, White-Westinghouse in appliances, and Penske Auto Centers in automotive services. Some private labels were discontinued after a review.

The goal of creating a quality image received a great deal of attention. Pro golfer Fuzzy Zoeller was engaged to promote golf equipment and other associated products. Mario Andretti, who raced in the Championship Auto Racing Teams' Indy car series, agreed to the cosponsorship of his car with associated promotion.

Kmart hired Martha Stewart, an upscale Connecticut author of lavish best-selling books on cooking and home entertaining, as its "life-style spokesperson and consultant." She was featured as a corporate symbol for housewares and associated products in advertising and in store displays. Management visualized her as the next Betty Crocker (a fictional character created some years ago by General Mills) and a representative of its interest in lifestyle trends. The "Martha Stewart Everyday" home fashion product line was introduced successfully in 1995 and expanded in 1996 and 1997. The company established a separate division to manage strategy for all Martha Stewart–label goods and programs.

The redesigned once-a-week Kmart newspaper circular featuring merchandise also carried the advertising theme: "The quality you need, the price you want."

To maintain "price leadership across America," the company reduced several thousand prices. As management noted, "it is absolutely essential that we provide our customers with good value—quality products at low prices." Although lower prices hurt margins and contributed significantly to a decline in earnings, management concluded that unit turnover of items with lowered prices increased sufficiently to "enable Kmart to maintain its pricing leadership that will have a most positive impact on our business in the years ahead."

A "centralized merchandising system" was introduced to improve communication. A computerized, highly automated replenishment system tracked how quickly merchandise sold, and just as quickly put fast-moving items back on the shelves. Satellite capability and a point-of-sale (POS) scanning system were introduced as part of the program. Regular, live satellite communication from Kmart headquarters to the stores would allow senior management to stay in touch with store managers and ask and answer questions. The POS scanning system made possible the recording of every sale and transmission of the data to headquarters. This enabled Kmart to respond quickly to what was new, what was in demand, and what would keep customers coming back.

A new corporate logo was designed to signify the changes taking place inside the stores. It featured a big red *K* with the word *mart* written in smaller white script inside the *K*.

The company opened its first Super Kmart Center in 1992. The format combined general merchandise and food. The centers ranged in size from 135,000 to 190,000 square feet and stressed customer service and convenience. The typical Super Kmart operated seven days a week, twenty-four-hours a day, and generated high traffic and sales volume. The centers also had wider shopping aisles, appealing displays, and pleasant lighting intended to enrich the shopping experience. Super Kmarts featured in-house bakeries, USDA fresh meats, fresh seafood, delicatessens, cookie kiosks, cappuccino bars, in-store eateries, food courts, and salad bars. In many locations, the centers provided customer services such as video rental, dry cleaning, shoe repair, beauty salons, optical shops, and express shipping services, as well as a full line of traditional Kmart merchandise. To enhance the appeal of the merchandise assortment, the centers emphasized "cross merchandising." For example, toasters stood above the fresh baked breads, kitchen gadgets hung across the aisle from produce, and baby centers offered everything from baby food to toys.

By 1998, the company operated ninety-nine Super Kmart Centers and served twenty-one states with this regionally based combination store format.

THE PLANNING FUNCTION

Corporate planning at Kmart was the result of executives, primarily the senior executive, recognizing change. The senior executive's role was to make others see that nothing is good forever. "Good planning" was perceived as the result of those who recognized that at some point they would have to get involved. "Poor planning" was done by those who didn't recognize the need for it. When they did, it was too late to survive. Good planning, if done on a regular and timely basis, was assumed to result in improved performance. Kmart's Michael Wellman, then director of planning and research, contended that

> . . . planning, as we like to stress, is making decisions now to improve performance tomorrow. Everyone looks at what may happen tomorrow, but the planners are the ones who make decisions today. That's where I think too many firms go wrong. They think they are planning because they are writing reports and are aware of changes. They don't say, 'because of this, we must decide today to spend this money to do this to accomplish this goal in the future.'

In the view of Kmart management, the firm had been very successful in the area of strategic planning. "When it became necessary to make significant changes in the way we were doing business," Wellman said, "that was accomplished on a fairly timely basis." When the organization made the change in the 1960s, it recognized that there was a very powerful investment opportunity and capitalized on it—far beyond what anyone else would have done. "We just opened stores," Wellman continued, "at a great, great pace. Management, when confronted with a crisis, would state, 'It's the economy, or it's this, or that, but it's not the essential way we are doing business.'" But he noted that, "suddenly management would recognize that the economy may stay like this forever," and it would decide to take action. Strategic planning was thought to arise out of some difficult times for the company.

Planning at Kmart was organized in a fairly formal way. It involved a constant evaluation of what was happening in the marketplace, what the competition was doing, and what kinds of opportunities were available. Management saw the need to diversify because a company would not be viable unless it was growing, and the Kmart format was unlikely to stimulate growth forever. It needed growth and opportunity, particularly for a company that was able to open 200 stores on a regular basis. Wellman recognized that "Given a corporate culture that was accustomed to challenges, management would have to find ways to expend that energy." "A corporation that is successful," he argued, "has to continue to be successful. It has to have a basic understanding of corporate needs and be augmented by a much more rigorous effort to be aware of what's going on in the external environment."

A planning group at Kmart represented a number of functional areas of the organization. Management described it as an "in-house consulting group" with some independence. Its members came from financial planning, economic and consumer analysis, and operations research. The CEO was identified as the primary planner.

REORGANIZATION AND RESTRUCTURING

Kmart financial performance for 1993 was clearly disappointing. The company announced a loss of $974 million on sales of $34,156,000 for the fiscal year ended January 26, 1994. Noting the deficit, the chairman, Joseph Antonini, concluded that it occurred primarily because of lower margins in the U.S. Kmart stores division. "Margin erosion," he said, "stemmed in part from intense industry-wide pricing pressure throughout 1993." He was confident, however, that Kmart was on track with its renewal program to make the more than 2,350 U.S. Kmart stores more "competitive, on-trend, and cutting merchandisers." Tactical Retail Solutions, Inc., estimated that during Antonini's seven-year tenure with the company, Kmart's market share in the discount arena fell to 23 percent, from 35 percent. Other retail experts suggested that because the company had struggled for so long to have the right merchandise in the stores at the right time, it had lost customers to competitors. An aging customer base was also cited.

In early 1995, following the posting of Kmart's eighth consecutive quarter of disappointing earnings, the company's board of directors announced that Joseph Antonini would be replaced as chairman. It named Donald S. Perkins, former chairman of Jewel Companies, Inc., and a Kmart director, to the position. Antonini relinquished his position as president and CEO in March. After a nationwide search, Floyd Hall, aged fifty-seven, a former chairman and CEO of the Target discount store division of Dayton-Hudson Corporation, was appointed chairman, president, and chief executive officer of Kmart in June of 1995.

In 1996, Kmart announced a restructuring of its merchandising organization aimed at improving product assortments, category management, customer focus, sales, and profitability. The company had also concluded the disposition of many non-core assets, including the sale of the Borders Group, OfficeMax, the Sports Authority, and Coles Myer. It had closed 214 underperforming stores in the United States, and cleared out $700 million in aged and discontinued inventory in the remaining Kmart stores.

The corporate mission was "to become the discount store of choice for middle-income families with children by satisfying their routine and seasonal shopping needs as well as or better than the competition." Management believed that the actions taken by the new president would have a dramatic impact on how customers perceived Kmart, how frequently they shopped in the stores, and how much they would buy on each visit. Increasing the frequency of customers' visits and the amount purchased on each visit were viewed as crucial to the effort to increase the company's profitability.

In 1996, Kmart converted 152 of its traditional stores to feature a new design that was referred to as the high-frequency format. These stores were named Big Kmart. The stores emphasized those departments that were deemed the most important to core customers and offered an increased mix of high frequency, everyday basics and consumables in the pantry area located at the front of each store. These items were typically priced at a 1 to 3 percentage differential from the leading competitors in each market and served to increase inventory turnover and gross margin dollars. In addition to the pantry area, Big Kmart stores featured improved lighting, new signage that was easier to see and read, and adjacencies that created a smoother traffic flow.

Floyd Hall felt Kmart's financial results for 1997 and early 1998 reflected the major financial restructuring that was underway at the company. Since he joined the company, his top priority had been to build a management team with "a 'can-do' attitude that would permeate all of our interaction with customers, vendors, shareholders, and one another." Major changes were made to the management team. Of the company's thirty-seven corporate officers, twenty-three were new to the company's team since 1995. The most dramatic restructuring had taken place in the merchandising organization where all four of the general merchandise managers responsible for buying organizations joined Kmart since 1995. In addition, fifteen new divisional vice presidents joined Kmart during

1997. Significant changes also were made in the board of directors: of the fifteen directors, nine were new to the company since 1995. (See Appendix for the board of directors and corporate officers at the beginning of 1998.) Hall argued that the company had turned a corner and that it was "finally and firmly on the road to recovery."

APPENDIX: KMART CORPORATION

Executive Directors 1997

The name, age, position and a description of the business experience for each of the executive officers of the company is listed below as of August 31, 1997. The business experience for each of the executive officers described below includes the principal positions held by them since 1992.

Floyd Hall (58)
Chairman of the board, president and chief executive officer since June 1995. Previously, he served concurrently as chairman and chief executive officer ofd the Museum Company, Alva Reproduction, Inc. And Glass Masters, Inc. From 1989 to 1995.

Warren Flick (53)
Director, president and chief operating officer, U.S. Kmart Stores since November 1996.

Laurence L. Anderson (55)
Executive vice president and president, Super Kmart since August 1997.

Warren Cooper (52)
Executive vice president, human resources & administration since March 1996.

Donald W. Keeble (48)
Executive vice president, store operations since February 1995.

Anthony N. Palizzi (54)
Executive vice president, general counsel since 1992.

Marvin P. Rich (52)
Executive vice president, strategic planning, finance and administration since 1994.

William N. Anderson (50)
Senior vice president and general merchandise manager, hardlines since September 1996.

Andrew A. Giancamilli (47)
Senior vice president, general merchandise manager, home and consumables since June 1997.

Ernest L. Heether (51)
Senior vice president, merchandise operations planning and replenishment since April 1996.

Paul J. Hueber (49)
Senior vice president, store operations since 1994.

Donald E. Norman (60)
Senior vice president, chief information officer since December 1995.

William D. Underwood (56)
Senior vice president, global sourcing since 1994.

Martin E. Welch III (49)
Senior vice president and chief financial officer since 1995.

Jerome J. Kuske (45)
Senior vice president, general merchandise manager, health and beauty care/pharmacy since June 1997.

James P. Mixon (53)
Senior vice president, logistics since June 1997.

E. Jackson Smailes (54)
Senior vice president, general merchandise manager, apparel since August 1997.

Board of Directors

James B. Adamson[4]#
Chairman and Chief Executive Officer
Flagstar Companies Inc.

Lilyan H. Affinito [1*,3,5,]
Former Vice Chairman of the Board
Maxxam Group Inc.

Stephen F. Bollenbach [4]#
President and Chief Executive Officer
Hilton Hotels Corporation

Joseph A. Califano, Jr. [4]
Chairman and President
The National Center on Addiction and Substance Abuse at Columbia University

Richard G. Cline [2*,3,5,]#
Chairman
Hawthorne Investors Inc., Former Chairman and Chief Executive Officer
NICOR Inc.

Willie D. Davis [2]
President
All Pro Broadcasting, Inc.

Enrique C. Falla [1]
Senior Vice President
The Dow Chemical Company

TABLE 2

Kmart Corporation, Consolidated Balance Sheets and Operating Statements, 1996–1997 (in millions, except per share data)

	Years Ended January 28, 1998, January 29, 1997, and January 31, 1996		
	1997	1996	1995
Sales	$32,183	$31,437	$31,713
Cost of sales, buying, and occupancy	25,152	24,390	24,675
Gross margin	7,031	7,047	7,038
Selling, general and administrative expenses	6,136	6,274	6,876
Voluntary early retirement program	114	—	—
Other (gains) losses	—	(10)	41
Continuing income before interest, income taxes and dividends on convertible preferred securities of subsidiary	781	783	121
Interest expense, net	363	453	434
Income tax provision (credit)	120	68	(83)
Dividends on convertible preferred securities of subsidiary, net of income taxes of $26 and $16	49	31	—
Net income (loss) from continuing operations before extraordinary item	249	231	(230)
Loss from discontinued operations, net of income taxes of $(3) and $(139)	—	(5)	(260)
Loss on disposal of discontinued operations, net of income taxes of $(240) and $88	—	(446)	(30)
Extraordinary loss, net of income taxes of $(27)	—	—	(51)
Net income (loss)	$ 249	$ (220)	$ (571)
Basic/diluted income (loss) per common share			
Continuing operations	$.51	$.48	$(.51)
Discontinued operations	—	(.01)	(.57)
Loss on disposal of discontinued operations	—	(.92)	(.06)
Extraordinary item	—	—	(.11)
Net income(loss)	$ .51	$ (.45)	$ (1.25)
Basic weighted average shares (in millions)	487.1	483.6	459.8
Dilute weighted average shares (in millions)	491.7	486.1	459.9

Joseph P. Flannery [3,4*,5]
Chairman of the Board, President and Chief Executive Officer
Uniroyal Holding Inc.

Warren Flick[#]
President and Chief Operating Officer, U.S. Kmart Stores
Kmart Corporation

Floyd Hall [3*] #
Chairman of the Board, President and Chief Executive Officer
Kmart Corporation

Robert D. Kennedy [4] #
Former Chairman and Chief Executive Officer
Union Carbide Corporation

J. Richard Munro [2,3,5*]

	As of January 28, 1998, and January 29, 1997	
	1997	1996
Current assets:		
Cash and cash equivalents	$498	$406
Merchandise inventories	6,367	6,354
Other current assets	611	973
Total current assets	7,476	7,733
Property and equipment, net	5,472	5,740
Property held for sale or financing	271	200
Other assets and deferred charges	339	613
Total assets	$13,558	$14,286
Current liabilities:		
Long-term debt due within one year	$78	$156
Trade accounts payable	1,923	2,009
Accrued payroll and other liabilities	1,064	1,298
Taxes other than income taxes	209	139
Total current liabilities	3,274	3,602
Long-term debt and notes payable	1,725	2,121
Capital lease obligations	1,179	1,478
Other long-term liabilities	965	1,013
Company obligated mandatorily redeemable convertible preferred securities of a subsidiary trust holding solely 7¾% convertible junior subordinated debentures of Kmart (redemption value of $1,000)	981	980
Common stock, $1 par value, 1,500,000,000 shares authorized; 488,811,271 and 486,996,145 shares issued, respectively	489	486
Capital in excess of par value	1,620	1,608
Retained earnings	3,343	3,105
Treasury shares and restricted stock	(15)	(37)
Foreign currency translation adjustment	(3)	(70)
Total liabilities and shareholders' equity	$13,558	$14,286

Source: Company Annual Reports.

Chairman of the Board
Gene tech, Inc.

Robin B. Smith[#]
Chairman and Chief Executive Officer
Publishers Clearing House

William P. Weber [1] [#]
Vice Chairman
Texas Instruments Incorporated

James O. Welch, Jr. [2] [#]
Former Vice Chairman
RJR Nabisco and Chairman
Nabisco Brands, Inc.

Committees:

1=Audit
2=Compensation & Incentives

TABLE 3

Kmart Corporation, Financial Performance 1988–1997
(in $ millions)

Year	Sales	Assets	Net Income*	Net Worth
1988	$27,301,000	$12,126,000	$803,000	$5,009,000
1989	29,533,000	13,145,000	323,000	4,972,000
1990	32,070,000	13,899,000	756,000	5,384,000
1991	34,580,000	15,999,000	859,000	6,891,000
1992	37,724,000	18,931,000	941,000	7,536,000
1993	34,156,000	17,504,000	(974,000)	6,093,000
1994	34,025,000	17,029,000	296,000	6,032,000
1995	31,713,000	15,033,000	(571,000)	5,280,000
1997	32,183,000	13,558,000	249,000	6,445,000

*After taxes and extraordinary credit or charges.
Data from 1995, 1996 and 1997 reflect disposition of subsidiaries.
Source: Fortune financial analysis and Kmart Annual Reports.

TABLE 4

Wal-Mart Stores, Inc., Financial Performance 1988–1997
(in $ millions)

Year	Sales	Assets	Net Income	Net Worth
1988	$ 20,649,001	$ 6,359,668	$ 837,221	$ 3,007,909
1989	25,810,656	8,198,484	1,075,900	3,965,561
1990	32,601,594	11,388,915	1,291,024	5,365,524
1991	43,886,900	15,443,400	1,608,500	6,989,700
1992	55,484,000	20,565,000	1,995,000	8,759,000
1993	67,344,000	26,441,000	2,333,000	10,753,000
1994	82,494,000	32,819,000	2,681,000	12,726,000
1995	93,627,000	37,541,000	2,740,000	14,756,000
1996	104,859,000	39,604,000	3,056,000	17,143,000
1997	117,958,000	45,384,000	3,526,000	18,503,000

Source: Wal-Mart Annual Reports and *Fortune* financial analysis.

3=Executive
4=Finance
5=Nominating
*=Committee Chair
#=Joined Board since 1995

References

Berner, Robert. "Kmart's Earnings More Than Tripled in First Quarter." *Wall Street Journal*, May 14, 1998, A13.

Brauer, Molly. "Kmart in Black 'in 6 Months.'" *Detroit Free Press*, January 26, 1996, E1.

Bussey, John. "Kmart Is Set to Sell Many of Its Roots to Rapid-American Corp's McCrory." *Wall Street Journal*, April 6, 1987, 24.

Carruth, Eleanore. "Kmart Has to Open Some New Doors on the Future." *Fortune*, July 1977, 143-150, 153-154.

Chakravarty, Subrata N. "A Tale of Two Companies." *Forbes*, May 27, 1991, 86-96.

Dewar, Robert E. "The Kresge Company and the Retail Revolution." *University of Michigan Business Review*, July 2, 1975, 2.

Duff, Christina, and Joann S. Lubin. "Kmart Board Ousts Antonini as Chairman." *Wall Street Journal*, January 18, 1995, A3.

Elmer, Vickie, and Joann Muller. "Retailer Needs Leader, Vision." *Detroit Free Press*, March 22, 1995, 1A, 9A.

Guiles, Melinda G. "Attention, Shoppers: Stop That Browsing and Get Aggressive." *Wall Street Journal*, June 16, 1987, 1, 21.

———. "Kmart, Bruno's Join to Develop 'Hypermarkets.'" *Wall Street Journal*, September 8, 1987, 17.

Ingrassia, Paul. "Attention Non Kmart Shoppers: A Blue-Light Special Just for You." *Wall Street Journal*, October 6, 1987, 42.

"It's Kresge…Again." *Chain Store Executive*, November 1975, 16.

Key, Janet. "Kmart Plan: Diversify, Conquer: Second Largest Retailer Out to Woo Big Spenders." *Chicago Tribune*, November 11, 1984, 1-2.

Kmart Corporation, Annual Reports, 1990, 1995, 1996, and 1997.

———. *Kmart Fact Book*, 1997.

"Kmart Looks to New Logo to Signify Changes." *Wall Street Journal*, September 13, 1990, 10.

"Kmart Will Expand Line With Purchase of Warehouse Club." *Wall Street Journal*, December 14, 1990, 4.

Main, Jerry. "Kmart's Plan to Be Born Again." *Fortune*, September 21, 1981, 74-77, 84-85.

Mitchell, Russell. "How They're Knocking the Rust Off Two Old Chains." *Business Week*, September 8, 1986, 44-48.

Rice, Faye. "Why Kmart Has Stalled." *Fortune*, October 9, 1989, 79.

Saporito, Bill. "Is Wal-Mart Unstoppable?" *Fortune*, May 6, 1991, 50-59.

Schwadel, Francine. "Attention Kmart Shoppers: Style Coming to This Aisle." *Wall Street Journal*, August 9, 1988, 6.

———. "Kmart to Speed Store Openings, Renovations." *Wall Street Journal*, February 27, 1990, 3.

Sellers, Patricia. "Attention, Kmart Shoppers." *Fortune*, January 2, 1989, 41.

Stavro, Barry. "Mass Appeal." *Forbes*, May 5, 1986, 128, 130.

Sternad, Patricia. "Kmart's Antonini Moves Far Beyond Retail 'Junk' Image." *Advertising Age*, July 25, 1988, 1, 67.

Wellman, Michael. Interview with Michael Wellman, director of planning and research, Kmart Corporation, August 6, 1984.

"Where Kmart Goes Next Now That It's No. 2." *Business Week*, June 2, 1980, 109-110, 114.

"Why Chains Enter New Areas." *Chain Store Executive*, December 1976, 22, 24.

Woodruff, David. "Will Kmart Ever Be a Silk Purse?" *Business Week*, January 22, 1990, 46.

CASE 23

The Cat Recovers: Caterpillar, Inc., in the Late 1990s

This case was prepared by M. Edgar Barrett of Thunderbird—The American Graduate School of International Management.

In early 1998, Donald V. Fites had reason to be more than just satisfied with the performance of Caterpillar, Inc. (Cat), under his leadership. Named chief executive officer in 1990, he had presided over a tumultuous—but highly successful—period in Cat's history. Sales had increased by approximately 85 percent between 1991 and 1997, with annual net income moving from a negative $404 million to a positive $1,665 million during the same period.

Nonetheless, he was concerned about the firm's likely future. The construction equipment industry was in the process of being both redefined and restructured, new competitors were emerging, and the rate of change seemed to be accelerating.

INDUSTRY BACKGROUND

The heavy construction equipment industry, with worldwide sales of $71 billion for 1996, was expected to continue its growth at about four percent per annum for the next four years.[1] Heavy construction equipment, ranging from the 240-ton off-highway trucks to mini-excavators, was being used all over the world for commercial and industrial construction, mining, transportation, forestry, road building, and many other applications. Five main categories made up the heavy construction equip-

ment industry: earthmoving equipment (loaders, scrapers, graders, rollers, and compactors); off-highway trucks; construction cranes; mixers, pavers, and related equipment; and parts and attachments (hoes, dragline buckets, winches, and so forth).

The construction equipment industry had experienced numerous changes over the last three decades. Rapid demand growth in the early 1970s was soon interrupted by world recessionary conditions caused by rising oil prices. After almost a decade of sluggish demand, construction equipment sales picked up. Demand growth in developing countries was expected to exhibit an above average rate as they set out to build basic infrastructure (see Tables 1 and 2). Developed nations, especially the United States, were expected to continue to show stable growth throughout the next decade.

These new conditions had created new challenges for construction equipment manufacturing firms. Growing Third World economies, primarily needing equipment for road building, housing, and mining, were expected to prefer used equipment coming from developed nations as they often lacked credit worthiness and were greatly concerned about investment costs. On the other hand, developed nations with fully developed infrastructures were expected to exhibit an increased level of demand for construction equipment for use in repairs and smaller construction projects. These combined effects were seen as resulting in strong growth for compact equipment within the developed world and larger machines for the developing nations.

Compact equipment generally had lower margins and faced stronger competition from regional

TABLE 1

Construction Equipment Industry: Supply and Demand by Region (in millions of U.S. $)

	Construction Equipment Demand				
	1987	*1992*	*1996*	*2001*	*2006*
North America	$10,950	$11,215	$19,660	$20,610	$24,680
Central and South America	2,500	2,605	3,660	5,050	6,600
Europe	17,320	17,945	17,935	22,230	26,700
Africa and Middle East	1,900	2,240	2,680	3,400	4,270
Asia and Oceania	10,010	18,390	27,340	35,330	45,730
Total	$42,680	$52,395	$71,275	$86,620	$107,980
	Construction Equipment Production				
	1987	*1992*	*1996*	*2001*	*2006*
North America	$10,240	$12,380	$19,755	$21,850	$27,800
Central and South America	1,415	1,419	1,923	2,710	3,610
Europe	19,890	20,027	21,017	26,275	31,940
Africa and Middle East	100	125	175	220	280
Asia and Oceania	10,565	16,179	26,955	34,145	43,160
Total	$42,210	$50,130	$69,825	$85,200	$106,790

Source: The Freedonia Group, Inc., July 1997.

construction equipment manufacturers. More than 200 participants were active in the mature U.S. market, although only a handful possessed extensive product lines and strong market share. The earthmoving business, although expected to grow at a slightly lower rate than the other segments, contributed almost half of industry sales. As shown in Table 2, demand for off-highway trucks, mixers, pavers, and related equipment was expected to climb at a faster rate than the other three categories.

Full-range suppliers such as Caterpillar and Komatsu offered a broad line of equipment for the construction industry around the world. In 1996, they commanded a 17.1 percent and 8.1 percent worldwide market share, respectively, of the heavy construction equipment industry. The next ten competitors, which included Case, Deere, Hitachi, Ingersoll-Rand, Liebherr, and Volvo, held 24.8 percent of the market.[2]

High rates of production volume were viewed as critical for construction equipment manufacturers as they allowed the spreading of high fixed overhead and research and development expenses across a larger number of units. Successful manufacturers had been implementing extensive cost-cutting measures and rationalization of production facilities to retain profitability in this increasingly competitive industry. A general trend toward outsourcing could also be seen throughout the industry, allowing equipment makers to focus on design and final assembly. In addition, manufacturers were reducing the number of suppliers in order to simplify supplier networks and promote cooperation.

Over the last decade, cooperative agreements had also become common. Collaboration took place either through joint ventures designed to share production facilities or through technology-sharing agreements. Joint ventures, such as the Caterpillar-Mitsubishi one in Japan, were being used to produce specific models for regional or worldwide sales. Examples of technology-sharing arrangements included Komatsu's 50/50 joint venture with Cummins Engine for the manufacture of diesel engines.

Historically, a strong dealer network has also been key in helping the company remain competi-

TABLE 2

Construction Equipment Industry: Demand for Specific Product Categories (in millions of U.S. $)

Demand for Earthmoving Equipment*	1987	1992	1996	2001	2006
North America	$5,255	$4,970	$9,848	$10,090	$12,070
Central and South America	1,279	1,308	1,768	2,495	3,290
Europe	8,964	9,203	9,031	11,125	13,290
Africa and Middle East	895	1,115	1,375	1,650	2,080
Asia and Oceania	4,609	8,941	13,459	17,140	22,070
Total	**$21,002**	**$25,537**	**$35,481**	**$42,500**	**$52,800**

Demand for Cranes	1987	1992	1996	2001	2006
North America	$961	$1,259	$2,372	$2,480	$3,035
Central and South America	139	134	224	275	350
Europe	1,905	1,996	2,083	2,620	3,160
Africa and Middle East	191	260	280	360	460
Asia and Oceania	764	1,531	2,291	2,955	3,795
Total	**$3,960**	**$5,180**	**$7,250**	**$8,690**	**$10,800**

Demand for Parts and Attachments	1987	1992	1996	2001	2006
North America	$3,517	$3,347	$4,750	$5,120	$6,120
Central and South America	612	604	912	1,240	1,590
Europe	4,637	4,884	4,965	6,145	7,375
Africa and Middle East	442	510	535	765	940
Asia and Oceania	2,917	4,947	7,012	9,080	11,735
Total	**$12,125**	**$14,292**	**$18,174**	**$22,350**	**$27,760**

Demand for Off-Highway Trucks	1987	1992	1996	2001	2006
North America	$526	$973	$1,519	$1,635	$1,935
Central and South America	331	410	550	745	985
Europe	747	719	671	830	1,015
Africa and Middle East	291	260	370	470	590
Asia and Oceania	1,091	1,702	2,607	3,540	4,655
Total	**$2,986**	**$4,064**	**$5,717**	**$7,220**	**$9,180**

Demand for Mixers, Pavers, and Related Equipment	1987	1992	1996	2001	2006
North America	$691	$666	$1,171	$1,285	$1,520
Central and South America	139	149	206	295	385
Europe	1,067	1,143	1,185	1,510	1,860
Africa and Middle East	81	95	120	155	200
Asia and Oceania	629	1,269	1,971	2,615	3,475
Total	**$2,607**	**$3,322**	**$4,653**	**$5,860**	**$7,440**

Source: The Freedonia Group, Inc., July 1997.
*Except off-highway trucks.

tive. Parts supply and equipment service are critical for customers due to high construction downtime costs. In turn, the sale of parts and attachments represented about one-fourth of industry sales. This highly profitable portion of the business generated important revenues for companies with a large installed base of construction equipment scattered throughout the globe. A strong service network could also be used to support the marketing effort of the equipment maker and provide it with valuable market information.

Most large and medium-size construction equipment makers offered both wholesale and retail financing. Wholesale financing is designed to allow distributors and dealers to maintain an adequate inventory of products and parts. Retail financing is used to assist end users with the purchase of equipment. This could be an important purchase variable for large construction projects or in cash-strapped, emerging markets.

The sale of heavy construction equipment often requires a substantial effort by dealers as well as by equipment makers. Relationships with large contractors and government officials are often critical, especially in developing nations, where large infrastructure projects are common. Large construction and engineering firms, as well as mine operators, frequently seek to limit the number of brands in their fleets in order to reduce training and maintenance costs at construction sites.

The retail price of heavy construction equipment had remained practically flat throughout the world during the last decade. Several reasons seemed to have produced this trend. Competition in medium- and small-sized equipment had dramatically increased. This was primarily due to the increasing number of equipment makers offering quality products. As the reliability of products from different equipment makers converged, brand loyalty decreased, especially for smaller projects, where each purchase could result in a reevaluation of the alternative sources of new equipment. New equipment also had to compete with longer-lasting used machinery that often sold at a 30 to 60 percent price discount. However, overall prices were expected to rise as equipment demand in developing countries outpaced the supply of used equipment coming from developed nations. The demand for new equipment was also likely to be affected positively as new credit, leasing, and renting options became available in the emerging world.

Equipment makers were constantly working on improving the quality of their products as a means of differentiation from both competitors and old machines. Onboard electronics provided continuous monitoring, thus optimizing performance and reducing repair costs. Features to enhance operator efficiency and comfort had also been added. These new features offered such benefits as improved maneuverability, quieter machines, reduced vibrations, and automatic transmissions.

CATERPILLAR: AN ENDURING LEADER

Caterpillar Incorporated, headquartered in Peoria, Illinois, had been the heavy construction industry leader since the mid 1920s. Its three main lines of business (machinery, engines, and financial products) all contributed to its $18.9 billion in sales for 1997 (see Table 3 for additional financial data). Caterpillar designed, manufactured, and marketed equipment for construction, earthmoving, mining, and agriculture. It was also a major manufacturer of forklifts, container handlers, and warehouse equipment. Cat engines were used to power on-highway trucks, ships and boats, locomotives, and other construction, mining, and agricultural equipment. Other power generating systems manufactured by Cat were commonly utilized as prime or standby sources of power for applications that ranged from off-shore drilling rigs to emergency power for factories and airports. Caterpillar's financial products complemented its manufacturing operations by offering a wide variety of financing options and insurance, both for its customers and for its worldwide network of distributors and dealers. (See Table 4 for data on the size and margins of the different business segments.)

Caterpillar, under the Caterpillar, Cat, Barber-Green, and Mak brand names, sold $18.1 billion worth of machinery and engines in 1997. Its full line of earthmovers included tractors, loaders, excavators, trucks, scrapers, paving products, motor graders, mining shovels, pipelayers, log skidders, log loaders, and related parts. As shown in Table 4, Cat's end users ranged from the energy industry and commercial and industrial construction to mining and transportation applications.

Engines and turbines provided Caterpillar with additional revenue growth that, in 1997, accounted for a quarter of Cat's net revenues. Additionally, the

TABLE 3

Caterpillar: Financial Highlights (millions of dollars unless indicated otherwise)

	1982	1983	1984	1985	1986	1987
(Year ended December 31)						
Sales and revenues	6,472	5,429	6,597	6,760	7,380	8,294
Sales of machinery and engines	6,469	5,424	6,576	6,725	7,321	8,180
Percent inside the United States	43%	54%	58%	58%	54%	52%
Percent outside the United States	57%	46%	42%	42%	46%	48%
Revenues of financial products	3	5	21	35	59	114
Profit (loss)	(180)	(345)	(428)	198	76	350
As a percent of sales and revenues	(2.8%)	(6.4%)	(6.5%)	2.9%	1.0%	4.2%
Profit (loss) per share of common stock	(2.04)	(3.74)	(4.47)	2.02	0.39	1.76
Dividends declared per share of common stock	2.40	1.50	1.25	0.50	0.31	0.28
Return on average common stock equity	(4.9%)	(10.1%)	(13.8%)	6.7%	2.4%	10.4%
Capital expenditures:						
Land, buildings, machinery and equipment	532	313	234	228	290	463
Equipment leased to others	3	14	23	55	41	30
Depreciation and amortization	505	507	497	485	453	425
Research and engineering expenses	376	340	345	326	308	298
As a percent of sales and revenues	5.8%	6.3%	5.2%	4.8%	4.2%	3.6%
Provision (credit) for income taxes	(303)	(264)	(115)	25	21	118
Wages, salaries, and employee benefits	2,474	2,142	2,426	2,173	2,184	2,284
Average number of employees	73,249	58,402	61,189	55,815	54,024	53,770
December 31						
Total receivables:						
Trade and other	965	1,451	1,133	1,296	1,755	2,044
Finance	64	74	66	117	466	795
Inventories	1,801	1,193	1,246	1,139	1,211	1,323
Total assets:						
Machinery and engines	7,153	6,849	6,084	5,951	6,134	6,647
Financial products	68	96	169	235	627	984
Long-term debt:						
Machinery and engines	2,389	1,894	1,384	1,177	963	900
Financial products	——	5	4	87	171	387
Total debt:						
Machinery and engines	2,612	2,247	1,861	1,404	1,582	1,484
Financial products	1	7	26	130	370	712
Ratios, excluding financial products						
Current assets to current liabilities	2.81	2.07	1.43	1.69	1.50	1.55
Percentage of total debt to total debt and stockholders' equity	42.8%	40.2%	39.5%	31.4%	33.4%	29.4%

Source: Caterpillar, Inc., Annual Reports.

machinery business benefited from advances in the power generation business, for Cat was seen as being in the forefront in efficiency and power in the engines and turbine businesses.

Caterpillar employed 59,860 people in manufacturing facilities around the world and in its numerous distribution centers. (See Table 5 for a list of manufacturing plant locations and employees.) Historically, one of Caterpillar's competitive advantages had been its strong international focus, which had contributed, over the last decade, to approximately 50 percent of total sales. Recent sales trends

1988	1989	1990	1991	1992	1993	1994	1995	1996	1997
10,435	11,126	11,436	10,182	10,194	11,615	14,238	16,072	16,522	18,925
10,255	10,882	11,103	9,838	9,840	11,235	13,863	15,451	15,814	18,110
50%	47%	45%	41%	45%	51%	51%	48%	49%	49%
50%	53%	55%	59%	55%	49%	49%	52%	51%	51%
180	244	333	344	354	380	465	621	708	815
616	497	210	(404)	(2,435)	652	955	1,136	1,361	1,665
5.9%	4.5%	1.8%	(4.0%)	(23.9%)	5.6%	6.7%	7.1%	8.2%	8.8%
3.04	2.45	1.04	(2.00)	(12.06)	3.21	4.70	5.72	7.07	4.44
0.43	0.60	0.60	0.53	0.30	0.30	0.63	1.30	1.55	4.37
16.0%	11.6%	4.7%	(9.4%)	(86.7%)	34.6%	37.4%	36.1%	36.3%	37.9%
732	984	926	653	515	417	501	464	506	824
61	105	113	121	125	215	193	215	265	282
434	471	533	602	654	668	683	682	696	738
334	387	420	441	446	455	435	532	570	700
3.2%	3.5%	3.7%	4.3%	4.4%	3.9%	3.0%	3.3%	3.4%	3.7%
262	162	78	(152)	(114)	42	354	501	613	796
2,643	2,888	3,032	3,051	2,795	3,038	3,146	2,919	3,437	3,773
57,954	60,784	59,662	55,950	52,340	50,443	52,778	54,263	54,968	58,366
2,349	2,353	2,361	2,133	2,330	2,769	3,096	2,657	3,084	3,465
1,222	1,498	1,891	2,145	2,525	3,140	3,988	4,820	5,646	6,541
1,986	2,120	2,105	1,921	1,675	1,525	1,835	1,921	2,222	2,603
8,226	9,100	9,626	9,346	10,979	11,131	11,582	11,238	12,156	13,001
1,460	1,826	2,325	2,696	2,956	3,676	4,668	5,592	6,572	7,755
1,428	1,797	2,101	2,676	2,753	2,030	1,934	2,049	2,018	2,367
525	491	789	1,216	1,366	1,865	2,336	1,915	2,514	4,575
2,116	2,561	2,873	3,136	3,271	2,387	2,037	2,219	2,176	2,474
1,144	1,433	1,848	2,111	2,401	3,041	3,866	4,181	5,283	4,575
1.76	1.78	1.67	1.74	1.57	1.53	1.62	1.78	1.68	1.62
34.0%	36.4%	38.8%	43.7%	67.5%	52.1%	41.2%	39.6%	34.6%	34.6%

(see Table 6) illustrated the relative growth of emerging regions of the world such as Asia-Pacific and Latin America, and a slowdown of business in Europe.

An extensive dealer network had led the company into its leadership position. The network of close to 200 dealers, 137 of which were located outside the United States, was unmatched by any other equipment maker. This allowed Cat to remain the market leader in every country in which it does business, with the exception of Japan. Cat's rival Komatsu led the industry in Japan.

TABLE 4

Caterpillar: Sales and Profit Composition by Segment (millions of U.S. $ unless indicated otherwise)

	1982	1983	1984	1985	1986	1987
Sales by Segment						
Machinery	4,795	4,211	5,053	5,208	5,761	6,529
Engines	1,674	1,213	1,523	1,517	1,560	1,651
Financial products	—	—	—	—	—	—
Total sales and revenues	6,469	5,424	6,576	6,725	7,321	8,810
Operating Profit by Segment						
Machinery	(78)	(29)	(52)	376	281	588
Engines	85	(64)	(74)	68	97	155
Financial products	—	—	—	—	—	—
Total operating profit	7	(93)	(126)	444	378	743
Profit Margin by Segment						
Machinery	(1.6%)	(0.7%)	(1.0%)	7.2%	4.9%	9.0%
Engines	5.1%	(5.3%)	(4.9%)	4.5%	6.2%	9.4%
Financial products	n.a.	n.a.	n.a.	n.a.	n.a.	n.a.
Weighted profit margin	0.1%	(1.7%)	(1.9%)	6.6%	5.2%	9.1%
New Machine Sales by End User						
Energy	22%	19%	20%	21%	18%	15%
Transportation	30%	28%	26%	29%	31%	27%
Housing and forest	17%	20%	22%	12%	13%	15%
Commercial and industrial construction	0%	0%	0%	9%	10%	13%
Mining	9%	11%	10%	10%	11%	11%
Food and water	6%	6%	6%	4%	4%	4%
Other	16%	16%	16%	15%	13%	15%

Source: Caterpillar, Inc., Annual Reports.

Profits for 1997 were at an all-time high, with a net profit margin of 8.8 percent. Years of investments in automation and cost reduction were instrumental in achieving these results. Cat's stock price reflected these financial results, showing an increase of nearly 300 percent from December 1992 to December 1997. But management was worried that changing consumer trends, labor disputes, and the increasing power of competitors might collectively serve to undermine the firm's achievements.

The Origins

Now the largest manufacturer of construction equipment in the world, Caterpillar was formed by the merger of Holt Manufacturing and C. L. Best Tractor companies in 1925. By the 1940s, Caterpillar had a product line that included track-type tractors, motor graders, blade graders, elevated graders, and terracers. Sales began to climb during World War II when track-type tractors were demanded by the Allies for pulling artillery and supply wagons through tough terrain. World War II also brought with it greater demand for construction equipment, resulting in a large number of pieces of Caterpillar equipment being dispersed throughout the world. Caterpillar quickly came to dominate the marketplace, commanding 50 percent of the earthmoving equipment market.

The 1980s

After a boom period in the 1970s, the world recession of the early 1980s severely affected Caterpillar's bottom line. The effects of the strong dollar

1988	1989	1990	1991	1992	1993	1994	1995	1996	1997
8,206	8,478	8,735	7,397	7,209	8,132	10,164	11,336	11,862	13,350
2,049	2,404	2,368	2,441	2,631	3,103	3,699	4,115	3,952	4,760
180	244	344	344	354	380	465	621	708	815
10,435	11,126	11,447	10,182	10,194	11,615	14,328	16,072	16,522	18,925
932	733	273	(281)	(107)	436	1,099	1,210	1,562	1,889
243	235	84	(10)	79	226	348	462	395	497
15	27	37	37	35	47	64	88	114	142
1,190	995	394	(254)	7	709	1,511	1,760	2,071	2,528
11.4%	8.6%	3.1%	(3.8%)	(1.5%)	5.4%	10.8%	10.7%	13.2%	14.1%
11.9%	9.8%	3.5%	(0.4%)	3.0%	7.3%	9.4%	11.2%	10.0%	10.4%
8.3%	11.1%	10.8%	10.8%	9.9%	12.4%	13.8%	14.2%	16.1%	17.4%
11.4%	8.9%	3.4%	(2.5%)	0.1%	6.1%	10.5%	11.0%	12.5%	13.4%
15%	16%	18%	20%	22%	19%	22%	12%	14%	13%
25%	25%	24%	25%	27%	28%	28%	23%	22%	24%
16%	15%	15%	14%	13%	15%	15%	15%	15%	15%
13%	11%	10%	9%	8%	9%	7%	12%	15%	15%
13%	13%	13%	13%	13%	12%	12%	20%	18%	17%
4%	4%	4%	5%	5%	5%	4%	6%	6%	6%
14%	16%	16%	14%	12%	12%	12%	12%	10%	10%

and depressed worldwide demand began to surface in 1982, when sales figures fell 29 percent compared with the previous year. The company registered a $180 million loss that same year, the second since its incorporation in 1925. (Caterpillar had registered a loss of $1.6 million in 1932.)

Caterpillar tried to alleviate the pressure on its cost structure by laying off 13,000 of its 47,000 U.S. hourly workers. Salaries for top management and other employees were cut by 10 percent and a range of 3 to 9 percent, respectively, affecting 13,800 employees. Additionally, salaries of 9,600 secretaries and technicians were frozen indefinitely. Capital expenditures were trimmed by 36 percent from the previous year's investment of $836 million. Debt soared to $2.6 billion, compared with $1.8 billion in 1981.

The United Auto Workers, representing about 13,000 employees in Caterpillar's U.S. plants, went out on strike in the second half of 1982 after talks broke down over new contract negotiations. The UAW asked for a continuation of the previous contract, while Caterpillar demanded wage freezes and a reduction in the cost-of-living adjustments (COLA) in light of the tough times. The strong dollar had produced huge wage differentials between Caterpillar and Japanese rival Komatsu, whose workers earned roughly half the pay of Cat's workers when expressed in dollar terms.

The strike ended in April 1983, after seven months of talks. Because Caterpillar had anticipated the strike and had expanded inventory levels, it was able to weather the long strike, although by April inventory levels were almost completely

TABLE 5

Caterpillar: Plant Locations and Employees

Plant Locations	
Inside the United States	*Outside the United States*

Manufacturing

California	Peoria	*North Carolina*	*Australia*	Peterlee	*Italy*
Gardena	Pontiac	Clayton	Burnie*	Skinningrove	Bazzano
San Diego	Sterling	Franklin	Cowell*	Stockton	Jesi
Florida	*Indiana*	Leland	Melbourne	Wolverhampton	Milan*
Jacksonville	Lafayette	Morganton	Perth	*France*	*Japan*
Georgia	*Kansas*	Sanford	*Belgium*	Grenoble	Akashi*
Jefferson	Wamego	*Oregon*	Gosselies	Rantigny	Sagamihara*
LaGrange	*Kentucky*	Dallas	*Brazil*	*Germany*	*Mexico*
Illinois	Danville	*Pennsylvania*	Piracicaba	Kiel	Monterrey
Aurora	*Michigan*	York	*Canada*	Wackersdorf	Tijuana
Champaign*	Menominee	*South Carolina*	Montreal	Zweibrucken	*Northern Ireland*
Decatur	*Minnesota*	Greenville	*China*	*Hungary*	Larne*
DeKalb	Minneapolis	Sumter	Guangzhuo*	Godollo**	*Poland*
Dixon	New Ulm	*Tennessee*	ErLiBan*	*India*	Janow Lubelski**
East Peoria	*Mississippi*	Dyersburg	Tianjin**	Bangalore*	*Russia*
Joliet	Oxford	Rockwood	Xuzhou**	Mumbai*	St. Petersburg
Mapleton	*Missouri*	*Texas*	*England*	*Indonesia*	*Sweden*
Mossville	Boonville	Houston	Leicester	Jakarta**	Soderhamn

Remanufacturing and Overhaul

Mississippi	*Australia*	*Indonesia*
Corinth	Melbourne	Bandung
Prentiss County	*Belgium*	*Malaysia*
Texas	Gosselies	Kuala Lumpur
De Soto	*Canada*	*Mexico*
Mabank	Edmonton	Nuevo Laredo

Full-Time Employees at Year-End						
	1992	*1993*	*1994*	*1995*	*1996*	*1997*
Inside the United States	37,311	38,103	39,749	39,978	38,571	39,722
Europe	8,011	7,999	8,146	8,413	11,953	12,627
Latin America	4,088	3,735	4,500	4,104	4,540	5,340
Asia-Pacific	1,155	1,235	1,383	1,630	1,746	1,843
Canada	97	91	117	121	127	219
Other	87	87	91	106	89	112
Outside the United States	13,438	13,147	14,237	14,374	18,455	20,141
Total	50,749	51,250	53,986	54,352	57,026	59,863

*Facility of affiliated company (50% or less owned).
**Facility of partially-owned subsidiary (greater than 50%, less than 100%).
Source: Caterpillar, Inc., Annual Reports and Form 10-K, 1997.

TABLE 6

Caterpillar: Sales Composition by Region (millions of dollars unless otherwise stated)

	1988	1989	1990	1991	1992	1993	1994	1995	1996	1997
Sales by Region										
United States	5,077	5,132	5,023	4,058	4,421	5,710	7,008	7,422	7,676	8,926
Asia-Pacific	1,113	1,472	1,595	1,411	1,309	1,612	1,964	2,290	2,560	2,474
Europe	1,875	1,939	2,049	1,780	1,785	1,578	2,078	2,686	2,366	2,619
Latin America	729	829	842	873	908	849	1,151	1,183	1,238	1,702
Africa and Middle East	720	732	922	1,148	892	802	753	914	1,151	1,183
Canada	741	778	672	568	525	684	909	956	823	1,206
Total Sales	10,255	10,882	11,103	9,838	9,840	11,235	13,863	15,451	15,814	18,110
Exports from the United States										
Asia-Pacific	781	1,002	1,130	1,023	948	1,191	1,359	1,527	1,753	1,693
Europe	684	693	833	739	698	745	973	1,176	1,240	1,331
Latin America	420	447	484	659	666	605	852	927	993	1,288
Africa and Middle East	439	488	630	781	606	577	522	644	767	757
Canada	606	661	608	503	416	625	806	852	748	1,049
Total Exports	2,930	3,291	3,685	3,705	3,334	3,743	4,512	5,126	5,501	6,118
Imports as Percent of Sales										
Asia-Pacific	70.2%	68.1%	70.8%	72.5%	72.4%	73.9%	69.2%	66.7%	68.5%	68.4%
Europe	36.5%	35.7%	40.7%	41.5%	39.1%	47.2%	46.8%	43.8%	52.4%	50.8%
Latin America	57.6%	53.9%	57.5%	75.5%	73.3%	71.3%	74.0%	78.4%	80.2%	75.7%
Africa and Middle East	61.0%	66.7%	68.3%	68.0%	67.9%	71.9%	69.3%	70.5%	66.6%	64.0%
Canada	81.8%	85.0%	90.5%	88.6%	79.2%	91.4%	88.7%	89.1%	90.9%	87.0%
U.S. Exports as Percent of Sales Abroad	56.6%	57.2%	60.6%	64.1%	61.5%	67.7%	65.8%	63.8%	67.6%	66.6%

Growth Rates

	1989	1990	1991	1992	1993	1994	1995	1996	1997	Comp. Annual
Sales by Region										
United States	1.1%	(2.1%)	(19.2%)	8.9%	29.2%	22.7%	5.9%	3.4%	16.3%	6.5%
Asia-Pacific	32.3%	8.4%	(11.5%)	(7.2%)	23.1%	21.8%	16.6%	11.8%	(3.4%)	9.3%
Europe	3.4%	5.7%	(13.1%)	0.3%	(11.6%)	31.7%	29.3%	(11.9%)	10.7%	3.8%
Latin America	13.7%	1.6%	3.7%	4.0%	(6.5%)	35.6%	2.8%	4.6%	37.5%	9.9%
Africa and Middle East	1.7%	26.0%	24.5%	(22.3%)	(10.1%)	(6.1%)	21.4%	25.9%	2.8%	5.7%
Canada	5.0%	(13.6%)	(15.5%)	(7.6%)	30.3%	32.9%	5.2%	(13.9%)	46.5%	5.6%
Total sales	6.1%	2.0%	(11.4%)	0.0%	14.2%	23.4%	11.5%	2.3%	14.5%	6.5%
Exports from the United States										
Asia-Pacific	28.3%	12.8%	(9.5%)	(7.3%)	25.6%	14.1%	12.4%	14.8%	(3.4%)	9.0%
Europe	1.3%	20.2%	(11.3%)	(5.5%)	6.7%	30.6%	20.9%	5.4%	7.3%	7.7%
Latin America	6.4%	8.3%	36.2%	1.1%	(9.2%)	40.8%	8.8%	7.1%	29.7%	13.3%
Africa and Middle East	11.2%	29.1%	24.0%	(22.4%)	(4.8%)	(9.5%)	23.4%	19.1%	(1.3%)	6.2%
Canada	9.1%	(8.0%)	(17.3%)	(17.3%)	50.2%	29.0%	5.7%	(12.2%)	40.2%	6.3%
Total exports	12.3%	12.0%	0.5%	(10.0%)	12.3%	20.5%	13.6%	7.3%	11.2%	8.5%

Source: Caterpillar, Inc., Annual Reports.

depleted. The parties agreed to wage freezes and reduction of bonus pay, maintaining COLA payments and pension and medical benefits. This lengthy strike was only the beginning of years plagued by disputes with the UAW.

In 1984, the U.S. market started to show signs of recovery, but demand abroad remained sluggish. Soft oil and gas prices severely affected petroleum-dependent emerging economies, hindering their infrastructure growth. Given its cash-strapped customers, Caterpillar set out to barter machinery for other products. Dealers in those regions were battling to keep inventory levels at an appropriate level. That same year, Cat created its financial products division in order to help these dealers and to provide financing for the equipment end buyers.

Miscalculating the length and effect of the world recession, Caterpillar, in 1984, found that it had 75 percent more capacity than in 1973, but only 25 percent more production. The strong dollar eroded overseas earnings and enabled foreign competitors, such as Komatsu and Italy's Fiatallis Europe, to wage a price war in the United States. At that time, PaineWebber estimated that each percentage-point fall in the yen-dollar exchange rate would result in a $0.10 reduction in Cat's earnings per share. In only eight months, from March to November 1984, the stock price fell from $52 to $31.

Caterpillar's CEO, George Schaefer, was clearly worried about Cat's condition. He outlined a series of initiatives designed to bring the company out of the hole. Caterpillar was to cut annual costs by 22 percent, or $2 billion, by the end of 1986. The plans included the shutting down of six plants and a job cut of 4 percent, on top of a 15 percent reduction since 1982. Schaefer also called for reducing the number of suppliers and seeking low-cost overseas sources. Capital expenditures were to be shaved an additional 26 percent, to $260 million. The company was to move away from competing in the area of advanced, large-sized machines sold at premium prices and pursue instead the often rejected smaller customers that demanded smaller, lower-priced earthmovers. That same year, Caterpillar signed an agreement with CMI Corp. in the United States and Franz Eder Maschinenfabrik in Germany to build small equipment to complement Cat's product line. Additionally, Caterpillar set out to develop new products to compete in the farm equipment market, a highly competitive, slow-growing industry led by Deere & Co.

At the same time, Cat's rival Komatsu was worried about possible U.S. protectionism and exchange rate swings. It responded by building its first U.S. assembly plant, Komatsu America Manufacturing Corp. Komatsu's weakest link in America was its distribution system. Komatsu, in the mid 1980s, garnered only 5 percent of the U.S. market, far behind Cat's leading position.

By 1985, Schaefer's plans were well under way. Caterpillar reached its cost-cutting goals one year ahead of schedule. It also reduced its work force and developed foreign sourcing agreements. Debt was trimmed to $1 billion, from $2.6 billion in 1982. Moreover, after three straight years of losses, the company regained its profitability.

Caterpillar developed a new backhoe loader and grouped it under the Century Line, targeting the same equipment market. This new product, built in a small lift-truck plant in Leicester, England, became an almost instant success after its 1985 introduction. Original sales were well above internally derived projections.

However promising the new line of products appeared, Cat was to directly compete with Case, which at the time held 50 percent of the backhoe loader market in the United States and had twice the number of sales outlets. Furthermore, this was a very price-sensitive market and offered substantially lower margins. Komatsu also jumped on the bandwagon and signed an agreement with Clark Equipment to market its line of mini-excavators under the Bobcat trademark.

Meanwhile, Caterpillar's sales to Asia were growing rapidly, accounting for one-tenth of total machinery sales in 1987. The Japanese market, however, was difficult to crack due to the strong position of Komatsu. Cat, nonetheless, announced an expansion of its joint venture with Mitsubishi Heavy Industries Ltd. Under the amended terms of the agreement, the Cat-Mitsubishi JV would make excavator equipment for Japan, as well as light construction equipment for the United States, and a broad line of products for the entire Pacific Rim.

Caterpillar continued to cut costs aggressively. By 1987, the work force had already been trimmed to 60 percent of the 1982 level, and nine manufacturing facilities had been closed. At the same time, Cat's product line had more than doubled from 150 products in 1984 and had grabbed 11 percent of the backhoe loader market. Cat products were still selling, however, at a 10 to 15 percent price premium over competitors. The recovering yen also benefited Caterpillar's position, as Komatsu was forced to increase prices in U.S. dollar terms. By 1988, Komatsu's dollar prices were 20 percent higher than in 1981, compared with Caterpillar's increase of only 9.5 percent during the same period.

In February 1988, Komatsu announced a 50/50 joint venture with Dresser Industries. The companies were to combine their construction equipment manufacturing and engineering facilities in the Americas. The joint venture appeared to be a sound opportunity for both Komatsu and Dresser. Komatsu could avoid building up facilities from scratch, while Dresser could utilize some of its 50 percent idle manufacturing capacity. Komatsu also acquired a 25 percent stake in Hanomag AG of Germany. At that time, Hanomag had a 30 percent share of market in Europe. This was to greatly benefit Komatsu's position in Europe.

Fearful of future exchange rate difficulties and impelled by Komatsu's success in automation of manufacturing facilities in Japan, Cat's CEO, Schaefer, announced an ambitious modernization program that would affect the majority of its thirty factories around the world. The new project, dubbed "Plant with a Future" (PWAF),[3] called for an investment of $1.8 billion and was to be completed by 1992.

Despite an overall success with the cost-cutting measures, Schaefer was still worried about Cat's future in this highly cyclical industry. Caterpillar's boom came after World War II, when its equipment was used to help rebuild Europe, roll out the United States interstate highway system, and build giant dams in the Third World. In the 1970s, rising oil prices sparked demand for Cat's oil field equipment and launched numerous massive construction projects in oil-rich economies. But in the 1980s, high interest rates and cheap oil prices had slowed the construction industry; housing development in the United States was stagnant; and construction and repair of the highway system was crimped by government budget cuts. In light of all this, Schaefer formed a committee of eight executives to study Caterpillar's position and consider diversification options.

CHANGING RULES OF THE GAME

Plant with a Future (PWAF)

Between 1982 and 1985, Caterpillar accumulated losses of almost $1 billion. Six plants were closed and employment was cut severely—44 percent

among hourly workers and 26 percent among salaried staff. Komatsu enjoyed lower labor costs because of the weaker yen. It had also engaged in an automation effort that further enhanced its competitive position.

The industry was expected to continue to suffer from excess capacity, making it imperative for Cat to have the ability to face Komatsu head-on. Furthermore, Cat's product line expansions toward the growing, low-margin, smaller-machine segment placed even heavier financial pressure on its manufacturing facilities.

In 1986, Schaefer launched a daring, factorywide plant modernization program termed "Plant with a Future," or "PWAF."[3] Initial forecasts estimated capital expenditures of $1 billion, which were later revised to $1.8 billion, spread between 1986 and 1992. The objective was to shift from traditional mass manufacturing to forms of advanced, flexible production through the use of just-in-time inventory techniques and sophisticated factory automation, resulting in estimated savings on manufacturing costs of 20 percent by late 1992. That would mean about $1.5 billion a year in savings. The long-standing "functional" arrangement of people and machines on the factory floor was to be dismantled. Instead, all manufacturing work was to be arranged in product and subproduct dedicated "cells," or modules.

As expressed by Pierre Guerindon, manufacturing executive vice president, in a meeting with stock analysts in 1988, "There are four basic elements of PWAF. First, we *consolidate* manufacturing space worldwide. Then we *simplify* product designs, manufacturing processes, and operating procedures. At the same time, we *automate* many machining and materials handling processes. And finally, we *integrate* the engineering, logistics, and shop floor functions into one single information system."[4] However, computer integration would be a long-term goal designed to gain an advantage over competitors. The benefits of cost reduction and customer responsiveness were to be realized within the earlier phases.

Donald V. Fites

Donald V. Fites, born on a farm in Tippecanoe, Indiana, was appointed CEO in 1990, succeeding Schaefer. His career at Caterpillar dated back to 1956. Straight out of Indiana's Valparaiso University, Don Fites started in Caterpillar as a district sales representative in South Africa, where he met and married his wife. He was later transferred to Germany and again to Switzerland. Fites returned to the United States in 1970 and was sent to MIT for a graduate degree in management. His thesis topic, "Japan Inc.: Can U.S. Industry Compete," reflected his fascination with Japan's industrial success. This, in turn, earned him a job as marketing director of Caterpillar's construction equipment joint venture with Mitsubishi in Tokyo, where he spent four and a half years.[5]

Fites's overseas experiences were a strong influence for the rest of his career. According to Fites, his first job as a sales representative taught him how stifling a large bureaucracy can be. He was impressed by the way unionized workers in Japan would sacrifice their interests for those of the company. He also admired the way Japanese companies rotated their managers through manufacturing, engineering, and sales to create better-rounded leaders.

Upon his return to Peoria in 1975, Fites applied Japanese-style management to Caterpillar's product development process by creating cross-functional teams including marketing, design, and manufacturing people. Results were impressive as development time was cut in half.

Recalling his frustrating experience with the central office when he worked overseas, Fites continued his reforms with Cat's worldwide marketing structure. After becoming executive vice president in 1985, he put more marketing staffers into the field and turned the authority for market-sensitive decisions, such as pricing, over to district offices. Additionally, he eliminated 100 management jobs that he considered to be redundant.

When he was elected CEO in 1990, Fites launched a three-point campaign. This campaign called for: decentralizing Caterpillar's top-down organizational structure and empowering lower management; setting clear return-on-assets targets, tied to incentive compensation plans; and trying to avoid massive layoffs. This ambitious program created tension within the ranks, but Fites was driven by the idea that "if you're not competitive everywhere, you're not competitive anywhere."[6]

In an effort to slash Cat's $2.2 billion in annual overhead costs, Fites reorganized the company into thirteen functionally independent profit centers and four service divisions (now seventeen and five), each of which would have its own budget and a before-tax return-on-assets target of 15 percent. Service operations and component supply segments would compete at market prices. Results were very favorable. In only four years, time to market of products was cut in half, to less than three years. Manufacturing process time for parts was cut from twenty-five days to six between 1987 and 1993. No official layoffs were announced during this time period. Caterpillar was able to make a profit in 1993 after two years of negative earnings.

But the true challenge for Fites appeared to be with the United Auto Workers.

United Auto Workers: Troubles Continue

By the early 1990s, Caterpillar had greatly improved its manufacturing processes, realigned its organizational structure, and was regaining market share lost in the 1980s to Komatsu. An important issue, however, remained unresolved. High labor costs and the relative lack of flexibility of union workers positioned Cat at a disadvantage relative to Japan's Komatsu. Cat's wages and benefits for an average hourly worker in 1991 of $31.74 were roughly the same as Komatsu's due to the weakening of the dollar. Fites, however, was worried that exchange rate fluctuations could quickly alter this (see Table 7). Almost 60 percent of Cat's sales of machinery and engines came from abroad in 1991. And 64 percent of those sales were exported from the United States.

With the UAW contract expiring on September 30, 1991, Fites pushed for a cut in health care costs. Cat's health care costs, including expenses for retirees, ran at about $9,000 per active employee per year. Health care costs had risen 14 percent the previous year and were expected to jump 75 percent by 1994 if the current contract was maintained. Fites also wanted to create a two-tier system, where new hires were locked into a lower pay scale. Furthermore, he wanted to eliminate companywide contract negotiations, allowing each profit center to use whatever work arrangements were best for its particular needs.

Caterpillar's contract negotiation problems stemmed from the fact that it wanted to tailor contracts for the company, while the UAW demanded a contract similar to those negotiated with the American automakers. Cat's position was further affected after Deere & Co. accepted the UAW's package later that same year—a package that included an immediate 3 percent wage hike, continued COLA adjustments, and improved health care benefits. But Fites,

TABLE 7

Yen/Dollar Exchange Rates, December 31

1971	1972	1973	1974	1975	1976	1977	1978	1979	1980
320	301	280	300	306	295	241	196	240	209
1981	**1982**	**1983**	**1984**	**1985**	**1986**	**1987**	**1988**	**1989**	**1990**
219	242	234	248	203	162	128	124	143	134
1991	**1992**	**1993**	**1994**	**1995**	**1996**	**1997**			
128	124	110	100	102	114	130			

Source: Federal Reserve Bank of St. Louis.

expecting a strike, had built up enough inventory to survive a six-month stretch. In November 1991, the UAW placed 2,400 members on strike in hopes of pressuring Cat. Cat retaliated by locking out 6,000 more workers and laying off 500.

Caterpillar's average worker at the time was forty-six years old, and more than 60 percent of the workers would be eligible for retirement within six years. The UAW appeared to be afraid that Cat would shrink its work force through retirement and, perhaps, fill some vacant positions with nonunion workers.

After enduring a five-month strike, Cat's management announced on April 1, 1992, that striking workers had to return to work by April 6 or risk losing their jobs to (permanent) replacement workers. Cat's human resources department estimated that it could interview no more than several hundred applicants per week and that it would take about two months to train new hires. So far throughout the strike, about 5,000 managers and office employees had replaced the striking workers in Cat's U.S.-based manufacturing facilities.

Eight days after the April 6 deadline, the UAW sent the strikers back to work. It did not, however, agree to sign the contract on Cat's terms. The union appeared to be worried that workers would cross picket lines once the new replacement workers arrived. It wasn't certain that the UAW workers would risk their $47,000-a-year jobs for $100-a-week strike pay. Cat's offer included a wage in-

crease limited to 13 percent over the life of the contract, as opposed to the 26 percent demanded by the UAW. This would save the company some $150 million over the life of the new contract, a figure that would merely compensate for the costs resulting from the five-and-a-half-month strike.

Workers stayed on the job without a contract for the next two years, only to walk out again on June 21, 1994. Over the two intervening years, Cat experienced several local walkouts after disciplining and firing workers for wearing T-shirts that disparaged the company, some with the slogan "Permanently Replace Fites." These continuing, low-level labor problems resulted in the National Labor Relations Board filing some 140 complaints against Cat, the largest number of complaints that had ever been issued to any one company.

For Caterpillar's management, the most important issue appeared to be its desire to avoid signing an agreement that would contain elements similar to the UAW's contracts with the American automobile manufacturers and other construction and agricultural equipment makers, such as Deere & Co. Fites argued that Caterpillar was different from both the auto companies and from Deere, which derived almost 70 percent of its revenue from sales in the United States and did not compete directly with strong Japanese equipment makers such as Komatsu. Cat's management also found it to be unacceptable that it could not make outsourcing decisions without consulting the union, which demanded that the number of jobs be guaranteed. Furthermore, Cat's UAW workers were paid an average of $19.60 per hour, plus overtime, compared with the national average manufacturing wage of $12.73 per hour.

Fites saw the union demands as constraining the company's ability to stay competitive and keep from collapsing in the next economic downturn. "What it is," said Fites, "is not so much a battle about economics as it is a battle of who's going to run the company. It's worth it. You know what you're doing is right for the company. What scares me is not being competitive in today's world."[7]

The UAW members returned to work in December 1995, after an eighteen-month strike. However, they refused to ratify Caterpillar's contract. It was a clear victory for the company. Thanks to Fites's organizational skills, the use of temporary workers, and the one-third of the Cat UAW workers that had crossed the UAW picket lines, Cat sales increased 23 percent in 1994 and 11 percent in 1995 despite the ongoing strike. Earnings rose 46 percent and 19 percent in the same time period.

After almost six and a half years without a contract, the UAW ratified a new six-year agreement with Caterpillar in March 1998, effective through April 1, 2004, covering approximately 12,000 Cat employees. In this new specially tailored contract, Caterpillar agreed to an immediate wage increase ranging from 2 to 4 percent depending on the worker's experience level. The agreement also provided for three lump-sum payments of 3 percent of earnings in 1999, 2001, and 2003. The cost-of-living allowance (COLA) was to be maintained for all workers, except for entry-level employees. Pensions were also revised to $38.50 per month per year of certified service. Decisions on where to source components and products remained solely with the company, and there was no set level of guaranteed employment.

Dealer Network

Caterpillar's management believed that it had enjoyed the benefits of engineering excellence, manufacturing efficiency, and quality products. But according to Fites, "the biggest reason for Caterpillar's success has been our system of distribution and product support and the close customer relationships it fosters."[8] With a backbone of 197 worldwide dealers, 132 of them outside the United States, Caterpillar had been able to maintain a close relationship with its customers and gain market insight and feedback on its products and services. Together, the 197 dealers owned 1,217 branch stores and employed about 79,900 people, or almost 20,000 more than Cat. The average dealer had annual revenues of $150 million. The combined net worth of the dealer network was about $5.68 billion in 1997.

Despite its overall good quality and reliability, construction equipment eventually wears out. Earthmovers have an operating life of up to thirty years. However, the equipment will most likely need to be repaired several times throughout its life, as a result of the tough operating environment and the regular wear and tear on its components. Caterpillar's manufacturing and distribution systems were designed so that any part, anywhere in the world, could be replaced in a maximum of forty-eight hours. Eighty percent of the time, however, parts were provided immediately from dealers' inventory.

Over the past decade, Caterpillar had also invested in an ambitious project to maximize equipment uptime and minimize customers' cost of service and repairs through the use of information technology. The system uses onboard sensors on each of Caterpillar's machines around the world that will automatically send an electronic alert to the local dealer's technicians when a problem is identified. The technician will connect to the Caterpillar machine via a laptop computer and use diagnostic software to identify the problem, without having to visit the customer and spend hours examining the machine. Once the problem is diagnosed and the needed parts are identified, a parts request will be generated through the system and an automatic search sequence based on proximity (starting with the dealer's inventory and the dealer's branch stores, and searching through Caterpillar's worldwide inventory, if necessary) will be triggered. This order will go into the system of factories or warehouses that can supply the parts, activating the printing of an order ticket and automatically setting into motion an automated crane that retrieves the parts from the storage rack. The parts will be immediately shipped to the dealer's pickup site (99.7 percent of the parts ordered from Caterpillar or the dealer were already being shipped the same business day).

By early 1998, most of the system was already in place: the onboard sensors; computers that diagnose problems and instruct on repairs; and the information system that links together Caterpillar's factories, distribution centers, and most of the 197 dealers. The two pieces still missing were the remote monitoring system and the worldwide sharing of inventories by Caterpillar and its dealers and suppliers. The company expected to spend about $250 million in completing the system. It hoped, however, to reduce both customer downtime and Cat's $2 billion parts inventory.

The extensive dealer network also provided Caterpillar with timely market intelligence and data about its products. Information about changing trends of the overall construction industry and of product use could be gathered through extensive communication with the dealer network. Dealers were also actively involved in programs of product quality and cost reduction with design engineers from Cat. This process was developed to more promptly respond to problems encountered by customers, making adjustments in the design and specifications of new machines.

Although all of their dealers were independent, Caterpillar tended to treat them as part of the family. Cat frequently helped dealers finance purchases by their own customers and offered advice on inventory management, logistics, equipment management, and maintenance programs. Financing had been especially important for dealers operating in emerging markets, where occasional economic crises had impaired the health of many construction equipment dealers. All five dealers operating in Mexico during a recent economic downturn survived a period when the construction industry practically came to a halt. In contrast, competitors' dealers struggled and many failed. These kinds of relationships had resulted in extremely low dealer turnover; the average dealer remained with Caterpillar for more than fifty years, with several predating the 1925 merger that created the company.

Cooperative Agreements and Joint Ventures

In 1963, Caterpillar and Mitsubishi Heavy Industries Ltd. formed one of the first joint ventures in Japan to feature partial U.S. ownership. Operations started in 1965 from a new plant in Sagamihara, 28 miles from Tokyo. The 50/50 joint venture was renamed Shin Caterpillar Mitsubishi Ltd. after the original agreement was expanded in 1987. By early 1998, primary production facilities were located in Kanagawa, Akashi, and Saitama. This permitted Cat to compete with Komatsu on its home ground with a Japanese product, although Komatsu continued to maintain its majority share of the market. In 1997, Cat entered an additional joint venture with Mitsubishi Heavy Industries Ltd. for the production of forklifts in Europe.

One of Caterpillar's primary market regions was Europe, which contributed about 15 percent of sales in 1997. Caterpillar expanded its European presence in the mid 1990s through various acquisitions. In 1995, it acquired Brown Group Holdings in the United Kingdom, a producer of heavy trucks. In 1996, Cat purchased Mak Maschinenbau GmbH, a diesel engine producer from Germany. Also in Germany, Cat formed a joint venture in 1997 with Claas KGaA for the sale and manufacturing of harvesters and rubber-belted agricultural tractors in North America and Europe. In February 1997, Caterpillar announced an agreement to acquire a majority share of Skogsjan AB, a Swedish manufacturer of "cut-to-length" forestry machines and equipment, including forwarders, wheel harvesters, and harvester heads. Cat entered into an agreement with Emerson Electric Company in 1995 for the production of diesel generator sets, acquiring a stake in Emerson FG Wilson Limited (UK) subsidiary.

Other cooperative agreements for the production of construction equipment included Caterpillar Xuzhou Limited, a joint venture formed in 1995 that produces hydraulic excavators for the Chinese market; and an 80/20, Caterpillar–PT Natra Raya (India) joint venture designed to produce crawler bulldozers, wheel loaders, and hydraulic excavators for the Asia-Pacific region.

Caterpillar also engaged in a series of cooperative agreements, acquisitions, and joint ventures for the design, production, and supply of engines. In January 1995, it announced a joint venture with Empresa Nacional Bazan Motores (Spain), for the production of a new, higher-powered, lightweight version of the Caterpillar 3600 family of engines. Caterpillar had been producing engines in India through its joint venture with Hindustan Powerplus Limited since 1989, although it did not start selling engines under Cat's brand until its ISO 9001 certification in 1996. A new venture in north cen-

TABLE 8

Komatsu, Ltd.: Financial Highlights (millions of yen unless otherwise stated)

	1984*	1985*	1986*	1987*	1988*
Net sales equipment and industrial machinery**					
Finance and interest income	27,692	28,698	31,517	33,217	5,907
Other income	713,472	796,235	788,726	740,599	174,599
Net sales	741,164	824,933	820,243	773,816	180,513
Cost of goods sold	502,813	582,362	591,478	555,146	128,866
Income before accounting changes	22,642	21,917	14,701	9,504	3,107
(Year ended March 31)*					
Cash and equivalents	24,365	26,436	33,738	42,779	43,668
Receivables	312,688	333,810	364,132	344,919	342,672
Inventories	172,488	175,044	155,383	152,998	164,395
Property, plant and equipment	20,693	21,414	156,908	156,714	157,211
Other current and noncurrent assets	413,572	446,856	273,521	330,065	325,770
Total assets	943,806	1,003,560	983,682	1,027,475	1,033,716
Short-term loans	228,811	262,182	246,395	274,600	277,431
Accounts payable	167,221	180,129	161,349	170,624	170,109
Long-term debt	80,722	73,143	65,182	61,676	61,507
Total liabilities	588,430	629,240	601,713	628,866	632,916
Stockholders' equity	355,376	374,320	381,969	398,609	400,800
Total liabilities and stockholders' equity	943,806	1,003,560	983,682	1,027,475	1,033,716
Cash flows from operations				35,981	5,147
Cash flows from investing activities				(71,042)	(3,236)
Cash flows from financing activities				44,318	(1,016)
Net increase (decrease) in cash***				9,041	889

*From 1960 to 1987, Komatsu ended its fiscal year December 31. Beginning in 1988, Komatsu ended its fiscal year in March 31.
  Figures for 1988 represent the transition period of January 1988 to March 1988.
 **Prior to 1989, sales of equipment and industrial machinery are included in other income.
***Includes the effects of exchange rates on cash.

tral China, Shanxi International Castings, Co., Ltd., was to manufacture engine-related castings for medium- and heavy-duty diesel engines. In December 1997, Caterpillar announced the acquisition of Perkins Engine, LucasVarity's diesel engine subsidiary, for $1.3 billion. Perkins engine, a leading manufacturer of small to medium-sized diesel engines (<200 hp) had sales of approximately $1.1 billion in the year ended January 31, 1997. The addition of Perkins offered Cat a position in smaller engines, both for powering Cat's products, as small and compact construction equipment became increasingly important, and for sale to OEM and end-user customers.

KOMATSU

Komatsu was the second largest player in the construction equipment industry, with a worldwide market share of 8.1 percent for 1996. (Financial data for Komatsu Ltd. is shown in Table 8.) It derived 65 percent of its sales from construction and mining equipment, which included the sale of hydraulic excavators, bulldozers, wheel loaders, dump trucks, cranes, road equipment, underground machinery, and other equipment. (See Table 9 for data on regional and industry segments sales.) The remaining 35 percent was derived from its business in civil engineering and construction (general civil

1989	1990	1991	1992	1993	1994	1995	1996	1997
592,541	657,380	747,132	667,243	603,908	586,593	647,607	772,718	860,595
27,129	31,936	39,633	54,606	43,133	29,141	35,911	31,710	18,919
200,268	229,728	241,765	252,510	266,020	259,260	271,303	226,609	238,321
819,938	919,044	1,028,530	974,359	913,061	874,994	954,821	1,031,037	1,117,835
590,550	657,554	718,714	689,039	662,408	649,512	702,416	763,045	827,665
20,833	27,282	31,258	10,898	3,037	1,303	10,225	14,291	18,160
59,770	37,520	28,593	24,635	21,504	22,192	27,285	82,553	87,827
364,060	412,357	457,284	407,053	370,833	419,013	418,564	442,104	463,001
132,292	152,895	184,483	171,051	155,524	176,888	181,899	188,054	193,798
149,801	178,494	217,896	261,211	260,999	260,720	257,219	264,842	299,098
423,034	449,370	430,933	588,868	515,100	497,153	657,005	615,450	469,006
1,128,957	1,230,636	1,319,189	1,452,818	1,323,960	1,375,966	1,541,972	1,593,003	1,512,730
213,026	209,410	213,886	306,310	244,628	307,410	348,887	305,855	281,743
203,700	252,511	247,206	194,523	176,496	179,039	199,990	220,731	234,306
127,640	109,900	171,899	222,088	207,027	142,578	140,550	140,208	163,590
683,982	740,040	794,399	929,431	807,551	870,095	966,438	986,559	970,797
444,975	490,596	524,790	523,387	516,409	505,871	575,534	606,444	541,933
1,128,957	1,230,636	1,319,189	1,452,818	1,323,960	1,375,966	1,541,972	1,593,003	1,512,730
61,960	63,808	(24,596)	55,144	65,675	70,545	54,210	55,424	67,919
(112,952)	(53,878)	(55,555)	(21,063)	13,315	(55,851)	(38,183)	71,083	(14,871)
67,202	(32,840)	71,361	(37,964)	(82,024)	(13,652)	(10,743)	(71,424)	(47,190)
16,102	(22,250)	(8,927)	(3,958)	(3,131)	688	5,093	55,268	5,274

engineering, prefabricated structures for commercial use, and real estate sales and leasing); electronics operations (for example, electronic control equipment, information equipment, and silicon wafers); industrial machinery (such as sheet-metal presses, industrial robots, and machine tools); and, other operations, including diesel engines, compressors, generator sets, and forklift trucks.

History in Brief

Komatsu Ltd. was established in 1921, resulting from the separation of Komatsu Ironworks and Takeuichi Mining Co. The company started producing sheet metal presses and, in 1931, introduced the first crawler-type farm tractor. This was the first Japanese agricultural tractor. In 1947, Komatsu began production of bulldozers and produced its first diesel engine the next year. By the early 1960s, Komatsu was already producing forklifts, motor graders, dump trucks, shovel loaders, and wheel loaders. Sales of 28 billion yen in 1960 were mostly confined to Japan. In 1961, Komatsu signed a diesel engine technology sharing agreement with Cummins Engine Co., Inc. (USA), with the objective of improving the quality of its products by ensuring access to the latest engine technology in a cost-effective way. Looking for expansion into global

TABLE 9

Komatsu, Ltd.: Sales Composition by Region and Segment (in millions of yen unless otherwise indicated)

	1993	1994	1995	1996	1997
Sales by Region					
Japan			608,187	660,948	687,459
The Americas			149,573	148,630	170,683
Asia-Pacific			76,423	104,724	126,812
Europe			72,741	70,378	87,047
Africa and Middle East			11,986	14,647	26,915
Total sales			918,910	999,327	1,098,916
Sales by Segment					
Construction equipment	549,198	536,294	619,113	642,804	716,932
Civil eng. and construction	100,076	101,266	104,123	114,821	99,801
Electronics	50,165	53,598	62,080	75,637	90,553
Industrial machinery	64,710	50,299	28,494	36,151	47,967
Others	105,779	104,396	105,100	129,914	143,663
Total sales and revenues	869,928	845,853	918,910	999,327	1,098,916

Source: Komatsu, Ltd.; *Fact Book 1997.*

markets, Komatsu opened its first operation abroad in 1967: Komatsu Europe S.A. in Belgium. By 1970, sales had shot up to 264 billion yen, or $734 million. However, Komatsu was still very far behind Cat's worldwide revenue in that same year. The quality of its products was also lagging, having a durability just over half that of Cat.

Komatsu's management focus at that time was both to improve the quality of its product and to expand internationally in order to achieve the economies of scale necessary to be able to compete with Cat. Shoji Nogawa, the president of Komatsu, referred respectfully to Caterpillar as "sendatsu," a Japanese word meaning pioneer or guide. But the rivalry between the number one and number two heavy construction equipment manufacturers was fierce.

Komatsu negotiated licensing arrangements with International Harvester Company and Bucyrus Erie to sell wheel loaders and excavators built from these firms' designs in Japan. After the agreements expired in 1982, Komatsu deepened its commitment to the U.S. market; it invested an estimated $200 million in a manufacturing facility in Chattanooga, Tennessee, and established Komatsu

America Manufacturing Corp., now Komatsu America International Company. This facility was to produce bulldozers, hydraulic excavators, and off-highway dump trucks to go head-to-head with Caterpillar on its home turf. As Nogawa acknowledged, "The United States is still the largest market in the world. We are not so strong there now, but we think we can increase our market share."[9] Despite sacrificing lower Japanese labor costs, Nogawa saw the move as insulation from possible U.S. protectionist policies and from future currency swings.

In 1984, Komatsu's U.S. market share was estimated at 5 percent, compared with Cat's 50 percent. Experts considered its dealer network as its weakest link. Komatsu had fifty U.S. dealers, compared with Cat's eighty-four. Furthermore, Komatsu's dealers were financially weaker than Cat's, and only a few carried Komatsu's equipment exclusively. As dealers heavily depend on parts and service revenues, they preferred to represent companies that sell the most machines.

At the same time, Komatsu was carrying out a massive automation effort, including computer-driven flexible manufacturing, to improve cost competitiveness. An estimated $80 million was destined for this effort, which was to result in further cost advantages over Caterpillar. At the time, Caterpillar had 40 percent higher labor costs, lower employee productivity, and lower inventory turnover.

Komatsu-Dresser

In 1988, Komatsu established a 50/50 joint venture with Dresser Industries, an energy-related firm that had moved into the construction equipment business by acquiring International Harvester's construction equipment business in 1983. Dresser's products included crawler dozers, crawler loaders, scrapers, and a complete line of underground mining equipment. The new venture was to combine the companies' manufacturing and engineering facilities in construction equipment in the Americas for the manufacture and marketing of crawler tractors, crawler loaders, hydraulic excavators, cranes, off-highway trucks, and electric-wheel mining trucks. Operating at 50 percent of capacity due to deteriorating sales, the Dresser JV would allow Komatsu to expand its U.S. presence without having to invest in building manufacturing facilities from scratch. Komatsu was to pour $300 million into the venture in an attempt to renovate Dresser's outdated and inefficient facilities. Initially, the venture was to be headed by a Dresser executive and the two firms were to maintain separate dealer networks. At the time, this represented a complete departure from Komatsu's traditional expansion policies of wholly owned subsidiaries and Japanese management leading the various operations.

The joint venture produced disastrous results, with aggregate losses of $125 million over the first four years of operation. The problems included a depressed construction machinery market, a costly reorganization of production lines, cumbersome distribution and dealer operations, and cultural misunderstandings between Japanese and American executives. However, sales of Komatsu-Dresser started to increase in 1993 as a result of the sharp rise in the overall U.S. construction equipment industry.

In 1993, Komatsu expanded its ownership position to 81 percent and in September 1994 bought the remaining 19 percent. At the time, North American facilities operated by Komatsu included Peoria, Illinois; Chattanooga, Tennessee; Galion, Ohio; and Quebec, Canada. In 1996, Komatsu Dresser Company was renamed Komatsu America International Company.

Komatsu's Position

Throughout the early and mid 1990s, Komatsu was unable to match the growth rate of its main competitor, Caterpillar. From 1990 to 1997, Komatsu managed a 21 percent growth rate in yen (or 55 percent in dollar terms), behind Cat's 63 percent increase. Despite continued diversification efforts, Komatsu remained heavily exposed to downturns in the Japanese economy, which represented 63 percent of its 1997 construction equipment sales revenues. Furthermore, its other divisions, with the exception of its electronics business, had shown unexciting growth and equally unexciting geographic diversification figures.

Nonetheless, Komatsu had slowly increased its presence in other areas of the world—in Europe, Asia, and North and South America. In 1996, Komatsu America generated revenues of $1.4 billion, making it one of the largest suppliers of construction equipment in the area. With a wide variety of products sold under the Komatsu, Dresser, Galion, and Haulpak brand names, Komatsu had been able to amass 20 percent of the hydraulic excavator and 13 percent of the wheel loader markets in the United States as of 1997.

KMS in Vernon Hills, Illinois, was established by Komatsu in April 1997. It is the second largest supplier of mining equipment in North America, manufacturing and marketing various mining products, including large-sized wheel loaders and large-sized dump trucks. Also in 1997, Komatsu agreed to extend its alliance with Cummins Engine, the largest producer of diesel engines above 200 horsepower, and form a third 50/50 joint venture company. The new venture, headquartered in Tochigi Prefecture, Japan, was to engage in engine development for construction equipment markets worldwide. The technologies developed were to be used by the two companies in their own manufacturing facilities. The increasing demand in the diesel engine industry, driven by increased customer expectations and new environmental standards, had motivated the two companies to cooperate in the past. This third joint venture would further benefit Komatsu's development effort relative to engine for construction equipment. Additionally, it had the potential to expand Komatsu's revenue base.

TABLE 10

Deere & Company: Financial Highlights* (in millions of U.S. $ unless otherwise indicated)

	1986	1987	1988	1989
Net sales of equipment	3,516	4,135	5,365	6,234
Finance and interest income	89	96	66	101
Other income	20	23	24	15
Net sales	3,625	4,253	5,454	6,350
Cost of goods sold	3,214	3,634	4,356	5,036
Income before accounting changes	(229)	(99)	287	380
(Year ended December 31)				
Cash and equivalents	182	116	49	57
Receivables	2,297	2,156	2,355	2,790
Inventories	483	465	708	711
Property, plant and equipment	951	982	944	982
Other current and noncurrent assets	1,062	1,040	1,189	1,372
Total assets	4,974	4,760	5,245	5,913
Short-term loans	396	356	477	640
Accounts payable	1,014	1,052	1,149	1,217
Long-term debt	1,280	1,052	805	824
Total liabilities	2,975	2,840	2,789	3,132
Stockholders' equity	1,999	1,920	2,456	2,780
Total liabilities and stockholders equity	4,974	4,760	5,245	5,913
Cash flows from operations				
Cash flows from investing activities				
Cash flows from financing activities				
Net increase (decrease) in cash**				

*Deere & Company Operations with Financial Services on the equity basis.
**Includes the effects of exchange rates on cash.
Source: Deere & Company, Annual Reports.

Komatsu also increased its commitment in Europe. In November 1995, Komatsu entered into a 50/50 joint venture with Mannesmann Demag (Germany) for the development, manufacture, and marketing of large and super-large hydraulic excavators. Furthermore, in June 1996, Komatsu increased its stake in Komatsu Hanomag AG to 98 percent from the 25 percent stake it had taken when it first invested in the corporation. High restructuring costs on top of weak demand in Europe, however, damaged Hanomag's profitability, resulting in losses of 4 billion yen in 1996 and forcing it to cut staff by nearly 30 percent. Other European operations included Komatsu UK Limited, FKI-FAI Komatsu Industries SpA (Italy), Moxy

Trucks AS (Norway), and Unex (Czech Republic).

Despite the slowdown, Asia was probably the most promising area because of its lack of infrastructure and perceived future potential growth. Komatsu, through joint ventures or wholly owned subsidiaries, operated manufacturing facilities in China, Thailand, Indonesia, India, Singapore, and Vietnam. Lower wage costs and proximity to markets were expected to favor future profit potential for Komatsu.

In an effort to catch up with Caterpillar's impressive systems infrastructure, in October 1997 Komatsu announced plans to standardize all its global affiliates on software developed by The Baan

1990	1991	1992	1993	1994	1995	1996	1997
6,779	5,848	5,723	6,479	7,663	8,830	9,640	11,082
112	116	99	84	81	105	121	115
19	21	23	23	24	28	29	48
6,910	5,985	5,845	6,587	7,768	8,964	9,789	11,244
5,430	4,904	4,902	5,381	6,033	6,944	7,486	8,499
411	(20)	37	184	604	706	817	960
26	99	40	72	104	531	625	411
3,281	3,242	3,187	3,436	3,267	3,437	3,418	3,477
678	538	525	464	698	721	829	1,073
1,135	1,220	1,287	1,216	1,282	1,295	1,301	1,479
1,652	1,831	1,870	2,431	2,359	2,481	2,595	3,045
6,771	6,930	6,908	7,618	7,710	8,464	8,768	9,484
850	881	856	476	54	396	224	171
1,297	1,334	1,319	1,533	1,617	1,860	1,975	2,134
804	1,018	1,234	1,069	1,019	703	626	540
3,764	4,091	4,258	5,533	5,153	5,379	5,211	5,337
3,008	2,836	2,650	2,085	2,558	3,085	3,557	4,147
6,771	6,927	6,908	7,618	7,710	8,464	8,768	9,484
		148	702	677	715	1,213	1,006
		(253)	(226)	(339)	(293)	(384)	(553)
		47	(443)	(308)	4	(735)	(664)
		(59)	31	32	427	94	(214)

Company, providing an infrastructure for managing the company's supplier network, production facilities, and distribution system. By 2000, Komatsu planned to implement a standard across its global network based on a fully integrated ERP system in an effort to be in a better position to respond to changing global market conditions.

Komatsu was also investing large sums of money in research and development in an attempt to improve the quality and features of its existing equipment and the design of new construction equipment. The company was expanding into growing lines of business such as machines for underground work, environmental preservation (for instance, trash crushers), and building demolition. Komatsu's R&D expense ratio of over 4 percent of sales was the highest in the industry.

OTHER IMPORTANT COMPETITORS

Deere & Company

Deere & Company, originally known as John Deere, was founded in 1837 in Grand Detour, Illinois, by a thirty-three-year-old blacksmith. Since then, it had grown to be the biggest agricultural equipment manufacturer in the world, with $11 billion in sales for 1997. (See Table 10 for financial highlights on the firm.) Deere historically competed with Caterpillar in several product lines, although its main focus had always been on agricultural equipment.

Over the past decade, Deere had increased its construction equipment business, which produced $2.3 billion in revenues and $216 million in operating profits in 1997, contributing 20 percent of Deere's total revenues. Construction equipment

TABLE 11

Deere & Company: Sales Composition by Region and Segment (in millions of U.S. $)

	1986	1987	1988	1989
Sales by Region				
United States	2,268	2,790	3,643	4,332
Canada	365	323	429	481
Europe, Africa, and Middle East	727	818	1,030	1,074
Latin America	122	106	134	159
Asia-Pacific	34	98	129	188
Total sales	3,516	4,135	5,365	6,234
Sales by Segment				
Agricultural equipment	2,648	3,224	4,203	4,110
Industrial equipment*	868	911	1,162	1,310
Commercial and consumer equipment**	—	—	—	814
Total sales and revenues	3,516	4,135	5,365	6,234

*Primarily construction equipment.
**Prior to 1989, commercial and consumer equipment is included in industrial equipment.
Source: Deere & Company Annual Reports; *Fact Book 1997.*

sold included crawler loaders, excavators, motor graders, scrapers, and backhoe loaders. In 1995, Deere started a four-year product development program that introduced thirty-nine new construction equipment products by 1997. Deere also competed with Caterpillar in the sale of diesel and natural gas engines. (See Table 11 for Deere sales by both geographic region and industry segment.)

As it was primarily focused on agricultural equipment, Deere faced less competition from large foreign rivals such as Komatsu, reducing its exposure to foreign exchange fluctuations. Deere sales were highly concentrated in the United States (65 percent) and in Europe (18 percent), although the company was slowly increasing its presence in Asia. By the end of 1997, Deere's dealer network in the United States included 1,700 dealers employing 25,000 people.

Deere had also teamed up with Hitachi Construction Machinery Co., Ltd. (Japan), to improve its position in Asia. They began the collaboration in 1988 by investing $58.8 million in a facility to produce hydraulic excavators in the United States, and the relationship contributed to more than a doubling of Deere's sales in Asia between 1993 and 1997. The partnership combined Deere's reliability and productivity with Hitachi's Asian market knowledge. Deere-designed four-wheel-drive loaders and other Deere-designed construction equip-

ment were also being manufactured and marketed by the Deere-Hitachi Construction Machinery Corporation for sale in the Far East.

Case Corporation

Case Corporation, with revenues of $6 billion in 1997, was also a leading manufacturer of agricultural and construction equipment. Construction equipment constituted approximately one-third of total sales for Case. Case was one of the world's largest manufacturers and distributors of light- to medium-sized construction equipment, marketed under the Case and Case Poclain brand names. The Case Poclain brand was the result of Case's acquisition of Poclain, the French firm, which was the largest manufacturer of hydraulic excavators in the world in the early 1970s. It derived 60 percent of its construction equipment sales from North America, 31 percent from Europe, 6 percent from Latin America, and 3 percent from Asia-Pacific. However, sales in Latin America climbed 19 percent in 1996, and the company had engaged in a joint venture in China (Liuzhou Case Liugong Construction Equipment Company) to further its growth in emerging markets.

In the early 1990s, Case was seen as inefficient, had excess capacity, was said to be building too many components in-house, and kept making un-

1990	1991	1992	1993	1994	1995	1996	1997
4,777	3,968	3,768	4,431	5,266	6,016	6,211	7,167
381	379	379	503	594	632	675	851
1,158	1,148	1,147	1,126	1,253	1,608	1,993	2,021
149	171	251	212	279	241	351	529
247	180	178	207	271	333	410	514
6,779	5,848	5,723	6,479	7,663	8,830	9,640	11,082
4,519	4,054	3,759	4,078	4,718	5,277	6,097	7,048
1,348	1,014	1,068	1,348	1,640	1,875	1,919	2,262
912	780	896	1,053	1,305	1,678	1,624	1,772
6,779	5,848	5,723	6,479	7,663	8,830	9,640	11,082

popular lines. In 1991, Case's parent corporation, Tenneco Inc., hired turnaround expert Michael H. Walsh as CEO. He, in turn brought in Dana G. Mead as CEO of Case. By 1993, Mead had moved Case into the black, up from a $1.3 billion loss in 1992. The firm's payroll was cut by 35 percent, 250 wholly owned dealers were sold, more than $2 billion in excess inventory was eliminated, and $920 million worth of fixed assets were written down. Between 1991 and 1995, G & A expense had fallen to 13 percent from 23 percent of sales, and gross margins had increased to 23 percent from 9 percent of sales.

Case also sent engineers and marketing managers to talk to 150 key customers and users of rival machines. With this information, it built a new family of backhoe loaders around a common platform where 75 percent of the parts were shared, up from 30 percent. By early 1998, Case was widely seen as being able to compete head-on with Caterpillar on both price and quality in the product categories where they overlapped.

FUTURE CHALLENGES FOR CATERPILLAR

While pleased with how well Caterpillar had been able to reposition itself as a firm over the last ten to fifteen years, Fites and the company's other senior managers clearly had reason to be concerned. The rate of change in this and other industries had clearly accelerated. Several of Cat's major competitors had become better focused, better managed, and more financially robust. Furthermore, the exact shape and size of the industry segments in which they competed were very hard to project. Competing in the new world economy did not look like it would be an easy process.

Endnotes

1. Forecasts presented are based on information provided by The Freedonia Group Incorporated, a leading international industry study/database company, in its report titled "World Heavy Construction Equipment to 2001," July 1997.
2. Freedonia Group, "World Heavy Construction Equipment Market Share, 1996" (July 1997).
3. This was almost immediately dubbed "Peoria Without a Factory," and several other less pleasant terms, by disgruntled workers in the Greater Peoria region.
4. P. Miller and T. O'Leary, "Accounting, 'Economic Citizenship' and the Spatial Reordering of Manufacture," *Accounting, Organizations and Society,* 19. No. 1 (1994), 15–43.
5. K. Kelly, A. Bernstein, and R. Neff, "Caterpillar's Don Fites: Why He Didn't Blink," *Business Week,* August 10, 1992.
6. J. Reingold, "CEO of the Year," *Financial World,* March 28, 1995.
7. Ibid.
8. D. V. Fites, "Make Your Dealers Your Partners," *Harvard Business Review* (March–April 1996), 83–95.
9. "Komatsu Digs Deeper into the U.S.," *Business Week,* October 1, 1984.

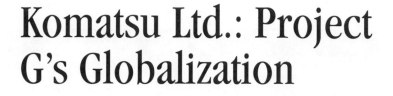

Komatsu Ltd.: Project G's Globalization

This case was prepared by Christopher A. Bartlett of Harvard Business School.

On a breezy spring day in 1991, passers-by on the bustling street in front of Komatsu's world headquarters stopped, pointed, and stared at the spectacle atop the building. Ten stories above, workers were dismantling one of central Tokyo's most notable landmarks—a giant, yellow Komatsu bulldozer precariously perched on a tall pole. For twenty-five years, this corporate icon had symbolized Komatsu's overriding strategic aim to surpass Caterpillar (Cat) and become the world's premiere construction equipment manufacturer.

President Tetsuya Katada had carefully timed the removal of this corporate symbol to mark recent changes in the company in preparation for Komatsu's spring celebration of its seventieth anniversary. Soon, a new electronic beacon would flash a new logo and a new corporate slogan ("The Earth Company, Unlimited"), confirming the changes in strategy and management practices that Katada and his management had started to implement. The new company president explained:

> Pulling down the bulldozer is just one example showing the strong determination of the president to outsiders and, more importantly, employees that we can't single-mindedly pursue production of the bulldozer. . . . Instead, we have challenged the organization with a new slogan, "Growth, Global, Groupwide"—or "the Three G's" for short. It's a much more abstract challenge than one focused on catching and beating Cat, but I hope it will stimulate people to think and discuss creatively what Komatsu can be.

This case is intended to be used as a basis for class discussion rather than as an illustration of either effective or ineffective handling of the situation. This case was prepared by Christopher A. Bartlett of Harvard Business School.

Katada's Three G's slogan challenged managers in all parts of Komatsu to reignite growth through a renewed commitment to global expansion, and an increase in groupwide leveraging of resources. For the core construction equipment business, it implied nothing less than a revolution. After three decades of focusing on the goal "to catch up and surpass Cat," this group was now being told to broaden its perspective and define the business on its own terms. In particular, Katada's challenge would require even further expansion of the company's three regionally based operations in the Americas, Europe, and Asia-Pacific. Furthermore, although several parts of this organization were new and untried, management felt it must try to integrate these operations more into a worldwide network of resources. Finally, those in Tokyo recognized that unless they began to elicit the ideas and leverage the expertise of these international operations, Project G would be little more than rhetoric.

KOMATSU COMPANY AND MANAGEMENT HISTORY

Established in 1921 as a specialized producer of mining equipment, Komatsu expanded into agricultural machinery during the 1930s and, during the Second World War, into the production of military equipment. The heavy-machinery expertise the company developed positioned it well to expand into earthmoving equipment needed for postwar reconstruction. Soon, construction equipment dominated Komatsu's sales.

In the high-demand and capital-constrained Japanese environment, Komatsu held a market share of more than 50 percent despite the low quality of its equipment at that time. This comfortable situation changed in 1963 when, after the government decided to open the industry to foreign investors, Cat announced it would enter the market in partnership with Mitsubishi. At this time, Komatsu had sales of $168 million and a product line well below world standards. Local analysts predicted three years of struggle before Cat bankrupted the puny, local company.

Emergence and Expansion: The Kawai Era (1964–1982)[1]

It was in this context that Ryoichi Kawai assumed the presidency of Komatsu from his father in 1964. The older man had prepared the company by initiating a Total Quality Control (TQC) program in 1961. Building on this base, Ryoichi Kawai's strategy for the company was straightforward—to acquire and develop advanced technology, to raise quality, and to increase efficiency to the level necessary to "catch up with and surpass Cat." To galvanize the company around his challenge and to focus management on his strategic priorities, Kawai introduced a style of management which he called "management by policy." Kawai explained the philosophy behind his strongly focused and directive approach:

> Personally, I believe that a company must always be innovative. To this end, the basic policy and value of the target must be clarified so that all the staff members can fully understand what the company is aiming for in a specific time period. This is the purpose of the management-by-policy system.

Under the umbrella of the TQC philosophy that was now deeply ingrained in Komatsu, management by policy began with Kawai's statement of an overriding, focused priority for the company. Launched the year after Cat announced its entry into the Japanese market, his first policy, "Project A," sought to raise the quality of Komatsu's middle-sized bulldozers to Cat's level. To support this goal, Kawai began an aggressive program to license technology from leading companies such as Cummins, International Harvester, and Bucyrus-Erie. As he implemented his "management-by-policy" approach, the young CEO instituted a new system of control, the "Plan, Do, Check, Act" (PDCA) cycle. Once Kawai announced the projects and priorities at the beginning of the year, the continuous PDCA cycle concentrated efforts within the company on attaining the broad policy objective until it was fully implemented (see Figure 1).

Kawai's new management approach, as reflected in Project A, was an immediate and outstanding success. Project A enabled Komatsu to double its warranty period within two years while cutting claim rates by two-thirds. And, in the face of Cat's entry into Japan, it triggered an increase in sales that raised Komatsu's market share from 50 to 65 percent by 1970, thereby confounding the experts' forecasts of an early demise.

An avalanche of policies followed, steering Komatsu through the turbulent environment. In response to the economic stagnation that hit Japan in 1965, Kawai targeted a "cost down" program at slashing costs. In 1966, his five-year "World A" campaign sought to make Komatsu internationally competitive in cost and quality, thus reducing Komatsu's potentially dangerous reliance on domestic sales. And, in rapid succession, Kuwai launched Projects B, C, and D to improve reliability and durability in large bulldozers and shovels, payloaders, and hydraulic excavators, respectively. Throughout the 1970s, not a year went by without a major project, campaign, or program aimed at catching and surpassing Cat.

By the early 1980s, Komatsu had emerged as the major challenger in the construction equipment industry, putting Cat clearly on the defensive (see Table 1). Nowhere were Cat's concerns clearer than in its 1982 annual report, which opened with a picture of a Komatsu bulldozer and a stern warning that Cat would not be able to compete against its Japanese rival at prevailing exchange and wage rates.

Struggle and Turmoil: The Nogawa Era (1982–1987)

Having guided the organization through an eighteen-year period of extraordinary growth, Ryoichi Kawai handed over operating leadership to Shoji Nogawa in 1982. Unfortunately for Nogawa, this date also marked the beginning of an era of falling demand, worldwide price wars, a rapidly appreciating yen, and heightened trade frictions throughout the industry.

Nogawa was an engineer who had risen through the manufacturing side of the construction equipment division. A reputed strong-willed, hands-on manager, he had high expectations of his managers, and drove them hard to meet those expectations. In spite of the growing challenges facing the industry, Nogawa was initially reluctant

FIGURE I

Company Description of "Plan, Do, Check, Act" Control Cycle

	Stage	Actual Activities
What is control? The term "control" is explained in the concept of a plan-do-check-act circle. Please understand that the concept of control is practice. 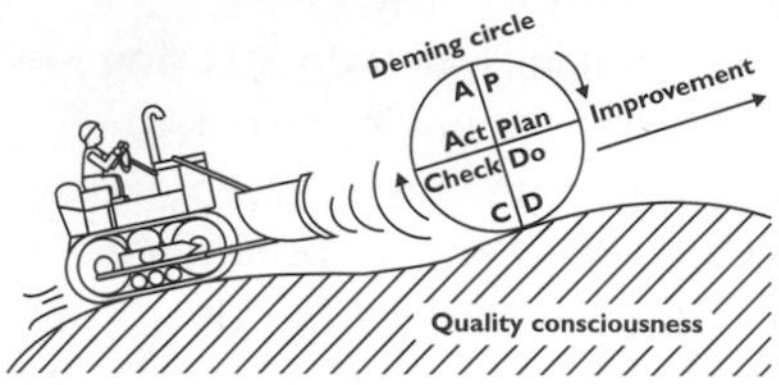 In short, control means the plan-do-check-act circle.	**Plan (P)**	• **In a work shop: arranging daily operation, preparing operation standards, equipment, jigs and tools, and planning for cost reduction.** • **In a technical department: planning for research and establishing design policy.** • **In a sales department: preparation of daily or monthly sales and visiting plans according to a given target.** • **Working out countermeasures for any defects or debts.** • **Understanding the problem through facts.** **One must grasp the facts of the matter in order to know the problem. Never adopt false data.** **To grasp the facts** • **See the place where the problem exists.** • **Observe the job and operation.** • **Investigate the actual problem.** • **Examine the data.** • **Listen to people.** • **Priority principle** **Treat the gathered facts and problem points on a priority principle, stressing those which are more important in view of expected effects. The Pareto diagram described later will be very helpful.** **-Maximum effect with minimum labor-** **70% of the problem is solved if the planning is properly done.**
	Do (D)	**Put the plan into practice and operate according to the rules and standards. This includes training on rules and standards.**
	Check (C)	• **It is your responsibility to check your own work.** **(Self inspection as well as error checks for drawings, documents, and business forms produce quality products.)** **Do not hand trouble on to the next person.** • **Check the result in comparison with the plan.**
	Act (A)	• **If a result deviates from the standard, correct it.** • **If any abnormality is found, investigate and remove the cause, and take action to prevent its reoccurrence.** **(Emergency and preventive measures are necessary.)**

Source: Company records

to change Komatsu's traditional policies, including the company's reliance on its highly efficient, centralized, global production facilities. As conditions worsened and external pressures increased (see Table 2), the new president seemed to focus more on cost-cutting and aggressive pricing than on shifting production overseas or reducing Komatsu's dependence on the stagnating construction industry. As the company implemented its aggressive sales strategy worldwide, political pressure mounted. Faced with several antidumping suits, Nogawa introduced new strategic goals in 1984, including faster product introduction and expansion of non-construction industrial machinery businesses.

The situation reached a crisis pitch in 1985 and 1986, when the value of the yen surged alarmingly. (See Table 2.) With domestic markets in turmoil, a 25 percent rise in the value of the yen in nine months exposed Komatsu's foreign exchange vulnerability, putting Nogawa under pressure to internationalize production more rapidly. His short-term strategy included raising prices abroad, expanding overseas parts procurement, and cutting production costs. His medium-term strategy called for developing more marketable construction equipment products through increased R&D spending and capital investments in manufacturing facilities. In the long-term, he told shareholders, "Komatsu is gearing itself toward new business areas of high-growth potential."

In addition, in 1985 he responded to the growing internal and external pressures for internationalization, approving the establishment of two important overseas plants—one in Chattanooga, Tennessee, and the other in a closed Cat facility in Birtley, United Kingdom. "As a drastic means of efficiently managing the sensitive trade friction and volatile foreign exchange environments," he told shareholders, "we have secured manufacturing bases in the world's major markets." Even after the plants were established, however, Nogawa seemed reluctant to embrace them fully into Komatsu's strategy. For example, when U.S. distributors began lobbying the head office to move additional production overseas, he rejected their proposals outright, finally relenting only when the yen appreciated even further, to ¥140 per dollar.

The rising tide of problems, rapidly deteriorating results, Nogawa's apparent resistance to faster and more dramatic change, and the deleterious influence of his unpopular autocratic management style eventually resulted in his replacement. Chairman Kawai explained: "With this serious appreciation of the yen . . . we have no time to lose. We need to have a complete change in people's attitudes so that we can build a new organization, aiming at progress in the 1990s and the twenty-first century."

Steadying the Ship: The Tanaka Transition (1987–1989)

In June 1987, Ryoichi Kawai chose Masao Tanaka to replace Nogawa as president. A former general manager of the domestic sales division and, more recently, three-year general manager of the overseas division, Tanaka responded quickly to the competitive crisis in the domestic market. Chosen, in part, for his diplomatic skills, Tanaka demonstrated his conciliatory approach by emphasizing the need to end price discounting and high-pressure sales practices. In one of his many public statements on the topic, he argued:

> Market share is certainly a source of profit, but there can be no such thing as market share that ignores long-term profitability. We are trying to establish a situation where we can recoup the money spent on development and investment. If Komatsu cannot do this, there is no other company in Japan that can. If business conditions become worse, we should cover this not by carrying out a price war, but by reducing production.

Slowly, the industry responded and Tanaka's efforts culminated in a spate of collective OEM supply agreements within the industry and the creation of the Japan Construction Equipment Manufacturers Association in March 1990. More important from Komatsu's perspective, restoring market order improved the bottom line. In the hydraulic excavator market segment alone, for example, while Komatsu's market share fell from 35 to 31 percent, overall profits rose.

Tanaka's pricing and sales policies were controversial within the company. When Komatsu developed the first mini-excavator that used advanced microelectronic controls, for example, some managers contended that with its traditional lower prices and aggressive sales methods, the company could capture a 50 percent market share. But Tanaka's philosophy prevailed, and the product was introduced at a 10 percent premium to existing prices.

TABLE I

Selected Data on Komatsu, Caterpillar, and Assorted Other Competitors
($ millions; fiscal year ends December 31 unless noted)

	1991	1990	1989	1988	1987	1986
Komatsu[a]						
Company sales	6,915	7,013	5,615	5,961	6,121	4,992
Construction equipment sales	4,356	4,685	3,824	4,131	4,389	3,592
Net income	82	222	173	157	79	93
Percent of sales outside Japan	30%	30%	31%	31%	39%	47%
Percent of sales from construction equipment	63%	67%	68%	69%	72%	72%
Caterpillar						
Sales (companywide)	9,838	11,103	10,882	10,255	8,180	7,321
Net income	(404)	21	497	616	350	76
Percent of sales from outside the United States	59%	55%	53%	50%	48%	46%
Sales of Other Major Construction and Agricultural Equipment Manufacturers						
Clark Equipment	1,190	1,445	1,392	1,278	1,055	954
Deere[b] (FY Oct. 31)	5,060	6,780	6,234	5,365	4,135	3,516
Hitachi Construction Machinery (FY Mar. 31)	1,812	1,780	1,777	1,725	1,195	824
Ingersoll-Rand[c]	1,363	1,445	1,328	1,140	969	865
International Harvester[b,d]						
J I Case (Division of Tenneco)	4,449	5,396	5,069	4,309	3,676	3,369
Shin-Caterpillar Mitsubishi (FY Mar. 31)	1,519	1,810	1,728			

Sources: Annual reports, Yamaichi Research Institute, company records, forms 10-K, Moody's Industrial Manuals, various years.
"NR" means business segment data not reported.
[a]Komatsu fiscal year ended on Mar. 31 between 1989 and 1991 and on Dec. 31 between 1975 and 1987. Data from 1988 are for the period April to March and correspond with January to December of other companies.
[b]Construction and agricultural machinery segments only.
[c]Standard machinery segment only. Includes some nonconstruction and agricultural equipment.
[d]J I Case acquired agricultural equipment division of International Harvester in 1985. Komatsu data are converted from yen-denominated data at fiscal year-end exchange rates.

Tanaka also pursued internationalization much more aggressively than his predecessor. More than internationalizing sales or market exposure, Tanaka wished to establish autonomous bases with regional capabilities in manufacturing, sales, and finance in the three core markets—Japan, the United States, and Europe. Explained Tanaka: "On the assumption that the yen will further appreciate to, let's say, ¥100 per U.S. dollar, I believe any extension of conventional measures such as management and production rationalization will no longer be effective." Extending its conservative domestic pricing strategy, in 1988 the company raised U.S. prices 7 percent, the seventh mark-up since Sep-

tember 1985. (Collectively, these represented a 40 percent aggregate price increase.)

Much of the driving force behind this emerging strategy came from Tanaka's director for corporate planning, Tetsuya Katada. Concerned about Komatsu's dwindling growth prospects in construction equipment and its dangerous reliance on domestic production, Katada pushed the company toward regionalizing production in Europe and the United States.

In Europe, Komatsu pursued a number of initiatives to reduce its yen exposure, respond to political pressure, and flesh out its product line. In response to an antidumping suit, the company

1985	1984	1983	1982	1981	1980	1979	1978	1977	1976	1975
3,581	2,831	3,235	3,434	3,199	2,944	2,736	1,999	2,118	1,680	1,506
3,023	2,177	2,585	2,733	2,488	2,338	2,214	1,597	1,655	1,252	1,137
110	90	113	138	141	126	116	82	66	63	60
49%	46%	54%	58%	49%	43%	37%	38%	42%	41%	45%
76%	77%	80%	80%	81%	79%	81%	80%	76%	75%	75%
6,725	6,576	5,424	6,469	9,154	8,598	7,613	7,219	5,849	5,042	4,964
198	428	345	180	578	564	491	566	445	383	399
44%	42%	46%	57%	57%	57%	54%	48%	51%	58%	57%
964	878	702	824	1,077	1,534	1,732	1,503	1,309	1,261	1,425
4,061	4,399	3,968	4,608	5,447	5,470	4,933	4,155	3,604	3,134	2,995
602										
929	876	771	988	1,292	772	686	676	676	615	529
	NR	NR	NR	NR	NR	4,069	3,200	3,065	2,930	2,992
2,697	1,741	1,752	NR	NR	NR	NR	1,386	1,149	1,054	964

began producing wheel loaders in its U.K. plant. It began sourcing mini-excavators for the European market—the subject of another antidumping suit—from the Italian company, FAI, using engines made by Perkins, a British diesel manufacturer. And it began sourcing articulated dump trucks from Brown (U.K.) and vibratory rollers from ABG Werke (Germany), marketing them around the world under its own name. It even imported backhoe loaders from FAI into Japan.

In the United States, the company's moves were even bolder. In September 1988, Komatsu's U.S. company entered into a 50/50 joint venture with Dresser, the American oil services company that had acquired International Harvester's construction equipment business in 1983. The new $1.4 billion company (Komatsu Dresser Corp., or KDC) combined the U.S.-based finance, engineering, and manufacturing operations for both companies, while maintaining separate sales and marketing organizations in KDC. Using all four of the two parent companies' plants in the United States and Brazil, the joint venture produced most major construction products, including hydraulic excavators, bulldozers, wheel loaders, and dump trucks.

The joint venture was controversial within Komatsu, partly because many within the company had heard the industry speculation that Dresser entered the joint venture as a means of exiting this money-losing business segment in which it had a neglected product line, lagging quality, and out-of-date plants. Furthermore, it represented a radical de-

TABLE 2

Conditions for Komatsu and the Japanese Construction Industry, 1966–1990

	1990[b]	1989[b]	1987	1986	1985	1984	1983	1982	1980	1970	1966
Average exchange rate (¥/$)	158	133	121	158	200	252	232	236	204	360	360
Domestic construction investment expenditures											
¥ trillion	72.6	67.4	61.5	53.6	50.0	48.5	47.6	50.2			
% of GNP	17.7	17.4	17.3	15.8	15.4	15.9	16.6	18.3			
Komatsu construction equipment (CE)											
• CE segment sales (¥ billion)	603.9	549.5	531.1	567.5	604.5	548.7	546.6	646.6	505.3	183.2	64.5
• Overseas CE production (% total CE)	30.2	12.2	8.9	2.4	3.2						
• Overseas share of CE sales (%)	40.9	38.9	47.9	55.4	58.5	54.3	62.8	67.0	43.3	13.9	10.2
• Japanese CE industry, export ratio	27.2	27.8	36.2	44.2	52.3	49.9	55.1	57.0	36.8	10.6	7.6
Global unit demand (excl. Japan) for selected types of CE[a]											
• Bulldozers	18,000	22,000	25,000	22,000	21,000	21,000	22,000	20,000			
• yearly % change	–18	–4	+14	+5	0	–5	+10				
• Hydraulic excavators	39,000	40,000	33,000	29,000	29,000	24,000	23,000	20,000			
• yearly % change	–3	+8	+14	0	+21	+4	+15				
Global unit demand (excl. Japan) all types of CE	110,500	121,000	112,000	104,000	107,000	98,000	96,000	86,000			
• yearly % change	–9	+3	+8	–3	+9	+2	+12				
Komatsu results:											
Sales (¥ billion)	887	793	741	789	796	713	751	810	648	264	28
Income (¥ billion)	27	21	10	15	22	23	26	33	28	13	2
Income (% of sales)	3.0	2.6	1.3	1.9	2.8	3.2	3.5	4.1	4.3	4.9	7.1

Sources: MITI, company records, *Komatsu Fact Book* (various years), Yamaichi Research Institute of Securities and Economics.

[a]Bulldozers are large pieces of equipment used primarily in road construction, earth moving, agricultural engineering, forestry, mining and waste management. Hydraulic excavators are lighter machinery used in these areas as well as river maintenance, building and demolition, water and sewer main construction, landscaping, and cargo-handling.

[b]Komatsu's results are for year ending December 31 up to 1987, and year ending March 31 from 1989 on.

TABLE 3

Komatsu Financial Highlights, 1982–1989 (consolidated, ¥ million)

	Fiscal Year Ended March 31			Fiscal Year Ended December 31					
	1991	1990	1989	1987	1986	1985	1984	1983	1982
Net sales	988,397	887,108	792,809	740,599	788,726	796,235	713,472	750,530	810,379
Net income	31,258	27,282	20,833	9,504	14,701	21,915	22,642	26,265	32,639
Net income per share	31.20	27.54	22.71	11.02	17.68	26.49	27.76	32.40	40.78
Total assets	1,319,189	1,230,636	1,128,957	1,027,475	938,682	1,003,560	943,806	894,549	930,685
Shareholders' equity	524,790	490,596	444,975	398,609	381,969	374,320	355,376	337,084	315,701
As a percentage of total assets (%)	39.8	39.9	39.4	38.8	38.8	37.3	37.7	37.7	33.9
Number of consolidated subsidiaries	51	43	37	37	35	36	35	33	30
Number of companies included in account	34	33	28	25	25	24	27	26	26
CE sales (as % total sales)	63.6	68.1	69.3	71.7	71.9	75.9	76.9	72.8	79.8

Source: Komatsu, *Fact Book,* 1992

SECTION B *Business Level: Domestic and Global Cases*

TABLE 4

Global Trends in Construction Equipment Demand by Region and Type of Equipment

Region	1991 Number of Units	1991 Growth Rate	1990 Number of Units	1990 Growth Rate	1989 Number of Units	1989 Growth Rate
The Americas	28,000	−30%	40,000	−22%	51,000	−6%
Europe	42,000	−7	45,000	−4	47,000	4
Middle East and Africa	9,000	0	9,000	29	7,000	0
Asia and Oceania	13,000	−24	17,000	6	16,000	33
Total	92,000	−17	111,000	−8	121,000	3

Equipment Type	1991 Number of Units	1991 Growth Rate	1990 Number of Units	1990 Growth Rate	1989 Number of Units	1989 Growth Rate
Bulldozers	14,000	−22%	18,000	−18%	22,000	−4%
Dozer shovels	2,000	−33	3,000	−40	5,000	−17
Wheel loaders	35,000	−10	39,000	−7	42,000	2
Hydraulic excavators	32,000	−20	40,000	0	40,000	8
Motor graders	7,000	−13	8,000	0	8,000	4
Dump trucks	2,000	−33	3,000	0	3,000	0
Motor scrapers	0	0	0	0	1,000	0
Total	92,000	−17	111,000	−8	121,000	3

Source: Komatsu, *Fact Book,* 1992.

Note: Figures in both tables exclude those for the Japanese market and show totals for bulldozers, dozer shovels, wheel loaders, hydraulic excavators, motor graders, dump trucks, and motor scrapers only.

parture from several of Komatsu's closely held strategic maxims and traditional management policies: centralized production, total control over product development, whole ownership of subsidiaries, and Japanese management throughout the Komatsu group. In this way, the KDC deal served notice that the company was committed to a major change in the way it managed its international operations

ENTERING THE 1990s

New Leadership: Tetsuya Katada

In June 1989, Masao Tanaka stepped down as president and was replaced by his internationally oriented vice president of corporate planning, Tetsuya Katada. With a degree from Kyoto University of Law, Katada had risen through Komatsu's ranks in

personnel, labor relations, and corporate planning. After thirty-six years in the company, Katada was well known. Colleagues saw him as a "quiet and cool-headed commander," who spoke freely and honestly with superiors and subordinates alike. His introduction in the press signaled that he intended to take bold action. In response to questions about yet another change in Komatsu's leadership, the new president differentiated his strategy and style from his predecessor's:

Mr. Tanaka placed defense above anything else in his management policy. [Defense] was necessary because of the persistent high-yen environment. I, however, will be on the offensive in my own management policy.

When pressed on his relationship with Ryoichi Kawai, Mr. Katada added: "I have never hesitated to talk straight with my superiors. . . . [Chairman] Kawai

CASE 24   *Komatsu Ltd.: Project G's Globalization*   **C339**

1988		1987		1986	1985	1984	1983	1982
Number of Units	Growth Rate	Number of Units	Growth Rate	Number of Units	Number of Units	Number of Units	Number of Units	Number of Units
54,000	−2%	55,000	10%	50,000	50,000	45,000	35,000	23,000
45,000	15	39,000	11	35,000	33,000	30,000	30,000	28,000
7,000	−13	8,000	−20	10,000	13,000	13,000	21,000	23,000
12,000	33	10,000	11	9,000	10,000	9,000	9,000	12,000
118,000	5	112,000	8	104,000	106,000	97,000	95,000	86,000

1988		1987		1986	1985	1984	1983	1982
Number of Units	Growth Rate	Number of Units	Growth Rate	Number of Units	Number of Units	Number of Units	Number of Units	Number of Units
23,000	−8%	25,000	14%	22,000	21,000	21,000	22,000	20,000
6,000	−14	7,000	0	7,000	6,000	6,000	6,000	5,000
41,000	14	36,000	6	34,000	37,000	34,000	34,000	31,000
37,000	12	33,000	14	29,000	28,000	24,000	22,000	19,000
7,000	−13	8,000	−11	9,000	10,000	8,000	8,000	7,000
3,000	50	2,000	0	2,000	3,000	3,000	2,000	3,000
1,000	0	1,000	0	1,000	1,000	1,000	1,000	1,000
118,000	5	112,000	8	104,000	106,000	97,000	95,000	86,000

is indispensable at Komatsu. He is, however, nothing more or nothing less than an important advisor."

Questioning the Past

The situation Katada inherited was anything but promising. Despite Komatsu's recent yet belated internationalization, sales were virtually unchanged from their level seven years prior, and profits were only half those of 1982 (see Table 3). This stagnation was made all the more painful by the incredible growth taking place all around Komatsu. In the same 1982 to 1989 period, while Komatsu's profits plunged, Japan's GNP grew 43 percent. Although the worldwide demand for construction equipment had rebounded since the 1982–1983 downturn, a simultaneous shift toward smaller, lighter, and therefore less expensive, equipment such as the hydraulic excavator and the mini-excavator had dampened the impact of the recovery (see Table 4).

Worse still, worldwide industry demand was expected to dip again, at least over the next few years (see Exhibits 2 and 5). With the global political economy in the midst of a major upheaval and large-scale development projects on the wane, Katada was concerned about the suitability of a strategy tightly focused on this declining sector:

There are doubts about the future demand for construction equipment. Central and South America and Africa are having problems with accumulated debt; the Soviet Union and China also have their problems; and the price of oil is [depressing demand for construction equipment.] In the places where there is latent demand, the market is dormant. As a result, 90% of our demand is in America, Japan, and Europe. . . .

We cannot hope for growth by relying simply on construction equipment. We need to take an objective look at the world economic situation and to discuss future moves within the company. In other words, I want everyone to stop concentrating simply on catching up with Caterpillar.

This call to abandon Komatsu's long-established competitive slogan surprised many observers. But Katada went even further. He openly challenged many of the company's deeply ingrained organizational processes and even much of the management philosophy that had made Komatsu the textbook example of management by "strategic intent."[2] The new president expressed his views openly:

The company is now stagnating. It has become stereotyped and bureaucratic. The spirit of enterprise and challenge has been lost.... When Mr. Kawai was president, the time and our situation allowed him to employ a top-down approach to lead the company. But times have changed.... First, the world economy is more and more borderless, and companies must play an important role in developing international harmony. Also, the values of the young people in Japan are changing, and increasingly they question narrow, top-down directions.

A New Culture; A New Direction

Managers at Komatsu confirmed that Katada was less autocratic than prior leaders. Said one colleague, "Mr. Katada believes that one can't manage from the top down, and that any important idea or concept should be fully understood by everyone before a campaign proceeds.... His style of free discussion is new in Komatsu."

In keeping with his participatory style, Katada encouraged debate about the company's future direction. In off-site meetings and other forums, he invited a broad spectrum of managers to help shape Komatsu's new mission. During a June 1989 off-site meeting (billed as a "directors' free-discussion camp-out"), Katada proposed a new slogan to help crystallize the nascent consensus of the company's new strategic thrusts: "Growth, Global, Groupwide," or the "Three G's." Katada explained:

Top-down management by policy is becoming obsolete. Although it is still useful, we can no longer have TQC at the center of the management process. The future outlook for the indus-

try is not bright. Managers can no longer operate within the confines of a defined objective. They need to go out and see the needs and opportunities, and operate in a creative and innovative way, always encouraging initiative from below....

Although the "three G" slogan is something I came up with when I became president, there's nothing new or unusual about it given the economic conditions we were in—stagnant sales and a bureaucratic and rigidly structured company. These three simple words were intended to promote discussions, directions and policies at the board level and throughout the organization. The slogan may seem abstract, but it was this abstract nature that stimulated people to ask what they could do, and respond creatively.

Stimulating New Initiatives

Stimulated by the new open organizational forums, and encouraged by Katada's participative and challenging management style, Komatsu executives struggled to give meaning and definition to the "Three G's" slogan in a series of meetings that cascaded down the organization from September 1989 to March 1990. By this time, Katada and his top team were ready to formally adopt the new slogan and operationalize it in a long-term strategic plan, known as "Project G."

The most basic element of Project G was that the organization committed itself to return to growth, the first of the three Gs. Following the months of intensive negotiation and debate during 1989–1990, Katada announced that the company would aim at achieving a sales level of ¥1,400 billion by the mid-1990s—a level almost double its 1989 revenue level.

The core task in achieving this objective was to begin to grow construction equipment sales that had been stagnating (as reported in yen) since the early 1980s. This was to be the company's major globalization task—the second G—and Katada predicted that by the year 2000, the overseas operations of this business would manufacture over half of Komatsu's total output. To signal his continued commitment to this core business, Katada announced plans to triple the company's capital investment in construction equipment to ¥50 billion per annum, and challenged his managers to develop the proposals to justify that commitment.

Beyond revitalizing construction equipment, the third major element in Project G was a belief that Komatsu had to reduce its dependence on its traditional business through the groupwide leveraging of existing assets and resources to apply them to new product and business opportunities. Katada planned to encourage his organization to grow business such as electronics, robotics and plastics, so that by the mid 1990s the nonconstruction part of Komatsu would account for 50 percent of its sales. (For a representation of Komatsu's diverse business holdings, see Figure 2).

To communicate this new vision, Katada began referring to the company not as a construction equipment manufacturer (and certainly not as one that defined itself in terms of its old rival Caterpillar), but rather as "a total technology enterprise." And the old Japan-centered, engineering-dominated organization was now redefined in futuristic terms as "a globally integrated high-tech organization that integrates hardware and software as systems."

GLOBALIZING CONSTRUCTION EQUIPMENT

The implications of Project G for Komatsu's core construction equipment business were profound. It implied a commitment to globalization that would build on and expand the thrust that had begun in the late 1980s under Katada's urging when he was director for corporate planning. Mr. Aoyama, Katada's new director for corporate planning, commented on the business's new long-term strategic objectives outside Japan:

We don't want our strategic position to depend just on exchange rate fluctuations or the latest trade frictions. We want a stable, perpetual system of being in the construction equipment business around the world in a more integrated way, starting from development through marketing and sales.

Katada wanted to change the way the construction equipment business was managed, loosening the traditional company policy of whole ownership and control over subsidiaries to allow much more flexibility and local participation. Under his guidance, Komatsu Dresser Corporation (KDC) had not only been structured as a 50/50 joint venture, but was managed jointly. Indeed, despite the fact that it contributed half of the joint venture's equity, Komatsu asked for only two seats on KDC's twelve-person board—and it asked Dresser to provide the

CEO. (It did, however, still maintain equal management representation on KDC's six-person management committee that oversaw operations and decided the basic policy for the joint venture.) Katada explained the change in thinking behind the new organization:

We have begun to doubt whether it is possible to become a "localized and international enterprise" using only the capital, management, and engineers of Komatsu. I consider the joint venture to be a combination of Japanese technology with American management and marketing. Of course, Japanese also have pride and confidence in their administrative and marketing skills, but these cannot be fully effective in an American environment. At the same time, Dresser is behind in development and capital investment, so we plan to combine Komatsu's design and development technology with American management and marketing to achieve localization.

With a major presence in North America, attention next focused on Europe. In July 1989, one month after Katada became president, Komatsu acquired an interest in the 154-year-old German niche producer of construction equipment, Hanomag. In addition, the company finalized a supply arrangement with FAI spa, the Italian producer of mini-excavators. Over the next three years, Komatsu signed no fewer than eighteen agreements establishing various partnerships and alliances with local firms. Again, the objective was to obtain a local marketing and management capability.

To oversee the growing number of operations, Katada agreed to the proposal to form Komatsu Europe International SA (KEISA) in November 1989 to develop a more integrated group of European operations, and to coordinate the "mutual supply" of parts and increasingly specialized products. Under KEISA's guidance, for example, Hanomag took over Komatsu U.K.'s (KUK) production of wheel loaders. This arrangement capitalized both on Hanomag's 20 percent share of the German market for wheel loaders and its 100-outlet-strong distribution network in Europe. It also freed KUK to specialize in hydraulic excavators. Extending the specialized sourcing network, Italian licensee FAI supplied mini-excavators to all European markets. Table 5 shows the resulting regionalization and specialization that emerged.

FIGURE 2

The Komatsu Group

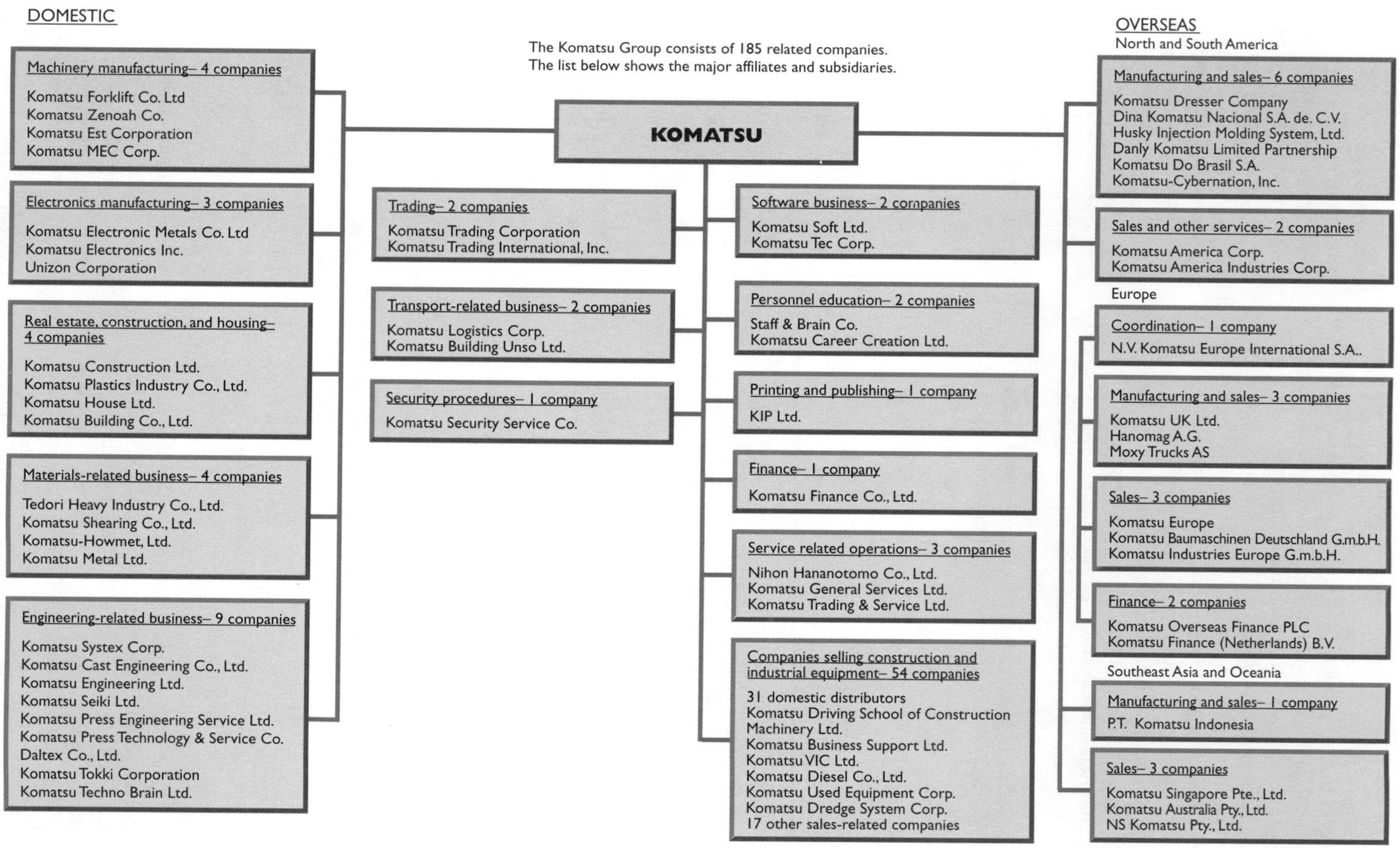

The Komatsu Group consists of 185 related companies.
The list below shows the major affiliates and subsidiaries.

KOMATSU

DOMESTIC

Machinery manufacturing— 4 companies
Komatsu Forklift Co. Ltd
Komatsu Zenoah Co.
Komatsu Est Corporation
Komatsu MEC Corp.

Electronics manufacturing— 3 companies
Komatsu Electronic Metals Co. Ltd
Komatsu Electronics Inc.
Unizon Corporation

Real estate, construction, and housing— 4 companies
Komatsu Construction Ltd.
Komatsu Plastics Industry Co., Ltd.
Komatsu House Ltd.
Komatsu Building Co., Ltd.

Materials-related business— 4 companies
Tedori Heavy Industry Co., Ltd.
Komatsu Shearing Co., Ltd.
Komatsu-Howmet, Ltd.
Komatsu Metal Ltd.

Engineering-related business— 9 companies
Komatsu Systex Corp.
Komatsu Cast Engineering Co., Ltd.
Komatsu Engineering Ltd.
Komatsu Seiki Ltd.
Komatsu Press Engineering Service Ltd.
Komatsu Press Technology & Service Co.
Daltex Co., Ltd.
Komatsu Tokki Corporation
Komatsu Techno Brain Ltd.

Trading— 2 companies
Komatsu Trading Corporation
Komatsu Trading International, Inc.

Transport-related business— 2 companies
Komatsu Logistics Corp.
Komatsu Building Unso Ltd.

Security procedures— 1 company
Komatsu Security Service Co.

Software business— 2 companies
Komatsu Soft Ltd.
Komatsu Tec Corp.

Personnel education— 2 companies
Staff & Brain Co.
Komatsu Career Creation Ltd.

Printing and publishing— 1 company
KIP Ltd.

Finance— 1 company
Komatsu Finance Co., Ltd.

Service related operations— 3 companies
Nihon Hananotomo Co., Ltd.
Komatsu General Services Ltd.
Komatsu Trading & Service Ltd.

Companies selling construction and industrial equipment— 54 companies
31 domestic distributors
Komatsu Driving School of Construction Machinery Ltd.
Komatsu Business Support Ltd.
Komatsu VIC Ltd.
Komatsu Diesel Co., Ltd.
Komatsu Used Equipment Corp.
Komatsu Dredge System Corp.
17 other sales-related companies

OVERSEAS

North and South America

Manufacturing and sales— 6 companies
Komatsu Dresser Company
Dina Komatsu Nacional S.A. de. C.V.
Husky Injection Molding System, Ltd.
Danly Komatsu Limited Partnership
Komatsu Do Brasil S.A.
Komatsu–Cybernation, Inc.

Sales and other services— 2 companies
Komatsu America Corp.
Komatsu America Industries Corp.

Europe

Coordination— 1 company
N.V. Komatsu Europe International S.A..

Manufacturing and sales— 3 companies
Komatsu UK Ltd.
Hanomag A.G.
Moxy Trucks AS

Sales— 3 companies
Komatsu Europe
Komatsu Baumaschinen Deutschland GmbH.
Komatsu Industries Europe G.m.b.H.

Finance— 2 companies
Komatsu Overseas Finance PLC
Komatsu Finance (Netherlands) B.V.

Southeast Asia and Oceania

Manufacturing and sales— 1 company
P.T. Komatsu Indonesia

Sales— 3 companies
Komatsu Singapore Pte., Ltd.
Komatsu Australia Pty, Ltd.
NS Komatsu Pty., Ltd.

TABLE 5

Specialization of Manufacturing Operations by Region and by Plant, 1992

Plant Komatsu Share (year stake taken)	Komatsu Ownership %	Number of Employees (= Japanese Expatriates)	Main Product	Local Content	Regions Supplied
Europe:					
Komatsu UK (1985)	100%	370 (12)[a]	Hydraulic excavators	70–75%	Europe, North Africa
Hanomag, Germany (1988)	64.1	1,600 (5)[a]	Wheel loaders	60–65	Europe, North Africa
FAI, spa, Italy (1991)	10	600	Mini-excavators	85	Europe, North Africa
Asia (non-Japan):					
Indonesia (1982)	50	530 (24)[a]	Bulldozers, wheel loaders	15–25	Indonesia, SE Asia, cast metal for Japan
			Hydraulic excavators, motor graders, casting and forging products, sheet metal (for Japan)		
Americas:					
Komatsu Dresser Corp. (1988)[b]	50	2779	Wheel loaders, hydraulic excavators, dump trucks, motor graders	50–65	U.S., Canada
Mexico (1974)	68.4	190 (15)[b]	Small pressers, sheet metal to USA	NA	Small presses to U.S.; sheet metal
Brazil (1973)	100	1,010 (10)[a] (10)[a]	Hydraulic excavators, bulldozers, wheel loaders, motor graders	8–95	South America, U.S., Indonesia

Source: Company records; Komatsu *Fact Book*, 1992.

[a]Number of Japanese employees as of year-end 1991.

[b]Includes companies in Peoria (1,020 employees), Chattanooga (261), Gallon (330), Candiac, Canada (110)

TABLE 6

Construction Equipment: Overseas Production (¥ million)

Overseas Production Subsidiaries	1986	1987	1988	1989	1990	1991	1992
Komatsu Dresser Co.					¥182,000[b]	¥199,000	¥136,000
Komatsu America Mfg. Corp.	NM[a]	¥600	¥17,100	¥25,400	NM	NM	NM
Komatsu Do Brasil SA	¥7,100	7,000	11,700	9,200	NM	NM	1,100[c]
Komatsu UK Ltd.	NM[a]	100	4,400	12,600	19,000	19,200	18,600
Dina Komatsu Nacional SA de CV	6,400	1,600	1,900	1,800	2,200	NM	NM
PT Komatsu Indonesia	3,100	2,400	6,400	5,500	8,600	11,600	9,300
Hanomag AG	NM	NM	NM	NM	NM	26,700	26,300
Overseas production	16,600	11,700	41,500	54,500	211,800	256,500	191,600
Domestic production	500,800	475,500	427,500	447,600	489,400	533,200	437,200
Overseas production as percentage of total production	3.2	2.4	8.9	12.2	30.2	32.5	30.5

Source: Company records.
"NM" = not meaningful (see notes below).
[a]Production began in the United States and the United Kingdom at the end of 1986.
[b]After 1989, Komatsu America Mfg. Corp. and Komatsu Brasil SA were reported as part of the Komatsu Dresser joint venture.
[c]In October 1991, Komatsu Brasil SA was again separated from Komatsu Dresser.

As a result of the aggressive expansion of off-shore operations, the company's overseas production of construction equipment rose from ¥11.7 billion, or 2.4 percent of total production in 1987, to ¥256.5 billion, or 32.5 percent of the total in 1991 (see Table 6). This growth in offshore production, together with an overall slowdown in the market, led to a major decline in the importance of parent company export sales. Accounting for 67 percent of sales at its peak in 1982 Komatsu Limited's export ratio had fallen to 37.7 percent by 1992. Nonetheless, exports still remained an important part of Komatsu's sales to all three global regions (see Table 7).

Expanding Overseas Responsibilities

Beyond developing its resource base abroad, the construction equipment management group also began to expand the roles and responsibilities of these offshore operations. With an overall vision of building a three-party, regional geographic structure, these overseas units began to develop not only manufacturing and sales functions, but also purchasing and development capabilities.

In the late 1980s, international production facilities mushroomed from a handful of offshore assembly plants to a worldwide network of sophisticated manufacturing facilities as described briefly above. Much more gradual was the shift in responsibilities for product design and development. The company's traditionally centralized development and applications policies were challenged when Hanomag's operations were found to have excellent engineering and development capabilities. The company decided to build on this asset by delegating clear development responsibility to the German company, and eliminating some duplication of effort with Tokyo. For example, management gave Hanomag full responsibility to develop all small wheel loaders for Europe, and a joint-development role with Tokyo on larger models.

In its U.K. company, however, the decision was a more basic one. Up until 1988, KUK had a three-person product engineering office headed by a Japanese manager, whose main task was to make minor modifications to Japanese drawings. Gradually, however, Komatsu began transferring responsibility for the redevelopment of the PW170 wheel excavator to a new development facility in KUK, expanding the department to include twenty-seven design engineers and twelve test engineers by 1992.

Such responsibility transfer had considerable immediate and tangible benefits. Starting with an

TABLE 7

Komatsu Financial Highlights, 1982–1989 (consolidated, ¥million)

	The Americas			Europe, Middle East, and Asia			Asia and Oceania			Total		
	Net Sales		Company	Company	Net Sales		Company	Net Sales		Net Sales		Exchange
	Yen in billions	U.S. $ In millions	Export Share (%)	Export Share (%)	U.S. $ in millions	Yen in billions	Export Share (%)	U.S. $ in millions	Yen in billions	Yen in billions	U.S. $ in millions	Rate (Yen/Dollar)
1979	¥49	$205	26.8	48.0	$367	¥88	25.2	$192	¥46	¥183	$764	240
1980	51	248	21.8	55.3	628	128	22.9	260	53	232	1,136	204
1981	57	261	18.7	66.0	920	203	15.3	214	47	307	1,396	220
1982	31	131	7.4	65.9	1,163	274	26.7	471	111	416	1,753	236
1983	41	177	10.9	71.3	1,157	268	17.7	288	67	376	1,621	232
1984	107	423	34.1	47.6	591	149	18.3	227	57	313	1,240	252
1985	103	517	31.8	44.4	723	145	23.8	388	78	325	1,627	200
1986	94	594	29.2	56.1	1,140	180	14.7	299	47	321	2,032	158
1987	87	718	36.3	41.1	812	98	22.6	445	54	239	1,976	121
1989	67	505	33.6	40.2	605	80	26.2	395	53	200	1,505	133
1990	61	385	28.1	37.4	513	81	34.5	472	75	216	1,370	158
1991	50	354	21.6	40.7	667	94	37.7	617	87	231	1,638	141
1992	38	282	19.2	49.7	728	97	31.1	456	61	195	1,466	133

Source: Company records.

Note: The exchange rate for each year reflects the Federal Reserve Bank of New York fiscal year-end average. This table excludes the three-month fiscal period ended March 31, 1988, because it represented an extraordinary term caused by the change in the fiscal period.

existing undercarriage from Europe, KUK engineers designed and modified a wheel excavator to satisfy European safety regulations and new work range requirements. Aware of strict local standards on braking and steering performance, these British engineers reduced the engine size and thus maximum speed, avoiding a far more costly redesign of the braking system. German engineers at Hanomag, too, modified basic product dimensions of a different vehicle to meet European roadwidth standards, creating a model better suited to local conditions than Tokyo's. Generally, local engineers were also able to simplify the manufacturing process design and bring the new product to market far faster than if it had been engineered in Tokyo. By operating according to centrally mandated standards covering parts and serviceability concepts, designers ensured that parts for the locally designed product were compatible with others in its product line. Said one former KUK manager:

> Before, if manufacturing had a concern about a drawing, they had no way to complain. Three engineers could not solve the problem. Information had to be transferred to Tokyo asking for a solution from the Osaka test center. Now, locals can decide on design changes as long as they meet commonality requirements.

KUK's recently opened test center, and its newly assigned responsibility for two additional projects, pointed to a continually expanding role for the group. The impact on local morale was immediate and visible.

Localizing Management

To have enduring value, it was clear to Komatsu's top management—and constantly emphasized by Katada—that this transfer of responsibility had to be accompanied by an equally strong commitment to the recruitment, development, and promotion of local managers. This strong belief was formalized in a July 1989 human resources policy that required a substantial increase in the number of foreign nationals in management positions. Komatsu Europe, for example, reduced the number of Japanese managers from 26 out of 180 employees in 1986 to 13 out of 260 by 1992, and planned to reduce that number to 6 within two years.

Despite the transfer of responsibilities and the replacement of expatriates with locals, Komatsu managers expressed surprise at how long the transition was taking. For example, their strong belief that "bottom-up problem solving" was an essential ingredient of the spirit of Komatsu led to frustration at the lack of initiative at the local level as responsibility was expanded. When one senior executive routinely began to answer employee reports of problems with the question, "How do you propose we fix it?" he was disappointed to find that typically the employees were surprised—and without answer. Other managers commented on fundamental differences in attitudes toward core values such as quality and customer service, and how long it took for such values to take deep root in Komatsu subsidiaries.

Those running the business found several causes of these problems and several areas where they needed to take action. Part of the challenge of localizing management entailed changing the way headquarters communicated with the subsidiaries. Mr. Suketomo, a director and former president of KUK, explained his difficulty in motivating non-Japanese employees in an environment where all high-level documents were written in Japanese:

> When I became KUK's president, there was a real difficulty with the language problem because all important communication with Tokyo was in Japanese. So my first job was to send a letter to Tokyo explaining that *all* communication from Tokyo would be in English, or I would ignore it! Soon, all official letters to me were in English. It not only allowed me to distribute copies to local managers, but more importantly, it forced expatriate staff to improve their English skills.

The other major problem was that many of the local nationals recruited in the earlier era were not strong managers. The main need prior to the late 1980s was for loyal implementers—"yes men," as one Japanese executive described them. As a result, many were not equal to the new challenges being given to them, and overseas units had to undertake major efforts to upgrade their personnel. In 1987, for example, Komatsu Europe had recruited only one university graduate; by 1991, it had recruited twenty-three, including its first two MBAs.

Localization created another unforeseen problem. As the number of Japanese nationals in the overseas operations decreased, the local entities' ability to coordinate their activities with the parent company—and even with each other—began to deteriorate noticeably. Numerous examples of miscommunication began to surface regularly, on issues ranging from market forecasts to product specifications. Said one observer:

> Just at the time they need more coordination than ever, they are reducing the number of Japanese managers abroad. For many Japanese companies, the most difficult task for local nationals has been to operate effectively in a linkage or coordinative role due to the high language and cultural barriers within the organization. As they increase their global integration, the intensity of such a role is going to increase dramatically.

Despite these difficulties in adjusting, in 1992 some managers believed that Japanese and Western management practices were converging, with each group learning from the other. Said one manager who spent four years in KDC:

> Our partner's style is very different from ours. The Komatsu style represents the typical Japanese emphasis on growth potential and market share for long-term survival. Dresser puts the highest priority on ROI and profit measures. Because of these differences, we encountered some friction at first. Recently, Komatsu managers have learned the importance of ROI; and those in Dresser came to understand that they must think beyond the short-term. In the future, I think we can expect a hybrid system of management.

Management also began to recognize that its localization program was only one step on a long road to fully internationalizing the management process. As Katada told the Japanese press in November 1990,

> Our goal is to transfer management from Tokyo to overseas outlets run by local nationals. As far as nationalities are concerned, this has already been accomplished in such key units as Komatsu Dresser and Hanomag. . . . But this is not enough for doing business. In this regard, what we really need to do is internationalize our headquarters in Tokyo.

Two full years later, Suketomo felt pride in the achievements, but echoed Katada's concerns:

> We have been successful increasing the local management of KUK, but there is a danger here in our thinking. If you ask, "Could the top of KUK or KDC become top of the home office in Japan, I would have to express my doubt. That reflects a limitation on our part, and I think we should see that as a challenge.

Achievements and Challenges

After three years of growth, Komatsu's construction equipment business experienced a sharp downturn in 1992. Overseas sales fell 10.6 percent to ¥246 billion, while domestic sales in this segment slipped even further, falling 13.5 percent to ¥334 billion. Worse, its operating income from construction equipment plummeted 60 percent.

Management attributed the setback to the downturn in industry demand associated with a recession that seemed to be deepening worldwide in 1992. To some industry observers, however, the continued performance problems also hinted at deeper problems with Komatsu's overall globalization strategy. Said one:

> There are clear risks in basing international expansion so heavily on joint ventures with and acquisitions of local and regional players each of which has different products, capabilities, and approaches. It's going to be hard for them to achieve the same product quality, efficiency, and strategic focus as they had a decade ago. The task is made all the more difficult if we continue to withdraw experienced Japanese expatriates from our overseas operations in the name of localization.

Nonetheless, Katada remained confident. In response to the downturn, he confirmed that Komatsu would continue its long-term globalization investments and its commitment to localization. In the short term, he was preparing a major new sales drive for hydraulic excavators, wheel loaders, and dump trucks in all three regional markets. He was clearly prepared to stay the course.

Endnotes

1. For a detailed description of the Kawai era, see "Komatsu: Ryoichi Kawai's Leadership," *Harvard Business School Case* No. 390-037.
2. See G. Hamel and C. K. Prahalad, "Strategic Intent," *Harvard Business Review* (May–June 1989), 63.

Kentucky Fried Chicken and the Global Fast-Food Industry

This case was prepared by Jeffrey A. Krug of the University of Illinois at Urbana–Champaign.

Kentucky Fried Chicken Corporation (KFC) was the world's largest chicken restaurant chain and third largest fast-food chain. KFC held more than 55 percent of the U.S. market in terms of sales and operated more than 10,200 restaurants worldwide in 1998. It opened 376 new restaurants in 1997 (more than one restaurant a day) and operated in seventy-nine countries. One of the first fast-food chains to go international during the late 1960s, KFC has developed one of the world's most recognizable brands.

Japan, Australia, and the United Kingdom accounted for the greatest share of KFC's international expansion during the 1970s and 1980s. During the 1990s, KFC turned its attention to other international markets that offered significant opportunities for growth. China, with a population of more than 1 billion, and Europe, with a population roughly equal to that of the United States, offered such opportunities. Latin America also offered a unique opportunity because of the size of its markets, its common language and culture, and its geographical proximity to the United States. Mexico was of particular interest because of the North American Free Trade Agreement (NAFTA), a free trade zone between Canada, the United States, and Mexico that went into effect in 1994.

Prior to 1990, KFC expanded into Latin America primarily through company-owned restaurants in Mexico and Puerto Rico. Company-owned restaurants gave KFC greater control over its operations than franchised or licensed restaurants. By 1995, KFC had also established company-owned restaurants in Venezuela and Brazil. In addition, it had established franchised units in several Caribbean countries. During the early 1990s, KFC shifted to a two-tier strategy in Latin America. First, it established twenty-nine franchised restaurants in Mexico following enactment of Mexico's new franchise law in 1990. This allowed KFC to expand outside of its company restaurant base in Mexico City, Guadalajara, and Monterrey. KFC was only one of many U.S. fast-food, retail, and hotel chains to begin franchising in Mexico following the new franchise law. Second, KFC began an aggressive franchise-building program in South America. By 1998, it was operating franchised restaurants in thirty-two Latin American countries. Much of this growth was in Brazil, Chile, Colombia, Ecuador, and Peru.

COMPANY HISTORY

Fast-food franchising was still in its infancy in 1952 when Harland Sanders began his travels across the United States to speak with prospective franchisees about his "Colonel Sanders Recipe Kentucky Fried Chicken." By 1960, "Colonel" Sanders had granted KFC franchises to more than 200 take-home retail outlets and restaurants across the United States. He had also succeeded in establishing a number of franchises in Canada. By 1963, the number of KFC franchises had risen to more than 300 and revenues had reached $500 million.

By 1964, at the age of seventy-four, the Colonel

had tired of running the day-to-day operations of his business and was eager to concentrate on public relations issues. Therefore, he sought out potential buyers, eventually deciding to sell the business to two Louisville businessmen—Jack Massey and John Young Brown Jr.—for $2 million. The Colonel stayed on as a public relations man and goodwill ambassador for the company.

During the next five years, Massey and Brown concentrated on growing KFC's franchise system across the United States. In 1966, they took KFC public and the company was listed on the New York Stock Exchange. By the late 1960s, a strong foothold had been established in the United States, and Massey and Brown turned their attention to international markets. In 1969, a joint venture was signed with Mitsuoishi Shoji Kaisha, Ltd., in Japan, and the rights to operate 14 existing KFC franchises in England were acquired. Subsidiaries were also established in Hong Kong, South Africa, Australia, New Zealand, and Mexico. By 1971, KFC had 2,450 franchises and 600 company-owned restaurants worldwide, and was operating in forty-eight countries.

Heublein, Inc.

In 1971, KFC entered negotiations with Heublein, Inc., to discuss a possible merger. The decision to seek a merger candidate was partially driven by Brown's desire to pursue other interests, including a political career (Brown was elected governor of Kentucky in 1977). Several months later, Heublein acquired KFC. Heublein was in the business of producing vodka, mixed cocktails, dry gin, cordials, beer, and other alcoholic beverages. However, Heublein had little experience in the restaurant business. Conflicts quickly erupted between Sanders, who continued to act in a public relations capacity, and Heublein management. Sanders became increasingly distraught over quality-control issues and restaurant cleanliness. By 1977, new restaurant openings had slowed to about twenty per year. Few restaurants were being remodeled and service quality had declined.

In 1977, Heublein sent in a new management team to redirect KFC's strategy. A "back-to-the-basics" strategy was immediately implemented. New unit construction was discontinued until existing restaurants could be upgraded and operating problems eliminated. Restaurants were refurbished, an emphasis was placed on cleanliness and service, marginal products were eliminated, and product consistency was reestablished. By 1982, KFC had succeeded in establishing a successful strategic focus and was again aggressively building new units.

R.J. Reynolds Industries, Inc.

In 1982, R.J. Reynolds Industries, Inc. (RJR), merged Heublein into a wholly owned subsidiary. The merger with Heublein represented part of RJR's overall corporate strategy of diversifying into unrelated businesses, including energy, transportation, food, and restaurants. RJR's objective was to reduce its dependence on the tobacco industry, which had driven RJR sales since its founding in North Carolina in 1875. Sales of cigarettes and tobacco products, while profitable, were declining because of reduced consumption in the United States. This was mainly the result of an increased awareness among Americans about the negative health consequences of smoking.

RJR had no more experience in the restaurant business than did Heublein. However, it decided to take a hands-off approach to managing KFC. Whereas Heublein had installed its own top management at KFC headquarters, RJR left KFC management largely intact, believing that existing KFC managers were better qualified to operate KFC's businesses than were its own managers. In doing so, RJR avoided many of the operating problems that plagued Heublein. This strategy paid off for RJR as KFC continued to expand aggressively and profitably under RJR ownership. In 1985, RJR acquired Nabisco Corporation for $4.9 billion. Nabisco sold a variety of well-known cookies, crackers, cereals, confectioneries, snacks, and other grocery products. The merger with Nabisco represented a decision by RJR to concentrate its diversification efforts on the consumer foods industry. It subsequently divested many of its nonconsumer food businesses. RJR sold KFC to PepsiCo, Inc. one year later.

PEPSICO

Corporate Strategy

PepsiCo, Inc., was formed in 1965 with the merger of the Pepsi-Cola Co. and Frito-Lay Inc. The merger of these companies created one of the largest consumer products companies in the United States. Pepsi-Cola's traditional business was the sale of soft drink concentrates to licensed independent and company-owned bottlers that manufactured, sold, and distributed Pepsi-Cola soft drinks. Pepsi-Cola's best known trademarks were Pepsi-Cola, Diet Pepsi, Mountain Dew, and Slice. Frito-Lay manufactured and sold a variety of snack foods, including Fritos Corn Chips, Lay's Potato Chips, Ruffles Potato Chips, Doritos, Tostitos Tortilla Chips, and Chee-tos Cheese Flavored Snacks. PepsiCo quickly embarked on an aggressive acquisition program similar to that pursued by RJR during the 1980s, buying a number of companies in areas unrelated to its major businesses. Its acquisitions included North American Van Lines, Wilson Sporting Goods, and Lee Way Motor Freight. However, these businesses did not prove as successful as the company had expected, mainly because PepsiCo lacked the expertise required to operate them.

Poor performance in these businesses led the then chairman and chief executive officer Don Kendall to restructure PepsiCo's operations in 1984. First, businesses that did not support PepsiCo's consumer product orientation, such as North American Van Lines, Wilson Sporting Goods, and Lee Way Motor Freight were divested. Second, the company sold its foreign bottling operations to local businesspeople, who better understood the culture and business environment in their respective countries. Third, Kendall reorganized PepsiCo along three lines: soft drinks, snack foods, and restaurants.

Restaurant Business and Acquisition of Kentucky Fried Chicken

PepsiCo first entered the restaurant business in 1977 when it acquired Pizza Hut's 3,200-unit restaurant system. Taco Bell was merged into a division of PepsiCo in 1978. The restaurant business complemented PepsiCo's consumer product orientation. The marketing of fast food followed many of the same patterns as the marketing of soft drinks and snack foods. Therefore, PepsiCo believed that its management skills could be easily transferred among its three business segments. This was compatible with the company's practice of frequently moving managers among its business units as a way of developing future top executives. PepsiCo's restaurant chains also provided an additional outlet for the sale of Pepsi soft drinks. Pepsi-Cola soft drinks and fast-food products could be marketed together in the same television and radio segments,

thereby providing higher returns for each advertising dollar. To complete its diversification into the restaurant segment, PepsiCo acquired Kentucky Fried Chicken Corporation from RJR-Nabisco for $841 million in 1986. The acquisition of KFC gave PepsiCo the leading market share in chicken (KFC), pizza (Pizza Hut), and Mexican food (Taco Bell), three of the four largest and fastest-growing segments within the U.S. fast-food industry.

Management

Following the acquisition by PepsiCo, KFC's relationship with its parent company underwent dramatic changes. RJR had operated KFC as a semiautonomous unit, satisfied that KFC management understood the fast-food business better than it did. In contrast, PepsiCo acquired KFC in order to complement its already strong presence in the fast-food market. Rather than allowing KFC to operate autonomously, PepsiCo undertook sweeping changes. These changes included negotiating a new franchise contract to give PepsiCo more control over its franchisees, reducing staff in order to cut costs, and replacing KFC managers with its own. In 1987, a rumor spread through KFC's headquarters in Louisville that the new personnel manager, who had just relocated from PepsiCo's headquarters in New York, was overheard saying that "There will be no more home grown tomatoes in this organization."

Such statements by PepsiCo personnel, uncertainties caused by several restructurings that led to layoffs throughout the KFC organization, the replacement of KFC personnel with PepsiCo managers, and conflicts between KFC and PepsiCo's corporate cultures created a morale problem within KFC. KFC's culture was built largely on Sanders's laid-back approach to management. Employees enjoyed relatively good employment stability and security. Over the years, a strong loyalty had been created between KFC employees and franchisees, mainly because of Sanders's efforts to provide for his employees' benefits, pension, and other non-income needs. In addition, the southern environment of Louisville resulted in a friendly, relaxed atmosphere at KFC's corporate offices. This corporate culture was left essentially unchanged during the Heublein and RJR years.

In stark contrast to KFC, PepsiCo's culture was characterized by a strong emphasis on performance. Top performers expected to move up through the ranks quickly. PepsiCo used its KFC, Pizza Hut, Taco Bell, Frito Lay, and Pepsi-Cola divisions as training grounds for its top managers, rotating its best managers through its five divisions on average every two years. This practice created immense pressure on managers to continuously demonstrate their managerial prowess within short periods, in order to maximize their potential for promotion. It also made many KFC managers feel that they had few career opportunities with the new company. One PepsiCo manager commented that "You may have performed well last year, but if you don't perform well this year, you're gone, and there are 100 ambitious guys with Ivy League MBAs at PepsiCo who would love to take your position." An unwanted effect of this performance-driven culture was that employee loyalty was often lost and turnover tended to be higher than in other companies.

When Kyle Craig, president of KFC's U.S. operations, was asked about KFC's relationship with its corporate parent, he commented as follows:

The KFC culture is an interesting one because I think it was dominated by a lot of KFC folks, many of whom have been around since the days of the Colonel. Many of those people were very intimidated by the PepsiCo culture which is a very high performance, high accountability, highly driven culture. People were concerned about whether they would succeed in the new culture. Like many companies, we have had a couple of downsizings which further made people nervous. Today, there are fewer old KFC people around and I think to some degree people have seen that the PepsiCo culture can drive some pretty positive results. I also think the PepsiCo people who have worked with KFC have modified their cultural values somewhat and they can see that there were a lot of benefits in the old KFC culture.

PepsiCo pushes their companies to perform strongly, but whenever there is a slip in performance, it increases the culture gap between PepsiCo and KFC. I have been involved in two downsizings over which I have been the chief architect. They have been probably the two most gut-wrenching experiences of my career. Because you know you're dealing with people's lives and their families, these changes can be emotional if you care about the people in your organization.

However, I do fundamentally believe that your first obligation is to the entire organization.

A second problem for PepsiCo was its poor relationship with KFC franchisees. A month after becoming president and chief executive officer in 1989, John Cranor addressed KFC's franchisees in Louisville, in order to explain the details of the new franchise contract. This was the first contract change in thirteen years. It gave PepsiCo greater power to take over weak franchises, relocate restaurants, and make changes in existing restaurants. In addition, restaurants would no longer be protected from competition from new KFC units, and PepsiCo would have the right to raise royalty fees on existing restaurants as contracts came up for renewal. After Cranor finished his address, there was an uproar among the attending franchisees, who jumped to their feet to protest the changes. The franchisees had long been accustomed to relatively little interference from management in their day-to-day operations (a tradition begun by Sanders). This type of interference, of course, was a strong part of PepsiCo's philosophy of demanding change. KFC's franchise association later sued PepsiCo over the new contract. The issue remained unresolved until 1996, when the most objectionable parts of the contract were removed by KFC's new president and CEO, David Novak. A new contract was ratified by KFC's franchisees in 1997.

PepsiCo's Divestiture of KFC, Pizza Hut, and Taco Bell

PepsiCo's strategy of diversifying into three distinct but related markets—soft drinks, snack foods, and fast-food restaurants—created one of the world's largest consumer products companies and a portfolio of some of the world's most recognizable brands. Between 1990 and 1996, PepsiCo grew at an annual rate of more than 10 percent, surpassing $31 billion in sales in 1996. However, the company's sale growth masked troubles in its fast-food businesses. Operating margins (profit as a percent of sales) at Pepsi-Cola and Frito Lay averaged 12 and 17 percent between 1990 and 1996, respectively. During the same period, margins at KFC, Pizza Hut, and Taco Bell fell from an average of more than 8 percent in 1990 to a little more than 4 percent in 1996. Declining margins in the fast-food chains reflected increasing maturity in the U.S. fast-food industry, more intense competition among U.S. fast-food companies, and the aging of the KFC and Pizza Hut restaurant base. As a result, PepsiCo's restaurant chains absorbed nearly one-half of PepsiCo's annual capital spending during the 1990s. However, they generated less than one-third of PepsiCo's cash flows. Therefore, cash was diverted from PepsiCo's soft drink and snack food businesses to its restaurant businesses. This reduced PepsiCo's return on assets, made it more difficult to compete effectively with Coca-Cola, and hurt its stock price. In 1997, PepsiCo spun off its restaurant businesses into a new company, called Tricon Global Restaurants, Inc. (see Figure 1). The new company was based in KFC's headquarters in Louisville, Kentucky. PepsiCo's objective was to reposition itself as a packaged goods company, to strengthen its balance sheet, and to create more consistent earning growth. PepsiCo received a one-time distribution from Tricon of $4.7 billion, $3.7 billion of which was used to pay off short-term debt. The balance was earmarked for stock repurchases.

FAST-FOOD INDUSTRY

According to the National Restaurant Association (NRA), food-service sales topped $320 billion in 1997 for the approximately 500,000 restaurants and other food outlets making up the U.S. restaurant industry. The NRA estimated that sales in the fast-food segment of the food service industry grew 5.2 percent, to $104 billion, in 1997, up from $98 billion in 1996. This marked the fourth consecutive year that fast-food sales had either matched or exceeded sales in full-service restaurants, which grew 4.1 percent, to $104 billion, in 1997. The growth in fast-food sales reflected the long, gradual change in the restaurant industry from an industry once dominated by independently operated sit-down restaurants to an industry fast becoming dominated by fast-food restaurant chains. The U.S. restaurant industry as a whole grew by approximately 4.2 percent in 1997.

Major Fast-Food Segments

Six major business segments made up the fast-food segment of the food service industry. Sales data for the leading restaurant chains in each segment are shown in Table 1. Most striking is the dominance of McDonald's, which had sales of more than $16 billion in 1996. This represented 16.6 percent of U.S. fast-food sales, or nearly 22 percent of sales among the nation's top thirty fast-food chains. Sales at McDonald's restaurants averaged $1.3 million per year, compared with about $820,000 for the average U.S. fast-food restaurant. Tricon Global Restaurants (KFC, Pizza Hut, and Taco Bell) had U.S. sales of $13.4 billion in 1996. This represented 13.6 percent of U.S. fast-food sales and 17.9 percent of the top thirty fast-food chains.

Sandwich chains made up the largest segment of the fast-food market. McDonald's controlled 35

FIGURE 1

Tricon Global Restaurants' Organizational Chart (1998)

Tricon Global Restaurants, Inc.
Corporate Offices
(Louisville, Kentucky)
Andrall Pearson, chairman and CEO
David Novak, vice chairman and president

Kentucky Fried Chicken Corporate
(Louisville, Kentucky)
Jeffrey Moody, chief concept officer
Charles Rawley, chief operating officer

Pizza Hut, U.S.A.
(Dallas, Texas)
Michael Rawlings, president and CCO
Aylwin Lewis, chief operating officer

Taco Bell Corp.
(Irvine, California)
Peter Waller, president and CCO
Thomas Davin, chief operating officer

Tricon Restaurants International
(Dallas, Texas)
Peter Bassi, president

TABLE 1

Leading U.S. Fast-Food Chains Ranked by 1996 Sales (in $ thousands)

Sandwich Chains	Sales	Share (%)	Family Restaurants	Sales	Share (%)
McDonald's	$16,370	35.0	Denny's	$1,850	21.2
Burger King	7,300	15.6	Shoney's	1,220	14.0
Taco Bell	4,575	9.8	Big Boy	945	10.8
Wendy's	4,360	9.3	Int'l House of Pancakes	797	9.1
Hardee's	3,055	6.5	Cracker Barrel	734	8.4
Subway	2,700	5.8	Perkins	678	7.8
Arby's	1,867	4.0	Friendly's	597	6.8
Dairy Queen	1,225	2.6	Bob Evans	575	6.6
Jack in the Box	1,207	2.6	Waffle House	525	6.0
Sonic Drive-In	985	2.1	Coco's	278	3.2
Carl's Jr.	648	1.4	Steak 'n Shake	275	3.2
Other Chains	2,454	5.2	Village Inn	246	2.8
Total	$46,745	100.0	Total	$8,719	100.0

Dinner Houses	Sales	Share (%)	Pizza Chains	Sales	Share (%)
Red Lobster	$1,810	15.7	Pizza Hut	4,927	46.4
Applebee's	1,523	13.2	Domino's Pizza	2,300	21.7
Olive Garden	1,280	11.1	Little Caesars	1,425	13.4
Chile's	1,242	10.7	Papa John's	619	5.8
Outback Steakhouse	1,017	8.8	Sbarros	400	3.8
T.G.I. Friday's	935	8.1	Round Table Pizza	385	3.6
Ruby Tuesday	545	4.7	Chuck E. Cheese's	293	2.8
Lone Star Steakhouse	460	4.0	Godfather's Pizza	266	2.5
Bennigan's	458	4.0	Total	$10,614	100.0
Romano's Macaroni Grill	344	3.0			
Other Dinner Houses	1,942	16.8	Chicken Chains		
Total	$11,557	100.0	KFC	$3,900	57.1
			Boston Market	1,167	17.1
Grilled Buffet Chains			Popeye's Chicken	666	9.7
			Chick-fil-A	570	8.3
Golden Corral	$711	22.8	Church's Chicken	529	7.7
Ponderosa	680	21.8	Total	$6,832	100.0
Ryan's	604	19.4			
Sizzler	540	17.3			
Western Sizzlin'	332	10.3			
Quincy's	259	8.3			
Total	$3,116	100.0			

Source: Nation's Restaurant News.

percent of the sandwich segment, while Burger King ran a distant second with a 15.6 percent market share. Competition had grown particularly intense within the sandwich segment as the U.S. fast-food market became more saturated. To increase sales, chains sought to win customers away from other sandwich chains by offering new products, introduced products traditionally offered by non-sandwich chains (such as pizzas, fried chicken, and tacos), streamlined their menus, and upgraded product quality. Burger King introduced its Big King, a direct clone of the Big Mac. McDonald's quickly retaliated by introducing its Big 'n Tasty, a direct clone of the Whopper. Wendy's introduced chicken pita sandwiches and Taco Bell introduced sandwiches called "wraps"—breads stuffed with various fillings. Hardee's successfully introduced fried chicken in most of its restaurants. Besides turning out new products, chains lowered prices, improved customer service, cobranded with other fast-food chains, and established restaurants in non-traditional locations (for instance, McDonald's installed restaurants in Wal-Mart stores across the country) to beef up sales.

The second largest fast-food segment was dinner houses, dominated by Red Lobster, Applebee's, Olive Garden, and Chili's. Between 1988 and 1996, dinner houses increased their share of the fast-food market from 8 to more than 13 percent. This increase came mainly at the expense of grilled-buffet chains, such as Ponderosa, Sizzler, and Western Sizzlin'. The market share of steak houses fell from 6 percent in 1988 to less than 4 percent in 1996. The rise of dinner houses during the 1990s was partly the result of an aging and wealthier population, which increasingly demanded higher-quality food in more upscale settings. However, rapid construction of new restaurants, especially among relative newcomers, such as Romano's Macaroni Grill, Lone Star Steakhouse, and Outback Steakhouse, resulted in overcapacity within the dinner house segment. This reduced per restaurant sales and further intensified competition. Eight of the sixteen largest dinner houses posted growth rates of 10 percent or more in 1996: Romano's Macaroni Grill, 82 percent; Lone Star Steakhouse, 41 percent; Chili's, 32 percent; Outback Steakhouse, 27 percent; Applebee's, 23 percent; Red Robin, 14 percent; Fuddruckers, 11 percent; and Ruby Tuesday, 10 percent.

The third largest fast-food segment was pizza, long dominated by Pizza Hut. While Pizza Hut controlled more than 46 percent of the pizza segment in 1996, its market share had slowly eroded because of intense competition and its aging restaurant base. Domino's Pizza and Papa John's Pizza have been particularly successful. Little Caesars is the only pizza chain to remain predominately a takeout chain, though it recently began home delivery. However, its policy of charging customers $1 per delivery damaged consumers' perception of it as a high value pizza chain. Home delivery, successfully introduced by Domino's and Pizza Hut, was a driving force for success among the market leaders during the 1970s and 1980s. However, the success of home delivery drove competitors to look for new methods of increasing their customer bases. Pizza chains diversified into non-pizza items (for example, chicken wings at Domino's, Italian cheese bread at Little Caesars, and stuffed crust pizza at Pizza Hut), developed nontraditional units (such as airport kiosks and college campuses), offered special promotions, and brought out new pizza variations with an emphasis on high-quality ingredients (for instance, Roma Herb and Garlic Crunch pizza at Domino's and Buffalo Chicken Pizza at Round Table Pizza).

Chicken Segment

KFC continued to dominate the chicken segment, with 1997 sales of $4 billion (see Table 2). Its nearest competitor, Boston Market, was second with sales of $1.2 billion. In 1998, KFC operated 5,120 restaurants in the United States, 8 fewer restaurants than in 1993. Rather than building new restaurants in the already saturated U.S. market, KFC focused on building restaurants abroad. In the United States, KFC focused on closing unprofitable restaurants, upgrading existing restaurants with new exterior signage, and improving product quality. The strategy has paid off. While overall U.S. sales during the last ten years remained flat, annual sales per unit increased steadily in eight of the last nine years.

Despite KFC's continued dominance within the chicken segment, it has lost market share to Boston Market, a new restaurant chain emphasizing roasted rather than fried chicken. Boston Market has successfully created the image of an upscale deli offering healthy, "home-style" alternatives to fried chicken and other fast-foods. It has broadened its menu beyond rotisserie chicken to include ham, turkey, meat loaf, chicken pot pie, and deli sandwiches. In order to minimize its image as a fast-food place, it has refused to put drive-throughs in its restaurants and has established most of its units in outside shopping malls rather than in freestanding units at intersections so characteristic of other fast-food restaurants.

In 1993, KFC introduced its own rotisserie chicken, called Rotisserie Gold, to combat Boston Market. However, it quickly learned that its customer base was considerably different from that of Boston Market's. KFC's customers liked KFC chicken despite the fact that it was fried. In addi-

TABLE 2

Top U.S. Chicken Chains

	Sales (in $ millions)						
	1992	1993	1994	1995	1996	1997	Growth Rate(%)
KFC	$3,400	$3,400	$3,500	$3,700	$3,900	$4,000	3.3
Boston Market	43	147	371	754	1,100	1,197	94.5
Popeye's	545	569	614	660	677	727	5.9
Chick-fil-A	356	396	451	502	570	671	11.9
Church's	414	440	465	501	526	574	6.8
Total	$4,758	$4,952	$5,401	$6,118	$6,772	$7,170	8.5
	Number of U.S. Restaurants						
KFC	5,089	5,128	5,149	5,142	5,108	5,120	0.1
Boston Market	83	217	534	829	1,087	1,166	69.6
Popeye's	769	769	853	889	894	949	4.3
Chick-fil-A	487	545	534	825	717	762	9.0
Church's	944	932	937	953	9,890	1,070	2.5
Total	7,372	7,591	8,007	8,638	8,795	9,067	4.2
	Sales per Unit (in $ thousands)						
KFC	$668	$663	$680	$720	$764	$781	3.2
Boston Market	518	677	695	910	1,012	1,027	14.7
Popeye's	709	740	720	743	757	767	1.6
Chick-fil-A	731	727	845	608	795	881	3.8
Church's	439	472	496	526	531	537	4.1
Total	$645	$782	$782	$782	$782	$782	3.9

Source: Tricon Global Restaurants, Inc., 1997 Annual Report; Boston Chicken, Inc., 1997 Annual Report; Chick-fil-A, corporate headquarters, Atlanta; AFC Enterprises, Inc., 1997 Annual Report.

tion, customers did not respond well to the concept of buying whole chickens for takeout. They preferred to buy chicken by the piece. KFC withdrew its rotisserie chicken in 1996 and introduced a new line of roasted chicken called "Tender Roast," which could be sold by the piece and mixed with its Original Recipe and Extra Crispy Chicken.

Other major competitors within the chicken segment included Popeye's Famous Fried Chicken and Church's Chicken (both subsidiaries of AFC Enterprises in Atlanta), Chick-fil-A, Bojangle's, El Pollo Loco, Grandy's, Kenny Rogers Roasters, Mrs. Winner's, and Pudgie's. Both Church's and Popeye's had similar strategies—to compete head-on with other "fried chicken" chains. Unlike KFC, neither

chain offered rotisserie chicken, and nonfried chicken products were limited. Chick-fil-A focused exclusively on pressure-cooked and char-grilled skinless chicken breast sandwiches, which it served to customers in sit-down restaurants located predominately in shopping malls. As many malls added food courts, often consisting of up to fifteen fast-food units competing side by side, shopping malls became less enthusiastic about allocating separate store space to food chains. Therefore, in order to complement its existing restaurant base in shopping malls, Chick-fil-A began to open smaller units in shopping mall food courts, hospitals, and colleges. It also opened freestanding units in selected locations.

Demographic Trends

A number of demographic and societal trends contributed to increased demand for food prepared away from home. Because of the high divorce rate in the United States and the fact that people married later in life, single-person households represented about 25 percent of all U.S. households, up from 17 percent in 1970. This increased the number of individuals choosing to eat out rather than eat at home. The number of married women working outside of the home also increased dramatically during the last quarter of the twentieth century, with about 59 percent of all married women having careers. According to the Conference Board, 64 percent of all married households will be double-income families by 2000. About 80 percent of households headed by individuals between the ages of twenty-five and forty-four (both married and unmarried) will be double-income. Greater numbers of working women increased family incomes. According to *Restaurants & Institutions* magazine, more than one-third of all households had incomes of at least $50,000 in 1996. About 8 percent of all households had annual incomes over $100,000. The combination of higher numbers of dual-career families and rising incomes meant that fewer families had time to prepare food at home. According to Standard & Poor's *Industry Surveys*, Americans spent 55 percent of their food dollars at restaurants in 1995, up from 34 percent in 1970.

Fast-food restaurant chains met these demographic and societal changes by expanding their restaurant bases. However, by the early 1990s, the growth of traditional freestanding restaurants slowed as the U.S. market became saturated. The major exception was dinner houses, which continued to proliferate in response to Americans' increased passion for beef. Since 1990, the U.S. population has grown at an average annual rate of about 1 percent and reached 270 million people in 1997. Rising immigration since 1990 dramatically altered the ethnic makeup of the U.S. population. According to the Bureau of the Census, Americans born outside of the United States made up 10 percent of the population in 1997. About 40 percent were Hispanic, while 24 percent were Asian. Nearly 30 percent of Americans born outside of the United States arrived since 1990. As a result of these trends, restaurant chains expanded their menus to appeal to the different ethnic tastes of consumers, expanded into nontraditional locations such as department stores and airports, and made food more available through home delivery and takeout service.

INDUSTRY CONSOLIDATION AND MERGERS AND ACQUISITIONS

Lower growth in the U.S. fast-food market intensified competition for market share between restaurant chains and led to consolidation, primarily through mergers and acquisitions, during the mid 1990s. Many restaurant chains found that market share could be increased more quickly and cheaply by acquiring an existing company than by building new units. In addition, fixed costs could be spread across a larger number of restaurants. This raised operating margins and gave companies an opportunity to build market share by lowering prices. An expanded restaurant base also gave companies greater purchasing power over suppliers. In 1990, Grand Metropolitan, a British company, purchased Pillsbury Co. for $5.7 billion. Included in the purchase was Pillsbury's Burger King chain. Grand Met strengthened the franchise by upgrading existing restaurants and eliminated several levels of management in order to cut costs. This gave Burger King a long-needed boost in improving its position against McDonald's, its largest competitor. In 1988, Grand Met had purchased Wienerwald, a West German chicken chain, and the Spaghetti Factory, a Swiss chain.

Perhaps most important to KFC was Hardee's acquisition of 600 Roy Rogers restaurants from Marriott Corporation in 1990. Hardee's converted a large number of these restaurants to Hardee's units and introduced "Roy Rogers" fried chicken into its menu. By 1993, Hardee's had introduced fried chicken into most of its U.S. restaurants. Hardee's was unlikely to destroy the customer loyalty that KFC long enjoyed. However, it did cut into KFC's sales, because it was able to offer consumers a widened menu selection that appealed to a variety of family eating preferences. In 1997, Hardee's parent company, Imasco Ltd., sold Hardee's to CKE Restaurants, Inc. CKE owned Carl's Jr., Rally's Hamburgers, and Checker's Drive-In. That same year, Boston Chicken, Inc., acquired Harry's Farmers Market, an Atlanta grocer that sold fresh quality prepared meals. The acquisition was designed to help Boston Chicken develop distribution beyond its Boston Market restaurants. Also in 1997, AFC Enterprises, which operated Popeye's and Church's, acquired Chesapeake Bagel Bakery of McLean, Virginia, in order to diversify away from fried chicken and to strengthen its balance sheet.

The effect of these and other recent mergers and acquisitions on the industry was powerful. The top ten restaurant companies controlled almost 60 percent of fast-food sales in the United States. The consolidation of a number of fast-food chains within larger, financially more powerful parent companies gave restaurant chains strong financial and managerial resources that could be used to compete against smaller chains in the industry.

International Quick-Service Market

Because of the aggressive pace of new restaurant construction in the United States during the 1970s and 1980s, opportunities to expand domestically through new restaurant construction in the 1990s were limited. Restaurant chains that did build new restaurants found that the higher cost of purchasing prime locations resulted in immense pressure to increase annual per restaurant sales, in order to cover higher initial investment costs. Many restaurants began to expand into international markets as an alternative to the United States. In contrast to the U.S. market, international markets offered large customer bases with comparatively little competition. However, only a few U.S. restaurant chains had defined aggressive strategies for penetrating international markets by 1998.

Three restaurant chains that had established aggressive international strategies were McDonald's, KFC, and Pizza Hut. McDonald's operated the largest number of restaurants. In 1998, it operated 23,132 restaurants in 109 countries (10,409 restaurants were located outside of the United States). In comparison, KFC, Pizza Hut, and Taco Bell together operated 29,712 restaurants in 79, 88, and 17 countries, respectively (9,126 restaurants were located outside of the United States). Of these four chains, KFC operated the greatest percentage of its restaurants (50 percent) outside of the United States. McDonald's, Pizza Hut, and Taco Bell operated 45, 31, and 2 percent of their units abroad. KFC opened its first restaurant outside of the United States in the late 1950s. By the time PepsiCo acquired KFC in 1986, KFC was already operating restaurants in 55

countries. KFC's early expansion abroad, its strong brand name, and managerial experience in international markets gave it a strong competitive advantage vis-à-vis other fast-food chains that were investing abroad for the first time.

Table 3 shows *Hotels'* 1994 list of the world's thirty largest fast-food restaurant chains (*Hotels* discontinued reporting these data after 1994). The seventeen largest restaurant chains of the thirty (ranked by number of units) were headquartered in the United States. The relative scarcity of fast-food restaurant chains outside of the United States had a number of possible explanations. First, the United States represented the largest consumer market in the world, accounting for more than one-fifth of the world's gross domestic product (GDP). Therefore, the United States was the strategic focus of the largest restaurant chains. Second, Americans were quicker to accept the fast-food concept. Many other cultures had strong culinary traditions that were difficult to break down. Europeans, for example, had a history of frequenting more mid-scale restaurants, where they spent several hours in a formal setting enjoying native dishes and beverages. While KFC was again building restaurants in West Germany by the late 1980s, it previously failed to penetrate the German market because Germans were not accustomed to takeout food or to ordering food over the counter. McDonald's had greater success penetrating the German market because it made a number of changes in its menu and operating procedures, in order to better appeal to German culture. For example, German beer was served in all of McDonald's German restaurants. KFC had more success in Asia and Latin America, where chicken was a traditional dish.

Aside from cultural factors, international business carried risks not present in the U.S. market. Long distances between headquarters and foreign franchises often made it difficult to control the quality of individual restaurants. Large distances also caused servicing and support problems. Transportation and other resource costs were higher than in the domestic market. In addition, time, cultural, and language differences increased communication and operational problems. Therefore, it was reasonable to expect U.S. restaurant chains to expand domestically as long as they achieved corporate profit and growth objectives. As the U.S. market became saturated, and companies gained

TABLE 3

The World's Thirty Largest Fast-Food Chains, Ranked by Number of Countries

		For the Year Ended December 31, 1993		
Rank	*Franchise*	*Headquarters Location*	*Units*	*Countries*
1	Pizza Hut	Dallas, Texas	10,433	80
2	McDonald's	Oakbrook, Illinois	23,132	70
3	KFC	Louisville, Kentucky	9,033	68
4	Burger King	Miami, Florida	7,121	50
5	Baskin Robbins	Glendale, California	3,557	49
6	Wendy's	Dublin, Ohio	4,168	38
7	Domino's Pizza	Ann Arbor, Michigan	5,238	36
8	TCBY	Little Rock, Arkansas	7,474	22
9	Dairy Queen	Minneapolis, Minnesota	5,471	21
10	Dunkin' Donuts	Randolph, Massachusetts	3,691	21
11	Taco Bell	Irvine, California	4,921	20
12	Arby's	Fort Lauderdale, Florida	2,670	18
13	Subway Sandwiches	Milford, Connecticut	8,477	15
14	Sizzler International	Los Angeles, California	681	14
15	Hardee's	Rocky Mount, North Carolina	4,060	12
16	Little Caesar's	Detroit, Michigan	4,600	12
17	Popeye's Chicken	Atlanta, Georgia	813	12
18	Denny's	Spartanburg, South Carolina	1,515	10
19	A&W Restaurants	Livonia, Michigan	707	9
20	T.G.I. Friday's	Minneapolis, Minnesota	273	8
21	Orange Julius	Minneapolis, Minnesota	480	7
22	Church's Fried Chicken	Atlanta, Georgia	1,079	6
23	Long John Silver's	Lexington, Kentucky	1,464	5
24	Carl's Jr.	Anaheim, California	649	4
25	Loterria	Tokyo, Japan	795	4
26	Mos Burger	Tokyo, Japan	1,263	4
27	Skylark	Tokyo, Japan	1,000	4
28	Jack-in-the-Box	San Diego, California	1,172	3
29	Quick Restaurants	Berchem, Belgium	876	3
30	Taco Time	Eugene, Oregon	300	3

Source: Hotels (May 1994); PepsiCo, Inc., 1994 Annual Report.

expertise in international markets, more companies turned to profitable international markets as a means of expanding restaurant bases and increasing sales, profits, and market share.

KENTUCKY FRIED CHICKEN CORPORATION

KFC's worldwide sales, which included sales of both company-owned and franchised restaurants, grew to $8.0 billion in 1997. U.S. sales grew 2.6 percent over 1996 and accounted for about one-half of KFC's sales worldwide. KFC's U.S. share of the chicken segment fell 1.8 points, to 55.8 percent, in 1997 (see Table 4). This marked the sixth consecutive year that KFC sustained a decline in market share. Market share fell from 72.1 percent of the market in 1988 to 55.8 percent in 1997, a total market share loss of 16.3 points. Boston Market, which established its first restaurant in 1992, increased its market share from zero to 16.7 percent

TABLE 4

Top U.S. Chicken Chains—Market Share (%)

	KFC	Boston Market	Popeye's	Chick-fil-A	Church's	Total
1988	72.1	0.0	12.0	5.8	10.1	100.0
1989	70.8	0.0	12.0	6.2	11.0	100.0
1990	71.3	0.0	12.3	6.6	9.8	100.0
1991	72.7	0.0	11.4	7.0	8.9	100.0
1992	71.5	0.9	11.4	7.5	8.7	100.0
1993	68.7	3.0	11.4	8.0	8.9	100.0
1994	64.8	6.9	11.3	8.4	8.6	100.0
1995	60.5	12.3	10.8	8.2	8.2	100.0
1996	57.6	16.2	10.0	8.4	7.8	100.0
1997	55.8	16.7	10.1	9.4	8.0	100.0
Change	−16.3	16.7	−1.9	3.6	−2.1	0.0

Source: *Nation's Restaurant News.*

over the same period. On the surface, it might appear that it did so by taking customers away from KFC. However, KFC's sales growth remained fairly stable and constant over the last ten years. Boston Market's success was largely a function of its appeal to consumers who did not regularly patronize KFC or other chicken chains that sold fried chicken. By appealing to a market niche that was previously unsatisfied, Boston Market was able to expand the existing consumer base within the chicken segment of the fast-food industry.

Refranchising Strategy

The relatively low growth rate in sales in KFC's domestic restaurants during the 1992–1997 period was largely the result of KFC's decision in 1993 to begin selling company-owned restaurants to franchisees. When Colonel Sanders began to expand the Kentucky Fried Chicken system in the late 1950s, he established KFC as a system of independent franchisees. This was done in order to minimize his involvement in the operations of individual restaurants and to concentrate on the things he enjoyed the most—cooking, product development, and public relations. This resulted in a fiercely loyal and independent group of franchises. PepsiCo's strategy when it acquired KFC in 1986 was to integrate KFC's operations into the PepsiCo

system in order to take advantage of operational, financial, and marketing synergies. However, such a strategy demanded that PepsiCo become more involved in decisions over franchise operations, menu offerings, restaurant management, finance, and marketing. This was met with resistance by KFC franchises, who fiercely opposed increased control by the corporate parent. One method for PepsiCo to deal with the conflict with KFC franchises was to expand through company-owned restaurants rather than through franchising and to use strong PepsiCo cash flows to buy back unprofitable franchised restaurants, which could then be converted into company-owned restaurants. In 1986, company-owned restaurants made up 26 percent of KFC's U.S. restaurant base. By 1993, they made up about 40 percent of the total (see Table 5).

While company-owned restaurants were relatively easier to control compared with franchises, they also required higher levels of investment. This meant that high levels of cash were diverted from PepsiCo's soft drink and snack food businesses into its restaurant businesses. However, the fast-food industry delivered lower returns than the soft-drink and snack foods industries. Consequently, increased investment in KFC, Pizza Hut, and Taco Bell had a negative effect on PepsiCo's consolidated return on assets. By 1993, investors became concerned that

TABLE 5

KFC Restaurants in the United States

	Company-Owned	%Total	Franchised/Licensed	%Total	Total
1986	1,246	26.4	3,474	73.6	4,720
1987	1,250	26.0	3,564	74.0	4,814
1988	1,262	25.8	3,637	74.2	4,899
1989	1,364	27.5	3,597	72.5	4,961
1990	1,389	27.7	3,617	72.3	5,006
1991	1,836	36.6	3,186	63.4	5,022
1992	1,960	38.8	3,095	61.2	5,055
1993	2,014	39.5	3,080	60.5	5,094
1994	2,005	39.2	3,110	60.8	5,115
1995	2,026	39.4	3,111	60.6	5,137
1996	1,932	37.8	3,176	62.2	5,108
1997	1,850	36.1	3,270	63.9	5,120

1986–1993 Compounded Annual Growth Rate

7.1%		−1.7%		1.1%

1993–1997 Compounded Annual Growth Rate

−2.1%		1.5%		0.1%

Source: Tricon Global Restaurants, Inc., 1997 Annual Report; PepsiCo, Inc., Annual Reports for 1994, 1995, 1996, and 1997.

PepsiCo's return on assets failed to match returns delivered by Coca-Cola. In order to shore up its return on assets, PepsiCo decided to reduce the number of company-owned restaurants by selling them back to franchisees. This strategy lowered overall company sales, but it also lowered the amount of cash tied up in fixed assets, provided PepsiCo with one-time cash flow benefits from initial fees charged to franchisees, and generated an annual stream of franchise royalties. Tricon Global continued this strategy after the spinoff in 1997.

Marketing Strategy

During the 1980s, consumers began to demand healthier foods, greater variety, and service in nontraditional locations such as grocery stores, restaurants, airports, and outdoor events. This forced fast-food chains to expand menu offerings and to investigate nontraditional distribution channels and restaurant designs. Families also demanded greater

value in the food they bought away from home. This increased pressure on fast-food chains to reduce prices and to lower operating costs in order to maintain profit margins.

Many of KFC's problems during the late 1980s stemmed from its limited menu and its inability to quickly bring new products to market. The popularity of its Original Recipe Chicken allowed KFC to expand through the 1980s without significant competition. As a result, new product introductions were never an important element of KFC's overall strategy. One of the most serious setbacks suffered by the company came in 1989 as it prepared to add a chicken sandwich to its menu. While KFC was still experimenting with its chicken sandwich, McDonald's test-marketed its McChicken sandwich in the Louisville market. Shortly thereafter, it rolled out the McChicken sandwich nationally. By beating KFC to the market, McDonald's was able to develop strong consumer awareness for its sandwich. This significantly increased KFC's cost of developing awareness for its own sandwich, which KFC introduced several months later. KFC eventually withdrew its sandwich because of low sales.

In 1991, KFC changed its logo in the United States from Kentucky Fried Chicken to KFC, in order to reduce its image as a fried chicken chain. It continued to use the Kentucky Fried Chicken name internationally. It then responded to consumer demands for greater variety by introducing several products that would serve as alternatives to its Original Recipe Chicken. These included Oriental Wings, Popcorn Chicken, and Honey BBQ Chicken. It also introduced a desert menu that included a variety of pies and cookies. In 1993, it rolled out Rotisserie Chicken and began to promote its lunch and dinner buffet. The buffet, comprising thirty items, was introduced into almost 1,600 KFC restaurants in twenty-seven states by year-end. In 1998, KFC sold three types of chicken—Original Recipe and Extra Crispy (fried chicken) and Tender Roast (roasted chicken).

One of KFC's most aggressive strategies was the introduction of its Neighborhood Program. By mid 1993, almost 500 company-owned restaurants in New York, Chicago, Philadelphia, Washington, D.C., St. Louis, Los Angeles, Houston, and Dallas had been outfitted with special menu offerings to appeal exclusively to the black community. Menus were expanded with side dishes such as greens, macaroni and cheese, peach cobbler, sweet-potato pie, and red beans and rice. In addition, restaurant employees wore African-inspired uniforms. The introduction of the Neighborhood Program increased sales by 5 to 30 percent in restaurants appealing directly to blacks. KFC then tested Hispanic-oriented restaurants in the Miami area, offering side dishes such as fried plantains, flan, and tres leches.

One of KFC's most significant problems in the U.S. market was that overcapacity made expansion of freestanding restaurants difficult. Fewer sites were available for new construction and those sites, because of their increased cost, were driving profit margins down. Therefore, KFC initiated a new, three-pronged distribution strategy. First, it focused on building smaller restaurants in nontraditional outlets such as airports, shopping malls, universities, and hospitals. Second, it experimented with home delivery. Home delivery was introduced

in the Nashville and Albuquerque markets in 1994. By 1998, home delivery was offered in 365 U.S. restaurants. Other nontraditional distribution outlets being tested included units offering drive-through and carryout service only, snack shops in cafeterias, scaled-down outlets for supermarkets, and mobile units that could be transported to outdoor concerts and fairs.

A third focus of KFC's distribution strategy was restaurant cobranding, primarily with its sister chain, Taco Bell. By 1997, 349 KFC restaurants had added Taco Bell to their menus and displayed both the KFC and Taco Bell logos outside their restaurants. Cobranding gave KFC the opportunity to expand its business dayparts. While about two-thirds of KFC's business was dinner, Taco Bell's primary business occurred at lunch. Combining the two concepts in the same unit could increase sales at individual restaurants significantly. KFC believed that there were opportunities to sell the Taco Bell concept in more than 3,900 of its U.S. restaurants.

Operating Efficiencies

As pressure continued to build on fast-food chains to limit price increases, restaurant chains searched for ways to reduce overhead and other operating costs in order to improve profit margins. In 1989, KFC reorganized its U.S. operations, to eliminate overhead costs and increase efficiency. This reorganization included a revision of KFC's crew-training programs and operating standards. The company renewed its emphasis on improving customer service, cleaner restaurants, faster and friendlier service, and continued high-quality products. In 1992, KFC reorganized its middle-management ranks, eliminating 250 of the 1,500 management positions at the corporate headquarters. More responsibility was assigned to restaurant franchisees and marketing managers and pay was more closely aligned with customer service and restaurant performance. In 1997, Tricon Global signed a five-year agreement with PepsiCo Food Systems (which was later sold by PepsiCo to AmeriServe Food Distributors) to distribute food and supplies to Tricon's 29,712 KFC, Pizza Hut, and Taco Bell units. This provided KFC with significant opportunities to benefit from economies of scale in distribution.

INTERNATIONAL OPERATIONS

The top ten fast-food chains owed much of their success to aggressive building strategies. Chains were able to discourage competition by building in low-population areas that could support only a single fast-food chain. McDonald's was particularly successful as it was able to expand quickly into small towns across the United States, preempting other fast-food chains. It was equally important to beat a competitor into more densely populated areas, where location was of prime importance. KFC's early entry into international markets placed it in a strong position to benefit from international expansion as the U.S. market became saturated. In 1997, 50 percent of KFC's restaurants were located outside of the United States. While 364 new restaurants were opened outside of the United States, only 12 new restaurants were added to the U.S. system in 1997. Most of KFC's international expansion was through franchises, though some restaurants were licensed to operators or jointly operated with a local partner. Expansion through franchising was an important strategy for penetrating international markets because franchises were owned and operated by local entrepreneurs with a deeper understanding of local language, culture, and customs, as well as local law, financial markets, and marketing characteristics. Franchising was particularly important for expansion into smaller countries such as the Dominican Republic, Grenada, Bermuda, and Suriname, which could support only one restaurant. Costs were prohibitively high for KFC to operate company-owned restaurants in these smaller markets. Of the 5,117 KFC restaurants located outside of the United States in 1997, 68 percent were franchised, while 22 percent were company-owned, and 10 percent were licensed restaurants or joint ventures.

In larger markets such as Japan, China, and Mexico, there was a stronger emphasis on building company-owned restaurants. By coordinating purchasing, recruiting and training, financing, and advertising, fixed costs could be spread over a large number of restaurants and lower prices on products and services could be negotiated. KFC was also better able to control product and service quality. In order to take advantage of economies of scale, Tricon Global Restaurants managed all of the international units of its KFC, Pizza Hut, and Taco Bell chains through its Tricon International division, located in Dallas, Texas. This enabled Tricon Global Restaurants to leverage its strong advertising expertise, international experience, and restaurant management experience across all its KFC, Pizza Hut, and Taco Bell chains.

Latin American Strategy

KFC's primary market presence in Latin America during the 1980s was in Mexico, Puerto Rico, and the Caribbean. KFC established subsidiaries in Mexico and Puerto Rico, from which it coordinated the construction and operation of company-owned restaurants. A third subsidiary, in Venezuela, was closed because of the high fixed costs associated with running the small subsidiary. Franchises were used to penetrate other countries in the Caribbean whose market size prevented KFC from profitably operating company restaurants. KFC relied exclusively on the operation of company-owned restaurants in Mexico through 1989. While franchising was popular in the United States, it was virtually unknown in Mexico until 1990, mainly because of the absence of a law protecting patents, information, and technology transferred to the Mexican franchise. In addition, royalties were limited. As a result, most fast-food chains opted to invest in Mexico using company-owned units.

In 1990, Mexico enacted a new law that provided for the protection of technology transferred into Mexico. Under this legislation, the franchiser and franchisee were free to set their own terms. The new law also allowed royalties. Royalties were taxed at 15 percent on technology assistance and know-how and at 35 percent on other royalty categories. The new franchise law resulted in an explosion of franchises in fast-food, services, hotels, and retail outlets. In 1992, franchises had an estimated $750 million in sales in more than 1,200 outlets throughout Mexico. Before the law was passed, KFC had limited its Mexican operations primarily to Mexico City, Guadalajara, and Monterrey. This enabled KFC to better coordinate operations and minimize costs of distribution to individual restaurants. The new franchise law gave KFC and other fast-food chains the opportunity to expand their restaurant bases more quickly to more rural regions of Mexico, where responsibility for management could be handled by local franchisees.

After 1990, KFC altered its Latin American strategy in a number of ways. First, it opened 29 franchises in Mexico to complement its company-owned restaurant base. Then it expanded its company-owned restaurants into the Virgin Islands, reestablished a subsidiary in Venezuela, and it expanded its franchise operations into South America. In 1990, a franchise opened in Chile, and in 1993 in Brazil. Subsequently, franchises were established in Colombia, Ecuador, Panama, and Peru, among other South American countries. A fourth subsidiary was established in Brazil, in order to develop company-owned restaurants. Brazil was Latin America's largest economy and McDonald's primary Latin American investment location. By June 1998, KFC operated 438 restaurants in thirty-two Latin American countries. By comparison, McDonald's operated 1,091 restaurants in twenty-eight countries.

Table 6 gives a count of KFC's and McDonald's Latin American operations. KFC's early entry into Latin America during the 1970s gave it a leadership position in Mexico and the Caribbean. It had also gained an edge in Ecuador and Peru, countries where McDonald's had not yet developed a strong presence. McDonald's focused its Latin American investment in Brazil, Argentina, and Uruguay, countries where KFC had little or no presence. McDonald's was also strong in Venezuela. Both KFC and McDonald's were strong in Chile, Colombia, Panama, and Puerto Rico.

Economic Environment and the Mexican Market

Mexico was KFC's strongest market in Latin America. Although McDonald's had aggressively established restaurants in Mexico since 1990, KFC retained the leading market share. Because of its proximity to the United States, Mexico was an attractive location for U.S. trade and investment. Mexico's population of 98 million was approximately one-third as large as that of the United States and represented a large market for U.S. companies. In comparison, Canada's population of 30.3 million people was only one-third as large as Mexico's.

TABLE 6

KFC and McDonald's Restaurants in Latin America (as of December 31, 1997)

	KFC			
	Company Restaurants	Franchised Restaurants	Total Restaurants	McDonald's
Argentina	—	—	—	131
Bahamas	—	10	10	3
Barbados	—	7	7	—
Brazil	6	2	8	480
Chile	—	29	29	27
Colombia	—	19	19	18
Costa Rica	—	5	5	19
Ecuador	—	18	18	2
Jamaica	—	17	17	7
Mexico	128	29	157	131
Panama	—	21	21	20
Peru	—	17	17	5
Puerto Rico and Virgin Islands	67	—	67	115
Trinidad and Tobago	—	27	27	3
Uruguay	—	—	—	18
Venezuela	6	—	6	53
Other	—	30	30	59
Total	207	231	438	1,091

Source: Tricon Global Restaurants, Inc.; McDonald's, 1997 Annual Report.

Because Mexico neighbors the United States, transportation between the two countries cost much less than shipments to and from Europe or Asia. This increased the competitiveness of U.S. goods in comparison with European and Asian goods; indeed, the United States was Mexico's largest trading partner. More than 75 percent of Mexico's imports came from the United States, while 84 percent of its exports went there (see Table 7). Many U.S. firms invested in Mexico in order to take advantage of lower wage rates. Produced in Mexico, U.S. goods could be shipped into the United States for sale or shipped to third markets at lower cost.

While the U.S. market was critically important to Mexico, Mexico still represented only a small percentage of overall U.S. trade and investment. Since the early 1900s, the portion of U.S. exports to Latin America had declined. Instead, U.S. exports to Canada and Asia, where economic growth outpaced growth in Mexico, increased more quickly. Canada was the largest importer of U.S. goods. Japan was the largest exporter of goods to the United States, with Canada a close second. U.S. investment in Mexico had also been small, mainly because of government restrictions on foreign investment. Most U.S. foreign investment was in Europe, Canada, and Asia.

The lack of U.S. investment in and trade with Mexico during this century was mainly due to Mexico's long history of restricting trade and foreign direct investment. The Institutional Revolutionary Party (PRI), which came to power in Mexico during the 1930s, had historically pursued protectionist economic policies, in order to shield Mexico's economy from foreign competition. Many industries were government-owned or controlled and many Mexican companies focused on producing goods for the domestic market without much attention to building export markets. High tariffs and other trade barriers restricted imports into Mexico, and foreign ownership of assets in Mexico was largely prohibited or heavily restricted.

Additionally, a dictatorial and entrenched government bureaucracy, corrupt labor unions, and a long tradition of anti-Americanism among many government officials and intellectuals reduced the motivation of U.S. firms for investing in Mexico. The nationalization of Mexico's banks in 1982 led to higher real interest rates and lower investor confidence. Afterward, the Mexican government battled high inflation, high interest rates, and labor unrest and lost consumer purchasing power. Investor confidence in Mexico, however, improved after 1988, when Carlos Salinas de Gortari was elected president and began an ambitious restructuring of the Mexican economy. He initiated policies to strengthen the free market components of the economy, lowered top marginal tax rates to 36 percent

TABLE 7

Mexico's Major Trading Partners (% of total exports and imports)

	1992		1994		1996	
	Exports	Imports	Exports	Imports	Exports	Imports
U.S.A	81.1	71.3	85.3	71.8	84.0	75.6
Japan	1.7	4.9	1.6	4.8	1.4	4.4
Germany	1.1	4.0	0.6	3.9	0.7	3.5
Canada	2.2	1.7	2.4	2.0	1.2	1.9
Italy	0.3	1.6	0.1	1.3	1.2	1.1
Brazil	0.9	1.8	0.6	1.5	0.9	0.8
Spain	2.7	1.4	1.4	1.7	1.0	0.7
Other	10.0	13.3	8.0	13.0	9.6	12.0
% Total	100.0	100.0	100.0	100.0	100.0	100.0
Value ($M)	46,196	62,129	60,882	79,346	95,991	89,464

Source: International Monetary Fund, *Direction of Trade Statistics Yearbook* (1997).

(down from 60 percent in 1986), and eliminated many restrictions on foreign investment. Foreign firms can now buy up to 100 percent of the equity in many Mexico firms. Previously, foreign ownership of Mexican firms was limited to 49 percent.

Privatization

The privatization of government-owned companies came to symbolize the restructuring of Mexico's economy. In 1990, legislation was passed to privatize all government-run banks. By the end of 1992, more than 800 of some 1,200 government-owned companies had been sold, including Mexicana and AeroMexico, the two largest airline companies in Mexico, and Mexico's 18 major banks. However, more than 350 companies remained under government ownership. These represented a significant portion of the assets owned by the state at the start of 1988. Therefore, the sale of government-owned companies, in terms of asset value, was moderate. Government-run companies controlled a large percentage of the remaining government-owned assets in certain strategic industries such as steel, electricity, and petroleum. These industries had long been protected by government ownership. As a result, until 1993 additional privatization of government-owned enterprises was limited. That year, however, President Salinas opened up the electricity sector to independent power producers, and Petroleos Mexicanos (Pemex), the state-run petrochemical monopoly, initiated a program to sell off many of its nonstrategic assets to private and foreign buyers.

North American Free Trade Agreement (NAFTA)

Before 1989, Mexico levied high tariffs on most imported goods. In addition, many other goods were subjected to quotas, licensing requirements, and other non-tariff trade barriers. In 1986, Mexico joined the General Agreement on Tariffs and Trade (GATT), a world trade organization designed to eliminate barriers to trade among member nations. As a member of GATT, Mexico was obligated to apply its system of tariffs to all member nations equally; consequently, it dropped tariff rates on a variety of imported goods. It also dropped import license requirements for all but 300 imported items. During the Salinas administration, tariffs were reduced from an average of 100 percent on most items to an average of 11 percent.

On January 1, 1994, the North American Free Trade Agreement (NAFTA) went into effect. The passage of NAFTA, which included Canada, the United States, and Mexico, created a trading bloc with a larger population and gross domestic product than the European Union (see Table 8). All tariffs on goods traded among the three countries were scheduled to be phased out. NAFTA was expected to be particularly beneficial for Mexican exporters because reduced tariffs made their goods more competitive in the United States compared with goods exported to the United States from other countries. In 1995, one year after NAFTA went into effect, Mexico posted its first balance of trade surplus in six years. Part of this surplus was attributed to reduced tariffs resulting from the NAFTA agreement. However, the peso crisis of 1995, which lowered the value of the peso against the dollar, increased the price of goods imported into Mexico and lowered the price of Mexican products exported to the United States. Therefore, it was still too early to assess the full effects of the NAFTA agreement.

Foreign Exchange and the Mexican Peso Crisis of 1995

Between 1982 and 1991, a two-tiered exchange rate system was in force in Mexico. The system consisted of a controlled rate and a free market rate. The controlled rate was used for imports, foreign debt payments, and conversion of export proceeds; it covered an estimated 70 percent of all foreign transactions. The free market rate was used for other transactions. In 1989, President Salinas instituted a policy of allowing the peso to depreciate against the dollar by one peso per day. The result was a grossly overvalued peso. This lowered the price of imports and led to an increase in imports of more than 23 percent in 1989. At the same time, Mexican exports became less competitive on world markets.

In 1991, the controlled rate was abolished and replaced with an official free rate. To limit the range of fluctuations in the value of the peso, the government fixed the rate at which it would buy or sell pesos. A floor (the maximum price at which pesos could be purchased) was established at Ps 3,056.20 and remained fixed. A ceiling (the maximum price at which the peso could be sold) was established at Ps 3,056.40 and allowed to move up-

TABLE 8

Selected Economic Data for Canada, the United States, and Mexico

	Percent of Annual Change				
	1993	*1994*	*1995*	*1996*	*1997*
GDP Growth					
Canada	3.3%	4.8%	5.5%	4.1%	—
United States	4.9	5.8	4.8	5.1	5.9
Mexico	21.4	13.3	29.4	38.2	—
Real GDP Growth					
Canada	2.2	4.1	2.3	1.2	—
United States	2.2	3.5	2.0	2.8	3.8
Mexico	2.0	4.5	−6.2	5.1	—
Inflation					
Canada	1.9	0.2	2.2	1.5	1.6
United States	3.0	2.5	2.8	2.9	2.4
Mexico	9.7	6.9	35.0	34.4	20.6
Depreciation Against $U.S.					
Canada (C$)	4.2	6.0	−2.7	0.3	4.3
Mexico (NP)	−0.3	71.4	43.5	2.7	3.6

Source: International Monetary Fund, *International Financial Statistics*, 1998.

ward by Ps 0.20 per day. This was later revised to Ps 0.40 per day. In 1993, a new currency, called the new peso, was issued with three fewer zeros. The new currency was designed to simplify transactions and to reduce the cost of printing currency.

When Ernesto Zedillo became Mexico's president in December 1994, one of his objectives was to maintain the stability of prices, wages, and exchange rates achieved by Salinas during his five years as president. However, Salinas had achieved stability largely on the basis of price, wage, and foreign exchange controls. While giving the appearance of stability, an over-valued peso continued to encourage imports which exacerbated Mexico's balance of trade deficit. Mexico's government continued to use foreign reserves to finance its balance of trade deficits. According to the Banco de Mexico, foreign currency reserves fell from $24 billion in January 1994 to $5.5 billion in January 1995. Anticipating a devaluation of the peso, investors began to move capital into U.S. dollar investments. To relieve pressure on the peso, Zedillo announced on December 19, 1994, that the peso would be allowed to depreciate by an additional 15 percent per year against the dollar compared with the maximum allowable depreciation of 4 percent per year

established during the Salinas administration. Within two days, continued pressure on the peso forced Zedillo to allow the peso to float freely against the dollar. By mid January 1995, the peso had lost 35 percent of its value against the dollar and the Mexican stock market plunged 20 percent. By November 1995, the peso had depreciated from 3.1 pesos to the dollar to 7.3 pesos to the dollar.

The continued devaluation of the peso resulted in higher import prices, higher inflation, destabilization within the stock market, and higher interest rates. Mexico struggled to pay its dollar-based debts. To thwart a possible default by Mexico, the U.S. government, International Monetary Fund, and World Bank pledged $24.9 billion in emergency loans. Zedillo then announced an emergency economic package called the "pacto," which included reduced government spending, increased sales of government-run businesses, and a freeze on wage increases.

Labor Problems

One of KFC's primary concerns in Mexico was the stability of the labor markets. While labor was relatively plentiful and wages were low, much of the work force was relatively unskilled. KFC benefited from lower labor costs, but labor unrest, low job retention, high absenteeism, and poor punctuality were significant problems. Absenteeism and punctuality were partially cultural. However, problems with worker retention and labor unrest stemmed primarily from workers' frustration over the loss of their purchasing power due to inflation and government controls on wage increases. Absenteeism remained high—at approximately 8 to 14 percent of the labor force—though it was declining because of job security fears. Turnover continued to be a problem and ran at between 5 and 12 percent per month. Therefore, employee screening and internal training were important issues for firms investing in Mexico.

Higher inflation and the government's freeze on wage increases led to a dramatic decline in disposable income after 1994. Furthermore, a slowdown in business activity, brought about by higher interest rates and lower government spending, led many businesses to lay off workers. By the end of 1995, an estimated 1 million jobs had been lost as a result of the economic crisis sparked by the peso devaluation. Industry groups within Mexico called for new labor laws that would give them more freedom to hire and fire employees and increased flexibility to hire part-time rather than full-time workers.

RISKS AND OPPORTUNITIES

The peso crisis of 1995 and the resulting recession in Mexico left KFC managers with a great deal of uncertainty regarding Mexico's economic and political future. KFC had benefited from economic stability between 1988 and 1994. Inflation had been brought down, the peso was relatively stable, there was little labor unrest, and Mexico's new franchise law had enabled KFC to expand into rural areas through franchises rather than company-owned restaurants. By the end of 1995, KFC had built twenty-nine franchises in Mexico. The foreign exchange crisis of 1995, however, had severe implications for U.S. firms operating in Mexico. The devaluation of the peso resulted in higher inflation and capital flight out of Mexico. Capital flight reduced the supply of capital and led to higher interest rates. To reduce inflation, Mexico's government instituted an austerity program that resulted in lower disposable income, higher unemployment, and lower demand for products and services.

Another problem was Mexico's failure to reduce restrictions on U.S. and Canadian investment in a timely fashion. Many U.S. firms experienced problems in getting required approvals for new ventures from the Mexican government. A good example was United Parcel Service (UPS), which sought government approval to use large trucks for deliveries in Mexico. Approvals were delayed, forcing UPS to use smaller trucks. This put UPS at a competitive disadvantage vis-à-vis Mexican companies. In many cases, UPS was forced to subcontract delivery work to Mexican companies that were allowed to use larger, more cost-efficient trucks. Other U.S. companies such as Bell Atlantic and TRW faced similar problems. TRW, which signed a joint venture agreement with a Mexican partner, had to wait fifteen months longer than anticipated before the Mexican government released rules on how it could receive credit data from banks. TRW claimed that the Mexican government slowed the approval process in order to placate several large Mexican banks.

A final area of concern for KFC was increased political turmoil in Mexico during the last several years. On January 1, 1994, the day NAFTA went into effect, rebels (descendants of the Mayans) rioted in the southern Mexican province of Chiapas, on the Guatemalan border. After four days of fighting, Mexican troops had driven the rebels out of several towns that the rebels had seized. Around 150 people—mostly rebels—were killed. The uprising symbolized many of the fears of the poor in Mexico. While Salinas's economic programs had increased economic growth and wealth in Mexico, many of Mexico's poorest felt that they had not benefited. Many of Mexico's farmers, faced with lower tariffs on imported agricultural goods from the United States, felt that they might be driven out of business because of lower priced imports. Therefore, social unrest among Mexico's Indians, farmers, and the poor could potentially unravel much of the economic success achieved in Mexico during the previous five years.

Moreover, Salinas's hand-picked successor for president was assassinated in early 1994 while campaigning in Tijuana. The assassin was a twenty-three-year-old mechanic and migrant worker believed to have been affiliated with a dissident group upset with the PRI's economic reforms. The possible existence of a dissident group raised fears of political violence in the future. The PRI quickly named Ernesto Zedillo, a forty-two-year-old economist with little political experience, as its new presidential candidate, and as mentioned earlier, he was elected president in December 1994.

Political unrest was not limited to Mexican officials and companies. In October 1994, between thirty and forty masked men attacked a McDonald's restaurant in the tourist section of Mexico City to show their opposition to California's Proposition 187, which would have curtailed benefits to illegal aliens (primarily from Mexico). The men threw cash registers to the floor, cracked them open, smashed windows, overturned tables, and spray-painted slogans on the walls such as "No to Fascism" and "Yankee Go Home."

KFC was still facing a variety of issues in Mexico and Latin America in 1998. Prior to 1995, few restaurants had been opened in South America.

However, KFC was now aggressively building new restaurants in the region. It had halted openings of franchised restaurants in Mexico, and all restaurants opened since 1995 were company-owned. KFC was more aggressively building restaurants in South America, which remained largely unpenetrated by KFC through 1995. Of greatest importance was Brazil, where McDonald's had already established a strong market share position. Brazil was Latin America's largest economy and a largely untapped market for KFC. However, the danger in ignoring Mexico was that a conservative investment strategy could jeopardize KFC's market share lead over McDonald's in a large market where KFC long enjoyed enormous popularity.

CASE 26

Outback Goes International

This case was prepared by Marilyn L. Taylor of the University of Missouri at Kansas City, George M. Puia of the Indiana State University, Krishnan Ramaya of the University of Southern Indiana, and Madelyn Gengelbach of the University of Missouri at Kansas City.

In early 1995, Outback Steakhouse enjoyed the position as one of the most successful restaurant chains in the United States. Entrepreneurs Chris Sullivan, Bob Basham, and Tim Gannon, each with more than twenty years experience in the restaurant industry, started Outback Steakhouse with just two stores in 1988. In 1995, the company was the fastest-growing U.S. steakhouse chain, with more than 200 stores throughout the United States.

Outback achieved its phenomenal success in an industry that was widely considered as one of the most competitive in the United States. Fully 75 percent of entrants into the restaurant industry failed within the first year. Outback's strategy was driven by a unique combination of factors atypical of the food service industry. As Chairman Chris Sullivan put it, "Outback is all about a lot of different experiences that have been recognized as entrepreneurship." Within six years of commencing operations, Outback was voted the best steakhouse chain in the country. The company also took top honors along with Olive Garden as America's favorite restaurant. In December 1994, Outback was awarded *Inc's* prestigious Entrepreneur of the Year award. In 1994 and early 1995, the business press hailed the company as one of the biggest success stories in corporate America in recent years.

In late 1994, Hugh Connerty was appointed president of Outback International. In early 1995,

Connerty, a highly successful franchisee for Outback, explained the international opportunities facing Outback Steakhouse as it considered its strategy for expansion abroad:

> We have had hundreds of franchise requests from all over the world. [So] it took about two seconds for me to make that decision [to become President of Outback International] . . . I've met with and talked to other executives who have international divisions. All of them have the same story. At some point in time the light goes off and they say, "Gee we have a great product. Where do we start?" I have traveled quite a bit on holiday. The world is not as big as you think it is. Most companies who have gone global have not used any set strategy.

Despite his optimism, Connerty knew that the choice of targeted markets would be critical. Connerty wondered what strategic and operational changes the company would have to make to assure success in those markets.

HISTORY OF OUTBACK STEAKHOUSE, INC.

Chris Sullivan, Bob Basham, and Tim Gannon met in the early 1970s shortly after they graduated from college. The three joined Steak & Ale, a Pillsbury subsidiary and restaurant chain, as management trainees—their first post-college career positions. During the 1980s, Sullivan and Basham became successful franchisees of seventeen Chili's restaurants in Florida and Georgia with franchise headquarters in Tampa, Florida.[1] Meanwhile, Tim Gannon played significant roles in several New Orleans restaurant

This case is intended to be used as the basis for class discussion rather than as an illustration of effective or ineffective handling of the situation. This case was prepared by prepared by Marilyn L. Taylor of the University of Missouri at Kansas City, George M. Puia of the Indiana State University, Krishnan Ramaya of the University of Southern Indiana, and Madelyn Gengelbach of the University of Missouri at Kansas City. Used by permission.

chains. Sullivan and Basham sold their Chili's franchises in 1987 and used the proceeds to fund Outback, their start-from-scratch entrepreneurial venture. They invited Gannon to join them in Tampa in the fall of 1987. The trio opened their first two restaurants in Tampa in 1988.

The three entrepreneurs recognized that in-home consumption of meat, especially beef, had declined.[2] Nonetheless, upscale and budget steak-houses were extremely popular. The three concluded that people were cutting in-home red meat consumption but were still very interested in going out to a restaurant for a good steak. They saw an untapped opportunity between high-priced and budget steakhouses to serve quality steaks at an affordable price.

Using an Australian theme associated with the outdoors and adventure, Outback positioned itself as a place providing not only excellent food but also a cheerful, fun, and comfortable experience. The company's Statement of Principles and Beliefs referred to employees as "Outbackers" and highlighted the importance of hospitality, sharing, quality, fun, and courage.

Catering primarily to the dinner crowd,[3] Outback offered a menu that featured specially seasoned steaks and prime rib. The menu also included chicken, ribs, fish, and pasta entrees, in addition to the company's innovative appetizers.[4] CFO Bob Merritt cited Outback's food as a prime reason for the company's success. As he put it,

> One of the important reasons for our success is that we took basic American meat and potatoes and enhanced the flavor profile so that it fit with the aging population. . . . Just look at what McDonalds and Burger King did in their market segment. They [have] tried to add things to their menu that were more flavorful [for example] McDonald's put the Big Mac on the menu. . . . as people age, they want more flavor. . . . higher flavor profiles. It's not happenstance. It's a science. There's too much money at risk in this business not to know what's going on with customer taste preferences.

The company viewed suppliers as "partners" in the company's success and was committed to work with suppliers to develop and maintain long-term relationships. Purchasing was dedicated to obtaining the highest quality ingredients and supplies. Indeed, the company was almost fanatical about

quality. As Tim Gannon, vice president and the company's chief chef, said, "We won't tolerate less than the best." One example of the company's quality emphasis was its croutons. Restaurant kitchen staff made the croutons daily on site. The croutons had seventeen different seasonings, including fresh garlic and butter, and they were cut by hand into irregular shapes so that customers would recognize they were handmade. At about 40 percent of total costs, Outback had one of the highest food costs in the industry. On Friday and Saturday nights, customers waited up to two hours for a table. Most felt that Outback provided exceptional value for the average entree price of $15 to $16.

Outback focused not only on the productivity and efficiency of Outbackers but also on their long-term well-being. Executives referred to the company's employee commitment as "tough on results, but kind with people." A typical Outback restaurant staff consisted of a general manager, an assistant manager, and a kitchen manager, as well as fifty to seventy mostly part-time hourly employees. The company used aptitude tests, psychological profiles, and interviews as part of the employee selection process. Every applicant was interviewed by two managers. The company sought to create an entrepreneurial climate where learning and personal growth were strongly emphasized. Sullivan explained:

> I was given the opportunity to make a lot of mistakes and learn, and we try to do that today. We try to give our people a lot of opportunity to make some mistakes, learn, and go on.

To make operations easier for employees, the company chose a restaurant design that gave 45 percent of the floor space to the kitchen area. Wait staff were assigned only three tables at a time. Most Outback restaurants were open only from 4:30 to 11:30 p.m. daily. Outback's wait staff enjoyed higher income from tips than the staff in restaurants that also served lunch. Restaurant management staff worked fifty to fifty-five hours per week, in contrast to the seventy or more common in the industry. Company executives felt that the dinner-only concept had led to effective utilization of systems, staff, and management. Outbackers reported that they were less worn out working at Outback and that they had more fun than when they worked at other restaurant companies.

Outback executives were proud of their "B-locations" (with) "A-demographics" location strategy.

They deliberately steered clear of high-traffic sites targeted by companies that served a lunch crowd. Until the early 1990s, most of the restaurants were leased locations—retrofits of another restaurant location. The company tried to choose locations where Outback's target customer would be in the evening. The overall strategy payoff was clear. In an industry where a sales-to-investment ratio of 1.2 to 1 was considered strong, Outback's restaurants generated $2.10 for every $1 invested in the facility. The average Outback restaurant unit generated $3.4 million in sales.

In 1995, management remained informal. Headquarters were located on the second floor of an unpretentious building near the Tampa airport. There was no middle management—top management selected the joint venture partners and franchisees, who reported directly to the president. Franchisees and joint venture partners in turn hired the general managers at each restaurant.

Outback provided ownership opportunities at three levels of the organization: at the individual restaurant level; through multiple store arrangements (joint venture and franchise opportunities); and through a stock ownership plan for every employee. Health insurance was also available to all employees, a benefit not universally granted to restaurant industry workers. Outback's employment and ownership opportunities for restaurant-level general managers were atypical in the industry. A restaurant general manager invested $25,000 for a 10 percent ownership stake in the restaurant, a contract for five years in the same location, a 10 percent share of the cash flow from the restaurant as a yearly bonus, opportunity for stock options, and a 10 percent buyout arrangement at the end of the five years. Outback store managers typically earned an annual salary and bonus of more than $100,000, compared with the industry average of about $60,000–70,000. Outback's management turnover of 5.4 percent was one of the lowest in its industry in which the average was 30–40 percent.

Community involvement was strongly encouraged throughout the organization. The corporate office was involved in several nonprofit activities in the Tampa area and also sponsored major national events, such as the Outback Bowl and charity golf tournaments. Each store was involved in community participation and service. For example, the entire proceeds of an open house held just prior to every restaurant opening went to a charity of the store manager's choice.

Early in its history, the company had been unable to afford any advertising. Instead, Outback's founders relied on their strong relationships with local media to generate public relations and promotional efforts. One early relationship developed with Nancy Schneid, who had extensive experience in advertising and radio. Schneid later became Outback's first vice president of marketing. Under her direction, the company developed a full-scale national media program, which concentrated on television advertising and local billboards. The company avoided couponing, and its only printed advertising typically came as part of a package offered by a charity or sports event.

Early financing for growth had come from limited partnership investments by family members, close friends, and associates. The three founders' original plan did not call for extensive expansion or franchising. However, in 1990 some friends, disappointed in the performance of several of their Kentucky-based restaurants asked to franchise the Outback concept. The converted Kentucky stores enjoyed swift success. Additional opportunities with other individuals experienced in the restaurant industry arose in various parts of the country. These multistore arrangements were in the form of franchises or joint ventures. Later in 1990, the company turned to a venture capital firm for financing for a $2.5 million package. About the same time, Bob Merritt joined the company as CFO. Merritt's previous IPO[5] experience helped the company undertake a quick succession of three highly successful public equity offerings. During 1994, the price of the company's stock ranged from $22.63 to a high of $32.00. The company's income statements, balance sheets, and a summary of the stock price performance appear as Tables 1, 2, and 3 respectively.

OUTBACK'S INTERNATIONAL ROLLOUT

Outback's management believed that the U.S. market could accommodate at least 550 to 600 Outback steakhouse restaurants. At the rate the company was growing (70 stores annually), Outback would near the U.S. market's saturation within four to five years. Outback's plans for longer-term growth hinged on a multipronged strategy. The company planned to roll out an additional 300 to

TABLE 1

Outback Steakhouse, Inc., Consolidated Statements of Income

	Years Ended December 31		
	1994	1993	1992
Revenues	$451,916,000	$309,749,000	$189,217,000
Costs and expenses			
Costs of revenues	175,618,000	121,290,000	73,475,000
Labor and other related expenses	95,476,000	65,047,000	37,087,000
Other restaurant operating expenses	93,265,000	64,603,000	43,370,000
General & administrative expenses	16,744,000	12,225,000	9,176,000
(Income) from oper. of unconsol. affl.	(1,269,000)	(333,000)	
	379,834,000	262,832,000	163,108,000
Income from operations	72,082,000	46,917,000	26,109,000
Non-operating income (expense)			
Interest income	512,000	1,544,000	1,428,000
Interest expense	(424,000)	(369,000)	(360,000)
	88,000	1,175,000	1,068,000
Income before elimination			
Minority partners' interest and income taxes	72,170,000	48,092,000	27,177,000
Elimination of minority partners' interest	11,276,000	7,378,000	4,094,000
Income before provision for income taxes	60,894,000	40,714,000	23,083,000
Provision for income taxes	21,602,000	13,922,000	6,802,000
Net income	$39,292,000	$26,792,000	$16,281,000
Earnings per common share	$0.89	$0.61	$0.39
Weighted average number of			
common shares outstanding	43,997,000	43,738,000	41,504,000
Pro forma:			
Provision for income taxes	22,286,000	15,472,000	8,245,000
Net income	$38,608,000	$25,242,000	$14,838,000
Earnings per common share	$0.88	$0.58	$0.36

350 Outback stores, expand into the lucrative Italian dining segment through its joint venture with the successful Houston-based Carrabbas Italian Grill, and develop new dining themes.

At year-end 1994, Outback had 164 restaurants in which the company had direct ownership interest. The company had six restaurants that it operated through joint ventures, in which the company had a 45 percent interest. Franchisees operated another 44 restaurants. Outback operated the company-owned restaurants as partnerships in which the company was general partner. The company owned between 81 and 90 percent, and the remainder was owned by the restaurant managers and joint venture partners. The six restaurants operated as joint ventures were also organized as partnerships in which the company owned 50 percent. The company was responsible for 50 percent of the costs of these restaurants.

Outback organized the joint venture with Carrabbas in early 1993. It was responsible for 100 percent of the costs of the new Carrabba's Italian Grills, although it owned a 50 percent share. As of year-end 1994, the joint venture operated ten Carrabba's restaurants.

The franchised restaurants generated 0.8 percent of the company's 1994 revenues as franchise

TABLE 2

Outback Steakhouse, Inc., Consolidated Balance Sheets

	December 31				
	1994	*1993*	*1992*	*1991*	*1990*
Assets					
Current assets:					
Cash and cash equivalents	$18,758,000	$24,996,000	$60,538,000	17,000,700	2,983,000
Short-term municipal securities	4,829,000	6,632,000	1,316,600		
Inventories	4,539,000	3,849,000	2,166,500	1,020,800	319,200
Other current assets	11,376,000	4,658,000	2,095,200	794,900	224,100
Total current assets	39,502,000	40,135,000	66,116,700	18,816,400	3,526,300
Long-term municipal securities	1,226,000	8,903,000	7,071,200		
Property, fixtures and equipment, net	162,323,000	101,010,000	41,764,500	15,479,000	6,553,200
Investments in and advances					
to unconsolidated affiliates	14,244,000	1,000,000			
Other assets	11,236,000	8,151,000	2,691,300	2,380,700	1,539,600
	$228,531,000	$159,199,000	$117,643,700	36,676,100	11,619,100
Liabilities and Stockholders' equity					
Current liabilities					
Accounts payable	$10,184,000	$1,053,000	$3,560,200	643,800	666,900
Sales taxes payable	3,173,000	2,062,000	1,289,500	516,800	208,600
Accrued expenses	14,961,000	10,435,000	8,092,300	2,832,300	954,800
Unearned revenue	11,862,000	6,174,000	2,761,900	752,800	219,400
Current portion of long-term debt	918,000	1,119,000	326,600	257,000	339,900
Income taxes payable			369,800	1,873,200	390,000
Total current liabilities	41,098,000	20,843,000	16,400,300	6,875,900	2,779,600
Deferred income taxes	568,000	897,000	856,400	300,000	260,000
Long-term debt	12,310,000	5,687,000	1,823,700	823,600	1,060,700
Interest of minority partners in					
consolidated partnerships	2,255,000	1,347,000	1,737,500	754,200	273,000
Total liabilities	56,231,000	28,774,000	20,817,900	8,753,700	4,373,300
Stockholders' equity					
Common stock, $0.01 par value,					
100,000,000 shares authorized for 1994 and 1993;					
50,000,000 authorized for 1992					
42,931,344 and 42,442,800 shares issues and					
outstanding as of December 31, 1994 and					
1993, respectively. 39,645,995 shares					
issued and outstanding as of					
December 31, 1992.	429,000	425,000	396,500	219,000	86,300
Additional paid-in capital	83,756,000	79,429,000	74,024,500	20,296,400	4,461,100
Retained earnings	88,115,000	50,571,000	22,404,800	7,407,000	2,698,400
Total stockholders' equity	172,300,000	130,425,000	96,825,800	27,922,400	7,245,800
	$228,531,000	$159,199,000	$117,643,700	36,676,100	11,619,100

TABLE 3

Outback Steakhouse, Inc., Selected Financial and Stock Data

Year	Systemwide Sales	Company Revenues	Net Income	EPS	Company Stores	Franchises & JVS	Total
1988	2,731	2,731	47	0.01	2	0	2
1989	13,328	13,328	920	0.04	9	0	9
1990	34,193	34,193	2,260	0.08	23	0	23
1991	91,000	91,000	6,064	0.17	49	0	49
1992	195,508	189,217	14,838	0.36	81	4	85
1993	347,553	309,749	25,242	0.58	124	24	148
1994	548,945	451,916	38,608	0.88	164	50	214

Outback Stock Data					
	High	Low		High	Low
1991			**1993**		
Second quarter	$4.67	$4.27	First quarter	22.00	15.50
Third quarter	6.22	4.44	Second quarter	26.16	16.66
Fourth quarter	10.08	5.5	Third quarter	24.59	19.00
			Fourth quarter	25.66	21.16
1992			**1994**		
First quarter	13.00	9.17	First quarter	29.50	23.33
Second quarter	11.41	8.37	Second quarter	28.75	22.75
Third quarter	16.25	10.13	Third quarter	30.88	23.75
Fourth quarter	19.59	14.25	Fourth quarter	32.00	22.63

fees. The portion of income attributable to restaurant managers and joint venture partners amounted to $11.3 million of the company's $72.2 million 1994 income.

By late 1994, Outback's management had also begun to consider the potential of non-U.S. markets for the Outback concept. Sullivan concluded that

> we can do 500–600 (Outback) restaurants, and possibly more over the next five years. . . . [However,] the world is becoming one big market, and we want to be in place so we don't miss that opportunity. There are some problems, some challenges with it, but at this point there have been some casual restaurant chains that have gone (outside the United States) and their average unit sales are way, way above the sales level they enjoyed in the United States. So the potential is there. Obviously, there are some distribution issues to work out, things like that. But we are real excited about the future internationally. That will give us some potential outside the United States to continue to grow as well.

In late 1994 the company began its international venture by appointing Hugh Connerty president of Outback International. Connerty, like Outback's three founders, had extensive experience in the restaurant industry. Before joining Outback, he developed a chain of successful Hooter's restaurants in Georgia. He used the proceeds from the sale of these franchises to fund the development of his franchise of Outback restaurants in northern Florida and southern Georgia. Connerty's success as a franchisee was well recognized. Indeed, in 1993 Outback began to award a large crystal trophy with the designation "Connerty Franchisee of the Year" to the company's outstanding franchisee.

Much of Outback's growth and expansion were generated through joint venture partnerships and franchising agreements. Connerty commented on Outback's franchise system:

> Every one of the franchisees lives in their areas. I lived in the area I franchised. I had relationships that helped with getting permits. That isn't any different than the rest of the world. The loyalties of individuals that live in their respective areas [will be important]. We will do the franchises one by one. The biggest decision we have to make is how we pick that franchise partner.... That is what we will concentrate on. We are going to select a person who has synergy with us, who thinks like us, who believes in the principles and beliefs.

Outback developed relationships very carefully. "The trust between (Outback) and the individual franchisees is not to be violated," Connerty said "The company grants franchises one at a time. It takes a lot of trust to invest millions of dollars without any assurance that you will be able to build another one."[6]

However, Connerty recognized that expanding abroad would present challenges. He described how Outback would approach its international expansion:

> There are some principles and beliefs we live by. It almost sounds cultish. We want international to be an opportunity for our suppliers. We feel strongly about the relationships with our suppliers. We have never changed suppliers. We have an undying commitment to them and in exchange we want them to have an undying commitment to us. They have to prove they can build plants [abroad].

He added that

> it would be foolish of us to think that we are going to go around the world buying property and understanding the laws in every country, the culture in every single country. So the approach that we are going to take is that we will franchise the international operation with companyowned stores here and franchises there so that will allow us to focus on what I believe is our pure strength, a support operation.

U.S. RESTAURANTS IN THE INTERNATIONAL DINING MARKET

Prospects for international entry for U.S. restaurant companies in the early 1990s appeared promising. Between 1992 and 1993 alone, international sales for the top fifty restaurant franchisers increased from U.S. $15.9 billion to U.S. $17.5 billion. Franchising was the most popular means for rapid expansion. Table 4 provides an overview of the top U.S. restaurant franchisers, including their domestic and international revenues and number of units in 1993 and 1994.

International expansion was an important source of revenues for a significant number of players in the industry. International growth and expansion in the U.S. restaurant industry over the 1980s and into the 1990s was largely driven by major fast-food restaurant chains. Some of these companies, for example, McDonald's, Wendy's, Dairy Queen, and Domino's Pizza, were public and freestanding. Others, such as Subway and Little Caesars, remained private and freestanding. Some of the largest players in international markets were subsidiaries of major consumer products firms such as PepsiCo and Grand Metropolitan PLC.[7] In spite of the success enjoyed by fast-food operators in non-U.S. markets, casual dining operators were slower about entering the international markets. (See Appendix A for brief overviews of the publicly available data on the top ten franchisers and casual dining chains that had ventured abroad as of early 1995.)

One of the major forces driving the expansion of the U.S. food service industry was changing demographics. In the United States, prepared foods had become a fastest-growing category because they relieved the cooking burdens on working parents. By the early 1990s, U.S. consumers were spending almost as much on restaurant fare as for prepared and nonprepared grocery store food. U.S. food themes were very popular abroad. U.S. food themes were common throughout Canada as well as Western Europe and East Asia. As a result of the opening of previously inaccessible markets such as Eastern Europe, the former Soviet Union, China, India, and Latin America, the potential for growth in U.S. food establishments abroad was enormous.

In 1992 alone, there were more than 3,000 franchisers in the U.S. operating about 540,000 franchised outlets—a new outlet of some sort

TABLE 4

Top Fifty U. S. Restaurant Franchises (ranked by sales in $ millions)

Rank	Firm	Total Sales		International Sales		Total Stores		International Stores	
		1994	1993	1994	1993	1994	1993	1994	1993
1	McDonald's	25,986	23,587	11,046	9,401	15,205	13,993	5,461	4,710
2	Burger King	7,500	6,700	1,400	1,240	7,684	6,990	1,357	1,125
3	KFC	7,100	7,100	3,600	3,700	9,407	9,033	4,258	3,905
4	Taco Bell	4,290	3,817	130	100	5,615	4,634	162	112
5	Wendy's	4,277	3,924	390	258	4,411	4,168	413	377
6	Hardee's	3,491	3,425	63	56	3,516	3,435	72	63
7	Dairy Queen	3,170	2,581	300	290	3,516	3,435	628	611
8	Domino's	2,500	2,413	415	275	5,079	5,009	840	550
9	Subway	2,500	2,201	265	179	9,893	8,450	944	637
10	Little Caesars	2,000	2,000	70	70	4,855	4,754	155	145
	Average of firms 11–20	1,222	1,223	99	144	2,030	1,915	163	251
	Average of firms 21–30	647	594	51	26	717	730	37	36
	Average of firms 31–40	382	358	7	9	502	495	26	20
	Average of firms 41–50	270	257	17	23	345	363	26	43

Non-Fast-Food Restaurants in Top Fifty

Rank	Firm	Total Sales		International Sales		Total Stores		International Stores	
		1994	1993	1994	1993	1994	1993	1994	1993
11	Denny's	1,779	1,769	63	70	1,548	1,515	58	63
13	Dunkin' Donuts	1,413	1,285	226	209	3,453	3,047	831	705
14	Shoney's	1,346	1,318	0	0	922	915	0	0
15	Big Boy	1,130	1,202	100	0	940	930	90	78
17	Baskin-Robbins	1,008	910	387	368	3,765	3,562	1,300	1,278
19	T.G.I.Friday's	897	1,068	114	293	314	NA	37	NA
20	Applebee's	889	609	1	0	507	361	2	0
21	Sizzler	858	922	230	218	600	666	119	116
23	Ponderosa	690	743	40	38	380	750	40	38
24	Int'l House of Pancakes	632	560	32	29	657	561	37	35
25	Perkins	626	588	12	10	432	425	8	6
29	Outback Steakhouse	549	348	0	0	NA	NA	NA	NA
30	Golden Corral	548	515	1	0	425	425	2	1
32	TCBY Yogurt	388	337	22	15	2,801	2,474	141	80
37	Showbiz/Chuck E. Cheese	370	373	7	8	332	NA	8	NA
39	Round Table Pizza	357	340	15	12	576	597	29	22
40	Western Sizzlin	337	351	3	6	281	NA	2	NA
41	Ground Round	321	310	0	0	NA	NA	NA	NA
42	Papa John's	297	NA	0	NA	632	NA	0	NA
44	Godfather's Pizza	270	268	0	0	515	531	0	0
45	Bonanza	267	327	32	47	264	NA	30	NA
46	Village Inn	266	264	0	0	NA	NA	NA	NA
47	Red Robin	259	235	27	28	NA	NA	NA	NA
48	Tony Roma's	254	245	41	36	NA	NA	NA	NA
49	Marie Callender	251	248	0	0	NA	NA	NA	NA

NA: Not ranked in the top 50 for that category

Source: "Top 50 Franchises," *Restaurant Business,* November 1, 1995, pp. 35–41).

opened about every sixteen minutes. In 1992, franchised business sales totaled $757.8 billion, about 35 percent of all retail sales. Franchising was used as a growth vehicle by a variety of businesses, including automobiles, petroleum, cosmetics, convenience stores, computers, and financial services. However, food service constituted the franchising industry's largest single group. Franchised restaurants generally performed better than freestanding units. For example, in 1991 franchised restaurants experienced per-store sales growth of 6.2 percent versus an overall restaurant industry growth rate of 3.0 percent. However, despite generally favorable sales and profits, franchiser-franchisee relationships were often difficult.

Abroad, franchisers operated an estimated 31,000 restaurant units. The significant increase in restaurant franchising abroad was driven by universal cultural trends, rising incomes, improved international transportation and communication, rising educational levels, increasing number of women entering the work force, demographic concentrations of people in urban areas, and the willingness of younger generations to try new products.[8] However, there were substantial differences in these changes between the United States and other countries and from country to country.

FACTORS AFFECTING SELECTION OF COUNTRY

Although Outback had not yet formed a firm plan for its international rollout, Connerty indicated the preliminary choice of markets targeted for entry as Canada, Hawaii, South America, and Asia for the first year. "At the second year," he said, "we'll begin a relationship in Great Britain and from there a natural progression throughout Europe. But we view it as a very long-term project. I have learned that people think very different than Americans." U.S. restaurant chains had to take into account numerous considerations when determining which non-U.S. markets to enter. Some of these factors are summarized in Table 5, and issues regarding infrastructure and demographics are discussed in the next section—including some of the difficulties that U.S. restaurant companies encountered in various countries. Profiles of Canada, South Korea, Japan, Germany Mexico, and Great Britain appear in Appendix B.

Infrastructure

A supportive infrastructure in the target country is essential. Proper means of transportation, communication, basic utilities such as power and water, and locally available supplies are crucial elements in the decision to introduce a particular restaurant concept. A restaurant must have the ability to get resources to its location. Raw materials for food preparation, equipment for manufacture of food served, employees, and customers must be able to enter and leave the establishment. The network that brings these resources to a firm is commonly called a supply chain.

The level of economic development is closely linked to the development of a supportive infrastructure. According to the U.S. International Trade Commission,

> Economic conditions, cultural disparities, and physical limitations can have substantial impact on the viability of foreign markets for a franchise concept. In terms of economics, the level of infrastructure development is a significant factor. A weak infrastructure may cause problems in transportation, communication, or even the provision of basic utilities such as electricity. . . . International franchisers frequently encounter problems finding supplies in sufficient quantity, of consistent quality, and at stable prices. . . . Physical distance also can adversely affect a franchise concept and arrangement. Long distances create communication and transportation problems, which may complicate the process of sourcing supplies, overseeing operations, or providing quality management services to franchisees.[9]

Some food can be sourced locally, some regionally or nationally, and some must be imported. A country's transportation and distribution capabilities may become a factor in the decision on the country's suitability for a particular restaurant concept.

Sometimes supply chain issues require firms to make difficult decisions that affect the costs associated with the foreign enterprise. Family Restaurants Inc. encountered problems providing brown gravy for its CoCo's restaurants in South Korea. "If you want brown gravy in South Korea," said Barry Krantz, company president, "you can do one of two things. Bring it over, which is very costly. Or, you can make it yourself. So we figure out the flavor

TABLE 5

Factors Affecting Companies' Entry into International Markets

External Factors

Country Market Factors
Size of target market, competitive structure—atomistic, oligopolistic to monopolistic, local marketing infrastructure (distribution etc.).

Country Production Factors
Quality, quantity and cost of raw materials, labor, energy, and other productive agents in the target country, as well as the quality and cost of the economic infrastructure (transportation, communications, port facilities and similar considerations).

Country Environmental Factors
Political, economic and sociocultural character of the target country—government policies and regulations pertaining to international business.
Geographic distance—impact on transportation costs.
Size of the economy, absolute level of performance (GDP per capita), relative importance of economic sectors—closely related to the market size for a company's product in the target country.
Dynamics including rate of investment, growth in GDP, personal income, changes in employment. Dynamic economies may justify entry modes with a high break-even point even when the current market size is below the break-even point.
Sociocultural factors—cultural distance between home country and target country societies. The smaller the cultural distance, the quicker the entry into these markets (e.g., Canada).

Home Country Factors
Big domestic market allows a company to grow to a large size before it turns to foreign markets. Competitive structure. Firms in oligopolistic industries tend to imitate the actions of rival domestic firms that threaten to upset competitive equilibrium. Hence, when one firm invests abroad, rival firms commonly follow the lead. High production costs in the home country are an important factor.

Internal Factors

Company Product Factors
Products that are highly differentiated with distinct advantages over competitive products give sellers a significant degree of pricing discretion.
Products that require an array of pre- and post-purchase services make it difficult for a company to market the products at a distance.
Products that require considerable adaptation.

Company Resource/Commitment Factors
The more abundant a company's resources in management, capital, technology, production skills, and marketing skills, the more numerous its entry mode options. Conversely, a company with limited resources is constrained to use entry modes that call for only a small resource commitment. Size is therefore a critical factor in the choice of an entry mode. Although resources are an influencing factor, it must be joined with a willingness to commit them to foreign market development. A high degree of commitment means that managers will select the entry mode for a target from a wider range of alternative modes than managers with a low commitment.

The degree of a company's commitment to international business is revealed by the role accorded to foreign markets in corporate strategy, the status of the international organization, and the attitudes of managers.

Source: Franklin Root, *Entry Strategies for International Markets* (Lexington, Mass.: Heath, 1987).

profile, and make it in the kitchen." Krantz concedes that a commissary is "an expensive proposition but the lesser of two evils."[10]

In certain instances, a country may be so attractive for long-term growth that a firm dedicates itself to creating a supply chain for its restaurants. An excellent illustration is McDonald's expansion into Russia in the late 1980s:

> . . . supply procurement has proved to be a major hurdle, as it has for all foreign companies operating in Russia. The problem has several causes: the rigid bureaucratic system, supply shortages caused by distribution and production problems, available supplies not meeting McDonald's quality standards. . . . To handle these problems, McDonald's scoured the country for supplies, contracting for such items as milk, cheddar cheese, and beef. To help ensure ample supplies of the quality products it needed, it undertook to educate Soviet farmers and cattle ranchers on how to grow and raise those products. In addition, it built a $40 million food-processing center about 45 minutes from its first Moscow restaurant. And because distribution was [and still is] as much a cause of shortages as production was, McDonald's carried supplies on its own trucks.[11]

Changing from one supply chain to another can affect not only the availability of quality provisions, but also the equipment used to make the food that is served. For example,

> Wendy's nearly had its Korean market debut delayed by the belatedly discovered problem of thrice-frozen hamburger. After being thawed and frozen at each step of Korea's cumbersome three-company distribution channel, ground beef there takes on added water weight that threw off Wendy's patty specifications, forcing a hasty stateside retooling of the standard meat patty die used to mass-produce its burgers.[12]

Looking at statistics such as the number of ports, airports, quantity of paved roads, and transportation equipment as a percentage of capital stock per worker can give a bird's-eye view of the level of infrastructure development.

Demographics

Just as in the domestic market, restaurants in a foreign market need to know who their customers will be. Different countries will have different strata in age distribution, religion, and cultural heritage. These factors can influence the location, operations, and menus of restaurants in a country.

A popular example is India, where eating beef is contrary to the beliefs of the 80 percent of the population that is Hindu.[13] Considering India's population is nearly one billion people, companies find it hard to ignore this market even if beef is a central component of the firm's traditional menu. "We're looking at serving mutton patties," says Ann Connolly, a McDonald's spokeswoman.[14]

Another area where religion plays a part in affecting the operation of a restaurant is the middle east. Dairy Queen expanded to the region and found that during the Islamic religious observance of Ramadan no business was conducted; indeed, the windows of shops were boarded up.[15]

Age distribution can affect who should be the target market. "The company [McDonald's in Japan] also made modifications [not long after entering the market], such as targeting all advertising to younger people, because the eating habits of older Japanese are very difficult to change."[16] Age distribution can also impact the pool of labor available. In some countries over 30 percent of the population is under fifteen years old; in other countries over 15 percent is sixty-five or older. These varying demographics could create a change in the profile for potential employees in the new market.

Educational level may be an influence on both the buying public and the employee base. Literacy rates vary, and once again this can change the profile of an employee as well as who comprises the buying public.

Statistics can help compare countries using demographic components like literacy rates, total population and age distribution, and religious affiliations.

Income

Buying power is another demographic that can provide clues to how the restaurant might fare in the target country, as well as how the marketing program should position the company's products or services. Depending on the country and its economic development, the firm may have to attract a different segment than in the domestic market. For example, in Mexico,

> major U.S. firms have only recently begun targeting the country's sizable and apparently burgeoning middle class. For its part, McDonald's

has changed tactics from when it first entered Mexico as a prestige brand aimed almost exclusively at the upper class, which accounts for about 5 percent of Mexico's population of some 93 million. With the development of its own distribution systems and improved economies of scale McDonald's lately has been slashing prices to aid its penetration into working-class population strongholds. "I'd say McDonald's pricing now in Mexico is 30 percent lower, in constant dollar terms, than when we opened in '85," says Moreno [Fernando Moreno, now international director of Peter Piper Pizza], who was part of the chain's inaugural management team there.[17]

There are instances where low disposable income does not translate to a disinterest in dining out in a Western-style restaurant. While Americans dine at a fast-food establishment such as McDonald's one or two times per week, lower incomes in the foreign markets make eating at McDonald's a special, once-a-month occurrence. "These people are not very wealthy, so eating out at a place like McDonald's is a dining experience."[18] China provides another example:

at one Beijing KFC last summer, [the store] notched the volume equivalent of nine U.S. KFC branches in a single day during a $1.99 promotion of a two-piece meal with a baseball cap. Observers chalk up that blockbuster business largely to China's ubiquitous "spoiled-brat syndrome" and the apparent willingness of indulgent parents to spend one or two months' salaries on splurges for the only child the government allows them to rear.[19]

Statistics outlining the various indexes describing the country's gross domestic product, consumer spending on food, consumption and investment rates, and price levels can assist in evaluating target countries.

Trade Law

Trade policies can be friend or foe to a restaurant chain interested in expanding to other countries. Trade agreements such as the North American Free Trade Agreement (NAFTA) and the General Agreement on Tariffs and Trade (GATT) could help allevi-

ate the ills of international expansion if they achieve their aims of

reducing or eliminating tariffs, reducing non-tariff barriers to trade, liberalizing investment and foreign exchange policies, and improving intellectual property protection. . . . The recently signed Uruguay Round Agreements [of GATT] include the General Agreement on Trade in Services (GATS), the first multilateral, legally enforceable agreement covering trade and investment in the services sector. The GATS is designed to liberalize trade in services by reducing or eliminating governmental measures that prevent services from being freely provided across national borders or that discriminate against firms with foreign ownership.[20]

Franchising, one of the most popular modes for entering foreign markets, scored a win in the GATS agreement. For the first time, franchising was addressed directly in international trade talks. However, most countries have not elected to make their restrictions on franchising publicly known. The U.S. International Trade Commission has pointed out that

Specific commitments that delineate barriers are presented in Schedules of Commitments (Schedules). As of this writing, Schedules from approximately 90 countries are publicly available. Only 30 of these countries specifically include franchising in their Schedules . . . The remaining two-thirds of the countries did not schedule commitments on franchising. This means that existing restrictions are not presented in a transparent manner and additional, more severe restrictions may be imposed at a later date. . . . Among the 30 countries that addressed franchising in the Schedules, 25 countries, including the United States, have committed themselves to maintain no limitations on franchising except for restrictions on the presence of foreign nationals within their respective countries.[21]

Despite progress, current international restaurant chains have encountered a myriad of challenges because of restrictive trade policies. Some countries make the import of restaurant equipment into their country difficult and expensive. The Asian region possesses "steep tariffs and [a] patchwork of inconsistent regulations that impede imports of commodities and equipment."[22]

OUTBACK'S GROWTH CHALLENGE

Connerty was well aware that there was no mention of international opportunities in Outback's 1994 Annual Report. The company distributed that Annual Report to shareholders at the April 1995 meeting. More than 300 shareholders packed the meeting to standing room only. During the question-and-answer period, a shareholder had closely questioned the company's executives as to why the company did not pay a dividend. The shareholder pointed out that the company made a considerable profit in 1994. Sullivan responded that the company needed to reinvest the cash that might be used as dividends in order to achieve the targeted growth. His response was a public and very visible commitment to continue the company's fast-paced growth. Connerty knew that international expansion had the potential to play a critical role in that growth. His job was to help craft a strategy that would assure Outback's continuing success as it took on the new and diverse markets abroad.

APPENDIX A: PROFILES OF CASUAL DINING AND FAST-FOOD CHAINS[1]

This appendix provides summaries of the 1995 publicly available data on (1) the two casual dining chains represented among the top fifty franchisers that had operations abroad (Applebee's and T.G.I. Friday's/Carlson Companies, Inc.) and (2) the top ten franchisers in the restaurant industry, all of which are fast-food chains (Burger King, Domino's, Hardee's, International Dairy Queen, Inc., Little Caesar's, McDonald's, Pepsico including KFC, Taco Bell and Pizza Hut, Subway, and Wendy's).

CASUAL DINING CHAINS WITH OPERATIONS ABROAD

Applebee's

Applebee's was one of the largest casual dining chains in the United States. It ranked twentieth in sales and thirty-sixth in stores for 1994. Like that of

1. Unless otherwise noted the information in this appendix was drawn from "Top 50 Franchisers," *Restaurant Business,* November 1, 1995. pp. 35–41; Hoover's Company profile Database, 1996, The Reference Press, Inc., Austin, Texas (from American Online Service); and various company listings.

most other casual dining operators, much of the company's growth had been fueled by domestic expansion. Opening in 1986, the company experienced rapid growth and by 1994 had 507 stores. The mode of growth was franchising, but in 1992 management began a program of opening more company-owned sites and buying restaurants from franchisees. The company positioned itself as a neighborhood bar and grill and offered a moderately priced menu, including burgers, chicken, and salads.

In 1995, Applebee's continued a steady program of expansion. Chairman and CEO Abe Gustin set a target of 1,200 U.S. restaurants and had also begun a slow push into international markets. In 1994, the company franchised restaurants in Canada and Curaçao and signed an agreement to franchise twenty restaurants in Belgium, Luxembourg, and the Netherlands.

Applebee's

Year	1989	1990	1991
Sales*	29.9	38.2	45.1
Net income*	0.0	1.8	3.1
EPS ($)	(0.10)	0.13	0.23
Stock Price Close($)	4.34	2.42	4.84
Dividends ($)	0.00	0.00	0.01
# Employees	1,149	1,956	1,714
Year	1992	1993	1994
Sales*	56.5	117.1	208.5
Net income*	5.1	9.5	16.9
EPS ($)	0.27	0.44	0.62
Stock Price Close($)	9.17	232.34	13.38
Dividends ($)	0.02	0.03	0.04
# Employees	2,400	46,600	8,700

*$m. **1994: Debt ratio 20.1%; ROE 19.2; Cash $17.2M; Current ratio 1.13; LTD $23.7.

T.G.I. Friday's/Carlson Companies, Inc.

T.G.I. Friday's was owned by Carlson Companies, Inc., a large, privately held conglomerate that had interests in travel (65 percent of 1994 sales), hospitality (30 percent), plus marketing, employee training, and incentives (5 percent). Carlson also owned 345 Radisson Hotels and Country Inns plus 240 units of Country Kitchen International, a chain of family restaurants.

T.G.I. Friday's

Year	1985	1986	1987	1988	1989
Sales*	0.9	1.3	1.5	1.8	2.0
Year	1990	1991	1992	1993	1994
Sales*	2.2	2.3	2.9	2.3	2.3

*$b; no data available on income; excludes franchisee sales.

Most of Carlson's revenues came from its travel group. The company experienced a surprise in 1995 when U.S. airlines announced that they would put a cap on the commissions they would pay to book U.S. flights. Because of this change, Carlson decided to change its service to a fee-based arrangement and expected sales to drop by $100 million in 1995. To make up for this deficit, Carlson began to focus on building its hospitality group of restaurants and hotels through expansion in the United States and overseas. The company experienced significant senior management turnover in the early 1990s, and founder Curtis Carlson, aged eighty, had announced his intention to retire at the end of 1996. His daughter was announced as next head of the company.

T.G.I. Friday's grew 15.7 percent in revenue and 19.4 percent in stores in 1994. With 37 restaurants overseas, international sales were 12.7 percent of sales and 11.8 percent of stores systemwide. Carlson operated a total of 550 restaurants in seventeen countries. About one-third of overall sales came from activities outside the United States.

THE TOP TEN FRANCHISERS IN THE RESTAURANT INDUSTRY

Burger King

In 1994, Burger King was number two in sales and number four in stores among the fast-food competitors. Burger King did not have the same presence in the global market as McDonald's and KFC. For example, McDonald's and KFC had been in Japan since the 1970s. Burger King opened its first Japanese locations in 1993. By that time, McDonald's already had over 1,000 outlets there. In 1994 Burger King had 1,357 non-U.S. stores (17.7 percent of systemwide total) in fifty countries, and overseas sales (18.7 percent) totaled $1.4 billion.

Burger King was owned by the British food and spirits conglomerate Grand Metropolitan PLC. Among the company's top brands were Pillsbury, Green Giant, and Haagen-Dazs. Grand Met's situation had not been bright during the 1990s, with the loss of major distribution contracts like Absolut vodka and Grand Marnier liqueur, as well as sluggish sales for its spirits in major markets. Burger King was not a stellar performer, either, and undertook a major restructuring in 1993 to turn the tide, including reemphasis on the basic menu, cuts in prices, and reduced overhead. After quick success, BK's CEO James Adamson left his post in early 1995 to head competitor Flasgston Corporation.

Domino's

Domino's Pizza was eighth in sales and seventh in stores in 1994. Sales and store unit growth had leveled off; from 1993 to 1994 sales grew 3.6 percent, and units only 1.4 percent. The privately held company registered poor performance in 1993, with a

Burger King

Year	1985	1986	1987	1988	1989	1990	1991	1992	1993	1994
Sales*	5,590	5,291	4,706	6,029	9,298	9.394	8.748	7,913	8,120	7,780
Net Income*	272	261	461	702	1,068	1,069	432	616	412	450
EPS($)	14	16	19	24	28	32	33	28	30	32
Stock Price—Close($)	199	228	215	314	329	328	441	465	476	407
Dividend/Share($)	5.0	5.1	6.0	7.5	8.9	10.2	11.4	12.3	13.0	14.0
Employees(K)	137	131	129	90	137	138	122	102	87	64

*Millions of sterling; 1994: debt ratio 47.3%; ROE. 12.4%; cash (Ster.) 986M; LTD (Ster.) 2,322M.
1994 Segments sales (profit): North America: 62% (69%); U.K. and Ireland 10% (10%); Africa and Middle East 2% (1%); other Europe: 21% (18%); other countries: 5% (2%).
Segment sales (profits) by operating division: drinks 43% (51%); food 42% (26%); retailing 14% (22%); other 1% (1%).

Domino's

Year	1985	1986	1987	1988	1989
Sales ($ millions)	1,100	1,430	2,000	2,300	2,500
Stores	2,841	3,610	4,279	4,858	5,185
Employees (K)	na	na	na	na	na

Year	1990	1991	1992	1993	1994
Sales ($ millions)	2,600	2,400	2,450	2,200	2,500
Stores	5,342	5,571	5,264	5,369	5,079
Employees (K)	100	na	na	na	115

0.6 percent sales decline from 1992. Observers suggested that resistance to menu innovations contributed to the share decline. In the early 1990s the company did add deep-dish pizza and buffalo wings.

Flat company performances and expensive hobbies were hard on the owner and founder, Thomas Monaghan. He attempted to sell the company in 1989 but could not find a buyer. He then replaced top management and retired from business to pursue a growing interest in religious activities. Company performance began to slide, and the founder emerged from retirement to retake the helm in the early 1990s. Through extravagant purchases of the Detroit Tigers, Frank Lloyd Wright pieces, and antique cars, Monaghan put the company on the edge of financial ruin. He sold off many of his holdings (some at a loss), reinvested the funds to stimulate the firm, and once again reorganized management.

Despite all its problems, Domino's had seen consistent growth in the international market. The company opened its first foreign store in 1983 in Canada. Primary overseas expansion areas were eastern Europe and India. By 1994 Domino's had 5,079 stores with 823 of these in thirty-seven major international markets. International brought in 17 percent of 1994 sales. Over the next ten to fifteen years, the company had contracts for 4,000 additional international units.[2] These units would give Domino's more international than domestic units. International sales were 16.6 percent of total, and international stores were 16.5 percent of total in 1994.

Hardee's

Hardee's was number six in sales and eleven in stores for 1994. In 1981 the large diversified Canadian company Imasco purchased the chain. Imasco also owned Imperial Tobacco (Player's and du Maurier, Canada's top two sellers), Burger Chef, two drugstore chains, the development company Genstar, and CT Financial.

Hardee's had pursued growth primarily in the United States. Of all the burger chains in the top ten franchises, Hardee's had the smallest international presence, with seventy-two stores generating $63 million (1.8 percent and 2.0 percent of sales and stores, respectively) in 1994.

Hardee's sales grew by about 2 percent annually for 1993 and 1994. A failed attempt by Imasco to merge their Roy Roger's restaurants into the Hardee's chain forced the parent company to maintain both brands. Hardee's attempted to differentiate from the other burger chains by offering an upscale burger menu, which got a lukewarm reception by consumers.

2. "Big News Over There!" *Restaurants and Institutions,* July 1, 1994.

Hardee's

Year	1985	1986	1987	1988	1989	1990	1991	1992	1993	1994
Sales*	3,376	5,522	6,788	7,311	8,480	9,647	9,870	9,957	9,681	9,385
Net income*	262	184	283	314	366	205	332	380	409	506
EPS ($)	1.20	0.78	1.12	1.26	1.44	1.13	0.64	0.68	0.74	0.78
Stock Price—Close ($)	13.94	16.25	12.94	14.00	18.88	13.81	18.25	20.63	20.06	19.88
Dividends ($)	0.36	0.42	0.48	0.52	0.56	0.64	0.64	0.68	0.74	0.78
Employees (K)	na	na	na	na	190	190	180	na	200	200

* $M— all $ in Canadian; 1994: Debt ratio: 38.4%; ROE. 16.1%; Current ratio: 1.37; LTD(M): $1,927;
1994 Segment Sales (Operating Income): CT Financial Services 47% (28%); Hardees 32% (11%); Imperial Tobacco 16% (20%); Shoppers Drug Mart 2% (9%); Genstar Development 1% (2%).

International Dairy Queen, Inc.

Year	1985	1986	1987	1988	1989	1990	1991	1992	1993	1994
Sales*	158	182	210	254	282	287	287	296	311	341
Net income*	10	12	15	20	23	27	28	29	30	31
EPS ($)	0.33	0.42	0.51	0.70	0.83	0.97	1.05	1.12	1.79	1.30
Stock Price—Close ($)	5.20	7.75	8.00	11.50	14.75	16.58	21.00	20.00	18.00	16.25
Dividends($)	-0-	-0-	-0-	-0-	-0-	-0-	-0-	-0-	-0-	-0-
Employees (K)	430	459	503	520	549	584	592	672	538	564

*$M; 1994: Debt ratio 15.3%; R.O.E. 24.4%; Current ratio 3.04; LTD $23M.
1994 Restaurants: U.S. 87%; Canada 9%; Other 4%; Restaurants by type: DQ's: franchised by company: 62%; franchised by territorial operators 27%; foreign 3%; Orange Julius: 7%; Karmelkorn 1%, Golden Skillet less than 1%); Sales by Source: Good supplies & equipment to franchises 78%; service fees 16%; franchise sales & other fees 3%; real-estate finance & rental income 3%.

International Dairy Queen, Inc.

Dairy Queen was one of the oldest fast-food franchises in the United States: the first store was opened in Joliet, Illinois, in 1940. By 1950, there were more than 1,100 stores, and by 1960 Dairy Queen had locations in twelve countries. Initial franchise agreements focused on the right to use the DQ freezers, an innovation that kept ice cream at the constant 23 degrees (Fahrenheit) necessary to maintain the soft consistency. In 1970, a group of investors bought the franchise organization; but the group has been only partly successful in standardizing the fast-food chain. In 1994 a group of franchisees filed an antitrust suit in an attempt to get the company to loosen its control on food supply prices and sources. DQ franchises cost $30,000 initially plus continuing payments of 4 percent of sales.

The company's menu consisted of ice cream, yogurt, and brazier items (hamburgers and other fast food). Menu innovations had included Blizzard (candy and other flavors mixed in the ice cream). The company had also acquired several other companies, including the Golden Skillet (1981), Karmelkorn (1986), and Orange Julius (1987).

In 1994, Dairy Queen ranked number seven in sales and six in stores. By that same year the company had expanded its presence into nineteen countries with 628 stores and $300 million in international sales. The year was an excellent one for DQ: sales were up 22.8 percent over 1993. This dramatic change (1993 scored an anemic 3.0 percent gain) was fueled by technology improvements for franchisees and international expansion. In 1992 Dairy Queen opened company-owned outlets in Austria, China, Slovenia, and Spain. DQ announced in 1995 that it had a plan to open twenty stores in Puerto Rico over a four-year period.

Little Caesar's

Little Caesar's ranked tenth in sales and eighth in stores for 1994. Sales growth had stopped: the 1992–1993 increase of 12.2 percent evaporated into no increase for 1993–1994. These numbers were achieved without a significant overseas presence. Of the top ten franchises, only Hardee's had a smaller number of stores in foreign lands. Little Caesar's received 3.5 percent of sales from foreign stores. Only 3.2 percent of the company's stores were in non-U.S. locations, namely, Canada, Czech and Slovak Republics, Guam, Puerto Rico, and the United Kingdom.

Little Caesar's

Year	1985	1986	1987	1988	1989	1990	1991	1992	1993	1994
Sales*	340	520	725	908	1,130	1,400	1,725	2,050	2,150	2,000
Number of stores	900	1,000	1,820	2,000	2,700	3,173	3,650	4,300	5,609	4.700
Employees	18,000	26,160	36,400	43,600	54,000	63,460	73,000	86,000	92,000	95,000

McDonald's

Year	1985	1986	1987	1988	1989	1990	1991	1992	1993	1994
Sales*	3,695	4,144	4,894	5,566	6,142	6,640	6,695	7,133	7,408	8,321
Net income*	433	480	549	656	727	802	860	959	1,083	1,224
EPS($)	0.56	0.63	0.73	0.86	0.98	1.10	1.18	1.30	1.46	1.68
Stock Price—Close($)	9.00	10.16	11.00	12.03	17.25	14.56	19.00	24.38	28.50	29.25
Dividends($)	0.10	0.11	0.12	0.14	0.16	0.17	0.18	0.20	0.21	0.23
Employees (K)	148	159	159	169	176	174	168	166	169	183

*$M; 1994: Debt ratio 41.2%; ROE.: 20.7%; Cash: $180M; Current ratio: 0.31: LTD $2.9M; Market Value: $20B

McDonald's

At the top in 1994 international sales and units, McDonald's Inc. was the most profitable retailer in the United States during the 1980s and into the 1990s. The company opened its first store in California in 1948, went public in 1965, and by 1994 had over 20 percent of the U.S. fast-food business. McDonald's opened its first international store in Canada in 1967. Growing domestic competition in the 1980s gave impetus to the company's international expansion. By 1994 there were over 15,000 restaurants under the golden arches in seventy-nine countries. The non-U.S. stores provided about one-third of total revenues and half of the company's profits. McDonald's planned to open 1,200–1,500 new restaurants in 1995—most outside the United States. International markets had grown into an attractive venue for the burger giant because there was "less competition, lighter market saturation, and high name recognition" in international markets.

The company's growth was fueled by aggressive franchising. In the early 1990s two-thirds of the McDonald's locations were franchised units, and franchisees remained with the company an average of twenty years. McDonald's used heavy advertising ($1.4 billion in 1994) and frequent menu changes and other innovations (1963: Filet-O-Fish sandwich and Ronald McDonald; 1968 Big Mac and first TV ads; 1972: Quarter Pounder, Egg McMuffin (breakfast); 1974: Ronald McDonald House; 1975: drive through; 1979: Happy Meals; 1983: Chicken McNuggets; 1986: provided customers with list of products' ingredients; 1987: salads; 1980s "value menus"; 1991: McLean DeLuxe, a low-fat hamburger—not successful—and experimentation with decor and new menu items at the local level; 1993: first restaurants inside another store, Wal-Mart). The company planned to open its first restaurants in India in 1996 with menus featuring chicken, fish sandwiches, and vegetable nuggets. There would be no beef items.

From 1993 to 1994, McDonald's grew 10.2 percent in sales and 8.7 percent in stores. Because of its extensive experience in international markets, international sales had grown to 42.5 percent of their total revenues and half its profits. Indeed, McDonald's was bigger than the twenty-five largest full-service chains put together.

PepsiCo: KFC and Taco Bell (Also Includes Pizza Hut which Is Not in the Top Fifty)

PepsiCo owned powerful brand names such as Pepsi-Cola and Frito-Lay and was also the world's

Pepsico

Year	1985	1986	1987	1988	1989	1990	1991	1992	1993	1994
Sales*	8,057	9,291	11,485	13,007	15,242	17,803	19,608	21,970	25,021	28,474
Net income*	544	458	595	762	901	1,077	1,080	1,302	1,588	1,784
EPS($)	0.65	0.58	0.76	0.97	1.13	1.35	1.35	1.61	1.96	2.22
Stock Price—Close($)	8.06	8.66	11.11	13.15	21.31	26.00	22.88	31.40	40.88	36.25
Dividends/Share($)	0.15	0.21	0.22	0.25	0.31	0.37	0.44	0.50	0.58	0.68
Employees (K)	150	214	225	235	266	308	338	372	423	471

*$M; 1994: Debt ratio 48.1%; ROE.: 27.0%; Cash: $1,488M; Current ratio: 0.96: LTD(M) $8,841.
1994 Segment Sales (Operating Income): Restaurants: 37% (22%); Beverages 34% (37%); Snack foods 29% (41%).

number one fast-food chain with its ownership of KFC, Taco Bell, and Pizza Hut.

KFC was third in sales and stores of the top fifty franchises in 1994. Active in the international arena since the late 1960s, KFC had been a major McDonald's competitor in non-U.S. markets. In 1994, the company had $3.6 billion in sales and 4,258 stores in other countries. McDonald's had been commonly number one in each country it entered, but KFC had been number two in international sales and had the number one sales spot in Indonesia. In 1994, KFC international revenues were 50.7 percent of sales with 45.3 percent of stores in international locations.

Taco Bell was fourth in sales and fifth in stores of the top fifty franchises in 1994. This ranking had been achieved with minimal international business to date. Taco Bell had $130 million in sales and 162 stores internationally. The company attempted to enter the Mexican market in 1992 with a kiosk and cart strategy in Mexico City. The venture did not fare well, and Taco Bell soon pulled out of Mexico.[3] In 1994, international revenues were 3.0 percent of sales and 2.9 percent of stores were international locations.

Subway

Founded more than twenty-nine years ago, Subway remained privately held in 1994.[4] The company had experienced explosive growth during the 1990s. It ranked ninth in sales and second in stores for 1994. Sales grew 13.6 percent from 1993 to 1994, and 26 percent from 1992 to 1993. Stores grew 17.1 percent from 1993 to 1994, and 15.3 percent from 1992 to 1993. In 1994, Subway overtook KFC as the number two chain in number of stores behind

McDonald's. The company attributed its growth at least partially to an exceptionally low-priced and well-structured franchise program. In addition, store sizes of 500–1500 square feet were small. Thus, the investment for a Subway franchise was modest.

The company's growth involved a deliberate strategy. The formula involved no cooking on site, except for the baking of bread. The company promoted the "efficiency and simplicity" of its franchise and advertised its food as "healthy, delicious, (and) fast." The company advertised regularly on TV with a $25M budget and planned to increase that significantly. All stores contributed 2.5 percent of gross sales to the corporate advertising budget. Subway's goal was "to equal or exceed the number of outlets operated by the largest fast-food company in every market that it entered." In most cases, the firm's benchmark was burger giant McDonald's.

International markets played an emerging role in Subway's expansion. In 1994, international sales were 10.6 percent of sales, compared to 8.9 percent the previous year. International stores were 9.5 percent of total in 1994, and 7.5 percent in 1993. Subway boasted a total of 9,893 stores in all fifty states and nineteen countries.[5]

Wendy's

Wendy's was number five in sales and number nine in stores for 1994. In 1994, after twenty-five years of operation, Wendy's had grown to 4,411 stores. This growth had been almost exclusively domestic until 1979, when Wendy's ventured out of the United States and Canada to open its first outlets in Puerto Rico, Switzerland, and West Germany. Wendy's granted JC Penney the franchise rights to France, Belgium, and Holland, and had one store opened in Belgium by 1980.

3. "US Operators Flock to Latin America," *Nation's Restaurant News,* November 17, 1994.
4. There is thus no publicly available financial data on Subway.

5. Subway's site on the Internet, accessed March 24, 1996.

Wendy's

Year	1985	1986	1987	1988	1989	1990	1991	1992	1993	1994
Sales*	1,126	1,140	1,059	1,063	1,070	1,011	1,060	1,239	1,320	1,398
Net income*	76	(5)	4	29	24	39	52	65	79	97
EPS($)	0.82	(0.05)	0.04	0.30	0.25	0.40	0.52	0.63	0.76	0.91
Stock price—close($)	13.41	10.25	5.63	5.75	4.63	6.25	9.88	12.63	17.38	14.38
Div/share($)	0.17	0.21	0.24	0.24	0.24	0.24	0.24	0.24	0.24	0.24
Employees(K)	40	40	45	42	39	35	39	42	43	44

*$M; 1994: Debt ratio 36.6%; ROE. 5.2%; Current ratio 0.98; LTD(M) $145

Wendy's still saw opportunities for growth in the United States. Industry surveys had consistently ranked Wendy's burgers number one in quality, but poor in convenience (Wendy's had one store for every 65,000 people while McDonald's, in contrast, had one for every 25,000). Growth was driven primarily by franchising. In 1994, 71 percent of the stores were operated by franchisees and 29 percent by the company. Company restaurants provided 90 percent of total sales while franchise fees provided 8 percent. The company had made menu and strategic changes at various points in its history. For example, in 1977 it first began TV advertising; in 1979 it introduced its salad bar; in 1985 it experimented with breakfast; in 1986 and 1987 it introduced Big Classic and SuperBar buffet (neither very successful); in 1990 it introduced grilled chicken sandwich and 99 cent Super Value Menu items; and in 1992, packaged salads.

Wendy's planned to add about 150 restaurants each year in foreign markets. With a presence of 236 stores in thirty-three countries in 1994, international was 9.1 percent of sales and 9.4 percent of stores that year.

APPENDIX B
COUNTRY SUMMARIES[1]

Canada

In the 1990s, Canada was considered an ideal first stop for U.S. business seeking to begin exporting. Per capita output, patterns of production, market economy, and business practices were similar to those in the United States. U.S. goods and services were well received in Canada: 70 percent of all Canadian imports were from the United States. Canada's market conditions were stable, and U.S. companies continued to see Canada as an attractive option for expansion.

Canada had one of the highest real growth rates among the OECD during the 1980s, averaging about 3.2 percent. The Canadian economy softened during the 1990s, but Canadian imports of U.S. goods and services were expected to increase about 5 percent in fiscal year 1996.

Although Canada sometimes mirrored the United States, there are significant cultural and linguistic differences between it and the United States and between the regional markets in Canada. These differences were evident in the mounting friction between the English- and French-speaking areas of Canada. The conflict had the potential of slicing Canada into two separate countries, and the prospect of such an outcome left foreign investors tense.

Germany

In the mid 1990s, Germany was the largest economy in Europe and the fifth largest overall importer of U.S. goods and services. Since reunification in 1990, the eastern part of Germany had continued to receive extensive infusions of aid from western Germany, and these funds were only just beginning to show an impact. The highly urbanized and skilled western German population enjoyed a very high standard of living, with abundant leisure time. In 1994, Germany emerged from a recession and scored a GDP of $2 trillion.

A unique feature of Germany was the unusually even distribution of both industry and population—there was no single business center for the country. This was a challenge for U.S. firms. They had to establish distribution networks that adequately covered all areas of the country. In Germany, there was little opportunity for regional concentration around major population centers as in the United States.

The country was a good market for innovative high-tech goods and high-quality food products. Germans expected high-quality goods and would reject a less expensive product if quality and support were not in abundance. The strongest competition for U.S. firms were the German domestic firms, not only because of their home-grown familiarity with the market, but also because of the consumers' widely held perception that German products were "simply the best."

A recurring complaint from Germans was the prevalent "here today, gone tomorrow" business approach of American firms. Germans viewed business as a long-term commitment to support growth in markets and did not always receive the level and length of attention necessary from U.S. companies to satisfy them.

Conditions in the former East Germany were not the doomsday picture often painted, nor were they as rosy as the German government depicts. It

---

1. The material in this appendix is adapted from the Department of Commerce Country Commercial Guides and the *CIA World Fact Book.*

would take ten to fifteen years for the eastern region of the country to catch up to the western region in terms of per capita income, standard of living, and productivity.

Japan

Japan had the second largest economy in the world. Overall economic growth in Japan over the past thirty-five years had been incredible: 10 percent average annual growth during the 1960s, and 5 percent in the 1970s and 1980s. Growth ground to a halt during the 1990s due to tight fiscal policy. The government tightened fiscal constraints in order to correct the significant devaluation of the real estate markets. The economy posted a 0.6 percent growth in 1994 largely due to consumer demand. The overall economic outlook remained cloudy, but the outlook for exports to Japan remained positive.

Japan is a highly homogeneous society, with business practices characterized by long-standing close relationships among individuals and firms. It took time for Japanese businessmen to develop relationships, and for non-Japanese businesspeople the task of relationship building in Japan was formidable. It was well known that Japan's market was not as open as that of the United States, but the U.S. government had mounted multifaceted efforts to help U.S. businesspeople "open doors." While these efforts were helpful, most of the responsibility in opening the Japanese market to U.S. goods or services remained with the individual firm. Entering Japan was expensive and generally required four things: (1) financial and management capabilities and a Japanese-speaking staff residing within the country; (2) modification of products to suit Japanese consumers; (3) a long-term approach to maximizing market share and achieving reasonable profit levels; and (4) careful monitoring of Japanese demand, distribution, competitors, and government. Despite the challenges of market entry, Japan ranked as the second largest importer of U.S. goods and services.

Historically, Japanese consumers were conservative and brand conscious, although the recession during the 1990s nurtured opportunities for "value" entrants. Traditional conformist buying patterns were still prominent, but more individualistic habits were developing in the younger Japanese, aged eighteen to twenty-one. This age cohort had a population of 8 million and boasted a disposable income of more than $35 billion.

Japanese consumers were willing to pay a high price for quality goods. However, they had a well-earned reputation for having unusually high expectations for quality. U.S. firms with high quality and competitive products had to be able to undertake the high cost of initial market entry. For those that could and were willing to do so, Japan could provide respectable market share and attractive profit levels.

Mexico

Mexico had experienced a dramatic increase in imports from the United States since the late 1980s. During 1994, the country experienced 20 percent growth over 1993. In 1994, Mexico's peso experienced a massive devaluation brought on by investor anxiety and capital flight. Although the Mexican government implemented tight fiscal measures to stabilize the peso, its efforts could not stop the country from plunging into a serious recession.

Inflation rose as a result of the austerity policies, and it was expected to be between 42 and 54 percent in 1995. Negative economic growth was anticipated in 1995 as well. The U.S. financial assistance package (primarily loans) provided Mexico with nearly $50 billion and restored stability to the financial markets by mid 1995. The government was taking measures to improve the country's infrastructure. Mexico's problems mask the fact that its government had, on the whole, practiced sound economic fundamentals.

Mexico was still committed to political reform despite the economic challenges. After ruling the country uninterrupted for sixty years, the PRI party had begun to lose some seats to other political parties. Mexico was slowly evolving into a multiparty democracy.

Despite the economic misfortunes of the 1990s, Mexico remained the United States' third largest trading partner. Mexico still held opportunities for U.S. firms able to compete in the price-sensitive recessionary market. Mexico had not wavered on the NAFTA agreement since its ratification, and in the mid 1990s 60 percent of U.S. exports to Mexico entered duty free.

South Korea

South Korea had been identified as one of the U.S. Department of Commerce's ten "Big Emerging Markets." Its economy overcame tremendous obstacles after the Korean War in the 1950s left the country in ruins. The driving force behind South Korea's growth was export-led development and energetic emphasis on entrepreneurship. Annual real GDP growth from 1986 to 1991 was over 10 percent. This blistering pace created inflation, tight labor markets, and a rising current account deficit. Fiscal policy in 1992 focused on curbing inflation and reducing the deficit. Annual growth, reduced to a still enviable 5 percent in 1992, rose to 6.3 percent in 1993. Fueled by exports, the 1994 growth was a heady 8.3 percent. South Korea's GDP was larger than that of Russia, Australia, or Mexico.

The American media had highlighted such issues as student demonstrations, construction accidents, and North Korean nuclear problem and trade disputes. Investors needed to closely monitor developments related to North Korea. However, the political landscape in South Korea had been stable enough over the 1980s to fuel tremendous economic expansion. The country was undertaking significant infrastructure improvements. Overall, South Korea was a democratic republic with an open society and a free press. It was a modern, cosmopolitan, fast-paced, and dynamic country, with abundant business opportunities for savvy American businesses.

There had been a staggering development of U.S. exports to South Korea: $21.6 billion in 1994 and more than $30 billion expected in 1995. While South Korea was twenty-two times smaller than China in terms of population, it imported twice as many U.S. goods and services than China in 1994.

Although South Korea ranked as the United States' sixth largest export market, obstacles for U.S. firms still remained. Despite the country's participation in the Uruguay Round of GATT and related trade agreements, customs clearance procedures and regulations for labeling, sanitary standards, and quarantine often served as significant non-tariff barriers.

The United Kingdom (or Great Britain)

The United Kingdom was the United States' fourth largest trading partner and the largest market for U.S. exports in Europe. Common language, legal heritage, and business practices facilitated U.S. entry into the British market.

The United Kingdom had made significant changes in its taxation, regulation, and privatization policies, which altered the structure of the British economy and increased its overall efficiency. The reward for this disciplined economic

approach had been a sustained, modest growth during the 1980s and early 1990s. The GDP grew 4.2 percent in 1994—the highest level in six years. The United Kingdom trimmed its deficit from $75 billion in fiscal 1994 to $50 billion in fiscal 1995.

The country had no restrictions on foreign ownership and movement of capital. There was a high degree of labor flexibility. Efficiencies had soared, and in the mid 1990s the country boasted the lowest real per-unit labor cost of the Group of Seven (G7) industrialized countries.

The United Kingdom's shared cultural heritage and warm relationship with the United States translated into the British finding U.S. goods and services to be attractive purchases. These reasons, coupled with a policy emphasizing free enterprise and open competition, made Britain the destination of 40 percent of all U.S. investment in the European Union.

The U.K. market was based on a commitment to the principles of free enterprise and open competition. Demand for U.S. goods and services was growing. The abolition of many internal trade barriers within the European Common market enabled European-based firms to operate relatively freely. As a result, U.S. companies used the United Kingdom as a gateway to the rest of the European Union. Of the top 500 British companies, one in eight was a U.S. affiliate. Excellent physical and communications infrastructure, combined with a friendly political and commercial climate, was expected to keep the United Kingdom as a primary target for U.S. firms for years to come.

Pizza Hut and Kentucky Fried Chicken, which had operations in more than sixty countries, and Taco Bell, which had operations in eleven countries, are owned by Pepsico.

Endnotes

1. All three Outback founders credited casual dining chain legend and mentor Norman Brinker with his strong mentoring role in their careers. Brinker played a key role in all of the restaurant chains Sullivan and Basham were associated with prior to Outback.
2. American consumption of meat declined from the mid 1970s to the early 1990s primarily as a result of health concerns about red meat. In 1976, Americans consumed 131.6 pounds of beef and veal, 58.7 pounds of pork, and 12.9 pounds of fish. In 1990, the figures had declined to 64.9 pounds of beef and veal, and 46.3 of pork, but rose to 15.5 of fish. The dramatic decrease in the consumption of beef and veal was attributed to consumer attitudes toward a low-fat, healthier diet. Menu items that gained in popularity

were premium baked goods, coffees, vegetarian menu items, fruits, salsa, sauces, chicken dishes, salads, and spicy dishes. George Thomas Kurian, *Datapedia of the United States 1790-10000* (Md: Bernan Press, 1994), p. 113.

3. Outback's original Henderson Boulevard Restaurant in Tampa, Florida was one of the few open for lunch. By 1995, the chain had also begun to open in some locations for Sunday lunch or for special occasions such as Mother's Day lunch.

4. Outback's signature trademark was its best-selling "Aussie-Tizer," the "Bloomin' Onion." The company expected to serve 9 million "Bloomin' Onions" in 1995.

5. Merritt had worked as CFO for another company, which had come to the financial markets with its IPO (initial public offering).

6. Outback did not grant exclusive territorial franchises. Thus, if an Outback franchisee did not perform, the company could bring additional franchisees into the area. Through 1994 Outback had not had territorial disputes between franchisees.

7. Pepsico owned Kentucky Fried Chicken, Taco Bell, and Pizza Hut; Grand Met owned Burger King.

8. Ref. AME 76 (KR).

9. "Industry and Trade Summary: Franchising," (Washington, D.C., U.S. International Trade Commission, 1995), pp. 15-16.

10. "World Hunger," *Restaurant Hospitality* (November 1994), p. 97.

11. *International Business Environments and Operations*, 7th ed., (1995), pp. 117-119.

12. "U.S. Restaurant Chains Tackle Challenges of Asian Expansion," *Nation's Restaurant News*, February 14, 1994, p. 36.

13. "India," *CIA World Factbook*, 1995.

14. "Big McMuttons," *Forbes*, July 17, 1995, p. 18.

15. Interview with Cheryl Babcock, professor at the University of St. Thomas, October 23, 1995.

16. "Franchise Management in East Asia," *Academy of Management Executive*, 4, No. 2 (1990), p. 79.

17. "U.S. Operators Flock to Latin America," *Nation's Restaurant News*, October 17, 1994, p. 47.

18. Interview with Cheryl Babcock.

19. "U.S. Restaurant Chains Tackle Challenges of Asian Expansion," p. 36.

20. "Industry and Trade Summary: Franchising," p. 30.

21. Ibid.

22. "U.S. Restaurant Chains Tackle Challenges of Asian Expansion," p. 36.

Corporate Level: Domestic and Global Cases

CASE 27

Nucor

This case was prepared by Frank C. Barnes of the University of North Carolina, Charlotte.

INTRODUCTION

Nuclear Corporation of America had been near bankruptcy in 1965, when a fourth reorganization put a thirty-nine-year-old division manager, Ken Iverson, into the president's role. Iverson began a process that resulted in Nucor, a steel mini-mill and joist manufacturer, which rated national attention and reaped high praise.

In a 1981 article subtitled "Lean living and mini-mill technology have led a one-time loser to steel's promised land," *Fortune* stated:

> Although Nucor didn't build his first mill until 1969, it turned out 1.1 million tons of steel last year, enough to rank among the top 20 U.S. producers. Not only has Nucor been making a lot of steel, it's been making money making steel—and a lot of that as well. Since 1969, earnings have grown 31% a year, compounded, reaching $45 million in 1980 on sales of $482 million. Return on average equity in recent years has consistently exceeded 28%, excellent even by Silicon Valley's standards and almost unheard of in steel. The nine-fold increase in the value of Nucor's stock over the last five years—it was selling recently at about $70 a share—has given shareholders plenty of cause for thanksgiving.[1]

The *Wall Street Journal* commented, "The ways in which management style combines with technology to benefit the mini-mill industry is obvious at Nucor Corp., one of the most successful of the

forty or more mini-mill operators."[2] Ken Iverson was featured in an NBC special, "If Japan Can, Why Can't We?" for his management approach. As the *Wall Street Journal* commented, "You thought steel companies are only a bunch of losers, with stodgy management, outmoded plants and poor profits?" Well, Nucor and Iverson were different.

However, the challenges hadn't stopped. The economy made the 1980s a horrible time for the steel industry. All companies reported sales declines, most lost profitability and some, in both major and mini-mill operations, closed or restructured. Nucor's 30 percent plus return on equity hit 9 percent. Iverson, however, was one of fifty-two recipients of the bronze model from *Financial World* in 1983 for holding on to profitability; it kept costs down but not at the expense of laying off its people—a near-religious commitment at Nucor.

By 1990, Nucor was the ninth largest steel producer in the United States and number 323 on the *Fortune* 500 list. But the easy gains scored by the new mini-mill operations over the integrated mills were over. The historical steel companies were awakening from their twenty-year slumber, adding modern technology, renegotiating with their equally aged unions, and closing some mills. They were determined to fight back. Mini-mill was fighting mini-mill, as well as imports, and a number had closed. Thus the industry faced a picture of excess capacity which would be the backdrop in the battle for survival and success over the next years.

Iverson and Nucor knew how to fight the battle. They invested $325 million in new processes in 1988. They went from $185 million in idle cash in 1986 to $180 million in debt by 1988. They had opened the first new fastener plant in the United States in decades, completed a joint venture with

This case is intended to be used as a basis for class discussion rather than to illustrate either effective or ineffective handling of the situation. This case was prepared by Frank C. Barnes, University of North Carolina, Charlotte. Used by permission.

the Japanese to build a plant to make structural steel products, and built the first mini-mill in the world to make flat-rolled steel, the largest market and major business of the integrated producers. They had broken away from the other mini-mills and had at least a three-year headstart in taking a share of this market from the integrated mills. Iverson believed with their new products they should double sales, and probably earnings, by 1991. Analysts predicted a jump to seventh largest among mills and doubling or tripling share price in the immediate future.

BACKGROUND

Nucor was the descendant of a company that manufactured the first Oldsmobile in 1897. After seven years of success, R. E. Olds sold his first company and founded a new one to manufacture the Reo. Reo ran into difficulties and filed for voluntary reorganization in 1938. Sales grew fifty times over the next ten years, based on defense business, but declined steadily after World War II. The motor division was sold and then resold in 1957 to the White Motor Corporation, where it operates as the Diamond Reo division. Reo Motors' management planned to liquidate the firm, but before it could do so, a new company gained control through a proxy fight. A merger was arranged with Nuclear Consultants, Inc., and the stock of Nuclear Corporation of America was first traded in 1955. Nuclear acquired a number of companies in high-tech fields but continued to lose money until 1960, when an investment banker in New York acquired control. New management proceeded with a series of acquisitions and dispositions: they purchased U.S. Semi-Conductor Products, Inc.; Valley Sheet Metal Company, an air conditioner contractor in Arizona; and Vulcraft Corporation, a Florence, South Carolina, steel joist manufacturer. Over the next four years, sales increased five times, but losses increased seven times. In 1965, a New York investor purchased a controlling interest and installed the fourth management team. The new president was Ken Iverson, who had been in charge of the Vulcraft division.

Ken Iverson had joined the Navy upon graduation from a Chicago-area high school in 1943. The Navy first sent him to Northwestern University for an officer training program but then decided it needed aeronautical engineers and transferred him

to Cornell. This had been "fine" with Iverson, because he enjoyed engineering. Upon receiving his bachelor's degree in 1945 at age twenty, he served in the Navy for six months, completing his four-year tour.

He wasn't too excited about an aeronautical engineering career because of the eight years of drafting required for success. Metals and their problems in aircraft design had intrigued him, so he considered a master's degree in metallurgy. An uncle had attended Purdue, so he chose that school. He married during this time, gave up teaching geometry so he could finish the program in one year, and turned down an offer of assistance toward a Ph.D. to "get to work."

At Purdue he had worked with the new electron microscope. International Harvester's research physics department had just acquired one and hired Iverson as assistant to the chief research physicist. Iverson stayed there five years and felt he was "set for life." He had great respect for his boss, who would discuss with him the directions businesses took and their opportunities. One day the chief physicist asked if that job was what he really wanted to do all his life. There was only one job ahead for Iverson at International Harvester and he felt more ambition than to end his career in that position. At his boss's urging, he considered smaller companies.

Iverson joined Illium Corporation, 120 miles from Chicago, as chief engineer (metallurgist). Illium was a sixty-person division of a major company but functioned like an independent company. Iverson was close to the young president and was impressed by his good business skill; this man knew how to manage and had the discipline to run a tight ship, to go in the right direction with no excess manpower. The two of them proposed an expansion, which the parent company insisted they delay three to four years until they could handle it without going into debt.

After two years at Illium, Iverson joined Indiana Steel products as assistant to the vice president of manufacturing, for the sole purpose of setting up a spectrographic lab. After completing this job within one year, he could see no other opportunity for himself in the company, because it was small and he could get no real responsibility. A year and a half later, Iverson left to join Cannon Muskegon as chief metallurgist.

The next seven years were "fascinating." This small ($5–6 million in sales and sixty-to-seventy people) family company made castings from special metals that were used in every aircraft made in the United States. The company was one of the first to get into "vacuum melting," and Iverson, because of his technical ability, was put in charge of this activity. Iverson then asked for and got responsibility for all company sales. He wasn't dissatisfied but realized that if he was to be really successful he needed broader managerial experience.

Cannon Muskegon sold materials to Coast Metals, a small, private company in New Jersey which cast and machined special alloys for the aircraft industry. The president of Coast got to know Iverson and realized his technical expertise would be an asset. In 1960 he joined Coast as executive vice president, with responsibility for running the whole company.

Nuclear Corporation of America wished to buy Coast; however, Coast wasn't interested. Nuclear's president then asked Iverson to act as a consultant to find metal businesses Nuclear could buy. Over the next year, mostly on weekends, he looked at potential acquisitions. He recommended buying a joist business in North Carolina. Nuclear said it would, if he would run it. Coast was having disputes among its owners and Iverson's future there was clouded. He ended his two years there and joined Nuclear in 1962 as a vice president, Nuclear's usual title, in charge of a 200-person joist division.

By late 1963, he had built a second plant in Nebraska and was running the only division making a profit. The president asked him to become a group vice president, adding the research chemicals (metals) and contracting businesses, and to move to the home office in Phoenix. In mid 1965 the company defaulted on two loans and the president resigned. During the summer Nuclear sought some direction out of its difficulty. Iverson knew what could be done, put together a pro-forma statement, and pushed for these actions. It was not a unanimous decision when he was made president in September 1965.

The new management immediately abolished some divisions and went to work building Nucor. According to Iverson, the vice presidents of the divisions designed Nucor in hard-working, almost T-group-type meetings. Iverson was only another participant and took charge only when the group couldn't settle an issue. This process identified Nucor's strengths and set the path for Nucor.

By 1966, Nuclear consisted of the two joist plants, the research chemicals division, and the nuclear division. During 1967, a building in Fort Payne, Alabama, was purchased for conversion into another joist plant. "We got into the steel business because we wanted to be able to build a mill that could make steel as cheaply as we were buying it from foreign importers or from offshore mills." In 1968 Nucor opened a steel mill in Darlington, South Carolina, and a joist plant in Texas. Another joist plant was added in Indiana in 1972. Steel plant openings followed in Nebraska in 1977 and in Texas in 1975. The Nuclear division was divested in 1976. A fourth steel plant was opened in Utah in 1981 and a joist plant was opened in Utah in 1982. By 1984, Nucor consisted of six joist plants, four steel mills, and a research chemicals division.

In 1983, in testimony before the Congress, Iverson warned of the hazards of trade barriers, that they would cause steel to cost more and that manufacturers would move overseas to use the cheaper steel shipped back into this country. He commented, "We have seen serious problems in the wire industry and the fastener industry." *Link* magazine reported that in the last four years, forty domestic fastener plants had closed and that imports had over 90 percent of the market.

In 1986, Nucor began construction of a $25 million plant in Indiana to manufacture steel fasteners. Iverson told the *Atlanta Journal,* "We are going to bring that business back."[3] He told *Inc.* magazine, "We've studied for a year now, and we decided that we can make bolts as cheaply as foreign producers and make a profit at it."[4] He explained that in the old operation two people, one simply required by the union, made one hundred bolts a minute. "But at Nucor, we'll have an automated machine which will manufacture 400 bolts a minute. The automation will allow an operator to manage four machines." Hans Mueller, a steel industry consultant at East Tennessee State University, told the *Journal,* "I must confess that I was surprised that Iverson would be willing to dive into that snake pit. But he must believe that he can do it because he is not reckless."[5]

Before making the decision, a Nucor task force of four people traveled the world to examine the latest technology. The management group was headed by a plant manager who joined Nucor after several years' experience as general manager of a bolt company in Toronto. The manager of manufacturing was previously plant manager of a 40,000-ton melt-shop for Ervin Industries. The sales manager was a veteran of sales, distribution, and manufacturing in the fastener industry. The plant's engineering manager transferred from Nucor R & D in Nebraska. The Touche-Ross accountant who worked on the Nucor account joined the company as controller. The first crew of production employees received three months of in-depth training on the bolt-making machines, with extensive cross-training in tool making, maintenance, and other operations. By 1988, the new plant was operating close to its capacity of 45,000 tons.

In what the *New York Times* called their "most ambitious project yet," Nucor signed an agreement in January 1987 to form a joint venture with Yamato Kogyo, Ltd., a small Japanese steel maker, to build a steel mill on the Mississippi River with a 600,000 ton per year capacity."[6] The $200 million dollar plant would make very large structural products, up to 24 inches. Structural steel products are those used in large buildings and bridges. Iverson noted, "These are now only made by the Big Three integrated steel companies." The Japanese company, which would own 49 percent of the stock, had expertise in continuous-casting in which Nucor was interested. Their 1985 sales totaled $400 million, with approximately 900 workers. They would provide the continuous-casting technology while Nucor would provide the melting technology and management style. The mill was completed in 1988 at a cost of $220 million for 650,000 tons of capacity. By the end of 1988, the plant was operating at 50 percent of capacity.

In August 1986, Iverson told Cable News Network, "We are talking about within the next two years perhaps building a steel mill to make flat roll products; that would be the first time a mini-mill has been in this area."[7] It was expected that approximately $10 million would be needed to develop this process. The thin-slab would also produce feed stock for Vulcraft's 250,000 tons per year steel deck operation. Although the project was considered pure research at the time and projected for "late 1988," the Division Manager stated, "The more we look into it, the more we feel we'll be able to successfully cast those slabs." This process would be the most significant development in the steel industry in decades and would open up the auto and appliance businesses to the mini-mills. Then in January 1987 plans were announced to build the $200 million, 800,000 ton mill for the production of high-grade flat rolled steel by the first half of 1989. They stated, "We've tested numerous approaches . . . this one is commercially feasible. It's been tested and it can do the job."[8]

The flat rolled steel was the largest market for steel products at 40 million tons in 1988 and 52 percent of the U.S. market. This is the thin sheet steel used in car bodies, refrigerators, and countless products. Making flat rolled steel required casting a slab rather than a billet and had not been achieved in the mini-mill. Nucor had invested several million in research on a process but in 1986 chose to go with a technology developed by SMS, a West Germany company. SMS had a small pilot plant using the new technology and Nucor would be the first mini-mill in the world to manufacture flat rolled steel commercially.

The plant would be built in Crawfordsville, Indiana, with an April 1988 start-up. It was expected that labor hours per ton would be half the integrated manufacturer's 3.0, yielding a savings of $50 to $75 on a $400 a ton selling price. If the project were completed successfully, Nucor planned to have three plants in operation before others could build. Investment advisers anticipated Nucor's stock could increase to double or triple by the mid 1990s. In July 1989, when Nucor announced a 14 percent drop in 2nd quarter earnings due to start-up costs, its stock went up $1.62, to $63. Iverson stated, "We hope this will map out the future of the company for the next decade."

However, it would not be as easy as earlier ventures. In April 1989, *Forbes* commented "If any mini-mill can meet the challenge, it's Nucor. But expect the going to be tougher this time around."[9] The flat-rolled market was the last bastion of the integrated manufacturers and they had been seriously modernizing their plants throughout the '80s.

In December 1986, Nucor announced its first major acquisition, Genbearco, a steel bearings manufacturer. At a cost of more than $10 million, it would add $25 million in sales and 250 employees. Iverson called it "a good fit with our business, our policies, and our people." It was without a union and tied pay to performance.

In October 1988, Nucor agreed to sell its Chemicals Division to a New York company for a $38 million gain.

Nucor's innovation was not limited to manufacturing. In the steel industry, it was normal to price an order based on the quantity ordered. In 1984, Nucor broke that pattern. As Iverson stated, "Some time ago we began to realize that with computer order entry and billing, the extra charge for smaller orders was not cost justified. We found the cost of servicing a 20 ton order compared with a 60 ton order was about 35 cents a ton and most of that was related to credit and collection. We did agonize over the decision, but over the long run we are confident that the best competitive position is one that has a strong price to cost relationship." He noted that this policy would give Nucor another advantage over foreign suppliers in that users could maintain lower inventories and order more often. "If we are going to successfully compete against foreign suppliers, we must use the most economical methods for both manufacturing and distribution."

THE STEEL INDUSTRY

The early 1980s had been the worst years in decades for the steel industry. Data from the American Iron and Steel Institute showed shipments falling from 100.2 million tons in 1979 to the mid-80 levels in 1980 and 1981. Slackening in the economy, particularly in auto sales, led the decline. In 1986, when industry capacity was at 130 million tons, the outlook was for a continued decline in per capita consumption and movement toward capacity in the 90–100 million ton range. The chairman of Armco saw "millions of tons chasing a market that's not there; excess capacity that must be eliminated."

The large, integrated steel firms, such as U.S. Steel and Armco, which made up the major part of the industry, were the hardest hit. The *Wall Street Journal* stated, "The decline has resulted from such problems as high labor and energy costs in mining and processing iron ore, a lack of profits and capital to modernize plants, and conservative management that has hesitated to take risks."[10]

These companies produced a wide range of steels, primarily from ore processed in blast furnaces. They had found it difficult to compete with imports, usually from Japan, and had given up market share to imports. They sought the protection of import quotas. Imported steel accounted for 20 percent of the U.S. steel consumption, up from 12 percent in the early 1970s. The U.S. share of world production of raw steel declined from 19 percent to 14 percent over the period. Imports of light bar products accounted for less than 9 percent of U.S. consumption of those products in 1981, according to the U.S. Commerce Department, while imports of wire rod totaled 23 percent of U.S. consump-

tion. "Wire rod is a very competitive product in the world market because it's very easy to make," Ralph Thompson, the Commerce Department's steel analyst, told the *Charlotte Observer.*[11]

Iron Age stated that that exports, as a percent of shipments in 1985, were 34 percent for Nippon, 26 percent for British Steel, 30 percent for Krupp, 49 percent for USINOR of France, and less than 1 percent for every American producer on the list. The consensus of steel experts was that imports would average 23 percent of the market in the last half of the 1980s.[12]

Iverson was one of very few in the steel industry to oppose import restrictions. He saw an outdated U.S. steel industry which had to change.

About 12% of the steel in the U.S. is still produced by the old open hearth furnace. The Japanese shut down their last open hearth furnace about five years ago.... The U.S. produces about 16% of its steel by the continuous casting process. In Japan over 50% of the steel is continuously cast.... We Americans have been conditioned to believe in our technical superiority. For many generations a continuing stream of new inventions and manufacturing techniques allowed us to far outpace the rest of the world in both volume and efficiency of production. In many areas this is no longer true and particularly in the steel industry. In the last three decades, almost all the major developments in steel making were made outside the U.S. There were 18 continuous casting units in the world before there was one in this country. I would be negligent if I did not recognize the significant contribution that the government has made toward the technological deterioration of the steel industry. Unrealistic depreciation schedules, high corporate taxes, excessive regulation and jaw-boning for lower steel prices have made it difficult for the steel industry to borrow or generate the huge quantities of capital required for modernization.

By the mid 1980s the integrated mills were moving fast to get back into the game; they were restructuring, cutting capacity, dropping unprofitable lines, focusing products, and trying to become responsive to the market. The president of USX explained: "Steel executives, in trying to act as prudent businessmen, are seeking the lowest-cost solutions to provide what the market wants." Karlis Kirsis, director of World Steel Dynamics at PaineWebber, told *Purchasing Magazine,* "The industry as we knew it five years ago is no more; the industry as we knew it a year ago is gone."[13]

Purchasing believed that buyers would be seeing a pronounced industry segmentation. There would be integrated producers making mostly flat-rolled and structural grades, reorganized steel companies making a limited range of products, mini-mills dominating the bar and light structural product areas, specialty steel firms seeking niches, and foreign producers. There would be accelerated shutdowns of older plants, elimination of products by some firms, and the installation of new product lines with new technologies by others. There would also be corporate facelifts as executives diversified from steel to generate profits and entice investment dollars. They saw the high-tonnage mills restructuring to handle sheets, plates, structurals, high quality bars, and large pipe and tubular products which would allow for a resurgence of specialized mills: cold-finished bar manufacturers, independent strip mills and mini-mills.[14]

Wheeling-Pittsburgh illustrated the change under way in the industry. Through Chapter 11 reorganization, it had cut costs by more than $85 per ton. It divided into profit centers, negotiated the lowest hourly wage rate ($18 per hour) among unionized integrated steel plants, renegotiated supply contracts, closed pipe and tube mills, and shut 1.6 million tons of blast furnace capacity in favor of an electric furnace with continuous casting.

PaineWebber pointed out the importance of "reconstituted mills," which it called the "People Express" of the industry. These were companies that had reorganized and refocused their resources, usually under Chapter 11. They included Kaiser Steel, the Weirton Works, Jones and Laughlin, Republic, Youngstown, Wheeling, LTV, and others.

Joint Ventures had arisen to produce steel for a specific market or region. The chairman of USX called them "an important new wrinkle in steel's fight for survival" and stated, "If there had been more joint ventures like these two decades ago, the U.S. steel industry might have built only half of the dozen or so hot-strip mills it put up in that time and avoided today's overcapacity." *Purchasing* observed, "The fact is that these combined operations are the result of a laissez-faire attitude within the Justice Department under the Reagan administration following the furor when government restrictions killed the planned USS takeover of National Steel (which later sold 50 percent interest to a Japanese steelmaker)."[15]

However, the road ahead for the integrated mills would not be easy. While it was estimated they would need $10 billion to improve their facilities, the industry had lost over $7 billion since 1982. *Purchasing* pointed out that tax laws and accounting rules are slowing the closing of inefficient plants. Shutting down a 10,000-person plant could require a firm to hold a cash reserve of $100 million to fund health, pension, and insurance liabilities. The chairman of Armco commented: "Liabilities associated with a plant shutdown are so large that they can quickly devastate a company's balance sheet."[16]

The American Iron and Steel Institute (AISI) reported steel production in 1988 of 99.3 million tons, up from 89.2 in 1987, and the highest in seven years. As a result of modernization programs, 60.9 percent of production was from continuous casters. Exports of steel were increasing, 2 million tons in 1988 and forecast to 3 in 1989, and imports were falling, expected to be less than 20 percent in 1989. Some steel experts believed the United States was now cost competitive with Japan. Several countries did not fill their quotas allowed under the five-year-old voluntary restraint agreements, which would expire in September 1989. The role of service centers in the distribution of steel continued with its fifth consecutive record year in 1988 of 23.4 million tons.

"If 1988 is remembered as the year of steel prosperity despite economic uncertainties, then 1989 is just as likely to go down as the year of 'waiting for the other shoe to drop,'" according to *Metal Center News* in January 1989.[17] The fears and the expectation of a somewhat weaker year arose from concerns about a recession, expiration of the voluntary import restraints, and labor negotiations schedules in several companies. Declines in car production and consumer goods were expected to hit flat-rolled hard. Service centers were also expected to be cutting back on inventories. AUJ Consultants told *MCN,* "The U.S. steel market has peaked. Steel consumption is tending down. By 1990, we expect total domestic demand to dip under 90 million tons."[18] Iverson expected 1989 to be mediocre compared with 1988.

THE MINI-MILL

A new type of mill, the "mini-mill," emerged in the United States during the 1970s to compete with the integrated mill. The mini-mill used electric arc furnaces to manufacture a narrow product line from scrap steel. In 1981, the *New York Times* reported:

> The truncated steel mill is to the integrated steel mill what the Volkswagen was to the American auto industry in the 1960's: smaller, cheaper, less complex and more efficient. Although mini-mills cannot produce such products as sheet steel [flat rolled] and heavy construction items, some industry analysts say it is only a matter of time before technological breakthroughs make this possible.[19]

Since mini-mills came into being in the 1970s, the integrated mills' market share has fallen from about 90 percent to about 60 percent, with the loss equally divided between mini-mills and foreign imports. While the integrated steel companies averaged a 7 percent return on equity, the mini-mills averaged 14 percent, and some, such as Nucor, achieved about 25 percent.

The leading mini-mills were Nucor, Florida Steel, Georgetown Steel (Korf Industries), North Star Steel, and Chaparral. Nucor produced "light bar" products: bars, angles, channels, flats, smooth round, and forging billets. It was beginning to make more alloy steels. Florida Steel made mostly reinforcing bar for construction (rebar) and dominated the Florida market. Korf Industries had two mini-mill subsidiaries, which used modern equipment to manufacture wire-rod.

The mini-mills were not immune to the economic slump in the early 1980s. Korf Industries, which owned Georgetown Steel, found its interest charges too large a burden and sought reorganization in 1983. In March 1983, Georgetown followed the historic wage cutting contract between the United Steel Workers of America and the major steel companies and asked its union to accept reductions and to defer automatic wage increases. In 1982, Nucor froze wages and executives took a 5 percent pay cut. Plants went to a four-day schedule in which workers would receive only base rate if they chose to work a fifth day doing cleanup.

Florida Steel, with two-thirds of its sales in Florida, also felt the impact. At its headquarters in Tampa, a staff of over 100 handled accounting, pay-roll, sales entry, and almost all other services for all its facilities. Their division managers did not have sales responsibilities. Florida Steel experienced a sales decline for 1982 of 22 percent and an earnings drop from $3.37 per share to a loss of $1.40. The next year was also a year of losses.

Florida Steel employees had faced periodic layoffs during the recession. The firm was non-union (although the Charlotte plant lost an election in 1973) and pay was based on productivity. A small facility at Indian Town, near West Palm Beach, never became productive, even with personnel changes, and had to be closed. A new mini-mill in Tennessee was completed in late 1983.

Mini-mills had tripled their output in the last decade to capture 17 percent of domestic shipments. PaineWebber predicted the big integrated mills' share of the market would fall to 40 percent, the mini-mills' share would rise to 23 percent, "reconstituted" mills would increase from 11 percent to 28 percent, and specialized mills would increase their share from 1 percent to 7 percent. Iverson stated mini-mills could not go beyond a 35 percent to 40 percent share due to technical limitations; mini-mills could not produce the flat rolled sheet steel used in cars and appliances.

Iverson told *Metal Center News* in 1983: "We are very interested in the development of a thin slab, which would then allow mini-mills to produce plate and other flat rolled products . . . actually, the thinnest slab that can now be produced is about 6 inches thick. . . . (That results in a plant that is too large.) There are a number of people working to develop the process. . . . We have done some work, but our primary efforts at the moment are in connection with other people who are working on it. . . . The likelihood is it would be developed by a foreign company. There are more efforts by foreign steel companies in that direction than in the United States. . . . I'd say probably a minimum of three to five years, or it could take as much as 10 to achieve this."[20]

In 1983, Iverson described the new generation of mini-mills he foresaw: "If you go way back, mini-mills got started by rolling reinforcing bar. With the advent of continuous casting and improvements in rolling mills, mini-mills gradually got into shapes. Now they have moved in two other directions: one being to larger sizes, and the other being a growing metallurgical expertise for improved product quality and production of special bar quality in alloys.

Both of these represent expansion of markets for mini-mills."

By 1986, the new competitive environment was apparent. Four mini-mills had closed their doors within the year and Iverson saw that more shutdowns were ahead. The overcapacity of steel bar products and the stagnant market had made it difficult for some companies to generate the cash needed to modernize and expand their product lines. "The mini-mills are going through the same kind of restructuring and rethinking as the integrated mill. They know the problem of overcapacity isn't going to go away quickly. And, for some of the remaining firms to survive, they will have to move into more sophisticated products like special quality and clean-steel bars and heavier structurals and, once the technology is perfected, flat-rolled products. You won't see the market growth by the mini-mills the way it was in the past until the overcapacity issue is resolved and the mills begin entering new product areas."

ORGANIZATION

Nucor, with its eighteen-person corporate office located in Charlotte, North Carolina, had divisions spread across the United States. The 15 divisions, one for every plant, each had a general manager, who was also a vice-president of the corporation, directly responsible to Iverson and Aycock. (See Figure 1.) The divisions were of two basic types, joist plants and steel mills. The corporate staff consisted of single specialists in personnel and planning and a four-person financial function under Sam Siegel. Iverson, in the beginning, had chosen Charlotte "as the new home base for what he had envisioned as a small cadre of executives who would guide a decentralized operation with liberal authority delegated to managers in the field," according to *South Magazine*.[21]

Iverson gave his views on organization:

You can tell a lot about a company by looking at its organization chart. . . . If you see a lot of staff, you can bet it is not a very efficient organization. . . . Secondly, don't have assistants. We do not have that title and prohibit it in our company. . . . In this organization nobody reports to the corporate office; the division managers report directly to me. . . . And one of the most important things is to resist as much as possible the number of management layers. . . . I've often

thought that when a company builds a fancy corporate office, it's on its way down.

Each division is a profit center and the division manager has control over the day-to-day decisions that make that particular division profitable or not profitable. We expect the division to provide contribution, which is earnings before corporate expenses. We do not allocate our corporate expenses, because we do not think there is any way to do this reasonably and fairly. We do focus on earnings. And we expect a division to earn 25 percent return on total assets employed, before corporate expenses, taxes, interest or profit sharing. And we have a saying in the company—if a manager doesn't provide that for a number of years, we are either going to get rid of the division or get rid of the general manager, and it's generally the division manager.

A joist division manager commented:

I've been a division manager four years now and at times I'm still awed by it: the opportunity I was given to be a Fortune 500 vice-president. . . . I think we are successful because it is our style to pay more attention to our business than our competitors. . . . We are kind of a "no nonsense" company. That is not to say we don't have time to play, but we work hard when we work and the company is first and foremost in our minds. . . . I think another one of the successes of our company has been the fact that we have a very minimum number of management levels. We've been careful to avoid getting topheavy and so consequently we put a great deal of responsibility on each individual at each level. It has often been said, jokingly, that if you are the janitor at Vulcraft and you get the right promotions, about four promotions would take you to the top of the company.

Mr. Iverson's style of management is to allow the division manager all the latitude in the world. His involvement with the managers is quite limited. As we've grown, he no longer has the time to visit with the managers more than one or twice a year. . . . Whereas in many large companies the corporate office makes the major decisions and the people at the operating level sit back to wait for their marching orders, that's not the case at Nucor. . . . In a way I feel like I run my own company because I really don't get any marching orders from Mr. Iverson.

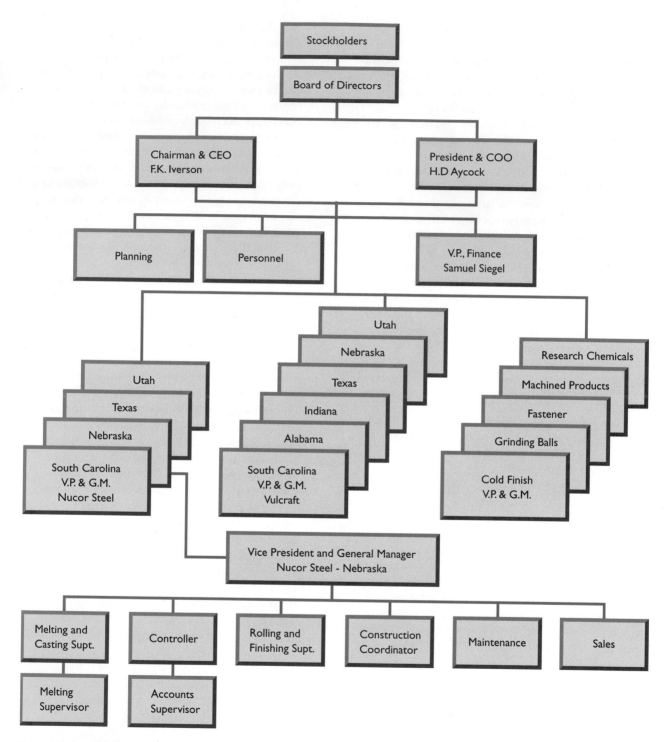

FIGURE I

Nucor Organizational Chart

He lets you run the division the way you see fit and the only way he will step in is if he sees something he doesn't like, particularly bad profits, high costs or whatever. But in the years I've worked with him I don't believe he has ever issued one single instruction to me to do something differently. I can't recall a single instance.

The divisions did their own manufacturing, selling, accounting, engineering, and personnel management. A steel division manager, when questioned about Florida Steel, which had a large plant 90 miles away, commented, "I really don't know anything about Florida Steel. . . . I expect they do have more of the hierarchy. I think they have central purchasing, centralized sales, centralized credit collections, centralized engineering, and most of the major functions." He didn't feel greater centralization would be good for Nucor. "The purchasing activity, for example, removed from the field tends to become rather insensitive to the needs of the field and does not feel the pressures of responsibility. And the division they are buying for has no control over what they pay. . . . Likewise centralized sales would not be sensitive to the needs of their divisions."[22]

South Magazine observed that Iverson had established a characteristic organizational style described as "stripped down" and "no nonsense." "Jack Benny would like this company," observed Roland Underhill, an analyst with Crowell, Weedon and Co. of Los Angeles; "so would Peter Drucker." Underhill pointed out that Nucor's thriftiness doesn't end with its "spartan" office staff or modest offices. "There are no corporate perquisites," he recited. "No company planes. No country club memberships. No company cars."[23]

Fortune reported, "Iverson takes the subway when he is in New York, a Wall Street analyst reports in a voice that suggests both admiration and amazement."[24] The general managers reflected this style in the operation of their individual divisions. Their offices were more like plant offices or the offices of private companies built around manufacturing rather than for public appeal. They were simple, routine, and businesslike.

In 1983, one of Iverson's concerns had been that as Nucor continued to grow they would have to add another layer of management to their lean structure. In June 1984 he named Dave Aycock president and chief operating officer, while he became chairman and chief executive officer—they would share one management level. Aycock had most recently been Division Manager of the steel mill at Darlington. But he had been with the company longer than Iverson, having joined Vulcraft in 1955, and had long been recognized as a particularly valued and close adviser to Iverson.

Iverson explained: "The company got to the size that I just wasn't doing the job that I thought should be done by this office. I couldn't talk to the analysts and everyone else I have to talk to, put the efforts into research and development I wanted to, and get to all the units as frequently as I should. That's why I brought Dave in. And, of course, he has been with the company forever." In a February 1985 letter, he told stockholders: "These changes are to provide additional emphasis on the expansion of the company's businesses."

"Dave is a very analytical person and very thorough in his thought process," another division manager told *33 Metal Producing,* a McGraw-Hill publication. "And Ken, to use an overworked word, is an entrepreneurial type. So, they complement each other. They're both very aggressive men, and make one hell of a good team."[25] Aycock stated: "I am responsible for the operations of all our divisions. To decide where we are going, with what technologies; what are our purposes. And what is our thrust. I help Ken shape where we are going and with what technologies. . . . I've been quite aggressive my whole career at updating, adapting, and developing new technology and new ideas in production and marketing. "Dave's the fellow who now handles most of the day-to-day operations," Iverson commented. "And he handles most of the employees who write to us"—about 10 to 15 percent of his time.[26]

DIVISION MANAGERS

The general managers met three times a year. In late October, they presented preliminary budgets and capital requests. In late February, they met to finalize budgets and treat miscellaneous matters. Then, at a meeting in May, they handled personnel matters, such as wage increases and changes of policies or benefits. The general managers as a group considered the raises for the department heads, the next lower level of management. As one of the managers described it,[27]

In May of each year, all the general managers get together and review all the department heads throughout the company. We have kind of an informal evaluation process. It's an intangible thing, a judgment as to how dedicated an individual is and how well he performs compared to the same position at another plant. Sometimes the numbers don't come out the way a general manager wants to see them, but it's a fair evaluation. The final number is picked by Mr. Iverson. Occasionally there are some additional discussions with Mr. Iverson. He always has an open mind and might be willing to consider a little more for one individual. We consider the group of, say, joist production managers at one time. The six managers are rated for performance. We assign a number, such as +3 to a real crackerjack performer or a –2 to someone who needs improvement. These ratings become a part of the final pay increase granted.

The corporate personnel manager described management relations as informal, trusting, and not "bureaucratic." He felt that there was a minimum of paperwork, that a phone call was more common and that no confirming memo was thought to be necessary. Iverson himself stated:

Management is not a popularity contest. If everybody agrees with the organization, something is wrong with the organization. You don't expect people in the company to put their arms around each other, and you don't interfere with every conflict. Out of conflict often comes the best answer to a particular problem. So don't worry about it. You are always going to have some conflict in an organization. You will always have differences of opinion, and that's healthy. Don't create problems where there are none.

A Vulcraft manager commented: "We have what I would call a very friendly spirit of competition from one plant to the next. And of course all of the vice presidents and general managers share the same bonus systems so we are in this together as a team even though we operate our divisions individually." The general managers are paid a bonus based on a total corporate profit rather than their own divisions' profits. A steel mill manager explained:

I think it's very important for the general managers to be concerned with contributing to the overall accomplishment of the company. There is a lot of interplay between the divisions with a flow of services, products, and ideas between di-

visions. Even though we are reasonably autonomous, we are not isolated. . . . We don't like the division managers to make decisions that would take that division away from where we want the whole company to go. But we certainly want the divisions to try new things. We are good copiers; if one division finds something that works, then we will all try it. I think that's one of our strengths. We have a lot of diverse people looking at ways to do things better.

Iverson revealed his view of management in his disdain for consultants:

They must have a specific job to do because they can't make your decisions. . . . The fellow on the line has to make decisions. . . . First he has to communicate and then he has to have the intestinal fortitude and the personal strength to make the decisions, sometimes under very difficult conditions. . . . A good manager is adaptable and he is sensitive to cultural, geographical, environmental, and business climates. Most important of all, he communicates. . . . You never know if someone is a good manager until he manages. And that's why we take people as young as we possibly can, throw responsibility at them, and they either work or they don't. In a sense it's survival of the fittest. But don't kid yourself; that's what industry is all about.

A steel division manager commented in comparing the Nucor manager with the typical manager of a large corporation:

We would probably tend to have managers who have confidence in their abilities and, very importantly, have confidence in other people in their division. And people who are very sensitive to the employees of their division. . . . But I think if you saw four or five different division managers, you'd have four or five different decision-making styles.

A Vulcraft general manager in his early forties who had been promoted to the division manager level nine years earlier said:

The step from department manager to division manager is a big one. I can't think of an instance when a general manager job has been offered to an individual that it has been passed up. Often it means moving from one part of the country to another. There are five department heads in six joist plants, which means there are 30 people who are considered for division manager slots at a joist plant. Mr. Iverson selects the division managers.

His own experience was enlightening:

When I came to this plant four years ago, we had too many people, too much overhead. We had 410 people at the plant and I could see, because I knew how many people we had in the Nebraska plant, we had many more than we needed. That was my yardstick and we set about to reduce those numbers by attrition. . . . We have made a few equipment changes that made it easier for the men, giving them an opportunity to make better bonuses. Of course the changes were very subtle in any given case but overall in four years we have probably helped the men tremendously. With 55 fewer men, perhaps 40 to 45 fewer in the production area, we are still capable of producing the same number of tons as four years ago.

The divisions managed their act with the corporate staff. Each day disbursements were reported to Siegel's office. Payments flowed into regional lock boxes. On a weekly basis, joist divisions reported total quotes, sales cancellations, backlog, and production. Steel mills reported tons-rolled, outside shipments, orders, cancellations, and backlog. Iverson graphed the data. He might talk to the division about every two weeks. On the other hand, Iverson was known to bounce ideas off the steel division manager in Darlington with whom he had worked since joining the company.

The Vulcraft manager commented on the communications with the corporate office: "It's kind of a steady pipeline. I might talk to the corporate office once a day or it might be once a week. But it generally involves, I would not say trivial information, just mundane things. Occasionally I hear from Sam or Ken about serious matters."

Each month the divisions completed a two-page (11 by 17 inches) "Operations Analysis" which was sent to all the managers. Its three main purposes were (1) financial consolidation, (2) sharing information among the divisions, and (3) Iverson's examination. The summarized information and the performance statistics for all the divisions were then returned to the managers.

VULCRAFT—THE JOIST DIVISIONS

Half of Nucor's business was the manufacture and sale of open web steel joists and joist girders at six Vulcraft divisions located in Florence, South Carolina; Norfolk, Nebraska; Ft. Payne, Alabama; Grapeland, Texas; St. Joe, Indiana; and Brigham City, Utah. Open web joists, in contrast to solid joists, were made of steel angle iron separated by round bars or smaller angle iron (see Figure 2).

These joists were costless and of lower greater strength for many applications and were used primarily as the roof support systems in larger buildings, such as warehouses and stores.

The joist industry was characterized by high competition among many manufacturers for many small customers. The Vulcraft divisions had over 3,000 customers, none of whom dominated the business. With an estimated 25 percent of the market, Nucor was the largest supplier in the United States. It utilized national advertising campaigns and prepared competitive bids on 80 percent to 90 percent of buildings using joists. Competition was based on price and delivery performance. Nucor had developed computer programs to prepare designs for customers and to compute bids based on current prices and labor standards. In addition, each Vulcraft plant maintained its own engineering department to help customers with design problems or specifications. The Florence manager commented, "Here on the East Coast we have six or seven major competitors; of course none of them are as large as we are. The competition for any order will be heavy, and we will see six or seven different prices."[28] He added, "I think we have a strong selling force in the marketplace. It has been said to us by some of our competitors that in this particular industry we have the finest selling organization in the country."

Nucor aggressively sought to be the lowest-cost producer in the industry. Materials and freight were two important elements of cost. Nucor maintained its own fleet of almost 100 trucks to ensure on-time delivery to all of the states, although most business was regional because of transportation costs. Plants were located in rural areas near the markets they served.

The Florence manager stated:

I don't feel there's a joist producer in the country that can match our cost. . . . We are sticklers

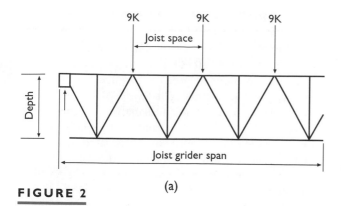

(a)

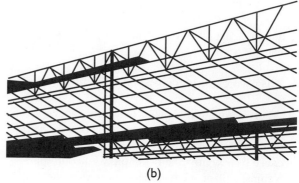

(b)

FIGURE 2

Illustration of Joists

Production

On the basic assembly line used at Nucor, three or four of which might make up any one plant, about 6 tons per hour would be assembled. In the first stage, eight people cut the angles to the right lengths or bent the round bars to desired form. These were moved on a roller conveyer to six-man assembly stations, where the component parts would be tacked together for the next stage, welding. Drilling and miscellaneous work were done by three people between the lines. The nine-man welding station completed the welds before passing the joists on roller conveyers to two-man inspection teams. The last step before shipment was the painting.

The workers had control over and responsibility for quality. There was an independent quality control inspector who had authority to reject the run of joists and cause them to be reworked. The quality control people were not under the incentive system and reported to the engineering department.

Daily production might vary widely, since each joist was made for a specific job. The wide range of joists made control of the workload at each station difficult; bottlenecks might arise anywhere along

about cutting out unnecessary overhead. Because we put so much responsibility on our people and because we have what I think is an excellent incentive program, our people are willing to work harder to accomplish these profitable goals.

the line. Each workstation was responsible for identifying such bottlenecks so that the foreman could reassign people promptly to maintain productivity. Since workers knew most of the jobs on the line, including the more skilled welding job, they could be shifted as needed. Work on the line was described by one general manager as "not machine type but mostly physical labor." He said the important thing was to avoid bottlenecks.

There were four lines of about twenty-eight people each on two shifts at the Florence division. The jobs on the line were rated on responsibility and assigned a base wage, from $6 to $8 per hour. In addition, a weekly bonus was paid on the total output of each line. Each worker received the same percent bonus on his base wage.

The amount of time required to make a joist had been established as a result of experience; the general manager had seen no time studies in his fifteen years with the company. As a job was bid, the cost of each joist was determined through the computer program. The time required depended on the length, number of panels, and depth of the joist.

At the time of production, the labor value of production, the standard, was determined in a similar manner. The general manager stated, "In the last nine or ten years we have not changed a standard." The standards list in use was over ten years old. Previously, they adjusted the standard if the bonus was too high. He said the technological improvements over the last few years had been small. The general manager reported that the bonus had increased from about 60 percent nine years earlier to

TABLE I

Tons per Manhour, Fifty-two-Week Moving Average

1977	.163
1978	.179
1979	.192
1980	.195
1981	.194
1982	.208
1983	.215
1984	.214
1985	.228
1986	.225
1987	.218

about 100 percent in 1982 and had stabilized at that point. Tables 1 and 2 show data typically computed on performance and used by the manager. He said the difference in performance on the line resulted from the different abilities of the crews:

> We don't have an industrial engineering staff. Our Engineering Department's work is limited to the design and the preparation of the paperwork prior to the actual fabrication process. Now, that is not to say that we don't have any involvement in fabrication. But the efficiency of the plant is entirely up to the manufacturing department.... When we had our first group in a joist plant, we produced 3½ tons an hour. We thought that if we ever got to 4 tons, that would

TABLE 2

A Sample of Percentage Performance, July 1982

		Line			
		1	2	3	4
Shift	1st	117	97	82	89
	2nd	98	102	94	107

be the Millennium. Well, today we don't have anybody who produces less than 6½ tons an hour. This is largely due to improvements that the groups have suggested.

Management

In discussing his philosophy for dealing with the work force, the Florence manager stated:[29]

> I believe very strongly in the incentive system we have. We are a non-union shop and we all feel that the way to stay so is to take care of our people and show them we care. I think that's easily done because of our fewer layers of management.... I spend a good part of my time in the plant, maybe an hour or so a day. If a man wants to know anything, for example, an insurance question, I'm there and they walk right up to me and ask me questions which I'll answer the best I know how.... You can always tell when people are basically happy. If they haven't called for a meeting themselves or they are not hostile in any way, you can take it they understand the company's situation and accept it.... We do listen to our people.... For instance last fall I got a call from a couple of workers saying that people in our Shipping and Receiving area felt they were not being paid properly in relation to production people. So we met with them, discussed the situation and committed ourselves to reviewing the rates of other plants. We assured them that we would get back to them with an answer by the first of the year. Which we did. And there were a few minor changes.

The manager reported none of the plants had any particular labor problems, although there had been some in the past.

> In 1976, two years before I came here, there was a union election at this plant which arose out of racial problems. The company actually lost the election to the U.S. Steelworkers. When it came time to begin negotiating the contract, the workers felt, or came to see, that they had little to gain from being in the union. The union was not going to be able to do anything more for them than they were already doing. So slowly the union activity died out and the union quietly withdrew.

He discussed formal systems for consulting with the workers before changes were made:

> In the economic slump of 1982, we scheduled our line for four days, but the men were allowed to come in the fifth day for maintenance work at base pay. The men in the plant on an average running bonus might make $13 an hour. If their base pay is half that, on Friday they would only get $6–$7 an hour. Surprisingly, many of the men did not want to come in on Friday. They felt comfortable with just working four days a week. They are happy to have that extra day off. Of course we're cautioned by our labor counsel to maintain an open pipeline to our employees. We post all changes, company earnings, changes in the medical plan, anything that might affect an employee's job. Mr. Iverson has another philosophy, which is, "Either tell your people everything or tell them nothing." We choose to tell them everything. We don't have any regularly scheduled meetings. We meet whenever there's a need. The most recent examples were a meeting last month to discuss the results of an employee survey and three months before was held our annual dinner meetings off site.
>
> We don't lay our people off and we make a point of telling our people this.

Recently the economic trouble in Texas had hurt business considerably. Both plants had been on decreased schedules for several months. About 20 percent of the people took the fifth day at base rate, but still no one had been laid off.

In April 1982, the executive committee decided, in view of economic conditions, that a pay freeze was necessary. The employees normally received an increase in their base pay the first of June. The decision was made at that time to freeze wages. The officers of the company, as a show of good faith, accepted a 5 percent pay cut. In addition to announcing this to the workers with a stuffer in their pay envelopes, meetings were held. Each production line, or incentive group of workers, met in the plant conference room with all supervision—foreman, plant production manager, and division manager. The economic crisis was explained to the employees by the production manager and all questions were answered.

STEEL DIVISIONS

Nucor had steel mils in five locations: Indiana, Nebraska, South Carolina, Texas, and Utah. The mills were modern mini-mills, all built within the last twenty years to convert scrap steel into standard angles, flats, rounds, and channels using the latest technology. Sales in 1988 were 1.44 tons, a 10 percent increase over those of 1987. This figure represented about 70 percent of the mills' output, the remainder being used by other Nucor divisions. In recent years, Nucor has broadened its product line to include a wider range of steel chemistries, sizes, and special shapes. The total capacity of the mills reached 2.8 tons in 1988.

A case writer from Harvard recounted the development of the steel divisions:

> By 1967 about 60% of each Vulcraft sales dollar was spent on materials, primarily steel. Thus, the goal of keeping costs low made it imperative to obtain steel economically. In addition, in 1967 Vulcraft bought about 60% of its steel from foreign sources. As the Vulcraft Division grew, Nucor became concerned about its ability to obtain an adequate economical supply of steel and in 1968 began construction of its first steel mill in Darlington, South Carolina. By 1972 the Florence, South Carolina, joist plant was purchasing over 90% of its steel from this mill. The Fort Payne plant bought about 50% of its steel from Florence. The other joist plants in Nebraska, Indiana and Texas found transportation costs prohibitive and continued to buy their steel from other steel companies, both foreign and domestic. Since the mill had excess capacity, Nucor began to market its steel products to outside customers. In 1972, 75% of the shipments of Nucor steel was to Vulcraft and 25% was to other customers.[30]

Iverson explained in 1984:

> In constructing these mills we have experimented with new processes and new manufacturing techniques. We serve as our own general contractor and design and build much of our own equipment. In one or more of our mills we have built our own continuous casting unit, reheat furnaces, cooling beds and in Utah even our own mill stands. All of these to date have

cost under $125 per ton of annual capacity—compared with projected costs for large integrated mills of $1,200–1,500 per ton of annual capacity, ten times our cost. Our mills have high productivity. We currently use less than four man hours to produce a ton of steel. This includes everyone in the operation: maintenance, clerical, accounting, and sales and management. On the basis of our production workers alone, it is less than three man hours per ton. Our total employment costs are less than $60 per ton compared with the average employment costs of the seven largest U.S. steel companies of close to $130 per ton. Our total labor costs are less than 20% of our sales price.

In contrast to Nucor's less than four man hours, similar Japanese mills were said to require more than five hours and comparable U.S. mills over six hours. Nucor's average yield from molten metal to finished products was over 90 percent compared with an average U.S. steel industry yield of about 74 percent, giving energy costs of about $39 per ton compared with their $75 a ton. Nucor ranked 46th on *Iron Age*'s annual survey of world steel producers. It was second on the list of top ten producers of steel worldwide based on tons per employee, at 981 tons. At the head of the list was Tokyo Steel at 1,485. U.S. Steel was seventh at 479. Some other results were: Nippon Steel, 453; British Steel, 213; Bethlehem Steel, 329; Kruppstahl, 195; Weirton Steel, 317; and Northstar Steel, 936. Nucor also ranked seventh on the list ranking growth of raw steel production. U.S. Steel was fifth on the same list. U.S. Steel topped the list based on improvement in tons-per-employee, at 56 percent; Nucor was seventh with a 12 percent improvement.[31]

THE STEEL-MAKING PROCESS

A steel mill's work is divided into two phases, preparation of steel of the proper "chemistry" and the forming of the steel into the desired products. The typical mini-mill utilized scrap steel, such as junk auto parts, instead of the iron ore that would be used in larger, integrated steel mills. The typical mini-mill had an annual capacity of 200–600 thousand tons, compared with the 7 million tons of Bethlehem Steel's Sparrow's Point, Maryland, integrated plant.

A charging bucket fed loads of scrap steel into electric arc furnaces. The melted load, called a heat, was poured into a ladle to be carried by an overhead crane to the casting machine. In the casting machine, the liquid steel was extruded as a continuous red-hot solid bar of steel and cut into lengths weighing some 900 pounds, called "billets." In the typical plant, the billet, about 4 inches in cross section and about 20 feet long, was held temporarily in a pit where it cooled to normal temperatures. Periodically, billets were carried to the rolling mill and placed in a reheat oven to bring them up to 2000°F, at which temperature they would be malleable. In the rolling mill, presses and dies progressively converted the billet into the desired round bars, angles, channels, flats, and other products. After being cut to standard lengths, they were moved to the warehouse.

Nucor's first steel mill, employing more than 500 people, was located in Darlington, South Carolina. The mill, with its three electric arc furnaces, operated twenty-four hours per day, five and a half days per week. Nucor had made a number of improvements in the melting and casting operations. The former general manager of the Darlington plant had developed a system that involved preheating the ladles, allowing for the faster flow of steel into the caster and resulting in better control of the steel characteristics. Less time and lower capital investment were required. The casting machines were "continuous casters," as opposed to the old batch method. The objective in the "front" of the mill was to keep the casters working. At the time of the Harvard study at Nucor each strand was in operation 90 percent of the time, while a competitor had announced a "record rate" of 75 percent, which it had been able to sustain for a week.

Nucor was also perhaps the only mill in the country that regularly avoided the reheating of billets. This saved $10–12 per ton in fuel usage and losses due to oxidation of the steel. The cost of developing this process had been $12 million. All research projects had not been successful. The company spent approximately $2 million in an unsuccessful effort to utilize resistance-heating. They lost even more on an effort at induction melting. As Iverson told *33 Metal Producing,* "That cost us a lot of money. Timewise it was very expensive. But you have got to make mistakes and we've had lots of failures."[32] In the rolling mill, the first machine was a roughing mill by Morgarshammar, the first of its kind in the Western Hemisphere. This Swedish machine had been chosen because of it lower cost, higher productivity, and the flexibility. Passing through another five to nine finishing mills converted the billet into the desired finished product. The yield from the billet to finished product was about 93 percent.

The Darlington design became the basis for plants in Nebraska, Texas, and Utah. The Texas plant had cost under $80 per ton of annual capacity. Whereas the typical mini-mill cost approximately $250 per ton, the average cost of all four of Nucor's mills was under $135. An integrated mill was expected to cost between $1,200 and $1,500 per ton.

The Darlington plant was organized into twelve natural groups for the purpose of incentive pay: two mills, each had two shifts with three groups—melting and casting, rolling mill, and finishing. In melting and casting there were three or four different standards, depending on the material, established by the department manager years ago based on historical performance. The general manager stated, "We don't change the standards." The caster, the key to the operation, was used at a 92 percent level—one greater than the claims of the manufacturer. For every good ton of billet above the standard hourly rate for the week, workers in the group received a 4 percent bonus. For example, with a common standard of 10 tons per run hour and an actual rate for the week of 28 tons per hour, the workers would receive a bonus of 72 percent of their base rate in the week's paycheck.

In the rolling mill there were more than 100 products, each with a different historical standard. Workers received a 4 percent to 6 percent bonus for every good ton sheared per hour for the week over the computed standard. The Darlington general manager said that the standard would be changed only if there was a major machinery change and that a standard had not been changed since the initial development period for the plant. He commented that in exceeding the standard the worker wouldn't work harder but would cooperate to avoid problems and move more quickly if a problem developed: "If there is a way to improve output, they will tell us." Another manager added: "Meltshop employees don't ask me how much it costs Chaparral or LTV to make a billet. They want to know what it costs Darlington, Norfolk, Jewitt to put a billet on the ground—scrap costs, alloy costs, electrical costs, refractory, gas, etc. Everybody from Charlotte to Plymouth watches the nickels and dimes."[33]

The Darlington manager, who became COO in 1984, stated:

> The key to making a profit when selling a product with no aesthetic value, or a product that you really can't differentiate from your competitors, is cost. I don't look at us as a fantastic marketing organization, even though I think we are pretty good; but we don't try to overcome unreasonable costs by mass marketing. We maintain low costs by keeping the employee force at the level it should be, not doing things that aren't necessary to achieve our goals, and allowing people to function on their own and by judging them on their results.
>
> To keep a cooperative and productive workforce you need, number one, to be completely honest about everything; number two, to allow each employee as much as possible to make decisions about that employee's work, to find easier and more productive ways to perform duties; and number three, to be as fair as possible to all employees. Most of the changes we make in work procedures and in equipment come from the employees. They really know the problems of their jobs better than anyone else. We don't have any industrial engineers, nor do we ever intend to, because that's a type of specialist who tends to take responsibility off the top division management and give them a crutch.
>
> To communicate with my employees, I try to spend time in the plant and at intervals have meetings with the employees. Usually if they have a question they just visit me. Recently a small group visited me in my office to discuss our vacation policy. They had some suggestions and, after listening to them, I had to agree that the ideas were good.[34]

THE INCENTIVE SYSTEM

The foremost characteristic of Nucor's personnel system was its incentive plan. Another major personnel policy was providing job security. Also all employees at Nucor received the same fringe benefits. There was only one group insurance plan. Holidays and vacations did not differ by job. The company had no executive dining rooms or restrooms, no fishing lodges, no company cars, or reserved parking places.

Absenteeism and tardiness were not problems at Nucor. Each employee had four days of absence before pay was reduced. In addition to these, missing work was allowed for jury duty, military leave, or the death of close relatives. After this, a day's absence cost them bonus pay for that week and lateness of more than a half hour meant the loss of bonus for that day.

Employees were kept informed about the company. Charts showing the division's results in return-on-assets and bonus payoff were posted in prominent places in the plant. The personnel manager commented that as he traveled around to all the plants, he found everyone in the company could tell him the level of profits in their division. The general managers held dinners at least twice a year with their employees. The dinners were held with fifty or sixty employees at a time. After introductory remarks, the floor was open for discussion of any work-related problems. The company also had a formal grievance procedure. The Darlington manager couldn't recall the last grievance he had processed.

There was a new employee orientation program and an employee handbook, which contained personnel policies and rules. The corporate office sent all news releases to each division where they were posted on bulletin boards. Each employee in the company also received a copy of the Annual Report. For the last several years the cover of the Annual Report had contained the names of all Nucor employees. Every child of every Nucor employee received up to $1,200 a year for four years if he or she chose to go on to higher education, including technical schools.

The average hourly worker's pay was $31,000, compared with the average earnings in manufacturing in that state of slightly more than $13,000. The personnel manager believed that pay was not the only thing the workers liked about Nucor. He said that an NBC interviewer, working on the documentary "If Japan Can, Why Can't We," often heard, "I enjoy working for Nucor because Nucor is the best, the most productive, and the most profitable company that I know of." [35]

"I honestly feel that if someone performs well, they should share in the company and if they are going to share in the success, they should also share in the failures," Iverson stated. [36] There were four incentive programs at Nucor, one each for production workers, department heads, staff people such as accountants, secretaries, or engineers, and senior management, which included the division managers. All of these programs were on a group basis.

Within the production program, groups ranged in size from twenty-five to thirty people and had definable and measurable operations. The company believed that a program should be simple and that bonuses should be paid promptly. "We don't have any discretionary bonuses—zero. It is all based on performance. Now we don't want anyone to sit in judgment, because it never is fair ...," said Iverson. The personnel manager stated: "Their bonus is based on roughly 90 percent of historical time it takes to make a particular joist. If during a week they make joists at 60 percent less than the standard time, they received a 60 percent bonus." This was paid with the regular pay the following week. The complete pay check amount, including overtime, was multiplied by the bonus factor. Bonus was not paid when equipment was not operating: "We have the philosophy that when equipment is not operating everybody suffers and the bonus for downtime is zero." [37] The foremen are also part of the group and received the same bonus as the employees they supervised.

The second incentive program was for department heads in the various divisions. The incentive pay here was based on division contribution, defined as the division earnings before corporate expenses and profit sharing are determined. Bonuses were reported to run as high as 51 percent of a person's base salary in the division and 30 percent for corporate positions.

Officers of the company were under a single profit sharing plan. Their base salaries were approximately 75 percent of comparable positions in industry. Once return on equity reached 9 percent, slightly below the average for manufacturing firms, 5 percent of net earnings before taxes went into a pool that was divided among the officers based on their salaries. "Now if return-on-equity for the company reaches, say 20 percent, which it has, then we can wind up with as much as 190 percent of our base salaries and 115 percent on top of that in stock. We get both."[38] In 1982 the return was 9 percent and the executives received no bonus. Iverson's pay in 1981 was approximately $300,000 but dropped the next year to $110,000. "I think that ranked by total compensation I was the lowest paid CEO in the *Fortune* 500. I was kind of proud of that, too."[39] In 1986, Iverson's stock was worth over $10 million. The young Vulcraft manager was likewise a millionaire.

There was a third plan for people who were neither production workers nor department managers. Their bonus was based on either the division return on assets or the corporate return on assets.

The fourth program was for the senior officers. The senior officers had no employment contracts, pension or retirement plans, or other normal perquisites. Their base salaries were set at about 70 percent of what an individual doing similar work in other companies would receive. More than half of the officers' compensation was reported to be based directly on the company's earnings. Ten percent of pretax earnings over a preestablished level, based on a 12 percent return on stockholders' equity, was set aside and allocated to the senior officers according to their base salary. Half the bonus was paid in cash and half was deferred.

In lieu of a retirement plan, the company had a profit sharing plan with a deferred trust. Each year 10 percent of pretax earnings was put into profit sharing. Fifteen percent of this was set aside to be paid to employees the following March as a cash bonus and the remainder was put into trust for each employee on the basis of percent of their earnings as a percent of total wages paid within the corporation. The employee was vested 20 percent after the first year and gained an additional 10 percent vesting each year thereafter. Employees received a quarterly statement of their balance in profit sharing.

The company had an Employer Monthly Stock Investment Plan to which Nucor added 10 percent to the amount the employee contributed and paid the commission on the purchase of any Nucor stock. After each five years of service with the company, the employee received a service award consisting of five shares of Nucor stock. Additionally, if profits were good, extraordinary bonus payments would be made to the employees. In December 1988, each employee received a $500 payment.

According to Iverson:

I think the first obligation of the company is to the stockholder and to its employees. I find in this country too many cases where employees are underpaid and corporate management is making huge social donations for self-fulfillment. We regularly give donations, but we have a very interesting corporate policy. First, we give donations where our employees are. Second, we give donations which will benefit our employees, such as the YMCA. It is a difficult area and it requires a lot of thought. There is certainly a strong social responsibility for a company, but it cannot be at the expense of the employees or the stockholders.[40]

Nucor had no trouble finding people to staff its plants. When the mill in Jewett, Texas, was built in 1975, there were over 5,000 applications for the 400 jobs—many coming from people in Houston and Dallas. Yet everyone did not find work at Nucor what they wanted. In 1975, a Harvard team found high turnover among new production workers after start-up. The cause appeared to be pressure from fellow workers in the group incentive situation. A survival-of-the-fittest situation was found in which those who didn't like to work seldom stuck around. "Productivity increased and turnover declined dramatically once these people left," the Harvard team concluded. Iverson commented: "A lot of people aren't goal-oriented. A lot of them don't want to work that hard, so initially we have a lot of turnover in a plant but then it's so low we don't even measure after that."[41]

The *Wall Street Journal* reported in 1981:

Harry Pigg, a sub-director for the USW in South Carolina, sees a darker side in Nucor's incentive plan. He contends that Nucor unfairly penalizes workers by taking away big bonus payments for absence or tardiness, regardless of the reason. Workers who are ill, he says, try to work because they can't afford to give up the bonus payment. "Nucor whips them into line," he adds. He acknowledges, though, that high salaries are the major barrier to unionizing the company.[42]

Having welcomed a parade of visitors over the years, Iverson had become concerned with the pattern: "They only do one or two of the things we do. It's not just incentives or the scholarship program;

it's all those things put together that results in a unified philosophy for the company."

Looking ahead, Iverson had said: "The next decade will be an exciting one for steel producers. It will tax our abilities to keep pace with technological changes we can see now on the horizon." Imports didn't have to dominate the U.S. economy. He believed the steel industry would continue to play a pivotal role in the growth of American industry. He pointed out comparative advantages of the U.S. steel industry: an abundance of resources, relatively low energy costs, lower transportation costs, and the change in the government's attitude toward business.

The excitement he had predicted had occurred. Imports were a challenge for steel, just as for textiles, shoes, machine tools, and computers. The old steel companies were flexing their muscle and getting back into the game. Overcapacity hadn't left the mini-mill immune; there was no safe haven for anyone. Nucor was no longer a small company, David, with free shots at Goliath.

The honeymoon appeared over. Wall Street worried about what Nucor should do. Cable News Network posed the position of some on Wall Street: "They say basically you guys are selling to the construction companies; you are selling to some fairly depressed industries. They also say, Nucor, they were a specialized little niche company. They did what they did very well; but now all of a sudden, they are going out, building these big mills to make huge pieces of steel and they are talking casted cold, all that stuff. They're worried that you may be getting into deals that are a little too complicated from what they perceive you as being able to do well."[43]

The *New York Times* pointed out that expansion would certainly hurt earnings for the next several years. They quoted a steel consultant: "It is hard to do all that they are trying to do and keep profits up. With the industry in the shape it's in, this is not the time to expand beyond the niche they've established."[44]

When they were sitting with $185 million in cash, Iverson told *Inc.*: "It (going private) has been mentioned to us by a number of brokerage firms and investment houses, but we wouldn't even consider it. It wouldn't be fair to employees, and I don't know whether it would be fair to the stockholders.... You're going to restrict the growth op-

portunities.... You either grow or die.... Opportunities wouldn't be created for people within the company."[45]

Iverson told CNN: "We've decided that really we want to stay in that niche (steel). We don't want to buy any banks.... All of the growth of the company has been internally generated. We think there are opportunities in the steel industry today. ... There are ample opportunities, although they are somewhat harder to find than they used to be."[46]

"Another of my strengths is the ability to stick to my knitting. The reason executives make a lot of mistakes is that sometimes they get bored—they think the grass is greener on the other side so they go out and buy a bank or an oil company or they go into business where they have no expertise.... I have never gotten bored with this company. I've done this job so long that I think I have some insight into the needs and the capabilities of the company. I'm not misled into thinking we can do something that we can't."[47]

An economics professor and steel consultant at Middle Tennessee State University told the *Times*, "You're not going to see any growth in the steel market, so the only way to make money is to reduce costs and have new technology to penetrate other company's business."[48]

The *New York Times* stated: "Critics question whether it is wise to continue expanding production capabilities, as Nucor is doing, when there is already overcapacity in the steel industry and intense competition already exists between the mini-mills." Iverson insisted the strategy would pay off in the long-term. He told the *Times*, "The company's strategy makes sense for us. To gain a larger share in an ever-shrinking market, you've got to take something from someone else."[49]

They had sold the chemicals division, gotten into the structural steel components business, into the fastener industry, and should soon be ready to go head-to-head with the major integrated producers for the lucrative flat-rolled market. Sales and earnings were projected to double in the next two years, as the stock price doubled or tripled.

Iverson's position was clear: "We're going to stay in steel and steel products. The way we look at it, this company does only two things well, builds plants economically and runs them efficiently. That is the whole company. We don't have any financial expertise, we're not entrepreneurs, we're not into acquisitions. Steel may not be the best business in the world, but it's what we know how to do and we do it well."

Endnotes

1. Richard I. Kirkland, Jr., "Pilgrims' Profits at Nucor," *Fortune,* April 6, 1981, pp. 43–46.
2. Douglas R. Sease, "Mini-Mill Steelmakers, No Longer Very Small, Outperform Big Ones," *Wall Street Journal,* January 12, 1981, pp. 1, 19.
3. Chris Burritt, "Foreign Steel Doesn't Scare Nucor's CEO," *Atlanta Journal,* August 24, 1986, pp. 1M, 5M.
4. "Steel Man Ken Iverson," *Inc.* (April 1986), 41–48.
5. Burritt, "Foreign Steel Doesn't Scare Nucor's CEO," pp. 1M, 5M.
6. "Nucor's Ambitious Expansion," *New York Times,* June 30, 1986, pp. D1, D3.
7. "Inside Business," interview with Ken Iverson, Cable News Network, August 17, 1986.
8. Jo Isenberg-O'Loughlin and Joseph J. Innace, "Full Steam Ahead on the Nucor Unlimited," *33 Metal Producing* (January 1986), 35–50.
9. R. Simon, "Nucor's Boldest Gamble," *Forbes,* April 3, 1989, p. 122.
10. Sease, "Mini-Mill Steelmakers," pp. 1, 19.
11. The *Charlotte Observer,* various issues.
12. "1985 Top 50 World Steel Producers," *Iron Age,* May 2, 1986, p. 48B1.
13. "Metals Report: Steel 1986," *Purchasing,* September 25, 1986, pp. 52–65.
14. Ibid.
15. Ibid.
16. Ibid.
17. *Metal Center News* (January 1989).
18. Ibid.
19. "The Rise of Mini-Steel Mills," *New York Times,* September 23, 1981, pp. D1, D6.
20. "Iverson Alloys Usher in New Era," *Metal Center News* (August 1987), 29.
21. Don Bedwell, "Nucor's Lean, Mean Management Team," *South Magazine* (August 1980), 50.
22. Interviews conducted by Frank C. Barnes.
23. Bedwell, "Nucor's Lean, Mean Management Team," p. 55.
24. "Pilgrims' Profits at Nucor," *Fortune,* April 6, 1981.
25. Isenberg-O'Loughlin and Innace, "Full Steam Ahead on the Nucor Unlimited," pp. 35–50.
26. "Ken Iverson," *33 Metal Producing,* 4.
27. All quotes are either from Ken Iverson or from interviews with Nucor managers conducted by Frank C. Barnes.
28. Interviews conducted by Frank C. Barnes.
29. Ibid.
30. Harvard Intercollegiate Case Clearing House, Harvard Business School.
31. "1985 Top 50 World Steel Producers," *Iron Age,* May 2, 1986, p. 48B1.
32. Isenberg-O'Loughlin and Innace, "Full Steam Ahead on the Nucor Unlimited," pp. 35–50.
33. Interview conducted by Frank C. Barnes.
34. Ibid.
35. Ibid.
36. "Nucor's Ken Iverson on Productivity and Pay," *Personnel Administrator* (October 1986), 46–108.
37. Ibid.
38. Ibid.
39. Ibid.
40. Ibid.
41. "A Calm Hand in an Industry Under the Gun," *The Business Journal,* September 5, 1986, p. 9.
42. Sease, "Mini-Mill Steelmakers," pp. 1, 19.
43. "Inside Business," Interview with Ken Iverson, Cable News Network, August 17, 1986.
44. "Nucor's Ambitious Expansion," *New York Times,* June 30, 1986.
45. "Steel Man Ken Iverson," p. 48.
46. "Inside Business."
47. "A Calm Hand," p. 9.
48. "Nucor's Ambitious Expansion."
49. Ibid.

CASE 28

Ups and Downs at Kodak

This case was prepared by Gareth R. Jones of Texas A & M University.

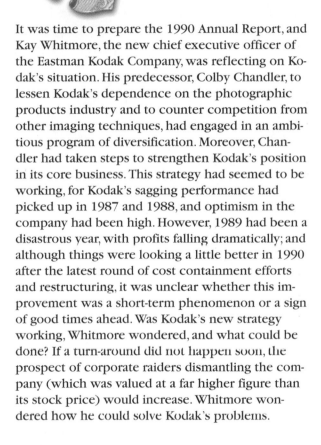

It was time to prepare the 1990 Annual Report, and Kay Whitmore, the new chief executive officer of the Eastman Kodak Company, was reflecting on Kodak's situation. His predecessor, Colby Chandler, to lessen Kodak's dependence on the photographic products industry and to counter competition from other imaging techniques, had engaged in an ambitious program of diversification. Moreover, Chandler had taken steps to strengthen Kodak's position in its core business. This strategy had seemed to be working, for Kodak's sagging performance had picked up in 1987 and 1988, and optimism in the company had been high. However, 1989 had been a disastrous year, with profits falling dramatically; and although things were looking a little better in 1990 after the latest round of cost containment efforts and restructuring, it was unclear whether this improvement was a short-term phenomenon or a sign of good times ahead. Was Kodak's new strategy working, Whitmore wondered, and what could be done? If a turn-around did not happen soon, the prospect of corporate raiders dismantling the company (which was valued at a far higher figure than its stock price) would increase. Whitmore wondered how he could solve Kodak's problems.

KODAK'S HISTORY

Eastman Kodak Company was incorporated in New Jersey on October 24, 1901, as successor to the Eastman Dry Plate Company, the business originally established by George Eastman in September

This case is intended to be used as a basis for class discussion rather than as an illustration of either effective or ineffective handling of the situation. This case was prepared by Gareth R. Jones, Texas A & M University. Used by permission.

1880.[1] The Dry Plate Company had been formed to develop a dry photographic plate that was more portable and easier to use than other plates in the rapidly developing photography field. To mass-produce the dry plates uniformly, Eastman patented a plate-coating machine and began to manufacture the plates commercially. Eastman's continuing interest in the infant photographic industry led to his development in 1884 of silver halide paper-based photographic roll film. Eastman capped this invention with his introduction of the first portable camera in 1888. This camera used his own patented film, which was developed using his own proprietary method. Thus, Eastman had gained control of all the stages of the photographic process. His breakthroughs made possible the development of photography as a mass leisure activity. The popularity of the "recorded images" business was immediate, and sales boomed. Eastman's inventions revolutionized the photographic industry, and his company was uniquely placed to lead the world in the development of photographic technology.

From the beginning, Kodak focused on four objectives to guide the growth of its business: (1) mass production to lower production costs, (2) maintaining the lead in technological developments, (3) extensive product advertising, and (4) the development of a multinational business to exploit the world market. Although common now, those goals were revolutionary at the time. In due course, Kodak's yellow boxes could be found in every country in the world. Preeminent in world markets, Kodak operated research, manufacturing, and distribution networks throughout Europe and the rest of the world. Kodak's leadership in the development of advanced color film for simple, easy-to-use cameras and in quality film processing was maintained by constant research and development in its many research laboratories. Its huge volume of production allowed it to obtain economies of scale. Kodak was also its own supplier of the plastics and chemicals needed to produce film, and it made most of the component parts for its cameras.

Kodak became one of the most profitable American corporations, and its return on shareholders' equity averaged 18 percent for many years. To maintain its competitive advantage, it continued to invest heavily in research and development in silver halide photography, remaining principally in the photographic business. In this business, as the company used its resources to expand sales and become a multinational enterprise, the name Kodak became a household word signifying unmatched quality. By 1990, approximately 40 percent of Kodak's revenues came from sales outside the United States.

Starting in the early 1970s, however, and especially in the 1980s, Kodak ran into major problems, reflected in the drop in return on equity. Its preeminence has been increasingly threatened as the photographic industry and industry competition have changed. Major changes have taken place within the photography business, and new methods of recording images and memories beyond silver halide technology have emerged.

THE NEW INDUSTRY ENVIRONMENT

In the 1970s, Kodak began to face an uncertain environment in all its product markets. First, the color film and paper market from which Kodak made 75 percent of its profits experienced growing competition from the Japanese when, led by Fuji Photo Film Co., they entered the market. Fuji invested in huge, low-cost manufacturing plants, using the latest technology to mass-produce film in large volume. Fuji's low production costs and aggressive, competitive price cutting squeezed Kodak's profit margin. Finding no apparent differences in quality and obtaining more vivid colors with the Japanese product, consumers began to switch to the cheaper Japanese film, and this shift drastically reduced Kodak's market share.

Besides greater industry competition, another liability for Kodak was that it had done little internally to improve productivity to counteract rising costs. Supremacy in the marketplace had made Kodak complacent, and it had been slow to introduce productivity and quality improvements. Further-

more, Kodak (unlike Fuji in Japan) produced film in many different countries in the world, rather than in a single country, and this also gave Kodak a cost disadvantage. Thus, the combination of Fuji's efficient production and Kodak's own management style allowed the Japanese to become the cost leaders—to charge lower prices and still maintain profit margins.[2]

Kodak was also facing competition on other product fronts. Its cameras had an advantage because of their ease of use as compared with complex 35mm single-lens reflex models. They were also inexpensive. However, the quality of their prints could not compare with those of 35mm cameras. In 1970 Kodak had toyed with the idea of producing a simple-to-use 35mm camera but had abandoned it. In the late 1970s, however, the Japanese did develop an easy-to-use 35mm pocket camera featuring such innovations as auto flash, focus, and rewind. The quality of the prints produced by these cameras was far superior to the grainy prints produced by the smaller Instamatic and disc cameras, and consumers began to switch to these products in large numbers. This shift led to the need for new kinds of film, which Kodak was slow to introduce, thus adding to its product problems.

Shrinking market share due to increased competition from the Japanese was not Kodak's only problem. In the early 1980s, Kodak introduced several less-than-successful products. In 1982 Kodak introduced a new disk camera as a replacement for the pocket Instamatic. The disk camera used a negative even smaller than the negative of the Instamatic and was smaller and easier to use. Four and a half million units were shipped to the domestic market by Christmas, but almost a million of the units still remained on retailers' shelves in the new year. The disk cameras had been outsold by pocket 35mm cameras, which produced higher-quality pictures.[3] The disk camera also sold poorly in the European and Japanese markets. Yet Kodak's research showed that 90 percent of disk camera users were satisfied with the camera and especially liked its high "yield rate" of 93 percent printable pictures, compared with 75 percent for the pocket Instamatic.

A final blow on the camera front came when Kodak lost its patent suit with Polaroid Corp. Kodak had foregone the instant photography business in the 1940s when it turned down Edwin Land's offer to develop his instant photography process. Polaroid developed it, and instant photography was wildly successful, capturing a significant share of the photographic market. In response, Kodak set out in the 1960s to develop its own instant camera to compete with Polaroid's. According to testimony in the patent trial, Kodak spent $94 million perfecting its system, only to scrub it when Polaroid introduced the new SX-70 camera in 1972. Kodak then rushed to produce a competing instant camera, hoping to capitalize on the $6.5 billion in sales of instant cameras. However, on January 9, 1986, a federal judge ordered Kodak out of the instant photography business for violating seven of Polaroid's patents in its rush to produce an instant camera. The estimated cost to Kodak for closing its instant photography operation and exchanging the 16.5 million cameras sold to consumers was expected to reach $800 million. In 1985 Kodak reported that it had exited the industry at a cost of $494 million.[4] However, the total costs of this misadventure were finally realized on July 15, 1991, when Kodak agreed to pay Polaroid a sum of $925 million to settle out of court a suit that Polaroid had brought against Kodak for patent infringement.[5]

On its third product front, photographic processing, Kodak also experienced problems. It faced stiff competition from foreign manufacturers of photographic paper and from new competitors in the film-processing market. Increasingly, film processors were turning to cheaper sources of paper to reduce the costs of film processing. Once again the Japanese had developed cheaper sources of paper and were eroding Kodak's market share. At the same time many new independent film-processing companies had emerged and were printing film at far lower rates than Kodak's own official developers. These independent laboratories had opened to serve the needs of drugstores and supermarkets, and many of them offered twenty-four-hour service. They used the less expensive paper to maintain their cost advantage and were willing to accept lower profit margins in return for a higher volume of sales. As a result, Kodak lost markets for its chemical and paper products— products that had contributed significantly to its revenues and profits.

The photographic industry surrounding Kodak had changed dramatically. Competition had increased in all product areas, and Kodak, while still the largest producer, faced increasing threats to its profitability as it was forced to reduce prices to match the competition. To cap the problem, by 1980 the market was all but saturated: 95 percent of all U.S. households owned at least one camera. Facing increased competition in a mature market was not an enviable position for a company used to high profitability and growth.

The second major problem that Kodak had to confront was due not to increased competition in existing product markets but to the emergence of new industries that provided alternative means for producing and recording images. The introduction of videotape recorders, and later video cameras, gave consumers an alternative way to use their dollars to produce images, particularly moving images. Video basically destroyed the old, film-based home movie business on which Kodak had a virtual monopoly. Since Sony's introduction of the Betamax machine in 1975, a video industry has grown into a multibillion-dollar business.[6] VCRs and 16mm video cameras are increasingly hot-selling items as their prices fall with the growth in demand and the standardization of technology. More recently, 8mm video cameras have been emerging—obviously much smaller than the 16mm version. The introduction of laser and compact disks has also been a significant development. The vast amount of data that can be recorded on these disks gives them a great advantage in reproducing images through electronic means, and it may be only a matter of time before compact disk cameras become available. It increasingly appears as though the whole nature of the recording industry is changing from chemical methods of reproduction to electronic methods. This transformation, of course, will undermine Kodak's edge in the market because its technical preeminence is based on silver halide photography.

Changes in the competitive environment have caused enormous difficulties for Kodak. Between 1972 and 1982 profit margins from sales declined from 15.7 percent to 10.7 percent.[7] Kodak's glossy image lost its luster. It was in this declining situation that Colby Chandler took over as chairman in July 1983.

KODAK'S NEW STRATEGY

Chandler saw the need for dramatic changes in Kodak's businesses and quickly pioneered four changes in strategy: (1) he strove to increase Kodak's control of its existing chemical-based imaging businesses; (2) he aimed to make Kodak the leader in electronic imaging; (3) he spearheaded attempts by Kodak to diversify into new businesses to create value; and (4) he embarked on major efforts to reduce costs and improve productivity. To achieve the first three objectives, he embarked on a huge program of acquisitions, realizing that Kodak did not have the time to venture new activities internally. Because Kodak was cash rich and had low debt, financing these acquisitions was easy.

For the next six years, Chandler acquired businesses in four main areas, and by 1989 Kodak had been restructured into four main operating groups: imaging, information systems, health, and chemicals. In a statement to shareholders at the annual meeting in 1988, Chandler announced that with the recent acquisition of Sterling Drug for $5 billion, the company had achieved its objective: "With a sharp focus on these four sectors, we are serving diversified markets from a unified base of science and manufacturing technology. The logical synergy of the Kodak growth strategy means that we are neither diversified as a conglomerate nor a company with a one-product family."[8]

Table 1 summarizes the four groups and their activities. The way these operating groups emerged over time is described below.

The Imaging Group

Imaging contains Kodak's original businesses, including consumer products, motion picture and audiovisual products, photofinishing, and consumer electronics. The unit is responsible for strengthening Kodak's position in its existing businesses. Kodak's strategy in its photographic imaging business has been to fill gaps in its product line by introducing new products either made by Kodak or bought from Japanese manufacturers and sold under the Kodak name. For example, in attempting to maintain market share in the camera business, Kodak introduced a new line of disk cameras to replace the Instamatic lines. However, in addition, Kodak entered into an agreement with Chinon of Japan to produce a range of 35mm automatic cameras under the Kodak name. This arrangement would capitalize on the Kodak name and give Kodak a presence in this market to maintain its camera and film sales. That venture succeeded; Kodak sold 500,000 cameras and had 15 percent of the market.

In addition, Kodak had developed a whole new range of "DX" coded film to match the new 35mm camera market—film that possesses the vivid color

qualities of Fuji film. Kodak had not developed vivid film color earlier because of its belief that consumers wanted "realistic" color.

Kodak also entered the electronic imaging industry through a joint venture with Matsushita. Matsushita produced a range of 8mm video cameras under the Kodak name. However, sales of these cameras never took off (some blame the outdated design of the camera), and in 1987 Kodak announced that it was withdrawing from the market.

Kodak has made major moves to solidify its hold on the film-processing market. It has attempted to stem the inflow of foreign photographic paper by gaining control over the processing market. In 1986 it acquired Texas-based Fox Photo Inc. for $96 million, becoming the largest wholesale photograph finisher. In 1987, it acquired the laboratories of American Photographic Group. In 1989, it solidified its hold on the photofinishing market by forming a joint venture between its operations and the photofinishing operations of Fuqua Industries. The new company, Qualex Inc., has ninety-four laboratories nationwide. These acquisitions provide Kodak with a large, stable "captive" customer for its chemical and paper products as well as control over the photofinishing market. Also, in 1986 Kodak introduced new, improved one-hour film-processing labs to compete with other photographic developers. To accompany the new labs, Kodak popularized the Kodak "color watch system," which requires these labs to use only Kodak paper and chemicals.[9] Kodak hoped that this would stem the flow of business to one-hour mini-labs and also establish the quality standards of processing.

As a result of these moves, Kodak gained strong control over the processing end of the market and made inroads into the film and camera end as well. In 1988, Kodak earnings were helped by the decline in value of the dollar, which forced Fuji Photo, its main competitor, to raise its prices. Consequently, Kodak was able to increase its prices. All these measures increased Kodak's visibility in the market and allowed it to regain strength in its existing businesses.

New and improved film products, including Kodak Gold Label film and Ektachrome film, were announced during 1988. Similarly, new types of 35mm cameras, some of which Kodak intended to make in its Rochester plant, were announced. Kodak also formed a battery venture with Matsushita. Matsushita produces a range of alkaline batteries for Kodak, and a gold-top battery is being exten-

TABLE 1

Kodak's Product Groups

Imaging	Chemicals	Health	Information Systems
Photographic products group Consumer imaging division Consumer services division Motion picture and television products division Professional photography division	**Eastman Chemical Company** Chemicals Plastics Fibers	Sterling Drug Inc. Health Sciences Division Clinical Products Lehn & Fink	**Commercial systems group** Copy products division Customer equipment service division Graphics imaging systems division Kodak apparatus division **Imaging information systems group** Business imaging systems division Federal systems division Image acquisition products division Integration and systems products division Mass memory division Printer products division

Source: Eastman Kodak Company, Annual Report, 1989.

sively advertised in opposition to Duracell's copper-top battery. In 1988, Kodak announced the introduction of new and improved Kodak Supralife and Ultralife batteries to be produced in a joint venture with Matsushita at a new battery-manufacturing facility built in Georgia, where production began in 1989. Moreover, Kodak internally ventured a new lithium battery, which lasts six times as long as conventional batteries. This was an opportunity for future growth because of the extensive use of the battery in cameras.

Kodak also engaged in a massive cost-cutting effort to improve the efficiency of the photographic products group. For the last six years it has introduced more and more stringent efficiency targets aimed at reducing waste while increasing productivity. In 1986, it established a baseline for measuring the total cost of waste incurred in the manufacture of film and paper throughout its worldwide operations. By 1987 it had cut that waste by 15 percent, and by 1989 it announced total cost savings worth $500 million annually.

Despite these strategic moves, the net earnings of Kodak's photographic business dropped dramat-

ically in 1989. Although Kodak's volume and sales of its products were up, profit margins were down. Polaroid with its new One Film product was advertising aggressively to capture market share. Fuji, realizing the strong threat posed by Kodak's reassertion of industry control, responded with an intense competitive push. Both Fuji and Kodak were spending massive amounts to advertise their products in order to increase market share. Kodak had 80 percent of the $7 billion film market in 1989 and Fuji had 11 percent, but Fuji increased its advertising budget by 65 percent in 1989 to increase its market share and simultaneously offered discount coupons on its film products. Moreover, Fuji announced plans for a major new film-making plant in Europe—a plant the size of its Japanese plant, which by itself can produce film for one quarter of the world market. The result has been a huge amount of excess capacity in film production, which raises costs and encourages competition. Fighting back, Kodak announced a fifteen-year agreement with the Walt Disney Company to use Disney characters in its advertising. Kodak also announced new multipacks and discounts on its products. However, these moves were very expensive for Kodak and cut into profits. They offset some of the prospective benefits from Kodak's cost-cutting efforts and led to the poor earnings results. Thus, growth in Kodak's photographic imaging business has been slow.

It was because of this slow industry growth that Chandler saw the need for diversification. Because sales increased only 5 percent a year and Kodak already had 80 percent of the market, it was tied to the fortunes of one industry. This fact, plus the increase in the use of other imaging techniques, led to Chandler's second strategic thrust: an immediate policy of acquisition and diversification into the electronic imaging business with the stated goal of being "first in both industries."[10]

The Information Systems Group

In 1988, when Sony introduced an electronic camera that could take still pictures and then transmit them back to a television screen, it became increasingly obvious that the threat to Kodak from new electronic imaging techniques would continue to increase. Although the pictures could not match the quality achieved with chemical reproduction with video film, the advent of compact disks offered the prospect of an imaging medium that could meet such standards in the future. To survive and prosper in the imaging business, Kodak realized that it required expertise in a broad range of technologies to satisfy customers' recording and imaging needs. Furthermore, it saw the electronic imaging business increasing and a large number of different types of markets emerging, including business and industrial customers. Electronic imaging had become important in the medical sciences and in all business, technical, and research activities, especially since the advent of the computer. Thus, Kodak began targeting electronics, communications, computer science, and various hard-copy-output technologies as being increasingly important to its future imaging products. To buy time until it could produce its own products, Kodak marketed the products of others under its own famous brand name—for instance, an electronic publishing system for corporate documents and an automated microfilm-imaging system.

Kodak's goal of reinvesting profits to build and extend its businesses could be seen in its move toward acquisitions and joint ventures. Growth of the Information Systems group has been due to several

acquisitions, including Atex Inc., Eikonix Corp., and Disconix Inc. Atex, acquired in 1981, makes newspaper and magazine publishing systems.[11] It sells versatile electronic publishing and text-editing systems to newspapers and magazines worldwide as well as to government agencies and law firms. Its list of customers include leading newspapers in such cities as Boston, Chicago, Dallas, Houston, Miami, New York, and Philadelphia; national magazines such as *Time, Newsweek, U.S. News & World Report, Forbes, Reader's Digest,* and *National Geographic;* and government customers such as the U.S. Supreme Court and the U.S. Government Printing Office.

Eikonix Corp. is a leader in the design, development, and production of precision digital imaging systems. Included in its range of commercial products are devices that scan and convert images into digital form and equipment to edit and manipulate color photographs and transparencies to produce color separations for printing and graphic arts applications. The Eikonix Designmaster 8000 allows users to proceed directly from artwork to printing plates with unmatched quality and flexibility.

Further growth within the Information Systems group came with the development of the Ektaprint line of copier-duplicators. The copiers achieved good sales growth and reached new standards for quality, reliability, and productivity in the very competitive high-volume segment of the copier marketplace. In 1988, Kodak announced another major move into the copier service business. It purchased IBM's copier service business and copier sales agreements in the United States. Kodak also announced that it would market copiers manufactured by IBM while continuing to market its own Ektaprint copiers. This service agreement was eventually extended to sixteen countries outside the United States.[12]

Kodak further enhanced its position in imaging with the announcement of two new image management packages: the Kodak Ektaprint Electronic Publishing System (KEEPS) and the Kodak Imaging Management System (KIMS). KIMS electronically scans, digitizes, and stores film images and transmits image information electronically. The system enables users with large, active databases to view and manipulate information stored on microfilm and magnetic or optical disks.[13] Presently, KIMS is being marketed by Digital Equipment Corporation in a joint venture. KEEPS is designed for use where there is a need for high-quality documents formed from text, graphics, and other images. The documents are reproduced by software designed specifically for electronic publishing. KEEPS has the ability to edit, print, and update text and graphics for publications. The computer comes from Sun Microsystems Inc. The software, enhanced by Kodak, is produced by Interleaf Inc., and the printer is manufactured by Canon (one of Kodak's Japanese competitors).[14] Kodak has also announced a new $500,000 imaging system that locates microfilm and scans it for computer use. This product is directed at the banking and insurance company markets. In 1988, Kodak announced that it would begin marketing a "VY-P1" printer developed in a joint venture with Hitachi. This printer can make high-quality still images from VCRs and camcorders.

With these moves, Kodak extended its activities into the electronic areas of artificial intelligence, computer systems, consumer electronics, peripherals, telecommunications, and test and measuring equipment. Kodak hoped to gain a strong foothold in these businesses to make up for losses in its traditional business. Kodak purchased companies that made products as diverse as computer workstations and floppy disks. It aggressively acquired companies to fill in its product lines and obtain technical expertise in information systems. After taking more than a decade to make its first four acquisitions, Kodak completed seven acquisitions in 1985 and more than ten in 1986. Among the 1985 acquisitions—for $175 million—was Verbatim Corporation, a major producer of floppy disks. This acquisition made Kodak one of the three big producers in the floppy disk industry.

Entry into the information systems market, like the expansion in its core photographic products business, produced new competitive problems for Kodak. In entering office information systems, Kodak entered areas where it faced strong competition from established companies such as Digital and IBM.[15] The Verbatim acquisition brought Kodak into direct competition with 3M. Entering the copier market brought Kodak into direct competition with Japanese firms such as Canon, which competitively market their own lines of advanced, low-cost products. Kodak was entering new businesses where it had little expertise, where it was unfamiliar with the competitive problems, and where there was already strong competition.

Kodak was forced to retreat from some of these markets. In 1990, it announced that it would sell Verbatim to Mitsubishi. (Mitsubishi was immediately criticized by Japanese investors for buying a company with an old, outdated product line.) Kodak has withdrawn from many other areas of business by selling assets or closing operations and taking a write-off. For example, to reduce costs, it sold Sayett Technology, Kodak Video programs and videocassettes, and Aquidneck Data Corporation. The decline in the performance of the Information Systems group, attributed to increased competition, a flat office systems market, and delays in bringing out new products, reduced earnings from operations from a profit of $311 million in 1988 to a loss of $360 million in 1989.

The Health Group

Kodak's interest in health products emerged from its involvement in the design and production of film for medical and dental x-rays. The growth of imaging in medical sciences offered Kodak an opportunity to apply its skills in new areas, and it began to develop such products as Kodak Ektachem—clinical blood analyzers. It developed other products—Ektascan laser imaging films, printers, and accessories—for improving the display, storage, processing, and retrieval of diagnostic images. However, Kodak did not confine its interests in medical and health matters to imaging-based products

In 1984, it established within the health group a life sciences division to develop and commercialize new products deriving from Kodak's distinctive competencies in chemistry and biotechnology. One of the division's objectives was to focus on product opportunities in markets with relatively few competitors and high profit potential—products such as nutritional supplements that can be delivered orally or intravenously, as well as nutrition products for sale over the counter to consumers. Another objective was to develop innovative ways to control the absorption of pharmaceutical drugs into the body so that a drug remains therapeutically effective for the optimum amount of time. A third objective involved developing new applications for existing products and processes. Kodak has in its files about 500,000 chemical formulations on which it can base new products.

Within life sciences was the bio-products division, which engaged in joint research with biotechnology companies such as Cetus Corporation, Amgen, and Immunex. Bio-Products pursued an aggressive strategy to scale up and commercialize products based on biotechnology derived from in-house as well as outside contract research. Ventures entered into by the bio-products division included an agreement with Advanced Genetic Sciences for the commercial production of SNOW-MAX, a product useful in making artificial snow for ski areas.[16]

Kodak began to enter into joint ventures in the biotechnical industry, both to build its business and to enter new businesses. In April 1985 Kodak and ICN Pharmaceuticals jointly announced the formation of a research institute that would explore new biomedical compounds aimed at stopping the spread of viral infections and slowing the aging process. Kodak and ICN were to invest $45 million over six years to form and operate the Nucleic Acid Research Institute, a joint venture located at ICN's Costa Mesa, California, facility. The institute would dedicate much of its research exclusively to preclinical studies of new antiviral and anti-aging substances.

However, these advances into biotechnology proved expensive, and the uncertainty of the industry caused Kodak to question the wisdom of entering this highly volatile area. In 1988, to reduce the costs of operating the bio-products division, a joint venture incorporating bio-products was formed between Kodak and Cultor Ltd. of Finland, and Kodak essentially left the market. The remaining parts of the life sciences division were then folded into the health group in 1988, when Chandler completed Kodak's biggest acquisition, the purchase of Sterling Drug for more than $5 billion.

The Sterling acquisition once again totally altered Kodak's strategy for the health group. Sterling Drug is a worldwide manufacturer and marketer of prescription drugs, over-the-counter medicine, and consumer products. It has such familiar brand names as Bayer aspirin, Phillips' milk of magnesia, and Panadol. Chandler thought this merger would provide Kodak with the marketing infrastructure and international drug registration that it needed to become a major player in the pharmaceuticals industry. With this acquisition Kodak's health group became pharmaceutically oriented, its mission being to develop a full pipeline of major prescription drugs and a world-class portfolio of over-the-counter medicine.[17]

Analysts, however, questioned the acquisition. Once again Chandler was taking Kodak into an industry where competition was intense and the in-

dustry itself was consolidating because of the massive cost of drug development. Kodak had no expertise in this area, despite its forays into biotechnology, and the acquisition was unrelated to the other activities of the health group. Some analysts claimed that the acquisition was aimed at deterring a possible takeover of Kodak and that it was too expensive.

The acquisition of Sterling dramatically increased the sales of the health group but dampened Kodak's earnings and helped lead to a reversal in profits in 1989. Moreover, by purchasing Sterling, Kodak had obtained Sterling's Lehn & Fink products division, which produced products as diverse as Lysol and Minwax wood-care products. Far from wishing to sell this division, Kodak believed that this acquisition would lead to long-term profits. Analysts asked whether this was growth without profitability.

The Chemicals Group

Established more than sixty-five years ago as a supplier of raw materials for Kodak's film and processing businesses, the Eastman Chemical Company has been responsible for developing many of the chemicals and plastics that have made Kodak the leader in the photographic industry. The company has also been a major supplier of chemicals, fibers, and plastics to thousands of customers worldwide. Kodak has been enjoying increased growth in its plastic material and resins unit because of outstanding performance and enthusiastic customer acceptance of Kodak PET (polyethylene terephthalate), a polymer used in soft-drink bottles and other food and beverage containers. The growth in popularity of 16-ounce PET bottles spurred a record year for both revenue and volume in 1985. Kodak announced the opening of a major new PET facility in England in 1988. In 1986, three new businesses were established within the chemicals group: specialty printing inks, performance plastics, and animal nutrition supplements. They all share the common objective of enabling the chemicals group to move quickly into profitable new market segments where there is the potential for growth.[18]

In its chemical business, too, Kodak has run into the same kinds of problems experienced by its other operating groups. There is intense competition in the plastics industry, not only from U.S. firms like Du Pont but also from large Japanese and European firms like Imperial Chemical Industries PLC and Hoech, which compete directly with Kodak for sales. In specialty plastics and PET, for example, volume increased but Kodak was forced to reduce prices by 5 percent to compete with other firms in the industry. This squeeze in profit margins also contributed to the reversal in earnings in 1989.

Logical Synergies?

With the huge profit reversal in 1989 after all the years of acquisition and internal development, analysts were questioning the existence of the "logical synergy" that Chandler, in his 1988 address to shareholders, claimed for Kodak's businesses. Certainly, the relative contributions of the various operating groups to Kodak's total sales differed from the past, and Kodak was somewhat less dependent on the photographic industry. But was Kodak positioned to compete successfully in the 1990s? What was the rationale for Kodak's entry into different businesses; what were the synergies that Chandler was talking about? Wasn't the improvement on profits in 1990 due to corporate restructuring to reduce costs?

CORPORATE RESTRUCTURING AND COST REDUCTION

As Chandler tackled changes in strategy, he also directed his efforts at reshaping Kodak's management style and organizational structure to (1) reduce costs and (2) make the organization more flexible and attuned to the competitive environment. Because of its dominance in the industry, in the past Kodak had not worried about outside competition. As a result, the organizational culture at Kodak emphasized traditional, conservative values rather than entrepreneurial values. Kodak was often described as a conservative, plodding monolith because all decision making had been centralized at the top of the organization among a clique of senior managers. Furthermore, the company had been operating along functional lines. Research, production, and sales and marketing had operated separately in different divisions. The result of all these factors was a lack of communication and slow, inflexible decision making that led to delays in making new product decisions. When the company attempted to transfer resources between divi-

sions, the separate functional operations also led to poor interdivisional relations, for managers protected their own turf at the expense of corporate goals. Moreover, there was a lack of attention to the bottom line, and management failed to institute measures to control waste.

Another factor encouraging Kodak's conservative orientation was its promotion policy. Seniority and loyalty to "mother Kodak" counted nearly as much as ability when it came to promotions. The company had been led by only twelve presidents since its beginnings in the 1880s.[19] Long after George Eastman's suicide in 1932, the company followed his cautious ways: "If George didn't do it, his successors didn't either."[20]

Kodak's technical orientation also contributed to its problems. Traditionally, its engineers and scientists had dominated decision making, and marketing had been neglected. The engineers and scientists were perfectionists who spent enormous amounts of time developing, analyzing, testing, assessing, and retesting new products. Little time, however, was spent determining whether the products satisfied consumer needs. As a result of this technical orientation, management passed up the invention of xerography, leaving the new technology to be developed by a small Rochester firm named Haloid Company (later Xerox). Similarly, Kodak had passed up the instant camera business. Kodak's lack of a marketing orientation allowed competitors to overtake it in several areas that were natural extensions of the photography business, such as 35mm cameras and video recorders.

Kodak's early management style, while profitable throughout the 1960s because of the company's privileged competitive position, was thus creating difficulties. With its monopoly in the photographic film and paper industry gone, Kodak was in trouble. Chandler had to alter Kodak's management orientation. He began with some radical changes in the company's culture and structure.

Firmly committed to cost cutting, Chandler orchestrated a massive downsizing of the work force to eliminate the fat that had accumulated during Kodak's prosperous past. Traditionally, Kodak had prided itself on being one of the most "Japanese" of all U.S. companies, hiring college graduates and giving them a permanent career. Now it had to go against one of its founding principles and reduce its work force. Kodak's policy of lifetime employment was swept out the door when declining profitability led to a large employee layoff.[21] Chandler instituted a special early retirement program, froze pay raises, and ordered the company's first layoffs in more than a decade. By 1985, the "yellow box factory" had dropped 12,600 of its original 136,000 employees. To further reduce costs in 1986, divisions were required to cut employment by an additional 10 percent and to cut budgetary expenditures by 5 percent. These measures helped, but because of Kodak's deteriorating performance, new rounds of cost cutting came in 1988 and 1989. Additional 5 percent reductions in employment aimed at saving $1 billion. The effect of these huge cuts was seen in 1990 when profits rebounded; however, it was not clear whether their effect on earnings would be short run or long run.

Although these measures had an effect on Kodak's culture, Chandler still needed to reshape Kodak's structure. In 1985 he began by shedding the old, stratified corporate structure for what he called an "entrepreneurial" approach. The first step was to reorganize the imaging group into seventeen operating units. Each of the seventeen line-of-business units now contains all the functions necessary for the success of the enterprise, including marketing, financial, planning, product development, and manufacturing. Each unit is treated as an independent profit center and managed by a young executive with authority over everything from design to production. All units have a common goal of improving quality and efficiency and eliminating problems in the transfer of resources and technology among operating groups. The purpose behind this change was to eliminate the old divisional orientation, which had led to competition and reduced integration within the company. Chandler hoped that the changes in organizational control and structure would promote innovation, speed reaction time, and establish clear profit goals.[22] With this restructuring, Chandler also reduced Kodak's top-heavy management in order to decentralize decision making to lower levels in the hierarchy. This reorganization was a sign that the company was at last shedding its paternalistic approach to management.[23]

In further attempts to bring costs more into line with those of foreign competitors who benefit from lower wage rates, favored government treatment, and currency advantages, Kodak instituted new control systems. In February 1986, operating groups were directed to reduce operating and expense budgets. In the move to maintain quality while keeping costs low, manufacturing plants have introduced stringent specifications that have improved both quality and efficiency. To compete effectively in a global marketplace, Kodak uses quality as the yardstick to measure its success.[24]

Relying on its new risk-taking attitude, Kodak also attempted to create a structure and culture to encourage internal venturing. It formed a "venture board" to help underwrite small projects and make conventional venture capital investments. In addition, the company created an "office of submitted ideas" to screen outside projects. Kodak received more than 3,000 proposals, although only 30 survived the screening process.[25] This aggressive research program led to a breakthrough in tubular silver halide grains, which improve the light-gathering capability of film. The discovery resulted in the new line of 35mm products.

However, Kodak's attempts to intrapreneurship have generally been unsuccessful. Of the fourteen ventures that Kodak created, six have been shut down, three have been sold, and four have been merged into the company; only one still operates independently.[26] One reason for this failure was that Kodak did not give managers an equity stake in the new ventures, so they felt that they had no stake in the ventures' success.

Having learned its lesson, Kodak announced that throughout the company pay would be more closely related to performance. For example, in 1989 as much as 40 percent of a manager's annual compensation was to be based on corporate performance. Even at the middle-manager level, 15 percent of compensation was to be linked to company results. Finally, at the level of wages, Kodak announced that it would link dividends paid to ordinary workers to the company's return on assets. It hopes by these measures to make the company more entrepreneurial and to move it along the cost reduction path. However, cost cutting will not be enough to turn Kodak around if its businesses do not generate increased revenues and achieve their profit potential.

Kodak also reorganized its worldwide facilities to reduce costs. International divisions were turning out identical products at higher cost than their counterparts in the United States. In a plan to coordinate worldwide production to increase productivity and lower costs, Kodak streamlined European production by closing duplicate manufacturing facilities and centralizing production and marketing operations, and it also brought some foreign manufacturing home. As a result, Kodak gained $55 million in productivity savings. However, the rise of the dollar boosted the cost of export products to foreign customers; thus, export expenses offset most of the gains.[27] Now that the dollar has fallen, these problems have been reversed, and profits from foreign operations are helping Kodak's earning figures as Kodak's international operations have regained their profitability. However, Fuji's new European facility will pose a severe challenge. Starting from scratch and employing production techniques learned from low-cost Japanese operations, Fuji will squeeze Kodak's profit margins and cause further changes in its European operations. In 1989, Kodak moved its international headquarters to London to decentralize authority to managers on the spot.

KODAK'S FUTURE

Whether Kodak has succeeded in its efforts to reorganize its strategy and structure has yet to be seen. Some analysts, pointing to the recent upswing in profits, are confident that the changes already made will restore Kodak's profitability. Others think that Kodak has done too little too late, that it has not achieved a clear rationale for its pattern of acquisitions, and that it still has many problems to deal with. They claim that Kay Whitmore needs to take a close look at Kodak's acquisitions and decide whether mistakes have been made and, if necessary, to divest acquisitions. On the other hand, given the investment in Sterling Drug and in other product lines, Whitmore needs to consider whether Kodak should make additional acquisitions to strengthen its stake in these new businesses so that it can deal with the fierce competition in the new product markets. Are there synergies to be achieved between operating groups? If there are, is the right structure in place to achieve them?

Kodak faces challenges in managing its new businesses. Given the failure of its intrapreneurship program, managing these ventures with a new entrepreneurial style rather than through the centralized, conservative approach of the past will not be easy. Already, difficulties have crept in. One example is Kodak's managing of Atex Inc., the manufacturer of desk-top publishing systems that Kodak bought in 1981. Because of Kodak's overbearing management style, the top executives and employees of Atex resigned, creating serious management problems for Kodak. The Atex executives claimed that Kodak executives were hard working but bureaucratic and did not understand the competitive nature of computer technology. Kodak managers should have been reacting to the computer marketplace weekly. They did not, and Atex executives could not handle Kodak's slow pace.[28]

What effects the reorganization of Kodak into four operating groups will have on performance remains to be seen. Even with reorganization, however, Kodak has moved into some uncertain environments in which the company has little experience and faces formidable rivals. Kodak faces competition from RCA and GE in consumer electronics, IBM and DEC in office systems. It must combat foreign competition from Fuji, Konica, Nikon, Canon, and Minolta in still cameras and copiers. It has already lost the battle with Matsushita, Sony, and Toshiba in video cameras and recorders and videotapes. Kodak also has the problem that entry into new businesses means lower profit margins. Ventures such as electronic imaging, magnetic tape, and floppy disks were in highly competitive industries that traditionally have lower profit margins than does chemical photography. Besides, new businesses are very expensive to enter, and Kodak's long-term earnings are heavily dependent on the future growth of these industries and on its ability to profit from this growth.

Venturing into the volatile biotechnology, pharmaceuticals, and office information systems business was obviously a gamble. However, Kodak had little choice because its existing business in mature and amateur and professional photography was a saturated market. Nevertheless, some analysts claim that Kodak should have stayed inside the imaging business and kept its activities closely aligned to its core skills. They argue that Kodak is still a one-business company and that its recent activities only disguise that fact. Indeed, they view the whole acquisition process over the last ten years as a way of fending off takeover attempts by companies competing for Kodak's huge cash flow. In 1990, they pointed to Kodak's creation of "tin parachutes" as yet one more way in which the company is fighting to maintain its independence. In the event of a takeover, Kodak has guaranteed all its employees large severance pay and other benefits. This plan makes Kodak a very expensive takeover target. Whether a takeover will occur depends on the outcome of the litigation with Polaroid. The amount of the settlement has yet to be announced. As soon as it is, analysts claim that takeover is a distinct possibility. Already a friendly takeover of Kodak by the Walt Disney Company has been suggested because of their fifteen-year marketing agreement. Would this add value to Kodak or to Disney? What should be done?

Can Kodak learn to play a different and tougher competitive game, or will it be taken over? The market has changed, and Kodak must play in businesses where it is no longer a worldwide leader and where it has neither a technological advantage nor a significant cost advantage. The question now is whether Kodak's moves under Whitmore can make Chandler's acquisition strategy bear fruit and whether Kodak can manage its new strategy and structure to fight off a takeover attempt. Financially, Kodak is still one of the top twenty-five U.S. companies. It is financially sound, with total assets of $25 billion. Kodak's brand name is also a major asset: it is one of the most recognized in the world. Can Kodak utilize these assets in the new competitive environment, or is it too late?

Endnotes

1. "Eastman Kodak Co.," *Moody's Industrial Manual,* 1 (1986), 3016.
2. Thomas Moore, "Embattled Kodak Enters the Electronic age," *Fortune,* August 22, 1983, pp. 120–128.
3. "Kodak's New Lean and Hungry Look," *Business Week,* May 30, 1983, p. 33.
4. Charles K. Ryan, *Eastman Kodak, Company Outline,* Merrill Lynch, Pierce, Fenner & Smith Incorporated, May 7, 1986.
5. Press release, Eastman Kodak Company, July 15, 1991.
6. John Greenwald, "Aiming for a Brighter Picture," *Time,* January 9, 1984, p. 49.
7. Barbara Buell, "Kodak Is Trying to Break Out of Its Shell," *Business Week,* June 10, 1985, pp. 92–95.
8. Eastman Kodak Company, *Kodak Highlights, First Quarter,* 1988, p. 7.
9. Taylor, "Kodak Scrambles," pp. 34–38.
10. Eastman Kodak Company, Annual Report, 1989.
11. Taylor, "Kodak Scrambles," pp. 34–38.
12. Eastman Kodak Company, *Kodak Highlights, Third Quarter,* 1988, p. 9.
13. Eastman Kodak Company, Annual Report, 1985, p. 5.
14. Barbara Buell, "Kodak Scrambles to Fill the Gap," *Business Week,* February 8, 1986, p. 30.
15. "Kodak's New Image: Electronic Imaging," *Electron Business,* January 1986, 38–43.
16. Eastman Kodak Company, Annual Report, 1986, p. 24.
17. Eastman Kodak Company, *Kodak Highlights, Third Quarter,* 1988, p. 5.
18. Eastman Kodak Company, Annual Report, 1986, p. 19.
19. Barbara Buell, "A Gust of Fresh Air for the Stodgy Giant of Rochester," *Business Week,* June 10, 1985, p. 93.
20. Moore, "Embattled Kodak," p. 120.
21. Buell, "A Gust of Fresh Air," p. 93.
22. Ibid.
23. "Yellow at the Edges," *Economist,* December 7, 1984, p. 90.
24. Eastman Kodak Company, Annual Report, 1985, p. 12.
25. Taylor, "Kodak Scrambles," pp. 34–38.
26. James S. Hirsch, "Kodak Effort at 'Intrapreneurship' Fails," *Wall Street Journal,* August 17, 1990, p. 32.
27. Eastman Kodak Company, Annual Report, 1985.
28. Moore, "Embattled Kodak," pp. 120–128.

CASE 29

Hanson PLC (A): The Acquisition Machine

This case was prepared by Charles W. L. Hill of the University of Washington.

INTRODUCTION

Hanson PLC is one of the ten biggest companies in Britain, and its U.S. arm, Hanson Industries, is one of America's sixty largest industrial concerns. A conglomerate with more than 150 different businesses in its portfolio, Hanson PLC has grown primarily by making acquisitions. By the end of 1989, the company had recorded twenty-six years of uninterrupted profit growth, cumulating in 1989 operating income of $1.61 billion on revenues of $11.3 billion and assets of $12.03 billion. The company's shareholders have been major beneficiaries of this growth. Between 1974 and 1989, the price of the company's shares on the London Stock Exchange increased eightyfold, compared with an average increase of fifteenfold for all companies quoted on the London Stock Exchange during this period.[1] Along the way, Hanson has gained a reputation for being one of the most successful takeover machines in the world. Its acquisitions during the 1980s included three American conglomerates (U.S. Industries, SCM Corporation, and Kidde) and three major British companies (London Brick, the Imperial Group, and Consolidated Gold Fields). So high is Hanson's profile that Oliver Stone, in his film *Wall Street,* reportedly used Sir Gordon White, head of Hanson Industries, as the model for the British corporate raider (the one who outmaneuvered the evil Gordon Gekko).

This case is intended to be used as a basis for class discussion rather than as an illustration of either effective or ineffective handling of the situation. This case was prepared by Charles W. L. Hill, University of Washington. Used by permission.

Despite this impressive track record, as Hanson enters the 1990s analysts increasingly wonder about the strategy of the company. There is speculation that the company may be on the verge of breaking itself up and returning the gains to shareholders. The age of the company's founders is fueling this speculation. The two men who built and still run the conglomerate, Lord Hanson and Sir Gordon White, are in their late sixties, and both have promised to consider retiring when they are seventy. As one insider put it, "The guys that started it off will finish it off."[2] Another factor is that Hanson is now so big that it would take some spectacular deals to continue its historic growth rate. According to many, including Harvard Business School strategy guru Michael Porter, there simply are not that many obvious companies for Hanson to buy. Thus, "even Hanson will be faced with poorer and poorer odds of maintaining its record."[3] On the other hand, at the end of 1989 Hanson had $8.5 billion in cash on its balance sheet. That, along with the billions it could borrow if need be (the company reportedly has a borrowing capacity of $20 billion), suggests that if Hanson and White should so wish, they could undertake an acquisition that would rival the RJR-Nabisco deal in size.

Other commentators question the long-term viability of the company. Some claim that Hanson PLC is little more than an asset stripper that in the long run will drive the companies it manages into the ground. According to one investment banker, "I'm not convinced that Hanson runs companies any better than anyone else. But I certainly know it squeezes them for cash, sucking the life from them."[4] Similarly, one former executive noted that "some of the incentive programs that they write for managers actually keep the company from growing. . . . They become so concerned with profit today that they don't re-invest for tomorrow."[5] The company disagrees. Sir Gordon White clearly sees Hanson PLC as reducing inefficiencies in the companies it acquires, not stripping assets. If anything is stripped away from acquisitions, according to White, it is unnecessary corporate bureaucracy, overstaffed head offices, and top-management perks, not assets. He steadfastly maintains that the company treats all acquired businesses as if it were going to keep them.[6]

With these issues in mind, in this case we consider the growth and development of Hanson PLC. We review the administrative systems that the company uses to manage its ongoing businesses, and we look at two acquisitions and their aftermath in depth: the 1987 acquisitions of SCM Corporation and the Imperial Group.

HISTORY

The origins of Hanson PLC go back to the port city of Hull in Yorkshire, England, in the 1950s.[7] At that time, James Hanson was learning his family's transportation business (the family operated a fleet of passenger coaches), and Gordon White was selling advertising for Welbecson Limited, a magazine printing company owned by his father. James Hanson's brother, Bill, was White's closest friend, and when Bill died of cancer at twenty-nine, James and Gordon became close friends. In the late 1950s, Hanson and White decided to team up in business. They formed Hanson White Ltd., a greeting card company. Although the company did well, the two soon became bored with the limited challenges and potential that the greeting card business offered, and in 1963 they sold out and began to look for acquisition opportunities.

Their first buy was Oswald Tillotson Ltd., a vehicle distribution company. This company was subsequently acquired by Wiles Group Ltd., a Yorkshire-based manufacturer of agricultural sacks and fertilizers. As part of the takeover deal, Hanson and White were given a substantial ownership position in the Wiles Group. Hanson and White soon gained management control of the Wiles Group, and in 1969, after deciding that James Hanson's name had a nicer ring to it than Gordon White's, they changed the name to Hanson Trust. Because of a series of small acquisitions, by the end of 1973 Hanson Trust owned twenty-four companies with combined sales of $120 million.

By 1973, however, the British economy was in deep trouble. The stock market had collapsed; the country was paralyzed by labor disputes; inflation was increasing rapidly, as was unemployment; and Prime Minister Edward Heath of the supposedly probusiness Conservative party had blasted conglomerate companies such as Hanson Trust as representing "the unacceptable face of capitalism." All of this prompted Gordon White to rethink his future. As White put it,

> I was disgusted with England at the time. Disgusted with socialism and unions and excessive, antibusiness government, disgusted with the way initiative was being taxed out of existence. . . . I'd done a lot of thinking. I told James (Hanson) that maybe we should just call it a day. I thought I'd try America.[8]

Hanson replied that there was no need to split up, and they agreed that Hanson would run the British operations while White tried to build operations in America.

White arrived in New York in the fall of 1973 in possession of a round-trip ticket, a one-year work visa, and $3,000 in traveler's checks, which was the most that British currency controls permitted a U.K. citizen to take abroad at that time. Moreover, because of British exchange controls, White could not gain access to Hanson's ample treasury without substantial penalties, and he had to struggle to convince banks that he was creditworthy. Despite this, in 1974 White managed to borrow $32 million from Chemical Bank to finance his first major U.S. acquisition, a friendly takeover of J. Howard Smith Company, a New Jersey-based processor of edible oils and animal feed that was later renamed Seacoast Products. The CEO of J. Howard Smith was David Clarke, whose family business it was. Clarke subsequently became White's right-hand man. He is now president of Hanson Industries and the most senior executive in the United States after White.

Over the next ten years, White made another six major U.S. acquisitions, all of them friendly (see Table 1). Then, in 1984, White was ready for his first hostile takeover, the $532-million purchase of U.S. Industries (USI). USI was a conglomerate that had grown by acquisitions during the 1960s and 1970s.

TABLE 1

U.S. Acquisitions, 1974–1990

Date	Acquisition	Cost (millions)	Businesses
1974	Seacost	$ 32	Fish processing, pet food
1975	Carisbrook	36	Textile manufacturing
1976	Hygrade	32	Castings and casing units
1977	Old Salt Seafood	2	Prepared foods
1978	Interstate United	30	Food service management
1978	Templon	7	Textile manufacturing
1981	McDonough	185	Cement, concrete
1984	U.S. Industries	532	33-company conglomerate
1986	SCM	930	22-company conglomerate
1987	Kaiser Cement	250	Cement plants
1988	Kidde	1,700	108-company conglomerate
1990	Peabody	1,230	Coal mining

Source: Adapted from Gordon White, "How I Turned $3,000 into $10 Billion," *Fortune,* November 7, 1988, pp. 80–89; and "Hanson PLC," *Value Line,* July 20, 1990, p. 832.

White became interested in the company when he read in a newspaper that management was putting together a leveraged buyout at $20 a share for a total purchase price of $445 million. He suspected that the company was worth more than that and quickly worked out how big a loan Hanson Industries could handle, using USI's projected cash flow to cover interest charges. To USI's pretax earnings of $67 million he added $40 million generated by depreciation and $24 million in savings that he thought Hanson could effect by removing USI's corporate headquarters. That yielded a total cash flow of $131 million, or more than $70 million after taxes. With interest rates running at 13 percent, White figured that Hanson Industries could afford a loan of $544 million. In what was to become standard White thinking, he also reckoned that even with a worst-case scenario, he could recoup his investment by selling off the disparate pieces of the company.

Hanson Industries began to buy USI shares and by April 1984 held 5 percent of the company. Hanson then made a $19 per share bid for the company, which was quickly rebuffed by USI management. Three days later White increased Hanson's bid to $22 per share. USI's management, which had yet to raise the financing for its own proposed leveraged buyout, responded by increasing the purchase price to $24 per share. Hanson responded by initiating a tender offer of $23 per share in cash. For stockholders, cash in hand at $23 per share was far more attractive than management's promise of $24 per share if financing could be arranged, and Hanson's bid quickly won the day.

After the acquisition was completed, Hanson Industries President David Clarke spent six months at USI's corporate headquarters reviewing operations. At the end of this period USI's corporate headquarters was closed down, the staff was laid off, and financial control was centralized at Hanson Industries' small headquarters. However, most of the operating managers in charge of USI's constituent companies stayed on, lured by Hanson's incentive pay scheme and the promise that they could run their own shows. In what was also typical Hanson fashion, nine of USI's operating companies were subsequently sold off to outside investors for a price of $225 million.

The acquisition of USI was followed by three other hostile takeover bids in the United States: for SCM Corporation, Kaiser Cement, and Kidde. Of these, the SCM bid was by far the most acrimonious. SCM took a poison pill and tried to protect

TABLE 2

U.K. Acquisitions During the 1980s

Date	Acquisition	Cost (millions)	Businesses
1981	Ever Ready	£95	Dry cell batteries
1983	UDS	£250	Retail operations
1984	London Brick	£247	Brick manufacturer
1984	Powell Duffryn	£150	Engineering, shipping, fuel
1986	Imperial Group	£2,500	Tobacco, brewing, food
1989	Consolidated Gold Fields	£3,610	Gold mining, building aggregates

Source: Various press reports.

its position through the law courts before Hanson finally won control over the company. (The SCM takeover is discussed in detail later in this case.)

While White was making these U.S. acquisitions, Hanson was not sitting idle in Britain. During the 1980s the company made a series of acquisitions in the United Kingdom. These are summarized in Table 2. The most notable were the 1983 acquisition of London Brick, Britain's largest brick manufacturer, against vigorous opposition from London Brick's incumbent management; the £2.36-billion acquisition of Imperial, the largest tobacco company in Britain and the third largest in the world; and the £3.61-billion acquisition of Consolidated Gold Fields, the second largest gold-mining business in the world. The acquisitions of Imperial and Consolidated Gold Fields were the two largest takeovers ever undertaken in Britain. (The Imperial takeover is discussed in detail later in this case.)

ACQUISITIONS PHILOSOPHY

Hanson PLC's acquisitions on both sides of the Atlantic are primarily overseen by Sir Gordon White. Lord Hanson is primarily responsible for the ongoing administration of the company. As Lord Hanson says of White, "He's the one with the gift for takeovers."[9] In turn, White says of Hanson, "James is a brilliant administrator and really knows how to run

a company."[10] White claims that many of his acquisition ideas, including the USI deal, come from the newspapers. Others are suggested to him by contacts in the investment banking community, particularly Bob Pirie, president of the Rothschild investment bank, with whom White has lunch once a week.

Whenever possible, White avoids working at the office, opting instead to work from one of his four houses. Unlike corporate raiders such as Saul Steinberg and Carl Icahn, White rarely reads annual reports or detailed stock reports on a target company, claiming that he can get all of the financial information that he needs from Standard & Poor's two-page summaries. In addition, his three-person takeover staff distills reams of financial data on a target and provides him with a short memo on the target company. Says White, "I'm like Churchill, tell me everything you can tell me. On one page."[11]

Under White's leadership, one of the things that has distinguished Hanson PLC from many other acquisitive conglomerates is its distinctive acquisitions philosophy (which is, in essence, White's philosophy). This philosophy appears to be based on a number of consistent factors that are found to underlie most of Hanson's acquisitions.[12]

1. *Target characteristics.* Hanson looks for companies based in mature, low-technology industries that have a less-than-inspiring record but show potential for improving performance.

Normally, the objective has been to identify a poorly performing target where the incumbent management team has gone some way toward improving the underlying performance but whose efforts have not yet been reflected in either the profit-and-loss account or, more importantly, the target's stock price.

2. *Research.* Although White claims that he does little reading on takeover targets, his takeover staff does undertake detailed research into the potential of target companies before any bid is made. The staff routinely investigates companies undertaking leveraged buyouts.

3. *Risk assessment.* One of White's most often quoted edicts is "watch the downside." What this means is that instead of considering the potential benefits of a deal, give consideration to what can go wrong and the likely consequences of a worst-case scenario. White will purchase a company only if he thinks that in a worst-case scenario he will be able to recover the purchase price by breaking the target up and selling off its constituent parts.

4. *Funding.* White was one of the early pioneers of the highly leveraged takeover deal. All of the U.S. acquisitions have been financed by nonrecourse debt, secured on the assets of the target. This enabled White to engineer substantial acquisitions when Hanson Industries itself had a very small capital base. The British acquisitions have been funded by a mix of cash, equity, convertible securities, and loan stock.

5. *Disposals to reduce debt.* After an acquisition has been completed, Hanson sends some of its own managers along with a group of external accountants to go through and audit the acquired businesses. After a thorough review, Hanson typically sells off the parts of the acquired company that cannot reach Hanson's stringent profitability targets. In the process, Hanson is able to reduce the debt taken on to fund the acquisition. The most outstanding example followed the purchase of SCM for $930 million. After the takeover, Hanson sold off SCM's real estate, pulp and paper, and food holdings for a price of $964 million while holding on to SCM's typewriter and chemicals business, which in effect had been acquired for nothing. Thus, within six months of the takeover's being completed, Hanson was able to eliminate the debt taken on to finance the SCM acquisition. Similar, although less spectacular, disposals have characterized almost all of Hanson's major acquisitions on both sides of the Atlantic.

6. *Elimination of excess overhead.* Another objective of Hanson's housecleaning of acquired companies is to eliminate any excess overhead. This typically involves closing down the corporate headquarters of the acquired company, eliminating some of the staff, and sending other staff down to the operating level. Before Hanson took over, SCM had 230 people in its corporate office, USI had 180, Kidde had 200, and Hanson itself had 30. Today the total headquarters staff for all four is 120.

Hanson also disposes of any management perks found either at the corporate or the operating level of an acquired company. For example, one of Kidde's operating companies had a collection of art and antiques, a hunting lodge, and three corporate jets. Hanson kept one jet and disposed of the rest, including the man at the top who had spent the money.

7. *The creation of incentives.* Hanson tries to create strong incentives for the management of acquired operating companies to improve performance. This is achieved by (a) decentralization designed to give operating managers full autonomy for the running of their businesses, (b) motivating operating managers by setting profit targets that, if achieved, will result in significant profit enhancements, and (c) motivating managers by giving them large pay bonuses if they hit or exceed Hanson's profit targets.

ORGANIZATION AND MANAGEMENT PHILOSOPHY

In addition to its acquisitions philosophy, Hanson is also renowned for its ongoing management of operating companies, of which there are more than 150 in the corporate portfolio. Although Hanson does have some interests elsewhere, the strategic development of the group has centered on the United States and Britain, where a broad balance has tended to exist in recent years. Hanson PLC looks after the British operations, and Hanson Industries, the U.S. subsidiary, manages the U.S. operations. Each of these two units is operated on an entirely autonomous basis. Only one director sits on the board of both companies. Hanson PLC is headed by Hanson; Hanson Industries is headed by White.[13]

There are two corporate headquarters, one in the United States and one in Britain. At both locations there is a small central staff responsible for monitoring the performance of operating companies, selecting and motivating operating management, the treasury function (including acting as a central bank for the operating units), acquisitions and disposals, and professional services such as legal and taxation.

Below each headquarters are a number of divisions (see Figure 1). These are not operating companies. Rather, they are groupings of operating companies. In 1988 there were four U.S. divisions (consumer, building products, industrial, and food) and four British divisions (again, consumer, building

products, industrial, and food). There are no personnel at the divisional level with the exception of a divisional CEO. Below the divisions are the operating companies. Each operating company has its own CEO who reports to the divisional CEO. The divisional CEOs in Britain are responsible to Lord Hanson; those in the United States are responsible to David Clarke, White's right-hand man. White himself is primarily concerned with acquisitions and leaves most issues of control to David Clarke. Indeed, White claims that he has never visited Hanson Industries' U.S. corporate headquarters and as a matter of policy never visits operating companies.[14]

The following principles seem to characterize Hanson's management philosophy.

■ *Decentralization.* All day-to-day operating decisions are decentralized to operating company

FIGURE I

Hanson PLC Organizational Structure

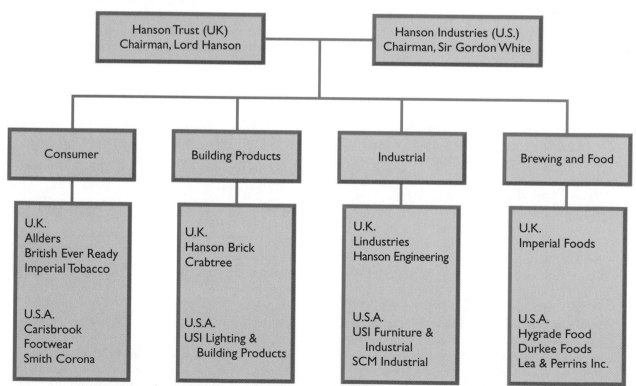

Source: Hanson Industries, Annual Report, 1986.

managers. The corporate center does not offer suggestions about how to manufacture or market a product. Thus, within the limits set by centrally approved operating budgets and capital expenditures, operating management has unlimited autonomy. As a consequence, operating managers are responsible for the return on capital that they employ.

■ *Tight financial control.* Financial control is achieved through two devices: (1) operating budgets and (2) capital expenditure policies. In a bottom-up process, operating budgets are submitted annually to the corporate center by operating company managers. The budgets include detailed performance targets, particularly with regard to return on capital employed (ROK). Corporate staff reviews the budgets and, after consultation with operating management, approves a budget for the coming year. Once agreed upon, the operating budget becomes gospel. The performance of an operating company is compared against budget on a monthly basis, and any variance is investigated by the corporate center. If an operating company betters its projected ROK, the figure used as the base for the next year's budget is the actual ROK, not the budgeted figure.

Any cash generated by an operating company is viewed as belonging to the corporate center, not to the operating company. Capital expenditures are extremely closely monitored. All cash expenditures in excess of $3,000 (£1,000 in Britain) have to be agreed upon by corporate headquarters. Capital expenditure requests are frequently challenged by headquarters staff. For example, a manager who contends that an investment in more efficient machinery will cut labor costs must even provide the names of the employees that he or she expects to lay off to achieve the savings. According to company insiders, when justifying a request for capital expenditure, a manager must explain every possibility. In general, Hanson looks for a pretax payback on expenditures of three years. The quicker the payback, the more likely it is that an expenditure will be approved.

■ *Incentive systems.* A major element of the pay of operating managers is linked directly to operating company performance. A manager can earn up to 60 percent of his or her base salary if the operating company exceeds the ROK tar-

get detailed in its annual budget. Bonuses are based strictly on bottom-line performance. As White puts it, "There are no bonuses for being a nice chap."[15] In addition, there is a share option scheme for the most senior operating company and corporate managers. More than 600 managers are members of the option scheme. The options are not exercisable for at least three years after they have been granted.

■ *Board structure.* No operating company managers are ever appointed to the board of either Hanson PLC or Hanson Industries. The idea is to eliminate any conflicts of interest that might arise over budgets and capital expenditures.

■ *De-emphasizing operating synergy.* In contrast to many diversified companies, Hanson has no interest in trying to realize operating synergy. For example, two of Hanson PLC's subsidiaries, Imperial Tobacco and Elizabeth Shaw (a chocolate firm), are based in Bristol, England, and both deliver goods to news agents and corner shops around Britain. However, Hanson prohibits them from sharing distribution because it reckons that any economies of scale that result would be outweighed by the inefficiencies that would arise if each operating company could blame the other for distribution problems.

THE SCM ACQUISITION

SCM was a diversified manufacturer of consumer and industrial products. SCM had twenty-two operating companies based in five industries: chemicals, coatings and resins, paper and pulp, foods, and typewriters.[16] Among other things, SCM was the world's leading manufacturer of portable typewriters (Smith-Corona typewriters), the world's third largest producer of titanium dioxide (a white inorganic pigment widely used in the manufacture of paint, paper, plastic, and rubber products), the sixth largest paint manufacturer in the world through its Glidden Paints subsidiary, and a major force in the U.S. food industry through its Durkee Famous Foods group (see Table 3).

Attractions to Hanson

The SCM group was first brought to White's attention by Bob Pirie, president of Rothschild Inc. in New York. Pirie thought, and Hanson's research

TABLE 3

SCM Divisional Results for the Year Ended June 1985

| Division | Revenues | | Profits | |
	$m	Percentage of Change from 1984	$m	Percentage of Change from 1984
Chemicals	$539.0	+49%	$73.7	−100%
Coatings and resins	687.0	+5%	49.9	−3%
Paper and pulp	362.0	+3%	23.1	+10%
Foods	422.0	+7%	23.0	+35%
Typewriters	176.0	−11%	(47.4)*	−200%

*Loss after a $35 million charge for restructuring.
Source: Data from Hanson Industries, Annual Report, 1986.

team soon confirmed, that SCM had a number of characteristics that made it a perfect Hanson buy.

1. *Poor financial performance.* Summary financial data for SCM are given in Table 4. Pretax profit had declined from a peak of $83.2 million in 1980 to $54.1 million in 1985. The 1985 return on equity of 7.7 percent was very poor by Hanson's standards, and earnings per share had declined by 19 percent since 1980.
2. *Beginnings of a turnaround.* There were signs that incumbent management was coming to grips with SCM's problems, particularly in the troubled typewriter operation, where the

1985 loss was due to a one-time charge of $39 million for restructuring. Financial performance had improved since the low point in 1983, but the benefits of this improvement were not yet reflected in the company's stock price.
3. *Mature businesses.* SCM's presence in mature, proven markets that were technologically stable fit White's preferences.
4. *Low risk.* Some 50 percent of SCM's turnover covered products well known to the U.S. consumer (for example, Smith-Corona typewriters, Glidden paint, Durkee foods). White felt that there would be a ready market for such highly

TABLE 4

Financial Data for SCM

	1980	1981	1982	1983	1984	1985
Net sales ($m)	$1,745.0	$1,761.0	$1,703.0	$1,663.0	$1,963.0	$2,175.0
Pretax profits ($m)	83.2	72.6	35.3	37.8	64.8	54.1
Earnings per share ($)—fully diluted	$4.76	$5.01	$3.20	$2.63	$4.05	$3.85
Return on equity	12.40%	12.00%	5.80%	4.90%	8.00%	7.70%

Source: Data from Hanson Industries, Annual Report, 1986.

branded businesses if Hanson decided to dispose of any companies that did not meet its stringent ROK requirements.

5. *Titanium dioxide.* Titanium dioxide was dominated by a global oligopoly. Hanson was aware of two favorable trends in the industry that made high returns likely: (a) worldwide demand was forecasted to exceed supply for the next few years, and (b) input costs were declining because of the currency weakness of the major raw material source, Australia.

6. *Corporate overhead.* A corporate staff of 230 indicated to White that SCM was "a lumbering old top-heavy conglomerate with a huge corporate overhead that was draining earnings."[17] He envisioned substantial savings from the elimination of this overhead.

The Takeover Battle

After reviewing the situation, in early August White decided to acquire SCM. He began to buy stock, and on August 21 Hanson Industries formally made a $60 per share tender offer for SCM, valuing the company at $740 million. SCM's top management team responded on August 30 with its own offer to shareholders in the form of a proposed leveraged buyout of SCM. SCM's management had arranged financing from its investment banker Merrill Lynch and offered shareholders $70 per share. On September 4 White responded by raising Hanson's offer to $72 per share.

SCM's management responded to White's second offer by increasing its own offer to $74 per share. To discourage White from making another bid, SCM's management gave Merrill Lynch a "lock-up" option to buy Durkee Famous Foods and SCM Chemicals (the titanium dioxide division) at a substantial discount should Hanson or another outsider gain control. In effect, SCM's management had agreed to give its crown jewels to Merrill Lynch for less than their market value if Hanson won the bidding war.

White's next move was to apparently throw in the towel by announcing withdrawal of Hanson's tender offer. However, in contrast to normal practice on Wall Street, White went into the market and quickly purchased some 25 percent of SCM's stock at a fixed price of $73.5 per share, taking Hanson's stake to 27 percent. Furious at this break with convention, SCM's lawyers drafted a lawsuit against Hanson charging that White's tactics violated ten-

der-offer regulations and demanding a restraining order prohibiting Hanson from making any further market purchases. Hanson quickly filed a countersuit, claiming that Merrill Lynch's lock-up option to buy the two SCM divisions illegally prevented the shareholders from getting the best price.

Hanson lost both suits in federal court in New York. White immediately appealed and on September 30 a U.S. court of appeals ruled in Hanson's favor. This, however, was not to be the end of the matter. On October 7 Hanson spent another $40 million to increase its stake in SCM to 33 percent, thereby effectively stalling the leveraged buyout plan, which needed approval by two-thirds of the shareholders. The following day Hanson revised its tender offer to an all-cash $75 per share offer, subject to SCM's dropping the "lock-up" option because the option had been triggered by Hanson's acquiring 33 percent of SCM.

Hanson's next move, on October 10, was to file a suit to prevent Merrill Lynch from exercising the right to buy SCM's crown jewels. On October 15 it followed this with a second suit against Merrill Lynch for conspiracy. A U.S. district court ruled on November 26 that the lock-up was legal and that Hanson had triggered its exercise by the size of its stake. Once again Hanson appealed to a higher court. On January 6, 1986, a U.S. court of appeals overturned the lower court ruling, granting to Hanson an injunction that prevented SCM from exercising the lock-up option. The following day Hanson Industries won control over SCM after further market purchases. The final purchase price was $930 million, which represented a price/earnings multiple of 11.5.

After the Acquisition

Having gained control of SCM, Hanson immediately set about trying to realize SCM's potential. Within three months, 250 employees were laid off, mostly headquarters staff, and the former SCM headquarters in New York was sold for $36 million in cash. At the same time, White and his team were using their new position as owners to thoroughly audit the affairs of SCM's operating companies. Their objective was to identify those businesses whose returns were adequate or could be improved upon and those businesses for which the outlook was such that they were unlikely to achieve Hanson's stringent ROK requirements.

At the end of this process, four businesses were sold off in as many months for a total amount that recouped for Hanson the original purchase price and left Hanson with the two best businesses in SCM's portfolio: Smith-Corona typewriters and the titanium dioxide business. In May 1986, SCM's paper and pulp operations were sold to Boise Cascade for $160 million in cash, a price that represented a price/earnings multiple of 29 and was 3 times book value. Hanson felt that the outlook for those operations was not good because of a depression in paper and pulp prices. Boise Cascade obviously thought otherwise. Shortly afterward, Sylvachem, part of SCM's chemicals division, was sold for $30 million, representing a price/earnings multiple of 18.5.

In August 1986 Glidden Paints was sold to the British chemical giant and Europe's largest paint manufacturer, Imperial Chemical Industries PLC (ICI) for $580 million. This represented a price/earnings multiple of 17.5 and was 2.5 times book value. The purchase of this operation enabled ICI to become the world's largest paint manufacturer. A few days later Durkee Famous Foods was sold to another British firm, Reckitt & Colman PLC, for $120 million in cash and the assumption of $20 million in debt. This represented a price/earnings multiple of 17 and was 3 times book value. This disposal served to withdraw Hanson from an area that was subject to uncontrollable and volatile commodity price movements. For Reckitt & Colman, however, which was already one of the largest manufacturers of branded food products outside the United States, it represented an important strategic addition.

The four disposals amounted to $926 million and were accomplished at an average price/earnings multiple of 19.5. Having recovered 100 percent of the purchase price paid for SCM within eight months, Hanson had effectively acquired for nothing a number of businesses that were projected to contribute around $140 million to net pretax profit for their first full year under Hanson's control.

Hanson retained the titanium dioxide business for two main reasons. First, with the industry operating at close to 100 percent capacity and with projections indicating an increase in demand through to 1989, prices and margins were expected to increase substantially. Although several companies had plans to expand global capacity, given the three- to four-year time lag in bringing new capacity on stream, this sellers' market was likely to persist for a while. Nor did it look as if the

additional capacity would outstrip the projected rise in demand. Second, two-thirds of world production of titanium dioxide is in the hands of global producers. SCM's business is ranked third with 12 percent of world capacity, behind Du Pont and Tioxide PLC. Given this oligopoly, orderly pricing in world markets seemed likely to continue.

Hanson also decided to retain SCM's typewriter business, despite the fact that in recent years it had been the worst-performing unit in SCM's portfolio. Hanson quickly realized that SCM management had in effect just completed a drastic overhaul of the typewriter businesses and that a dramatic turnaround was likely. In the two years prior to Hanson's acquisition, SCM's management had undertaken the following steps:

1. A new line of electronic typewriters had been introduced to match the increasingly sophisticated Japanese models.
2. Capacity had been reduced by 50 percent, and six U.S. production facilities had been consolidated into a single assembly plant and distribution center in New York to manufacture all electronic models.
3. As a result of automation, economies of scale, and labor agreements, productivity at the New York plant had increased fourfold since 1984, and unit labor costs had declined by 60 percent.
4. The manufacture of electric models had been moved offshore to a low-cost facility in Singapore.
5. Smith-Corona had just introduced the first personal word processor for use with a portable electronic typewriter, and it retailed at slightly less than $500.

As a result of these improvements, the Smith-Corona business seemed ready to become a major profit producer. Hanson forecasted profits of $30 million for this business during 1986–1987, compared with an operating loss of $47.4 million in financial year 1985.

THE IMPERIAL ACQUISITION

On December 6, 1985, while still engaged in the SCM acquisition, Hanson opened another takeover battle in Britain by announcing an offer of £1.5 billion for Imperial Group PLC.[18] Imperial Group was one of the ten largest firms in Britain. Imperial was

TABLE 5

Imperial Divisional Results for the Year Ended October 1985

Division	Revenues £m	Percentage of Change from 1984	Profits £m	Percentage of Change from 1984
Tobacco	£2,641	+7%	£123.1	+11%
Brewing and leisure	974	+8%	97.0	+20%
Foods	719	+4%	33.0	+5%
Howard Johnson	617	+11%	11.1	−40%

Source: Data from Hanson Industries, Annual Report, 1986.

Britain's leading tobacco manufacturer and the third largest tobacco company in the world. Its Courage Brewing subsidiary was one of the "big six" beer companies in Britain. Its leisure operations included 1,371 public houses (taverns), 120-plus restaurants, and more than 750 specialized retail shops. Imperial manufactured more than 1,000 branded food products. (See Table 5 for a breakdown of Imperial's divisional results.) In September 1985 Imperial had sold its fourth business, the U.S. motel chain Howard Johnson, to Marriott. Howard Johnson had been purchased in 1980 and was widely regarded as one of the worst acquisitions ever made by a major British company.

Attractions to Hanson

Hanson's interest in Imperial was prompted by the news on December 2, 1985, of a planned merger between Imperial and United Biscuits PLC, a major manufacturer of branded food products. The financial press perceived this measure as a defensive move by Imperial. However, despite its well-documented problems with Howard Johnson, Imperial's financial performance was reasonably strong (see Table 6). What factors made Imperial an attractive takeover target to Hanson? The following seem to have been important.

- *Mature business.* Like SCM's businesses, most of Imperial's businesses were based in mature, low-technology industries. There is little prospect of radically changing fashions or technological change in the tobacco, brewing, and food industries.

- *Low risk.* Most of Imperial's products had a high brand recognition within Britain. Thus, Hanson could easily dispose of those that did not stand up to Hanson's demanding ROK targets.

TABLE 6

Financial Data for Imperial

	1981	1982	1983	1984	1985
Revenues (£m)	£4,526	£4,614	£4,381	£4,593	£4,918
Pretax profits (£m)	106	154	195	221	236
Earnings per share (pence)	12.8	16.4	18.0	20.3	22.4
Return on capital (%)	12.7%	17.9%	20.4%	21.1%	18.1%

Source: Data from Hanson Industries, Annual Report, 1986.

■ *Tobacco cash flow.* Imperial's tobacco business was a classic cash cow. The company had 45 percent of the tobacco market and seven of the ten best-selling brands in 1985. Although tobacco sales are declining in Britain because of a combination of health concerns and punitive taxation, the decline has been gradual, amounting to 29 percent since the peak year of 1973. Given Hanson's emphasis on ROK and cash flow, this made Imperial particularly attractive to Hanson. Imperial had arguably squandered much of this cash flow by using it to underwrite unprofitable growth opportunities, particularly Howard Johnson.

■ *Failure of Imperial's diversification strategy.* Imperial's recent track record with respect to diversification was poor. In 1978 it bought a construction company, J. B. Eastward, for £40 million. After four years of trading losses, Eastward was sold in 1982 for a total loss of £54 million. In 1979 Imperial paid $640 million for Howard Johnson, the U.S. motel and restaurant chain. In 1985, after six years of declining profits, this business was sold for $341 million. These losses suggested a fundamental weakness in Imperial's top management in an area in which Hanson was strong: diversification strategy. Moreover, the failure of Imperial's diversification strategy probably resulted in Imperial's shares being discounted by the stock market.

■ *Inadequate returns in brewing and leisure.* Imperial's brewing and leisure operations earned an ROK of 9 percent in 1985. This return was considered very low for the brewing industry, which was characterized by strong demand and was dominated by a mature oligopoly that had engineered high prices and margins. Hanson thought that this return could be significantly improved.

The Takeover Battle

The planned merger between Imperial and United Biscuits PLC (UB), announced on December 2, 1985, gave rise to considerable concern among Imperial's already disgruntled shareholders. Under the terms of the proposed merger, UB, although contributing just 21 percent of net assets, would end up with a 42 percent interest in the enlarged group. The implication was that Imperial's shareholders would experience significant earnings dilution. In addition, it was proposed that the corporate management of the enlarged group would primarily come from UB personnel. These factors prompted a reverse takeover by UB of the much larger Imperial group. See Table 7.

Hanson's interest was sparked by this controversy. Hanson's corporate staff had been tracking Imperial for some time, so when the for-sale sign was raised over Imperial, Hanson was able to move quickly. On December 6, 1985, Hanson made a 250-pence per share offer for Imperial, valuing the group at £1.9 billion. This offer was rejected out of hand by Imperial's management.

The next major development came on February 12, 1986, when the British secretary of state of trade and industry referred the proposed Imperial/UB merger to the Monopolies and Mergers Commission for consideration. Britain's Monopolies and Mergers Commission has the authority to prohibit any merger that might create a monopoly. The referral was due to the recognition that an Imperial/UB group would command more than 40 percent of the British snack-food market.

On February 17, Hanson took advantage of the uncertainty created by the referral to unveil a revised offer 24 percent higher than its original offer, valuing Imperial at £2.35 billion. On the same day, UB announced a bid of £2.5 billion for Imperial and indicated that, if the offer was successful, Imperial's snack-food businesses would be sold, thus eliminating the need for a Monopolies and Mergers Commission investigation. Imperial's board duly recommended the UB offer to shareholders for acceptance.

Many of Imperial's shareholders, however, were in no mood to accept Imperial's recommendation. Under British stock market regulations, once the Imperial board accepted UB's offer, Imperial's shareholders had two months in which to indicate their acceptance or rejection of it. If the offer was rejected, then the shareholders were free to consider the hostile bid from Hanson. What followed was an increasingly acrimonious war of words between Hanson and Imperial. Hanson charged Imperial with mismanagement. Imperial responded by trying to depict Hanson as an asset stripper with no real interest in generating internal growth from the companies it owned. In the words of one Imperial executive during this period, Lord Hanson "buys and sells companies well, but he manages

TABLE 7

Hanson PLC—Financial Data

Income Data (million $)*

Year Ended Sept. 30	Revs.	Oper. Inc.	% Oper. Inc. of Revs.	Cap. Exp.	Depr.	Int. Exp.	Net Bef. Taxes	Eff. Tax Rate	Net‡ Inc.	% Net Inc. of Revs.
1989§	$11,302	$1,609	14.2%	$2,141	$200	$533	$1,718†	23.6%	1,313	11.6%
1988§	12,507	1,561	12.5%	724	215	485	1,488†	23.2%	1,143	9.1%
1987‖	10,975	1,230	11.2%	522	172	493	1,217†	22.8%	939	8.6%
1986‖	6,196	713	11.5%	848	105	359	667	22.5%	517	8.3%
1985	3,771	477	12.7%	84	74	172	356	23.5%	272	7.2%
1984	2,930	303	10.3%	61	55	119	208	25.7%	154	5.3%
1983	2,226	207	9.3%	59	47	81	137	30.2%	94	4.2%
1982	1,952	NA	NA	NA	NA	NA	NA	NA	72	3.7%
1981	1,549	NA	NA	NA	NA	NA	NA	NA	62	4.0%

Balance sheet data (million $)*

Sept. 30	Cash	Assets	Curr. Liab.	Ratio	Total Assets	% Ret. on Assets	Long-Term Debt	Common Equity	Total Inv. Capital	% LT Debt. of Cap.	% Ret. on Equity
1989	$8,574	$12,038	$5,278	2.3	$17,482	8.5%	$8,028	$1,689	$10,683	75.1%	47.6%
1988	6,527	10,413	4,165	2.5	13,210	9.4%	3,592	3,707	7,878	45.6%	33.5%
1987	5,025	8,236	3,422	2.4	10,471	9.3%	2,837	2,841	6,151	46.1%	37.5%
1986	2,509	7.977	3,572	2.2	9,577	7.6%	2,834	2,068	5,252	54.0%	29.1%
1985	1,659	2,908	1,277	2.3	4,021	7.7%	903	1,376	2,563	35.2%	27.7%
1984	641	1,775	925	1.9	2,638	9.0%	981	505	1,540	63.7%	36.7%

*Data as originally reported; prior to 1986 data as reported in the 1985 Annual Report (prior to 1984, data are from the listing application of November 3, 1986), conversion to U.S. dollars at year-end exchange rates. †Includes equity in earnings of nonconsolidated subsidiaries. ‡Before specific item(s) in 1989, 1988, 1986. §Excludes discount operations and reflects merger or acquisition. ‖Reflects merger or acquisition.
Source: Standard & Poor's, *Standard & Poor's NYSE Stock Reports,* Vol. 57, No. 54, Sec. 12, p. 1096. Reprinted by permission of Standard & Poor's, a division of The McGraw-Hill Companies, Inc.

them jolly badly. He buys, squeezes and goes on to the next one. The only way to grow is by bigger and bigger acquisitions. Like all great conglomerate builders of the past, he's over the hill."[19]

Imperial's management failed to win the war of words. By April 17, UB had secured acceptances for only 34 percent of Imperial's shares, including 14.9 percent held by UB associates. The UB offer lapsed, leaving the way clear for Hanson. On April 18 Hanson secured acceptances for more than 50 percent of Imperial's shares, and its offer went uncondi-

tional. At £2.5 billion, the takeover was the largest in British history; it implied a price/earnings multiple of 12.3 on Imperial's prospective earnings.

After the Acquisition

After the acquisition Hanson moved quickly to realize potential from Imperial. Of the 300 staff at Imperial's headquarters, 260 were laid off, and most of the remainder were sent back to the operating level. In July Imperial's hotels and restaurants were sold to Trusthouse Forte for £190 million in cash, representing a price/earnings multiple of 24 on prospective earnings and amounting to 1.7 times book value. That sale was followed in September 1986 by the sale of the Courage Brewing operations, along with a wine and spirits wholesaler and an "off-license" chain (liquor stores) to Elders IXL, an Australian brewing company, for £1.4 billion in cash. The price/earnings multiple for that deal amounted to 17.5 times prospective earnings and represented a premium of £150 million over book value. It was quickly followed by the sale of Imperial's Golden Wonder snack-food business to Dalgety PLC, a British food concern, for £87 million in cash, representing a price/earnings multiple of 13.5 over prospective earnings.

As a result of these moves, by the autumn of 1986 Hanson had raised £1.7 billion from the sale of Imperial's businesses. Effectively, Hanson recouped 66 percent of the total cost of its acquisition by selling companies that contributed slightly more than 45 percent of Imperial's net profit forecasted for the year to October 1986. The net cost of Imperial on this basis had fallen to £850 million, with a consequent decline in the price/earnings multiple on prospective earnings from 12.3 to 7.6.

This was followed in 1988 by the sale of Imperial's food businesses for £534 million, along with the sale of various other smaller interests for £56 million. By the end of 1988, therefore, Hanson had raised £2.26 billion from the sale of Imperial's assets. It still retained Imperial Tobacco, by far the largest business in Imperial's portfolio, which it had in effect gained for a net cost of £240 million—this for a business that in 1988 generated £150 million in operating profit.

LATER DEVELOPMENTS

Following the SCM and Imperial acquisitions, in 1987 Hanson acquired Kidde, a 108-company U.S. conglomerate, for $1.7 billion. Kidde seemed set for the "Hanson treatment." Its headquarters was closed within three months of the takeover, and a series of disposals was arranged. These were followed in 1988 by continuing disposals of operations acquired in the Imperial and Kidde acquisitions. In total, they amounted to $1.5 billion.

In mid 1989 Hanson embarked on its biggest takeover ever, the £3.61 billion ($4.8 billion) acqui-

sition of Consolidated Gold Field PLC (CGF). In addition to being the second largest gold-mining operation in the world, CGF also owns a large stone and gravel operation, ARC Ltd., with major holdings in Britain. CGF came to Hanson's attention following an abortive takeover bid for the company from South African-controlled Minorco.

Hanson bought Minorco's 29.9 percent minority stake in CGF and launched its own takeover bid in July 1989. After raising its bid, Hanson won control of CGF in August. CGF also seemed set to be broken up. About half of CGF's value consists of minority stakes in publicly quoted mining companies in the United States, South Africa, and Australia. These stakes range from 38 to 49 percent, enough to hold the key to control in many of the companies. Thus, Hanson should be able to extract a premium price for them. Initial estimates suggest that Hanson should be able to raise $2.5 billion from the sale of CGF's minority holdings.[20] Indeed, by February 1990 Hanson had reportedly recouped about one-third of the purchase price of CGF through disposals and was looking to sell additional operations while gold prices remained high.[21]

The CGF deal led directly to the June 1990 acquisition of Peabody Holdings Co., the largest U.S. coal producer, for a total cost of $1.23 billion in cash. CGF had a 49 percent stake in Newmont Mining Corp., the biggest U.S. gold-mining concern. In turn, Newmont owned 55 percent of Peabody. In April 1990 Hanson purchased the 45 percent of Peabody not owned by Newmont from three minority owners. Then in June it outbid AMAX Corporation for Newmont's stake in Peabody.

The attraction of Peabody to Hanson lies in two factors: (1) the company owns large deposits of low-sulfur coal, which is increasingly in demand because of environmental concerns; (2) the company has recently invested heavily to upgrade its plant. As a result, in the past four years labor productivity has increased 50 percent.[22] In addition, analysts speculate that the deals, by improving Newmont's financial position (Newmont has used the cash to reduce its debt), may make it possible for Hanson to sell off its 49 percent stake in Newmont for a reasonable premium.

Endnotes

1. "The Conglomerate as Antique Dealer," *Economist,* March 11, 1989, pp. 71–73.
2. Quoted in ibid.

3. Quoted in John Byrne and Mark Maremont, "Hanson: The Dangers of Living by Takeover Alone," *BusinessWeek*, August 15, 1988, pp. 62–64.

4. Quoted in Andrew Marton, "The Buccaneer from Britain," *Mergers and Acquisitions* (February 1987), pp. 141–146.

5. Quoted in Byrne and Maremont, "Hanson: The Dangers."

6. Gordon White, "How I Turned $3,000 into $10 Billion," *Fortune*, November 7, 1988, pp. 80–89.

7. The material in this section is based on the following sources: White, "How I Turned," pp. 80–89; Marton, "The Buccaneer from Britain," pp. 141–146; and Hope Lampert, "Britons on the Prowl," *New York Times Magazine*, November 29, 1987, pp. 22–24, 36, 38, 42.

8. White, "How I Turned," p. 81.

9. Quoted in Lampert, "Britons on the Prowl," p. 36.

10. Quoted in White, "How I Turned," p. 81.

11. Quoted in Lampert, "Britons on the Prowl," p. 24.

12. The material in this section is based on the following sources: White, "How I Turned," pp. 80–89; Lampert, "Britons on the Prowl," pp. 22–24, 36, 38, 42; and Mark Cusack, *Hanson Trust: A Review of the Company and Its Prospects* (London: Hoare Govett Limited, 1987).

13. The material in this section is based on the following sources: Cusack, *Hanson Trust;* "The Conglomerate as Antique Dealer," pp. 71–73; Byrne and Maremont, "Hanson: The Dangers," pp. 62–64; and Gordon White, "Nothing Hurts More Than a Bogus Bonus," *Wall Street Journal*, July 20, 1987, p. 18.

14. White, "How I Turned," p. 81.

15. White, "Nothing Hurts More," p. 18.

16. Most of the detail in this section is drawn from two sources: Cusack, *Hanson Trust;* and Lampert, "Britons on the Prowl," pp. 22–24, 36, 38, 42.

17. White, "How I Turned," p. 84.

18. The material in this section is based on the following sources: Cusack, *Hanson Trust;* and Lampert, "Britons on the Prowl," pp. 22–24, 36, 38, 42.

19. Quoted in Philip Revzin, "U.K.'s Hanson Trust Aims for Big Leagues in Takeovers," *Wall Street Journal*, February 25, 1986, p. 30.

20. Mark Maremont and Chuck Hawkins, "Is Consgold Just an Appetizer for Hanson?" *BusinessWeek*, July 10, 1989, pp. 41–42.

21. Joann Lubin, "Hanson to Buy Peabody Stake for $504 Million," *Wall Street Journal*, February 16, 1990, p. A4.

22. "Hanson PLC," *Value Line*, July 20, 1990, p. 832.

CASE 30

Hanson PLC (B): Breaking It Up

This case was prepared by Charles W. L. Hill of the University of Washington.

INTRODUCTION

During the 1970s and 1980s, Hanson PLC put together one of the most impressive growth stories of any industrial company in the world. Under the leadership of James Hanson and Gordon White, Hanson PLC made its name by acquiring poorly run conglomerate companies in both Britain and America at prices that were often below their book value. In quick order Hanson would then change the senior management of the acquired company, sell many of the company's assets to other enterprises, typically for a considerable profit, and impose tight financial controls on what remained in order to maximize profitability and cash flow. The locus classicus was Hanson's 1986 acquisition of the Imperial Group, a diversified British tobacco, brewing, and food conglomerate, where some £2.4 billion of the £2.5 billion purchase price was recouped from asset disposals, leaving Hanson with the cash-generating tobacco business intact. The results of this strategy were nothing short of stunning. Between 1973 and 1991, Hanson put together twenty-nine years of uninterrupted profit growth to build a diversified company with revenues of £7.69 billion ($12.3 billion) and operating income of £1.33 billion ($2.13 billion). Hanson's stock price appreciation was also spectacular, increasing more than a hundredfold between 1973 and 1991.

However, 1991 may have been the high-water mark of Hanson's growth story. In 1990 Hanson took a 2.9 percent stake in the British chemical and

This case is intended to be used as a basis for class discussion rather than as an illustration of either effective or ineffective handling of the situation. This case was prepared by Charles W. L. Hill, University of Washington. Used by permission.

pharmaceutical company, Imperial Chemical Industries (ICI). Many saw this as a prelude to yet another Hanson acquisition, but ICI was not about to be taken over. After a bitter public relations battle during which ICI characterized Hanson's management as having a short-term orientation and criticized them for failure to add value to the companies they acquired, Hanson sold its stake in May 1991. While the stake was sold for a profit of £45 million ($70 million), the public relations battle damaged Hanson's image. A year later Hanson was outbid for a British food company, RHM, by a smaller conglomerate run by a former Hanson manager. These two failures raised questions as to whether Hanson's two founders, who were now both in their seventies, were still up to the rough game of hostile takeovers. To compound matters further, for the year ending in September 1993, with many of its cyclical businesses suffering from the effects of a recession in both Britain and America, Hanson reported a 33 percent decline in after-tax profits to $1.5 billion, the first such decline in its history. Reflecting these problems, Hanson's stock price peaked in early 1991 and remained flat over the next few years, while the equity markets in Britain and America boomed.

A NEW DIRECTION?

In 1992 the leadership mantle at Hanson started to pass from the company's charismatic founders, the now ennobled (Lord) Hanson and White, to Derek Bonham and David Clarke, who were then forty-eight and fifty, respectively. Bonham took over as CEO with primary responsibilities for Hanson's

British-based operations, while Clarke succeeded White as president of Hanson's substantial American operations. Lord Hanson remained on in the chairman's role, while White continued as the company's senior person in charge of mergers and acquisitions. (White died in 1995.)

Although both long-time Hanson employees, Bonham and Clarke clearly lacked the predatory thirst that had driven Hanson and White. Early in his tenure Bonham admitted that Hanson had become "too much of a mishmash" and stated that he hoped to correct that by focusing management's attention on improving the performance of its core businesses in building materials, chemicals, tobacco, and natural resources (primarily timber and coal). While this might require "bolt on acquisitions," Bonham seemed to be signaling that the swashbuckling days of hostile acquisitions and quick asset disposals to pay down debt were over.[1]

Another signal of a shift in management's philosophy came in May 1994, when Hanson announced that it would lengthen the payback period required of new capital investments from three or four years to five or six years. The company stated that it had lengthened the required payback period to take advantage of low interest rates and continuing low inflation. However, many also saw the shift as an attempt to allay fears in the financial community that Hanson's management style was too focused on the short term. Moreover, the move seemed to be consistent with Bonham's stated goal of increasing internal investments as a way of generating growth.[2] The growth that Bonham was talking about, however, was a far cry from the 20 percent annual rate achieved under the leadership of Hanson and White. According to Bonham, "The reality is that we are living in a low growth, low inflation climate. To suggest that you can continue to grow by 20 percent is out of line."[3]

Both Bonham and Clarke repeatedly stated that they saw Hanson growing at about twice the rate of inflation during the 1990s, which suggested a growth rate of around 6 percent, given British and American inflation rates.

Acquiring Quantum

The first significant strategic move under Bonham occurred on June 31, 1993, when Hanson an-

nounced that it had reached an agreement to purchase Quantum Chemical Corp., the largest U.S. producer of polyethylene plastics, in a stock swap that valued Quantum at $20 per share, or $720 million. The purchase price represented a premium of 60 percent over Quantum's closing price of $12.50 on June 30. Hanson also stated that it would assume all of Quantum's $2.5 billion in debt. The acquisition added to Hanson's U.S. chemical operations, which included SCM Chemicals, the world's third largest producer of titanium dioxide.

According to observers, the acquisition represented a strategic bet by Hanson that a protracted cyclical downturn in the polyethylene business was nearing an end. At the peak of the last plastics cycle in 1988, Quantum earned $760 million. However, Quantum had saddled itself with the $2.5 billion debt load in a 1989 restructuring, undertaken while plastics prices were at their previous cyclical peak. Massive debt service requirements and a slump in polyethylene prices had left Quantum with a 1992 loss before accounting charges of $118.4 million, or $3.98 per share. One immediate financial benefit of the acquisition was that Hanson was able to use its superior credit rating to refinance Quantum's debt (much of which was in the form of junk bonds with an average yield of more than 10 percent) at rates closer to Hanson's 5 percent borrowing costs. This move alone cut Quantum's $240 million annual interest bill in half.[4]

In retrospect the Quantum acquisition turned out to be particularly well timed. Prices for low density polyethylene bottomed out in the summer of 1993 at $28 per gallon. By the end of 1994 they had risen to $33 per gallon.[5] Quantum's profits turned out to be highly leveraged to prices. As a result of this leverage and lower interest payments, Quantum's chemical operations earned almost $200 million in fiscal 1994, more than $300 million ahead of its 1992 results. Quantum's results helped Hanson to rebound from its poor showing in 1993. For 1994 it reported a 32 percent rise in pretax profits and a record operating profit of £1.23 billion ($1.92 billion).[6]

1993–1994 Disposals

Throughout 1993 and 1994, Hanson proceeded with a series of relatively minor asset disposals. The objectives of these disposals were twofold: first, to focus the company on its core businesses and, second, to help pay down Hanson's enormous debt load, the legacy of its acquisitions including Quantum. In fiscal 1993 Hanson's long-term debt stood at £7.22 billion ($11.5 billion), and its debt to equity ratio was 1.83 (see Table 1). This debt load was beginning to trouble the financial community, who were starting to question the ability of Hanson to maintain its historically high dividend. In a previous era Hanson had quickly paid down debt from

acquisitions by raising cash through asset disposals, but there had been little movement in this direction since the late 1980s.

Between January 1993 and August 1994, Hanson sold more than fifteen companies for a total of £815 million ($1.3 billion). These disposals included its Beazer home building operations in both the United States and the United Kingdom; an office supply business; and Axelson, an oil industry equipment group.[7]

TABLE I

Hanson PLC—Financial Data

Income Data (million £)*

Year Ended Sept. 30	($) Per Pound†	Revs.	Oper. Inc.	% Oper. Inc. of Revs.	Cap. Exp.	Depr.	Int. Exp.	Net Bef. Taxes	Eff. Tax Rate	Net Inc.‖	% Net Inc. of Revs.	Cash Flow
1994	1.509	11,199	1,633	14.6	293	401	545	1,346	20.9%	1,065	9.5	1,466
1993	1.523	9,760	1,288	13.2	301	310	600	1,016	27.8%	734	7.5	1,044
1992	1.822	8,798	1,322	15.0	279	254	777	1,286	15.3%	1,089	12.4	1,343
1991‡	1.820	7,691	1,327	17.3	266	216	741	1,319	21.5%	1,035	13.5	1,251
1990‡	1.700	7,153	1,236	17.3	247	180	638	1,285	24.4%	971	13.6	NA
1989‡	1.690	6,998	996	14.2	192	124	330	1,064	23.6%	813	11.6	NA
1988‡	1.770	7,396	923	12.5	198	127	287	880	23.2%	676	9.1	NA
1987§	1.560	6,682	749	11.2	151	105	300	741	22.8%	572	8.6	NA

Balance Sheet Data (million £)*

Sept. 30	($) Per Pound†	Curr. Cash	Curr. Assets	Curr. Liab.	Curr. Ratio	Total Assets	% Ret. on Assets	Long-Term Debt	Common Equity	Total Inv. Cap.	% LT Debt of Cap.	% Ret. on Equity
1994	1.566	6,815	9,933	6,704	1.5	21,536	4.7	5,038	4,598	9,768	51.6	24.9
1993	1.525	8,067	11,636	7,065	1.6	24,057	3.3	7,221	3,953	11,266	64.1	18.0
1992	1.779	8,445	11,204	6,386	1.8	20,541	5.9	5,069	4,224	9,430	53.8	28.9
1991	1.750	7,771	9,955	4,751	2.1	16,583	6.6	4,880	3,325	8,351	58.4	33.6
1990	1.870	6,883	8,993	4,226	2.1	14,754	7.6	4,258	2,834	7,222	59.0	50.1
1989	1.620	5,309	7,454	3,269	2.3	10,825	8.7	4,971	1,046	6,133	81.1	50.1
1988	1.690	3,860	6,158	2,463	2.5	7,812	9.5	2,124	2,192	4,659	45.6	34.1
1987	1.630	3,059	5,014	2,083	2.4	6,375	8.8	1,727	1,730	3,745	46.1	35.5

*Data as originally reported; prior to 1988 as reported in 1987 Annual Report. Based on UK GAAP.
†Average exchange rates for income data; fiscal year-end exchange rates for balance sheet.
‡Excludes discretionary operations and reflects merger or acquisition.
§Reflects merger or acquisition.
‖Before special items.

Spinning off U.S. Industries

The next big strategic move occurred in February 1995, when Hanson announced that it would spin off thirty-four of its smaller American-based companies into a new entity called U.S. Industries under the leadership of David Clarke. Hanson would retain ownership over several of its larger U.S. operations, including Quantum Chemical and Peabody Coal. The new company was to include such well-known brand names as Jacuzzi whirlpools, Farberware cookware, Ames garden tools, Rexair vacuum cleaners, and Tommy Armour golf clubs. In 1994 the thirty-four companies had sales of $3 billion and operating profits of $252 million. The company was to be responsible for $1.4 billion of Hanson's debt. According to one analyst,

> For Hanson, it achieves a one shot divestiture of a number of companies they may have struggled to sell independently, not because the individual assets are unattractive, but because it's messy to sell so many of them. They are able to divest in a tax efficient way and at the same time take a lot of cash out, leaving them with the ability to buy something else.[8]

The spinoff was completed on June 1, 1995. At the time, David Clarke stated that the new company's first objective would be to reduce its debt load, primarily by selling off a number of companies valued at $600 million.[9]

Acquiring Eastern Group

On July 31, 1995, Hanson announced that it would acquire Eastern Group, one of Britain's major electric utilities, for £2 billion ($3.2 billion). Eastern, which was privatized in 1990, has a customer base of 3 million and is responsible for 15 percent of the electricity produced in Britain, primarily for natural gas-fired generating facilities. Eastern is also the seventh largest natural gas supplier in the country. In the year ending March 31, 1995, Eastern's earnings were up 15 percent to £203 million ($324 billion) on revenues of £2.06 billion ($3.2 billion).[10]

Hanson stated that it was attracted to Eastern by its steady earnings growth. However, critics noted that the deal yet again stretched Hanson's balance sheet, which once more had begun to look solid after the U.S. Industries spinoff. The debt-financed purchase of Eastern caused Hanson's debt-to-equity ratio to shoot up from 37 percent to 130 percent, once more raising concerns that Hanson might not be able to service its historically high dividends. A partial response to these concerns came in December 1995, when the company announced plans to dispose of two additional U.S. subsidiaries—Suburban Propane and Cavenham Forest Industries—for £1.5 billion ($2.4 billion). The proceeds were to be used to pay down Hanson's debt load. Analysts calculated that the cash raised from these spinoffs would reduce Hanson's debt-to-equity ratio to around 90 percent.[11]

THE DEMERGER

By late 1995 it was becoming increasingly clear within Hanson's senior management team that drastic action would be required to boost the company's lagging share price.[12] As the British and American economies continued in their long recovery from recession, Hanson's cyclical business staged a significant performance improvement, with operating profits increasing by 44 percent for the fiscal year that ended in September 1995. Despite this performance, the company's share price had been essentially flat since the early 1990s (see Figure 1). Over the same period both the London and New York stock markets had increased substantially. By the end of 1995 the price-to-earnings ratio of Hanson's shares was 30 percent below that of the average stock on the London exchange, while Hanson's dividend yield at over 6.5 percent was among the highest offered by any company. It seemed that nothing could move the stock price, not the strong profit performance, not the spinoff of U.S. Industries, not the Eastern acquisition, and not the recently announced disposals.

It was against this background that Hanson stunned both London and Wall Street with its January 29 announcement that it would divide the company up into four independent businesses, effectively dismantling the conglomerate assembled by Hanson and White. Hanson stated that it would split into a chemicals business, an energy company, a tobacco company, and a building materials enterprise. Imperial Tobacco would be the

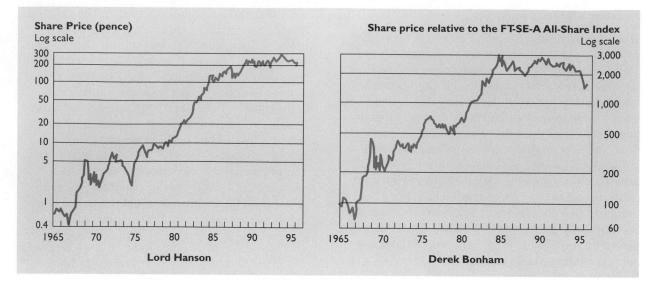

FIGURE I

Hanson PLC

largest company, with sales of £3.57 billion ($5.37 billion). The energy business, which would include Hanson's coal and electric businesses, would have sales of £3.5 billion ($5.27 billion). The chemicals business would have sales of £2 billion ($3.04 billion), while the building materials group would have sales of £2.3 billion ($3.48 billion).[13] Bonham was to run the energy business, while Hanson was to take over the building materials group until his retirement. The company estimated that the demerger would be completed by early 1997.

Hanson's stock price initially surged 7 percent on the news, but it fell later the same day and ended up less than 0.5 percent. The lack of a sustained positive reaction from the stock markets on both sides of the Atlantic puzzled Hanson's managers. Over the last few years, a number of diversified companies had announced demergers—including ITT, AT&T, and Sears—and their stock prices had almost always responded in a very positive fashion. In Hanson's case, however, this did not occur.

One possible explanation for the lack of a favorable reaction came from Moody's Investor Service, which put Hanson's debt under review for a possible downgrade one day after the breakup was announced. Moody's noted that "this is a highly complex sequence of transactions which are at an early stage and which will require various approvals."[14] Among the concerns expressed were that the demerger might raise Hanson's borrowing costs. The tax consequences of the demerger were also not immediately apparent, although there were some indications that there might be some one-time capital gains tax charges. Moreover, several stock analysts commented that the demerged Hanson units might not be able or willing to maintain Hanson's historically high level of dividends. One influential London-based stock analyst also noted that unlike most conglomerates that were demerging, there were few if any hidden assets at Hanson. This analyst calculated that Hanson's constituent parts should be valued at 194 pence, which was below the 212 pence price that Hanson's stock closed at on January 30, 1996.[15]

As a further prelude to the demerger, in March 1996 Hanson announced the sale of its remaining U.S. timberland operations to Willamette Industries for $1.59 billion. This sale followed Hanson's disposal of Cavenham Forest Industries in December

1995, and it completed Hanson's exit from the timber business. The cash generated from the sale was to be used to pay down Hanson's debt.[16]

Endnotes

1. R. A. Melcher, "Can This Predator Change Its Stripes?" *BusinessWeek,* June 22, 1992, p. 38; J. Guyon, "Hanson Crosses the Atlantic to Woo Investors," *Wall Street Journal,* December 6, 1983, p. 7D.
2. R. Rudd, "Hanson Increases Investment Payback Time," *Financial Times,* May 16, 1994, p. 15.
3. P. Dwyer and J. Weber, "Hanson Looks for a Hat Trick," *BusinessWeek,* March 14, 1994, pp. 68–69.
4. S. McMurray, "UK's Hanson to Buy Maker of Polyethylene," *Wall Street Journal,* July 1, 1993, p. A3.
5. D. Wighton, "Conglomerate's $3.2 Billion Gamble Pays Off," *Financial Times,* December 2, 1994, p. 23.
6. "Hanson Posts 32% Rise in Pre Tax Profits," *Wall Street Journal,* December 2, 1994, p. B3.
7. P. Taylor, "Hanson Lifted by Quantum Chemical," *Financial Times,* August 17, 1994, p. 13.
8. R. W. Stevenson, "Hanson Plans to Spin Off 34 U.S. Companies," *New York Times,* February 23, 1995, p. C1.
9. L. L. Brownless and J. R. Dorfman, "Birth of U.S. Industries Isn't Without Complications," *Wall Street Journal,* May 18, 1995, p. B4.
10. D. Wighton, "Hanson Plugs into New Current," *Financial Times,* July 31, 1995, p. 15.
11. D. Wighton, "Hanson Seeks £1.5 Billion from U.S. Disposals," *Financial Times,* December 21, 1995, p. 13.
12. "Widow Hanson's Children Leave Home," *Economist,* February 3, 1996, pp. 51–52.
13. R. Bonte-Friedheim and J. Guyon, "Hanson to Divide into Four Businesses," *Wall Street Journal,* January 31, 1996, p. A3.
14. Bonte-Friedheim and Guyon, "Hanson to Divide into Four Businesses."
15. D. Wighton, "Centrifugal Forces That Pulled Hanson Apart," *Financial Times,* January 31, 1996, p. 18.
16. "Hanson to Sell Mills," *Wall Street Journal: Money & Investing Update,* March 12, 1996.

CASE 31

First Greyhound, Then Greyhound Dial, Then Dial, Now What?

This case was prepared by Gareth R. Jones of Texas A & M University.

It was July 1996, and John Teets, the chairman, president, and chief executive officer of the Dial Corporation, was under increasing attack from Michael Price, president of Heine Securities Corp. Price was the adviser to the Mutual Series Funds, a large mutual fund company that owned 9.9 percent of Dial's stock. Teets had announced in February 1996 that he had decided to break Dial up into two companies to try to increase the company's earnings and boost its lackluster performance. Price, along with other analysts, however, argued that this move would reduce, not increase, value for shareholders and that what Teets should do was to divest Dial's many different businesses and return the proceeds to shareholders. Who is correct? To try to answer this question, it is necessary to understand the way that Dial's strategy has evolved over time under a succession of different CEOs.

GREYHOUND'S EARLY HISTORY AND GROWTH

Greyhound was founded in Hibbing, Minnesota, in 1914. Its first business was providing bus transportation to carry miners to work at the Mesabi Iron Range. Because Greyhound was the sole provider of bus service for these workers, it was immediately successful. In its very first year, the new corporation started expanding its routes and

acquiring interests in bus companies operating near Chicago. For the next sixteen years, the young company continued purchasing interests in bus companies, extending its route structure from New York to Kansas City. In 1930, the name *Greyhound Corporation* was adopted, and the now-familiar running-dog logo was painted on the buses.[1]

For the next twenty-seven years, Greyhound continued to acquire bus interests in order to consolidate its routes and link its various bus operations. Growth proceeded sometimes by purchase, sometimes by stock swaps, and sometimes by merger. However, the result was always the same to the traveling public: it saw more and more of the familiar running dog. By 1960, Greyhound had substantially achieved its objective of operating a bus system that could carry passengers to most destinations in the continental United States and Canada.

By 1962, however, Greyhound was facing the prospect of increasingly limited opportunities to expand its route system. In the company's favor was the fact that bus operations were generating large sums of excess cash, which could fund expansion into new businesses. So Greyhound's board of directors decided to diversify into operations outside of the bus transportation industry.

In that same year, Greyhound began the program of acquisition that turned it into a conglomerate. It solidified its bus-manufacturing operations into Motor Coach Industries, which became the foundation of Greyhound Dial's transportation manufacturing operating division. Also in 1962, the corporation acquired Boothe Leasing Company, an enterprise that specialized in equipment leasing. Boothe Leasing was renamed Greyhound Leasing

This case is intended to be used as a basis for class discussion rather than as an illustration of either effective or ineffective handling of the situation. This case was prepared by Gareth R. Jones, Texas A & M University. Used by permission.

and became the core business around which Greyhound's financial services division was to be built. Thus, by the end of 1963, Greyhound Corporation was operating in three major businesses: bus transportation, bus manufacturing, and financial services. Bus manufacturing supplied buses to bus transportation as well as to other bus companies.

ACQUISITIONS BETWEEN 1966 AND 1970

Gerry Trautman was appointed CEO in 1966, and he wasted no time in accelerating Greyhound's new strategy for expansion and growth.[2] From Trautman's installation as CEO until 1970, Greyhound acquired more than thirty widely different companies and formed a new operating division, services: it specialized in managing transportation-related businesses, such as Border Brokerage Company, which operated two duty-free shops at the Canadian border, and Florida Export Group, which also handled duty-free commerce. In addition, the services division included Manncraft Exhibitors, a company that specialized in building displays for major exhibitions; Nassau Air Dispatch, a Caribbean shipping company; and Freeport Flight Services, a Bahamian aircraft-servicing business. Trautman also brought in a line of cruise ships in the Caribbean, the Bahama Cruise Line Company.[3] Then he added companies as diverse as Ford Van Lines of Lincoln, Nebraska, a company specializing in furniture moving; Red Top Sedan Service, a Florida limousine service; two regional intercity bus lines; Washington Airport Transport, a commuter carrier from the Washington, D.C., suburbs to Dulles Airport; and Gray Line New York Tours Corporation, a sightseeing bus line. Furthermore, he added Hausman Bus Parts to the bus-manufacturing unit.[4]

Not all the companies that Trautman acquired proved to be as profitable or as manageable as he had hoped. What he was looking for was value as well as some synergy with Greyhound's existing transportation activities. However, as the acquisition process continued, synergy became a secondary objective. When Trautman became dissatisfied with an acquisition, he would divest it as quickly as he had acquired it, and many companies were spun off. Near the end of his tenure as CEO, Trautman would boast that Greyhound had achieved "diversification within diversification."[5]

What he meant was that in his view the operating groups had become diversified, so that each individually was recession-proof and all were enhancing the financial strength of the holding company.

Trautman's boldest maneuver and biggest acquisition came in 1970. He acquired Armour & Co., another large conglomerate that had many diverse business interests in food and consumer products. Trautman paid $400 million in cash, notes, and stock to take over Armour, which was primarily a large meat-packing company with more than $2 billion of sales in marginally profitable businesses. However, Armour also had interests in pharmaceuticals, cosmetics, and consumer products, such as soap, through its very profitable Dial division.

Trautman knew that it appeared as though he had overpaid for Armour–Dial. However, he soon reduced the price of the acquisition by selling off, for some $225 million, a number of Armour's divisions that he considered to be peripheral to Armour's core food and consumer businesses. In 1977, he sold off Armour's pharmaceutical division for $87 million, reducing Greyhound's net investment to $88 million.[6] What remained after the divestitures were Armour's food operations and Armour's Dial division, from which would emerge Greyhound Dial's consumer products operating division.

Trautman hoped that his new acquisition would be more recession-proof than the bus business, if not countercyclical to it. However, the Armour acquisition brought to Greyhound new businesses that had management problems of their own—in areas in which Greyhound had no experience, such as the price of pork bellies, cycles for meat packers' contracts, and foreign competition.

TRAUTMAN'S ACQUISITIONS AND DIVESTITURES BETWEEN 1970 AND 1978

For the next eight years, Greyhound under Trautman continued buying businesses and increasing the size of the operating divisions in its corporate portfolio. By 1978, Greyhound's holding company consisted of five operating divisions: transportation, bus manufacturing, food and consumer products, financial, and services/food service. Each of these operating divisions acquired many new businesses, so Greyhound was still undergoing "diversification within diversification." Many of the new acquisitions, however, were failures. Businesses as diverse as a chicken hatchery, a European acquisition to expand the financial services group, and various transportation businesses (Caribbean Gray Cruise Line, Ltd., VAVO Greyhound N.V. of Schoonhoven, Netherlands, Shannon-Greyhound Coaches, and Hausman Bus Parts) proved unprofitable.[7]

Greyhound's portfolio of businesses kept changing during this period, and Trautman continued to feel that he was shaping a diversified company that would have a powerful base in many lines of business. He was willing to take the risk of acquiring some companies that would be failures as long as the overall health of the company was strengthened. However, Greyhound became more and more distant from its core business—bus transportation.

In April 1978, Trautman engineered another major acquisition by acquiring 97 percent of the stock of Verex Corporation, the largest private insurer of residential mortgages in the United States. The Verex acquisition was intended to strengthen the operations of Greyhound's financial operating division. Verex insured first mortgages on residential real estate generally having loan-to-value ratios in excess of 80 percent.

By 1978, Greyhound had grown nearly as large as it would grow under Trautman's leadership. The collection of businesses that he had assembled—some by acquisition, some by internal growth, and some by selling off pieces of larger businesses—was designed to make Greyhound more resistant to economic downturns. The activities of Greyhound's five major operating divisions are summarized below.

- *Transportation.* This operating division comprised the intercity services division and the travel services division. Transportation operated regularly scheduled passenger bus service between most metropolitan areas in North America and engaged in related operations, such as package shipping, sightseeing services, airport ground transportation, and deluxe tour and charter bus services.

- *Bus manufacturing.* The largest maker of intercity buses in North America, the bus-manufacturing division had operations that were vertically integrated to fabricate bus shells of in-

tercity design, assemble buses, and manufacture bus parts for final assembly. In addition, this operating division warehoused and distributed replacement parts to meet its own requirements and the larger requirements of the bus industry. Greyhound bus manufacturing was the principal U.S. supplier of buses to charter operators and sightseeing companies.

- *Food and consumer products.* The companies in this operating group manufactured and marketed products to independent retailers under private-label arrangements and distributed several products under their own trademarks. These trademarks included Dial, Tone, and Pure & Natural soaps, Armour Star and Armour Tree canned meat and meat food products, Dial antiperspirants and shampoos, Appian Way pizza mixes, Parsons' ammonia, Bruce floor care products, Magic sizing and prewash, and Malina handknitting yarns and needle products.

- *Services/food service.* Companies in this operating division provided a broad range of services directed primarily to business markets, although duty-free shops located at airports and on cruise ships were targeted toward the consumer market. Greyhound convention services (GCS) specialized in designing, fabricating, warehousing, shipping, and setting up exhibits for trade shows, conventions, and exhibitions. GCS also served as a decorating contractor at conventions and trade show sites. The Food Service division, generally known as Greyhound food management (GFM), served approximately 400 locations in industrial plants, bus terminals, airports, office buildings, schools, colleges, and other facilities.

- *Financial.* This operating division consisted of Greyhound Computer Corporation, a company specializing in computer leasing and sales in the United States, Canada, Mexico, and Europe; Greyhound Leasing and Financial Corporation, a company specializing in worldwide industrial equipment leasing; Pine Top Insurance, an entity that reinsured commercial property and provided excess casualty insurance for large policyholders; and Verex Corporation, the leading private insurer of highly leveraged residential mortgages for primary lenders. Travelers Express Company, Inc., another company in the financial division, specialized in providing traveler's checks and check-cashing services in 32,000 retail establishments and financial institutions in the mainland United States and Puerto Rico.

Together, those five operating divisions were generating combined revenues of nearly $4.5 billion. Trautman had accomplished his objective of using profits from the bus operations to move Greyhound into other businesses.

TRAUTMAN SELECTS TEETS TO TAKE OVER GREYHOUND

Serious problems became apparent at Armour when the food and consumer products operating division went from a profit of $22 million in 1979 to a loss of $1.7 million in 1980. Armour's problems came at a very inconvenient time for Trautman because he had planned to retire in 1980. Trautman wanted to solve Armour's difficulties while he kept business rolling at Greyhound's other groups and prepared a successor to take over the collection of companies that he had assembled. That successor was to be John Teets.

Teets was very different from Trautman. His background did not include Harvard Business School or law practice. Instead, Teets had learned to be an effective hands-on manager by staying as close to the action as possible. He had worked for his father's construction company but decided that he wanted to operate a restaurant. He borrowed money, started his own restaurant, and quickly made it successful. However, soon after he had paid back his loan money and his restaurant was earning a profit, it burned to the ground. In search of a new business opportunity, Teets answered a newspaper advertisement about a position managing a Greyhound food service concession stand at the New York World's Fair in 1964.

After joining the services/food service operating group, Teets quickly distinguished himself as a tight-fisted cost cutter who could make money on a miserly budget. He seemed to have a talent for squeezing every last penny out of everything he managed. Teets moved up quickly, gaining a reputation as an extremely effective manager. By 1975, he was put in charge of the food service group, which primarily operated a conglomeration of marginally profitable, obscure, franchised restaurants. His aggressive management style produced quick results, and in 1980 he was named the outstanding execu-

tive in the food industry. Also in 1980, in addition to Teets' responsibilities as CEO of the food service group, Trautman named Teets to head Armour and turn around the division's performance.

In 1981, Armour's major problem, as Teets saw it, was its paying from 30 to 50 percent more in wages and fringe benefits than its competitors. Teets asked Armour's unions for immediate wage concessions. He told the unions that if he failed to get the concessions, he would have to start closing plants. After a bitter strike, wage concessions in excess of 15 percent were obtained. Given these concessions, the cost cutting from plant closings, and more efficient operating procedures, it looked as though Armour had bought itself some time.

With Armour running more efficiently, the bus business cruising along on excess profits because of the recession and energy crunch in 1979–1980, and high profits in its financial operating division generated by high interest rates in the early 1980s, it looked as though the stage was set for Trautman's retirement. In fact, all that remained to be done was to formally select a successor. It was not difficult for Trautman to make up his mind about who should be his successor. He was impressed with Teet's successes in managing the services/food service group and also with the way in which Teets had dominated Armour's labor unions.

TEETS SEEKS SOLUTIONS

In 1981, John Teets succeeded Gerry Trautman as the chief executive officer of the Greyhound Corporation. The challenge facing Teets was to manage Greyhound's diverse businesses so that he would be able to achieve at least a 15 percent return on equity. However, many problems on the horizon might hinder the achievement of this goal. Some were the direct consequence of Trautman's ambitious expansion and diversification efforts. Others resulted from changes in environmental factors and consumer preferences. Still others stemmed from internal inefficiencies that Teets hoped he would be able to remedy.[8]

Two challenges in particular caused Teets to feel uneasy about the corporation's overall profit picture. The first problem was Armour's high production costs, which made it a weak competitor. The second was the challenge faced by Greyhound Bus Lines: the need to compete in a newly deregulated bus transportation market. He knew that if he did not find solutions for these two problems, they would seriously diminish the Greyhound Corporation's earnings. The contribution of each operating division to Greyhound's total sales revenues in 1981 is presented in Figure 1.

Dealing with Armour's High Production Costs

Having been president of Armour, Teets was very familiar with the division's problems: its high production costs, the reluctance of union leadership and rank-and-file workers to agree with Greyhound's assessment of Armour's problems, and its utter inability to successfully change its marketing orientation in order to compete effectively. In addition, Teets was concerned about Armour's inefficient plants and volatility of hog and pork-belly prices, which cyclically depressed Armour's 1981 profit of $9 million and represented a profit margin of less than 0.39 percent on sales of more than $2.3 billion.[9] Teets sensed that it was not going to be easy to make Armour a low-cost leader. Thus, he decided to divest Armour.

In preparation for the sale, he separated the Armour Food Company from Armour-Dial. On December 18, 1983, the food company was sold to ConAgra, Inc., for $166 million. With the Armour

sale, Teets was chopping off nearly half of Greyhound's business. Nevertheless, even with Greyhound's revenues dropping from $5 billion in 1982 to less than $3 billion in 1984 without Armour, the sale gave Teets the opportunity to put Greyhound in better shape than it had been in years.

The Bus Line Divestiture

Teets was also concerned about the 1981 passage of House bill H.R. 3663, which deregulated the intercity bus business. Greyhound Bus Lines had based its route system on the competitive conditions that had existed in the earlier business environment. Teets, however, sensed that future success in the bus business would be based not on the extensiveness of Greyhound's route system or its fifty years of experience in operating in a regulated industry but on its ability to make money by charging competitive fares.

With the beginning of deregulated competition in the intercity bus business and declining passenger revenues resulting from the end of the energy crunch, Greyhound found itself paying wages and benefits that were from 30 to 50 percent higher than those paid by its competitors. Furthermore, its chief competitor, Trailways, having negotiated signif-

FIGURE 1

Greyhound in 1981

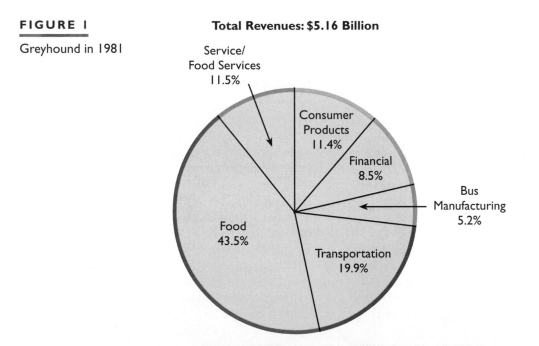

Total Revenues: $5.16 Billion

Service/Food Services 11.5%

Consumer Products 11.4%

Financial 8.5%

Bus Manufacturing 5.2%

Food 43.5%

Transportation 19.9%

Source: Data from Greyhound Dial Corporation, Annual Report, 1990.

icant wage concessions from the Amalgamated Transit Union, had immediately passed the savings on to customers in the form of lower fares. Trailways' action was a frontal assault on Greyhound's most lucrative routes in an attempt to gain market share. Greyhound's response was to match every one of Trailways' price cuts. Although Greyhound preserved its market share, it lost millions of dollars.

For Greyhound Bus Lines, the legacy of deregulation was a total inability to be a low-cost provider of bus transportation. Deregulation had brought about the emergence of lower-cost competitors in regional markets, competitors that were able to be responsive and flexible in pricing and in reacting to Greyhound's actions. As a result, Greyhound lost its competitive edge.[10] In 1986, in an effort to save the bus lines, Teets converted 120 company-owned terminals to commission agencies, trimming a huge overhead burden. He also created four stand-alone regional bus companies and a new travel and charter company. Finally, he franchised several of Greyhound's least profitable routes to independent operators, licensing them to use the Greyhound logo and trademark.

However, the one factor that Teets could not control was winning a new labor contract. In February 1986, an offer to freeze wages was rejected by the union. In October, in a deteriorating market, a second offer involving concessions was presented with the understanding that its rejection would prompt the sale of the company. The offer was subsequently rejected, and fifteen days later Teets announced the sale of Greyhound Bus Lines for approximately $350 million to an investor group headquartered in Dallas. Teets claimed that the actions taken by management in an effort to salvage the bus business were exactly the ones that made it an attractive acquisition for the Currey Group in Dallas.

The sale of Greyhound Bus Lines brought in $290 million in cash and equivalents, including a 22.5 percent interest in a new holding company established by the Dallas investor group.[11]

Divestitures in the Financial Operating Division

Besides selling Greyhound Bus Lines in 1987, Teets also sold Greyhound Capital Corporation (GCC). The decision to sell GCC reportedly reflected Teets's conviction that "some businesses just fit better into Greyhound's plans than others."[12] What this statement really meant was that GCC had become an underperformer in the face of lowered interest rates and changes in the tax laws that disallowed investment tax credits. GCC was sold for $140 million, realizing a one-time gain of $79.7 million for Greyhound.

In early 1987, Greyhound announced its intention to sell Verex. The timing of the acquisition had been a disaster, given the recession in the real estate market caused by the oil bust in the early 1980s. Verex suffered huge losses generated by insurance claims from business generated before 1985. These claims were originating in states where severe downturns in farming, auto production, and oil drilling had led to a widespread inability to keep up with mortgage payments.

Not surprisingly, Teets could not find a buyer for Verex. In January 1988, Greyhound announced that it had stopped taking applications for new mortgage insurance and that it was discontinuing its mortgage insurance business. It also announced that 1987 results would reflect a one-time after-tax charge of $45 million as a result of reclassifying Verex as a discontinued operation; then Greyhound would manage Verex's existing portfolio to minimize continuing losses from the company's operations. Management hoped the remnants of Verex would not be a drain on corporate resources.

With the sale of Greyhound Bus Lines, Greyhound Capital Corporation, and Armour, and with the discontinuation of Verex, Teets announced that he was near the end of his mammoth task of restructuring Greyhound and shedding businesses that seemed to lack sufficient growth potential. By late 1987, Greyhound Corporation was primarily a consumer products and services company. Figure 2 summarizes the contribution of the different operating groups to total revenues in 1988. Compare the Greyhound Corporation that Teets structured (Figure 2) with the corporation he inherited in 1982 (Figure 1).

TEETS'S NEW MOVES

With the restructuring in place, Wall Street looked for an improvement in Greyhound's performance. However, it soon became obvious that the stack of businesses created by Teets was not proving much

FIGURE 2

Greyhound 1988

Total Revenues: 3.3 Billion

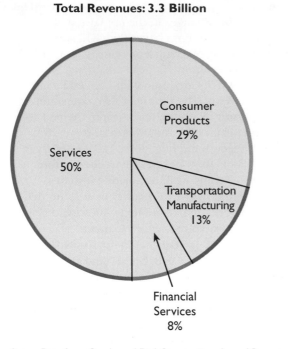

Source: Data from Greyhound Dial Corporation, Annual Report, 1990.

more profitable than the ones he had divested. There was only an 8.8 percent return on equity in 1987, and net income after nonrecurring losses was $25.1 million, the lowest for many years. Revenue was $2.5 billion. Teets maintained that the problems with Greyhound's various divisions could not have been foreseen as the restructuring was taking place but that Greyhound was set for "substantial profits in the future." Teets began a program of acquisitions and new product developments to strengthen Greyhound's presence in the four business areas identified in Figure 2 and begin the turnaround process.

Consumer Products

In the midst of the divestiture of Armour and Greyhound Bus Lines, Teets had made one major acquisition. On February 21, 1985, Teets an-

nounced the purchase of Purex Industries and its thirty household cleaning products for $264 million. Teets's aim with this acquisition was to boost profits in Greyhound's Consumer Products operating division (principally composed of the old Dial division) by using the Dial sales force and marketing expertise to sell Purex products— Purex bleach, Brillo soap pads, Old Dutch cleanser, and Sweetheart and Fels-Naptha soap, among others.

The Purex acquisition drew mixed reviews from Wall Street. It did not meet Teets's goal of a 15 percent return, but Teets believed that it would by 1988. Analysts were also unimpressed with the purchase because Greyhound had not been successful in managing Armour. Teets responded that Dial was capable of marketing consumer products, although it had not been successful at developing its own lines. He cited as evidence the fact that Dial was marketing the number one deodorant soap in its Dial brand. Analysts did concede that Teets should be able to realize increased profitability by using the same sales force to sell Purex and Dial products. Along with Purex's household cleaners, Greyhound also got Elio's Pizza as part of the Purex acquisition. Teets was enthusiastic about expanding this frozen pizza business nationwide from its East Coast base. This was to be done by means of the Dial sales force.[13]

The Dial operating division, as it was now known, became the center of Teets's attention and the flagship of the Greyhound Corporation. In the past Dial had not had much success in launching new products, but Teets was determined to change the situation, recognizing that growth in revenue had to come from the manufacture and marketing of new products. The first product introduced by the Dial division was Lunch Buckets, a range of microwavable meals with a stable shelf life of two years. This was a new market segment. Previously all microwavable meals had been frozen. Lunch Buckets meals were very successful and surpassed early expectations by a wide margin. By 1988, they had national distribution. By 1990, they had seized a 30 percent market share, becoming the market leader. In 1990, Dial announced new low-calorie Lunch Buckets.

Another new product introduced in 1987 was Liquid Dial antibacterial soap. This product, too, was very successful, and by 1990 it had achieved a

20 percent market share and was the second best-selling liquid soap in the market, after Procter & Gamble's Ivory liquid. Another successful new product was Mountain Fresh Dial, a highly scented version of Dial's deodorant soap. Additional developments were liquid Purex detergent and other cleaning products.

In 1988, Teets acquired the household products and industrial specialties businesses of the 20 Mule Team division of United States Borax and Chemical Corporation. Teets announced a new advertising campaign to reestablish the market presence of Borax bleaches and cleaning powders. Teets's formula for increasing the Dial division's market share called for

> further extensions of the Dial brand, further extensions of the Purex brand name, Parsons' ammonia working in those various regional markets. Finding new products that fit in those product niches that will augment the major shares that we have already, that will have a high enough dollar price on them to add to our income.[14]

The Emergence of Greyhound Dial

On June 4, 1990, Teets learned that Greyhound Bus Lines, the bus transportation company that he had sold in 1987, had declared bankruptcy and Greyhound's stake was now valueless. To distance his "new" company from Greyhound, he changed the company's name to Greyhound Dial in February 1990. The name change also marked the company's new focus on its consumer products division. However, the price of Greyhound Dial's stock, which had been more or less unchanged for the last six years, started to plunge in 1990 after Greyhound Dial reported a loss. Analysts wondered whether Teets would ever be able to improve the company's profitability.

In September 1990, another consumer products acquisition was announced: Breck hair care products. Breck had 1989 revenues of $60 million. Teets announced that integrating Breck into Dial would result in annual sales of more than $1 billion for the Dial division. Teets said that "Breck has been a household name for 60 years. It's a perfect fit with our other Dial products and under Dial management the power of the Breck name will flourish."[15] Under its previous owners, Breck had languished.

Teets hoped to turn the product around by applying Dial's marketing skills.

From the changes he had orchestrated, Teets was hoping for sizable revenue growth and profit from the Dial division, and in March 1991, as an indication of the company's future strategy, the company's name was again changed, to the Dial Corporation.

Services

By 1987, Greyhound's restaurant food services division was contributing the most to total revenues. It was natural, therefore, that Teets should seek to strengthen food operations. In 1987, Greyhound purchased the nation's second biggest airline catering and airline retailing business. The new operation had three units: Dobbs International Services, the nation's second largest provider of in-flight meals for airlines; Dobbs Houses, the operator of restaurants at many airports; and Carson International, which operated the food and beverage concession at Chicago's O'Hare Airport. In 1990, Teets announced that Dobbs had had a record year—the company had served sixty scheduled airlines in forty cities. Moreover, it had added five new accounts, including Houston International Airport.

Teets commented about Greyhound's food service businesses as follows:

> I see major changes in the food service business. We are exiting the service businesses that require a great deal of marketing, i.e., pizza and hamburger businesses. And, Greyhound is now primarily in the contract feeding business, be it Dobbs Houses or Restaura, our in-house catering business. Our operations in airports are primarily captive audiences. We also perform contract feeding for General Motors, IBM, office buildings, and banks.[16]

Teets strengthened Greyhound Dial's Travelers Express money order business with the purchase of Republic Money Orders, Inc., of Dallas. This acquisition made Greyhound Dial the leader in the money order business, ahead of the U.S. Postal Service. Teets had returned to the cruise-ship industry in 1984 with the takeover of Premier Cruise Lines. In 1986, he negotiated an agreement with the Walt

Disney Company that made Premier Disney's exclusive cruise-ship line, with three- and four-day sailing to the Bahamas from Cape Canaveral in Florida. The cruise-lines business enjoyed record sales, and in 1989 another line was added.

THE NEW LOOK OF THE DIAL CORPORATION

The new look of Dial's businesses after the acquisitions and divestitures is shown in Table 1. Teets acknowledged the wide diversity of businesses in the company's portfolio. However, he contended that the businesses did fit together. In his words, "We are a multiservice business. We operate in niches and were number one or two in most of these niches. From a recession standpoint, I think we're going to feel it less than most major companies."[17] Teets argued that Greyhound Dial was making acquisitions to strengthen its presence in existing niches. By concentrating on a niche, the corporation avoided going head-to-head with major competitors. Moreover, the niches were recession-proof, small-ticket items such as Lunch Buckets and

TABLE I

Greyhound's Businesses

Consumer Products	Services	Transportation Manufacturing	Financial Services
The Dial Corporation	Brewster Transport Company, Ltd.	Motor Coach Industries (MCI)	Greyhound Financial Corporation
Food	Consultants and Designers, Inc.	Transportation Manufacturing Corporation (TMC)	Greyhound Financial and Leasing
Personal care	Carson International, Inc.	• Custom Coach	Greyhound Financial Services, Ltd.
Laundry and household	Dobbs Houses, Inc.		Greyhound Bank PLC
	Dobbs International Services, Inc.		

Greyhound Airport Services Companies

Greyhound Exhibitgroup, Inc.

Greyhound Exposition Services, Inc.

Greyhound Food Management, Inc.
- Faber Enterprises, Inc.
- Glacier Park, Inc.
- GFM Engineering and Design Group
- GFM Fast Food Division
- GFM Public Service Division
- GFM Truckstop Systems
- Restaura
- Restaura, S.A.

Greyhound International Travel, Inc. (GITI)

Greyhound Leisure Services, Inc. (GLSI)
- Florida Export Warehouse
- International Cruise Shops
- Greyhound Leisure Services Duty-Free Shops
- Premier Cruise Lines, Ltd.

Greyhound Lines of Canada, Ltd.

Travelers Express Company, Inc.
- Republic Money Orders, Inc.

Universal Coach Parts, Inc.

Source: Greyhound Dial Corporation, Annual Report, 1990.

TABLE 2

The Dial Corporation: Consolidated Balance Sheet
(000 omitted, except per share data)

	Year ended December 31		
	1995	*1994*	*1993*
Revenues	$3,575,070	$3,546,847	$3,000,342
Costs and expenses			
Costs of sales and services	3,271,151	3,216,627	2,725,049
Restructuring charges and asset write-downs	191,100		
Unallocated corporate expense and other items, net	43,194	43,938	42,734
Interest expense	75,994	61,195	57,292
Minority interests	4,346	3,392	3,618
	3,585,785	3,325,152	2,828,693
Income (loss) before income taxes	(10,715)	221,695	171,649
Income taxes (benefit)	(11,852)	81,384	61,376
Income from Continuing Operations	1,137	140,311	110,273
Income from discontinued operations			32,120
Income before extraordinary charge and cumulative effect of change in accounting principle	1,137	140,311	142,393
Extraordinary charge for early retirement of debt, net of tax benefit of $11,833			(21,908)
Cumulative effect, net of tax benefit of $7,544, to January 1, 1995, of initial application of SFAS No. 121, "Accounting for the Impairment of Long-Lived Assets and for Long-Lived Assets to Be Disposed Of"	(17,696)		
Net income (loss)	$ (16,559)	$ 140,311	$ 120,485
Income (Loss) per Common Share			
Continuing operations	$0.00	$1.61	$1.28
Discontinued operations			0.38
Income before extraordinary charge and cumulative effect of change in accounting principle	0.00	1.61	1.66
Extraordinary charge			(0.26)
Cumulative effect, to January 1, 1995, of initial application of SFAS No. 121	(0.20)		
Net income (loss) per common share	$ (0.20)	$ 1.61	$ 1.40

soap, not refrigerators and cars. Teets argued that Greyhound Dial was positioned for growth and that management expected revenues to increase steadily over the next few years. See Table 2.

Some analysts, however, felt that the organization was still a hodgepodge of different businesses in need of rationalization. They pointed to the lack of fit between a cruise-ship line and hotel operations in Glacier National Park and contract cater-

ing, saying that Greyhound Dial was still a collection of companies with no real connection. They also argued that Greyhound Dial's breakup value was more than $60 a share, while its stock price had been in the range of $25 to $35 for years. Teets agreed that some minor divestitures were necessary, but he believed that the best way to proceed was to stay in the same niches and manage the existing businesses more efficiently.

Dial in the 1990s

In 1991, it appeared that, at last, things were going Dial's way. Dial's share price, which had plummeted to less than $10 a share at the end of 1990, rose to almost $25 a share by the end of 1992. This turnaround occurred for several reasons. First, Dial had finally spun off its loss-making financial services group to stockholders so that the liabilities of the new "Finova" Company no longer affected its balance sheet. Second, its consumer products group, and in particular the Dial soap division, was performing strongly. Dial had become the number one selling deodorant soap in the United States, with more than 20 percent of the market. Third, Teets had orchestrated a major downsizing, or what he had called "rightsizing," reducing the number of corporate managers from 400 to 300. Also, all of Dial's different businesses were subjected to close scrutiny to try to reduce costs, and employment was reduced across the board, even in the successful Dial division. Teets also reduced corporate debt from a high of $850 million to $550 million by the sales of certain assets such as Dobbs House, its airport catering company. Analysts hoped that all these events were the first signs of a turnaround in the company's performance.

These hopes were doomed, however, by a series of problems that emerged in Dial's various businesses. In the 1990s, businesses in Dial's transportation manufacturing unit began to perform poorly, draining the company's profits. In 1993, Teets decided to dispose of it. Also, its washing Purex bleach business was doing poorly and losing money. It began to seem that just when Dial was making strides in one of its businesses, problems in another were wiping out the effects of the improvement. Investors began to wonder again about Teets's claims for his recession-proof niche strategy.

By 1995, major problems were affecting many areas of the company, including the pivotal Dial division. Teets, desperate to increase the company's return on equity and stock price, which had been flat since its high in 1992, began again to slash costs. One way he slashed costs was by reducing the advertising budget for Dial soap products from $8.7 million to $4.9 million. However, this was something that no niche player could afford to do when battling such industry giants as Procter & Gamble and Unilever, whose new soap Lever 2000 made major inroads into sales of Dial soap. Dial soap's market share dropped to 17.6 percent from 19.7 percent of the market in 1995, which was a severe blow to the Dial Corporation's most important product line and a disaster for the company.

The Purex division also was not performing well. The Purex bleach line was phased out in 1995 because of mounting losses. Purex detergents, the low-priced detergent that had been selling well, came under intense pressure from Procter & Gamble, which introduced a competing low-priced brand, Ultra Bonus, that was aimed directly at Purex late in 1995. Dial was forced to slash the price of Purex by 10 percent to compete, further cutting into the company's profits. Furthermore, Dial's successful Lunch Buckets, the line of microwave products, had generated a host of imitators from major food companies that quickly introduced their own competing products. Having lost this niche and no longer able to compete, Dial phased out Lunch Buckets in 1995. It began to seem to Dial's managers that even when they found a winning strategy their larger competitors just stole the idea away from them.

Dial's other businesses were also suffering problems. Its cruise-ship line, Premier Cruise Lines, which had formed an agreement with the Walt Disney Company to operate Disney's theme cruises in the Big Red Boat, lost its license in 1995 when Disney decided that it would launch its own cruise line. With four aging ships, and lacking any differentiated appeal in the increasingly competitive cruise-ship industry in the 1990s, the company put its ships up for sale and withdrew from the cruise-ship business—one more recession-proof niche gone.

Then, Dial's airline food business began to suffer in the 1990s when, to cut down on costs in an increasingly competitive airline industry, the major airlines cut back on the quality of the food they offered their customers. Airlines that had offered full meals began to offer snacks, and airlines such as Southwest offered passengers nothing. In airports, too, there had been a move to allow fast-food chains to set up their franchises on-site to increase the variety of foods offered to customers. All this hurt Dial's catering businesses.

It was becoming increasingly obvious to industry analysts that Dial was nothing more than a hodgepodge of different businesses that had nothing in common, were not recession proof, and did not even have a secure niche.

NOW WHAT?

With its profits flat or eroding and no turnaround in sight, the question became how to create new value from Dial's different businesses. The movement of many diversified companies to break up their operations and let individual businesses go it alone in the early 1990s gave Teets his answer. He would split apart Dial's consumer products and services operations—thus dismantling the empire he had built since 1984—into two different companies. One, which will still be known as the Dial Corp., would consist of all its consumer products interests and have revenues of about $1.3 billion. The other, to be called Viad Corp., would manage its remaining financial, catering, and exhibition businesses and have revenues of about $2.2 billion.

Initially, analysts thought that the breakup would allow the two new companies to realize more value. For example, by operating separately, a downturn in the business of one division would no longer hurt the performance of the other. Moreover, after the breakup managers would be able to make decisions that could promote their own businesses, not corporate interests. However, analysts later came to realize that in the future there would be two sets of managers who would have to be paid to manage the two companies and two sets of overhead costs. Moreover, the question arose as to whether there was any value to be created by the breakups because all of Dial's businesses were under threats from more efficient and aggressive competitors.

Analysts came to believe increasingly that more value could be made for shareholders if the company dismantled itself and sold off its assets to the highest bidder. A bidder could then merge a particular Dial business into its own operations and thus reduce manufacturing, distribution, or marketing costs or even use its skills to increase the division's differentiation advantage. Of course, the selloff would mean that many of Dial's managers might find themselves out of well-paying jobs, including Teets who had earned many millions of dollars over the years. On the other hand, these managers had not created much value for their shareholders.

In 1996, Teets answered his critics with half-page ads in the *Wall Street Journal* arguing that his strategy was a "strategy for empowered growth" that would allow each of the two new companies to "aggressively pursue acquisition opportunities without worry about upsetting the balance in Dial's existing mix of business." However, he did not explain how new value would be created by the two companies or how the proposed acquisitions might create value. Since Teets's acquisition strategy has met little success for the last twelve years, what reason would shareholders have to suppose it would improve in the future?

In July 1996, Michael Price, seeking to prevent the split-off by arguing that it was not in the best interests of shareholders, filed a claim with the Securities and Exchange Commission. A Dial spokesperson immediately responded that Dial felt that a delay was not in the best interest of Dial's shareholders and that the company still planned to go ahead with the split-off, which was scheduled for sometime in the fall of 1996.

Endnotes

1. *Moody's Transportation Manual,* 1987.
2. A. Stuart, "Greyhound Gets Ready for a New Driver," *Fortune,* March 3, 1966, pp. 34–38.
3. Greyhound Corporation, Annual Reports, 1966–1970.
4. Ibid.
5. Greyhound Corporation, Annual Report, 1980.
6. "Greyhound: A Big Sell-off Leaves It Built for Better Speed," *BusinessWeek,* July 25, 1983, pp. 88–90.
7. Greyhound Corporation, Annual Reports, 1970–1978.
8. "Greyhound's New Strategy: Slimmed Down and Decentralized, It's After More Market Share, 15% on Equity," *Dun's Business Month* (February 1984), 66–68.
9. "Greyhound: A Big Sell-off."
10. "Greyhound's New Strategy."
11. Greyhound Corporation, Annual Report, 1986.
12. Ibid.
13. S. Toy and J. H. Dobrzynski, "Will More Soap Help Greyhound Shine?" *BusinessWeek,* March 11, 1985, pp. 73–78.
14. "The Greyhound Corporation," *Wall Street Journal Transcript,* February 5, 1990, pp. 96, 204.
15. Greyhound Dial News Release, September 10, 1990.
16. "The Greyhound Corporation," pp. 96, 204.
17. Ibid.

Enron International in India

This case was prepared by Charles W. L. Hill of the University of Washington.

INTRODUCTION

Back in 1990, Enron, a Houston-based independent power company, established a subsidiary, Enron International, and gave it the mission of building and running power generation projects in the developing world. Enron's chairman appointed one of his protégés, Rebecca Mark, then only thirty-six years old, as CEO of the new unit. By 1997, the outspoken and photogenic Mark, who was fast gaining a reputation as one of the most dynamic businesswomen in America, had built Enron International into a global operation with sales of $1.1 billion, annual profits of $220 million, and a backlog of international energy projects worth more than $20 billion. The potential jewel in Enron International's crown was a growing presence in India. By the end of 1997, Enron International had plans to invest $20 billion in India. Getting to this point, however, had severely tested Mark's diplomatic skills and political acumen.

ENRON'S INDIA STRATEGY

Enron's interests in India date back to 1991, when the country's former prime minister, Narasimha Rao, visited the United States to seek help with India's economic development. Rao asked Enron if it was interested in independent power projects in the country. This request signaled a shift of policy in India. Since independence from Britain in 1947, political opinion in India had by and large been op-

This case is intended to be used as the basis for class discussion rather than to illustrate either effective or ineffective handling of the situation. This case was prepared by Charles W. L. Hill of the University of Washington. Used by permission.

posed to significant foreign direct investment on anything other than terms that were highly favorable to the host country. Indeed, for almost half a century, Indian politics had been strongly influenced by Gandhi's doctrine of *swadeshi*, or self-reliance. This had been translated into a presumption against foreign investment and a desire to see India build its own domestic industries under the protection of restrictions on foreign investment and high import tariffs.

However, by the 1990s the winds of ideological change were blowing through India. The national government seemed to be embracing a free market approach, which included substantial deregulation and the loosening of rules on foreign direct investment. Consistent with this, in October 1991 Rao's government liberalized India's domestic power-producing sector, allowing private developers, both Indian and foreign, to build and operate independent power projects with no restrictions on foreign equity ownership.

India's need for power was obvious. A plentiful supply of electric power is a key requirement for economic development, but India was suffering from chronic power shortages. At peak periods, demand for electricity often exceeded available power supply by more than 20 percent. Moreover, the installed capacity in the early 1990s, which amounted to around 80,000 megawatts, was working at only about 60 percent efficiency. Forecasts suggested that an extra 140,000 megawatts of capacity would be needed by 2005, but public money to finance such massive investments in infrastructure was scarce. In the mid 1990s, around 70 percent of India's electricity supply was being produced by state-owned electricity generation and distribution boards, which collectively were running up losses of more than $2 billion per year. Clearly, they could not afford to fund the required expansions in capacity.

Mark jumped on Rao's offer but quickly discovered that India's energy problems involved more than a simple lack of generating capacity. The country also lacked adequate supplies of fuel. To help solve these problems, Mark articulated a strategic vision that was audacious in scope. The vision called for Enron to invest up to $20 billion to become the largest distributor and consumer of liquefied natural gas (LNG) in India by 2010. Under the plan, Enron would set up two LNG terminals and regassification units in India, one at Dabhol in the state of Maharashtra, and one at Ennore in the state of Tamil Nadu. The company would construct two gas-based power-generating plants near the terminals. Enron would also build a network of pipelines to pipe the gas to its LNG terminals from oil and gas fields near Bombay, and then onward to its own and other power plants around the country. The Bombay fields, however, were not large enough to supply India's projected LNG needs, so the company also planned to import LNG from a facility that it was building in the Gulf State of Qatar. The Qatar facility would cost $4 billion to complete, and was being funded by a group of investors including the state-owned Qatar Gas & Pipeline Co., Enron International's parent company, and Royal Dutch Shell. Enron International had promised investors in the Qatar facility a 15 percent annual growth in shareholders' income. Achieving this goal, however, depended on the success of Mark's India strategy. Without India, Enron might lack sufficient customers to absorb the LNG output from its Qatar facility.

THE DABHOL PROJECT

By mid 1992, Mark was moving forward with the first stage of her plan. She was deep in negotiations with the Indian federal government and the government of the state of Maharashtra where Enron's Dabhol power plant was to be constructed. The Dabhol project was bold; Enron was to develop a 2,015-megawatt power plant that would be fired by LNG. The total cost for the project was well over $2 billion, making the Dabhol project the single largest foreign investment ever committed to India and the biggest independent power project in the world.

The choice of Dabhol for Enron's first investment in India was dictated by a number of factors. Located on India's western seaboard, the state of Maharashtra and its capital, Bombay, were enjoying a sustained period of political stability and economic growth. This had enabled the state to attract industry from other areas of India, such as the traditional industrial heartlands of Calcutta and eastern India. Economic growth in these regions had suffered under successive Communist governments at the state level. The Western seaboard was also closer to the Gulf States, and Qatar in particular, which would lower the costs of shipping LNG. Moreover, the state of Maharashtra was at that time governed by the Congress Party, the same party that governed the nation. Mark reasoned that Prime Minister Rao would be able to pressure the local state government to approve the project.

Mark was alert to the basic political realities in India. While the federal government in Delhi might in principle approve the project, she realized that Enron would also have to win approval from the Maharashtra state government and cultivate the approval of key players in India's extensive civil service. To get the Dabhol project approved, the company needed to get 170 different state and federal permits, to sort through fifty complicated legal questions, and to deal with a complex web of state and federal taxes. Reflecting on this process, Mark reported that

> I've had tea with every bureaucrat in India.... People (foreigners) don't understand how to get things done in India. Politicians lay out a plan, but that's different from working through the system. There's only one political level approval—that of the foreign investment board. But then there are all sorts of channels and procedures needed. Politicians will never intervene and force a bureaucrat to make a decision when an issue of process is at stake. This is where companies mess up and are confused.[1]

By early 1995, Enron had received full approval for the project and was proceeding with the initial construction. However, storm clouds were gathering on the political horizon of Maharashtra, and they spelled trouble for Enron. Throughout the negotiations, Maharashtra had been controlled by the Congress Party. Its local leader, Sharad Pawar, was a big supporter of Enron's Dabhol project. Unfortunately, during 1994 and early 1995 the popularity of the Congress Party started to decline. In 1994, a series of ethnic riots swept through Bombay. Anti-Muslim hysteria had been whipped up by Shiv Sena, a local militant Hindu nationalist party. The party was led by Bal Thackery, a former political cartoonist and an admirer of Adolf Hitler. To fight upcoming state elections in February 1995, Shiv Sena formed an alliance with a less extreme Hindu nationalist party, the BJP. In the event that the alliance won the state elections, Shiv Sena would control the local administration in Maharashtra, while the BJP would occupy any seats won by the alliance in the national parliament.

During the election campaign, Shiv Sena seized on the Dabhol project and used it to attack the Congress Party and its leader, Sharad Pawer. Shiv Sena claimed that Pawer had been bribed by Enron to support the Dabhol project. This played well in the court of public opinion in India, where in the words of one observer, "the popular belief is that any dealings with foreigners are bound to be either crooked or disadvantageous. Maybe 9 times out of 10 this is correct."[2] The BJP also warmed to this theme as the election campaign progressed, and began to champion the Gandhi doctrine of *swadeshi*. Both the BJP and Shiv Sena successfully contrasted their defense of Indian rights and Indian self-reliance with what they depicted as the corrupt machinations of Enron, Pawer, and the Congress Party.

Fuel was added to this fire when an Enron official, in testimony before a committee of the U.S. Congress that was dealing with foreign aid allocations, revealed that Enron had spent $20 million to educate Indians about the benefits of its various power projects in the country. (The Enron official made the apparently innocent suggestion that the U.S. government might want to use its foreign aid help with such educational campaigns). Elements of the Indian press, in concert with Shiv Sena, seized on this "revelation" to claim that the $20 million had been used primarily to "educate" corrupt officials such as Pawer in order to win approval for the Dabhol project—in other words, that much of the $20 million had been in the form of bribes. In the heat of the election campaign, it apparently mattered little that there was no evidence whatsoever that Enron had bribed anyone. Mud sticks, and the charges proved to be powerful ammunition. As a result, in February 1995 Pawer and the Congress Party were swept from power in the state of Maharashtra to be replaced by Shiv Sena and its new chief minister, Manohar Joshi.

After the election, the new government set up a committee, under the leadership of Gopinath Munde, the BJP deputy minister in the coalition, to review the Dabhol project. The committee was to review the charges of corruption and abuse that had been leveled at Enron during the election campaign. However, Rebecca Mark felt she was on solid ground. Enron had not done anything wrong, contracts had been signed, construction work on the project was under way, India clearly needed the power, and the agreements protected Enron from any unilateral breach of contract. If the state canceled the project, it would be hit with a $200 million cancellation fee.

In mid 1995, the state government committee reviewing the Dabhol project finished its report. The report was never published, although excerpts were leaked to the press and in them Enron was accused of deception and cost padding. Enron vigorously denied these charges. On the cost padding charges, Rebecca Mark later noted that "In India you are supposed to have a 20 percent import duty on equipment. But when it comes right down to it, very common in a project is that it doesn't end up being 20 percent but whatever the customs inspector wants it to be on the day you get there. So you have to price that risk in."[3] The implication was that a risk premium had been built into Enron's contract with the state of Maharashtra.

The report also criticized the previous administration for not putting the Dabhol project out to competitive bid. Privately, Enron officials noted that this was an absurd charge. After all, Enron had been invited to the country by Prime Minister Rao, it was Enron that had first suggested the Dabhol project, and Enron was the only foreign power producer apparently willing to shoulder the risk associated with such a large investment in the country. Reflecting this, Bob Pender, an independent lawyer who specializes in financing energy projects, noted that the lack of competitive bidding "was the opportunity cost of getting a company to come and create an industry."[4]

Significantly though, the committee was not able to uncover any evidence of corruption on the part of either Enron or Indian political officials. However, after having made such an issue of the project during the election, the Shiv Sena/BJP coalition was not yet ready to back down. On August 3, 1995, the state government issued a work stoppage order on the deal, after Enron had already spent $100 million.

Two days later, Enron served the state government with legal notice that it would pursue arbitration in London. The Maharashtra state government was now facing damages of at least $300 million, with the possibility of another $500 million on top of that. On August 12, Little & Co, which had acted as the lawyers for the Maharashtra state government for the previous twenty years, resigned and stated off the record that the state's position was indefensible. Top civil servants in the state also reportedly told Munde and Joshi that the government's position was untenable.

Simultaneously, Enron mounted a public relations campaign of its own. Enron ran full-page advertisements in Indian newspapers publicizing the benefits to India of its Dabhol project. It also prevailed on U.S. president Bill Clinton to call the Indian premier to try and get the project started again. By September, public opinion polls showed that 80 percent of the people in Maharashtra and 60 percent of those in India wanted the project restarted.

Despite rising pressure to restart the project, the Shiv Sena/BJP coalition government was unwilling to back off without getting something in return. By this point, however, it was clear that the best interests of all parties would be served by a compromise. Enron wanted to get the project back on track. It still had big plans for India, and then there was that plant in Qatar whose output was projected for India. The Maharashtra government, for its part, was facing the potential of heavy damages, and was rapidly losing support for its position. At the same time, the government needed evidence that its efforts had not been for naught; it needed to save face.

That fall Mark returned to the bargaining table, and a settlement was worked out. Enron agreed to cut the price it charged for power generated by the Dabhol project by 22.6 percent. In return, Enron walked away with a deal for a 2,450-megawatt plant, 450 megawatts bigger than the initial plant. According to Enron, the larger plant would realize much greater scale economies and allow Enron to maintain its projected rate of return on investment while simultaneously cutting prices.

AFTERMATH

Reflecting on her Indian experience, Mark suggests that the key to Enron's success was its intention to help India solve a problem and to stay engaged in the country for the long term. She and her colleagues have spent six years coming to India, meeting with the same people, talking about the same projects. Says Mark, "I don't think that anyone who works with us doubts our intentions, goodwill, or long term commitment to India. We've earned a place on the list of friendlies."[5] Mark also believes that Enron's appeal to the people of India ultimately served the company well. She concludes that "Our experience tells us that India's a good environment for foreign investment, and a market where foreign investors are seen as necessary. If anything, our experience proves the strength of the system in India to withstand a lot of assaults from different places. Even though the political system is shaky, the judiciary and the business system work."[6]

In February 1997, Enron reaffirmed its commitment to India when it submitted a proposal to build five to seven more power plants in the country at a total cost of $10 billion. As for the Dabhol plant, the first phase of the project, which will generate 740 megawatts of power, was completed in December 1998, three months ahead of schedule.

For India's part, there is little doubt that Enron's experience with the Dabhol project was something of a public relations setback. Although ultimately the outcome reaffirmed the country's commitment to encouraging foreign direct investment, the perception has been created that the shifting political landscape, bureaucratic rules, and the crosscurrents between national and state governments, make India a difficult place in which to invest. As noted by a former U.S. ambassador to India, William Clark, the Dabhol incident "Sends the right signals, but unfortunately it sent off the wrong signals for a while. Just like a retraction in a newspaper, it will take a long time for people to notice."[7]

Endnotes

1. From C. Hill, "How Rebecca Mark Solved India," *Institutional Investor* (January 1998), 28G.
2. B. Edwards and M. Shukla, "The Mugging of Enron," *Euromoney* (October 1995), 28–33.
3. P. Sibbald, "You Have to Be Pushy and Aggressive," *Business Week*, February 24, 1997, p. 56.
4. Edwards and Shukla, "The Mugging of Enron."
5. Hill, "How Rebecca Mark Solved India."
6. "It's a Done Deal," *Journal of Commerce*, December 20, 1996, p. 7B.
7. Ibid. The following sources were also used in the preparation of this case: T. Mack, "High Finance with a Touch of Theater," *Forbes*, May 18, 1998, p. 140–154; G. McWilliams, "More Power to India," *Business Week*, January 22, 1996, p. 62; and M. Nicholson, "Dabhol Plant Finally Gets Green Light," *Financial Times*, January 9, 1996, p. 6

Nestlé: Global Strategy

This case was prepared by Charles W. L. Hill of the University of Washington.

INTRODUCTION

Nestlé is one of the oldest of all multinational businesses. The company was founded in Switzerland in 1866 by Heinrich Nestlé, who established Nestlé to distribute "milk food"—a type of infant food that he had invented that was made from powered milk, baked food, and sugar. From its very early days, the company looked to other countries for growth opportunities, establishing its first foreign offices in London in 1868. In 1905, the company merged with the Anglo-Swiss Condensed Milk, thereby broadening its product line to include both condensed milk and infant formulas. Forced by Switzerland's small size to look outside for growth opportunities, Nestlé established condensed milk and infant food processing plants in the United States and Britain in the late nineteenth century, and in Australia, South America, Africa and Asia in the first three decades of the twentieth century.

In 1929, Nestlé moved into the chocolate business when it acquired the activities of a Swiss chocolate maker. This was followed in 1938 by the development of Nestlé's most revolutionary product, Nescafé, the world's first soluble coffee drink. In the period after the second world war Nestlé continued to expand into other areas of the food business, primarily through a series of acquisitions that included Maggi (1947), Cross & Blackwell (1960), Findus (1962), Libby's (1970), Stouffer's (1973), Carnation (1985), Rowntree (1988), and Perrier (1992).

As a result of this growth strategy, by the late 1990s Nestlé had 500 factories in 76 countries and sold its products in a staggering 193 nations—just about every country in the world. In 1998, the company generated sales of close to CHF 72 billion ($51 billion), only 1 percent of which were made in its home country. Similarly, only 3 percent of its 210,000 employees were located in Switzerland. Nestlé was the world's biggest maker of infant formula, powdered milk, chocolates, instant coffee, soups, and mineral waters. It was number two in ice cream, breakfast cereals, and pet food. Roughly 38 percent of its food sales were made in Europe, 32 percent in the Americas, and 20 percent in Africa and Asia.

A GROWTH STRATEGY FOR THE TWENTY-FIRST CENTURY CHALLENGES TO GROWTH

Despite its undisputed success, by the early 1990s Nestlé realized that it faced significant challenges in maintaining its growth rate. The large western European and North American markets were now mature. In several countries, population growth had stagnated, and in some there had been a small decline in food consumption. Moreover, the retail environment in many Western nations had become increasingly challenging, and the balance of power was shifting away from the large scale manufacturers of branded foods and beverages and toward nationwide supermarket and discount chains.

Increasingly, retailers found themselves in the unfamiliar position of being able to play off manufacturers of branded foods against each other, bargaining down prices in the process. Particularly in Europe, this trend was enhanced by the successful introduction of private label brands by several of Europe's leading supermarket chains. The results included increased price competition in several key segments of the food and beverage market, such as cereals, coffee, and soft drinks.

At Nestlé, one response to these developments has been to look toward emerging markets in eastern Europe, Asia, and Latin America for growth possibilities. The logic is simple and obvious—a combination of economic and population growth, when coupled with the widespread adoption of market-oriented economic policies by the governments of many developing nations, makes for attractive growth opportunities. Many of these countries are still relatively poor, but their economies are growing rapidly. For example, if current economic growth forecasts come to pass, by 2010 there will be 700 million people in China and India that have income levels approaching those of Spain in the mid 1990s. As income levels rise, it is increasingly likely that consumers in these nations will start to substitute branded food products for basic foodstuffs, thereby creating a large market opportunity for companies such as Nestlé.

In general, the company's strategy has been to try and enter emerging markets early—hopefully before competitors—and build up a substantial position by selling basic food items that appeal to the local population base, such as infant formula, condensed milk, noodles, and tofu. By narrowing its initial market focus to just a handful of strategic brands, Nestlé claims it can simplify life, reduce risk, and concentrate its marketing resources and managerial effort on a limited number of key niches. The goal is to build a commanding market position in each of these niches. By pursuing such a strategy, Nestlé has taken as much as 85 percent of the market for instant coffee in Mexico, 66 percent of the market for powdered milk in the Philippines, and 70 percent of the market for soups in Chile. As income levels rise, the company progressively moves out from these niches, introducing more upscale items, such as mineral water, chocolate, cookies, and prepared foodstuffs.

Although the company is known worldwide for several key brands, such as Nescafé, it uses local brands in a wide range of local markets. Indeed, although it owns 8,500 brands, only 750 of them are registered in more than one country, and only 80 are registered in more than ten countries. While Nestlé will use the same "global brands" in multiple developed markets, in the developing world it focuses more effort on trying to optimize ingredients and processing technology to local conditions, and then using a brand name that resonates locally. Customization rather than globalization, therefore, is the key to its strategy in emerging markets.

EXECUTING THE STRATEGY

Successful execution of the strategy for developing markets requires a degree of flexibility, an ability to adapt in often unforeseen ways to local conditions, and a long-term perspective that puts building a sustainable business before short-term profitability. In Nigeria, for example, a crumbling road system, aging trucks, and the danger of violence forced the company to rethink its traditional distribution methods. Instead of operating a central warehouse, as is its preference in most nations, it has built a network of small warehouses around the country. For safety reasons, trucks carrying Nestlé goods are allowed to travel only during the day, and frequently under armed guard. Marketing also poses challenges in Nigeria. With little opportunity for typical Western style advertising on television or billboards, the company has resorted to hiring local singers to go to towns and villages offering a mix of entertainment and product demonstrations.

China provides another interesting example of local adaptation and a long-term focus. After thirteen years of talks, Nestlé was formally invited into China in 1987 by the government of Heilongjiang province. Nestlé opened a plant to produce powdered milk and infant formula there in 1990 but quickly realized that the local rail and road infrastructure was totally inadequate and inhibited the collection of milk and delivery of finished products. Rather than try and make do with the local infrastructure, Nestlé embarked an ambitious plan to establish its own distribution network, known as "milk roads," between twenty-seven villages in the region and factory collection points, called "chilling centers." Farmers brought their milk—often on bicycles or carts—to the centers, where it was weighed and analyzed. Unlike the government, Nestlé paid the farmers promptly. Suddenly, the farmers had an incentive to produce milk, and many bought a second cow, increasing the cow population in the district by 3,000 to 9,000 in eighteen months. Area managers then organized a delivery system that used dedicated vans to deliver the milk to Nestlé's factory.

Although at first glance this might seem to be a very costly solution, Nestlé calculated that the long-term benefits would be substantial. Indeed, Nestlé's strategy is similar to that undertaken by many European and American companies during the first waves of industrialization in those countries. There, too, companies often had to invest in infrastructure that we now take for granted in order to get production off the ground. Sure enough, once the infrastructure was in place, production took off. In 1990, 316 tons of powdered milk and infant formula was produced. By 1994, the output exceeded 10,000 tons, and the company decided to triple capacity. Based on this experience, Nestlé has decided to build another two powdered milk factories in China and is aiming to generate sales of $700 million by 2000.

Nestlé is pursuing a similar long-term bet in the Middle East—an area that most multinational food companies have little presence in. Collectively, the Middle East accounts for only about 2 percent of Nestlé's worldwide sales, and the individual markets are very small. However, Nestlé's long-term strategy is based on the assumption that regional conflicts will subside and intraregional trade will expand as trade barriers between countries in the area come down. Once that happens, Nestlé's factories in the Middle East should be able to sell throughout the region, thereby realizing scale economies. In anticipation of this development, Nestlé has established a network of factories in five countries in hopes that each will someday supply the entire region with different products. The company currently makes ice cream in Dubai, soups and cereals in Saudi Arabia, yogurt and bouillon in Egypt, chocolate in Turkey, and ketchup and instant noodles in Syria. For the present, Nestlé can survive in these markets by using local materials and focusing on local demand. The Syrian factory, for example, relies on products that use tomatoes, a major local agricultural product. Syria also produces wheat, which is the main ingredient in instant noodles. Even if trade barriers don't come down anytime soon, Nestlé has indicated that it will remain committed to the region. By using local inputs and focusing on local consumer needs, it has been able to earn a good rate of return in the region, even though the individual markets are small.

Despite its successes in places such as China and parts of the Middle East, not all of Nestlé's

moves have worked out so well. Like several other Western companies, Nestlé has had its problems in Japan, where a failure to adapt its coffee brand to local conditions meant the loss of a significant market opportunity to another Western company, Coca-Cola. For years, Nestlé's instant coffee brand was the dominant coffee product in Japan. In the 1960s, cold canned coffee (which can be purchased from soda vending machines) started to gain a following in Japan. Nestlé dismissed the product as just a coffee-flavored drink, rather than the real thing, and declined to enter the market. Nestlé's local partner at the time, Kirin Beer, was so incensed at Nestlé's refusal to enter the canned coffee market that it broke off its relationship with the company. In contrast, Coca-Cola entered the market with a product developed specifically for this segment of the Japanese market, Georgia. By leveraging its existing distribution channel, Coca-Cola was able to capture a 40 percent share of the $4-billion-a-year market for canned coffee in Japan. Nestlé, which failed to enter the market until the 1980s, has only a 4 percent share.

While Nestlé has built businesses from the ground up in many emerging markets, such as Nigeria and China, in others it will purchase local companies if suitable candidates can be found. The company pursued just such a strategy in Poland, which it entered in 1994 by purchasing Goplana, the country's second largest chocolate manufacturer. With the collapse of communism and the opening up of the Polish market, income levels in Poland have started to rise, and so has chocolate consumption. Once chocolate was a scarce item, but the market grew by 8 percent per annum throughout the 1990s. To take advantage of this opportunity, Nestlé has pursued a strategy of evolution, rather than revolution. It has kept the top management of the company staffed with locals—as it does in most of its operations around the world—and carefully adjusted Goplana's product line to better match local opportunities. At the same time, it has pumped money into Goplana's marketing, which has enabled the unit to gain share from several other chocolate makers in the country. Still, competition in the market is intense. Eight companies, including several foreign-owned enterprises, such as the market leader, Wedel, which is owned by PepsiCo, are vying for market share, and this has depressed prices and profit margins, despite the healthy volume growth.

MANAGEMENT STRUCTURE

Nestlé is a decentralized organization. Responsibility for operating decisions is pushed down to local units, which typically enjoy a high degree of autonomy with regard to decisions involving pricing, distribution, marketing, human resources, and so on. At the same time, the company is organized into seven worldwide strategic business units (SBUs) that have responsibility for high-level strategic decisions and business development. There is, for example, a strategic business unit that focuses on coffee and beverages. Another one focuses on confectionery and ice cream. These SBUs engage in overall strategy development, including acquisitions and market entry strategy. In recent years, two-thirds of Nestlé's growth has come from acquisitions, so this is a critical function. Running in parallel to this structure is a regional organization that divides the world into five major geographical zones, such as Europe, North America, and Asia. The regional organizations assist in the overall strategy development process and are responsible for developing regional strategies (an example would be Nestlé's strategy in the Middle East, which was discussed earlier). Neither the SBU nor regional managers, however, get involved in local operating or strategic decisions on anything other than an exceptional basis.

Although Nestlé makes intensive use of local managers, to knit its diverse worldwide operations together the company relies on its "expatriate army." This is a cadre of managers who spend the bulk of their careers on foreign assignments, moving from one country to the next. There are around 700 individuals in this group. Selected primarily on the basis of their ability, drive, and willingness to live a quasi-nomadic lifestyle, these individuals often work in half a dozen different nations during the course of their career. Nestlé also uses management development programs as a strategic tool for bringing together managers and creating an *esprit de corps*. At Rive-Reine, the company's international training center in Switzerland, the company brings together managers from around the world, at different stages in their careers, for specially targeted development programs of two to three weeks' duration. The objective of these programs is to give the managers a better understanding of Nestlé's culture and strategy, and to give them access to the company's top management.

The Research and Development operation has a special place within Nestlé, which is perhaps not surprising for a company that was established to commercialize innovative foodstuffs. The R&D function comprises eighteen different groups, which operate in eleven countries throughout the world. Nestlé spends approximately 1 percent of its annual sales revenue on R&D and has 3,100 employees dedicated to the function. Around 70 percent of the R&D budget is spent on development initiatives. These initiatives focus on developing products and processes that fulfill market needs, as identified by the SBUs, in concert with regional and local managers. So, for example, Nestlé instant noodle products were originally developed by the R&D group in response to the perceived needs of local operating companies through the region. The company also has longer-term development projects, which focus on new technological platforms, such as non-animal protein sources or agricultural biotechnology products.

References

Hall, W. "Strength of Brands Is Key to Success." *Financial Times*, November 30, 1998, p. 2.

"How to Conquer China (and the World) with Instant Noodles." *Economist*, June 17, 1995.

Lorenz, C. "Sugar Daddy." *Financial Times*, April 20, 1994, p. 19.

Michaels, D. "Chocolate Giants Worldwide Find Themselves Sweet on Polish Market." *Wall Street Journal*, December 12, 1997.

Nestlé. Key Facts and History (www.nestle.com).

Rapoport, C. "Nestlé's Brand-Building Machine." *Fortune*, September 19, 1994, p. 147.

Steinmetz, G. and T. Parker-Rope. "All over the Map." *Wall Street Journal*, September 26, 1996, p. R4.

Sullivan, M. "Nestlé Is Looking to Coffee Market in Russia for Sales." *Wall Street Journal*, August 7, 1998, p. B7.

CASE 34

Pharmacia & Upjohn

This case was prepared by Gareth R. Jones of Texas A & M University.

In September 1995 the Upjohn Company, one of the largest pharmaceutical companies in the United States, announced that it was merging with Pharmacia, the largest Swedish pharmaceutical company. With Upjohn's annual sales of $3.3 billion and Pharmacia's of $3.6 billion, the merger created the ninth largest pharmaceutical company in the world, Pharmacia & Upjohn. What prompted Upjohn's management to seek a merger that would change the future of the company forever? To answer this question, it is necessary to study Upjohn's history and its performance in the turbulent pharmaceutical industry of the last decade.

HISTORY

For the first seventy-three years of its existence, the Upjohn Company was a family-owned and -operated, domestic pharmaceutical company. In 1885, W. E. Upjohn was granted a patent on a manufacturing process that produced a "friable" pill. The new pill disintegrated rapidly in the body to speed the release of medication. This friability contrasted with the hardness of many of the mass-produced pills of the day, which often passed through the body without releasing their contents. This manufacturing process and the secrecy that surrounded it fueled the early growth of the company and made it difficult for other companies to imitate the popular product. The founder speeded the company's growth with a policy of selling his pills at

about half the price of the old-style, mass-produced pills, generating considerable hostility from competitors in doing so. The company expanded its product line quickly, offering 500 products by 1892 and 2,000 by 1900.

By 1900, the new technology of compressed tablets superseded the friable pill, and Upjohn had to imitate the innovations of other companies and produce the new tablets. Tablets that disintegrated rapidly in the body were much easier to mass-produce. The company began featuring tablets and created a tablet department to speed product development.

From its beginnings, Upjohn was strongly aware of the need to develop marketing strengths to complement the company's research and development and manufacturing skills. Realizing early that the profit potential from mass-produced tablets would be low, Upjohn emphasized the need to develop and market quality-based, high-price drug products that would give higher profit margins. Perceiving the company as operating in a luxury market, he had the insight to switch its focus from pills to tablets and to emphasize product characteristics. For example, he pioneered the development of pleasantly flavored drugs to suit consumers' tastes. One result was an important innovation called phenolax, a sweetly flavored laxative. It proved to be a big seller for more than forty years.

In the next two decades, Upjohn added a number of promising research areas. In 1912, bacterial vaccines became part of the company's product line. Research was begun in endocrinology and digitalis extracts for heart failure in 1914. A pleasant-tasting alkalizer called Citrocarbonate was introduced in 1921 and reached $1 million in annual sales by 1926, the first Upjohn product to do so. This product and the intensive sales effort that accompanied it marked the emergence of the company as a first-class pharmaceutical house. A succession of other introductions followed, including new flavored versions of cough syrup, cod liver oil, and Kaopectate, still a best-selling antidiarrhea product. Each of these research efforts was stimulated by a perceived need to respond to the demands of the medical community for improved drug products.

Upjohn was always sensitive to the needs of its main "distributor," the doctors who prescribed its products. An aggressive sales push directed toward pharmacists and doctors helped the company to grow through the tough 1930s and into the years of World War II. The medical department was created in 1937 by a member of the founding family, Gifford Upjohn, to upgrade the company's contacts with physicians. This focus became a hallmark of sales efforts at Upjohn. Through the decades that followed, the company continued to differentiate its products and match its sales strategy to the changing composition of the medical profession.

Much of the company's growth through the 1930s and 1940s was tied to vitamins. In 1929, Upjohn was the first to produce a standardized combination of vitamins A and D in the United States. Vitamins accounted for half of the $40 million in sales in 1945 and marked the company as a leader in nutritional supplements. Other products critical to Upjohn's growth included Kaopectate, estrogenic hormone products introduced in the 1930s, antibiotics, and an antidiabetic drug brought out in the 1940s and 1950s.

By 1952, the research department had 421 employees, who viewed their research output as second in quality only to that of Merck & Co. among domestic pharmaceutical companies. The department began to establish broad research areas, which are still important to the company today: antibiotics, steroids, antidiabetes agents, nonsteroidal anti-inflammatory drugs, and central nervous system agents.

The progress of the company's research efforts led to increasing demand for specialty chemicals to manufacture new drug introductions. The company had purchased standardized chemicals in the past, but the growing need for unique materials led to the establishment of the fine chemicals manufacturing division in 1949 to supply the company with its own products. The division expanded into external sales, and by 1984, 40 percent of its production was for other companies.

After World War II, the Upjohn Company continued a modest export program, sending most of its foreign sales representatives to Central and South America. The creation of the export division in 1952 was the first strong corporate signal that management was committed to competing globally. The division was formed in reaction to the globalization strategies of the leading domestic drug companies, which recognized the potential in developing a worldwide market for their products.

In 1958, the twenty-member board of directors, eleven of whom were related directly or by marriage to the founder, voted to recommend public ownership. The following year, the Upjohn Company was formally accepted for listing and trading on the New York Stock Exchange. The decision to go public did not end the involvement of the extended family of the founder, W. E. Upjohn, but it did give the company the additional financial resources it needed to become a stronger force in the global pharmaceutical market.

The company continued to expand its international scope quickly to include sales subsidiaries in Canada, England, and Australia. Through the 1960s and 1970s, it added more subsidiaries and sales offices and built two major production facilities outside the continental United States: one in Belgium in 1963 and the other in Puerto Rico in 1974. By the mid 1980s these plants, in combination with the principal facility in Kalamazoo, Michigan, produced pharmaceuticals for sale in more than 150 countries.

Upjohn's first large venture out of pharmaceuticals came via its entry into animal health products in the late 1940s, when it repackaged several human products, such as antibiotics, for animal use. New products specifically for animals began flowing in 1952, and a sales force targeting veterinarians was established, growing from 1 person in 1956 to 20 in 1957. The sales force gradually increased to 130 by the mid 1980s.

Other agricultural products were added over time. After deciding against entry into fertilizers, the company acquired its core seed company, Asgrow Seed Company, in 1968 to develop new, improved strains of seeds. It added another top-ten domestic seed company, O's Gold, in 1983. The latter was chosen because its sales force and products complemented Asgrow's. In 1974, Upjohn acquired Cobb Breeding Corporation, a producer of chicken broiler breeders, to continue its expansion into animal drugs. In 1986, the company formed a joint venture with Tyson Foods, Inc., to further expand its broiler operations.

Nonagricultural diversification began in the 1960s. The company started manufacturing polymer chemical products in 1962, with the purchase of the Carwin Company, which was combined with the fine chemicals manufacturing operations. The company entered cosmetics in 1964, when several other pharmaceutical companies were doing likewise. In 1969, it entered home nursing services when it purchased Homemakers, Inc.

The chemicals business was profitable for many years. After profits peaked in 1979, however, rapid decline set in because of a down cycle in the principal markets for chemicals. The polymer chemicals operation was sold in 1985, but the fine chemicals manufacturing division was retained. The cosmetics business never proved very profitable and was liquidated in 1974. The home nursing service business was renamed Upjohn Healthcare Services. It quickly added new locations and became the market leader in 1974.

By the mid 1980s, Upjohn had become a global, research-based manufacturer and marketer of pharmaceuticals, chemicals, agricultural seeds and specialties, and health services. In 1987, it had research, manufacturing, sales, and distribution facilities in more than 200 locations worldwide. The company generated almost $2.3 billion in sales in 1986, its centennial year, from two broad industrial segments. First, Upjohn's World-wide Human Health Care Businesses, which concentrates on the development, manufacture, and marketing of drug products globally, accounted for almost 82 percent of total sales in 1986. Second, the agricultural division, which develops and supplies seeds and drugs for use in agriculture and animal production, accounted for slightly more than 18 percent of the company's sales.

Globally, in 1986, 67 percent of Upjohn's sales revenues were generated in the United States, 15 percent in Europe, and 18 percent were scattered elsewhere across the world. By 1986, Upjohn's share of the worldwide pharmaceutical market was 1.5 percent, and top management's ambition was to achieve a minimum of 2 percent of the market by 1990. The realization of this goal would move

Upjohn from among the top-fifteen to among the top-ten drug companies globally.

The middle to late 1980s proved to be a turning point in Upjohn's history, however, as a result of changes in both the domestic and global pharmaceutical industry and because of a series of internal problems that became evident in the company at this time. These problems were to plague Upjohn for the next decade, and it was the attempt to resolve them that led Upjohn's management to seek the merger with Pharmacia in 1995.

THE PHARMACEUTICAL INDUSTRY ENVIRONMENT

By the late 1970s and early 1980s, important changes were reshaping competition in the domestic and global pharmaceutical markets. First, more countries were imposing greater regulation on the drug approval process. In the United States, the Kefauver-Harris amendment of 1962 placed major new constraints on pharmaceutical manufacturers. They required that companies set forth substantial proof that a drug was safe and effective before the FDA could allow it on the market. As a result of this legislation, the new-drug introduction process became considerably longer and more expensive, which was viewed by many as the single most important nonscientific event to affect the industry since World War II.

The Kefauver-Harris amendment marked the beginning of substantially increased regulation of the domestic pharmaceutical industry. As drug approval time lengthened, valuable years of patent protection were being eroded. The Waxman-Hatch Act of 1984 reflected the tremendous growth in domestic political influence of the Generic Pharmaceutical Industry Association (GPIA).

Another major thrust of the bill was to speed the introduction of generic drugs after patent expiration in order to reduce their price. This put increasing pressure on the profits of the company that developed a new drug. Development costs were estimated to approach $100 million for each new drug introduced in 1986, and they are $150 million today. To placate the large drug companies, the bill guaranteed several drug companies, including Upjohn, the exclusive rights for five years beyond normal patent length to market four major drugs each. These patent extensions were to compensate for the FDA's slow handling of drug registrations over the previous few years.

However, by 1990 approvals for generic copies of patent-expired drugs were being issued at a very rapid pace, and the large drug companies were experiencing price competition on many fronts. Large pharmaceutical companies, including Upjohn, came under intense pressure during the 1990s. In the early 1990s, for example, Upjohn faced the prospect of a loss of patent protection on four of its major revenue-generating drugs: Xanax, an antidepressant; Halcion, a sleeping pill; Micronase, a treatment for diabetes; and Ansaid, an anti-inflammatory agent. Upjohn lost more than $400 million in annual revenues as generic drug companies began producing their own versions of these drugs. In fact, Upjohn avoided losing more money only because it began to produce a generic version of its own drug, Xanax, allowing it to keep 80 percent of prescriptions of the drug. This marked a major move for Upjohn into the production of low-priced generic drugs and over-the-counter drugs sold under its own brand name.

Similar legislative pressures to reduce drug prices were mounting in many other countries. Between 1981 and 1984, the Japanese government ordered price reductions on drugs averaging 40.1 percent. Such legislation marked an industry trend toward, as Upjohn's president and chief operating officer, Lawrence C. Hoff, put it, a "two-tier industry with innovators in one group and a large number of generic manufacturers in the other segment, competing fiercely on the sole basis of price." In the 1990s, many drug companies such as Upjohn have been fighting to gain a foothold in both markets to increase their revenues in a more competitive marketplace.

Many countries also had begun protectionist campaigns, restricting drug marketing to products manufactured by the domestic industry. Furthermore, many foreign companies benefited from development support from their respective governments, allowing them to avoid the full cost of their research efforts. Since regulatory procedures, processes, and time orientations differ considerably from one country to another, domestic companies often experienced difficulty in obtaining information on how drugs move through foreign regulatory agencies. Although an attempt to achieve standardization of clinical procedures and disseminate intelligence on postmarketing response of users through an international information network was under way in the 1980s, it never came to fruition.

With increasing competition in research and increasing difficulty and costs in achieving regulatory approval, drug companies began concentrating their research in specific fields of medicine in order to reduce the cost of developing new drugs. To maintain their profitability, companies began specializing in the world's three most lucrative markets for new drugs: heart disease, anti-inflammatory agents and analgesics, and antibiotics. This concentration of resources by major companies in a few specific areas was suggested by an Upjohn spokesperson to be the cause of the scarcity of new drugs classified as breakthrough developments by the FDA in recent years. However, the slowdown in drug innovation seems to be on the verge of reversal. The advent of biotechnology has fueled a surge in new global pharmaceutical products as cures and medications for major diseases begin to appear, albeit at a slower pace than expected.

Another major environmental threat to Upjohn arose from the changing U.S. pharmaceutical environment in the 1990s. In the early 1990s, the new Clinton administration championed the introduction of a national health care system and also proposed that in the future drug companies should be strictly regulated in the amount they could charge for new and existing drugs. Because this would obviously eat into the profits of the large drug companies, their stock price declined.

Although these proposals eventually came to nothing, another major trend was developing in the 1990s: the emergence of managed health care by health maintenance organizations (HMOs). HMOs are national chains of medical and health centers that employ doctors and buy drugs in huge quantities from major pharmaceutical companies. Because they buy in such bulk, HMOs can bargain with pharmaceutical companies for lower prices, and this occurred during the 1990s and squeezed the profit margins of these companies. Moreover, besides pressures from HMOs, mail-order drug companies, such as Medco, sprang up. By virtue of their national customer base and huge buying power, they were also able to bargain with the large drug companies for lower prices by threatening to switch suppliers.

Finally, global competition became intense in the 1990s as the increasing costs of developing drugs, combined with reduced patent protection and competition from generic drug makers, put pressure on pharmaceutical makers to recoup their investments on a global level. In the 1990s, drug companies could only hope to be as profitable as they have been in the past if they could successfully market a drug on a global level.

Thus, pharmaceutical companies have experienced significant environmental challenges in the last decade, challenges that are still becoming stronger. First, there has been increasing price competition in the health care industry from the rapid growth of generic drug companies. Second, there has been an increase in legislative pressures on new drug development, both at home and abroad. Third, there has been an increase in global competition as drug companies vie with each other on a worldwide basis.

In response to all these pressures, a wave of merger activity occurred in the pharmaceutical industry in the 1990s. Merck bought Medco, the national mail-order drug supply company mentioned earlier, for $6.6 billion in 1993; American Home Products bought American Cyanamid for $9.6 billion in 1994; Eli Lilly bought PCS Health Systems, another mail-order drug company, for $4 billion; and Wellcome bought Glaxo Holdings in 1995 for $14.2 billion. The increasing consolidation of the global pharmaceutical industry is still continuing as companies fight to position themselves for the events in the next century. Clearly, the problem facing Upjohn's management was how to maintain its growth in the domestic and international markets in the face of this increasing industry competition and regulatory pressure. Upjohn, with its very small share of the global market, realized it had to find a global partner if it was to stay in the big league.

UPJOHN'S NEW CORPORATE STRATEGY

In 1990, Upjohn stated that its pharmaceutical business strategy to the year 2000 was to ensure that it delivered the greatest volume of quality pharmaceuticals to the greatest number of people globally and, at the same time, maintained an appropriate return on investment to ensure its continued growth. Three goals were particularly stressed: (1) sales growth (with concurrent market share growth); (2) a continuing growth in return on investment; and (3) competition based on high quality rather than low price.

The aggressive nature of this approach was indicated by Upjohn's quest to become one of the

top ten drug companies by the mid 1990s. During the early 1990s, however, it became clear that achieving these goals would be difficult because of a number of internal problems that had arisen at this time.

One of its first problems was that the number of new promising drugs waiting in its product-development pipeline for FDA approval dropped off precipitously in the 1990s. Its previous blockbuster drugs, such as Xanax and Halcion, were losing their patent protection, and these drugs had not been followed by new blockbusters. As a result, during the early 1990s, Upjohn faced the prospect of flat revenues, which would not help it to achieve its ambitious goals.

The lack of new drugs in the pipeline was not the result of a lack of investment in research and development. Upjohn continued to invest heavily in R&D. For example, Upjohn invested heavily in biotechnology as a way of promoting new product development. Dr. Ralph E. Christofferson, a long-time consultant, was hired by the company, assigned a budget, given a custom-constructed facility, and instructed to hire the best people in the field. The 150-person staff began working with research professionals in Upjohn's other businesses to show them how the new technology could help applied-research efforts in both human health services and agriculture. However, the pace of new product development was disappointing, and costs were rising. Under any circumstances, the development of new drugs is a very uncertain and risky process, and it has been estimated that only one out of ten to fifteen drugs that start the development process come to the market—hence, the high prices that drug companies are forced to charge.

Besides the lack of new products in the pipeline, Upjohn's previous strategies of vertical integration and diversification were causing problems. Vertical integration had been a part of Upjohn's strategy since its inception. Upjohn pursued backward integration into the production of fine chemicals so that it could maintain quality control from initial chemical manufacture to the final packaging of its products in order to protect the quality of its drugs. Upjohn's production unit purchased most of its bulk chemicals from Upjohn's chemicals unit. In the 1990s, however, vertical integration was proving an expensive strategy that raised costs and did little to increase the bottom line. It had become clear that in many cases it was now cheaper to buy rather than make many of the chemicals that the company needed, so that the costs of vertical integration were now outweighing the benefits.

Similarly, Upjohn's diversification efforts had not produced the gains that had been expected. Its Asgrow seeds division, while profitable, was far removed from its core pharmaceutical business, and few synergies had been obtained. Its home health care business was similarly far removed from the company's core activities. The costs associated with managing all these different businesses were rising, sucking up a lot of top management's time, and did not seem to promise much of a return.

In the early 1990s, Upjohn's top management began to realize that its diversification efforts were not helping the company and were unlikely to help it achieve its central mission of becoming a top-ten global pharmaceutical company. So it sold off various of its chemicals businesses and its home health care business. However, the turning point for Upjohn came in 1994, when Theodore Cooper, Upjohn's long-time CEO, died and was replaced by John L. Zabriskie, one of Merck's former top managers. Zabriskie took a long, hard look at Upjohn's current strategy, and he immediately decided that Upjohn's strategy of using acquisitions to achieve its objectives of diversification and expansion in health and agriculture was not working. Zabriskie decided that he needed to restructure Upjohn, and he moved quickly to do so.

In early 1994, Zabriskie sold off what were now regarded as noncore assets, such as Asgrow Seeds and the chicken-breeding venture with Tyson Foods, among others, getting the company out of the agricultural business. He also eliminated 1,400 managerial jobs by restructuring and consolidating Upjohn's manufacturing and sales and marketing operations. For example, he decreased the number of Upjohn's global manufacturing sites to reduce excess capacity and operating costs in the years ahead. Then, he restructured its U.S. pharmaceutical sales and marketing efforts to focus solely on large customers such as health care systems, HMOs, and insurance providers. Because of Upjohn's new strategy, sales for 1994 reached $3.3 billion, slightly below 1993 sales, but net earnings jumped by 25 percent as costs fell.

Zabriskie then turned his attention to the company's research and development operations. He realized that it was here, in the development of important new pharmaceutical products, that the company's future lay. He decided to refocus the company's R&D efforts on developing thirty major products aimed at product markets that seemed to offer the greatest prospects for future new-product development. Many other R&D programs were terminated to save money. Then, Zabriskie pumped more money into R&D to promote these thirty new products. The company spent more than $600 million in 1994, which represented more than 18 percent of sales and was above the industry average, to speed the development of new products to the marketplace.

In the process of refocusing Upjohn's efforts, however, Zabriskie realized that, at best, all that these remedies offered was a short-term fix for the company's problems. It had become clear to him that, especially in view of the wave of mergers taking place within the industry, Upjohn was increasingly becoming a prospective takeover target for another pharmaceutical company seeking a quick way to become a major player. Zabriskie had to find a means of raising Upjohn's global presence and speeding the new-product development process. So even before he had finished with these major restructuring efforts, he convened a meeting of the company's top twenty executives in the summer of 1994 to develop a plan to take Upjohn into the next century as one of the top ten global pharmaceutical companies.

It became clear from this meeting that none of these executives thought that Upjohn could become a major global player on its own and that the company could not wait for its next generation of drugs to be approved for sale over the next five to ten years if it was to avoid being taken over. Zabriskie and his managers decided that Upjohn must seek a merger partner, one that could remedy Upjohn's weaknesses with its strengths. Accordingly, Zabriskie began to analyze the global pharmaceutical companies that had not yet been taken over to find a potential partner.

Enter Pharmacia

Jan Ekberg, chief executive of Pharmacia, was also very aware of the merger movement proceeding in the pharmaceutical industry. Since 1992, when the previously state-owned company had been privatized, he had been approached by several other European pharmaceutical companies about a possible merger. These companies had realized the potential of Pharmacia, because it had a very strong product-development process, with several promising new drugs in the pipeline. Ekberg was not tempted by these merger opportunities because he saw that Pharmacia's major weakness was its lack of developed sales and marketing channels in the United States, the world's biggest drug market. He realized that to become a global player, Pharmacia would need a strong presence in the U.S. market and that the way to do this was to search for a U.S. partner.

When Zabriskie took over at Upjohn, Ekberg saw an opportunity for a distribution deal between the two companies. He saw that Pharmacia's well-developed sales and marketing operations in Europe could efficiently handle the sales of Upjohn's products in Europe, and he saw that Upjohn's U.S. sales and marketing network would provide an avenue to distribute Pharmacia's new drugs in the United States. Ekberg called Zabriskie to discuss the distribution agreement, but Zabriskie, on the lookout for a merger partner, was thinking along different lines.

Like Ekberg, he saw that a combined distribution operation between Pharmacia and Upjohn would allow both companies to offer a much wider product line to HMOs and national drug-supply companies throughout the United States and Europe. Combined distribution operations and a larger presence would give them a better bargaining position and an opportunity to increase global sales volume. However, Zabriskie also saw that, in the short run, the many new drugs in Pharmacia's drug pipeline would compensate for the lack of new drugs in Upjohn's and remedy Upjohn's major weakness in this area. Given his recent cost-cutting efforts, he also saw that there might be many other areas in which a combined Pharmacia and Upjohn could reduce costs. Pharmacia began to look like the ideal merger partner.

Zabriskie proposed a meeting in Washington, D.C., which quickly led to a whole string of meetings across Europe as a surprised Ekberg began to warm up to the idea of a formal merger rather than just a strategic alliance through a distribution agreement. After some negotiations, both men bought into the idea and began the process of convincing their major stockholders to agree to the merger. They pointed out that after a merger a combined Pharmacia and Upjohn would allow major cost savings in marketing and sales, manufacturing, and research and development. Each of these activities could be sourced on a global level to the country where factor skills or costs were most fa-

vorable, for example, and they announced that they expected to be able to reduce staff by 4,000 people, or 12 percent of the work force. Alongside this, of course, they expected sales revenues to increase because of the combined company's ability to serve the global marketplace better, so that they saw big profits ahead.

Moreover, the two CEOs also pointed out that the continuing wave of merger activity implied that if they did not agree to a merger now, both companies might be the object of unfriendly takeover attempts. A combined Pharmacia and Upjohn, and a new place as the ninth largest pharmaceutical company in the world, would better position the company and make it a global player by the year 2000.

In August 1995, the two companies announced a tax-free stock swap that would result in a merger of equals. The new company would have its headquarters in London. Zabriskie would be the new CEO, and Ekberg would be the nonexecutive chairman. The company would have an R&D budget of more than $1 billion a year, equal to any major global pharmaceutical company.

In 1996, it was not clear what the future would hold for Pharmacia & Upjohn. Would the new company be able to combine the strengths of both companies, eliminate their weaknesses, and develop a sustainable pipeline of important new drugs so that the company becomes a truly global player? Alternatively, would Upjohn's new research and development efforts come to nothing so that the short-term boost to revenues brought about by Pharmacia's new drug pipeline would fizzle out? If this happens, the combined company may itself become a takeover target in the next few years, as the global pharmaceutical industry continues to consolidate. Zabriskie clearly does not believe in this latter scenario. In a public announcement, he claimed that

This is a merger that truly constitutes far more than the sum of the parts. The new company will be able to take full advantage of uniquely complementary geographic reach, product portfolio, pipeline, and R&D strengths. As a result of the merger, Pharmacia & Upjohn will have extensive financial and operating resources, market scope, and earnings potential. Consequently, we fully expect the new company to achieve additional growth in expected 1996 earnings per share (EPS) as well as acceleration of future earnings growth.

CASE 35

Monsanto: Building a Life Sciences Company

This case was prepared by Charles W. L. Hill of the University of Washington.

INTRODUCTION

As Monsanto approached the new millennium, Bob Shapiro, Monsanto's CEO, reflected on how much the company had changed during the last quarter of a century, and the vast opportunities and daunting challenges now confronting the enterprise. Monsanto was established in 1901 when John Queeny, a chemicals salesman, invested $5,000 in manufacturing facilities to produce saccharin, a synthetic sweetener. Over the next half a century, Monsanto moved into raw materials production, becoming an integrated chemical manufacturer. By the early 1970s, Saint Louis–based Monsanto was one of the world's largest producers of high-volume, commodity chemical products. Then the first OPEC oil shock hit and Monsanto saw its margins drastically compressed by rising raw material prices and plunging demand.

It was at this point that Monsanto started on a journey that was to transform the company into a life sciences behemoth. From small beginnings, the company had grown to become one of the world's leading producers of agricultural and animal biotechnology products. Along the way, the company had acquired G. D. Searle, a second-tier pharmaceutical firm, thereby adding human life sciences to its animal and agricultural life science businesses. By the late 1990s, twenty years of investment in life sciences seemed to be paying off. Monsanto had introduced genetically altered cotton, potatoes, corn, and soybean seeds. These seeds were engineered to produce natural herbicides

This case is intended to be used as the basis for class discussion rather than as an illustration of either effective or ineffective handling of the situation. This case was prepared by Charles W. L. Hill, University of Washington. Used by permission.

and/or to resist damage from Roundup, Monsanto's best selling chemical herbicide; their sales were growing rapidly as farmers recognized their potential to boost crop yields. Furthermore, Monsanto had plans to roll out forty new genetically altered seed products during the 1999–2002 period.[1] Meanwhile, under Monsanto's tutelage, Searle had assembled one of the best new product pipelines in the pharmaceutical industry, and expected to launch more than two dozen new products between 1999 and 2002, led by Celebrex, the first in a class of new painkillers.[2] To complete the transformation of Monsanto from a chemical to a life sciences company, in September 1997 Monsanto spun off its chemical operations as an independent company, Solutia. What remained was a company with sales of more than $9 billion that analysts thought could grow its earnings at an annual compound rate of 20 percent for years to come.

Despite the growth potential of the new Monsanto, however, Shapiro had more than a few worries. Getting Monsanto to this position had been an expensive endeavor that had left the company straining under an $8.2 billion debt load and a debt to equity ratio of 1.25 and a $360 million annual interest bill. Given its debt, some analysts questioned whether Monsanto had the financial resources, and the marketing and sales muscle, to maximize the potential of its pharmaceutical and agricultural biotechnology pipelines. To address these concerns, in June 1998 Monsanto announced an agreement to merge with American Home Products. Many saw the potential merger as an ideal marriage of complementary assets, with AHP's financial resources and strengths in pharmaceutical distribution being a good match for Monsanto's bulging new product pipeline. However, in October 1998 the merger talks broke down, reportedly due to disagreements between senior executives at the two companies over operations and strategy. Now Shapiro had to devise an alternative strategy to maximize the value of Monsanto's pipeline.

If this were not enough, in September 2000 Monsanto's U.S. patent on glyphosate, the key ingredient in Roundup, would expire. Roundup was Monsanto's best-selling product, accounting for over $1.5 billion of its $4 billion in 1998 sales to agricultural markets. In countries outside of the United States where the patent had already expired, prices for Roundup had been cut in half. Many analysts believed that the same was about to occur in the United States. Of course, Shapiro's hope was that the slack would be taken up by the increased sales of Roundup-ready seeds, which should also boost demand for Roundup. Here, too, however, there was a problem, for there was growing opposition to genetically engineered foodstuffs among the environmental community, which referred to transgenic crops as a form of "genetic pollution."[3] The resistance was strongest in Europe, where in response to public disquiet, the European Union had considered blocking imports of genetically altered agricultural products.[4]

BUILDING LIFE SCIENCES AT MONSANTO

The life science business at Monsanto was constructed over a quarter of a century during the tenure of three CEOs: John Hanley, Richard Mahoney, and Robert Shapiro. At the outset of this twenty-five-year odyssey, Monsanto was a major chemical company with substantial sales from low-margin, capital-intensive, commodity chemical operations that produced fibers, plastics, and agricultural chemicals. The main raw material input for these products was petrochemicals, leaving Monsanto highly vulnerable to fluctuations in the price of oil. Pushed by the OPEC oil price hikes of 1973 and 1979, both Hanley and Mahoney repeatedly emphasized the need for Monsanto to migrate its revenues away from low-margin commodity business toward proprietary, high-margin businesses. In the words of Richard Mahoney in a 1989 article,

> Our current strategy at Monsanto began to emerge in the mid 1970s, undertaken because we realized that, after 30 years of growth, many

of our traditional chemical markets were maturing. In addition, oil companies and oil producing nations were crowding into these markets. Not wanting to become a me-too player, we began to evaluate potential new directions. That decision liberated us to look at other technologies. Underlying that search was a determination to find technologies that would present whole new families of opportunities to exploit. We dedicated ourselves to becoming one of the truly great industrial enterprises by the early 1990s. In financial terms that means a 20% return on equity consistently, year after year.[5]

Hanley, who ran Monsanto from 1972 to 1983, made the first moves into biotechnology. Mahoney, his successor, built on this over the next ten years, and in addition, steered the company toward human pharmaceuticals with the 1985 acquisition of G. D. Searle. Shapiro, who succeeded Mahoney in 1993, completed the process.

Establishing Competencies in Biotechnology

The genesis of life sciences at Monsanto can be traced to a 1973 decision to fund a small biotechnology skunkworks to carry out cellular research.[6] The skunkworks was the brainchild of Ernie Jaworski, a senior research scientist at Monsanto. Jaworski had been following developments in plant genetics among the academic community. Like many other scientists, he had been stunned by the news in early 1973 that two California scientists, Stanley Cohn and Herbert Boyer, had managed to isolate fragments of a gene from one bacterium and insert them into another to create a bit of living cellular material that had never before existed.[7] Jaworski reasoned that it might be possible to use the Cohn-Boyer method—referred to as recombinant DNA technology—to genetically alter crop seeds to make them resistant to herbicides. The herbicides could then be used to kill the weeds around the crops as they were growing, without fear of harming the crops. This would help boost demand for one of Monsanto's newest products, the herbicide Roundup. Approved for market introduction in 1974, Roundup was a proprietary, environmentally friendly herbicide developed by Monsanto. At the time, Roundup could only be applied before crop growth since it failed to discriminate between weeds and crops. Another possibility might be to genetically alter crops so that they expressed proteins that functioned as "natural" insecticides, repelling harmful pests. An example would be the cotton bollworm, which ate cotton plants and forced cotton farmers to spend significant sums on insecticides.

Jaworski proposed his idea to Hanley, Monsanto's new CEO who joined Monsanto from Procter & Gamble in 1972. Hanley agreed to fund the establishment of the skunkworks, and Jaworski set up the operation with a staff of thirty-five scientists. The main focus of Jaworski's skunkworks was on understanding cell biology with a view to creating crops with innate herbicide resistance. At the same time, Jaworski was cognizant of the opportunities that might exist if animal proteins could be produced using recombinant DNA technology. Back in the 1930s, Russian scientists had extracted growth hormone from the pituitary glands of slaughtered pigs and cows. They found when injected into live animals, the hormone could accelerate growth and, in the case of cows, increase milk production. However, the process was too expensive, and the technology required to mass-produce growth hormone proteins did not exist at that point in time, so for decades growth hormone remained little more than a scientific curiosity.[8] Now Jaworski realized that recombinant DNA technology might be used to mass-produce animal growth hormones, so he authorized research into growth hormones, but progress was hindered by a lack of resources.

In 1976, Jaworski tried to persuade Monsanto to invest in Genentech, one of the first biotechnology start-ups. Herbert Boyer, one of the inventors of recombinant DNA technology, was one of the two founders of the company. At the time, Genentech was seeking initial venture capital to finance basic research aimed at producing human proteins using recombinant DNA technology. Jaworski believed that Genentech might be an interesting way for Monsanto to get a foothold in this emerging field. However, Monsanto's top management was enamoured of the growth possibilities that might be had producing silicon for semiconductors, and expressed no interest in Jaworski's proposal. In retrospect, this proved to be a mistake.

In 1978, Genentech produced the first human protein (somatostatin) in a microorganism (*E. coli* bacterium). Also in 1978, it succeeded in cloning human insulin using the same technology. The method involved using recombinant DNA technol-ogy to insert the piece of human DNA that carries instructions for producing the desired human protein (for example, the gene to produce insulin) into the DNA of a microorganism (usually *E. coli* bacterium or some form of yeast). Because it now contains the gene for making the human protein, the microorganism will express (produce) this protein. Cultures of the microorganism are then placed in fermentation tanks where they multiply and produce more of the desired protein. The microorganism is then harvested, and the desired protein is removed and converted into a drug, such as human insulin, that can then be injected into people who lack the protein (diabetics, in the case of insulin).[9] In 1979, Genentech used this technology to engineer microorganisms to produce human growth hormone. The company went public in 1980 with an offering that leapt from $35 a share to a high of $88 after less than an hour on the market. At the time, this was one the largest stock run-ups ever.[10]

Against the background of rising interest in biotechnology, in 1979 Hanley hired Howard Schneiderman to head Monsanto's R&D efforts. At the time he was hired, Schneiderman was the dean of biological sciences at the University of California, Irvine. As a member of the National Academy of Science and a recognized expert in the techniques of genetic engineering, Schneiderman struck Hanley as the ideal person to oversee Monsanto's biotechnology efforts. As Schneiderman later recalled it, Hanley posed a question to Schneiderman: "We spent $170 million on research in 1978. We probably should have spent $275 million. Do you have any good ideas?"[11] Schneiderman was instantly sold. "If you are a red-blooded American who has chosen research as a career, and a guy comes along and says 'Do you have any good ideas for $100 million worth of research?' it's a fantastic temptation."[12] At Irvine, Schneiderman had administered an $8 million budget.[13] Hanley made Schneiderman senior vice president for research and development and gave him the charter to make Monsanto a "significant world force in molecular biology."[14]

Schneiderman moved quickly. Jaworski's group was transferred into central R&D under Schneiderman's direction. Jaworski was made the director of biological sciences within the corporate R&D staff, and given free rein to go on a hiring spree to attract brilliant young researchers. It wasn't easy; a surge of new biotechnology start-ups offering attractive stock options contracts to scientists competed with Monsanto for scarce talent. Monsanto had an advantage, however. Its financial resources offered scientists the opportunity to engage in long-term research projects, free from financial worries. Schneiderman's reputation also helped, and the company hired 135 Ph.D.'s in the first three years of his tenure. What also helped was the company's decision to invest $165 million to build a life sciences research center on a 210-acre campus 25 miles west of downtown Saint Louis. Referred to within Monsanto as "the house that Howard built," the research center was a powerful symbol of Monsanto's commitment to basic biotechnology research. By 1990, the facility had 250 laboratories and 900 research scientists, making it one of the most powerful concentrations of life science research effort anywhere in the world.[15]

Research Alliances

Despite Monsanto's aggressive investment in R&D, Schneiderman was the first to admit that Monsanto could not do it all alone. Within three months of joining the company, Schneiderman entered into an alliance with Genentech. By this time, Genentech had already figured out how to use recombinant DNA technology to mass-produce human growth hormone. Monsanto was interested in using the same technology to mass-produce animal growth hormones. In return for the rights to the bovine somatotropin growth hormone (BST), Monsanto paid Genentech $990,000, agreed to make several subsequent milestone payments, and promised royalties on future sales of BST. Genentech delivered the first 600 milligrams of BST in December 1981, and initial tests showed that the product worked like natural BST.[16]

In 1982, Monsanto forged an alliance with nearby Washington University in order to get access to leading-edge academic research on molecular biology. This was Monsanto's second big involvement with a university. Back in 1974, the company had entered into a twelve-year, $23-million agreement with Harvard Medical School for research on the molecular basis of organ development. However, Monsanto was not satisfied with this arrangement. A major problem had been that the Harvard researchers refused to give Monsanto access to research findings until they had

been published in academic journals. Moreover, the company had found it was unable to direct or influence the course of research at Harvard.[17]

This time, Monsanto structured the agreement to give it greater access to research results and a greater ability to direct the research process. The agreement called for Monsanto to invest $23.5 million over five years for biomedical research into teins and peptides, small proteins that modify the behavior of cells. About one-third of the effort was to be directed toward basic research, and the rest toward new pharmaceutical products aimed at treating a variety of ailments, including allergies. The contract specified that faculty members participating in projects funded by Monsanto would be free to publish all results of their findings and that Washington University would hold any resulting patents. Monsanto, on the other hand, would have exclusive marketing rights to such patents. Projects to receive funding would be selected by a committee that included four university and four Monsanto scientists. Monsanto scientists would be able to work side by side with university researchers in university labs, and vice versa.

This agreement raised concerns in some quarters that it might violate fundamental principles of academic research and freedom. Albert Gore Jr., then a Democratic representative from Tennessee and chairman of the Investigation and Oversight Subcommittee of the House Committee on Science and Technology commented that "You don't have to know algebra to figure out how that committee works. No research can be done unless the company gives permission."[18] In reply, Schneiderman insisted that "everything is carefully designed to enable the university to be true to its fundamental purpose."[19]

The Washington University deal was followed by a series of other research deals structured along similar lines. These included a $5-million, five-year agreement with Oxford University in the United Kingdom to sequence the structure of certain plant proteins and a $4-million, five-year agreement with Rockefeller University to investigate the structure and regulation of plant genes involved in photosynthesis. Smaller agreements were also signed with the California Institute of Technology, the University of California (San Francisco), and Harvard University. In 1985, the Washington University agreement was extended to cover eight and a half years, and the total funds committed increased to

$62 million, making it the largest collaborative agreement of its kind.[20] According to Schneiderman, such contracts provide "a powerful insight into the future," fund research that is "more likely to make a leap," keep Monsanto researchers "in the front line of academic research," and "can be a magnet for attracting good people to Monsanto."[21]

Acquiring Searle

As Monsanto embarked on its journey into the life sciences business, it was not altogether clear exactly what the focus of the company would ultimately be. Jaworski's skunkworks, and many of the scientists hired after Schneiderman arrived, focused primarily on applying the principles of molecular biology to plants. This made good sense, given Monsanto's strong position in agricultural herbicides—a position that was getting stronger all the time due to the success of Roundup. In the early 1980s, this herbicide was generating more than $500 million a year in sales and was Monsanto's most profitable product.[22] On the other hand, the alliance with Genentech signaled an interest in animal proteins, and the agreement with Washington University was in large part directed at producing human pharmaceuticals.

Within Monsanto, the debate was not so much about whether the company should leverage its growing life science expertise to enter the human pharmaceutical business as it was about how best to achieve this. By 1983, Monsanto, in collaboration with its university partners, was beginning to identify some interesting candidates for clinical investigation. An example was atrial peptide, a human protein that had been isolated from the atrium of the heart by researchers at Washington University. The protein dilates the vascular system, and Monsanto believed that it might have value as a drug for controlling blood pressure.[23] However, Monsanto lacked both the regulatory experience with the FDA and the distribution network required to maximize the potential of such pharmaceuticals.

The slow pace of Monsanto's move away from its low-margin commodity chemicals business added urgency. By 1984, the company was still generating 60 percent of its sales from its traditional chemical operations, even though 65 percent of its operating profits came from agricultural chemicals, and most of those could be attributed to just two products, Roundup and another herbicide, Lasso

(the patent on Lasso was set to expire in 1988). Monsanto's new CEO, Richard Mahoney, wanted to accelerate the shift away from commodity chemicals, and simultaneously gain a pharmaceutical distribution network. To further the attainment of these objectives, in 1983 Monsanto hired the investment banker Goldman, Sachs & Co. to identify acquisition candidates in the pharmaceutical business. In 1984, Monsanto acquired a small Belgian drug company, Continental Pharma, but a large acquisition candidate eluded it. G.D. Searle was on the list compiled by Goldman, Sachs, but the company was 34 percent owned by the Searle family, and it seemed unlikely to sell. This changed in 1984 when the Searle family indicated that it wanted to sell its stake, effectively putting Searle on the block. Searle's pharmaceutical business had been a lackluster performer in recent years. The company had not introduced a significant new drug for eight years. It did, however, have a powerful anti-ulcer drug, Cytotec, in late-stage clinical trials. There were also a number of interesting drug candidates farther down the product development pipeline. Searle also had aspartame (NutraSweet), the artificial sweetener that generated $600 million in annual sales—roughly half of Searle's total revenues. However, the patent on aspartame was due to expire in 1992. Initially, Monsanto wanted to purchase Searle's pharmaceutical business, leaving Searle with NutraSweet, but Searle refused to deal and negotiations broke down.

In 1985, Monsanto approached Searle again, this time with an offer to buy the entire company. The change in Monsanto's position was in part due to a reassessment of the value of NutraSweet. Searle had just won regulatory approval to use 100 percent NutraSweet in diet soda. Mahoney believed that this would expand sales for NutraSweet to close to $1 billion before the patent expired, throwing off significant free cash flow in the process. In Mahoney's words, "NutraSweet brings a very interesting earnings stream in the time between now and when our biotechnology begins to pay off."[24]

In July 1985, Monsanto announced that it had agreed to purchase Searle for $2.7 billion, or about seventeen times Searle's estimated 1985 earnings. While many analysts commented that the acquisition was too expensive and that Monsanto was paying a hefty premium for a mediocre drug company, which had not introduced any significant new products for some time, Monsanto seemed pleased with its purchase. One business development executive in the company noted that "Searle's marketing and distribution operations will be the vehicle by which we can go forward and commercialize new products worldwide. Now Monsanto has the infrastructure to realize the benefits of biotechnology."[25] Mahoney also noted that "Searle has done a very good job of finding product leads of its own. We are engaged in a long term strategic move to have Searle's and Monsanto's strengths melded together."[26] In fact, by mid 1986, Searle had twenty-one new chemical or biological entities in various stages of clinical development—one of the best pipelines in the pharmaceutical industry. These included cardiovascular drugs for hypertension and irregular heartbeat; central nervous system drugs for depression, epilepsy, and pain; immuno-inflammatory drugs for arthritis; and an ulcer medication.[27] However, most of these products were still in the early stages of clinical testing, there was no guarantee that they would show the desired combination of efficacy and manageable side effects in clinical trials, and even if they did, they were years from market introduction.

DEVELOPING PRODUCTS

With the 1985 acquisition of Searle, Monsanto had assembled the main building blocks required to embark on the transformation from a major chemical company into a life sciences concern. At the time, Jaworski commented that "by 1990 Monsanto will be the greatest biotechnology company in the world."[28] Executives in other biotechnology firms characterized such comments as "absolutely ridiculous" and an "extraordinary boast."[29] They noted that it was small entrepreneurial biotechnology enterprises such as Amgen, Genentech, and Biogen that had succeeded in moving biotechnology products to market, not large corporations like Monsanto. Large companies, the critics noted, lacked the required sense of urgency, drive, and creativity of smaller biotechnology enterprises. In 1986, only two biotechnology products were on the market, insulin and human growth hormone. Genentech, not a large pharmaceutical firm, produced both of these. Moreover, all five biotechnology products then in phase III (final stage) clinical trials belonged to entrepreneurial biotechnology companies, not large pharma-

ceutical enterprises. More than anything else, the critics felt that Monsanto was underestimating the problems involved in developing biotechnology products and bringing them to market.

Ps–3732

By 1986, Monsanto was already beginning to get a taste of the problems involved in developing biotechnology products. On May 20 of that year, the Environmental Protection Agency turned down an application from Monsanto to field-test its first genetically altered microbe, dealing a body blow to one of the company's most advanced agricultural biotechnology research projects.[30] The microbe in question was a genetically engineered bacterium that produced a protein that functioned as a natural insecticide and was capable of killing insects that fed on corn. In denying the company's request to proceed with field testing, the EPA was bowing to pressure from environmental activists, who had criticized Monsanto's testing procedures and questioned the safety of releasing genetically altered organisms into the environment.

The research project that produced the bacterium was begun in 1980 when a twenty-person team of scientists, led by thirty-two-year-old Robert Kaufman, received approval for research to develop microbes that produced "natural" insecticides. The thinking was straightforward; farmers around the world were spending about $7 billion on chemical pesticides, but these pesticides also killed animals, polluted ground water and rivers, and showed up in traces in foods. Surely, Monsanto executives believed, farmers would buy a genetically engineered product that was cheaper, easier to use, and did not harm the environment or human health.

By late 1982, after collecting and analyzing hundred of bacteria that colonized the roots of corn, Dr. Kaufman and his team isolated a single microbe, dubbed Ps–3732, capable of mass reproduction and able to compete with other microorganisms for space around the roots of corn plants. The team had also identified a natural toxin capable of killing caterpillar-type pests and generated by one of the 3,000 to 5,000 genes in the chromosomes in another common bacterium, Bacillus thuringiensis. By the end of 1983, the team had isolated the gene and succeed in inserting it into the chromosomes of Ps–3732 using recombinant DNA technology.

The team now believed that it had a means to deliver a natural insecticide. The plan was to sell corn seeds coated with the genetically modified bacteria. After the farmer planted the seeds, the bacteria would multiply in the soil and form a barrier around the roots of the corn, preventing damage from cutworms, a common pest. Before field-testing the bacteria, Kaufman's team undertook seventeen safety studies, designed to establish the environmental impact of the genetically modified Ps–3732. The bacteria were fed to mice, quail, and fish, and bees and a wide variety of plants were exposed to it. No adverse effects were observed. Armed with this data, Monsanto submitted a request to the EPA to move forward with a field test.

At this point, Jeremy Rifkin entered the picture. A well-known radical activist, Rifkin was president of the Foundation for Economic Trends, a policy study group largely funded from sales of Rifkin's own books. Rifkin had already established a reputation as a vocal and effective critic of the imperialism of modern science in general, and biotechnology in particular. In Monsanto's request, he saw an opportunity to nip the emerging agricultural biotechnology movement in the bud.

Rifkin's attack on Monsanto had two thrusts. First, he argued that once released into the environment, genetically altered bacteria could spread uncontrollably. Such "genetic pollution" might cause problems that had not yet been identified. Second, he requested from the EPA access to all of Monsanto's data on safety studies. He then had these data reviewed and critiqued by several ecologists and microbiologists that he had worked with for several years. These experts criticized Monsanto's safety studies as poorly conducted and scientifically inconclusive. Armed with this finding, Rifkin formally petitioned the EPA to deny Monsanto a permit to field-test Ps–3732.

The EPA subsequently issued a report on Monsanto's safety study tests. Written by microbiologists on the EPA's staff, the report stated that thirteen of the seventeen studies were either inconclusive or scientifically flawed. Kaufman acknowledged that some of the safety studies were scanty, but argued that Monsanto was breaking new ground, that many of the tests were the first of their kind, and that the EPA ignored a lot of good data and instead simply focused on those tests where there was some question about the sample design. Kaufman subsequently met with the EPA's advisory panel—which was composed of independent academic advisers—after which the panel indicated that it would "reverse" the staff evaluation and recommend that the EPA allow Monsanto to proceed with the experiment. In reaching its decision, the panel acknowledged that some of Monsanto's safety studies were poorly designed but added that it had enough data from other sources to know that if Monsanto's microbe were released into the environment, it would not be a hazard.

Unfortunately for Monsanto, the panel's advice is not binding, although reversal of the panel's recommendation is a rare event. Alerted by EPA insiders as to what the panel recommendation would be, Rifkin continued to put pressure on the EPA, indicating that he would sue the agency if it approved the field test. This put Dr. John Moore, the head of the EPA, in a difficult position. Although privately he acknowledged that Monsanto's microbe was in all probability not harmful, he recognized that a lawsuit would give Rifkin the opportunity to probe Monsanto and the EPA in public. Cognizant of Rifkin's eloquence and his influence among certain members of Congress and aware of the holes in some of Monsanto's studies, Moore decided to deny the request, although he urged the company to undertake several safety studies and resubmit the request. In a short letter to the company, Moore wrote, "I believe that it is in the best interests of Monsanto and the EPA that the general public develop a feeling of trust and confidence that all decisions to permit experiments of this sort be based on expert evaluation of reliable data." Later, Moore pointed out that "we do not have the knowledge to completely understand the interactions of organisms in the environment. I think caution is absolutely justified."[31] Commenting on the decision, Rifkin stated that "we owe it to ourselves and the next generation to raise these issues and ask these questions. We are talking about the ability to change the genetic code of life, and that's ominous power. We ought to have a thorough, reasonable, and well thought out public debate. It ought not to be left in the hands of Monsanto."[32]

In the aftermath of the EPA's decision, Kaufman resigned from Monsanto to join a start-up biotechnology company, his team was reassigned, and

Monsanto decided to shelve the project and pursue other avenues in the agricultural biotechnology research arena.

Genetically Altering Plants

One of the other avenues that the company was pursuing was the genetic manipulation of plant DNA. Unknowingly, human beings have been manipulating plant DNA since the dawn of the agricultural revolution thousands of years ago, but they have done it through the slow and highly imprecise methods of selective breeding and hybridization. By harnessing biotechnology, Monsanto hoped to dramatically reduce the time required to produce new varieties of crops, and to design crops that had specific desirable traits. To this end, in 1981 a twenty-eight-year-old scientist within Monsanto, Robert Fraley, was put in charge of the plant molecular biology group and given the task of developing better crops through genetic engineering.[33]

Fraley's group first had to confront the problem of how to alter a plant's DNA. They settled on the novel approach of harnessing bacteria that have the natural ability to invade plant cells without destroying the cells. The bacterium they chose, *Agrobacterium tumefaciens*, invades a plant's cell and produces tumorous crown galls on infected species. The utility of this bacterium as a gene transfer system was first recognized when it was demonstrated that the crown galls were actually produced as a result of the transfer and integration of genes from the bacterium into the genome of the plant cells. The scientists theorized that if they could disable the disease causing genes in *Agrobacterium*, it would prove to be a useful vector for transporting foreign genes into the DNA of a plant.[34]

It took two years to disassemble *Agrobacterium*'s genetic code and remove the regions of DNA that produced crown gall. They then took another bacterium, *E. coli*, and isolated the gene that made *E. coli* resistant to an antibiotic called kanamycin. They cut the kanamycin-resistant gene out of the *E. coli* and spliced it into the DNA of the *Agrobacterium*. They then infected cells from a petunia plant with the modified *Agrobacterium*. The significance of this is that kanamycin is normally lethal to petunias. When they exposed *Agrobacterium*-infected petunia cells to kanamycin, however, the petunia cells continued to divide. In 1983, Fraley announced that Monsanto

had produced a kanamycin-resistant petunia that was the world's first genetically engineered plant.[35] Subsequent experiments found that traits introduced into the DNA of host plants were stable over multiple generations during crossbreeding.[36]

Fraley then used the same methodology for more elaborate, and commercially important, plant transformations. The first successful gene-altering experiment with a staple crop came in 1987, when Fraley's group succeeded in modifying soybeans to resist damage from glyphosate, the active ingredient the company's best-selling herbicide, Roundup. The glyphosate gene had been isolated from bacteria and then inserted into the cells' genetic structure of soybeans using recombinant DNA technology.

While Monsanto claimed Roundup-resistant plants would boost yields, critics in the environmental community opposed Monsanto's attempt to create crops resistant to Roundup. Because Roundup does not discriminate between weeds and crops, farmers must use it with extreme care and avoid it altogether in soybean, corn, and cotton fields. The development of Roundup-resistant crops, however, allows farmers to spray the herbicide freely—a fact that troubled environmentalists. As one put it, "Monsanto's rhetoric is low or no pesticide agriculture, but in fact what they are delivering is a whole new generation of herbicide tolerant plants that will shackle us to chemicals for the foreseeable future."[37] For its part, Monsanto pointed out that Roundup is an environmentally friendly herbicide. Glyphosate becomes inert on contact with the soil, breaking down into nitrogen and other nontoxic elements that are naturally found in the soil.

A series of other crop modifications followed the creation of Roundup-resistant soybeans. These included the engineering of an array of crops— tomatoes, potatoes, alfalfa, tobacco, and cucumbers—that were resistant to viral infections. By 1990, the company had also succeeded in engineering transgenic cotton, tomato, and potato plants that contain genes from bacteria that produce proteins fatal to budworms, bollworms, and other common farm pests.[38] The insect-resistant crops were based on genes from a family of bacteria called *Bacillus thuringiensis*, commonly referred to as *Bt*. The *Bt* genes are a code for assembling proteins that can kill certain pests while having no effect on beneficial insects and animals. *Bt*'s have been used in sprays for decades, mostly by organic farmers who forgo the use of manmade chemicals. But the sprays were not effective enough to make much of a dent in the chemical-pesticides market. Monsanto wanted to change that, in the process saving farmers millions of dollars per year in spending on insecticides. Once more, however, the environmental community protested loudly. A big concern is that over time common pests will develop resistance to the *Bt* protein. In particular, environmentalists worry that insects and weeds will quickly build up resistance to the transgenic plants and the herbicides used in conjunction with them, possibly leaving farmers worse off than before after a short burst of extra productivity.[39]

BST

Monsanto licensed the rights to bovine somatotropin growth hormone (BST) from Genentech in 1981 and received the first batch of BST in December of that year. Monsanto planned to perfect BST so that it could be used to boost milk production in dairy cattle (subsequently, studies at universities and at dairy farms have found that the drug increases milk production 10 to 20 percent in well-managed herds). It took twelve years and an estimated $300 million in R&D before the company finally won approval to sell BST in the marketplace.[40]

Monsanto's product is made by inserting the BST gene from cows into *E. coli* bacteria, which are then multiplied in fermentation tanks. The bacteria are then harvested, the BST protein is removed, purified, and converted into the drug that can be injected into cows. This process might sound straightforward, but it is not. It took several years for Monsanto's scientists to find the ideal environment in fermentation vats for the care and feeding of the BST-producing *E. coli. E. coli* turned out to be difficult to mass-produce, requiring just the right amount of oxygen and nutrients and the correct temperature. If any one of these variables was not right, other bacteria could swamp *E. coli*, dramatically lowering BST yields from the fermentation process. Then researchers ran into problems when they tried to kill the bacteria and "crack open" the organisms. Cracking open bacteria involves submitting the organisms to very high pressure, and then releasing that pressure. The sudden drop in pressure causes the bacteria to pop open and release their contents. Monsanto found that the BST-laden bacteria quickly wore down the stainless steel

valves on pressure equipment. The reason was that BST protein particles have the consistency of superhard grains of sand. As a result, the pressure equipment was breaking down constantly. Solving the problem required the invention of ceramic valves that could withstand the wear and tear from BST. After cracking, Monsanto found that it needed to conduct a further seven purification steps to separate the BST molecules from thousands of other proteins, fats, and carbohydrates in the *E. coli* mix. To perfect the purification process, Monsanto had to develop special filters that prevented BST from becoming contaminated.

Another problem was finding the correct formulation of the drug. Early BST tests required scientists to inject cows every day, but Monsanto concluded that such a regime would be too expensive and cumbersome for farmers, and it developed a formulation that only needed to be injected weekly. Then there was also the issue of where to produce BST. United States regulations prohibit the export of drugs that have not been approved for marketing by the Federal Drug Administration (FDA) in the United States. Monsanto reasoned that it might get approval to market BST from foreign regulators before it received FDA approval (correctly as it turned out), so the company decided to locate the manufacturing facilities in Austria.

Difficult as they were, however, solving all of these production problems was a minor matter compared with the political and regulatory problems that Monsanto had to solve before BST could be marketed. The problems started in 1985, when researchers at Cornell University reported the results of early field trials that found the drug increased milk production by as much as 40 percent. The widely publicized results dismayed dairy farmers in New York, Wisconsin, Minnesota, and other milk-producing states. They came at a time when large dairy surpluses were pushing prices down, forcing family farms out of business. Thousands of farmers in the Upper Middle West joined with Jeremy Rifkin in a grassroots campaign that in 1990 succeeded in persuading the state legislatures of Wisconsin and Minnesota to enact temporary moratoriums on the use of the drug in the event it was approved. The moratoriums expired in 1991. In the same year, an unprecedented review by a panel of experts convened by the National Institutes of Health declared the drug safe.

In November 1993, the FDA got its turn. After extensive testing and review, the FDA approved Monsanto's BST. This was the first time that the government was allowing food to be produced using a genetically engineered drug. The decision was made by Dr. David A. Kessler, the commissioner of food and drugs, who noted that "There is virtually no difference in milk from treated and untreated cows. In fact, it's not possible using current scientific techniques to tell them apart. We have looked carefully at every single question raised, and we are confident this product is safe for consumers, for cows and for the environment." Jeremy Rifkin was defiant in his response: "We have said since 1986 that if the F.D.A. ever approved this drug that the final battleground would be the grocery stores, restaurants and convenience stores. This is the beginning of food politics in this country. If Monsanto succeeds with this product, they open the floodgates on the biotechnology age. If we succeed, it will send a chilling message through the agricultural business that people don't want genetically engineered foods."[41]

COX–2 Inhibitor

In 1999, Monsanto's Searle unit introduced Celebrex, the first in a new class of pain treatments for arthritis that offers the same benefit as existing pain relief medications for arthritis (such as aspirin), but with a sharp reduction in the harmful, and often dangerous, side effects of stomach irritation, ulcers, and internal bleeding. The product was the result of a fifteen-year quest by Philip Needleman to understand the role of cyclo-oxygenase (COX) enzymes in the regulation of prostaglandins, hormone-like fatty acids that are crucial to the body's maintenance.[42] As a researcher in the medical school at Washington University, Needleman studied complex chemicals that act as on and off switches in the body. Needleman and a colleague discovered a chemical inhibitor that affects prostaglandins. He learned more from an English researcher, who discovered that aspirin and aspirin-like drugs block the production of prostaglandins and thus reduce pain. But too much blocking is dangerous. Prostaglandins help regulate blood flow through the kidneys and aid in blood clotting. Without prostaglandins producing a protective coating, the stomach would eat itself due to the acid it secretes during digestion. As a result of this effect, patients taking drugs that block COX en-

zymes, such as aspirin, can suffer from serious stomach lesions. The resulting internal bleeding contributed to the death of some 16,000 people a year in the United States alone.

Needleman found that there are two COX enzymes: COX-1 handles the body's housekeeping; injury or disease triggers COX-2. Aspirin and other similar painkillers, referred to as nonsteroidal anti-inflammatory drugs (NSAIDs), block both enzymes—hence the side effects. Needleman wanted to block just COX-2. If that could be achieved, it would be possible to develop a pain medicine that lacked the side effect profile of NSAIDs. By the late 1980s, Needleman was convinced that this was possible, but he did not have the resources to do much about it. At this point he was also chair of the department of pharmacology at Washington University. In this role, he had helped negotiate the original Monsanto–Washington University research agreement and now helped the company allocate funds to Washington University researchers. The company was looking for a successor to Schneiderman and was favorably disposed toward hiring another academic. Needleman had the combination of scientific credentials and leadership skills that Monsanto was looking for, and he was also a known quantity to the company. Like Schneiderman before him, Needleman found the possibilities enticing; "I became enthralled with the idea of what it's like to have all of the people and resources to attack a problem."[43] In 1989, he joined the company as chief scientist.

At Monsanto's Searle division, Needleman found a company that had a long history of household-name products, but the new product pipeline seemed relatively bare to him, and he found the research effort to be diffused. Moreover, Needleman was aware of the costs and risks involved in bringing a new drug to market. Producing human pharmaceuticals is, if anything, a more expensive and risky business than producing transgenic crops. On average, it can take twelve years and cost $300 million to take a drug from the laboratory to the marketplace. To make matters worse, some 80 percent of products that enter clinical trials fail to make it to the market. A drug candidate must go through three sets of increasingly expensive clinical trials to test for safety, dosage, and efficacy (referred to as phase I, II, and III trials). The drug then faces a rigorous review by the FDA. On average, 70 percent of drug candidates that enter into phase I trials make it through to phase II, 47 percent entering phase II make it to phase III, and

82 percent entering phase III make it to the FDA, where 74 percent are approved.[44]

Realizing that Searle lacked the resources of its larger pharmaceutical industry rivals, Needleman developed a two-pronged strategy for Searle's R&D.[45] First, he directed research effort toward three main therapeutic areas: arthritis, oncology, and cardiovascular problems. By concentrating resources, Searle could match or exceed the dollars spent per therapeutic area by larger rivals. In 1998, for example, Searle spent $280 million per therapeutic area, compared with $250 million at Pfizer and $200 million at Merck.[46] Second, Needleman developed the discipline of ending drug development projects early if they didn't survive what he characterizes as "killer experiments."

As part of this strategy, Needleman "exploded the budget for COX-2." The search for a COX-2 inhibitor became the biggest project Searle had ever undertaken. For three years, a team of thirty chemists and thirty biologists examined 2,000 chemical compounds in the quest to find a COX-2 inhibitor. Urgency was added to the quest by the fact that Merck was also racing to develop a COX-2 inhibitor. When the Searle team found the compound that that eventually became Celebrex, they submitted it to a "killer experiment" while it was being tested in phase I trials as an arthritis treatment. The killer experiment was to discover whether the drug relieved severe tooth pain. Needleman reasoned that if the drug alleviated dental pain, it would also ease the pain of arthritis. Celebrex survived the experiment, and the phase I and II trials suggested that the drug not only relieved pain, but also had none of the dangerous side effects associated with other treatments. After an 8,000-patient phase III trial produced favorable results, Searle, in August 1998, filed for FDA approval to market the drug. Because the drug was the first COX-2 inhibitor to come up for review, the FDA granted Celebrex a proprietary review, which meant that it would announce a decision within six months (normally, FDA approval can take as long as twelve months). Approval was granted in December 1998, and Celebrex was launched in mid January 1999, the first in a new class of "super aspirin" painkillers.

PRODUCT LAUNCHES

Monsanto launched BST in February 1994. It was to be the first in a series of new product launches over the next five years that was to finally generate significant revenues for the company—almost a quarter of a century after Jaworski's skunkworks started Monsanto down the biotechnology road.

BST

By early 1999, BST, which Monsanto sold under the brand name Posilac, was being regularly injected in some 30 percent of dairy herds in the United States. Follow-up data showed that BST boosted milk production by about 10 percent on average. Robust demand for milk and milk products in the United States has meant that the supply glut feared by dairy farmers had not materialized. Monsanto and the FDA continued to monitor BST for possible adverse effects. As of 1999, the FDA continued to state that milk from BST-treated cows poses no health risks. The American Medical Association, the World Health Organization, and the National Institutes of Health have issued similar findings. According to Monsanto, BST has enjoyed robust sales gains, and in 1998 passed 100 million doses—at $5.80 per dose.[47]

Despite its success in the United States, however, Monsanto has still not been able to get the product approved for sale in either Canada or the European Union. In early 1999, Health Canada, the Canadian version of the FDA, rejected Monsanto's application to market BST. While a review of existing data by Canadian scientists found no significant risk to human beings who ingest products from animals treated with BST, they noted that short-term tests on lab rats suggest that further study is needed. Health Canada concluded that there was sufficient concern to warrant not approving the drug.[48]

In 1989, the European Union imposed a moratorium on the use of animal growth hormones and the sale of products produced by those hormones, on the grounds that European farmers were already producing too much milk and beef and there was no need for greater production. The moratorium was extended in 1996 and 1997. The current version is due to expire at the end of 1999. In early 1999, the animal health and welfare committee of the European Union concluded that BST should not be injected into cattle. Its report cites increased likelihood of mastitis, foot problems, and injection site reactions, which would also lead to welfare problems besides human health risks. In contrast, another European Union committee, the committee for veterinary medicinal products, had ruled in 1998 that BST was perfectly safe.[49] More generally, public opinion in the European Union seemed to be strongly against not just BST, but genetically modified foods in general. In the United States, the Clinton administration was considering appealing to the World Trade Organization on the grounds that the European Union ban on BST represented an unfair restraint of trade that was at variance with WTO rules, of which the European Union was a signatory.

Genetically Modified Crops

Following regulatory approval, in 1996 Monsanto introduced the first wave of its genetically modified crops; Roundup-ready soybeans, Bollgard insect-protected cotton, and New Leaf insect-protected potatoes. Getting to this point had required sixteen years of research and according to various estimates, cost between $300 million and $500 million in R&D spending. A series of other products were scheduled to follow over the next few years, including Roundup-ready canola, cotton and rape seed, Yield Guard insect-protected corn, insect-protected tomatoes, corn rootworm-protected cotton, and Roundup-ready insect-protected soybeans (which adds *Bt* to Roundup-ready soybeans to provide both insect resistance and herbicide tolerance).

Although it was acknowledged as a technology leader and the first to bring a substantial number of products to market, Monsanto did not have the field entirely to itself. Monsanto faced the prospect of competition from several large companies, including Du Pont and Swiss-based Novartis. Du Pont had developed soybeans that tolerated the company's powerful Synchrony herbicide. Novartis had genetically altered corn seed so that it produced a protein that killed a common pest, the European corn borer. Both companies also had active research programs that promised to produce a range of genetically modified crops over the next decade.

Several smaller agricultural biotechnology companies had also been developing genetically altered crops, including DeKalb Genetics and Calgene. Calgene had introduced the first genetically engineered crop the previous year, a tomato that ripened more slowly and would stay fresh longer on supermarket shelves. Calgene was also developing a variety of soybean that was resistant to glyphosate, the active ingredient in Roundup. Simi-

larly, DeKalb was developing corn seed that was resistant to glyphosate. Monsanto purchased Calgene in April 1997 for $240 million.

Distribution Agreements   The delivery vehicle for all of Monsanto's genetic improvements was seed. However, the company had not traditionally been a strong player in the seed business. Thus, to produce and deliver genetically modified seed to farmers, Monsanto needed to find a way to participate in the seed industry. Companies in this industry grow seeds and then distribute them to farmers. The issue was further complicated by the fact that the genes that Monsanto created provided only one specific trait to the farmer. It was crucial that Monsanto's genes be incorporated in the best germplasm available, necessitating that Monsanto find some way to cooperate with leading seed companies. In its 1998 Annual Report, the company explained the issue as follows:

> Seed is the delivery vehicle for biotechnology traits. Integrating seed into our life sciences system will accelerate the development of new traits and their introduction into new varieties. The combination of breeding and genomics will accelerate the development of new varieties with better quality. Germplasm, the basic genetic structure of a plant, determines the characteristics of that variety, such as yield potential or drought resistance. Germplasm is crucial to grower acceptance; our traits must be available in the varieties that growers prefer. While we license our technology for use in other companies' germplasm—and that's an integral part of our overall strategy—we need to be involved from the start in developing new varieties that include the best traits.

The seed industry itself was highly concentrated, with a small number of players dominating the market. Different seed companies also focused on different product and vertical segments of the seed market. For example, Delta and Pine Land had a 55 percent share of the U.S. market for cotton seeds, but a zero percent share of the market for corn seeds, and only 1 percent of the market for soybean seeds. In contrast, Pioneer Hi-Bred had a 44 percent share of the market for corn seeds, a 19 percent share of the soybean market, and no position in the market for corn seeds. Other large seed companies included DeKalb Genetics, Northrup

King (owned by Sandoz), Cargill, Ciba Seeds (owned by Ciba-Geigy), Asgrow (owned by ELM of Mexico), and Holden's Foundation Seeds. DeKalb Genetics and Holden's were among the companies that focused on producing seeds, which they then sold to distributors.

Monsanto's initial approach was to explore a variety of relationships with seed companies. It decided to license its Roundup-ready soybean technology to a broad range of seed companies. In contrast, it entered into an exclusive licensing agreement with Delta Pine & Land to produce and market Bollgard cotton. In early 1996, the company acquired a minority position in DeKalb, which would produce Monsanto's Yield Guard corn. Independently of Monsanto, DeKalb Genetics had developed a strain of corn that was resistant to glyphosate. This was followed in September 1996, when Monsanto acquired one of its Roundup-ready soybean technology licensees, Asgrow, for $240 million. At the time of the acquisition, Asgrow ranked second among U.S. soybean seed companies, with an 18 percent market share for licensed and proprietary products. Monsanto stated that it would continue to license its technology to other soybean seed companies

In January 1997, Monsanto acquired Holden's Foundation Seeds and Corn States Hybrid Service and Corn States International, which marketed Holden's products worldwide, for around $1 billion. Like DeKalb, Holden's specializes in developing corn germ plasma, the genetic foundation for seed corn varieties. It licenses the germ plasma to independent companies, which in turn create corn hybrids for commercial use. Although Holden's doesn't sell seeds directly to farmers, it supplies one-third of the corn seed parent stock planted in the United States every year. Along with DeKalb and leading corn seed seller Pioneer Hi-Bred International, Holden's owns one of the three largest pools of corn genetics in the world. It is stored in the form of millions of kernels in cooled storage rooms. According to Monsanto's CEO, Holden's would give Monsanto "an excellent delivery mechanism for our biotechnology innovations in corn. These acquisitions mean the latest technological advances will be made available to the greatest possible number of seed companies of all sizes with unparalleled speed."[50] Holden's had been the subject of acquisition rumors for months before the Monsanto takeover. The company reportedly got bids or inquiries from several multinational companies that were moving into agricultural biotechnology, including DuPont, Dow-Elanco, AgrEvo and Novartis.[51]

The acquisition spree continued in 1998 when Monsanto purchased DeKalb Genetics outright for $2.3 billion, Delta and Pine Land for $1.3 billion, wheat seed company AgriPro, and the international seed business of Cargill. As a result of these acquisitions, Monsanto controlled an estimated 86 percent of the U.S. cotton seed market and nearly 50 percent of the corn and soybean seed markets.[52] To finance these acquisitions, Monsanto offered about $1.5 billion in common and preferred stock, and took on $2.5 billion in long-term debt, adding significant leverage to its balance sheet.[53] Monsanto's view of the industry value chain in early 1999, and its position in it, is summarized in Figure 1. The companies listed under the "seed" box in Figure 1 are biotechnology companies with which Monsanto had research alliances in 1999.

Monsanto was not alone is buying its way into the seed business. In May 1997, Du Pont invested $1.7 billion to acquire a 20 percent stake in Pioneer High Breeds, the largest seed producer in the United States. Like Monsanto, Du Pont made the purchase in order to speed up the process of commercializing its discoveries in agricultural biotechnology, and bring genetically altered seeds to market more rapidly. Many independent observers worried that in their race to become the Coke and Pepsi of agricultural biotechnology, Monsanto and Du Pont were fast creating an oligopolistic situation in the seed business.[54] Their fears intensified in March 1999, when Du Pont offered $7.7 billion to purchase all of Pioneer. If regulators approve the Du Pont–Pioneer deal, three companies—Du Pont, Monsanto, and Novartis—will control two-thirds of the North American seed corn market and 45 percent of the soybean seed market, and 85 percent of the U.S. cotton seed market.[55]

Pricing Strategy A big issue for Monsanto was how to price genetically altered seeds to capture the value implied by its proprietary position, and years of heavy investment in R&D. With regard to Bollgard cotton, which was distributed by Delta and Pine Land, Monsanto decided to price the seed at market rates but to tack on a separate technology fee of $32 per acre, which the farmers had to

FIGURE I

The Value Chain for
Transgenic Crops

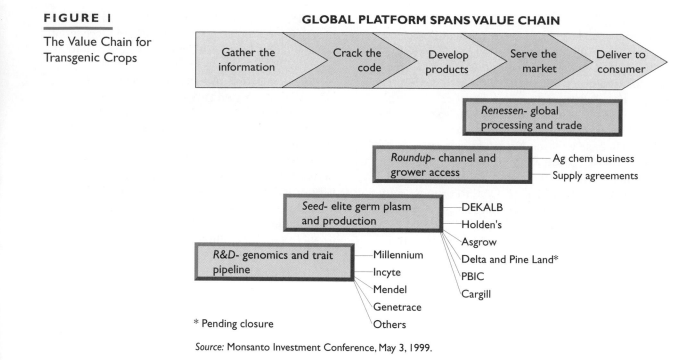

Source: Monsanto Investment Conference, May 3, 1999.

pay directly to Monsanto. The pricing strategy presented farmers with something of a gamble: would it cost more to fight pests using traditional methods, or should they pay the fee to Monsanto? And would the cotton survive if they didn't use Bollgard? Depending on the year, most farmers estimate that they spend anywhere from $20 to $100 per acre spraying against pests. While some of this cost is saved if they plant Bollgard cotton, they might still have to use some sprays to fight other pests.[56]

According to Monsanto, in its first full year, 1996, more than 5,700 U.S. farmers purchased Bollgard cotton and planted 1.8 million acres, or 13 percent of the total cotton acres in the United States. Approximately 60 percent of Bollgard users were able to totally eliminate insecticides, saving the average grower $33 per acre on land planted with Bollgard. Crop yields from fields planted with *Bt* cotton increased by 8 to 10 percent. Four out of five users said they were either satisfied or very satisfied with the cotton's overall performance. Only 2 percent said that they would not use it again.[57]

With regard to Roundup-ready soybeans, Monsanto decided to charge a technology fee of $5 per 50-pound bag of seed. A 50-pound bag of soybean

seeds was selling for between $13 and $15 in 1996. Roundup-ready soybeans cost between $18 and $20 per bag, depending on the seed company (Monsanto did not control the retail price; distributors did). Monsanto also required farmers to sign an agreement promising not to reuse the patented seed—which annoyed many farmers who were in the habit of doing so. Furthermore, the farmers had to agree to use Roundup, and not any competing glyphosate-based herbicide. In addition, the contract also allowed Monsanto to visit their farms for three years to make sure they kept their promise. In response to numerous complaints, Monsanto later dropped the requirement that farmers allow the company to inspect their operations but raised the technology fee to $6.50 per bag in 1998.[58]

Monsanto's marketing pitch for Roundup-ready soybeans emphasized two things. First, the company extolled the virtues of being able to use the environmentally friendly broad-spectrum Roundup herbicide to control weeds *after* crops began to sprout, rather than more expensive crop-specific herbicides. The company estimated that this would save farmers $12 to $16 per acre in reduced weed control costs, which of course had to be offset against the $5 technology fee. Second, Monsanto emphasized that if farmers made greater use of Roundup, they could reduce their use of traditional deep tillage weed control methods. This would have a long-term benefit in terms of reduced soil erosion. Put differently, it would facilitate the adoption of conservation tillage methods.

Roundup Strategy If Monsanto's push into Roundup-ready crops generated the sales that the company hoped for, the result would be a substantial surge in demand for Roundup that should succeed in expanding sales past the expiration of its U.S. patent on glyphosate in September 2000. By 1996, Roundup was generating more than $1 billion in annual sales for Monsanto. To ensure that revenue growth was not held back by volume constraints, in 1996 Monsanto embarked on a $200-million project to expand production capacity for Roundup over three years. To help protect its proprietary position, the company developed a new formulation of Roundup, Roundup Ultra, and applied for a patent on Ultra. Roundup Ultra contained surfactants and additives that that improved the herbicides absorption by weeds. This means that Ultra has less chance of being washed away by rain—it is absorbed by weeds in one to two hours, whereas basic Roundup takes six hours. The company estimated that 90 percent of Roundup users would switch to Ultra by 1997, primarily because of the convenience (prior to Ultra, they had to purchase surfactants and additives separately and add them to Roundup).[59]

At the same time, Monsanto continued a move begun ten years previously to price Roundup aggressively. Between 1992 and 1998, Monsanto reduced the price of Roundup by 9 percent in the U.S. market. This, coupled with the tie-in to sales of Monsanto's genetically altered crops, produced a 201 percent increase in the volume of Roundup sales. Even larger volume increases were observed in other nations where Monsanto's patent had already expired. In Brazil, for example, Monsanto cut the price of Roundup by 45 percent between 1992 and 1998 and was rewarded by a 685 percent surge in volume. In Canada, a 34 percent reduction in price over the same time period led to a 310 percent increase in Roundup volume.[60]

In 1998 and 1999, Monsanto took additional steps to deal with the increased threat of competi-

tion after the U.S. patent on glyphosate expired. The catalyst was an attempt by Zeneca, to test its own brand of glyphosate-based herbicide, Touchdown, on Monsanto's Roundup-ready soybeans. Zeneca already sold Touchdown outside of the United States and was preparing to sell in the United States after September 2000. In mid 1998, Monsanto sued Zeneca, saying it illegally acquired Roundup-ready soybean seed for testing Touchdown. The British company responded by suing Monsanto, charging that the company's requirement that farmers use its brand of glyphosate on Roundup-ready crops was anticompetitive. In March 1999, the companies dropped their law suits against each other. In exchange, Monsanto agreed to allow Zeneca to use its Touchdown on seeds using Monsanto's Roundup-ready herbicide-tolerant technology. In return, Zeneca agreed to pay Monsanto an unspecified licensing fee.[61]

While the lawsuits were still pending, Monsanto entered into a number of separate agreements to sell glyphosate to five other agricultural chemical companies, including Dow Chemicals and Novartis. Under the terms of these agreements, which extended for five years and could be renewed thereafter, Monsanto also agreed to allow U.S. farmers to use glyphosate herbicides from these companies on Roundup-ready cotton and soybeans in 2000, and corn in 2001. Commenting on the Dow deal, a Monsanto spokesman noted that "We were concerned that Dow would go and build glyphosate plants and engage in a price war. By having Monsanto provide supplies of glyphosate, Dow will have better costs of production."[62]

Early Results and Looking Ahead Since 1996, the use of transgenic seeds has increased exponentially, from 4 million acres planted in 1996 to 70 million acres in 1998. In 1997, sales of transgenic crops totaled $4 billion. The worldwide market is projected to double by 2002. In 1996, only 1 million acres of Monsanto's Roundup-ready soybeans were planted. In 1998, around half of the U.S. 75-million-acre soybean crop will be Roundup-ready. If growth continues, in 1999 Monsanto will have earned almost $300 million in royalties from sales of soybean seeds alone. *Bt* cotton is also expected to be used on more than half of the U.S. cotton acreage planted in 1999. Moreover, adoption is also occurring quickly overseas. China will use Mon-

FIGURE 2

Major Players in the
Agricultural Seed and
Chemical Industry:
Projected 1999
Revenues

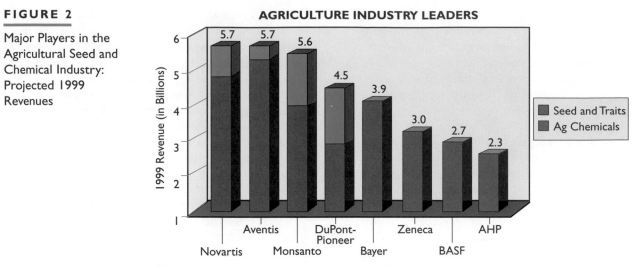

AGRICULTURE INDUSTRY LEADERS

Source: Monsanto Investment Conference, May 3, 1999.

santo's *Bt* cotton for about a quarter of its planting
in 1999. Of the nearly 70 million acres planted with
genetically modified crops worldwide in 1998,
Monsanto varieties accounted for more than 70
percent. Monsanto claims that it could have sold a
lot more if it had the seed (see Figure 2 for
details).[63]

Human Pharmaceuticals

During the 1990s Monsanto's Searle unit launched
a number of products, cumulating in the launch of
Celebrex, the COX–2 inhibitor, in early 1999. The
first of these, Ambien, a treatment for insomnia,
was introduced in 1993 and by 1998 was generating more than $450 million in annual revenues.
This was followed by Daypro, a once-a-day NSAID
treatment for osteoarthritis and rheumatoid arthritis, which generated annual sales of $308 million in
1998, and Arthrotec, another NSAID drug that also
has ulcer prevention properties, which generated
revenues of $346 in 1998. Revenues from all three
of these drugs, however, could well be dwarfed by
sales of Celebrex.[64]

Aware that Merck's competing COX–2 inhibitor, Vioxx, would probably be on the market by
mid 1999, Searle entered into a co-marketing agreement with Pfizer. The goal was to leverage the
reach of Pfizer's large sales force, reckoned by

many to be among the best in the industry. To
jump-start market adoption, Searle and Pfizer sent
45,000 "patient starter kits" to physicians and phar-
macies. In each free kit there were ten bottles, each
containing a twenty-five day supply of Celebrex.
Using a sophisticated data base, Searle gave its samples to doctors who most often prescribe arthritis-
related painkillers (NSAIDs)—rheumatologists,
orthopedic surgeons, and podiatrists. Searle also
aimed the kits at physicians in big medical practices who prescribe large amounts of NSAIDs.[65]

As might be expected, the marketing pitch emphasized that Celebrex offers the same pain relief
as traditional NSAIDs but causes fewer side effects,
such as intestinal bleeding and ulcers. Pricing was
perhaps the most difficult issue. Searle and Pfizer
tested some 700 different pricing models before
settling on a cost to consumers of about $2.42 per
day. This was significantly more than generic
NSAIDs, which can cost as little as 10 cents per day,
but less than most analysts had initially expected. In
part, the lower price was a concession to managed
care organizations that were trying to get control of
soaring prescription costs. Following a formal
launch meeting of February 22, hundreds of sales
representatives from both companies fanned out to
doctors offices in what was one of the most intense
marketing efforts ever. The aim was to acquaint the
nation's 150,000 doctors with the virtues of Cele-

brex within six months. This was to be followed by a consumer advertising blitz. The cost of this effort was forecasted to exceed $100 million.[66]

The initial results from this launch effort were nothing short of spectacular. By April, Searle was reporting that it had already directly contacted 70 percent of the nation's doctors. According to independent research data, two months after the launch, about 100 percent of rheumotologists surveyed were aware of the drug and 98 percent had prescribed it. This compared with averages of 85 and 54 percent for new arthritis treatments.[67] It was soon apparent that Celebrex was experiencing the second fastest sales ramp-up of any drug product launch in U.S. history, outpaced only by sales of Pfizer's male impotence drug, Viagra. Two months after the launch, analysts were predicting first-year sales in excess of $550 million, and sales of $3 billion annually by 2002. To put this in context, in 1998 Monsanto's total sales were $8.65 billion, and that of its Searle unit $2.42 billion.

LOOKING AHEAD

In September 1997, Monsanto confirmed its commitment to life sciences when it spun off its commodity chemical businesses to stockholders as an independent unit with sales of close to $3 billion. What remained of Monsanto was focused on agricultural and human life sciences. In both areas, the company had ambitious long-term plans.

Agriculture

The success of the first wave of Monsanto's transgenic crops was based on the benefits farmers gained in the form of improved yield and economies in the use of inputs. Although these products offered no direct benefits to consumers, there was an indirect benefit from the increase in productivity; consumers needed to spend less of their disposable incomes on food. The second wave of transgenic crops, which Monsanto and others were set to introduce in the 1999–2004 time period, offered quality and nutrition traits—in other words, value-added outputs. Examples include oilseed rape with high lauric, stearate, oleic and GLA contents (all nutritionally beneficial), soy-

beans containing proteins that reduce cholesterol or have a medical value in combating osteoporosis or hormonal cancer, maize with enhanced oil and protein contents, and high-starch potatoes, which would take up less fat when fried. The last of these was a Monsanto product scheduled for market introduction in 2000. Monsanto had altered the genetic sequence of the potatoes to make them higher in starches and lower in water. When cut into french fries, the potato absorbs less fat in the deep fryer. The result is that the fries taste the same but have fewer calories and a better texture.[68]

A third wave of genetically modified crop products further down the pipeline could best be described as "plants as factories." Examples under development at Monsanto, Du Pont, and Novartis included using tobacco plants to produce albumin and growth hormones, corn to produce humanized monoclonal antibodies for treating diseases, and transgenic oilseed rape for producing modified fatty acids. Rape could also be modified to produce high levels of beta carotene—much greater than the amounts produced in crops such as carrots. This could be significant for meeting dietary deficiencies in some developing countries. There is also research under way to engineer plants that produce fibers, polymers, or intermediaries that otherwise could come from petrochemicals.

To accelerate the process of developing new transgenic crop varieties, in 1997 Monsanto entered into an alliance with Millennium, a biotechnology firm with expertise in screening genes to identify the causes of diseases—an area known as genomics. The terms of the deal called for Monsanto to pay Millennium $118 million over five years for *exclusive* access to Millennium's gene research in agriculture. In addition, Monsanto stated that it would start a gene research unit in Cambridge, Millennium's base, which would employ up to 150 scientists by the end of 1998. Millennium will hire most of the staff. According to a Monsanto spokesman, "By greatly increasing the speed and precision with which we can analyze new product leads, this agreement will help us rapidly bring future Monsanto life sciences products to market,"[69] The Millennium announcement came one day after Monsanto said it was extending an existing collaboration with another genomics firm, Incyte Pharmaceutical, also in agricultural genetics.

FIGURE 3

COX–2 Technology
Platform

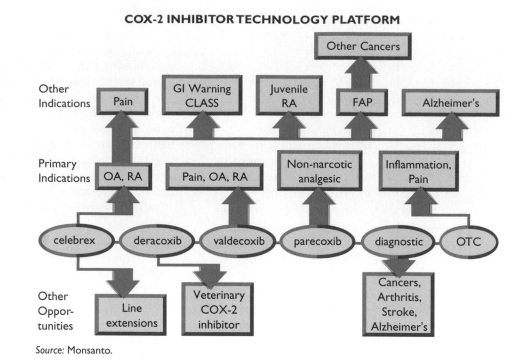

COX-2 INHIBITOR TECHNOLOGY PLATFORM

Source: Monsanto.

Pharmaceuticals

In pharmaceuticals, Monsanto has set itself the goal
of continuing to grow its product portfolio and development pipeline in arthritis, oncology, and cardiovascular by adding one new chemical or
biological entity to the pipeline every year (on average), and one new "technology platform" every
three years. The concept of a technology platform
refers to the notion of adding multiple indications
for the same drug, or using an understanding of a basic biological process to develop a family of drugs.

The concept of technology platform can best be
understood by considering how Monsanto hopes to
exploit its technology platform in COX–2 inhibitors
(see Figure 3). COX–2 enzyme expression is suspected of playing a role in Alzheimer's disease and
some cancers, such as colon cancer (FAP). This raises
the possibility that a COX–2 inhibitor, such as Celebrex, might be a useful treatment for these diseases.
Searle is conducting phase III trials to explore the
use of Celebrex in treating FAP, has data from a phase
II trial using Celebrex to treat Alzheimer patients,
and on the basis of this intends to move forward
with a phase III Alzheimer trial later this year. Searle
is also looking at producing different COX–2 in-

hibitors, such as deracoxib for the veterinary
market, or valdecoxib, a second generation COX–2
inhibitor.

The Concerns of Analysts

While impressed by Monsanto's plans, analysts worried that the company lacked the resources required to grow its business, given its debt load. Of
particular concern was the pharmaceutical area,
where Monsanto was still a small player relative to
industry leaders. There were fears that Searle, with
its smaller research budget and sales force presence, would not be able to fully exploit and extend
its strong product pipeline.

In mid 1998, Monsanto seemed to have found a
solution to these issues when it announced a
merger with American Home Products (AHP). AHP
had a world-class pharmaceutical sales force and a
strong financial position, but lacked Monsanto's
deep product pipeline. However, the merger talks
collapsed in October 1998, reportedly due to
clashes between the top management of both companies over layoffs and attitudes to R&D spending
and risk taking. In the aftermath of the collapse,
Monsanto's management vowed to go it alone. [70]

TABLE I

Monsanto's Financial Position, 1996–1998

A: Statement of Consolidated Income (dollars in millions, except per share)

	Three Months Ended December 31		Twelve Months Ended December 31	
	1998	*1997*	*1998*	*1997*
Net sales	$ 2,148	$ 1,820	$ 8,648	$ 7,514
Costs, expenses, and other:				
Cost of goods sold	971	749	3,593	3,091
Selling, general, and administrative expenses	675	557	2,421	2,023
Technological expenses	391	326	1,358	1,044
Acquired in-process research and development	213	75	402	684
Amortization of intangible assets	281	59	487	173
Restructuring and other special charges—net	307		272	
Interest expense	98	59	312	170
Interest income	(11)	(9)	(50)	(45)
Other expense—net	69	7	96	8
Income (loss) from continuing operations before taxes	(846)	(3)	(243)	366
Income taxes	(243)	(8)	7	72
Income (loss) from continuing operations	(603)	5	(250)	294
Income from discontinued operations				176
Net income (loss)	$ (603)	$ 5	$ (250)	$ 470
Basic earnings / (loss) per share				
Continuing operations	$(1.00)	$ 0.01	$(0.41)	$ 0.50
Discontinued operations				0.30
Total	$(1.00)	$ 0.01	$(0.41)	$ 0.80
Diluted earnings / (loss) per share				
Continuing operations	$(1.00)	$ 0.01	$(0.41)	$ 0.48
Discontinued operations				0.29
Total	$(1.00)	$ 0.01	$(0.41)	$ 0.77
Weighted average common shares—basic (in millions)			603.5	590.2
Weighted average common shares—diluted (in millions)			603.5	610.5
Earnings before interest and Tax expense (EBIT)	$ (748)	$ 56	$ 69	$ 536

B: Segment Data (dollars in millions)

	EBITDA[1]			
	Three Months		Twelve Months	
	1998	*1997*	*1998*	*1997*
Segment				
Agricultural products	$ 35	$(11)	$1,092	$ 939
Nutrition and Consumer Products	88	109	405	440
Pharmaceuticals	222	197	451	422
Corporate and other	(25)	(26)	(183)	(94)
Total	$ 320	$ 269	$1,765	$1,707

[1]EBITDA (earnings before interest expense, taxes, depreciation and amortization excluding unusuals) is EBIT excluding depreciation, amortization, and the effects of unusual items.

C: Statement of Consolidated Financial Position (dollars in millions)

	December 31, 1998	December 31, 1997
Assets		
Current assets:		
Cash and cash equivalents	$ 89	$ 134
Trade receivables	2,404	1,823
Prepaid assets and other receivables	1,141	692
Deferred income tax benefit	567	243
Inventories	2,004	1,374
Total current assets	6,205	4,266
Net property, plant and equipment	3,254	2,400
Intangible assets	6,047	2,837
Investment and other assets	1,233	1,271
Total assets	$16,739	$10,774
Liabilities and Shareowners' Equity		
Current Liabilities		
Payables and accruals	$ 2,998	$ 1,813
Short-term debt	1,069	1,726
Total current liabilities	4,067	3,539
Long-term debt	6,259	1,979
Postretirement liabilities	871	735
Other liabilities	536	417
Shareowners' equity	5,006	4,104
Total liabilities and shareowners' equity	$16,739	$10,774
Working capital	$ 2,138	$ 727
Debt to capital ratio	59%	47%

Endnotes

1. J. Vorman, "China Seen Swiftly Adopting Transgenic Cotton," *Reuters*, April 26, 1999.
2. Monsanto, "In the Pipeline" (www.monsanto.com).
3. J. Rifkin, "Perils of Unnatural Science," *Financial Times*, June 20, 1998, p. 9.
4. C. Blackledge, "Benefits That Go Against the Grain," *Financial Times*, March 15, 1999, p. 4.
5. R. J. Mahoney, "The Player's Point of View," *Institutional Investor*, June 1989, p. 23.
6. D. Leonard Barton and G. Pisano, "Monsanto's March into Biotechnology," *Harvard Business School Case* 9-690-009.
7. K. Schneider, "Betting the Farm on Biotechnology," *New York Times* Business World Magazine, June 10, 1990, sec. 3, pt. 2, p. 26.
8. R. Steyer, "BST Is Monsanto's Splice of Life," *St. Louis Post Dispatch*, April 25, 1994, p. 12.
9. K. Drlica, *Understanding DNA and Gene Cloning* (New York: Wiley, 1997).
10. Company history (summarized at www.gene.com).
11. Schneider, "Betting the Farm."
12. Ibid.
13. "Offer of Top R&D Post Lured Him Off Campus," *Chemical Week*, January 23, 1980, p. 48.
14. "The Reworking of Monsanto," *Chemical Week*, January 12, 1983, p. 42.
15. Schneider, "Betting the Farm."
16. Steyer, "BST Is Monsanto's Splice of Life."
17. E. B. Fiske, "Monsanto Research Pact Aims to Cut Academic Controversy," *New York Times*, June 4, 1982, p. 21A; D. Sanger, "Corporate Links Worry Scholars," *New York Times*, October 17, 1982, sec. 3, p. 4.
18. Ibid.
19. Fiske, "Monsanto Research Pact."
20. B. J. Spalding, "Monsanto's Bid for the Lead in Biotechnology," *Chemical Week*, June 11, 1986, p. 41.
21. Ibid.
22. "The Reworking of Monsanto," *Chemical Week*, January 12, 1983, p. 42.

23. "Monsanto-Searle: A Biotech Coupling," *Chemical Engineering*, August 19, 1985, p. 26.
24. J. E. Ellis and E. K. Spragius, "Why Monsanto is Bucking the Odds," *Business Week,* August 5, 1985, p. 76.
25. "Monsanto-Searle: A Biotech coupling."
26. Ibid.
27. Spalding, "Monsanto's Bid for the Lead in Biotechnology."
28. Ibid.
29. Ibid.
30. K. Schneider, "Biotech's Stalled Revolution," *New York Times*, November 16, 1986, sec. 6, p. 43.
31. Ibid.
32. Ibid.
33. Schneider, "Betting the Farm."
34. C. S. Gasser and R. T. Fraley, "Genetically Engineering Plants for Crop Improvement," *Science*, June 16, 1989, p. 1293.
35. "Plant-Genetics Advance; Antibiotic-Resistant Petunias," *Popular Science*, 222, (April 1983), p. 19.
36. Gasser and Fraley, "Genetically Engineering Plants for Crop Improvement."
37. Schneider, "Betting the Farm."
38. Ibid.
39. B. J. Feder, "Out of the Lab, a Revolution on the Farm," *New York Times*, March 3, 1996, p. 3.
40. Steyer, "BST Is Monsanto's Splice of Life."
41. K. Schneider, "U.S. Approves Use of Drug to Raise Milk Production," *New York Times*, November 6, 1993, p. 1.
42. R. Steyer, "Discovery of Arthritis Drug Began in WU Lab," *St. Louis Post Dispatch*, April 6, 1998, p. A1.
43. Ibid.
44. These figures come from the FDA's own data base and were compiled by Analysis Group Economics, a drug industry consulting firm.
45. T. M. Burton, "A Pharmaceutical Plumb in Monsanto's Basket," *Wall Street Journal*, June 2, 1998, p. B1.
46. Figures come from Monsato's May 3, 1999, presentation to securities analysts (posted at www.monsanto.com).
47. M. Groves, "Canada Rejects Hormone That Boosts Cow's Milk Output," *Los Angeles Times*, January 15, 1999, pt. C, p. 1.
48. Ibid.
49. K. O'Sullivan, "EU Scientific Committee Casts Doubt on Safety of Injected Hormone Used to Boost Milk Yield," *Irish Times*, March 17, 1999, p. 2.
50. J. Swiatek, "Business of Seeds Changing in Big Ways," *Indianapolis Star*, January 12, 1997, p. E1.
51. R. Steyer, "Monsanto Buys Seed Corn Firm," *St. Louis Post-Dispatch*, January 7, 1977, p. C6.
52. P. Downs, "Badseed: Company Has Near Monopoly on the Seed Industry," *Progressive*, 63 (February 1999), 36.
53. T. M. Burton, "Monsanto's Cost Cutting Steps to Raise Cash for Seed Company Acquisitions," *Wall Street Journal*, November 12, 1998, p. A4.
54. S. Kilman and S. Warren, "Old Rivals Fight for New Turf Biotechnology Crops," *Wall Street Journal*, May 27, 1998, p. A4.
55. R. Steyer, "DuPont's Purchase of Pioneer Validates Big Bet Monsato Made on Seed Companies," *St. Louis Post Dispatch*, March 21, 1999, p. E1.
56. S. J. Willis, "Farmers Torn Over Use of Pest Fighter," *Arizona Business Gazette*, May 29, 1997, p. 16.
57. Monsanto, Bollgard Cotton Update (March 1997).
58. R. Steyer, "Super Soybean," *St. Louis Post Dispatch,* February 25, 1996, p. E1.
59. R. Steyer, "Monsanto Reports Success for New Roundup," *St. Louis Post Dispatch*, December 22, 1996, p. 1E.
60. Figures come from Monsato's May 3, 1999, presentation to securities analysts (posted at www.monsanto.com).
61. R. Steyer, "Monsanto, British Firm End War Over Herbicides," *St. Louis Post-Dispatch*, March 19, 1999, p. C9.
62. R. Steyer, "Monsanto Will License Roundup Rights to Dow," *St. Louis Post Dispatch*, January 20, 1999, p. C1.
63. R. F. Service, "Chemical Industry Rushes Toward Greener Pastures," *Science*, October 23, 1998, p. 608; J. Vorman, "China Seen Swiftly Adopting Transgenic Cotton," *Reuters*, April 26, 1999.
64. Data from Monsanto's May 3, 1999, presentation to securities analysts (posted at www.monsanto.com).
65. "Safe Painkiller Set to Launch Pharmaceuticals World War," *Financial Times,* February 5, 1999, p. 26.
66. A. Barrett and R. A. Melcher, "Why Searle Is Feeling No Pain," *Business Week*, February 15, 1999, p. 36.
67. Data from Monsanto's May 3, 1999, presentation to securities analysts (posted at www.monsanto.com).
68. R. Lenzner and B. Upbin, "Monsanto v. Malthus," *Forbes*, March 10, 1997, p. 58–60.
69. R. Rosenberg, "Millennium Inks Pact Worth as Much as $218M," *Boston Globe,* October 29, 1997, p. C2.
70. T. M. Burton and E. Tanouye, "Another Drug Industry Megamerger Goes Bust," *Wall Street Journal*, October 14, 1998, p. B1.

CASE 36

Tyco International

This case was prepared by Cynthia Montgomery, Robert Kennedy, Lisa Chadderdon, and Harold F. Hogan, Jr., of Harvard Business School.

On October 6, 1995, Tyco International, a diversified U.S. conglomerate, received some very unflattering news. A respected investor monitoring organization, the Council of Institutional Investors (CII), had included the firm in its list of the twenty worst-performing S&P 500 companies. CII generated its list annually, based on a mechanical formula that calculated total shareholder returns over a five-year period.[1] One commentator described the annual rankings as "the corporate equivalent of being put on the school detention list."[2]

The choice of Tyco as one of the twenty culprits was quickly challenged. Tyco's own management described the result as an artifact arising from an abnormally high share price during a narrow window at the start of CII's measurement period. Robert Monks, head of Lens, Inc., an activist money management firm and former member of Tyco's board of directors, also took exception to the report. In a letter of protest to the executive director of CII, Monks asserted that based on his own experience, he believed Tyco was a responsible company fully committed to enhancing shareholder value. He wrote:

> On balance we conclude that this is a first-rate company successfully adding value in the difficult mode of a conglomerate. Our criteria [for evaluating] companies ultimately is—what can we, as informed and effectively involved own-

ers, do to enhance value? Our answer in the case of Tyco is—virtually nothing. What are we missing? [See Appendix].

Was Monk's belief in Tyco justified? Or had the conglomerate form of organization in fact become outdated?

TYCO'S BUSINESSES

Tyco International was a diversified manufacturer based in Exeter, New Hampshire. In fiscal 1996, it had sales of $5 billion and net income of $310 million, up 12 percent and 45 percent, respectively, from the previous year. The company operated more than 300 individual profit centers in over sixty countries. Until recently, many people had been unaware of Tyco's existence, and many still confused it with a toy maker of the same name. In the last few years, however, Tyco had begun to make bids for more visible companies, such as American Standard and ADT, and had gained greater recognition in the press and on Wall Street. In 1997, *Business Week* described Tyco as one of the "stars you may never have heard of" and listed it among its top fifty companies.[3]

Traditionally, Tyco thrived in converter businesses, producing finished goods from raw materials. Each year the company purchased over 1 million tons of steel, 24 million pounds of cotton, and 1 billion pounds of polyethylene. Tyco generally ran its machines and factories twenty-four hours a day, seven days a week, and most of its businesses had at least a 50 percent share of their respective markets. The combination of volume purchasing, efficient production, and dominant market positions helped

Tyco become a low-cost producer and price leader in each of its core industries.

In 1997, the company had six primary operating divisions:[4]

- *Fire protection.* Manufactured, installed, and maintained detection systems, sprinklers, extinguishers, hydrants, hazardous equipment, and other related products. Major company: Grinnell.

- *Flow control.* Manufactured a variety of pipes, fittings, meters, valves, and other pipe-related products. Major companies: Grinnell; Allied Tube and Conduit; Mueller.

- *Disposable medical products.* Produced disposable medical supplies such as gauze; incontinence, urological, and anesthetic supplies; vascular therapy products; and medical electrodes. Major company: Kendall International.

- *Simplex Technologies, Inc.* Produced transoceanic fiber optic cable, underwater power cable, flexible pipe, and other undersea cable products.

- *Packaging materials.* Manufactured a wide variety of packaging materials for industrial and commercial use. Major companies: Armin Plastics; Ludlow Laminating and Coating; Carlisle Plastics.

- *Specialty products.* Described by one company executive as Tyco's "catch-all group, the pieces of the business that didn't really fit with anything else, a conglomerate within a conglomerate." Major companies: Earth Tech (environmental); Tyco Printed Circuit Board Group (printed boards); Twitchell (fabrics); Accurate Forming (metal parts).

Each of the six divisions was headed by its own president, who, in many ways, functioned as a CEO. The presidents were responsible for developing group-level strategy and building sets of related businesses within their respective domains.

There were very few transactions or resource flows among Tyco's divisions. Brad McGee, president of the specialty products division, commented:

> Across the six divisions, there's very little synergy. If you look at the percentage of things that are synergistic versus the size of the businesses, it's really just tiny little opportunities that we find here and there. And where those do occur, it's generally just because we happen to belong to the same company and somebody out at a factory finds something that could make sense. For example, someone from one of my companies buys something from Kendall.... It's done only if they get a better price than in the market, and only because they happen to know they [Kendall] are there.[5]

The closely related fire protection and flow control divisions ("fire/flow"), which until 1993 had been one large segment, were the exception to this rule. The synergies between these divisions were multifold. Many of the flow control products manufactured by Grinnell, for instance, were used in the installation of the systems sold by the fire protection division. Nevertheless, both divisions were encouraged to negotiate the best terms available in the marketplace, and occasionally would buy from another company.

When Tyco's chairman, L. Dennis Kozlowski, was asked why Tyco ran its six divisions under one umbrella instead of spinning them off as independent companies, he responded:

> If at any time there was better value to be created for the shareholders by spinning off a business or breaking up the company, we would do that in a heartbeat. I own a million shares of the stock—I'm a big stockholder—so if a $70 share price would become a $100 share price, I wouldn't even hesitate—I'd do it right away.
>
> At least once a year we bring in someone from the outside who is highly incentivized to break up the company—for instance someone from J.P. Morgan, Merrill Lynch, or Goldman Sachs—and we tell them, "take a good look at us, break us up, and tell us what we're going to get per share for it. Then tell us if you think we should break up." It's the only way to get an objective look at it. And they have always said that we should stay as we are. Then I take what they say and give it to the Board.
>
> Looking at these factors, I come to the conclusion that the sum of the parts here is a lot less than the value of the whole. And it usually goes the other way for a diversified company. Someday breaking up the company may be the right thing to do. When I took over the company at the beginning of fiscal 1993, our market capital was 1.2 billion dollars. When we finish all these deals now, it will be about 20 billion

dollars—that's four years later. We have created an awful lot of value in the marketplace. I think if we can continue to do that, we will continue to be rewarded.[6]

THE MAKING OF A CONGLOMERATE

Tyco, Inc., was founded by Arthur J. Rosenberg in 1960 as a research and development laboratory. The company went public in 1964, and Rosenberg pursued a vision of rapid growth through acquisitions. By 1973, Tyco had completed twenty acquisitions, sales had increased to over $40 million, and the company had been transformed from an R&D provider into a manufacturing concern.

Inconsistent stock performance and widespread operational problems led to a change in management, and in April 1973, Joseph P. Gaziano was named president, chairman, and CEO. Gaziano established the goal of making Tyco a $1 billion company by 1985. It soon became clear that he intended to pursue his vision through a series of aggressive acquisitions. The business press observed that he made "a habit of hostile raids before that was the fashion."[7]

Gaziano's favored method of takeover was to begin buying a target company's stock on the open market. While he often failed to win the company, several of his aborted takeover attempts left Tyco with handsome profits. For example, a hostile bid for the electronics company Leeds and Northrup ended in failure, but still garnered Tyco $6.4 million in profit. In another instance, Gaziano bought 4.9 percent of the stock in Trane, a manufacturer of air conditioners. When confronted by Trane's chairman, Gaziano agreed to sell back the stock—for 21 percent above the market price. Three failed attempts in the 1970s alone added $15 million to Tyco's earnings.[8] Gaziano soon acquired a reputation as a corporate raider, which made him angry. "Nobody likes to be called nasty names,' he says, 'but it's like saying a linebacker hits too hard. What's too hard?"[9]

By 1982, Gaziano had transformed Tyco from a small, $41 million manufacturer to a $574 million conglomerate with substantial market share in a variety of industries. The story, however, was not universally positive. One commentator described the company as a "glamorous, shoot-from-the-hip buyer of small companies—a kind of mini-conglomerate long after conglomerates had gone out of fashion."[10] The recessions of 1979 and 1982 also hit Tyco hard, with profits falling more than 20 percent between 1980 and 1982.

JOHN FORT, 1982–1992

Gaziano did not live to see the day that Tyco reached $1 billion in revenue. He died unexpectedly of cancer in 1982 and was succeeded by John F. Fort, an aeronautical engineer with degrees from Princeton and MIT. Fort had started working at Simplex in 1965 and was president when Tyco acquired the business in 1974. Soon afterward, Fort was named Tyco's COO.

The company Fort inherited in 1982 was "choking on high debt and chaotic management."[11] Fort discarded Gaziano's goal of becoming a $1 billion company and instead strove for improved operating performance. He implemented numerous cost-cutting measures, eliminating perks like corporate jets and apartments, and reducing the staff at corporate headquarters to thirty-five people. *Financial World* reported that "under Fort, all the glamour is gone. So are the jets, and so is much of the management. With the loss of the old management's glamour has come renewed respect from Wall Street."[12]

Fort also pruned nonproductive assets from Tyco's portfolio. He sold $68 million in equity accumulated during eight failed takeover attempts. In one transaction alone, he liquidated over 500,000 shares of Allied Corporation for $54.3 million and netted $11.3 million in profit.[13] At the same time, he jettisoned a number of unrelated businesses, and used some of the proceeds to reduce Tyco's heavy debt. Between 1982 and 1985, the company's long-term debt dropped from 119 to 8 percent of shareholders' equity.[14]

Fort reorganized the firm into three core business segments, each centered on a leading company: fire protection flow control (Grinnell); packaging materials (Armin and Ludlow); and electronic and electrical components (Simplex and the Printed Circuit Board Group).

Building a Disciplined Organization.

Fort focused on careful growth and disciplined, lean operations. Early on, he restructured the compensation system to create powerful incentives and

CASE 36 Tyco International

Stock Price Analysis for
Alternative Corporate
Structure

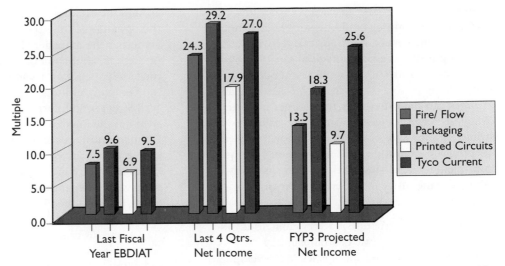

Three investment banks conducted independent analyses to determine whether Tyco's shareholders would
be better off if the company was split into several pieces. All three investment banks used similar methodologies. They valued each of Tyco's four business segments using market multiples for similar companies. The
studies concluded that Tyco trades at a higher multiple than comparable firms in the printed circuit board
and fire/flow industries, and at a multiple slightly below firms in the packaging industry. Thus, the analysts concluded that spinning off Tyco's business segments would not create value for shareholders.
aMarket capitalization/(*relevant measure*) based on closing stock prices on April 2, 1993.
The comparable companies were the following:
Fire/flow: Amcast Industrial, BWIP Holding, Duriron Company, Gould Pumps, Graco Incorporated, IDEX Cor-
poration, Keystone International, Mark Controls, Watts Industries, Central Sprinkler, and Figgie International.
Packaging: Ball Corporation, Bemis Company, Engraph, Inc., PCI Services, Inc., Sealed Air Corporation, and
Sonoco Products Company.
Printed circuits: Altron Incorporated, Benchmark Electronics, Circuit Systems, Diceon, Hadco Corporation,
Micronics Computers, and VLSI Technology.

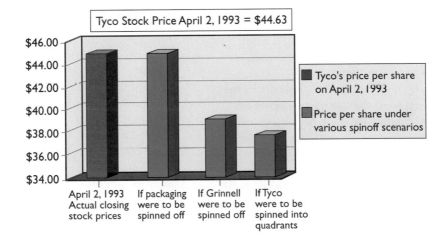

long-term thinking. Base salaries were set low, but performance bonuses could be very high. When an executive took over a division, a target was set for operating profit as a percentage of sales. Going forward, that person's bonus would be a percentage of operating profits above that target. As long as executives ran their divisions, their target rates never changed. Performance bonuses were paid in restricted shares, which vested slowly over time, thus keeping the executive team focused on continued improvement. Fort viewed this system as a way to mimic the incentives that leverage-buyout firms offered their managers:

> Our corporate structure is a very capitalistic system. There is very little central planning. We don't tend to set up a lot of rules. We develop incentives for our people, and it works. All of the earnings and incentives are geared to a higher stock price. Top management receives straight salary and stock options. Middle managers receive a percentage of profits from the profit centers they manage. You have to provide that—the greatest competition for good managers today is the entrepreneurial world. The way to hold onto them is to give them a business of their own within your business.[15]

Fort built a powerful controllers' organization as a complement to the decentralization effort. Managers had great freedom to improve performance, but they had to account for every dollar. Fort's focus on earnings was legendary. He once said, "The reason we were put on earth is to increase earnings per share."[16]

Based on his own experience as president of the fire/flow unit, Kozlowski explained the impact on executives: "... while they have the backing of an old-line, financially secure, capable company, they have all the entrepreneurship of a small entrepreneur who can go out and do what needs to be done without all the encumbrances by the corporation."[17]

Fort's Acquisition Policies

Fort's approach to acquisitions was radically different from his predecessor's. "Joe had a terrific instinct for acquisitions," Fort explained less than a year after becoming CEO. "But my background is in operations. I think we'll use a little more analysis now."[18] Fort believed that a good acquirer had to really understand a target. Someone had to walk around the factories, talk to the workers, and assess the operations. Only then could one decide "whether the managers know what they are doing, or don't. It's not something you can record on a piece of paper. It's very important to get a feel for the company, to judge what you can do with it."[19] Wall Street seemed to agree. Edward Cimilluca, who ran the Special Situations Group for Shearson Lehman Brothers commented, "Fort is a guy who knows how a factory works. He's not romanced by investment banking. His notion of making a company work is to get the best out of what Tyco owns. In doing that, he's completely changed the corporate culture of the place."[20]

During his tenure, Fort made several large acquisitions in the fire/flow division including Grinnell (1986), Hersey Water Meters (1986), Allied Pipe (1987), and Mueller (1988). The acquisitions were designed to make the firm a single source of manufacturing, contracting, and supply for its customers. In 1990, Tyco's fire/flow unit expanded overseas when it acquired Wormald, a manufacturer of fire protection equipment with operations in Europe, Australia, and New Zealand. This significantly expanded Tyco's worldwide presence in fire protection equipment, giving it more than 200 offices in thirty countries. By 1991, the fire/flow group had grown to nearly 80 percent of Tyco's sales.

Performance Under Fort

During Fort's eight years at the helm, Tyco's return on equity averaged 18 percent, and EPS increased an average of 25 percent per year. Tyco's stock price on the NYSE stood at $1.55 in January 1982 and was $29.56 in July 1990, a 41 percent compound growth rate. Total sales hit $1 billion in 1988, $2 billion in 1990, and $3 billion in 1991.

After this phenomenal growth, Tyco was again jolted by recession. The company's fire/flow business was hit particularly hard, as it depended on the highly cyclical construction industry. Between July and October 1990, Tyco's stock price declined 35 percent, to $19.19. EPS decreased from a high of $2.90 in fiscal 1990 to $1.58 in June 1993.

From the very beginning of his chairmanship, Fort had made it known that he planned to step down after ten years. He kept this promise and passed the leadership of the firm to L. Dennis Kozlowski on July 1, 1992.

TABLE I

Tyco's Consolidated Statement of Income (in thousands, except per share data)

	Year Ended							
	June 30, 1997	June 30, 1996	June 30, 1995	June 30, 1994	June 30, 1993	June 30, 1992	June 30, 1991	May 31, 1990
Sales	$6,597,629	$5,089,828	$4,534,651	$3,262,832	$3,114,500	$3,066,485	$3,107,891	$2,102,740
Costs and Expenses:								
Cost of sales	4,751,987	3,692,885	3,313,301	2,534,322	2,428,406	2,390,218	2,406,077	1,603,054
Selling, general, and administrative	1,066,991	814,179	735,917	482,490	467,404	455,906	438,893	271,256
Merger and restructuring costs			37,170		39,325	25,612		
Interest	90,762	58,867	63,385	45,017	50,453	63,261	73,856	41,256
	5,909,740	4,565,931	4,149,773	3,061,829	2,985,588	2,934,997	2,918,826	1,915,566
Income before income taxes and extraordinary items	687,889	523,897	384,878	201,003	128,912	131,488	189,065	187,174
Income taxes	268,887	213,750	168,285	76,441	56,532	36,222	71,580	68,055
Net income before extraordinary items	419,002	310,147	216,593	124,562	72,380	95,266	117,485	119,119
Extraordinary items			(2,600)		(71,040)[b]			
Net income	419,002	$310,147	$213,993	$124,562	$1,340	$95,266	$117,485	$119,119
Net Income Per share:[a]								
Before cumulative effect of account changes	$2.61	$2.03	$2.87	$2.70	$1.58	$2.06	$2.57	$2.90
Cumulative effect of accounting changes			(0.3)		(1.55)[b]	1.58		
Net income	2.61	$2.03	$2.83	$2.70	$.03	$2.06	$2.57	$2.90
Common equivalent shares	160,268	152,862	75,509	46,062	45,750	46,290	45,760	41,020
Cash dividends per common share	$.20	$.20	$.40	$.40	$.38	$.36	$.35	$.31

Note: All figures as reported each year. They are not restated for merger activity or stock splits. See Table 2 for restated figures.
[a]Two transactions significantly affected the number of shares outstanding: In October, 1994 Tyco issued 30.4 million shares as part of its merger with Kendall. On October 18, 1995, the company announced a two-for-one stock split effected in the form of a stock dividend.
[b]Effective July 1, 1992, Tyco adopted the provision of Statement of Financial Accounting Standards ("SFAS") 109 " Accounting for Income Taxes" and SFAS 106 "Employers' Accounting for Post-Retirement Benefits Other than Pensions." These accounting changes resulted in a $71.04 million charge to earnings.
Source: Company documents.

DENNIS KOZLOWSKI, 1992–1997

L. Dennis Kozlowski joined Tyco in the mid 1970s. Within a few years, he had become president of the packaging business; he later headed the fire/flow division; and became Tyco's COO in 1989. In these roles he had worked closely with John Fort. Although he would make a number of changes as CEO, many of Fort's innovations and institutions would remain intact. As Senior Vice President Irving Gutin, a seventeen-year veteran at Tyco, explained, "We are very much the same, and we have changed dramatically at the same time."[21]

During Kozlowski's first year as CEO, the company's name was changed to Tyco International in order to better reflect its evolution into a world-wide provider of branded industrial products and services. The fire/flow division, which was four times as large as the other two divisions combined, was split into two independent segments, creating four divisions in all.

Shortly after he became CEO, Kozlowski initiated a strategic planning process. The end result was to set out two goals for the company: doubling EPS to $5 per share in five years (coined "five in five"), and reducing Tyco's operating cyclicality. Looking back at that period, CFO Mark Swartz commented:

> During the 1980s, we grew the fire/flow division, but electrical and packaging really became the stepsisters of the company. Tyco really was not a diversified company in 1991—it was almost entirely fire and flow. During the recession, we saw that it was in the electrical and packaging areas that we were able to continue 15% earnings growth year over year, while fire and flow were more cyclical. The goal since then has been twofold: to build those other two segments and make them strong, sequel partner businesses that can continue to grow during an economic downturn; and to increase the non-cyclical parts of fire/flow [i.e., service].[22]

Finding Growth   Because Tyco's core businesses were not expanding at a 15 percent rate, achieving that level of earnings growth would require cost cutting or acquisitions. Although Kozlowski was a fervent cost cutter, he believed that alone would not be sufficient to meet the firm's targets. Instead, he believed that sustained growth would require a number of acquisitions. In the fire/flow division,

Tyco had been pursuing a strategy of industry consolidation through acquisition. These acquisitions were designed to achieve economies of scale and to improve Tyco's relative competitive position. Kozlowski explained:

> If you look at our businesses, we're in industries for the most part that are consolidating—consolidating in manufacturing, distribution, and aftermarket. And so we have no one big competitor or one big customer in any one of our businesses. So that puts us in a very opportune position to continue this and consolidate more.[23]

In addition to pursuing this strategy in the firm's existing core businesses, Kozlowski was also eager to extend it to other industries ripe for consolidation.

Reducing Cyclicality   The recession-induced earnings plunge was also a pressing concern for Kozlowski when he took office. He commented on the problem:

> After years of earnings growth in the eighties, Tyco hit a wall in 1991. We hit the wall because nonresidential construction was down in every English-speaking country in the world . . . and at that point in time we were highly dependent on nonresidential construction. Our investor group looked at us and said, "Oh my gosh—I didn't know we had a cyclical diversified company here, I thought we had a long-term sustainable diversified company." . . . So, having faced the cyclicality issue, I really thought we could add a lot of value in Tyco over the long term by addressing that issue. I wanted new growth [acquisitions] to be in long-term, sustainable businesses over the long term.[24]

One effort to address the cyclicality issue was to increase Tyco's service offerings in core businesses. Kozlowski explained:

> We want to service everything we sell in the aftermarket. Service is something that other competitors don't necessarily want to fool around with. There's a 24-hour-a-day, 365-days-a-year commitment, and you need to have infrastructure—the trucks, the systems, the communications—to do that. So we now pursue servicing on a worldwide basis, and will continue to pursue it. Service also happens to carry a margin in excess of 20%, probably 25%–30%.[25]

Service, which was only 15 percent of Tyco's fire protection business in 1993, grew to 45 percent of that business's revenues by 1997. Tyco also combated cyclicality through geographic expansion, so that it was unlikely that a recession in one part of the world would drive down performance across all of its businesses.

When interviewed in 1997, Kozlowski firmly believed that reduced cyclicality led to a premium for the company's stock. CFO Swartz agreed: "if you were to look right now at each of the single line businesses we're in, take the average multiple for each of those businesses and add it all up, you wouldn't come up with [our current] stock price."[26]

Corporate Headquarters

To achieve the firm's goals, Tyco's corporate executives, like its business managers, were expected to perform in ways that boosted shareholder value. This involved oversight and control of the businesses, allocating capital, and managing the firm's compensation system. Corporate headquarters also facilitated the mergers and acquisitions process, provided a minimum of overhead functions, and fulfilled the legal reporting requirements and investor relations needs of a large public company. One division president remarked, "Tyco takes care of a lot of things for us. They provide insurance, treasury functions and cash, investor relations and stock issues. Since I don't have to be concerned with those things, that allows me to really focus on growing my business."[27]

The headquarters of the $6 billion company was located in a small, two-story wooden building. Consistent with the company's philosophy and strategy, headquarters staff and overhead were kept to a minimum. The staff, including secretarial assistants, totaled 50—only 0.1 percent of Tyco's 40,000 employees. Although Tyco had experienced explosive growth for two decades, the corporate staff had increased only slightly. Tyco's had always been keen to eliminate bureaucracy, and headquarters reflected that antibureaucratic zeal. Meetings were kept to a minimum, and communication was direct and efficient—telephone calls or face-to-face discussions were far more common than memos. Formal support staff for senior executives was limited to a single shared secretarial assistant, although the CEO had a dedicated assistant.

Corporate executives were expected to be intimately familiar with the operating businesses. Jack Guarnieri, the corporate controller, explained: "We don't manage at arm's-length. We are making judgments all the time. When I first came [to Tyco] ... the one thing that struck me was how much the corporate people knew about the businesses. And I don't think we've lost a lot of that over the years."[28] Corporate executives came from a variety of backgrounds, including accounting, engineering, and law. Something they all had in common, however, was that they spent a considerable amount of time away from headquarters, traveling to Tyco divisions, working with managers, and assessing potential acquisitions.

There was no general charge on divisions to help cover the costs of corporate overhead, nor was corporate overhead in any way built into the divisions' budgets. Divisions were only billed by corporate for identifiable services, such as the provision of an outside environmental consultant or a lawyer to handle a specific problem. Beginning in 1995, all businesses were charged for the capital they employed and goodwill amortization on acquisitions. The cost of capital uniform across divisions was competitive with market rates.

Control and Compensation

Control of capital was highly centralized at Tyco. Cash was swept daily from the bank accounts of the divisions, and held in a central corporate account. Businesses were not paid interest on the monies held at corporate, and there were no guarantees that the divisions generating the cash would later be able to spend it. Capital expenditures between $100,000 and $150,000 required the approval of the corporate controller, between $150,000 and $500,000 that of the CFO, and beyond $500,000 the approval of the CEO and board of directors.

Under Kozlowski's leadership, decentralization and financial control continued to be at the core of Tyco's approach. The company used financial systems to push responsibility and accountability deep into the organization. Prior to joining Tyco, many of the companies' businesses had been unable to track profitability by product line. Senior Vice President Gutin emphasized the critical role of the company's financial controls: "Our systems are extremely important to us. I think they're our lifeline, our bloodline, because they enable us to know at each one of these 300-odd profit centers what's happening very quickly. Our systems are focused on the bottom line, on earnings. The numbers are very clear and specific."[29]

Given the importance of Tyco's financial systems, corporate management felt it was absolutely critical to have a first-rate controller staff, both at headquarters and within the operating units. One corporate officer noted:

> I would characterize the controller group as being stronger than in most other companies. Generally speaking, in the larger divisions, we try to put someone in the controller job who really is partnering up with the person running the operation. They're not considered bookkeepers. Ninety-nine percent of the ideas that we have for acquisitions surface from the business units and we expect a lot of input from the controllers on the local level before that information gets here. And you really can't do that if you are just keeping the books.[30]

Budgeting

Tyco's budgeting process was top-down, and budgets for the divisions were renegotiated from scratch each year. Since EPS had to increase 15 percent annually in order to reach the "five in five" goal, the budgets in aggregate had to yield that number. This did not translate into automatically setting a 15 percent earnings target for each division. Rather, budgets were set individually, reflecting Tyco's varying goals for each division. Some divisions had earnings targets of 25 percent, others of 12 percent. Additionally, since each business group was expected to strive to be the leader in its industry, each was expected to outperform its industry average in any given year. Swartz commented:

> We try to instill throughout the corporation that our goal is year in, year out to deliver to shareholders a minimum of 15% growth in earnings at the corporate level. We want all our people to really be reaching in the budgeting process. If we had a 15% across the board budgeting plan, I don't think we'd be getting all the potential from the ones who are growing faster. Plus, we have to consider the ones who are in a tough business environment. There might be a business in which being flat year to year would be a success.[31]

The process of setting budgets was rigorous and engaging. One division president, who headed a conservative, risk-averse company Tyco had recently acquired, described his first encounter with the process:

> Dennis [Kozlowski] was taking the group to an off-site strategic planning meeting in the middle of the budgeting process. He said, "You know, we're going to do the budget at this meeting and I expect everyone to meet the levels we've set." He told us he wanted a 15% increase, saying "I don't want to fight with you or any of the other guys. Just come down and show me how you get 15. If you think you can't get it, I want a one-on-one meeting with you—no finance guys."
>
> Well, I knew we were hitting a tough pocket here at my business. Although we were in the process of making an acquisition that was going to help tremendously, it was part of our culture historically that if you give a number when forecasting and setting budgets, you have to know there's a road map to get you there ... So we never put in new products, never put in acquisitions, when we calculated our budgets—those were support. I decided I needed to have a meeting with Dennis because I couldn't in good faith say that I was going to get 15% growth.
>
> So I called Dennis maybe a week later and set up an appointment. He called me back two days before the meeting. He wanted to find out why I was coming down, because I don't meet with him very often—primarily when they bring us in for meetings. I said, "Well, this is in response to your request that we meet with you if we can't bring 15% growth to the off-site we're having." He said, "Well, what do you mean, what's the problem?" And I said, "Well, I just have some trouble." He said, "Where are you now?" I said, "somewhere around 5 percent." And he said, "You don't want to come down here and meet with me and tell me that. It's just not a good thing for you to do. . . . It would be an ugly meeting." He went on to say, "This is when I have trouble with management. It's always around budget time. Management says one thing and I need something else, and then it's at the end of the day that we have to make fundamental changes."
>
> When I heard that, I just gulped, and said "maybe we ought to make sure we have this meeting because I don't think it would make

sense for me to go to the off-site meeting and find out there needs to be a fundamental change." Dennis finally agreed and we had the meeting. He listened to the issues and saw that there were some things that were really preventing us from getting to that number. He took these into consideration when setting our target, but I think the actual number was about 12 percent.

So, he's tough, but he did give in a little. But, you know, we do the same thing here in our business. We try to intimidate the folks into thinking that they have to do their best or incur the wrath of God. Dennis seems to be more effective at this than I am, though. [Laughter] I don't think that anyone here feels like I did after that phone call. But he simply said, "You've got to make sure these things happen. That's your job. And that's what you are doing—[building the business], acquisitions, cost reductions."

Dennis puts you out there. We're more at risk than we were before we were acquired by Tyco. If you can operate in a pressure cooker environment, though, you really get high rewards. But you're really out there. I know that if I don't deliver that number, I don't think there will be a lot of longevity.[32]

Once budgets were finalized, division presidents independently determined how to pass the budgets down to their direct reports. The budgets would continue to be passed down in this fashion to the line managers at each of Tyco's profit centers.

Remuneration Complementing Tyco's control systems was an incentive system that provided high rewards for outstanding performance. Base salaries for operating managers were relatively low, but bonuses could be large. Unlike Fort, Kozlowski revised incentive plans annually. CFO Swartz commented on the change:

> Dennis thought that the old compensation system (which rewarded managers on the cumulative performance of their businesses) may have boosted an entrepreneurial spirit, but it didn't take into account the money corporate had invested in a business and the return that was required, nor did it provide a powerful incentive for managers to maintain a high-level of performance. What we are supposed to do is grow the business for the shareholders every year—year in, year out. We are not supposed to be paying managers in down years and up years. That's

why we put into place a compensation plan that is focused on year over year results, with a built-in consideration of the costs of generating those results.[33]

Bonuses were based on operating performance, measured against three plateaus.[34] The first plateau was set at the level a manager had to reach to get any bonus, and usually was reached when there was minimal growth over the prior year's earnings. The second plateau was set at the level corporate believed the business should get, without anything going "incredibly right or wrong." Although significant variations existed, in the typical business this plateau was generally set at a 15 percent earnings increase. The third plateau was set at a point at which managers dramatically exceeded expectations. This could occur, for example, if they moved more quickly than expected on the integration of facilities, or put into place new capital expenditures to create additional earnings. Often this plateau coincided with an increase in earnings of 22 percent or greater.

Bonuses escalated rapidly as managers achieved higher performance plateaus. Bonuses for level one were approximately 10 to 20 percent of salary; for level two, 80 percent of salary; and for level three, bonuses increased from there. Management was quick to point out that managers who performed at level one for several years were unlikely to keep their jobs—that, they said, was "the ultimate discipline."

Plateau levels were announced after budgets for each of the operating divisions were determined. When asked about the degree of correspondence between incentive plateaus and budgets, managers differed in their views. Some at headquarters claimed that the linkage was relatively straightforward:

> [Businesses] are going to generate what they generate, regardless of what the budget ends up saying—because the budget is a game of cat and mouse. Tyco may agree to a lower budget for a business if the company insists that it can't make a higher one—but the plateaus will be based on corporate's level of expectation at the higher budget level. We pretty much know the plateaus before the budgets are finalized, based on the investments we've put into them, as well as what the competition is doing.[35]

Others claimed that the relationship was less direct. One even praised this ambiguity: "I think the fact that bonus plateaus are a bit of a mystery is one of the strengths of the system. It's very flexible. It can change." Kozlowski himself subscribed to this view and emphasized that there was no direct correlation between incentive plateaus and budgets:

If you talk to the operating people, they might tell you that their budget is important to their incentive plan. I maintain that it isn't. I never wanted budgets to be part of what a person was going to negotiate for their incentives. That would make the budget take on a whole different view. That makes them think, "How many cookies can I keep under the rug to guarantee that I'm going to max out in the process?" I know—when I was in their position—I would lowball my budget as much as possible, and argue violently for it. So for the operating people, we get their levels of performance over the prior year, and they don't know what the bonus plans are going to be until after their budgets are approved.[36]

Since its inauguration, management believed that the system had been working well. One corporate executive noted:

To date, there haven't been any catastrophic events that have driven a change in a budget for a business. There have been skirmishes that have broken out, but when that happens, there are other things one can do to make up for that, through cost reductions elsewhere, or moving more quickly to put in new technology to lower costs. Managers are expected to take such steps.

Dennis wants everybody operating at the maximum all the time. So he pushes people to make an aggressive commitment—not an unrealistic one, but an aggressive one—and then he pushes them hard to come up with the results."[37]

Stock was an important element of compensation plans. For corporate executives, earned bonuses were paid 90 percent in stock; for division heads, the percentage was 60 to 70 percent; and for operating managers in individual profit centers, 10 percent. These bonuses often accumulated to large shareholdings. By 1996, seven Tyco executives had accumulated more than $1 million in stock.

The Acquisition Process

Acquisitions were a key activity at Tyco, and one in which the firm had a significant amount of expertise. For most acquisitions, the process started when a division recommended an acquisition to corporate. Division President Brad McGee explained:

Generally, a lot of the acquisition process takes place in a decentralized fashion. So the guy that runs fire protection in Europe, who reports to the global president of fire protection, is always on the lookout for ways that he can enhance his business. He's always asking, "where are the gaps in my product line, and how can I fill those gaps?" When he finds an opportunity, he brings it back to the worldwide president, and they talk about where else that potential acquisition might fit into the organization. How would it benefit fire protection in Asia? How would it

TABLE 2

Selected Data from Consolidated Statements of Income, 1991–1996 (in millions, except per share amounts)

	1997	1996[a]	1995	1994[b]	1993[b]	1992	1991
Sales	6,598	$5,090	$4,535	$4,076	$3,919	$3,066	$3,108
Net income	419	310	214	189	21	95	117
Per share, net income	2.61	2.03	1.42	1.28	0.14	1.03	1.28

Note: Restated to reflect hypothetical combined operations prior to the Kendall acquisition—for FY 1993 and 1994—and stock splits.
[a]On October 18, 1995, the Company announced a two-for-one stock split effected in the form of a stock dividend. Results for all years presented have been restated to reflect the split.
[b]On October 19, 1994, a wholly owned subsidiary of Tyco merged with Kendall International, Inc. in a transaction accounted for as a pooling of interests. The financial results of Tyco and Kendall have been restated for fiscal years 1993 and 1994 to reflect this pooling.
Source: Company documents.

TABLE 3

Tyco's Consolidated Balance Sheet (in thousands, except per share data)

	Year Ended							
	June 30, 1997	June 30, 1996	June 30, 1995	June 30, 1994	June 30, 1993	June 30, 1992	June 30, 1991	May 31, 1990
Current Assets	2,446,524	1,695,524	1,451,901	1,048,404	1,133,105	1,107,262	1,097,940	732,424
Long-Term Assets								
Property and equipment, net	1,020,457	725,742	658,471	407,200	418,497	413,715	423,197	303,669
Goodwill and other intangible assets	2,106,900	1,232,617	1,004,463	864,416	832,561	910,070	859,082	362,257
Reorganization value in excess of identifiable assets	96,179	102,591	108,801	—	—	—	—	—
Deferred income taxes	58,183	69,823	101,678	65,610	60,281	—	—	—
Other assets	160,086	127,639	56,147	30,748	14,897	20,490	12,747	18,206
Total Assets	5,888,329	$3,953,936	$3,381,461	$2,416,378	$2,459,341	$2,451,537	$2,392,966	$1,416,556
Current Liabilities	1,735,265	1,291,810	1,084,715	810,683	868,541	832,984	854,713	512,651
Long-Term Liabilities								
Deferred income taxes	24,728	19,226	9,599	13,698	8,032	26,791	23,847	26,755
Long-term debt	919,308	511,622	506,417	412,913	562,059	534,951	609,255	269,776
Other liabilities	157,451	192,839	146,049	100,025	100,999	16,260		
	1,101,487	723,687	662,065	526,636	671,390	578,002	633,102	296,531
Shareholders' Equity								
Common stock at par value	84,203	76,488	38,183	23,176	23,161	23,503	23,527	21,018
Capital in excess of par value	1,412,041	627,985	620,633	371,785	366,278	377,634	370,628	119,334
Currency translation adjustment	(100,395)	(34,571)	(9,451)					
Retained earnings	1,655,728	1,268,537	985,316	720,991	614,967	631,679	553,347	459,265
	3,051,577	1,938,439	1,634,681	1,079,059	919,710	1,040,551	905,151	607,374
Total Liabilities and Shareholders' Equity	5,888,329	$3,953,936	$3,381,461	$2,416,378	$2,459,341	$2,451,537	$2,392,966	$1,416,556

Source: Company documents.

benefit the U.S.? The operating managers don't just think about their individual regions.[38]

After potential acquisitions were identified by operating managers, Tyco's corporate headquarters employed a structured evaluation process. Corporate headquarters started by projecting adjusted EBIT and ROI for the acquisition. The ROI hurdle was generally set in the high teens. Two additional criteria were also important. Only friendly deals were considered and all acquisitions had to be *immediately* accretive to earnings. Acquisitions that hurt short-term EPS were never considered. Kozlowski emphasized that the process was very conservative:

> We do not use revenue enhancements as part of the return. We *want* revenue enhancements—we push them—but that's on *our* account for *our* shareholders, and we refuse to pay somebody else for our ability to increase revenues. Chances are we're going to share some cost reductions in the pricing of the business, but we *know* we're going to get the cost reductions. We will not miss on those because they're laid out—either you're going to consolidate this manufacturing facility, you're going to consolidate this distribution facility, or do away with dual HQ—you know those things are going to happen. But you're not always sure about revenue enhancements. So as a result, we don't use those. And we're absolutely not afraid at all to walk away from a marginal deal.[39]

When a potential candidate had passed the preliminary tests, operating people and corporate personnel began due diligence. In most cases the process was completed in a week to ten days, and sometimes even faster. If the acquisition passed this hurdle, operating managers immediately began to plan how the company would be folded into Tyco. Estimates were made of how many people would be laid off, which plants would be closed, and where the greatest synergies could be exploited. McGee noted:

> In acquisitions done to build existing divisions, we're either trying to use a common distribution channel, or maybe a common sales force, or we're looking for common manufacturing so that we can close down some manufacturing plants. In every acquisition, there's always something that we're going to force the acquired company to do that they did not do before so that we can reduce costs.[40]

While the operating divisions were developing these plans, corporate initiated the negotiation process. To ensure that the lowest price was paid, operating divisions were never involved in the actual negotiations. One senior executive explained,

> It's discipline. You don't let emotions get in the way. You don't let egos get in the way. You don't throw another million, 5 million, or 10 million bucks at a deal once you've set down what it's worth. If someone else tops your bid, you walk. We keep the discipline, and we therefore have a very good record of acquisitions with very strong rates of return.[41]

Tyco's key negotiator for all deals was Senior Vice President Gutin, whom many of his coworkers described as the best negotiator they had ever known. Kozlowski joked, "Irving was born to negotiate—he wakes up negotiating in the morning."[42]

Every acquisition required a corporate "champion" to see the deal through. Most often, the champion was the president of the division into which an acquisition would be folded. Sponsoring an acquisition carried with it a high level of commitment and accountability. The champion, in essence, pledged his or her bottom line that the promised cost reductions and performance levels relating to that acquisition would be met. When an acquisition was completed, the incentive plateaus for the sponsoring division president would be adjusted accordingly.

Growing by Leaps and Bounds

Since 1992, Tyco had completed more than seventy acquisitions. Most of these were "bolt-on acquisitions," undertaken to strengthen Tyco's leadership position in one of its existing core businesses. Examples include Keystone International, bolt-on to flow control, and AT&T's Submarine Systems, a bolt-on to Simplex.

Tyco also made several "platform" acquisitions that provided new opportunities for long-term growth and reduced Tyco's exposure to the business cycle. One of these was the acquisition of Kendall International, a $816 million health care products company. Kozlowski described the merger as one which "turned us overnight into a global force in the expanding market for disposable medical products."[43] The acquisition came at a time when the healthcare industry was on the

TABLE 4

Tyco's Acquisitions

Calendar Year	Selected Bolt-ons	Platforms
1990	National Pipe & Tube Allied Tube & Conduit Wormald and 2 others	
1991	Canvil Anvil Fluorotec	
1992	Neotecha U-Brand Machine shops and 3 others	
1993	Hindle Cockburns Charles H. Winn Stanley Flagg and 13 others	
1994	Preferred Pipe Medical Products Division of Labeltape Meditect and 10 others	Kendall International, Inc.
1995	Smith Valve Tectron Unistrut Automatic Sprinkler and 12 others	
1996	Star Sprinkler Nashua Corp. Betham Corp. Sentry Medical Products Thorn Security ARBO Group Stockham Valves & Fittings Rochester Corp. Triangle Wire & Cable Zettler GmbH and 24 others	Earth Technology Carlisle Plastics
1997 (through May)	Electro Star Babcock Sempell Valve American Fence Sherwood Medical AT&T Keystone Inbrand and 5 others	ADT

Source: Company documents.

verge of a major consolidation and restructuring. A smaller "platform" acquisition was Earth Technology Corp., purchased in January 1997. Earth Tech, a $108 million firm, was involved in both environmental consulting and the development of water and wastewater treatment facilities.

In 1997, Tyco consummated its largest acquisition ever when it bought ADT Ltd., a $1.7 billion home security systems provider.* ADT's business complemented Tyco's service operations in the fire protection sector and would allow Tyco to offer one source to customers for both security and fire monitoring.

After a spate of sizable acquisitions in 1997, some analysts warned that Tyco's pace was not sustainable. Board member Phil Hampton stated: "As you get larger, it takes more to keep producing the same kind of percentage returns. Either you do lots of small deals or you have to find larger ones that make sense. Those are harder to do because there are fewer of them and there is greater risk in each of them."[44]

---

*Tyco's acquisition of ADT was structured as a reverse merger. This means that, technically, ADT purchased Tyco and then changed its name to Tyco International. The purchase was structured in this manner for tax reasons. Tyco executives assumed all key executive positions in the new company.

WHAT'S SPECIAL ABOUT TYCO?

Under Kozlowski, revenues had grown by 66 percent, and earnings by 226 percent between 1992 and 1996. During this period, the company's market capitalization had increased from $1.60 billion to $6.23 billion. In January 1992, a Lehman Brothers analyst report concluded that "Tyco has the strongest fundamentals and best business mix of the diversified companies in our universe."

What *was* so special about Tyco? What accounted for its success? Here is what some people had to say in response to this question:

Corporate Controller Jack Guarnieri:

> Everything here at corporate is done in controllable elements, and the people who run the individual businesses really feel like entrepreneurs. The decision levels are pushed down, everything's within the control of the people who run the business. The compensation system reflects [this fact], and people in the businesses make a considerable amount of money. That's what drives the whole place.[45]

The president of the specialty products division, Brad McGee:

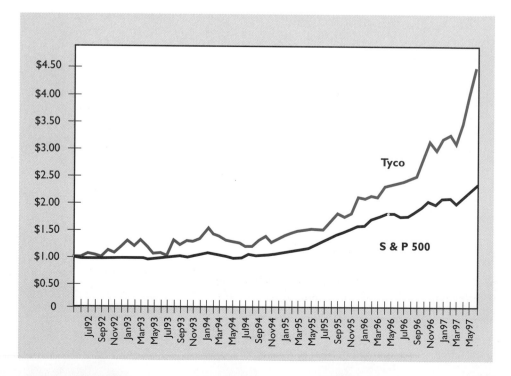

FIGURE 2

Tyco International versus S&P 500 Total Monthly Returns, July 1992–June 1997

Everybody within the organization understands what Tyco is trying to do . . . we are focused on consistent EPS growth. We do whatever it takes to get there. Earnings per share drives the budgeting process, and since the businesses know that, it also drives their individual acquisition strategies, and their quest for growth. It also drives their desire to have the leanest cost structure, because the first place they can get earnings growth is through cost reduction. But, as Dennis has said before, nobody ever cuts their way to greatness. And so what people focus on most is "how are we going to get growth in this business?"[46]

CEO L. Dennis Kozlowski:

There are a few reasons why no one else is doing what we're doing. Most of the companies we buy are competitors. If you look at our businesses, we're in industries for the most part that are consolidating—consolidating in manufacturing, distribution, and aftermarket. And so we have no one big competitor or one big customer in any one of our businesses. So that puts us in a very opportune position to continue this and consolidate more.

Also, it's boring. It's not as glamorous as other things to tell someone you make fire hydrants and sprinkler heads. I've had a lot of very capable MBAs who have responded to the effect, "I've got a lot of education here, so I'm really not that interested in making fire hydrants or adhesive bandages—that's just not where I see my world." That's an advantage for somebody like us. Everybody wants to be the next Cisco Systems, so everybody is chasing that. In the meantime, we're quietly grinding it out in Rust Belt America. You know, if Bill Gates or other people like that got involved in our kind of businesses, we'd probably be in trouble. But fortunately there aren't a whole lot of people bothering us in our markets, and it's a real advantage.[47]

A VIABLE ORGANIZATION FORM?

Many in academic and business circles debate the viability and merit of conglomerates. In addressing this issue, John Thackeray wrote:

One could easily fill a football stadium with business academics and consultants who deride the strategy of diversification—unrelated diversification, that is to say, like a steel company running a pizza chain, or a real-estate firm owning a baseball team. And to back up their case, they can point to half a dozen studies in the past decade that document the wastefulness of most diversification, which in big companies is invariably done via acquisition.

On the other hand, the number of academics who believe in unrelated diversification could just about fill a phone booth. The conventional wisdom is emphatic: the massive diversification by U.S. business in the '60s, '70s, and early '80s was a red herring. What companies should have been doing instead was improving the global competitive positions of their original businesses.

Analysts and institutional investors have seen it happen a thousand times. A company unravels its diversification through disinvestment and, bingo, the stock price goes up. Which leads the moneymen to think that any management that clings to a passionate attachment to diversification must be wacko.

So, who's right and who's wrong? Perhaps, neither side. The answer seems to be relative: the oft-cited studies against diversification tend to look at the average outcomes—which are indeed lackluster—and don't focus on the few companies that have talent in this type of endeavor. Some years back, Stephen C. Coley of McKinsey & Company isolated a group of large companies that have got to be among the best managed in the country. All with sales of more than $500 million, they've earned a return on equity of more than 15% in every year from 1970 to 1988. There are only 30 of them. Of these, 13 were multibusiness companies. What's more, when all 30 are ranked for total shareholder return, in every five-year period since 1970 the multibusiness companies win hands down. Says Coley: "I suspect that the people who are good at diversifying do it all the time. They have mechanisms in place, they've been through the process a number of times. They know what kinds of business they can and can't manage."

It is the neophytes who push up the casualty rates. Which is why companies recently released from the straitjacket of regulation—notably those in the transportation, telecommunications, and power utilities industries—have squandered billions of their shareholders' money in recent years.

TABLE 5

Tyco's Sales and Operating Income by Segment, 1989–1996 as Reported Each Year
(in $ thousands)

	Year Ended June 30				
	1996	*1995*	*1994*	*1993*	*1992*
Fire protection					
Sales	$1,991	$1,703	$1,526	$1,588	$1,616
Operating income	128	86	69	47	84
Flow control					
Sales	1,159	1,014	914	745	721
Operating income	114	90	70	38	33
Electrical					
Sales	481	430	437	413	392
Operating income	88	76	70	67	53
Disposable and safety products[a]					
Sales	1,459	1,387	—	—	—
Operating	292	261	—	—	—
Packing material[a]					
Sales	—	—	386	368	337
Operating income	—	—	54	45	41

[a]Following the Kendall acquisition in October 1994, the packaging business segment was combined with Kendall to create the disposable and safety products division.
Source: Company documents.

. . . There are many pathways to triumph through unrelated diversification. Successful diversification is like great art. It knows no rules. But its presence is unmistakable.[48]

APPENDIX: LETTER FROM ROBERT MONKS OF LENS, INC., TO THE COUNCIL OF INSTITUTIONAL INVESTORS (OCTOBER 6, 1995)

"The Council of Institutional Investors' ("CII") annual list of 'focus companies' is an important event. We spend much energy and time in trying to identify such companies. The 1995 CII list includes one company in particular which we evaluate very differently—**TYCO INTERNATIONAL**. I am writing to learn about differences in our methodologies—to find out what we don't know, so to speak.

"I know Tyco well. Indeed, I served as a direc-

tor for ten years, from 1985 till 1994. Since that time I have only the information available to all shareholders. In our analysis there are at least three aspects of Tyco that bring it into our preliminary pool of potential 'focus companies':

"First, its five year total return is in the lowest decline of all companies we follow. As I look back five years to the third calendar quarter of 1990, I recollect the acquisition of Wormald—the largest transaction the company had ever entered into and one which made Tyco a worldwide business. . . . The stock price soared—briefly—up to a high of $60^{7/8}$ on July 25, 1990. . . . Thereafter, cyclical downturn of the nonresidential construction business resulted in a reduction of earnings and lowering stock price down to a low of $31^{3/4}$ (July 27) in the summer of 1992 which happened to be the time the current chief executive officer took his position. Our own calculations indicate an annual return (calculated on a "total return" basis) for hold-ers of Tyco stock on September 19, 1995 . . . of 35.4% for the previous year; 20.9% for three years; and 3.1% for five years. . . .

"Second, Tyco is a multi-industry company—a traditional conglomerate. Our experience (Litton in the 1960s, ITT in the 1970s, Sears and others in re-cent times) suggests that this is a commercial mode in which it is extremely difficult to add value com-petitively over a long period of time. Some compa-nies manage it—most notably GE under Jack Welch. Is Tyco a GE or an ITT? This is a question that the directors asked often and pointedly. We pe-riodically engaged independent investment bankers—DLJ was the most recent—to analyze the 'spin off' values available to shareholders and com-pare them with the current market. . . . It is appar-ent that this company has achieved an enviable record of increasing earnings, cash flow, and earn-ings per share over a decade. It has made a great deal of money for its owners save only those who bought between June and September 1990.

"Third, the Board contains in addition to the CEO, the former CEO and the general counsel, result-ing in three out of eight members being "insiders." . . . The Tyco directors for many years have invested their entire compensation in common stock. The av-erage value of the shareholdings of each of the seven 'nonmanagement' directors is in excess of $1 mil-lion. . . . For several years, United Shareholders of America ranked the largest American companies with a composite measure containing equal weight-ing for 'governance' and for 'performance.' On two occasions, Tyco was ranked in the top ten compa-nies in the country and publicly given appropriate awards. . . . It is probably the only company incorpo-rated in the Commonwealth of Massachusetts to have timely opted out of the statutory requirement for staggering election to boards of directors (dis-gracefully rushed through the legislature to "save" the Norton Company in 1988) . . .

"On balance we conclude that this is a first rate company successfully adding value in the difficult mode of a conglomerate. Our criteria for 'focus companies' ultimately is—what can we, as in-formed and effectively involved owners, do to en-hance value. Our answer in the case of Tyco is—virtually nothing. What are we missing?"

Source: Company documents.

Endnotes

1. CII used the following methodology to determine which companies were listed: First, a list of S&P 500 companies that underperformed their industry median in five-year and one-year total returns were identified. Those that outperformed the S&P 500 average for five-year total shareholder returns were dropped from the list. For the remaining companies, the difference between the industry's median five-year returns and each company's five-year returns was calculated to estab-lish ranking. The lowest 20 firms were selected for the list.
2. Richard Thomson, "An Investor Calls," *Management Today,* December 1995, p. 62.
3. "The Business Week 50," *Business Week,* March 24, 1997, p. 79.
4. For external reporting purposes, Tyco divided its businesses into only four segments.
5. Interview with Brad McGee, April 28, 1997.
6. Interview with Dennis Kozlowski, June 23, 1997.
7. Laura Jereski, "Synergy, synergy, synergy," *Forbes,* November 14, 1988, p. 194.
8. Mitchell Lynch, "Tyco's Success Acquisition Still Leaves Questions About Gaziano's Grand Design," *Wall Street Jour-nal,* August 27, 1981, p. 21.
9. Aimee Morner, "The Man Who Would Be Geneen," *Fortune,* March 12, 1979, p. 108.
10. Stephen Kindel, "The Guy Who Knows Factories," *Financial World,* June 30, 1987, p. 36.
11. "Tyco: Pursuing Profits as Relentlessly as It Once Pursued Growth," *Business Week,* March 5, 1984, p. 96.
12. Kindel, "The Guy Who Knows Factories," p. 36.
13. "Turning the Tables at Tyco," *Business Week,* August 29, 1983, p. 65.
14. Dougald MacDonald, "Grinnell Acquisition Pushes Tyco Rev-enue Past $1 Billion Mark," *New England Business,* Febru-ary 3, 1986, p. 32.
15. "John Fort: CEO, Tyco Laboratories," *The Business of New Hampshire* (February 1991), 38.
16. John Thackray, "Diversification: What It Takes to Make It Work," *Across the Board* (November 1991), 17.
17. Mark McLaughlin, "Flat and Happy at the Top," *New Eng-land Business* (March 1990), 19.
18. "Tyco Official Adds Post of Chairman," *New York Times,* July 14, 1983, sec. D, p. 2.
19. Thackray, "Diversification," p. 17.
20. Kindel, "The Guy Who Knows Factories," p. 36.
21. Interview with Irving Gutin, April 25, 1997.
22. Interview with Mark Swartz, June 12, 1997.
23. Interview with Dennis Kozlowski, June 23, 1997.
24. Ibid.
25. Ibid.
26. Interview with Swartz.
27. Interview with Tyco executive.
28. Interview with Jack Guarnieri, May 9, 1997.
29. Interview with Gutin.
30. Interview with Tyco executive.
31. Interview with Swartz.
32. Interview with Tyco executive.
33. Interview with Swartz.
34. Two calculations were used to determine the level of com-pensation each division head would receive. The first was a

straightforward EBIT calculation. If certain target EBIT levels, called plateaus, were met, a percentage of base salary was awarded as a bonus. Second, a cash flow modifier was included. Corporate headquarters looked at inventory, receivables, contracts in process, payables, and accrued expenses on a quarterly basis to determine if cash flow trailed or exceeded its projected target. The EBIT-based bonus was then adjusted by a multiple of this percentage variation. If a business made an acquisition during the year, the target was reset to reflect the acquisition, but only at the acquisition's pre-Tyco level of performance.

35. Interview with Tyco executive.
36. Interview with Kozlowski.
37. Interview with Tyco executive.
38. Interview with Brad McGee, April 28, 1997.
39. Interview with Kozlowski.
40. Interview with McGee.
41. Interview with Tyco executive.
42. Interview with Kozlowski.
43. 1995 Tyco Annual Report, p. 4.
44. "Corporate Focus: Tyco International Isn't Playing, It's Out on the Prowl," *The Wall Street Journal,* Jan. 17, 1997, p. B4.
45. Interview with Jack Guarnieri.
46. Interview with McGee.
47. Interview with Kozlowski.
48. John Thackray, "Diversification: What It Takes to Make It Work," p. 17.

CASE 37

Philips Versus Matsushita: Preparing for a New Round

This case was prepared by Christopher A. Bartlett of Harvard Business School.

Throughout their long histories, N.V. Philips (Netherlands) and Matsushita Electric Industrial (Japan) had followed very different strategies and emerged with very different organizational capabilities. Philips built its success on a worldwide portfolio of responsive national organizations while Matsushita based its global competitiveness on its centralized, highly efficient operations in Japan.

During the 1980s, both companies experienced major challenges to their historic competitive positions and organizational approaches that forced major changes, and throughout the 1990s, both companies were struggling to reestablish their competitiveness. With the twenty-first century around the corner, observers were divided on the effectiveness of the massive strategic and organizational changes both companies had implemented, and how it would affect their long-running competitive battle.

PHILIPS: BACKGROUND

In 1892, Gerard Philips and his father opened a small light bulb factory in Eindhoven, Holland. When their venture almost failed, they recruited Gerard's brother, Anton, an excellent salesman and manager. By 1900, Philips was the third largest light bulb producer in Europe.

From its founding, Philips developed a tradition of caring for workers. In Eindhoven, it built com-

This case is intended to be used as a basis for class discussion rather than as an illustration of either effective or ineffective handling of the situation. This case was prepared by Christopher A. Bartlett, Harvard Business School. Used by permission.

pany houses, bolstered education, and paid its employees so well that other local employers complained. When Philips incorporated in 1912, it set aside 10 percent of profits for employees.

Technological Competence and Geographic Expansion

While larger electrical products companies were racing to diversify, Philips made only light bulbs. This one-product focus and Gerard's technological prowess enabled the company to create significant innovations. Company policy was to scrap old plants and use new machines or factories whenever advances were made in new production technology. Anton wrote down assets rapidly and set aside substantial reserves for replacing outdated equipment. Philips also became a leader in industrial research, creating physics and chemistry labs to address production problems as well as more abstract scientific ones. The labs developed a tungsten metal filament bulb that was a great commercial success and gave Philips the financial strength to compete against its giant rivals.

Holland's small size soon forced Philips to look beyond its Dutch borders for enough volume to mass produce, and in 1899, Anton hired the company's first export manager. Soon the company was selling into such diverse markets as Japan, Australia, Canada, Brazil, and Russia to establish new markets. In 1912, as the electric lamp industry started to show signs of overcapacity, Philips started building sales organizations in the United States, Canada, and France, and other cartel-free countries. All other functions remained highly centralized in Eindhoven. In many foreign countries, Philips created joint ventures with domestic companies to gain acceptance in local markets.

In 1919, Philips entered into the "Principal Agreement" with General Electric, giving each company the use of the other's patents. The agreement also divided the world into "three spheres of influence": General Electric would control North America; Philips would control Holland; but both companies agreed to compete freely in the rest of the world. (General Electric also took a 20 percent stake in Philips.) After this time, Philips began evolving from a highly centralized company whose sales were conducted through third parties to a decentralized sales organization with autonomous marketing companies in 14 European countries, China, Brazil, and Australia.

During this period, the company also broadened its product line significantly. In 1918, it began producing electronic vacuum tubes; eight years later its first radios appeared, capturing a 20 percent world market share within a decade; and during the 1930s, Philips began producing x-ray tubes. The Great Depression brought with it trade barriers and high tariffs, and Philips was forced to build local production facilities to protect its foreign sales of these products.

PHILIPS: ORGANIZATIONAL DEVELOPMENT

One of the earliest traditions at Philips was a shared but competitive leadership by the commercial and technical functions. Gerard, an engineer, and Anton, a businessman, began a subtle competition where Gerard would try to produce more than Anton could sell and vice versa. Nevertheless, the two agreed that strong research was vital to Philips' survival.

During the late 1930s, in anticipation of the impending war, Philips transferred its overseas assets to two trusts, British Philips and the North American Philips Corporation; it also moved most of its vital research laboratories to Redhill in Surrey, England, and its top management to the United States. Supported by the assets and resources transferred abroad, and isolated from their parent, the individual country organizations became more independent during the war.

Because waves of Allied and German bombing had pummeled most of Philips' industrial plant in

the Netherlands, the management board decided to build the postwar organization on the strengths of the national organizations (NOs). Their greatly increased self-sufficiency during the war had allowed most to become adept at responding to country-specific market conditions—a capability that became a valuable asset in the postwar era. For example, when international wrangling precluded any agreement on television transmission standards, each nation decided at different times whether to adopt PAL, SECAM, or NTSC standards. Furthermore, consumer preferences and economic conditions varied: in some countries, rich, furniture-encased TV sets were the norm; in others sleek, contemporary models dominated the market. In the United Kingdom, the only way to penetrate the market was to establish a rental business; in richer countries, a major marketing challenge was overcoming elitist prejudice against television. In this environment, the independent NOs had a great advantage in being able to sense and respond to the differences.

Eventually, responsiveness extended beyond adaptive marketing. As NOs built their own technical capabilities, product development often became a function of local marketing conditions. For example, Philips of Canada created the company's first color TV; Philips of Australia created the first stereo TV; and Philips of the United Kingdom created the first TVs with teletext.

While NOs took major responsibility for financial, legal, and administrative matters, fourteen product divisions (PDs), located in Eindhoven, were formally responsible for development, production, and global distribution. (In reality, the NOs' control of assets and the PDs' distance from the operations often undercut this formal role.) The research function remained independent and, with continued strong funding, set up eight separate laboratories in Europe and the United States.

While the formal corporate-level structure was represented as a type of geographic/product matrix, it was clear that NOs had the real power. NOs reported directly to the management board, which Philips enlarged from four members to ten to ensure that top management remained in control of the vital NO operations. The board encouraged interaction with the highly autonomous NOs, and each NO regularly sent envoys to Eindhoven to represent its interests. Top management, most of whom had careers including multiple foreign tours of duty, made frequent overseas visits to the NOs. In 1954, the International Concern Council was established to formalize regular meetings among the principal managers from all the NOs and the board of management.

Within the NOs, the management structure mimicked the legendary joint technical and commercial leadership of the two Philips brothers. NOs were led by a technical manager and a commercial manager. In some locations, a finance manager filled out the top management triad that typically reached key decisions collectively. This cross-functional coordination capability was reflected throughout the NOs organization. On the front lines, product teams, comprising junior managers from the commercial and technical functions, set product policies and carried out administrative functions. Cross-functional coordination also occurred at the product group level through group management teams, whose technical and commercial members met monthly to review progress and resolve inter-functional differences. Finally, the senior management committee of each NO (with top commercial, technical, and financial managers) reviewed progress to ensure that product group directions fit with national strategies and priorities.

The overwhelming importance of foreign operations to Philips, the commensurate status of the NOs within the corporate hierarchy, and even the cosmopolitan appeal of many of the offshore subsidiaries' locations encouraged many Philips managers to take extended foreign tours of duty, working in a series of two- or three-year posts. This elite group of expatriate managers identified strongly with each other and with the NOs as a group, and had no difficulty representing their strong, country-oriented views to corporate management.

PHILIPS: ATTEMPTS AT REORGANIZATION

In the 1960s, the creation of the Common Market eroded trade barriers within Europe and diluted the rationale for maintaining independent, country-level subsidiaries. New transistor- and printed circuit-based technologies demanded larger production runs than most national plants could justify, and many of Philips' competitors were moving

production of electronics to new facilities in low-wage areas in East Asia and Central and South America. Despite its many technological innovations, Philips' ability to bring products to market began to falter. In the 1960s, the company invented the audiocassette but let its Japanese competitors capture the mass market. A decade later, its R&D group developed the V2000 videocassette format—superior technically to Sony's Beta or Matsushita's VHS—but could not successfully market the product. Indeed, North America Philips rejected the V2000, choosing instead to outsource, brand, and sell a VHS product under license from Matsushita. Within three years, Philips was forced to abandon V2000 and produce a VHS product.

Over three decades, six chairmen experimented with reorganizing the company to deal with its growing problems. Yet in the late 1990s, Philips's financial performance remained poor and its global competitiveness was still in question. (See Tables 1 and 2.)

Van Reimsdijk and Rodenburg Reorganizations, 1970s

Concerned about what *Management Today* described as "continued profitless progress," newly appointed CEO Hendrick van Reimsdijk created an organization committee to prepare a policy paper on the division of responsibilities between the PDs and the NOs. Their report, dubbed the "Yellow Booklet," outlined the disadvantages of Philips' matrix organization in 1971:

> Without an agreement [defining the relationship between national organizations and product divisions], it is impossible to determine in any given situation which of the two parties is responsible. . . . As operations become increasingly complex, an organizational form of this type will only lower the speed of reaction of an enterprise.

On the basis of this report, van Reimsdijk proposed rebalancing the managerial relationships between PDs and NOs—"tilting the matrix" in his words—to allow Philips to increase the scale of production, decrease the number of products marketed, concentrate production, and increase the flow of goods among national organizations. He proposed closing the least efficient local plants and

TABLE 1

Philips Group Summary Financial Data, 1970–1997 (millions of guilders unless otherwise stated)

	1997	1996	1995	1990	1985	1980	1975	1970
Net sales	F76,453	F69,195	F64,462	F55,764	F60,045	F36,536	F27,115	F15,070
Income from operations (excluding restructuring)	5,065	2,537	4,090	2,260	3,075	1,577	1,201	1,280
Income from operations (including restructuring)	4,960	1,812	4,044	–2,389	N/A	N/A	N/A	N/A
As a percentage of net sales	6.5%	2.6%	6.3%	–4.3%	5.1%	4.3%	4.5%	8.5%
Income after taxes	3,278	685	2,889	F–4,447	F1,025	F532	F341	F446
Net income from normal business operations	3,291	723	2,684	–4,526	n/a	328	347	435
Stockholders' equity (common)	19,457	13,956	14,055	11,165	16,151	12,996	10,047	6,324
Return on stockholders' equity	16.6%	5.0%	20.2%	–30.2%	5.6%	2.7%	3.6%	7.3%
Distribution per common share, par value F 10 (in guilders)	F2.00	F1.60	F1.60	F0.0	F2.00	F1.80	F1.40	F1.70
Total assets	59,441	55,072	54,683	51,595	52,883	39,647	30,040	19,088
Inventories as a percentage of net sales	18.6%	17.9%	18.2%	20.7%	23.2%	32.8%	32.9%	35.2%
Outstanding trade receivables in month's sales	1.7	1.7	1.6	1.6	2.0	3.0	3.0	2.8
Current ratio				1.4	1.6	1.7	1.8	1.7
Employees at year-end (in thousands)	270	263	265	273	346	373	397	359
Wages, salaries and other related costs				F17,582	F21,491	F15,339	F11,212	F5,890
Exchange rate (period end; guilder/$)	2.02	1.74	1.60	1.69	2.75	2.15	2.69	3.62
Selected Data in Millions of Dollars								
Sales	$39,207	$40,944	$40,039	$33,018	$21,802	$16,993	$10,098	$4,163
Operating profit	2,543	1,072	2,512	1,247	988	734	464	NA
Pretax income	2,174	541	2,083	–2,380	658	364	256	NA
Net income	2,940	(349)	1,667	–2,510	334	153	95	120
Total assets	29,426	31,651	32,651	30,549	19,202	18,440	11,186	5,273
Shareholders' equity (common)	9,632	8,021	8,784	6,611	5,864	6,044	3,741	1,747

Source: Annual Reports; Standards & Poor's *Compustat*; Moody's Industrial and International Manuals.

TABLE 2

Philips Group, Sales by Product and Geographic Segment, 1985–1997 (million guilders)

	1997		1996		1995		1990		1985	
Net Sales by Product Segment										
Lighting	F10,024	13%	F8,860	13%	F8,353	13%	F 7,026	13%	F 7,976	12%
Consumer electronics	23,825	31	24,039	35	22,027	34	25,400	46	16,906	26
Domestic appliances	—		—		—				6,644	10
Professional products/systems	12,869	17	11,323	16	11,562	18	13,059	23	17,850	28
Components/semiconductors	15,003	20	11,925	17	10,714	17	8,161	15	11,620	18
Software/services	13,009	17	11,256	16	9,425	15				
Miscellaneous	1,723	2	1,783	3	2,381	4	2,118	4	3,272	5
Total	76,453	100%	69,195	100%	64,462	100%	F55,764	100%	F64,266	100%
Operating Income by Sector										
Lighting	1,151	23%	702	39%	983	24%	419	18%	F 910	30%
Consumer electronics	772	16	10	1	167	4	1,499	66	34	1
Domestic appliances	—		—		—		—		397	13
Professional products/systems	502	10	0	0	157	4	189	8	1,484	48
Components/semiconductors	2,262	46	1,496	83	2,233	55	–43	–2	44	13
Software/services	1,173	24	490	27	886	22				
Miscellaneous	188	4	199	11	423	10	218	10	200	7
Increase not attributable to a sector	(1,090)	(22)	(1,085)	(60)	(805)	(20)	–22	–1	6	0
Total	4,960	100%	1,812	100%	4,044	100%	2,260	100%	F3,075	100%

Notes: Totals may not add up due to rounding.
Product sector sales after 1988 are external sales only; therefore no eliminations are made. Sector sales before 1988 include sales to other sectors; therefore eliminations are made.
Data are not comparable to consolidated financial summary due to restating.
Source: Annual Reports.

converting the best to International Production Centers (IPCs), each supplying many NOs. In so doing, van Reimsdijk hoped that PD managers would gain control over manufacturing operations. Due to the political and organizational difficulty of closing local plants, however, implementation was slow. By the end of the decade, several IPCs had been established, but the NOs seemed as powerful and independent as ever.

In the late 1970s, his successor as CEO, Dr. Rodenburg, continued this thrust. He reinforced matrix simplification by replacing the dual commercial and technical leadership with single management at both the corporate and national organizational levels. Yet the power struggles continued.

Wisse Dekker Reorganization, 1982

Unsatisfied with the company's slow response and concerned by its slumping financial performance, upon becoming CEO in 1982, Wisse Dekker outlined a new global strategy. Aware of the cost advantage of Philips's Japanese counterparts, he created more IPCs and closed inefficient operations—particularly on the Continent where 40 of the company's more than 200 European plants were shut. He focused on core operations by selling some businesses (for example, welding, energy cables, and furniture) while acquiring an interest in Grundig and Westinghouse's North American lamp activities. Dekker also supported technology-sharing agreements and entered alliances in offshore manufacturing.

To deal with the slow-moving bureaucracy, he continued his predecessor's initiative to replace dual leadership with single general managers. He also continued to "tilt the matrix" by giving PDs formal product management responsibility, but leaving NOs responsible for local profits. And he energized the management board by reducing its size, bringing on directors with strong operating experience, and creating subcommittees to deal with difficult issues. Finally, Dekker redefined the product-planning process, incorporating input from the NOs, but giving global PDs the final decision on long-range direction. Still sales declined and profits stagnated.

Van der Klugt Reorganization, 1987

When Cor van der Klugt succeeded Dekker as chairman, Philips had lost its long-held consumer electronics leadership position to Matsushita, and

was one of only two non-Japanese companies in the world's top ten. Its net profit margins of 1 to 2 percent not only lagged behind General Electric's 9 percent, but even its highly aggressive Japanese competitors' slim 4 percent. Van der Klugt set a profit objective of 3 to 4 percent and made beating the Japanese companies a top priority.

As van der Klugt reviewed Philips's strategy, he designated various businesses as core (those that shared related technologies, had strategic importance, or were technical leaders) and non-core (stand-alone businesses that were not targets for world leadership and could eventually be sold if required). Of the four businesses defined as core, three were strategically linked: components, consumer electronics, and telecommunications and data systems. The fourth, lighting, was regarded as strategically vital because its cash flow funded development. The noncore businesses included domestic appliances and medical systems, which van der Klugt spun off into joint ventures with Whirlpool and GE, respectively.

In continuing efforts to strength the PDs relative to the NOs, van der Klugt restructured Philips around the four core global divisions rather than the former fourteen PDs. This allowed him to trim the management board, appointing the displaced board members to a new policy-making group management committee. Consisting primarily of PD heads and functional chiefs, this body replaced the old NO-dominated international concern council. Finally, he sharply reduced the 3,000-strong headquarters staff, reallocating many of them to the PDs.

To link PDs more directly to markets, van der Klugt dispatched many experienced product line managers to Philips' most competitive markets. For example, management of the digital audio tape and electric shaver product lines was relocated to Japan, while the medical technology and domestic appliances lines were moved to the United States.

Such moves, along with continued efforts at globalizing product development and production efforts, required that the parent company gain firmer control over NOs, especially the giant North American Philips Corp. (NAPC). Although Philips had obtained a majority equity interest after World War II, the U.S. company did not always respond to directives from the center. Referring to its much publicized choice of Matsushita's VHS video cassette format over its parent's V2000 format, NAPC's chairman said, "We made the best decisions for the parochial interests of our stockholders. They were not always parallel with those of Philips worldwide." To prevent replays of such experiences, in 1987 van der Klugt repurchased publicly owned NAPC shares for $700 million.

Reflecting the growing sentiment among some managers that R&D was not market-oriented enough, van der Klugt halved spending on basic research to about 10 percent of total R&D. To manage what he described as "R&D's tendency to ponder the fundamental laws of nature," he made R&D the direct responsibility of the businesses being supported by the research. This required that each research lab become focused on specific business areas (see Table 3).

Finally, van der Klugt continued the effort to build efficient, specialized, multimarket production facilities by closing 75 of the company's 420 remaining plants worldwide. He also eliminated 38,000 of its 344,000 employees—21,000 through divesting businesses—shaking up the myth of lifetime employment at the company. He anticipated that all this restructuring would lead to a financial recovery by 1990. Unanticipated lossed for that year—more than 4.5 billion Dutch guilders ($2.5 billion)—provoked a class-action lawsuit by angry American investors, who alleged that positive projections by the company had been misleading. In a surprise move, on May 14, 1990, van der Klugt and half the management board were replaced.

Timmer Reorganization, 1990

The new president, Jan Timmer, had spent most of his thirty-five-year Philips career turning around unprofitable businesses. In an early meeting with his top 100 managers he distributed a hypothetical—but fact-based—press release announcing that Philips was bankrupt. (There had already been rumors of a takeover or a government bailout.) "So what action can you take this weekend?" he challenged.

Under "Operation Centurion," headcount was reduced by 68,000, or 22 percent, over the next eighteen months, earning Timmer the nickname "The Butcher of Eindhoven." Because European laws required substantial compensation for layoffs—Eindhoven workers received fifteen months' pay, for example—the first round of 10,000 layoffs alone cost Philips $700 million. To spread the burden around the globe, and to speed the process, Timmer asked his PD managers to negotiate cuts with NO managers. According to one report, however, country managers were "digging in their heels to save local jobs." But the cuts came—many from overseas operations. In addition to the job cuts, Timmer vowed to "change the way we work." He established new performance rules and asked hundreds of top managers to sign contracts that committed them to specific financial goals. Those who broke those contracts were replaced—often with outsiders.

To focus resources further, Timmer sold off various businesses, including integrated circuits to Matsushita, minicomputers to Digital, defense electronics to Thomson, and the remaining 53 percent of appliances to Whirlpool. Yet profitability was still well below the modest 4 percent on sales he promised. In particular, consumer electronics lagged with slow growth in a price-competitive market. The core problem was identified by a 1994 McKinsey study that estimated that value added per hour in Japanese consumer electronic factories was still 68 percent above that of European plants.

TABLE 3

Philips Research Labs by Location and Specialty, 1987

Location	Size (Staff)	Specialty
Eindhoven, The Netherlands	2,000	Basic research, electronics, manufacturing technology
Redhill, Surrey, England	450	Microelectronics, television, defense
Hamburg, Germany	350	Communications, office equipment, medical imaging
Aachen, W. Germany	250	Fiber optics, X-ray systems
Paris, France	350	Microprocessors, chip materials and design
Brussels, Belgium	50	Artificial intelligence
Briarcliff Manor, New York	35	Optical systems, television, superconductivity, defense
Sunnyvale, California	150	Integrated circuits

Source: Philips, in *Business Week,* March 21, 1988, p. 156.

In this environment, most NO managers kept their heads down, using their distance from Eindhoven as their defense against the ongoing rationalization.

After three years of cost-cutting, in early 1994 Timmer presented a new growth strategy to the board. His plan was to expand software, services, and multimedia to become 40 percent of revenues by 2000. He was betting on Philips' legendary innovative capability to restart the growth engines. Earlier, he had recruited Frank Darrubba, Hewlett-Packard's director of research, and encouraged him to focus on developing fifteen core technologies. The list, which included interactive compact disk (CD-i), digital compact cassettes (DCC), high definition television (HDTV), and multimedia software, was soon dubbed "the president's projects." But his earlier divestment of some of Philips' truly high-tech businesses and a 37 percent cut in R&D personnel left the company with few who understood the technology of the new priority businesses.

By 1996, it was clear that Philips's HDTV technology would not become industry standard, that its DCC gamble had lost out to Sony's Minidisc, and that CD-i was a marketing failure. While costs were lower, so too was morale, particularly among middle management. Critics claimed that the company's drive for cost cutting and standardization had led it to ignore new worldwide market demands for more segmented products and higher consumer service. When Timmer stepped down in October 1996, the board decided to replace him with a radical choice for Philips—an outsider whose expertise was in marketing and Asia rather than technology and Europe.

Boonstra Reorganization, 1996

Cor Boonstra was a fifty-eight-year-old Dutchman whose years as CEO of Sara Lee, the U.S. consumer products firm, had earned him a reputation as a hard driver and a marketing genius. Joining Philips in 1994, he had headed the Asia Pacific region and the lighting division before being tapped as CEO. Unencumbered by tradition, he immediately announced sweeping changes. "There are no taboos, no sacred cows," he said. "The bleeders must be turned around, sold or closed. And we must change an organization that has been a closed system."

Within six months Boonstra had sold off eighteen businesses he described as "bleeders" and had reduced commitments to thirteen more perpetual loss makers, including a withdrawal from troubled

German giant Grundig. To reach his target of increasing return on invested capital from 17 to 24 percent by 1999, he also initiated a major restructuring of Philips's worldwide operations, promising to transform a structure he described as "a plate of spaghetti" into "a neat row of asparagus." He said:

> How can we compete with the Koreans? They don't have 350 companies all over the world. Their factory in Ireland covers Europe and their manufacturing facility in Mexico serves North America. We need a more structured and simpler manufacturing and marketing organization to achieve a cost pattern in line with those who do not have our heritage. This is still one of the biggest issues facing Philips.

Within a year, he had begun to rationalize the global structure and redeploy its resources. Over and above the restructuring, 3,100 jobs were eliminated in North America and 3,000 employees were added in Asia Pacific during 1997, emphasizing Boonstra's determination to shift production to low-wage countries and his broader commitment to Asia. ("With Europe's slow growth, Asia is key to our rebuilding task," he said.) And he restructured the company around 100 business units, each responsible for its profits worldwide, effectively eliminating the old PD/NO matrix. Finally, to the shock of most employees, he announced that the 100-year-old Eindhoven headquarters would be relocated to Amsterdam.

By early 1998, he was ready to announce his strategy. Despite early speculation that he might abandon consumer electronics, he proclaimed it as the center of Philips's future. Betting on the "digital revolution," he planned to focus on established technologies such as cellular phones (through joint ventures with Marantz and Lucent), digital TV, digital videodisc, and web TV. More radically, he committed major resources to marketing, including a 40 percent increase in advertising to raise awareness and image of the Philips brand.

Record profits for 1997 boosted spirits in Philips, but, as the *Financial Times* pointed out, from such a low profit base, "the first few percentage points are comparatively easy to achieve."

MATSUSHITA: BACKGROUND

In 1918, Konosuke Matsushita (or "KM" as he was affectionately known), a twenty-three-year-old inspector with the Osaka Electric Light Company, invested ¥100 to start production of double-ended sockets in his modest home. The company grew rapidly, expanding into battery-powered lamps, electric irons, and radios. On May 5, 1932, Matsushita's fourteenth anniversary, KM announced to his 162 employees a 250-year corporate plan broken into 25-year sections, each to be carried out by successive generations. His plan was codified in a company creed and in the "Seven Spirits of Matsushita" (see Table 4), which, along with the company song, continued to be woven into morning assemblies worldwide and provided the basis of the "cultural and spiritual training" all new employees received during their first seven months with the company.

TABLE 4

Matsushita Creed and Philosophy (Excerpts)

Creed
Through our industrial activities, we strive to foster progress, to promote the general welfare of society, and to devote ourselves to furthering the development of world culture.

Seven Spirits of Matsushita
Service through Industry
Fairness
Harmony and Cooperation
Struggle for Progress
Courtesy and Humility
Adjustment and Assimilation
Gratitude

KM's Business Philosophy (Selected Quotations)
"The purpose of an enterprise is to contribute to society by supplying goods of high quality at low prices in ample quantity."

"Profit comes in compensation for contribution to society. . . . [It] is a result rather than a goal."

"The responsibility of the manufacturer cannot be relieved until its product is disposed of by the end user."

"Unsuccessful business employs a wrong management. You should not find its causes in bad fortune, unfavorable surroundings or wrong timing."

"Business appetite has no self-restraining mechanism. . . . When you notice you have gone too far, you must have the courage to come back."

Source: "Matsushita Electric Industrial (MEI) in 1987," *Harvard Business School Case* No. 388–144.

In the postwar boom, Matsushita introduced a flood of new products: TV sets in 1952; transistor radios in 1958; and color TVs, dishwashers, and electric ovens in 1960. Capitalizing on its broad line of 5,000 products (Sony produced 80), the company opened 25,000 domestic retail distribution outlets. With more than six times the outlets of rival Sony, the ubiquitous "National Shops" represented about 40 percent of all appliance stores in Japan in the late 1960s. These not only provided assured sales volume, but also gave the company direct access to market trends and consumer product reaction.

When postwar growth slowed, however, Matsushita had to look beyond its expanding product line and excellent distribution system for growth. After trying many tactics to boost sales—even sending assembly line workers out as door-to-door salesmen—the company eventually focused on export markets.

The Organization's Foundation: Divisional Structure

Plagued by ill health, KM wished to delegate more authority than was typical in Japanese companies. In 1933, Matsushita became the first Japanese company to adopt the divisional structure, giving each division clearly defined profit responsibilities while creating a "small business" environment to maintain growth and flexibility. This divisional structure generated competition among divisions, spurring them to drive growth by leveraging their technology assets into new products. After the innovating division had earned substantial profits on its new product, however, company policy was to spin it off as a new division to maintain the "hungry spirit."

Under the "one-product-one division" system, each product line was managed almost like an independent corporation. Corporate management provided each autonomous division with initial funds, deliberately underestimating working capital requirements to motivate it to work hard to generate retained earnings. Divisional profitability was determined after deductions for central services such as R&D and interest on internal borrowings. KM expected uniform performance across the company's thirty-six divisions, and division managers whose operating profits fell below 4 percent of sales for two successive years were replaced.

Matsushita ran its corporate treasury like a commercial bank, reviewing divisions' loan requests for which it charged slightly higher-than-market interest, and accepting deposits on their excess funds. Each division paid 60 percent of earnings to headquarters and financed all additional working capital and fixed asset requirements from the retained 40 percent. Transfer prices were based on the market and settled through the treasury on normal commercial terms.

While basic technology was developed in a central research laboratory (CRL), product development and engineering occurred in each of the product divisions. Matsushita intentionally underfunded the CRL, forcing it to compete for additional funding from the divisions. Annually, the CRL publicized its major research projects to the product divisions, which then provided funding in exchange for technology for marketable applications. While it was rarely the innovator, Matsushita was usually very fast to market—earning it the nickname "Manishita," or copycat.

MATSUSHITA: INTERNATIONALIZATION

Although the establishment of overseas markets was a major thrust of the second 25 years in the 250-year plan, in an overseas trip in 1951 KM had been unable to find any American company willing to collaborate with Matsushita. The best he could do was a technology exchange and licensing agreement with Philips. Nonetheless, the push to internationalize continued.

Expanding Through Color TV

In the 1950s and 1960s, trade liberalization and lower shipping rates made possible a healthy export business built on black and white TV sets. In 1953, the company opened its first overseas branch office—the Matsushita Electric Corporation of America (MECA). With neither a distribution network nor a strong brand, the company could not access traditional retailers, and had to resort to selling its products under their private brands through mass merchandisers and discounters.

During the 1960s, pressure from national governments in developing countries led Matsushita to open plants in several countries in Southeast Asia and Central and South America. As manufacturing costs in Japan rose, Matsushita shifted more basic production to these low-wage countries, but almost all high-value components and subassemblies were still made in its scale-intensive Japanese plants. By the 1970s, projectionist sentiments in the West forced the company to establish assembly operations in the Americas and Europe. In 1972, it opened a plant in Canada; in 1974, it bought Motorola's TV business and started manufacturing its Quasar brand in the United States; and in 1976, it built a plant in Cardiff, Wales, to supply the Common Market.

Building Global Leadership: Dominating through VCRs

The birth of the videocassette recorder (VCR) propelled Matsushita into first place in the consumer electronics industry during the 1980s. Recognizing the potential mass-market appeal of the VCR—developed by the Californian broadcasting company Ampex in 1956—engineers at Matsushita began developing VCR technology. After six years of development work, Matsushita launched its commercial broadcast video recorder in 1964 and introduced a consumer version two years later.

In 1975, Sony introduced the technically superior "Betamax" format, and the next year JVC launched a competing "VHS" format. Under pressure from MITI, the government's industrial planning ministry, Matsushita agreed to give up its own format and adopt the established VHS standard. During Matsushita's twenty years of VCR product development, various members of the VCR research team had moved from central labs to the product divisions' development labs and eventually to the plant. In 1976, as sales at home and abroad began to take off, Matsushita celebrated the unit's first profitable year.

The company quickly built production to meet its own needs as well as those of OEM customers like GE, RCA, and Zenith that decided to forgo self-manufacture of VCRs. Between 1977 and 1985, capacity was increased thirty-threefold, to 6.8 million units (In parallel, the company aggressively licensed the VHS format to other manufacturers, including Hitachi, Sharp, Mitsubishi, and eventually, Philips.) Increased volume enabled Matsushita to slash prices 50 percent within five years of product launch, while simultaneously improving quality. By the mid 1980s, VCRs accounted for 30 percent of sales—over 40 percent of overseas revenues—and provided 45 percent of profits.

MATSUSHITA: MANAGING INTERNATIONAL OPERATIONS

In the mid 1980s, the growing number of overseas companies reported to Japan in one of two ways: wholly owned, single-product global plants reported directly to Matsushita's product divisions, while overseas sales and marketing subsidiaries and overseas companies producing a broad product line for local markets, reported to Matsushita Electric Trading Company (METC), a separate legal entity. (See Figure 1 for METC's organization.)

Changing Systems and Controls

Throughout the 1970s, the central product divisions maintained strong operating control over their offshore production units. Overseas operations used plant and equipment designed by the parent company, followed manufacturing procedures dictated by the center, and used materials from Matsushita's domestic plants. Growing trends toward local sourcing, however, gradually weakened the divisions' direct control. By the 1980s, instead of controlling inputs, they began to monitor measures of output (for example, quality, productivity, inventory levels).

About the same time, product divisions began receiving the globally consolidated return on sales reports that had previously been consolidated in METC statements. By the mid 1980s, as worldwide planning was introduced for the first time, corporate management required all its product divisions to prepare global product strategies.

Headquarters-Subsidiary Relations

Although METC and the product divisions set detailed sales and profits targets for their overseas subsidiaries, local managers were told they had complete autonomy on how to achieve the targets. "Mike" Matsuoko, president of the company's largest European production subsidiary in Cardiff, Wales, however, emphasized that failure to meet

FIGURE 1

Organization of METC, 1985

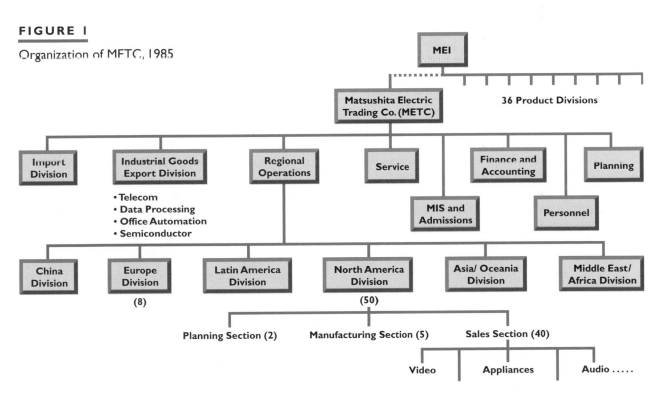

Note: ( ) = number of people.
Source: Harvard Business School Case No. 388–144.

targets forfeited freedom: "Losses show bad health and invite many doctors from Japan who provide advice and support."

In the mid 1980s, Matsushita had more than 700 expatriate managers and technicians on foreign assignment for four to eight years but defended that high number by describing their pivotal role. "This vital communication role," said one manager, "almost always requires a manager from the parent company. Even if a local manager speaks Japanese, he would not have the long experience that is needed to build relationships and understand our management processes."

Expatriate managers were located throughout foreign subsidiaries, but there were a few positions that were almost always reserved for them. The most visible were subsidiary general managers, whose main role was to translate Matsushita philosophy abroad. Expatriate accounting managers were expected to "mercilessly expose the truth" to corporate headquarters; and Japanese technical managers were sent to transfer product and process technologies and provide headquarters with local market information. These expatriates maintained relationships with senior colleagues at headquarters, who acted as career mentors, evaluated performance (with some input from local managers), and provided expatriates with information about parent company developments.

General managers of foreign subsidiaries visited headquarters at least two or three times each year—some as often as every month. Corporate managers reciprocated these visits, and on average, major operations hosted at least one headquarters manager each day of the year. Face-to-face meetings were considered vital: "Figures are important," said one manager, "but the meetings are necessary to develop judgment." Daily faxes and nightly phone calls between headquarters and expatriate colleagues were a vital management link.

Yamashita's Operation Localization

Although international sales kept rising, as early as 1982, growing host country pressures caused concern about the company's highly centralized operations. In that year, newly appointed company president, Toshihiko Yamashita, launched "Operation Localization" to boost offshore production from less than 10 percent of value-added to 25 percent, or half of overseas sales, by 1990.

To support the target, he set out a program of four localizations—personnel, technology, material, and capital.

Over the next few years, Matsushita increased the number of local nationals in key positions. In the United States, for example, U.S. nationals became the presidents of three of the six local companies, while in Taiwan, the majority of production divisions were replaced by Chinese managers. In each case, however, local national managers were still supported by senior Japanese advisers, who maintained a direct link with the parent company. To localize technology and materials, the company developed its national subsidiaries' expertise to source equipment locally, modify designs to meet local requirements, incorporate local components, and adapt corporate processes and technologies to accommodate these changes.

By the mid 1980s, offshore production subsidiaries were free to buy minor parts from local vendors as long as quality could be assured, but still had to buy key components from internal sources. They could also carry out routine production tasks independently, calling on corporate technical personnel when plans called for major expansion or change. And sales subsidiaries had more choice over the products they sold. Each year the company held a two-week internal merchandising show and product-planning meeting, where sales subsidiary managers negotiated over features, quantities, and even prices of the products they wanted to buy from the parent's product divisions. Corporate managers, however, could overrule the subsidiary if they thought introduction of a particular product was of strategic importance.

The overall localization thrust sparked opposition from managers in Japan. In a low-growth environment, increased foreign production would come at the expense of export sales. "What will that mean for employment in Japan?" said one senior manager. "Protecting the interests of employees is one of our greatest moral commitments. We cannot sacrifice that for any reason." Even some foreign subsidiary managers feared localization would reduce their access to central resources and expertise. If localized operations caused export income to contribute less, they reasoned, the central product division managers could give priority to domestic needs over foreign operations.

Nonetheless, between 1980 and 1988, Matsushita added twenty-one manufacturing companies and twelve sales companies abroad to bring those respective totals to sixty and forty-one. In 1990, Matsushita employed 50,000 workers overseas, twice the number of a decade earlier. Despite these efforts, in 1990 overseas production stood at only ¥600 billion—still less than half Matsushita's 25 percent target.

Yamashita's greatest wish was that Operation Localization would help Matsushita's overseas companies develop the innovative capability and entrepreneurial initiatives that he had long admired in the national organizations of rival Philips. (Past efforts to develop such capabilities abroad had failed. For example, when Matsushita acquired Motorola's TV business in the United States, its highly innovative technology group atrophied as American engineers resigned in response to what they felt to be excessive control from Japan's highly centralized R&D operations.) In an unusual act for a Japanese CEO, Yamashita publicly expressed his unhappiness with the lack of initiative at the TV plant Cardiff. Despite the transfer of substantial resources and the delegation of many responsibilities, he felt that the plant remained too dependent on the center.

Tanii's Integration and Expansion

Yamashita's successor, Akio Tanii, expanded on his predecessor's initiatives. In part because Matsushita's product divisions received only 3 percent royalties for foreign production against at least 10 percent return on sales for exports from Japan, he felt that product divisions were not giving their full attention to developing operations outside Japan. To correct the situation, he brought all foreign subsidiaries of Matsushita under the control of METC in 1986, thus consolidating the company's international operations in one administrative entity. To further integrate domestic and overseas operations, in April 1988, Tanii merged METC into the parent company. Then, to shift operational control nearer to local markets, he relocated major regional headquarters functions from Japan to North America, Europe, and Southeast Asia. Yet still he was frustrated that the overseas subsidiary companies acted as the implementing agents of the Osaka-based product divisions.

Through all these changes, however, Matsushita's worldwide growth continued generating huge reserves. With $17.5 billion in liquid financial assets at the end of 1989, the company was referred to as the "Matsushita Bank." Several top executives felt that if they could not develop innovative overseas companies, they should buy them. Flush with cash and international success, in early 1991 the company acquired MCA, the U.S. entertainment giant for $6.1 billion, with the objective of obtaining a media software source for its hardware. Within a year, however, Japan's economic bubble had burst, plunging the economy into recession. Almost overnight, Tanii had to shift the company's focus from expansion to cost containment.

Morishita's Restructuring

Despite Tanii's best efforts to cut costs, the problems ran too deep. The company's huge capacity, its full line of products, and its network of 27,000 retailers turned from assets to liabilities. With 1992 profits less than half their 1991 level, Tanii was forced to resign in February 1993.

His replacement, Yoichi Morishita—at fifty-six the most junior of the firm's executive vice presidents—immediately implemented a major restructuring designed "to eliminate laxness and extravagance." Central to his effort was a commitment to cut headquarters staff and decentralize responsibility to operating units, including overseas companies. Under the slogan "simple, small, speedy and strategic," over the next eighteen months he eliminated a layer of management and transferred 6,000 corporate staff to operating jobs. To the shock of many, he even began questioning the sanctity of lifetime employment. By contrast, he consolidated twenty research centers into nine, centralizing decisions to speed up new product introductions. Unwilling to respond to MCI's management pressure for more funding and greater independence, Matsushita sold off 80 percent of the company to Seagram at a $1.2 billion loss in early 1995.

Meanwhile, stimulated by a rising yen that raised the export prices, product divisions were aggressively moving value-added offshore, particularly to Southeast Asia. Attracted by booming markets, lower costs, and strong local partners, the company began investing in major production facilities, not just the knockdown assembly plants of the 1970s and 1980s. For example, production of all 1.5 million of Matsushita's export air conditioners was transferred to Malaysia. In that country alone,

TABLE 5

Matsushita, Summary Financial Data, 1970–1997[a]

	1997	1996	1995	1990	1985	1980	1975	1970
In billions of yen and percent:								
Sales	¥7,676	¥6,795	¥6,948	¥6,003	¥5,291	¥2,916	¥1,385	¥932
Income before tax	332	77	232	572	723	324	83	147
As % of sales	4.3%	1.1%	3.3%	9.5%	13.7%	11.1%	6.0%	15.8%
Net income	¥138	¥(58)[b]	¥90	¥236	¥216	¥125	¥32	¥70
As % of sales	1.8%	(0.8%)	1.3%	3.9%	4.1%	4.3%	2.3%	7.6%
Cash dividends (per share)	12.50	12.50	13.50	¥10.00	¥9.52	¥7.51	¥6.82	¥6.21
Total assets	8,696	8,011	8,202	7,851	5,076	2,479	1,274	735
Stockholders' equity	3,696	3,398	3,255	3,201	2,084	1,092	573	324
Capital investment	415	381	316	355	288	NA	NA	NA
Depreciation	345	292	296	238	227	65	28	23
R&D	435	399	378	346	248	102	51	NA
Employees (units)	270,651	265,538	265,397	198,299	175,828	107,057	82,869	78,924
Overseas employees	116,279	107,530	112,314	59,216	38,380	NA	NA	NA
As % of total employees	43%	40%	42%	30%	22%	NA	NA	NA
Exchange rate (fiscal period end; ¥/$)	124	106	89	159	213	213	303	360
In millions of dollars:								
Sales	$61,902	$64,102	$78,069	$37,753	$24,890	$13,690	$4,572	$2,588
Operating income before depreciation	3,015	2,495	2,924	4,343	3,682	1,606	317	NA
Operating income after depreciation	2,678	723	2,609	2,847	2,764	1,301	224	NA
Pretax income	1,112	(536)	1,017	3,667	3,396	1,520	273	408
Net income				1,482	1,214	584	105	195
Total assets	70,128	75,583	92,159	49,379	21,499	11,636	4,206	2,042
Total equity	29,804	32,053	36,575	20,131	10,153	5,129	1,890	900

[a]Data prior to 1987 are for the fiscal year ending November 20; data 1988 and after are for the fiscal year ending March 31.
[b]1996 results include a write-off of ¥164 billion in losses stemming from the sale of MCA in June 1995.
Source: Annual reports; Standard & Poor's *Compustat*; Moody's Industrial and International Manuals.

TABLE 6

Matsushita, Sales by Product and Geographic Segment, 1985–1997 (billion yen)

	1997		1996		1995		FY 1990		FY 1985	
By Product Segment:										
Video equipment	¥1,342	17%	¥1,225	18%	¥1,272	18%	¥1,598	27%	¥1,947	37%
Audio equipment	576	8	518	8	555	8	561	9	570	11
Home appliances	1,026	13	914	13	916	13	802	13	763	14
Communication and industrial equipment	2,492	32	2,013	30	1,797	26	1,375	23	849	16
Electronic components	1,055	14	1,020	15	893	13	781	13	573	11
Batteries and kitchen-related equipment	472	6	405	6	374	4	312	5	217	4
Others	710	9	700	10	530	8	573	10	372	7
Total	7,676	100%	6,795	100%	6,948	100%	¥6,003	100%	¥5,291	100%
By Geographic Segment:										
Domestic	4,046	53%	3,727	55%	3,455	50%	¥3,382	56%	¥2,659	50%
Overseas	3,630	47	3,068	45	3,493	50	2,621	44	2,632	50

Notes: Total may not add due to rounding.
Source: Annual Reports

Matsushita had established sixteen companies producing a wide range of products and employing 20,000 people. Subsequently, the air conditioning and television companies expanded their commitment by establishing substantial Malaysian design and development centers. Similar levels of commitment were also being made to facilities in China, India and Vietnam.

By fiscal year 1997, profit margins had risen from 2.8 percent when Morishita took over to 4.3 percent. Besides restructuring the company, he had successfully repositioned its product portfolio, reducing low margin consumer electronics from 50 to 35 percent of sales and moving into digital technologies such as cellular phones, digital cameras, and digital video discs. Yet Morishita was discouraged that still less than half of its overseas sales were manufactured abroad. Equally troubling was the company's slow transition to local senior-level management in its overseas companies, and the even less successful attempts to integrate foreign managers at senior levels in the parent company.

ABB in China: 1998

*This case was prepared by Suzanne Uhlen, Lund University (Sweden),
under the supervision of Professor Michael Lubatkin of the University of
Connecticut.*

"I want to make ABB a company that encourages
and demands innovation from all of its employees,
and a company that creates the environment in
which teamwork and innovation flourish," declares
ABB's CEO Göran Lindahl. In seeking new growth,
Lindahl is moving out of the long shadow of his
predecessor, Percy Barnevik, considered one of
the most successful international managers in
Europe.

Technology giant ABB, the world leader in electrical engineering, is a $35 billion electrical engi-
neering group, with companies all over the globe.
It operates primarily in the fields of reliable and
economical generation, transmission, and distribution of electrical energy.[1] Much has been written
about the worldwide company. In 1996, ABB was
ranked in the top forty of the first 500 companies
listed by *Fortune* magazine. Recently, the company
has announced its newest reorganization, which
will make it more up-to-date globally according to
Lindahl.[2] Lindahl took over from Barnevik as CEO
in 1997.

ABB has different priorities in different markets.
Western Europe and North America are the company's biggest markets. However, the high-potential
markets are the Middle East, Africa, Latin America,
and Asia. These markets are growing fast, and ABB
expects to have half of its customers in these regions not long into the next century. The priority is
on building local manufacturing, engineering, and
other forms of added value. ABB wants to integrate

these operations into the global networks to get
full synergy effects and scale economies.

During 1998, the industrial production in
OECD countries, in which ABB performs about 75
percent of its total business, has continued to grow,
although at a slower pace than the strong growth
rates of the previous year. Overall, industrial production in Europe is lower than a year ago, but still
high compared with historical levels. Current economic activity in North America is slowing compared with the strong economy of recent years. In
Latin America, high interest rates are delaying the
financial closing of projects in an environment of
reduced economic activity. The Indian economy is
slowing, also due to reduced exports as a result of
its strong currency compared with others in the region. Southeast Asia is gradually stabilizing at a low
level, with reduced consumption and investments.

As a result of the ongoing economic uncertainty, overall global demand is forecast to remain
soft in the near future. ABB expects to benefit with
its well-established local presence around the
world from higher demand in various industries
and world markets. Appropriate cost cutting, continued selective tendering, and successful working
capital reduction programs are expected to continue contributing positively to the ABB Group results. The company recognizes the world to be
rapidly changing and increasingly unpredictable. Efforts have paid off and the group has taken advantage of opportunities in Asia and positioned itself
for future growth in what is seen to be "the world's
most dynamic market over a long term—China."[3]

The interest in China is growing steadily, and
companies in Japan, the western European countries, the United States and elsewhere today view
the Chinese market as having enormous potential.

This case was prepared by Suzanne Uhlen (Lund University,
Sweden) under the supervision of Professor Michael Lubatkin
(University of Connecticut). The case is intended to be used as
a basis for classroom discussion rather than to illustrate either
effective or ineffective handling of the situation. Used by
permission.

Given China's population of a billion and a growing economy, it has appeared to be worthwhile to make a major effort to gain a foothold in the market.[4] On the one hand, China represents a huge and largely untapped market. It is potentially bigger than that of the United States, the European Community, and Japan combined. On the other hand, China's new firms are proving to be very competitive, and China's culture is quite different from that of the West. However, in the Chinese market the growth remains at a relatively good level for enterprises such as Procter & Gamble, Motorola, Nestlé, and ABB. This market is regarded as a lifeboat to a lot of worldwide companies suffering from the financial crisis in the rest of Southeast Asia. Nevertheless, there is talk about China devaluing its currency, which might also drag China down into the crisis. However, the country has not shown any visible scratches from the surrounding crisis. China seems to be unshakable, and analysts are still valuing China as the country of the future.[5] Thus, the changes in China are creating both opportunities and threats for established worldwide companies. According to *Management Today,* China will be one of the top ten economies in the world by the year 2010.[6]

CHINESE INFLUENCE

A recruiters' guide to the country proclaims that "China will enter the next century as the rising power in Asia after two decades of astonishing economic growth that has transformed the country and that has given rise to new challenges."[7] Many cities in China have more than 5 million inhabitants. China has had a growing economy that cannot be compared with any other country's economy during almost three decades.[8] It is argued that China is not like any other developing country because of the rapid changes that are taking place in certain areas. In some areas, such as home electronics,[9] the development has surpassed the development in western countries, while in other areas China lags far behind.

The Chinese culture and society stretch back more than 5,000 years. There is a unique cultural heritage of philosophy, science and technology, societal structures, and traditional administrative bureaucracy.[10] With this in mind, it is no wonder, according to researchers, that conflicts often occur between Chinese and foreign cultures. Foreign managers are

accustomed to other values and norms, some of which may hardly be acceptable in China.[11]

In the current half-year reports from worldwide companies, a distinct trend is noticeable, according to Dagens Industri.[12] The more focus that the companies have put on basic industry, the more the Asian crisis tends to affect these companies. However, China is the country that can save these companies and others, but especially those companies operating in the business of infrastructure.[13] Now that the Cold War with China has ended, economic growth is stabilizing and the country is demanding a speedy reconstruction. The country has begun to enjoy unprecedented strategic latitude for the first time in 200 years and it no longer faces the threat of aggression from superior powers.[14] This has enabled it to focus on economic developments as the driving force of both its domestic and foreign policies. According to Professor Michael Yahuda, China's leaders also have come to base their legitimacy on providing the conditions of stability in which people can look forward to continued high levels of prosperity. The need for economic development is fueled by many other factors, such as providing employment for a vast population that increases by some 15 million a year. Additionally, there are significant regional inequalities that can only be addressed by further economic development.[15]

China is expected to evolve into a hybrid system of authoritarianism, democracy, socialism, and capitalism. Also recognized are the internal problems the country faces such as environmental disasters, political struggles, and tensions between the emerging entrepreneurial economy and the vast parts of China still under state control.[16] Today China receives the most direct investment and foreign aid of any developing country. Many companies are eager to establish their presence in China, which, it is argued, attracts more than its proportionate share of investments.[17] However, concluding remarks are, ". . . westerners cannot expect to know how China will develop and need to expect that the Chinese will always be different from them. Instead of trying to change China, they should look for positive steps that take their differences into account."[18]

According to China's Premier Zhu Rongji, China is indeed the largest market in the world. However, because of duplicate construction, there is a problem of oversupply in some areas. Nevertheless, the premier states that the market is far from being saturated.[19] Since China opened its doors to the outside world in the late 1970s, a large number of foreign investors have gained rich returns from their investments, yet some have ended in failure. The *China Daily* offers this guideline for ensuring business success in China:[20]

- Make long-term strategies for the Chinese market. Competition is intensifying and market exploitation needs time and patience. Foreign companies eager to get a quick return are usually disappointed at the results.

- Localize staff. They are familiar with the local business environment.

- Be aware of changes in policies and regulation. China is in the process of transforming from a planned economy to a market economy. Various policies and regulations are being revised and replaced, while new ones are being issued. Foreign investors must keep informed of the ongoing changes.

- Undertake practical market research. Because of social, economic, and cultural differences, practical and down-to-earth market research is a must before and during investment in China.

CHINESE CULTURAL INFLUENCE

There is a consensus among several authors that the Chinese have a traditional respect for age, hierarchy, and authority.[21] It originates from the Confucian concept of *li* (rite, proprietary), which plays an important role in maintaining a person's social position. *Li* can be seen today in the existing traditional bureaucracy and in vertical relationships concerning centralization of decision making, and in corruption to some extent, which is acceptable in such a cultural context.[22]

Second, the family is viewed as an essential social unit and there is a strong tendency to promote the collective or the group. Members within the family or group must maintain harmonious relationships and these social relations are seen as more important than the individual.[23] Thus, the family or clan norms are adopted as the formal code of conduct, and members are bound to these standards. Other research has found that in modern China, business and industrial enterprises were perceived as an extension of the family system.[24]

Third, the concept of *mianzi* ("face") is seen as an important characteristic. As Yanan Ju has noted, the general idea of *mianzi* is related to "a reputation achieved through getting on in life through success and ostentation."[25] *Mianzi* also serves to enhance harmony within the family or group, so that the positive is expressed publicly and any conflicts remain private.[26] Yung Lee Hong has found that the concept of *mianzi* still plays an important role in social relationships and organizational behavior.[27] However, Lu Yuan points out that there are two sides to this concept.[28] The first includes the individual's moral character, and the strong fear of losing this limits the person's behavior. The second aspect of *mianzi* involves assertions about a person, which is not seen quite as serious as the loss of face.[29]

The importance of personal relations (*guanxi*) is the fourth characteristic. According to Hong, persons with *guanxi* usually share a common birthplace, lineage, surname, or experience, such as attending the same school, working together, or belonging to the same organization.[30] A comparative study of decision making in China and Britain has revealed that Chinese managers use their personal *guanxi* more widely to exchange information, negotiate with planning authorities, and accelerate decision-making processes than managers from British firms.[31] As it is, the network transmits information, and because contacts and co-operation are built on trust, it is seen as very serious if that trust is broken. If a trust is broken the whole network will soon know about the incident and the person involved will have a hard time doing business again.[32]

ABB has been doing business in the Chinese market since 1919. At that time this was the first product delivery to China, and it was not until 1979 that ABB established its first permanent office. Nearly eleven years later hearing the words *Asia* and *electricity* made the heart pound with excitement in almost every chairman of an energy company. There were billions to be had from the booming demand for electricity in Asia.[33] But in recent years, the emerging Asian market has slowed down due to the financial crisis in the area. At the moment it seems as though China is the only country not affected by this financial crisis, and consequently, there are many companies that are now trying to be successful in China.

ABB is argued to be a company with a good position on the Chinese market due to good performance, delivery, autonomy, and also its good name. Today the company has nine representative offices and fifteen joint ventures; the number of employees has grown in four years from approximately 1,000 to 6,000 employees in China.

LOCAL ROOTS

The strategy of ABB is to use its global strength to support the needs of its local customers around the world. However, in China, ABB has a fairly high import duty on its products, which limits how much the company can sell. The idea of setting up local production in China was to increase market share, due to the fact that most Chinese customers do not have foreign currency[34] and are consequently forced to buy locally produced goods with the local currency. The reason for ABB to localize in China was not to achieve lower production costs, as some locally supplied components are more expensive in China than elsewhere. It was rather to be closer to the local market, and therefore facilitate a few local modifications to the products and provide shorter delivery times to the customer.

The phrase "think global, act local" is said to reflect ABB's fundamental idea of strong local companies working together across borders to gain economies of scale in many areas.[35] In spite of ABB claims to be able to respond swiftly and surely to market conditions,[36] some of the products in China are not truly adapted to the local market. Most of the products are designed for the IEC—international standard association based in Europe. The company manufactures products, which have to be tested according to different norms and standards. For example, North America ABB follows the ANSI-standard and in Canada the CSA-standard.

However, some of ABB's products would not pass a type test based on the Chinese standards. That is not because the quality is too low; on the contrary the quality of ABB products is sometimes too high. The quality of some of the products has evolved far beyond the requirements of Chinese standards—therefore these ABB products cannot meet the standards. The Chinese standards are based on what the local manufacturer can produce because the country does not have much other information. As one manager at ABB in China stated,

We are not going to redesign our products in order to meet the standards for the obvious rea-

sons, why should we take our quality out, why shall we take the advances out? It does become an issue from time to time, Chinese are very risk averse, if we have not done the type test in China. It is more to cover themselves in case something goes wrong.

Some other managers said that though ABB tries to adapt the products to the Chinese local standard there was a negative response because customers regard Western standards as superior and are asking for the superior product. The Chinese customers are seen as tough and sometimes demand more tests than ABB's products have gone through. Furthermore, insufficient feasibility studies for new joint ventures set up in China delay work when new information has to be collected about market conditions. This problem arises from the speed of changes in China and the difficulty for a company to catch up with what is going on.

However, when the so-called type tests of the product have been done, the company cannot change the design because of the high costs involved in this test. Some critics have suggested that ABB should adapt more to the Chinese situation, but then the tests would have to be redone. For some products, though as one manager said, the company must "adapt to the configurations the customers have a demand for, because they have an option—go to the competitor."

Still, in most cases, the local ABB companies in China are not allowed to change the products other than according to agreements with the licensee. The reason for that is that the technology partners[37] have the overall view of the quality and performance. The ABB corporation does not want to have different product performance for different countries. To be seen as the same product all over the world, the products must have the same descriptions. Consequently, the local ABB company can do only a few modifications to the standard product for the specific customer and cannot change the technology involved. The technology partners have a few alternatives that meet the demands of the Chinese customers and these products are also tested, but do not necessarily meet the Chinese standards.

The local ABB company tries to follow the ABB Group's policy, to be close to the customer and responsive to his or her needs.[38] In China, however, contracts are not commonly used, and this frequently obstructs satisfying the many customer demands.

> They keep on saying this is China and you should adapt to the Chinese way: Ok, if you want to buy a Chinese product that's fine, but this is our product—here are the terms and conditions. You can't just give in to that; otherwise you will kill your company, because they expect you to accept unlimited liability and lifetime warranty and the risks to which you would expose your company would eventually lead to its shutting down, so you just cannot do that.

The ABB view is that being close to the customer is the best guarantee that local requirements will be met.[39] However, the headquarters in Zurich has also set up some rules about the kind of contracts that the local subsidiaries shall sign worldwide. In China, contracts are something new and many Chinese customers do not want them. Consequently, some ABB companies in China do not use the standard ABB contract and are actually responsive to the customers' needs. When another ABB company comes to the same customer to set up a standard contract, the customer will point out that the previous ABB company did not seem to find the contract necessary.

PROFIT CENTERS

ABB's strategy is to take full advantage of its economies of scale while at the same time being represented by national companies in many home markets where some 5,000 entrepreneurial profit centers serve local customers. These companies are quite independent and have to stand on their own economically. In addition, the individual company's profit can easily be compared with revenue. In other words, the individual ABB company is measured on its own performance and needs, a profit when selling products or parts, even though it is within the ABB Group. It is recognized that the profit centers are efficient for decentralization and that the organization can act relatively fast. This also enables the company to be sensitive and responsive to potential problems. Each company has a fair amount of autonomy, which in turn makes the individual company flexible in the decision-making process. Even though ABB brochures state that the strategy of having profit centers enables

the easy transfer of know-how across borders,[40] it is argued that the direction is pretty much one way—from the technology partners, business areas, and country level to the subsidiary—rather than a two-way exchange.

Nevertheless, some conflicts of interest have occurred. For example, the local ABB company and all other licensees are more or less dependent on their licensors in Europe.[41] In the local ABB company's case, a factory in X-city that is one of its technology partners is measured, like everyone else, on its performance and on its profit. If it gives the local ABB company support, it will cost the former money, and likewise, if it sells the local ABB company components, it wants to make a profit. The consequence is that it is charging the local ABB company 25 to 100 percent over and above the cost of its parts.

> So in the end you end up calling them as little as possible and we end up buying parts from local suppliers that probably we should not buy from local suppliers. And we reduce our quality. They have great profit figures, we have some profit figures but there are some real serious problems along the way.

The technology partner argues, on the contrary, that the prices are high because it first has to buy from its supplier and then sell to the local ABB company, which makes the products more expensive. Besides, the technology partners pay for the type tests and all the product development.[42]

Such disagreements or conflicts have been occurring for a long time within ABB, but nobody has yet found a solution. It is said to be difficult for a company, like ABB, which is working with so many different products, markets, and in different cultures to have anything else than sole profit centers. If the profit centers did not aim for a profit when selling within the ABB Group, it is argued that the companies would no longer be independent companies. Being independent is seen as a strength, and therefore it would be against the laws of nature if the companies were not always aiming for a profit. Nonetheless, among these independent companies with profit centers there are some extreme examples:

> Our partner in Y-country was selling the finished product in China before. Now he sells the parts to the joint venture in China and wants to charge more for the parts than he did for the finished

product, and that is because it is in his interest and he will be evaluated on his performance. If he does not do that, his profits will be too low and he will be blamed for it. So he has got to do what he has got to do. That is what he is motivated to do and that is what he is going to do.

To some extent the technology partners are even selling indirectly to the Chinese market using nonofficial agents to avoid a high import tax and slip under the high market price that exists on the Chinese market. ABB China has sought to stop the use of these agents and is trying to force ABB companies to use only two official channels for ABB goods into the Chinese market. They are to rely on goods produced locally by the local ABB company and on direct imports from a technology partner.

STRUCTURE

ABB is a huge enterprise with dispersed business areas. They encompassed three segments—power generation, transmission and distribution, and industrial building systems—but these segments have recently been divided into six. Before the reorganization every country had its national ABB head office, with a country management that dealt with all the company business in that particular country. The other dimension of the matrix structure reflects the clustering of the activities of the enterprise into thirty-six business areas (or BAs). Each business area represents a distinct worldwide product market. Simplified, each BA is responsible for worldwide market allocation and the development of a worldwide technical strategy for that specific product line. Additional responsibilities for the BA are to coordinate who shall supply or deliver where, and also to work as a referee in potential disagreements between companies within the ABB Group.

In China, however, as in most developing countries, there is no BA in place and the decision power of the country management is consequently closer at hand. Hence, it is argued, decisions tend to be made at the country level rather than at the BA level. Disagreements between licensees in Western countries and subsidiaries in China have been, and are occurring, due to different business orientations. The local subsidiary in China has two or more licensors in Western countries, from which it buys components. Some of the licensees sold these

components themselves before the local subsidiary was taken up in China. Some licensees feel that the market in China was taken from them and that they therefore can compensate for potentially lost sales only by charging the Chinese subsidiary a higher cost. Consequently, if the disagreeing partner seeks the BA as a referee in this kind of case, the following happens, as one manager explains:

The BA are looking at the global business—we can increase our global business if we set up a joint venture in China. But the technology partner can't increase their business if we set up a joint venture in China. If we set up a joint venture in China the technology partner wants to increase its business also, they are going to do some work, and of course want something for it. The BA is really powerless to push those along.

To date, the licensors have also been paying for all the technology development, which is, from their point of view, the reason for charging a higher price for the components they are selling. Because the enterprise is divided into 5,000 profit centers and because each of these profit centers wants a profit when selling a component or product, there have been some shortcomings in the coordination and cooperation between the licensors and the local Chinese subsidiary.

For example, the licensor in X-country makes the same breakers that the local ABB company does. When the licensor runs into a quality problem, it is ineffective at informing its licensee in China, which will probably also run into the same quality problem in the near future. The problem may be discussed at the local ABB company, but if it suggests changes to the licensor, the licensor will evaluate the situation on the basis of benefits to itself. Since it is going to invest its own resources, it is, of course, going to invest in areas beneficial to itself first or charge the local ABB company extra. Thus, "We have had some things that would really help us here in China. But I don't even bother, because I know the reaction."

More than eighty percent of what the Centers of Excellence produce is going to be exported,[43] which makes it especially important that the partners of the licensor can manage the contemporary challenges and opportunities that can emerge. However, the BA divides the world markets into different areas in which the specific ABB companies are to be a so-called first source.[44] Between some of the licensors and the local ABB company this has resulted in certain disputes. For example,

> We are responsible for the Peoples Republic of China's market and are supposed to be the sole source (or rather first source) because we have the expertise for this market. Our technology partner in X-country quotes into this market on a regular basis, does not inform us, and competes against us, and takes orders at a lower prices. This can destroy our position in the market place.

According to the licensor, it does not quote in the local ABB company's market because if the final customers have foreign currency, they will prefer imported products. The licensor states that it does not go into the Chinese market and offer its products, but does get inquiries from ABB in Hong Kong and delivers to that company. The Hong Kong Company in turn sells the products directly to the Chinese customer after having increased the original price up to the market price, which is often several times higher in China than in Europe, for example. It is a decision of the ABB China management that the Hong Kong coordinated sales force shall sell the local ABB company's products on the Chinese market among imported products and those of the local joint venture. It is argued that it helps to have sales coordination, that is the decision as to whether the products should be imported or not.

The technology is owned today by the Centers of Excellence in Europe, the licensors, which are also the ones paying for all the product development. ABB has chosen these licensees to be responsible for becoming the company's world source of this specific technology. These units are responsible for developing new products and ensuring quality by arranging technical seminars about the technology and by keeping special technology parts—so-called "noble parts"—only at their factory. The strategic decision to keep special parts and the drawings of these parts at only one chosen factory enables the company to secure itself against competitors copying its products. Consequently, these parts will not be localized or purchased in China. However, for one product group (THS) there has been an organizational change, including the establishing of a unit called CHTET, which shall now own all new technology that is developed and also pay for the product development. This change now involves all product groups.

MULTICULTURAL

The current fashion, exemplified by ABB, is for firms to be "multicultural multinationals," which means that the company must be very sensitive to national differences.[45] Barnevik, the former CEO, has argued that a culturally diverse set of managers can be a source of strength. According to Barnevik, managers should not try to eradicate these differences and establish a uniform managerial culture. Rather, they should seek to understand these cultural differences, to empathize with the views of people from different cultures, and to make compromises for such differences. Barnevik believes that the advantage of building a culturally diverse cadre of global managers is to improve the quality of managerial decision making.[46]

ABB in China is typified by a culturally diverse set of managers, with a mixture of managerial ideas derived from the different managers' national backgrounds, different values, and different methods of working. It then depends on which stage in personal development the manager has reached if he or she is going to be influenced by and absorb the new climate. As one manager said, "If you are close to being retired you might not change so much, there isn't much point. But you can't work in the same way as you do at home—it just wouldn't work."

According to another manager, ABB is a very international company with a great deal of influence from Scandinavian culture. However, it is a mixture of many cultures, and the mix depends on where the ABB company is located. In China, the ABB culture is influenced by Chinese culture, by the environmental circumstances, and by the laws. It is stricter in China than it is, for example, in Europe, because there are more rules. In spite of that, the managers do not feel that the result is a subculture of the ABB culture, but rather a mixture of managers from different cultures—"we are a multidomestic company."

The top level of the ABB management, however, is seen as far away from the daily life at the subsidiary level in China, such as at the local ABB company. According to one of the managers, "between that level and here, it's like the Pacific Ocean." Most of the managers say, though, that what the top level, including Barnevik and Lindahl,[47] says sounds very good and that is how it should be. Some disagree:

> Sounds like I'm working for a different ABB than these guys are. What they talk about is re-

ally good and that is how it should be. But then when I sit back and go into the daily work and say that's not at all how it is. Somewhere along the line something gets lost between the theory and ideas at that level which is quite good. But when you get down to the working level and have to make it work something really gets lost along the way.

EXPATRIATES

It is the BA with its worldwide networks that recommends, after suggestions from local offices, who is going to be sent as an expatriate to China or any other country. Thereafter, the BA and the country level cooperate, but it is the latter that finally decides which potential foreign expatriate is appropriate. The expatriate must be able to fit into the system in China, for the costs involved are very high. It is estimated that an expatriate costs the company about $250,000 a year, due to the high taxes the company is paying to have a foreign employee.

As a corporation, ABB's identity is supported not only by its possession of a coordinating executive committee but also by an elite cadre of 500 global managers, which the top management shifts through a series of foreign assignments. Their job is intended to knit the organization together, to transfer expertise around the world, and to expose the company's leadership to differing perspectives.[48] However, ABB in China is not yet a closely knit country unit, for several reasons. First, the expatriates come from the outside and most of their contacts are back in the home country. Most expatriates claim that the home office does not understand how difficult it can be to work abroad and that they need support. As one expatriate put it, "sometimes it just feels like I'm standing in the desert screaming." The home office, on the other hand, often views the expatriates as a burden because they need so much support. The home office, along with the BA, chooses the candidates for foreign placement, even though it is argued it has little knowledge, or no knowledge at all, of how it really is to work in a given country. But it would be almost impossible for all the local offices to have insight into the working conditions in other countries.

As to growing a strong country unit, the expatriates themselves say that they are stationed in China for a relatively short time and thus are less able to build up informal networks. Apparently, little effort is made to establish an informal network because the few contact persons the managers have today will return home after a while and there is no formal way of contacting the replacing person. The formal LOTUS notes, a computer-based network that includes all managers worldwide, cannot compensate for this deficiency and help build the preferred strong country unit within China. Finally, the managers do not feel that they can offer the time, or the effort, to establish informal networks if these have to be rebuilt every two to three years due to the replacement of expatriates. A worldwide policy within the company limits the expatriates to operating as such for not more than five years at a time. Executives have questioned this policy, for, they say, "It is during the first year you learn what is going on and get into your new clothes. During the second year you get to know the people and the system, the third year you apply what you learned and the fourth year you start to make some changes—and this is very specific for developing countries."

Three years ago, the expatriates did no get any information or education about the country-specific situation before being sent out to ABB's subsidiaries in China. Today, when there are about 100 expatriates of twenty-five different nationalities in China, the approach has changed to some degree, but it is still mostly up to the prospective expatriate to collect material and prepare so that the acclimatization works out. Within the worldwide corporation, there is no policy of formal training for foreign assignments; rather, it is up to the expatriate's home office to prepare individuals. Some argue that "you could never prepare for the situation in China anyway, so any education wouldn't help." Others say that this attitude has resulted in a lot of problems with the expatriates, raising the company's costs even higher if the expatriate fails.

When it is time for the expatriates to return to the home office, they may feel unsure whether there are jobs for them back home. Thus, it is argued that it is very important for the expatriate to have as close a contact with the home office as possible and also to make use of the free trips home offered by the company.

THE CHINESE CHALLENGE

According to ABB, it wants to send out managers with preferably ten to fifteen years of experience. The task, however, is difficult, especially when the location may be in a rural area overseas and most managers with ten to fifteen years' experience have families, which are less likely to want to move to these areas. Sometimes, apparently, a manager gets sent to China rather than being fired—"they send the manager to where the pitfalls are greater and challenges bigger and potential risks are greater."

Research indicates that most expatriates have strong feelings about living in and adapting to the new environment in China. Newly arrived expatriates seem to enjoy the respect they get from the Chinese, and several managers said delightedly, "I love it here, and how could you not, you get a lot of respect just because you're a foreigner and life is just pleasant."

Some of the expatriates got to dislike the situation greatly after a longer stay, and a number of expatriates have asked to leave because their expectations about the situation in China have not been fulfilled.[49]

Some country-specific tasks have to do with teaching the Chinese employees to work in teams. The worldwide company ABB is especially focusing on creating an environment that fosters teamwork and promotes active participation among its employees.[50] This is, however, a big challenge for Western managers (the expatriates) because, it is argued, the Chinese employees have a hard time working in a group due to cultural and historical reasons. Some of the local ABB companies are said to have failed radically in their attempt to create teams, ad hoc groups, and the like because they have been in too much of a hurry. As was pointed out, "Here in China the management needs to encourage the teamwork a little bit, because it is a little against the culture and the nature of the people. This is not a question of lack of time for the managers, but I do not think we have the overall commitment to do it. Some of us feel strongly that we should, others that we can't." Because the expatriate management does not have the understanding or the commitment to teach local employees the company values, the quality at some companies has not been acceptable.

It is stated that ABB has a great advantage compared with other worldwide companies because of its top priority of building deep local roots by hiring and training local managers who know their local markets.[51] Replacing expatriates with local Chinese employees, where the local employees are set to be successors to the expatriates after a certain amount of years, shows the commitment to

the philosophy of having a local profile. However, as the Chinese employees are coming from an extremely different system from that of the Western expatriates, it is argued that it takes them quite a long time to get exposed to Western management practices. To ease this problem, and to teach Western management style, ABB China, among other companies, has recently set up an agreement with a business school in Beijing to arrange training for Chinese employees with good management potential. This is in a way specific for ABB China because in developed countries the employees are responsible for their own development.[52] Just recently ABB had its own school in Beijing for Chinese employees to learn ABB culture and management. The school had to close, however, because of the profit center philosophy that required the school to charge the individual ABB companies for teaching their employees. As few companies wanted to pay for the education, the school had to close.

ABB is also regularly sending about 100 local Chinese employees to an ABB company in a Western country every year. Having had several employees quit after the invested training, ABB has now taken precautions against this risk with a service commitment. It requires that the employee (or the person's new employer) pay back the training investment if he or she quits or sign an agreement to continue working for ABB a certain number of years. The problem of local employees quitting after ABB's investment in their training is evidenced by the personnel turnover rate—approximately 22 percent within ABB China. Many local employees seek the experience of working for an international company such as ABB and then move on to another job, which might be better paid.

However, by having local employees, the local ABB company is responsive to local conditions and sensitive to important cultural objectives, such as the Chinese "guanxi."[53] It has been decided that the local employees should take care of the customer contact since the expatriates are usually only stationed for a few years at one location and are consequently not able to build up strong connections with customers.

REORGANIZATION

ABB is a decentralized organization, based on delegated responsibility and the right to make decisions in order to respond quickly to customers' requirements. In the core of this complex organization are two principles: decentralization of responsibility and individual accountability. These principles have been very relevant in China, which is a relatively young country for ABB to be operating in.[54] Decentralization is highly developed and the expatriate[55] managers have a wide responsibility that would normally demand more than one specialist in a Western company. However, in some instances the organization is criticized for being too centralized, such as that the country manager needs to accept if an employer is flying overseas.

The changes in China happen very fast, and according to ABB brochures, the greatest efficiency gains lie in improving the way people work together.[56] Within the ABB China region, communication has, however, its shortcomings when companies with overlapping products or similar products do not exchange their information to any large degree or coordinate their marketing strategies. On the technical side, communication is frequent: a manager during one day usually receives up to 100 E-mails from other ABB employees. But procedures for building up effective informal communication are lacking between most ABB companies operating in China. The distances are large, and so a meeting demands a greater effort than in almost any other country in the world.

According to the former CEO, Percy Barnevik, the aim of the matrix organization is to make the company more bottom heavy than top heavy—"clean out the headquarters in Zurich and send everybody out, have independent companies operating in an entrepreneurial manner," as one respondent mentioned. It is further maintained in the company brochures, that these entrepreneurial business units have the freedom and motivation to run their own business with a sense of personal responsibility.[57]

However, the result from the matrix organization in China is that the ABB subsidiaries have ABB China's objectives (the country level) and the business area's (BA) objectives to follow. ABB China is measuring how the different companies are performing within China. The BA, on the contrary, is measuring how the specific products are performing on a worldwide basis and what the profitability is for the products. Each BA has a financial controller, and each country level also has one. "Rarely are the two coordinated, or do they meet. So you end up with one set of objectives from each . . . Duplication! Which one shall you follow?"

According to the ABB Mission Book, the roles in the two dimensions of the ABB matrix must be complementary.[58] It demands that both the individual company and headquarters are flexible and strive for extensive communication. This is the way to avoid the matrix interchange becoming cumbersome and slow. It is seen as the only way to "reap the benefits of being global (economies of scale, technological strength, etc.) and of being multidomestic (a high degree of decentralization and local roots in the countries in which we operate)."

For many years, ABB was widely regarded as an exemplary European company, yet it is undergoing a second major restructuring within four years. CEO Lindahl's restructuring is aimed at making the organization faster and more cost efficient.[59] Due to the demands of a more global market, there are reasons for getting rid of the regional structure and to concentrate more on the specific countries. The reorganization has basically dismantled one half of the matrix: the country management. Henceforth, the BAs will manage their businesses on a worldwide basis, and it is said that there will no longer be the confusion between BA and country management setting different objectives. At the same time, segments are split up (many BAs form a segment) to make them more manageable (for example, the transmission and distribution segment has been split into two segments: transmission and distribution). Thus, the general managers of the individual joint ventures and other units will have only one manager above them in the organization who has a global view of the business. In China, it also means the dismantling of the Hong Kong organization as well as the Asia Pacific organization.

According to Lindahl, the reorganization is preparation for a much faster rate of change in the markets and for the company to be able to respond more effectively to the demands of globalization. It is seen as an aggressive strategy to create a platform for future growth.

FUTURE VISION

CEO Lindahl's view of the future is that it can no longer be extrapolated, but has to be forecasted by creativity, imagination, ingenuity, and innovation, leading to action based not on what was, but on what could be. The corporate culture needs to be replaced by globalizing leadership and corporate values. ABB is focusing on this by creating a unified organization across national, cultural, and business borders.

On the path toward the next century, ABB is going to focus on several essential elements: a strong local presence; a fast and flexible organization; the best technology and products available; and excellent local managers who know the business culture, are able to cross national and business borders easily, and can execute the company's strategy faster than the competition.[60] The company's view is that "We are living in a rapidly changing environment, and our competitors will not stand still. In the face of this great challenge and opportunity, enterprises that adapt quickly and meet customer needs will be the winner, and this is the ultimate goal of ABB."[61]

Endnotes

1. "100 Years of Experience Ensures Peak Technology Today," ABB STAL AB, Finspong.
2. *Dagens Industri,* August 13, 1998, p. 25.
3. Ibid.
4. Jean-Claude Usunier, *Marketing Across Cultures.*
5. *Dagens Industri,* July 2, 1998.
6. David Smith, *Management Today* (April 1996), 49.
7. Ahlquist, Magnus, as editor; *The Recruiters' Guide to China,* by preface of Professor Michael Yahuda.
8. *Bizniz,* September 30, 1997.
9. Examples include VCD-player, CD-ROM player, mobile telephones, beepers, and video cameras.
10. Jeffrey E. Garten, "Opening the Doors for Business in China," *Harvard Business Review* (May–June 1998), 160–172.
11. *Månadens Affärer,* No. 11, November 1996 (searched through AFFÄRSDATA via http://www.ad.se/bibsam/).
12. *Dagens Industri* August 19, 1998 (searched through AFFÄRSDATA via http://www.ad.se/bibsam/).
13. Ibid.
14. Ahlquist, Magnus, as editor; *The Recruiters' Guide to China,* by preface of Professor Michael Yahuda.
15. Ibid.
16. Garten, "Opening the Doors for Business in China," pp. 167–171.
17. See the report from *Economist,* October 1998 (www.economist.com).
18. Hong Yung Lee, "The Implications of Reform for Ideology, State and Society in China," *Journal of International Affairs,* 39, no. 2, pp. 77–90.
19. An interview with Premier Zhu Rongji in *China Daily,* March 20, 1998, p. 2.
20. *China Daily, Business Weekly,* Vol. 18, No. 5479, March 29–April 4, 1998, p. 2.
21. Hoon-Halbauer, Sing Keow; *Management of Sino-Foreign Joint Ventures.*
21. Yuan Lu, *Management Decision-Making in Chinese Enterprises.*
22. Ibid.
23. Jun Ma, *Intergovernal Relations and Economic Management in China.*
24. Oiva Laaksonen, *Management in China during and After Mao in Enterprises, Government, and Party.*
25. Yanan Ju, *Understanding China,* p. 45.
26. Quanyu Hwang, *Business Decision Making in China.*
27. Hong Yung Lee, "The Implications of Reform."
28. Yuan Lu, *Management Decision-Making in Chinese Enterprises.*
29. Ibid.
30. Hong Yung Lee, "The Implications of Reform."
31. Yuan Lu, *Management Decision-Making in Chinese Enterprises.*
32. *Månadens Affärer,* No. 11, November 1996.
33. *Economist,* Oct. 28, 1995 (searched http://www.economist.com).
34. Because China is still a quite closed country, Chinese people are not able to obtain foreign currency except in very limited amounts.
35. ABB, "The Art of Being Local," ABB Corporate Communications Ltd., printed in Switzerland.
36. ABB brochure, "You Can Rely on the Power of ABB," ABB Asea Brown Boveri Ltd., Department CC-C, Zurich.
37. Technology partner (in this case) = Center of Excellence (CE) = Licensors.
38. ABB's Mission, Values, and Policies.
39. HV Switchgear, ABB, ABB Business Area H. V. Switchgear, printed in Switzerland.
40. ABB, "You Can Rely on the Power of ABB."
41. Licensing is defined here as a form of external production where the owner of technology or proprietary right (licensor) agrees to transfer this to a joint venture in China, which is responsible for local production (licensee).
42. During the study, this has changed to some degree due to a unit called CHTET being introduced.
43. http://www.abb.se/swg/switchgear/index.htm (November 1997).
44. First source = you are the first source, but if you cannot meet the customer's requirements the second source steps in.
45. *Economist,* Jan. 6, 1996 (searched from http://www.economist.com)
46. ibid.
47. Göran Lindahl is the present CEO and chairman of the board.
48. *Economist,* Jan. 6, 1996.
49. There are two types of common but false expectations expatriates have when coming to China. Either they believe they are going to make a lot of money or they think they are going to experience the old Chinese culture—a culture that most of the time does not correspond to the culture of today's China.
50. ABB's Mission, Values, and Policies, Zurich, 1991.
51. ABB, "The Art of Being Local."
52. ABB's Mission, Value, and Policies.
53. Guanxi = connections, relations.
54. ABB set up its first office, a representative office, in 1979.
55. Expatriate is a person who has a working placement outside the home country.
56. ABB, "You Can Rely on the Power of ABB."
57. Ibid.
58. ABB's Mission, Values, and Policies.
59. *Dagens Industri,* August 13, 1998, p. 25.

60. "Meeting the Challenges of the Future," presentation given to the Executives' Club of Chicago, October 16, 1997.
61. ABB, "Leading the Way in Efficient and Reliable Supply of Electric Power," ABB Transmission and Distribution Ltd., Hong Kong.

APPENDIX

Motorola

Motorola was involved with their business in Russia and faced some problems with Glasnost and the decline of the country. At that time, the founder of the company, Galvin, realized that there was no future in Russia and declared that China was the country where the growth was to be. Consequently, Motorola established its first representative office in China in 1987, and has grown very fast ever since. Today, China generates more than 10 percent of Motorola's sales and the company has its major businesses in China.

Motorola has found that modernization in China happens very fast and all its competitors are present in the country, but it is still predicting China to be the potential leader in Asia for its kind of business. The customers also have high expectations of the products Motorola is offering because the products are considered very expensive. However, the problem the company is facing in China "is that Motorola is growing very fast and it is like chasing a speeding train and trying to catch up with it."

At present, Motorola has 12,000 employees and 200 expatriates in China, whereas the goal is that Chinese successors will take over the job of the expatriates. The expatriates are sent out on assignments for two to three years, with the possibility of renewal with a one-two rotation, but limited to a maximum of six years as an expatriate. The expatriates must meet high demands and cope with the difficulties of teaching teamwork to local employees. That aspect is very important within the company since all the strategy planning is done in teams. When the contract time for the expatriate has expired,

> You have done your job when the time comes and you have left the company and everything is working smoothly, but if everything is falling apart, you are a failure as an expatriate and have not taught a successor.

However, progress has been made in developing the company's local employees. Motorola has set up training abroad. The training, nevertheless, is preferably held within China, with rotation assignments and training at Motorola University. This company university was set up in 1994 when the company found that the Chinese universities did not turn out sufficiently well-trained students. Within the company there is, however, a requirement that every employee worldwide shall have at least forty hours of training, which is argued to possibly be exceeded in China. The view is that there must be a combination of good training and mentor development to get successful people. Motorola admits that it does make a mistake by not providing enough training for foreign expatriates before they come to China. It is also said that they have noticed that overseas Chinese often do not do well fitting into the system, even though they speak Chinese, or as quoted: "You get more understanding if you look like a foreigner and make some mistakes than if you don't. Overseas Chinese are measured through other standards than other foreigners."

Other problems the company is facing concerning expatriation, is that some expatriates just cannot handle the situation in China. If an expatriate fails, this has to be handled with care; otherwise the person looses face when coming back to the home office. The company also has pointed out that it needs expatriates with ten to fifteen years of experience in order to teach the local employees the company values and to transfer company knowledge. However, the people who are willing to change addresses and move to China are the younger employees with less than five years of experience.

The expatriates are often responsible for transferring technology knowledge and helping to get projects started, especially in the case of the newly set-up Center of Excellence in Tianjin, where $750 million was invested. This was Motorola's first manufacturing research laboratory outside the United States. In all the company has invested $1.1 billion in China and plans to invest another $1 to 1.5 million. Motorola has also set up two branches of worldwide training universities to educate customers, suppliers, and government officials, as well as its own employees. The money invested in China is said to be from the earnings within the whole enterprise, with the motivation that the Chinese market is going to be huge. Sincere commitment has been made and the present CEO, Gary Tucker, is said to have expressed the following:

"When Motorola has come to your country they never leave ... We manufacture in China, because this is where our market is. We get wealth by going to a lot of countries around the world and then doing well in that country."

The expansion strategy in China is through joint ventures. However, since it is important that the Chinese partners bring something of value, they have to be approved by the CEO. Other than that, it is argued that the company has become "so decentralized that it has become bad," and that the company desires to reorganize more along customer than product lines. A practical reorganization has taken place to move everybody operating in Beijing to the same newly built headquarters. However, entrepreneurial activities are also argued to be of importance, but difficult in practice due to financial motivation and autonomy.

In China the products are localized by having Chinese characters on the cellular phones and pagers. In 1987, Motorola started selling pagers and thought there would not be a big market because the telephone network was not well established, but then the company invented codebooks, which made possible two-way communication, and it also worked in Hong Kong, Singapore, and Taiwan. After five years of operation in China, the company has not yet been able grow deep roots in the market. Nevertheless, the investments in the country and efforts to make the company a Chinese one are argued to be the reason for the depth of the localization and make the company unshakable. To show its seriousness about putting in deep roots in China, Motorola has invested huge sums in sponsoring environmental protection, providing scholarships to students, building labs at universities, and donating money to primary schools in rural areas.[1]

The worldwide organization is seen as a "pyramid," with the corporate on top and business units underneath—"then put the apex at the bottom." The corporate office works as the glue that holds the organization together. In 1997, Motorola conducted a reorganization to better reflect the global nature of the business.[2] The coordination is also said to be safeguarded by this new formal structure. However, the informal information flow is argued to be better, but pointed out as probably overused. The information flow is mostly through E-mails. A manager gets approximately 70 to 100 a day, of which less than 30 percent are regarded as really useful.

All the controllers or general managers in the joint ventures get together quarterly to counsel, to solve problems, and give support to each other. Information is encouraged, but no system is developed to track what is going on in all the six districts in China where the company is operating. Competition between the different units is a common problem and is said to confuse customers. This problem cannot be solved because of the matrix organization.

What makes Motorola a worldwide company is argued to be that it has a set of key common beliefs or guiding principles from the role model and father figure of the company, Galvin: "uncompromising integrity and constant respect for people— that is what makes us Motorola." This is the principal code of conduct that Motorola practices, and which the management has to reread and sign every two years.

Motorola has made it clear that it has had to change the way it does things because it is operating in the Chinese market: it needs to show face, build relations, and have its people go to ceremonial meetings. Regarding relations, it is essential to make sure that the partner is reliable, that the business makes sense, and that it is legal, which is pointed out to be opposite from the West. However, it is then stated that the Motorola company always looks the same all over the world; it is the expatriates and their families that have made an effort to adapt to the surroundings.

China is a very difficult country for a huge company like Motorola to be operating in "because they would like to control the system and everything takes a long time because they will make sure that you are not cheating. You must be able to work with all the people that come from different departments and to let them trust you. Ordinary things like getting water, electricity, etc. is a huge problem. Doing business in the Chinese system is a challenge and therefore creates pressure because you get frustrated.

Procter & Gamble

In August 1998 China's largest international employer had been in China for ten successful years. Procter and Gamble, or P&G, has approximately 5,000 employees and 100 expatriates spread over eleven joint ventures and wholly owned enterprises in the country. This year it was ranked on *Fortune* magazine's "World's Most Admired Companies" list. Currently, the biggest market for the company is China, where new companies are being established. Before establishing companies in China, P&G did a feasibility study. However, as with most other feasibility studies done in China, the information was outdated even though it was only a year old, and people were criticized for not having sufficient knowledge about the country's specific situation.

The expatriates sent to China for the P&G account are said to have no other preparation than the company's deep culture, which will support them. Furthermore, a constant effort is being made within the company to put different cultural backgrounds together. Cultural values are also written down and are consistent all over the world. However, due to that, the different expatriates have a wide variety of cultural backgrounds and their management style is colored by their culture. It is pointed out that this mixture of management styles might confuse the local Chinese employees.

The main benefit gained for an expatriate is the one offered in the daily work. One exception are the expatriate salespeople, who get a whole year of orientation and language training. In line with the localization demands, the number of expatriates is decreasing. Because of the high costs involved of having expatriates, who are mostly three to four levels up in the organization, one of the key strategies is to develop local employees. Everybody who is an expatriate for P&G has a sponsor back home, a contact. It is deemed essential to keep in touch with the sponsor, and people are also encouraged to go back home once a year at the company's expense. There is no official limit in expatriate policy within the company on the length of stay for expatriates, but most of them are on a three-year contract. The expatriates are said to be a very close group—"we are all in this together and we have a common vision"—although as yet there is no expatriate network.

The optimal goal for P&G is to develop the organization so that it can be a Chinese-run company. Today, everything is made in the Chinese P&G factories for internal use and, just a couple of months ago, the company opened up a research center in Beijing, in cooperation with a prominent university.[3] A reason for opening a research center in Beijing is a bet on the future that the world's largest group of consumers will have a large say on how P&G will market and develop in the rest of the world. If the company has developed a good idea in China, the company will analyze how to reapply those ideas in the rest of the world. The same would be true of ideas developed at the headquarters in Cincinnati or in the previous Center of Excellence in Brussels.

Counterfeits are the greatest competition for the company, and an extensive problem. However, P&G does not sell all its products in China, and the quality of the products sold is not as high as it is in Western countries. The Chinese customers are said to be unable to pay for better value. Nevertheless, the company is trying to offer a consistency of quality the Chinese consumers are willing to pay for.

In the Chinese P&G organization, fewer layers are developed and the decision making takes a shorter time within the organization, because the company evolved very quickly and the market is said to be so dynamic and changing that P&G has not had the time to implement the layer. Consequently, the Chinese organization and structure are not the same as in other countries, but it is argued that the Chinese organization is, by all accounts, more efficient and that P&G will implement some of its features in other countries. At the current time a reorganization is taking place within the worldwide P&G, and the culture and reward system are being changed as well—all to make the company more flexible.[4]

As for the Chinese situation, "*guanxi*" is mentioned, which is said to be difficult for the expatriates to establish and consequently the company relies on the local staff. The local employees get an immense amount of education at P&G's own school. Also, expatriates at the company have the explicit responsibility to deal with company principles, values, and all the technical specifics for P&G. However, "they are so into running the business that sometimes the coaching of the locals is not possible."

One of the challenges Procter & Gamble faces in China is the difficulty in dealing with the government. The company has dealt with this by searching for a sophisticated government-relations manager who shall report not only to the head of operations in China but also to the chief executive of the company.[5]

Nestlé

In the beginning of the 1980s, China asked the world's largest food company, Nestlé, to come build "milk streets" in the country. China was unfamiliar with how to produce milk and turned to Nestlé, whose core business is actually milk powder. From that time the company has grown strongly in China and now has almost 4,000 employees, 200 of them foreign expatriates.

Today, Nestlé is regarded as having come from Swiss roots and turned into a transnational corporation.[6] The company has a history of being locally adaptive. During the First World War, Nestlé gave its local managers increasing independence from the beginning, to avoid disruptions in distribution.[7] This resulted in a great deal of Nestlé's operations being established at other locations than at their headquarters in Switzerland. Another cause was the company's belief that the consumers' taste was very local and that there were no synergy effects to be gained by standardizing the products. However, in 1993 the company started to rethink its belief in localization due to the increasing competition in the industry. Nestlé has acquired several local brands, influenced by its own country culture, which has caused it to standardize wherever possible.[8]

However, although the company is growing in China, it must be pointed out that it is not always selling products with as much margin as desired. The company is said to have as high a quality of products as they have in other countries, but the downside is that they must have lower margins in order to be competitive, which might not always be profitable. On the question "Why Nestlé has to be in China"? the following was expressed:

> "It is because China is a large country and if you have a company that is present in more than 100 countries, you see it as a must for all international companies to be present there. We supply all over the world and it is our obligation to bring food to the people—which is the company's priority."

Nestlé entered China with a long-term strategy to be in the country for a long period of time and from then the strategy was always set to focus on the long-run perspective. Nestlé's overall approach is "Think global and act local!" The company's strategy is guided by several fundamental principles, for instance, that "Nestlé's existing products will grow through innovation and renovation while maintaining a balance in geographic activities and product lines."[9]

With regard to the local Chinese employees, they get a few days of Nestlé education to learn about the Nestlé culture, but the expatriates have less training about going to another country. It is

up to the home country to decide if it is necessary to train expatriates before sending them on an often three-year foreign assignment. However, leadership talent is highly valued within the company and consequently Nestlé has developed courses for this. The managers can independently develop their leadership talent, without any connection with the specific company style or culture. Community centers have been established to help expatriates with their contacts, supporting these expatriates psychologically and even offering language training.

In 1997, Nestle's "The Basic Nestlé Management and Leadership Principles" was published. It aims to make "the Nestlé spirit" generally known throughout the organization by means of discussions, seminars, and courses.[10] According to the CEO of Nestlé China, Theo Klauser, this publication is the key factor in Nestlé's corporate culture and started the company's international expansion 130 years ago.[11]

Within the organization of Nestlé China, the company has developed a specific structure due to the joint venture configuration. The information flow is seen as easy and smooth between these regions, thanks to the company concentrating its activities in only three regions in China. However, communication is said to be on a very high level, although it is argued that it is not even necessary to get all levels involved. As an example, only one unit in China takes care of all the marketing. At the same time each Nestlé company in China is responsible for its own turnover rate, which is said to create the flexible and decentralized company Nestlé is today. Quite unique for a worldwide company, Nestlé does not have any external E-mail network, and this is believed to concentrate the flow of information within the company.

A major challenge indicated for Nestlé in China is the effort in building long-term relationships to establish Nestlé as the leading food company. The difficulty is bringing the products to a more acceptable level in terms of profitability. Legal difficulties are also more important than in any other country. Other challenges are the issues concerning change, summed up as follows:

> Change happens every couple of months here, that is how the environment is, a lot of employees come from other more stable countries and sometimes find it difficult with all the changes. Change is how things are in China—it is nor-

mal. It is when something doesn't change, that is when you get worried! It is expected to change! Different from other countries where changes can be difficult to get.

Appendix Endnotes

1. Jeffrey E. Garten, "Opening the Doors for Business in China," *Harvard Business Review* (May-June 1998), 174-175.
2. Motorola Annual Report, 1997.
3. Qinghua University.
4. Procter & Gamble Annual Report, 1998.
5. Garten, "Opening the Doors for Business in China," *Harvard Business Review* (May-June 1986), 59-60.
6. http://www.Nestlé.com/html/home.html (September 1998).
7. J. A. Quelch and E. J. Hoff, "Customizing Global Marketing," *Harvard Business Review* (May-June 1986), 59-60.
8. Brorsson, Skarsten, Torstensson; *Marknadsföring på den inre markanden—Standardisering eller Anpassning,* Thesis at Lund University, 1993.
9. http://www.Nestlé.com/html/h2h.html (September 1998).
10. Nestlé Management Report, 1997.
11. Interview with CEO of Nestlé China, Theo Klauser, *Metro* (July 1998), 27.

Sandvik AB (A)

This case was prepared by Robin Teigland, Assistant Professor Julian Birkinshaw, and Professor Roderick E. White of the Richard Ivey School of Business, The University of Western Ontario, Canada.

In the fall of 1996, Clas Åke Hedström, CEO of the Sandvik Group, was reviewing the progress of the three initiatives he had undertaken since assuming leadership of the group in 1994. First, his push for corporatewide profitable growth, helped along by a strengthening global economy, had been successful. During 1995, revenues rose by 17 percent, while net profits went up by 54 percent. Further growth was expected. Second, Hedström had also changed the group's conservative financial policy. Dividends were increased to 50 percent of net profits over the business cycle. Third, Hedström was actively pushing for greater synergies among the six Sandvik business areas. But here progress was proving more difficult to measure.

All of these initiatives were intended to enhance shareholder value. Sandvik was viewed by most investors as a highly dependable, if unglamorous, asset. (See Figure 1 for shareprice performance.) As explained by one analyst,

> Sandvik is reliable . . . year after year, Sandvik's results are on the plus side of our expectations . . . it is seldom exciting, it never surprises by bolting in some unexpected direction, nor does management make the kind of bold plays that put butterflies in the stomach.

At the same time, Sandvik received its share of pointed questions. For example, what did management intend to do with its cash hoard? An analyst stated:

> We expect more action from an essentially debt-free company with liquid assets exceeding SEK 5 billion . . . we wonder if Sandvik has ever heard of something called "leverage" to enhance return on shareholders' equity.

Hedström had taken action on this matter by increasing the dividend, lifting the overall growth ambition for the Sandvik Group and putting plans in place for a share repurchase.

Another line of inquiry was directed at Sandvik's portfolio of businesses. Some observers saw Sandvik as six stand-alone businesses, several with few, if any, operational links to the others. In many countries, the corporate strategy of unrelated diversification had become decidedly unpopular. A wave of corporate refocusing, sell-offs, and demergers resulted.[1] It was suggested that Sandvik could enhance shareholder value by selling one or more of its business areas. Indeed, takeover, or the threat of takeover, had forced some major corporations to restructure their business portfolios. Even though there was not as active a market for corporate control in Sweden, Sandvik did have reason to be concerned about changes in ownership and control. Sandvik's largest shareholder (25 percent) had recently announced its intention to sell its Sandvik holding. (See Table 1).

Sandvik's six businesses shared a common history, corporate culture, and corporate identity. While there was a historical relationship (see Figure 2), their activities had diverged over time. Since 1984, Sandvik's different business areas had operated with

FIGURE I

Monthly Share Price
Performance for
Sandvik, 1986–1996

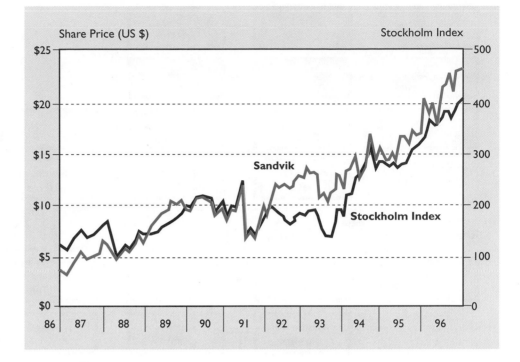

a very high level of autonomy. Even so, Sandvik corporate management was averse to any suggestions that the group be broken up. "You would not put these six businesses together today, but that does not mean you should break them up either," explained Leif Sunnermalm, the executive vice president. It was believed there were many benefits for Sandvik businesses to be part of the group, and

there were many other areas where additional benefits could be gained. These potential benefits lay behind the current drive for greater cooperation among businesses. But Hedström recognized that if the benefits of being part of the group could not be realized, then the argument for breaking the group apart became more compelling. The whole had to be worth more than the sum of its parts.

TABLE I

Largest Shareholders of Sandvik AB as of December 1995

	Percentage of Voting Rights	Percentage of Shares
Skanska AB	26.1	20.3
Investment funds of the Swedish savings banks	10.4	10.1
National Swedish pension fund	7.8	6.2
Svenska Handelsbanken pension foundation	5.0	3.9
The Swedish staff pension foundation	3.9	3.6
SEB Investment funds	2.7	2.3
Folksam	2.4	1.9
National Swedish pension insurance fund	2.3	1.8
Labor market insurance AB	2.2	1.8
Skandia	1.9	1.8
Svenska Handelsbanken's investment funds	1.8	1.7
Nordbanken's investment funds	1.5	1.2

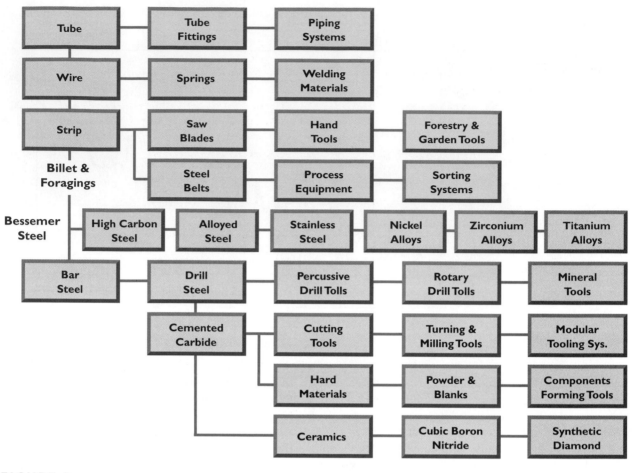

FIGURE 2

The Sandvik Evolution

Hedström and the executive group had begun to look for ways of achieving synergies among the businesses *without* centralizing decision making. At every opportunity, the executive group communicated its belief that Sandvik had to become a more integrated organization, to ensure that "the whole was greater than the sum of the parts." The corporate executives' enthusiasm for building an integrated Sandvik was tempered by a recurring worry: that employees throughout the company would see the changes as a step backward, as a reestablishment of central control over the six autonomous business areas. While this was not the intention, corporate management recognized the need to proceed very carefully, ensuring that the push for synergies did not jeopardize the effectiveness of Sandvik's existing organizational structure.

The process of change would not be easy because many managers at all levels did not see the need for greater integration. Hedström and his team began to consider the best ways of moving ahead.

SANDVIK HISTORY

The Early Years—1862 to 1941

Sandvik AB had its origins in a small steel company, Göransson Högbo Stål & Jernwerks, founded in 1862 in the town of Sandviken, 200 kilometers north of Stockholm, Sweden. The company was the first in the world to manufacture and sell steel using the Bessemer method. A reorganization of the company in 1868 led to the establishment of Sandvikens Jernverks AB, which was renamed Sandvik AB in 1972.

From its historical roots in steel and in a provincial Swedish town, Sandvik developed over the next century into a global materials technology engineering company, and one of Sweden's largest exporters. In 1995, Sandvik comprised more than 200 companies and employed more than 30,000 people in 130 countries. Its sales were SEK30 billion (approximately $4.5 billion), with 90 percent of sales outside of Sweden. (See Table 2)

Like many other Swedish industrial firms, Sandvik had developed an export orientation and an innovation-driven business philosophy. The company's operating philosophy evolved during the late nineteenth century. It could be summarized as

1. a conscious striving for the manufacture of high value-added products, which could bear the costs of transportation.
2. a firm commitment to R&D.
3. the identification of global needs for advanced niche products, which could be standardized to provide economies of scale but were uninteresting for bulk steel producers.
4. product development in close cooperation with customers.
5. the marketing of products through its own distribution channels, either wholly owned subsidiaries or exclusive agents.

Throughout its history, Sandvik had remained true to these principles.

TABLE 2

Sandvik Financial Results, 1990–1995*

	1995	1994	1993	1992	1991	1990
Invoiced sales, SEK M	29,700	25,285	21,770	17,217	17,558	18,256
Operating profit before depreciation and financial increase	6,265	4,550				
Profit after financial income and expenses, SEK M	5,620	3,811	1,764	1,486	1,776	2,842
as % of invoicing	19	15	8	9	10	16
Net profit for the year, SEK M	3,727	2,436	1,069	1,112	1,248	2,380
Earnings per share, SEK	13.40	8.75	3.85	4.05	4.55	8.70
Dividend per share (1996: as proposed), SEK	6.00	3.75	2.25	1.90	1.80	1.70
Pay-out ratio, %	45	40	58	47	40	20
Equity capital, SEK M	18,503	16,013	14,364	13,538	12,693	11,928
Equity ratio, %	64	59	60	59	57	54
Debt/equity ratio, times	0.1	0.2	0.2	0.2	0.3	0.4
Liquid assets, SEK M	6,893	6,591	5,171	4,864	4,814	5,251
Return on equity capital, %	21.6	16.0	7.7	8.5	10.1	21.8
Return on net assets, %	28.0	21.7	12.0	10.4	12.9	19.2
Investment in property, plant, and equipment, SEK M	2,050	1,229	886	886	1,021	1,161
Total investments, SEK M	2,092	1,575	964	1,311	1,761	1,715
Cash flow, SEK	164	1,215	1,425	1,645	882	1,486
Number of employees, 31 Dec.	29,946	29,450	26,869	28,617	26,237	25,781

*Key figures for 1994 and earlier have been adjusted to reflect the revised definitions that have been applied from 1995.

Around the turn of the century, Sandvik's emphasis on high-value added products led the company to expand from its base in Bessemer steel production into the emerging markets for specialty steel. For example, the company moved into markets that required hardness, cleanliness, dimensional stability, and blemish-free surfaces. End products made with Sandvik steel included corsets, gramophone needles, pens, umbrellas, and pocket watches. One important new product introduced in this era was Sandvik's cold-rolled strip steel, which became widely used for the manufacture of wood saws. This led to the development of a large saw product line. It eventually became the Saws and Tools Business area. Sandvik was one of the first companies to produce steel conveyer belts. Steel belts became a major product line and provided the base for the creation of a distinct business area, Process Systems.

International growth developed rapidly, and by 1914, 80 percent of Sandvik's sales occurred outside Sweden. The company experienced a downturn during the First World War and in the interwar period, but export levels remained high. By 1937, the company had established subsidiaries in thirteen countries in Europe and North America.

Diversification and Growth—1941 to 1981

In 1941, the management group made the critical decision to invest in an emerging technology called cemented carbide. Cemented carbide is a powdered metallurgical product, made primarily of tungsten, carbide, and cobalt, and it has a hardness approaching that of diamonds.[2] One of Sandvik's key competitors, Fagersta Bruks AB, had already begun experimenting with cemented carbide. It appeared to have great potential in the metalworking, mining, and forestry industries. Sandvik acquired the necessary cemented carbide technology. The new business, named Coromant, was placed under the direction of Wilhelm Haglund.

For the first few years, Coromant struggled to commercialize its cemented carbide technology. The Sandvik board even considered shutting down the business. But Haglund's foresight and determination were eventually rewarded, and cemented carbide rapidly became one of Sandvik's core technologies. By the 1980s, the Coromant business area was the largest and most profitable in the Sandvik Group. In addition, the Hard Materials and Rock

Tools business areas both evolved out of the group's cemented carbide technology.

While the cemented carbide product lines began to flourish, the steel operations experienced a downturn in demand during the 1950s. In order to reduce the effect of future downturns, Sandvik decided to focus on value-added steel products. One of these was seamless stainless steel tubes. After big investments during the 1960s, it became an important product for the Steel business area.

Throughout the 1950s and 1960s, Sandvik experienced a high level of growth, driven both by increased demand for cemented carbide products and by further internationalization. Under Haglund's leadership, the company increased the number of its foreign subsidiaries from thirteen in 1957 to thirty-five in 1967. In the 1970s and early 1980s, Sandvik continued to grow, but with an increasing reliance on acquisitions, which were typically relatively small companies in closely related areas of expertise. By 1980, Sandvik had 33,289 employees. However, in 1981 the world economy experienced the worst industrial recession since the 1930s. Sandvik was severely affected, and its profits fell from SEK746 million in 1979 to SEK310 million in 1982.

Crisis and Renewal—1982 to 1994

In order to return Sandvik to previous profit levels, the management group realized that significant changes needed to be made. In addition to reducing the work force to 24,000, management proposed some major organizational changes. For a long time Sandvik had been structured into divisions under a parent company. Managers reported to division management, as well as to functional management in the parent company. This dual reporting system had created a high level of bureaucracy, and delayed decision making.

In 1983 a decentralized organizational structure was established. Six independent business areas, two service companies, and three regional companies for peripheral markets were established. The organization structure still closely resembled the one created in 1984 (see Figure 3). The parent company was reduced to a management group with a staff of just fifty people. Sandvik announced to the public, "Our goal with the new structure is to delegate responsibility as well as to achieve an awareness of results and costs at all levels and a decreased bureaucracy with shorter decision routes."

FIGURE 3

The Sandvik Organization

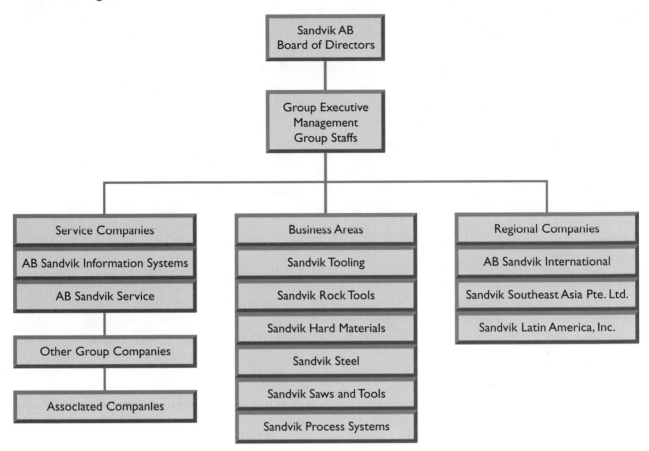

The structure of the Sandvik organization is shown in the diagram above. The underlying principle was established in 1983 and it consists of six separate business areas that are responsible for development, production, and sales of the group's products. Each business area has subsidiaries, or divisions, within joint Sandvik companies, in all major markets.

Outside the main markets, Sandvik's products are marketed by three regional companies that operate through local subsidiaries, sales offices, and agents.

Two companies provide general services; their principal customers are the Sandvik units in Sweden, but they also sell services to subsidiaries outside Sweden and to external customers.

Sandvik's organization also comprises a number of associated companies whose operations generally pertain to one of the business areas. The other group companies sector includes companies or groups of companies whose marketing strategies differ from those of the six business areas.

However, the financial problems were not over. In August 1983, Sandvik lost SEK219 million largely due to an unforeseen rise of the dollar against the Swedish krona. The company's major shareholder, Skanska AB, decided that it needed to take a stronger stand regarding the management of Sandvik. In 1984, Skanska increased its holding in Sandvik from 11 to 37 percent. Percy Barnevik, a former Sandvik employee and at that time CEO of ASEA, was appointed nonexecutive chairman, and Per-Olof Eriksson, formerly president of Seco Tools, was named CEO.

With the new organization and management team, Sandvik quickly returned to profitability.

Eriksson emphasized the need for clearly defined accountability. Each business was assessed on its return on net assets worldwide. Foreign-based businesses reported directly to their respective business heads, with only a token line of reporting into their country operation (in order to satisfy legal requirements). The corporate staff was kept very small.

Unlike his predecessors, Eriksson saw profitability as his primary objective, and growth as secondary. He became known as a cost-conscious leader, careful to avoid unnecessary expenditures and cautious in his growth plans. He was also visibly frugal in his own lifestyle and was frequently seen cycling to work from his home in Sandviken. Under Eriksson's leadership, Sandvik became a consistent performer, with ten unbroken years of profitable growth. In 1994, Eriksson retired and was replaced by Hedström, president of Sandvik Coromant since 1980.

SANDVIK'S BUSINESSES

There were six principal business areas and a number of service and regional companies. Sandvik Steel and Sandvik Tooling were by far the largest, with 33 percent and 32 percent of net sales, respectively. Rock Tools, Hard Materials, Saws and Tools, and Process Systems were the remaining business areas, each with between 9 and 15 percent of net sales. (See Tables 3 to 5.)

Sandvik Tooling

Sandvik Tooling had three parts: Sandvik Coromant; CTT Tools; and a small automation business.

Coromant   Coromant was consistently the highest return business in the Sandvik Group. It provided a product line of cemented carbide tools and tooling systems for metalworking products. These products had a very high value-to-weight ratio, and were typically transported by airfreight. The company supplied all major markets. In the United States, Coromant had two major competitors, Valenite and Kennametal. These competitors were expanding their activities through acquisitions in Europe, where Coromant was the market leader. Coromant was also the most solidly established non-Japanese competitor in Japan.

Coromant was recognized as the leading global player in its industry. In large part, this leadership

position stemmed from a stream of product and process innovations. Products introduced during the last five years accounted for approximately 50 percent of total sales. Coromant was also the first company to introduce industry-scale diamond-coated carbide cutting inserts. Six per cent of annual turnover was invested in R&D.

Coromant was considered innovative in order processing, production, and logistics. Starting in 1984, a team developed a computer-aided purchase processing system (CAPP), which streamlined the entire order, design, and production process.[3] At the same time, Coromant introduced flow groups at its worldwide manufacturing facilities in order to promote flexibility. These changes enabled the company to reduce lead time from 50 days in 1984 to 2.3 days in 1995. A further aspect of Coromant's strategy was the development of its direct delivery system. In 1995, a change in the roles of the two European central warehouses (Gimo, Sweden, and Schiedam, the Netherlands) made possible a faster and more reliable supply of products to continental Europe and U.S. customers. Deliveries were made directly to the end users, generally within twenty-four hours.

In 1995 Coromant introduced its *CoroKey* program, to simplify the sales of Coromant's products. The program included a catalogue with a condensed product program, packaging with essential cutting data printed on the label, and coding and marking of the inserts to facilitate identification and ensure optimal use. Coromant also led the industry in information technology developments. In 1996, the company developed an extensive Intranet application, which provided immediately feedback on the relative cost and service levels of the different plants around the world. The CAPP system also speeded up the processing of tailored customer orders.[4]

In order to meet increasing demand, the business area made a substantial number of investments in 1994 and 1995. Management expanded the Gimo and U.S. facilities, acquired MKTS, a Russian cemented carbide company, and established a wholly owned production facility in China.

CTT Tools   CTT Tools was acquired in 1993 from the Swedish ball-bearing manufacturer SKF. CTT complemented Sandvik's cemented carbide product line with high-speed steel cutting tools and tooling systems. CTT Tools had approximately 10 percent of the global market. A comprehensive rationalization and restructuring program was performed at CTT between 1992 and 1994. Positive

TABLE 3

Key Figures for Sandvik Business Areas
(in SEK millions)

I. Tooling	1995	1994	1993	1992	1991
Invoiced sales	9576	8178	7184		
Profit before financial items	2436	1509	972		
Investment	747	397	240		
Number of employees	11010	10995	9919		
Ia. Coromant					
Invoiced sales	7184	6124	5287	4584	4884
Investment	616	364	200	218	332
Number of employees	7892	7911	6606	7186	7783
Ib. CTT Tools					
Invoiced sales	2334	2050	1897		
Investment	129	33	40		
Number of employees	3047	3084	3313		
II. Rock Tools					
Invoiced sales	2015	1955	1812	1510	1579
Profit before financial items	219	219	130	—	—
Investment	49	45	29	45	31
Number of employees	1877	1814	1840	1894	2063
III. Hard Materials					
Invoiced sales	1224	1029	893	808	655
Profit before financial items	185	135	51	—	—
Investment	102	60	46	73	43
Number of employees	1447	1446	1390	1574	1316
IV. Steel					
Invoiced sales	9807	7752	6450	5267	5570
Profit before financial items	1623	1014	461	159	279
Investment	452	293	289	253	277
Number of employees	7257	6903	5951	5917	6178
V. Saws and Tools					
Invoiced sales	2674	2583	2363	2049	1437
Profit before financial items	184	185	3	−82	−16
Investment	102	86	74	117	136
Number of employees	2998	3050	3060	3275	3676
VI. Process Systems					
Invoiced sales	1810	1603	1190	1190	1290
Profit before financial items	101	156	43	21	166
Investment	65	44	48	37	49
Number of employees	888	1037	789	755	755

TABLE 4

Overview of Sandvik's Business Areas

Hard Materials
R &D   Stockholm, Coventry (England), France
Manufacturing   United Kingdom and Denmark: two large highly specialized units for global market
                    10 local manufacturing units to supply customized production locally (five in Europe, five in
                    rest of world)
Sales   Direct market coverage in 50 countries (own units in 25, direct sales in 25)

Rock Tools
R&D   Stockholm
Manufacturing   In 13 countries with 30% of total production in Sweden
Sales   Direct market coverage in 50 countries

Coromant
R&D   Stockholm
Manufacturing   Main production in Gimo, Sweden
                    In 20 countries, including the United States (Fairlawn, N.J.), the United Kingdom (Feather-
                    stone), Russia, Poland (JV)
Sales   Direct market coverage in 60 countries

CTT Tools
R&D   Stockholm, Halmsted, Frankfurt, Zell, Sheffield (each brand has its own development)
Manufacturing   13 units, 10% within Sweden
Sales   Direct market coverage in 30 countries (12 units), and indirect via agents in most other
                    countries

Steel
R&D   Sandviken
Manufacturing   Main production in Sandviken
                    16 units, in Canada, Argentina, Czech Republic, Spain, United Kingdom, France, Brazil, India,
                    Finland
                    JV in Brazil, the United States (Scranton, Pa.), with Sumitomo, China
Sales   Direct market coverage in 55 countries

Saws and Tools
R&D   No central R&D; product development conducted at 8 product centres in Sweden (4),
                    Switzerland, Germany, the United States, and Portugal
Manufacturing   15 plants in 7 countries
Sales   Direct market coverage in 40 countries

Process Systems
R&D   Sandviken
Manufacturing   x units, including Korea

Sales   Direct market coverage in 25 countries

TABLE 5

The Competitive Environment of Sandvik's Business Areas

Tooling	***SEK 70 billion world market***
Cemented carbide	Sandvik about 20% market share
	Kennametal, Valenite (U.S.)
	Mitsubishi, Toshiba, Sumitomo (Asia)
	Number of local companies in Europe
High-speed steel	Sandvik about 10% market share
	Few large producers, but many small ones
Rock Tools	***SEK 8 billion world market***
Top hammer drilling	Sandvik, Uniroc (Sweden), Boart (S. Africa) with 67% of market
	10 companies with remaining 33%
Mineral tools	Kennametal, American Mine Tool
Down-the-hole drilling	Ingersoll-Rand (U.S.)
	Atlas Copco (Sweden)
	Large number of local suppliers
Hard Materials	***Sandvik Largest in Industry with 15% share***
	Four major competitors in Europe (Sandvik, Ceremetal, Plasee, Hertel), plus 50 small-medium firms
	Similar concentration in North America and Asia, but different competitors in each case
Process Systems	***Large Number of Companies, Limited Geographically or by Product Segment***
Steel	
Seamless tubes	Sumitomo (Japan), DMV (Europe)
Wire and bar	Ugine
	Number of smaller independent drawing mills
Strip	Hitachi Metals (Japan), Daido, Böhler Uddeholm
	Number of independent cold-rolling mills
Saws and Tools	***SEK 100 Billion World Market***
	Sandvik, Stanley and Falcon share 15% of market in Europe; remaining 85% is split among 500 competitors. U.S. market is more consolidated. Five competitors account for 50% of market. Remaining 50% is split among hundreds of smaller firms (including Sandvik)

effects of this program were achieved in 1995 since CTT was able to reduce costs as well as increase sales, partly due to its entrance into new markets provided by Coromant's global marketing organization.

Management worked to exploit synergies between the two companies in logistics, distribution, and product development. Dormer, one of the CTT Tools' companies, established a central warehouse with Coromant in the Netherlands. But some syner-

gies were difficult to realize because of operational differences. As Coromant's president stated, "The devil hides in the details." One example was customer distribution. Seventy-five percent of Coromant's sales were direct, while only 30 percent of CTT's sales were direct and these were primarily to one customer.

Automation   Automation accounted for SEK58 million in sales in 1995. The business area was responsible for developing and marketing products such as computer systems for tool monitoring, tool administration, and production follow-up.

Sandvik Steel

Sandvik Steel was more of an engineering company than a conventional steel company. It developed, manufactured, and marketed only about 200,000 tonnes of specialty steel products annually. The steel business's main operations and R&D were located in Sandviken. In 1995, Sandvik Steel sold SEK 9.8 billion in stainless and high-alloy steel strips, wire, bars, and seamless tubes. The company was the world's largest producer of seamless tubing and rock-drilling steel. The products were used in a wide range of applications, from knives to surgery equipment and airplanes.

This business experienced an upsurge in demand in 1994. Invoiced sales increased by 20 percent in 1994 and 27 percent in 1995, resulting in a backlog of orders. In order to meet demand, capacity was expanded in Sweden and NAFTA. A tube mill was acquired and expanded in the Czech Republic and a jointly owned company (60 percent) was established in Quingdao, China. A joint venture was also developed in Brazil in 1994. Avesta Sandvik Tube, owned 25 percent by Sandvik Steel, grew substantially in this period due to access to Sandvik Steel's sales channels, particularly in Europe and Asia.

Although many of the business areas within Sandvik required steel in their product line, the Steel business area supplied only limited amounts to other Sandvik businesses. Steel provided 2,000 tonnes of steel to Saws & Tools, which was about 50 percent of the steel required in its saws, and SEK20–30 million value added to the Process Systems business area. As the world's largest producer of drill steel, the steel business provided a considerable amount of steel to Rock Tools, and to Rock Tools' competitors. The Steel business also shared the same trucking and shipping services with Rock Tools and Saws and Tools for its products from Sandviken to Europe.

Saws and Tools

The Saws and Tools area manufactured and marketed saws and hand tools for use in engineering, construction, metalworking, forestry, and horticulture. Eighty percent of product sales were to industrial and professional customers; the remaining sales were to individuals for personal use. With 1995 sales of SEK2.7 billion, the company was one of the largest in the hand tools industry, which was highly fragmented. The Saws and Tools business represented 9 percent of the group's total sales.

Competitive advantage in the saws and tools industry depended primarily on product adaptations and improvements rather than on basic research. In 1994, for example, Saws and Tools introduced the Ergo product line, which utilized a new design process to create ergonomically superior tools.[5] But some basic materials research was conducted in cooperation with the steel business and Coromant.

In order to improve profitability and delivery reliability, a series of productivity improvement programs and a new production organization were introduced between 1990 and 1994. The flow group organization was adapted from Coromant and was implemented at the production unit in Bollnäs, Sweden.

The hand tool industry experienced a rationalization during the 1994–1995 period, particularly with respect to the distribution system. The Saws and Tools area adapted Coromant's centralized warehousing concept and built a central European warehouse in the Netherlands, close to Coromant's Schiedam facility. Northern Europe was served by the Sandviken warehouse. North American distribution was being consolidated in a facility near Scranton, Pennsylvania.

Rock Tools

Representing 7 percent of the group's sales in 1995, the Rock Tools business area produced cemented carbide and steel-tipped rock-drilling tools for use in mining, civil engineering, and water-well drilling. Rock Tools was the only company in the rock-drilling industry that supplied a full line of rock-drilling tools.

The industry was mature, with Rock Tools and one or two other companies controlling the main markets. Continuous product improvement was essential to remain competitive. There was a trend toward increasing mechanization and more sophisticated, capital-intensive machinery. As a measure of progress, drilling speed increased from 10 meters per hour in the 1940s to 160 meters per hour in the 1990s. Rock Tools was able to lead the industry in technology development due to its membership in the Sandvik Group. The group had substantial research, development, and production of both cemented carbides and special steels, the materials that accounted for most of the components in rock-drilling tools. Rock Tools conducted its cemented carbide research in Stockholm in the same building as the Coromant and Hard Materials research teams, and also pooled its resources with the Steel business area in Sandviken.

In 1988, Rock Tools terminated its forty-one-year distribution agreement with Atlas Copco. Atlas Copco had purchased Fagersta, Rock Tools' main competitor. As a result, Rock Tools was left overnight without a sales and distribution organization. However, within three months Rock Tools was able to leverage the group's worldwide presence and build a new sales force of 200 people (many coming from Atlas Copco). Rock Tools was able to regain its market share and endure the subsequent price war, although with reduced margins. During this period, the Sandvik Group bought 25 percent of Tamrock, a Finnish producer of rock-drilling machinery and a competitor of Atlas Copco. This holding was increased to 49 percent in 1996.

In addition to product development and marketing support, Rock Tools also benefited from a series of best practices developed in the Coromant business area. When Lars-Anders Nordqvist was transferred from Coromant logistics and production to become the president of the Rock Tools business area, he brought with him the CAPP system as well as the logistics system. The introduction of a new work organization (self-managed flow groups) on the shop floor, together with new logistic systems for production loading and other improvements, led to a 60 percent rise in productivity from 1990 to 1996.

In order to achieve better market coverage, Rock Tools expanded its operations in Asia, Eastern Europe, and Latin America during 1995. A number of new development projects were also initiated with Tamrock.

Process Systems

Process Systems had 1995 sales of SEK 1.8 billion, 6 percent of the total for the group. The business originated in the early 1900s when the Steel business area began to make steel belts for chemical processing. In the early 1970s Process Systems

was moved to Stuttgart, in order to be closer to the heart of the worldwide chemical processing industry. However, Process Systems developed applications for a wide variety of industries, including goods sorting and food processing in many countries, notably in the United States, Japan, and other parts of Asia. In 1996, the decision was made to relocate the head office for Process Systems back to Sweden.

In 1995, Process Systems delivered the world's largest package sorting system to UPS in Chicago (180,000 packages per hour). A new chemical processing production center was established in Korea for deliveries in Southeast Asia and China. In order to further broaden its product line, the business area acquired CML, an Italian company providing high-speed sorting systems of postal packages, magazines, and newspapers, in 1995. Other developments included the introduction of a new steam cooker as well as a dryer for the food processing industry.

The outlook for Process Systems was mixed. The competitive environment had become more difficult in the last few years. While the business continued to be profitable, management warned in the 1995 Annual Report that "weaker demand will be countered with continuing rationalization measures."

Hard Materials

The Hard Materials business area accounted for 4 percent of the Sandvik Group's total sales in 1995 and was the largest company in the hard materials industry. Hard Materials was formally created as a result of the 1984 reorganization, at which point it defined its product portfolio as "all cemented carbide applications not provided by Rock Tools and Coromant." Over time this definition became more focused, so that by 1996 Hard Materials competed in three areas: mechanical components, blanks for toolmakers, and rolls for the steel industry. This business needed finer grades of cemented carbide than either Rock Tools or Coromant. It was also involved in research into biocompatible ceramics. As a result, Hard Materials undertook much of its own research, in Stockholm, England, and France, though there were also frequent cooperative projects with Coromant and Rock Tools.

Hard Materials sold a small percentage of its products to other Sandvik businesses, for example, drill bits and carbide blanks to Sandvik Tooling, but most were to external customers (which were sometimes competitors of other Sandvik businesses). Hard Materials worked to coordinate purchases of tungsten and cobalt with Coromant and Rock Tools.

In the period 1991 to 1993, the hard materials industry experienced a recession and many companies became unprofitable. As a result, there were a number of bankruptcies and shutdowns. Sandvik made several acquisitions during this time (and in the years before 1987), including companies in the United Kingdom, France, and the United States. Subsequent to these acquisitions, Hard Materials underwent a restructuring of its manufacturing activities that resulted in a specialization of its European activities around five product centers. Currently, this business area was experiencing high demand as cemented carbide replaced steel in many industrial applications. In order to improve

its competitiveness, Hard Materials planned to further increase its R&D programs and accelerate the introduction of new materials and processes.

Corporate-Level Activities

Sandvik had a corporate staff consisting of approximately fifty people. The executive group comprised Hedström, the president and CEO; Leif Sunnermalm, executive vice president and CFO; and Lars Östholm,[6] executive vice president. In addition there were corporate managers responsible for Human Resources, Research and Development, Finance, and Corporate Relations (See Table 6).

Finance was one function that had always been performed centrally. A group of seven people in Sandviken, plus six in Switzerland and two in Singapore, were responsible for cash management, lend-

TABLE 6

The Sandvik Management Group

- *Clas Åke Hedström,* chief executive officer. Prior to being elected to CEO in 1994, Hedström was president of Sandvik Coromant, with a total of twenty-nine years of experience within the Sandvik Group.
- *Leif Sunnermalm,* executive vice president and chief financial officer. Sunnermalm joined the Sandvik Group in 1971 and moved from EVP in Coromant to EVP for the group in 1994.
- *Lars Östholm,* executive vice president, R&D. Östholm was employed by the Sandvik Group in 1958 and worked for it continuously except for the period 1971–1977, when he worked for ABB Steel. Prior to becoming EVP, he worked at Rock Tools.
- *Gunnar Björklund,* president, Sandvik Steel. Björklund joined Sandvik in 1959 and was elected to this position in 1982.
- *Göran Gezelius,* president, Sandvik Saws and Tools since 1988. Member of the Sandvik Group since 1982.
- *Lars-Anders Nordqvist,* president, Sandvik Rock Tools. Nordqvist started with Sandvik in 1967 and was elected president in 1991. Prior to this position, he was responsible for logistics and production at Sandvik Coromant.
- *Lars Pettersson,* president, Sandvik Coromant. Prior to joining Coromant, Pettersson worked in Steel. He was promoted to president in 1994.
- *Lars Wahlqvist,* president, Sandvik Hard Materials. Wahlqvist joined Rock Tools in 1969, left Sandvik to join Esab in 1975, and rejoined Sandvik in 1981. President of Hard Materials since 1984.
- *Roland Setterberg,* president, International Operations. Setterberg joined Hard Materials in 1986 after working with British Oxygen and Cabot Corporation. He became president of International Operations in 1997.
- *Rune Nyberg,* head, Human Resources. In 1983 Nyberg was hired by Sandvik into Coromant. After Nyberg had been two years outside Sandvik, Hedström recruited him to headquarters.
- *Peter Lundh,* head, Information Services. Member of Sandvik group since 1983.
- *Anders Illstam,* president, CTT Tools since its start in 1990. Previously president of SKF Tools.

ing and investments, and foreign exchange activities. The individual businesses were responsible for screening investment opportunities, presenting them to the board for approval.

Information systems (IS) had not been completely decentralized in 1984. Each business unit was made fully responsible for its IS needs. This meant businesses could establish their own resources, acquire external resources, or utilize the central IS function. The central IS function provided IT-services to the business units but also handled some of the common resources (the network, central operation, and so forth) in order not to lose scale and synergy effects. The decentralization of IS was not uniform. Most notably, Coromant built its own information systems group in 1988 by taking over its development resources from the central IS function. By 1996, Coromant had almost 65 people working in IS, compared with 170 in the central group. Other business areas still relied on the central resource and had smaller numbers of IS employees.

There was also a central component to the management of the group's technology. Sandvik's technology base had evolved over the years. In 1996, the company was positioned as "materials-driven," with technological strength in three areas:

1. Steel and alloyed steel
2. Cemented carbide and other hard material
3. Materials coatings

These technologies, in various combinations, formed the foundation for the six business areas.

While all R&D occurred in the business areas, there was a small technical advisory group responsible for the strategic direction of Sandvik's R&D. This group consisted of Lars Östholm, a staff researcher, and the heads of research from Tooling, Steel, Hard Materials, and Rock Tools. The advisory group met every three months to evaluate strategic R&D projects and to support projects that "fell between the lines" of the business areas or were pure research projects outside the company's mainline interests.

The executive group was also responsible for business development activities that fell beyond the boundaries of the existing six business areas. The possibility of a seventh Sandvik business, for example, had not been ruled out, but as Leif Sun-nermalm explained, "It would have to meet some very strict criteria, in terms of core technologies, customer base, expected return on investment, and growth opportunities."

Other Sandvik Operations

Sandvik had three regional companies. Sandvik International was responsible for exporting into Africa, the Middle East, and parts of the former USSR. Sandvik South East Asia and Sandvik Latin America, based in Singapore and Miami, respectively, were responsible for coordinating marketing activities in their particular regions. There were also two service companies: Sandvik Central Service, responsible for various support activities in the Sandviken area, and Sandvik Information Systems (see above).

Foreign Subsidiaries

Sandvik had extensive operations throughout the world, with approximately 200 foreign affiliates in 130 countries (see Table 7). In most of the smaller country markets, Sandvik had a single holding company, which represented all six business areas. Infrastructure and support functions were often shared, but the country manager had little or no influence over the day-to-day running of the various businesses. In the larger markets, such as the United States, the United Kingdom, and France, the business areas were more separate from one another. In these countries, there was little attempt made to share support functions or infrastructure. Following the 1984 reorganization, the country manager job was no longer a full-time responsibility. This role was usually assumed by the head of the largest business area in each country.

THE SANDVIK CULTURE

In many ways, Sandvik was the quintessential Swedish industrial company. The company was built on technological innovation around the turn of the century, and it rapidly gained a major overseas presence. Sandvik was also very "Swedish" in its style of doing business: conservative, understated and rather traditional, but with a strong work ethic and a strong corporate culture. As

TABLE 7

Geographic Distribution of Sales

	Invoiced Sales by Market Area (SEK million)		
	1995	1994	1993
Sweden	2370	1807	1494
European Union, excluding Sweden	13755	11506	9110
Rest of Europe	1419	981	1428
Total, Europe	17544	14294	12032
NAFTA	5626	5361	4572
South America	1422	1359	1210
Africa, Middle East	763	641	651
Asia, Australia	4345	3630	3305
Group Total	29700	25285	21770

	Invoiced Sales in the Ten Largest Country Markets (SEK million)		
	1995	1994	1993
United States	4863	4657	3872
Germany	4016	3453	3015
France	2533	2096	1857
Sweden	2370	1807	1494
Italy	2193	1658	1332
Great Britain	1893	1576	1263
Japan	1510	1307	1309
Brazil	831	752	682
Australia	817	748	623
Canada	620	587	543

stated by Percy Barnevik, "Sandvik cannot be described as a company given to excesses—put simply, the company does a darn fine job without a lot of fuss and without seeking any particular recognition for it." Sandvik was far and away the largest employer in the small town of Sandviken, two hours' drive north of Stockholm. Almost all senior managers were Swedes, and many had also grown up in Sandviken or the surrounding towns.

THE SEARCH FOR SYNERGIES

When Hedström was appointed CEO of the Sandvik Group in 1994, he brought with him an expansionist attitude. In addition to a goal of a 2 percent return on net assets over a business cycle, he set a goal for annual sales growth at 6 percent for a ten-year period (compared with 4 percent in the past). In order to reach the aggressive growth goals, he encouraged managers to focus in particular on Asia, Central and East Europe, and the North American Free Trade area.

A key item on Hedström's agenda was to create greater synergies between the business areas and more value added by the corporate headquarters. To assist him, Hedström appointed Sunnermalm, a former colleague in the Coromant business area, as an executive vice president, and Rune Nyberg, an ex-Coromant manager, as corporate head of human resources. In the years following the 1984 reorganization, the six business areas had been encouraged to optimize their own profitability, with the result that the cooperative links between them had lessened over the years. Thus, while there were historical ties between the business areas, the current linkages were very mixed. Rock Tools, Hard Materials, and Tooling, for example, all drew from Sandvik's cemented carbide technology, but Saws and Tools and Process Systems were relatively independent of their sister business areas. Table 8 lists some of the synergies that were currently being exploited.

Hedström and his colleagues in the executive group were keen to see much greater synergies between the business areas. They felt there was considerable potential for cost savings if more activities were coordinated or combined, and also

TABLE 8

Existing and Potential Synergies in the Sandvik Group

Management and Administration	Profitability focus Use of management by objectives technique Parenting synergies Worldwide use of Sandvik IT network (common order, invoicing and financial) Group financing Shared back-office functions at smaller-scale subsidiaries Tax management
Human Resources	Common management planning system Internal career market Availability of corporate expatriate management Intercompany task forces (e.g., U.S.) Creating "center of excellence" Incentive system
Marketing and Sales	Sandvik brand Joint advertising and trade shows Joint customer education Customer file swapping Package sales to big customers and distributors
Logistics and Purchasing	Coromant and some CTT products sharing logistics Steel and Rock Tools sharing shipping Common purchasing of raw materials for the Group Coordinate purchase of travels, telecommunications, etc.
Production	Technology for Coromant, Rock Tools, and Hard Materials Manufacturing equipment for same Joint manufacture of carbide powder Flow-group concepts (developed by Coromant) CAPP system for Coromant, Rock Tools, and CTT
Research and Development	Materials research for Coromant, Rock Tools, Hard Materials, and partially for CTT Steel research for Rock Tools Steel grades with optimum machinability together with Coromant Boundless sharing of materials and application know-how

some opportunity for sales growth through, for example, cross-selling products between business areas. In order to get things moving, the Sandvik Group management put forward organizational initiatives in Human Resources and Information Technology. In the United States, a task force was formed to look for synergies among the sixteen U.S. operations. It was headed by Jim Baker, manager for Coromant's U.S. operations.

The U.S. Task Force

Of Sandvik's sixteen companies in the United States, many had been established through acquisition. Hedström convened a meeting of the sixteen company presidents in November 1995 to discuss the need to build synergies between these businesses. They identified purchasing, marketing, and human resources as areas where the greatest potential for synergies existed. Three task forces were set up, each headed by one of the company presidents and with representatives from each company. Jim Baker, the head of Coromant U.S., took overall responsibility.

A follow-up meeting between the U.S.-company presidents in December 1996 indicated that good progress had been made. As Baker observed, "we have 95 percent commitment to use the programs." The purchasing task force had looked at common purchasing agreements in all areas. They had in place agreements that were expected to save $13 million annually. The marketing task force agreed on standardized logos and a joint presence at trade shows. They also planned to launch a corporate advertising campaign in 1997 directed at senior managers in major user companies. The HR task force wanted to make movement of people between the Sandvik companies "seamless," and to this end it began the difficult task of harmonizing the different benefits packages in the sixteen companies. A further review was scheduled for June 1997, to look for further synergies in these areas and to consider other areas in which similar task forces could be established (for example, logistics, IT, distributor representation).

Human Resources

Rune Nyberg, the newly appointed corporate vice president of human resources (HR), observed that HR had "no co-ordination whatsoever." In an at-

tempt to develop greater cooperation among the business areas, Nyberg organized a conference in March 1996 for sixty senior HR managers from around the world. They discussed the key HR issues facing Sandvik as a group and identified six specific areas in which groupwide systems could be developed, such as compensation and benefits packages and benchmarking practices. International project groups were created to develop state-of-the-art systems in each area and establish "competence centers" that other parts of the Sandvik group could then draw on. While some systems, such as the new compensation and benefits system, would be mandatory, most would be at the discretion of the business areas. Nyberg's hope was that the involvement of these managers would encourage them to make use of the competence centers as they became established and to maintain relationships between one another. Nyberg also started a corporate HR newsletter to share the results of the project teams' research and to foster a dialogue between participants.

Another important issue was career management. Most managers had traditionally followed careers exclusively in a single business area. By 1996 only about 20 percent of managers had experience outside their current business areas. Hedström and Nyberg both felt that this proportion had to be increased in order to enhance the opportunities for cross-fertilization of ideas.

The Information Technology Council

Since 1984, some business areas had invested in their own proprietary information systems. As a result, the central IS group's ability to control groupwide systems was seriously compromised. In 1996, the Data Council, which had been established in 1985, was reorganized and given more precise tasks. At the same time a cooperation committee—the Information Technology Council—was formed. This council consisted of the president of Sandvik Information Systems and the heads of the IS groups in each business. Together they were responsible for defining policies and procedures, and analyzing major investments to ensure one set of standards, while not taking away each business area's responsibility for adapting these standards to its specific needs. The head of IT stated, "It has now dawned on many of the business units that there are significant opportunities for a common approach towards the setting of standards." The council met once a month and reported to the Sandvik Group Data Council.

INSTILLING THE NEED FOR CHANGE

Hedström hoped that the business area managers would see the changes he was putting forward as positive for the Sandvik Group and that they would also attempt to explore further synergies between the business areas. However, he realized that the business area presidents saw differing levels of potential and had different priorities. Gunnar Björkland, the former vice president of Sandvik Steel, believed that there might be distribution synergies for the various businesses due to a common customer base. However, he stated, "I can get more out of talking to Sumitomo with whom we do not directly compete than by talking to Coromant." Lars Wahlqvist, president of Hard Materials, observed that a "formal integration process is often rather less effective than an informal one." Göran Gezelius, president of Saws and Tools, went further when stating that "the search for synergies should not drive a major reorganization."

Hedström had several concerns about the search for greater synergies. First, it was not clear where the most valuable potential synergies lay. Hedström was aware of many of the obvious opportunities—hence the initiatives in HR, IT, and the U.S. task force—but many others would only be apparent to frontline managers in Sandvik's 200 international affiliates when they focused on identifying and exploiting the possibilities. Second, promised synergies often proved to be less significant than first anticipated, as the CTT-Coromant *relationship* had shown.[7] Finally, the exploitation of synergies was never costless. Lars Pettersson, president of Coromant, pointed out the possibility of conflicting needs between business areas, meaning that the optimum course of action for one business area could negatively impact another. The decision by Saws and Tools to build a new warehouse facility in the Netherlands, rather than build on Coromant's existing facility in Schiedam, was often cited as an example of business area needs taking precedence over group synergies. But Gezelius disagreed: "The fact is that we would have used the Schiedam facility, but the building was too small, there was no room to extend it, and Schiedam itself is extremely congested. In addition, Saws and Tools have very

different warehousing requirements from Coromant—we have pallet goods, they don't; we ship products in one to three days, they air-freight products within 24 hours. Once again, the devil hides in the details."

There were also concerns about the transfer of best practices between business areas. Historically, many innovative practices had come from Coromant. Thus, for the other business areas, adopting Coromant's practices meant "identifying a need and being humble enough to copy." Some business areas, such as Rock Tools, had been very good at this, but others had preferred to develop their own systems.

An underlying reason for most managers' concerns about the changes was the worry that increased synergies between the businesses would lead to a de facto recentralization of power and a corresponding loss of autonomy in the six business areas. The executive group was fully aware of this concern. As explained by Sunnermalm, "We are raising a warning flag as we proceed. Are we making roles unclear? Are we damaging the clear accountability that has served us so well? We need to move forward very carefully." The actions taken by the executive group had been focused on communication and voluntary cooperation. Hedström, Sunnermalm, and Östholm all traveled frequently to Sandvik's operations around the world, explaining the need for greater synergies between business areas and emphasizing that they were not trying to move back to the centralized approach of the early 1980s.

But they recognized that the "preaching stage" may not be sufficient to create and sustain the changes in behavior that were being sought. The goal was to get Sandvik employees acting with regard to their business *and* the group, rather than just their business. The U.S. task force and the HR and IT initiatives represented specific steps toward this goal. But Hedström felt that further changes were needed to expand and sustain the search for and exploitation of synergies within the Sandvik group. He pondered what further actions he should take.

Endnotes

1. The United States (e.g., 3M, AT&T) and the United Kingdom (e.g., ICI, Hanson) were two countries in which demergers and spinoffs were being increasingly employed to drive corporate restructuring and refocusing. However, there were

also signs of such things happening in Sweden, with Trelleborg's demerger of Boliden and Volvo's sale of its food and beverages businesses.

2. Tungsten and other carbides such as titanium were ground into powder and mixed with another metallic powder, usually cobalt. The powder was then pressed into the desired form and exposed to high temperatures. The result was a material which was both hard and durable for use in metal cutting.

3. Using this system, a salesperson entered an order in the company's computer, and it was then directly transmitted to the production floor, bypassing any administrative personnel.

4. Customers could input specifications for a desired product with the help of a Coromant representative. Within ten minutes, the customer would receive by fax a scale drawing of the product, as well as delivery and cost information.

5. Ergonomic tools were designed to reduce the risk of workplace injuries and promote greater productivity.

6. Gunnar Björkland, president of Sandvik Steel, was due to join the executive group in early 1997 when Lars Östholm retired.

7. Coromant and CTT had almost 100 percent overlap in customer groups, but on closer inspection Coromant had about 70 percent direct sales and 30 percent distributors, while CTT had the reverse.

CASE 40

PBS (A): The Joint Venture Decision

This case was prepared by Stanley D. Nollen, Karen L. Newman, and Jacqueline M. Abbey of Georgetown University.

Richard Kuba had brought a decision to his board of directors. A joint venture proposal between První Brněnská Strojírna (PBS), of which he was the general manager, and Asea Brown Boveri (ABB), the Swiss-Swedish engineering company, was on the table. Kuba had worked more than a year on these negotiations. A majority of his board members had been opposed to a joint venture with ABB and had initially rejected it. Now ABB had a new proposal to offer. Kuba and his board would reconsider the joint venture decision in a new board meeting. It was the board's decision to make, and it would not be easy.

As the general director (chief executive officer) of a sizable Czech company struggling to make the transition from central planning to a market economy, Kuba was in uncharted managerial waters. He believed that PBS had to take a decisive step to adapt to the challenge of international competition in the post-Soviet era. He felt responsible for the welfare of his employees and fellow managers, and he had a sense of national duty. PBS, a power plant equipment engineering and manufacturing company, had a continuous history from its founding in 1814 (the company name means "First Brno Machinery") through two world wars and the recently ended communist period. Now PBS once again had to adapt in order to survive.

PBS

The Company's Business

At the time of the Velvet Revolution, PBS's principal business was the manufacture of turbines and boilers, which accounted for a large majority of its revenue. (See the Appendix for a description of the change in government and general business conditions under central planning.) The company also built complete power and heating plants, serviced and reconstructed old plants, and manufactured miscellaneous industrial parts. The company listed its product lines as follows:

- *Turbines.* Steam turbines for industrial heating and power plants, small to mid-size gas turbines, turbochargers, and accessories.

- *Boilers.* Oil-fired, gas-fired, and coal-burning industrial boilers and accessories.

- *Power plants.* Complete power and heating plants made on a turnkey basis; service and reconstruction of existing plants.

- *Other products.* Burners, heaters, railcar shock absorbers, power plant measurement and regulation instruments, gas meters, castings, and forgings.

In 1992, PBS booked orders worth Kč 4,857 million (about $175 million (Table A-1) and earned revenue of Kč 3,472 million (about $125 million). Profit was Kč 365 million ($13 million). The level of employment was just under 8,000 and falling steadily (Table A-2).

The company's headquarters and most of its manufacturing facilities were in Brno, where it had made steam turbines for ninety years and gas tur-

TABLE A-1

PBS Sales Booked by Product Line, 1990–1992
(Kč million current)

Product	1990	1991	1992
Total sales	1,484	3,307	4,857
Turbines	527	1,080	782
Steam turbines	234	270	557
Gas turbines	63	54	27
Turbochargers	230	756	198
Boilers	549	724	1,823
Industrial boilers	415	563	1,099
Piping	134	161	724
Assemblies	85	288	299
Repairs	171	191	162
Central heating equipment	68	111	119
Aircraft equipment	101	14	18
Other (see text)	282	898	1,653

Notes: Freeing of prices in 1991 resulted in price inflation in Czechoslovakia of 58 percent in that year. Gas turbines includes expansion turbines.
Source: První Brněnská Strojíma (PBS), Annual Report, 1992.

TABLE A-2

Selected Financial and Operating Data for PBS, 1990–1992
(Kč million current except where indicated otherwise)

Variable	1990	1991	1992
Total revenue	2,052	3,412	3,472
Production revenue	1,842	3,207	3,255
Profit	224	369	365
Total assets	3,338	5,399	6,187
Fixed assets	2,246	2,688	2,972
Trade receivables	377	1,411	1,635
Trade payables	322	814	857
Bank loans	752	1,107	931
Exports as percent of booked sales—to COMECON	20	19	10
Exports as percent of booked sales—worldwide	24	28	53
Employees (number)	9,564	8,857	7,946
Labor productivity (Kč 000 revenue per employee)	215	385	437
Average monthly wages (Kč)	3,629	4,410	5,299

Notes: Data include the Velká Bítes plant. Figures for revenue in this table do not match sales figures in Table A-1 because the figures in Table 1 represent sales orders booked, not revenue received.
Source: První Brněnská Strojírna (PBS), Annual Report, 1992; and communication with PBS managers.

bines for thirty-five years. Four plants were located in smaller towns in Moravia, dating from post–World War II years. The plant in Trebič made boilers and accessories (burners, heaters), and the plant in Mikulov made blades for turbines. The plant in Velká Bíteš made turbochargers and had received most of the new capital investment that came to PBS from the central planning authorities during the 1980s. This plant's output was exported mostly to the Soviet Union until its breakup in 1991; this business then fell by 80 percent. The plant in Oslavany made a variety of products and parts, such as railcar shock absorbers, nuts, bolts, and screws that were not central to PBS's main turbine and boiler businesses.

By 1992, PBS had begun to concentrate on environmentally friendly power plant and heating plant systems. Much of its recent boiler business was to overhaul and reconstruct existing boilers to meet higher regulatory standards. In precommunist Czechoslovakia, PBS was a leader in the power generation equipment industry, with a reputation for good products and service. The early years of central planning were economically satisfactory as well. However, relative competitive decline set in at PBS after the "normalization" that followed Prague Spring in 1968. Investment in plant and equipment and in new technology was insufficient for more than twenty years. By 1992, PBS product quality was below Western standards, concern for the customer was low, and employee willingness to take initiative was lagging.

Yet PBS was better off than many other Czech companies that also suffered from little investment, aging capital equipment, and outdated products. Unlike most companies during central planning, PBS had its own engineering capabilities in-house, and as a result had developed its own coal-fired boiler and steam turbine technology. In addition, PBS had a long-standing but small turnkey business. It not only made boilers and turbines, but it also did all the work necessary to construct or reconstruct complete electric power generation plants and steam-heating plants. PBS was not just a manufacturing plant.

Distribution

Before 1989, PBS used two state trading companies for export sales: Škoda-export and Technoexport. Exports accounted for about one-quarter of PBS business, about three-quarters of which went to So-

viet bloc countries. Domestic sales of turbines and boilers were uncomplicated, partly because the product was tailor-made; also, there were few potential customers, orders were big, and there were no direct domestic competitors. PBS customers were the contractors that built the power plants or end users (usually companies or city governments) if PBS did the project on a turnkey basis.

Employee Wages and Production Costs

Wage rates at PBS as in all Czech companies were quite low—an average of Kč 5,400 per month in 1992 (about $190). The skill level of the work force was very good. However, productivity was also quite low because, PBS managers asserted, of the lack of investment in recent years. However, PBS did not have a production cost advantage compared with German companies. As Kuba said,

> We figured the German company's hourly rate for value added to engineer and produce turbine blades. We added up their wage rates and rental rates and depreciation rates, but we excluded the price of raw materials and parts they purchased from outside suppliers. Then we did the same calculation for ourselves. We found that our hourly rate was one-third of theirs. But then we looked at how long it took the Germans to make the turbine blades compared to how long it took us. It turned out that the German company used one-third the time that our company used. So our production costs were about the same as theirs.

Managers

The top managers at PBS were mostly technically educated (as expected in Czech industrial companies), and most had been employed at PBS for their entire careers. Kuba, the first post-revolution general manager, fit this pattern.

He had joined PBS in 1965 after graduating from Brno Technical University, where he studied power generation and turbine design. Early in his career, he spent some time in PBS's turnkey business. In 1968, Kuba began to attend economics courses from the Prague School of Economics, but when Prague Spring was crushed and tighter government control reasserted, he dropped his studies.

Kuba's ascent to the upper levels of PBS management was slow because he chose not to join the Communist Party. Despite his refusal to join the party, he was given the opportunity to travel abroad and work with foreign customers in Bulgaria, Romania, Sweden, and Syria. After completing graduate studies in power grid management in 1989, he was promoted to director of the engineering department in the power plant division. His promotion to general manager in 1990 at the age of forty-seven (he was selected by the head of Škoda Konzern) came as a surprise, even to Kuba himself.

Corporate Culture

The PBS corporate culture was influenced strongly by the requirements of central planning. PBS was the monopoly producer of boilers and turbines in its size range (small to medium sizes) in the Czech/Socialist Republic. There was no competition. Producing to meet a plan was the most important criterion of success. Cost control did not matter, and costs and prices were determined by central planners rather than market forces.

The work force was dominated by engineers. Boilers and turbines were over-engineered to stand up under extremely adverse conditions. Building a tough, sturdy, long-lasting product was far more important than building efficiently. PBS collaborated with the local technical university on research and development and took pride in its ability to design sophisticated equipment. More employees than necessary worked for PBS, a function of the government's full-employment policy. The enterprise was driven by production and engineering concerns. Employees were more excited about a well-engineered boiler than financial results.

The Investment and Finance

During the years of central planning, investment decisions from the Czechoslovak government were heavily influenced by the needs of major national or Soviet projects (for example, the development of nuclear energy or the construction of a natural gas pipeline). Profits earned by enterprises were remitted to the state and new investment capital came from the state, but there was no linkage between the two. In the case of PBS, most of the investment that came to it went into the outlying plants, especially the plant at Velká Bíteš which made turbochargers, mainly for the Soviet Union. However, these investments were of little value in 1992 because they were designed for the Soviet market that diminished so rapidly and dramatically.

Conversion of these plants to meet Western needs was difficult and costly because of differences in product specifications.

Interest rates were quite high in Czechoslovakia during this time, even in real terms, and loanable funds were very scarce. Short-term finance was also difficult to obtain, and a liquidity crisis ensued during 1992 and 1993. Since trade credit was scarcely available, many companies responded by simply not paying their bills. In PBS's case, trade receivables at their worst exceeded payables by a factor of two, and were Kč 1,635 million ($57 million) at the end of 1992, just below half of that year's sales revenue (Table A-2).

Privatization

The Czechoslovak government's objective for privatization was to transfer most of the country's large enterprises to widespread private ownership quite quickly. Because local citizens did not have the financial resources to "buy the economy" overnight, much of it was "given away." Under voucher privatization, each adult citizen was entitled to buy a book of vouchers containing 1,000 points for Kč 1,000 (which in early 1992 was an average week's wages). The voucher holder could bid for shares of individual companies or spend voucher points on mutual funds that in turn bought shares of companies. Other methods of privatization included auction (for smaller companies), tender offers (usually with conditions attached about future employment levels), management buyouts, direct sale to a predetermined buyer, transfer at no cost to a municipality, and restitution to the family from which property had been confiscated by the state.

PBS was converted to the legal form of a joint stock company to become PBS a.s. in 1991. All of the shares in the company were owned by the National Property Fund (NPF), which was the Czech government agency established to hold shares of enterprises until they could be sold to private buyers. The company, which had the usual functional structure of large enterprises in centrally planned economies (Figure A-1), reorganized into a divisional structure of product-centered businesses (Figure A-2). The Ministry of Industry put PBS a.s. into the first wave of voucher privatization in 1992. Thirty-six percent of PBS a.s. shares were purchased by individuals and investment funds; 60 percent remained with the NPF; and 4 percent were set aside for restitution, which was the standard practice. The

FIGURE A-1

PBS Organization Chart (partial) in 1989

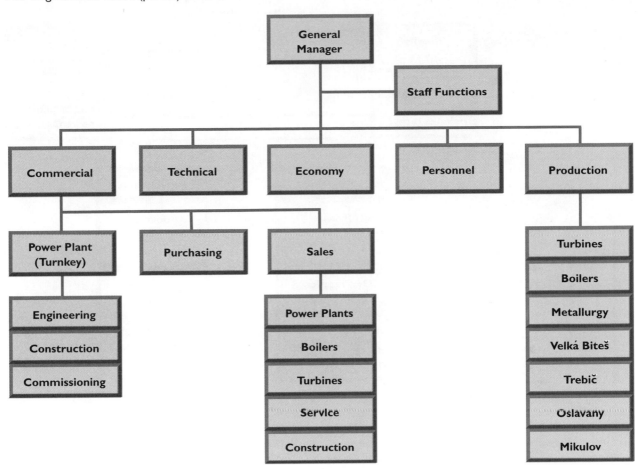

Source: První Brněnská Strojírna (PBS), Annual Report, 1991; and communication with PBS managers.

fact that the NPF held the majority of PBS shares meant that privatization was not complete and that further ownership changes would occur.

The Search for a New Business Strategy

To successfully make the transition from central planning and become competitive in world markets, PBS managers proposed two different types of strategies. PBS had been an industry leader before the central planning era. Some managers believed it could regain this position through increased efficiency and product innovation. These people, who included most of the deputy

general directors and department heads, placed their hopes for PBS in an ambitious new business strategy that called for maintaining independence and becoming more competitive by increasing quality standards, cutting production costs, producing products to meet international environmental standards, improving the fuel efficiency of products, and creating a climate for change within the company.

Financing this strategy, however, was a problem. There was very little capital available from Czech banks in the form of multiyear loans at reasonable interest rates, and PBS had not met with success in finding affordable financing from Western banks.

FIGURE A-2

PBS Organization
Chart in 1992

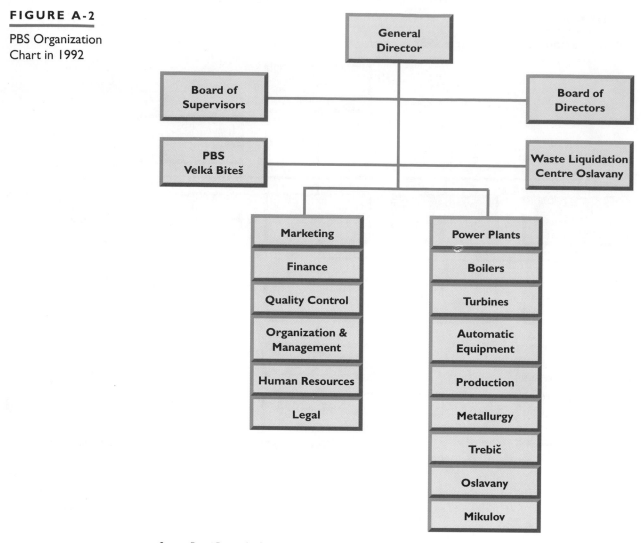

Source: První Brněnská Strojírna (PBS), Annual Report, 1992.

Other managers believed the choice was to decide which among several alternative relationships with other companies was best. They thought a go-it-alone approach could not succeed. The range of possibilities included some type of technology licensing or manufacturing link with a foreign company, some type of marketing agreement, a strategic alliance of some sort that would have technology transfer gains for PBS, the establishment of a joint venture with a foreign or domestic company, or purchase by a foreign or domestic company. When several Western companies—including General Electric, GEC-Alsthom, Deutsche Babcock, Siemens, and ABB—discussed business relationships with PBS beginning in 1991, PBS management listened, but only reluctantly.

THE JOINT VENTURE NEGOTIATIONS

Points of View and Kuba's Role

When foreign companies initially discussed partnership proposals with PBS, managers were ambivalent. They knew they needed capital to modernize, to gain access to Western technology, and to get assistance in developing export markets. But they also had a strong wish to remain independent and not lose their brand name. PBS was, according to the Czechoslovak Ministry of Privatization, the "family silver." Most managers were unwilling to consider breaking up the company or entering into a relationship that rendered PBS "just an equipment manufacturer." Many of the initial partnership proposals from Western companies would have led to one or both of these unattractive outcomes. Some PBS managers declared that the company had operated successfully for nearly two centuries and could survive without any Western equity partners. The trend toward environmentally clean power plants and heating plants by itself would bring substantial new business to PBS's repair and reconstruction unit. The PBS order book was full in 1991. Maybe no foreign partner was needed.

Kuba, however, thought differently. He knew that PBS did not have the latest technology. He discovered that Western companies could deliver a product in 25 percent less time than PBS could. While Kuba thought that PBS could upgrade its technology by itself, it would take more than five years because the investment capital was not available. With a foreign partner, it would go faster. In addition, turnover among young engineers at PBS was making internal technology development harder.

Kuba also believed PBS did not have the market economy experience to implement the company's strategy for improving its international competitiveness. In 1991 and 1992, he visited several PBS customers in foreign countries such as Pakistan and Iran.

They knew about Škoda Plzen and Škodaexport, but not about us. Škoda Plzen had ten businesses. If one of their businesses fails, they have nine others. We had one, and we had no name. ...There are four big international companies—General Electric, Siemens, ABB, and Mitsubishi—that control a big majority of the world market. There are tens of smaller companies like us, and some will not survive.

As Kuba saw it, these two facts—that PBS was not diversified and that world markets did not know his product—were as important as the need for technology updates.

The Czechoslovak economy, with economic reforms initiated in January 1990, was still getting worse. Industrial production had fallen about 40 percent since the Velvet Revolution, and GDP was off 26 percent (Table A-3). An upturn in business conditions was not predicted until 1994.

Kuba came to believe that it would be necessary to bring in a foreign investor, for both technological and market reasons.

I was not enthusiastic about bringing in a foreign investor, but I knew that we had to do it if we wanted to keep the company whole and not split it up. To keep the company together was more important than keeping it independent.

TABLE A-3

Economic Conditions in Czechoslovakia, 1989–1992

Variable	1989	1990	1991	1992
Gross domestic product, real % change[a]	0.7	−3.5	−15.0	−7.1
Industrial production, real % change	0.9	−3.7	−23.1	−12.4
Consumer price inflation, %	1.4	10.0	57.8	11.5
Interest rate %[b]	5.5	6.2	15.4	13.9
Exchange rate, Kč/$, annual average	15.1	18.0	29.5	28.3
Unemployment rate, %	na	0.3	6.8	7.7

[a]Net material product.
[b]Lending rate to state enterprises.
Sources: Economist Intelligence Unit, *Country Report: Czech Republic and Slovakia,* 2nd quarter 1993. 2nd quarter 1990. London, 1993, 1990. International Monetary Fund, *International Financial Statistics,* March 1994. Washington, D.C., 1996, 1994.

Although the company could survive for several more years on the strength of its existing assets, order book, work force, and customer base, he thought that only a strong Western partner could ensure that PBS would flourish and remain the pride of Czechoslovakia.

As was common practice in the centrally planned Czechoslovakian economy, the general director of PBS decided most issues of company policy himself within the framework of the five-year plan. In 1992, Kuba was, in theory, accountable to a board of directors elected by the shareholders of PBS and to the state. In practice, however, these bodies had little experience with corporate governance. Committing the assets of PBS to a venture with a Western company that meant a foreign ownership stake was a controversial decision with major ramifications. Kuba expected to be criticized no matter which course the company chose. Therefore, he would not make this decision alone.

The International Finance Corporation

At the recommendation of the Ministry of Industry, which was keenly interested in the fate of PBS, Kuba met with advisers from the International Finance Corporation (IFC), the consulting arm of the World Bank. The first meeting occurred in March 1992. Kuba was impressed with the work the IFC advisers had done earlier in the Czech Republic, particularly in facilitating the conclusion of Škoda Plzen's joint venture negotiations. Kuba hired the IFC to structure a tender process and oversee negotiations for a joint venture.

The IFC advisers made two important recommendations to Kuba. First, PBS should secure government approval to enter into a joint venture with a Western partner in advance of negotiations. This would ensure that PBS, not the state, would be the ultimate decision maker. PBS acted on this recommendation immediately.

Second, the IFC advised that PBS should separate its turbine, boiler, and turnkey businesses from its other activities. Only by packaging the core businesses together, without adding in peripheral businesses and unrelated assets of dubious value, would PBS attract a Western partner. The advisers explained that they were trying to create an auctionlike situation, and in order to do that they had to package the most valuable parts of the company separately from the rest. Though most managers and board members were very skeptical, Kuba con-

vinced them to allow the IFC advisers to restructure the company on paper in order to find the best potential partners.

Kuba remained noncommittal throughout the discussions, supporting the IFC advisers and facilitating negotiations but always in the name of "exploring options." He communicated that he was willing to take a risk to improve the company's prospects, but he did not challenge the sometimes passionate objections of his fellow managers to the need for a foreign investor in the company.

As the discussions continued, General Electric proposed to license technology to PBS, but General Electric would have imposed conditions that were unattractive and would not have invested any equity. The other potential partners fell into secondary positions. Siemens, GEC Alsthom, and Deutsche Babcock did not put forward sufficiently comprehensive proposals, or they did not offer enough technology transfer. The remaining contender was ABB.

ABB

ABB, formed by the merger in 1988 of Asea of Sweden and Brown Boveri of Switzerland, was one of the world's major engineering and industrial equipment companies. It had revenue of $29.6 billion in 1992 and net income of $505 million, which gave it a return on equity of 11.8 percent (from ABB web site http://www.abb.ch/abbgroup/investor). The company, with 213,000 employees, came out on top of both the 1994 and 1995 Financial Times–Price Waterhouse polls of European executives as the most respected company in the world (*Financial Times,* September 19, 1995).

The ABB corporate culture was more market- and efficiency-oriented than PBS's. Operating throughout the world in competitive markets, ABB's emphasis was on high quality at the right price. The customer dictated technical specifications as much as design engineers in ABB. ABB was accustomed to competing against other industry giants on big contracts. The firm was lean, renowned for having one of the smallest corporate staffs of any firm its size. Subsidiaries generally were given semiexclusive rights to a geographic area, but if the subsidiary failed to win bids or failed to make a profit, its geographic area might be changed or it might be sold.

ABB had five main businesses: industrial and building systems, power generation, power transmission and distribution, transportation, and financial services. The power generation business, into which PBS's business would fall, was the second largest of ABB's businesses, accounting for one-quarter of all ABB revenue. This business had experienced rapid growth; it had nearly tripled its revenue since 1988, despite declining prices. ABB's main competitors in its main businesses were Siemens of Germany, GEC Alsthom of Britain and France, Mitsubishi of Japan, and General Electric of the United States.

ABB was an example of a truly global corporation. The company had product-oriented business units with worldwide responsibilities ranging from design through manufacturing to marketing and customer service. ABB had a very small headquarters group in Zurich and dozens of wholly owned or majority-owned companies on six continents.

ABB was no stranger to negotiating foreign joint ventures. Its approach to negotiations—which emphasized relationship building, patient persistence, and resolving issues one at a time—had been honed through experience. In the power generation business, its corporate strategy was to locate the complete range of boiler production, turbine production, and power plant design activities into each of several ABB companies around the world rather than to separate boilers from turbines and put them in different companies. This approach allowed ABB to reduce the high costs of engineering labor and to compete in the high-value-added turnkey plant market.

Drawn by the country's skilled work force, low relative labor costs, proximity to western Europe, and successful conservative government, the company began investing in the Czech Republic in 1991. PBS would be the fourth and largest of seven Czech companies in the ABB network; other acquisitions had already been made in Poland, Hungary, and Romania.

In particular, ABB identified four main attractions of a joint venture with PBS:

1. ABB expected the market for power plants in the Czech Republic and in other central and east European countries to develop over time and become large, stimulated by the effort to clean up old plants; ABB wanted to be a "local" company inside this market.
2. ABB needed to develop a low-cost export platform—to export components to other ABB companies and to export complete products to other countries. Low-cost east European components could be combined with high-cost German or Swedish components to make an attractive total product package.
3. PBS had boilers and turbines in one company (one location), while ABB did not have boiler capacity in Europe. (It is easier to build a power plant if boiler and turbine production are located together because they frequently communicate with each other.)
4. PBS had considerable installed capacity to service; this would provide good short-run business even though the Czech Republic was not a major growth market in the power plant business at present.

ABB gave no thought to a licensing arrangement. According to an ABB negotiator,

> It is not the ABB way. We wanted equity. Anyway, in this case, we wanted just about the whole company, and that is not as easy to license as, say, the production of gas turbines like General Electric does. . . . We wanted to develop the power generation business in east and central Europe, and that required the hands-on management that only a controlling interest in a joint venture allowed.

The ABB team made it clear that it sought to buy into both the turbine and boiler businesses and to expand the turnkey operations. The other bidders were interested in smaller segments of the business. The ABB team's desire to incorporate both the turbine and boiler business made it more attractive to PBS management. ABB presented opportunities for technology transfers, training, market access, and investment capital that could build up PBS instead of simply absorbing it.

ABB sent representatives from its Power Ventures unit to negotiate the deal. Their task was to establish the joint venture and to manage its startup. The representatives had contact with PBS management and employees at different levels. Meetings with ABB's top corporate executives, including a lunch in Zurich with Percy Barnevik, the chief executive officer, were arranged for Kuba. ABB also engaged the head of its Prague office to emphasize to PBS management the advantages that ABB offered as a joint venture partner and ABB's vision for creating with PBS an efficient engineering firm capable of serving the turbine, boiler, and turnkey markets using advanced technologies and creative engineering solutions. ABB recognized PBS's capabilities in coal-fired power plants and intended to keep the joint venture a full-fledged company, not just a manufacturing plant. ABB also included environmental indemnifications in its offer. Substantial sums were invested in developing and presenting the pitch.

Among all potential western partners, only ABB was seemingly unfazed by PBS's lack of unified commitment to the concept of a joint venture. ABB sought to identify specific concerns of PBS management and responded with detailed presentations.

THE DECISION

After several months of negotiations, PBS managers had all the information needed to make a decision and several proposals before them to consider, the most attractive of which was from ABB. The meeting of the PBS board to decide on the proposals was held in late December 1992; it lasted twelve hours and became contentious. Everyone realized the gravity of the situation.

The board members returned to the issue of whether PBS should enter into a joint venture with a large western partner. Strong concerns were voiced; many of the managers had worked for PBS for decades and feared that PBS was inviting ruin by surrendering its independence. They feared the intrusion of western management. They saw the joint venture proposals as giving up, and they weren't ready to do that. Finally, after several hours, one member stood up and said "I'm going to say what I think everyone else is afraid to say—we don't like it. We don't want a deal." The board took a poll and decided that PBS should reject all joint venture proposals.

After the poll, the IFC advisers addressed the board for a further six hours, emphasizing that PBS's negotiating position was not likely to improve with time. Its market position would decline in the absence of needed investment and technology improvement. Further, if they simply broke off negotiations with the companies courting them now, they should expect that any future discussions on cooperation would meet with a much less favorable response. In short, PBS's negotiating leverage would steadily decrease over time and eventually, given its economic prospects, the company

would be forced to accept a much less desirable arrangement than was currently available. The time to form a joint venture was now or never; the company needed to decide now whether it would pursue its business objectives without a foreign partner or tell the existing bidders why their proposals were not satisfactory and invite revised bids. After further deliberation, the board resolved to solicit improved bids.

ABB responded quickly with a multifaceted approach, directing its attention not only to the board members but also to managers at lower levels and employees whose voices they knew could flow upward to persuade board members to change their minds in favor of a deal. Several ABB executives and engineers arrived in Brno the weekend following the marathon board meeting to address the issues that PBS had identified as most troublesome. They arranged to meet with employees at several different levels in order to hear and address the most common concerns. They believed it was important to provide a formal avenue for these employees to express their fears and reservations.

The ABB team presented a new proposal within a few days. A new board meeting was scheduled in which a decision would be made.

APPENDIX: BUSINESS UNDER CENTRAL PLANNING AND THE VELVET REVOLUTION

The Czechoslovak economy was nearly totally state-owned and mostly closed to trade and investment with the West from 1946 until the end of 1989. Most industries had only a few large enterprises, and in many instances they were monopoly producers of individual products. This meant that enterprises were typically very big (relative to the size of the market) and specialized in the production of just one product or a narrow product line. Enterprises in an industry were typically combined under a single "koncern." PBS was part of the Škoda Koncern group of companies, which consisted of Škoda Plzeň (a heavy machinery maker with 30,000 employees), PBS (10,000 employees), CKD (a maker of railroad cars with 4,000 employees), SES (a Slovak company with 8,000 employees), and several smaller companies. Škoda Koncern was organized differently from most other Czech industrial groups insofar as it did not separate research and engineering into an enterprise apart from manufacturing units. Each company was a stand-alone enterprise.

The needs of the Soviet Union shaped the production program of many enterprises. Producers in centrally planned economies typically were only manufacturing plants (an enterprise was termed a "statni podnik" or state plant). They were producers, but they did not do other business functions, such as marketing and finance. Distribution and sales were handled by separate state-owned trading companies, research and development was either centralized or assigned to a separate enterprise, and capital investment decisions were made by the state. Banks disbursed funds and collected "profits" but did not make lending decisions. There were no capital markets.

The goal of the firm that all managers understood was to meet the production plan set by the central ministry. Successful managers were those who could skillfully negotiate a favorable plan and who knew how to produce the required quantity. Another goal imposed on firms by the state was to provide employment for everyone. There was little concern about costs, prices, money, or profits. Most managers were technically trained, and all top managers were necessarily members of the Communist Party; selection depended on political as well as business considerations.

Enterprises were centralized and hierarchical and typically had a functional organizational structure in which the production function was the biggest and most important. Other functions usually included a technical function, a commercial function (this was mainly order-filling and shipping), an economy function (mainly financial recordkeeping), a personnel function, and others depending on the company's type of business. Large enterprises during the socialist era typically provided a wide range of housing, recreation, education, and medical services to their employees.

The Velvet Revolution occurred in late November 1989 in Czechoslovakia, a few months after the fall of the Berlin Wall. The name, Velvet Revolution, comes from the fact that the existing Communist government resigned without bloodshed, after massive peaceful demonstrations in Prague, giving way to a democracy almost overnight. The first post-Communist government was led by Václav Havel, a playwright who had been imprisoned under the former regime for his political views. Havel, though inexperienced in government, was a strong symbol of the moral underpinnings of the Velvet Revolution and the future for Czechoslovakia. One of the first orders of business was rapid transformation of the economy (one of the ten largest in the world between World Wars I and II) from the most thoroughly state-owned of all Soviet bloc economies to a market economy based on private ownership of property. Many of the people who rose to power in companies had been active in the "Prague Spring" of 1968, a period of liberalization. The reforms were put down by an invasion of troops and tanks from Russia and other Soviet client states in August 1968. Many business leaders who sympathized with Prague Spring reforms were demoted.

PBS (B): The ABB PBS Joint Venture in Operation

The PBS board meeting to make the decision whether to accept the ABB proposal for a joint venture lasted eighteen hours. In the end, the PBS board voted in favor and the joint venture was agreed to. Several legal and contractual issues were quickly resolved, and the deal was signed in late December 1992.

STRUCTURE AND ORGANIZATION

ABB První Brněnská Strojírna Brno, Ltd. (ABB PBS) was a joint venture in which ABB had a 67 percent stake and PBS a.s. had a 33 percent stake. The PBS share was determined nominally by the value of the land, plant and equipment, employees, and goodwill. ABB contributed cash and specified technologies and assumed some of the debt of PBS. The new company started operations on April 15, 1993.

The ABB PBS company was a joint venture in its formal structure and governance. PBS a.s. had seats on the board, had part ownership, and was a supplier to the joint venture. The core operations of PBS a.s. were its Brno-based power generation business, its experience with turnkey operations, and its engineering and manufacturing capabilities with its customer base of installed equipment. The joint venture included the turnkey power plant business, boilers, and turbines (but not turbochargers). All of the PBS facilities in Brno and the outlying plant in Mikulov that made turbine blades went into the joint venture (refer to Table A-2). In sum, about 4,000 employees from PBS a.s. went to the joint venture; about 3,400 remained in PBS a.s. About 80 percent of the revenue of PBS a.s. became part of the joint venture.

Profit was to be divided in 2/3 to 1/3 shares according to ownership when it was earned and distributed; initial plans called for reinvestment of all profits and no dividends paid out to corporate parents.

ABB PBS was organized by product lines: power plants, turbines, boilers, and external services (the latter was added in 1995). Centralized functions such as marketing, finance, human resources, quality control, and information systems reported vertically to the general director and were matrixed horizontally with the business units or product divisions. The internal service division (maintenance) served the four product divisions. Each product division also had some of the same functions (Figure B-1).

ABB PBS was assigned geographic regions as its market territories by the ABB power generation segment and used the ABB selling network in these territories. Other ABB companies in the same lines of business had other territories, so head-to-head competition among ABB sister companies for the same customers was minimized.

The ABB regional selling network assisted ABB PBS in identifying business opportunities. ABB PBS was the prime contractor for the projects obtained. For turbines and boilers that were not part of a turnkey project, or in cases in which another ABB company was the primary contractor, ABB PBS participated as a subcontractor. ABB PBS had its own vice president for export sales and an export sales force for direct selling, as well as selling in cooperation with the ABB regional network.

In the domestic market, ABB PBS continued to use its own sales force and customer contacts. There were two domestic competitors, Škoda Turbiny (a company in the Škoda Koncern) and Vitkovice, whose principal business was steel.

FIGURE B-1

ABB PBS Organizational Chart in 1995

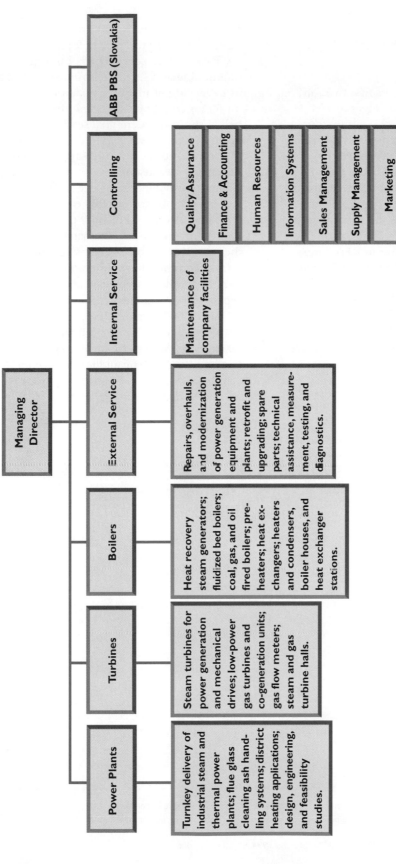

Source: ABB PBS, Annual Report, 1995.

BUSINESS RESULTS

Financial Performance

Business for the joint venture in its first two full years was good in most aspects. Orders received in 1994, the first full year of the joint venture's operation, were the highest in the history of PBS. Orders received in 1995 increased 7 percent over 1994 in nominal terms. Revenues for 1995 were two and a half times those in 1994 (Table B-1). The company was profitable in 1995 and ahead of 1994 results with a rate of return on assets of 2.3 percent and a rate of return on sales of 4.5 percent (Table B-2).

The 1995 results showed substantial progress toward meeting the joint venture's strategic goals adopted in 1994 as part of a five-year plan. One of the goals was that exports should account for half of total orders by 1999. (Exports had accounted for more than a quarter of the PBS business before 1989, but most of this business disappeared when the Soviet Union collapsed.) In 1995, exports in-creased as a share of total orders to 28 percent, up from 16 percent the year before.

The external service business, organized and functioning as a separate business for the first time in 1995, did not meet expectations. It accounted for 5 percent of all orders and revenues in 1995, below the 10 percent goal set for it. The retrofitting business, which was expected to be a major part of the service business, was disappointing for ABB PBS, partly because many other small companies began to provide this service in 1994 (including some started by former PBS employees who took their knowledge of PBS-built power plants with them). However, ABB PBS managers hoped that as the company introduced new technologies, these former employees would gradually lose the ability to perform these services and that the retrofit and repair service business would return to ABB PBS.

ABB PBS dominated the Czech boiler business with 70 percent of the Czech market in 1995, but managers expected this share to go down in the future as new domestic and foreign competitors ap-

TABLE B-1

Orders and Revenues for ABB PBS Businesses in 1994 and 1995

Business	1994		1995	
	Kč million	% of total	Kč million	% of total
Power plants				
Revenue	490	23	3,062	52
Orders	3,230	49	3,687	47
Turbines				
Revenue	707	34	1,118	19
Orders	938	14	1,389	18
Boilers				
Revenue	900	43	1,353	23
Orders	2,439	37	2,452	31
Services				
Revenue	(not reported separately		314	5
Orders	in 1994)		381	5
Total	2,097	100	5,847	100
	6,607	100	7,909	100

Notes: Kč are in nominal terms. The sum of revenues and orders across businesses in this table exceeds the total revenue and orders figures reported in the income statement data in Table B-2; the percent distributions in this table are figured on the sum of revenues and orders in this table.

Source: ABB První Brněnská Strojírna s.r.o., 1995 Business Report and 1994 Business Report.

TABLE B-2

Selected Income Statement, Balance Sheet, and Other Operating Data for ABB PBS, 1994 and 1995
(Kč million current)

Variable	1994	1995
Revenue	1,999	5,015
Orders received	6,208	7,088
R & D expenditure	29	64
Investment	435	388
Total assets	5,115	9,524
Fixed assets	1,773	2,186
Trade receivables	451	509
Trade payables	197	817
Bank loans	690	710
Equity	1,130	1,110
Exports (percent of orders)	16%	28%
Employees (number)	3,600	3,235
Labor productivity (value added/salaries)*	Kč109/Kč	Kč 163/Kč

*Value added is revenue minus purchased inputs. The labor productivity figures are not meaningful as absolute numbers but rather are used for overtime comparisons.
Sources: ABB První Brněnská Strojírna s.r.o., 1995 Business Report and 1994 Business Report.

peared. Furthermore, the west European boiler market was actually declining because environmental laws caused a surge of retrofitting to occur in the mid 1980s, leaving less business in the 1990s. Accordingly, ABB PBS boiler orders were flat in 1995.

Top managers at ABB PBS regarded business results to date as respectable, but they were not satisfied with the company's performance. Cash flow was not as good as expected. Cost reduction had to go further. "The more we succeed, the more we see our shortcomings," said one official.

Restructuring

The first round of restructuring was largely completed in 1995, the last year of the three-year restructuring plan. Plant logistics, information systems, and other physical capital improvements were in place. The restructuring included the following:

■ Renovating and reconstructing workshops and engineering facilities

■ Achieving ISO 9001 for all four ABB PBS divisions (awarded in 1995)

■ Transfer of technology from ABB (this was an ongoing project)

■ Installation of an information system

■ Management training, especially in total quality assurance and the English language

■ Implementing a project management approach

A notable achievement of importance to top management in 1995 was a 50 percent increase in labor productivity, measured as value added per payroll crown. However, in the future, ABB PBS expected its wage rates to go up faster than west European wage rates (Czech wages were increasing about 15 percent per year), so it would be difficult to maintain the ABB PBS unit cost advantage over west European unit cost.

The Technology Role for ABB PBS

The joint venture was expected from the beginning to play an important role in technology development for part of ABB's power generation business worldwide. PBS a.s. had engineering capability in coal-fired steam boilers, and that capability was expected to be especially useful to ABB as more countries became concerned about air quality. (When asked if PBS really did have leading technology here, a boiler engineering manager remarked, "Of course we do. We burn so much dirty goal in this country, we have to have better technology.")

However, the envisioned technology leadership role for ABB PBS had not been realized by mid 1996. Kuba, the ABB PBS managing director, realized the slowness with which the technology role was being fulfilled, and he offered his interpretation of events:

> ABB did not promise to make the joint venture its steam boiler technology leader. The main point we wanted to achieve in the joint venture agreement was for ABB PBS to be recognized as a full-fledged company, not just a factory.... We were slowed down on our technology plans because we had a problem keeping our good, young engineers. The annual employee turnover rate for companies in the Czech Republic is 15 or 20 percent, and the unemployment rate is zero. Our engineers have many other good entrepreneurial opportunities. Now we've begun to stabilize our engineering workforce. The restructuring helped. We have better equipment and a cleaner and safer work environment.... We also had another problem, which is a good problem to have. The domestic power plant business turned out to be better than we expected, so just meeting the needs of our regular customers forced some postponement of new technology initiatives.

ABB PBS had benefited technologically from its relationship with ABB. One example was the development of a new steam turbine line. This project was a cooperative effort among ABB PBS and two other ABB companies, one in Sweden and one in Germany. Nevertheless, technology transfer was not the most important early benefit of the ABB relationship. Rather, one of the most important gains was the opportunity to benchmark the joint venture's performance against other established western ABB companies on variables such as productivity, inventory, and receivables.

MANAGEMENT ISSUES

The toughest problems that ABB PBS faced in the early years of the joint venture were management issues. There were two: How to relate to ABB sister companies in other countries and how to transform the human capital of the company.

Relationships with Other ABB Companies

Managing a joint venture company was always difficult, and joining a global corporation compounded the start-up challenges. The Czech managers at ABB PBS had to learn fast. One set of problems arose from the relationship of ABB PBS to its ABB sister companies. Kuba and his colleagues were accustomed to working together with other companies on big projects; before the Velvet Revolution, PBS worked with other companies in the Škoda group. But ABB was different. Cooperation coexisted with competition, and that was outside Kuba's experience. Sibling rivalry among companies was very much a fact of business life, he discovered. After relating an unhappy episode about his company's unfamiliarity with these business relationships, he commented:

> We underestimated the cultural differences between Czechs and other west European people. We have to learn how to say "no." We have to be better in claim management. We have to fight more in order to succeed in this environment.

This fact of corporate life was confirmed by Erik Fougner, the ABB country manager in the Czech Republic, who also noted that excess capacity in Europe caused the older ABB companies to be particularly anxious about the arrival of the Czech newcomer. Some were concerned that there would not be room for three ABB power generation industry companies in Europe in the future.

Human Capital Transformation

The physical and organizational restructuring of ABB PBS was nearly completed by 1996. The transformation of the thinking and behavior of employees had just begun. The ways that were adaptive, or at least tolerated, under central planning would not succeed in a competitive market economy. Changing employees' "mentality"—the term used by Czech managers—was human capital restructuring. It was proving very difficult to do, and it was going very slowly.

In several respects, ABB PBS was nicely positioned to accomplish human capital restructuring. The top management of the joint venture was stable; it was thoroughly Czech but with a keen awareness of the mentality issues; and the ABB parent company tried to offer assistance in a variety of ways. Czech management was supported by two or three expatriates taking nonexecutive positions in project management, supply management, and workshop planning.

The ABB PBS managers believed a background of knowledge of local history, culture, and business practices was essential. These Czech managers, as in most Czech companies, knew they had to change the attitudes and behaviors of their employees. Kuba said,

> It is easy to change the structure of the company, and it is easy to change the facilities, but it is not easy to change people's minds.... Employees don't yet understand the consequences of their actions. They don't take responsibility. There is low unemployment so they can leave and get a less stressful job instead of taking responsibility here.

ABB PBS had never laid off any employees for lack of work. Managers appreciated the good reputation this brought the company, but they also wondered if it dampened employees' motivation to work hard. Without the threat of layoff, would managers' human resource initiatives be followed?

Fougner, a Norwegian located in Prague since 1992, saw the same "mentality" problem:

> This is a bigger challenge than I thought it would be. The first level of change in Czech companies comes easily. To make nice new offices and new factory layouts is quite simple. But the transfer of real human resource learning is slow.... Responsibility and initiative are poor because it was not rewarded for two generations in these formerly centrally planned economies. Under central planning, you were given a task, you did it, and nothing bad would happen to you. The tasks themselves were compartmentalized—I did mine and you did yours. I did my duty so I'm okay. Even managers did not see the whole picture and could not take responsibility for it. The functional organization of companies [with the archetypal "functional chimneys"] made it worse.

What could be done? The company took three approaches. At the corporate level, ABB PBS tried to instill a sense of mission. The annual report for 1995 noted the efforts of top management to find agreement on corporate goals and values in order

to strengthen employee identification with the company.

ABB, the parent company, tried to assist, but did not want to send too many expatriates to ABB PBS. Rather, local managers had to bring about the mentality changes themselves. ABB loaned some of the people from its internal consulting unit to the joint venture on a part-time basis. Their job was to train the (local) trainers and to sit beside the production and engineering managers and supervisors and work through attitude change material with them. Line managers were the ones who would implement the human capital restructuring, not personnel managers.

The compensation system was the third line of attack. Before the Velvet Revolution, factory-worker pay at PBS was based on a piece rate system that was surprisingly common in the Czech Republic. However, it was badly manipulated so that it did not motivate workers to raise output. Real or imagined equipment problems or shortages of parts—both of which occurred frequently—would excuse workers from meeting desired rates of output, or workers would stockpile output and then slack off. The system fostered the attitude among some workers that "you get a wage to show up, and anything extra you do gets you extra pay." This attitude reflected working conditions under communism, where wages were an entitlement rather than a payment for labor services rendered.

ABB PBS introduced a new incentive pay scheme, which was not without its problems. Employees were accustomed to stability and predictability in earnings. Another problem was that the time horizon for the incentive pay was too long—year-long profit-sharing schemes were too distant for production workers because they could not see the link between their performance and their reward that far ahead. The scheme was modified in 1996 to reintroduce some smaller discretionary bonuses, which were granted when the bonus-worthy work took place.

THE FUTURE

The ABB PBS joint venture was only three years old in the spring of 1996. By that time, the legal privatization of industry in the Czech Republic was essentially completed. The first five years of the transition from central planning to market economy for Czech companies was over. This meant

TABLE B-3

Economic Conditions in the Czech Republic, 1993–1995

Variable	1993	1994	1995
Gross domestic product, real % change	−0.9	2.6	4.6
Industrial production, real % change	−5.3	2.3	9.0
Consumer price inflation, %	20.8	10.0	8.9
Interest rate, %	14.1	13.1	12.8
Exchange rate, Kč/$, annual average	29.3	28.8	26.3
Unemployment rate, %	3.5	3.2	3.0

Sources: Economist Intelligence Unit, *Country Report: Czech Republic and Slovakia,* 1st quarter 1996; 2nd quarter 1994. International Monetary Fund, *International Financial Statistics,* March 1996, January 1994. Washington, D.C., 1996, 1994.

that some of the most extreme external stresses on companies, such as loss of markets and lack of finance, were behind them. The Czech economy appeared to be strong and growing (Table B-3).

By 1996, most of the major restructuring of ABB PBS was completed. Most of the easier internal changes had been made. Plant and equipment had been improved, and product quality was in good shape. Kuba and his colleagues had accomplished a lot, but they were not satisfied. Some of the hard changes were yet to be made, and the outlook for the company was mixed.

Doing business in competitive western markets was much more rugged than Kuba expected. Financial results were sufficient, given the difficult busi-

ness conditions the company faced, but they were not good enough for a mature market economy. Kuba knew there was overcapacity in the industry worldwide. There were tons of relatively small companies like his, and some of them would not survive. Belonging to the ABB network had advantages of course, but it also brought problems. Cooperation with ABB sister companies in marketing and technology was mirrored by competition and sibling rivalry with companies from cultures with which Kuba and his colleagues were unfamiliar. Internally, the transformation of ABB PBS's considerable human capital required renewed focus. Kuba could not rest easily yet.

CASE 41

The Boeing Company: The Merger with McDonnell Douglas

This case was prepared by Isaac Cohen of San Jose State University.

On December 10, 1996, Boeing CEO Philip Condit and McDonnell Douglas CEO Harry Stonecipher met in a hotel suite in Seattle to negotiate what *Fortune* magazine called "the sale of the century." Approved by both boards four days later, the merger of Boeing and McDonnell Douglas ended the longest-running rivalry in the aerospace industry. Boeing offered the McDonnell Douglas shareholders a stock swap that amounted to a premium of 21 percent over the price of McDonnell stock on the New York Stock Exchange—the equivalent of $14 billion in company stock. McDonnell Douglas's shareholders readily accepted the offer.[1]

To Stonecipher, the merger with Boeing represented an opportunity. With only one-third of its revenues and almost no earnings derived from its commercial products, McDonnell Douglas's commercial aircraft business was fast declining. The rapid consolidation of the defense business in the hands of a few large corporations (Lockheed Martin, Raytheon, Northrop Grumman, Boeing), coupled with the steady shrinkage of the defense budget, seriously threatened McDonnell Douglas's defense business. To survive, McDonnell Douglas had to merge with other defense firms. Stonecipher, therefore, was faced with a difficult decision: should McDonnell Douglas buy other defense businesses and pay a premium to the seller, or should it merge with the leading commercial aircraft maker and one of the largest defense companies, and be paid a premium by the buyer? Clearly, the high pre-

mium offered by Boeing tipped the balance in favor of a Boeing–McDonnell Douglas merger. Following the deal, Stonecipher became Boeing president.[2]

To Condit, the takeover of McDonnell Douglas also represented an opportunity. Because the commercial aircraft industry was subject to deep cyclical movement of booms and busts, and because the demand for defense products was relatively stable, Boeing could have benefited from the acquisition of a major military aircraft maker. Recalling two major slumps in Boeing's history, Condit explained:"We found ourselves moving in a direction ... of 80 percent commercial 20 percent defense and space, and at 20 percent, defense doesn't provide much pad for the next downturn on the commercial side."[3]

Condit acquired McDonnell Douglas just four months after he made a successful bid to purchase Rockwell's military and space division for $3.2 billion. He made both acquisitions during his first year at Boeing's helm, departing from Boeing's long-standing tradition of relying on in-house expansion rather than outright acquisition.[4] Condit continued serving as Boeing CEO following the takeover of McDonnell Douglas.

Although top management at Boeing and McDonnell Douglas had been discussing the possibilities of a merger for nearly three years, Condit's decision represented a strategic gamble. Would the Boeing Aircraft Company gain or lose from the merger with McDonnell Douglas? Would the merger enhance Boeing's worldwide competitive position relative to Airbus Industrie (a consortium formed by aerospace firms in four European countries), its only remaining rival? Or would it rather result in climbing costs and diminishing profits, because of the difficulties in integrating the two companies?

This case is intended to be used as the basis for class discussion rather than as an illustration of either effective or ineffective handling of the situation. This case was prepared by Isaac Cohen of San Jose State University. Used by permission.

THE AEROSPACE INDUSTRY

Commercial Aircraft

The structure of the commercial aircraft industry resembled that of a pyramid, with a few airframe integrators at the top, dozens of primary subcontractors at the middle, and thousands of secondary subcontractors at the base. Subcontracting of aircraft production had grown in importance as aircraft components became more and more complex. In the 1930s, subcontracting made up less than 10 percent of the industry's operation; in the 1950s, 30 to 40 percent; and by the 1970s, subcontractors fabricated between 60 and 70 percent of the value of American airframes.[5] As aircraft production became increasingly more risky, subcontracting became associated with risk sharing. Over time, aircraft manufacturers extended subcontracting throughout the world, partly as a result of the demand made by foreign customers and their governments. As overseas carriers bought aircraft, their governments required airframe integrators to share design work and production with overseas firms.[6]

Entry into the business of manufacturing large commercial aircraft had always been very limited. One barrier to entry was the high and increasing cost of product development. The Boeing 747, for example, cost $1 billion to develop, the Boeing 767 cost $1.5 billion, the Airbus A320 cost $2.5 billion, and the total cost of developing the Boeing 777 in the early 1990s exceeded of $5.5 billion.[7]

Another entry barrier was the need to establish learning curves and achieve economies of scale. To break even on an entirely new aircraft, it took sales of 400 to 500 units and a minimum of fifty sales per year. Not only was it necessary for a company to wait up to ten years in order to reach the break-even point, but there was no guarantee that the company would ever break even, let alone make profits. As one group of industry analysts concluded, "economic failure is the norm in the civil aircraft business."[8]

The need to control costs gave rise to the "family concept" in aircraft design. Producing families of planes rather than single models, aircraft manufacturers built flexibility into the design of a given aircraft so that the fuselage could be stretched in the future to add more passenger seats in the cabin. Pioneered by Boeing, model stretching did play an important role in enhancing aircraft productivity.

These cost-cutting measures notwithstanding, commercial aircraft makers were unable to survive without government support. In the past, military contracts were extremely beneficial to commercial aircraft and engine makers, especially insofar as expensive new technologies like jet propulsion and swept wings were concerned. Since the mid 1960s, however, military and commercial developments had diverged, and consequently, government support to commercial projects declined. The Department of Defense continued to fund research with potential military implications, but by the late 1980s such funding amounted to less than 5 percent of Boeing's research and development. NASA also provided some direct funding, but again, only for technology development, not commercial product development.[9]

An additional factor that influenced the dynamics of the aircraft industry was airline deregulation. Deregulation of the domestic airlines in 1978 resulted in a substantial increase in air travel, intense air-fare competition among carriers, the entry of new low-cost, low-capacity airlines into the industry, and the growing utilization of the hub-and-spoke system by the major carriers. On the one hand, the explosion in air travel led to a steep growth in demand for new aircraft of all kinds. On the other, the proliferation of low-cost, short-haul airline companies (for example, Southwest Airlines, American West), combined with the extensive use of hubs by the large carriers, brought about an increased demand for short-range, single-aisle airplanes like the Boeing 737, the McDonnell Douglas MD80, and the Airbus A320. Additionally, the deregulatory environment shifted the focus of airline competition from performance to cost and from service to price. As Frank Shrontz, Boeing CEO between 1988 and 1996 observed, "In the old days airlines were infatuated with technology for its own sake. Today the rationale for purchasing a new plane is cost savings and profitability".[10]

In Europe, too, the airline industry experienced progressive deregulation during the 1980s and 1990s. By 1998, about one half of all worldwide air travel took place within a competitive, deregulated environment.[11] Such a trend—which was expected to continue—was likely to encourage foreign air carriers to become more cost conscious and more profit oriented in the future. Thus, in both the domestic and foreign markets, the economic deregulation of airline travel promoted increased competition among aircraft manufacturers.

Defense and Space

The defense and space industry differed from the commercial aircraft industry in three important respects. First, the U.S. government was the only primary customer for noncommercial aerospace products and services, and consequently, the total output of the industry was determined by political considerations. On the one side, the production of domestic military aircraft, missiles, and space products and services was subject to congressional debate over the budget; on the other, foreign military sales were restricted by the administration's foreign policy.[12]

Second, the defense and space industry operated under favorable contractual arrangements with the government. Unlike investments in commercial aircraft manufacturing, investments in defense and space were neither subject to excessive risks nor to volatile changes in market demand. The potential for unforeseen obstacles in developing defense and space products was so large that cost estimates prior to production were almost impossible to obtain. Accordingly, the government provided contractors with a special shelter—a contractual arrangement known as "cost plus," under which a defense contractor was guaranteed fixed profits regardless of the level of the final costs. Contractors competed for projects by submitting bids, but such bids were later supplemented by additional funds to cover overrun costs.[13] To control cost overrun, the U.S. government introduced "fixed-price contracts" in the late

1980s, but as a result of intense lobbying efforts on the part of the defense contractors, the fixed price contracts were replaced again by "cost reimbursement contracts" in the early 1990s.[14]

Third, the government's importance as a customer for aerospace products and services had diminished (Table 1). With the breakup of the Soviet Union in 1990, the Cold War was over and projected defense spending plummeted. Between 1987 and 1997, the Pentagon budget declined by 30 percent and its weapon procurement budget declined by 54 percent in 1997 dollars.[15] The shrinking defense budget led to large-scale mergers and acquisitions among defense contractors and to the growing consolidation of the industry. (Table 2). Following the merger of Boeing and McDonnell Douglas, four defense and space conglomerates ruled the aerospace industry: Lockheed Martin, Boeing-McDonnell Douglas, Raytheon, and Northrop Grumman. All four competed for leadership, and all were joined in a dense web of alliances and subcontracting arrangements that allowed each to prosper.[16]

HISTORY OF THE BOEING-DOUGLAS RIVALRY

In 1917, William Boeing founded the Boeing Airplane Company in Seattle, Washington. Three years later, Donald Douglas established what would become in 1926 the Douglas Aircraft Company. During the early 1920s, both companies were building

TABLE 1

U.S. Aerospace Industry Sales by Customer, 1982–1996, Selected Years

Year	Total Sales	% of Total Sales to U.S. Government	% of Total Sales to Other Customers
1982	56.4 billion	69.0%	31.0%
1984	69.6	74.9	25.1
1986	88.5	73.9	26.1
1988	95.5	72.6	27.4
1990	112.0	63.9	36.1
1992	115.5	55.7	44.3
1994	92.1	60.5	39.5
1996	93.9	54.6	45.4

Source: Aerospace Facts and Figures, 1997–98 (Washington: Aerospace Industries Association of America, 1997), p.13.

TABLE 2

The Ten Largest Defense Mergers and Acquisitions, 1992–1996

- March 1993   Lockheed acquired General Dynamics' aircraft and military businesses for $1.52 billion.
- April 1993   Martin Marietta acquired General Electric's aerospace assets for $3.05 billion.
- December 1993   Loral Corporation Acquired IBM's Federal Systems' Division for $1.57 billion.
- May 1994   Northrop Corporation acquired Grumman Corporation for $2.17 billion.
- December 1994   Martin Marietta merged with Lockheed in a transaction valued at more than $10 billion.
- April 1995   Raytheon Company acquired E. Systems for $2.3 billion.
- March 1996   Northrop Grumman acquired the defense electronics business of Westinghouse for $3.2 billion.
- April 1996   Lockheed acquired most of the assets of the Loral Corporation for more than $9 billion.
- August 1996*   Boeing acquired the defense business of Rockwell International Corporation for $3.2 billion.
- Dec. 1996**   Boeing acquired McDonnell Douglas for $14 billion.

*Sources: Wall Street Journal, December 16, 1996, *New York Times, December 16, 1997; **Business Week, December 30, 1996, p.38.*

a variety of flying machines—made of wood and fabric—for the military. The market for commercial aircraft evolved during the 1930s. As Boeing supplied United Airlines with its first sixty B–247s, Douglas went ahead with the development and production of a similar but superior aircraft: the DC1 (Douglas Commercial). The DC1 served as a prototype, but the larger DC2 outclassed the B–247, and the improved DC3 established Douglas as the world's largest manufacturer of commercial aircraft.[17]

Unable to compete with Douglas in the commercial aircraft business, Boeing redirected its efforts toward the military. Boeing's principal success during World War II was the development and production of the B–17 "Flying Fortress"—a giant four-engine bomber. Douglas, too, put its resources into the war effort, building attack bombers (A-20 Havoc) and Navy bombers (SBD Dauntless) and suspending its commercial production.[18]

The steep decline in military orders at the end of the war brought the aircraft industry to the verge of collapse. Douglas met the crisis by reestablishing itself as the world's largest manufacturer of commercial aircraft, producing the last great American piston transports: the DC6 and DC7. Boeing survived the downturn by producing an early gen-

eration of jet aircraft for the military: the B–47 and B–52 strategic bombers.[19] Having stayed out of civil aviation for more than ten years,[20] Boeing reentered the air transport market only after the jet had become operational for commercial use.

Boeing's first jet, the 707, followed closely the design of the military tanker KC-135, which Boeing had first produced under government contract. Douglas had no such advantage. By contrast to the Boeing 707, Douglas's first jet, the DC8, was a financial disaster: the company did not sell a sufficient number of units to recover its development cost.[21] Douglas's second jet, the smaller DC9, also failed to compete successfully with its rival, the Boeing 727. Altogether, twice as many 727s as DC9s were delivered (Table 3), Douglas's expenses were higher than Boeing's, and Douglas was selling the DC9 below cost. To avoid bankruptcy, Douglas merged in 1967 with the stronger McDonnell Aircraft Corporation, a defense contractor.[22]

The newly formed McDonnell Douglas Corporation became the largest manufacturer of military aircraft in the United States. McDonnell's premier aircraft in the 1960s and early 1970s was the F-4 Phantom, the Air Force's top fighter in Vietnam. To replace the Phantom, the McDonnell Douglas Corporation developed and produced the Air Force F-15 Eagle Attack fighter (1972), and the Navy

TABLE 3

Total Number of Best Selling Commercial Airplanes Delivered by Boeing and McDonnell Douglas, 1959–1997

Boeing		McDonnell Douglas	
B–707	1,010 (retired)	DC–8	556 (retired)
B–727	1,831 (retired)	DC–9	976 (retired)
B–737	2,975	MD80/90	1,221
B–747	1,136	DC–10	446 (retired)

Source: Boeing, Commercial Airplane Group, *Announced Orders and Deliveries as of 12/31/97.*

F/A–18 Hornet strike fighter (1978). Both fighters were still in production in the 1990s, both were used in the Gulf (1991) and Kosovo (1999) wars, and both were principal contributors to McDonnell Douglas's revenues on the eve of the merger with Boeing. On the eve of the merger, the McDonnell Douglas Corporation also produced the C–17 Globemaster—the Air Force's most advanced military transport, first introduced in 1995. Other defense products manufactured by McDonnell Douglas at the time of the merger included attack jump jets for the Marines (AV–8B Harrier), training aircraft for the Navy (T–45 Goshawk), attack helicopters (AH–64 Apache), and guided missiles (Harpoon, Cruise, and Tomahawk Cruise). In 1993 and 1994 respectively, foreign orders of F/A–18s (Switzerland) and F–15 (Israel) boosted the company's military business.[23]

In contrast to its defense sector, McDonnell Douglas's commercial business lagged far behind Boeing's. Between 1959 and 1996, Boeing produced 8,200 commercial jetliners and Douglas only 3,300. Defined by range of travel, Boeing families of airframes included the 737 for short-range, the 757 and 767 for medium-range, and the 747 and 777 for medium- to long-range travel. Boeing's most successful models were the 737 and 747 series. Going into service in 1967, the B–737 had become the top-selling commercial jetliner in history, with 3,300 units delivered by early 1999. Boeing offered the 737 in a variety of models of different ranges (2,000 to 3,200 miles) and different seat capacities (108 to 189 seats).[24]

The 747 family was introduced in 1970. Its development and tooling costs had almost bankrupted the company, but by 1978 sales reached the break-even point and thereafter the 747 became Boeing's most profitable aircraft.[25] Responding to Boeing's challenge, both the McDonnell Douglas and the Lockheed corporations launched a new wide-body aircraft, and both failed. The DC10, like the L1011, carried only two-thirds of the passenger load of the 747, cost two-thirds as much, and had one-half the travel range of the 747; besides, the market for such an airplane could not sustain two competing models. Lockheed exited the market in 1981 after selling only 244 units, and Douglas rolled out the last passenger version of the DC10 in 1980, unable to recover the airplane's high development costs.[26]

Still, McDonnell Douglas introduced two other commercial aircraft models. To compete with the B–737, Douglas upgraded and stretched the DC9 into the MD–80 (1980) and MD–90 (1995). Although an initial success, the MD–80/90 series did not generate sufficient orders to sustain sales (Table 4). By 1996, less than 150 units were on order (against more than 750 B–737 units on order),[27] sales were slowing down, costs were going up, and the MD program was losing money. After the merger with McDonnell Douglas, Boeing decided to discontinue manufacturing the two MD models, effective in 1999.[28]

Finally, McDonnell Douglas made one last effort to enter the market for large wide-body aircraft. In 1989, the company put into service the three-engine

TABLE 4

Shipments of Large (over 33,000 lbs.) U.S.-manufactured Civil Transport Aircraft During the Five years preceding the Boeing–McDonnell Douglas Merger, 1992–1996

Company and Model	1992	1993	1994	1995	1996
B 737	218	152	121	89	76
B 747	61	5	40	25	26
B 757	99	71	69	43	42
B 767	63	51	40	36	42
B 777	—	—	—	13	32
Boeing total	441	330	270	206	218
MD–11	42	36	17	18	15
MD–80	84	42	22	18	12
MD–90	—	—	—	14	24
McDonnell Douglas total	126	78	39	50	51
Total	567	408	309	256	269

Source: Aerospace Facts and Figures, 1997–98, p.34.

("tri-jet") MD–11, a derivative of the DC10.[29] Again, sales of the MD–11 languished, and Douglas soon faced competition from Boeing's newest jetliner, the 777. Entering into service in 1995, the 777 outsold the MD11 by a margin of 2 to 1 within a year (Table 4). Following the merger with McDonnell Douglas, Boeing management decided to limit future production of the MD11 to its freighter version.[30]

Product Development

Product development in the commercial aircraft industry had long been the preferred growth strategy undertaken by competing manufacturers. The occasional development of a new family of planes was essential for securing market share in the future, and accordingly, both Boeing and McDonnell Douglas undertook such a strategy in the 1990s. Yet only Boeing managed to deliver the new product.

Early in 1996, McDonnell Douglas announced a plan to develop a new twin-engine, wide-body aircraft. Named the MD-XX, the new jetliner (8,000-mile range, 300 to 400 seats) was intended to broaden the McDonnell Douglas product line and thereby reestablish the company's role as a major player in the commercial aircraft industry in the twenty-first century. During the spring and summer of 1996, engineers at Douglas facilities in Long Beach, California, worked on the design of the MD-XX, the company received orders for forty to fifty units from customers, and it made preparations to launch the new aircraft at the end of the year. Yet, on October 24, it decided to terminate the project. Stonecipher, McDonnell Douglas's CEO, urged the company board to forgo the development of the MD-XX because of its prohibitive cost: the project would have required an initial investment of $3 billion and an additional capital of $12 billion spent over a ten-year period. "Fundamentally, it wasn't an MD-XX decision," Stonecipher admitted, "it was a question of how far, how fast, and at what rate" Douglas could compete in the commercial aircraft business. "The market may be too tough for us to battle through" and "I have . . . other alternatives." Six weeks later, Stonecipher negotiated with Philip Condit the sale of McDonnell Douglas to Boeing.[31]

Condit led the 777 program to completion. Condit's role in developing the 777 paved his way to the top: Midway through the 777 development program, Boeing's board of directors elected him president and gave him a seat on the board. Four years later, in 1996, the board promoted Condit to CEO.

Launching the Boeing 777 in 1990, Boeing management sought to ensure the company's future.

"This is an offensive, not a defensive strategy," Condit noted, predicting that the 777 family would remain in production for fifty years. A wide-body aircraft with two gigantic jet engines ("the most powerful ever built"), the 777 went into service two years after Airbus had introduced its own new wide-body models: the two-engine A320 and the four-engine A340.[32]

Competition—and Cooperation—in Space

Boeing and McDonnell Douglas had long competed over NASA contracts, but such competition did not rule out partnership. On the contrary, the typical NASA project was extremely demanding and therefore required the joint efforts of several competing contractors. In the 1960s, Boeing built the lunar orbiters that circled the moon and the first stage of the rockets used in the Apollo space program; McDonnell created the Mercury and Gemini capsules; and Douglas developed the Delta expendable launch vehicle, the world's most reliable space launcher. Following the successful moon mission, both Boeing and McDonnell Douglas competed for NASA's contract to build Skylab, America's first space station, and McDonnell Douglas won. In the 1980s, the Rockwell Corporation led the development of the space shuttle program, with Boeing and McDonnell Douglas as key partners. Boeing produced the upper stage of the shuttle, and McDonnell Douglas provided the structural parts for the booster that lifted the shuttle into space.

In the 1990s, Boeing was in charge of leading the development of the International Space Station—the largest and most complex structure ever assembled in space—and McDonnell Douglas served as a subcontractor to Boeing, responsible for producing the station's structural backbone. As the two companies merged in 1997, the International Space Station contract was a major contributor to Boeing's revenues, just as the Delta II space launcher contract was a principal contributor to McDonnell Douglas's revenues. After its merger with Rockwell (1996) and McDonnell Douglas, the new Boeing became NASA's single largest contractor.[33]

The Challenge of Airbus Competition

The new Boeing had one formidable rival: Airbus Industrie. While Airbus's production rates in the 1980s were still low, its booking of new aircraft orders skyrocketed, and subsequently, the consortium was fast expanding its capacity. Airbus orders surpassed those of McDonnell Douglas in 1986, and its deliveries exceeded those of McDonnell Douglas in 1991. As Airbus gained, Boeing's new orders fell below the 50 percent mark for the first time in more than two decades. In 1990, the 777 launch year, Boeing booked 45 percent of the total industry orders, Airbus 34 percent, and McDonnell Douglas 21 percent. In 1996, the year in which Boeing announced its merger with McDonnell, Airbus booked nearly 50 percent of the worldwide industry orders, and delivered close to one-third of the worldwide output of commercial jetliners (Table 5). The merger created a duopoly, which was supposed, in theory, to reduce competition and give each of the two companies a price advantage in a seller's market. On the contrary, however, the merger intensified the battle between Boeing and

TABLE 5

Market Share of Actual (1992–1998) and Forecast (1999–2000) Shipments of Commercial aircraft, Boeing, McDonnell Douglas(MD), and Airbus.

	1992	1993	1994	1995	1996	1997	1998	1999	2000
Boeing	61%	61%	63%	54%	55%	67%	71%	68%	61%
MD	17	14	9	13	13				
Airbus	22	25	28	33	32	33	29	32	39

Sources: Aerospace Facts and Figures, 1997–98, p. 34; Wall Street Journal, December 3, 1998, and January 12, 1999; The Boeing Company 1997 Annual Report, p. 19; data supplied by Mark Luginbill, Airbus communication director, November 16, 1998.

Airbus, leading each company to slash aircraft prices by as much as 20 percent.[34]

In 1970, aerospace companies in France, Germany, Britain, and Spain had formed Airbus. Pooling their resources together to create a consortium, the participating companies served as both shareholders of and subcontractors to Airbus. The participating companies competed with each other over the development and production of particular aircraft components, and thus different shares of a given program were distributed among the partners. The partners, in addition, received generous subsidies from their governments to finance Airbus projects and ensure the consortium's long-term survival. Airbus received nearly $10 billion in government assistance for the development and manufacture of its first three models, and an additional $4–5 billion for initial work on its A330/340 models. These subsidies led to a trade war. The United States government, together with representatives of Boeing and McDonnell Douglas, claimed that Airbus' subsidies violated the General Agreement on Tariffs and Trade (GATT), and called for their removal. Again and again, the parties failed to reach a compromise. In 1992, at long last, Airbus and Boeing signed a bilateral agreement that limited government subsidies to 33 percent of Airbus's total development costs. In exchange, the agreement limited federal indirect R&D funds to 3 percent of the total revenues received by American aircraft manufacturers. In 1995, after twenty-five years of losses, Airbus finally generated profits.[35]

Although government assistance helped Airbus stay in the aircraft industry for the long haul, the consortium's success was impossible to understand without considering its strategy. In developing its long-term plans, Airbus sought to build on Boeing's rich experience, mimicking three elements of the old Boeing strategy: technological leadership, cost controls, and the development of families of planes.

Technological Leadership   "You cannot compete with a dominant . . . player if you don't offer something different," former Airbus President Roger Beteille said. He added that to persuade the major airlines to switch to a new supplier, Airbus had to differentiate itself from Boeing by incorporating the most advanced technology into its planes.

Among Airbus's technological firsts, the fly-by-wire system was perhaps the most famous. Introduced in 1988, the A–320 was the world's first fly-by-wire commercial aircraft, an aircraft controlled by a pilot transmitting commands to the rudder and flaps electrically, not mechanically.[36]

Cost Controls   As competition with Boeing intensified during the recession of the early 1990s, Airbus sought to reduce costs through deep cuts in jobs, the streamlining of the production process, and the speed-up of deliveries. Each of the consortium's partner companies participated in these cost-cutting efforts. In Britain, British Aerospace cut its wing-production time by 50 percent in two years while trimming its Airbus work force from 15,000 to 7,000 in five years. In Germany, Daimler-Benz (later Daimler-Chrysler), which built fuselages, reduced its production costs by 33 percent and production time by 50 percent, in six years (1992–1998). And in France, state-owned Aerospatiale, which produced cockpits, reduced its work force by 17 percent between 1993 and 1996.[37]

Families of Planes   Boeing was the first company to use the family concept in aircraft design. Airbus made the concept the foundation of its manufacturing and marketing strategy. A family of planes was made up of derivative jetliners built around a basic model. Since all derivatives of a given model shared maintenance, training, and operation procedures, as well as replacement parts and components, the use of such derivative airplanes to serve different markets enabled airline carriers to cut costs. Airbus used this family-based strategy in two ways. First, it produced and marketed derivative jetliners, and second, it introduced common design features ("commonalities") across the entire range of its models, not just the members of a single family, thus providing airline carriers with additional sources of savings.[38]

Airbus's strategy served the consortium well. By the mid 1990s, Airbus competed with Boeing in every travel market except the one served by the 747. The A320 family challenged the 737 in the short-range 120-plus seat market, the A300/A310 family competed with the 757 and 767 in the medium range 200+ seat market, and the

A330/A340 family went after the market for medium- to long-range travel, anticipating the coming of the 777.

THE RESULTS OF THE MERGER

The Boeing–McDonnell Douglas merger was completed on August 1, 1997, eight months after Condit and Stonecipher had originally announced it. Upon the completion of the merger, Boeing became the world's largest producer of military aircraft and the second largest supplier to the U.S. Department of Defense. The newly merged company quickly consolidated its holdings. It turned McDonnell's Saint Louis headquarters into Boeing's headquarters for military aircraft and missile program, put Boeing's space division (based in Seal Beach, California) in charge of all Boeing and McDonnell Douglas space-related programs, and developed detailed plans to phase out the McDonnell Douglas commercial aircraft business.[39]

Yet the merger failed to produce the expected results. In 1997, Boeing recorded a net loss of $178 million, the worst financial performance in fifty years. In 1998, a United Airlines executive called Boeing a "dysfunctional organization,"[40] a *Wall Street Journal* reporter described Boeing's revised projections for 1999–2000 (Table 6) as "shock[ing],"

and Boeing President Harry Stonecipher conceded that the crisis was likely to last from "two to five" years.[41] Over a two-year period following the announcement of the merger, Boeing shares lost one-third of their value.[42] What, then, was the source of Boeing's post-merger difficulties?

Defense and Space

Boeing's defense and space business units had performed well right from the early days of the merger. Defense and space revenues accounted for 39 percent of the total company sales in 1997, up from 25 percent in 1996, 23 percent in 1994, and 20 percent in 1992.[43] The Defense Department was Boeing's largest customer, spending nearly four times as much as NASA (Table 7). Boeing's Defense and Space Group was profitable in 1997, generating a 7.3 percent return on sales and thus offsetting, almost entirely, the large loss incurred by the company's Commercial Airplane Group. As shown in Table 6, Boeing's defense and space business units were profitable in 1998 and were expected to continue generating profits through the year 2000, with the group's margins steadily improving.

Boeing Defense and Space Group gained from recent changes in the defense budget. Following a decade-long decline in U.S. military spending, the

TABLE 6

Highlights of Boeing's Financial and Operation Data: Actual (1997–1998) and Projected (1999–2000)

	1997	*1998*	*1999*	*2000*
Operating revenues (bm)	$46	$56	$58	$50
R&D spending (bm)	$1.9	$1.9	$1.6–1.8	$1.5–1.7
Comm. aircraft shipped	374	559	620	490
Employment (thousands)	238	231	200–210	185–195
Profit margins:*				
Comm. aircraft	– 6.6%	0%	2%–3%	1%–3%
Defense and space**	7.3%	7.7%	7%–9%	8%–10%

*Operating earnings returns on sales.
**Including "Information."
Sources: For 1997 and 1998, The Boeing Company 1997 Annual Report, pp. 19, 24, 35, 72, and The Boeing Company 1998 Annual Report, pp. 35, 51, 76; for 1998–2000, Frederick M. Biddle and Andy Pasztor, "Boeing May Be Hurt Up to 5 Years," *Wall Street Journal,* December 3, 1998.

TABLE 7

Boeing's Defense and Space Group:*
Sales by Customer, 1997

Air Force	30%
Navy	18%
Army	6%
NASA	15%
Foreign	22%
Other	9%
Total	$18 billion

* Including information.
Source: The Boeing Company 1997 Annual Report, p. 24.

defense budget stabilized in 1997 at about $250 billion and was expected to increase moderately between 1998 and 2003. NASA's budget was expected to remain flat on an inflation-adjusted basis.[44] With no further spending cuts projected in either defense or space, and with a slight increase in the military procurement budget, the prospects of the industry were fast improving. Lockheed Martin, Raytheon, and to a lesser extent, the Northrop Grumman Corporation, were Boeing's principal competitors in this segment.

The largest defense contractor, Lockheed Martin, was a highly diversified company, producing a well-balanced mix of aircraft, electronics, and missiles. Lockheed held the most lucrative Defense Department contract in the 1990s: the development and production of the Raptor fighter jet (F-22), a successor to McDonnell Douglas's "still unchallengeable" F-15. The Pentagon ordered 340 F-22s at a "minimum" cost of $75 million each. In 1997, Lockheed delivered the first test model to the Air Force, but the Raptor was not expected to go into full production until 2004. Although Lockheed was the project's prime contractor, Boeing served as a subcontractor to Lockheed, producing about one-third of the Raptor, including the wings and the aft fuselage.[45]

Raytheon was Boeing's major competitor in aerospace electronics. Of the total cost of a given fighter aircraft, electronics made up one-third; the airframe and engine accounted for the remaining two-thirds. Raytheon had acquired Hughes electronics in 1997 and as a result became a powerful rival to Boeing, specializing in the development

and production of radar systems, night vision equipment, avionics gear, and missiles.[46]

Northrop Grumman was a much smaller company than either Lockheed or Raytheon. Building one of the last B-2 Stealth bombers in 1997, Northrop had become the industry's principal subcontractor and Boeing's single largest supplier. Northrop manufactured the aft fuselage for the Navy's Super Hornet fighter and the tail assembly and surface controls for the C-17 military transport, both produced by McDonnell Douglas, later owned by Boeing. In addition, Northrop served as a major supplier to Boeing Airplane Commercial Group, building half of the 747's fuselage and the doors for most of Boeing's passenger jetliners, including the 747.[47]

Boeing's position in the industry was unique. Boeing had no recent experience in building fighter jets and therefore its merger with McDonnell Douglas was critical, especially insofar as long-term government contracts were concerned. First, McDonnell held the second largest Defense Department contract in the industry: the production of the Super Hornet F/A18E/F aircraft fighter, the latest addition to the Navy fleet. The Navy ordered a total of 500 Super Hornets at a cost of $45 million each. Production of the F/A18E/F had begun in 1997 and was expected to continue until 2010.[48]

More important, the merger strengthened Boeing's competitive position in the contest over the richest military-aircraft contract ever: the development and production of the Joint Strike Fighter (JSF), a successor to Lockheed's F-16. In October 1996, the Defense Department selected Boeing and Lockheed, not McDonnell, to compete for the JSF project. The exclusion of McDonnell Douglas played a key role in Stonecipher's decision to sell the company to Boeing. A multipurpose low-end fighter, the JSF was expected to cost less than half as much as the high-end Raptor, yet the sheer size of the Pentagon's projected order was staggering: 2,850 JSFs in three different versions (Air Force, Navy, and Marine models) at the total estimated cost of more than $200 billion. The fly-off contest between Boeing and Lockheed was scheduled for 2001, and according to defense analysts, Boeing had the edge both because it was better equipped to master the complex manufacturing process required and because it was able to control costs better, having had the discipline of the commercial marketplace. In 1999, Lockheed reported a $150 million cost overrun for work on the design of an entrant to the JSF fly-off competition, a problem that was likely to hurt the company's prospects of winning the contract.[49]

The merger with McDonnell Douglas also provided Boeing with ample engineering and manufacturing resources. In the long run, the potential of transferring technological know-how back and forth between commercial and military business units gave Boeing an enormous advantage over its rivals, as even Boeing's competitors acknowledged. To mention one example, Boeing had developed expertise in composite materials while working on the B–2 bomber and then used this expertise to build the tail wing of the 777, which, in turn, was used to develop its advanced wing design for the proposed JSF jet.[50]

Commercial Aircraft

Boeing Commercial Aircraft Group lost $1.8 billion in 1997, the first year of the merger. In 1998, the group barely generated any profits, and during the next two years (1999–2000), its profits were expected to remain low, with the margins ranging from 1 to 3 percent (see Table 6).

One source of Boeing's post-merger troubles was its acquisition of the McDonnell Douglas MD model series. At the time of the merger, McDonnell's commercial jetliner business was losing money, and consequently, Boeing's management decided to phase it out, taking a special $1.4 billion pretax charge[51] which resulted in a larger than expected reported loss in 1997 (see Table 6).

Another source of difficulties was Condit's neglect of Boeing's commercial aircraft business. A newly promoted CEO, Condit focused almost exclusively on expanding Boeing's military business. He developed a long-term strategy of turning Boeing into the world's largest aerospace and defense company and implemented it at once, first buying Rockwell's military units, and then the McDonnell Douglas Corporation. Eager to complete the deal with McDonnell and preoccupied with lobbying the U.S. government for its approval, he overlooked mounting assembly-line problems that crippled Boeing Commercial Airplane Group. When it became apparent in the summer of 1997 that Boeing's assembly line was falling behind, Condit still underestimated the problem, acknowledging just a month-long delay in deliveries of commercial jets.[52]

But Boeing production problems were serious. A rapid ramp-up in aircraft production led to shortages of raw materials (aluminum, titanium, and other composites) and to delays in deliveries of parts and subassemblies. The hiring of thousands of inexperienced, "green," workers resulted in productivity inefficiencies.[53] So severe were the shortages and inefficiencies that the company was forced to shut down its 737 and 747 production line for one month in order "to bring work back into sequence."[54] Although largely unrelated to the Boeing–McDonnell Douglas merger, these problems did affect the post-merger results.

Other problems affected the post-merger results as well. Increased competition with Airbus drove Boeing's management to protect the company's market share at almost any cost. Caught in the competition, Boeing's management overlooked expenses, slashed prices, and gave up technological leadership. In the market for single-aisle, narrow-body aircraft, for example, Boeing competed with Airbus on price rather than technology, often selling the B–737 below cost. Because the A–320 was slightly more advanced than the B–737 (and its cabin a bit larger), a growing number of airline carriers favored the first over the second, citing passengers' preferences as the reason. United Airlines' 1996 decision to extend an Airbus A–320 order was a case in point.[55]

Still, Boeing's most pressing problem was cost escalation. In 1998, Boeing used 20 to 30 percent more labor hours to produce a jetliner than it had done in 1994.[56] As the company's four-year efforts to contain costs had stalled, Boeing lost $1 billion on the sale of its first 400 new-model 737s.[57] Although the company had launched a two-year program to modernize production, it continued to operate 400 separate computer systems that were not linked together.[58] While Airbus had already adopted a flexible, lean-production manufacturing system, Boeing was still utilizing a standardized, mass-production system that had barely changed since World War II. Hence the gap in labor productivity. In 1998, Boeing employed 211 workers for every commercial aircraft (560 jets made by 119,000 employees), and Airbus just 143 (230 jets produced by 33,000 workers).[59]

Finally, the merger of Boeing and McDonnell Douglas coincided with the Asian economic slump. The slump prompted the Asian airlines to cancel or defer aircraft orders. The slump affected both Airbus and Boeing, but not in the same way. On the one hand, Asian orders of wide-body jets were the most vulnerable and the first to be canceled; on the other, Airbus booked fewer such orders than did Boeing. Since Boeing, unlike Airbus, was highly dependent on the Asian market for the sale of its wide-body jets, the 747 and 777, Boeing's potential losses were greater than those of Airbus.[60]

CULTURE AND LEADERSHIP

The merger of Boeing and McDonnell Douglas posed a challenge to the new Boeing of integrating the two companies' corporate cultures and leadership styles. To be sure, both Boeing and McDonnell Douglas were aerospace firms dominated by an engineering culture. Their respective corporate images embodied the values and attitudes of engineers, that is, logic, precision, professionalism, and authority. Their professional work force was made up, first and foremost, of engineers, and their skilled work force of aircraft mechanics.

Still, there was a difference. According to industry analysts, McDonnell had long been known for its top-down management style, which had been formed through close alliance with the defense industry. Its organizational structure was rigid, its decision-making procedure centralized, and its chain of command quasi-military. Boeing, by contrast, had developed a more progressive management structure, based partly on team work and partly on employees' participation in decision making.[61] Boeing's management practices were shaped, above all, by the need to compete in the marketplace.

Condit's leadership style reflected Boeing's managerial tradition. An inspirational leader endowed with exceptional social skills, Condit led by example. Always preferring to work in groups, he regularly assigned tasks to teams rather than individuals. To promote camaraderie, loyalty, and a strong sense of bonding among Boeing's executives, he developed a ritual. Periodically, he would invite a new group of managers to his house to sit around the fire and tell anecdotes about their experience at Boeing. Each executive would than write on a piece of paper a positive and a negative story about Boeing, toss the paper with the negative story into the fire, and keep the paper with the positive story to carry it around and show others.[62]

Stonecipher's style was different, reflecting, to some extent at least, McDonnell's managerial philosophy. A strong executive with a track record of corporate turnaround, downsizing, and outsourcing, Stonecipher was a blunt talker and an aggressive leader, feared by his subordinates and highly respected on Wall Street. A nonplayer, he led by explicit command rather than persuasion. Asked once (in 1998) to compare his managerial style with that of Condit, he replied: "I'm more likely to shoot you and then ask your name; Phil is likely to ask your name and then shoot you."[63]

Condit had joined Boeing in 1965, after receiving a master's degree in aeronautical engineering from Princeton University. A gifted engineer, he rose quickly at Boeing, becoming vice president in 1983, president in 1992, and CEO in 1996.[64] Stonecipher had spent twenty-seven years at General Electric, rising through the ranks to become head of GE's jet engine division. He subsequently spent seven years at the Sunstrand Corporation (a military contractor making aerospace components), turning the company around, and three years at McDonnell Douglas, improving the firm's financial performance before selling it to Boeing.[65] At Boeing, Stonecipher served as president and as a director of the board.

The contrast between Condit's and Stonecipher's leadership styles raised an interesting question: Would the two executives cooperate successfully during the post-merger years or would they clash? Apparently, as Boeing's financial performance worsened, Stonecipher had gained power relative to Condit. Stonecipher was now one of Boeing's largest shareholders—Condit owned a relatively small amount of stock—and he enjoyed wide support among the company's investors. Nevertheless, he had two handicaps. First, he lacked the backing of Boeing's board of directors. Only four of Boeing's thirteen board members (including Stonecipher and John F. McDonnell, son of the company's founder) were McDonnell Douglas affiliates, and fully eight directors represented the old Boeing and were loyal to Condit. Second, he was sixty-three years old (in 1999) and Boeing's top executives were required to retire at sixty-five.[66]

TURNAROUND

As Boeing's crisis deepened, Condit, Stonecipher, and other top executives laid out a turnaround strategy. The strategy was based on a combination of four elements: the reorganization of Boeing's two major product groups, the replacement of the executive responsible for running the company's commercial airplane division, the introduction of radical cost-cutting measures, and the hiring of a new chief financial officer from outside the company.

On September 1, 1998, Condit ousted Ronald Woodward, head of Boeing's Commercial Airplane Group, who was next in line to become CEO, and replaced him with Alan Mulally. Mulally, who had served as Condit's chief engineer on the 777 project, had a reputation of a skillful team leader and headed Boeing's Defense and Space Group after the merger with McDonnell Douglas.

In consolidating the businesses of Boeing and McDonnell, Mulally quickly reorganized the Defense and Space Group. Taking a page from Alfred Sloan's reorganization of General Motors in the 1920s, he grouped all products and services into separate, autonomous divisions, drew carefully the divisional boundaries, and rendered each division responsible for its own financial performance. He then took charge of Boeing's Commercial Airplane Group and did the same. He reorganized it into three independent divisions: one responsible for single-aisle (narrow-body) planes, one for twin-aisle (wide-body) planes, and one for customer service. Again, each division was expected to generate its own profits, and each was responsible for its own loses. In the past, Boeing's executives rarely knew the exact cost of the planes they produced. Now they were fully accountable.[67]

Next, Boeing undertook several steps to cut costs, the most significant of which was downsizing. During the two-year period 1999–2000, Boeing planned to cut 30,000 to 50,000 jobs (see Table 6), most of them in the commercial aircraft division. Early in 1999, Boeing introduced a new computerized system designed to control the supply and stock of parts and components, and thereby reduce inventory costs. At the same time, Boeing renewed its efforts to build a flexible, integrated production-management system that would link its separate computer systems. In addition, the company was trying to reduce the number of special features it introduced into a variety of aircraft models sold to different airlines, and by so doing, cut its expenses further (without, of course, turning away customers).[68]

Lastly, in December 1998, in a move initiated by Stonecipher, Deborah Hopkins, former chief finan-

cial officer at General Motors, Europe, replaced Boeing's chief financial officer for thirty-two years, Boyd Givan. A forty-four year-old financial analyst, Hopkins was the youngest senior executive at Boeing, and the only woman occupying such a high position. She spelled out her plans at once. To help Boeing recover, she sought first to obtain more accurate cost data and deliver the data to line supervisors in a timely fashion; second, to determine the risks of undertaking large projects in a more methodical way; third, to discontinue unprofitable projects; and fourth, to increase Boeing's reliance on the outsourcing of aircraft components, systems, and equipment. "Teaching the business" to Boeing managers and workers, she had quickly proved she could deliver, helping the company improve its financial results.[69]

Hopkins's early success at Boeing raised the issue of succession. On the one side, Alan Mulally represented the traditional CEO candidate. A Boeing engineer groomed and promoted by Condit, he occupied the immediate position leading directly to the top. On the other, Deborah Hopkins embodied anything but the traditional. An outsider brought in by another outsider, she was a woman working in a company dominated by a tribal culture of white male engineers. An ambitious and outspoken executive, she said she was interested in running the company following Condit's retirement, a statement that created some tension within the leadership.[70] Whoever succeeded Condit, the rivalry between Mulally and Hopkins was likely to underlie Boeing's difficult journey to recovery and comeback.

FUTURE CONCERNS

Despite its initial promise, Boeing's turnaround strategy failed to adequately address two major concerns that could have affected its recovery. One concern pertained to the state of labor relations, and the other to the prospects of product development.

Labor Relations

Following the merger of Boeing and McDonnell Douglas, about half of all Boeing's employees were covered by collective bargaining agreements. Boeing's two largest unions were the International Association of Machinists (IAM), representing 30 percent of its employees, and the Seattle Professional Engineering Employees Association (SPEEA), representing 12 percent of the employees. In 1999, Boeing was expected to negotiate new union contracts with 54,000 machinists, 24,000 engineers, and 8,000 other workers, the vast majority of whom were employees of the old Boeing, working in four states (Washington, Oregon, California, and Kansas). In 2001, Boeing was scheduled to negotiate an additional IAM contract with 10,000 machinists, all of whom were former employees of McDonnell Douglas in the Saint Louis area.[71]

During the 1995–96 round of union negotiations, just before the merger, both Boeing and McDonnell Douglas experienced bitter and costly strikes. In 1995, the Boeing machinists struck for sixty-nine days, and a year later, the McDonnell machinists struck for ninety-nine days. The two strikes erupted over the issue of job security.

At Boeing, the machinists had voted down two proposed contracts before ratifying a third with an approval rating of 87 percent. Described by analysts as "overly generous," the Boeing IAM 1995 agreement provided the machinists with the best job security provisions in the industry (management was required to discuss outsourcing decisions with the union before implementing them) and with excellent health benefits. Financially

weak, Boeing was unwilling to undergo another lengthy strike with the engineers. Instead, it offered the SPEEA a labor agreement closely modeled on the IAM's.[72]

At McDonnell Douglas, the striking machinists ratified the contract with only 68 percent of the vote. Described by some analysts as "rich," the McDonnell Douglas–IAM agreement, like Boeing's contract a year earlier, contained several clauses restricting the company's ability to subcontract jobs. In addition, the agreement required McDonnell management to compensate displaced workers with adequate job training and/or limited severance pay.[73]

Following the strikes of the mid 1990s, negotiations in 1999 were particularly difficult because of Boeing's commitment to produce a record of 620 commercial jets throughout the year—a goal that enhanced the union's bargaining power relative to management's. Still, as the IAM contract expired in the summer of 1999, Condit and his team managed to avoid a Boeing strike, reaching an agreement with the machinists on a three-year contract. Ratified by the majority of the membership, the agreement provided the machinists with job security (no layoffs as a result of outsourcing), while granting the company the right to decide which jobs should be outsourced. Both the union president and a Wall Street analyst praised Condit for the successful ne-

TABLE 8

Highlights of Financial and Operating Data for Boeing Before the Merger with McDonnell Douglas (1994–96) and After the Merger (1997–98) (in $ millions except per share data)

	After merger		Before merger		
	1998	*1997*	*1996*	*1995*	*1994*
Sales and other Operating Revenues:					
Commercial jets	$35,545	$26,929	$16,904	$13,933	$16,851
Defense and space	19,872	18,125	5,777	5,582	5,073
Other revenues	730	745			
Total	56,154	45,800	22,681	19,515	21,924
Net earnings (loss)	$1,120	($178)	$1,095	$393	$856
Earnings per share (loss)	1.16	(0.18)	3.19	1.15	2.51
R & D expense	1,895	1,924	1,200	1,267	1,704
Number of employees	231,000	238,000	112,000	109,000	119,000

Source: Boeing Annual Report for 1996, p. 64; Boeing Annual Report for 1998, p. 78.

gotiations of the agreement; yet in the long run, the contentious issue of outsourcing had not been resolved.[74] Because Boeing was fast increasing its reliance on subcontracting and at the same time was reluctant to give union leaders a greater voice in outsourcing decisions, labor relations at the company were likely to remain strained as it entered the twenty-first century.

Product Development

Similarly, Boeing's decision not to develop a new aircraft had far-reaching implications on the long-term competitive advantage of the company. Historically, the aviation industry had rewarded risk taking. On the eve of the jet age, Boeing upstaged Douglas with the 707, gambling the entire company on the success of the jet technology. In the 1970s, Boeing revolutionized air travel with the introduction of the 747, taking another huge risk and leaving McDonnell Douglas further behind. At the dawn of the twenty-first century, Boeing suddenly turned conservative. Not only was the company reluctant to develop a new family of planes, but its R&D budget was shrinking: between 1998 and 2000, Boeing's research and development spending was projected to decline from $1.9 billion to as low as $1.5 billion (see Table 6).

Airbus, in the meantime, was developing an entirely new aircraft, the "super jumbo" A3XX. A giant double-decker designed to carry 550 to 650 passengers, or 230 more than the largest standard 747, the A3XX was projected to go into production in 2000 and into service in 2005, at the earliest. Airbus intended to use the A3XX to compete with the 747 "from above."[75]

During the twenty-year period 1999–2019, Airbus management forecasted a need for 1,400 "super jumbos" valued at $300 billion. Boeing disputed these figures, contending that about three-quarters of Airbus's projected demand for the "super jumbo" was, in fact, a demand for the 747. Given its projections, Boeing management concluded that there was no justification for spending more than $10 billion (Airbus's estimate of the project's cost) on replacing the jumbo. Instead, Boeing decided to introduce derivative airplanes built around the 747. Looking for ways to stretch and upgrade the thirty-year-old jumbo, Boeing engineers were examining a 550-seat 747 equipped with improved wing aerodynamics and a fly-by-wire technology.[76]

Boeing also decided to delay another project, its most ambitious one: the development and production of a supersonic jet. In November 1998, Boeing postponed until the year 2020 the date on which its projected supersonic jetliner would enter service. A 300-foot-long mockup built in 1970—now under restoration in a San Francisco museum—represented the most advanced progress Boeing had ever made toward completing the project.[77]

Endnotes

1. David Whitford, "Sale of the Century," *Fortune*, February 17, 1997, p. 100; Andy Reinhardt, "Three Huge Hours in Seattle," *Business Week*, December 30, 1996, p. 38; Jeff Cole, "Air Power: Boeing Plan to Acquire McDonnell Douglas Bolsters Consolidation," *Wall Street Journal*, December 16, 1996.
2. *Fortune*, February 17, 1997, pp. 96, 98, 100; Anthony Velocci, "Vertical Integration Looming Larger at McDonnell Douglas," *Aviation Week and Space Technology*, March 6, 1996, pp. 58–59.
3. Quoted in *Fortune*, February 17, 1997, p. 96.
4. Lawrence Fisher, "Boeing Chairman Offers 'Exuberance and Dynamism,'" *New York Times*, December 16, 1996.
5. David C. Mowery and Nathan Rosenberg, "The Commercial Aircraft Industry," in Richard R. Nelson, ed., *Government and Technological Progress: A Cross Industry Analysis* (New York: Pergamon Press, 1982), p. 116; Michael L. Detrouzos, Richard K. Lester, and Robert M. Solow, *Made in America: Regaining the Productive Edge* (New York: Harper-Perennial, 1990), p. 204.
6. Mowery and Rosenberg, "The Commercial Aircraft Industry," p. 116; Dertouzos et al., *Made in America*, p. 204.
7. David C. Mowery and Nathan Rosenberg, *Technology and the Pursuit of Economic Growth* (New York: Cambridge University Press, 1989), p. 172. For the Boeing 777, see Eugene Rodgers, *Flying High: The Story of Boeing* (New York: Atlantic Monthly Press, 1996), p. 431; and for the A320, Eric Vayle, "Collision Course in Commercial Aircraft: Boeing—Airbus—McDonnell Douglas, 1991 (A)," *Harvard Business School Case* No. 9-391-106, October 1993, p. 3.
8. Dertouzos et al., *Made in America*, p. 203.
9. Ibid., pp. 206, 214.
10. Quoted in Janet Simpson, Lee Field, and David Garvin, "The Boeing 767: From Concept to Production," *Harvard Business School Case* No. 9-688-040, p. 6.
11. The Boeing Company 1998 Annual Report, p. 45.
12. For more on this argument, see Barry Bluestone, Peter Jordan and Mark Sullivan, *Aircraft Industry Dynamics: An Analysis of Competition, Capital, and Labor* (Boston: Auburn House, 1981), pp. 9–10.
13. Ibid., pp. 163–164.
14. Form 10-K of the Boeing Company for the Year Ended December 1, 1997, p. 3.
15. Lee Smith, "Air Power: Warplane Contracts Give a Lift to the New Aerospace Conglomerates," *Fortune*, July 7, 1997, p. 136.
16. *Fortune*, July 7, p. 135.
17. John B. Rae, *Climb to Greatness: The American Aircraft Industry, 1920–1960* (Cambridge Mass.: MIT Press, 1958), pp.

9-11, 63-72, 171; Boeing Commercial Airplane Group, *Backgrounder*, August 1997, p. 2.

18. Irving B. Holley, *Buying Aircraft: Material Procurement for the Army Air Force* (Washington: GPO, 1964), pp. 550, 576-77.

19. Rae, *Climb to Greatness*, p. 206.

20. Almarin Phillips, *Technology and Market Structure: A Study of the Aircraft Industry* (Lexington, Mass.: D.C. Heath, 1971), p. 110.

21. Rodgers, *Flying High*, p. 199.

22. Ibid., pp. 225-26.

23. Rae, *Climb to Greatness*, pp. 187-188; *Aerospace Facts and Figures, 1997-98*, pp. 47, 52-54; Boeing, *Backgrounder*, August 1997, pp. 5, 7-8; *Hoover's Handbook of American Business, 1997* (Austin: Hoover's Business Press, 1997), pp. 892-93.

24. Boeing, *Commercial Airplane Group, Announced Orders and Deliveries as of 12/31/97*, p. 1, in conjunction with The Boeing Company 1997 Annual Report, p. 19, and *Aerospace Facts and Figures 1997-98*, p. 35.

25. Rodgers, *Flying High*, pp. 287-88; Boeing, *Backgrounder*, August 1997, p. 6.

26. Rodgers, *Flying High*, pp. 284-85.

27. *Aerospace Facts and Figures 1997-98*, p. 33.

28. The Boeing Company Annual Report, p. 23.

29. Rodgers, *Flying High*, p. 413.

30. The Boeing Company 1997 Annual Report, p. 35.

31. Anthony L. Velocci, "MD-XX Termination May Seal Douglas' Fate," *Aviation Week and Space Technology*, November 4, 1996, pp. 24-25. See also *Fortune*, February 17, 1997, p. 98; and Bruce Smith, "Douglas Looks at Twin-Engine Design," *Aviation Week and Space Technology*, September 2, 1996, p. 78.

32. The quotations are from Jeremy Main, "Betting on the 21st Century Jet," *Fortune*, April 20, 1992, pp. 103-104, but see also Rodgers, *Flying High*, p. 420.

33. *Hoover's Handbook of American Business, 1997*, pp. 272-73, 892-93; Boeing, *Backgrounder*, August 1997, pp. 8-9; Rodgers, *Flying High*, p. 327; Form 10-K of the Boeing Company for the Year Ended December 31, 1997, p. 3.

34. *Rodgers, Flying High*, p. 422; Dertouzos et al., *Made in America*, p. 208; Vayle, "Collision Course in Commercial Aircraft," p. 18.

35. Dertouzos, et al., *Made in America*, pp. 210-214; Rodgers, *Flying High*, chap. 12; "Airbus 25 Years Old," *Le Figaro*, October 1997 (reprinted in English translation by Airbus Industrie), p. 6.

36. Equally important, Airbus made an aggressive use of composite materials to reduce aircraft's weight and simplify aircraft's construction (for example, it used composites to build a vertical fin, reducing the fin's parts-count from 2000 to 100). Similarly, in the area of aerodynamics, Airbus designed a wing that featured a distinct twist at the root to reduce drag, and a gust alleviation system to improve efficiency in cruise as well as reduce passenger discomfort in turbulence. "Airbus Industrie: 25 Flying Years," Airbus Industrie, 1997, pp. 13, 14, 17; Dertouzos et al., *Made in America*, pp. 212-213.

37. Together, these efforts enabled Airbus to slash its deliveries "lead time" (the period lasting from the time a customer gave specifications until delivery) from fifteen to nine months (single aisle) and from eighteen to twelve months

(wide body), and thereby reduce costly inventories by 30 percent. Charles Goldsmith, "Re-engineering: After Trailing Boeing for Years Airbus Aims at 50% of the Market," *Wall Street Journal*, March 16, 1998.

38. Dertouzos et al., *Made in America*, p. 212. A typical Airbus ad read: "Airbus' unique use of the latest fly-by-wire technology ... enables airlines to operate ... a whole set of aircraft types ranging from 120 to over 400 seats in capacity.... with a single pool of pilots" at a saving of "$1 million per aircraft per year." "Airbus: the Airbus Family," Airbus Industrie, 1997.

39. The Boeing Company 1997 Annual Report, p. 3; Jeff Cole, "Boeing Names New Managers, Alters Structure," *Wall Street Journal*, August 7, 1997.

40. Lawrence Zuckerman, "Boeing's Man in the Line of Fire," *New York Times*, November 8, 1998.

41. Frederick Biddle and Andy Paszor, "Boeing May be Hurt Up to 5 Years," *Wall Street Journal*, December 3, 1998.

42. "Fearful Boeing," *Economist*, February 27, 1999, p. 59.

43. The Boeing Company 1997 Annual Report, p. 72.

44. Jeanne Cummings, "President, in State of the Union Address, Offers Most Ambitious Agenda Since 1995," *Wall Street Journal*, January 20, 1999; The Boeing Company 1997 Annual Report, p. 27; *Fortune*, July 7, 1997, p. 134.

45. *Fortune*, July 7, 1997, pp. 133-136.

46. Ibid., p. 136.

47. Ibid.

48. The Boeing Company 1997 Annual Report, p. 25; *Fortune*, July 7, 1997, p. 136.

49. *Fortune*, February 17, 1999, p. 100, July 7, 1997, p. 136; Jeff Cole, "Lockheed Warplane has Racked Up Cost Overruns," *Wall Street Journal*, February 5, 1999.

50. Adam Bryant, "Boeing Offering $13 Billion to Buy McDonnell Douglas," *New York Times*, December 16, 1996.

51. The Boeing Company 1997 Annual Report, p. 36; Frederick Biddle, "Boeing Is still Waiting for the Merger Results to Take Off," *Wall Street Journal*, March 2, 1998.

52. Frederick Biddle and John Helyar, "Flying Low: Behind Boeing's Woes: Clunky Assembly Line, Price War with Airbus," *Wall Street Journal*, April 24, 1998.

53. Form 10-K of the Boeing company for the Year ended December 31, 1997, p. 4; Form 10-Q of the Boeing Company for the Quarterly Period ended June 30, 1998, pp. 14-15.

54. "Out-of-sequence work is an especially costly problem on an aircraft assembly line," says The Boeing Company 1997 Annual Report (p. 3), "as it causes efficiency to plummet to a small fraction of what it should be." See also p. 37.

55. "Bouncing Boeing," *Economist*, June 13, 1998, p. 72; *Wall Street Journal*, April 24, 1998.

56. According to Harry Stonecipher, cited in the *New York Times*, December 3, 1998.

57. "Aircraft Making: Boeing Woeing," *Economist*, August 8, 1998, p. 55, June 13, 1998, p. 72.

58. *Wall Street Journal*, April 24, 1998.

59. "Aerospace: Hubris at Airbus, Boeing Rebuilds," *Economist*, November 28, 1998, p. 65. My figures are slightly different from those of the *Economist* because I used the actual number of jets produced and the *Economist* used the projected number.

60. *Wall Street Journal*, December 3, 1998.

61. *Business Week*, December 30, 1996, p. 39.

62. Rodgers, *Flying High*, pp. 428–430.

63. Laurence Zuckerman, "Boeing's Leaders Losing Altitude," *New York Times*, December 13, 1998.

64. Rodgers, *Flying High*, pp. 427–28.

65. *New York Times*, December 13, 1998.

66. *New York Times*, December 13, 1998; Seanna Brower, "Comeback: Boeing Breathes Easier," *Business Week*, May 3, 1999.

67. *New York Times*, November 8, 1998; *Economist*, November 28, 1998, p. 65.

68. *Economist*, November 28, 1998, p. 65.

69. Jeff Cole, "New CEO's Assignment: Signal a Turnaround," *Wall Street Journal*, January 26, 1999.

70. Ibid.

71. The Boeing Company 1998 Annual Report, p. 39; Jeff Cole, "Boeing Co. May Give Unions Say on Subcontracts," *Wall Street Journal*, April 5, 1999.

72. Rodgers, *Flying High*, pp. 449–62; for the quotation see Anthony Velocci, "Healing Begins at McDonnell Douglas as Strikers Return to Work," *Aviation Week and Space Technology*, September 16, 1996, p. 90.

73. Robert Rafalko and James Fisher, "Business as Warfare at McDonnell Douglas Corporation," Paper presented at the 1998 meeting of the North American Case Research Association, Durham, New Hampshire, pp. 1–7. For the quotation, see *Aviation Week and Space Technology*, September 16, 1996, p. 90.

74. *Wall Street Journal*, April 5, 1999; Ann Marie Squeo, "Boeing, Union leaders Reached Pact on Contract," *Wall Street Journal*, August 30, 1999.

75. Frederic Biddle, "Pulled Off Its Cloud, Boeing Suspends Quest for the Next Generation Jumbo Jet," *Wall Street Journal*, December 3, 1998; "Airbus May Be About to Challenge the Jumbo Jet's 30-Year-Old Monopoly," *Economist*, March 27, 1999, pp. 61–62.

76. *Economist*, March 27, 1999, pp. 61–62.

77. *Wall Street Journal*, December 3, 1998.

INDEX

CLOSING CASES

PRACTICING STRATEGIC MANAGEMENT

Small-Group Exercise
Short experiential exercise that asks students to work in groups and discuss a scenario concerning some aspect of strategic management.

Article File
An exercise that requires students to search business magazines to identify a company facing a particular strategic management problem.

Strategic Management Project
A semester-long project that asks students to select a company and analyze it using a series of questions at the end of every chapter. At the end of the course, students might write a case study of their company and present it to the class.

Exploring the Web
An Internet exercise that requires students to go beyond the text by exploring a web site and answering chapter-related questions.